Chronicle of Britain and Ireland

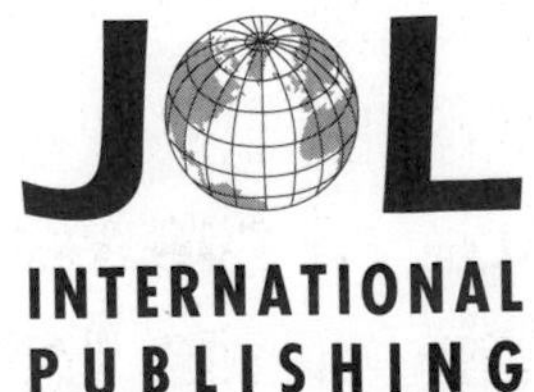

Notes about chief consultants

Dr Jeremy Black, Reader in History, Durham University
Dr Ciaran Brady, Senior Lecturer in Modern History, Trinity College, Dublin
Dr S P Brindle, Historian, London Region of English Heritage
Dr Keith Brown, Lecturer, Stirling University
Professor L A Clarkson, Professor of Social History, Queen's University of Belfast
Dr Barry Coward, Reader in History, Birkbeck College, London
Dr David Crouch, Senior Lecturer in History, University College, Scarborough
Dr David Englander, Senior Lecturer in European Humanities Studies, The Open University
Chris Going, Freelance archaeologist based in Cambridge
Dr Steven Gunn, Fellow and Tutor in Modern History, Merton College, Oxford
Dr Colin Haselgrove, Senior Lecturer in Archaeology, University of Durham
Dr Felicity Heal, Tutor in History, Jesus College, Oxford
Dr Rosemary Horrox, University of Cambridge
Simon Loseby, Junior Research Fellow, St Anne's College, Oxford
Jonathan Luke, PhD student in English Literature
Dr Diarmaid MacCulloch, independent Lecturer, Bristol University
Professor Joan Perkin, part-time Professor in History, Northwestern University, Evanston, Illinois, USA
Dr Jonathan Phillips, Honorary Research Associate, Royal Holloway and Bedford New College, University of London
Dr Roy Porter, Reader in the Social History of Medicine at the Wellcome Institute for the History of Medicine, London
Professor Michael Prestwich, Professor of History, Durham University
Dr John Spurr, Lecturer in History, University College of Swansea
Dr Pauline Stafford, Senior Lecturer, University of Huddersfield
Dr Julian Thomas, Lecturer in Archaeology, St David's University College, Lampeter, Dyfed
Leslie Webster, Deputy Keeper of Mediaeval and Later Antiquities in the British Museum
Dr C J Woods, Assistant to the Royal Irish Academy

Illustrations inside front and back covers show examples of the earliest and the most recent human settlements in the British Isles. Front: Dun Conor, Inishmann (the second largest of the Aran Islands, off the west coast of Ireland). Back: London docklands housing development at Free Trade Wharf, Wapping.

lished in 1992 by Chronicle Communications Ltd,
House, 16 Invincible Road, Farnborough,
GU14 7QU, England
78000 Fax: 0252 373222

amendments 1993

35-8

Legrand SA International Publishing, Paris, for World English Rights
Communications Ltd, England
unication, Dortmund, for the Chronicle system

Louis-Jean, Gap, France
Beauclair, Paris – Tipsa, Paris – MCP, Orléans – Point 11, Paris
pols, Turnhout, Belgium

Distributor for England:

Random Century Group
20 Vauxhall Bridge Road
London SW1V 2SA
United Kingdom
Tel.: (44) 71 973 9000.
Fax: (44) 71 233 6058

USA:

JL International Publishing Inc.
244 West Mill Street
Liberty – Missouri
64068 USA
Tel.: (1) 816 792 19 81
Fax: (1) 816 792 19 32
Distribution by Macmillan, NY

Distributor for Canada:

Raincoast Books Distribution Ltd.
112 East 3rd Avenue
V5T 1C8 – Vancouver
British Columbia – Canada
Tel.: (1) 604 873 65 81
Fax: (1) 604 874 27 11

Distributor for Australia:

Penguin Books Australia Ltd.
487 Maroondah Highway
PO Box 257 – Ringwood
3134 – Victoria
Australia
Tel.: (63) 3 871 24 00
Fax: (63) 3 870 96 18

Chronicle of Britain and Ireland

Editor: Henrietta Heald

Picture Editor	Ruth Darby
Assistant Editor	Chris Jackson
Chief Consultants	Dr Jeremy Black, Dr Ciaran Brady, Dr S P Brindle, Dr Keith Brown, Professor L A Clarkson, Dr Barry Coward, Dr David Crouch, Dr David Englander, Chris Going, Dr Steven Gunn, Dr Colin Haselgrove, Dr Felicity Heal, Dr Rosemary Horrox, Simon Loseby, Jonathan Luke, Dr Diarmaid MacCulloch, Professor Joan Perkin, Dr Jonathan Phillips, Dr Roy Porter, Professor Michael Prestwich, Patricia Reed, Dr John Spurr, Dr Pauline Stafford, Dr Julian Thomas, Lorraine Ward, Leslie Webster, Dr C J Woods (see note on consultants, opposite page)
Additional Consultants	John Bently, Dr Simon Esmonde Cleary, Eric Grove, Peregrine Horden, Dr R A Houlbrooke, David Keys, Dr John Lowe, Gordon Marsden, Charles Messenger, Dr Peter Northover, Philip Waller, Dr Graham Webster
Writers	Bruce Arnold, Frank Barber, Peter Bently, Ray Boston, Patrick Brogan, Jerome Burne, Carol Dix, Christopher Dobson, David Gould, Jonathon Green, Derek Hall, Robert Jones, Charles Langley, Peter Lewis, John Miller, Rupert Morris, Tony Pearce, Charles Phillips, Denis Pitts, Richard Trench, Barry White, Peter Wilsher
Chronologies	Bronwen Lewis
Research	Joan Thomas (manager), Hazel Bedford, Rob Crow, Marion Dain, Jason du Sautoy, Dr Judith Ford, Eva O'Cathaoir, Mark Piachaud, Susan Pitt, Caroline Prentice, Carl Röhsler, N C Vincent
Picture Research	Susanna Harrison, Jane Lewis, Francesca Odell
Production	Catherine Balouet (manager), Marie Dautet, Linda Pasteuning, Paige Rosenberg
Editorial Production	Martine Colliot, Nathalie Cox, Laurel Sherrer (managers), Chris Allman, Pat Harper, Barbara Levinson, Alistair Mansfield, Gillian Mercer
Style Editor	Laura Hicks
Indexers	Tony Bastow (manager), Judith Brody
Artwork	Colin Salmon; Mike Saunders; Andrea Fairbrass at Swanston Graphics Ltd; Jonathan Preston and Julian Baker at the Maltings Partnership; typesetting: Shaku Woodrow and Gabriella Markus at the Right Setting.

Editor-in-chief: Derrik Mercer
Publisher: Jacques Legrand

A woman on horseback with flowing robes forms part of the elaborate floor mosaic uncovered at the Roman villa at Littlecote, in Wiltshire.

A section of the Bayeux Tapestry depicting the jubilant Norman soldiers at a celebratory banquet following their defeat of the English at Hastings.

Acknowledgements

The principal contributors to this book are credited on page 5, and the agencies that supplied the illustrations on pages 1293-96. A book of this kind is inevitably a team operation, and there are certain other individuals and organizations to whom gratitude is due. First, however, I would like to express particular thanks to Derrik Mercer, our editor-in-chief, who provided great wisdom and inspiration through all the stages in the preparation and production of this book. Jerome Burne also deserves a special mention for putting together our team of expert advisers and initiating the research with his accustomed vigour.

As ever, we subjected photographic agencies to a barrage of detailed requests; we would like to thank them for the speed and diligence with which they responded. Thanks to all at the Bridgeman Art Library, Mary Evans Picture Library, Popperfoto and Topham Picture Library; Lucy Bunning at English Heritage, Simon Cobley at Weidenfeld Archives, Helen Henderson at Edinburgh Photographic Library, Ben Hopkins at Hulton Picture Library, David Lyons, Gavin Morgan at the Museum of London, Kelly Preedy at the National Trust Photo Library and Mick Sharp. In addition, Helen McCurdy and Robert Stewart made a valuable contribution as textual fact-checkers. We would also like to thank the numerous libraries throughout the British Isles who provided information on local history.

The responsibility for what appears in this book rests with us. We have tried, with the help of expert advisers, to ensure that it is accurate. But even experts can make mistakes or, more probably, disagree. Picture captions supplied by agencies can be inaccurate. If, in word or illustration, errors have evaded our scrutiny, we apologize - but ask to be told so that they can be corrected for future editions.

The west front of Wells Cathedral, with its impressive towers and sculpted façade, is a fine example of early English "gothic" architectural style.

The English fleet engages in battle with the Spanish Armada, valiantly fighting off the threat of an invasion by King Philip II of Spain.

Contents

"The cast-iron bridge near Coalbrookdale" by William Williams, 1780. The bridge, an early icon of the Industrial Revolution, was completed in 1779.

A spectacular view of the south side of the Crystal Palace. It was designed and built to house the Great Exhibition, planned by Prince Albert, in 1851.

"The Battle of Marston Moor" by James Ward (1769-1859): the battle, in 1644, was a great victory for Oliver Cromwell (centre) over King Charles I.

Thundering through the peaceful Scottish countryside: one of British Rail's impressive high-speed 125 trains rushes on towards its destination.

Introduction

Some 8,500 years ago the British Isles were cut off from the continent of Europe by rising sea levels – caused by the melting glaciers of the last "ice age". In 1993 this physical isolation is set to end with the completion of the Channel tunnel. In the distinctive *Chronicle* style – vividly reporting events of the past as though they had just happened – this book covers the key developments in our islands' history during the intervening millennia, with a strong emphasis on the past 200 years. It recounts events in every part of England, Scotland, Wales and Ireland. This entirely fresh approach to history – brought alive as never before with the aid of more than 3,000 stunning illustrations – is intended to open new doors on the past and lead the way to a deeper understanding of the parade of remarkable characters who have made their marks in these islands over the centuries. The combination of national and local coverage and the juxtaposition of momentous political happenings with social developments and advances in fashion, science and the arts allow the reader to view events in context and to embark on a rediscovery of our shared heritage.

In the early 1530s, for example, when Henry VIII of England was forging ahead with the campaign that resulted in the English church's split with Rome, James V of Scotland was completing the transformation of Holyrood Abbey into a royal palace. English power was being extended in Wales and the Marches at the same time as a rebellion was simmering in Ireland under "Silken Thomas" FitzGerald. Tin-miners in the English West Country were attempting to reassert their ancient rights and privileges, and sheep-farmers in East Anglia were grappling with a new law banning anyone from owning more than 2,000 sheep. Meanwhile, an explosion in demand for sweet European wines led the English parliament to fix the price of wine at a shilling [5p] a gallon.

In 1887, when Queen Victoria celebrated her golden jubilee, *The Times* newspaper accused Charles Stewart Parnell, the Irish nationalist politician, of complicity in the Phoenix Park murders. Welsh farmers mounted a campaign against land taxes, and Lancashire women marched to London demanding to be allowed to exercise their right to work as miners. The fictional detective Sherlock Holmes made his first appearance in print.

This is a book in which the reader provides the analysis. From the high ground of hindsight, it is possible to look back and comprehend better the world in which we live today. For example, many echoes of the past can be heard in recent events. Protests against the "poll tax" had their forerunner in the campaign mounted in 1381 against a similar measure. The fact that our age has no monopoly on financial corruption is illustrated by the infamous South Sea "bubble" of 1720 – a scam on a grand scale that bankrupted thousands and came within an ace of toppling the government.

One subject that provides a recurrent theme throughout this book is the tortured relationship over the centuries between Britain and Ireland. So closely are the islands' histories interwoven that no chronicle of Britain would be complete that did not also attempt to deal with events in Ireland. We have tried to be fair in our coverage and, in order to provide a context for developments, to give attention to the history of Ireland even where this does not interact directly with that of Britain. We have been helped enormously in this task by our distinguished consultants in Ireland, but we accept that – on account of the very nature of Ireland's relationship with Britain – this may be an area in which queries about the selection, and possibly the slant, of material may arise.

This book aims to present history in a way that is not only authoritative but also fun and uniquely accessible. Rising to this challenge has proved an exhilarating experience. The sense of excitement and discovery that accompanied the book's creation is – we hope – destined to catch the imagination of every reader, young and old alike.

Henrietta Heald, August 1992

Henrietta Heald

A warning about dates

During certain periods of history covered by this book, the use of dates must be treated warily. Many of the stories reported up to around AD800 reflect what the best-informed archaeologists and historians believe happened, which may not be the same as what really did happen. This is because written records are non-existent or partial, or were set down long after the events to which they refer actually occurred. Most of the dates given before the arrival of the Romans – and the first extant written records – have been identified by the technique known as radiocarbon dating, and "calibrated" to correspond with ordinary calendar years. Specialists may be interested to know that the calibration curve used here is one derived from oak trunks preserved in Irish bogs, produced by scientists at Belfast University in 1986.

For the two centuries after Britain ceased to be part of the Roman Empire, great caution is necessary. Fifth-century events, recorded by the British historian Gildas in the 540s, were based on information passed to Gildas up to a century after they happened. The *Anglo-Saxon Chronicle* – based on other written and oral traditions – was first compiled only in the ninth century, some 300 years after Anglo-Saxons started to settle in England. As history progresses through the mediaeval era and into the Tudor, Stuart and later periods, dates become less of a problem, but differentiating between fact and fiction, between propaganda and bias, remains a constant difficulty for the historian. There are no such things as historical facts – just witnesses to events. Even a bare chronology is a selection from a great number of events. To say anything about what happened involves interpretation – and interpretation is rarely, if ever, neutral. One final point to note is that, until 1752, when Britain and Ireland officially adopted the Gregorian calendar, "old-style" dates derived from the Julian calendar are given.

Opposite page: a 15th-century representation of George, the patron saint of England. His origins, possibly in Palestine in the third century, are obscure. The slaying of the dragon, shown here, was attributed to him in the 12th century. During the reign of Edward III (1327-77) he replaced Edward the Confessor (1042-66) as patron saint of England; his feast day is 23 April. Since c.750 the patron saint of Scotland has been the fisherman Andrew the Apostle, the brother of St Peter; his feast day is 30 November. David, the patron saint of Wales, died c.600 at Mynyw (St David's). He founded 12 monasteries and reputedly became primate of Wales; his feast day is 1 March. Ireland's patron saint, Patrick, who was born near Carlisle, was captured by pirates at the age of 16 and taken to Ireland. He later became a missionary and converted many Irish to Christianity; he died c.490, and his feast day is 17 March.

Two million years ago: the dawn of the 'ice age'

Taking a snapshot of the British Isles of two million years ago, at the start of the "ice age", is not easy. The evidence that exists is patchy, confused and hard to interpret.

To start with, the scientific record, incomplete as it is, shows that the term "ice age" is something of a misnomer. There were certainly massive expansions of the earth's icecaps: during the deepest freeze, about one-third of the earth's land surface was covered with ice, compared with around one-tenth now. Vast areas as far south as the Mediterranean experienced conditions similar to those in Arctic Norway today. However, there were also warmer times, some even warmer than the present day. So "ice age" refers not to one long big freeze but to a period of frequent and sometimes rapid climatic shifts.

Attempts to reconstruct what happened in the British Isles are dogged by sheer lack of evidence and uncertainty as to how to interpret what little evidence is available. Piecing together the history of this period has been compared to trying to complete a jigsaw puzzle with most of the pieces missing and the rest dirty, torn and twisted.

Not surprisingly, more is known about the most recent glaciation than any other. The last expansion of the ice sheet, which had reached its maximum extent about 20,000 years ago, left behind abundant deposits within the range of certain important dating methods. These enable scientists to map out the advance of the ice and to attempt to calculate the size, shape, growth and direction of the ice sheet.

Such reconstructions are subjected to repeated refinements as new information becomes available. For example, it was long assumed that the ice covering Britain was part of a continuous sheet stretching all the way to Scandinavia. But recent investigations of the North Sea bed – stimulated largely by oil and gas exploration – suggest that the sea was open during the last glaciation.

There has been much controversy over the number, duration and dates of the glaciations that affected the British Isles, and there are enormous gaps in the record of up to a million years wide. There is broad agreement, however, on at least two big glacial periods – the most recent one, and one believed to date from between 300,000 and 250,000 years ago. There is some scanty evidence for six other glaciations affecting the British Isles. One seems to have occurred between about 480,000 and 430,000 years ago; beyond this little is certain.

However, a recent important scientific advance is shedding more light on the ice age. Called "oxygen isotope signal dating", it assesses climatic change by examining fossilized dead plankton – microscopic sea creatures – which have dropped to the sea bed for millions of years. It should soon be possible to arrive at a more reliable picture of the changing climate of the British Isles and, indeed, of the Earth.

Flora and fauna are shaped by climate

The mild weather conditions now enjoyed by the British Isles are not typical of the last two million years. The climate has changed repeatedly between periods of glaciation and warmth [*see report above*].

Before the "ice age" the islands were host to sub-tropical flora such as nypa palm, hickory, hemlock and magnolia, and animals such as elephants, porcupines, hyaenas, tapirs and turtles. Now, compared with neighbouring parts of Europe, the islands' plant and animal life is relatively impoverished. The climatic swings may have set off great migrations across the landbridge linking Britain to Europe, many of the species then adapting to other regions and not returning when the climate again changed. Of the species that did return, those able to migrate more quickly and colonize more effectively survived best.

The history of human occupation [*see report alongside*] very likely followed a similar pattern. Each warm climatic phase saw an expansion of dense forests throughout Europe, which may have deterred certain types of game and humans alike. But some species of game were probably more abundant in the less dense forest edges, such as in Britain. This may have lured humans to Britain in the first place.

Half a million years ago: humans make their first appearance

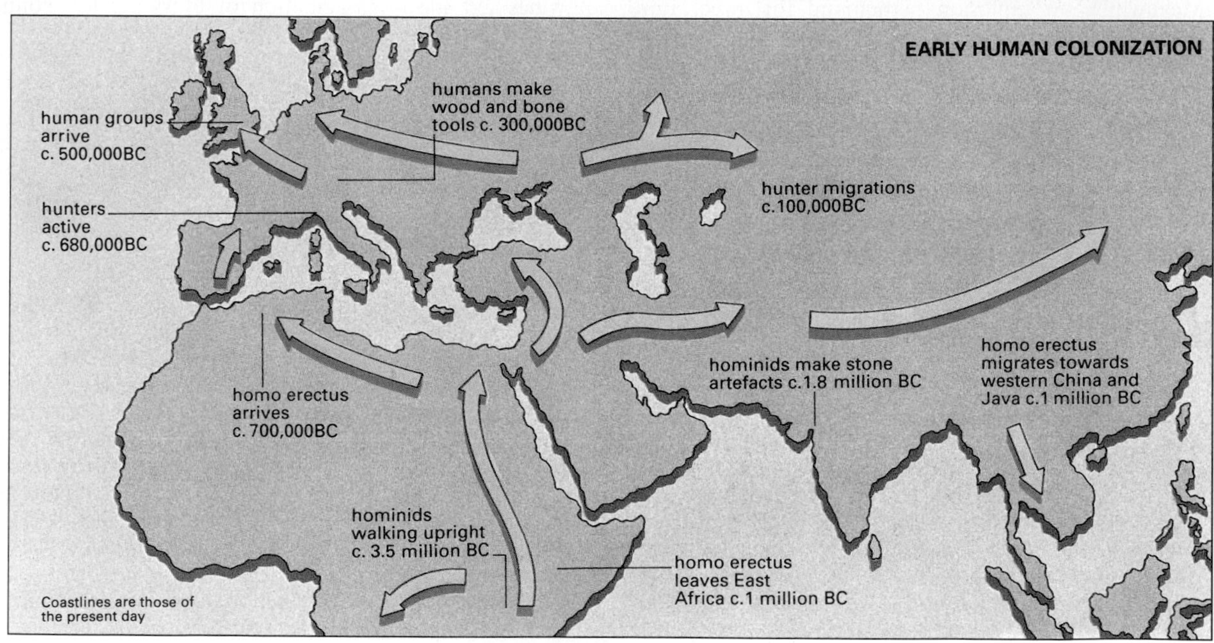

Humans arrive in Britain, in the context of their migrations from Africa into neighbouring continents.

Around 500,000 years ago a new species arrived to join the hordes of rhinoceroses, sabre-toothed cats, elephants and other beasts which roamed the British Isles. The newcomers were *homo erectus*, early humans, walking upright on two legs, with heavy jaws, receding brows and no chins. They had arrived in Europe 200,000 years previously from Africa, where they evolved [*see map above*].

The first humans to arrive settled in East Anglia, the river valleys of the English Midlands and the southern English coastal plain. They survived in their new home, which for a long time had been enjoying a hot climate, by killing game – including deer, elephant, rhinoceros and horse – and scavenging from the kills of other animals, as well as by gathering edible plants. They lived in semi-permanent dwellings or, especially when they moved south during the cold periods, caves.

Humans were distinguished from other beasts by their highly developed intelligence. This gave them the ability to plan ahead and to organize socially in small groups to obtain and share food, putting themselves at the top of the food chain. They also used small stone tools and had begun to learn how to make and use fire [*see reports opposite*]. In short, they were the only creatures able to initiate deliberate changes to the natural order. The adaptable, versatile humans lost no time in bringing about radical alterations to the new environment.

First inhabitants learn how to live

Fire makes survival easier for settlers

After an arduous day spent hunting game and gathering plants for food, keeping out the cold at night would have been a big problem for the first humans who settled in Britain half a million years ago. Lighting a fire must have been a frustrating business, but some people at least had learnt how to kindle, maintain and regulate a flame. By a lake at High Lodge in Suffolk, for example, wood was burnt on a round patch of ground, close to where flint tools [*see report below*] were made.

The first fire that humans encountered was probably some natural phenomenon such as a forest blaze caused by lightning. They may have discovered how to make their own by observing the sparks made when pieces of flint were struck together, but however the skill was acquired it proved to be an invaluable asset. As well as providing heat on cold days and nights it could also be used to cook the flesh of animals caught on their hunting trips in the valleys and coastal plains of southern Britain. It would also have been a way of scaring off those marauding animals for which humans were themselves prey.

Around 350,000 years ago fires swept through the forests of East Anglia over an area from Mark's Tey in Essex to Hoxne in Suffolk. Whether the blazes were started naturally or by humans, they offered new opportunities for hunting deer, horse, bison and other beasts which emerged from the forests to graze on young shoots in new clearings. This may also explain why, at about the same time, humans began to venture away from previously favoured river- and lakeside clearings like those at Hoxne, Clacton in Essex and Swanscombe in Kent.

An artist's impression of hunters at Swanscombe in Kent, c.400,000BC.

Mushrooms, ferns, mammoth on menu

The early inhabitants of the British Isles enjoyed a wide-ranging diet. Mammoth, bison, pike, ferns and willow shoots were all on the menu for a society of hunter-gatherers for whom getting and preparing food was a full-time activity.

Every adult needed to consume about a kilo of boneless meat a day, so hunters were obliged to pursue big game in order to keep their group alive. A bull provided 40 people with enough meat for three days, while the tonne of flesh from a mammoth would probably keep them going for a month. The fishers in the tribe would use clubs or spears to catch basking fish such as pike, and traps made of interlaced branches for smaller fry. While some people hunted, others would gather all sorts of vegetation, such as ferns and mushrooms, to bolster their diet.

Meat was probably smoked or left to cook slowly, either on a flat stone next to the fire or in the embers, as roasting directly makes it shrink. Food was also wrapped in leaves or cooked on spits.

Flint is fashioned into tools for job

The people who settled at Boxgrove, near Chichester in West Sussex, around 450,000 years ago found that the area offered two advantages: easy access to game and, below the cliffs, an abundance of flint for making handaxes – the all-purpose choppers, cutters and scrapers essential as everyday tools.

To make a handaxe, a Boxgrove toolmaker used one stone as a hammer to chip or "knap" a lump of flint into the basic flattish, almond shape. Flint was a particularly good material to use, because if hit at the right angle flakes would come off, and a skilled worker could soon fashion the handaxe and its sharp edge. The tool would have been trimmed and finished with a bone, antler or small stone to remove smaller flakes and give a smoother finish. The chipped-off flakes were not necessarily wasted. Settlers at High Lodge in Suffolk used flakes to produce an extensive variety of more specialist tools that included knives, serrated cutters and scrapers for removing fat and hair from animal skins.

In due course the basic handaxe itself became more sophisticated as skills improved. A particularly fine handaxe shows that one of the new breed of expert craftsmen or craftswomen lived at Furze Platt in Berkshire around 350,000 years ago. The 30-cm-long tool was shaped, trimmed and finished into a strikingly even symmetrical form, with a fine continuous edge and a thickening towards the base for better balance. It shows a profound understanding of the qualities which make the handaxe such a useful tool; such care has gone into it that the expert toolmaker appears to have taken pride in his or her skill for its own sake.

Handaxes were basic all-purpose tools; these are from Hoxne in Suffolk.

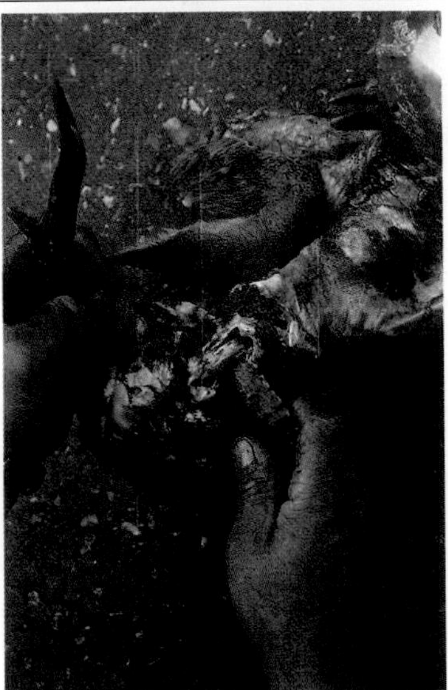

One use for a handaxe: butchery.

People acquire a sense of the beautiful as the toolmaker's craft reaches new levels

A handaxe from Swanscombe, Kent, adorned with the fossil of a sea urchin.

Flint tools from Baker's Hole, Kent.

A flint cut by a Crayford toolmaker: used to butcher rhinoceros flesh.

By about 225,000 years ago flint-toolmaking was well established as a highly developed craft, as is shown by the fine implements and weapons made in Kent at Baker's Hole and Crayford. The Crayford makers' blades were so good that they were used for butchering the tough flesh of the local woolly rhinoceroses brought back by hunters. Both groups of Kentish workers were helped by easy access to a supply of good-quality flint, which was essential for the best products. Other workers, such as those at Caddington in Bedfordshire, faced problems with the poorer raw materials at their disposal.

At around the same time some toolmakers were clearly fashioning flint with a care that went beyond mere functionality. Another Kentish maker, at Swanscombe, chipped and trimmed a handaxe with great expertise to preserve the fossil of a sea urchin, which served no useful purpose and seems purely decorative. Another sign that people were acquiring an aesthetic sense – a preference for the *look* of one thing over that of another – comes from Caddington. Here holes in naturally perforated stones were enlarged and the stones strung together, probably on sinew, to form necklaces and bracelets. Elsewhere the daisy-like coral fossils in a flake of pink chert – a type of stone – obviously caught someone's eye. It originated in Wiltshire but was carried halfway across the south of England to end up in Kent.

New humans develop

The growing sophistication of the toolmakers of Britain of 225,000 years ago [*see report left*] may have had something to do with the fact that the shape of humanity itself was changing – literally.

In the long term these changes proved quite dramatic, as can be seen in the skull of a woman – the lack of muscle markings suggests a female rather than a male – who lived around that time at Swanscombe in Kent. From the size of her skull she must have had a bigger brain than earlier humans, and although the face is missing it appears to have been broad, with quite large eyebrow ridges, a receding forehead, heavy jaws and big teeth. Overall her appearance would have been markedly more like modern humans than that of her forebears. This new strain of more intelligent humans is called *homo sapiens*; it is also called Neanderthal, from the valley near Düsseldorf in western Germany where other remains have been found.

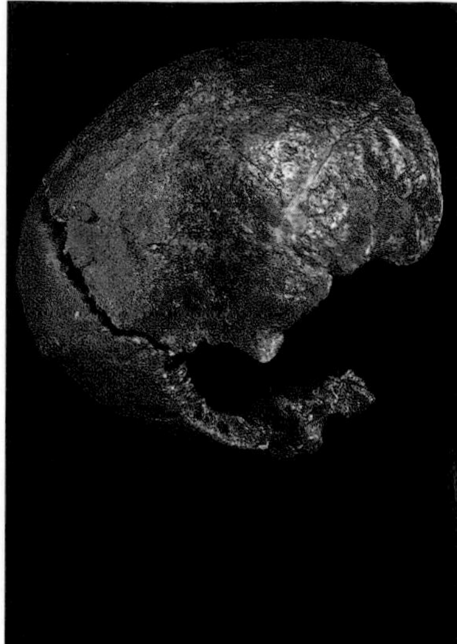
The Swanscombe woman's skull.

The hardiness and resourcefulness of these early modern humans is shown by a Neanderthal cave near Pontnewydd in Clwyd. The local stone, a tough igneous rock, was a hard material to make tools from, but this does not seem to have put off the cave dwellers, who probably used the cave as a temporary shelter during hunting expeditions. It would have offered a good base to look out for the many animals which passed through the valley.

Thames is home to hippos in baking heat

Between 130,000 and 118,000 years ago the British Isles were in the grip of a great thaw after a period of glaciation. Melting ice raised sea-levels to cut off the islands from the rest of Europe and end the migration of returning animals and people. At the same time, warm sea currents and high summer temperatures meant a climate similar to that of the Mediterranean today. The summers in this post-glacial era appear to have been hotter than they had been for hundreds of thousands of years.

The new conditions provided lush vegetation for the hippopotamuses and other beasts, such as lions, hyaenas and rhinoceroses, which had migrated north as the ice receded. Giant elephants also appeared in place of the woolly mammoths of colder times, and cave bear, horse, musk-ox and deer were also widespread. The hippos, which had last been in evidence hundreds of thousands of years earlier, found ample supplies of food around their homes in the fresh water and thick mud of the Thames valley. For the humans, now increased in number and possessing even more refined hunting skills than before, there was a rich abundance of game in the new landscape.

Giant elephant: artist's impression.

Technocrats displace Neanderthals

At some time around 34,000BC a new breed of human began to displace the Neanderthals who had first become established in the British Isles some 225,000 years ago [*see report on page 12*]. These newcomers, distinguished by their superior technological abilities, were of the type known as *homo sapiens sapiens* – modern humans.

As a result of intervening periods of glaciation the Neanderthals would have been unable to maintain an unbroken habitation of the islands, but until this time they appear to have returned during warmer intervals.

With the men of the new breed averaging about 1.65 metres (5 feet 5 inches) in height, *homo sapiens sapiens* was taller than the short-limbed, heavily built Neanderthals. Their ancestors, like those of the Neanderthals, seem to have evolved in Africa but to have started their migration to Europe at a much later date, first arriving there in approximately 40,000BC.

Technological innovations that had developed over a long time enabled the new people to be more effective than the Neanderthals at surviving in what was by that time a chilly climate. For example, they used hafted spears and traps to hunt large game, such as mammoth, woolly rhino, ox, horse and reindeer. Some were adept at fishing, using lines, hooks, harpoons and possibly even nets and boats. Other tools which they produced were more specialized than those of their predecessors – scrapers, engraving tools, knives and borers.

The Neanderthals may simply have succumbed in the face of such competition, forced to leave their hunting grounds, isolated and left to starve. However it happened, by about 30,000BC they had disappeared from the scene.

How Neanderthals – not the dimwits of popular legend – may have looked.

People find homes in nature's prefabs

By the time that the breed of people known as *homo sapiens sapiens* arrived in the British Isles [*see report left*], caves were well established as practical human shelters. For a start, they provided literally rock-solid protection from the bitter winds during spells of cold weather, and in milder times they were convenient places from which to look out for prey or hide from marauding beasts.

The most favoured caves were those with fairly narrow entrances. Heaps of dried fungus were kindled inside to provide light and warmth, to roast meat or to repel unwelcome carnivores. Those who occupied the caves would establish their chief living areas inside them, near the entrances. People left the caves to pursue the mammoths, bison and woolly rhinoceroses which migrated across the tundra landscape of southern Britain.

However, in spite of the popularity of caves as places of human habitation, some hunters preferred to build huts or tents with animal-bone frames and skin covers.

A young hunter is buried in South Wales with unusual ritual

The chance discovery of a skeleton in a cave at Paviland, in West Glamorgan, gives a fascinating insight into some of the burial rites that were practised around 24,000BC. The cave was located 9 metres up a sheer cliff face, the entrance marked by an elephant's skull staring out from the cave mouth. Behind it, in the cave's dark recesses, lay the body of a young man, probably put there by his fellow-hunters.

The body, which was covered in red ochre, lay in a simple face-upwards attitude on the west side of the cave. The ochre may have been used to soften the skins he wore, but the amount used suggested that it was deliberately applied to his body and may have had some symbolic significance for his people.

The young man wore ivory bracelets, and cylindrical ivory rods were laid on his chest. A necklace made from the teeth of wolves and reindeer adorned his neck. Ochre had also been mixed with a handful of small shells placed in a pocket against his right thigh, and his body was covered with earth.

Burials like this one at Paviland evidently did not happen very often, and the fact that the man was singled out for such remarkable treatment implies that he was highly regarded by those people who laid him to rest. Elaborate burials with ochre and shell ornaments were not confined to Britain, however. Similar rituals were carried out in the south-west of France and at Grimaldi in north-western Italy.

An artist's impression of how a young hunter was honoured at Paviland.

Hunters head south as ice age worsens

By around 16,000BC the British Isles were little more than a frozen waste, and few humans could exist in the constant sub-zero temperatures. For about 2,000 years the ice had covered everywhere north of a line drawn between the Severn and the Wash, and the small, roaming bands of hunters in the sub-Arctic south, which were all that remained of the human population, had long since left. They had headed across the landbridge to the near continent and turned south in search of a more hospitable climate.

Few animals remained in the tundra landscape of the ice-free south, with its long, harsh winters. Many indigenous smaller animals had left, so that there would have been little to hunt even if the humans had stayed. It was mainly the hardy larger mammals such as reindeer which stayed to survive on the few plants that could withstand the freezing temperatures.

Settlers move north as ice age comes to an end

Rising waters spur people into migration

The last ice age before modern times finally came to an end between 11,000BC and 8000BC. As the great ice sheets melted and sea levels rose, the landbridge between Britain and the rest of Europe began once more to shrink. Eventually it would be totally submerged, creating more or less the familiar shape of the British Isles and cutting families off both from their kin and from the latest technological ideas in north-west Europe.

But the retreating ice also opened up new regions for settlers. This was just as well, for many settlements faced submersion in the thaw. Intrepid pioneers established camps at Kirkhead Cave and Lindale Low Cave, near Morecambe Bay in north-western England, in around 10,000BC, when the great valleys and peaks of the Lake District were still covered with ice. As the ice receded, more people began to explore further north, and by 7000BC the first settlers had moved into southern Scotland and the lower Bann valley and Lough Neagh areas of Northern Ireland.

As they migrated along the coast and inland up the great estuaries and river valleys, people would have discovered an abundance of game and fish to keep them sustained during their trek.

Victoria Cave above Settle in North Yorkshire, whose occupants were forced to decamp by the threat of rising meltwaters during the post-glacial thaw.

Tools and weapons are more refined

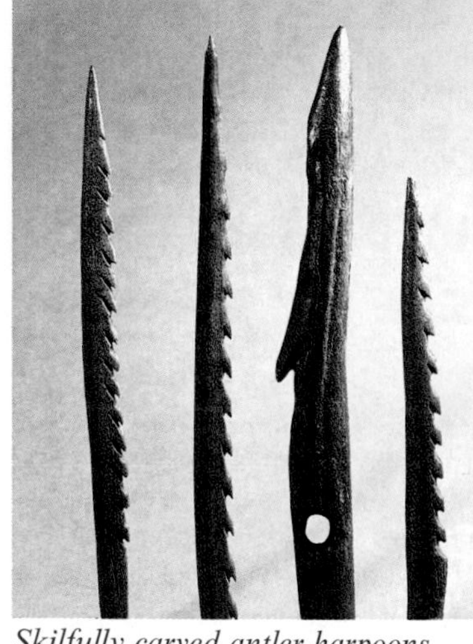

Skilfully carved antler harpoons.

The tools of around 11,000BC were being made with more refinement than ever before. All over southern Britain people made specialized implements with greater skill from longer and thinner pieces of flint. These were mass-produced with much less waste, allowing hunters to head into areas where replacement flint was otherwise scarce.

The human toolkit was also being supplemented by a greater use of bone and antler. Barbed points, which were probably used as harpoons, were an important recent development, and bone was also used for making awls and needles.

Wandering hunters show signs of more sophisticated culture

A group of hunters living in Somerset in around 11,000BC found it easier than most to keep track of time – all because of a hare's leg. For thousands of years people had probably planned their lives, especially hunting, by the phases of the moon. As an aid to working out when these changes were due, a hunter at Gough's Cave, near Cheddar, notched a lunar calendar into the shinbone of an Arctic hare.

Gough's Cave was used by small family groups during the hunting season, when red deer, antelope and horses were attracted to the nearby spring and waterhole. It may have had some special significance, because the skeletons of at least seven people – dismembered after death in what looks like a sophisticated funeral rite – have also been found in the cave. Perhaps the person who made the calendar was a special figure involved in special rituals. Whoever did it was a remarkably accurate observer, cutting notches into the hare bone in monthly sets of 28 or 29 – the average lunar month lasts 29½ days.

Cresswell Crags in Derbyshire provide further proof of how sophisticated the first post-glacial Britons were. A local hunter of around 8000BC found time to make a very fine engraving of a horse's head on a piece of animal bone. It represents the forequarters, neck and head of a horse in profile, facing right. The piece, its quality comparable to that of the wonderful contemporary carvings and paintings of south-western France, is remarkable in that it attempts a realistic representation of an animal. Other works of art produced at around the same time tended to be more enigmatic, like the chevron designs on a horse's jawbone found in Kendrick's Cave near Llandudno, in Gwynedd, which appears to be an abstract decoration.

Many of the objects which people decorated also served as tools or other implements. Some were no more than notched tallies, perhaps of days or kills, while others may have been decorated either simply for pleasure or for complex ritual or spiritual reasons.

The bone lunar calendar discovered at Gough's Cave, near Cheddar.

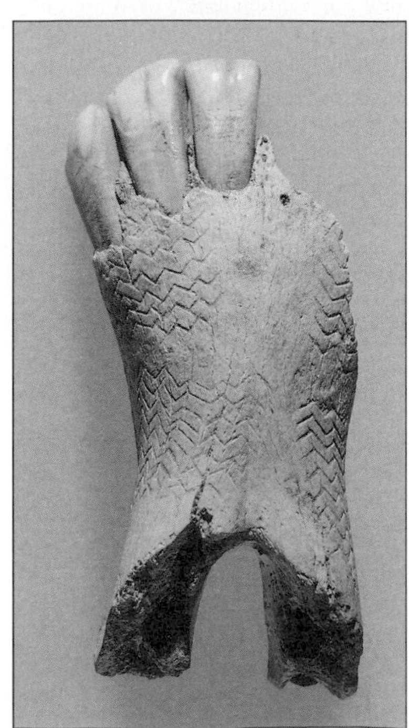

Chevron design on a horse's jawbone from Kendrick's Cave, Gwynedd.

Skin, bone and sinew keep out the cold and wet

The people living and hunting in the cold northern winters in the period around 8000BC would have worn fur and leather. The ability to sew, which had been practised by humans for more than 23,000 years, was an essential skill for making the clothes to keep out the chill winds blowing off the retreating glaciers.

The raw material – literally – for the post-glacial tailor was skin, bone and sinew – just about every bit of an animal that was not eaten. Once they had been removed from the carcass and scraped clean of remaining flesh, fur and skin went to form the greater part of people's clothing, including tunics (which may also have had hoods) and trousers for the men, and apron-like skirts for the women. Hareskin proved to be an especially convenient material from which to make footwear.

Needles and thread, the basic equipment needed for tailoring, were made respectively from larger animal bones, which were polished down and then fashioned so that they had a point at one end and a hole at the other, and tough, stringy animal sinews. It is possible that needles developed as a by-product of the bone harpoons and spearheads which were widely used in hunting.

To facilitate the task of stitching together the different parts of a garment, the tailor used a pointed flint or bone as an awl to pierce the fur and leather, allowing the needle to pass through easily. Those people who liked their clothes to have a more distinctive look could commission a plain fur or leather tunic to be embellished with shells across the chest or shoulders.

The Neanderthal predecessors of the people who wore such personalized attire generally went around in skin tunics and fur mantles. Humans even earlier had managed with simple unstitched skin wraps, aprons and capes to keep the harsh wintry weather at bay.

Warm weather alters hunting tactics

The increasingly warmer climate as the glaciation ended made the movements of game more and more unpredictable, and humans had to face up to changes in their hunting techniques. Previously, deer and aurochs – giant bison – had used the same migration routes in both spring and autumn, and hunters had simply lain in wait.

One particularly rich hunting ground proved to be the narrow Goring Gap, part of the Thames valley near Reading in Berkshire, through which herds of reindeer passed when the ice began to melt. Another was Cheddar Gorge in Somerset, where seasoned hunters, who had brought their flint from as far away as Pewsey in Wiltshire, would lie in wait in the surrounding caves for passing prey.

However, milder winters and more abundant vegetation meant that animals took to foraging over wider areas, making their routes harder to predict. Hunters could not take the risk of broken weapons when they had to pursue game for some distance, and so they developed spears with barbed flint heads with which to kill more surely. They also carried tools for emergency repairs to their equipment.

The red deer: pursued by hunters.

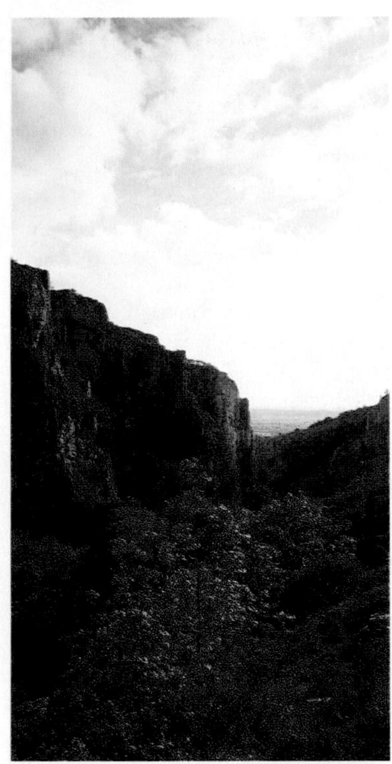

Cheddar Gorge: hunting grounds.

Bow and arrow is latest lethal weapon in the hunter's armoury

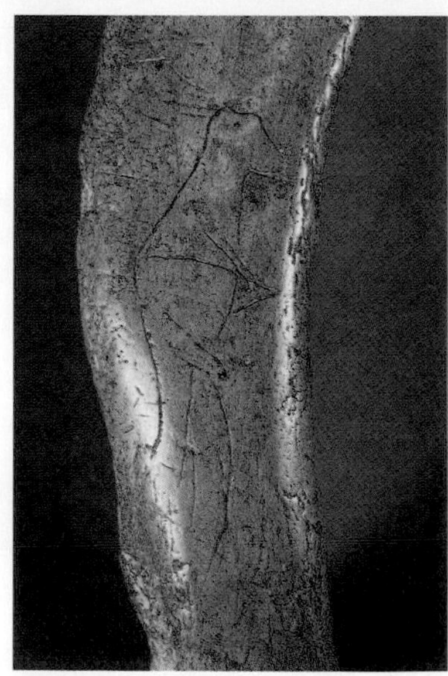

A carving of a human on a bone.

A hunter wearing deer antlers as he stalks his prey: an artist's impression.

In about 7000BC hunters at Star Carr camp, near Pickering in North Yorkshire, were using a new weapon that had proved to be far more adaptable than the spear: the bow and arrow. A flexible rod made of wood, with a tight line attached to the ends, was used to propel an arrow – in effect a stick with a small, sharpened piece of flint attached to the end. When used by a skilful hunter the weapon was deadly accurate, with the power to penetrate even the thick hide of a large animal, such as a horse or deer.

The bow and arrow is thought to have been developed by hunters seeking an effective way of attacking their prey in wooded areas, where the presence of trees made it difficult to use spears. Among other early users of the bow and arrow were hunters who used an important camp on Hampstead Heath, in London, as a base for expeditions into the surrounding countryside.

Star Carr appears to have been a summer hunting camp. The people there also developed fertility rituals involving the use of deer antlers.

The Early Island Peoples

6500-70BC

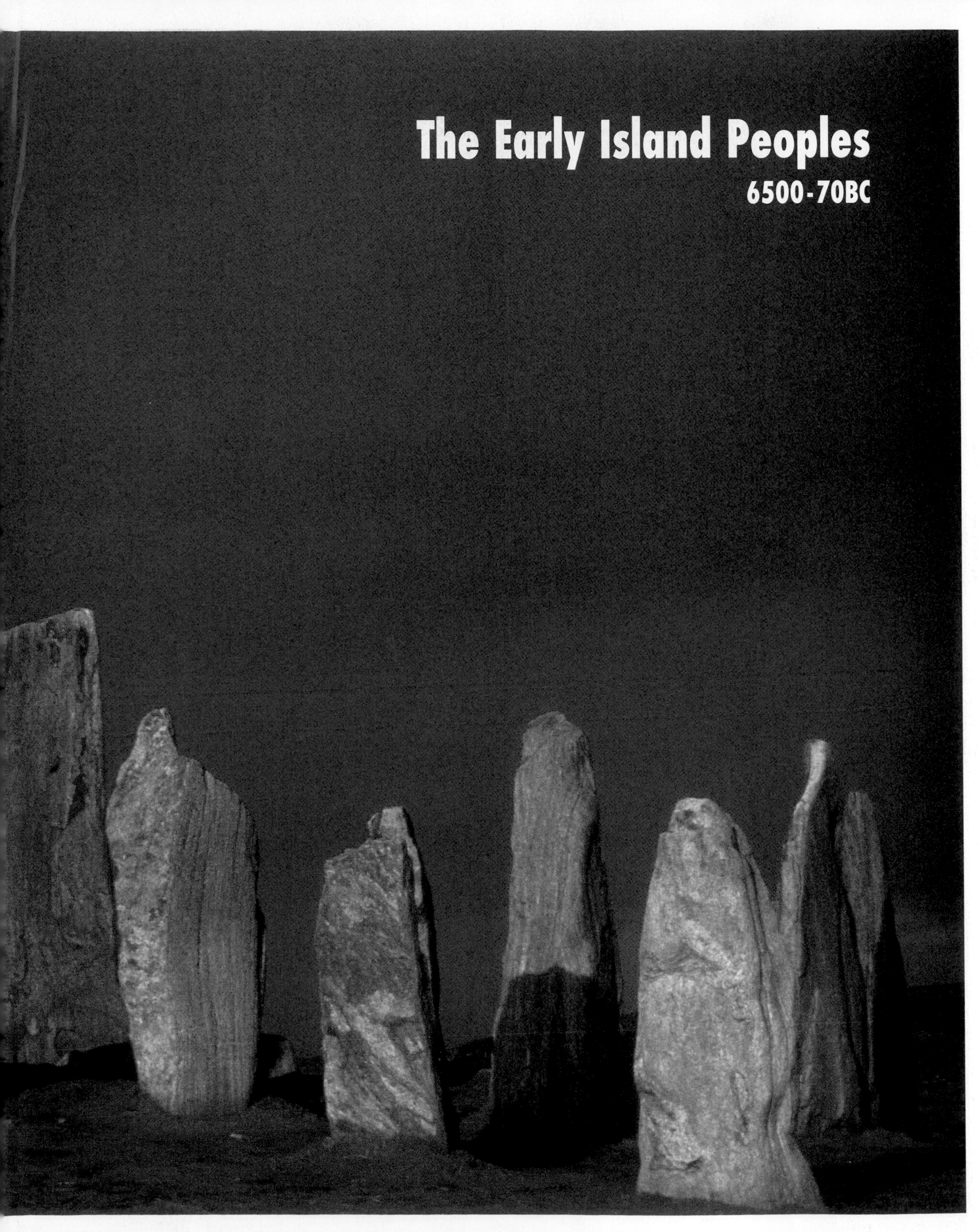

6500 - 4400BC

British Isles, c.6500BC. A nomadic life of hunting and gathering persists in the islands and in much of the European continent; by contrast, some human groups in south-eastern Europe have begun to clear the forests in order to grow plants and herd cattle, establishing a more settled lifestyle.→

Co Antrim, c.6100BC. Human groups who have appeared at Newferry are using a new type of tool, the polished stone axe; they depend for food on catching eel and salmon.

Essex, c.6000BC. Hunting communities on the Essex coast build timber platforms which help them to hunt the seals living in the Blackwater estuary.

North-western Europe, c.6000BC. The ritual burial of the dead is becoming more important as the building of burial chambers increases. In Britain, however, the dead are still simply placed in the ground (→ c.4400BC).

Dorset, c.6000BC. Settlers start to excavate chert stone, which is local to Dorset, for toolmaking. The tools are used mainly for hunting purposes, and they spread widely across the country as the hunters move around (→ c.4400BC).

Britain, c.5800BC. As people become more settled, definite tribal identities are emerging within the different regions across the country; groups begin to adapt to their own environments, making the best use of what is available and developing their own tools and communities.

Fife, c.5500BC. Settlers living on the Scottish coast are successfully supplementing their diet with fish, caught from small vessels (→ c.4300).

Surrey, c.5500BC. New building techniques are evident as people become more settled; skin tents are being erected on open sites, with sunken floors to provide a more substantial form of shelter.

Co Sligo, c.4400BC. A huge burial ground, containing more than a hundred tombs, has been created at Carrowmore.→

West Sussex, c.4400BC. Flint for toolmaking is excavated on a large scale at Church Hill, Findon (→ c.4300BC).

Wiltshire, c.4400BC. Many people have been taking part in ritual feasting and sacrificial burying on a hillside above the river Avon (→ c.4100BC).

Sea rise creates islands

British Isles, c.6500BC

Britain is now an island. The marshy land which for so long has formed a bridge from south-eastern England to the rest of Europe has finally been swamped by the sea, which has been swollen steadily by the melted waters of the retreating ice sheets.

Indeed, as the ice sheets and glaciers have melted, the British Isles as a whole have been taking on a new shape, with many coastal areas flooded. Nomadic hunters have been deprived of many of their most fertile hunting grounds, such as now-submerged areas of Lincolnshire and Yorkshire.

Britain and Ireland – whose former land-link with Scotland has also been severed since the last ice age – are now likely to develop culturally in ways distinct from those of their European neighbours. But of more immediate concern will be the need to secure new sources of food. One answer will be to exploit inland resources more effectively; another will be to look for more food from coastal areas and the sea. Seafaring itself is increasing – humans returning to Ireland in recent centuries may well have arrived by sea – and this may yet provide Britain with a lifeline to mainland Europe to replace the land-link lost under the waves.

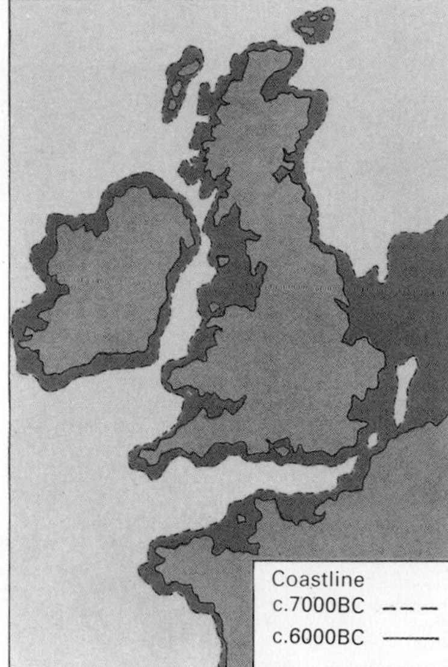

A hypothetical reconstruction of the coastlines of Britain and Ireland.

Forests burnt down to encourage game

Pennines, c.6500BC

People living in the Pennines have worked out two ways of easing the endless task of obtaining food: to burn down part of the forest, and to give wild animals a chance to breed. They have noticed, in addition, that cereals and berries grow more plentifully in open countryside cleared of dense woodland, and that the juicy green plants which grow after a forest fire lure deer and wild cattle for the hunters. Burning must happen every few years if the new clearings are to be maintained, but much of the high moorland is already open.

Yet the success of the hunters can pose problems. Some people have realized the serious consequences of allowing wild beasts to be killed faster than they can breed; as a result they are starting to conserve them to keep up numbers. This means that communities must cooperate if the novel idea of deciding who should look after which wild herd is not to cause serious disagreements (→ c.4500BC).

Hunter-gatherers spread over a wide area

Mount Sandel on the river Bann: a favoured location for campsites.

British Isles, c.6500BC

Groups of hunters and gatherers now occupy the whole of the British Isles. There has been intermittent human occupation of the islands over hundreds of thousands of years, but the latest inhabitants arrived in southern Britain from continental Europe only as the ice began to retreat northwards some 5,000 years ago. During the past millennium humans have explored further afield, moving into Scotland and Ireland. Favoured sites for camps in the north-east of Ireland have included the lower Bann valley and the Lough Neagh area. Subsistence here depends on fishing, hunting small game and collecting nuts and seeds (→ c.4400BC).

Seafood is on the menu – but no elk

Devon, c.5700BC

Britain's inhabitants are eating a varied diet – particularly if their campsites are close to the sea. Judging by the refuse dumped on a beach at Westward Ho! in north Devon, food includes crab, limpet, periwinkle, whelk, oyster and lobster, as well as fish such as wrasse, saithe and ling which are caught with net and spear in shallow waters. People are hunting inland as well, for red deer and wild pig, found on the uplands of Exmoor.

There are similar dumps at Portland in Dorset, on Caldey Island off South Wales, and, in great numbers, on Oronsay in the Hebrides. The ready availability of these foods explains why so many people are moving to seaside locations.

In fact, the range of food has changed little since Britain became cut off from the continent as the last ice sheets melted. There is one casualty, though: elk has vanished from the diet (→ c.5500BC).

Farming alters pattern of human life

Britain, c.4400BC
Hunting, gathering and foraging are no longer the only means of subsistence for people living in the British Isles. Slowly but surely, in the woodland clearings, river valleys and coastal plains of Britain, more and more land is being devoted to farming and herding; agriculture is here to stay.

The idea of deliberately growing plants and keeping livestock for food has come to Britain from north-eastern continental Europe. Where these practices have been adopted, there seems to be a link between production and prestige. Eating, meanwhile, has developed into more of a communal and ceremonial occasion.

So far the changes are modest enough. Cereals such as emmer wheat and barley, and pulses such as peas and beans, are being grown in small gardens rather than in any large-scale way in fields. Neither cereals nor pulses yet contribute more to the average diet than the fruits of wild plants – hazelnuts or crabapples, for instance – simply gathered from the ground. But the attraction of creating a permanent, nearby source of staple food is clear, and it could make a big impact on Britain's physical and social landscape.

Axes and hammers are being put to new uses in agricultural settlements.

So, too, could the domestication of livestock. Cattle are the most prized beasts, although not solely for food: dead cattle are used for ceremonial purposes, live cattle as a means of payment between communities. Although hard to digest as a drink, cows' milk can be used for making cheese or yoghurt.

There are signs that farming is giving people new roles. Men now spend their time tending the herds rather than hunting; women generally look after the small patches of land where cereals and plants are grown, while continuing to collect the wild foods which remain crucial to the diet (→ c.4100BC).

Tombs of stone constructed as a mark of respect to the dead

British Isles, c.4400BC
The business of dying has gained new life as continental ideas are taken up in Britain and Ireland. Until recently burial was a fairly straightforward business, with bodies simply being covered in earth. Now, though, dying has become a more sophisticated matter altogether, and tombs are being built to hold several bodies. This is because the dead are no longer just corpses but revered ancestors and the most senior people – albeit dead – in society.

Death has thus become an important communal activity. Bodies are "stored" together in tombs and brought out to "witness" ceremonial occasions before being laid to rest. Then the tombs are sealed and buried under earth.

There are two main sorts of tomb: the chambered tomb, such as that at Wayland's Smithy in Berkshire, which is usually a rectangular box made of rock slabs 2 or 3 metres long and about a metre high, and a similar structure made of wood where stone is scarce, such as at Fussell's Lodge, in Wiltshire. Both types are buried within a long mound known as a "barrow". A more settled lifestyle has encouraged the building of timber houses for single families.

An imposing home for the dead: a burial chamber at Pentre Ifan, in Dyfed.

Farmers in the north-west of Ireland have created what is believed to be the biggest burial ground in Europe. The cemetery at Carrowmore, in Co Sligo, contains over a hundred tombs, mainly chambers built of stone. Here the bodies are usually burnt and the ashes buried in the stone chambers, along with tools and other possessions. Each tomb is marked by a large stone or dolmen, and many are built to face the rising sun (→ c.4200BC).

Most of landscape dominated by rich cover of woodland

British Isles, c.4500BC
Two thousand years of relatively stable climate have resulted in the British Isles being covered by woodland. Only the highest mountains, the extreme north and coastal dunes and marshes lack the rich and varied range of trees which began to recolonize the land after the last ice age. Settlements based on clearings in the woodland have made little overall impact: the humans are too few, their tools too puny and the trees too difficult to burn.

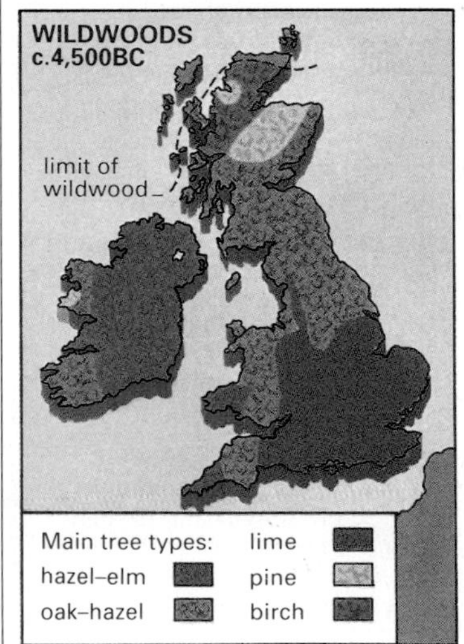

Rising temperatures as the ice age ended enabled trees to grow in Britain and Ireland once more. The first to return were those which could prosper in colder climates, such as birch, aspen and sallow. Then, over a period of several thousand years, came trees which needed a warmer climate – pine, hazel, alder and oak were among the first of these; hornbeam and maple came later. Different species of trees have come to dominate different areas [*see map*] in naturally regenerating "wildwoods". Even areas as high as the Pennines and most of the Lake District fells have become covered by trees. Human settlements use woods for hunting and gathering; any moves to cultivate land would entail a larger-scale threat to the wildwoods (→ c.4100BC).

4400 - 3400BC

Cornwall, c.4300BC. Hard rock found in the region of the Lizard peninsula is being transformed into stone axes, which are put to use primarily as tools but also have a value as an exchange for cattle and other goods (→ c.4000BC).

Surrey, c.4100BC. Settlers at Runnymede are making and using clay pots as storage and cooking vessels (→ c.3000BC).

British Isles, c.4100BC. Human death and burial have acquired symbolic significance in many places, and burial grounds are being lavishly marked by the erection of henges, large circular monuments of stones or wood which are surrounded by earth banks (→ c.3600BC).

Dorset, c.4100BC. A great rectangular monument, or cursus, has been created by enclosing earlier monuments within one huge compound.→

Ireland, c.4000BC. Solitary burials with a pot or bowl as an offering are taking place in the east of the island.

Britain, c.4000BC. Farmers are clearing large areas of forest, by either using handaxes or burning or simply killing the trees by stripping away the bark, for crop cultivation and cattle raising (→ c.2100BC).

England, c.4000BC. New farming practices, including the use of ploughs and draught animals, reach southern England from Europe. Prior to this, crops were cultivated with digging sticks (→ c.3700BC).

Europe, c.4000BC. Settlers have mastered a new technique, that of fashioning tools from metal. Stone is still the most popular material in the British Isles.→

Powys, c.3900BC. Large round burial chambers are erected in place of long barrows (roughly rectangular mounds covered with earth). Most contain underground inner chambers, reached by a long passage. The body is surrounded by polished tools and bowls in preparation for burial (→ c.3700BC).

Co Meath, c.3700BC. The inhabitants of Newgrange habitually gather in a passage-tomb to watch the sun rise at the winter solstice (→ c.3600BC).

Dorset, c.3500BC. People are carving cosmological symbols on the walls of a ditch surrounding an enclosure as part of a fertility ritual linking death and rebirth. Similar symbols are found in Ireland.

Marsh roads bring people closer together

Somerset Levels, c.4300BC
People in Somerset have devised a way to keep their feet dry when crossing the marshes. They now build wooden causeways, up to 10 km (6 miles) long, to connect their isolated settlements.

High ground near the rivers is ideal for settlements and agriculture, but communications across the swamps have always been both difficult and dangerous. The new causeways permit people to move around the marshes easily, and there has been a great increase in mobility from one settlement to another. The roads across the wetlands have also boosted trade in the region, since axe-traders from the north and flint-traders from the east can now reach some of the remotest Somerset settlements.

The causeways are built of planks and upright poles. For some time, people have been managing the woods and coppices to grow long, straight, regularly sized ash or oak, which are needed for the poles used in causeways and other building operations. The posts are driven through the marsh into the underlying clay, to serve as guides for the upper part of the causeway. The planks which form the surface are held in place by wooden pegs driven in crossways.

A model of a wooden causeway.

Stews added to the diet as new fashion for pots is adopted

British Isles, c.4300BC
Stews and casseroles are introducing a new variety into the diet of the inhabitants of the British Isles, as fresh ideas about food and its preparation are absorbed from continental Europe. For the first time people in Britain and Ireland are using clay pots in both cooking and eating food, and as a consequence are beginning to adopt a more experimental approach to what they consume.

In Europe these round-bottomed capacious pots have been in use for some time. Often as large as 30 cm across, and between 15 and 30 cm in height, they are built up slowly from long coils of clay, which are wound one on top of another to form the shape of the pot and then worked together with the hands to a smooth surface. The containers are then fired on a simple clay clamp over flames (→ c.4100BC).

Corpses picked clean as death rituals grow more sophisticated

The ritual centre at Windmill Hill.

An artist's impression of the long barrow at Hazelton, in Gloucestershire.

Southern England, c.4200BC
Rituals linked with death, when people join their revered ancestors, are becoming more intricate. At Hambledon Hill in Dorset, for example, where a big regional cult centre has developed, corpses are picked clean of flesh by birds of prey before burial. The Hambledon centre covers 8 hectares (20 acres) and, like similar sites at nearby Windmill Hill and elsewhere in southern England, has an inner area surrounded by several rings with deep ditches between them. Human heads are put into the ditches, along with the occasional whole corpse, and exposed to the birds. The dead are thought to exert power beyond the grave, and "shamans" – people purporting to intercede between the living and the dead – are becoming influential.

At Hazelton in Gloucestershire, where a barrow has been in use for centuries, the bodies of the prominent dead are laid in the entrances of huge communal tombs, and those left behind gather to light fires and feast on roast pig. Corpses are left to decompose until only their bones remain, when they are carried into the tombs' inner chambers.

After death, the progression from dead relative to the much more significant status of ancestor corresponds with the change from corpse to skeleton. This process is complete when the most powerfully symbolic part of the skeleton – the skull – joins others along one wall of an inner chamber (→ c.4000BC).

Cattle bosses win power

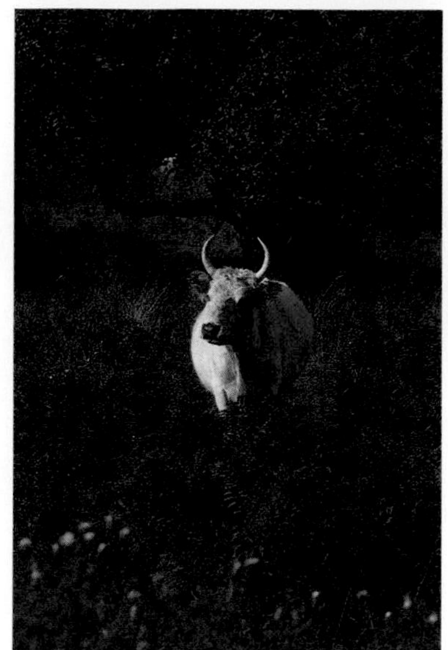
Cattle: key to wealth and prestige.

Southern England, c.4100BC
As more and more of the ancient forest is cleared to make way for pasture and crop-growing, and farming becomes established as the key to prosperity and prestige, certain powerful cattle-herders have embarked on a policy of expansion and control over neighbouring groups, or tribes. In one part of Dorset the new cattle bosses have seized a swathe of land containing many tribes' tombs and have built vast earthworks and ditches around them to form a huge rectangular compound, or cursus, 10 km (6 miles) long. The cursus is aligned with the sun's course on midsummer's day, and is believed to have important ritual significance.

Dorset's Hambledon Hill and other such ringed enclosures have also become targets for the ambitious herders, who are apparently seeking to exploit the symbolic power of these spiritual and trading centres and turn them into bases for their own control of the surrounding areas.

It seems that these aggressive new activities are largely carried out by the male members of the tribe, who generally run the pastures and roam far and wide with their herds. This reflects a change of emphasis in the performance of the everyday tasks required for survival. The former equality of status between the sexes has been shifting ever since men turned their attention from hunting to herding, and women began to spend more time on small-scale cultivation rather than gathering (→c.4000BC).

Axemakers risk their lives to get stone

The Pike of Stickle summit shows the indentations created by axemakers.

Cumbria, c.4000BC
Intrepid axemakers are climbing some of the highest, most hazardous crags in the English Lake District in order to quarry stone for the blades of their axes. A favoured source of stone is the Pike of Stickle summit at the head of the Langdale valley. Here fire is used to crack the mountain-peak rock, which is made up of compressed volcanic ash and is extremely hard. Axes are vital tools for people trying to clear dense virgin forest to create land for fields and pasture. They are used in tasks involving woodworking, such as the building of houses or fences.

Axes are also important for ceremonial purposes, with finely chiselled examples being used as offerings or smashed as part of burial rituals. It is for these special axes that the axemakers risk their lives, for the stones gathered from the highest places are believed to have mystical qualities (→c.2700BC).

Tomb-building is a fine art in Fenland

Cambridgeshire, c.4000BC
The increasing reverence accorded to ancestors can be seen in the effort put into the construction of their resting-places – as exemplified at a cemetery on the edge of the Fens. The tombs at Haddenham in Cambridgeshire consist of foyers and burial chambers in which the dead are laid with various possessions. The completed structures are then covered with earth.

The chambered tombs at Haddenham resemble those seen elsewhere, except that they are of wood rather than stone – virtually unobtainable in this part of the country. Great skill is needed to fashion oak slabs up to 4.8 metres long, 1.2 metres wide and 10 cm thick. These form the bodies of the tombs, which often have ornate façades and projecting arms of oak leading to the entrances (→c.3900BC).

For making tools or weapons, flint is the most flexible material

British Isles, c.4000BC
The most prized skill for the people of Britain and Ireland is the one on which all other skills depend: how to make tools and weapons. Wood, bone and antler are used for some implements, but for jobs where a tool or weapon needs to be made of harder stuff – such as stabbing, striking, scraping and slicing – it has to be stone or flint. Suitable rock for stone axes is found in the north and west of Britain, but flint occurs in quantity only in the chalk regions of the south and east, where extensive mining is now under way.

Flint can be fashioned into utensils such as arrowheads, axes and sickles, and miners will dig many metres into the ground to find the best-quality material.

The basic technique for turning a flint lump into a thin, delicate (and lethal) arrowhead is knapping: if it is hit, say with another piece of flint or an antler used as a hammer, chips flake off. Experts know at just what angle and with what pressure to knap flint to remove the right amount and are making things with ever more precision and delicacy (→c.2700BC).

A flint sickle used by farmers.

A barbed flint arrowhead.

Pioneer farms are established in the northern regions

Northern Britain, c.4000BC
As pioneer farming spreads throughout Britain, scattered permanent settlements are being established in northern England and Scotland as well as in more southerly areas. Even places as far north as the Orkney and Shetland Islands, which have so far been only sporadically visited, are now being colonized.

Like their counterparts further south, these small northern communities have begun to domesticate plants and animals such as sheep and cattle. They make pottery and polished stone axes, and they build monuments to honour their dead. However, as elsewhere in the country, the new farmers continue to hunt, gather and forage for food in the traditional way. The rich coastal fringe resources in the far north and west, for example, provide a thriving existence for such groups.

The inhabitants of the settled northern communities have developed certain distinct traits. They attach great importance to portable artefacts as symbols of alliance and affiliation, and they place less value than southerners on monuments as sites for communal gathering. Some burn their dead in great pyres beneath earthen mounds fed by flues; others bury prominent individuals alone under small round mounds. At Rudston, in Humberside, the locals have set up a huge standing stone at a point where four processional ways meet, forming a centre for pilgrimage.

Another place of religious pilgrimage has developed in Wales, on the island of Anglesey, where large standing stones dominate the landscape. A power struggle is believed to be in progress here between local families, who boast of their contacts with influential dynasties in Brittany or Ireland which bring them exotic stone axes and secret knowledge which they use in monument building.

Vast tomb complex built

The passage-tomb at Newgrange presents an impressive aspect to onlookers.

Boyne Valley, Co Meath, c.4000BC
A tribe living in the valley of the river Boyne has built three colossal tombs as the last resting-place for its honoured dead. Nearby – all within three miles – stand forty other monuments in what is one of the largest concentrations of funerary buildings in Ireland, a special landscape which symbolises the power of those who control it.

The tombs, at Knowth, Dowth and Newgrange, are used for elaborate rituals by those who built them, as well as for burying the dead. The bones of the tribe's ancestors lie in recesses off the tomb-chambers, and homage is paid to them on special occasions, particularly during both the solstices and the equinoxes.

The tombs have been built with both great artistic and great architectural skill. At Newgrange, the most striking feature is an opening over the doorway; it is capped by an elaborately carved stone, and every year, at the winter solstice, the stone can be removed to allow the rays of the rising sun to strike through the opening and down the passage beyond to light up the burial chamber 19 metres (21 yards) distant.

There are two chambers in the tomb at Knowth, orientated towards the spring and autumn equinoxes, 34 and 40 metres long respectively. Two-thirds of the way down the passages, the ceiling rises before opening into the vast space of the tomb-chamber. The tomb at Dowth is similar in construction.

The tomb chambers and the passages leading to them are built of stone, much of it finely carved. Over these the builders piled huge earth mounds, and they set up more carved stones in front to form a kerb (→ c.3700BC).

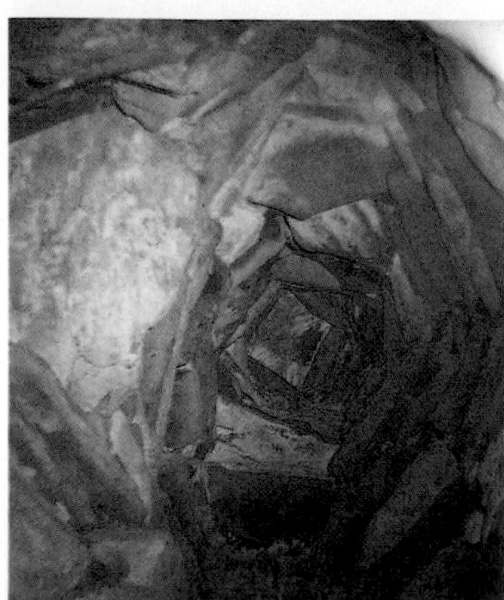

Newgrange: the main chamber ceiling (l) and the carved passage walls.

Tribes now led by warrior-chieftains

Southern England, c.4000BC
The rivalry of wealthy cattle magnates has come to a head in the emergence of a new class of warrior-chieftains. These tribal leaders have taken over as their headquarters old ringed enclosures such as Hambledon Hill in Dorset – attractive not only on account of their powerful spiritual and symbolical value but also because their structure of rings and ditches makes them easily defendable. Crickley Hill in Gloucestershire has been elaborately fortified by the construction of stone walls, earthworks, ditches and a palisade.

Communal burials are giving way to individual ones, with the new leaders getting the pick of the old tombs. The dead and their graves are still revered, but now they contain not several tribal ancestors but one – the chief of the tribe. Such leaders are buried with a number of the fine possessions, such as polished flint knives and jet belt-sliders, which in life had been signs of their power (→ c.3900BC).

Warlords linked to symbols of disorder

Etton, Cambridgeshire, c.4000BC
Ritual burials representing death as a descent into chaos have taken place at a settlement at Etton, near Peterborough. Some burials consist of a human head, a cremated body, broken pots arranged in a pattern, an upturned wooden bowl, cattle bones and the antlers of a deer. Others have a dog's head set upside down with broken deer antlers or crushed stone axes.

In the middle of the burial site, which is made up of linked rings and ditches around a central area, is an upturned grinding stone with a pestle trapped beneath, buried in a pit. The symbolic representation of an overturning and breaking-up of the ordered world may be linked to the current rise of a new class of aggressive warrior chiefs.

The Etton settlement seems to be divided, with one half for the living and the other for the dead. Some dwellings are apparently occupied only during the summer, possibly for crop cultivation (→ c.3900BC).

Ferocious tribal rivalry threatens might of chieftains as settlements are attacked

Southern England, c.3900BC
The prospect of rich pickings from cattle-owning warlords has sparked ferocious tribal warfare that threatens to topple them from power. Bands of raiding warriors are now mounting well-organized attacks on rich settlements such as Crickley Hill in Gloucestershire, looking for plunder and, especially, for cattle which can easily be driven away. It appears that the conspicuous wealth of such settlements has aroused resentment in other groups; in establishing their pre-eminent social position the cattle bosses seem to have overstepped the mark.

The attacking warriors are armed with spears, bows and arrows and axes. Fire is also a weapon, with the attackers trying to burn down defensive palisades while deluging the defenders with flint-headed arrows. The defenders reply with their own lethal rain of arrows, and have organised their defences so that the attackers are drawn into ambushes where they can be struck down from behind cover.

Although the defenders sometimes manage to bury their fallen comrades in hastily dug graves, they are often forced to leave the dead lying in ditches. At Hambledon Hill in Dorset, the scene of fierce fighting, one terrified woman has been found struck down with a baby lying beneath her.

When the attackers succeed in making a breakthrough, the fighting becomes hand-to-hand, raging through the huts within the defences. In victory, the attackers butcher all the men and seize the women and cattle. Occasionally the victors will move in and take over a captured settlement; usually, they burn it to the ground.

Hambledon Hill, Dorset: the scene of fierce fighting between rival warlords.

Farmers flourish in the Irish countryside

Ireland, c.3700BC
The farming revolution is now well under way in Ireland, and farmers and herders have developed an extensive system of fields. The development of the system began a couple of centuries ago when tracts of the vast forests which cover the island were cleared. Stones were gathered to build walls dividing the cleared areas into irregular enclosures. Some large fields, covering up to 6 hectares (15 acres), are used to raise livestock, while grain for bread and winter fodder for the animals is grown in smaller fields. The farmers' diet is augmented by coastal fishing.

The farming communities live in large round thatched huts within the field walls. The roofs are raised on pine posts, and openings over the middles of the huts allow smoke from central hearths to escape. The farmers have built granaries for storing and grinding grain. They work with tools of stone, bone and antlers (→c.2400BC).

Barrows sealed as fear of death grows

These rocks bar the way: West Kennet long barrow at Avebury, in Wiltshire.

Western Britain, c.3600BC
A growing fear of death could be behind the closure of tombs which have been communal burial places for centuries. Passages and tomb-chambers of long barrows and stone tombs are being filled in and entrances are being blocked off.

The tombs of the Kennet valley in Wiltshire, along with those in other places such as the Black Mountains in Wales, have been important ritual centres for many years, used by the whole community for ceremonies honouring their ancestors. It is possible that ancestors are now regarded as so remote that they can only be approached by an élite class of people, which may want to restrict access to the tombs in order to enhance its own powers. Or perhaps people have begun to look on death with more anxiety and are closing old tombs to help to shut out their worries about their own mortality (→c.3100BC).

New ritual centre constructed in Wiltshire

Stonehenge, Wiltshire, c.3600BC
A new-style place of worship has been built on Salisbury Plain to play its part in a new type of communal ritual. The large, circular monument is a henge, a development of enclosures ringed with ditches. It is 90 metres (100 yards) across and is made up of a bank and a ditch surrounding several rings of wooden posts which represent a wooden temple. The bank has one entrance, in the north-east, guarded by two large standing stones; three more stones have been erected just outside.

The middle of Stonehenge seems to be an area where people can take part in more structured and continuous worship. The observance of rituals has become more formal, possibly under the controlling eye of a new priestly caste. Life and the sun are now more revered than death, which is feared and shut out from the "temple" (→c.3000BC).

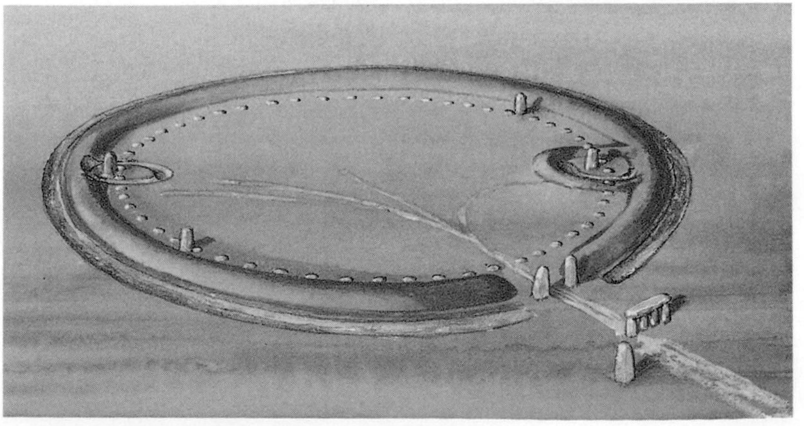

3400 - 2300BC

Orkney, c.3300BC. Two large henge monuments – the Stones of Stenness and the Ring of Brodgar – are constructed on the island of Mainland (→ c.3000BC).

North Yorkshire, c.3300BC. A community at Duggleby Howe has erected a huge monument on the chalk hills, at a point where four processional ways meet. The monument has become the central point for all ceremonial activity in the region (→ c.3100BC).

Shepperton, Surrey, c.3000BC. An enormous henge monument devoted to the worship of the sun has been constructed by local people.→

Europe, c.3000BC. People are only now coming to recognize the importance of the horse for its strength and meat. Wild horses are still being hunted, but a widespread domestication of the animal is under way.

Dorchester, Oxfordshire, c.2900BC. Small pits and circular burial mounds are being dug alongside existing monuments and are being used for the disposal of cremated bodies (→ c.2800BC).

Wiltshire, c.2800BC. The people in West Kennet are taking part in elaborate rituals involving the offering of human and animal bones, pots and weapons, all of which are then scattered in burial tombs to commemorate their ancestors (→ c.2200BC).

Cumbria, c.2700BC. Craftsmen have mastered a new technique for fixing highly polished stone axeheads onto wooden shafted handles (→ c.2600BC).

Wiltshire, c.2600BC. People whose pottery is marked with distinctive grooves have been filling pits with their pots and other material, including old animal bones and weapons, as part of a ritual offering to the gods.→

Southern England, c.2500BC. An attractive new type of pottery, believed to have originated in the Low Countries, is catching on. These articles are bell-shaped beakers or drinking cups; they have become widely prized possessions and are being used in burial rituals in many communities.→

Cambridgeshire, c.2400BC. Farmers living in the region of the Fens have constructed a complex system of paddocks which has made possible improvements to their system of rearing cattle (→ c.1550BC).

Orkney villagers live in peace and plenty

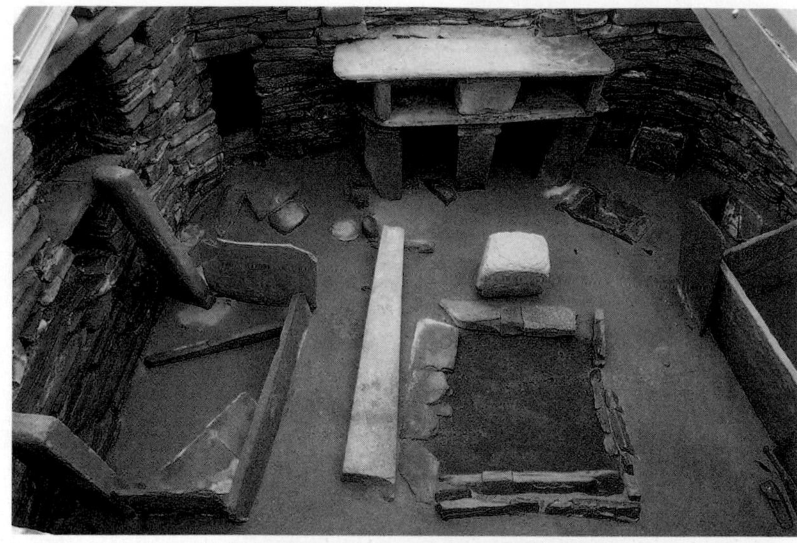

Remains of settlers' belongings at Skara Brae include stone beds and a hearth.

Orkney, c.3300BC

Permanent housing is catching on in the Orkneys, where small, self-contained villages are springing up. While people on the mainland continue to live a semi-nomadic sort of life, Orcadians are building houses in groups of six or more, partly underground and connected by passageways and communal drainage systems. Ten or 15 families live in each "village" and share the tasks of building and getting food. One such village is Skara Brae.

The houses are solidly built in stone, with their outer walls protected by rubbish and earth, and with thatched roofs made with beams cut from driftwood in the general shortage of trees. They are sunk into the ground for extra protection from the bitter Orkney wind; the builders enlarge natural hollows for this purpose. The houses all have one large principal room, and a series of cells leads off it. The cells are used for storage or as workshops, and one in each house is used as a lavatory. A drain from the lavatory leads out to a communal sewer running under the village's main passageway. Inside, the basic furniture is built of stones the same as those used for the walls. The houses have formal dressers opposite the main door, on which the residents can arrange their most valued possessions, and box beds. There is a stone hearth in the middle of the room, and there are clay-lined tanks for water.

The villages live side by side peacefully in a landscape which provides enough for a generous subsistence. There is rich pasture for cattle and sheep; Orcadians also grow wheat and barley and catch fish from the sea (→ c.1185BC).

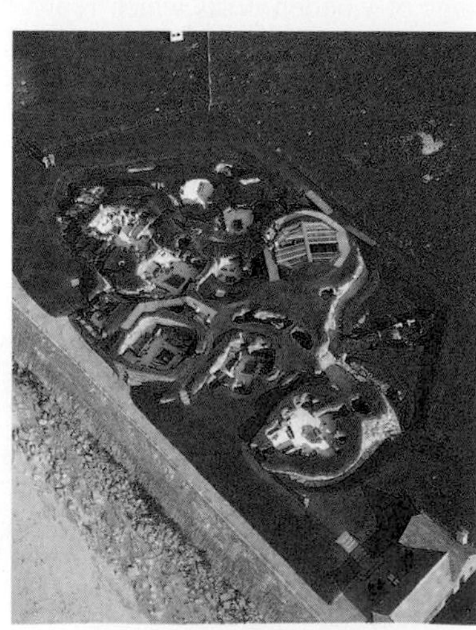

An aerial view of Skara Brae.

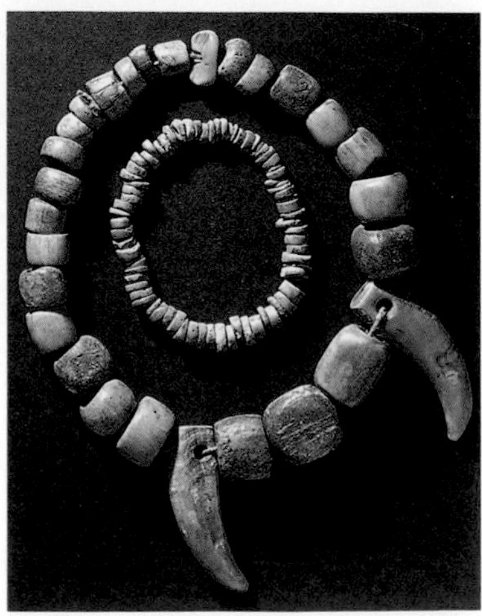

Pendants made at Skara Brae.

Rich Yorkshire folk go it alone in death

North Yorkshire, c.3100BC

Mass burials are being abandoned in favour of individual graves by well-to-do families at Duggleby Howe on the Yorkshire Wolds. The bodies are placed in shaft-graves at a depth of about 2.7 metres (nine feet), often with the heads pointing due east, and are accompanied by polished flint tools, arrowheads, boar tusks or sections of antler.

A high level of infant mortality is indicated by the numerous graves of children. The remains, placed in the graves in a crouched position, appear not to be accompanied by the valuable artefacts provided for adults (→ c.2900BC).

A burial hoard at Duggleby Howe.

Hebrideans hole up on artificial island

Western Isles, c.3300BC

A fortified island has been built in a loch at North Uist, in the Outer Hebrides. It is about 22 metres (25 yards) across, with substantial stone foundations, and contains dwellings of stone and wattle for some 20 people, probably an extended family.

The island, linked to the mainland by a wooden bridge, offers a refuge from marauding bands. It is stocked with food, tools, pottery and other household items, as well as sexual symbols, including pottery phalluses, which are used in fertility rites (→ c.700BC).

Fine artefacts are distributed through wide trade contacts

Jadeite axes from the Borders area: prized artefacts symbolizing power.

British Isles, c.3000BC
A variety of fine-quality artefacts are becoming widely distributed through trading contacts between some of the most powerful tribes in Britain and Ireland.

Highly polished jadeite axes, decorated maceheads, pendants and necklaces of bone beads are the treasured possessions of families in Orkney, other settlements in Scotland and parts of Ireland. Similar articles, possibly made by the same craftsmen, are owned by families as far apart as Yorkshire and East Anglia. As symbols of power these artefacts are used to seal marriages or alliances formed by privileged groups, and protect their status, although little is known of the trading routes (→c.1800BC).

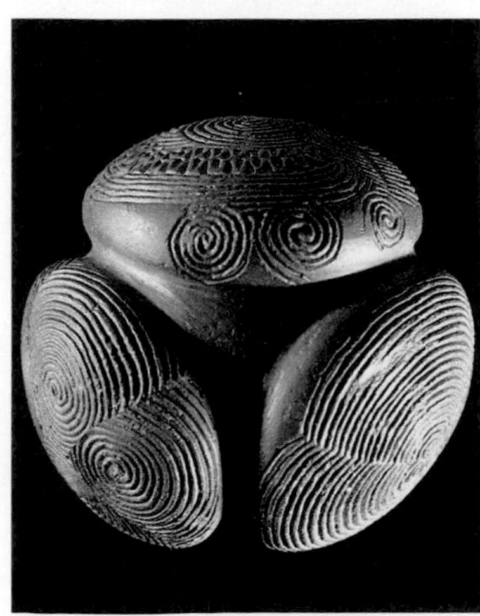

A stone ball from Grampian.

Magnificent stone circles and henges are built as temples of a new religion as people turn to worshipping moon, sun and earth

High in the hills: Castlerigg stone circle, erected in a prominent position overlooking Derwent Water.

Cumbria, c.3000BC
Huge stones left behind by the glaciers have been set up to form an imposing circle at Castlerigg, overlooking Derwent Water in Cumbria. Such stone circles – and similar monuments known as henges, which are made from great circular earthworks – are becoming common sights across the British Isles. They are the temples of a new religion.

Over the last thousand years a great change has taken place among the British tribes. Instead of worshipping their ancestors in tombs filled with skulls, as for countless years past, they have turned to new gods: the sun, the moon and the earth. At the same time a new group of people – priests – has emerged to interpret these mysteries.

Midwinter sun: the magnificent Ring of Brodgar, in the Orkney Islands.

There are many local variations to this new religion. At some sites worshippers have sacrificed their fellow humans, perhaps as a means of sanctifying the temple. People living at the Curragh in Co Kildare buried a young woman alive in their henge enclosure. In other places, chalk phalluses and cups, which may represent a woman's sex organs, have been buried, probably as part of a fertility cult. The monuments are very often constructed to align with the movements of the sun and moon which signal the changing seasons. The great circle at Stonehenge in Wiltshire is laid out to greet the midsummer sunrise. Many stone circles in north-eastern Scotland contain long blocks positioned so that the most southerly summer moon will rise or set above them.

The temples function as focal points for their communities. On the Orkney Islands, the entire local population of some 9,000 clubbed together to build two stone circles on Mainland, the largest island of the group. One of these, the extraordinary Ring of Brodgar, is built of 60 stones and measures 100 metres across.

Such magnificent structures take many years – possibly centuries – to build, and represent a huge investment of manpower and social organization. It is likely that the "blueprint" for each monument is handed down from generation to generation, and that apprentice workers are trained in the necessary skills. The earliest stone circles were built by hand, but more recently workmen have used sturdy oxen in transporting stones and moving earth (→c.2500BC).

▷

Norfolk flint-miners dig deeper than ever before

A seam of flint together with picks fashioned from antlers at Grime's Graves.

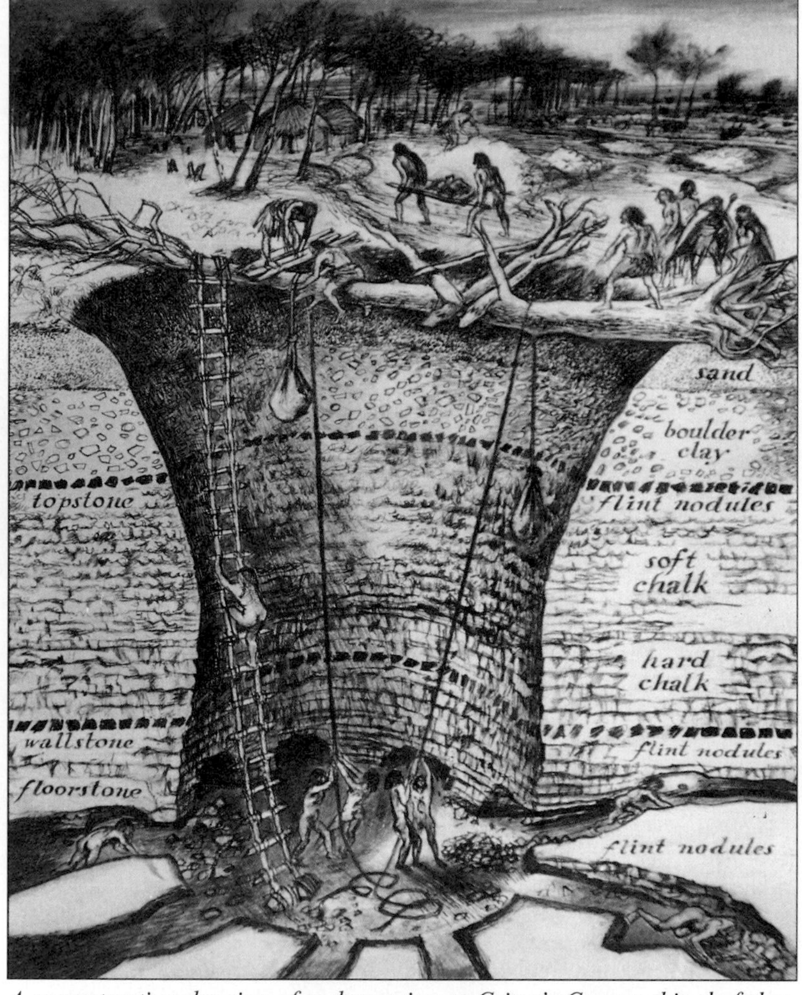

A reconstruction drawing of a deep mine at Grime's Graves; this shaft has a simpler system for raising flints to the surface than that used elsewhere.

Thetford, Norfolk, c.2600BC
Makers of tools and weapons in Norfolk have sunk huge mining shafts in the search for more and better flint, their essential raw material. The 300 shafts at the Grime's Graves mine go down further than anyone has dug before, even as far as around 12 metres (40 feet) in some cases. Greater teamwork and coordination is now required between those who go down the mines and those who supply them with their tools and work their products.

When opening a shaft the miners first have to remove the topsoil and then the chalk covering the flint deep under ground. As they go down they construct a sort of platform at intervals across the shaft. Ladders placed at angles of 45 degrees connect the various platforms, which both protect the miners from falling debris and act as places to put extracted flint and chalk waste.

Careful thought has gone into this arrangement. The angle of the ladders is the ideal one for climbers bearing a load. A platform system is also quicker and more efficient than one using ropes and pulleys to haul out baskets of rubble. Work at the face is equally methodical, and galleries are patiently dug out from the main shaft to exploit the main seams of flint.

A team of perhaps six prises out lumps of flint with picks made from antlers, a specialized tool for this sort of work. The lumps are smashed into manageable pieces with large flint blocks. Another team of six or seven carries the material to the surface, where yet another group works the flint into various tools.

The miners work with digging tools such as the antler picks as well as antler rakes, shovels made from animal shoulder-blades and small lamps hollowed out of lumps of chalk. Flint is extracted in great quantities before being fashioned into axes and knives. These are traded with other communities some distance away rather than used locally, perhaps a sign that they are in some way specialized.

Other such complexes are known to exist at Cissbury and Blackpatch Hill, in West Sussex (→c.2500BC).

Pots with spiral grooves used by powerful priests in magic rituals

Britain, c.2600BC
A new type of pot decorated with spiral-grooved designs is being distributed among influential people from Orkney to East Anglia, from Yorkshire to Wessex. The flat-bottomed vessels are thought to have originated in Orkney but are now being made by local craftsmen in different parts of Britain. Only the most important people have access to these wares, so that to own one is regarded as a symbol of high status. It seems likely that the pots are being manufactured specially for use at ritual magic centres by the increasingly powerful "priests" who mediate between the human and the divine. The carvings are thought to refer to the heavens and their varied influences on people's lives (→c.2500BC).

A pot with a grooved design used at Durrington Walls, in Wiltshire.

Stone supremacy is challenged by Irish chopper of copper

South-western Ireland, c.2500BC
Artisans in Ireland have made a discovery which could challenge the positions of stone and flint as the most popular materials for tools and weapons in the British Isles: how to work metal. The first Irish axes of copper, a fairly soft metal, have begun arriving in Wales and western England. Flat with thick butts, they are made by smelting copper ore, which is then cast and cooled in one-piece stone or pottery moulds.

Among the places in Ireland where copper mines can be found is Mount Gabriel in Co Cork, where at least two dozen shafts have been sunk; here, long low approach galleries lead down to mining chambers. The copper ores are extracted from the seams by the application of fire and pounding with heavy stone hammers.

There are indications that these techniques of mining and metal-working are also being adopted on the other side of the Irish Sea, although the sophistication and quality of the objects produced here does not match that of the highly prized ornaments and small tools – awls, needles, knives – which have been arriving in southern England from continental Europe. But copper has been recognized as having great potential. It can be melted down and re-used, unlike flint, and recycling centres are springing up which are spreading metalworking skills (→c.2150BC).

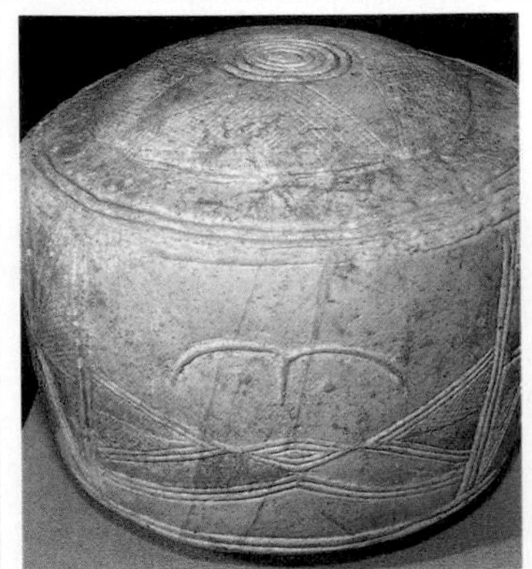

One of three carved chalk drums buried in a child's grave at Folkton Wold, in Humberside.

Cult of wealth spurs spiritual revival

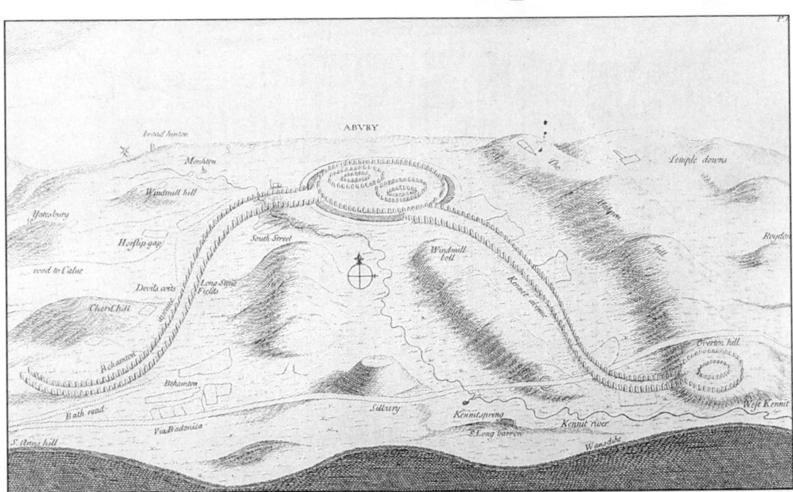

An 18th-century archaeologist's view of the Avebury henge monument.

Work at Silbury Hill, near Avebury.

A standing stone at Avebury henge.

Materialism threatens communal values

Britain, c.2500BC
Old communal values are coming under increasing threat from a new class of aggressive aristocrats to whom personal success and material wealth appear to be more important than spirituality. These people are distinguished by the prestige that they attach to exotic foreign possessions, which are being brought into the island from continental Europe. The list of these fancy imports is headed by beautiful vessels, probably beakers for drinking, and objects made from copper and gold.

Some of the finest beakers are in the shape of inverted bells. They may be decorated by pressing twisted cords onto the damp clay, by grooving, or by making patterns with comb-like implements. Perhaps designed for use in some cult practice or ritual, their quality is far superior to other contemporary British pottery.

The beaker users are particularly prevalent in Wessex and the upper Thames valley, as well as in East Anglia and eastern Scotland. They have counterparts all over Europe, from Scandinavia to the Mediterranean, although the precise connection between the British inhabitants and their continental cousins is not clear.

The new individualism of these people seems to be part of a male-orientated culture. This is suggested by the fact that knives and daggers are among their favourite copperware; they also insist on the finest wristguards and flint arrowheads (→c.2100BC).

Imposing centres of worship assert old religious traditions

Wiltshire, c.2500BC
People in Wessex, the heartland of the old communal traditions, are fighting back against the spread of individualist values by the "beaker" aristocrats. The focus of this spiritual revival is the old religious centre at Avebury, which is undergoing a transformation. The idea behind it resembles that which inspired earlier generations to devise the Dorset cursus [*see page 21*]: lots of individual monuments are incorporated in one awe-inspiring complex.

At Avebury several tombs have been sealed, while some existing monuments have been taken into the one large design. The old central circular area, or henge, has been upgraded with more stone and wooden buildings to become one of the largest ceremonial structures in Europe – the ditch and outer bank enclose more than 11 hectares (28 acres). Sandstone blocks ring the inside of the ditch, and on the central plateau stand two smaller rings, each 90 metres (100 yards) across. The centre is approached by a mile-long processional avenue.

Another vast henge has been built at Durrington Walls to the south of Avebury. It consists of a chalky earth bank and ditch ringing a central area nearly 500 metres across. Its most unusual feature is the two large circular wooden buildings in the middle. Supported on stout timber posts, they may be used as a combination of a dwelling and a ritual centre. Pottery and fine arrowheads also have a role at Durrington, which, as a focal point for the community, may double as an important trading centre. Much of the ritual conducted here involves the slaughter of animals, particularly bulls. To accompany the ceremonial there is much feasting on roasted young pigs, which are bred for the feasts and consumed in large numbers.

Similar henges are appearing all over this area: two are at Marden, in the Vale of Pewsey, and Mount Pleasant in Dorset (→c.2100BC).

2300 - 1500BC

Ireland, c.2200BC. Funeral ritual has become very lavish with regard to the gifts with which the dead bodies are adorned; most have gold jewellery and decorated beakers similar to those prized in Britain (→ c.2000BC).

Southern England, c.2000BC. Wooden circles within many existing monuments are being replaced by stone in an attempt to make them more permanent. Unlike the posts which formed the wooden circles, the stones in the new ones are widely spaced. They are unlike any other British monuments (→ c.1500BC).

Britain, c.2000BC. Cremation of the dead is increasingly popular; the ashes are placed in collared urns, which appear to be unique to Britain, unlike the highly decorated beakers which are widespread in Europe (→ c.1900BC).

Charterhouse Warren Farm, Somerset, c.1900BC. A large number of animal bones have been thrown down a natural well-shaft in a cave, possibly as part of a ritual ceremony practised by locals.

Methilhill, Fife, c.1900BC. Some of the ritual drinking cups buried with male corpses are being filled with a strong fermented liquor (→ c.1550BC).

Britain, c.1800BC. The development of trade routes has helped to spread the knowledge and use of metals. New links with Brittany enable groups in Britain to use bronze weaponry (→ c.1100BC).

Ilkley Moor, West Yorkshire, c.1700BC. The inhabitants decorate stones with engraved circles and dots as part of a symbolic burial ritual.

Wilsford, Wiltshire, c.1600BC. A 33-metre-deep well-shaft is being dug through the chalk earth in an attempt to find fresh water.

Isles of Scilly, c.1550BC. Farmers are carving a granite statue 60 cm high, the top 25 cm of which represent the facial features of a human. The neck is indicated by an indentation which runs round the circumference of the pillar. This is similar to other statues found in Europe, but is thought to be the first of its kind in Britain.→

Ireland, c.1550BC. The funerary ritual of surrounding bodies with pots and beakers seems to be dying out after about 700 years (→ c.1500BC).

Stonehenge seized for 'beaker' cult site

Stonehenge: rebuilt to alter its alignment with the midsummer sun's rising.

Stonehenge, Wiltshire, c.2100BC
Wealth-loving warlords have struck a blow at the spiritual revival which inspired the building of great "temples" such as Avebury and Durrington. "Beaker" users [*see report on page 27*] have seized Stonehenge, another ancient site, and turned it into a temple for the glorification of their own cult of individualism.

As befits people to whom outward show means so much, the new-look Stonehenge is a stunning sight. The entrance has been widened, with the gatestones moved and part of the existing ditch filled with soil from the old bank. As if to outdo the mile-long avenue at Avebury, an avenue flanked by ditches stretches for two miles in a straight line from the entrance down to the river Avon. Most impressive of all, in the centre of the henge, work has begun on erecting a double circle of 82 massive bluestones which came originally from Prescelli mountain in south-western Wales, probably deposited locally by glaciers thousands of years ago. If they were not, bringing them to Salisbury Plain has been an amazing feat: each stone weighs up to five tonnes.

In a more direct spiritual snub, the rebuilders of Stonehenge have slightly altered the alignment of the henge with the rising of the midsummer sun. Now they seem to take more account of the moon, which rises at right angles to the sun at midsummer (→ c.2000BC).

Woodland bows to demands of grazing

Southern England, c.2100BC
Across much of southern England dense woodland is being replaced by turf grazing-land as the result of intervention by the "beaker" users, who have made great strides in domesticating animals to supplement food from hunting. These powerful individualists are fast gaining the upper hand in the struggle between their own lifestyle and that of the older priestly caste. In addition to Stonehenge, they are trying to take over many ancient spiritual centres, such as Mount Pleasant and Maiden Castle in Dorset and Avebury in Wiltshire.

A granite statue from the Isles of Scilly, the first of its kind.

Large palisaded enclosures reflect more violent times

Wessex, c.2000BC
A huge new palisade has been built to surround the important spiritual centre at Mount Pleasant in Dorset – with a similar structure, of two linked enclosures, going up at West Kennet, near Avebury, in Wiltshire. The palisades appear to have been erected for defensive purposes, in reaction to a growing tide of violence and lawlessness as materialist "beaker" users struggle with supporters of traditional spirituality for the leading role in society. On the other hand, the high walls may be intended simply to conceal the sacred ceremonies held at these places from the eyes of the outsiders.

Whatever its purpose, the palisade at Mount Pleasant is an impressive creation, enclosing some 4.5 hectares (11 acres). It is oval shaped, 800 metres (880 yards) long, and made up of about 1,600 solid oak posts – representing 360 hectares of oak forest. The structure is six metres high, over 40 cm thick and surrounded by a ditch about three metres deep. Clearly a huge labour force must have been assembled to build it (→ c.1900BC).

Stone coffin burial for Scots chieftain

Orkney, c.2000BC
A tribal chief has been buried here in an elaborate stone coffin placed in a specially built tomb cut out of the rock. And, in a startling break with tradition, his coffin has been constructed in such a way as to allow it to be re-opened and used for a second burial.

First a large pit some two metres deep by approximately 3.3 metres square (just over six feet deep by 10 feet square) was cut into the rock. Within this the stone coffin was constructed from slabs jointed together with great skill, so that one side of it remained moveable. The rest of the pit was then roofed over with large capstones, which can easily be removed if and when people from a local settlement wish to re-use the burial site (→ c.1900BC).

Tough metal discovered

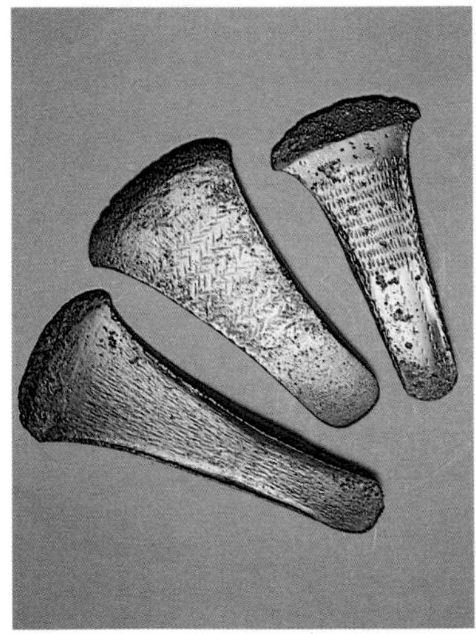
Sharp axes from the new metal.

South-western England, c.2150BC
Axes and daggers sharper than any made before could become a reality following the discovery of a new type of metal: bronze. Prospectors looking for gold and copper have uncovered rocks which yield tin, a light-coloured metal. This is remarkable in itself, except that on its own tin seems to have little practical application, except perhaps for decoration.

The big news, though, is the discovery that when molten tin is mixed with molten copper the result is bronze, a metal which is actually harder than either of the two metals from which it is made. Handling and working bronze is more difficult than working softer copper, because it must be heat-treated in order to achieve the strength and hardness which can make a blade at least twice as keen as one made from plain copper. If this process goes wrong the new substance is liable to crack. However, the prospect of more efficient tools and weapons – such as axes which can cut wood across the grain as well as split it – makes the effort worthwhile (→c.1900BC).

Old priestly caste toppled by newcomers

Southern England, c.1900BC
The materialist warriors identified by their fondness for fine beakers have wrested the most prominent position in society from the old priestly class; conspicuous consumption now looks to be the order of the day.

Nowhere is this seen more clearly than in the way these ambitious aristocrats carry their ostentation to the grave: they are buried with their favourite ornaments and wristguards, and new, highly decorated beakers are often placed at the feet of the corpses. Such beakers used to be imported from continental Europe; now, however, a local industry has been established under the control of the warlords.

Strangely, the women afforded "beaker" burials have their heads pointing south, as opposed to north for men. This distinction may reflect differing female and male roles in a warrior society (→c.1550BC).

Two grave daggers, copper and flint.

A highly decorated funeral beaker.

Irish gold craze catches on in Cornwall

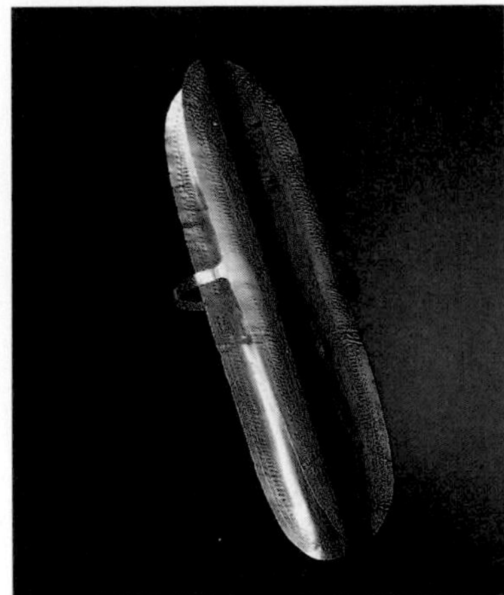
A collector's golden hair-clip.

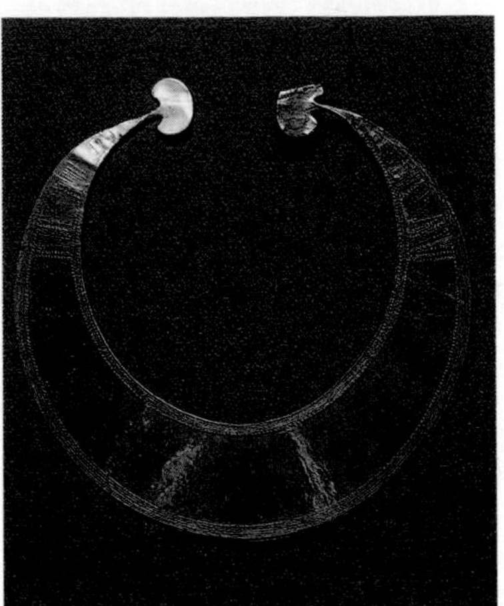
A beautifully fashioned gold lunula.

Ireland and Cornwall, c.2000BC
The Irish "beaker" users' love of gold has proved infectious. Their one-piece, crescent-shaped gold necklaces have found their way into key markets in Britain. At Harlyn Bay in Cornwall, for instance, one rich person owns two of these gold gorgets, one of them imported from Ireland. He may have traded it for another precious commodity: tin.

Renowned for their artistry, the goldsmiths of south-western Ireland beat single sheets of gold into crescent shapes, or *lunulae*, and then incise intricate, zoned geometrical patterns – similar to those found on their pottery – onto the gold. Finally, the crescent is carefully twisted at the ends to form a simple clasp. This characteristic geometric patterning is ushering in a new era in design. As beakers and pots decorated in this way have spread among the powerful and influential, goldsmiths have caught on to the craze and incorporated it into their work.

In Ireland – just as in Britain – decorated beakers have been used in burials, but they have very often been placed on their own in old tombs, rather than used in lavish individual burials. In the Irish tradition such decorated goods are clearly not just a status symbol for the wealthy, but possess some religious aura.

The enchanting decorated Irish necklaces are mainly produced for domestic consumption, but traders bring the odd gold *lunula* to Britain. Such is the demand that British goldworkers are also mastering the skills of burnishing and decoration (→c.1700BC).

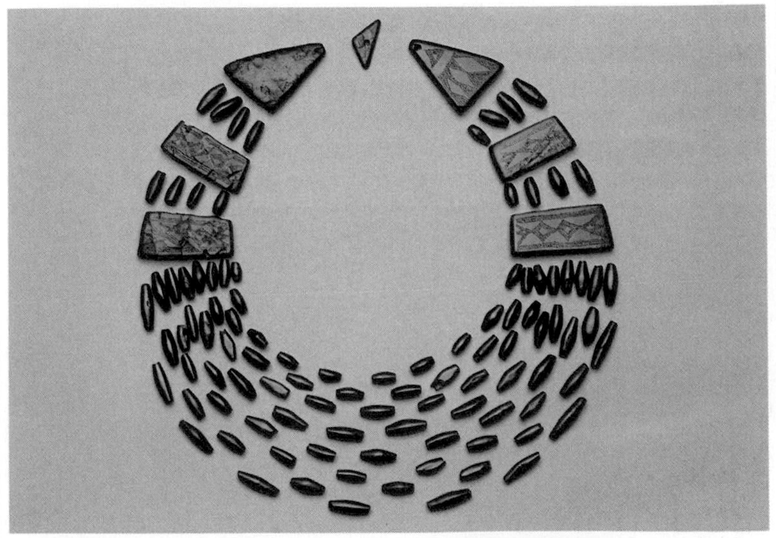
As elaborate decoration becomes more popular, craftsmen are producing complex jewellery such as this necklace of jet, a material rare in Britain.

Competition hots up between bronze and flint in toolmaking

British Isles, c.1900BC
The steady growth of metal production in Britain is heralding a major revolution in technology, as stone tools are being phased out in favour of ones made from the new material. Metalwork from western Europe, where the industry first appeared 2,000 years ago, includes needles, knives, awls and ornaments, some made of gold. But it is the use of metal for making tools that is exciting most interest.

A rich seam of ore deposits in the south-west of Ireland, where metal-making first began in the British Isles, has continued to yield large amounts of copper each year. The molten metal is cast in stone or pottery moulds to make axes, daggers and halberds. Until now, copper tools have not been used in preference to stone, because copper's softness does not make it very durable. But developments in the production of bronze – an alloy of copper and tin, and an even stronger metal than either – has led to tools being made with longer-lasting and harder cutting edges. Metal is also a material that can easily be recycled – melted down and recast.

Flint dagger shaped like a metal one.

Mining and smelting of copper is now thriving in south-eastern Wales, and supplies of tin ore are also abundant in the south-west of England. Thus the future of bronze seems to be assured (→c.1600BC).

Wealthy chiefs go for gleaming gold

British Isles, c.1700BC
People in Britain and Ireland are panning for gold, and skilled workers are making it into beautiful objects, in what amounts to a gold rush. The gold industry, which has flourished here for the last 600 years, seems to be reaching its peak.

The precious metal is valued for its rarity, weight and malleability, but above all, perhaps, because its yellow glint echoes the shining sun – the source of warmth, life and power. For that reason it is especially valued by kings and chiefs, like the warrior who has been buried at Mold, in Clwyd, wearing his cape of solid gold.

But it is the ruling élite of the Wessex region who have chosen to express their wealth and power with flamboyant displays of exquisitely crafted gold. At Bush Barrow in Wiltshire, for example, a chief has been buried wearing two beautiful lozenges of delicately incised sheet gold; a stunning gold hook fastens his belt, and his dagger handle has been decorated with thousands of minute gold pins forming a chevron pattern. Others have been buried with objects made of gold combined with exotic substances such as amber and shale.

Such wealthy and powerful individuals, whose burials proclaim their admiration for costly goldwork, no doubt encourage such innovation by their generous patronage of goldworkers. What is more, they have important personal, trade and cultural connections with their counterparts in Germany, Brittany and Ireland: rich sources of new decorative ideas. And so the jewellery workshops of Wessex set the trend for the rest of Britain. Dagger decorations, lozenges and gold discs from as far away as Norfolk, Orkney and Tayside carry echoes of the inimitable Wessex style.

In Ireland, a long period of prosperous stability has encouraged innovations in the well-established and technically advanced goldworking industry. The specialist art of making *lunulae* (crescent-shaped neck ornaments of beaten gold), for example, is now very sophisticated, with three distinct schools emerging. More and more gold jewellery, of ever-improving design, is being made (→c.1500BC).

This gold funeral cup buried at Rillaton, in Cornwall, demonstrates the wealth of the deceased.

A beaten gold breastplate from Bush Barrow, in Wiltshire: the work of the influential Wessex goldsmiths.

A chest ornament made from sheet gold in the Wessex style with geometric decorations, probably a sign of rank; from Little Cressingham, in Norfolk.

The sheet-gold cape worn proudly by a warrior at Mold, in Clwyd: carrying the warmth – and power – of the sun even into his grave.

Bronze industry spreads from old centres as tin mines boom in Cornwall and Devon

British Isles, c.1600BC
As bronzeworking continues to spread throughout the British Isles, the demise of flint as the pre-eminent material for making tools and weapons looks inevitable. At Arreton Down on the Isle of Wight, for instance, there are flourishing groups of metalworkers who are producing bronze daggers, axes and spearheads in several designs.

Metalworking has spread here from the old population centres on the mainland in Wessex, and elsewhere in the country there are now many bronzeworking centres, including bronze foundries in Gloucestershire, the Thames valley and East Anglia. There is also a thriving trade in bronze imports from continental Europe. But bronze is not confined to the south of England. As well as production sites in Lancashire, Cheshire and Shropshire there are large areas of workings in Ireland and Strathclyde and in Wales, with copper mines at such places as Parys Mountain in the north and Cwmystwyth in Dyfed.

The booming market in bronze, meanwhile, has firmly established the tin-mining industry of Devon and Cornwall at the centre of a growing economy. To make bronze one needs tin and copper. Although copper has been found throughout the British Isles, from southern Ireland to central Scotland, the only known sources of recoverable tin are in Devon and Cornwall, and demand for it is now far exceeding supply. Techniques for extracting the metal are crude and laborious. Once a promising vein is identified a fire is built to heat the rock. When water is flung against the heated stone it shatters, and the miners can then pound the fragments further with stone mauls, or heavy hammers, to a rubble fine enough for smelting in shallow pits about 30 centimetres across.

If the ore discovered is particularly rich the miners may dig deeper, although the shafts rarely extend further than a worker can reach. The demand is such that tin ore may be traded anywhere where bronze is worked, linking the tin-miners of south-western England with far-flung corners of the British Isles. Those people who have mastered the techniques of metal production and distribution now wield great influence (→c.1450BC).

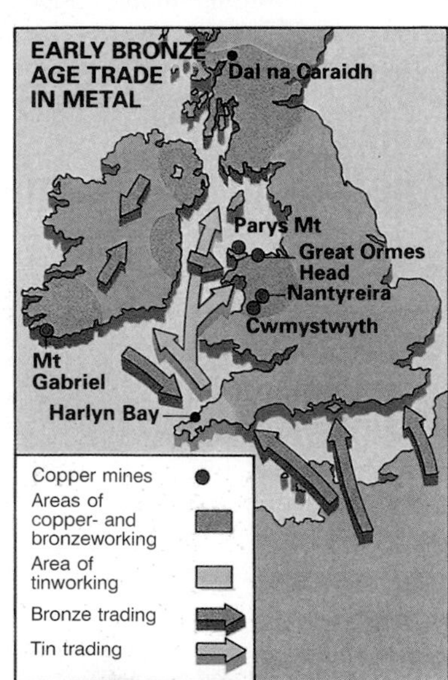

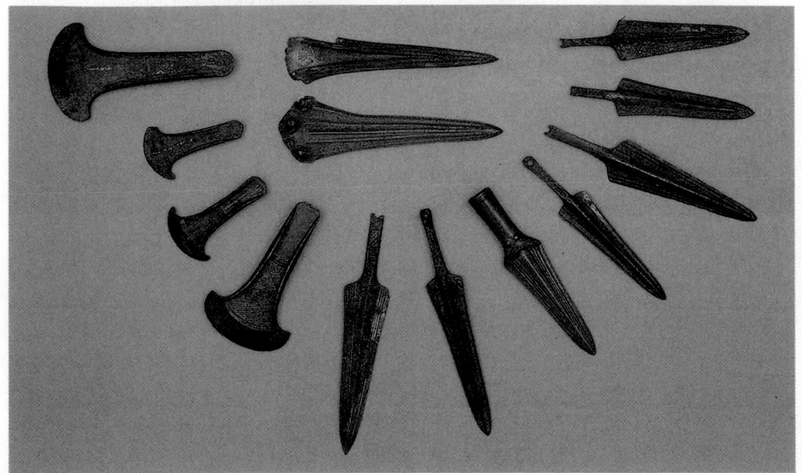
Varied bronze weapons attest to the skill of the workers at Arreton Down.

Miles of stone walls erected on Dartmoor

Grimspound, on Dartmoor: enclosure and settlement of an area of moorland.

Dartmoor, Devon, c.1550BC
An intention to organize and regulate the use of land within communities seems to be behind the decision by people on Dartmoor to build 120 miles of stone walls to separate their fields. These metre-thick walls mark the boundaries between huge pasture meadows for sheep and cattle – some more than 200 hectares (500 acres) in area. Most of them, such as those at Dartmeet and Rippon Tor, stretch right up to the steep and rugged moorland which is valued as grazing land in spite of its exposed and bleak position.

Some of the walls follow the natural contours of the landscape – which implies that they may have been planned as broad frontiers rather than simply boundaries between the pastures of peaceful farmers. However, at only two or three feet in height, the walls would do little to discourage aggressive neighbours from attempting to expand their territorial influence.

The people who live in this part of south-western England have built themselves substantial houses on stone foundations. Typically these are grouped together, creating villages of between six and 15 houses often sited in pairs some 250 metres (275 yards) apart. Near the houses there are numerous small fields, while larger ones belonging to the same community are situated further away.

Villages develop on the chalk downlands

Southern England, c.1550BC
Farming is now taking over completely from the old hunting and gathering lifestyle, and more and more agricultural communities are beginning to emerge on the chalk downlands of southern England such as Salisbury Plain and the Marlborough Downs in Wiltshire. Houses in these villages are grouped together and are often surrounded by large enclosed fields.

Within the communities there is a high degree of organization. The continual tilling of the large fields requires the disciplined following of an agricultural cycle to give the land a chance to recover from each year's crop. The large areas under cultivation require plough teams to be assembled with the latest in bronze implements.

These communities are extended but nevertheless very closely knit. They are probably bound by kinship links, especially the exchange of women – who are regarded as part of a man's wealth – as wives. The villages are prosperous enough to produce a food surplus, allowing some people to concentrate on metalworking and pottery production. Bronze tools, weapons and ornaments, with designs like that on the pottery, are used (→c.1400BC).

1500 - 1100BC

Britain, c.1500BC. As the demand for jewellery grows, goldsmiths are hard at work making items such as diadems, necklaces, pins and bracelets The most highly regarded workers export their wares to mainland Europe (→c.850BC).

Newquay, Cornwall, c.1500BC. A ritual burial ground with elaborately engraved quartz paving stones has recently been constructed by people living in the area. The paved area, or courtyard, is surrounded by five substantial wooden buildings where ritual feasts are to be held (→c.1400BC).

Essex, c.1500BC. Communities are becoming more permanent as the inhabitants concentrate on increasing their agricultural production and defending their settlements from outsiders.

Dorset, c.1400BC. The increasingly rare practice of burning bodies and removing the bones from the funeral pyre, for burial in a pit or long barrow (rectangular burial mound), is still taking place here (→c.900BC).

Dorset, c.1400BC. Shearplace Hill settlement is a typical example of the field systems and enclosures which are rapidly spreading across the country; there are two main buildings, a working area and a pond within the boundaries of the settlement (→c.1200BC).

Derbyshire, c.1300BC. The hilltop at Mam Tor is fortified by a timber palisade which will protect the settlers within who feel the growing need for defence from outsiders.

Orkney, c.1185BC. Settlers are erecting a new building around a large stone trough which will be used for heating water. For cooking purposes hot stones will be thrown in, and animals will be boiled in it in preparation for communal feasts (→c.100BC).

England, c.1150BC. New eastern European techniques of sheet-metalmaking reach Britain via the metal-trade routes. With these new methods, toolmakers are able to make thinner sheet metal and create better tools with which to make a wide variety of articles (→c.1100BC).

East Anglia, c.1150BC. Bronze vessels are being used for cooking and serving food. Large cauldrons, drinking cups and forks are made for everyday use, with rather more elaborate vessels being made for ceremonial purposes.→

Warriors strive to revive fading glory

An amber cup buried in a rich grave.

Southern England, c.1500BC
The old "beaker" aristocrats are struggling to keep up their power and prestige in their Wessex heartland by turning back to the custom of rich burials. They are using the old-style pomp and ceremony in a desperate attempt to demonstrate that their status remains untouched by the social and economic changes spreading through the country.

It looks like being a forlorn hope, however, for many of the great monuments, the henges and the barrows, are falling into disuse. The landmarks in the southern English countryside now are not religious monuments but agricultural features, because field systems, farms and hillforts have sprung up to supplant the henges.

More fundamentally, though, the centre of economic power in southern England has moved away from Wessex to the Thames valley and the south-east. Here a new type of society is evolving, which is based on the establishment of permanent farming settlements rather than warrior prestige (→c.1400BC).

An ornate cup from a Wessex grave.

Wales becomes hub of bronze industry

Wales, c.1450BC
Despite its isolated situation on the western coast, the Welsh bronze industry has risen to supremacy in an increasingly important and sophisticated British trade which can compete with the continental mainland on even terms. The bronzeworkers of Wales are clustered mainly around the mines of Snowdonia, and the Great Orme on the coast, where skilled miners are digging for copper in shafts up to 12 metres deep. The landscape here is bleak, and the workers' lives are harsh and uncomfortable.

Part of the key to the success of the Welsh industry is its development of the skill of smelting copper and tin ores together to produce a reliable quality of bronze. A further innovation has consolidated its position: the creation of bronze moulds from which 50 or more axes can be cast before the moulds need replacing.

The basic product of these Welsh workshops is a large heavy axe which is exported as far afield as the Low Countries and elsewhere in Europe. Even the best bronze axeheads become blunt eventually, but the Welsh ones are traded with local smiths who either rework them into smaller axes or use them as a source of raw material for their own bronze goods (→c.1150BC).

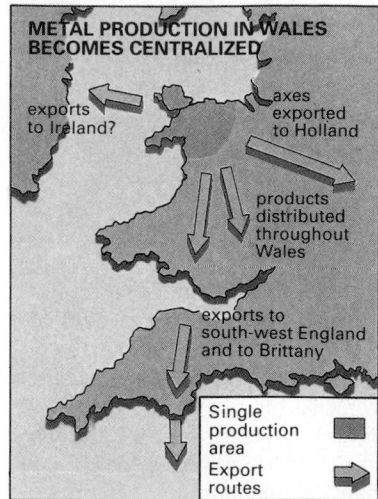

METAL PRODUCTION IN WALES BECOMES CENTRALIZED
exports to Ireland?
axes exported to Holland
products distributed throughout Wales
exports to south-west England and to Brittany
Single production area
Export routes

Small-scale skirmishing is on the increase

Tormarton, Avon, c.1150BC
The bodies of two young men have been discovered lying in a ditch. It is clear from their injuries that they met violent ends: both have been impaled with spears, while one of the victims had also received a doubtless fatal blow to the head, possibly with a sword. The two corpses are a gruesome illustration of a society where feuding and small-scale skirmishes are increasingly common. Settlements that were once undefended have now been provided with ramparts. One influence on the violence is the improvement in weaponry with the advent of bronze technology and new swords which are beginning to replace the rapier.

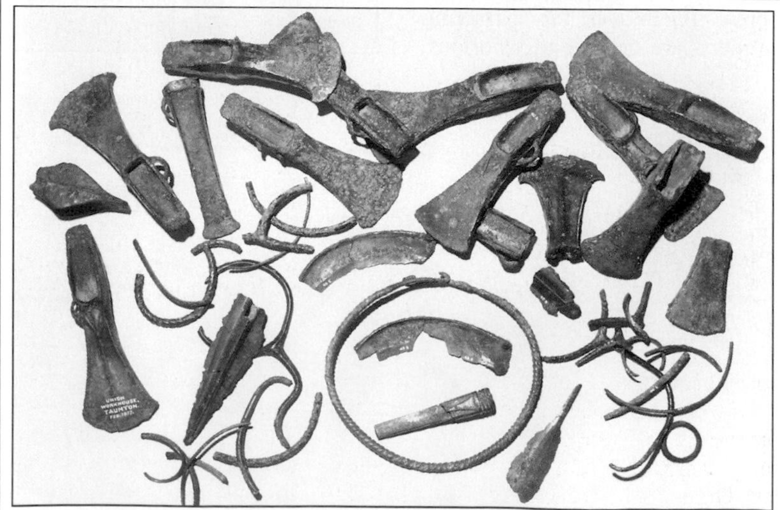

Various bronze weapons and ornaments, from a store of scrap metal carefully put aside for future re-use at Taunton, in Somerset, c.1300BC.

Scotland hit by volcano

Fire from below: a 20th-century photograph of an active volcano in Iceland.

Scottish Highlands, c.1150BC
Northern Scotland has been hit by a colossal eruption of Mount Hekla in Iceland. A huge column of volcanic dust has blotted out the sun, ruined the harvest and made large areas of the region uninhabitable. Northern England, Ireland and Wales have also been affected.

In the highlands thousands of people have left their homes and are streaming south in search of lowland areas where conditions are kinder. On the island of North Uist alone, 15 villages and hamlets have been abandoned. At Strath of Kildonan, in Highland, 80 hamlets have been left deserted by their fleeing inhabitants. Refugees from the highland areas have come into conflict with people living further south, often forcing them to leave and become refugees themselves.

These migrations have caused widespread devastation, leaving nothing but abandoned homes and villages in the uplands, while in the lowlands, further south, settlements are being fortified against likely attack. At Eildon Hill on the Scottish borders, and Broxmouth, in Lothian, for instance, the inhabitants of open settlements have constructed sturdy palisades for protection.

French cargo ship is wrecked near Dover

A ship of the type sunk (on a bowl found near Caergwrle Castle in Clwyd).

Kent, c.1150BC
A ship transporting bronzeware from northern France has sunk in strong winds off Langdon Cliff, near Dover. The cargo of axes, daggers, spearheads and chisels was destined for a community in southern England. Despite the dangers of the sea there is a thriving cross-Channel trade in bronze. A curious feature of this trade is that perfectly good foreign material is treated as scrap. Smiths prefer to recast imported material according to local tastes; an ornate axehead is simply a lump of metal to importers.

Agriculture transforms face of landscape as large areas of woodland are cleared

How a typical farming village might have looked. Each hut would probably serve a different function: for example, one might be used as a dwelling, another for housing animals, another for work or for food preparation.

Britain, c.1200BC
Farming is taking a heavy toll of the British landscape, as large areas of wildwood are cleared to make way for crops and herding. Parts of East Anglia, the south-west and the coast around the Lake District have been practically denuded. The same process is at work on high ground and along river valleys.

It has not been an easy task. British trees – apart from pine – cannot be burnt standing, so it is impossible simply to set light to them. Nor will they burn where they lie – they have to be chopped up and stacked. Stumps then have to be removed, and the danger of regrowth has to be avoided, usually by allowing cattle, sheep and goats to graze on the cleared land.

People are changing not just the countryside but also their way of life. While hunting requires cooperation with a large number of others, farming shrinks society to the immediate family of parents, children and grandparents. Such a family will manage its own farm, cultivating barley, wheat, beans and other vegetables, as well as producing meat from sheep and cattle. The traditions of hunting and gathering have not been entirely abandoned, however. People still go out to harvest sloes, blackberries, hazelnuts and edible weeds such as goosegrass from wildwoods near the farmstead; they may gather hedge mustard and hedge garlic for flavouring. Coastal dwellers take advantage also of shellfish, seaweed and plants growing along the shore.

A pot used in the preparation and eating of communal family meals.

Roles are also becoming more formalized, the men looking after the ploughing and wood clearance while the women prepare food and care for the children. Women and children also do the gathering and help with the harvesting (→c.900BC).

1100 - 700BC

London, c.1100BC. The inhabitants throw offerings of weapons and human remains into the Thames to appease the gods and demonstrate their own warlike power (→ c.900BC).

Edinburgh, c.1000BC. A base has been established on a huge rock overlooking a loch. The settlement consists of wooden buildings.

Southern England, c.1000BC. A new alloy, leaded bronze, which is a combination of copper, tin and lead, has come into use (→ c.900BC).

Orkney, c.900BC. Weapons and domestic vessels are being made from wood, as a consequence of the lack of metal in the area.

Runnymede, Surrey, c.900BC. A large established riverside settlement has opened up extensive trade links with Europe through the success of its metal industry (→ c.750BC).

Orkney, c.900BC. Wooden weapons are being habitually thrown into the peat moss as offerings designed to placate the gods (→ c.650BC).

Co Armagh, c.850BC. A circular settlement is built on a hilltop at Emain Macha. Hilltop sites are easily defendable and are increasingly being chosen as settlement locations (→ c.465BC).

Ireland, c.850. Golden ornaments of all kinds are proliferating, many of them made from gold imported from Spain or central Europe (→ c.400BC).

Northern Welsh Marches, c.850BC. Communities are being fortified by their inhabitants as a result of increased instability in the relations between different groups and frequent outbreaks of violence.

Britain, c.750BC. A new type of metalwork which began in southern Europe over 200 years ago is gradually reaching Britain. The abundant sources of iron in Europe have led to its gradually replacing bronze as the most popular material for weapons (→ c.675BC).

Tayside, c.700BC. Farming communities by Loch Tay are building islands on the loch. Surrounded by water, they are very easy to defend.

Scotland, c.700BC. A varied, healthy diet for loch farmers includes a combination of berries, nuts and fungi which supplement the meat and cereal that they farm.

Weaponmakers in urgent design race

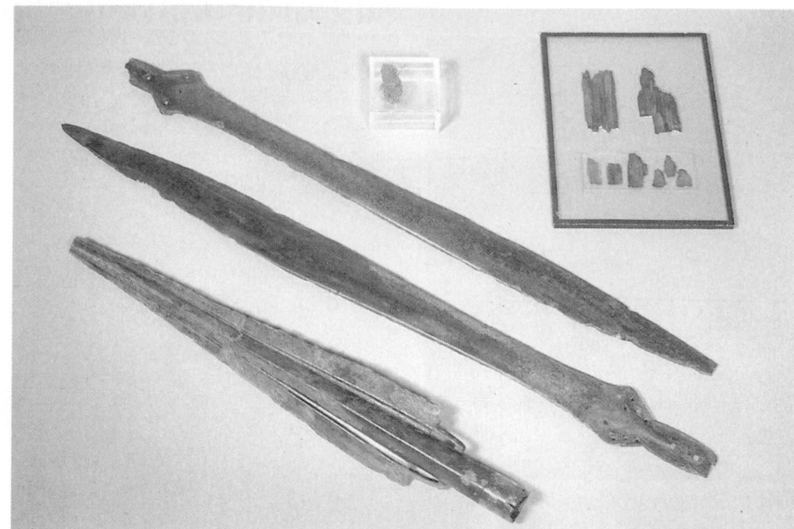

The arms race: the design of socketed axes such as these has been improved.

Southern England, c.1100BC
The weaponsmiths of Britain are involved in a hectic arms race as the instruments of war enter one of the most lively periods of development since the first copper axeheads were produced more than a thousand years ago.

The various schools of the craft are competing to be the first to come up with the best combination of lightness, strength and effectiveness for a bronze sword, speartip or axehead. Some design innovations are being copied from the continent, while others are original to British weaponmakers. In swords, the long, thin rapier shape is increasingly being superseded by the elegant leaf-shaped blade, with or without a protective guard on the hilt. A common feature of the most successful new designs is a distinct ridge down the centre of the blade to help give the weapon a dual slash and stab function.

New and revised forms of spearhead are appearing, including a new version of the pegged leaf-shaped blade, and fresh work is also being done on the design of sickles and axeheads (→ c.1000BC).

Plank-boats drift down the Humber

Humberside, c.950BC
Settlers at Ferriby, on the Humber estuary, are getting about on the water by wooden boat. The vessels, which they have constructed from large wooden planks – rather than digging out a single tree-trunk – may have a variety of functions, including the hunting of wildfowl and the transportation of everyday materials, as well as being a means of communication. These skilfully built boats, with their many uses, are probably propelled and steered by means of paddles. They are completely transforming the river-dwellers' relationship with their environment (→ c.250BC).

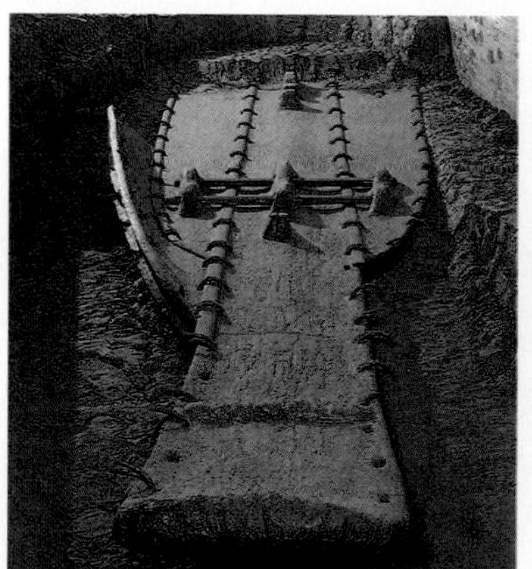

A replica of a river plank-boat.

Salt from the sea makes villagers a living

Brean Down, Avon, c.1100BC
The people at Brean Down, near the mouth of the river Avon, are getting a name as producers of salt. Making good use of the most plentiful natural resources possible – the sea – they have built their modest settlement around this small village industry.

Sea-water is initially allowed to stand in large open pans until most of the water has evaporated. Then villagers take this concentrated brine and reduce it further by boiling over an open fire.

Communities such as Brean Down, dedicated to a particular craft or skill, are now increasingly common throughout Britain, and groups from different areas are beginning to establish a network through which they can exchange their goods (→ c.500BC).

A reconstruction of the huts at Brean Down, showing a domestic hearth.

Farming disrupted by climate change

British Isles, c.900BC
A gradual worsening of climatic conditions in Britain and Ireland over the past century has caused widespread disruption to formerly settled communities. Rainfall and wind have increased, and annual average temperatures have fallen by a few degrees. Farmers in upland and marginal lowland areas have been especially badly hit. The growing season has become shorter, soils have been leached of minerals, and many areas of previously fertile land have been waterlogged, with blanket bogs forming on Dartmoor, for example, and in upland parts of Wales. Some low-lying settlements have been destroyed by floods, forcing their inhabitants to retreat to higher ground (→ c.600BC).

Advances boost mass arms production

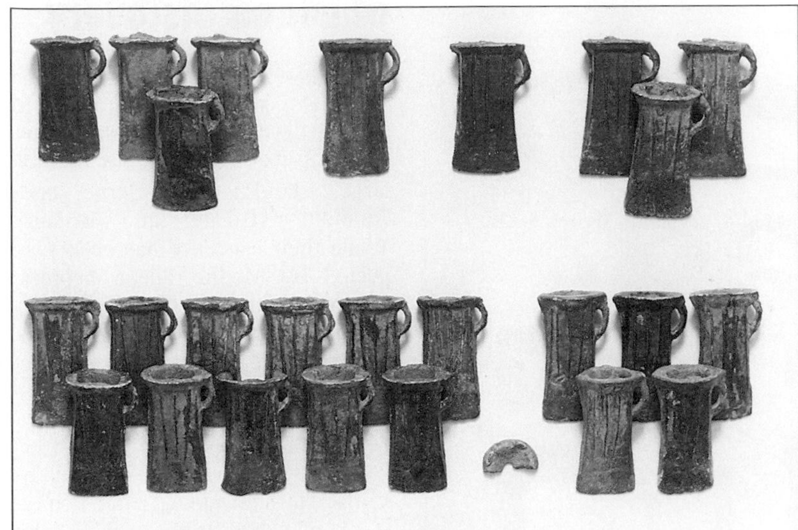

Production advances are leading to radically improved weapons.

British Isles, c.900BC
New techniques developed in Britain have transformed the production of bronze weapons and look likely to increase dramatically the supply of the most effective instruments of war yet developed. Enormous increases in efficiency have been achieved by a combination of improved technology and reorganized methods of production.

By using an alloy in which lead has been added to the tin and copper, a bronze with a lower melting point is obtained. In addition to making it flow more easily into complex moulds, this makes it much easier to pour the melt into several moulds at a time.

Combining this with improved designs of mould in stone and bronze, which are often pre-heated to inhibit solidification before pouring is complete, the bronze-weaponsmiths can turn out relatively large numbers of almost identical weapons which require a minimum of finishing.

To maximize output, the hardening process is carried out to an acceptable minimum rather than to the maximum still sought for one-off castings (→c.750BC).

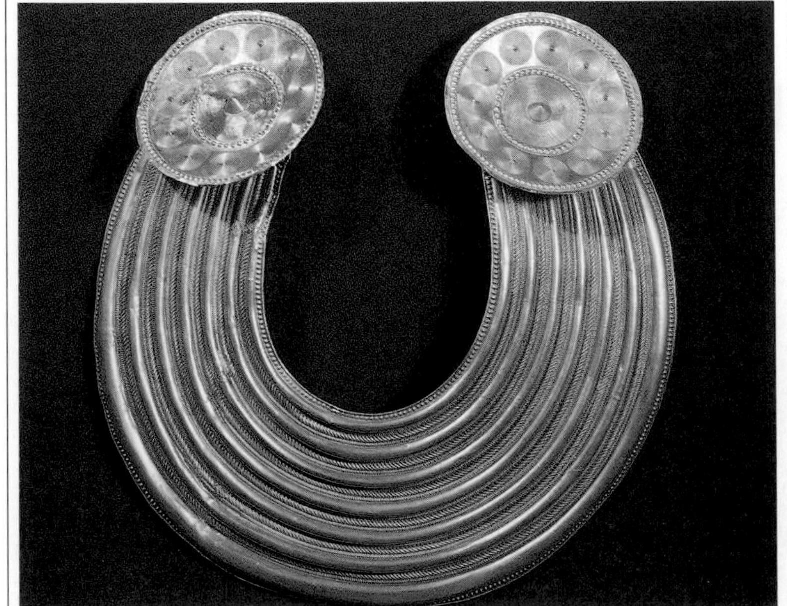

Golden neck armour from Gleninsheen, Co Clare, reflects the prosperity of Ireland, based on agriculture. In Co Kildare bronze sickles have boosted harvests, while bronze tools make possible sophisticated woodwork.

Bodies of humans and animals involved in ritual sacrifice during river ceremonies

Cambridgeshire, c.900BC
Human and animal corpses have been thrown into the water in ritual sacrifices on an artificial island at Fengate, near Peterborough. The bodies are followed by bronze swords, daggers, knives and jewellery which have been ceremonially broken up.

Formed by some two million long timber stakes driven deep into the clay and gravel, the island is said to be considered the temporary abode of the dead during the transition to the next world. It has seven rectangular buildings, or temples, and is joined to the mainland by a sacred avenue some 820 metres (900 yards) long. It was built in the belief that the next world lies beneath the water and that spirits dwell just below the surface. Human sacrifices, with the bodies being placed in marshlands and rivers along with weapons or household items, also take place in other parts of Britain.

River ceremonies have recently occurred along the banks of the Thames, with hundreds of bodies, and bronze weapons, being cast into the river during rites of passage into the next world. The funerals of prominent warrior-heroes have often been the occasions for these sacrifices (→c.250BC).

An artist's impression of funeral rites on the banks of the river Thames.

Plymouth prospering as a trading port

South-western England, c.700BC
With trading ships plying from Spain and France, the western settlement of Mount Batten [Plymouth] has become Britain's largest port. It is a thriving harbour which exports precious metals brought from the moors rich in ore a few miles to the north and west.

These exports include tin, silver, copper and gold, all of which are traded for bronze tools and other finished metal products from the other side of the channel and Spain.

The port is also involved in the manufacture of hides, fleeces and food – with the slaughter of pigs and cattle taking place on the promontory, possibly for the coastal trade if not for barter to the continent. Jewellery is being fashioned in the Spanish or French styles. Wool is another export.

The port is helped by a strange but well-known local phenomenon: at high tide certain areas of the coastline become islands, and Mount Batten, one of these areas, is then easily accessible by ship. Greek travellers and traders who have come this way speak enthusiastically of a port called Ictis, which may well be Mount Batten. It is certainly a vibrant trading post, which locals say has been active for 200 years (→c.500BC).

700 - 450BC

Britain, c.675BC. A new type of sword has arrived from continental Europe. Made totally from bronze, it is longer and far more effective as a weapon. Its appearance seems related to an increase in warlike activities in both Europe and Britain (→ c.650BC).

Glamorgan, c.650BC. Lavish offerings are being made to the mountain-lake gods by local tribes. The gifts thrown to the gods are frequently the rich spoils of successful raids into wealthier areas of southern Britain (→ c.500BC).

British Isles, c.600BC. Bronze production declines with the increased use of the new metal, iron; bronze seems now to be very scarce (→ c.500BC).

South-eastern England, c.600BC. The sword is going out of fashion in some parts of the region. Its replacement is the iron dagger, which is shorter and easier to use. The majority of daggers in Britain, originally European imports, are now locally made. They are extremely highly prized and are frequently used as offerings (→ c.325BC).

Cornwall, c.600BC. Farmers are clearing fields and paddocks of stones to intensify crop cultivation. The field boundaries are marked out by the stones which are piled into drystone walls (→ c.400BC).

Wiltshire, c.550BC. Pottery is becoming a major industry in and around the Salisbury area. The distinctive ware is made of local brick-earth clay, producing a shiny red finish which is decorated with scratch marks and coated with haematite (→ c.200BC).

Crickley Hill, Gloucestershire, c.500BC. The hillfort settlement has been attacked and overrun. The victorious tribe is now remodelling the existing site with stronger defences of massive stone ramparts and an elaborate entrance gate.

South-eastern England, c.500BC. Many luxury goods, some totally new to Britain, have begun to appear by means of the complex trade routes established within Europe. The items, or their decorative motifs, are adapted or copied by expert workers and incorporated into British-made goods (→ c.300BC).

Co Armagh, c.465BC. A hilltop site at Emain Macha is chosen as the capital of the Ulaid tribe.→

Iron succeeds bronze

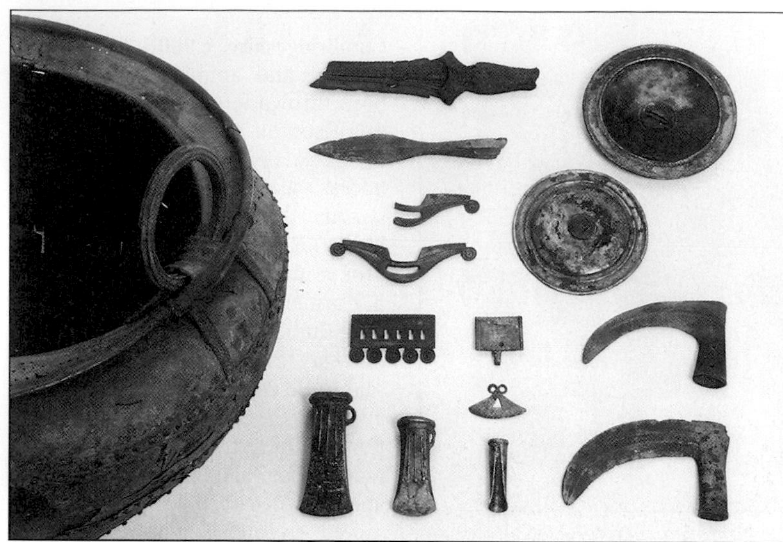

Iron and bronze objects were stored together at Llyn Fawr in Glamorgan.

British Isles, c.650BC
Metal weapons and tools which are stronger, harder and more abundant than anything yet seen in bronze are becoming increasingly evident as people take to a new metal: iron.

Iron is the unexpected by-product of the search for a substitute for leaded bronze (an alloy of copper, tin and lead), the standard metal, which is now in short supply. Iron ore is relatively common throughout the British Isles, but it is much harder to extract a usable metal from it. Unlike bronze smelting, in which the molten metal drips through the fire to collect in the bowl of the furnace, the extracted iron fuses to form a "bloom" which is then hammered repeatedly on a stone anvil. To melt it so that it could be poured like bronze would require far higher temperatures than furnaces can produce.

Provided this stage is carried out successfully, the metal can then be reheated and hammered several times, often on an anvil dusted with charcoal which combines with the iron to make a harder surface without losing its malleability. Apart from plugging the bronze gap, an iron sword is stronger and more flexible than a bronze one, and can be given a sharper edge (→ c.600BC).

Greek sailor tells of island discovery

Marseilles, France, c.530BC
A Greek sailor, returning from a voyage beyond the Straits of Gibraltar, has written a report of two large islands called Ierne and Albion – Ireland and Britain. While their existence has been suspected by Mediterranean peoples for some years, this is the first time that their names have been written down in the Greek language. The sailor did not visit the islands himself but heard of them when on a trading voyage to the city of Tartessos on the Atlantic coast of Spain. He was told that the Tartessians traded with people in Brittany, who in turn traded with two islands further north (→ c.325BC).

Trader's booty: an Iberian clasp.

Ireland's smiths get hooked on ironwork

Ireland, c.500BC
Ireland's metalworkers are gradually overcoming their reluctance to make the switch from bronze to iron, as trade brings examples of the latest designs from Britain and the European mainland for local smiths to copy. The modern Irish iron sword now clearly shows the influence of long-bladed foreign weapons, and smiths are now attempting to make a full range of metal objects in iron: pins, ornaments, buckets and hooks as well as swords, daggers and spearheads. However, they are having some difficulty adapting designs developed for casting in bronze to forging techniques used when working in iron (→ c.325BC).

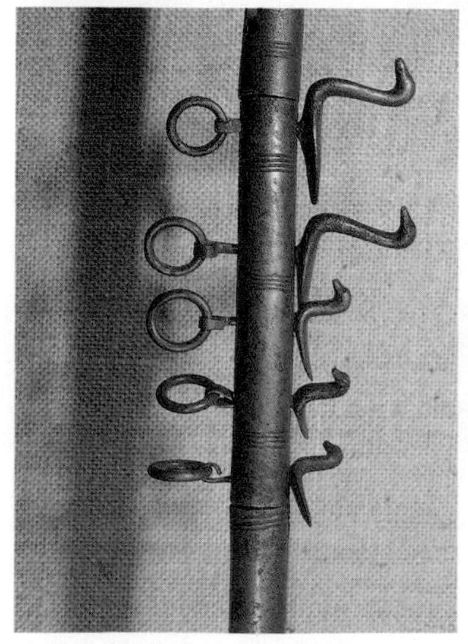

A flesh-hook from Co Antrim.

Salt is being traded all over Midlands

Hereford and Worcester, c.500BC
Salt trading has become an important industry in the English Midlands and the Severn valley. The salt is extracted from saltwater springs surfacing near the river Salwarpe at Droitwich, where it is collected in specially dug evaporation pits. The salt is stored and distributed in distinctive clay vessels, made by the salt panners from coarse local clay. About 20 cm (eight inches) high, and with narrow bases and wide necks, these salt containers are traded among the hillforts and settlements up to 36 miles (60 km) to the north, south and west of Droitwich.

Massive hillforts built across England and Wales

Population pressures fuel land conflicts

The steep slopes of this hillfort in the Welsh Marches would deter attackers.

Southern Britain, c.550BC
Huge hillforts are springing up the length and breadth of England and Wales as population pressures lead to mounting conflicts over scarce agricultural land. To withstand prolonged attacks and sieges, certain forts have walls up to 4.5 metres (15 feet) high; others have been given steep ramparts over six metres high, in front of which are deep V-shaped ditches.

Some forts, which may contain upwards of 50 round houses including grain stores, can sustain populations of around 200, who work on land within a five-mile (eight-km) radius. The defenders rely on spears, bows and arrows and stones to scatter the attackers, as they pile brushwood against the wooden gates and put it to the torch.

Despite their formidable defences, many hillforts have been captured, sacked and burnt, with the men being killed and the women often being carried off. Almost always the forts are rebuilt, and the chiefs and their followers, if they have survived, take over again. But they are not likely to be left in peace (→c.500BC).

Tribes have a head for grisly spoils of war

Hereford and Worcester, c.500BC
Grisly trophies greet the visitor to Bredon hillfort: rotting human heads stuck onto poles. These novel spoils of war are gaining currency among local tribespeople, who hold that the human head has magical powers and is therefore suitable for adorning hillforts such as those here or at Maiden Castle in Dorset.

Stories are told of severed heads uttering prophecies or warnings, often in groups of three (believed to be a magic number). Heads may be cast into a lake or a river as part of a ritual associated with the gods; some 20 skulls have been placed in a cave at Wookey Hole in the Mendip Hills of Somerset.

Another feature of tribal beliefs is the ritual pit or well, about 27 metres (30 yards) deep and 1.8 metres wide, into which are cast broken spears and swords, dead ravens, hares and cocks. A favourite offering is a dog's body, associated by the tribes with their god of healing. Some tribes also carve their own stone heads, which may represent tribal deities (c.300BC).

A 20th-century artist's view of the hillfort at Maiden Castle, in Dorset.

An imported bronze ribbed pail from Weybridge, in Surrey, made by a European metalworker during the sixth century BC.

Irish tribes establish an important new settlement on hilltop site

Co Armagh, c.465BC

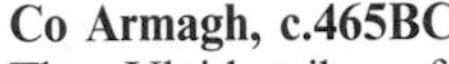

The Ulaid tribe of north-eastern Ulster has chosen a hilltop a few miles west of Armagh for its new central base, or capital. A bank and a ditch at Emain Macha enclose an area of some seven hectares (17 acres), and within this circle round houses of wattle or planks, nine metres (10 yards) across, have been built. Bronze has been widely used in the fashioning of artefacts for the capital, which stands on the site of an earlier settlement. A tiny bronze axe, a bronze socketed sickle and bronze trumpets have been made for use by members of the Ulaid here. Plans are also under way for using the central area of the enclosure for religious ceremonies.

A natural monument to a people: the hilltop at Emain Macha in Co Armagh where the Ulaid tribe set up the capital of its flourishing tribal kingdom.

Britain, c.400BC. The warmer, drier climate lengthens the growing season, meaning that more marginal upland areas can be turned into arable land.→

Box, Wiltshire, c.400BC. Finely crafted brooches with catchplates are the latest fashion and are used as cloak or dress fasteners (→c.75BC).

Rome, c.390BC. The Gauls sack the city, much to the horror of the Romans, who vow to set up a proper defence system and fortify their settlement against any such future attacks.

Highland, c.375BC. The wooden ramparts of a hillfort are destroyed by fire. This is not the first time that fire has broken out here or in other Scottish forts, and may indicate a design flaw.

British Isles, c.325BC. Pytheas, a Greek explorer based in Marseilles, makes a circumnavigation (→c.AD82).

Britain, c.300BC. Flour production has been revolutionized by the rotary quern, a new grinding method. It consists of two large stones pivoted together: the grain is poured in down the sides of the pivot as the top stone is turned and runs out as flour between the stones (→c.275BC).

Britain, c.300BC. The influence of a new learned priestly caste, the Druids, is growing. Druidic teachings and rites spread to Gaul (→c.70BC).

West Sussex, c.275BC. The immediate success of the quern, the new flour-grinding device, has led to the creation of specialist quern factories to meet the increase in demand from farmers.

Southern England, c.250BC. Metalworking increases, bringing a specialization of both tools and products. The metalworking tools available are more refined, ranging from tongs and chisels to hammers and anvils, all of which produce a wide variety of goods (→c.10BC).

Kingston upon Hull, Humberside, c.250BC. A large boat made from a dug-out log, heavily laden with rough-cut timber and meat, sinks in the river Foulness.

Cleveland, c.200BC. The forest is cleared at Thorpe Thewles to make way for a new farmstead. Farmers make the heavy clay soil more workable by the use of a drainage system dug around the farm.

Harvests grow as farming flourishes

A 20th-century reconstruction of a well-established farming community.

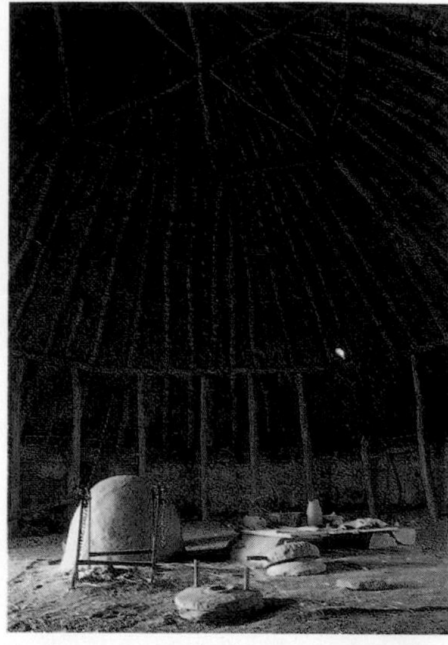

A clay oven, with domestic objects.

Britain, c.400BC

Farms are flourishing throughout lowland areas of the country, where iron tools and improved agricultural techniques have brought bigger harvests, a better diet and a settled population. Barley and wheat are now the staple crops, and farmers are able to cultivate less-fertile land thanks to the increased number of sheep – their manure has enriched much poor land – and to the development of an iron tip for the ard, a plough that breaks the ground rather than turning it. The expansion of crop growing allows farmers to produce approximately a tonne of grain per hectare (2.5 acres); they cut the crop with iron sickles.

In some areas farms are regularly spaced just over half a mile (1.5 km) apart and grouped around a hill-fort. In the forts grain is stored in large underground pits, or in wooden granaries raised on posts above the ground.

Pigs are kept for meat; cattle and sheep are primarily for milk, cheese and wool – bigger sheep-flocks have boosted the production of wool – and are rarely slaughtered before old age or disease make it necessary. Horses and dogs, sometimes eaten during rituals, are not in the usual diet (→c.AD1).

Sword and dagger fashions change as iron adapts to weapons

British Isles, c.325BC

Iron and bronze implements are now considered essential for most modern forms of skilled work and to arm a warrior. However, the supply is still extremely limited, and metal artefacts of all sorts remain beyond the reach of most of the estimated half a million people who live in the British Isles.

For the rich and powerful, however, ornate metal objects in both iron and bronze are as much a symbol of their status as metal weaponry is the foundation of their power. Iron is now clearly the preferred material for practical objects, but bronze is used for personal items and in decorative roles such as an ornate sheath for an expensive iron dagger.

A horse's bit cast in bronze, together with a guiding ring and various moulds.

Large metal objects such as buckets, cauldrons and shields are a real test of the smith's art and are more important for prestige than for usefulness, but tools such as chisels, axes, razors and knives made of iron are now essential equipment for any community. Improving the manufacture of swords and daggers, the principal iron weapons, remains the leading edge of technological development, although the common style of iron sword with a ridged leaf-shaped blade, forged complete and with a small pommel, is now almost universal in the British Isles. Decoration has become more individual and often shows signs of contact with the styles of the Mediterranean, northern Europe and the mountains of central Europe (→c.250BC).

Radical strengthening of hillfort defences betrays settlers' fears of imminent attack

Hampshire, c.400BC
The need to concentrate food stocks and improve defences appears to lie behind the massive reconstruction of the Danebury hillfort, near Andover, which is now nearing completion. Such is the scale of the rebuilding programme that a number of smaller forts nearby have been abandoned as work at Danebury has progressed.

The rampart at Danebury has been raised and the surrounding ditch redug into a steep V-shape; the entrances have been rebuilt to improve their defendability. New roads have been laid out, many new houses erected and large granaries constructed to provide a storage capacity which is far more than would be required to satisfy the immediate needs of local people. These granaries seem to be owned, or at least managed, by groups operating from within the fort itself rather than outside in the farming community. This could mean that the chief and his nobles have been assuming ever more autocratic powers over subservient peasant farmers who supply their grain.

There were ritual pits at Danebury well before the first hillfort was built. Now the central area has been levelled and four large rectangular buildings have been put up to serve as shrines and give new vigour to old customs (→c.75BC).

Tin ingots shipped from Cornwall to Gaul

A tin ingot made in Cornwall.

Cornwall, c.300BC
The steady demand for tin in European markets has put Cornish tin bosses in the forefront of a well-established trade network which stretches right down to the Mediterranean and the fringes of the political hotbeds of Asia Minor. The miners extract the tin and work it into small irregular ingots, similar in form to knucklebones. These are then carried across at low tide to St Michael's Mount, from whence merchants ship them across the Channel. Once safely landed, the ingots go south by pack-horse and along the great rivers of Gaul – the Loire, the Rhône and the Gironde – to their destinations all around the northern shores of the Mediterranean Sea (→c.100BC).

Yorkshire leaders interred with carts

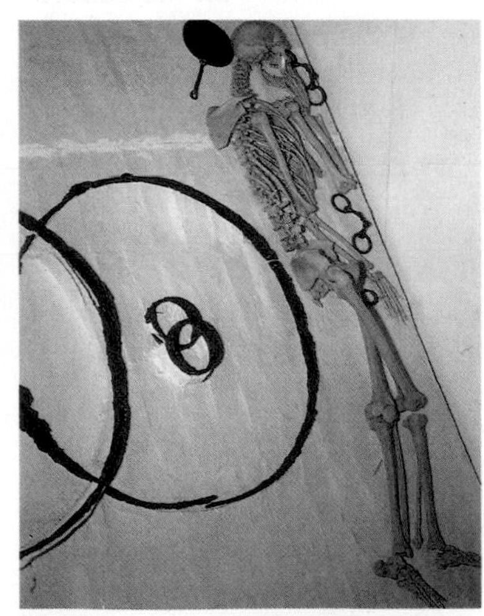
A woman buried with chariot wheels.

Yorkshire, c.250BC
Local leaders are facing death equipped with shields, swords and objects of value and accompanied by their carts or chariots. They are honoured with large burial pits, in which each is stretched out, often in the box of the cart, on top of the wheels of the dismantled vehicle, laid flat. Warriors have been entombed with spears, swords and scabbards, and one man in this area has been laid out beneath a chain-mail tunic. Some of the dead are buried with parts of horse harnesses or with objects such as mirrors; occasionally a corpse is interred with a side of pork (→c.60BC).

Regions develop their own distinctive styles for pottery decoration

England, c.200BC
Distinctive regional styles are emerging in the pottery now being made in the British Isles. In southern England, for instance, the characteristic form is a pot shaped like a saucepan, with vertical sides. There are variations in the decorative styles, though, even within this region.

In Hampshire, for example, the potters seem to favour horizontal areas with diagonal hatching, sometimes bordered by dots, whereas their Wiltshire counterparts often use an arc motif with indentations at the intersections. The straight-sided southern pots are in contrast to the rounder bowls with ring ornamentation found in the English Midlands. These pots also have patterns of scoring which differ from those predominating further south.

Yet these regional motifs originate from the same technique: potters use the tips of bones to incise geometrical lines and dots on vessels which generally have a smooth and evenly fired black surface. This "shallow-tooled" form of decoration on hardened vessels is thus used to enhance a sense of regional identity, even when the basic shape of the pot is the same (→c.90BC).

A decorated pot from Dorset.

Art has been developing in similar styles in three different areas of western Europe. Above left is a detail of a bronze ceremonial jug from Gaul, alongside an ornamented Irish necklace. The British shield (right), also made of bronze, was thrown as an offering into a river near Lincoln.

200 - 70BC

English Midlands, c.190BC. Currency bars made of iron ore are being used by local people as a means of valuing goods (→ c.125BC).

Cornwall, c.150BC. A new method of cold storage is in use in the village of Carn Euny. It is a form of large underground passage, or *fogou*, and is used for storing food or, in times of attack, to hide the locals.

Kent, c.125BC. The use of gold coins as a method of payment has spread to south-eastern England from northern Gaul. The coins are based on Greek ones which Gallic soldiers would have been accustomed to using in the Mediterranean (→ c.110BC).

Bardsey Sound, North Wales, c.120BC. A foreign trader is wrecked. The ship's route is uncertain, but she may have been following the tin trade route to south-western Britain and been blown off course.

Kent, c.110BC. Bronze coins being minted here are similar to the Greek coinage in use at Marseilles and have a high tin content which gives them a silvery appearance (→ c.70BC).

Tre'r Ceiri, Gwynedd, c.100BC. An isolated mountaintop settlement of 19 stonewalled houses has been built. It may be used only seasonally or as a temporary refuge.→

Orkney, c.100BC. A new type of settlement, dominated by thick-walled, circular, two-storey stone buildings, or *brochs*, has been established.→

Haddenham, Cambridgeshire, c.100BC. The rising water level in the Fens is threatening the isolated community living at Haddenham which breeds cattle and beaver and grows crops suited to wet land.

Wessex, c.90BC. Potters are able to imitate the pottery of northern Gaul with the introduction of the potter's wheel to their craft (→ c.40AD).

South-eastern England, c.80BC. Diviciacus, the king of the Suessiones and the most powerful ruler in northern Gaul, is recognized as overlord by the Belgae, northern Gallic immigrants to southern England (→ c.57BC).

Danebury, near Andover, Hampshire, c.75BC. The long-established hillfort settlement is destroyed by fire and abandoned; there are no plans to rebuild it.

Prosperity sows the seeds of instability

Southern Britain, c.120BC
Southern Britain has been thrown into turmoil by a series of burnings, massacres and pillagings. As a consequence of the unrest, people are building more massive ramparts on their hillforts and making extensive use of the slingshot – a lethal weapon in expert hands.

Such widespread disturbances seem unwarranted in a region which has enjoyed relative affluence for centuries. But this very prosperity has sown the seeds of instability. The population has risen to record levels, while farmlands have become steadily more exhausted and livestock diseases have been on the increase. In a society in which conspicuous consumption adds to prestige, the pressure to maintain one's standing – by fair means or foul – appears to be fuelling the tension.

A sinister development is the growth in child burials, indicating that people are also taking drastic action to curb the number of mouths to feed.

Growing influence of Rome boosts trade

British export: a bronze plaque.

South-western England, c.100BC
The growing influence of Rome in the Mediterranean is giving a boost to trade with distant lands such as Britain. The Roman move into southern Gaul, especially, is forcing Gallic tribes further north and west to adjust their trading habits and open up new markets.

This probably lies behind the flourishing trade between south-western and western Britain and north-western Gaul which has grown up around the bustling port of Hengistbury Head in Dorset. A prime mover in this trade is a Gallic tribe from south-western Brittany, known as the Veneti, which has built up the largest merchant fleet in the region and has a reputation for producing highly skilled mariners.

The Veneti have become the chief middlemen between Hengistbury and mainland Europe: their vessels arrive at Hengistbury laden with local Gallic goods such as fine black pottery and coins, and goods from the Roman world, especially wine, which is usually transported in large pottery jars known as *amphorae*. The ships return to Gaul with a range of goods from all over south-western Britain.

Hengistbury is home to a thriving metalworking industry, and metals – tin, copper, lead, iron, gold and silver – are its chief exports; other goods destined for overseas may also include shale, salt, corn, cattle and hides, together with slaves and hounds (→ c.55BC).

Somerset fair is famous for its jewellery

Somerset, c.150BC
People from near and far are flocking to a great annual trade fair at Meare, a marsh settlement not far from Glastonbury. Coming on foot or by horse, cart and log-canoe across the boggy surrounding land, men and women gather to feast and exchange wares, many made at Meare itself. On offer are ladles, baskets and pots as well as axes, sickles, saws, files and knives. Weaving is also common. However, Meare's speciality is the manufacture of brightly coloured glass beads, which make attractive necklaces. Colours include blue, yellow and blue-green.

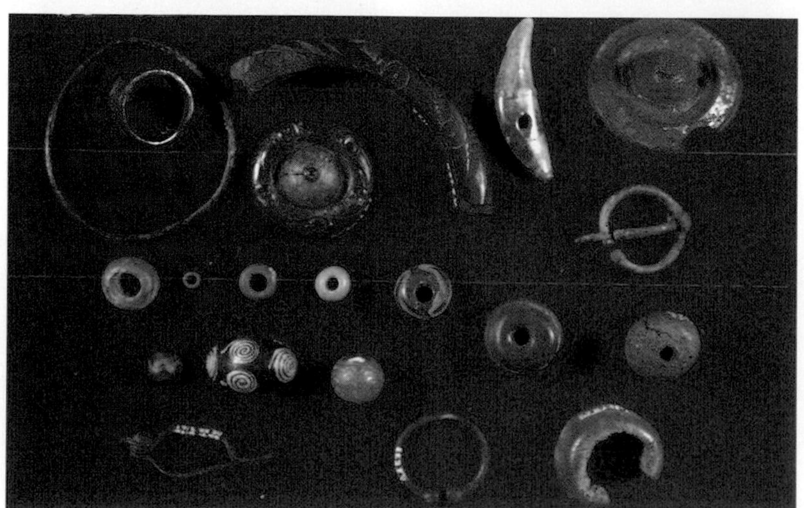

Attractive and highly coloured wares for sale at the fair.

Gallic tribes cross Channel for pillage

Southern England, c.100BC
Newcomers – and not always welcome ones – are arriving in Britain from across the Channel. The immigrants are believed to be Belgae, members of tribes from northern Gaul, who speak a Celtic tongue like their British counterparts.

The original aim of the Belgae was apparently to pillage captives and livestock in order to supply the lucrative market in the Roman-influenced south of Gaul. There, to the delight of Italian traders, the Gauls will reportedly pay one slave for an *amphora* of wine – a huge price. Now, however, the Belgae are coming to stay, possibly in fear of Roman expansion.

Contacts between Britain and northern Gaul have have led to a number of changes, including the use of gold coinage and sophisticated wheel-made pottery. Social habits have also been influenced, as in the trend towards burning rather than burying the dead (→ c.80BC).

Gold neck-rings all the rage in Norfolk

Exquisite craftsmanship: a British neck-ring from Snettisham, in Norfolk.

Norfolk, c.75BC
Members of the status-conscious élites at the top of society place great value on ornamentation. Fine metalwork heads the list of desired accessories, and, for those who can afford them, the most beautiful personal luxuries are twisted neck-rings, or torcs, which are being produced with exquisite craftsmanship in East Anglia. Torcs are often made of electrum, an alloy of gold and silver, and decorated with characteristically British spiral designs. Other goods eagerly sought by better-off Britons include finely embellished weapons, brooches, mirrors and horse-fittings.

Southern goldsmiths copy imported coins

Southern England, c.70BC
Gold coins from mainland Europe are prompting English imitations. Used primarily as gifts and for warrior payments, the original coins are thought to have been introduced by Belgic tribes from northern Gaul, perhaps as early as 125BC. They are common in areas of Belgic settlement such as Kent and Essex. Gold coins are now made as far away from direct Belgic influence as Dorset or Lincolnshire. Meanwhile, coins for use as currency are being made from less rare metals such as tin and bronze.

Sacrificial offerings are made in watery places as Druids intercede with the gods

British Isles, c.70BC
In many parts of the British Isles influential priests known as "Druids", whose training may last more than 20 years, have become established as the chief mediators between the human and the divine. They give guidance about the fantastic array of gods and goddesses, heroes, sacred animals and birds, which in their many guises are believed to rule over the natural world – and which must be venerated or appeased in open-air shrines, springs and sacred rivers.

Among the divinities most important to the Britons are the three "mother goddesses", who promote fertility, childbirth and, sometimes, war. Others, such as Alator, Teutates ("the Ruler of the People"), Camulos, Nemetius ("the Sacred") and Nodens ("the Cloudmaker"), protect their tribes and supporters in war and in their daily lives. The animal kingdom comes under the protection of Cernunnos, "the Lord of the Beasts", and animals like the bull, the stag and the boar are regarded as sacred. The flight of birds such as the raven and the crane is used to make prophecies.

According to the Druids, the soul survives death, passing into the "otherworld" beyond. The seat of the human soul is the head, which is worshipped and treated as a powerful charm. The heads of enemies defeated in war are much prized and regarded as potential offerings to the gods. Many are left in sacred oak groves or rivers. In this warrior society weapons are also thought to be worthy objects of sacrifice. They, too, are left in watery sites – in bogs such as Llyn Cerrig Bach on the island of Anglesey, in streams and, in particular, in the sacred river Thames (→AD55).

Bronze shield cast into the Thames.

House styles: a hut squats beneath forbidding stone ramparts (left) at Tre'r Ceiri hillfort in the Llyn peninsula in Gwynedd, one of a series of fortress settlements being built in the hills of north Wales. Further north, at Gurness in the Orkneys, the islanders have been gathering in a new type of building (right) – a thick-walled stone tower known as a "broch" which also offers better protection for communities in the event of an attack.

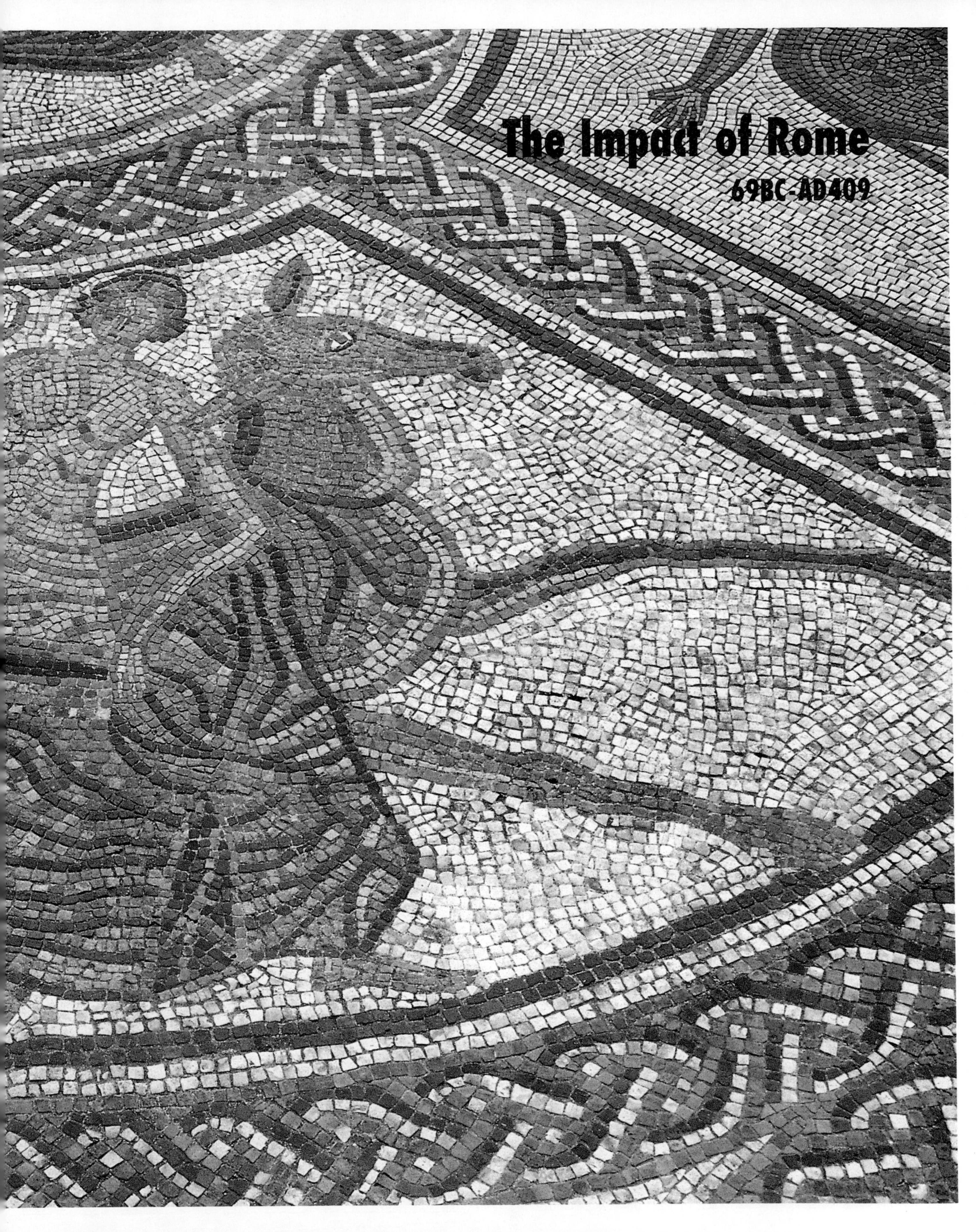

The Impact of Rome

69BC-AD409

69-54BC

St Albans, Herts, c.60BC. Residents in the area are getting a taste for wine as it arrives in Britain via new trade routes with Italy (→c.AD55).

Gaul [France], c.58BC. Having won control of the provinces of Cisalpine Gaul, Transalpine Gaul and Illyricum, Julius Caesar, the Roman military leader, opens a new campaign in Gaul, conquering the Gallic tribe known as the Helvetii at Mont Beuvray.

Kent, c.57BC. Refugees from Gaul arrive following Caesar's defeat of the Belgic tribes in Picardy (→c.51BC).

Gaul, 56BC. Caesar sets up a firm base on the Channel coast.

Channel, summer 56BC. On Caesar's orders, a warship commanded by Gaius Volsenus reconnoitres the southern English coast for possible landing places (→27/8/55BC).

Gaul, August 56BC. Wary of Rome's military build-up on the northern coast of Gaul, British envoys arrive to offer submission to Caesar. They return home with Commius, whom Caesar has made king of the Gallic tribe known as the Atrebates (→28/8/55BC).

Brittany, 56BC. Gallic merchants trading across the Channel with south-western Britain call for British military assistance in the struggle against the Romans (→c.55BC).

Kent, 28 August 55BC. Commius, the king of the Gallic Atrebates, who was arrested when he came to Britain last year as an envoy of Caesar, is freed (→51BC).

Southern Britain, c.55BC. Trade in copper with Gaul has been halted by the outbreak of war between the Romans and Gallic tribes (→cAD10).

South-eastern England, 54BC. The king of the Trinovantes tribe has been killed by a neighbouring ruler, Cassivellaunus; his son Mandubracius flees to Gaul and surrenders to Caesar.

Gaul, June 54BC. Caesar assembles a huge fleet to invade Britain again (→8/7).

South-eastern England, July 54BC. Cassivellaunus, the strongest ruler, is chosen to lead the British coalition against the Romans (→21/7).

Britain, autumn 54BC. Caesar takes hostages and imposes an annual levy on the Britons before moving back to Gaul with his troops (→c.46BC).

Romans turn their thoughts to Britain

Gaul [France], c.60BC
Roman forces now consolidating their hold on Gaul are starting to turn their attention to the island, and its peoples, on the other side of the Channel. For centuries there has been a thriving seaborne trade (and piracy) between Britain and its neighbours, through which Roman leaders such as Julius Caesar, a prominent and ambitious general, have acquired some knowledge of the land which some believe will be their next target for colonization as the Roman Empire expands. In spite of reports that they dye their bodies with woad, giving them a blue colour, Caesar regards these painted Britons as reasonably civilized (→56BC).

Painted Britons (17th-century view).

Cremation of dead is new burial trend

South-eastern England, c.60BC
Britons in south-eastern England are burning the bodies of their dead rather than exposing them or burying them whole in coffins. This new trend in burials is concentrated in areas south of the Thames, although it occurs occasionally north of the river, too. The ashes of the dead person are usually buried in, or with, a ceramic urn or similar container. Simple graves may hold nothing but the ashes and urn, but wealthier people are dignified by the personal ornaments buried with them, such as decorated bronze vessels or wine buckets (→c.30BC).

Caesar's legions meet a fierce resistance

Slaves man the oars below, while Roman soldiers on deck present arms.

Kent, 27 August 55BC
Roman troops led by Julius Caesar, the conqueror of Gaul, today landed on British soil. The 10,000-strong 7th and 10th Legions were fiercely resisted as they came ashore, but tonight they have secured a beach-head between Deal and Walmer. Caesar had set sail at midnight from near Boulogne, and by nine o'clock this morning was in sight of Dover, where the cliffs were lined by armed Britons. After waiting until afternoon for more ships, Caesar headed northwards before running his fleet ashore. At first the Romans were in difficulties, fighting from the water, but responding to skilful leadership they put the British to flight.

Invaders retreat under cover of darkness

Kent, September 55BC
The Romans have abandoned their toehold in Kent after British tribes broke a truce agreed following the invasion last month. With their fleet badly damaged in a Channel storm – and reinforcements from Gaul forced to return to port – the Roman 7th Legion was ambushed by a British force which included cavalry and chariots. The Britons were driven off and again sued for peace. Poor weather prevented renewed fighting, but Caesar knew that he remained vulnerable. Under cover of darkness, he and his troops slipped across the Channel in hastily repaired ships (→6/54BC).

Rome reigns supreme in the known world

Rome, 55BC
Four and a half centuries ago Rome was no more than a small community in central Italy, a fledgeling republic born of the farming villages that had grown up around the river Tiber. Now it is the uncontested master of the known world. Having subdued northern Italy and the Greek colonies of the south, including Sicily, Rome has come to dominate large parts of North Africa, Asia Minor and Europe.

The structure of the Roman republic is complex, organized around a senate, magistracy and various popular assemblies; it is also under strain, for a number of reasons. Not least of these is the class struggle between the underprivileged masses, the "plebs", and the ruling élite or patricians. Then there is the mutual rivalry of the men at the top, such as Pompey, Crassus and Julius Caesar.

Such rivalry may explain why Britain has aroused Caesar's interest. Afraid of returning from his campaign in Gaul to Rome, where he fears that Pompey and Crassus are plotting against him, Caesar has decided to invade, claiming that Britons are supplying his enemies in Gaul.

Opposition crumbles as Romans return in force

Attackers advance after Kent landing

Kent, 8 July 54BC
The Romans have returned. They landed yesterday in far greater numbers than last year and have already penetrated further inland. Tonight Julius Caesar, again in command, is fortifying his position.

Caesar left Boulogne two days ago with at least 800 ships carrying five legions and 2,000 cavalry. The scale of the armada appears to have unnerved the Britons, who put up little resistance. The Romans again landed on the beaches near Deal and by midday yesterday – with the Britons having withdrawn inland – the entire Roman army was ashore and a base camp built.

Caesar then marched 12 miles by night to a ford on the river Stour [Canterbury], surprising the British defenders, who retreated to a hill-fort at nearby Bigbury. The fort entrances had been blocked, but the Romans made a makeshift causeway and then men of the 7th Legion, shields locked over their heads, stormed the fortress with few casualties. Many Britons were killed or put to flight.

Julius Caesar, who led an invasion force of five legions and 2,000 cavalry.

Resistance leader offers peace terms

Hertfordshire, 29 August 54BC
Roman forces have stormed the headquarters of their greatest opponent, Cassivellaunus. With the failure, too, of an attack on Caesar's beach-head, Cassivellaunus is now suing for peace. The war is over.

Cassivellaunus had kept up a series of guerrilla attacks on the Romans as they headed northwards to the Thames. These tactics slowed the advance, but Caesar was still able to cross the river in the London region. His advance was slow but brutal; his troops laid waste great areas.

This devastation, allied to the tribal rivalries of the Britons, persuaded several tribes, led by the Trinovantes, to offer their support to Caesar in return for protection. Their envoys told Caesar where to find the cleverly hidden stronghold of Cassivellaunus. It was well fortified, but attacks on two sides forced the defenders to flee. Caesar is likely to accept his foe's bid for peace, not least because he plans to withdraw to Gaul [France] for the winter (→ autumn 54BC).

Chariots defeated by Roman cavalry

Kent, 21 July 54BC
The Romans have been confronted by a new challenge: mastering the art of chariot warfare. Yesterday, while the invaders prepared to head north, British forces under Cassivellaunus – the leader of a powerful tribe based in Hertfordshire – sent out raiding parties of cavalry and charioteers, disorientating the legionaries in their heavy armour. Each chariot has a driver and a soldier; they attack at speed, throwing javelins at their foe, after which the warrior dismounts to fight hand to hand while the driver waits to aid a retreat.

Emboldened by their success the British today attacked again, but three legions and Caesar's entire cavalry were waiting. The Britons fled, with the enemy in hot pursuit.

Julius Caesar leads his troops into uncharted enemy territory

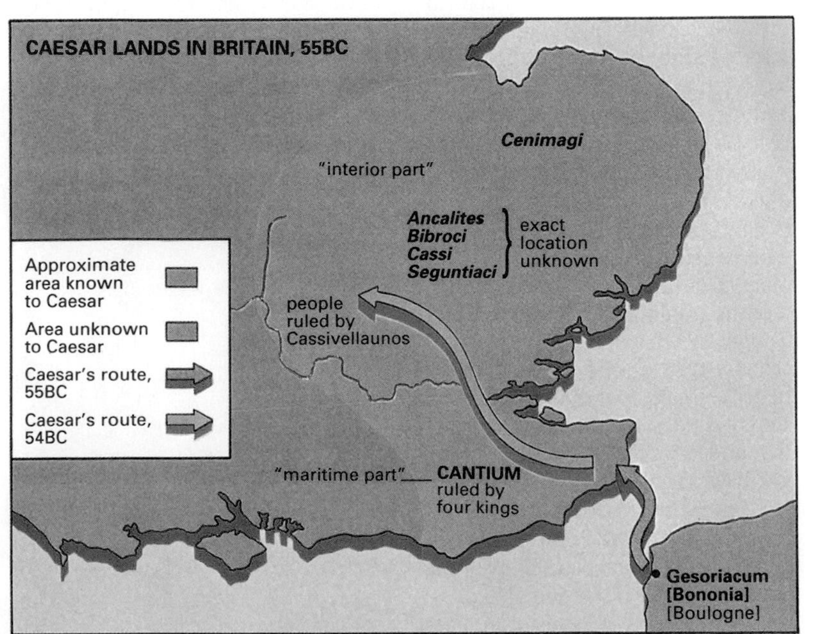

Julius Caesar's view of Britain and its tribes, and his invasion routes. He designates the area beyond the south-east "terra incognita" [unknown land].

Kent, summer 54BC
All military commanders need to have reliable knowledge of the land that they will lead their men through, as well as the strength and position of potential enemies. Julius Caesar lacked all of this in his first invasion of Britain last year and is not much better informed this time.

Although there is much trade between northern Gaul [France] (now under Roman occupation) and southern Britain, hardly anything is known about the island. No one even knows for sure how big it is. Caesar has been led to believe, nonetheless, that Britain consists of a stable agricultural zone near the sea (which he calls the "maritime part") and a wild pastoral hinterland (the "interior part"). He also knows the names of a few tribes but has only a general idea of the areas which they control.

53BC - AD30

Gaul [France], 52BC. Commius, Caesar's former ally, falls out with Rome when he supports a Gallic rebellion against Roman rule (→ 51BC).

Ireland, c.50BC. Tribes in central Ireland are building a huge earthen wall along the river Shannon, to keep out the warring tribes from the north.

Britain, c.46BC. Caesar's plans for a permanent occupation are postponed by the renewed outbreak of revolt in Belgic (northern) Gaul (→ c.44BC).

Rome, c.44BC. Julius Caesar is assassinated by political rivals.

Rome, c.27BC. Following his defeat of Marcus Antonius (Mark Antony) in Egypt in 31BC, Octavian, Caesar's adopted nephew, becomes emperor and is given the title "Augustus [sacred]" by the senate (→ 27BC).

Gaul, c.27BC. Emperor Augustus postpones invasion plans for Britain while unrest continues here (→ 19/08/AD14).

Southern England, c.20BC. Tincommius, the son of Commius, is made king of the Atrebates (→ c.15BC).

Lexden, Essex, c.15BC. Addedomaros, the king of the Trinovantes, recently allied with Rome, is buried near Colchester with all the pomp of a Roman leader (→ c.AD150).

Britain, c.10BC. Objects are being made out of brass, an alloy of copper and zinc introduced by the Romans and originally imported as jewellery and currency (→ c.AD10).

Barton Court Farm, Abingdon, Oxfordshire, c.AD1. Farmers have started to grow a new type of wheat for making bread (→ c.AD35).

Southern England, c.AD10. Two new rulers emerge: Verica, the grandson of Commius, based at Silchester, and Cunobelinus, who is at Colchester (→ c.AD16).

Braughing, Hertfordshire, c.AD10. A trading post is founded which is used by traders from the Mediterranean.→

Rome, 19 August AD14. Augustus dies and is succeeded as emperor by his stepson Tiberius (→ 16/03/37).

East Anglia, c.AD16. The survivors of a shipwreck, who include Roman soldiers, are given safe passage back to Gaul at the instigation of Cunobelinus, the ruler of the Trinovantes (→ c.AD30).

Fugitive chieftain plans new kingdom

South-eastern England, c.51BC
The Gallic chieftain Commius has fled across the Channel with a band of supporters, intent on forging a new kingdom in south-eastern England. Commius was sent to Britain by Julius Caesar before the Roman invasions to try to win over some of the British tribes, but his mission was a failure and he was temporarily held prisoner before returning to Gaul. He fell out of favour with Rome last year after supporting a rebellion against Roman rule by the Gallic resistance leader Vercingetorix.

Caesar had made Commius king of the Atrebates, a tribe with lands in both Britain and Gaul. The British Atrebates are weaker, which lessened Commius's significance as a potential ally in 55BC, but which may now enable him to emerge as their leader. He has established a base at Silchester, in Hampshire, and plans to unite several tribes into a major force from the Thames to the south coast (→ c.20BC).

Silchester: the foundations of a rectangular house and a pre-Roman well.

Silchester remodelled in the Roman style

Hampshire, c.15BC
The Atrebates – now a powerful confederation of tribes in south-eastern England led by Commius's son, Tincommius – are transforming their settlement at Silchester, founded over 30 years ago. Traditional round houses, haphazardly arranged, are being superseded by Roman-style rectangular ones built on a grid of straight, cobbled roads. The Romans may have gone, but the élite ruling this new town wants to imitate the fashionable architecture of the Mediterranean and its ancestral Gaul [France] (→ c.AD85).

Caesar carries out reform of calendar

Rome, 46BC
Julius Caesar, now the most powerful man in the Roman Empire, has resolved the discrepancy between the lunar and solar years by reforming the calendar. In the British Isles, as in many parts of the known world, time is reckoned according to lunar phases. Each month is divided on the basis of the moon's waxing and waning. A year is also divided into two parts – a dark and a light (corresponding to autumn and winter, and spring and summer). The lunar year consists of 12 months totalling 355 days, ten and a quarter days shorter than the solar year [the time the earth takes to make one revolution around the sun]. To keep the two in line, every two and a half years a 13th month is added to the calendar.

Caesar has introduced to the Romans a year of 365 days. April, June, September and November have 30 days; all others have 31, the only exception being February, which has 28 (except every fourth year, when it will have 29) (→ c.540).

Rich are buried with worldly treasures

Hertfordshire, c.30BC
Concern with prestige does not end with death for top Britons, who fill their graves with high-class goods such as bronze vessels and tankards, *amphorae* [tall wine jars] and silver cups – all of them testifying to their owners' wealth and power. Recent grave goods at Welwyn and Baldock included a board-game and a bronze nail-cleaner. The nobles belonged to local dynasties which control the movement of luxury goods from continental Europe, in particular from central Italy and Belgic (northern) Gaul (→ c.15BC).

Varied goods from a Welwyn grave bear witness to an aristocrat's wealth.

Ousted leaders seek refuge with Romans

A coin showing Augustus enthroned.

South-eastern England, c.AD5
The emergence of a powerful tribe as the dominant power in south-eastern England is giving the Romans food for thought. This tribe – which is known as the Catuvellauni – is centred on Hertfordshire and has been steadily encroaching on the territory of its neighbours. The Catuvellauni have already begun unseating their rivals. One of these is Tincommius, the leader of the Atrebatic confederation of tribes centred on Hampshire, whose father Commius founded the kingdom after he fell out with Rome.

Tincommius, however, seems to be better disposed towards the Romans, perhaps because he has benefited from cross-Channel trade. In any case, he and Dubnovellaunus, another ousted ruler, probably from the Trinovantes tribe based in Essex, have sought refuge with Emperor Augustus in Rome, and the Romans have treated their arrival as support for the claim that Augustus is overlord of Britain. This claim is chiefly for propaganda purposes – at least for the moment (→c.AD30).

Roman luxuries popular with aristocracy

Britain, c.AD10
In spite of their continuing independence from Rome, tribes of central and southern Britain are acquiring a taste for the Roman high life and forging ever-closer trading connections with the Mediterranean world.

British aristocrats are importing silver- and bronzeware from Italy and olive oil and wine from Spain, together with high-quality tableware from Gaul [France], just across the Channel. The Romans seem to prefer trading to raiding. After all, it is cheaper to raise heavy customs duties than to maintain an army which has to levy tribute. Britain also conveniently supplies Rome with cattle, hides and vital raw materials such as gold and silver, as well as slaves.

Southern British kings, apparently keen to imitate Roman fashion, have also started to issue coins in the Roman imperial style, with portraits resembling Emperor Augustus (→c.AD85).

'King' Cunobelinus rules

A gold coin struck in the name of Cunobelinus, who calls himself "king".

South-eastern England, c.AD30
Much of the richest part of Britain is now effectively under one ruler: Cunobelinus, or Cunobelin, whose capital is at Colchester. His power and influence extends from Bedfordshire to the Sussex coast and from Berkshire to Kent.

Cunobelinus claims on his coins to be the son of Tasciovanus, the ruler of the powerful Catuvellauni tribe until about 20 years ago, although his first coins were minted at Colchester when it was in Trinovantian territory. So either he overthrew the Trinovantes and ruled them for his father, or he is a Trinovantian who overthrew the Catuvellauni and calls himself the "son" of their old ruler to appear more legitimate.

Cunobelinus has made a point of having close contacts with Rome. His coins use Latin words such as *rex* [king], and under his rule the quantity of Roman imports has grown while British goods have begun making their mark on the continent. And when a number of Roman troops were shipwrecked off the coast of East Anglia about 14 years ago, it was probably Cunobelinus who ensured their safe return to Roman territory (→39).

A glimpse of Britain's tribal society

Britain, c.AD30
If Julius Caesar were today planning to invade Britain, he would be far better informed about the tribes that live here. While the picture is still incomplete, it is now clear that tribal groups are bigger than in Caesar's day [*see map on page 49*]. This presents the military with two possibilities: either resistance to any future invasion will be better co-ordinated, or else Rome might be able to play off one tribe against another – divide and rule, a classic Roman strategy.

An important power bloc lies north of the Thames, where the Trinovantes and Catuvellauni form a large confederation. They are at odds with another confederation in southern Britain, led by the Atrebates – to the west of whom are the Durotriges and the Dobunni. Other confederations exist in Wales, such as that of the Demetae. The Brigantes control central Britain, while in the very north there are numerous tribes, many grouped together as the Caledonii.

The Romans think the south-eastern tribes "civilized", as they have adopted continental ideas and wares, while those of the north and west are thought backward. The latters' assessment of Rome is not recorded.

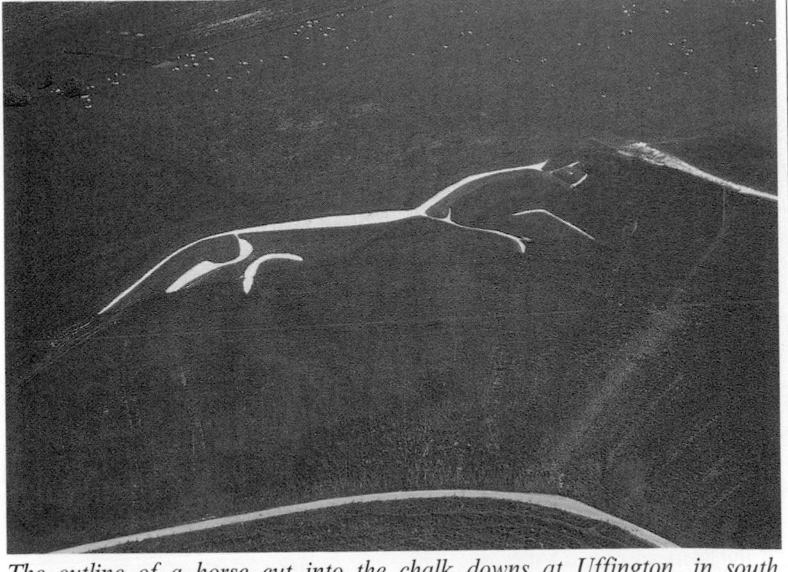

The outline of a horse cut into the chalk downs at Uffington, in south Oxfordshire, is like horses on coins of both the Dobunni and the Atrebates.

31 - 43

Nottinghamshire, c.35. Farmers are beginning to lay out fields in a regular pattern as a means of improving crop growth and emphasizing land ownership (→c.135).

Italy, 16 March 37. Emperor Tiberius dies; he is succeeded by his great-nephew Gaius, nicknamed "Caligula [Little Boot]" – derived from his childhood fondness for the army (→spring 40).

Canterbury, Kent, c.39. In a big tribal split Cunobelinus, the ruler of south-eastern England, expels his son, Adminius, the former regent in Kent, who flees to take refuge with Caligula in Rome (→41).

Rome, 24 January 41. After a reign characterized by cruelty and depravity, and shortly after declaring himself a god, Caligula is murdered by two of his Praetorian Guard (→25/01).

Rome, 25 January 41. Claudius, Caligula's uncle, who has long been believed to be mentally unsound, is discovered by the Praetorian Guard hiding in the palace. Despite his own republican leanings and those of most senators, he is declared emperor by the troops and is recognized by the senate (→43).

Colchester, Essex, 41. Cunobelinus, the most powerful British ruler in south-eastern England and a long-time ally of Rome, is dead. Over the last 25 years he has gradually extended his rule beyond his original power base north of the Thames, taking over large areas formerly belonging to the Cantii and Atrebates tribes based on Kent and Hampshire respectively. He is succeeded by his sons Togodumnus and Caratacus, who are thought not to share his pro-Roman views (→42).

South-eastern England, 42. King Verica of the Atrebates is expelled from his kingdom by Caratacus and Togodumnus and flees to Claudius in Rome for help (→c.43).

Kent, summer 43. The Roman commander Aulus Plautius lands at Richborough at the head of a 40,000-strong invasion force.→

Kent, summer 43. Togodumnus, joint ruler with Caratacus, is killed as their forces withdraw after a battle at the river Medway.→

Rome, 43. Claudius leaves the imperial administration in the hands of Lucius Vitellius during his visit to Britain.→

I came, I saw – I took home sea shells

Caligula on his horse Incitatus.

Boulogne, Gaul, spring 40
The young Emperor Gaius – nicknamed "Caligula [Little Boot]" since childhood because of his fondness for dressing up as a soldier – has called off a planned invasion of Britain in the face of what appears to be a near mutiny among his troops. In disgust he has ordered them to go home laden with the spoils of war they deserve – sea shells from the Channel shore.

The cancellation is a bitter personal blow to the volatile 28-year-old emperor, who had desperately wanted to cross the Channel in the footsteps of his ancestor Julius Caesar. Moreover, Caligula had his excuse in the person of the British prince Adminius, who fled to Gaul [France] last year after being exiled by his father, Cunobelinus, and persuaded Caligula that Britain was ripe for plucking.

Caligula, in Gaul on a campaign against Germany, headed for the Roman base at Boulogne, and is even reported to have set sail himself, eventually turning back when he saw that no one wanted to follow (→24/01/41).

Grand temples replace traditional shrines

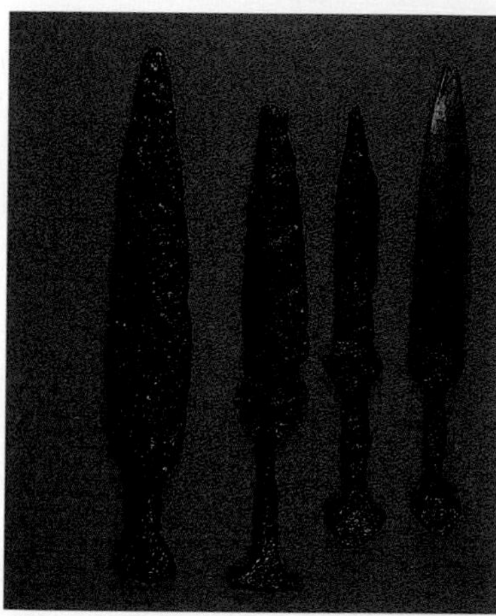

Tiny iron swords found at Harlow.

Hampshire, c.40
Plans to build a large stone temple in Roman style are soon to be put into effect on Hayling Island. A temple already exists there, but it is a more modest, wooden structure sacred to the local tribe, the Atrebates. The project appears to be the initiative of the Atrebates' king, Verica, who is also constructing a palace on the mainland. The new temple will be built on top of the present one and follow the existing layout – a circular tower within a rectangular enclosure.

The Catuvellauni tribe is planning a similar development on one of its sacred sites at Harlow, in Essex. Elsewhere the story is different. Smaller village shrines are being left as they are. It seems that British tribes are concentrating on their holiest religious centres to build prestigious temples. The tower at Hayling Island, however, looks as though it will outdo them all. When finished it will stand some 15.2 metres (50 feet) high and be decorated with painted wall plaster in a variety of colours (→55).

Potters throw in their lot with revolutions

South-eastern England, c.40
A dramatic rise in the number of commercial potteries is taking place to cater for an ever-increasing demand for fine tableware and other pottery. This has been made possible by the arrival from Gaul [France] of the potter's wheel, allowing the making of vessels in shapes almost impossible to make by hand alone. Today's potters can make things such as platters, dishes and flagons, formerly available only as Gallic imports (→c.85).

Ejected British king seeks aid in Rome

A coin showing Verica "Rex".

Southern England, c.43
Tension between Britain and Rome has grown since the death about two years ago of Cunobelinus, the king of the Catuvellauni and Trinovantes, and the succession of his sons Caratacus and Togodumnus. Like their father they have pursued expansionist policies, and they have ejected King Verica of the Atrebates, a tribe of Gallic origin in Hampshire, Sussex and Surrey.

Verica has fled to Emperor Claudius for help, and as he is evidently a friend of Rome – he uses the Latin title *rex* [king] – his plea is likely to be listened to. Besides, Claudius needs to prove that he is fit to be emperor, and Roman prestige is still smarting from the farcical invasion bid in 40. Then, Caligula used as his pretext the grievances of Adminius, another son of Cunobelinus who had been exiled, possibly in a row with his brothers – the same men who have now expelled Verica. Claudius needs no more excuses.→

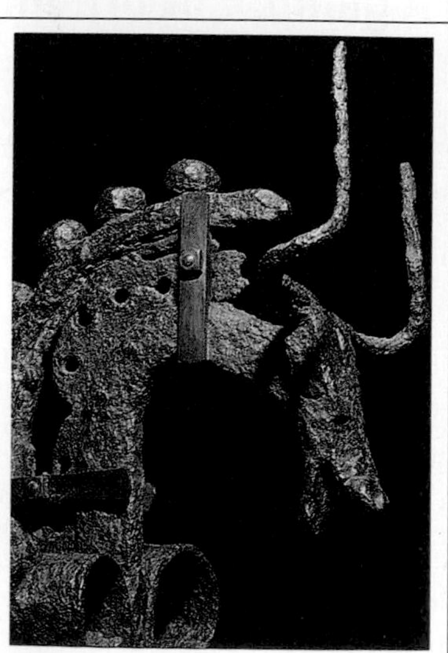

"Fire-dog": used to hang utensils above fires in British homes.

Massive Roman invasion stuns British defenders

Scale of landings causes fast retreat

Kent, summer 43
The Romans have invaded. With an estimated 40,000 troops in the invasion force the front-line troops have disembarked at Richborough and have already seen off the Britons in two skirmishes. The Romans crossed the Channel in three successive waves, all apparently planning to land at the same destination. The British leaders, Caratacus and Togodumnus, have fallen back into the interior, with the Romans, led by the veteran Aulus Plautius, a former governor of Pannonia [Hungary], in pursuit.

An invasion was planned three years ago, when Caligula faced a near mutiny as he urged his troops to set sail from Gaul. But this time the army is backing Caligula's uncle, Emperor Claudius, even though he had to send Narcissus, a former slave, to spur on the troops. They embarked amid disgruntled cries of "Hooray for Saturnalia!" – a reference to the Roman festival when masters do the bidding of their slaves.

Britons outwitted by enemy tactics

Kent, summer 43
The Romans have won a crucial two-day battle on the river Medway. Togodumnus, a British resistance leader, died in the fighting, while his brother, Caratacus, has fled north-westwards with their surviving troops. Sure that the Romans would try to cross the river by a bridge, Caratacus and Togodumnus had set up camp on the opposite bank. But Roman auxiliary troops moved upstream to ford the river and launch a pre-emptive strike, shooting down the horses of the feared British charioteers.

Legionaries under Flavius Vespasianus (Vespasian) and his brother Sabinus then crossed the river to strong resistance, but a Roman offensive under Hosidius Geta the next morning finally put the Britons to flight.

Badbury Rings fortress, in Dorset, is among those captured by the Romans.

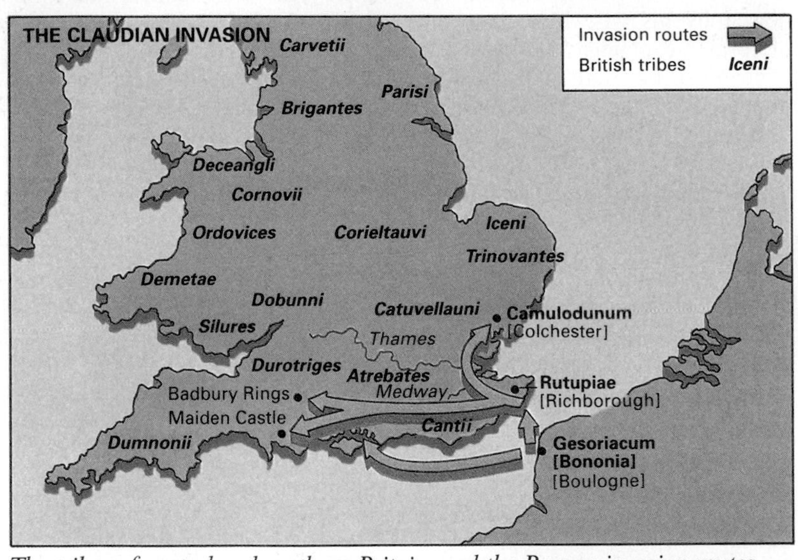

The tribes of central and southern Britain, and the Roman invasion routes.

Invaders continue to advance westward

Dorset, late summer 43
With the south-east securely under Rome's boot, the main area of continuing opposition to the enemy advance in southern Britain is the west country, where the Durotriges tribe of Dorset and the western part of the Atrebates tribe in particular still refuse to come to heel. Further west still, the Dumnonii tribes of Devon and Cornwall remain outside Roman control.

However, with Emperor Claudius still in Britain, the 2nd Legion under Vespasian is conducting a fierce campaign in the west. Vespasian – who conquered the Isle of Wight following the victory at the Medway – is making deep inroads into British resistance here and is becoming skilled at attacking the imposing earthwork hillfortresses typical of this undulating region. First an artillery barrage showers the defenders with a lethal iron rain, forcing them off the ramparts and laying them open to the direct infantry assault which follows. Twenty forts have so far fallen, including Badbury Rings and the great stronghold of Maiden Castle. It seems probable that the total surrender of the tribes cannot be long delayed.

Emperor celebrates as tribes surrender

Essex, summer 43
British resistance in the south-east has ended. To mark the Roman victory, Emperor Claudius himself has presided at an awesome surrender ceremony at Colchester, the capital of the defeated Trinovantes tribe and the legendary seat of the great British war-god Camulos. The emperor led a grand parade which included members of the Praetorian Guard (his personal bodyguard) and key senators – he was too canny to leave Rome without them – as well as elephants.

Resistance crumbled weeks ago, when Aulus Plautius, the Roman leader, reached the river Thames. He sent for Claudius, who wanted to take the final prize, Colchester, in person. Now Claudius has accepted the surrender of the south-eastern tribes which led the British resistance, and received homage and peace offers from ten tribal chiefs, including representatives of the Atrebates, Cantii, Durotriges and Iceni. But most exotic was an embassy from the king of the Orkney Islands, more than a thousand miles north of here. Clearly news of the conquest has reached the furthest quarters of Britain. But it is not thought likely that the Romans will occupy these distant islands, at least for the moment, for there is still fighting in the west, and still one British leader who will not submit: Caratacus (→48).

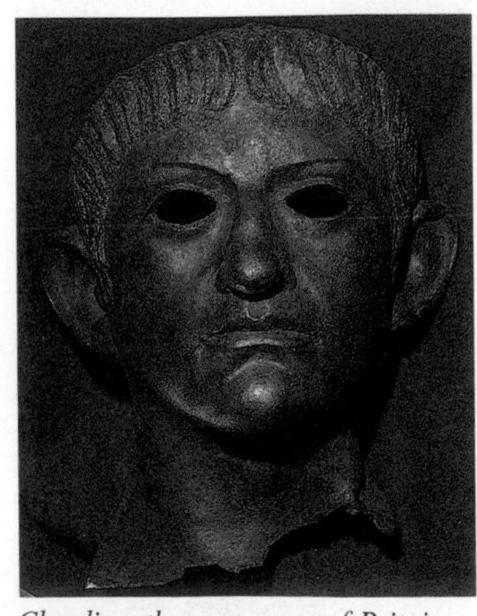

Claudius, the conqueror of Britain.

44-59

Rome, 44. The senate is to build two triumphal arches, in Rome and Gaul, to mark the submission of ten British kings.

South-eastern England, 45. Land occupied by the Trinovantes and Catuvellauni tribes is being garrisoned with Roman forts as the army moves inland (→ 46).

Chichester, West Sussex, c.45. A supply base is being built here to supply the expanding nearby town.

Peterborough, Cambs, c.46. A fort is being built for the 19th Legion at Longthorpe (→ 60).

Rome, 47. Aulus Plautius, the commander of the invasion forces and first Roman governor of Britain, retires with great military honours for his services. He is replaced by Publius Ostorius Scapula.

Britain, 48. Rebel tribes in the west, led by Caratacus, launch raids against the Romans (→ 51).

Gloucester, 48. The Roman governor, Scapula, and the 20th Legion move to a new fortress at Kingsholm to begin the campaign against the rebels in Wales (→ 67).

Central England, c.50. A communications line between Exeter and Lincoln [the Fosse Way] is being built, probably to mark the boundary of areas under Roman occupation.

Wales, 51. Caratacus moves north in an attempt to escape but is defeated in a clash with Scapula and seeks refuge with Cartimandua, the queen of the Brigantes. Probably under Roman pressure, she hands him over to Scapula.→

Rome, 51. Emperor Claudius stages a great display to mark the capture of Caratacus and his family, including a parade of the captives.→

London, 52. Exhausted by the struggle against Caratacus in Wales, Scapula dies suddenly.

Britain, 52. Aulus Didius Gallus, an experienced soldier, is appointed governor (→ 58).

Rome, 13 October 54. Emperor Claudius dies after eating mushrooms, possibly poisoned, and is succeeded by Nero, his 17-year-old adopted son (→ 4/69).

Britain, 58. After the sudden death last year of Quintus Veranius, just months after he arrived to succeed Didius Gallus, Gaius Suetonius Paulinus becomes governor. He plans to continue the campaign in Wales (→ 60).

New province welcomed with 'triumph'

A Roman "triumph", as imagined later by Peter Paul Rubens (1577-1640).

Rome, 44

Claudius has celebrated his British victory with a lavish "triumph", or celebratory parade. Heading the vast, glittering procession was the emperor himself in a chariot, followed by his wife Messalina and decorated campaign veterans. As is demanded by tradition, Claudius mounted the steps of the Capitol on his knees, supported by his sons-in-law. The emperor has decreed Victory Games for the people and an *ovatio*, his own mini-"triumph", for Aulus Plautius, the successful campaign commander and first governor of the new province of "Britannia", whom Claudius personally welcomed at the gates of the imperial capital (→ 51).

Client rulers govern under eye of Rome

Sussex, 45

A British chief who has lived in Rome and is steeped in Roman ways has been appointed by Emperor Claudius to rule as a client king in southern Britain. He is called Tiberius Claudius Cogidubnus (he has adopted the first two names in honour of the emperor), and his capital will be at Chichester.

Cogidubnus succeeds Verica, the king of the Atrebates tribe based in Sussex and Hampshire, whose flight to Rome after a revolt persuaded Claudius to invade Britain. Cogidubnus was made a Roman citizen, and he is developing his capital into something more suitable for a Roman-backed ruler. He joins other client rulers of areas not under direct Roman rule, chief of whom are Queen Cartimandua of the northern Brigantes tribal confederation and King Prasutagus of the Iceni in East Anglia (→ 47).

The hard life of men in the Roman army

Britain, c.45

Life for the 40,000 Roman troops now in Britain can be tough. Raw recruits train from dawn to dusk over a four-month period and learn their drill with 50-pound packs on their backs, while trained troops do drill every morning and go on five-hour, 20-mile route marches three times a month. Sloppy discipline is punished by a whack from the baton of a centurion, the commander of 80 men and a senior NCO. Duties (for defaulters) also include guard duty, weapons cleaning and horse grooming, as well as barrack-room, bath-house and latrine fatigues. There are frequent manoeuvres and exercises.

A Roman centurion: artist's view.

Four of Rome's 30 legions are serving in Britain: the 2nd Augusta, the 14th Gemina, the 20th Valeria Victrix and the 9th Hispana. Of these, the first three were transferred from the Rhine armies and the last from Pannonia on the Danube. The nominal strength of a legion is around 5,000 infantry, plus around 120 cavalry, all under the *legatus* [legate], the legionary commander. Legionaries, who are all Roman citizens, sign up in their teens, even as young as 15, for 20 years' service on a basic pay of 225 *denarii* per annum, paid into an account three times a year. From this account sums are deducted for bedding, rations, footwear, weapons and burial. On retirement, legionary troops get pensions and grants of land. Auxiliary (non-citizen) units, which make up about half the army, are paid perhaps half as much as legionaries and may serve 25 years, but on discharge they will receive Roman citizenship, so their sons can join the legions. Serving soldiers may not marry.

Tribal uprising is suppressed in east

Cambridgeshire, 47

The Romans have quelled a revolt by the Iceni and neighbouring tribes in a battle at Stonea Camp fort on a small natural island in the Fens, near March. Trouble erupted after the new Roman governor, Ostorius Scapula, ordered the disarming of tribes in the south and east. The Iceni resented this insensitivity to their status as a client kingdom, not a captive one, but their revolt was swiftly crushed by Roman auxiliaries (→ 55).

A Briton's bronze harness mount.

Fortress becomes a Roman showpiece

Colchester, Essex, 49
Engineers and soldiers are busy demolishing ramparts and filling in ditches here as the Romans create a showcase town. Existing buildings are already being turned over to army veterans and others. At present the living accommodation is spartan, making use of the old barrack blocks, but a new civic centre east of the old fortress is planned as the focus of a large new town called "Colonia Claudia Victricensis" [The Victory Colony of Claudius], which is likely to be the province's administrative capital (→55).

Lead mines go for private investment

Somerset, c.50
Lead mining has begun at Charterhouse, in the Mendip Hills, in the territory of the Dobunni tribe. According to the Roman historian Strabo, Britain is rich in mineral resources and this was one of the reasons behind the Roman conquest. At present the mines are all under military control, but as Roman rule becomes better established in the region civilian prospectors, working on behalf of Roman investors, are being encouraged to play their part (→c.91).

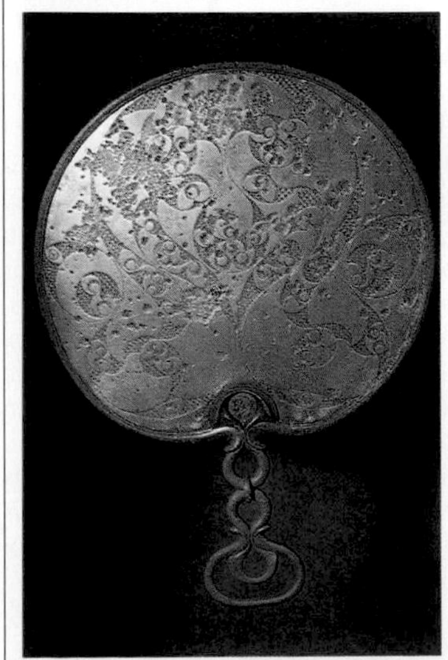

British art is developing in an exuberant fashion: a highly polished bronze mirror from Desborough, Northamptonshire.

Rebel leader betrayed by wily queen

Caratacus handed over to the Romans

Central Wales, 51
Caratacus, the leader of British resistance to Rome, has been betrayed by his compatriot, the client-queen Cartimandua of the Brigantes, and handed over to the Roman governor in chains.

Caratacus's many victories and his prestige as the son of the late King Cunobelinus of the Catuvellauni tribe had won him the position of national leader of British opposition, first among the Silures of south Wales and then among the Ordovices further north. But he was finally outmanoeuvred on the river Vrynwy, south of Oswestry, when the Romans penetrated the defences of his redoubt on the Llanymynech mountain.

The British hillfort was backed by steep cliffs and fronted by the river, at a site difficult to cross. Ostorius Scapula, the Roman governor, was dismayed by the river and overhanging cliffs, which were ferociously defended, but his legionaries crossed the river and, after suffering casualties at the ramparts, pressed forward under interlocking shields. Caratacus escaped, though his family was captured, and briefly found shelter in the north with the Brigantes. But their queen, a Roman ally, surrendered him to the enemy.

Scapula, the governor of Britain.

A gold coin struck by Emperor Claudius to celebrate his British triumphs.

Chained captive impresses the emperor

Rome, 51
The captive Caratacus, paraded through Rome, has caught the imagination of the emperor and the crowds with a defiant speech: "I had horses, men, arms and wealth – are you surprised that I am sorry to lose them? Had I yielded without a blow, neither my downfall nor your triumph would have been famous. If you execute me they will be forgotten." Claudius ordered his chains to be struck off, saying that he and his family could live freely in Rome. Impressed by the city, the Briton then asked: "Why, when you have all this, do you envy us our poor huts?"

Cartimandua is rewarded for her loyalty

North Yorkshire, 51
Queen Cartimandua of the Brigantes, the ruler of the largest British tribal confederation still outside direct Roman rule, has been well rewarded by Rome for her loyalty in handing over Caratacus. In particular, she can expect to receive more Roman subsidies and imports of luxury goods.

But there are rumblings that Cartimandua may not enjoy the wholehearted backing of her subjects, especially some younger Brigantians, who are repelled by her pro-Roman policy and her Romanized tastes. Regarded as even more intolerable, though, are her sex – there is a strong faction that opposes female rule – and her betrayal of Caratacus to the Romans. For the moment, however, she can rely on the promise of Roman help if rebellion occurs, and on the military skill of her husband, Venutius (→56).

Brigantia, goddess of the Brigantes. ▷

Rebel tribes continue to fight in the hills

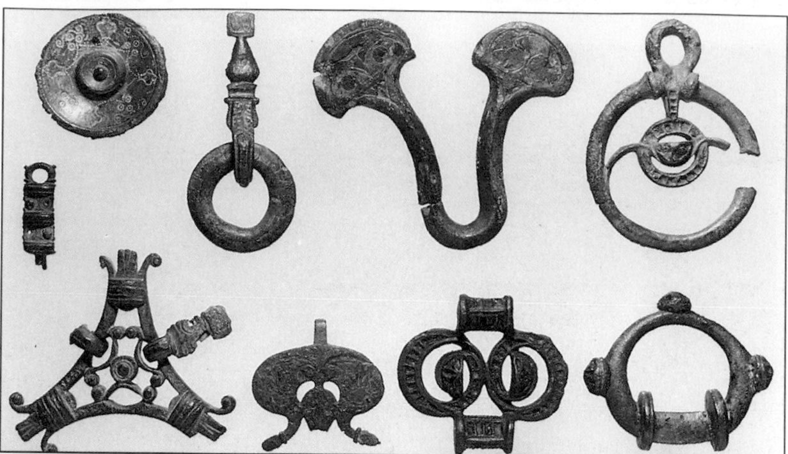

A hoard of Roman harness fittings captured and buried by the Silures.

South Wales, 55
Since they lost the leadership of Caratacus four years ago, members of the Silures tribe of south Wales have harassed and often defeated the Roman occupation forces. They have preyed on troops building forts, inflicting heavy casualties, and Roman horsemen have been put to flight when attempting to rescue their comrades. Skirmishes generally go in favour of the natives, as the Roman army is unfamiliar with the terrain.

The Silures were enraged by the remark of the Roman governor Ostorius Scapula, condemning them either to extermination or to transportation to Gaul [France]. They rejoiced when Scapula died, worn out by his responsibilities and their harassment, in 52.

When his successor, the elderly Didius Gallus, arrived he found that the situation had deteriorated – the tribe had defeated a detachment of the 20th Legion under Manlius Valens and begun offensive raids, plundering the surrounding country at will. The first act of Didius Gallus was to drive it back into its own territory, but as yet he has advanced no further. South Wales remains a dangerous region where marauders can easily disappear into the hills when pursued. The frontiers of Roman Britain are still by no means secure (→ 58).

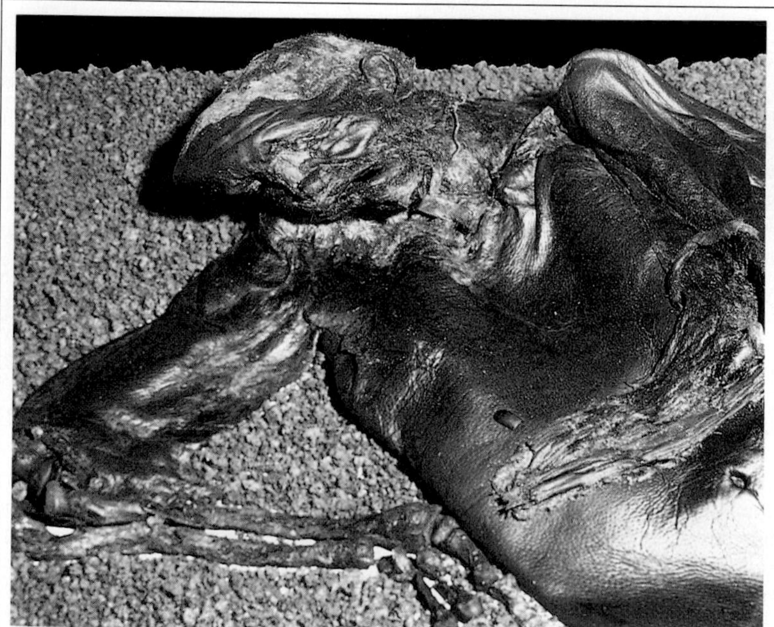

Alderley Edge, Cheshire, c.55. A 25-year-old man, probably a priest, who was painted blue, green and red, then garrotted and had his throat cut before being hit on the head and pressed into a bog in a Druid ritual (→ 60).

Imposing temple planned at Colchester

Colchester, Essex, 55
Two massive trenches, both 32 metres (35.2 yards) long, have just been completed on the edge of the six-year-old Roman town of Colchester which is growing up out of the former military fortress. The wooden shuttering is already in position, and soon the foundations will be laid for the temple which will dominate the town and dwarf the houses of the retired army veterans, which are still little more than converted barracks.

The temple will be in classical style, 32 by 25 metres, fronted by a flight of steps three metres high. There will be eight columns along the front, each a metre in diameter, made out of brick and faced with stucco. In front of them will be an open-air altar, and the south side will be faced with an ornamental screen.

However, there is some controversy over the use of this temple, which many local Britons think is intended for the worship of the emperor himself; they find the prospect deeply offensive, as they do not approve of worshipping mortals. In fact, the temple is for the Imperial cult – the worship of the guiding spirit of Claudius's family (→ 79).

A 20th-century model of the planned temple of Claudius at Colchester.

Imperial wines flow into the new colony

Colchester, Essex, c.55
Wine, regarded as a luxury before the Romans came, is now freely available in Roman towns such as this – to those with enough money to spend. All told, wine from 19 different regions of the empire is available. Nearly half comes from Italy, though an increasing share of the market is being taken by wines from Spain, of which two regions, Tarraconensis and Baetica, are stepping up production. The best, though, are reputed to be Falernian and Caecuban from Pompeii, near Naples, in southern Italy. For those with a leaner purse there is everyday wine from the Greek island of Rhodes, a favourite with the army. The island also produces a popular dessert wine (→ c.150).

Civil war sparked by marital conflict

Pennines, 56
The Romans have stepped in to secure the position of their ally Queen Cartimandua after the outbreak of civil war among her people, the Brigantes. Her chief opponent in the conflict was her husband Venutius, who decided to take up arms against the pro-Roman contingent in the tribal confederation after being alienated from his wife. There are suggestions that his group of young supporters was motivated by a hatred of female rule.

After Cartimandua took his brother and other relatives captive, Venutius invaded her kingdom. His ambitions were thwarted when the Romans, who appear to have foreseen the move, sent in a legion to put down the rebellion (→ 69).

60 - 70

Lincoln, 60. The Romans have pushed further north, and a fortress is being built here for the 9th Legion (→c.67).

East Anglia, 60. Prasutagus, the king of the Iceni tribe and a client of Rome, dies, leaving half his kingdom to the emperor and the other half to his wife and two daughters. Catus Decianus, the chief Roman financial official in Britain, tries to seize the whole kingdom, causing the Iceni to rebel. Decianus flees to Gaul.→

Exeter, Devon, 60. The Romans are building a bath-house.

Wales, 60. The governor of Britain, Gaius Suetonius Paulinus, abandons his campaign on Anglesey and marches to London to tackle the Iceni rebellion.→

Exeter, Devon, 60. Poenius Postumus, the chief of staff of the 2nd Legion, commits suicide after failing to obey an order to march 200 miles to meet Paulinus at Mancetter.→

London, 60. Gaius Julius Alpinus Classicianus, a Gaul, is appointed the new Roman procurator fiscal (chief financial official) to replace the disgraced Decianus.→

England, 61. Following the failure of the Iceni revolt, the people now face a poor harvest as few crops were planted during the rebellion.

London, 63. Trebellius Maximus, a career administrator, replaces Petronius Turpilianus as governor (→4/69).

Wroxeter, Shropshire, 66. Nero sends the 14th Legion to serve against tribes rebelling in the Near East (→69).

Gloucester, 67. The 20th Legion has moved into a new fortress, abandoning its fort at Kingsholm (→96).

Britain, 69. Emperor Vitellius returns the 14th Legion, which backed his rival Otho, to Britain, from where it was withdrawn by Nero. This puts a possible source of opposition to his rule at a safe distance.

Britain, 69. Vitellius appoints Vettius Bolanus governor. Bolanus, a former consul, has served as a legion commander at the other end of the empire, in Armenia (→71).

Norfolk, 70. A new town, Caistor St Edmund, is being built as the capital of the *civitas* [administrative district] of the Iceni tribe (→c.140).

Flogged queen leads tribes in revolt

Colchester, Essex, 60

The newly built Roman town at Colchester, once King Cunobelinus's capital and now a colony created to show Britons the supposed advantages of Roman rule, has been razed to the ground and its inhabitants butchered by forces led by Queen Boudica of the Iceni tribe. The Iceni revolted after their king, Prasutagus, a client of Rome, died, leaving half his estate to the emperor and half to his wife Boudica and their two daughters. When Catus Decianus, the procurator fiscal (chief Roman financial official in Britain), arrived to divide the goods, the Iceni protested at his troops' rough behaviour. Decianus's response was to declare all Iceni property forfeit to Rome, and to tell his troops to grab what they wanted. Boudica was flogged. Her daughters were raped. Homes and estates were plundered.

British defiance: a statue of Queen Boudica, or Boadicea, erected in 1902.

Boudica had no trouble finding British allies; she soon gathered an army estimated at 120,000 strong. According to one account she addressed them, spear in hand, thus: "Some of you may have been duped by the Romans' tempting promises. Now you have learned the difference between foreign tyranny and the free life of your ancestors. Have we not suffered every shame and humiliation?" Colchester was her first target, and the news is on its way to the Roman governor who is in Wales [*see report below*].→

Romans attack Druids and storm the island sanctuary of Anglesey

Anglesey, Gwynedd, 60

The new Roman governor, Gaius Suetonius Paulinus, has set out to destroy the Druids by capturing their island sanctuary of Anglesey. Since the Roman conquest, the Welsh mainland and Anglesey have served as refuges for rebels of all kinds, including the Druids. These are the priests and seers whom tribes rely on to divine the future, which depends on their observation of the death struggles of sacrificial victims, often human. One type of sacrifice involves burning a person alive in a wicker basket.

Druids are also the repository of the oral history, law and traditions of the people; novices must learn these by heart rather than commit secrets to writing. They regard the oak tree and the mistletoe that grows on it as sacred and conduct their rites in oak groves. Mistletoe, which is cut with a golden sickle, is believed to be a cure for poisoning and barrenness. Druids also believe in the transmigration of souls.

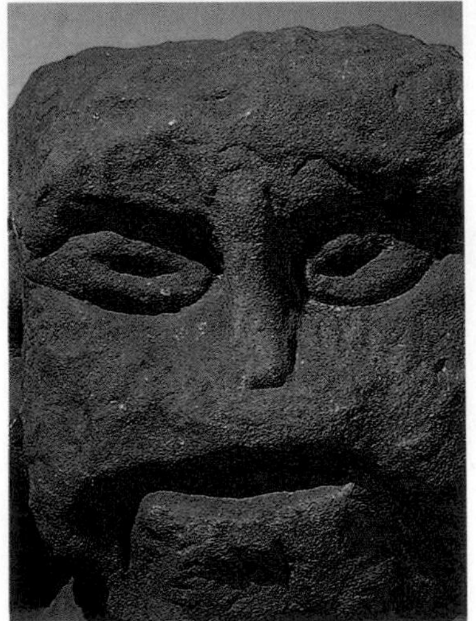

Head-worship in a pagan shrine.

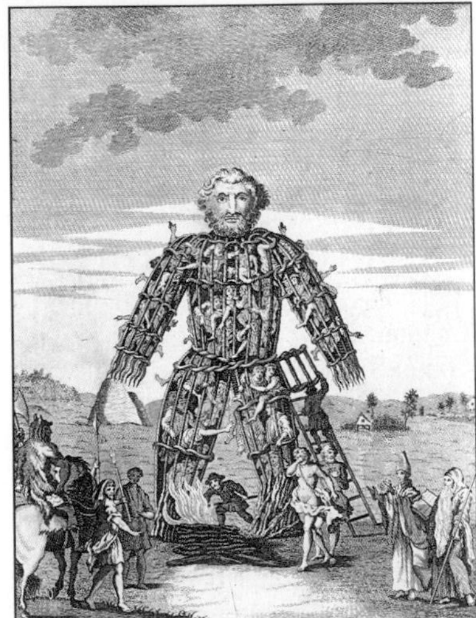

Wicker man: Druids burn victims.

When the Romans under Suetonius reached the Menai Strait, the infantry were ferried across in flat-bottomed boats while the cavalry swam across with their horses. They were thunderstruck by what greeted them: the shore was lined with armed men and women in black robes, brandishing torches above dishevelled heads. The white-robed Druids stood near at hand raising their hands to heaven and screaming curses on the invaders.

Urged by their commander not to fear a horde of women, the Romans engulfed them in the flames of their own torches. Then the sacred groves were cut down and the blood-stained altars demolished (→79).

Britain rocked by rebellion led by Queen Boudica

Rebels unleash their wrath on London

Revenge for the Iceni as the inhabitants of London are put to the sword.

London, 60
Following the mayhem wrought at Colchester, Boudica has turned her wrath on London. The town has seen scenes similar to those at Colchester, where she unleashed an orgy of burning after cutting to pieces part of the 9th Legion which was hurrying to the town's rescue.

London was her main prize. It has recently taken over from Colchester as the administrative capital of the province and is the headquarters of Catus Decianus, the hated procurator fiscal. The Roman governor, Suetonius Paulinus, also racing for London, arrived first. London is unwalled, and, deciding that he could not defend it against the rebels, he left for the Midlands, leaving London to its bloody fate. Exaggerated estimates put Roman deaths since the revolt began at around 70,000. Reports from London tell of women being mutilated or impaled on stakes – Boudica's answer to her daughters' violation.

Boudica is pursuing Suetonius, sacking St Albans on the way, with the Trinovantes in her army exacting revenge on their old masters, the pro-Roman Catuvellauni tribe.

Revolt is crushed: '80,000 Britons die'

Warwickshire, 60
The Romans have crushed the British revolt in a decisive battle in the English midlands. Boudica has taken her own life, and the Romans are now exacting vicious revenge after the rout near Watling Street.

The governor, Gaius Suetonius Paulinus, who had been forced to abandon London and St Albans to Boudica, had eventually met up with the bulk of his army in the Midlands. Recognizing a good defensive position – a funnel-like valley – he disposed his army of 10,000 across it, with the neck of the valley behind him, to face the confident Britons, who had brought their families to watch from carts to their rear – an error, because it hindered a retreat.

Boudica is reported to have told her army: "I fight not for my kingdom or booty, but for my lost freedom, my bruised body, my outraged daughters. We will win this battle or perish! That is what I, a woman, will do; men may live in slavery!" Suetonius's own rallying address exploited all the stories his men had heard about the Britons: "Come, my fellow soldiers! Come, Romans! ... It is better for us to fall fighting manfully than to be captured and impaled, to see our own entrails cut from us ... Let us therefore either conquer them or die!" The British advanced with shouting and war-songs, but the Romans were silent and orderly until their javelins were within range. They kept in tight formation until the British were upon them; then out from behind the Roman shields darted the lethal blades of their short swords. In such close fighting the Britons could do little with their long swords, and after many hours the contest turned into a rout; some Roman sources put British losses at 80,000, compared with under a thousand Romans (→ 61).

Mounted Roman; defeated Briton.

Emperor Nero recalls 'brutal' governor

London, 60
Gaius Suetonius Paulinus, the governor of Britain and the man who put down Boudica's revolt, has been recalled, ostensibly because of some shipping losses, but in reality because he has lost the confidence of Rome. The rift began when Gaius Julius Alpinus Classicianus, the newly appointed procurator fiscal (chief Roman financial official), fell out with Suetonius over the brutal Roman "scorched-earth" policy pursued after the uprising. This involved slaughtering everyone who had sworn loyalty to Boudica, and laying waste tribal lands.

Classicianus, whose predecessor Catus Decianus sparked off the revolt, saw that hunting down every last rebel was unlikely to lead to the peace and reconciliation which, coming from a recently absorbed province – Gaul [France] – he realized was essential. He also feared that, with food stocks low because little was sown during the revolt, the governor's actions could stir up further unrest.

Classicianus appealed to the emperor to intervene in the dispute, and Nero despatched one of his top civil servants, the freedman (ex-slave) Polyclitus, to gather the full facts. A face-saving formula has been devised so that Suetonius, whose term is nearly over anyway, is not totally disgraced, and thus the official reason for his departure is given as shipping losses (→ 62).

Britons lose an outspoken peacemaker

Classicianus's tomb in London.

London, 62
The man who did most for reconciliation after Boudica's revolt, Gaius Julius Alpinus Classicianus, has died. He is to be buried in a cemetery near Aldgate in London, says his wife India Pacata. As the procurator fiscal (chief financial officer) of the province he was subordinate to the governor but answerable only to Rome – a notoriously sensitive position with a high probability of falling out with the governor, which he did in a dramatic way [*see story left*].

As a Gaul he probably had some sympathy with the rebels, but he had to walk a tightrope between financial probity and the bitter feelings of the defeated British.

Governor flees mutiny

One year, but three emperors: left to right, Galba, Vitellius and Otho.

Britain, April 69
The power struggle being played out in Italy for the imperial throne has claimed the British governor, Trebellius Maximus, who has been forced to flee by the hostility of his troops. Robbed of army support, Maximus is on his way to Vitellius, the governor of Lower Germany, who has followed Galba and Otho as the third Roman emperor this year since Nero committed suicide in the face of revolt.

Although military sympathy in most of the British garrison also appears to be with Vitellius, the basis of their dispute with Maximus is less political than economic. The troops are claiming that they cannot live on their salaries, and that in recent years they have been deprived of their traditional perk – plunder – because of the official "softly-softly" policy towards the Britons following the withdrawal of a previous governor, Gaius Suetonius Paulinus, in 60 after Boudica's revolt.

Maximus's departure leaves Britain in the hands of a committee of its legionary commanders under Roscius Coelius, the commander of the 20th Legion. Meanwhile Vitellius has withdrawn 8,000 men from Britain, and a clash with another imperial challenger, Vespasian, a popular commander and distinguished veteran of the Roman invasion of Britain in 43, cannot now be far off (→ 70).

Brigantian queen is dethroned by consort

Yorkshire, summer 69
Cartimandua, the queen of the Brigantes of northern Britain and a client of Rome, has been dethroned by her estranged consort, Venutius. He has taken advantage of the confusion in Roman imperial politics to seize power over the largest confederation of British tribes still outside direct Roman rule. The conflict between the queen and her partner had been brewing for 15 years, erupting at one point into civil war. Initially pro-Roman, Venutius resented her betrayal of the resistance leader Caratacus in 51 and seems to have been influenced by Brigantians opposed to female rule. Matters were not improved when the queen took Venutius's armour-bearer, Vellocatus, as her lover.

Vettius Bolanus, the new Roman governor, has used auxiliary troops (considered more loyal than the legions) to restore control, but he has only managed to rescue the queen. She remains powerless (→ c.73).

A bronze mount of the Brigantes.

Power to select the next emperor now held by provinces

Rome, 1 January 70
One thing has become clear from the the bloody turmoil of what has been called the "Year of the Four Emperors": any provincial governor, backed by a strong army, has the means to seize power for himself. When one or all of the four emperors who followed the late and unlamented Nero – Galba, Otho, Vitellius and Vespasian – chose to march on Rome, the central government could do little to stop them. That the British garrison of 40,000 did not put up an imperial candidate of its own is fortunate; had it done so the province might have again been plunged into violence and turmoil.

New emperor has British connection

Victorious challenger: Vespasian.

Britain, 70
News has just reached here of the crowning of Vespasian as emperor last December, so ending a year-long power struggle which has seen the deaths of his rivals Otho, Vitellius and Galba. Vespasian is the first emperor not to emerge from the patrician Julian line of Caesar and Augustus. His accent is rustic rather than aristocratic, and he has risen to the top through sheer ability. Britons know him well. He served with distinction in the 43 invasion of the island (→ 23/6/79).

Roman goal is to win 'hearts and minds' of young

Southern Britain, c.70
A generation has now grown up in Britain of young men and women who have no memory of life before the Roman conquest, but they certainly remember the battles, deaths, shortages and violent changes caused by Britain's occupation, and they were on the brink of adolescence when Boudica's great uprising almost threw off the Romans.

After a decade of peace, old wounds are beginning to heal. Families divided into pro- and anti-Roman factions are beginning to be reconciled, and memories are dulling; this senior generation is now ripe to be given responsibility for the good conduct and order of the tribes. But it is the hearts and minds of the young, born in the years since the revolt, that the Romans must win, for they are the key to the peaceful transition of the island from its mosaic of kingdoms into a fully fledged imperial province.

Recent governors such as Trebellius Maximus unleashed a "charm offensive" in the later 60s, and this policy is pursued elsewhere when there is trouble. In north-eastern Gaul in 69, a former commander in Britain, Petillius Cerialis, paraded the advantages of Roman life to the Lingones and Treviri tribes, who had threatened revolt, in words which could have been addressed to the British: "Everything ... is shared ... You are not excluded from anything ... The good that flows from the emperor reaches everyone." But it will take more than luxury goods. While some Britons can read and write, far more must do so if a provincial "middle class" is to be created. Most still speak Celtic tongues, but education in Roman ways is the key, and those who master Latin may win opportunities for advancement not dreamt of by their parents – not least the prize of Roman citizenship, and its status symbol of a three-part name (→ 84).

71-80

London, 71. Vettius Bolanus is replaced as governor by Petillius Cerialis, a relative of Vespasian, who was proclaimed emperor in 69 after defeating and killing Emperor Vitellius (→ 74).

North Yorkshire, c.73. The Brigantes tribal confederation is forced to abandon its main stronghold at Stanwick, leaving a huge new area open to direct Roman control (→ 77).

Britain, 74. Julius Frontinus, who has replaced Cerialis as governor, begins his term of office with a campaign in Wales against the Silures tribe. A fortress is built at Caerleon for the 20th Legion (→ 77).

Southern England, c.75 Earthwork defences are constructed at the towns of Silchester, Winchester, Chichester and St Albans (→ 79).

London, 77. Gnaeus Julius Agricola becomes governor, replacing Frontinus. Agricola plans to continue the movement of troops into northern Wales and northern England against the Brigantes.→

Chester, c.78. The 2nd Legion moves to the new fortress begun by Frontinus (→ 79).

Cutilia, Italy, 23 June 79. Emperor Vespasian dies at the age of 69. He is succeeded by his elder son Titus, aged 40, who was responsible for Roman military success in Judaea [Palestine] in 70. Titus appoints his younger brother Flavius Domitianus (Domitian) as his heir (→ 1/9/81).

Solway/Tyne line, late 79. At the end of the campaigning season, Agricola, the governor, and his army have reached the northern fringes of the Brigantes' tribal area (→ 80).

St Albans, Herts, 79. The new civic centre begun about four years ago is complete (→ c.156).

Scottish Lowlands, 80. Julius Agricola seeks permission from Emperor Titus to launch an attack on the northern tribes. By the end of the year he has reached the river Tay (→ 81).

Colchester, Essex, 80. A ceremonial gate is erected at the entrance to the town. It incorporates a triumphal arch built by the Romans in 75.

Bath, Avon, c.80. A temple in the Roman style is being constructed at the hot-water springs as the fame of this religious site, which is dedicated to the British water god Sul, spreads (→ c.100).

Welsh tribes surrender

St Mary's, Conwy valley, where Caerhun Roman fort was built c.78.

Julius Agricola: a later impression of Britain's triumphant governor.

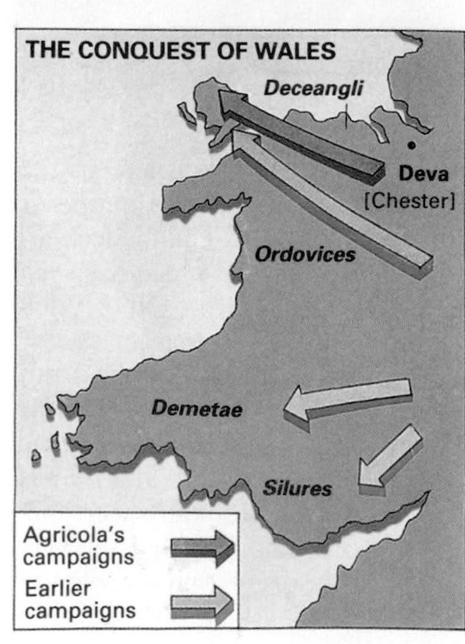

Northern Wales, 77
Wales is now firmly in Roman hands following a lightning campaign by Britain's new governor, Julius Agricola, which began as an attack on British tribes who had attacked a Roman cavalry unit stationed at Chester.

The tribes, led by the Ordovices, had hoped to take advantage of the handover period between the governorships of Julius Frontinus, who three years ago subdued the Silures tribe in southern Wales, and Agricola. But Agricola, who knows this territory well after serving as an officer with the 20th Legion at Wroxeter, was swift to act. He attacked the Ordovices and, according to reports, "cut to pieces the entire tribe" before proceeding to the Irish Sea. His devastating push through Snowdonia made Agricola the first Roman commander to see the shores of northern Wales since his predecessor Gaius Suetonius Paulinus in 60. Under Suetonius, the Romans had devastated the Druid stronghold of Anglesey before being forced to withdraw by the great revolt of Boudica.

Lacking proper naval support, Agricola ordered his men to swim the narrow Menai Strait and thereby gain a foothold on the island of Anglesey. Faced with this rate of advance, the British tribes had no alternative but to surrender. To secure their position the Romans are now building forts at places such as Caerhun, Caernarfon and Pen Lustyn (→ c.78).

Romans set out to confront Brigantes

Northern England, summer 78
Fresh from his success in crushing the Ordovices and their allies in Wales, Julius Agricola has turned his attention to another continuing threat to Roman power, the Brigantes, the great northern tribal confederation centred on the Pennines. It was partially subdued six years ago by Petilius Cerialis, the then governor, but remains a force to be reckoned with.

Agricola has set out from the new legionary camp at Chester with the 2nd Legion. He plans to attack the northern territory of the Brigantes, which straddles a line running between the mouths of the rivers Tyne and Solway [*see report opposite*], drive routes across the hill passes and then join up with his forces from York.

Islanders' belief in magic elicits scorn

Rome, 79
Gaius Plinius (Pliny), the Roman historian, has attacked the British for their superstition and belief in magic, comparing them to the Persians, who are notorious for their practice of necromancy. Roman writers have long been intrigued by the Druids and their powerful hold over the British aristocracy. The Druidic training takes place by word of mouth, from master to pupil, and the belief in souls passing to other bodies on death inspires bravery in battle (→ c.100).

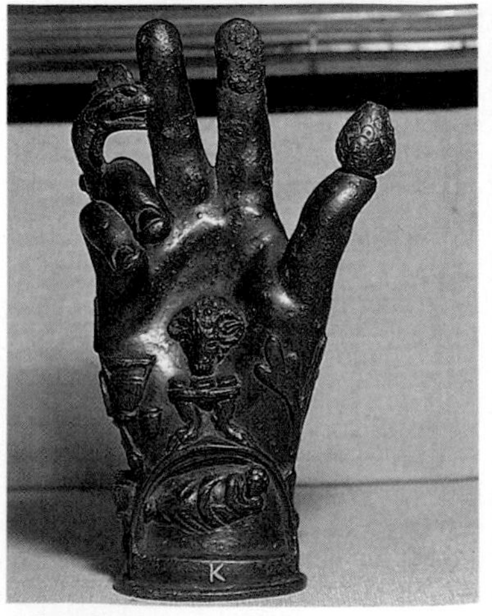

A hand used to avert the evil eye.

Conquerors move inexorably northwards

Worn by a northern warrior: a bronze collar from Dumfries and Galloway.

Eildon Hill, Borders, 79
The Britons north of the Tyne and Solway are mustering for what may be their last stand as Roman legions under the command of Britain's governor, Julius Agricola, make their way towards the northern hill-fort of Eildon Hill at Newstead, a base of the Selgovae tribe.

Never has Rome penetrated so far north, although the tribes which are readying themselves for the assault – the local people of the Selgovae, Votadini, Novantae and Dumnonii – already know much of imperial power. The famous stories of Caratacus's defiance and Boudica's revolt are still strong, as are the tales of refugees who fled north after the Brigantes too failed to hold off the Romans. Forts and settlements are being strengthened, cattle and sheep hidden away, and barley is being hoarded. Meanwhile the Romans are moving inexorably northwards, preparing for battle with those whom they know only as "barbarians".

So far it is only the lowland tribes, whose territories reach as far north as the Clyde, which are under threat. But if Rome, as many fear, proves too strong, the tribes north of the Forth/Clyde line – called "Caledonii" by the Romans – will be under threat as well (→81).

Tribes given local autonomy in south

Southern England, 80
A new system of administration, modelled on the way in which Rome rules Gaul, is taking root in southern England as it emerges from more than a generation of military rule by Roman soldier-governors. Now, with Rome's troops occupied in the north, pursuing the conquest of tribes beyond the Forth, the towns of southern England are returning to civilian rule as tribal elders and Roman advisers combine their individual methods to create, in the *civitates* [administrative districts], a new form of government for the province.

Two basic forms of settlement exist: the *colonia* or colony (a plantation of Roman army veterans) and the *municipium* (a "chartered" town, such as Verulamium). Administration is centred on the *ordo*, a council of some 100 members, known as *decurions*, who must have a certain amount of property to stand for election. From their ranks come officers responsible for justice, public buildings and local finance. The *civitates peregrinae* are largely rural districts with no big settlements, of which most of southern England is made up. Also self-governing, they are often named from the dominant local tribe. The hallmark of self-government, whatever its size, is the civic centre consisting of the *forum* [council offices plus shopping centre], *basilica* [law courts] and temple (→c.90).

Cultures clash on the role of women

Southern Britain, c.80
Now that southern Britain at least has been absorbed into the Roman Empire, cultural clashes between the Celtic and Roman worlds are evident. One of the most awkward of these concerns the place of women.

Traditional Celtic society assigns women prominent roles in legal, religious and military affairs. Marriage does not demand subservience to the husband, and women can divorce. Hereditary issues are often determined by the female line of descent, and, as the Romans have found, Britain's tribal queens can be extremely skilful in exploiting changes in the political arena, and formidable foes in war.

A bone hairpin from Leicester.

By contrast – although they have honoured religious roles, as vestal virgins and oracles – women in Rome have no political status nor vote. They have little say in legal matters and are forbidden to join the army. A family is run by the father, who has control over his wife, children and slaves. Women in Britain raised in the Celtic tradition now face a struggle to avoid being relegated to secondary positions in public and private life.

Roman governor to be granted a luxurious palace at London

London, c.80
The Roman governor is to get a splendid new palace on the west bank of the Walbrook stream which runs down into the Thames at London. The building, to the west of the *forum*, will cover 1,300 square metres (a third of an acre) and be arranged around a large courtyard with fountains and an ornamental pool. It will be lavishly decorated with both paintings and mosaics. As well as living space there will be offices and reception rooms in the palace, which will be the seat of power for the governor of Britain and should be ready for Julius Agricola's successor.

A 20th-century reconstruction of the Roman governor's palace at London.

81-85

Italy, 1 September 81. Emperor Titus dies at Cutilia of the plague. He is succeeded by Domitian, his 30-year-old brother (→ 82).

Britain, 81. Julius Agricola, the governor of Britain, consolidates Roman control of the whole island except for the areas in the hands of the Caledonii.→

Rome, 82. Emperor Domitian agrees to Agricola's request to move into north-eastern Scotland, but takes large detachments from all four of the legions in Britain for his own invasion of Germany and planned campaign against the Chatti tribe (→ c.83).

The Minch, Highland, c.82. The fleet supporting Agricola and his expeditionary force completes an exploratory voyage around the western isles.→

Germany, 83. Julius Frontinus, a former governor of Britain, joins Emperor Domitian as a senior officer on his German expedition.

Inchtuthill, Tayside, c.83. A fortress is under construction on the river Tay to serve as a base for the 20th Legion. It will be the most northerly legionary fortress yet built in Britain (→ 84).

Mons Graupius [Bennachie? In the Grampians], 84. Agricola inflicts a crushing defeat on a force of Caledonii during a mountain engagement. Britons fight on the Roman side for the first time.→

Scotland, 84. Emperor Domitian, possibly through jealousy at Agricola's success in the north compared with his own failures in Germany, recalls Agricola to Rome after seven years as governor, an unusually long term. He is awarded high military honours but is effectively retired. Sallustius Luculluss succeeds him as governor (→ 98).

Thames estuary, 85. A small freighter transporting wares including *mortaria* – bowls used for grinding up food – from a Kentish pottery to London has foundered and sunk off Whitstable after leaving the port of Richborough (→ c.170).

Staines, Middlesex, c.85. Experiments in pottery technology have succeeded in producing a ware with a glossy lead glazing. The new luxury vessels are expected to compete with imported Samian pottery or metal containers (→ c.126).

Forth/Clyde line marks the new frontier

A fierce Caledonian warrior (from a 16th-century English travelogue).

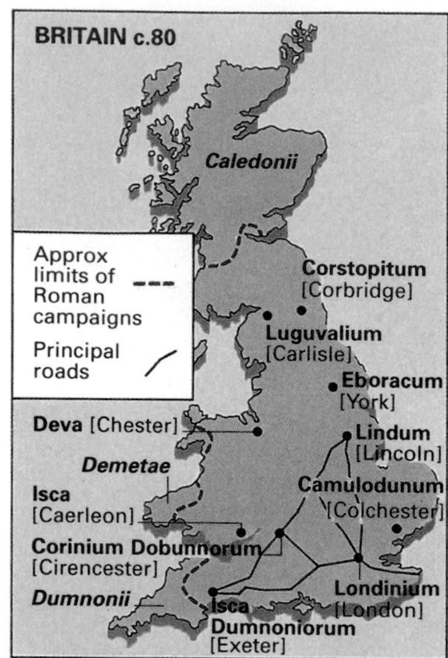

Chief Roman centres of influence and limits of Roman campaigns.

Scottish Lowlands, 81
Julius Agricola, the governor of Britain, is consolidating Roman strength in central Scotland. Garrisons are now being established in the valleys of the rivers Clyde and Forth. These will be the most northerly outposts of the Roman Empire.

After last summer's successful advances as far as the Tay, the 20th Legion headed north from Carlisle and the 9th Legion from Corbridge, joining forces on the Forth at Inveresk. Now, in line with his customary practice, Agricola is setting up forts in positions that he hopes to hold throughout the coming winter. Whether he plans to move even further north is not clear. If not, these forts will become the new frontier of Roman Britain, keeping the Caledonii of the far north at bay. Agricola may also be contemplating using such forts as bases for raids on Ireland.

Apart from the territory of the Caledonii, the entire island of Britain is now under Roman control. Two regions, however, appear to have escaped direct military intervention: the south-western peninsula, inhabited by the Dumnonii, and south-western Wales, the land of the Demetae (→ c.82).

Gold sows thoughts of conquest of Ireland

Dumfries and Galloway, c.84
Following Julius Agricola's success in northern Britain, the Romans are considering the conquest of Ireland, which can be faintly seen from Galloway. There are fears that the island may become a haven for discontented Britons, who are believed to be of similar stock to the people across the sea. There is even said to be an Irish tribe called the Brigantes, which may have links with the British tribe of the same name. More importantly, the Romans believe that Ireland has large reserves of gold. Agricola reckons he needs only one legion plus auxiliaries to take Ireland. He also holds hostage an Irish prince who has fled from a rebellion (→ c.250).

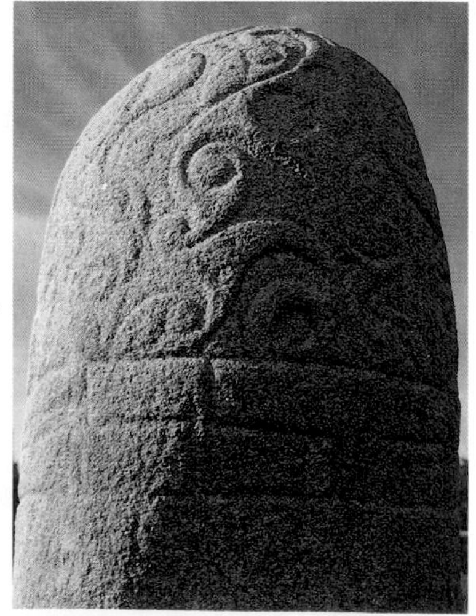

The Turoe Stone, in Co Galway: art flourishes in independent Ireland.

Top Britons adopt 'civilized' attitudes of Roman overlords

Britain, 84
During his seven-year governorship Julius Agricola has produced a dramatic change in the attitudes of leading Britons towards Roman ways. The nobility are now seeking fluency in Latin, for example, because of the career advantages it offers, and have taken to wearing Roman clothing such as the toga. They are also beginning to appreciate the luxuries of Roman life, such as wine and hot baths.

In recent speeches Agricola has gone out of his way to say that the natural ability of the British is greater than that of the Gauls, many of whom have been employed in Britain in top posts in the legions and the civil service. This is clearly a hint that he would like to see greater local involvement in British affairs, both to wean tribes from their hostility to Rome and to keep down the cost of running Britain.

A later view of Romanization.

The governor is therefore creating self-governing administrative districts based on tribal areas. He has also given encouragement to building works, whether they be temples, public squares or houses. St Albans and Colchester, for example, old tribal centres which almost 25 years ago witnessed great savagery in Boudica's revolt, both have new civic centres, each focused on a *forum* comprising council offices, shopping centre and a public meeting-place (→ 90).

Caledonian tribes fail

Grampian, 84
The Caledonian tribes have failed to stem the Roman tide. Some 30,000 northern tribesmen met a matching Roman force – which for the first time included auxiliaries – at a mountain called Mons Graupius [possibly Bennachie in the Grampians] and were completely routed. The survivors scattered into the forests. Julius Agricola showed himself far more skilful than his adversary Calgacus. At one stage his auxiliaries had advanced so fast that they found themselves stranded in a sea of Caledonii, but the arrival of the cavalry clinched the victory and the Britons broke and ran.

In the end Mons Graupius was a victory for Roman technology as well as strategy. The opposition was armed with small shields and long slashing swords; against them the Romans carried short stabbing swords and large shields. In the thick of battle, these proved much the superior weapons. It has been, nonetheless, as bitter a victory as it has been a defeat. As the Romans advance into Caledonian territory they have found little to please them: preferring to deny their conquerors an easy occupation, the tribespeople have conducted a scorched-earth policy, destroying their own homes, cattle and crops themselves, rather than letting the Romans do it. For, as Calgacus is reported to have said to his troops before the battle: "[The Romans] rob, kill and rape and call it Roman rule. They make a desert and call it peace" (→c.86).

Romans find that Britain is an island

Dumfries and Galloway, c.82
Sailors operating with the Roman fleet in support of Julius Agricola's invasion of the far north of Britain have made two fascinating discoveries: firstly, that Britain really is an island, as they had always suspected, and secondly, that the Greeks got there first. The men claim to have discovered an ancient Greek inscription on the coast near Gatehouse of Fleet – a carved stone referring to the hero Odysseus – when making a routine landing. Many are taking the find as proof that the famous Greek explorer Pytheas passed this way some 500 years ago (→c.150).

London becomes a major trading port

London, 85
The landing stages of the port of London are being dismantled although they are only 20 years old. Bigger and stronger structures are now required to cope with the sheer volume of goods and freight which come in and out of the port daily.

British trade has expanded many times over as the province has become integrated into the Roman empire, and London has become Britain's commercial hub. Large box-framed wharves are being constructed and filled with earth upstream and downstream of the new Thames bridge, and behind the new quays a series of warehouses is being built. They stand two storeys high and have broad loading doors which open right out into the docks.

Monument to mark site of the invasion

Richborough, Kent, c.85
The old Roman invasion base at Richborough has been selected as the site of a great victory monument to commemorate the conquest of 43 and to serve as a symbolic gateway to the province of Britain. The monument will take the form of a four-square triumphal arch and will be faced with marble imported from the European mainland. It will be adorned with columns in the Doric and Corinthian orders and topped with statues symbolizing the conquest of the god Oceanus, the ocean.

The arch will be a useful landmark for mariners making their way up the coast towards the Thames; it will help them to avoid the Goodwin sands which have claimed many ships (→c.275).

South-eastern landowners move from tribal huts to opulent country houses

A 20th-century impression of the lavish palace built in the Roman style at Fishbourne, near Chichester; craftsmen came here from Rome.

South-eastern England, c.85
Tribal landowners in the rich south-east of England are building villas, or country houses, in the Roman style and starting to live in the manner of their Gallic cousins. Although the first villas were modest affairs, several large houses are now being built on the river Colne in Essex, most likely as second homes for wealthy people from the important town of Colchester.

Substantial new dwellings are being erected in Kent as well, at Darenth and Eccles, and along the Sussex coast at Angmering and Bignor. They are expensive to build, which indicates just how much British landowners – many of whom would have been born in simple tribal-style huts – have been assimilated into Roman society. Their new homes have many of the Roman trappings: several large communal rooms, en suite bathrooms, mosaic floors, glazed windows and lavish interior decoration.

However, the most ambitious project in progress at present is the large house at Fishbourne, near Chichester, for which craftsmen have been imported from Rome. With its formal garden, stucco decoration, mosaics and fine wall-paintings, Fishbourne is fit to be the governor's winter palace. For one class in Roman-occupied Britain life is improving, but the homes of the poor remain unaltered (→c.150).

This decorative floor mosaic forms part of a breathtaking room in the Fishbourne palace; fine wall-paintings add to the feeling of opulence.

86 - 104

Dacia [Romania], 86. The Romans suffer a serious setback and Cornelius Fuscus, the commander of the Praetorian Guard – the imperial household division – is killed (→ 89).

Dacia, 89. Despite the extra troops from Britain, the Romans have failed to wipe out the Dacian army. Emperor Domitian is forced to sign a humiliating peace treaty with the king, Decebalus (→ 18/9/96).

London, 90. The governor, Sallustius Lucullus, is executed on Domitian's orders – apparently for the crime of naming a new military javelin after himself.

Gwynedd, c.90. Following successful raids by the Ordovices tribe, a new building programme is begun at the fort of Caer Llugwy (→ c.100).

Yorkshire, c.91. The Romans are exploiting the lead ores found in the territory of the northern Brigantes tribes to such an extent that stringent legal restrictions on licences are being introduced.

Lincoln, c.95. The old fortress on the ridge, built by the 9th Legion and later used by the 2nd Legion, is being turned into a *colonia* [army veterans' colony] (→ 100).

London, c.95. Bath-houses are being built at Cheapside and Huggin Hill (→ c.105).

Rome, 18 September 96. Domitian, who has conducted a three-year reign of terror, is assassinated in a plot organized by his wife, Domitia. He is succeeded by Nerva Cocceus, aged 65 (→ 27/10/97).

Gloucester, 96. The old fortress is turned over for civilian settlement (→ 100).

Rome, 27 October 97. To placate the Praetorian Guard and the legions in Germany, Emperor Nerva adopts, as his son and successor, the general Marcus Ulpius Trajanus (Trajan), a Spaniard by birth and the governor of Upper Germany (→ 28/1/98).

Cologne, Germany, 28 January 98. Following Nerva's murder earlier this month, Trajan is declared emperor (→ 110).

Gloucester, Lincoln and Winchester, 100. New civic centres (complexes of *forum, basilica* and temple) are being built (→ 110).

Caerleon, Gwent, c.100. The legionary fort is being rebuilt in stone (→ c.254).

Northern tribes are left in peace as legions leave for continent

North-eastern Scotland, c.86

The Romans are withdrawing from the northern provinces, leaving forts unmanned and settlements undeveloped. The northern tribes, whose struggle was crushed so ruthlessly on the slopes of Mons Graupius, are to be left in peace – for now. Emperor Domitian needs extra troops for his current campaign in Romania, has ordered a halt to further advances, and has commanded his troops to return to a line drawn between Newstead and Dalswinton, establishing that as the northern limit of Roman rule. Nothing is to be left, however, and at Inchtuthill even the nails used to build the fort are to be buried in great pits.

There are rumours that Domitian has always been jealous of the achievements of the man responsible for Roman successes in northern Britain, Julius Agricola, who had served as governor for almost twice as long as any of his predecessors before his recall to Rome in 84. Domitian, whose own military exploits in Germany were undistinguished to say the least, may have feared a popular and successful general so far from Rome (→ 89).

The Roman army is shown here at its most ruthless, fighting German warriors.

British and Roman gods enjoy harmony in earthly coexistence

A bronze head of a Roman god found at Felmingham Hall, Norfolk.

Offerings to Mars Alator dedicated in a temple at Barkway, in Hertfordshire.

Southern England, c.100

In matters of religion, the Romans are showing a pragmatic tolerance as long as local practices do not clash with their own interests, as was the case with the Druids. At the most important British shrines, the Romans encourage the joint worship of both the native and the Roman god or goddess. For, in Roman eyes at least, the myriad gods and spirits worshipped by the British [*see page 41*] are identifiable with the Roman gods. The British god of war Camulos, for example, is readily equated with the Roman god Mars. The main difference in observance is that the Romans tend to venerate their more important gods in temples, while Britons prefer to worship in open-air sanctuaries and sacred groves. There are some shrines to British deities, however.

Now the pattern of worship is changing, it seems, with the construction of temples at formerly important British sites, such as Harlow in Essex and Hayling Island in Hampshire. Harlow uses a plan first developed in Gaul, for a small square building with an outer corridor and an inner sanctum; in Hampshire, the temple takes the form of a large tower-like building which betrays an origin in Gallic and, ultimately, classical architecture. The classical Roman temple, such as those for the Imperial cult at Colchester and at London, is still very rare, but lately work has begun on one at Bath, dedicated jointly to the British god Sul and the Roman goddess Minerva (→ c.180).

Local councils deal with roads and law

England, c.90
The council known as the *curia* is in session. At one end of the *forum*, councillors are debating the construction of a new bath-house and the cost of an aqueduct to serve it. A tax will need to be raised; and who is going to pay for the resurfacing of the streets?

At the other end, magistrates are dealing with civil disputes, petty crime and matrimonial affairs, handing out fines in some cases and confiscating property in others. It has not taken long for the conquerors to set up a form of local government in Britain. The south of the country has largely accepted domination by far-away Rome.

At least ten new *civitates* [administrative areas] have been established, their development fostered by the Romans to encourage acceptance of the new ways. All are based on earlier tribal areas, with powers of self-government, each with its own administrative capital – often an existing settlement. The magistrates are elected by the council, although most of them are expected to be benefactors (→c.125).

Biography delayed by a fear of death

Rome, 98
The famous historian and senator Cornelius Tacitus has had to wait until after the death of Emperor Domitian, assassinated two years ago, before he could safely publish his biography of the celebrated Julius Agricola, governor of Britain from 77 to 84.

Agricola, who died in 93, was Tacitus's father-in-law. He served in the campaign against Boudica in 60 and commanded the 20th Legion in the north from 70 to 73. He extended the northern Roman frontier to the Forth and Clyde and beyond, but was recalled by Emperor Domitian and retired, on the grounds, it is widely believed, of simple jealousy. Tacitus obviously takes this view: he describes his father-in-law's achievements as being "thrown away". Such criticism of Domitian while he was alive would probably have meant death.

Gladiators attract enormous crowds as the Romans import their favourite public diversion and construct vast amphitheatres

A Roman's bronze helmet.

A reconstruction of the Roman theatre at St Albans, Hertfordshire.

A mosaic (c.350) representing two gladiators in close and bloody conflict.

A gladiator carved in ivory.

Southern England, c.100
The Romans have imported their favourite public diversion, and now there is nothing quite like a good fight between gladiators to pull in the crowds. The seats and stands are free, with amphitheatres at Cirencester and Dorchester holding up to 2,500 people each.

The entertainment usually starts with conjurors and acrobats. Boxing, a bloody affair with metal-thonged "gloves", follows. Gladiators will then pit their skills against wild boars, bulls and wolves brought from the far north before the main attraction: death matches between gladiators. These men are stars in their own right. They have come a long way from their origins as slaves, prisoners of war and petty criminals – and now their young fans scribble adoring *graffiti* to them on the walls of the theatres.

Chariot races, held on flat land near the towns, also pull in large crowds, with teams – usually the reds, blues, greens and yellows – battling in brightly decorated chariots, each pulled by four mighty horses.

Another attraction at the amphitheatre is the public execution. Criminals convicted of offences against the state may face formal execution, but often they are thrown to wild animals. Prisoners are either tied to a stake in the centre of the arena, into which the animals are released, or thrust naked, shivering and unarmed into the theatre.

105 - 125

Lincoln, c.105. Public baths are under construction in the town (→c.108).

Northern Britain, c.105. Roman forts are seriously damaged at Newstead, High Rochester, Glenlochar and Cappuck in a series of successful raids by the Selgovae tribe (→c.108).

York, c.108. The fortress, one of the three permanent legionary bases in Britain, is being rebuilt in stone (→c.110).

London, c.110. A fortress is being built on the western edge of the town, to house troops seconded for duties connected with town administration (→c.130).

Cirencester, Glos, c.110. The town's amphitheatre is being remodelled in stone (→c.120).

Near East, 110. Emperor Trajan launches a new campaign in Mesopotamia [Iraq]. Such initiatives mean that Britain has slipped down the agenda of urgent imperial matters (→117).

Syria, August 117. At the end of a successful eastern campaign that has taken Roman power down to the Persian Gulf, the dying Trajan names Publius Aelius Hadrianus (Hadrian) as his successor. To establish peace on the empire's frontiers, Hadrian abandons Trajan's far-flung conquests in Mesopotamia (→122).

Dover, Kent, c.117. The Romans are building a new port as the home base for their British fleet.→

Northern England, 118. Following an unsuccessful revolt by the Brigantes tribal confederation, which is contained by Pompeius Falco, the new governor of Britain, Hadrian commemorates his success by a gold coin (→c.143).

Colchester, Essex, c.120. The town's earthwork defences are being replaced by the building of a stone wall (→c.160).

Britain, 122. Emperor Hadrian visits Britain as part of a tour of his frontier provinces. He brings with him a new governor, the Spanish-born Aulus Platorius Nepos.→

Northern England, 122. On Hadrian's orders construction begins on a frontier wall between the Roman province and the unconquered northern tribes. It will stretch from the Solway Firth to the mouth of the river Tyne.→

Navy headquarters is sited at Dover

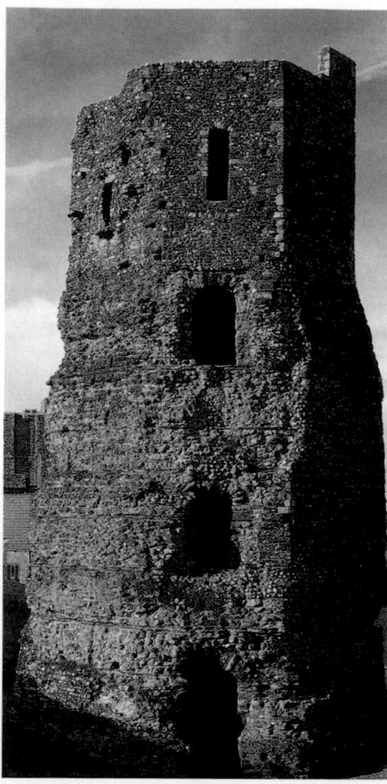

Remains of the lighthouse at Dover.

Dover, Kent, 117

Work has begun on a major naval base which will be the headquarters of Rome's *classis Britannica* [British fleet]. When completed, the base at Dover will operate with Boulogne, its counterpart in Gaul, to provide escorts for official sea traffic between Gaul and Britain and to the Rhine with its own fleet, as well as providing support for military expeditions in northern Britain.

Engineers are surveying the difficult sloping site into which the one-hectare (2.5-acre) fort must be squeezed; when finished it will contain barracks and stores for at least ten ships (→c.135).

Great wall built in north

Northern England, 122

Determined to stamp his authority on the northernmost part of the empire, Emperor Hadrian has ordered the building of countless monuments during his current tour of Britain. But none of them can match in scale or size his most ambitious plan yet: a great wall across the neck of Britain, snaking 73 miles (117 km) from the Solway Firth to the mouth of the Tyne.

Although the wall will serve as a defensive line against any invasion from the north, its main purpose is to split the troublesome Brigantes from the Selgovae and Novantae tribes to the north. The emperor himself surveyed the terrain, and now legionaries and slaves are moving thousands of tonnes of stone to create the 2.4-metre-thick wall, which stands 3.7 to 6.1 metres high. To the south a "dead zone" is being built, a ditch between two earthen ramparts; 16 forts are to be built into the wall, with smaller fortlets every mile. Look-out towers will enable the defenders to scan vast areas of country, while warning beacons will be used to summon assistance, which will move rapidly along a new road system.

The wall zone will be manned by 11,500 troops, mainly auxiliaries (non-citizen troops), and the headquarters will be at Carlisle, where a cavalry unit 1,000 strong is to be housed, with the main legion bases at Chester and York (→c.132).

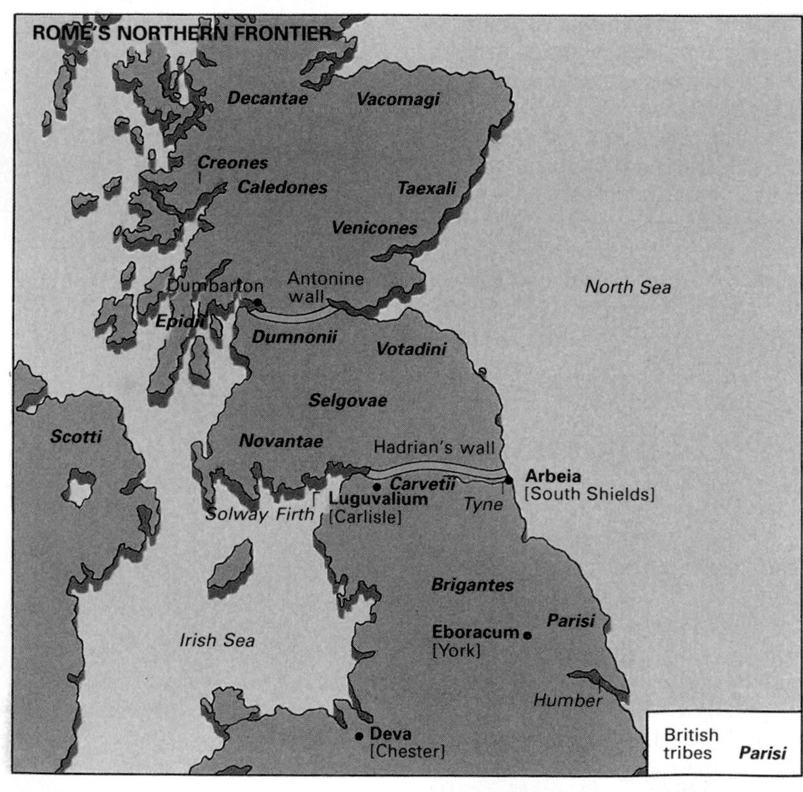

Life on the northern frontier: cold, pink-eyed and short of cash

Northumberland, c.110

What does a Roman soldier wear under his skirt? Letters from the fort of Chesterholm in this remote northern outpost of the Roman empire reveal the answer to this – underpants – and to many other questions about life in the frontier lands. A soldier begs his old messmates to send him new underpants and woolly socks to fend off the bitter chill of a northern British winter. The wife of the commander of Chesterholm writes to her friend, the wife of the commander of the neighbouring fort, hoping that she is in good health and inviting her to come and pay a visit.

The *medicus* [the unit's medical officer] reports that 30 soldiers are suffering from "pink eye" (conjunctivitis); military intelligence notes that the local "little Brits" fight with chariots – a method of warfare no longer used on the continent but still clearly to be found in this distant part of the empire. "Send money – quickly, please" is the plea of a merchant called Octavius with a shipment of goods on his hands who finds himself short of cash. He cannot move his load – the roads are too bad (→c.125).

Hadrian plans new era

A reconstruction of a bath-house and hostel at Wall, in Staffordshire.

Britain, c.125

It is not just for his wall that Britons will remember the bearded Emperor Hadrian. Preceded by legionaries, and accompanied by his bodyguard and a retinue of officials, Hadrian is sweeping around Britain clearly intent on massive reorganization.

Together with his planned military changes, Hadrian is determined to revitalize and extend the scheme of civil self-government awarded to a number of tribal regions in the south in the latter part of the last century. The Cornovii tribe is to be provided with a *civitas* [administrative region] capital at Wroxeter, complete with a civic centre including a *forum* [council offices and shopping centre] and a *basilica* [law courts], as are the Corieltauvi, or Coritani, at Leicester. A *forum* is being completed at Caistor St Edmund for the Iceni, 65 years after their revolt under Boudica. Grants of self-government are likely to be given to some tribes in Wales, although some military supervision will probably continue.

In addition, Hadrian is taking steps to improve the official communications network in the province, ordering the building of official posting houses in towns such as Chelmsford and Wall (→ 10/7/138).

Chariots to drive on left down new roads

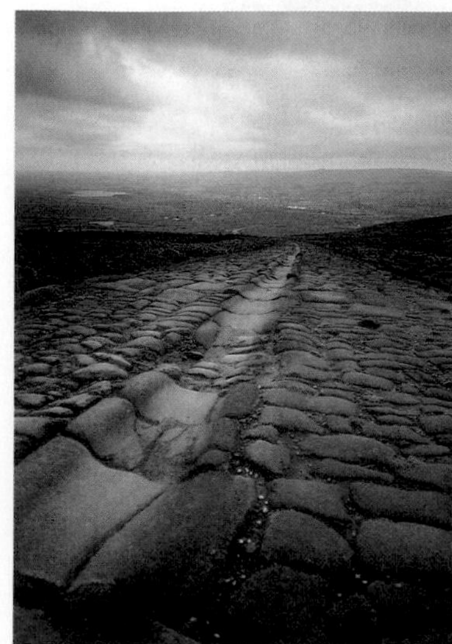

The Roman Pennine road at Blackstone Edge, north of Manchester.

Britain, c.120

Tired of stumbling over the rough network of tracks and paths that served as highways for the Britons, the Romans have embarked on a major road-building programme in the north. Communications will be transformed by these superbly engineered roads with cambers, drainage ditches and causeways across marshes.

Colchester was the first centre of road construction, followed by London as the hub of a radiating network. Although many of these new roads offer long straight routes for traffic, they are also constructed to negotiate gradients with the minimum of effort. Mile-posts record distance between towns, and traffic drives on the left (→ 225).

Britons encouraged to join Roman army

The army on the move: soldiers bearing standards cross a pontoon bridge.

Britain, c.125

Work on the northern wall is making big demands on the Roman army in Britain, since there is a need for guards as well as construction workers. As a result, many Britons are being encouraged to join up as troops.

The army in Britain falls into three sections: at the top are the legionaries, who are all Roman citizens; then come the auxiliaries, Britons pressed into front-line service; last are the *numeri*, natives generally reserved for routine occupations such as that of frontier guard. Many legionaries who arrived in 43 stayed on and settled down after completing 20 years' service. In old garrison towns such as York and Caerleon, they opened bars and brothels. Their British children are Roman citizens, and eligible to join up as legionaries.

For many Britons, joining the army is an attractive prospect, for on retiring an auxiliary becomes a citizen, with legal and voting rights. Less willing members of conquered tribes are often pressed into service as *numeri* and packed off to places such as Germany.

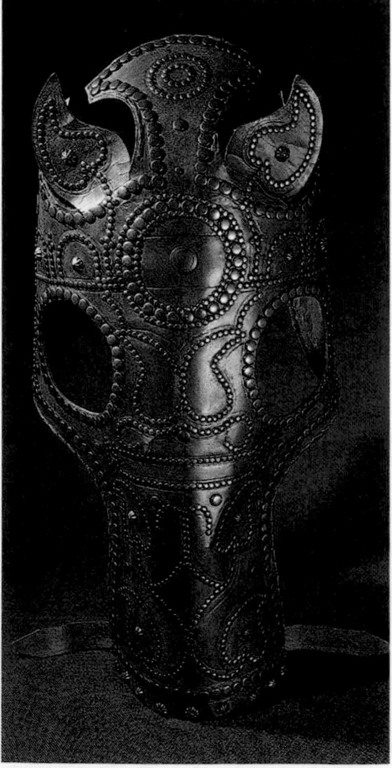

A reconstructed leather mask for a horse, from an army camp.

A bronze statuette, c.100-200, of a legionary warily "at ease".

126 - 154

Dorset, c.126. Basic kitchenware pottery from the south-west of Britain is being made for Roman units in the north (→c.150).

London, c.130. About 26 hectares of the provincial capital is destroyed in a serious fire (→c.195).

Northern England, c.132. Hadrian's wall is completed (→c.139).

Britain, 132. Sextus Julius Severus, who became governor just last year, is transferred to Judaea [Palestine] to quell a Jewish revolt. His replacement is Mummius Sisenna.

Dover, Kent, c.135. The Roman *classis Britannica* (British fleet), which has been restrengthening the wall around the port, begins work on a second fortress (→c.160).

Baiae, Italy, 10 July 138. Emperor Hadrian dies of the painful wasting disease from which he has suffered for the last three years. His successor is his adopted son, the 51-year-old Titus Aurelius Antoninus (→139).

Rome, 139. Emperor Antoninus appoints Quintus Lollius Urbicus, a native of the Roman province of Africa [Tunisia and Libya], as the new governor of Britain.

Hadrian's Wall, c.139. The Roman governor, Urbicus, re-establishes the old supply base which was built by Emperor Agricola at Corbridge in 84 and prepares the army to advance northwards from the wall (→145).

Caistor St Edmund, Norfolk, c.140. The forum complex is under construction, with plans to build a bath-house (→c.195).

Essex, c.140. A great villa is being built at Rivenhall.

Northern England, c.143. The governor, Urbicus, suppresses a revolt by the Brigantian tribal confederation which began last year. Emperor Antoninus issues a coin to commemorate this victory in the province of Britain.

London, c.145. Marcus Maenius Agrippa is appointed by the emperor as the new procurator fiscal (chief financial official) of Britain. He may remain as commander of the Roman *classis Britannica* [British fleet].

Cambridgeshire, c.150. The production of fine tableware pottery is a major industry at Water Newton (→c.160).

Fens are fields as wetlands reclaimed

East Anglia, c.135

Substantial areas of the northern fenland of East Anglia are being settled and reclaimed for agriculture, following major construction programmes which have transformed this marshy and once sparsely populated landscape. Canals and drainage ditches have lowered water-levels which were already beginning to fall naturally; roads have been added and field systems developed to exploit land which, once drained, is highly fertile. As a result this area of East Anglia has experienced a sudden and large growth of population.

Hundreds of villages and farms have been established over the past 15 years. The houses are mostly the simple dwellings of peasants working the land or making salt from the saline marshes. One larger settlement is Stonea, once a gravel island surrounded by watery fens, which was the scene of a major battle by local tribes against the Romans in 47. Now Stonea is being transformed into an administrative centre for the emerging fenland.

The scale of these changes indicates considerable official planning, and could even reflect Emperor Hadrian's interest in the reclamation of marginal agricultural land. Certainly the massive scale of the engineering works and transformation of the landscape are in keeping with his style (→c.150).

Romans advance north to new frontier

Hadrian's wall, abandoned by the army as it moves north to a new frontier.

Northern Britain, 145

Barely a decade after the completion of Emperor Hadrian's mighty wall, the great bulk of its Roman garrison has left to march northwards to a new frontier built by his successor, Antoninus. The *vallum*, the earthwork defence to the south that marks the edge of the military zone, is being decommissioned, and more bridges are being thrown across it to allow free access.

Overturning Hadrian's plan to halt Roman expansion at his wall, Antoninus advanced north to the valley formed by the rivers Forth and Clyde that marked the boundary for Julius Agricola, who governed Britain in the last century. There he ordered the construction of a new wall – at 40 miles (64 km) half the length of Hadrian's – with the aim of keeping the Caledonian tribes out of southern Scotland. The new wall is built of turf and clay in some places rather than stone, with stone foundations. There are forts at intervals along the wall.

A ditch has been dug to the north of the wall and, unlike at Hadrian's wall, the forts are linked by a roadway, which will lead to a harbour at Dumbarton. The new wall will be manned by about 7,000 troops, more per mile than Hadrian employed, but there will be proportionately fewer cavalry (→c.156).

Efficient functioning of economy depends on network of slaves

Heavy load: a female slave at work.

Britain, c.140

The efficient functioning of the British economy today depends heavily on the contribution made by slaves. Slavery existed in Britain before the Roman invasion – the historian Strabo listed slaves along with hunting dogs among Britain's exports 200 years ago – but it is an institution with which the Romans feel very much at home. The supply of slaves is not a problem: some are born into it, others are prisoners of war or are driven into it by debt. The great agricultural estates need thousands of them. Here females are less prized than males, so baby girls are sometimes killed at birth. Because of a constant fear of revolts, the males are often kept shackled. Living quarters may be dark and unhealthy. Being the property of their master, who can buy, sell or kill them, slaves are ruthlessly exploited.

They do have some rights, however. They can take concubines, lease shops, rent land or even own slaves themselves. Those who are able to amass enough money can buy their freedom. Sometimes slaves are freed on their owner's death. An owner may decide to set a slave free, or a master may release his slave-girl to marry her. A slave freed by a citizen also becomes a citizen but is barred from the upper ranks of society.

Life and death a hundred years after the invasion

Good life enjoyed by the upper class

St Albans, Hertfordshire, c.150
The big town house built by the family of Paternus and Sabina at St Albans is a striking example of the gracious living enjoyed by upper-class Britons since their country became a Roman province. The house has a central suite of rooms with wings at each end enclosing a garden. A central-heating system serves the dining room and bathing suites.

While the mass of the people working on the land remain as poor as ever, many others have shared in the wealth generated by the trades and industries brought over by the Romans. Tribal leaders and other Britons who have learnt to speak Latin have enthusiastically embraced the lifestyle of their colonial masters. They decorate their homes with Roman-style mosaics and furnishings, give fashionable dinner parties and applaud the gladiatorial combats at the local amphitheatre.

Many, like Paternus, have acquired country estates as well as town properties and serve as magistrates. The half-dozen or so slaves who are kept in the St Albans home to care for Paternus, Sabina and their two children are well treated and reasonably content.

At the heart of the farm: an artist's view of the villa at Gorhambury, Herts.

Boost for harvests from new technology

Britain, c.150
The heavy demands for regular food supplies by the army of occupation, along with the development of large farming estates to achieve economies of scale, have transformed British agriculture under the Romans. New crops, new tools and new techniques have been imported from Rome and Gaul.

The ancient iron plough is still widely used, but its efficiency has been improved by the fitting of the blade-like coulter to cut into the soil ahead of the ploughshare which turns the furrow. A two-handed scythe enables hay to be cut more rapidly, and a new balanced sickle has made reaping easier, while spring-handled shears have eased the task of sheep shearing. An iron-shod spade is now in general use, and better-quality axes and saws have eased scrub-clearing.

The Romans have opened up more upland areas, and by better management they ensure that food is not wasted. Harvests are now brought in more rapidly, and overall yields have risen. People are becoming used to seeing cabbages, carrots, celery and parsnips on the menu, not to mention apples, plums, mulberries and walnuts. Other crops – flax, rye and oats – have also been introduced (→c.450).

Dead sent off with food and valuables

Essex, c.150
An elaborate mausoleum, one of the most splendid in Britain, is being built at West Mersea for a well-off local family. Its magnificence reflects the way in which death has come to be regarded as an occasion for ostentatious display in the Roman province: many monuments show the deceased accompanied by servants, household goods and the tools of a trade. Often the dead person's age is given in multiples of five, since the precise age is a matter of guesswork.

Many rituals from pre-Roman times have been carried over by the native Britons. Cremation is the general rule for funerals; after being loudly mourned, the body of the deceased is burned on a pyre and the ashes are buried in containers of pottery, or sometimes of glass and lead. The wealthier burials often have wooden caskets with bronze and iron fittings. Most graves are furnished with food and drink, and some have glass vessels for eating and drinking, and even clothes and a pair of shoes for the journey into the next life. Sometimes a lamp, still burning, is sealed in the tomb. People die young, most often between 30 and 40, though occasionally a few live to 80 (→353).

Fine living: an ornate candlestick.

Reclining diners enjoy luxurious dinners

Southern England, c.150
Upper-class Britons such as Paternus and Sabina [*see report above left*] can throw a fine dinner party these days. In the spacious dining-room, where couches are laid out around three sides of a square before fine place settings, slaves serve up a luxurious meal in several courses.

After hors d'oeuvres, the first dish may well be shellfish, with oysters in sauce a particular favourite, or fresh fish such as herring or grey mullet. A fish sauce known as *liquamen* is widely used in the preparation of these meals. It is made by mashing small fish, such as sprat, with the entrails of larger fish to create a mixture which is then left to mature in the sun. The resulting juice is strained off and is a staple in the kitchen.

The main course may be beef or veal, roasted and dressed with a sauce made of *liquamen*, pepper and oil, and served with vegetables, possibly leeks and onions. Fresh fruit and pastries commonly round off the feast.

The meal is accompanied by fine wines imported from continental Europe. Much in demand is the red Falernian wine from Campania in southern Italy, but vintages from Bordeaux and the banks of the Moselle are also popular. Some guests prefer beer or mead.

Beautiful wares: jug and glass bowl. ▷

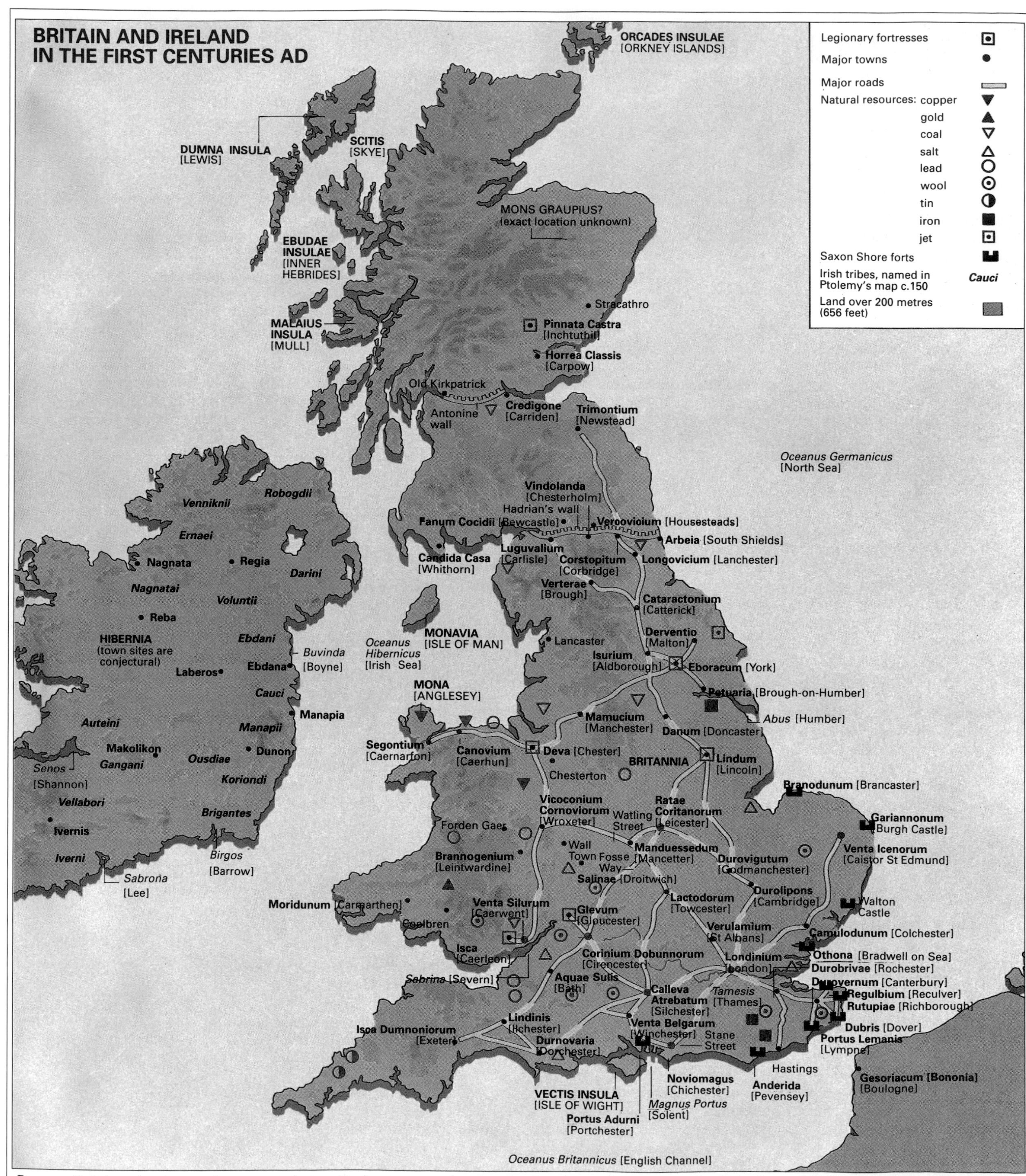
BRITAIN AND IRELAND
IN THE FIRST CENTURIES AD
Legionary fortresses
Major towns
Major roads
Natural resources: copper
gold
coal
salt
lead
wool
tin
iron
jet
Saxon Shore forts
Irish tribes, named in Ptolemy's map c.150
Cauci
Land over 200 metres (656 feet)
ORCADES INSULAE
[ORKNEY ISLANDS]
DUMNA INSULA
[LEWIS]
SCITIS
[SKYE]
EBUDAE
INSULAE
[INNER
HEBRIDES]
MONS GRAUPIUS?
(exact location unknown)
MALAIUS
INSULA
[MULL]
Stracathro
Pinnata Castra
[Inchtuthil]
Horrea Classis
[Carpow]
Old Kirkpatrick
Antonine wall
Credigone
[Carriden]
Trimontium
[Newstead]
Oceanus Germanicus
[North Sea]
Vindolanda
[Chesterholm]
Hadrian's wall
Fanum Cocidii [Bewcastle]
Vercovicium [Housesteads]
Arbeia [South Shields]
Candida Casa
[Whithorn]
Luguvalium
[Carlisle]
Corstopitum
[Corbridge]
Longovicium [Lanchester]
Verterae
[Brough]
Cataractonium
[Catterick]
Derventio
[Malton]
Lancaster
Isurium
[Aldborough]
Eboracum [York]
Petuaria [Brough-on-Humber]
Abus [Humber]
MONAVIA
[ISLE OF MAN]
Oceanus
Hibernicus
[Irish Sea]
MONA
[ANGLESEY]
Mamucium
[Manchester]
Danum [Doncaster]
Segontium
[Caernarfon]
Canovium
[Caerhun]
Deva [Chester]
BRITANNIA
Lindum
[Lincoln]
Chesterton
Branodunum [Brancaster]
Viroconium
Cornoviorum
[Wroxeter]
Watling
Street
Ratae
Coritanorum
[Leicester]
Gariannonum
[Burgh Castle]
Forden Gaer
Wall
Town
Fosse
Way
Manduessedum
[Mancetter]
Venta Icenorum
[Caistor St Edmund]
Brannogenium
[Leintwardine]
Durovigutum
[Godmanchester]
Salinae [Droitwich]
Durolipons
[Cambridge]
Lactodorum
[Towcester]
Walton
Castle
Moridunum [Carmarthen]
Venta Silurum
[Caerwent]
Glevum
[Gloucester]
Coelbren
Verulamium
[St Albans]
Camulodunum [Colchester]
Isca
[Caerleon]
Corinium Dobunnorum
[Cirencester]
Othona [Bradwell on Sea]
Londinium
[London]
Durobrivae [Rochester]
Sabrina [Severn]
Aquae Sulis
[Bath]
Calleva
Atrebatum
[Silchester]
Tamesis
[Thames]
Durovernum [Canterbury]
Regulbium [Reculver]
Rutupiae [Richborough]
Lindinis
[Ilchester]
Venta Belgarum
[Winchester]
Stane
Street
Dubris [Dover]
Portus Lemanis
[Lympne]
Isca Dumnoniorum
[Exeter]
Durnovaria
[Dorchester]
Hastings
Noviomagus
[Chichester]
Anderida
[Pevensey]
Gesoriacum [Bononia]
[Boulogne]
VECTIS INSULA
[ISLE OF WIGHT]
Magnus Portus
[Solent]
Portus Adurni
[Portchester]
Oceanus Britannicus [English Channel]
Venniknii
Robogdii
Ernaei
Nagnata
Regia
Darini
Nagnatai
Voluntii
Reba
HIBERNIA
(town sites are conjectural)
Ebdani
Buvinda
[Boyne]
Laberos
Ebdana
Cauci
Auteini
Manapia
Manapii
Makolikon
Gangani
Dunon
Ousdiae
Senos
[Shannon]
Koriondi
Vellabori
Brigantes
Ivernis
Iverni
Birgos
[Barrow]
Sabrona
[Lee]

Roman Britain, showing major towns, legionary fortresses and other landmarks and (where applicable) their modern equivalents. The map of Ireland locates the Irish tribes identified by the Greek geographer Ptolemy in his chart of the British Isles (see reports on facing page).

Britain put on the map

Alexandria, Egypt, c.150
The first detailed chart of the British Isles has been produced by a man who has never visited them. He is the celebrated Greek geographer Claudius Ptolemaius (Ptolemy), who lives at Alexandria, in Egypt, the home of the famous library of some 700,000 volumes.

Britain and Ireland feature in Ptolemy's massive geography of the world as it is known to the Greeks and Romans, from Taprobane [Sri Lanka] in the east to the Fortunate Islands [Canaries] in the west. It lists the latitude and longitude of over 8,000 named places, from which a map can be plotted. Earlier map-makers and explorers were inclined to exaggerate the size of Britain, and they liked to place Ireland somewhere between Spain and Britain. Ptolemy has, oddly, turned Scotland at right angles, so that it runs east-west rather than north-south.

There are a few other slips. Calleva [Silchester, in Hampshire] is placed north-west of London, and Mona [Anglesey] appears to be confused with Monavia [the Isle of Man] as one island in the Irish Sea. Hadrian's wall, which was begun in 122 and completed in the mid-130s, is not on the map. The new wall recently begun by Emperor Antoninus is probably too new for inclusion.

In the preparation of his massive work, Ptolemy made substantial use of the information provided by official and military sources as well as data assembled by historians such as Marinus of Tyre (→ c.550).

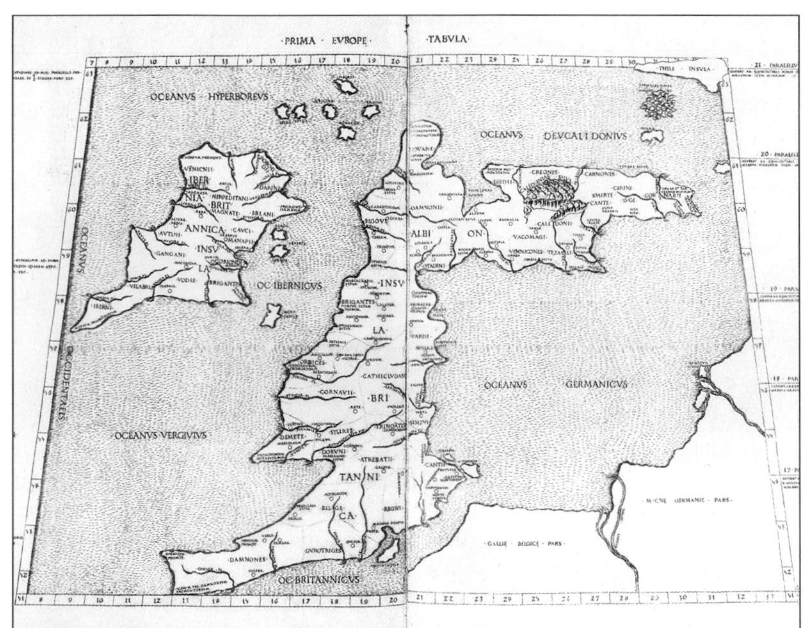

A reconstructed version of Ptolemy's map of Britain, with Ireland to the west.

How the Greek map-maker sees Ireland

Alexandria, Egypt, c.150
Ptolemy's chart is the first attempt to map Ireland and the first to locate it correctly – both the Romans and the Greeks believed that it lay between Britain and Spain.

Working from reports of seamen who would have given names in their own dialects, Ptolemy names several rivers, including the Buvinda [Boyne], Sabrona [Lee], Senos [Shannon] and Birgos [Barrow], and a number of tribes including peoples of the interior and west coast such as the Nagnatai of Galway and the Vellabori of the south-west, as well as those of the better-known east coast such as the Cauci and Darini, and the Robogdii in the north.

Intriguingly, a tribe called the Brigantes is mentioned in the south-east, suggesting that there may be an Irish branch to this thorn in the Roman side and that it speaks the same language (→ c.250).

Wine shops and restaurants win growing popularity as civic centres are redesigned

Reconstruction of the bath-house at Wroxeter shows a rare open-air pool.

Britain, c.150
The bustling centres of the larger civic settlements are being redesigned and enlarged. At Wroxeter, in Shropshire, large new public baths and shops are being built, and a new *forum* has recently been finished. In London, a huge new *forum* has been constructed, and the baths have been enlarged at Huggin Hill. New developments are modifying Roman practice to suit the colder, wetter British climate. Covered buildings known as *palaestrae* are under construction at Wroxeter and Caerwent so that people can exercise in shelter, instead of in open-fronted premises.

On a typical day in a place like Wroxeter the town centre is packed with shoppers, while farm bailiffs and others crowd into wine shops and inns. The bath-houses are always busy. Here people come to keep fit, as well as for social contact. Afterwards some may gamble in the exercise yard. Dice are popular, as well as "twelve-lines", a form of backgammon, and a board-game similar to draughts, known as "soldiers".

The bath-houses, together with inns, restaurants and private houses, need an enormous amount of water. Town centres are often serviced by aqueducts – channels dug through the ground, possibly lined with clay. The aqueduct at Wroxeter is capable of delivering two million gallons of water a day. Timber-lined drains have also been built in many towns, and in some places heavy stone sewers carry away the town's waste (→ c.165).

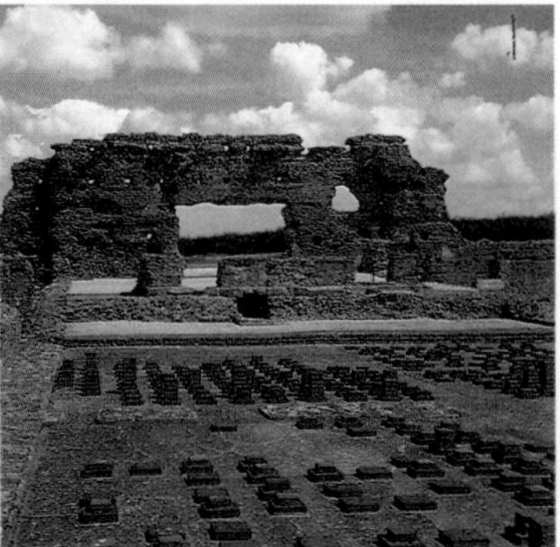
Wroxeter: the remains of the large and luxurious bath-house.

A Roman god of the sea: detail from a pavement at St Albans.

155 - 175

Northern Britain, 155. Julius Verus, a general from the province of Lower Germany, the new governor of Britain, subdues the Brigantes and reasserts control of land south of Hadrian's wall temporarily lost to Rome (→c.156).

St Albans, Herts, c.156. A fire destroys much of the town; work on the earthwork defences is abandoned (→c.160).

Carmarthen, Dyfed, c.156. The old fort site is being redeveloped as a new town with a formal street grid and an amphitheatre (→c.165).

Scotland, 159. The Antonine wall is re-garrisoned following the ruthless suppression of the recent Brigantian revolt (→163).

Leicester, c.160. The building of public baths and an aqueduct has been completed.→

Colchester, Essex, c.160. The town's defence wall is being reinforced with an internal earth ramp (→c.180).

Italy, 7 March 161. Emperor Antoninus dies; he is succeeded by Marcus Aurelius, who grants Lucius Verus, his adopted brother, the powers of a tribune and makes him co-emperor. For the first time imperial powers are fully shared.

Britain, 161. Statius Priscus Licinius Italicus is appointed governor. He was highly decorated in the Jewish rebellion before his promotion to the senate and the governorship of Dacia [Romania] (→163).

Britain, 163. Statius Priscus is transferred to the eastern provinces.

Scotland, 163. After only a brief reoccupation, the Antonine wall is abandoned. Troops are withdrawn southwards to Hadrian's wall.→

Wroxeter, Shropshire, c.165. A fire has destroyed the civic centre. The rebuilding includes plans for a temple (→c.195).

Welsh Marches, c.165. The Romans, fearing an outbreak of trouble from the Ordovices tribe of north Wales, regarrison Forden Gaer and Coelbren and begin building new forts at Wall town and Leintwardine (→c.240).

Italy, 166. Germanic tribes invade northern Italy.

Thames estuary, c.170. A freighter laden with Samian pottery from Gaul [France] founders en route to London.

Troops withdrawn from Antonine wall to tackle rebellion

Northern Britain, c.156

A serious rebellion by the ever-troublesome Brigantian people of the Pennines has forced the Roman governor of Britain, Julius Verus, to evacuate the Antonine wall only a few years after its construction was completed. The move demonstrates the over-ambitious nature of the project, since the trouble has occurred to the south of Hadrian's wall – in an area which the Romans believed to have been firmly under their control.

The governor will derive no comfort from the knowledge that it was the depletion of Roman troops in the Brigantian country, in order to garrison the Antonine wall, that gave the Brigantes the opportunity to revolt. The number of troops stationed among the Brigantes, whose capital is at Aldborough, had been reduced once before when the legionaries were sent north to serve on the newly completed Hadrian's wall. That too led to a revolt, which was decisively quelled by the year 143.

To punish the Brigantes the present emperor, Antoninus, incorporated much of their territory into an imperial estate, at the same time bringing in troops from legions in Upper and Lower Germany to regarrison the tribal lands (→159).

A brooch from the Brigantes' land.

Iron industry boom gives fleet new role

Sussex, c.160

Rome's *classis Britannica* [British fleet] has taken on a new role in the wake of greatly increased demand for tools, weapons and armour in the military zones of northern Britain, which has led to a boom in the iron-producing areas of the thickly wooded Kent and Sussex Weald, where dozens of new smelting sites have been opened.

The iron industry in this area was well established at sites near Hastings and Battle before Julius Caesar's raids of 55 and 54BC. In the century since the Roman occupation, however, it has been expanded, and there are at least 40 sites being worked, some under direct imperial control and others leased to civilian ironworkers.

The fleet appears to have taken over the control and distribution of this expansion. The role of the fleet is to distribute the products by taking the raw iron from the small ports around Romney Marsh to its main bases such as Dover. From there it is shipped to the army in northern Britain and also to the empire's troops stationed on the lower Rhine (→c.244).

Relax and chat at the local bath-house

Cleaning up: life in the local bath-house, as imagined by a 20th-century artist.

Britain, c.160

The public baths recently constructed at Leicester, like those in other large towns, represent an important element of Roman-style living in the province of Britain. Usually close to an open complex in the centre of the town – the *palaestra*, where sports and games are held – the baths provide one of the commonest forms of relaxation after work has finished for the day. While open-air ones are known, closed baths are understandably more popular in the unpredictable British climate.

As most people work from dawn until noon and then finish for the day, the bath-house is usually open in the afternoons, and it is popular with all classes of people. Bath times may be staggered and the sexes segregated, but quite often bathing is a mixed affair, with the bath-house becoming a centre for both social and business gatherings, a place for negotiations between merchants or simply gossip among friends.

Inside is a warm, steamy hubbub of men, women and children bathing, relaxing and talking, while around them teems a diverse array of food-sellers, hawkers, pedlars, servants and slaves, serving their customers or masters.

Bathers can proceed from the *tepidarium* [warm room] to the *calidarium* [hot room] before finishing with a plunge into a pool of cold water in the *frigidarium* [cold room]. After this there is the opportunity to be massaged and rubbed with oils, which are afterwards scraped from the skin with a tool called a *strigil*.

Hadrian's wall to be the frontier again

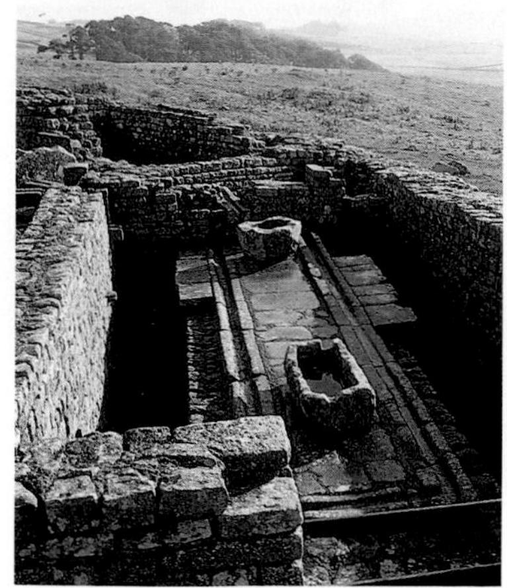
Hadrian's wall: Housesteads fort.

Antonine wall, 163
The death of Emperor Antoninus has led to the abandonment of the Antonine wall, only four years after it was reoccupied on his orders. Now that he is gone, the new governor of Britain, Calpurnius Agricola – backed by the new emperor, Marcus Aurelius – has decided that it is too costly to hold, and has ordered the regarrisoning and refortification of the area south of Hadrian's wall. The territory between the two walls is the homeland of the Selgovae and Votadini tribes, and the Brigantes also occupy some land in this region.

The recent troubles in the region [*see report on page 68*] have been put down only at the cost of many Roman deaths. Now the frontier will be resealed; the gates of the mile-castles along the wall are being rehung and causeways across the deep *vallum*, the defensive earthwork to the south, dug up.

Some forts are still being held north of the wall, among them Newstead, but Hadrian's wall is again to be the main linear defence for the Romans in northern Britain. At least 30 forts are being regarrisoned, while on the wall itself the garrison has been brought up to 10,000 men. Defences along the Cumbrian coast and Solway Firth, however, seem likely to be less well guarded than in the past (→190).

Potters launch threat to Gallic imports

A leaping stag: detail from a red-glazed Samian-ware pot found in England.

Colchester, Essex, c.160
For the first time British potters are mounting a competitive challenge to the luxury red glossy-glazed Samian tableware produced across the Channel. In Gaul [France] potters such as Cinnamus of Lezoux have giant workshops that turn out thousands of Samian pots a month, but the standard of their product has been falling in recent years. This has given the British a chance to enter the market. Now Acceptus and Cunopectus of Colchester are carrying out the first experiments in producing a British version of Samian.

It may not be terribly good, but they hope to improve it and, by using what are in effect factory methods of manufacture, to provide a cheap alternative and create a home market as prosperity grows in Roman Britain (→c.300).

Trade enriches London

An artist's impression of traders of the period operating from London docks.

Southern England, c.170
London and other administrative centres are flourishing after a century of self-government under Roman rule and are enjoying the benefits of integration into the empire. Direct military rule has dwindled, and towns and villages are expanding as agricultural advances take hold [*see report on page 65*].

With urban growth comes a demand for luxuries. French and Spanish wine flows into Britain. From Cologne comes the green glassware to put it in; from Spain, olive oil, from Gaul [France], prestigious red Samian pottery, and from Britain itself the finest cultivated oysters in the empire.

While other ports benefit from the growth in trade, most activity is centred on the capital, London, which began its rise in the boom years of the late first century AD, after taking over from Colchester as the administrative capital of the province. The town boasts a town-hall complex which includes what some say is the largest building north of the Alps. With its unrivalled port facilities and permanent garrison, London has attracted merchants of all kinds, and its river estuary – facing towards the mouth of the river Rhine with its huge traffic from the continent – make it a ready market for all sorts of exotic goods which literally span the globe. The fabulously rich silks worn only by the richest have come by road, and port to port, all the way from China (→c.195).

Emperor diverted by Danube 'barbarians'

Danube region, c.175
Britain is low on the imperial agenda at the moment because war has broken out again on the Danube frontier. Emperor Marcus Aurelius has hastened to Pannonia [Hungary] to deal with renewed hostility on his eastern borders from the Germanic tribes known as the Quadi and Marcomanni.

Eight years ago "barbarian" tribes broke through Roman defences on the Danube and briefly threatened Italy itself. Marcus Aurelius was set to counter-attack when he was forced to deal with a revolt by one of his own generals, Avidius Cassius, the governor of Syria, who proclaimed himself emperor. At that stage Marcus Aurelius bought a fragile peace with the German tribes, and he has since been determined to reassert Roman authority in the region.

In the past Roman policy towards the tribes pressing on the boundaries of the empire has been to bring them inside and settle them in border regions. Once there they were required to provide men for the legions and to secure the border. Now Marcus Aurelius has decided to solve the frontier problem by annexing tribal territory and creating new buffer provinces across the Danube (→17/3/180).

176 - 193

Vienna, 17 March 180. On the death of Emperor Marcus Aurelius from the plague, his adopted son and successor Commodus makes peace with the Marcomanni tribe on the Danube, abandoning plans for conquering them (→31/12/192).

Kent, c.180. As an offering for the newly built Romano-British temple at Spring Head, the bodies of four children are buried in the four corners of the building (→c.190).

Lincoln, c.180. Earthwork defences are being built around the city (→c.195).

Britain, c.181. Commodus appoints Ulpius Marcellus as governor. His first task is to quell the trouble at Hadrian's wall (→184).

Rome, 184. To commemorate the victory over the tribes of northern Britain, Emperor Commodus strikes a new coin and assumes the commemorative title "Britannicus [British]" (→185).

Britain, 185. Marcellus is recalled to Rome, due to his unpopularity. His replacement is Publius Helvius Pertinax, a man who has risen through the ranks; he served as consul in Britain in 174-75 (→186).

Britain, 186. A new coin issue – the *concordia militum* [harmony of the troops] – marks the end of troubles within the Roman army (→187).

Britain, 191. Clodius Albinus, a commander from Germany, succeeds Pertinax as governor (→31/12/192).

Rome, 31 December 192. The mentally unstable Emperor Commodus is assassinated in a palace plot. Earlier this year he renamed Rome after himself and claimed to be the reincarnation of Hercules. He is succeeded by the city prefect and former British governor, Pertinax (→28/03/193).

Rome, 28 March 193. The Praetorian Guard assassinates Pertinax, the former British governor, after he has been emperor for only three months and chooses Marcus Didius Julianus to succeed (→02/06).

Rome, 2 June 193. Julianus is murdered and Septimius Severus, who was chosen as an imperial claimant last month by the army in Pannonia [Hungary], is proclaimed emperor (→12/193).

Britain, 193. The governor, Albinus, is given the title *caesar* [deputy emperor] by Emperor Severus (→12/93).

Mutiny compels governor to resign

Britain, 187

After only two years in office, punctuated by violent army unrest, the governor of Britain, Helvius Pertinax, has resigned and asked Emperor Commodus to replace him. Although Pertinax started his governorship well, he soon won a reputation as a strict disciplinarian, and opposition to him within the legions has been steadily mounting.

Rome's relations with the army in Britain have been strained for the best part of a decade. The worst trouble may be dated to 182, when Commodus appointed a Praetorian prefect called Perennis. In his role as administrator, Perennis downgraded the social rank from which legionary officers are drawn. This incensed the British legions, which sent a 1,500-strong delegation to Rome in 185 demanding that Perennis be sacked. Commodus agreed to this and replaced Britain's governor, Ulpius Marcellus, with Pertinax in an attempt to restore order. At first Pertinax appeared to have reached a settlement of sorts, quelling army support for a rival imperial claimant and refusing the same honour himself. But the army, still deeply discontented, mutinied and almost killed him.

As army discipline and respect for the emperor and his governors seems to be breaking down, Commodus must choose Pertinax's successor with some care (→191).

Villas and town houses furnished with lavish interior design

Autumn: a mosaic at Cirencester.

Sea leopard: from a mosaic at the palace of Fishbourne, near Chichester.

Britain, c.190

The peace and stability brought by the Romans has transformed living conditions for the wealthier people in society. There has been a notable expansion in the number of large and comfortable town houses and villas, many of them luxuriously furnished and decorated.

Walls are often adorned with paintings of landscapes and domestic scenes and portraits of the owner, his family and friends. In the most prosperous houses there are marble panelling and tapestry hangings, although some of the finer colours and textures can be hard to see as the thick green window glass casts a dull, blue-green light over everything.

Floors are generally made of small tiles, but in the formal rooms – particularly the dining room – mosaics and carpets are to be found, and everywhere there are festoons of flowers and greenery hanging from the walls and ceilings. In the bedrooms, even of the very rich, bedclothes tend to be utilitarian, with a heavy quilt to cover the owner and his wife and a simple bolster for their heads.

Some houses are kept warm by hypocausts (underfloor heating), with warm air distributed by ducts and vents. Others have fireplaces that burn wood, or sometimes coal from opencast mines. Lighting usually comes from oil lamps, but candles and rushes dipped in fat are also used (→c.370).

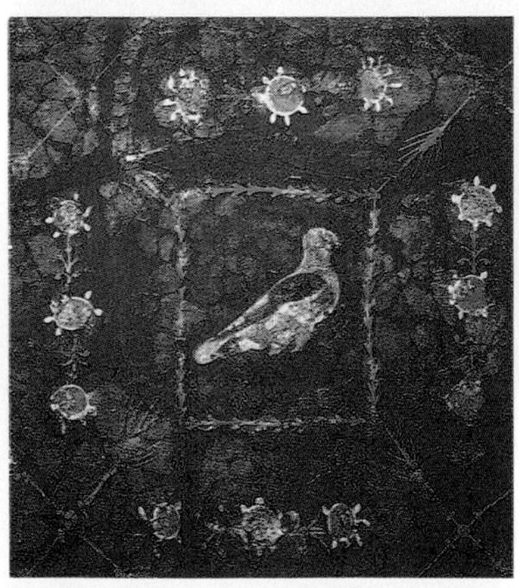

Ceiling design at a St Albans villa.

Tiles from a house at Wall, Staffs.

Northern tribes gang up

The type of northern fortification known as a "broch": Dun Telve, Highland.

Northern Britain, c.190
Following the trouble in the north in the past decade, there is growing concern among Roman commanders of the wall garrison at the increasing tendency of the tribes to the north of the Antonine wall to form alliances and other power groups. As a result they have taken steps to ensure that the power of these groups is not allowed to go unchallenged.

The foremost group in the north is the Caledonii, which has managed to unite most of the other tribes of the north and west under it, forming a formidable power bloc. For the moment it is bound by treaties which were thrashed out with the retired governor, Marcellus, but this alone is not enough to guarantee Roman security.

In addition, a second confederation, the Meatae, has been formed – with Roman encouragement – in lowland Scotland. This grouping, made up of tribes such as the Selgovae, the Novantae and the Verturiones, is intended to act as a buffer between the British province and the Caledonii. To improve matters further, another tribe in this area, the Votadini, has an existing treaty with Rome.

Obedience to the Romans has been made an attractive prospect for the tribes of the new grouping. In return for their support, the Romans have granted increased autonomy to these lowland peoples, who were previously under direct military rule. Sometimes, too, the army also withdraws from its outpost forts in the tribes' territories – and thus removes the threat of attack (→c.197).

New emperor emerges from year of crisis

Antioch, Syria, December 193
Septimius Severus, the African-born ex-governor of Pannonia [Hungary], is the undisputed emperor after a bitter power struggle reminiscent of the strife of 69. It began with the murder of Emperor Commodus last year. His mistress Marcia had him strangled by members of the Praetorian Guard while he was drunk, after discovering that the mentally unstable emperor planned to execute her.

The senate elected in his place the elderly Pertinax, a former governor of Britain, but after a reign of only three months he was also murdered by the Praetorian Guard, which then auctioned the throne to the highest bidder. This was the senator Didius Julianus, whose ambitions proved greater than either his abilities or his pockets.

After only a few months both his money and his luck ran out, and Septimius Severus was declared emperor by the legions in Pannonia. He had rivals in the governors of Britain and Syria, but he marched to Rome and put Julianus to death. To appease the British governor, Severus has made him his deputy with the title of *caesar* (→194).

A bust of Severus, the new emperor.

Leisure thrives on six-hour working day

Britain, c.190
The Romans have divided the day into twelve hours – dawn to dusk – but with the exception of the slaves most people work for six hours, from dawn until noon; after that the day is their own.

For the most part, entertainment for working people is fairly modest; a board-game, a little music, a little dancing and a few jugs of ale are the norm, although the theatre, the baths and the sports grounds are always available. Gladiatorial shows with wild beasts at the amphitheatre are a rare event. They take place only when paid for by a notable who is seeking office and hoping to curry favour with the populace.

The rich enjoy the usual pursuits that go with their favoured positions. Hunting, as ever, is popular: wild boar and deer are plentiful, bears becoming less so. In the evenings there are dinner parties, which are partly meals and partly social gatherings, rounded off with after-dinner entertainments, readings and music.

Curses and cures are on offer at Bath

Bath, Avon, c.190
"I curse Tretia Maria and her life, mind and memory." So begins a bitter curse called down on a woman in the spa town of Bath, which has become famous for the curative effect of its hot springs. People come from all over Britain and Gaul [France] to seek cures in its waters, but sometimes there is a dark intent behind a visit to the Roman temple and its springs. The temple has become a recognized centre for invoking powerful curses by those seeking revenge. Temple scribes write out the curses on lead tablets (neat writing is more expensive), and the tablets are then nailed up in the temple. How long a curse remains on show depends on how much the purchaser can afford; when the money runs out, it is taken down and buried. The curse on Tretia Maria concludes: "Thus may she be unable to speak what things are concealed" (→c.220).

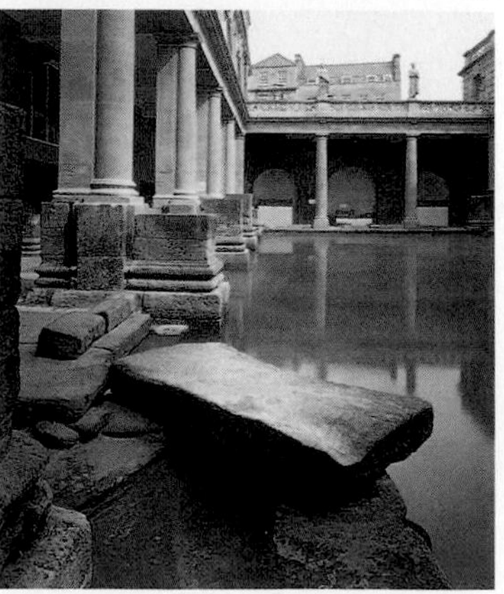
The ornate remains of the baths which give Roman Bath its name.

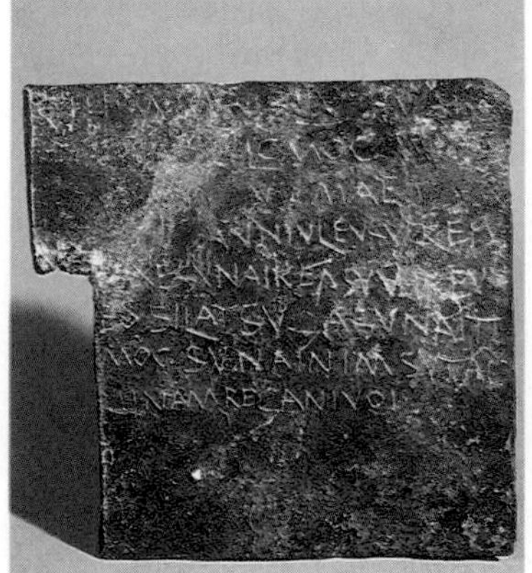
A lead tablet carrying a curse; well-written curses cost more.

194-210

Syria, 194. Septimius Severus, the new emperor, campaigns against Pescennius Niger, the governor of Syria, who was proclaimed emperor of the east by his troops last year.

Britain/Gaul, 194. While Severus marches east to meet Niger, Clodius Albinus, the governor of Britain and *caesar* [deputy emperor], prepares his own attempt on the imperial throne.→

Norfolk, c.195. A bad fire has destroyed Caistor St Edmund civic centre (→c.215).

Gaul, 196. In an attempt to secure the support of the German legions for his imperial claim, Albinus, who has been declared *augustus* [emperor] by the army in Britain, crosses to Gaul [France] (→19/02/197).

Gaul, 19 February 197. With the defeat of his last rival, Albinus, at Lyons, Severus reunites the Roman Empire. Niger, the former emperor of the east, has committed suicide.→

Northern Britain, 197. The Meatae tribal alliance, taking advantage of the absence of the governor, Albinus, and the Roman army, has moved south across Hadrian's wall (→205).

Rome, 197. Severus passes a law permitting serving soldiers to marry.

London, 197. Sextus Varius Marcellus, a Syrian by birth and a relative of Severus, is appointed procurator fiscal [chief provincial finance officer] for Britain.

Britain, 202. Virius Lupus ends his term as governor. He is replaced by Valerius Pudens, the governor of Lower Germany (→c.207).

Northern England, c.207. Alfenius Senecio, who replaced Valerius Pudens as governor in 205, has begun a massive fort-building project and requested more military support from Rome. Emperor Severus, keen for military renown and glad to remove his family from the vituperative atmosphere of Rome, prepares to move to Britain (→208).

London, 208. Geta Caesar, the younger son of the emperor, is appointed governor of the new province of Upper Britain by his father (→4/2/211).

Northern Britain, c.208. The Romans advance beyond both Hadrian's wall and the Antonine wall into the far north (→210).

Governor gambles on Caledonian loyalty

York, 194

Clodius Albinus, governor of Britain, deputy emperor and a contender for the top job in Rome, has made a treaty with the tribes north of Hadrian's wall so that his three legions are free to march on Rome. Shocked by the assassination of the reforming Emperor Pertinax and by the ignominious sale of the empire by the Praetorian Guard, he is resolved to free Rome of corruption and establish himself as emperor.

He is one of the empire's most respected governors, a protégé of Marcus Aurelius who offered him the succession, a dangerous honour which he wisely declined. He is popular with his troops, and when he reminded them of the ancient liberties of republican Rome they greeted him with acclaim.

In stripping the northern frontier of most of its defensive troops, Albinus is taking a calculated risk that the tribes will honour their agreement to remain loyal and that the Caledonii will not attack across the new buffer zone. It is a considerable gamble, but behind it lies a brutally simple reckoning: if he secures the imperial throne he can dispatch someone northwards from Rome to regain the frontier; if he loses, it will not be his problem – for he will be dead (→196).

A soldier's bronze cheekpiece.

'Public enemy' kills himself after a rout

Gaul [France], 19 February 197

Clodius Albinus, the British governor, has taken his own life after being overwhelmed by Septimius Severus's Illyrian and Pannonian legions. While Severus took Rome and confronted threats from Syria, he flattered Albinus, offering him the succession and the title of *caesar* [deputy emperor]. Once secure, Severus declared Albinus a public enemy. Albinus crossed to Gaul with his three legions to find all of Severus's legions against him. The result was inevitable, and the governor's army was routed.

Clodius Albinus: took his own life.

London surrounded by sturdy fortifications

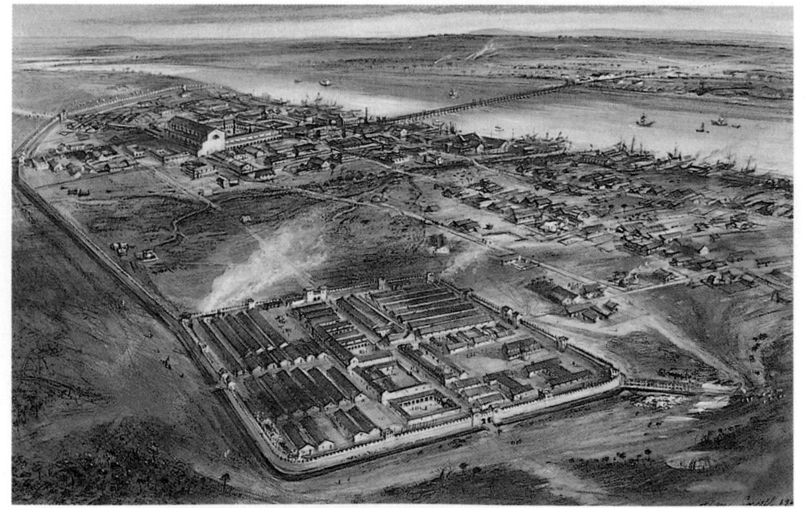

Fortified town: an artist's view of London, protected by a firm stone wall.

London, c.195

London is to plug a weak spot in its defences by building a wall along the Thames bank, thus giving the city a complete circuit of fortifications. They currently run in a bow from the marshy south-east corner, across the Walbrook stream, then west to the garrison's barbican. From there they turn south, following the valley of the river Fleet down to the Thames. The defences are broken by gates on the roads to Colchester, York and St Albans. Attacks by northern tribes have concentrated minds, and already other towns are improving their fortifications. Many are building earthwork defences, but few boast stone walls like the capital (→c.226).

Reforming emperor cuts Britain in two

York, 208

Emperor Septimius Severus has arrived in Britain, and has set about perhaps the most radical shake-up of how the territory is run since the Roman occupation began. Determined to re-establish Roman authority in northern territories which have been ravaged by rebellion and tribal invasions, Severus has set up court at York.

He has swept through civil and military bureaucracies with zeal. Hadrian's wall is to be refurbished, as will some forts to the north of it. This is to enable the legions to adopt a forward policy north of the wall, with the northern lowlands being depopulated and the tribes there relocated.

Most radically, Britain is to become two provinces. One is "Britannia Inferior" [Lower Britain], under a military governor at York; the other is "Britannia Superior" [Upper Britain], under a civil governor based at London with legions at Chester and Caerleon (→208).

Cult of Christ is adopted

Hadrian's wall, 205
Accounts are reaching the northern Roman frontier posts that the cult of Jesus Christ – the leader of a Jewish breakaway sect who was executed in Palestine in the time of Tiberius – is now establishing itself among the tribes north of Hadrian's wall.

"Christianity" – barely tolerated in the empire – may have been practised in Britain for some time, but followers have been few. Now it seems to be gaining influence. Tertullian, a Christian apologist in Carthage, has even claimed that "parts of Britain inaccessible to the Romans have been subjected to Christ". The authorities are worried about the spread of a religion that shows scant respect for the imperial cult (→22/6/208).

'Miracles' surround death of Christian

Hertfordshire, 22 June 208
Rumours are rife of "miracles" at today's execution of a Christian Briton. A man from Verulamium [St Albans] is said have hidden a Christian priest from the authorities. When the priest was found, his host, Albanus (Alban), donned the priest's robes and surrendered in place of him; he was then tortured before being put to death. Witnesses say that Alban's calm during his ordeal was supernatural, and that he made a local river run dry so that he could walk dry-shod to his death. The first executioner, they say, refused to strike, and as soon as a stand-in dealt the fatal blow his eyes fell from their sockets (→c.250).

Alban's death: a 16th-century view.

Christian worship is a focus of suspicion

Britain, 205
Although their numbers are growing, the Christians are not well understood by most people in the Roman Empire. They worship in private houses, are not keen to serve in the army, stay away from gladiatorial combat in the arenas and are rumoured to indulge in secret vice. They also avoid honouring the cult of the emperor, for which they are accused of being subversive. Suspicion has on occasion led to bloody persecution, such as that in southern Gaul [France] in 177 and only three years ago in Carthage.

They worship one god, like the Jews among whom they originated in first-century Palestine. They also worship Jesus Christ, who is called the "Son of God" and whose death and resurrection are taken as signs of a new relationship between man and God, based on the forgiveness of individuals' sins and the promise of eternal life. Personal morality is stressed by Christians. Charity to the poor and needy – putting faith into practice – is proof of this morality and a major reason for the sect's expansion.

Christianity now extends from Arabs in Palestine to footholds among Celts and Romans in Britain. It has followers in Syria, Asia Minor and the Mediterranean area, including Roman North Africa, Gaul and parts of Spain. Strong among the poor, it also attracts intellectuals such as Tertullian (Carthage), Irenaeus (Lyons) and Clement (Alexandria) (→22/6/208).

Sick emperor leads army into far north of Britain to subdue recalcitrant tribes

An inscription from an outpost fort built by the 20th Legion at High Rochester.

Northern Britain, 208
Emperor Septimius Severus – over 60 years old, stricken by gout and carried on a litter – has crossed the walls of Hadrian and Antoninus at the head of the 6th Legion and is pressing far into northern Britain. He plans to depopulate the region and relocate its tribes, but he will be facing hardy warriors, especially the alliance known as the Meatae. So far, however, no major army has taken him on, the tribes retreating into the mountains and opting for protracted guerrilla warfare.

Since the rebellion of the then governor, Albinus, in 196, the northern tribes have raided what is now the new province of "Britannia Inferior" [Lower Britain, as the Romans call northern England], with impunity. Severus's first governor, Virius Lupus, had to pay the Meatae tribes to go away. They soon came back and were reported to be "overrunning the country, carrying off booty and destroying almost everything". Now Severus has taken personal charge of the campaign. To supply his advancing legion he has built a vast base at Corbridge, in Northumberland, and a second is under construction at South Shields (known as Arbeia, a name derived from Arabia, because of the origin of a special unit of longshoremen based here).

Elsewhere large stores are going up and a naval base has been built at Cramond, on the Forth, so that supplies can elude ambushes and come direct by sea (→210).

Severus leaving Rome for Britain.

Severus plans new campaign in the north

York, 210
Two years after his indecisive campaign beyond the Antonine wall, Emperor Severus faces winter with his health failing and his business with the belligerent British tribes of the north still unfinished.

The long thrust into northern territory, which reached almost to Aberdeen, ended in a kind of peace, despite the lack of a conclusive battle. The tribes submitted to the emperor and ceded valuable land to Rome; the Votadini tribe may be rewarded with fertile territories around Fife, confiscated by the legions. But the peace was shortlived, and within a year revolt had broken out again. Severus took firm action, and the British paid dearly for their challenge. Yet the emperor has returned to winter quarters sure that a follow-up campaign next spring is necessary (→4/2/211).

211 - 225

York, 4 February 211. Emperor Septimius Severus, who had planned to join his son Caracalla with the Roman army further north, dies before he can do so. Caracalla and Severus's other son, Geta, succeed him as co-rulers.→

Northern Britain, late 211. Caracalla, having suffered heavy losses in a new campaign in the north, makes peace with the British tribes and returns south to York to meet his brother, Geta, and his mother, Julia Domna. The family sets out for Rome (→2/212).

Northern Britain, c.213. Units of British troops take an oath of loyalty to Caracalla, who became sole emperor last year after ordering the brutal murder of his brother, Geta. Loyal units are allowed to take the title *antoniniana* (from the emperor's real name, Marcus Aurelius Antoninus).

Germany, 213. A campaign is mounted by Caracalla against the Alamanni, a Germanic tribe which is posing a threat to the Alpine province of Rhaetia (→c.216).

Godmanchester, Cambs, c.215. The civic authorities are building a *basilica* (→c.220).

Rome, c.216. Caracalla sets off on a campaign to the Near East, in emulation of Alexander the Great of Macedonia (→217).

Mesopotamia [Iraq], 217. Following the assassination of Caracalla, the Praetorian prefect, Marcus Opellius Macrinus, a Moorish officer implicated in the killing, becomes the first emperor of equestrian (rather than senatorial) rank (→15/5/222).

Canterbury, Kent, c.220. The earthen amphitheatre is being remodelled in stone.

Rome, 15 May 222. Elagabalus, the illegitimate son of Caracalla, emperor since the murder of Macrinus in 218, is stabbed to death. He is succeeded by his adopted nephew, Severus Alexander (→10/5/238).

Hadrian's Wall, c.222. Netherby fortress is being rebuilt to include an exercise hall (→c.240).

Southern England, c.225. The threat of coastal raids by Germanic pirates has persuaded the Romans to embark on a new fort-building programme (→c.230).

Emperor dies at York between campaigns

York, 4 February 211
Far from his birthplace in the Roman province of Africa [Tunisia and Libya], Emperor Septimius Severus died today on the wintry northern fringes of the empire which he ruled for 18 years. He came to Britain in 208 with his wife and family, and for three years he governed Rome from this remote outpost while campaigning against British tribes.

Severus will be mourned by his legions – the foundation of his power, as they are of most emperors' – whom he always paid well. There are now worries about a struggle for the succession between his sons, Marcus Aurelius Antoninus (nicknamed "Caracalla" on account of his long-hooded Gallic cloak) and Geta. Severus's last words to them are reported to have been: "Do not fall out with each other; pay the army enough, and scorn everyone else." But Caracalla's ambitions are thought to be high: whether he will be content to share authority with his brother is uncertain (→2/212).

Battlefield medicine helps the Britons

A surgeon's instruments: box for drugs, bleeding-cup, scalpel and probes.

London, c.215
Over 40 years after the revolution in medicine started in Rome, Britons are benefiting from the new discoveries. Before the invasion, medicine in Britain relied largely on prayer, helped by the use of herbs. Even now, doctors are not highly regarded and are often the butt of jokes. But army surgeons have won a good deal of anatomical knowledge on the battlefield, and medical progress has been driven by the need to service the imperial troops.

In terms of learning, the guiding light has been Galen of Pergamon, in Asia Minor [Turkey], a Greek who died a few years ago in Rome. Physician to several emperors, he spread medical knowledge through public lectures on vivisection and in some 500 treatises.

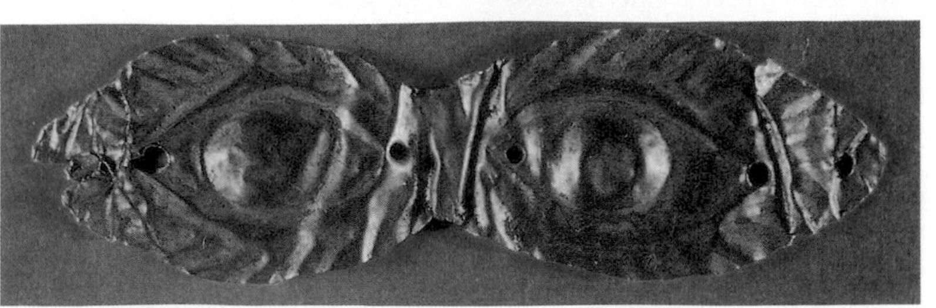

Gold eyes found at Wroxeter: a talisman for a patient seeking a cure?

Greedy ruler orders murder of brother

Severus and family: the face of the murdered Geta has been removed.

Rome, February 212
Caracalla is now sole ruler of the empire following the murder of his brother Geta, killed by Caracalla's agents in the arms of their mother, Julia Domna. Caracalla has ordered her to show only joy, on pain of death, and that Geta's name and image be everywhere erased.

When their father, Septimius Severus, died at York last year, Caracalla at once tried to persuade the army to recognize him as sole emperor. When this failed, he made peace with the British tribes in the north and evacuated their territory. But even as the family returned to Rome Caracalla was establishing his dominance (→213).

Empress gets as good as she gives

Britain, 211
Empress Julia Domna left for Rome on the death of her husband after angering the wife of a Caledonian chieftain, Argentocoxus. Implying that British women were too generous with their favours, Julia Domna asked Argentocoxus's wife "about the free intercourse of her sex with men". The reply was blunt: at least local women "consort openly with the best men, whereas you [Roman women] let yourselves be debauched in secret with the vilest". The empress – who set new fashions during her time in Britain – had been voicing a general Roman belief that British women commonly sleep with men other than their husbands.

All free Britons granted Roman citizenship

Free to pay: the empire's new citizens will add to the imperial coffers.

Britain, 213
All free Britons are to become Roman citizens, following a decree published in Rome by Emperor Caracalla. He has extended the privileges of citizenship to almost all free inhabitants of the empire within a year of seizing sole power through the murder of his brother and after a period of repression which has left some 20,000 dead.

It is not clear what prompted such a decision by an emperor not noted for his magnanimity. The distinctions between citizen and non-citizen have been greatly eroded in recent times, and the imperial edict is a natural culmination of that process. The more cynical of the newly created citizens, however, are pointing out that there is a catch to Caracalla's gesture, because all citizens are fully liable to pay taxes. But Romans are still stunned by the ruthlessness with which Caracalla acted after his father's death in Britain, and opposition is likely to be muted (→215).

Bizarre new cults imported by Romans

Britain, c.220
While many Roman gods and goddesses have their counterparts among British divinities, the Romans have also imported some cults wholly foreign to Britain. The first of these was the public cult of the divinity of the emperor; these days, though, clandestine cults involving exotic and even terrifying rituals are more usual. These include binding oaths of secrecy, and it is hard to estimate numbers involved.

However, there is little doubt that since the visit here of Emperor Severus these secretive religions have enjoyed a revival throughout Britain. The cult of Mithras is popular in the Roman army, and other deities have their devotees. The late Empress Julia Domna, Severus's wife, was said to be a devotee of the fertility goddess Cybele, whose son and lover, the castrated Attis, also has his followers. Some of these sects seem to strike a chord with Britons, but their spread is primarily due to the Roman army and to traders with Near Eastern links (→c.230).

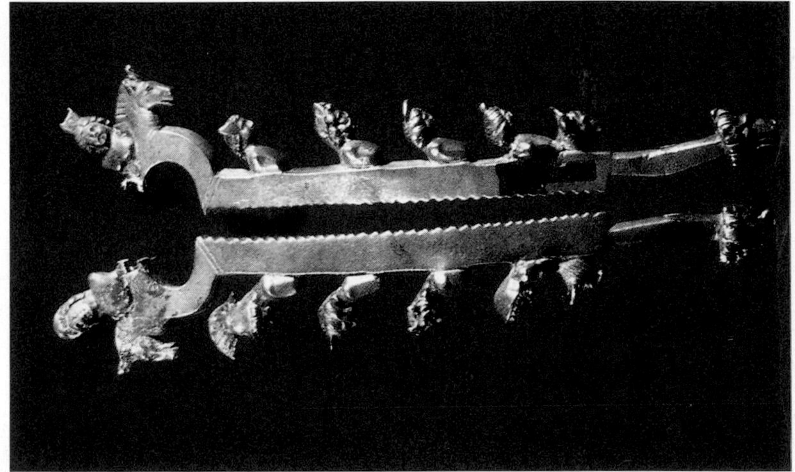

Castration clamps. Castration was practised by followers of Cybele.

New coin brings in inflationary fears

Rome, 215
In the first key change to the currency since Emperor Nero ordered that the number of *aurei* made from one pound of gold should be raised from 84 to 96, a new coin has been introduced in the Roman Empire. The *antoninianus* is named after Emperor Caracalla (Marcus Aurelius Antoninus), who increased the number of citizens liable to pay tax by his decree of 213. It is notionally worth two old *denarii*. But since the coin weighs only as much as one and a half *denarii* the effect is likely to add further to the already worrying level of inflation.

Nero effectively devalued the *denarius* by dropping its weight from 40 to 45 to the pound, but it seems probable that this more drastic move will either fail to gain acceptance or debase the existing coinage further (→290).

Travelling made easier by map of main routes of the empire

Rome, 225
Travellers to Britain should find it easier to get around from now on, following the publication of a new official guide to the important land and sea routes of the Roman Empire. Compiled over the past ten years, the Antonine Itinerary (named after Emperor Antoninus, or Caracalla) shows the *cursus publicus*, the inspection route of high Roman officials. It includes 225 of the major roads of the empire, listing the places and distances along them. The British section describes 15 routes and records more than one hundred place names. The routes zig-zag across the country by way of important centres such as Chester and York; most of them pass through London (→c.250).

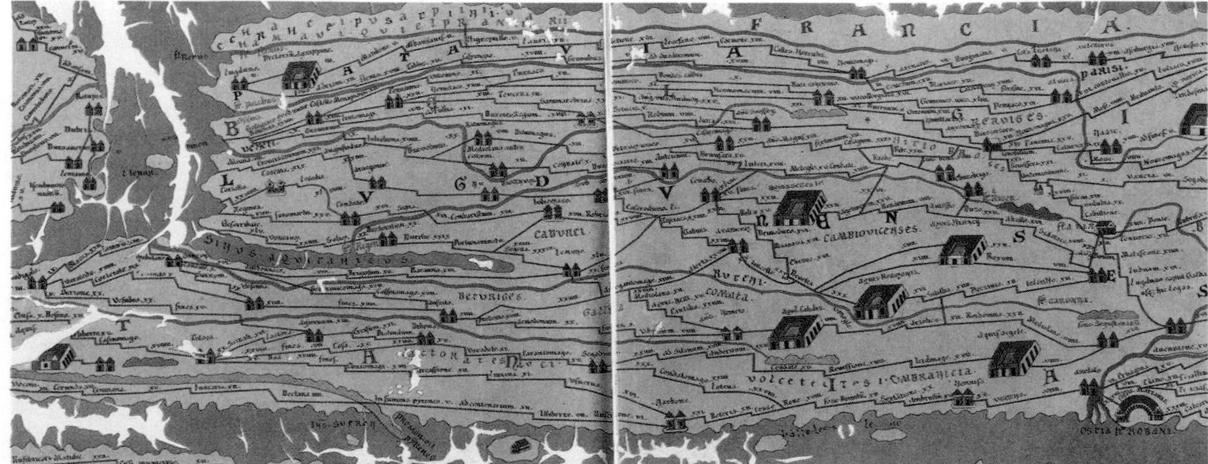

Part of a road map of the Roman Empire. This is a later version of one compiled in the fourth century.

226 - 260

London, c.226. Major new dock facilities are being built (→ c.260).

Aquileia, Northern Italy, 10 May 238. Maximinus, emperor since 235 when he conspired to murder Severus Alexander, is killed by his own troops. A power struggle ensues (→ 244).

Co Durham, c.240. The disused Lanchester fort is being rebuilt and regarrisoned (→ c.300).

Carlisle, Cumbria, c.240. The Carvetii tribe is given *civitas* [administrative district] status.

Mesopotamia [Iraq], 244. Philip, the Arab Praetorian prefect, is proclaimed emperor on the murder of Gordian III, emperor since 238 (→ 249).

Dover, Kent, c.244. The Romans are reorganizing their British fleet's base (→ 255).

Italy, 249. Emperor Philip dies in a clash with the commander in Dacia [Romania], Decius, who becomes emperor (→ 251).

Rome, c.250. Christians are persecuted by Emperor Decius, who has decreed that everyone must make a pagan sacrifice or be punished (→ 259).

Britain, c.250. A road-building programme is planned for Britain, together with repairs and improvements (→ 307).

Dacia [Romania], 251. Emperor Decius and his son are defeated and killed by the Goths under Kniva. Gallus, the governor of Moesia, becomes emperor (→ 253).

Balkans, 253. While attacking Aemilianus, the new governor of Moesia, Gallus is killed by his own troops. Aemilianus becomes emperor (→ 9/253).

Rome, September 253. Following Aemilianus's death in a mutiny, Valerian is recognized as emperor (→ 260).

Gaul [France], 253. Two German tribes, the Franks and the Alamanni, invade (→ c.255).

Caerleon, Gwent, c.254. The fortress of the 2nd Augusta Legion is remodelled as the garrison is reduced (→ c.280).

Britain, c.255. Units of British troops are withdrawn to assist Gallienus, the son of Valerian, against the Alamanni (→ 256).

Milan, Italy, 256. Gallienus defeats the Alamanni (→ 262).

Rome, 260. Gallienus, sole emperor since the murder of his father, Valerian, this year, issues an edict of tolerance of the Christians (→ 303).

Temple is dedicated to all-male cult

London, c.230

A new temple dedicated to Mithras, the Persian god of light and truth, at which the secret ceremonies of the all-male cult are to be performed, is being built in London. The cult was introduced to Britain and other western provinces of the empire by the Roman army. Troops came into contact with the cult when they were serving in the Near East, and its doctrine of loyalty, courage, physical and moral strength and rigorous adherence to fasting and continence appeals to their disciplined society. It also excludes women, so it was ideal for military life, in which marriage has only been permitted in the last thirty-odd years.

Rituals at Mithraic temples centre on a statue of Mithras killing a bull, because an essential part of the cult is the belief that Mithras slaughtered a sacred bull in a grotto and fertilized the earth with the bull's blood. Temples are small, slightly sunken buildings with little light and air, representing the atmosphere of the grotto in the legend. Membership of each temple is limited to 20 or 30 men divided into seven grades with names like the Raven, the Lion, the Soldier and the Persian. To ascend through the grades the devotees must undergo ordeals to prove their courage and endurance. Prayers and hymns follow the ceremonies, with the members reciting the Mithraic prayer: "Thou shalt see a young god, fair of aspect with flaming locks, clad in white robe and scarlet cloak and having a crown of fire ..." They then join in a ritual feast.

A reconstruction of the Mithraic temple at Carrawburgh, in Northumberland.

Before anyone is admitted to membership of a temple he must prove his courage worthy of the god. For the initiation ritual, members of the temple arrive in twos and threes and don the masks of their grades in the antechamber of the temple. They then wait for the novice to arrive with his sponsors, and he is asked to swear an oath that he will keep secret all the rites and ceremonies of the cult. Before the novice can enter the main part of the temple, he is taken to a two-metre-long pit next to the fireplace. He is told to lie down as if in a grave and is then covered with stone slabs, so that he experiences at the same time the heat of the fire and the cold of the grave.

The new temple in sophisticated London promises to be more richly endowed than those already established in the frontier forts in Wales and on Hadrian's wall. Like most Mithraic temples, it is a rectangular building with a central nave and an apse containing altars at which ceremonies take place (→ 331).

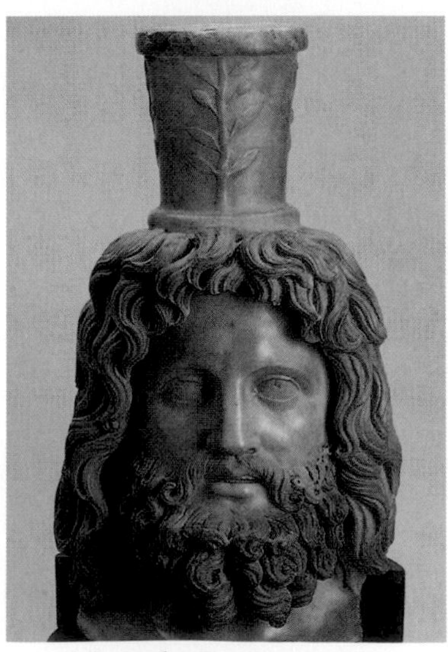

A god from the London temple.

Mithras is born, armed with a sword.

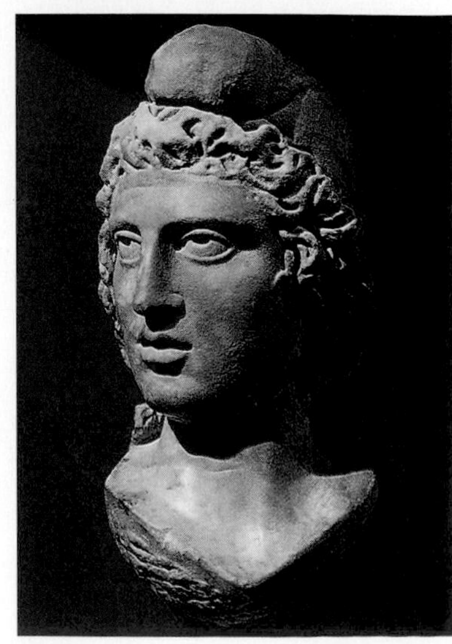

The god in his traditional cap.

Romans to stiffen coastal defences as pirate raids mount

Kent, c.230
The threat of raids by Germanic pirates is forcing the Romans to reconsider their defence policy for Britain. The increasingly frequent attacks across the North Sea mean that guarding the northern and western frontiers will have to take second place to defending vulnerable points on the south-eastern and eastern coasts.

At Reculver, on the north Kent coast, the first of what may eventually be a chain of coastal forts is being built. It will be manned by troops at present serving on Hadrian's wall, who will receive support from Rome's British fleet. Vulnerable rivers and coastal areas on the Norfolk coast will be protected by additional forts being built at Brancaster and at the mouth of the river Yare to augment the existing naval defences at Dover and across the Channel at Boulogne. Officials hope that this will be enough to see off the "barbarian" threat (→c.275).

London docks face shortage of water

London, c.260
The docks authorities in London have a headache – they are short of water. For years the high-water level of the Thames has been falling as a consequence of falling sea-levels. The high-tide mark has dropped by almost two metres in the 200 years since the first docks were built and is at present at about the same level as the first-century low-tide mark.

Since the river is shallow-sided with a deep trench in the middle, ships have to remain at anchor in midstream until their cargoes can be unloaded into lighters, causing traffic jams in the river. Although an attempt has been made to solve the problem by building new wharves on the foreshore, this is an expensive exercise, and in the long term the wharves have to be renewed in turn at substantial cost. One definitive solution could be to create new port facilities to the east of London (→275).

British Christians suffer new persecution

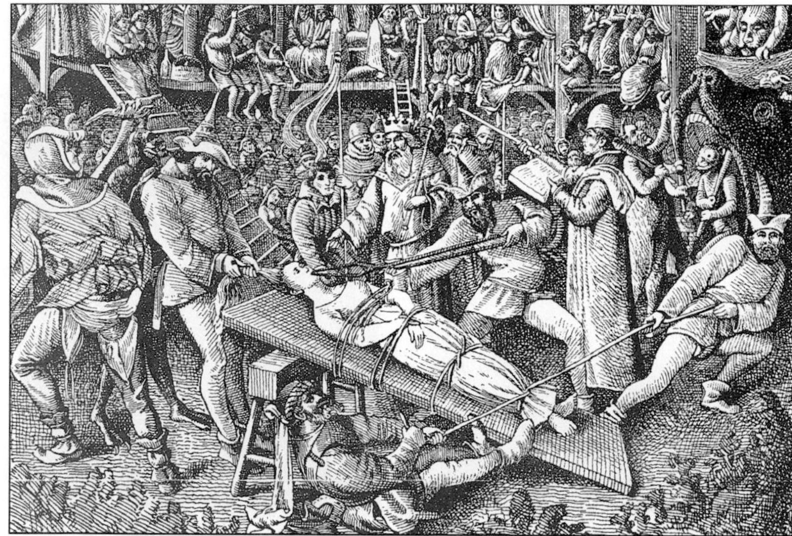

A Christian martyred by the Romans, as imagined by a 17th-century artist.

Britain, 259
Britain's tiny, urban, secretive and probably largely foreign Christian community has suffered in the last decade from renewed persecution under Emperors Decius and Valerian. There are reports this year, for example, of two British Christians, called Julius and Aaron (the latter probably a converted Jew), who are believed to have been put to death for their faith at Caerwent, in southern Wales. Other sects will pay respects to the traditional Roman gods as well as to their own deities, but not the Christians; this lays them open to trumped-up charges of disloyalty and makes them frequent scapegoats for civil strife (→260).

Irish isolation allows culture to flourish

Ireland, c.250
While Ireland lies close to Britain, it remains essentially untouched by the influence of the mighty Roman Empire. Contacts with Britain are restricted mainly to trade; ties may be stronger across the narrow seas between north-eastern Ireland and south-western Scotland. Unlike in the "civilized" parts of Britain, tribal relationships here are dominated by traditional feuding, and the priestly caste is strong. But Ireland's isolation means that art and architecture draw on an unbroken tradition for inspiration and are developing to a standard not seen across the water in Britain (→c.260).

A reconstruction of an Irish lake-village at Craggaunowen, in Co Clare.

Province of Britain becomes part of a rebel Gallic empire

Gaul [France], 260
In a dramatic turn of events, Britain has become part of a breakaway Roman empire. Marcus Postumus, the governor of Gaul, has rebelled against Emperor Gallienus, murdering Gallienus's son, Salonus, and the praetorian prefect Silvanus.

Supported by the western Roman provinces, Postumus has declared himself emperor of a separatist "*imperium Galliarum*" [Gallic empire], which consists of Britain, Gaul, Germany and Spain. Meanwhile Gallienus – who has recently put down a rebellion in Pannonia [Hungary] – continues to rule the eastern part of the empire.

Neither emperor can feel safe, however. "Barbarians" are threatening Postumus's line along the Rhine, and the Romans have virtually abandoned their military-agricultural settlements to the east of the river, in the face of fresh attacks from German tribes. At the same time Gallienus faces a threat in the east, where his father and co-ruler, Valerian, was defeated, captured and flayed alive this year by the Persian king Shapur. With neither emperor in a position to do much about his rival, the empire looks set to remain split (→274).

Wily Roman writer peddles tall stories

Ireland, c.260
Colourful, if not entirely accurate, descriptions of Ireland are being circulated by a Roman geographer, Solinus. His tales are a curious mixture of truth and speculation, culled from genuine second- or third-hand accounts and spiced by his own imagination, about an island as remote as anywhere in Europe from Rome. Solinus claims that Irish warriors drink the blood of the slain and smear it on their faces. He says that there are no snakes in Ireland and few birds. He also gives an account of how a mother who has given birth to a son places the first bit of food on her husband's sword and gently introduces it into the child's mouth (→c.420).

261 - 286

Italy, 262. Germanic tribes have crossed into northern Italy. The Romans begin to build defences around major cities to try to stop the "barbarians" advancing (→271).

Lancaster, c.265. The fortress is being refortified as a precaution against raiders from across the Irish Sea.

Italy, September 268. Emperor Gallienus is assassinated while attacking Aurelos, the leader of rebel troops. He is succeeded by one of his chief officers who becomes Claudius II (→270).

Rome, 270. Emperor Claudius II, nicknamed "Gothicus" for his victory over the Goths last year, has died of plague. He is succeeded by Lucius Domitius Aurelianus (Aurelian), an army officer (→c.271).

Rome, c.271. Emperor Aurelian orders the construction of a wall 11 miles (18 km) long around the city as a means of defence against "barbarian" attack.

Gaul [France], 274. The Gallic empire is reunited with Rome by Aurelian after Tetricus, who was proclaimed emperor by his troops in 270, is deserted by the same troops.→

Richborough, Kent, c.275. Defence ditches are being built around the monument at the spot where the Roman invasion is thought to have begun. The monument is now used as a watchtower (→c.280).

Britain, c.275. Many people are hoarding coins, worried by the threat of unrest (→c.277).

Gaul, 277. Marcus Aurelius Probus, who became sole emperor last year, liberates Gaul from the Franks and the Alamanni, who invaded in 275.

Caerleon, Gwent, c.280. Large parts of the fortress are being demolished to prepare for the withdrawal of part of the 2nd Augusta Legion, which will probably be sent to Richborough, in Kent.→

Rome, 20 November 284. Diocletian, the commander of the emperor's bodyguard, is proclaimed emperor by his soldiers, ending a period of instability.

Gaul, 285. Maximian, the *caesar* [deputy emperor], orders the execution of Carausius, the commander of the *classis Britannica* [British fleet], for dereliction of duty – he is alleged to have kept pirate booty (→12/286).

Treasure is buried to thwart plunderers

Mercury adorns a silver dish.

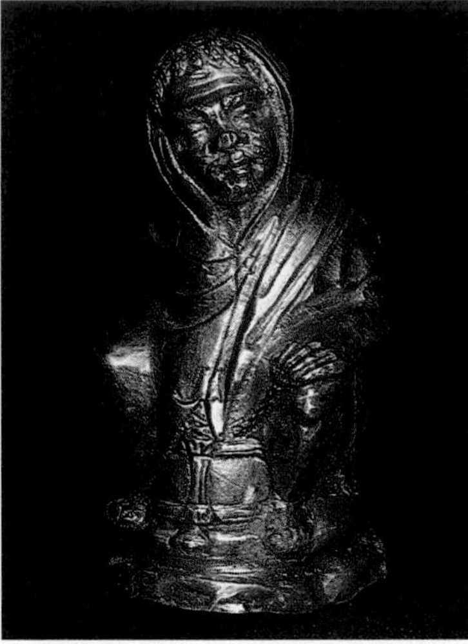

A silver piece representing a slave.

Southern England, c.270

Villa owners in the wealthy south of England – fearing an imminent Roman assault to reunite the empire – have started to bury their riches under trees and in hedgerows. They pack coins and precious jewellery into earthenware vessels and hide them to stop them falling into the hands of looters. Temple treasures, including beautiful works of votive art, are also being buried by priests. Another purpose of the caches is to provide instant sources of money if their owners should have to flee and their houses and property be destroyed – although there is a danger that they may be dug up by robbers or have to be abandoned (→274).

Breakaway Gallic empire is crushed

Central Gaul [France], 274

Aurelian, the latest in a long line of Roman emperors elevated to power by their troops, has reunited the domains of Rome by putting an end to the separatist Gallic empire and taking captive its ruler, Tetricus, in a battle outside Châlons. He has thereby brought Gaul, Spain and Britain back into the imperial fold out of which they were led by Marcus Postumus 14 years ago [*see report on page 77*].

Postumus, like so many soldiers hailed as emperors by their men, was also killed by them while putting down a revolt in c.269, the year before Aurelian's accession. He was succeeded as Gallic emperor first by Victorinus, then by Tetricus, but meanwhile the central government was recovering under an emperor determined to restore unity and security. Aurelian, who has also destroyed Queen Zenobia's Palmyran army in the east, plans a great "triumph" in Rome at which he will display his captured rivals (→277).

Stone walls built to boost city defences

London, 275

Groups of workers have been gathered together to build up the defences of London, the capital of the province of Britain, and other towns in south-eastern England to ward off the threat of attacks by "barbarians". The old earthwork defences are being faced with massive stone walls some 3 metres thick and 6 metres high. In London, special precautions are being taken against hostile landings from the Thames, with defensive walls being built along the banks of the river.

This activity reflects the fear of the "barbarians" which is spreading through the empire. Not even Rome itself is thought safe; Emperor Aurelian is building a huge city wall to surround the heart of Roman power. In Gaul [France], however, which has proved particularly vulnerable to attack – over 50 towns have fallen into "barbarian" hands in recent years – few fortifications are in progress, perhaps because of a lack of funds (→c.340).

'Barbarian' troops to put down rebellions

A barbarian in Roman service.

London, c.277

Germanic prisoners of war have arrived in Britain as a potential standby force to put down rebellions against Emperor Probus and Roman central control. The move follows a recent uprising by a governor of Britain which may have been intended as a bid to secure the imperial throne – the emperor had to send forces led by a Moorish officer named Victorinus to suppress the revolt.

This coup attempt was Probus's second headache linked with Britain in three years. The first was a failed attempt to restore the separatist "Gallic empire" (suppressed in 274) by the commander of Rome's Rhine fleet at Cologne, Bonosus, whose father was British and mother Spanish. One of Bonosus's aims seems to have been to save himself from almost certain execution after his ships had been destroyed by Germanic raiders.

The decision to move Germanic prisoners – known as Burgundians and Vandals – to Britain kills two birds with one stone. It keeps them out of the way at a time when their kindred are frequently assaulting Rome's German frontier, and it provides (or will do when they are turned into effective Roman army units) useful reinforcements for deployment against further unrest in the island (→1/4/286).

Western empire is given its own ruler

Diocletian (left) and Maximian.

Milan, Italy, 1 April 286
Britain gained a new overlord today with the appointment of Marcus Maximianus (Maximian) as *augustus* [co-emperor] of the western empire. Last year Emperor Diocletian made Maximian *caesar* [deputy emperor], with responsibility for the defence of the west, including Britain. Maximian aims to restore order on the northern and western fringes of the empire. He will also assume some of Diocletian's formal duties in the west, allowing his colleague more time to concentrate on Rome's troublesome eastern provinces. The *augusti* will share equal power, but Maximian will remain the junior partner (→12/286).

Why east is east and west is west

Nicomedia, Asia Minor, 286
A massive restructuring of the Roman Empire is under way. In order to ease the bureaucratic burden, Diocletian has decided to split the empire into two parts – a Latin west and a Greek east. The division will be made by drawing an imaginary line running from north to south down the Adriatic sea. Diocletian, as emperor, or *augustus*, will rule the eastern half from Nicomedia, in Asia Minor [Turkey], and Maximian, his nominated co-emperor, also *augustus*, will rule the west from Milan – a better site than Rome for defending the empire's northern frontier (→1/4/286).

Condemned admiral seizes power

London, December 286
Britain is once again in the control of a Roman regime independent of the central government. Mausaeus Carausius, the commander of the imperial British fleet – who eluded a death sentence passed on him last year by Emperor Maximian – has seized power in the province and set himself up as emperor.

He has also seized a large part of north-western Gaul as a first step towards recreating the breakaway Gallic empire which was reunited with Rome only 12 years ago. With his powerful fleet Carausius can thereby control the Channel and prevent any counter-coup by Maximian, the co-emperor of the western empire. Indeed Maximian, who is now preoccupied fighting the Franks along the river Rhine, has realized that he cannot, for the time being, budge his rival by intrigue or military means.

Just a few months after his appointment as commander of the British fleet last year, Carausius was sentenced to death for treason and gross dereliction of duty. He had been accused of keeping booty recovered from Germanic pirates in the Channel for his own use. There were even rumours, probably false, that he had prior knowledge of the raiders' attacks.

Although of lowly birth – by origin a Menapian of the Low Countries – Carausius has proved himself a first-class soldier, and he has the support of legions in Gaul and Britain which are prepared to fight to maintain their independence. He seems to be genuinely admired for his part in protecting Britain against raiders, and there was little opposition to his coup. He is a good administrator, the civil service works, he can pay his soldiers and is tackling the problem of debased coinage which undermined the Gallic empire (→289).

Carausius and those he claims as brothers, Diocletian and Maximian.

Shore-fort garrisons are modernized with larger stone defences

Richborough, Kent, c.280
A chain of massive stone forts intended to keep out the Saxon raiders is being constructed along the British coast from the Wash in the east to Portchester on the Solent. At Richborough, for instance, one such fort will replace the 30-metre-high monumental archway built in the confident early days of Roman occupation as the ceremonial *accessus Britanniae* [gateway to Britain]. The archway – its gilded bronze statuary weathered and its Italian marble facing chipped and decaying – is being demolished after having served as a watchtower for the past few years.

The forts incorporate the latest advances in military architecture, and when the chain has been completed it will guard all the major estuaries with paired forts and defended harbour sites. The garrisons in these forts are being drawn from troops stationed along Hadrian's wall and detachments from Chester and Caerleon, the bases of the 2nd and 20th Legions. They will coordinate with naval detachments to pursue and round up raiders who penetrate the fortress screen and manage to get ashore (→c.310).

Fortifications against the Saxons: a view of Richborough Castle today.

Soldiers' loss: gems from Caerleon.

287 - 304

Gaul [France], 289. Maximian, the *augustus* [co-emperor] of the west, fails in an attempt to dislodge the forces of the usurper Carausius, who now rules Britain, from their base at Boulogne (→ 293).

Nicomedia, Asia Minor [Turkey], March 293. Emperor Diocletian appoints two *caesars*, Galerius and Constantius Chlorus, to join the two *augusti* [co-emperors] as rulers (→ 296).

Gaul, 293. Constantius Chlorus, the new *caesar*, captures Boulogne from the forces of Carausius, eliminating the usurper's foothold on this side of the Channel.→

Britain, 293. Carausius, who proclaimed himself emperor of Britain and northern Gaul seven years ago, is murdered by Allectus, his finance minister, who succeeds him.→

Gaul, 296. Constantius Chlorus establishes the imperial capital of the west at Trier.

Britain, 296. Constantius Chlorus crosses to Britain; his forces defeat and kill Allectus, ending Britain's ten years of independence from central Roman control.→

Britain, 296. Britain is divided into four separate provinces, with capitals at London and Cirencester, and possibly at York and Lincoln.→

Gaul, 297. Constantius Chlorus returns to Gaul to challenge the Germanic tribe known as the Alamanni (→ 298).

Gaul, 298. A large number of skilled men are brought over from Britain by Constantius Chlorus to restore the city of Autun, badly damaged in recent conflicts (→ 355).

Northern England, c.300. Under the direction of Constantius Chlorus, a major building programme is under way to restore Rome's northern defences.→

Nicomedia, Asia Minor, November 301. Diocletian limits by edict the prices of goods and the cost of wages.→

Rome, 20 November 303. The two *augusti* and their *caesars*, all together for the first time, celebrate the 20 years of Diocletian's reign (→ 1/5/305).

Nicomedia, Asia Minor, 303. On the advice of Galerius, Diocletian proclaims an empire-wide persecution of Christians, but this is not implemented in the west by Constantius Chlorus (→ 2/311).

Equality, fraternity claim on new coins

London, 290

Carausius, the commander of the British fleet, who seized power and declared himself emperor of Britain, has opened Britain's first mint since 225, when the last one was transferred to a new imperial mint at Byzantium in Asia Minor [Turkey]. So far his mint in London has produced silver *denarii* (which people are bound to hoard against future devaluations) and bronze *Antoniniani*, improvements on issues under the old Gallic empire. One coin shows Carausius as an equal and brother of the two official *augusti* or co-emperors, Maximian and Diocletian, perhaps suggesting to his imperial "colleagues" a peaceful way out of his secession. They are unlikely to agree (→ 314).

Rebel admiral loses key port in Gaul

Gaul [France], 293

The heavily fortified port of Boulogne, the key to Carausius's control of the Channel, has fallen to the forces of Constantius Chlorus, the newly appointed *caesar* [deputy emperor] of the western empire. Constantius cut off the town by building a mole across the harbour-mouth, thus preventing Carausius's galleys from bringing in supplies and reinforcements.

Once the garrison surrendered the town gave up, and Constantius now controls this strategic stretch of coast. The way is open for him to cross the Channel – evading the British ships, which cannot maintain a solid blockade owing to the limitations of oar-power – and land his legions on the south coast. There are also signs that Carausius's personal popularity is waning: Allectus, his finance minister, is said to be in the ascendant.

A British coin showing a galley.

Firstly, however, Constantius is likely to deal with the Rhineland Franks who have been cooperating with Carausius. Having secured his rear, he will turn to Britain (→ 296).

Pottery industry adopts mass production as economy prospers

Britain, c.300

The economy is booming. The Picts may be threatening in the north, and sea raiders may be ravaging the east coast, but for the past few decades the conditions have been far better than they were 80 years ago.

A money economy has really only taken off in the last 30 years, and the expansion of the money supply has brought in its wake extensive economic growth and an expansion of goods and services of all kinds.

The pottery industry, for example, is undergoing a revolution. Earlier in the century it was in the doldrums, but now, following the collapse of the continental Samian pottery industry, it has stepped up production substantially. The old British village potter is disappearing, replaced by large establishments producing hundreds of jugs, plates, bowls and jars every day.

In some places, such as the Nene valley in Cambridgeshire, dozens of potteries have sprung up, especially around Water Newton, where the industry is concentrated in a few hands. The kilns are owned by magnates who live in spacious villas and usually house their workforces in half-timbered cottages. The most impressive of the 20 or 30 potteries in the area is probably the one at Castor, where the proprietor has built a big luxurious house with painted walls and mosaics. Other industries are expanding almost as quickly – two of them, in Oxfordshire and Hertfordshire, making imitation Samian wares.

A New Forest pottery vessel.

In other areas, such as the New Forest and the lower Thames valley, the independent potter still survives, but even he employs middlemen who transport the earthenware all over Britain by donkey caravan.

Wealthier individuals can set their sights on something grander than ceramics and are investing in metal table goods made of pewter (using lead from the mines in the Mendips), bronze and glass. There is also a lot of money being spent on improving and expanding the big town and country houses. Schools of mosaicists and interior decorators are flourishing.

Mass-produced: Oxfordshire pots.

The question remains as to how long it will all last. The separatist empire of Carausius, in common with any other empire, is unlikely to endure for ever, and the current scourge of inflation may soon tip over into recession (→ 575).

Britain is reconquered

Conquering hero: a coin showing Constantius at the gates of London.

London, 296
Britain, independent for ten years, has been reconquered and returned to central Roman control. Allectus, who overthrew and murdered the rebel emperor Carausius in 293, has been killed fighting the invading army of Constantius Chlorus, the *caesar* of the western empire.

Constantius sailed with his fleet from Boulogne and cruised in mid-Channel while another fleet under Julius Asclepiodotus slipped past the Isle of Wight in thick fog and landed troops near Southampton Water. Allectus rushed his forces, mainly Frankish mercenaries and troops from Hadrian's wall, to meet Julius's army in a decisive clash near Silchester, in Hampshire. As the remnants of Allectus's army fled to London they met Constantius, who had landed his own force and occupied the capital with little resistance. The rout was complete. Constantius was welcomed by Londoners, who had feared that their city would be looted by the Frankish mercenaries as they headed east to flee Britain by sea (→c.300).

Britain is now divided into four provinces

Britain, 296
Following its decade of secession Britain now consists of four provinces, instead of two. "Britannia Superior" has been split into "Britannia Prima" and "Maxima Caesariensis", run from Cirencester and London, while "Britannia Inferior" becomes "Britannia Secunda" and "Flavia Caesariensis", run from York and Lincoln. The governor of each province is responsible to a *vicarius* [vicar, or imperial representative] in London, who is answerable to the prefect of Gaul, at Trier, who is responsible to the emperor (→c.300).

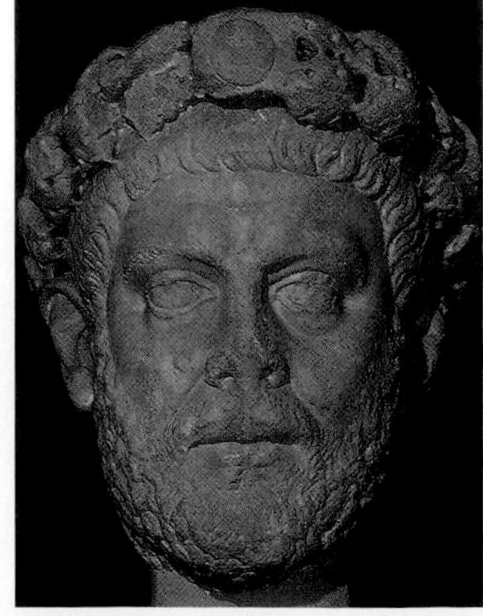

Diocletian: an ardent reformer.

Major works begin at Hadrian's wall to repair damage from neglect and vandalism

Northern England, c.300
Britain's return to the imperial fold and the presence in the island of Constantius Chlorus, the *caesar*, have inspired a reconstruction of its northern defences. It is 60 years since major works were carried out on Hadrian's wall: it has suffered from neglect and vandalism. In some areas locals have stolen tiles and stones for building, while outposts, as one observer noted, "have been covered with earth and fallen down through age".

The wall's condition was not improved by the withdrawal of much of the garrison in 296 to fight for the British usurper Allectus against Constantius. Now the troops are back, and repair work is under way at Birdoswald and Housesteads, where dormitories for a hundred men are being replaced by smaller chalet-type buildings. These could be married quarters now that serving soldiers are allowed to have wives. Outpost forts to the north, such as Risingham, Bewcastle and High Rochester, are also being extensively refurbished.

York, to the south, which has been chosen as the capital of the new province of Britannia Secunda [*see report below left*], is receiving lavish additional defences which will dominate the river and constitute an impressive piece of political architecture (→370).

These carved figures from near Hadrian's wall may have been house deities.

Wages and prices frozen to beat inflation

Asia Minor, November 301
To alleviate the distress caused by the collapse of the currency and rampant inflation, Emperor Diocletian has launched an assault on prices and incomes. His aim is to stabilize the cost of everyday goods throughout the Roman Empire and to restrain rising wages. An edict issued from his base at Nicomedia, in Asia Minor [Turkey], lays down maximum prices for all major and many minor commodities.

An egg is to cost one *denarius*; a lemon is to cost 24 *denarii*; a chicken 30; a male slave 30,000; a racehorse 100,000. The costs of labour are also fixed: farm workers will be paid up to 25 *denarii* a day; bakers 50; scribes will get 25 for every 100 lines; teachers 50 a month per pupil. Profiteers who overcharge or withhold goods will be executed or exiled.

But observers are doubtful about how well the new edict will work in practice. Certainly it has opened the door to corruption; for example, civil servants who had prior knowledge of the details of the price changes have turned the information to their own financial advantage. Many goods have disappeared from normal outlets only to resurface on the black market at prices higher than the edict allows; people have no choice but to pay these inflated prices (→c.310).

305 - 324

Rome, 1 May 305. Emperor Diocletian abdicates.→

Britain, spring 306. Constantius Chlorus, the new *augustus*, begins attacking the northern tribes.

York, 26 July 306. Constantius Chlorus dies; his 32-year-old son Constantine is proclaimed *augustus* by his troops, in defiance of Flavius Severus, Constantius's deputy and rightful heir.→

Rome, 28 October 306. The Praetorian Guard proclaims Maxentius, the son of the former *augustus* Maximian, as western *augustus* (→28/10/312).

Northern England, 307. A massive programme of road improvements is begun.

Milan, Italy, February 311. Licinius, who succeeded Flavius Severus as western *augustus* when he was killed by the usurper Maxentius in 306, and his deputy Constantine agree on more tolerance for Christians (→28/10/312).

Italy, 28 October 312. Constantine, having invaded Italy, defeats the usurper Maxentius in battle at the Milvian Bridge outside Rome, and is recognized as absolute ruler of the western empire.→

Milan, Italy, 8 February 313. Constantine and Licinius, now *augustus* of the east, issue a further edict of tolerance of Christians (→1/8/314).

London, 314. The London mint issues coins which may mean that Constantine intends to visit; there may be unrest among the troops (→326).

Rome, July 315. A triumphal arch and *basilica* are completed and dedicated to Constantine as a monument to his victory over Maxentius.

Rome, c.318. Constantine has assumed the title of *Britannicus Maximus*, possibly after some victory in Britain.

Rome, 3 July 321. Constantine makes Sunday a day of rest throughout the empire.→

Rome, 25 December 323. Constantine passes a law imposing severe punishments on anyone found forcing Christians to take part in pagan rituals (→20/5/325).

Asia Minor [Turkey], 18 September 324. After inflicting a series of defeats by land and sea, Constantine captures and executes Licinius, proclaiming himself sole ruler of the Roman empire (→25/7/326).

Top ruler abdicates to cultivate garden

Milan, Italy, 1 May 305

After a 21-year reign, and probably prompted by a recent severe illness, Emperor Diocletian, the supreme ruler of Britain, has abdicated. The 60-year-old senior *augustus* [co-emperor] is retiring to his home at Split in Dalmatia [Yugoslavia] and plans to spend his time gardening, growing cabbages and refurbishing his palace. Maximian, the junior *augustus*, has also abdicated under pressure from Diocletian. The new *augusti* will be the current *caesars* [deputy emperors]: Constantius Chlorus for the western empire, including Britain, and Galerius for the east (→26/7/306).

Soldiers hail new emperor at York

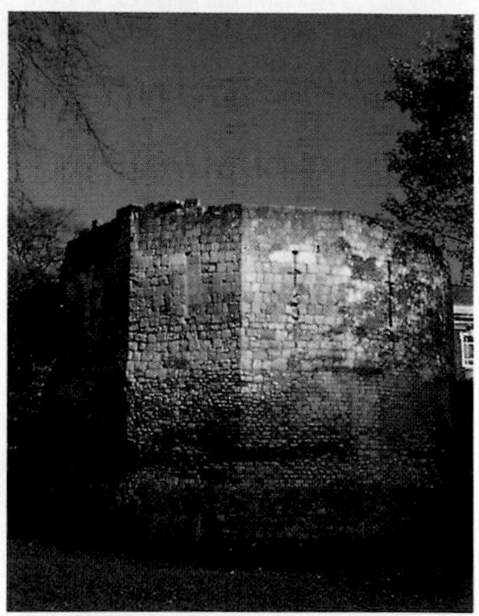

A look-out tower at York fortress.

York, 26 July 306

For the second time in almost 100 years a Roman emperor has died at York. Constantius Chlorus, who was made western *augustus* [co-emperor] in May last year, had just returned from the first major Roman campaign north of the Forth since that of Septimius Severus – who also died at York – a century ago. Constantius's son, Constantine, has been proclaimed *augustus* by the army in York, instead of Constantius's *caesar* [deputy], Flavius Severus. Constantine seems prepared to compromise, but the rules of tetrarchy (four-man government) set up by Diocletian have been breached (→28/10).

Army plans crack units for rapid reaction

Roman soldiers attacking a city, from the Arch of Constantine in Rome.

Britain, c.310

The nature and purpose of the Roman army here is to undergo a dramatic change, following a full-scale review of military tactics by Emperor Constantine. This follows the crisis brought about by the increasing severity of "barbarian" attacks on the imperial frontiers.

The key concept in the new thinking is mobility. No longer will troops stay immobile in forts defending the frontiers. Instead, the front-line troops will be downgraded while special crack units of "fire-fighting" legions, reinforced with cavalry, will be formed and held at central points ready to march to trouble at a moment's notice, led by the emperor or one of his deputies.

Constantine is completing reforms begun by Diocletian, who set out to separate the civil and military branches of provincial administration. Whereas in the past attacks by tribesmen on Britain's northern or western borders would have been dealt with by the provincial governors, often with troops of variable quality, it is now intended that a central force will be able to respond to trouble with greater speed and efficiency (→342).

Imperial armour together with the "fasces", a symbol of high Roman office.

Taxes may be paid in kind, not in cash

Roman Empire, c.310

A system by which taxes are paid in kind rather than in money – devised by Emperor Diocletian – is proving a boon for the imperial government. Where taxes used to be levied in an arbitrary manner, they are now strictly imposed on provinces, cities and individuals.

The levies are based on a census in each part of the empire, and everybody is required to contribute. Wheat, wine, oil, horses, recruits, labourers – all are demanded by the tax collectors. The taxpayers' burden is heavy, but the new system means that the state can function without using the debased currency which in the past only fuelled inflation. Because they are now better able to predict the income into the imperial treasury, the Roman administrators can draw up a proper annual budget.

Constantine hails the Christian god

Rome, 28 October 312
In a development that could have important ramifications throughout the empire, Constantine today became the first Roman emperor to acknowledge publicly the power of the Christian god. Last year Constantine and Licinius, his pagan co-emperor in the east, agreed at Milan to adopt a policy of neutrality towards Christians, and Constantine's new position will bring further succour to those believers who have suffered periodic persecution under imperial rule.

Constantine's statement came after he had invaded Italy and seen off the usurper Maxentius in a great battle at the Milvian Bridge outside Rome, establishing himself as supreme in the western empire. Once a worshipper of *sol invictus* [the unconquered sun], Constantine – who has been at the top of the imperial ladder for six years – proclaimed that he was led to victory by the Christian god. On the night before the battle he dreamt that he saw a Christian symbol in the sky over the battlefield. This was the third time that he had had the dream during the Italian campaign. The symbol was a monogram of the Greek letters *chi* [ch] and *rho* [r], the first two letters of the word "Christ". He told his soldiers to put it on their shields before going into combat (→8/2/313).

A hanging bowl from a collection of Christian silver found in Cambridgeshire.

British 'bishops' attend church convention

Gaul [France], 1 August 314
Representatives from Britain are among those attending the first major council of the western Christian church, at Arles in Gaul.

Although Britain has not so far been widely influenced by Christianity, three leading churchmen known as "bishops" have been sent to the council, from London, Lincoln and York. Emperor Constantine, the leader of the western empire, has summoned hundreds of bishops to debate church matters just over a year after his edict of Milan proclaimed official toleration for Christians. Now that persecution has ended in the western empire, he and church leaders hope to resolve questions of doctrine and discipline in order to bring about Christian unity (→3/7/321).

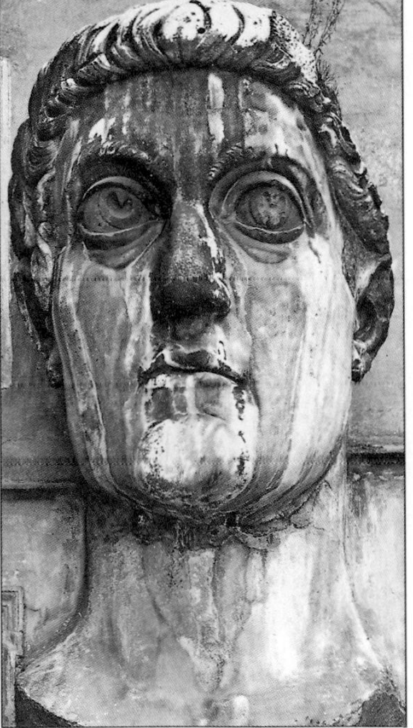

Constantine: a Christian convert.

Sunday is set aside as a day of rest and of Christian worship

Rome, 3 July 321
Emperor Constantine has proclaimed that *dies solis*, Sunday, will be a day of rest and Christian observance. In 312 he had already set aside the day, dedicated to his protector *sol invictus* [the unconquered sun], as one on which his own Christian soldiers might attend services of worship, and pagan troops might be allowed to offer prayers to their own gods.

Constantine, supreme leader of the western empire since 312, has often cited his faith in Christ as the basis of his success. He is now acting in accordance with the Bible, the sacred Christian writings, by identifying Sunday with the seventh day of creation, on which God the Father himself rested. His decision to make it a holy day will have profound economic and social repercussions throughout the empire.

No business will be conducted, nor will legal actions be permitted, and manufacturing industries must pause. Nor will there be any amusements. However, one area of exception is agriculture. If the weather is fine, harvests may be reaped. Another exception is that slaves may be freed in Christian churches on Sundays.

In Britain – where pagan cults still flourish alongside the new faith – Constantine's ruling will be welcomed by the growing numbers of town-dwellers who are turning to Christianity (→25/12/323).

Coats and rugs are British hits abroad

Britain, c.320
Gaul [France], as is well known, provides the empire with its finest wine, but Britain has its own speciality: textiles. Woollen products such as the heavy overcoat known as *byrrus Britannicus*, developed for an unpredictable climate, and the woollen rug (*tapete Britannicum*) have made British craftsmen – and their sheep – famous.

Such materials as tweed and Otterburn cloth have become staples of British manufacture, thanks to the exploitation of the large flocks of sheep that dominate the farming landscape. Towns in East Anglia such as Great Chesterford and Caistor St Edmund have developed into great centres, making woollen items and conducting a thriving export trade with the continent. Some of the best products command high prices and were included in the empire-wide *edictum de pretiis* [edict of prices] that Emperor Diocletian issued nearly 20 years ago (→480).

A carving shows Roman cloth merchants examining a length of material.

325 - 353

Byzantium [Istanbul, Turkey], 325. Emperor Constantine bans the arena sport of gladiator fighting.

Rome, 25 July 326. Following the execution of his son, Crispus, for plotting against him, Constantine – now the sole emperor, or *augustus* – visits Rome for celebrations of his victory over Licinius and his 20 years in power. He offends the senate by refusing to carry out the traditional pagan sacrifices at the temple of Jupiter.

Byzantium, 11 May 330. The new capital of the Roman Empire, which Constantine decided in 324 should be built here and which is already known as the "New Rome", is dedicated and called Constantinopolis [Constantinople: city of Constantine] after the emperor.

Constantinople, 331. Constantine orders all pagan temple treasures throughout the empire to be confiscated and vigorously promotes the Christian faith (→22/5/337).

Nicomedia, Asia Minor [Turkey], 22 May 337. After being baptized on his deathbed, Constantine dies at the age of 64 (→359).

Constantinople, 9 September 337. Constantine's three sons are declared *augusti*, or co-emperors. Constantine II and Constans are to share the western empire; Constantius II is to rule the east (→3/340).

Italy, March 340. After defeating and killing his brother Constantine II, Constans proclaims himself the sole ruler of the west (→350).

London, c.340. Cemeteries in the capital are being plundered for stone to use in the construction of interval towers along the eastern city wall. Among the tombs used is that of Classicianus, the chief Roman financial official after Boudica's revolt of 60 (→352).

Britain, 342. General unrest in the island prompts an imperial midwinter visit by the western emperor, Constans.

Mursa [Osijek, Yugoslavia], 28 September 351. Magnentius, the rebel leader, is defeated by Constantius II, the emperor of the east (→8/353).

Gaul [France], August 353. Magnentius, pursued by Constantius II, is defeated in battle at Seleucis and commits suicide. Constantius becomes sole emperor (→8/11/355).

Compromise looks set to unify church

A Christian mosaic in the Roman villa at Hinton St Mary in Dorset.

Asia Minor [Turkey], 20 May 325
Britain's bishops have again been summoned to a major church convention, following Emperor Constantine's decision to call together bishops from every part of the empire for an ecumenical council on a major dispute. The council, opened today at Nicaea, in Asia Minor, will be presided over by the emperor himself who, although converted 13 years ago and nominally a Christian, has still not been baptized.

The dispute is over the nature of Christ: is he the equal of God, as the "orthodox" maintain, or is he inferior, a creation of God and not part of his substance, as the theologian Arius of Alexandria believes? Constantine favours a formula stating that Christ is "of one substance" with the Father (→331).

Rampant inflation shuts mint in London

London, 326
From now on Britons will no longer see the mark of the London mint on their new coins. The mint, set up nearly 40 years ago by the imperial usurper Carausius to fund his short-lived bid for independence from Rome, was kept on by Diocletian when he reconquered Britain. Now it is being abolished as part of a package of fiscal reforms by Constantine in yet another attempt to deal with the raging inflation that has plagued the empire for years.

The first part of the reforms came a couple of years ago when two new silver coins – the *miliarensis* and the *siligua* – were introduced. Made of almost solid silver and worth their bullion value, they were intended to replace the virtually worthless plated coins, many of them forged, which were circulating as a result of inflation.

The next step has been to rationalize the imperial mints, closing down several others elsewhere in the empire and opening a central mint in the emperor's new capital at Byzantium. The treasury in London will remain, however, to oversee the extraction of silver from the lead mines in the Mendips and gold from the Welsh mountains.

There is also a political reason for the closure. Challenges to the imperial throne need money to keep troops loyal. The absence of a mint in London will make the funding of rebellious troops much harder.

Some observers can see no other benefit. They point out that coins will have to be imported from continental mints such as Trier, which will mean long delays, in turn leading to coin shortages, which encourage forgeries, which fuel inflation. It seems likely that, despite punishments such as having molten lead poured down their throats, forgers will still be in business (→405).

Ironmaking forges ahead as basilica is converted to foundry

Silchester, Hampshire, 325
Travellers visiting the important town of Silchester may be in for a surprise when they arrive at the *forum* and *basilica*, the civic complex which is usually at the heart of life in a Roman town, combining shopping and administrative areas.

Instead of the usual mix of a bustling market and the quiet hum of people waiting while justice is administered and taxes are being paid, they will encounter the smoke, dirt and noise of an iron foundry, which has been set up on the ground floor. At the moment the foundry is producing bronze nails, but reliable reports say that coins were being forged here some years ago. The bureaucracy still goes about its business – upstairs.

General's coup ousts licentious emperor

Gaul [France], 350
After a 10-year rule as emperor of the west, Constans, the youngest son of Constantine the Great, has been assassinated at Autun by one of his army commanders, Magnentius, who has proclaimed himself emperor. Constans was away hunting when Magnentius, of "barbarian" descent, staged his coup; the emperor fled for his life but was captured by the rebels in Spain and subsequently murdered.

Constans came to power in the west after murdering his elder brother and co-ruler, Constantine II; his rule rapidly degenerated into vice and unbridled oppression. His overthrow has been widely welcomed, especially in Britain, where the father of Magnentius is said to have been born.

How long Magnentius will be able to survive as emperor is far from clear. He has a rival would-be emperor in Illyria [Yugoslavia], where the soldiers have chosen one of their generals, Vetranio. But the real threat to Magnentius is posed by another of Constantine's sons, Constantius, who is emperor of the east (→28/9/351).

A bust of the usurper Magnentius.

Towns fortified to combat threat of raids

A tower to strengthen the wall: a reconstruction of London's defences.

London, 352
With coastal piracy and raids by the Picts on the increase, and the Roman garrison in Britain below strength after last year's defeat of the usurper Magnentius, an extensive programme for reinforcing town defences is being mounted. A few of the more important towns, such as St Albans, have been well fortified for many years. Now London, Chichester, Brough (on the Humber), Caerwent and Great Casterton will have towers added to their walls for defenders to deliver enfilading fire against attackers.

Much of the material for this work is being taken from demolished buildings. In London, though, the new towers are being constructed with stones taken from local cemeteries. Even the tomb of Alpinus Classicianus, the emperor's chief financial official in Britain after Boudica's revolt, has been raided (→400).

Christian burial becomes fashionable as pagan observances fall into disrepute

Britain, 353
Anyone caught offering a pagan sacrifice or worshipping household gods faces execution, on the orders of Emperor Constantius II, a devout Christian. This new ruling ends a brief period of freedom for pagan worship under the usurper Magnentius. Magnentius killed himself this year after suffering defeat in 351 at Mons Seleucis in Gaul [France] – leaving Constantius, a son of Constantine the Great, in the position of master of the empire in north-western Europe.

As pagan observances fall into increasing disrepute across the empire, and Christianity takes a firmer hold, traditional burial rites are giving way to a new style. This development is evident even in Britain, in spite of its great distance from the centre of imperial life. The past century has seen the gradual decline of the once universal practice of cremation in favour of burial. Now the dead are placed in coffins, often massive, which are fashioned from wood, stone or even lead.

While such burials have taken over from pagan funeral pyres, some customs persist. As in the past, all but the poorest Britons are buried with a variety of grave offerings, often pots, and sometimes even a coin, reflecting Greek custom – it is thought necessary to have money to pay Charon, the boatman who is believed to ferry the dead across the river Styx to Hades.

The wealthy take with them the same material splendours as they possessed on earth. Their grave goods are far more extravagant than those of their poorer neighbours: men and women are both dressed in their finery, the women with their hair carefully combed and pinned into place. Yet these customs too are fading, and the Christian practice of abandoning all of one's worldly goods when one is buried is gaining popularity. Devout Christians have no grave goods, and they are covered with simple shrouds (→c.625).

The victorious Constantius II, a fervent supporter of the new faith.

A lead coffin found in London.

354 - 364

Britain, 354. Martinus, the vicar (imperial governor-general) of the British diocese (group of provinces), commits suicide after trying to end a brutal purge.→

Cologne, Germany, 8 September 355. Silvius, a Roman military commander proclaimed emperor by his troops in August this year, is killed by German tribesmen.

Milan, Italy, 8 November 355. Constantius II proclaims his cousin Julian, aged 24, *caesar* [deputy emperor] of the western empire, of which Britain is a part (→25/9/357).

Gaul [France], 355. The Alamanni, a Germanic tribe, cross the Rhine into eastern Gaul (→25/9/357).

Gaul, 25 September 357. Julian defeats the Alamanni at Strasbourg and drives them back across the Rhine.→

Gaul, February 360. Julian, who as *caesar* had subdued the Alamanni and successfully driven them back across the Rhine, is proclaimed *augustus* by his army (→3/11/361).

Britain, 360. The Roman expeditionary force under Lupicinus, sent to deal with attacks by tribes in the north which have breached terms previously imposed upon them, is withdrawn to support Julian's bid for the throne.→

Cilicia [southern Turkey], 3 November 361. Constantius II dies of fever while marching to meet Julian, who is advancing with his army from the Rhine frontier (→11/12/361).

Constantinople [Istanbul, Turkey], 11 December 361. Julian, a pagan, is proclaimed emperor by the senate.→

Chalcedon [Kadikoy, Turkey], January 362. Paulus "the Chain", who conducted a savage purge in Britain in 354, is among officials executed for excesses during the rule of Constantius II.

Britain, c.362. The edict passed by Julian tolerating all forms of religion has caused an increase in pagan worship, and new temples are being built in many areas of Britain (→c.380).

Constantinople, 364. Emperor Jovian, who came to the throne on the death of Julian in August last year, dies after less than eight months in office. His successor Valentinian goes to confront the "barbarian" threat on the Rhine (→367).

Suspects arrested in reign of terror

Britain, 354

The emperor's representative in Britain has killed himself after attempting to end the reign of terror instigated by an agent of Emperor Constantius II. The imperial notary, Paulus, a Spaniard, arrived to root out army supporters of a pretender to the throne, Magnentius, but launched a round-up of all suspected opponents. The vicar (imperial governor-general) of Britain, Flavius Martinus, ordered Paulus – nicknamed "the Diabolic" and "the Chain" – to stop. In a bitter row, Martinus tried to kill Paulus, but failed and committed suicide. Paulus is now taking hundreds of prisoners to Gaul [France] for trial and almost certain death (→1/362).

Young deputy wins a triumph for Rome

Philosopher and soldier: Julian.

Strasbourg, Gaul [France], 357

In what is being hailed as Rome's greatest triumph for generations, Julian, the 26-year-old *caesar* [deputy emperor] of the western empire, including Britain, has inflicted a heavy defeat on the German Alamanni tribe. Although heavily outnumbered, Julian risked all with his 13,000-strong force; he slaughtered some 3,000 enemy troops and captured their king, Chnomodar. The battle took place on the empire's German frontier.

Julian has gained the nickname "Victorinus" [Victorious] – an epithet sure to win the displeasure of his jealous cousin, Emperor Constantius II, who sent Julian to Gaul to restore order after the civil war instigated by the imperial usurper Magnentius (→359).

British bishops described as 'pigheaded'

A fresco of a Christian monogram at Lullingstone Roman villa, in Kent: British Christians complain that their church is afflicted by poverty.

Rimini, Italy, 359

Travelling expenses have become the focus of a row between British and Gallic bishops at a council in Rimini called by Emperor Constantius II to settle a long-running debate over the "heresy" of Arianism. The British contingent accepted the emperor's offer to cover its costs, angering the Gauls on the grounds that it would put the British in his pocket. The British pointed out how poor their church was in comparison with the continental one, and were charged with being "pigheaded". The emperor wants western churchmen to accept Arianism – the doctrine, popular in the eastern empire, that Christ and God the Father are similar but not "of one substance" (→c.360).

A Christian priest at Lullingstone.

Grain shipped to continent to feed troops

Gaul, 359

An enormous fleet of 600 vessels has been put together to carry shipments of grain from Britain to the Roman army on the German frontier. Granaries are being constructed on the rivers Rhine, Meuse and Scheldt as part of a plan by the deputy emperor and commander-in-chief, Julian, to overcome the problem of food shortages for soldiers facing the threat from "barbarians" on this frontier.

The shortages are believed to have been engineered in Rome by the praetorian prefect, Florentinus, in an attempt to discredit Julian and curry favour with Emperor Constantius II. Florentinus said that the army would have to bribe the Franks to allow the ships to use the waterways that the Franks control.

Julian promptly launched an attack on them and forced them to come to terms, taking hostages as a guarantee of their good faith. Julian's men are pleased with their commander's efforts to feed them. The British – who will now be forced to tighten their belts – are less happy (→2/360).

Cruel commander dispatched to curb Picts

London, 360
A top Roman officer renowned for his cruelty and high-handedness has arrived from Gaul with four army units to halt new incursions into Roman territory in northern Britain. Lupicinus was sent to Britain by Julian, the deputy emperor, in response to reports of plundering raids by northern tribes, including Picts and Scots from Ireland. Julian, preoccupied with unrest on the German frontier and the emperor's jealousy at his successes, decided against leading an expedition to Britain in person. Lupicinus has travelled first to London in order to gather intelligence and replenish his supplies before continuing northwards (→365).

Druid curse is blamed for death of king

Ireland, c.360
Christianity is beginning to reach Ireland, probably through traders, and stories are increasingly circulating of the fate of Cormac mac Airt, a third-century king and warrior who quarrelled with the local Druids. After shocking them by revealing that he had become a Christian, he choked to death on a salmon bone. Now some say that his death was no accident, but that the Druids had cast a spell on him. Cormac's story is popular in Ireland, where he is seen as an heroic figure. But sceptics suspect that his deeds are exaggerated (→431).

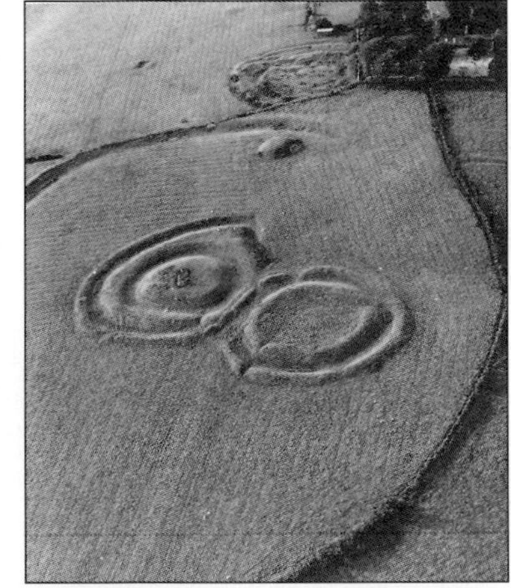

Seat of kings: Tara, Co Meath.

Pagan emperor to ban Christian teaching

Constantinople, 11 December 361
Julian, the former commander-in-chief and *caesar* [deputy emperor], whose brief included Britain, today made a triumphant entry into Constantinople as sole emperor at the age of 30. His predecessor and cousin, Constantius II, died last month aged 44 on his way to fight Julian for the imperial crown.

But in a shock revelation Julian has disclosed that although he was brought up a Christian he has abandoned the faith and become a devotee of the old pagan religions. The new emperor will not actively persecute the faithful, but he intends to ban the teaching of Christianity and sack Christian teachers.

In Britain, news of the return to paganism will be widely welcomed, since away from the towns the new faith has not taken hold among the mass of the people and, despite the edicts of Christian emperors, pagan cults have continued to flourish. Temples which have been allowed to fall into decay are to be restored and new ones are planned, such as in the old tribal hillfort of Maiden Castle in Dorset (→362).

Offerings continue at pagan altars.

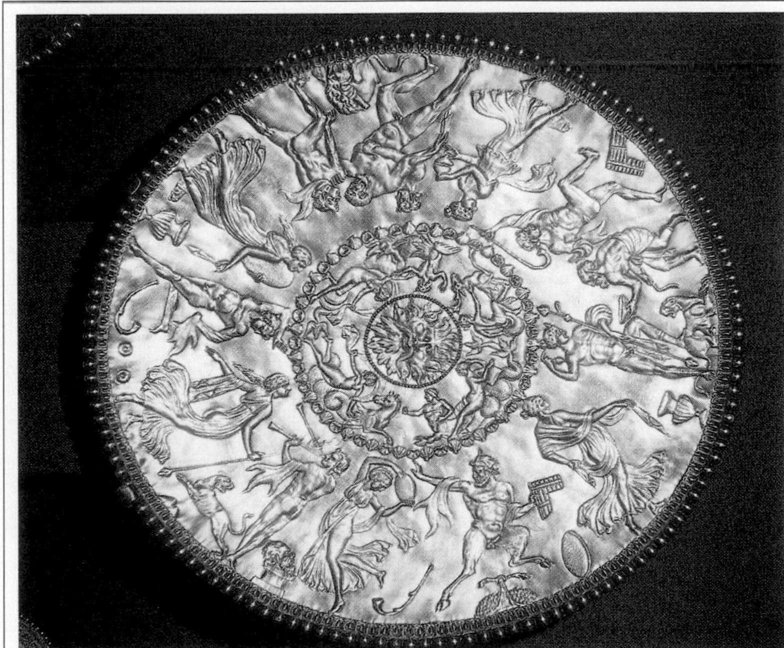

A magnificent silver dish from a hoard buried at Mildenhall in Suffolk in the mid-fourth century, probably by wealthy landowners who intended to return and collect their treasures. This dish, which weighs more than 7 kg, was imported from southern Europe, and was possibly made in Rome. Its pagan decoration features the victory of Bacchus, the god of wine, over Hercules. Elated in victory, Bacchus (to the right) rests his foot on a panther, while Hercules (centre, top) has been undone by wine and is being supported by satyrs. The sea god Oceanus looks out from the centre.

This decorated silver platter is from the same hoard. It features two worshippers of Bacchus who have broken away from the main gathering of revellers. Such fabulous silverware as that found at Mildenhall reflects an extravagance and wealth to which very few British families could rise.

Britain, 365. The Roman provinces are simultaneously attacked by the Picts, Scots and Attacotti (→367).

Trier, Gaul [France], 367. Emperor Valentinian, who is seriously ill, learns of discussions about who is to succeed him and nominates his eight-year-old son Gratian as his successor (→17/11/375).

Gaul, 367. News of the unrest in Britain reaches Valentinian, who, despite sending troops, is unsuccessful in quelling the trouble.→

Gaul, 368. Following a long campaign against the Alamanni, Valentinian finally defeats them and turns his attention to the worsening problems posed by "barbarians" in Britain.

London, 368. Theodosius, the Spanish-born commander of four field-army units, reaches the city and makes a base to campaign against the "barbarians".→

Britain, 372. The Alamannic chieftain Fraomar is sent to Britain to command units of his compatriots serving in the Roman army (→383).

Pannonia [Hungary], 17 Nov 375. Outraged by "barbarian" envoys, Emperor Valentinian dies of apoplexy. He is succeeded by his 16-year-old son, Gratian (→19/1/379).

Dalmatia [Yugoslavia], 19 January 379. Gratian appoints Theodosius, the son of the commander who was sent to Britain, as the new *augustus* [co-emperor] of the eastern empire (→383).

Constantinople [Istanbul, Turkey], c.380. Theodosius issues a constitution, also adopted by Gratian, which recommends that all subjects adopt the Christian faith, all others being banned (→385).

Gaul, 25 August 383. Magnus Maximus, proclaimed emperor by his troops in Britain, invades Gaul. Gratian, the western emperor, is killed, and Maximus is appointed emperor by the army (→384).

Britain, 384. Magnus Maximus returns to carry on the fight in the north (→385).

Trier, 385. Maximus sets up court, is baptized and accepts Theodosius as senior *augustus* [co-emperor] (→388).

Rome, c.385. Pelagius, a British law student, decides to abandon law to take up theology (→391).

Fears grow of 'barbarian conspiracy'

Romans shocked by coordinated attacks

Britain, 367

"Barbarian" raiders have exploited the temporary weakness of the empire – caused by yet another imperial succession crisis – to launch a coordinated attack on the Roman provinces of Britain. The simultaneous assault from all sides by Picts, Scots and Attacotti, all of whom have made regular raids in recent years, has horrified the Romans, who are talking with alarm of a "barbarian conspiracy".

Their anguish appears justified, especially as Gaul [France] has been attacked at the same time by Franks and Saxons. So far, two senior Roman military commanders in Britain, Fullofaudes and Nectaridus, are reported to have been lost in the onslaught, and the "barbarians" are now believed to be fanning out in search of plunder.

The emergency has grave implications. How did Rome, with its vast intelligence network, fail to learn of the plot? Is there some brilliant "barbarian" commander behind it? Rome has always feared a concerted attack on its frontiers. Its leaders must answer these questions to prevent such a thing from happening again (→368).

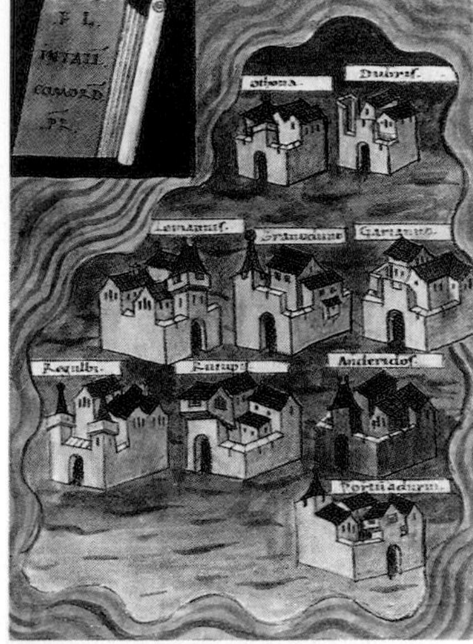

A Roman map showing forts built to keep out Saxon raiders: a later copy.

Defenders muster to quell incursions

London, 368

Theodosius, the Roman general sent to subdue the "barbarians", has entered London in triumph. His force of four top field-army units now plans to head into the provinces to drive out the invaders, who last year launched attacks by both land and sea; they put the Roman commander Fullofaudes out of action and killed Nectaridus, another commander – apparently aided by an army mutiny which had support in governing circles.

After it had made a successful landing at Richborough, in Kent, Theodosius's force set out for the capital, attacking the bands of barbarians roaming south-east England and winning local support by returning captured booty. Deserters from the Roman army are now being pardoned as Theodosius musters his forces to confront the invaders elsewhere in Britain (→369).

Failed rebellion led by European exile

Britain, 369

Roman forces have crushed a revolt masterminded by Valentinus, an exile from Pannonia [Hungary] sent to Britain as a punishment for having committed serious crimes. Valentinus rallied considerable support among other exiles, and took advantage of the army discontent that has rumbled on ever since the mutiny of two years ago.

Theodosius, who was sent to restore order in the British provinces last year, has proved to be equally successful in meeting this new threat. Valentinus and others now face execution. However, in contrast to the reprisals after past mutinies, Theodosius has decided to adopt a generally lenient approach on this occasion in order to avoid further trouble.

Valentinus is the brother-in-law of Maximinus, a barrister known in Rome as the scourge of the aristocracy. The nature of the crimes that led to his exile is not known (→370).

Fortified watch-towers to line east coast

A lookout post near Scarborough: coastal defences are being strengthened.

Northern England, 370

The Romans are refortifying parts of Hadrian's wall damaged in 367 in the "barbarian" attacks, and more troops have been sent to man the northern forts as part of a drive to secure Roman-held territory.

New defences are planned for the north-east coast of England, with fortified watch-towers stretching from Filey to Huntcliff, near Saltburn, in response to the growing threat from seaborne Saxon invaders. Until now the only coastal defences linked to the wall were those built on the Solway Firth in the west some two centuries ago. The new defences are to give early warning of attack to the Roman land forces based at York and Malton. Inland city fortifications are also being strengthened (→397).

Exotic arrivals from Spain upset peace of the Scilly Isles

Isles of Scilly, 370
The tranquillity of the Scilly Isles, one of the westernmost outposts of the Roman empire, has been disturbed by two exotic arrivals from Spain: Bishop Instantinus and an aristocrat called Tiberius. Following a crackdown on heretics, the two men have been exiled here for membership of an esoteric sect. Their leader Priscillian has been executed for "studying magic, obscene doctrines, frequenting nocturnal meetings of infamous women and praying naked". Britain has long been used by the Romans as a dumping-ground for powerful undesirables, but since the revolt last year led by the exiled Pannonian Valentinus the authorities have decided that the mainland is not remote enough for such a purpose.

Troops in Britain back imperial rival

A gold coin of Magnus Maximus.

Britain, 383
Roman troops in Britain have proclaimed Magnus Maximus, one of their generals, as emperor. Maximus came to prominence last year when he defeated an attempted invasion by Picts. With his position secure in Britain, Maximus plans to invade Gaul [France] and build up his strength in the western empire. It is not clear whether he intends to challenge directly the power of Emperor Theodosius, the son of the general who helped to repel the "barbarians" from Britain a decade and a half ago (→25/8).

New building boom brings wealth to the Cotswolds while demand soars for decorative multicoloured patterns for floor mosaics

England, c.370
In spite of the continuing threat posed by "barbarian" attacks and social upheaval, much of England has been seeing a boom in the construction of villas, or country houses, usually some 5 to 10 miles outside major towns. In the Cotswolds, for example, a great deal of building work has been in progress in the region around Gloucester, Bath and Cirencester, and further south near Ilchester.

The term "villa" denotes not just a house but an estate where wheat and barley are grown, cattle and sheep are kept or horses bred. Barns, dairies, smithies and potteries often form part of the villa complex, constructed around a large courtyard. Near the main house lie the vegetable garden and orchard. Villas frequently have underfloor (hypocaust) central heating, and all have hot-water baths.

The building boom has spurred demand for interior decoration, particularly floor mosaics. At least four mosaic schools are prospering: at Cirencester, Dorchester (in Oxfordshire), Chesterton (in the Nene valley) and Brough (on the Humber).

To make a mosaic, pieces of coloured stone are first cut into tiny cubes (*tesserae*): sandstone and limestone for yellows, ironstone for reds and browns, slate for blue and black, and marble or chalk for white. The expert mosaicist outlines in a layer of cement the pattern into which these cubes will be laid, and other skilled workers cover the cement with a solution of lime and water. Into this they painstakingly place the cubes, using perhaps 120,000 pieces to cover a floor of 2.8 by 4.5 metres.

While the designs are usually geometrical, rich patrons may commission more complex naturalistic scenes. Fine examples include the "Four Seasons" at Chedworth, Gloucestershire. One of the largest is at Woodchester, near Gloucester. Its theme of Orpheus also occurs at Littlecote in Wiltshire.

A 20th-century reconstruction of the villa at Littlecote, in Wiltshire.

A mosaic showing Orpheus and animals, from the villa at Littlecote.

The figure of Spring, from a mosaic at Chedworth villa, in Gloucestershire.

386 - 408

Northern Italy, 388. Following his invasion of Italy and expulsion of the western co-emperor, Valentinian II, last year, Magnus Maximus, the Roman general from Britain, gives himself up to Theodosius and is executed. Britain is restored to central imperial control (→ 392).

Italy, 392. Valentinian II, restored to the western throne, is killed, probably by Arbogast, a military commander. Eugenius is proclaimed emperor (→ 6/9/394).

Italy, 6 September 394. The usurper Eugenius is defeated and killed in battle at the river Frigidus, leaving Theodosius as sole emperor. The death of Eugenius ends a two-year period during which Britain was again free from central imperial control (→ 17/1/395).

Milan, Italy, 17 January 395. Emperor Theodosius dies and is succeeded by his two sons – Honorius in the west, Arcadius in the east – once again dividing the empire (→ 406).

Northern Britain, 397. Flavius Stilicho, the supreme Roman military commander in the western empire, spearheads a campaign to deal with renewed outbreaks of trouble (→ 1/400).

Ravenna, Italy, 402. Stilicho defeats Alaric and forces the Visigoths out of Italy. For safety the imperial court, which had been based at Milan, is now moved to Ravenna (→ 406).

Britain, 406. A soldier named Marcus is proclaimed emperor by a mutinous faction in the army (→ 407).

Britain, 407. Following the murder of Marcus by the very troops who elevated him last year, a civilian Briton named Gratian is proclaimed emperor by the army; he too is deposed and murdered after a reign lasting only four months.

Gaul [France], 407. The usurper Constantine III leaves Britain, where he has been declared emperor by the army, and takes control of Gaul after fighting off "barbarian" invaders and loyal imperial troops (→ 408).

Spain, 408. Constantine III's son, Constans, and his army commander, Gerontius, bring Spain under Constantine's control (→ 409).

Britain, 408. Lack of defensive troops allows fierce "barbarian" raids on the south and east coasts (→ 409).

Emperor outlaws all forms of pagan ritual and worship

Roman Empire, 391
Emperor Theodosius has issued a decree outlawing all forms of pagan worship. Temples are to be closed, statues destroyed and hefty penalties imposed upon anyone breaking the law. Even pagan rituals which are performed in private are banned under the new imperial decree, which reflects the determination of Theodosius that the Roman empire should be Christian.

Although the emperor has been personally tolerant of pagans as individuals, he has been persuaded by the archbishop of Milan to adopt this new tougher line. The archbishop favours further measures, such as laws against honouring traditional household gods and the death penalty for practising pagan rites. This first decree should therefore be seen as possibly only the first step in an imperial war against all forms of paganism. One casualty of the decree has been the Altar of Victory in the Senate in Rome. Incense was burnt here before the start of each session, but now the altar has been removed.

The imperial decree enhances still further the growing power of the Christian church, yet it will not make Theodosius immune from political attack. Magnus Maximus, who eight years ago was proclaimed a rival emperor after his military success in Britain, was also a fervent Christian (→ 20/12/415).

Pagan jewellery from Britain.

Imperial control looks increasingly shaky

Human heads on a pagan British pot from Burgh-by-Sands, Cumbria.

Britain, January 400
Roman Britain is entering the fifth century to rousing claims that imperial control is secure and that the "barbarian" threat has been rebuffed. Flavius Stilicho, the Roman strongman in the west, was praised this month by the poet Claudian for banishing fear of the Picts, Scots and Saxons after it had seemed that Britain might "succumb to the attack of neighbouring peoples".

However, the threat has not gone away, and there are signs that Rome's hold on its island outpost remains fragile. In 367 "barbarian" attacks brought Roman rule to the point of collapse. A task force under Theodosius imposed order and, with fortifications and town walls strengthened, the "barbarians" were kept at bay to leave Britain generally peaceful and prosperous.

Yet sporadic Pictish attacks continue in the north, and in the west where some loyalty lingers in Wales to Magnus Maximus, the general who briefly ruled Britain as a rival emperor. Some Welsh forts, and some in the Pennines, have recently been abandoned by the Romans. The 20th Legion has also been withdrawn from Chester. The imperial hold may thus be more precarious than it seems, especially as Roman armies are increasingly using "barbarians" as mercenaries recruited into their ranks (→ autumn 401).

Irish establish colonies in western Britain

Ireland and Britain, c.400
Irish raids on the western seaboard of Britain have grown in frequency as Roman power has weakened, and now the Irish have begun to establish a more permanent presence on the other side of the Irish Sea, from Cornwall to places as far north as the Hebrides.

In Wales, the Deisi tribal group from south-eastern Ireland has established a large colony in Dyfed, and the Laigin of Leinster have a colony in the north based around Anglesey and the Lleyn peninsula, which is now named after them. Colonists of the Ui Liathin dynasty, probably from east of Cork, have settled in Devon and Cornwall, and further north invaders from the Dal Riata group of dynasties in Ulster, called "Scots" [pirates] by the Romans, have a strong foothold on the west coast of Britain beyond Hadrian's wall.

Wherever the Irish go, they take their distinctive culture. They also put up stone – mainly granite – pillars which bear inscriptions in "ogham", an alphabet of lines and notches, cut into the edges. Ogham is the first attempt to write Irish, and the letters that it represents are based on those of Latin; it is thus one of the fruits of direct contact with the Roman world, either through the longstanding, if limited, trade relations between Ireland and Roman Britain or through the newer settlements (→ 405).

Roman troops leave to defend Italy

Britain, autumn 401
Roman soldiers are being withdrawn from Britain to help Flavius Stilicho, the supreme commander of imperial forces in the western empire, to resist "barbarian" attacks in northern Italy. Visigoths led by Alaric have now penetrated the Alps, and Stilicho is amassing an army from several parts of his beleaguered empire. The walls of Rome itself are being strengthened against possible attack.

The decision to concentrate defences upon Italy will inevitably imperil frontier territories, such as Britain, from which troops are being removed. It is not clear exactly how many men have left Britain, or when the withdrawals began – some sources have claimed that there were troop movements to Gaul [France] as long ago as 398. Certainly, the Roman authorities think that they have contained the attacks by Picts, Scots and Saxons that marked the later years of the last century.

The Romans also believe that their hold on Britain will have been strengthened by the improvements to military fortifications which have been in progress over the last 30 years. But decisions have been taken to abandon some minor forts, and many Britons will be uneasy at the prospect of substantial troop withdrawals.

The northern and western borders of Rome's sphere of influence are likely trouble spots, and some "barbarians" may be given land in return for defensive assistance as Roman mercenaries (→402).

Supreme commander: Stilicho.

Bartering is back as coin supply fails

Britain, 405
Britain is suffering from a shortage of coins – a development which has fuelled fears about the extent of Rome's commitment to and control of its far-flung British provinces. The most obvious consequence of the shortage is a return to bartering as a means of trade.

No Roman coins have been minted in the island since the reign of the usurper Magnus Maximus in the last century, and none has been imported for at least three years. The coins were used for paying the troops – those who remain are understandably frustrated – and widely in general trade. The lack of coins is threatening to cause a recession: the potteries in particular are badly hit (→c.425).

A reconstruction of the kitchen of a typical Roman villa or town house.

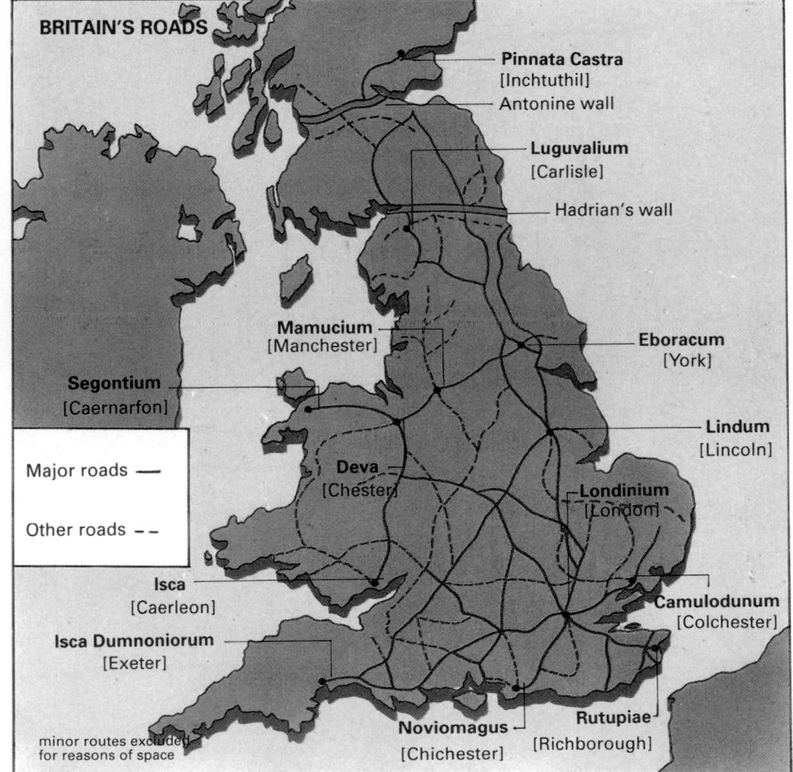

Britain faces power vacuum after three and a half centuries of Roman dominance

Britain, c.405
For more than 350 years much of Britain has been under the domination of Rome. Now, as the empire decays, Britons face a power vacuum such as no one has ever known. New enemies, meanwhile, are at the gates.

Under Roman control Britain has become a group of provinces within an empire stretching as far as the Caucasus in the east and the African Atlantic coast in the west. The Romans have introduced new methods of government, new legal systems, a new language and two new religions, the more recent being the Christian faith.

A road network links all parts of the country with its provincial capitals. The island's east and west coasts are lined by fortifications against "barbarian" attack. Large estates flourish, particularly in the west. Agriculture has been improved, great buildings have been constructed, and Britons have access to the latest medical ideas. Water-mills grind corn, large potteries make goods for local markets. There are doctors, lawyers, professional soldiers, theologians, bishops and priests, merchants.

The lives of ordinary Britons, however, are probably much the same as they were before the Romans arrived. If the withdrawal now under way proves permanent, this, combined with increasing emigration, will create a shortage of talented people capable of continuing effective government. The *civitates* – the self-governing tribal areas set up by the Romans – may again fragment into warring kingdoms.

FECERVN: PRANDIVM:

Saxons, Vikings and Normans

409 - 1153

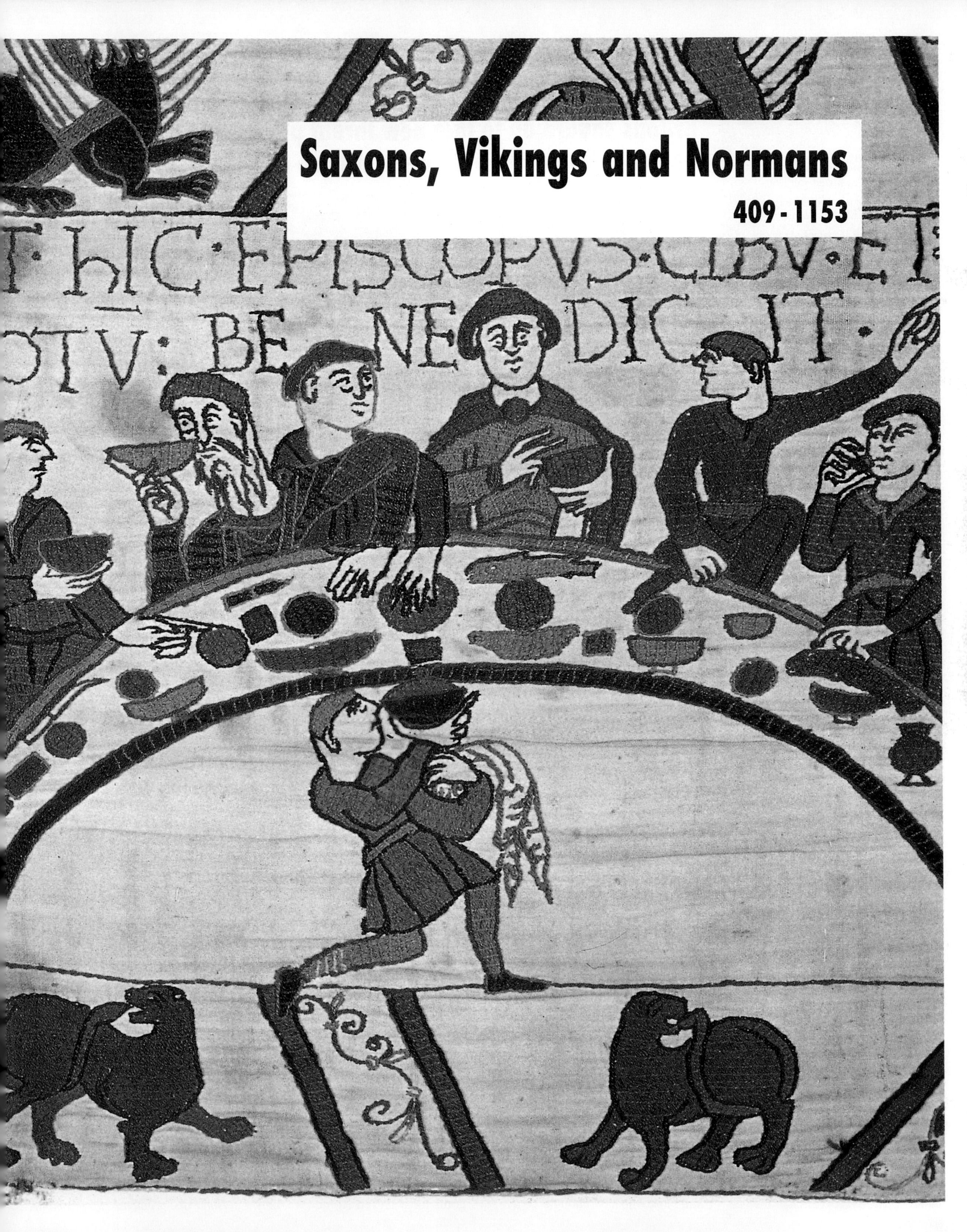

409 - 448

Ravenna, 409. Constantine III is recognized by Emperor Honorius as his co-ruler.→

Rome, August 410. The city is sacked by the Visigoths.→

Arles, Gaul [France], 411. The usurper Constantine III is captured by Honorius's troops and killed.

Rome, 30 April 418. The theologian Pelagius, welcomed by Pope Zosimus on his return last September, is expelled as a heretic (→c.429).

East Anglia, c.420. Groups of Saxon migrants arrive from the North Sea coast intent on settlement (→c.425).

Southern England, c.429. Bishops Germanus and Lupus from Gaul arrive on a mission designed to combat the Pelagian heresy.→

Britain, c.430. Bartering has completely taken over as money loses its value.

Southern England, c.430. Vortigern, a British leader, recruits German mercenaries to fight against their fellow-"barbarians" (→c.446).

Ireland, 431. Pope Celestine sends a deacon, Palladius, to act as bishop to "the Irish believing in Christ" and to combat Pelagianism.→

Britain, c.432. Patricius (Patrick), a north Briton, returns from Gaul, where he has fled to escape slavery in Ireland. He begins to train as a deacon (→c.448).

Britain, c.437. There are rumours of a battle between Romano-British factions at a place called Guolloppum.

Britain, 443. Plague is endemic; its consequences contribute to an acceleration of urban decay (→537).

Britain, c.445. A reported revival of Pelagianism prompts Bishop Germanus to embark on a second mission to the island, this time with Bishop Severus of Trier. The heretics are banished (→c.450).

Leinster, 446. "High king" Niall of the Nine Hostages kills King Mac Cairthinn mac Coelboth at a place called Femen (→c.453).

Britain, c.446. An appeal, "the groan of the Britons", is sent in vain to Aetius, the Roman commander in Gaul, for aid against the Saxons (→449).

Ireland, 27 November 448. The missionary bishop Sechnall (Secundinus) dies (→c.460).

Britons square up to face new threat posed by Saxon raiders as era of Roman rule draws to a close and officials depart

Britain, December 409

Nearly four centuries of Roman rule in Britain are over. The end came not with a dramatic battle or on a specific day, but gradually over this past year as native Britons decided to oust Roman officials and themselves square up to the threat presented by their new adversaries: the Saxons.

Roman troops began to withdraw in large numbers from Britain in 401, in order to strengthen imperial defences in northern Italy, which was being harassed by "barbarians". The pace quickened two years ago, after a rebel Roman soldier was proclaimed Emperor Constantine III by a dissident army faction in Britain. His elevation followed the violent deaths of two other men proclaimed emperor in the same way.

Forces under the command of Constantine left for Gaul [France] and won control of much of the country after fighting off "barbarian" invaders and loyal imperial troops. By leaving Britain undefended, Constantine, who has now been recognized by Honorius as co-emperor in the west, lost control of the province.

This year, as Saxon attacks have increased, Britons have been encouraged by a series of reverses suffered by the co-emperor to abandon loyalty to him. His commander in Spain, the Briton Gerontius, rebelled and marched into Gaul to defeat and kill Constantine's son.

Roman officials left in Britain are being expelled or persuaded to back the British cause as Britons take control of the Roman administration and raise militias to fight the Saxons. Now their example is being followed in northern Gaul (→410).

British shores under threat: an artist's view of Saxon raiders at Scarborough.

Empire shocked by the sack of Rome

Rome, 410

The sack of Rome by hordes of "barbarians" has sent shockwaves across the empire it once ruled. "The world has been beheaded," says the Christian scholar Jerome. Imperial authority has never been so rudely shattered as at Rome, where for three days the Germanic people known as the Visigoths burnt and pillaged this great city. Led by Alaric, the Visigoths had posed an internal threat to the empire since being given sanctuary in 375 from the advancing Huns.

The news will doubtless be a shock to some in Britain – now in practice independent, even though Emperor Honorius may still regard the island as part of his empire. However, one Briton living in Sicily is quite phlegmatic. He writes home: "The world is coming to an end. So what?" The world is unjust anyway: "Mankind is divided into three classes – the rich, the poor and those who have enough" (→476).

'Defend yourselves' insists the emperor

Ravenna, Italy, 410

Emperor Honorius has written to tell the Britons that they must fight the "barbarians" without help from Rome. His letter – addressed to the cities, as there is no longer any official civil or military imperial authority in Britain – will come as a blow only to the few British loyalists. Since last year, when they ejected the administrators of the usurper Constantine III, local leaders have been running the country and fighting for survival without central assistance.

What prompted the letter is not known – although it is rumoured that one of the embattled British cities had appealed for help – but the emperor clearly has more urgent problems to worry about closer to home. His rival Constantine III is holding out in his capital at Arles against Gerontius, his rebellious former army chief; "barbarians" are at large in Gaul; Spain, like Britain, has slipped from imperial control; worst of all, the Visigoths have sacked Rome (→c.420).

Honorius: problems close to home.

Radical theologian argues the case for his belief in free will

"Pelagianism" is shown to make the stars fall and the waters bitter.

Palestine, 20 December 415
The British-born theologian Pelagius today convinced a council of bishops at Diospolis that he is not a "heretic". Pelagius, who is popular in Britain, believes that everyone can choose whether or not to sin. This doctrine of free will, or "Pelagianism", has been denounced by the influential Bishop Augustine of Hippo, in Africa [Tunisia and Libya], and by other church leaders. They maintain that no one can escape "original sin" [according to the Christian Bible, the state of sin inherited by all humans from Adam and Eve] without the grace of God, and that the only way to obtain this – and salvation – is through confession and absolution by a priest. But Pelagius, a fine debater, has won, despite being denounced by the acerbic theologian Jerome as a "corpulent dog" (→ 30/4/418).

Anarchy and fear cause urban chaos

Britain, c.425
Economic decline, the collapse of law and order and the disappearance of a central administration have combined to make city life across the country increasingly uncomfortable. In the east, some cities (Caistor St Edmund, for example) have been abandoned altogether by the locals through fear of marauding Anglo-Saxon raiders. The chaos has caused concern about food supplies, and parts of towns have been given over to agriculture. Other areas are derelict deathtraps, littered with debris from abandoned buildings. Disease is rife.

The decaying cities have spawned a new generation of local leaders, who are trying to establish order over their towns and the surrounding areas. They have recruited Germanic mercenaries to protect them against raiders. But lack of military coordination has resulted in the abandonment of vital coastal and frontier defences.

Fine Roman silverware from a hoard found at Traprain Law, Lothian.

People who grew rich under the Romans have not remained immune from insecurity. The material trappings of the extravagant lifestyle which they used to enjoy have become increasingly irrelevant. For example, silver plate once flaunted as a mark of success is now more likely to be hidden or buried to keep it safe from the Saxons (→ c.430).

Pope sends delegate to care for 'the Irish believing in Christ'

Pagan idols like these from Co Fermanagh are worshipped in sacred groves.

Ireland, c.431
Irish Christians are to have their first bishop, following the decision by Pope Celestine, the head of the Roman church, to send Palladius, at present believed to be a deacon at Auxerre in France, to care for "the Irish believing in Christ". He will probably be based in the south-east of the island, where the Christian influence is strongest. Two years ago Palladius urged the pope to send the bishop of Auxerre to Britain to fight the Pelagian "heresy" [*see report below left*]. Rome may now be worried about the spread of the heresy to Ireland (→ c.439).

Crusading bishop routs Picts and Saxons

Central Southern England, c.429
The mission to Britain of Bishop Germanus of Auxerre and Bishop Lupus of Troyes to counter the Pelagian "heresy" [*see report above*] has been a resounding success.

By chance – some say a miracle – they escaped a shipwreck on the way, and they have toured town and country preaching the "true faith". One one occasion, it is said, Germanus cured a girl of blindness. The Britons, impressed, asked him to bless the army that they were about to send against an alliance of Picts and Saxons. Germanus himself took command and led an ambush in a narrow valley. Under the direction of the bishop, the Britons joined in a great cry of "Alleluia", which so alarmed the Saxons and Picts that they fled. This triumph is being celebrated as the "Alleluia Victory". But now the bishops have left, and the Britons must cope alone once more (→ c.440).

Ireland is put between Britain and Spain

Spain, c.420
The Spanish churchman and writer Orosius has included a survey of Ireland in the geographical essay with which he prefaces his great work *Historia adversus paganos* [*A history condemning the pagans*]. He calls the country "Hibernia" and places it, as other geographers have done before him, between Britain and Spain.

Orosius stresses that Hibernia is smaller than Britain, but observes that the land is of greater value because of its favourable climate and soil. He locates the river Shannon, which he calls "Scena" (his greatest predecessor, the Greek Ptolemy, called it "Senos"), and says that Hibernia is inhabited by tribes of Scots. Although his history chronicles the activities of the usurper Constantine III on the European continent, Orosius has no comment to make about the internal affairs of Britain (→ c.550).

449 - 489

Rome, 455. Pope Leo promulgates a new method for calculating the date of Easter; this method is adopted by Christians in Britain (→c.540).

Aylesford, Kent, c.455. Horsa is killed by Vortigern's troops. Asc now succeeds him as co-ruler with his father, Hengest (→c.456).

Crayford, Kent, c.457. Hengest and Asc kill an estimated 4,000 Britons; the rest flee to London, and Kent is thus abandoned to the invading forces (→465).

Co Kildare, c.460. Auxilius, a Roman missionary bishop who founded the church at Killashee, has died (→c.470).

Southern England, 465. Twelve British chieftains are killed during a battle with Hengest and Asc at a place called Wippedesfleot (→c.477).

Strathclyde, c.470. The Christian king of Strathclyde, Coroticus, is excommunicated by Bishop Patricius (Patrick) of Ireland for seizing Irish Christians whom he subsequently sells into slavery (→c.490).

Gaul [France], 476. Euric, the king of the Visigoths, conquers the remainder of Gaul, extending his rule up to the Italian frontier (→481).

Rome, 476. The boy emperor Romulus Augustulus is forced to abdicate by the Germanic leader Odoacer, who has no plans to appoint a replacement. The western empire thus ceases to exist.

Sussex, c.477. Saxon warriors under the leadership of the chieftain Aelle and his sons land on the south coast, killing many Britons at a place called Cymenesora; the survivors of the battle flee into the Weald. The kingdom of the South Saxons is formed (→c.480).

Gaul, 481. Childeric, the great warrior leader of the Franks, dies at his capital, Tournai, and is succeeded by his son Clovis (→486).

Ireland, c.483. Cremthann mac Endae Chennselaig, the king of Leinster, is assassinated by Finchad mac Garrchon, who then succeeds him in the kingship (→c.516).

Gaul, 486. Clovis, the king of the Franks, defeats Syagrius, the leader of a Roman-controlled enclave in Gaul, in battle at Soissons; he conquers much of northern Gaul except for Armorica [Brittany].

Rebel 'Stallion' and 'Horse' ride high

Kent, 449
The defence policy of Vortigern, one of the most powerful Romano-British leaders, has been smashed to pieces by the Jutish mercenaries whom he employed to defend Kent against the Picts. The mercenaries – led by two brilliant generals known to their growing number of followers as Hengest [Stallion] and Horsa [Horse] – summoned reinforcements and made an alliance with the Picts before taking control of eastern Kent and driving back the Britons.

Their success may set off a chain reaction throughout eastern Britain, as waves of German migrants from the continent (including Jutes, Angles, Saxons, Frisians, Franks) exploit British confusion to plunder or settle this fertile and ill-defended land. The Britons are confronting serious losses, and Vortigern's policy of paying mercenaries to fight his enemies in exchange for permission to settle in eastern Britain lies in tatters.

Vortigern's supporters say that he was only following the old Roman practice of employing federate troops to bolster his own limited forces. There can be no doubting his initial success, for the Picts were driven back. But his critics accuse him of taking too many risks by giving power to soldiers whose loyalty could not be trusted (→c.455).

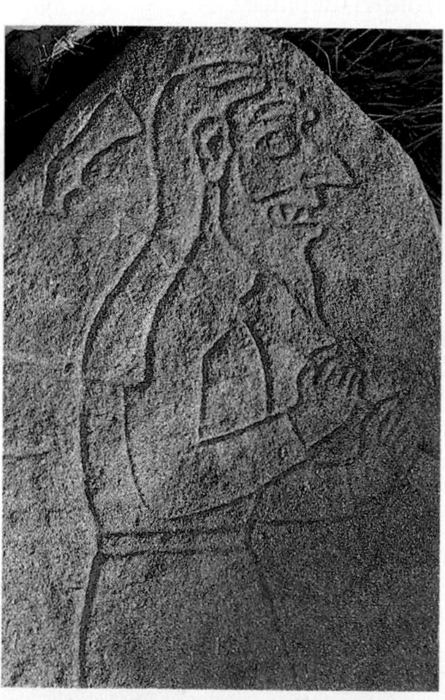

A carved Pictish figure, perhaps a warrior, at Rhynie, in Grampian.

Mercenaries turn swords to ploughshares

A reconstruction of the halls with thatched roofs at West Stow, in Suffolk.

Eastern England, c.450
A thriving community which has been established at West Stow in Suffolk in many ways typifies the growing number of small Anglo-Saxon settlements in the fertile, sheltered valleys of eastern rivers such as the Lark, Blackbourn, Waveney and Ouse. Further north, the Wash and Humber estuaries have also become popular.

At West Stow three or four families, together with their attendant slaves, live in wooden halls with thatched roofs supported by internal posts. This living accommodation is surrounded by outhouses for servants, manufacturing and storage. Taking advantage of the easily worked land, the inhabitants are self-sufficient, growing wheat, barley, rye and peas, and rearing livestock. They also hunt and fish to vary their diet.

Many of the new settlers in these river valleys are Anglo-Saxon mercenaries once in the pay of the Roman Empire, together with new arrivals from across the North Sea. Other newcomers have settled in the Thames valley – not only at strategic points on its estuary, such as Mucking, but also far upriver in a series of new communities as far inland as Oxfordshire. Some have set up homesteads on land near deserted Roman towns such as Caistor St Edmund (→c.480).

Christianity gains ground in Galloway

Dumfries and Galloway, c.450
Christianity is spreading among the British tribes who live in south-west Scotland. At Whithorn a church and monastery have been founded which are thought to be the first Christian institutions established in the north of Britain since the Romans left over 40 years ago.

A pioneer of the Christian gospel in this area was a British monk called Ninian. He had made the arduous journey to Rome to complete his Christian education before returning to his native land charged with spreading the faith. He died about 18 years ago, but his link with the monastery established later at Whithorn, at around 440, is not entirely clear (→c.612).

Death of Irish king who took hostages

Ireland, c.453
Niall, the "high king" of Ireland renowned for his penchant for taking hostages in order to further his aims, has died. He acquired the nickname "Niall of the Nine Hostages" after his spectacular feat of holding hostage a member of each of the ruling dynasties of Ireland at the same time.

The "high-kingship" of Ireland – which is often more a claim to lordship over the myriad petty rulers in the island than a reality – has never been held by one particular tribe. However, Niall's dynasty, the Ui Neill, which controls a wide area of northern and central Ireland, seems determined to try to hold on to it (→482).

Irish dynasties fight over 'high-kingship'

Ireland, 482
With its defeat of King Ailill Molt in battle at Ochae, in the south-eastern Irish region of Leinster, the Ui Neill tribe of the north appears to be well on its way towards securing control of the so-called "high-kingship" of Ireland centred on Tara [*see map on page 110*].

Although claims to the office of high king have repeatedly given rise to disputes, Ailill Molt was clearly regarded as its rightful holder. This was borne out by his celebration of the important Feast of Tara in either 467 or 470. His death is variously attributed to his Ui Neill successors, or to the king of the Dal nAraidi in the northern region of Ulster, or to the king of Leinster. One thing is certain, however. The death of Ailill Molt ends his family's control of the high-kingship of Tara and gives control of Leinster to the Ui Neill.

The nature and influence of the office of high king depends very much on the ability of the claimant and is not even a rank recognized in law. In fact, many consider the king of Cashel, in the south-western region of Munster, to be Ireland's greatest king. But the Ui Neill have upset the ancient division of Ireland into five regions by setting up new kingdoms in the north and the midlands, and the Ui Neill over-king has habitually called himself "king of Tara". The death of Ailill Molt thus secures the position which the Ui Neill have always believed was rightfully theirs (→c.483).

A latchet dress-fastener from Co Offaly, made of copper alloy and enamel.

Trading flourishes at Cornish settlement

Tintagel, Cornwall, 480
The people of Tintagel, perched on a steep headland jutting out from the north Cornish coast, have developed close trade links with the continent. Merchants bring wine and oil in exchange for slaves and tin from local mines, and supply the Cornish market with high-quality pottery from Gaul [France] or even North Africa and Asia Minor. Tintagel is also patronized by the local British kings, the rulers of Devon and Cornwall, who sometimes use it as the seat of their kingdoms. Its position affords great security – attackers from the land would have to pass along the narrow spine that links the headland to the coast, to be faced by a broad ditch overlooked by a steep bank (→c.580).

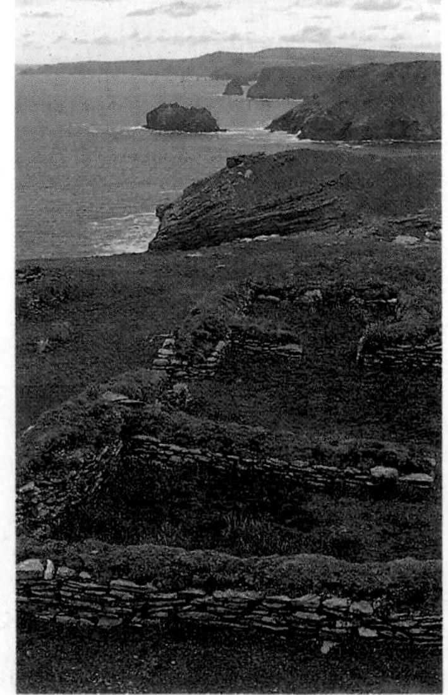

Remains of a Tintagel monastery.

Germanic tribes known as the Angles, Saxons and Jutes settle down in Britain

A bronze pot-lid from Norfolk, a popular region for settlement.

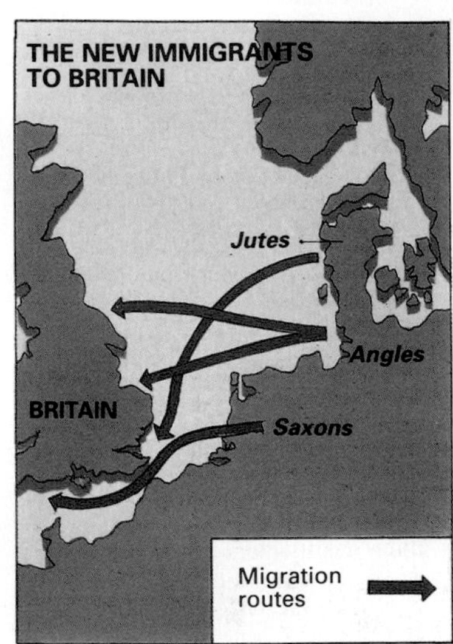

England, c.480
Over the past few decades migrants from continental Europe, driven by population pressures, have been arriving in England in droves and are now consolidating their settlements in the east and pushing westwards. The former Romano-British policy of "guided settlement" of mercenaries has long since broken down as new arrivals, settlers and ex-mercenaries have joined in a combination of peaceful settlement and violent conquest.

The newcomers derive from a variety of Germanic tribes but fall into three principal groups: Angles, Saxons and Jutes. They are readily distinguishable from one another by their dress, personal equipment, pottery and burial customs, although there is already some intermingling both among these groups and with the native British population.

The Jutes, originally from Jutland in Denmark, have mainly settled in Kent, the Isle of Wight and southern Hampshire. The Saxons, who have their roots in northern Germany, have settled in coastal regions and river valleys in the south-east not under Jutish sway. The West Saxons are concentrated in Hampshire and Wiltshire near the river Avon. Saxons are also spreading out over Sussex from a power base around the rivers Ouse and Cuckmere, established recently by their leader Aelle, to occupy the South Downs, and in addition have settled in parts of the Thames valley.

East Anglia – which has long been a popular focus for Saxon migrants – has become the destination for the third main Germanic group, the Angles. They are dominant further north, have colonized the Wash and Humber estuaries, and have pushed on across Lincolnshire and down the river Trent into the Midlands (→c.491).

Gilt saucer-brooches, made by a craftsman from Mildenhall in Wiltshire.

490-555

Southampton, c.495. Cerdic, a Saxon chief, and his son Cynric land on the coast and fight the Britons for control of the area (→c.500).

Ireland, c.497. Cormac, the bishop of Armagh, who is known as *heres Patricii* [the heir or successor of Patrick], dies (→c.520).

Leinster, c.500. Laidcenn mac Bairchedo compiles one of the first collection of poems about the Irish dynasties.

Hampshire, c.508. Cerdic and Cynric, the West Saxon leaders, kill Natanleod, a British king, and 5,000 of his men in battle (→c.519).

Leinster, c.516. The Laigin, the ancient rulers of Leinster, are defeated in battle at Druim Derge by the Ui Neill (→562).

Hampshire, c.519. Cerdic and Cynric fight the Britons at Charford, on the Avon. A Saxon kingdom is taking shape around this river (→c.530).

Isle of Wight, c.530. Cerdic and Cynric are reputed to control the island (→c.534).

Southern England, c.534. Cerdic dies; he is succeeded by Cynric, who rules over the Hampshire and Wiltshire area (→c.539).

Scotland, c.537. Comgall, the king of the Scots, dies after a peaceful 30-year reign (→c.538).

Ireland, c.537. Following a bad harvest and famine, plague sweeps the country (→555).

Lothian, c.538. The Gododdin, a British tribe based at the fortress of Din Eidyn [Edinburgh], are defeated by the Scots in a raid on the Forth valley (→558).

Western Britain, 539. Welsh sources report the deaths of the British leaders Arthur (who some believe may have led the British forces to victory at Mount Badon) and Medraut in battle against the Saxons at Camlann (→c.547).

Derry, c.546. The missionary Colum Cille (Columba) founds a monastery (→c.549).

Leinster, c.549. The scholar and churchman Ciaran, who founded a monastery at Clonmacnoise in Co Offaly two years ago, dies (→c.555).

Salisbury, Wiltshire, c.552. Following an attack by Cynric, the West Saxon leader, the Britons flee (→c.556).

Ireland, 555. A new plague, smallpox, is spreading.

'Apostle' to Ireland dies

Ireland, c.490
Patricius (Patrick), the missionary who converted many Irish to Christianity, has died. He was born in about 415 near Carlisle; his father was a Romano-British civic official and a Christian deacon. Patrick was seized by pirates at the age of 16 and taken to Ireland to be sold into slavery. After six years, guided by a vision, he escaped and sailed to Gaul [France], eventually returning to his family to train as a deacon.

In his *Confession* he tells how he had a second vision in which he saw a letter, entitled *The voice of the Irish*, and heard "the voices of those who dwelt beside the forest of Foclut which is near the western sea, and thus they cried, as if with one mouth, we beg you, holy youth, to come and walk among us again". With his knowledge of Latin and Irish, Patrick was a natural choice to be consecrated by the British church as bishop of Ireland, where Christianity had made little progress, especially in the north.

He set off with great zeal, baptizing converts of all classes countrywide. When the raiding soldiers of Coroticus, the British king, killed some of his converts, Ireland's "apostle" excommunicated them. This ruffled relations between Patrick and his homeland and, in his *Confession*, he was forced to justify his conduct. But in Ireland his legacy of religious communities and native clergy testify amply to the scale of his achievement (→c.497).

An early Irish image of Patrick.

British victory may have been secured by shadowy Arthur

South-western England, c.500
Reports are circulating in this region of a decisive victory for the Britons over an Anglo-Saxon force at a place called Mount Badon. If these reports are true, this is the latest, and perhaps the most significant, of a string of British successes. It is unclear who led the Britons: the Romanized general Ambrosius Aurelianus and a shadowy commander called Arthur are possible candidates for a triumph which many believe will stem the Germanic tide.

The social impact of Saxon, Pictish and Irish incursions, however, lingers on. Former Roman towns have continued to decline as British leaders have taken to the hills, occupying natural strongholds such as Dumbarton ["the fortress of the Britons"] in Strathclyde, the Mote of Mark in Dumfries and Galloway, Deganwy in Gwynedd and Chun Castle in Cornwall. Some of these fortresses date from before the Roman conquest, and have been refurbished. The old defences of South Cadbury in Somerset, for example, have been upgraded to a stone and timber rampart enclosing 7 hectares (18 acres). Despite this, many Britons have decided to emigrate, to Armorica in western Gaul [France], which is itself becoming known as "Britannia" [the land of the Britons] (→c.508).

Christianity gains acceptance in Ireland

Ireland, c.490
Little is known about the origins of Christianity in Ireland, although Germanus, the bishop of Auxerre, is thought to have had an Irish disciple earlier this century. Certainly the first missionaries in recent times came from Gaul [France], where the Christian church has been well organized for some time and where the decision was clearly made to take responsibility for Ireland.

Missionaries have also come from Britain, the most famous of them being Patricius (Patrick). He introduced the monastic life into Ireland and wrote with gratitude of the great numbers of converts embracing it, and he practised the episcopal system of church government that he had seen in operation in Britain and Gaul. Most of his work took place north of a line from Galway to Wexford.

Christianity is now becoming widely accepted in Ireland. And while paganism seems prepared to put up a stiff fight before being overthrown, this seems so far to be the only country in western Europe whose conversion has produced no martyrs (→c.497).

Saxons win control of south coast area

Pevensey, East Sussex, c.491
Britons besieged in an old Roman fort here have been massacred by their Saxon enemies. The chieftain of the South Saxons, Aelle, stormed the fort – which, ironically, had been built to keep his compatriots out of Britain – along with one of his sons, Cissa. Neither is a stranger to battle. When they arrived on the south coast 14 years ago they killed a large number of Britons at a place called Cymenesora. The survivors fled into the Weald, allowing Aelle to win control of the whole south coast area (→c.495).

Monastic centre is founded in Ireland

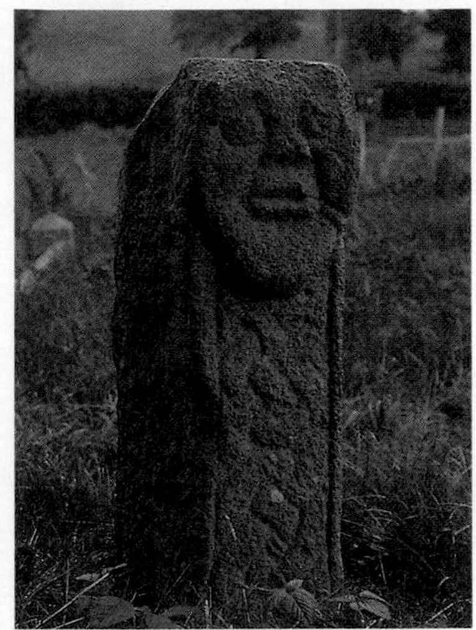

A Christian stone: of pagan origin.

Co Meath, c.520
The missionary Finnian has returned to Ireland from Wales, where he has been working in monasteries founded by renowned priests such as Gildas and Cadoc.

Inspired by the achievements of these men, Finnian has established a monastic centre at Clonard. It is expanding rapidly, with a student population numbering some 3,000, who receive instruction in the open air. They live in huts of wattle and clay, although some permanent stone housing is being built. They fish, sow their own corn and milk their own cows. Finnian's work will not stop here: he intends to send out "apostles" to spread the Christian message (→ c.546).

Anglian chief claims descent from a god

Bamburgh, Northumberland, c.547
A stronghold has been set up on the rock of Bamburgh, on the Northumbrian coast, by Ida, an Anglian leader. He is strengthening the natural defences of the rocky fortress in preparation for an attempt by the British kings of the north to oust him. At the same time he is keen to legitimize his rule and win support by claiming descent from a line of Germanic deities and legendary figures. If he is to be believed, the god Woden was his great-great - great - great - great - great-great-grandfather (→ c.552).

Irish fall out with Rome

Ireland, c.540
A rift has developed between the Irish church and the pope, the head of the Roman church, over the pivotal feast in the calendar: Easter, when Christians celebrate the resurrection of Christ from the dead following his crucifixion. The problem is when to date it.

This is no simple matter, because the timing of Easter derives from the dating of the Jewish Passover, which is calculated by reference to the lunar calendar. The lunar calendar must be combined with the everyday Julian calendar, established by Julius Caesar in 46BC [*see report on page 46*], to fix the day on which Easter falls. Because the two calendars cannot be made to match, the computations can be very complex. The Irish church has chosen a different way from Rome of setting the date of Easter, and it is now being put under pressure to adopt the Roman method.

The practices of the Christian church have always varied from one area to another, but many are coming to see diversity on the Easter issue as a matter of faith, and nonconformity as a sin. The signs are that the Irish will not budge: an unholy row is looming (→ 600).

Missionary tells of islands of ice and fire

Co Galway, c.555
Brendan, a missionary from Kerry, is the latest eminent Irish churchman to found a major monastery, at Clonfert. During a colourful life, he claims to have made a magical voyage to a place he calls Hy Brasail, to the west of Ireland. Guided by a miraculous current, Brendan set out westwards from Ireland and saw "wondrous things" such as one island made of ice and another of fire. Educated by the scholar Bishop Ere, Brendan is said to have gone to Brittany where he founded a monastery in memory of a friend who was drowned at sea (→ c.560).

Brendan is sorely tempted by a siren.

Byzantine writer's odd view of Britain

A mosaic of Emperor Justinian.

Constantinople [Istanbul], c.550
Opposite the mouth of the Rhine is a great island, divided down the middle by a wall. To the east of this wall the land is fertile; to the west there are only wild beasts, and the air is so foul that no creature from the east can survive there. The islanders, who always fight on foot because they have no horses, are reputed to be extremely formidable in battle. The name of this land – according to Procopius of Caesarea, the official historian to Emperor Justinian – is Britain. In fact, from what Procopius has heard there are two islands to the west of mainland Europe, one called "Brittia", which lies opposite the Rhine mouth, and another opposite Spain called "Bretannia".

Priest rails against immorality and evil

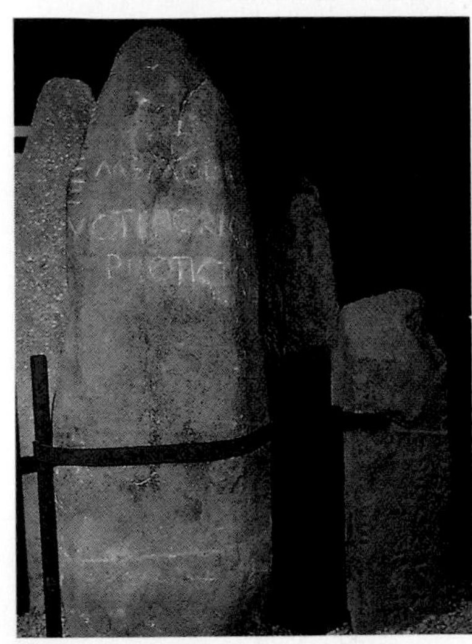

The tombstone of King Vorteporix.

Western Britain, c.540
"Britain has kings, but they are tyrants ... Britain has priests, but they are fools," according to a controversial priest, Gildas. In his diatribe, *The Ruin of Britain*, Gildas rails against the immorality and corruption that he sees as endemic in British society.

He reserves some of his fieriest prose for five British kings, whose sins he spells out: Constantine of Devon and Cornwall – adulterer and sacrilegious murderer; Aurelius Caninus of the Severn estuary – parricide and fornicator; Vorteporix of Dyfed – rapist of his daughter; Cuneglasus of mid-Wales – violent maniac, adulterer and opponent of holy men. Then, "last in my list but first in evil", Gildas singles out Maelgwyn of Gwynedd, a lapsed monk who killed his uncle to seize power, then murdered his own wife and nephew and married the nephew's widow.

Gildas accuses Britain's clergy of being vicious, worldly and greedy; kings and clerics alike are warned of dire consequences unless they mend their ways and renounce sin. He claims that the Saxon invasion was divine vengeance for the sinfulness of Britons following the Roman withdrawal. British resistance, culminating in the famous victory of Mount Badon, may have restored order for a while, but now a new generation has forgotten the lessons of that bitter war and returned to sin. Worse retribution may follow, he warns (→ 597).

556-580

Wiltshire, c.556. Cynric and Ceawlin, the West Saxon leaders in this area, fight the Britons at Barbury Castle, near Swindon (→c.560).

Tayside, 558. Bridei mac Maelchon, the king of the Picts, goes to war with the Dal Riata Scots from Ireland and defeats them in battle (→c.581).

Thames valley, c.560. Ceawlin succeeds to the leadership of the West Saxons in the middle and upper Thames area (→568).

Highland, c.560. Stories are circulating of a strange and fearsome monster reported to have been seen in Loch Ness.

Co Down, c.560. The missionary monk Comgall founds a monastery at Bangor (→c.562).

Northern England, c.560. Aelle becomes king of Deira, the Anglian kingdom which is developing between the rivers Humber and Tees, following the death of Ida, king since 547 (→c.560).

Kent, c.560. The Cantwara, as the Jutish people of Kent are known, have a new king, Athelbert (→568).

Ireland, c.562. The influential churchman Colum Cille (Columba) is involved in a controversy over his role in a battle at Cul Dreimne and is placed under threat of excommunication. He is exiled and, accompanied by 12 supporters, heads for the island of Iona, off the west coast of Scotland (→13/5/563).

Co Londonderry, c.562. The Ui Neill dynasty is victorious in battle at Moin Dairi Lothair and expands its boundaries further to the west and south, encroaching on the territory of the former Cruthin dynasty of Ulster (→581).

Kent, 568. After defeat by the West Saxon leaders Ceawlin and Cutha at a place called Wibbandun, Athelbert has to retreat here. Two princes, Oslac and Cnebba, were killed in the battle (→c.570).

Southern England, c.571. Cuthwulf, a West Saxon leader who fought the Britons earlier this year and captured Limbury, Aylesbury, Eynsham and Bensington, dies (→c.575).

Northumberland, c.575. The Anglian leader Theodoric is besieged for three days on Lindisfarne by Urien, the ruler of the British kingdom of Rheged [Cumbria] centred on the Solway Firth (→577).

Irish monk sets out to save the Picts

Intrepid churchman arrives in Scotland

Iona, Strathclyde, 13 May 563

Today is the Christian festival of Pentecost (Whitsun), and the controversial Irish churchman Colum Cille (Columba), who landed here after leaving his native Ireland, has chosen to celebrate the occasion by establishing a monastery on this small and remote island off the west coast of Scotland. Colum Cille, who is 42 years old, travelled here with 12 companions aboard a *currach* made of wickerwork and hides. Himself a man of deep spiritual conviction, he clearly intends to restore the flagging spirits of the tiny Irish colony already here.

However, rumours are rife as to his reasons for leaving Ireland. It is said by some church and secular leaders that he caused a bloody battle at Cul Dreimne, in north Sligo, and that he has to win for Christ as many souls as were lost in the battle. Colum Cille himself would probably say that he left Ireland of his own accord, having long felt the call to extend his missionary work abroad, and that Scotland was a convenient destination.

His first problem is Bridei, the king of the Picts, whose forces have recently attacked Iona. Colum Cille will have to establish good relations with him if the new foundation on Iona is to survive, let alone become the key Christian centre in the British Isles which Colum Cille wants it to be (→565).

Colum Cille: an early 20th-century view of the leading Irish missionary.

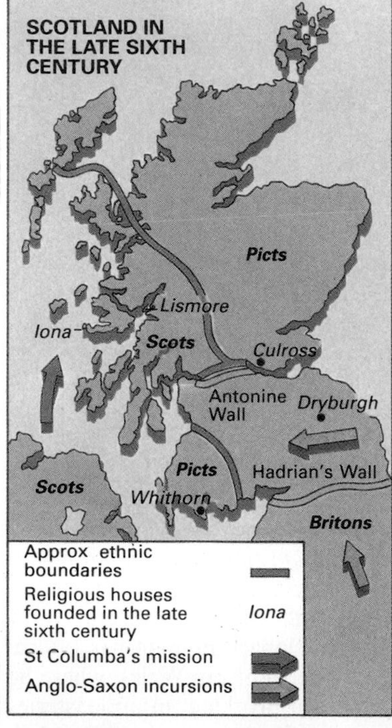

Pictish king impressed by newcomers

Inverness, Highland, 565

Colum Cille (Columba), the Irish missionary, has been received here by Bridei, the king of the Picts. Bridei has tolerated Christian missionaries since he granted the island of Iona to Colum Cille's community in 563, and this visit suggests that he is open to Christian teachings himself. It could mean the recognition of Christianity as the official religion of his kingdom. There is even a rumour that when Colum Cille arrived at Bridei's residence he caused the gates to open by making the sign of the cross. Colum Cille was born in Donegal of Irish royal blood. He entered the local monastery at Moville where he was taught by the saintly Finnian, then left to sit at the feet of the Leinster hermit Gunmon before returning to the monastic life at Clonard. From there he founded a community at Derry before setting sail for Iona.

With his royal links, Colum Cille had no difficulty in dealing with Bridei, who is impressed by his monks' energy in clearing forests and draining land (→c.575).

Monastic movement burgeons in Ireland

Ireland, 565

The monastic movement is making great strides in Ireland where, in spite of the persistence of pagan beliefs, Christianity is now firmly established. Twelve disciples of the missionary monk Finnian of Clonard, who died about 15 years ago, have been responsible for creating a boom in the number of monasteries. Among their foundations are Moville, set up in 540 by another influential Finnian; Clonmacnoise, founded in 541 by Ciaran; Derry, founded in 546 by Colum Cille (Columba); Clonfert, founded by Brendan in 552; and Bangor, founded by Comgall in 558.

The inhabitants of these monasteries – which are commonly regarded as retreats from the world – are committed to following increasingly strict regimes as asceticism gains in popularity. The most significant reforms, which derive in part from British monastic customs, are regarded as those requiring the separation of the communities from the local laity, and the segregation of the sexes (→597).

A sixth-century Anglo-Saxon disc-brooch of "Kentish" type.

Immigrants forge a patchwork of states

England, c.570
Anglo-Saxon immigrants from continental Europe now occupy a large area, possibly the greater part, of England, and the political map of the region has developed into a patchwork of statelets under the command of chieftains.

Typically, these states are named after their leader or his earliest remembered ancestor. For example, the Haestingas of Sussex are "Haesta's people" and the Woccingas of Surrey are "Wocca's people". However, not all of those living in such an area are necessarily related by blood or are even Germanic in origin: there are many Romano-British among them – as intermarriage has the effect of destroying social, cultural and linguistic distinctions.

British resistance over the last 50 years has prevented the Germanic peoples from penetrating further west. But their very success in holding off the migrants may rebound on the Britons for, as new waves continue to arrive, competition for land and resources in the east of the country is intensifying. This has resulted in the forging of broader, more powerful, confederations from the petty states. The leaders of these confederations are beginning to call themselves "kings", and the most successful are extending their power (→c.571).

Anglo-Saxon ornament from Lincs.

Royal wedding affirms cross-Channel ties

A gold pendant from Faversham.

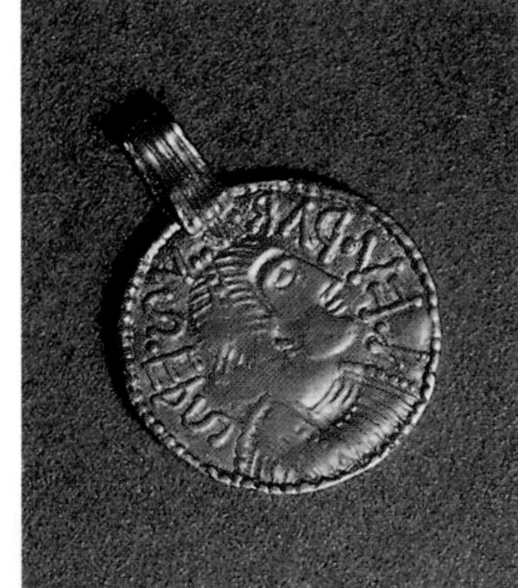
A gold medal of Bishop Liudhard.

Canterbury, Kent, c.580
Long-standing links between Kent and the Franks across the English Channel have been cemented by the wedding of a Kentish royal and a Frankish princess.

The marriage of Athelbert and Bertha, the daughter of the late King Charibert and his first wife Ingoberga, reaffirms the decades-old cross-Channel relations between Kent and the Franks.

Trade with Europe had existed for centuries before the Romans conquered Britain, and more recently this has made Jutish Kent the wealthiest of England's Germanic states. Frankish weapons, jewellery and glass are increasingly common in Kent, and luxury goods from the Mediterranean arrive here via the Frankish lands. Kentish jewellery, a distinctive fusion of Anglo-Saxon animal ornament and the garnet inlay fashionable among the Franks, is now exported to the Franks.

However, perhaps Kent's biggest export commodity is human. The slave trade brings wealth to the most established families of Kent and enhances the influence of Kentish rulers, who are rapidly becoming the most powerful kings in southern England.

The marriage has a condition attached to it: Bertha must keep her Christian faith in this pagan kingdom. As a result of this, Bishop Liudhard has come as her personal chaplain, and a building east of Canterbury, which is believed to be an old Roman church, has been put at their disposal (→c.597).

Rivals reconciled by Irish missionary

Co Londonderry, c.575
As a result of skilful negotiation, the Irish missionary Colum Cille (Columba) has brought about an alliance between two rivals, the king of the Dal Riata – the dynasty of Ulster Scots which has established itself in north-western Britain – and the king of the powerful Ui Neill dynasty which dominates the northern central part of Ulster [*see map on page 110*].

The deal was struck at Druim Cett, and one of its consequences is to give protection to the increasingly influential monastic community created by Colum Cille on the island of Iona. In part this has been achieved because of the warm relations between Aedan mac Gabrain, the king of the Dal Riata Scots, and Colum Cille – who consecrated the king in a solemn ceremony on Iona last year. This was the first time that a ruler in Britain had been officially blessed by the Christian church since the departure of the Romans, and Colum Cille looks destined to become the chief churchman in the Scots kingdom, and probably the most important figure in the entire Celtic church.

With Iona's influence assured, and as a result of his strengthened position, Colum Cille is now intent on establishing new monastic foundations, both in Scotland and in his native Ireland (→c.587).

Pots are showing influence of continent

Eastern England, c.575
The German settlers of Britain are beginning to get a name for developing new techniques of pottery manufacture and decoration. The majority of the pottery made by the Anglo-Saxons is basic and coarse, made locally for everyday use. It is handmade, generally quite soft, and ranges from black to a brownish grey. However, in some areas pottery is more sophisticated, such as in Kent, where a reddish flask-shaped pot is common and reflects the kingdom's close ties with mainland Europe. Specialists are also starting to produce finer pottery for particular occasions, such as the cremation urns of the Illington-Lackford workshop in Suffolk.

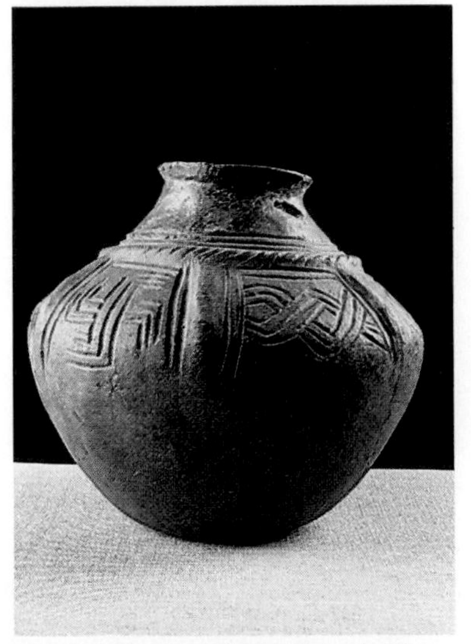
A cremation urn from East Anglia.

Saxon victory splits British lands in two

Dyrham, Gloucestershire, 577
The Britons of Wales have been cut off from those of Devon and Cornwall by a Saxon victory at Dyrham. Three British kings, Conmail, Condidan and Farinmail, died in the battle against Saxon forces under Ceawlin and Cuthwine. The West Saxons, especially those of the upper Thames valley under Ceawlin, have been winning land from the Britons in recent years, and this victory puts the great Romano-British cities of Bath, Gloucester and Cirencester in their hands. It opens up much of the Cotswolds to German colonization and drives a wedge between British-held lands (→c.584).

581 - 597

Ireland, 581. Baetan mac Cairill, the king of Ulster and self-proclaimed "high king" of Ireland, has died after a nine-year reign (→ 598).

Scotland, c.581. Aedan mac Gabrain, the king of the Dal Riata Scots, conquers the Orkneys and expands his kingdom northwards (→ c.583).

Isle of Man, c.583. Following his successful invasion last year, Aedan mac Gabrain wins a battle and thus controls the island (→ c.585).

Oxfordshire, c.584. Cutha and Ceawlin, West Saxon leaders, fight the Britons. Cutha is killed; Ceawlin has to retreat with much spoil (→ c.585).

Scotland, c.585. Bridei mac Maelchon, the king of the Picts, has died. Despite many attempts by Colum Cille (Columba) to convert him to Christianity, he remained a pagan (→ c.590).

Co Offaly, c.587. Colum Cille (Columba) founds an offshoot of Iona at Durrow (→ 9/6/597).

English Midlands, c.588. Creoda, the king of the "Mierce" [the people of the Marches], dies and his son, Pybba, succeeds him (→ 590).

Lindisfarne, Northumberland, 590. King Urien of Rheged [Cumbria] is killed following his betrayal by a fellow chieftain, Morcant (→ c.593).

Scotland, c.590. King Aedan mac Gabrain of the Scots successfully carries out a raid against the Picts (→ c.600).

Ireland, c.590. Columbanus, a monk, sets off on the first Irish monastery-founding mission to Europe (→ c.600).

Wessex, c.593. A power struggle occurs between Ceawlin, Cwichelm and Crida, West Saxon rulers in Wiltshire, Hampshire and the Thames valley areas (→ c.594).

Northern England, c.593. Athelfrith, Athelric's son, becomes king of Bernicia (northern Northumbria) and embarks on an expansion campaign (→ c.594).

English Midlands, c.594. Cearl emerges as king among the Mercians (→ c.597).

Rome, 597. The churchman and scholar Augustine is sent by Pope Gregory to evangelize the Anglo-Saxons.→

Wessex, c.597. Ceolwulf gains control of the West Saxon kingdom from the Thames valley to Hampshire (→ c.611).

Frontier lands face up to menace posed by fierce Mercians

English Midlands, c.585

The Britons have been obliged to confront a new threat following the rise of a powerful warlord on the borders of the British and Anglo-Saxon kingdoms. This bellicose adversary is Creoda, an Angle whose great-grandfather, Icel, was (he claims) the first of his family to settle in Britain and a descendant of the great war-god Woden.

Creoda and his people have pushed westwards from their original settlements near the Wash and upper Trent, along the extensive Trent valley river-system and into Leicestershire, Derbyshire, Staffordshire, and now Warwickshire. They raid extensively on the British borderlands, and hence they are called the "Mierce" [people of the Marches], or Mercians. These borderlands are the belt of high land that runs from the hills of Cannock Chase to the forest of Arden. On the western side of this belt stretch those forests that remain under Celtic control.

The Mercians are a branch of the Angles, who came to this country from the southern part of Denmark and some of the Danish islands. They are a fiercely independent people, as determined to stand up to pressure from other Germanic settlers in England as from the indigenous Celts (→ c.588).

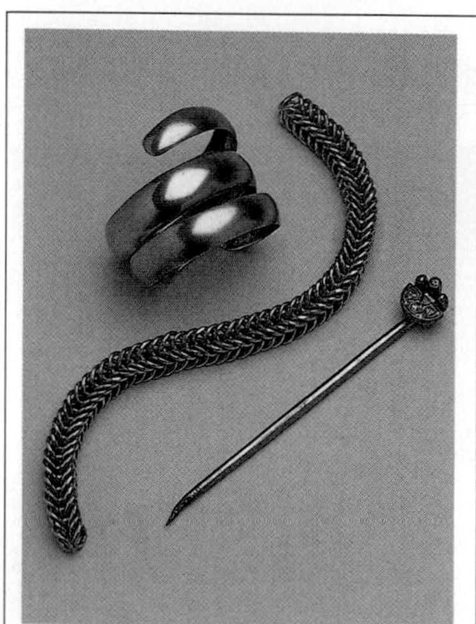

Northern ornamentation typical of the late sixth century: a silver bracelet, a chain and a pin with swirling Celtic-style decoration, found at Ley, in Grampian.

Christians land in Kent

Augustine: leader of papal mission.

Kent, 597

A mission from Pope Gregory has arrived in Kent intent on converting the Anglo-Saxons to Christianity [*see reports below*]. Headed by Augustine, an Italian monk, the 40 monks in the mission set out from Rome last year and landed on the isle of Thanet after a journey of several months. Athelbert, the king of Kent, told them to await his arrival on the island and then insisted on meeting them in the open air in case they practised sorcery on him indoors.

The missionaries came before the king bearing a silver cross and an icon of Christ painted on wood. The court listened to what they had to say. Although a pagan, Athelbert is no stranger to the church since his wife, Bertha, the daughter of a Frankish king, is a Christian [*see report on page 101*]. He is not yet convinced that his people should abandon their old religious wisdoms, but he has acknowledged the missionaries' sincerity and allowed them to preach in his kingdom.

The mission has established itself at Canterbury in an old Roman Christian church dedicated to St Martin and is already winning converts (→ 7/598).

Pope shows interest in 'angelic' Angles

Rome, 597

Gregory, a one-time Roman prefect turned monk, was elected pope in 590 for his intellectual as well as his spiritual gifts. He is the author of biblical commentaries, saints' lives and laws for the clergy. His *Dialogues* and *Pastoral Care* in particular are widely read. Gregory also has a missionary zeal to convert the tribes on the borders of the Roman Empire.

He is keenly interested in the Anglo-Saxons, having met some slave-boys in Rome calling themselves "Angli [Angles]". Gregory punned that with their fair complexions they were not Angles but "*angeli Dei* [angels of God]". On hearing that they were from Deira (southern Northumbria), he said that they would be saved "*de ira Dei* [from God's wrath]" (→ c.710).

Papal mission led by a fellow-Italian

Kent, 597

Pope Gregory looked to one of his protégés when he chose Augustine to be a missionary to the Anglo-Saxons. A fellow Italian, Augustine had been prior of St Andrew's on the Coelian Hill in Rome – Gregory's own monastery.

Augustine has been wise to head for a major centre such as Canterbury and deal directly with the king. Missions to other Germanic tribes have shown that, if the king converts, the people soon follow. In addition, Queen Bertha of Kent is a Christian and has a Frankish bishop, Liudhard, with her [*see report on page 101*]. No doubt Augustine is aware that in 497 the king of the Franks, Clovis, was converted under the influence of his Christian queen, Clotilda – Bertha's great-grandmother (→ 7/598).

Monk Colum Cille dies

Colum Cille in stained glass.

Iona, Strathclyde, 9 June 597
The great Irish churchman Colum Cille (Columba) died today at the age of 76, in the monastery which he established on this island of Iona. Descended from royal households on both sides of his family, Colum Cille was born in December 520, in Donegal. He attended a number of monastic schools and was later ordained into the priesthood. At some time around 546 he founded the monastery of Derry, and later one at Durrow, his most important foundation in Ireland.

In 561 Colum Cille was accused, for reasons which are obscure, of causing a bloody battle. He decided, or was obliged, to leave Ireland and, with 12 disciples, founded the monastery on Iona which has grown to become perhaps the most influential Christian centre in the British Isles, with offshoots across Scotland and Ireland.

Some time after 585 Colum Cille returned to Ireland, where he visited the monastic settlement at Clonmacnoise. Kind, scholarly and shrewd, he was quick to detect those of little worth. Although people have spoken with awe of his imposing presence, he was readily accessible to the poor.

Celts hold true to their Christian faith

British Isles, 597
Augustine, Pope Gregory's missionary to Britain, has not arrived in a pagan country. The Anglo-Saxons – who are comparative newcomers to the island – do not follow the Christian religion, but many among the native Celtic population have long been Christian. Some Britons were converted as long ago as the second and third centuries AD, and the Irish had their first bishop, Palladius, in 431.

Irish Christians in particular have preserved a superior Latin culture, while the British churches are in retreat from the pagan immigrants. Indeed, for decades now Irish monasteries have been true beacons of learning. Patricius (Patrick), a British missionary bishop in Ireland a century ago, used to complain that he was looked down on there for his mediocre education. Ireland has itself produced missionaries such as Colum Cille (Columba) – and Ninian before him – who worked among the native people, or Picts, of northern Britain, as well as among Irish settlers in the north-west, who are called "Scotti" [pirates] by the Romans (→c.600).

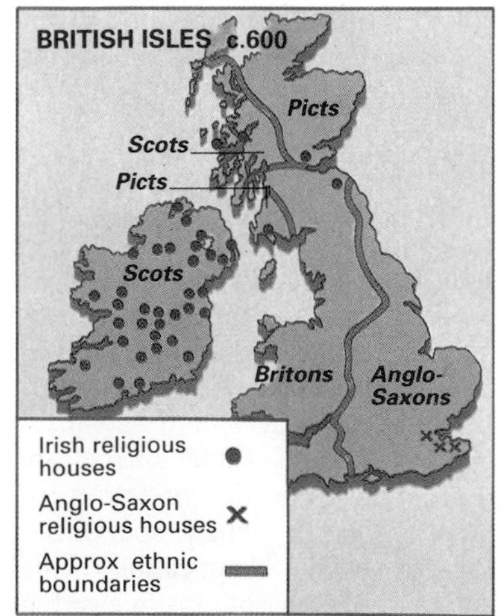

Bold and stylized animal forms adorn the creations of Anglo-Saxon jewellers

The "Strickland fibula", a silver and gold brooch with animal decoration.

Anglo-Saxon Kingdoms, c.590
Anglo-Saxon jewellers are winning wide repute for the skill and verve of their animal representation. The style is bold, usually depicting creatures whose features are so distorted as to become no more than pure pattern. Heads and limbs, teeth and tails intertwine in elaborate, flowing shapes that cover every available inch of space. The Anglo-Saxons probably learnt this style in past generations from artists in the south of Scandinavia, near their ancestral homelands. In Kent and East Anglia there is a vogue for rich, multicoloured jewellery. Flat-cut stones and glass are set on bases of gold foil in compartments made of gold or silver. Between the compartments are laid panels of filigree wire, which is also used to build up a border for the jewel.

Anglo-Saxons skilled at working metal have not hesitated to borrow from the repertoire of Celtic artists. Familiar Celtic styles such as boar-motifs are used on weapons, while intricate spiral patterns are carved onto the hanging bowls that adorn aristocratic halls (→c.930).

A copper wrist-clasp, from West Heslerton, in North Yorks.

A mount decorated with a long-beaked bird's head, from Kent.

598 - 608

Rome, July 598. Pope Gregory writes to the patriarch of Alexandria in Egypt to report that Augustine's mission to England has so far resulted in 10,000 converts to Christianity in Kent (→c.600).

Ireland, 598. Aed mac Ainmerech, the "high king" of the Ui Neill dynasty, is killed in battle at Dun Bolg by Brandub mac Echach, the king of Leinster (→600).

France, c.600. The Irish missionary Columbanus founds a monastery at Luxeuil in Burgundy (→610).

Ireland, c.600. Monks produce the *Cathach*, a psalter of Colum Cille (Columba), adorned with decorative illuminations (→c.650).

Kent, c.600. King Athelbert accepts Christianity and is baptized. Augustine returns from France, where he has been made archbishop of the Anglo-Saxons – France is the nearest place with the necessary bishops to consecrate him – and writes to the pope of his mission's success.→

Ireland, 602. A big earthquake is reported in the Mourne mountains in Ulster.

Co Down, 603. Comgall, who founded the abbey at Bangor in 558 and was Columbanus's teacher, dies aged 88 (→610).

Canterbury, Kent, 604. Augustine establishes a new see at Rochester and appoints Justus bishop. He also ordains, as bishop of London, Mellitus, who founds a church of St Paul and begins converting the East Saxons (→c.605).

Canterbury, c.605. Augustine dies and is buried beside the nearly completed church of St Peter and St Paul, into which his remains will eventually be transferred. Before his death he made Laurentius his successor (→610).

Canterbury, 605. Laurentius and his colleagues urge the British and Irish bishops to accept the Roman dating of Easter. They refuse (→4/640).

Strathclyde, 608. Aedan mac Gabrain, the king of the Dal Riata Scots, who have become the most powerful force in western Scotland, dies at over 70 years of age. He ruled for 34 years, and often fought against the neighbouring Picts, Angles and Britons (→638).

Ireland, 608. Brandub mac Echach, the king of Leinster, is killed (→625).

Kentish king christened

Remains of the church of St Pancras at Canterbury, used by King Athelbert.

Canterbury, Kent, c.600
Augustine has won a big prize in his mission to Britain: the conversion of the pagan King Athelbert of Kent. Letters have arrived from the pope in Rome sending his blessing to the king, together with gifts.

The king's conversion and baptism are likely to have a great influence on his subjects. Augustine, who was consecrated bishop of the Anglo-Saxons in 597, is now to become their "archbishop" with his seat at Canterbury. Pope Gregory has urged Athelbert to extend Christianity among his people and to suppress the worship of idols. His plan for the future organization of the church in Britain is to have 12 bishoprics under two archbishops with seats at Canterbury and York.

The king has granted more property in Canterbury to the missionaries but is unlikely to ban pagan worship. The pope has advised Augustine to purify existing pagan temples and convert them into churches, adapting their rites to Christian worship so that the people may be drawn gradually into the new faith; but the old idols must be destroyed.

The pope also discussed some of the questions raised by Augustine himself, such as whether menstruating women should be allowed into church, and what the punishment should be for church robbers (→601).

Irish hunger strikers have right to justice

A royal image from Co Westmeath: Irish kings are above the law.

Ireland, c.600
Irish law is being written down for the first time, and tracts are appearing that formalize the rights of each section of society. The Irish kings, traditionally judges and law-makers as well as overall rulers, are transferring the interpretation of these rights to a new specialized class of lawyers. Application of the law depends on status – measured in units of cattle. As far as a king is concerned, "his honour is too great to be claimed against"; this puts him above the law. But sometimes the king may be "fasted against" in an appeal for justice, and he would lose face if he failed to respond to a hunger strike (→602).

Easter row between Celtic church and Rome is intensified

Rome, 600
The row between Rome and the Celtic church over the dating of the Christian festival of Easter has taken a new twist. Frankish bishops have joined the dispute with their own ideas on the question, and the renowned and fiery Irish missionary Columbanus has appealed directly to Pope Gregory for a ruling on the matter – but has received no reply to his letter.

Columbanus is currently the most famous Irishman in Europe because of the tireless zeal with which, since leaving Ireland about ten years ago, he and his followers have founded flourishing monasteries – such as those at Fontaines and Anegray in France – and also for his stubborn insistence, in the face of the full weight of the papacy, on the Irish church's method of dating Easter.

Pope Gregory: ruling on Easter?

Reckoning the date of Easter – the festival to commemorate the resurrection of Jesus Christ from the dead following his crucifixion – is complex. The calculations involve reconciling the lunar and solar calendars. Basically, the Celtic method of calculation means that Easter can fall on any day of the week, while Rome – and the rest of Christendom – holds that the resurrection should always be celebrated on a Sunday (→4/640).

Britons massacred by 'Twister' forces

North Yorkshire, c.600

In a pitched battle fought near Catterick, Northumbrian forces under Athelfrith – known as "the Twister" to the Britons – have thwarted an attempt to overthrow their kingdom.

An army of more than 300 warriors had set out from Manau, a British kingdom around Edinburgh; unnerved by what they saw as the growing threat from Northumbria, the Gododdin – as they are called – had decided to take the fight to the enemy's camp. It proved to be a costly error. Barely a handful of men survived the encounter with Athelfrith's forces.

Northumbria, recently formed into one kingdom by Athelfrith from his own kingdom of Bernicia and that of Deira to the south, looks now to be dominant from the Humber to the Forth. His victory also puts him within raiding distance of the Dal Riata kingdom in western Scotland (→603).

Man who converted most of Wales dies

Dewi: a 20th-century statue.

Dyfed, c.600

Dewi, or David, a leading figure in the monastic movement that has swept through Ireland, Scotland and Wales over the past century, has died at Mynyw, or Menevia [St David's], the seat of his bishopric.

Born in Dyfed, the son of a British prince, Dewi was educated by Illtud, the head of the great monastic school at Llantwit Major in South Glamorgan. From there he travelled through the south-west of Britain, founding 12 monasteries, including those at Bath, Leominster and Glastonbury, where the monks follow strict rules prescribing an ascetic life of compulsory manual labour and regular prayer. Speech is forbidden unless absolutely necessary. The meagre diet consists of bread and vegetables.

Dewi – a notable orator – played a leading part in the Synod of Brevi, which determined the course of Welsh Christianity, and was chosen to be the primate of Wales in succession to Dyfrig, or Dubricius (→603).

Culprits must make amends under new law code for Kent

Kent, c.602

King Athelbert has issued the first law code to be written down in the Anglo-Saxon language. Its guiding principle is compensation to the injured party by the wrongdoer, according to the scale of both the crime and the status of the victim. Penalties are graded according to whether the sufferer is royal, noble, a free man, half-free or a slave.

Theft of church property must be repaid at 12 times its value, whereas the king himself is compensated only ninefold. Compensation for offences against women depends on their lords' status. "If anyone lies

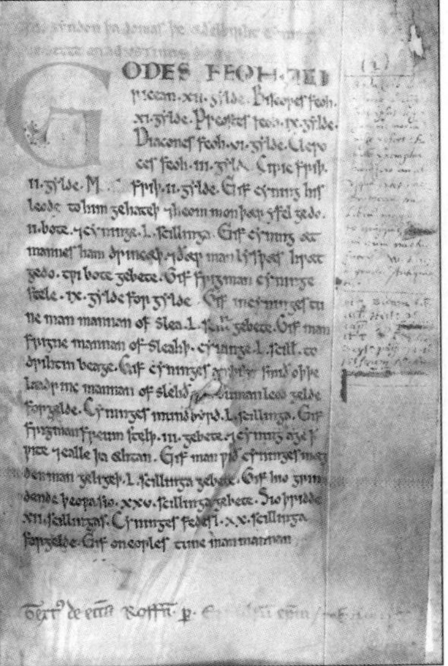

A page from Athelbert's law code.

with a maiden belonging to the king, he is to pay 50 shillings", but if she is merely the serving-woman of a noble the fine is 20 shillings. If the required compensation is not paid, the family of the injured party may exact vengeance.

In common with other immigrant Germanic tribes from the continent, the Anglo-Saxons who came to this country brought with them an elaborate legal system. They passed this on orally, and it is only because of church influence that laws are now being written down. The church is a new dimension to life in Kent, and churchmen – who belong to a written, not an oral, culture – want to set down the laws that touch them (→680).

Northumbrian king sees off new threat

Borders, 603

Only three years after his defeat of the British Gododdin at Catterick, King Athelfrith of Northumbria has thwarted another attempt to contain his expanding realm. His army was attacked at a place called Degsastan in Liddesdale by Aedan mac Gabrain, the king of the Dal Riata Scots in western Scotland and Athelfrith's most powerful enemy.

The Northumbrian victory owes a lot to confusion in the Celtic ranks. Aedan had forged an alliance between his own forces, neighbouring British tribes and Irish forces from Ulster. All were meant to launch a simultaneous attack on Athelfrith, but the British failed to appear, and Aedan and the Irish were overwhelmed by Athelfrith's counter-attack.

Aedan had hoped to block Northumbrian expansion into the Scottish lowlands. Now, however, he has lost his own son, as well as the majority of his army, and Athelfrith seems free to advance further north and west (→c.608).

Bishops reject the authority of Augustine

Gloucestershire, 603

A dispute has erupted over the varying practices of the Roman and old British churches. Two conferences held near the river Severn between Augustine of Canterbury and the leaders of the church in west Britain have ended in failure.

Seven British bishops and monks from Bangor met Augustine but refused to accept the authority that Pope Gregory has given him over them. British clergy have developed their own traditions, and they refuse to obey certain Roman practices. Nor will they join Augustine in preaching to the Anglo-Saxons, preferring instead the teachings of their own holy men such as Gildas, Dewi (David) and Illtud (→604).

A circular gold pendant, finely ornamented with a flowing abstract design and a milled border, made by an Anglo-Saxon metalworker.

609 - 626

Rome, 610. Bishop Mellitus of London visits Pope Boniface IV to report on the success of his Christian mission to the Anglo-Saxons (→c.619).

France, 610. Columbanus, the Irish missionary, is welcomed by King Clothar II of Neustria [north-western France] following his expulsion from the Frankish kingdom, and more recently from Burgundy, for his outspoken views on the dating of Easter (→612).

Wessex, c.611. Cynegils becomes king of the West Saxons (→614).

Italy, 612. Columbanus founds a monastery at Bobbio, in Lombardy, where his austere rule of penances, beatings and fasts is popular among new inmates (→23/11/615).

Strathclyde, c.612. Kentigern, a popular British monk known to many of his followers as "Mungo [dear friend]", has died, aged over 90. He founded several churches, including one at Glasgow (→616).

Bindon, Devon, 614. Over 2,000 Britons have been killed in battle by West Saxons under their leaders Cynegils and Cwichelm (→c.615).

Canterbury, 24 February 616. King Athelbert of Kent dies; he will be buried with Queen Bertha in a chapel of the church of St Peter and St Paul.

Scotland, 617. Following the death of King Athelfrith of Northumbria in battle against his rival Edwin last year, his three sons seek asylum with the Scots and Picts (→626).

Canterbury, c.619. Archbishop Laurentius dies and is succeeded by Mellitus, the bishop of London (→624).

Canterbury, 624. Archbishop Mellitus dies and is succeeded by Justus, the bishop of Rochester (→625).

Ulster, 625. Mongan, the son of the king of Ulster, dies in battle against the Britons of Strathclyde (→639).

Northumbria, 625. King Edwin of Northumbria marries Athelburga, the daughter of the late King Athelbert and Queen Bertha of Kent. She is accompanied north by Paulinus, one of the Roman missionaries, who was made bishop of York before leaving Kent (→11/4/627).

Mercia, c.626. Penda, a member of the Mercian royal family, the Iclingas, comes to prominence in Mercia (→628).

Monks are butchered in battle at Chester

Chester, c.615
Up to 1,200 monks were savagely butchered by King Athelfrith of Northumbria before his armies vanquished the Britons of the kingdom of Powys in a key battle here. The horrific bloodbath was ordered when, before the battle, Athelfrith noticed a host of British monks, said to have come from the nearby monastery of Bangor-is-Coed, assembled apart from the main body of British forces. He asked what they were doing and was told that they were praying for a British victory over the Northumbrians. The king, incensed, chose to regard them as participants and ordered the first attack to be made on them.

A certain Brocmail, the Briton charged with the protection of the monks, fled with his men before the attack, and only 50 monks escaped the ensuing slaughter. In the resounding defeat for the British which followed, the many dead included Solomon, the son of the king of Powys.

The strategic blow to the Britons is incalculable: Athelfrith has cut off the British kingdoms of Wales from their counterparts of Rheged [Cumbria] and Strathclyde to the north (→616).

Exiled heir beats and kills his persecutor

This gilt bronze-winged dragon probably adorned the shield of Radwald.

West Yorkshire, 616
Edwin, the rightful heir to Deira, the southern part of the kingdom of Northumbria, has won power over the whole kingdom by killing his persecutor, King Athelfrith, in battle on the river Idle. Edwin had spent years in exile before the warlike Athelfrith sent envoys to the latest ruler to give him asylum, the powerful Radwald of East Anglia, threatening hostilities and offering bribes for Edwin's execution. Radwald was tempted, but his queen talked him out of it. Instead he decided to help Edwin to power and raised a large army to march on Northumbria. It will now be the turn of Athelfrith's three sons to head into exile (→617).

Archbishop's scars turn king to Christ

Kent, 616
In a dramatic attempt to win over a new king to Christianity, an archbishop stripped to the waist to reveal what are said to be "terrible scars". Laurentius of Canterbury told King Edbald of Kent that the lashes were inflicted by St Peter in a vision because he was abandoning his mission. Edbald rejected Christianity on the death this year of his father, King Athelbert, and married his stepmother. But he was so moved by Archbishop Laurentius that he abandoned his wife and accepted baptism. Meanwhile, in Essex, the three sons of the late King Sabert have remained pagans. Many missionaries have fled to France in despair (→c.619).

Controversial Irish monk dies in Italy

Northern Italy, 23 November 615
The Irish missionary Columbanus has died at the monastery which he founded at Bobbio, in Lombardy. Held in awe by many because of his stern, fiery and somewhat severe nature, he was the most internationally famous Irishman of his time.

Born in Leinster, south-eastern Ireland, between 539 and 554, Columbanus founded monasteries in Ireland and Scotland and then moved on to north-eastern France and Switzerland. He introduced the Irish monastic system into France, insisting that his abbots should have total control and allowing no interference from the bishops. He was also responsible for introducing penitential practices into his monasteries, and severe punishments were inflicted on wrongdoers. He was famous for his outspokenness on the still unresolved question of dating Easter, which has divided the Irish and Roman churches for many years.

A Christian figure from Ireland.

King avenges bid to murder him by agent of rival ruler

Wessex, 626

King Edwin of Northumbria has scored a spectacular victory over the West Saxons. Five Wessex leaders have died, and their people have been forced to submit to his authority. The attack was launched after an assassination attempt on Edwin by an agent of the Wessex king Cwichelm, who sent to Edwin's palace a man named Eumer.

Eumer arrived on Easter day and asked to see Edwin, claiming to have an important message from Cwichelm. But when he saw Edwin, Eumer suddenly drew a poisoned dagger from beneath his cloak and lunged at him. Edwin would undoubtedly have died but for prompt action by one of his lords, Lilla, who threw himself in front of the king and took the blow.

Eumer's blow was so powerful, however, that the blade pierced Lilla's body and wounded Edwin. In the fight that followed, another lord, Forthhere, died before Eumer was finally overpowered and killed.

That same night Edwin's Kentish queen, Athelburga, gave birth to a daughter. King Edwin allowed Bishop Paulinus, one of the missionaries from Rome who came with the queen from Kent, to baptize the baby; he then promised to be baptized himself if the Christian god would give him victory over Cwichelm (→ 11/4/627).

Sheep row prompts massacre on Eigg

Highland, 17 April 617

A dispute over the grazing of sheep led to the horrific deaths today of the Irish missionary monk Donnan and nearly 150 of his followers on the small Scottish island of Eigg. They were burnt to death by Picts from the Isle of Skye who had come to exert the rights of the local Pictish queen over the sheep on Eigg. The massacre took place shortly after Donnan and his community had celebrated Sunday Mass in the church built by Donnan when he came to Eigg some years ago.

Lavish royal burial at Sutton Hoo

Sutton Hoo: a solid gold buckle.

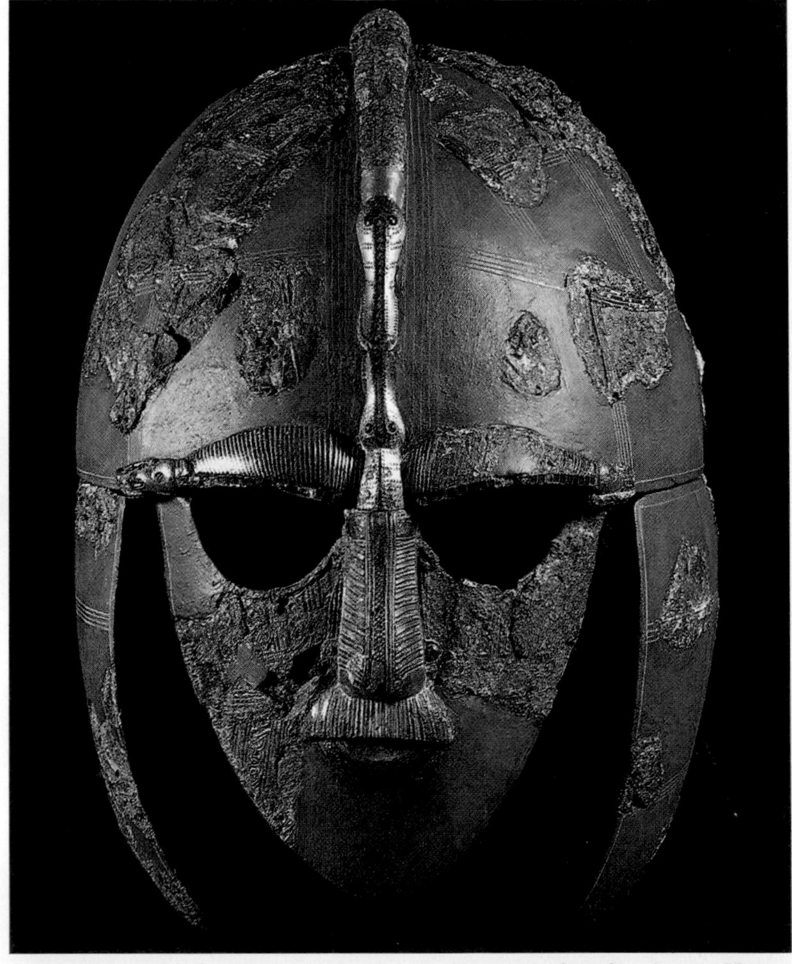

A warrior's iron helmet reconstructed from fragments found at Sutton Hoo.

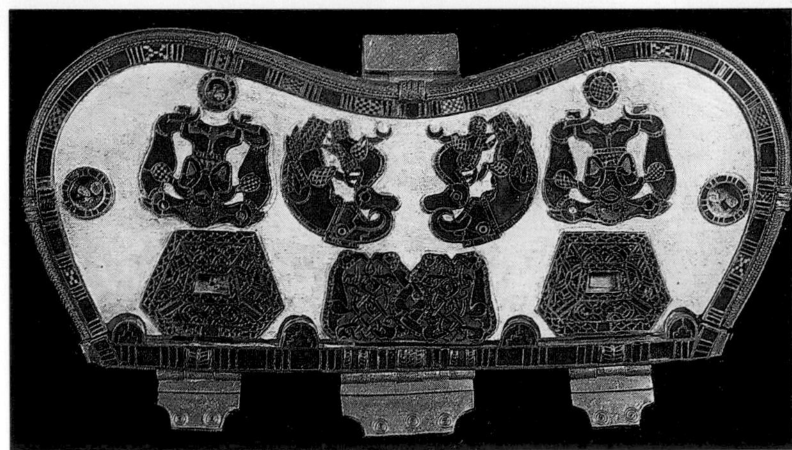

A purse lid of gold, decorated with garnets and enamels, from Sutton Hoo.

Sutton Hoo, Suffolk, c.625

King Radwald, once the strongest monarch in southern England, has been given a spectacular funeral with a display of pomp and ceremony that is bound to leave a lasting impression of the power and magnificence of his royal dynasty, the Wuffingas of East Anglia.

A ship 27 metres (30 yards) long was dragged to the royal burial ground on top of a high bluff overlooking the Deben estuary. In a chamber at the centre a magnificent array of wealth – an amazing collection of items, remarkable for their beauty and splendour – was laid out before the ship was buried under a huge earth barrow. Among the grave goods are a great silver dish from Byzantium and a bronze bowl from Alexandria. There are weapons from Sweden and coins from the domains of the Franks, coats of mail and personal ornaments of gold, drinking horns, dishes, armour – all the work of smiths of unrivalled skill.

To afford the king every comfort in the other world there are also domestic and luxury items of every sort. Into the ship went hanging bowls and cauldrons, maplewood bottles with silver mounts, a lyre to make music, shoulder clasps, belt buckles and ornaments of garnet-encrusted gold. The king's weapons of war go with him: a sword, a shield, a helmet of fine workmanship, spears, an axe-hammer and a gigantic four-sided whetstone, its ends carved with human faces surmounted by red-painted knobs encased in bronze.

Only a great king could have acquired such wealth. During his lifetime, Radwald was one of the few men to have exercised overlordship over all the Anglo-Saxon kingdoms south of the Humber. He played a major role in helping Edwin to defeat Athelfrith and gain power in Northumbria [*see report on page 106*]. Radwald was converted to Christianity at the court of King Athelbert of Kent, but relapsed following his return to East Anglia.

627 - 635

York, 11 April 627. King Edwin of Northumbria and many of his people are baptized by Bishop Paulinus on the eve of Easter.→

Canterbury, Kent, 10 November 627. Honorius becomes archbishop following the death of Justus (→628).

East Anglia, 627. Eorpwald, the new king, is persuaded by Edwin of Northumbria to abandon the pagan beliefs of his late father, King Radwald, and adopt Christianity (→c.628).

Cirencester, Glos, 628. King Penda of Mercia fights and defeats Cynegils, the king of Wessex, and his son Cwichelm to win territory (→630).

Lincoln, 628. Honorius, the new archbishop of Canterbury, is consecrated by Bishop Paulinus (→c.630).

East Anglia, c.628. King Eorpwald, a recent convert to Christianity, is murdered and the kingdom reverts to paganism (→c.634).

Anglesey, Gwynedd, 630. King Cadwallon of Gwynedd, who was besieged at Priestholm following the invasion of Gwynedd by King Edwin of Northumbria, is forced into exile in Ireland (→12/10/633).

Kent, c.633. Bishop Paulinus flees from Northumbria with Queen Athelburga, and becomes bishop of the vacant see of Rochester (→c.635).

Northumbria, 633/4. Cadwallon of Gwynedd eliminates King Edwin's successors, Osric of Deira (southern Northumbria), Edwin's cousin, and Eanfrith of Bernicia (northern Northumbria), the son of Athelfrith, his predecessor.

Northumbria, c.634. Oswald, the brother of King Eanfrith of Bernicia, returns from exile among the Scots and defeats Cadwallon to become king of all Northumbria.→

Dorchester, Oxfordshire, c.635. Birinus, who arrived from Italy last year to convert the Anglo-Saxons, baptizes the West Saxon king, Cynegils, and becomes bishop (→640).

Lyminge, Kent, 635. Queen Athelburga of Northumbria, King Edwin's widow, is appointed abbess of a monastery founded by her brother Edbald.

East Anglia, c.635. King Sigebert enters a monastery. His kinsman Egric succeeds him (→c.637).

Northumbrians embrace Christianity

A Victorian view of King Edwin of Northumbria being baptized at York; Queen Athelburga looks on.

York, 11 April 627

True to his word – that he would become a Christian if he defeated the West Saxons – King Edwin of Northumbria was today baptized at York by the missionary Bishop Paulinus. The ceremony took place in a wooden church hastily built for the purpose, with many of Edwin's subjects following their king in embracing the new faith.

The most dramatic conversion was that of Coifi, Edwin's pagan high priest, who declared that, although he might now be the gods' keenest devotee, many other people were luckier: "If these gods were good for anything they would help their worshippers!" Then he rode to nearby Goodmanham, hurled a spear into the pagan temple there, which he himself had dedicated, and ordered it to be burnt down.

Christianity has clearly struck a chord among Northumbrians. One lord put it eloquently to Edwin: "The life of man, O King, seems as a sparrow's flight through the hall when you are sitting at dinner in winter ... The sparrow flies in at one door and tarries for a moment in the light and heat of the hearth, and then flying out of the other vanishes into the wintry darkness whence it came. So tarries for a moment the life of man in our sight, but what is before it, what after it, we do not know. If this new teaching tells us anything certain of these things, then let us follow it."

Paulinus, a striking figure – tall, slightly stooped, with black hair and aquiline features – will continue his missionary work, initially south of the Humber (→628).

Edwin vastly extends the influence of the kingdom of Northumbria

York, 12 April 627

At 42, King Edwin of Northumbria is arguably the most powerful man in England. He has extended the boundaries of the kingdom inherited from his father, Aelle, so that he now rules directly or through client kings from Berwick to Cornwall.

Edwin holds sway over West, East and South Saxons as well as the Mercians and the Angles of central and eastern England. Only Kent has clung on to its independence – although it has an alliance with Edwin, who is married to King Edbald's sister, Athelburga. Edwin's climb to power has also won him many enemies. Cwichelm, the king of the West Saxons, tried to have Edwin assassinated last year. The attempt failed; the rivalry that prompted it remains (→630).

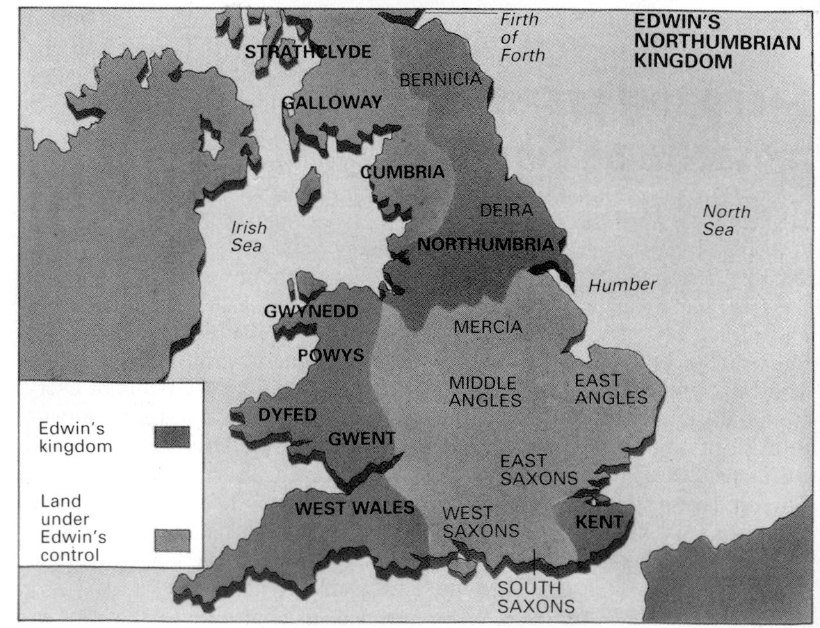

Missionary wins souls with royal blessing

A 20th-century view of Bishop Paulinus preaching to crowds at Yeavering.

Northumberland, c.630
Bishop Paulinus, one of the missionaries sent from Rome, has just completed a remarkable stint of 36 days spent instructing and baptizing the people of Bernicia (northern Northumbria) from his base around King Edwin's great timber hall at Yeavering, 20 miles from Bamburgh.

Since accompanying the king and his Kentish bride northwards in 626, Paulinus has done little else but preach the message of the gospel, and the locals have flocked to hear him and be baptized in the nearby river Glen. Now that his mission has royal backing from the recently converted Edwin, the bishop is making rapid progress.

York, in Deira (southern Northumbria), is Edwin's chief city, but Yeavering is one of a number of royal centres which he visits on tours of his lands. The purpose of these is to allow people to come before him, and to tap the resources of his sprawling kingdom – the biggest yet in Britain – in the form of food dues to maintain his court.

Edwin's power is such that he has even ordered posts with brass bowls hanging from them to be set up beside roadside springs for thirsty travellers: no one dares to steal or abuse these bowls, because he is so respected. His authority as acknowledged overlord stretches deep into the south, and as far west as Anglesey and Man (→c.633).

King and monks in conversion drive

East Anglia, 634
Following the conversion of King Sigebert, Christianity is taking hold in his kingdom of East Anglia. Two years ago Sigebert returned from exile in France, where he had been baptized, to spread the word of Christ. He was helped in his task by Felix, a cleric from Burgundy, who had been sent by Archbishop Honorius of Canterbury. Since establishing a bishopric at Dunwich, Felix has won many converts and is setting up a Christian school for young boys. More recently Fursa, a learned Irish ascetic and preacher famous for his visions, has arrived in East Anglia and founded a monastery in the Roman fort at Burgh Castle (→c.635).

Monastery to grace isle of Lindisfarne

Lindisfarne, Northumberland, 635
Oswald, the king of Northumbria, has granted his bishop, Aidan, an island off the north-eastern coast of England on which to found a monastery and establish his episcopal seat. Cut off twice a day by the tide, Lindisfarne is ideal for monastic seclusion and within convenient reach of the king's capital at Bamburgh. The monk Aidan left Iona in response to Oswald's request for a bishop and has won great popularity. A humble, holy man, he is indifferent to worldly status but strict with his brothers, who fast regularly and learn the scriptures. Celtic missionaries from far and wide are coming to spread the word in Northumbria (→31/8/651).

Strongest king toppled

South Yorkshire, 12 October 633
King Edwin of Northumbria has fallen in a fierce battle at Hatfield Chase with the rampaging forces of King Cadwallon of Gwynedd and his ally King Penda of Mercia. This unholy alliance of British Christian and Anglo-Saxon pagan rulers has toppled the strongest king in Britain. Cadwallon is unlikely to resist this opportunity to take revenge for Edwin's ventures into his territory. Penda, meanwhile, will be seeking as much plunder as possible in order to bolster his shaky hold on Mercia.

A gold cross from Wilton, Norfolk.

Northumbria also faces internal conflict. With Edwin, the unifier of the kingdom, dead, the rival royal houses of Deira (southern Northumbria) and Bernicia (northern Northumbria) seem likely to split the kingdom. The sons of the late King Athelfrith have been in exile among the Picts and Scots since Edwin toppled their father from the Northumbrian throne, and will be keen to reassert their hereditary rights in Bernicia. In Deira, where Edwin came from, his successor is in doubt. One son, Osfrith, died in the battle; another, Edfrith, surrendered to Penda.

Finally, further prospects for Paulinus's mission must be poor. Although Cadwallon is a Christian, the missionaries can expect little sympathy from him, for he aims to destroy Northumbria (→633/4).

Pious exile returns to end reign of terror

Northumberland, c.634
Oswald, a son of the late King Athelfrith of Northumbria, has returned from exile in Scotland to wipe out King Cadwallon of Gwynedd, who killed King Edwin last year. At a place called Denisesburna, near Hexham, Oswald has crushed a superior army which the British king had boasted was invincible. Oswald's victory ends the brutality which followed Edwin's death, when Cadwallon set about devastating Northumbria. Oswald was converted to Christianity in exile; some put the victory down to his prayers and a cross which he erected before the battle (→c.636).

Drinking horns elaborately decorated with animal motifs from Taplow, Bucks, which were made in the last few decades. They are probably for ceremonial use at the grand feasts where warriors toast their exploits.

636 - 651

Kent, c.636. Athelburga of Northumbria sends her son and grandson to the Frankish King Dagobert for safety from King Oswald of Northumbria, whose father King Edwin killed (→ 638).

East Anglia, c.637. Sigebert, the ex-king, is dragged from his monastery to fight the Mercians. He refuses to fight and is killed, as is his successor, Egric. Anna, the nephew of the late King Radwald, succeeds (→ c.641).

Din Eidyn [Edinburgh], 638. King Oswald of Northumbria captures the fortress of the British Gododdin tribe (→ 642).

Kent, 640. King Edbald dies. His son Eorconbert succeeds.→

Wessex, c.641. King Cynegils dies. His pagan son Cenwalh succeeds (→ 645).

France, c.641. Erchinoald, the chief minister of Neustria [north-western France] buys an Anglo-Saxon slave, Balthild, from pirates. He gives her to the young King Clovis II, who marries her (→ 657).

Northumbria, 643. King Oswy, the successor and brother of Oswald, marries Eanfled, the late Edwin's daughter (→ 644).

Rochester, Kent, 644. Bishop Paulinus, the missionary who came to Britain from Rome in 601, dies. He is succeeded by Ithanar, the first native Anglo-Saxon bishop (→ 650).

Northumbria, 644. Oswin, of King Edwin's line, succeeds to the throne of Deira (southern Northumbria), again dividing the kingdom (→ 20/8/651).

Wessex, 645. King Penda of Mercia drives King Cenwalh into exile in East Anglia after Cenwalh rejected his wife, Penda's sister, for another woman (→ 648).

Winchester, 648. Cenwalh, converted in exile, founds a minster after regaining his kingdom (→ 658).

Hartlepool, 649. Hild, a princess of Deira, founds a monastery (→ 657).

Wessex, 650. Agilbert, a Frank, succeeds Birinus as the West Saxons' bishop (→ 651).

Co Kildare, c.650. The first biography of Brigit, the holy woman whom many regard as a "saint", has been commissioned by the monastic community that she founded.

Lindisfarne, Northumberland, 651. Finan, also from Iona, succeeds Bishop Aidan (→ 660).

Scots lose Irish lands

Co Down, 639
Domnall mac Aedo, the Irish high king, has seen off a joint threat to his dominance of north-eastern Ireland. In an encounter at Mag Rath [Moira] he has killed the Ulaid leader Congal Cloe and deprived the king of the Dal Riata, Domhnall Brecc, of his dynasty's Irish lands. The Dal Riata must now concentrate on Scotland [*see below*].

Congal was fostered by Domnall mac Aedo at Tara, the seat of the high kings. One day, it is said, a bee stung him in the eye, damaging his sight and preventing him from becoming high king, since no one with a blemish may succeed. He bore a grudge against Domnall mac Aedo not only for this but also because the latter broke a promise to restore Ulaid lands in Ulster (→ 702).

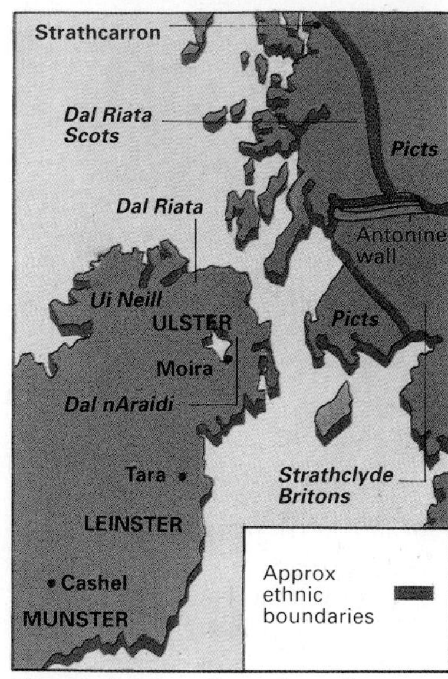

The Dal Riata Scots have been cut off from their homelands in Ireland.

Humiliating defeat puts the Britons on top

Central [Scotland], 642
The Dal Riata Scots, the powerful dynasty which originated in Ireland, have been humbled in battle by the Britons of Strathclyde. The encounter, at Strathcarron, deep inside Dal Riata territory, saw the death of the Scots' king, Domhnall Brecc, concluding a reign that coincided with a steep decline in Dal Riata power and culminated in four major military defeats. The Strathclyde Britons, under King Owen, are now the dominant power north of the Anglo-Saxon kingdoms, especially as the British Gododdin tribe, based around Edinburgh, is a spent force (→ 653).

Idols banned from Kent and fasting made obligatory

Kent, 640
The king of Kent, Eorconbert, has become the first Christian Anglo-Saxon ruler to impose a total ban on idol-worship and a compulsory fast during Lent, the period leading up to the Christian festival of Easter. He has ordered the destruction of idols throughout the realm, signalling the end of organized pagan worship in Kent. But superstition and magic will probably continue to thrive – the legacy of Anglo-Saxon settlers who nurtured their beliefs in a number of Germanic gods, many of the most popular of which were war gods. One of these, Woden, has been claimed as an ancestor by several Anglo-Saxon kings. He, like other deities, has a day (Wednesday) named after him.

Christian missionaries are trying to rid people of the belief that they can take personal possessions with them to the afterlife. (Women are cremated or buried with pins and spindles, the rich with jewellery, warriors with their weapons and craftsmen with their tools.) The missionaries are also attempting to replace pagan festivals as nearly as they can by Christian ones (→ 644).

Irish church is divided in two on the issue of dating Easter

A Celtic church in Kerry: the Irish church is split over the dating of Easter.

Armagh, April 640
Pope John IV has dispatched an outspoken letter to Tommene, the bishop of Armagh, insisting that the northern Irish church should step into line over the dating of Easter [*see page 99*]. A deputation from the Irish church is preparing to leave at once for Rome to plead its case with the papacy.

Following an earlier intervention by Pope Honorius, the southern Irish church agreed to abandon the Celtic way of working out when Easter should fall in favour of Roman custom, but the northern church has resolutely adhered to the Celtic method. The members of the northern deputation to Rome realize that they are unlikely to elicit a positive papal response but seem determined to stick to their beliefs. Pope John's letter is not expected to have much effect (→ 664).

The 'bright blade' of Oswald cut down

Welsh Marches, 642
King Oswald of Northumbria has been defeated and killed in battle by his rival King Penda of Mercia at Maserfeld [possibly Oswestry]. The king, who was 38 and nicknamed "Bright Blade", was beheaded, and his head and forearms were set up on a stake as trophies of Penda's triumph. Survivors of the battle said that the king was heard to pray for the souls of his men as the enemy closed in for the kill. Oswald was as powerful as he was devout, a king who reigned for less than a decade but restored Northumbrian overlordship in large areas of Britain. He worked closely with Bishop Aidan of Lindisfarne to boost the spread of Christianity. The unity of Northumbria may again be vulnerable – as it proved to be after the death of King Edwin in 633.

Eowa, the Mercian warleader's brother, also died in the battle, leaving Penda firmly in control of the territory and free to indulge his expansionist plans (→643).

Oswald: a 12th-century view.

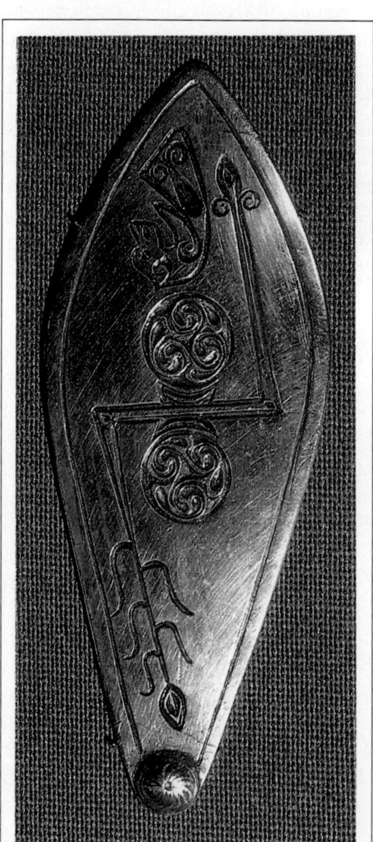
A fine silver plaque fashioned by a Pictish craftsman in northern Britain. The Picts have been busy resisting encroachments on their territory by the Dal Riata Scots.

Northumbrian ruler is fatally betrayed

North Yorkshire, 20 August 651
The cold-blooded assassination at Gilling of King Oswin of Deira (southern Northumbria) by his enemy, King Oswy of Bernicia (northern Northumbria), has brought their rivalry to an abrupt end.

The dispute between the two men began when King Oswald of Northumbria was killed in 642 by King Penda of Mercia, and the kingdom was split. Bernicia passed to Oswy, Oswald's brother, and Oswin assumed control of Deira. Recently, battle had seemed ever more likely. Hoping to reunite the kingdom, Oswy invaded Deira, and Oswin, realizing that his forces were not up to the task, fled to a friend, who subsequently betrayed him. To widespread disgust, Oswy ordered Oswin's execution.

At a recent dinner attended by Oswin, Bishop Aidan of Lindisfarne confided to his chaplain that he feared for the king, for he had never known such a humble ruler: his anxiety was justified. Oswin was courteous and popular, and Oswy may rue his death (→653).

Acclaimed bishop of Lindisfarne, who gave royal gifts to the poor, dies near Bamburgh

Northumberland, 31 August 651
Aidan, the Irish-born bishop of Lindisfarne, died today at a royal residence near Bamburgh. His body will be taken back to the monastic community on Lindisfarne, where he first set up his mission when he was sent from Iona 17 years ago.

Although no stranger to high society, the peace-loving Aidan always retained the common touch. His church at Lindisfarne is only a rough wooden building, and he was always concerned about poverty. He gave away the gifts of kings and nobles, including a fine horse from King Oswin, to the needy people whom he met on his travels.

He had no estates of his own, except for a few fields on Lindisfarne, and depended on royal help in his work of conversion, using royal centres such as Bamburgh as bases for his preaching tours. Rank did not impress him, and he never thought twice about rebuking the mighty. As a member of the Celtic church Aidan celebrated Easter at a different time from Rome, but he won the goodwill of prominent churchmen such as Archbishop Honorius of Canterbury (→660).

Lindisfarne church: reconstruction.

Missions end for émigré envoys of Christ

England, 651
Bishop Aidan [*see report above*] was the fourth great foreign missionary to be lost to the Anglo-Saxon church in recent times. Another great Irish cleric, Fursey, died last year in France. An ascetic monk hailing from an aristocratic family, he decided to win souls for Christ abroad. Fursey was active in East Anglia and established a monastery in an old Roman fort, Burgh Castle, in the 630s.

Gall, a disciple of Columbanus, died last year in Switzerland. He too belonged to the band of talented and zealous Irishmen who have forsaken the wealth and security of their native church to lead the monastic life abroad. The Irish are winning a wide reputation as particularly talented religious leaders.

The Italian missionary and first bishop of York, Paulinus, died only seven years ago. Paulinus came from Rome in 601 on the orders of Pope Gregory to help Augustine's mission in Kent. He later moved to Northumbria, where he converted King Edwin. After Edwin was killed Paulinus returned south to become bishop of Rochester, where he remained until his own death. His fellow-Italian Birinus, the first bishop of Wessex, also came to England on a papal mission, in 634. He converted King Cynegils and made his see at Dorchester in Oxfordshire. Birinus died three years ago (→30/9/653).

St Matthew the Evangelist.

652 - 663

Canterbury, Kent, 30 Sept 653. Honorius, the last of Augustine's companions to be archbishop, dies (→ 26/3/655).

Northumbria, 653. Peada, the son of King Penda of Mercia, is baptized while on a visit to win the hand of King Oswy's daughter Alhfled (→ 654).

France, 653. The Northumbrian nobles Benedict Biscop and Wilfrid set off on a pilgrimage to Rome (→ c.660).

Northumbria, c.653. King Oswy, driven north by Penda, fails to buy off the Mercian king (→ c.654).

Northumbria, 654. Penda of Mercia launches a fresh campaign to oust Oswy from Northumbria (→ 15/11/655).

East Anglia, c.654. King Anna is killed in battle by Penda of Mercia.

Canterbury, 26 March 655. Deusdedit, an Anglo-Saxon, is consecrated as the sixth archbishop (→ 14/7/664).

Mercia, Easter 656. King Oswy of Northumbria takes control of Mercia following King Peada's murder (possibly by his wife, Alhfled, Oswy's daughter) (→ c.658).

Grampian, 657. King Talorgen of the Picts dies after a four-year reign (→ 671).

France, 657. King Clovis II dies. His widow, Queen Balthild, an Anglo-Saxon ex-slave, becomes regent of Neustria [north-western France] (→ 665).

Mercia, c.658. Wulfhere, a son of Penda, who has been kept in hiding since his father's death, expels King Oswy's men and is proclaimed king (→ 661).

Somerset, 658. King Cenwalh of Wessex defeats the Britons, expanding his kingdom west to the river Parret (→ 682).

Northumberland, 660. Bishop Finan of Lindisfarne dies; Colman succeeds him (→ 664).

Ripon, North Yorkshire, c.660. Alchfrith, King Oswy's son, gives the monastery to Wilfrid, who became a monk at Lyons while living in France after his visit to Rome (→ 664).

Essex, c.660. The pious King Sigebert of the East Saxons is killed by two kinsmen because he forgave his enemies; Swithhelm succeeds him (→ 665).

Southern England, 661. King Wulfhere of Mercia takes the Isle of Wight and some of the West Saxons' land (→ 15/2/670).

East Saxon ruler is converted to Christ

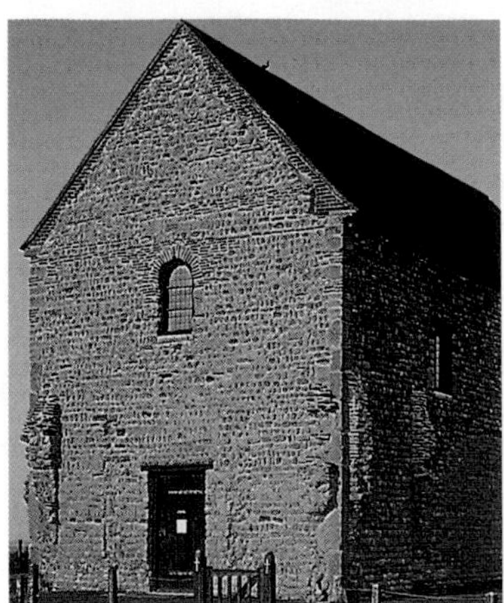

The church of St Peter on the Wall, at Bradwell-on-Sea, built by Cedd.

Essex, c.654

The East Saxon king, Sigebert, has been converted to Christianity and baptized. He has also asked King Oswy of Northumbria for missionaries to spread the Christian gospel, the "good news", in his kingdom.

The merits of Christianity were explained to Sigebert in the course of his many visits to Oswy, who diverted the missionary Cedd to Essex. Cedd, originally from Northumbria, had been working among the Middle Angles, whose land is now a sub-kingdom of Mercia [*see map on page 108*].

Recently made bishop of the East Saxons, Cedd has established monasteries at Tilbury and Bradwell-on-Sea and won many converts. Other Northumbrians are doing the same in Middle Anglia, whose pagan overlord, King Penda, does not object – as long as the converts are sincere (→ c.660).

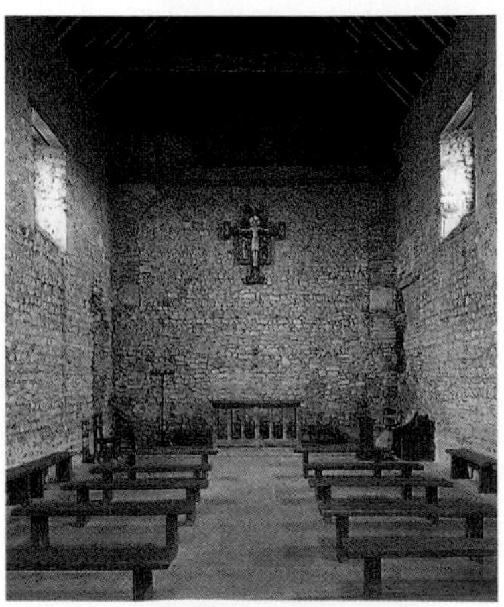

Interior of St Peter on the Wall.

Northern Picts choose Anglo-Saxon prince

A mounted warrior and his helpless opponent: detail from a helmet plaque.

Grampian, 653

In a surprising development, the nephew of King Oswy of Northumbria has emerged as king of the Picts in the far north of Britain [*see map on page 100*]. The new king, Talorgen, is the son of Eanfrith, who fled with his brothers, Oswy and Oswald, after their father, King Athelfrith of Northumbria, had been overthrown and killed by his rival Edwin in 616.

Following their father's downfall, Oswy, the present king, and Oswald, his predecessor, took refuge among the Scots. Eanfrith lived with the Picts, and it was during this period that a Pictish princess gave birth to their son, Talorgen. In 633 Eanfrith returned south to claim his throne, but he met his death a year later.

Although little is known about the Picts [*see report on page 117*], it is believed that, when the succession to their kingdom is in doubt, they tend to choose a king from the female rather than the male royal line. The accession of Talorgen is clearly also due to his uncle's influence. Facing a constant threat from King Penda of Mercia to the south, Oswy is keen to keep the Picts to the north on his side (→ 657).

A brooch of the sixth or seventh century from Kingston Down, in Kent, of enamel inlaid with garnet, glass, white shell and gold filigree panels. Only the wealthiest families can afford such ostentatious jewellery.

Hundreds drown as Oswy brings down mighty pagan foe

West Yorkshire, 15 November 655
King Oswy of Northumbria has defeated and killed the fearsome King Penda of Mercia in a battle near Leeds. Many of Penda's men drowned in the swollen river called the Winwed as they fled.

Although the pagan Penda went into battle at the head of a much superior force to that of the Christian Oswy, he and almost all of the 30 royal leaders with him, many of them minor kings who recognized Penda's overlordship, are dead.

In expanding his territory in the English Midlands, Penda killed three kings of East Anglia, bringing the minor kingdoms between East Anglia and Mercia under his control as Middle Anglia [*see map on page 108*]. He also drove out successive rulers of Wessex, securing the lower Severn area, and allied with the British kings of Gwynedd and Powys to gain control of minor kingdoms to the west around Hereford and Worcester. Penda eventually acquired the power to take on his arch-enemy, Northumbria, in a continuing border war: he killed two of its kings, Edwin and Oswald, with British help. His death gives Oswy the chance to go on the offensive (→ Easter 656).

Chief champion of 'penitentials' dies

Iona, Strathclyde, 662
The death of the abbot of Iona removes the most prominent exponent of the "penitential" system in Irish monasteries. This system has been devised by concerned Christians in an effort to combat the immorality and wickedness which they see all around them.

"Penitentials" grew out of the rigorous asceticism for which Celtic Christianity is famous. Every imaginable sin is written down, and the guilty face a range of rigorous punishments and penances for wrongdoing. Unfortunately, some sinners believe that their crimes will be forgiven if they carry out a suitable penance, but this is not the official church view (→ c.680).

Abbess establishes monastery at Whitby

Cleveland, 657
Hild, the abbess of the monastery at Hartlepool, has been appointed to run a new community on a clifftop estate at Whitby founded by her kinsman King Oswy of Northumbria. It will be a double monastery of both men and women – a concept borrowed from France, where male communities become attached to female monasteries in order to perform activities that are closed to women, such as administering the sacraments and manual labour.

A double monastery is usually run by an abbess, a position increasingly seen as fitting for Anglo-Saxon royal or noble women [*see report below*], who until recently normally went to France. Hild herself, from the Deiran (southern Northumbrian) royal house, set off to do the same, but Bishop Aidan persuaded her to return. She lived a monastic life by the Wear before running Hartlepool, founded about a decade ago by Northumbria's first nun, Heru. At Whitby, as at Hartlepool, Hild intends to forbid the ownership of private property.

Many women carry keys attached to their girdles by means of a ring.

Her royal birth and reputation for holiness and wisdom have already drawn the humble and the powerful to seek her guidance. At a time when literary and artistic activity is beginning to flourish in monasteries, the Whitby foundation is in a good position to attract rich endowments (→ c.670).

Men and women are equal before the law

Anglo-Saxon women are permitted many advantages under the law.

England, c.660
In common with many other Germanic peoples, the Anglo-Saxons – at least as far as the upper classes are concerned – prefer to treat men and women as equals. Noblemen's wives are by no means limited to a life of domesticity. They can hold land in their own right and dispose of it as they, rather than their husbands, desire; they can defend their rights in the courts; and they have the power to release their own slaves.

Marriage and divorce are both areas where English women enjoy many rights. When a man marries, he makes a *wed* [pledge] and pays the woman a "bride-price", or sum of money, that she is allowed to keep. She also keeps the "morning-gift", her husband's present to her on the day following the wedding. Law codes vary, but generally if a wife then leaves her husband, taking her children, she is entitled to half the household goods. And a widow is allowed to make her own decision about whether or not to embark on a second marriage.

Inheritance – a crucial aspect of the law – also affords women fair treatment. Should her husband die, a woman is allowed to keep usually a third, sometimes half, of his property. If there are children, a widow may be able to keep everything, as long as she does not remarry.

Schooling, too, is open to the girls of noble families. Like boys, they can learn to read and write, going on, if they wish, to a career in the church as nuns or abbesses.

The most powerful kings to have led the Anglo-Saxons

Hengest and **Horsa**: led Jutes in Kent against the Britons, 449.

Aelle: king of Sussex c.447-491.

Cerdic: king of Wessex 495-534.

Ida: king of Bernicia (northern Northumbria) 547-c.560.

Aelle: king of Deira (southern Northumbria), died c.588.

Ceawlin: king of Wessex c.560-593.

Athelfrith: king of Northumbria 593-616. United Deira and Bernicia.

Athelbert: king of Kent 560-616. Accepted Augustine's Christian mission and himself took the new religion.

Radwald: king of East Anglia, died c.627. Killed Athelfrith. Converted to Christianity but later relapsed.

Edwin: king of Northumbria 616-633. Accepted Paulinus's mission and became a Christian.

Penda: king of Mercia 633-655. Fought against Edwin, 633.

Oswald: king of Northumbria 634-642. Killed by Penda, 642.

Oswy: king of Northumbria 642- . Founded Whitby and other monasteries.

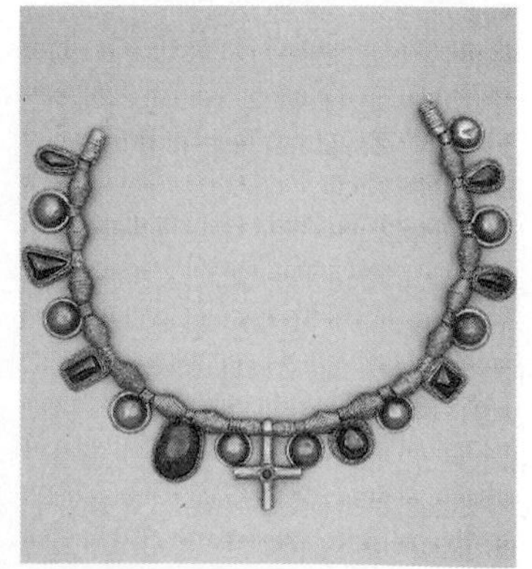

A necklace worn by a Christian.

664 - 678

Canterbury, 14 July 664. Archbishop Deusdedit and King Eorconbert of Kent die. Egbert succeeds the king, but the see of Canterbury remains vacant (→ 669).

North Yorkshire, 664. At a synod held at Whitby, Celtic churchmen have agreed to follow the Roman method of dating Easter, thus resolving a bitter dispute between the two traditions.→

York, 664. Wilfrid, recently ordained priest, is made bishop of the see of Northumbria, which is now to be based at York. As there is at present no archbishop of Canterbury, he goes to France to be consecrated (→ c.665).

York, c.665. King Oswy of Northumbria, impatient at Wilfrid's absence in France, consecrates Chad, the abbot of Lastingham and the late Bishop Cedd's brother, bishop of York (→ 669).

Co Mayo, c.668. Colman, the ex-bishop of Lindisfarne, founds a monastery on the isle of Inishboffin (→ 750).

Canterbury, Kent, 669. The new archbishop, Theodore of Tarsus, arrives in Britain after being detained in Paris on suspicion of spying, and replaces Chad as bishop of York with Wilfrid. Chad is appointed bishop of Mercia, Middle Anglia and Lindsey, based at Lichfield (→ 672).

Ireland, 670. A severe winter follows a great famine (→ c.795).

Northumbria, 15 February 670. Oswy dies; his son Egfrith succeeds him (→ 674).

Scotland, 671. Drest, the king of the Picts and a nephew of the late King Oswy of Northumbria, is exiled (→ 672).

Lichfield, Staffordshire, 672. Bishop Chad dies.

Tyne and Wear, 673. King Egfrith gives the nobleman Benedict Biscop an estate at the mouth of the Wear for a new monastery (→ 23/4/685).

Mercia, 674. King Wulfhere's coalition against Northumbria is defeated (→ c.679).

Northumberland, 675. Wilfrid founds a monastery at Hexham on land given by Egfrith's ex-queen, Athelthryth (→ 678).

Frisia [Netherlands], 678. En route to appeal to the pope following a quarrel with Egfrith and his deposition as bishop of York, Wilfrid begins preaching to pagans (→ 680).

Celtic church loses debate at Whitby

North Yorkshire, 664
The Celtic church has lost the long-running row with Rome over the dating of Easter [*see report on page 99*]. A synod held at Whitby and presided over by King Oswy of Northumbria has come down firmly on the side of the Roman calculation for the feast which lies at the heart of the Christian faith. In recent years the Easter question has split not only leading churchmen but also the Northumbria court, where both the Roman and Celtic churches have been influential.

Key supporters of the Roman view at Whitby were Agilbert, the former bishop of the West Saxons, and a Northumbrian named Wilfrid whom Agilbert had just ordained priest at Ripon. On the Celtic side stood the powerful figure of Bishop Colman of Lindisfarne, who like his predecessors Aidan and Finan is an Irishman trained at Colum Cille's (Columba's) foundation on Iona. Next to him were two prominent pro-Celtic Northumbrians, Abbess Hild and Bishop Cedd of the East Saxons, brought up to follow the teachings of Aidan.

Amid much debate Wilfrid argued that his Easter was that of St Peter the apostle, the holder of the keys to heaven. After checking with Colman that St Peter's authority was genuine and above Colum Cille's, Oswy opted for the Roman Easter: "Otherwise, when I come to the gates of heaven, there may be no one to open them" (→ 690).

Detail from a headstone showing Christ surrounded by symbols of the four evangelists, who wrote the biblical Gospels: (from left) Mark, represented as a lion; Matthew, as a winged man; John, as an eagle; Luke, as a bull.

Bishop of Lindisfarne resigns in disgust

Northumberland, 664
Bishop Colman has resigned as bishop of Lindisfarne in a move widely expected after the Synod of Whitby earlier this year. The synod decided to adopt the Roman way of determining when Easter should fall, rather than continuing with the Irish way, of which Colman was the chief proponent.

Colman has returned to his native Ireland with fellow dissenters. King Oswy of Northumbria, who chaired the synod and took the final decision in favour of the Roman Easter, has the highest regard for his chief churchman and was sorry to see him go. Before Colman left Oswy agreed to his choice of Eata, the abbot of Melrose in Bernicia (northern Northumbria), to succeed Colman as head of the monastic community on the isle of Lindisfarne. Eata's colleague Cuthbert was chosen to be prior.

Colman's successor as Northumbria's bishop was Tuda, who died shortly after his appointment. The new bishop – who will be based at York – will now be the energetic Wilfrid, who has headed a monastery at Ripon since 660 (→ c.668).

A symbolic eagle from the "Book of Durrow", an Irish Gospel-book.

A stone marked with the cross and a pilgrim's name at Kilcoman, in Co Kerry.

Heathen revival is sparked by plague

Essex, 665
Jaruman, the bishop of the Mercians, is making for home after suppressing a revival of paganism among the East Saxons. The pagan upsurge was sparked by the current devastating epidemic of plague, which has claimed many leading churchmen in the last couple of years, including Cedd, the bishop of the East Saxons.

Mercia's King Wulfhere, the overlord of Essex, decided to send his own bishop, Jaruman, to bring all of Essex back to the faith. The mission has proved a success, but the plague, which has also devastated many monasteries, continues.

The crisis is such that the priest Wilfrid – who was chosen to replace Tuda, another plague victim, as bishop of Northumbria – has travelled to France for consecration. He does not want the ceremony performed by Celtic bishops, who do not conform to Roman ways, but there are no orthodox Roman bishops in England. The last one, Archbishop Deusdedit of Canterbury, died last year (→669).

Picts crushed in battle

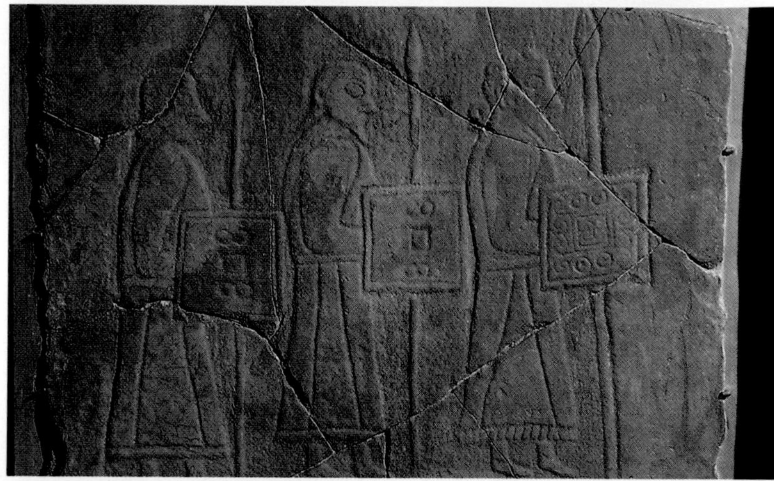

Ready for battle: three warriors on a Pictish stone from Birsay, in Orkney.

Scotland, 672
King Egfrith of Northumbria has crushed the Picts in a bloody battle on Pictish territory. The king led his warriors north after a faction of the Picts ousted his cousin, King Drest, because it resented his status as a client of the Northumbrians.

Drest, like his brother and predecessor Talorgen, was a nephew of the late King Oswy, under whom Northumbria exerted considerable influence over internal Pictish affairs for some 20 years. But Oswy's death two years ago encouraged the Picts to expel Drest and replace him with Bridei, the younger brother of the late King Owen of the Strathclyde Britons [*see map on page 117*]. In fear of expansionist aims on the part of the new Pictish king, Egfrith, Oswy's son and successor, decided to re-establish Northumbrian power by force (→682).

Archbishop asserts Canterbury's strong influence on church

Hertford, September 672
Anglo-Saxon bishops have come together for the first time under the direction of Canterbury. The archbishop, Theodore of Tarsus, has called a synod here to promote unity and agree on fixed rules for church administration. Only four bishops have appeared in person, however. Among the absentees was Wilfrid of York, who opposes any division of his huge diocese which would reduce his power and status.

Theodore wants to appoint many new bishops, and give them smaller sees which they can cover adequately. The synod has avoided a commitment on this issue, but accepted Theodore's proposals on church discipline. Among the latter are a number of strictures on Christian marriage, including bans on incest and on the abandonment of wives for any cause except adultery. But Theodore is still determined to set up new sees and to halt the Anglo-Saxon tendency for bishoprics to be kingdom-sized (→c.675).

Slave who became French queen is ousted

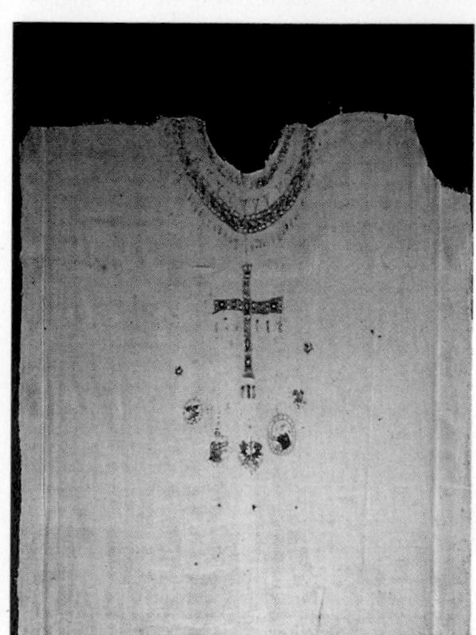

One of Queen Balthild's robes.

France, 665
Balthild – the Anglo-Saxon slave who became a formidable Frankish queen – has been forced into retirement in a palace coup engineered by her chief minister. She will now spend the rest of her days at her favourite monastery of Chelles.

Sharing a fate suffered by more than a few of her compatriots, Balthild was captured by pirates in 641. She was taken across the Channel from England and sold as a slave to Erchinoald, the chief minister of Neustria [the Frankish kingdom in north-western France]. Erchinoald married her off to the feeble boy king Clovis II.

When Clovis died eight years ago, aged only 23 – soon followed by Erchinoald himself – Balthild took power as regent in the name of her young son, Chlothar III. She proved a highly intelligent, and ruthless, ruler, in spite of concerted opposition from nobles and bishops, some of whom she executed.

Now her adversaries have succeeded in bringing off a campaign to remove her. There are, however, signs that the pious Balthild may welcome the chance to devote herself to the religious life at Chelles, one of the many monasteries and churches of which she was a great benefactor (→c.680).

One-time cowherd is now celebrated poet

North Yorkshire, c.670
A cowherd turned poet has become one of the most celebrated monks at Whitby Abbey. Once ashamed of his inability to sing, Caedmon is said to have dreamt that he was ordered to sing the story of the Creation. When he awoke, he told the dream to Abbess Hild. He then demonstrated his new-found poetic gift to the monks, who regarded him as divinely inspired. He has since been busy composing poems on biblical themes. They are the first Christian poems in the Anglo-Saxon language (→17/11/680).

Brixworth church, in Northamptonshire, built by a community of monks from Peterborough, partly with material from old Roman buildings.

679 - 685

River Trent, c.679. King Athelred of Mercia, who succeeded his brother Wulfhere in 675, defeats King Egfrith of Northumbria. Archbishop Theodore draws up a long-term peace treaty (→ 697).

Whitby, North Yorkshire, 17 November 680. Abbess Hild dies; she is succeeded as abbess of Whitby by King Oswy's daughter, Alffled.

Kent, c.680. Hlothere and Edric, the kings of Kent, issue a law code (→ c.690).

Northumbria, 680. Wilfrid returns from Rome with the pope's judgement in his favour but is imprisoned by King Egfrith (→ 681).

France, c.680. Balthild, the Anglo-Saxon slave who became queen of Neustria [north-western France], dies at her monastery at Chelles.

Mercia, c.680. Archbishop Theodore divides the Mercian see into three bishoprics, based at Leicester, Hereford and Worcester (→ 681).

Northumbria, 681. Theodore consecrates two new bishops, at Hexham and Abercorn, making five sees of Wilfrid's diocese (→ 26/3/685).

Dunbar, Lothian, 681. Egfrith releases Wilfrid from nine months' imprisonment when his wife, Queen Eormenburg, falls seriously ill (→ 682).

Orkney, 682. King Bridei of the Picts subdues the islands (→ 20/5/685).

Ireland, 684. King Egfrith of Northumbria sends troops to raid Ireland, where his exiled brother and British refugees have sought asylum. His men ravage Meath (→ 685).

Kent, 6 February 685. King Hlothere dies of wounds received in battle with his nephew King Edric, who now takes over the whole of the kingdom (→ 686).

York, 26 March 685. Theodore consecrates Prior Cuthbert, who has been living as a hermit on the Farne Islands, as bishop of Lindisfarne. Cuthbert – reluctantly – assents (→ 20/3/687).

Northumbria, 685. Following the death of King Egfrith, Aldfrith, his bastard half-brother, returns from exile on Iona to rule (→ 686).

Sussex, c.685. The exiled West Saxon Cadwalla invades, killing King Athelwealh. He then takes over Wessex (→ 686).

Abbess, twice forced to wed, dies at Ely

Ely, Cambridgeshire, 679
Getting out of unhappy marriages has never been easy for women, but the recent growth in the number of nunneries offers at least one escape route, because the desire to become a nun is an acceptable ground for divorce. This certainly helped the abbess of Ely, Athelthryth, who died this year of a tumour under her jaw. She founded Ely Abbey seven years ago after her husband Egfrith had agreed to divorce her on the grounds of the non-consummation of their marriage and her devotion to the religious life.

The daughter of King Anna of East Anglia, she was forced by her parents to marry a princeling in 652; but she kept her virginity, and when he died in 655 she withdrew to the Isle of Ely, which he had given her. Then, in 660, her family pushed her into marrying Egfrith, the 15-year-old son of King Oswy of Northumbria, but for 12 years she shunned sexual contact and stuck to her devotions (→ 695).

'Punishment' blaze wrecks monastery

Borders, c.680
The monastery of Coldingham is in ruins, destroyed by a great fire. Some would ascribe this to carelessness, but others believe that the fire is God's punishment. The community, they say, was simply too wicked.

Not that it was ignorant of the danger. It is rumoured that an Irish member of the community, one Adamnan, who lived a life of great austerity, eating but twice a week and often spending whole nights in prayer, was visited during a vigil by a mysterious stranger.

The stranger congratulated him on his piety, but warned that the rest of the community, which included both monks and nuns, was asleep, or awake only to sin. The members' cells, meant for prayer, were used for eating, drinking and worse. Their punishment, promised the stranger, would come in the form of a devastating fire.

When the abbess, Abbe, heard Adamnan's story, she was deeply shocked and ordered all members of the community to do penance. This they did, but on her recent death they allegedly relapsed into their sinful ways. The fire, it is said, was their promised retribution.

A surviving arch at Coldingham.

Irish lawyers seek to define bishops' role

Munster, 680
An important law tract has been written by Aimirgein mac Amalgado, a poet from Munster. It both adds to the continuing codification of Irish written law and increases the power and influence of a small band of scholar-clerics who are trying to define church power, especially that of the bishops.

The code is mainly concerned with the church and its government by the bishops. It also says that monks must live either in monastic communities which impose rules, especially rules of poverty, or as hermits. In addition, the laws cover the life and behaviour of vagabonds and impose punishments on those guilty of "running around among women, telling stories, living under no rule, and being occupied with secular affairs". The lawyer-clerics face a potential conflict between the role of the bishops, who claim to be all-powerful, and the growing influence of the monasteries and their abbots (→ c.720).

Rainmaker bishop saves Sussex souls

Sussex, 682
Wilfrid, the former bishop of York who has been exiled from Northumbria, has begun a crusade to convert this largely heathen part of the Anglo-Saxon kingdoms.

Sent into exile last year in the latest chapter of a turbulent career, Wilfrid was turned away by both King Athelred of Mercia and King Centwin of Wessex, whose queens are the sisters of, respectively, King Egfrith and Queen Eormenburg of Northumbria. But he found refuge with King Athelwealh of Sussex, who was baptized in Mercia some time ago but whose people remain heathen – it was on the Sussex coast that Wilfrid and his companions were attacked by pagans on their way back from France in 666.

Wilfrid arrived at a time of great famine, caused by a drought. Sometimes, it is said, 40 or 50 people would join hands and jump off the cliffs rather than face starvation. On the very day that Wilfrid began baptizing converts, however, it began to rain, saving the new harvest. He has also taught the people how to fish: previously they could catch only eels.

Wilfrid, regarded as the people's saviour, is now hugely popular. More converts are being won, and the king has given him an estate at Selsey for a new monastery (→ 686).

Wilfrid's statue in the cathedral at Ripon, where he began his career.

Jarrow church dedicated

Centre for learning: a 20th-century model of the monastery at Jarrow.

Tyne and Wear, 23 April 685
King Egfrith of Northumbria attended the consecration today of the church of the lavish new monastery at Jarrow. Benedict Biscop, the founder and abbot of the monastery and its twin at Wearmouth, intends the church, which is dedicated to St Paul, to be a centre for Christian learning throughout Northumbria.

Biscop has visited Rome four times and has brought back a large library, vestments and many relics and icons of saints for his communities. He has also brought John, the pope's own choirmaster, to teach Roman-style chant. All in all, Jarrow should be one of the finest monastic schools in England.

The monasteries have been richly endowed by King Egfrith and other members of his family. The land for Wearmouth was granted in 673 and that for Jarrow seven or eight years later. Between them they will house over 600 monks and lay brothers, who will live under a moderate rule based on that of St Benedict of Nursia.

Biscop has brought masons and glaziers from France so that his buildings will be of fine stone and richly decorated "in the Roman manner". The monastery will have a *scriptorium*, where books will be copied, and the fine library, unparalleled elsewhere in Britain, will be increased further (→12/1/689).

A decorated letter in a manuscript of St Mark's Gospel, from Jarrow.

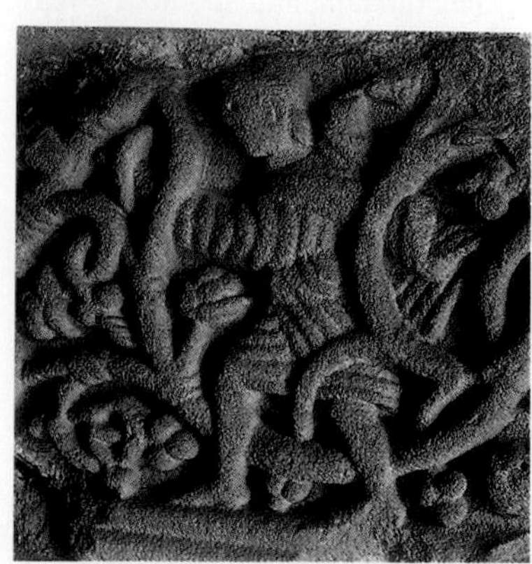
A carved fragment, probably from Benedict Biscop's church of St Paul.

Northumbria's expansion plans shattered

Tayside, 20 May 685
The Picts have avenged the defeat inflicted on them 13 years ago by King Egfrith of Northumbria. Egfrith and most of his army have been slaughtered after being lured into a mountain ambush at Dunnichen Moss, near Forfar.

The battle is a personal triumph for King Bridei of the Picts, who has spent the years since the disaster of 672 consolidating his power and extending his influence northwards. King Egfrith has paid the penalty for his ruthless expansionist policies to the north and west. Advisers criticized last year's unprovoked attack on Ireland, in which many churches were looted, and several also spoke out against his advance into Pictish territory.

Egfrith miscalculated by ordering his army to cross the Tay into the Picts' heartland, plundering as it went. When the invaders had been drawn into the Sidlaw Hills, Bridei cut off their rear and attacked. Survivors of the rout and other Northumbrian refugees, including the bishop of Abercorn, are now pouring south. One of Egfrith's advisers, Bishop Cuthbert, who is visiting the queen at Carlisle, is said to have had a vision of the defeat just as it was taking place (→693).

A mighty kingdom: Northumbria in the late seventh century.

Sexual wrongdoers to endure penances

Canterbury, Kent, c.680
"If any woman puts her daughter upon a roof or into an oven for the cure of a fever, she shall do penance for five years." This is just one of the hundreds of punishments prescribed in an exhaustive new guide to sin and penance written by a Northumbrian priest following a series of interviews he conducted with Theodore, the archbishop of Canterbury.

The penances in question generally consist of periods of austerity and fasting. The guide, or "penitential", covers subjects ranging from general church rules to drinking and sexual activities. Sex with a virgin earns one year's penance; with a married woman, four. A man who "fornicates with a man" faces ten years of penance, but a woman practising "vice with a woman" gets off with three. Even thinking about sex has its price, for, says the guide: "He who amuses himself with libidinous imagination shall do penance until the imagination is overcome" (→770).

Uttermost north is homeland to Picts

Scotland, c.680
The regions far to the north of Hadrian's wall are home to two Celtic groups: Britons, related to the tribes further south, and other tribes – the most powerful being the Caledonii – called the Picts. Their lands stretch, roughly, from Fife to the Pentland Firth.

The Picts are largely a mystery. Their name at least tells us something: it comes from the Latin word *picti*, meaning painted people. The Romans gave them this nickname because of the war-paint with which they decorate their bodies.

The Picts also have an artistic streak: skilled carvers produce stone engravings showing bulls, boars, eagles, wolves and other animals, or otherwise they carve strange symbolic shapes such as discs, crescents and rectangles. No one knows what these scenes mean – and the Picts are not telling.

686 - 690

Northumbria, 686. Adomnan, the abbot of Iona, arrives at the court of King Aldfrith to negotiate for the release of prisoners taken by Aldfrith's predecessor, Egfrith, on his punitive raid into Ireland two years ago (→ 14/12/704).

Kent, 686. King Edric's death throws the kingdom into turmoil as rivals contend for the throne (→ c.690).

London, 686. Archbishop Theodore and Bishop Wilfrid are reconciled. Theodore writes to King Athelred of Mercia, King Aldfrith of Northumbria and Abbess Alffled of Whitby, urging them to accept Wilfrid as bishop of York (→ 686/7).

Northumbria, 686/7. King Aldfrith summons Bishop Wilfrid back to his original, though much-reduced, see of Ripon (→ 691).

Kent, 687. Mul, the brother of the West Saxon leader Cadwalla, and 12 of his men are burnt to death in retaliation for the recent savage West Saxon attack on Kent. Cadwalla goes on a campaign of devastation through the kingdom in revenge (→ 688).

Isle of Wight, 687. After its conquest by the West Saxon leader Cadwalla, the island is the last area of the Anglo-Saxon kingdoms to become Christian (→ 688).

Wessex, 688. Cadwalla abdicates and sets out for Rome to be baptized. He is succeeded as West Saxon ruler by Ine, his distant royal kinsman (→ 20/4/689).

Jarrow, Tyne and Wear, 688. Adomnan, the abbot of Iona, decides at a conference to accept the Roman way of dating Easter (→ 690).

Germany, 689. The Irish pilgrim monk Kilian is martyred at Wurzburg in Franconia.

Frisia [Netherlands], 690. The exiled Northumbrian monk Willibrord, a former pupil of Wilfrid at Ripon and of their compatriot Egbert in Ireland, arrives at the mouth of the Rhine on a mission to convert the Frisians (→ 21/11/695).

Kent, c.690. Wihtred, King Edric's brother, emerges as king of Kent. He rules jointly with Swaebhard (→ 694).

Wessex, c.690. King Ine of the West Saxons issues a law code (→ 6/9/695).

Pagan island falls to campaign of terror

Cadwalla (right) meets Bishop Wilfrid: a 16th-century view.

Isle of Wight, 686
Cadwalla, an exiled member of the royal family of the West Saxons, has annexed the Isle of Wight, the last remaining Anglo-Saxon pagan kingdom. It becomes the latest kingdom of southern England to fall to Cadwalla since he became king of Wessex two years ago.

From his exile in the Chilterns and the Weald, Cadwalla struck first at Sussex, killing Athelwealh, its king, and devastating much of the countryside before being driven out. He then established his rule over Wessex, as he was now the strongest member of its royal dynasty. Surrey and Sussex were the next to be attacked and subjugated. With his brother, Mul, he has also ravaged as far as Kent.

Cadwalla was hurt in the fighting for the Isle of Wight, but his victory was never in doubt. The Saxon king has been followed to the island by preachers sent by Bishop Wilfrid, who backed Cadwalla after his patron, King Athelwealh of Sussex, died. Cadwalla, although not yet baptized, has sworn to give a quarter of the island to God in return for victory (→ 687).

West Saxon king dies after baptism

Rome, 20 April 689
Cadwalla, once the king of the West Saxons, died today just a week after being baptized by Pope Sergius. He was believed to be about 30 years old, and the cause of his death is not known. The ex-king was wearing the white gown of the newly baptized when he died.

He had gone to Rome as a pilgrim after abdicating the throne of a kingdom which he had ruthlessly extended [*see map on page 131*]. Cadwalla was converted to Christianity in Britain but had never been baptized and wanted to be received into the church at the shrine of St Peter. Pope Sergius gave him the baptismal name of Peter after the prince of the apostles in whose church he will be buried. The archbishop of Milan is writing a verse epitaph for his tomb (→ 710).

Weapons are vital key to supremacy

England, c.690
Among the crucial factors which make the Anglo-Saxon warriors such fearsome adversaries are the quality of their weapons and their skill in using them.

The fundamental combat weapon is the sword. When the Anglo-Saxons first came to Britain their swords were mostly double-edged with flat blades, although the *scramaseax*, a long-handled sword which resembled a large knife, was single-edged. Present-day swords are all double-edged, with a groove or blood-channel down the middle; the blades are sometimes constructed of iron and steel in alternating patterns. They often have elaborate hilts.

Other weapons are the spear, the bow and arrow and the *francisca*, a deadly throwing axe.

Armagh makes bid for supremacy as Easter row goes on

Ireland, 690
The church of Armagh is mounting a campaign to establish its supremacy over the entire Irish church. The move is thought to stem from the Synod of Whitby in 664, which favoured the Roman method of dating Easter, annoying Armagh, which supported the Celtic method. Armagh lawyers are basing their claim to the primacy on a life of Patricius (Patrick), the reputed founder of the Armagh bishopric, written by Muirchu Tireachan, which assigns absolute authority to Patrick's heir as bishop. They also claim that the holding of relics in Armagh entitles them to superior honours and places their church court above Irish courts.

Celtic church: a Crucifixion plaque.

Armagh's move contrasts with the decision two years ago by Adomnan, the abbot of Iona, at a conference in Northumbria, to abandon the Celtic method of setting the date of Easter and accept the Roman calendar. Northumbria, which was strongly influenced by the Celtic church, accepted the Roman Easter at the Synod of Whitby, while Iona and the Irish churches stuck to the Celtic Easter. Adomnan's change of heart has proved influential. He is a distinguished scholar and churchman and is related to Iona's founder, Colum Cille (Columba) (→ 692).

Three inspirational giants are lost to the church

Animal-loving monk dies in hermitage

Northumberland, 20 March 687
Bishop Cuthbert, aged 53, died today at his hermitage on Farne island, 2 miles off the coast of north-east England. Monks visiting him lit torches to signal the news to his monastic community on Lindisfarne, a few miles north.

Cuthbert was a shepherd in northern Northumbria when he saw a vision of Bishop Aidan of Lindisfarne. In 651 he became a monk at a community at Melrose which upheld the traditions of Irish monasticism. From here he preached and taught all over the region. The abbot of Melrose, Eata, who had been a pupil of Aidan, was to exercise a lasting influence on Cuthbert's life. Cuthbert followed in Eata's footsteps by becoming prior of Lindisfarne in 664.

About 12 years ago Cuthbert retired to Farne island, where he lived alone until King Egfrith of Northumbria came to him to persuade him to become a bishop. Cuthbert reluctantly agreed, and in 685 he was consecrated at York as bishop of Lindisfarne.

In that same year, while he was at Carlisle, Cuthbert saw a vision of King Egfrith's defeat and death in a distant battle with the Picts [*see report on page 117*]. Cuthbert won a reputation for his visions and prophecies and for his performance of "miracles".

He made numerous missionary journeys across northern Britain. It was reputed that birds and animals came to him fearlessly. In an incident at Coldingham a priest claimed that he saw otters leave the sea to dry Cuthbert's feet.

Cuthbert returned to Farne just after Christmas. Cut off by storms, he suffered five days of agony before his monks sailed over to find him at death's door (→20/3/698).

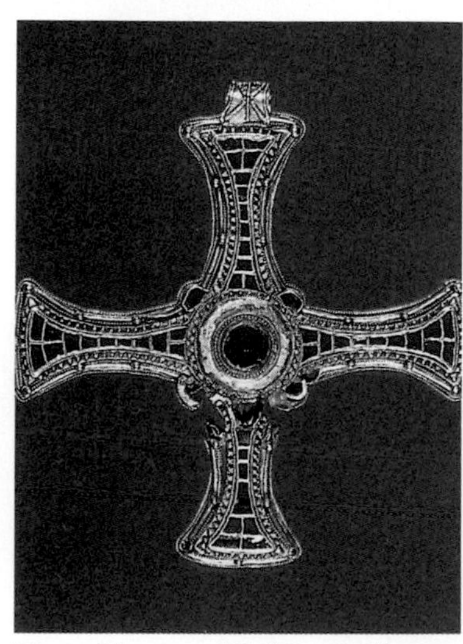
The gold cross of Bishop Cuthbert.

An artist's reconstruction of Cuthbert's isolated dwelling on Farne island.

End of the journey for traveller Benedict

A Northumbrian-style Madonna.

Jarrow: reconstructed stained glass.

Tyne and Wear, 12 January 689
Benedict Biscop, the inveterate traveller and founder of two great monastic houses, has died aged about 60 at Wearmouth in his native Northumbria. Born into a noble family as Biscop Baducing, he took the name Benedict after the saint whose rule he admired and adapted. In 653 he went on the first of five pilgrimages to Rome, and in the early 670s, after his third trip, King Egfrith of Northumbria was so impressed by the books and relics which he had brought back that he granted him land at Wearmouth for a new monastery. To build his church in true Roman style Benedict brought furnishings, masons and glaziers from France, reintroducing windows to Britain for the first time for centuries.

After the fourth visit, Egfrith granted land for a new monastery at Jarrow, to be twinned with Wearmouth, and Benedict went on a fifth visit to Rome in 685 to furnish it. But he fell ill and, with death near, he told his monks to stick to his monastic rule and to appoint abbots on grounds of merit, not birth. Almost his last act was to make Ceolfrith, the abbot of Jarrow, head of both foundations (→25/9/716).

Doughty champion of Roman church dies

Canterbury, Kent, 690
Theodore of Tarsus, the archbishop of Canterbury, has died at the age of 88. The most active and successful primate since Augustine, he was already 66 when Pope Vitalian sent him to Canterbury but set about extending his authority vigorously.

Theodore was born in Tarsus, in Asia Minor [Turkey]. He was a monk and a scholar and was appointed to Canterbury when the archbishop-elect died of the plague in Rome. Theodore travelled all over the Anglo-Saxon lands and called the first general council of the English church. One of his main feats was to break up the large Anglo-Saxon dioceses based on kingdoms into smaller bishoprics. He split the diocese of Mercia into five sees and did the same in Northumbria, despite Bishop Wilfrid's opposition. Theodore was a great church legislator, skilfully adapting Greek and Roman practices to local conditions, and an administrator of genius. He set up the first school in the Anglo-Saxon kingdoms, at Canterbury (→1/7/692).

691 - 699

Iona, Strathclyde, 16 September 691. Six monks drown when their ship sinks in a great storm.

Northumbria, 691. Bishop Wilfrid is exiled by King Aldfrith as the dispute over his diocesan powers continues. He takes refuge in Mercia (→702).

Canterbury, Kent, 1 July 692. Bertwald, the abbot of the monastery at Reculver in Kent, is elected archbishop, following the death of Theodore in 690 (→29/6/693).

Iona, 692. Bishop Adomnan, the abbot, who has recently completed his biography of Colum Cille (Columba), plans to leave for Ireland following his failure to have the Roman Easter accepted (→697).

London, 30 April 693. Bishop Eorcenwald of London, who founded big monasteries at Barking and Chertsey, dies.

Lyons, France, 29 June 693. The consecration of Bertwald as archbishop of Canterbury takes place (→709).

Iona, 693. Bridei, the British-born king of the Picts, dies after a 21-year reign and is buried here (→698).

Kent, 694. Wihtred, Edric's younger brother, becomes the sole ruler. He makes peace with King Ine of Wessex by paying 30,000 pence in compensation for the burning, in 687, of Mul, the brother of King Cadwalla, Ine's predecessor (→23/4/725).

Ely, Cambs, 695. Abbess Sexburga of Ely has the allegedly intact body of her saintly predecessor Athelthryth, who died in 679, brought into the church from its grave outside.

Mercia, 697. Queen Osthryth, the wife of King Athelred of Mercia and daughter of the late King Oswy of Northumbria, is murdered by the Mercian nobility (→704).

Lindisfarne, Northumberland, 20 March 698. Cuthbert's body is transferred to a shrine in the church, in a ceremony marking the 11th anniversary of his death which amounts to declaring him a saint.→

Lindisfarne, May 698. Bishop Edbert dies. He is succeeded by Edfrith, who made the Lindisfarne Gospels (→c.700)

Strathclyde, 698. Ainbcellach, the king of the Scots, who succeeded only last year, is deposed by Fiannamail and imprisoned in Ireland (→711).

Wessex plans new port for Channel trade

This Coptic bowl from Egypt is typical of sought-after luxury imports.

Southampton, Hampshire, c.695
A major trading port is being established on the coast of Wessex, on the Solent estuary. The site chosen for the new settlement lies on the western bank of the river Itchen, downstream of the former Roman fort and harbour of Clausentum. Five thousand people could live in this new town, which is being called Hamtun [Southampton]. Its size reflects the ambitions of the increasingly powerful kings of Wessex.

In the last ten years Kings Cadwalla and Ine have greatly expanded Wessex. The new port – close to the capital at Winchester, along the Itchen – will give them a commercial centre from which to conduct trade with ports on the European mainland. Boats will be beached on the mudflats along the Itchen where they can benefit from the sheltered tidal patterns of the Solent estuary, protected from the open sea by the Isle of Wight.

It is alongside the mudflats that the building work has now begun. A deep ditch has been dug to form an enclosure of 45 hectares (114 acres) within which a grid of roads is being created. Many of the buildings under construction will house industrial activities as well as the new inhabitants themselves. Metalworking, including iron, lead, silver and bronze, is widespread, as are carpentry, textile manufacture and pottery.

When remodelling is completed, Hamtun is likely to be the biggest manufacturing centre in southern England, yet its primary role is to act as a trading centre with ports across the Channel. In addition to manufactured goods, agricultural products will be exported in return for luxury items made of gold, silver, glass and pottery sought by the royal and church households in Winchester. Tolls on sea-borne trade may also be used to boost the royal coffers.

Hamtun is not the first trading centre to be developed in Anglo-Saxon kingdoms separately from the royal and episcopal capital, but it is the first to be planned on such a scale. Ports such as Ipswich in East Anglia and Fordwich in Kent play a significant role in the economies of other kingdoms but are much smaller. In some cases former Roman centres continue to combine administrative and commercial functions. The prime example of this is London, in the kingdom of the East Saxons.

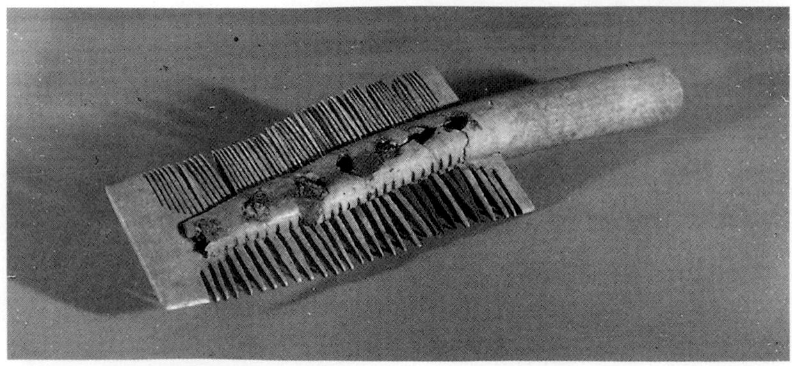

A bone comb produced in the commercial centre at Hamtun [Southampton].

Church is exempted from taxation by written legal code

Kent, 6 September 695
King Wihtred of Kent has followed the lead of King Ine of the West Saxons and issued a written code of laws, imposing a legal framework on existing social practices.

The move follows an assembly of nobles and church leaders at Bearsted, including Archbishop Bertwald of Canterbury and Bishop Gefmund of Rochester, to agree the proposals. A major aim of both Wihtred's and Ine's codes is to support the church, whose exemption from taxation is now formalized in writing. There are also cash penalties for such offences as unlawful marriage, eating meat during fasts, failing to observe Sunday and sacrificing to devils.

An intricately decorated necklace pendant from Milton Regis, in Kent.

However, Ine has gone further and established fixed penalties for many varieties of secular offences, from fighting and stealing to the illegal felling of trees. Foreigners are not forgotten: any who stray off the beaten track without shouting or blowing a horn risk being put to death as thieves.

The new codes reflect the hierarchy of Anglo-Saxon life: a king's or bishop's word is enough to establish innocence; leading churchmen and royal *thegns* [noble retainers] are believed if they swear an oath, while clerics and *churls* [ordinary free men] must be backed by three of their peers (→c.720).

Church leaders try to stop war crimes

Leinster, 697
Church leaders have drawn up a code of war in an attempt to curb the violence that has savaged Ireland for much of this century. Bishops and abbots meeting in conference at Birr have agreed to impose severe penalties for acts of violence against non-combatants, especially women and children. In defining what they see as "war crimes", the churchmen hope that the spiritual authority of the monks will restrain, or deter, violence.

The declaration marks a significant intervention by the church in secular affairs. It was called the "Law of Adomnan" after its principal instigator, Adomnan, the abbot of Iona and biographer of Columba, who is also playing a leading role in seeking to persuade the Irish church to accept the Roman method for dating Easter, the most important event in the Christian calendar. The rest of the Celtic church bowed to Rome at the 664 Synod of Whitby (→704).

Northumbrian sent to convert pagans

Rome, 21 November 695
Willibrord, a Northumbrian monk, was today consecrated bishop of pagan Frisia [in the Netherlands] by the pope. The appointment was requested by the ruler of Austrasia [eastern France], Pippin II, who is gradually extending his authority over Frisia and hopes that the conversion of the Frisians will assist in their pacification.

The new bishop was educated under the controversial churchman Wilfrid at Ripon, where he became a monk. He then spent 12 years studying in Ireland with the Northumbrian scholar Egbert before deciding to work on the European continent as a Christian missionary. Five years ago he crossed to the mouth of the Rhine with 11 companions and began preaching to the Frisians – for which he obtained the sanction of both Pippin and the pope. Today's consecration recognizes the growing respect with which his missionary work is regarded (→739).

Monk completes gospel masterpiece

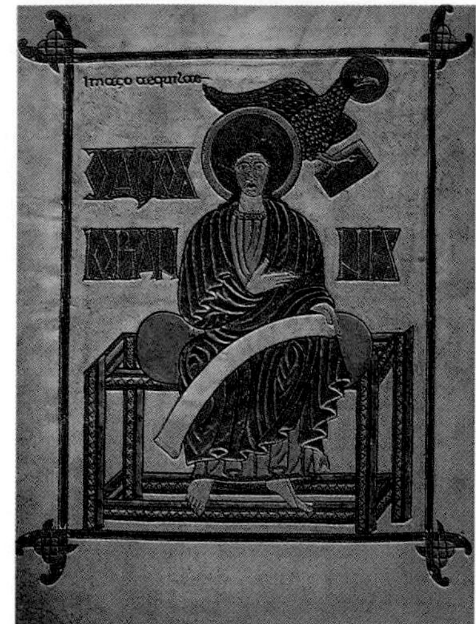

St John the Evangelist, by Edfrith.

Northumberland, 20 March 698
A magnificent Gospel-book has been completed in time for the removal of the much-loved Bishop Cuthbert's remains from the cemetery at Lindisfarne to an oak chest in the church, an act which amounts to a formal declaration of his sainthood.

The book was made by a single scribe, Edfrith, over several years, and has been bound by his colleague Athelwald. It is perhaps the finest so far of the many masterpieces of manuscript art currently being produced in the great Northumbrian monasteries such as Lindisfarne, Wearmouth-Jarrow, Hexham, Whitby and Ripon.

The Latin text of the Gospels is from the Vulgate translation by St Jerome, with introductions and lists of passages for readings, which Edfrith copied from an Italian example probably borrowed from Benedict Biscop's library at Wearmouth and Jarrow. He has written in a fine, regular script of Irish origin, two columns to a page of white vellum (dried calf's skin). But Edfrith's stunning illuminations are the book's most dazzling feature, in colours including red, yellow, indigo, pinks, purples and even lapis lazuli from the Himalayas. Apart from portraits of the evangelists, which are distinctively adapted from Mediterranean models, the decoration is purely ornamental, wonderfully fusing Celtic motifs such as spirals and trumpets with animal ones derived from Germanic metalwork (→5/698).

A masterpiece of manuscript illumination: Edfrith used the rarest colours, including lapis lazuli, here, for the hair and beard of St Matthew.

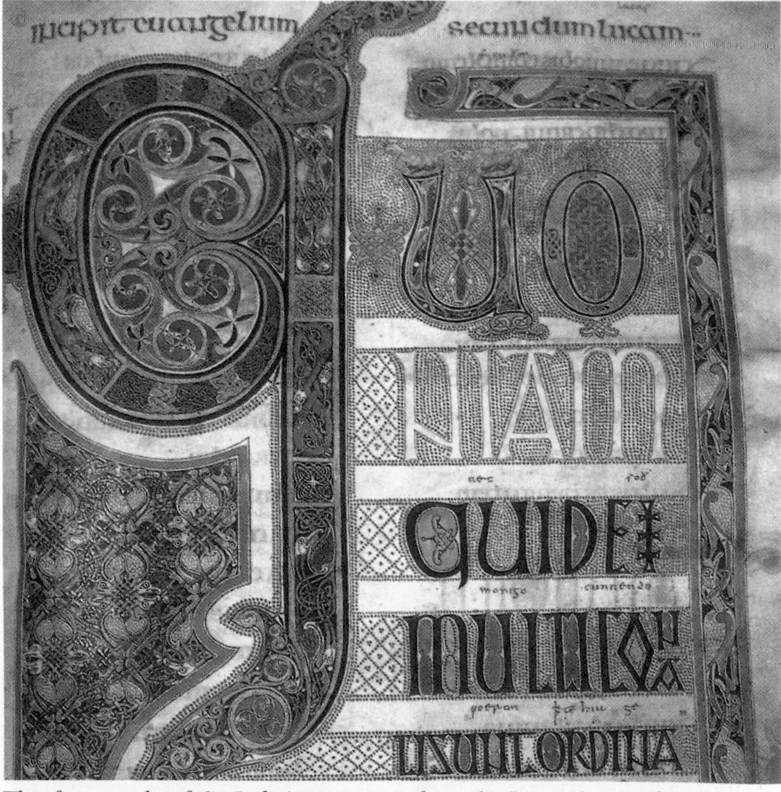

The first words of St Luke's narrative from St Jerome's translation of the Bible into Latin, magnificently illuminated by Edfrith for his Gospel-book.

700 - 716

Lindisfarne, Northumberland, c.700. A life of St Cuthbert is written (→ 721).

Wimborne, Dorset, c.700. Cuthburh, the sister of King Ine of Wessex, founds a monastery.

Isle of Man, 702. The king of Brega, in eastern Ireland, is killed in a British raid on Irish-held lands here (→ 737).

South Yorkshire, 702. On papal advice a synod is held at Austerfield to settle the case of Bishop Wilfrid. It finds against him; he sets off once more to appeal to the pope (→ 706).

Iona, Strathclyde, 23 September 704. A year after writing *De Locis Sanctis* [On the Holy Places], dedicated to King Aldfrith of Northumbria, Abbot Adomnan dies, aged 77.

Ireland, 704. A church synod accepts the Roman method for dating Easter (→ 717).

Mercia, 704. King Athelred abdicates to become a monk; his nephew Cenred succeeds him (→ 709).

Driffield, Humberside, 4 December 705. Aldfrith of Northumbria dies; he is succeeded by his son Osred, aged eight.→

North Yorkshire, 706. In a compromise agreed at a synod on the river Nidd under Archbishop Bertwald, Wilfrid is restored to his monasteries as bishop at Hexham. Its current bishop, John, moves to the see of York (→ c.707)

West Sussex, c.707. A new South Saxon see is established at Selsey (→ 12/10/709).

Mercia, 709. King Cenred abdicates and goes to Rome with Offa of Essex. His son, Ceolred, succeeds him (→ 716).

South-western England, 710. West Saxons control is ensured by the defeat of King Geraint of Dumnonia [west Somerset, Devon and Cornwall] (→ 721).

Whitby, North Yorkshire, c.710. A life of Pope Gregory, who began the conversion of the Anglo-Saxons, is compiled.

Borders, 711. A Northumbrian army defeats the Picts under King Nechtan; their expansion south is halted (→ 724).

Crowland, Lincs, 11 April 714. Guthlac, the warrior turned hermit, dies (→ 716).

Northumbria, 716. King Osred, an unpopular ruler who killed many nobles, is murdered. He is succeeded by Cenred (→ 732).

Church deprived of more top figures

Wilfrid: evangelist who trod on toes

Northamptonshire, 12 October 709
Bishop Wilfrid, one of the most influential and controversial figures in the Anglo-Saxon church of the last 50 years, died today visiting his monastery at Oundle. He was 75.

Much of his life was shaped by the events of one year, 664, when he led the pro-Roman party at the Synod of Whitby and was promoted to be bishop of York. He founded great monasteries at Ripon and Hexham but then quarrelled with King Egfrith of Northumbria and was forced into exile. Wilfrid spent much of his life trying to reassert his authority, twice appealing in person to the pope for support; the backing of Northumbrian kings and churchmen, or of archbishops of Canterbury, was more elusive. During years of exile south of the Humber he set up many more monasteries to which he introduced the Rule of St Benedict and an evangelistic ethos. Three years ago he was allowed to return to Hexham.

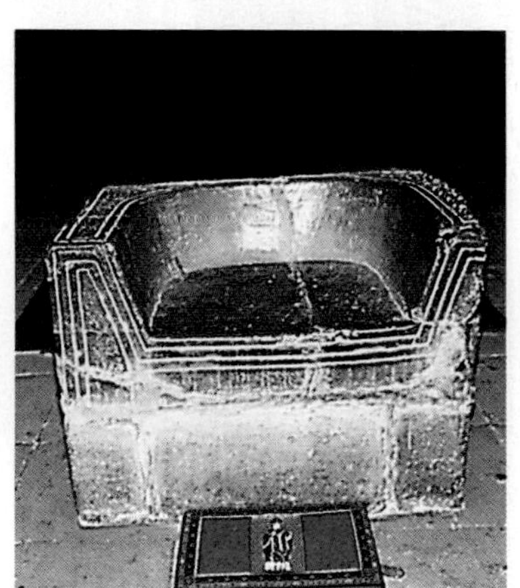
Wilfrid's throne at Hexham Abbey, which the great bishop founded.

A man of great learning and energy, he was an inspirational preacher who converted Sussex to Christianity. He was a keen builder, restoring the ruined church at York and erecting many others. Wilfrid is leaving a quarter of his riches to Rome and a quarter to the poor. He also leaves a lasting mark through his monasteries from Selsey to Hexham, in which he is being hailed as a saint.

Hadrian: last Mediterranean missionary

The missionaries' work bears fruit: an 8th-century Anglo-Saxon whalebone casket shows a Germanic legend (r) alongside the Adoration of the Magi.

Canterbury, Kent, 709
Abbot Hadrian of the school here has died after almost 40 years in charge of the monastery of St Peter and St Paul. When the pope was looking for an archbishop for the Anglo-Saxons he nominated Hadrian, the North African-born abbot of a monastery near Naples, known for his administrative skills.

Considering himself unworthy, Hadrian declined the offer and proposed Theodore, agreeing to go with him to England. Hadrian and Theodore established a school of learning at Canterbury, founded on scripture and the writings of the church fathers but including many other skills, such as Latin, Greek and the rules of religious poetry and music, along with mathematics, law, rhetoric and medicine.

Hadrian's death leaves no continental missionaries active in England, but his legacy of scholarship means that there is now no shortage of equally learned Anglo-Saxons in the country (→ 7/5/721).

Aldhelm: poet and champion of virginity

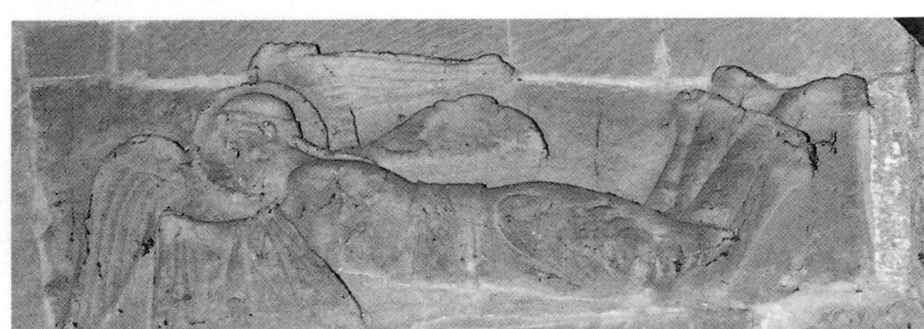
A carved angel from the church of St Laurence, Bradford-on-Avon, which is attributed by many experts to Aldhelm, reported to have built a church here.

Somerset, 23 May 709
Bishop Aldhelm of Sherborne, who died today at Doulting aged about 70, was famous for writing prose and verse treatises in praise of virginity in Latin so difficult that few people could understand it. He studied at the school of Abbot Hadrian in Canterbury and was its most accomplished graduate so far, being renowned as a teacher himself. He was a monk at Malmesbury for many years before becoming abbot there, and he visited Rome, bringing back a marble altar and a chasuble. He became bishop of Sherborne four years ago when the diocese of Wessex was split up.

Aldhelm's Latin style was extraordinarily complex and obscure; he delighted in what he called "a dense forest of Latinity". He also wrote Christian poetry in Anglo-Saxon and, in addition to his more serious works, produced collections of riddles and acrostics.

Well-paid noble retainers are key to court security

Britain, c.710
There are few certainties in the hurly-burly of politics today, but one enduring feature of public life at each royal court is the king's retinue of warriors. The king lives surrounded by a group of nobles who feast with him and sleep in his hall, who are retained to fight for him and if necessary to die in his cause.

For these men, life in royal service may be bloody, dangerous and short, but it offers rapid advancement in honourable status and in wealth. For the king, the number and ability of his retainers is both a status symbol and a deterrent to challengers for power in an unstable political environment.

A king able to make valuable gifts to his followers can attract warriors from neighbouring regions and so boost his standing and his local power base. His army may draw recruits from fighting men who are on the road for a variety of reasons; young soldiers are often found travelling from one kingdom to another to seek their fortunes, while older warriors are sometimes forced to follow their destinies abroad if they or their leaders are driven into exile.

A sensible king gives generously and needs a solid base of wealth with which to honour his men. But gifts are not a merely a matter of material reward; a warrior who is chosen to receive a beautifully made weapon, a hefty piece of armour or an extravagant ring or brooch is widely celebrated and respected by his companions.

Life at court centres on communal ritual, and in feasting and drinking these men accept a natural hierarchy among themselves, determined by prowess in battle. Acts of cowardice and desertion are reviled, and the warrior in society is taught to be unafraid of death. He and his fellows believe that a warrior's path to true greatness lies in honesty and fearless loyalty.

Royal succession fulfils hermit's prophecy

Guthlac building a chapel, from an 11th-century biography of the seer.

Mercia, 716
The death of Mercia's dissolute King Ceolred, who became insane after having a fit at a banquet, has cleared the path to the throne for his relative Athelbald – as prophesied by the hermit Guthlac.

Athelbald, seen as a rival and exiled during the reign of Ceolred, was a frequent visitor to the hermit, who told him of his prediction. Then, a year after Guthlac died in 714, his body, apparently undecayed, was moved to a shrine. Athelbald came to mourn; one night the hermit is said to have appeared and insisted that Athelbald would be king of Mercia within a year.

Guthlac was born into the Mercian royal house and became a famous warrior, but he decided to abandon his worldly goods and enter the monastery at Repton. He gave up drink, to the initial disgust of his brethren, whom he soon won over by his sincerity. After two years he went off alone to the allegedly demon-haunted island of Crowland in the Fens. He lived in a simple hut, fighting off temptation and despair and increasingly visited by pilgrims (→ 733).

Culture blooms under Northumbrian king

From a Northumbrian manuscript.

Northumbria, 4 December 705
Northumbria has enjoyed a golden age of art and learning under King Aldfrith, who died today. Educated in exile in Ireland and on Iona, he was a noted scholar and writer of Irish verse and a friend of Abbot Adomnan of Iona, Abbot Aldhelm of Wessex and the late Benedict Biscop, who founded the monastery at Wearmouth-Jarrow, home to sculptors and to scholars such as Bede. Other great regional centres include Lindisfarne, with its scribes and illuminators, and Whitby, which under Hild and Alffled has produced many bishops (→ 716).

Wearmouth-Jarrow abbot bequeaths a splendid new bible

France, 25 September 716
Ceolfrith, the retired abbot of the twin monastery of Wearmouth-Jarrow, has died at Langres in France on his way to Rome. The magnificent bible that he commissioned in honour of St Peter will however be taken on to be presented to the pope. It is one of three identical examples made by around 600 of his monks. The task has been huge: some 1,500 calves were killed to provide the skin for the vellum. The writing is executed in a stately script, and the pages are richly decorated in the Italian style.

Although the Christian religion is based on a person, Jesus Christ, and led by the Holy Spirit, believers attach great importance to the word of God transmitted to man in the pages of the Bible. The "Old Testament" contains the story of the Hebrew people, while the "New Testament" records the life of Christ and the writings of important figures in the earliest Christian communities. Originally written in Greek, the New Testament exists in various Latin translations. Parts have also been translated into English, in which it is called the "gospel [*god spell*]" or "good news" (→ 721).

An Old Testament prophet at work: the frontispiece of the new bible.

717 - 732

Rome, 15 May 719. The Wessex-born monk Wynfrith, who has a papal commission to preach to the Rhineland heathens, is rechristened Boniface (→ 30/11/722).

Humberside, 7 May 721. John, who retired as bishop of York four years ago, dies in his monastery at Beverley (→ 727).

Jarrow, Tyne and Wear, 721. The scholarly monk Bede, who was made a priest in 703, writes a fuller version of the *Life of St Cuthbert* at the request of the Lindisfarne monastery (→ 725).

Cornwall, 721. The expansion of the West Saxons under King Ine is abruptly halted when they are defeated by Britons of Cornwall on the Hayle estuary. The West Saxons are believed to have brought all of Devon under their control (→ 726).

Grampian, 724. King Nechtan of the Picts is forced to abdicate and retire to a monastery. Civil war erupts between the four rivals to succeed him (→ 12/8/729).

Kent, 23 April 725. King Wihtred, who brought stability to Kent, dies. The kingdom is split among his sons Edbert, Athelbert and Alric (→ 762).

Wessex, 726. Athelheard succeeds to the throne, ending the confusion and fighting that followed Ine's abdication.→

Rochester, Kent, 727. Eldwulf becomes the new bishop after the death of Tobias, a Greek and Latin scholar (→ 30/7/734).

Iona, Strathclyde, 24 April 729. Bishop Egbert, who in 716 persuaded the monks of Iona to accept the Roman Easter, dies aged 90 (→ 731).

Tayside, 12 August 729. The Pictish civil war, which has raged since Nechtan abdicated in 724, ends when a claimant, Oengus, defeats and kills his cousin Drest. He becomes unchallenged king (→ 736).

Jarrow, 731. Bede completes his *Ecclesiastical History of the English People*. It is dedicated to King Ceolwulf of Northumbria (→ 25/7/735).

Northumbria, 732. King Ceolwulf, who came to the throne following the death of King Osric in 729, retains control of his kingdom despite being seized and tonsured as a monk by his enemies (→ 737).

Rhineland, 732. Bishop Boniface, the Wessex-born missionary to the Rhineland, is made an archbishop (→ c.747).

Monks out as Picts renounce Celtic rite

The Pictish "Glamis Stone".

Iona, Strathclyde, 717

Monks on Iona who refuse to abandon Celtic religious customs have been expelled by King Nechtan of the Picts. The dispute began last year when Nechtan wrote to Abbot Ceolfrith of Jarrow in Northumbria for a defence of Roman practice, especially on dating Easter.

As a result of Ceolfrith's reply, Nechtan insisted that clerics in his lands switch from Celtic to Roman usage. He seems sincere, but many think that he is cultivating a leading Northumbrian like Ceolfrith to bolster his domestic position. Nechtan succeeded his brother Bridei in 708 in breach of the custom of electing the king from among a number of families; his defeat by Northumbria in 711 further eroded his popularity (→ 24/4/729).

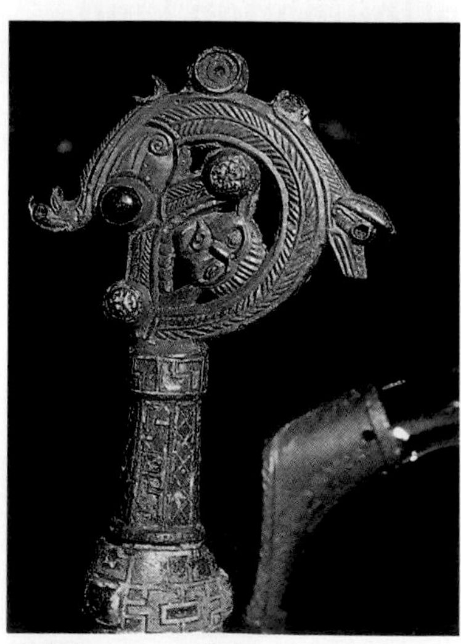

Eighth-century Celtic church art.

Aged Irish bishop's life ends in Lombardy

Bobbio, Northern Italy, 720

Bishop Cummian, an Irish churchman who left his homeland for the first time when he was in his late seventies, has died aged 95. He ended his days at Bobbio, the monastery in Lombardy founded in 612 by his great compatriot Columbanus.

Cummian was 78 when he decided to travel to Italy on a pilgrimage, following in the footsteps of the many Irish ecclesiastics who are famous throughout western Europe for their missionary zeal and monastic foundations. The fame of the Irish church is likely to continue with the current compilation of the *Collectio Canonum Hibernensis* [Irish Collection of Canons], the most wide-ranging and systematic Irish law code to date. It will bring together all Irish law on church and most other matters in one treatise. The respect in which Irish scholarship and the Irish church are held abroad means that the *Collectio* is almost certain to be influential in Europe (→ 753).

A house-shaped shrine in a distinctive Irish style, from Siena, in Italy.

Law code puts price on bishop's head

Ireland, c.720

Anyone in Ireland thinking of killing a bishop should make sure that he can afford a hefty penalty, following the appearance of a new law code that sets out the punishments applicable to those who cause harm to the church and its employees. The treatise also lays down the penalty for injuring a bishop, an abbot or – in a piece of self-interest by the work's writers – a scribe, as well as for insulting, injuring or killing those attached to a bishop's retinue. Theft from a holy shrine or a church treasury is also met with stiff penalties.

The code, called *Tres Canones Hibernici* [Three Irish Canons], indicates the growing power of ecclesiastical control and the dominance of church law within Irish society. It also deals with the question of church tithes, or taxes of one-tenth, which are imposed on livestock, and even on human beings, as well as on first fruits. Other matters covered include the need for priests to reject "the gift of the wicked" and the need for a signature in business dealings (→ c.750).

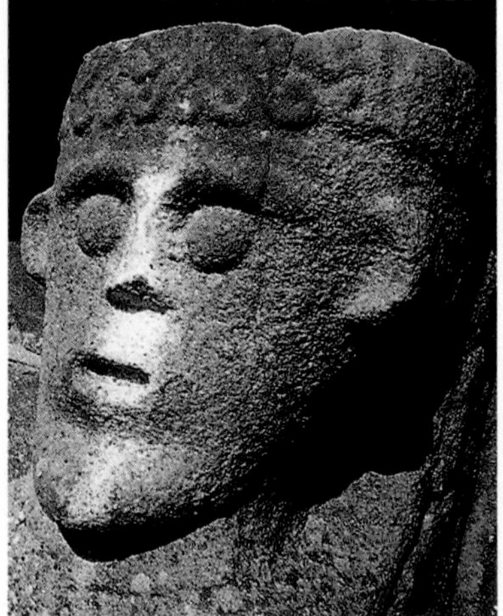

Christian statues from Lough Erne.

Anglo-Saxon pilgrims journey to Rome

Wessex, c.726
Another Anglo-Saxon king has chosen abdication and a pilgrimage to Rome, to stay for the rest of his life. Ine of Wessex, for much of his 38-year reign the strongest ruler in southern England, follows others such as his predecessor Cadwalla and Cenred of Mercia.

Ine extended his kingdom southwestwards at British expense, bringing Devon under his control and expanding into Cornwall. He fought off Mercian attempts to move south of the Thames, and for many years he controlled Surrey and the sub-kingdom of Sussex [*see map on page 131*].

Although the journey south is perilous, more and more Anglo-Saxons are setting out to offer their prayers and gifts at the tombs of the saints – the most exalted members of the Christian church – in the hope of winning their blessing on earth and in the world to come. A Saxon quarter is even developing in Rome to cater for the pilgrims. Some go to learn and return home; others die there, and many are robbed or killed on the way (→752).

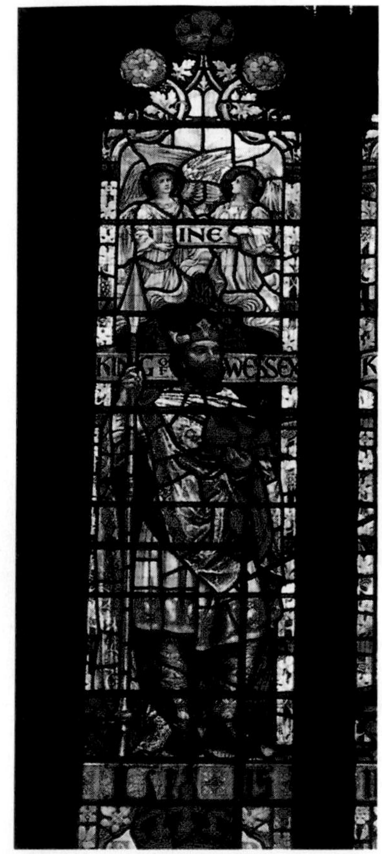
Pilgrim bound for Rome: King Ine.

Wessex man made bishop to Germans

Rome, 30 November 722
A missionary born in Wessex has been consecrated by the pope as bishop to the heathen inhabitants of Germany east of the river Rhine. Boniface, formerly Wynfrith, was a monk at Exeter in his youth, and he went on to achieve renown as a scholar and a teacher of grammar at another monastery at Nursling on Southampton Water. During this period he was sent by King Ine of Wessex on an important diplomatic mission into Kent.

In 716, however, when he was about 40 years old, Boniface gave up his promising career in the English church to become a missionary. He worked with the Northumbrian monk Willibrord in Frisia [in the Netherlands] and in neighbouring parts of northern Europe. His success in winning converts led Pope Gregory II to summon him to Rome. He was rechristened Boniface, after one of the martyr saints, by the pope (→732).

Bede reckons time from birth of Christ

Jarrow, Tyne and Wear, 725
The scholar Bede has added to his already prodigious literary output by completing an intriguing treatise on the Christian calendar entitled *De temporum ratione* [*On the calculation of time*]. It is an elaboration of his *De temporibus*, an elementary manual of chronology that was written in 703.

In his new work Bede revives a system devised two centuries ago in Rome, but long disregarded by the church, for reckoning years from the era of Christ's incarnation. He includes a "chronicle" of historical events, both secular and sacred, in the known world – a list of dates with the corresponding events of the year in question entered against each date. Bede believes that the study of chronology, which involves the laborious reconciliation of different systems of dating, can help him and other Christians to a better appreciation of God's purpose in the world (→24/4/729).

Beowulf is triumphant in monstrous saga

England, c.725
The poem *Beowulf*, a Germanic tale of heroism, monsters and dragons which has long been recited in banqueting halls of the mighty, has been written down for the first time. In more than 3,000 rhythmical, moving lines in Anglo-Saxon, it tells of Beowulf and his struggles with evil.

Beowulf is the nephew of the king of the Geats (in Gotland, Sweden), and in his youth he visits the Danish king Hrothgar. Hrothgar's court is deserted, because a fierce swamp-demon called Grendel stalks the land by night, slaying sleeping warriors and eating them. Beowulf sets out to kill the fiend, and one night wrenches off its arm.

Grendel flees, and Hrothgar rewards Beowulf. But one night Grendel's monstrous mother kills the king's best companion in revenge. Beowulf tracks the mother to a cave at the bottom of a black lake and slays her. He takes her head to the king, who gives a great feast. Beowulf returns home and slays an evil dragon, but, as he had foreseen, is mortally wounded. His body is burnt on a headland, and his pyre is visible far out to sea. *Beowulf* deals with the supernatural and refers to real rulers of the past while reflecting the values of its warrior audience – kinship, treasure-giving, loyalty and heroism – along with Christian piety and a belief in the futility of earthly treasure.

Warrior on a bronze matrix used for Swedish helmet plaques.

Fierce beasts confounded: this bronze matrix for making decorative plaques for helmets was, like the one above, found at Tors Lunda, Sweden.

733 - 748

Somerset, 733. King Athelbald of Mercia becomes the direct ruler of a large part of Wessex beyond Selwood after capturing Somerton from the West Saxons under King Athelheard (→ 736).

Canterbury, Kent, 30 July 734. Archbishop Tatwin, who succeeded Bertwald on his death in 731, dies. Nothhelm, from London, succeeds (→ 735).

York, 735. The pope upgrades York to an archbishopric, making it independent of Canterbury (→ 740).

Strathclyde, 736. King Oengus of the Picts defeats the Dal Riata Scots, who have been leaderless since the death of King Eochaid in 733. He captures the fortress of Dunadd and imposes his overlordship (→ 750).

Northumbria, 737. King Athelbald of Mercia ravages the north of England (→ 743).

Northumbria, 737. King Ceolwulf abdicates after a troubled reign to become a monk at Lindisfarne. He is succeeded by his cousin Edbert, the brother of the archbishop of York (→ 750).

Terryglass, Co Monaghan, 737. Aed Allan mac Fergaile and Cathal mac Finguine, who are the most powerful rulers in the north and south of Ireland respectively, reach an agreement to settle their territorial differences. The south also agrees to recognize the primacy of Armagh over the Irish church (→ 19/8/738).

Canterbury, 740. Cuthbert, the bishop of Hereford, succeeds Nothhelm. He is the third consecutive Mercian to hold the position of archbishop of Canterbury (→ 23/4/741).

York, 23 April 741. York Minster, which was built by Bishop Wilfrid, is destroyed by fire (→ c.760).

Welsh Marches, 743. King Cuthred of Wessex, who succeeded Athelheard in 740, fights with King Athelbald of Mercia against the Welsh Britons (→ 747).

Mercia, 747. King Athelbald receives a letter from Boniface, the archbishop of Mainz, and seven other leading bishops criticizing him for violating ecclesiastical privilege and for misbehaviour with nuns (→ 749).

Rhineland, c.747. The Wessex-born missionary Boniface has his archbishopric permanently based at Mainz (→ 5/6/754).

Greatest Anglo-Saxon scholar dies

Tyne and Wear, 25 May 735
Bede, the greatest Anglo-Saxon scholar of his generation, died today in his simple monk's cell at Jarrow monastery. This morning he rose to dictate the last chapter of his Anglo-Saxon translation of St John's Gospel. "Take up your pen and ink and write quickly," Bede told his scribe. Six hours later, after distributing his meagre possessions, he knelt down to pray and died. He was in his early sixties.

Born at Wearmouth, Bede was seven when he entered the church there, later moving to the new foundation at Jarrow. Soon afterwards only he and the abbot, Ceolfrith, survived a plague outbreak. A deacon at the age of 19 and a priest at 30, Bede devoted his life to study, teaching and writing. His vast output is dominated by masterly Bible commentaries but also includes hymns, epigrams, a Latin grammar and lives of churchmen.

He made popular a method of dating by reference to the birth of Christ [the BC and AD system] and can even claim to be the first Anglo-Saxon scientist. Though he never left Northumbria, Bede's fame and network of contacts enabled him to gather copious material for perhaps his greatest work, the *Ecclesiastical History of the English People* – see reports below.

A Victorian view of Bede's death.

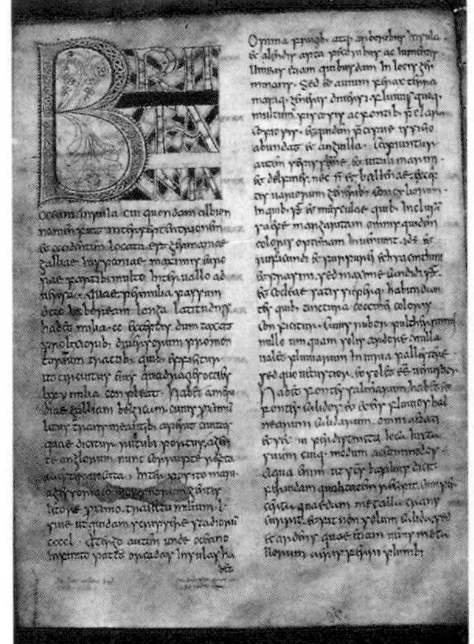
A text composed by the great Bede.

Bede was a stern critic of abuses within the church. Only last year he wrote to his ex-pupil Bishop Egbert of York urging reform in the monasteries, most of which, he said, were "useful neither to God nor man". Since the death of King Aldfrith of Northumbria in 705, Bede noted, more and more nobles had avoid military service and taxation by turning their estates into monasteries where they continued to live secular lives and where the so-called "monks" and "nuns" habitually married and reared children. Bede also criticized some bishops for being more interested in feasting and drunkenness than in prayer.

Some villagers in the north of England had never seen a teacher, let alone a bishop, he said. Bede recommended increasing the number of bishops in Northumbria to 12, with smaller sees on land taken from bogus monasteries, so that communities could be visited by a bishop at least once a year (→ 1022).

The earth is round, says scientist Bede

Tyne and Wear, 735
His book *De rerum natura* [*On the nature of things*] marks Bede out as the first Anglo-Saxon scientist. In its compilation, Bede, a master of Latin, made extensive use of a library brought from Rome; he knew of Greek science only from Latin translations. His ideas came mainly from the church fathers and from writers such as Isidore of Seville and the Roman encyclopaedist Pliny. Bede said that the earth is a sphere, surrounded by seven heavens: air, ether, Olympus, fiery space, the firmament of heavenly bodies (which revolves around the earth), and the heavens of angels and the Trinity. Four elements make up the earthly world: earth, water, air and fire, which, with light and the human soul, were made by God at time of the Creation.

Bede recounts in his monastic cell the earliest tales and legends of his people

Tyne and Wear, 735
Bede's reputation as a scholar has reached far beyond the British Isles to Europe, where his *Commentaries*, *Martyrology* and other writings are already seen as indispensable works of reference. Yet it is the *Eccelesiastical History of the English People* (731) that has brought him widest admiration. In its five books Bede rescues from oblivion the earliest memories of Celtic Britain and Saxon England.

Encouraged to write a history by Abbot Albinus of Canterbury, Bede preferred not to give just a dry chronology of events. Instead he scoured every source he could lay hands on, going by spoken as well as written accounts and keeping to local traditions where possible. It was a task that no one in this country had set himself before.

Bede made use of copies of documents from the pope's archives in Rome, while bishops and monks around the country sent him information he wanted concerning their own churches. As far as he could, Bede checked facts – even when it came to writing about his native Northumbria, about which he naturally knew most.

Above all, Bede brings to life the people who have forged the English nation. Whether recalling the selfless lives of the Celtic saints or the savage rivalry of Saxon kings, Bede makes us aware that the past is a force that continually shapes the future.

Fighting in Leinster destroys hopes for Irish peace pact

Leinster, 19 August 738
Peace in Ireland looks as remote as ever today following a battle at Ballyshannon in Co Kildare from which the "high king", Aed Allan mac Fergaile of the Ui Neill dynasty, emerged victorious.

The object of the battle, instigated by Aed Allan, the most powerful ruler in the north of Ireland, was to crush opposition emanating from Leinster to a pact agreed last year at Terryglass in Co Monaghan. Under the settlement, reached between Aed Allan and Cathal mac Finguine, the top ruler in the south, it was agreed to resolve long-standing territorial differences between the north and south of the island. In a major breakthrough, the south also agreed for the first time to recognize the primacy of Armagh over the Irish church, bolstering church unity.

Reports from today's battle indicate that there has been a heavy loss of life, with the dead including a number of Aed Allan's leading opponents such as Aed mac Colggen and Bran Bec. Following Aed Allan's defeat of the Ulaid dynasty of the north-east three years ago at Faughart, the victory at Ballyshannon is seen as a decisive assertion of Ui Neill authority (→743).

Dynastic rivalry mounts in Ireland

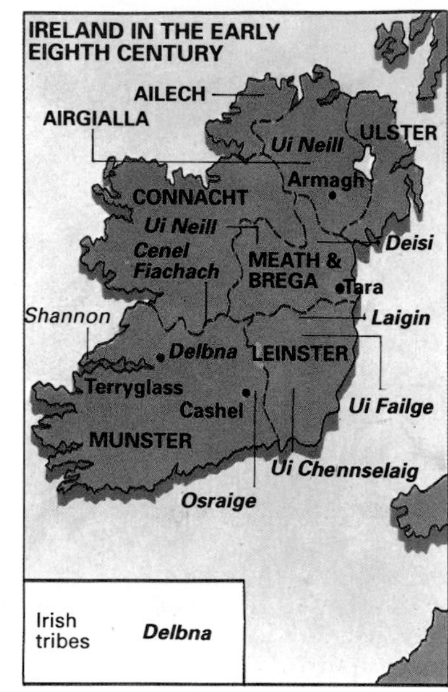

A highly decorated gold brooch of the early eighth century, found at Tara.

Co Meath, 743
Aed Allan mac Fergaile, the ruler of the Ui Neill dynasty and the most powerful man in the north of Ireland, has been defeated and killed in battle at Seredmag in Co Meath by the king of Meath, Domnall Midi.

With the death of Aed Allan, it would appear that his dynasty's claim to the "high-kingship" of Ireland, centred on Tara, has ended – – for the time being at least – especially since Domnall Midi is now determined to seek this position for himself. The high-kingship is still coveted as a important prize [*see report on page 97*], in spite of the decline in its influence that has led to a strengthening of the position of some provincial dynasties in the island.

The Laigin of Leinster, for example, are enjoying the benefits of strong rule under Muiredach, the son of Bran Bec who was killed at the Battle of Ballyshannon [*see report left*]. The Ui Chennselaig in the south and the Ui Failge in the west – while busy consolidating their territorial gains – seem to be on course for a period of comparative peace. The same cannot be said, however, of the Osraige, who hold land to the west of the Ui Chennselaig.

The Osraige have wielded little influence under previous rulers, but the situation has been transformed by the accession of Anmchaid, the son of Cu Cerca. Anmchaid has already crushed the Delbna and the Cenel Fachach, who inhabit the territory between the Ui Failge and the Shannon and now seems determined to extend his domains by making further raids on the Deisi in Co Louth (→824).

I am king of Britain, says Mercian ruler

Hereford and Worcester, 736
In a charter founding a monastery beside the river Stour, King Athelbald of Mercia has grandly styled himself "*rex Britanniae* [king of Britain]". During his 20-year reign, Athelbald has extended his dominions to make himself the most powerful ruler south of the Humber. He has annexed Middlesex and the flourishing port of London from the East Saxons, brought large areas of West Saxon territory under his control and raided deep into Wales [*see map on page 131*].

But Athelbald, despite the title which he claims, has no authority north of the Humber. In fact, *rex Britanniae* signifies less than it seems; it is a Latin rendering of the Anglo-Saxon term *bretwalda* [wide ruler], applied to those who have become overlords of southern England. In his history of the English the scholar Bede lists seven such kings, including Oswy of Northumbria and Aelle of Sussex (→737).

A Victorian fake of a silver coin of King Athelbald of Mercia's reign.

Light of the pagans fades out, aged 81

Luxembourg, 739
Willibrord, the monk from Northumbria revered for his pioneering missionary work on the continent, has died in retirement at the Echternach monastery given to him by the Frankish leader, Pippin II. He was 81 and had served as archbishop of the people of Frisia [in the Netherlands] for four decades.

Born in 658, Willibrord was educated at Ripon under Wilfrid and went to Ireland when he was about 20, spending a dozen years there as the pupil of the Northumbrian missionary Egfrith before embarking on his work in Europe. Following his consecration as archbishop in 695 [*see report on page 121*], Willibrord, at Pippin's instigation, made Utrecht the base for his operations, and the Frankish leader also helped Willibrord to establish the monastery at Echternach where he spent his last days.

For the rest of his long life Willibrord worked among the Frisians, whose similar language and culture makes them an appropriate target for Anglo-Saxon missions. He had plans for working further afield, among the Danes and also in central Germany, where his one-time assistant, the Wessex-born Boniface, has continued his work.

Boniface, who has set up several monasteries, terrified local pagans on one occasion by chopping down the sacred oak of Woden at Geismar in Germany. His work is attracting many new volunteers from England (→c.795).

Strathclyde, 750. King Edbert of Northumbria takes control of Kyle from the Strathclyde Britons (→ 10/8/756).

Strathclyde, 750. Teudubr, the son of King Bili of the Strathclyde Britons, becomes overlord of the Picts; he beat King Oengus at Mugdock, near Glasgow (→ 761).

Wessex or Mercia, 752. King Cuthred of Wessex defeats King Athelbald of Mercia, throwing off Mercian overlordship (→ 756).

Strathclyde, 10 August 756. Unexpected losses force the Northumbrian army to withdraw south to Kyle only nine days after imposing their rule on the Strathclyde Britons. King Oengus, the Northumbrians' Pictish ally, has also withdrawn (→ 758).

Wessex, 756. King Cuthred dies and is succeeded by his kinsman Sigebert (→ c.757).

Canterbury, Kent, 756. A terrible fire destroys the city.

Wessex, 757. The principal nobles, under Cynewulf, deprive Sigebert of all his realm apart from Hampshire "for unlawful actions". Cynewulf rules the remainder but has to acknowledge Mercian overlordship (→ c.760).

York, 758. Edbert of Northumbria abdicates to become a monk in his brother Archbishop Egbert's minster at York. Oswulf, his son, succeeds him (→ 5/8/759).

Northumbria, 5 August 759. Athelwold Moll is the new king (→ 9/8/761).

Canterbury, c.760. Archbishop Cuthbert dies and is buried in his new church to the east of the cathedral. He is succeeded by Bregowin (→ 9/11/766).

East Anglia, c.760. King Beonna issues new coins like those minted by King Pippin of the Franks (→ 792).

Wessex, c.760. King Sigebert, expelled from Hampshire for killing an important noble, is murdered (→ 772).

Northumbria, 9 August 761. King Athelwold Moll defeats his rival for the throne, Oswin, in a battle at a place called Adwinesclif (→ 30/10/765).

Tayside, 761. King Oengus of the Picts dies after a troubled reign of 32 years (→ 789).

Kent, 762. King Athelbert of Kent dies. Last of the old royal line, he leaves Kent ruled by several petty kings (→ 776).

Mercian ruler tries to heal church rift

Leicestershire, 749

At a council held at Gumley, King Athelbald of Mercia has told the churches of his kingdom that from now on they will be free from all public duties except for the basic tasks of maintaining fortresses and repairing bridges. The move seems to be an attempt to meet criticisms levelled at him two years ago by eight top bishops including Boniface, the Wessex-born missionary who is now archbishop of Mainz.

In 747 Athelbald, the dominant figure in southern England for some 30 years, was at the centre of a scandal involving sexual misbehaviour with nuns – who were said to be giving birth to babies and then killing them – and the misappropriation of church funds.

The bishops wrote the king a letter condemning his licentiousness and fornication with women consecrated to God. Athelbald was praised for his almsgiving, but at the same time he was accused of violating church privileges, helping himself to church revenues and using clerics as forced labour to build military fortifications. The bishops drew attention to the abysmal example that the king was setting to his people. Athelbald responded by calling a council of churches to make reforms (→ 757).

Irish abbots challenge bishops for power

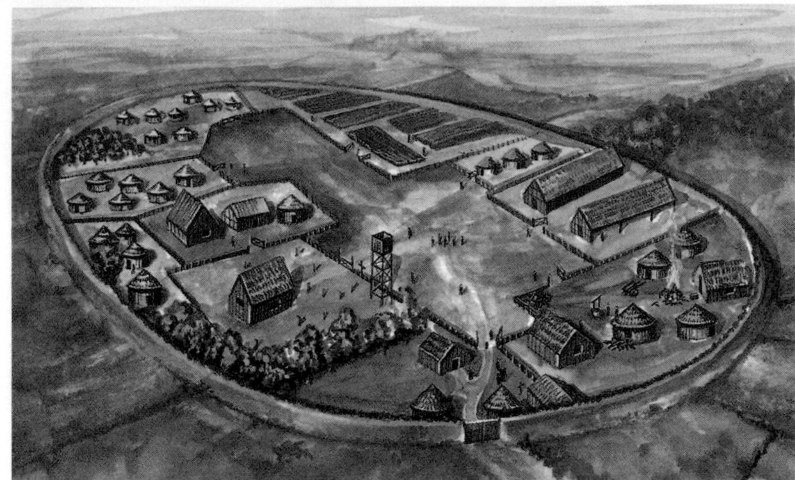

A reconstruction of an open-plan monastery in Ireland, enclosed by a ditch and a bank. The church and graveyard are to the south-west, beside the wooden belfry and look-out tower; the kitchen buildings lie to the south-east.

Armagh, 750

The death of Bishop Congus of Armagh, the seat of the traditional *coairbe* [the heir of St Patrick], has confirmed a shift in church power. Congus's successor as *coairbe* is Cele Petair, an abbot [monastery superior] rather than a bishop, and the change reflects a growing challenge to the power of the bishops, whose ecclesiastical jurisdiction is confined to the geographical boundaries of their sees.

Through the acquisition of land through gift or bequest, the influence of individual monasteries has been extended not just through Ireland but into Britain, and sometimes as far as the continent. This has led to monastic overlordship and to abbots moving from one property to another, sending out monks to create new settlements that owe their allegiance to the parent monastery.

The abbot of Iona was one such leader who regularly visited subsidiary establishments. Sometimes confrontation was avoided, as in the case of Lindisfarne, where Bishop Aidan shared power amicably with the abbot. But in most cases the power shift has been real, and irreversible (→ 770).

London expands to become the 'market-place of many peoples'

London, c.750

London, or Lundene as the Anglo-Saxons call it, is now the largest city in Britain, with a port that has no equal in the island. Such is its reputation that Bede, the late Northumbrian chronicler – who never travelled south of the river Humber – described it as "the market-place of many peoples coming by land and sea".

For decades after the departure of the Romans, London suffered a period of decline and depopulation, with many of its buildings falling into ruin. By 604, however, it had revived sufficiently for Mellitus, a monk from Rome, to be ordained as its first bishop by Augustine. Mellitus went on to build St Paul's church on the city's east hill, but a few years later the people of London reasserted their independence by driving him out and reverting to heathenism.

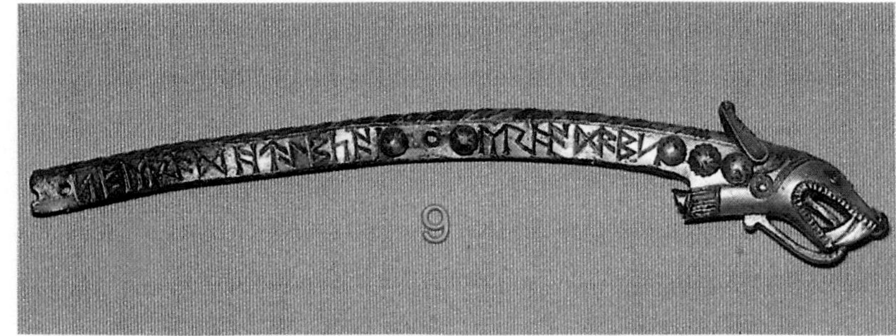

A silver-gilt mount of the eighth century, cast into the Thames at London.

Although London lies within the domain of the East Saxons, it is controlled by Mercia, which rules indirectly through dependent East Saxon sub-kings. The city stretches along the north bank of the Thames at a bend in the river between two tributaries, the river Tyburn to the west and the river Fleet to the east. Its western boundary is marked by the church of St Martin and its eastern boundary by St Bride's. Downstream, within its ancient walls, lies Roman London, now largely empty of life.

Mercia is seized by Offa

A later mural showing King Offa.

Mercia, 757
Offa – who claims descent from a brother of King Penda – has won control of the kingdom of Mercia in the English midlands after six months of civil war and anarchy. His rise to the kingship follows the murder of King Athelbald, who was stabbed to death by his own bodyguard at Seckington near Tamworth. The motive behind the murder is unclear, but during his 41 years on the throne Athelbald had made plenty of enemies.

On Athelbald's death a certain Beornred claimed to be his legitimate successor, but he was quickly challenged by Offa – even though Offa's relationship to Athelbald was no closer than that of first cousin twice removed. Because both he and Athelbald were apparently descended from Eowa, the brother of King Penda who died just over a hundred years ago, that sufficed to give Offa a strong claim.

The struggle between Beornred and Offa was typical of those disputes that arise from the fact that Anglo-Saxon monarchies have no strict rules governing succession. Although kingship usually passes from father to son, anyone who can claim, or manufacture, a link with the royal house, even if it goes back some generations, may feel justified in making a bid for the throne.

The disorder following Athelbald's death has resulted in the disintegration of the confederacy that he forged in southern England, and Offa now faces a hard task in recreating Mercian hegemony (→771).

Dual law codes cause confusion in Ireland

Ireland, c.750
Irish law tracts have been gathered together in an attempt to define church law and to strengthen the power of the church. This process began some two centuries ago when the church was operating in the midst of an essentially pagan society while trying to establish its own laws. Traditionally, in the dozens of Irish *tuaths*, or petty kingdoms, the basic legal unit was the kinship (extended family) group, rather than the individual, and the law depended on "honour" and its loss. The implementation of a system that has evolved from these tenets side by side with the ecclesiastical one has caused widespread confusion.

Further complications, created by the conflict between the monastic system and the power of the bishops, have slowly been resolved, with the monasteries now seeming to come out on top (→806).

Pagan mob kills preacher Boniface

Dokkum, Netherlands, 5 June 754
Archbishop Boniface, the 78-year-old British missionary, was martyred near here today with 53 of his companions. They were cut down by pagans after sailing through the Zuider Zee on a missionary expedition into the heartland of the Frisians.

At first all went well and thousands were baptized, but this morning Boniface and his companions awoke to find a huge crowd of armed pagans descending on their camp. Boniface ordered his followers not to resist, shouting: "Render not evil for evil. Fear not them that kill the body since they cannot kill the soul."

Using only a book to protect himself, Boniface was cut down. His body has been taken to his monastery at Fulda in Germany, and the book, torn by sword cuts, has gone with him.

Irish artisans show off their superb skills

An elaborate eighth-century paten (for Communion bread). It was buried as part of a hoard of churchware at Derrynaflan, in Munster.

Ireland, c.750
The skills of Irish metalworkers and sculptors have attained extraordinary heights of sophistication under the patronage of the church and rich aristocrats. Ecclesiastical equipment such as chalices and patens (vessels for the communion wine and bread) display astonishing skills in the handling of gold, silver and alloys, and are often richly ornamented with, for example, intricate filigree and enamel panels, frequently depicting human and animal figures. The church has also been responsible for erecting carved stone crosses, with patterns resembling those of fine metalwork.

The aristocratic patrons of smiths also favour brooches for pinning clothes; these are often penannular (in open-ring form) and can be finely decorated with complex ornament (→c.795).

Sumptuous decoration: detail of an Irish metal shrine-mount.

A copy of a silver brooch found at Loughmoe, in Munster.

764 - 790

Northumbria, 30 October 765. King Athelwold Moll is deposed by Alhred, who claims to be a descendant of Ida, the founder of the royal line of Bernicia (southern Northumbria) (→ Easter 774).

York, 19 November 766. Albert, the learned head of the cathedral school, is to succeed its founder Egbert, who has died, as archbishop (→ 778).

Wales, 768. The Welsh church is submitted to the authority of Rome by Bishop Eidfodd.

Sussex, 771. By a victory at Hastings, Offa now controls the whole of Sussex (→ 772).

Bexhill, East Sussex, 772. Offa issues a land-grant witnessed by King Cynewulf of Wessex. Wessex remains independent, but Sussex no longer exists as a separate kingdom (→ 779).

York, Easter 774. Alhred is overthrown by Athelred, the son of the deposed Athelwold Moll, and flees (→ 779).

Otford, Kent, 776. A Kentish revolt throws off Mercian overlordship (→ 785).

York, 778. Albert resigns and is succeeded as archbishop by his pupil Eanbald (→ 780).

Benson, Oxfordshire, 779. Offa defeats Cynewulf of Wessex, regaining control of the upper Thames valley (→ 784).

Sockburn, Co Durham, 780. Higbald is consecrated as bishop of Lindisfarne on the resignation of Cynewulf (→ 786).

Wales, 784. Offa attacks Wales and ravages large areas (→ 785).

Kent, 785. Offa reasserts his overlordship of Kent (→ 787).

Wessex, 786. Beortric becomes king following the murder of Cynewulf.→

Mercia, 787. Offa has his son Egfrith anointed as king to try to ensure his succession (→ 789).

Northumbria, 23 September 788. King Alfwold is murdered and buried in Hexham church. His nephew, Osred, succeeds him (→ c.790).

Western Scotland, 789. Following the death of the Pictish King Talorgen, his successor Conall mac Tadc is defeated by Constantine mac Fergus (→ 820).

Northumbria, c.790. King Osred is tricked by his nobles, imprisoned and tonsured as a monk. He flees into exile on the Isle of Man; the former king, Athelred, returns to claim his throne (→ 14/9/792).

Freeze sparks fires and thwarts scribes

Britain, 764

The country is slowly recovering from a cruel winter; trees and crops have died under a pall of snow and ice, and there have been disastrous fires among the closely packed wooden houses in the cities. London, Winchester and York have all suffered. One scribe wrote of the season: "An immense snowfall, hardening into ice, unparalleled in all former ages, oppressed the land from the beginning of winter almost until the middle of spring." He did not write much because the weather was so severe that he and his fellow scribes found it too cold to write; even sea mammals, such as seals, froze to death.

'God's companions' launch attack on sin

Dublin, 770

A fresh attack on sin is being launched with the emergence of a strict new monastic order known as the "Culdees", or companions of God. The leader of this ascetic reform movement is Mael Ruain, the abbot of Tallaght, near Dublin.

The Culdees regard the body and all its natural functions as providing constant occasions for sin. Women, too, are a serious source of danger and not to be trusted. Sunday is kept sacred; banned pursuits on that day include work or worldly activities of any kind, cooking and food preparation, and all journeys except those to attend Mass or visit the sick. The Culdees emphasize the importance of prayer as the central duty of believers (→ 807).

An Irish copper-alloy figure of an angel from the late eighth century.

Leading intellectual joins brain drain

Eighth-century Northumbrian text.

Aachen, Germany, 782

A leading Northumbrian scholar and intellectual, the monk Alcuin, is rapidly becoming one of the most influential brains in Europe after leaving York to become head of a school of thinkers established here at the court of King Charles of the Franks. With his friend Albert, the archbishop of York, Alcuin had helped to build up a great library, and the two men had turned York into the major centre of learning in England. Now that Albert has died Alcuin has gone abroad, contributing to a brain drain that has bedevilled the Anglo-Saxon church throughout the century (→ c.795).

Third coup in five years hits Northumbria

Northumbria, 779

A coup has brought five years of strife to a head, with matters set to get worse as three rival dynasties vie for control of the kingdom.The new ruler, Alfwold, has deposed King Athelred, the tyrant who had several of his top noblemen executed for treachery. Alfwold's coup brings the number of kings to have reigned in Northumbria to four in 14 years, three of them in the last five years. In 774, while he was celebrating Easter at York, King Alhred was driven out by Athelred, the son of Athelwold Moll, the man whom Alhred had deposed.

Athelred began ruthlessly removing his potential rivals, but now he in turn has been dispatched by Alfwold, the grandson of King Edbert, whose successful reign is still clearly remembered. In spite of all this internal conflict and instability, Northumbria remains a prosperous region, still too strong for the ambitious King Offa of Mercia to risk an attack (→ 23/9/788).

Pope demands halt to pagan traditions

Mercia, 786

Two papal legates, Bishop George of Ostia and Bishop Theophylact of Iodi, have just completed a tour of Mercia, Wales and Northumbria. Their mission is to enforce papal reforms in the way that the church and the laity lead their lives.

They insist on an end to such pagan practices as slitting the nostrils of horses, fastening their ears and docking their tails, eating horsemeat and deciding lawsuits by casting lots. The pope's demands have been well received by the English kings, not least because they insist on the sanctity of kingship and ban plots against monarchs and the succession of bastards (→ 792).

King killed while visiting mistress

Wessex, 786

King Cynewulf of Wessex has been murdered while visiting his mistress. The killers were led by Cyneheard, a brother of the former King Sigebert of Wessex, who believed that Cynewulf was preparing to exile him. Knowing that the king would have only a small escort, the assassins surrounded the bedchamber. Cynewulf defended himself bravely; before he died he managed to wound Cyneheard so severely that he could not be moved. The next day many of the dead king's men arrived to demand his surrender. Cyneheard offered them bribes to support him, but they killed him and most of his men (→ 815).

Offa builds giant dyke

Part of Offa's great dyke near Mainstone, in Shropshire: a 20th-century view.

Welsh Marches, c.789
King Offa is building a massive earthwork to cut off the whole of Wales from his Mercian kingdom. Planned to run "from sea to sea", from the Severn in the south to the Dee in the north, it will be nearly 160 miles (240 km) long – a greater length than the two Roman walls in northern Britain put together.

Thousands of men are digging a ditch 1.8 metres (6 feet) deep on the Welsh side of the dyke, while behind it an earth rampart 18 metres across and 7.5 metres high is being thrown up, with palisades of timber and, in parts, a stone wall to strengthen it. The design is intended to make it as difficult as possible for the Welsh to ride their horses up the steep bank, and even harder for them to drive rustled cattle down it on the way home. The huge undertaking is not made any easier by the deliberate policy of constructing the dyke to run along the highest parts of the border, allowing the Mercians to dominate the high ground and increase the dyke's defensive capabilities. At some points the men are struggling to cut their way across hills more than 300 metres high.

Offa is able to summon huge numbers of people because of his right to demand his subjects' labour on public works, a duty that extends even to monks. Each community is given its own section of dyke to build under the direction of the king's officials. Villages have to supply oxen and carts to shift the earth and stones, as well as providing shelter and food for the work-gangs (→ 790).

Snub to Canterbury wins papal blessing

Chelsea, London, 787
King Offa has achieved a great political victory at the end of a stormy synod here. Despite vigorous protests he has won agreement to create a new archbishopric at Lichfield, a town only a few miles from his favourite seat at Tamworth, in Mercia.

The move is politically motivated, designed to undercut the power of the archbishop of Canterbury – towards whom Offa feels deep antagonism – and put the king in a position to appoint an archbishop sympathetic to his own views. The pope is backing the move as a vote of confidence to Offa, who supported the papal legates when they came to Britain last year to demand reforms.

The new archbishop, Hygebert, will take over responsibility for all the sees of Mercia from Archbishop Janbert of Canterbury, whose supporters are furious at what they see as a considerable reduction of their authority over the English church. But, confronted by the combined opposition of king and pope, they found themselves eventually forced to concede (→ 792).

Offa dominates England south of Humber as Mercia goes from strength to strength

Mercia, c.789
No Anglo-Saxon king has made his mark as powerfully as Offa. Since fighting his way to the throne in 757, Offa has striven to forge a unified kingdom in middle England.

Offa's is the most successful of the some 30 tribes of Mercia. The heart of their kingdom lies in the land of a tribe called the Tomsaetan, stretching from Breedon-on-the-Hill (south of Derby) to King's Norton (south-west of Birmingham). Offa has a royal church in this area, at Repton, and his main residence at Tamworth. He has created an archbishopric at Lichfield to rival Canterbury.

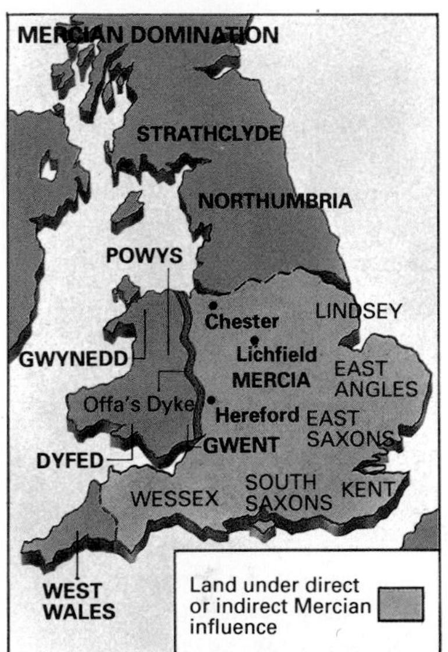

Mercia has no capital, however. Offa keeps on the move, travelling between the farms and estates of his subordinates. With him go his chief men, his bishops and his officials. Accompanied by a baggage train of carts and horses, the royal retinue moves along old Roman roads such as the Fosse Way, collecting tribute and in return granting privileges. Over the three decades that he has reigned, Offa has made Mercia the greatest of the Anglo-Saxon kingdoms. Having consolidated his lands in central England, he has gone on to subdue first Kent and then Wessex. With the exception of East Anglia, all England south of the Humber is now Offa's (→ 790).

Royal marriage row hits Channel trade

A likeness of King Charles, c.1350.

Tamworth, Staffordshire, 790
Two envoys from King Charles of the Franks have been trying to end a dispute between him and King Offa. The two envoys are well known to both kings. Alcuin is a Northumbrian scholar who has been the head of Charles's fine court school, while Gervold is the official responsible for much of the toll collection at Frankish ports.

Cross-Channel trade has been badly hit by the row, which began when the Frankish king proposed that his son Charles should marry one of Offa's daughters. Offa refused to agree to this unless Charles also agreed to let his daughter Bertha marry Offa's son Egfrith.

Furious at what he saw as Offa's impertinence, Charles imperiously ordered all his continental ports to close to English shipping – a move that has severely damaged the prosperity of London, Ipswich and other English ports.

Offa too is angry. He descends from the Mercian royal line of kings, which he feels is more than a match for Bertha and Charles, who come from a line of mere dukes. More seriously, Charles has begun to allow exiles from Mercia to settle in France. These include Egbert – who is a rival to Offa's son-in-law, Beortric, for the throne of Wessex (→ 794).

791-800

Northumbria, 14 September 792. The exiled King Osred returns but is killed by King Athelred (→ 29/9).

Catterick, North Yorkshire, 29 September 792. Athelred marries Alffled, the daughter of King Offa (→ 18/4/796).

Southern England, c.792. Offa reforms the coinage, increasing the amount of silver in it.

Canterbury, Kent, 792. Janbert, who became archbishop in 765, dies. He is succeeded by Athelheard, the abbot of Louth in Lincolnshire, who, unlike Janbert, has good relations with Offa (→ 803).

Sutton Walls, near Hereford, 794. King Athelbert of East Anglia is killed on the orders of Offa (→ 796).

Iona, Strathclyde, 795. Vikings raid the monastery (→ 806).

France, c.795. Alcuin, the Northumbrian monk, writes verse and prose versions of a *Life of St Willibrord* (→ 796).

Mercia, 796. Offa and King Charles of the Franks agree to provide protection for merchants on both sides of the Channel (→ 29/7/796).

France, 796. Alcuin becomes abbot of St Martin's abbey at Tours (→ 5/804).

Northumbria, 18 April 796. Athelred is murdered and succeeded by Osbald, one of those who had plotted against him (→ 26/5/796).

Northumbria, 26 May 796. After ruling for 27 days, Osbald is forced to flee into exile. He is replaced by Eardwulf (→ 2/4/798).

Mercia, 29 July 796. Offa dies; his only son Egfrith, anointed his successor in 787, takes over (→ 12/7/796).

Kent, late 796. After Offa's death an ex-priest, Edbert Praen, leads a revolt. Archbishop Athelheard of Canterbury, a Mercian, has to flee (→ 798).

Northumbria, 2 April 798. Eardwulf defeats the nobles responsible for the murder of Athelred (→ 799).

Kent, 798. Cenwulf of Mercia invades and captures the rebel Edbert, who is blinded and maimed. Cenwulf instals his brother, Cuthred, as king, and Archbishop Athelheard is restored to his see (→ 807).

Northumbria, 799. Eldred, Athelred's murderer, dies in a revenge killing (→ 810).

Viking raiders from Scandinavia attack isle of Lindisfarne

Northumberland, 8 June 793
Viking raiders from Scandinavia [*see report on page 138*] have laid waste to the island of Lindisfarne. Storming ashore from their longships they razed the monastery, killed many of the monks and carried off others as slaves.

It is the first major raid by the Norsemen and has been presaged by many reported omens: lightning, whirlwinds, fiery dragons in the sky and a rain of blood that fell on York Minster. The people were already worried by these portents before the first Norseman set foot on the land; now they are in terror.

The Norse, who are heathens, left little untouched on Lindisfarne, a place so revered that Christians call it Holy Island. They despoiled the altars, seized precious treasures, and butchered and drowned the monks. Many see their actions as manifestations of God's anger at the fornication, theft and violence in society and the wearing of luxurious dress and "pagan" hairstyles. There is a growing clamour for moral reform.

The vikings have been making small forays for the past four years, probing defences and finding them lacking. The attack on Lindisfarne by a fleet of longboats marks a new phase of detailed organization and planning (→ 875).

Disasters treated as divine punishment

Ireland, c.795
A relentless succession of natural disasters through much of the past two decades has left Ireland in a state of near-panic. Disease, drought, famine, thunderstorms and gales have created a widespread belief that the displeasure of God has been incurred and that divine retribution is at hand. Since the early 770s there have been severe storms and outbreaks of dysentery, rabies and smallpox. The cattle have been struck by attacks of cattle murrain, and there have been an eclipse of the moon, famine and floods (→ 17/3/803).

Stone crosses offer new outlet for artists

A cross at Ahenny, in Munster.

A cross at Rothbury, Northumbria.

Britain and Ireland, c.795
Artistic expression has found a distinctive and durable new outlet in recent decades with the erection of numerous carved-stone crosses in Ireland and parts of northern Britain. A form of free-standing cross with relief sculpture which blends continental and Celtic influences has emerged in the islands. In the absence of a church, the crosses serve as symbols of religious faith and as points at which travelling preachers and bishops can address local communities. They are also used for memorial purposes.

The stone crosses usually consist of rectangular sections divided into panels on which figures or decorations are sculpted. There are considerable geographical variations. In Ireland, wheel-headed crosses are particularly popular; some of the most bold and subtle carving can be seen on those at Ahenny, in Munster.

In Britain, stone-carving is a northern speciality – the legacy of the craftsmen who built the monasteries of Benedict Biscop and Wilfrid in Northumbria more than a century ago. There is a fine cross at Bewcastle in Cumbria, while one of the largest is at Ruthwell, in Dumfries and Galloway. It is 5.6 metres (18 feet) high and has scenes from the life of Christ and passages from *The Dream of the Rood*, a poem in which the Cross itself describes Christ's suffering. Accompanying this are pre-Christian-type images of birds and beasts (→ c.930).

The Ruthwell cross: fine carving.

The cross at Bewcastle, Cumbria.

Ambition of Offa to create a dynasty dies with his son

Mercia, December 796
King Egfrith has followed his illustrious father Offa to the grave after a reign of just 141 days, and the kingdom of Mercia is in disarray. Determined that the kind of damaging civil war that often follows the death of a strong monarch should not trouble his son, Offa – builder of the great dyke – had Egfrith consecrated as his successor during his lifetime, a religious act designed to stress the sanctity of kingship. However, there was another inheritance problem that had to be overcome.

Anglo-Saxon kings have no set rules about the system of inheritance, with the result that anyone with a blood relationship to the royal house, no matter how distant, can lay claim to the throne. To stop this, Offa set about murdering his way through generations of his relatives to make sure that there were no other claimants. So effective was this bloody purge that with the unexpected death of Egfrith the throne has passed to Cenwulf, a cousin whose relationship to his predecessor was too distant to have been thought a threat.

The sudden death of his son has frustrated Offa's wish to found a dynasty, reflecting a rare failure by the mightiest king that the English have yet seen. Offa restored Mercia to a great power [*see report on page 131*] and, in spite of his ruthless ambition, was a responsible and efficient Christian ruler. His actions included taking over the mint at Canterbury and organizing a reform of the coinage (→823).

A silver penny in the name of Offa of Mercia, reformer of the coinage.

Irish art reaches new heights at Kells

Leinster, c.800
The art of Celtic manuscript illumination has flowered into a triumphant exaltation of God's glory with the creation of the magnificent Book of Kells, a Latin manuscript of the Christian Gospels. The beginning of each Gospel and each chapter is illustrated, and the borders and paragraph openings are superbly decorated.

The intricate designs are full of surprises which need much study and good eyesight to be appreciated. They testify to the extraordinary skill and patience of the scribes and illuminators who have devoted many years of their lives to the book's creation.

The Gospel According to St Matthew, for example, has a page based on the letters XP, the first two letters of the Greek word *Christos*. The swirling design of scrolls and spirals is artistically pleasing, but what first meets the eye is only the top layer of design. Within each scroll, within each swirl, there are secrets to discover.

Animals peep out of the pages. Two cats play peaceably with four mice. An otter swallows a fish, the symbol of Christianity. There are moths and angels. All but two of the book's 680 pages are produced in vivid colour, and many of them are decorated with gold leaf. The Book of Kells is one of the most ornate editions of the Gospels ever made and, as long as it can be kept safe from raiders, is destined to remain an outstanding treasure of the Irish church (→939).

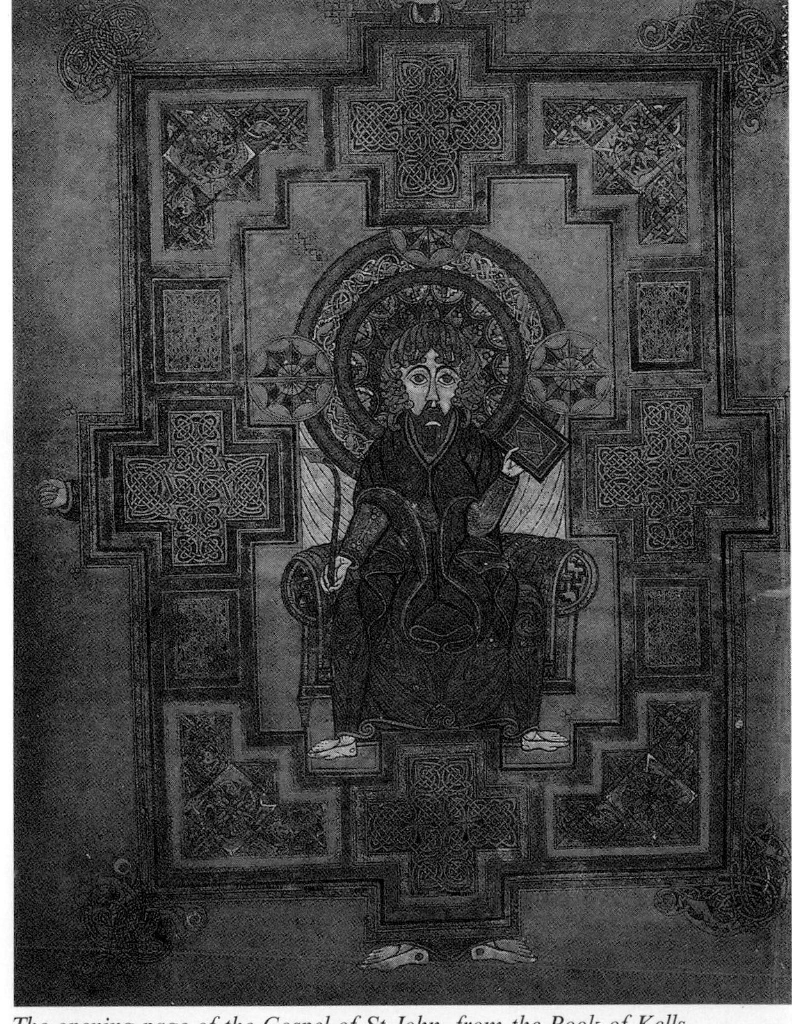
The opening page of the Gospel of St John, from the Book of Kells.

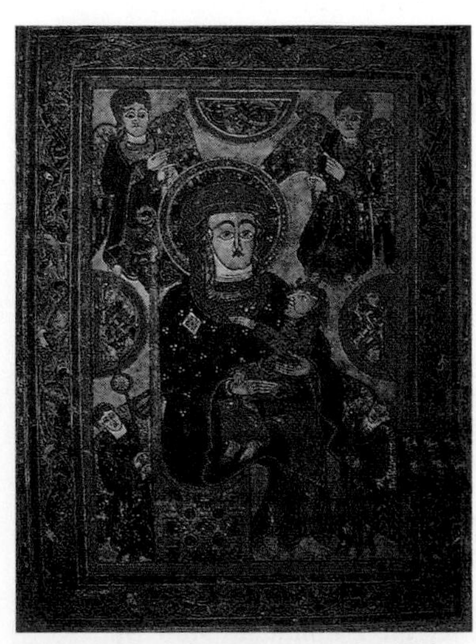
Portrayal of the Virgin and Child.

Intricate design: a text page and illumination from the Kells Gospel-book.

The land the Anglo-Saxons have made their own

England, c.800
For over 300 years the Anglo-Saxons have spread across the land that they call *Angelcynn*, "Angle-race" [England]. The Celtic population has either retreated before them or found a means of coexistence. Apart from the area of the East Angles and East Saxons, most of England is now under the sway of the Anglo-Saxon kingdoms of Mercia and Northumbria [*see map on page 131*], although Mercia's hold over Wessex looks shaky. The Scots, Welsh, Cornish and Irish have kept the Anglo-Saxons at bay.

Anglo-Saxon place names have proliferated. Villages near fords may be named after the nature of the crossing, for example. *Stanford* [Stamford] is the "stony" ford; *Gyldeford* [Guildford] is the ford by the marigolds; *Heorotford* [Hertford] and *Oxnaford* [Oxford] are the crossings for harts and oxen. Some names derive from the kind of land settled. An enclosed area or farm is a *tun*. *Hamtun* [North- and Southampton] may be "home farm" (*ham tun*) or "farm in an enclosed water-meadow" (*hamm tun*). *Aet Heantune* [Wolverhampton] means "(at the) high farm". A large fortified settlement is called a *byrig*: *Cantwarabyrig* [Canterbury] is the *byrig* of the people (*wara*) of Kent (*Cant*). Some such places are close to the remains of a Roman fort or *ceaster*, such as *Hrofesceaster* [Rochester], the "fort belonging to a man called Hrofe". Places are also named after the people – or their leader – who live there. *Godmunddingaham* [Goodmanham] means the "home of the people of Godmund"; *Folcanstan* [Folkestone] is the "stone (where the local assembly is held) of Folca".

Celtic traces remain, however, in river names such as *Afene* [Avon], *Esce* [Exe], *Saefern* [Severn] and *Temese* [Thames]; the first two of these mean just "water". Towns which have Celtic names include *Loidis* [Leeds], *Lundene* [London] and *Mameceaster* [Manchester], whose first element (*Mame-* is from a word meaning "breasts", defining the shape of the hill on which the town was first built (→c.900).

Key to map on facing page [map is not comprehensive]

Aethelinga-eig Athelney, Som.
Afene River Avon.
Andredesweald The Weald of Kent and Sussex.

Baddanbyrig, aet Badbury Rings, Dorset.
Badecanwiellon, to Bakewell, Derbyshire.
Bancornaburg Bangor-is-y-coed, Clwyd.
Bardanstapol Barnstaple, Devon.
Basengum, aet Basingstoke, Hampshire.
Bathum, aet Bath, Avon.
Bearwe, aet Barrow upon Humber, Humberside.
Bebbanburh Bamburgh, N'thd.
Bedanford Bedford.
Beoforlic Beverley, Humberside.
Bruneswald Bromswold Forest, Cambridgeshire.
Brycgstow Bristol, Avon.
Buccingahamm Buckingham.
Buttingtun Buttington, Powys.

Cantwarabyrig Canterbury, Kent.
Carrum, aet Carham, N'thd.
Ceoddor Cheddar, Som.
Cetreht Catterick, North Yorks.
Ciltern Chiltern Hills.
Cirenceaster Cirencester, Glos.
Cisseceaster Chichester, W Sx.
Colneceaster Colchester, Essex.
Corebricg Corbridge, N'thd.
Cridiantun Crediton, Devon.
Cynibre Kinver Forest, Staffs.
Cwatbrycg Bridgnorth, Salop.

Deoraby Derby.
Devennport Davenport, Ches.
Dofran Dover, Kent.
Dorcanceaster Dorchester-on-Thames, Oxfordshire.
Dornwaraceaster Dorchester, Dorset.
Dunholm Durham City.

Eamotum, aet Eamont Bridge, Cumbria.
Earden Arden, Forest of [English midlands].
Elmete Elmet, Pennines.
Elmham North Elmham, N'fk.
Eoforwic York.
Escanceaster Exeter, Devon.
Esce River Exe.

Farne Farne Islands.
Folcanstan Folkestone, Kent.

Gefrin Yeavering, Northum.
Gipeswic Ipswich, Suffolk.
Gleawanceaster Gloucester.
Glestingabyrig Glastonbury, Somerset.
Godmunddingaham Goodmanham, Humberside.
Grantanbrycg Cambridge.
Grenewic Greenwich, London.
Gyldeford Guildford, Surrey.
Gyruum, in Jarrow, Tyne and Wear.

Haestingas Hastings, E Sussex.
Hamtun Northampton.
Hamtun Southampton, Hants.
Heantune, aet Wolverhampton, West Midlands.
Hefresham Heversham, Cumbria.
Heorotford Hertford.
Hrofesceaster Rochester, Kent.
Hrypadun Repton, Derbyshire.
Hrypum, in Ripon, N Yorks.
Humbre River Humber.
Huntandun Huntingdon, Cambridgeshire.
Hwiccawudu Wychwood Forest, Oxfordshire.
Hwitern Whithorn, Dumfries and Galloway.

Laestinga eu Lastingham, North Yorkshire.
Laewes Lewes, East Sussex.
Legaceaster Chester, Ches.
Liccidfeld Lichfield, Staffs.
Ligoraceaster Leicester.
Lindcylene Lincoln.
Lindisfarnea Lindisfarne, Northumberland.
Loidis Leeds, West Yorks.
Luel Carlisle, Cumbria.
Lundene London.

Maerse River Mersey.
Magilros Melrose, Borders.
Mameceaster Manchester.
Medeshamstede Peterborough, Cambridgeshire.
Miodowaege River Medway.
Moerheb Morfe Forest, Salop.

North-sae Bristol Channel.
Northwic Norwich, Norfolk.

Oxnaford Oxford.

Pefenesea Pevensey, E Sussex.
Peoclond The Peak, Derbyshire.
Portesmutha Portsmouth, Hampshire.
Raegeheafde, aet Gateshead, Tyne and Wear.
Readingum, to Reading, Berks.
Reculf Reculver, Kent.
Rumcofa Runcorn, Cheshire.

Saefern River Severn.
Sanctae Albanes stow St Albans, Hertfordshire.
Sanctae Eadmundes stow Bury St Edmunds, Suffolk.
Sanctae Germane St Germans, Cornwall.
Sceapig Sheppey, Kent.
Sceobyrig, to Shoeburyness, Ex.
Scirwudu Sherwood Forest, Nottinghamshire.
Scrobbesbyrig, on Shrewsbury, Salop.
Sealwudu Selwood [SW Eng].
Searoburg Salisbury, Wiltshire.
Snotingaham Nottingham.
Staengfordesbrycg, aet Stamford Bridge, Humberside.
Staethford Stafford.
Stanford Stamford, Lincs.
Streonaeshalch Whitby, N Yks.
Suthriganaweorc Southwark, London.

Tamoworthig Tamworth, Staffs.
Temese River Thames.
Tese River Tees.
Theodford Thetford, Norfolk.
Tiouulfingacaestir Little-borough, Nottinghamshire.
Tottaness Totnes, Devon.
Treante River Trent.
Tuidi River Tweed.

Use River Ouse.

Waege River Wye.
Waeringwicum, aet Warwick.
Weogorenaleag Wyre Forest, Hereford and Worcestershire.
Weogornaceaster Worcester.
Westmynster Westminster.
WihT Isle of Wight.
Wintanceaster Winchester, Hampshire.
Wiuraemuda Monkwearmouth, Tyne and Wear.
Wreocen The Wrekin, Salop.

Ylig Ely, Cambridgeshire.

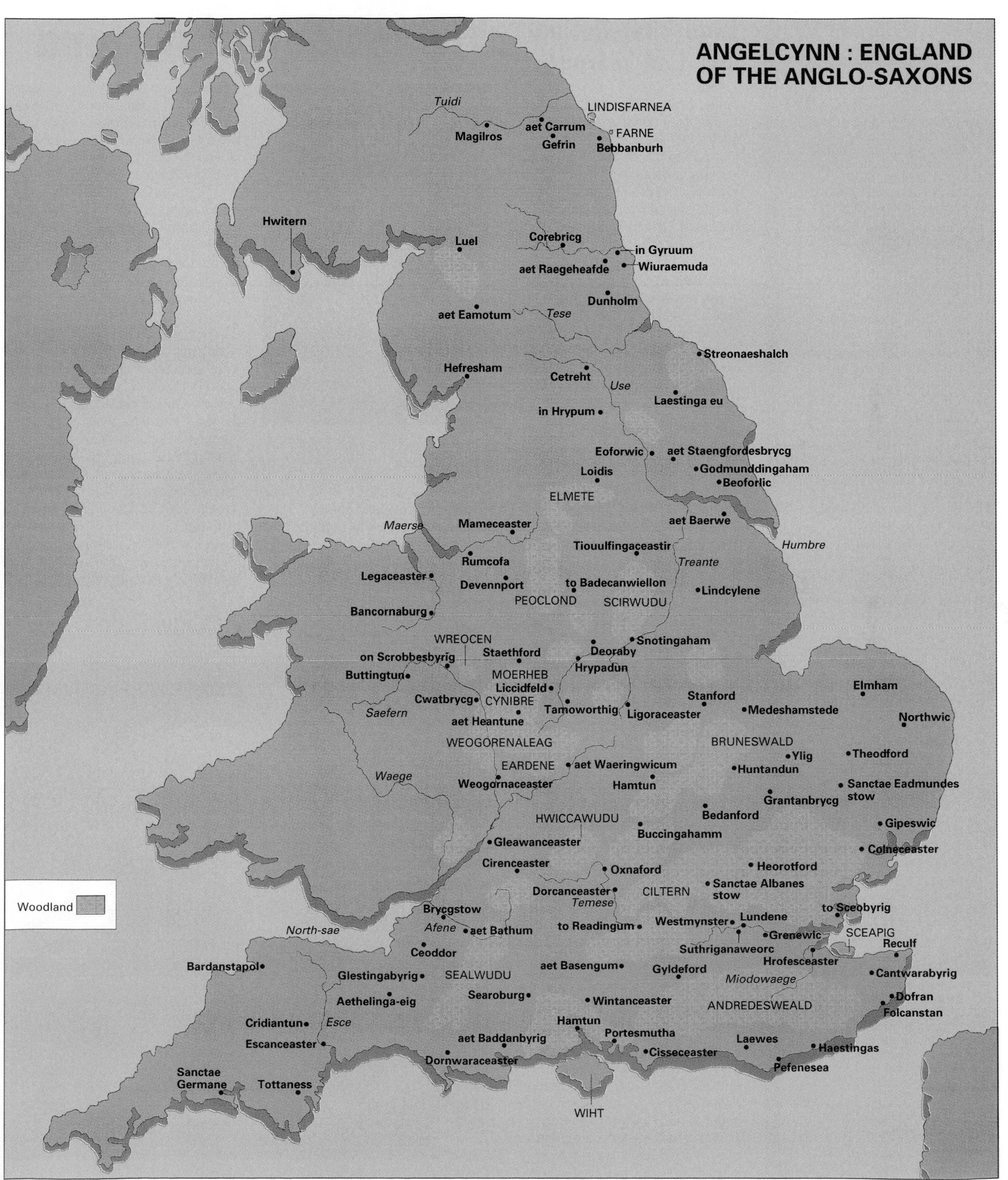
ANGELCYNN : ENGLAND OF THE ANGLO-SAXONS
Woodland
Tuidi
LINDISFARNEA
FARNE
Magilros
aet Carrum
Gefrin
Bebbanburh
Hwitern
Luel
Corebricg
in Gyruum
aet Raegeheafde
Wiuraemuda
Dunholm
aet Eamotum
Tese
Streonaeshalch
Hefresham
Cetreht
Use
Laestinga eu
in Hrypum
Eoforwic
aet Staengfordesbrycg
Godmunddingaham
Beoforlic
Loidis
ELMETE
aet Baerwe
Maerse
Mameceaster
Tiouulfingaceastir
Humbre
Rumcofa
Treante
Legaceaster
Devennport
to Badecanwiellon
Lindcylene
PEOCLOND
SCIRWUDU
Bancornaburg
WREOCEN
Snotingaham
on Scrobbesbyrig
Staethford
Deoraby
Hrypadun
Buttingtun
MOERHEB
Liccidfeld
Elmham
Stanford
Cwatbrycg
CYNIBRE
Saefern
Tamoworthig
Ligoraceaster
Medeshamstede
aet Heantune
Northwic
WEOGORENALEAG
BRUNESWALD
Ylig
Theodford
EARDENE
aet Waeringwicum
Huntandun
Waege
Weogornaceaster
Hamtun
Sanctae Eadmundes stow
Grantanbrycg
Bedanford
HWICCAWUDU
Gipeswic
Buccingahamm
Gleawanceaster
Colneceaster
Cirenceaster
Heorotford
Oxnaford
Sanctae Albanes stow
Dorcanceaster
CILTERN
Temese
to Sceobyrig
Brycgstow
Lundene
Westmynster
North-sae
Afene
aet Bathum
to Readingum
Grenewic
SCEAPIG
Reculf
Suthriganaweorc
Ceoddor
Hrofesceaster
Bardanstapol
aet Basengum
Gyldeford
Cantwarabyrig
Glestingabyrig
SEALWUDU
Miodowaege
Aethelinga-eig
Searoburg
Wintanceaster
Dofran
ANDREDESWEALD
Folcanstan
Cridiantun
Esce
Hamtun
Portesmutha
Escanceaster
aet Baddanbyrig
Laewes
Haestingas
Cisseceaster
Dornwaraceaster
Pefenesea
Sanctae Germane
Tottaness
WIHT

801 - 829

Co Clare, 17 March 803. More than 1,000 people are killed in storms on the west coast of Ireland (→ 11/11/892).

England, 803. A synod at a place called Clovesho re-establishes, on papal orders, the power of Canterbury, suppressing the rival archbishopric set up by King Offa at Lichfield (→ 8/805).

Canterbury, Kent, August 805. Bishop Wulfred succeeds Athelheard, who died earlier this year, as archbishop (→ 824).

Iona, Strathclyde, 806. Vikings ravage the island for a third time, killing 68 monks and laymen.→

Co Meath, 807. Monks from Iona found a church at Kells on land given by the see of Armagh (→ 851).

Kent, 807. King Cuthred, the brother of King Cenwulf of Mercia, dies. Baldred succeeds him (→ 825).

Northumbria, 810. Eanred becomes king following the death of King Eardwulf last year (→ 1/11/866).

Dunkeld, Tayside, 811. Constantine, who proclaimed himself king of Dal Riata this year, establishes a new church to replace Iona as the spiritual centre of his realm (→ 906).

Cornwall, 815. King Egbert of Wessex, who succeeded in 802 on the death of Beortric, ravages the area (→ 825).

Tayside, 820. Oengus II succeeds as king of the Picts and Scots on the death of his brother, Constantine. Because of a renewed threat from Norse raiders the kingdom is based at Forteviot (→ 834).

Northumbria, c.820. Athelwulf, the poet, finishes his poem *De abbatibus* [*On the abbots*], a history of the island of Lindisfarne.

Mercia, 823. Ceolwulf, king since 821, who last year sacked Deganwy and ravaged the kingdom of Powys, is deposed by Beornwulf (→ 830).

Southern England, 825. King Egbert of Wessex reigns over southern England, excluding Cornwall, following victories at Galford and Wroughton, where he regained control of Kent and drove out its king, Baldred, and at Swindon, where he killed the Mercian king, Beornwulf (→ 838).

Iona, 825. Vikings savagely kill Blathmac, the head of the community.→

English intellectual has died in France

Tours, France, May 804

Alcuin of York, the great English intellectual who played an important role in the revival of European learning which was fostered by King Charles of the Franks (Charlemagne), has died at the abbey of St Martin in Tours, where, as abbot, he occupied one of the top ecclesiastical posts in the Frankish kingdom. He was 69.

He was a man of many parts – scholar, teacher, poet, theologian – and when he was invited to Charles's glittering court he gathered round him a group of cosmopolitan thinkers who moulded the Frankish king's ideas into practical form. He became master of the court school and urged the establishment of schools throughout the kingdom. He also supervised the revision of the Latin Bible, and yet he had time to write hundreds of letters, some of them in verse, to his friends. Perhaps his best-known work is an epic poem celebrating York, where he was educated.

Vikings devastate Iona

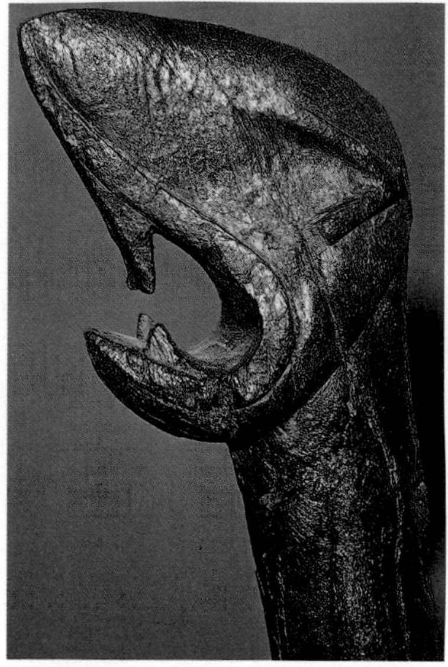

Adorning a ship: a sea monster.

Iona, Strathclyde, 806

In a savage attack on Iona, viking raiders from Scandinavia have butchered 68 monks and laymen and burnt the abbey built by the great Irish missionary St Colum Cille (Columba). It was the third such raid on the island in 11 years and the most devastating yet. It has also proved to be the last straw for Abbot Cellach, who has decided to abandon the island, taking with him the remains of Iona's library. He hopes to found a new monastic community at Kells in the Irish kingdom of Brega [in Leinster].

The monastery on the tiny island of Iona was founded over 200 years ago when Colum Cille arrived with 12 companions to bring Christianity to far northern Britain. He became known as the apostle of Caledonia and is reputed to have converted all of northern Scotland.

Abbot Cellach's decision to pull out has caused considerable dismay in the Hebrides, where the community is held in high regard by local chiefs, many of whose ancestors are buried on Iona. In the circumstances, a small number of monks have decided not to leave with the abbot; they will seek to keep the faith alive on the island despite the near certainty that the pagan vikings will return (→ 825).

Feuding neighbours risk losing all under new Irish law code

Ireland, 806

Neighbours who go to war with each other could lose everything if they breach a new law code promulgated this year by High King Aed Oirdnide of the Ui Neill dynasty. The new code, called the "law of Patrick" after the great missionary saint, resembles legal codes in other Irish provinces, which are a collaboration of ecclesiastical and secular authorities to cut down lawlessness.

The codes cover areas which include crimes against women, the clergy and cattle, the protection of non-combatants in warfare, and sinning on Sunday. The penalties for law-breaking consist for the most part of a system of fines and compensation. Details of how this works in practice are not completely clear, but the basic principle is simple: the greater the crime the more severe the compensation. People who fight with their neighbours do so knowing that if, for example, they harm church property or non-combatants they may lose all they own in fines (→ 891).

Church property: a chalice of c.800 buried at Derrynaflan, in Co Tipperary.

Raiders hit Irish coasts

A settlement on Skellig, Co Kerry.

Co Kerry, 824
The viking terror has struck again and Skellig Rock, off the west coast of Ireland, has been attacked by raiders. They captured the hermit Etgal, who died shortly afterwards of hunger and thirst. This is only one of a series of isolated attacks which the vikings have made on Ireland in the past 30 years, starting with the destruction of the church on Lambay Island, off Dublin, in 795. Only last year the vikings raided Bangor in the north-east with devastating results. Many bishops and scholars were killed, and the shrine of the great missionary and teacher Comgall was destroyed.

Each raid follows a predictable pattern. The vikings, or Norse [*see report on page 138*], concentrate on coastal areas easily accessible in their swift longboats, and there is rarely any warning of a strike. They arrive and leave with great speed, killing and taking prisoners as they go, and are interested only in acquiring valuable objects. The wealthy monastic settlements, with their concentrated populations, valuable stock and churches filled with precious ornaments, bear the brunt of the attacks. Because of the constant threat many communities live in a permanent state of terror, especially those near monasteries and the sea. The rest of the population, fully occupied with the hardships of daily life, seems largely unmoved by viking atrocities (→ c.837).

Silent monk is torn apart by vikings

Iona, Strathclyde, 825
The pagan vikings have returned to the island of Iona for another orgy of slaughter, looting and destruction. Among their victims is Blathmac, the Irishman who headed the small monastic community which remained after the devastating raid of 806.

Blathmac is said to have had a vision warning him of the raid but to have chosen to stay and face martyrdom. When they landed, the vikings demanded to know the whereabouts of the shrine of St Colum Cille (Columba), the founder of the monastery on Iona, which they wanted to plunder. Blathmac refused to divulge the information they wanted and was torn apart for his pains.

Blathmac's bravery is not of the sort to impress vikings, however, because Christianity stands for everything that their ethical code tells them to despise: peace and humility as opposed to war and heroism (→ 849).

Irish dynasties fight over Armagh abbot

North-eastern Ireland, 827
The defeat in battle at Leth Caim of the king of Airgialla, in north-eastern Ireland, marks another milestone in the development of the relationship between church and state in Ireland. The conflict was triggered by a disagreement between Eogan Mainistrech, the abbot of Armagh, and the king, who drove Eogan from the abbacy and replaced him with own half-brother. Niall Caille, the king of the rival Cenel nEogain dynasty, went to the aid of Eogan and, following a war against Airgialla, succeeded in reinstating him.

The abbots of Armagh – which is in effect the ecclesiastical capital of Ireland – have tended to be more astute in their dealings with local rulers than have their counterparts in parts of the country. They have recognized and supported the growing power rise of the Cenel nEogain, quickly spotting the value to the church of influential royal patronage (→ 848).

Archbishop is forced to submit to the king

Mercia, 824
A long dispute between the kings of Mercia and Archbishop Wulfred has been settled. The archbishop will yield to the king a large estate in Oxfordshire and pay him a fine of £120. In return, the king is to restore Wulfred's estates in Kent.

King Cenwulf suspended Wulfred for six years after he tried to take control of two monasteries owned by the king's daughter. The settlement means that the church has accepted that lay people, particularly royals, will continue to control church land. Since he became archbishop of Canterbury, in 805, Wulfred has tried to strengthen the powers of bishops over church property but has lost the battle, at least for now. The kings have shown that to control land they will go to any lengths, including deposing an archbishop (→ 27/8/833).

Under the symbol of St Luke: a decorated bible made at Canterbury 800-850.

Different grades of king rule in Ireland

Ireland, c.825
Ireland is in disarray, with many factions vying for supremacy – a situation complicated by the different grades of kings who control the royal dynasties. The lowest are the kings of local tribal regions. Next in the hierarchy come the "great kings", or overlords of the tribal kings. At the top are usually the kings of provinces, including the so-called "high king of Ireland" – whose title is more a claim than a reality. In Ireland a king is believed to be sacred. In some inauguration rites, a white mare is killed and the king undergoes symbolic union with it by bathing in its broth and drinking it. A poet then recites the king's genealogy and sings his praises (→ 827).

830-851

Mercia, 830. King Wiglaf of Mercia regains his throne after being driven out last year by King Egbert of Wessex (→ 840).

Canterbury, Kent, 27 Aug 833. Ceolnoth becomes archbishop after the deaths of Wulfred and his successor Feolgild earlier this year (→ 870).

Fife, 834. King Oengus II of the Picts and Scots, who founded the church at St Andrews, dies (→ 839).

Cornwall, 838. King Egbert, defeated by the Norse in 836, beats a Cornish/Norse alliance at Hingston Down (→ 839).

Scotland, 839. Eoganan, the successor of Oengus II as king of the Picts and Scots, is killed at sea by the Norse (→ c.840).

Kent, 839. Athelwulf, the new king of Wessex, grants control of Kent to his eldest son, Athelstan.→

Strathclyde, c.840. Kenneth mac Alpin, an ally of the Norse, seizes control of the Scots after the death of Eoganan (→ c.844).

Dublin, 841. A Norse settlement has sprung up at Dubh linn [Black pool], which is at the mouth of the river Liffey (→ 848).

South-eastern England, 842. Norse raiders ravage London and Rochester (→ 865).

Gwynedd, 844. Rhodri succeeds Merfyn "the Freckled" as king (→ 853).

Leinster, 848. The Dublin Norse are defeated by High King Mael Sechnaill, who drowned Thorgest, one of their leaders, in 845.→

Iona, Strathclyde, 849. Because of the Norse threat the remains of St Colum Cille (Columba) are moved for safe keeping (→ 1037).

Co Louth, 850. Over 260 people hiding in a church at Trevet are burnt by Cinead mac Conaing, the king of Brega [in Leinster], who allies with the Norse against High King Mael Sechnaill (→ 851).

North-eastern Ireland, 851. High King Mael Sechnaill of the Ui Neill dynasty, who executed his rival Cinead earlier this year, is recognized as overlord by the powerful Ulaid dynasty (→ 861).

Thanet, Kent, 851. A permanent viking settlement is established (→ 865).

Sandwich, Kent, 851. King Athelstan of Kent defeats a viking fleet at sea (→ 856).

Norse terror raids spread as invaders sail up Irish rivers

Norse plunder: Irish metal figure.

Eastern Ireland, c.837

The Norse assault on Ireland has intensified. A fleet of 60 ships has sailed up the river Boyne, and another fleet, almost as large, has reached the river Liffey. Fierce raids have been carried out along the Liffey valley and in the plains of Meath, with many people being killed and property looted.

This development is viewed with great alarm. Until now raids by the Norse, or vikings [*see report right*], have been limited to coastal areas and the islands, but clearly the leaders are learning the geography of the country and the location of its harbours and navigable rivers. This means that they can spread their reign of terror further inland.

Last year the Norse sailed up the river Shannon and devastated large areas of Connacht in the west of Ireland. They have also established themselves at Arklow and Louth, from where they raid the surrounding countryside. These settlements provide permanent bases for bands of trained fighting men, representing a new threat to the Irish. However, native rulers, nearly powerless against swift seaborne attacks, should at least stand a chance against land-based forces (→ 841).

Newcomers put down roots in Scotland

Northern Scotland, 837

After decades of terrifying, brutal raiding, the pagan Norse and their families from Scandinavia are now swarming into northern Scotland and the Hebrides to settle on the very lands which they had devastated. In many places they already outnumber the native Gaelic speakers, who now refer to the Hebrides as "Innse Gall" [Islands of the Foreigners]. The long Norse homesteads are rapidly replacing the smaller native dwellings, Scandinavian dialects are driving out Gaelic, and places that have had Celtic names for a thousand years are vanishing under the impact of the colonists. The Pictish region of Cait, for example, has become Katanes [Caithness] and the Norse term for farm, *stadir*, is now widely used on Orkney and Shetland.

For the colonists, most of whom are farmers or fishermen, northern Scotland and the Western Isles offer a nostalgic reminder of the mountains and fjords of their native Scandinavia. At home, Scandinavian tribal chiefs are exploiting the overseas settlements to seize control of the trade routes which link Scandinavia to Ireland via the Orkneys and Hebrides (→ 839).

Welsh historian blends fact and legend

Wales, c.835

A Welsh scribe has gathered together fact and hearsay to write a history of his people. The *Historia Britonum* [*History of the Britons*], attributed to one Nennius, covers the origins of the Britons and the Roman occupation and ends with King Arthur's victories over the Saxon invaders. The history, as Nennius admits, combines popular legend and hard fact, drawn "from the annals of the Romans, the writings of the Holy Fathers, the annals of the Irish and the Saxons and our own traditions". Typical of the blend is the treatment of two British kings, Vortigern and Arthur. Vortigern has a basis in fact while Arthur is drawn from legend – yet both receive equal attention (→ 893).

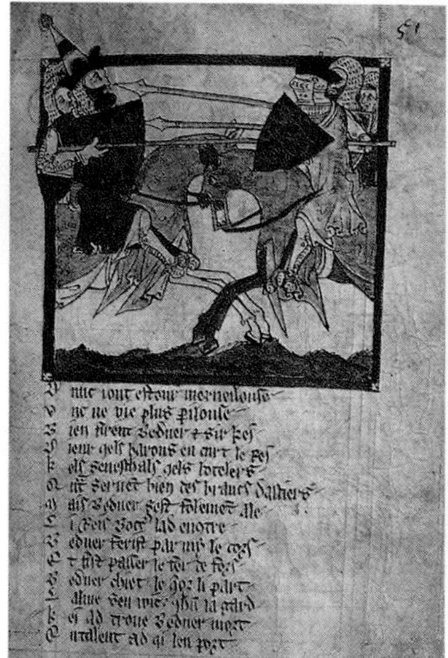

King Arthur: a 13th-century view.

Rampaging Norse known by many names

British Isles, c.840

Everywhere they go – and they go virtually all over the known world – those terrifying freebooters of the north, the Norse, are identified by special names. The Anglo-Saxons call them *wicingas* or *Dene*, vikings or Danes (even when describing Norwegians or Swedes). Latin chroniclers in Britain and on the continent use *nordmanni* [northmen], the Arabs of Spain *al-majus* [heathen], the Germans *ascomanni* [shipmen], and the Greeks of Constantinople *Rus* or *varangoi*, names of uncertain origins. They themselves prefer *Northmenn* or *vikingar* – vikings, a name that may mean originally someone lurking in a bay (*vik*), or a fighter, or even a trader. For those on the sharp end of an attack, however, only one translation fits – "raiders".

In fact, they are people from the petty kingdoms of Scandinavia. Whether Danish, Norwegian or Swedish, they "go viking" as a means to the good life. Trade, piracy and land-taking are all grist to the mill – and woe betide anyone who gets in their way (→ c.900).

Power of Wessex is vastly greater as eventful reign ends

Egbert: a 19th-century engraving.

Wessex, 839
King Egbert of Wessex has died after a long and turbulent reign which saw his realm grow vastly in influence. The son of a Kentish sub-king, Egbert lost out to Beortric – a protégé of King Offa of Mercia – in a dynastic quarrel for the throne of Wessex; he was forced to flee to the court of the Frankish King Charles (Charlemagne) until his rival died in 802.

On his return to England Egbert took the throne in a rebellion against Mercian sovereignty. He then embarked on an expansionist policy, striking west against the Britons of Cornwall in 815. Next, in 825, he waged a campaign against Mercia and defeated its king, Beornwulf, at the Battle of Ellendun. Turning eastwards, he took control of Kent and East Anglia.

Egbert drove out Beornwulf's successor Wiglaf in 829 and turned north to subdue Northumbria. He was recognized as overlord of all the English kingdoms, but in 830 Wiglaf regained Mercia and at the same time Egbert faced the growing threat of invasion by vikings. They defeated him in 836, but two years later he got his revenge by beating a combined army of Britons and vikings at Hingston Down in Cornwall. It was to be the warrior-king's last battle (→851).

Mausoleum constructed for Mercian ruler

Derbyshire, 840
The kingdom of Mercia is mourning its ruler, King Wiglaf, who held out against repeated attacks by King Egbert of Wessex. The king is to be buried in the Mercian royal mausoleum in the convent at Repton, which is one of the largest in Mercia; the late king deeply revered its abbess and nuns.

Mercia almost disintegrated in the infighting that followed the death of King Cenwulf in 821. King Egbert of Wessex, Mercia's powerful neighbour to the south, exploited the kingdom's instability to launch aggression, defeating King Beornwulf in 825.

Beornwulf died later that year, and Wiglaf came to the throne in 827 after Beornwulf's successor Ludeca was killed in battle. Although Egbert drove Wiglaf into exile in 829, Wiglaf recovered his throne in 830 and held it for ten years despite continuing pressure from Wessex. He reasserted Mercian authority over Kent, where Archbishop Wulfred had taken advantage of the earlier disarray in Mercia to recover lost lands.

A coin struck in the name of Wiglaf.

The Mercian-controlled port and city of London, strategically positioned as it is between Mercia, Kent and Wessex, remains an important base. Despite this, however, Wiglaf was not able to restore Mercia to the position which it had enjoyed under King Offa. Mercia and Wessex continue to fight over the upper Thames valley, and the future looks unstable, with a growing viking threat and dynastic disputes within Mercia itself (→869).

Norse get a taste of their own medicine

Ireland, 848
At last the Irish kings are turning the tables on the Norse invaders, a task made easier since the Norse now operate from fixed bases and are no longer mobile targets. High King Mael Sechnaill of the Ui Neill dynasty has been harrying the Norse for a number of years since they carried out a series of raids in the Shannon valley. In 845 he defeated them and had Thorgest, one of their leaders, drowned in the river Owel. This year Mael Sechnaill has also destroyed the Norse settlement at the mouth of the Liffey with the help of another Irish king. Cooperation between rulers is becoming an effective tool against the Norse (→851).

Irish thinker writes on things to come

Ireland, c.851
The eminent Irish scholar, metaphysician and thinker Johannes Scotus Eriugena has written a major theological tract called *De praedestinatione* [*On predestination*]. Although little is known of his early life, Eriugena visited France some time around 847 and later became a close friend of King Charles "the Bald" of the Franks. He is known to be well versed in logic, but his views are seen as controversial and unorthodox. He is one of the founders of the philosophical school of Realists, believing that "Everything is God, God is everything" (→893).

The famous scholar: a later portrait.

First 'king of Scots and Picts' emerges from arduous war

Scotland, c.844
After a devastating seven-year war, Kenneth mac Alpin, the ruler of Dal Riata, the south-western Scottish kingdom, has united his kingdom with that of the Picts, who dominate the north-east. Kenneth seized power in Dal Riata after a viking invasion and, joining forces with the Hebridean vikings, turned on the Picts. As the struggle dragged on, Kenneth set out to rally his troops with an ingenious trick: he made one of his servants dress up as an angel and appear before the men with a promise that if they held fast God would soon give them victory over the Picts.

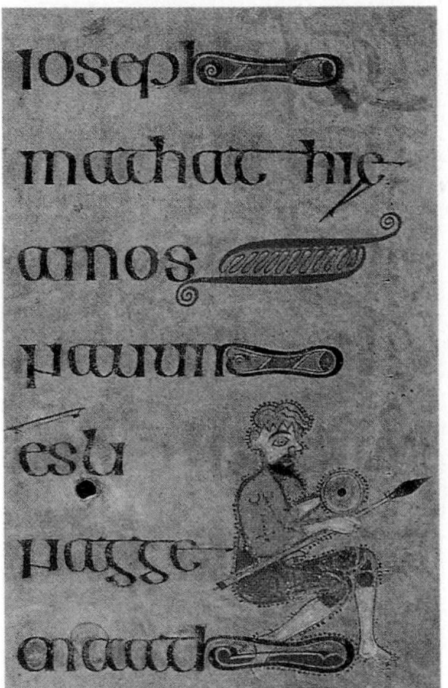
A Scots warrior (Book of Kells).

In the event, Kenneth's victory had its roots in another piece of treachery. He organized a "peace banquet" to which chiefs from both sides were invited. The Pictish leaders were greeted as heroes and seated on special benches set up over concealed pits. On a given signal the benches were overturned; the helpless Picts fell into the pits and were hacked to pieces by the triumphant Scots. Kenneth now presents himself as the first king of Scots *and* Picts. Earlier rulers have claimed to be overlords of both peoples, but his ruthless determination means that a unified kingdom may now be a lasting reality (→858).

852 - 869

Wales, 853. Burgred, king of Mercia since 852, and King Athelwulf of Wessex subdue the southern kingdoms (→856).

Orkney, 853. The Norse chief known as Olaf "the White" launches a bid to be king of the Dublin Norse from a new base in Orkney (→857).

Gwynedd, 856. King Rhodri is dubbed "Mawr [the Great]" by his followers after defeating the Norse warrior Orm and his "Black Army" (→c.872).

Western Isles, 857. Olaf the White defeats the Hebridean Norse under an ex-ally, Ketil Flatnose, who had proclaimed himself king of the islands in defiance of Olaf (→866).

Iona, Strathclyde, 858. Kenneth mac Alpin, the king of both the Scots and the Picts, dies (→13/4/862).

Wessex, 858. Athelwulf dies. His son Athelbald succeeds and controversially marries his father's widow, Judith (→860).

Wessex, 860. Athelbald dies; his wife Judith returns to her native France and his brother Athelbert succeeds (→871).

Dublin, 861. The Norse establish an alliance with the Irish chief Aed Findliath against High King Mael Sechnaill II (→27/11/862).

Scotland, 13 April 862. King Donald II, Kenneth mac Alpin's successor, dies (→866).

Ireland, 27 November 862. High King Mael Sechnaill dies and is succeeded by his enemy Aed Findliath (→863).

Co Meath, 863. Norsemen sack the ancient Boyne tombs (→866).

North-eastern Ireland, 866. Aed Findliath destroys Norse settlements to avenge raids in the Boyne valley (→868).

Northern Scotland, 866. Olaf the White's Dublin Norse ravage Pictish lands (→870).

York, 1 Nov 866. The Norse sack the city (→23/3/867).

Humberside, 867. A Norse fleet arrives in the Humber estuary (→869).

North Yorkshire, 867. The Norse destroy Whitby Abbey (→869).

Co Louth, 868. High King Aed Findliath defeats a force of Norsemen and Leinstermen at Killineery (→877).

Nottingham, 869. Burgred surrenders the town to the Norse (→7/871).

'Great army' lands in East Anglia

East Anglia, 865
In the latest threat to Britain from the warlike Scandinavian peoples, a "great army" of Norse has landed in East Anglia, led by Ivar "the Boneless" [*see report on page 142*] and his brother Halfdan, the sons of Ragnar Lothbrok. This is more than a raid: the brothers are seeking conquest, and their army is planning to stay.

The landing follows a treacherous act by another group of Norse in Kent earlier this year. A large force arrived at Thanet and made a truce with the Kentish people, promising in return for money not to attack them. In spite of this, the Norse stole out at night and ravaged wide areas of eastern Kent.

Much of western Europe, from northern Scotland to the Mediterranean, is now being harassed by these ambitious warriors. They come from Norway, Sweden and Denmark, and although they recognize differences in origin among themselves, these are rarely appreciated by their victims. [The Scandinavians are often referred to collectively as "Norse", "Danes" or "vikings", regardless of their exact place of origin; see report on page 138]. A common language and culture, despite regional variations, make joint expeditions between Norse armies relatively easy, while their enemies are often weak and fragmented culturally, linguistically and politically (→866).

Tools of the fierce invaders: a group of Norse weapons from London Bridge.

Norse gilt-bronze bird figures, used as brooches or harness mountings.

Child bride for king in bid for French ally

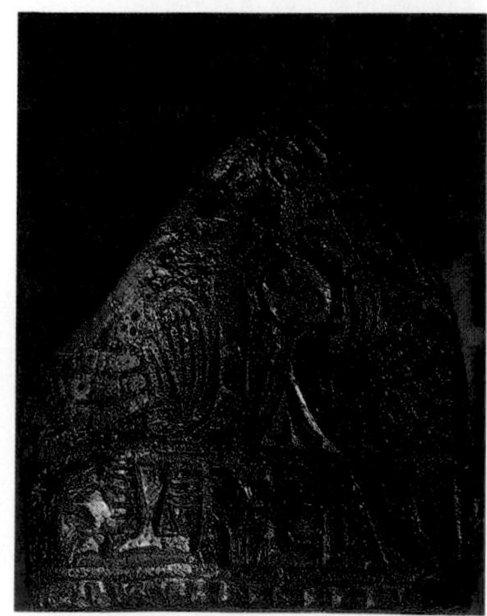

A decorated ring belonging to the 50-year-old Athelwulf of Wessex.

Wessex, 856
Athelwulf, the king of Wessex, has married Judith, the 12-year-old daughter of the Frankish king, Charles the Bald, on his way back from a pilgrimage to Rome. She is 38 years his junior. The marriage creates a diplomatic link between Wessex and Charles's kingdom but, ironically, threatens Athelwulf's rule. For Athelbald, his eldest son, fears that a stepmother and future stepbrothers backed by Frankish power will threaten his succession, and he is prepared to take up arms against his father. Reports from France suggest that the king will compromise, dividing Wessex in order to avoid war (→858).

A sculpted Pict wears trousers similar to those of the ancient Scythians of eastern Europe.

York falls to the Norse

York, 23 March 867
York, the chief city of Northumbria, has fallen to the Norse "great army", and the two rival kings of Northumbria, Aella and Osbert, have died in a joint attempt to retake it. Osbert was killed in the fighting, while Aella has been sacrificed to the Norse god Odin in a gruesome ritual.

Exploiting a civil war between Aella and Osbert, the Norse leader Ivar "the Boneless" [*see report on page 142*] – whose army had been wreaking havoc further south since its invasion in 865 – first seized York last November. The city's capture followed some crafty manoeuvring by the Norse, which included winning Aella's confidence and bribing some of the Northumbrian nobility to stand aside if Ivar were to make a bid for the throne. The Northumbrian response was delayed until Aella and Osbert could patch up their dispute and mount a joint attack.

At first they did well and fought their way through the city's old Roman defences, but soon the Norse began to get the better of them. They were forced back and defeated, and Osbert fell in battle. Aella, meanwhile, was betrayed to and captured by the Norse and subjected to the horrifying ritual of the "blood eagle": his ribs were hacked from his spine, and his lungs were torn out and arranged on his back to resemble the wings of an eagle. Ivar claims that his father, Ragnar Lothbrok, was killed when Aella threw him into a pit of vipers. The story is untrue, but Ivar has used it as a justification for killing Aella in such a manner (→869).

'Blood eagle' rite claims East Anglian ruler

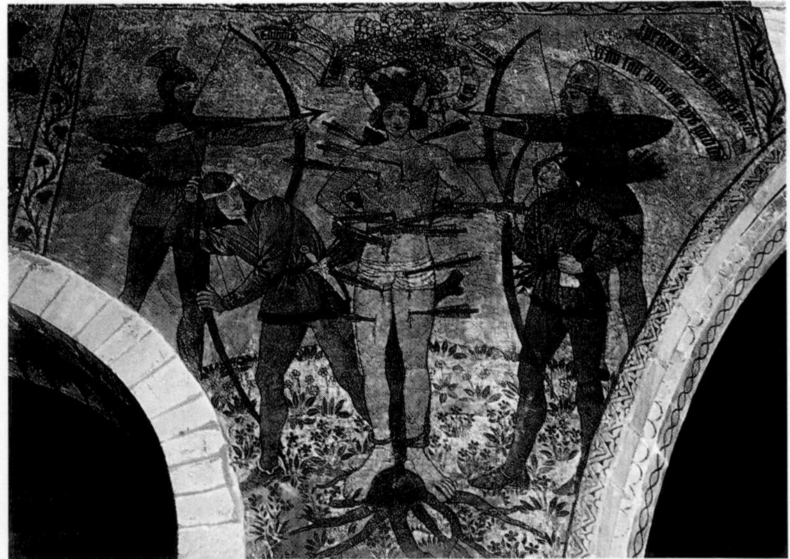

The death of Edmund of East Anglia, as imagined by a 15th-century artist.

East Anglia, 869
Defeated and captured by the Norse leader Ivar "the Boneless", King Edmund of East Anglia has suffered the same gruesome fate as Aella of Northumbria [*see above*].

Anxious to avoid a battle that he thought he would lose, the pious Edmund tried to negotiate with Ivar but made the mistake of stipulating that he must convert to Christianity. Ivar had no reason to abandon the Norse god Odin; since bringing his "great army" to England four years ago, Ivar has achieved victories in Odin's name over kings whose own god has let them suffer defeat.

In gratitude to Odin, Ivar likes to offer him the highest sacrifice: a king's life. Aella fell victim to this desire, and Edmund has now gone the same way. He was beaten, tied to a tree and shot full of arrows. Still alive, he was cut down, subjected to the "blood eagle" rite and beheaded. His head and body were thrown into a wood (→870).

Speedy longships are ideal vessels for viking campaigns of raiding and plunder

Scandinavia, c.865
The key to the success of the Norse, or vikings, is their perfection of the fast, light, easily built vessel known as the longship, by which they have launched raids all over Britain and Ireland [*see map below*]. A typical one is 25 to 30 metres (28 to 33 yards) long by 6 wide, and just over 2 metres from the bottom of the keel to the top of the gunwale. It draws only a metre when carrying a crew of about 40 plus food and equipment; each extra ton of cargo increases the draft by only a couple of centimetres, so the vessel is ideal for plunder.

The ships are built of oak planks about 2.5 centimetres thick, fastened to the ribs with twine or wooden pegs. A longship can sail 90 km (55 miles) in 24 hours and can be rowed in calm conditions. Its steering oar allows it to sail equally well in a tailwind or a crosswind (→899).

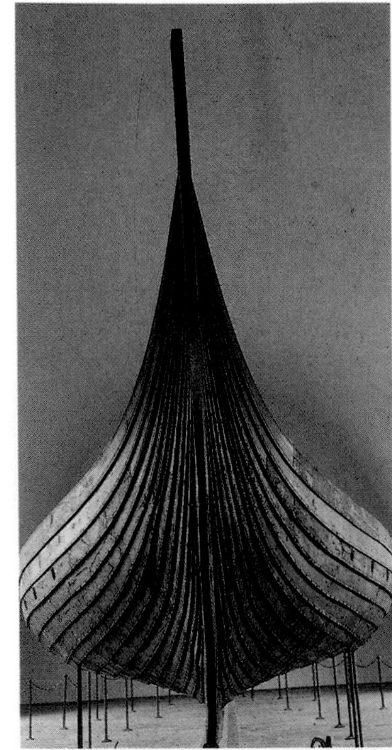

A viking longship, made of oak, found at Gokstad, in Norway.

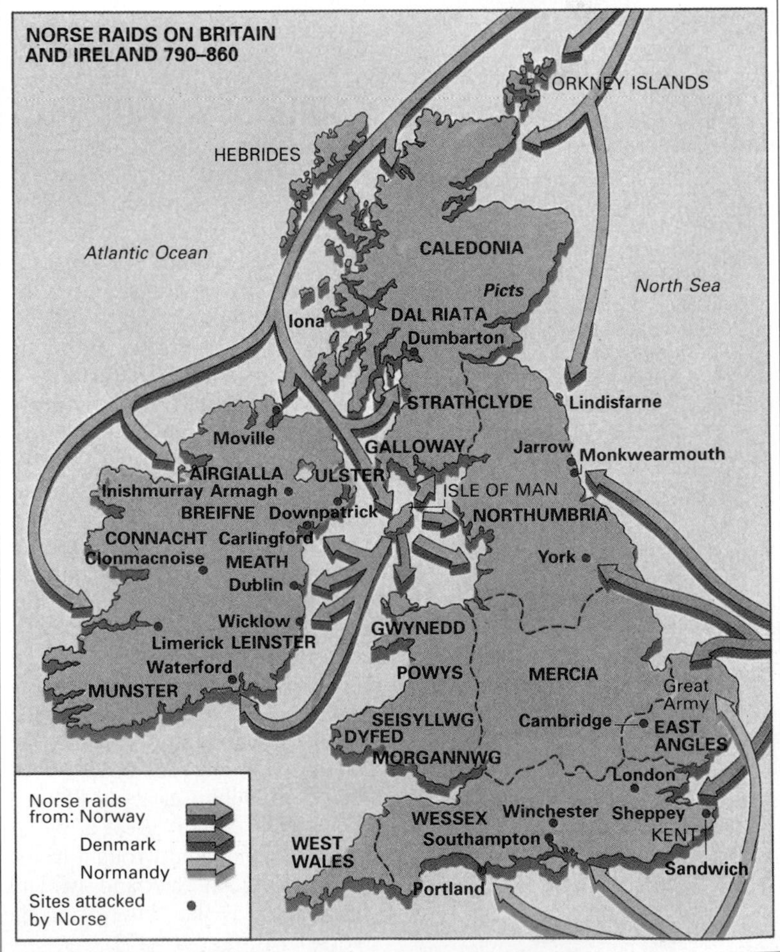

870-879

Cambridgeshire, 870. The monks of Peterborough Abbey are slaughtered by Norsemen.

Canterbury, Kent, 870. Ceolnoth dies; Athelred succeeds as archbishop (→ 890).

Reading, Berkshire, 871. King Athelred of Wessex and his brother Alfred launch a raid on the new Norse base.→

Dorset, April 871. Alfred succeeds as king of Wessex on the death of his brother Athelred (→ late 871).

London, July 871. The Mercians surrender to a new Norse army led by the warlord Guthrum, who means to ally with the "great army" (→ 872).

Scotland, 871. King Constantine of the Scots and the Picts has King Artgal of Strathclyde, who fled from the Norse last year, killed (→ 875).

Lincolnshire, 872. The Norse "great army" moves north from London to deal with a Mercian rebellion (→ 873).

Dyfed, c.872. King Rhodri "the Great" of Gwynedd now controls most of north and west Wales (→ 878).

Ireland, 873. Ivar "the Boneless" dies; his brother Halfdan, at York, succeeds him (→ 875).

Central [Scotland], 875. Halfdan, who last year led half the Norse "great army" to the Tyne, ravages a force under Constantine at Dollar (→ 877).

Lindisfarne, Northumberland, 875. The monks leave in the face of the viking threat, taking the remains of St Cuthbert for safety (→ 882).

Wareham, Dorset, 876. King Alfred makes oaths of peace to Guthrum, the leader of the Norse army in the south, following a defeat (→ 878).

Co Down, 877. The Norse leader Halfdan is killed in battle at Strangford Lough by the Dublin Norse (→ 885).

Southern England, 877. The Norse "great army" raids Wessex and forces King Ceolnoth of Mercia to divide his kingdom (→ 886).

Fife, 877. Following Halfdan's death his army, returning to York, defeats and kills King Constantine of the Scots and the Picts (→ 889).

Wiltshire, 878. King Alfred defeats Guthrum at Edington and imposes peace terms at Wedmore, allowing the Norse to stay in East Anglia (→ 880).

Dumbarton Rock submits after siege

Strathclyde, 870
Dumbarton Rock, the imposing fortress capital of the Britons of Strathclyde, has fallen to Norse invaders. The Britons surrendered to the Norse king of Dublin, Olaf the White, and his ally Ivar "the Boneless" after a long siege. Numerous Britons and Picts, probably destined for the slave market, have been taken back to Dublin in the viking longships, together with huge quantities of booty. Artgal, the king of Strathclyde, however, managed to escape.

The warlord Olaf, who led the attack, has been recognized as the king of Dublin – where the Norse first established a settlement some 30 years ago – since about 856. From there he has launched raids on various parts of Ireland and northern Britain, recently ravaging Pictish lands. His accomplice Ivar [*see report below*] has been waging a similar campaign all over Britain and Ireland for much of the past two decades; his strategy has included forging links between Norse communities in the islands. For the attack on Dumbarton, the Norse brought up a fleet of 200 longships and laid siege to the fortress for four months. They succeeded in cutting off the water supply to the fortress, and having "wasted the people who were in it by hunger and thirst" they forced the Britons to surrender. Such an unprecedented attack demonstrates the emphasis which the Norse place on controlling the Firth of Clyde, which forms an important part of the trade route between York and Dublin (→ 871).

Dumbarton Rock: a 20th-century view of the base of the Strathclyde Britons.

'Boneless' Ivar, warrior and seer, can wriggle out of any corner

Strathclyde, 870
The Norse strongman Ivar is one of the most extraordinary characters of the age. Dubbed "the Boneless" for his ability to wriggle out of any corner, Ivar has not lost a battle for almost 20 years. Soldier, priest and seer, he is as admired for his wisdom as he is feared for his savagery.

In Ireland his power has earned him the title of "Ivar the Great of the Wise Judgements". But his sacrifices to the Norse god Odin of at least three kings – of Munster, Northumbria and East Anglia [*see reports on page 141*] – horrified Christians and will not easily be forgotten. It may be that Ivar has the status of a pagan priest-king, and he is held in awe for his reputed gifts of sorcery and prophecy.

Ivar's first recorded battle was an attack on Dublin in about 850. He brought the Norse "great army" to England in 865 and wrought havoc, taking York in 867 and winning recognition as the "king of all the Norse in Britain" (→ 873).

A fierce face: detail from a warrior's carved helmet from Vendel, Sweden.

Saxon army routs Norse

Arms for the opposing warriors: the heads of Anglo-Saxon and viking swords.

Berkshire, 871
The Wessex Saxons, fighting under the command of Alfred, the youngest son of the late King Athelwulf, have won a great victory against the Norse at Ashdown, near the royal estate at Reading. The Norse – who moved their army to Reading from its base at Thetford, in East Anglia, at the end of last year – had already engaged the Saxons in several skirmishes in the area. On this occasion, led by two kings, they split their forces into two divisions, forming shield-walls of equal size. Seeing this, the West Saxons also divided their army into two parts. It was planned that the first, under King Athelred, would attack the Norse kings while the other, under Alfred, Athelred's brother, kept the remaining Norse forces busy.

When the time came for the Saxons to take the field, however, Athelred was at prayer in his tent and refused to leave until he had heard Mass, saying that he would not forsake divine service for that of men. Alfred, already on the battlefield, was put on the spot: he had to flee or attack without the king. He chose to attack. The Norse had the better position, occupying the high ground, but Alfred went at them, in the words of one account, "like a wild boar".

The fighting raged around a solitary, stunted thorn tree. It was bloody work with swords and battle-axes. First one side, then the other, was dominant as the shield-walls clashed. Eventually, inspired by the bravery of Alfred, the Saxons drove the Norse from the field.

There was a great slaughter as the Saxons harried their defeated enemies across country, cutting them down as they fled to the safety of their camp. Only nightfall stopped the killing. Among the Norse warriors who died were a king and at least five earls (→4/871).

Norse bribed to leave Saxons in peace

Wessex, late 871
The Norse have ceased hostilities against Alfred, following the West Saxon king's payment to them of a large sum of money, and are turning their attention to the kingdom of Mercia [*see report above right*].

Alfred must know that he has only bought a breathing space and that the Norse will be back, but there was little else that he could do. The Saxon superiority achieved by their victory at Ashdown, near Reading, earlier this year proved fleeting. Alfred and his army are now exhausted after a momentous few months which have brought his accession on the death of his elder brother, King Athelred, and seen nine major encounters with a reinforced enemy, including a serious defeat at Wilton (→876).

Invaders set up winter base at Repton

Repton, Derbyshire, 873
The kingdom of Mercia has come under attack from the Norse "great army" and is now facing the prospect of disintegration. Norse troops have set up winter quarters in an enormous D-shaped fortification at Repton in the heart of the kingdom. One side of the 1.5-hectare (3.5-acre) fortification is formed by the bank of the river Trent, into which the Norse have cut a dock to enable them to haul out and repair their ships during the winter. The leader of the "great army", Ivar "the Boneless", has gone to Ireland and left the force under the command of his brother, Halfdan.

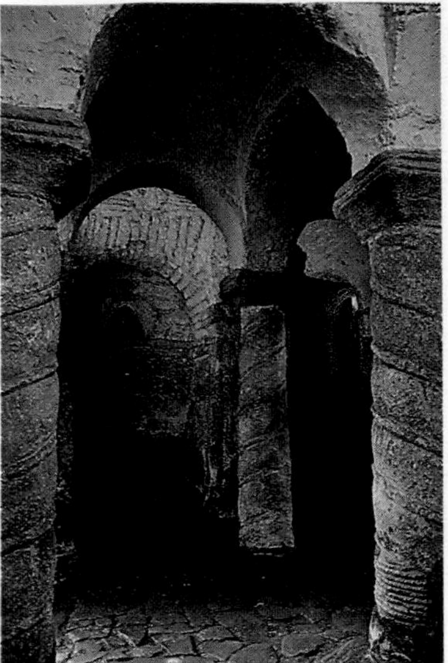
The Anglo-Saxon crypt at Repton.

The new Norse stronghold has powerful symbolic associations for the Mercians. A site of Christian worship for two centuries, and a major political centre, Repton is where the Mercian kings have their mausoleum, and it has developed into a place of pilgrimage. In recent months heavy fighting is reported to have taken place in the area, which saw the death of an important Norse chief. He was buried in the mausoleum, and around his body were stacked the bones of 250 men, all picked clean by carrion and bearing signs of battle (→877).

King who briefly united Wales has died

Wales, 878
The first Welsh ruler to bring most of Wales under his control has died fighting the Anglo-Saxons. Rhodri "the Great", who had been king of Gwynedd since 844, extended his kingdom to include Ceredigion [western central Wales] and Powys. His reign coincided with the appearance in Wales of Norse raiders, who swept down on lonely farmsteads to seize crops and drive off cattle. Gold altarpieces were looted from the monastery on Caldey Island. Anglesey, though devastated by repeated raids, was the scene of Rhodri's greatest victory when he killed the Norse leader Horn.

Rhodri's domain has now been shared out between his sons, who are already at war with southern Welsh kingdoms (→c.881).

Alfred distracted as the cakes burn

Athelney, Somerset, 878
King Alfred of Wessex, attacked by the Norse under cover of a truce, has fled his estate at Chippenham in Wiltshire for the Somerset marshes. Among tales told of his life as a fugitive, it is said that he took shelter at a swineherd's hut where his host's wife asked him to mind some cakes she was baking. Alfred absentmindedly let them burn and she, ignorant of his true identity, scolded him furiously.

Burnt cakes: 18th-century view.

880 - 888

Canterbury, Kent, c.880. An *ealdorman* [king's deputy], Alfred, and his wife buy back a beautiful Gospel-book that was looted by the Norse in one of their many raids on Wessex lands.→

Wales, c.881. King Anarawd of Gwynedd defeats King Athelred of Mercia, avenging the death of his father, Rhodri "the Great", in battle against the Anglo-Saxons (→ 882).

Co Durham, 882. The Lindisfarne monastic community, which has been homeless for many years after savage viking attacks, settles at Chester-Le-Street (→ 934).

South Wales, 882. The kings of Dyfed, Brycheiniog and Glywising, faced with a constant threat of attack from Gwynedd in the north, seek the protection of King Alfred of Wessex.→

Rome, 883. Pope Maurius frees the English school in Rome from its heavy burden of taxation at the request of King Alfred of Wessex, to whom he sends many valuable and beautiful gifts (→ c.885).

Rochester, Kent, 885. King Alfred rescues the city and its besieged citizens from a Norse invasion.

East Anglia, 885. King Alfred moves north from Kent, attacking and defeating Norse settlers (→ 886).

York, 885. Guthfrith, the Norse king of York, who has succeeded on the death of Halfdan, allies with King Anarawd of Gwynedd against the other Welsh kings, who are themselves allied with King Alfred of Wessex (→ 890).

Wessex, c.885. King Alfred commissions a translation into Anglo-Saxon of the *Historia Mundi [History of the World]* by the Roman writer Orosius. He adds to it the accounts of two voyagers, the Norse trader Ohthere and the Anglo-Saxon Wulfstan (→ c.890).

Wessex, c.885. With the introduction of walrus ivory by people like the Norse voyager and trader Ohthere, workers are becoming more skilled at carving this material into jewellery and other beautiful objects.

London, 886. King Alfred of Wessex gives control of the city to his client and ally King Athelred of Mercia, after he receives the submission of the citizens not under Norse domination.→

Alfred ejects the Norse from Wessex

Wessex, 880
King Alfred of Wessex has completely turned the tables on the Norsemen. In just two years he has defeated them in battle, forced them to agree terms, brought their pagan king to baptism and cleared them out of Wessex.

This remarkable change in the once-fugitive king's fortunes followed the spread of the news that he was still alive, despite every effort of the invading Norse army under King Guthrum to finish him off. This put fresh heart into the battered Wessex levies and provided them with a much-needed rallying-point just as they reached their lowest ebb.

Since the spring of 878 the king had been gathering troops around his headquarters in the marshes of Athelney, whence they sallied forth to carry on a disruptive guerrilla war against the Norse. In May of that year Alfred left his marshy fastness and was received with great joy by the men of Somerset, Wiltshire and Hampshire. Gathering his army he fell on the vikings at Edington in Wiltshire and defeated them, and then besieged their camp at Chippenham, his old estate, forcing them to surrender unconditionally and give hostages.

Under the terms of the treaty, known as the Peace of Wedmore, King Guthrum agreed to be baptized and was sponsored by Alfred, who bestowed lavish gifts on him. Guthrum's army was allowed to winter at Cirencester before falling back into East Anglia. The Norse have begun settling in that region, but few believe that the struggle is over. The king has fought back hard, but there could be a lot more fighting to come (→ 883).

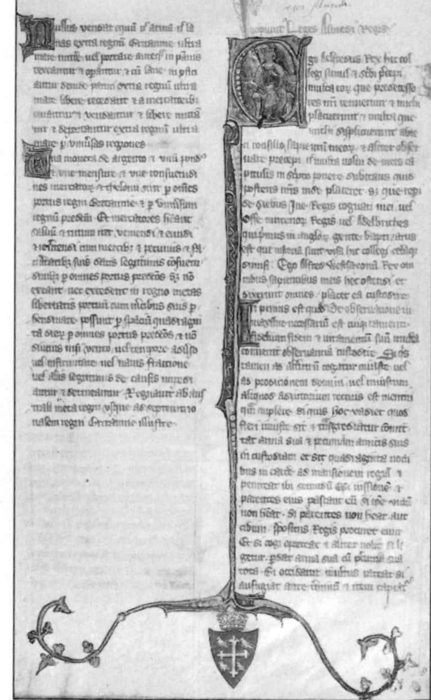

A copy of the Peace of Wedmore.

Noble buys back looted book from Norse

Canterbury, Kent, c.880
Alfred, a Kentish *ealdorman* or king's deputy, and his wife Werburh have retrieved a masterpiece of Anglo-Saxon craft from the Norsemen who had stolen it. The thieves have been paid gold, appropriately enough, for the return of the beautifully illustrated *Codex Aureus* [*Golden Book*]. Alfred intends to present the book to Christchurch, Canterbury.

While the Norse were only interested in a good business deal Alfred and his family acted because they could not bear to see heathens in possession of a holy book. They also hope that their good deed will bring eternal benefits for their souls.

The Codex Aureus: an inscription records its purchase from the vikings.

Alfred seen as the lesser of two evils

A ninth-century Saxon brooch.

Wales, 882
The sons of Rhodri "the Great", who inherited the kingdom of Gwynedd four years ago, have alarmed their southern neighbours so much that the latter have turned to the Saxon enemy for assistance. In anticipation of aggression from Gwynedd, the kings of Glywising, Brycheiniog and Dyfed have asked King Alfred of Wessex for protection. The move is highly unusual given the traditional Welsh mistrust of their neighbours to the east. One recent Welsh chronicle speaks of a victory over the Saxons as "God's vengeance" (→ 885).

Defence shake-up meets viking threat

Wessex, 883
As part of his plans to strengthen defences against the Norse threat, King Alfred has created a network of *burhs* [fortified places] stretching through much of the kingdom of Wessex [*see map on page 141*]. The site for each *burh* has been selected with long-term strategy in mind. The fortresses guard every main route across Wessex and are situated so that most people live no further than 20 miles from one.

The *burhs* vary in size and design. Some, such as those at Bath, Exeter and Alfred's capital of Winchester, incorporate the remains of Roman walls, while others have been built from scratch to form large rectangular enclosures surrounded by earthworks. Those based on existing towns have been planned to combine a defensive function with everyday commercial activities.

The creation of the *burhs*, which is similar to measures taken by King Charles of the Franks, is paralleled by Alfred's reorganization of his army. Now half the troops stay at home while the others remain on active service, including those who have been selected to garrison their local *burh*. For every "hide" of land the garrison needs one man. A hide is the area which can support a free man and his dependants, and it ranges from 24 to 48 hectares (60 to 120 acres). On that basis Wessex needs an army of some 27,000 men (→885).

London is wrested back from Norse

London, 886
King Alfred has taken London from the Norse after a short siege. The city, which has changed hands several times since first falling to the Norse in 871, is now firmly back under Anglo-Saxon control.

Alfred was joined in the siege by King Athelred of Mercia, who accepted his overlordship three years ago. The retaking of London was vital to both kings. Its strategic position on the river Thames made it a perfect base from which seaborne Norse armies could attack either of their kingdoms. Now Alfred plans to hand the city to Athelred, an astute move which respects its former status as a Mercian town. Its recapture has brought renewed confidence to the Anglo-Saxons, and it seems likely that all England, outside the Norse-controlled areas, will now accept Alfred as overlord (→888).

King Alfred imagined in London.

A second English queen dies in Italy

A gold ring belonging to Athelswyth, Alfred's sister, who has died in Italy.

Pavia, Italy, 888
King Alfred's sister Athelswyth, the widow of King Burgred of Mercia, has died on a pilgrimage to Rome. Her loss recalls the death here a century ago of a less revered Anglo-Saxon queen: Edburh, the wife of Beortric of Wessex, who was accused of debauchery and of poisoning her friends and husband. She fled to a nunnery but was forced to leave after a sexual scandal and ended her days begging in Pavia, accompanied by a single slave boy. She left such a mark that the wives of Wessex kings are no longer allowed the title of queen.

A wealthy trader from the Arctic north spins travellers' tales for King Alfred

A chalice from a viking hoard.

A Danish amber playing-piece.

Winchester, Hampshire, c.885
Not all the Norse are fierce warriors wallowing in beer and blood. Many, such as Ohthere from the far north of Norway, prefer to trade. Ohthere – the Anglo-Saxon version of his Norse name, Ottarr – is currently the guest of King Alfred at Winchester, where he has come with a cargo of walrus tusks for the king.

No one, Ohthere claims, lives further north than him apart from a few Lapps. Once, he decided to discover how far the land in fact stretched beyond his own home. He sailed due north for six days until the land ended, and then east and south [around North Cape and as far as the White Sea], following the coast but finding only Lapp hunters, fishermen and bird-catchers.

Ohthere is a rich man, boasting a herd of 600 reindeer and also some farmland. Most of his wealth, however, comes as tribute from the Lapps – hides, down, furs and whalebone, some of which he uses in turn as merchandise.

The trader seems quite unlike some of his more brutal compatriots, but many Norse are indeed like this – hard-headed, prudent people who take precautions and live by their wits. For instance, when Ohthere found that he was heading into hostile territory during his trip through the far north, he turned back.

Like many other peoples, the Norse turn some of their practical wisdom into verse maxims. The advice is blunt: "Do not praise the day until evening, a wife before she dies, a sword till it is tested, a girl before she is married, ice till it is crossed, beer till it is drunk." And as for death and glory, there is this salutary reminder: "A corpse is no use to anyone."

A neatly carved walrus ivory of the sort traded at the Anglo-Saxon court.

889 - 893

Canterbury, Kent, 888. A new law is passed stipulating that all new buildings must have at least a 60-cm (2-foot) space all around them to allow water to drip from the eaves.

Winchester, Hampshire, 888. King Alfred rewrites his will, confirming the exclusion of his nephews from the throne in an attempt to pass the crown to his own son Edward (→ 892).

Tayside, 889. Donald "the rough one", the son of the late King Constantine of the Scots and Picts, kills King Giric of Scots in battle at Dundurn to become King Donald II. Giric had killed Constantine's successor Aed in 878 (→ 900).

Strathclyde, 889. Eochaid, the king of the Britons of Strathclyde, is exiled by King Donald II of Scots, who has annexed his kingdom (→ 890).

Canterbury, 890. Plegmund is made archbishop, following Athelred's death in 889 (→ 909).

Gwynedd, 890. Eochaid, the exiled king of the Britons of Strathclyde, is allowed to settle on the borders of Gwynedd by King Anarawd, on condition that his men will destroy any Anglo-Saxon colonists (→ 893).

British Isles, 10 May 891. The appearance of a comet causes great concern (→ 995).

Cornwall, 891. Three Irishmen in an oarless boat arrive on the coast on a mission to see King Alfred of Wessex.

Highland, 891. The Norse leader Sigurd "the Powerful", the earl of Orkney, dies at Strath Oykel after defeating his enemies in battle. He is believed to have died from an infected leg wound inflicted by the tooth of a dead rival whose head hung from his saddle after the battle (→ 936).

Ireland, 11 November 892. Freak winds destroy forests, churches and houses (→ 965).

Kent, 892. Viking fleets arrive opposite Sheppey and at Lympne, and settlements are built at Milton and Appledore.→

Gwynedd, 893. King Anarawd of Gwynedd breaks off his eight-year-old alliance with the Norse to make peace with King Alfred of Wessex.→

Surrey, 893. Returning from an unsuccessful offensive into Berkshire, the Norse based at Appledore in Kent are defeated by the West Saxons at Farnham. The Norse had been trying to join up with their colleagues at Milton (→ 6/893).

Alfred spearheads revival of learning

Winchester, Hampshire, c.890
King Alfred has brought to his court a number of scholars from other kingdoms in England and the European continent to begin a much-needed revival of reading, writing and learning. With the damage caused by the vikings to the monasteries, which provide the only centres of worship and learning, there are few people north or south of the Humber still capable of understanding Latin, the common language of the educated classes of Europe.

South of the Thames, an area that includes Wessex, there is not a single clerk who can understand the language. However, Alfred intends to turn this to advantage by popularizing the use of Anglo-Saxon English as an alternative written language for the first time. He is also bringing in other trappings of civilization, such as fine cloth and embroidery.

While some attribute the decay of learning to the terrible scourge of the vikings, the king sees matters in a different light. He believes that the viking terror is divine retribution, a punishment for the failure of his people to equip themselves with the means to study the works of learning and of God.

By restoring the knowledge of reading and writing, King Alfred hopes to strike at the heart of the problem. He is himself translating a number of Latin works into the Anglo-Saxon language [*see report below*] with the intention of distributing these to his bishops. In this way books will be made available in all parts of the country.

Alfred has declared his intention to "bring it to pass that all the youth now in England born of free men may be devoted to learning until they can read English" (→ 893).

A manuscript in Frankish style.

A king presented with a work of art.

Beautiful bookmarks reflect new thinking

"Alfred had me made": this may be the head of one of the king's "aestels".

Winchester, Hampshire, c.890
King Alfred has sent out beautifully made *aestels*, or bookmarks, of enamelled gold and crystal to every bishopric in his kingdom. They are to be used with the Anglo-Saxon translations of the best Latin works [*see above*]. Each *aestel* carries the inscription "Alfred had me made", a message reflecting the king's devotion to learning and desire to strengthen the church by educating the clergy. Alfred, illiterate in his own language until he was 12, has now set up a court school similar to that of the late King Charles of the Franks (Charlemagne) at which both adults and children are taught. One of his projects is a great chronicle of the Anglo-Saxons (→ 893).

King reveals his tenets of wise rule

Winchester, Hampshire, c.890
In a translation into Anglo-Saxon English of a learned work in Latin, *On the Consolation of Philosophy* by Boethius, King Alfred has set out his ideas about society and how to rule it. In the same way that a craftsman needs his tools, he writes, so a king needs three sets of people: churchmen, soldiers and labourers. Without the support of these subjects he cannot rule, but he can keep them happy only if he gives them land to live on, weapons, clothes, food and drink – all their basic requirements.

Alfred warns, however, that kingship is more than simply materials. It also calls for wisdom. Power is to be exercised honourably, and not for its own sake. As for himself, Alfred wishes only that in years to come he might be remembered for his good works (→ 26/10/899).

New invasion fleet sails up Kent river

Kent, 892
A viking force of some 250 ships has arrived in Kent, sailing up the Lympne estuary and casting anchor at the east end of the great forest of the Weald. The vikings made their first attack on a *burh* [fortified place] located in the marshlands along the river. This was a half-built fort, garrisoned by a few men; they were unable to put up any real resistance to the Norsemen, now encamped at Appledore.

Despite King Alfred's insistence on improving the national defence system of his kingdom, some of his subjects have failed to take his demands seriously; the ease with which the vikings overran this inadequate fort proves the folly of such half-heartedness. The vikings have obviously taken note of such weak spots. A second expedition, led by one Hastein, landed near the Isle of Sheppey shortly afterwards; it is now well established in a fort at Milton (→893).

A picture stone shows viking sailors.

Alfred's tactics keep enemy pinned down

A representation of one of the "burhs" which perform a key defence role.

Wessex, June 893
The two Norse armies which landed last year are finding the going tougher than they bargained for, owing to the skilled generalship of King Alfred. The swift seaborne invasion forced Alfred immediately onto the defensive, but with his son Edward and his ally King Athelred of Mercia he has kept the Norse pinned down. By dividing his army into two halves, only one of which fights at a time, the task of keeping troops loyal is made easier.

Alfred has put his force in striking distance of both armies, so that the Norse have only been able to make two major expeditions from their bases at Milton and Appledore in Kent. They have amassed much booty, but Alfred has turned the tables on them by successful attacking their fort at Benfleet in Essex (→894).

History of England to be written down

Wessex, 893
The history of England from the time of Julius Caesar to the present day is to be set down for the first time. King Alfred's desire to promote works in Anglo-Saxon has prompted the collection of the annals of the West Saxons and of other kingdoms, to create one work that will be known as the *Anglo-Saxon Chronicle*. For centuries scribes have compiled records of events in Latin, but never before have these been brought together and translated into Anglo-Saxon English to form a continuous chronological history. Important events will be added yearly.

In another important literary development, Asser, the Welsh-born bishop of Sherborne, has this year been commissioned to write a life of Alfred – of whom he is a close friend – aimed at convincing readers in Wales of the king's good character and intentions (→1136).

Reinforced Norse army is defeated

Powys, 893
Despite gaining substantial reinforcements from their allies in Northumbria and East Anglia, the Norse have been defeated at Buttington, on the river Severn. The reinforcements arrived while King Alfred was occupied in the defence of Exeter.

The combined force then sailed up the Severn, but was opposed by Anglo-Saxon lords who had gathered troops from many *burhs* [fortified places], especially those north of the Thames and west of the Severn. A number of Welsh troops joined the Anglo-Saxon force.

This host besieged the Norse in their stronghold at Buttington until, weakened by famine, the Norse tried to break out and in the end were soundly defeated (→c.904).

Many Irish die in clash of dynasties

Ireland, 893
The celebrations of the Christian festival of Whitsun at Armagh have been marred by a major clash between the Cenel nEogain (a subdynasty of the Ui Neill) and the Ulaid, their Ulster rivals. Many have been killed on both sides and Aitith, the king of the Ulaid, has been forced to pay compensation to the abbot of Armagh. This is in keeping with Irish law which lays down that payment can atone for almost any crime. Payment is based on the honour-price of the victim, which makes the killing of a person of high rank a very costly business, and often involves the culprit's relatives if he cannot pay (→908).

New laws are drawn up to deal with treachery against the king

Wessex, c.891
King Alfred has become the first West Saxon king to issue a code of laws since the days of King Ine nearly 200 years ago. For the first time laws have been passed against treason, leaving no one in any doubt about the dangers of plotting against the king.

Anyone who plots, or connives with a plotter, or helps men exiled by Alfred, will lose both his property and his life. The king has made sure that the laws extend the same protection to his lords. Alfred has also laid down standard penalties that depend on the nature of the crime rather than its exact form. Previously, stealing horses, stealing gold or stealing a hive of bees had each attracted different fines; now all are classed as theft, and each is punishable by a 120-shilling fine. Crimes committed on Sundays or on religious holidays such as Easter and Christmas attract double punishment.

There is some attempt to set compensation levels for accidents. The code declares: "If a man unintentionally kills another by letting a tree fall on him, the tree is to be given to the kinsmen" (→935).

A fine Irish silver brooch (replica).

894-908

Mersea Island, Essex, 894. Norsemen land in search of a place of refuge and winter quarters (→ 9/895).

England/Flanders, 895. To strengthen the Channel alliance, King Alfred arranges his daughter Alfthryth's wedding to Count Baldwin II of Flanders. Baldwin is the stepson of Judith, the former wife of both King Athelwulf of Wessex and his son King Athelbald of Wessex, Alfred's father and brother respectively.

Mersea Island, September 895. Alfred orders the building of two forts, forcing the Norse to abandon their ships.

London, September 895. After a failed attack on the Norse earlier this year, Londoners destroy many ships in another attempt (→ 26/10/899).

Chichester, West Sussex, 895. The city successfully holds off a Norse attack.

Wessex, 26 October 899. Edward, the son of Alfred, succeeds on his death. His cousin Athelwold – following an unsuccessful revolt against Edward – is recognized as king by the Northumbrian Norse.→

English Lake District, 900. Over 900 Norse settle, farming the area with a breed of sheep called Herdwick.

East Anglia, 902. Athelwold and his Norse allies challenge Edward. The Norse are victorious, but Athelwold is killed, ending the real challenge to Edward (→ 906).

Dyfed, c.904. Hywel ap Cadell, the grandson of Rhodri "the Great", becomes king (→ c.920).

Strathearn, Tayside, 905. Fighting at the cross of St Colum Cille (Columba), the Scots, led by Constantine II, defeat and kill Ivar II, the king of the Dublin Norse (→ 918).

Scone, Tayside, 906. King Constantine II and Bishop Cellach of St Andrews make an agreement to enforce church laws (→ 963).

Leighton Buzzard, Bedfordshire, 906. King Edward signs the Treaty of Tiddingford, making peace between Wessex, East Anglia and Northumbria (→ 6/8/910).

Chester, Cheshire, 907. Athelfled, the daughter of the late King Alfred of Wessex and the wife of Athelred of Mercia, refortifies the city after a raid (→ 6/8/910).

Alfred, the 'saviour of his kingdom', dies

Wessex, 26 October 899
King Alfred died today, aged 50. Born at Wantage in 849, he came to the throne aged 21 at a critical moment, when Wessex was about to be overwhelmed by Norse invaders. Before he was 30 he had saved his kingdom, and he spent the rest of his reign reinforcing that victory.

Plagued for much of his life by illness, he nonetheless led his armies to a series of unequalled victories over the Norse. Yet he was a scholar and thinker who could manage the revenues of his kingdom, redraft its laws and organize the translation from Latin into Anglo-Saxon of many books, some of which he translated himself.

He had a capable and inquiring mind – not many kings have taught themselves Latin at the age of 38 – and held a strong conviction that a life without knowledge or reflection is unworthy of respect. With his translations he made every effort to give his countrymen the means to acquire this knowledge. Alfred was also lucky in that he had no strong rival for the throne. At a time when Wessex needed all its strength to repel the invader, a dynastic quarrel such as has beset many other English kingdoms could have been disastrous (→ 902).

A Victorian image of King Alfred.

Wessex inherits strong and efficient navy

Specially designed ships of the kind introduced into King Alfred's navy.

Wessex, 899
As part of his overall plan to improve defences against the Norse, King Alfred ordered the building during his reign of a number of new ships, which have been incorporated into a reformed and more efficient navy. These longships have 60 oars and are of a new style, built on neither the traditional Frisian nor the Danish pattern but according to a design that Alfred judged appropriate to English waters. However, they have not been an unqualified success. Several ran aground on their first outing, and the design has proved unsuitable for tight manoeuvres in coastal waters – although the ships operate satisfactorily on the open sea.

King of Scots is enthroned at Scone in secret ceremony

Scone, Tayside, 900
King Constantine II of Scots has been consecrated at Scone in a secret ceremony which has its origins in the practices of the ancient Picts. The king was "married" to the land and people of Scotland in a pagan ritual.

In past years, elements of the symbolic marriage included the sacrifice of a horse to the earth-goddess, a feast on its flesh, and a ritual bath by the new king. It is also customary for the ancient genealogy of the king to be recited and for the nobles present to demonstrate their obeisance.

Reports from this year's ceremony have not revealed whether these heathen rites have been maintained. What is known is that the king sat on a sacred "stone of destiny" and was invested with a sceptre and ceremonial robes. There is no Scottish crown, so King Constantine was not crowned.

The ceremony took place at the Moot Hill, which is an ancient Pictish burial mound, perhaps the tomb of an early king of Scots. It is known as "the Place of the Melodious Shields", on account of the traditional practice whereby the clansmen clash their shields when the ceremony is over in a ritual greeting to the new king. Constantine succeeded his cousin, the late King Donald VI (→ 905).

Woman is drowned for being a witch

London, 900
A widow from the Ailsworth estate in Northamptonshire has been drowned in the Thames at London Bridge in punishment for her conviction on a charge of witchcraft. The accusation was originally laid against the woman when an effigy of her neighbour, Alfsige, was discovered in a closet at her house with an iron pin driven through its heart. Her estate has been transferred to the victim and will pass to his son, Wulstan Uccea. Meanwhile, the widow's son has been branded as an outlaw.

Dublin Norse take their money and run

Dublin, 902
The Norse have finally been pushed out of their former stronghold of Dublin after holding sway in Ireland for a hundred years. Cearbhall, the Irish king of Leinster, has sacked the town with its fine commanding position on the Irish Sea, and the Norse holdings on the coast as far as Waterford are now under his influence.

Cearbhall was provoked by constant Norse meddling in Irish political affairs, in which they sought to play off the different kings and tribes against each other. Having stirred up trouble, the Norse would then hire themselves out as mercenaries to one or other of the opposing sides – a clever and lucrative operation. Ireland has become something of a milch cow to the Norse. It is a source of slaves for use in colonizing other places, especially Iceland, and it also serves as an indispensable base and haven for attacks on England and Wales. Nevertheless they have made no serious attempt to conquer the entire island, which would probably have overstretched them.

The Dublin Norse have made off for north-western England and south-western Scotland, carrying a remarkable silver hoard weighing 41 kilograms (90 lbs) and containing 7,000 coins as well as brooches, arm-rings and silver scrap (→919).

Part of a hoard of Norse silver buried c.900 near the river Ribble, Lancs.

Irish scholar-king is consigned to history

Co Carlow, 908
Flann Sinna, the overlord of the Ui Neill dynasty and high king of Ireland, has defeated and killed King Cormac mac Cuilennain of Munster at a place called Belach Mugna [in Co Carlow]. Cormac's campaign against the Ui Neill peaked last December, when he used a fleet based on the river Shannon to subdue Connacht and the Irish midlands. His death removes not only a king but also a remarkable cleric and scholar who will be remembered for *Cormac's Glossary*, an account of Irish history (→25/5/916).

A stone cross from western Ireland.

Norse settlers dominate central swathe of England and put down roots elsewhere

British Isles, c.900
The Norse have now established small communities among the Celts of Ireland, Wales, the Isle of Man and the north-western coast of Britain, while a large slice of England, stretching from the Tyne to near London, has in effect been yielded to those forsaking their homelands in the far north of Europe. This latter area has been open to strong Danish influence since 878, when King Alfred made a treaty with the then leader of the Danes, Guthrum. (The Norwegians tend to prefer the northern fringes of the British Isles.) Danish nobles have taken over from English ones in these lands, and Danish law is in force there.

Among the new place names introduced by the settlers are *Northmanna byr*, "village of the Norse" [Normanby], *Dena byr*, "village of the Danes" [Denby] and *Ira byr*, "village of the Norse from Ireland" [Irby]. On occasion the name of the founder is part of a settlement's name, as at *Grims byr*, "Grimr's village" [Grimsby] or *Thorsteins tun*, "Thorsteinn's farm" [Thurstaston]. A site may be identified by what goes on there, as in the case of *Thingvellir*, "assembly plains" [Dingwall].

A brook near birch trees is a *birkibekkr* [Birkbeck]. An orchard is an *apaldrsgarthr* [Applegarth]. The Norse feel at home everywhere – in a wood or *skogr* [Myerscough], by sandbanks or *melar* [Meols], on a high ridge or *hryggr* [Crossrigg], or near a spring or *kelda* [Trinkeld]. Their influence is also clear in names that include, for example, "dale" or "gill" [both meaning valley], "fell" [large hill], "thrope" [hamlet] or "wick" [creek or bog] (→c.1000).

909 - 930

Tettenhall, Mercia, 6 August 910. King Edward of Wessex defeats the Northumbrian Norse in Mercia (→911).

Mercia, 911. Athelred of Mercia dies; his widow Athelfled rules alone (→915).

Canterbury, Kent, 2 August 914. Archbishop Plegmund dies. His successor is Athelhelm (→29/5/931).

Mercia, 915. Athelfled fortifies the borders at Runcorn in Cheshire and Chirbury in Shropshire (→916).

Ireland, 25 May 916. Niall Glundub mac Aeda, the son of Aed Findliath, succeeds Flann Sinna mac Maelsechnaill as high king (→summer).

Llangorse Lake, Powys, 916. After Welsh raiders kill a Mercian abbot, Athelfled seizes King Tewdur of Brycheiniog's wife (→918).

Northumberland, 918. King Constantine II of Scots defeats the Norse leader, Ragnald, at Corbridge (→12/7/927).

England/France, c.919. Edward of Wessex's daughter Edgifu is married to King Charles "the Simple" of the Franks (→923).

Dyfed, c.920. King Hywel ap Cadell creates the new kingdom of Deheubarth in South Wales (→c.943).

Armagh City, 10 November 921. The Dublin Norse, led by Guthfrith, the brother of Sigtrygg, raid the city (→938).

York, 921. Sigtrygg succeeds his brother Ragnald as king of the Dublin Norse (→30/1/926).

Northern France, 923. On the imprisonment of her husband, Charles "the Simple", Edgifu flees to her father, King Edward of Wessex (→926).

Nottinghamshire, 17 July 924. King Edward dies; his son Alfward succeeds him (→8/924).

Kingston Upon Thames, Sy, August 924. Edward's illegitimate son Athelstan becomes king after Alfward's sudden death (→12/7/927).

Tamworth, Staffordshire, 30 January 926. Athelstan's sister Edith marries Sigtrygg, the Norse king of York (→934).

England, 926. Athelstan's sister Edhild marries Hugh, the count of Paris (→936).

Cumbria, 12 July 927. A peace with Constantine II and Owen of Strathclyde ensures Athelstan their support against Guthfrith (→12/927).

Church is target of sweeping reforms

A silver penny in Plegmund's name.

Canterbury, Kent, 909
Archbishop Plegmund has launched a sweeping reorganization of the church. He is splitting up two huge dioceses centred on Winchester and Sherborne, conducting a campaign against married clergy, and sending missionaries to convert the Norse-dominated parts of England. Plegmund intends the new measures to revive standards of education, particularly in Latin, which are deplorable even in Canterbury because of the many teaching monasteries destroyed by the Norse invaders.

Plegmund was elevated to Canterbury in 890 and worked closely with King Alfred on the king's new law codes. He hopes to convert the Norse to Christianity (→2/8/914).

Irish king to revive great rural festival

Leinster, summer 916
To general rejoicing, High King Niall Glundub mac Aeda has decided to revive the *Oenach Tailten* [Fair of Teltown]. This great gathering, held annually in Meath, was a major event in the rural calendar until Norse raids stopped it in 876. Traditionally the Irish high king comes from Tara to preside.

The *Oenach Tailten*, which includes games and horse-racing, is seen as an important popular assembly. It also serves a political purpose, giving the king an opportunity to promise the people that he will implement certain laws or emergency measures in times, for example, of plague, defeat or foreign invasion (→919).

Norse bow to Wessex

England, December 918
After a two-year Saxon onslaught, most of the southern lands under former Danish control [*see map on page 149*] have recognized the overlordship of Edward of Wessex, whose authority now runs from the English Channel to the Humber estuary. The campaign was conducted jointly by the king and his sister Athelfled, the ruler of Mercia.

Edward: Wells Cathedral window.

Edward's strategy against the many disunited Danish armies was to build fortresses, known as *burhs*, which they had no means of overrunning. He began at Towcester, the old Roman station on Watling Street, and built another at a place called Wigingamere. Danish attacks on both strongholds were repulsed. His sister pursued a similar policy in Mercia.

Next Edward overcame the Danish-held towns of Tempsford, east of Bedford, and Colchester, killing the Danish king of East Anglia. This left only four Danish armies south of the Humber – at Leicester, Stamford, Nottingham and Lincoln. After Northampton and Huntingdon submitted to Edward, Athelfled marched on Derby and Leicester, which gave in without a fight.

On 12 June this year, when she was about to receive the submission of York, Athelfled died at Tamworth, ending an extraordinary life. The daughter of King Alfred of Wessex, she married Athelred, the lord of Mercia, to cement a military alliance, and became active in the politics of Mercia, succeeding her husband as its ruler in 911. Known as "the lady of the Mercians", she will be remembered for her prowess in battle, especially in the struggle against the Danes. Since her death, Stamford, Nottingham and Lincoln have surrendered, leaving all Mercia under Edward's rule (→920).

A romanticized view of "the lady of the Mercians" at the head of her army.

Irish Norseman is declared king of York

A Norse cross from Cumbria.

York, 919
Ragnald, a Dublin Norseman, has captured York – which last year agreed to submit to Wessex overlordship – and declared himself king. This move follows an infiltration by the Norse of north-western England from their settlements in Ireland, the Isle of Man and southern Scotland while King Edward of Wessex was securing his position south of the Humber. They have occupied the Wirral and the coastline to the north of it; indeed, the border between the English and the Norse now stretches from the Humber to the Mersey.

In the west the English have boosted their defences at Chester, Thelwall and Runcorn. Edward has also occupied Manchester and is repairing the old Roman fortifications to prevent the Norse from penetrating Mercia and cutting the direct road to York (→921).

The Irish Norse influence: a carved hog-back tomb at Heysham, Lancs.

Norse plan to unite Dublin and York under one ruler after regaining power in Ireland

Norse graffiti: a picture of a viking ship etched on a plank found in Dublin.

Ireland, 919
In an attempt to quell a resurgence of Norse power in Ireland, High King Niall Glundub mac Aeda of the Ui Neill has died in battle against a Norse army at Islandbridge, near Dublin. Several other Ui Neill leaders fell with him.

The Norse began to return in strength to Ireland five years ago, when a great fleet anchored at Waterford. More arrived the following year, launching attacks on Munster and Leinster and plundering monasteries. Niall led an Irish counter-attack with little success. Last year he fought a campaign to free Munster from the invaders, but this too ended in failure.

The Norse are now left in undisputed control of Dublin, which has come to be regarded as a state in its own right. They are believed to be planning to unite Dublin and York under the same ruler, to create a powerful axis which will be maintained by their mighty sea-power.

Many of the Irish rulers have no wish to drive out the Norse, preferring to use them as mercenaries to further their own political ambitions (→10/11/921).

Leading rulers pay homage to Wessex

Bakewell, Derbyshire, 920
King Edward of Wessex has taken a major step towards establishing the West Saxon monarchy as the premier force in the whole of Britain. After effectively annexing Mercia on the death of his sister Athelfled in 918 [*see report on page 150*], he has built a fortress on the river Trent at Nottingham and another at Bakewell, in Derbyshire, which dominates all routes to the north and north-west.

All the leading kings have come to pay homage, including those of the Scots and of Strathclyde, who want his protection from the Norse raiders. One Norseman, Ragnald, came too. After taking York last year, he wants Edward's recognition (→17/7/924).

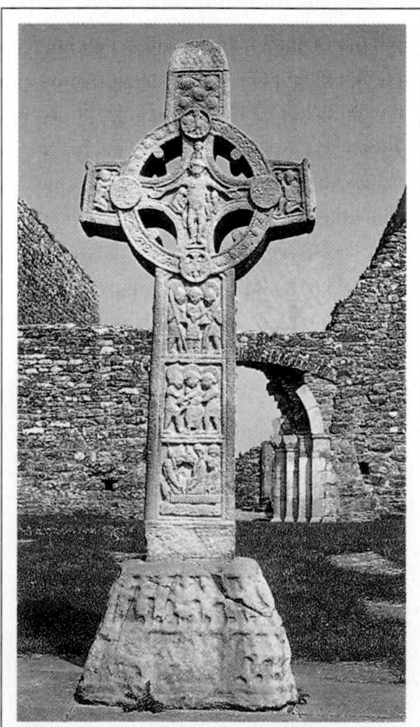
The west side of the four-sided stone cross at Clonmacnoise, Co Offaly, showing Christ's passion.

York is recaptured by King Athelstan

York, December 927
The Dublin Norse have been ousted from York by Athelstan, king of Wessex and Mercia since 924, and their leaders, Olaf and Guthfrith, have fled to Ireland. Olaf is the son of Sigtrygg, the Norse king of York who died earlier this year. On Sigtrygg's death, his brother Guthfrith, the king of the Dublin Norse, came over from Ireland to support Olaf. Athelstan responded by invading Northumbria, securing recognition of his supremacy from the kings of Scotland and Strathclyde and the English lord of Bamburgh. Having put his Norse foes to flight, Athelstan took possession of York, establishing himself at the head of a larger English kingdom than any of his predecessors ruled (→934).

Local governors are appointed by king

England, c.930
King Athelstan has solved the problem of how to administer the many provinces of his realm by appointing *ealdormen* [king's deputies] as governors of large, self-contained areas. The *ealdorman* acts as army commander, administrator and patron for his area.

The king's method of maintaining central control of government is to travel around his kingdom holding councils which are attended by the *ealdormen* as well as by bishops, *thegns* [noble retainers] and nobles. Some 50-60 councillors advise him on law and policy and witness his grants of lands and privileges. Several *ealdormen* are Danes, sons of the men who fought Athelstan's father, Edward (→23/3/931).

Artistic creativity finds many forms of expression

British Isles, c.930

The past two centuries have seen a great artistic outburst among the peoples of the British Isles. From the early part of this period, the fertile marriage in the Anglo-Saxon kingdoms of late Romano-Christian art and motifs with Germanic spiral ornament spawned magnificent works in many media, including religious manuscripts, sculpture and fine metalwork. One late-classical motif, the "inhabited vine" – a symbol of Christ's union with creation – finds expression in many forms, as on the silver-gilt Ormside bowl. The dominant feature of secular metalwork is elegant animal interlace decoration such as that on the Witham pins. More recently, a general decline in monasticism has been detrimental to book art, but the cultural renaissance under King Alfred has revived interest in this area, with works such as the Athelstan Psalter being imported from the continent and modified in England. Irish craftsmen have won wide renown for their metalwork [*see report on page 129*], which has proved influential in the development of Pictish art, also noted for its vigorous sculpture. Although many works have been lost through viking depredations, Norse settlers have themselves introduced new artistic influences, reinforcing the popularity of animal and foliage ornament.

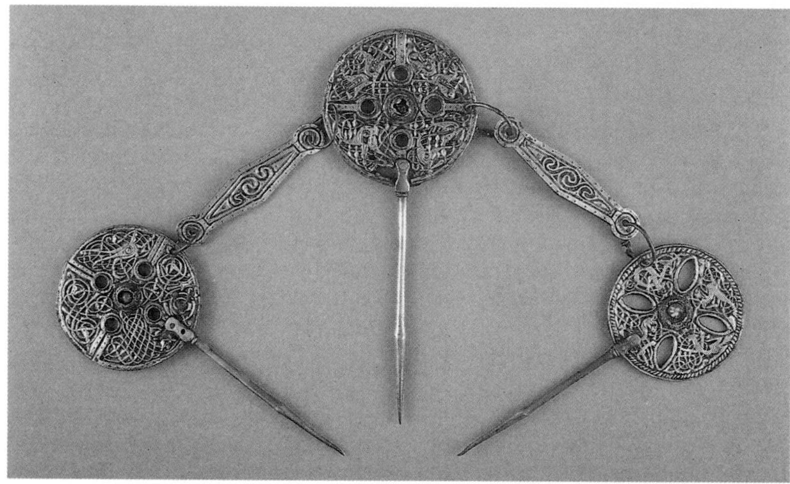

Late eighth-century silver-gilt pins, found in the river Witham, Lincolnshire.

An English addition to a psalter given by Athelstan to the Winchester monks.

A silver-gilt bowl adorned with an "inhabited vine", from Ormside, Cumbria.

A Pictish silver brooch of the eighth century, found at Rogart, Highland.

A house-shaped reliquary from Monymusk, in Grampian, of wood covered with silver and copper-alloy sheets; it combines Irish and Pictish features.

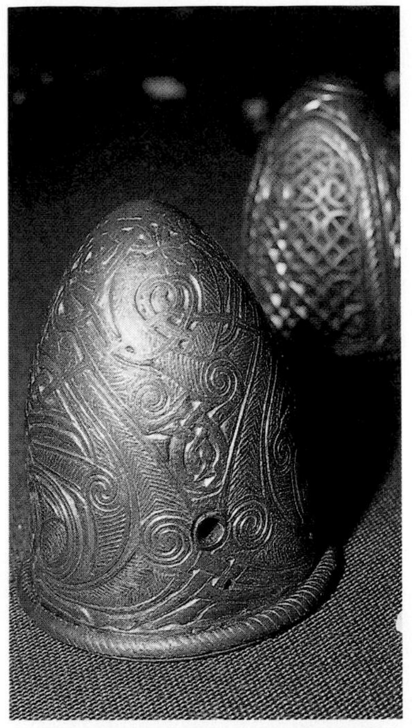

Pictish silver mounts from the eighth century (St Ninian's Isle, Shetland).

A ninth-century Irish harness mount from Markyate, in Hertfordshire.

A stone grave-marker from Lindisfarne. Sculpted in the late ninth century, it commemorates one of the many attacks on the island by viking raiders.

Relief of huntsmen and wild animals from a Pictish sarcophagus of the tenth century. On the right is the biblical figure of Samson with a lion.

The head of a viking axe intricately decorated with animal motifs; as well as fear and destruction, the Norse brought with them new artistic influences.

A ninth-century viking silver cup inlaid with bird and foliage designs.

Silver brooches buried at Pentney, in Norfolk, for fear of viking raids.

931-941

Winchester, Hampshire, 29 May 931. King Athelstan consecrates Beornstan as bishop (→ 12/2/942).

Colchester, Essex, 23 March 931. In an attempt to break down the provincial barriers in England King Athelstan holds a national assembly in which every local interest is represented.

Scotland/Ireland, 934. Olaf, the son of Guthfrith, the king of the Dublin Norse, marries King Constantine II of Scots' daughter to stop King Athelstan of Wessex's expansion north.→

Dunnottar, Grampian, summer 934. King Athelstan invades Scotland by land and sea in retaliation for the Scots-Irish alliance (→ 937).

France, 936. Louis, the exiled son of the deposed King Charles, who has been brought up at the court of Athelstan, his half-uncle, is recalled by Count Hugh of Paris to claim his throne (→ 937).

France, 937. King Louis IV escapes from the clutches of Count Hugh of Paris; he begins to plan how to reclaim his kingdom (→ 939).

Dublin, 938. High King Donnchad Donn mac Flainn and Muirchertach mac Neill, his chief warrior who defeated Halfdan, the Norse leader, in 926, lay siege to the city (→ 941).

Armagh City, 939. Donnchad Donn lavishly enshrines the Book of Armagh.

Beverley, Humberside, 939. King Athelstan of Wessex refounds the minster.

English Channel, 939. Athelstan, supporting the claims of his exiled half-nephew, Louis, to the French throne, attacks the French coast.

English Midlands, 940. King Olaf Guthfrithsson of the Dublin Norse captures the north-eastern midlands, helped by his cousin, Olaf Sigtryggsson (→ 941).

Northumbria, 941. The people rebel against the young King Edmund. They seek Olaf Guthfrithsson as ruler, and on his death his brother, Blacair, succeeds him as king (→ 942).

Munster, 941. Muirchertach mac Neill, campaigning on behalf of High King Donnchad Donn mac Flainn, forces the submission of Cellachan, the king of Cashel (→ 26/2/943).

Athelstan is called 'king of All Britain'

London, 933
On King Athelstan's orders, the English coinage – complicated by the introduction of Scandinavian marks and ore – is to be reformed. In future there will be only one currency and coins may be struck only by authorized moneyers in certain towns – eight in London, seven in Canterbury, six in Winchester and two in each of seven other towns spread across the realm.

Athelstan, king of Wessex and Mercia since 924, brought Northumbria under his sway in 927 and has since secured the promise of a yearly tribute from most of the Welsh princes. In keeping with the status he has won both at home and abroad, where he is accepted as the senior ruler in western Europe, all the new coins struck in his reign will carry words describing him as "king of All Britain" (→ 973).

A new coinage for King Athelstan.

Dublin Norse build powerful new fleet

Dublin, 934
The drumbeat of war is beginning to sound through Ireland after the death this year of Guthfrith, the king of the Dublin Norse. His son, Olaf, is poised to regain lands in northern England once held by his family which he thinks were stolen when Guthfrith was ousted from the area by King Athelstan in 927.

Olaf, regarded as the leader of all the Norse now based in eastern Ireland, is building the most powerful fleet in the Irish Sea. He has potential allies in Scotland among those who already fear Athelstan's growing power, and conflict seems inevitable (→ 937).

King presents gifts at northern shrine

Royal gifts: the embroidered maniple (l) and stole donated by Athelstan.

Co Durham, 934
The community of St Cuthbert at Chester-le-Street, which brought the saint's body here from Lindisfarne to escape the viking raids, has received a visit from King Athelstan himself. He brought a richly inscribed manuscript of Bede's *Life of St Cuthbert*; its frontispiece depicts the king presenting the work to the saint. Among other gifts from the king are a stole and maniple embroidered in silk with figures of saints, worked at the request of Alffled, his stepmother; they join the Lindisfarne Gospels. Athelstan's court is regarded as so highly civilized that an anonymous poet sings:

With festive treat the court abounds,
The brisk wine foams, the hall resounds,
The pages run, the servants haste,
And food and verse regale the taste
(→ 999).

Harsh new laws aim to keep the peace

Thunderfield, Surrey, 935
King Athelstan and his council, or *witan*, have issued a law code dealing with theft and law enforcement. From now on everyone is to be organized into groups of ten, or *tithings*, which are sworn to be accountable for each other and to pay four pence a head annually for the common benefit. Penalties are harsh, including death. Previously vengeance has been a matter for the victim; now, however, "if anyone slays anyone in the act of vengeance, he shall forfeit his life and all he possesses, unless the king is willing to pardon him".

Compensation for theft, to be paid by the culprit, is fixed by the law: "We reckon a horse at half a pound; but if it is less valuable, it shall be paid for by its appearance, unless its owner can produce evidence that it is as good a horse as he says." A cow is valued at 20 pence, a slave at half a pound (→ 961).

'Torf' Einar, Norse ruler of Orkney, dies

Orkney, 936
The Norseman "Torf" Einar has died after ruling Orkney for some 40 years. He earned a reputation for being tough to enemies but caring to his people – although he deprived Orkney farmers of some of their land-holding rights.

Einar was the illegitimate son of a slave-girl and Earl Rognvaldur, who was burnt alive by Halfdan Highleg, the son of a Norwegian king. But Einar revenged himself by capturing Halfdan and sacrificing him to the Norse god Odin in the "blood eagle" rite. Severing his ribs he spread out Halfdan's lungs as eagle's wings. Einar was nicknamed "Torf" after he organized the cutting and transport of peat [*torf*] to Orkney from as far away as Tarbat Ness in Easter Ross (→ 1008).

Gory win for Athelstan

England, 937
Anglo-Saxon forces under King Athelstan have repelled an invasion by Norse warlords and Scots in a bloody confrontation at a place called Brunanburh [somewhere between the Mersey and the Solway]. An anonymous English poet describes the battlefield as "slick with men's blood", with "numberless slain among shipmen and Scots" before the invaders fled. Five kings and seven earls from Ireland, as well as a son of the Scottish king, have been killed.

It was a crushing victory which saw Mercians and West Saxons sink their traditional rivalries under the leadership of Athelstan and his brother Edmund. Confronting them at Brunanburh was formidable force. The Norse of Ireland, led by Olaf, had allied with Scots, led by Constantine II, and Strathclyde Britons under Eugenius.

Olaf, the son of King Guthfrith of Dublin, was aiming to recover the kingdom of Northumbria, from which his father had been expelled ten years before. He arrived in Britain with a large fleet and joined forces with the men from Scotland, who were determined to check further English expansion. They were met by Athelstan and Edmund, and battle was joined. After fighting had raged all day the invaders were put to flight, and those who had come by sea rushed in disarray to board their ships. Other survivors were hotly pursued until stopped by nightfall (→27/10/939).

Lines from the "Anglo-Saxon Chronicle" on the Battle of Brunanburh:

And the host from the ships fell doomed.

The field grew dark with the blood of men after the sun, that glorious luminary, God's bright candle, rose high in the morning above the horizon, until the noble being of the Lord Eternal sank to its rest.

There lay many a warrior of the ... north, torn by spears, shot o'er his shield; likewise many a Scot, sated with battle, lay lifeless ... The sorry Norsemen who escaped the spears set out upon the sea, making for Dublin o'er deep waters, ashamed and shameless back to Ireland.

York kingdom recaptured by Irish king

A two-edged decorated iron sword.

York, December 939
Within two months of King Athelstan's death, York is once again in the hands of the Norse. Olaf of Dublin entered the city – the capital of the Northumbrian kingdom from which his father, Guthfrith, was driven 12 years ago – without meeting much resistance.

Olaf seized the chance to attack before Edmund, Athelstan's 18-year-old half-brother, could establish himself firmly on the throne. Edmund had fought alongside Athelstan at the Battle of Brunanburh two years ago when Olaf and his supporters from Scotland had been all but annihilated by the combined forces of Wessex and Mercia.

The swift success of the Norse in regaining York exposes the fragility of Athelstan's kingdom and the extent to which it had depended on his own exceptional qualities. Olaf is now poised to strike south in the direction of the formerly Norse-dominated boroughs of Leicester, Lincoln, Nottingham, Stamford and Derby. For 12 years these have been ruled by Athelstan, and many of Norse descent have attended the councils which he established for local administration. Now Edmund, a forceful prince, faces a fight to retain their loyalty (→940).

Athelstan's mighty reign draws to a close

Athelstan: a 14th-century view.

Gloucester, 27 October 939
King Athelstan, the man who forged a powerful kingdom covering most of England, died today. He was 44, and in 14 years on the throne he had established himself as the dominant English figure of his time; he was the first Anglo-Saxon king to ally with leaders in France, Germany and Norway.

Athelstan, a flaxen-haired man who combined courage and intellect, consolidated the union of Wessex and Mercia, reclaimed Northumbria from the Norse and secured the allegiance of Welsh princes and the Britons of Cornwall. This alliance was responsible for his victory at Brunanburh two years ago [*see report above*]. The title he often used, "King of the English and Ruler of All Britain", was at least partly justified.

The West Saxon king was more than simply a warrior. He set up many councils in southern England backed by royal charters, a device that enabled nobles and churchmen to work together in government and allowed new views and ideas to be aired. He also devised detailed new law codes (→12/939).

York prospers under control of the Norse

York, December 939
The city of York, which was recaptured this month by the Norse, is once again a pivotal point in the battle for power in Britain. Here Roman emperors once sat in state in the *principia*, a headquarters building which still stands. Later, York became the chief city of the mighty Anglo-Saxon kingdom of Northumbria. But it has grown most rapidly since falling to the Norse in 867.

The Norse have expanded the city south of the Roman fortress towards the river Foss, creating a network of new streets, including Coppergate with its densely packed houses and workshops. Meanwhile, the numerous cargo ships berthed at the new wharves are evidence of a thriving trade with Europe and Ireland. Some estimate that the population is as high as 30,000, including craftsmen of all descriptions, producing work of the highest standard that reflects the vigorous traditions of both English and Norse.

A pot from the Norse city of York.

St Peter's, constructed on the site of churches erected by King Edwin of Northumbria and St Wilfrid, is the most important of York's many ecclesiastical buildings.

942 - 957

English Midlands, 942. King Edmund retakes Mercia, seized two years ago by King Olaf Guthfrithsson of the Dublin Norse (→ 16/8/946).

Canterbury, Kent, 12 February 942. Oda succeeds Wulfhelm as the first Norse archbishop of Canterbury (→ 943).

Ardee, Co Louth, 26 February 943. Muirchertach mac Neill, High King Donnchad Donn mac Flainn's chief warrior, is killed by the Dublin Norse under King Blacair (→ 944).

Ireland, 944. King Congalach mac Mael Mithig of Brega and King Braen mac Mael Morda of Leinster raid Dublin. The high-kingship is in dispute after the death of Donnchad Donn (→ 948).

Dublin, 945. Olaf Sigtryggsson, the deposed king of York, ousts Blacair of Dublin (→ 948).

Cumbria, c.945. Edmund cuts the Norse route to Northumbria by accepting King Malcolm of Scots (→ 949).

Kingston Upon Thames, Sy, 16 August 946. Following the murder of Edmund earlier this year, Edred succeeds him as king of Wessex (→ 947).

Tanshelf, West Yorkshire, 947. Northumbria, under Archbishop Wulfstan of York, submits to Edred (→ 948).

Ripon, North Yorkshire, 948. The minster is destroyed when Edred expels Eric Bloodaxe, who became king of York last year (→ 952).

Ireland, 948. Blacair of Dublin is killed by Congalach, who seizes the high-kingship (→ 951).

Northumbria, 949. King Malcolm of Scots invades in support of his ally King Olaf Sigtryggsson of Dublin (→ 954).

Co Clare, 951. High King Congalach Cnogba fights the Dal Cais dynasty after the death of Ruairi ua Canannain of the Cenel Conaill, his rival for the high-kingship (→ 956).

Northumbria, 952. Archbishop Wulfstan is imprisoned for obeying Eric Bloodaxe, who has expelled Olaf (→ 954).

Stainmore, Cumbria, 954. Eric Bloodaxe is killed in an ambush (→ 957).

Somerset, 23 November 955. Edred dies; his nephew Edwy succeeds him as king (→ 956).

Leinster, 956. Congalach is killed by the Dublin Norse; Domnall ua Neill, the son of Muirchertach, succeeds (→ 963).

Most of Wales is united

Wales, c.943
The dynastic feuds that have bedevilled Wales for generations appear to have come to an end – at least for the time being. A new leader of rare talents, Hywel ap Cadell – also known as Hywel "Dda [Good]" – has succeeded in establishing himself as master of almost all of the country, apart from the south-east.

Hywel, the grandson of Rhodri "the Great" – the first king to unite Wales – has rescued his country from near anarchy by means of both an astute marriage and ruthless military campaigning. He gained control of Dyfed by taking Elen, the daughter of Llywarch ap Hafaidd, the king of the region, as his bride. Gwynedd and Powys have now fallen under his sway following the death of their ruler, Idwal "the Bald". The only areas to remain outside Hywel's control are Glamorgan and Gwent.

Hywel cultivated close relations with the English King Athelstan, who died three years ago, and – unlike other recent Welsh rulers – he has been deeply influenced by English life and methods of government. He is drawing up a legislative programme based partly on procedures which he admires in the kingdom of Wessex; this will codify laws for Dyfed, Gwynedd and Powys, all of which at present operate according to their different customs. Hywel is also contemplating issuing his own coinage; if he goes ahead with this plan, he will be the first Welsh king to do so (→ 999).

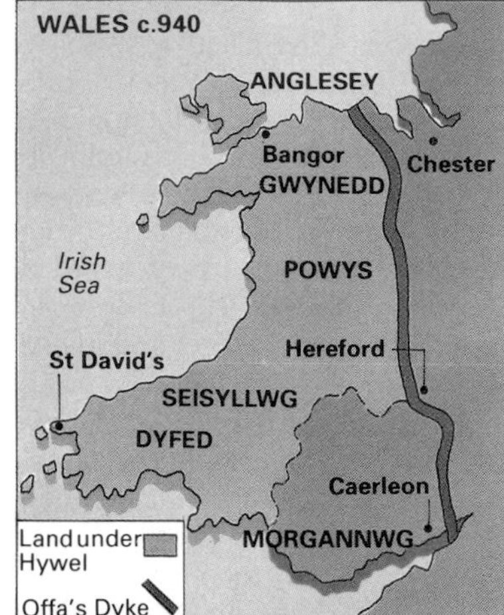

A coin of King Hywel of Dyfed.

Bell tower fails to protect scholar monk

Leinster, 950
Striking out from their Dublin stronghold, the Norse have raided Slane in Co Meath, burning alive a scholar named Caenechair in the round bell tower here – which was built to offer protection against just such an attack.

These tall, tapering towers, with entrances constructed high above the ground, have become a distinctive feature of monastic sites in Ireland. The monks use them as watchtowers and as refuges. When a monk on lookout duty observes signs of an imminent Norse attack, a handbell is rung from the top of the tower as a warning to colleagues, who swiftly make their way into the tower, pulling their ladder up behind them.

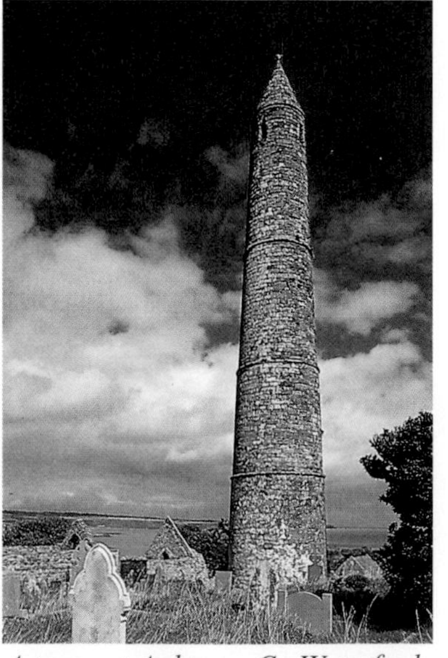
A tower at Ardmore, Co Waterford.

Glastonbury Abbey is made to follow strict new regime

Glastonbury, Somerset, 943
Since becoming abbot of Glastonbury three years ago, Dunstan – whose friends say that he speaks "face to face" with God – has transformed life here by the introduction of a strict Benedictine rule. Dunstan deplores the decline of British monasticism since the great age of Bede and Aldhelm. In his view, many old minsters – especially those that sprang up around shrines such as St Frideswide's at Oxford or St Cuthbert's at Chester-le-Street – have become mere hostels manned by loose groupings of clerics following slack routines. Glastonbury was one such institution – albeit blessed with a superb library. But now St Benedict's regime, in use throughout Europe, imposes high standards of behaviour here and a demanding timetable: eight prayer meetings and only two meals in a day that starts at 2am and ends at 8pm.

Dunstan kneels at the feet of Christ.

Dunstan is also close to King Edmund of Wessex, to whom he owes his abbacy. Born into a well-connected aristocratic family, Dunstan grew up at the court of King Athelstan before becoming a monk. He is well suited to the hurly-burly of politics, and Edmund relies on his advice, especially in financial matters. In addition, the abbot is a talented musician (→ 2/6/958).

Scots king swaps palace for monk's cell

A hunter carved on a stone coffin at Constantine's new home, St Andrews.

Fife, 943
King Constantine II of the Scots has abdicated to enter the monastery of St Andrews, exchanging a king's palace for a monk's cell after four decades on the throne. For the first 37 years of his reign he held the balance of power in Britain, allying himself with the vikings against King Athelstan's Wessex and maintaining indirect control over the whole of Scotland. Athelstan's growing power upset this balance, and when Constantine tried to contain him, with an alliance of Scots, Irish and vikings, his army was decimated at Brunanburh six years ago. Since then Constantine has slowly declined, and he has now apparently lost the will to rule (→945).

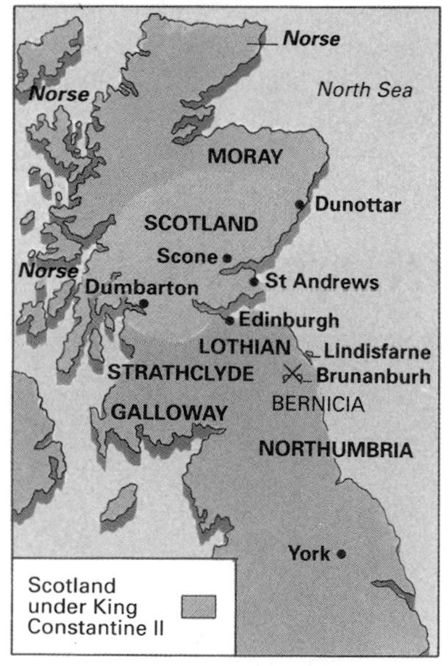

Boy king provokes anger by abandoning his coronation feast for sexual diversion

Surrey, 956
Orgiastic scenes have marred the coronation of King Edmund's 15-year-old son Edwy – who has succeeded his childless uncle, Edred, as king of Wessex amid family quarrels. Edgifu, Edwy's mother, is particularly furious about her son's recent marriage to Alfgifu, which endangers the rights of his brother Edgar to the throne.

Showing no signs of concern about the controversy, Edwy left his coronation feast at Kingston Upon Thames with a noblewoman and her daughter to enjoy some sexual diversions in his bedchamber. The two women were already well known to the young king, having some time ago seduced him in order to try to forge a marriage alliance. The nobles were outraged by the king's departure from the feast, and Archbishop Oda gave orders for him to be brought back. At first, fearful of incurring Edwy's anger, everyone was reluctant to intervene. Seeing this, the archbishop appointed Dunstan, the abbot of Glastonbury, and Cynesige, the bishop of Lichfield, to go to bring him back by force if necessary.

The two men burst into the royal bedchamber, where they found the crown lying on the floor and Edwy wallowing between the two women "as if in a vile sty". The clerics demanded that he return; when he refused, Abbot Dunstan dragged him off the bed, jammed the crown back on his head and forced him back to the table. In return for Dunstan's pains, the king has now exiled him (→957).

Edwy: a controversial boy king.

Dunstan denies Edwy's pleasure.

Men of Moray kill Scottish king in battle

Fife, 954
King Malcolm of Scots has been killed in a skirmish at Kincardine on the banks of the river Forth. His killers are men from Moray in the north-east, the annexation of which by Malcolm was his first victory after he succeeded Constantine II on the throne.

In spite of this early triumph, and the subsequent expansion of his kingdom into Cumbria, Malcolm's reign has to be accounted unsuccessful in terms of Scots power. He was unable to curb the growing power of Wessex to the south, and his alliances with Olaf Sigtryggsson and Eric Bloodaxe, the Norse kings of Dublin and York, only weakened his kingdom.

At first his reign appeared full of promise. Two years after his accession in 943 he made peace with Wessex, gaining Cumbria in return for maintaining peace on the border between the two kingdoms. But five years later he reneged on this pledge and invaded English territory, only to be defeated. He is succeeded by his cousin, Indulf (→962).

Edwy's brother takes half his kingdom

Wessex, 957
Edwy's catastrophic reign, dogged by opponents who insist that he is morally bankrupt and politically incompetent, has reached a new crisis with the appointment of his younger brother and rival Edgar to the kingdom of Mercia and the division of his inheritance. South of the Thames, Edwy still rules, but the area north of the river has transferred its allegiance to Edgar. Half of Edwy's noblemen have accordingly deserted him for Edgar's court. Worse still for Edwy, who had a reputation for sleazy sexual adventures even before he was crowned, Archbishop Oda of Canterbury has moved to separate him from his wife Alfgifu because they are linked by blood.

They are distantly related, she being descended from Athelred of Wessex, into whose family Edwy's grandfather had married; but Oda's intervention seems motivated by a desire to undermine Edwy, whose moral turpitude contrasts markedly with his brother Edgar's piety (→959).

958 - 969

Canterbury, Kent, 2 June 958. Archbishop Oda, the first Norse leading churchman, dies. He is succeeded by Alfsige (→ 21/10/960).

Wessex, 959. Mercia and Northumbria are reunited with Wessex on Edwy's death, when his brother Edgar becomes king (→ 964).

Canterbury, 21 October 960. Bishop Dunstan of Winchester is consecrated as archbishop, replacing Alfsige who died shortly after his own consecration (→ 961).

London, 961. St Paul's cathedral is destroyed by fire and rebuilt in the same year.

Strathclyde, 962. Norsemen fleeing from York kill King Indulf, who in 958 seized Edinburgh and Lothian from the Norse. Dub, the king of Strathclyde, succeeds him as king of Scots (→ 966).

Winchester, Hampshire, 29 November 963. Athelwold, the abbot of Abingdon and a former pupil of Dunstan, becomes bishop (→ 964).

Co Armagh, 963. High King Domnall ua Neill establishes a claim to southern Ulster.

Cashel, Co Tipperary, 963. Mathgamain mac Cennetig, the leader of the Dal Cais dynasty, resists the claims of King Fergal ua Ruairc of Breifne and Connacht and proclaims himself ruler (→ 968).

Iona, Strathclyde, 963. Bishop Fothad mac Briain, who began a Christian revival here by converting the invading Norse, dies (→ 986).

Ireland, 965. Famine is spreading through the country.

York, 966. Oslac, a Fenland nobleman and an outsider, is appointed by King Edgar as the leader of the city in an attempt to put the north under southern control (→ 966).

Grampian, 966. The body of the kidnapped King Dub is found in a ditch at Kinross. It is thought that his murderers acted on the orders of Culen, who is next in line for the succession (→ 971).

Winchester, 966. Edgar grants a charter to the new minster, confirming that its reform will comply with the Benedictine order under the control of Bishop Athelwold (→ 972).

Co Tipperary, 968. Mathgamain mac Cennetig defeats the Norse at Sologhead and captures Limerick (→ 971).

Campaign to wipe out monastic laxity is boosted by new Worcester appointment

Worcester, 961
Monastic reformers have acquired a powerful new ally with the appointment of Oswald as bishop of Worcester. He was promoted at the request of Dunstan, who became archbishop of Canterbury last year following his recall from exile by King Edwy in 957 [*see report on page 157*].

As a young man Oswald was installed by his uncle Oda, the first Norse archbishop of Canterbury, at the head of a small monastery at Winchester, where he was scandalized by the slackness and self-indulgent luxury which was taken for granted there. Eventually he travelled to France to experience at first hand the new movement for monastic reform that is spreading throughout Europe.

While Dunstan, at home in Wessex, was applying zealous principles similar to those practised in France, Oswald was earning a reputation for holiness and humility in France which he has brought with him to Worcester. Already the talk is of establishing a new monastery near Worcester and sending for French monks to help to build the new house on firm foundations of reformed monastic rule that will end the abuses (→ 29/11/963).

From the Ramsay Psalter: Oswald founded Ramsey Abbey, Cambs.

New local courts to boost royal power

London, c.961
Edgar, who rules Wessex north of the Thames, has set out the functions of the new "hundred" courts which are being used to extend royal control in the countryside.

The hundreds are subdivisions of English administrative districts known as "shires", each of which is dependent upon a particular town or important royal estate; in Wessex, where shires have been in existence since before the eighth century, "Hamtunscir" and "Wiltunscir", for example, are governed from Southampton and Wilton. Each hundred court has jurisdiction over its own particular territory. The court meets monthly to administer justice and mediate in tax disputes. It receives collective fines from wrongdoers. The court is presided over by a king's *reeve*, or representative, who can guide but not control deliberations.

The hundred court has evolved from the semi-official system of *tithings*, which under Athelstan, king of Wessex until 939, managed to impose some sort of order in a time of banditry. However, the *tithings* were only groups of kinsfolk charged with policing duties. They formed posses to ride after cattle rustlers and act against family groups harbouring thieves (→ 1006).

The king and his legal advisers.

Lay sister rejected as king remarries

Winchester, Hampshire, 964
King Edgar, who was widowed two years ago, has been accused of remarrying for political advantage in order to secure his position in south-western England. His new wife – Alfthryth – is the daughter of Ordgar, the properous *ealdorman* [king's deputy] of Devon, and the widow of Athelwold, the former *ealdorman* of East Anglia. Edgar's first wife, Athelfled, died giving birth to their son, Edward.

Disquiet about the marriage has been fuelled by the king's recent rejection of Wulfthryth, a former lay sister, by whom he had a daughter last year. Edgar's relationship with Wulfthryth has thrown into doubt the legitimacy of any children who may be born to him and his new wife (→ 965).

Property is prime factor in marriage

England, c.960
Despite a small increase in the number of couples seeking a priest's blessing for their wedding, this is not necessary to the legality of the marriage, and family and property considerations still play the major role in any settlement. A man must be seen to be able to provide for his wife before her family will consent to his proposal and the feasting and celebrations can begin.

The price of a bride can be extraordinarily high and may take years to accrue, while some men may never be able to afford to marry. It is common practice for a groom to give his bride both a morning-gift at the time of consummation and a dower to keep her in widowhood. He must also make some sort of payment to her family and assent to a contract assuring her parents that, even if the couple choose to live far away from them, they may have no fears for their daughter's wellbeing.

Women today have great freedom to hold and dispose of land. Among the upper classes, agreements are often drawn up on marriage about succession to land and goods on the death of either partner of the marriage.

Greedy clerics expelled

A superb Winchester manuscript showing the abbey's patron, King Edgar.

Winchester, Hampshire, 964
A group of clerics with a name for drunkenness, gluttony and lechery is being expelled from Winchester as part of a new drive to enforce stricter codes of behaviour in English monastic life. The man behind the expulsions is Athelwold, who was appointed bishop of Winchester last year by King Edgar of Wessex. Winchester, the royal capital, is the seat of a council called by King Edgar in 963 to devise a set of regulations for all monks and nuns in his lands, so it is not surprising that the town has been chosen as a target for the reformers.

According to some reports, many clergy at Winchester's new minster are ill-mannered and more keen on alcohol, eating and the pleasures of the flesh than on celebrating Mass. The wayward clerics have been given a clear choice: become monks and fall into line, or get out. Those who go will be replaced by monks from the abbey at Abingdon in Oxfordshire, of which the energetic and increasingly respected Athelwold is abbot (→966).

Legitimacy of king's new son challenged

Winchester, Hampshire, 966
The birth of a son to King Edgar and Queen Alfthryth of Wessex has been celebrated by one of the greatest royal family gatherings ever seen in the kingdom. But some still doubt the validity of Edgar's marriage two years ago and believe that the boy, Edmund, is a bastard. Edgar has therefore made all those present sign their names as witnesses. This commits them to recognizing Edmund's legitimacy, and thereby his right to succeed.

Edgar has also told Athelwold, the bishop of Winchester, to draft a charter confirming Edmund as heir, undermining the claims of Edward, the king's elder son by his first marriage, to Athelfled (→971).

Widespread slave trade and hierarchy of peasants underpin economy of England

Land labour: peasants hard at work tending their flocks. Many small farmers pay part of their "rent" by working for the lord of the manor.

Southern England, c.960
Much of England's economy is underpinned by the slave trade. However, slavery is not an irreversible state, nor is it necessarily entered into forcibly, although the vikings are notorious for selling captives as slaves abroad. It is not rare for slaves to be freed, nor for free men, in times of hardship, to sell themselves and their families into slavery to avoid starvation. Slaves are often freed during public celebrations or on the deaths of their masters. The recent death of King Edwy, for example, was marked by the freeing of his slave Lethelt and her children.

While the slave is at the bottom of the social ladder, the *gebur* – the lowest peasant – is not much further up. Struggling to feed his family on a little land provided by his lord, he pays for the use of the land partly in money, partly in kind and partly in work. He frequently spends two days a week working the lord's land, as well as making payments of corn, chickens, lambs and sometimes money.

The *villein* and the *sokeman* rank above the *gebur*, but not far. They farm bigger holdings, perhaps 12 hectares (about 29 acres), but as the *sokeman* owes less service he outranks the *villein*. Above them all are free men, owing their lord only military service. But for them all life is tough. A popular Latin grammar puts imaginary words into the mouth of a landless ploughman: "It's hard work, sir, because I am not free" (→c.1005).

A detail of "Abraham and the sacrifice of Isaac" from a manuscript. The figures in this biblical tale, such as the servant carrying his master Abraham's sword, are drawn from contemporary Anglo-Saxon life.

970 - 987

Lothian, 971. King Culen of Scots is killed by Riderch of Strathclyde in revenge for having raped his daughter.→

Wessex, 971. Edmund, the five-year-old son and heir of Edgar and Alfthryth, has died. All their hopes now lie with Athelred, who was born in 968 (→ Whitsun 973).

Bath, Avon, Whit Sunday 973. Edgar is crowned "emperor of Britain".→

Armagh/Munster, 973. Mathgamain mac Cennetig, the king of the Dal Cais dynasty, decides in favour of the abbot of Armagh in the latter's claim to supremacy over the abbot of Munster. This decision not only settles the dispute but also gives Mathgamain influence in the north (→ 976).

Munster, 976. Mathgamain is killed by Mael Muad mac Brain, who claims the high-kingship of Ireland (→ 978).

England, 976. Following the death of Edgar last year his son Edward (by his first wife Athelfled) has become king after a power struggle with supporters of his half-brother, Athelred (→ 18/3/978).

Kingston Upon Thames, Surrey, 14 April 978. Athelred becomes king following the ugly murder of his half-brother, Edward (→ 979).

Shaftesbury, Dorset, 979. Alfhere, the *ealdorman* of Mercia, a supporter of the new king, Athelred II, moves the bones of the murdered Edward for honourable burial (→ 983).

Irish and North Seas, 980. The Norse launch attacks on Britain (→ 981).

Padstow, Cornwall, 981. Irish Norsemen sack the town and ravage the Cornish and Devon coastline (→ 988).

Dublin, 981. The town is captured by the Irish high king, Mael Sechnaill II, who came to the throne on the death of his father, Domnall ua Neill, in 980, after defeating a Norse alliance at Tara. Its leader, Olaf Sigtryggsson, fled to Iona (→ 989).

Mercia, 983. Alfhere of Mercia, King Athelred II's main supporter, dies (→ 990).

Winchester, Hampshire, 984. Archbishop Athelwold has died (→ 19/5/988).

Iona, Strathclyde, 986. Following attacks last year, the Norse have killed the abbot and 15 monks in further raids.

Irish women and children burnt alive

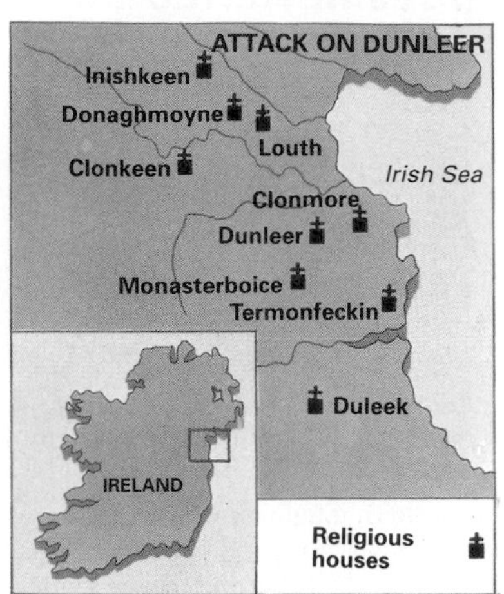

Warriors with shields and drinking horn: from a stone cross in Co Louth.

Co Louth, 971

Three hundred and fifty men, women and children have been burnt alive in the refectory of Dunleer monastery. It is the worst of the atrocities arising from the recent battles between High King Domnall ua Neill and his rivals.

The powerful Ui Neill dynasty is believed to be responsible for this outrage. And the perpetrators face stiff penalties if caught, because crimes against women are punished severely. This is not because a woman herself is regarded as sacrosanct, but because such crimes are considered to be against her husband, father and sons as well as the head of her kinship group. The culprit must pay these guardians an "honour-price".

Church law treats the crime of killing a woman as more serious than that of killing a man. Under the code of St Adomnan, the murderer may have a hand and a foot cut off before being executed, while his relations must pay compensation to the victim's family. Alternatively, woman-murderers may choose to do 14 years of a penance such as fasting and pay double compensation. If a woman has been raped, the rapist must pay the honour-price of her husband, father or son (→ 973).

English monasteries swept up in European reform movement

Winchester, Hampshire, c.970

A transformation is taking place in English monasteries as part of a Europe-wide movement to revitalize monastic life. New monasteries are being founded, old ones are expanding, and reformers are enlisting royal help to regulate the lives of monks and nuns to a greater degree than ever before. The reforms are also intended to ensure the security of monasteries by recovering land and influence lost over the years to local landlords.

In the forefront of the reform movement are men such as Archbishop Dunstan of Canterbury, Bishop Oswald of Worcester and Bishop Athelwold of Winchester, backed by their equally zealous patron King Edgar.

From a Winchester manuscript.

From Athelwold's "benedictional".

The culmination of their work comes in a new code of practice for monks and nuns, the product of a council, appointed by Edgar, which has sat at Winchester since 963. The *Regularis Concordia* [*Agreement of the Rule*] lays down a way of life based on the rule of St Benedict. To protect abbey property it invokes royal patronage and makes it difficult for abbots and abbesses to bequeath abbey lands. Celibacy is called for, and there is a detailed daily timetable which involves rising at about 1.30am in the summer (2.30am in winter) and going to bed at 8.15pm (6.15pm in winter). There is one secular treat in the monastic day: a drink of beer in the early evening (→ 984).

Edgar is now 'emperor'

Bath, Avon, Whit Sunday 973
Fourteen years after establishing himself as ruler of England, Edgar has been crowned "emperor of Britain" in a spectacular ceremony at Bath conducted by Archbishop Dunstan of Canterbury. In a city redolent with the imperial grandeur of Rome, Edgar has achieved greater authority than any other British ruler for more than 500 years. His coronation is a formal sanction of his position by the church and heralds a new phase of his reign.

Edgar is the second son of King Edmund of Wessex, and in 957, at the age of only 14, he – or possibly nobles acting in his name – rebelled against his elder brother, Edwy, securing for himself control of Northumbria and Mercia; two years later, Edwy's death made Edgar ruler of virtually all of England. Already anointed king, he has now, at the age of 29, been crowned emperor.

King Edgar's authority is wide-ranging. Acting under his patronage, Archbishop Dunstan has led a revival of Benedictine monasticism and reform of the church. The increased power that Edgar has allowed the clerics has buttressed that of the monarch. Ecclesiastical reform has been matched by changes to the administration of local government, involving a clarification of shire boundaries and new law codes [*see report on page 158*]. Edgar's reign has been mostly peaceful and prosperous, with Danish-dominated areas of the country more assimilated into the English kingdom (→ spring).

Edgar takes his entire navy to Chester for conference with other British kings

A Victorian impression of Edgar being rowed in triumph on the river Dee.

Chester, spring 973
At least six kings from northern and western kingdoms of Britain have met King Edgar in a ceremony here and apparently pledged their support for him. Edgar had travelled to Chester with his entire naval forces, fresh from the pomp of his coronation at Bath.

Detailed reports of the event are still confused. Some say that eight kings were present, others that there were six. It is also said that, as an act of subservience, the kings rowed Edgar in a boat along the river Dee. A less fanciful view is that this was just a conference about borders, during which Edgar recognized Scottish rule over Lothian and in turn the Scots recognized English influence over Bernicia (northern Northumbria).

Among the kings and princes said to have been there were Kenneth of Scots, Iago of Gwynedd and his rival Hywel, Malcolm of Cumbria, Dunmail of Strathclyde and Maccus of the Western Isles. One or more of the Norse princes who rule parts of Ireland may also have added assurances that they would be Edgar's allies (→ autumn 975).

Fourth Scots king in a row dies violently

Lothian, 971
King Culen of Scots has been assassinated by Riderch, the sub-king of Strathclyde, in punishment for crimes committed during a Scottish campaign to assert control over Strathclyde. He is the fourth Scots king in a row to die violently.

In 954 King Malcolm was killed in the Mearns [in Grampian] by the people of Moray, whom he had subjugated on coming to power in 943. Under the "tanistry" system – by which the succession, in theory, alternates between two branches descended from King Kenneth mac Alpin – Malcolm was succeeded by his cousin Indulf.

Malcolm's son Dub came to the throne in 962, after the Danes killed Indulf. Four years later his body was found in a ditch at Kinross. He had been kidnapped by men apparently acting for Culen, Indulf's son – who has himself now met a similarly bloody fate (→ 994).

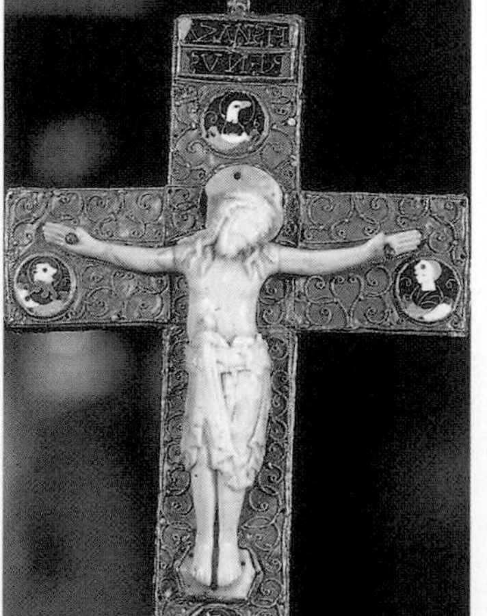

A late tenth-century crucifix: the body, of walrus ivory, covers a cavity used to contain holy relics.

Oswald is appointed archbishop of York

York, 972
In a move as much political as religious, Bishop Oswald of Worcester has been appointed archbishop of York. His predecessor Archbishop Wulfstan was put in prison in 952 for supporting a take-over of York by the Norse. King Edgar needed to find someone whose loyalty could be counted on and yet who would be acceptable to the Mercians, in whose territory York lies. Oswald seems a perfect choice. He is Mercian by birth and Danish by descent, but as a southern bishop from a well-connected family he can be relied on to keep the north in check (→ c.975).

King orders reform of the English coinage

Edgar's head adorns the new coins.

Lincoln, 973
King Edgar has ordered that all coins currently in circulation in England be withdrawn and new coins struck. A silver penny will be the main coin, with around 40 towns licensed as sites for royal mints. On one side of the coin will be the king's head and title, on the other the name of the mint and a design which will change every six or so years. The central government will determine the design and weight of each new coinage and will be in a position to profit financially each time a new coin is minted.

Since England has few internal sources of silver, the bullion for the new coins – which may number up to ten million at any one time – will have to be imported in exchange for products such as wool. Edgar's reform reflects not only a desire to symbolize the king's prestige but also the current strength of England's economy (→ 992).

Sons fight as Edgar dies

King Edgar seated between Dunstan, the archbishop of Canterbury, and Athelwold, the bishop of Winchester (from the "Regularis Concordia").

Southern England, autumn 975

Two sons of King Edgar are locked in a power struggle for the throne of England following his death on 8 July at the age of only 31. The figureheads of the row are 12-year-old Edward, Edgar's son by his first wife, and seven-year-old Athelred, Edgar's second son by his second wife. Athelred's full brother, Edmund, died in 971 at the age of five. Doubts about the legitimacy of Edgar's second marriage [*see report on page 158*] and claims that the late king favoured one son or the other have fanned the dispute between the two half-brothers. There seems no prospect of a compromise, such as a sharing of the kingdom between the two boys.

The division at court is being exploited by those who see a chance to regain the power lost when Edgar increased the authority and land-holdings of the churches and monasteries. Attacks on church property have occurred from Kent to Northumberland and from the Severn to the Fens, wherever churchmen have been accused of using their power to expand their personal wealth.

Money and religion are not the only causes of the conflict. In northern areas the hostility has been compounded by the traditional fears of southern domination, in this case by a king of Wessex. Here archbishops are frequently seen not only as land-grabbing churchmen but also as agents of southern rule. Edgar kept such fears in check, presiding over a kingdom which was apparently united in its peace and prosperity.

Only two years ago, when rival kings and princes agreed at Chester to give their support to Edgar, the power of Wessex had never seemed more formidable. Now the unity looks in danger of being shattered for good (→976).

This elegy for Edgar appears in the "Anglo-Saxon Chronicle" for 975:

In this year Edgar passed away,
Ruler of the English,
Friend of the West Saxons,
And protector of the Mercians.
That was known far and wide
Throughout many nations.
Kings honoured the son of Edmund
Far and wide over the gannet's bath,
And submitted to the sovereign,
As was his birthright.
No fleet however proud,
No host however strong,
Was able to win booty for itself
In England, while that noble king
Occupied the royal throne.

Strongman emerges in southern Ireland

Munster, 978

Reports are spreading throughout Ireland that a powerful chieftain, Brian Boruma mac Cennetig of the Dal Cais dynasty, has seized the kingship of Munster. Clearly the Dal Cais have turned the internal stuggles of the Ui Neill, the dynasty which dominates much of the north and east of the island and claims the high-kingship, to their advantage.

While the northern and southern branches of the Ui Neill struggle for supremacy in the Ui Neill lands, the Dal Cais have stepped in to forge their own power base in Munster. Brian Boruma is reputed to have been an indefatigable fighter against the Norse and to have carried on the struggle against them from amongst the hills and woods north of the Shannon estuary.

His brother, Mathgamain, was king of the Dal Cais until brutally murdered by a rival, Mael Muad. Already a well-established leader, Brian succeeded to the kingship and was determined to kill those responsible for his brother's death. Last year he killed the king of the Norse. This year he fought a great battle at a place called Belach Lechta [in Co Cork] in which Mael Muad was killed and his army, which may have included Norsemen, was defeated. Brian is now likely to spend some time consolidating his position in Munster (→981).

King is dragged to death by bolting horse

King Edward dies outside a poor country hovel: an engraving of 1792.

Corfe, Dorset, 18 March 978

King Edward, the elder son and heir of the late King Edgar, is dead. The teenage monarch was treacherously murdered today at his stepmother Queen Alfthryth's castle at Corfe. Alfthryth is suspected of instigating the assassination plot to gain the throne for her nine-year-old son, Athelred.

It happened when Edward paid a visit to the castle to see the queen and his stepbrother. He was travelling informally, without his bodyguard. When he arrived unexpectedly at the castle, one of Alfthryth's lords offered him a welcome cup. Still on his horse, Edward reached down to take it but was seized from behind by several of her retainers. "What are you doing?" he cried. "You are breaking my arm!" Then he was stabbed in the back. Trying to break through the ring of assassins, he was pushed from his horse. One observer said that a lord then twisted one of the stirrups, trapping Edward's foot, and the horse bolted, dragging him to his death. Athelred will now be crowned, but his reign is starting in an atmosphere of suspicion that will surely damage the prestige of the crown (→14/4/978).

988 - 995

Watchet, Somerset, 988. Norse attacks are becoming more frequent along both the southern and the western coasts of England (→991).

Canterbury, Kent, 19 May 988. The successor to Archbishop Dunstan is Athelgar.→

Dublin, 989. High King Mael Sechnaill II raids the town again, levying a gold tax on the Dublin Norse (→993).

Ireland, 990. Airbertach mac Coisse Dobrain, the geographer and scholar, is captured by the Norse at Roscarbery and held to ransom.

Canterbury, 990. Athelgar dies after only two years as archbishop. He is succeeded by Sigeric (→29/2/992).

England, 990. The queen mother, Alfthryth, who lost influence under the rule of her son, Athelred II, is allowed to return to court life (→993).

Southern and eastern England, 991. A Norse offensive begins with the arrival of a fleet of 93 ships led by Olaf Tryggvason, a Norwegian prince. They are concentrating on the areas of Maldon, Sandwich and Ipswich (→August).

York, 29 February 992. Archbishop Oswald dies.→

Ulster, c.993. Aed Ua Neill is crowned king of Ailech by Muirecan mac Ciaracain, the abbot of Armagh (→994).

Winchester, c.993. The scholar Alfric publishes *Lives of the Saints*, a translation of sermons in Latin (→1005).

Dublin, 994. King Sigtrygg Silkbeard of the Dublin Norse, the successor to Olaf Sigtryggsson, is deposed (→997).

West Midlands, 994. Wulfrun endows the monastery at Hamton, which will be known from now on as "WulfrunHamton" [Wolverhampton].

Northumberland, 994. The Scots, led by King Kenneth, raid south to reassert their claim on Bernicia but are repulsed by Earl Uhtred, its ruler (→995).

Canterbury, 28 October 994. Sigeric, archbishop since 990, dies (→995).

Britain, 995. A comet has appeared in the sky; it is being called "the long-haired star".

London, 995. Wulfstan is consecrated as bishop of London (→1002).

Archbishop and top royal mentor dies after great career

Canterbury, Kent, 19 May 988
Dunstan, archbishop of Canterbury for the past 28 years and a leading counsellor to several kings, has died shortly before reaching his 80th year. For much of his life Dunstan was at the centre of English affairs both spiritual and temporal, and he will be sorely missed by both church and state.

Born into an aristocratic Somerset family, Dunstan was educated at Glastonbury, where he was appointed abbot by King Edmund in 940. He was an influential figure at court during the reigns of Edmund and his brother Edred, but he was briefly exiled to Flanders in 955 after supporting the claims of Edgar to the throne against his brother Edwy. Recalled by Edgar, Dunstan became successively bishop of Worcester, bishop of London and, in 960, archbishop of Canterbury. Among Dunstan's achievements was his reformation of monastic life by enforcement of the strict Benedictine rule. He created a group of reformed monasteries, including Westminster and Bath, which looked to Glastonbury for inspiration.

As adviser to Kings Edgar and Edward he helped to draft key legislation and organize important financial reforms. A generous patron of the arts, he will also be remembered for his skills as teacher, artist, musician and poet (→990).

Archbishop Dunstan on his throne: mourned by both church and state.

Monastic reform sparks revival of arts

From a psalter made at Canterbury.

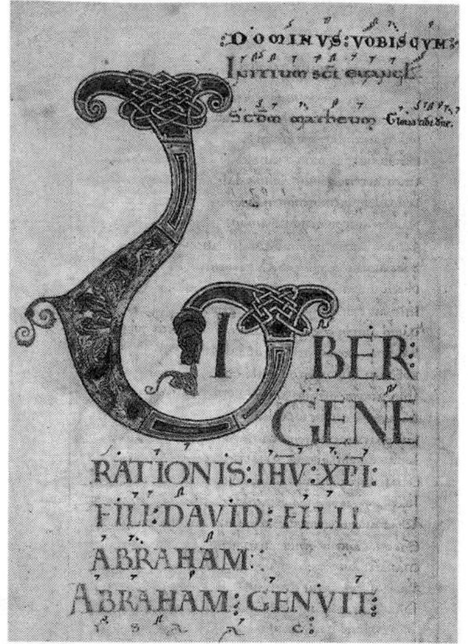

From a Winchester Gospel-book.

Southern England, c.990
The movement which has invigorated English monastic life in the past few decades has also breathed new life into the arts. Under the influence of its bishop, Athelwold, Winchester has been in the vanguard of this revival. The fine illustrated books produced at this old royal city are exemplified by the benedictional (a book containing the blessings said by a bishop during Mass) made for Athelwold himself. Its majestic, richly coloured pages show the influence of French art but have a particularly English liveliness. Musical knowledge has also increased following the appointment of a French music master at Winchester.

In monastic institutions elsewhere many illustrated Gospel-books and psalters have appeared. An especially magnificent example is a psalter produced at Canterbury, probably for the late Archbishop Dunstan himself, containing hymns and canticles as well as all the important texts which make up the Benedictine office.

Monks have also been collecting into a single book manuscripts containing the finest examples of Anglo-Saxon poetry. Among the most memorable and poignant of these are *The Wanderer*, *The Seafarer* and *The Wife's Lament*, as well as longer religious poems, notably *Guthlac*, *Christ* and *The Phoenix*.

Alongside these serious works are a number of bawdy and irreverent riddles. One of these asks what is "the strange thing that hangs by a man's thigh under its master's clothes ..." and which is "pierced in front" and "stiff and hard"? The answer, of course, is a key. Then there is the strange beast that leaps from the imagination of a monk to haunt the pages of the new book. "Two ears it has and one eye only. Two feet and 1,200 heads, one back, one belly, a brace of hands, a pair of sides and shoulders, and arms and a neck. Name please?" Although it sounds monstrous, the creature described turns out to be nothing more fearsome than a one-eyed garlic-seller.

An artist may have kept his quills in this delicately carved ivory case.

▷

East Saxons suffer heroic defeat at Maldon at hands of mighty Norse invasion fleet

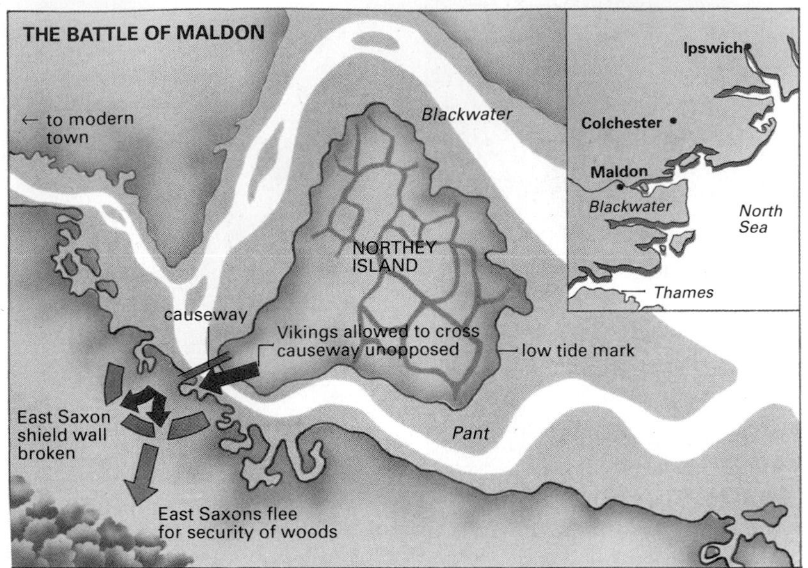

At low tide, the vikings crossed the river Pant and broke the East Saxon lines.

Maldon, Essex, August 991
The *ealdorman* [king's deputy] Byrtnoth, the royal representative and man in charge of the eastern militia, has been killed, along with a large number of men, in battle with the Norwegian prince Olaf Tryggvason.

The viking fleet – numbering over 90 ships – had been ravaging the Thames estuary and raiding up the east coast as far as Ipswich. It was sighted entering the Blackwater estuary and occupying Northey island, east of Maldon; from here, the only access to the mainland is provided by a causeway which is flooded at high tide.

In control of the landward end of the causeway, Byrtnoth drew up the East Saxon levy on the shore. Shouting across the water, which was running high, the Norse threatened to attack unless they were bought off with silver, but Byrtnoth refused. As the tide ebbed, the raiders began to stream out along the causeway, where they were initially held at bay by three of Byrtnoth's retainers.

Fearing that the Norse might sail away to strike elsewhere, the *ealdorman* decided to let them cross unhindered to the mainland so that battle could be joined on equal terms. It proved a disastrous move. In a desperately hard fight he and many of his men were cut down and killed. A particularly brave group of English warriors stood and died to the last man rather than survive their fallen leader. However, the Norse were also badly mauled, and they had hardly enough survivors in their ranks to sail their ships away.

Byrtnoth, *ealdorman* of Essex since 956, had been closely involved with the late King Edgar's policy of reviving monastic life and was a generous benefactor of the monasteries of Ely and Ramsey (→994).

Lines from the poem "The Battle of Maldon", c.1000:

Then Byrtwold spoke, shook ash-spear, raised shield-board. In the bravest words this hoar companion handed on the charge: "Courage shall grow keener, clearer the will, the heart fiercer, as our force faileth. Here our lord lies levelled in the dust, the man all marred: he shall mourn to the end who thinks to wend off this war-play now. Though I am white with winters I shall not away, for I think to lodge me alongside my dear one, lay me down by my lord's right hand."

Godric likewise gave them all heart, Athelgar's son, sending spears, death-darts, driving on the Danish ranks.

Mercian promoted to powerful office

Northern England, 993
The Mercian nobleman Alfhelm, who is an experienced statesman, has been appointed by King Athelred as Northumbria's *ealdorman* [king's deputy]. It is a prestigious appointment, bringing with it responsibilities and powers second only to those of the king.

The position which Alfhelm is to occupy is one which was originally granted to either a descendant or a successor of a royal line. However, with not only his own wide-ranging experience in Anglo-Danish affairs but also the influence of a wealthy brother, Wulfris Spot, Alfhelm has found his lack of royal ancestry to be of little consequence.

At one time each shire had its own *ealdorman*, but the last hundred or so years have seen quite a change in the importance of the position. Today the holder of the office is likely to have power over a number of shires, and Alfhelm, by his appointment here, has effectively become vice-regent for the whole of Northumbria.

As King Athelred's representative in the area, Alfhelm is entitled to official estates and the right to claim hospitality for his officials. He can summon levies from his shires and lead them into battle. Routine duties, however, can be delegated to his assistant officers, who are known as *reeves* (→1006).

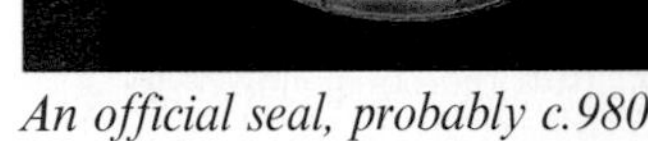
An official seal, probably c.980.

First mint in Dublin is set up by Norse

One of the Norse coins from Dublin.

Dublin, 992
Norse settlers here have opened a mint to produce silver pennies, becoming the first people in Ireland to make their own currency. Some English coins have been circulating in Dublin since the 920s, but these merely formed part of a system of barter by which the silver was weighed rather than counted. The pennies being minted now are modelled on English ones, so the new currency should help trade with England (→1000).

Last of trio who led church reform dies

York, 29 February 992
Oswald, archbishop of York since 972, died today. With Bishop Athelwold of Winchester and Archbishop Dunstan of Canterbury, both of whom predeceased him, Oswald was at the forefront of the vigorous reform movement which has transformed church life over the past few decades.

Deeply influenced by his time at the French monastery of Fleury, on the Loire, which followed the rule of St Benedict, the English-born Oswald returned in 959 to teach true monastic observance in his native land. At Dunstan's instigation he became bishop of Worcester in 961 – an office he held for the rest of his life. Oswald established many monastic foundations in the diocese of Worcester, including those at Westbury-on-Trim, Winchcombe, Pershore and Evesham, but he was most closely attached to the great abbey that he founded at Ramsey, near Peterborough (→28/10/984).

Opposition mounts to policy of appeasing aggressors by the payment of 'Danegeld'

Southern England, 994
Viking forces have returned to England, attacking London and the south coast under the leadership of Olaf Tryggvason of Norway and King Svein of Denmark. The raiders could not breach London's defences, but along the coasts of Essex and Kent, and inland in Sussex and Hampshire, they caused extensive destruction, using stolen horses to move through the countryside in an orgy of looting, burning and killing. King Athelred has now secured peace for his kingdom with a tribute of 16,000 pounds of gold and silver. This is not the first time that the king has been forced to buy off the vikings in this way.

In another incident, a Danish raiding party recently threatened to burn down Christchurch in Canterbury unless they were paid a large sum. In desperation Archbishop Sigeric turned to Bishop Ascwig of Dorchester, who lent him 90 pounds of silver and a considerable quantity of gold to satisfy the aggressors. Such tributes – which have come to be known as "Danegeld" – offend many in England. There are fears that they will encourage others to make equally extortionate demands (→997).

A marginal drawing shows the great Olaf in close combat with a wild boar.

Irish king breaks Norse hold on Dublin

An exquisite Viking architectural wood-carving found in Dublin.

Dublin, 995
High King Mael Sechnaill II has consolidated a victory at Tara in 980 over King Olaf Sigtryggsson of the Dublin Norse by taking Dublin after a siege. It is the third time that the Ui Neill high king has been in control here; this time he has exacted a heavy penalty from his foes.

Following his defeat at Tara, King Olaf fled to the island of Iona, off Scotland's west coast, leaving behind his Irish wife, the Leinster princess Gormlaith, and several sons. He died on Iona in 981, the year when Mael Sechnaill first took Dublin. The high king returned briefly two years ago, but this time he may finally have broken the Norse stranglehold on the town. He has forced the Norse to hand over the two most famous insignia of their rulers: the gold ring of Tomar, which weighs 560 grams (20 ounces), and the sword of Carlus.

The ring of Tomar lay on the altar at pagan ceremonies, and oaths were sworn on it during sacrifices. However, the Norse appear increasingly sceptical of their pagan tradition, and the loss of the ring may not cause great concern (→993).

Eat, drink and mind the silver tableware in nobleman's hall

East Anglia, 993
Athelwin, the *ealdorman* [king's deputy] of the East Angles, has died, and his luxury life-style has died with him. From now on the king intends to divide this large area among several administrators who will be expected to pursue less ostentatious lives.

The centre of Athelwin's imposing estate was a timber-built hall about 30 metres (100 feet) long. It was furnished with trestle tables and fixed benches, the beautiful silver tableware was imported from continental Europe, and the walls were hung with elaborate gold-woven tapestries. It was here that Athelwin entertained his many followers, including chaplains who doubled as secretaries, feeding them with enormous quantities of food served from a kitchen block some 18 metres away.

The long winter evenings were passed in harp-playing, singing and heavy drinking. Dicing and chess were popular, and during the day stag- and fox-hunting and hawking were favourite outdoor activities for which Athelwin retained his own huntsmen and wildfowlers. The duties of an *ealdorman*, however, embrace more than eating, drinking and enjoying himself. In time of war he is a military commander, and in peace he must attend many legal, political, royal and religious occasions.

Hawking: one of the favourite outdoor activities on a nobleman's estate.

Widow wills eight estates to the king

England, c.995
Alffled, the widow of Byrtnoth, the *ealdorman* [king's deputy] who fell at the Battle of Maldon, has died, leaving substantial property and land in her will. Among much else she bequeaths to King Athelred eight estates, two armlets of silver weighing together over a kilo, two drinking cups and some silver plate.

It is not unusual for women from upper-class families to be great heiresses, and Alffled amassed land and money from Byrtnoth's family as well as her own. While her husband was alive he exercised control over their joint estates, but on his death she took charge.

In a break with custom, Alffled has left estates to both her family and that of her husband. A woman who has inherited land from one member of her family is often expected to leave it to another, to keep the family's wealth intact (→999).

996 - 1001

South-western England, 997. A newly arrived Norse army rampages through Cornwall, Devon and Somerset before moving on to harry southern Wales. The towns of Tavistock, Lydford and Watchet are burnt to the ground (→ 998).

Orkney, 997. Sigurd "the Stout", the earl of Orkney, has converted to Christianity as a condition of his ransom imposed by King Olaf of Norway (→ 1008).

Isle of Wight, 998. A Norse base is established on the island following a raid (→ 999).

St David's, Dyfed, 999. Maredudd ab Owain, the grandson of King Hywel "the Good" of Dyfed who briefly united the realms of Gwynedd and Deheubarth, has been killed in a Norse raid (→ 1022).

Southern England, 999. The Norse army that arrived in 997 launches raids in Kent. Last year it ravaged Dorset before moving eastwards through Hampshire and Sussex.→

Bocking, Essex, 999. King Athelred II refuses to confirm the will of a local noble accused of helping Svein of Denmark to land. His widow has to purchase the aid of the archbishop of Canterbury before she can get her land.

Co Dublin, 999. King Brian Boruma defeats King Mael Morda of Leinster and King Sigtrygg Silkbeard of the Dublin Norse in battle at a place called Glenn Mama [near Saggart] (→ 1/1000).

Dublin, January 1000. Brian Boruma captures the town; Sigtrygg Silkbeard is forced to submit to his rule (→ 1002).

Bristol, Avon, 1000. Athelred establishes a mint in the town, and gold coins are struck.

England/Normandy, 1000. Athelred II renews Anglo-Norman relations, re-forming an old alliance with Duke Richard II (→ 1002).

England, 1000. An anonymous author writes *The Battle of Maldon*, describing the events of the battle in 991 and the defeat and death of the English leader.

Waltham, Essex, 1001. Continuing their rampage, the Norse burn and destroy the town (→ 23/5).

Hampshire, 23 May 1001. The Norse defeat the British in battle at Dean (→ 13/11/02).

Scottish royal feud claims new victims

A Pictish horseman hunting deer: detail from a carved stone from Montrose.

Tayside, 997

The increasingly bitter dispute over the Scottish succession [*see report on page 161*] has claimed another victim, with the death of King Constantine III in a civil war with rival members of the royal family. This latest fatality comes just two years after the mysterious murder of King Kenneth II at Fettercairn in the Mearns [in Grampian], near the east coast of Scotland.

Kenneth had been trying to persuade the Scottish nobility to agree that the royal succession should pass to the eldest son when he was lured to the home of a noblewoman named Finvela, who had promised to reveal the names of traitors. Before his death Kenneth was apparently entertained at a great feast at which wine flowed freely. Some say that he was then taken to a room containing a booby-trapped statue. When he touched the statue, the king activated several hidden crossbows and died in a hail of bolts. But this story may have been invented by the king's bodyguard to conceal its own negligence as well as Kenneth's dalliance.

Kenneth's desire to secure the throne for his son died with the accession of Constantine, a distant relative, ensuring the continuation of Scotland's bloody feud (→ 1005).

Two rival leaders agree to split Irish rule between them

Ireland, 997

Brian Boruma, the king of Munster, and Mael Sechnaill II, the high king of Ireland, have agreed at a meeting near Clonfert to divide Ireland between them, Mael Sechnaill taking the northern half of the island and Brian the southern half.

Hostilities between the two men began in 980, when Mael Sechnaill succeeded his father, Domnall. Renowned as a fierce fighter, Mael Sechnaill attacked the Dal Cais of northern Munster – Brian's dynasty – felling the sacred tree under which their kings were inaugurated. The following year Brian placed a large fleet on the Shannon and attacked Connacht, capturing Gilla Patraic, the king of Osraige, and taking hostages. In 984 he joined forces with the Waterford Norse for a major attack on Leinster and Dublin in which he burnt churches and devastated the countryside. Mael Sechnaill responded to a later assault on Connacht and Meath by invading Munster; Brian, in return, began to attack Leinster.

These skirmishes have continued over the years, with neither side claiming victory. But once Brian had secured his position in the east Mael Sechnaill was forced to recognize his supremacy not only in Munster but throughout the southern half of Ireland (→ 999).

New Durham church is built by fugitives

Durham, 999

A new church has been dedicated at Durham by the Northumbrian bishop Aldhun, following his flight here four years ago to escape the Norse threat. He came to Durham with his supporters from Chester-le-Street, where a see was created in 882 after the arrival of monks from Lindisfarne. The monks had been driven out of their monastery by an earlier Norse attack. Taking with them the body of St Cuthbert, the head of St Oswald and their Gospels, they wandered around Northumbria for seven years before finding a secure base (→ 1022).

These Norse coins, minted in England in the late tenth century, may form part of a tribute extorted from the English. The payment of such tributes – known as "Danegeld" – has been branded as foolhardy appeasement.

Isle of Man comes under attack from rattled English king

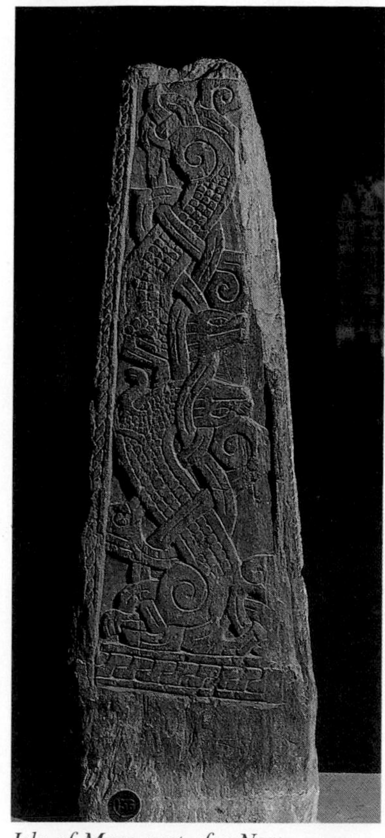

Isle of Man: part of a Norse cross.

Isle of Man, 1000
Goaded by a series of attacks on Wales and north-western England, King Athelred II has led a retaliatory raid against Norse settlements on the Isle of Man. The raid was preceded by others against similar targets in Cumbria. Athelred badly needs a victory over the Norse following several humiliating defeats and bungled attempts at gathering an adequate defensive force.

The Isle of Man has served the Norse for some years as a convenient base for attacks into Wales. Naturally the areas nearest to Man – Anglesey and Gwynedd – have borne the brunt of this aggression. Twenty-eight years ago Anglesey was in fact briefly held by Guthfrith Haraldsson of Man.

The English want to make sure that the vikings cannot establish themselves near Chester, an important commercial centre. The experience of recent years shows that once settled on an offshore island they can exact a heavy toll on mainland communities (→23/5/1001).

Norse culture takes hold in islands

British Isles, c.1000
Just when it seemed that 200 years of viking attacks were over for good, the longboats are once more at work spreading terror around the coastlines of Britain and Ireland. The new onslaught obscures the fact, however, that many Norse have made a permanent home in the islands, either bringing over their families to settle or marrying local women.

While their hold on some places, particularly in Ireland, is insecure, elsewhere the Norse have set down deep roots. In Northumbria, eastern Mercia and the lands of the East Angles there has been a huge influx of settlers, and in these areas their laws and language prevail.

They divide up the land into "weapontakes" instead of English hundreds, and in the York and Lindsey areas they have introduced their customary division into "ridings" or "thridings", from *thrithjungr* [a third part]. But more pervasive than these legal changes are the words that the English are slowly picking up from their Norse neighbours. These range from the particular – law, by-law, outlaw and husting – to everyday words such as husband, sister, fellow, happy, ill, take, want and even they, them and their.

Kent is latest victim of viking savagery

Kent, 999
The people of Kent have become the latest victims of the Norse marauders who have plagued England since the vacillating King Athelred II came to the throne in 978. England has been under constant attack in the last few years, and Athelred has twice had to pay a fortune to get rid of the fearsome northern warriors – most recently in 994, when Olaf Tryggvason of Norway and Svein Forkbeard of Denmark mounted a joint invasion.

Two years ago another Danish sea-borne army arrived to pillage the coasts of Wessex. Based in the Isle of Wight, this year it sailed round the Kent coast and up the Medway to Rochester, where there was a clash with local troops. The Kentish men were forced to flee through lack of support (→1000).

The silver hilt of a viking sword.

Icelandic poet wins the king's approval

Southern England, 1001
Following a prolonged visit to King Athelred, Iceland's celebrated poet Gunnlaug has embarked for home. His dignified bearing made a great impression on all who met him.

During his stay at court, Gunnlaug was granted an audience to read a poem he had written for the king. It ended with the refrain: "All the host of the generous and dauntless prince fears England's lord as a god, and the sons of men do homage to Athelred."

The king thanked him with the gift of a fur-lined scarlet cloak, and made him his retainer throughout the winter. On parting, Gunnlaug was given a gold ring weighing almost 170 grams (6 ounces) and was invited to return when he could.

York, 1002. Wulfstan, the bishop of London, is consecrated as both archbishop of York and bishop of Worcester (→ 1006).

England/Normandy, 1002. The alliance between the countries is strengthened by Athelred II's marriage to Emma, the sister of Duke Richard II of Normandy (→ 1005).

Exeter, Devon, 1003. The city is sacked by a force of raiders under the leadership of King Svein of Denmark (→ 1004).

Co Antrim, 14 September 1004. Aed Ua Neill, the king of Ailech and claimant to the kingship of Ulster, kills Eochaid mac Ardgail, the king of Ulster, in battle at Crew Hill before he himself is also killed (→ 1006).

Norfolk, 1004. Svein, following his total destruction of Norwich three weeks ago, has moved on to Thetford; despite accepting peace money from the East Angles, he has ransacked it (→ 1006).

England, 1005. A great famine spreads across the country (→ 1/5/1048).

Islip, Oxfordshire, 1005. Edward, the first son of Athelred II and his Norman wife Emma, is born (→ 1008).

Tayside, 1005. King Malcolm II of Scots kills his last rivals to his throne, Kenneth III and his son Giric, at Monzievaird. The succession to the throne is now secure (→ 1006).

Ireland, 1006. Brian Boruma mac Cennetig, the king of Munster, is recognized as high king of Ireland; last year he was accepted as overlord in Ulster and confirmed the supremacy of Armagh over the Irish church (→ 1013).

Canterbury, Kent, 1006. Bishop Alfheah is consecrated as the new archbishop, following the death last November of Archbishop Alfric, who had succeeded to the office on the death of Sigeric 12 years ago (→ 9/1011).

Wallingford, Oxfordshire, 1006. The town is sacked and the castle destroyed by King Svein of Denmark after raids on Reading, Sandwich and Winchester (→ 1007).

Isle of Wight, 1007. Following further attacks on the English in Berkshire and Wiltshire, the Danes rejoin their ships after receiving tribute money amounting to 36,000 pounds of silver (→ 1009).

Thousands of Danes are massacred

Wrist-wear: a massive tenth-century silver bracelet from Falster, Denmark.

Oxford, 13 November 1002

Thousands of Danes – men, women and children – have been put to the sword in some of the most violent massacres England has ever seen. Since dawn today, St Brice's day, all over central and western England defenceless families have been dragged from their homes and hacked to pieces.

Here in Oxford the terrified Danes fled for sanctuary to the monastery of St Frideswide [Christ Church]. When the mob failed to break in, it burnt the church and the entire Danish community in Oxford with it. The rich and noble have fared no better than the poor and the peasants. In London the dead include Gunnhild, the sister of King Svein Forkbeard of Denmark. Svein has sworn vengeance, and England can only wait as he gathers his ships and men.

There is no doubt that King Athelred II instigated the massacre. Only a few days ago he announced a "Danish conspiracy" to assassinate him and take over the country. His subjects eagerly completed what his soldiers had started after being the victims of countless Danish raids for so many years. Athelred's motives are threefold: to avenge the Danish sea-raids on England, to show himself a strong king, and to gain popularity with his subjects, who are dubious about his controversial accession after the murder of his half-brother, King Edward (→ 1003).

Made by Danes: a tall stone cross.

Southern king lays claim to all of Ireland

Tara, Co Meath, 1002

High King Mael Sechnaill II has abdicated in favour of Brian Boruma, the king of Munster, whose spectacular rise to power could finally bring about the union of all Ireland under one ruler. Three years ago, Leinster joined forces with the Dublin Norse to attack Brian, who under an agreement with Mael Sechnaill had been recognized by the high king as overlord in the south of Ireland. Brian defeated the allies and went on to plunder and burn Dublin.

After this victory Brian decided to break his agreement with Mael Sechnaill, under which he had also recognized the high king as overlord in the north of Ireland. To try to win the north he gathered a large army – including Dublin Norsemen – and marched to the seat of the high kings at Tara. There he was met by an advance force of Norse and Leinstermen; although he defeated them, he was uncertain as to whether he had won a complete victory.

Last year Brian planned a campaign against Mael Sechnaill, who had joined with the king of Connacht in building a barrier across the Shannon at Athlone to stop Brian's advance. Brian marched on Athlone, took hostages from both kings and defeated them. Overpowered as he was, and without the help of the northern branch of his dynasty, the Ui Neill, Mael Sechnaill had no choice but to submit. The ancient title "high king of Ireland" could now, at long last, become a reality (→ 14/9/04).

The opening to the Gospel of Matthew in a beautiful Gospel-book from Kells, Co Meath. It was probably made in the abbey at Iona and brought to Ireland.

Literary abbot with royalist leanings is appointed to head monastery at Eynsham

Part of an illustrated manuscript of the "Hexameron", showing Noah's Ark.

Oxfordshire, 1005
Alfric, one of Britain's most gifted writers of English prose, has been appointed abbot of Eynsham, the newly established monastery in Oxfordshire. Educated by Bishop Athelwold at Winchester, where he was a Benedictine monk, he has become a formidable scholar and a powerful voice within the church. A man of strong convictions, Alfric denies the immaculate conception and disputes the doctrine of transubstantiation. Much of his literary output is designed for the guidance of clergy and laity alike.

His association with Athelweard, the chronicler, while at Winchester brought Alfric into contact with patrons of enormous wealth and influence. When Athelweard's son Athelmer founded a monastery at Cerne Abbas in 987, it was Alfric who became head of teaching there.

Alfric's prose is distinguished by its clarity – unpretentious and plainly stated, but with a vigour that makes its meaning clear. His works include a Latin grammar, a Latin primer and his *Colloquy*, which are among the first textbooks of their kind in the country [*see report right*]. Between 989 and 992 he finished the *Catholic Homilies*, two books of sermons, and in the next seven years he translated six books of the Old Testament into English – the *Hexameron* – and wrote *The Lives of the Saints*.

An ardent royalist, Alfric singles out for particular praise the English kings Alfred, Athelstan and Edgar. He believes that successful rule always depends on "those who work, those who fight, those who pray". If any of these three supports breaks down, he argues, a reign is doomed (→ 1020).

Scots suffer heavy defeat at Durham

Durham, 1006
A force of Scots under King Malcolm II has been heavily defeated by the English at Durham. The battle signalled a bloody end to a Scottish-Northumbrian peace that had lasted for a generation.

The English were commanded by Earl Uhtred, who gathered men from all over the region to oppose Malcolm's advance. Uhtred is descended from a family which has ruled Bernicia (northern Northumbria) with a large measure of independence from the English kings for at least a century. He has been rewarded for his success by being given control of all English territory north of the Humber.

Malcolm – who was lucky to escape from the battle at Durham with his life – became king of Scots last year after killing his cousin Kenneth III and Kenneth's son Giric, the last surviving contender for the throne, at Monzievaird. He decided to take advantage of the current insecurity of King Athelred of England by advancing into northern Northumbria.

The encounter with Uhtred has claimed thousands of lives. The heads of the dead Scots have been cut off and placed around the walls of Durham, where local women wash them and comb their hair – in return for payment (→ 1018).

Top official killed on orders of king

Athelred's head on a silver penny.

Surrey, 1006
In a purge against English nobles, Alfhelm, the *ealdorman* [king's deputy] of York, has been murdered at Kingston-upon-Thames on King Athelred's instructions. His sons were ordered to be blinded.

Athelred, always on his guard for treachery, real or imagined, is moving to abolish many of the large *ealdormanries*. They are being subdivided into a number of units, each under the control of a lesser official, the high *reeve*. Such a policy parallels that pursued by Athelred's father, Edgar, who systematically removed all *ealdormen* south of the Thames. Some, however, see Athelred's purges more as a reflection of his limited political skills, his weakness of character and his well-known inability to choose good men and hold their loyalty (→ 1013).

English working boys face hard daily slog

Oxfordshire, c.1005
The daily slog of working boys provides the inspiration for Alfric's *Colloquy*, a Latin dialogue with English translation between a teacher and his pupils. The boys' frank replies to the teacher's questions give a telling insight into their lives.

The hardest lot falls to the ploughboy. His day starts at dawn when the oxen have to be driven down to the fields – in all weathers. "There is no winter so severe," he groans, "that I dare stay at home for dread of my master." Once he has yoked up the oxen, he begins his daily task of ploughing a full acre or more. Another lad helps him, prodding the oxen with an iron goad and growing hoarse from shouting at them. Work is not finished till the oxen are led back, watered, fed and mucked out.

Another boy, who fishes for a living, seems to have a better time. He usually fishes in rivers because "sea-fishing involves too much rowing", although it does provide a more varied catch, including herring, sturgeon, lobsters and even dolphins.

A pupil training to be a monk also rises at dawn, when the tough routine of seven or more services a day starts. But at least the food is good; the novice's diet includes vegetables, eggs, fish, cheese, butter and beans.

1008 - 1015

England, 1008. King Athelred II declares that 18 March will be kept as a special day in memory of his murdered half-brother, Edward (→ 1009).

Scotland, 1008. Sigurd "the Stout", the earl of Orkney and ruler of the Western Isles, marries the youngest daughter of Malcolm II of Scots (→ 1005).

Isle of Wight, August 1009. The Danish leader Thorkell "the Tall" and his men have built a base here after successful raids on southern England (→ 1010).

East Anglia, 1010. Thorkell's Danish troops sack Ipswich and burn Thetford and Cambridge (→ 1011).

England, 1011. Athelred II sues for peace after Danish raids in the south (→ 4/1012).

Canterbury, Kent, September 1011. Archbishop Alfheah is captured and held to ransom by the Norse (→ 4/1012).

England, April 1012. Athelred II pays "Danegeld" of 48,000 pounds of silver (→ 5/1012).

Kent, May 1012. Thorkell "the Tall" and his troops ally with Athelred, instead of Svein Forkbeard (→ 8/1013).

Sandwich, Kent, August 1013. Svein Forkbeard returns to England (→ 12/10/13).

Leinster, 1013. High King Brian Boruma builds a fortress against attacks by the Dublin Norse and Sigurd "the Stout" of Orkney (→ 23/4/14).

Canterbury, 1013. Lyfing replaces the martyred Alfheah as archbishop (→ 1014).

England, 3 February 1014. King Svein Forkbeard dies; his son Harald, the elder brother of the Danish leader in England, Cnut, succeeds him (→ spring 1014).

England, spring 1014. Athelred, who fled to Normandy last year when Svein usurped his throne, is restored to it by the *witan* [royal council].

Lincolnshire, 1014. Cnut is driven out by Athelred, who attacks in revenge for his exile. Cnut mutilates all hostages before fleeing (→ 1015).

Oxford, 1015. Edric Streona, the most powerful Mercian, kills the nobles Sigeferth and Morcar for treachery.→

England, 1015. Edmund, the successor to Athelred's throne, marries Sigeferth's widow and flees north.→

'God help us' prays king

A Norse warrior armed to the teeth.

An 11th-century Anglo-Saxon ship.

Bath, Avon, 1009
King Athelred II and his councillors have called on the English people to do penance and pray for God's help against Norse depredations. Enraged by the murder of his sister Gunnhild in the St Brice's day massacre at Oxford in 1002 [*see report on page 168*], Svein Forkbeard, the king of Denmark, has been mounting repeated revenge attacks on England. Athelred would rather pay "Danegeld", or tribute-money, than fight. Two years ago he paid Svein the enormous sum of 36,000 pounds of silver, the equivalent of three or four years of the national income, but it bought only a short respite. Thorkell "the Tall", a Danish noble, has now arrived with a large army, and the English forces are in such disarray that Athelred has turned to prayer to try to stop the pillaging.

He has ordered the people to fast for three days on bread, herbs and water, while "every man is to come barefoot to church without gold and ornaments" and go to confession. They are also to parade the holy relics and call on Christ from their "inmost hearts".

Athelred has also ordered the collection of alms and taxes "to the end that Almighty God may have mercy on us and grant that we may overcome our enemies". These provisions reflect the view that the Norse are a plague visited on the English in punishment for their failure to pay church taxes. So now any man who does not pray or pay his taxes will be punished. *Thegns* [noble retainers] will be fined 30 shillings and free men 30 pence; slaves will be flogged (→ 8/1009).

Archbishop is felled by single axe-blow

Greenwich, London, April 1012
Alfheah, the archbishop of Canterbury, has been cruelly murdered by the Danes. Captured in Canterbury last year, when the raiders sacked the city, he was later brought north to their Greenwich camp. Some 48,000 pounds of silver was paid by the English as the usual tribute to buy the Danes off, but they demanded a separate ransom for Alfheah, which he would not allow anyone to pay.

The result was that a drunken mob grabbed the archbishop and pelted him with cattle bones. One of the Danes then finished him off with a single axe-blow. Thorkell "the Tall", a Danish leader who tried to save Alfheah's life, was so disgusted that he is said to be about to join the English side (→ 1013).

An ivory panel from Canterbury.

'Leech Book' advocates herbal remedies for common complaints

England, c.1010
Remedies for everything from the common cold to smallpox have been gathered together in Bald's *Leech Book*, the most extensive medical work available today. It is especially useful for women, who have a high mortality rate, as a consequence of the general risks involved in pregnancy and childbirth. The book recommends giving up alcohol during pregnancy; advises using warm poultices and hot herbal drinks if periods have stopped; and tells how to make special charms to prevent miscarriages.

Herbal remedies are the most commonly suggested cures, aimed at everyday complaints such as earache, toothache and headaches, although the book says that surgery is necessary for more serious matters, such as gangrene and abscesses on the liver. There are also recipes for salves for burns and wounds as well as astringents for common parasites such as lice.

Most people cannot read, however, and rely on ancient charms for good health. The charms are short poems against all manner of ailments – tumours, convulsions, or simply a sudden stitch, when a bystander has to chant, amongst other things: "Out, little spear, if herein thou be!" (→ c.1200).

London surrenders to the Danes, who now rule length and breadth of England

A 15th-century picture of Svein Forkbeard's triumphal return to England.

London, December 1013
London has surrendered to Svein Forkbeard, and the Danish king now rules all England. Athelred bought him off in April last year with a ransom of 48,000 pounds of silver. This was on top of the 36,000 pounds of silver that he had given him in 1007, and means that Athelred has paid Svein the equivalent of ten years of the national income – but he has still returned to conquer.

Svein came with a great fleet of longships. After pausing at Sandwich, he sailed north to disembark 20 miles up the Trent at Gainsborough in Lincolnshire. There, the Danes who had settled in the area now known as the "Danelaw" [*see map on page 149*] flocked to his standard. Indeed, Northumbria and the whole of the Danelaw south of the Wash acknowledged him as king without a blow being struck. He gathered men, horses and supplies and moved south-westwards into Mercia. Only then did he allow his men to rape and pillage.

So great was the fear that spread before Svein's advance that there was little opposition. Oxford surrendered, as did Winchester, and it was only when he reached London that he met stout resistance. The Londoners fought off his men, many of whom drowned in the Thames.

After this Svein marched west to receive the surrender of Bath, while Athelred fled to Normandy. Isolated, London could no long resist and has accepted Svein as master of all England (→3/2/14).

England is entirely divided into shires

England, 1013
All of England is now divided into administrative units known as shires, centred on major towns. The Wessex shires – Hampshire, Wiltshire, Dorset, Somerset and Devon – date from the eighth century, when each had an *ealdorman* [king's deputy] at its head. Those of Kent, Essex and Sussex are based on former kingdoms. The midland shires are newer, created without regard to the ancient divisions of Mercia. In the eastern midlands the typical shire derives from the settlement of a Danish army, such as the armies of Leicester, Northampton, Bedford, Cambridge and Huntingdon. An *ealdorman*'s territory now extends to several shires (→1189).

Giants fight at Clontarf

Ireland, 23 April 1014
A great battle has been fought today, Good Friday, at Clontarf, near Dublin, between High King Brian Boruma and the men of Sigtrygg, the Norse king of Dublin. Losses have been heavy. Brian, his son Murchad and grandson Tordelbach have all been killed, as has their enemy Mael Morda, the king of Leinster, who had lined up with the Norsemen. Despite this the battle is being seen as a victory for Brian, putting a decisive halt to Norse ambitions in Ireland.

The battle at Clontarf is more importantly an internal struggle for sovereignty, in particular a revolt of the men of Leinster against Brian's dominance of their territory. Brian blockaded Dublin last year, and since the Leinstermen and their Norse allies feared renewed attacks this spring they looked for support to their kinsmen in Scotland. Sigurd, the earl of Orkney, agreed to come to Dublin, as did Brodir, a viking leader in Man. Brian originally had the support of Mael Sechnaill II, the king of Meath, and a fine band of his warriors, but on the eve of battle a dispute arose and Mael Sechnaill departed with his men, leaving Brian to fight alone.

An armed Irish footsoldier.

Brian's death is sure to weaken further the power of the Munster kings. As a result Mael Sechnaill could well regain the high-kingship of Ireland from which he abdicated in favour of Brian (→1022).

Norse sent by God to 'punish' English

York, 1014
In his *Sermo Lupi ad Anglos* [*Sermon of the Wolf to the English*], Archbishop Wulfstan of York has savaged the decline in English society and morals. The title of his homily includes a Latin translation of part of Wulfstan's name.

According to the sixth-century writer Gildas, Wulfstan recalls, the Anglo-Saxons were sent as a reflection of God's judgement on the early Britons. In the same way, the archbishop says, the coming of the Norse reflects God's judgement on today's English. "Understand well ... that for many years now the devil has led astray this people ... If we are to experience any improvement, we must deserve better of God."

Wulfstan aims to lay down standards for both public and private morality. He believes in one source of morality for kings and commoners alike: God's word (→12/6/20).

Deputy from Mercia defects to the Danes

Mercia, 1015
Edric Streona, the *ealdorman* [king's deputy] of Mercia, has treacherously gone over to Cnut, the younger son of Svein Forkbeard. The reason for his defection lies in the turmoil following Svein's death last year, only weeks after he became ruler of all England.

The Danish army in England then declared its allegiance to Cnut, but King Athelred returned from his Norman exile to fight him. Athelred is old and sick, however, and unlikely to live long.

Then, earlier this year, Edric killed his rivals Sigeferth and Morcar, but Edmund Ironside, Athelred's son, freed Sigeferth's imprisoned widow and married her. He has also raised an army in the lands of the murdered men. Edric has joined Cnut because he fears for his life if Edmund succeeds his ailing father as king (→early 1016).

1016 - 1023

Mercia, early 1016. Having formed an alliance with Earl Uhtred of Northumbria, Edmund Ironside, Athelred's son, ravages the lands of Edric Streona, the Mercian who allied last year with the Danish leader Cnut (→ 23/4).

Alney, Gloucestershire, November 1016. After many attempts by both Edmund, king since the death of Athelred II in April this year, and the Danish leader Cnut to control England, they agree to divide the kingdom. The Londoners buy peace (→ 30).

Somerset, 30 November 1016. King Edmund Ironside dies at Glastonbury. Cnut rules the whole kingdom (→ 1017).

Strathclyde, 1016. King Owen "the Bald" dies in battle at Carham. Duncan, the grandson of King Malcolm II of Scots, succeeds him (→ 1031).

England, 1017. Cnut divides his kingdom into four earldoms. He will rule Wessex; Edric Streona takes Mercia; Thorkell "the Tall" and Eirik of Hlathir rule East Anglia and Northumbria respectively. Cnut has killed Edwy, Edmund's brother, in an attempt to remove claimants to the throne.→

England, 1018. Cnut orders all but 40 of his ships to return to Denmark (→ 1019).

Canterbury, Kent, 12 June 1020. Lyfing dies; Athelnoth is the new archbishop (→ 1023).

Ashingdon, Essex, 1020. Cnut builds a minster as a memorial to those killed in battle (→ 1021).

England, c.1020. Alfric the monk, best known for his *Catholic Homilies*, dies.

England, 1021. Cnut outlaws Thorkell "the Tall" (→ 1023).

Durham, c.1022. The bones of Bede, the scholar, are moved into the cathedral along with those of St Cuthbert (→ 1094).

Glamorgan, 1022. Eilaf, a Norse sailor, ravages southern Wales as far west as St David's, in Dyfed (→ 1039).

Ireland, 1022. King Niall mac Eochada of Ulster beats the Dublin Norse at sea (→ 1023).

Denmark, 1023. Cnut makes peace with Thorkell, who will rule in his absence (1039).

Munster, 1023. King Tadg mac Briain of Munster, the son of Brian Boruma, is killed in battle by his brother, Donnchad, who takes his title.→

Londoners acclaim 'Ironside' as king

London, 23 April 1016
Edmund Ironside was acclaimed as king by Londoners today following the death of his father, Athelred II – restored to the throne two years ago in succession to Svein Forkbeard. Still in his early twenties, Edmund, a renowned warrior, will need all his battle prowess to hold together the unhappy kingdom left by his ill-fated father.

Last year Edmund, in an effective rebellion against his father, won the submission of the Danish-dominated "five boroughs" of Lincoln, Stamford, Leicester, Derby and Nottingham. Conflict looms, however, as much of England backs the rival claim to the throne of Svein's son Cnut (→ 10/1016).

Athelred: Winchester stained glass.

England faces partition

A horseman with a spear: a carved tombstone from Sockburn, in Co Durham.

Ashingdon, Essex, October 1016
King Edmund Ironside has been defeated by Cnut, the leader of the Danes in England, in a great battle that took place near here today. Edmund fought well but was hamstrung by jealousies between his nobles. Edric Streona of Mercia, who turned back to Edmund's side earlier this year, once again defected to Cnut, an act of treachery that ensured a Danish victory.

Thorkell "the Tall", the Danish turncoat, had already deserted Edmund in favour of Cnut, while Earl Uhtred of Northumbria, another former ally, had been assassinated at York [*see report below*]. Edmund was then forced to turn to the Welsh princes for armed support.

Yet with both sides weary of war and increasingly aware that a decisive victory is impossible, there are reports that Cnut and Edmund are planning to put down their swords and meet in Gloucestershire to partition England along the line of the Thames. Cnut would probably get the east and north, Edmund the south and west (→ 11/1016).

Earl assassinated after Scots win Lothian

Northumbria, early 1016
King Malcolm II of Scots has scored a double success in a campaign to extend and consolidate his southern border. By defeating Earl Uhtred of Northumbria at Carham on the river Tweed, he has consolidated firm Scots control of Lothian, for many years part of Northumbria. Furthermore, the death at Carham of King Owen of Strathclyde has allowed Malcolm to impose direct Scottish rule on Strathclyde, formerly a semi-independent kingdom under Scots overlordship.

After his defeat Earl Uhtred was assassinated at Wighill by Thurbrand, one of his own noblemen. It was an act of pure deceit. Uhtred entered the hall where the Danish leader Cnut – against whom he had campaigned – was staying, in order to make peace with him. But before Uhtred had a chance to speak, Thurbrand's men raced out from a hiding place and killed him where he stood.

Although Thurbrand had a personal vendetta against Uhtred, it seems that he was acting on orders from Cnut – against whom Uhtred had backed first Athelred and then the latter's son Edmund Ironside. One of Cnut's closest henchmen, Eirik of Hlathir, is now in charge of Northumbria (→ 10/1016).

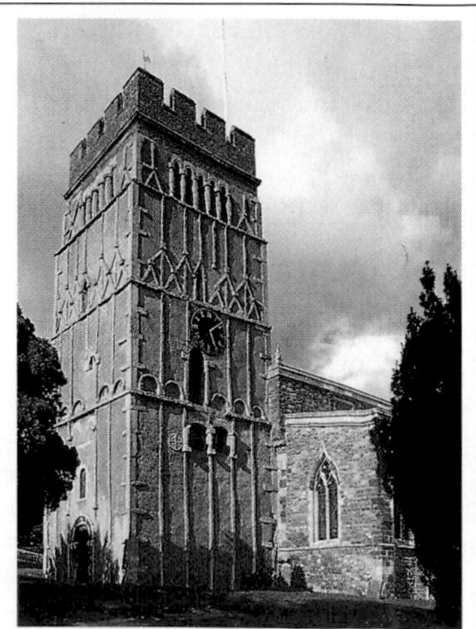
All Saints tower, Earls Barton, Northants: strip decoration is a feature of Saxon architecture.

Cnut says he will keep the faith of Christ

Oxford, 1018
Cnut – now undisputed king of England [*see report below*] – has given his support to a remarkable agreement reached by a great council at Oxford. The Danes and the English have decided to live by the code of laws that obtained 50 years ago in the days of King Edgar. Under the pact Cnut, ruling as a Christian king, has pledged that he and his men will "duly love and honour one God and steadfastly hold one Christian faith and diligently avoid every heathen practice".

In the wake of so many years of strife Cnut wants England to remain happy and prosperous and "love him with due loyalty", while he turns his attentions elsewhere. He has already returned most of his longboats to Denmark (→c.1072).

Danish influence: a dragon cut on a London tombstone in Cnut's reign.

Athelred's widow marries King Cnut

London, 1017
Cnut, who was accepted as king of all England following the death of Edmund only a few weeks after their agreement at Alney to partition the country, has consolidated his grip by marrying Emma, the widow of Athelred II and stepmother of Edmund. This is an important political marriage: Emma is the sister of Duke Richard II of Normandy. By marrying her, Cnut has pre-empted any action by the duke on behalf of Emma's two sons by Athelred, Edward and Alfred, who have fled to Normandy. Yet Cnut also has a relationship with the beautiful aristocrat Alfgifu of Northampton, by whom he already has a son, Harald [*see family tree on page 181*] (→1018).

Death of high king leads to tribal war

Ireland, 1023
Dynastic strife is breaking out following the death last year of high king Mael Sechnaill. He resumed his title after the death of Brian Boruma, in whose favour he had previously abdicated, at the Battle of Clontarf in 1014, but he left no obvious successor. Brian's son, Donnchad, has had Tadg, his rival and half-brother, assassinated and is trying to establish supremacy in Munster. He has marched into Connacht and taken hostages in Meath and Leinster. But the people of Osraige, north of Waterford, with the Eoganacht of Cashel, have made successful raids against him. They now hold part of east Munster, and Donnchad's claim to the title looks far from secure (→1038).

Cnut secures Denmark

Denmark, 1019
King Cnut has crossed the North Sea with a fleet of only nine ships and established himself as ruler of Denmark. After the recent death of his elder brother Harald, he had to move swiftly before any rival seized the throne.

That he has been able to do so bears testimony to the settled state of England now that it is united under his rule. Cnut was confident enough to leave the country under the rule of his viceroy, Thorkell "the Tall", who has alternately backed and opposed Cnut but is now earl of East Anglia.

Nevertheless, Cnut is keeping a watchful eye on England and has sent Thorkell a directive, addressed to all his people, in which he restates the obligation that he undertook at Oxford "steadfastly to observe Edgar's laws".

In the directive he explains his absence from England: "I was informed that greater danger was approaching us than we liked at all; and then I went myself with the men who accompanied me to Denmark, where the greatest injury had come to you, and with God's help I have taken measures so that never henceforth shall hostility reach you from there as long as you support me rightly and my life lasts."

King Cnut (manuscript illustration).

He also commands Thorkell to "cause evildoers to do right and drive those that refuse out of the land". It is a confident, carefully written document reflecting Cnut's growing power (→1020).

Archbishop Wulfstan – 'the wolf' – dies

York, 1023
Wulfstan, the archbishop of York and one of the finest intellects in Europe, has died. He was the author of the sternly moralistic *Sermo Lupi ad Anglos* [*Sermon of the Wolf to the English*], and his life illustrates the influence that a man steeped in God's word can have on national affairs. He served jointly as bishop of Worcester and archbishop of York, where he combined his ecclesiastical duties with political ones and drafted two codes of laws, one each for Athelred and Cnut.

In a society nearing disintegration in the face of continuous Norse attack, Wulfstan preached the necessity of both established hierarchies and social ranks and orders which, he argued, must be accepted. The king should be advised by his churchmen, whom Wulfstan set above the king in importance to highlight the king's position as a ruler ordained by God and thus subordinate to him. Rebellion would therefore be a blow not just against earthly monarchy but against God himself (→26/3/27).

St John the Evangelist, from an 11th-century Latin Gospel-book.

1024 - 1039

Ireland, 1024. The poet Cuan Ua Lothchain is murdered by a gang.

Southern Sweden, 1026. King Cnut joins battle against Olaf Haraldsson, the king of Norway, and Onund Jacob, a king of the Swedes (→ 1023).

Normandy, 1027. Fearing invasion by Athelred II's sons Edward and Alfred, who fled to Normandy in 1017, Cnut considers marrying his sister Estrid to Robert "the Devil", the duke of Normandy (→ 1035).

Scotland, 1031. Cnut invades and regains Bernicia (northern Northumbria) to stop King Malcolm II of Scots aiding the Norwegians (→ 1034).

Scotland, 1034. Malcolm II is killed at Moray; his grandson Duncan, the ruler of Strathclyde, succeeds to a larger inheritance than any of his predecessors (→ 1039).

Irish Sea, 1034. The lector of Kells, Macnia Ua hUchtain, drowns while taking the relics of the saints Colum Cille (Columba) and Patrick from Scotland to Ireland (→ 1036).

Normandy, 1035. William, the illegitimate son of Duke Robert of Normandy and Arlette, a tanner's daughter, inherits the dukedom (→ 1047).

Norway, 1035. Magnus, the son of Olaf, who was deposed by Cnut in 1028, drives out Alfgifu and Svein, and Cnut loses the kingdom (→ 12/1035).

Dublin, 1036. Christchurch cathedral, founded in 1028, is completed (→ 1074).

Wessex, 1037. Emma, the widow of both Athelred II and Cnut, has fled to Flanders. Last year she tried to oust Harald Harefoot, Cnut's son by his common-law wife Alfgifu, helped by Edward and Alfred, her own sons by Athelred. The attempt failed, and Harald is king (→ 12/1037).

Beverley, Humberside, 1037. John of York, who died in 721, is canonized (→ 25/7/44).

Dublin, 1038. Ivar Haraldsson is king of the Norse, deposing Echmarcach Ragnaldsson, who deposed Sigtrygg Silkbeard in 1036 (→ 1042).

Rhyd-y-Groes, nr Welshpool, Powys, 1039. Gruffudd ap Llywelyn, made king of Powys and Gwynedd this year, expels English who have settled near the river Severn (→ 2/1055).

Durham, 1039. Duncan of Scots fails in an attack (→ 1040).

Pope receives plea to lift 'unjust tolls'

Rome, 26 March 1027
Visiting Rome for today's Easter coronation of Holy Roman Emperor Conrad II, King Cnut has seized the opportunity to ease the lot of English pilgrims and traders in their travels across Europe. Cnut said that his people encountered many difficulties during their journeys to Rome, and he appealed to Pope John XIX, Conrad and the many princes present to lift the "barriers and unjust tolls" imposed on his people and allow them to travel in peace.

Cnut also complained about the "immensity of the sums of money" demanded from the English archbishops when they collected their episcopal vestments from the pope. The pope said he would put a stop to this, but that tithes and other dues must still be paid to Rome.

In a lengthy letter to the English archbishops and noblemen, telling them of his successful negotiations, Cnut promises to try harder to rule justly and to remedy any wrongs done "through the intemperance of my youth or through negligence". He also begs all his "sheriffs and reeves" not to use "unjust force" in extracting money from the people.

Cnut's visit to Rome and letter home are seen as bids to restore his authority after the shocks of the past year, during which he was defeated in battle in Denmark by the Norwegian and Swedish kings while his brother-in-law Ulf, his regent in Denmark, treacherously defected to the enemy (→ 1037).

Emperor Conrad with his falcons.

Anglo-Danish fleet defeats Norwegians

A Swedish runestone with a cross.

Norway, 1028
Cnut has avenged his defeat two years ago by the kings of Norway and Sweden. With a combined English and Danish fleet he has conquered Norway, having taken the precaution beforehand of paying generous bribes to the local princes and lords to persuade them to betray their king.

One disapproving poet, Sighvat Thordarson, said that Cnut's men were "walking about with open purses", but "everyone knows that he who takes gold for the head of his good lord has his place in the midst of black hell ... the deep-lying world of flaming fire". The gold handed out so freely in Norway had been amassed in England where Cnut's exactions, and the violence that goes with them, are causing deep resentment (→ 1035).

Monk's flight ends with heavy landing

Malmesbury, Wiltshire, 1030
An English monk, Eilmer, has made a valiant attempt to fly, but his enterprise – like that of many others who have looked to the birds for inspiration – has ended in misfortune. He has broken both his legs and may never be able walk again. It was nevertheless a determined and not wholly unsuccessful effort. Eilmer attached wings to his arms, climbed up the tower of Malmesbury Abbey and, after waiting for a strong gust of wind, leapt into space.

Eilmer's "flight" – if it may be so described – lasted for a distance of almost 200 metres (just over 200 yards), although how much was simply a slow glide to the ground and how much could be attributed to genuine propulsion remains open to question. He blames his failure on the lack of a tail.

Eilmer: Malmesbury stained glass.

Converted Dublin king founds cathedral

Ireland, 1028
Sigtrygg Silkbeard, the king of the Dublin Norse, has founded a cathedral, Christchurch, in Dublin. After surviving the Battle of Clontarf, some 14 years ago, he went on a pilgrimage to Rome with a number of Irish lords and became a convert to Christianity. Dublin's first bishop is to be Dunan.

Sigtrygg's conversion is not unprecedented among the Norse, although many of them still believe in their deities – whether they be the gods of myth and legend, such as Odin and Thor, or the nature spirits who control fertility and good fortune. Christianity has long been making inroads into these ancient beliefs; Iceland formally adopted the faith at the turn of the century, while Norway and Denmark can boast a succession of kings who have called themselves Christian. Missionaries – many of them English – are active in Sweden (→ 1034).

Family feud over throne

Winchester, December 1035
Following his untimely death at Shaftesbury on 12 November – of natural causes – Cnut's burial in the old minster here has served as prelude to a bitter dynastic feud. At the centre of the struggle are Cnut's two wives and three sons.

Cnut, who was aged 40, had two sons, Svein and Harald "Harefoot", by his common-law wife, Alfgifu of Northampton. Before he died, she and Svein were sent to rule Norway. Emma, his lawful wife, was meanwhile sent to rule Denmark with her son by Cnut – and the king's choice as successor in England and Denmark: Harthacnut. That left Harald in England with his eye on the English throne.

But Emma will have none of that. She claims that Alfgifu was only Cnut's concubine and that, in any case, Harald is not Cnut's son but the son of a cobbler, smuggled into the palace in a warming-pan, and so not even of royal blood.

The succession struggle is further complicated by the fact that, before her marriage to Cnut, Emma had been married to Cnut's predecessor Athelred II, by whom she had two sons, Edward and Alfred, both of whom are also laying claim to the throne.

The claims of Edward and Alfred have found little support among the magnates who prospered under Cnut. Essentially the struggle is between Emma's son Harthacnut and Alfgifu's son Harald. For the time being at least a compromise has been worked out in Oxford by English nobles: the area north of the Thames will go to Harald, and that south of the river to Harthacnut, who has still to return from Denmark. The division has been officially marked by the issue of different coinages for the two kingdoms [*see family tree on page 181*] (→1037).

Cnut: shown as a good Christian.

How the Norse make their lasting marks

England, c.1030
Norse settlers here are keen to keep their traditional culture, including their writing system. They are still using the runic ABC or *futhark* of their ancestors [*see below*]. A similar system used by the Anglo-Saxons was largely abandoned after the introduction of Roman letters by Christian missionaries. While a Christian scribe has to prepare a sheep's skin for writing on, as well as ink and a quill, a Norseman needs only a knife to carve his message on wood, metal or stone. Norse runes, of which there are only 16, are used for all kinds of purposes, from sending messages (on wooden staves called *runakeflir*) to inscribing monuments to the dead.

ᚠᚢᚦᚬᚱᚴ:ᚼᚾᛁᛅᛋ:ᛏᛒᛘᛚᛦ

f u th o r k h n i a s t b m l R

England's new king is the fittest survivor

England, December 1037
It must be with profound relief that Harald, nicknamed "Harefoot", ends the year king of England: the fight to secure the backing of parties, factions, kingdoms, mothers and half-brothers has been fierce [*see family tree on page 181*].

Harald's brother Svein died soon after their father, Cnut, leaving Harthacnut, their half-brother, the main contender. Although Harthacnut was backed by his mother Emma, and by two of the most powerful earls in England, Leofric of Mercia and Siward of Northumbria, he was stuck in Denmark, fearing an invasion from Norway.

Emma's sons by Athelred II, Edward and Alfred, were living as exiles in Normandy. Alfred was rash enough to come over to England last year – whereupon Earl Godwin of Wessex, a supporter of Harald, connived at Alfred's murder. So, with all contenders either dead or abroad, Harald was promoted from regent to king earlier this year. At last he can settle down to enjoy his patrimony (→17/3/40).

British Isles given their place in Europe

Canterbury, Kent, 1030
Using the most up-to-date knowledge available, experts here have produced a pictorial representation of the known world which gives the clearest view yet of the British Isles' place in Europe.

The map-makers have drawn on major journeys such as that which Archbishop Sigeric made to Rome 40 years ago to collect the *pallium*, or stole of his office. A record was made of the 80 stages by which he made his way from the Channel to Rome – a necessary journey in an age when Rome is the centre of religious life, although it still takes six months. Britain and Ireland are recognizable as islands at the bottom left of the picture (→1280).

Britain and Ireland (bottom left) have found a place in the world picture.

1040 - 1051

London, 17 March 1040. King Harald "Harefoot" dies; his half-brother, Harthacnut, claims the throne (→ 8/6/42).

Ireland, 1042. Sigtrygg Silkbeard, deposed as king of the Dublin Norse in 1038, dies (→ 1046).

Winchester, Hants, 2 April 1043. Edward, the son of Athelred II and Emma, is crowned king (→ 16/11).

Winchester, 16 November 1043. King Edward accuses his mother of treason and deprives her of all lands (→ 1047).

Ramsey, Cambs, 25 July 1044. Alfward, the bishop of London and abbot of Evesham, dies. He is succeeded by a Norman, Robert of Jumièges (→ 3/1051).

Tayside, 1045. Macbeth, who killed King Duncan in 1040, consolidates his rule by killing Abbot Crinan of Dunkeld, Duncan's father (→ 1050).

Dublin, 1046. Ivar Haraldsson, the king of the Dublin Norse, is deposed by his own men, who reinstate Echmarcach Ragnaldsson (→ 1058).

Ireland, 1047. A major famine in Ulster provokes migration to Leinster and Connacht.

Flanders, 1047. Sweyn, the son of Earl Godwin of Wessex, flees here from England after kidnapping Edgifu, the abbess of Leominster (→ 1049).

England, 1047. Edward refuses to help Svein Estridsson to regain the Danish throne from King Magnus Olafsson of Norway, who deposed him last year (→ 25/10).

English midlands, 1 May 1048. Derby and Worcester are hit by the worst earthquake in memory (→ summer 1078).

Flanders, 1049. Duke William of Normandy is betrothed to a noblewoman, Matilda (→ 1051).

England, 1049. Earl Sweyn Godwinson, returned from exile, has murdered his cousin, Earl Beorn (→ 9/1051).

Rome, 1050. On a pilgrimage here, King Macbeth of Scots has made a great impression with his generosity (→ 7/1054).

Canterbury, Kent, March 1051. Robert of Jumièges, the bishop of London, is the new archbishop following the death last year of Edsige (→ 1052).

England, October 1051. Edward begins divorce proceedings against his wife, Edith, the daughter of the outlawed Earl Godwin.→

Duncan's failed attack in the mountains leaves Macbeth at the helm in Scotland

Macbeth: now king in Scotland.

King Duncan: Macbeth's victim.

Grampian, 1040
The six-year reign of King Duncan has come to a violent end in the mountains of north-eastern Scotland. Duncan was killed leading an attack against Macbeth, a rival claimant to the throne.

Macbeth has until now held the title of *mormaer*, or steward, of Moray. His claim to be king is based on his marriage eight years ago to Gruoch, the granddaughter of Kenneth III who was murdered in 1005 by Malcolm II, cousin to Kenneth and grandfather to Duncan. It was expected that when Malcolm died the succession would revert to Kenneth's side of the family. Succession in the direct line has not been the rule in Scotland for some 200 years.

Yet it was Duncan who became the next king. With sons of his own he wanted to make sure that there would be no one else waiting to be king after him, and so he moved against Macbeth – a fatal blunder, leaving Macbeth with the crown and Duncan's sons refugees with kinsmen in Northumbria (→ 1045).

Scandinavian kings fight for supremacy

England, 25 October 1047
Fears of a Scandinavian invasion receded today with news of the death of King Magnus of Norway, a claimant to the throne. This ends the immediate threat of a resurgence of Cnut's dynasty here; Scandinavia, meanwhile, is threatened with conflict between Magnus's maternal uncle, Harald Hardrada, and Svein Estridsson of Denmark.

Harald, while ambitious for the throne of England, is consolidating his kingdom in Norway as well as coveting Denmark. He is a formidable foe: a physical giant, he has fought in great battles from Poland to Constantinople [Istanbul], from Sicily to Palestine (→ 1051).

An early 11th-century Anglo-Saxon plaque, made of walrus ivory, shows Christ enthroned and holding a staff and a book.

Poison may have caused royal death

Lambeth, London, 8 June 1042
The English court has been left stunned at the sudden death of King Harthacnut. He had spent today drinking with his retainers when suddenly he collapsed in convulsions and was carried from the hall gasping for breath. He died soon afterwards. Nobody is mourning him, however: he was a ruthless man who preferred drinking to attending to the affairs of state.

Some suspect that the king was handed a poisoned cup by his half-brother, Edward, the son of Cnut's predecessor, Athelred II. Even if this is true – and few believe it is – Edward is bound to be the next king. He may be a penniless bachelor with scant military experience, but the only other serious candidate is a foreigner: King Magnus of Norway (→ 3/4/43).

A silver coin of Harthacnut's reign.

King Edward looks to Bretons for aid

England, 1047
The elevation of Ralph de Mantes, King Edward's Breton nephew, to an earldom has set tongues wagging furiously at court. Ralph is the first foreigner to be honoured in this way, and the king's motive may be to irritate the influential Godwin family – perhaps even to punish his own wife Edith (herself a Godwin) for failing to produce an heir.

There has been a marked rise in "foreign appointments" under Edward, particularly in the church. Worry about the "Scandinavian connection" and the Cnut legacy is thought to have induced the king to look across the Channel for moral and religious support (→ 1047).

Ancient sagas and legends of Ireland are written down

An ornate Irish church service-book.

Ireland, c.1050

The victory of the late Brian Boruma over the Norse at Clontarf in 1014 [*see report on page 171*] is proving to have been a turning-point in literary, as well as political, history. Brian was a patron of religion and education as well as a soldier. By thwarting Norse attacks he inspired scholars to turn their thoughts to Ireland's heritage. The sagas of ancient times have been written down, and religious works have also been assembled and written in both Gaelic and Latin.

Brian's influence is especially notable in the monastic settlement at Clonmacnoise, second only to that at Armagh for its piety and learning. Under his patronage it became the chief centre for scribal activity and the powerhouse of Ireland's literary energies.

Brian also instituted new schools of learning. Formerly, Gaelic literature was studied only in the monasteries, but he preferred the idea of establishing learned families whose duty it would be to protect historical, genealogical and poetical traditions for future generations.

Poets and story-tellers also tell tales in prose and ballads about Fionn mac Cuail and his legendary band of followers – tales known as the "Fenian cycle". The poets used to prefer the "red cycle", which told of ancient northern battles, but since the victory at Clontarf the broader Fenian cycle seems more appropriate to the times (→1134).

Anti-Norman agitators forced to flee

West Sussex, September 1051

Earl Godwin of Wessex, an opponent of increasing Norman influence at court, has fled the country. He left Bosham, in West Sussex, this month on his way to the continent after falling out with the king over a recent incident at Dover, a town under Godwin's jurisdiction. Edward's brother-in-law Eustace, the count of Boulogne, was returning home after a visit to London when his men got into a fight with locals at the port. Eustace fled for protection to the king at Gloucester. Godwin was incensed both by the violence and by Edward's order that he harry Dover in retaliation.

Godwin prepared for a showdown with the king, who had called on the earls Siward and Leofric for help, but both sides backed off. When, however, Godwin refused talks with the king, Edward outlawed him and his sons, who have also fled. There had already been ill-feeling over the appointment of a Norman, Robert of Jumièges, as archbishop of Canterbury – seen as part of a plan to secure Norman succession to the throne (→1052).

King Edward and his nobles are waited upon at a royal banquet.

Taking a tough line: King Edward.

Mystery surrounds fate of 'virgin' queen

England, October 1051

Although her whereabouts remains a mystery, it is clear that Queen Edith has been banished by her husband, King Edward. As the eldest daughter of the rebellious Earl Godwin, who has just fled the country, she was seen as a possible focus for Godwin's anti-Norman faction. Some say that she has been sent to her old school, the convent at Wilton, "with an imperial escort and royal honour". Others allege that she has lost all her possessions and been sent to the king's sister, the abbess of Wherwell, "without honour and with only one maid".

Edith was a clever and beautiful 25-year-old on her marriage six years ago to the king, who was then 40. Edward's concern at the time was to provide himself with an heir, and Edith's failure to produce one has left her the target of conflicting rumours. It is said either that she has had a number of lovers, or that she is still a virgin because the king has taken a vow of celibacy.

Yet the couple were close – like father and daughter, according to some. Although ostentatiously modest – she often sat at the king's feet rather than at his side on the throne – Edith was recognized as powerful. Edward finds ceremonial occasions difficult, and it was because of her influence that he appeared at them suitably dressed (→1200).

William of Normandy rumoured to be in line for English throne

London, 1051

Rumours are rife that King Edward has made a secret deal with Duke William of Normandy, promising him the throne of England on his death. If the story is true, it is a coup for both the Norman archbishop of Canterbury, Robert of Jumièges – who apparently passed Edward's offer to William while travelling to Rome to accept his *pallium* [stole of office] – and the whole pro-Norman party. It is equally a disaster for their opponents, led by the outlawed Earl Godwin and his sons.

Edward's preference is easy to understand. He is half-Norman – his mother, Emma, was the daughter of Duke Richard I of Normandy – and he was brought up there along with his brother Alfred. The deal gives Edward a continental ally against Count Baldwin V of Flanders, host to Godwin and three of his sons since they left England. (Another son, Harold, has fled to Ireland.) Edward is also using his lack of a direct heir as a diplomatic weapon; the duke will probably be played off against other claimants such as King Svein Estridsson of Denmark (→1052).

1052 - 1063

Isle of Wight, 1052. Earl Harold meets his father Godwin, the earl of Wessex, who plans to return from exile in Flanders (→ 14/9).

Canterbury, Kent, 1052. The Norman archbishop, Robert of Jumièges, flees (→ 10/1052).

Southwark, London, 14 September 1052. Godwin tries to invade London (→ 10/1052).

Canterbury, October 1052. Stigand replaces Robert of Jumièges as archbishop, but the pope will not recognize the appointment (→ 30/11/66).

Winchester, 15 April 1053. Godwin, who was reconciled with King Edward last year, dies; the earldom of Wessex passes to Harold, until recently exiled in Ireland (→ 1054).

Tayside, July 1054. King Macbeth is defeated in battle at Dunsinane by Earl Siward of Northumbria, whose nephew Malcolm – the son of the late King Duncan – takes control of Lothian and Strathclyde (→ 15/8/57).

Hereford, February 1055. After the death in battle of the city's bishop, Leofgar, Gruffudd ap Llywelyn makes peace with the earls of Wessex and Mercia (→ 24/10).

Grampian, 15 August 1057. Macbeth dies after clashing with Malcolm. Lulach, Macbeth's stepson, succeeds as king (→ 17/3/58).

Coventry, West Midlands, 30 October 1057. Leofric, the earl of Mercia and husband of Godiva, dies. His son Alfgar becomes earl (→ 10//1065).

England, 1058. Edward, the son of King Edmund II Ironside, returns from exile in Hungary but dies soon afterwards (→ 1064).

Munster, 1058. King Donnchad mac Briain is challenged by his nephew Toirrdelbach ua Briain and Diarmait mac Mael na mBo, the king of Leinster (→ 1059).

Grampian, 17 March 1058. Malcolm becomes king of Scots after killing Lulach.→

Westminster, London, 1059. Work begins on rebuilding the abbey (→ 28/12/65).

Munster, 1059. Donnchad mac Briain submits to Aed ua Conchobair, the king of Connacht (→ 1063).

Northern England, 1061. Malcolm III of Scots raids the territory of his ally Earl Tostig of Northumbria (→ 1068).

Emma, wife of two kings, dies alone

Emma is offered her "Encomium".

Winchester, Hampshire, 1052
England is mourning the death of Emma, the wife and queen first of Athelred II and then of Cnut, and the mother of King Edward. She has died in relative obscurity despite being politically active for most of her life.

Emma, the daughter of Duke Richard of Normandy, was married to Athelred as his second wife in an attempt to form an anti-Norse alliance between England and the duchy. When England was under acute Norse threat in 1013, it was to Normandy that Emma fled with Edward and Alfred, her sons by Athelred.

After Athelred's death Emma became the second wife of Cnut, who needed both her expertise in English politics and a regent for England during his absences in Scandinavia. Emma worked hard for her children, ensuring the accession of Harthacnut, her son by Cnut, in Denmark.

When Cnut died unexpectedly in 1035 Emma invited Edward back to England (his brother Alfred had been murdered by this time), but far from being grateful he dispossessed her. Emma retired to the religious life; her life and times are contained in the *Encomium Emmae* [*In praise of Emma*] (→ 1064).

Rebels return after ravaging south coast

London, October 1052
Earl Godwin of Wessex is back in London, just a year after he and his family were outlawed and fled the country. King Edward was powerless to prevent their return after Godwin and his second son Harold ravaged the south coast of England with their fleet. But Godwin also owes his success to a fear among other magnates in England that to fight him would mean civil war – costly in itself, and an open invitation to any Norse warlord with an eye on the English throne to launch an invasion.

Godwin wants not only to regain his immense wealth in England but also to thwart the hopes of the pro-Norman party – which includes the king – of placing a candidate of theirs on the throne when Edward dies. So far his plans are proceeding well: he has recovered his lands, while the influential Norman bishops of London and Dorchester as well as Robert, the archbishop of Canterbury, have now fled. Meanwhile, Godwin's daughter Edith, King Edward's wife, who was banished last year, has been recalled to court (→ 15/4/1053).

The Nativity: a missal belonging to Archbishop Robert of Jumièges.

Harold pins his hopes on exiled prince

England, 1054
Eldred, the bishop of Worcester, is back after a year in Germany trying to make contact with Edward the Atheling [royal prince], the son of King Edward's half-brother Edmund Ironside. When Edmund died in 1016 the Atheling was sent to Hungary so that he should not fall into Cnut's hands. Now, in the absence of a more direct descendant, he is the heir to the throne.

Eldred and Earl Harold hatched the plan as a way to thwart a Norman succession. Yet despite spending a year in Cologne and sending messengers into Hungary, Eldred has returned alone (→ 1058).

Southerner becomes earl of Northumbria

A sundial from St Gregory's Minster, Kirkdale, rebuilt in Tostig's time.

Northumbria, 1055
Tostig, the third son of Earl Godwin, has become the first southerner to be made earl of Northumbria. His promotion comes just three years after his return from exile in Flanders. It is thought that the appointment is a political initiative by King Edward, who wants to exercise greater control over an unruly province that has until now been governed – in so far as it has been governed at all – by local aristocrats. But bypassing powerful families may cause more problems than it solves (→ 1065).

Gruffudd unites Wales

A carved stone head from Anglesey.

A page from a bible of Earl Alfgar.

Hereford, 24 October 1055
Gruffudd ap Llywelyn – the first man to unite Wales under one rule – sacked Hereford today. He was aided by the Englishman Earl Alfgar of East Anglia, who was outlawed last year for treason. Some 500 people were killed and an unknown number taken off as slaves. The Norman earl of Hereford, Ralph, had put his faith in a new style of defences borrowed from the Normans which involved cavalry. But his men, unused to fighting on horseback, turned tail almost as soon as fighting began.

The charming but ruthless Gruffudd has shown that his power is now great enough to take on the English. The son of Llywelyn ap Seisull, who seized power in Gwynedd in 1018, Gruffudd was a slow developer who, guided by an omen, has eventually reached the top.

One New Year's night, young Gruffudd was driven out of doors by the taunts of his sister and hid under the eaves of the cookhouse, where he heard the cook remark: "It's curious, but there is one piece of meat that no matter how much I push it down always comes to the top again." Seeing this as a portent, Gruffudd changed his ways, and by 1039 he had seized power in Gwynedd and Powys. Immediately afterwards he routed an Anglo-Saxon army at Rhyd-y-Groes, a ford on the Severn near Welshpool. He recently disposed of his southern rival Gruffudd ap Rhydderch and now rules the whole country (→ 1058).

Malcolm Canmore comes out on top in a battle with Macbeth for the Scottish throne

Grampian, 17 March 1058
Just seven months after the death of his stepfather, Macbeth, King Lulach has fallen in battle against Malcolm Canmore [the great head, or chief]. Malcolm ambushed Lulach at Essie, in Strathbogie, and has thereby become king of all Scotland, the ambition he had nursed ever since his father, King Duncan, was killed by Macbeth in 1047.

Macbeth's fledgling dynasty took a heavy blow on 27 July 1054, when Earl Siward of Northumbria defeated him in battle at Dunsinane and installed Malcolm, Siward's own nephew, as lord over Lothian and Strathclyde. Until then he had known only success, beating off several challenges to his rule. By 1050 he felt secure enough to go on pilgrimage to Rome, where he reputedly scattered alms "like seed".

Then, on 15 August last year, Malcolm clashed with Macbeth at Lumphanan, 20 miles west of Aberdeen. Soon afterwards Macbeth died of his wounds. He left a widow, Gruoch, Lulach's mother (by a previous marriage), a pious woman who helped to give land on Loch Leven to monks (→ 1061).

Norse invaders join forces with the Welsh

Wales, 1058
A large fleet of Norsemen has crossed the Irish Sea and landed in Wales. It is commanded by Magnus, the son of King Harald "Hardrada" of Norway, but includes elements from various Norse colonies such as the Orkneys, Dublin and the Hebrides. Magnus has secured the help of Gruffudd ap Llywelyn, the king of all Wales, which might result in a repeat performance of Gruffudd's raid on Hereford three years ago, when he allied his own forces with those of Earl Alfgar of East Anglia and others from Ireland.

King Edward is at present in Hereford, no doubt hoping that the threatened raid can be bought off with "Danegeld". But he fears that Magnus wants to help his father's ambitions. Harald considers himself to have a claim on the English throne inherited from his nephew and predecessor, Magnus Olafsson. In 1038 Magnus agreed with the then king of Denmark, Harthacnut, that if either party died without an heir, his kingdom should pass to the other. As Harthacnut claimed both Denmark and England, Harald is now pursuing exactly the same goals for himself (→ 1063).

An 11th-century Norse crucifix.

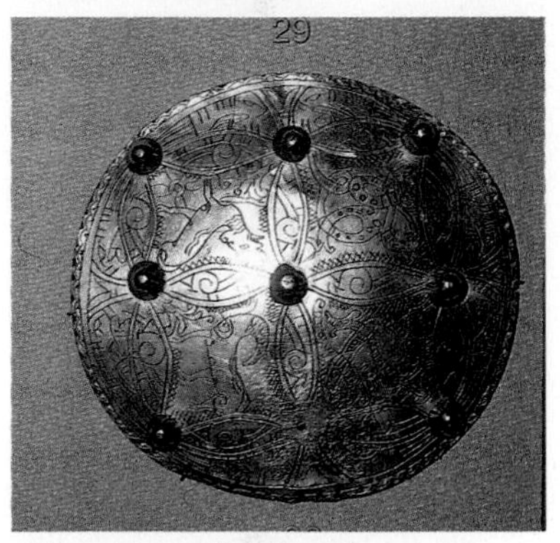
A fine Norse disc-brooch.

Fugitive Welsh king killed by own men

Gwynedd, 5 August 1063
King Gruffudd ap Llywelyn of Wales has been killed by his own men today after months on the run from Harold Godwinson, the earl of Wessex. His head was cut off and brought to the earl, who is expected to pass on this grisly trophy to King Edward.

Gruffudd had been a fugitive since Earl Harold launched a surprise attack on his headquarters at Rhuddlan in the depths of last winter. He managed to escape, but his earls betrayed him, joining forces with Harold who, supported by his younger brother Earl Tostig of Northumbria, launched a brilliant campaign. While Tostig attacked overland from Chester Harold ravaged the coast around Anglesey. Within less than three months they have succeeded in destroying Gruffudd's power base (→ 1067).

King of Munster is forced to abdicate

Ireland, 1063
Donnchad mac Briain, the youngest surviving son of Brian Boruma, has abdicated under pressure from Toirrdelbach ua Briain, who now becomes king of Munster. Donnchad took control of the Dal Cais, the ruling dynasty in Thomond, after his father's death. His greatest rival was his brother Tadg, and so in 1060 Donnchad had him killed.

King Donnchad then engaged in skirmishes with his neighbours but failed to gain control over the people of Osraige, who have grown extremely powerful in recent years and have now allied with the Eoganacht of Cashel to raid territory in Munster. Donnchad has only been able to retain a fitful authority over Munster. Now he has been challenged successfully by Toirrdelbach, the son of his murdered brother (→ 1064).

1064 - 1066

Europe, 1064. Donnchad mac Briain, the king of Munster who abdicated last year, dies on pilgrimage to Rome.

Ireland, 1064. King Ardgar mac Lochlainn of Ailech dies, leaving the kingdom in chaos (→1068).

France, 1064. Harold Godwinson, the earl of Wessex, joins forces with Duke William of Normandy against the Bretons (→11/1065).

York, October 1065. Morcar, the brother of Edwin of Mercia, becomes earl of Northumbria following the expulsion of Tostig (→1067).

Birsay, Orkney, 1065. Earl Thorfinn of Orkney dies; his burial will take place at the church of Christ that he founded (→7/1181).

London, 28 December 1065. The new abbey at Westminster, built by King Edward at great cost, is consecrated. The king, who suffered a stroke four days ago, is too ill to attend the ceremony (→6/1/66).

England, January 1066. King Harold II, the son of Godwin and earl of Wessex, marries Edith, the widow of King Gruffudd ap Llywelyn of Wales and sister of Earls Edwin and Morcar.

Normandy, 1066. Duke William sends Gilbert, the archdeacon of Lisieux, to Rome in order to gain papal blessing for his forthcoming expedition to England.

Rome, 1066. Pope Alexander II declares King Harold to be a usurper and proclaims William the lawful claimant to the English throne (→8/1066).

London, 8 September 1066. The English fleet sails to London after four months off the Isle of Wight. In the move many ships are destroyed in a storm (→13/10).

Hastings, East Sussex, 15 October 1066. Gytha, the mother of the dead King Harold, offers his body weight in gold to Duke William in order to bury him. It is refused, and Harold is buried on the shore (→1068).

England, October 1066. Edgar the Atheling [royal prince], aged 14, an English heir to the throne, is chosen as king by Earls Morcar and Edwin (→30/11).

Wallingford, Oxon, December 1066. Stigand, the archbishop of Canterbury, surrenders to the Normans (→29/8/70).

Visit to Normandy cloaked in mystery

London, 1064
Mystery surrounds a visit to Normandy by Earl Harold Godwinson of Wessex, the brother-in-law of the king and one of the most powerful men in England. While there, he is said to have delivered a message from King Edward telling Duke William of Normandy that he is now heir to the English throne. The Normans claim that Harold swore allegiance to William as his future king, but Harold claims that the oath was obtained by deception and cannot be considered binding.

One report talks of a shipwreck and the arrest of Harold by Count Guy of Ponthieu. Another speaks of a near-disaster in Normandy and Harold's rescue of endangered Norman knights, while a third says that Harold joined William in an expedition against Dinan Castle in France and was knighted for his valour. Whatever the truth, it seems unlikely that Harold will allow Duke William a throne which he covets himself (→25/12).

Northern rebellion topples Earl Tostig

England, 1065
Tostig, the earl of Northumbria and brother of Harold Godwinson, has been forced into exile by a rebellion of his *thegns* [noble retainers]. The rebels marched halfway across England to demand Tostig's exile and were met at Oxford by King Edward, who eventually agreed to their demands. Tostig has now fled to the continent cursing his brother Harold for refusing to help.

Tostig was hunting with King Edward in Wiltshire when news broke that the Northumbrians had marched on York, killing most of Tostig's private army and plundering his armoury and treasury. They proclaimed Earl Morcar as their leader and followed him south to Northampton, where they are said to have caused "much damage".

Tostig is now accusing Harold of fomenting the uprising, a charge vehemently denied by Harold, who mediated between Tostig and his former *thegns* but yet refused to involve his own army (→25/9/66).

Confessor's brother-in-law seizes power amid controversy over deathbed wishes

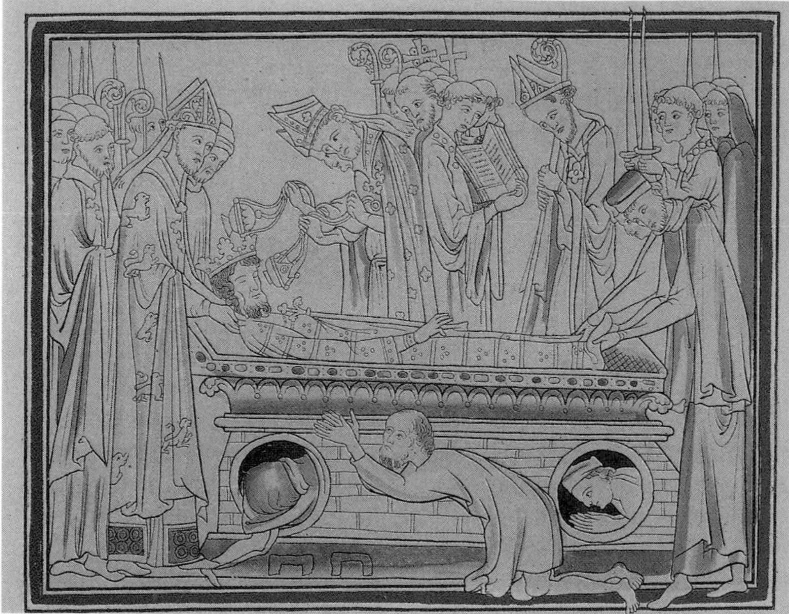

Churchmen perform the last rites at the burial of Edward the Confessor.

London, 6 January 1066
King Edward, who died yesterday, has been buried in the newly completed abbey church of Westminster, to whose construction he had devoted the last 15 years. It replaces the wooden church of St Peter that had stood here since early Saxon times and for the last hundred years had been home to a small Benedictine community. Westminster – so called because it stands to the west of the city of London – is an imposing building in stone from Caen in Normandy.

Hard on the heels of the king's death, Harold Godwinson, the brother of Edward's wife Edith, today had himself crowned in a staggering coup. He claims that Edward, for his saintliness nicknamed "the Confessor", made a deathbed promise that the crown was his. This is an almost unbelievable reversal of Edward's pro-Norman policy, according to which Duke William was to be king.

Archbishop Stigand of Canterbury supports Harold's story – but he owes his appointment to Harold and so cannot be regarded as unbiased. Meanwhile Duke William claims that Edward promised the throne to him two years ago – and that it was Harold who conveyed that promise to him (→8/1066).

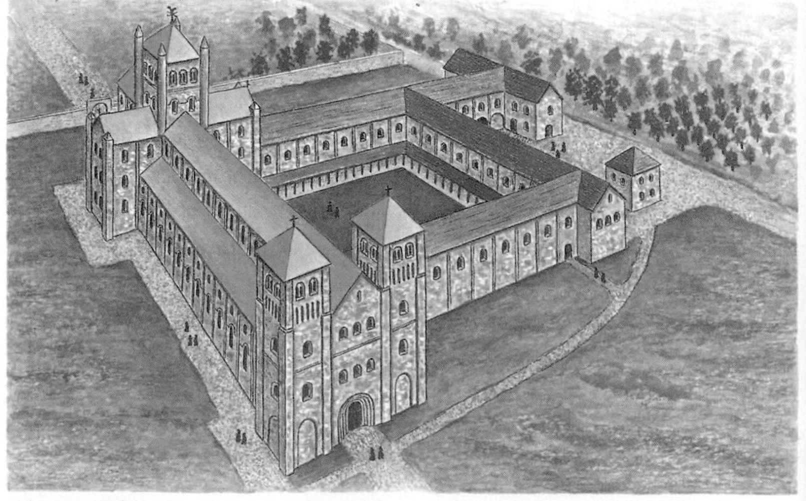

The new abbey at Westminster, consecrated on 28 December 1065.

English king menaced from both north and south

Duke William awaits a change in the wind

Provisioning the fleet that will sail on England: from the Bayeux Tapestry.

Normandy, August 1066
Disgusted at what he sees as King Harold's treachery, William of Normandy is ready to fight for the throne of England. He will invade, and all he is waiting for now is a change in the wind that has been blowing constantly from the north. Norman harbours have echoed all year to the sounds of axe and adze as shipbuilders fashion a great fleet capable of carrying to the beaches of southern England not only men and their weapons but also supplies and cavalry horses.

Fighting men, both mercenaries and volunteers, have crowded into Normandy from all over Europe, some of them impressed by the papal blessing on this invasion. Duke William of Normandy is now seeking to fashion them into a cohesive and disciplined army. Many more of those archers and spearmen who practise their skills on open spaces from St Malo in the west to the Flanders border in the east are attracted by the idea of plunder in England. The duke "utterly forbade pillage" here in Normandy, however, and the corn grows well, untrampled by the soldiery. By invoking papal patronage for his invasion William appears to have gained the moral ground.

Meanwhile in England Harold is waiting, but if William does not come soon he may have to disband his army, which cannot be held in levy indefinitely. Only that northerly wind is holding up William's invasion, for now he is moving his fleet to St Valéry in the Somme estuary. England's destiny depends on the weathercock of St Valéry parish church (→ 8/9).

The Bayeux Tapestry shows Harold swearing an oath of fealty to William.

Harold kills Hardrada at Stamford Bridge

York, 25 September 1066
In a brutal and desperate fight between kings and brothers at Stamford Bridge near here today, the king of Norway, Harald Hardrada, and Tostig, the exiled brother of King Harold of England, have both been killed.

Hardrada came to England intending to rule and brought with him his wife, his mistress and most of his household. With his allies from Scotland, Ireland and Iceland, the Norwegian king joined the renegade Tostig at the mouth of the Tyne. Together they ravaged the Cleveland coast and burnt much of Scarborough. The fleet then sailed up the Humber and along the Ouse to land near the village of Ricall, nine miles from York.

It was not until the invaders reached the village of Fulford that the first clash took place, when two armies led by English earls challenged them. With his standard – the "Landwaster" – flying, Hardrada charged the English flanks and drove them into the river with terrible casualties. Shortly afterwards York submitted.

Five days later, an army led by Harold of England suddenly appeared at York after a forced march from the south. In today's battle, Harold has slaughtered his enemies and ended this northern challenge to his power (→ 30).

Competition hots up for English throne

London, 30 September 1066
King Harold is adamant that his late brother-in-law Edward the Confessor bequeathed him the throne of England. Yet Duke William of Normandy is bitterly opposed to Harold. William asserts that, in 1064, Edward dispatched Harold to Normandy to confirm an earlier promise (by the king) that the duke would succeed him. Harold is said to have sworn an oath of homage to William, pledging to secure the throne for the duke. This he has now broken. Furthermore, the duke claims kinship with the late king – through Edward's mother Emma, the daughter of Richard I of Normandy, William's own great-grandfather.

With Harald Hardrada dead, the other claimants are Edgar the Atheling, the grandson of Edmund Ironside, and King Svein Estridsson of Denmark. Neither has much chance: Edgar is only in his teens, while Svein is too busy with internal affairs to interfere (→ 13/10).

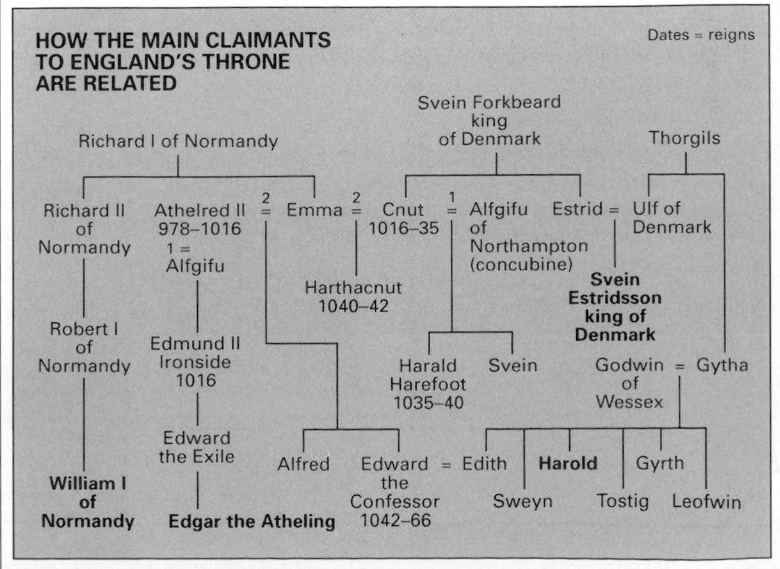

English forces are cut down in Hastings carnage

English army races south to head off Norman invasion

East Sussex, 13 October 1066
Darkness had fallen by the time that advance units of an exhausted English army took up their positions here tonight after a frantic 100-km (60-mile) forced march from London. Many are veterans of the recent battle at Stamford Bridge, where King Harold brilliantly defeated a Norwegian invasion [*see report on page 181*]. Now he must face another, potentially disastrous, threat to England from Duke William of Normandy, whose army is well rested after its Channel crossing of 27/28 September. The Normans have fortified Hastings and await their opponents.

Harold's chances of another victory so soon after his last battle are not high. The speed of his return from the north has forced him to leave behind much of his infantry and many archers, although he has received some reinforcements from the midlands as he marched southwards and from Wessex as he waited in London.

His only hope is to achieve the same surprise that crushed the Norwegians in Yorkshire. A sudden attack could cause havoc in the Norman positions and cut William off from his ships. But the English badly need rest and are in no shape for a sudden offensive. A determined William, meanwhile, will not easily be taken by surprise (→ 14).

The noble general: King Harold.

Norman cavalry make a lethal assault: a 20th-century artist's view.

Men and horses fall amid the slaughter at Hastings: the Bayeux Tapestry.

The Bayeux Tapestry shows a warrior shot in the eye. Was it Harold?

Harold falls under a relentless hail of Norman arrows

Hastings, 14 October 1066
After a day of savage fighting on the Sussex downland, an English army has been vanquished by an invading force of Normans, Frenchmen, Bretons and mercenaries led by William, the duke of Normandy. Harold, the king of England, lies dead on the battlefield.

As dusk fell, mercifully hiding the carnage, only the cries of the wounded attested to the horror that was Hastings today. The English forces were tired even before the battle started, many of them having marched through the night to reach the spot. As a consequence of exhaustion they were not drawn up to face the Norman onslaught until nine o'clock in the morning.

The English formed tight ranks near the top of a hill, armed with lances and axes. The Normans attacked first, with archers raining arrows while the armoured infantry charged uphill. For much of the day King Harold's tactic of holding the upper ground succeeded, and William made little progress.

Then the Norman foot fell back and the English levies raced down after them. William was knocked off his horse, and panic ran through the Norman ranks as the cry went up that he was dead. At this moment of crisis, William managed to remount and lift his helmet to show that he was still alive. The Norman line steadied and the cavalry, moving up to cover the fleeing foot-soldiers, caught the charging English in the flank and proceeded to butcher them. William then organized a series of feints that tempted the English to break ranks, only to be ambushed by the cavalry.

Yet it was dusk before the Normans were close enough for their archers to use high-angle fire, forcing the defenders to raise their shields, while the Norman horse charged in to stab beneath them. Some reports say that Harold was then struck in the eye with an arrow. This cannot be confirmed, but he is certainly dead (→ 15).

England yields to Norman conqueror

Horses and arrows proved the keys to William's success

Hastings, 14 October 1066
It was William of Normandy's shrewd use of cavalry and archers that gave him the vital edge in today's battle over the static mass of English foot-soldiers, who had to rely on spears and battleaxes for close-range work. William staked a great deal on his highly trained cavalry. Other Norman leaders have used similar forces in previous campaigns in Sicily and Apulia. At Hastings, they acted with great discipline, feigning the retreats that succeeded in fatally confusing the English infantry.

Against these formidable fighters, ably supported by skilled archers, Harold's heavily armed *housecarls* were backed up by a hastily assembled defensive force wielding a motley collection of weapons. These mainly local men followed the classic English tactic of forming a defensive shieldwall. Lined up on the summit of a slope looking down towards the Norman lines, they were sadly under-armed. Few had swords, bows or battleaxes; instead, some had javelins, while others had only hatchets or sledgehammers which were most useful at close quarters.

Harold's static battleplan – to defend the hill, and the road to London, at all costs – contrasted with William's dynamic leadership. During the battle the English king failed to capitalize on his initial success, while the Norman duke turned an early reverse into a triumph (→ 15).

A later statue of Duke William.

English homes are set alight as Norman soldiers enjoy the taste of victory.

Normans ravage south-eastern England

Southwark, 30 November 1066
Duke William of Normandy and his army are for the moment encamped here, just across the Thames from London. In the six weeks since their victory at Hastings the Normans have ravaged south-eastern England, exacting tribute from the towns.

William has sacked the Channel ports, taking Romney and Dover. An outbreak of dysentery forced his army to halt for some weeks near Canterbury, but the townspeople were so cowed by reports of enemy brutality that they surrendered without a fight. Those who backed the wrong candidate – the late King Harold – are meanwhile busy changing sides. Archbishop Stigand, for example, who only a month ago was supporting Edgar the Atheling, the Saxon heir apparent to the crown [*see family tree on page 181*], has defected to William. Queen Edith, the widow of Edward the Confessor and sister of the late King Harold, has promised not to encourage resistance to the Norman take-over. William has sent a detachment to receive her surrender at Winchester.

He now plans to continue laying waste to the countryside around London until the city is forced to give in (→ 25/12).

Victorious duke is crowned in London

Westminster, 25 December 1066
The coronation of Duke William of Normandy here today nearly descended into farce. Shouts of acclamation that rang through the abbey as Eldred, the archbishop of York, anointed the king caused troops on security duty outside to think that a riot was starting. They promptly retaliated by setting fire to neighbouring houses. Panic spread into the abbey, and many of the congregation fled.

The bishops and clergy, however, stayed by the duke and completed the coronation, which effectively legitimizes his invasion of the country. The service laid great stress on his "right of blood" to the throne: his relationship is to Emma, the daughter of Duke Richard I of Normandy and mother of Edward the Confessor.

Yet Edgar the Atheling [royal prince], the young English candidate as king, is much closer to the line of succession: he is the grandson of King Edmund Ironside, who died in 1016 and was the half-brother of Edward the Confessor. Despite this, William's victory at Hastings enables him to impose his claim ahead of Edgar's. Today's anointing gives William the dignity of kingship and the church's confirmed backing (→ 16/12/67).

William is offered throne by royal council

Hertfordshire, December 1066
At a meeting at Berkhamsted, 20 miles north-west of London, Duke William has been offered the throne of England. He was approached by a delegation comprising Edgar the Atheling [royal prince], his only remaining legitimate challenger, members of the *witan* [royal council] and leading Londoners.

Edgar, the 15-year-old grandson of Edmund Ironside, was elected king by the *witan* last month, but, unsettled by Duke William's advance, his supporters failed to have him crowned. Then, after deciding against a direct attack on London [*see report above*], William moved westwards, crossing the Thames at Wallingford. Confronted by a renewed campaign of destruction, his remaining opponents were eventually prompted to submit.

Recent events have highlighted the key role played by the *witan* in state affairs, especially kingmaking. Such a council has existed in England for some four centuries and is made up of a cross-section of powerful interest groups. It may include members of the royal family, earls (whose role as regional governors is almost identical to that of the *ealdormen* they have superseded), *thegns* [royal retainers], bishops and abbots (→ 1068).

William: the new king is crowned.

1067 - 1070

Canterbury, Kent, 6 December 1067. On the day of King William's return to his kingdom after a triumphant tour of Normandy, the cathedral burns down.→

Northumbria, 1067. William sells the earldom to Gospatric of Bernicia (northern Northumbria) (→1070).

Northern England, May 1068. Robert de Commines, a Flemish noble elevated to an earldom by William, arrives to build Norman power in the region (→3/1069).

Westminster, London, 11 May 1068. Eldred, the archbishop of York, crowns William's wife, Matilda, as queen of England (→12/1068).

Munster, 1068. King Toirrdelbach ua Briain, who last year aided Aed Ua Ruairc to claim his throne in Connacht, has issued a law against cattle-rustling (→1069).

England, 1068. Gytha, King Harold's mother, prepares to flee to Flanders. Edgar the Atheling, the English heir to the throne, his mother and sisters also leave, and go to the court of King Malcolm III of Scots (→3/1069).

Humberside, December 1069. Danes and their English allies based on the Isle of Axholme have been driven out by the Normans, who are trying to establish themselves in the north (→1/1070).

Devon, 1069. An Irish fleet, led by sons of King Harold, lands at the mouth of the river Taw. The attempted invasion is foiled by Count Brian of Brittany, who compels the invading forces to retreat (→7/2/72).

Wallingford, Oxfordshire, 1069. An 8pm curfew imposed by William in an attempt to prevent rebellious meetings is altered to 9pm because of the warm welcome given here to the king (→1/1070).

Selby, North Yorkshire, 1069. William founds an abbey, the first monastic house in Yorkshire (→1070).

Pennines, January 1070. King William marches to put down a revolt which is based in the Welsh border towns of Chester and Shrewsbury (→2/1070).

Dunfermline, Fife, c.1070. Margaret, the sister of Edgar the Atheling, the English heir to the throne of England, is married to King Malcolm III of Scots.→

Castles planned to subdue the Welsh

Chepstow, Gwent, 1067

The new earl of Hereford, William fitz Osbern, the lord of Breteuil, hereditary steward of Normandy and a cousin of King William, is helping to extend Norman rule into the border area of Wales. He has already crushed a revolt by Mercian nobles who, allied to the Welsh, attempted to fend off the advance of Norman rule, and he is now making sure that in Hereford, as elsewhere, that rule is obeyed.

Central to his plan is the building of a string of castles, securing strategic points along the border; notable among them is the fortress at Chepstow. These castles are basic constructions: a fortified enclosure called a bailey is linked to a "motte" – a mound on which a watch-tower or keep is built. These can be built quickly of earth and timber and rebuilt later, if necessary, in stone (→1071).

Triumphant William returns to England

England, 6 December 1067

King William has returned to England after spending the summer in a triumphant tour of Normandy. In William's absence his two regents – William fitzOsbern and Bishop Odo of Bayeux – have kept up Norman rule. Meanwhile William has made sure that his Norman subjects, like the English, are left in no doubt as to his power.

Leaving England in March, William staged a great assembly in Fécamp on Easter day (8 April). Nobles from all over France gazed on the duke's "prisoners", among them Edgar the Atheling, the heir apparent of the Anglo-Saxon kings, Archbishop Stigand and the earls Edwin and Morcar.

William's progress combined the display of captives with the donation of gifts, especially to religious foundations at Fécamp and Jumièges (where a new abbey church was consecrated on 1 July), and the filling of church appointments.

It is clear to all that William has reached a new peak of glory, and that he wishes the world to bear witness to it (→3/1068).

City of London granted special privileges

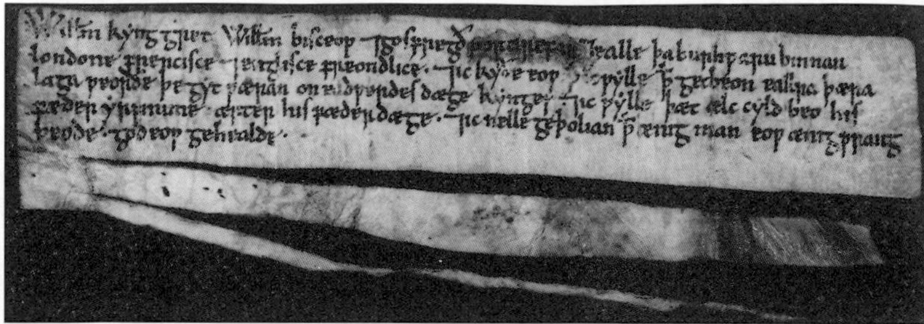

"God keep you": King William's charter to all the citizens of London.

London, 1067

London has been accorded special privileges by King William, who has granted the city a charter, confirmed the liberties it received under Edward the Confessor, and endowed its burgesses with hereditary powers. In the charter, which addresses both Norman and English citizens of the capital, William says: "I will not suffer that any man offer you any wrong."

The king makes it clear how much he values London, both for its wealth and for its support of his claim to the throne. He is obviously keen to demonstrate his desire that, in London at least, the Normans and the English should live in harmony.

This munificence is in stark contrast to his dealings with other towns. While London has survived largely unscathed, other areas of England, especially its wealthy churches, have suffered systematic looting. Their treasures have been exported to France, where many churches have benefited from these involuntary gifts (→1078).

Norman wives demand knightly cuddles

Norman women have been left to tend the home hearth: the Bayeux Tapestry.

Normandy, 1068

An unexpected problem of a rather personal nature has resulted from the length of the Norman stay in England. Wives of King William's knights are demanding that their men be sent back because, they say, they are fed up with sleeping alone.

The women feel left out in the cold – certainly they have been left in Normandy – and miss the warm comfort of their husbands' arms. Now they want them back so that they can enjoy conjugal rights. Desperate messages have been sent across the Channel urging the men to return home, and threatening that if they do not the Norman ladies will seek comfort elsewhere. At least one bishop has already condemned what he calls "the lustfulness" of these women, but the messages keep coming.

Afraid of English rebellion and of being labelled deserters, or traitors, most of William's men are staying put for the present. Those who have heeded their wives' calls and returned to Normandy are unlikely to retain their English estates.

William keeps firm grip on restless new kingdom

Castle-building key to William's control

England, 1068
The Norman tactic of constructing castles to hold down occupied lands has been widely in evidence since the battle at Hastings. Motte-and-bailey castles have been built all over the country, but particularly in the south where the Normans are most firmly established.

King William's priority has been to secure the south-coast ports that guard his lines of communication with Normandy. Immediately on landing he built a rough fortification at Pevensey, and he quickly followed it with a better one at his main base at Hastings. Soon after the battle Dover was fortified, and castles have now been built at London, Winchester and Arundel, while those at Hastings and Pevensey have been strengthened. Now almost all the important river estuaries of Sussex are guarded by loyal Norman lords.

William has had to intervene to put down various local risings, and has built castles to guard Exeter, Warwick, York, Lincoln, Huntingdon and Cambridge. Others are being constructed as quickly as possible by his lieutenants (→ 1071).

The motte-and-bailey castle at Thetford, in Norfolk: a 20th-century view.

Exeter siege ended by deal with the king

Exeter, Devon, March 1068
The siege of Exeter, the first city to rise against William of Normandy, has ended after 18 days. Many Englishmen joined the army that William raised against the city, but despite heavy casualties on both sides Exeter was not defeated and has won good terms from the king.

The citizens of Exeter have only obeyed their English kings when it suited them, so this revolt was no surprise. But the Normans' determination to crush opposition led to William's decision to deal with the insurrection himself. Another reason was the presence in Exeter of the late King Harold's mother, Gytha, and the citizens' robust response to William's demand for fealty. "We will neither swear fealty nor admit him within our walls," they replied, "but we will pay tribute to him according to ancient custom."

William's response was predictable. "It is not my custom to have subjects on such terms," he said, and marched on the city. The siege ended when the city asked for peace and William, aware of the strength of its walls, agreed. He confirmed all the city's privileges, then built a small castle and left (→ 1115).

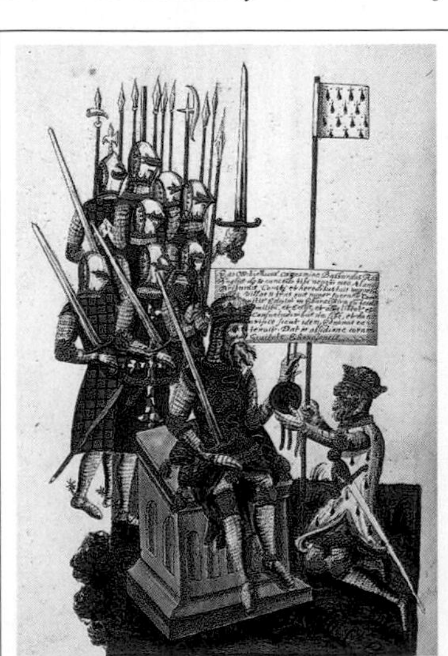
Keen to transfer land to French nobles, King William grants the estates of a Yorkshire rebel to Alan "the Red" of Brittany.

Exiled heir apparent backs revolt in north

York, March 1069
King William has crushed a serious rising in northern England sparked by the massacre of a new Norman governor, Robert de Commines, and 500 of his men. Arriving in Durham on 28 January, the Normans went on a drunken spree of rape and looting. A furious posse of local men ambushed and killed all but two of them. The news reached Edgar the Atheling, the exiled heir apparent to the throne of England, in Scotland; he moved south to join the citizens of York and besiege the newly built Norman castle there. Answering an urgent summons, William took the besiegers by surprise, showing no mercy in killing those who did not flee (→ 1070).

Robert's men drinking at Durham.

Rebellions against Normans crushed

Norman soldiers armed for battle.

England, December 1068
The country has been simmering with discontent all year, and rebellions against the foreign rulers have broken out in many places. The Welsh King Bleddyn, for one, marched with a great army to aid the rebel earls Morcar of Northumberland and Edwin of Mercia. Edgar the Atheling, the Saxon heir apparent to the English throne, preferred to flee to Scotland with his mother and sisters, where they were well received by King Malcolm III. Pleas for help have none the less been sent to King Svein Estridsson of Denmark, himself once a contender for the throne of England.

Violent disturbances occurred north of the Humber. The city of York in particular was a centre of revolt, and the woods, marshes and hills have filled with rebels, many of whom refuse to sleep in houses for fear of being taken unawares.

To counter the unrest William has moved remarkably swiftly – first to Warwick, where he built a castle to stop Edwin and Morcar's Anglo-Welsh troops linking up with the northern rebels. This forced the earls to surrender. Then he moved to Nottingham, York – where he is constructing a new castle – and Lincoln, making it utterly clear that he is in charge now (→ 12/1069).

English north laid waste

Northern England, December 1069
The north of England has been devastated under the full force of Norman revenge. The discontent that has repeatedly spilt over into rebellion here has provoked William to drastic measures over recent months. He has ordered his men to use all means necessary to ensure that the countryside can never support a hostile army. Villages have been torched, herds slaughtered, crops destroyed and ploughs smashed. Large numbers of people who faced starvation as a consequence of these actions have preferred to sell themselves into slavery.

William faced a serious challenge to his authority here in September, when a Danish fleet under Osbern, the brother of King Svein Estridsson of Denmark, and a rebel Northumbrian army under Edgar the Atheling conquered York, having first burnt much of the city to the ground. The Normans themselves burnt down houses adjoining their two new castles, fearing that they would be demolished and the rubble used to fill in the moats.

The enraged citizens had their revenge when both castles fell. More than 3,000 Normans were killed, although their commander, William Malet, and his family were spared. But more of William's men marched up to York and routed the Danes and Northumbrians.

Edgar submitted to William at the end of 1066, but last year he fled to the court of King Malcolm III in Scotland. This brief foray into England may prove his last: humiliated by William's men, he has had to flee north again (→ 1070).

Norse god Odin: a Cleveland cross.

A brooch probably looted from York.

English infantry falls as Norman cavalry attacks: the Bayeux Tapestry.

Jewish financiers brought to London

London, 1070
A community of Jewish financiers from Rouen has been imported into England by King William. Their expertise is vital to the king's economic plans, especially in the expansion of trade and the building of new castles and monasteries. Canon law bans Christians from lending money at interest, but the king needs loans and "his" Jews are there to provide them. In any case, the king has forbidden them to practise any profession than this and medicine.

As well as financing royal projects, the Jews have substantial dealings with the church and the nobles. Despite the influence that all this confers upon them, the Jews form an isolated community, living mainly around the brothel district of the city, safely housed in sturdy stone buildings under the personal protection of the king (→ c.1140).

Scottish king raids south of the border

Northern England, 1070
Forces led by the Scottish king, Malcolm III, have struck south in a ferocious assault on William of Normandy's newly won English kingdom. Although he is host to a claimant to the English throne, Edgar the Atheling, Malcolm had refused to back a northern revolt against William, so his attack has come as a surprise – and a bloody one, too, as the Scots ravaged towns as far south as Cleveland.

Many people have been killed and many more taken prisoner. St Peter's at Monkwearmouth is among the churches plundered and destroyed. Only Earl Gospatric in Bamburgh has yet offered much resistance, attacking Malcolm's territory in Cumbria. William is sure to retaliate, however. His hold on the north of England has been too precarious for him to brook any competition here (→ 1072).

Epic winter march ends Welsh revolt

Chester, February 1070
King William has crushed a revolt in Cheshire and the Welsh borders, where rebels against his rule had besieged the town of Shrewsbury. William now plans to tighten his grip by building castles here and at Stafford, with garrisons to command the unruly Welsh Marches.

The king had marched his forces over the Pennines from York in the depths of winter, inspiring them to overcome fears of the wild terrain. He led his soldiers across mountains, valleys and rivers which no army had tackled before. Sometimes their only food was horses that had perished in bogs (→ 4/1071).

An early Norman font in St Nicholas's church, Curdworth, Warwickshire, decorated with primitively carved but inspired figures of Christ. Many churches are being remodelled and refitted according to Norman taste.

Normans move to increase church control

A manuscript psalter from Winchester c.1060 shows King David at his harp.

Winchester, Hampshire, April 1070
William has been crowned by two Roman cardinals at an Easter synod here that aims to boost Norman control of the English church. Major reforms are expected to result from the conference, with Archbishop Stigand of Canterbury a potential victim of King William's determination to place his supporters in key positions.

The cardinals – sent to Winchester for the synod by Pope Alexander – were the first papal legates to have performed an English coronation, but this symbolic rite merely confirmed the authority established by William's military victories. After the ceremony, the synod swiftly moved on to a discussion of church reform. An alleged lack of chastity by some priests is being used to justify a widespread purge – as a result of which few English-born churchmen survive in high office.

The most vulnerable are Stigand and his brother, Bishop Athelmer of East Anglia. Stigand – who backed Edgar the Atheling's claim to the throne before submitting to William – has recently resumed his duties as archbishop after a spell as a captive in Normandy. Stigand's fate will be decided here; that of the others will be resolved at Whitsun when a second council is convened at Windsor (→29/8).

Abbey to be built where Harold fell

East Sussex, 1070
King William is to found an abbey on the battlefield near Hastings where his invasion force defeated Harold four years ago. Battle Abbey, as the monastery is to be known, is to be built on the site where Harold fell.

Whether the abbey is seen by the Conqueror as a memorial to his victory or an act of atonement for so many deaths is not known. But William is a pious man, anxious to secure spiritual salvation as well as earthly power. Religion thus plays a prominent part in his life; a patron of many churches, he hears Mass each day and is always accompanied by chaplains (→4/1070).

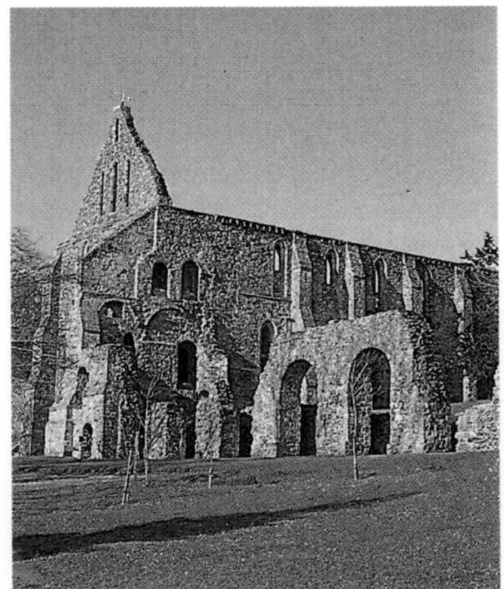

Battle Abbey: a 20th-century view.

Anglo-Danish army sacks Peterborough

Cambridgeshire, 2 June 1070
A combined force of Danes and English rebels today attacked and plundered Peterborough Abbey, burning the buildings and fleeing tonight to Ely with their booty. The abbey's treasures – crosses and crucifixes made of gold and silver, as well as money and books – have been stolen in an attack that poses a direct challenge to the authority of King William.

A Danish fleet mustered off the Humber earlier this year and secured a truce with the local people. Buoyed by this success, the Danes sailed south towards the Wash under the command of King Svein Estridsson. His soldiers landed and, building up a base in the Isle of Ely, were joined by English renegades still determined to resist Norman rule. Among them is a *thegn* from Lincolnshire called Hereward.

The combined rebel army marched on Peterborough, where William had just appointed a Frenchman, Turold, as abbot in place of the English incumbent, Brand. Turold was given 160 troops to help control the area, but they arrived too late to thwart the attack on the abbey. The rebels' success seems certain to win them further support, especially as William is preoccupied with attacks on the continent (→4/1071).

Norman abbot is appointed to Canterbury

Canterbury, Kent, 29 August 1070
Lanfranc, the abbot of St Stephen's at Caen, has today been consecrated archbishop of Canterbury, setting the seal upon the Norman conquest of the English church. The new primate – an Italian – is Normandy's most distinguished lawyer, diplomat and teacher. He is unshakeably loyal to King William.

The king has appointed many Norman prelates to English sees after dismissing their English incumbents – including, in April, Archbishop Stigand. The king has high hopes that Lanfranc will reform the church and help him to administer his new kingdom. The archbishop, who at first resisted his nomination to Canterbury, is a brilliant administrator (→1071).

Lanfranc, the new archbishop.

1071 - 1073

Flanders, 20 February 1071. William fitzOsbern, the earl of Hereford, dies in battle at Cassal. King William loses an ally, and Flanders becomes hostile under the rule of Robert the Frisian (→4/1080).

Northern England, April 1071. William receives the head of Edwin, the earl of Mercia, who was murdered on the way to Scotland by his own men following his flight from the Norman court (→14/5/80).

Ely, Cambridgeshire, April 1071. Morcar, the former earl of Northumbria, who fled from William's court with Edwin of Northumbria, has joined the English resistance forces led by Hereward (→27/10).

Richmond, North Yorkshire, 1071. Alan "the Red", the brother of Brian, the count of Brittany, has commissioned the building of a castle above the river Swale on land given by William (→1073).

Co Meath, 7 February 1072. King Conchobar Ua Mael Sechlainn kills King Diarmait mac Mael na mBo of Leinster in battle near Navan.→

Winchester, Hants, April 1072. William decides to give Canterbury primacy over York, finally ending the long-running dispute between Archbishop Lanfranc and Bishop Thomas (→1074).

South Wales, 1072. With Norman help, Caradog ap Gruffudd, the ruler of Gwent, kills his rival King Maredudd of Deheubarth on the banks of the Rhymney river (→1073).

Northern England, 1072. William, keen to gain the support of the English, replaces Gospatric as earl of Northumbria with Waltheof. Gospatric flees north to the court of King Malcolm III of Scots (→15/8).

Scotland, 1072. King Malcolm orders Bishop Fothad of St Andrews to submit to the archbishop of York (→1087).

Exeter, Devon, 1072. A manuscript of poems is bequeathed to the cathedral on the death of Bishop Leofric.

Rome, 30 June 1073. Gregory VII is elected pope (→2/1076).

Wales, 1073. Irish and Hebridean Norsemen ravage Bangor, in Gwynedd, and St David's, in Dyfed (→1075).

Rhuddlan, Clwyd, 1073. Robert of Rhuddlan builds a castle at the ford over the river Clywd (→1075).

William deals with rivals and rebels

Hereward is betrayed by monks at Ely

Ely, Cambs, 27 October 1071
The Fenland revolt is over, and with it the spirited campaign of resistance by English rebels against Norman rule. King William today entered the Isle of Ely, the heart of a – till now – independent England ruled by Earl Morcar and the Lincolnshire warrior Hereward.

The rebels had withstood fierce land and sea attacks by William's forces, but the revolt was fatally undermined by the surrender of monks from Ely Abbey after the king had seized their lands beyond the Isle of Ely. Morcar is now a prisoner, but Hereward escaped, and already his defence of Ely is acquiring the hallmark of legend. Several times, it is said, Hereward used disguises to enter the king's camp and discover enemy plans.

Hereward first came to prominence last year when he backed a Danish force that landed in East Anglia. The abbey at Peterborough was sacked, and the Fenland uprising got under way, gaining many influential supporters; recruits came from many parts of an England still smarting from Harold's defeat at Hastings.

William scored a diplomatic coup by enticing the Danes into a truce, as a result of which they left Ely and sailed for home. But the isle, surrounded by marsh and water, posed a daunting military challenge for the Normans. Ships attacked from the sea, and soldiers began building a two-mile causeway of stones, timber and earth across the marshes from Aldreth towards Ely. Yet for months the Normans could not break through, until the capitulation of the monks led to the surrender of all the rebels except Hereward and his closest followers, who have escaped capture and still roam free (→28/4/1074).

Scottish king pays homage to William

Abernethy, Tayside, 15 August 1072
King Malcolm III of Scots, who has again tried to invade Northumbria in his bid to annex northern England, has met King William here in the shadow of a Pictish tower.

In the face of William's superior force, Malcolm agreed to submit to his rival, withdrawing his men and handing over his son, Duncan, as a hostage. This, the fifth attempt made by Malcolm to invade England, forced William to take a land and sea campaign to Scotland in order to assert his authority.

William has felt uneasy with his Scottish neighbour ever since Malcolm's marriage in c.1070 to Margaret, the sister of Edgar the Atheling, posed a potential threat. Malcolm has now agreed to expel Edgar, who fled to the Scottish court four years ago (→1074).

Earl of Shrewsbury leads Norman advance further into Wales

William's army – on the hoof.

William fitzOsbern's base for conquering Gwent: Chepstow Castle.

Welsh Marches, 1071
King William aims to strengthen his hold on the Marches, the border country between England and Wales. Chester, Shrewsbury and Hereford have therefore been selected as the headquarters for a three-pronged campaign to bring the disputed and unruly borders under Norman control and establish a springboard for advance. This year the king appointed his friend and adviser Roger of Montgomery to the earldom of Shrewsbury to control the central border region. It was only last year that Shrewsbury itself was besieged by Welsh rebels, but the earl now plans to implement an aggressive strategy based on castles at Montgomery, Oswestry and Shrewsbury. Further north Hugh "the Fat" d'Avranches, the earl of Chester, intends to subdue northern Wales, aided by his ruthless nephew Robert of Rhuddlan.

The southern member of this triumvirate was, until his death this year, William fitzOsbern, a cousin of the king. As earl of Hereford fitzOsbern built castles at places such as Chepstow and Wigmore. Gwent is already under Norman control (→1072).

See of Canterbury flexes its muscles

William: a 13th-century portrait.

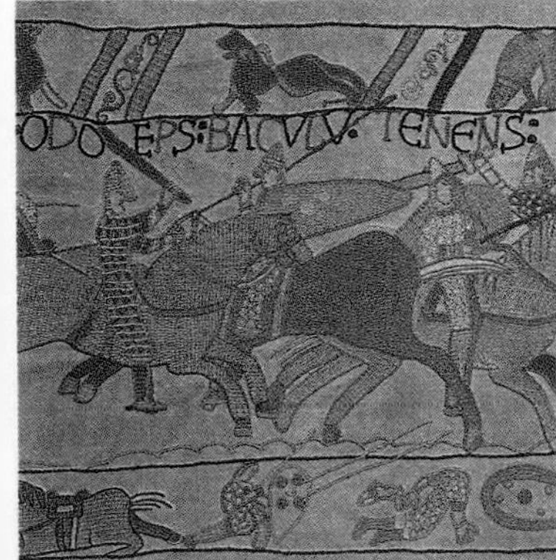

Saxons and Normans: a hard fight.

England, 1071
Lanfranc, the new archbishop of Canterbury, has refused to enthrone Thomas of Bayeux as archbishop of York unless he first recognizes the primacy of Canterbury over the whole English church. He has thus reasserted claims going back to St Augustine, and it seems that King William will support him.

The king has appointed Norman bishops and abbots in England, and has given Norman monasteries great tracts of English land. His own half-brother, Bishop Odo of Bayeux, has been made earl of Kent. Clearly William's way of reforming the church is to make sure that he controls it himself.

The king counts on Lanfranc and the new bishops to help administer his kingdom. York has special importance in this aim because the king has not yet conquered the north of England. One way of exerting control is through the archbishop, who will in turn be subject to Canterbury.

Under William and Lanfranc, Canterbury is becoming one of the most powerful sees in the western church. But elevating Canterbury to such a position might bring it into conflict with the pope, whose policy is to centralize control of the church at Rome (→4/1072).

Challenge to Normandy is repressed

Normandy, 30 March 1073
King William is back in Normandy for a lightning campaign against Count Fulk IV of Anjou, known as "the Repulsive". Last year Fulk exploited William's absence to take Maine, a province on Normandy's southern border which had been under William's control for the last ten years.

William had to move quickly to remove this threat to his continental possessions. He led his army of Norman and English soldiers in a series of swift, knock-out attacks on Fulk's strongholds in Maine. William offered the citizens of the capital, Le Mans, two choices: surrender or be put to the sword. They wisely chose to hand over the keys of the city. With the immediate danger out of the way William can breathe more easily – until the next threat (→10/1076).

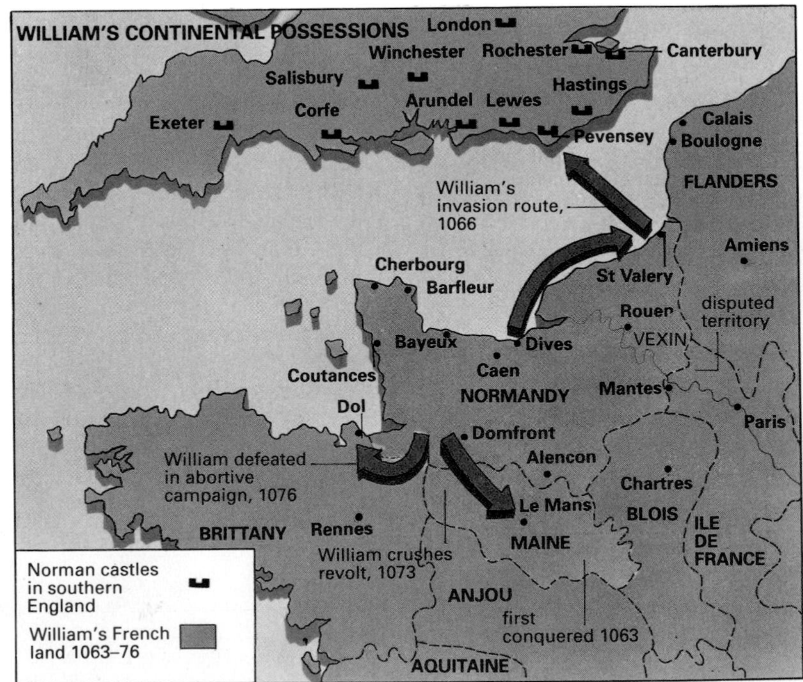

New laws raise cost of killing Normans

London, c.1072
Killing a Norman could cost everyone dear, according to a new law passed by William to protect his countrymen. The lord of anyone who murders a Norman has to bring him to justice before five days are up, and if he fails to do so then he has to pay the fine for the murder himself. At present this stands at a considerable sum: 46 marks of silver [£28].

The bad news for people living where the crime took place is that they have to pay whatever the lord cannot afford. Although this will probably raise some money for the king it will do nothing to curb the resentment that leads Englishmen to kill their new, foreign masters in the first place (→25/1/1130).

High king laid low in battle at Odba

Ireland, 7 February 1072
King Diarmait mac Mael na mBo of Leinster has been killed in battle at a place called Odba [near Navan]. Known as "high king with opposition", a new title devised for kings who control the greater part of the country but not the whole island, he had been a dominant influence since 1042. He controlled the Norse cities within Leinster and placed his allies in strategic positions of influence.

His power increased steadily: by 1054 he was king of Leinster and had established control over Meath; six years later he defeated the Dublin Norse and became king there. He later conquered Munster and made his protégé Toirrdelbach ua Briain king (→1073).

Dynasties decline after Irish king's death

Ireland, 1073
Following the death of King Diarmait mac Mael na mBo, and the succession of Toirrdelbach ua Briain as high king with opposition [*see left*], there has been much juggling for power amongst the stronger dynasties. These divisions have prevented the warring factions from offering any serious opposition to Toirrdelbach's triumphal progress; for example, he seized Connacht through the permanent struggle for its kingship between the Ui Flaithbertaig, Ui Ruairc and Ui Conchobair dynasties.

Potential opposition from the north has been neutralized. The Cenel nEogain are torn apart by vicious struggles, leaving them much weakened, and the once-powerful Ui Neill dynasty is also in disarray. Even the king of the Ulaid, a still-formidable northern power, has travelled south to submit to Toirrdelbach, who seems now to be unstoppable and is being referred to by many as "the magnificent king of Ireland" (→1074).

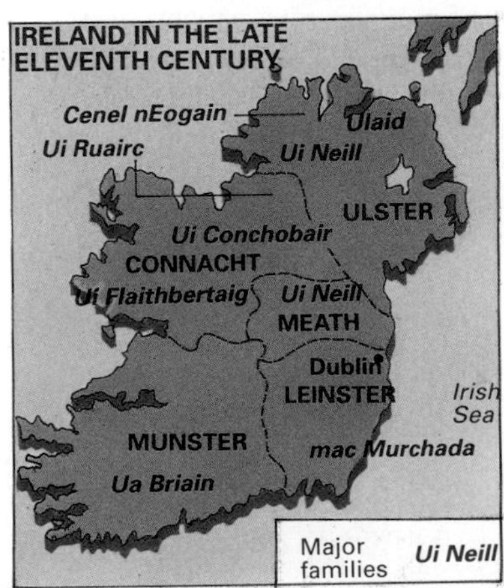

1074 - 1077

Denmark, 28 April 1074. Svein Estridsson, the king, dies. He is succeeded by his son, Harald III (→ 1075).

Edinburgh, 1074. King Malcolm III of Scots begins the refortification of both the castle and the city (→ 1078).

Ireland, 1074. Dunan, the first bishop of Dublin, dies. He is succeeded by Gilla Patraic (Patricius), who is consecrated by Lanfranc, the archbishop of Canterbury.→

Ireland, 1074. High King Toirrdelbach ua Briain expels Gofraid, the king of Dublin, and instals his own son, Muirchertach (→ 1078).

Northern England, 1074. Monasteries have been founded at Durham, Whitby and York by three Mercian monks, following an expedition that led them to believe that monastic life barely survived in Northumbria (→ 1076).

Winchester, Hampshire, 19 December 1075. Edith, the widow of King Edward the Confessor, dies. She will be buried alongside her husband in Westminster Abbey (→ 1102).

Deganwy, Gwynedd, 1075. Robert of Rhuddlan builds a castle on the Conwy estuary to push Norman influence further into the northern Welsh kingdom of Gwynedd.

Wales, 1075. Trying to regain power in Gwynedd, Gruffudd ap Cynan recruits Norse troops from Dublin (→ 1078).

York, 1075. Cnut, a son of King Svein Estridsson of Denmark, arrives in England with a fleet of 200 ships. The Danes sack the church of St Peter in York (→ 1080).

Rome, February 1076. Pope Gregory VII excommunicates Holy Roman Emperor Henry IV in a clash over papal authority (→ 20/1/77).

Kent, 1076. Archbishop Lanfranc of Canterbury wins a case against Bishop Odo, the earl of Kent and half-brother of William. He claimed that Odo had stolen church land; after the trial, he reclaims 25 manors in Kent (→ 1/4).

Rome, 28 January 1077. The pope lifts his excommunication of Henry IV after the emperor stands barefoot in the snow outside the pope's residence for three days in penance (→ 1080).

Normandy, 1077. William makes peace with Count Fulk IV of Anjou and King Philip of France (→ 4/1080).

Archbishop urges Irish church reform

Ireland, 1074

Lanfranc, the archbishop of Canterbury, has written to Toirrdelbach ua Briain, the king of Munster and high king of Ireland, urging reforms within the Irish church. He has asked for the elimination of simony (the selling of church offices), the proper administration of the sacraments, and correction of the laws that currently allow divorce and marriage within relationships forbidden by canon law. He is also seeking assurances that no bishop will be consecrated except to a fixed see. These letters reflect the growth of close links between Canterbury and the Irish church, with Canterbury leading the way towards reform.

Lanfranc had also written to King Gofraid of Dublin about the same reforms. But he could have saved his vellum: Toirrdelbach has now marched on Dublin, ousted Gofraid and replaced him by his own son, Muirchertach. There seems little to stop Toirrdelbach's successes. His power is growing in Meath and Connacht, and he has appointed Domnall, the brother of his late predecessor, Diarmait mac Mael na mBo, to rule Leinster [*see report on page 189*] (→ 10/10/84).

The bell shrine of St Cuilleann.

William's son dies in riding accident

A spear-carrying riding party, from an 11th-century manuscript.

Winchester, Hampshire, c.1074

The court is in mourning at the news that Prince Richard, King William's second son, is dead. Richard, who was still only in his teens, has died of injuries received in a riding accident a few days ago.

The prince was hunting in the forest near Winchester when he collided with a tree and received terrible injuries. Prince Richard's shocked companions acted swiftly to bring him back to Winchester where he could be cared for. But all the frantic attentions of the members of his household and the advice of doctors were not enough to save the wounded prince. After confession and absolution, and having taken the last sacrament of Holy Communion, he died.

William is devastated, for he has fallen out with his ambitious eldest son, Robert Curthose, now living in exile in William's duchy of Normandy. But he still has two younger sons on whom to rely: William Rufus and Henry (→ 1/1079).

Saxon pretender gives in to William

Normandy, 1074

King William has received his long-term enemy and rival Edgar the Atheling [royal prince] into his court here. He seems thus to have neutralized the Englishman, who only this summer was one of those planning to ally against William.

On 8 July Edgar travelled from Flanders, where he has had to take refuge for the last two years, back to the court of King Malcolm III of Scots. He was received with great honour – in open contravention of Malcolm's 1072 peace treaty with William [*see report on page 188*]. While Edgar was in Scotland, King Philip of France sent to him, offering him a castle at Montreuil-sur-Mer, between Boulogne and Dieppe. From this site Edgar could have launched raids into William's Norman territories or even threatened England.

Edgar and his men set out for France, but on the way their fleet was wrecked in a terrific storm. A dejected Edgar trailed back to Scotland with the survivors. At this juncture Malcolm advised Edgar to make peace with William, and the Atheling sent to the Norman court in submission. William gladly accepted and invited Edgar, at one time considered the rightful heir to the English crown, to cross the Channel once more (→ 1078).

Cleric speaks out on school beatings

Bec, Normandy, c.1076

Monastic schools must become less harsh and their teaching more inspirational if scholars are to fulfil themselves. So says Anselm, the influential prior of Bec Abbey. Born in Aosta, near Piedmont in Italy, he spent three years wandering in Burgundy and France before taking his vows at the age of 26.

Within three years he had succeeded Lanfranc as prior of Bec. The harsh discipline in the schools, with children learning by rote and regularly beaten, has shocked him. "With what good profit do you expend your substance in nurturing human beings till they become brute beasts?" he asks.

Revolt by earls crushed

The plot was laid at a wedding feast: 11th-century revellers at a banquet.

England, 1075
King William's deputies have crushed a major uprising in his absence. The attempted coup, led by Earl Ralph of Norfolk and Suffolk and Earl Roger of Hereford, had the backing of Cnut, the son of the late King Svein Estridsson of Denmark and a rival claimant to the English throne.

The plot was hatched at a feast for Ralph's marriage to Roger's sister Emma. It was to be massive: in addition to Danish support, the half-Breton Ralph was to involve many of his countrymen now settled in England. Yet as trouble brewed, King William kept in touch from Normandy, where Archbishop Lanfranc suggested that he should stay. Everything was soon under control. Men loyal to William contained Roger within his Herefordshire lands, while Ralph was defeated near Cambridge and forced to flee to Brittany. The Danish expedition arrived too late to be of any help.

Although this revolt was so swiftly put down, trouble may lie ahead. Roger is under arrest, but Ralph is at large in Brittany (→31/5/76).

Normans create a new order in England

England, c.1075
The powerful grip that the Normans have on England is especially clear when it comes to land ownership. It is with land that William rewards his henchmen, having no qualms about ousting the native holders: the English upper class is being dispossessed by the immigrants.

Land is split up into estates called "manors", held by the lord or baron from the king in return for "homage", "fealty" – demonstrations of obedience, dependence and fidelity – and military service. The baron in turn parcels out land to his dependent subordinates or vassals. This so-called "feudal" system resembles the Anglo-Saxon custom whereby *thegns* were the baronial class and *ceorls* the vassals. So while life remains much the same for those at the bottom of the ladder, those at the top have lost their privileges.

Normans are also taking over senior posts in the church, while the law is moving away from the traditional notion of compensation for victims of crime to punishment of those found guilty. Court business is no longer spoken in English but in French, and written in Latin. Words derived from French – such as county, village, justice, prison, money and rent – are even creeping into everyday speech.

Revenge execution settles an old score

Winchester, Hants, 31 May 1076
Earl Waltheof of Northumbria today earned himself an unenviable distinction: he became the only English aristocrat whom King William has executed. The death penalty was passed for Waltheof's complicity in last year's revolt [*see report left*]. His wife Judith, the king's niece, testified against him, but many people insist that he was the victim of a powerful group of Normans after his lands.

The beheading took place on St Giles's Hill outside the town, for fear that local people might cause trouble. The few witnesses report that the earl asked for time to say the Lord's Prayer but was so overcome by emotion that he could not finish. At this the executioner lost patience and carried out the sentence with a single blow. A rumour is spreading that the head then completed the prayer, saying: "... deliver us from evil. Amen" (→10/76).

William's prestige takes a bad knock

Brittany, October 1076
King William has suffered a serious blow at the castle of Dol near the Norman frontier, where Ralph of Gael, the rebel earl of Norfolk and Suffolk, continues to pose a threat. Earl Ralph, the sole remaining ringleader of the conspiracy that William put down last year [*see report far left*], retreated here to join an attack against the count of Brittany, Hoël of Cornouailles. The king saw this as an indirect challenge to him, especially as his enemy Count Fulk IV of Anjou sent reinforcements to Ralph.

Last month William, acting in concert with Hoël, laid siege to Dol. The castle held out long enough for King Philip of France to intervene and lift the siege; William was forced to retreat with heavy losses. It is his first setback in France for 20 years, and the damage to his prestige will take a long time to heal (→late 1077).

No sex allowed for men of the cloth

A beautifully carved ivory comb customarily used in church ceremonies.

Winchester, Hants, 1 April 1076
While conceding that priests who already have wives may keep them, Archbishop Lanfranc's third ecclesiastical council has decreed that all other members of the priesthood must adopt celibacy. This is only one of several reforms introduced by the Italian-born primate, who has campaigned against corrupt practices in the church. Lanfranc has also sought to reform Normandy, where John, the archbishop of Rouen, was appointed through his efforts. When John tried to separate his priests from their concubines, they stoned him. He fled, reportedly quoting from the psalms: "O God, the heathen are come into thine inheritance" (→1080).

1078 - 1080

England, summer 1078. Fires resulting from a long dry period of weather destroy many villages and devastate crops (→ 11/8/89).

Wales, 1078. Rhys ap Twdwr becomes king of Deheubarth [in southern Wales] (→ c.1080).

Grampian, 1078. King Malcolm III of Scots expels Maelsnechtai, the leader of Moray and son of the former Scottish king Lulach (→ 9/1079).

London, 1078. King William commissions Gundulf, the Norman monk who last year was made bishop of Rochester, to begin the construction of a tower fort to be made of white stone (→ 1087).

Ireland, 1078. King Donn Sleibe mac Eochada of Ulster offers allegiance to the Irish high king, Toirrdelbach ua Briain (→ 1079).

Northern England, September 1079. Malcolm III of Scotland breaks the Peace of Abernathy, which he made with William in 1072, and storms across the border; he raids the lands of Bishop Walcher of Durham, who controls the earldom of Northumbria, as far as the Tyne river (→ 9/1080).

Leinster, 1079. The warlord Conchobar Ua Conchobair lays claim to the kingship of Leinster (→ 1085).

Normandy, April 1080. King William finally agrees terms for peace with Count Robert II of Flanders at an Anglo-Norman assembly convened at Rouen (→ 1081).

England, 8 May 1080. Hubert, a legate from Rome, arrives with letters from Pope Gregory VII on a secret mission. He is to try to persuade William to become a papal vassal.→

Lewes, East Sussex, 1080. The first Cluniac monastery in England is built by William of Warenne, one of the king's most trusted nobles (→ 8/5).

Rome, 1080. Holy Roman Emperor Henry IV is excommunicated again by Pope Gregory VII (→ 8/5).

Dyfed, 1080. The Dublin Norse ravage the countryside, killing the bishop of St David's (→ 1081).

Wales, c.1080. King William of England has recognized Rhys ap Twdwr as ruler of Deheubarth. In return, Rhys has agreed to pay William £40 a year as rent for his kingdom (→ 1081).

Turbulent events leading to the Norman conquest caught in beautiful embroidery

Recent events recalled: the Bayeux Tapestry records the movements of armies.

Bayeux, Normandy, 1077
The women of St Augustine's abbey at Canterbury have recorded the events leading up to the Norman conquest of England in a huge masterpiece of embroidery. The so-called "Bayeux Tapestry" is made of coloured wool stitched onto a strip of linen 70 metres (230 feet) long and 50 cm (20 inches) high. Created in Canterbury, it is now proudly displayed at the new cathedral here in Bayeux.

The work was commissioned by William's half-brother, Bishop Odo of Bayeux, and tells the story of Harold Godwinson's rise and fall in a series of separate scenes, with only brief Latin captions to help to identify the participants. The narrative is acted out by stiffly posed yet expressive figures in the main frieze.

The embroiderers, working with great gusto and humour, pay close attention to details such as architecture, armour, clothing and hairstyle. Some episodes – for example, the building and sailing of William's fleet – are sewn with special clarity and liveliness. Blue horses and men with green hair help to keep things colourful.

Decorative margins along the top and bottom of the embroidery show foliage, plants, animals (real and imaginary) and scenes that provide an occasionally ribald diversion from the main story. Some, indeed, are obscene, with naked lovers running eagerly into each others' arms.

All the principal events of recent years are here. Of the highest importance are the scenes showing Harold making an oath to William over holy relics at Bayeux itself. It was at this point, William claims, that the throne of England was promised to him. The embroidery is in a sense, therefore, part of William's propaganda machine. The central political message is clear: Harold's death, and his dynasty's loss of the kingdom of England, were God's punishment for his breaking the oath.

A 19th-century representation of the women sewing the Bayeux Tapestry.

Trade in England is largely untouched by Norman regime

England, c.1080
In spite of the Norman occupation, England's industries have hardly changed since the reign of Edward the Confessor. The country's industries are centred on the manor, the village and the town. All of these units are virtually self-sufficient, and many have their own watermills. Any necessities that they cannot produce themselves are bought at fairs or markets or from itinerant pedlars.

Communications are mostly by river. Only the old Roman roads – Watling Street, Ermine Street and the Fosse Way – provide efficient land communications, in spite of the potholes and the clusters of weeds breaking through their surfaces after centuries of neglect. Iron-mining continues in the Forest of Dean, where forges make nails, picks, shovels and horseshoes. Lead-mining still flourishes around Alston Moor on the borders of Northumbria and Cumbria. Worcestershire and Cheshire produce most of the nation's salt, although the trade has been depressed since the Norman campaigns against Waltheof's rebellion in the north.

Eleventh-century builders at work.

English trade with Scandinavia remains strong. Ships from Norway and the Baltic regularly sail up the Thames, where they berth beside trading vessels from the Rhine, Flanders, Normandy and even the Mediterranean (→ c.1100).

'New forest' is created

Winchester, Hampshire, 1078
A huge area of southern England is being turned into a royal hunting preserve for King William, enforced with ferocious forest laws. The king has created a "new forest" for game by clearing away a great deal of the ancient forest, destroying many Saxon villages as well as some churches.

William is not the first king of England to change the landscape for his sport, or to impose savage penalties for those found guilty of poaching the royal game: Cnut and Edward the Confessor were both keen hunters. The protected animals include red deer, fallow deer, roe deer and wild boar. A poacher who kills a deer will be put to death. For shooting at a deer he will have his hands cut off, while just for disturbing one of the animals he can be blinded. There are also tough penalties for setting snares for birds, knotting nooses, enticing animals by music, or laying any sort of trap.

The depopulation of the villages, the destruction of churches and the oppressive regime imposed on commoners in the New Forest have done nothing to improve William's image. But it is said that he is a powerful and accurate shot with a bow from the back of a fast-moving horse (→c.1130).

A royal party out hunting: the chase is one of William's great passions.

William humiliated on Normandy frontier

Normandy, January 1079
King William has suffered the greatest humiliation of his career at the hands of his belligerent son and heir Robert Curthose. It was a double blow for the king. Not only was he defeated by the rebel force, but Robert himself knocked him from his horse and wounded him in the hand. He was only saved from death by one of his English followers, Toki, the son of Wigod, who was himself killed as he brought the king another horse.

For three weeks the king had besieged his son at Gerberoi, a castle east of Normandy placed at Robert's disposal by King Philip of France. The garrison came out and took on the besieging army which – unexpectedly – was beaten. Another casualty of the battle was the king's younger son, William, wounded as he fought alongside his father. Robert has been a thorn in his father's side since the king refused to give him authority in Normandy and Maine (→30/11/83).

King William with Robert Curthose.

William and pope clash over who is boss

London, 8 May 1080
King William has curtly rejected a demand from Pope Gregory VII that he should submit himself to the overlordship of Rome. While he acknowledges the pope's spiritual leadership, William is adamant that the church, which is an essential instrument of government, remains firmly under his control. The pope sent a legate to England with a dual demand: William should pay regularly an annual sum known as Peter's Pence to the papacy, and he should at the same time do homage and become the pope's vassal for the English kingdom.

In replying, William has stressed that he would continue to make cash payments, as has been done by previous English rulers, but added: "I have not consented to pay fealty, nor will I now because I never promised it, nor do I find that my predecessors ever paid it to your predecessors." The pope maintains that in seeking and receiving papal approval for the 1066 invasion, the king had become Rome's dependant; this William emphatically denies. In spite of this correspondence it is unlikely that the dispute will sour the generally extremely cordial relations between William and Pope Gregory. Only recently the pope referred to the Conqueror as "a jewel among princes". William has striven for years to foster clerical reforms and has pursued policies of special concern to the papacy – celibate clergy, the collection of outstanding tithes – as well as encouraging the general welfare of the church (→1083).

Pope Gregory: a later engraving.

Bishop of Durham murdered by mob

Tyne and Wear, 14 May 1080
In a furious outburst of intercommunal violence Walcher, the Norman bishop of Durham, has been killed. The local people were convinced that he had connived at the murder of his own chief adviser, the English *thegn* Ligulf.

As well as being bishop, Walcher also controlled the secular earldom of Northumbria, forfeited in 1076 by the rebel Waltheof [*see report on page 191*]. He tried honourably to govern according to English law but failed to control the violent behaviour of his Norman knights. Things came to a head when Ligulf was murdered by Gilbert, a relative of the bishop's. An assembly was held today at Gateshead to settle the matter, but Ligulf's kinsmen and supporters began a fight. Walcher, Gilbert and others took refuge in the church, but it was set on fire. As they emerged the Northumbrians killed them all (→1/8/86).

Anglo-Scottish pact feared by Normans

Newcastle upon Tyne, Sept 1080
A powerful fortress has been built here on the river Tyne by King William's son Robert Curthose – now reconciled with his father – as a bastion against two formidable foes: the Scots and the northern English. The Normans face tenacious resistance in the further reaches of Northumbria from English people grown self-confident from years of fighting the Scots without seeking any outside help. The Scots themselves not only cling to the far north but also control the west of the country as far south as a mere two days' ride from York.

The Normans' daunting task in facing two such stubborn groups is being complicated by a new development. Some Northumbrian leaders, believing the Scots to be less of a threat than the Normans to their way of life, are linking up with them to form a combined front against the foreign invader (→1087).

1081 - 1085

Denmark, 1081. King Harald III, the son of Svein Estridsson (who was once a claimant to the English throne), dies; he is succeeded by his brother Cnut "the Good" (→ 1085).

Gwynedd, 1081. Following the victory at Mynydd Carn of Gruffudd ap Cynan, the prince of Gwynedd, he is taken prisoner by Hugh "the Fat", the earl of Chester.→

Maine, France, 1081. Fulk IV of Anjou attacks and captures William's stronghold of La Flèche. William is forced to cross the Channel and make peace with him (→ 10/1086).

Bermondsey, London, 1082. Monks from Charité-sur-Loire found a Cluniac monastery.

Normandy, winter 1083/84. William's eldest son, Robert Curthose, is left without allies after the death of his mother, Matilda, and the imprisonment of Bishop Odo at Rouen in 1082. Living in self-imposed exile in Normandy, he attempts to win support from European nobles (→ 5/1086).

Rome, 31 March 1084. Pope Gregory VII has been forced to flee by Holy Roman Emperor Henry IV. His replacement is the anti-pope, Clement III, whose legitimacy William is considering recognizing (→ winter 1085).

Irish Sea, 10 October 1084. Bishop Gilla Patraic (Patricius) of Dublin is drowned (→ 1086).

England, 1084. William, under the threat of a Norse invasion or a second rebellion by his son Robert Curthose, raises a heavy land tax which proves extremely unpopular (→ 1085).

Canterbury Kent, 1084. Archbishop Lanfranc, who earlier this year founded St Nicholas's leprosy hospital at Harbledown, founds St John's hospital and the priory of St Gregory.

Hereford, 27 March 1085. Walter of Lacy, the founder of St Peter's church, falls to his death from the church tower while on a tour of inspection.

London, winter 1085. Archdeacon Maurice of Le Mans, William's chancellor, becomes bishop of London in succession to Bishop Hugh Orival, who died earlier this year of the incurable disease of leprosy (→ 25/12).

Munster, 1085. High King Toirrdelbach ua Briain falls ill with the great sickness sweeping across the country.→

William asserts authority in Wales

Dyfed, 1081

Following a major clash between the Welsh princes, King William of England has paid his first visit to Wales, travelling to St David's. The fighting, at Mynydd Carn, north of St David's, led to the death of Caradog ap Gruffudd, the dominant power in Morgannwg [Glamorgan], and left the joint victors, Gruffudd ap Cynan and Rhys ap Twdwr, presiding over an uneasy peace. Yet the battle has improved stability in Wales. Caradog had sought to add Rhys's kingdom of Deheubarth [in south Wales] to his possessions, and several of Wales's other princes soon joined in. Three of them died, and this alone has helped to reduce tension.

Although some parts of Wales are under Norman occupation [*see map*], and many castles have been built to secure the approaches to Welsh territory, large tracts of the region remain outside Norman control. By his visit, however – during which he established good relations with Rhys ap Twdwr – King William has penetrated further into Wales, and put himself in a stronger position here, than any of his predecessors in England (→ 3/7/93).

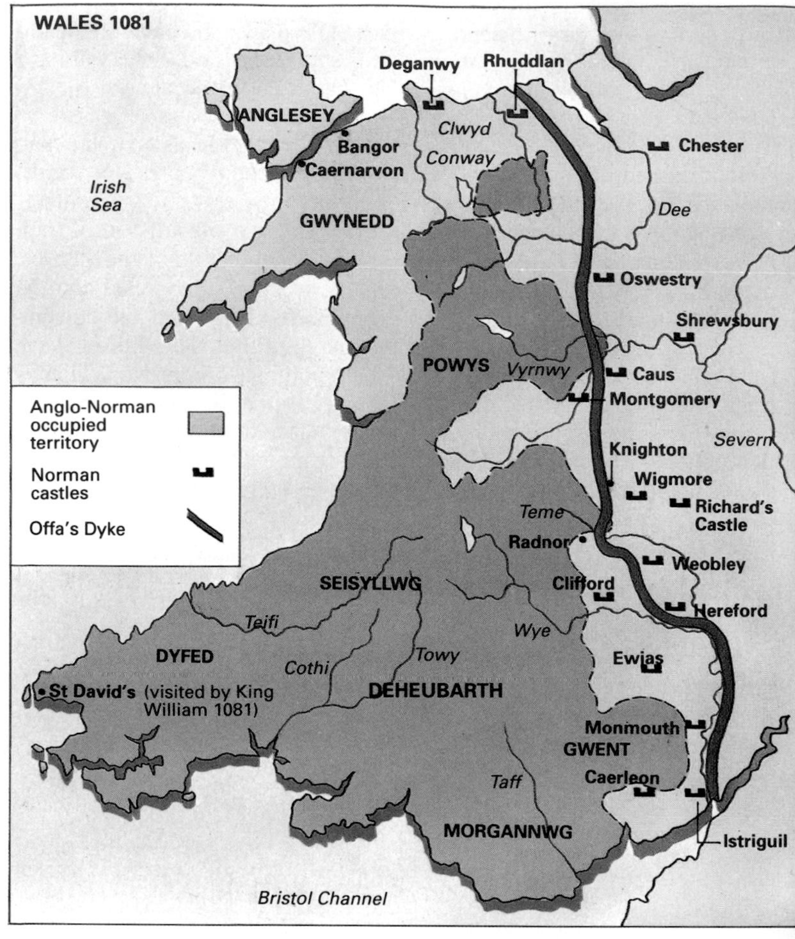

Normans relax playing odd board game

Gloucester, 1081

Norman administrators and troops based in the castle at Gloucester – where King William holds one of his three vast annual councils – are relaxing in their off-duty moments by playing a board game involving 29 carved pieces known variously as tablesmen, stones or counters. The game appears to be similar to one played by the Romans some 600 years ago; this was called *ludus duodecim scriptorum* [the game of the twelve scribes]. The modern version being played in Gloucester is known locally as the "tables" game.

Players move their pieces in turn according to a set of simple rules, in order to try to remove their opponents' pieces from the board. The tablesmen are carved to resemble animals, either real or mythical, and many also feature designs based on seasonal events in the calendar. Most of the tablesmen are circular in shape, averaging 45 mm (1.75 inches) in diameter, and between 7 and 10 mm thick. The carving is quite elaborate and appears to have been done by hand rather than by lathe.

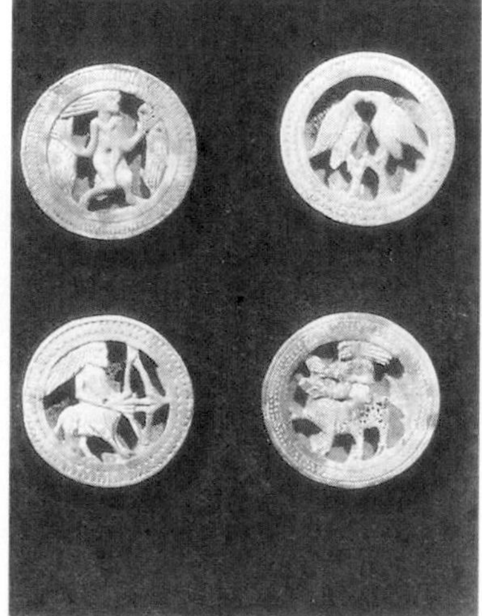

Bone pieces used by game-players.

Norman bishop in jail for disloyalty

Normandy, 1082

King William has seized his half-brother Odo, the bishop of Bayeux and earl of Kent, and flung him into prison. The king has accused Odo of disloyalty and maladministration during his regency in England, but it was the bishop's attempt to woo some of William's senior vassals to go with him on an expedition to Italy that has most inflamed the king's anger.

Some reports say that Odo, a man of immense energy, ability and ambition, had set his sights on seizing the papacy by force. He had recruited a number of distinguished knights, including Earl Hugh of Chester, with promises of rich pickings in Italy, but the king intercepted the force as it was about to set off from England. Although Odo is now in jail, he has not forfeited his possessions (→ 1088).

Challenger to Irish throne killed in battle

Ireland, 1085
Hostilities have broken out between Toirrdelbach ua Briain of Munster, the high king, and Donnchad Ua Ruairc, the militant leader of one of the Connacht dynasties [*see map and reports on page 189*].

While Toirrdelbach's army was marching into Meath, Donnchad took advantage of his absence to attack the Munster region of Thomond, burning monasteries and making off with booty. Emboldened by this success, Donnchad led his forces on to invade Leinster. But he was met near Leixlip, outside Dublin, by Muirchertach, Toirrdelbach's son, whose large army inflicted a crushing defeat on the men from Connacht. Donnchad was killed and his head taken to Limerick to go on show (→ 14/7/86).

The 11th-century shrine of Cathac: carried into battle to ensure victory.

Monks massacred on orders of abbot

Glastonbury, Somerset, 1083
Three monks have been murdered and 18 seriously wounded at the abbey here after Abbot Thurstan, an appointee of Archbishop Lanfranc, called in armed retainers to quell growing discontent.

Trouble has been brewing at the abbey for some time as a consequence of Thurstan's autocratic rule and his harsh treatment of the monks. It was his recent attempt to replace the monks' preferred Gregorian chant with a new one from Fécamp that led to a heated argument and an exchange of blows.

When the soldiers arrived many of the monks had locked themselves in the church. The soldiers forced their way in and killed three of the monks on the steps of the altar as they prayed. The remainder were wounded in an uncontrolled frenzy of bloodletting (→ 31/3/84).

Formidable queen buried at convent

Normandy, 30 November 1083
Matilda, King William's queen, has died after a protracted illness. She was given the last sacrament before her death on 2 November and was buried between the choir and the altar at Holy Trinity, Caen, in the nunnery she had founded in 1063.

In addition to the monks, abbots and priests attending her funeral, there was a large gathering of the poor – people who, throughout her lifetime, revered the queen for her Christian beneficence towards the disadvantaged. A monument is to be erected over her grave, engraved in letters of gold.

Matilda may have been small in stature – little more than 1.2 metres (four feet) tall – but she was a formidable woman who had played a significant role in her husband's life since their marriage over 30 years ago (→ winter 1083/84).

Wealth of England to be investigated

Gloucester, 25 December 1085
King William today announced an extensive survey into the wealth and potential income of his new realm of England. After exhaustive discussions at Gloucester, the king "sent his men over all England into every shire and had them find out how many hundred hides there were in the shire, or what land and cattle the king himself had in the country, or what dues he ought to have in twelve months from the shire. Also he had a record made of how much land his archbishops had, and his bishops and his abbots and his earls ...what or how much everybody had who was occupying the land in England, in land or cattle, and how much money it was worth" (→ 1/1086).

William depicted in stained glass.

Heavy tax levied to meet invasion threat

England, 1085
To meet the cost of a threatened invasion by King Cnut "the Good" of Denmark, King William is levying a heavy tax on landowners and has brought with him to England the biggest force of cavalry and infantry ever to have been seen in the country.

Mercenaries have been allocated to the estates of William's vassals across the country, who must provision them according to the size of their land – a ruling that is arousing outrage. William has also ordered large stretches of English coast to be laid waste so that provisions are unavailable to enemy forces which make a successful landing.

Cnut wants to revive the Scandinavian claim to the English throne made by his father, King Svein. He has enlisted the support of Robert, the dissident count of Flanders, King Philip of France and William's eldest son, Robert Curthose, also pose a threat to the English ruler (→ 7/1086).

A reconstruction of the priory on Lindisfarne island, in Northumberland, which was founded by Benedictine monks sent from Durham by the new Norman bishop of Durham, William of St Calais; building began in 1083.

1086 - 1087

Lismore, Armagh, 16 January 1086. Mael Isu Ua Brolchain, the celebrated religious poet, dies.

Westminster, Whitsunday 1086. King William bestows a knighthood on his youngest son, Henry.→

Denmark, July 1086. The threat of a Norse invasion of England is removed by the assassination of King Cnut "the Good" (→1/8).

Munster, 14 July 1086. High King Toirrdelbach ua Briain dies. His two sons, Muirchertach and Diarmait, both seek the kingship of Munster (→1087).

England, October 1086. After signing the Oath of Salisbury, King William leaves for the Isle of Man to travel to Normandy to face the invasion threatened by his son Robert Curthose, King Philip of France and Count Robert of Flanders, who have joined forces against him on the Norman borders (→7/87).

Hereford and Worcester, 1086. The great survey of England reveals that Droitwich is the largest producer of salt.

Kent, 1086. According to the survey the population is estimated at 13,000 people.

Ireland, 1086. Donnchad mac Domnaill Remair ("the Fat"), the king of Leinster, grants Clonkeen in Co Dublin to Christchurch Cathedral following his victory at Clonliffe over the forces of the kingdom of Brega (→2/1101).

Mantes, France, July 1087. The city falls to William after a surprise attack (→12/9).

Normandy, October 1087. Henry, the youngest son of the Conqueror, remains in Normandy. He acquires from his eldest brother, Robert Curthose, bishoprics and lands belonging to Coutances and Avranches, and assumes the title of count (→7/1088).

Connacht, 1087. Ruaidri Ua Conchobair becomes king of Connacht (→1089).

Scotland, 1087. After 15 years as a hostage to the English, Duncan, the son of King Malcolm III of Scotland, is released and knighted by Robert Curthose (→2/1091).

London, 1087. Following the plague which has raged here for the last two years, a great fire destroys St Paul's Cathedral and many other buildings (→10/1091).

Conqueror exacts loyalty oath from leading landholders

Salisbury, Wilts, 1 August 1086
In an impressive show of power, King William today exacted oaths of allegiance and loyalty from England's most important landholders and top military tenants. The oaths were sworn at a special council called by the king at Salisbury, at the ancient hillfort site of Old Sarum, where a royal castle now stands. Although this is a bleak and windswept place with few urban amenities, the see of Sherborne was moved here a decade ago, and a small cathedral is now under construction.

The Salisbury oath confirms the close ties between the king and the country's leading men as a possible challenge to William's authority gathers momentum on the borders of Normandy. The council proceedings were clearly designed to reinforce the dominant position of the king in his lands.

Meanwhile, threats from another quarter have vanished with the recent murder of King Cnut of Denmark, ending Danish plans for the invasion of England (→10/1086).

Prince learns arts of peace and war

London, Whitsunday 1086
Henry, the king's youngest son, has been knighted in recognition that he has completed his training for future kingship. The 17-year-old boy has endured a rigorous regime dictated by his father, who sought to mould a rounded character schooled in the elements of letters, religion and arms. Tutors were appointed to ensure that the boy acquired the outline of a literary education. Royal chaplains have instructed him in the basics of the Christian religion: the creed, the ritual and some of the psalms.

Hunting and military exercises, which he started at the age of 12, are more to Henry's taste. He rode with boys of his own age and learnt to school his horse, brandish his spear, manage his shield, and strike and not be struck. He was rarely outclassed (→10/86).

Great inquiry launched

England, January 1086
The most ambitious survey ever undertaken of England gets under way this year. Commissioners working to the king's barons will be dispatched to most parts of the country [*see report below*] for an inquiry which could lead to even higher taxes being levied by the king. Money is at the heart of the inquiry – a survey not only of England but also of the value of estates and their capacity to help the royal treasury. This help could be in the form of more taxes or by billeting more troops as the king expands his army to counter the threat of attack by the Danes. William also wants to legalise the dramatic changes of ownership of land which have occurred since he won the throne. When the survey is completed the king will know more about his kingdom than any previous king did.

The plough is the essential agricultural tool: from an 11th-century calendar.

England is divided into seven 'circuits'

Ely, 1086
England has been divided into seven areas for the great stocktaking inquiry ordered by the king. In theory at least, the same questions are to be asked by the king's commissioners in each of the areas or "circuits". These circuits are:

1. South-east England.
2. South-west England.
3. East Midlands.
4. Central Midlands.
5. West Midlands.
6. North Midlands, Lincolnshire and Yorkshire.
7. East Anglia.

The inquiry is concentrating on the areas of England where William's rule is most secure. This means that it will stop at the Welsh border and roughly at the line of the River Tees in northern England. The scale of the inquiry is still awesome in both the detail sought and the deadline of completion this year.

Just how ambitious the inquiry is can be seen from a summary of the questions prepared at Ely. These begin by seeking the name of an estate and its owner now and at the time of King Edward's reign before asking a series of more detailed questions, including: how many ploughs, how many free men and slaves, how much woodland and pasture, how many mills, how many fishponds. The inquiry must then seek to value the estate, including, according to the Ely summary, "whether it is possible that more [revenue] could be taken from the estate than is being taken now".

Although most available land is cultivated, sheepfarming remains popular.

William documents the riches of his kingdom

Pigs are favoured as herd animals because they can forage in woodland.

Arable land can support 81,000 ploughs

England, 1087

The great survey of England which was ordered by the king a year ago has revealed a country populated by between one and one a half million people. East Anglia is the most heavily populated area, with between 40 and 50 people per square mile compared with barely four per square mile in northern counties.

The English are living in a land of which about 35 per cent is arable, based on the acreage which can be attributed to the total of 81,000 ploughs reported by the survey. A further 30 per cent of the land is used for pasture, with around 15 per cent reported to be woodland. This leaves approximately one-fifth of England south of the Tees as anything from mountains, moorland or marsh to houses and gardens. This last 20 per cent is also assumed to include large areas in counties such as Yorkshire which were left as "waste" after the king had crushed revolts against his rule.

Although the inquiry began with one aim and essentially one set of basic questions, the degree of detail in the results varies. Some counties were not covered at all – Northumberland and Durham – and there was little on Westmorland, Cumbria, Lancashire and parts of Herefordshire. Some commissioners provided unasked-for details on, for instance, churches, but elsewhere towns as large as London and Winchester were omitted altogether. More generally the survey omitted to record most commercial activity that was not directly related to the land – fishing and mining, for instance. The inconsistencies mean that figures for total population and land use can only be estimates; but they are more accurate than any available previously.

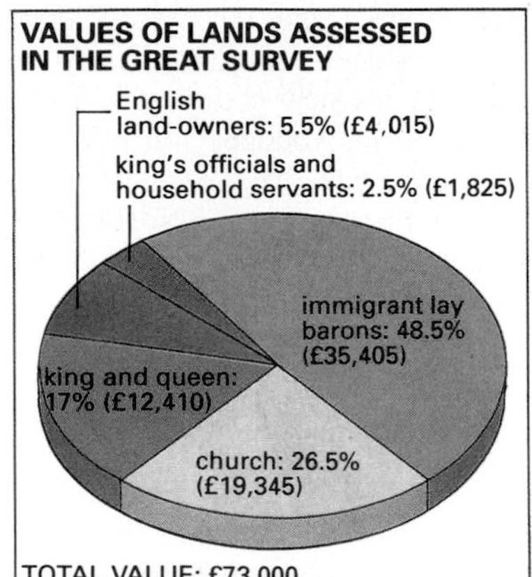

In the regions covered, apart from church property, only 5.5% of land remains in native English hands.

Threshing and winnowing: the annual struggle to secure a good harvest.

East Anglia is the most populous region

England, 1087

The king's survey of England offers the most comprehensive and authoritative picture of the country yet compiled. It reveals a land where villages are the most common form of settlement in the more populous southern and eastern counties, but hamlets and scattered homesteads predominant in large areas of the north and west. These broad conclusions can be drawn from reports of unprecedented detail about individual estates; for instance, one Cornish estate is summarised thus: "Richard holds Thersent from Count Mortain. Alwin held it in the time of King Edward & paid geld for 1 hide. But there are 2 hides there. There is land for 12 ploughs. In demesne are two ploughs & 6 slaves & 5 villeins & 11 bordars with 5 ploughs. There is pasture 3 leagues long & 2 leagues wide. Wood 1 league long and half league wide."

What the king was seeking was an assessment of the value of the estates, but his diligent commissioners have also produced a picture of his kingdom in terms of both its people and its landscape.

East Anglia is the most populous region, with some 95,000 people in Norfolk and 70,000 in Suffolk. Other counties with populations estimated to be over 50,000 are Lincolnshire (90,000), Devonshire (70,000) and Essex and Somerset with between 50,000 and 60,000 each. In contrast Yorkshire, a large county but one hit hard by William's harsh punishments, seems to have fewer than 30,000 inhabitants.

The survey is less reliable in suggesting the populations of towns. London was left out – perhaps because of the serious fire in the summer – but one estimate of its population puts it at around 25,000. Elsewhere the survey names 112 places which appear to be towns. Winchester and York are among the largest, with populations of around 6,000.

Most people, though, live in the countryside. The villages of southern and eastern England are usually surrounded by two or three open fields, and beyond these are areas of uncultivated marsh and woodland. In the northern and western counties of England people are more likely to live in smaller communities, hamlets rather than villages, and often in scattered individual farmsteads in more remote regions. Here fields are smaller and more land is given over to pasture for grazing livestock.

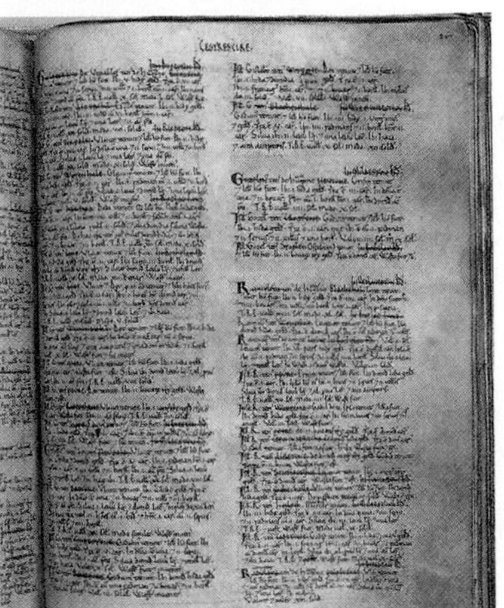

A survey page, covering Cheshire.

The less fertile land of the north and west is the most important cause of the different patterns of settlement revealed by the survey. Yet it also shows that farmers are becoming more ambitious in their attempts to bring land into cultivation. In Devon the survey reports farmers on land as high as 360 metres (1,200 feet) on Dartmoor and Exmoor. Elsewhere marshland in areas such as Romney Marsh, the Pevensey Levels, the Fens and Holderness are being reclaimed, although the survey records tidewater regularly flooding most of these areas. More generally, it is woodland which is under attack.

Woodland and wood pasture cover roughly 15 per cent of the area surveyed, a lower proportion than is thought to cover countries such as France. Of 12,580 settlements for which full details are given, only 6,208 have woodland. The Weald is the most wooded area. Others with significant woodland are the Chilterns, North Worcestershire, East Cheshire, East Derbyshire and South-east Staffordshire; but the primaeval wildwood has virtually gone.

Mighty Conqueror dies

Caen, France, 12 September 1087
Duke William of Normandy, the conqueror and king of England, was buried here today in a chaotic ceremony at the monastery of St Stephen which he himself had founded. He was hurt some days ago in a bizarre battle accident while attacking the French garrison at Mantes to punish it for its raid against Normandy. His horse shied at a burning ember, throwing him against his saddle pommel and causing serious internal injuries. He died early on 9 September.

Today's disastrous funeral was hardly one fit for a king. First a fire broke out as William's body was being carried to the monastery, and the mourners had to abandon the coffin to fight the blaze. Then a man named Ascelin interrupted the ceremony, shouting that William had no right to be buried there since he had stolen from him the land on which he had built the monastery. As this was true the chief mourners were forced to bribe him to allow the funeral to continue.

The final indignity was that the stone sarcophagus proved too small, so that the bearers were forced to manhandle the corpse, which burst open, releasing a stench so dreadful that the priests had to rush through the rest of the service. Yet the king who came to such an undignified end will without doubt be remembered as a great ruler. A stern and often ruthless man, he succeeded in the immensely difficult task of consolidating his conquest of England after 1066. He was also a superb legislator who brought order to his new territories. Last year he instigated an unprecedented survey of his English lands in the Domesday Book (→ 26).

Caen, where William was buried.

Durham prior lauds Scots queen's piety

Fife, 1087
The new prior of Durham is Queen Margaret of Scotland's confessor, Turgot. He is a Benedictine monk at Dunfermline Priory which was founded by the English-born queen and her husband King Malcolm. Now he has paid tribute to his patron's great goodness.

Turgot says that Margaret is known throughout the kingdom for her good works. She has been a generous backer of the church in Fife, supporting the communities at St Andrews and Loch Leven, and creating the Queen's Ferry across the Forth for pilgrims. She has also campaigned for reform of the Scottish church, urging conformity with Rome on issues such as the date of Lent and participation in Easter Communion (→ 20/6/1107).

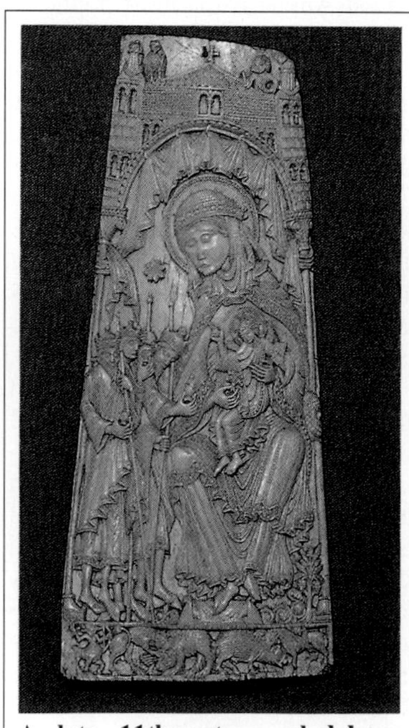
A late 11th-century whalebone ivory showing "The Adoration of the Magi", carved by a Norman artist practising in England.

William Rufus crowned king of England in haste, as his brother inherits Normandy

Westminster, 26 September 1087
William Rufus, the son of the Conqueror, was crowned king of England today in Westminster Abbey by Archbishop Lanfranc. The coronation took place soon after William's arrival in England, for fear of a rival claim from his elder brother Robert Curthose. Indeed, such was the need for haste that William left to claim the throne before his father was actually dead.

The new king was given the crown by his father as William lay on his deathbed in Rouen less than three weeks ago. In accordance with Norman tradition, the dying man left his new conquest – England – to his younger son and his inherited lands to his eldest son. Thus Robert inherits Normandy, despite his persistent disloyalty in allying with his father's enemies in northern France. The Conqueror had sought to avoid splitting England from Normandy, fearing that this would weaken both countries and lead to conflict. But given the crisis of his decline – and the solid support for Robert in Normandy – he found that his hands were tied.

Now the immediate future looks very difficult. The tough Norman lords know that they can manipulate the weak Robert, and there are moves afoot to place him on the throne of England as a puppet ruler. Robert himself is not strong enough to rule alone, nor to resist the blandishments of those who want to use him. A dynastic war between the brothers is looming.

England's new king, who takes after his father in looks, is a thickset muscular man with a protruding belly. He wears his long blond hair parted in the centre and his forehead bare, diplaying the choleric red complexion that led to the nickname "Rufus" (from the Latin for red). He is every inch a soldier, sometimes violent, sometimes swollen with anger and self-importance. He has many weaknesses, but his personal courage and determination are not in doubt (→ 10/1087).

A coin struck for William Rufus.

A seal used by the new king.

Treasure distributed to poor and clergy

Westminster, October 1087
King William II – who has enjoyed a peaceful start to his reign – is carrying out the instructions that he was given by his dying father and has started to distribute part of the Conqueror's treasure to the churches and poor people of England. His first action after the coronation was to take control of the royal treasury at Winchester where he found the enormous wealth accumulated by William I in the course of his long and successful career: vast amounts of gold, silver and plate as well as precious stones and costly robes.

Under the terms of the late king's will, every minster in England will receive money to say prayers for his soul. Some of these will be granted ten marks of gold, others six. Each country church will receive 60 pence, and every shire £100 to be spent on alms for the poor and needy (→ 1088).

1088 - 1091

Worcester, April 1088. Bishop Wulfstan, a supporter of King William II of England, has foiled an attempt to capture the city by the lords Bernard of Neufmarché and Osbern fitzRichard, who following their capture of Hereford had marched on it (→ 24/6).

Lewes, East Sussex, 24 June 1088. William of Warenne, the earl of Surrey, one of the king's followers, dies of wounds which he received at the siege of Pevensey fighting against Bishop Odo (→ 7/1088).

Normandy, July 1088. Duke Robert Curthose, the king's brother, plans to cross the Channel to give support to Bishop Odo and the besieged city of Rochester (→ 15).

England, 15 July 1088. Henry, the king's younger brother, crosses the Channel to claim lands belonging to their late mother, Matilda. These are refused to him, and he returns to Normandy (→ 9/1088).

Rouen, Normandy/Maine, France, September 1088. The exiled Bishop Odo urges Duke Robert Curthose to assert his power over England (→ 2/11).

England, 11 August 1089. A massive earthquake affects the whole country (→ 10/1091).

Warwick, 1089. William II appoints one of his supporters, Henry of Beaumont, as the first earl and gives him custody of the royal castle (→ 2/1090).

Rochester, Kent, 1089. The king commissions Bishop Gundulf to build a new castle.

England, February 1090. William II plans to claim Normandy from his brother Robert Curthose (→ 3/11).

Leinster, 1090. King Domnall Mac Lochlainn of Ailech, who has defeated Muirchertach Ua Briain, the claimant to the thrones of Dublin and Leinster, fails in his bid for the high-kingship (→ 1092).

Normandy, February 1091. Following the peace between William and Robert, which deprived Edgar the Atheling of some lands, Edgar flees to his brother-in-law, King Malcolm III of Scots (→ 10/1091).

Winchester, Hants, Nov 1091. William II and Robert Curthose abandon plans to pacify and reclaim the duchy of Maine (→ 12/93).

England, 23 December 1091. Robert, again at odds with his brother William, sets sail with Edgar for Normandy (→ 5/92).

Rebellion by Bishop Odo is a failure

Winchester, Hampshire, 1088
King William II has beaten off a determined challenge to his rule after only a few months in power. He has moved decisively against his uncle, the ambitious and worldly Bishop Odo of Bayeux, and a handful of Norman barons who had planned to replace him by Robert Curthose of Normandy, his brother.

The revolt centred in Kent, where Odo was regaining control of his earldom after a period of imprisonment for rebelling against King William I [*see report on page 194*]. The key engagement took place at Rochester. Royal forces blockaded the castle, and the rebels were forced to surrender after suffering from terrible disease and starvation. Duke Robert failed to commit his army from the continent, and the uprising failed. Bishop Odo's plans to incite a rising in London and the Channel ports came to nothing. He has now fled to Normandy after being stripped of his riches (→ 4/1088).

Odo at table: the Bayeux Tapestry.

Kingship of Leinster and Dublin seized

An Irish warrior fells a sacred tree.

Ireland, 1089
A succession row has broken out between the two sons of Toirrdelbach ua Briain following their father's death three years ago. Muirchertach banished Diarmait and assumed the kingship of Munster, whereupon Diarmait took his revenge by allying himself with the men of Leinster and trying unsuccessfully to defeat his brother.

Muirchertach then turned his attention to Connacht; he sailed up the river Shannon with his fleet and then cut down the sacred tree at Roveagh, but was subsequently defeated in a skirmish. His attempts to subdue Leinster and Meath were more successful; he killed Donnchad mac Domnaill Remair "the Fat", the king of Leinster and Dublin, and then seized the kingship (→ 1090).

Archbishop, loyal servant to crown, dies

Canterbury, Kent, 28 May 1089
Archbishop Lanfranc has died at the age of 74. He was born in Pavia, the son of a lawyer, and studied law in Italy before going to Normandy and becoming a monk, and subsequently a notable theologian, teacher and administrator.

He was one of the key figures in setting up the new regime. William I conquered England by force, but held it by policy and good government. Lanfranc not only brought the English church firmly under Norman control but also established the primacy of the see of Canterbury over its rival at York. He was completely loyal to the late king, and has also been so to his son, William Rufus (→ 4/12/93).

Treacherous bishop flees to Normandy after losing castle

Salisbury, Wilts, 2 November 1088
After a long and complex trial, a court has found William of Saint-Calais, the bishop of Durham, guilty of perjury and treachery against the king. He has been ordered to hand over his castle to King William of England.

The bishop had been close to the king and supported him during the rebellion led by Odo of Bayeux, but when asked to fight with him against the rebels he deserted and fled to Durham. His action shook the king – vassals and barons have military duties and strong ties of obligation, even if they prefer not to engage actively in fighting.

A long legal wrangle followed between William and the bishop, who insisted that he had to be tried by bishops under canon law and not by laymen under feudal law. At the trial, in Salisbury Castle, he put up a spirited defence and refused to accept the judgement of a "king's court". He also said that he intended to visit the pope to discuss the case and his treatment.

Eventually, overcome by threats from William, he agreed to surrender his castle. Harassed to the end, he was allowed to sail to Normandy (→ 1089).

An 11th-century bishop's crozier.

Royals clash over Rouen

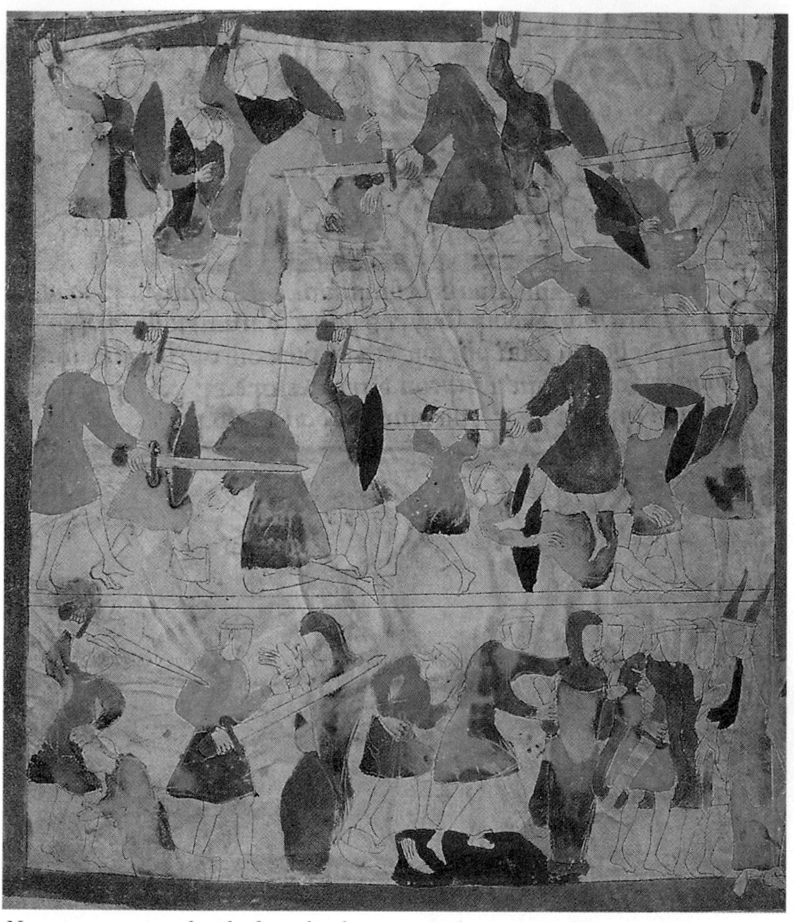

Norman warriors battle fiercely, from an 11th-century old testament.

Normandy, 3 November 1090
King William II of England has come off worst in a trial of strength with his brothers, Robert Curthose and Henry. During a day of bloody fighting at Rouen, Henry – the only one of them to see action – has proved a merciless foe.

William intervened in Normandy after Norman churchmen appealed to him to stop a campaign of harassment by Robert, but his real aim was to settle old scores with his elder brother. He had clashed with his younger brother, Henry, after trying to buy the allegiance of some barons in upper Normandy.

Last month William's allies, led by Conan, a rich merchant's son, rebelled in Rouen. The English king sent 300 knights to take the city. But Robert and Henry had already occupied the castle, and their relief forces arrived to beat off the enemy. Conan was captured with many others. Henry led him through the castle, jeering at him. Conan begged for mercy, but Henry threw him from a tower window. He plunged to his death (→2/1091).

Buildings topple as storms lash London

London, October 1091
Devastating gales have scythed across London, bringing widespread destruction to property. More than 600 buildings have been flattened, many of them churches. A single gust of a ferocious south-easterly ripped off the roof of St Mary-le-Bow, and two men sheltering inside were killed. The wind was so fierce that four rafters from another building, each about 7.5 metres long, hit the ground vertically with such violence that only short lengths were left protruding from the muddy street. Dazed residents of the city are saying that the storms are the work of the devil. More destruction and greater evils are in store, they predict (→1097).

Scots king forced to do homage to English following his invasion of Northumbria

Lothian, October 1091
For the second time in his reign King Malcolm III of Scots has been forced to do homage to an English king. His public show of obedience to William II is part of a settlement arranged by William's brother, Robert Curthose of Normandy.

Malcolm launched an opportunist invasion of Northumbria in May, when William was in Maine. The English king returned at once and marched north with a powerful army, but the loss of his fleet in a freak storm [*see report below*] hampered his plans. Although Malcolm and his troops then faced up to the English in Lothian, both sides were keen to take up Robert's offer of negotiations. Malcolm has agreed to go through the motions of paying homage and swearing fealty, while William has promised to restore Malcolm's right to 12 English villages and to pay him 12 marks per year. It remains to be seen whether this apparent diplomatic victory will be any more lasting for William than that of his father over Malcolm in 1072, when the Scottish king also made a show of doing homage (→23/12).

Malcolm III: forced to do homage.

Mystery surrounds loss of royal fleet

Tynemouth, 30 September 1091
King William II's fleet has been wrecked off the north-eastern coast of England. On a calm sea and in fine weather, the ships ran onto rocks before being swamped by waves which seemed to swell up from nowhere. The sailors, heading north to join a campaign against the Scots, were reported to have gone wild yesterday, rampaging around the Tynemouth area. Some of them, it seems, stole a piece of cloth from an old woman, who appealed to St Oswy for vengeance. Locals are now saying that the saint, whose shrine is in a local priory, drove the evildoers to a watery death.

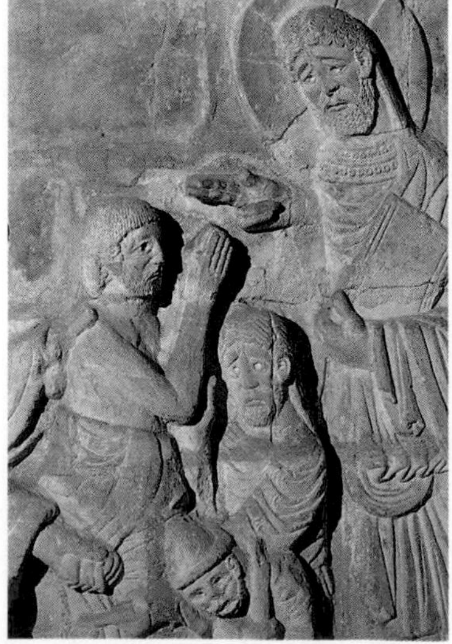

Details of stone reliefs from Chichester Cathedral, West Sussex (11th or 12th century): Christ's entry into Jerusalem (l) and the raising of Lazarus.

Carlisle, May 1092. King William II begins work on a royal castle following his takeover of Cumbria in which he expelled Dolfin, the son of Gospatric, a former earl of Northumbria, who ruled it as a vassal of King Malcolm III of Scots (→ 6/3/93).

Lothian, May 1092. Following his expulsion from Cumbria, Dolfin is given extensive lands in Dunbar by King Malcolm (→ 8/1093).

Bangor, Gwynedd, 1092. In an attempt to bring the churches of England and Wales closer together, Hervey, a Breton clerk, is made the first French bishop in Wales (→ 18/9/1115).

Connacht, 1092. Dynastic warfare continues as King Ruaidri Ua Conchobair of Connacht is captured and blinded by King Flaithbertach Ua Flaithbertaig of West Connacht (→ 1093).

Winchester, Hampshire, 8 April 1093. The new cathedral is formally opened.

Wiltshire, August 1093. King Malcolm removes his 12-year-old daughter Edith from the nunnery at Wilton after a visit from King William, who is said to be looking for a wife (→ 13/11/1093).

Scotland, November 1093. Donald Bane, the brother of the late Malcolm, succeeds to the Scottish throne.→

Fife, 17 November 1093. Margaret, the pious queen of Scotland, dies at Dunfermline four days after her husband's murder. She was already weakened by fasting and ill-health; the news brought on her sudden death (→ 1094).

Canterbury, Kent, 4 Dec 1093. Archbishop Anselm, formerly the abbot of Bec in Normandy, is enthroned (→ 11/12/94).

Gloucester, December 1093. Duke Robert Curthose of Normandy notifies William that their peace treaty will end unless the king helps him to recapture the duchy of Maine. The king, in an attempt to help his brother, levies a huge tax to fund an army (→ 10/1094).

Connacht, 1093. Muirchertach, ua Briain, the son of the late High King Toirrdelbach ua Briain, reconciled with his brother Diarmait in his own bid for the high-kingship of Ireland, has crushed a revolt by King Flaithbertach of West Connacht and subdued King Domnall Ua Mael Sechlainn of Meath (→ 1094).

1092-1093

Bishops use king's illness to secure reforms of the law

A seal belonging to William II.

Gloucester, 6 March 1093
King William of England has found that there is nothing like the threat of death to persuade a man to change his ways. He is at present seriously ill and confined to bed in Gloucester Castle. His bishops have told him that he is being punished by God. The only medicine that can save him now, they say, is spiritual; he must confess his sins.

Although he does not usually burn with religious zeal, William is scared enough to heed this advice and has promised major reforms. There will be an amnesty for all the king's prisoners. All unjust laws will be abolished and good ones made and enforced, he says. People owing money to the king will have their debts cancelled, while those who have sinned against him will be pardoned.

The bishops and abbots summoned to Gloucester have convinced the king that by swearing to defend the church he will avert the wrath of God. He has also promised to end the practice of buying and selling vacant posts in the church.

The clergy's greatest coup, however, is its success in persuading William to appoint Anselm, the brilliant abbot of Bec in Normandy, to the vacant archbishopric of Canterbury. Until now its lands and money have been in the king's own possession. Today Anselm, who was visiting England solely on abbey business, was literally dragged by a gang of bishops to the king's bedside and forced to receive the staff of office (→ 12/93).

Malcolm Canmore fatally betrayed during his fifth invasion of English-held territory

Northumberland, 13 Nov 1093
King Malcolm III of Scotland, known as Malcolm Canmore (the great chief), has been treacherously killed while raiding English lands. The king and his party were ambushed near the river Aln by men working for Robert of Mowbray, the earl of Northumberland. Malcolm was killed by his "sworn brother" Arkil Morel, who is also the earl's nephew. After the battle the king's body was carried off to Tynemouth for burial. His son, Edward, also died in the fighting.

Malcolm's fifth invasion of England follows his trip in August to Gloucester, where he had gone to confront William over the English king's failure to honour their treaty of 1091. On that occasion, in what can only be interpreted as a calculated insult, William refused to speak to him and rejected Scottish demands for a mixed commission to adjudicate on the matter, offering only a judgement by his own court. An enraged Malcolm set out for the north to raise his forces and launch this latest attack.

It is 35 years since Malcolm became king after defeating and killing Macbeth. His determination to hold on to territory in Cumbria and Northumberland brought him into frequent conflict with England, but he failed completely in his policy, losing out in the struggle for the disputed land and ending his life as a client ruler (→ 17).

Norman lord loses his head on sea-shore

A reconstruction drawing of Robert's castle at Rhuddlan, on the Clwyd.

Deganwy, Gwynedd, 3 July 1093
Robert of Rhuddlan, who for 20 years had waged war against the princes of northern Wales, died today at their hands. He was captured and then beheaded by raiders under the command of Gruffudd, the dispossessed king of Gwynedd who has only just been released from prison by Robert's uncle and mentor, Earl Hugh "the Fat" of Chester.

The raiders had landed in three ships near Robert's castle at Deganwy, on the river Conwy. Woken from a midday sleep, a furious Robert raced down to a beach beneath the Great Orme where Gruffudd was preparing to leave. But with only one companion he was defenceless, and those still in the castle watched in horror as their leader's head was severed and fixed to a mast.

Robert had been the principal lieutenant of the Earl of Chester in northern Wales, carrying the attack to the Welsh rulers. Using his recently built castles at Rhuddlan and Deganwy, Robert laid claim to Welsh territory. Embarking on a campaign of raids, he had gradually extended Norman influence deeper into north Wales, although his death might delay any further advances (→ 1094).

1094 - 1095

East Sussex, 11 February 1094. Archbishop Anselm of Canterbury consecrates the church founded by King William I to mark the site of the Battle of Hastings (→23).

Scotland, May 1094. King Donald Bane, who succeeded his brother Malcolm III last November, is deposed. His nephew Duncan, Malcolm's son and a client of King William II of England, becomes king (→12/11).

Shrewsbury, Shropshire, 27 July 1094. The earl, Roger of Montgomery, dies. He is buried in the abbey which he founded, and his second son, Hugh, succeeds him.

Scotland, 12 November 1094. Donald III resumes the throne following the murder by his supporters of his nephew, Duncan II (→7/1095).

Normandy, 29 December 1094. William II sets sail for Dover after his Normandy campaign. He returns to confront the problem of Welsh attacks and his continuing dispute with Archbishop Anselm (→27/5/95).

North Wales, 1094. Cadwgan ap Bleddyn of Powys and Gruffudd ap Cynan of Gwynedd launch a series of successful attacks against Earl Hugh "the Fat" of Chester and Normans in Conwy (→9/1095).

Normandy, April 1095. William's younger brother, Henry, is sent by the king to fight their eldest brother, Duke Robert Curthose of Normandy (→11/1097).

Canterbury, Kent, 27 May 1095. Anselm, who became archbishop last December, receives his *pallium* [stole of office] from Rome (→1096).

Scotland, July 1095. Following Donald Bane's alliance with Robert of Mowbray, the earl of Northumberland, William II of England, claiming to act as overlord, gives Scotland to Edgar, a younger son of Malcolm III (→10/1097).

Wales, October 1095. King William of England invades northern Wales in a not entirely successful attempt to put down the tide of insurrection that began last year (→7/1097).

Berkshire, December 1095. During his Christmas court at Windsor, the king gives orders that the plotters in the revolt lead by Robert Mowbray, the earl of Northumberland, are to be harshly punished (→1/1096).

Fighting fund splits king and archbishop

East Sussex, 23 February 1094
A furious row has erupted between Archbishop Anselm of Canterbury and King William II of England. It started when Anselm offered to contribute £500 towards William's latest expedition against his brother Robert Curthose in Normandy. William demanded more, and when Anselm hesitated the king told him to go away and take his money with him.

Relations have gone downhill ever since. Today, Ash Wednesday, Anselm gave a verbal roasting to the king and his men, who have assembled at Hastings on their way to Normandy. Anselm condemned their long, girlish hair and limp-wristed manners. He went on to lash out against the Normans' rampant immorality and accused them of sexual perversion. William is livid with the archbishop and has ignored his request for a general council to discuss these and other matters. Anselm is indignant that the king has tried to seize church lands to raise money for his expedition. The bishops want Anselm to placate William by handing over his donation of £500, but it now seems probable that William would not accept the money even if it were offered (→29/12/95).

Anselm: a 12th-century manuscript.

Northerners ally against Irish strongman

Ireland, 1094
After ten years of fighting, Muirchertach Ua Briain is dominant in Munster and Leinster. This year he expelled Gofraid Meranach, the king of Man, from Dublin, where he had been in power for the past three years, and put to death the king of Meath, Domnall Ua Mael Sechlainn, partitioning the kingdom between the dead king's two sons. He is now preparing to crush resistance in Connacht. But the northern dynasties are determined to stand up to him. Last year Domnall Mac Lochlainn of the Cenel nEogain of Ailech and Donnchad Ua hEochada of the Ulaid of Ulster met and agreed to ally against him (→22/12/1101).

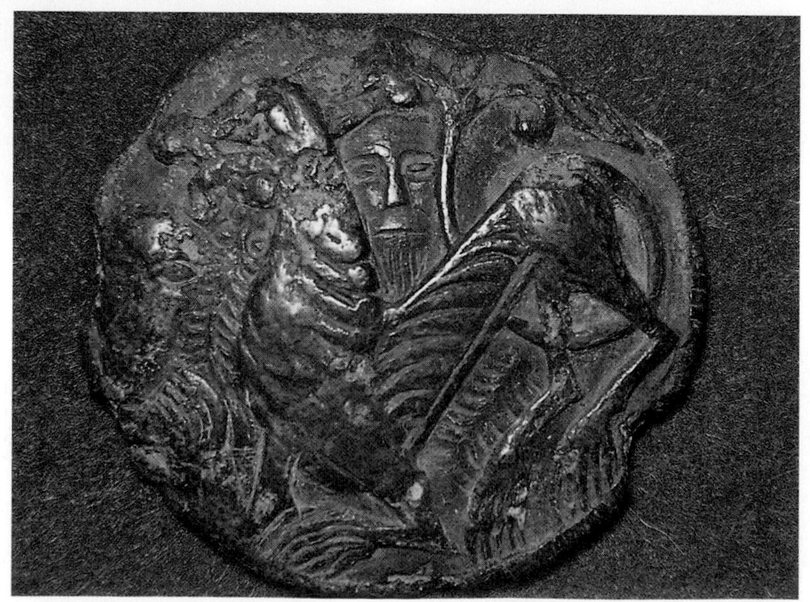
Metalwork from the Isle of Man, whose king has been driven out of Dublin.

Cathedral to reflect might of Normans

Durham, 1094
Norman power in stone: that is what the vast cathedral now being built at Durham will represent. King William has planned it as a symbol of his domination of northern England. Durham will be his administrative centre here, defended by the castle begun in his father's reign, and all trace of the town's Saxon past will be erased. The cathedral, which may take 40 years to finish, will be a spectacular showpiece; timber trusses and panels will be dispensed with for the first time, and the whole structure will instead be clad in stone (→c.1193).

An 11th-century text from Durham.

William loses land in lower Normandy

Normandy, October 1094
King William faces defeat in a new campaign against Robert Curthose, his land-hungry elder brother. They have been fighting since March, after Robert claimed that William had broken a pact on their respective rights in Normandy. Following early successes by William, Robert captured land in lower Normandy and took 800 of William's men prisoner. The king also faces anger at home over taxes to finance an army of 20,000 men which never crossed the Channel. William has summoned his younger brother Henry from Domfront to his headquarters in Eu, but Henry has gone to England instead (→4/1095).

Pope calls for crusade

France, 27 November 1095
In a call that will be answered by those all over Europe seeking new adventures, Pope Urban II has urged a crusade to free the Holy Land from the grip of the "infidel" Moslems. In a sermon at Clermont, he appealed to "everyone, no matter what class, be he knight or footman, rich or poor" to go to take up the sword for Christ. "All men going there who die untimely deaths, whether on the journey by land or by sea or while fighting the pagans, will immediately have their sins remitted," he promised.

This follows an appeal for help made in March by an ambassador to Italy from the Byzantine empire who said that the infidel had taken most of Asia Minor and would soon be at Constantinople (→6/1096).

The French monk Peter the Hermit preaching in favour of a crusade.

King moves fast to crush attempted coup

Northumberland, 1095
King William has threatened to gouge out the eyes of Robert of Mowbray, the rebellious earl of Northumberland, unless his men besieged in Bamburgh Castle surrender. Robert was trying to escape from the siege when he was caught.

Robert's revolt started early this year when he stole the merchandise of four Norwegian trading ships and refused the king's demand to hand it back. Backed by several disenchanted nobles, including the Herefordshire baron Roger de Lacy and the king's kinsman Count William of Eu, Robert planned to kill the monarch and replace him by his cousin Stephen of Aumale.

King William conducted a lightning campaign to crush the first signs of revolt. He outflanked Robert's brother at Newcastle, captured a rebel stronghold at Morpeth and built a castle across from the one at Bamburgh. The rebels are expected to submit before long. If Robert is not put to death at once, he will probably spend the rest of his life in captivity (→12/95).

Fashions at William's court condemned by moralists and clergy as 'effeminate'

A long-haired lord goes hawking.

England, c.1095
Moralists and members of the clergy have been denouncing the latest fashions at the court of King William. A new, extravagant and even outrageous way of dressing has replaced the comparatively austere clothing seen during the reign of his father, William the Conqueror. The present king has started rumours that he is homosexual by encouraging a trend in men's appearance and clothing that has been condemned as effeminate. In contrast with the traditional Norman preference for clean-shaven faces and short hair, young men at court now sport little beards and grow their hair – which is frequently combed and curled – long.

The most distinctive feature of women's clothing is the vogue for wide, voluminous sleeves – sometimes so wide that they have to be knotted up to prevent them from trailing on the ground. Men are mimicking this fashion in their generously cut robes and mantles, as well as wearing long, tight-fitting shirts and tunics. These long-line clothes, made in luxurious and flamboyant fabrics, are complemented by shoes with long points stuffed with wool and curling at the toes. The clothes are sometimes worn so tight that courtiers have to walk with a mincing gait (→9/4/1105).

Women are sporting voluminous, intricately knotted sleeves; this view of extravagant fashions at court is engraved after a 12th-century psalter.

1096 - 1097

Berkshire, 2 January 1096. William of St Calais, the bishop of Durham and one of King William II's leading councillors, dies at Windsor.

Waterford, 27 December 1096. Mael Isu Ua hAinmere is consecrated as the first bishop of the new see by Anselm.

Norwich, Norfolk, 1096. A cathedral is commissioned.

Cerne Abbas, Dorset, 1096. Archbishop Anselm tells Bishop Osmund of Salisbury of his concern about monks who plan to go on the crusade, which is forbidden unless their seniors permit it (→ 5/1097).

Berkshire, April 1097. Delayed by the weather, William arrives at Windsor from Normandy just before Easter. He will hold his court here (→ 2/8/1100).

Welsh Marches, July 1097. William launches a second campaign into Welsh territory; in spite of help from local guides it is not successful, and his troops are forced to retreat to the border (→ 1098).

Winchester, Hampshire, October 1097. After a long dispute with Archbishop Anselm of Canterbury, the king finally permits him, on pain of permanent exile, to visit the pope. William takes personal control of the see of Canterbury (→ spring 1099).

England, 11 October 1097. A rare star has been visible in the skies for the last week; many believe it to be a comet.

Tayside, October 1097. King Donald III of Scots is defeated in battle at Rescobie by Edgar, his nephew. The latter, the son of Malcolm III and Queen Margaret, supported by money from William of England and his maternal uncle Edgar the Atheling, succeeds to the Scottish throne (→ late 1097).

Normandy, November 1097. Following his return to the duchy, William sets out to reclaim the eastern border area of the Vexin. He starts to build a castle at Gisors, on the river Epte (→ 9/1098).

Westminster, 1097. Rebuilding work begins on the wall around the city, which was destroyed in floods earlier this year. Work also starts on a new hall for the king's palace.→

Scotland, late 1097. Following his coronation, King Edgar settles Robert fitzGodwin in Scotland. He is the first Anglo-Norman noble to be settled here officially (→ 1098).

England backs crusade

A 14th-century miniature showing knights as they embark for the crusades.

Winchester, Hants, October 1096
England is putting money and men behind a crusade to free the Holy Land from the Moslem Turks. Following the pope's appeal to princes and knights to make peace with one another in order to make war on the "heathen", King William and his brother, Duke Robert Curthose of Normandy, have done a deal.

Robert has "taken the Cross" (the term used for those going on crusade) either because he is ruined and sickened by the civil war and feuds in his duchy or because he is attracted by the lure of adventure and forgiveness of his sins. But as he has no money to pay for his part in the crusade he has struck a bargain with his brother. William is paying him 10,000 marks (£6,666) in silver in return for the custody of Normandy for three years. This is a good investment for the English king – the sum is less than a quarter of his annual income. He would gain control of the duchy if Robert died on the crusade. And he has secured the agreement of their younger brother Henry to the deal by handing over a couple of French counties to him.

William raised the money from his unwilling subjects during the summer; the sum, contained in 67 barrels, was handed over at Rouen. Robert has left for Constantinople by way of the main road of pilgrimage to Rome and Norman Italy. He is one of a party of distinguished princes which includes his kinsmen and neighbours as well as a few of William's vassals and allies. It is also expected that around 30 ships from England will operate in the eastern Mediterranean (→ 15/7/99).

Higher taxes for crusade spark protests

London, June 1096
Rich and poor throughout the land are almost literally up in arms over new taxes set by the king's financial adviser, Ranulf Flambard. The taxes are being imposed to raise the 10,000 marks (£6,666) that William has agreed to lend his brother Robert Curthose to enable him to go on crusade to Jerusalem. Land rents have already doubled, but still more money has to be raised.

The church is particularly enraged. Formal complaints from abbots and bishops have been made in the courts, but to no effect. Many of them have no choice but to melt down the church silver and to loot sacred shrines for the gems that adorn them. Naturally this has led to great bad feeling among churchmen. Archbishop Anselm has been accused of despoiling the church at Canterbury because he has handed over gold and silver worth over 200 marks. Abbot Godfrey of Malmesbury, who is seriously ill, is said to be sick as a divine punishment for stripping shrines and gospels of their jewels.

The aristocracy are also being hit hard. They are trying, however, to pass the tax burden on to those below them. This often means that the people who can least afford the new taxes – farm tenants – are the ones who are squeezed the most. The king is convinced that he at least is getting a good deal: Robert has in effect pawned Normandy to him, since the duchy is the security for the loan (→ 10/1096).

Cruel punishments dealt out to rebels

Salisbury, Wiltshire, January 1096
William, the count of Eu, has died from the mutilations he received after suffering defeat in a formal trial by battle. Implicated in last year's conspiracy against the king, the rebel William was accused and challenged to a fight here by Geoffrey Baynard, the former sheriff of Yorkshire. Geoffrey won the combat, and the loser was condemned in traditional fashion to castration and having his eyes put out.

That such a cruel punishment should be meted out to someone of William's high social standing has made a powerful impression on those who might have felt sympathy with last year's plotters. However, there is a widespread belief that in condemning William of Eu's cousin and steward, William of Aldrie, to death by hanging the king has gone too far.

It is a measure of the strength of the king's position that he now feels able to settle old scores in such a high-handed fashion (→ 4/1097).

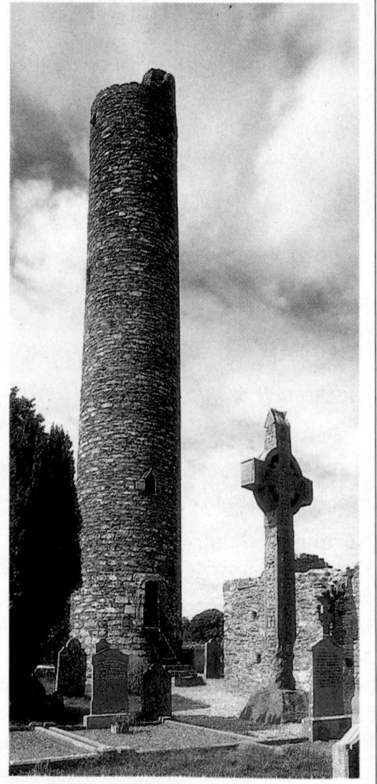

Remains of a round tower at the monastery of Monasterboice, Co Louth, which was founded in the sixth century. In 1097 the tower was badly damaged in a fire.

Towering above London

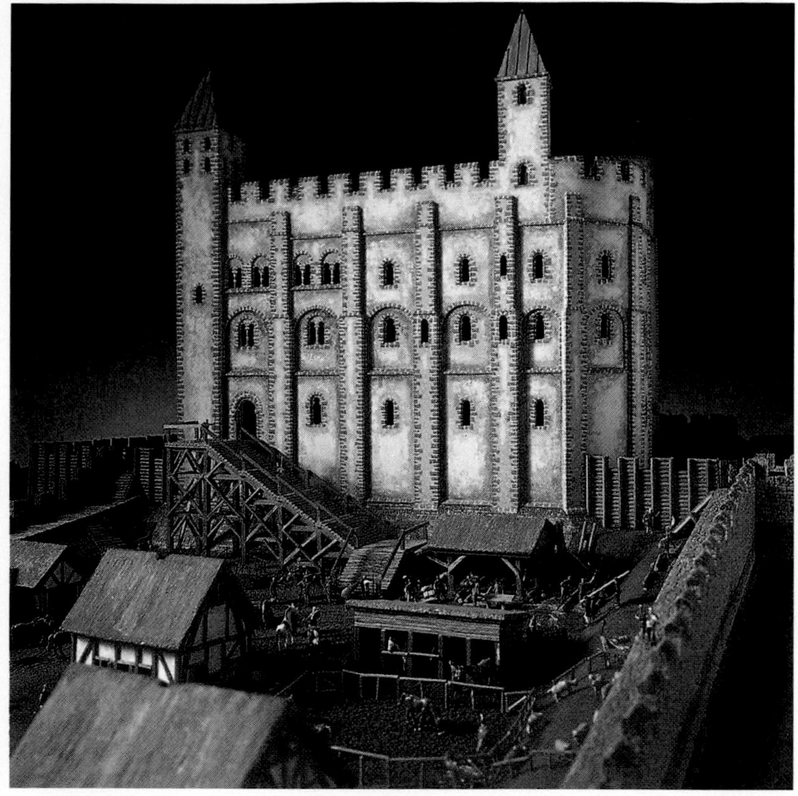

A 20th-century reconstruction model of the riverside White Tower.

London, 1097
The great White Tower beside the Thames, commissioned by William I, is almost finished. It is the biggest castle in England and has taken 20 years to build. From floor to battlements it rises 28 metres, soaring high above the walled city, just within the eastern Roman wall.

Gundulf, the Norman bishop of Rochester, has supervised its building as well as that of Rochester Castle. The walls of the White Tower, built of Caen stone, are 3.3-4.5 metres (11-15 feet) thick. Although it looks square, all the walls are of different lengths, enclosing a space more than 93 square metres (1,000 square feet) in area which is divided by a massive internal wall.

There are three apartments on each floor, including a banqueting hall, a council chamber and royal apartments. The main chamber is the chapel of St John, whose apse with its massive columns projects along the eastern wall. In addition to this, there are two square corner towers and one round one. All are white-washed (→ 1099).

Row erupts between king and archbishop over a church council on moral reforms

Windsor, Berkshire, May 1097
Sexually active priests are just one of the problems facing the church, according to Archbishop Anselm of Canterbury. He has come to the king's court here to press for a reform council. Other matters for discussion are married priests, the buying and selling of jobs in the church, and such perceived social ills as incestuous marriages, long hair and homosexuality.

King William is against the idea, saying that he is too busy defending the realm to waste time on church councils. Anselm has retaliated by appealing to the pope for help over the king's head, provoking a serious row between crown and church. As usual William is ready to go to the brink, and he has threatened to oust Anselm from Canterbury for good if he dares to go to Rome.

Anselm is not worried by this threat. He never wanted to be archbishop in the first place and is sick of being caught between duty to king and duty to God (→ 10/1097).

Anselm: 20th-century stained glass.

Eel is prize catch at freshwater fisheries

England, 1097
The freshwater fisheries of England are thriving, and nothing in the catch is as highly prized as eel. Fisheries are commonly associated with watermills, and when the miller has to pay his taxes in kind it appears that he often hands over more eels than grain.

The heartland of the inland fishing industry is the Fens, especially Cambridgeshire. Doddington alone harvests more than 27,000 eels a year. In neighbouring Huntingdon the local abbots send out their boats in order to profit from the plentiful eels.

Maintaining the fisheries is an important part of peasant life. The labourers must look after their weirs and turn over 50 per cent of their catch to the lord of the manor. No one can trade in fish without his authority (→ 1238).

King's uncle dies on his way to Jerusalem

Palermo, Sicily, February 1097
Bishop Odo of Bayeux, the half-brother of William I, has died here, reportedly on his way to a crusade in Jerusalem. At first he was a trusted ally of the king, helping to organize the conquest and administration of England, but William imprisoned him in 1082 and then expelled him. Officially the charge was maladministration. However, at the time Odo had a bold plan to seize the papacy, with help from Anglo-Norman knights, which the king did not like. Odo also fell out with his nephew William, the present king, and gathered nobles and a large army at Rochester to oppose his succession in 1087. William II defeated Odo after building two siege towers outside the town.

Since then Odo, who was also the earl of Kent, had been living in Normandy. His decision to go on a crusade followed the arrival in Normandy last September of the English king, who had not forgotten Odo's revolt against his father.

An English watermill: these are often linked with freshwater fisheries.

1098 - 1100

Normandy, November 1098. Following the capture of Maine two months ago, King William II of England acquires a powerful new ally: William, the duke of Aquitaine and count of Poitou (→ 5/1199).

Scotland/Norway, 1098. King Edgar of Scotland negotiates an important alliance with King Magnus "Barefoot" of Norway (→ c.1100).

Rome, spring 1099. Pope Urban II again forbids churchmen to pay homage to laymen, even kings (→ 10/1100).

Westminster, London, May 1099. William returns from Normandy after making peace with the French (→ 7/1099).

Westminster, May 1099. Bishop Ranulf Flambard, the king's chief minister, is allowed to buy the vacant bishopric of Durham in reward for his loyal service (→ autumn 1100).

Rome, 29 July 1099. Pope Urban II, who initiated the crusade, dies without hearing of its recent success only two weeks ago (→ 19/5/1147).

Holy Land, September 1099. Duke Robert Curthose of Normandy begins his return to Europe in triumph (→ 5/1100).

Wales, 1099. The princes Gruffudd ap Cynan of Gwynedd and Cadwgan ap Bleddyn of Powys, who fled to Ireland last year from King Magnus of Norway's invasion, return and make peace with the Normans (→ 1102).

Hampshire, May 1100. Richard, the bastard son of Robert Curthose, dies in a hunting accident in the New Forest (→ 2/8/01).

England, autumn 1100. Bishop Ranulf Flambard, the chief minister of King William II, is dismissed. King Henry's closest adviser will be his chaplain, Bishop Roger of Salisbury (→ 1101).

England, October 1100. The exiled archbishop, Anselm, returns to be welcomed by Henry, although, following the pope's orders, he does not pay the new king homage (→ 1102).

England, 11 November 1100. King Henry marries Edith, the sister of King Edgar of Scots. The new queen will be known as Matilda or Maud, which are easier for the Normans to pronounce (→ 1102).

Scotland, c.1100. The deposed king, Donald III – blinded on the orders of his nephew, King Edgar – dies (→ 8/1/1107).

England extends influence on continent

Maine, France, September 1098
William II of England has secured his most important victory since becoming king: the conquest of Maine, the area between Normandy and Anjou [*see map on page 189*]. He has been campaigning here for the past seven months against Count Fulk IV of Anjou. In July he defeated Fulk and – imitating his father's ceremonial takeover of the city in 1063 – entered the capital, Le Mans, in a procession of great pomp and triumphalism.

Now that he has won the war, William has to win the peace. In other words, he has to persuade the people of Maine that he will be a just ruler. Consequently one of Fulk's supporters, a local magnate called Helias of La Flèche, has been let off lightly.

At a meeting in Rouen, Helias – a prisoner of the king – asked to be given back the title of count and offered to serve William. The king could have had him killed but instead has allowed him to return to his lands in southern Maine. At one point Helias threatened to recover his lost honour and possessions. Incensed, the king grabbed hold of him and shouted: "Get out! Sod off! You can do whatever you like!" – not gracious words, but vanquished enemies can usually expect to feel the rough edge of someone's sword, rather than simply of his tongue (→ 11/1098).

William: from a manuscript c.1250.

William dashes to rescue of Le Mans

Maine, France, July 1099
Cities in flames and countryside laid waste are again familiar sights here since King William II of England began a campaign against his old rival Helias of La Flèche. A year ago Helias was a prisoner of the king, but was freed to return to his lands in southern Maine [*see report left*]. He has repaid the king's generosity by seizing Le Mans, the capital of Maine, and burning it.

William learnt the news earlier this month while hunting in the New Forest. Infuriated, he immediately broke off the hunt and rode hell for leather to the coast. He took passage to Normandy and, with bewildering speed, raised an army and marched down to Le Mans. Helias withdrew to Mayet, a short way to the south, burning two major towns as he went to deny their aid to William. Although the king failed to take Mayet he has contained Helias and retreated to Le Mans, ravaging the countryside on his way (→ 1110).

Norman advance in Wales is repulsed

Anglesey, Gwynedd, 1098
The earl of Shrewsbury has died while fighting a campaign to assert Norman control of north Wales. He was felled by an arrow shot by Magnus Barefoot, the king of Norway. The earl, Hugh of Montgomery, had led an expedition with the earl of Chester to reclaim land west of the Conwy [*see map on page 194*]. Two Welsh leaders, Gruffudd ap Cynan and Cadwgan ap Bleddyn, withdrew across the Menai Strait to Anglesey where they had recruited Norse mercenaries from Ireland. But the Norsemen then switched sides, forcing the Welsh princes to flee.

Fortune seemed to be smiling on the Normans, but then Magnus arrived with a fleet, intent on plunder. He struck the earl clean through the eye as he was riding along the sea-shore. Magnus left soon after the killing, as did the Normans. So, with their enemies gone, it is the Welsh who – for now – control Gwynedd (→ 1099).

Massacre and looting as Holy City falls

Jerusalem, 15 July 1099
The crusaders took the Holy City today, restoring it to Christian hands by putting the Moslem defenders to the sword. Today's bloodbath marks the climax of a long campaign by Duke Robert Curthose of Normandy, the brother of William II of England, and a force of largely French knights.

The crusaders arrived outside Jerusalem six weeks ago but had to wait for English and Genoese ships to bring supplies. Wood was found to build siege towers and a battering ram as the onslaught continued. Invoking God's help, the knights preceded their attack by visiting sacred sites outside the city walls and listening to sermons on the Mount of Olives.

Godfrey de Bouillon's men were the first to bridge the gap between their tower and the heavily fortified wall. The first knights actually to cross it were from Tournai. With a mighty surge, the crusaders poured over the wall and also through a breach made by the battering ram. Moslem fighters retreated from the wall to Solomon's Temple, where they were massacred. In the aftermath of the battle the victors looted gold and silver in an orgy of pillaging. Soldiers and knights ransacked houses for holy relics, now destined for churches in England and France (→ 29).

Knights setting off for battle.

Arrow kills hunting king

Hampshire, 2 August 1100
King William II of England has been shot dead. He was hunting in the New Forest when a French knight, Walter Tirel, hit him with an arrow. Tirel fled from the scene and is thought to be heading back to France.

Although some suspect murder, others are saying that the death was a terrible accident. It was late in the afternoon when a stag was flushed out and ran between William on the one side and Tirel on the other. The king let fly an arrow but missed. A second deer then charged through the same spot, and this time Tirel shot, missing the animal but striking William in the chest. He fell forward onto the arrow, and the tip pierced his heart. Death followed within seconds.

William's body, still dripping blood, has now been transported by cart to Winchester, where he will be buried tomorrow in the old minster. His brother Henry is also in Winchester and is already claiming the right to succeed to the throne.

To some, the manner of William's death was God's judgement on an immoral ruler, an alleged homosexual who provided a good living for no one but mercenaries and whores. Others will remember him as a rough but fair, often magnanimous, king who took chances and often won, and who kept hold of his father's lands in England and on the continent (→ 5/8).

Henry crowned in haste to thwart brother

Westminster, 5 August 1100
Henry, the youngest son of William I, was crowned in haste here today before his brother, Duke Robert Curthose of Normandy, could return home from a crusade and assert his own claim to the throne of England. When William II – the second of the Conqueror's three surviving sons – fell dead in the New Forest [*see report left*], Henry went straight to Winchester to seize the castle and the royal treasury.

In his coronation charter Henry promised to treat the church better than did his brother William, who farmed its revenues and sold its benefices. Henry has also sent messengers to Anselm, the exiled archbishop of Canterbury, inviting him to return from Normandy (→ 11/11).

Henry's coronation: he succeeds his brother William as England's king.

Enormous new hall built at Westminster

The hall built by William II at Westminster: a 20th-century reconstruction.

London, 2 August 1100
William II's most imposing memorial is a huge new hall at Westminster, completed last year on a site alongside the palace laid out by Edward the Confessor shortly before the Norman invasion. This was William's biggest building project; it followed a wall to surround the White Tower, as well as major repairs to London Bridge, which had been damaged by flood water.

The hall is the largest in England, possibly indeed in Europe. It is nearly 72 metres (240 feet) long and over 20 metres wide. With its auxiliary buildings it is, in effect, a new palace; in fact, it is to be known as "the New Palace at Westminster". There has been a certain amount of haste in the work – the buttresses are 1.2 metres out of phase – but the hall is a magnificent creation, with 12 bays lit by round-headed windows in an arcaded wall gallery.

While William was inspecting the hall for the first time some courtiers observed that it was large enough, while others suggested that it was too large. The king remarked that it was only a bedroom in relation to the palace which he had originally had in mind (→ 1114).

Peasantry marked by complex hierarchy

England, c.1100
Peasant life may be low on comforts, and by their very numbers peasants may appear to be no more than an undifferentiated mass of village-dwellers – some farmers, some working in mills or smithies – but the peasantry, which makes up the bulk of the population in England, is marked by complex relationships.

As far as dependent peasants are concerned, "villeins" are at the top of the heap. They are duty-bound to offer their services to their lords as "week work", providing regular help – perhaps three days each week – with harvesting, ploughing and sowing. In addition they pay rents in both cash and kind. A villein might hold 12 or even 40 hectares (30 to about 100 acres).

Below the villeins are found "bordars", cottagers with smallholdings, and "cottars", responsible for only 1.5 hectares (about 4 acres) or less each. Lowliest of all are "serfs", mere slaves to their lords. Outside the dependent peasantry come "sokemen" such as, typically, the miller and the smith. While rarely better off than villeins, they may sell their land and move around the country at will. They may have to lend their oxen to help in the lords' fields (→ 1200).

The fruit of their labours: an 11th-century view of peasants harvesting.

1101-1105

Dover, Kent, 10 March 1101. On the return of Duke Robert Curthose of Normandy from the crusade, King Henry renews his agreement with Count Robert II of Flanders, ensuring the support of the latter for the price of 400 marks a year (→ 9/1118).

Chester, 27 July 1101. Earl Hugh "the Fat" of Chester dies in the monastery which he founded. His heir, Richard, is aged seven.

Ireland, 22 December 1101. Muirchertach Ua Briain, the claimant to the high-kingship, moves his campaign from Connacht to Ailech, forcing King Domnall mac Lochlainn of Ailech to free King Donnchad Ua hEochada of Ulster (→ 5/8/03).

London, 1101. Bishop Roger le Poer of Salisbury is made justicar and given the royal seal to keep (→ 1110).

Ireland, 1102. Archbishop Anselm, attempting to reform the Irish church through Muirchertach Ua Briain, brings the English and Irish kings into contact (→ 1107).

England, February 1102. Queen Matilda gives birth to a daughter, who is also named Matilda (→ 8/1103).

England, 1102. Henry arranges the marriage of Mary, the sister of King Edgar of Scots, to the count of Boulogne, improving Anglo-French links (→ 5/5/08).

Normandy, March 1103. Sybil of Conversano, the wife of Robert Curthose, dies; she gave birth to a son, William Clito [prince], on 25 October 1102 (→ 1104).

England, 27 April 1103. Anselm leaves for Rome to end a dispute between the pope and King Henry (→ 22/7/05).

England, August 1103. Queen Matilda gives birth to William, the heir to the throne (→ 1108).

Normandy, 1104. Henry of England accuses Robert Curthose of breaking their 1101 agreement. Robert tries to strike a bargain but loses an important supporter, Count William of Evreux, who swears allegiance to Henry (→ 4/1105).

Normandy, April 1105. Henry invades Bayeux and Caen but fails to reach peace terms with Robert (→ 10/1106).

Dyfed, 1105. Gerald, the constable of Windsor, is to represent King Henry of England in west Wales (→ 1107).

War averted by a kiss

Alton, Hampshire, 2 August 1101
The brothers Henry of England and Robert Curthose of Normandy met face to face surrounded by their armies today. They kissed one another and agreed to be reconciled, thereby averting war. In return for a handsome pay-off, Robert has promised to drop his claim to the English throne.

Duke Robert's army landed at Portsmouth a short time ago. "I demand the right due to me as the eldest son," he declared. He had been provoked into the expedition by Bishop Ranulf Flambard, recently escaped from imprisonment in London's White Tower. Henry had placed him there because, as William II's favourite and chief minister, Flambard had backed the late king's plundering of England.

Flambard escaped from the White Tower by ordering his butler to bring in a very long rope concealed in a wine cask. When his guards were drunk, he fastened the rope to a window mullion and let himself down. As he slid the great distance, his hands were lacerated by the roughness of the rope and he fell heavily. Friends were waiting for him at the foot of the tower with horses, and they fled to Normandy, where Duke Robert gave the bishop refuge and in return received advice on how to seize England from his younger brother.

A later engraving of Duke Robert.

Henry would have been foolish to take the threat lightly. Duke Robert is a skilled soldier who has led assaults on Jerusalem and Antioch. But today the planned seizure came to nothing when he renounced his claim to England and, in reciprocation, Henry gave up his claim to the Cotentin peninsula in Normandy. Henry also made a promise to pay Robert £2,000 a year in order to assuage his thwarted ambition (→ 3/1103).

Earls forced to flee after Welsh-backed revolt is put down

Shrewsbury, Shropshire, 1102
King Henry has put down a rebellion by Robert of Bellême, the earl of Shrewsbury, and his brother Arnulf, the earl of Pembroke, who had attempted to rally Welsh support against the English king. Henry had been warned of the plot; 45 charges of treachery were prepared, and Robert was summoned to appear at court.

But the earl did not attend and began to build up his defences in castles at Arundel, Tickhill, Bridgnorth and Shrewsbury. His brother gave support from Pembroke in Dyfed. The English castles were soon taken, but those in Wales and the Marches posed a greater challenge. Both sides looked for allies. The king urged the Norman army to act against the rebels' holdings in France; Robert rallied support among the Welsh, while Arnulf also sought help from Ireland.

In the autumn Henry moved into the Marches with a large army. Bridgnorth fell after a siege. Robert yielded Shrewsbury without a fight, symbolically handing over the keys of the town to his conqueror. The brothers have now been exiled and their lands confiscated (→ 1105).

Irish church poised for sweeping change

A bronze reliquary made c.1100 to house a bell used by St Patrick.

Munster, February 1101
The synod which is now taking place at Cashel is proving to be a momentous landmark in the history of the Irish church. Presided over by Muirchertach Ua Briain, the king of Munster, the synod was convened as a direct result of the wish for reform expressed in letters from Lanfranc and Anselm, the previous and present archbishops of Canterbury.

The synod proposes to free the church from secular obligations, to protect its rights of sanctuary from abuse, to restrict the marriage laws, and to regulate ecclesiastical appointments.

Most surprising of all, perhaps, has been Muirchertach's outright gift of Cashel, the capital of the old Eoganacht dynasty, to the religious of Ireland (→ 1102).

Priests must forgo long hair and sex

Westminster, London, 1102
Sex, drink and sodomy were among the topics on the agenda of a synod held at Westminster Abbey in London. This was a personal triumph for Anselm, the archbishop of Canterbury and president of the synod: for years the late King William II forbade church councils to discuss the nation's morals.

All priests must now be celibate; those with wives or mistresses must leave them. They are also banned from attending drinking parties. Priests must shave their heads, while laymen are to style their hair so that it lies above the eyes and covers only part of the ears: long hair is considered a sign of loose living. Anselm also forbids homosexual acts (→ 27/4/03).

Munster king fails to win control of north

A 12th-century Irish reliquary: warlike Ireland is still producing great art.

Ireland, 5 August 1103
Muirchertach Ua Briain, the king of Munster, has made yet another attempt to defeat Domnall Mac Lochlainn, the king of Ailech, and achieve his long-standing ambition to dominate the north. After skirmishes between the two men over several years, Domnall decided to attack the Ulaid in Ulster [*see map on page 214*].

Seizing his opportunity, Muirchertach assembled a huge force and marched to Armagh to assist the Ulaid. Since previous efforts to defeat Domnall had been foiled by the intervention of the abbot of Armagh, Muirchertach offered the latter gold in a placatory gesture and then went off to attack the Dal nAraidi while awaiting developments in Armagh, leaving some of his forces at Mag Coba, outside Newry. In his absence, Domnall reappeared at Mag Coba and inflicted a crushing defeat on his old enemy, seizing much plunder, including the royal tent (→1114).

The death of St Atheldreda: a fine carved capital [head to a column] from Ely Cathedral. Abbot Simeon, the brother of Bishop Walkelin of Winchester, began rebuilding the abbey church in 1083, and by the early 1100s he was at work on the astonishing 13-bay nave and the west front.

Courtiers agree to cut their flowing locks

Carentan, Normandy, 9 April 1105
King Henry of England, castigated today by a Norman prelate for the "unseemly and detestable" way in which he and his followers wear their hair, agreed to have an immediate and drastic haircut. Henry is staying here after crossing the Channel in response to calls for help to counter the misgovernment of his brother Robert Curthose.

Condemnation of the long-haired styles at present fashionable in the English court, despite Anselm's ruling in 1102, came from Serlo, the bishop of Seez, before he conducted the Easter day service in the village church. "All of you", the bishop told his congregation, "wear your hair in woman's style, which is not seemly for you who are made in the likeness of God and ought to use your strength like men."

Bishop Serlo said that long hair was a true glory for a woman, but for a man it led to sin and apostasy, and called on the king to set an example to his subjects. Henry promptly consented to be shorn of his long tresses by the bishop. His retinue quickly followed suit, shearing their own hair and treading the once-cherished locks underfoot (→c.1120).

French foppery: a later reconstruction of effeminate 12th-century fashion.

'Miracle' occurs as royal tomb opened

London, October 1102
The body of Edward the Confessor, which had lain in state behind the high altar of Westminster Abbey for 36 years, has been exhumed. As Bishop Gundulf of Rochester and Abbot Gilbert Crispin of Westminster watched, the top of the sarcophagus was removed. A sweet fragrance filled the air, according to witnesses. Not a limb had decomposed, not a hair had withered, they claim. Beside the king lay his crown and sceptre.

The corpse's immaculate preservation is only one among a number of miracles that have been attributed by ordinary people to the old king. The body was subsequently returned to the tomb, although the crown and sceptre had gone missing – only to reappear in the abbey's treasury (→13/10/63).

King does deal on question of homage

Laigle, Normandy, 22 July 1105
Archbishop Anselm held talks with King Henry of England here today in order to solve a long-running dispute between church and crown. The king is fighting a tough campaign to conquer Normandy, where hostilities with his brother, Robert Curthose, flared up again last year. Seeking papal support in the campaign, Henry agreed to concede on the question of whether clerics may receive bishoprics from the hands of laymen, including kings.

The church believes that the king owes obedience to the church; the king thinks that the church owes homage to him when he invests a new bishop with his ring and staff. Anselm and Henry agreed to drop the investiture but to allow the king to keep his right to homage from a bishop or abbot (→23/3/06).

1106 - 1112

Rome, 23 March 1106. Pope Paschal II, eager for King Henry of England's support in crusades, agrees to compromise on royal power to command homage from clergy (→ 1/8/07).

Grampian, 1107. The new king, Alexander, crushes a rebellion in Moray (→ 1112).

St Andrews, Fife, 20 June 1107. Prior Turgot of Durham, formerly confessor to Queen Margaret, takes the bishopric, vacant since the death of Fothad in 1093 (→ 1114).

South Wales, 1107. After the death of King Hywel ap Goronwy, King Henry of England seizes Carmarthen, leaving Gower and Kidwelly to be ruled by the earl of Warwick and Bishop Roger of Salisbury (→ 1108).

Winchester, Hants, 1107. The tomb of King William II is damaged when the great tower above the minster collapses.

France, 5 May 1108. King Philip dies; his son, Louis "le Gros [the Fat]", is the new king (→ 3/1109).

York, 21 May 1108. Gerard, archbishop of York since 1101, dies in odd circumstances. He is suspected of dabbling in the occult, and the canons of York refuse to bury him within the cathedral (→ 1260).

London, 1108. Henry backs Anselm's renewed attacks on clerical marriages, fining all clergy found guilty (→ 21/4/09).

Normandy, March 1109. Anglo-French relations break down when Louis VI of France demands that Henry abandon Gisors Castle (→ 3/1113).

Canterbury, Kent, 21 April 1109. Anselm's death leaves the archbishopric vacant, to the pope's dismay (→ 26/4/14).

Pembroke Castle, Dyfed, 1109. Owain ap Cadwgan, the prince of Powys, abducts Nest, the wife of Gerald of Windsor, the king's constable (→ 1114).

Maine, France, 1110. On the death of Count Helias of La Flèche, its ruler, the county passes to his daughter, Eremburga, who is married to Count Fulk V of Anjou, who takes control against the wishes of King Henry of England (→ 3/1113).

Normandy, 4 November 1112. Robert of Bellême, once a supporter of King Henry and now a follower of Duke Robert Curthose, is imprisoned by Henry when he pleads for Robert's release (→ 3/1113).

English king secures control of Normandy

Lisieux, Normandy, October 1106
The king of England has established his rule throughout Normandy at a council of magnates held here this month. His brother Robert Curthose, who ruled the duchy for so long and so ineffectively, is now a prisoner and likely to remain so for the rest of his life.

The quarrel between the brothers has dragged on for years. Robert invaded England in an unsuccessful attempt to take the crown in 1101. Last year Henry invaded Normandy, taking Caen and Bayeux. This summer he returned and, with the counts of Maine and Brittany, besieged the castle of Tinchebrai.

Duke Robert arrived to relieve it, threatening that if Henry did not raise the siege he would declare war. Henry countered by demanding half the duchy and its castles. The duke and his council rejected this with scorn and a pitched battle ensued, but by the end of it Robert had been captured along with 400 knights and 10,000 men (→ 4/11/12).

Limerick bishop plans church revolution

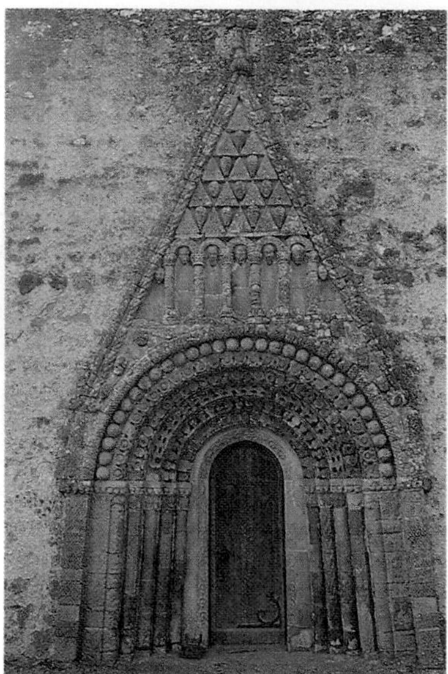
Irish Romanesque: Clonfert.

Ireland, 1107
The reform of the Irish church, begun at the Synod of Cashel [*see report on page 208*], is being encouraged by Gilbert, the first consecrated bishop of Limerick. A friend of Anselm of Canterbury, Gilbert has been appointed papal legate and has written a treatise on the theory of reform, *De statu ecclesiae* [*Concerning church order*].

Gilbert's design for church hierarchy envisages dioceses ruled by bishops, under whom priests will run parishes; monasteries will be ruled by celibate abbots. The bishops will be subject to an archbishop, who is subject to the primate, over whom presides the pope. This implies a complete overthrow of the traditional system (→ 1111).

Scots king who was given a camel dies

Edinburgh, 8 January 1107
King Edgar of Scotland has died at the age of 33. The son of Malcolm III and the saintly Queen Margaret, Edgar won a succession struggle with his uncle Donald Bane, defeating him in battle at Rescobie in Fife in 1097 with the help of William II of England. The late king pursued pro-English policies, settling the first English knight in Lothian in 1097 and marrying his own sister to King Henry. A calm, godly man, Edgar endowed many churches. A few years ago he received the present of a camel, the first seen in Scotland, from an Irish lord. He is succeeded by his brother Alexander, a more warlike character (→ 1112).

Welsh deplore new tide of immigration

Dyfed, 1108
More newcomers are now following the Normans into south-western Wales: many people from Flanders are arriving in the areas of Rhos and Daugleddau near Pembroke, apparently with the backing of the English king. Land is being given to Wizo, the leader of the Flemings, and to other Flemish knights and their followers.

King Henry hopes that colonization will benefit agriculture, woollen manufacture and trading links. Although this venture is commercial rather than military, the Welsh deplore it. Some are losing land, and all risk seeing their established culture supplanted (→ 1109).

Royal dispute with church resolved by council at London

London, 1 August 1107
A council of England's top clerics and nobles has met to smooth over problems between King Henry and the church. For the last five years at least they have been at loggerheads; the dispute primarily concerns the appointment of abbots and bishops.

Until now the king has granted bishoprics and abbacies "by gift of staff and ring". This means that the new appointee is in effect a vassal of the king and has to do him homage. Churchmen – not least among them Anselm and Pope Paschal II – have complained because under the present arrangement they appear to recognize a worldly power, the king, as their ultimate authority. For his part, the king has clung on to this tradition because he does not want to seem to have no spiritual power in the realm.

A compromise has been reached, however. Investiture by the king or any other layman is now forbidden, but bishops and abbots will still do the king homage for the lands that they hold (→ 1108).

A decorated English cross, c.1100.

Women and hunting offer royal diversion

Henry pictured in bed with the Welsh princess Nest, one of his many lovers.

England, 1108
Hailed as "*rex Norman-Anglorum* [king of the Normans and the English]", Henry is now consolidating control of his domains both here and across the Channel. His ambitious brother Robert Curthose is held in comfortable captivity at Devizes Castle, and the royal dispute with the church has been settled [*see reports on facing page*]. Henry's marriage in 1100 to Matilda, the daughter of Malcolm III of Scotland, enhanced the security of his throne, but the English king, who boasts over 20 illegitimate offspring, is an inveterate womanizer.

With a temperament that blends piety and ruthlessness, Henry is an active man who loves to hunt; he has claimed the hunting rights throughout England for himself alone. He is of medium height with black hair and a bushy beard – but not as bushy as it was since a Norman bishop condemned the fashion for full beards and long hair as inappropriate for Christians. Henry at once offered to trim his beard; his nobles did the same (→ 7/1/14).

Scotland is next to ride the Norman tiger

Scotland, 1112
Alexander, the king of Scotland since 1107, has proved himself adept at humouring his powerful Norman neighbour to the south. Realizing that Henry of England would have no qualms about invading Scotland, Alexander has actually invited Norman knights to settle in his lands, offering them inducements. He permits them considerable freedom, thus denying Henry any reasonable excuse for war.

While their foothold here is not yet strong, the Normans have started to introduce into Scotland their "feudal" system for holding land [*see report on page 191*]. They are also encouraging the building of castles in their favoured style.

These are often simple earthworks made up of a "motte" [tall mound] topped by a wooden tower known as a "donjon" [keep]. Around that is a courtyard or "bailey", and around the brow of the motte is usually a timber palisade. These castles – and mounted knights – form the basis of Norman military success. No wonder that Alexander is building one on the 75-metre (250-foot) crag above the Forth near Stirling (→ 12/1113).

Irish reforms are agreed

Ireland, 1111
Major church reforms have been agreed at the Synod of Raith Bressail, held near Cashel in Munster. The delegates included an impressive array of bishops (among them Bishop Gilbert, the papal legate), some 300 priests, 3,000 clerics and many Munster nobles, most notably King Muirchertach Ua Briain.

Continuing the work begun at the Synod of Cashel and following the suggestions of Bishop Gilbert [*see report on page 210*], the council took the first step towards the creation of a national diocesan hierarchy. It also decided that the churches of Ireland should be given over entirely to the bishops. The country is to be divided into two provinces. Armagh will take the northern half, and its overall superiority has been recognized by the designation of its archbishop as primate. Cashel will lead the southern half.

A strange omission from the 25 named dioceses is that of Dublin, a diocesan centre for over 50 years. It seems to be regarded with suspicion fuelled by the animosity between it and Armagh. Under the new plan, it belongs to the diocese of Glendalough in Co Wicklow (→ 1124).

Tablecloth is key to the new 'Exchequer'

Westminster, 1110
An ingenious accounting system for calculating the royal revenues has been adopted by the most able of King Henry's ministers, Bishop Roger of Salisbury. A table 1.5 by 3 metres (5 by 10 feet), covered with a cloth marked out in large black-and-white columns, is used to record payments from the royal manors collected by local sheriffs.

As a clerk reads out the amount due from each sheriff, counters are placed in the various columns representing pounds, shillings and pence. Different counters are used for deposits and outgoings, and the final calculation is made by subtracting one from the other.

Because of the chequerboard appearance of the tablecloth, the new system has come to be known as the "Exchequer". It meets twice a year, at Easter and Michaelmas, and gives the king a more exact picture of the royal finances. It has certainly made it easier for debts to be calculated and collected (→ 1123).

England's accounts: a 20th-century artist's view of the "Exchequer".

1113-1117

England, December 1113. David, the brother and heir of King Alexander of Scotland, marries the widowed Maud de Senlis, a great-niece of William the Conqueror. By the union David receives the earldoms of Huntingdon and Northampton (→ 1114).

Worcester, 1113. Fire destroys the city, the cathedral and the castle (→ 4/8/16).

Germany, 7 January 1114. Matilda, the daughter of King Henry of England, is married to Holy Roman Emperor Henry V (→ 5/1118).

Canterbury, Kent, 26 April 1114. Bishop Ralph d'Escures of Rochester is elected archbishop. Thurstan, the king's chaplain, is to be appointed to the archbishopric of York, succeeding Thomas, who died in March (→ 4/2/23).

St Andrews, Fife, 1114. Bishop Turgot retires to the monastery at Wearmouth, in north-eastern England, following a dispute with Alexander over his obedience to York, which the king has forbidden (→ 1120).

Wales, 1114. The princes of Gwynedd and Powys, Owain ap Cadwgan and Gruffudd ap Cynan, swear oaths of allegiance to King Henry of England (→ 1116).

London, 1114. A record ebb-tide has meant that people can cross the Thames with water below the knee (→ 1170).

Scone, Tayside, 1115. An Augustinian priory is founded by King Alexander. A prior and six canons arrive from the Yorkshire community of Nostel (→ 1128).

Normandy, 1115. King Henry of England forces the Normans to swear allegiance to his son and heir, William the Atheling [royal prince] (→ 4/1117).

Peterborough, Cambridgeshire, 4 August 1116. A huge fire destroys most of the monastery and parts of the town (→ 1207).

Powys, 1116. Prince Owain ap Cadwgan, who abducted and seduced the wife of Gerald of Windsor in 1109, dies fighting for King Henry of England against Prince Gruffudd ap Cynan of Gwynedd.→

Ireland, 1116. Muirchertach Ua Briain, who last year was restored to power in Thomond after recovering from a two-year illness, relinquishes his claim as high king in favour of his brother Diarmait before retiring to Lismore (→ 1118).

Henry gains more lands from France

King Louis of France's official seal.

Gisors, France, March 1113
Two kings, Louis of France and Henry of England and Normandy, have agreed here to end their territorial squabbles. Louis, who had already recognized Henry's conquest of Normandy, yielded to him the suzerainty of Brittany and Maine [*see map on page 222*] and the town of Bellême in southern Normandy.

Fulk V of Anjou had inherited Maine in 1110; he refused to do homage to Henry for it, so Henry attacked Anjou. A rebellion broke out in Normandy led by Robert of Bellême, whom Henry arrested. Last month Fulk sued for peace, paid his homage and betrothed his daughter, Matilda, to Henry's son, William. When Count Alan Fergant of Brittany did homage to Henry, the king betrothed his daughter to Alan's son (→ 1115).

Deranged priest kills infant Scottish heir

Edinburgh, 1114
A baby boy who was second in line to the Scottish throne has been murdered by a deranged priest. The infant, Malcolm, was the son of David, the earl of Huntingdon, who is the brother and heir of King Alexander of Scots. His mother is the rich heiress Maud de Senlis, who married David only last year.

The murderous priest had been taken into the earl's household as an act of charity following a horrific episode in Norway, when he was blinded and had his hands and feet cut off in punishment for sacrificing a fellow priest at a black mass. But the man repaid David's hospitality by killing Malcolm, tearing open the child's abdomen with two fingers of his artificial iron hands. A grief-stricken David has ordered him to be pulled apart by being tied to wild horses. In recognition of his status, Earl David has recently been granted by his brother huge estates and wide powers in southern Scotland, where last year he endowed an abbey at Selkirk (→ 12/6/22).

Kelso Abbey: founded by David at Selkirk and later moved to Kelso.

Armagh archbishop creates Munster truce

Ireland, 1113
In an attempt to quell the turmoil that is currently besetting Ireland, Cellach, the archbishop of Armagh, has spent 13 months journeying to and fro to establish peace between the warring factions. In particular, the domination of Toirrdelbach Ua Conchobair of Connacht over the whole country is bitterly resented, especially in Munster.

Cellach tried to induce King Cormac Mac Carthaig of Desmond, who had been living in a monastery in Lismore, to return. He reluctantly agreed. His brother and rival, Donnchad, was expelled, and Munster was then united under Cormac. In response Toirrdelbach brought a fleet of ships down the Shannon and devastated Co Limerick, but Cormac and his ally, Conchobar Ua Briain, stationed their fleet on Lough Derg and eventually drove him out. Cormac then accepted Cellach's peace moves and has agreed to a year's truce with both Munster kings (→ 1116).

England's first zoo is established at Woodstock hunting estate

Woodstock, Oxfordshire, c.1115
King Henry is collecting a menagerie here at Woodstock containing some of the most extraordinary animals ever seen in England. From the hunting lodge that he has built in the nearby Forest of Wychwood, the king and his court delight in the sight of lions, leopards, lynxes and camels.

It is known that the king is pleased to receive such gifts, and Earl Paul of Orkney is one of those attempting to gain his favour by sending him these wonderful creatures. So far the most amusing animal the king has been confronted with is an African porcupine, a gift of William of Montpellier (→ 1256).

Lions are prominent among the animals resident in the King Henry's menagerie at Woodstock.

First non-Welsh bishop elected in Wales

London, 18 September 1115
Norman power in Wales received a significant boost today with the election of the first Norman cleric to be bishop of St David's in Dyfed. The new bishop, Bernard, will be consecrated at Westminster today by the archbishop of Canterbury.

He succeeds Wilfrid, a Welshman like all his predecessors. Bernard is reputed to be a scholarly and courtly figure, but his election will be resented in Wales as evidence of King Henry of England's plan to bring Wales under his control. By appointing his own men as feudal overlords and church leaders he has enhanced his powers in the Welsh Marches. Last year a major – and successful – expedition was mounted in Powys and Gwynedd. Now a Norman occupies the most important Welsh bishopric (→ 1134).

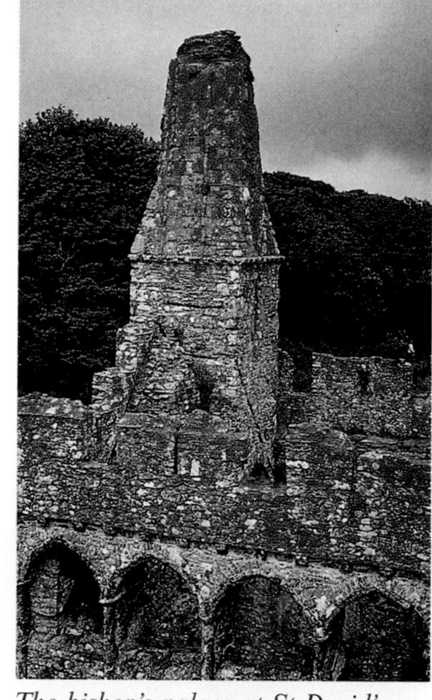

The bishop's palace at St David's.

An ornate candlestick given to the abbey at Gloucester (now the cathedral of St Peter) by Peter, Gloucester's abbot 1104-1113.

Castles and forts spring up in Wales

Wales, 1116
For half a century castles have been the symbol of the Norman drive to conquer Wales. Now they are being built by the Welsh themselves. This year Uchdryd ab Edwin of Powys completed a castle at Cymmer in the area known as Meirionydd [in Mid-Glamorgan] – one of the new native-built castles in Wales. Even before this project another Welsh lord, Cadwgan ap Bleddyn, erected his own Norman-style fort at Trallwng Llywelyn [near Welshpool].

Until now Welsh leaders have preferred to rely on ancient earthworks for defence and have even tended to destroy captured castles, as happened at Gwynedd in 1096. Yet in the long term this development, while a back-handed compliment of sorts to the Normans, may not prove to be the guarantee of military success that its supporters claim.

Certainly in the short term it has not helped the pioneering Uchdryd: his castle has already been attacked and set ablaze by rival Welsh princes, who have now captured his territory. But the politics of Wales are aggressively competitive, and every leader has to do what he can to ensure his survival (→ 1136).

Foundation of hospital for lepers signals changing attitudes to the care of the sick

London, 1117
Matilda, the wife of King Henry of England, has founded a hospital for London's lepers. To be called the hospital of St Giles, it will be sited half a mile west of Holborn village.

The hospital is one of many being built to give refuge to sufferers from leprosy, the most feared disease in Christendom. The spectre of the ragged outcast with bell and begging bowl can terrorize entire towns, and the last few years have seen a growing hostility to lepers. Drawing on the Old Testament book of Leviticus, some see them as morally "unclean". St Giles's – like Lanfranc's hospital of St Nicholas near Canterbury, and Count Robert of Flanders's hospital at St Omer – will reflect Christian compassion while providing a sop to those who are calling for lepers to be rigorously isolated.

The foundation of the hospital also marks a change in the Norman nobility's attitude to the care of the sick. A generation ago rich men left their money for the founding of monasteries. Today their sons might leave money for the building of hospitals and hospices (→ 1123).

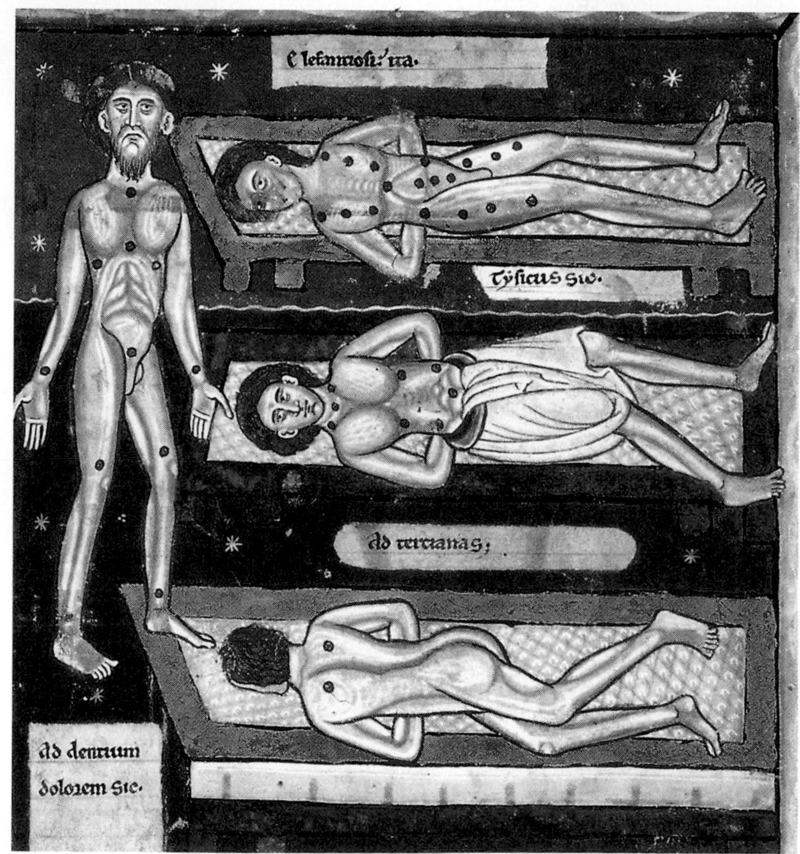

Patients prepared for examination (from a 12th-century medical text).

Henry supports two nephews in France

France, April 1117
King Henry of England is at war with the king of France in support of Count Theobald of Blois and his brother Stephen. Theobald and Stephen are the sons of Henry's sister Adela. When Theobald rebelled against the king of France last year, Henry sent him troops. Now the king of France has sworn to take Normandy from Henry and give it to William Clito [prince], the son of Henry's brother, Robert Curthose.

Brought up at the English court, Stephen is a particular favourite with Henry, who made him count of Mortain (in Normandy) as well as giving him English lands. Stephen is poised to become one of England's chief magnates (→ 1118).

1118 - 1122

Normandy, September 1118. Count Baldwin of Flanders, unlike his predecessors hostile to King Henry of England's rule in Normandy, is wounded invading the duchy (→ 6/1119).

Munster, 13 March 1119. Muirchertach Ua Briain, who abdicated as self-styled high king of Ireland in 1116, dies at Killaloe (→ autumn 1119).

Flanders, June 1119. Count Baldwin dies of wounds which he received during his unsuccessful invasion of Normandy in 1118 (→ 20/8).

Normandy, September 1119. Despite a defeat last month, King Louis VI of France again invades the duchy (→ 20/11).

Gisors, France, 20 November 1119. Pope Calixtus II, on hearing of King Louis VI's appeal against Henry, arranges a peace between them (→ 1120).

Ireland, 1120. Toirrdelbach Ua Conchobair, the king of Connacht, who claimed Munster on the death of Muirchertach last year, revives the old festival known as the *Oenach Tailten* [Fair of Teltown] (→ 1122).

France, 1120. William the Atheling, the son of King Henry, pays homage to Louis VI for the duchy of Normandy in place of his father (→ 26/11).

Fife, 1120. Eadmer, the new bishop of St Andrews, is sent from Canterbury at the request of King Alexander (→ 1124).

England, 29 January 1121. After the death of his son William the Atheling, recently married to Matilda of Anjou, King Henry marries Adelaide, the daughter of Count Godfrey VII of Louvain (→ c.1123).

Reading, Berkshire, 18 June 1121. King Henry founds a Cluniac abbey (c.1128).

Lothian, c.1121. Alexander founds the first royal burgh in Scotland at Berwick-Upon-Tweed, in the hope that the privileges granted to its merchants will increase international trade (→ c.1125).

Ireland, 1122. Toirrdelbach Ua Conchobair of Connacht proclaims himself high king of all Ireland (→ 1127).

Tayside, 12 June 1122. Queen Sybilla, the wife of King Alexander and illegitimate daughter of King Henry of England, dies suddenly at Loch Tay. She was said to be immodest and lacking in refinement (→ spring 1124).

Ambitious Connacht king bids for the top

Ireland, autumn 1119
Muirchertach Ua Briain, the king of Munster, has died, and his kingdom is threatened by a vigorous onslaught from Toirrdelbach Ua Conchobair, the young and ambitious king of Connacht. Toirrdelbach has invaded Munster with his allies and camped at Killaloe, and is reputed to have "hurled Kincora [where the Ua Briain lived], both stone and wood, into the Shannon" to show his contempt for the once-powerful family.

He then proceeded to destroy the Ua Briain crops, and later plundered Cashel and Ardfinnan with such severity that Munster is said "to have cried aloud". He has since divided Munster between Tadg Mac Carthaig of Desmond and the sons of Diarmait Ua Briain of Thomond. Toirrdelbach has secured the support of enough petty kingdoms to qualify as high king, and plans to enforce the prerogative of this office by celebrating the festival of the *Oenach Tailten* [Fair of Teltown].

Toirrdelbach, a fierce fighter and skilled strategist, seems determined to make Connacht a bastion from which to dominate the rest of Ireland. The brutal logic of conquest means that he has to reduce the power of other kingdoms to ensure the supremacy of his own (→ 1120).

'Merciful' Henry blinds and castrates rebel

Normandy, 1118
In the midst of his war with the king of France, Henry of England has uncovered a plot against his life from within his own household. One of his favourites, Herbert, the treasurer, has been caught plotting to assassinate the king and has confessed his crime. Herbert is a man of modest origins whom the king had been pleased to advance at court. His motive for plotting against the king's life is unknown. Yet because of his affection for him, King Henry has shown what passes for mercy. Instead of having him hanged – which would have been the normal penalty – the king has decreed that Herbert should suffer the lesser punishment of having both his eyes put out and being castrated (→ 9/1118).

'Good Queen Maud' is buried at abbey

Westminster, May 1118
Following her death on 1 May the funeral has taken place of one of the most outstanding women of recent times. Queen Matilda, who was not quite 40 years old when she died, was the wife of King Henry of England. The founder of the Augustinian priory of Holy Trinity at Aldgate, she now lies here at Westminster Abbey – a fitting place of rest for such an honourable queen.

Edith, as this daughter of King Malcolm III and Queen Margaret of Scotland was known in her own country, was educated by the nuns at Wilton and Romsey, but despite her caring and kind nature she made it clear that she did not wish to follow in her teachers' footsteps.

In any case, she suddenly found that, at the age of twenty, she had a suitor: Henry, the son of the Conqueror. Edith was a wise diplomatic match, being descended from the Saxon kings. She bore Henry two surviving children, William and Matilda.

Preferring a devout life in the world to one of seclusion, Matilda became known, through her good works and concern for the welfare of society, as "Good Queen Maud". She will be especially remembered as the founder of the leper hospital of St Giles-in-the-Fields of Holborn and of the Aldgate priory, so far the only major religious house in the City of London (→ 29/1/21).

One of 40 full-page miniatures from the St Albans Psalter [book of psalms], assembled by Abbot Geoffrey of St Albans c.1120.

French assault on duchy of Normandy put down by English

Normandy, 20 August 1119
King Henry of England has won a decisive victory over Louis VI, the king of France, in battle at Brémule near Noyon. Henry, with 500 knights, and Louis, with 400, were seeking each other in the field when the French burnt a barn and the English rode for the rising smoke.

Henry was accompanied by two of his illegitimate sons, Robert and Richard, while Louis had with him William Clito, the son of Robert Curthose of Normandy, eager to avenge his father, whom Henry took prisoner in 1106. The French knights launched a furious assault, but their horses were brought down and they were surrounded. But when their leader, William de Crispin, caught sight of Henry, whom he hated, he penetrated the mêlée and struck the king on the head with his sword. The blow was hard enough to force the king's helmet down on his forehead. Blood gushed from the wound.

Roger, one of the king's knights, struck down the assailant and managed to take him captive. Before long the French decided to abandon the struggle, leaving some 140 knights as prisoners of the triumphant English (→9/1119).

Heir dies in shipwreck

Normandy, 26 November 1120
King Henry sailed from the Norman port of Barfleur last night for England, leaving his sons and a great company of friends to follow in a new vessel called the *White Ship*. The king landed safely, but the *White Ship* foundered on a rock just offshore, capsized and sank.

No one has yet dared to tell the king that his son and heir, Prince William, and a younger, illegitimate, son, Richard, appear to have perished with all their friends – some 300 people in all. To make the tragedy worse, it appears to have been the result of drunkenness and recklessness.

Prince William ordered large supplies of wine for the ship's company, which became a party of wild and headstrong young men. Priests who came to bless the ship were received with rude guffaws.

Thomas, the ship's master, vowed to overtake the king's fleet, and the *White Ship* raced out, only to be run onto a submerged rock by her drunken helmsman. The ship capsized without warning. Those who had seen off their friends heard cries out at sea, but the night was dark and they could not see what had happened. Today one of only two survivors, a butcher from Rouen named Berold, was picked up clinging to a spar (→3/8/1124).

Henry in mourning (14th century).

Curative waters of Bath attract crowds as new city arises

Bath, Avon, December 1122
A new city is growing up among the ruins of this ancient spa, the "Aquae Sulis" of the Romans, set on a bend in the river Avon. The work was the inspiration of Bishop John of Tours, who has just died. When he arrived in Bath, in 1088, the main chamber enclosing the warm water spring was clogged with sand, and its vaulted roof had collapsed.

The bishop and the monks of Bath refurbished the spring as a bath, building niches against the inner face of the thick Roman-built walls of the enclosure, and also erected new edifices throughout the city. Former Roman underground channels have been re-excavated to bring water into the main reservoir, and there the lame, the sick, the mad and the fashionable frolic in the bubbling waters, hoping to be cured of their ailments.

Bishop John, who before coming to Bath was the king's chaplain, was rumoured to be an alcoholic. He died very suddenly, suffering a heart attack after eating his Christmas dinner. The medical skill that he possessed was said to have been acquired through practice rather than by training.

Moralists lambast women who let fashion go to their heads

High-born Anglo-Norman women demonstrating how to wear wimples.

London, c.1120
Ladies of fashion do not know what to do with their hair. While some are flaunting it, braiding it, dyeing it and even wearing wigs, others are hiding it behind wimples, the new headdresses from France.

Moralists pour scorn on women who expose and dye their hair or wear wigs. Women who wish to be seen as pure hold up the wimple – a veil of fine white linen or silk draped over the bosom, with its end drawn up and pinned to the hair, framing the face – as a mark of modesty. It is particularly favoured by widows and religious women. The effect is not always that which is apparently intended, however. As with any item of dress, it is not what is worn but how it is worn that is more revealing (→c.1155).

The Munster shrine of St Lachtin's arm, made of bronze with silver inlay to hold relics, c.1120.

1123 - 1128

Canterbury, Kent, 4 February 1123. William of Corbeil becomes archbishop following the death of Ralph d'Escures last year (→ 1/1127).

Scone, Tayside, spring 1124. King David bestows lands in Annan on his friend Robert de Brus [Bruce], a Norman noble who is now resident in Yorkshire (→ c.1140).

Normandy, 3 August 1124 King Henry of England secures a crushing victory over Norman insurgents at Bourgthéroulde (→ 22/7/28).

Fife, 1124. Prior Robert of Scone is the new bishop of St Andrews (→ 7/7/36).

Bangor, Co Down, 1124. Malachy, a reformer, is made both abbot and bishop of Down and Connor (→ 1/4/29).

Scotland, c.1125. David founds burghs at Dunfermline, Perth, Edinburgh and Stirling (→ 1175).

Windsor, Berkshire, 1 January 1127. English barons and nobles swear to recognize Henry's daughter Matilda as heir should he not have another son. David of Scotland was the first to promise support (→ 5/1127).

Rome, January 1127. William of Corbeil is made papal vicar and legate for life by Pope Honorius II, ending the primacy dispute between York and Canterbury (→ 4/1136).

Normandy, May 1127. Henry of England's daughter Matilda is betrothed to Geoffrey Plantagenet, the son of the count of Anjou (→ 17/6/28).

Dublin, 1127. Conchobar Ua Conchobair, the king of Leinster and Dublin, is ousted by the Dublin Norse.

Ireland, 1127. Toirrdelbach Ua Conchobair, aiming for the high-kingship, continues his country-wide attacks (→ 1128).

Leinster, 1128. After his ambush of Archbishop Cellach, King Tigernan Ua Ruairc of Breifne and Meath is defeated by Magnus Mac Lochlainn at Ardee (→ 1130).

Edinburgh, 1128. David founds Holyrood Abbey (→ 1136).

England, 1128. Hugh de Payns, the founder of the Order of the Temple, which protects Holy Land pilgrims, arrives to recruit (→ 3/1185).

Flanders, 27 July 1128 William Clito, the claimant to the English throne, dies of battle wounds (→ 8/9/31).

Salisbury bishop takes over government

London, June 1123

With the new Exchequer as his power base [*see report on page 211*], Bishop Roger of Salisbury has become the dominant influence in the king's entourage – to the extent that Henry has given him the job of governing England while he himself goes off to Normandy to put down a rebellion. Among Roger's many tasks as regent is to punish anyone who seeks to adulterate the coinage. The bishop has also adopted a much tougher policy of extracting donations from sheriffs, the men responsible for royal government in the shires.

Roger's influence with the king was demonstrated last year when a royal charter was granted to Merton priory. For several years Gilbert, the local sheriff, had been seeking a charter, which confers important privileges, but the king had always turned him down. Gilbert appealed to the bishop, who persuaded Henry that by granting the charter he would be "giving freely to God". Even so, Gilbert had to pay a stiff price (→ 5/1/25).

A carved fragment from Salisbury.

Earl of Huntingdon is new Scottish king

Stirling, 23 April 1124

King Alexander is dead, and since he has no legitimate children he is to be succeeded by his brother David, the earl of Huntingdon. King David is the sixth and youngest son of the great Malcolm Canmore and will be the fourth Scottish king to be enthroned at Scone.

Like most of Queen Margaret's children, he is known for his godly and pious life. He has a reputation already for generosity to the church in Scotland. Aged about 44, he has been married for 11 years to Maud de Senlis, the daughter of Waltheof, the earl of Huntingdon, who was executed for rebellion by William I of England in 1076.

David has considerable experience of the English court, where he lived first as an exile in the mid-1090s and then as a self-styled "brother of the queen" under King Henry. He was trained as a knight in an English household and probably fought under King Henry in the latter's successful campaigns in Normandy.

The new king is the greatest landowner in Scotland, and throughout Alexander's reign he has been the designated heir. It seems unlikely that his succession to the throne now will be met with any serious opposition (→ 1130).

Hospital is founded after saintly vision

London, 1123

Canon Rahere, a former courtier and jester of King Henry, has built a hospital and priory at Smithfield in the City of London. Rahere amassed a small fortune as a highly placed clerk at the court. Some years ago he fell ill on a journey of penance to Rome and made a vow that, if his life were spared, he would establish a hospital for the poor on his return. St Bartholomew appeared to him in a vision and named Smithfield as the site. The complex is dedicated to the saint, and it is said that his divine power is responsible for the recovery of the patients.

Formidable daughter of William the Conqueror opts for seclusion

France, c.1123

In common with growing numbers of her contemporaries [*see report on facing page*], Adela of Blois, the daughter of William the Conqueror, has decided to become a nun, retiring to the Cluniac priory at Marcigny-sur-Loire after a remarkable life. Her marriage to Count Stephen of Blois and Chartres in 1081 was one of convenience – being French, he was seen as a useful ally for the Normans against the French king.

If Adela had not been a woman she might have followed in her father's footsteps as a soldier and have become a crusader. Instead, she had to make do with tales of her husband's battles detailed in his letters to her. She then transformed these tales into brilliant tapestries and hung them in her bedroom. She reminded Stephen of his cowardly flight from the siege of Antioch and urged him to redeem his honour by taking the cross again.

When Stephen died in battle Adela continued to act as regent and bring up their eight children, which she did with great success. The eldest son, William, was never considered worthy of the inheritance, and with Adela's diligent manoeuvring Theobald, the next in line, became the beneficiary. Stephen and Henry, the other two sons, have made their fortunes in different areas with her help. Stephen became a warrior at his uncle King Henry of England's court, while Henry became a monk and, with his great intellect, is tipped to become a leading churchman (→ 1/1/27).

A crusader: the crusade provided Adela with artistic inspiration.

Minters who debased coins are castrated

The king sits in judgement at the Exchequer, from a 12th-century psalter.

Winchester, Hants, 5 January 1125
Bishop Roger of Salisbury tonight completed his grim task of punishing 94 minters judged guilty of debasing the royal currency. They were rounded up over Christmas and have been blinded and castrated on the orders of King Henry.

Henry, away in Normandy to put down a rebellion, had found himself confronted by enraged knights complaining that they were being paid in worthless coins made almost entirely of tin instead of silver. The king has been obliged to mount repeated campaigns against debasers of the coinage. Some 50 or more mints have been operating, and more than 240 coiners have been identified.

In Leicestershire last year, after a bad harvest and widespread famine, the circuit judge hanged 44 men and blinded and castrated six others. It is generally accepted that counterfeiters have never been more active. Many a man with a pound in his pocket found that it bought less than a pennyworth of goods at the market (→c.1180).

King's daughter marries a Plantagenet

Anjou, France, 17 June 1128
Matilda, the 26-year-old daughter and sole legitimate heir of Henry, the king of England, was married today at Le Mans to Geoffrey Plantagenet, the 15-year-old son of Count Fulk V of Anjou. (It was Fulk's daughter, also called Matilda, who was the wife of King Henry's ill-starred son, William.) This is Matilda's second marriage, her first having been to the late Holy Roman Emperor Henry V [*see family tree below*].

Her father hopes that this calculating political union will make for better relations with Anjou, but the English and Norman barons are unhappy. Having sworn over a year ago to accept Matilda as ruler after her father's death, they detest the idea that the son of a mere count is to join the royal family and stake a claim to the throne (→27/7).

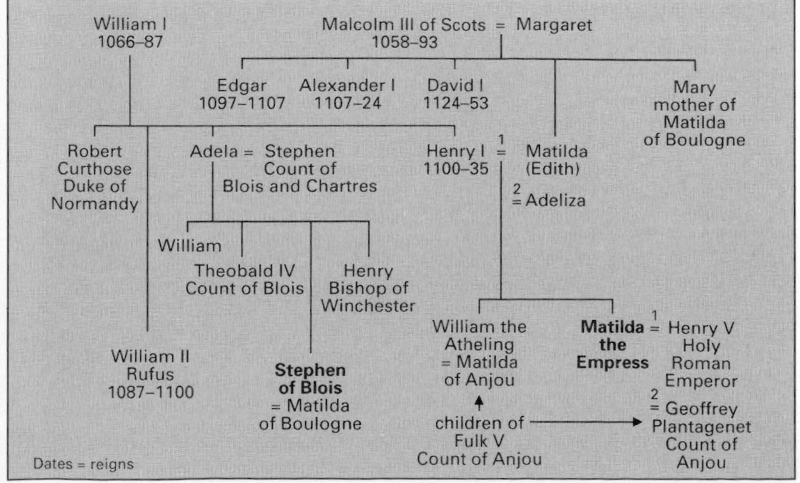

More and more men and women seek refuge from the world in houses of God

Britain, c.1128
Europe's fastest-growing monastic order is to build its first abbey in Britain. The Cistercians have chosen Waverley, in a remote part of Surrey, for the site. They are moving in under the guidance of the bishop of Winchester, William Gifford.

The Cistercians, founded at Cîteaux (*Cistercium* in Latin) near Dijon in 1098, are ascetics who wear habits made from coarse, undyed wool – for which they are nicknamed the White Monks. The simple life that they prefer is inspired by the sixth-century Rule of Benedict which prescribes hard manual labour and spartan, unadorned places of worship. Unlike other monastic orders they do not levy tithes or manorial rents, and they keep away from towns. The intellectual leader of the order is Bernard, the abbot of Clairvaux, who joined it 15 years after its founding. The abbot of the mother house in Cîteaux is an Englishman, Stephen Harding.

Another development among Britain's powerful and multiplying monasteries is the advent of foundations for women only. Some 25 Benedictine and three Cluniac nunneries have been set up during the last half century. Designed to promote piety and worship, "nunneries" also act as refuges for widowed, abandoned or persecuted women.

Bernard of Clairvaux at prayer.

They are as varied as the foundations for men. Some, such as Wilton, are attached to homes of aristocrats and offer a luxurious lifestyle. Others, such as those established by the fiercely misogynistic St Gilbert – who saw women as unclean beings – are rather primitive. But whatever the regime, nunneries, with their opportunities for learning as well as refuge, open up new paths for women (→9/5/31).

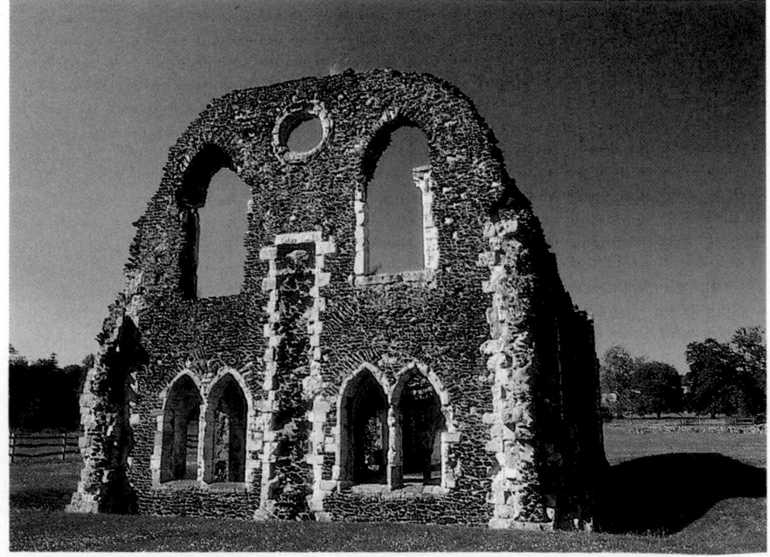

The remains of Waverley Abbey, the first Cistercian house in Britain.

1129-1134

Munster, 1 April 1129. Archbishop Cellach of Armagh, who mediated between High King Toirrdelbach Ua Conchobair and the Mac Lochlainn dynasty, dies (→ 1132).

Hampshire, 1129. Henry of Blois is consecrated as bishop of Winchester (→ 1/3/39).

Worcester, 25 January 1130. The efficacy of "trial by hot iron" – whereby defendants are forced to carry red-hot irons to determine a verdict – is questioned after three dubious acquittals (→ 1/1166).

Western Ireland, 1130. Toirrdelbach and his fleet ravage the coast. Tigernan Ua Ruairc, the king of Breifne, kills King Diarmait Ua Mael Sechlainn of Meath (→ 1131).

Grampian, 1130. A rebellion breaks out in Moray while King David is in England acting as a judge at a conspiracy trial of his brother-in-law, King Henry (→ 1131).

Gloucestershire, 9 May 1131. Walter fitzRichard de Clare, the lord of Chepstow, founds a Cistercian abbey at Tintern, in the Wye valley (→ 1146).

Northampton, 8 September 1131. The barons renew their allegiance to Matilda, the daughter of Henry and wife of Geoffrey of Anjou (→ 8/1133).

Scone, Tayside, 1131. Queen Maud, the pious English wife of King David, dies (→ 1134).

Ireland, 1132. Toirrdelbach invades Munster and establishes Muirchertach Ua Mael Sechlainn as king of Meath (→ 1136).

Co Kildare, 1132. Diarmait Mac Murchada, the king of Leinster, rapes and deposes the abbess of Kildare (→ 1136).

Armagh, 1132. Malachy, the abbot and bishop of Down and Connor, is consecrated archbishop (→ 1134).

Normandy, August 1133. King Henry of England visits his duchy following the birth at Le Mans in March of his grandson, Henry, to Matilda and Geoffrey (→ 3/2/34).

South Glamorgan, 3 February 1134. Duke Robert Curthose of Normandy, King Henry of England's brother, dies at Cardiff, having been held captive since 1106 (→ 10/1135).

Roxburgh, Borders, 1134. The rebel Malcolm mac Heth, the illegitimate nephew of David, is imprisoned (→ 5/2/36).

Lost secrets of the ancients uncovered

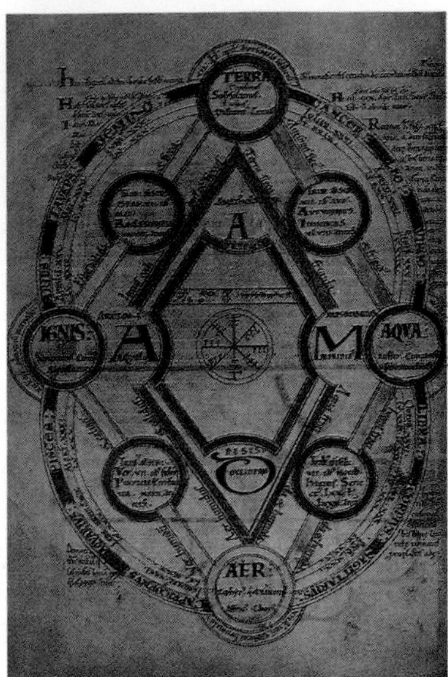

A planetary chart: aid to wisdom.

England, c.1130

The lost wisdom of the ancients in manipulating numbers is being rediscovered, thanks to Adelard, a monk from Bath. He is busy translating the works of the most sophisticated mathematicians of Arab civilization into Latin, making them more accessible to those in England who can read.

Adelard is also popularizing the insights of the ancient Greek mathematical masters – for example, he is translating the 13 books of mathematical propositions by Euclid, who taught in the legendary library of Alexandria some 1,300 years ago. In the process Adelard is devising a new sort of language allowing scholars to describe the world in terms of numbers (→ 1148).

Royal fun protected

England, c.1130

Much of England is being set aside for the pleasures of the king's hunt. "Forests" – which need not be woodland – are carved out of common land and filled with boar and deer, protected by savage penalties from would-be poachers. Forest law, such as that applied in the New Forest in the south, is basically the king's arbitrary word and is much resented. Beasts which prey on royal forest game are to be killed, as are the outlaws who often take refuge there.

Alliance against savage raider collapses

Ireland, 1131

An alliance forged between Munster, Leinster, Meath and the Norse – in order to ward off savage raids against them by King Toirrdelbach Ua Conchobair of Connacht – has collapsed, bringing the welcome relief to Toirrdelbach of a year's truce. The past ten years have not brought Toirrdelbach the prize which he has so eagerly sought: to be acknowledged as the high king of Ireland, not just "high king with opposition". That he has achieved countless victories cannot be denied, but he has failed to break the power of the other kingdoms by mobilizing his cavalry and his river and sea fleets to crush resistance in one concerted effort (→ 1132).

A cross made for Toirrdelbach.

Written code of courtly customs published

England, c.1134

King Henry has set a precedent in the ordering of his household. He has had its regular customs set down in writing and published as the *Constitutio Domus Regis [Establishment of the Royal Household]*, dividing the household into five main administrative departments: chapel, chamber, hall, buttery and constabulary-marshalsea.

The chapel staff are entrusted with the king's spiritual and secretarial needs. At their head is the chancellor, and beneath him are the master of the writing office and several chaplains, who oversee the production and ordering of the ever-growing flow of government documents. The chamber, which once dealt only with a king's domestic affairs, now deals with the whole system of royal finances, providing money for the king's immediate needs. It is headed by a master-chamberlain and a treasurer.

The hall and buttery deal with the provision of refreshments. The constables and marshals see to the running of the outdoor staff; constables also act as hunting officials so that the king can enjoy his sport. Altogether the household provides employment for the great officers of state, men with the ear of the king and upon whose advice he depends.

Royal wedding: a manuscript illustration representing the marriage feast for King Henry's daughter Matilda and Holy Roman Emperor Henry V.

Welsh archbishop dies while in Rome

Rome, 1134
Archbishop Urban of Llandaff has died in Rome shortly after appealing to Pope Innocent II to restore to him large areas of the dioceses of St David's and Hereford which, he alleged, were stolen from Llandaff. The pursuit of this claim occupied Urban for 30 years, amounting to an obsession.

Urban travelled to Rheims in 1119 to present his grievances to Pope Calixtus II, then twice went to Rome to petition Calixtus's successor, Honorius II. However, in 1131, Innocent II referred the case to a church commission which ruled against him. Urban then set out on his last journey to Rome. Although Urban's critics accuse him of tampering with the evidence in putting forward his case, he demonstrated a compelling determination to regain his church's lands (→23/4/88).

Intriguing chapel is built at Tipperary

Munster, 1134
Cormac's chapel has been consecrated at Cashel, in Co Tipperary. Begun in 1127 by Cormac Mac Carthaig after he was restored to the throne of Desmond, it has aroused interest because of its ornamental design, largely derived from foreign influences. The great north door, decorated with carved tympana, is perhaps its most impressive feature. Upset that this religious centrepiece has been sited in Munster, the clergy of Connacht refused to attend the consecration (→1136).

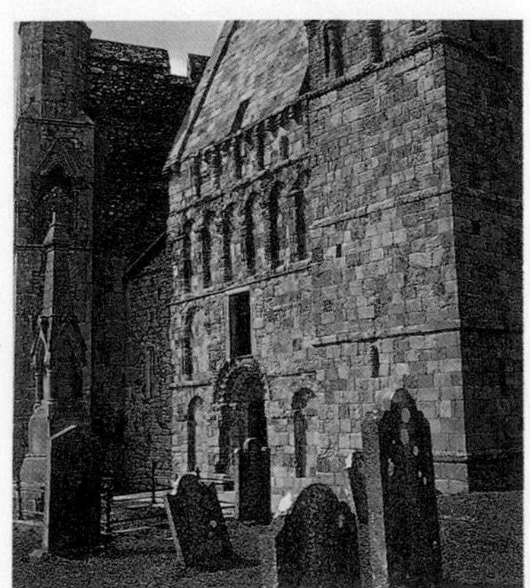
Cormac's Romanesque chapel.

Norman ingenuity is set in stone for all time as England is adorned by the vaulted splendour of massive new cathedrals

Durham, c.1133
High on a promontory above the river Wear, one of the greatest buildings in Europe soars into the sky. The first stone of the church of the abbey of Durham was laid on 11 August 1093, and now, 40 years on, the structure is nearing completion.

Durham is in the Norman style, characterized by arcades of round arches on stout pillars, massive walls and chevron [zigzag] ornament, but with some striking new features, especially in the vault of the nave. Rather than spanning each section of the vault between two pillars directly opposite each other, in the manner of a bridge, the architect has thrown the arches crossways between diagonally opposite pillars. This idea is not new but has never before been used for such a high vault. The chevron-decorated ribbed arches – ribs are another "first" for Durham – create a vault that needs far less stone for stability. The crossways-ribbed arches are separated by other single arches.

Although Durham stands in a class of its own, it is part of a wider development. Edward the Confessor used Norman models when planning his abbey at Westminster around 1050, and ever since 1066 the Normans, who found Anglo-Saxon church buildings uninspiring, have been involved in a vast ecclesiastical rebuilding programme, financed by the new bishops. Archbishop Lanfranc had Canterbury rebuilt, while Bishop Walkelin at Winchester and his brother Abbot Simeon at Ely proved enthusiastic architects. It was Simeon who commissioned Ely's massive nave with its 13 bays. Impressive new cathedrals are also being built at Norwich, Peterborough in Cambridgeshire and Southwell in Nottinghamshire.

The Normans' ultimate inspiration derives from Roman public buildings such as the basilica. The spirit of these cathedrals, like that of the Roman Empire itself, is of unchallengeable strength (→5/9/74).

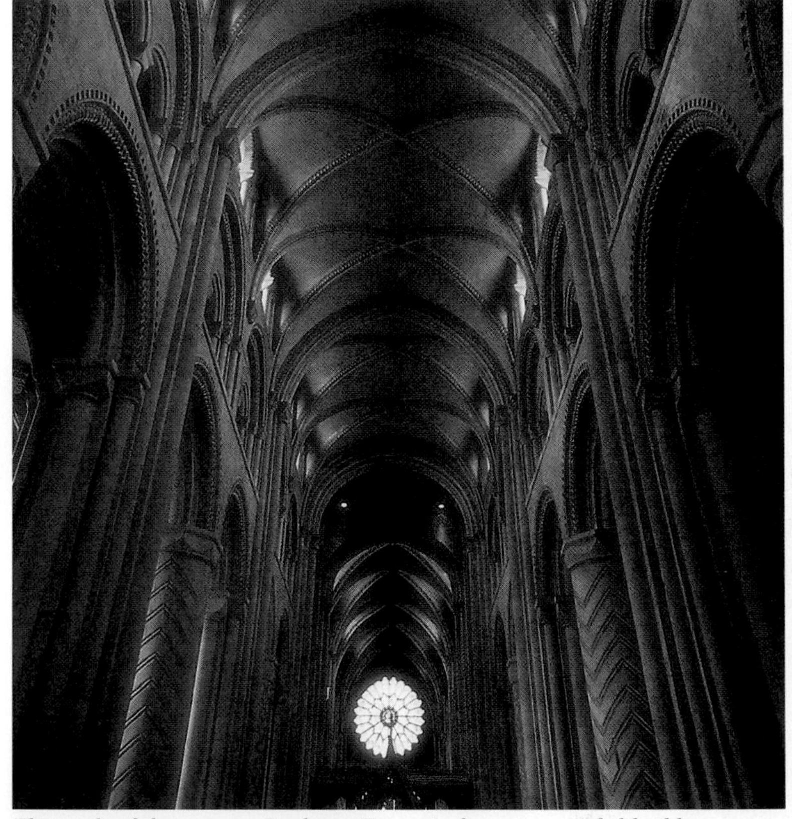
The vault of the nave at Durham, Europe's first stone-roofed building.

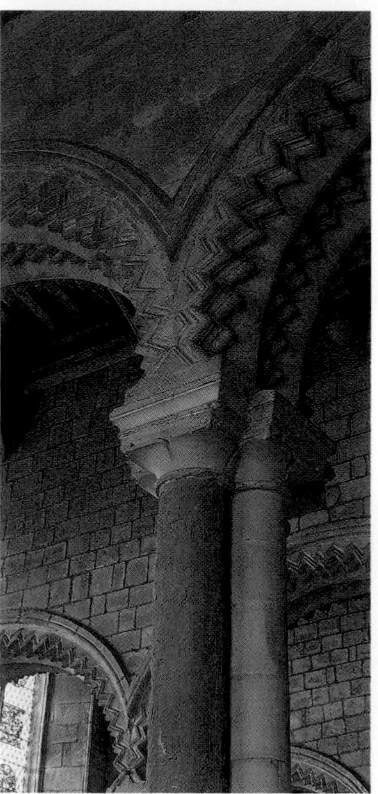
The Galilee chapel at Durham: arches with chevron decoration.

Southwell Minster, Notts, begun in 1108: the striking west front.

1135 - 1136

Normandy, 25 November 1135. Henry, the king of England and duke of Normandy, falls violently ill at his hunting lodge at Lyons-la-Forêt, near Rouen (→ 1/12).

Rouen, Normandy, 2 December 1135. The body of King Henry is embalmed in St Mary's cathedral and prepared to be taken to England for burial in Reading (→ 20).

Normandy, 20 December 1135. Empress Matilda, the daughter of Henry, seeks the support of her cousin Count Theobald IV of Blois in her claim to the English throne, only to learn that his younger brother, Stephen, has claimed the throne for himself (→ 22/12).

Normandy, December 1135. Empress Matilda loses the support of Earl William of Warenne, who seizes Rouen, and her half-brother Robert, the earl of Gloucester, who seizes the treasury at Falaise (→ 4/2/36).

Reading, Berks, 4 February 1136. The body of King Henry is buried in the Cluniac abbey which he founded (→ 4/1136).

Cardigan, Dyfed, 1136. The sons of Gruffudd ap Cynan retake the town from the Normans (→ 4/1136).

Durham, 5 February 1136. David, the king of Scotland, and Stephen, the new king of England, sign a treaty which settles their dispute over land in England. David's son receives the earldom of Huntingdon, but Stephen keeps Northumberland (→ 4/1138).

Usk valley, Gwent, April 1136. The murder this month of the Norman noble Richard fitzGilbert de Clare by the brothers Morgan and Iorwerth, the heirs to the royal line of Glamorgan, has led to general unrest against rule by the Normans (→ 8/1136).

Normandy, April 1136. King Stephen sends his friend Count Waleran of Meulan to deal with the revolt in favour of Geoffrey of Anjou (→ 3/1137).

Glasgow, 7 July 1136. The cathedral is consecrated in King David's presence (→ 1142).

Ireland, 1136. Dynastic clashes occur following the illness of Toirrdelbach Ua Conchobair of Connacht, the "high king with opposition" (→ 1141).

Armagh, 1136. Malachy is ousted from his archbishopric by Abbot Niall mac Aeda and retires to Down (→ 6/3/52).

'Angevins' make bid for English throne

Northern France, October 1135
The succession to the crown of England has been thrown into chaos by a sudden war between King Henry and the "Angevins", a dissident faction in Normandy whose leaders include Count Geoffrey of Anjou and his wife Empress Matilda, the king's daughter, the principal contenders for the throne. Matilda is being kept in the background, but Geoffrey is not hiding his ambition to claim Normandy and England.

Geoffrey's campaign is a brutal one – he has burnt villages and aroused considerable discontent. As part of Matilda's marriage dowry the count has demanded certain castles in Normandy which he would probably use as a power base. Wisely, Henry has refused to agree to this and is attempting to keep the succession under his control. The king is furious at this challenge to his authority from his son-in-law, and to deal with the threat he has seized land from rebel supporters. Having acquired the castle of Alençon, he is fortifying it, filling the people with fear of a devastating war to follow (→ 25/11).

Succession crisis looms

Normandy, 1 December 1135
Henry, the king of England, died aged 67 at the hunting lodge of Lyons-la-Forêt near Rouen today. He had arrived a week ago to go hunting but fell ill after eating lampreys. He confessed his sins and told his illegitimate son Robert to take £60,000 from his treasury to pay his household and soldiers. His body is to be taken to the monastery that he founded at Reading, if it can be preserved for long enough.

The problem of the succession is that Henry's only legitimate son – there are plenty of illegitimate ones – was drowned in the *White Ship* 15 years ago. Although the king remarried following the death of Queen Matilda, the marriage was childless.

Henry, by Matthew Paris (c.1250).

Henry's only legitimate descendant is his daughter Matilda, who was married to Holy Roman Emperor Henry V, who died in 1125. [*see family tree on page 217*]. Henry made his barons swear to receive her as Lady of England in 1127, and the next year she married Geoffrey Plantagenet, now count of Anjou. But Henry crucially failed to provide them with control of any of the castles of England or Normandy – indeed he had recently quarrelled with both of them. As a consequence the Norman barons are divided into two camps: those who support Geoffrey and Matilda, and those who had remained loyal to Henry. The legacy of the master-politician of the age is, ironically, a dangerous power vacuum (→ 2/12).

Arthurian legend published in 'History of the Kings of Britain'

England and Wales, 1136
Geoffrey of Monmouth, a Welsh churchman and renowned scholar, has included an elaborate account of the exploits of "King Arthur" in his *History of the Kings of Britain*, a chronicle of events from prehistoric times to the year 800. Until now the legend of Arthur – apparently based on the shadowy British leader who flourished some time around 500 [*see page 98*] – has only been a part of other tales.

The Welsh chronicler describes deeds both heroic and lurid; bravery and fine feelings alternate with violence and cruelty. The portentous prophecies of a wizard, Merlin, jostle with vivid accounts of battles, where soldiers "vomit forth their souls with their life blood". Geoffrey claims that his work is based on written sources and oral tradition; critics, however, say that it is "romance masquerading as history" and accuse him of trying to give Britain a glorious past (→ c.1168).

Arthur kills the Saxon leader Hengist at Badon: a 15th-century depiction.

King's nephew in dash to seize crown

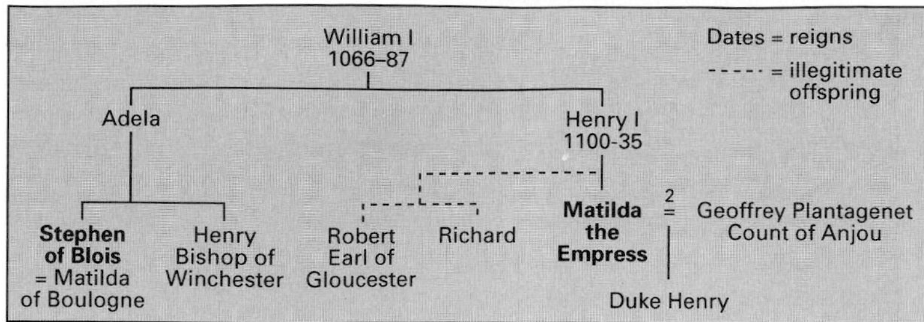

A 14th-century image of Stephen.

London, 22 December 1135
A hectic dash across the Channel, shrewd diplomacy and a dubious oath have secured the crown of England for Stephen of Blois, the late King Henry's nephew. Stephen was anointed king by the archbishop of Canterbury today.

When Henry died of food poisoning on 1 December the question of the succession was unresolved. The "official" candidate was the king's daughter, Matilda, but her husband, Geoffrey, the count of Anjou, is a traditional enemy of the Normans – indeed he is at war with Normandy.

Stephen wasted no time. He was in Boulogne when the news of Henry's death in Rouen was received, and he set sail immediately. He hurried to London, where he was received as king.

Stephen's subsequent move was crucial: a fast ride to Winchester, where his brother Henry, the bishop, agreed to induce Bishop Roger of Salisbury to recognize his claim. As justiciar, Roger controls the government of England. Henry also used his influence with William Pont de l'Arche, the keeper of the royal treasury.

With these all-important men willing to support him, Stephen returned to London. The suspicious archbishop was won over when one of Stephen's supporters, Hugh Bigod, swore that he had witnessed a death-bed change of mind by King Henry. Matilda, however, has yet to be persuaded. The widow of Holy Roman Emperor Henry V, now married to Geoffrey of Anjou, she is a formidable woman no less hungry for power than her cousin, Stephen, and is certain to be a focus of opposition to him (→4/2/36).

Welsh nationalists rise up to throw out Anglo-Normans

Wales, August 1136
Welsh nationalists have taken advantage of the death of King Henry of England and Stephen's *coup d'état* to launch a series of uprisings against their Anglo-Norman masters. Rebellions have broken out in Gower, Kidwelly, Gwent, Brecon and the area known as Ceredigion. In April, Richard fitzGilbert, the Norman lord of Ceredigion, died at the hands of the Welsh in the Usk valley. The Normans now confront the serious possibility of losing the whole of Ceredigion with its vital castles.

The power of the rebellion has staggered the occupiers: at Crug Mawr, north of Cardigan, a powerful Anglo-Norman and Fleming force was annihilated in a massive battle.

The Anglo-Norman "colonization" of Wales depends largely on the continued momentum and confidence of the occupying force. Many Normans feel "disinherited" in the wake of Stephen's sudden takeover, and morale is low. Welsh leaders – particularly those from the kingdoms of Gwynedd, Deheubarth and Morgannwg – have not hesitated to seize the opportunity to profit from this (→1137).

Pledge of religious freedom wins ovation

An enamel plaque by a French goldsmith c.1150 of Bishop Henry of Blois.

England, April 1136
King Stephen has made a ringing declaration of religious freedom to bishops and clergy at the Easter royal court. Simony – the buying and selling of church posts and fake holy relics – is now illegal, he announced, and also said that "jurisdiction and power over churchmen and all clerks and their property and the distribution of the goods of the church are in the hands of the bishops". Stephen has granted all property held by the churches on the day of William the Conqueror's death "in free and absolute possession", and promised to look into complaints. Churches are still liable to be plundered when bishoprics are vacant, and bishops (in their capacity as barons) are still subject to royal justice (→9/1/39).

Cistercian abbey is set up in Scotland

Melrose, Borders, 1136
King David has announced the foundation of the first Cistercian abbey to be established in Scotland. The new abbey will be located here in the Scottish borders on the site of an earlier monastery dedicated to St Cuthbert. David appears to have heard of the Cistercians through a relative who is a lord in Yorkshire, where the monastic order has established an abbey at Rievaulx. Its commitment to simplicity and to manual labour such as sheep rearing impressed the king, who has lent support to several monastic bodies.

Richard, the abbot of the abbey at Melrose, himself comes from Rievaulx, as do many of the monks who will be joining him in Scotland. Until now it has been the Benedictine priory at Dunfermline – where David's mother, Queen Margaret, is buried – that has benefited the most from royal patronage (→1160).

The patriarch Moses at rest, as drawn by Master Hugo, from a superbly illuminated bible made at Bury St Edmunds c.1135.

Normandy, March 1137. King Stephen of England makes peace with his elder brother, Count Theobald IV of Blois, at Bayeux (→ 5/1137).

Normandy, May 1137. Stephen is recognized as king of England by King Louis VI of France (→ 6/1137).

Carmarthen, Dyfed, 1137. Owain and Cadwaladr, the sons of Gruffudd ap Cynan, continue the revolt against Norman rule.→

Northumberland, April 1138. King David of Scotland invades to support his niece Matilda, the late King Henry of England's daughter, in her claim to the throne (→ 9/6).

Lancashire, 9 June 1138. An English army is defeated at Clitheroe by William, David's nephew (→ 22/8).

Cumbria, 26 September 1138. After King David's defeat at the Battle of the Standard, Alberic, the bishop of Ostia and papal legate, negotiates a treaty for David and King Stephen at Carlisle (→ 11/11).

Wark, Northumberland, 11 November 1138. The castle surrenders to the Scots (→ 1139).

Normandy, November 1138. Waleran of Meulan and William of Ypres, allies of Stephen, besiege Robert of Gloucester at Caen after forcing out Geoffrey of Anjou (→ 6/1139).

Canterbury, Kent, 9 January 1139. Abbot Theobald of Bec becomes archbishop (→ 1148).

England, 1 March 1139. Henry of Blois, the bishop of Winchester, who has designs on the archbishopric of Canterbury, is made papal legate (→ 7/4/41).

Leeds, West Yorkshire, 1139. Stephen seizes the castle in his march on the Scots (→ 9/4).

Bodmin, Cornwall, January 1140. Stephen quells a revolt by Earl Reginald, one of King Henry's bastard sons, and makes Count Alan of Brittany earl of Cornwall (→ 1/1140).

England, January 1140. Stephen's ally Waleran of Meulan pillages the Vale of Evesham in reprisal for attacks by Empress Matilda's supporters in England and Normandy (→ 2/1140).

England, February 1140. Eustace, the son of King Stephen, is betrothed to Constance, the sister of Louis VII of France (→ 6/1/41).

Distrust of mercenaries weakens army

Livarot, France, June 1137

Convulsed by internal feuds, King Stephen of England's army came close to disintegration here as barons collected their vassals and left the camp. One reason for the conflict, which has left many dead, is the distrust between Norman barons and Stephen's Flemish mercenaries led by William of Ypres.

From the moment of King Henry's death Normandy has been in chaos, and great hope had been placed in Stephen as a peacemaker. He certainly made peace with his brother Theobald – a former claimant to the English throne – with a substantial pension.

Stephen has also formed an alliance with the king of France, Louis VI, and would have turned his army on that of Geoffrey of Anjou – who is married to Matilda, Stephen's principal rival for the English throne – but for these internal problems (→ 11/1138).

An effigy of Geoffrey of Anjou.

STEPHEN'S CONTINENTAL POSSESSIONS, 1137

COUNTY OF BOULOGNE
belongs to Stephen through marriage
St Valery
Amiens
Cherbourg
English Channel
Barfleur
Eu
Rouen
Dives
Seine
Bayeux
Caen
Meulan
Coutances
Falaise
NORMANDY
Mantes
Paris
BRITTANY
Domfront
Alencon
Chartres
MAINE
BLOIS
ILE DE FRANCE
Le Mans
belongs to Stephen's elder brother Count Theobald
ANJOU
Stephen's lands in France
Allied territory

William I 1066–87
William II Rufus 1087–1100
Henry I 1100–35
Adela
Matilda = Geoffrey of Anjou
Stephen 1135–54

Scots routed at 'Battle of the Standard'

Yorkshire, 22 August 1138

The barons of Yorkshire have routed a huge army under King David of Scotland, who has been forced to retreat to Carlisle. All year northern England has been suffering violent raids by the Scottish king, thought by some to be in support of his niece Empress Matilda's struggle to gain the English crown. This latest campaign began in July after David rejected English terms for peace.

At Cawton Moor near Northallerton, Archbishop Thurstan of York had a ship's mast set up as an emblem for the English. To it were tied church banners and a silver casket holding the consecrated bread for Holy Communion. (Because of this, the struggle has been dubbed "the Battle of the Standard".) The Scots' attack was led by men of Galloway who, although brave, were cut down by the better-equipped English. Today's defeat is a terrible blow for Matilda. The campaigns of her uncle have only succeeded in uniting the barons of Yorkshire against her (→ 26/9).

Welsh ruler's death may spur rebellion

Gwynedd, 1137

The death of Gruffudd ap Cynan marks the end of an era. For more than 40 years he has not only ruled this region but also towered over all the warring princes of Wales. He lived through a period when Norman power was making massive inroads into Wales.

Gruffudd decided that the Normans were too powerful for him to fight them, so he played the role of client prince. He showed a huge talent for compromise. Under him there was peace; the economy prospered as never before, and there was a flowering of church architecture and a renaissance of poetry and music. In the last two years, as Norman power has waned, there have been sporadic revolts by Welsh princes. With Gruffudd dead, this process is likely to accelerate and fragment the country (→ 1146).

Jewish community expands in England

England, c.1140

England's Jewish population, while by no means large, has established itself as a permanent and important part of the national life, both intellectual and economic. Jews, who first settled in London, and whose largest concentration is still there – in Westcheap close to St Paul's – are now spread throughout the country, in places such as Lincoln, Oxford, Norwich, Bungay and Cambridge.

Jews are the only people permitted to trade as moneylenders, and as such their fortunes, which are sometimes quite substantial, are vital to the king and his magnates, all of whom need a ready source of cash. In return the king has granted them his own protection, or placed them under that of a local lord. Anyone molesting a Jew therefore runs the risk of incurring royal displeasure.

That is the theory, but it is not for nothing that the Jews are noted as among the first to be building stone houses – they need them for protection. Wealth makes for jealousy which in turn provides a ready excuse for attacks (→ 3/9/89).

Scots king bounces back from defeat to strike a diplomatic bargain with England

Durham, 9 April 1139
In a treaty signed here today King David of Scots has been allowed to keep the lands won when he broke another treaty signed with King Stephen of England three years ago and invaded England in support of Empress Matilda. Stephen, for his part, will get the security on his northern border that he badly needs in his battle against Matilda.

King David was actually defeated last August [*see report on page 222*], but his powerful army has remained in control of much of the north, forcing Stephen to negotiate. David's eldest son, Henry, has been given the earldom of Northumberland (but not the castles of Newcastle and Bamburgh) and keeps that of Huntingdon. In return David has recognized Stephen as king of England, promised to keep the peace and agreed to give hostages to ensure that he does not break his word again.

Earl Henry will probably follow Stephen south to support him against the empress, and there is even talk of his marrying into one of the families which support the king (→28/5/41).

Stephen launches onslaught on bishops

West-country stronghold: 20th-century view of Sherborne Old Castle, Dorset.

Devizes, Wiltshire, June 1139
One of England's principal bishops – Roger le Poer of Salisbury, who is also the justiciar – was held prisoner in a cowshed near here as his nephew defied the king from the battlements of the local castle.

Roger and his nephews, Nigel and Alexander, had been ordered to King Stephen's presence at Oxford. Fighting broke out between the king's men and the bishop's escort – few doubt that Stephen deliberately provoked the trouble – and Roger and Alexander were arrested. Nigel escaped and rode to Devizes Castle, one of several owned by Roger. After three days of siege, Stephen produced Roger and threatened to starve him to death if Nigel did not surrender. The attempt failed. Only a threat to hang Roger's son ended the siege.

The show-down with Bishop Roger is part of a much wider struggle for power. The king is unhappy with the influence that bishops wield – especially ones such as Roger, who has collected a formidable retinue and built several strong castles. To avoid direct confrontation Stephen has tried to weight the dice in his own favour by creating a host of new earldoms and giving them to his own men, despite the fact that only one, Geoffrey de Mandeville, has any administrative experience (→10/1139).

'Normanization' of Scotland is intensified

Strathclyde, c.1140
King David's policy of "Normanizing" the Scottish nobility continues to attract land-hungry settlers from England. They arrive not through military conquest but at the king's invitation and are soon the happy recipients of crown lands and possibly titles.

This peaceful feudal settlement has been going on for years now. A major Yorkshire baron, Robert de Brus [Bruce], was given a huge land grant in Annan when David became king in 1124. Parts of Lothian and elsewhere have been given to Hugh de Morville, whose estate lies in Huntingdon. More recently Walter fitzAlan, the younger son of a Breton noble living in Shropshire, received both land and the title of "steward of the household", a new post in Scotland based on Norman custom.

These men and many others are introducing Norman-style feudalism, parcelling out land to inferiors in return for services, particulary military. This pattern, along with "motte-and-bailey" castles, is gradually spreading throughout the Scottish lowlands (→c.1150).

Religious art of the 12th century: a Herefordshire ivory (left) shows an emaciated Christ lowered from the cross, while the Shaftesbury Psalter (right) has the three Maries, in fashionable wimples, at the empty tomb.

Empress rallies supporters in south-west

West Sussex, October 1139
Despite the growing threat to his throne, King Stephen has allowed his rival, Empress Matilda, safe conduct across the south of England to Bristol following the threat of military action here. Along with her illegitimate half-brother Robert, the earl of Gloucester, Matilda arrived at Arundel Castle last month at the invitation of King Henry's widow, Queen Adeliza (married last year to William d'Aubigny, the earl of Arundel) – clearly with an eye to rallying support against Stephen.

No one expected such a fast reaction from the king, whose army marched to Arundel and immediately got ready to besiege the castle. Robert had already managed to slip away to Bristol, and the garrison, suspecting that it had little or no chance, gave up the empress at once – only for Stephen to let her go.

It seems that the king's clemency was prompted by the advice of his brother, Bishop Henry of Winchester. Yet even as Matilda heads westwards, at least two leading noblemen, Brian fitzCount of Wallingford and Miles, the sheriff of Gloucester, are preparing to rise against Stephen.

Some observers are saying that Stephen is not ruthless enough for the fight lying ahead of him. Although Robert is the real leader of his opponents, Matilda is already attracting other malcontents like moths to a candle. The great danger is that such people can use Matilda's cause to claim that their own rebellion is legitimate (→1/1140).

1141 - 1142

Lincoln, 6 January 1141. Earl Ranulf of Chester seizes the castle and lays claim to the city (→ 2/1141).

Winchester, Hampshire, 7 April 1141. Empress Matilda is declared "Lady of the English" by Henry of Blois as a preliminary to being crowned in London (→ 6/1141).

Scotland, 28 May 1141. King David breaks his two-year-old treaty with King Stephen of England and heads south to support Matilda (→ 1144).

England, September 1141. Stephen's main supporter, Count Waleran of Meulan, the earl of Worcester, defects to Matilda's side (→ 14/9).

Winchester, 3 November 1141. Peace talks break down completely. An exchange is agreed whereby Stephen is released from Bristol and Robert of Gloucester from Rochester (→ 25/12).

Canterbury, Kent, 25 December 1141. Stephen and his queen, Matilda, are crowned again by Archbishop Theobald (→ 5/1142).

Dublin, 1141. Conchobar Ua Briain, the co-ruler in Munster, lays claim to the kingdom of Dublin (→ 1142).

Northampton, May 1142. Stephen falls ill. Matilda, who is based in Oxford, sends word to her husband, Geoffrey of Anjou, for aid in a last attempt to seize power (→ 6/1142).

Wareham, Dorset, June 1142. Earl Robert of Gloucester, the illegitimate half-brother of the empress, takes ship for Normandy (→ 9/1142).

Oxford, September 1142. King Stephen, having seized Wareham, besieges Matilda in Oxford Castle (→ 11/1142).

Wareham, November 1142. Robert returns with the empress's nine-year-old son, Henry (→ 12/1142).

Highland, 1142. Bishop Wimund of the Isles has been tricked into surrendering after a rebellion by an offer of peace. In punishment for his actions King David blinds and castrates him (→ 8/11/76).

Co Louth, 1142. Ireland's first Cistercian abbey is founded at Mellifont at the request of Malachy, the former archbishop of Armagh (→ 1148).

Munster, 1142. King Conchobar Ua Briain, who last year claimed Dublin, dies at Killaloe (→ 1143).

England rent by turmoil of civil war

The royal army prepares for the battle at Lincoln: a picture made c.1200.

First blood of the conflict shed at Lincoln

Bristol, Avon, February 1141
Stephen, the king of England, is today a prisoner here in the castle of Earl Robert of Gloucester after being captured in battle at Lincoln. He was there fighting Earl Ranulf of Chester when Robert took him unawares and overwhelmed his forces. Now he has been brought before Empress Matilda, Robert's half-sister, who claims the English throne as her own.

Stephen fought valiantly, laying about him with a two-headed axe. When that broke he used his sword to equal effect until one of Robert's men hit him on the head with a stone. It was another of Robert's vassals who then shouted: "Here, everyone, here! I've got the king!"

Trouble started when Stephen gave Cumberland to Henry, the son of King David of Scots, ignoring the claims of Ranulf, the heavily moustached earl of Chester. Ranulf and his half-brother William captured Lincoln Castle to register their annoyance. It was while Stephen was trying to dislodge Ranulf that he found his own army under attack by Matilda's forces, led by Robert (→ 7/4).

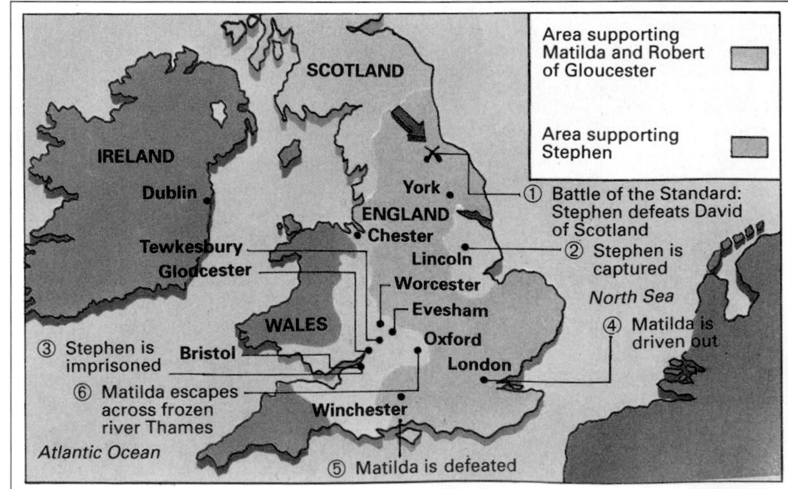

This map lists in numerical order the principal events of the conflict of 1139-42 between King Stephen of England and the Empress Matilda, his cousin and rival for the throne.

Empress forced to flee London's fury

London, June 1141
A sudden uprising by the citizens of London has made it necessary for Empress Matilda to flee to Oxford just as she was on the point of being crowned queen of England. She was lucky to escape with her life when the mob stormed a banquet at Westminster, which had been intended as a pre-coronation feast. The presence on the south bank of the Thames of an army led by her rival Queen Matilda, the wife of King Stephen, had emboldened the Londoners to attack.

The empress believes that her claim to the English crown is better than that of Stephen, whom she is holding captive in Bristol [*see report*

King Stephen and Queen Matilda: the empress's rivals on a coin.

left], or of his queen, Matilda. Her personality is so overbearing, however, and her political judgement so poor that she has alienated many of her supporters. She dismisses lords and bishops with contempt and refuses all advice. By treating Londoners with similar disdain she has stirred their fury and lost herself the crown.

The empress had sought huge sums of money from the Londoners. When told that they could not afford to pay because the war had made them poor, she lost her temper and refused to lower her demands. This, coupled with the appearance of the queen's army on the south bank, has made London regret that it ever backed her bid for the throne (→ 9/1141).

Matilda's forces are routed at Winchester

Winchester, Hants, 14 Sept 1141
Empress Matilda narrowly escaped capture here today when her army was expertly trapped while besieging the castle of Henry of Blois, the bishop of Winchester and brother of King Stephen. Fleeing on horseback, she was forced to run the gauntlet of enemy lines before escaping with a few loyal knights.

Matilda had arrived in the town with a strong army under the command of her half-brother Robert, the earl of Gloucester, and accompanied by her uncle, King David of Scotland, and six other earls. She immediately summoned Henry, who was perfectly well aware that this would be simply a prelude to his arrest.

The bishop promptly fled to his own small castle of Wolvesey, in the south-eastern corner of the city, and sent pleas for help to his brother's wife, Queen Matilda. The queen responded at once by dispatching her army under the command of William of Ypres, a professional soldier, whose instructions were to take prisoner the defiant empress and her men.

Earl Robert and the empress were engaged in attacking the bishop's castle when they discovered that William of Ypres had succeeded in blocking all routes in and out of the city. What happened next was a complete rout in which it was every man for himself – apart from Robert, who held off the attackers.

David was taken captive three times, and three times secured his escape by the payment of a ransom. The earl of Hereford threw away his armour to hide his identity and walked home half naked to Gloucester, while Robert was surrounded and captured alive at Stockbridge in Hampshire (→3/11).

Hiding place: a reconstruction of the old bishop's palace at Wolvesey.

Brave escape made across frozen Thames

Oxford, December 1142
Stephen, freed from captivity in a prisoner exchange and crowned king for a second time at the end of last year, has again been given the slip by his rival for the throne, Empress Matilda. He had her under siege here but, with only four knights, she escaped over the frozen Thames in darkness, right through the ranks of Stephen's men.

To camouflage themselves in the snow, Matilda and her knights donned white cloaks before stealing from the castle and crossing the ice-bound river on foot. They passed unhindered through the king's pickets, who were too busy shouting, singing and blasting on trumpets to each other to notice them.

This marks a serious setback for Stephen, as the empress is bound to continue the war from the many other castles that remain loyal to her. As well as a suggestion that treachery may have aided her escape, the damage to Stephen's prestige is huge. Although it is a case of bolting the stable door after the horse has fled, Stephen may draw comfort from the fact that Oxford Castle has now fallen (→1143).

Normans raise castles to leave people in no doubt about who is giving the orders

A 20th-century reconstruction of Pickering Castle, in North Yorkshire.

England, c.1140
The current hostilities in England have given the biggest boost to castle-building since the Conquest. Some have gone up in response to local uprisings, such as those in south-western England and the Welsh Marches, while others stand simply as a symbol of aristocratic power, aimed at intimidating local populations.

William the Conqueror's castles in London testify to this will to impress. The White Tower in the heart of the city was begun as soon as he took the capital. This vast structure, standing 27 metres (90 feet) high, is almost impregnable. King Stephen has regularly held court here during the present unrest.

Other notable Norman castles in the London region are Baynard's Castle, on the north bank of the Thames near the city, and Windsor Castle far to the west. Since the days of King Henry, Windsor has boasted a chapel and royal quarters in addition to the original "motte-and-bailey" construction. A new keep at Rochester Castle in Kent was completed three years ago.

Castle-building requires both forced labour and the mass destruction of property: Lincoln lost 160 houses to make way for its castle, and Oxford about half of 100 properties listed in the great survey of 1086. Typically, castles are vast, square-based and several storeys high, with thick walls and turrets at the corners. The keep at Hedingham in Essex, built by the de Veres, is remarkable. On the second of four floors it has a hall 9 metres high spanned by a huge arch.

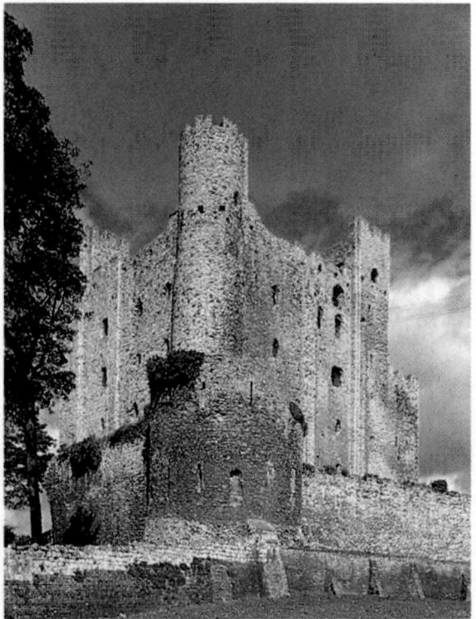
The castle at Rochester, in Kent.

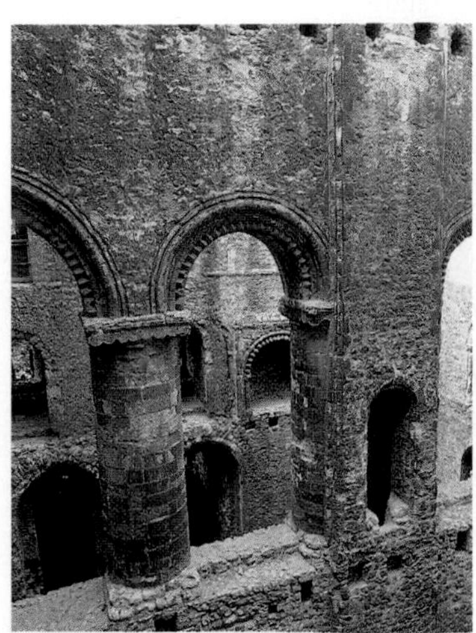
Inside the keep at Rochester.

1143 - 1148

Connacht, 1143. King Toirrdelbach Ua Briain of Munster invades in pursuit of his claim to the high-kingship, which is held by Toirrdelbach Ua Conchobair (→1144).

St Albans, Herts, 1143. King Stephen arrests Geoffrey de Mandeville, the earl of Essex, for his support of Empress Matilda; he is freed in exchange for Waldon and Pleshey Castles and the White Tower (→1/7/43).

Wilton, Wiltshire, 1 July 1143. Stephen is saved from capture by his steward, William Martel (→16/9/44).

Scotland, 1144. King David's son, Earl Henry of Huntingdon and Northumberland, is made "designated king" (→5/1144).

Durham, May 1144. William Comyn, the chancellor of Scotland, has to abandon the castle given to him two years ago by Matilda (→22/5/49).

Cambridgeshire, 16 September 1144. Geoffrey de Mandeville dies at Burwell; he is denied a church burial (→1145).

Munster, 1144. A church council tries to mediate between Ua Briain and Ua Conchobair in their claims to the high-kingship (→1145).

Faringdon, Oxon, 1145. Stephen seizes the castle built by Robert of Gloucester, who supports Matilda. Robert's son Philip joins Stephen (→5/1147).

Rufford, Lancashire, 1146. Earl Gilbert de Gant of Lincoln founds a Cistercian abbey (→1160).

Dublin, 1146. Ragnall, the *mormaer* [steward], is killed in a clash with forces of the kingdom of Brega (→1148).

England, May 1147. Henry Plantagenet, Matilda's son, returns to Normandy after a failed attempt to claim the throne (→31/10).

Lisbon, 25 October 1147. Following the capture of the city from the Moors by a force of English, Normans, Flemings and Germans, the English cleric Gilbert Hastings is elected bishop (→3/1185).

England, 31 October 1147. Robert of Gloucester dies and with him Empress Matilda's hopes for the crown. His son William succeeds him (→1/48).

Co Wicklow, 1148. Diarmait Mac Murchada, considered by Bernard of Clairvaux "king of Ireland", founds a Cistercian abbey at Baltinglass (→1157).

Warfare covers 'trembling sod' of Ireland

Ireland, 1145
Ireland – in common with many other European countries – is now in a state of constant warfare, and has been described as resembling "a trembling sod". Certainly dynastic strife has been prevalent for most of this century, and, while often seen as a succession of aimless acts of violence, the march and countermarch of succeeding generations of Irish provincial kings across the country have always been aimed at securing them the high-kingship. None of the attempts has so far been successful. The dynasty of Ua Mael Sechlainn in Co Meath has failed to achieve dominance despite its central position, which includes Dublin. As a consequence, greedy pretenders to the high-kingship have carved up areas of this ancient kingdom for themselves. This policy of partition has caused Meath to become the focus of a number of warring factions (→1146).

Gold's secret comes closer to discovery

Chester, 1144
Hopes are rising of a breakthrough in the search for the secret of transforming base metals such as lead into the most precious substance of all: gold. Experimenters in this field now have access to a handbook of alchemy that has just been translated by Robert of Chester. The theory is simple: since all creation is composed of the basic elements – earth, air, fire and water – it must be possible to rearrange their proportions and change a common form of matter into something higher and rarer. Although nobody has yet achieved total success, Robert details – for the first time in Europe – those furnaces and chemicals which have shown the most promising results so far.

Purifying fires: a woodcut of alchemists at work (from the 16th century).

European crusaders set off for Lisbon

Crusaders: a 19th-century view.

Dartmouth, Devon, 19 May 1147
A multinational force of knights from England, Scotland, Flanders, Normandy and Cologne set sail today on a new crusade, with the first stop being Portugal in order to help King Alfonso in his war against the Moslems. This campaign involves up to 13,000 crusaders, mostly seafaring men, who left in some 165 ships.

The crusaders are destined for Palestine, the Holy Land, but they have decided to help the king to mount a siege of Lisbon in exchange for the right to plunder the city when it is taken. They also expect to be offered land in Portugal. There is no leader of this Second Crusade, but a strict code of upright behaviour is expected to be enforced. Each ship has its own priest (→25/10).

Barons set to lose castles whichever side they support

Normandy, 1145
Following a recent victory, the duchy of Normandy has passed into the hands of Geoffrey of Anjou – to the great discomfiture of many of the barons who are fighting his wife, Matilda, for control of England. All the barons in England own extensive estates in Normandy, which they are now in danger of losing if they continue to oppose Matilda in her war to dethrone King Stephen. Should they switch sides, Stephen will then deprive them of their English estates.

To many barons, their Norman estates are their ancestral property and the land from which they draw their identity. The earl of Worcester, for instance, is better known as Waleran of Beaumont, the count of Meulan, the greatest landowner in Normandy. The lord of Hastings is John, the count of Eu (in northern Normandy), and there are many more in the same position. To these men the loss of their Norman lands is the more serious because it means loss of prestige and family identity, even though their English holdings may be bigger. It also means that from now on whoever holds Normandy can incite treachery to England by offering to return confiscated estates to some of the greatest lords there (→5/1147).

Christ in majesty: a mural from the 12th century, restored in the 20th, in Copford church, Essex.

Welsh oust Normans

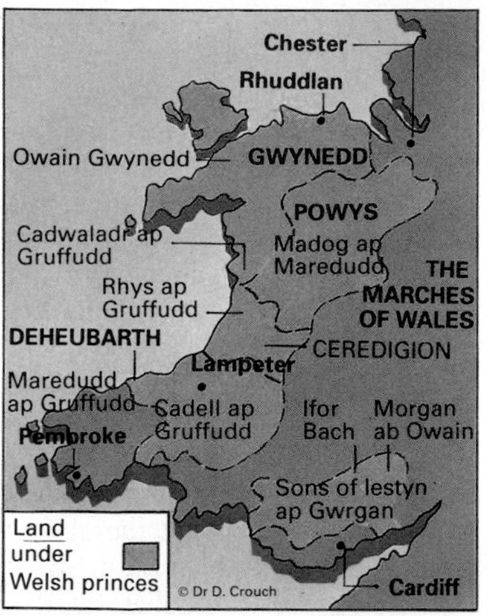

Lampeter, Dyfed, 1146

Cadell, one of the four sons of Gruffudd ap Rhys, has routed the Normans and captured the castle here, and his brother Maredudd is tackling the Normans in Pembroke. This is a remarkable turn of fortune in less than a decade. The four have been determined to regain control of the southern part of the realm of Deheubarth from the Normans and have almost succeeded. Revolts began in many different parts in 1136 and 1137. In Gwynedd, Owain has fought the Normans, unlike his father, Gruffudd ap Cynan, who appeased them. Owain has not only recovered most of Gwynedd but has also installed his brother Cadwaladr as ruler in the area of Deheubarth known as Ceredigion and captured other northern parts of the realm.

In Powys the Welsh successes have been less extensive, but the leader, Madog ap Maredudd, has done wonders for morale. He is known for his love of the hunt and the stud and has set up an impressive court. The court poet calls him "a firm anchor in a deep sea".

The success of the Welsh irks some of the Norman barons. The earl of Chester proposed that King Stephen of England should lead a campaign against the Welsh. This has been stopped by some of the king's advisers who fear that the proposal is a plot to ambush and kill Stephen (→ 1157).

Growth in literacy boosts private schools

London, 1148

Education is on the increase in England, with an ever growing number of people who can read and write – especially in the upper classes, and among women, who have no military preoccupations. Private schools are emerging to complement the more official ones associated with the church.

A pioneer in private schooling was Robert de Bethune, the bishop of Hereford, who died this year. He became a teacher at the turn of the century and made a considerable living from satisfying the growing desire for education among the landed classes. With his income he was able to set up his nieces in suitable marriages and purchase places in monastic houses for his nephews. At the same time some of the leading knights in the country are engaging tutors for the education of their children.

Almost all traditional school classes take place in churches and are usually conducted by officials or servants of those churches. The elementary schoolmaster is commonly the village or town priest. He is expected to teach all ages reading, writing and grammar – that is to say, Latin grammar – from the youngest to the oldest.

Scholars engaged in a debate.

Basic education is now available to most of those who want it, and the clever poor can often be educated free. Hundreds of people are able to express legal transactions in good Latin (→ 1209).

Irish north divided into smaller kingdoms

Ireland, 1148

King Muirchertach Mac Lochlainn of the northern Cenel nEogain kingdom of Ailech has partitioned the north. It now consists of two provinces – "the North", covering Derry and West Antrim, and "Ulster", which includes Down and Connor – within which are four sub-kingdoms. Muirchertach himself will be the overall ruler.

The Cenel nEogain have controlled what is now "the North" for some time. In 1113 the then king of Ailech, Domnall Mac Lochlainn, one of the claimants to the high-kingship of Ireland, had partitioned Ulster after deposing Donnchad mac Duinn Sleibe who was ruling it from Downpatrick.

Domnall died in Derry, his base for many years, in 1121, and since then there have been constant battles between the leaders of the two northern territories. Conchobar Mac Lochlainn, Domnall's successor, invaded Ulster in 1127, taking hostages and forcing Bishop Malachy to flee to Lismore (→ 1151).

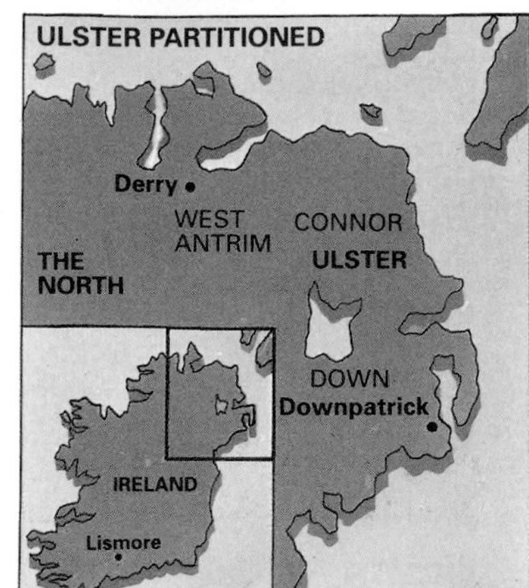

Matilda abandons her claim to throne

Normandy, January 1148

Empress Matilda has left England and returned to Normandy, controlled for the last three years by her husband, Geoffrey of Anjou. Her attempts to win back England from her cousin Stephen have failed after a bitter civil war that, at one time, she almost won. It seems that she is relinquishing her claim: with the recent death of her half-brother and loyal supporter Earl Robert of Gloucester she has little option. But all may not be lost. Henry Plantagenet, Matilda and Geoffrey's 15-year-old son, may wish to pursue the claim (→ 9/1149).

Empress Matilda: defeated in war.

Archbishop defies king and is exiled

Canterbury, Kent, 1148

The archbishop of Canterbury has been exiled for disobeying the king's order not to attend the Council of Rheims, in France, summoned by Pope Eugenius III. It is the latest move in a long fight between the crown and the church, with King Stephen striving to keep the English church under his thumb and restrict the power of the pope.

When the summons arrived the king appointed a delegation of three bishops – of Chichester, Hereford and Norwich – to go in the archbishop's stead. Many believe that he did this to weaken Theobald's standing with the pope and to please his own brother, Henry of Blois, the bishop of Winchester, a rival of Theobald's.

As Stephen expected, Theobald disobeyed. With his clerk Thomas Becket he braved the March storms and slipped away in a boat so small and unseaworthy that he was lucky to survive the crossing. At Rheims the pope chose to excommunicate Stephen; the ceremony had already begun when Theobald begged Eugenius to stop. The pope reluctantly agreed, but the archbishop's charity has done him no good; no sooner had he returned than he was exiled to France (→ 6/4/52).

1149 - 1153

Normandy, September 1149. King Louis VII of France recognizes Geoffrey of Anjou, Matilda's husband, as duke in return for the surrender of the strategically important area of the Vexin (→ 1/1150).

Normandy, January 1150. Duke Geoffrey declares his and Matilda's son Henry Plantagenet to be of age and gives the duchy of Normandy to him (→ 1151).

Rome, 1151. Pope Innocent II vetoes King Stephen's plans to crown his son Eustace as king of England (→ 8/1151).

Paris, August 1151. Henry Plantagenet makes peace with King Louis VII (→ 7/9).

Anjou, France, 7 September 1151. A succession crisis follows the death of Geoffrey Plantagenet (→ 3/5/52).

Leinster, 6 March 1152. At a synod held at Kells, the papal legate, Cardinal Paparo, attempts a full diocesan reorganization of the Irish church (→ 1158).

London, 6 April 1152. Theobald, the archbishop of Canterbury, flees to France, refusing to pay homage to Stephen's son Eustace as heir to the throne (→ 1/1155).

England, 3 May 1152. Stephen is devastated by the death of his wife, Matilda (→ 18/5).

Scotland, 12 June 1152. Henry, the recently deceased earl of Northumberland and Huntington, and only son of King David, is buried at Kelso Abbey. David's 11-year-old grandson, Malcolm, is now heir to the throne (→ 24/5/53).

Dorset, January 1153. Henry Plantagenet lands at Wareham with a small army; he and his forces head for Devizes in Wiltshire (→ 5/1153).

Gloucester, May 1153. Many back Henry Plantagenet, but only Earl Robert of Leicester, the strongest landowner in the English midlands, joins him from the king's side (→ 17/8).

Wallingford, 17 August 1153. Following the death of his son Eustace, Stephen negotiates with Henry Plantagenet to guarantee the succession of William, his younger son, to Boulogne and Mortain (→ 6/11).

Ireland, 1153. King Toirrdelbach Ua Conchobair of Connacht returns the wife of King Tigernan Ua Ruairc of Breifne, abducted last year by King Diarmait Mac Murchada of Leinster (→ 31/1/55).

Scots rule extended deep into England

The formidable King David of Scotland seated beside his grandson Malcolm.

Carlisle, 22 May 1149
King David of Scots has pulled off a major diplomatic coup in a meeting here with Henry Plantagenet, his great-nephew and a likely successor to the English throne. Henry, the son of Empress Matilda, has promised that he will in future recognize that it is the king of Scotland who rules Cumberland and Northumberland from the Tyne to the Tees. This is the price that Henry paid for being knighted by David at today's meeting. No Scottish king has ruled a kingdom as large as David's; yet this is just one of his achievements.

Since coming to the throne in 1124 David has revolutionized government in Scotland, bringing in a new post of chancellor and the writing of charters, adopted from Anglo-Norman custom. He has also embraced the Normans' feudal system, whereby all land belongs to the king who gives it out in return for service. He is interested in spiritual issues, too, welcoming Cistercians, Augustinians and other monastic orders (→ 12/6/52).

Irish king's wife is kidnapped in feud

Ireland, 1152
Diarmait Mac Murchada, the king of Leinster, has abducted Derbforgaill, the wife of Tigernan Ua Ruairc, the king of Breifne. It is said that Derbforgaill was a willing accomplice in the abduction and had agreed to be the kidnapper's prize. Others blame her brother, Donnchad Ua Mael Sechlainn, saying that he persuaded her to go with Diarmait in retaliation for Tigernan's cruel treatment of her.

It is more likely that the abduction is as cynical a political act as was the rape of the abbess of Kildare by King Diarmait two decades ago. Diarmait had old scores to settle with Tigernan and has done so by besmirching his honour as a husband.

Despite his reputation as a savage warlord, Diarmait has another side to his character. He has established friendly relations with the great religious leader Bernard of Clairvaux, who has granted him confraternity with the Cistercian monks. Diarmait is a generous patron of monks and nuns, and six years ago he founded the great Arroasian abbey of St Mary de Hogges in Dublin (→ 1153).

Cork battle is the century's bloodiest

Munster, 1151
In what has been called the bloodiest battle of the century in Ireland, King Toirrdelbach Ua Briain of Thomond in northern Munster has been crushed at Moin Mor [in northern Co Cork] and forced to flee Munster. This has been a catastrophic setback for Thomond, 7,000 of whose men lie dead.

Toirrdelbach was challenged by Toirrdelbach Ua Conchobair, the king of Connacht, and Diarmait Mac Murchada, the king of Leinster, who support the Mac Carthaig of Desmond in southern Munster. The Mac Carthaig were Munster's leading family until the Dal Cais of Thomond won the over-kingship in the reign of Brian Boruma. Partly restored to power in 1118, they moved south from their ancestral lands in Tipperary (→ 1152).

English heir weds French king's ex-wife

Poitiers, France, 18 May 1152
The marriage today of Eleanor, the duchess of Aquitaine, to Henry Plantagenet, the count of Anjou and duke of Normandy, has sent shockwaves through the French establishment. It comes a mere two months after the divorce of Eleanor from King Louis VII of France.

Since the marriage was unauthorized, the court views it as a slight on the royal dignity: by feudal custom Eleanor should have sought the king's consent. Besides, although consanguinity was the reason given for the divorce, she is as closely related by blood to Henry as she is to Louis.

At 30, the duchess is 11 years older than her new husband. Although the newlyweds have met only once before, at peace talks in Paris last summer, the wedding was probably arranged in secret last Christmas, when King Louis first indicated that he wished to annul his marriage to Eleanor. In 14 years of marriage the duchess had borne only two daughters and no son and heir (→ 1/1153).

King Louis VII of France.

Scotland will never be the same after good King David

Carlisle, Cumbria, 24 May 1153
David, king of Scotland since 1124, died today in his 69th year. His successor is his 12-year-old grandson Malcolm, designated after the death of David's son Henry last year. The youngest son of King Malcolm Canmore and Queen Margaret, David inherited a devout nature from his mother. A great patron of the church, he ruled with a civilized hand, establishing a much-admired framework of laws.

Scotland's public life has been transformed under David. He surrounded himself with close friends and supporters within a formal power structure; in return for the right to rule prescribed areas he demanded that the nobles should support the royal army and castles. Civil government has been reorganized, with the establishment of burghs and sheriffdoms (→ 1157).

England's civil war splutters to a halt

Hampshire, 6 November 1153
The English civil war ended at last today with the conclusion of a treaty at Winchester between King Stephen and Duke Henry of Normandy, the son of Empress Matilda and the late Geoffrey Plantagenet, the count of Anjou and duke of Normandy. Stephen has accepted Henry as the heir to the throne of England, and the two sides are to cooperate in restoring order and dismantling the many castles built during the 12 years of conflict.

Having inherited Normandy from his father and gained Aquitaine by his marriage to its duchess, Eleanor, last year, Duke Henry came over to England to continue the bitter campaign against Stephen that had been begun by his mother.

In the late summer he put Bedford to the torch but failed to take its castle. From there he then went via Stamford to Nottingham, where he suffered a further military setback when the castle's defenders burnt the town and forced him to retire from the siege. By now war-weariness was beginning to overtake both sides, and there was an increasing reluctance to fight on. In any case peace negotiations had already been opened by Archbishop Theobald and Bishop Henry of Winchester, Stephen's brother, and a meeting was arranged between the parties. After some hard bargaining, in which neither side was strong enough to force the issue, terms were agreed today that both the king and the duke have found acceptable (→ 13/1/54).

Winchester's 13th-century hall.

Henry Plantagenet's inheritance.

Fate of England, Scotland and Wales is inextricably bound up with that of France

Britain, c.1150
In the years since the Norman conquest, England, Scotland and Wales have gradually been drawn out of their seclusion into contact with the rest of Europe. In particular, their fate is now bound up with that of France.

The effect of this has been most radical in England. No English king since Harold has had English as his mother tongue. The nobility and the leaders of the church – a dominant player in the national power game – speak French. Many of both groups come from, or hold land, across the Channel. The clerics belong to a Europe-wide church centred in Rome but not recognizing national borders.

Unlike England, Scotland has not been conquered, but it has accommodated an alien (Anglo-Norman) aristocracy within the country, such as the Balliol and Brus [Bruce] families. (The latter, for example, originated in Brix, in western Normandy.) Rigid central government does not exist yet, but King David's policies [*see report above*] have moved southern Scotland decisively in that direction. In addition, new monastic orders have taken root and royal burghs have been established.

Wales has proved a tougher nut to crack. So far the mountainous central and northern regions have mounted the greatest resistance, but the Normans have barely a foothold even in the lowlands of the south.

Apart from their influence on architecture, the Normans have encouraged the arts and town planning. The excellence of book illustration is clear from the psalter [book of psalms] created at Canterbury by the scribe Edwin, and sculpture is also of high quality, as the Winchester font shows. New boroughs have been built to increase trading possibilities, some of them on a grid plan rather than on the pre-Conquest triangular layout (→ 1200).

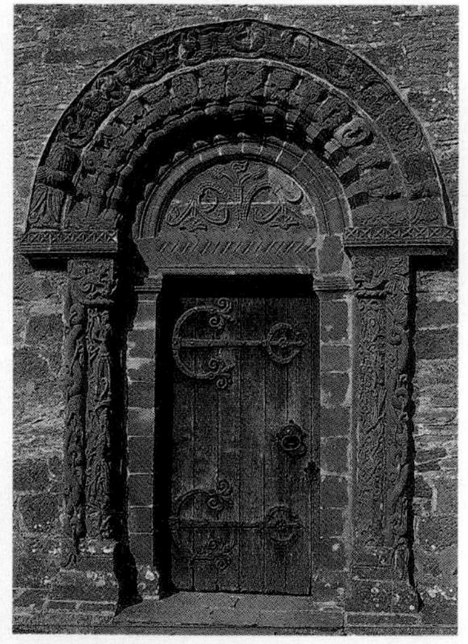
The Romanesque south door of Kilpeck church, near Hereford.

A self-portrait of the scribe Edwin from the Canterbury psalter.

A carved font of black Tournai marble, made at Winchester in Norman style; among the baptismal party is a lord with his hunting-bird.

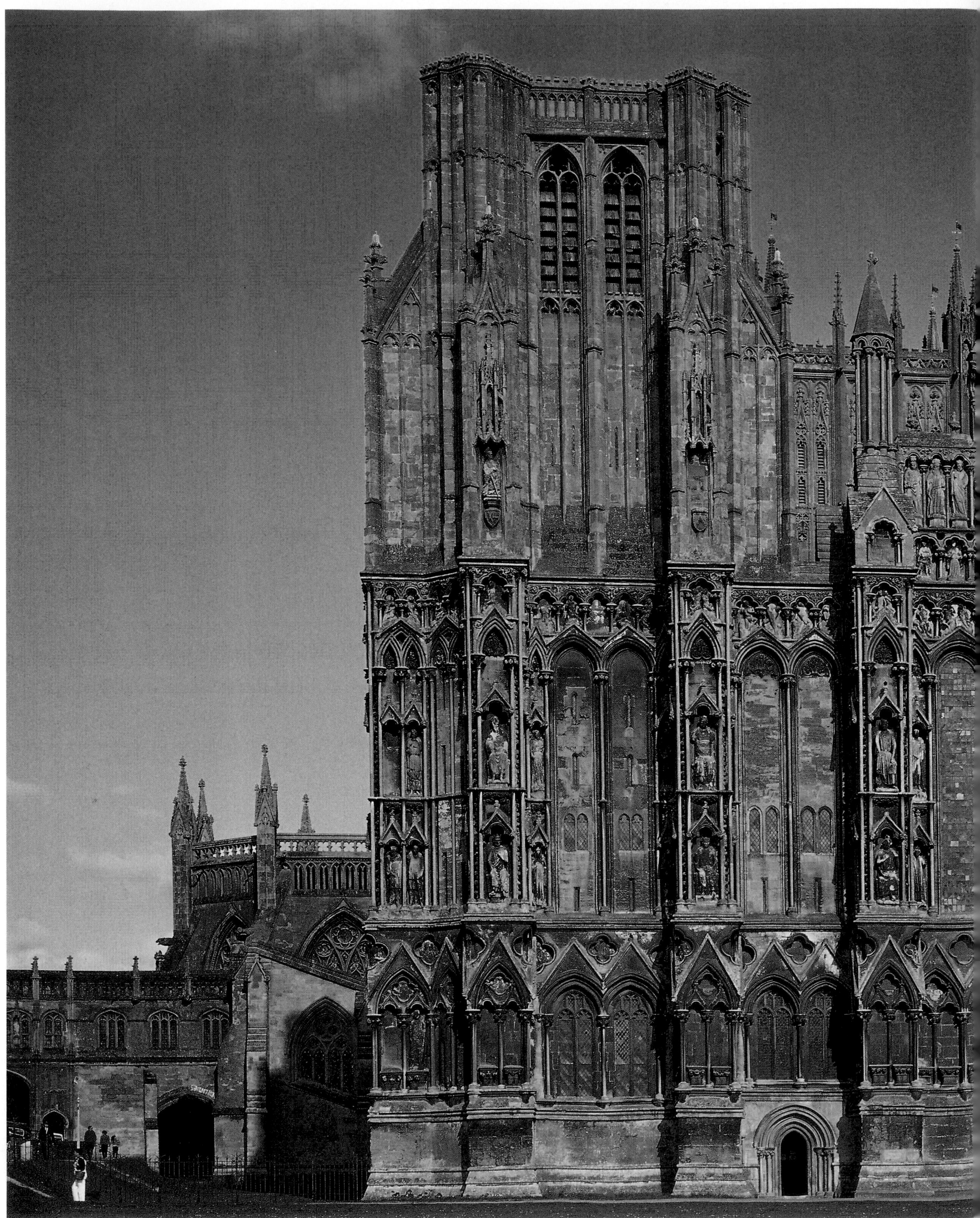

The Middle Ages
1154-1485

1154 - 1157

Strathclyde, January 1154. Somerled, the lord of Argyll, and his nephews, the sons of the rebel Malcolm mac Heth, revolt against King Malcolm IV of Scots (→ 1156).

Oxford, 13 January 1154. Henry Plantagenet and King Stephen of England meet to ratify the terms of the Treaty of Winchester, which made Henry Stephen's heir (→ 25/10).

Kent, 25 October 1154. King Stephen dies. He will be buried at a Cluniac monastery that he founded at Faversham (→ 8/12).

Hampshire, 8 December 1154. Henry Plantagenet arrives to claim his throne (→ 19/12).

Co Meath, 31 January 1155. King Mael Sechlainn Ua Mael Sechlainn is poisoned (→ 1156).

London, 28 February 1155. Henry II's second son, Henry, is born (→ 10/4).

England, 10 April 1155. The barons accept Henry II's sons William and Henry as rightful heirs to the throne (→ 7/1155).

Shropshire, July 1155. Henry subdues the last rebel baron, Hugh Mortimer, confiscating the castles of Wigmore and Bridgnorth (→ 10/9/67).

Rome, 1155. John of Salisbury, the archbishop of Canterbury's clerk, visits Pope Adrian IV. He is presented with a papal bull, *Laudabiliter*, sanctioning Henry II of England to invade Ireland (→ 11/9/59).

Winchester, Hampshire, 1155. Henry of Blois, the bishop of Winchester and brother of the late King Stephen, flees to France.→

Bristol, Avon, 1155. The city is awarded a royal charter.

England, 1155. Henry II appoints Robert of Beaumont, the earl of Leicester, justiciar and viceroy (→ 28/2).

Roxburgh, Borders, 1156. The rebel Malcolm mac Heth and his son Donald are imprisoned by Malcolm IV (→ 1158).

Ailech, 1156. King Muirchertach Mac Lochlainn claims the high-kingship of Ireland (→ 1158).

Chester, 1157. Henry breaks his treaty of 1149 with the Scots and forces Malcolm to yield both Northumberland and Cumbria (→ 1159).

Newry, Co Armagh, 1157. Muirchertach Mac Lochlainn, the high king of Ireland, grants a Latin charter to the Cistercian abbey (→ 1160).

A peaceful succession

The new English king, Henry II, beside his wife, Eleanor of Aquitaine.

Westminster, 19 December 1154
Henry Plantagenet, the son of Empress Matilda and Geoffrey of Anjou, has been crowned Henry II of England after the longest interval between the death of one English king and the coronation of another for over 100 years. His queen is Eleanor of Aquitaine, the former wife of Louis VII of France, and the succession brings with it vast areas of land in continental Europe, including Anjou and Aquitaine (also known as Gascony).

Henry's delay contrasts with the dash made by Stephen after the death of Henry I (the new king's grandfather), and that of Henry I after the death of William II – whose danger from rivals was such that his grab for the throne began before his father, William the Conqueror, was actually dead. The aim is no longer to choose the most eligible heir – usually the one with the largest army – but the man with the best hereditary claim.

Henry was in Normandy besieging a vassal when the news that he was king reached him in October. He ended the siege, settled affairs in the duchy and arrived in England on 7 December with his wife, Eleanor. She is 32, he 21 (→ 1155).

The dominions of King Henry II of England at their greatest extent.

Breakspear elected first English pope

Rome, 25 December 1154
Cardinal Nicholas of Albano became the first English pontiff today when he was enthroned as Pope Adrian IV. Recognized as a skilful diplomat, Adrian IV faces a barrage of challenges to papal authority from the republican movement in Rome, from King William in Sicily and from Greece.

Born in Abbot's Langley in Hertfordshire, Nicholas Breakspear, to give him his family name, was still a boy when his father joined the monastery of St Albans. Surviving on alms, Nicholas made his way to France – in common with many young people in search of a good education. He studied at Arles before entering a house of canons at St Ruf, near Avignon, where he rose to become abbot.

When the canons sent a second complaint to Rome about his strict discipline, Pope Eugenius III promoted him to cardinal and in 1152 dispatched him on a mission to Scandinavia. He was so successful in affirming Rome's presence in that region that, on his return earlier this year, he was dubbed "the apostle of the north".

Such is the background of the new pope, a man of whom it is said that St Albans Abbey refused him admittance when he failed a literacy test. Since then his career has been one of uninterrupted success, and it is that record which secured his unopposed election (→ 1155).

London's youth is devoted to fashion

London, c.1155
Rich young Londoners seem set on aping every fashion that crosses the Channel from France and Italy. Women's gowns are now so long that they trail along the ground, while their bell-shaped sleeves have to be tied with knots in case the wearer trips over them. By contrast bodices cling tightly to the torso, revealing every contour. Fashion-conscious men grow hair to their waists, adopt the fad for voluminous sleeves and sport jewel-studded gloves. Shoes are commonly worn long and pointed.

Thomas Becket is appointed chancellor

London, January 1155
Thomas Becket, the archdeacon of Canterbury and trusted emissary of Archbishop Theobald, has been appointed chancellor by the newly crowned King Henry II. Becket, also known as Thomas of London, comes from a solid Norman family which owns property in the city of London. He worked as a notary before joining Theobald's household where he distinguished himself by carrying out delicate diplomatic missions. His official function will be to act as the chief ecclesiastical servant of the royal household, in charge of the chapel royal and the writing office. He will be paid five shillings a day.

It is thought at court, however, that he will remain Theobald's man and will keep the archbishop well informed and ably represented on the king's councils (→ 9/1158).

Nobles get short shrift under new regime

Winchester, Hampshire, 1155
By the act of razing the castles of earls associated with the late King Stephen's side in the civil war, King Henry II has served notice on the great barons of England that their power, swollen in the chaotic struggles between two royal houses, must now acknowledge a greater authority: that of the king.

Demonstrating an enormous energy and capacity for hard work, Henry has kept his court in constant activity since arriving in England last December. Apart from repairing the royal finances, an urgent task, there are many outstanding disputes to be resolved dating from the time when both he and Stephen claimed the right to issue royal grants.

A 20th-century reconstruction of a 12th-century castle at Scarborough.

The signs at the moment are that Henry intends to administer a justice which, if rough, ready and long-winded, is not too divisive. But those who rely on charters granted by Stephen during the civil war can expect little – as the loss of his castles has taught Henry of Blois, the bishop of Winchester, Stephen's brother (→ 28/2).

Henry's first Welsh foray ends in a draw

Gwynedd, 1157
Anxious to reassert Anglo-Norman power in Wales, Henry II of England has met several reverses in the first royal expedition here since 1121: a naval force sent to attack the Welsh in the rear was routed at Anglesey, and an army contingent was ambushed by the Welsh near Hawarden. But overall Owain, the prince of Gwynedd, can claim no more than a draw.

The English king has reimposed some degree of overlordship. Owain has been forced to accept the return of his estranged brother, Cadwaladr, from exile in England, and has also been compelled to deliver hostages to the king and to surrender the territory known as Tegeingl. Henry is a long way from conquering the Welsh, but it is possible that that was not his intention. He has skilfully exploited the divisions between the Welsh. He took Madog of Powys with him to Gwynedd. While Owain was preoccupied by talks with Henry, Madog recovered his former territory of Iâl [in north-eastern Powys] and destroyed Owain's castle there.

Henry seems to be seeking to restrain the more powerful princes by building up some of their potential enemies. And he expects them all to bow to him as overlord (→ 1158).

Church rethinks marriage: true wedlock exists when women genuinely want it

England, c.1155
The need to obtain a woman's consent to wedlock is winning wide recognition by the church – even if this is so more in theory than in practice. Not long ago marriage was simply a civil contract with its origins in Roman law, when a woman was handed over to a man like a piece of property. But canonists have fought to introduce an element of female consent to a marriage contract. If a woman wishes to obtain an annulment from a church court, she can cite absence of consent in her support. The recent case of Christina of Markyate illustrates the point. As a young girl Christina vowed to pursue a life of celibacy but was forced into an arranged marriage. She refused to consummate it and eventually obtained an annulment from Archbishop Thurstan of York.

Another recent scandal demonstrates the church's determination to ensure that the marriage laws are strictly enforced. Richard of Anstey succeeded in claiming an inheritance from his uncle, William de Sackville, on the grounds that the original intended beneficiary – William's daughter from his second marriage – was illegitimate. The claimant's success sprang from the fact that de Sackville had failed to annul his first, unconsummated marriage before taking a new wife (→ 1172).

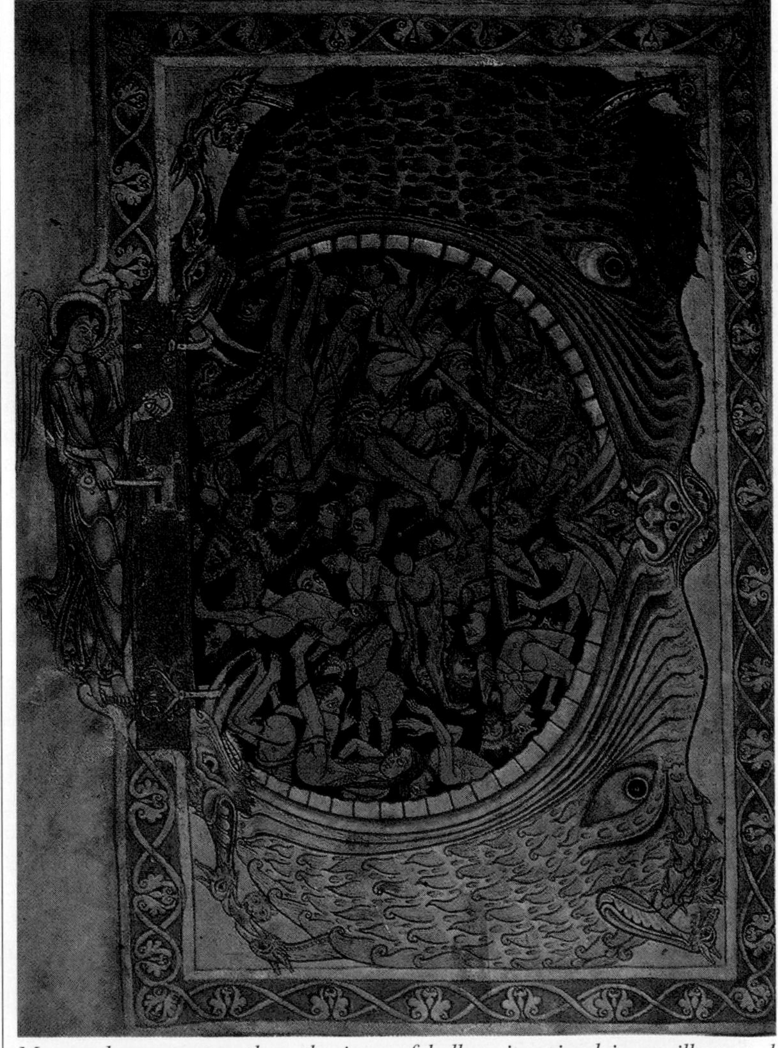
Men and women together: the jaws of hell as imagined in an illustrated psalter c.1140-60 belonging to Henry of Blois, the bishop of Winchester.

1158 - 1163

Normandy, 27 July 1158. King Henry II gains Nantes and lands of his brother Geoffrey on the latter's death (→ 1159).

Ireland, 1158. King Toirrdelbach Ua Briain of Munster blinds two of his cousins to try to stop inter-family fighting (→ 1159).

Breemount, Co Louth, 1158. The papal legate gives certain abbots episcopal status in the Irish church (→ 6/9/81).

Wales, 1158. Morgan ab Owain, the king of Glamorgan, is killed in an ambush (→ 1160).

Isle of Man, 1158. Somerled, the lord of Argyll, defeats King Godfrey, completing his conquest of the islands off Scotland (→ 12/1160).

Norwich, 1158. The city receives a royal charter.

France, 1159. King Malcolm IV of Scots accompanies Henry II to Toulouse and is knighted by him (→ 1162).

Perth, Tayside, December 1160. Somerled, the lord of Argyll, makes peace with Malcolm IV (→ 1164).

Dumfries and Galloway, 1160. Malcolm IV subdues Fergus, the lord of Galloway, forcing him to retire to a monastery and dividing the lordship between his sons (→ 1174).

Canterbury, Kent, 23 June 1162. Thomas Becket is consecrated as archbishop following the death last year of Theobald (→ 19/5/63).

France, 18 September 1162. Henry II of England and Louis VII are reconciled at a meeting in the Loire valley (→ 25/1/63).

Scotland, 1162. Count Florence of Holland arrives to marry Ada, the elder sister of Malcolm IV, whose younger sister married Duke Conon of Brittany in 1160 (→ 1/7/63).

Southampton, Hampshire, 25 January 1163. Henry II returns from France (→ 1167).

Oxfordshire, 1 July 1163. Malcolm of Scots and the Welsh princes Owain Gwynedd and Rhys ap Gruffudd pay homage to Henry and his son Henry at Woodstock.→

Doncaster, South Yorkshire, August 1163. Malcolm IV falls seriously ill on his return from Woodstock (→ 9/12/65).

Westminster, 14 October 1163. Following a disagreement in council in May, Henry takes his young son from Becket's care (→ 30/7/64).

Splendour of Becket embassy stuns Paris

Paris, September 1158
Thomas Becket, King Henry II's chancellor, has stunned Paris by the magnificence of his mission to King Louis VII of France. The wealth he displayed was far greater than that of Henry's own cavalcade when the two kings met last month by the river Epte to betroth Louis's infant daughter from his second marriage, Margaret, to Henry's three-year-old son, also called Henry.

The chancellor has come to Paris to iron out the details of the marriage contract, and he is determined to leave the French in no doubt about the power and wealth of England. He has brought with him 200 men from his household, each with their own servants all dressed in new livery, and he has no fewer than 24 sets of the most elegant clothes.

Becket also has hawks and hounds fit for a king. Eight of his dozen pack-horses are laden with the gold and silver plate of his office. The others carry his altar vessels and money for day-to-day use. Each horse has a groom at its head and a monkey on its back. As this procession made its way through the countryside towards Paris, people marvelled at its splendour: "What a wonderful king he must be to have such a great chancellor" (→ 23/6/62).

Becket: 12th-century stained glass.

Pope who sought Irish invasion dies

Anagni, Italy, 11 September 1159
Adrian IV, the English-born pope enthroned in 1154, died today in southern Italy after falling victim to an attack of quinsy. His five years in office were marked by a three-cornered power struggle in which the Roman church was alternately pitched against William, the Norman king of Sicily, in the south and Holy Roman Emperor Frederick Barbarossa in the north.

In May this year, wary of Frederick's growing ties with the republican movement in Rome, Adrian IV withdrew to Anagni, some 30 miles (48 km) to the south-east, to be nearer William's protection. At the time of his death he was preparing to excommunicate Frederick.

In England, Adrian IV will be remembered for authorizing Henry II to invade Ireland. His move sprang from Rome's claim on all islands converted to Christianity, according to the *Donation of Constantine*, a document forged in the eighth century (→ 11/11/71).

New tax reforms to replace 'Danegeld'

England, 1159
With the continued decline of the "Danegeld" – the method of raising revenue begun in England during the time of the Danish invasions – a new system of taxation is to be introduced. Ever since the reign of William the Conqueror, an increasing number of anomalies have affected methods of tax assessment throughout England, some parts of the country having to pay considerably more than others. At one time the county of Kent paid only half as much Danegeld as Sussex, a county of similar size.

The number of people claiming reductions and in some cases being granted total exemption from the tax, as well as the administrative problems associated with its collection, have fuelled the need for urgent reform.

The alternative method of raising revenue, favoured by the king, is likely to be by the adoption of "scutage" – a payment of money in lieu of military service.

Rivals vie for high-kingship of Ireland

Ireland, 1159
Much of Ireland remains in turmoil, and Muirchertach Mac Lochlainn, the king of the Cenel nEogain in the north, has been "high king with opposition" for three years now. He has forced other leaders to submit to him, most notably Tigernain Ua Ruairc in Breifne, Diarmait Ua Mael Sechnaill in Meath and Diarmait Mac Murchada in Leinster. In addition, Ruaidri Ua Conchobair of Connacht has been quick to recognize Muirchertach's supremacy. Beset by dynastic difficulties at home, he has agreed to submit to Muirchertach, hoping to ward off a threatened invasion of his kingdom (→ 1166).

Five heirs to share Welsh prince's land

Powys, 1160
Madog ap Maredudd, who ruled Powys for 28 years, is dead. He not only regained the territory lost to the Normans but also pushed into England. In 1149 he seized Oswestry, and in 1152 his son killed the Norman lord of Montgomery. In the course of the last three years Madog had bowed to the power of Henry II of England, letting himself be used in the latter's campaign against Gwynedd. The future is uncertain because Powys is to be divided between five heirs (→ 1/7/63).

The day of reckoning: enamel decoration, on a copper panel, of the Last Judgement, c.1150-60.

Monastic expansion centred on Yorkshire

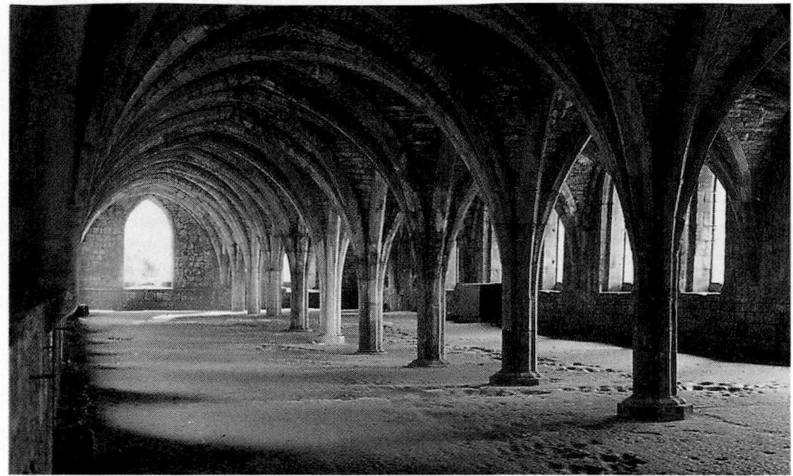

Fountains Abbey, Yorkshire: the undercroft, used by the lay brothers.

Ripon, North Yorkshire, 1160
Yorkshire has become the spearhead of the Cistercian movement in Britain [*see report on page 217*]. Rievaulx, in the valley of the river Rye, was founded in 1132 under the direct sponsorship of Bernard of Clairvaux. Its abbot, Ailred, now boasts some 140 monks and over 500 lay brothers. Nearby is Fountains Abbey, founded by a group of dissident Benedictine monks.

There are now some 330 Cistercian houses in Europe. There are about 50 in the British Isles, many of them in the west, including Tintern in the Wye valley and Neath and Margam in West Glamorgan. Scotland received its first Cistercian abbey in 1136 [*see report on page 221*] and Ireland in 1142, after Archbishop Malachy of Armagh had visited Clairvaux and been moved by the monks' austere piety.

The rugged terrain of Wales and Yorkshire is ideal for the Cistercians, who lead an ascetic life away from the luxuries of towns. They believe that hard physical labour develops spiritual thinking. So successful are they at their chosen vocation of sheep-farming that they now rank among the country's leading wool producers (→1211).

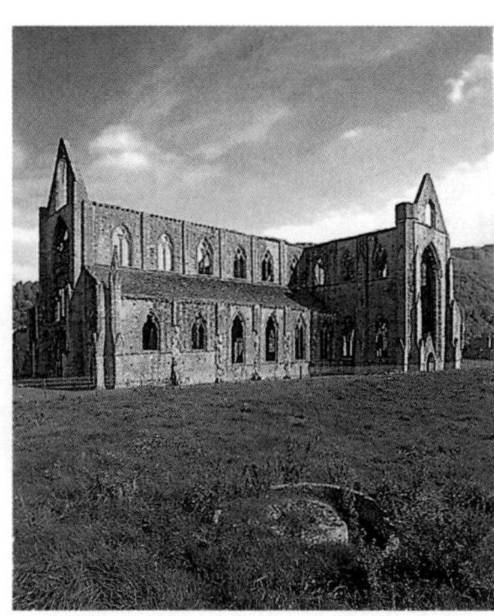

Tintern Abbey, in the Wye Valley.

The remains of the Cistercian foundation at Rievaulx Abbey, Yorkshire.

Henry's advance halted in French south

Southern France, 1159
King Henry of England's expensive expedition to win the county of Toulouse in the south of France and extend his writ as far as the Mediterranean is petering out. His huge army – the feudal barons reinforced by mercenaries paid for by levies on towns, moneylenders and, to its annoyance, the church – is now ravaged by sickness.

To compound Henry's troubles, Louis VII, the king of France and Henry's overlord in his duchy of Normandy, has obstinately installed himself in Toulouse and made an announcement that he has taken charge of its defence. This means that Henry dare not mount a decisive attack.

Henry's main strategy was to intimidate Count Raymond V of Toulouse into surrendering. To that end Henry sent his knights to take castles and major towns around Toulouse and so break the count's will. But now the intervention of Louis has sunk that plan, and the English king's army is expected to withdraw, giving up its gains. Henry's claim to Toulouse derives from that of his wife, Eleanor of Aquitaine, to inherit it. Although it is not a particularly powerful claim, it is hard to write off entirely since Louis himself tried to press the same claim when he was married to Eleanor (→18/9/62).

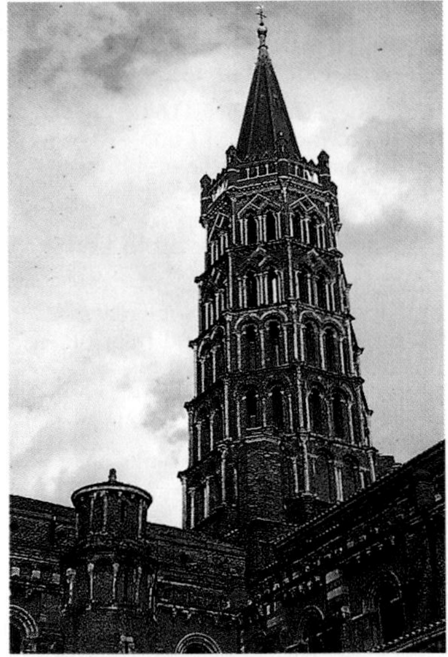

Toulouse: the church of St Sernin.

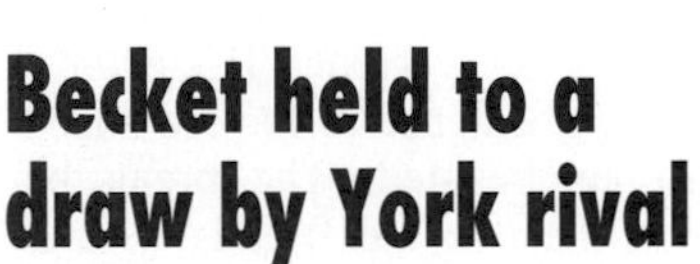

Becket held to a draw by York rival

Tours, France, 19 May 1163
Thomas Becket, the archbishop of Canterbury, has been received with much honour at the council summoned by Pope Alexander III here, on the border between the French and English realms. It has not, however, been an entirely happy occasion for the archbishop. He could only achieve a draw in an argument over precedence with Roger, the archbishop of York, and his antagonist proved himself superior as both a Latin scholar and an ecclesiastical lawyer (→14/10/63).

New shrine for body of the Confessor

Westminster, 13 October 1163
The body of Edward the Confessor, who was canonized only two years ago, was moved today to a new shrine in Westminster Abbey. King Henry and senior noblemen bore the coffin through the cloisters to its final resting-place, with a service conducted by Thomas Becket, the archbishop of Canterbury. Afterwards, the general assembly discussed the king's dissatisfaction with the soft sentences given by church courts to priests and clerics found guilty of crimes (→6/7/1245).

Henry's hard line with Wales stirs revolt

Oxfordshire, July 1163
Pursuing his campaign to restore Norman supremacy in Wales, Henry II has returned from a successful expedition to crush the rebellion of Rhys ap Gruffudd of Deheubarth [*see map on page 236*] and now intends to teach all Welsh leaders a lesson. He has forced Rhys, Owain Gwynedd and five others to come to Woodstock to pay homage to him. The English barons have been given similar treatment because Henry wants to limit their power too. But today's ceremony may backfire. The Welsh do not take kindly to humiliation; a new revolt is brewing (→summer 1165).

1164 - 1169

Wiltshire, 30 July 1164. A church council at Clarendon discusses the privileges of clerical life (→ 14/10).

France, December 1164. Following his flight into exile, Thomas Becket, the archbishop of Canterbury, settles in the Cistercian monastery at Pontigny under the protection of King Louis VII (→ 22/5/65).

Strathclyde, 1164. Somerled, the lord of Argyll and ruler of the Scottish isles, and his son are killed during their invasion of Renfrew (→ 16/5/1212).

Germany, 22 May 1165. King Henry II of England's clerks swear allegiance to Paschal III, the anti-pope [ie, his election as pope is disputed] (→ 24/4/66).

Wales, September 1165. On the withdrawal of Henry II's troops, Rhys ap Gruffudd, the ruler of Deheubarth, seizes castles and land in the area known as Ceredigion (→ 1170).

France, 24 April 1166. Pope Alexander III makes Thomas Becket his legate, in response to Henry II of England's loyalty to the anti-pope, Paschal III (→ 14/6/70).

Winchester, spring 1166. The new Scots king, William, provokes a row with Henry II by demanding the restoration of Northumberland (→ 15/6/70).

Ireland, August 1167. Diarmait Mac Murchada, the former king of Leinster, returns from exile with troops from Wales, recruited with the permission of Henry II of England, to whom he has sworn fealty. He re-establishes himself in the Ui Chennselaig kingdom (→ 1168).

Normandy, 10 September 1167. Empress Matilda, the daughter of King Henry I of England, mother of Henry II and a former claimant to the English throne, dies at Rouen aged 65 (→ 11/6/72).

France, 1167. Henry II of England and Louis VII make peace after the betrothal of Duke Richard of Aquitaine, Henry's son, to Alice, Louis's daughter (→ 7/4/68).

Poitou, France, 7 April 1168. The English governor, Earl Patrick of Wiltshire, is murdered (→ 1/1169).

Ireland, 1168. High King Ruaidri Ua Conchobair divides the kingdom of Meath with his ally King Tigernan Ua Ruairc of Breifne (→ 1/5/69).

Ireland, 1 May 1169. Robert fitzStephen lands at Bannow Bay, Co Wexford (→ 23/8/70).

Becket flees to France

Northampton, 14 October 1164
Thomas Becket, the archbishop of Canterbury, fearing arrest by his erstwhile friend King Henry II, has fled the king's council here and is believed to be making his way to France. His flight follows a quarrel between these two powerful, arrogant men which sprang to life when Henry made Becket archbishop two years ago.

Becket, when chancellor, had been Henry's boon companion. But the moment he was consecrated the merry chancellor became a rigorous archbishop, jealous of his church's privileges. He challenged the king over properties that he considered had been taken illegally from Canterbury and insisted that clerics could be tried only by (more lenient) ecclesiastical courts, even for secular offences.

He thus set himself on a collision course with King Henry, who was determined to win back powers lost by the crown to the church under his weak predecessor, Stephen. The king drew up the "Constitutions of Clarendon", designed to restore his "grandfather's [Henry I] customs" of total obedience to the crown.

Becket resisted. The break between the two old friends became complete, and at Northampton last week Becket was sued for the return of land and ordered to account for royal money which he swore that he had spent on behalf of the king. It was becoming clear that Henry intended to demand his resignation. Following alleged threats of violence, the archbishop fled early this morning (→ 12/1164).

An engraving of Becket's mitre.

Scottish king who stood up to English suffers early death

Borders, 9 December 1165
The 24-year-old Scottish king, Malcolm IV, has died at Jedburgh after a long illness. Excessive fasting – Malcolm was a deeply religious man – is thought to be the cause of his early death. Malcolm's great achievement during his 12-year reign was to resist Henry II of England's bullying. Although he had to give up Northumberland and do homage for his lands in Huntingdon, he never did homage for his kingdom. In other words, he never recognized the authority of an English king over Scotland.

Malcolm made shrewd marriage alliances for his sisters with Holland and Brittany to secure his independence from Henry. At home he was a good administrator and a generous patron of the church, especially of monastic orders. He was also a gifted campaigner, defeating both Fergus, the lord of Galloway, and the rebel Somerled of Argyll, the lord of the Isles, whom he crushed last year. Although Malcolm was said to have a bastard son – somewhat at odds with his reputation for celibacy – his successor will be William, his more worldly brother (→ spring 1166).

Humiliated Henry is finally forced to negotiate in Wales

Wales, summer 1165
In brutal retaliation for the failure of his military expedition to put down a rising in Wales which began in 1163, King Henry II of England has had 22 young Welsh hostages held at his court since then mutilated and killed. The rising followed the Council of Woodstock, in July of 1163, before which Henry had taken Rhys ap Gruffudd of Deheubarth prisoner for attempting to seize the strategic castle of Llandovery.

The Woodstock conference ended with Malcolm IV, the king of Scotland, Rhys, the prince of southern Wales, and Owain Gwynedd of northern Wales doing homage to the king of England. But the terms of this homage defined Henry's overlordship of Wales in a way that was particularly demeaning. Almost at once the entire region rose up in arms.

The king prepared his response with care. In October 1164 his barons promised to supply him with the infantry for a hill campaign. In July of this year the army marched towards Corwen along the traditional invasion route known as the English Road, and it was here that the plan began to go horribly wrong. Unseasonable rainstorms turned the summer moors into bogs. Biting winds and attacks by elusive enemies eroded morale, and when supplies ran low the decision to retreat was inevitable.

Henry has pressing concerns across the Channel, but after this year it is likely that any attempt to deal with the Welsh must involve him in negotiations. Both Rhys and Owain are free now to reassert their own power, and the Norman barons of the south-west of Wales are rumoured to be setting their sights on what they hope will be an easier target – Ireland (→ 9/1165).

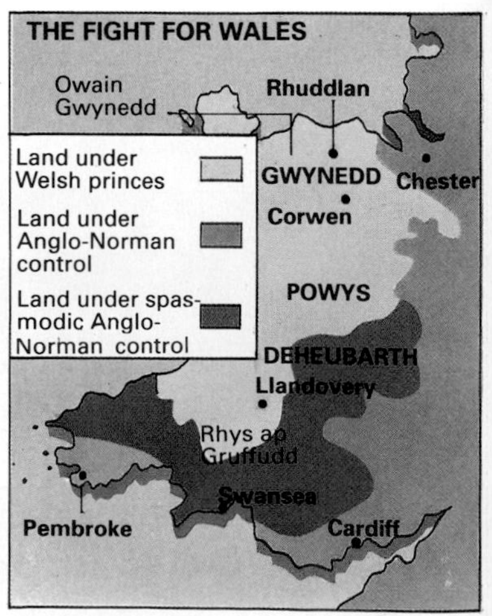

Irish high king dies

Three vivid male figures adorn a house-shrine from Drumlane, Co Cavan.

Ireland, 1166
Muirchertach Mac Lochlainn, who has dominated the Irish political struggle for the past ten years, has been killed by King Tigernan Ua Ruairc of Breifne and King Donnchad Ua Cerbaill of Airgialla. He had tried and failed to dominate both the Cenel Conaill in the west and the Ulaid in the east of his northern territory.

In an incident which caused intense revulsion, Muirchertach took captive King Eochaid Mac Duinn Sleibe of the Ulaid and blinded him. His enemies, notably Ruaidri Ua Conchobair of Connacht, who has succeeded him as "high king with opposition", seized the opportunity to destroy him. Muirchertach's allies soon deserted him, and he died defending his kingdom.

Ruaidri's sudden rise to power has altered the position of Muirchertach's chief ally, King Diarmait Mac Murchada of Leinster. His fate has been sealed by a revolt against him by the Leinstermen and the Dublin Norse, who have razed to the ground his stone house at Ferns and expelled him from royal office. Deprived of support, Diarmait has sailed to England in search of allies (→1167).

The knight, the queen and the bishop: three carved walrus-ivory chessmen of the late 12th century, from Uig, Isle of Lewis, Western Isles.

New law reforms curb barons' power

Wiltshire, January 1166
King Henry II has called his barons to a conference at Clarendon, near Salisbury, to hammer out major law reforms. Sheriffs (royal officers of shires, or counties) will acquire increased powers – at the barons' expense – and juries will be introduced into every hundred (the basic unit of local government).

Sheriffs appointed by the king will investigate robbery, murder, theft and arson. They will arrest suspects and bring them to trial. Barons and towns, until now enjoying the right to try criminals, must give this up to the king's officers.

Twelve-man juries, which originate in pre-Conquest times, will also have wider powers. Juries will examine crimes, and those indicted must be brought to trial. Those convicted will lose their land, which reverts to their lords, and their moveable property, which is to be sold. The proceeds go to the king.

Richard of Lucy, the justiciar, or king's chief deputy, and Geoffrey de Mandeville, the earl of Essex, are to tour the country to implement the new system (→26/1/76).

England and France put down weapons

Montmirail, France, January 1169
Henry II of England and Louis VII of France seem to have brought their bloody quarrel to an uneasy peace at this small border town. But some uncertainty remains.

Henry has announced arrangements for the division of his "empire" after his death in order to allay Louis's fears of the growing influence throughout his kingdom of the Angevins [the descendants of Geoffrey of Anjou, Henry's father]. England, Normandy and Anjou are to go to Henry's eldest son, also Henry, while 11-year-old Richard will rule Aquitaine [*see map on page 232*]. With Henry already married to one of Louis's daughters from his second marriage, and Richard betrothed to another, Henry has in effect asked Louis to divide France between their families, and the two boys have paid him homage.

A reminder, however, that another bitter quarrel also had a part in the recent conflict came from Archbishop Thomas Becket, who refused to settle his dispute with Henry despite the efforts of his present protector, Louis (→22/8/79).

Tales of King Arthur spread far and wide

England, c.1168
"Who is there, I ask, who does not speak of Arthur the Briton? The Eastern peoples speak of him as do the Western." The anonymous writer's words illustrate the current craze for the Arthurian legend.

It has reached such a pitch that the "prophecies of Merlin" are treated with deadly seriousness. John Marshal, an acquaintance of the legend's first chronicler, Geoffrey of Monmouth [*see page 220*], was recently charged with treason for reporting that a "prophet" had denied the legend that Arthur, who led the Britons against the Anglo-Saxons at Mount Badon and Camlann the early sixth century, would not return alive.

The legend is popular in France, where a translation of Geoffrey and a new version, the *Roman de Brut* by the poet Wace, introducing Arthur's Knights of the Round Table, appeared around 1150. Chrétien de Troyes, a clerk at the court of Champagne, is re-inventing the story, adding a quest for the Holy Grail and an affair between a new knight, Lancelot, and Guinevere, a queen for Arthur (→c.1190).

Manuscripts spread Arthur's fame.

Westminster, 14 June 1170. In defiance of Thomas Becket, the exiled archbishop of Canterbury, Henry, the eldest living son of King Henry II of England, is crowned heir to the throne of England, Normandy and Anjou by Roger, the archbishop of York (→ 1/12).

London, 15 June 1170. King William of Scotland, as an English landowner, and the barons of England are forced by Henry II to swear allegiance to "Young King" Henry (→ 10/1173).

Munster, 23 August 1170. Richard "Strongbow" fitzGilbert, the earl of Striguil [Chepstow], lands near Waterford with 200 knights and 1,000 men in support of Diarmait Mac Murchada's attempt to take the high-kingship (→ 1/5/71).

Sandwich, Kent, 1 December 1170. Following his reconciliation with Henry II, Thomas Becket returns to England after six years' exile and is reinstated as archbishop of Canterbury (→ 3).

Canterbury, Kent, 3 December 1170. Becket excommunicates clerics opposed to him, including the archbishop of York and the bishops of London and Salisbury, all involved in crowning Young King Henry (→ 18).

Southwark, London, 18 Dec 1170. After an enthusiastic reception from the city of London, Becket is ordered by Young King Henry at Woodstock to return to his church (→ 25).

Normandy, 25 December 1170. Henry II of England is infuriated by news from the excommunicated clergy of Becket's actions (→ 29).

Gwynedd, 1170. On the death of Owain Gwynedd, his lands are divided between his sons and grandsons. Rhys ap Gruffudd, the lord of Deheubarth [in south Wales], is now the most powerful man in the country (→ 17/4/72).

Rome, April 1171. Pope Alexander III interdicts King Henry II of England for the murder of Archbishop Thomas Becket (→ 21/2/73).

Ferns, Co Wexford, 1 May 1171. Diarmait Mac Murchada, the king of Leinster, dies. Richard Strongbow, as his daughter Aife's husband, inherits his kingdom (→ 11/11/71).

Archbishop murdered on holy ground

Kent, 29 December 1170

Thomas Becket, the archbishop of Canterbury, was murdered in his own cathedral by four of King Henry's knights this evening, only four weeks after his return from six years of exile in France. He was 50.

His death drowns in blood the fragile peace made by Henry and his former friend at the French town of Fréteval on 22 July and confirms Becket's own foreboding. "I go to England," he had said, "whether to peace or to destruction I know not; but God has decreed what fate awaits me." He made no attempt to avoid that fate, rushing at it head-on and causing turmoil in England. He processed proudly through London, scattering alms to the cheering crowds. He also inflicted punishments, sanctioned by the pope, on his enemies in the church, especially the bishops who had officiated at the crowning in June of Henry's young son as king-in-waiting, a privilege that Becket insisted belonged to Canterbury.

News of his behaviour, undoubtedly embellished, was carried to King Henry in France by the archbishop of York and the bishops of London and Salisbury whom he had excommunicated. Becket, they said, was ready to "tear the crown from the young king's head".

Henry was enraged. On Christmas day he erupted. "What a pack of fools and cowards have I nourished in my household," he cried, "that not one of them will avenge me of this turbulent priest."

This was enough for four of the knights who surrounded him. William de Tracy, Reginald fitzUrse, Hugh de Murville and Richard le Breton rode hard for the coast and took ship to England, arriving last night at Saltwood Castle in Kent, the home of Becket's enemies, the de Brocs. This afternoon they rode to the archbishop's palace where he was talking with his advisers. A terrible quarrel ensued between the angry knights and Becket.

The knights left after ordering some monks to guard Becket, who ran after them shouting: "I have not returned to Canterbury to run away. You'll find me here. And in the Lord's battle I will fight hand to hand, toe to toe." The knights armed themselves for battle in a garden and returned to the palace, breaking in through a window. The archbishop was ushered to sanctuary in the holy ground of the cathedral, but the knights hunted him down and, after another furious altercation during which they tried to arrest him, they struck out with their swords, cutting off the crown of his head so that his brains fell onto the floor. He is being buried tonight near where he fell (→ 4/1171).

Prince Henry is crowned, from a 13th-century "Life of Becket".

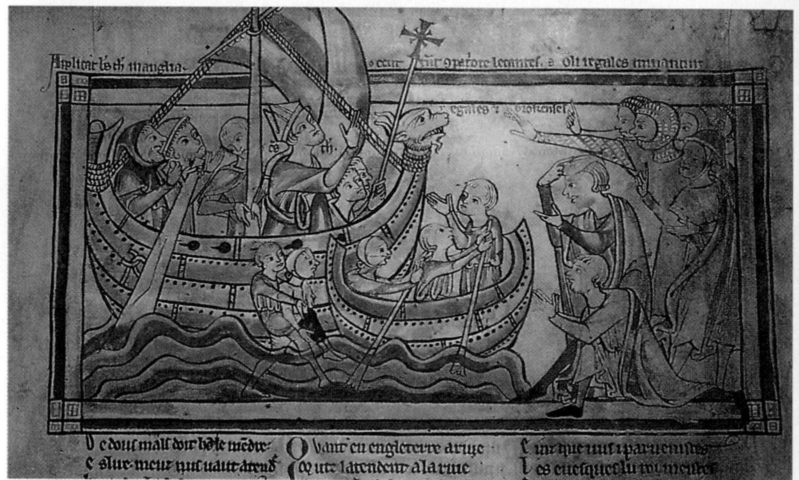

Thomas returns from his French exile (from the "Life of Becket", above).

The archbishop slain: Becket's murder, as illustrated in a manuscript c.1180.

London thrives as population grows to exceed 30,000

London, 1170

Many houses have recently been completed for London's burgeoning population of more than 30,000. Now indubitably England's greatest city, its boundaries stretch as far as Ludgate and Newgate to the west, Cripplegate and Bishopsgate to the north and north-east, the river Thames to the south, and the White Tower to the east.

Buildings for the aristocracy – barons, bishops and abbots – have paved courtyards, huge halls and spacious gardens. They are not confined to one quarter of the city but

London: 13th-century baron's seal.

are scattered about, surrounded by smaller houses which are designed as combined shops and living quarters for the merchant classes, with rear extensions for outhouses and cesspits. Much has yet to be done to improve the humble dwellings of the unskilled workers. A large suburb has sprung up outside the city wall running as far as the palace of Westminster. London boasts over 100 churches amid the muddy, garbage-strewn streets and bustling markets. The Jewish quarter is well served with synagogues.

To meet popular demand, a public cookhouse has opened beside the Thames, serving fish and game dishes. To lessen the fouling of the streets, a riverside public lavatory is in operation. The large fields adjoining the hospital and priory of St Bartholomew, the site of colourful weekly horse sales, are under consideration for development. Nearby is access to woodlands containing deer, wild boars and bulls (→1281).

Ireland bows the knee to England

Dublin, 11 November 1171

Less than a month after his arrival in Ireland, King Henry II of England has marched here from Waterford to receive the submission of the kings of north Leinster, Breifne, Airgialla and Ulster. (Ruaidri Ua Conchobair, the high king, has not submitted.) Dublin has been granted to Henry's knights from Bristol while Henry controls the seaports. Having held out for nearly a century, much of Ireland now lies within the Anglo-Norman world.

The roots of today's events go back to when Diarmait Mac Murchada was ousted from Leinster in 1166 [*see report on page 237*]. He went to Bristol, Aquitaine and then Wales seeking Norman help to regain his kingdom. Chief among his recruits was Richard fitzGilbert de Clare (nicknamed Strongbow), the earl of Striguil [Chepstow], enticed by the offer of Diarmait's daughter, Aife, in marriage, in addition to all of Leinster on Diarmait's death. Other recruits were Robert fitzStephen and his half-brother, Maurice fitzGerald, who were promised Wexford.

These and others, among them Raymond "le Gros" fitzWilliam, landed in Ireland between May 1169 and August 1170. By 21 September 1170 Diarmait, aided by his Norman allies, had taken Dublin and reconquered Leinster. But when Strongbow inherited Leinster on Diarmait's death on 1 May this year, King Henry – whose right to rule Ireland was granted by Pope Adrian IV in 1155 – moved swiftly

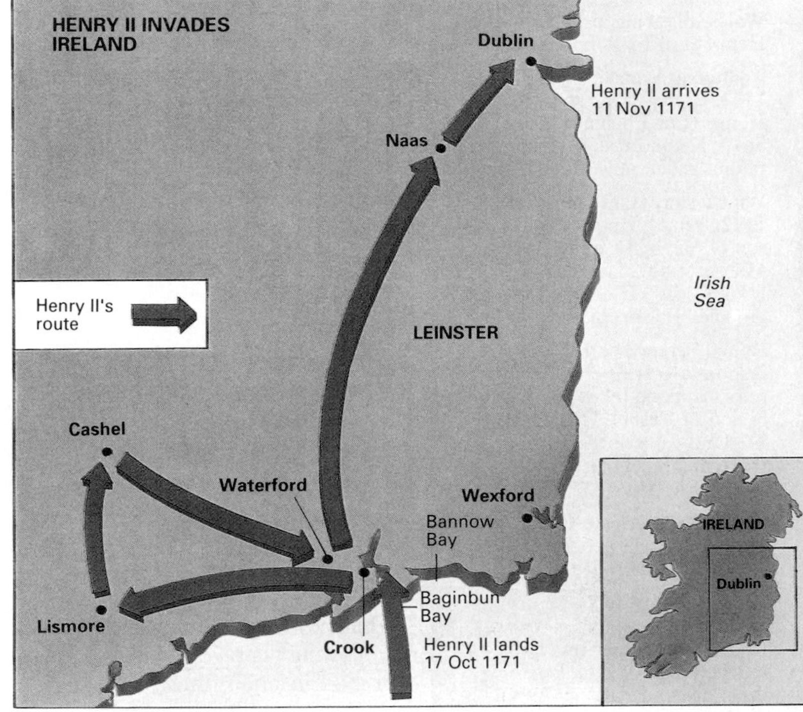

to prevent the establishment of a rival Norman kingdom here. He landed on 17 October, having already agreed terms with Strongbow – who keeps Leinster as a fief.

In recognizing Henry as overlord, Irish leaders have something to gain: protection against Strongbow and his ilk. They have not lost sovereignty but have simply transferred allegiance from the high king to the "son of the empress [Matilda]". Henry may now attempt to introduce church "reform" here (that is, conformity with English church customs) to give his actions a pious sheen (→9/1172).

Robert fitzStephen at Wexford.

Steps to invasion

1 May 1169: Robert fitzStephen lands at Bannow Bay.
May 1169: Diarmait Mac Murchada and Norman allies take Wexford.
May 1170: Raymond "le Gros" fitzWilliam lands at Baginbun.
25 Aug 1170: Richard Strongbow, who landed two days ago, takes Waterford with Raymond fitzWilliam and marries Aife.
21 Sept 1170: Diarmait and Norman allies take Dublin.
17 Oct 1171: Henry II lands at Crook, near Waterford.

Welsh baron's ambition sparked action

Ireland, 1171

Richard Strongbow is a central figure in the events leading to King Henry II of England's invasion of Ireland. His role began when, as a top baron in Wales – he is the earl of Striguil [Chepstow] – he was approached by Diarmait Mac Murchada for help to regain his lands in Leinster. As a result, Strongbow was by this autumn master of Dublin, Waterford and Wexford – and married to Aife, Diarmait's daughter. He had also inherited Leinster – Diarmait had died in May. But Henry had awakened to the danger of an independent Norman kingdom on his western seaboard. He embargoed all shipping to Ireland and prepared to invade.

Realizing that a decisive curb was about to be placed on his ambitions, Strongbow had better sense than to fight. Instead he begged for forgiveness and, although having lost everything else, has at least been allowed to keep Leinster as a fief. Strongbow had claimed Meath as well, but Henry has appointed his own man, Hugh de Lacy, as justiciar (king's deputy) and viceroy and given him all of Meath.

1172 - 1174

Laugharne, Dyfed, 17 April 1172. Rhys ap Gruffudd is appointed justiciar of south Wales following a treaty with Henry II of England (→ 6/1175).

Aquitaine, France, 11 June 1172. Richard, the son of Henry II of England, becomes duke. His mother, Eleanor, retains much power (→ 21/8).

Winchester, Hants, 21 August 1172. Young King Henry, the son of Henry II, and his wife, Margaret, the daughter of King Louis VII of France, are crowned (→ spring 1173).

Rome, September 1172. In response to Irish church reforms made by the 1171 Synod of Cashel, Henry II of England's overlordship of Ireland is recognized by Pope Alexander III (→ 1174).

Rome, 21 February 1173. Thomas Becket is canonized by Pope Alexander III (→ 12/7/74).

France, spring 1173. Henry II's three eldest sons, Henry, Richard and Geoffrey, having rebelled against him, base themselves in Paris (→ 29/9).

Lothian, October 1173. King William of Scots offers to back King Henry II of England against his sons in return for control of Northumberland. When the offer is refused, he invades (→ 14/7/74).

Italy, 7 April 1174. Richard, the prior of Dover, is consecrated as archbishop of Canterbury (→ 18/8/91).

Canterbury, Kent, 12 July 1174. Henry II walks barefoot through the city, prays in the cathedral and is scourged for the death of Becket (→ 28/5/75).

Hartlepool, Cleveland, July 1174. The fleet of Count Hugh of Bar, which landed to aid King William of Scots in his invasion of England, returns to Flanders on learning of the capture of William (→ 29).

Huntingdon, Cambridgeshire, 29 July 1174. After the surrender of Earl David of Huntingdon, the brother of King William of Scots, Henry II's men defeat Earl Hugh Bigod of Norfolk and force him to do homage (→ 30/9).

Galloway, 1174. Uhtred, the son of Fergus, the late lord of Galloway, is killed by his brother Gilbert in a quarrel over their inheritance (→ 1186).

Leinster, 1174. In an anti-Norman rising, the native Irish under Ruaidri Ua Conchobhair destroy Norman forts at Trim and Duleek (→ 1175).

Three sons plot to undermine position of the English king

Facing a family fight: King Henry.

Chinon, France, November 1173

Following the revolt by King Henry II of England's three eldest sons, their mother Queen Eleanor – implicated in the revolt – has been arrested. She tried to escape from Chinon disguised as a man but was caught by her husband's officers.

The eldest of the rebels, Henry, who is 18, is the titular king of England and duke of Normandy but protests that his father allows him no real authority in either place and denies him the revenues that should go with his titles. Richard, the second rebel son, aged 15, the titular duke of Aquitaine, and Geoffrey, the third son, to whom the barons of Brittany swore allegiance in 1169, have the same complaint. They also oppose Henry's wish to give considerable lands to the youngest son, John.

What all this amounts to is a family conspiracy against the king to strip him of his powers and possessions. King Louis VII of France has incited Young King Henry against his father. Louis, whose daughter Margaret is the young king's wife, used himself to be married to Eleanor; they were divorced in 1152. Henry II has now interned her in a castle. The queen, 11 years older than her husband, is a strong woman who resents the strict discipline imposed on her, allowing her no independence at all. Although she has borne Henry eight children he has now taken a mistress, Rosamund Clifford (→ 29/7/74).

Rebel earls crushed at Bury St Edmunds

Suffolk, 29 September 1173

Barons loyal to King Henry have won a great victory over rebels near Bury St Edmunds in Suffolk. An army of Flemish mercenaries led by Earl Robert of Leicester and Earl Hugh Bigod of Norfolk has been destroyed. Local peasants drove the Flemings into the bogs and slaughtered them.

Robert and Hugh are the leading supporters in England of Henry's vengeful sons. (Hugh of Cyveiliog, the earl of Chester, also rebelled.) After their allies on the continent, Count Philip of Flanders and Louis VII of France, were defeated by the king last month, the earls launched a new offensive in England. They marched on Leicester, besieged by Richard of Lucy, England's justiciar (king's chief deputy), who remains loyal to Henry. Lucy had gone north to deal with an invasion of Northumberland by William of Scotland, who has been driven back across the border (→ 11/1173).

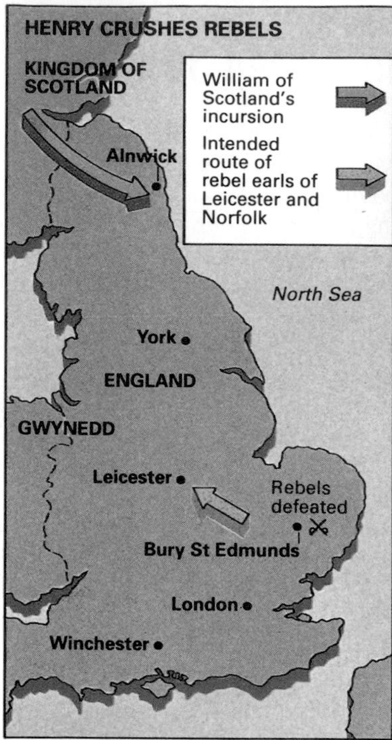

Attacked on two fronts: Henry is threatened by Scots and earls.

Woman fights to maintain forced marriage

England, 1172

In a far-reaching decision, Pope Alexander III has validated the disputed marriage between Aubrey de Vere, the earl of Oxford, and his young wife Agnes. Childless from two previous marriages, de Vere married Agnes ten years ago by arrangement, when she was 12. Less than a year later he was contesting the union – on tenuous grounds, claiming that Agnes was already betrothed to his own brother at the time of the wedding. Agnes always denied this allegation and appealed to the bishop of London and to Pope Alexander. She has won; Alexander has ordered de Vere to treat Agnes as his wife before God. What this bizarre episode proves is that women have so few options that marriage – even an arranged one to a reluctant husband – is better than being left single (→ 1185).

This "lunette" above the south porch of St Mary's Abbey at Malmesbury in Wiltshire depicts six seated apostles with an angel flying above them. The scene was carved c.1160-70 in the Romanesque style and is considered to be one of the finest examples of its kind in England.

Scots king taken captive

Alnwick Castle (a 20th-century view), near which King William was captured.

North Yorkshire, 14 July 1174
Under close guard and shackled to a horse, Scotland's King William, known as "the Lion" or "the Brawny", was brought to Richmond, in North Yorkshire, today and handed over to King Henry of England. The war in northern England, which had been going very well for William until recently, may be about to end. As the news of his capture spreads, church bells are ringing out across England.

William was taken prisoner yesterday near Alnwick Castle, which is under siege by the Scots. A party of some 400 English knights – who had set out from Newcastle under the command of Robert of Estouteville, the king's sheriff, hoping to inflict some damage on the Scots – surprised William and his escort of 60 knights resting in a meadow. The Scots put up a tough fight until all of them were either slaughtered or captured. William's horse was killed under him; he was thrown to the ground before being seized.

For the past few years Henry has faced formidable enemies in both England and France. In some parts of England there has been virtual open rebellion. The Scots have raided as far south as Yorkshire in pursuit of William's claim to Northumberland (→ 8/12).

England and Scotland agree peace terms

King William "the Lion" of Scotland: a 17th-century engraving.

Normandy, 8 December 1174
After being held in chains since his capture in July, Scotland's King William has made peace with King Henry II of England. The Treaty of Falaise, signed today, gives Henry overlordship of Scotland, but William can return home.

The Scots also have to accept the subjugation of their church to that of England. William's major castles have been handed over, and he has lost all his land in England. And some important hostages are to be sent to England to ensure the good behaviour of the Scots, including the king's brother. Territory is not Henry's main concern. What he wants from the treaty is security on his northern border (→ 10/8/75).

Henry pardons sons to promote harmony

France, 30 September 1174
King Henry of England has made peace with his rebellious sons at Montlouis in Touraine, bringing an end to the civil war. He has pardoned them, and most of their followers, in the hope of restoring peace to the land.

He has not, however, pardoned Queen Eleanor, who remains under house arrest. The eldest rebel son, Henry, the "Young King", and the second one, Richard, have both been given castles and revenues. One reason for their revolt was that the king had refused to give them incomes sufficient for their needs. King William of Scots, captured at Alnwick in Northumberland last July, will be required to swear allegiance to the king before he is released. As for France, Henry has decided to restore the status quo and will not attack King Louis VII.

Henry has ordered all the English rebels' castles to be demolished and has also decided to demolish many of his supporters' castles as well. They are a menace to the peace and an incitement to rebellion. He has pardoned his most dangerous opponents, Earl Robert of Leicester and Earl Hugh Bigod of Norfolk, and his sons have also agreed to pardon barons who stayed loyal to the king (→ 1/4/75).

Canterbury Cathedral destroyed by fire

Restoration work: a late 12th-century fresco of St Paul from Canterbury.

Kent, 5 September 1174
A devastating fire has swept its way through Canterbury Cathedral during the night and has caused enormous damage, particularly to the east end of the building. Monks have spent the night tearing down hangings and metalwork to cheat the fire's advance. Attempts have also been made to collect the highly venerated relics of saints that had been scattered around the altar. So extensive is the damage that it is thought unlikely that the old framework of the building can be reused, and there is talk of bringing in a French architect, William of Sens, to design a new choir. If that plan were to go ahead, then this cathedral, built by Lanfranc, its first Norman archbishop, would be one of the first English buildings to feature the new Gothic style so popular in northern France (→ c.1200).

1175 - 1179

Strathclyde, 1175. King William grants the bishop of Glasgow a royal burgh (→ 1191).

Leinster, 1175. High King Ruaidri Ua Conchobair ends his campaign in Meath, giving the Normans a chance to rebuild their forces (→ 6/10/75).

Normandy, 1 April 1175. Young King Henry, following his brothers Richard and Geoffrey, pledges allegiance to King Henry II of England, his father, at Bur-la-Roi (→ 1176).

Canterbury, Kent, 28 May 1175. King Henry, Young King Henry and his brothers arrive on a pilgrimage (→ 1176).

Gloucester, June 1175. King Henry II meets the Welsh princes and betroths his half-sister, Emma, to Dafydd ab Owain, the prince of Gwynedd, at a council (→ 1177).

Wales, June 1175. William of Briouze and Richard Strongbow fall from Henry II of England's favour after their actions against the nobles of Gwent (→ 1177).

Leinster, 1176. William fitzAudelin, who is to be procurator of Ireland, and John de Courcy arrive to further the Anglo-Norman conquest of Ireland (→ 20/4/76).

Ulster, 1177. John de Courcy invades, captures Downpatrick and builds a castle.

Oxford, 1177. The Welsh princes swear allegiance to King Henry II (→ 9/1184).

Connacht, 1177. Ruaidri Ua Conchobair defeats the Normans, led by Miles de Cogan and his own son, Muirchertach (→ 5/1177).

Oxford, May 1177. With the pope's authority Henry II proclaims his ten-year-old son John lord of Ireland (→ 1181).

Newcastle upon Tyne, 1178. The fortress begun by King Henry I is completed.

Scotland, 1178. Countess Ada, the mother of King William, dies (→ 1179).

Woodstock, Oxfordshire, 6 August 1178. Henry II knights his son Geoffrey (→ 1/4/80).

Highland, 1179. William leads an expedition against the rebel Donald mac William, the grandson of the deposed Donald II (→ 7/1181).

Rheims, France, 1 November 1179. Young King Henry, as co-king of England, attends the coronation of Louis's son, Philip (→ 13/9/80).

Scots do homage to Henry of England

York, 10 August 1175
King William of Scots has today sworn loyalty to King Henry of England before all the major Scottish lords and leading clergy. Scotland's political leaders then followed him in doing formal homage to Henry under the Treaty of Falaise.

Along with Henry's lordship, the Scots have had to accept the subjection of their church to that of England. William has lost all his English lands, including the earldom of Huntingdon, and any chance of regaining Northumberland, the initial cause of his attack on Henry. He has also agreed to hand over all the major castles in the south of Scotland.

A number of hostages are to be sent to England, including the king's brother, Earl David. Henry sees no need to subject Scotland to full military occupation (→ 1178).

Ireland treaty is sealed

A 12th-century cross from Co Clare.

Berkshire, 6 October 1175
The Treaty of Windsor has been sealed five days after the Normans, aided by High King Ruaidri Ua Conchobair, seized the town of Limerick. It establishes, for the first time, a constitutional relationship between Anglo-Norman and Gaelic rulers in Ireland. The guiding influence in promoting the treaty is thought to have come from Irish church leaders anxious for both peace and church reform.

Ruaidri must now submit to King Henry II of England, pay him an annual tribute and accept his direct jurisdiction over Meath, Leinster and areas between Dublin and Waterford which are held in the king's name. Outside Henry's jurisdiction Ruaidri is recognized as high king, and his traditional rights are acknowledged. The success of the treaty will depend on his effectiveness as high king (→ 1176).

England's grip on Ireland grows at Strongbow's death

Ireland, 20 April 1176
The Anglo-Norman commander Richard fitzGilbert, who was popularly known as "Strongbow", has died of gangrene aged 47. He came to Ireland in 1170 at the invitation of Diarmait Mac Murchada, the exiled king of Leinster, who had sought help from King Henry II of England to regain his kingdom.

Diarmait won Leinster back shortly before his death in 1171, after which it passed to Strongbow – by then his son-in-law – as arranged, even though Diarmait had a son still living. After lengthy arguments with Henry, Strongbow agreed to hand over to him Dublin and the seaport towns. In 1173 he was appointed *custos* [keeper] of Ireland. In that post he strengthened the Anglo-Normans' hold: he consolidated his position in Leinster and pushed west into Munster and north into Ulster.

Strongbow is to be buried in Christchurch Cathedral in Dublin. Since his two children are under age, his lands now come into the king's wardship (→ 1177).

Poetry and music festival held in Cardigan

Cardigan, Dyfed, 1176
A festival of poetry and music has been held at Cardigan, arranged by Lord Rhys ap Gruffudd of Deheubarth. It was designed to bring together two sorts of entertainers – the musicians, whether playing the pipes, the harp or other stringed instruments, and the bards and poets. To attract entrants Rhys offered substantial cash prizes, as well as sponsorship for the future efforts of the winners. Two chairs were set up to enthrone the overall victors. On the day a young man from Rhys's own court carried off the prize for playing the strings, while a poet from Gwynedd was judged to have produced the finest verses.

A musician playing his harp.

Henry appoints new justices for England

Northampton, 26 January 1176
King Henry II today strengthened the crown's hold on the administration of justice by decreeing at a special assize here that the kingdom be split into six districts, to each of which will be assigned three royal judges. Henry, who is a keen lawyer, aims to bring a truer justice to the people than that at present meted out by local courts, which invoke old-established and haphazard local customs, invariably favouring the richest and the strongest.

The justices, mostly chosen from trusted barons, bishops and abbots, will make regular circuits of their areas to preside at trials. At the same time they will be expected to collect outstanding crown revenues to go to the exchequer (→ 1179).

London plans Becket memorial bridge

The old timber bridge over the Thames at London (artist's reconstruction).

London, 1176
Plans have been agreed for the construction of a bridge to span the river Thames in London. It will be a memorial to Thomas Becket – the archbishop of Canterbury who was brutally murdered on the altar steps of his cathedral six years ago.

The enterprise is the brainchild of Peter de Colechurch, the parish priest of St Mary's church in Cheapside. So many of the city's previous bridges, built of timber, have been destroyed by fire or flood; Colechurch's plan is to build one of Kentish ragstone and furnish it with houses, the rent being used to pay for maintenance work.

The Bridge House Trust has been set up by Colechurch, raising funds from charitable organizations. It is expected that the bridge might take up to 30 years to complete, starting with a chapel, in the new Gothic style which is becoming popular on the continent, to give the bridge a religious significance. It should be a fine memorial to a much-loved Londoner and a former parishioner of Cheapside (→25/10/80).

Scots church keeps its independence

Rome, 8 November 1176
A refusal by the Scottish bishops to submit to the English church has been upheld by Rome. The demand for submission was made in January at Northampton by Henry II of England as a condition of the treaty which brought about King William's release last year. Both parties then appealed to Rome.

The pope sent a legate to deliver a denunciation of Henry's interference in church affairs. Archbishop Roger of York was forbidden to exercise any authority over the Scottish episcopate, which now appears to have put paid to this latest attempt by York to impose dominance north of the border (→1182).

Rumour surrounds royal lover's death

Oxford, 1176
Henry II's favourite mistress, Rosamund Clifford, has been buried at Godstow nunnery, Oxford. The king – who met Rosamund six years ago, when he was 40 and she was still a girl – has ordered her tomb to be set before the high altar and draped with a silken pall.

Some say that Rosamund was poisoned by Queen Eleanor; the most fanciful story has it that Henry kept Rosamund in a bower near Woodstock, hidden in a labyrinth to which he alone held the secret. But, the story continues, the queen found her way in after attaching a silken thread to her husband's heel (→13/11/77).

A wedding to unite England and Sicily

Palermo, Sicily, 13 February 1177
The good relations that England has always enjoyed with the Norman kingdom of Sicily were today strengthened by the marriage of Joan, the youngest of King Henry of England's three daughters, to King William II of Sicily.

It was a splendid ceremony, and Joan has joined her sisters in being married off to a suitable husband. Her eldest sister, Matilda, is married to Duke Henry "the Lion" of Saxony, and Eleanor is married to King Alfonso VIII of Castile. They are all comfortable marriages rather than unions of any great political significance (→6/8/78).

Land disputes to be resolved by juries

Windsor, Berkshire, 1179
In the latest round of legal reforms, King Henry II has introduced "trial by jury" as an alternative to trial by battle to settle land disputes. Under this new procedure, a number of carefully chosen knights of the shire consult widely before reporting to the royal justices which party has the *maius ius*, or greater right, to the land. This experiment is not thought to be suitable to deal with Britain's crime epidemic. Juries are used to indict criminals, but ordeal by water is the standard trial. Those who fail it face execution, banishment or mutilation of the foot (→c.1180).

French king is first to land in England

Canterbury, Kent, 22 August 1179
King Louis VII of France has made a pilgrimage to the shrine of St Thomas Becket and in so doing has become the first reigning French king to set foot on English soil. Louis, aged 60, was hoping to have his 14-year-old son Philip crowned as co-king this month, but Philip fell seriously ill and his father had a dream that he should pray at the shrine of St Thomas. King Henry II has received Louis, and he stayed at court for five days. Henry's acquisition of parts of Aquitaine has discomfited the French king, but for now territorial quarrels have been set aside (→1/11/79).

The sign of the goat: a beautifully drawn illustration of Capricorn, from an English psalter [book of psalms] made at York in about 1170.

1180 - 1184

Reading, 1 April 1180. Young King Henry arrives to pay homage to his father, Henry II (→ 28/7/81).

Paris, 13 September 1180. Louis VII of France, who surrendered his throne to his son Philip after a stroke earlier this year, dies (→ 28/7/81).

England, 28 July 1181. At a conference involving Henry II of England, William "the Lion" of Scotland, Philip II of France and Young King Henry, Henry II surrenders Normandy to his son the Young King (→ 12/1182).

Highland, July 1181. In the absence of King William, a rebellion led by Donald mac William and Harald Maddason, the earl of Orkney, breaks out in Ross (→ 1186).

Dublin, 6 September 1181. John Cumin becomes archbishop in succession to Lorcan Ua Tuathail, who died last year (→ 14/1/1217).

Ireland, 1181. Hugh de Lacy, who married the daughter of High King Ruaidri Ua Conchobair last year, becomes the first Anglo-Norman *custos* [keeper] of Ireland (→ 1183).

Normandy, December 1182. Matilda, the daughter of Henry II of England, and her husband, Duke Henry V of Saxony and Bavaria, flee to safety after their expulsion from Germany for inciting rebellion (→ 11/6/83).

Scotland, 1182. King William, who was excommunicated last year when he refused to accept Pope Lucius III's nominee, John the Scot, as bishop of St Andrews, is readmitted to the church and receives a golden rose of honour after a mission to the pope by his loyal churchmen (→ 11/3/92).

France, September 1183. After the death of Young King Henry, Henry II of England requests his son Richard, now his heir, to give his own duchy of Aquitaine to his brother John; Richard refuses (→ 6/12).

Normandy, 6 December 1183. Henry II of England settles his disputes with Philip II of France and pays him homage at Gisors (→ 27/4/86).

Wiltshire, 1183. Henry II transforms an old hunting lodge at Clarendon, near Salisbury, into one of England's greatest palaces.

Glastonbury, Somerset, 1184. The abbey is destroyed by fire (→ c.1190).

Amorous knight cuts a tournament dash

Battle with honour: Young King Henry's champion has defeated all-comers.

Lagni, France, November 1180
At a spectacular tournament on the banks of the river Marne, William Marshal, the champion of Young King Henry (the son and crowned successor of Henry II of England), has defeated all who rode against him. The tournament – organized by the count palatine of Champagne and Brie, a keen patron of chivalry – was held to celebrate the accession of Philip II as king of France following the death of Louis VII in September.

The Young King, attending the festivities on behalf of his father – who for once was generous with his purse – arrived with 200 knights and barons. They included Robert, the count of Dreux, David, the earl of Huntingdon and brother of King William of Scotland, and the counts of Eu and Soissons.

In the contest that followed, William Marshal broke every lance that was levelled against him. To men, he is the very model of knightly strength. In women's eyes (not least, it is said, those of Margaret, the wife of the Young King), he epitomizes a romantic ideal. His rise has been extraordinary for a landless man and seems likely to provoke enmity (→ 25/12/82).

Frenchman mints new coin for England

In the king's name: a new penny.

England, 1180
Philip Aimer, a French goldsmith from Tours, has designed a new coin with well-defined edges and a standard weight of between 22 and 23 grains. This "short cross" penny will be minted at 11 major towns in England. Coins will be hand-struck between two iron dies, in the traditional way, and tight central control will be reimposed to prevent variations in shape and weight that have crept in over recent years.

Introduction of the new coinage is overdue. The 1158 so-called "Tealby" type was carelessly struck on square or polygonal flans, often too small to receive more than a partial impression of the dies. It also proved quite easy to forge.

Profits from wool have provided the main strength of the English coinage, although the system fell apart during the civil war between Stephen and Matilda. It is hoped, however, that the new currency will be safeguarded under the watchful eye of King Henry II. From now on, all merchants coming to England will be obliged to exchange their coins for pennies bearing the legend "Henricus Rex" (→ 10/1251).

Fatal ambush halts Irish land-grabbing

Ireland, 1181
Miles de Cogan and Ralph FitzStephen have been attacked and killed by Mac Tire, the chieftain of Imokilly in Co Waterford. The two Norman knights had been successful in grabbing much of the land around Cork and were planning further assaults on Waterford when they were ambushed.

The men of Munster have revolted against the Anglo-Norman assaults, and Raymond "le Gros" has been summoned to restore order to the district. Meanwhile King Henry II of England has ordered Richard de Cogan to Ireland to replace his brother Miles (→ 1183).

John of Salisbury, philosopher, dies

Chartres, France, 25 October 1180
John of Salisbury, an Englishman who was at the forefront of European learning, died today, having been bishop here since 1176. No other contemporary writer could match his classical scholarship. He has bequeathed his library to his cathedral, along with a phial of the blood of Archbishop Thomas Becket, whom he accompanied on his return to Canterbury and eventual murder in the cathedral there. One of John's literary works was a life of Becket, his friend (→ 7/7/1220).

The story of David: a single leaf from a bible made at Winchester Cathedral priory c.1160-80.

Connacht invasion prompts abdication

Ireland, 1183
Ruaidri Ua Conchobair, the king of Connacht and high king of Ireland, has had to abdicate and retire to the abbey of Cong in Co Mayo. By the Treaty of Windsor, which he and Henry II of England signed in 1175, Ruaidri's sovereignty over Ireland, with the exception of the area around Dublin, was recognized in return for an annual tribute which he had to collect from the lesser Irish kings. But in 1179 Henry gave Connacht to William FitzAdelm, and Ruaidri's sons – including his successor in Connacht, Conchobar Maenmaige – joined William in invading the province, forcing their father to abdicate (→25/4/85).

Christmas banquet at court disrupted

The symbolic cup-giving ceremony.

Normandy, 25 December 1182
There has been upheaval at the court of Henry II of England and his sons at Caen. Their Christmas feast was disrupted by William Marshal [*see page 244*] and his cousin William de Tancarville, a disgraced chamberlain, who arrived unannounced. De Tancarville demanded his right as chamberlain to present the king with silver cups, while Marshal, alleged to have slept with Young King Henry's wife, Margaret, insisted on proving his innocence by trial by battle. Henry is wisely ignoring them (→7/1190).

Fate resolves family war

Brutal fighting: a battle scene from a book made at Durham c.1170-80.

Aquitaine, France, 11 June 1183
The sudden death today of 28-year-old Young King Henry, the eldest son of Henry II of England, has given the troubled empire of Anjou the unexpected prospect of a clear resolution to its recent messy wars. The Young King died of dysentery and a fever at Martel during a somewhat aimless campaign in southern Aquitaine, which was undertaken following his failure to get back into the besieged principal town of Limoges.

The various barons and parties who joined the Young King in the revolt against his brother Richard's overlordship in Aquitaine had various motives, but the central issue was always the succession to Henry II. Richard is the king's second eldest son and is now, with his brother dead, first in line to the throne of England as well as the realms of Normandy and Anjou.

Militarily the revolt was always a lost cause. The people of Limoges, while holding out against Henry II, had also rejected Young King Henry, stoning him from the walls and shouting: "We will not have this man to rule over us." Richard had already begun mopping up the motley forces of mercenaries and knights who had caused disorder throughout Aquitaine without raising a general rebellion. There are reports that he is dealing severely with captives, some of whom have been butchered or blinded. Until fate intervened, however, the consequences of this filial revolt might have been both bloody and long-lasting (→9/1183).

Wales proves too tough a nut to crack

Welsh Marches, September 1184
The Anglo-Normans are failing to make much headway in Wales. The Marches, or border areas between Wales and England, have been subject to sporadic attempts at domination, but most of this Celtic land is still largely under native control.

In some places, such as Haverford and Pembroke, the Normans are firmly in command, but they move outside these safe havens at their peril. This month, for example, Welsh raiders burnt Cardiff and Kenfig in a typical foray to ruffle Norman feathers. Henry II of England's justiciar [chief deputy], Ranulf de Glanville, has been sent to restore order but can do little. Fortunately for the Welsh, there is no coordinated Norman policy to deal with them (→1194).

Henry lays down the 'common law'

England, c.1180
In an attempt to fight growing administrative corruption, Henry II has thoroughly purged local government and tightened control of the shires by appointing many new sheriffs, most of whom have links with the court and the Exchequer (which keeps the royal accounts).

The office of sheriff, which was instituted in the tenth century and won higher status under Henry I, has become more onerous during the present reign. As chief officer of a shire, or county [from the Norman French *comté*], the sheriff takes responsiblity for the collection of royal revenue and general administration in his area; in addition he now plays a key role in implementing Henry's important legal reforms. Perhaps Henry's greatest achievement is to have established a system of so-called "common law", standardizing legal practices across the whole country, in place of various sets of laws based on local customs. Enforcement has been improved by "assizes" (procedural instructions given by the king to his judges and courts), particularly those of Clarendon in 1166 and Northampton in 1176 [*see pages 237 and 242*]. Since last year private property cases have been judged by the "Grand Assize" of Windsor, which introduced the jury trial as an alternative to trial by battle (→1215).

Trial by battle: no longer the only method of settling land disputes.

1185-1188

England, March 1185. Henry II declines the offer made by Jerusalem's patriarch, Heraclius, that he could succeed to that kingdom. Heraclius asked him in January to help with a crusade against Saladin, the Moslem ruler of Palestine (→11/1187).

Lincoln, 15 April 1185. The cathedral is destroyed by an earthquake (→2/8/1279).

Ireland, 25 April 1185. John, the lord of Ireland, lands at Waterford and sets about reasserting English royal authority by granting lands to supporters (→25/7/86).

England, 1185. Henry II restores the earldom of Huntingdon to King William of Scotland (→5/9/86).

Southampton, 27 April 1186. Henry II returns after dividing the Aquitainian castles to the disadvantage of his son Richard of Poitou (→17/2/87).

Leinster, 25 July 1186. Hugh de Lacy, who became the first Anglo-Norman *custos* [keeper] five years ago, is killed (→1189).

Woodstock, Oxfordshire, 5 September 1186. William of Scotland marries Ermengarde of Beaumont, a cousin of Henry II of England (→1188).

Carlisle, Cumbria, 1186. Roland, the nephew of the rebel Gilbert of Galloway who died last year, agrees with William of Scotland to abide by the laws of Henry II of England's court and is made lord of Galloway (→1187).

Dover, 17 February 1187. Henry II sets sail for France in preparation for war (→5/1187).

Brittany, 29 March 1187. Constance, the widow of Henry II of England's son Duke Geoffrey, who was accidentally killed while jousting, gives birth to his son, Arthur (→27/5/99).

Châteauroux, France, May 1187. The city is besieged by Philip II, who takes Issoudun and Fréteval (→18/11/88).

Scotland, 31 July 1187. Roland of Galloway gives William the head of Donald mac William (→16/7/1235).

Aquitaine, November 1187. Duke Richard, on hearing of the fall of Jerusalem, plans to become a crusader (→22/1/88).

France, 22 January 1188. Henry II of England, Philip II of France and Philip of Flanders agree to support the planned crusade (→21/1/89).

Crown profits from a market in brides

England, 1185

Business is booming in the marriage market these days, with the crown enjoying a virtual monopoly on the profits. The most valuable commodities are widows and heiresses with land over which the king enjoys seigneurial rights. These women are being literally sold by the crown in marriage to the highest bidder, or to the king's friends, with their land as a dowry.

Any woman refusing to play the marriage game has to pay a heavy fine to the crown for the right to remain single as long as she wishes or to choose her own husband. The bride's "market rate" is fixed according to her age, the number and ages of any children she has, the size and value of her property and the quantity of livestock on her land. Itinerant justices collect these facts, which are kept up to date by each county in "rolls of ladies, boys and girls in the king's gift".

Typical of this year's returns is the case of a 30-year-old widow from Cambridgeshire, Eugenia Picot, who has a manor house and grounds worth £25 a year, three sons and a daughter, and is "in the gift of the lord king". The king has already given her daughter to one of his friends (→1261).

Outspoken Welsh commentator provokes anger by his harsh portrayal of the Irish

Hereford, 23 April 1188

Archbishop Baldwin of Canterbury today completed a 48-day tour of Wales to recruit men for a new crusade to the Holy Land. He was helped by Gerald, the 42-year-old archdeacon of Brecon, who is emerging as a key royal adviser on Wales and Ireland.

Gerald of Wales, as he is sometimes known, became a royal clerk four years ago and has often acted as an intermediary within Wales, being a Marcher of mixed Norman and Welsh descent. In 1185 he accompanied the king's son, John, on a tour of Ireland, about which he has now written two books.

The *Expugnatio Hibernica* covers the Anglo-Norman campaign of conquest that began in 1169, while the *Topographia Hiberniae* deals with Irish history, geography, wildlife and customs. Gerald is now renowned as the author of this pioneering work. His descriptions of birds such as ospreys and blackbirds are highly detailed, but some Irish have taken exception to themselves being portrayed as treacherous, ill-tempered and violent. They may, though, have the last laugh. It seems that Gerald naïvely believed many folk-tales, including one that Irish shoelaces release poison. Gerald now plans a book on his travels in Wales with the archbishop. It was an arduous journey, and once they almost came to grief. Heading in the direction of Swansea they wandered into quicksands in the Neath estuary. One of their horses was sucked down and was only rescued, Gerald relates, "after much hard and dangerous work, though not without damage to my books and belongings" (→1191).

A picture from the "Topographia".

Father and son fall out over succession

Bonmoulins, France, 18 Nov 1188

Knights are said to have reached for their swords today as the third attempt this year to patch up the quarrel over the succession between Richard and his father Henry II of England nearly ended in violence. Then, dramatically, Richard knelt before King Philip II of France and did him homage for Normandy and Aquitaine, swearing fealty against all men "save only the fealty which I owe to my father the king".

The gesture was doubtless born of Richard's frustration at Henry's continued refusal to acknowledge his right to inherit the kingdom, but some will think that it plays into the hands of Philip, whose wish to see the break-up of Angevin dominions is no secret. Even Philip, however, is reluctant to take on Henry's power directly and must once again look for a negotiated peace. Judging by the end of today's meeting, when father and son walked away in opposite directions as the meeting broke up, it promises to be a long search (→1/1189).

A rival lord: King Philip of France.

William 'the Lion' refuses to pay tax

Scotland, 1188

William "the Lion", the king of Scots, has delivered a defiant snub to Henry II of England. With the full backing of his barons, he is refusing a request to raise a tax in Scotland to subsidise the English king's proposed crusade to the Holy Land. There is a further slap in the face for Henry: his embassy to Scotland has been denied entry into the country.

Instead of paying taxes, William wants to renegotiate the 1175 Treaty of Falaise by which, among other things, he surrendered a number of important castles. Now William is offering to buy them back, which is a more advantageous way for him to donate money to the English Exchequer (→5/12/89).

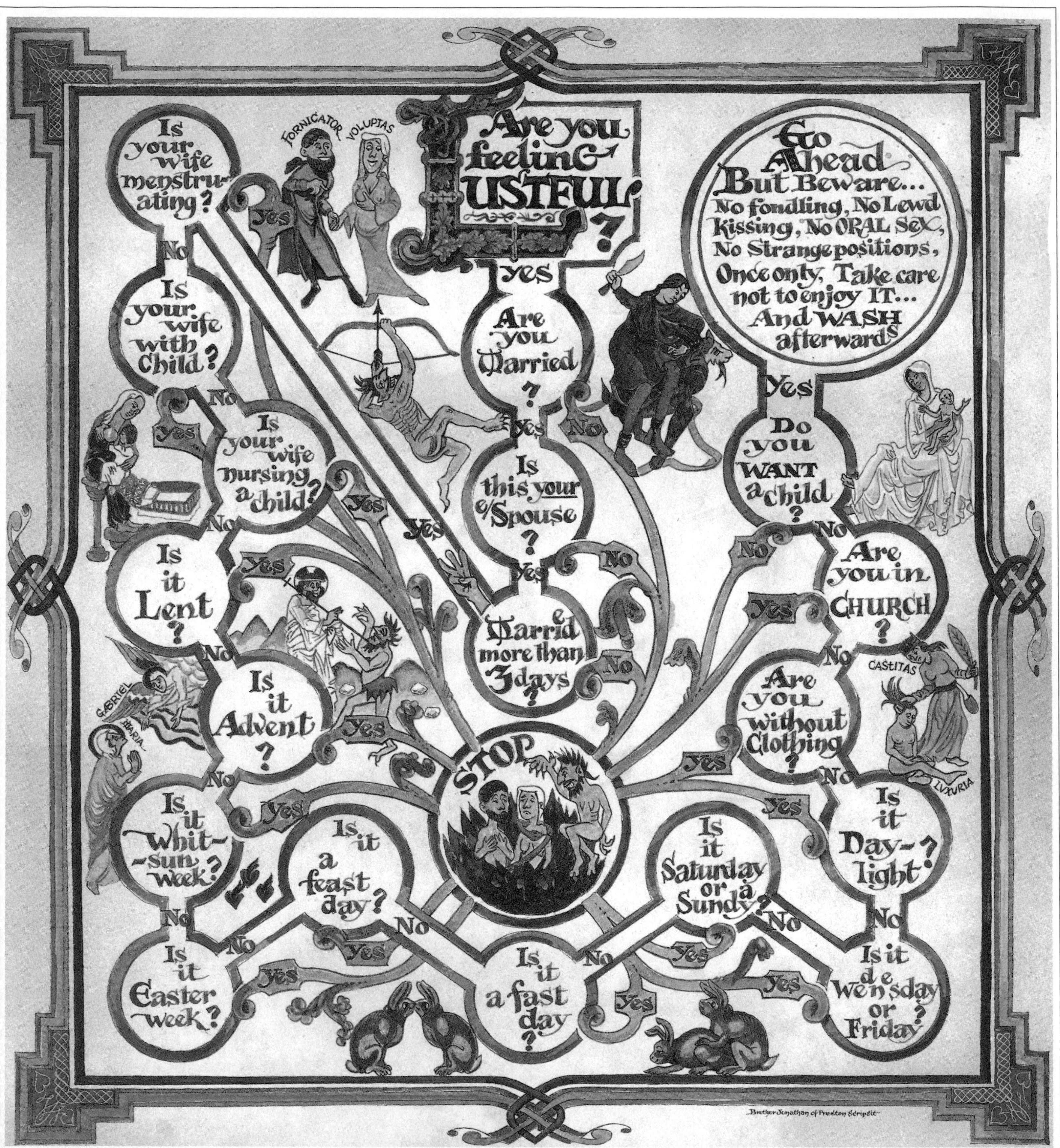

An illuminated manuscript page (by a 20th-century artist) illustrates Christian sexual tenets typical of the 12th century. It is based on contemporary penitentials – books listing sinful acts and the penances, or punishments, for those committing them. A penance might require a sinner to fast on bread and water for a prescribed period or, for more serious transgressions, to go on a pilgrimage. Sex was allowed only under strict conditions. A wrong answer to any of the questions shown above [starting in the centre at the top and moving anti-clockwise around the page] meant that a Christian had either to stop or to fall into sin and suffer the consequences. Essentially the church allowed sex solely for the purpose of procreation within wedlock.

1189-1190

Brittany, January 1189. King Henry II of England falls seriously ill, and the duchy rebels (→5/1189).

Europe, 21 January 1189. The rulers of Europe assemble troops for the Third Crusade (→6/10/90).

La Ferté-Bernard, France, May 1189. Henry II of England, a sick man, fails to make peace with his son Richard and Philip II of France (→2/7).

Saumur, France, 2 July 1189. Philip of Flanders, Archbishop William of Rheims and Duke Hugh of Burgundy make peace with Henry II, who fled here when Le Mans fell in June (→3).

Tours, France, 3 July 1189. Philip storms the city; Henry finally surrenders to him (→6).

Rouen, Normandy, 20 July 1189. Richard is consecrated as duke of Normandy and discusses his long-delayed plans to marry Alice, Philip II's sister (→13/8).

Portsmouth, 13 August 1189. Richard claims his throne, proclaiming his mother, Eleanor of Aquitaine, as regent in England (→6/6/90).

England, 29 August 1189. John, the brother of King Richard, marries Isabella of Gloucester and is put under papal ban for marrying his second cousin (→7/1199).

Cork City, 1189. Count John grants a charter.

Lincolnshire, 1189. Gilbert, the rector of Sempringham, the founder of the Gilbertine order, dies at the age of 100.

Connacht, 1189. A succession crisis follows the murder of King Conchobar Maenmaige Ua Conchobair (→1193).

England, 6 June 1190. Bishop William Longchamp of Ely, who yesterday became papal legate, arrests his fellow justiciar, Bishop Hugh le Puiset of Durham, for exceeding his authority and becomes the sole holder of the office (→7/1190).

Sicily, Italy, 6 October 1190. En route to Jerusalem, Richard of England makes a treaty with King Tancred for the return of the dowry of Richard's sister, Joan, the widow of the previous king (→5/1191).

Scotland, 1190. David, the earl of Huntingdon and brother of King William, marries Matilda, the sister of Earl Ranulf of Chester (→6/1195).

Henry II dies abandoned in France

Chinon, France, 6 July 1189

Harried by his sons and humbled at the last by Philip II of France, Henry II of England ended his 34-year reign today in this rocky fortress in the duchy of Anjou. Henry, who was 56 years old, died having alienated everyone around him: first Thomas Becket, then Queen Eleanor and finally his sons. The king's body will be taken to the abbey church of Fontevrault.

The latest war with Richard and Philip hastened Henry's end, but he was already worn down by the endless disputes over his successor. In June, against all advice, Henry turned back from Normandy and travelled to the fortress of Chinon in southern Anjou. He was going home to die.

While he lay sick, Philip besieged Tours. On 3 July it fell, and the next day Henry met the French king at nearby Ballan, where he promised to pay homage to Philip for his French lands and to grant England and the Plantagenet lands to Richard. He then discovered that his favourite son, John, whose loyalty he had counted on, was chief among Richard's supporters. It was the final blow.

Only time will tell whether Richard can hold together the domains that sapped his father's prodigious energies. First the new king's eyes are turned towards the Holy Land and a new crusade (→20).

King Richard's coronation procession, from a 15th-century manuscript.

Jews are brutally attacked at coronation

Westminster, 3 September 1189

Three weeks after landing from France, Duke Richard of Aquitaine has been crowned king of England in a glittering ceremony in Westminster Abbey. People have high hopes of him, particularly since his first gesture after the death of his father, Henry II, has been to free all those imprisoned merely on the king's orders. Richard, who will be 32 years old in five days' time, swore to honour both God and his church, seek justice for all and root out corrupt customs.

The coronation banquet was magnificent, but trouble began when Jewish leaders from the City arrived to pay their respects. This contravened the king's decree that no Jew should attend his coronation, and the group was bundled out. Most of its members were beaten and some were killed, sparking anti-Jewish rioting in the capital. Richard has ordered the arrest of the ringleaders; since Jewish money-lenders will help to fund his proposed crusade Richard wants to keep in with them (→16/3/90).

Eleanor freed from long house arrest

England, 1189

After 16 years of house arrest Eleanor of Aquitaine has been released following the recent death of her second husband, Henry II. Eleanor's problems began when she found that Henry was having an affair with Rosamund Clifford, a nobleman's daughter, for whom he refurbished the Oxfordshire palace of Woodstock. Thus betrayed, Eleanor could no longer support her husband, and so, when Young King Henry rebelled, she sided with her son. Knowing that a divorce would lose him Aquitaine, Henry chose to make his wife a prisoner instead. Yet Eleanor has remained popular, and it is unlikely that the public will now turn against her.

Eleanor, who was taken captive in 1173 after rebelling against Henry.

'Mayor' elected to speak for citizens

London, 1189

The first man to become "mayor" of London is Henry fitzAilwin, whose family has long associations with the city. It is not clear how someone of English rather than Norman descent came to be chosen, but he has the support of leading citizens and the new king. Mayors are being appointed in many towns as citizens' spokesmen, able to report to the king and be answerable for their fellows' behaviour, like village headmen. Yet fitzAilwin is likely to be more than a headman, since the king needs a man in the capital who is able to maintain the people's trust in him.

Jews massacred during rampage at York

York, 16 March 1190
More than 150 Jews are reported either to have been massacred or to have committed suicide in York. This is by far the bloodiest example of the anti-Jewish rioting that has continued sporadically throughout England since the disturbances in London last year at King Richard's coronation banquet [*see report on page 248*]. Jews are targeted as being the only significant religious and racial minority here as well as for their work as money-lenders.

Although the king, after having three of the original rioters hanged, kept the Jewish population under his protection – chiefly in recognition of their usefulness in financing his crusader army – he left for France last December. The mob seems meanwhile to have rampaged unrestrained through this city, which had one of the biggest and most prosperous Jewish communities in the land.

Some 150 of the Jews escaped and took refuge in the royal castle. There they were besieged by an angry crowd which told them that unless they converted to Christianity they would be killed. When they realized that no help would arrive, most of the Jews defiantly killed their own wives and children, to save them from the evil of forced conversion, before taking their own lives. The few who accepted the crowd's terms came out of the castle only to be butchered (→1255).

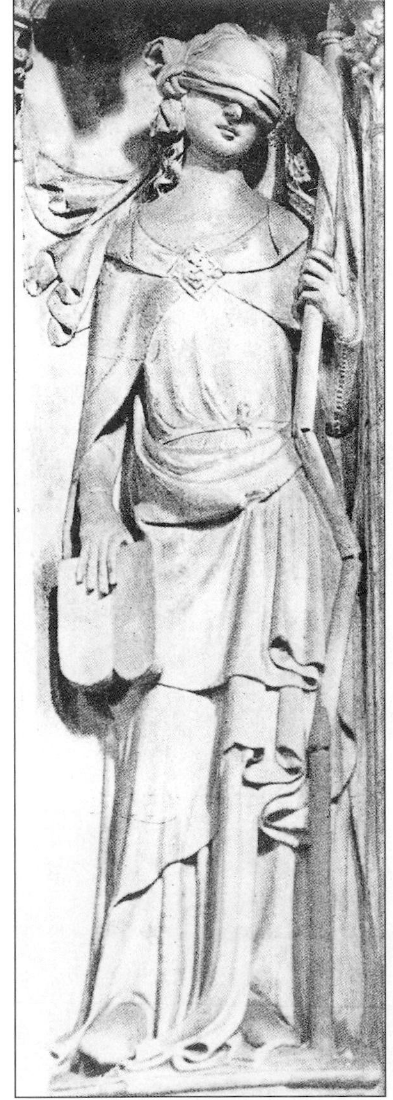

A statue from Rochester synagogue.

Monks at Glastonbury claim to have found the last resting-place of legendary Arthur

Glastonbury, Somerset, c.1190
As the Arthurian legends are retold and embroidered [*see report on page 237*] – and intertwined with other romances, such as the love affair of Tristan and Iseult – monks at Glastonbury have made a startling find in their churchyard. Inside a hollowed oak they have unearthed a man's skeleton, which they claim to be that of Arthur. Beneath it was a leaden cross with a Latin inscription reading: "Here lies buried the famous King Arthur with Guinevere his second wife in the island of Avalon." The coffin also contained the bones of a woman, a lock of whose golden hair was lifted out only to fall to dust. The man's bones, which are huge, show ten wounds, the last unhealed.

There is a political side to this apparently innocent story. Fearing that the Welsh might use Arthur as a figurehead in a rebellion, English kings would prefer to prove that he is dead and buried – since so many of the legends about him say that he will one day return. Henry II suggested to the monks of Canterbury that perhaps Arthur's grave was there. Glastonbury was considered a possible site because of its ancient holy associations; the Welsh themselves sometimes call it "glass island" (once an island, it is still criss-crossed by dykes) (→c.1235).

The lovers Tristan and Iseult, from a 15th-century French manuscript.

Scots win diplomatic victory over English

Canterbury, 5 December 1189
King William of Scotland has won an impressive victory over the English at the negotiating table. At a meeting here Richard of England has agreed to scrap the Treaty of Falaise signed between his father, Henry II, and William in 1174 [*see report on page 241*].

Today's decision, which has been dubbed the "Quitclaim of Canterbury", puts an end to 15 years of English political overlordship of Scotland. It also signals the surrender by England of one of the leading aims of the old treaty: the submission of the Scottish church to its southern neighbour.

There is of course a price to be paid: William has to hand over 10,000 marks to the English crown. He also has to pay homage to Richard – but, crucially, only for the lands that he holds in England. The important thing, however, is that the ignominy of the past 15 years has been dispelled: under the old treaty William had to ask his English liege lord permission even to quell a rebellion in his own country.

This surrender of England's long-standing claim to subjugate Scotland is a measure of Richard's burning desire to start his crusade against the Moslems in what Christians call the Holy Land. William's money is no doubt intended to be used as part of the finance behind this project (→1190).

Deputies take control in king's absence

Jerusalem, the crusaders' goal: from a 13th-century French manuscript.

England, July 1190
King Richard of England departed from France last month for the Holy Land. In accordance with a tradition well established since the reign of Henry I, England is being run in the king's absence by his justiciar [chief deputy], William Longchamp. Four further deputies – William Brewer, Hugh Bardolf, Geoffrey fitzPeter and William Marshal – have been appointed, but there are fears that they may be unable to restrain Longchamp if he abuses power. He has already arrested his former fellow justiciar, Bishop Hugh le Puiset of Durham.

These appointments seem a hasty device to buttress the arrangement for government set up by Richard during his four months in England, one aspect of which is the meteoric rise of the Marshal family. William's brother John is now sheriff of Yorkshire and had the honour of carrying a pair of golden spurs before the king at his coronation. Perhaps ominously, however, the Marshals are thought to be close to Richard's brother John (→27/6/91).

1191 - 1196

Cyprus, May 1191. On his way to the crusade, Richard of England takes control after marrying Berengaria, the daughter of King Sancho of Navarre (→ 2/9/92).

England, 27 June 1191. Archbishop Walter of Rouen and the king's mother, Eleanor of Aquitaine, arrive with Richard's secret order for Walter to replace the justiciar, William Longchamp, if necessary (→ 14/9).

Tours, France, 18 August 1191. Geoffrey, the illegitimate half-brother of Richard, is finally consecrated archbishop of York after being elected two years ago (→ 7/11/93).

Dover, 14 September 1191. Archbishop Geoffrey is seized by Longchamp's men, giving Richard's brother John a chance to take power (→ 8/10).

London, 8 October 1191. Longchamp is deposed and John takes power (→ 7/1193).

Tayside, 1191. A royal burgh is granted at Dundee (→ c.1200).

Scotland, 13 March 1192. A papal bull, *Cum universi*, declares the Scottish church subject directly to the pope, thus thwarting the claims of York (→ 21/11/1218).

Holy Land, 9 October 1192. Richard leaves Acre and heads for England at the end of the Third Crusade (→ 28/12).

England, July 1193. Bishop Hubert Walter of Salisbury returns from Germany with news of Richard's release. John flees to France (→ 17/4/94).

Canterbury, 7 November 1193. Hubert Walter is enthroned as archbishop (→ 12/1206).

Mellifont, Co Meath, 1193. Derbforgaill, Tigernan Ua Ruairc's widow, dies (→ 1196).

Conwy, 1194. Dafydd ab Owain, the prince of Gwynedd, is defeated by his nephews, loses his throne (→ 1197).

England, 1194. Richard issues a decree licensing tournaments, banned by his father, Henry II, as dangerous (→ 1219).

Scotland, June 1195. King William is seriously ill. He leaves his throne to Otto, the son of Duke Henry V of Saxony and Bavaria, provided that Otto marries William's eldest daughter (→ 24/8/98).

France, 13 January 1196. After Richard of England's attempts to regain lost Norman lands, he and Philip II seal a treaty at Louviers (→ 6/4/99).

Crusaders talk peace

Christian world view: a wide-ranging map from a 13th-century manuscript.

Holy Land, 2 September 1192
The Third Crusade, which began three years ago, has failed in its main goal: to recapture Jerusalem (taken by the Moslems in 1187) and restore the Christian kingdom set up there during the First Crusade in 1099. The instigator of the present crusade, Holy Roman Emperor Frederick, died in 1190, and his son, Duke Frederick of Swabia, fell last year. Richard of England, who then led the campaign with Philip II of France, has today brought off the best deal he could with the Moslem leader, Saladin.

Richard arrived in Palestine on 8 June last year. He successfully besieged Acre and, in September, defeated Saladin at Arsuf. He came within sight of Jerusalem in June of this year but thought better of an attack. Saladin then made his move and took Jaffa in July. Although Richard won it back, the point had been made: he had to compromise rather than conquer. Today's peace treaty, to run for three years, allows the Christians control of the coastal strip from Tyre to Jaffa. They are also to have access as pilgrims to Jerusalem.

On his way to the crusade, Richard travelled to Sicily, where he agreed with Philip of France a settlement of their territorial disputes. Negotiations were prompted by Richard's wish to end a 20-year betrothal to Philip's sister Alice in order that he might marry Berengaria, the daughter of King Sancho of Navarre. While apparently advantageous to Richard, the treaty heralds the break-up of the empire ruled for so many years by his father, Henry II (→ 9/10).

Spartan Welsh love to fight – and sing

Wales, 1191
If the English ever wonder why the Welsh are so difficult to subdue, they could do worse than consult a new book, the *Description of Wales*. Its author, Gerald of Wales, is the talented archdeacon of Brecon who has travelled widely here and in Ireland [*see report on page 246*]. He says that his compatriots are "totally dedicated to the practice of arms" and that they have a passionate devotion to their freedom and the defence of their country.

But the Welsh are not depicted as a violent people. They willingly extend hospitality to strangers – who should not, however, expect luxury. The diet is plain, consisting of meat, oats, dairy produce and a little bread; guests have to sleep in the same bed as everyone else. At least there is free entertainment, including harp-playing by women. Choirs are especially popular; they sing not in unison but in an intricate variety of parts – as many as there are performers (→ 1203).

English king taken captive by Austria

Vienna, 28 December 1192
Duke Leopold of Austria has announced that he has taken King Richard of England prisoner here. The news ends weeks of speculation about Richard's fate. Richard was apparently on his way home from the crusade in Palestine when he learnt that his brother John, backed by Philip II of France, had seized power in England. He therefore planned to skirt France by heading through Germany.

Shipwrecked near Venice and travelling overland disguised as a pilgrim, he was picked up here with his small party after arousing suspicion. One story claims that he tried to pass himself off as as a kitchen-hand while wearing a ring that would have been worth many years' wages. As a crusader, Richard is technically under the protection of the pope, but Leopold and his lord, Holy Roman Emperor Henry VI, are unlikely to give up such a powerful political card except for a great price (→ 7/1193).

Hostage Richard returns to claim crown as his treacherous brother flees to France

Winchester, Hants, 17 April 1194
Richard of England is back at the reins of power. First crowned in 1189, he has been re-affirmed as king in a "crown-wearing" ceremony here presided over by the new archbishop of Canterbury, Hubert Walter. Those attending included the leading nobles and clergy of the land and Eleanor of Aquitaine, Richard's mother, still a formidable woman at the age of 72.

Today sees the end of a turbulent period in Richard's life. For half a year from December 1192 he was the hostage of first Duke Leopold of Austria and then Holy Roman Emperor Henry VI. His release came only after the payment to Henry of a ransom of 100,000 marks. But a stern test of leadership awaited his subsequent return to England: while he was away his brother John had seized power.

Luckily, John fled for France as soon as he heard that Richard was on his way home. The careworn crusader landed at Sandwich, in Kent, on 13 March this year and took little time re-establishing his authority. He has been magnanimous in victory, too: next month he intends to cross the Channel and make peace with John (→12/5).

Enthroned in state: King Richard surrounded by his leading barons.

Richard gets his revenge on the French

Normandy, 12 May 1194
Richard of England has uncovered the hiding place of his rebel brother John here at Lisieux and, in a gesture at once generous and deeply patronizing, forgiven him. When John was brought to him, Richard said: "Think no more of it, John. You are only a child who has had evil counsellors." John, aged 27, is only ten years Richard's junior.

Meanwhile, the remarkable way in which Richard has gone about reasserting mastery of his domain has only enhanced the fear and respect in which he is held. Although himself brave almost to the point of recklessness, he conducts his campaigns with an eye to avoiding full-scale battle and heavy casualties.

Within weeks of landing from England Richard had routed Philip II of France's army, capturing prisoners, arms and much treasure, and was heading south to punish rebels in Aquitaine. Now he is planning a long-term campaign to invade the lands held by the French king, and in this he can expect the support of Holy Roman Emperor Henry VI, to whom he has acknowledged fealty as part of the ransom deal that secured his release [*see report above*] (→13/1/96).

Popular astrology spreads from the east

Guidance in the stars: a manuscript picture of the constellation Leo.

England, 1194
Firmly back on the English throne after what is recognized as his triumph in the Third Crusade, King Richard may find time to reflect on the predictions of the astrologer-hermit Joachim of Fiore. Joachim, a Cistercian abbot from Calabria in southern Italy, met Richard three years ago during the king's journey to the Holy Land and foretold the imminent fall of the Moslem leader, Saladin, at Richard's hand. The prophecy sprang from a complex, revolutionary theory of history, devised by the hermit, which is winning widespread popularity. Indeed, more and more people across Europe are turning to interpretations of the stars for the answers to life's problems.

For many years now Arab texts explaining the relationship between the stars and events on earth have been translated and eagerly studied both here and on the continent. Experts in the science of astrology use it for telling the future and even for diagnosing illnesses and prescribing treatment. Some astrologers are also dabbling in religion and politics; they are tolerated by the church so long as they do not challenge orthodox belief (→c.1450).

Anti-tax riot leader hanged in London

London, 1196
Anger at the unfair distribution of taxes paid by Londoners has boiled over into serious rioting that ended only when the populist leader William fitzOsbern was captured and hanged at Tyburn. Led by the merchants, the city élite had been avoiding the payment of royal taxes by passing on the main burden to the poorer sections of society. It was largely as a consequence of this that fitzOsbern was able to swear in an army of 52,000 Londoners under his leadership.

After some serious rioting fitzOsbern was cornered in the church of St Mary le Bow and captured. With his hands tied behind his back he was dragged naked behind a horse to Tyburn, where he was hanged in chains so that he would not die too quickly (→7/1198).

Settlers' advances checked in Ireland

Ireland, 1196
Norman settlers in the south-west of Ireland received a violent check to their ambitions this year when Domnall Mor Mac Carthaig, the king of Desmond, raided their settlements in Munster. He was helped by the king of Connacht, Cathal Crobderg Ua Conchobair. Domnall is now the dominant Irish leader in Munster, where the Normans have made gradual advances in recent years. These have mostly been peaceful, effected through marriages and political deals.

King Domnall's goal was to stop the Normans establishing themselves in the important town of Limerick, opened up to them by his rivals, the Ua Briains of Thomond. It is unlikely, however, that the Normans will have been deterred for very long (→2/11/98).

1197 - 1200

France, 31 January 1197. Bishop William Longchamp of Ely, the chancellor and former chief justiciar of England, dies at Poitiers.

Limerick City, 18 December 1197. A royal charter is granted.

Powys, 13 August 1198. An English force led by Geoffrey fitzPeter defeats Prince Gwenwynwyn at Paincastle, in the south (→ 11/7/1201).

Lothian, 24 August 1198. A son, Alexander, is born to King William (→ 26/11/1200).

Connacht, 2 December 1198. Ruaidri Ua Conchobair, the former high king, dies.→

Orkney, 1198. Earl Harald Maddason, who refused to make peace with King William last year and was imprisoned, has been released. He defeats Harald Ungi, who tried to take control of his earldom (→ 1201).

Normandy, 25 April 1199. John, who succeeds Richard as king of England, is invested as duke of Normandy (→ 27/5).

England, 28 May 1199. Hubert Walter, the archbishop of Canterbury, becomes chancellor (→ 12/1199).

Normandy, July 1199. King John, on his return from England, angers the pope by having his marriage to Isabella of Gloucester annulled in the hope of contracting a more elevated alliance (→ 24/8/1200).

Beverley, Humberside, 18 April 1200. King John grants to the people of Beverley a charter of free passage throughout the land with the exception of London.

Aquitaine, September 1200. Eleanor, the dowager queen of England, gives her duchy to King John (→ 10/1200).

England, October 1200. John embarks on a tour of his newly acquired kingdom, leaving his child-bride, Isabella of Angoulême, behind (→ 1/10/07).

France, October 1200. Hugh "le Brun" of Lusignan appeals to Philip II over the recent wedding of John to Isabella of Angoulême, to whom he had been betrothed (→ 3/1201).

Lincoln, 22 November 1200. William of Scots reasserts his claim to Northumberland at a meeting with John (→ 28/11/01).

Lincoln, 26 November 1200. Hubert Walter reconciles King John and the Cistercian monks, who had quarrelled over money (→ 1220).

Family feuds imperil Welsh lord's legacy

Deheubarth, Wales, 1197

Lord Rhys, the dominant figure in Welsh politics in the last quarter of the century, has died. He had re-established the kingdom of Deheubarth – stretching from the Tawe valley to Cardigan Bay – as the most powerful force in Wales, successfully resisting further encroachment by either the English crown or Marcher barons.

His military success began when he was still in his teens, and his power was recognized in 1171-2 by King Henry II of England, who extended his protection to Lord Rhys, or Rhys ap Gruffudd as he was also known, as the ruler of the revived kingdom of Deheubarth. This alliance was maintained until Henry's death in 1189, creating a period of stability that enabled Rhys to reform the administration, revise the legal system, encourage the arts via an *eisteddfod* and enhance the status of St David as well as that of Welsh monasteries. After Henry's death Rhys maintained his authority by a series of raids on Anglo-Norman lords throughout south Wales. But these latter years also exposed family feuds – he had at least 18 children – which now imperil his legacy (→ 13/8/98).

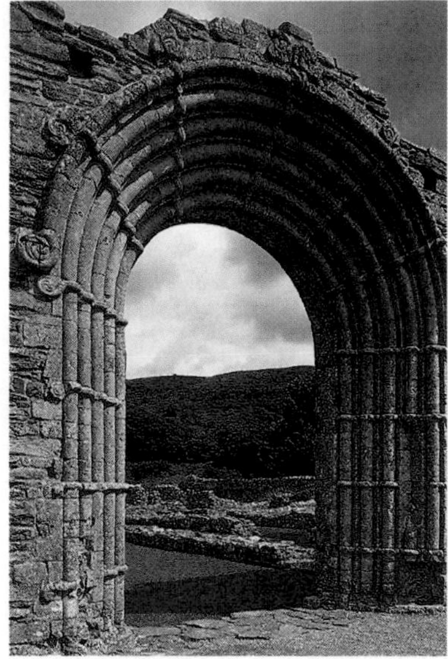

Rhys was lord of this Dyfed abbey.

Minister resigns in row over sacrilege

London, July 1198

After fewer than five years in office Hubert Walter has resigned as justiciar, the king's chief agent for all administrative, financial and judicial matters. His departure follows a furious row over an act of sacrilege at Bow church, in London.

Walter's henchmen crushed a violent campaign against new taxes led by William fitzOsbern, who took refuge in the church. Walter, who is also archbishop of Canterbury, had fitzOsbern smoked out and dragged to the gibbet. This provoked Walter's enemies, the Canterbury monks, into persuading Pope Innocent III to invoke a canon law banning a high-ranking cleric from serving in a secular job.

Walter, from a Norfolk baronial family, had served his king well, devising ingenious ways of imposing new taxes and getting knights in the shires to undertake many new duties unpaid (→ 12/1199).

Cathedral windows tell biblical stories

Windows in the choir at Canterbury.

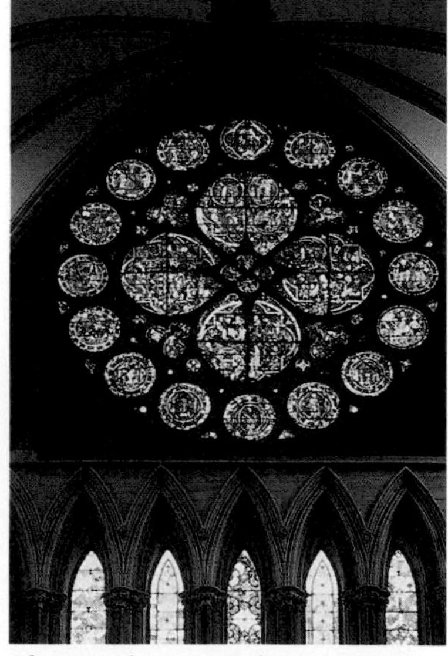

The superb rose window at Lincoln.

Canterbury, Kent, c.1200

The new choir at the eastern end of Canterbury Cathedral, now nearing completion after the almost total destruction by fire in 1174 of its predecessor, is being fitted out with elaborate stained-glass windows on a scale and of a quality unrivalled in England. The first windows in the choir went into the upper part or clerestory – literally, a "clear storey" designed to let in more light – in about 1178, while the scaffolding was conveniently still in place. They depict Christ's ancestry, beginning with a wonderfully lively picture of Adam, and are interrupted by new windows in the very latest style showing scenes from the life of Christ (→ 1218).

Death of high king marks end of era

Ireland, 2 December 1198

The one-time high king of Ireland, Ruaidri Ua Conchobair, has died. He became king of Connacht in 1156 and ten years later won recognition as high king. But the arrival of the Normans two decades ago sounded his political death-knell, and in 1175 he acknowledged Henry II of England as his overlord. In 1183 he had to leave public life and retreat to the abbey of Cong.

Political reality in Ireland has changed dramatically since the Normans came. The feudal system has been introduced wherever they are in control, with land split up into manors which, ultimately, belong to the lord of Ireland – Henry's son John. However, it does not amount to a re-run of England's subjugation a century ago.

Neither Henry II nor Richard has wielded the direct control that the Conqueror did. Large areas are in the hands of powerful Norman lords who are jealous of their independence, while others have been won piecemeal by similarly independently minded settlers (→ 1202).

'Lionheart' dies of crossbow wound

Limousin, France, 6 April 1199
Hit by a chance crossbow bolt in a trivial dispute with the rebellious count of Limoges, the warrior-king Richard is dead. He was 41 years old. After fighting with such valour in many great wars, he has been killed in an encounter for which he did not even feel it was worth putting on his armour.

Richard was besieging the unimportant castle of Chalus when, on 26 March, a defender shot him in the shoulder. The wound festered, and today the king died at Chalus-Chabrol here in the Limousin in central France. He will be buried in the tomb of the Plantagenets at Fontrevault in Normandy, where his father lies.

In ten years' reign he spent just six months in England, but he twice drained its resources to the limit, the second time to raise his own ransom. Richard will none the less be remembered as a dashing, exciting figure, as his nickname "the Lionheart" testifies. His brother John succeeds him (→25).

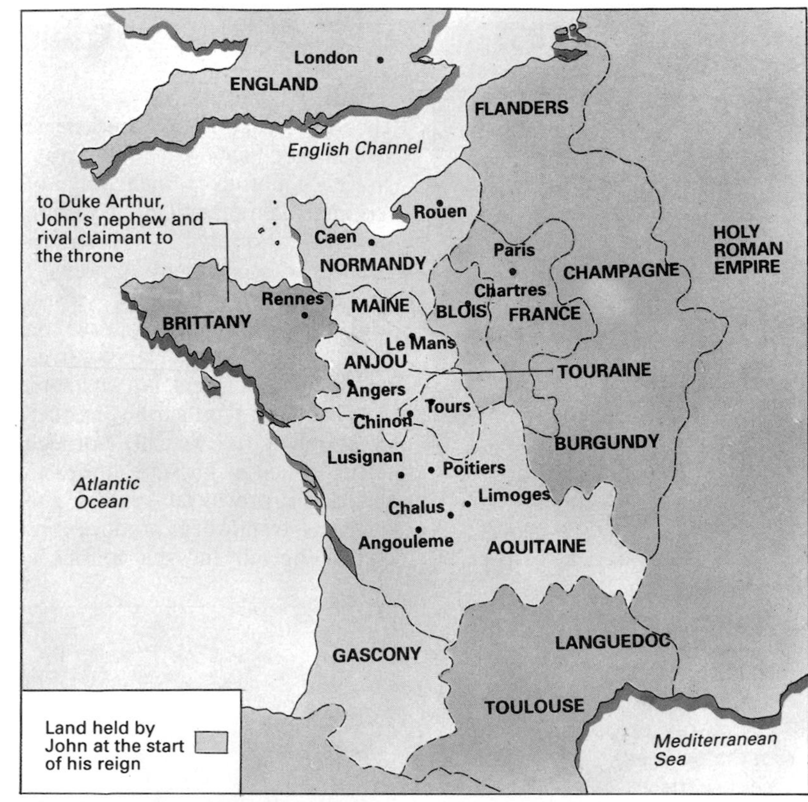

The European continental lands bequeathed by King Richard of England.

Irish poets speak out against settlers

Ireland, c.1200
Poets are being enlisted by their patrons to decry the invasion of Ireland and extol those leaders (the same patrons) who fight the Normans. A special focus of hope is the king of Connacht, Cathal Crobderg O'Connor [Ua Conchobair]. One of Cathal's predecessors was the last high king, Rory O'Connor [Ruaidri Ua Conchobair], and some of the glory of the high-kingship is rubbing off onto Cathal. One bard, in a poem called *A fir na suidh arin sith* [*Man, do not sit on the mound*], sees Cathal and Rory as noble salmon – a symbol of wisdom in Celtic mythology – attacked by monster *gairbheisc*, or rough fish, identified as the Welsh, the English and the French.

In spite of the upheavals of recent years, the indigenous literary tradition in Ireland is stronger than ever. The Irish language itself, and even spelling, are conforming more and more to well-regulated and consistent standards (→c.1325).

Ambitious brother arrives to claim throne

Westminster, 27 May 1199
The untimely death of King Richard has created confusion in his "empire" of England, Aquitaine, Anjou and Normandy [*see map above*]. His younger brother John, the count of la Marche (part of Aquitaine), was staying with their nephew Arthur of Brittany, a rival claimant to the throne, when news reached them of Richard's death. Six weeks later John arrived in England to claim the throne.

Hubert Walter, the archbishop of Canterbury, wanted the throne to go to Arthur, but his advisers opposed this, arguing that it was John who was the nearest heir to the land that had belonged to his father and elder brother. "So be it then," said the archbishop, "but mark my words, you will never regret anything in your life as much as this." So today John was crowned in Westminster Abbey, on the feast of the Ascension. The new king is leaving England at once in a bid to hold on to his Angevin empire, where hostile Bretons have seized control of the main roads (→7/1199).

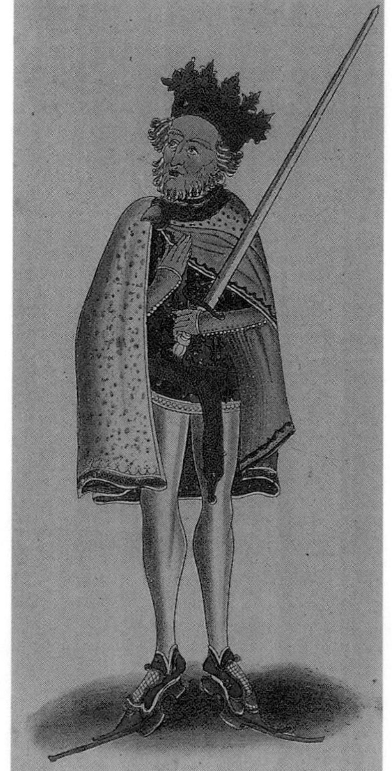
John, the new king of England, who faces the break-up of his empire.

Land tax is levied to oil war machine

London, December 1199
Less than a year after being forced into resigning as justiciar, Hubert Walter, the archbishop of Canterbury, is back in office, this time as chancellor, and serving with Geoffrey fitzPeter, the earl of Essex, who succeeded him as chief royal deputy [*see report on page 252*].

Walter is determined that every aspect of the king's administration shall be placed on record. More scribes have been recruited to compile lists of fines, plough-teams and tax records. Records are now being kept – in triplicate – of all loans made by Jewish businessmen, in order to maximize the taxes on their lucrative transactions.

To fund the king's Norman war, Walter has imposed a tax of five shillings on every piece of land that can be tilled in a year by one plough and eight oxen. This looks like the old "Danegeld" in a new form, and Walter's agents are having much trouble collecting it. Local knights are especially bitter (→c.1200).

King John takes a 12-year-old bride

Bordeaux, France, 24 August 1200
At the conclusion of his tour of Aquitaine, King John of England today married Isabella, the 12-year-old daughter and heiress of Audemar Taillefer, the count of Angoulême and a claimant to the county of la Marche. It is a shrewd match: John has drawn to his side a family that caused his brother Richard more than a few problems. Today's is John's second marriage; the first, to Isabella of Gloucester, was annulled earlier this year on grounds of close relationship.

The union has, however, angered Hugh "the Brown", the count of Lusignan, another claimant to la Marche. Isabella was once betrothed to him, and out of thwarted ambition he may want to stir up trouble. For now, however, John is planning to return to England for the coronation of his new wife in Westminster Abbey next month. He hopes to make another tour of France early next year to explore his entire inheritance (→9/1200).

Peasants reap the corn, kings reap the taxes

Sheep are the secret of England's success

The key to prosperity: women at work in the open air weaving wool.

England, c.1200
It may sound strange, but it is true: England's prosperity walks around on four legs and bleats. Over six million sheep, producing 50,000 sacks of wool a year, are the source of half the country's wealth. The export trade is thriving: English wool is highly prized on the continent for its high quality and good value. The main destination for exports is Flanders, where Europe's cloth-weaving industry is based. After it has been woven, the cloth is re-exported to lucrative markets in southern Europe.

The aristocracy, with its massive land-holdings, has taken to large-scale sheep-rearing. Even monastic communities, which moved to bleak valleys and wolds in search of isolation, now find themselves perfectly placed for rearing sheep and are growing exceedingly wealthy from the proceeds.

Yet the riches that nature gives the king usually takes away. The Plantangenet kings have raked off huge amounts of money in taxes to fund their military expeditions. When Henry II imposed a tithe in 1188 to pay for a crusade, for instance, it brought in £70,000. It was deeply unpopular but was levied all the same – with violence when necessary. Treaty payments to the king of France have to come from somewhere; in 1189 Salisbury had to provide a total of £25,000 – a staggering sum (→26/11).

"God speed the plough": peasants and animals cultivating the fields.

Irish economy is boosted by immigration

Ireland, c.1200
The Irish economy is experiencing radical modifications as the Anglo-Normans introduce their ways of farming and trading. On the eastern lowlands, where their grip is strongest, a market economy is growing up in place of traditional subsistence methods of farming. Rotation of crops is now used in lands carved up by the colonizers into manors. This creates a food surplus marketed through the small borough towns, which in turn are linked to the larger provincial centres and the ports, from where produce travels to England and the continent.

Huge social changes are also under way. All sorts of newcomers continually arrive; the merchant guild of Dublin boasts immigrant traders from all over England, Wales, France and even Flanders.

Norman French is widely spoken in towns; one poet working here in this language has made a *chanson de geste* (an epic poem in the French manner) about the invasion of Ireland, *The Song of Dermot and the Earl*. The native Irish tenantry in Norman-controlled areas are tied to the soil as serfs. Only a tiny number have gained entry to the land-owning feudal aristocracy.

An image of life in Ireland: a pair of coracle paddlers from Connacht.

'Burghs' are Scotland's new trade centres

Scotland, c.1200
Gradual but important changes are under way in Scotland's economy. People are tending to raise sheep rather than cattle and then selling the fleece not for other goods but for cash. The past 50 years have seen a large increase in the number of silver coins in circulation. A steadily growing population means that more land must go under the plough to feed the extra mouths. Often it is the monasteries that are leading the way in land clearance.

Settlements known as "burghs", which enjoy specific legal rights to trade, are at the forefront of expansion; they have strong links with the surrounding countryside, on which they depend for raw materials. Burghs also serve as places of royal residence or sites for royal mints. The most important of these centres are Berwick and Perth, both of which export cloth to Flanders (cloth and leather are Scotland's biggest industries, but many other crafts thrive). Each burgh has a church, a market cross and a "tolbooth" [town hall]. Burghs are run on hierarchical lines, with burgesses who can take part in town government at the top and the mass of unfree labourers at the bottom (→1203).

Wherever you are, life is sweetest at the top

Feudal customs are thriving in Scotland

Scotland, c.1200
As in other places, life in Scotland depends on one's station in society. At the top there are native Gaelic lords, along with Anglo-Norman immigrants who began settling here around a hundred years ago. Some of the native families, such as the *mormaers* [stewards] of Fife, have adapted well to the new feudal fashions; they are now earls of Fife, holding their land from the king by feudal charter. Among the immigrants there is a strong movement to integrate with the native Scots. The most successful in this respect have been the powerful Comyn, Bruce and Stewart families, all colonists from the early years of the past century.

The majority of the population lives under far less favoured circumstances than the lords, native or foreign, to whom different kinds of dues are owed. Some people pay traditional ones – *cain*, a food payment, or *conveth*, free hospitality for their lord. While these are based on personal loyalty to the lords, the newer feudal obligations are based on land tenure.

The lesser nobility might, for instance, hold their land from a lord in return for military service, while "bondimen" and "cottars" are peasants who are allowed to work the soil. In return they have to pay rent to their lord, are obliged to use only his mill and are not allowed to move away from his land. Their vulnerability is underlined by the fact that, when they want to settle any dispute, it is their lord's barony court to which they have to go for justice. Bondimen also have to serve in the king's army if he requires them to.

Their living conditions are meagre. They and their families live in "farm towns". These are small rural townships of perhaps no more than a dozen households. While the nobles construct "motte-and-bailey" castles for themselves – and some are now building in stone rather than wood – the peasantry make do with poor housing of clay, turf, wattle and wood.

Grape-pickers: a superb 12th-century window in Canterbury Cathedral.

English cooking meets continental cuisine

England, c.1200
Anyone dining today at one of the great houses of the landed gentry can be sure of the most tempting spread. England's choice of cuisine has greatly expanded as a result of its strong links with continental Europe. Game and wild bird – even wild boar and occasionally bear – are cooked with home-grown herbs or spices from the East. From the sea there is a choice of sturgeon, salmon and lobster. This is all washed down with plenty of ale and beer, although the rich prefer wine.

Aristocratic menus are more elaborate than those of the average household, but unless there is a famine – when peasants suffer the greatest hardship – most people have fairly healthy diets (→c.1390).

Holy days provide peasants' only rest

England, c.1200
The drudgery of ploughing, sowing and harvesting makes up the peasants' lot. Their year follows the seasons, beginning with winter, from Michaelmas (29 September) to Christmas, when wheat and rye are sown. Between Christmas and Easter is Lent, when such "Lenten seeds" as barley, beans, peas, oats and vetch are planted. Then comes summer, which continues until 1 August; and so the year ends with Harvest, at Michaelmas.

The only rest comes on holidays, or "holy days" to mark church festivals – times of riotous excess when the Lord of Misrule turns the world upside down and the "villein" may dine with his lord. The festivals include Christmas, Easter, Mayday (a time to celebrate fertility), the Rogation days (when a village goes in procession to "beat its bounds"), Midsummer (24 June) and Lammas (1 August, the end of the wheat harvest), each celebrated with its special rituals.

Elaborate herbal remedies form the core of medical treatment

Europe, c.1200
Elaborate herbal remedies, prayer and a dash of common sense form the core of the medical services now generally available throughout Europe – for rich and poor alike. Some things produce the desired effect – a herb called feverfew certainly cures headaches – but as the causes of disease are scarcely understood the doctor can do little but guess at the problem, and "cures" are often little more than spells. A typical remedy for headache and pains in the joints recommends:

"Take helenium and radish, wormwood and bishopwort, cropleek and garlic and hollowleek, of each an equal amount. Pound up. Boil in butter and with celandine and red nettle. Put in a brazen vessel and leave therein until it be dark coloured. Strain through a cloth and smear the head and limbs where they be sore." However, in some places a more professional approach has been adopted, for example at the medical school founded at Salerno, in Italy, in the ninth century. Scholars there blend ancient Greek learning with contemporary medical science, particularly that from Moorish Spain, where Arab physicians are making great progress in understanding anatomy and optics (→c.1246).

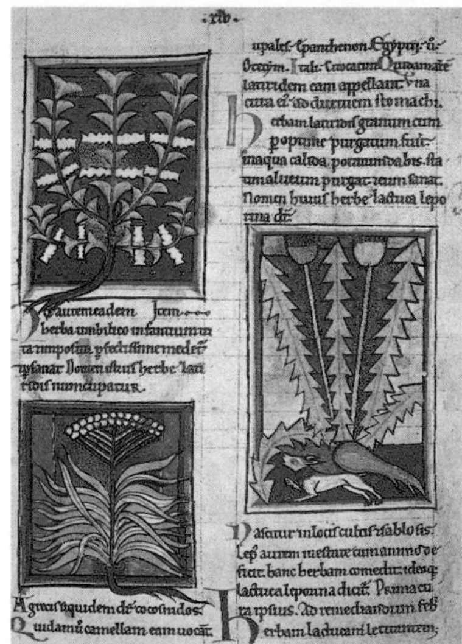

Herbs used for medicinal purposes.

A page from a textbook on surgery.

1201 - 1203

Normandy, March 1201. John of England faces a revolt here begun by Hugh "le Brun" of Lusignan in Aquitaine after John's marriage to his own former fiancée, Isabella of Angoulême (→ 8/1201).

France, March 1201. Queen Eleanor of England retires to the abbey of Fontevrault where her husband, Henry II, is buried (→ 1204).

Brittany, August 1201. Duke Geoffrey's widow, Constance, dies. Her son Arthur is left under the protection of Philip II of France (→ spring 1202).

Lothian, 28 November 1201. Scottish nobles swear fealty to Alexander, the three-year-old heir to the throne, at Musselburgh (→ 7/8/09).

Leicester, 1201. The barons of England, opposed to the rule of King John, meet (→ 12/1205).

France, spring 1202. After John of England's refusal to account for attacking Hugh "le Brun" of Lusignan and his brother Ralph, the count of Eu, Philip II makes John's French land forfeit (→ 7/1202).

Mirebeau, France, July 1202. The recently knighted Arthur of Brittany, betrothed to Philip II's daughter, joins Hugh "le Brun" against John (→ 1/8).

Anjou, France, August 1202. William des Roches rebels against John, who refuses to release Duke Arthur of Brittany (→ 1/1203).

Powys, 8 September 1202. Llywelyn of Gwynedd marches on Prince Gwenwynwyn of Powys; a settlement is made, but Powys is now a second-class principality (→ 1208).

Alençon, Normandy, January 1203. John of England's attempt to relieve Chinon is abandoned with the desertion of some Norman nobles to Philip II (→ 4/1203).

Normandy, August 1203. Philip continues to attack John, besieging his stronghold of Château Gaillard (→ 5/12).

Normandy, 5 December 1203. John secretly sails to England from Barfleur (→ 3/1204).

Strathclyde, 1203. A royal burgh is erected at Ayr beside the new royal castle (→ 1207).

Ireland, 1203. William de Burgh leads Norman forces in Connacht and builds a castle at Meelick; John de Courcy retreats to Tir Eogain after defeat at Downpatrick by Hugh de Lacy (→ 29/5/05).

Gwynedd is now the leading Welsh force

Gwynedd, 11 July 1201
John of England has recognized the power of Llywelyn ab Iorwerth, who, in less than a decade, has risen to be the dominant figure in north Wales. Today's treaty not only acknowledges Llywelyn's authority in the area he now controls but also agrees that any disputes will be settled in accordance with Welsh law.

Llywelyn has moved ruthlessly and with great speed to reintegrate the kingdom of Gwynedd. Victory in a battle at the mouth of the river Conwy in 1194 was followed by the expulsion of certain members of his family and the subordination of others to his rule. Just two years ago he described himself as "prince of the whole of north Wales".

With Deheubarth to the south falling apart after Lord Rhys's death, and Gwenwynwyn of Powys lacking resources, Gwynedd is emerging as the most powerful force in Wales – as King John has implicitly acknowledged by his sealing of today's treaty (→ 8/9/1202).

Scots hostage has both eyes put out

Borders, 1201
King William of Scots has finally lost patience with Harald Madasson, the earl of Orkney, and inflicted a terrible punishment on his son, Thorfinn. As revenge for an attack this year by Harald on Caithness, in which the bishop there was mutilated, William has ordered Thorfinn to be blinded and castrated.

Thorfinn has been a hostage at William's castle in Roxburgh for the last three years to ensure his father's good behaviour – in vain, as things turned out. In 1197 the earl was himself captured by the ageing king while campaigning in Caithness. After a year he was freed in exchange for Thorfinn. Earl Harald then returned home to Caithness where he killed his rival Harald Ungi at Wick. He continued to fight to reverse the losses suffered earlier at William's hands, and it was at this point that the decision was made to make the hostage pay (→ 1210).

'Troubadours' sing of love and longing

The troubadours, or minstrel poets: from a 14th-century French ivory.

Europe, 1201
"Troubadours" are flourishing at the courts of Europe, and some of them are aristocrats, even kings. The first troubadour – from a Provençal word meaning "to invent" – was the duke of Aquitaine, the great-grandfather of Richard of England, who inherited his ancestor's songwriting talent.

While in captivity in the Holy Roman Empire, Richard composed a song about his unhappiness and urgent need for money. "I have many friends," it ran, "but their gifts are few." The French minstrel Blondel, who was with him on crusade in Palestine, is said to have discovered where Richard was imprisoned by singing outside the walls a song that they had jointly written and hearing his answering voice.

Most of the troubadours compose love poems to be sung to the viol, expressing devoted obedience and longing in honour of an idealized lady. The fact that the object of his desire may be married only increases the poet's anguish (→ c.1235).

Norman barons on the make in Ireland

Connacht, 1202
The people of Connacht are hoping that stability will soon return after months of warfare now that Cathal Crobderg O'Connor has been reaffirmed as king of the province by John of England. Cathal first took power here in 1195 but was ousted two years ago by the O'Briens in alliance with the Norman baron William de Burgh.

Recent events show clearly how Norman warlords are quick to exploit internal rivalries in Ireland to their own advantage. After he was ousted, for instance, Cathal Crobderg fled to Ulster where the Norman barons John de Courcy and Hugh de Lacy (a namesake of the Hugh who died in 1186) offered military aid. They had no sanction from King John for this but were looking to expand their own influence. John decided, however, to back Cathal Crobderg against his rival Cathal Carrach, and de Burgh has had no option but to restore him to the throne (→ 1203).

John exults in victory over French rivals

Knights in close combat: a scene from a biblical picture book, c.1325.

Aquitaine, France, 1 August 1202
King John of England has scored a great victory over his rivals in France after a forced march to the castle at Mirebeau where his mother, Eleanor of Aquitaine, was being besieged. In an exultant message to his barons in England, John reports that he has captured more than 250 knights, as well as Arthur, his nephew and rival for power in the French possessions. Arthur's hopes of becoming king of England are now dead and buried.

The immediate background to this victory is the fight between John and Hugh "le Brun [the Brown]" of Lusignan, who was also captured today [*see report on page 253*]. Philip II of France used John's aggression against Hugh, one of his own men, as an excuse to enter the war, but when he heard of John's victory he pulled out. John is meanwhile taking his prisoners back to Normandy in chains.

The war is certain to be resumed, however, since John still refuses to accept Philip as overlord in France. John says that he, as king of England and duke of Normandy, owes no allegiance to Paris. Yet Philip argues that John, as the count of Aquitaine, is obliged to attend court in Paris and submit there to judgement on his actions (→ 8/1202).

"The Ladder of the Salvation of the Human Soul, and the Road to Heaven": a magnificent wall-painting made c.1200 in the church of St Peter and St Paul at Chaldon, Surrey. The lower half represents the punishments of the wicked; the upper, the deliverance of the blessed.

Patriotic Welsh cleric gives up the fight with Canterbury over religious home rule

St David's, Dyfed, 1203
The church in Wales has finally bowed to the authority of Canterbury. For five years Gerald of Wales, the influential archdeacon of Brecon, has been waging a campaign to revive the claims of St David's to be supreme within Wales, but successive archbishops of Canterbury have been equally determined to stamp their authority over Wales and exact oaths of obedience from bishops there. Now Gerald has at last abandoned his campaign.

The dispute goes back much further than the last five years, however. English claims to rule the ecclesiastical roost were trumpeted by archbishops of Canterbury such as Lanfranc and Anselm nearly a hundred years ago. They saw Canterbury as the mother church of Britain, and when they spoke about "England", for example, they meant Wales as well. Kentish clerics have not been above falsifying records, either. Around fifty years ago a record was made up to show that the bishops of Llandaff and St David's had been consecrated at Canterbury as long ago as the tenth century.

Quarrels and rivalry between Welsh bishops helped Canterbury's cause, but in the end it was the belief that an independent church would foster the desire for political independence that always made English kings throw their weight behind the "mother church" of Canterbury (→ 1223).

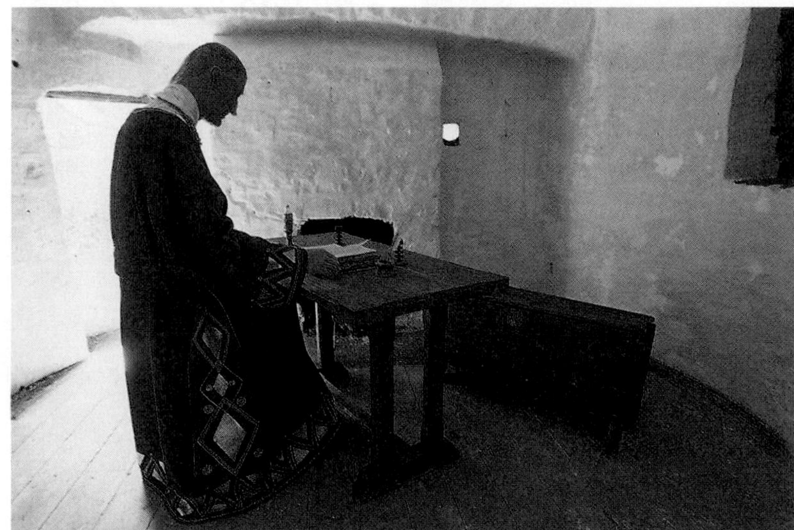

A reconstruction of Archdeacon Gerald's study at Manorbier, Dyfed.

King's nephew mysteriously disappears

Rouen, Normandy, April 1203
Arthur, the 16-year-old nephew of King John of England and his rival for power, has vanished in mysterious circumstances and is believed to have been murdered. He was captured by John's forces in the Battle of Mirebeau last year [*see report above left*] and was being held in the castle of Hubert de Burgh, the royal chamberlain, at Falaise.

Arthur, the son of Geoffrey and Constance of Brittany and a grandson of Henry II of England, is a hero to the Breton people, and his imprisonment caused widespread unrest. John then ordered him to be blinded and castrated – a barbarous plan frustrated by Hubert.

Hubert hoped to calm things down by announcing that Arthur had died of a broken heart. When he then changed his story and said that Arthur was still alive, nobody believed him. It is now being said that John took his nephew to Rouen and after dinner one evening, when he was drunk and possessed by the devil, killed Arthur with his own hands and cast him into the river Seine, where a fisherman found the body (→ 8/1203).

1204 - 1209

France, March 1204. King Philip II of France refuses to make peace with King John of England until John releases Arthur, the duke of Brittany, who mysteriously vanished last year (→1/4).

Normandy, 1 April 1204. Philip II of France controls the whole region apart from Gascony (→24/6).

France, spring 1205. Earl William Marshal of Pembroke, a favourite of John of England, does homage to Philip II of France for his French fiefs and then refuses to fight the French (→1207).

Anjou, France, April 1205. Philip II captures John of England's last castles, Chinon and Loches (→12/1205).

Ulster, 29 May 1205. John of England grants the earldom to Hugh de Lacy (→18/4/08).

Waterford City, 2 July 1205. King John of England grants a charter.

France, December 1205. The English lords in Poitou resist attempts by John of England to fight in France (→8/12/12).

France, 24 October 1206. John of England and Philip II of France call a truce (→4/5/12).

Leinster, February 1207. William Marshal, the earl of Pembroke, still out of favour with the English king, retires to his Irish lordship (→9/1207).

Woodstock, Oxon, Sept 1207. William Marshal is recalled from Ireland to explain a dispute with the justiciar, Meiler fitzHenry (→13/1/17).

Winchester, 1 October 1207. Queen Isabella gives birth to a son, Henry, the heir to the throne (→28/10/16).

Borders, 1207. A fire destroys much of the important burgh of Roxburgh.

Ireland, 18 April 1208. John of England, who last month confirmed Leinster to William Marshal, gives Meath to Walter de Lacy (→6/1208).

Ireland, June 1208. Meiler fitzHenry, defeated in March at Tipperary, is replaced as justiciar by Bishop John of Norwich (→2/7/10).

Aberystwyth, Dyfed, 1208. Llywelyn ab Iorwerth of Gwynedd seizes control of north Ceredigion (→10/1208).

Shrewsbury, Shropshire, October 1208. King John arrests Gwenwynwyn of Powys and seizes his land (→c.1210).

England loses its foothold in Europe

Rouen, Normandy, 24 June 1204
This wealthy trading city has fallen to Philip II of France. Now all the lands of the duchy of Normandy, except for the Channel Islands, are lost to the English crown. The barons here deserted King John of England at the first opportunity.

Two years ago John was riding high, but since then he has relied on mercenaries paid by England to cling on to the remnants of his Norman lands. When the final blow came he was, in fact, in England seeking funds for a new army. In response to urgent appeals from Rouen's defenders, he answered that everyone should do what seemed best; to avoid devastation they surrendered (→4/1205).

Influential queen dies at age of 82

Fontevrault, France, 1204
Eleanor of Aquitaine, the wife of first Louis VII of France and then Henry II of England, who was perhaps the most influential queen of modern times, has died at the age of 82. The inheritance she brought to her marriage to the future Henry II in 1152 greatly increased his powers. In 1173, however, she incited three of her sons to rebel against Henry. She was later held under house arrest in punishment for her betrayal. Despite this setback Eleanor succeeded in securing the English throne for her favourite son, Richard; 11 years later, having retired from public life, she returned to it to ensure the accession of her youngest son, John.

Irish courts forced to heed English law

Ireland, 2 November 1204
King John of England seems to be determined to consolidate his position in Ireland. In August he ordered a castle to be built in Dublin, not only as a fortress and the seat of justice but also to house the treasury. Clearly, Dublin Castle is set to become the centre and symbol of English authority in Ireland.

John has now decided to extend to Ireland English laws relating to questions of property and inheritance. The creation of a judicial system introducing the common law to Ireland seems bound to have far-reaching consequences. It is the first authoritative declaration that Irish courts are to use English law (→29/5/05).

Prestige of Oxford attracts new scholars

Academic centre: students at Oxford university attending a lecture.

Oxford, 1209
The prestige of Oxford as a centre of academic excellence is attracting scholars from all over Europe, where the university's reputation is well established. There are 70 masters and 200 students here, studying Roman and canon law, the liberal arts, theology and medicine. To meet the need for accommodation, townsmen and masters have set up a committee to fix the rents of available houses. Some scholars have this year settled at Cambridge, also an established place of learning.

Scholarly activity began in Oxford with the French schoolmaster Theobald of Etampes, a teacher here for about 30 years from 1095. The demand of nearby monasteries for literate recruits led to his school's success. Then in less than a century Oxford's ecclesiastical courts saw the city's rise as a judicial centre. With so many adjacent schools and courts, the system of sharing knowledge and experience and combining instruction with practice has given Oxford an enviable reputation. Since grammar schools can no longer provide enough recruits for higher posts in government, students are turning to the university (→1209).

Beastly fables said to hold divine truth

England, c.1205
The popularity of books known as "bestiaries" is scaling new heights. Bestiaries are manuscripts of fables about animals and birds, beautifully illustrated with drawings of beasts both real and imaginary. In the past century bestiaries were modest books with line drawings, but now they are illustrated by the best artists of the day. The strange allegorical texts are imbued with moral meanings mirroring theological truth (→1250).

A page from a bestiary, c.1210.

England caught up in feud with Rome

Pope's man forced on English bishops

Rome, December 1206
Pope Innocent III has intervened to settle the dispute between King John of England and the monks of Canterbury over who should succeed the late archbishop, Hubert Walter. When Hubert died last July the monks tried to pre-empt the king by secretly electing on 11 November one of their number, a sub-prior called Reginald.

They sent him to Rome with orders not to reveal his election unless it became clear that the pope was about to agree to the king's choice, Bishop John of Norwich. Reginald disobeyed, however, and announced his election the moment that he set foot in Rome. English bishops, in alliance with the king, disputed this claim, and Innocent ordered an inquiry.

King John, furious, went to Canterbury, but the monks denied electing Reginald and obligingly elected John. This simply confused matters even more; the pope, losing patience, ordered the king, the bishops and the monks to send their representatives to Rome to decide the case. Innocent has resolved matters by imposing his own candidate: Stephen Langton, a cardinal-priest who is active in the pope's own court (→ 24/3/08).

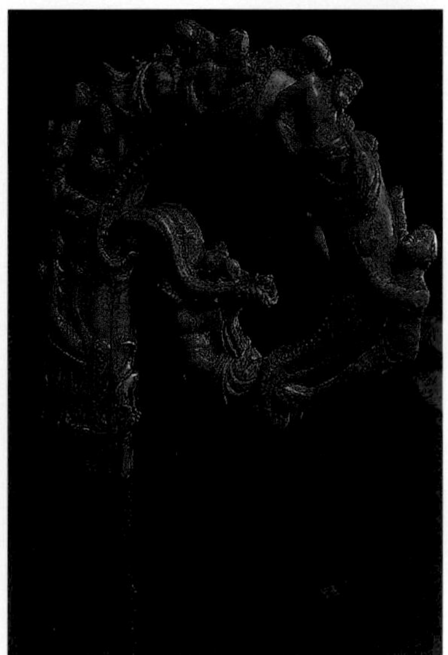

Church rule: a bishop's staff c.1180.

A pope and his cardinals in conference, from a 14th-century manuscript.

Church in turmoil as pope orders 'strike'

Rome, 24 March 1208
Pope Innocent III has issued an order called an "interdict" to force King John of England to accept his own nominee, Stephen Langton, to the most important ecclesiastical appointment in the country – the archbishopric of Canterbury. Under the terms of the order, the clergy of England are forbidden to carry out any ecclesiastical office "save the baptism of infants and the confession of the dying".

The king has retaliated by sending in royal officers to seize the property of any cleric who obeys the interdict. The monks of Canterbury, where the whole dispute began [*see report left*] have been singled out for special treatment: they are to be expelled from the city and treated as public enemies. This move can only exacerbate the quarrel between John and Innocent III, the gravest that there has ever been between an English monarch and the papacy.

Trouble started when the pope attempted to resolve the problem of who should be appointed archbishop. John, furious that his own man, Bishop John of Norwich, failed to get the job, spurned Langton, claiming that he had lived among enemies and was not known in England. Pope Innocent, although sorely tried, waited a year for the king to bend to his will, but he has now lost patience and means to force John to submit (→ 11/1209).

Key Welsh nobles lose royal support

South Wales, 1207
King John of England has crushed the growing power of William Marshal, the earl of Pembroke, and his southern Marcher colleague William of Briouze. After a period of humiliation, during which he lost most of his royal posts, Marshal has negotiated a settlement with the king. Briouze's place as bailiff of Glamorgan has been taken by another Norman, Fawkes de Bréauté, a man noted – like his predecessor – for his brutality (→ 2/1207).

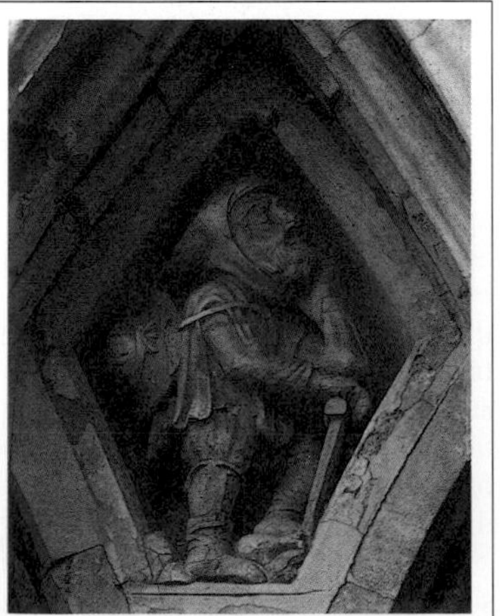

A resting pilgrim: a carving on the exterior of Lincoln Cathedral.

English and Scots seal border dispute with peace treaty

Northumberland, 7 August 1209
In the border castle of Norham today Scotland's King William "the Lion" has again submitted to an English king. Faced with the threat of invasion by King John's army, he has agreed to terms that include dropping claims for the return to the Scottish crown of Northumberland, lost some 50 years ago.

John had been fortifying his northern border in anticipation of a Scottish attack and had built a new castle at Tweedmouth, near Berwick. William decided that this was provocative and destroyed it, thus bringing John and his army north. He must now pay compensation of £10,000 and hand over two of his daughters, Margaret and Isabel, to be married to John's eldest son, Henry, and another Englishman. John has now secured his frontiers with Wales and Scotland (→ 4/3/12).

The seal of William "the Lion".

Defiant King John is excommunicated

Westminster, November 1209
In a climax to England's four-year feud with Rome [*see reports above left*], Pope Innocent III has taken the drastic step of excommunicating King John – rumoured to be an agnostic. This follows the king's campaign, begun last year, against the papal "interdict" on the English church. Very profitably for the crown, John has systematically confiscated the property of churchmen obeying the pope and made the church buy it back (→ c.1210).

1210 - 1213

Co Meath, 2 July 1210. John of England captures Walter de Lacy's castle at Trim (→24/8).

Powys, November 1210. To lessen the power of Llywelyn of Gwynedd, John of England reinstates Gwenwynwyn, who was deprived of his land in the south last year (→7/1211).

Scotland, 1210. Hakon IV of Norway re-establishes Norwegian overlordship of Orkney and the Western Isles and levies taxes (→1212).

Connacht, 1210. The justiciar John de Grey, the former bishop of Norwich, makes peace with Cathal Crobderg O'Connor, the tributary king, at Athlone (→23/7/13).

Shropshire, August 1211. After a second successful attack by John at Oswestry, Llywelyn of Gwynedd submits and swears that his lands will revert to the king should he die without a legitimate heir (→14/8/12).

France, September 1211. William of Briouze, exiled for his rebellion last year during which his wife Matilda was captured by King John's men, dies at Corbeil (→28/10/16).

London, 4 March 1212. John knights Alexander, the Scottish heir, after renewing his 1209 agreement with King William of Scots (→4/12/14).

London, 4 May 1212. John, hoping to regain land in France, signs the Treaty of Lambeth with the count of Boulogne, agreeing not to make peace with Philip II of France (→5/1213).

Chester, 14 August 1212. Before invading Wales after Llywelyn's recent uprising, King John orders 28 hostages who were imprisoned last year to be hanged (→12/1215).

England, 8 December 1212. An assassination plot against King John is discovered (→1/2/14).

France, 18 December 1212. Archbishop Geoffrey of York dies (→15/5/13).

Grampian, 1212. The rebel Guthred mac William, who frustrated King William's campaign against him last year, is betrayed by his own men, captured and then beheaded (→16/5).

Portsmouth, May 1213. John prepares the fleet for his invasion of France (→30).

Ireland, 23 July 1213. Henry of London, the archbishop of Dublin, is made justiciar (→5/7/15).

Llywelyn creates power base in Gwynedd

North Wales, c.1210

A court poet in the powerful kingdom of Gwynedd has called the sudden rise of the present king, Llywelyn ab Iorwerth, "a swirling windstorm". The grandson of the great Owain Gwynedd, Llywelyn restored order here after the instability following Owain's death in 1170. In 1194 Llywelyn defeated his uncle, Dafydd ab Owain; three years later he exiled him to England. Llywelyn has not balked at flouting the traditional laws of inheritance: kinsmen in his way have either lost their lands or been made to accept client status. He has further strengthened his position by a treaty in 1201 with John of England, whose illegitimate daughter Joan he married in 1205. Now that he dominates Powys and even parts of the central March, his power seems unassailable (→11/1210).

Monks thrive whether saints or sinners

Every monk has a task: the cellarer keeps the keys and samples the wine.

England, 1211

The monastic movement is still thriving, despite occasional laments about the less than pure lives of some monks. A state of near anarchy, for example, reigned in the monastery at Bury St Edmunds in Suffolk when Abbot Sampson, who died this year, took it over. Debts had grown and grown, while the sacristan was a drunk and the other monks just idle. It was not, perhaps, an exceptional scene: as long ago as 1177 Gerald of Wales was astonished, on a visit to Canterbury, to find the monks there filling their bellies with all kinds of sumptuous food. He was particularly irritated by the florid gestures used at table when, to get round their vow of silence, they signalled for food or drink to be passed.

Yet most monasteries remain sober centres of learning and art. Monks compile and illustrate with superb skill not only religious works but also the nation's chronicles. They provide social welfare, dispensing alms and even medical care. The national economy benefits from their skills in farming; certain monasteries have become expert in rearing sheep, whose wool is a mainstay of England's wealth [*see report on page 254*] (→1216).

A prior's seal, Coldingham, c.1200.

Church makes big gains as property is redistributed

A 12th-century knocker on the north door of Durham Cathedral.

England, c.1210

There has been a massive redistribution of wealth since the Norman Conquest – which has brought great benefits to the church but not to the laity. William the Conqueror and his successors took all the land owned by the Anglo-Saxon nobility and distributed it among their own favourites. About half is now held by the new barons of Norman descent, and most of that by the ten richest barons.

Land reverts to the crown on a death. It usually goes to the eldest son, but if there is no male heir the king grants it to new favourites. Kings have on occasion forced female heirs to marry royal favourites.

Churchmen have been far more successful in staving off this royal interference. A small part of church land is now in the name of abbots and bishops. The great majority of it, however, is held by congregations of monks. In legal terms such bodies never die, so the king is not in a position to redistribute their lands according to his whim. In effect this has given the church, which now possesses a quarter of all the country's land, everlasting property rights and has also provided continuity of economic management, enabling the church to make considerable advances in farming methods (→18/12/12).

King John subdues his British empire

Anglo-Norman settlers tamed in Ireland

A 19th-century view of the de Lacys' castle at Carrickfergus, Co Antrim.

Ireland, 24 August 1210
King John of England has been here since 20 June fighting a successful campaign to tame the Anglo-Norman barons and impose his own authority. With the help of Cathal Crobderg O'Connor, the king of Connacht, and certain other Gaelic Irish lords, John has broken and expelled the de Lacy brothers – Walter, the lord of Meath, and Hugh, the earl of Ulster – whose newly completed castle at Carrickfergus fell on 28 July. John has also taken hostages from William Marshal, the lord of Leinster. There are now very few barons here who are not dependent on John's favour and from whom he does not exact feudal dues. By curbing them John wishes to be seen as establishing his domination of Ireland, both Gaelic and Norman.

John de Grey, the justiciar (and bishop of Norwich), is well trained in English law and financial practice. Under him Anglo-Norman Ireland is bound to be governed even more from the mainland; local kings may even be allowed into the baronage to effect this. Yet he controls only two thirds of the country; the north and west remain mostly independent (→ 23/7/13).

Welsh in disarray as English invade

Gwynedd, July 1211
King John of England has scored a crushing victory over the Welsh in the first expedition into Wales by an English monarch since 1171. His men penetrated deep into the north, torching Bangor and forcing Llywelyn, the once-mighty leader of Gwynedd, to cede land between the river Conwy and Chester as well as further south, near Aberystwyth. Hostages were taken, along with innumerable cattle and horses.

A first foray into Gwynedd two months ago failed, but this month better military preparations were coupled with political success in detaching most native Welsh rulers from Llywelyn. Now John plans to build castles to consolidate his triumph (→ 8/1211).

The great seal of Prince Llywelyn.

Seafaring king of Man is forced to pay homage to England

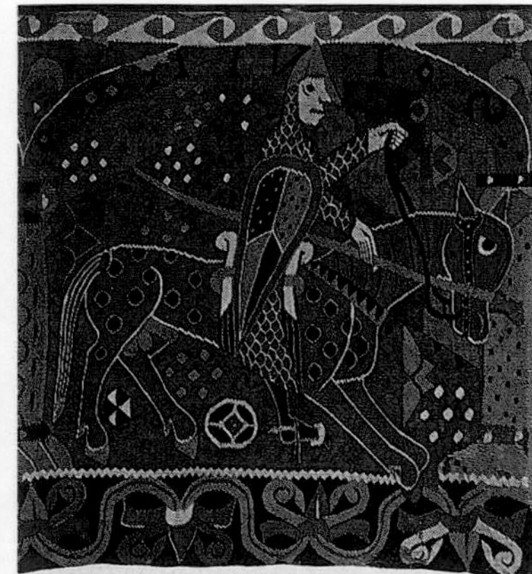

A warrior from Norway, which has long exerted control over Man.

Isle of Man, 16 May 1212
Reginald, the king of the Scottish isles and the Isle of Man, has been forced to travel to England to pay homage to King John for the second time in his reign. England is trying to assert its strength over Ireland, Man and the Scottish isles – an expansion that is being resisted by the kings of Norway, traditionally the overlords of the region.

Reginald is no powerful warlord but rather an aggressive sea-king of the old school, whose main preoccupations in life have been raiding, piracy and fighting with his brothers over their inheritance. It is rumoured – perhaps somewhat improbably – that he once spent three years with his ships without being under a roof ashore for a single hour.

Yet he has discovered that trying to balance the growing power of England with the waning strength of Norway is not easy; John was, not surprisingly, furious to discover that Reginald had done homage to Norway in 1210. This was only four years after Reginald had paid homage to him. It was only to be expected, therefore, that Reginald would be summoned to England to kneel before John again (→ 15/6/15).

Royal capitulation keeps pope happy

London, 15 May 1213
King John, who once brazened out a papal "interdict" and sentence of excommunication, has now caved in to Pope Innocent III – or rather to the possibility of a French invasion backed by the pope's military and spiritual powers. To escape the consequences of his defiance of Rome in refusing to accept Stephen Langton as archbishop of Canterbury [*see reports on page 259*], John has said that he will agree to anything that the vicar of Christ (as Innocent styles himself) suggests. The pope has not minced words, telling John that this "concerns not merely the church of Canterbury but the whole English church, which by your impious persecutions you are trying to enslave".

Already faced with internal problems caused by rebellious barons, John has decided to grovel. Today he offered to make England a fief of the papacy, to pay an annual tribute of 1,000 marks and to do homage to the pope. Innocent is delighted and has graciously forgiven the penitent king (→ 2/7/14).

Fleet victory denies gift to French heir

Portsmouth, 30 May 1213
The English fleet won a stunning victory over the French today and lifted the threat of invasion by King Philip II of France. Philip had planned to give England to his son, Louis, as a present.

Two days ago a fleet of 500 ships carrying 700 knights and a strong force of mercenaries under the command of William Longsword, the earl of Salisbury, left Portsmouth for the Flemish coast and entered the Zwyn estuary, where it found the harbour of Damme crowded with 1,700 ships assembled to transport the French army to England. The ships, laden with stores, were virtually unguarded. The English looted many of them and set them on fire. Hundreds more were set adrift, and others were captured. The landing party had to flee when the French army arrived, but it had done its job. Philip cannot invade now (→ 2/7/14).

1214-1215

France, 2 July 1214. After a successful campaign in Poitou, King John of England takes Angers and besieges Roche-au-Moine, thus enhancing his rule in Aquitaine (→ 27).

Rome, 2 July 1214. The pope lifts the interdict on King John of England after John pays his debts to the church (→ 10/5/15).

France, 18 September 1214. After the failure of his allies at the Battle of Bouvines, King John of England is forced to make peace with Philip II of France at Chinon (→ 9/1215).

Northampton, 27 April 1215. In revolt at John's refusal either to listen to or act on their reforms, the barons seize Northampton (→ 12/5).

Reading, 10 May 1215. In vain, Archbishop Stephen Langton tries to mediate with the barons (→ 28/8).

England, 12 May 1215. John orders the sheriffs to confiscate all the rebels' lands (→ 17).

Grampian, 15 June 1215. A rebellion against the new king, Alexander, is crushed. Loyalists kill the leaders, Donald Ben mac William and Kenneth mac Heth (→ 9/1222).

Co Meath, 5 July 1215. John of England reinstates Walter de Lacy to his lordship (→ 13/9).

Oxford, 16 July 1215. As a result of the slowness of John's reforms the barons refuse to restore London (→ 9/1215).

Surrey, 28 August 1215. After a meeting of the bishops and barons at Staines, a papal mandate excommunicates all who opposed John (→ 9/1215).

Ireland, 13 September 1215. John of England ratifies Cathal Crobderg O'Connor's claim to the Connacht kingship (→ 1219).

Canterbury, September 1215. Langton is suspended by the pope for not excommunicating the barons (→ 29/5/16).

London, September 1215. After besieging Oxford, the barons return to London hoping to meet Louis, the son of Philip II of France, whom they want as king (→ 25/12).

Northumberland, 22 October 1215. King Alexander II of Scots, besieging Norham Castle, receives the homage of the northern barons (→ 1/1216).

Hampshire, 25 December 1215. John, who took the fortress at Rochester in Kent two weeks ago, after a siege of several weeks, captures Winchester (→ 3/1216).

Scotland loses 'the Lion' after longest reign in its history

King William's tomb at Arbroath.

Tayside, 4 December 1214
William "the Lion", the king of Scots, has died at the age of 71, ending a reign of 49 years – the longest in Scotland's history. He stamped his authority on Galloway, put down rebellion in Ross and kept the Norse earls of Orkney in their place. A good campaigner, he was also a skilled administrator, setting up sheriffdoms and burghs as part of a programme to broaden the modern government practices begun by King David.

Although he will be remembered as a strong king, William failed to recover Northumberland, lost to England by his brother Malcolm IV. He also bequeathes instability to his 16-year-old son, Alexander. To the south John of England is a growing threat; on the western coast Hakon IV is trying to build up Norwegian power. William will be buried at his greatest religious foundation, Arbroath Abbey (→ 22/10).

The seal of the new king, Alexander.

Recovery of Normandy: hopes dashed

Flanders, 27 July 1214
King John of England, mockingly known as "Softsword" for his lack of martial success, has met with disaster at Bouvines. His plan to crush King Philip II of France came to nothing this morning when Philip routed William Longsword, the earl of Salisbury, and John's allies, Holy Roman Emperor Otto (his nephew) and the counts of Boulogne and Flanders.

John now has no hope of recovering Normandy or other French possessions. The hammer that should have pounded the French forces against the anvil of his own army advancing from Poitou was broken when the attack through north-eastern Normandy by Longsword and Otto failed. John was also in difficulties. After driving French forces away from his base at La Rochelle, he was held up at the fortress of Roche-au-Moine. Philip's son Louis relieved it, and John prepared to attack, but the barons from Poitou who had joined him refused to fight Louis. John had to retreat to La Rochelle (→ 18/9).

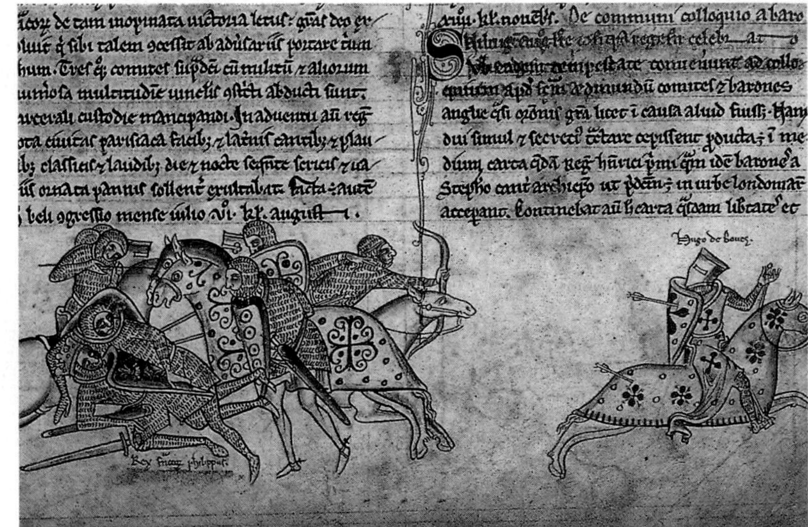

Close combat at Bouvines, by the 13th-century chronicler Matthew Paris.

Choice of deputy is set to stir up fury

London, 1 February 1214
Bishop Peter des Roches of Winchester has been made justiciar [king's deputy], the highest post in the royal administration; he succeeds Geoffrey fitzPeter, who died last year. Originally from Touraine, des Roches was a soldier before he decided to take holy orders.

His appointment will be deeply resented by the English barons, who see him as part of the powerful "Poitevin" party at court, a cabal from Poitou with scant regard for English laws and customs. Many barons are already near rebellion after the king's demands for money for his French campaign, and some – especially in the north, where they have no trust in "French" kings – have refused to serve in his latest expedition (→ 27/4/15).

Welsh prince leads stunning campaign

Dyfed, December 1215
Welsh forces, led by Llywelyn ab Iorwerth of Gwynedd with the support of dissident Marcher lords and 11 other Welsh princes, have conquered seven castles in a three-week onslaught that has stunned the English. Carmarthen (under English royal control for 120 years) and Cardigan are the greatest prizes in the campaign, which has succeeded in restoring the authority lost by Llywelyn during King John's attacks four years ago [*see report on page 261*]. Troubles with his barons prevented the king from returning to the attack, enabling Llywelyn to re-emerge as the undisputed leader of the Welsh. In May he succeeded in taking Shrewsbury, and now the English are in full retreat (→ 1216).

John holes up in Tower as barons take over London

London, 17 May 1215
King John has lost control of London to his rebellious barons. He has taken refuge in the White Tower, but the barons, riding out from Baynard's Castle, the stronghold of Robert fitzWalter, have struck a shrewd blow against the king.

FitzWalter is a violent man and has gathered round him a company of hotheads who have been spoiling for a fight ever since the king returned, defeated, from France and demanded the payment of a special tax by those barons who had refused to fight for him. The tide of rebellion, which was at first strongest in the north, then turned south to strike at the heart of the king's power. He, with his usual cunning, is trying to outmanoeuvre the barons while gathering a mercenary army from France.

John has taken the vows of a crusader and as such has invoked the sentence of excommunication on his rebellious subjects. The pope, to whom John surrendered his kingdom in 1213, fully supports the wily monarch, and John is trying to split the church from the barons. Yet Archbishop Langton, whose election in 1206 was the cause of the great quarrel between the king and the pope, is playing a careful game. He has advised the barons to base their demands not only on their own selfish interests but also on ancient law and custom in a charter similar to the one promulgated at the coronation of Henry I. With the barons in control of the capital, John will find it difficult to resist agreeing to such a charter (→15/6).

An engraving of Duke Robert's seal.

'Magna Carta' signed

King John confirming the great charter, as imagined by a later artist.

Runnymede, Surrey, 15 June 1215
King John has at last bowed to his rebel barons and consented to the terms set out in their "Articles of the Barons". The agreement was signed this morning at a tense meeting of barons, churchmen and the king on the great meadow here, by the river Thames between Staines and Windsor. Not all the rebels were present – rebellion is, after all, a capital offence. Some, however, are king's men who only went over to the rebels after they seized London last month.

The barons, having set up a tent and a small throne for the king, waited for him to arrive, with their mailed and armed men kept at a respectful distance. Then, in the distance, a small cavalcade was seen approaching from Windsor. King John rode in front of Stephen Langton, the archbishop of Canterbury, the papal legate, several bishops and the royal officials. They all dismounted, and the king walked hurriedly into the tent. The archbishop then read out the articles; the king agreed to them immediately and set his royal seal in a lump of wax to signify that he had "signed" them. Barely able to contain his anger, he then rode away to Windsor.

Many of the barons can hardly comprehend what they have accomplished. The articles, meanwhile, are being drafted into 63 clauses to form a *Magna Carta* committing the king to observing the barons' privileges (→16/7).

Barons and church secure privileges

Runnymede, Surrey, 1215
In its 63 clauses *Magna Carta*, the Great Charter, safeguards the privileges of the church and barons of England. It is not a law and says nothing specifically about the rights of the mass of the population.

Under *Magna Carta* it is now cheaper for a baron's heir to buy his right to inherit: the new £100 fee is much less than King John used to demand. The king needs the barons and leading churchmen to agree if he wants new taxes. Meanwhile the baronial party's supporters, the citizens of London, have their own privileges confirmed.

Some of the élite's gains are designed to "trickle down": the barons should extend liberties granted to them in turn to their tenants. Yet there are some important principles: the king is forbidden to deny justice to anyone, and no one may be jailed unless the law prescribes it. To that end royal judges are to visit each county regularly. In such measures may lie a germ of protection for the individual against arbitrary rule (→12/11/16).

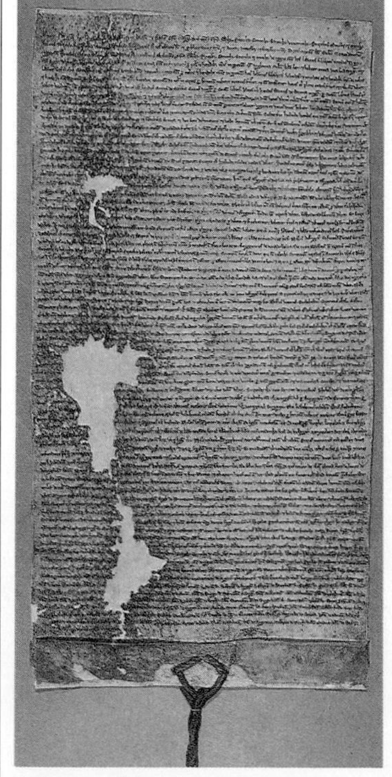
"Magna Carta": an extract.

1216 - 1218

Lothian, January 1216. King John of England, furious at the invasion of King Alexander II of Scotland, moves his troops north (→2/1216).

Cumbria, February 1216. The area is harried by the Scots on King John's retreat (→9/1216).

Essex, March 1216. John captures Colchester Castle before moving to Dover to prevent French aid from reaching London (→14/4).

Thames valley, 14 April 1216. John offers safe conduct to those rebels who are prepared to make peace (→5/1216).

Rome, 29 May 1216. Louis Capet, the son of Philip II of France, who arrived in London three days ago to be hailed as king of England, is excommunicated, and an "interdict" is put on London and his French lands (→18/10).

Dover, September 1216. Following the surrender of Carlisle, Alexander II of Scots comes south to pay homage to Louis Capet for the northern counties of England (→5/1217).

England, 12 November 1216. The regents of Henry III, the nine-year-old new king, revise *Magna Carta* (→6/11/17).

Cambridge, 13 January 1217. Following a Christmas truce, a second one is agreed between Louis Capet and the regent, William Marshal (→23/4).

Ireland, 14 January 1217. A royal mandate bans Gaelic Irishmen from cathedral benefices (→26/1/56).

Sandwich, Kent, 23 April 1217. After seeking aid from his father, Philip II of France, Louis Capet returns to find his support dwindling (→20/5).

Northumberland, May 1217. Alexander II of Scots besieges Mitford Castle (→19/12).

London, 12 September 1217. Louis Capet and the regents make peace (→14/7/23).

England, 6 November 1217. *Magna Carta* is reissued in its revised form (→4/10/78).

Northampton, 19 December 1217. Alexander II of Scots pays homage to Henry III for his English lands only (→1219).

Worcester, March 1218. Llywelyn of Gwynedd accepts Henry III of England as his overlord (→5/5/20).

Rome, 21 November 1218. Pope Honorius III takes the Scottish church under his protection (→1225).

Louis of France seizes White Tower

London, May 1216
Invited last September by the rebel barons to take King John's throne, Louis Capet, the son of Philip II of France, has seized the White Tower and Westminster Palace. The barons, infuriated by John's reluctance to implement the reforms of *Magna Carta*, have sworn allegiance to the French prince, whose claim to the English throne is through his wife Blanche, the granddaughter of Henry II. He now controls most of the southern counties following his invasion of England on 14 May. Even John's half-brother, William Longsword of Salisbury, one of the king's chief commanders, is supporting Louis.

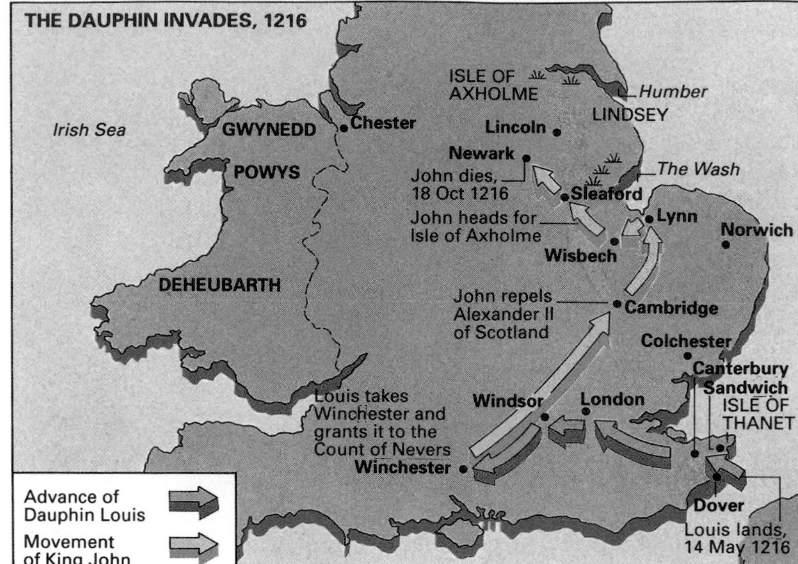

John hoped to prevent Louis's arrival, but a storm wrecked the English fleet and Louis landed at Dover virtually unopposed. John watched him come ashore but then withdrew to Winchester without joining battle.

Louis is not, however, having everything his own way. Up and down the country pockets of royalist support thrive, following the king's raids through rebel territory last winter. John's men control Dover and Windsor. The English bishops are still loyal to their king, who also has the backing of Pope Innocent III. Despite this the immediate future still looks bleak; as if one invader were not enough, Alexander II of Scots has advanced deep into England (→29/5).

Dysentery finishes off England's 'soft and cowardly' king

Nottinghamshire, 18 October 1216
King John died of dysentery in the bishop of Lincoln's castle at Newark today. He was 48. He bade farewell to his captains and dictated a brief will, saying that he relied for its execution on the "fidelity and discretion of my faithful men whose names are written below".

Misfortune dogged him to the end. Last month he went on the offensive against the rebel barons and the would-be usurper Louis Capet of France and made good progress, lifting the siege of Windsor Castle. At Lynn, however, he ate and drank too much at a civic reception when he was tired from long days in the saddle and contracted dysentery. Nevertheless, he continued with his campaign, crossing the Wash to Wisbech.

Here disaster overtook him when his baggage train, stuck in the sand, was overwhelmed as the tide raced in and many of the royal jewels were lost. By this stage he could hardly ride. He rested at Sleaford, and then moved on to Newark, where he could go no further. He died while a great storm raged.

A favourite royal pastime: a manuscript illustration shows King John enjoying the chase as he rides with his hounds in pursuit of a prize quarry – a stag.

John's worst failing was that he inspired no affection. An impatient, tactless – though able – man, he had an often tempestuous relationship with the English barons who forced *Magna Carta* upon him. The troubadour Bertrand de Born wrote of this unpopular king: "No man may ever trust him, for his heart is soft and cowardly" (→28).

Henry III is crowned at nine years of age

Gloucester, 28 October 1216
Last week a nine-year-old boy was playing contentedly in the garden of a Wiltshire castle when a noble messenger came for him. That boy – whose father, John, died ten days ago – was today crowned Henry III, king of England, in the abbey church at Gloucester.

With Louis Capet of France eager for the English throne, the barons have wasted no time in crowning King John's successor. A knight was sent to Devizes to bring Henry to Gloucester, where coronation garments were sewn. Before the coronation the boy was first knighted by William Marshal, the earl of Pembroke, who described him as "a fine little knight".

The barons are keen for Marshal to be regent, but he wants time to think it over. Meanwhile the battle-torn country is in an unpredictable and dangerous state. Even as the nobles feasted after the coronation, Welsh troops were attacking nearby Goodrich Castle (→ 13/1/17).

Gwynedd's success proves unstoppable

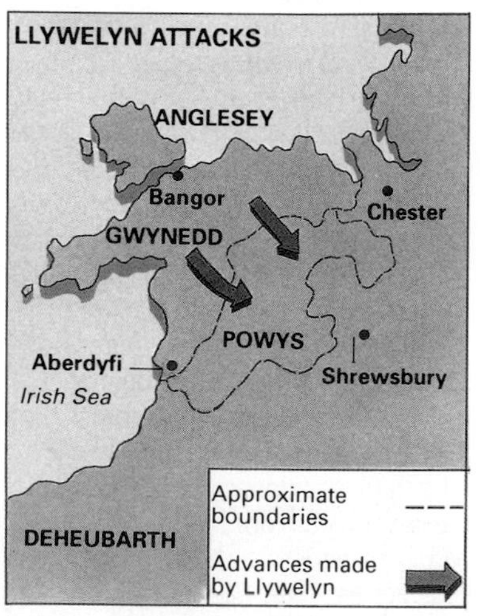

Powys, 1216
Llywelyn of Gwynedd has seized the region of Powys in central Wales and dubbed its ruler, Gwenwynwyn, a traitor. When he learnt that Gwenwynwyn had entered an alliance with the English king, John, Llywelyn tried the prince of Powys for treachery in his absence. Then he summoned the other princes of Wales to him and proceeded to overrun the realm.

Since 1211, when he suffered a crushing defeat by the English, Llywelyn ab Iorwerth has hardly put a foot wrong. He campaigned successfully a year ago [*see report on page 262*], and this year, when conflict broke out among the princes of Deheubarth, in the south of Wales, he summoned the squabbling rulers to an assembly at Aberdyfi and divided their lands. In this way Llywelyn has succeeded in redrawing the map of Wales in his own best interests (→ 3/1218).

Abbots are ousted in Irish 'conspiracy'

Ireland, 1216
The chief Cistercian monastery in the country has been the unlikely setting for a bitter and unChristian struggle dubbed "the conspiracy of Mellifont". Special agents called "visitators" arrived at Mellifont, near Drogheda, and Jerpoint, near Kilkenny, to depose the Gaelic abbots on the orders of the Cistercian general chapter at Clairvaux, in France. They are to impose on these and other Cistercian monasteries here the manners and mores of the Anglo-Norman church: arrogantly, they consider native Gaelic customs inferior (→ 1221).

Rebels defeated in streets of Lincoln

Lincoln, 20 May 1217
King Henry III's armies have won a decisive victory here over the "Capetians", who back Louis Capet of France's claim to the English throne. The Capetians were at Lincoln awaiting reinforcements when Henry's soldiers, led by the regent William Marshal, scaled the walls and wrought havoc among the cavalry inside. Meanwhile other men broke down the town gates, allowing Marshal himself to lead his cavalry through the centre of the city. Knights charged hell for leather at each other through the narrow streets as if at a tournament.

Louis is at present in Dover, but today's defeat will probably persuade him that his best bet now is to make a stand in London (→ 24/8).

French routed off Dover

A great victory: the English rout the French fleet off the coast of Kent.

Dover, 24 August 1217
With Louis Capet of France now trapped in the White Tower in London, to which he retreated from Dover after his forces in Lincoln crumbled back in May [*see report below left*], forces loyal to the boy king Henry III look confident of victory. A bid to resupply Louis was crushed today when a French fleet coming to his aid fell foul of an English force led by Hubert de Burgh, the justiciar [king's chief deputy] of England.

Early this morning the French fleet was spotted leaving Calais. De Burgh sailed his ships across the French line as though he were heading for Calais. De Burgh was in fact seeking to gain the weather advantage: once he had the wind behind him he turned to the attack.

Several French ships managed to escape, but the flagship – heavy with treasure and knights with their horses – was surrounded by English vessels, whose crews hurled pots of finely pulverized lime, creating a cloud to blind the defenceless French. Their commander, Eustace the Monk, was found hiding in the bottom of the ship and put to death. With his supply lines cut, Louis – said to be mad with rage and grief – has little choice now but to sue for peace (→ 12/9).

Vast new cathedral is planned at Salisbury

A view of Bishop Richard Poer's cathedral and settlement at Salisbury.

Salisbury, Wiltshire, 1218
A vast new cathedral is to be built at Salisbury, just over 2 miles (3 kilometres) from the present building at Old Sarum. Richard Poer, who was appointed bishop of Salisbury last year, has endorsed plans for a move from the traditional hilltop site, which has long been bedevilled by a poor water supply. Instead, a new cathedral will be built in fields near the river Avon. Here, too, there will be a new episcopal palace and other buildings associated with the church. In effect, a new town will grow around the cathedral, and the bishop plans to approach the king to secure a charter for the settlement, which will be called New Sarum.

The building will probably follow the recent trend for ever bigger and better cathedrals. In northern France colossal designs for cathedrals have been begun or are at the planning stage – for example, at Chartres, Bourges, Rheims, Beauvais and Amiens (→ 1220).

1219 - 1222

England, 14 May 1219. William Marshal, the earl of Pembroke and regent to King Henry III, dies (→ 30/5/21).

Scotland, 1219. Earl David of Huntingdon, the uncle of King Alexander II, dies (→ 1221).

Ireland, 1219. John de Courcy, the former justiciar, dies (→ 8/1220).

Shrewsbury, Shropshire, 5 May 1220. Work begins on rebuilding the town walls.

Gwynedd, 5 May 1220. Dafydd, Llywelyn's only legitimate son, is recognized as his heir by King Henry III of England's government (→ 1222).

Westminster, 17 May 1220. Following a papal order, Henry III is recrowned by Archbishop Stephen Langton of Canterbury (→ 1228).

Canterbury, 7 July 1220. St Thomas Becket's body is translated from its grave to an elaborate shrine designed by Elias of Dereham, the steward and royal architect (→ 1245).

Ireland, August 1220. Walter de Lacy, the lord of Meath, returns and opens a campaign against Cathal O'Reilly, the king of Breifne (→ 1222).

Oxford, 15 August 1221. A small group of Dominican friars bases itself at the university (→ 10/9/24).

York, 1221. King Alexander II of Scots marries Joan, the sister of King Henry III of England (→ 5/1222).

Rome, 1221. Pope Honorius III refuses to grant Alexander II of Scots the right to be crowned and anointed, following intense English lobbying (→ 1225).

York, 1221. Margaret, the sister of King Alexander II of Scotland, marries Hubert de Burgh, the powerful justiciar of England (→ 1222).

Strathclyde, May 1222. A rebellion in Argyll is quashed by Alexander II, who increases his authority (→ 6/7/35).

Rome, 1222. Llywelyn of Gwynedd persuades Pope Honorius III to confirm his son, Dafydd, as his rightful heir (→ 1223).

Leinster, 1222. Peace talks begin at Dundalk to end the fighting between the justiciar, Archbishop Henry of Dublin, and Hugh de Lacy, the earl of Ulster (→ 1223).

Dublin, 1222. Wine is taxed for the first time (→ 1278).

Canterbury Cathedral restored to glory

Canterbury, 1220
The completion of a magnificent shrine for the body of St Thomas Becket marks the final stage of the restoration of Canterbury Cathedral after the disastrous fire of 1174. The fire gutted the entire choir (eastern end) of the cathedral.

The rebuilding was entrusted to a French master-mason, William of Sens, an architect of exceptional skill, and has been funded largely by revenue from thousands of pilgrims to the tomb of St Thomas, who was canonized in 1173. William had built most of the choir in the latest pointed style by 1179 when a fall from faulty scaffolding left him severely injured (he died a year later). His successor, called William the Englishman to distinguish him, added the Trinity chapel for Thomas's shrine, which will be the cathedral's focal point (→ 7/7).

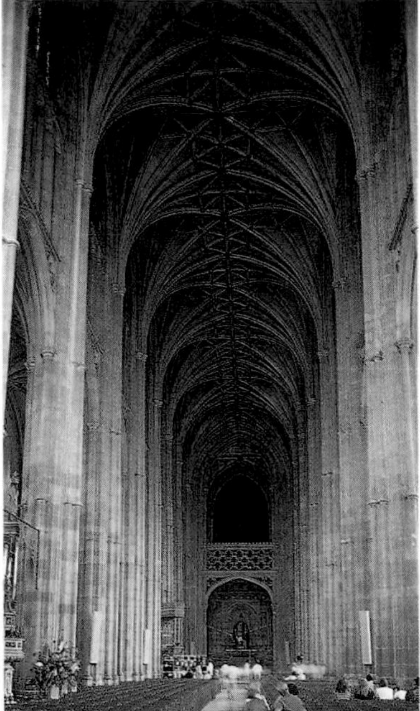

The superb nave at Canterbury.

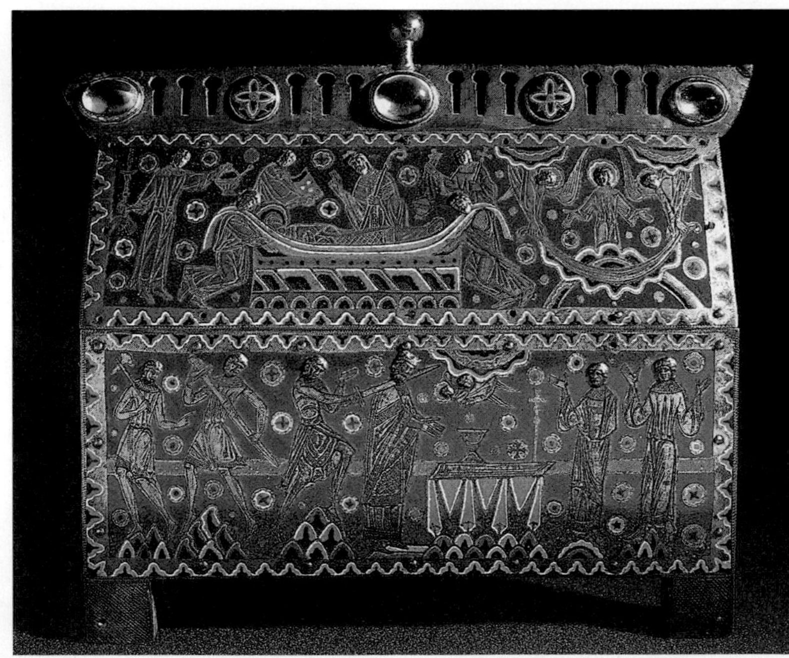

A decorated cask of 1190 containing the remains of St Thomas Becket.

New tax regime helps the rich get richer

England, 1220
The aristocracy of England has taken more than a few hard knocks in recent years, thanks to a succession of kings who have milked it for taxes. Kings cost money, after all – which means that they have to tax their subjects. At least after the great storm of protest leading to *Magna Carta* these demands have eased somewhat; but in any case, it has not all been bad. Baronial revenues have never been so high: the crown's taxes and bad harvests have forced the aristocrats to improve the way in which they run their estates to get the most from them. The one group in society for whom this is not such good news is the peasant majority, whose toil, as ever, supplies the foundation for baronial riches (→ 4/1275).

Black-robed friars preach God's word among the poorest

England, 1221
A religious group which shuns the sheltered life of the monastery has arrived here from France to preach the word of God while living among the people in the poorest districts of the towns. The black-robed friars, who call themselves Dominicans, were received by Stephen Langton, the archbishop of Canterbury. Impressed by their sincerity and eloquence, he has extended his patronage to them. Monks in the closed houses, however, regard the newcomers as sensation-seekers.

The friars follow the teaching of a Spanish intellectual, Dominic, who died this year. Dominic was strongly influenced by the self-denial of an Italian, Francis of Assisi, and his adherents are dedicated to poverty and chastity; they have to desire to own no land and wish to beg for their sustenance.

The Dominicans, who are both scholars and trained speakers, are giving vivid sermons that have had a marked impact on slum-dwellers, who had previously absorbed little Christianity from parish priests. Many aristocrats have also been swayed by their learning. But the friars are criticized by the established orders for asserting that faith needs to be allied with logic for a true understanding of heaven to be reached (→ 15/8).

Dominic, founder of the new order.

Pro-French barons forced to toe line

Winchester, 30 May 1221
The leading noble Peter de Maulay, once a staunch supporter of the late King John, attended the Whitsun feast at the palace here today unaware that he was to be charged with treason for conspiring with Philip II of France. De Maulay was lured into the king's chamber, where he was put in chains.

De Maulay will be forced to surrender his castles at Corfe and Sherborne, where he has been holding a number of hostages on King Henry III's behalf – without passing the ransoms on to the king.

The move by Henry's regents follows the recent siege of the rebellious William de Forz, the count of Aumale, at his castle at Bytham, in Lincolnshire. Slowly but, it seems, surely, the king's supporters are gaining ground against the pro-French barons who held half of Henry's kingdom at the time of his accession (→1222).

Rioting in London alarms government

London, 1222
Serious pro-French rioting in London has raised the spectre of yet another civil war and greatly alarmed the men running King Henry III's government during his minority. The leader of the rioters was Constantine fitzAthulf, who raised the old French battle-cries of "Mountjoy, Mountjoy" and, even more provocatively, "Let God and our Lord Louis [of France] help us". The unrest stems from the government's decision to make the citizens of London pay 2,000 marks for the lifting of the interdict imposed on them during the war.

The king's justiciar, Hubert de Burgh, rode to London and after summoning the mayor and citizens demanded to know who was responsible for the trouble. When Constantine fitzAthulf stepped forward, de Burgh had him arrested and hanged the next day without trial (→8/1224).

Wind power raises East Anglian corn yield

Tall sails: a working windmill.

Ely, Cambridgeshire, 1222
Four splendid windmills can now be seen from the belfry of the cathedral here. These strange creaking giants with their cloth and lattice-work sails are now a dominant feature of the landscape throughout East Anglia; the first ones were built in Norfolk nearly 40 years ago. Pope Celestine III (1191-98) gave the archdeacon of Ely permission to levy tithes on them.

Traditional water-powered mills are totally unsuited to the East Anglian terrain: the ground is just too flat to give power to them. The windmill, however, incorporates the power train of the water mill while adding an air-screw attached to a revolving post. The miller moves this around so that it catches the wind whatever its direction. He can also adjust the amount of cloth in the sail so as to make the most of light winds.

The flat fenland around here, which gives the wind ample opportunity to build up its force, is ideal for windmills, and, as a result of their success, East Anglia is fast becoming the best corn-producing region in England. There is another big concentration of windmills in Yorkshire and Northumberland, where many streams often dry up in the hot, rainless summers.

Orkney ruler flees in wake of murder

Highland, September 1222
John, the earl of Orkney, has fled Scotland in the wake of the savage murder of the bishop of Caithness. He got away in time to avoid King Alexander II, who has come north to investigate the events of Sunday 11 September, when Bishop Adam was killed at his house in Haukirk by men of the diocese believed to be acting on John's orders.

The attack seems to have arisen from a quarrel between John and Bishop Adam over the collection of tithes. The men who broke into the house first murdered the chaplain, Serlo, by way of persuading the bishop to renounce his claim to the tithes. When this failed to have the desired effect they tortured Bishop Adam with darts and stones. Losing patience, they then tied him to a doorpost in the kitchen, after which the house and its owner were put to the torch.

In bloody retribution, Alexander has taken 80 men present at the atrocity and had their hands and feet cut off. Many have since died of this mutilation (→1230).

Never mind the glamour: jousting is now a business enterprise

England, 1219
The idealized view of a knight jousting for honour and a token from his lady was given the lie by William Marshal the Elder, the earl of Pembroke and regent of England, who died this year. His experiences show jousting as it is: a business enterprise whose aim is to win as much booty as possible in the form of ransoms, horses and equipment.

During the 1170s William made a fortune. Along with another knight he captured 103 knights with all their belongings over a ten-month period. When William lay dying, the church – having banned jousts – said that his winnings were a form of robbery and that he ought to make restitution to the church or the victims. He declined.

William was representative of his kind: a nobleman's younger son without an inheritance who saw jousting as a way to fame and, with a bit of luck, the hand of a wealthy widow. This search has been given a romantic glow by the tales of knights, ladies

Jousting knights competing at a tournament, from a later manuscript.

and courtly love that started to appear in the 1170s and were encouraged by Eleanor of Aquitaine, Henry II's queen.

For all their popularity, tournaments have other opponents as well as the church, which has declared that those killed jousting should not be permitted church burials. A common complaint is that jousters ruin crops and do serious damage to the land they fight over. King Richard did something to control the sport by licensing only five sites where it could take place and excluding foreign knights to stop political rivalry (→1292).

1223 - 1230

France, 14 July 1223. Philip II dies; his son becomes King Louis VIII (→ 13/8/24).

Leinster, 1223. Henry III of England prepares for war with Hugh de Lacy, the earl of Ulster, who has allied with King Aed Meith O'Neill of Tyrone [Tir Eogain] (→ 1224).

Connacht, 1224. King Cathal Crobderg O'Connor dies; his son Aed succeeds him (→ 2/5).

Ireland, 2 May 1224. William Marshal the Younger is appointed justiciar (→ 5/1227).

France, 13 August 1224. Louis VIII controls Poitou after the fall of La Rochelle (→ 2/1225).

England, February 1225. Richard, the earl of Cornwall, Henry III's younger brother, is made count of Poitou (→ 1227).

Scotland, 1225. The church receives from Pope Honorius III the right to hold provincial councils (→ 19/6/50).

Rome, 1226. Joan, King John of England's illegitimate daughter, the wife of Llywelyn of Gwynedd and mother of his son and heir Dafydd, is declared legitimate by Pope Honorius III (→ 2/5/30).

England, January 1227. Henry III declares himself of age and assumes full powers (→ 19/2).

Connacht, summer 1227. King Aed O'Connor flees to Tyrconnell [Tir Conaill]; Richard de Burgh installs Rory O'Connor's son, also Aed, as king (→ 13/2/28).

France, 1227. Richard, the brother of Henry III of England, loses Poitou (→ 1230).

Ireland, 13 February 1228. Richard de Burgh becomes justiciar (→ spring 1228).

Ireland, spring 1228. The deposed king of Connacht, Aed O'Connor, is murdered in his bath (→ 27/4/30).

Wales, 1228. Hubert de Burgh, who last year became earl of Kent and was granted land in the Marches, conducts a disastrous campaign against Welsh lords (→ 30/10/33).

Canterbury, 10 June 1229. Richard Weathershed succeeds Archbishop Stephen Langton, who died last year (→ 2/4/34).

Ireland, 27 April 1230. Henry III of England requisitions the treasury (→ 1232).

Poitou, France, 1230. Henry III of England invades but retakes only the isle of Oleron, a vital trading link (→ 1242).

South Wales conquered

Built by the victorious earl of Pembroke: the castle at Cilgerran, in Dyfed.

South Wales, 1223
William Marshal, the young earl of Pembroke (and son of the William Marshal who died four years ago), has overturned Llywelyn of Gwynedd's dominance in south Wales, seizing the vital castles at Cardigan, Carmarthen and Kidwelly.

After wintering in Ireland to raise an army William landed at St David's, and on Easter Monday, 24 April, he struck, taking Cardigan; two days later Carmarthen fell. At Kidwelly on Carmarthen Bay Llywelyn's son Gruffudd counter-attacked, but the day-long battle was inconclusive. William made repairs to the castle at Carmarthen and began a new one just south of Cardigan at Cilgerran before finally seizing Kidwelly in July.

The campaign reverses Llywelyn's invasion of Pembroke three years ago, which isolated the Marshal family. The wider importance, however, is that Cardigan and Carmarthen are now officially in the hands of the English king (→ 1226).

Welsh churchman and historian dies

St David's, Dyfed, 1223
Born 77 years ago, the son of a Norman Marcher lord and a Welsh mother, the learned cleric and writer Gerald of Wales died this year. He was a towering influence upon Welsh life without ever achieving his greatest ambition – to see St David's an archbishopric with himself the incumbent. Gerald remained the archdeacon of Brecon, unable to persuade the pope that Canterbury should not lord it over the Welsh church. Yet it might be said that in one sense he secured a place at St David's: it now holds his tomb.

A scribe, from one of Gerald's texts.

As a royal chaplain Gerald travelled widely between 1184 and 1192 in Ireland and Wales. The books that he subsequently wrote describing his travels brought a scholar's mind – he was educated in Paris as well as England – to the topography, history and culture of these countries. He spent his latter years writing an autobiography (among other works) which provides a vivid, if necessarily partial, view of his colourful life (→ 31/3/1406).

Bedford surrender makes young king secure in his realm

Bedford, August 1224
Just two months from his 17th birthday and nearly eight years since he was first proclaimed king of England, Henry III is at last secure in his realm. Pro-French barons have till now posed an implicit and sometimes actual threat to Henry's reign, but with the fall this month of Bedford Castle royal government is restored.

The castle's commander, William de Bréauté, together with more than 80 knights and sergeants, have been hanged following an eight-week siege. Although de Bréauté and his men threw themselves at the king's feet to beg for mercy, only three were saved from the gallows.

King Henry III, by Matthew Paris.

The castle's owner, de Bréauté's brother Fawkes, sought refuge in Cheshire during the siege, but he has now emerged to hand all his possessions over to the crown, including £698 and his castles at Plympton and Stogursey. It was the length of the Bedford siege that guaranteed the death sentences for its garrison. Other sieges – at Bytham and Newark, for instance – lasted only a few days. The credit for the campaign's success goes to Hubert de Burgh, the justiciar and regent to the king since the death five years ago of William Marshal, the earl of Pembroke (→ 1/1227).

Franciscan monks arrive from Pisa

Holy simplicity: Francis, a saint here, with the Virgin and Child and St John.

London, 10 September 1224
Wandering preachers who belong to a new order, the Friars Minor, are reaching England from Italy, where they have been brought together by a remarkable social reformer called Francis of Assisi. The friars, nicknamed Franciscans, are going about the country in pairs, especially during Advent and Lent. They follow a radical doctrine of poverty and so travel in truly biblical simplicity, walking barefoot even in deep winter. Their activities are directed by a group of enlightened bishops who are working for moral and disciplinary reforms within the church. Yet the Franciscans are no social reformers. On the contrary theirs is a traditional message, asking the rich to give alms and the poor to be patient (→ 1245).

Connacht kingdom falls to the English

Connacht, May 1227
The western province of Connacht has been granted to Richard de Burgh by Henry III of England; the whole area has now been overrun by the English. The Gaelic king of Connacht, Aed, the son of Cathal Crobderg O'Connor, has fled, and the province has been taken without much opposition.

Aed, although at one time supported by the English, had many enemies ready to dispute his succession. Two years ago Aed Meith O'Neill, the king of Tyrone [Tir Eogain], gave the throne of Connacht to Turlough O'Connor, the son of the late High King Rory O'Connor. Aed O'Connor rallied support and managed to oust Turlough, but last year his luck ran out.

On 30 June Aed received a mandate from London telling him to surrender Connacht to Richard de Burgh. Not unreasonably, Aed refused to attend a tribunal in Dublin in April of this year, and today, three years since Aed became king, de Burgh has been granted Connacht as a fief (→ summer 1227).

Norse invaders put to flight from Bute

Strathclyde, 1230
Alan, the lord of Galloway, has rooted out Norse invaders on the island of Bute. The royal castle at Rothesay, on the island's eastern coast, had fallen to a combined assault by Uspak, the Norse king of the Hebrides, and Olaf, the king of the isles. Uspak was killed during this campaign, and now Olaf, with the news of Alan's arrival, has fled south to Man with his fleet.

This is the first set-back that Olaf has suffered in his struggle to establish himself as a local warlord. Only last year, in a fierce battle at Tynwald, he defeated and killed his brother Reginald whom he had thrown out of Man in 1226, thereby bringing to a bloody conclusion a long-standing feud over their inheritance. Olaf felt that his brother was denying him his fair share of the islands. Six years ago he captured his nephew, Godfrey, blinding and castrating him. Olaf now has to cling on to his independence from Scottish, Norwegian and English claims to the overlordship of his "kingdom" (→ 1231).

Canterbury loses another turbulent priest

England, 1228
This year has seen the death of the controversial archbishop of Canterbury, Stephen Langton. His appointment was doggedly contested by King John, who found himself as a result at odds with Pope Innocent III. Stephen was therefore at the heart of a dispute that saw relations between England and the papacy sink to new depths [*see reports on pages 259 and 261*].

Born into a well-off English family around 1150, Stephen was sent to Paris to study at the university there. His rise in the ranks of the church started in 1206 when Pope Innocent, who had studied with Stephen at Paris, made him a cardinal and offered him a post in his household. Innocent consecrated him as archbishop of Canterbury on 27 June 1207, with the consequences already reported.

Stephen was the pope's man only until, in 1213, John accepted him. He later refused to publish the excommunications sent by the pope against the English barons. It was, after all, they who had backed him against John. Innocent suspended him from his duties in 1215, but three years later Pope Honorius III reinstated him (→ 10/6/29).

Langton with the English barons.

Welsh prince strings up his wife's lover

Gwynedd, 2 May 1230
William of Briouze, the Marcher lord of Brecon, was executed today after being discovered in bed with Princess Joan, the wife of Llywelyn ab Iorwerth, the prince of Gwynedd. Briouze was dragged out and publicly hanged after Llywelyn encounted the couple making love in a chamber of one of his houses.

As today's events show, Llywelyn is a man with a fiery temper. Yet it may not simply be a case of his anger getting the better of him: as a Marcher lord Briouze posed a potential threat to Gwynedd's increasing power in central Wales. At first he was placated by diplomatic means, as when Llywelyn shrewdly married off his only legitimate son and designated successor, Dafydd, to Briouze's daughter Isabella a year ago. The incident that has resulted in Briouze's execution could have provided Llywelyn with an excuse to deal with his rival in a more brutal – and definitive – way (→ 6/1231).

The stone coffin of Princess Joan, the wife of Llywelyn of Gwynedd.

1231 - 1235

England, 4 April 1231. William Marshal the Younger, the earl of Pembroke and brother-in-law of the king, dies (→ 3/8).

Westminster, 3 August 1231. Richard Marshal, the brother of William Marshal the Younger, is invested as earl of Pembroke (→ 24/6/33).

Westminster, 13 August 1231. Simon de Montfort arrives from France to claim the earldom of Leicester by right of his grandmother (→ 1/1238).

Orkney, 1231. Earl John of Orkney and Caithness is murdered in Thurso by Hanef the Young, King Hakon of Norway's cupbearer (→ 1239).

Ireland, 2 September 1232. Maurice fitzGerald is appointed justiciar (→ 1233).

Oxford, 24 June 1233. Earl Richard Marshal leads a conference of barons who are keen to rid the king of the Poitevin influence (→ 4/1234).

Connacht, 1233. Felim O'Connor destroys several Anglo-Norman castles after the murder of King Aed O'Connor (→ 27/9/34).

Oxford, March 1234. Simon de Montfort is called in to settle riots between the students and burgesses (→ 1249).

Canterbury, 2 April 1234. Edmund Rich becomes archbishop (→ 1235).

Gloucester, 27 May 1234. Henry III, who last month dismissed Peter des Roches, the pro-Poitevin bishop of Winchester, makes peace with Hubert de Burgh, the earl of Kent (→ 30/7/35).

Connacht, 27 September 1234. Henry III of England restores the kingdom to Richard de Burgh (→ 6/1235).

Ireland, June 1235. Maurice fitzGerald launches a major campaign against the Gaelic Irish in Connacht, defeating Felim O'Connor, the rebel leader (→ 1237).

Dumfries and Galloway, 16 July 1235. Alexander II puts down a rebellion by Thomas, the bastard son of the late lord of Galloway, who raised native support against the division of the lordship among his father's daughters and their English husbands (→ 6/1237).

Worms, Germany, 30 July 1235. The elaborate wedding of Holy Roman Emperor Frederick II and Isabella, Henry III of England's sister, takes place (→ 20/1/36).

Welsh ruler regains his lands and power

South Wales, June 1231

Llywelyn ab Iorwerth of Gwynedd again controls much of south Wales after a devastating campaign that has seen him overthrow the towns of Brecon and Caerleon and retake Kidwelly. With characteristic cunning Llywelyn seized the opportunity afforded him by the recent death of William Marshal the Younger, the earl of Pembroke, to regain the initiative in the south and win back territory lost over the last ten years. Llywelyn launched a massive attack across the length and breadth of Wales. He first set about raiding Montgomery and then proceeded southwards to Gwent and westwards through Glamorgan.

For the English it represents, like the 1228 campaign botched by Hubert de Burgh, another military failure against the Welsh. But, despite Llywelyn's raids, they have clung on to Montgomery, from which they could in future penetrate central and northern Wales. Their sights are also set on the region around Chester. Control of that would offer a vital base for confronting the power of Gwynedd head on (→ 21/6/34).

England to control finances of Ireland

Ireland, 1232

King Henry III of England is tightening his control over the Irish exchequer. In a move designed partly to thwart any justiciar [king's deputy] tempted to line his pockets with royal revenues, he has now instituted a chancery in Dublin, with its own staff and records to act as watchdog over the exchequer. The new chancellor, for example, will have his own clerk who will keep an independent financial record to check against the treasurer's at the exchequer.

A chancery staffed with skilled professionals is also needed because the post of justiciar is becoming increasingly complex. The office demands the combined talents of a soldier, administrator, judge and diplomat. Furthermore, appointees need solid professional support in order to do the job well (→ 2/9).

Top official on the run

De Burgh begs for sanctuary.

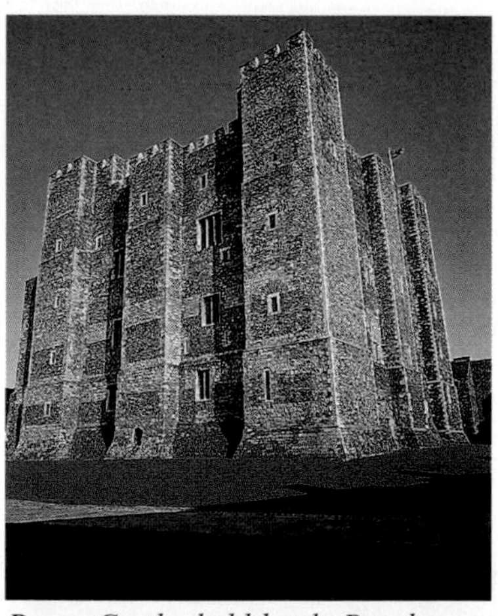

Dover Castle, held by de Burgh.

Chepstow, Gwent, 30 October 1233

Once one of the most powerful men in England, Hubert de Burgh, arrived here today as a prisoner on the run. His career first faltered when King Henry III became suspicious of him, and then his bitterest rival, Peter des Roches, exploited that suspicion for his own ends.

Justiciar of England from June 1215 until 29 July last year, de Burgh loyally supported first King John and then his son Henry. In the civil war he defended Dover Castle against Louis Capet of France, whose navy he defeated in 1217 [*see report on page 265*]. But then military success eluded him, beginning with the failures of both the expedition to Wales of 1228 and that to Poitou and Gascony in 1230.

King Henry blamed de Burgh for these defeats and also suspected him of defrauding the exchequer. Then Peter des Roches, the bishop of Winchester, persuaded Henry to sack de Burgh and confiscate his castles. De Burgh fled but was caught and put in the White Tower.

Although imprisoned early this year at Devizes he escaped to take sanctuary in the church of St John. After he had been dragged back to his cell the bishop of Salisbury intervened, and de Burgh was allowed back to the church; Henry then ordered him to be starved out. But today 100 knights led by Richard Siward, an enemy of des Roches, rescued him and took him to Chepstow Castle, where he will await the king's next move (→ 27/5/34).

Oxford author is the new bishop of Lincoln

Lincoln, 1235

The new bishop of Lincoln is an intellectual, Robert Grosseteste, a former chancellor of Oxford university where he was the first teacher of theology in the school of the Franciscans there. A pious man who has many admirers, Grosseteste has written on a wide variety of fascinating topics.

He has an especially keen interest in the sciences, and among his best known works are a study of Aristotle's *Physics* (as well as a number of other translations from the Greek) and a study of the Creation, entitled the *Hexameron*. Yet his most important work so far concerns optical phenomena. In fact Grosseteste has single-handedly elevated this subject from near-total oblivion.

His books on optics include *On lines, angles and figures* and *On the rainbow*, which links the rainbow to the study of perspective. Other works include *The refractions and reflections of rays*, *On the Sphere* and *On colour*. In all of them Grosseteste attempts to expain the way in which the science of optics forms the basis for the way in which we understand our whole material world (→ 1/2/41).

Truce brings an end to Welsh hostilities

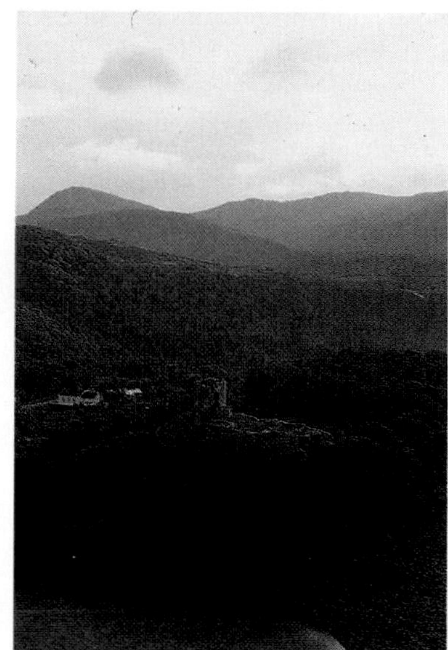
Llywelyn's castle at Dolbadarn.

Shropshire, 21 June 1234
Peace finally returned to the Welsh Marches today when Archbishop Edmund of Canterbury brokered a truce between Henry III of England and Llywelyn ab Iorwerth of Gwynedd. The treaty ends a year of troubles in the region, fuelled by the decision last June of Richard Marshal, the earl of Pembroke, to rise against King Henry. Richard, the brother of William Marshal the Younger, formed a confederacy of earls and barons in protest against the king's reliance on the pro-French, Poitevin [of Poitou] faction at court. In response the royal army besieged Richard's castle at Usk, in Gwent, prompting Richard to offer the surrender of his castle for 15 days as a token of submission. But he later went back on his word and rallied his troops to recapture Usk.

Having made an alliance of convenience with Llywelyn, Richard attacked large parts of Gwent and Glamorgan while Henry, who had not the money to sustain his army, sat idle in Gloucester. Richard also sent Richard Siward, one of his followers, on daring raids into England. The targets were usually lands belonging to Poitevin supporters such as Peter des Roches, the bishop of Winchester and an enemy of both the earl and Siward.

Early this year peace negotiations were started at the prompting of the archbishop. Richard Marshal was subsequently killed in Ireland [*see below*], so the treaty has been made just with Llywelyn (→ 4/1240).

Royal connection in plot to murder earl

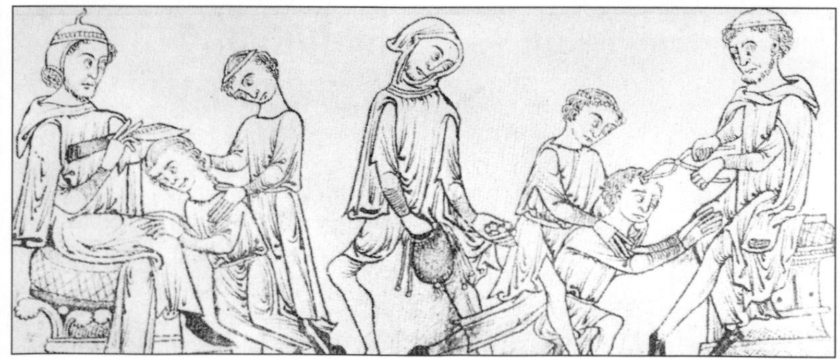
Under the surgeon's knife: an experience revealed to hold new dangers.

Leinster, April 1234
Controversy surrounds the death today of Richard Marshal, the earl of Pembroke. On 1 April Richard was wounded in battle at Kildare against allies of his old enemy, Peter des Roches, the Poitevin [of Poitou] bishop of Winchester; he had returned to Ireland in February to protect lands of his ravaged by the de Lacys. He was recovering in Kilkenny Castle when, on 16 April, a surgeon allegedly murdered him with a heated knife under the pretence of cauterizing his wounds. Suspicion is falling on the Poitevins, whose influence at court Richard had been striving to limit – and therefore it is also falling on King Henry III himself.

Local opinion, which sees this murder as nothing less than heinous, is convinced that the justiciar, Maurice fitzGerald, is deeply implicated as well – one of his clerks, Henry Clement, is openly boasting of his part in the plot to kill Marshal (→ 24/12/45).

Poems of chivalry and romance are the favourite reading of England's nobility

The dreamer in "Le Roman de la Rose" enters the garden of love.

England, c.1235
Continental writers are the ones favoured at court – not surprisingly, since the language and outlook here are French. Whatever the language, the kind of writing preferred is "romance", concerning deeds of chivalry or love among the high-born, such as Gottfried von Strassburg's account of the star-crossed lovers Tristan and Isolde [Iseult].

The most recent such works include *Le Roman de la Rose* [*The Romance of the Rose*], by the Frenchman Guillaume de Lorris, a poem of some 4,000 lines in the style of courtly love, which the poets call *fine amour* (in French) or *amor honestus* (in Latin). On the surface the *Rose* tells of a young man who dreams that he enters a walled garden presided over by the god of love. The dreamer aims to find a glorious rosebud that he has seen, whereupon the god of love explains how he must proceed to win his goal.

Guillaume's story is an allegory and so has to be understood not just literally but in a number of different ways. On one level the dreamer is searching for the love of a woman, represented by the rosebud; on another level he is perhaps seeking the love of the Christian God – also the rosebud. There are no "real" characters. Instead Guillaume gives them names such as Oiseuse [Idleness] or Raisoun [Reason] to make it clear that they represent certain values (→ 1349).

A scene from von Strassburg's story of Tristan and Isolde

1236 - 1244

Scotland, June 1237. King Alexander II recognizes Robert Bruce of Annandale as his heir (→ 9/1237).

York, September 1237. Henry III and Alexander II fix the border between England and Scotland (→ 4/3/38).

Ireland, 1237. The O'Briens of the kingdom of Thomond revolt against the justiciar, Maurice fitzGerald (→ 1241).

England, January 1238. Simon de Montfort marries Eleanor, the sister of Henry III, who was married to the late earl of Pembroke, William Marshal the Younger (→ 2/1238).

London, February 1238. A coup by Richard of Cornwall, the brother of Henry III and rival of Simon de Montfort, fails (→ 9/6).

London, 4 March 1238. Queen Joan of Scotland dies while paying a visit to her brother, Henry III (→ 15/5/39).

Surrey, 9 June 1238. The Poitevin bishop of Winchester, Peter des Roches, dies at Farnham (→ 9/8/39).

Westminster, 17 June 1239. A son, Edward, is born to Henry III and Eleanor (→ 16/1/45).

France, 9 August 1239. Simon de Montfort and his wife, Eleanor, flee here after Henry III accuses him of seducing her before the wedding (→ 1242).

Western Isles, 1239. Harald, the king of the isles, is restored after recognizing the Norwegian king, Hakon IV, as his overlord (→ 1249).

Gwynedd, 15 May 1240. Dafydd succeeds his father, Llywelyn ab Iorwerth (→ 1241).

Canterbury, 1 February 1241. Bishop Boniface of Savoy, an uncle of Queen Eleanor, is elected archbishop (→ 1249).

Borders, 4 September 1241. A son, Alexander, is born at Roxburgh to Alexander II and his second wife Marie, the daughter of Enguerrand de Courcy, whom he married just over two years ago (→ 14/8/44).

London, December 1243. Richard, the earl of Cornwall, Henry III's brother, marries Sanchia of Provence (→ 1/5/48).

Ulster, 1243. Hugh de Lacy, the earl of Ulster, dies; the earldom reverts to the English crown.→

Gwynedd, 1244. Dafydd ap Llywelyn leads a united Welsh campaign to regain lands lost recently to England (→ 8/1245).

Eleanor of Provence is crowned queen

London, 20 January 1236
The city was thronged with people today as thousands turned out for the crowning of their new queen, 19-year-old Eleanor of Provence, and to celebrate her marriage to Henry III, aged 28, which took place at Canterbury six days ago. Banners and flags decked the streets, while rubbish was removed from gutters to aid the progress of the glittering 1,000-strong procession to Westminster, where the ceremony was held.

Before the coronation itself – presided over by Edmund, the archbishop of Canterbury – almost every nobleman and priest in the land attended a magnificent banquet, where the royal couple and their retinue feasted on venison, fish and fine wines.

The archbishop also officiated at the royal wedding last week, immediately after Eleanor's arrival from France. The new queen could hardly be better connected there: her elder sister Margaret is married to King Louis IX. The French monarch and over 300 knights escorted her to England (→ 17/6/39).

Great Welsh leader buried at Aberconwy

Llywelyn's sons mourn his death.

Conwy, Gwynedd, April 1240
The great Llywelyn of Gwynedd, for 22 years the *de facto* ruler of much of Wales, has been buried here in the Cistercian abbey of Aberconwy which was founded by his dynasty. He was 45. The bards hailed him as "the great head of Wales and all its orderliness", although he made no attempt to forge a unified realm. He ruled his dependants with patriarchal authority and won fame as a builder of castles and religious houses.

Llywelyn understood that his supremacy depended on his ability to contain the lords of the Welsh Marches. In this area he displayed a shrewd diplomacy that was typical of his political life, making use of alliances and marriages to build understanding. But he was also a great soldier and leader, veteran of a number of brilliant campaigns which established his territory. He used diplomacy to consolidate in peace what he had won in war.

His reign also saw considerable change to the government of Gwynedd, which he modelled on that of a great English earldom, and where he established a civil service with posts for chancellors, bailiffs and seneschals [household stewards].

Llywelyn was determined to safeguard his achievements and twice, in 1226 and 1238, he summoned the Welsh lords to swear allegiance to his designated heir, his son Dafydd. But towards the end of his life he became apprehensive about the future. In large part, he knew, his great success had depended on the weakness of his opponents in both Wales and England (→ 15/5).

Mongol threat boosts Norfolk fish trade

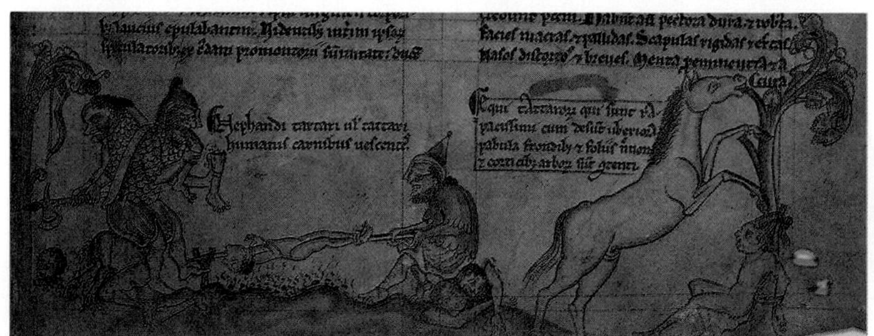

Mediaeval propaganda: the Mongols are portrayed as fierce cannibals.

Great Yarmouth, Norfolk, 1238
As a somewhat improbable consequence of their migration far away from their native lands in central Asia, the Mongols are unwittingly benefiting the fishermen of Norfolk. This year there has been an exceptionally rich harvest of herring to be gathered off the coast of East Anglia – and the Mongols are responsible.

The Mongols are advancing far and wide in their campaign. Russia and several countries in eastern Europe have experienced at first hand the thunder of their cavalry. As they spread further, fishermen from Gotland and Friesland in northern Europe have stopped raiding the fishing grounds off Norfolk in case they too are attacked by the Mongols. What they used to take is now reaped by East Anglian boats.

The Mongols' successes are also leading to intense diplomatic activity. The Saracens are suggesting that England and France join with them to form a common front.

Irish defeat seals the fate of dynasty

Ireland, 1241
A decisive battle has been fought at a place called Caimeirge [near Maghera, Co Londonderry] between Donal Mac Lochlainn and Brian O'Neill. Brian has become king of Tyrone [Tir Eogain], and the power of the Mac Lochlainn dynasty has been shattered.

The battle ends a struggle that has been going on for some 70 years. In 1167 the O'Neills, whose base was at Tullaghogue in Tyrone, were granted the southern part of Tyrone by the then high-king of Ireland, Rory O'Connor. But the northern part was granted to the Mac Lochlainns, who contested the kingship of the whole with the O'Neills. Now that he has established control over all of Tyrone, Brian O'Neill will probably take the opportunity to confront the Anglo-Norman presence in the north-east of the country (→ 1243).

King smiles again on disgraced lord

France, June 1242
Henry III's brother-in-law, Simon de Montfort, is back in royal favour. De Montfort, who is in his mid-thirties, fled here with his wife in August 1239 when Henry accused him of sleeping with her before the marriage. Yet Henry has turned to him for help in the campaign here [*see story right*]. De Montfort was on crusade two years ago and is an excellent soldier.

Until 1239 de Montfort's rise seemed unstoppable. A younger son from an aristocratic family in northern France, he offered to fight for the English king in 1230. He was high steward at the coronation of Eleanor of Provence in 1236 and in the king's council a year later. Then, in January 1238, he married Henry's sister, Eleanor, and on 11 April Henry made him earl of Leicester. Yet he has enemies: many English barons, increasingly suspicious of foreign influence in home matters, resent Eleanor's marriage to a Frenchman (→ 12/1243).

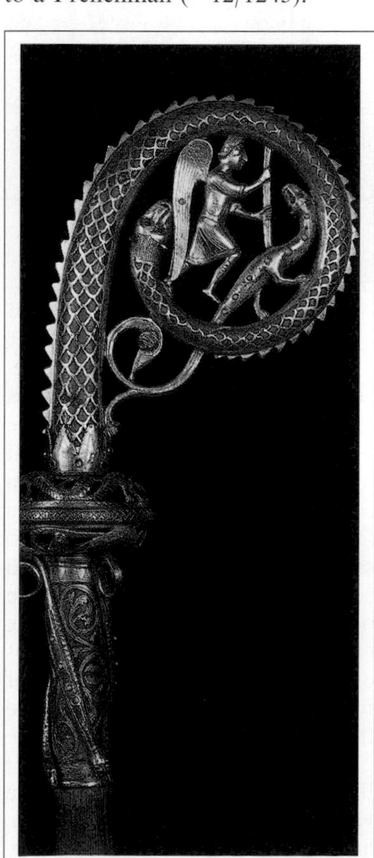

A 13th-century bishop's crozier from Wells Cathedral, which was consecrated on 23 October 1239.

Shortage of funds leads to disaster for England in its campaign against France

Weapons of war: armoured knights with axes, spears, swords and knives.

Gascony, France, 1242
Prolonged delays while Henry III of England worked to raise a fighting fund and concluded alliances have led to disaster in a campaign against his rival, King Louis IX of France. Shortage of money has dogged Henry from the very beginning of this war, initiated because he wanted to recover the region of Poitou, an English possession in the west of France lost by his brother Richard some 15 years ago.

Between May and the middle of July, Henry spent over £22,000 in wages for his army and bribes for his supporters. By the time he actually arrived to fight Louis he had spent everything and was forced to borrow money from his supporters. Bonds were issued against £5,000 in loans, yet these remain unpaid as Henry's army gets ready to leave.

Militarily the campaign has been equally costly. Far from regaining Poitou, Henry has lost Saintonge, a region to the north of the duchy of Gascony, to which he has retreated. Gascony is his last secure foothold in France (→ 6/1242).

English and Scots agree to stand-off

Northumberland, 14 August 1244
Henry III of England and Alexander II of Scots have met at Newcastle to renew the truce sealed between them in September 1237. Today's diplomatic efforts bring to a peaceful conclusion a tense summer of threatening gestures from both sides.

The truce of seven years ago fixed the Anglo-Scottish border (running from just south of Gretna to just north of Berwick), while Alexander also renounced his claim to Northumberland. But ill-feeling between the two countries has persisted, not least because the English have been suspicious of both Alexander's relations with Louis IX of France and his menacing – to their eyes – reinforcement of border defences.

The outbreak of peace was not entirely unforeseen, however. Richard, the earl of Cornwall and brother of King Henry, has acted skilfully as a mediator; in any case, the English barons were not particularly keen to take on Alexander. Some people also expect the imminent announcement of a royal betrothal to cement the agreement: that of Henry III's daughter Margaret, who is three years old, to the Scottish heir, Alexander, who will be three next month (→ 8/7/49).

Balance of power changes in Wales

Powys, 1241
At long last Prince Gruffudd ap Gwenwynwyn has taken up his inheritance in southern Powys. For a quarter of a century he has been denied his lands because of the strength of the rulers of Gwynedd, but the death of Llywelyn ab Iorwerth last year has opened the way for him come to power as a protégé of King Henry III of England.

In the short term Gruffudd is consolidating his position before, he hopes, expanding east into Gorddwr near Montgomery and gaining influence in Cedewain and Ceri, respectively north and south of the Severn. But he also wants to be a great patron, aping the splendour of the rulers of Gwynedd (→ 8/1245).

Ireland falls further under English shadow

Ireland, 1243
King Henry III of England has marked a new phase in the gradual domination of Gaelic Ireland by sending out commissioners charged with extending English landholdings here. This follows other moves to tighten control over the country, such as requisitioning the treasury (in 1230) and setting up a chancery to monitor the Dublin exchequer (in 1232) [*see report on page 270*].

The justiciar, Maurice fitz-Gerald, has added force to administrative control, as when he crushed opposition in Connacht in 1238. Yet the great flaw in Anglo-Irish relations is that Henry never comes here. He planned to do so this year and in April ordered the building of a great hall for himself at Dublin Castle. He did not come. But a personal visit would help him to keep an eye on independently minded barons and disillusioned Gaelic lords. One previous rebel, Hugh de Lacy, died this year (→ 4/11/45).

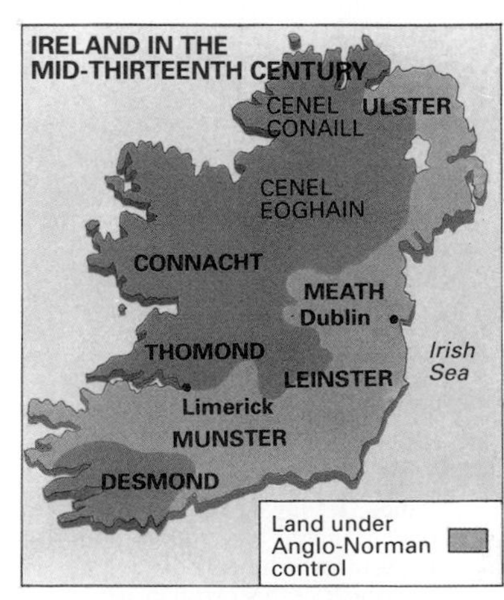

1245 - 1248

England, 16 January 1245. A second son, Edmund, is born to Henry III and Eleanor of Provence (→1247).

Gwynedd, August 1245. Henry III of England's army, reinforced with Irish troops led by the justiciar, Maurice fitzGerald and the Gaelic king, Felim O'Connor, moves to crush the Welsh revolt led by Dafydd ap Llywelyn; Henry builds a new castle at Deganwy (→25/2/46).

Ireland, 4 November 1245. The new justiciar is John fitzGeoffrey (→1247).

England, 24 December 1245. Anselm, the only remaining son of William Marshal the Elder, the earl of Pembroke, dies childless. The Marshal family inheritance is divided between the daughters, breaking up one of the most powerful Marcher earldoms.

Shrewsbury, Shropshire, 1245. Franciscan monks arrive from Italy (→9/11/51).

England, 1245. Elias of Dereham, the architect of both Salisbury Cathedral and St Thomas Becket's shrine in Canterbury Cathedral, dies (→6/7).

England, 1245. Alexander of Hales, the philosopher and theologian, dies.

Wales, summer 1246. Nicholas de Molis, King Henry III of England's steward for Carmarthen and Cardigan, successfully attacks Welsh forces in a campaign from Carmarthen to Deganwy (→spring 1247).

Wales, spring 1247. The revolt begun by Dafydd in 1244 ends as Owain and Llywelyn ap Gruffudd, the heirs to Gwynedd, submit to Henry III of England (→4/1247).

Oxfordshire, April 1247. The rulers of Gwynedd are forced into a treaty at Woodstock by which much of the late Dafydd's principality goes to Henry III (→6/1255).

Ireland, 1247. Maurice fitzGerald defeats a Gaelic Irish force at Ballyshannon; the O Reilly dynasty expels the Anglo-Norman rulers of Breifne (→21/7/53).

France, 1 May 1248. Henry III of England appoints Simon de Montfort, the earl of Leicester and his brother-in-law, as his viceregent in Gascony for seven years, with full powers to collect and levy taxes (→1/1251).

Revival of Welsh fortunes falters with prince's death

Gruffudd dies fleeing the Tower of London (Matthew Paris, c.1250).

Wales, 25 February 1246

Dafydd ap Llywelyn, the first of his dynasty to use the title "prince of Wales", has died fighting against King Henry III of England. His loss, just five and half years after he succeeded his father, Llywelyn ab Iorwerth, is a great blow to the Welsh in their struggle against English claims on their lands.

Henry launched a Welsh offensive in April 1240, immediately after the death of Llywelyn. The king humiliated Dafydd, who had to do homage for his landholdings, and at negotiations at Gwerneigron and London in 1241 Henry forced him to give up all lands won by Llywelyn since 1215. Dafydd's illegitimate elder brother Gruffudd was left in London as a hostage.

When Gruffudd was killed escaping from the White Tower in 1244 an allegedly outraged Dafydd hit back, recovering much of the land that he had lost three years previously. But Dafydd's untimely death robs this successful campaign of its figurehead. He leaves no direct heir, and so his nephew, Llywelyn ap Gruffudd, will be his successor (→summer 1246).

English lords grow angry with king over alleged favouritism to French immigrants

Westminster, 1247

King Henry III's four French half-brothers have come to England, and no sooner have they arrived than he has started showering them with gifts, lands and titles. This is the second wave of royal foreigners to arrive: the first consisted of Queen Eleanor's relatives from Savoy.

The four are the sons of the late King John's widow, Isabella of Angoulême. After the king died in 1216 she married Hugh "le Brun [the Brown]" of Lusignan, the head of a prominent family in Poitou, to whom she had previously been betrothed. Isabella died last year and was buried in the Plantagenet mausoleum at Fontevrault in Normandy; now her sons have come to seek their fortunes in England.

They belong to the "Poitevin" faction [people of Poitou], as distinct from the "Savoyards" [people of Savoy], who are already well established. For instance, the queen's uncle, Boniface, was consecrated archbishop of Canterbury in 1241, while another Savoyard, Piers, was created earl of Richmond seven years ago. Anti-foreign prejudice is growing among the English barons, who are unhappy with the king's openhandedness towards these penniless new arrivals.

Monk explains all the body's ailments

The doctor at work: illustrations from a medical volume by Rogier de Salerne.

England, c.1246

A pioneering new encyclopaedia on clinical medicine has been completed by Bartholomew Anglicus ["the Englishman"], a Franciscan monk. Much has been written about surgery in the past, but this is the first full account of illnesses and their treatments. Bartholomew has never trained as a physician; he says that his book, which runs to 19 volumes, is meant for the general public, and that it should not be seen purely as a reference book for the medical profession.

Not one to mince his words, Bartholomew writes in the chapter on halitosis that "stinking of the mouth comes sometimes from a corruption of the teeth, sometimes from infection of the gums, but also sores of various kinds in the mouth ...". He mentions that such an odour may spring from a simple cause such as eating garlic, onions or leeks, but he stresses that, for more serious complaints, tooth extraction may be the only cure.

Not surprisingly for a work of this size, the book covers a wide variety of ailments – from colic and dysentery, dropsy and leprosy, catarrh and epilepsy to the frightening convulsions and twitchings that may be caused by various kinds of intestinal worms (→1349).

Church architecture advances into a golden age

Henry III supervising the work of masons rebuilding Westminster Abbey.

The west front of Wells Cathedral, built in Early English Gothic style.

Westminster, 6 July 1245
King Henry III today laid the foundation stone for what will be a complete rebuilding of Westminster Abbey, begun two centuries ago by the king's personal patron saint, Edward the Confessor. The work, entrusted to the French master mason Henry of Rheims (who built the cathedral there), will be at Henry's own expense.

The abbey will be built in the Gothic style, which is highly popular in northern France. With its pointed arches and ribbed vaults it is in striking contrast to the simple round-arched Romanesque style. Architects and stonemasons skilled in the Gothic style are much in demand. For example, construction has been in progress throughout this century of cathedrals at Wells and Lincoln, where the love of decoration typical of the new style has been indulged.

At Wells, which was consecrated in 1239, the master mason Thomas Norreys and the sculptor Simon have created nearly 180 statues to adorn the west front, while the new abbey at Peterborough boasts almost frivolously intricate ribbing and, in the central bay, foliage motifs never before used in English architecture. Scottish churchmen also favour Gothic, albeit a less ornate version – introduced by the Cistercians – in keeping with the preceding Romanesque of churches such as that at Leuchars in Fife. Bishop William de Bondington has commissioned beautiful stonework in Glasgow Cathedral, while in Orkney, outside Scotland proper, a new Gothic cathedral dedicated to St Magnus has been built at Kirkwall. Yet the greatest achievements in Alexander II's kingdom are the cathedral at St Andrews, the largest ever built here, and the Augustinian abbey at Jedburgh (→ 13/10/69).

Peterborough's cathedral church.

Romanesque: Leuchars, in Fife.

The restrained Gothic of St Magnus's Cathedral at Kirkwall, in Orkney.

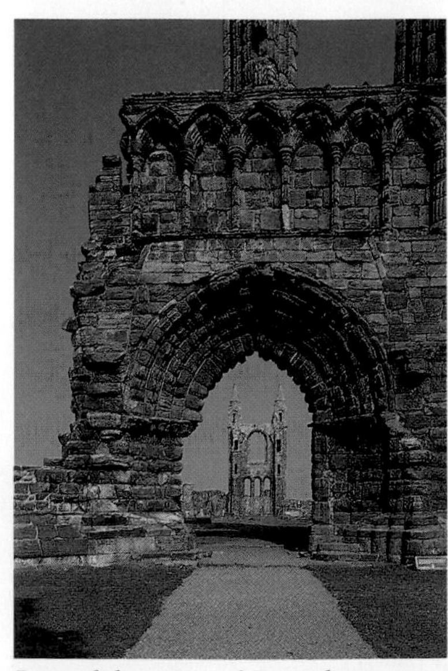

Part of the ruins of St Andrews.

1249 - 1253

Scotland, 8 July 1249. King Alexander II dies.→

Oxford, 1249. University college is founded (→ 1274).

Canterbury, 1249. Boniface of Savoy, appointed to the see in 1141 but unable to fulfil his duties owing to military commitments, is finally enthroned (→ 13/10/52).

Orkney, 1249. Harald, the king of the isles, and his wife Ceilia, the daughter of King Hakon IV of Norway, are drowned returning from their wedding in Norway (→ 2/10/63).

Ireland, 16 June 1250. Churchmen are to preach a crusade to the Holy Land with the permission of Henry III of England and the authority of Pope Innocent IV (→ 19/8/70).

Fife, 19 June 1250. The body of the recently canonized Queen Margaret, the wife of Malcolm III, is enshrined in the church of the Holy Trinity at Dunfermline (→ 24/2/1310).

Gascony, France, January 1251. The nobles rebel against Simon de Montfort, Henry III of England's viceregent, claiming that his taxes and rule are unjust (→ 8/1252).

Dublin, October 1251. A mint is opened (→ 8/1/54).

Gloucestershire, 9 Nov 1251. Richard of Cornwall, the brother of Henry III, attends the consecration of the new Cistercian abbey that he has built at Hailes (→ 1/4/89).

Gascony, August 1252. Following much unrest, Simon de Montfort leaves his viceregency in return for 7,000 marks and retires into France.→

London, 13 October 1252. Robert Grosseteste of Lincoln leads a council of bishops in refusing to pay a tenth of its money to the king, as Pope Innocent IV ordered (→ 1253).

Oxford, 1252. Irish students riot in protest against discrimination (→ 1284).

Ireland, 21 July 1253. The justiciar, John fitzGeoffrey, receives a royal mandate to colonize all waste land in the country (→ 30).

Ireland, 30 July 1253. A royal mandate prevents anyone from interfering with the decisions and rule of Connor O Brien, the king of Thomond (→ 11/8).

Ireland, 11 August 1253. Henry III of England requisitions the exchequer to finance his campaign in Gascony (→ 1255).

Fever claims the life of Scotland's peace-making king

Scotland, 8 July 1249
Alexander II of Scots has fallen sick with a fever and died on Kerrera island, near Oban. He was king for the last 34 of his 50 years. His death has come in the middle of an expedition which he was leading against Norwegian earls here. His aim was to establish Scottish control of Argyll and the western isles, long a source of contention between Scots and Norwegians.

Alexander won the respect of his nobles here, while in England he enjoyed good relations with Henry III, whose sister Joan (the younger of that name) he married. Known as "the Peaceful", Alexander won peace through being a skilful campaigner, subduing a number of rebellions early in his reign. He successfully extended his power into Caithness and westwards into Galloway and Argyll.

He was not only a good soldier but also a good diplomat, successfully negotiating a settlement of the Anglo-Scots border with Henry of England in 1237. Government improved under his guidance; laws were collected and codified to modernize the administration of justice. Alexander will be buried at Melrose; he is succeeded by his young son, also Alexander (→ 26/12/51).

De Montfort sacked

Westminster, August 1252
King Henry III has dismissed Simon de Montfort as his viceregent in Gascony. The earl was acquitted of charges of corruption and treason at a trial here in May and June this year, but the king was not satisfied and has now ended his commission. De Montfort has been paid off with 7,000 marks. King Louis IX of France has meanwhile offered him the regency of his realm while he goes on crusade, but the offer has been turned down.

Affairs in Gascony remain dangerous. Conflicts with the king of France and the Spanish kingdoms threaten, as well as with the nobles of south-western France. In such circumstances it is not clear who might do better than de Montfort, and it is perhaps surprising that Henry may send the 13-year-old Lord Edward to rule in Gascony.

De Montfort is Henry's brother-in-law, but he is now seen as an important figure among the baronial party in England which accuses the king of a high-handed style of rule. De Montfort's troubles in Gascony were partly due to confusion over his authority. Henry gave him a seven-year term as his representative in Bordeaux, with powers equal to those of a king, yet always meant to supervise his actions and constantly interfered – much to De Montfort's resentment.

The seal of Simon de Montfort.

Henry, depicted on a silver penny.

Giving vent to his anger, he once said in public that the king should be locked up, as happened to Charles "the Simple" of France; the insult has not been forgotten. De Montfort still professes loyalty to his king, but a full reconciliation will be difficult (→ 11/8/53).

Scotland and England are linked by youthful marriage alliance

York, 26 December 1251
In the early hours of this morning – a time chosen to avoid popular protests – Alexander III, the king of Scots, married King Henry III's daughter Margaret in the abbey here for a dowry of 5,000 marks. Yesterday Henry knighted Alexander, who is just ten years old, along with 20 other young noblemen. Margaret is only 11 years old.

Today there was fury among the Scots when, at a banquet after the wedding, Alexander was nearly tricked into doing homage for the English lands that he holds. Henry tried also to get Alexander to do homage for the kingdom of Scotland itself. But the boy has been well schooled: he answered that he had come to York to marry and not to "answer about so difficult a matter". With remarkable presence of mind for one so young Alexander went on to say that he had in any case not "taken full deliberation" with his nobles.

Henry had the good sense to accept this evasive reply, but he still seems determined to interfere in his son-in-law's official appointments. He is demanding the resignation of some officers and their replacement by men who will look after the interests of Queen Margaret.

Alexander, whose royal genealogy traces his descent back to Scota, the daughter of an Egyptian pharaoh, has been king for just over two years. He will have to wait for another ten before he can rule in his own right (→ 20/9/55).

A portrait of King Alexander III of Scots as he appeared in later life.

Church loses its philosopher-bishop

Lincoln, 1253
Robert Grosseteste, the bishop of Lincoln, has died aged 78. He was an influential churchman and a valued adviser to Simon de Montfort, whose sons he tutored. Grosseteste had already been chancellor of Oxford university and held several church offices when, in 1235, he succeeded Hugh de Wells at Lincoln, the largest diocese in the country. His clerical success was matched by his scholarly work, notably in the science of optics [*see report on page 270*]. Yet there was a darker side to Robert: Henry III forbade him to set up an inquisition in his diocese last year, denouncing it as "an unprecedented harassment of the poor and defamation of good Christians" (→18/3/77).

English king makes peace, not war

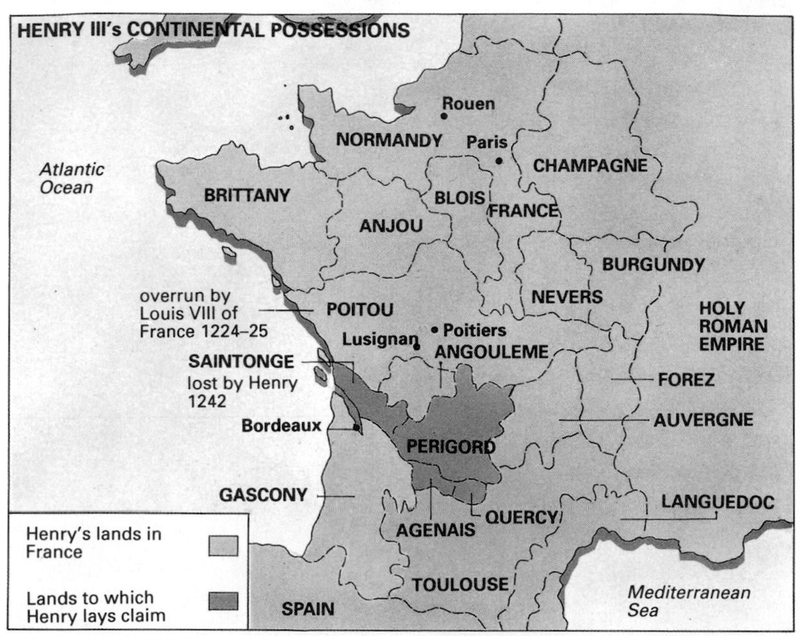

Bordeaux, France, 20 August 1253
King Henry III of England has come to Gascony to settle its troubles, pursuing a policy of conciliation instead of the high-handed violence of his former lieutenant here, Simon de Montfort [*see report on page 276*].

Next year Henry will marry off his eldest son, Edward, to his cousin, Princess Eleanor of Castile, the sister of King Alfonso X of Castile. Henry will grant Edward, who is 14 years old, the whole of Gascony, most of Ireland and great lands in England. Alfonso will meanwhile help the king against rebel Gascon nobles such as Gaston de Béarn, who is in control of the Pyrenees. Henry has also made peace with Louis IX of France and plans to visit him soon (→10/1254).

Monk-artist illustrates history in books

St Albans, Hertfordshire, 1250
Matthew Paris, an illustrator and chronicler who works with a team of artists, has this year produced a magnificently illustrated chronicle of English history, *Chronica Majora*. He is a monk at the Benedictine abbey here and is maintaining for St Albans the pre-eminence as a centre of learning that it won in the time of his predecessor as chronicler, Roger of Wendover.

Paris produces vivid illustrations that capture the humanity of his historical characters, who are often engaged in everyday activities. He has also drawn several beautiful maps, including one of Britain with decorative symbols to mark the cities [*see illustration far right*].

It is not simple chance that a Benedictine house should be responsible for this type of work. The Bendictine Rule balances work, prayer and study in such a way that makes it easy to pursue learning; the Cluniacs are too preoccupied with liturgy, and the Cistercians with manual labour. Another notable centre for book production and illumination is to be found at the Benedictine cathedral-monastery at Winchester, which made a magnificent bible for King Henry II. Other centres are at Canterbury and at Oxford, where William de Brailes is a particularly fine illuminator of psalters.

De Brailes's "Last Judgement".

In producing books the scribe and the illustrator are usually different monks. The illustrator may, like Paris, have assistants who copy his style, so not all of the drawings in the *Chronica Majora* are by Paris (→c.1290).

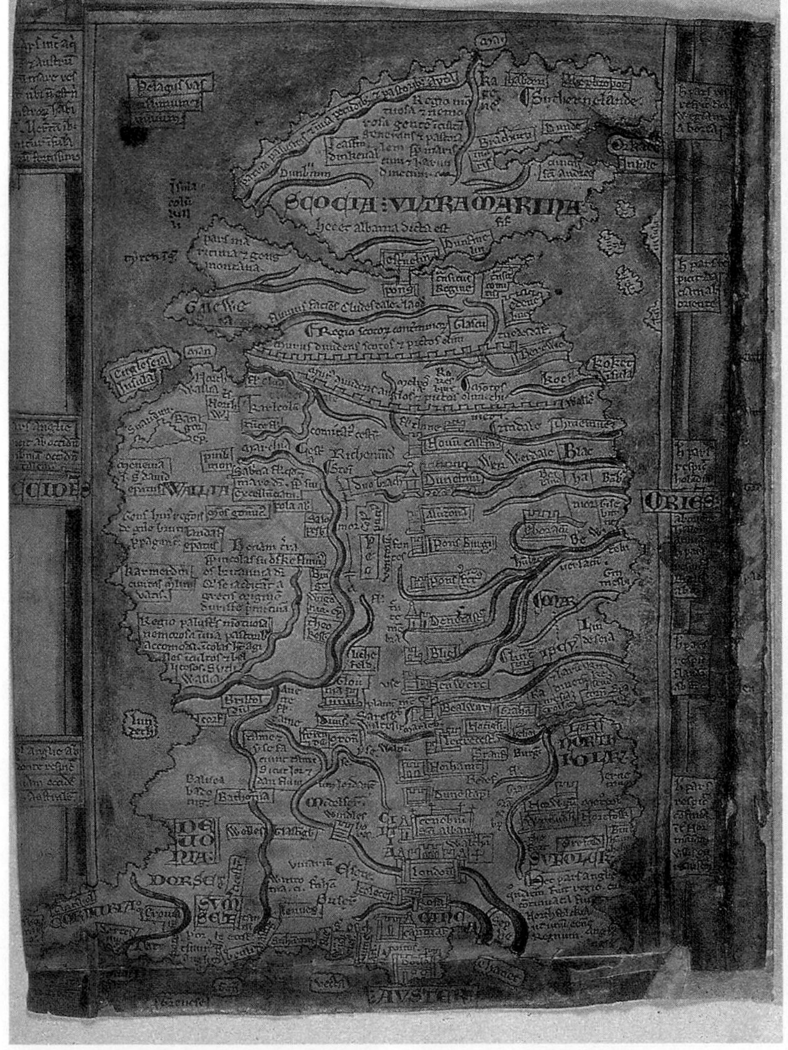
The magnificent map of Britain drawn c.1250 by Matthew Paris.

1254 - 1257

Dublin, 8 January 1254. The mint, which opened three years ago, is closed down (→ 18/6).

Spain, October 1254. King Alfonso X of Spain renounces all claims on Gascony in favour of England following the wedding of Lord Edward, the eldest son of King Henry III of England, to Eleanor of Castile (→ 4/12/59).

Dublin, 1254. St Patrick's Cathedral is dedicated (→ 26/1/56).

Gwynedd, June 1255. Llywelyn ap Gruffudd of Gwynedd, the grandson of Llywelyn the Great by his eldest illegitimate son, defeats his brothers at Bryn Derwen, becoming ruler of Gwynedd (→ 8/1256).

Borders, 20 September 1255. A new council of regency (or government) is formed at Roxburgh after a coup planned by the English and the arrival in northern England of Henry III and his army (→ 28/10/57).

Leicester, 1255. All Jews are expelled (→ 10/1275).

Ireland, 1255. Aed O'Connor, the son of Felim, the Gaelic Irish leader of Connacht, attempts to make peace with the northern kings (→ 3/5/56).

Co Leitrim, 3 May 1256. The O'Reilly dynasty is left in chaos when Cathal O'Reilly is killed by Aed O'Connor in battle at a place called Mag Slecht (→ 1257).

Chester, August 1256. Lord Edward, the eldest son of Henry III, becomes earl of Chester and visits lands in north Wales given to him by his father (→ 6/1257).

Westminster, 1256. Philip Lovell, the treasurer, is ordered to find money to finish the hall (→ c.1325).

England, April 1257. Despite money from the clergy, the nobles refuse to pay for Henry III's son Edmund to claim the throne of Sicily (→ 4/12/59).

Germany, 17 May 1257. Richard of Cornwall, the brother of Henry III of England, and his wife are crowned king and queen of the Romans at Cologne (→ 28/1/59).

Ireland, 27 May 1257. Maurice fitzGerald, the long-serving justiciar, dies (→ 16/5/60).

Wales, June 1257. After besieging Gruffudd of Powys at Welshpool, Llywelyn ap Gruffudd of Gwynedd ravages Glamorgan and Pembrokeshire to establish himself (→ 18/3/58).

'Parliament' is summoned to vote taxes

Richard's coat of arms: detail from a tiled pavement at Cleeve Abbey, Glos.

Westminster, 11 February 1254
King Henry III's brother, Earl Richard of Cornwall, who has been appointed regent during the king's absence in Gascony, has used his powers to summon the knights of the English shires to a "parliament" at Westminster to vote taxes. Each shire court will elect two knights who will join the barons at council here to raise money for the defence of Gascony. This is the first time that such a parliament – the term derives from the French word for "discussion" – has been called to win consent for taxation, though knights of the shires attended similar assemblies during King John's reign for other purposes.

Usually the king consults only his royal councillors and powerful members of the clergy. It was Richard's decision to involve shire representatives on this occasion. The new assembly will meet for the first time at Easter (→ 30/4/58).

Irish bishops take complaints to pope

Ireland, 26 January 1256
Archbishop Florence MacFlynn of Tuam, Co Galway, and Sean O'Laidig, the bishop of Killala, Co Mayo, have visited King Henry III of England to present a list of grievances on behalf of the Irish clergy. They have also sent representatives to Rome to lobby for support from Pope Alexander IV.

The prelates believe that they are being denied justice by the operation of the common law. Like their colleagues in England they have protested vigorously against alleged violations of ecclesiastical liberty and what they regard as a usurping of ecclesiastical jurisidiction by the crown.

Like many of his predecessors, Archbishop Florence has frequently complained about the existence of the neighbouring diocese of Annaghdown, and he has made unsuccessful attempts to absorb it. He has also objected to royal officials molesting both his clergy and his tenants, and he fiercely resents the seizure of the property of clergy convicted of criminal acts. His current visit to the English king represents a more thorough airing of these existing grievances.

The churchmen are also expected to tell Henry III that his judges are corrupt, negotiating with litigants for personal gain (→ 13/11/71).

London-based Italian bankers fined for abusing royal mint

Oiling the wheels of trade: bankers at work in Siena, in central Italy.

Westminster, 18 June 1254
Several prominent London bankers have been fined 200 marks each for breaking the rules of the mint. Among those fined are two Italian firms, those of the Cahorsins and the Ultramontanists.

A general reissue of the coinage was begun in 1247, with a new design for the silver penny. Each coin has the name of both moneyer and mint on the back, so that the maker can be identified if the coin's purity or weight is questioned. Fining the bankers is not only a means of preserving the value of the coinage but also a way of raising money. King Henry III also plans to issue a gold coinage for the first time. One gold penny would be worth 20 silver pennies (→ 10/1278).

Feast of art greets monks as they dine

Wall art: from Easby Abbey, Yorks.

Norfolk, c.1255

Monks sitting down to eat in the Benedictine priory at Horsham St Faith will now be able to feast their eyes as well as their stomachs. The walls of their refectory have just been adorned with a superb series of paintings in a style similar to that of the St Albans artist Matthew Paris. In many places the artist has painted simulated stonework, nowadays quite a common feature. St Albans is outstanding, but other abbeys also house works of art; among them is Easby Abbey, near Richmond in North Yorkshire.

English king faces growing opposition of barons and clergy over Sicilian adventure

Westminster, March 1255

Henry III's second son, Edmund, has been granted the kingdom of Sicily in a deal with Pope Alexander IV. The pope has agreed that conquering the kingdom, which includes southern Italy, will count as a crusade, thereby freeing the English king from his vow to go to the Holy Land. Henry has agreed to pay the pope's expenses and to send troops to confront the Moors in Sicily by next year. If he fails, he will be excommunicated. Taxes raised to pay for the original crusade will now go to the Sicilian foray.

The English barons and clergy are furious. They will have to pay large sums of money to finance a venture that does not interest them. The clergy were ready to back a crusade but not to further the king's Mediterranean ambitions.

For decades Italy has been at the centre of a fierce territorial dispute. While Holy Roman Emperor Frederick II sought to unite Italy under his rule, the papacy was attempting to annex Naples and Sicily. After the emperor's death in 1250, Pope Innocent IV offered Sicily first to Richard of Cornwall, King Henry's brother, then to Charles of Anjou, the French king's brother – both of whom declined – and finally to Henry III himself. Innocent's successor, Alexander IV, renewed the offer, and the king has now accepted on behalf of his ten-year-old son, Edmund. But Sicily will have to be conquered. It is held by Frederick's bastard son Manfred in the name of the late emperor's infant grandson, Conradin.

Henry: bargaining with the pope.

The English clergy are refusing to pay the taxes, and the barons are equally restless. They blame Henry's French and Italian relatives for leading him into the Sicilian quagmire. Serious opposition to the king is mounting in England (→ 4/1257).

'Rebel' lords seize young Scottish king

Tayside, 28 October 1257

Alexander III, the 16-year-old king of Scotland, was seized today at Kinross by leaders of a family ousted two years ago from the council of regency: Walter Comyn, the earl of Menteith, and William Comyn, the earl of Buchan.

The Comyns are now intending to re-establish their control over the Scottish government until King Alexander comes of age in 1262. They were removed from power in the wake of an English-engineered coup; a new government was then formed dominated by noblemen more amenable to English control.

The latest move by the Comyn faction is certain to infuriate Henry III of England, whose daughter, Margaret, married Alexander in 1251 [*see report on page 276*]. It was Henry's professed concern for his daughter and son-in-law that led him to threaten aggressive action against the Scottish leaders in 1255. The young couple had complained about their treatment by the Comyns, who had been suspicious of the growing English influence at the Scottish court.

Henry encouraged the regents' overthrow by assembling an army in northern England while offering to give his protection to the new councillors if they managed to oust the "rebels" (→ 1/1258).

First elephant in England draws large crowds to royal menagerie

London, 1256

A barn 12 metres long and 6 metres wide (40 by 20 feet) is to be built at the Tower to house King Henry III's elephant. The animal, the first seen in England, is suffering from cold, damp, and cramped quarters and is showing signs of depression. The elephant, a gift from Louis IX of France, arrived two years ago and is one of the sights of London. It is the latest addition to Henry III's exotic royal menagerie. The king had a similiar barn built for his two leopards in 1237. The elephant has drawn even more crowds than the polar bear, the zoo's other great attraction, which arrived in 1252 and captured the hearts of Londoners, who gather daily to watch it hunt fish in the Thames.

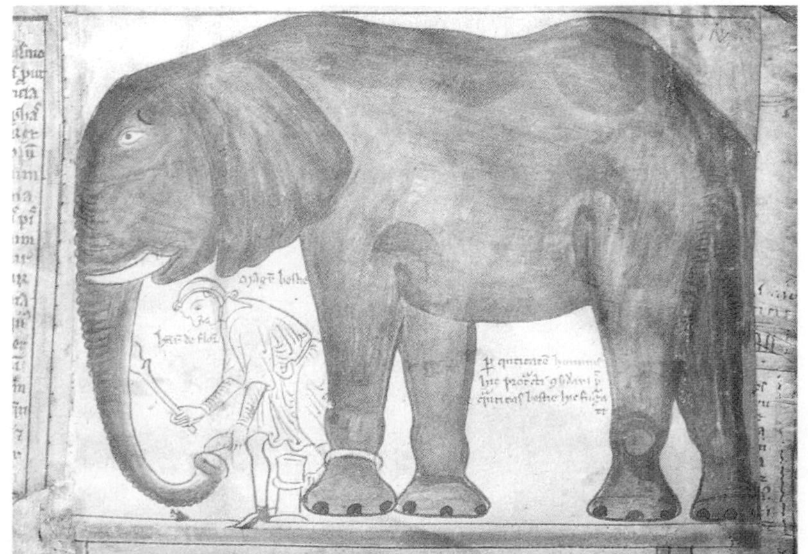

Henry III's elephant, drawn by the contemporary chronicler Matthew Paris.

English earl elected king of the Romans

Germany, 4 January 1257

Earl Richard of Cornwall, the brother of Henry III of England, has been elected king of the Romans and emperor-elect of Germany. The electors were well paid to vote for him. Richard and his wife, Sanchia, will be crowned in the spring. Richard's and Henry's sister was married to the late Holy Roman Emperor Frederick II, and there are close trade links between the Rhineland and England, based on wool. Richard, who is 48 this month, has no possessions in Germany and may prove to be no more than titular emperor. He will only become emperor formally if the pope crowns him in Rome (→ 17/5).

1258 - 1263

England, January 1258. Henry III prepares to march against the "rebels" who seized the Scottish king, Alexander III, last year (→ 9/1258).

Wales/Scotland, 18 March 1258. Llywelyn of Gwynedd, the self-proclaimed prince of Wales, signs a treaty with Walter Comyn, the Scots baron who seized power last year (→ 17/6).

Oxford, 17 June 1258. Henry III, facing domestic difficulties as his council meets to talk about reforms, agrees to a truce with Llywelyn of Gwynedd (→ 11/1262).

Borders, September 1258. Alexander III presides over negotiations at Jedburgh which leave the Comyn faction dominant but reconciled with their rivals and with England's Henry III (→ 11/1258).

Westminster, November 1258. Queen Eleanor, Alexander Comyn and the bishop of St Andrews are among ten people named to care for Alexander III in a proposal which ends Henry III's dispute with Scotland (→ 13/2/60).

Dover, 28 January 1259. Richard, the king of the Romans, Henry III's brother, swears to keep the "Provisions of Oxford" (8/1269).

Oxford, 1260. The Franciscan philosopher Roger Bacon flees to Paris to escape the furore stirred up by his controversial scientific theories (→ 1268).

England, 2 May 1262. Henry III, backed by Louis IX of France and the pope and amid dissension from his barons, annuls the "Provisions of Oxford" (→ 3/7).

London, 3 July 1262. Queen Eleanor sails for France with Henry III to arbitrate in a long-running dispute between Henry and Simon de Montfort over the dowry of Simon's wife, Henry's sister, also Eleanor (→ 4/1263).

Wales, November 1262. The four-year-old truce between Llywelyn of Gwynedd and Henry III of England ends as Llywelyn exploits an uprising to take Gwent (→ 6/1263).

England, April 1263. Simon de Montfort joins the rebel barons against Henry III after his annulment of the "Provisions of Oxford" (→ 9/7).

Shropshire, June 1263. Troops sent by Llywelyn of Gwynedd join Simon de Montfort's men at Bridgnorth (→ 19/6/65).

English barons air their grievances

Westminster, 30 April 1258

A deputation of barons confronted King Henry III in Westminster Hall today and demanded that he hand over the government to a council of 24 peers. The barons left their swords outside and professed their loyalty to the king, but their demands represent the strongest challenge to monarchical power since King John was forced to approve *Magna Carta* over 40 years ago. The king, facing fresh trouble from the Scots and Welsh plus widespread opposition to his proposed intervention in Sicily, has bowed to the baronial demands.

A council of 24 members – 12 nominated by the king and 12 by the peers – is to be charged with reforming the troubled state of England, at home and abroad. Henry and his heir, Edward, have agreed to accept the council's proposals. Among the first targets for the barons will be the king's four French half-brothers, who are likely to be expelled.

Seven leading barons swore an oath on 12 April to act together when parliament opened. They were the earls of Gloucester, Norfolk and Leicester, Peter of Savoy, Hugh Bigod, John fitzGeoffrey and Peter de Montfort. They claim to be loyal supporters of the king, who has promised that no more taxes will be levied for his unpopular Sicilian policy without the consent of parliament (→ 6/1258).

Confrontation at Westminster: the barons put their demands to Henry.

Barons plan curbs on royal power in new 'Provisions of Oxford'

Oxford, June 1258

Radical changes in the ways in which England is governed are proposed by the 24-man council set up here by the king at the instigation of his barons. Three parliaments are to be held each year, and their powers are to be extended over the chancellor, the treasury and certain forms of patronage. Two new organs of government are recommended in these "provisions" – a council of 15 members and a legislative commission of 12 members. These will come under the joint direction of king and peers, which the barons claim will safeguard the role of the monarchy. King Henry III appointed half the council and has promised to accept its proposals.

The council meeting here has also revived the post of justiciar, or king's chief deputy. Hugh Bigod, the spokesman for the barons in their meeting with Henry on 30 April, is to hold it and has been given custody of the Tower of London. Royal castles are also to go to new holders, all sworn to loyalty by the council, not the king (→ 2/5/62).

England loses key French possessions

Paris, 4 December 1259

Henry III of England has today renounced claims to the lands of Normandy, Maine, Anjou and Poitou in France which his father John lost 50 years ago. He also paid homage for the duchy of Aquitaine to France's King Louis IX.

The treaty was a family affair as it involved royal interests in many parts of France. Signatories are therefore not only Henry but also his brother Richard, the king of the Romans, and their sister Eleanor, the wife of Simon de Montfort, the earl of Leicester, himself a leading participant in the negotiations. In exchange for these important concessions Louis has agreed to support the English claim on Sicily and cede lands north and east of Gascony. The tenants of these lands will not be pleased (→ 26/1/76).

Matthew Paris: a self-portrait of the versatile writer, illustrator and Benedictine monk from St Albans Abbey who died c.1260.

Ulster chiefs suffer Downpatrick defeat

Co Down, 16 May 1260

The first attempt to restore the high-kingship since the Normans invaded Ireland almost a century ago has ended in disaster today at the battle of Downpatrick. Brian O'Neill, the king of Tyrone, has been killed, along with many chiefs of both Ulster and Connacht.

O'Neill had formed a confederacy to oppose attempts by Lord Edward, Henry III of England's son, to extract forced rents from Ulster chiefs. Early this month the chiefs marched on Downpatrick, the earldom's capital. They were met at Drumderg by an English force led by the justiciar, William of Dene. A fierce battle ensued in which the English were victorious. Aed Buide ["the Yellow-haired"] has become chief of the O'Neills following Brian's death (→ 18/6/64).

Rebel peer blocks king's links to France

Romney, Kent, 9 July 1263
Simon de Montfort, the earl of Leicester and brother-in-law of the king, has acted to force Henry III to uphold the "Provisions of Oxford". Simon backed the rebels in April, having failed to make the king reverse his annulment of the provisions, under which the monarchy ruled through parliament. Now he has cut Henry's links with France, and the kingdom is sliding towards all-out civil war.

Marching swiftly with a small force, Earl Simon avoided the royal army and today reached Romney, where he was welcomed by the knights of Kent and the seamen of the Cinque Ports [the chief ports of Kent and Sussex which traditionally perform ship service for the king]. The king's men still hold Dover Castle, but reinforcements can no longer reach Henry from France. He relies so heavily on his French relatives for support – much to the anger of the English barons – that this is a grievous blow. Much now depends on what happens in London where the king, not a martial man, is living in the Tower. Many leading citizens, fearing an outbreak of mob rule, have already made it clear to Henry that he ought to abide by the provisions and so bring peace (→25/1/64).

The seal of Henry III, 1259-72.

The countess who held the purse strings

Independence – for some women.

Wiltshire, 1261
The death this year of Ela, the countess of Salisbury, has highlighted the rise of a new kind of woman: the wealthy, independent widow. Ela was the sole heiress to the earldom of Salisbury, but she decided not to remarry after the death of her husband, William Longsword, King John's half-brother. Instead she took on the hereditary office of sheriff of Wiltshire, becoming one of the few women ever to have held high government office. She also hired a large staff of knights and professionals, and in 1238 she founded the abbey at Lacock, in Wiltshire, where she was abbess until 1257.

Only a few decades ago Ela could have been married off by the king against her will – as she was to Longsword – or forced to pay substantial fines for the right to remain single. However, since the signing of *Magna Carta* the rights of women to their own land and money have improved greatly. Increased security has allowed some widows to enjoy holding the purse strings. Whether, like Ela, they choose to remain single or, like her contemporary Countess Isabel of Warenne, the heiress to the earldom of Surrey, they pass from husband to husband, they ensure that their rights are respected by men. But for most women life offers little more than toil, child-bearing, arranged marriages or nunneries (→1281).

Norwegian king abandons campaign as Scots counter-attack in battle at Largs

Strathclyde, 2 October 1263
In a long-expected trial of strength between King Hakon IV of Norway, the ruler of the Western Isles, and the mainland Scots, the Norwegians have been soundly defeated at Largs on the west coast. Hakon is retreating northwards, still master of the islands but with his credibility greatly undermined.

The Norwegian empire, which extends from the Orkneys to the Isle of Man, has faced a growing challenge from Scotland in recent years. Tension rose two years ago when a Scottish envoy, sent to ask Hakon to cede the Western Isles, was arrested.

Hakon and the Scots began to launch raids on each other's territories until, in July, Hakon set sail with a large fleet. Islay and Kintyre were plundered; Rothesay Castle on Bute was captured. Negotiations broke down. King Hakon, based on Arran, planned to raid the Ayrshire coast, where King Alexander III hoped to counter-attack.

Hostilities came to a head two nights ago when four Norse ships were stranded at Largs after a storm. Local Scots launched an attack, and Hakon arrived with 1,000 troops to defend and salvage his ships. A Scottish force commanded by Alexander Stewart of Dundonald then intervened, routing the Norsemen and forcing Hakon to withdraw. The defeat has raised serious questions about the Norwegian king's ability to defend his scattered empire (→16/12).

The two sides of the great seal of Alexander III, the triumphant Scots king.

Hakon dies, and with him Norse power

Orkney, 16 December 1263
King Hakon IV of Norway died today at Kirkwall, where he was wintering after his defeat at Largs in October. His death has increased Scottish hopes that four centuries of Norse threats to Scotland may now be over. Hakon's successor, Magnus, is thought likely to favour a peaceful settlement.

Scotland was among the first targets for Norse adventurers. The islands north and west of the Scottish mainland were within easy reach of the Norse longships and proved ideal bases for first raids and then settlements. Although the Scottish kings of the ninth and tenth centuries thwarted a complete Norse or Viking conquest, the islands of the Hebrides, Orkney and Shetland became permanent colonies of the Scandinavians.

In these islands a distinct culture and language have emerged as, in time, the raiders became farmers with land divided into strips under Norse rather than Scottish feudal law. This practice, and the Norse words in everyday use, seem likely to outlast Norwegian rule now that Hakon's ambitions appear to have died with him (→1264).

1264 - 1267

Oxford, 25 January 1264. After his annulment of the "Provisions of Oxford", King Henry III summons all barons believed to be loyal (→ 14/5).

Scotland, January 1264. Queen Margaret, who had a daughter four years ago, gives birth to a son, Alexander, the heir to the throne (→ 9/8/74).

Kildare City, 18 June 1264. The first Irish parliament convenes (→ 6/12).

Western Isles, 1264. King Alexander III of Scots assembles an army and fleet to overawe the island chiefs and weaken their loyalty to Norse rule (→ 2/7/66).

London, 14 January 1265. The new English parliament reconciles the barons to ruling together (→ 28/5).

Connacht, 1265. Aed O'Connor succeeds his late father Felim as king (→ 19/5).

Dublin, 19 May 1265. The Anglo-Irish magnates discuss peace with the justiciar, Maurice fitzGerald (→ 1267).

Pipton, Powys, 19 June 1265. After their joint attack on Montgomery on 13 December, Simon de Montfort recognizes Llywelyn of Gwynedd as prince of Wales (→ 25/9/67).

Welsh Marches, July 1265. Simon de Montfort, cut off from supporters in England, escapes over the Severn (→ 4/8).

Evesham, 31 August 1265. A cult is growing up around the memory of Simon de Montfort, the remains of whose dismembered body were buried at Evesham Abbey by the monks following his death in battle here this month (→ 1290).

Perth, 2 July 1266. Norwegian envoys sell the Western Isles to Scotland, ending 400 years of Norse domination there.

Warwickshire, 31 October 1266. The "Dictum of Kenilworth", passed by the new parliament, forces Henry III to offer good terms to those barons who surrender (→ 14/12).

London, 6 June 1267. Gilbert de Clare and royalist supporters, who seized Westminster Palace in March because the government had failed to keep the "Dictum of Kenilworth", are reconciled with parliament (→ 1269).

Ireland, 1267. Earl Walter de Burgh of Ulster leads Anglo-Norman campaigns against Gaelic lords in Co Sligo and Roscommon (→ 1272).

King captured at Lewes

East Sussex, 14 May 1264

Simon de Montfort, the earl of Leicester, and his barons have won a stunning victory over King Henry III at Lewes, destroying his army and capturing both the king and his warrior son, Edward.

Earl Simon, the king's brother-in-law, is now the most powerful man in England. He seized the advantage with one of his surprise marches, occupying high ground outside the town of Lewes early this morning. Still unable to ride because of a leg broken in a fall from his horse, he was carried into battle in a brightly decorated litter. This litter became the target for the dashing 24-year-old prince, Lord Edward, but Simon, wisely, had abandoned it. Edward's impetuosity may well have cost the king the battle, for when the untrained Londoners on Simon's left flank broke before his charge he chased them so far that by the time he returned to the battlefield the fight was over.

Simon had laid a trap, allowing the royal forces to advance in the centre and then crushing them with attacks from both flanks by armoured cavalry. The victory was total. Few knights, encased in their armour, were killed, but all the important royalists were taken prisoner apart from a handful who escaped to France. Tonight details of a peace settlement are being worked out to ensure the safety of the prisoners taken by Simon and those taken earlier by the king. The release of the "Marcher lords", in order to protect England's western counties from the Welsh, is especially important (→ 23/6).

Seizing power: Simon de Montfort.

Simon de Montfort summons barons to radical parliament

London, 23 June 1264

Simon de Montfort, with both King Henry III and his heir, Edward, in his power, has called the barons and four knights elected from each shire court to a parliament to deal with the affairs of the land. It is hoped that a provisional government will be approved by this more representative parliament, under which the king will govern through a council of nine which would, in effect, be the ultimate authority.

Earl Simon is anxious to restore order and unity to the kingdom. He has already taken other radical steps, handing over royal castles to baronial keepers and banning armed travel without special permission. He has also sought to restore the confidence of the business community by encouraging foreign trade. The parliament will not be an easy affair, however. Some barons are upset by Simon's commitment to the peace treaty agreed after the battle at Lewes to arrange for the exchange of all prisoners without ransom. There is also the threat of Louis IX of France invading to rescue the royal hostages (→ 14/1/65).

Irish justiciar seized and taken prisoner

Ireland, 6 December 1264

The widespread disturbances which have been taking place in Ireland over the past months have culminated in an infamous incident during which the justiciar, Richard de la Rochelle, has been seized at Castledermot by the FitzGerald family and held prisoner in a castle.

The outrage took place while the justiciar [king's chief deputy] and other noblemen were attending a council meeting. The explanation is thought to lie in the rivalry between two powerful families – the de Burghs and the FitzGeralds – and the seizure by Walter de Burgh of Geraldine castles and manors in Connacht.

The situation is seen as so serious that as soldiers seek to maintain order preparations are being made at Dublin Castle, the headquarters of English rule in Ireland, to withstand a siege (→ 1265).

Arms at the ready: an Irish soldier.

Welsh prince wins English recognition

Montgomery, 25 September 1267

King Henry III of England today acknowledged the authority of Llywelyn, the prince of Wales, by an agreement here conferring greater power on the Welsh prince than has been enjoyed by any of his predecessors since the Normans invaded England two centuries ago.

In return for homage and money, Llywelyn has won English backing for his claims to large swathes of Welsh territory extending far beyond his Gwynedd power base in Snowdonia. Llywelyn initially exploited divisions among the English lords in the Marches along the Welsh border. However, his victories eventually forced most of the Marcher lords into the royal camp during the baronial wars, so they now pose a more formidable barrier to Welsh ambitions (→ 11/4/68).

Henry fights back against the English barons

Edward escapes as barons' split grows

Hereford, 28 May 1265
Lord Edward, Henry III's son and heir, escaped from Simon de Montfort's clutches today while riding outside Hereford with the men charged with his care – Thomas de Clare, the brother of the earl of Gloucester, and Simon's son, Henry. De Clare now appears to have been involved in the plot. Edward had edged away from Henry when, at a signal from a horseman in the distance, he spurred his horse off, followed by de Clare. The guards gave chase but could not catch him.

The escape was carefully planned, and it was clearly a mistake for Edward to have been put in the charge of de Clare, whose brother has quarrelled with de Montfort. The quarrel, arising from squabbles over the ransoming of barons and knights captured at the Battle of Lewes, reflects the growing disenchantment of the barons with de Montfort's control of the kingdom and the outbreak of jealousies between the powerful rival families.

The escape heightens the danger for de Montfort, as Edward could join forces with the barons of the Marches who, led by Roger Mortimer, are defying orders to hand over their castles (→7/1265).

A bloody end: Simon de Montfort is struck down in battle at Evesham.

De Montfort slain in battle at Evesham

Evesham, Worcs, 4 August 1265
Simon de Montfort, who has ruled England in the name of King Henry since the Battle of Lewes, was killed here today when his army was overwhelmed by the forces of Lord Edward, the earl of Gloucester and the Marcher barons. Henry, held by de Montfort, was wounded in the fray and escaped death only by crying: "Slay me not. I am Henry of Winchester, your king." But there was no way out for de Montfort. His Welsh soldiers ran away, and in the murk of a sudden storm he formed a ring of his knights and fought to the end. His body was dismembered and his head sent to the wife of Roger Mortimer, the Marcher lord who had helped to thwart de Montfort's plans for a new way of governing (→14/9).

Lands seized as the king takes revenge

Windsor, 30 September 1265
Henry III, meeting his closest counsellors here, has moved quickly to consolidate his victory in the battle at Evesham over the forces of Simon de Montfort. All lands held by supporters of de Montfort are to be taken over by the king, according to an ordinance issued on 17 September. Some of these lands and other holdings have already been distributed to the king's supporters.

The tough line has quashed talk of an amnesty for the supporters of de Montfort, who professed to the end that they were supporters of the king. Forty Londoners who sought a peaceful settlement have been arrested, and the city has been threatened with attack if it resists the king's authority. Harsh revenge is stiffening resistance, whereas some generosity might have brought compliance.

Simon de Montfort, the son of the late earl, has released the king's brother Richard but refuses to surrender Kenilworth Castle. And while the victorious royalists are quarrelling over their booty, the bitter men whom they have dispossessed are turning outlaw, roaming the forests and making the land unsafe for travellers (→31/10/66).

Henry calls parliament to annul the acts of de Montfort's rule

Winchester, 14 September 1265
King Henry III, barely recovered from the wounds he received at Evesham [*see report above*], has gathered his councillors and loyal barons around him in a parliament to undo many of the laws enacted in his name while he was in the power of Simon de Montfort.

He has revoked all letters, charters and writings, and all grants of land made during the period of his captivity from the Battle of Lewes in May last year. He also intends to exact his revenge on the supporters of de Montfort, although it is typical of this unmartial king that he is treating with great chivalry the womenfolk of the "outlaws" who died at Evesham (→9/1265).

King Henry III and his barons.

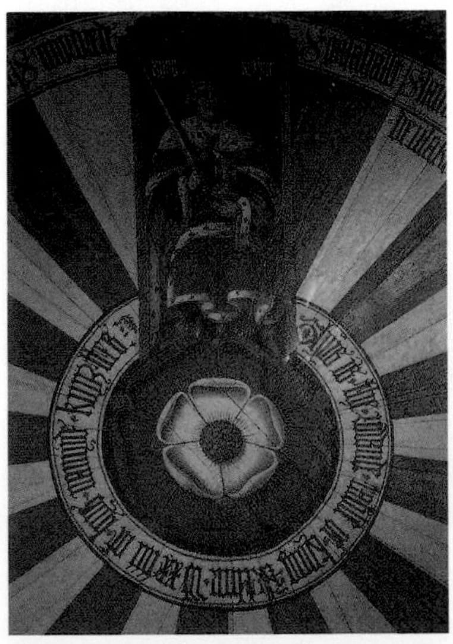

The round table at Winchester.

Castle siege brings the final surrender

Warwickshire, 14 December 1266
Simon de Montfort, the son of the earl killed at Evesham in August last year, has surrendered Kenilworth Castle, besieged by Lord Edward, Henry III's son. Simon is to be given a pension in return for an oath of loyalty. The success of the siege shows the importance of this form of warfare. Castles are the source of the barons' strength, and this can only be removed by besieging them. If time is not critical, the besieger will simply starve the garrison out, however long this might take. Otherwise, giant catapults will be used to hurl rocks at the walls to weaken them (→6/6/67).

1268 - 1273

Mid Glamorgan, April 1268. Gilbert de Clare, the earl of Gloucester, begins building a castle at Caerphilly (→ 1269).

England, August 1269. Owing to the ill health of Henry III, his brother Richard, the king of the Romans, returns to assist as regent (→ 13/3/71).

Gwynedd, 1269. Llywelyn, the prince of Wales, restores to his brother, Dafydd, his share of Gwynedd according to the terms of the 1267 Treaty of Montgomery (→ 12/1270).

Derby, 1269. Robert de Ferrers, the earl, is tricked out of his lands by Henry III; they are combined with land belonging to the late Simon de Montfort to create a new earldom, of Lancaster, which is given to Edmund, Henry's second son (→ 3/2/94).

Dover, 19 August 1270. Edward, the eldest son of Henry III, leaves on the first stage of a crusade; he is going to Tunis to join his uncle, Louis IX of France (→ 6/1271).

Gwent, October 1270. Gilbert de Clare, the earl of Gloucester, deposes Maredudd ap Gruffydd, the last remaining member of the Caerleon dynasty, in revenge for attacks made by Llywelyn, the prince of Wales, on Glamorgan (→ 6/1273).

Holy Land, June 1271. Lord Edward of England launches his first raid, on a small enemy fortress 15 miles (24 km) east of Acre (→ 9/1271).

Westminster, 1 August 1271. John, the eldest son of Lord Edward and Eleanor of Castile, dies aged five (→ 19/8/74).

Holy Land, September 1271. Edmund, the second son of Henry III of England, joins his brother, Edward, with reinforcements (→ 24/9/72).

Norwich, 1271. The cathedral and monastery are destroyed by rioting monks (→ 1280).

Athlone City, 1272. Aed O'Connor, the king of Connacht, destroys the bridge and castle (→ 3/5/74).

Holy Land, 24 September 1272. Following an attempt on his life three months ago, Lord Edward of England sails for Europe (→ 11/1272).

Dolforwyn, Powys, June 1273. Llywelyn, the prince of Wales, who has ignored a summons by England's rulers to do homage to the absent King Edward, is ordered to stop building a castle (→ 11/1274).

Outspoken scientist seeks pope's backing

Paris, 1268

Roger Bacon, the exiled scientist who is regarded as one of the leading English intellectuals of the present day, has appealed to the pope for backing in his often controversial research. Bacon, now based in Paris, left Oxford eight years ago after criticism that his study of nature owed too much to non-Christian thinking such as that of Arab and ancient Greek culture.

He has now sent Pope Clement IV the results of his work, his *Opus Maius*, which sets out in great detail his theories of mathematics, optics and physiology. With it goes an impassioned plea to reform the study of nature throughout Christendom and develop a science which is a match for that of the Arab cultures of the East. His letter begins: "For 20 years I have laboured specifically in the pursuit of wisdom, abandoning the opinions of the vulgar." He also complains of the high cost of research, saying that he has spent £2,000 on books and instruments.

Pope Clement: judging the dispute.

His challenge to conventional thinking is not some dry-as-dust dispute between academics but has far-reaching practical implications. Building on the work of the great Moslem philosopher and scientist Alhazen, he asks for mathematics to be applied to a full-scale reform of the "manifest and palpable errors" of the Christian calendar, now so badly out of kilter with such self-evident facts of nature as the moon's phases (→ 18/3/77).

King's nephew dies in revenge attack

Viterbo, Italy, 13 March 1271

Henry of Almain, the son of Earl Richard of Cornwall and nephew of Henry III of England, was murdered by his cousins Guy and Simon de Montfort here today while at Mass in the parish church of St Silvestro. After striking Henry with his sword, Guy dragged his body out of the church and mutilated it.

It appears that the murder was not premeditated but was a hot-headed act of revenge for the death and mutilation of their father at Evesham in 1265. The brothers had never forgiven Henry for deserting their father's cause and going over to Lord Edward, the king's heir.

Ironically Edward, on his way south to fulfil his great ambition of going on crusade, had sent Henry (also *his* cousin), to Viterbo on a mission of reconciliation. He had learnt that two of the de Montfort brothers were nearby, serving in the army of Charles of Anjou, the king of Sicily. Now they have fled to Tuscany to find refuge (→ 2/4/72).

Marriage celebrations degenerate into boisterous brawls

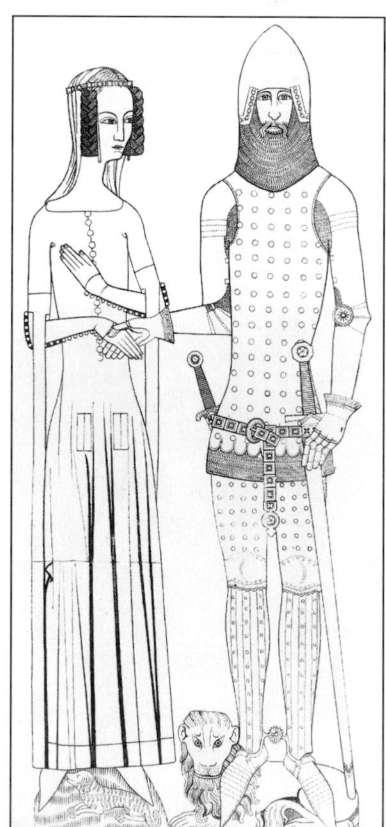

Courtly union: a knight and bride.

North Yorkshire, 1268

Marriages may begin in church, but the celebrations are increasingly ending in violence. The trend towards over-boisterous festivities has been more evident recently, and this year reached a new low with a death reported after fighting broke out at a wedding in Byram.

One man was killed and many others were injured in clashes between a wedding party and local villagers. Eaxctly what caused the violence is unclear, although the fighting appears to have involved two groups of villagers as well as the wedding guests themselves. The confrontation was certainly bloody – bows and arrows were even used.

Such incidents are unfortunately not uncommon, however, with festivities often turning into drunken brawls. The fact that weddings become so boisterous could be due to the timing of the celebrations. It is usual to get married during the seasons of revelry, such as January (the month of fertility rites) or October and November (the time for the harvest and butchering feasts).

A violent wife, from a later psalter.

England sends army against Welsh prince

Chester, 29 August 1277
After a short and carefully planned campaign, England's King Edward is confident that he will bring the Welsh prince Llywelyn to heel. Llywelyn is expected to sue for peace as a huge English army with more than 15,000 foot-soldiers, many of them recruited in Wales, advances north of Snowdonia towards Caernarfon and Anglesey.

Even before the whole weight and panoply of the English army was displayed as it began to muster at Worcester on July, Llywelyn must have considered negotiation. Five important Welsh leaders all did homage to Edward in that month, and the English king, eager to exploit what was clearly a near-civil war in Wales, gave his support to Dafydd, Llywelyn's brother, and Gruffud ap Gwenwynwyn, who had both plotted to kill Llywelyn.

The invasion of Wales became inevitable after Llywelyn's steadfast refusal to attend Edward at Westminster, despite frequent invitations since the coronation. Even the imprisonment by Edward of Llywelyn's intended bride failed to persuade the Welsh prince to pay homage. Llywelyn feared that his life would be endangered if he attended the English court, but Edward took his absence as a challenge to his authority (→3/9).

King Edward and his loyal knights.

Welsh prince yields to English fire-power

Fierce resistance: a Welsh archer.

Gwynedd, 9 November 1277
A humiliated prince of Wales has agreed at Aberconwy today to pay a "fine" of £50,000 for his "disobedience" and to swear allegiance to the king of England. Few doubted that Llywelyn would yield when King Edward attacked this year, and peace terms were agreed almost a year to the day after he had been branded a rebel. The Welsh prince has been forced to abandon claims to all lands seized by Edward – except Anglesey, for which he will be obliged to pay rent. Hostages will now be returned, including Eleanor de Montfort, whom he proposes to marry (→13/10/78).

English church curbs scientific theory

Oxford, 18 March 1277
Robert Kilwardby, the archbishop of Canterbury, has brought Oxford university into line with current developments in France by issuing his own restrictions on the speculations of philosophers. Earlier this month church leaders meeting in Paris effectively threw a boundary round Aristotelian thought, by insisting that further than this no one might go, on pain of excommunication.

For instance, it is now heretical to state that a vacuum is impossible – since nothing is impossible for God. Conservatives are afraid that science will undermine Christian doctrine (→1292).

The reeve, ploughman and dairymaid: divisions of labour in an English manor

England, c.1275
Decisions by manorial courts around the country show how rural communities in 13th-century England are organized. The courts are involved when disputes arise: peasants charged with bad ploughing, perhaps, or the parson who lets his cow stray into the lord of the manor's meadow. In one case, the whole village of Little Ogbourne was fined 6s 8d [33p] for failing to help to wash the lord's sheep.

For the lord, the key decision in a successful manor is selecting the right overseers, the most important of which is the "seneschal", or steward. As holder of the purse-strings, a good seneschal will keep a daily tally on both household expenses and farm income. He is also responsible for keeping everyone else in order, from the under-bailiffs to the cook. A high level of loyalty is also demanded of the "bailiff", the head man on the estate. Getting up before dawn, he must do a daily round of the fields, woods, orchards and pastures. His assistant, the "hayward", keeps him informed of the whereabouts of all the lord's animals.

The "reeve", elected by the villagers, is often the star tiller in the village. It is a sought-after job; the holder must "strive unceasingly for his lord's profit" and check that threshers and winnowers do not steal corn.

Ploughmen are expected to treat the oxen well, stay with them at night and give them encouragement during ploughing by singing plenty of jolly songs. Carters should do the same with the horses. Other specialist occupations are those of shepherd, baker and dairymaid. The latter is the best job for women on the farm. To qualify, they need to be not only honest and thrifty but also chaste (→1285).

Striving for profit: the reeve rides out to spy on his fellow-workers.

Watching the bread rise: a baker on duty at the oven door.

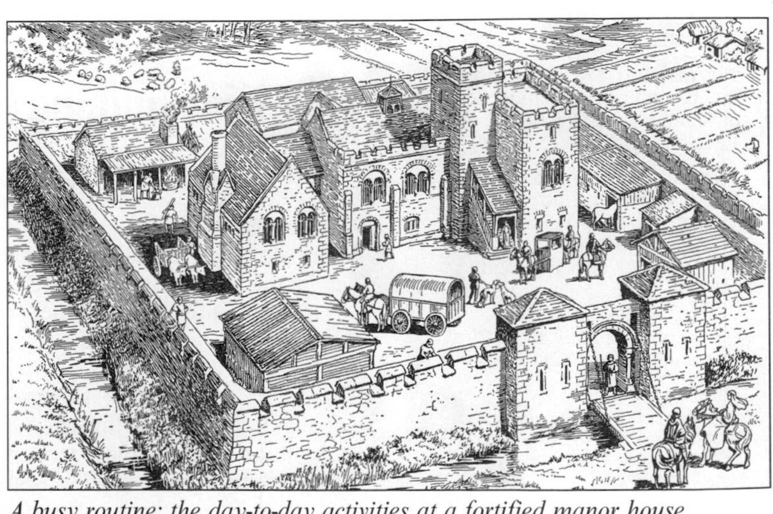
A busy routine: the day-to-day activities at a fortified manor house.

1278 - 1281

England, 4 October 1278. Parliament enacts the Statute of Gloucester for King Edward, providing a variety of measures and challenging the exercise of judicial rights by nobles (→ 12/10/83).

Worcester, 13 October 1278. Llywelyn ap Gruffudd, the prince of Wales, marries Eleanor de Montfort, the daughter of the late Simon de Montfort and a cousin of King Edward of England (→ 10/1281).

England, October 1278. King Edward has many Jews and goldsmiths arrested for coin-clipping (→ 4/8/79).

Dingle, Co Kerry, 1278. A tax is raised on wine (→ c.1330).

Rome, 12 March 1279. John Pecham, a Franciscan friar, is consecrated as archbishop of Canterbury (→ 11/1279).

Gascony, April 1279. King Edward of England reaches an agreement with the rebel Gaston de Béarn, whose lands are restored to him (→ 24/6).

England, 24 June 1279. King Edward returns from a successful trip to Ponthieu, in France, to claim the hereditary rights of his wife, Eleanor of Castile (→ 13/5/86).

East Anglia, 2 August 1279. A terrible storm, lasting a day and a night, causes extensive damage and widespread flooding (→ autumn 1316).

England, 4 August 1279. The first new coins of Edward's reign are issued (→ 10/1294).

Exeter, 1280. Work begins on a new nave for the cathedral.

Ireland, 1281. The kingdom of Thomond is divided among the O'Briens under the overlordship of Thomas de Clare (→ 1/10).

Stirling, June 1281. David, the younger son of King Alexander III, dies (→ 7/1281).

Norway, July 1281. Margaret, the daughter of Alexander III of Scotland, marries King Eirik II (→ 15/11/82).

Powys, 9 October 1281. Llywelyn ap Gruffudd, the prince of Wales, makes a pact with Roger Mortimer, a powerful Marcher lord and former enemy, for mutual support in war and peace against all but King Edward of England (→ 31/3/82).

London, 1281. The river Thames freezes over, and five piers of London Bridge collapse under pressure from ice (→ 30/6/85).

New 'mappa mundi' drawn for cathedral

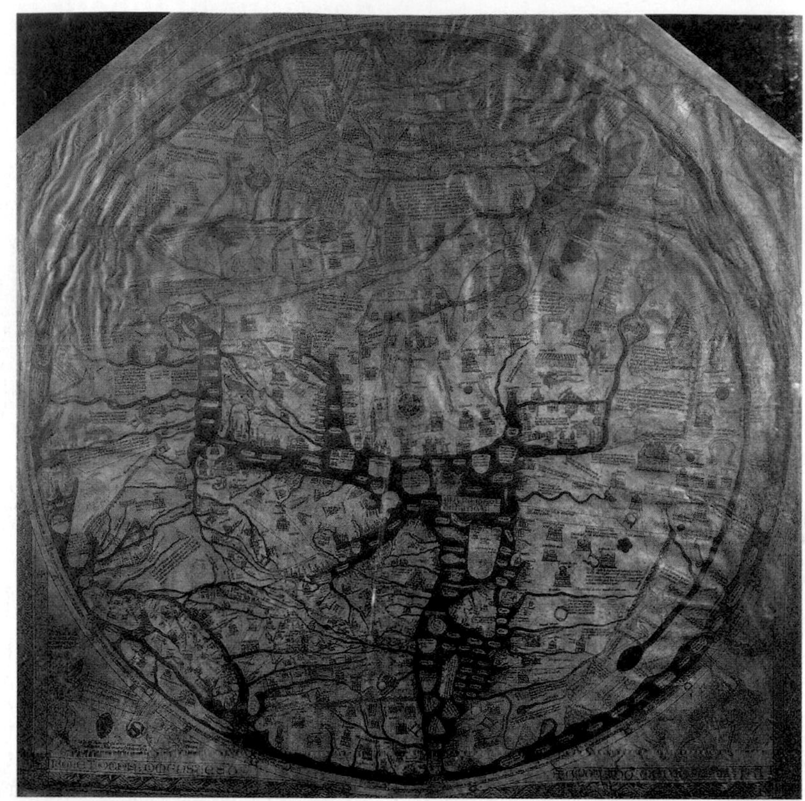

The "mappa mundi", or map of the world, drawn for Hereford Cathedral.

Hereford, 1280
The world is round and flat, with Jerusalem at its centre, according to the new *mappa mundi* [map of the world] recently drawn for Hereford Cathedral. Colourfully illustrated, the map has east at the top.

Hereford's *mappa mundi*, like the similar one at Westminster made for the king, has been admired for not only its geographical precision but also its spiritual and artistic qualities. Jerusalem, where Christ died, is the heart of the Holy Land fought over by the crusaders, so its central position on a Christian map is not really surprising. Maps are good opportunities for artists to show off their talents by illustrating the various wonders of strange and distant lands.

The artist Matthew Paris, who died about 20 years ago, included several maps in his varied output (the Westminster *mappa mundi* is "in the manner of Matthew Paris"). He used different colours for mountains, rivers and seas; to indicate towns he drew special symbols with towers and walls, and he included such exotic things as a camel, a turtle and other beasts.

Scottish king snubs 'homage' proposal

Westminster, 28 October 1278
A serious breach between Scotland and England was narrowly averted today when Alexander III of Scots met Edward, his English counterpart. The Scottish king had paid homage to Edward, his brother-in-law, for his lands in England when the bishop of Norwich suggested that Alexander should also acknowledge that he held Scotland, too, only with the English king's consent. Brusquely Alexander replied: "To homage for my kingdom of Scotland, no one has right except God alone, nor do I hold it except of God alone." Edward did not press the matter, but it has chilled relations between them (→ 6/1281).

Land row puts laws of Wales in doubt

Powys, October 1281
A dispute between Llywelyn, the prince of Wales, and Gruffudd ap Gwenwynwyn over the ownership of the district of Arwystli in mid-Powys has brought into question the validity of Welsh law. It is three years since the prince laid claim to the land, which he sees as a strategically important border territory.

The dispute centres on the legal status of Gruffudd. As a baron of the Marches, he claims not to be subject to Welsh law. King Edward of England has angered Llywelyn by ordering an inquiry into the justness of these laws. Other Welsh barons see the issue as one which could threaten their way of life (→ 9).

King wins backing to impose controls on land grants to church

Westminster, November 1279
King Edward has won another round in his battle to limit the rise in the church's wealth and power. The Statute of Mortmain approved this month brings the endowment of church lands under royal supervision. The citizen's right to make donations is preserved, but he must win royal consent for the size and terms of the gifts. These reforms are further evidence of Edward's desire to oversee far-reaching reforms in conjunction with his councils and parliaments. The 1275 Statute of Westminster [*see page 286*] was followed by one at Gloucester last year which sought to define the power of the barons. Now it is the church which faces new legal curbs. Edward realized that if no action was taken the church would continue to amass ever greater wealth. The Statute of Mortmain is a blow for Archbishop Pecham, who made clear at a church council at Reading in July his desire to limit royal power over the church (→ 11/1296).

King Edward's great seal (1276).

Irish justiciar quits on health grounds

Ireland, 1 October 1281
Robert d'Ufford, who as King Edward of England's justiciar [chief deputy] was the top administrative officer in Ireland, has been forced by ill health to retire. However, he hopes to continue working on his commentary on Irish society, seen from the perspective of an English gentleman. D'Ufford had worked hard to promote the king's economic interests in Ireland since the mandate allowing foreign merchants to come here and trade freely was issued. This has resulted in a greatly increased revenue for Edward and has shifted the burden of taxes, which before this came almost exclusively from the land, to the merchants.

Stephen de Fulbourn, the bishop of Waterford, must take some of the credit for the improved receipts at the exchequer. De Fulbourn acted as treasurer during d'Ufford's period as justiciar and succeeds him in that office. However, doubts have been raised about de Fulbourn's financial integrity. Despite his being a highly trusted servant of the crown, many complaints have been made against him, and irregularities and omissions are suspected in his accounts. It is thought that he may owe King Edward a great deal of money (→ 1285).

Lincoln Cathedral renovations completed

The fabulous, five-bay Angel Choir at Lincoln Cathedral, finished c.1280.

Lincoln, 1280
It has taken almost 90 years to complete, but now the renovation of the cathedral here has been brought to a splendid conclusion. Work was commissioned in 1192, after the earthquake of 15 April 1185 had almost destroyed the old cathedral. Perched on a ridge, dominating the town and surrounding country, the new building is a stupendous sight. From a distance it appears to be perfectly balanced on each side of the central tower, and closer up a dazzling display of decorative carving becomes apparent (→ 1287).

How widows lose their inheritances

Hereford and Worcester, 1281
A decision of the manor court at Hales this year exemplifies how the laws of inheritance are implemented when a wife outlives her husband. The lord of the manor has approved a court decision that the recently widowed Agnes Bird must hand over the land left to her on her husband's death to her eldest son, Thomas. According to the agreement certain conditions will have to be met by Agnes's son. He has to provide her with a house plus money and food at various intervals throughout the year. She will, of course, be able to reclaim the land should Thomas fail to keep up with these terms.

A widow with land is often obliged to surrender it in this way; it is unlikely that any lord will allow land to deteriorate if she cannot maintain it herself. However, if a widow decides to remarry this will not necessarily mean that she can hold on to her land. Earlier this year at Mapledurham, Hampshire, an inquest decided that Richard, the brother of Walter le Hurt, had more right to the dead man's land than his widow, Lucy, who had recently remarried. So even if it is a husband's intention to provide for his wife after he dies, it does not always work out (→ 1345).

Cleanliness is new fashion among rich

England, c.1280
The art of cleanliness is becoming increasingly prized among the more prosperous people in England. Soap is manufactured from goats' tallow and beech ash (although olive oil is also popular as an ingredient), with sponges and perfumes imported from the Mediterranean. Public bath-houses provide a focus for this new fashion. Such establishments are sometimes visited for medicinal purposes, but for many people they also serve as places to meet friends and perhaps to enjoy a drink or some food. Most bathers use individual wooden tubs, although grander bath-houses boast larger marble versions, with water heated in cauldrons over log fires.

Edward devotes thousands to strengthening Tower of London

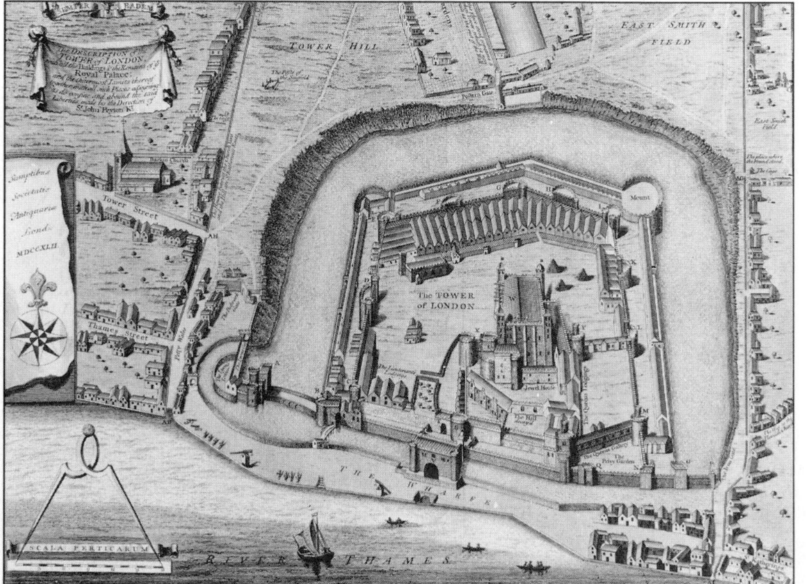

A later view of the Tower of London showing Edward's improvements.

London, c.1280
Thousands of royal pounds are being spent to improve and enlarge the Tower of London, already one of the strongest castles in the kingdom. The 28-metre (90-foot)-high White Tower was built by William the Conqueror. Successive kings added extra features, but under Henry III the Tower was transformed into a fortress by the addition of a dozen small towers and a surrounding curtain wall. Now King Edward is constructing a wide moat and outer wall and rebuilding the western defences. The improved western entrance will comprise inner and outer gatehouses, with a huge barbican beyond. St Thomas's Tower, a new watergate, will replace an earlier one now left high and dry (→ 1281).

1282 - 1285

Wales, 20 May 1282. Eleanor, the wife of Prince Llywelyn, dies in childbirth (→ 6/11).

Gwynedd, 6 November 1282. Many English troops, trying to invade the Welsh mainland from Anglesey, die crossing the Menai Strait (→ 11/12).

Borders, 15 November 1282. Alexander, the heir of King Alexander III, weds Margaret, the daughter of Count Guy de Dampierre of Flanders, at Roxburgh (→ 9/4/83).

Gwynedd, 18 January 1283. Edward of England's seizure of Dolwyddelan Castle, the centre of Welsh power, allows him to consolidate his rule (→ 6/1283).

Norway, 9 April 1283. Queen Margaret, the daughter of Alexander III of Scotland, dies in childbirth, leaving a daughter, Margaret (→ 25/2/84).

Wales, June 1283. After the surrender in April of the last Welsh-held castle, Castell-y-Bere, Edward begins building new castles (→ 27/8/83).

Clwyd, 27 August 1283. King Edward and Queen Eleanor of England escape as Caergwrle Castle catches fire (→ 3/10).

Shropshire, 3 October 1283. Prince Dafydd of Gwynedd, who was captured in June, is hanged and quartered at Shrewsbury (→ 5/1285).

England, 12 October 1283. The Statute of Acton Burnell [in Shropshire] is enacted, making it easier to recover debts (→ 4/1284).

Tayside, 25 February 1284. After the death in January of Alexander, the only son and heir of Alexander III, parliament swears at Scone to accept the ten-month-old Margaret of Norway as heir presumptive (→ 14/10/85).

Gwynedd, 25 April 1284. Edward, the heir to the English throne, is born at Caernarfon (→ 17/2/90).

Cambridge, 1284. Hugh de Balsham founds Peterhouse college (→ 1312).

Wales, May 1285. Edward of England sets about anglicizing his new territories (→ 5/9/87).

Borders, 14 October 1285. Alexander III marries Yolande, the daughter of Count Robert of Dreux, at Roxburgh (→ 20/3/86).

Ireland, 1285. Stephen de Fulbourn, the justiciar, denounces the Dominicans and Franciscans for their use of the Irish language (→ Easter 1297).

Welsh princes raise flag of rebellion

Edward determined to crush the revolt

Denbigh, Clwyd, 31 March 1282

A new uprising is sweeping northern Wales following an attack by Prince Dafydd on the castle at Hawarden, near Chester. Dafydd had been invited to an Easter banquet at the castle in Clwyd, but he arrived in the company of an armed band which set about killing and looting. It was the signal for another Welsh uprising against the English. Within days castles at Ruthin, Hope and Dinas Bran were taken, and a "parliament" at Denbigh committed the Welsh to war.

Dafydd has travelled south to raise the banner of a revolt which has taken King Edward of England by surprise. Only four years ago Dafydd defected from the Welsh cause to join Edward and bring about the defeat of his brother, Prince Llywelyn, in a war that left Llywelyn confined to Snowdonia and subordinate to English rule.

Dafydd, feeling that Edward had shown insufficient gratitude for his support, has now initiated a rebellion that leaves Llywelyn little alternative but to join the anti-English forces. Disputes over English laws and taxes have menwhile created a groundswell of support for the rebellion.

Edward's father, Henry III, had recognized Llywelyn as prince of Wales, and Edward had hoped to establish smooth working relations with the two Welsh brothers while reserving the right to assert his overall responsibility. The English king is particularly angered by what he sees as Dafydd's betrayal and is already laying plans for an army of paid soldiers and a navy to attack the Welsh rebels from both land and sea (→ 20/5).

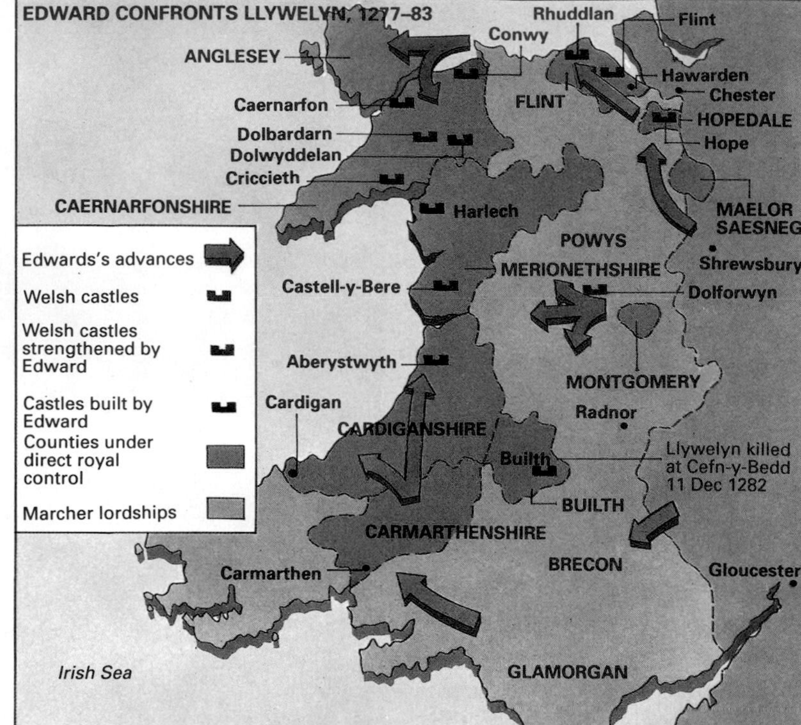

Prince of Wales killed as Edward's forces consolidate victories

Powys, 11 December 1282

Prince Llywelyn was killed today, a month after rejecting surrender terms negotiated by church leaders. His death will be a blow to Welsh rebels already reeling under a land and sea onslaught. King Edward of England had marshalled an army of 10,000 men plus a navy to take Anglesey. Having won control of the south and west of Wales, Edward sent his men north. Llywelyn, encouraged by the death of a key Marcher lord, Roger Mortimer, and the failure of an attempted landing from Anglesey, broke out of his Snowdonia stronghold. He drove towards mid-Wales but was surprised and killed by the English near Builth. His head is to be set on a pike at the Tower of London while his brother, Dafydd, fights on in the mountains (→ 18/1/83).

A later view of Llywelyn's last stand: the Welsh prince was killed by an English squire, Stephen de Frankton, who had failed to recognize him.

Survey launched to boost royal coffers

Rhuddlan, Powys, March 1284
King Edward is set to launch yet another nationwide survey. The first, the "Hundred Rolls" inquiry of 1274-75, led to a tightening of legal administration around England. The new survey will be less ambitious in scope but more narrowly focused on finance.

A statute agreed here appoints commissioners headed by John Kirkby, the royal treasurer, to find out how payment of debts owed to the crown could be enforced. The king is anxious to boost the exchequer after officials reported that crown revenues amounted to no more than £26,828 a year. Earlier enquiries have revealed some corruption in the administration of crown debts, so the commissioners want more detailed information on money owed by knights, sheriffs, bailiffs and other landholders.

The king, who needs money for his army as well as for himself and his family, hopes that his Statute of Rhuddlan will ensure not only that future debts are paid but also that old and until now largely unrecovered debts are reclaimed. Relations between local officials in the shires and the exchequer are also likely to be reformed (→1285).

King moves to curb London prostitutes

London, 1284
King Edward has launched a new drive to clean up what he regards as the shocking state of morals in London. He has issued a decree banning prostitutes from living in the capital on pain of imprisonment. The decree claims that "houses of women of evil life" encourage thieves and murderers. Moves are also planned against crime generally in the royal-backed campaign for law and morality.

New city laws against prostitutes forbid them to live within the city walls, with penalties of 40 days in jail for any "common woman" found in London. The measure follows a similar one in 1272 and subsequent anti-vice orders. They seem to have had little effect in discouraging brothels, which are concentrated around the "Bordhawe" [brothel area], in the heart of the city, on land leased from St Paul's Cathedral.

Prostitutes and clients wishing to avoid the decree can simply cross the Thames to Bankside in Southwark, outside the city's jurisdiction. Here, trade at the licensed brothels and "stews" (which are ostensibly bath-houses) can expect a boost from the king's campaign (→c.1290).

Edward's statute backs hereditary rights

King Edward: the lawmaker.

Westminster, 1285
King Edward has submitted the most intensive body of law reform of his reign to parliament this year. Under the statutes agreed here the law relating to the inheritance of land is established in a way that confirms hereditary family rights. Following closely upon statutes on criminal law agreed earlier this year at the Winchester parliament, this new Statute of Westminster also confirms the English king's reputation as a law reformer.

However, Edward has been motivated by a desire for efficient administration rather than by crusading zeal. The first Statute of Westminster (1275) followed the "Hundred Rolls" inquiry and tried to eliminate inconsistencies unearthed by the inquiry. A statute to define the powers of barons followed in 1278, and one a year later to control gifts of land to the church. This year's Statute of Winchester focused on criminal law, appointing justices of the peace and giving penalties for such crimes as robbery, rape, poaching and murder. The provisions can be quite specific: undergrowth must be cut back 60 metres (200 feet) from roads to deny robbers a hiding place.

Yet the second Statute of Westminster, dealing with ownership of land, could be the most significant reform yet. Previous legislation on gifts of land made it possible for a son or daughter to sell to a third party land which, if certain conditions designed to keep it in the family had not been met, was due to revert to the father's estate. Donors will now have full rights to recover all lands irregularly sold. And a tenant is only a tenant for life, with no rights of ownership (→1288).

Survey reveals contrasting lifestyles of merchants and craftsmen

King's Lynn, Norfolk, 1285
The marked difference in living standards between the aspiring merchant class and the humbler craftsman has been highlighted in inventories of the population's goods and chattels recently compiled here for tax purposes. The listings indicate that a wealthy merchant has household possessions valued at £75 or more. Those of craftsmen such as carpenters and glaziers amount to about £3.

The merchant owns expensive clothing, armour, bedding, period tapestries and other hangings, silver plate and jewels, and a stock of foodstuffs in the larder. He also has merchandise stored in a warehouse or aboard ship. Most of a craftsman's income goes on food, bedding and coarse clothes. Only the most prosperous have some silver plate (→autumn 1316).

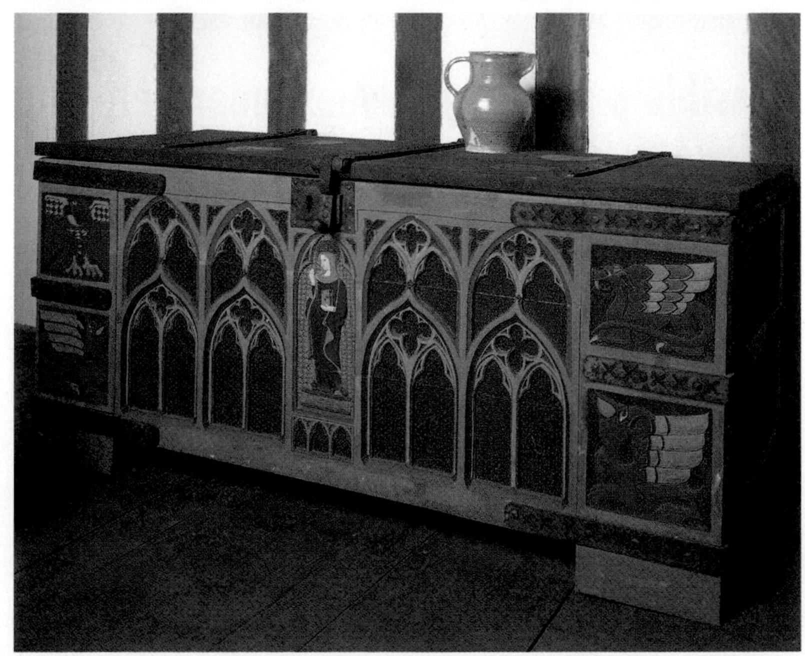

A decorated chest, from the house of a well-off merchant (reconstruction).

Mayor is ousted by Edward in London

London, 30 June 1285
King Edward has taken control of the city of London in swift response to a gesture of revolt by the mayor and his aldermen. After some rioting a few weeks ago the king proclaimed the St Paul's area to be a haunt of thieves and vagabonds and appointed a commission to investigate. This was deemed an insult to the city's autonomy, and Gregory of Rokesley, the mayor, led a protest to one of the commissioners, John Kirkby, the king's treasurer. Gregory appeared without his official seal of office, allowing Kirkby to claim that the city was without a mayor and to take London formally under royal control. The king plans to rule through a warden, with royal ordinances to maintain law and order (→15/10/1326).

1286 - 1290

Scone, Tayside, 2 April 1286. Parliament appoints six guardians to rule the kingdom following the death last month of King Alexander III.→

Dover, 13 May 1286. King Edward and Queen Eleanor leave to pay homage to Philip IV of France for lands in Gascony (→27/10/93).

Strathclyde, 20 September 1286. Robert Bruce, the 75-year-old lord of Annandale, and his supporters draw up a bond in preparation for making a claim to the throne (→1/1287).

England, 2 May 1287. Jews are imprisoned, to be freed only if they pay £12,000 (→18/7/90).

East Sussex, 1287. Following a great storm in which many coastal ports were destroyed, King Edward orders the building of a new town at Winchelsea, to be designed on a grid system.

Hereford, 1287. The brass tomb of St Thomas Cantilupe in the cathedral is finally completed (→1322).

England, 1288. New courts known as "piepowder" courts, with juries which are made up of merchants, are established to try offenders at village fairs (→30/11/89).

Rome, 1 April 1289. The pope, Nicholas IV, denounces the custom whereby only native Scots are permitted to serve in religious foundations in Scotland (→6/1291).

Tayside, August 1289. Duncan, the earl of Fife, one of the six guardians of Scotland, is killed at Brechin (→6/11).

Wiltshire, 6 November 1289. A treaty is sealed at Salisbury between the Norwegians, acting for Margaret "the maid of Norway", King Edward (Margaret's great-uncle) and the Scots (→26/9/90).

Orkney, 26 September 1290. Margaret, the seven-year-old "maid of Norway", the heir to the Scottish throne, dies on her way to Scotland.→

Worcestershire, 1290. Twenty-five years after the death of Simon de Montfort, the earl of Leicester, over 200 miracles have been attributed to him, although devotion to his memory is now waning.

England, 1290. Ecclesiastical law orders any sodomites to be buried alive, although secular authorities appear to be hanging anyone convicted of the crime (→1329).

Scots king dies in riding accident

Kinghorn, Fife, 20 March 1286
Alexander III, the king of Scotland, was killed in a riding accident here last night. The tragedy occurred when the 45-year-old king was returning home from Edinburgh to Queen Yolande in Dunfermline Palace. Alexander had reigned for 36 years, and his death seems certain to cause controversy over the succession to the throne.

The king had attended a meeting of the royal council in Edinburgh before setting out for home. After crossing the Forth at the Queen's Ferry, he was separated from his party in stormy, misty conditions. As he rode alone along a clifftop path, it appears that his horse lost its footing in the dark. This morning courtiers found the king's body at the foot of the cliffs. No foul play is suspected; it seems that the king was thrown by his horse.

Alexander's accident is the latest in a succession of disasters to hit the royal household in recent years. Since the death of the king's first wife, Margaret, in 1275, all three of their children have died. The last remaining member of a dynasty established by Malcolm III in the 11th century is Alexander's two-year-old granddaughter, Margaret, who is currently living with her father, King Eirik II of Norway. Her claim to the throne was recognized by parliament two years ago, but female succession is unpopular and could prove divisive (→2/4).

Alexander III killing a stag, as portrayed by Benjamin West (1738-1820).

Bruce leads revolt in south-west Scotland

Strathclyde, January 1287
A rebellion led by Robert Bruce, the 75-year-old lord of Annandale, has broken out in the south-west of Scotland. Bruce is one of the most powerful Scottish lords, and in the parliament which met last April he contested the right of Margaret of Norway, as a female, to inherit the kingdom of her late grandfather, Alexander III. However, parliament rejected Bruce's claim to the succession – he is descended from King David – and appointed six guardians to rule the kingdom. They were to exercise power until Margaret (or any child of Queen Yolande) came of age. It was the choice of guardians which first angered Bruce, since his traditional enemies, the Comyns, were included at his expense.

Now that it is clear that Yolande is not pregnant, Margaret is again the heir, and Bruce's party has been plotting to seize power. Attacks on royal officials and sporadic fighting have been reported this winter, although it is difficult to see how Bruce can impose his will on the wider community still committed to Margaret (→8/1289).

Possible pregnancy delays succession

Scone, Tayside, 2 April 1286
Six guardians drawn from powerful Scottish families were today appointed to rule the kingdom by a meeting of parliament called to discuss the succession to the throne. Margaret of Norway, the granddaughter of the late King Alexander, who will be three next week, was recognized as heir two years ago, but her succession was not confirmed today because of the possibility that Queen Yolande might be pregnant. She and Alexander were married last October; any child of theirs would take precedence over "the maid of Norway" (→20/9).

Alexander's era of peace and prosperity

Dunfermline, Fife, 20 March 1286
The tragic death last night of King Alexander III has ended a highly successful reign. For his people he brought peace and increasing prosperity. Most Scots still live by farming or fishing, but towns are now richer and better administered. Many were given the status of burghs by the king, with provosts presiding in burgh courts to control business and everyday life. Merchants prospered, whether exporting wool to Flanders and Italy or importing wine and metal craftwork for wealthy consumers. Prosperity reflected 25 years of good government by Alexander after he assumed power in 1261.

His greatest achievement was to consolidate the unity of the Scottish kingdom by ending four centuries of Norse dominance in the Hebrides. A Norwegian military challenge in 1263 was defeated at Largs, leading to the 1266 Treaty of Perth which gave Scotland control over the Western Isles and the Isle of Man. Peaceful relations were also maintained south of the border, although Alexander insisted that he paid homage to King Edward only for his lands in England, not those in Scotland.

Welsh stronghold falls

Siege war: the defenders strike back.

Dyfed, 5 September 1287
Another Welsh revolt effectively ended today when English-led forces recaptured the castle at Dryslwyn, east of Carmarthen. The lord of Dryslwyn, Rhys ap Maredudd, had rebelled in June, seizing several castles and attacking large areas of south Wales. Rhys was loyal to the English in the wars against Prince Llywelyn, but he has become a disappointed and embittered man.

Rhys was publicly humiliated by Edward for taking possession of lands granted to him without waiting for the official investiture. He has been harassed by English officials; judicial immunities granted to him by the king were ignored; he has been the victim of financial extortion and ordered to observe English, not Welsh, laws.

Last June he seized Llandovery Castle and other English strongholds. With Edward in France, his regent, Edmund of Cornwall, mustered an army of 24,000; most were paid, and most were Welsh. They soon forced Rhys to retreat and last month began not only besieging Dryslwyn but also bombarding it with a huge stone-throwing "siege engine". Rhys and his wife and followers have fled to the hills (→ 1292).

Chief justice exiled in corruption probe

England, 30 November 1289
About 1,000 judges and royal officials have been accused of corruption in what is widely seen as a purge instigated by King Edward. The most prominent victim to date is Thomas de Weyland, the chief justice of common pleas, who has been exiled for protecting two of his men from facing a murder charge.

The king, who returned from Gascony three months ago to face financial worries, renewed rebellion in the Welsh Marches and arrears of cases from the *Quo Warranto* campaign [*see report right*], was determined to stamp out abuses in government. In September de Weyland was found guilty of corruption and his estates were confiscated. He was made to choose between exile and life imprisonment.

A commission, consisting of the bishop of Winchester, the earl of Lincoln and three noblemen, was appointed last month to hear complaints against royal officials. To date 1,000 defendants have been named in 670 actions, including some senior judges (→ 6/1290).

New laws approved on feudal holdings

Westminster, June 1290
The campaign by King Edward to simplify the complex landholding arrangements which have grown out of the feudal system has borne fruit this month with the issue of the important new statute *Quia Emptores*. This is intended to stamp out the alienation of feudal rights by subtenants, who have devised clever ways of regranting the land they hold in order to deprive England's main landowners of their feudal rights. In future, says the new law, land may only be granted out providing the new tenant holds it directly from the original lord.

It follows the statute of *Quo Warranto* two months ago, which regulated the king's tenants-in-chief – accused of usurping the king's rights. In 1278 Edward began using the writ of *Quo Warranto* which required feudal magnates to explain by what right they held land. Its heavy-handed application by justices led to howls of protest from the gentry. Now they simply have to show continuous use of a franchise since 1189 (→ 11/1295).

Royal edict expels Jews from England

Crude religious intolerance: Jews are burnt at the stake as heretics.

England, 18 July 1290
The Jews are to leave England. A community that has played a major part in the economy is to be expelled under a new edict ordered by King Edward. It comes as the climax to a century of increasing persecution which has combined pressure on Jewish finances with such anti-Semitism as the massacre of the Jews of York in 1190. All Jewish property will be forfeit. One reason for the new law is that a succession of enforced loans, high taxes and property confiscations have left the 3,000-strong Jewish community with nothing more to give. A second reason is that the Jews failed to comply with a 1275 statute requiring them to abandon their traditional role as money-lenders. The last reason is simply prejudice. Many charges are made about atrocities by Jews; there is no proof that any have occurred, but the stories are widely believed.

Bible's last book inspires art revelations

Rich in detail and colouring: an illustration from the Trinity Apocalypse.

England, c.1290
For as long as half a century the Revelation of St John, the last book of the Bible, has inspired stained-glass windows, wall-paintings and illustrated manuscripts. One of the most notable books, *The Trinity Apocalypse*, seems to have been made at the Westminster court for a wealthy lay client. Its illustrations are very rich in detail and colouring, although its human figures are traditional, with elongated bodies quite often in contorted positions, red cheeks and staring eyes.

Artists are starting to find ways to breathe new life into traditional scenes. A book designed for King Edward and Queen Eleanor in about 1270, *The Douce Apocalypse*, features startling new techniques which create a sense of depth in the pictures and remarkable naturalism in landscapes (→ c.1330).

Impressive new castles are built in Wales

The castle at Conwy, Gwynedd, built by King Edward between 1283-7.

Wales, June 1290
Edward of England's determination to subdue Wales, following his defeat of Prince Llywelyn, has resulted in an impressive collection of castles after a massive building programme.

The first group to be finished – at Flint, Rhuddlan, Aberystwyth and Builth – incorporated fortified towns built onto the castles and protected by them, on the French pattern. After the death of Llywelyn in the second rising of 1282, Edward commissioned four more castles to dominate Llywelyn's territory of Gwynedd at Caernarfon, Conwy, Criccieth and Harlech.

He chose as architect Master James of St George, who had revolutionized castle-building in Savoy. Instead of a central keep James is fond of high enclosure walls, studded with projecting round towers, from which the defenders can command the approaches on all sides. Some castles have two concentric circles of fortifications.

The cost is formidable – not far short of £80,000. The most costly, at £27,000, is Caernarfon, which is to be the seat of government as well as a large fortified town. The labour force of masons, carpenters, diggers, smiths and carters amounts to between 2,500 and 3,500 men from all over England. James directs operations from Harlech Castle, so well sited that it can be defended by a mere 37 men. He has been made its constable.

The last great castle of Edward's 1282-3 campaign: Caernarfon.

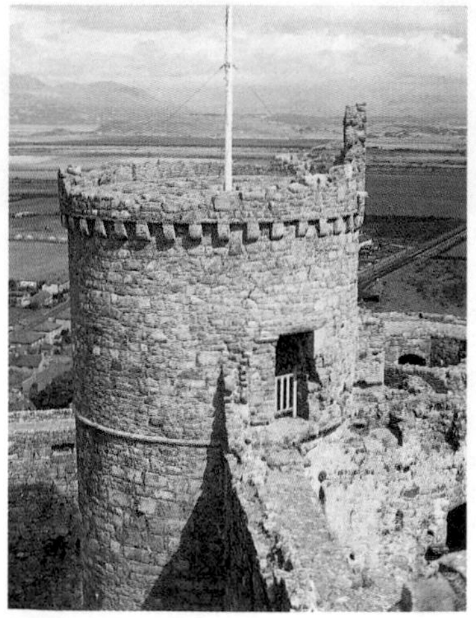
Harlech Castle, in Gwynedd, built by Master James in 1283.

Girl queen dies without seeing Scotland

Orkney, 26 September 1290
Scotland's seven-year-old queen, Margaret, has died as she travelled from her home in Norway to claim the kingdom she never saw. "The maid of Norway", as she was called, became ill during a rough sea crossing and was dead by the time she arrived in Kirkwall. Her body is to be returned to Norway, where her father is king, for burial.

Margaret became queen on the death of her grandfather, Alexander III, in 1286. Fierce rows ensued between rival Scottish families as six guardians took control in her name. Just two months ago a treaty with England's King Edward arranged her eventual marriage to his son, but her death throws the succession to the Scottish throne open again (→ 2/8/91).

The land that Margaret never saw.

Westminster burial for Queen Eleanor

Westminster, 17 December 1290
After a long and emotional journey the body of Queen Eleanor of Castile, the wife of King Edward, has finally come to rest at Westminster, following her death at Harby, in Nottinghamshire, on 28 November. She was 54. Edward was devoted to his wife and is said to be shattered by his loss. The king has ordered a lavish display more monumental than anything built before for a dead king or queen. It is understood that Edward intends to erect elaborate memorial crosses at each of the 12 places where the queen's funeral cortège stopped on its journey to London (→ 17/7/1307).

A cross to honour Queen Eleanor.

1291 - 1294

Cork, June 1291. A dispute between Irish and Anglo-Irish Franciscans leaves 16 dead (→ 9/2/1310).

Northumberland, 2 August 1291. Edward of England, who assumed the role of Scottish overlord on 11 June at Norham, opens a law suit at Berwick-Upon-Tweed to determine the succession dispute (→ 17/11/92).

York, April 1292. The Welsh loyalist Rhys ap Maredudd, who rebelled in 1287, is caught and executed. His death ends the ruling dynasty of Deheubarth (→ 10/9/45).

Oxford, 1292. Roger Bacon, the Franciscan philosopher who suffered from church persecution and lived in exile for a time because of his devotion to science, dies (→ 1335).

England, 1292. King Edward issues a statute to regulate tournaments and the chaos surrounding them.

Scotland, 2 January 1293. John Balliol, the king of Scotland, who paid homage to King Edward of England last December, acknowledges in writing that Edward is released from the Treaty of Birgham which ensured Scottish independence (→ 11/1293).

Paris, 27 October 1293. King Philip IV of France summons King Edward of England to appear before him to account for England's total destruction of the Norman fleet off the coast of Brittany earlier this year (→ 3/2/94).

London, November 1293. King Edward's court finds King John of Scotland in contempt for refusing to answer an appeal in person; he loses three of Scotland's major castles to England (→ 6/1294).

Paris, 3 February 1294. Edmund of Lancaster, the brother of Edward of England, meets Philip IV. He arranges a temporary transfer to the French of Bordeaux and some Gascon fortresses (→ 5/1294).

Portsmouth, 14 June 1294. Edward orders feudal tenants to prepare for war with France on 1 September (→ 8/1294).

England, June 1294. King John of Scotland agrees to do military service for England against France (→ 1295).

England, August 1294. Edward makes a alliance treaty with Adolf de Nassau, the king of Germany (→ 9/10/95).

John Balliol named as Scottish king

King John with Queen Isabella.

Northumberland, 17 Nov 1292

After two years of legal wrangling over the succession, King Edward of England has finally arbitrated in favour of John Balliol as Scotland's new king. This was announced at Berwick-Upon-Tweed today after Edward had swung the balance of power in a court of 104 auditors which had been set up to adjudicate between the hereditary claims of the two main contenders, John Balliol and Robert Bruce [*see family tree on page 294*].

King John is 42, the son of an English baron, John de Balliol, and Devorguilla, a daughter of Alan, the lord of Galloway. He, like his rival Robert Bruce, is descended from daughters of Earl David of Huntingdon, a grandson of King David (1124-53). Balliol won on the grounds that he is descended from the earl's eldest daughter whereas Bruce traces his lineage to the second daughter. The English king has skilfully exploited the rivalry to enhance his own position, persuading both claimants to recognize him as their lord.

King John has large estates in England and is little known in his new kingdom, although his sister is married to one of the Comyns, the most powerful family in Scotland. His success as king depends on how skilfully he can play off Edward's demands against patriotic sensibilities in Scotland. He will be crowned at Scone next month (→ 2/11/93).

England imposes power on Marches

Welsh Marches, 1292

King Edward of England is asserting his authority over the Welsh Marches – traditionally ruled by their own lords independently of the English crown. He has imposed a royal tax of one-fifteenth and created a precedent for further taxation. In a separate move he summoned the earls of Hereford and Gloucester, the lords of the Brecon and Glamorgan Marches, to Westminster to be charged with flouting his authority by making war on each other. They were sentenced to imprisonment and had their estates confiscated, but were later freed after paying fines (→ 4/1292).

London bank crisis

London, October 1294

Lombard Street, the centre of the Italian banking houses in London, is in confusion following King Edward's dramatic break with the House of Riccardi, the Lucca-based bank that has dominated English finance for two decades. Edward had entrusted the collection of money for a projected crusade to Riccardi. This month he seized the bank's assets in Ireland, claiming that it is unable to meet its debts. Now he is expected to seize its English assets (→ 3/1344).

English king spurned by French princess

King Edward rides to London, from an illustrated manuscript made in 1338.

Westminster, May 1294

King Edward has been spurned as a suitor for Blanche, the sister of the king of France, Philip IV "the Fair". Their marriage was to have been part of a deal under which Edward acknowledged Philip's jurisdiction over the English lands in Gascony which Edward inherited from his father, Henry III.

Philip had given an oath that after 40 days the lands, including Bordeaux, would be restored to the English king as part of Princess Blanche's dowry. A day had been fixed for the two kings to meet at Amiens to settle their disputes and to contract the marriage. But now it is reported that Blanche has written to inform Edward that "she does not wish ever to marry any man, especially such an old one".

Edward, who is 55, was trying to avoid a war with France, but he has resigned himself to raising an army to fight for his territories in Gascony in south-west France. He has called a parliament to authorize an expedition to recover his French lands (→ 14/6).

1295 - 1299

Strathclyde, 1295. Robert Bruce, the lord of Annandale, King John's rival for the succession, dies (→ 23/10).

Scotland, 23 October 1295. King John, prevented by his government from serving under Edward of England against the French, makes a pact with Norway and France against England (→ 3/1296).

Scotland, early March 1296. John renounces his homage to Edward of England, who prepares to invade (→ 30).

Northumberland, 30 March 1296. Berwick-Upon-Tweed refuses to open its gates to Edward, provoking an assault; it is stormed and sacked with great slaughter (→ 27/4).

Lothian, 27 April 1296. King Edward of England's advance guard easily defeats the Scots at Dunbar (→ 10/7).

Suffolk, November 1296. The clergy of Bury St Edmunds, obeying Pope Boniface VIII's bull *Clericis Laicos* which bans the taxation of clergy in England and France without authority, refuse to be taxed by King Edward (→ 31/7/97).

Dublin, Easter 1297. Parliament forbids Irish dress for the Anglo-Irish (→ 1303).

Scone, Tayside, May 1297. The English justiciar, William Ormsby, is put to flight by Sir William Douglas and William Wallace, who recently murdered the English sheriff of Lanark (→ 7/7).

Strathclyde, 7 July 1297. Aristocratic support for Scotland's growing popular revolt collapses when leading noblemen agree terms with the English at Irvine (→ 31/8).

Rome, 31 July 1297. Under pressure from Philip IV of France, the pope abandons *Clericis Laicos* (→ 18/6/1300).

Stirling, 31 August 1297. Wallace leaves his base in Selkirk forest to join Andrew Murray's army (→ 11/9).

Rome, 1298. Pope Boniface VIII arranges marriages between King Edward of England and Margaret, the sister of King Philip IV of France, and Edward, the prince of Wales, and Isabella, Philip's daughter (→ 3/1298).

Scotland, September 1298. Sir William Wallace resigns his guardianship to John Comyn of Badenoch, ex-King John Balliol's brother-in-law, and Robert Bruce, the earl of Carrick (→ 10/5/1300).

England is ready to fight for Gascony

England, 9 October 1295
The first of three expeditionary forces to Gascony left England today after a summer of feverish military and diplomatic activity by King Edward. The English king is preparing for war with King Philip IV of France who on 19 May "confiscated" the lands in Gascony claimed by Edward. As moves began to raise an army, the count of Flanders became embroiled in the dispute. The Welsh revolt has distracted the king, and possibly delayed the departure of the first force, but Edward is set on fighting even though some barons object and the clergy are refusing to pay taxes demanded for the war (→ 1298).

Scots king abdicates

Tayside, 10 July 1296
John Balliol gave up his crown and his kingdom today in a humiliating ceremony at Kincardine Castle. His submission to King Edward of England follows a short-lived rebellion when his forces were swept aside by English forces at Dunbar in April. With a significant number of Scottish nobles backing Edward, John had no alternative but to seek peace on English terms.

The former king was deprived of his dignity as well as his kingdom; he was decked out in his robes, then symbolically stripped of the crown, sceptre, sword, rings and all other royal trappings. John and his family are to be taken south as prisoners of Edward (→ 28/8).

Humiliated: John Balliol gives up both his crown and his kingdom.

King and bishops: at odds over war.

Scottish leaders submit to English king

Northumberland, 28 August 1296
King Edward of England today received the formal homage of some 2,000 Scottish leaders at a parliament at Berwick. The submission of lay and clerical landowners seals the conquest of Scotland. Edward had already demonstrated this on 8 August by the symbolic act of removing the legendary enthronement stone of Scottish kings – the "stone of destiny" – from Scone.

Edward's dominance over the Scots is complete, for now at least. After receiving the surrender of the former King John last month, Edward headed as far north as Elgin before returning south in triumph. He is determined to control affairs in Scotland. Although local government is likely to be left in native hands, national administration will be headed by the earl of Surrey and other English officials.

The English king, who had effectively chosen John Balliol as king in 1292, has no desire to see a new monarch in Scotland. He rejected a claim by Robert Bruce, the son of John's late rival for the throne, asking: "Have we nothing to do but win realms for you?" (→ 5/1297).

Third Welsh rebellion brought to an end

Conwy, Gwynedd, 10 April 1295
The third Welsh revolt of King Edward of England's reign is over after eight months in which the king has been fully stretched, with an army of 35,000 men, in reasserting his hold on the country. The Welsh, angered by Edward's taxes and enlistment of men to fight in France, rose up and attacked his castles. Caernarfon, Ruthin and Denbigh fell and others were besieged as Madog ap Llywelyn, the son of a lord of Meirionydd, proclaimed himself prince of Wales.

Edward relieved several castles from the sea, but in January he was forced to abandon an advance on Bangor, retreating to the castle at Conwy where he spent the rest of the winter. Emboldened by this success, and anticipating an English counter-attack, Madog moved south into Powys and met disaster.

On 5 March his forces were encircled at Maes Moydog near Montgomery by a 2,500-strong army led by the earl of Warwick. Madog escaped, but many of his men were killed and his revolt was in tatters.

Today Edward set forth from Conwy on a victory march around the country designed to assert his authority and to crush any lingering resistance. The first stop is Bangor, and then Anglesey, where a new castle is to be built at Beaumaris (→ 7/12/1301).

Edward summons a new parliament

Westminster, November 1295
King Edward, needing money to fight his war with France and to pay for putting down the recent rebellion in Wales, has summoned parliament. He has asked the clergy to attend, as "what touches all should be approved by all" – a Roman law phrase which will be familiar to them. As well as barons, the king is calling two knights from each shire and two citizens from each town. They are to have full powers to "do what shall be ordained by common counsel", a development of the formula used last year (→ 10/10/97).

Armies wage bloody battle for power in Scotland

Stirling: Scots win convincing victory

Stirling, 11 September 1297
Scottish forces today ambushed the English on the bridge over the Forth and won a battle which has shocked King Edward's court. The earl of Surrey's professional army of 300 cavalry and 10,000 infantry was routed by forces led by William Wallace and Andrew Murray, Scottish nobles of low rank.

Hugh Cressingham, the king's treasurer in Scotland, has been killed in the fighting; Wallace boasts that he is going to make a swordbelt out of his skin. English soldiers who crossed over to the north side of the Forth have been massacred; those who were not killed on the end of the Scots' long spears drowned in the river, dragged down by the weight of their armour. Surrey himself has fled.

The Wallace rebellion is the focus for Scottish anger over not only specific English demands but also Edward's claiming Scotland at all. Recruitment of soldiers to fight for England, plus taxation, fuelled the anger before Wallace started the uprising by murdering the sheriff of Lanark. As his followers started to force English officials out of office, Murray started another rising. The English response was hesitant and indecisive until Surrey, ordered by the king to deal with the challenge, met disaster today (→22/7/98).

Hero to one nation, enemy to another: William Wallace goes into battle.

Falkirk: English hit back against Scots

Falkirk, Central, 22 July 1298
King Edward of England has crushed William Wallace's Scottish army after a long, fierce battle here. Since 25 June, when they invaded Scotland at Roxburgh, the English had plundered Lothian and won back some castles but had been unable to bring Wallace to battle. The Scots' scorched-earth approach, and mistakes made by English suppliers, had left morale and food low; then Edward heard that Wallace was at Falkirk.

There, on a hillside, Wallace had arranged his spearmen in four "schiltrons" – circular, hedgehog formations surrounded by a defensive wall of wooden stakes. But Wallace's order of battle collapsed. Edward's cavalry attacked first, mowing down the Scottish archers; the Scottish knights fled, and then Edward's men laid siege to the schiltrons. Some reports say that the infantry, which rained bolts, arrows and even stones onto the hapless spear-carriers, played the key role; according to others, an attack by the cavalry from the rear was decisive. Either way, there were soon gaps wide enough for the English to wade in and smash any lingering resistance. Scottish losses were very heavy. Wallace has escaped with his life, but his military reputation lies in shreds (→9/1298).

King bows to pressure over 'Magna Carta'

Westminster, 10 October 1297
While King Edward is away at war in Flanders, his quarrels with the barons and the bishops have come to a head. Parliament met on 30 September to discuss grievances which arise mostly from the king's demands for his European wars. His seizure of the wool crop has caused particular anger, but the discontent has widened to embrace complaints that Edward is failing to observe the charter agreed between King John and the barons in 1215.

Today the regency council, ruling England in Edward's absence abroad, agreed that that charter [*Magna Carta*] and the Charter of the Forest should be renewed as charters of the liberties of the kingdom of England. In addition, it was agreed that new taxes or demands could be imposed only "with the common consent of the whole kingdom". The agreement should be confirmed by Edward in Ghent next month. The defeat of his army in Scotland last month, on top of his expensive European expedition, gave him no choice but to bow to pressure. The wool tax is to be abolished, but in return the barons and clergy will back moves to boost the royal exchequer (→28/3/1300).

England pays price of war on three fronts

Westminster, March 1298
The war between King Edward and King Philip IV of France is over, with most of Gascony remaining under French control. Edward still hopes that the current truce will enable him to regain through diplomatic means the titular hold on Gascony that his military attempts failed to recover. It was distractions in the British Isles – wars against what he sees as rebels in Wales and Scotland – that undermined English efforts in Europe. Fighting on three fronts at once has also put him deep in debt. His military outlay amounts to the colossal sum of £750,000 in the past four years.

His attempts to raise so much money have caused great unpopularity. A wool export tax, originally 6s 8d [33p] a sack, was increased to 40s [£2] and was known as the *maltote* or "bad tax" until it was remitted last year. His demands for a tax of a fifth of the clergy's income led to a papal bull forbidding them to contribute. Defiant clergy were outlawed until the pope withdrew the bull "in emergencies", and the clergy granted him a tenth of their income following the overall settlement with parliament last year (→1/1302).

1300 - 1305

England, 28 March 1300. King Edward reissues the Charter of the Forest, adding several new clauses. Knights will enforce *Magna Carta*, and sheriffs will be elected to rule in their own counties (→ 20/3/10).

Strathclyde, 10 May 1300. Following a violent quarrel between the Scottish guardians at Peebles last August, Robert Bruce, the earl of Carrick, is replaced by Sir Ingerman Umfraville, one of the rival Comyn faction, at Rutherglen (→ 30/10).

Scotland, 31 May 1301. The Anglo-Scottish truce expires (→ 24/9).

Strathclyde, 24 September 1301. Bothwell Castle falls to the English (→ 16/2/02).

France, January 1302. John Balliol, the deposed king of Scotland, is freed and goes to Bailleul, in Picardy (→ 11/7).

Flanders, 11 July 1302. The French defeat at Courtrai leaves the Scots without hope of further help in their fight with the English (→ 20/5/03).

Ireland, 1303. Peter de Paris, the first admiral, transports a huge Irish army, led by Richard de Burgh, to help King Edward of England to fight the Scots (→ 31/5/15).

Lothian, 24 February 1303. John Comyn, the earl of Badenoch, who has resumed his role as guardian of Scotland, routs an English army led by John Segrave at Roslin (→ 3/1304).

France, 20 May 1303. Gascony is returned to the English as the French make peace, abandoning the Scots and John Balliol, the former Scottish king (→ 4/1313).

St Andrews, Fife, March 1304. Edward of England, successful in his bid to reconquer Scotland, holds a parliament which most of the Scots magnates attend after their surrender last month (→ 11/6).

Central, 11 June 1304. Robert Bruce, the head of the Bruce family after his father's death, reaches a secret agreement at Cambuskenneth with the bishop of St Andrews about his claim to the throne (→ 3/5/05).

Strathclyde, 3 May 1305. Sir William Wallace is captured (→ 24/8).

London, 15 September 1305. A council of 21 Englishmen and ten Scots meets to draw up ordinances for the government of Scotland (→ 10/2/06).

Scots seek pope's help to rebuff English power in Scotland

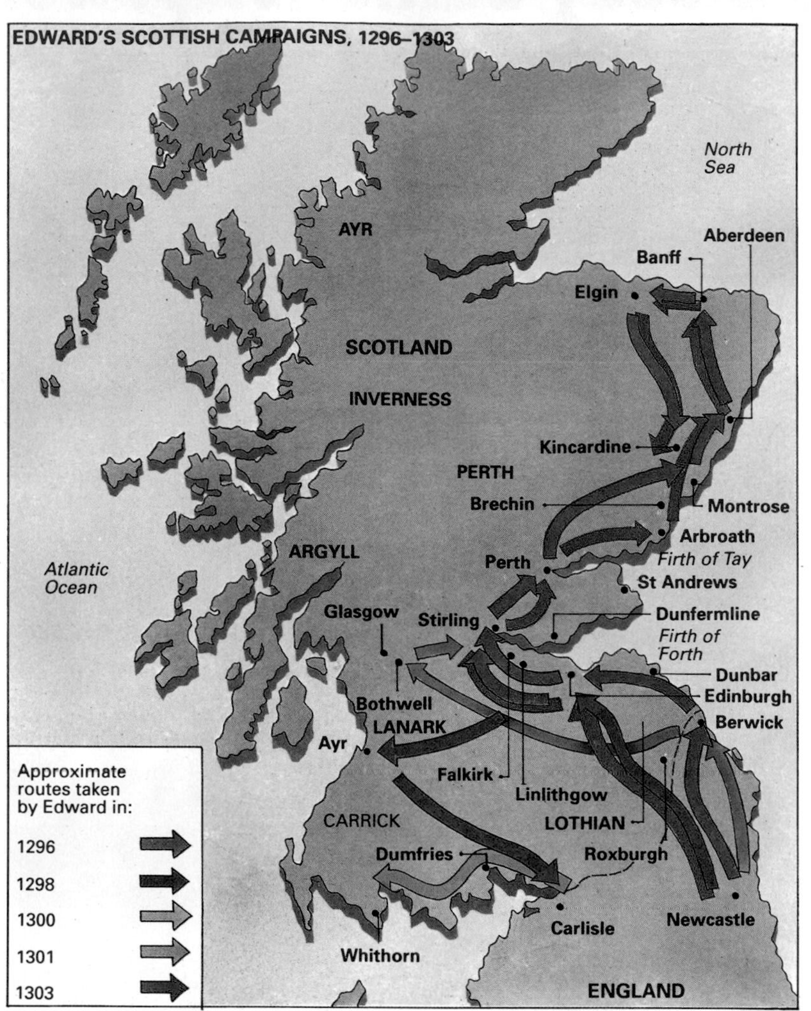

Rome, May 1301

The Scots appear to be winning the sympathy of Pope Boniface VIII as the church attempts to arbitrate over English claims to Scotland. The pope became embroiled in this dispute after England and France accepted his offer of arbitration as part of a wider resolution of their conflict during which the Scots had been allies of France.

In January King Edward wrote to the pope arguing that English claims to the Scottish throne sprang from the days when fugitives from Troy – the supposed ancestors of the English – had exterminated the giants of Albion. The Scots, led by Baldred Bisset, a graduate of Bologna, countered with more recent events, asking how it was that a descendant of William of Normandy could have any connection with the ancient Britons, let alone any Trojan ancestors.

Besides, argues Bisset, the Scots are descended from Scota, an Egyptian pharaoh's daughter, and have an even older claim to the throne. Appeals to natural law, based on the tenet that one kingdom cannot subjugate another, have been spiced with charges of chicanery, bullying, lying and forgery, stirring papal criticism of the English (→ 31).

Durham Cathedral besieged by bishop

Durham, 18 June 1300

King Edward today sought to resolve a bitter dispute here between the bishop, Antony Bek, and Richard de Hoton, the prior of the cathedral convent. Last month Bek appeared at the priory gates with an army of followers to make an official visitation. There was a fierce argument over the form that the bishop's visit should take, as a result of which de Hoton and his monks were excommunicated and imprisoned in their own priory.

De Hoton then sought Edward's intervention. The king is an old ally of Bek, but he rejected the bishop's plea to stay out of the dispute. Edward met the monks today, and they promised to accept whatever the king ruled. Edward will put his peace formula to the bishop in two days' time (→ 11/5/13).

New English throne will upset the Scots

Galloway, 30 October 1300

Under pressure from the pope and France, King Edward of England has agreed to grant the Scots a truce. English forces advanced into south-western Scotland last July, swiftly capturing Caerlaverock Castle in Galloway and then defeating a Scottish army led by John Comyn, the earl of Badenoch, on the river Cree. These victories confirmed Edward's strength but gave him little tangible reward for the expedition. In a move calculated to symbolize English authority in Scotland – and one which will infuriate Scots – Edward has ordered the construction of an ornate new coronation chair to house the "stone of destiny" upon which Scottish kings have been enthroned for centuries at Scone. Edward seized the stone in 1296 (→ 5/1301).

Bruce makes peace with English king

Scotland, 16 February 1302

Robert Bruce, the grandson of the unsuccessful rival claimant to John Balliol for the Scottish throne in 1292, has made his peace with King Edward of England. Bruce, the earl of Carrick, is a more aggressive character than his father, the lord of Annandale, and his apparent acquiescence in English rule will be a boost to Edward. He was one of two joint guardians of Scotland who were appointed after Wallace had been defeated at Falkirk in 1298. The other was John Comyn, the earl of Badenoch, with whose family the Bruces had a longstanding rivalry. Bruce was ousted as a guardian in 1300 by a supporter of the exiled King John and the Comyns. John was last month freed by the French and has retired to a castle in Picardy (→ 24/2/03).

Eldest son of king of England is to be the prince of Wales

Lincoln, 7 February 1301
Edward, King Edward's heir apparent, was today proclaimed the first English prince of Wales. He will be presented to the people of Wales as a prince born in the principality – at Caernarfon on 25 April 1284 – although since then he has had few known connections with his birthplace. However, the new prince (who also became earl of Chester today) is expected to tour Wales later this year.

He has already shown his mettle in the Scottish wars, taking part in the capture of Caerlaverock Castle last July. He has been ruthless in terrorizing the Scottish countryside. When he was 13 he acted as regent during the king's war in Flanders, signing the reconfirmation of *Magna Carta* in 1297.

A Gascon squire, Piers Gaveston, served with the king in Flanders. On his return to England Edward placed him in his son's household, where he has become a great favourite (→ 1309).

'Outlaw' Wallace dies horrific death

London, 23 August 1305
William Wallace, the scourge of English rule in Scotland, was executed for treason today, dying an horrific death intended by King Edward to be both a punishment and a warning to other potential Scottish rebels. Tonight his head is transfixed to a spike on London Bridge, with his limbs dispatched for grisly displays in Newcastle, Berwick, Edinburgh and Perth.

Wallace shot to fame eight years ago when he defeated an English army at Stirling and led a devastating raid on northern England. His power waned after a defeat at Falkirk in the following year, but he defied English rule by seeking continental support for the Scots and by heading what Edward regarded as a band of treacherous outlaws. He spurned peace moves which reconciled Robert Bruce and the king until he was captured near Glasgow by Sir John Menteith, a Scot loyal to Edward, last May.

Yesterday Wallace arrived in London to confront a public which for years had been fed stories of his alleged atrocities against the English. He was paraded today at a show trial in Westminster Hall, forced to wear a crown of laurel leaves and given no chance of answering the charges of treason hurled at him. These included accusations that he killed anyone speaking English, including children, widows and nuns. But the central charge was his rebellion against the king. As Wallace never acknowledged Edward's authority the verdict of the court was never in doubt, and he was taken to be hanged and then cut down to be disembowelled while still alive (→ 15/9/05).

William Wallace's trial, by the Victorian artist Daniel Maclise (1806-70).

How naval designers can turn merchant vessels into warships

England, 1300
England's ship designers have devised a simple yet effective way of converting the country's merchant fleet into an "instant" navy. By the addition of towering structures – "fore- and after-castles" – for spear-throwers and archers at either end of the ship, a trading vessel can, whenever necessary, join Edward's fleet as an effective warship within a matter of weeks.

Other significant changes in ship design have made naval warfare a far more sophisticated business. William the Conqueror had to wait for a favourable wind for his invasion; today's ships with their deep-draught hulls, bowsprits and stern rudders – replacing the inefficient "steerboard" or steering oar – can take advantage of any wind. But the method of fighting remains the same, with archers and crossbowmen taking the initial toll until grappling hooks bring the ships together and the hand-to-hand slaughter begins (→ 8/1436).

A later coloured engraving shows the new "fore- and after-castles" on ships.

Sea battle: sailors prepare for hand-to-hand combat as two ships manoeuvre.

English king loses treasure in robbery

London, 26 April 1303
Edward's treasure has been stolen in a daring robbery carried out at Westminster Abbey. Silver and gold plate and other valuables said to be worth £100,000 were taken. The king has ordered an inquiry into the robbery, and several arrests have already been made.

Among those held is Richard Pudlicote, a merchant, who says that he spent months tunnelling through a stone wall to get to the wardrobe treasury located in a crypt under the chapter house. He spent two days in the crypt gloating over the treasure before taking away as much as he could carry. Bits and pieces have already been fished out of the Thames and found in nearby fields and churchyards.

There is growing suspicion, however, that this could have been an inside job, and that the abbot and many monks and laymen were also closely involved (→ 1315).

1306 - 1311

Dumfries, 10 February 1306. Robert Bruce, the earl of Carrick, murders John Comyn of Badenoch (→ 27/3).

Tayside, 19 June 1306. Robert Bruce, the newly crowned king, flees north after defeat at Methven by Aymer de Valence of Pembroke, King Edward of England's lieutenant (→ 11/8).

Central, 11 August 1306. King Robert, defeated at Strathfillan by John Lorne, the son of Alexander MacDougall of Argyll and a kinsman of the murdered John Comyn, flees the country (→ 7/11).

Strathclyde, 10 May 1307. Robert defeats Aylmer de Valence at Loudon Hill for his second victory over an English army in a month (→ 25/8).

Dumfries, 6 August 1307. Edward II of England creates his favourite, Piers Gaveston, earl of Cornwall (→ 25/2/08).

Strathclyde, 25 August 1307. Edward II of England leaves Scotland (→ 25/12).

Grampian, 25 December 1307. Robert defeats John Comyn, the earl of Buchan (→ 15/9/08).

Strathclyde, 15 September 1308. Robert crushes his last rival, Alexander MacDougall of Argyll, at the Pass of Brander (→ 16/3/09).

Fife, 16 March 1309. Robert calls his first parliament at St Andrews, establishing the Bruce claim to the throne and stating that John Balliol was illegally made king (→ 12/8/11).

Chester, 27 June 1309. Piers Gaveston, sent to Ireland as lieutenant a year ago, is greeted by Edward II as his brother on his return despite baronial opposition (→ 4/11/11).

Powys, 1309. Gruffudd ab Owain, the last prince, dies. Despite opposition to female inheritance, Powys passes to the Charlton family into which his daughter married (→ 1318).

Ireland, 9 February 1310. Parliament at Kilkenny forbids Anglo-Irish religious houses to accept Irish members (→ 1329).

Dundee, 24 February 1310. The Scottish clergy agree to back King Robert (→ 9/1378).

London, 20 March 1310. Parliament insists on a council and ordainers to rule the country (→ 27/9/11).

Cumberland, 12 August 1311. Robert of Scotland crosses the Solway in the first Scottish invasion of England for 15 years (→ 1312).

Robert Bruce is new Scottish king

Robert Bruce, whose accession poses a challenge to English authority.

Tayside, 27 March 1306
Robert Bruce, the earl of Carrick, was today proclaimed king of Scotland in a ceremony at Scone which directly challenges the authority of England's King Edward. The coronation ends the four-year pact which Bruce concluded with the English king and threatens to unleash a fresh wave of blood-letting.

Bruce moved quickly to have himself crowned following six weeks of turmoil. At Dumfries on 10 February a long simmering rivalry with John Comyn of Badenoch flared into violence. Comyn refused to abandon Scotland's imprisoned King John in favour of Bruce, and in the heat of the argument Bruce stabbed Comyn. Bruce's supporters finished Comyn off and also killed his uncle, Sir Robert Comyn.

Since then Bruce has consolidated his power base in the south-west and – despite the censures of King Edward and the church – had himself crowned today by Isabel, the countess of Buchan, who claimed the "Macduff right" to set the king on his throne. King Robert, as his supporters now call him, was born near Chelmsford in 1274 and is the grandson of the Robert Bruce who challenged for the Scottish throne 15 years ago (→ 1305).

Scots king's family and friends undergo savage punishments

London, 7 November 1306
Further savage punishments were meted out today to the family and friends of King Robert of Scots. Simon Fraser, one of the victors of Roslin, has been hanged, drawn and beheaded, with his head placed on a pole beside what remains of that of William Wallace on London Bridge. And the earl of Atholl, who claimed kinship with King Edward of England, was hanged before being beheaded and burnt.

The vengeance visited by Edward on the Bruce family and its supporters have seen Neil Bruce, the brother of the Scottish king, put to death along with many others at Berwick, while Robert's brother-in-law, Christopher Seton, was butchered at Dumfries. Sixteen people were slaughtered at Newcastle. Even the female members of the family have been cruelly punished. Queen Elizabeth is under house arrest at Burstwick in Holderness, and Christian Bruce, the king's sister, has been sent to a nunnery. His other sister, Mary, and Isabel, the countess of Buchan, who crowned him king, are to be held in cages of wood and iron which have been specially constructed within the towers of Berwick and Roxburgh Castles. Marjorie, Robert's 12-year-old daughter, is to be kept in the Tower of London where only the constable may speak to her.

Robert himself is being pursued by English forces, intent on curbing a revolt which Edward thought he had ended when he reached an agreement with Bruce and others in 1302, ending four years of rebellion, and captured Wallace in 1305. But Robert is equally determined to retain the throne he claimed earlier this year (→ 10/5/07).

On show: the countess of Buchan is displayed in a cage at Berwick.

England gets new knights as prelude to Scottish battles

Armed knights: bound by honour.

Westminster, 13 May 1306
In an unprecedented display of chivalry King Edward has knighted 300 of the country's most noble young men – including his own son – as a prelude to his new war against the Scots. They are now pledged to appear before him in Scotland on 8 July to give battle to Robert Bruce, who has been crowned king of Scotland against Edward's wishes.

The royal palace of Westminster proved too small for the huge crowd, so walls were demolished and the apple trees at the nearby New Temple cut down to make room for pavilions and tents for the new knights, for whom Edward had provided golden robes. There was still such a crush at the ceremony that two knights died and several fainted. Nevertheless, the banquet that followed was a great success, with its centrepiece of roast swans decorated with golden nets in a bed of gilded reeds (→ 19/6).

Warrior-king dies on way to battle

Edward I dies after reign of 34 years

Cumbria, 7 July 1307
King Edward is dead. The king who waged wars in Wales, Scotland and Gascony was heading north to join battle once again with the Scots. But "the hammer of the Scots" did not die in battle; he died at Burgh-by-Sands, near Carlisle, of dysentery. He was 68 and had reigned for almost 35 years.

He leaves a formidable legacy as a law reformer through the statutes and parliaments of his reign, but it has been his wars which have dominated his years as monarch. He died having made Wales firmly subject to English rule and with his lands in Gascony restored to him by Philip IV of France. European peace has been sealed by the betrothal of his son Edward, the prince of Wales (who now becomes King Edward II), to Isabella of France, Philip IV's daughter.

Only in Scotland was he still at war. Robert Bruce was last year crowned Scottish king at Scone and defeated an English army at Loudoun Hill. It was to engage him that the king, already ill with dysentery, was marching. His last wish was for his bones to be carried by his army on the expedition into Scotland, but his body is to be taken to lie at Waltham Abbey until the campaign is over (→ 6/8).

Ceremony at court: the marriage of King Edward and Queen Isabella.

Coronation rocked by rows over favourite

Westminster, 25 February 1308
The coronation of Edward II and his 12-year-old queen, Isabella of France, took place today. It was a political disaster for Edward thanks to the leading role played by his favourite, the Gascon knight Piers Gaveston, whom Edward has made earl of Cornwall.

Gaveston's hold over the king is detested by the barons, and his short period of regency, while Edward was in France to marry Isabella, has done nothing to endear him to them. This morning the barons threatened to stop the ceremony unless Edward agreed to banish Gaveston as his father had done once before. But the king agreed only to honour whatever they decided at the next parliament. When the coronation began Gaveston appeared carrying the crown – much to the disgust of the barons, among others.

At the banquet later Gaveston came dressed in imperial purple trimmed with pearls. This ostentation, coupled with Edward's unwavering attention to him, so outraged the queen's French relatives that they walked out (→ 2/6/09).

King yields to the demands of barons

London, 27 September 1311
In an historic compromise King Edward has accepted the "Ordinances", the demands of the barons who have threatened civil war if he does not comply. They insisted on the banishment of the king's favourite, Piers Gaveston, and that of a member of the Florentine banking family, the Frescobaldi, charged with fraud; the abolition of customs duties introduced in 1303; an independent treasury, into which all customs dues will be paid; and the right to conduct foreign policy and choose officers of state (→ 4/11).

Gaveston goes into exile once again

London, 4 November 1311
Piers Gaveston, the king's favourite, has finally been forced into exile, four days later than the deadline agreed between King Edward and his barons. Gaveston is understood to have sailed for France, even though King Philip IV detests him and is likely to imprison him. Edward was forced to expel his friend, with whom he is suspected of having a homosexual relationship, by pressure from barons who resent Gaveston's influence over him. But Gaveston has been exiled before – and returned (→ 19/6/12).

A tin-lead badge for a pilgrim, showing the Virgin and Child.

1312 - 1314

Durham, 1312. King Robert storms the town, surprising the citizens. A truce is then agreed at Hexham (→ 3/1312).

Dundee, March 1312. The city falls to the Scots, leaving Perth as the only English garrison north of the Forth (→ 6/12).

London, 13 November 1312. Edward II calls a parliament and prepares for battle against the barons (→ 14/10/13).

Lothian, 6 December 1312. A Scottish assault on Berwick Castle is foiled by the barking of a dog (→ 7/1/13).

Oxford, 1312. Hertford college is founded (→ 4/4/14).

France, April 1313. John Balliol, the deposed Scottish king, dies on his estate at Bailleul (→ 9/1319).

Canterbury, 11 May 1313. Thomas Cobham is elected archbishop on the death of Robert Winchelsey; Edward II asks the pope to confer the title on his clerk, Walter Reynolds, the bishop of Worcester (→ 1328).

Stirling, 23 June 1313. Edward Bruce, the king's brother, and the commander of the English garrison besieged at Stirling Castle, agree that the castle will be yielded to the Scots if it has not been relieved by midsummer 1314 (→ 19/12/14).

England, 14 October 1313. Edward II and his earls are formally reconciled (→ 8/1316).

Borders, 19 February 1314. Scots led by James Douglas and disguised as black cattle make a successful night raid on Roxburgh Castle (→ 14/3).

Edinburgh, 14 March 1314. Thomas Randolph, the earl of Moray, captures the castle (→ 17/6).

Oxford, 4 April 1314. Bishop Walter Stapledon of Exeter founds Stapledon hall (→ 1326).

Lothian, 17 June 1314. Edward II of England leaves Berwick Castle with 15,000 men on route for Stirling to relieve Sir Philip Mowbray and prevent the castle from being surrendered to the Scots (→ 24).

Scotland, October 1314. King Robert's wife, Elizabeth, his daughter, Marjorie, and Bishop Wishart of Glasgow are exchanged for the earl of Hereford, one of the English nobles captured at the Battle of Bannockburn. The king has not seen his wife and daughter since they were imprisoned eight years ago (→ 27/4/15).

Noblemen put style before speed when they travel abroad

England, c.1312

Rich noblemen are increasingly to be found travelling to European cities. Ghent, Bruges, Toulouse and Bordeaux all have populations as big as London's – believed to be in the region of 40,000 – while Paris and Venice are even bigger. Travel is now also more common within England, where it is remarkable for rigour rather than speed.

Most nobles are not unduly bothered about speed. They are more concerned to be able to take ample supplies of their favourite foods, to say nothing of their favourite ladies and musicians. This means that the speed of the journey is dictated by the luggage carts and the chariots and litters that carry the ladies. Those who like to take foot archers can do no more than 12 miles a day, while the fastest carts average only 20 miles a day. Most great nobles take at least 50 or 60 people. They prefer to stay in the castles of foreign lords when possible, and they like to take musicians, young girls and jesters to help provide the evening entertainment, but sometimes they have to stay in inns and endure beds used for sleeping three or four.

Main roads are about 9 metres (30 feet) wide, with a few surviving Roman roads twice that width. But there are hazards: mud in winter, dust in summer, highwaymen and wild animals in the forests, broken bridges and flooded fords. Bad weather can thwart any traveller.

Knights Templar punished for life

England, May 1312

Pope Clement V has abolished the Order of the Knights Templar, and, as has happened across Europe, the knights here are to be arrested and their property shared between the pope and the king – in this case, Edward II. The attack has little to do with the Templars' position in England, where they have worked usefully as bankers and archivists. Rather, it comes as a result of pressure from the French. None the less the English knights must suffer too.

Barons order death of king's favourite

Under arrest: Piers Gaveston.

Warwickshire, 19 June 1312

Piers Gaveston, the favourite of King Edward II, was murdered today on the orders of four leading barons including the earls of Warwick and Lancaster. Three times he had been banished from the royal court – twice by Edward II, once by his father – and three times he had returned. Ten days ago he was kidnapped and held at Warwick Castle from where he was marched, barefoot, to his death on nearby Blacklow Hill. There, on land owned by the earl of Lancaster, he was beheaded by two of the earl's men. Told that he was to die, Gaveston sighed and replied: "Let the will of the earls be done" (→ 13/11).

Last English fort north of Forth captured

Tayside, 7 January 1313

Leading his men through a moat of freezing water, King Robert of Scotland has stormed the English garrison at Perth. After the fall of Dundee last March this was the only garrison remaining in English hands north of the river Forth.

Robert had been besieging Perth for some considerable time when he appeared to withdraw. The garrison's commander, Sir William Oliphant, was lured into lowering his guard, thinking that the siege was over, so the king's surprise attack caught him napping.

The Scottish king, carrying his own rope-ladder, waded through water up to his throat before scaling the castle walls. Robert was the second man over the walls, and so great was the surprise of his men's attack that the castle fell with little fighting (→ 23/6).

Hunting the fox: a scene from the 14th-century manuscript of "Phoebus", which shows horsemen, hounds and their foot-followers in full cry.

English forces routed in battle at Bannockburn

A fatal stroke: King Robert kills an English knight in the battle at Bannockburn, where the Scots – although outnumbered – routed the English.

Stirling, 24 June 1314
The English army has been routed by the Scots near Stirling, and King Edward II is tonight fleeing for his life. Two days of fighting have ended with a total victory for the forces of King Robert, despite being outnumbered by the large English army of 2,500 professional knights on horseback and 15,000 men-at-arms as infantry.

For four years Robert had tried to avoid pitched battles with the English. Then, with Edward heading towards Stirling, he was forced to make a stand, but he chose his battleground with care. The high and wooded slopes of New Park outside Stirling gave cover for his own troops, while pits and spikes forced the English to bunch at a narrow spot where the road from Falkirk crosses a stream, the Bannock burn. Robert rallied his forces to "fight for the honour of their nation" and said that England wished to "obliterate our whole nation".

'Edward had fought bravely, but tonight he is on the run, fleeing for his life'

Whether the Scots were inspired by their king's oratory or by his military skill, round one went to them, with the English cavalry yesterday forced to retreat. Surprised by the Scottish tactics, the English then settled for the night on peaty marshlands beside the river Forth, with their backs to the Bannock burn. This position gave them water for their horses but left them dangerously exposed on the tightly constricted ground above the burn. At dawn today the Scottish battalions of spearmen broke their "schiltrons" – circular defensive formations – to attack, again surprising the English.

In an attempt to repel the Scots the earl of Gloucester led a cavalry charge, but he was killed and the counter-attack failed. The Scots then pressed into the mass of English knights, with their spears taking a heavy toll of the horses. The English archers, arriving belatedly, were driven off by a flank charge from Scottish light cavalry. Then Robert's own schiltron attacked.

Compressed into the tight area between river, burn and marsh, the English were forced back by the Scottish spears, and fears arose in the English camp for the safety of their king. His death would have been a disaster, his capture potentially worse. Although the English forces had lacked clear leadership, Edward had fought bravely – one horse was killed beneath him – and was reluctant to leave the battlefield. But his knights insisted that he fled, and the king made for Stirling Castle surrounded by horsemen. His departure triggered a final panic amongst the remnants of the army, and, as the Scottish camp-followers swept forward, thousands of soldiers were killed.

Meanwhile Edward is still on the run. At Stirling he was told that the castle would be surrendered to the triumphant Robert, leaving him to head south on a circuitous route, probably for Dunbar (→ 10/1314).

1315-1318

Ayr, 27 April 1315. Parliament agrees on the succession of the Scottish crown to King Robert's brother Edward rather than to his daughter Marjorie (→ 1/8).

Co Louth, 29 June 1315. Edward Bruce sacks Dundalk after a victory over the English at Moiry Pass (→ 10/9).

Carlisle, 1 August 1315. King Robert of Scotland abandons his ten-day siege (→ 2/3/16).

Co Antrim, 10 Sept 1315. Edward Bruce defeats the earl of Ulster at Connor (→ 1/2/16).

Co Kildare, 1 February 1316. Edward Butler, the justiciar of Ireland, is defeated at Skerries, near Ardscull, by Edward Bruce, opening the way for an attack on Dublin (→ 2/5).

Strathclyde, 2 March 1316. Robert's daughter Marjorie, who last year married Walter "the Stewart", dies in a riding accident at Paisley (→ 1/4/18).

Co Galway, 10 August 1316. Richard de Burgh, the earl of Ulster, defeats and kills Felim O'Connor of Connacht at Athenry (→ 1/3/17).

York, August 1316. The earl of Lancaster, who became "chief councillor" in February, leaves parliament after a violent quarrel over Scotland with Edward II (→ 6/1317).

West Yorkshire, June 1317. The earl of Lancaster blocks Pontefract bridge to troops going north to join Edward II's forces at York (→ 9/8/18).

Ireland, 1317. King Donal O'Neill of Tyrone and other Irish leaders send Pope John XXII a remonstrance of grievance against Anglo-Norman massacres of Gaelic Irish (→ 5/1317).

Northumberland, 1 April 1318. Twenty-two years after Edward I of England sacked Berwick, it returns to Scottish control (→ 3/12).

Munster, 10 May 1318. Richard de Burgh is killed by Murtough O'Brien in battle at Dysert O'Dea (→ 14/10).

Scone, Tayside, 3 December 1318. After Edward Bruce's death, the Scottish parliament names Robert's heir as Walter "the Stewart" (→ 20/9/19).

Cardiff, 1318. Llywelyn Bren, a Welsh landowner who revolted in 1314 and was imprisoned after surrendering to the English in 1316, is executed by Hugh Despenser the younger (→ 7/1378).

Scots open Ulster front

Larne, Co Antrim, 31 May 1315
Edward Bruce, the brother of the Scottish king, who landed at Larne on 26 May with an army of 6,000 well trained soldiers, is preparing to invade Ulster. This new front against England's King Edward II has scored early successes: local armies of the Ulster colonists have been beaten, and a number of chiefs have joined the Scottish forces.

It is believed that the invasion resulted from an invitation to Edward Bruce by Donal O'Neill, the king of Tyrone and an enemy of the pro-English Richard de Burgh, the earl of Ulster. O'Neill seems prepared to surrender his hereditary claim to the high-kingship of Ireland in favour of the Scottish king's brother. This would suit King Robert, who has been wanting a crown for the brave Edward (→ 29/6).

Invader: a Scottish foot soldier.

Edward Bruce is crowned king of Ireland

Dundalk, Co Louth, 2 May 1316
Edward Bruce has been crowned king of Ireland on the hill of Knocknemelan, near Dundalk, watched by crowds of his Irish supporters. His invasion of Meath and subsequent victory at Kells ensured the support of Walter and Hugh de Lacy, who brought over to his side at least 70 Meath noblemen and four Gaelic chiefs. Edward's crowning has caused consternation among the Irish lords. Although they boasted that they could defeat the new king, they seemed incapable doing so. Nor have they received much help from Edward II of England, whose feeble government placed the burden of saving the state on them, creating several earldoms to encourage expressions of loyalty. Meanwhile a rising of the Gaelic Irish has caused uproar and disturbance (→ 10/8).

Wine and gifts flow despite cash deficit

England, 1315
This year's royal expenditure was £66,000, outstripping income by £6,000. Much of this went on fighting the Scots, but the king clearly has not stinted on luxuries. Critics claim that he has wasted money on over-lavish clothes and feasting while squandering vast sums on friends and favoured courtiers. The royal household's bill for wine was more than £4,000 this year; gifts accounted for over £3,000, and clothes and jewels cost nearly £1,000. Alms totalled a mere £194.11s. By comparison, a ploughman can expect to earn 12 or 13 shillings [60-65p] a year.

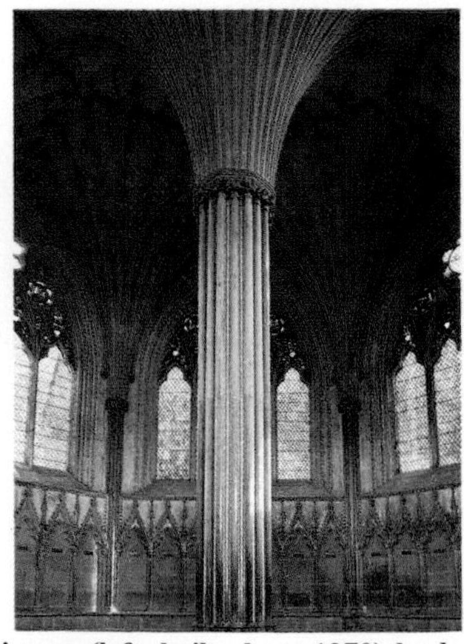

The irregular sweep of the prior's staircase (left, built about 1270) leads up to the remarkable chapter house (right, completed in 1315) at Wells Cathedral, in Somerset. The ceiling here is delicately patterned, with the supporting ribs which emanate from the sturdy central pillar shown.

Famine worsens as harvests fail again

England and Wales, autumn 1316
Hopes of avoiding a serious famine have finally collapsed following reports from the countryside that this year's harvest will be at least as bad as last year's and in some areas may be even worse. Unrest is growing, with riots in Bristol and revolts in Wales and Lancashire.

Last year's harvests were ruined throughout Europe by torrential rain. One Yorkshire churchman spoke of misery "such as our age has never seen", and there were reports of men eating dogs and horses. This summer the downpours returned, bringing serious flooding and reducing crops to only a quarter of their normal levels.

The price of grain is already reaching record levels. A quarter of wheat, which would have fetched less than six shillings [30p] only a few years ago, is now being offered for more than 26 shillings. But it is not just grain for which prices have soared: salt now costs as much as wheat. Attempts at price controls by the government have failed, with some dealers withdrawing goods from the market altogether. Even the king is affected. When he visited St Albans this autumn, his courtiers found it difficult to buy bread for the royal household. The poor, of course, have no hope of affording today's prices, and many will die of starvation (→ c.1336).

Dublin is set ablaze to thwart Scots

Robert Bruce: back in Scotland.

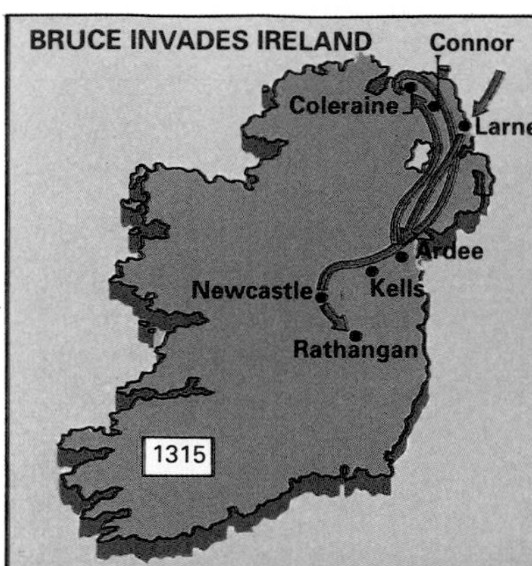

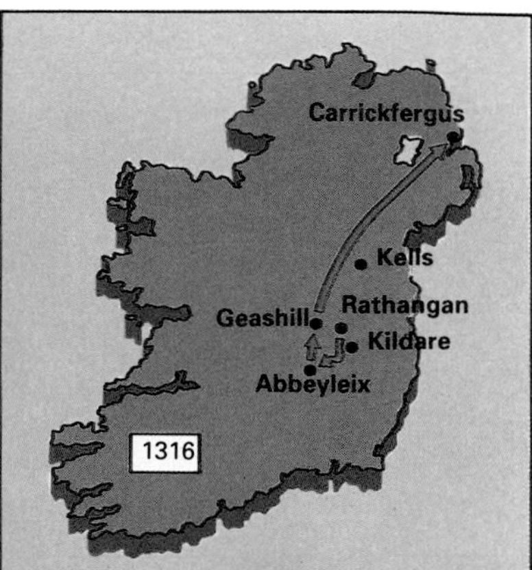

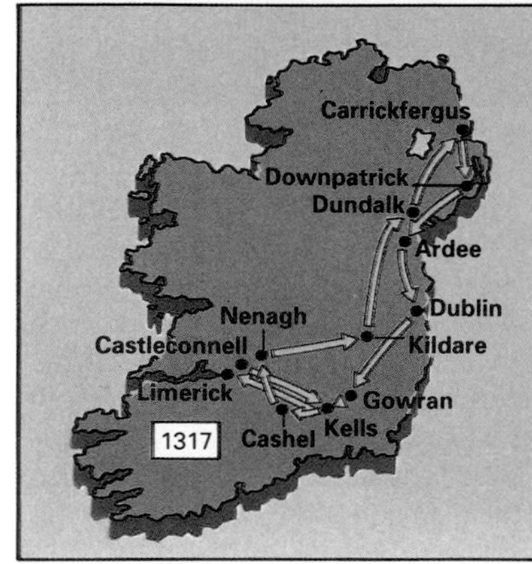

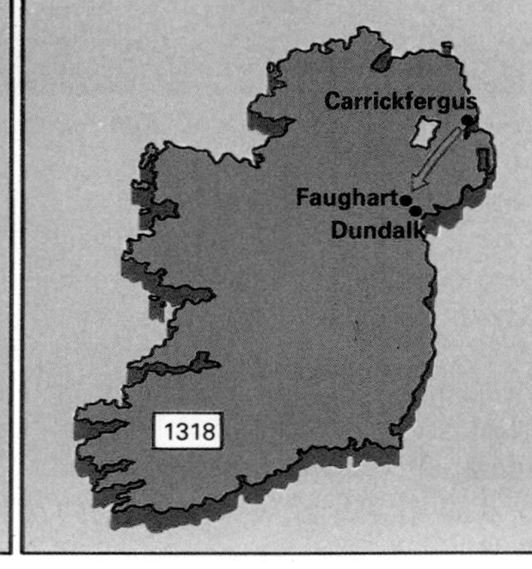

Ireland, May 1317
King Robert Bruce of Scotland has returned home after an abortive attempt to help his brother Edward to capture Dublin. Robert arrived last December, and after lifting the siege of Carrickfergus the brothers assembled a huge army which included many Ulster Irish. They invaded the midlands and reached Slane, burning and devastating the countryside as they went. This, combined with the poor harvests of recent years, is expected to result in famine and disease.

The two kings then advanced on Dublin expecting an easy victory. On 23 February they paused at Castleknock, just outside the city, hoping that, since they had no artillery, Richard de Burgh, the earl of Ulster, the commander-in-chief of the royal [English] forces who is also Robert's father-in-law, might deliver the capital to them. The earl had sought refuge in the city as the Scots forces advanced. But the mayor, Robert Nottingham, suspecting that the earl might indeed surrender the city, had bravely arrested him and imprisoned him in the castle two days earlier.

At this point the citizens of Dublin took matters into their own hands. They demolished a church, using its stones to extend the city wall to the north. They then set fire to Thomas Street, but the blaze got out of control and soon spread to the suburbs. The sight of the blazing buildings, the determination of the townspeople and the imprisonment of the earl made the Bruces realize that Dublin was impregnable. They therefore abandoned their plans to capture it and set off on a path of destruction through Limerick and Castleconnell, and back through Cashel to Kells.

The earl of Ulster was released by a royal [English] order on 10 May, but he has not been reinstated as the commander of the royal forces. Deeply humiliated, he has retired to his estates (→10/5/18).

Edward and barons strike a deal over new royal council

Nottinghamshire, 9 August 1318
A treaty was sealed at Leake today which is intended to heal the continuing breach between Edward II and many of his most powerful barons. The treaty provides for a standing council to advise the king and replace the courtiers whom some barons regard as "evil counsellors". The king also undertakes to summon a parliament, to observe the "Ordinances" of government agreed earlier in his reign [*see report on page 301*] and to pardon the earl of Lancaster, who has been his strongest opponent. It was on Lancaster's land that Edward's favourite, Piers Gaveston, was murdered six years ago.

However, the earl also seems to have lost by the treaty. Although he is the most powerful of the Marcher lords, and the man at the heart of the opposition to the court, he is not among the earls and bishops who will make up the formal council of royal advisers.

What Lancaster has gained is a pardon for himself and some 600 followers, plus assurances that the "Ordinances" will be observed. What the treaty also makes clear is the king's own weakness, obliging him to reach yet another deal with his barons in preparation for further Scottish battles (→5/1319).

Edward Bruce's Irish kingdom ends with his death in battle

Co Louth, 14 October 1318
Edward Bruce, the king of Ireland, has been killed in battle at the hill of Faughart, near Dundalk. A large army, drawn from the gentry and militia of Meath and Drogheda and led by John de Bermingham, had marched north determined to demolish the Scottish lion.

Robert Bruce had promised to join his brother, and Edward was expected to defer the battle; but he decided not to wait and to pit his 3,000 Scots and Irish allies against the larger force. However, the Scots experienced their first and last defeat, and the head of Edward Bruce was sent in triumph to Edward II of England. Yet it is hard to imagine how Bruce would have ruled Ireland had he lived, apart from giving the country a Scottish aristocracy instead of an English one.

If he had been a better strategist, subduing the major towns in a well-planned campaign and sparing the country his useless and destructive marches, Bruce might have established a secure base in Ulster from which he could have ruled Ireland. But even before he died famine and slaughter had exhausted the land, and his staunchest allies were disillusioned by the constant bloodletting and burning. In the end a chance victory restored Ireland to the Anglo-Irish lords and re-established the titular authority of England's king (→9/9/25).

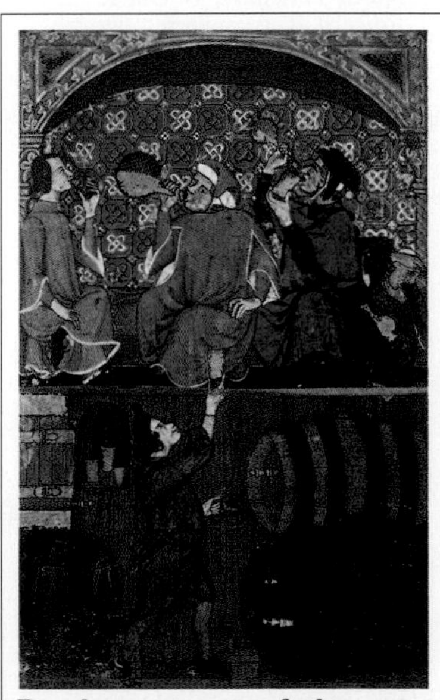

Drunkenness, one of the seven deadly sins: a 14th-century view.

1319 - 1324

England, May 1319. Thomas, the earl of Lancaster, demands the right to appoint the steward of the royal household (→ 1/1320).

France, September 1319. King Philip V demands that King Edward II of England pay homage in person for French land (→ 1/9/24).

England, January 1320. The earl of Lancaster refuses to attend parliament (→ 1/1321).

Scone, Tayside, 4 August 1320. Sir William de Soulis is jailed and four others are executed for complicity in a plot to kill King Robert (→ 7/1322).

Welsh Marches, January 1321. Hugh Despenser and his son, also Hugh, becoming increasingly unpopular, fortify their castles (→ 24/5).

West Yorkshire, 24 May 1321. The earl of Lancaster assembles the magnates of the north at Pontefract to agree a mutual defence pact (→ 19/8).

Gloucestershire, 20 December 1321. Edward II prepares an attack on the Marcher lords at Cirencester (→ early 1322).

Lancashire, July 1322. King Robert of Scotland, who broke his truce with Edward II in January, invades over the border as far south as Preston and Lancaster (→ 14/10).

Welsh Marches, early 1322. Edward II, after his success against the Marcher lords, recalls the Despensers from exile and heads north to confront the earl of Lancaster, whom he suspects of treason, and Robert of Scots (→ 16/3).

North Yorkshire, 14 Oct 1322. Edward II, his men retreating from a fruitless campaign, only just escapes a fierce Scots attack at Byland (→ 3/3/23).

Cambridgeshire, December 1322. Repair work is under way at Ely Cathedral, whose central tower collapsed on 12 February. It will be replaced by a timber-and-lead octagonal lantern (→ 1350).

York, 1324. Peace talks break down between Edward II and Robert of Scots, in spite of last year's 13-year truce (→ 5/3).

Fife, 5 March 1324. A son and heir, David, is born to King Robert (→ 1/2/27).

England, 1 September 1324. Gascony is threatened by French invasion; in return the French-born Queen Isabella's lands in England are seized by the Despensers (→ 26/4/26).

English forces abandon Berwick siege

Holding the high ground: a 20th-century view of the old castle at Berwick.

Northumberland, 20 Sept 1319
King Edward II's attempt to regain Berwick has ended in another military disaster. With Edward's army of 8,000 men dug in around Berwick's town and castle, King Robert of Scotland staged a bold diversionary attack which ultimately obliged the English to abandon their siege today.

Robert sent a Scottish force led by Thomas Randolph, the earl of Moray, and Sir James Douglas south to try to capture Queen Isabella at York. She escaped, but Archbishop Melton of York tried to intercept the Scots with local citizens and clergy. This inexperienced force was scattered at Myton-on-Swale, with English losses estimated at 3,000. When news of this reached Berwick northern earls decided to abandon the siege and defend their own homes (→ 6/4/20).

Scots urge pope to back their freedom

Arbroath, Tayside, 6 April 1320
Scottish nobles, under the guidance of King Robert, have written to Pope John XXII urging him to recognize the justice of the Scots' claims to independence. The document, drawn up by Bernard of Linton, the abbot of Arbroath, is a declaration of nationhood. It outlines the Scots' ancient roots, their 113 kings, their early conversion to Christianity and their determination to fight for freedom from England's interference. It states: "For so long as there shall but one hundred of us remain alive, we will never consent to subject ourselves to the dominion of the English. For it is not for glory, it is not riches, neither is it honour, but it is liberty alone that we fight and contend for, which no honest man will lose but with his life." King Edward II of England has also written to the pope saying that the Scots are his subjects, but the reality is that Robert rules Scotland (→ 4/8).

Pope John XXII (15th century).

Barons force king to banish his friends

London, 19 August 1321
King Edward II has today bowed to the will of parliament and banished two of his leading supporters, Hugh Despenser and his son, also Hugh. The younger Despenser especially had aroused the hostility of many barons, who claimed that he was using his closeness to the king to advance his landholdings in Wales and the Marches. With rebel armies controlling much of his capital, the king had little choice but to comply when the earl of Pembroke urged him to save his throne by agreeing to the banishment of the Despensers. They are to be exiled as "evil counsellors", and in return the barons are to drop some of their more stringent demands for a curb on royal power. Edward has also agreed to issue pardons to the earl of Lancaster and 500 of his supporters for their action in opposing the king and the Despensers in clashes earlier this year (→ 10/1321).

Irish pilgrim friars struck by painted chamber at Westminster

Ireland, c.1324
Two friars who returned last year from pilgrimage to the Holy Land have set about writing an account of the wonders that they saw on their journey, among which they include the marvellous painted chamber of the English royal palace of Westminster. The two friars, Simon FitzSimon and Hugh "the Illuminator", visited Westminster Abbey, beside which, they say, "stood the celebrated palace of the kings of England, in which is that famous chamber on whose walls all the warlike stories of the whole Bible are painted with wonderful skill and explained by a complete series of texts, accurately written in French, to the great admiration of the beholder and with the greatest royal magnificence".

The chamber, which includes the king's bed, was badly damaged by fire in 1263, and the paintings began as part of the redecoration. They include Old Testament war scenes of King Hezekiah and the destruction of Sennacherib and of Nebuchadnezzar and Jehoiachin.

Civil war looms as Edward besieges castle

Besieged by King Edward II: a 20th-century aspect of Leeds Castle, in Kent.

Leeds Castle, Kent, October 1321
The long-running power struggle between King Edward II and his barons is now closer than ever to civil war. Tension has been heightened by a clash involving a former steward of the royal household, Bartholomew, Lord Badlesmere. Now constable of Leeds Castle, he has been a supporter of the earl of Lancaster, the most powerful of the king's noble opponents. Badlesmere became embroiled in a confrontation with the king when, in his absence, his wife refused Queen Isabella admission to Leeds Castle.

In a fight between Isabella's servants and the armed defenders of the castle, several of the queen's servants were killed. Badlesmere is not a leading member of the peerage, but the insult to the queen gave the king a pretext for raising an army to combat the power of the barons. Many earls backed the king, and together they mustered a force to besiege the castle.

Some Marcher lords rallied to Badlesmere's side and assembled an army to challenge the royalist forces, but they had only reached Kingston Upon Thames when they heard that Leeds Castle had fallen to the king. Any possibility of a continuing advance to challenge the king's army was scotched by the opposition of the earl of Lancaster. He has withdrawn to the north, where he plans to call a "counter-parliament" next month (→20/12).

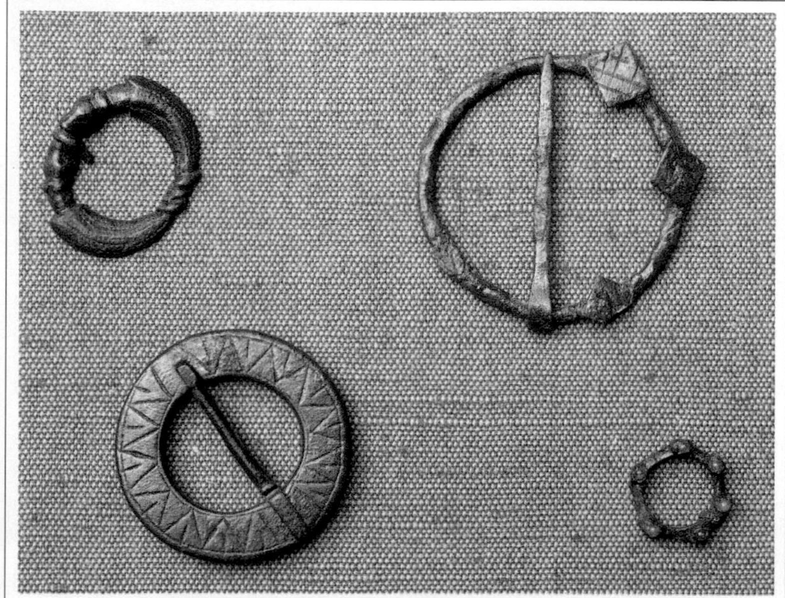
Contemporary design: four finely decorated ring-brooches from Norfolk.

Rebel leader taken by royalist forces

North Yorkshire, 16 March 1322
The end of the civil war is in sight with the defeat and capture of the leader of the anti-royalist forces, the earl of Lancaster, today. The earl had retreated northwards with only the remnants of his army, probably less than 700 men, after the Marcher lords had capitulated to Edward earlier this year. He had reached Boroughbridge and may have been trying to reach Scotland when he was intercepted by forces led by a veteran of the Scottish wars, Sir Andrew Harclay,.

Before the battle Lancaster tried both bribery and argument to get Harclay to switch sides, but Harclay was not tempted. To add to Lancaster's troubles Harclay's army was bigger and well-trained, while many of his own men deserted during the night. Lancaster split his forces in two, but to no avail. His ally the earl of Hereford was killed, and, surrounded and outnumbered, Lancaster himself surrendered. He was taken to York.

Without Lancaster it is difficult to see how the barons' revolt can continue. Given his apparent willingness to link with King Robert of Scotland and the king's desire for revenge over Lancaster's role in the murder of his favourite courtier Piers Gaveston ten years ago, it seems likely that Lancaster will lose his head for treason (→21/9/25).

Earl loses favour – and his head

Carlisle, 3 March 1323
Sir Andrew Harclay, the earl of Carlisle and a royal hero at last year's Battle of Boroughbridge, was today hanged, drawn and quartered for treason after making a secret visit to King Robert of Scotland to negotiate a peace treaty without King Edward II's knowledge. Under its terms Bruce agreed not to invade England, to pay 40,000 marks in return for Edward's renunciation of his claim to the Scottish throne and to allow Edward to choose a wife for Bruce's heir. The treaty could hardly have been more favourable, but the king was furious at not being told in advance (→1324).

Shocking witchcraft trial grips Ireland

Co Kilkenny, 2 July 1324
In a sensational trial which has attracted huge interest, Dame Alice Kyteler and ten of her associates have been found guilty of heresy. Dame Alice is a rich woman from an Anglo-Norman family who has added to her wealth by marrying four husbands. She and a son by her first marriage, William Outlaw, are disliked intensely by her stepchildren, who have claimed that Dame Alice killed some of their fathers by witchcraft and so infatuated others that they gave her all their money and disinherited their rightful heirs. They also accused Dame Alice of attempting to murder her present husband, Sir John le Poer, by administering powders which destroyed his nails and left him in a wasted condition and without hair on his body.

A secret art: two witches at their pot.

Rumours abound that sackfuls of horrible objects have been found by Dame Alice's maid and sent to Bishop Richard Leatherhead for examination, and she and her associates have been accused of demon worship and of boiling evil substances in the skull of a decapitated burglar. Her private demon is said to be a cat or a Negro who drinks the blood of cocks. The associates have been burnt alive or excommunicated, but Dame Alice has escaped to England (→13/11/1441).

1325 - 1327

Co Clare, 9 September 1325. Armed retainers of Maurice fitz Thomas FitzGerald, the earl of Desmond, seize Bunratty Castle (→ 12/7/27).

France, 21 September 1325. Queen Isabella, the estranged wife of Edward II of England and lover of Roger Mortimer, an old enemy of his, allies herself with enemies of the king (→ 25/8/26).

Ireland, c.1325. *The Book of Kildare* – a collection of poems and prayers – is completed (→ 1373).

France, 26 April 1326. The Franco/Scottish alliance is renewed by the Treaty of Corbeil (→ 6/6/29).

France, 25 August 1326. Queen Isabella of England betrothes Edward, the heir to the English throne, to Philippa, the daughter of the count of Hainault. She then gathers an army, led by John, the count's brother, and Roger Mortimer, to invade England (→ 9/1326).

Oxford, 1326. Archdeacon Adam de Brome of Stowe founds Oriel college (→ 1340).

Westminster, 1 February 1327. Edward III is crowned after the deposition of his father, Edward II. The real power and wealth pass to his mother, Queen Isabella (→ 4/1327).

Northumberland, 1 Feb 1327. As Edward III is crowned, King Robert of Scots attacks Norham Castle (→ 8/1327).

Gloucester, April 1327. Queen Isabella and Adam Orleton, the bishop of Hereford, have the former King Edward II kidnapped and imprisoned in Berkeley Castle (→ 22/9).

Co Antrim, 12 July 1327. King Robert of Scots, who landed at Easter, forces Ireland's English government to agree to a humiliating truce (→ 11/1327).

Northumberland, August 1327. Following Edward III's narrow escape from the Scots at Stanhope, Robert again attacks Norham Castle, planning to annex the county (→ 26/10).

Grampian, 26 October 1327. Queen Elizabeth, Robert's wife, dies at Cullen (→ 17/3/28).

Gloucester, 21 December 1327. The body of the murdered Edward II is buried in the abbey (→ 30/1/28).

Scotland, 1327. Prosperity returns slowly; wool exports have reached a record high of 5,000 sacks (→ 1407).

English queen challenges kingdom

Queen Isabella flees to France.

Paris, September 1326

Queen Isabella of England has signalled her intention to return home and declare war on the court favourite, Hugh Despenser. She has been in Paris since last year and is living openly with her lover Roger Mortimer, a lord from Wigmore in the Marches. She has now become the focus of a powerful opposition to her husband, which includes leading bishops and peers.

The queen, the sister of King Charles IV of France, was sent here as an ambassador to sort out a rapidly escalating dispute over English lands in France and homage due to the French king from Edward II. She has long been an enemy of Despenser, blaming his close, possibly homosexual, relationship with Edward for her own estrangement from him. "Someone has come between my husband and myself," she has said. "I shall assume the robes of widowhood and mourning until I am revenged."

Despenser and his father were banished by the king under baronial pressure in 1321 but allowed to return after the Battle of Boroughbridge in 1322. When a French war looked likely Isabella's estates were seized, and Despenser's wife was put in charge of them – another factor in their enmity. With the queen is 13-year-old Edward, the heir to the throne (→ 15/10).

Public support grows for Isabella as king and Despenser flee

London, 15 October 1326

Queen Isabella, the estranged wife of the king, has returned to England with an army of mercenaries, intent on overturning the influence of Edward II's principal courtier, Hugh Despenser. Her mercenary force is backed by several bishops and barons who have long opposed Despenser's influence on the king; these include the earl of Leicester, the earl marshal, as well as Isabella's lover, the formidable Roger Mortimer of Wigmore.

Within days of the queen's arrival at Orwell, in Suffolk, there was a groundswell of public support for her. Sailors in the royal fleet at Portsmouth mutinied, and rioting has broken out here in the capital as citizens rebel against the king. An orgy of murder, rioting and looting is under way, with suspected royal supporters receiving brutal treatment. The bishop of Exeter, Walter Stapledon, had been put in charge of London by the king – and paid the price of loyalty today: he was executed with a butcher's knife [*see report below*].

The archbishop of Canterbury, Walter Reynolds, escaped a similar fate by commandeering horses belonging to the elderly bishop of Rochester (who escaped on foot). Edward and Despenser are heading for Caerphilly to organize a defence of their kingdom. Isabella is not far behind. She is now at Gloucester assembling her army (→ 24/11).

Isabella lands with her supporters.

Mob murder shows greater political power of English capital

London's Bankside: reconstruction.

London, 15 October 1326

The growing political power of London was bloodily apparent today when a howling crowd besieged the Tower and hacked off the head of Walter Stapledon, the bishop of Exeter, with a butcher's knife. The murder of the bishop – who had been put in charge of the city by Edward II – demonstrates the unwillingness of Londoners to tolerate the slightest taint of what they perceive as royal tyranny.

London is by far the kingdom's principal city. Its population is vast – perhaps as many as 80,000 – and it plays host to every great English institution, such as parliament and the law courts. Its prosperity boosted by the boom in the woollen trade, London is now larger than Rome, Bruges and many other top European cities; only Paris and Venice are bigger.

Its significance continues to increase, and immigrants from all ranks of society inevitably go there. Whether they are nobles investing in luxurious town houses, or peasants seeking fortunes that could never be found in the country, all see it as the place to be (→ 10/1382).

Edward's favourite suffers a gruesome death before queen

The execution of Hugh Despenser.

Hereford, 24 November 1326
Hugh Despenser, the close friend and adviser of King Edward II, was today executed in a most grisly manner before the woman who had brought his downfall – Isabella, the estranged wife of the king.

Despenser's father, the earl of Winchester, was first to be captured by Isabella's army. A "trial" in Bristol last month ordered that he should be "drawn for treason, hanged for robbery, beheaded for misdeeds against the church". His son was captured with the king at Neath Abbey on 16 November after bad weather thwarted attempts to escape by sea to Ireland. Edward has been taken to Kenilworth.

Isabella wanted Despenser executed in London, but he had refused food since his capture and was said to be very weak. On the approach to Hereford he was stripped and crowned with nettles. Trumpets blared and the crowd made a tremendous din as four horses drew him to a 15-metre (50-foot)-high gallows. A fire was lit in front of him, and then his genitals were cut off – because of his allegedly "unnatural practices with the king" – before he was disembowelled and forced to watch his own entrails being burnt. Then his head was cut off and the rest of his body was quartered (→ 24/1/27).

English king forced to resign throne

Westminster, 24 January 1327
To cries from his people of "Let it be done!" Edward II, the king of England, was deprived of his crown here today. The king himself had no say in the matter: he is being held prisoner by his wife and her lover at Kenilworth Castle in Warwickshire.

Isabella and Roger Mortimer, the Marcher lord who is her lover, had plotted Edward's fall long before they returned to England last October at the head of a mercenary army to overthrow the Despensers. Isabella and Mortimer believe it to be essential that any move against the king should appear wholly legal and that the reputation of the crown should not suffer.

The king's son, Prince Edward, had already been "elected" as "guardian" at a meeting in Bristol attended by several barons and knights and the bishop of Bristol. The prince's seal was used to summon parliament – the plotters alleging that the king was out of the kingdom. Although no official record has been kept of this assembly, well-informed sources have revealed that representatives met on 7 January and that members of the London mob were allowed to attend – watched throughout by men loyal to Roger Mortimer. Few doubt that the king has been kept deliberately from the proceedings lest he should challenge their legality; technically, he would have the right to overturn any verdict, although in reality he is powerless and with little choice but to abdicate in favour of his son (→ 1/2).

King Edward II: now deposed.

Queen linked to English king's cruel death

The sunny cell in Berkeley Castle where Edward II met his horrific end.

Gloucestershire, 22 Sept 1327
Edward II, the deposed king, was tortured to death in a Gloucestershire castle tonight – almost certainly at the behest of his wife, Isabella. Mystery surrounds Edward's movements since his arrest and incarceration early this year – some reports speak of attempted rescues by his former supporters – but it is known that he was brought to Berkeley Castle, overlooking the Bristol Channel, in July.

Reports suggest that the former king, aged 43, was well treated until a few days ago when his murderers – apparently misunderstanding a letter from Adam Orleton, the bishop of Hereford – locked Edward in a secure chamber and began systematic torture. His horrific end came tonight when cushions were held over his head and a plumber's soldering iron was thrust into his bowels. The former king's cries were reputedly heard in both the castle and the town of Berkeley. The identity of Edward's killers remains a mystery, although the names of both Sir John Mautravers and Sir Thomas Gurney are being mentioned (→ 21/12).

Mortimer seeks to restore Irish peace

Ireland, November 1327
The influence of Roger Mortimer, the powerful Marcher lord and lover of Queen Isabella of England, is beginning to make itself felt in Ireland at a time when disturbances in Munster are increasing.

Mortimer's Irish connections have predisposed him to take a keen interest in affairs here. He was appointed king's lieutenant in Ireland in 1316, with the responsibility of organizing Anglo-Irish resistance to Edward Bruce, and in 1318 he became justiciar [king's chief deputy] in the island. In addition to his two periods of office here, he has spent time in Co Meath where his wife owned considerable property. Mortimer now faces a difficult task: to solve the continuing conflicts between the Anglo-Irish lords while ensuring that their leaders respect his authority and English laws are enforced.

The new English government has moved swiftly to increase its influence over the development of Irish affairs. The 15-year-old earl of Ulster has been given custody of his lands, and both he and his powerful uncle, Edmund, have been granted dispensations from the pope to encourage them to marry Englishwomen (→ 3/3/31).

1328 - 1332

York, 30 January 1328. Edward III marries Philippa of Hainault (→ 10/1328).

France, 25 May 1328. Simon de Meopham is consecrated at Avignon as archbishop of Canterbury after the death last year of Archbishop Walter Reynolds (→ 20/12/49).

Northumberland, 12 July 1328. Four-year-old David, the son and heir of King Robert of Scotland, is married to Joan, Edward III's seven-year-old sister, at Berwick (→ 7/6/29).

England, October 1328. Roger Mortimer is made earl of March (→ 19/3/30).

Amiens, France, 6 June 1329. Edward III of England pays homage to Philip VI for Aquitaine (→ 30/4/31).

France, 13 June 1329. Pope John XXII permits King David II of Scotland the privileges of coronation and unction. Last year he lifted the sentence of excommunication imposed in 1306 on David's father Robert (→ 25/8/30).

Berwick-Upon-Tweed, 1329. Augustinian friars set up their first Scottish friary (→ 1338).

England, 19 March 1330. Isabella has Edmund of Kent executed. Although loyal to her over the deposition of his brother Edward II, he was too close to Edward III (→ 19/10).

Oxfordshire, 15 June 1330. Queen Philippa gives birth to Edward, the heir to the throne, at Woodstock (→ 3/1337).

Spain, 25 August 1330. Sir James Douglas, a loyal supporter of the late King Robert of Scots, is killed while on a crusade; he had Robert's heart with him (→ 24/11/31).

London, 29 November 1330. Despite Isabella's pleas for clemency, Roger Mortimer, the earl of March, is hanged and drawn at Tyburn (→ 3/1340).

France, 30 April 1331. Edward III of England travels in disguise to discuss peace terms with Philip VI (→ 5/1334).

Tayside, 24 November 1331. King David II is crowned at Scone (→ 11/8/32).

Tayside, 24 September 1332. Edward Balliol is crowned king of Scotland at Scone after defeating the earl of Mar at Dupplin Moor (→ 3/1333).

Co Donegal, November 1332. William de Burgh, the earl of Ulster, starves Walter de Burgh to death at Greencastle (→ 3/5/36).

Independent Scotland recognized

Robert grants Edinburgh a charter.

Edinburgh, 17 March 1328
Scotland has won its independence after a war that has lasted for most of the last 32 years. Peace terms have been hammered out in Edinburgh, and the signing of the treaty effectively means that the Scots have won and the English have lost.

Political instability within England and pressure from France and the pope, plus relentless Scottish raids over the border, have forced Edward III to agree that Robert "the Bruce" is king of Scotland and not his vassel. The English king has renounced forever any claim to feudal superiority. With this concession, which alone makes Scotland independent, all the other major demands have also been met. In future the English will respect Scotland's alliance with France, and the two countries are to be allies. To cement the treaty a marriage is to take place between Edward's sister, aged seven, and Robert's son, aged four.

Robert is now seriously ill with leprosy, but he has lived to see his life's work completed. The irony is that he and the earls who fought so hard for Scots freedom shared the same ancestry as Edward and his barons. In fact they are all Normans, with both Edward and Robert tracing their ancestries to villages in Normandy that lie just a few miles apart (→ 7/6/29).

Robert, saviour of Scotland, is dead

Strathclyde, 7 June 1329
King Robert has died, and the whole of Scotland is in mourning for the man who brought freedom to the nation. He died at his favourite residence of Cardross on the north shore of the Clyde.

Robert, who was 55, had been seriously ill for two years and appears to have known that he was dying. He had just completed a painful pilgrimage to the shrine of St Ninian at Whithorn in Galloway. On his deathbed he told his family of his wish to go on crusade. The late king's embalmed heart will be taken to the Holy Land while his body is buried at Dunfermline.

Already Robert's life is the stuff of legend. One of the most popular tells how, as a fugitive in the Western Isles, he drew inspiration to press on with the war against Edward I from a spider which tried eight times to complete its web before succeeding. There are some who will remember Robert as a bloody man who murdered John Comyn in Dumfries, put to death the de Soulis conspirators and terrorized the north of England. But to most Scots he is the man who saved them from bondage to England, and he will be associated for ever with the great victory at Bannockburn in 1314. Robert is succeeded by his five-year-old son, who becomes David II (→ 13/6/29).

Church ponders rules for sex and wedlock

Canterbury, 1329
In a frontal attack on "clandestine" marriages, currently estimated at one in four, Simon Meopham, the archbishop of Canterbury, has ordered the calling of banns for three consecutive weeks before all weddings. By making the process more public, he hopes to reduce disputes over dowries and legacies.

Recent church edicts say that marital sex is not as sinful as it was previously thought to be, but many rules are still insisted on. Some only allow sex for procreation, or to avoid worse sins such as unfaithfulness or masturbation. The usual yardstick is the intent: pleasure as the motive for sex is sinful, but as the by-product it is condoned by the church. Doctors also uphold sexual pleasure for health reasons.

All churchmen ban sex on Sundays; some also on Wednesdays, Fridays and Saturdays. One treatise recommends that a woman lie absolutely still during intercourse and not let her thoughts wander in case, in thinking about cows, she conceive a cow-like child. Kissing and fondling are only allowed as preludes to intercourse.

Despite the restrictions, all agree that sex is essential to marriage. Some English courts employ "honest women" to test a husband's potency. If all their skills fail, a divorce will be granted (→ (1/1353).

With the church's backing: a bishop ceremonially blesses the marriage bed.

English king seizes queen mother's lover

Bedroom battle: a romanticized view of Roger Mortimer's bloody arrest.

Nottingham, 19 October 1330
Roger Mortimer, the earl of March and the queen mother's lover, is being rushed to London tonight to face trial and certain execution for his "notorious" crimes. It was a yeoman of the household, William Montagu, who engineered the earl's downfall, persuading both King Edward III and Pope John XXII at Avignon that it was time to attack, before Mortimer himself struck at the king and the establishment. A meeting of the great council here at Nottingham presented the necessary opportunity.

Montagu was told of a secret passageway into the castle where Mortimer and Queen Isabella were staying. Joined by the king, Montagu and other conspirators struck down two knights who were guarding the queen and her lover and dragged Mortimer away to face his fate, despite the protests of the screaming Isabella (→29/11).

Irish to be subject to laws of England

Ireland, 3 March 1331
Ordinances have been passed by the Westminster parliament declaring that all free Irishmen are to be subject to English law. They also revoke all grants made when the late Roger Mortimer, the earl of March, was in charge of Irish affairs.

Since Mortimer's fall last year the English authorities have sought to reassert their authority, and the new ordinances place a limited date on the power of the justiciar [the king's chief deputy, or law officer] to pardon offences. They also entrust the enforcement of the legislation to new Irish ministers.

All this will have serious implications for those Anglo-Irishmen who accepted Mortimer's patronage. The changes are taking place in the shadow of King Edward III of England's planned visit to Dublin in the autumn of next year. His proposed expedition is thought to be favoured by William de Burgh, the earl of Ulster, who is anxious to gain the upper hand in his tussles with his Anglo-Irish competitors and has also been blessed by the pope. But the Irish lords regard it with foreboding (→11/1332).

Scots defeated by a mercenary army backed by England

Tayside, 11 August 1332
Scotland has been shocked by the surprise defeat of the Scottish army on Dupplin Moor at the hands of Edward Balliol, the son of the deposed King John, and an expeditionary force of adventurers and mercenaries. Balliol, who has been living in England for the last eight years, drew support from men disinherited by the late King Robert. With the covert help of King Edward III of England, he set sail from Ravenspur in Yorkshire with an army of 1,500 men. He landed at Kinghorn in Fife five days ago and set out towards Perth.

With Scotland's king, David II, still a child, the Scottish forces were commanded by Donald, the earl of Mar. He was elected guardian only nine days ago following the death of the earl of Moray. Mar occupied the high ground on the north of the river Earn, but his forces were over-confident. This morning Mar woke up to discover that Balliol had forded the river and taken up a good defensive position. A shambolic Scottish attack and the effect of the English archers led to confusion, panic and heavy losses among the Scots. Mar was among those killed (→24/9).

Skilful artists at work in Fenlands

East Anglia, 1330
Artists of exceptional skill are producing beautifully illustrated manuscripts in the relative obscurity of the Fenlands. They are being hired by monasteries at places such as Peterborough and Ormesby, or by wealthy families such as the St Omers of Norfolk, to decorate holy books. Most of these works are psalters [copies of the Book of Psalms]. The artists fill the borders around the text with grotesque creatures intertwined with biblical scenes.

The fact that these are religious books does not stop the illustrators having some fun. On a typical page, such as one from the St Omer Psalter, one can see rabbits basking in the sun, a couple lying naked, and even a game of piggyback (→c.1410).

Musicians and monarchs: an illuminated initial from the St Omer Psalter.

Brewing becomes a woman's business

England, c.1330
Ale is now the most commonly consumed liquid in the country, and home brewing for commercial purposes is an everyday activity. In many cases the brewers are women, working from their homes while their menfolk work in the fields. Women also make up a large proportion of the vendors of ale, often supervising a corporate household activity with other family members helping out when necessary. The work of the ale-wives tends to be sporadic and is seen as a way of supplementing the annual family income. In towns ale is consumed at taverns; elsewhere brewing and drinking are more likely to take place in people's homes.

1333 - 1338

Northumberland, March 1333. Edward Balliol, forced to flee by nobles loyal to King David II, leads an English army to besiege Berwick (→ 29/7).

France, May 1334. David Bruce, the deposed king of Scotland, is welcomed by King Philip VI (→ 8/1337).

Northumberland, summer 1334. The English are driven back at Berwick after a Scottish offensive (→ 25/11).

Borders, 25 November 1334. After the English retreat in the summer, Edward III invades, taking Roxburgh (→ 18/8/35).

Oxford, 1335. William Heytesbury, a fellow of Merton college, publishes *Rules for Solving Sophisms*, developing his mean speed theorem – the ratio of distance and time (→ 1349).

Perth, 18 August 1335. The Scots accept English terms and recognize Edward Balliol as king; Balliol has paid homage to Edward III of England and declared him overlord of Scotland (→ 30/11).

England, March 1337. The king's eldest son, Edward, created earl of Chester in 1334, is made duke of Cornwall; six new earls are also created – of Huntingdon, Northampton, Suffolk, Derby, Salisbury and Gloucester (→ 12/5/43).

England, August 1337. Edward III declares war on France after Philip VI confiscates Aquitaine (→ 7/10).

France, 10 November 1337. England and France are at war after English troops sack Cadzand (→ 4/1338).

Scotland, 1338. Sir Andrew Murray, the guardian of Scotland, who took Bothwell Castle last year, dies; his successor is Robert "the Stewart", the heir to the throne (→ 17/8).

Ireland, 3 March 1338. King Enri O'Neill of Tyrone is allowed to hold much of Ulster during the minority of Elizabeth, the heiress of the late earl of Ulster, William de Burgh, who was murdered in 1333 (→ 2/7/41).

England/France, April 1338. Fighting continues in Gascony, despite last year's truce; the French raid the Isle of Wight and Portsmouth (→ 20/9/39).

Perth, 17 August 1338. The last English stronghold north of the Forth surrenders to the Scots; the surrounding area is wasted (→ 16/4/41).

Scotland comes under English control

Scotland, 29 July 1333
Scotland is under English rule. With the Scottish army routed by Edward III of England's forces at Halidon Hill ten days ago, and many noblemen killed, Edward Balliol is in control north of the border in the name of the king of England.

Balliol, the son of King John who was deposed in 1296, was crowned at Scone last September after his defeat of the Scottish army at Dupplin Moor. Having proclaimed the overlordship of Edward III he found himself challenged by a number of Scottish lords who killed his brother Henry and forced Edward himself to flee to Carlisle.

Since March, Edward Balliol had been laying siege to Berwick, while the Scots forces had regrouped under Sir Archibald Douglas. But Edward III's army arrived from England in time to stop the Scots raising the siege. On 19 July Sir Archibald Douglas's army was obliged to attack the English from an inferior position at Halidon Hill, outside Berwick.

Edward III relied on his archers, who hit many of the Scots before they could get to close quarters. A bloody battle ended in catastrophe for the Scots, with heavy casualties. The few survivors were hounded for miles; prisoners were summarily executed (→ 25/11/34).

King Edward III takes Berwick, from the chronicles of Jean Froissart, c.1400.

Scots fight back against English rule

Grampian, 30 November 1335
David, the earl of Atholl, has been killed and his army destroyed at Culbean, in Mar, in the latest outbreak against English rule in Scotland. A mere three months ago many leading Scottish nobles accepted the overlordship of Edward III of England at Perth, but Sir Andrew Murray was in an English prison at the time.

Once released, Murray broke off peace talks with the English and hurried north to relieve his wife, Christian Bruce, who was holding Kildrummy Castle against Atholl. The earl was the principal supporter of Edward Balliol, the English king's nominee as Scottish monarch. His death and the defeat of his army by Murray throw Scotland's future into doubt (→ 1338).

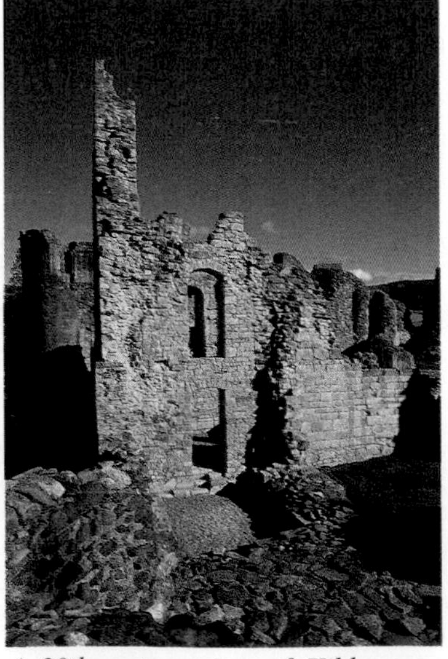
A 20th-century view of Kildrummy Castle, defended against Atholl.

English population and poverty grow

England, c.1336
While the severe harvest failures and livestock epidemics of some 20 years ago are fading in public memory, the country's peasants are still finding life hard. Their hunger for land is being met by landlords concerned with the high level of wages and anxious to cut back. But more often than not it is the poorest, least productive land that is being sold off. Grain prices, in fact, are some 20 per cent lower than they were in the 1280s, and the wheat yield is just below four times the seed sown. The number of poor people in villages is a sign of the times. England's population, which has been expanding rapidly, is probably about seven million (→ 1346).

English king lays claim to French throne

London, 7 October 1337
The 25-year-old Edward III of England has given a new twist to the already strained relations with his distant cousin, Philip VI of France, by claiming the French crown for himself.

Edward is the son of Isabella, the sister of Charles IV of France. When Charles died his first cousin, Philip, succeeded, and Edward was not even considered. But now, in a letter to Duke John of Brabant, his ally in the Low Countries, Edward accuses the French of intransigence and is seeking John's help in a fight for the French crown.

The quarrel between the two kings stems from Edward's position as duke of Gascony. Last May Philip, claiming that Edward was giving asylum to his enemies, sent in an army and annnexed the duchy for himself (→ 10/11).

Edward III: the king as an old man.

England extends plans for Irish reform

Dublin, 3 May 1336
In a significant move which indicates his intention of extending his control in Ireland, King Edward III of England has sent a set of "articles" to Dublin designed "for the reform of the state of Ireland and the direction of his affairs there and the punishment of malefactors and delinquents" for the Irish parliament to implement.

These ordinances are thought to be intended for use within Dublin Castle. Their conventional, somewhat bureaucratic outlook is seen to reflect the contribution of Ireland's treasurer, John Ellerker – who has considerable influence with the king.

The export of corn from Ireland is to be controlled. Debts are to be rigorously collected, and the leasing of the king's demesnes is to be investigated, as is the suspected chicanery over the allocation of the royal alms (→ 3/3/38).

Monastic life covers a multitude of sins behind the closed doors of monasteries

Exeter, Devon, 1338
An alarming decline in standards of monastic life has been revealed by a series of visitations – official inspections by bishops – to various religious establishments in England. Buildings in a state of disrepair, economic inefficiency, lax morals and in some cases a drift from the true vocation of monasticism paint a gloomy picture of modern life which is far from the Christian ideal.

Fifteen years ago the registrar for Exeter, John de Stapleton, reported that he had found the prior of Bodmin to be aged, blind, infirm and weak in the head. At Hartland Abbey neglect had the dormitory in a state of collapse, the lavatory out of order, the lantern leaking, and pigs rooting around in the area enclosed by the cloisters. These were two of many similar examples.

Monks spy on their brothers at play.

John de Grandison, de Stapleton's present-day successor, finds little to suggest that things have altered. At Tavistock, five years ago, the abbot was removed from office for waste and misconduct. John Courteney was appointed in his place, but he, too, has proved to be disastrous, living extravagantly at the expense of his monks and the abbey fabric.

A lunatic prior has left St James in ruins; St Michael's Mount is in serious debt; and at Totnes a weak and worldly prior has allowed his relations to live in the priory with their hawks, hounds and horses. The prior of Launceston, despite repeated warnings for absence and immorality, has been sacked. But although he is a sick man, the prior and his friends have fought with the administrators and repossessed the building. Scandal still overshadows Merton Abbey, distressing locals for more than nine years.

All this damages the concept of monastic life, bringing it into disrepute. Bishops believe that this decline must be halted if monasticism is not to lose its meaning (→ 1383).

Bloody combat: a crowded scene from an English manuscript bible of c.1320-30 ["the Holkham Bible"] which retells the history of mankind, from the Creation to the Last Judgement, in 231 miniature illustrations.

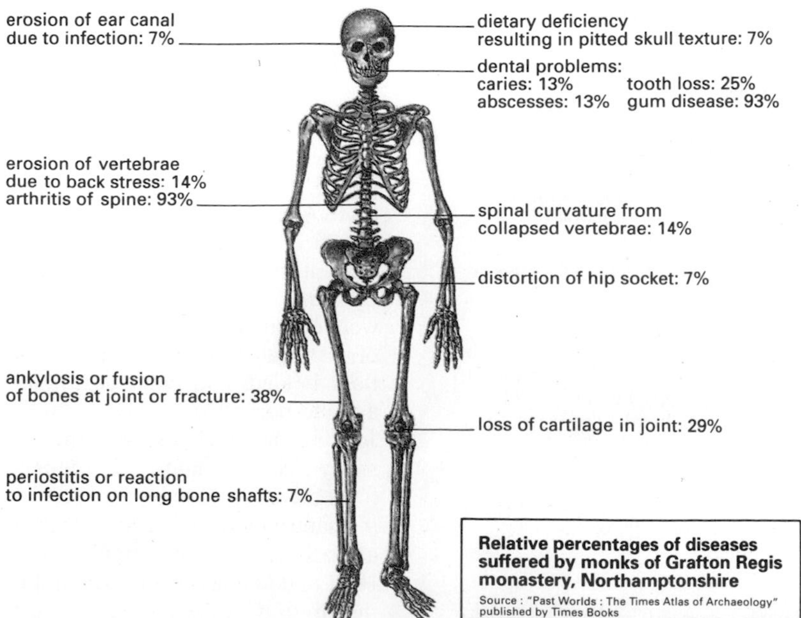

Relative percentages of diseases suffered by monks of Grafton Regis monastery, Northamptonshire
Source : "Past Worlds : The Times Atlas of Archaeology" published by Times Books

1339 - 1345

Flanders, October 1339. In order to raise money for the war in France, Edward III of England offers the crown to the archbishop of Trier as surety for £3,000 (→ 1340).

Flanders, 1340. David II Bruce, the exiled king of Scotland, joins Philip VI of France in a campaign against the English. The Anglo-French war has taken much pressure off the Scots (→ 26/1).

Low Countries, 26 Jan 1340. Edward III of England formally assumes at Ghent the arms and title of king of France, much to the rage of Philip VI of France (→ 24/6).

England, March 1340. Edward III returns from France to raise more money for the war and solve problems of home government; he agrees to the formation of a council to rule the country in his absence (→ 30/11).

England, 30 November 1340. Edward III, bankrupt and in a truce agreement with France for one year, returns and blames his bankruptcy on the treasurer and chancellor. The earls of Derby and Salisbury are held in Brussels as hostages for Edward's debts.→

Oxford, 1340. Queen's college is founded by the clerk Robert de Eglesfield, confessor to Queen Philippa (→ 1352).

Edinburgh, 16 April 1341. The Scots regain the castle from the English (→ 10/4/42).

Ireland, 27 July 1341. An ordinance excludes everyone from royal office except English-born clergy (→ 1345).

Scotland, 10 April 1342. After David II's return Roxburgh, Stirling and other strongholds surrender (→ 6/10/46).

France, 19 January 1343. A three-year truce is signed between England and France at Malestroit (→ 6/1345).

Westminster, 12 May 1343. Edward, the king's son, is invested as prince of Wales (→ 12/7/46).

England, March 1344. New gold coins are issued (→ 1346).

France, June 1345. After the execution of leading Bretons by Philip VI, and a French threat to Flanders, Edward III of England breaks the truce made last summer (→ 26/7/46).

Co Kildare, 1345. The FitzGeralds of Desmond rebel unsuccessfully against the English justiciar (→ 17/10/51).

English terror tactics hit French hard

France, 20 September 1339
Edward III of England and his German and Flemish allies, pursuing Edward's claim to the French crown, have unleashed a campaign of wholesale plunder in northern France, destroying homes, crops and cattle. Over a distance of some 15 miles (24 km)the air is thick with the pall of smoke. A French cardinal, Bertrand de Montfaucon, climbed a high tower to gaze on a scene of such devastation that he collapsed from grief and shock.

The city of Cambrai, however, has been heavily fortified by King Philip VI of France and has so far withstood the siege mounted by Edward's allies. With autumn on the way and the weather deteriorating, a frontal assault on the city is ruled out; the English hope to win by starvation.

For Edward, a more urgent problem is the wavering loyalty of his ally from the Low Countries, Duke John of Brabant. Edward still owes most of the £60,000 promised when the duke joined his side and has told John that he will pay the balance in three instalments of Florentine florins. He has named the archbishop of Canterbury and a motley collection of bishops and earls as guarantors. But John fears that Edward will abandon him and return home – so he keeps in touch with Philip (→ 10/1339).

English soldiers attack a fortress.

How England's king raised the money for the war in France

A gold coin of King Edward.

London, 30 November 1340
In a desperate attempt to raise money for his war with France, Edward III has given his allies – and creditors – in the Low Countries the slip and arrived secretly in London to vent his anger on the tax collectors and merchants whom he blames for his lack of funds.

He began the war three years ago with an elaborate scheme for a royal monopoly on the export of wool, which he believed would raise some £200,000 in the first year. But the wool sold for less than expected, and he had to go back to the Florentine bankers for further loans. They demanded as security future consignments of wool.

Still short of funds, Edward gave orders that all fees and pensions in England must be suspended except for people with no other sources of income. By now the king's war debts have mounted to £300,000 for a military campaign that has so far achieved nothing. Edward may succeed in squeezing more cash out of his people, but tax evasion is now widespread (→ 3/1348).

Lord mayor builds palatial manor house from his wool riches

Penshurst, Kent, 1340
Sir John de Pulteney, a draper and merchant and four times the lord mayor of London, has built here a manor house richer than many a palace. The hall is 18.6 metres long by 13.6 metres wide (62 by 39 feet), dignified by four deep bays. Underneath its magnificent roof of crown-post and collar-beams resting on wooden caryatids are wall paintings of men-at-arms and crusaders. The floor is tiled, and entry is through a grand porch two storeys high. Sir John is the wealthiest of London's newly rich merchants. With money from the wool trade he has founded a chantry at St Paul's Cathedral and a Carmelite friary in Coventry. His London house is the grandest in the city.

The great hall at Penshurst Place, with its superb hammerbeam roof.

English forces step up French wars

Men's fashions can reveal (nearly) all

London, c.1340
Fashionable men's clothing can rarely have been more revealing than it is today. Jackets are so short that men are exposing not only the lines of their thighs but also their genitals and buttocks. Ironically, while clothes are getting tighter they are also far more extravagant in their use of material, with flowing sleeves and "castellated" edges. The greatest waste is in footwear. Pointed shoes have become so exaggerated, sometimes extending half a metre (2 feet) beyond the toes, that they are turned up like ram's horns, attached to the knee by neat little silver chains (→1363).

Courtiers sporting the new fashions.

Thousands of French sailors are slaughtered at the Battle of Sluys.

French fleet destroyed in Channel battle

Sluys, Flanders, 24 June 1340
With a hastily assembled fleet of some 250 merchantmen and a few galleys, Edward III of England has virtually wiped out the French navy in a two-day battle off the Flemish coast. A Genoese contingent supporting the French escaped.

For the past three years French men-of-war have been roaming the Channel at will. When Edward heard that a great fleet had assembled off Sluys, at the mouth of the river Zwin, he combed England's east-coast ports for ships and embarked with a force of bowmen and men-at-arms. The French ships, crowded together, could not manoeuvre. With wind and tide behind him and the sun full in the faces of the enemy, Edward attacked, the bowmen causing carnage even before the men-at-arms swarmed aboard. The battle went on into the night by the light of burning French ships. Although the French fought gallantly, they were soundly defeated. More than 200 ships were captured, and over 20,000 French are thought to have died (→9/1342).

Edward fights for power in Brittany

Brittany, September 1342
The disputed succession to the duchy of Brittany has given King Edward III of England a new ally and an excuse for renewing the war against Philip VI of France. When John, the duke of Brittany, died, Philip's nephew, Charles of Blois, claimed the title, having married the daughter of one of Duke John's brothers. But another of the duke's brothers, John de Monfort, turned to Edward, recognized him as king of France and in return was recognized as the new duke.

However, the unlucky de Montfort was captured by the French, and his wife Margaret was left to carry on the struggle, backed by Edward and his forces, which overran most of the duchy until they came up against a sizeable French army at Vannes.

The stage was set for a decisive battle, but it is now late September and the weather is deteriorating. Neither Philip nor Edward is willing to risk all in such circumstances. When a delegation sent from Avignon by Pope Clement VI arrived in Brittany to plead for peace, the two kings were glad to agree to a truce. Edward is returning to England, resolved to restart the war when he has recovered his strength (→19/1/43).

Lack of education limits women's work

Scotland, 1345
Seven years after defending her lord's castle at Dunbar against King Edward III of England's soldiers, "Black Agnes", the countess of March, is a local legend and shining example of a good and faithful wife.

An aristocratic noblewoman is expected to be an efficient manager of her husband's estate and even to take up arms in his absence. If a noblewoman is not married by the age of 14, she will most likely go into a nunnery, where she is expected to become a good administrator. Some city women have joined trades guilds as shoemakers, chandlers, gilders, spicers or embroiderers. But this is usually only possible for the wives or daughters of members. Many women are skilled at medicine, especially midwifery. Yet male doctors have kept them from professional practice, branding them as ignorant or even as witches. Poor education is a major problem. Although a noblewoman might be taught at home or by the nuns, the peasant woman is usually illiterate, her career limited to dairying, brewing and spinning (→1431).

Women at work in the fields, from a psalter written and illuminated in the 1340s for Sir Geoffrey Luttrell of Irnham, in Lincolnshire.

1346 - 1350

Italy, 1346. Excessive loans made to King Edward III of England bankrupt the Bardi company (→ 1373).

Normandy, 12 July 1346. Edward III knights his son the prince of Wales at St Vaast-la-Hogue (→ 3/11/53).

Normandy, 26 July 1346. The English seize Caen (→ 27/8).

Perth, 6 October 1346. King David II prepares to invade England (→ 17).

Scotland, late October 1346. Robert "the Stewart" is elected king's lieutenant after David's capture at Neville's Cross (→ spring 1347).

Flanders, 28 April 1347. The count of Flanders flees after breaking his betrothal to Isabella, Edward III of England's daughter (→ 4/8).

Perth, spring 1347. Edward Balliol, the son of John Balliol, the former claimant to the Scottish crown, forces the Scots into a truce (→ 27/3/52).

England, March 1348. Parliament grants taxation for three years, but the king accepts that there should be no taxes without parliamentary consent (→ 22/2/77).

England, 11 June 1348. The Anglo-French truce ends (→ 6/4/54).

Dorset, 24 June 1348. Plague breaks out near Weymouth (→ 8/1348).

Ireland, August 1348. Plague reaches Howth and Drogheda.

Gloucester, August 1348. To stop the spread of plague, all contact with Bristol is forbidden (→ 1/1349).

London, January 1349. Parliament is postponed owing to the spread of plague, which reached London in November (→ summer 1349).

London, 20 December 1349. After the plague deaths of John Stratford and his elected successors as archbishops of Canterbury, John de Offord and Thomas Bradwardine, a new archbishop, Simon Islip, is consecrated (→ 6/6/74).

English Channel, 29 August 1350. Edward III captures a Spanish fleet (→ 1362).

Norwich, 1350. The city has become a centre for the manufacturing of "worsted", a cloth named after the village of Worstead (→ 2/1443).

Norfolk, c.1350. Flooding of empty peat pits creates broad expanses of water.

England gains key victories in France

Massed knights: the English and French armies do battle at Crécy.

Longbows prove decisive in Crécy battle

Crécy, France, 7 August 1346
Edward III of England has won a devastating victory over the French under their king, Philip VI. The English took up position at Crécy, 10 miles north of Abbeville, early yesterday. Some French generals had urged Philip to delay an attack, in order to rest their men, but the French knights swept caution aside, charging to disaster at the hands of the English longbowmen.

At about 4pm the French, advancing from Abbeville, began to close. Two hours later there was a sudden thunderstorm, after which the sun came out, shining directly into the eyes of the French as their Genoese crossbowmen attacked. When they came within range the English longbowmen opened fire; the Genoese, short of arrows, were forced to retreat, with many falling to their deaths under their own side's cavalry. The French knights also suffered grievously from the English arrows as they charged. Fifteen times the French attacked, but they all met the same fate.

On one of the few occasions when the French were able to close with the English line 16-year-old Edward, the prince of Wales, was in danger of being overwhelmed. His father refused to send more than 30 knights to help him, saying "let the boy win his spurs".

Today upwards of 10,000 French corpses lie on the field of Crécy. Among them is the cream of the French nobility. One body is that of the blind King John of Bohemia who rode into battle tied on each side to a knight. King Philip himself, although he had had his horse shot under him and received an arrow in the neck, survived and has fled to Amiens. The English lost little more than a hundred men; Edward now intends to march on the port of Calais (→ 28/4/47).

Crossbowmen defeated.

Calais succumbs to a year-long siege

Calais, France, 4 August 1347
A triumphant King Edward III of England today entered Calais, having accepted its total surrender after a siege lasting nearly a year, during which Philip VI of France arrived with 200,000 men, then lost his nerve and decamped.

Edward had deployed his forces with great skill. He used his fleet to stop a French relief force advancing along the cliffs, and he had seized the only bridge across the impassable ditches and bogs inland.

These moves largely counterbalanced the numerical superiority of the French. Philip sent emissaries to Edward inviting him to come out and do battle in the open, but the English king knew that all he needed to do was to bide his time, and Calais would be starved into submission. When Philip saw reinforcements arriving for Edward he set fire to his tents and retreated.

The burning tents told the people of Calais that they had been abandoned. Six of the most wealthy citizens presented themselves to Edward, offering themselves as hostages. Edward was at first inclined to execute them, but then he responded to the entreaties of his queen, Philippa, and sent them to England (→ 11/6/48).

Philippa pleads for the hostages.

Scotland's invasion of England turns into a disaster as King David II is captured

Durham, 17 October 1346
King David II of Scotland has been taken captive and his army badly defeated by the English at Neville's Cross near here today. David had invaded England in support of his ally Philip VI of France, and he led one of three battalions which met the English forces in wet and foggy conditions today.

The English forces, which had been assembled by the archbishop of York, were superior in numbers and in the power of their archers. As the first two Scottish battalions, led by the earl of Moray and the king, came under heavy attack, the third under Robert "the Stewart" fled without engaging the enemy. David fought with great courage; although wounded by an arrow in the eye, he had to be forced to join his army's retreat. Then, overtaken by the English, he took on his captor, John Coupland, in single combat and knocked out two of his teeth before being overpowered. Scottish losses are high: the king and four earls are prisoners, while the earl of Moray is among several powerful Scottish nobles who were killed (→late 10/1346).

The battle at Neville's Cross: a view which puts art before foggy reality.

What it costs a nobleman to live in style

Gloucestershire, 1346
An annual budget compiled last year by Thomas de Berkeley, a baron with a castle north of Bristol, gives an insight into what it costs for a nobleman to live in style these days. He spent £1,308, of which more than half – £742, or 57 per cent – went on household food: a lot, but the baron entertains often. Eleven per cent, about average for households which need to travel, was spent on keeping his horses. Of this, most went on feed, with straw bedding, harness and riding tackle among other costs. Buying new horses and falcons took 2 per cent of the budget, or £26.

The baron is a lavish dresser and his personal clothing bill came to 11 per cent, or £142, considerably more than the £45 that went on household linen and silver. Wax alone consumed almost 2 per cent, or £21, exactly the same as the total spent on building. Legal fees were relatively modest at 1 per cent, but pensions and gifts to relatives accounted for 5 per cent. Finally, the extras: alms, boots, shoes and wages, in that order, came to 6 per cent, or £86 (→1351).

A million die of plague

The grim reality of life in a country at the mercy of the Black Death.

British Isles, summer 1349
The first hint of near-certain death is a large painful white lump – a buboe – in the armpit. A rash follows, then coughing, chest pains, a terrible fever and finally vomiting of blood. This is the plague – the "Black Death" that has cost nearly a million lives in these islands alone in 12 horrific months.

The disease spread from Asia into southern Europe, carried by rat-infested ships, and then westwards until it reached southern England in June last year. Bristol was the first sizeable centre to suffer its horrors, with a death rate of more than 40 per cent of the city's population, and by November of last year London was also being hit. At Clerkenwell, on a site outside the city walls, 50,000 corpses were buried in a mass grave on 13 acres of land. The city echoed with the tolling of the death-knell from every church, the cries of mourners and the dread call of "bring out your dead" from men pulling wagons piled with plague victims. The stench of death was everywhere. The plague continued to rampage across the nation, wiping out entire villages, and leaving fields and livestock untended.

This year has seen it spread northwards from southern England and southern Wales to engulf most of the British Isles. Only northern Scotland and the north of Ireland so far remain immune, but it seems only a matter of time before they, too, succumb.

The cause of the Black Death has been baffling doctors throughout Europe. Some blame a conjunction of three planets – Saturn, Mars and Jupiter – for causing a corruption of the air; others claim that a spate of earthquakes has released noxious fumes from the earth's core; and there are those who see the plague as a judgement of God against sin.

Treatments are equally varied, ranging from blood-letting (to clear the veins of wormlike organisms), through starving, to burning aromatic woods, poulticing and purging. Villages have cut themselves off from their neighbours, but still the disease spreads, with no sign that it has run its course (→1351).

Clean flames: survivors burning plague-infected clothes in an oven.

▷

Abbey vault is built for Edward II's tomb

Gloucester, 1350
A stunning architectural development has been exciting the attention of visitors to Gloucester Abbey. Since King Edward II was buried here after his murder in 1327, the constant stream of pilgrims to his grave has brought wealth, and the construction of a royal tomb, commissioned by Edward III, has been accompanied by the rebuilding of the old Norman abbey.

The tomb itself supports a lifelike effigy in alabaster of the dead king, lying with his head on a cushion beneath an elaborate stone canopy. The masons did not stop there; they lifted the roof of the chancel to an unprecedented height of 27.6 metres (92 feet) and at the east end installed the largest stained-glass window in England. This is a memorial to the victory at Crécy, an expanse of glass divided into three sections by vertical columns so slender that people marvel that they support the roof. This is a complex network of ribs curving and intersecting one another. Each intersection is adorned with a carved and gilded boss, in the shapes of stars, leaf fronds, animal heads and, over the altar, angels playing music. The effect is like looking up into a sky full of suns. Beneath it the Norman walls of the chancel and transepts are overlaid by a delicate stone tracery like the window's, with slender clustered columns fanning out to support the roof (→1370).

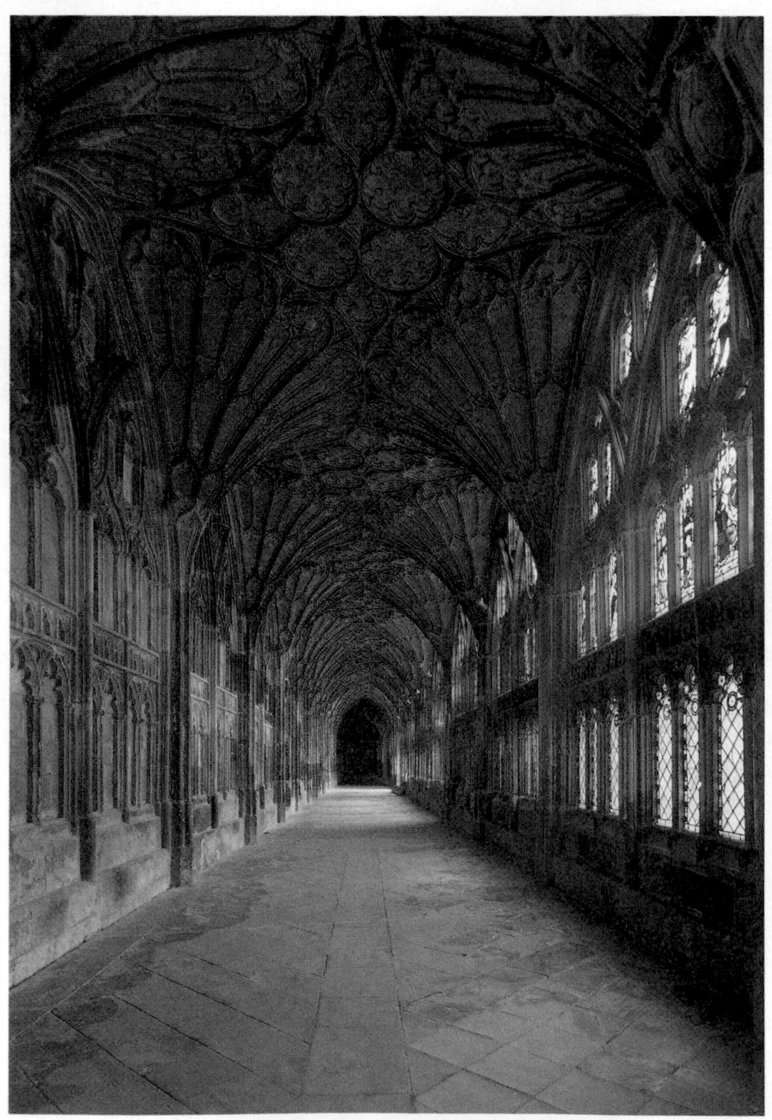

Intricate designs: the vaulted roof to the cloisters at Gloucester.

Controversial philosopher dies of plague

Munich, Germany, 1349
The Black Death has claimed one of its most celebrated victims. It has taken the great English philosopher William of Ockham. In 1328 this Franciscan scholar fled the papal court in Avignon, where he had been summoned in 1324 to answer charges of heresy, and sought protection in Germany. Before then, in Oxford, he had contributed to the struggle to reconcile the theology of the church with Aristotle's teachings about nature. He challenged theologians by arguing that the mysteries of God were matters of faith, not human enquiry, and urged scholars to focus on observable phenomena (→9/3/1457).

William of Ockham: philosopher.

English king founds new order of chivalry

Edward as a knight of the Garter.

Windsor Castle, 1348
After his victories at Crécy and Calais, Edward III has returned to England to found a new order of chivalry, and most of its members are knights who fought alongside the king in his campaigns in France. The patron saint of the new Order of the Garter is the fourth-century soldier-martyr St George.

Edward had been contemplating creating a new order for some years when he began refurbishing the castle at Windsor with thoughts of creating a new Arthurian Round Table. Members of the new order will attend a Mass each year at Windsor in a specially dedicated chapel (→1386).

Diseases given profit and loss diagnosis

England, 1349
A medical book has recently been written by John of Gaddesden, the prebendary of St Paul's Cathedral, which appears to focus as much on the financial rewards a physician can hope to expect from his expertise as on advice for the poorly.

Rosa Angelica is a compilation from other published sources dealing with everything from epilepsy to apoplexy; for example, a treatment using a red light is suggested for smallpox. The book has not been received with universal acclaim, however. Many of the remedies have been described as the crassest quackery and childish superstitions; many are of Arabic origin, and they are often extraordinarily repulsive. Perhaps more interestingly, the book looks at the pecuniary side of medicine in 14th-century England.

The book advises physicians to arrange for their pay in advance and goes as far as naming the diseases that are likely to bring a doctor hardly any profit; it draws a distinction between remedies suitable for the poor and those suitable for the better off. And finally, Gaddesden says that "because too great familiarity breeds contempt" a distance should be kept between doctors and patients (→c.1400).

1351 - 1354

England, February 1351. Parliament passes the Statute of Labourers by which wages are set at pre-plague rates, and all workmen must fulfil their contracts (→ 1357).

Dublin, 17 October 1351. The great council discusses ways of stopping Anglo-Irish lords integrating with the native Irish community (→ 1352).

Devon, 1351. The area has suffered greatly from the plague of 1349. Over half the clergy have died, tin-mining has ceased, and much of the land is deserted (→ 1360).

Scotland, 27 March 1352. King David II of Scotland returns to his homeland by permission in an attempt to negotiate the terms of his release (→ 8/1352).

Windsor, April 1352. The first mechanical weight-driven striking clock is in use.

Ireland, 1352. Succession to the kingship of Tyrconnell is contested after the murder of King Angus O'Donnell by Magnus O'Donnell (→ 10/1353).

Cambridge, 1352. Corpus Christi college is founded (→ 28/2/55).

Ireland, 1352. Aed O'Connor, the son of Turlough, the king of Connacht, destroys Ballindoon Castle (→ 10/1353).

England, January 1353. Wheat prices continue to fall following a massive import of wheat from Ireland and the Low Countries.

Westminster, January 1353. Prostitutes are forbidden by parliament to wear hooded garments unless made of striped material (→ 7/1385).

Borders, August 1353. Sir William Douglas of Liddesdale, recently freed by King Edward III after agreeing to serve him, is ambushed and killed in Ettrick Forest by his godson, William, the lord of Douglas (→ 20/1/56).

Dublin, October 1353. Parliament opens (→ 27/7/60).

Waterford City, 1353. Two heretics are burnt.

Flanders, 6 April 1354. A draft treaty is drawn up at Guines; Edward III of England will keep sovereignty of Aquitaine, Poitou, Anjou, Maine, Calais and Touraine, on condition that he abandons claims to the French throne (→ 24/6/55).

France/Scotland, 1354. The Franco-Scottish alliance is renewed (→ 17/1/57).

Peasants shake off past servility to win wage rises in wake of the 'Black Death'

Peasants at work: life is easier for them in the wake of the Black Death.

England, 1351
England may be facing the end of the rural system that has served its landowners so well for centuries. As the country begins to recover from the human toll of the Black Death, the rural economy is in a state of chaos. Peasants are able to shake off the servility of centuries and demand higher wages – often three or four times as high as those of a year ago.

With lower rents and greatly reduced prices for most commodities, farmworkers are enjoying a standard of living that no one dreamt possible two years ago – and a freedom of movement unfamiliar until now, with labour in such universal demand. A horse once worth 40 shillings [£2] can be bought for as little as 6s 8d [33p], a fat ox for four shillings and a cow for a mere one shilling.

Many landowners are facing great difficulties, with smaller profits from wool, wheat and other produce, and are tending to seek a return from their land by leasing smaller plots to the more ambitious peasants – who, in turn, are able to invest their newfound wealth by lending it to equally industrious neighbours. Landowners are fighting back, however, demanding action by king and parliament to check increased wages and the free movement of labour (→ 2/1351).

Statute defines the nature of 'treason'

England, 1352
A new treason statute drawn up by parliament has been well received by Edward III. Until now accusations of high treason have rested on the concept of "encroaching on the royal power" – an idea so vague that it has given rise to explosive disputes. But now treason will have to be an "open act" aimed at killing the king or his highest officials, raping his wife or eldest daughter, or making war on the crown. Highway robbery and riot are among the offences which are no longer acts of treason (→ 24/5/76).

Edward: in favour of new law.

Heroic duke offers religious diagnosis

Lancaster, 4 December 1352
Henry of Grosmont, the duke of Lancaster, has added to his remarkable reputation this year by writing a book, *Livre de Seyntz Medicines*, in which sinful humanity is compared to a diseased body, desperate for the cure that only the "divine physician" Christ can provide. The duke has long been a close companion of the king, a hero of his French and Scottish wars, but he is also known for his piety, crusading in Poland and Prussia last year and founding a college at Leicester, of which he was previously earl. In his book Henry draws upon contemporary folklore to suggest pious remedies for what the Bible identifies as the seven deadly sins (→ 1361).

England to challenge Bruges wool trade

The seal of a Bruges corporation.

England, April 1354
A new set of rules governing the wool trade has been set down by parliament in the Statute of Staples: the old staple or commercial centre at Bruges in Flanders is to be abandoned and new staples established in England in its place.

This has brought an important trade closer to home, but English merchants are frustrated by their exclusion from the lucrative export market. Internal trading is open to all, but once the wool – highly prized in Europe – is brought to a staple town for export, it must be turned over to foreigners, who have a monopoly in selling it abroad.

While growers and small merchants are undoubtedly aggrieved, the new policy suits national interests. Relations between England and Flanders have been deteriorating, and traders have suffered too. Under the new system, however, losses at sea or in Flanders itself will cost England and its merchants nothing (→ 12/1382).

1355 - 1363

Oxford, 28 February 1355. Riots which began with a tavern brawl on 10 February have lead to an exodus of students to Reading and Cambridge (→ 1387).

Europe, 24 June 1355. With last year's Treaty of Guines unratified, an Anglo-French truce breaks down (→ 3/11).

Borders, 20 January 1356. Edward III of England, having retaken Berwick, lost to the Scots last year, receives the Scots crown at Roxburgh from Edward Balliol (→ 17/1/57).

Normandy, 5 April 1356. On capturing the king of Navarre, Edward III sends troops to fight the French (→ 18/6).

Normandy, 18 June 1356. The English begin to amass troops under Henry of Grosmont, the duke of Lancaster, at St Vaast-La-Hogue (→ 19/9).

Scotland, 17 January 1357. The Scots, on the capture of John II of France by the English, negotiate for the release of David II (→ 7/10).

England, 7 October 1357. King David II is free after 11 years' imprisonment; the Scots will pay 100,000 marks in ransom over a decade (→ 1358).

Scotland, 1358. The Scottish government raises the customs rate on a sack of wool from 6/8d [33p] to £1 to pay the king's ransom (→ 1360).

Paris, 19 May 1359. The French reject a draft treaty by which John II had agreed to pay England a huge ransom and cede half his kingdom in return for freedom (→ 13/4/60).

Kilkenny City, 27 July 1360. A great council asks Edward III to appoint an English lord as lieutenant of Ireland (→ 1361).

Calais, October 1360. John II of France is finally freed; Edward III drops the title of king of France (→ 19/7/62).

Lothian, 1360. Katherine Mortimer, the mistress of King David II, is stabbed to death by noblemen jealous of her influence (→ 1363).

Westminster, 19 July 1362. Edward III grants the prince of Wales the kingdom of Gascony (→ 1/1369).

England, 1362. John of Gaunt, the fourth son of Edward III, succeeds to the duchy of Lancaster (→ 3/4/67).

Scotland, 1363. David II quells a rebellion led by magnates in protest at the abandonment of hostages in England (→ 4/3/64).

French towns fall to English prince

English advance in Gascon campaign

Bordeaux, 3 November 1355
Striking out from his headquarters here, Edward, the prince of Wales, has led a 7,000-strong army of English, Welsh and Gascon troops deep into the rich lands of the count of Armagnac, seizing castles and looting and burning towns. The prince, now aged 25, was sent to Gascony by his father, Edward III of England, to recover territory lost to the French over the years, but he has gone far beyond the old borders.

The count of Armagnac remained shut up in the walled city of Toulouse confident that the prince would be forced to halt when he came to the wide Garonne river, because all the bridges were down.

Victor: Edward, prince of Wales.

Yet, with the audacity and courage for which the young prince is renowned, he led his men and horses into the river to ford it south of Toulouse. From there the prince, easily recognizable on account of his distinctive black armour, headed into Languedoc where, as he reported, "the land was very rich and plentiful and there was not a day but towns, castles and strongholds were taken" and "many goodly towns and strongholds destroyed".

When he came to the "fair and great" city of Carcassonne, the citizens offered the prince the huge sum of 250,000 gold *écus* [the local currency] if he would spare it. He spurned the offer and burnt the city to the ground (→ 5/4/56).

English bowmen help to send the French army towards defeat at Poitiers.

French king captured in battle at Poitiers

Poitiers, 19 September 1356
In a three-hour battle outside the city of Poitiers, Edward, the prince of Wales, has inflicted a crushing defeat on the French and captured King John II. The French king is being sent to England to be imprisoned in the Tower of London.

The prince had set out from his headquarters at Bordeaux, moving north with the intention of joining his cousin, the duke of Lancaster. But at Tours, where the prince pitched his tents, he found that the French had slipped past him and were heading for Poitiers in his rear. The prince moved swiftly, deploying his forces outside Poitiers, many behind hedges and ditches out of sight of the enemy. The English bowmen played a decisive role in breaking the French attacks, which had been launched by dismounted cavalry – on the advice of an old adversary of the English, the Scot William Douglas.

The prince, roaring defiance, drove at the French with his sword, killing all who came at him. At a crucial point in the battle the prince's Gascon ally, the Captal de Buch, attacked the French from the rear, causing them to break and run for Poitiers (→ 19/5/59).

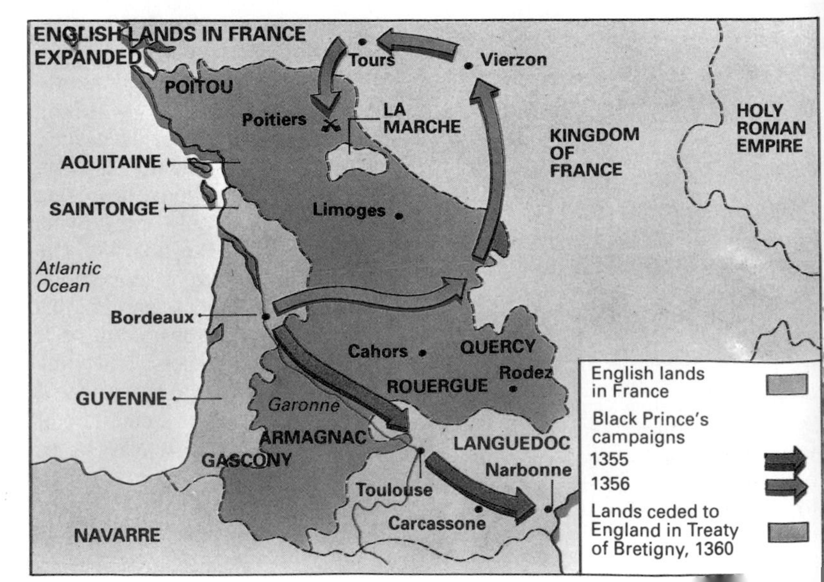

England calls off war against France

Chartres, France, 13 April 1360
After witnessing the devastation caused by today's raging storm, Edward III of England has listened to the advocates of peace and decided to abandon his attempts to subdue the French. Huge hailstones pounded his forces, killing so many horses that the whole army is immobilized. The troops are calling the day Black Monday.

Edward believed that French power had been broken by English victories at Crécy and Poitiers and the capture of King John II. He demanded a crippling ransom for the king and vast territorial concessions. His original intention was to capture Rheims and have himself proclaimed king of France in the city where, for centuries, all French kings had been crowned. But it resisted his siege, and he moved on to Paris, only to find the capital heavily fortified and well stocked.

In six months of campaigning, Edward never managed to force the French to fight. Charles, the *dauphin* [French royal heir], acting as regent, had learnt from Crécy and Poitiers, where pitched battles gave the English victory. Now the duke of Lancaster has told the king that he must come home or "we could lose more in one day than we have gained in 20 years" (→8/5).

Edward III at the siege of Rheims.

Irish blame Edward for recurrence of the dreaded plague

Ireland, 1360
A recurrence of the terrible plague which first swept through the country in 1349 has caused so much loss of life that people are saying that the end of the world is near and everyone will die. The plague is even being described as *"Cluiche an Riogh"* – the king's game – a reference to Lionel, the duke of Clarence and son of Edward III of England, who is to be sent to Ireland as lieutenant and who is being blamed for the outbreak.

The plague seems to have caused the most havoc among the Anglo-Irish, in the towns and manors and in major centres of population, where low standards of hygiene are encouraging rats to breed. But its long-term effects could be even more disastrous. Many towns and villages have been totally destroyed, and the widespread fear of death has caused many skilled workers to emigrate to England. High wages are on offer there to skilled artisans, thereby creating a scarcity of labour in Ireland (→1375).

French king to be released as Edward negotiates a peace treaty

John II of France: the price to be paid for his freedom has been cut.

Chartres, France, 8 May 1360
With his army ravaged by sickness and his supplies lost in heavy storms, Edward III of England was only too glad to open peace talks with the French. A truce has been agreed and a provisional treaty worked out during meetings in the hamlet of Brétigny, south-west of Paris, near Chartres.

Edward will renounce his claim to the French throne in return for sovereign rights over a Gascony enlarged by French territorial concessions. Edward retains Calais and gains the port of La Rochelle, the centre of the salt trade. He has ceded Brittany, which he had occupied for the past 18 years, and he has renounced sovereignty over Anjou, Normandy, Touraine and Maine. The ransom for King John II has been reduced from four million gold *écus* to three million.

The two sides have also made a deal to abandon the allies that they had been using to cause trouble for each other. Edward has dropped the Flemings, and John will abandon the Scots.

After less than a week the talks were concluded, and the duke of Lancaster for the English and the bishop of Beauvais for the French exchanged sworn documents. The treaty will be ratified by the two kings later this year, when John has been released after part of the ransom has been handed over to the English (→10/1360).

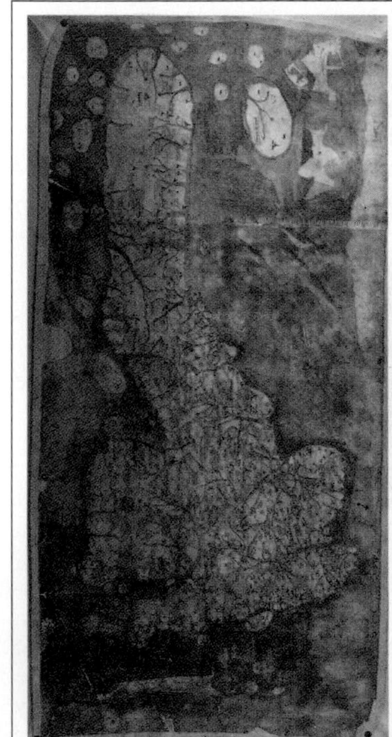

This map of c.1360 is the first known attempt by contemporary cartographers to show the road system of Britain in its entirety.

Seashore death highlights the dangers facing child labourers

England, 1357
Child labour is a regular cause of accidents in England, where peasant boys are expected to help out fishing, herding and minding sheep and geese. One casualty this year, for instance, was 12-year-old William Baly, who was swept out to sea while collecting cockles. Girls also work in the fields, although more do housework. In the upper classes, young children are not sent out to work, but many go to live in other households; this has led an Italian to comment on "the want of affection in the English" towards their children (→1370).

A hard life in the country: peasants at work harvesting the crops.

Years of war transform the English army

England's war machine in action: archers and soldiers besieging a city.

London, 1360

England's war machine has been transformed by the long years of fighting both the French and the Scots. Battlefield tactics developed in the Scottish wars have been used with devastating effect against the French, troops are better equipped and, under Edward III, a more sophisticated military administration has made service in the king's forces increasingly popular.

Uniforms have begun to appear. The prince of Wales has arrayed his archers in green-and-white coats and hats. Outdated equipment, including padded coats of mail and vast iron helmets, has been replaced by suits of light plate armour and close-fitting helmets of light steel.

On the battlefield the army is arrayed in three battalions of dismounted men-at-arms, with archers on the flanks at an angle to fire at the enemy from the side. After receiving the first charge with their lances the men fight back-to-back for mutual protection.

Rates of pay and rules for the division of spoils are now set out in voluntary contracts which the king makes with his captains, who take responsibility for recruiting the rank and file.

King's son alarms Anglo-Irish nobles

Dublin, 1361

Edward III's son Lionel, the duke of Clarence, is creating anxiety among members of the Anglo-Irish nobility as he settles into his role as lieutenant of Ireland. They fear that the real motive behind his arrival in September is the recovery of Leinster, where the Irish have reconquered the lands held by the crown and where two leading families, the Butlers and the Geraldines, have appropriated much of Kilkenny and Carlow. The duke's behaviour has added to these fears. He has forbidden anyone of Irish birth to approach his English camp and is preparing a strong campaign on behalf of the crown (→19/2/66).

Secret wedding is surprise to court

Windsor, 10 October 1361

The prince of Wales has secretly married his cousin, Joan of Kent. The bride, renowned for her looks, has been romantically linked in the past to the prince's father, Edward III, and has been married twice before. As a young girl she wed Sir Thomas Holland in secret, in 1339, only to be forced by her family a year later to marry William, the earl of Salisbury, while Sir Thomas was fighting abroad. A papal dispensation enabled Joan to be reunited with Sir Thomas, who died nine months ago. Now the prince is entranced, putting love before any talk of a dynastic marriage to a foreign princess (→6/1/67).

Archery kicks football off the royal pitch

Archery, once England's favourite sport, is falling out of favour now.

England, 1363

Sports such as football, handball, cock-fighting and stickball [a kind of cricket] have been forbidden on feast days and public holidays by royal decree, under penalty of two years' jail or a fine of £10. The king wishes his subjects to practise the art of archery on their days off, believing that his military successes against the French and Scots have stemmed largely from the prowess of the English bowmen.

Archery has been the national sport of most Englishmen, from noblemen to commoners, since the reign of Edward I, but in recent years its popularity has dwindled. This has displeased the king, who has long espoused the virtues of practising archery skills. Now Edward III has sent a writ to every sheriff in the land ordering them to ensure that no "worthless" games such as football are played on holidays, which should be kept for archery. A skilled longbowman can shoot ten or 12 arrows a minute with the six-foot-long yew or oak bow; this can penetrate chain mail, with a maximum range of almost 360 metres (400 yards).

English told to tighten their fashion belts

England, 1363

Despite the lack of funds of King Edward III's court the English have taken up foreign fashions in such a big way that a sumptuary law [against excessive apparel] has been introduced to curb overspending. Not only are moralists outraged by the elaborateness of today's new styles but the ridiculous extravagance and high costs have also been severely criticized.

The Sumptuary Statute approved by parliament this year is concerned also with the appropriateness of fashions for particular classes of society. It attempts to divide English society into seven classes and then lays down the kind of clothing deemed to be suitable for each class. Clear budget limits are set out for each class, with the penalty of forfeiting one's wardrobe for serious over-indulgence – a sanction more likely to be invoked for the *gens de mestere* [merchants and burgesses] than the *garçons* [agricultural workers and others with goods worth less than £2].

For the rich, wool and other workaday fabrics made into voluminous gowns have given way to a new, tighter fit, with a widening of women's necklines, and shortened men's tunics, made in silks, adorned with gold and silver threads, precious stones and furs (→1410).

Elaborate: imported fashions.

1364 - 1368

Scotland, 4 March 1364. Parliament upholds the right of Robert "the Stewart", rather than Edward III of England, to inherit the crown, should King David II die without an heir (→ 1369).

England, 8 April 1364. King John II of France dies. He returned to captivity in England last year of his own free will, after discovering that his son, Charles, had failed to fulfil the terms of his release agreed four years ago (→ 1366).

Westminster, 1365. Parliament passes a statute of *praemunire* forbidding appeals to the pope in disputes concerning church patronage. This and another such measure passed in 1353 are to strengthen the position of lay courts (→ 4/11/66).

Westminster, 4 November 1366. Simon Langham, a former bishop of Ely and chancellor of England, receives the *pallium* [stole of office] as archbishop of Canterbury. He succeeds Simon Islip, archbishop since 1349, who died on 26 April (→ 6/6/74).

Gascony, 6 January 1367. A second son, to be named Richard of Bordeaux, is born to Edward, the prince of Wales, and his wife Joan; he is third in line to the English throne (→ 8/6/76).

Gascony, 10 January 1367. Honouring an alliance forged in 1362 with King Pedro of Castile, Edward, the prince of Wales, and his brother, John of Gaunt, the duke of Lancaster, depart with an army for Castile; they intend to restore Pedro, who was ousted last year (→ 3/4).

Lincolnshire, 3 April 1367. Blanche, the duchess of Lancaster, has a son, who is to be called Henry Bolingbroke. Blanche, the daughter of Henry of Grosmont, the previous duke of Lancaster, married John of Gaunt, Edward III's fourth son, in 1359 (→ 10/1/67).

Winchester, 1367. William of Wykeham, a close adviser of Edward III, who became bishop here last year, succeeds Simon Langham as chancellor of England (→ 27/9/1404).

Edinburgh, 1367. David II begins work on major fortifications at the castle.

England, 17 October 1368. Lionel, the earl of Ulster and duke of Clarence, who returned from Ireland two years ago, dies (→ 3/3/69).

English prince aids ousted Spanish ally

Don Henry at his coronation.

Bordeaux, 1366
King Pedro of Castile, an ally of Edward, the prince of Wales, has been deposed by a mercenary army that included many English and French knights and replaced by his rival Don Henry of Trastamare. Pedro is unreliable, and not for nothing is he known as "the Cruel". Some of the prince of Wales's knights fought in the army that ousted Pedro, but his appeal for help was answered by Edward, who sent a ship to bring him here to Aquitaine. Edward's council wants him to have nothing to do with the king, but Pedro is offering 550,000 florins cash for his restoration, plus massive land and trade deals. The prince may be tempted (→ 10/1/67).

Spanish usurper is beaten by Edward

Navarre, 3 April 1367
Edward, the prince of Wales, has achieved a stunning victory here today, defeating the army of the usurper King Henry of Castile in spite of a gruelling march through the Pyrenees. Abandoning a strong position, Henry's army advanced across the Najerilla river to meet the forces of the prince of Wales, who had come to restore the legitimate king, Pedro, to his throne. During the night Edward led his men round the side of a mountain to catch the Castilians unawares, forcing Henry's army back to the banks of the Najerilla where it was cornered and massacred (→ 1372).

Ireland's royal lieutenant seeks to keep Irish 'enemies' beyond English zone

Kilkenny City, 19 February 1366
Parliament has been summoned here by Lionel, the duke of Clarence, to pass 35 enactments which are, for the most part, anti-Irish in sentiment. It is being heralded as the most significant event of Lionel's five-year rule as the English king's lieutenant in Ireland.

Lionel, King Edward III's third son, arrived in Ireland in September 1361 to head a concerted campaign to bring the Anglo-Irish nobles under firmer English control [*see report below*]. Yet what are being called the Statutes of Kilkenny are more an admission of his failure than an affirmation of victory in his war against the Irish people.

Beyond English rule: Edmund Albanach, the independent head of the de Burghs [Burkes] of Connacht.

A large part of Ireland is to be abandoned to the Irish people (who are called "enemies"), with English language, race and law confined to the area of English lordship. In this "obedient" land, along the east coast and including Carlow, Kilkenny and Tipperary, the purity of the English tradition will be protected and preserved. The English are forbidden to marry the Irish or to foster children with them. They must not sell horses or weapons to the Irish nor entertain Irish minstrels or story-tellers. The Irish who live in this area are obliged to speak English and observe English customs. The Statutes of Kilkenny represent an outlawry of the Irish living beyond the area of English lordship. They will be barred from church office and from any contact with the king's officials.

Yet this attempt to defend English traditions from "degenerate" influences could prove even more divisive and add further fuel to existing feuds between the two races (→ 11/1366).

English lose campaign to colonize Irish

Dublin, November 1366
The five-year reign of Lionel, the duke of Clarence, as lieutenant of Ireland ended this month with his departure for England. Lionel, who is the third son of King Edward III, came to Dublin intent on reasserting English control. He had arrived with a force of 1,500 men, but neither this army nor his royal lineage have been able to put a stop to the steady erosion of English authority in Ireland.

Normans who acquired territory in Ireland have become progressively more sympathetic to Irish culture in the course of the past century. The present generation were mostly born in Ireland, and many rule like native chieftains; native customs and language have been adopted, to the dismay of King Edward's English court. The Anglo-Irish families also challenged the authority of the justiciars, or law officers, appointed by Edward – not because they were seeking independence but because they believed themselves better qualified to rule on behalf of the king than English-born officials.

Edward sent Lionel to signify his refusal to let Anglo-Irish families control the government in Dublin. Declining crown revenues and continuing feuds with landowners culminated, however, in the Statutes of Kilkenny this year, which effectively conceded defeat in any attempt to colonize the island of Ireland as a whole (→ 17/10/68).

1369 - 1372

Paris, January 1369. After a summons to the court of Charles V of France, to answer charges of high taxes levied on his kingdom, Edward, the prince of Wales, has his lands confiscated (→ 9/1369).

Ireland, 3 March 1369. William of Windsor becomes lieutenant of Ireland (→ 7/1370).

England, August 1369. Queen Philippa, the wife of King Edward III, dies (→ 1375).

England, September 1369. Edward III, who this year returned Charles V's envoys, sends his son John of Gaunt and Humphrey de Bohun, the earl of Hereford, to reclaim his crown in France (→ 1370).

Scotland, 1369. King David II divorces his second wife, Margaret Drummond, who flees to Avignon to solicit the pope's support (→ 22/2/71).

England, 1369. Geoffrey Chaucer, a poet and civil servant, writes *The Book of the Duchess*, an elegy for Blanche, the duchess of Lancaster, who died this year (→ 12/7/89).

Munster, July 1370. The O'Brien dynasty of Thomond rebels against William of Windsor (→ 23/3/72).

England, January 1371. After handing over Aquitaine to his brother John of Gaunt, the prince of Wales returns to England afflicted by infectious dysentery and dropsy (→ 1372).

Tayside, 27 March 1371. Robert "the Stewart", the grandson of Robert Bruce, is crowned Robert II at Scone. His eldest son, John, the earl of Carrick, is recognized as his heir despite doubts over his legitimacy (→ 1382).

Ireland, 23 March 1372. After several failed campaigns and the suspension of all taxes last year, Edward III of England loses faith in William of Windsor and removes his right to the royal seal (→ 29/9/73).

Aquitaine, August 1372. Owain ap Thomas ap Rhodri, the great-nephew of Llywelyn ap Gruffudd, who has declared an aim to recover Wales, leads a French force against the English, taking La Rochelle and imprisoning the Captal de Buch, a Gascon knight on the English side (→ 7/1378).

Castile, 1372. John of Gaunt, who married Constance, the daughter of the former King Pedro of Castile, last year, assumes the title of king of Castile (→ 22/6).

A leaner economy arises from plague

England, 1370

With the country recovering from a fresh outbreak of both bubonic and pneumonic plagues, England's population has fallen to fewer than two and a half million, and the cost of labour continues to rise despite the 1351 Statute of Labourers introduced in the interest of landowners after the "Black Death".

Recovery has been faster than anyone could have imagined during that first fearful year of mass burials and villages made empty. Despite the statute, the peasant classes suddenly find themselves in a powerful position. Wages are high, food is cheap, and only manufactured goods have increased in value.

Perhaps most significant since that first huge loss of life has been the steady, stealthy emergence of radical thinkers such as John Wyclif, whose "Lollard" [from the Dutch *lollen*, applied to mutterers of prayers] movement is challenging aspects of religious thinking and the worldliness of the clergy.

The succession of plagues has acted as a social as well as an economic catharsis. Women now carry out much of the work previously done almost exclusively by men. Their wages have risen significantly more than those earned by men. Better management techniques are also helping to create a more efficient workforce (→ 6/1381).

In the fields: work goes on, but the quality of life is improving.

Prince leaves his sickbed to raze Limoges

The English army is on the move.

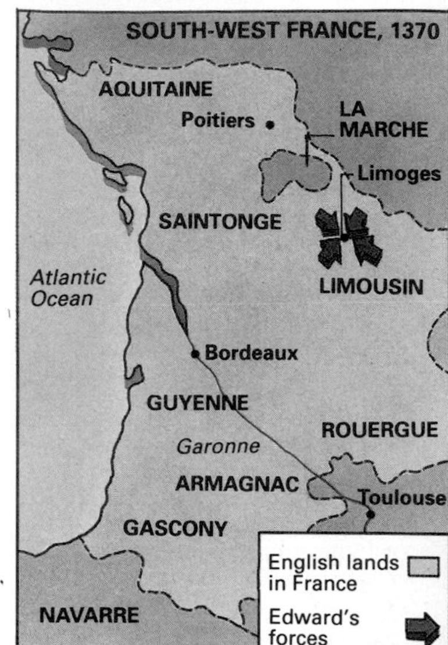

France, 1370

Edward, the prince of Wales, has carried out the most terrible massacre of men, women and children at Limoges after the city fell to him at the end of a siege lasting a month. Estimates vary, but it seems that at least 300 people have been slaughtered as the prince and his brother John of Gaunt try to stem the French advance into Aquitaine with a show of strength.

The prince has been seriously ill for some time, and the French have taken advantage of this to push into Aquitaine, using guerrilla tactics that avoid meeting the English in battle. But when the prince heard that his friend John le Cros had "turned French" and surrendered Limoges, he was so angry that he rose from his sick bed to do battle.

Too ill to ride, he was carried to the city where he found the French garrison well supplied and determined to resist. Eventually the English undermined the walls to create a gap through which they poured into the city massacring the people. Ironically, John le Cros, who had so angered the prince, was himself spared (→ 1/1371).

Modern kitchen stands alone at abbey

Somerset, 1370

The recently completed kitchen at Glastonbury Abbey is exciting the interest of architectural enthusiasts of all persuasions. It already seems destined to become an important addition to one of England's most revered monasteries.

Unlike smaller religious houses, where the kitchens are integrated within the main buildings, at Glastonbury the abbot's kitchen stands on its own. From the outside it is seen as a square-shaped building, but fireplaces set diagonally across each of the four corners create an octagonal interior.

Arches spring from the corners to support a vaulted roof that can be seen from the outside as a stone-clad pyramid, crowned with a pair of lanterns – a larger one topped by a smaller (→ 1390).

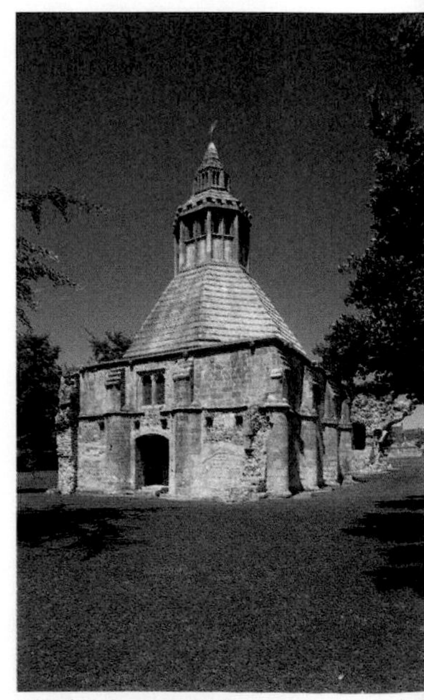

The kitchen: a 20th-century view.

Robert II succeeds his uncle, David II, to found a new Stewart dynasty in Scotland

King David II of Scotland.

Edinburgh, 22 February 1371
King David II, Scotland's ruler for over 40 years, died unexpectedly at the castle here today at the age of only 46. As he has failed to leave an heir – he had been contemplating a third marriage – the crown now passes to his half-nephew, Robert "the Stewart", who is eight years older than the late king.

David succeeded his father on the throne in 1329, but he spent much of his reign as a minor and for 11 years was held a prisoner in England. This was when Scotland was again plunged into a ruinous war with England and David's crown was threatened by both the pretender Edward Balliol and King Edward III of England.

After being freed in 1357 David showed himself to be an able king, tough in his dealings with England and his own magnates. He was not vindictive, however; those found guilty of political offences lost their lands, but they were not executed. His relations with his nephew, the new Robert II, were not always easy. Robert was imprisoned after offending Queen Margaret, David's second wife, and David did not really want to accept him as his successor. But at least Robert will not leave Scotland without an heir.

The new king has five surviving sons and seven daughters; his accession thus creates a new Stewart dynasty in Scotland (→27/3/71).

English fleet routed by Spanish galleys

The earl of Pembroke and his men are routed by the Spaniards at La Rochelle.

La Rochelle, France, 22 June 1372
Castilian galleys today routed, burnt and sank an English fleet sailing into this Bay of Biscay harbour with vital reinforcements for the hard-pressed duchy of Aquitaine. The losses, which included a vital £20,000 to pay 3,000 soldiers for a year, will seriously weaken England's hold on the region.

The defeat off La Rochelle has demonstrated the potency of the alliance against the English between Charles V of France and Henry of Trastamara, who regained the throne of Castile in 1369 when the pro-English Pedro "the Cruel" was murdered. English fortunes have waned since Edward, the prince of Wales, returned home unwell last year. In today's sea battle the English ships were no match for the Spaniards' galleys of 200 tonnes, propelled by 180 oars manned by free men and commanded by a professional sailor. The English ships were under the command of the young earl of Pembroke, who had no previous naval experience.

As he sailed into the bay the Castilians rammed his ships and then sprayed the rigging and decks with oil set alight by flaming arrows. Stone cannon-balls were rained down on the English archers from the galleys' high poops. The earl, who was due to take over as the new lieutenant of Aquitaine, was taken prisoner (→25/12/73).

Leading Welsh poet leaves rich legacy

Dyfed, 1370
Wales is mourning the death of a man regarded by many as its greatest poet – Dafydd ap Gwilym, the "nightingale of Dyfed". He was a supreme master of the Welsh language and wrote according to the strict and elaborate *cywydd* metre – that is, in couplets of seven-syllabled rhyming lines. His example inspired a golden age in Welsh poetry, with many poets of the first rank practising their art for their patrons among the gentry and in the Cistercian abbeys.

Although he was violently anti-English, which was natural since his uncle had been murdered by an English official, Dafydd changed the course of Welsh poetry by introducing new themes, notably subjects drawn from nature – he did not like towns – rather than writing the conventional eulogies of the living and the dead.

Dafydd came from a noble family and travelled widely throughout Wales. He wrote much about love in both romantic and humorous vein. He made fun of jealous husbands, reluctant mistresses and lovesick suitors who pined away to literal skin and bone yearning for the impossible favours of unattainable loved ones, whose praises they never tired of singing. His is a personal poetry, warm and informal, full of vitality and humour.

Plowman's progress recorded in poetry

A Franciscan friar illustrates a later edition of William Langland's work.

London, c.1370
A remarkable portrait of society which strongly attacks church bureaucracy is contained in a poem, *Piers Plowman*, which has been written recently. The author of this allegorical work in alliterative verse is believed to be William Langland, a former member of a priory now living in London. The narrator of the poem, Will, uses dreams to range over time and space, analyzing Christian society – in theory and practice – and focusing on corruption in clerical and ecclesiastical affairs. Langland uses Latin and English in a variety of ways to make the spiritual visual, peppering his text with puns and metaphors.

1373 - 1375

Bristol, 1 September 1373. The town is granted county status by King Edward III.

Ireland, 20 September 1373. William of Windsor is reappointed as justiciar of Ireland (→ 27/5/74).

Scotland, 1373. A devaluation of the Scottish currency brings to an end its long established parity with English sterling; a new exchange rate of 3:4 is established.

Ireland, 1373. Adam O'Keenan, the poet and scholar who chose to retire to a life of monasticism at Lisgoole, dies (→ 1392).

Kilkenny City, 27 May 1374. The great council meets (→ 18/6/75).

London, 6 June 1374. The archbishop of Canterbury, William of Whittlesea, dies at Lambeth. He succeeded Simon Langham in 1369 (→ 5/1375).

England, August 1374. Despite his superiority over the French forces, Edward III is ready to call a truce because of the great expense of remaining at war (→ 27/6/75).

Canterbury, May 1375. Simon of Sudbury, the bishop of London, becomes archbishop of Canterbury (→ 1376).

Ireland, 18 June 1375. Edward III of England appoints Nicholas Dagworth to secure increased Anglo-Irish financial support for England's war in Ireland (→ 8/1375).

Ireland, August 1375. William of Windsor, the justiciar, undertakes a campaign with the Anglo-Irish in Thomond (→ 6/10).

Ireland, 6 October 1375. Parliament opens at Kilkenny; all Anglo-Irish representatives are summoned to appear before a council in England (→ 1375).

Grampian, 1375. John Barbour, the archdeacon of Aberdeen, finishes his poem *The Bruce* – 13,000 lines of couplets glorifying King Robert I (→ 1477).

London, 1375. Alice Perrers, Edward III's ambitious mistress, is the main attraction at a week of jousting tournaments (→ 24/5/76).

England, 1375. An epidemic of plague breaks out (→ 1479).

Co Down, 1375. Niall Mor O'Neill, the recognized king of Tyrone, defeats a force of Anglo-Irish in battle at Downpatrick (→ 1376).

English forces hit by starvation in France

John of Gaunt is entertained by the king of Portugal on a later expedition.

Bordeaux, 25 December 1373
The remnants of John of Gaunt's army struggled into the city today in the most desperate state imaginable. Half the men and almost all the horses have died of starvation, and the rest are reduced to beggary.

The condition of the army has been brought about not by military defeat, for it has not fought a battle, but by continuing too long on a raid deep into French territory that at first promised well.

John of Gaunt, the duke of Lancaster and fourth son of King Edward III, landed at Calais in July with about 5,000 men. He began a long march to Aquitaine through Champagne and Burgundy, raiding and pillaging as he went.

The plan was to reduce the pressure on Aquitaine while at the same time forcing a pitched battle that the English were likely to win. In both of these objectives it failed. The French refused to give battle, and by November the army found itself isolated on the windswept plains of the Auvergne.

Far from home and with time and food running out, knights without horses plodded on foot and discarded their rusting armour. By the time they reached Aquitaine they were forced to beg for bread in the village streets (→ 8/1374).

Gaunt seals temporary truce at Bruges

Low Countries, 27 June 1375
England and France today sealed a one-year truce at Bruges. After his disastrous march through France two years ago that ended with half his army starving to death, John of Gaunt has taken to diplomacy to solve England's problems on the continent and has proved himself remarkably adept at it.

England's holdings in France have been reduced to an area around Calais, a strip of coastland between Bordeaux and Bayonne and a few isolated castles, but England can still threaten mightily. The French know that another invasion is already being prepared across the Channel and are glad enough to agree to Gaunt's truce (→ 24/6/77).

France's Charles V: now an ally.

Miraculous cure is claimed by mystic

Norwich, 13 May 1373
Julian the Anchorite, a Norwich mystic, has been miraculously cured of an apparently fatal illness after seeing a series of divine visions. The 30-year old holy woman had been critically ill for three days and had received the last rites when she experienced 16 revelations about the nature of God and Jesus Christ. She says that she had no feeling left in any part of her body and could feel her life "ebbing away" when the visions began to emanate from a cross in her sick room. "Suddenly all my pain was taken from me," Julian says.

She believes that the experience was granted in answer to her prayer to receive the three graces of God: the recollection of Christ's passion, bodily sickness, and God's gift of three wounds. Little is known of the reclusive Julian, but she is thought to have grown up in a convent and now belongs to a community of nuns (→ 9/1417).

Lincoln court fails to identify killer

Lincoln, 1375
The bloody murder of Sir William Cantilupe, a Lincolnshire knight of some stature in his home county, is baffling judges and jurors here. Though several people have been charged and brought to trial, it has proved difficult to make the cases against them stick.

Sir William was murdered in his own bed. The murderers put the body naked into a sack, carried it for 4 miles, reclothed it in fine garments, with spurs and belt, and threw it into a field – apparently to suggest that he had been killed by footpads or highwaymen.

A dozen members of the knight's household, including his own wife and her maid, were indicted, as well as a landowning neighbour. Some were acquitted and others outlawed, but it is likely that all will soon secure pardons.

The killing of a master by his servants or a husband by his wife is technically one of petty treason. An uncommon offence, it is regarded as particularly heinous.

London, 10 July 1376. Richard, the son of Edward, the late prince of Wales, is declared heir to the throne of England (→ 21/6/77).

England, 1376. The "Lollard" leader John Wyclif preaches on civil jurisdiction over church property (→ 10/1378).

Westminster, 21 June 1377. King Edward III dies (→ 16/7).

England, 24 June 1377. The truce with France expires (→ 10/1378).

Warwickshire, August 1377. John of Gaunt, excluded from Richard II's governing council because of his unpopularity, retires to his castle at Kenilworth (→ 13/3/83).

Scotland, September 1378. The Scots give their support to the Avignon pope, Clement VII, following a great schism in the Roman church.

Gloucester, October 1378. The English government gives its support to Urban VI, the pope in Rome (→ 1381).

France, September 1379. Anglo-French talks reopen at Calais (→ 8/1380).

Munster, October 1379. James Butler, the earl of Ormond, quells a revolt by the O'Byrnes and the O'Tooles (→ 4/1380).

Ulster, May 1380. Edmund Mortimer, the lieutenant of Ireland, campaigns against Niall Mor O'Neill (→ 3/11).

Kent, August 1380. Gravesend is sacked by a fleet from Castile (→ 1/1384).

Northampton, October 1380. The new poll tax is passed; at one shilling [five pence] per man, it is three times more than in 1377 (→ 15/6/81).

Ireland, 3 November 1380. Parliament at Dublin confirms the 1366 Statutes of Kilkenny (→ 26/12).

Canterbury, 1381. William Courtenay is consecrated as archbishop after the death of Simon of Sudbury (→ 5/1381).

England, May 1381. John Wyclif publishes his openly heretical work *Confessio* (→ 26/12/84).

Leinster, 26 December 1381. Edmund Mortimer, the lieutenant of Ireland, dies from a sickness caught during a long summer campaign against the O'Byrnes (→ 23/10/85).

England, 1381. The Navigation Act requires the English to use English ships to export and import (→ 1430).

Parliament mounts opposition to taxes

Westminster, 24 May 1376
In the first parliament summoned since 1373, members of the House of Commons have offered unprecedented opposition to King Edward III. After days of secret deliberation they joined the Lords in the Parliament House of Westminster Palace to answer the king's request for taxes.

Sir Peter de la Mare, a knight from Herefordshire, was chosen by the Commons to be their speaker. He declared the taxes unreasonable, arguing that there would be no need for them had the king spent his treasure wisely and without waste. Sir Peter added: "He has with him certain counsellors who are not useful or loyal, and they have taken advantage by their cunning to deceive the king." He named Lord Latimer, the chamberlain, and Richard Lyons, a merchant, who have lent the king £13,000 at 50 per cent profit to themselves when others had offered the money interest free, to be repaid out of the wool customs.

The Commons demanded that these "evil counsellors" be removed along with Dame Alice Perrers, the king's mistress (→ 22/2/77).

Prince of Wales dies

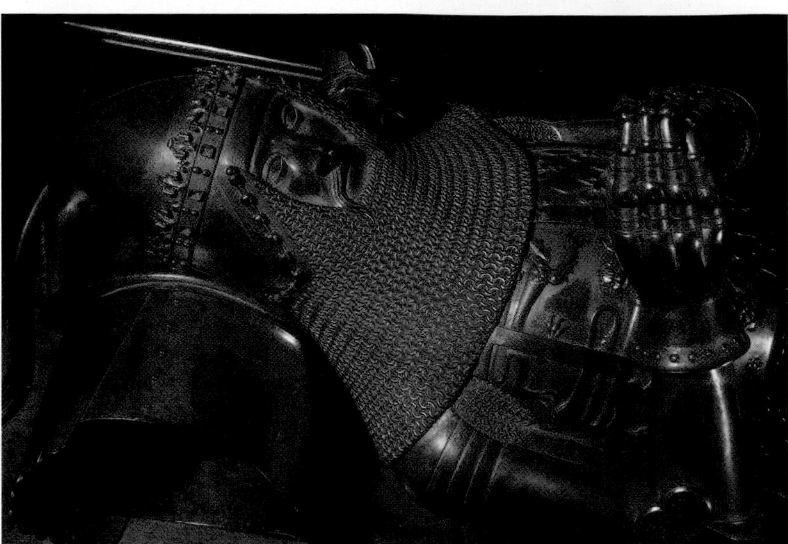
Finally at rest: the effigy of Edward in Canterbury Cathedral, Kent.

Westminster, 8 June 1376
The prince of Wales is dead. At 46, the man who struck fear into his opponents in Europe has lost his final battle against the illness which forced him to return from France in 1371. His son, Richard, is now the heir to the throne.

Edward, recognizable by his distinctive armour, was fearless in battle and ruthless in pursuit of his enemies; when citizens of Limoges rose in protest against heavy English taxes, the ailing prince ordered the city to be razed. Yet neither military victories nor campaigns of terror were able to arrest the loss of English holdings in France.

The prince who had revelled in war and tournaments spent his final years on a sickbed. When he was asked by the bishop of Bangor to forgive all his enemies, the prince refused through gritted teeth until the last moment, when he finally repented (→ 10/7).

Edward withdraws his Irish lieutenant

Dublin, 1376
A second spell as King Edward III's lieutenant in Ireland has come to an end this year for William of Windsor. William, the husband of the king's mistress Alice Perrers, was first sent to Ireland in 1369, but he found it difficult to assert royal authority even within the area of English lordship. His policy of raising taxes for the crown was unpopular, and his lack of social status further offended the Anglo-Irish nobles. Their complaints led Edward to withdraw William in 1371 and to defer the imposition of certain taxes. Three years later, however, William was reappointed with a mandate to impose the taxes but was no more successful than before; complaints of corruption led to his withdrawal, this time, it seems, for good (→ 10/1379).

Pro-royal parliament approves a 'poll tax'

Westminster, 22 February 1377
The new parliament summoned last month was dissolved today, having undone most of the work of last year's "Good Parliament". It has meekly agreed to the king's demand for finance to resume the French war by voting in a "poll tax" of fourpence a head from all lay people, men and women, over the age of 14. Only beggars are exempt.

The parliament also petitioned for pardons for those impeached last year. Lord Latimer and Richard Lyons have already been restored to their offices by John of Gaunt, acting as virtual regent for the sick king. All acts of the "Good Parliament" are annulled and its speaker, Sir Peter de la Mare, has been jailed. Alice Perrers, the king's mistress, has returned to court.

John of Gaunt: a regent's role.

William of Wykeham, the bishop of Winchester and an opponent of Gaunt, was banished from the precincts of the court, but the convocation of Canterbury has refused to grant a poll tax on the clergy until his position is restored. Riots have meanwhile forced John of Gaunt to flee his London palace (→ 10/1380). ▷

Richard II crowned king

A romanticized view of the young king (left) from later in his reign.

Westminster, 16 July 1377
In the first coronation ceremony in England for 50 years, the ten-year-old grandson of Edward III was crowned Richard II in the abbey today. The boy was so exhausted by the elaborate ceremony of anointing, robing and crowning that he had to be carried from the abbey into Westminster Hall for his coronation banquet on the shoulders of his tutor, Sir Simon Burley. On the way one of his red shoes fell off and was never found.

One of the first acts of the young king before his coronation was to make peace between the citizens of London and his uncle, John of Gaunt. He also freed Peter de la Mare, the former speaker of the Commons, from imprisonment in Nottingham Castle.

Yesterday, as a prelude to the coronation ceremonies, the king rode in a great procession from the Tower of London to Westminster through streets decked in cloth of gold and silken hangings. At its head was a band made up of the citizens of Bayeux wearing livery, followed by the City liverymen. The earls and barons, knights and squires followed, all dressed in white to show the king's innocence.

Wine flowed from the pipes of a conduit throughout the procession, but at Cheapside the citizens had set up an effigy of Sir Thomas Belknap, the chief justice, who had insulted them when they asked for their traditional office of butlers at the royal banquet – he had suggested that they might wash up the pots and goblets. When the procession arrived at Cheapside, the effigy vomited wine from its mouth.

The pageantry of these days is the work of John of Gaunt, the young king's uncle and steward of England, who walked beside Richard carrying the sword *Curtana.* But he is too unpopular to be accepted as regent; a "continual council" of 12 has been appointed, excluding Gaunt who is going to his castle at Kenilworth (→ 8/1377).

The ten-year-old king: Richard II.

English spy stabs last Welsh prince

France, July 1378
Owain ap Thomas ap Rhodri, the last claimant to the Welsh throne, has been assassinated at Mortagne-sur-Mer. His killer, James Lambe, believed to be an English spy who had infiltrated Owain's household as his squire, stabbed him as he combed his hair.

Owain, who had been brought up in exile in the French court, was one of France's most flamboyant mercenaries, notching up victories from the Pyrenees to Flanders. But in 1372 he led an ill-fated expedition to Wales. It was supported by France, which wanted to create a diversion for the English forces, but the expedition got no further than Guernsey. Owain smartly defeated the English there, but he never moved on to Wales. However, his prowess on the battlefield and the fear that he might return to Wales made him a serious menace to England. Despite this, most English knights are shocked by the killing and see it as a breach of etiquette that could lose them sympathy in the war against France (→ 10/1400).

No more money for war, say Commons

Gloucester, October 1378
Parliament, meeting at St Peter's Abbey here to avoid interference from the citizens of London, has strongly resisted pleas for more money to be raised for the war in France. Progress in the war, parliament was told, was unsatisfactory, but the Commons reminded the chancellor that they had been promised last year that the king would in future finance the war on his own.

Since the war began again in 1369 the English have lost so much ground to the campaigns of the constable of France, Bertrand de Guesclin, that little remains in their hands beyond Calais, some fortresses in Brittany and the Bordeaux region of Gascony.

Two ports, Brest and Cherbourg, have been ceded to the English on lease, but John of Gaunt's two-month siege of St Malo has failed, and the earl of Arundel failed to take Harfleur in Normandy. One plan now is to obtain and defend a ring of castles around the French coast (→ 9/1379).

English embroidery wins acclaim abroad

A fine example of "Opus Anglicanum": a priest's embroidered vestment.

England, c.1380
The art of embroidery has been scaling new heights of sophistication in England during the past century. English needlewomen are widely recognized as the finest in Europe, and orders for rich copes and chasubles come to London merchants from the papal court at Avignon and great churches on the continent as well as from churches at home. The requests from the continent are for what is called *Opus Anglicanum* [English work].

Among the characteristic features of this work is the liveliness of the beasts and Biblical figures depicted amid decorative frameworks and motifs of silver and gold thread.

Poll tax anger sparks peasants' revolt in London

London, 15 June 1381
Angry mobs – "commoners" from Kent, Essex and London itself – are making their way home tonight after three days and nights of bloody anarchy. The archbishop of Canterbury was murdered, along with other royal officials, and much of London has been looted and burnt, but King Richard II survived after bravely meeting the rebels in a showdown ending with the death of their leader, Wat Tyler.

The rising began as a protest against the poll tax, a levy of one shilling on every adult, but was widened to embrace demands for laws about serfdom to be abolished and for reforms in the church and at court. Rebels from Kent struck first, burning the Marshalsea prison before marching on London Bridge and into the City. Their progress through London was peaceful until they reached Fleet Street where they burnt shops and finally Savoy Palace, John of Gaunt's house. Blood began to flow at St Martin-le-Grand where the mob dragged a judge, Roger Legett, from the altar and beheaded him. The boy king had moved to the security of the Tower and watched the burning before calling a crisis meeting of lords and advisers. Yesterday Richard went to negotiate with the rebels at Mile End, promising to meet their demands.

While the king was away some of the mob broke into the Tower where they seized Simon of Sudbury, the archbishop of Canterbury, as he sang the seventh of seven psalms in the tower's chapel. It took eight blows of the axe to sever the archbishop's head, which was paraded to Westminster before being placed on a stake over London Bridge, a red mitre nailed to the skull to prove its owner. In the bloodbath that followed at least 150 people were to die in a day and night of violence.

It was the teenage king who made the first move today when he rode with his retinue from Westminster to Smithfield where Wat Tyler and a crowd of 60,000 were waiting. Much to the surprise of the people, the king acceded to their demands. The meeting would almost certainly have brought the rebellion to a peaceful conclusion had not Tyler not stepped up his demands in a rude and menacing manner. Angered, the mayor of London, William of Walworth, unsheathed his sword and ran Tyler through. Tyler's supporters moved towards the royal party, but Richard rode towards them. "Sirs, will you shoot your king?" he asked. "I am your captain, follow me."

The young king's bravery, his acceptance of their demands and his offer of a pardon to all rebels carried the day, and the mob is tonight dispersing. Wat Tyler's head has now replaced that of the archbishop on London Bridge (→ 1399).

The rebellious peasants outside the Tower, as imagined by a later artist.

The king goes to meet the rebels (from Froissart's Chronicles, c.1400).

Rebellion spreads throughout England

Artisans of all types were involved.

England, June 1381
News of the London insurrection has spread rapidly across the country, with riots at York, Scarborough and Beverley in the north and "mirror-image" atrocities at St Albans, in Hertfordshire, and in East Anglia. The worst of these horrors is reported from Bury St Edmunds, in Suffolk, where a mob led by a renegade priest, John Wraw, captured Sir John Cavendish, the chief justice of the kingdom, beheaded him and placed his head on the pillory. Later rioters beheaded the prior, John of Cambridge, and paraded both heads on poles as though they were puppets.

Why the people rose against the poll tax

England, June 1381
The tax that provoked this month's uprising was the third of its kind to be imposed in four years, and the most uncompromising. Underlying the unrest were social grievances rooted in the hierarchical system of serfs, merchants and landowners, but the tax itself – requiring each person over the age of 14 to pay a shilling [five pence] – has been perceived as grossly unfair because it takes no account of means. The insensitive behaviour of collectors, who had to compile details of personal circumstances, has caused much resentment, and there has been widespread evasion (→ c.1440).

Wat Tyler kills a tax collector.

1382 - 1386

Westminster, 20 January 1382. Richard II, aged 15, marries Anne of Bohemia (→ 6/1394).

London, October 1382. John of Northampton, the mayor of London, enacts a statute forbidding any member of the victualling guilds to hold judicial office (→ 1385).

Flanders, December 1382. England's and Scotland's lucrative wool trade with Flanders, the chief source of royal revenue, has virtually come to a halt after a series of military advances by the French in Flanders (→ 9/1383).

Borders, 1382. The earl of Dunbar defeats an English army led by Lord Greystoke at Benrig (→ 3/1384).

London, 13 March 1383. Michael de la Pole, an old adherent of John of Gaunt, the duke of Lancaster, is appointed chancellor (→ 1386).

East Anglia, 1383. King Richard II and Queen Anne make a tour of their abbeys in the region (→ 3/3/1415).

London, 1383. John of Northampton is replaced as mayor by Nicholas Brembre, a grocer, who annuls all the recent radical reforms (→ 1385).

France, January 1384. Following the failure of the Norwich "crusade" a nine-month truce is agreed between England and France (→ 4/1386).

Dublin, 23 October 1385. The great council of Ireland asks Richard II of England for a powerful lord to subdue the Anglo-Irish and Gaelic Irish (→ 2/1/87).

London, 1385. The first custom house is built in the City, to the east of London Bridge (→ 1394).

Scotland, 1385. Feuding within the royal family and council continues with a furious attack on Alexander, the "wolf of Badenoch", one of Robert II's sons (→ 8/1385).

France, April 1386. The French royal council makes preparations for an invasion of England (→ 8/7/86).

Plymouth, Devon, 8 July 1386. John of Gaunt, the duke of Lancaster, sets out to claim the Castilian throne with the support of Pope Urban VI (→ 11/1386).

London, 13 October 1386. Richard II promotes his favourite, Robert de Vere, from marquis to duke of Ireland (→ 4/1387).

'Crusade' fails to protect wool trade

London, September 1383
An ill-conceived raid on the French in Flanders – granted the status of a "crusade" by Pope Urban VI – has ended in fiasco. One of its main aims was to re-open access to Flemish markets for the English wool trade. They remain firmly closed off. The leader of the expedition, Henry Despenser, the bellicose bishop of Norwich, has returned here in disgrace with the remnants of his rabble force.

Instead of trying to take Bruges, where French control threatens the future of the English wool staple at Calais, Despenser besieged Ypres. Half of his badly trained army soon deserted. Despenser was allowed to leave only after financially expensive mediation with the French.

The pope receives supplicants.

Scots end 14-year truce with England

Edinburgh, March 1384
Fourteen years of peace between England and Scotland are at an end. Following extensive military preparations on both sides the Scots initiated hostilites on 4 February, two days after the expiry of a truce made by King David II before his death in 1371. They quickly seized Lochmaben Castle [in Dumfries and Galloway] and expelled the English from Annandale. The duke of Lancaster has now camped outside Edinburgh and extorted a ransom from the burgh (→ 1385).

John Wyclif, champion of Lollards, dies

A Victorian view of John Wyclif reading his translation of the Bible.

Leicester, 31 December, 1384
John Wyclif, the intellectual inspiration of the Lollard movement, now widely regarded as heretical, is dead. He was struck down by an acute paralysis three days ago while taking Communion in his parish of Lutterworth, 15 miles from here. He fell just as the host was elevated and has been unable to speak or move much ever since.

Wyclif was primarily a theorist, who developed his ideas in the cloistered atmosphere of Oxford. He believed that the ordinary man should be able to judge the scriptures for himself and pioneered the translation of the Bible into English. He opposed the prevailing practices of buying penances, going on pilgrimages and paying church tithes. His suggestion that priests be judged by their piety rather than simply accepted because of their office won him many enemies. After the 1381 revolt he was condemned by the Black Friars in London at the so-called "Earthquake Council", but he was not excommunicated.

He retired to live quietly and discreetly as Lutterworth's vicar, but his ideas have spread among the independently minded men of the Midlands. Though the majority, even here, are quite happy with the pope's church, the Lollards will probably continue to operate as an influential minority (→ 9/3/92).

London vice ring run by alderman's wife

London, July 1385
Elizabeth Moring, the apparently respectable wife of a London alderman, Henry Moring, has been found guilty of keeping a brothel and sentenced to three years' exile from London.

The key evidence against Mrs Moring was given by Johanna, her serving woman, who described how she had been forced to "consort" with friars, chaplains and others in the house which Mrs Moring had claimed was used for an embroidery business. The young girls who came into her care as apprentices were all forced into the vice ring. Mrs Moring herself also received clients, it was alleged. On 4 May, Mrs Moring sent Johanna to spend the night with a chaplain in his lodgings. When she returned empty-handed the following morning, Mrs Moring sent her back for another night with orders to steal anything she could lay her hands on.

Following the recent crackdown in London, many prostitutes have moved outside the City boundaries. The flocks of girls on Southwark streets are known as "the Winchester geese" because so many live in property owned by the diocese of Winchester (→ 1422).

Border war fizzles out in a stalemate

Scotland, August 1385
The Anglo-Scottish border war, which has been fought throughout the summer, would appear to have fizzled out, with neither side able to claim victory. In May the Scots were reinforced by a French expeditionary force of more than a thousand knights, men-at-arms and armaments. In July the Franco-Scottish army invaded Northumberland, capturing Wark and two other castles. But when Richard II of England approached with an army led by John of Gaunt, the duke of Lancaster, the Scots withdrew. It was an act that disgusted the French, who were eager for a fight to win battle honours.

As the Scots were using their "scorched-earth" tactics, Richard marched on Edinburgh burning a number of churches and abbeys in the region. It was only due to the intervention of John of Gaunt that Holyrood was spared devastation.

The Scottish strategy worked, however, as a lack of provisions forced the English to retreat, and in mid-August the Scots resumed the offensive, raiding Cumbria and Durham with even greater ferocity. Despite this counter-attack the French are reported to be unhappy with the unchivalrous nature of the war and the lack of deference shown to their knights by the Scottish peasantry (→ 6/8/88).

French abandon plans to invade England

An impressive fleet: French sea power is widely feared and respected.

Antwerp, November 1386
It was hailed by the French as the greatest invasion fleet "since God created the world". All summer the shipbuilders had been busy as the armada was marshalled in the sheltered estuary of the Scheldt. Almost 100,000 men were assembling to launch an invasion of England, but the attack has now been called off, a casualty of worsening weather and chronic indecision.

Officially the invasion has only been postponed to next year, but whether it can be reassembled must be doubtful. At its peak the army had 40,000 knights and squires, 50,000 horses and 60,000 foot soldiers, with a navy of 1,200 vessels. Taxes were levied to pay for a cornucopia of supplies ranging from 200,000 arrows to 1,000 barrels of French wine (not forgetting 857 barrels from other countries). There was even a portable wooden town to house the invaders in England.

The delay in embarkation was blamed variously on the weather or the non-arrival of a key French lord, the duc de Berry. His delay sowed doubts about the unanimity of support for the invasion. He turned up three weeks ago, but this month 150 ships' captains said that the rough Channel seas now made an invasion impossible (→ 8/5/89).

English chancellor faces impeachment

London, 1386
The martial aristocracy and an overtaxed parliament have combined to humiliate King Richard II. The magnates, led by the young king's uncle, the duke of Gloucester, have forced Richard to dismiss his chancellor, the earl of Suffolk, and parliament has impeached the earl for mismanaging the nation's affairs.

When the magnates first made their demands for the dismissal of Suffolk, the king replied disdainfully that he would not sack a single kitchen scullion at their request. Military power, however, is in the hands of the magnates, and when Gloucester made a threatening speech including a thinly veiled allusion to the awful fate of the effeminate King Edward II, who was murdered by a red-hot poker, the king's defiance crumbled.

It is the effeminate nature of his court which has much to do with the anger of the old warriors. They point to men like Robert de Vere, the king's closest friend, and jeer that they are "rather knights of Venus than of Bellona".

It seems that Suffolk has been impeached as a scapegoat, for there are guiltier men than him at court. He will not be the last to feel the lash of the council, headed by Gloucester, which has been set up with great powers over all matters of state (→ 13/10).

Knights go to battle over coats of arms

At arms: King Edward III's shield.

England, 1386
A case is being heard at the court of chivalry that highlights the cult of chivalry which has developed since King Edward III founded the Order of the Garter in 1348. Two knights, Sir Richard Scrope of Yorkshire and Sir Robert Grosvenor of Cheshire, are each contesting the right to use the arms "azure a bend or". Both men plan to call witnesses who will back their claims to precedence. Whoever wins the case, which could last for as long as three years, it shows how successful Edward was in fostering a pride in the martial traditions of noble families which now zealously strive to protect their coats of arms against usurpers.

Christ in majesty: two scenes from the beautiful wall painting of the Apocalypse of Saint John, from the chapter house at Westminster Abbey. Its Italianate style was popular right across Europe at this time.

1387 - 1390

England, 2 January 1387. King Richard II orders the arrest of Anglo-Irish spies (→20/2/91).

Wales, April 1387. Robert de Vere, the duke of Ireland and a favourite of Richard II, plots with him to murder Thomas, the duke of Gloucester, and his allies, the earls of Arundel, Warwick, Nottingham and Derby (→14/11).

Hertfordshire, November 1387. At Waltham Cross, Richard II reaches a truce with the barons until the next parliament, accepting an appeal by the duke of Gloucester and his allies, who accuse the king's advisers, Robert de Vere, Michael de la Pole and the chief justice Robert Tresilian, of treason (→20/12).

London, 26 December 1387. The "lords appellant" – those who oppose the king's advisers – threaten to depose the king unless he fixes a date for parliament to hear their charges of treason (→1/1388).

Hampshire, 1387. A school is founded at Winchester by the bishop, William of Wykeham (→27/9/1404).

Flanders, January 1388. After his escape at Radcot Bridge from the "lords appellant", Richard II's favourite Robert de Vere, the duke of Ireland, takes refuge here (→2/1388).

England, 1388. Parliament petitions for anyone levying taxes on the clergy without the king's permission to be classed as a traitor (→11/1415).

Scotland, June 1389. The Scots join the Anglo-French truce which was agreed last month; it is designed to last for three years (→5/1393).

England, 12 July 1389. The poet Geoffrey Chaucer is made clerk of the king's works (→1392).

Strathclyde, 19 April 1390. King Robert II dies, aged 74, at Dundonald Castle in Ayrshire (→17/6).

Grampian, 17 June 1390. Alexander, the earl of Buchan and younger brother of King Robert III, burns Elgin Cathedral in order to warn his brothers against interfering in the region (→14/8).

Tayside, 14 August 1390. Robert III, formerly John, the earl of Carrick, is crowned king of Scotland at Scone and confirms his brother Robert, who is the earl of Fife, as guardian (→9/1396).

Barons defeat the king's auxiliaries

Oxfordshire, 20 December 1387
Robert de Vere, the newly created duke of Ireland, was defeated at Radcot Bridge yesterday as he made for London to support King Richard II in his quarrel with the barons and parliament. The royal favourite was trapped by the baronial forces led by the duke of Gloucester, who is determined to impose his will on his nephew, the king.

De Vere apparently fled when he saw that he was trapped, rejecting pleas from his soldiers to stand and fight. In his seized baggage letters have been found from the king telling him to hurry to London with a large army. The barons claim that these letters are proof of Richard's untrustworthiness (→26).

Royalists are convicted of treachery after being tried by 'the merciless parliament'

London, February 1388
From the moment when the five "lords appellant" dressed in golden surcoats walked arm in arm into a crowded Westminster Hall on the third of this month, it was clear that a crucial meeting of parliament was to take place. First, the duke of Gloucester, the king's uncle and senior lord appellant, knelt before Richard and denied any intention of deposing him. The king declared his uncle blameless, and parliament began its main business: the lords' accusation of treachery against the king's friends and advisers.

The five lords – Gloucester, Arundel, Warwick, Derby and Nottingham – argued that civil law did not apply in this case, and that only the lords of parliament could judge cases involving the king. Parliament agreed and convicted the alleged traitors – winning itself the label "merciless". the five condemned men were the earls of Suffolk and Oxford, Sir Robert Tresilian, the chief justice, the archbishop of York and Sir Nicholas Brembre.

The earls and the archbishop have fled abroad, but Tresilian was hanged after being found hiding in Westminster Abbey. His crime had been to support royal supremacy against a parliament controlled by nobles. Brembre was refused permission for trial by battle, and, although few thought him guilty, he too died at Tyburn (→3/5/89).

Scots victorious in battle at Otterburn

A later engraving of the clash at Otterburn when Scotland won the day.

Newcastle upon Tyne, 6 Aug 1388
The Scots won a great victory near here last night, killing at least 1,500 of an English army led by Henry Hotspur, the son of the earl of Northumberland, who was among those captured. The Scottish leader, the earl of Douglas, was fatally wounded at the moment of victory.

The Scots were at dinner when a messenger brought news of the English army nearby. Douglas led his best men to Otterburn through thickets and thorn brakes to burst upon the English just as the sun was setting. Caught off guard, the much bigger English force was slaughtered in the moonlight.

Ironically, the victory was won by a decoy force. The main Scottish army under the earl of Fife was on the other side of the country. Hotspur first went to intercept them but doubled back when he found that Fife had more men. He planned to attack Douglas's smaller army, but Fife had sent a messenger to warn Douglas. The Scots were therefore able to surprise the English while they were resting (→1/12).

Heir loses power in Scottish reshuffle

Scotland, 1 December 1388
Further quarrelling within the reigning Stewart family has led to a reshuffle in the Scots government. King Robert II has removed his eldest son, John, the 49-year-old earl of Carrick, from his position as lieutenant and replaced him with his second son, Robert, the earl of Fife, who is appointed guardian.

Four years ago Carrick became lieutenant in a palace coup during which the king's age – he was 68 at the time – and his apparent inability to enforce law and order were used as excuses to transfer executive authority to Carrick. The new lieutenant was also concerned at the favour being shown to another brother, Alexander, the earl of Buchan. Buchan has recently been sacked from his office as justiciar north of the Forth.

Last August Carrick was left lame after being kicked by a horse. This gave Fife the opportunity to persuade the council that his elder brother should be retired. However, Carrick remains the heir. In contrast to feuding with his sons, Robert has maintained good relations with the Scots nobility by generous grants of land, pensions and privileges. Several of his seven daughters have also married prominent nobles (→6/1389).

Richard takes personal control of England

William Wykeham, the bishop of Winchester: the new chancellor.

London, 3 May 1389
After a year of licking his wounds while the "lords appellant" ruled the nation, King Richard II has today struck back in a dramatic style which bodes ill for the men who have humiliated him and judicially murdered his friends. Summoning the great council, to Westminster, he asked how old he was. The puzzled councillors told him that he was 22. He then declared that as he had come of age he meant to take control of "my house and household, not to mention my kingdom".

This bold stroke took the council by surprise, and Thomas Arundel, the archbishop of York, meekly surrendered the great seal of office as chancellor. Bishop Gilbert of Hereford and Bishop Waltham of Salisbury, respectively the treasurer and the keeper of the privy seal, followed his example.

The king then handed the seal to the elderly William of Wykeham, the bishop of Winchester, appointing him chancellor. The equally venerable bishop of Exeter was made treasurer, and the privy seal was given to Edmund Stafford, a young man of a noble house.

To accompany these appointments Richard has sent the sheriffs writs proclaiming that he has taken the government of the realm "upon his own person" (→22/11/92).

Cathedral painting hailed as masterpiece

Norwich, 1390
A splendid altarpiece, recently finished and now in place at Norwich Cathedral, seems destined to be regarded as a masterpiece of 14th-century panel painting.

The altarpiece (or "retable") is divided into five vertical panels depicting the scourging of Christ, Christ carrying the cross, the Crucifixion, the Resurrection and the Ascension. Included in the decorative border surrounding the altarpiece are the armorials of Henry Despenser, the bishop of Norwich. The iconographical style of the altarpiece has links with Bohemian painting in the way in which the figure of the resurrected Christ is shown. The crowding of the slender figures in the foreground, with their arched eyebrows, marks a new style in East Anglian painting (→1412).

The crucifixion panel at Norwich.

Blancmange highlights a culinary craze as cooks add spices to the dining tables

The nobleman's table: a reconstruction of mealtime in the great hall.

Kitchen skills: the cook's talent is to liven up a repetitive menu.

England, c.1390
God sends food, and the Devil sends cooks, as the proverb puts it, but the cooks, at least those working for the rich, are doing their best to improve their image. Rarely, not perhaps since the Romans, has cookery inspired such inventiveness, such elaborate dishes and such colour, complexity and sheer cost of ingredients.

Great roasts, luscious pies, cunningly assembled sauces, mouthwatering desserts, all laden with a wide variety of exotic spices and flavourings, make the nobleman's table full of temptations. Few, even the most pious, are immune. If a man has the money and his cook the skill, then both are exploited fully. Even the duke of Lancaster, in his *Livre de Seyntz Medicines*, a book that castigates such sins as gluttony, says that all should indulge "as their estate demands".

Typical of today's dishes is the blancmange: a mixture of shredded chicken and rice, boiled in almond milk and seasoned with aniseed. Much of this spicing and saucing is born of necessity. Fresh ingredients are frequently hard to come by, and salted meat and fish and dried vegetables are found in the most prosperous larder. The cook must mask these monotonous staples with every artifice – in taste and appearance – that he can devise (→14/5/1413).

A reconstructed kitchen.

1391 - 1398

Flanders, 22 November 1392. Robert de Vere, the former duke of Ireland and favourite of Richard II of England, dies in exile (→1/1397).

England, 1392. Geoffrey Chaucer, the poet, completes the "Prologue" to his *Canterbury Tales* (→25/10/1400).

Co Sligo, 1392. A luxuriously illuminated manuscript, the *Yellow Book of Lecan*, is compiled by Giolla Iosa Mor Mac Fir Bhisigh of Lecan.

France, May 1393. Anglo-French peace talks, which collapsed in April 1392, resume at Ponthieu (→8/7/95).

England, 1393. The third Statute of Praemunire limits papal power in England (→31/7/96).

Leinster, 30 October 1394. Richard II of England defeats the forces of Art MacMurrough (→1397).

Surrey, 9 April 1395. Richard II orders the destruction of Sheen Palace (→1/1397).

England, 8 July 1395. Richard II proposes his marriage to Isabelle, the six-year-old daughter of Charles VI of France (→9/3/96).

Paris, 9 March 1396. An Anglo-French truce is agreed (→11/1396).

Canterbury, 31 July 1396. Thomas Arundel, a "lord appellant", succeeds William Courtenay as archbishop (→26/2/1401).

Tayside, 28 September 1396. King Robert III watches a clan combat at Perth which sees the deaths of 19 men of Clan Chattan and 29 of Clan Kay (→28/4/98).

London, January 1397. Parliament legitimizes the children of John of Gaunt, the duke of Lancaster, by his wife and former mistress Katherine Swynford (→25/9).

Ireland, 1397. Niall Mor O'Neill, the king of Tyrone, resigns in favour of his son, Niall Og (→20/7/98).

Scotland, 28 April 1398. Robert III creates the dukedom of Rothesay for his eldest son David and that of Albany for his own younger brother Robert (→27/1/99).

Co Carlow, 20 July 1398. The lieutenant, Roger Mortimer, the earl of March and of Ulster, dies in an attack by the O'Tooles and the O'Byrnes of Leinster (→29/5/99).

Rule of Ireland is subjected to review

Ireland, 20 February 1391
King Richard II of England has ordered an inquiry into the conduct of his government in Ireland. The situation here has been deteriorating since the king's decision to free himself of the burden of Ireland and govern it by contract instead. However, Sir John Stanley's period in office as lieutenant has been a disaster. He has failed to curb the power of Irish chieftains, most notably the O'Neills in Ulster, and this, coupled with his alleged incompetence, has greatly angered the king (→30/10/94).

In full cry: an Irish chieftain.

English king hits earl at queen's funeral

London, June 1394
King Richard II, heartbroken by the death of his beloved queen, Anne of Bohemia, flew into a rage today when the earl of Arundel arrived late for her funeral at Westminster Abbey. Seizing a steward's wand of office, he struck Arundel in the face and drew blood. There was a gasp of horror from the congregation, and the clerics believe that this act of violence has polluted the abbey. The magnificent state funeral ran its course, however, and Richard and Arundel appear to be reconciled. But there is great anger seething beneath the glittering surface (→9/4/95).

Queen Anne on her deathbed.

Lollard leader hides in the Welsh Marches

Hereford, 9 March 1392
King Richard II has today given the go-ahead for Bishop John Trefnant to arrest and imprison the leading Lollard preacher in the county, William Swinderby. Trefnant summoned Swinderby to Hereford for judgement last October. Swinderby stuck by his views that monks should live in poverty, not luxury, and that the pope had no right to sell indulgences.

After that excommunication was certain, and Swinderby fled to the Welsh hills without waiting for the verdict. He is no stranger to persecution. He began preaching in Leicester and became leader of a small group of heretics in the chapel of St John the Baptist near the leper hospital. He was condemned by the bishop and forced to recant in 1392. He moved to Worcester, but the bishop there prohibited him from preaching in August 1387.

His eloquence has won him many converts around here, and they will protect him. The bishop will not find it easy to catch him if he stays in the Welsh Marches (→1393).

Richard marries his French child bride in extravagant ceremony

A diplomatic marriage: Richard weds the seven-year-old Princess Isabelle.

Calais, France, November 1396
Richard II has married his child bride, Princess Isabelle of France, the eldest daughter of Charles VI. By the time Isabelle is crowned in London next January the English king will have spent £200,000 – far more than her dowry – on gifts and lavish ceremonies on both sides of the channel.

The marriage is unpopular in England because of Isabelle's age and nationality. But Richard obviously hopes that the marriage will not only set the seal on the recent truce with France but also boost his own authority in dealing with recalcitrant English lords. He is said to be fond of the French child and prepared to wait the years it will take before she can produce an heir. His first queen, Anne of Bohemia, died two years ago (→7/2/1403).

Vengeful English king is increasingly tyrannical

The king's vengeance: Gloucester in custody after his arrest by Richard.

Homage to a despot: four Irish kings kneel before King Richard in 1395.

Lords executed as Richard exacts revenge

London, 25 September 1397
King Richard II has today taken a fearsome revenge on the barons who humiliated him and forced the execution of his court officials and the banishment of his friends over nine years ago. At a parliament held in a specially erected building in the palace yard at Westminster, the three principal "lords appellant" – the duke of Gloucester, the earl of Arundel and the earl of Warwick – have been found guilty of treason and sentenced to be hanged, drawn and quartered.

Arundel was taken immediately to the Tower for the sentence to be carried out; the king allowed him only the mercy of being beheaded instead of being hanged. Warwick, who confessed to everything in abject fashion, had his sentence commuted to banishment for life on the Isle of Man. The king is satisfied with this punishment because Warwick's confession gave him the justification for his revenge on the other lords.

Gloucester, the king's uncle, has already been disposed of. Arrested by Richard himself, he was taken to Calais and there murdered by the king's men. It is said that he was smothered with a mattress. The king, nevertheless, needed to have him found guilty of treason to justify his death. The king has prepared for this day with great secrecy and cunning. He now rules unchallenged (→16/9/98)

Parliament deprived of long-held rights

London, 16 September 1398
The rule of King Richard II is growing increasingly despotic. He holds many feasts on holy days at which he sits on a high throne, saying nothing but seeing everything, and when he looks at anyone that person, whatever his rank, must bend his knee in submission or incur the king's wrath.

Richard has gathered power into his hands by persuading parliament to hand over its decision making to a committee of 18, all of them his men. He has thus taken control of the rights and liberties won by parliament over the last century.

He travels around the country guarded by his rough bowmen from Cheshire, spending his time at feasts and tournaments and leaving the running of the country to minor officials in Westminster. The people are being heavily taxed to pay for his extravagance, and there is much grumbling in the country.

Today he has enraged both Henry Bolingbroke, the son of John of Gaunt, and Thomas Mowbray, the duke of Norfolk. Bolingbroke had accused Mowbray of using treasonable language against the king, and it was arranged that they would meet in trial by battle. A huge crowd gathered, but when the pair entered the lists the king forbade them to fight and exiled Mowbray for life and Bolingbroke for ten years. He has made a dangerous enemy of Bolingbroke (→3/2/99).

Royal arts patron

Westminster, 25 December 1396
A series of banquets is being laid on to celebrate rebuilding work on the 37-metre (120-foot)-long hall at Westminster. Richard II is presiding over the festivities, which include indoor jousts. The remodelling of the hall has created an architectural wonder: a number of giant hammerbeam trusses to support the 660-tonne roof and leave a vast open floor space without supporting columns (→c.1405).

A discerning patron of the arts: (left) a small devotional painting made for the king shows Richard, kneeling, as he is presented by his favourite saints to the Virgin and Child and a group of angels wearing his badge of the White Hart; (right) Westminster Hall with its superb hammerbeam roof, whose rebuilding Richard commissioned.

1399 - 1400

Scotland, 27 January 1399. King Robert III replaces his brother Robert, the duke of Albany, as guardian by David, the duke of Rothesay, his own eldest son (→ 22/3).

England, 18 March 1399. King Richard II announces that the exile of his cousin, Henry Bolingbroke, the son of the late John of Gaunt, the duke of Lancaster, is to be permanent; all the lands of the duchy of Lancaster will return to the crown (→ 4/7).

Scotland, 22 March 1399. Anglo-Scots peace talks open (→ 18/2/1400).

South Yorkshire, 4 July 1399. Henry Bolingbroke lands at Ravenspur to take possession of his father's lands (→ 13).

South Yorkshire, 13 July 1399. Henry Bolingbroke joins forces at Doncaster with Henry Percy, the earl of Northumberland, Henry Percy the younger, Ralph Neville, the earl of Westmorland, and others who are opposed to Richard II (→ 11/8).

Conwy, Gwynedd, 11 August 1399. Richard II returns from Ireland to face the invasion of Henry Bolingbroke (→ 20).

Ireland, 11 October 1399. The earl of Desmond, John fitz Gerald FitzGerald, drowns at Ardfinnan returning from a campaign against the Butlers (→ 8/12/1407).

Westminster, 13 October 1399. Henry Bolingbroke is crowned Henry IV of England (→ 15).

Westminster, 15 October 1399. Henry IV makes his son Henry prince of Wales (→ 4/1/1400).

Lothian, 18 February 1400. George Dunbar, the earl of March, asks Henry IV to intervene in his row with Robert III of Scotland over the betrothal dowry of Dunbar's daughter to David of Albany, who has married a daughter of Archibald "the Grim" without returning the dowry (→ 23/8).

Edinburgh, 23 August 1400. On the refusal of Robert III to pay homage to Henry IV, Henry tries unsuccessfully to storm the castle (→ 10/1400).

Borders, October 1400. Anglo-Scots peace talks fail when Robert III questions Henry IV's right to the English throne (→ 5/1402).

London, 21 December 1400. Henry IV meets the Byzantine emperor, Manuel II, at Blackheath, during Manuel's tour of western Europe.

John of Gaunt, the loyal uncle, is dead

London, 3 February 1399

John of Gaunt, one of the richest and most powerful noblemen in the kingdom, died today and is to be buried with due ceremony in St Paul's Cathedral. He was 59. The duke of Lancaster was the son of one king and uncle of the present monarch. He virtually ruled England during the minority of King Richard II and, although unpopular, never faltered in his loyalty to the king. He is succeeded as duke by his son, Henry Bolingbroke, exiled by Richard last year. The court is now waiting to see if the king will allow his cousin to return (→ 18/3).

John of Gaunt: the heraldic arms.

Richard leads new offensive in Ireland

Co Waterford, 1 June 1399

King Richard II of England arrived here today to begin the second Irish expedition of his reign. The king was angered by a renewed challenge by an Irish chieftain, Art MacMurrough. Four years ago Richard, accompanied by leading English nobles, had forced MacMurrough and other rebels into submission. MacMurrough forfeited his lands in Leinster but was given a knighthood by Richard. Following the death of the earl of March, the king's lieutenant, MacMurrough took back his lands, claiming that he was Ireland's rightful king. Despite the uncertainty in England, Richard decided to return to Ireland (→ 11/10).

King surrenders to his cousin Bolingbroke

A treacherous pact: Richard meets Henry Percy, who later betrayed the king.

Gwynedd, 20 August 1399

Richard II agreed to surrender today to Henry Bolingbroke, the duke of Lancaster. It is just 47 days since the exiled duke landed at Ravenspur in Yorkshire claiming that he wanted only the restoration of the lands left him by his father, John of Gaunt, which had been seized by Richard, his cousin.

Henry had a force of only 300 men, but he rapidly gathered support from discontented northern magnates, including Henry Percy, the earl of Northumberland. He met hardly any opposition because the king, over-confident, was in Ireland. By the time Richard returned, delayed by storms, he found that his support had melted away.

He might have held out here in Conwy Castle but Percy and Thomas Arundel, the brother of the executed earl of Arundel, offered him terms under which he would remain king. He accepted, but was taken prisoner when he left the castle (→ 30/9).

A marginal illustration to a book of hours commissioned by the de Bohun family, which has exerted an enormous influence in patronizing the arts. Eleanor de Bohun, who continued the tradition of patronage established by her father Humphrey, the sixth earl of Hereford, died in 1399.

Captive monarch forced to abdicate

Westminster, 30 September 1399
This morning, before an empty throne in Westminster Hall, Henry Bolingbroke laid claim to the crown of England. A parliament summoned in the name of Richard II was told that the king, held by Henry's supporters in the Tower of London, had abdicated. It is highly unlikely that Richard, a champion of the monarch's absolute powers, would have chosen such a course voluntarily. However, parliament deposed Richard after hearing 33 charges against him. Henry, his cousin, then formally claimed the throne "by right line of blood" and, more persuasively, because the kingdom was "almost undone for default of government and undoing of good laws". He will be crowned Henry IV next month (→13/10).

A new beginning: Henry of Lancaster is crowned as King Henry IV.

Mystery surrounds English king's death

West Yorkshire, 14 February 1400
There are conflicting reports at Pontefract about the death of the deposed King Richard II. Some say that he died violently today at the castle, others that he was slowly starved to death on the orders of King Henry IV.

According to one report, Henry sent a knight, Sir Peter Exton, to the castle with a party of seven armed men, who rushed into Richard's cell armed with axes while he was at dinner with his squire. When Richard saw them he threw back the table, snatched an axe and set about defending himself with such courage that four of his attackers were killed. Whatever the truth, Richard is definitely dead, and his body is to go on display (→21/7/03).

Medical handbook uses signs of zodiac

Oxford, c.1400
Physicians, mathematicians and astronomers have joined forces to produce a medical handbook that will provide ground rules for the treatment of illness.

A table of eclipses opens the book, followed by a table of the planets and a coloured drawing of the zodiac man, which depicts parts of the body and their relationship to the zodiac.

Man is a microcosm composed of four elements – earth, water, air and fire – varying in temperature and moisture, which can accentuate any of the four moods – sanguine, choleric, phlegmatic or melancholic. Illness is a result of an imbalance in these humours.

The handbook goes on to deal with blood-letting, which is the most usual treatment. Blood can be taken either from the seat of pain or from an opposite point and must only be done when the planets are favourably positioned. The book also includes a colour chart which gives instructions on interpreting urine colour (→1421).

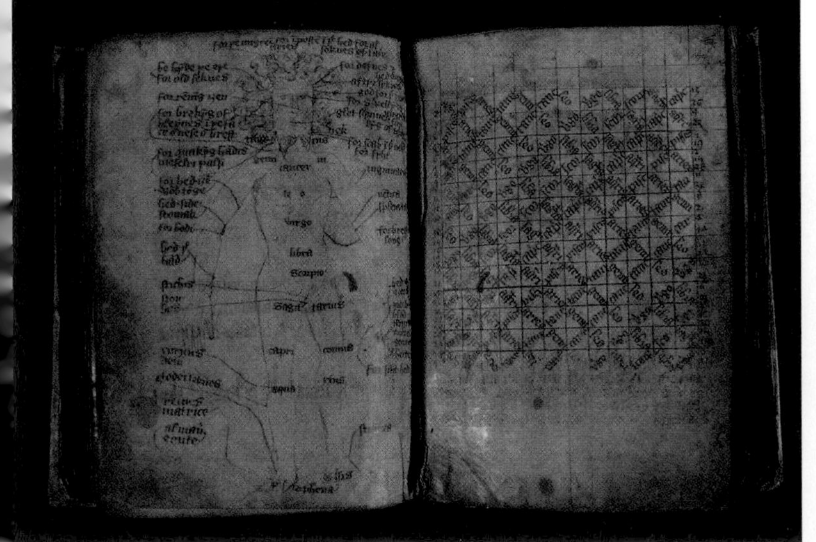

The zodiac man (left) links the planets to different parts of the body.

Plot by rebel earls is foiled by tip-off

Windsor, 4 January 1400
Rebel barons hold the castle here, but a plot to kill Henry IV and restore Richard II appears to have been betrayed. The conspirators included the earls of Rutland, Kent and Huntingdon and a man called Richard Maudelyn, who looks sufficiently like Richard to impersonate him. The barons planned to seize the king, but early this morning Henry collected his sons and set out in great haste for London and help. It seems certain that Henry must have been told of the plot, some say by Rutland, his cousin (→14/2).

The funeral of the deposed king.

Welsh finally submit to king's authority

Shropshire, October 1400
King Henry IV of England has returned to Shrewsbury from an expedition into north Wales confident that he has stamped out the rebellion launched last month by Owain Glyndwr, a lord in the Upper Dee valley who had proclaimed himself "prince of Wales".

The revolt was sparked off by a dispute with an English neighbour, Reginald Grey, the lord of Ruthin. Angered by what he regarded as Grey's victimization of him, Glyndwr soon gathered supporters among Welshmen increasingly hostile to English rule. On 18 September they attacked, burning Ruthin before launching raids on Denbigh, Rhuddlan, Flint and other towns as far west as Anglesey and as far south as Oswestry.

But as Henry marched towards Wales, an English force under Hugh Burnell defeated Glyndwr on 24 September near Welshpool. Glyndwr withdrew into the hills, leaving the king to lead a brief, punitive raid into Wales to reassert his authority (→3/1401).

Holy shrines attract pilgrims and inspire writers

Canterbury pilgrims: from a collection by contemporary poet John Lydgate.

Great poet Chaucer closes his last book

London, 25 October 1400
Geoffrey Chaucer, the greatest English poet of the last century, has died, aged about 60. Chaucer led a full life even without his writing: he fought with English forces in France, undertook diplomatic missions in Europe, represented Kent in one parliament and held offices in the royal court. Yet he still had time to be a prodigious scholar who read widely in Latin, French and Italian and studied science.

He published first *The Book of the Duchess*, on the death of the wife of John of Gaunt, his patron, then the humorous *Parliament of Fowls* and his great poem of tragic love *Troilus and Criseyde*. His last 15 years were spent on the unfinished *Canterbury Tales* (→ 1478).

Geoffrey Chaucer: learned poet.

'Tales' cover wide range of English society

Tellers of tales: the merchant ...

... and the oft-married wife of Bath.

England, 1400
At his death Geoffrey Chaucer left the manuscript of 24 of his popular *Canterbury Tales*. A long "Prologue" tells how 30 pilgrims, meeting at the Tabard inn in Southwark to set out on the journey to the shrine of St Thomas Becket in Canterbury, were invited by the host of the inn to tell two stories each along the way. He would give a free supper for the best storyteller.

The pilgrims Chaucer describes with humour are a cross-section of society. Among the better-off are a chivalrous "perfect gentle knight" with his ardent young squire, a franklyn [freeholder], at whose open house it "snowed with meat and drink", and a wife of Bath who had "had five husbands all at the church door" and done very well out of them.

The religious ones include a nun speaking dainty French, a hunting monk with his greyhounds, a merry friar and a pardoner who sells indulgences. Lower in the scale, a miller, a reeve [estate steward], a cook (who gets drunk), a sea captain and a threadbare Oxford student relate some of the very bawdiest tales.

Shrines at the end of the pilgrims' travels

Gloucester, 1400
Thomas Becket's shrine at Canterbury is not the only place drawing "*folk to goon on pilgrimages*". Some go for the papal indulgences, others for a holiday. St Michael's Mount in Cornwall, where St Michael is said to have appeared in 495, Walsingham in Norfolk, where the Virgin Mary appeared in 1061, Glastonbury, where King Arthur, Joseph of Arimathea, and maybe Christ Himself, came, and where the Holy Grail is reputedly buried, attract tens of thousands.

Among the more recent shrines drawing thousands of pilgrims is Gloucester Abbey, where Edward II is buried. In spite of the discouragement given by Gloucester's monks, the common people are convinced that he is a saint.

Two badges worn by pilgrims to signal to fellow travellers their devotion.

1401 - 1406

London, 2 March 1401. William Sawtre is burned for heresy, the first victim of a new statute (→ 8/6/05)

Welsh Marches, March 1401. New laws restrict Welsh land rights (→ 18/10).

Powys, 18 October 1401. Owain Glyndwr kills Lord Charlton of Powys in a raid on Welshpool (→ 30/11/02).

Winchester, 7 February 1403. Henry IV marries Joan, the dowager duchess of Brittany, and daughter of King Charles II of Navarre (→ 10/8/12).

Wales, May 1403. Henry, the prince of Wales and its newly appointed lieutenant, begins raiding the country (→ 29/8/04).

Shrewsbury, 23 July 1403. Thomas Percy, the earl of Worcester and uncle of Henry "Hotspur", seized in the revolt against Henry IV, is beheaded (→ 11/8).

York, 11 August 1403. Henry Percy, the earl of Northumberland, submits to Henry IV, repudiating the revolt in which his son and brother died (→ 3/11).

York, 3 November 1403. Henry IV orders that Henry "Hotspur's" head be returned to his widow (→ 8/2/05).

Normandy, 29 August 1404. After the alliance between Glyndwr and Charles VI of France, Henry IV of England halts a French fleet bound for Wales at Harfleur (→ 8/1405).

England, 27 September 1404. William of Wykeham, the bishop of Winchester and founder of New College, Oxford, dies (→ 13/7/39).

Gwynedd, 28 February 1405. Owain Glyndwr, Edmund Mortimer and Henry Percy, the earl of Northumberland, agree at Aberdaron to partition England (→ 23/5).

Hereford, 23 May 1405. Henry IV abandons his Welsh invasion to head north to combat a revolt led by the earl of Northumberland (→ 6/1405).

Scotland, June 1405. The earl of Northumberland seeks refuge from Henry IV of England (→ 8/1405).

Hereford and Worcester, August 1405. Owain Glyndwr retreats from a clash with Henry IV at Woodbury (→ 19/9/07).

North Sea, 14 March 1406. James, the 11-year-old son of Robert III of Scots, is seized on his way to France (→ 4/4).

Scottish heir died of 'natural causes'

Ailing ruler: King Robert III.

Lothian, May 1402
A verdict of death by "divine providence" was delivered today, by a narrow margin, at the inquiry into the death of David, the duke of Rothesay, the eldest son of the king. The council rejected the claim by Rothesay's friends that the heir to the Scottish throne was starved to death at Falkland Castle on the orders of the king's brother, Robert, the duke of Albany. It was Albany who had persuaded the ailing King Robert to jail his own son in order to punish his corruption. Albany now becomes king's lieutenant in Rothesay's place (→ 14/9).

'Hotspur' wins crushing victory over Scots

Northumberland, 14 Sept 1402
The earl of Northumberland and his son Henry Percy – nicknamed "Hotspur" – have inflicted a crushing defeat on the Scottish army at Homildon Hill, overlooking the small town of Wooler on the edge of the Cheviots.

The Scots, under the earl of Douglas, had invaded England together with some 30 French knights and plundered as far south as Newcastle upon Tyne. Northumberland barred their way home, and at midday battle commenced. The Scots, numbering about 10,000, established themselves high on the hill. The 7,000-strong corps of English archers bombarded them mercilessly from a sheltered position, inflicting a terrible toll.

Although Douglas rallied his knights for a charge against the archers, the rain of arrows made this impossible. Douglas was hit, lost an eye and was taken prisoner; the Scots broke up in disarray. Five hundred of them drowned trying to cross the Tweed. English losses were slight (→ 14/3/06).

The fierce battle at Homildon Hill, as imagined by a later artist.

Penalty for heresy to be death by burning

A heretic does public penance.

London, 26 February 1401
The death penalty is to be used against heretics. William Sawtre, a Lollard preacher who was condemned for heresy and dismissed from the priesthood by an ecclesiastical court three days ago, has been sentenced to be burnt to death.

For the bishops, who have been campaigning for the death penalty against the Lollards for five years, this is a victory. Pope Gregory XI condemned John Wyclif in 1377 for his criticisms of clerical abuses and of the church as an institution, in particular its hierarchy and its wealth. In these attacks, Lollardy has threatened the ecclesiastical order. Now the bishops have persuaded the state that it threatens the secular order, too (→ 2/3).

Scholars and clerks in front of New College, Oxford, where new cloisters were finished in 1400.

Bloody battle ends revolt by 'Hotspur'

Shrewsbury, 21 July 1403

"Hotspur" – Henry Percy, the son of the powerful earl of Northumberland – is dead. He was among hundreds of knights and soldiers who died today in a day-long battle of the utmost ferocity which leaves Henry IV as the undisputed master of England. The king had moved quickly when he got news that Hotspur was in open revolt in Cheshire. Henry took just three days to join the prince of Wales's small force at Shrewsbury, thus catching the rebels by surprise.

By moving quickly Henry had also forestalled the arrival of reinforcements for Percy in the shape of his father, the earl of Northumberland, and the Welsh led by Owain Glyndwr. The armies were drawn up about two miles north-east of the town, near a little hamlet called Berwick. Henry sent the abbot of Shrewsbury with an offer to hear Hotspur's grievances, but it was too late; Percy had already openly challenged the legitimacy of Henry's coronation, backing instead the rival claim of the infant earl of March.

Battle began at midday. Twice Hotspur's men struck down a knight dressed as the king, and the cry went up: "Henry Percy, king!" But as night fell Hotspur was surrounded and cut down, and the shouts turned to: "Henry Percy, slain!" Disheartened, the rebels decided to flee, leaving a battlefield strewn with corpses for some 5km (3 miles) (→23).

Glyndwr intensifies challenge to Henry

Rebel prince: Owain Glyndwr.

Wales, 30 November 1402

The rebellion of Owain Glyndwr, the self-styled prince of Wales, today gathered further momentum with the marriage of his daughter to Edmund Mortimer, the uncle of a claimant to the English throne, the infant earl of March. Mortimer was captured by Glyndwr during the battle at Pilleth, in Powys, during June. Henry IV of England resisted ransom pleas, saying that he was not paying money to strengthen his enemies. Glyndwr exploited this refusal by winning Mortimer's support for his claim to rule Wales, with March to reign in England. This pact follows a year of military success for Glyndwr (→5/1403).

Son's capture is blamed for king's death

Strathclyde, 4 April 1406

King Robert III died at Rothesay Castle on the Isle of Bute today, aged 69. He had been lame for the past 18 years and was living in semi-retirement. He died less than a fortnight after receiving the news that his only surviving son, 11-year-old Prince James, had been captured by English pirates. Those close to the king say that he simply lost the will to live and stopped eating.

Prince James's elder brother, the duke of Rothesay, died in suspicious circumstances four years ago [*see report on page 339*], and Robert decided to send James to France for his own safety. Once at sea the prince's ship, *The Maryenknyght*, was boarded by Great Yarmouth pirates on 14 March. The possibility that the English were tipped off while James lingered on the Bass Rock has not been discounted in the Scottish court. Although Scotland and England are at present enjoying a truce, King Henry IV has placed Prince James in the Tower of London.

This latest disaster seems to have proved to be too much for Robert III to bear. His ambitious and able younger brother Robert, the duke of Albany, retains the governorship of Scotland.

Robert III: lost the will to live.

The late king, whose life was blighted by family feuding and his own physical disability, once said that he would be content to be buried in a midden with the epitaph "Here lies the worst of kings and the most wretched of men in the whole realm" (→3/1409).

Archbishop is executed for joining rebels

York, 8 June 1405

Despite a last-minute plea from the archbishop of Canterbury, and in defiance of those who thought he would never have the audacity to go through with it, King Henry IV has executed the archbishop of York, Richard Scrope. Scrope, who had been archbishop since 1398, had been caught by trickery when he led a citizens' army to press grievances which had previously been nailed to church doors in the city.

Ralph Neville, the earl of Westmorland, met the prelate at Shipton Moor, six miles outside York. At the parley Neville agreed to support these claims, and then he persuaded the delegation to show their friendship by drinking together in the open. As they did this the rebel forces dispersed back to York, and it was then, ten days ago, that the archbishop was taken prisoner.

Henry arrived here two days ago and today ordered a court to condemn Scrope, Thomas Mowbray, the earl marshal, and Sir William Plumpton to death as traitors. They were then taken just outside the walls at Skeldergate, close to the river, and beheaded (→8/1407).

Trading guilds boost London's prosperity

Trading centre: a reconstruction drawing of a market at St Paul's, London.

London, c.1405

The streets of London may not be paved with gold, but large amounts of wealth are being amassed in the city thanks to the triumph of the trading guilds – those of the Mercers, Drapers, Grocers and others – which, together with associations such as the Merchant Adventurers, have organized and now dominate home and overseas trade. Trading wharves are sprouting up by the river, with 30 or 40 woolships alone setting out daily for the continent, and dozens of ships of other trades putting in and going out. Indeed, the city is now one of the greatest ports in western Europe. Its population has risen steadily since the Black Death in the last century and is now believed to number some 50,000 people (→23/1/37).

1407 - 1409

Dyfed, 12 September 1407. Supporters of Owain Glyndwr, besieged in Aberystwyth Castle by Henry IV's eldest son, Henry, the prince of Wales, agree to surrender if Glyndwr fails to relieve the garrison by 1 November (→ 19/2/08).

Ireland, 8 December 1407. James Butler, the "white earl" of Ormond, is made deputy (→ summer 1408).

London, 1407. Bethlehem hospital, better known as "Bedlam", becomes an institution for the insane.

West Yorkshire, 19 Feb 1408. Henry Percy, the earl of Northumberland, dies in battle against King Henry IV at Bramham Moor (→ 1/1409).

Leinster, summer 1408. Plague kills Sir Stephen le Scrope, the lieutenant in Ireland; he is replaced by one of King Henry IV of England's sons, Thomas of Lancaster (→ 12/8).

Ireland, 12 August 1408. Thomas of Lancaster, the new lieutenant, who arrested the earl of Kildare in Dublin shortly after arriving, is injured in an attack on the Irish at Kilmainham (→ 1/8/12).

London, 21 January 1409. King Henry IV, who has been seriously ill, makes his will at Greenwich in the presence of both Archbishop Arundel and his own son, Thomas of Lancaster (→ 21/12).

London, January 1409. Archbishop Arundel of Canterbury holds a meeting at St Paul's Cathedral to discuss methods of ending the papal schism (→ 26/6).

Dumfries and Galloway, March 1409. Archibald Tyneman, the earl of Douglas, breaks his parole to Henry IV of England and fails to return to England (→ 7/5).

Borders, 7 May 1409. The Scots destroy the last English stronghold in the country, at Jedburgh (→ 5/3/11).

Pisa, Italy, 26 June 1409. A church council deposes the rival popes, Benedict XIII and Gregory XII, and elects Alexander V to reunite the church (→ 5/3/10).

Canterbury, 21 Dec 1409. Archbishop Arundel resigns as chancellor. The king's worsening health has increased the influence of Henry, the prince of Wales, and his allies the Beauforts (→ 23/10/11).

Dublin, 1409. Thomas Cusack is appointed as the first mayor.

Archbishop begins drive to crush the 'heresy' of Lollards

Canterbury, August 1407

Thomas Arundel is making his most determined effort since he became archbishop of Canterbury to stamp out the Lollard heresy. He is running a show trial in his palace at Saltwood near here. In the dock is William Thorpe, one of the most eloquent Lollard preachers from the Welsh Marches; he is accused of heresies in a sermon he delivered at St Chad's, Shrewsbury.

Arundel's attack focuses on theological issues. He hopes to stamp out the suggestion that the Holy Sacrament remains bread and wine even after the consecration, and is also trying to stop the attacks on pilgrimages. The real threat of the Lollards is as much political as theological, however. Their puritanism and populism threaten the alliance between king and church. Pilgrimages, penances for rich sinners and the tithe system, which Lollards attack, ensure a good income for the church. And the king does not like the attack on priestly luxuries because rich livings are such an effective form of patronage.

Arundel fears the influence of such men as Sir John Oldcastle, a friend of the prince of Wales, who is married to a daughter of Lord Cobham, an important Kent landowner (→ 1/1409).

Arundel: attacking the Lollards.

Harlech Castle is taken

A 20th-century view of Harlech Castle, which has fallen to the English.

Harlech, Gwynedd, January 1409

Months of sustained bombardment have brought victory to the English army besieging Harlech Castle after forces loyal to Owain Glyndwr surrendered. The self-styled "prince of Wales" escaped, but his wife and daughters were captured. His son-in-law, Edmund Mortimer, had starved to death.

The rebels had been blockaded in the castle for several months, pounded by heavy cannons, fired upon by archers and taunted by the smell of meat being roasted by the 900-strong English forces under the leadership of John Talbot. With Aberystwyth also captured, the English controlled the land and sea approaches to Harlech where the dream of Welsh freedom disintegrated amid disease and starvation.

Four years ago the challenge posed to English rule by Glyndwr appeared to be considerable, with the French offering support against King Henry IV. But now Henry plans to exploit his success by offering other Welsh leaders pardons and rewards, aiming to leave Glyndwr a fugitive with only a handful of followers (→ 1410).

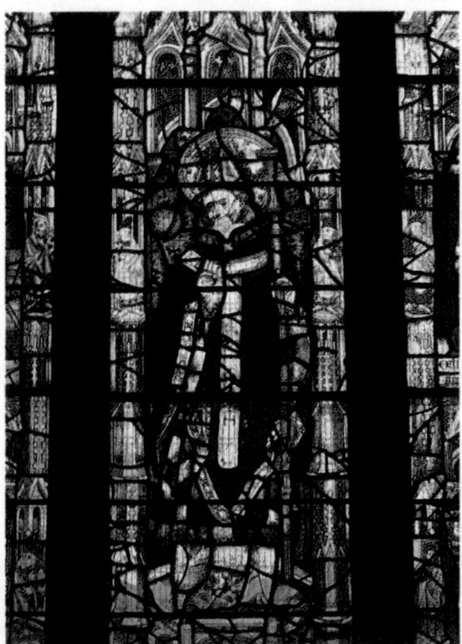

Imposing stained glass from York, a centre of the finest glass-painting in England, where the numerous glaziers have formed their own craft guild. The vast east window at York Minister, created by John Thornton of Coventry, was completed in 1408. The illustrations show windows from the churches of St Martin-le-Grand (l) and of All Saints, North Street.

1410-1414

Shropshire, 1410. Owain Glyndwr, the native "prince of Wales", loses his closest allies, including his cousin Rhys ap Twdwr, in a raid on the English; all are executed (→7/1415).

England, 1410. The latest haircut is the "bowl-crop": shaped like an inverted bowl, with the rim touching the ears and brushed forwards to create a circular fringe (→c.1480).

Glasgow, 1410. The old wooden bridge across the Clyde is replaced with an eight-arch stone bridge.

Fife, 28 February 1411. Bishop Henry Wardlaw founds the first Scottish university, at St Andrews (→1450).

London, 9 September 1411. Henry IV backs a proposal by Thomas Arundel, the archbishop of Canterbury, to investigate heresy at Oxford university (→19/10/13).

London, 23 October 1411. Six servants of Henry, the prince of Wales, who said that Henry IV should abdicate in favour of his son, are jailed (→21/10/12).

Scotland, 1412. Donald, the lord of the Isles, is forced to surrender to Robert, the duke of Albany (→30/1).

London, 30 January 1412. King James of Scotland, held captive by Henry IV since 1406, accuses his uncle Robert, the duke of Albany, of failing to secure his release (→6/1415).

London, 1 August 1412. Henry IV summons his son Thomas, the lieutenant of Ireland, and Thomas Butler, the earl of Ormond, to account for their rule of Ireland (→13/5/1513).

Westminster, 21 October 1412. Henry IV is reconciled with the prince of Wales (→20/6/13).

Gloucester, 1412. The cloisters at the cathedral are completed.

England, 13 May 1413. Parliament orders the expulsion of Irish people from the country (→summer 1415).

London, 19 October 1413. Sir John Oldcastle, the Lollard sympathizer arrested last month and sentenced to death for heresy, escapes (→13/1/14).

London, 20 December 1413. Henry V orders that Richard II, buried at Kings Langley, Hertfordshire, be reburied at Westminster (→5/8/15).

Canterbury, 19 February 1414. Thomas Arundel is succeeded as archbishop by Henry Chichele (→14/12/17).

Outspoken Lollard is burned at the stake

London, 5 March 1410
John Badby, an artisan and a layman, who became one of the most outspoken propagandists for the Lollard heresy, was burnt at the stake at Smithfield today. He died in front of his most distinguished audience ever. It included bishops, earls, the chancellor, the archbishop of York and the prince of Wales. Both clergy and the prince made last-minute attempts to get Badby to recant. When he cried out as the flames licked his body the prince stopped the burning. But Badby had cried from pain, not repentance, and the burning was soon resumed.

Those who saw his trial at the convocation in St Paul's Cathedral did not expect him to recant. He put the Lollard belief that anything created by God is more worthy of worship than a man-made image in the crudest terms. He also said that the Eucharist was of less value than a toad or spider. Badby was not a very important Lollard. Compared with William Thorpe, the preacher who was tried at Canterbury three years ago, his influence was minimal. Thorpe escaped with his life.

A romanticized view of Badby's end.

The fact that Badby has been executed shows how worried the king and the bishops now are about the spread of Lollard ideas. They were determined to make an example of him (→9/9/11).

Advance by lord of the Isles is checked

Grampian, 5 March 1411
In a fierce battle at Harlaw, 20 miles from Aberdeen, the advance of Donald, the lord of the Isles, has been checked by Alexander Stewart, the earl of Mar.

Since 1402 Donald has been trying to gain control of the earldom of Ross, but he has been opposed by the duke of Albany, who has custody of the heiress to the land, Euphemia Leslie.

The Stewarts already held five earldoms in the Highlands and had a number of lordships, keeping the lord of the Isles at bay until, finally, Donald became frustrated with their tactics and invaded the earldom, capturing Inverness and marching on Aberdeen.

It turned out to be an unwise move, for Mar rallied his men and marched out to meet Donald at Harlaw. Accounts of the battle are still confused, but Donald is in retreat tonight (→1412).

King's son leads English army in France

Knights in battle: the English army has now intervened in France.

France, 10 August 1412
After months of confusion and manoeuvring English forces have landed in France under the command of Henry IV's second son Thomas, now the duke of Clarence.

The expedition follows the agreement made at Bourges last year by which leaders of the Armagnacs, who support the duke of Orleans, agreed to help the English king re-establish his control over Aquitaine if he assisted them against the duke of Burgundy. The French king's incapacity has led to civil war between Orleans and Burgundy.

But since the duke of Clarence left London the French princes have been persuaded to go back on their agreement. If any English territory is to be recovered it will only be by force (→10/8/14).

Daily feasts offered by Suffolk hostess

Suffolk, 14 May 1413
A well-to-do English household can get through over 70 loaves of bread in a single day, according to the household book of Dame Alice de Bryene of Acton in Suffolk.

Today she provided breakfast for six people, dinner for 26 and supper for 20, and between them they consumed 66 white loaves and eight black. Catering for so many diners, who include family friends and household staff, is not unusual for Dame Alice, who routinely entertains large numbers of guests.

She runs a tight regime in which fast days are strictly observed and Saturday is kept as a fish day in addition to Wednesday and Friday. Since today is a Sunday, the menu comprises a quarter of beef, a quarter of bacon, one capon and 20 pigeons. There is ale and wine to drink. Chicken and mutton are also staples that would be eaten on other meat days. On a typical fish day, Dame Alice might serve up to 50 red and white herrings, half a saltfish, a couple of crayfish and half a dozen crabs (→1467).

King Henry IV is dead

Westminster, 20 March 1413

After King Henry IV fainted while he was making an offering at Edward the Confessor's shrine in Westminster Abbey, his life has finally ebbed away. He was 45. In recent years the king's bouts of illness had become more severe and more frequent, but he leaves the kingdom more united than at any time in his 13-year reign.

The cause of the king's decline from such an admirable vigour at the start of his reign are ascribed by some to the burden of feeling twin guilts: at having both usurped a crown and executed an archbishop. It is said that his confessor, John Tille, urged him on his deathbed to repent of both, but Henry refused. He said that his sons would not permit him to repudiate his claim to the throne, and that the pope had absolved him of guilt in executing the archbishop of York, Richard Scrope, in 1405 for conspiracy.

He is succeeded by his son, also Henry, who was with the king as he slipped into unconsciousness in the "Jerusalem Chamber" of the abbot's house here. At one point, thinking that the king had died, the prince took the crown and left the room. But Henry revived and ordered him back; he then gave him his blessing, and died (→20/12).

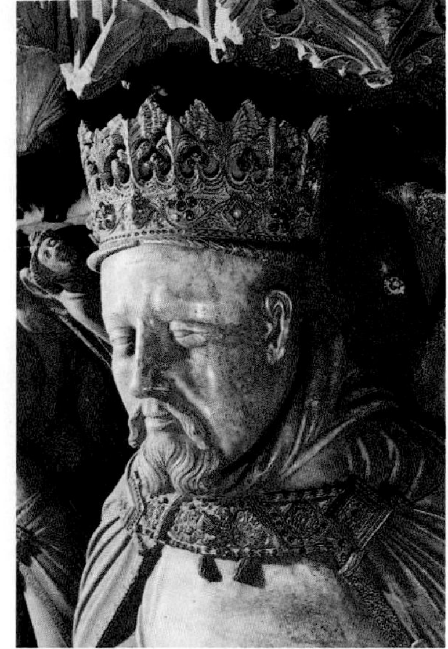

The effigy on King Henry's tomb.

England formally claims throne of France

Paris, 10 August 1414

After months of negotiations, Henry V of England's envoy to the French has made clear the price of peace. Henry will marry Princess Catherine, the youngest daughter of King Charles VI of France, provided that the crown and kingdom of France are yielded to England.

His claim derives from the fact that his great-grandfather, Edward III of England, had a mother who was the daughter of Philip IV of France and rests on ignoring the "Salic Law" which debars succession through the female line. Henry's demand would seem to make war inevitable, but the diplomats still hope to avert conflict.

Bishop Courtenay, who is leading the English negotiators, has made it clear to the French that Henry's real territorial ambitions concern the lands specified in the 1360 Treaty of Brétigny after King John II of France was taken prisoner at Poitiers. The English king is also asking for the balance of John's ransom of £500,000. England has requested Normandy, Anjou, Touraine, Flanders, Brittany, Maine and the old duchy of Aquitaine, but the French insist that the marriage must be discussed first. Despite suggestions that the French are treating Henry's claim with derision, they have indicated flexibility and seem to be prepared to be make concessions over Aquitaine. For now, both sides are prepared to talk rather than fight (→13/3/15).

Henry V (left) when prince of Wales.

Lollard supporters hanged in London

London, 13 January 1414

Sixty Lollard rebels were hanged on the king's orders here today. They were the core of the group who made the abortive coup attempt earlier this week. The leader, Sir John Oldcastle, has escaped.

Oldcastle, a longstanding personal friend of King Henry V, is an unlikely rebel. However, in recent months Archbishop Arundel has determined to make him recant of his Lollard beliefs. The pressure has been increasing month by month. First it was intended to stop Oldcastle appointing Lollard priests; then it was pressure to recant his own private beliefs.

The king did his best to smooth the argument between his old friend and the primate, but Oldcastle would not recant. He was excommunicated last September and put in the Tower accused of planning the king's death. Oldcastle did not wait to hear his sentence from the king. He escaped and mounted the coup (→19/2).

Manuscript art scales new peaks in illustrated 'books of hours'

England, c.1410

The illumination of manuscripts has reached the highest standards seen since Anglo-Saxon days. Limners – as the illustrators who work on manuscripts are called – are usually not monks but lay artists based in studios in towns such as Oxford, Cambridge, Norwich or York. Powerful patrons, in particular the de Bohun family [*see page 336*], have played an important role in this development.

The commonest illuminated manuscripts are devotional texts such as psalters and "books of hours", a form of prayer book containing a series of short services which are designed to be recited at different times of the day and night.

Books used for the public services of the church, such as missals, are also popular, as are bestiaries and lives of saints. The missal illuminated for the Benedictine monks of Sherborne Abbey in Dorset is a rich example, painted by the Dominican friar John Siferwas.

French, Italian and Flemish influences have played a crucial role in the evolution of English illumination. Some continental artists are presently at work in this country; for example, Herman Scheere from Flanders has just finished what is being hailed as an outstanding book of hours for the Beaufort family.

The Sherborne Missal: brightly coloured marginal illustrations.

A page from an English "book of hours" (early 15th-century).

1415

Middlesex, 3 March. Henry V founds Syon, the first Bridgettine house in England, for both nuns and priests, at Twickenham (→ 7/5/21).

France, 13 March. Envoys sent by Henry V of England, on the advice of Thomas Chaucer, one of his ministers, arrive to negotiate Henry's rights to land in France by peaceful means (→ 11/4).

England, 11 April. Henry V announces that he will attack the forces of the Armagnac faction in France (→ 1/5).

England, 1 May. The Anglo-French truce is extended to let French envoys negotiate with Henry V in England (→ 6/7).

England, June. Murdoch Stewart, the eldest son of Robert, the duke of Albany and regent in Scotland during King James's captivity in England, is kidnapped by Lollards while under guard; he is promptly rescued and returned to the custody of Henry V (→ 7/1415).

London, 6 July. Anglo-French talks break down (→ 14/8).

Borders, July. The Scots break a truce with England which had three years to run and raid across the border (→ 28/2/16).

Wales, July. Owain Glyndwr, the leader who threatened English rule before turning fugitive, may have died (→ 1421).

Ulster, summer. Sir John Talbot, the new lieutenant of Ireland after the death last year of John Stanley, wages a successful campaign against the O'Mores and the O'Connors before going north to subdue Ulster (→ 31/12/16).

Normandy, 17 August. Henry V of England and his troops march to Graville, 4 miles west of Harfleur (17/9).

Normandy, 17 September. The earl of Suffolk, Michael de la Pole, dies of dysentery, an epidemic of which has hit the English during their siege of Harfleur (6/10).

Normandy, 6 October. After over a month of siege, Harfleur surrendered to Henry V two weeks ago. Henry begins the long march across Normandy towards Calais, the closest English-occupied town (→ 25).

Dover, 16 November. Henry V returns and is met by the Cinque Port barons (→ 23).

London, November. Parliament grants Henry V the customs revenues for life.

King's treacherous enemies executed

Southampton, 5 August

A plot to assassinate Henry V and proclaim the earl of March as king has been foiled. It was the earl who tipped off the king as he waited in Southampton to begin his expedition to France. The principal plotters – Richard, the earl of Cambridge, Henry, Lord Scrope of Masham, and Sir Thomas Grey – were seized and have met swift retribution. All three men have been convicted of treason and executed.

Although they were sentenced to be hanged, drawn and beheaded, the earl of Cambridge and Lord Scrope were spared the worst penalties and only beheaded today. Sir Thomas Grey has already died, and his head is to be displayed at Newcastle upon Tyne.

The earl, a brother of the duke of York, had confessed to plotting the death of Henry and his brothers. Lord Scrope maintained that he never meant the king to die and, like the earl, demanded his right of trial by his fellow peers. With much of England's nobility gathered in the town to go to war it was a simple matter to assemble a jury competent to judge them unanimously guilty of treason. The abortive coup is the latest sign of disaffection within the House of York. Cambridge's elder brother, Edward, although not involved this time, was prominent in early opposition to Henry IV (→ 31/8/22).

Interior design: the production of carved and decorated floor tiles is a local industry in Norfolk.

Henry V lands in France

A travelling army at war: English forces besieging a French city.

Normandy, 14 August

The long struggle between England and France has entered a new phase. Today Henry V arrived at the little port of Chef de Caux at the mouth of the river Seine with an army of some 10,000 men. His aim is nothing less than the seizure of the French crown.

The English claim to the French throne is, of course, not new. Henry's great-grandfather Edward III justified it through his mother and could have secured it, having captured the French king and his son after the Battle of Poitiers in 1356. Instead he chose to ransom them in return for appearing to give up his claim. Since then the matter has surfaced on a number of occasions and in recent years has, with the civil war in France between the Burgundians and the Armagnacs, assumed increasing prominence.

When Henry came to the throne two years ago he did so determined to resolve the situation once and for all. Last year he sought to use diplomacy to achieve his ends, but all the time he has been preparing for the eventuality of renewed hostilities. The manufacture of cannon was stepped up both at the Tower of London and at Bristol, and the king also prohibited the export of any arms from England. He has strengthened the fleet, both by increased warship construction and by obtaining ships from the Netherlands and Spain – some 1,500 vessels were used in the task of transporting the army across the English Channel.

The king's army, too, is drawn from many quarters. He has his Welsh longbowmen, English yeomen – largely lured by the prospect of ransom money – German gunners and miners from Liège, as well as somewhat undisciplined Irish troops. All this has cost money, and Henry has even been forced to pawn his own crown. The country, however, is behind him.

Now that he has landed, Henry intends to capture the nearby major port of Harfleur and use it as a base for subsequent operations. He then plans to march on Paris. While the Burgundians are, as a result of the alliance made with their duke in May 1413, unlikely to oppose him, the Armagnacs, under the constable of France, Charles d'Albret, have considerable forces at their disposal and could well outnumber Henry's army.

The youthful English king – he is still only 27 – will therefore have seize Harfleur and then advance on Paris before the opposition is able to concentrate (→ 17).

Well disciplined English victorious at Agincourt

French attack meets lethal arrow-storm

Arras, 25 October
The village of Agincourt, three miles north-west of here, has been the scene this St Crispin's day of a remarkable English victory.

Misfortune had dogged Henry V since he landed in France in August. Although Harfleur finally fell after a five-week siege, the cost was high. Dysentery reduced his army by a third and put paid to an advance on Paris. The king's advisers wanted him merely to garrison Harfleur and return home, but he was intent on a more spectacular conclusion to his expedition. Hence his decision to march the 240km (150 miles) to English-held Calais. Yesterday, however, the English found their way barred by a French force numbering some 20,000 men.

Last night morale among the English was low. Hungry, tired and realizing that they were outnumbered by ten to one, they had defeat staring them in the face. Just after dawn the king deployed 5,500 men in a single defensive line. Most of them were dismounted, and longbowmen made up the largest part of the force. The French were in three massive divisions, but the woodland meant that they could only attack on a narrow front.

For three hours the two armies faced each other, neither making a move. Then, at 9am, Henry ordered his men forward, telling them "all England prays for us". The French attacked but ran into a storm of arrows. The constricted space meant that the heavily armoured French horsemen were unable to manoeuvre, and their casualties grew. Their second division ran into the first and made matters worse.

After three hours the French forces began to withdraw, leaving some 6,000 dead, including prisoners who had been taken early in the battle; English casualties were fewer than 500. The English guns may have battered Harfleur into submission, but it was the longbows which won Agincourt. The road to Calais now lies open (→16/11)

An heroic English victory: King Henry's men routed a superior French force in a constricted "bottleneck" at Agincourt.

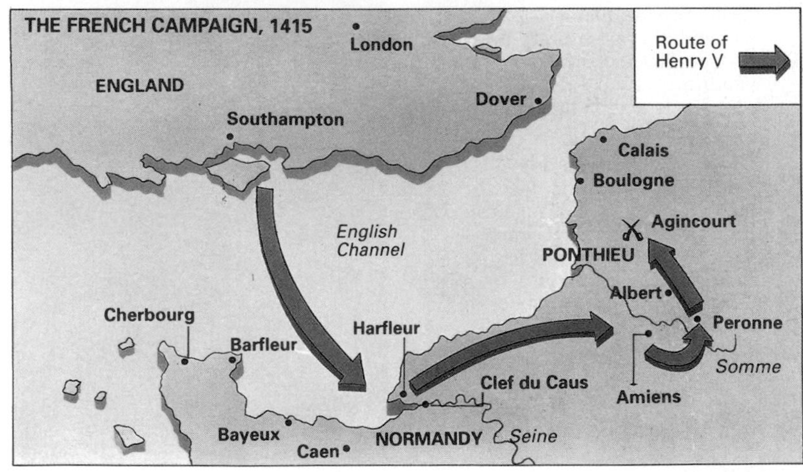

French prisoners are put to death.

Wildly cheering crowds hail Henry's triumphal return to London

London, 23 November
London showed its brightest face, and its wealth, when the City turned out to welcome King Henry V back from France and the great victory at Agincourt last month.

First thing this morning the city's mayor rode out to Blackheath with 24 aldermen in furred scarlet gowns to accompany the king back into London. Henry's party was made up of a few officers of his household and some of the more prominent French prisoners, but the watching crowds were so noisily enthusiastic and so vast that it took the procession more than five hours to reach Westminster.

The arches and gateways along the route had been decorated, and choruses of dancers and musicians had been arranged at strategic points. As the king approached London Bridge he was greeted by giant effigies offering him keys and bearing the slogan "A giant full grim of sight to teach the Frenchmen courtesy". The grip on the national imagination exercised by the victory at Agincourt was shown by the frequent shouts of: "Welcome to the fifth Henry, king of England and France!"

After kissing the altar at St Paul's, where he was greeted by 18 bishops as the great bells rang out, Henry rode along the banks of the the Thames to Westminster Abbey to make an offering at the shrine of Edward the Confessor before leaving the crowds and entering the palace (→24/5/16).

1416 - 1422

London, 28 February 1416. Murdoch Stewart, the heir of Robert, the duke of Albany and Scots regent, is held to ransom by Henry V (→ 3/9/20).

Canterbury, 15 August 1416. Holy Roman Emperor Sigismund agrees to help Henry V against France.

Normandy, 15 August 1416. The duke of Bedford, the brother of Henry V, defeats the French at the Seine, lifting the siege of Harfleur and returning the English Channel to England's control (→ 4/9/17).

Ireland, 31 December 1416. The king of Leinster, Art MacMurrough, dies; his son, Donough, succeeds (→ 26/6/18).

Normandy, 4 September 1417. The town of Caen falls to Henry V (→ 30/7/18).

England, 14 December 1417. John Oldcastle, the Lollard leader, is executed (→ 5/1431).

Ireland, 26 June 1418. Sir Thomas Talbot, the Irish lieutenant, arrests the earl of Kildare and his allies on charges of treason (→ 18/1/25).

Normandy, 30 July 1418. Henry V lays siege to Rouen (→ 19/1/19).

Perth, Tayside, October 1418. Scotland, the last country loyal to Pope Benedict XIII, withdraws its support from him, finally ending the papal schism (→ 13/8/72).

France, 25 December 1419. Henry V and Philip II, the duke of Burgundy, ally against Charles, the *dauphin* [French royal heir], after the murder of Philip's father John, the previous duke, in September by the *dauphin*'s men (→ 21/5/20)

France, 2 June 1420. After signing the Treaty of Troyes, recognizing him as heir to the French throne, in May, Henry V of England weds Catherine of France (→ 22/3/21).

France, 22 March 1421. Henry V's brother and heir, Thomas, the duke of Clarence, is killed by a Franco-Scots army at Baugé in Anjou (→ 2/5/22).

England, 23 April 1421. Henry V knights the imprisoned King James of Scotland (→ 28/3/24).

Wales, 1421. Maredudd, the son of Owain Glyndwr, accepts the pardon offered in 1417, ending Welsh unrest (→ c.1430).

France, 2 May 1422. The city of Meaux falls after a siege in which many English, including King Henry V, contracted dysentery (→ 4/1423).

Besieged Rouen surrenders to the English

Normandy, 19 January 1419
Help having failed to arrive by the agreed date, and after six months' siege, the city of Rouen has surrendered to the English army. This brings the whole of Normandy under King Henry V's control and marks the climax of a successful campaign that has been marked as much by French internal divisions as by the undoubted martial qualities of the English forces.

While Henry was manoeuvring to subdue the other castles and towns of the region, John, the duke of Burgundy, was marching on Paris. As Henry finally felt able to settle into a prolonged siege last July, with the surrender of the garrison at Pont de l'Arche, John was preoccupied with keeping control in the country round the capital.

By the end of the year the captain at Rouen, Guy le Boutellier, was compelled to begin negotiations. The city was so hungry that he had already ejected many of the older and poorer citizens to starve in the defensive ditch. Angry townsfolk forced him to sue for terms. As well as submitting, Rouen has agreed to pay 300,000 crowns (→ 25/12).

Henry wins promise of French kingdom

Founding a dynasty: the warrior-king and his French bride, Catherine.

Troyes, France, 21 May 1420
The treaty between Henry V of England and Charles VI of France sealed here today would appear to give Henry everything he wants. He will marry Princess Catherine and inherit the whole kingdom of France when Charles dies.

It is complex document, as it must be to specify the terms on which the English king will fight the French king's quarrels and rule his domain while the French king remains on the throne, but the most surprising thing is that it comes only a year after it seemed that the French were about to unite against the English for the first time.

That hope was broken by the Armagnac axe which killed John, the duke of Burgundy, last September and drove his son Philip to make common cause with Henry in order to track down and punish his father's killers. But there is a shadow over Henry's triumph. He, Charles and Duke Philip are the only parties to Troyes. Charles's son, the *dauphin* [French royal heir], whom it disinherits, and the Armagnacs are excluded. Henry still has enemies in France (→ 2/6).

Doctors bid to be all-male preserve

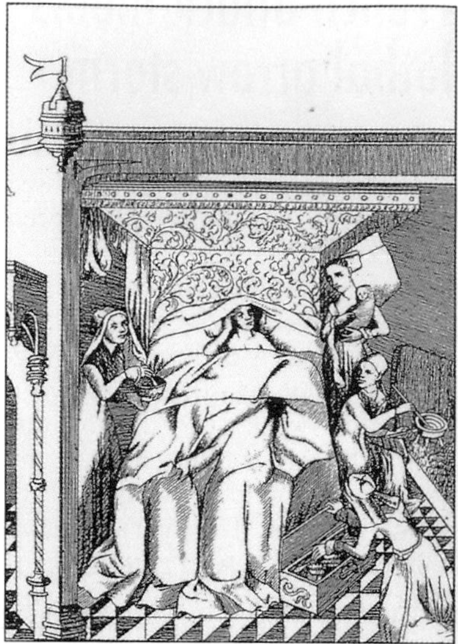

Women in attendance at childbirth.

England, 1421
Physicians have been petitioning parliament with a plea to limit the practising of medicine to university-trained graduates and to prevent women completely from caring for the sick. Female physicians and healers have been practising in this country for some time and offer enormous help in society to women who feel uneasy about seeking male advice on certain illnesses peculiar to the female sex. Some women are reluctant to reveal gynaecological problems to men. But whatever the outcome of the petition, it is certain that the majority of medical care will remain in the hands of untrained people (→ 1430).

Roman emperor is new English knight

Windsor, 24 May 1416
Holy Roman Emperor Sigismund was invested here today by King Henry V as a knight of the Garter. He was also honoured with an award of the gold livery collar of the House of Lancaster. Henry is anxious to impress Sigismund with the justice of his claim to the kingdom of France and to sign with him a treaty of mutual help. The emperor has been given the royal palace of Westminster as a residence during his stay and is being entertained by the usually frugal Henry in a lavish manner (→ 15/8).

Legal loophole gives respite to brothels

London, 1422
Some London brothels are beyond the law, thanks to a legal quirk, and prostitutes, whom the city fathers were attempting to ban, are laughing all the way to the bedroom.

Following a crackdown on brothels inside the city walls, "unseemly" characters have moved to Trimillstreet outside. Now an ordinance to abolish "stews" – public baths which have become synonymous with brothels – has become a joke since it was discovered that Trimillstreet is owned by the king of Scotland and so outside the city's jurisdiction. However, the drive against moral and physical filth seems certain to be pursued; it began with an investigation two years ago after the chaplain to the fishmongers' guild was "taken in adultery" and a liveryman and councillor was indicted for being a "common bawd".

The investigation reported that Ebgate and Woolgate Lanes were full of human filth, while the public toilet at Ludgate was "defective and perilous". Woodstreet brothel was "a great resort of thieves and priests and their concubines".

Market scene: a reconstruction drawing of London's bustling shambles.

Duke dies who held Scotland together

Stirling, 3 September 1420
Robert, the duke of Albany, second son of Robert II and governor of Scotland, has died here at Stirling Castle. He was over 80 years old.

The duke has been the effective ruler of Scotland since 1388. The only challenge to his authority came from his nephew, the duke of Rothesey, who died in his custody in 1402. King James, a prisoner, accused Albany of doing little to secure his release and contrasted it with the efforts Albany made to secure the freedom of his own son, Murdoch. He was indulgent of his family's violence, ambitious and corrupt. But he avoided clashes with the nobility, courted the lower orders, and, above all, he held Scotland together (→ 23/4/21).

English king plans monastery reforms

Westminster, 7 May 1421
A broad programme of reforms within the Benedictine order was announced today by King Henry V. More than 260 senior clergy attended a meeting at which the king was anxious to answer growing criticisms of the state of England's monasteries.

Henry proposed 13 articles of reform, none revolutionary but all stressing the importance of the monastic traditions of abstinence and piety. Reminding the monks of their origins, he called for more prayer and less interest in worldly goods.

Monks must give up the growing habit of mixing in secular society and should devote more time to God than to hoarding, feasting and entertaining women guests (→ 1433).

Soldier-king Henry dies

King Henry V: his early death has plunged England into a protectorate.

Bois-de-Vincennes, 31 August 1422
Henry V, the king who embodied so much that is glorious about the martial life, has finally succumbed to the most humbling of the perils a soldier faces. The dysentery that he contracted at the siege of Meaux this May conquered him in the early hours of this morning. Before he died he had bravely tried to go to the aid of the Burgundian garrison at Cosne-sur-Loire, but he was unable to ride.

Henry's son, born to his wife Catherine on 6 December last year, inherits the kingdom not only of England but also, when Charles VI dies, as he must soon, France. Yet with the *dauphin* [French royal heir] pursuing his own claims to France, and powerful rivalries among the English nobility, the future looks bleak for the infant king.

Before he died, Henry apparently made his brother Humphrey, the duke of Gloucester, the child's protector, and asked Thomas Beaufort, the illegitimate son of Henry's grandfather, John of Gaunt, to arrange his upbringing (→ 26/2/24).

Mystic Margery cleared of heresy charge

Leicester, September 1417
Margery Kempe, a mystic and pilgrim, has been acquitted of several charges of heresy and deception after a heated trial at All Saints church at Leicester. The 44-year-old mother of 14, who took a vow of chastity after 20 years of marriage, was arrested after she was heard weeping and shrieking uncontrollably at another Leicester church. A well-known visionary, Margery is renowned for such fits and is reputed to have had as many as 14 in one day during her travels around Europe and the Holy Land. After her arrest by the mayor of Leicester she was kept overnight in the city jail, where there were no separate facilities for women, and where she claims the city's steward tried to rape her.

The mayor's case is that Margery, who cuts a striking figure in her flowing white robes, is a heretic who aims to lure away the wives of the dignitaries of Leicester. Her honesty and frankness persuaded the court that there was no case to answer. They accepted the holy woman's word that she spoke for God and released her.

1423 - 1429

France, April 1423. John, the duke of Bedford and regent of France, marries Anne, the sister of Duke Philip II of Burgundy, enhancing Anglo-Burgundian links (→ 17/8/24).

London, 26 February 1424. John Mortimer is executed for plotting to murder Humphrey, the duke of Gloucester, brother of the late Henry V and regent of Henry VI, and put Edmund Mortimer, the earl of March, on the throne (→ 30/10/25).

Durham City, 28 March 1424. England and Scotland agree a seven-year truce (→ 5/4).

Scone, Tayside, 26 May 1424. King James imposes a 5 per cent tax to pay his ransom; this is the first tax in Scotland for 50 years (→ 25/5/25).

France, 17 August 1424. An Anglo-Burgundian force, led by John, the duke of Bedford, defeats a Franco-Scots force at Verneuil (→ 10/1424).

France, October 1424. The duke of Gloucester invades Burgundian Hainault to claim his wife's inheritance, thus upsetting the Anglo-Burgundian alliance (→ 7/1428).

Ireland, 18 January 1425. Edmund Mortimer, who defeated the O'Donnells and O'Neills last year, dies of plague; his heir is his nephew, Richard, the duke of York (→ 5/12/28).

Perth, 1426. Parliament makes all Scotland subject to the same law (→ 1428).

Calais, 25 March 1427. Henry Beaufort, the bishop of Winchester, who left on a pilgrimage following a long dispute with Humphrey, the duke of Gloucester, is made a cardinal (→ 5/1428).

France, July 1428. A marriage contract is made for Louis the *dauphin* [French royal heir] and Margaret, the daughter of James of Scotland (→ 8/5/29).

Dublin, 5 November 1428. Parliament backs the justiciar, James Butler, the earl of Ormond, against his rival, Sir John Talbot (→ 10/1/30).

Inverness, 1428. King James arrests over 50 Highland chiefs as they arrive for a meeting called by him (→ 27/8/29).

Lothian, 27 August 1429. Alexander, the lord of the Isles, who was one of the 50 Highland chiefs arrested at Inverness last year, submits to King James and is imprisoned in Tantallon Castle (→ 1430).

Mayor Whittington turns for last time

Whittington: three times mayor.

London, 1423
Richard Whittington, one of the most powerful men in the public and commercial life of London, has died. Three times mayor of London, he was also twice mayor of Calais where he ran the lucrative wool monopoly.

The third son of minor Gloucester gentry, he came to London in about 1371 and was apprenticed to a mercer. He supplied cloth to Richard II's extravagant favourite Robert de Vere and in the 1390s was a chief supplier to the king. First elected mayor in 1397, he advanced large loans to both Henry IV and Henry V.

Merchants such as Whittington have great political power in London; many are aldermen who, since 1395, serve for life unless there are exceptional circumstances. Whittington leaves rich endowments to Christ's Hospital and to found Whittington College.

James sees his kingdom

Borders, 5 April 1424
King James of Scotland returned to his kingdom today for the first time for 18 years. At the age of 11 James was sent to France for his own safety [*see page 340*], but on the way he was kidnapped by pirates off Flamborough Head and then imprisoned in the Tower of London by Henry IV. He remained a captive of the English until this year.

Most of this exile was spent in various English castles – Nottingham near Sherwood Forest was a favourite – but he also went with Henry V on his expedition to France in 1420. Discussions began about James's release, although Henry died before a treaty was sealed last year in which James promised to pay a ransom of £40,000 in instalments. James has since married Joan Beaufort, a relative of the English king.

In James's absence Scotland was first governed by his uncle, the duke of Albany. James feels that Albany did too little to secure his release and in 1416 was angered when Albany's son, Murdoch, was freed from being held in England. Murdoch succeeded his father in 1420 and will be the first target of James as he returns to Scotland (→ 26/5).

James is received on a visit to Italy.

Scottish king executes his cousin in purge

Stirling, 25 May 1425
King James has purged a rival faction within his own family and executed his cousin Murdoch, the duke of Albany. The king had nursed a serious grudge against Murdoch, the former governor, ever since he returned to Scotland last year. James had for long believed that Albany and his father deliberately left him to languish as a prisoner in England, and he was also envious of the family's great wealth.

On 21 March the duke was arrested for the second time with his eldest son, Walter Stewart, his wife and members of his household. In early May Albany's other son, James Stewart, retaliated by burning Dumbarton and killing John, the "Red Stewart" of Dundonald, the king's illegitimate uncle. Yesterday parliament tried Murdoch and his family. They were found guilty of extortion, and Walter Stewart was beheaded in front of Stirling Castle. Today Albany himself and his father-in-law, the earl of Lennox, were put to death. James Stewart has fled (→ 1426).

Londoners called to arms as royal guardians battle for power

London, 30 October 1425
Bitter enmity between Humphrey, the duke of Gloucester, and Henry Beaufort, the bishop of Winchester, brought thousands of Londoners close to a pitched battle on London Bridge today. Henry V had named Gloucester as protector until Henry VI comes of age, but the duke has clashed with Beaufort, the chancellor, as the two men sought to dominate the council of regency. Beaufort, determined to challenge the duke's claim to be regent of his nephew's country, assembled a large force of his men-at-arms and archers brought from Windsor behind barricades on the southern end of the bridge and was clearly intent on a fight.

John Coventry, newly elected as London's mayor, was sitting down for his election feast when he received a summons from the duke of Gloucester, in his capacity as protector, claiming that the bishop of Winchester, as chancellor, wanted to seize the king and take over the government. The gates to London bridge were closed as thousands of Londoners lined the banks of the Thames preparing to fight at the barricades. Beaufort has become increasingly unpopular as chancellor for his support of foreign merchants (→ 25/3/27).

Earl of Warwick is 'master' of boy king

A genealogy of the earls of Warwick: Richard Beauchamp holds Henry VI.

England, May 1428
Henry VI, the seven-year-old king of England and France, is to be given a "master", Richard Beauchamp, the earl of Warwick. The boy king is clearly destined to be taught the arts of war and chivalry. Warwick, a distinguished soldier, has been approved by the king's council for not only military prowess but also his "loyalty, knowledge, wisdom, good breeding, prudence and discretion".

Warwick was named as "master" in Henry V's will. In 1418 the adventurous earl had battled his way across France to arrange Henry's marriage with the boy's mother. One report suggests that the earl has already commissioned the making of a suit of armour for the young king with a set of miniature swords "to learn the king to play at his tender age".

The earl's terms of reference are also to train the boy in the moral virtues, literacy, languages, discipline and courtesy, to hold before him examples of times past, of virtuous kings who came to good ends and those who came to bad. Warwick can "chastise the boy for refusal to learn or other disobedience". In an emergency – such as plague – he can move his charge wherever he wishes (→6/11/29).

Maid triumphs in France

Orleans, France, 8 May 1429
A slender 17-year-old girl, the daughter of a peasant family, has inspired a major change in military fortunes here in France. Wearing a full suit of armour, clutching a small axe and mounted on a black charger, Joan from the village of Arc led an army of 4,000 men into Orleans today, relieving the city after months of siege by the English and their Burgundian allies.

A later view of the maiden warrior.

The extraordinary claims of this deeply religious girl have transformed the French army, which was badly demoralized after a string of defeats, and it is now the English forces which have been put on the defensive.

Joan passed a message via a local commander to the *dauphin* [French royal heir] that from the age of 13 she had been hearing mysterious voices – she says that they are Saints Michael, Margaret and Katherine. They have told her that it is the will of heaven that the English be thrown out of France, and that the *dauphin* must be anointed with holy oil at Rheims, after which victory would be assured. Her apparent sincerity convinced the *dauphin*, and suddenly the whole character of the war has changed.

Joan was given command of the army here at Orleans and has shown a formidable capacity for leadership. Strict discipline was enforced. Swearing was forbidden, and camp-followers were banished. No one doubted that Joan's voices were real and that victory was assured. Joan was supreme in her confidence. Illiterate she might be, but she dictated a letter to the duke of Bedford, the English commander, making no bones about her demands. The noble duke, accustomed to the niceties of diplomacy, was to read: "Take yourself off!"

Victory came when Joan led an attack on an isolated English fort at Saint Loup. It was not an important win, but it had a tremendous effect on French morale. A succession of victories followed until the earl of Suffolk, the English commander, gave up the siege (→24/5/30).

Boy King Henry crowned at Westminster

Westminster, 6 November 1429
Eight-year-old Henry, the son of Henry V, was crowned king of England in the abbey here today – and given jelly at the sumptuous feast that followed. He deserved his favourite treat after undergoing what was clearly a gruelling ordeal.

The crown was so heavy for the small boy that it had to be supported while the bishops of Chester and Rochester sang a litany over him and the archbishop of Canterbury read not one but "many" collects. The feast also included "roast meat fritters", which are said to be favourites of the young king who is shortly to be crowned again, this time in Paris (→6/11/31).

A portrait of Henry later in life.

Hatred of foreigners spread from pulpits

London, 1424
How do the common folk of England – the merchant classes, the villeins and serfs – learn of battles fought in distant places on the other side of the Channel?

Propaganda and disinformation have become important weapons in the art of managing the war, particularly when it comes to justifying the struggle on moral and legal grounds.

Such justification is commonly set forth in long Latin tracts by the learned for the learned. News about victories (and other matters) is reported in appropriate tones from the pulpits for the masses. It is only 50 years since the bishop of Rochester told his congregation that God was an Englishman – and that it was right, therefore, that Englishmen should fight for him.

Hatred of foreigners is spread from the pulpits on both sides of the Channel. The French are taught that the English are arrogant and have tails; the English are told that the French are effeminate and deceitful. All foreigners are subject to hostility; thus Thomas Hoccleve, a clerk in the privy seal office, states simply: "I am an Englishman and I am your foe".

1430 - 1435

Ulster, 10 January 1430. The lieutenant, John Stanley, reports unrest after the defeat of the Anglo-Irish by Donal O'Neill, the lord of Tyrone (→ 1436).

France, 24 May 1430. Joan of Arc is captured at Compiègne by Burgundians (→ 30/5/31).

York, 15 December 1430. The Anglo-Scots truce is renewed for five years (→ summer 1431).

England, c.1430. Owain ap Maredudd ap Twdwr, a Welsh squire, marries the dowager Queen Catherine (→ 3/1/37).

Oxfordshire, May 1431. Humphrey, the duke of Gloucester, stops a Lollard plot led by William Perkins at Abingdon Abbey (→ 4/12/57).

Highland, summer 1431. A royal army is defeated at Inverlochy by the army of the lord of the Isles (→ 1433).

England, 6 November 1431. The duke of Gloucester claims that Henry Beaufort should have resigned his see of Winchester on his appointment as cardinal (→ 16/12).

Paris, 16 December 1431. Henry of England is crowned king of France (→ 21/2/32).

London, June 1432. The dispute between Gloucester and Beaufort is settled in parliament (→ 12/1433).

Scotland, 1433. King James is forced to pay back a tax raised for an embassy to France after public protests (→ 10/1433).

Scone, Tayside, October 1433. The Scots refuse peace with England to keep their French allies (→ 8/1436).

Westminster, December 1433. John, the duke of Bedford and regent of France, who returned to raise money for the defence of Normandy, is to stay in England as head of the government (→ 6/7/34).

Co Clare, 1433. The MacNamaras found Ireland's first Franciscan house of Observants, at Quin (→ c.1445).

England, 6 July 1434. The duke of Bedford, after a row with his brother, the duke of Gloucester, over who should go to France, returns to negotiate, on money lent by Cardinal Beaufort (→ 27/5/44).

France, 21 September 1435. Burgundy allies with France as the latest peace talks between England, Burgundy and France break down a week after the death of John, the duke of Bedford (→ 5/1436).

Scottish football hooligans and drinkers feel lash of law-reforming parliaments

Football in the 15th century: a distraction from defensive archery skills.

Scotland, 1430
King James has presided over another session of the Scottish parliament which has demonstrated his close interest in every detail of his people's lives. New laws approved in this session include curbs on football ("the king fobiddes that na man play at the fut ball") and drinking after 9pm. Scots have also been ordered to wear clothes appropriate to their social status, and unemployed people who fail to seek work face imprisonment.

The new legislation is the latest attempt to enforce strong government in Scotland. Since his return from captivity in England six years ago James has put new life into the moribund parliament; it had not sat for 18 years before that. On that occasion James made it plain that he intended to crack down on law and order; he also secured a 5 per cent tax in a country where taxes were rare. Laws have since been passed restricting the nobility, suppressing local laws and regulating the right to attend parliament. Football has incurred the royal displeasure because it distracts people from archery, and because matches often end in bloodshed, sometimes even death (→ 15/12).

Court criticized for Icelandic trade curb

London, 1430
English merchants are angry and bitter over a treaty secured with Denmark aimed at preventing them from trading with Iceland. Several towns, including King's Lynn and Hull, have sent delegates to London to try to put pressure on king and parliament to revoke it.

England's trade with Iceland, which is effectively ruled by the Danish king, has been growing. Fishermen and merchants, looking for new supplies and markets, have established links with the remote, cold and fog-shrouded island. This trade has been boosted by progress in the arts of navigation.

The trade links have irritated King Eirik of Denmark, who asked London to sever them. An act of parliament has since been regulating all legitimate English traffic with Iceland. Ships and their cargoes have been seized, warnings issued, commissions appointed, and traders and fishermen fined and imprisoned. There is annoyance that England appears to be giving in to the wishes of Denmark. King Henry VI's advisers have promised remedies and to send envoys to Denmark to discuss the treaty.

English court poet offers medical and scientific advice in verse

London, 1430
John Lydgate, the prolific court poet, has just published *Pageant of Knowledge*, a verse compendium of medical and scientific knowledge. Among many other works, Lydgate has previously written in praise of the monarchy and of city corporations as well as a *Treatise on Laundries* and *Nine Properties of Wine*.

In the *Pageant* he links medicine with astrology. Good health depends upon a clear understanding of the effects of the zodiac and the four elements: fire, water, earth and air. Lydgate follows Aristotle in recommending moderation in eating, sleeping and drinking, and also avoidance of bad weather, infected places and black mists. He has also written *Dietary and a Doctrine for Pestilence* to help people to escape the plague. He says: "Be clean, keep warm, avoid dissipation and take moderate exercise."

The poet John Lydgate presenting a book of his work to King Henry VI.

Joan is burnt at stake

Convicted: the men crowd round to watch as Joan is tied to the stake.

Rouen, Normandy, 30 May 1431
Despite her protestations of purity and intense love of France, Joan of Arc was led to the stake in the market place here today and burned as a witch. To ensure that the body of this peasant girl – who had led French armies in outstanding victories – will never become a national rallying point, the duke of Bedford, the English regent, has ordered her ashes to be scattered.

Joan was captured by Burgundian forces at Compiègne and sold to the English for 10,000 gold crowns. Brought to Rouen, she was questioned by the Burgundian Bishop Cauchon in an examination based on the rites of inquisition. The dice were loaded against Joan. French aristocrats were jealous of her success; courtiers resented her influence on the king; and the church saw her as a heretic. King Charles VII did nothing.

Joan conducted her own defence, but this was a political trial and she stood no chance. She was sentenced to life imprisonment for heresy. She had promised to stop wearing men's clothes as part of her agreement to renounce heresy. When she resumed wearing them it was interpreted as heresy, and she was burnt as a lapsed heretic. Her last word was "Jesus" (→21/9/35).

Anne, the duchess of Bedford, kneels to the Virgin: from a prayer book given to her by her brother, Philip of Burgundy.

Treasury unable to meet defence bill

London, 11 August 1433
A new treasurer took office today determined to put England on a firm financial footing. Lord Cromwell has inherited a financial crisis of the gravest magnitude and immediately took steps to suspend assignments – promises of payment from future royal revenue – in order to ensure a payment of £2,000 for the king's personal expenses and those of the royal household. The recent coronation was hideously expensive, and there is no way in which the expenses of government can be met. Huge debts for the war are also beginning to loom, with no way of meeting them either, said Cromwell (→1458).

Royal welcome for king of two nations

London, 21 February 1432
King Henry VI returned to London from France today, and rarely has the City seen such a display of colour and pageantry. For this was the king of England *and* France: is he not the most powerful monarch in the world?

The cost of the war which is threatening to cripple the king's realm was forgotten as the king entered Blackheath to be met and escorted by the mayor clothed in crimson velvet with a great baldrick of gold around his neck. From then on it was cheering all the way, the streets lined with people.

As the royal procession neared London Bridge it was greeted by the king's champion, a giant with drawn sword swearing death to the king's enemies. Three women in diaphanous white with blue girdles represented Nature, Grace and Fortune, and seven virgins in white silk with gold coronets presented Henry with token gifts representing royal requirements – guile, intelligence, sapience, strength, pity, dread and lowliness. More virgins presented more gifts. White doves were released, and then the king crossed into the city to be met by his judges, his serjeants-at-law [sic] and three more ladies representing Mercy, Truth and Cleanliness.

The conduit at Cheapside flowed with red and white wine for all to drink. It was a day for all of London to remember (→6/1432).

The young Henry VI is crowned king of France at Saint-Denis, near Paris.

Feminist works fuel debate about women

France, 1431
The influence of another remarkable Frenchwoman, the writer Christine de Pisan, who died this year aged 67, has fuelled a debate in European literary circles about the nature and role of women. Appropriately, de Pisan's last work was a celebration of her famous compatriot, *The Tale of Joan of Arc.*

Born in Venice, Christine de Pisan was brought up in France and married at 15. After the death of her husband in 1389, when she was 25, de Pisan supported herself, her three children and other members of her family by writing – a highly unusual career for a woman.

She produced over 15 major works, including biography, history, philosophy and poetry, from which she emerges as an energetic champion of her sex. Two of her most significant allegorical works, *The Book of the City of Ladies* and *The Book of the Three Virtues*, deal with women's importance in history and identify ways in which women of every class can contribute usefully to their society (→1442).

1436 - 1442

France, May 1436. Richard, the duke of York and regent of France, leads an army to defend Normandy (→ 25/6).

France, 25 June 1436. Louis, the 13-year-old *dauphin* [royal heir], marries Margaret, the ten-year-old daughter of James of Scotland (→ 29/7).

France, 29 July 1436. Burgundian forces besieging Calais withdraw when the duke of Gloucester's army approaches (→ 18/7/39).

Borders, August 1436. King James abandons his siege of Roxburgh owing to unrest within his army (→ 21/2/37).

Co Meath, 1436. The O'Connors of Offaly attack the Anglo-Irish, avenging the capture of Niall O'Donnell.

London, 23 January 1437. The city gate on London Bridge collapses into the frozen Thames.

England, 23 March 1437. Jacquetta, the widow of the late duke of Bedford, is fined £500 for marrying Richard Woodville without a royal licence (→ 1/5/64).

Scotland, 25 March 1437. James II, aged six, is crowned at Holyrood Abbey, the first king not to be crowned at Scone. On the same day, the earl of Atholl, his grandson, Sir Robert Stewart, and Sir Robert Graham, the assassins of James I, are executed at Perth (→ 3/8/39).

France, 18 July 1439. A truce is agreed between England, Burgundy and France; England will continue to hold French lands, but Henry VI will lose the title of king of France (→ 30/8).

Stirling, 3 August 1439. Sir Alexander Livingstone jails Queen Joan, taking custody of James II (→ 24/11/40).

England, 30 August 1439. Henry VI, obeying his council, refuses to give up his French title (→ 25/6/41).

Normandy, 25 June 1441. Richard, the duke of York, and his wife, Cecily Neville, arrive at Rouen with a huge army (→ 10/1442).

France, October 1442. Charles VII attacks Gascony (→ 6/2/43).

London, 1442. James Butler, the earl of Ormond and lieutenant of Ireland, is summoned to the court on charges from his rival, Sir John Talbot, the earl of Shrewsbury (→ 18/11/45).

English power linked to control of seas

England, August 1436

An anonymous pamphlet is circulating, stressing the importance of preserving English sea-power and, by implication, criticizing the policy of pursuing claims for sovereignty of France. The *Libel [Book] of English Policy* comprises nearly 1,200 lines of verse, addressed to the lords of the council. It is well-informed and timely, since an English fleet arrived in the nick of time on July 29 to end the siege of Calais by Philip of Burgundy.

Attributing Denmark's decline to the destruction of its merchant class, the book warns against neglecting trade and emphasizes the importance of safeguarding links with Flanders and Ireland. Its author could be Adam Moleyns, the clerk to the council.

Forging international links: traders loading up a merchant ship with goods.

King's cousins help assassins of James

Tayside, 21 February 1437

James, the king of Scots, was today assassinated by members of his own family. The 42-year-old king was staying in the Dominican priory at Perth when the assassins broke in and murdered him.

The killers gained entry through the help of James's own chamberlain and cousin, Sir Robert Stewart; he bridged the ditch surrounding the priory with planks and unlocked the doors. Stewart was vengeful because his father died while a hostage in James's custody.

Sir Robert Graham, who lost *his* father as a hostage and had been arrested for opposing the king's behaviour, led the eight killers. The portly king used a poker to lever up floorboards and let himself down into a vault beneath his chamber.

Queen Joan was injured when the men burst into the chamber as she and her ladies tried to bar the door. The king, unable to escape through a sewer because of his obesity, was hacked to death after a struggle. The killers escaped but are now being pursued into the highlands.

The murder comes as no surprise to informed observers. The king's avaricious policies and harsh treatment of the nobility, and a recent military disaster, have all fuelled his growing unpopularity (→ 25/3).

Secret marriage is revealed at death

London, 3 January 1437

The death today of the 36-year-old queen mother, Catherine of France, at Bermondsey Abbey has exposed a secret. For the past seven years she had been married to Owain Twdwr, a Welsh gentleman. They had three sons and a daughter.

They were married without the king's permission, necessary for the remarriage of any dowager queen. The queen was able to protect Owain from the consequences of his indiscretion, but now he is in grave danger and may be arrested. The council kept Catherine in England after the late king died to look after their son, Henry VI. She will be buried in Westminster Abbey, next to King Henry V (→ 3/11/56).

'God's House' to be a training college

Cambridge, 13 July 1439

King Henry VI has granted a licence for the foundation of a new Cambridge college to be devoted to the teaching of grammar school masters. The founder is William Byngham, the rector of the church of St John Zachary, in London.

Byngham comes from a far humbler background than that of the founders of the eight existing colleges, most of whom were bishops, noblemen or heiresses. He believes passionately in education; "God's House", as the new college is to be called, is the outcome of a 12-year campaign to improve standards by training teachers. The king's licence makes provision for 24 places for training masters in grammar.

Sitting in judgement: the court of the king's bench seen here during the reign of King Henry VI.

English heir's wife convicted of witchcraft

Witches at work: conjuring rain.

London, 13 November 1441
Eleanor Cobham, the second wife of Humphrey, the duke of Gloucester, uncle of the king and heir to the throne, has walked the streets of London with a burning taper in her hand, doing public penance like a common prostitute.

Her crime is witchcraft and treason. Throughout the year, as her husband lost influence with the young king, she conspired with astrologers, necromancers and priests in the "black arts", first to become pregnant and bear a future king and then to predict the king's death. Amongst those arrested with her are Roger Bolingbroke, the rector of St Stephen's Walbrook, Thomas Southwell, the Gloucesters' chaplain, and Mary Jourdemain, a well-known witch from Westminster.

Four weeks ago Southwell died in the Tower, and Mary Jourdemain was burnt at Smithfield. Eleanor's royal status has saved her from a similar fate, but she faces life imprisonment.

Court backs war widows in legal battle

Gloucestershire, 1442
A group of widows in Painswick has won a legal battle against the lord of the manor, John Talbot, the earl of Shrewsbury. The earl had taken 16 of his tenants to the war in France, but only five had returned. The widows of the dead men complained that they had lost not only their husbands but also their landholdings. In the resulting inquest, the widows won the right to their husbands' holdings for life and the freedom to choose themselves second husbands.

The case follows other rulings in favour of women. In the Worcestershire village of Sedgebarrow a widow succeeded in getting the lord of the manor to order a certain John Cayn to marry her after he had slept with her and then refused to make the union official. And in Cleeve Prior, Isabel Edmond managed to get permission for her lover to marry her and hold her land. Even so, the law remains very restrictive of women's rights.

A truce in the battle of the sexes.

Scottish brothers killed by king's captor

Edinburgh, 24 November 1440
The earl of Douglas and his younger brother have been murdered by the Scottish chancellor, Sir William Crichton. He is the commander of Edinburgh Castle and is guarding the ten-year-old James II, whom he kidnapped last September. The earl was 17 and, with his brother, had been invited to the castle to dine. At the end of the meal the servants laid the head of a black bull on the table. It was the signal. Crichton's men rushed in, and seized the two boys. They were subjected to a mock trial and executed. Crichton feared that Douglas, the head of a powerful family, might challenge his position as the king's guardian (→ 8/1444).

Life gets better for farm labourers as attitudes harden towards sin of poverty

Scenes from a 15th-century calendar showing the labours of the year.

England, c.1440
Life is getting better in the country, especially for anyone who has a job or a bit of land. A labourer doing building work or threshing earns about fourpence, while for those who have money to lend the going rate of interest is 300 per cent, usually paid in kind. By comparison a monastery might spend five shillings a week feeding a prior, 2s 6d on a monk and tenpence on a groom. Tallow candles cost a penny halfpenny a pound, and both a two-pound loaf of bread and a pint of beer cost about a farthing.

A farthing is also often the daily rate handed out to the poor who are on some sort of relief; for the lucky ones who have a place in one of the almshouses, however, the daily rate can be as much as a penny. Attitudes towards the poor have hardened though; when the Franciscan friars first appeared, about two hundred years ago, their vow of poverty made them hugely popular and turned them into a living criticism of the extravagant ways of the church. But now the wealthy are striking back, and many bishops claim that property can be found in paradise, and that it is poverty rather than wealth that is the product of sin.

There is also growing concern in some quarters that financial aid should only go to the deserving poor who are genuinely unable to work, not to the growing number of *pauperes superbi*, or proud beggars, who are thought to be too proud or lazy to work. Others point to the requirements of Christian charity and to the fact that even with almshouses, parish relief, monasteries and the occasional hand-outs from wills or the great houses the need is still vast.

Amongst those who are working accidents are common. The most dangerous time of the year is between June and September, when 47 per cent of all men's accidents happen while they are doing the dangerous jobs of harvesting, carting and storing grain: scythes are lethal weapons, carts and ladders unstable.

For the over-45s January is the cruellest month, with many deaths being recorded from exposure or falling into water. Dawn is also a hazardous time: 20 per cent of all male accidents occur before breakfast (→ 1496).

1443 - 1448

England, 6 February 1443. Lack of money to defend both Gascony and Normandy starts a government row (→ 8/1443).

Tours, France, 22 May 1444. William de la Pole, the duke of Suffolk, arranges for Henry VI to wed Margaret, the daughter of René of Anjou (→ 22/4/45).

Dorset, 27 May 1444. John Beaufort, the duke of Somerset, who returned to England in disgrace after his campaign failed, dies at Wimborne (→ 5/8/44).

Scotland, August 1444. Civil war erupts; Sir William Crichton, the dowager Queen Joan and Bishop Kennedy of St Andrews combine against William, the earl of Douglas (→ summer 1445).

Westminster, 30 May 1445. Queen Margaret of Anjou is crowned (→ 22/12).

Lothian, 15 July 1445. Queen Joan, the mother of James II, dies at Dunbar (→ 23/10/48).

Ireland, 18 November 1445. James Butler, the earl of Ormond, is cleared of charges of maladministration during his lieutenancy (→ 12/1447).

England, 22 December 1445. Henry VI submits to his wife, Margaret, and surrenders Maine to her father, René of Anjou (→ 24/12/46).

England, 24 December 1446. Richard, the duke of York, is replaced as lieutenant of France by Edmund Beaufort, the marquis of Dorset (→ 27/7/47).

Suffolk, 18 February 1447. On royal orders the duke of Suffolk's rival, Humphrey, the duke of Gloucester and uncle of Henry VI, is arrested at Bury St Edmunds (→ 11/4).

Winchester, 11 April 1447. Cardinal Beaufort, the long-time enemy of the duke of Gloucester, dies (→ 14/7).

London, 27 July 1447. Henry VI promises French envoys that he will cede Maine by November (→ 16/3/48).

Ireland, December 1447. Richard, the duke of York, is made lieutenant (→ 10/3/48).

London, 10 March 1448. Henry VI pays the earl of Shrewsbury half the sum owed to him for his costs in the Irish government (→ 6/7/49).

Dumfries and Galloway, 23 October 1448. Hugh Douglas, the earl of Ormond, defeats an English army at the river Sark, in Annandale (→ 1/4/49).

Troops sent to quell rioters in Norwich

Scene of the troubles: a 20th-century view of the Guildhall in Norwich.

Norwich, February 1443

Troops have reoccupied Norwich after it had been in the control of rioters for a week. Eight ringleaders have been arrested and imprisoned in the Tower of London.

As the capital of the wool industry, Norwich is the second largest city in England. The chief quarrel there is between the rich merchants and leading men, who are supported by the earl of Suffolk and the royal council, and the lesser craftsmen. There were riots in 1433 and 1437. Unrest leading up to the recent crisis had also been exacerbated by a dispute over the right to tax church property.

A group of tradesmen stormed the guildhall on 25 January, and when the prior arrested two debtors the crowd attacked the priory. Having failed to break in, they dug trenches and brought up guns. The rebels seized a veteran of the French wars and, by threatening to throw him out of the guildhall windows, forced him to prepare the guns. The priory then surrendered. Order has now been restored following the intervention of the duke of Norfolk (→ 18/6/69).

Troops prepare to renew French wars

Cherbourg, France, August 1443

The duke of Somerset landed here earlier this month with a force of at least 8,000 men, a train of heavy artillery and a great deal of siege and bridging equipment for what is hoped will be a conquest of new areas of France. The English territories in Normandy and Gascony are under pressure from France, but it has been decided to try to conquer the lands between them, particularly Alençon, rather than go to the military relief of either.

So far the English campaign has not been a success. It began late, it appears to have no clear plan, and Somerset is not a healthy man, having undergone bouts of serious illness before arriving in France.

However, the greater part of the English forces already gathered in Normandy have come to join the duke, raising the size of the army to more than 10,000. Unfortunately, despite long delays in England, no plan had been made to feed, accommodate or move such a large force once it had disembarked. Somerset has sought to provide for his men by levying unauthorized taxes on local people and commandeering their horses and carts (→ 22/5/44).

King's critic gets last-minute pardon

Reading, 5 August 1444

Thomas Carver, the abbot of Reading's bailiff, who was sentenced to be hanged, drawn and quartered for treason, has been reprieved at the last moment. He was cut down from the gallows and hustled off to prison. Carver had said that the *dauphin* [French royal heir] was a better man than King Henry VI, and all the force of the law was visited upon him. Henry is set on asserting his right to the crowns of both the kingdoms won by his father, Henry V, and grandfather, Henry IV. After sentence Carver was dragged through Reading and Maidenhead on a hurdle and then hanged until near death. The king pardoned him in honour of the Assumption, but the pardon is to be kept secret so that Carver's fate may serve as a warning (→ 18/2/47).

Monasteries are under fire for alleged sins

Penance: punishment for a sinner.

England, c.1445

Some English monasteries, far from maintaining the standards of piety and self-denial for which such foundations were originally set up, have been alleged in a recent report to be hotbeds of abuse and corruption. The monks, and indeed the nuns, are better known for self-indulgence and excess than for prayer and purity.

Adultery, fornication, gambling, hunting and hawking, feasting and drinking – all are claimed to be part of a monastic life that was once believed to be dedicated to prayer and abstinence. Some observers have even found that often Mass is said incorrectly, if at all. Nor are convents any better. Many nuns are truly pious, but a significant number are not. Supposedly virgin sisters have produced children, some of whom have been fathered by priests (→ 1458).

English king weds a French princess

Charles VII: the French king has agreed to uphold a two-year truce.

Hampshire, 22 April 1445
Henry VI's marriage to Margaret of Anjou, the French king's niece – which took place today at Titchfield Abbey – is expected, at least temporarily, to halt Anglo-French hostilities. Following the failure of the military expedition to France two years ago, its leader, the duke of Somerset, returned to England sick and in disgrace. With the king's finances in difficulty, and lawlessness increasing in the country, the earl of Suffolk, the leader of the council, was delegated to strike the best possible deal. Seeking a peace treaty, he managed to negotiate the royal marriage and a two-year truce (→30/5).

Death of a dowager queen stirs tension

England, summer 1445
Tension on the Anglo-Scottish border has risen following the death in July of Queen Joan, the mother of James II of Scotland. The death of Joan (who, as a Beaufort, was also a member of the English royal family) has made possible a Franco-Scottish alliance. The tension now highlights the families which compete to control northern England: the Percies and the Nevilles.

England's interests in the north were represented at the beginning of the century by the Percy family, through the appointment of the earl of Northumberland as warden of the west march, and his son, Henry Percy (known as "Hotspur"), as the warden of the east march.

Since 1420 Richard Neville, the earl of Salisbury, has held the west wardenship – apart from a seven-year military campaign in France on the king's behalf – and has gradually acquired more land and influence. His differences with his half-brother Ralph, the earl of Westmorland, were settled in 1443. Salisbury has since increased his influence through his uncle, Cardinal Beaufort, who is King Henry VI's banker, and through his brothers in important bishoprics.

Civil war broke out in Scotland last year in which Queen Joan backed one side against the earl of Douglas, the lieutenant-general, and the Livingston family (→15/7).

English lose French land

Armed power: the English have suffered a further setback in France.

Le Mans, France, 16 March 1448
The on-again off-again war between England and France that has lasted for more than a hundred years took a dramatic turn today when the city of Le Mans, the capital of Maine, surrendered, and the whole province was handed over to the French king, Charles VII.

English power in France has been in decline since the peasant girl Joan of Arc triumphantly rode to the relief of Orleans in 1429. For more than two years Henry VI of England has actually been trying to return Maine to Charles, his uncle, but has encountered fierce resistance from powerful magnates. All those associated with the idea of surrender were vilified; the powerful marquis [formerly earl] of Suffolk felt obliged to swear a solemn oath in the presence of the king and a group of peers that he had never advocated the surrender of Maine. The diehards in Le Mans stubbornly frustrated Henry's policy until Charles lost patience and surrounded the city with 7,000 troops, forcing its surrender (→29/10/49).

The cathedral at Canterbury, where Henry Chichele, archbishop since 1414, died on 12 April 1493. He founded All Souls' College, Oxford.

Dramatic reprieve for Gloucester's friends

London, 14 July 1447
The illegitimate son of the late duke of Gloucester and three of his men were dragged through the streets to Tyburn today to be hanged and disembowelled, only to be dramatically pardoned at the last minute on the orders of King Henry VI.

Their crime was loyalty to the duke, who was the king's uncle and heir presumptive to the throne. The king and his chief minister, the marquis [formerly earl] of Suffolk, detested Gloucester and plotted his downfall. He had opposed the king's vacillating and unsuccessful policies in France. Last February they summoned parliament to Bury St Edmunds, Suffolk's stronghold, and surrounded it with troops.

When the duke arrived, he was immediately arrested. Gloucester died on 23 February, although foul play was not suggested (→19/2/50).

1449 - 1450

Flanders, 1 April 1449. Following the renewal of the Franco-Scottish alliance last December, a marriage alliance is arranged between King James II of Scots and Mary of Guelders (→15/11).

Ireland, 27 August 1449. The northern Gaelic lords submit to Richard, the duke of York, at Drogheda (→28/7/50).

France, 29 October 1449. The French capture Rouen from the English (→1/1/50).

Borders, 15 November 1449. The Anglo-Scots truce is renewed (→4/1451).

France, 1 January 1450. Harfleur falls to the French (→1/7).

England, 19 February 1450. The carrying of weapons is forbidden in the south-east following anti-royalist riots in London last month (→12/3).

London, 12 March 1450. William de la Pole, the duke of Suffolk, denies charges of treason and responsibility for the loss of Maine; he puts his fate into the hands of King Henry VI (→17).

Westminster, 17 March 1450. The duke of Suffolk is exiled by Henry VI (→2/5).

London, 17 June 1450. Kentish rebels, under the leadership of John (Jack) Cade, demanding redress of their grievances from the king, are dispersed on Blackheath by royal troops (→2/7).

France, 1 July 1450. The duke of Somerset surrenders Caen to the French (→12/8).

London, 2 July 1450. After the defeat of royal troops in Kent, Jack Cade leads the rebels to Southwark (→4).

East Sussex, 12 July 1450. The rebel leader Jack Cade is killed by the sheriff of Kent at Heathfield.

Ireland, 28 July 1450. Richard, the duke of York, retains the services of James Butler, the "white earl" of Ormond, for life; he is to receive an annual payment of 100 marks (→23/8/52).

Gwynedd, early September 1450. Richard, the duke of York, lands at Beaumaris, in Anglesey, having returned from Ireland to clear himself of any link with the rebels led by Cade (→29).

London, 29 September 1450. The duke of York receives a warm welcome from King Henry VI (→11/2/51).

New universities open in Scotland

St Andrews, Fife, 1450
The European vogue for schools and universities is starting to be taken up with enthusiasm in Scotland. The college of St Salvator has this year been founded at St Andrews by the local bishop, James Kennedy. It is situated in the town's North Street. University teaching has in fact been going on at St Andrews since 1410, when it was again the local bishop, Henry Wardlaw, who set things up.

Yet another bishop, William Turnbull of Glasgow, plans to open a university in that city next year. It will be built on a site in the High Street, not far from the cathedral. The proposed annual intake of just ten students will be expected to study a basic curriculum of grammar (ie Latin and Greek), logic and rhetoric.

The two English universities, at Oxford and Cambridge, are organized into various colleges. Originally intended to provide accommodation for scholars, the colleges are tending more and more to provide teaching as well. Last year a new college was begun in Cambridge with royal support (→1451).

Duke of Suffolk loses his head off Dover

Executed at sea: in this view Suffolk is beheaded with an old axe.

Dover, 2 May 1450
William de la Pole, the duke of Suffolk, for more than 20 years a loyal servant of Henry VI, believed that he was going into exile when he set sail from Ipswich for Burgundy on 30 April. But yesterday in Dover Roads a gang of sailors intercepted his ship, and today, throwing their prisoner into a small boat, they beheaded him with a rusty axe. His body has been dumped on Dover beach. Suffolk, who was 53, had been accused of conspiring with the French enemy and losing Henry's possessions in Normandy, which have fallen one after the other to Charles VII of France.

On 28 January Suffolk was sent to the Tower and, following a charge against him of treason, was banished for five years by the king on 17 March – probably in an attempt to spare his life. But the duke's enemies have proved to be determined men (→17/6).

The duke of York arrives in Ireland

Ireland, 6 July 1449
Richard, the duke of York, has arrived to take up the post of lieutenant of Ireland to which he was appointed two years ago. Some are saying that he has been "exiled" here by the leader of the court faction, William de la Pole, the duke of Suffolk, who sees York as a focus for opposition to King Henry VI. Far from being pushed, it is more likely that York jumped.

York has many vested interests in Ireland. Heir to the earldom of Ulster and the lordship of Connacht, he already holds the lordships of Trim and Laois. As most of this property is in the hands of so-called "rebels", York will have to campaign to get hold of the revenues due to him. He stands to make a lot of money if successful, since he does not have to account to Henry for his Irish revenues (→27/8).

English colonizers in Ireland continue to cling onto the gradually shrinking 'Pale'

Ireland, c.1450
Over the last few years the English colony on the east coast of Ireland has acquired a new name – "the Pale". Its boundaries mark the extent of English royal authority here.

The Pale is shrinking. In 1300 it extended from Dundalk in the north to Waterford in the south and as far west as Athlone. Yet so much has been reclaimed by the Gaelic Irish and Anglo-Irish that nowadays only a short journey south of Dublin takes a traveller into land where King Henry VI's writ means nothing.

Part of the reason for this decline is lack of money. For decades the colony has been a much lower priority for Westminster spending than France, Scotland and Wales. Lieutenants of Ireland have had to raise most of their salary from within the country, rather than relying on Westminster to foot the bill. The debts that they have run up by living off credit to feed their soldiers and households were reckoned by Archbishop Swayne of Armagh in 1428 to be £20,000.

Certain Gaelic Irish lords seemed to retreat when the present lieutenant, Richard, the duke of York, led successful campaigns against them last year. Yet in June of this year he told his brother-in-law, Richard Neville, the earl of Salisbury, that "my power cannot stretch to keep [the colony] in the king's obedience". In September he returned to London to clear his name of complicity in John [Jack] Cade's rebellion.

Rebels murder sheriff

John (Jack) Cade: raising support.

London, 4 July 1450
London is today under the control of rebels. Angry mobs have been roaming round the city, looting and burning and calling for the punishment of those royal servants whom they call "traitors". The sheriff of Kent, William Crowmer, has been killed by the rebels and his head stuck on a pike. His father-in-law, Lord Saye, the chamberlain of the royal household, met the same fate. The mob cheered when the lifeless heads were made to kiss.

Trouble began six weeks ago when, during Whitsun religious gatherings in Kent, Sheriff Crowmer threatened to lay waste the whole county as punishment for the murder of Henry VI's long-time servant, the duke of Suffolk, whose headless body had just been found on Dover beach [*see report on page 356*]. Unrest soon became a full-scale rebellion led by a local soldier of fortune, John (Jack) Cade. Thousands of armed men marched on London to put their grievances to King Henry VI. He responded by sending troops to crush the rebels. When even his own men turned mutinous he fled to Kenilworth Castle in the Midlands.

The rebels are mostly respectable citizens dismayed at England's loss of its French possessions and angry at the widespread corruption in the government (→7).

Calais is England's only foothold in the north of France after Cherbourg's fall

A view of Calais, England's last stronghold in the north of France.

Cherbourg, France, 12 August 1450
A tough year-long campaign by a combined French and Breton force of 30,000 men reached its climax today when the port of Cherbourg, England's last stronghold in Normandy, surrendered. The duchy's links with England, which go back four centuries, are now broken, and refugees are fleeing across the Channel. The Channel Islands and Calais remain in English hands, but English power in northern France has been effectively wiped out. Although Gascony in the south-west of the country still holds out, its position is precarious. It is probable that Charles VII, the French king, will open up a new campaign there next spring.

The military balance between England and France changed radically following the army reforms introduced by Charles, who abandoned the traditional practice of raising a force only when war was likely. He now keeps his troops on in peacetime, pays them regularly and enforces discipline. By contrast the English garrisons in Normandy were ill-paid and had become mutinous (→30/6/51).

Unpopular queen crushes London rebels

Cade's rebels are punished.

London, 7 July 1450
Queen Margaret of Anjou, who is widely disliked for her French origin and her association with the late duke of Suffolk, is playing a key role in bringing to an end the rebellion led by John (Jack) Cade.

Two days ago the rebels were routed after a bloody all-night battle with a joint force of citizens and the Tower of London garrison. During the truce that followed the 20-year-old queen, who had remained at Greenwich while her husband, Henry VI, fled to Kenilworth Castle, suggested that the rebels lay down their arms in return for a royal pardon. Some 3,000 accepted the offer, but Cade and a small group of supporters spurned it and have retreated into Kent, where they are threatening a last-ditch stand. Among those who accepted the pardon are 18 squires, 74 self-styled gentlemen, 500 yeomen and hundreds of tradesmen, brewers, innkeepers, butchers, tailors and sailors (→12).

Brass gadget helps to plot the heavens

England, c.1450
A gadget currently popular with the intelligent layman is the astrolabe, used for studying the movements of the stars. It is a hand-held brass disc engraved with a terrestrial sphere (only the ignorant think the earth is flat) first developed by the Arabs. A rotating star grid and a pointer or *aldade* is used to check the altitude of a star above the horizon. While astronomy is respectable, astrology is still controversial: churchmen see it as a black art. Yet it is studied at the universities and is favoured by politicians (such as, ironically, the late duke of Suffolk) keen to see into the future.

Decorative style: the Beauchamp chapel, St Mary's church, Warwick.

1451 - 1454

Ireland, 11 February 1451. Richard, the duke of York, is confirmed as lieutenant of Ireland (→ 5/1541).

Dumfries and Galloway, April 1451. James II fights William, the earl of Douglas, whose lands he has seized (→ 28/6).

Westminster, May 1451. Thomas Yonge, the MP for Bristol, proposes that the duke of York be made heir to King Henry VI (→ 9/1451).

Edinburgh, 28 June 1451. King James II is reconciled with William, the earl of Douglas (→ 22/2/52).

France, 30 June 1451. The English surrender Bordeaux (→ 9/1453).

France, 21 September 1451. Edmund Beaufort, the duke of Somerset, is made captain of Calais (→ 5/1458).

Glasgow, 1451. Pope Nicholas V and Bishop Turnbull found a university (→ 6/2/95).

London, 10 March 1452. The duke of York takes an oath of loyalty to Henry VI (→ 25).

Stirling, 17 March 1452. James, the earl of Douglas, denounces James II for the murder of Douglas's brother, William (→ 18/5).

Tayside, 18 May 1452. Alexander Gordon, the earl of Huntly, defeats a pro-Douglas army led by Alexander Lindsay, the earl of Crawford, at Brechin (→ 3/6).

Fife, May 1452. Queen Mary gives birth to a son, James.

England, 3 June 1452. Henry VI negotiates with the earl of Douglas (→ 16/1/53).

Ireland, 23 August 1452. James Butler, the "white earl" of Ormond, dies; his son, James, the earl of Wiltshire, succeeds him.

Canterbury, 24 September 1452. Cardinal Kempe is made archbishop after the death in May of John Stafford.

France, September 1453. The English finally lose Bordeaux, retaken last year, and with it the hundred-year war against France (→ 28/8/57).

England, 13 October 1453. Queen Margaret gives birth to a son, Edward.

England, 27 March 1454. The duke of York is made protector of England (→ 23/5).

London, 23 May 1454. The duke of Somerset is sent to the Tower (→ 1/1455).

Earl of Douglas is brutally murdered during negotiations

Hot-tempered: King James II.

Stirling, 22 February 1452
William, the earl of Douglas, has been murdered by King James II at Stirling Castle. During discussions with Douglas, the hot-tempered king drew his dagger and plunged it into the 27-year-old earl. Royal courtiers joined the butchery, after which the earl's body, stabbed 26 times, was thrown out of a window. James's quarrel with the earl began when Douglas gained control of the government while the king was a minor (James is now 21 years old). Douglas, who was lieutenant-general of the kingdom, had recently allied himself with the earl of Crawford and others against the court party (→ 17/3).

Duke of York steps in to halt family feud

Taunton, September 1451
Richard, the duke of York, heir apparent to the English crown and widely seen as a threat to Henry VI's position, has dramatically demonstrated his political power by intervening in the feud between Thomas Courtenay, the earl of Devon, and his bitter enemy William Bonville. While Henry was still trying to assemble a force to quell this private war, York rode into the west country and personally persuaded the earl to abandon his siege of Bonville in Taunton Castle.

Devon and Cornwall are among the most lawless regions in England; murder, abduction and the seizure of property are commonly used to resolve disputes. The war between Bonville and the aristocratic Devon family broke out after one of the Bonvilles married – in the earl's view – above his station: his bride was the earl's aunt. For years the two families have raised armed bands to pursue their feud and ignored royal orders to stop.

York became involved after Bonville found favour in court circles. The earl of Devon reacted by joining the rival Yorkist faction and resolved to bring matters to a head by force – a rebellion defused only by York's dashing intervention.

York and Henry VI are both descended from Edward III. Henry is descended in the male line from Edward's fourth son, John of Gaunt, the duke of Lancaster. York is descended in the male line from Edward's fifth son, Edmund, the duke of York, and in the female line

Richard: a stained glass portrait.

from Edward's second son, Lionel, the duke of Clarence, through Anne Mortimer, Clarence's great-granddaughter. Despite York's proclaimed loyalty to Henry VI, suspicion lingers that he has his eye on the throne. Last year, after the rebellion led by John (Jack) Cade – who claimed Yorkist support – York returned to England in defiance of a royal command.

So long as Henry remains childless, York remains heir apparent. But Henry's wife, Margaret of Anjou, might still bear him a son. At 40 years of age, York is ten years older than King Henry and unlikely to gain the crown by outliving him (→ 10/3/52).

Lancastrian court completes tour for support against Yorkists

King Henry and his court at prayer.

London, 6 September 1452
With the end today of a triumphant six-week tour, first of the west country and then northwards to Kenilworth and nearby Coventry, accompanied by judges and peers of the realm, and receiving the homage of knights and bishops along the way, King Henry VI has given an impressive demonstration of his authority in the face of challenges by Richard, the duke of York.

Notably absent from the king's entourage were York and his supporters, although much of the journey took the royal party into strongly pro-Yorkist territory. The king is now planning another foray into Yorkist strongholds in England's eastern counties.

Earlier this year Richard established himself at Dartford with a force of more than 10,000 men and demanded that the king get rid of Edmund Beaufort, the duke of Somerset, whom he blames for the loss of Normandy. At first the king seemed to be conciliatory, but when Richard arrrived at the royal tent at Blackheath he was arrested. Taken to London, he was made to swear an oath of loyalty to Henry in St Paul's. But nobody believes that the Yorkists have accepted defeat.

Defeat ends English rule in France

English forces (left) lock spears with the French at the siege of Castillon.

GASCONY UNDER ATTACK
Gironde
Jean Bureau lays siege
Castillon
Bordeaux
Atlantic Ocean
finally lost to French, 1453
land under Charles VII of France
GASCONY
Saint Sever
Dax
Bayonne
lost to French, 1442
NAVARRE
ARMAGNAC
French forces
Land held by English since 1429, lost by 1453

Castillon, France, 17 July 1453
English fortunes in the century-long struggle against France have been dealt a possibly final blow. French forces have been converging since April on English-held Gascony. John Talbot, the 69-year-old earl of Shrewsbury, leading the smaller Anglo-Gascon army, knew that he could only skirmish with the French and avoid being drawn too far from the capital, Bordeaux. Yet his strategy changed after a French column under Jean Bureau – who, with his brother Gaspard, has totally reformed the French army – besieged Castillon, 30 miles from Bordeaux, last week [*see map above*].

The inhabitants of Castillon pleaded with Shrewsbury at Bordeaux to relieve them. Against his better judgement he relented, and yesterday he set out with 4,500 men, hoping to surprise the French. Bureau was, however, expecting an attack and had fortified his camp with no fewer than 300 cannon. After a gruelling night march, but encouraged by a mistaken report that the French were withdrawing, Shrewsbury attacked this morning, only to witness his men being mown down by the French guns. Both Shrewsbury and his son John, Lord Lisle, were killed fighting a desperate rearguard action.

Not only the fate of Castillon but also that of Bordeaux is now sealed. The fall of the capital would mark the end of the 300-year English hold on Gascony (→ 9/1453).

Government crisis in England as king suffers breakdown

Windsor, 25 March 1454
The king of England has gone mad. That is the conclusion of a delegation from the House of Lords which came here today to urge King Henry VI to resolve the constitutional impasse following the death three days ago of Cardinal Kempe, the lord chancellor.

Mental illness set in last August at the royal hunting lodge at Clarendon when Henry learnt of the annihilation of the English army at Castillon [*see report left*]. Since then he has sunk into a lethargy and lost all sense of time, memory and even the knowledge that he is king. A delegation of doctors which visited him recently envisaged little chance of recovery. Until Kempe's death some semblance of normality was possible with the council ruling in the king's name.

Margaret: focus for opposition.

Yet only the king can appoint a new chancellor. If Henry is unfit to do so, the only alternative is to appoint a "protector" of England to exercise royal authority during the king's illness. The obvious candidate is the king's cousin, Richard, the duke of York. But he is the acknowledged enemy of Henry's close associates, the Beauforts, who are therefore unlikely to welcome his appointment. They might prefer to see power pass to the queen, as regent for her new-born son, but that would certainly be unacceptable to the rest of the council. An embarrassing power struggle seems inevitable (→ 27).

Uneasy peace agreed in Scottish civil war

Scotland, 16 January 1453
A fragile peace has been reached in the continuing feud between King James II and James, the earl of Douglas. Douglas swore to avenge the murder of his elder brother, William, at the king's hands in February of last year [*see report on page 358*]. Today's settlement will give Douglas some satisfaction, in that it leaves him in possession of his brother's entire inheritance. The apparent generosity of this concession is being taken by some observers as a sign of the guilt that James feels over the murder.

The violence is not just, however, a minor feud: it is in fact civil war – and the most serious crisis that the Stewart monarchy has yet had to face. It has been waged on both diplomatic and military fronts. Last March Douglas led an army to Stirling, denounced the king for violating his brother's safe-conduct and then sacked the burgh. James's response was to attack Douglas castles and make parliament accuse the murdered Douglas of a conspiracy against him.

It is unlikely that today's peace will last very long: the Douglases represent too potent a threat to the Stewarts. As a way of containing that threat, the king may seek to exploit the division between the "Red" and the "Black" Douglases. His enemies are on the Black side of the house. The Red Douglases, the earls of Angus, are descended from an illegitimate son of the second earl of Douglas, and the present earl shows signs of supporting the king rather than his kin (→ 3/1455).

Monks, like the ones in this early 16th-century French manuscript, were paid to pray for people's souls after they died to shorten their stay in purgatory.

1455 - 1456

London, January 1455. King Henry VI receives his ministers after recovering from his mental illness (→ 6/2).

London, 6 February 1455. Edmund Beaufort, the duke of Somerset, is freed from the Tower (→ 18/5).

London, February 1455. Richard, the duke of York, resigns as protector (→ 18/5).

Scotland, March 1455. James II attacks Archibald Douglas, the earl of Moray (→ 1/5).

Dumfries and Galloway, 1 May 1455. The Black Douglases are defeated at Arkinholm on the Esk; the earl of Moray and his brother, Hugh Douglas, the earl of Ormond, are killed (→ 7/1455).

Westminster, 18 May 1455. The duke of York and the earls of Salisbury and Warwick march south to confront the duke of Somerset and the king (→ 21).

London, 21 May 1455. The duke of Somerset and the royal household leave for St Albans on their way to a council meeting at Coventry (→ 22).

London, 23 May 1455. The duke of York returns with Henry VI (→ 9/7).

London, 9 July 1455. Henry VI, now under the control of the duke of York and ill again, opens parliament (→ 19/11).

Dumfries and Galloway, July 1455. The last stronghold of the Black Douglas clan, Threave Castle, surrenders to James II (→ 4/8).

Ulster, July 1455. Owen O'Neill, the lord of Tyrone, is forced to resign by his son, Enri (→ 28/5/56).

Westminster, 19 November 1455. Henry VI confirms the duke of York as protector once more (→ 25/2/56).

Westminster, 25 February 1456. The duke of York is dismissed as protector when he alienates the lords of England by urging the cancellation of royal grants (→ 17/8).

Borders, July 1456. James II, against whom the duke of York is raising troops, attacks Roxburgh Castle (→ 16/8).

Northumberland, 16 August 1456. James II of Scotland and his army invade (→ 2/1457).

Warwickshire, 17 August 1456. While the duke of York makes military preparations against the Scots, Queen Margaret takes Henry VI to Kenilworth for safety (→ 14/9/57).

Civil war looms in battle for throne

England, 1455
The struggle for control of King Henry VI has brought the country perilously close to the brink of civil war and reopened doubts about the legitimacy of the Lancastrian title to the throne.

The origins of these doubts go back a long way. When Richard II was deposed in 1399, the succession went to Henry IV, the elder son of John of Gaunt, the duke of Lancaster. This is contested by those who are insisting that it should have gone to Edmund Mortimer, the son-in-law of Lancaster's elder brother Lionel, the duke of Clarence [*see family tree on page 363*].

Yet all this was not considered an issue until serious doubts began to be raised about Henry VI's fitness to rule. A weak and vacillating man, he is reported to agree with whoever is his most recent adviser. As if this were not bad enough, there is also considerable worry about the soundness of the king's health. Henry, who is 34 years old, has recently suffered from a period of mental illness. Although he is now recovered, there are fears that his mental state could deteriorate at any moment.

Henry's staunchest supporter is his queen, Margaret of Anjou, the daughter of the titular king of Sicily, René of Anjou. She is an unpopular figure because of both her French origins and her overbearing nature. Two years ago she finally presented Henry with an heir, Edward. She can be relied upon to go to any lengths to ensure her son's succession. Henry's other backers include the 49-year-old duke of Somerset, Edmund Beaufort, and his two sons, Henry and Edmund. Further support comes from 62-year-old Henry Percy, the earl of Northumberland, and his son, who is also called Henry. Then there are the Twdwrs from Wales. Owain Twdwr was the second husband of Catherine of France, who is the mother of Henry VI. Owain's sons, Edmund and Jasper, are therefore half-brothers to the king. They have recently been made the earls of Richmond and Pembroke respectively, and Edmund is now married to Margaret Beaufort, the niece of the duke of Somerset.

As for the opposition, Henry's fiercest critic is Richard, the 44-year-old duke of York, who is also the heir to the Mortimer claim to the throne through his mother, Anne Mortimer. Until the birth of King Henry's son, Richard was the next in line to the throne. A short and dark-complexioned man, he is said, like the king, to be easily swayed by his counsellors. Richard is backed by his two eldest sons, Edward and Edmund, and also by the members of the Neville family – whom he helped in their long-running feud with the Percys – Richard Neville, the 55-year-old earl of Salisbury, and his sons Richard, the charismatic earl of Warwick, and John. By an interesting irony the earl of Salisbury is in fact of Lancastrian lineage: his mother, Joan Beaufort, was a legitimated daughter of John of Gaunt and his third wife.

Richard, the duke of York: focal point of opposition to King Henry.

Henry VI: doubts are growing about his competence to rule England.

The family of the power-broker Richard Neville gather at prayer.

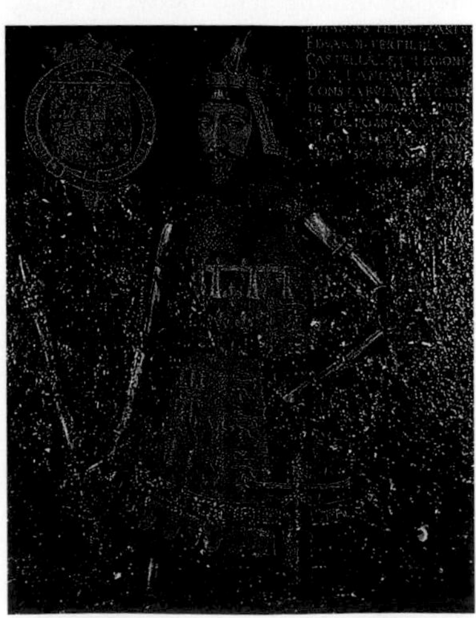
Lancastrian figure-head: John of Gaunt, the duke of Lancaster.

Richard II: the present dispute goes back to his fall 56 years ago.

Douglas clan meets a savage downfall at Stewart hands

Edinburgh, 4 August 1455
The downfall of the Black Douglases has been completed by parliament. The leading members of this once powerful family are now either dead or in exile, their castles hammered into submission by King James II's heavy artillery, and their estates, mostly in the south-west of the country, forfeited and split up between the king and his supporters. The distribution will bring some £2,000 of regular income into the royal purse.

Douglas fortunes reached their nadir on 1 May this year when a force under Archibald Douglas, the earl of Moray, was defeated by a small army of borderers at Arkinholm on the river Esk (Dumfries and Galloway). The earl was killed in the battle and his severed head presented as a gruesome trophy to James II. Hugh Douglas, the earl of Ormond and younger brother of Archibald, was taken prisoner but has since been executed. By the end of July the last Douglas stronghold, Threave Castle, had been battered into surrender to the king.

Parliament has also passed an act of annexation preventing the king from alienating his lands or other forms of income in the future without parliament's prior consent. The goal is to reduce the political instability that has dogged Scotland over the last 20 years, during which time both James I and James II have sought to increase their wealth by attacking certain prominent noblemen.

Despite this gesture at clipping the royal wings, the Stewarts are enjoying great success. Their popularity is clear from the fact that it took only three months to crush their chief rivals decisively. No one wanted to defend the Douglases against the Stewart onslaught. The ground for this victory was well laid: seven new "lords of parliament" – a new title – have been created by the king over the last three years in order to win aristocratic support away from the Douglases. Blessed with both diplomatic success and an heir (the three-year-old James), the king seems to have a bright future (→7/1456).

Lancaster and York do battle at St Albans

The battle in the streets of St Albans, as imagined by a later artist.

St Albans, Herts, 22 May 1455
Richard, the duke of York, has crushed the Lancastrian forces of King Henry VI in a short but decisive brawl in the streets of St Albans. The king's men reached the town first and fortified the centre. At first their barricades kept out the Yorkists, but Richard Neville, the earl of Warwick, led his soldiers through the back doors of houses to fall on the defenders and rout them.

Taken by surprise, many of the Lancastrian leaders had not donned their full armour and were struck down with arrows. The king himself was wounded in the neck. Edmund Beaufort, the duke of Somerset, trapped in the Castle inn, charged the besiegers and killed four men before he was himself hacked down. Lord Clifford and Henry Percy, the earl of Northumberland, are also among the dead.

York found the wounded king in the house of a tanner and, after pledging his allegiance, escorted him to the abbey, where he remains entirely in York's power. They will ride to London tomorrow.

The fight between the Yorkists and the Lancastrians became inevitable once the king recovered from his bout of madness and, urged on by Queen Margaret, resolved to treat York as a traitor (→23).

Irish lords battle for power outside Pale

Ireland, 28 May 1456
In the continuing struggle for power in Ulster, Enri O'Neill, the lord of Tyrone, has killed Donal O'Donnell, the lord of Tyrconnell. The O'Neills and the O'Donnells have long been rivals for dominance in Ulster; at present the O'Neills are winning. In this part of Ireland – as in most of the country – power struggles are local. Chieftains aim not for domination of the whole country but for lordship over their own provinces. English influence is hardly felt. In fact lords of English descent outside the Pale, such as the Burkes (or de Burghs) of Connacht, are increasingly accepted as Irish (→4/12/59).

Lancastrians mourn loss of Welsh ally

Carmarthen, 3 November 1456
Edmund Twdwr, the half-brother of Henry VI, who was appointed last year to reassert royal authority in Wales, has died of plague in the castle here. He is a sad loss to the Lancastrian cause. Edmund had partly succeeded in overcoming abuses of power by local landowners who have been taking advantage of absentee English lords. He was married to Margaret Beaufort, the niece of Edmund, the duke of Somerset. Margaret, although just 13, is pregnant: Edmund, who was 26, impregnated her at the earliest possible moment to guarantee his hold on her land (→28/1/57).

Rigged murder trial

Devon, 26 October 1455
A grim parody of justice took place in Tiverton today when Thomas Courtenay, the 23-year-old son of the earl of Devon, callously conducted a mock inquest into the death of Nicholas Radford, declaring that Radford, a lawyer and supporter of the earl's rival, Lord Bonville, had "killed himself". This was far from true. In fact Courtenay and 60 armed men broke into Radford's house three days ago, stole valuable property and then, in cold blood, murdered the old man.

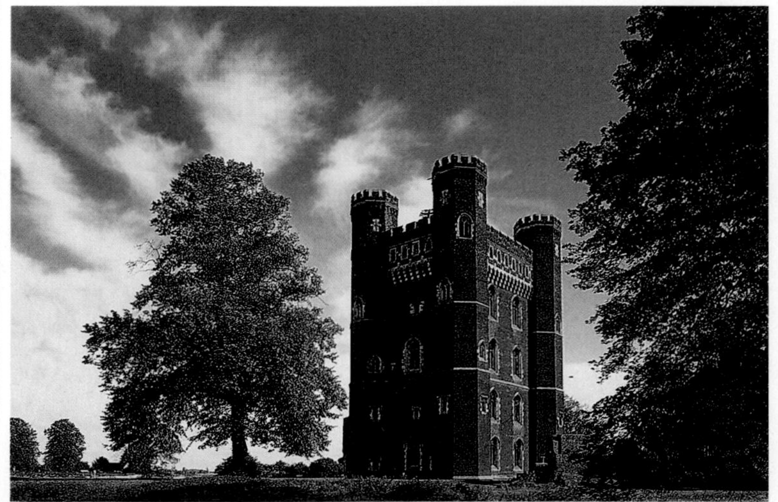

The keep of Tattershall Castle, Lincolnshire: the castle, completed in the mid-1450s, was begun in 1434 by Ralph Cromwell, who served as lord treasurer under King Henry VI. It was one of the first castles in England to be built in brick, which, although a poor defensive material, is now increasing fashionable, as the popularity of stone castles ebbs.

1457 - 1459

Dyfed, 28 January 1457. Henry Twdwr, the son of Edmund, the late earl of Richmond, is born at Pembroke (→ 12/1463).

Northumberland, February 1457. James II of Scots tries in vain to take Berwick (→ 1457).

Kent, 28 August 1457. The French launch a raid on the port of Sandwich (→ 8/10/63).

Coventry, 14 September 1457. Margaret of Anjou and King Henry VI, who is clearly under her control, are welcomed by the city (→ 27/1/58).

Dumfries and Galloway, 1457. English raiders burn Kirkcudbright in retaliation for a Scottish attack on the Isle of Man two years ago (→ 1458).

Edinburgh, 1457. A huge siege gun, nicknamed "Mons Meg" after its place of manufacture, is received at the castle; it is a gift to James II from his nephew-by-marriage, Philip "the Good" of Burgundy.

Westminster, 27 January 1458. Henry VI, in remission from his illness, addresses his council (→ 24/6/59).

France, May 1458. Richard Neville, the earl of Warwick, seizes a Spanish fleet off the coast of Calais in order to pay the English garrison in the town (→ 20/11/59).

Co Fermanagh, 1458. A fire destroys the monastery and library at Aghavea (→ 1/1481).

Coventry, 24 June 1459. The great council, summoned by the queen, meets without the duke of York, who remains in his castle at Ludlow (→ 23/9).

Shropshire, 23 September 1459. The earl of Warwick defeats the Lancastrians in battle at Blore Heath while on his way to link up with the Yorkists (→ 12/10).

Ludlow, Shropshire, 12 October 1459. The duke of York flees to Ireland after a failed confrontation with Henry VI and his army at Ludford Bridge (→ 20/11).

France, 20 November 1459. The earls of Warwick, Salisbury and March, the Yorkist allies who fled from Ludlow, hold out at Calais against Lancastrians (→ 1/7/60).

Ireland, 4 December 1459. With Richard, the duke of York, in disgrace, James Butler, the fifth earl of Ormond, is appointed lieutenant by King Henry VI of England (→ 8/2/60).

Money worries overshadow Scots success

Edinburgh, 1458

Although James II is finding it hard to organize his country's economy, at least his foreign policy is going well. He crushed the threat to his power from the Douglas family three years ago, and since then he has raided Northumberland, Roxburgh, Berwick and the Isle of Man. He is negotiating with Norway over the future of the Western Isles, while in the growing civil unrest in England he has thrown his weight behind the Yorkist cause against King Henry VI.

James II of Scots later in life.

The Edinburgh parliament this year commended James's valour, but it also raised criticisms of his financial policies. The economy is in bad shape: poor harvests last year prompted a rise in inflation so serious that parliament has forbidden the striking of new coins. (The coinage was also devalued in 1451.)

It is no surprise that parliament is blocking James's plan to reorganize land tenure. James favours the "feuing" of land, whereby tenants would have more rights than before and landlords' incomes would be higher. What worries parliament – many of whose members hold land – is that these incomes are vulnerable to inflation (→ 3/8/60).

Anti-Lollard bishop falls foul of church

London, 4 December 1457

Reginald Pecock, the bishop of Chichester, made a public renunciation of his theological views today in St Paul's churchyard. Four of his books were then burnt. There to hear him were the archbishop of Canterbury and the bishop of London. Pecock is the oddest victim of the attempt to stamp out Lollardy, a religious movement critical of the pope and many church traditions. Pecock's books were meant to refute Lollard beliefs, but the church interpreted them as attacks on the true faith. Pecock was given the choice of recanting or death by fire. He chose the former.

Purifying flames: here seven believers are martyred for their faith.

Economists turn to alchemy for help

London, 9 March 1457

It is an outstanding example of optimism over experience: a royal commission has been appointed to investigate the possibility of using the science of alchemy to restore the national economy.

Alchemy, which seeks by closely guarded secret processes to transmute such base metals as lead into the most valuable of precious metals, gold, has long fascinated both European and Arab scientists.

The idea underlying it is that all matter, whether animate or not, has a "spirit" that persists no matter what form it takes. Therefore, given the right chemical processes (and planetary influence), one metal, such as lead, might be turned into gold, another metal. Some of the greatest minds have wrestled with alchemy, searching to create the "philosopher's stone" that will ensure the metamorphosis.

An alchemist at his secret work.

Avicenna, Albertus Magnus, St Thomas Aquinas and Roger Bacon have all considered alchemy. Their problem has been that the more detailed their researches, including the testing of alleged alchemical gold, the more they have begun to doubt that alchemy is a "true" science. Such doubts are not helped by a vulnerability to fraud. For every sincere alchemist there are many impostors only too ready to take advantage of the greedy and the credible (→ 9/1507).

Lancastrians enlist parliament to crush Yorkists

York and his allies declared traitors

Coventry, 20 November 1459
Richard, the duke of York, and his allies have been denounced by parliament. Meeting at St Mary's Priory and packed with King Henry VI's supporters, it has ordered the execution of the "traitors" and the attainder, or confiscation, of their estates. This new penalty, which involves not only the seizure of all property but also the disinheritance of the culprits' heirs, aims at destroying the Yorkists by ruining their families. It is much disliked by many English noblemen who still look upon certain land rights as sacrosanct, even against the charge of treason.

These parliamentary moves follow recent military developments. At the Battle of Blore Heath, in Cheshire, on 23 September the Yorkists, under Richard Neville, the earl of Salisbury, brushed aside the king's forces and killed their commander, Lord Audley. Another clash was narrowly averted at Ludford Bridge, in Shropshire, on 12 October, when the king himself was present. The Yorkist leaders were unwilling to risk the charge of treason that they would have incurred by fighting Henry in person, so they slipped away. The duke of York has fled to Ireland, while the earl of Salisbury and his son Richard, the earl of Warwick, have decamped to Calais along with York's son Edward, the earl of March (→12/1459).

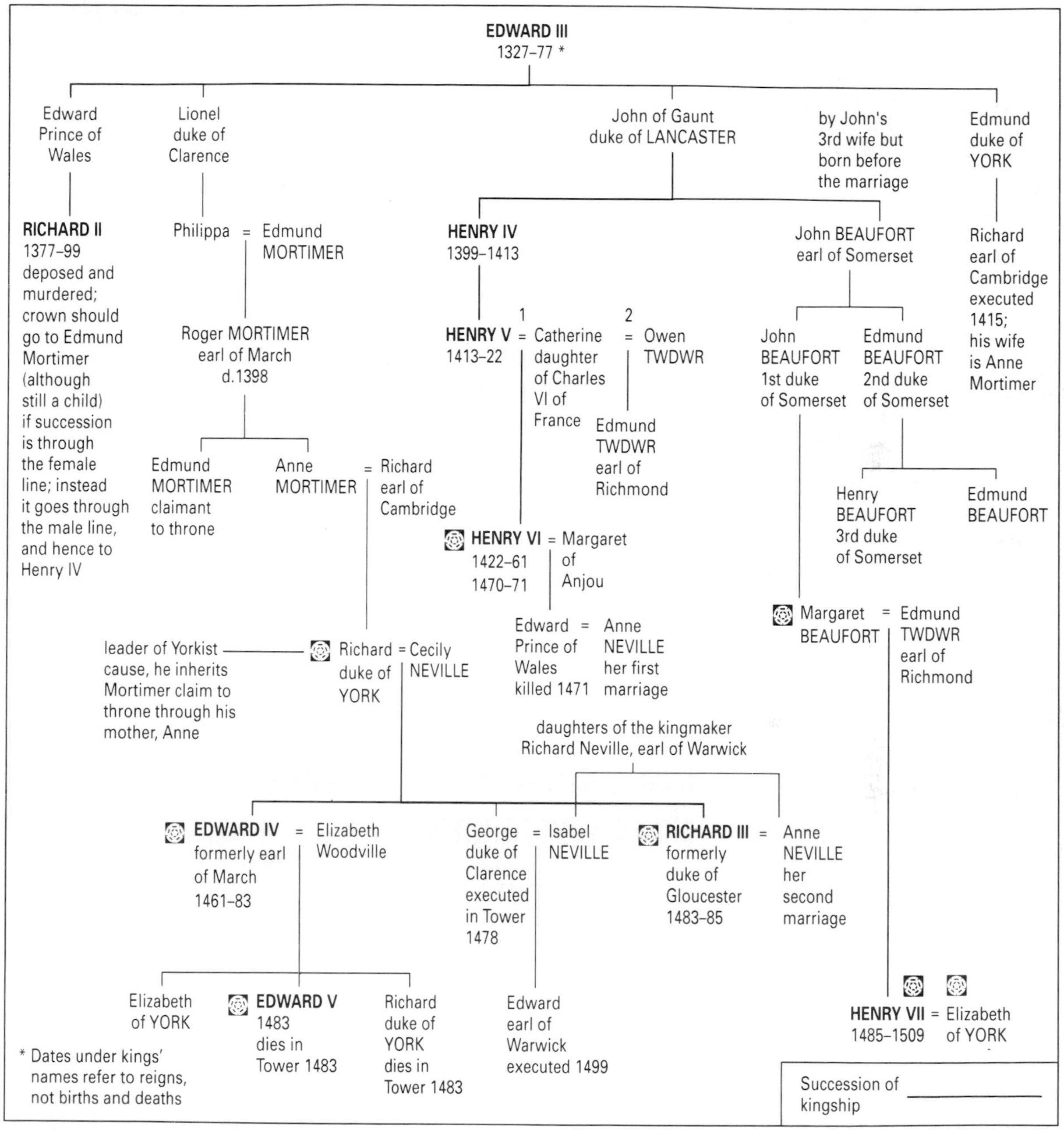

EDWARD III
1327–77 *

Edward Prince of Wales

RICHARD II
1377–99
deposed and murdered; crown should go to Edmund Mortimer (although still a child) if succession is through the female line; instead it goes through the male line, and hence to Henry IV

Lionel duke of Clarence

Philippa = Edmund MORTIMER

Roger MORTIMER
earl of March
d.1398

Edmund MORTIMER claimant to throne

Anne MORTIMER = Richard earl of Cambridge

leader of Yorkist cause, he inherits Mortimer claim to throne through his mother, Anne — Richard duke of YORK = Cecily NEVILLE

John of Gaunt duke of LANCASTER

HENRY IV
1399–1413

HENRY V = (1) Catherine daughter of Charles VI of France (2) = Owen TWDWR
1413–22

Edmund TWDWR earl of Richmond

HENRY VI = Margaret of Anjou
1422–61
1470–71

Edward Prince of Wales killed 1471 = Anne NEVILLE her first marriage

by John's 3rd wife but born before the marriage

John BEAUFORT
earl of Somerset

John BEAUFORT
1st duke of Somerset

Edmund BEAUFORT
2nd duke of Somerset

Henry BEAUFORT
3rd duke of Somerset

Edmund BEAUFORT

Margaret BEAUFORT = Edmund TWDWR earl of Richmond

Edmund duke of YORK

Richard earl of Cambridge executed 1415; his wife is Anne Mortimer

daughters of the kingmaker Richard Neville, earl of Warwick

EDWARD IV = Elizabeth Woodville
formerly earl of March
1461–83

George duke of Clarence executed in Tower 1478 = Isabel NEVILLE

RICHARD III = Anne NEVILLE her second marriage
formerly duke of Gloucester
1483–85

Elizabeth of YORK

EDWARD V
1483
dies in Tower 1483

Richard duke of YORK dies in Tower 1483

Edward earl of Warwick executed 1499

HENRY VII = Elizabeth of YORK
1485–1509

* Dates under kings' names refer to reigns, not births and deaths

Succession of kingship ———

Arms of Henry VI and Margaret.

Margaret of Anjou emerges as the key to success of Lancaster

London, December 1459
King Henry VI made a wiser match than perhaps he was aware when, 14 years ago, he married Margaret of Anjou. Then only 16 years old, Queen Margaret has grown into a woman of formidable ability and great determination. While Henry has dithered or simply been too ill to rule she has kept everything under control, especially during this last, troubled decade.

Margaret is the daughter of René, the duke of Anjou who is the titular king of Sicily, and is also a niece by marriage to the French king, Charles VII. It was this relationship that made her a good prize for Henry: the marriage symbolized a longed-for truce between England and France. Among her personal qualities Margaret also displayed an intelligence to equal that of her husband.

Concern over her choice as queen grew over the first eight years of the marriage, however, as Margaret failed to produce the male heir seen as vital to the survival of the Lancastrian dynasty. Then, six years ago, she gave birth to a son, Edward. Margaret is utterly determined that Edward will succeed to the throne.

This desire has led her into a fierce struggle of wills with Richard, the duke of York, who governed the country while the king was too ill to rule. The Lancastrian alliance that has recently triumphed in the exile of York and his followers was forged largely through Margaret's efforts (→6/1462).

1460 - 1462

Southwark, 1 July 1460. Yorkist troops, who landed at Sandwich from Calais on 26 June, arrive (→ 10).

Northampton, 10 July 1460. Henry VI is defeated and captured by Yorkists (→ 16/10).

Borders, 10 August 1460. James III, aged eight, is crowned king (→ 1/1461).

Westminster, 31 October 1460. Henry VI accepts the duke of York as his heir (→ 30/12).

Scotland, January 1461. In return for military aid from James III of Scots and his mother, Mary of Guelders, Margaret of Anjou, the queen of England, agrees to a marriage alliance and the surrender of Berwick (→ 23/2).

Lothian, 23 February 1461. Mary of Guelders wins custody of James III (→ 3/1462).

Westminster, 4 March 1461. Edward, the son of the late Richard of York, proclaims himself Edward IV (→ 29/3).

Lothian, April 1461. On the loss of Berwick-Upon-Tweed, Henry VI, Margaret, Prince Edward, the duke of Somerset and other Lancastrians flee to Scotland (→ 28/6).

Ireland, 1 May 1461. Thomas fitz Maurice FitzGerald, the earl of Kildare, is appointed justiciar (→ 28/2/62).

Westminster, 28 June 1461. Edward IV is crowned in the abbey (→ 8/10/63).

Ireland, 28 February 1462. The new lieutenant is a minor: George, the duke of Clarence, the third son of Richard, the late duke of York (→ 2/8).

Scotland, March 1462. James, the earl of Douglas, agrees to fight James III with English backing (→ 7/1463).

France, June 1462. Margaret, the wife of Henry VI of England, enlists the aid of Louis XI (→ 25/10).

Connacht, 2 August 1462. Edward IV grants James fitz Gerald FitzGerald, the earl of Desmond, the stewardship of the province (→ 1462).

Northumberland, 25 October 1462. Margaret of Anjou lands at Bamburgh with a French army (→ 4/11).

Northumberland, 4 November 1462. Margaret and Henry VI flee again to Scotland.

Co Durham, November 1462. Edward IV's anti-Lancastrian campaign ends (→ 5/1/63).

Blast kills James, king of Scotland

Borders, 3 August 1460
James II, the 29-year-old king of Scotland, was killed today by one of his own guns. It is an ironic death for a man who did much in his 23-year reign to strengthen his country's military power.

The accident happened at the siege of the English Yorkist garrison inside Roxburgh Castle. A special salvo from the royal artillery was arranged to mark a visit to the siege by the queen, Mary of Guelders, but one of the cannon blew up, killing James outright.

Although it is likely that the castle will soon fall, James's death casts long shadows over Scotland's long-term prospects. Once more the throne goes to a minor: the late king's heir, who is also called James, is only eight years old. James II was himself six years old when he became king. His minority saw the country sink into an intermittent civil war that ended only five years ago, when the Black Douglases were crushed (→ 10).

York claims the throne

Westminster, 16 October 1460
Richard, the duke of York, has formally submitted his claim to the throne of England by right of inheritance and demanded an immediate answer from parliament. His demand confirms the impression given by what can only be described as his royal progress to London after landing from Ireland last month. Richard flew the royal standard, his wife was borne to meet him on a blue velvet chair, trumpets heralded his approach, and he took possession of the queen's apartments in the palace.

Richard has refused to call on King Henry VI, saying: "I know of no person in this realm whom it does not behove to come to me and see my person rather than that I should go and visit him." He is determined to depose the king and sit on the throne in his stead. This has dismayed Yorkist lords such as Richard Neville, the earl of Salisbury, and even York's own heir, Edward, the earl of March, who defeated the Lancastrians at Northampton in July and captured the king. Throughout their campaign, after returning from their French exile in June, these lords gathered support by claiming that they were devoted to King Henry and sought only to save him from evil advisers. They want to control the king, not depose him (→ 31/10).

The white rose and crown of York.

Irish parliament to claim sovereignty

Co Louth, 8 February 1460
The Irish parliament, summoned to Drogheda by Richard, the duke of York, has confirmed him as lieutenant and made it treasonable for anyone to challenge his authority.

Believing the Anglo-Irish loyal to his cause, Richard fled here after the stand-off with the Lancastrians at Ludford Bridge in Shropshire last October. For the moment, at least, the authority in Ireland of King Henry VI of England appears undermined.

Essentially, Ireland has declared itself to be a separate entity, bound only by laws accepted and passed by its own parliament. In other words English law is inapplicable here. To underline this, parliament has introduced measures to regulate the currency and provide for a distinctive Irish coinage, consisting of "Irelands", "groats" and "Patricks". These enactments reflect a growing consciousness among the Anglo-Irish of their own traditions and institutions (→ 16/10).

Lancastrian forces kill rebel duke of York

York, 30 December 1460
The leader of the Yorkist challenge to King Henry VI is dead. Richard, the 49-year-old duke of York, took on a Lancastrian force near Wakefield today but was cut down in the ensuing battle. Tonight his severed head, mockingly adorned with a paper crown, glowers down from the gates of York.

His 17-year-old son, Edmund, the earl of Rutland, was also killed, caught as he fled the field by John, Lord Clifford, who was determined to avenge his father's death at St Albans in 1455. "By God's blood," said Clifford, "thy father slew mine; and so will I do thee, and all thy kin."

Duke Richard had marched north at the beginning of December with 6,000 men when he learnt that Queen Margaret, determined to fight for her son's succession, was gathering an army under Henry Beaufort, the duke of Somerset. The Yorkists fought off attempts to halt their progress, but when they arrived at Sandal Castle outside Wakefield they found the countryside in Lancastrian hands. They spent a miserable Christmas inside the castle while Richard was forced to disperse his troops in foraging parties. Today, when he did venture out, he was overwhelmed.

Queen Margaret can now march on London to regain control of both King Henry and the government of the country (→ 17/2/61).

Rutland is killed: a romantic view.

York and Lancaster battle for the English throne

Savage battle once more at St Albans

Hertfordshire, 17 February 1461
Five and a half years after their first clash here the forces of York and Lancaster met again at St Albans today. This time the Lancastrians have triumphed. Queen Margaret's army inflicted a bloody defeat on Richard Neville, the earl of Warwick, wounding him and slaughtering half his army.

She has also recovered her husband, King Henry VI, who had been carried to the battlefield by Warwick and placed under a large tree to watch the battle. He had been put in the care of two knights whose orders were to ensure that he was not harmed. It is a measure of the ferocity with which this dynastic war is being fought that both these knights have been executed on the queen's orders, despite the pleas of her husband.

The Lancastrians arrived here after a long march from their victory at Wakefield seven weeks ago, when they killed Richard, the duke of York. If they move south swiftly they will be able to occupy London without opposition: stories of the savagery of these northerners and their Scottish allies are already spreading terror along their route.

To punish towns such as Grantham and Stamford, which supported the Yorkists, Queen Margaret's soldiers have been given free rein to loot and pillage. So great has the destruction been that some of the Scottish soldiers have abandoned the war to hurry back home with their booty.

News of the queen's advance has meanwhile reached Edward, the eldest son of the slain duke of York, who defeated a Lancastrian force at Mortimer's Cross near Hereford on 2 February. As at St Albans no quarter was given in this battle.

So many leading nobles have died in the war that both sides are now commanded by young men thirsting to avenge fathers and elder brothers. Edward, who has inherited his father's dukedom at the age of 18, is one such. He is now marching on London to confront Queen Margaret (→4/3).

Queen Margaret at her prayers: now she has proved herself a ruthless leader.

A winter battle: the Yorkists grab victory in a snow blizzard at Towton.

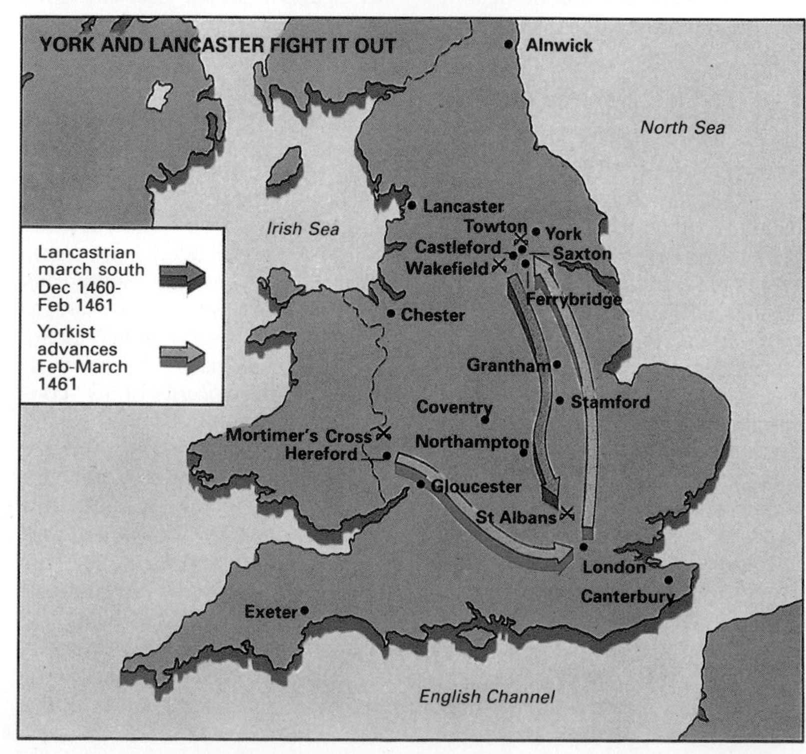

Decisive Towton victory for Yorkists

North Yorkshire, 29 March 1461
While others were at their Palm Sunday prayers today, the armies of Lancaster and York fought a pitched battle in blizzard conditions at Towton, some 10 miles (16km) east of Leeds. Victory has gone to the Yorkists, whose leader, Edward, marched into London a month ago to have himself proclaimed king.

Edward, who will be 19 years old next month, inherited the claim to the throne established by his father, Richard, the duke of York. Unlike his father, however, he has achieved his aim. Perhaps he has simply been luckier. Edward's campaign was certainly helped by Queen Margaret's decision to return northwards rather than march on London after her victories at Wakefield, when Duke Richard was killed, and then at St Albans.

Nine days after taking London himself, Edward set off north to pursue the Lancastrians. Today he caught up with them. The deposed king, Henry VI, will probably seek refuge in Scotland along with Queen Margaret and their seven-year-old son, Edward (→4/1461).

England's civil war spills into Ireland

Co Kilkenny, 1462
Thomas FitzGerald, the earl of Desmond, has inflicted a major defeat on Sir John Butler, the earl of Ormond, in a battle at Piltown in Co Kilkenny. Ormond, a staunch Lancastrian, was found guilty of treason last year, and his English and Irish properties were both forfeited to the new Yorkist king, Edward IV. Hoping not only to regain his lands but also to launch a counter-offensive against the king, Ormond invaded Ireland with a huge force of Lancastrian Englishmen and captured Waterford town.

Desmond, a Yorkist, has crushed this nascent threat to Edward's reign. While his enemy Ormond has gone into exile, Desmond can expect to be rewarded (→1/4/63).

1463 - 1467

Northumberland, 5 January 1463. Richard Neville, the earl of Warwick, retreats from the siege of Alnwick as the Lancastrians arrive (→ 7/1463).

Ireland, 1 April 1463. Thomas FitzGerald, who became earl of Desmond earlier this year, is made deputy to George, the duke of Clarence (→ 1466).

Northumberland, July 1463. James III of Scots retreats from Norham on the arrival of the earl of Warwick and his younger brother, John Neville, Lord Montagu (→ 9/12).

Flanders, 8 October 1463. Louis XI of France agrees peace terms with Edward IV of England (→ 3/7/68).

York, 9 December 1463. An Anglo-Scots truce is signed; Edward IV abandons support for the earl of Angus, and James III abandons the Lancastrians (→ 12/1463).

Wales, December 1463. Henry Beaufort, the duke of Somerset, returns to the Lancastrian cause and joins Jasper Twdwr, who was stripped of the earldom of Pembroke in 1461 (→ 15/5/64).

Northumberland, 1464. John Neville, Lord Montagu, ambushed at Hedgeley Moor on his way to Scottish peace talks, fends off Lancastrians under the leadership of the earl of Somerset (15/5).

York, 27 May 1464. Edward IV creates Montagu earl of Northumberland (→ 11/6).

York, 11 June 1464. A 15-year Anglo-Scots truce is agreed (→ 13/10/66).

York, 15 March 1465. George Neville, another of Warwick's brothers, is made archbishop of York, increasing Neville family power in the north (→ 8/6/67).

England, 22 March 1466. Negotiations begin for a marriage between Margaret, the sister of Edward IV, and the heir to the duchy of Burgundy, Charles (→ 3/7/68).

Ireland, 1466. Plague breaks out in Meath, Leinster and Dublin (→ 10/1467).

York, 8 June 1467. Edward IV dismisses George Neville, the archbishop of York, from his position as chancellor; the rift between the king and the Neville family becomes even wider (→ 25/4/72).

Ireland, October 1467. John Tiptoft, the earl of Worcester, who was made deputy this spring, arrives (→ 1468).

Scotland is now left entirely in the care of regency council

Scotland, December 1463

Mary of Guelders, Scotland's dowager queen, has died. She outlived her husband, James II, by less than three and a half years. After his death Mary kept custody of their child, James (the present king), although the regency was denied her. She also maintained control of the most important fortresses, which meant that she continued to wield considerable power.

The niece of Philip "the Good" of Burgundy, Mary was a woman with a lively mind and strong convictions. As such she was bound to clash with Bishop Kennedy of St Andrews, who has dominated the council of regency that rules the country during James III's minority and who thinks women should not be in positions of authority.

Mary was a tough campaigner, successfully concluding the Roxburgh siege that cost her husband his life. She was also a skilful politician, who backed the Lancastrians in return for the surrender of Berwick and Carlisle. Her reputation was however dented when she became the mistress of Adam Hepburn, Master of Hailes and a married man. Her death leaves Bishop Kennedy in control of both the king and the nation at large (→ 11/6/64).

Edward IV makes secret marriage public

Edward and his queen, Elizabeth: stained glass in Canterbury Cathedral.

Reading, 28 September 1464

King Edward IV has caused uproar among his lords by admitting that he has been secretly married since May to Elizabeth Woodville, the widow of Sir John Grey, a Lancastrian knight who died fighting for Henry VI at St Albans in 1461.

She is said to be extremely good-looking and chaste, but, at 27 years old, she is five years older than the king and already has two young sons. She also has five brothers and seven unmarried sisters who must be provided for.

Gossip has it that Edward, a notorious womanizer, wanted only to seduce her. Even when he put a dagger to her throat she resisted his advances. At last she gave in to him on condition that he marry her – which, on 1 May this year, he did. There is much sneering at court about her lowly status for, although her mother is Jacquetta of Luxembourg, the widow of Henry V's brother, John, the duke of Bedford, her father is Sir Richard Woodville, John's chamberlain. Sir Richard, who courted and won Jacquetta after her first husband's death, is snobbishly thought not to have the rarefied lineage necessary to provide a queen of England.

What could prove even more embarrassing, however, is that Edward kept his marriage secret from Richard Neville, the earl of Warwick, while his powerful supporter was deeply involved in negotiating a political marriage for him with a French princess (→ 2/11/70).

Turncoat duke killed after Hexham battle

Northumberland, 15 May 1464

A Lancastrian force under Henry Beaufort, the turncoat duke of Somerset, was defeated in battle here today by the Yorkist commander John Neville, Lord Montagu. Somerset was captured and executed on Montagu's orders, putting an end to a life that deserves to be called dramatic even by the standards of these extraordinary times.

Somerset was one of the chief architects of the great Lancastrian victories at Wakefield in 1460 and St Albans in 1461. After the defeat at Towton the duke retreated to continue the struggle for the deposed Henry VI from the north of England. In 1462 he was forced to surrender to Edward IV at the siege of Dunstanburgh and Bamburgh Castles and might well have expected to die on the block then.

But Edward, anxious to pursue a policy of conciliation, not only pardoned him but also restored his honours and estates. In return, Somerset went over to the Yorkists and swore allegiance to Edward. He proved the sincerity of his "conversion" by joining the siege of the Lancastrian garrison at Alnwick Castle. Edward showered favours on his latest recruit, making him captain of the king's bodyguard and holding a tournament in his honour. Yet Edward's old supporters felt that their lord was being too trusting – and so it has proved to be. Somerset fled to Wales last December and once again took the field for Henry VI (→ 27/5).

Well-born ladies of this time wear full, high-bodiced dresses.

Fugitive Henry betrayed

King Henry VI: taken captive.

Lancashire, 13 July 1465
King Henry VI, a fugitive in the north of England since the collapse of Scottish support for him following the death of Mary of Guelders in 1463, has been taken captive a few miles west of Clitheroe. With him was a meagre entourage of two clergymen and a groom.

Henry, who is 43 years old, has been wandering from one safe house to another, sometimes disguised as a monk, while Edward IV's spies searched for him. He found sanctuary near to where he was captured at Waddington Hall, the home of Sir Richard Tempest. But as he sat at dinner a few days ago Sir Richard's brother, John, burst into the room with a group of armed men and attempted to seize him. It seems more than likely that Sir Richard was involved in the plot, for he did nothing to protect his royal guest. Fortunately for Henry others did intervene, enabling him to make his escape.

He might have got away to resume his wanderings, but he was betrayed again, this time by a monk of Abingdon. Henry was finally taken without a struggle. Tonight he is being led back to London in the power of the Yorkists. His journey will be a slow and ignominious one on horseback, with his feet tied to the stirrups and another rope tied around his body. His future is extremely bleak, with his queen, Margaret of Anjou, and his only child, Edward, languishing in exile in France.

Scots king says he was not kidnapped

Edinburgh, 13 October 1466
James III has issued a statement that the Boyd family acted under his instructions in removing him to their custody in Edinburgh. On 9 July Sir Alexander Boyd took the 14-year-old king out hunting during an exchequer audit at Linlithgow. This was, however, just a cover for his abduction; James was taken to Edinburgh Castle, of which the Boyds are the keepers.

Behind this plot is Robert, Lord Boyd, whose ambitions for his family include the marrying of his eldest son, Thomas, to James's sister, Lady Mary. Although James is known to be against such an alliance, for the time being he has no choice but to play along with his captors. The Boyds, for their part, are exploiting the power vacuum that has existed since last year, when the head of Scotland's government, Bishop Kennedy of St Andrews, died (→ 10/7/69).

Edward suspicious of younger brother

Coventry, 26 December 1467
Edward IV has summoned his 18-year-old brother, George, the duke of Clarence, here in order to keep an eye on him. The reason for this is that George has come under the influence of Richard Neville, the earl of Warwick, whose daughter, Isabel, he plans to marry despite Edward's objections.

The king and "kingmaker" have clashed over foreign policy, Warwick working for an alliance with France but Edward for one with Burgundy – to be sealed by the marriage of his sister, Margaret, to the duke of Burgundy. Warwick has retired in fury to his estates in Yorkshire and refuses to respond to an accusation that he has contacted Margaret of Anjou, the wife of the deposed Lancastrian king, Henry VI. While this accusation seems unfounded, Warwick may be persuading Clarence to think of taking the throne himself (→ 10/7/69).

Rich, highly spiced dishes are popular as English palates grow more sophisticated

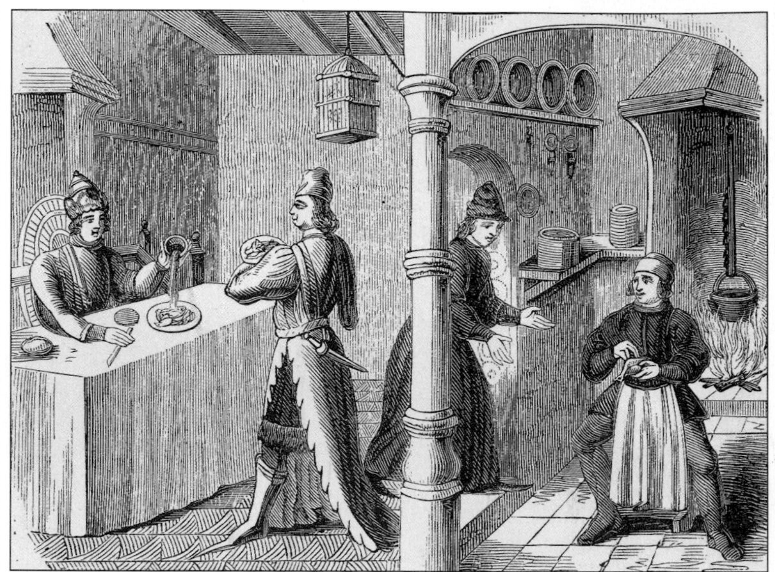
Servants hard at work preparing a meal in a 15th-century kitchen.

England, 1467
If the regular diet of most people in the country is somewhat dull, based on an repetitive round of grain and vegetables, that of the nobility has much more to offer, as exemplified by recent banquet held at the Neville household.

At a feast to celebrate the appointment this year of George Neville as archbishop of York, his brother Richard, the earl of Warwick, entertained on a huge scale. More than 60 cooks prepared, among other items, 104 oxen, 1,000 sheep, 2,000 pigs – and 13,000 desserts, all washed down with 300 large casks of ale and 100 casks of wine.

The Nevilles are typical in spurning simple peasant food. No nobleman would dream of eating vegetables or bacon. Rich dishes are preferred, especially now that spices are more easily obtainable. English palates are becoming accustomed to costly imports such as cloves, ginger, cinnamon, pepper and sugar, in addition to currants, figs, raisins and almonds. Spices and herbs are combined with wine, cream and eggs to add flavour to all kinds of meat dishes (→ 6/1520).

In contrast to the banquets of the nobility, most people enjoy a simple diet.

1468 - 1470

Wales, 1468. The Lancastrian supporter Jasper Twdwr sacks Denbigh (→ 8/9).

Norwich, 18 June 1469. King Edward IV stops here on his way to attack the rebel leader Sir John Conyers of Hornby, also known as "Robin of Redesdale" (→ 26/7).

Edinburgh, 10 July 1469. James III, aged 17, marries Margaret, aged 12, the daughter of King Christian of Norway (→ 11/1469).

Oxfordshire, 26 July 1469. Edward IV's troops are defeated by Redesdale's rebels, backed by Warwick and Clarence, at Edgcott, near Bicester (→ 8/1469).

Coventry, 12 August 1469. Pro-Warwick rebels execute Anthony Woodville, Earl Rivers, and Sir John Woodville, the father and brother of Edward IV's queen.

Northamptonshire, August 1469. Edward IV is captured by Archbishop George Neville of York, Warwick's brother (→ 10/9).

York, 10 September 1469. Edward IV escapes from his captors (→ 31/3/70).

Edinburgh, November 1469. Parliament declares Scotland a free imperial monarchy and convicts Lord Boyd and his sons of treason. Sir Alexander Boyd, who kidnapped James III in 1466, is executed, but his father and brother escape into exile (→ 17/3/73).

Nottingham, 31 March 1470. Warwick and Clarence are proclaimed traitors by Edward IV (→ 20/4).

France, July 1470. Warwick, who fled here with Clarence in April, makes his peace with Margaret of Anjou, the wife of Henry VI; her son, Edward, will marry Warwick's daughter, Anne (→ 13/9).

Devon, 13 September 1470. Warwick and Clarence land at Dartmouth and declare Henry VI the rightful king (→ 6/10).

London, 6 October 1470. Warwick and Clarence free Henry VI (→ 11/10).

England, 18 October 1470. John Tiptoft, the earl of Worcester, who was promoted from deputy to lieutenant of Ireland in March, is executed (→ 18/2/71).

Westminster, 2 November 1470. Elizabeth Woodville gives birth to Edward IV's son, Edward (→ 16/6/83).

French slanders fail to halt royal wedding

Damme, Netherlands, 3 July 1468
Margaret of York, the sister of King Edward IV of England, has been married here to Charles, the duke of Burgundy, despite scurrilous rumours about the bride spread throughout Europe by ambassadors of the duke's rival Louis XI, the king of France.

It is now two weeks since Margaret landed here with a party of more than 1,800 courtiers and attendants. Edward had undertaken to supply the necessary plate and finery and devoted all of £2,450 6s 8d to his sister's expenses. He even provided two of his own fools to keep the wedding guests entertained as they sailed from Margate.

The port of Sluys was torch-lit, with bonfires blazing, when Margaret's fleet arrived. Once the wedding party was ashore, pageants – *Jason and the Golden Fleece* among them – were presented in the market square.

On the following Monday the duke arrived to see his bride-to-be for the first time. Charles had been distinctly cool about the prospect of this marriage, but Margaret's beauty overwhelmed him, and the delighted duke kissed her openly. The feasting and pageantry are expected to last for nine days, with daily jousting in the market place at Bruges. Anthony, the illegitimate brother of Duke Charles, had planned to defend his title and break 101 lances; but he has broken his knee instead (→ 14/4/71).

The duke and courtiers on a hunt.

Rebellion provoked by earl's execution

Ireland, spring 1468
There has been a violent reaction in Ireland to the execution on 4 February of Thomas FitzGerald, the earl of Desmond. He was deputy lieutenant of Ireland until replaced last year by John Tiptoft, the earl of Worcester. Desmond's brother, Gerald, has invaded Meath with over 20,000 men; there has also been fierce fighting in Ulster, Louth, Cavan and Leinster.

Edward IV is paying a heavy price for his decision to replace Desmond with Tiptoft, a ruthless man known as "the butcher". He lost no time in attacking Desmond and accusing him of treason. Eventually he had Desmond arrested and executed. It is assumed that the king is responsible for Desmond's death, possibly believing that the confiscation of his estates will enhance his power in Ireland. But both the king and Tiptoft miscalculated the power of the FitzGerald earls, especially the earl of Kildare, whom Tiptoft is having to placate in order to restore order (→ 18/10/70).

Raglan Castle is home to the new and powerful earl of Pembroke

Gwynedd, 8 September 1468
The grasping and ambitious William Herbert secured an important accolade today when King Edward IV of England gave him Jasper Twdwr's earldom of Pembroke. It was Herbert's reward for forcing the Lancastrians to surrender Harlech Castle on 14 August.

Herbert's rise to eminence has been spectacular, exemplifying the rewards that can be gained from backing the Yorkist king. The new earl, who is 45 years old, has benefited enormously from the king's patronage in terms of the wholesale redistribution of land in both Wales and the Welsh Marches.

No Welshman has ever achieved such power and authority – or such a high income. Herbert earns more than £2,000 a year, and his power centre, Raglan Castle, south-west of Monmouth, is an impressive building with gardens, walks, fountains and courtyards. In a shrewd propaganda move, Herbert has engaged itinerant Welsh poets to espouse the Yorkist cause and has established Herbert Court as a Welsh literary centre.

A forbidding gateway: a 20th-century view of the splendid Raglan Castle.

One poet has described Herbert as Edward's "master-lock", or linchpin, in Wales; the authority vested in him is a marked departure from the policy of earlier English kings, who relied on absentee aristocrats to run the principality.

Herbert's rise to power really began in May 1461 when he was made chief justice and chamberlain of south Wales and received seven castles as well as custody of Henry, Edmund Twdwr's son – whom he has earmarked as his future son-in-law. As Lancastrian opposition continued in Wales more and more property was conveyed to Herbert, and he was appointed constable of Harlech, although it was four years before he could successfully attack the castle, the last Lancastrian stronghold in Wales (→ 9/1471).

Rebel earls issue a warning from across the sea

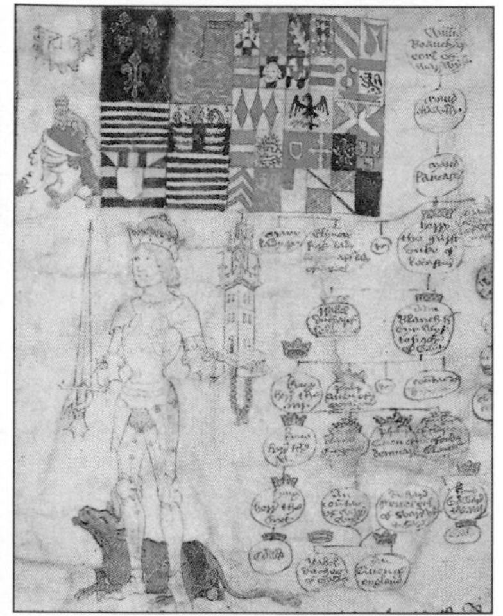
Rebel leaders: duke of Clarence ...

Calais, France, 12 July 1469
Richard Neville, the earl of Warwick, and George, the duke of Clarence, have dropped all pretence of loyalty to the king and called their supporters in England to arms at Canterbury in four days' time.

In company with sympathizers such as Archbishop George Neville of York, Warwick and Clarence have played shadowy roles in a rebellion against Edward IV in the north of England. The rebel leader is Sir John Conyers of Hornby, an ally of Warwick, who styles himself "Robin of Redesdale". In their manifesto – which appears in the form of an open letter – Warwick and Clarence complain of their exclusion from the king's secret council. They also draw unflattering comparisons between the king's present advisers and those of three of his predecessors, Edward II, Richard II and Henry VI, who cost those kings their thrones. They then stated their intention to lay their proposals for a "remedy and reformation" before the king.

Warwick has also told his supporters of Clarence's marriage here yesterday to Isabel, one of Warwick's daughters. It was a family affair: Warwick's brother, the archbishop of York, presided over the ceremony (→26).

... and Richard, earl of Warwick.

Power struggle swings towards Edward IV

Southampton, 20 April 1470
King Edward IV arrived here today chasing Richard Neville, the rebel earl of Warwick, only to find he had already slipped back across the Channel to France with his ally, George, the duke of Clarence. At least they are no longer in England where, ever since their return late last July, they led opposition to the king. But by last October Edward had started to regain control. Peace talks got under way in February, but last month another rebellion broke out in Lincolnshire. Edward swiftly put it down, prompting Warwick and Clarence to take to their boats (→7/1470).

Edward IV: now he is fighting back.

Betrayed English king flees into exile

The Hague, 11 October 1470
Edward IV of England and his party reached the safety of The Hague tonight after a hectic dash across Lincolnshire – in which Edward IV came close to drowning in The Wash – and an equally hazardous voyage across the North Sea.

The king has miscalulated badly. Expecting his foes, Richard Neville, the earl of Warwick, and George, the duke of Clarence, to land from France in the north, where their support is greatest, Edward left the south coast unprotected. But last month the rebels landed at Dartmouth, declared for Henry VI and called all able-bodied men to join them. Edward headed for London, pausing at Doncaster for reinforcements from John Neville, the marquis of Montagu (a title he was given on 25 March). But then Edward learnt that Montagu had defected to his brother, Warwick. Edward immediately headed with his nobles to King's Lynn, where shipping could be found.

They were pursued by a hostile squadron of ships belonging to the north German Hanseatic trading league, but they got to the Dutch coast near Alkmaar. The king of England is now penniless and could only pay the master of the ship with a furred gown (→2/3/71).

Writer convicted of violent crimes completes 'Morte d'Arthur'

England, 1469
Sir Thomas Malory, a convicted criminal, has this year completed his *Morte d'Arthur*, a new account of the rise and fall of the court of King Arthur and the Knights of the Round Table. Sir Thomas, who has spent several of the past 19 years in prison on a range of charges, including rape, has devoted most of his time behind bars to the work.

Malory's text draws on earlier French Arthurian narratives but brings a new complexity to the tale. Now 70 years old, the author was formerly a respected gentleman-soldier. But his reputation plummeted after he was first sentenced to prison.

A legendary king: a manuscript illumination of Arthur's coronation.

Viscount is stabbed in 'private' battle

Avon, 20 March 1470
Two private armies joined battle today at the village of Nibley Green. Victory was secured by William Berkeley over his arch-rival, Thomas, Viscount Lisle. The fighting began after 19-year-old Lisle challenged Berkeley to either single combat or a pitched battle to resolve a legal row between them. A mob of small boys climbed into the trees to watch the two armies clash. Berkeley had recruited miners and foresters led by "Black Will", an expert bowman. One of his arrows felled Lisle, who was then swiftly knifed to death.

1471 - 1475

Ireland, 18 February 1471. George, the duke of Clarence, is reappointed lieutenant (→4/1471).

Netherlands, 2 March 1471. Edward IV of England sets sail to reclaim his lost throne (→15).

Humberside, 15 March 1471. Edward IV, stating that he has arrived only to reclaim the duchy of York, heads for York itself (→2/4).

Warwick, 2 April 1471. Edward IV is joined by George, the duke of Clarence, who has deserted his former ally, the earl of Warwick (→11).

London, 11 April 1471. Edward IV and his brothers enter London and take possession of Henry VI (→14).

Co Tyrone, April 1471. Enri O'Neill, the lord of Tyrone, captures Omagh from Clann Airt Ui Neill (→12/1471).

Tewkesbury, Gloucester, 7 May 1471. The Yorkists capture Margaret of Anjou, in hiding in a nunnery since the battle here on 4 May (→21).

London, 21 May 1471. Edward IV enters the city; Henry VI, aged 49, dies in the Tower in the evening (→6/1473).

Wales, September 1471. Jasper Twdwr takes his nephew Henry Twdwr to France for safety (→6/1473).

Ireland, December 1471. Thomas FitzGerald, the earl of Kildare, is appointed deputy (→1472).

Hertfordshire, 25 April 1472. George Neville, the archbishop of York, is arrested for a plot against Edward IV (→8/7/76).

St Andrews, 13 August 1472. The bishopric of St Andrews is raised to a metropolitan archbishopric; Scotland's first archbishop is to be Patrick Graham (→9/1/78).

Ireland, 1472. Enri O'Neill defeats the lord of Tyrconnell, Aodh Ruadh O'Donnell, at Castlemoyle (→25/3/78).

Scotland, 17 March 1473. Queen Margaret gives birth to a son, James, the heir of James III (→26/10/74).

Lothian, 26 October 1474. A marriage is agreed between Cecily, the daughter of Edward IV of England, and James, the Scots heir; the 1419 peace treaty is renewed (→7/1476).

Bruges, Low Countries, 1474. William Caxton prints the first book in English, the *History of Troye* (→9/1476).

Lancastrians fall in Easter bloodbath

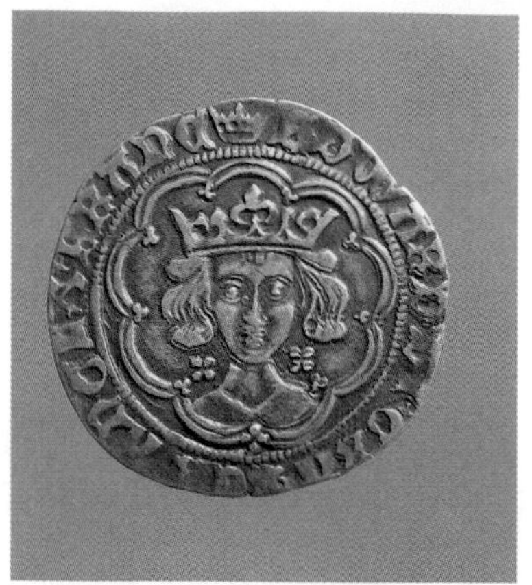

A coin issued in Edward's name.

London, 14 April 1471
Richard Neville, the 42-year-old earl of Warwick, has been killed in a battle north of London. For Edward IV, whom Warwick supported until their alliance started to turn sour four years ago, this was the longed-for victory to bring him back the throne. Having returned last month from his exile in the Low Countries, Edward arrived in London on 11 April only to learn that Warwick was marching on the capital. Yesterday Edward moved up to Barnet, 10 miles (16km) north of the city, to block Warwick's advance. Today, Easter day, Edward's men attacked. Losses have been heavy on both sides, but it was Edward's Yorkists who carried the day. Both Warwick and his brother John, the marquis of Montagu, were killed. Their bodies, now lying in St Paul's Cathedral, have been saved from dismemberment on Edward's orders.

Edward's battles are not yet over. Henry VI's queen, Margaret of Anjou, landed today at Weymouth in Dorset. The Yorkists have now to confront her and the remaining Lancastrian noblemen (→4/5).

Duke of Burgundy backs Edward in his claim to English throne

Burgundy, 14 April 1471
News of the victory won today near London by the Yorkist king, Edward IV, will be received with great interest on this side of the Channel, where the dynastic conflict between York and Lancaster has drawn into its embrace the king of France, Louis XI, and his leading opponent, Charles, the duke of Burgundy. Both have sought to exploit an alliance with England in their struggle against each other.

Louis has for years grappled with a problem with which Henry VI of England would easily sympathize: disenchanted noblemen forming alliances against him and running amok all over his lands. Over recent years he has stabilized the situation, but the duchy of Burgundy remains a thorn in his side. Louis's concern is that Burgundy will join forces with England to divide his own kingdom.

Louis has always put his money on the Lancastrian cause, so today's news will cause him more than a little distress. He gave shelter and military support to Henry VI's wife, Margaret of Anjou, when she fled to his kingdom in March 1462. Similarly when Richard Neville, the earl of Warwick, who had turned against Edward IV, took refuge in France for the second time last summer, Louis sent him assurances that he was the best friend that Warwick had in the world. Louis even promised to fit him out with an invasion fleet. All Warwick had to do in return was to ally with France in a war against Burgundy.

King Edward's backer: Charles, the duke of Burgundy, with his council.

His reward would be Holland and Zeeland, both now under Burgundian rule.

This was just the sort of talk to give Duke Charles sleepless nights. His diplomatic insurance against such an alliance was his marriage to Margaret, Edward IV's sister. This, however, depended on the assumption that Edward would stay on the throne. Charles was therefore somewhat distraught to learn, in October of last year, that Edward had arrived on the Dutch coast, having been ejected from his own kingdom. Charles had no choice but to support Edward: the return of Henry VI to the throne could only mean that Louis's hand had been greatly strengthened. So it was with Charles's help that Edward set off last month from Flushing across the North Sea in his bid to regain the crown (→4/5).

Lancaster annihilated

Gloucestershire, 4 May 1471
Just three weeks after his victory at Barnet [*see report on opposite page*] Edward IV's Yorkist army crushed Margaret of Anjou's Lancastrians at Tewkesbury today. For Margaret it is a bitter end to her long expected return from France. Landing at Weymouth on 14 April (the same day as the battle at Barnet), she quickly raised a large force in the west country and by the end of the month had entered Bristol.

Margaret planned then to cross the Severn and recruit more men in Wales. Edward, meanwhile, was marching down from London and reached Cirencester on 29 April. He had heard that Margaret intended to meet him on the Bristol-to-Malmesbury road. In fact she wheeled north, and Edward, in hot pursuit, sent messengers ahead to Gloucester warning the townsfolk not to receive her. Frustrated there, Margaret moved to the next crossing over the Severn at Tewkesbury, where Edward arrived today to annihilate her army. Among the dead is Margaret's only son, 17-year-old Prince Edward. Margaret and Edmund Beaufort, the duke of Somerset, have sought refuge in religious houses, but Edward is unlikely to respect any claims to sanctuary. He knows that the Lancastrian cause lacks just one thing now – the *coup de grâce* (→ 7).

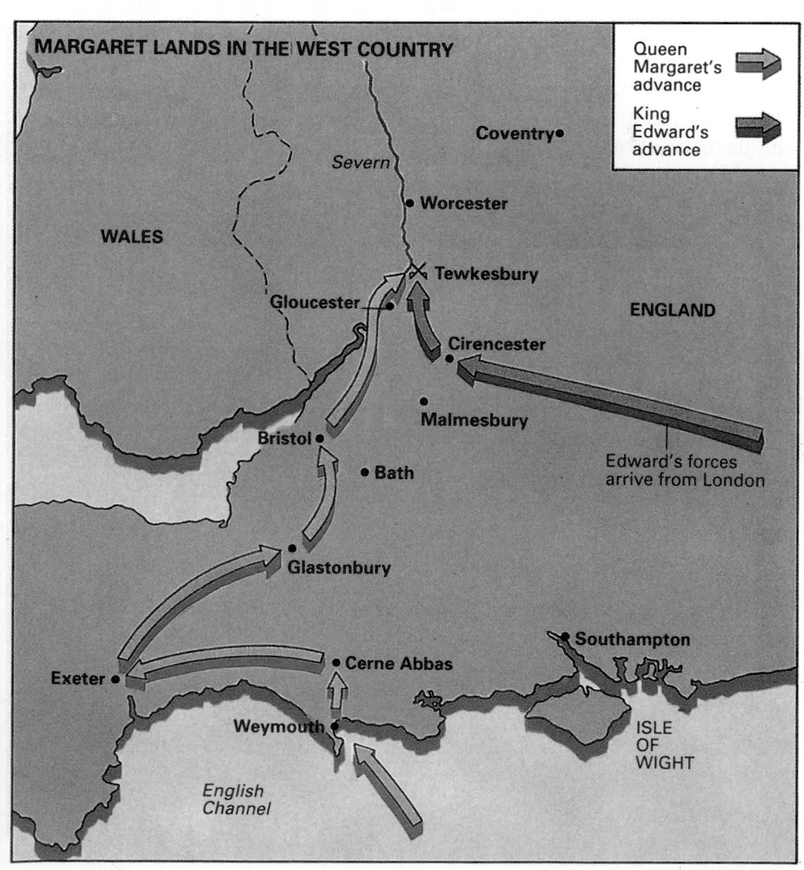

Shake-up looms for English rule in Wales

Shrewsbury, June 1473
Determined to impose full authority in Wales, Edward IV has called his Marcher lords to a meeting at Shrewsbury to demand promises that they will carry out their traditional responsibities.

In the meantime Edward, the king's two-year-old son, has been created prince of Wales. A council of 15 men has duly been appointed to administer the principality until the prince reaches the age of 14. This council, operating from a headquarters in Ludlow Castle, will also supervise the courts in Wales, the Marches and the English border shires (→ 10/1483).

Phoney French war ends well for English

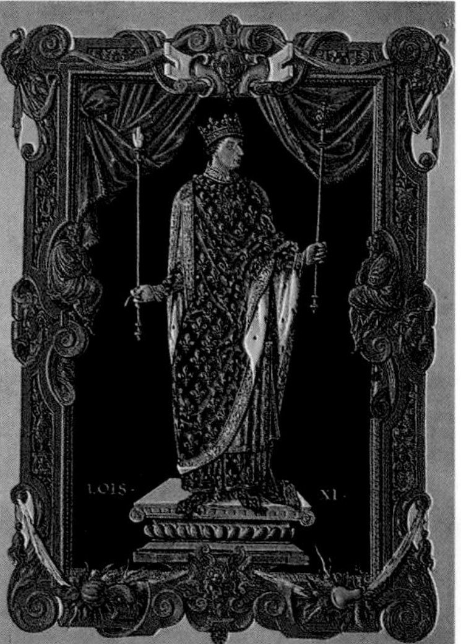

King Louis: a 16th-century view.

France, 29 August 1475
Edward IV of England's great campaign against Louis XI of France, who backed Edward's Lancastrian opponents in the civil war, has proved a non-event. Instead of glorious deeds on the field of battle, negotiators have hammered out a peace deal in the Somme village of Pecquigny, some 70 miles (112km) south of Calais. Speaking through a protective trellis on a bridge over the river Somme, both kings have agreed on a seven-year truce with barely a shot having been fired. The trellis was a security measure in case of assassination attempts.

Edward has promised to leave France peacefully on payment to him of £15,000. The treaty also arranges for the marriage of the Charles, the French royal heir, to Edward's daughter, Elizabeth of York, as well as an annual pension to Edward of £10,000 a year.

Edward arrived in Calais last July at the head of an invasion fleet as large as his ambition: to make himself king of France. Yet his ally, Charles, the duke of Burgundy, turned up in Calais with little more than a bodyguard. Without Burgundy's help, Edward knew that he could not fight Louis head-on and so, thwarted of a victory on the battlefield, decided to barter for one instead. Fortunately for the English, it appears that Louis was not aware of Edward's military disadvantages and was himself more than eager to talk (→ 1/1482).

Bitter dispute arises over marriage plans

Surrey, February 1472
A dispute between King Edward IV's brothers over the huge wealth accumulated by the Neville family has been resolved at Sheen Palace. George, the duke of Clarence, has agreed to concede the marriage of his wife Isabel's sister, Anne Neville, to Richard, the 19-year-old duke of Gloucester.

Anne is the sister of Clarence's wife, Isabel, and the daughter of the late earl of Warwick, Richard Neville. She was, furthermore, the wife of Henry VI's son Edward who was killed at Tewkesbury last year. After the battle Gloucester abducted Anne from Clarence's custody. Although the relationship between Anne and him is so close – several times within the prohibited degrees – that a church dispensation to marry will be difficult to acquire, Gloucester sees it as his best chance of getting some of the Warwick inheritance.

Clarence had objected that much of this inheritance was his for helping King Edward regain the throne.

Richard and Anne: happy couple?

He has agreed to drop some of his demands but says that he will not accept the division of the estate. Gloucester has already been given Warwick's northern land and Clarence wants to keep the rest. It is hardly surprising that the inheritance should be contentious: it is, after all, the combined wealth of three of England's greatest families – the Beauchamps, the Nevilles and the Despensers (→ 12/5/77).

1476 - 1479

England, 22 January 1476. Margaret of Anjou, the widow of Henry VI, is to renounce all claims to the throne and return to her native France (→25/8/82).

England, 8 July 1476. Archbishop George Neville of York, freed from prison in 1474, dies.

Lothian, July 1476. John, the lord of the Isles, who lost the earldom of Ross in December for treasonable dealings with Edward IV of England, submits to James III (→4/1479).

Westminster, September 1476. William Caxton sets up a printing press in the chapter house of the abbey (→1478).

France, 7 January 1477. Charles "the Bold", the duke of Burgundy, is killed in battle at Nancy (→2/1477).

England, February 1477. The royal council plans an English marriage for Mary, Charles of Burgundy's heiress (→18/8).

England, 12 May 1477. John Stacey, an astronomer, and Thomas Burdett, an esquire of the duke of Clarence, are accused of treason (→19/1/78).

Low Countries, 18 August 1477. Mary of Burgundy marries Maximilian of Austria, the son of Holy Roman Emperor Frederick III, at Ghent (→1/1482).

Lothian, 1477. Henry the Minstrel, nicknamed "Blind Harry", writes *The Wallace*, eulogizing Sir William Wallace (killed by the English in 1305) and criticizing James III's pro-English policy (→1508).

Westminster, 19 January 1478. The duke of Clarence is to be tried for treason (→18/2).

Ireland, 25 March 1478. The justiciar Thomas fitz Maurice FitzGerald, the earl of Kildare, dies; he is succeeded by his son, Gerald [Gearoid Mor] (→5/5/79).

Ireland, 5 May 1479. Richard, the duke of York, the second son of Edward IV, aged five, is appointed lieutenant (→1480).

Edinburgh, April 1479. Alexander, the duke of Albany, accused of conspiracy by his elder brother, James III, flees to France (→12/1479).

Lothian, December 1479. John, the earl of Mar, the youngest brother of James III, is executed for treason (→4/1480).

Windsor, 1479. Edward IV begins the rebuilding of the chapel.

Caxton prints epic work

Westminster, 1478
Chaucer's epic poem *Canterbury Tales* has appeared in print, the first original work of English literature ever to be set in type. The printer is William Caxton, a man originally from Kent who set up his wooden printing-press near the chapter house at Westminster Abbey two years ago.

Caxton, at one time an apprentice in the mercer's trade, went to Cologne to learn the new art of printing with movable type, begun about 1450 by Johannes Gutenberg, whose Bible appeared in 1455.

Caxton moved to Bruges where he set up a press and produced the first book printed in English, his own translation of the *History of Troye*, followed by *The Game and Playe of Chesse*. The first book he printed in England was *The Dictes and Sayings of the Philosophers* two years ago. But *Canterbury Tales* is by far his most ambitious publication to date. An illustrated second edition may follow.

Many of the patrons of both authors and printers are high-born women. For example, Margaret of York, now the duchess of Burgundy, helped and encouraged Caxton with his translation of the history of Troy. His next big project is a *Chronicle of England* and also Sir Thomas Malory's prose romance *Morte d'Arthur*, which gathers into one epic the mass of French tales of Arthurian chivalry (→1485).

Caxton presents a book to a patron.

¶And ſayd/he that gedreth and aſſembleth moche ſiluer
ought not to be called riche/but he that diſpendeth it wor
ſhipfully and laudably. ¶And ſom aſked him howe one
might kepe him from nede/and he anſwered if men be riche
let hem lyue temperately/and ſobrely. and if they be pouer
lete hem laboure diligentely/Than ſome axed him of howe
moche goode a man ought to be content/And he anſwered
to haue ſo moche as he nedeth nat to flatre nor borowe of o
ther ¶And ſayd to his diſciples/Whan ye ſhalbe wery

From the "Sayings of the Philosophers", the first book printed in England.

Scottish archbishop made to suffer the disgrace of prison

Fife, 9 January 1478
Patrick Graham, the archbishop of St Andrews, has been deprived of his see and imprisoned at Inchcolm. Graham, who has held the bishopric of St Andrews since 1465, when he was only 30 years old, became Scotland's first archbishop in 1472. Yet Pope Sixtus IV's policy of using Archbishop Graham to prevent what he sees as James III's interference in church appointments has failed. Instead, the king has prevented Graham from exercising any metropolitan authority.

Archbishop Graham's predicament shows how difficult it can be for a modern state to draw a line between the authority of the church and that of the king. The particular problem in this case is that the church, in the person of the pope, is claiming the right not just to confirm the appointment of bishops to sees but to appoint lower clergy directly to other posts when a see falls temporarily vacant. King James, like his father and grandfather before him, has determined to tackle the pope head on.

Sadly, the victim of this dispute is the man in the middle: Graham himself. On top of everything else he has found himself deeply in debt to the papal *curia* [court], and he was excommunicated three years ago when a papal commission of inquiry found him guilty of heresy and blasphemy. The sentence so shocked Graham that he suffered a nervous breakdown. It is unlikely that the archbishop, who is still afflicted by mental illness, will ever be freed (→4/1504).

Corpus Christi guild statutes confirmed by archbishop of York

York, 1477
Thomas Rotherham, the archbishop of York, has confirmed the statutes of the guild of Corpus Christi. The York guild, which is the best-known religious fraternity in the north of England, was formed in 1408 and has many leading landowners amongst its members. The guild is dedicated to "the praise and honour of the most sacred body of our Lord Jesus Christ" – hence the Latin name, which means "the body of Christ". Members are "to keep a solemn procession, the sacrament being in a shrine borne in the same through the city yearly, the Friday after Corpus Christi day", and the day after to have a "solemn Mass dirge".

The celebrated mystery plays for which York is famous will continue to be performed on Corpus Christi itself – the Thursday after Trinity Sunday. On this day the pageants, staged on mobile tiered platforms, tour the city, stopping at certain "stations" to attract an audience. Performed by members of all the city's craft guilds, the cycle of 48 plays – presenting a Christian view of history from the creation to the last judgement – begins at 4.30am and goes on throughout the day, with occasional intervals for refreshments (→1495).

Royal duke may be dead after secret execution in Tower

London, 18 February 1478
According to reports from the Tower of London, George, the 28-year-old duke of Clarence, has been drowned in a malmsey wine butt. George, the younger brother of Edward IV and third in line to the throne, was sentenced to death for treason ten days ago; some believe that he has been executed in secret to spare him the shame of a public execution.

Edward himself had Clarence put on trial, accusing him of conspiracy against him. There has been a lot of mistrust on Edward's side ever since, in 1469, George went over to his brother's enemy, the earl of Warwick, during the civil war. The two men were later reconciled but suspicions returned when, in 1477, the recently-bereaved duke wanted to marry Mary, the duchess of Burgundy. Edward forbade the union: Mary is descended from John of Gaunt, and so she could have revived a Lancastrian claim to the throne.

Clarence: drowned in a wine butt.

Clarence's final downfall came after the execution last year of an Oxford astrologer, John Stacey, and one of Clarence's own esquires, Thomas Burdett, for casting the king's horoscope – a treasonable offence. When Clarence came forward to protest the men's innocence he was sent to the Tower, to await what turned out to be a show trial (→12/5/80).

Recurrence of plague intensifies preoccupation with mortality

The way of all flesh: the gruesome tomb effigy of Alice de la Pole.

The gravedigger is always busy.

England, 1479
A recurrence this year of the bubonic plague or the "black death" has deepened the preoccupation with mortality that has grown over the past century or more. Since the catastrophic arrival of the plague in 1348 there have been sporadic epidemics, particularly among children and young people who have low resistance to infection.

But those who survive youth now live longer than their predecessors did before the plague. Those who reach 20 can expect to live into their mid-fifties instead of their mid-forties. About 10 per cent of the population reach the age of 60 or more. This is an indirect result of the reduction by plague of the population to about three million, leaving more land to go round. Many farmers have switched from arable to raising cattle; more people are eating meat, and housing has also improved.

The omnipresence of death makes people aware of the fickleness of fate, for which the Wheel of Fortune is a favourite literary image. Life is seen as a game at which one can lose without warning, as it says in the poem *Farewell to this World*:

This life, I see, is but a cherry fair
All things pass on and so must I;
Today I sat full grandly in a chair
Till cunning Death knocked at my gate
And unforeseen he said to me "Checkmate!"

Even the details of bodily decay after death may be carved on the tombs of the upper classes. When Alice de la Pole, the countess of Suffolk (Geoffrey Chaucer's granddaughter), died in 1475, the effigy of her in life was mirrored below her catafalque in a detailed carving of her decomposing corpse [*see picture above left*]. The "Dance of Death", in which skeletons dance with all ranks of men and women and lead them to the grave, is painted in the cloister of St Paul's Cathedral in London and can also be found on the walls of many English churches.

Grim realism: an Italian fresco representing the triumph of death.

1480 - 1482

England/Scotland, April 1480. Scheming by Louis XI of France leads to a breakdown in relations between James III and Edward IV; fighting breaks out on the Anglo-Scottish border (→ 12/5).

Ireland, 1480. Conn, the son of Enri O'Neill and the foremost Gaelic lord, marries Eleanor, the daughter of Thomas FitzGerald, the earl of Kildare and the foremost Anglo-Irish lord (→ 7/2/83).

London, January 1481. Edward IV offers the order of Observant Franciscan Friars a House at Greenwich.

Lothian, May 1481. Sir Andrew Wood attacks the English, who have raided in the Firth of Forth (→ 11/1481).

Borders, November 1481. James III prepares to relieve an English siege of Berwick, but the nobility refuse to fight and the army is disbanded; the siege fails (→ 3/5/82).

England, January 1482. Burgundian envoys appeal in vain to Edward IV for aid against France (→ 23/12).

London, 3 May 1482. Edward IV receives Alexander, the duke of Albany and younger brother of James III of Scotland (→ 11/6).

Northamptonshire, 11 June 1482. It is agreed at Fotheringhay that Albany will, in exchange for Edward IV's support against James III, cede Berwick and the disputed border lands, pay homage to Edward and, if possible, marry his daughter, Cecily (→ 7/1482).

Lothian, July 1482. Richard, the duke of Gloucester, and Albany march on Edinburgh with 20,000 men (→ 4/8).

Edinburgh, 4 August 1482. Gloucester and Albany make peace with the opposing Scottish factions (→ 24).

Northumberland, 24 August 1482. Berwick falls to a renewed English siege (→ 29/9).

France, 25 August 1482. Margaret of Anjou, the widow of Henry VI of England, dies, aged 53, at Château de Dampière, near Saumur.

Edinburgh, 29 September 1482. James III's uncles, the earls of Atholl and Buchan, agree to free the king, who has to make peace with Albany (→ 11/12).

Edinburgh, 11 December 1482. Parliament asks James III to appoint Albany lieutenant-general (→ 8/7/83).

King's lieutenant gathers men in north

Close to the king: the duke of Gloucester (in cap and robe) at court.

Westminster, 12 May 1480
Edward IV has made his brother Richard, the duke of Gloucester, lieutenant-general of the north of England, which he is to defend against the Scots. The king fears an invasion from Scotland, but, if there is a war, he hopes to recover Berwick-Upon-Tweed, lost by the English 20 years ago.

Gloucester has strong family links with the north. His mother, the dowager duchess of York, is a Neville, as is his wife, Anne. Her father was Richard Neville, the earl of Warwick, who was killed at Barnet in 1471. The Gloucesters have inherited much of the Nevilles' immense possessions in Yorkshire and have close links with other northern magnates, including the Stanleys and the Percys.

Duke Richard's power base in the north of England has been made even greater with his new appointment. The north is a poor but warlike region where the duke could easily raise a large army. Yet there appears to be no danger to the state. The duke has always professed loyalty to the king and his heir, Prince Edward (→ 1/1482).

Son battles father to be lord of Isles

Inner Hebrides, 1481
A sea battle off Tobermory on the isle of Mull has led to the defeat of John MacDonald, the lord of the Isles, by his illegitimate son Angus Og. By his victory at "the Bloody Bay" Angus is now certain to take over from his father as effective head of the MacDonald clan.

The power struggle between Angus and John over who rules in Duart Castle, the ancient stronghold of the lord of the Isles, has gone on for five years. Its origins lie in John's decision to submit to James III in Edinburgh after coming under suspicion of treasonable dealings with the English king, Edward IV. Although, when he appeared before James to answer the charges, an earlier forfeiture was overturned, he was still punished by losing the earldom of Ross.

His vast following in the clan was appalled that he had surrendered without a fight. The lordship has since then been racked by a series of internal quarrels with the MacDonald chiefs, who came to believe that other clans, particularly the Macleans and the Macleods, were being favoured by John at their expense. Angus Og became the focus of the disquiet at the policies pursued by the lord of the Isles. Twice in the last four years he and his men have sailed to the Isle of Arran where they have plundered crown lands (→ 5/1493).

Atlantic exploration voyage funded by merchants of Bristol

Bristol, 1481
Enterprising merchants in Bristol have financed a new endeavour to explore the Atlantic westwards, seeking new fishing grounds, new islands and a new land-mass.

English traders already sail to the Iberian islands of Madeira and Canary to the south, and they recently opened commercial links with Oran in North Africa. The new voyage coincides with a suggestion this year from the Spanish, who want to partner England in a venture to West Africa, where the Portuguese have already succeeded in sailing down the coast as far as the island of Sao Tomé, just above the Equator (→ 6/8/97).

English ships on the high seas: now traders are exploring further afield.

Nobles lead successful coup in Scotland

Borders, 22 July 1482
James III of Scotland has been ousted by a cabal of nobles, led by John Stewart, the earl of Atholl, and his younger brother James, the earl of Buchan. The king's army is in disarray. An English invasion, led by Richard, the duke of Gloucester, looks set to engulf Berwick.

The king was surprised at Lauder, 25 miles (40km) south-east of Edinburgh, by the two earls, his half-uncles. He was imprisoned, and several of his household were hanged. The rebels are capitalizing on resentment at James's debasing of the coinage to pay for the war with England and his determination to risk a battle to save Berwick. They may also simply be tired of his capricious behaviour (→4/8).

A map of Scotland, made c.1480, with the capital, "Edenburgh".

England gets squeezed out of Europe

Arras, France, 23 December 1482
Much to the fury of England's Edward IV, France and its rival Burgundy have made peace today with the Treaty of Arras. Edward is now likely to lose the £10,000 annual pension from Louis XI of France agreed by the 1475 Treaty of Pecquigny, and there will be no marriage between Edward's daughter, Elizabeth of York, and the *dauphin* [French royal heir], Charles [*see report on page 371*].

England's standing is suddenly very low in Europe. Edward is so enraged that he thinks of nothing but vengeance – even of invading France again. He had promised Holy Roman Emperor Maximilian and the rulers of Burgundy, that he would invade last summer – but was unable to because of his conflict with Scotland.

Now he is out of the diplomatic game. The *dauphin* will marry Maximilian's daughter, Margaret, while Burgundy and Artois will recognize French authority. This makes the outlook for the English enclave at Calais extremely bleak: France will now control its hinterland, Artois (→1/1483).

'Courtesy Books' offer guide to etiquette

London, c.1480
There is currently much amusement in the halls of the aristocracy and among the families of well established English merchants at the spate of new books directed at the *nouveau riche*, instructing them how to behave in polite society.

While both the "black death" and years of war have decimated many of the old Anglo-Norman dynasties, new and wealthy families anxious to be accepted by the nobility, squirearchy and merchant classes are beginning to emerge. Their great social ambition is, of course, to marry their offspring into the upper orders. So, as a wise precaution to ensure that eventual weddings between new money and old cause no embarrassment, ambitious burghers are buying "Courtesy Books" – which may be the only books they own except for the Bible – to teach them how to behave amongst their betters.

The etiquette of the banquet hall is a particularly sensitive matter that has to be fully mastered. Members of the socially ambitious middle class are taught that they should always let their social superiors serve themselves at table first, never wipe their noses on the tablecloth and avoid drawing attention to their spittle. It is also deemed prudent not to relate dirty jokes, scratch or break wind.

Fashion rules in the fairest of courts

London, c.1480
Never has an English court been clothed so sumptuously as that of Edward IV. The king himself, now 39 years old, leads the way, wearing garments lined in rare furs; more fur, hanging from his shoulders like a cape, is there to enhance his stature – literally and metaphorically.

While Edward's courtiers wear their hair long, their doublets are so short as to be positively obscene. Sleeves, meanwhile, are slashed to show off the richness of the courtiers' shirts, and shoes taper into exaggeratedly long points. The women of the court are clothed no less splendidly than the men. Bodices cling tightly to torsos, necks and cleavages are bare, the better to display gold necklaces, and sleeves are edged with fur. The ladies also wear striking headdresses which are shaped like steeples, horns, chimney-pots and even butterflies.

The English court is not only fashionable: it is licentious too. For Edward, a change in style usually means a change in concubine as well as dress. Yet it is Mistress Elizabeth Shore, the longest-lasting of the king's bed companions, who chooses the new styles for him. It is also to Mistress Shore – quick, witty and trustworthy – that the king always returns after letting his carnal curiousity wander.

Apart from the mere frivolity of fashion, clothes have an important social function: they let people know the wearer's station in life. English society being so rigidly divided, this means that anyone who dresses like his betters is asking for trouble. In fact parliament passed a law in 1463 to stop precisely this sort of upstart behaviour. Members from constituencies relying on the wool trade were especially keen on this measure, which stipulates who can wear what. Gold, purple or sable cloth is, for instance, only to be worn by lords. Velvet, satin and silk are the preserve of knights; squires may wear damask, while commoners must forgo scarlet or imported cloth, and any fur but sheepskin.

Dressed to kill: ladies hunting.

Courtiers show off their figures.

Nobles revel in exotic headgear.

1483

England, January. Edward IV prepares for war with the French, who have broken the Treaty of Pecquigny (→ 9/4).

Limerick City, 7 February. The Irish parliament passes an act for transfer of unclaimed absentee lands in Carlow and Kildare to Gerald fitz Maurice FitzGerald [Gearoid Mor], the earl of Kildare (→ 19/7).

Windsor, 20 April. Edward IV is buried (→ 29).

Northampton, 29 April. Richard, the duke of Gloucester, plots with his ally, Henry Stafford, the duke of Buckingham, to make himself protector (→ 30).

London, 4 May. Gloucester arrives with the young King Edward V (→ 6).

Westminster, 6 May. The duke of Gloucester is made protector for the duration of the king's minority; the coronation is rescheduled for 16 June (→ 13/6).

London, 13 June. William, Lord Hastings, an old friend of the late Edward IV, is executed for conspiracy to murder Gloucester.

Westminster, 16 June. The dowager Queen Elizabeth, who sought sanctuary in the abbey with her children, is persuaded to allow her second son, Richard, the duke of York, to join his brother, Edward V, for the coronation. Gloucester postpones its date for a second time (→ 10/1483).

London, 22 June. Today was to have been the coronation of Edward V, but some now claim that Edward IV's sons are illegitimate and that Gloucester should himself be king (→ 25).

Westminster, 25 June. Parliament petitions Richard of Gloucester to take the crown (→ 26).

Westminster, 6 July. Gloucester is crowned Richard III of England (→ 10/1483).

Ireland, 19 July. Richard III of England makes his son, Edward, lieutenant (→ 9/4/84).

Lincoln, 11 October. Richard III orders his troops to move against his former ally, the duke of Buckingham (→ 2/11).

Brittany, 25 December. In a ploy to associate himself with Yorkist sentiment, Henry Twdwr says that if he becomes king he will marry Elizabeth of York, the daughter of Edward IV (→ 7/8/85).

Edward IV dies of stroke

The late King Edward and his two sons: from Canterbury Cathedral.

Westminster, 9 April

King Edward IV has died, ten days after suffering a stroke. He was 40 years old. He is succeeded by his 12-year-old son, Edward V, but real power during the boy's minority will lie with either his mother's relatives, the Woodvilles, or his paternal uncle, Richard, the duke of Gloucester.

In his last days Edward decided that there should be no delay in crowning the prince. Although the council is split over the issue of who exactly should have control of him, it has obeyed the late king's wishes, and the coronation is to take place on 4 May. The new king, Edward V, is at the moment in Ludlow with his maternal uncle, Anthony Woodville, Earl Rivers. The duke of Gloucester is in the north of England but plans to return soon to London – as does Rivers.

Edward IV was daring and ruthless. He is believed to have had Henry VI and his own brother, Clarence, murdered to assure his hold on the throne. He married Elizabeth Woodville secretly in 1464 when he was 22 and she a 27-year-old widow with two sons. The Woodville family made enemies during its rise to power, including William, Lord Hastings, and Henry Stafford, the duke of Buckingham. But Gloucester has always been the queen's friend (→ 30).

Scots duke is made to forfeit his lands

Edinburgh, 8 July

After the blow to his power – and self-esteem – last summer, when a coup nearly toppled him [*see report on page 375*], James III seems at last to be enjoying some success. Alexander, the duke of Albany, who is both James's brother and his chief enemy, has today forfeited his title and lands for treason. The wheel of fortune has swung fully round for him: last July he seemed to have James on the run. Now he is in disgrace.

Albany attempted yet another coup on 3 January, but it was soon foiled. Then, in April, he invited English troops to his castle at Dunbar. It seems that James has now decided that his brother can no longer be trusted (→ 13/3/84).

The peacemaker king: James III.

Royal guardians arrested on way to London coronation

Buckinghamshire, 30 April

Richard, the 30-year-old duke of Gloucester, has taken captive his nephew, Edward V. The king's guardian Anthony Woodville, Earl Rivers, who is his mother's brother, and Richard Grey, her son, have also been arrested and sent to the north of England under guard.

The young king and his half-brother Grey were travelling to London for the coronation, planned for 4 May. The duke of Gloucester had arranged to meet them here in the village of Stony Stratford with an armed escort for their security as they journeyed to London. So far, so kind: but Gloucester had somehow forgotten to mention that he intended to arrest Earl Rivers before meeting the royal party.

Edward V: seized by his uncle.

Along with his close ally, Henry Stafford, the duke of Buckingham, Gloucester gave Rivers a warm welcome at a Northampton inn last night. But when Rivers awoke this morning, he found to his astonishment that the door to his room at the inn was locked – he was under arrest.

Then Gloucester and Buckingham proceeded to Stony Stratford, where this morning they found the young king and his retinue, two of whom – Richard Haute and Thomas Vaughan – were immediately arrested on charges of conspiracy. Edward is now in Gloucester's hands (→ 4/5).

Richard, duke of Gloucester, seizes English crown

Richard: he has seized power.

London, 26 June
Richard, the 30-year-old duke of Gloucester, became king of England today when he usurped the throne of his 12-year-old nephew, Edward V. Richard's opponents – chiefly the Woodvilles – are now in the political wilderness. Edward and his younger brother, Richard, the duke of York, have been confined in the Tower of London.

Richard's rise to power began in April when he seized the young king and made himself protector. Edward's mother, Elizabeth Woodville, fled to sanctuary in Westminster Abbey with her children, but Richard forced her to give the younger boy up. On 13 June, during a meeting of the council in the Tower, William, Lord Hastings, was arrested. He was loyal to the young king, and so he was taken out and beheaded.

Richard then made his case for the throne. He said that Edward IV's marriage to Elizabeth was invalid, because he was already engaged to another woman, Lady Eleanor Butler. His children by Elizabeth were therefore bastards. (He also hinted that Edward IV was himself illegitimate.) Richard argued that his brother Clarence's son, Earl Edward of Warwick, had no claim to the throne either, because Clarence had been convicted of treason.

Richard claimed that the Woodvilles were corrupt, greedy and incompetent, and had plotted against his life. The queen's brother, Anthony Woodville, Earl Rivers, and Richard Grey, her youngest son by her first marriage, were executed in Pontefract Castle yesterday, and other members of the family have fled the country.

However ruthless this campaign has been, it cannot alter the fact that Richard is well liked among his followers – a rare thing in an age when most people follow their lords out of naked self-interest. In the north of England, the heartland of Richard's influence, he is considered a just and open-handed leader and an effective soldier. He has certainly brought to the region a stability that it has not known for many years. Whether he will be able to achieve the same for the country as a whole remains to be seen (→ 6/7).

Deposed boy king and brother are feared to have been murdered

London, October
It is being widely rumoured that the deposed king, Edward V, and his brother Richard, the duke of York, have been murdered on the order of their uncle, Richard III. The two boys, who are respectively 12 and ten years old, have been confined in the Tower of London since June. They may have been killed after a conspiracy in July which aimed to overthrow Richard and restore the young Edward.

Edward's brief reign lasted from the death of his father, Edward IV, on 9 April until Richard seized the throne on 26 June. The princes have been seen a few times playing in the gardens of the Tower, but recently even these glimpses of them have stopped.

Rumours of the boys' deaths have been given greater credence with the news that one of Richard's allies, Henry Stafford, the duke of Buckingham, has turned against him and is backing a new claimant to the throne, 26-year-old Henry Twdwr. A rival candidate would be unthinkable, some say, if the princes were still alive. Henry's claim is through his mother, Margaret Beaufort, who is descended from Edward III on the Lancastrian side. Henry hopes to gain political credibility by marrying Elizabeth of York, the elder sister of the vanished princes (→ 11).

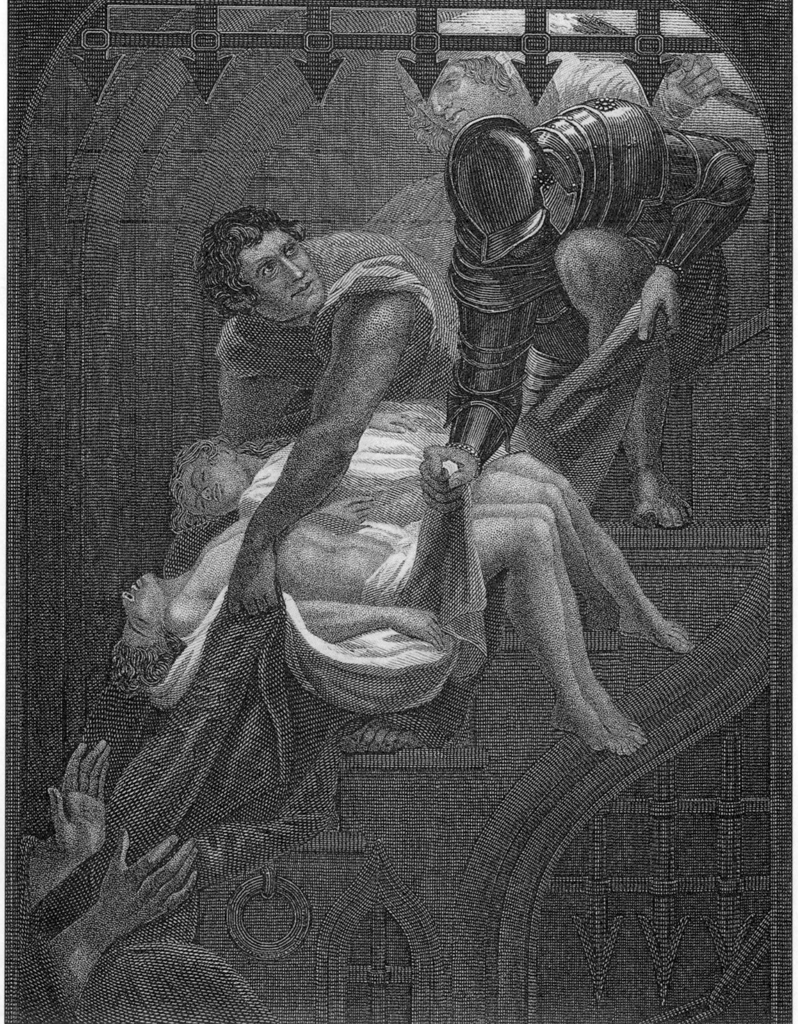
A dark secret: a later picture of the princes' presumed fate.

Execution of rebel leader Buckingham

Salisbury, 2 November
Henry Stafford, the duke of Buckingham, was executed here today for rebelling against his one-time ally, Richard III. He was 28.

Buckingham, who was Richard's key supporter when he took the throne, seems to have repented of his actions and rebelled last month; he tried to raise the English midlands and Wales, but failed. He had hoped that Henry Twdwr, a new claimant to the throne, would come with an army from Brittany, where he has been in exile since the Lancastrian defeat at Tewkesbury in 1471. Unhappily for Stafford, Henry was unable to land and returned across the English Channel.

It may be that Buckingham had hoped to win the throne for himself (he was descended from Edward III) but more probably he wanted greater power with Henry Twdwr as king than he enjoyed under Richard III. Either way, he miscalculated. When Buckingham declared himself, the king marched west from London and overawed the rebels. Deserted by even his own servants, Buckingham was captured and summarily executed. Now, with the rebels dispersed and Twdwr in Brittany, it seems that Richard can settle down to a more stable future (→ 25/12).

1484 - 1485

Westminster, 1 March 1484. Elizabeth Woodville, the widow of Edward IV, and her daughters leave their sanctuary in the abbey (→18/1/86).

Scotland, 13 March 1484. The Franco-Scottish alliance is renewed (→22/7).

North Yorkshire, 9 April 1484. Edward, Richard III's only son, dies at Middleham Castle, aged ten (→16/3/1485).

Dumfries and Galloway, 22 July 1484. Alexander, the duke of Albany, is defeated at Lochmaben; James, the earl of Douglas, is imprisoned (→21/9).

South Yorkshire, July 1484. Richard III sets up a northern council at Sandal under his nephew John de la Pole, the earl of Lincoln (→3/1485).

Ireland, 21 August 1484. Richard III of England appoints the earl of Lincoln lieutenant (→9/1484).

Nottingham, 21 September 1484. A three-year Anglo-Scots truce, with a marriage alliance between Richard III's niece, Anne de la Pole, and James III's son, James, is agreed (→3/7/86).

Ireland, September 1484. Thomas Barrett, the bishop of Annaghdown, treats with Gaelic lords and Gaelicized Anglo-Irish lords (→11/3/86).

France, March 1485. Richard III appoints his bastard son, John of Gloucester, captain of Calais (→16).

Dyfed, 7 August 1485. Henry Twdwr lands at Milford Haven (→17).

Nottingham, 20 August 1485. Richard III marches on Leicester (→22).

London, 23 August 1485. Henry Twdwr has the Yorkist heir, Edward, the earl of Warwick and son of the late duke of Clarence, put in the Tower (→30/10).

Westminster, 30 October 1485. Henry Twdwr is crowned Henry VII of England (→7/11).

Westminster, 7 November 1485. Henry VII calls his first parliament (→5/8/1503).

England, 1485. Henry VII forms the Yeomen of the Guard.

Scotland, 1485. James III's new coinage shows him with the arched imperial crown, in the Italian style (→1534).

Paris, 1485. Alexander, the duke of Albany, is killed accidentally at a tournament.

Printer brings Canterbury pilgrims to life

Edward IV is given a printed book.

Aesop, in an edition by Caxton.

Westminster Abbey, 1485
William Caxton, the pioneering printer, has produced an illustrated edition of Geoffrey Chaucer's *Canterbury Tales*. The book contains rough but lively woodcuts of the pilgrims who feature in the various poems which together make up the whole work.

Caxton's first edition of the *Tales* appeared – without pictures – in 1478 [*see page 372*]. Since then he has kept busy, turning out from his London press not only books in English but also some translated by himself from other languages. In March 1480 he published *The Mirrour of the World*, the first book with illustrations to be printed in this country. It had the further distinction of being Caxton's own translation of the *Speculum Historiale* by the Frenchman Vincent of Beauvais. This year he has printed an edition of *Morte d'Arthur* by Sir Thomas Malory (→1504).

English succession suffers a new blow

Westminster, 16 March 1485
Richard III has lost his queen. Anne Neville died here today during an eclipse of the sun. She was 29. Her untimely death comes barely a year after that of her only son, Edward, the prince of Wales. The king is now left with neither a wife nor an heir.

Anne was a daughter of Richard Neville, the earl of Warwick, and was first married to Henry VI's son, Edward, who was killed at Tewkesbury in 1471. She then married Richard when he was still the duke of Gloucester – a somewhat unlikely match, considering that he had had a part in the deaths of her father, husband and father-in-law.

It is already being suggested that Richard might marry his niece, Elizabeth. In that way he could make his peace with the Woodvilles and also foil any plan to marry the princess to his rival, Henry Twdwr. The marriage would, however, be unpopular with Richard's northern supporters, who hate the Woodvilles. The king might therefore prefer to look for a bride from a European royal family, a move that would help to give his shaky hold on power wider credibility (→7/8).

Experts in heraldry are recruited to found a new 'college of arms'

London, 2 March 1484
King Richard III has given his 12 heralds and pursuivants a formal identity as a "college of arms". He has also, obligingly, given them Coldharbour, a grand house in Thames Street, to serve as their headquarters.

Ever since Henry I knighted Geoffrey Plantagenet in 1127 and hung around his neck a shield decorated with golden lions, coats of arms have become increasingly important symbols among the nobility. They are displayed at tournaments and are worn by heralds on their wide-sleeved tabards, or surcoats. Since arms are symbols of aristocratic lineage, the right to bear them can on occasion lead to disputes. This may happen, for example, when two families claim the right to bear the same arms. The heralds are now the recognized authorities to settle such matters.

Heraldic colours: noblemen take pride in displaying their coats of arms.

Plantagenets crushed at Bosworth

Henry rallies wide support in Wales

Staffordshire, 17 August 1485
King Richard III is facing a new Lancastrian threat to his position. His rival for the throne is the 28-year-old Henry Twdwr, who has arrived here in Stafford with an army of 5,000 men just ten days after sailing to England from Normandy. Henry fled to Brittany with his uncle, Jasper, in 1471 after the Lancastrian defeat at Tewkesbury. Two years ago he made an abortive attempt to land in England; this time he has had better luck.

Landing at Milford Haven, Henry has made his way from Haverfordwest to Cardigan, then along the coast to Aberystwyth, before swinging east into the hills around Machynlleth. His initial force of 2,000 men was then joined on 12 August by 2,000 men of Rhys ap Thomas, the leading Welsh figure in the region. A day later many more Welsh chieftains met him at Welshpool with their men.

Yet the Lancastrian force is barely half the size of the Yorkist army that Richard III is bringing down from Nottingham. On top of this Richard and his men are veterans, while Henry has never commanded an army, and most of his men have never fought a battle. While it may not be the greatest solace for those facing death or maiming in combat, Henry's men have been assured by the Welsh seer Dafydd Llwyd that victory will be theirs (→20).

A 16th-century portrait of King Henry VII, from the English school.

King Richard (l) leads from the front in the battle at Bosworth field.

Lancaster is the final victor at Bosworth

Leicestershire, 22 August 1485
Richard III has been defeated and killed by Henry Twdwr. He was 32. After a savage battle fought here at Bosworth field, 12 miles (19km) west of Leicester, the royal crown was recovered and placed on Henry's head. After the first skirmishes Richard led a charge against Henry's position, getting close enough to kill his standard-bearer. But the Lancastrians rallied, and Richard, isolated with only a handful of his Yorkist soldiers, was cut down. He had been abandoned by the disenchanted Stanley family, whose forces stayed out of the fight until Richard's final charge, when they chose, crucially, to throw in their lot with Henry Twdwr (→23).

Verdict on Richard left to the historians

England, 22 August 1485
The death of Richard Plantagenet today on Bosworth field brings to an end the royal house of Plantagenet that first came to the English throne in 1154 with Henry II. All that remains is to write the history – which probably means continuing on the printed page the war that has just ceased on the battlefield.

Henry Twdwr has only a tenuous claim to the throne through his mother, Margaret Beaufort, and he may therefore want to add a righteous sheen to his ambition by painting Richard as a villain. Certainly there is scope to do just that: no one can survive as king without getting blood on his hands sooner or later.

Yet Richard deserves better than this. He was by all accounts a generous lord to those who served him faithfully. A good military man – despite the manner of his death – he was also cultured; for example, his court attracted fine musicians. He was also a benefactor of the church and of education (→23/8).

Three centuries of Plantagenet rule draw to a close

British Isles, 1485
Of the many changes that have taken place in 300 years of Plantagenet rule in England, one of the most significant has been the slow erosion of French influence. Nearly all the lands in France that were once held by kings of England have now been lost. French used to be the language of both the court and the cultured élite – Henry IV (1399-1413) was the first king after the Conquest whose mother tongue was English – but now the native language is gaining a new respectability.

Scotland, beyond the writ of Plantagenet kings but well within the scope of their ambitions, has grown since the 12th century into a far more united kingdom than it had been previously. The Scots have also managed to fight off English encroachments on their independence. Life here is distinguished by an openness towards continental (particularly French) influences, in both trade and culture.

The Welsh came close to maintaining their own independence from the Plantagenets, but the Glyndwr rebellion, which was crushed at the beginning of this century, changed all that. Now Wales is forced into getting the best deal that it can within the framework of English politics. It may be some small consolation that the new king, Henry Tudor [Twdwr], is a quarter Welsh.

Ireland has changed radically since Henry II of England's invasion in 1171. The country is now effectively split into two parts. There is the "Englishry", which is itself divided into that region where Anglo-Irish lords hold territories in fief from the English king and another of more direct English rule known as "the Pale", centred on Dublin. Then there is the "Irishry", comprising most of the north and west of the country, where Gaelic lords still rule according to Irish custom.

Reformation and Renaissance

1486-1603

1486 - 1494

Westminster, 18 January 1486. Henry VII marries Elizabeth of York (→ 20/9).

Ireland, 11 March 1486. Jasper Tudor, the duke of Bedford, is appointed lieutenant (→ 1488).

London, 3 July 1486. A three-year Anglo-Scots truce is agreed (→ 4/3/92).

Stirling, July 1486. Queen Margaret dies (→ 11/6/88).

London, 20 September 1486. Queen Elizabeth gives birth to a son, Arthur (→ 17/3/89).

Stoke-on-Trent, 16 June 1487. A royal army defeats forces led by the pretender Lambert Simnel, who landed at Furness on 4 June (→ 3/11/92).

Co Leitrim, 1488. Firearms are used for the first time in Ireland, by troops of Aodh Ruadh O'Donnell, the lord of Tyrconnell (→ 1489).

Spain, 17 March 1489. Ferdinand of Aragon agrees to marry his daughter Catherine to Prince Arthur, Henry VII's son (→ 29/11).

Strathclyde, 19 July 1489. James IV acts to quell rebels in Renfrewshire (→ 12/1489).

Westminster, 28 November 1489. Queen Elizabeth has a daughter, Margaret (→ 25/6/95).

England, 29 November 1489. Prince Arthur is created both prince of Wales and earl of Chester (→ 14/11/1501).

Strathclyde, December 1489. Dumbarton Castle, the last major rebel stronghold, finally surrenders to King James IV (→ 11/8/90).

England, 28 June 1491. Queen Elizabeth has a second son, Henry (→ 12/9/94).

Glasgow, 9 January 1492. Robert Blackadder becomes the city's first archbishop.

Scotland, 4 March 1492. James IV ratifies a Franco-Scottish alliance against England (→ 25/6/93).

Ireland, 30 March 1493. Henry VII pardons Gerald fitz Maurice FitzGerald [Gearoid Mor], the earl of Kildare, of suspected treason (→ 12/9/94).

Scotland, May 1493. The lordship of the Isles is made forfeit, so ending this rebellious fiefdom (→ 22/4/1500).

Edinburgh, 25 June 1493. The Anglo-Scots truce is extended to April 1501 (→ 30/9/97).

Ireland, 12 September 1494. Henry VII appoints his son, Henry, lieutenant (→ 1/12).

Tudor asserts authority

The king's triumph: the marriage medal struck for King Henry VII.

York, October 1486
England's new king, Henry VII, having inherited a land still divided between the rival claims of York and Lancaster for the crown, is working to resolve that rivalry. His marriage in January to Elizabeth of York is one way. Another is simply to make his presence felt, as he has done this month at York.

York was the bedrock of Richard III's support, and despite his death at Bosworth last year it is still home to supporters of his cause. As one of the leading cities of the realm and a potential focus for rebellion, York has to be won over by Henry. So his state entry here was intended to show that he is very much in control – and the message seemed not to be lost on the crowds who came out to see him.

No king is ever invulnerable, especially if – as in Henry Tudor's case – he is trying to establish a new dynasty rather than perpetuate an existing one. Only last April, Francis, Lord Lovel, was discovered to be plotting against Henry. Action was swiftly taken: Lovel, who fought for Richard III at Bosworth, has escaped to Flanders, while his ally, Humphrey Stafford, was executed in July (→ 24/5/87).

English pretender crowned in Ireland

Dublin, 24 May 1487
Lambert Simnel, the ten-year-old son of an Oxford joiner, has been crowned "Edward VI" at Christ Church, Dublin. Simnel is posing as Edward Plantagenet, the earl of Warwick, who, as a nephew of Edward IV, remains a Yorkist rival for Henry VII's throne. (The real Warwick is now in the Tower of London.) Simnel's sponsors are Gerald fitz Maurice FitzGerald, the Yorkist earl of Kildare, and John de la Pole, the earl of Lincoln. This month has also seen the arrival in Ireland of 2,000 German mercenaries; it is thought that they will invade England with Simnel in a bid for the English crown (→ 16/6).

Rebel sponsor: Lincoln and his wife.

Scottish rebel lords sort out their grievances on the battlefield

A King James silver penny, or groat.

Stirling, 11 June 1488
James III has been killed at Sauchieburn, near Stirling, fighting rebels under the nominal command of his son, James, the duke of Rothesay. The king's body has been recovered close to a mill; it seems that he was cut down while trying to make his escape. Near the body was the sword of Robert the Bruce, with which James made his last stand.

Duke James is said to be shocked and angry. His supporters are insisting that the battle orders explicitly forbade any violence against the king's person. None the less, today's events are a boon to the rebel programme, and the duke can now be declared king.

James, who is 15 years old, recently deserted his father when the latter's enemies persuaded him that the king was favouring the prince's younger brother. On 2 February he was taken to join the rebels at Stirling Castle by James Shaw of Sauchie. There he became a useful puppet for those nobles with various axes – literal and metaphorical – to grind with King James III.

Their complaints were numerous. Chief among them was that the king had debased the coinage; he was also accused of neglecting justice, and of having subordinated the nobility's interests to those of his personal favourites. James's peaceable policy towards England was another cause for discontent. With their protégé now set to become King James IV, the rebels will be expecting the removal of some of these grievances (→ 19/7/89).

Rebel Irish lords turn their backs on Yorkist pretender

An Irish lord displays his arms.

Ireland, 1489
Gerald fitz Maurice FitzGerald [Gearoid Mor], the earl of Kildare, has publicly repented of his flirtation with rebellion. Two years ago Kildare was a principal backer of the pretender to the English crown, Lambert Simnel [*see report on previous page*]. But Simnel's expedition met a bloody and conclusive end when he, masquerading as "Edward VI", was defeated and captured in battle with Henry VII.

Early this year Kildare and a number of Yorkist lords of the Pale were summoned to a reconciliation banquet with Henry at Greenwich, near London. It must have been, to say the least, one of the less agreeable dates in their social calendars. Henry rubbed salt in his guests' wounds by making Simnel himself wait on them at table.

Irish support for Kildare and the Yorkist rebels was far from unanimous. Waterford, the midlands and Dublin, along with much of the Pale, came out for Henry. Then in June 1488 Henry's agent, Sir Richard Edgecombe, arrived in Ireland with 500 men and began taking oaths of allegiance to the present king, culminating on 21 July with Kildare's own submission. Yet for all his public announcements there must remain serious doubts as to whether Kildare is truly reconciled with Henry (→12/9/94).

Anglo-French pact is a blow to Warbeck

France, 3 November 1492
Henry VII's expedition to France with an army has ended surprisingly well for the English king, and without bloodshed. Henry had been drawn into the campaign by a promise to aid the duchy of Brittany in its war against Charles VIII of France. But a treaty signed today at Etaples brings peace and the offer of large reparations to defray the cost of the English intervention (the figure of 745,000 gold crowns has been given). The French king has also agreed not to support any pretenders to Henry's throne. Charles, whose attention is focused on a coming struggle in Naples, had no desire to be distracted by the English invaders.

Peacemaker: Charles of France.

But for Perkin Warbeck, known to his supporters as the duke of York and King Richard IV of England, today's treaty will come as a severe blow. Charles has been supporting his claim to Henry's crown, and Warbeck is now being maintained by Charles in some style at the castle at Amboise. Unless the pretender can engineer a swift escape from France, the agreement states that Charles must hand him over to King Henry (→12/1493).

Trade war opens over bogus duke of York

London, December 1493
Henry VII has opened economic warfare with Holy Roman Emperor Maximilian. English merchants are now forbidden to trade with Antwerp and the Low Countries in a retaliatory measure for Maximilian's recognition of a new claimant to the Tudor throne of England – Perkin Warbeck.

Accompanied by Yorkist agents, Warbeck turned up at Cork, in Ireland, in November 1491 claiming to be Richard, the duke of York, escaped from the Tower. Although it is widely believed that the duke and his brother, Edward V, are either dead or still in the Tower, Margaret of Burgundy, Edward IV's sister, together with the kings of Scotland and France, accepted Warbeck's claim last year. But then Charles VIII of France, who until recently entertained Warbeck at Amboise Castle, agreed to hand him over to Henry under the treaty signed last year at Etaples [*see above*]. Warbeck, who is 19, is now in Vienna with the emperor, presumably planning his next move (→3/7/95).

Irish laws are to be vetted by England

Ireland, 1 December 1494
Rattled by Irish support for the Yorkist pretenders Lambert Simnel and Perkin Warbeck, Henry VII has ordered Sir Edward Poynings, the deputy of Ireland since 13 September, to establish here a "whole and perfect obedience". Poynings' parliament at Drogheda has now found Gerald fitz Maurice FitzGerald, the great earl of Kildare, guilty of treason. Kildare did nothing to hinder Warbeck back in 1491. Then, in July last year, his men brawled with men of the earl of Ormond; in November Kildare was called to the English court.

Parliament also passed "Poynings' Law", whereby bills accepted by the Irish executive must be vetted by the English council before being discussed by the Irish parliament. The aim is to stop Kildare using the executive to suit himself. Irish parliament are also forbidden to offer a native earl, a Yorkist claimant, a Scottish or French king, the crown of Ireland (→5/3/95).

Scots and English fight it out at sea

Fife, 11 August 1490
A dramatic and bloody sea-battle in the Firth of Forth has ended with a victory for the Scots over a well-armed English squadron under the command of Stephen Bull. He has since been taken into captivity by the enemy, and all three of his ships have been seized.

Bull had been lying in wait for Sir Andrew Wood, the Scottish privateer who defeated another English squadron last year. Wood and his ships, the *Flower* and the *Yellow Carvel*, were returning with their cargoes from Flanders yesterday morning when they were subjected to an English attack.

The battle raged throughout the day, drawing crowds of onlookers from the shore. Wood had the advantage in the close-quarter combat, during which guns, crossbows, swords and lime pots were employed. By this morning the English ships had drifted north to the Tay, where the aggressors realized that they had no alternative but to surrender and allow their vessels to be towed into Dundee as prizes.

This incident is only the latest in a succession of violent encounters at sea which have taken place in spite of an Anglo-Scottish truce, supposed to have been operative since 1486 (→4/3/92).

A silver-gilt Irish chalice of 1494 betrays strong English influence.

1495 - 1500

Rome, 6 February 1495. Bishop William Elphinstone of Aberdeen, gets agreement from the pope to build a university, to be called King's College, in Aberdeen (→ 6/1496).

Dublin, 5 March 1495. Gerald fitz Maurice FitzGerald, the earl of Kildare, arrested for treason on 27 February, is sent to England (→ 12/1495).

England, 25 June 1495. Negotiations begin for a marriage between James IV of Scots and Margaret, the daughter of Henry VII (→ 8/8/1503).

Deal, Kent, 3 July 1495. Perkin Warbeck's invasion fails, and he flees to Scotland for refuge (→ 2/1496).

Ireland, December 1495. Edward Poynings returns to England (→ 1/1/96).

Ireland, 1 January 1496. Henry Deane, the bishop of Bangor, becomes the new justiciar (→ 17/9).

Flanders, February 1496. An Anglo-Burgundian trade treaty, the *Magnus Intercursus*, denies Perkin Warbeck sanctuary in his native Flanders (→ 26/9).

London, 18 March 1496. A daughter, Mary, is born to Henry VII's queen, Elizabeth (→ 17/12/1508).

Portsmouth, 7 April 1496. The first dry dock here opens.

Scotland, June 1496. A new act requires barons and freeholders to send their eldest sons to grammar schools.

Dublin, 17 September 1496. The earl of Kildare, cleared of treason and now married to a ward of Henry VII of England, returns from England and is made deputy (→ 1/3/99).

Cork City, 26 July 1497. Perkin Warbeck arrives to raise support for his claim to Henry VII's throne (→ 7/9).

London, 17 July 1497. Royal troops defeat Cornish rebels at Blackheath (→ 7/9).

Land's End, 7 September 1497. Perkin Warbeck lands, with Geraldine supporters, hoping to exploit local unrest (→ 5/10).

Dublin, 1 March 1499. The first parliament to be held under "Poynings' Law" is opened (→ 26/9/03).

Scotland, 22 April 1500. Archibald Campbell, the earl of Argyll, is given viceregal powers over the former lordship of the Isles.

Sexual disease takes hold in Scotland

One cure for syphilis was thought to be the application of mercury.

Scotland, 1497
Syphilis, a sexual disease apparently brought to Europe by sailors returning with Christopher Columbus from the New World in 1493, has broken out in Scotland. Whatever the origins, the symptoms are extremely unpleasant. Victims first suffer ulceration of the skin and then inflammation of the eyes and bones. Finally the heart and nervous system become so damaged that death inevitably follows.

The disease seems to have reached Scotland through some of Columbus's sailors who enlisted in a siege of Naples over 1494/95 and passed it on to Neapolitan women, who in turn infected mercenary soldiers from all over Europe engaged in the siege. When Perkin Warbeck, the pretender to the English throne, came to Scotland at the end of 1495, his mercenaries included men who had been at Naples. These men, garrisoned at Aberdeen, have now spread syphilis here. James IV has ordered all syphilitics to assemble for treatment on Inch Keith in the Firth of Forth.

Cecily, mother of two kings, is dead

Hertfordshire, 31 May 1495
Cecily Neville, the 80-year-old dowager duchess of York, has died in her castle at Berkhamsted. Her whole life was linked to the great conflict between York and Lancaster. The youngest daughter of Ralph Neville, the earl of Westmorland, Cecily had for her mother Joan Beaufort, the half-sister of the Lancastrian king, Henry IV. When only nine years old, Cecily married Richard, the duke of York and until his death in 1460 the leader of the Yorkist cause. She was to bear him two kings of England, Edward IV and Richard III. She was also grandmother to a third, Edward V, as well as to the present queen, Elizabeth.

Her family has suffered much: her husband, sons and grandsons – bar Edward, the earl of Warwick, now a prisoner in the Tower of London – are all dead. Yet Cecily remained a lady of great piety, like her cousin and rival, Margaret Beaufort, Henry VII's mother. Cecily divided her time between her castle here and her London home, Baynard's Castle. She performed many good works, attended to her household's spiritual welfare and bore misfortune with great stoicism.

Venetian ambassador is shocked at hardness of English hearts

England, 1496
The Venetian ambassador's visit to London this year has resulted in some critical observations of the way in which the English upper classes treat their children. In particular the practice of placing them, from the age of seven or eight, in others' homes as domestic servants is regarded as a "want of affection in the English".

The reason given for the custom – that the "children might learn better manners" – is regarded with some cynicism. The ambassador suspects that the real motive is that parents "like to enjoy all their comforts themselves, and that they are better served by strangers than they would be by their own children".

The text of these observations, written down by the ambassador's secretary, accuses the English of being "avaricious by nature" and indulging in fine food themselves while giving lesser members of the household – other people's offspring – only the coarsest bread and beer. The author suggests that if the children were sent away to learn virtue and good manners, and were welcomed home again once the apprenticeship was over, the severity of the practice might be excused. But the parents know that after seven to nine years in service their children rarely, if ever, return: the boys invariably get married, while the girls stay with their patrons.

As if all these remarks were not damning enough, the ambassador adds that, although Englishmen are licentious, he has not noticed anyone "either at court or among the lower orders, to be in love".

Young girls attend to the chores.

Pretender let down by Scottish allies

Warbeck: the failed pretender.

Borders, 26 September 1496
Perkin Warbeck, the claimant to the crown of Henry VII of England, has been badly let down by his backer, James IV of Scots. James is returning to Edinburgh after a brief raid into northern England that Warbeck believed was going to be a serious challenge to Henry's forces. The 22-year-old Warbeck, who says he is Edward IV's son Richard, the duke of York, was until recently in Vienna at the court of Holy Roman Emperor Maximilian, but in July of last year he attempted to land at Deal, in Kent. Repulsed from there he came north to James's court, where on 20 November he was accepted as "Richard IV of England". Since then he has even been married off to James IV's cousin, Catherine Gordon. Today shows that there are, however, limits to how far James will back Warbeck (→26/7/97).

Warbeck captured after failed revolt

Cornwall, 5 October 1497
Following another doomed attempt to invade England, the pretender Perkin Warbeck has been captured at Taunton and thrown himself on King Henry VII's mercy.

After the failure of his "invasion" from Scotland last year [*see report left*], Warbeck sailed in July to Ireland, where he won at least promises of support from, among others, Gerald fitz Maurice FitzGerald, the earl of Kildare, and Maurice fitz Thomas FitzGerald, the earl of Desmond. Warbeck then set sail for England early last month and put in at Whitesand Bay, near Land's End, with some 120 men.

By the time he reached Bodmin on 7 September his following had swelled to a more menacing 4,000. There he proclaimed himself King Richard IV. His next move was to attack Exeter, but he was driven off and retired to Taunton. Although by this time his army had grown to around 8,000, it was little more than a rabble with little or no military ability.

With Henry VII fast approaching at the head of some of the best troops in the country, Warbeck and his associates lost their nerve and were captured in Taunton without a fight. Warbeck might have expected justice at the end of a rope, but Henry has – so far – spared his life in return for a confession that he is not Richard IV but simply the person he in fact is: Piers Osbeck, or Warbeck, a poor Fleming from Tournai. His next residence is likely to be the Tower (→28/11/99).

Explorer John Cabot returns from voyage across Atlantic with tales of new lands

The king's explorer: John Cabot departing from Bristol on his voyage.

Bristol, 6 August 1497
John Cabot, the Genoese navigator, has returned in triumph from an expedition to America licensed by Henry VII of England. From the newly discovered lands of the north-east of the continent he brings the promise of magnificent fisheries and the possibility of a new route to Asia.

Although Cabot was born in Genoa and has Venetian citizenship, he settled in Bristol about ten years ago to raise support for a transatlantic voyage. On 5 March last year Henry granted him £10 for the voyage from the privy purse, plus an annuity of £20. Cabot set sail from Bristol on 2 May this year, and it was on 24 June that his ship, the *Matthew*, reached the coast of Nova Scotia, where he planted the Tudor flag and the standard of St Mark, the symbol of Venice.

His journey was quicker than that of Columbus four years ago and vindicated his decision to explore a more northerly crossing.

However, the expedition contravened an agreement, made in 1494 with Pope Alexander VI's approval, granting Spain exploration rights in that area. Cabot is already planning a return trip.

Scots and English give peace a chance

Borders, 30 September 1497
James IV, the 23-year-old Scottish king, has agreed another truce with England. Following the breach of an earlier truce, extended in 1493, this one is meant to last for seven years. The treaty, signed today at Ayton, comes in the wake of several successful border raids into England carried out by James over recent months. In June, for example, an English force was defeated at Duns, while in August James saw off a counter-attack by Thomas Howard, the earl of Surrey. James's success should come as no surprise. He is respected for his personal courage and reputedly obsessed by the arts of war – but he is also a man of great learning and culture.

As befits a king whose court is full of accomplished academics and poets, James is an avid reader with a prodigious memory. He is also a skilled linguist who not only speaks the language of diplomacy, Latin, but is also competent in Danish, German, Flemish, Italian, French and Gaelic, spoken by his remote northern subjects (→24/1/1502).

Holy Trinity, Long Melford, Suffolk: one of the many churches built in East Anglia to celebrate the prosperity brought to the area by the wool trade. It was completed in 1496, but the tower is a 20th-century addition.

Death sentences are carried out on two more claimants to the throne of England

Publicly shamed: a later view of Perkin Warbeck in the pillory.

London, 28 November 1499
Edward, the earl of Warwick and a claimant to the throne of England, has been beheaded for treason just five days after another pretender, Perkin Warbeck, was hanged for plotting to escape from the Tower.

Since surrendering to Henry VII at Taunton two years ago, Warbeck had been treated not as a prisoner but as a member of the court. Henry seemed content with his public confession that he was not the duke of York – one of Edward IV's sons held in the Tower – and so not the rightful king of England.

But then Warbeck escaped. Recaptured on 9 June 1498, he was confined once more in the Tower with the earl who, as the son of the late duke of Clarence, was the main Yorkist candidate for the throne. Whether the two really plotted together is unknown, but Warbeck was found guilty of planning to escape again and Warwick of treason. Whatever their guilt, Henry is now free of two rivals (→6/5/1502).

Irish look to 'tower-houses' for safety

Ireland, c.1500
For some decades now both Gaelic and Anglo-Irish lordships have witnessed a vogue in castle-building. In the absence of a strong central authority, local property-holders have to protect themselves against riot and robbery, and the favoured defensive structure now is the tower-house. A typical example, such as that built by Cormac MacCarthy at Blarney, in Co Cork, stands in a walled enclosure called a "bawn" and is four or five storeys high. Two of these storeys are usually vaulted, while the others have floors and ceilings of wood. The ground floor serves as a cellar, and the top floor as a hall (→26/9/03).

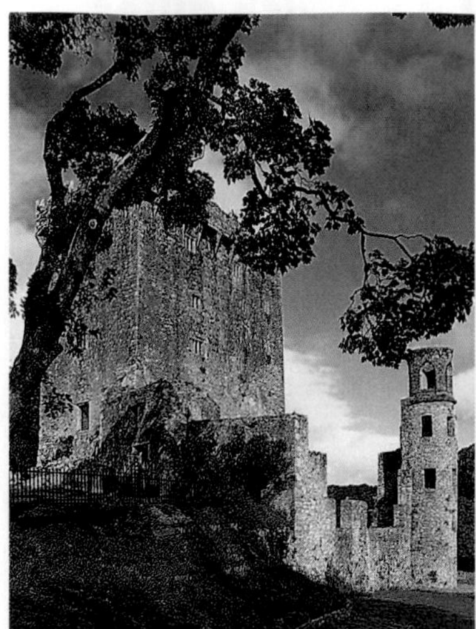
Blarney tower-house, built c.1480.

Flemish ingenuity hired to stop fen floods

Lincolnshire, 19 February 1500
A prominent Flemish engineer, Matthew Hake, contracted today with the crown to build a huge sluice and dam on the river Witham at Boston to stem the serious flooding of the northern fenlands around Lincoln. Hake plans to lay a stone pier in the middle of the Witham. Doors on each side of it will close against other piers at the side of the river, all of them being connected at the top to form a walkway over the whole construction.

Hake's commissioning follows pressure by Margaret Beaufort on her son, King Henry VII. She has several properties in the area that are regularly damaged by flooding. Her commercial revenues from Boston will also suffer if the harbour declines.

Hake brings with him advanced designs developed in Flanders, where sluices have been widely used since the 11th century. He expects to complete his task with a workforce of 14 masons, 24 labourers and a master carpenter and his assistants. Hake's bill will mostly be met by Margaret or Henry; the rest will be raised locally.

A 19th-century depiction of one of the Coventry mystery plays.

Playful morality saga draws the crowds

England, 1495
The morality play *Everyman*, already popular in Europe, has been performed for the first time in England. Translated from a Dutch original called *Elckerlijc*, the play is an allegory of human life and death in which the leading character Everyman, is summoned by Death and invites – among others – Good Deeds, Knowledge, Beauty, Possessions and Strength to join him on the journey. Only Good Deeds goes with him.

Morality plays, which personify virtues and vices, have been popular for a century or more. They have developed from the plays based on biblical stories performed in the open air by the guilds or "mysteries" of craftsmen. The responsibility for staging these cycles of plays, whose subjects range from the Creation to Doomsday, is shared among the trade guilds of large towns. The bakers, for instance, create *The Last Supper*, while the nailmakers put on *The Crucifixion*. The plays are in English, rather than Latin, and are written partly by the craftsmen themselves, who stage them on wagons that are wheeled through the streets from one station to the next. The York cycle, in which characters such as Satan, the Serpent and Herod have some of the best lines, is especially popular.

A character from a morality play, as viewed by a later artist.

Red brick is the height of architectural taste

An imported style: the extravagant red-brick palace at Richmond, built for King Henry in the manner of the grand houses of Flanders and Burgundy.

Athelhampton, near Dorchester, Dorset: one of a new kind of country house for the well-to-do. On view here are the battlements and the great hall.

England, 1500
The royal house of Tudor has initiated a new and splendid style of architecture in England. Henry VII is building the greatest and costliest palace yet seen in this country to replace the old Thames-side palace of Sheen, a few miles west of London, which burnt down during the Christmas revels of 1497, sending the king and his courtiers fleeing into the night.

The new Sheen palace is to be called Richmond, meaning "Rich Mount" – appropriately enough, since it will cost some £15,000 for the structure alone. The chief reason for the name, however, is probably that "Richmond" was Henry's title before he succeeded. A notable feature of Sheen is the great number of glazed windows, including large and costly bay windows, never before seen in England.

The design and furnishing of the palace are the last word in luxury. There is a library, and a covered "long gallery" surrounds an ornamental garden. Then there are vast windows of Flemish stained glass, and Flemish tapestries and paintings in the great hall, together with rich Burgundian furnishings and gold plate. The completion date has been advanced for the forthcoming wedding of Prince Arthur and the *infanta* [Spanish royal heir], Catherine of Aragon, at which Henry intends to demonstrate the magnificence of the Tudor court.

On a humbler scale, a distinctive "Tudor style" has become established in the houses of the prosperous wool and cloth merchants in East Anglia and the south-west. At Coggeshall, in Essex, the cloth merchant Thomas Paycocke has built himself a magnificent mansion whose beams and timbers are decoratively carved to beautiful effect, while William Grevel has constructed an equally splendid house at Chipping Camden, in Gloucestershire, from his wool profits.

The village of Lavenham in Suffolk, one of the country's leading cloth towns, can boast whole streets of carved, timber-framed houses with overhanging upper floors. Kent is also rich in substantial yeomen's houses such as those at Smallhythe, near Tenterden.

Country gentlefolk are building impressive fortified manor houses – intended more for decoration than defence. For example, an attractive red-brick house at Compton Wynyates, in Warwickshire, sports turrets and towers but is actually more a home than a castle. Athelhampton, near Dorchester, in Dorset, was built in the mid 1480s by Sir William Martyn. It is in the same style, if on a more modest scale, with a small range of battlements and a great hall (→ 1501).

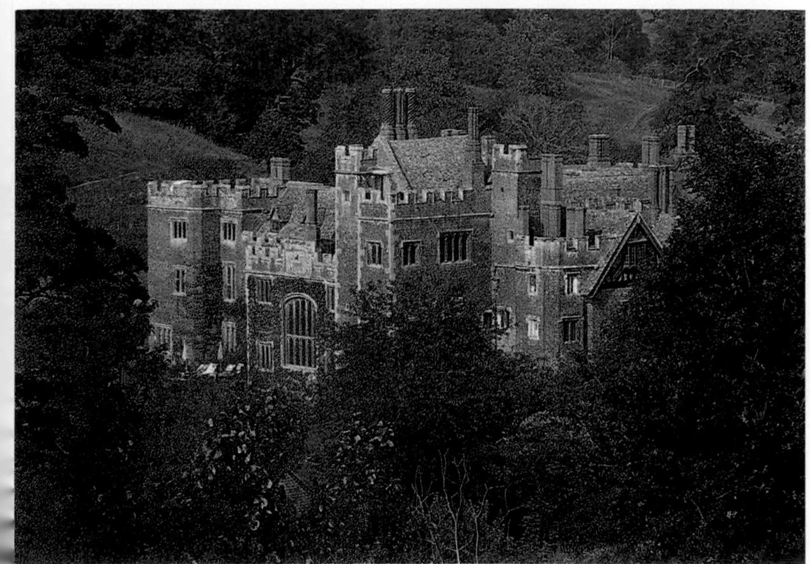

Decorative defences: Compton Wynyates manor house in Warwickshire.

A house built by cloth merchant Thomas Paycocke at Coggeshall, Essex.

1501 - 1503

Canterbury, 26 May 1501. Henry Deane, the bishop of Salisbury, is the new archbishop (→ 15/2/03).

Grampian, 11 August 1501. James IV grants Alexander Gordon, the earl of Huntly, viceregal powers in the north of Scotland (→ 10/1501).

Highland, October 1501. A rebellion breaks out against royal policies here (→ 24/1/02).

London, 1501. Henry VII makes Baynard's Castle, on the north bank of the Thames, his principal London residence (→ 1508).

Surrey, 1501. Henry VII's new palace at Richmond is completed.

Stirling, 1501. James IV founds the Chapel Royal.

Surrey, 24 January 1502. The Anglo-Scots truce of Ayton becomes a treaty of perpetual peace, the first since 1474, at Richmond; James IV is to marry Margaret, the daughter of Henry VII (→ 8/8/03).

England, April 1502. Prince Henry succeeds his brother, Arthur, the prince of Wales, as duke of Cornwall (→ 23/6/03).

Scotland, May 1502. James IV sends a small force to aid King Hans of Denmark against Norwegian rebels (→ 25/12/03).

Suffolk, 26 December 1502. At Ipswich, Edmund de la Pole, the earl of Suffolk, is proclaimed an outlaw for treason (→ 4/5/13).

Bradford, 1502. Mining for coal begins in the area.

London, 11 February 1503. Queen Elizabeth dies nine days after giving birth to her seventh child, Katherine; the baby is unlikely to live.

Lambeth, 15 February 1503. Henry Deane, the archbishop of Canterbury, dies (→ 29/11).

Ulster, 26 September 1503. Gerald fitz Maurice FitzGerald, the earl of Kildare, burns Belfast Castle in his campaign against Gaelic Irish lords here (→ 19/8/04).

Rome, 29 November 1503. William Warham is given papal approval to be the new archbishop of Canterbury (→ 9/3/04).

Highland, 25 December 1503. Rebels attack lands around Badenoch belonging to James IV's lieutenant, the earl of Huntly (→ 9/1506).

Lothian, 1503. Edinburgh high school is founded (→ 1506).

Heir to throne marries a Spanish princess

Arthur, the prince of Wales.

Princess Catherine of Aragon.

London, 14 November 1501
St Paul's Cathedral was the scene today for the marriage of Henry VII's eldest son Arthur, the prince of Wales, to Princess Catherine of Aragon. After the ceremony, which was presided over by both English archbishops and witnessed by the dignitaries and nobles of the realm, there was a wedding feast of a magnificence not usually associated with this reign.

For the crowds of Londoners who turned out when Catherine was brought into the city two days ago, five weeks after her arrival in England, there will be ten days of spectacle, with jousting, dancing, plays and music. These splendid festivities reflect the importance Henry attaches to the match, which comes more than ten years after the betrothal was first mooted.

The negotiations have been long and complicated, but the bride's father, Ferdinand of Aragon, may also have encouraged delay until he was certain that Henry's grip on the English throne was secure. That the wedding has gone ahead sends a message to Europe that the house of Tudor is here to stay. And with bride and groom just 15 years old, there is every hope that the succession is secure for at least another generation (→ 4/4/02).

Confessed killer of princes executed

London, 6 May 1502
Sir James Tyrrell, the commander of the town of Guines in the Calais area, has been executed for plotting against Henry VII. Tyrrell was arrested earlier this year along with other Yorkist sympathizers, including William, the brother of the earl of Suffolk, Edmund de la Pole – who apparently masterminded the plot to overthrow the king. Edmund and William's mother, Elizabeth, was a sister of the Yorkist king Richard III. The earl has, wisely, fled abroad.

Tyrrell is also said to have confessed to killing the young princes, Edward V and his brother Richard, the duke of York. This confession seems to lend credence to the belief that the boys, whom Richard III put in the Tower in June 1483, were killed on Richard's orders. Yet suspicion lingers around Henry, too. It is strange, for instance, that when Henry passed an act condemning Richard he made no mention of the princes' deaths. Furthermore, in order to unite York and Lancaster by his marriage to Elizabeth of York, Henry repealed an act that had made her and her brothers, the princes, illegitimate. As the new act thus made the princes legitimate, their sister Elizabeth could not represent York so long as they were alive. It would then have been necessary to get rid of them (→ 26/12).

Succession imperilled on death of Arthur

Greenwich, 4 April 1502
Henry VII's personal confessor today brought the king the shocking news of the death of Prince Arthur. The prince, who died two days ago at Ludlow Castle in Shropshire, was only 15 years old; there is, however, no suggestion of anything suspicious about his death. Two years ago Henry lost his third son, Edmund, at the age of just 16 months.

What had seemed so settled five months ago at the time of Arthur's grand marriage to Catherine of Aragon [*see report above*] – a prince of Wales well married and a second son, Henry, in the wings – now looks vulnerable to both fate and plots. The king is apparently overwhelmed with grief. First he sent for his wife Elizabeth, saying that they would face their sorrow together. Elizabeth has been comforting the king, reminding him that God has still spared him a fair prince (Henry) and two princesses (Margaret and Mary). But when she was alone the queen was herself overcome with sadness; it was then Henry's turn to go to her.

Although he is only 45 years old King Henry is not in good health himself, and so he must turn his attention all the more urgently to the problems of succession – the new heir, Henry, is a boy of ten – and also of what to do with a Spanish princess who, at 16, has just become a widow (→ 23/6/03).

Prince betrothed to brother's widow

Richmond, Surrey, 23 June 1503
Prince Henry, the heir to the English throne, who will be 12 years old in a few days' time, is to marry Catherine of Aragon, the 17-year-old widow of his brother Arthur. A treaty signed here today with Spain provides for the marriage to take place once Henry reaches his 15th year. A papal dispensation will be needed as, through her marriage to Arthur, Catherine became related to Henry in the "first degree of affinity". Before agreeing to the contract, Henry VII considered marrying Catherine himself. Elizabeth of York, his wife, died in February (→ 18/2/04).

English rose marries Scottish thistle

Edinburgh, 8 August 1503
Lavish celebrations at Holyrood Palace marked the wedding today of King James Stewart IV to Princess Margaret Tudor, the 13-year-old daughter of Henry VII of England [*see below*]. The marriage, along with the treaty of perpetual peace signed between England and Scotland last year, ushers in a new era of stability after two centuries of intermittent war. The symbolic union of Stewart thistle and Tudor rose has been set to verse by one of Scotland's foremost poets, William Dunbar. In *The Thrissil and the Rois* Dunbar fulsomely praises his patron, James, and refers to Margaret's "angelic beauty". With the recent deaths of Henry's wife and eldest son, Margaret is second in line to the throne (after her brother, Henry); should anything happen to Henry, James Stewart would become king of England (→9/1506).

James IV and his new queen, Margaret Tudor, process on horseback through Edinburgh to the accompaniment of court musicians (left).

European fashions dazzle Scots at magnificent royal wedding

Edinburgh, August 1503
European fashions, never seen in Scotland before, have dazzled court and country at the sumptuous wedding at Holyrood Palace between King James IV of Scotland and Princess Margaret, the daughter of King Henry VII of England [*see report above*].

The bride wore a wedding gown of white damask and crimson velvet lined with taffeta; her train was made of cloth of gold. The bridegroom, weighed down by jewellery, wore velvet, satin, silk and cloth of gold, bordered with ermine.

Members of Margaret's entourage, who brought with them jewels, silver plate and beautifully wrought gold, were almost as richly clad as she was. Her men wore satin, velvet and damask, the fabric cut in the Italian style with doublets padded at the shoulder and symmetrically slashed sleeves showing off shirt sleeves of contrasting colours. The doublets ended at the waist, below which richly decorated cod-pieces acted as keystones to the multi-coloured hose. Their shoes were broad duck-billed affairs which, had they been worn by less illustrious feet, would have looked ridiculous. The women, meanwhile, were decked out in crimson and velvet. The low *décolletages* of their bodices were sometimes square, sometimes rounded, and sometimes revealingly V-shaped. Their trains were luxurious, closely fitting at the top, then spreading out, with fur, velvet or embroidered borders. There was hardly a "steeple" or a "butterfly" headdress among them. Instead the women favoured mantillas and bonnets, richly embroidered on the hems and displaying the front of the hair, which was parted down the middle of the head in the new style.

Queen Margaret adores the new Italian fashions and has declared that the only thing that cheers her up, whenever she has to stay in her chamber because of sickness, is having her gowns of silk, velvet and cloth of gold laid out on her bed, where she can gaze at them.

The new styles: long trains for the women, padded tunics for the men.

Financial genius makes last account

Windsor, 5 August 1503
Sir Reynold Bray, one of England's most distinguished administrators and a close friend of King Henry VII, died at the castle here today. He will be buried in the beautiful chapel of St George, to which he was a generous benefactor.

Sir Reynold, who owned land in 11 different counties, came from an honourable old Northamptonshire family whose ancestors came over to England from France at the time of the Norman Conquest. He found employment as a steward in the household of Henry's mother, Margaret Beaufort, and over the years proved himself to be a loyal servant of the Tudors. Sir Reynold fought alongside them in the Battle of Bosworth field in 1485. It is sometimes alleged – perhaps unreliably – that after the fighting it was he who discovered the crown of King Richard III concealed in a hawthorn bush.

Sir Reynold rose to become Henry's chief financial adviser and ultimately directed the entire revenue machinery of the kingdom. His success as chancellor of the duchy of Lancaster reflected the achievements of the king's land-revenue policy. During his 18 years of public service he served on over a hundred government bodies. He was rewarded with liberal grants of land, but, as shrewd a businessman as he was an administrator, he also made money from activities such as the wool trade (→4/1504).

Nicholas Kratzer, astronomer to King Henry VII, as depicted by Hans Holbein the Younger.

1504 - 1507

England, 18 February 1504. Prince Henry, the duke of Cornwall, is created both prince of Wales and earl of Chester (→ 27/6/05).

Canterbury, 9 March 1504. William Warham is enthroned as archbishop (→ 14/10).

Fife, April 1504. On the death of his brother James, the archbishop of St Andrews, James IV appoints to the see his own 11-year-old bastard son, Alexander, (→ 18/3/07).

Highland, May 1504. James IV campaigns from Dumbarton, in Strathclyde, against rebels active in the western highlands and islands (→ 9/1506).

Kent, 14 October 1504. John Fisher is appointed bishop of Rochester.

Spain, 26 November 1504. Queen Isabella of Castile dies, leaving Henry VII of England in a difficult position as his allies, Philip, the duke of Burgundy, and Ferdinand of Aragon are rivals for the regency of Castile (→ 25/5/05).

London, 1504. Henry VII appoints a royal printer to add to his newly created office of royal librarian (→ 1507).

Europe, 25 April 1505. Henry VII lends £108,000 to Philip, the duke of Burgundy, to support Philip's claim to Castile (→ 30/4/1506).

Lothian, May 1505. Building of a dockyard at Newhaven, near Leith, starts (→ 12/10/11).

Surrey, 27 June 1505. Henry, the prince of Wales, protests at Richmond against his betrothal to Catherine of Aragon despite receiving a papal dispensation to marry (→ 24/4/09).

Edinburgh, 1505. The Royal College of Surgeons is founded (→ 23/9/18).

Highland, September 1506. Stornoway Castle, the last rebel stronghold, falls to Alexander Gordon, the earl of Huntly (→ 1510).

Cambridge, 1506. Margaret Beaufort, the mother of Henry VII, founds Christ's College at the university (→ 1/6/09).

Dumfries and Galloway, 18 March 1507. James IV completes a 120-mile (192-km) eight-day pilgrimage on foot from Edinburgh to Whithorn (→ 1509).

Co Kildare, 1507. Gerald fitz Maurice FitzGerald meets Aodh Dubh O'Donnell, the lord of Tyrconnell, at Maynooth (→ 28/7/09).

Parliament wins row over spending plans

Westminster, April 1504

The present session of parliament, which closes this month, has witnessed unprecedented opposition to the king's financial plans. Henry VII has been offered a greatly reduced grant of £40,000 instead of the £113,000 that he had been asking for. Chastened by this experience, Henry will in fact take only £30,000 of the grant.

Although Henry expected some cuts, this was still a remarkable flexing of parliamentary muscle, perhaps provoked by the king's claim that he needed the money after the expense of knighting his son Arthur and marrying off his daughter Margaret. But since Arthur, who died two years ago, was knighted back in 1489, and Margaret married James IV of Scotland a whole year ago, parliament suspected that the real aim was to bolster royal finances and create new registers of landowners' wealth.

Henry is reported to have paid close attention to the part played in this wrangle by a parliamentarian called Thomas More. Although only 26, this rising lawyer is credited with providing most of the arguments against the royal demands, although he wisely avoided attacking the king directly, which would have cut short his promising career. So, with the crown having a healthy surplus, and in the absence of a war, Henry will think hard before calling a parliament again (→ 30/3/12).

An expert lawyer: Thomas More.

The power of money: tax collectors, as seen by Pieter Brueghel the Elder.

Scottish king's friend fails to take wing

Stirling, September 1507

An Italian alchemist escaped death by inches today when he plunged from the battlements of Stirling Castle during an attempt to fly. John Damien, a close friend of King James IV, aimed to fly to France, but he only got as far as the castle midden, some one hundred metres below. Undaunted, he plans to review the design of his wings. Damien's ignominious landing elicited peals of laughter from the assembled courtiers, many of whom are thought to resent the Italian's intimacy with the royal family. The king has funded Damien's – so far unsuccessful – experiments in alchemy since he arrived at court four years ago.

Gaelic Connacht is crushed in battle by deputy, Kildare

Co Galway, 19 August 1504

One of the toughest battles to be fought in Ireland since the time of Strongbow in the late twelfth century has taken place at Knockdoe, outside Galway, with terrible loss of life. The battle is being seen as a culmination of the feuds that have gone on for the past 50 years between the western Gaelic lords.

The battle was between Gerald fitz Maurice FitzGerald [Gearoid Mor], the earl of Kildare and deputy of Ireland, and Ulick Burke, the earl of Clanricard, who is married to Kildare's daughter, Eustasia. Kildare claimed that Ulick's power in Connacht threatened Henry VII's authority there, especially when, earlier this year, Ulick seized Galway town – one of the king's own. Yet it was really Kildare's own power – the huge extent of which Henry may not fully appreciate – that was in jeopardy.

All was set for today's showdown at Knockdoe. In a spectacular demonstration of his authority throughout the country, Kildare led an alliance of his own soldiers, Ulster forces and men of the Pale against Ulick, who was soundly defeated. Kildare, now redeemed from past disgrace, will send the chancellor, Walter FitzSimons, to give the good news to Henry in London (→ 1507).

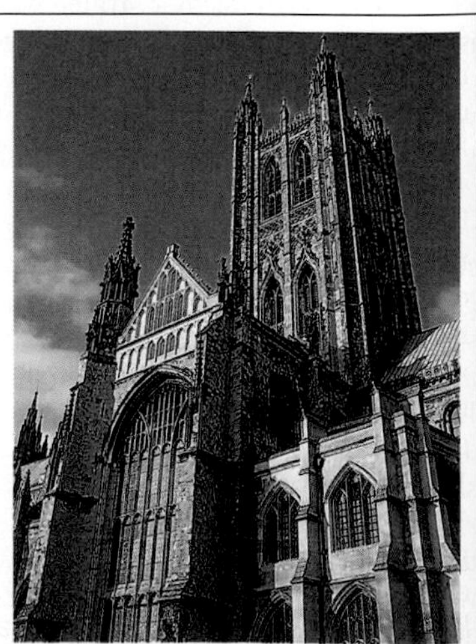

The construction of the grand Harry Tower of Canterbury Cathedral in Kent, designed by John Wastell, was finished in 1504.

Negotiations with Europe open the way for English merchants to make a killing

Westminster, 30 April 1506
Three months of tough negotiating have won Henry VII a trade agreement from Philip, the duke of Burgundy, that is extremely favourable to England's interests. The negotiations began after the duke and his fleet were forced ashore at Weymouth by Channel storms while on their way to Spain.

Henry has also signed a treaty of mutual defence with Burgundy and has been promised the hand of Duke Philip's sister, Margaret of Savoy; their father is Holy Roman Emperor Maximilian. Everything is going Henry's way: last month Philip's men handed over to the English at Calais the Yorkist heir, Edmund de la Pole, the one-time earl of Suffolk. Edmund, who fled from England in 1501, is now in the Tower.

Philip will soon leave once more for Spain to claim Castile in the name of his wife, Joanna, the daughter of King Ferdinand of Aragon and Queen Isabella of Castile, and has authorized commissioners to settle outstanding commercial disagreements between England and Burgundy, which also involve the vital trading partners of Flanders and the Netherlands. This will prove particularly important for wool merchants, who can expect confirmation of their rights to sell freely throughout the areas covered by the trade treaty of 1496 called the *Magnus Intercursus*, with some significant extension of their trading area as well. They also hope to reduce the tariff advantages which the German Hanseatic League is at present enjoying over English merchants (→17/12/08).

Philip with English merchants.

First printing press set up in Scotland

Edinburgh, 1507
James IV has granted a patent to two businessmen to set up the first printing press in Scotland. It will be sited here in the capital. While many European countries have been installing the new technology, this is the first time that a king has been personally involved.

The two men, Walter Chepman and Andrew Myllar, have been asked by the king "for our pleasure, the honour and profit of our realm [to] furnish and bring home a printing press with all stuff belonging thereto and expert men to use the same". Instructed to print books "for competent prices", they have in fact been granted a monopoly. The option of printing books abroad and merely selling them in Scotland has been outlawed.

James is well known as a patron of the arts. Poets, known as *makars* because they "create" words, are particularly encouraged. One such is William Dunbar, who wrote a charming allegory called *The Thrissil and the Rois* for James's wedding to Margaret Tudor. This year he has written an altogether different work, *The Dance of the Sevin Deidly Synnis*, in which the devil summons the souls of those who have died unconfessed. Another fine poet of the king's circle was Robert Henryson, who died in 1490. One of his most popular works was the *Morall Fabillis of Esope*, which tells in 13 stories of the harsh realities of animal life, such as that of birds who are trapped and beaten by the fowler, the "bloody butcher". Henryson's best known work is, however, *The Testament of Cresseid*, which is a sophisticated re-working of the English poet Geoffrey Chaucer's *Troilus and Criseyde*.

James and his wife: literary types.

Brewer promises influence in high places to boost business

Canterbury, 1507
A local brewer has hit on a novel way of increasing his trade with the alehouse-keepers. William Crompe is promising them that if they become his customers he will be "their very good master in whatsoever they have to do in the court-hall"; in other words, he will bribe magistrates for them. He is giving out more than a broad hint that his help will be extended particularly whenever keepers are brought before a court for such offences as giving short measure.

The move clearly reflects the vigorous competition within the city's growing band of brewers. Many are already doing favours for alehouse-keepers, such as tiding them over debts or obtaining trading licences for them. Crompe is in a good position to make his promises sound credible: he is at present the mayor of Canterbury.

The beer business: a German engraving representing the evils of drink.

Magnate pays the penalty for rioting

Kent, 24 December 1507
It is going to be a bleak Christmas for the Kentish magnate George Nevill, Lord Abergavenny. In a settlement signed today with Henry VII, he has submitted to a crippling fine of £70,650 and is to start paying it off at a rate of £500 a year for the next ten years. This is his punishment for having a private army and instigating a riot four years ago at Horsmonden, 10 miles (16 kilometres) south-east of Tonbridge, when one of his men, Robert Tykhill, attacked local rivals who were also officers of the crown. Although a free man for now, Abergavenny may go to prison at a moment's notice until the fine is paid off. His treatment is eloquent testimony to Henry's policy of coming down hard on noblemen who step out of line.

1508 - 1511

Cambridge, 1508. A fan vault in perpendicular style is designed for King's College chapel (→ 1512).

Scotland, 1508. The poet William Dunbar writes *The Golden Targe*, a dream allegory (→ 1522).

Oxford, 1 June 1509. William Smyth, the bishop of Lincoln, lays the foundation stone of Brasenose College (→ 4/1511).

London, 11 June 1509. Henry VIII weds Catherine of Aragon, his brother's widow, at Greenwich (→ 31/1/10).

Ireland, 28 July 1509. Gerald fitz Maurice FitzGerald, the earl of Kildare, is summoned to the English court; earlier this year he burnt Omagh in support of the sons of Conn O'Neill, who dispute the succession to the lordship of Tyrone (→ 8/11/10).

London, November 1509. Henry VIII promotes Thomas Wolsey, the dean of Lincoln, to the position of almoner (→ 15/9/14).

Grampian, 1509. William Elphinstone, the bishop of Aberdeen, completes the *Aberdeen Breviary*, containing over 70 Scottish saints (→ 1512).

London, 31 January 1510. Catherine of Aragon delivers a stillborn daughter (→ 22/2/11).

Ireland, 8 November 1510. The earl of Kildare, who returned to Ireland earlier this year and campaigned against Gaelic lords in Munster, is confirmed as deputy by Henry VIII of England (→ 3/9/13).

Scotland, 1510. Prince Arthur, the only son of King James IV, dies (→ 10/1412).

Surrey, 22 February 1511. Henry VIII's son, Henry, the duke of Cornwall, dies at Richmond .

Cambridge, April 1511. John Fisher, the bishop of Rochester, founds St John's College (→ 5/6/12).

Europe, 17 November 1511. England joins the Holy League against Louis XII of France; it was formed last month by Pope Julius II, the Venetian Republic and Ferdinand of Aragon after Louis held a schismatic general council of the church in May (→ 4/1514).

Greenwich, London, 1511. Henry VIII sets up a royal armoury at Greenwich Palace after being given a suit of armour by Holy Roman Emperor Maximilian.

Tudors link their fate to Habsburgs

Mary: an important marriage.

Richmond, Sy, 17 December 1508
With a solemnity befitting the dynastic significance of the alliance, Henry VII of England has been celebrating the formal betrothal of his 12-year-old daughter Mary to - Prince Charles, the son of Duke Philip of Burgundy and grandson of Holy Roman Emperor Maximilian of Habsburg.

While Henry entertained the embassy from Flanders with grand ceremonial, the various terms were hammered out by nobles and clergy from both sides. Then the leader of the embassy, Lord Bergues, standing in for the young prince, spoke the contract of matrimony with Mary, and she reciprocated to him. He then put a gold ring on her finger, and the court moved into the king's chapel to celebrate Mass. A banquet will take place tonight, followed tomorrow by jousting.

The betrothal caps Henry's tortuous manoeuvrings to construct secure alliances for the house of Tudor on the shifting dynastic sands of Europe. Now the king who snatched a crown on the battlefield has linked his line to the greatest inheritance in Europe. Despite the burden of a 50,000-crown loan to Maximilian (which may never be repaid), Henry is greatly pleased by an alliance that includes the Habsburg lands, the Netherlands and the Spanish kingdoms (→ 17/11/11).

Spendthrift earl receives broken bones on top of money worries

London, June 1508
It is not unusual for a courtier to suffer a metaphorical downfall, but this month Richard Grey, the earl of Kent, has suffered a literal one as well. An experienced tournament rider, he was teaching the chivalric art of jousting to Prince Henry Tudor, the 17-year-old son of Henry VII, when his pupil unhorsed him so forcefully that he fell and broke his arm. It is just possible that Grey's mind was on something else – he has been in serious financial straits and appears to be hoping that Henry VII will be able to help him out.

The courtly sport of jousting: Prince Henry has proved a good horseman.

Grey is a vivid example of a man smaller than his office, and his links with the Tudor court cast a rather unflattering light on the way it operates. A spendthrift and a gambler, he has left himself so much at the mercy of grasping courtiers that over the last four years he has given away, or sold, most of the lands he inherited from his father, George. Perhaps out of gratitude for the loyal service that George Grey bore him till his death five years ago, the king has in the past helped the present earl out of his troubles and may do so again. After all, he has benefited from them by picking up Grey's manors on the cheap.

Scots celebrate the launch of the most powerful warship afloat

Lothian, 12 October 1511
Amid colourful celebrations James IV has launched his latest ship, the *Michael*, at Newhaven, near Leith. This latest addition to the king's powerful fleet is reputedly the greatest ship afloat and has taken five years to complete at a cost of nearly £30,000. Almost 55 metres (180 feet) long, the *Michael* has needed vast amounts of timber, most of it imported from Norway. She carries 27 cannon of varying sizes as well as 300 smaller guns.

James inherited an interest in the navy from his father, James III, who was impressed by the achievements of Christopher Columbus and other navigators in discovering and exploring lands in the New World over the last twenty years. He also appreciated the huge trade benefits that have flowed to Spain as a result. Closer to home he was also keen to develop the naval means to enforce his rule on the remote and frequently unruly Western Isles.

With tension rising as England heads towards war with James IV's ally, Louis XII of France, it may not be long before the *Michael* sees action (→ 13/6/14).

Reins of power pass to Henry VIII

Enemies held after a secret accession

London, 24 April 1509
Today, just three days after the death of his father died, the young Henry Tudor, now the new king of England, rode to the Tower of London with a strong escort of noblemen led by John de Vere, the earl of Oxford. Because of fears of public unrest a watch was kept in every ward while the young king, whose 18th birthday is on 28 June, remained in the city.

So unstable was the throne in the last years of Henry VII that for two days his death was kept a secret from his court at Richmond Palace. He died there at 11pm on Saturday 21 April, whereupon Prince Henry immediately acceded; yet the death was not announced until yesterday evening, by which time the new regime had got rid of anyone who might have sought to stand in its way. Henry Stafford, the brother of Duke Edward of Buckingham, is already under arrest. Early this morning, meanwhile, two of Henry VII's officials, the despised tax collectors Sir Richard Empson and Edmund Dudley, were sent to the Tower for allegedly plotting against Henry's succession.

Henry VII's body is being kept at Richmond until his new chapel at Westminster Abbey is ready to receive it. The new king, Henry VIII, whom the Venetian ambassador has approvingly described as "magnificent, liberal and a great enemy of the French", plans to marry his brother's widow, Catherine of Aragon, in order to secure the Spanish alliance (→11/6).

A joint ceremony: the coronation of King Henry and Queen Catherine.

Pageantry marks beginning of new reign

Westminster, 24 June 1509
Westminster Abbey was the scene today for the magnificent coronation of England's second Tudor king, Henry VIII. The transfer of power from Henry's late father to him has so far gone peacefully, to the relief of those who remember the savage struggle for the throne between York and Lancaster in past decades.

Enthroned beside Henry was his queen, Catherine, whom he married on 11 June – Pope Julius II had granted him a dispensation to marry the widow of his brother, Arthur. That marriage had lasted only five months, and Catherine says that it was unconsummated; Arthur was only 15 when he died.

Yesterday Henry and Catherine left the Tower to process to Westminster. The streets were hung with tapestries and cloth of gold, while members of each craft guild, dressed in livery, lined Cheapside. Today – Midsummer day – the king wore a robe of crimson velvet trimmed with ermine and beneath it a jacket embroidered with diamonds, rubies, emeralds and great pearls. His horse was draped in gold damask, and the barons of the Cinque Ports bore a canopy over his head. The queen was borne in a litter by two white palfreys.

Henry is generally well-liked. "His goodly personage, his amiable visage, his princely countenance, known to every man, needeth no rehearsal," writes the chronicler Edward Hall, describing the procession. The king loves hunting, jousting, music and dance; one of his many tutors was the poet John Skelton (→31/1/10).

Scholar with taste for satire moves to Cambridge college

Cambridge, August 1511
Desiderius Erasmus, a humanist scholar who trained as an Augustinian monk, has joined Queen's College as professor of Greek and Divinity for Cambridge University. The appointment was made by the university chancellor, John Fisher, the bishop of Rochester. Erasmus, who is 45, is the first to be given the newly created chair.

Born in the Netherlands, Erasmus has a European-wide reputation, having taught and studied in France and Italy. A skilled linguist and biblical scholar, he is above all a humanist thinker. Humanists are scholars who stress the value of the Greek and especially Roman civilizations that were superseded by Christianity. Erasmus's *Enchiridion* of 1503, for instance, argues that a grounding in classical literature is a necessary preparation for understanding the Bible – a sentiment that would have been anathema to many church fathers.

Erasmus: scholar and satirist.

Yet apart from purely academic works Erasmus also enjoys highbrow satire. In 1509 he wrote the *Encomium Moriae*, aimed at the follies of public life and conceived while he was travelling to see his great friend, the lawyer Sir Thomas More. The punning title can be translated as either *Praise of folly* or *Praise of More*.

Two-day tournament celebrates birth of a son to Henry VIII

Westminster, February 1511
An immensely lavish tournament is being held this month to celebrate the birth at Richmond Palace on 1 January of Henry, King Henry VIII's son by Catherine of Aragon. The cost is estimated at £4,000. Processions through the City, bonfires and free wine will mark this national celebration. The king himself is to take part in the jousting.

Court celebration: the tournament marking the birth of the king's son.

1512 - 1513

Westminster, 30 March 1512. Parliament closes after granting taxes for a war with France (→ 5/1513).

Scotland, 10 April 1512. Queen Margaret gives birth to a son and heir, James (→ 21/9/13).

London, April 1512. King Henry VIII declares war on France (→ 25/4/13).

Scotland, May 1512. John Barton, the captain of James IV's ship the *Margaret*, captures several Flemish privateers and sends the king barrels filled with the pirates' heads.

Fife, 1512. Alexander Stewart, the archbishop of St Andrews, founds St Leonard's College for the education of 20 poor clerics (→ 19/6/20).

Scotland, March 1513. Nicholas West, the dean of Windsor, asks James IV to stay neutral in the war between the Holy League and France (→ spring 1513).

Ulster, spring 1513. Carrickfergus Castle is bombarded by a Scots fleet en route to Normandy to support Louis XII of France (→ 8/5).

Europe, 25 April 1513. Holy Roman Emperor Maximilian joins the Holy League against France (→ 30/6).

London, 4 May 1513. Edmund de la Pole, the earl of Suffolk, imprisoned in the Tower since 1506, is executed without trial as Henry VIII prepares to invade France.

France, 8 May 1513. Louis XII promises to pay James IV of Scots for equipping his navy with ships and seamen (→ 9/9).

North Yorkshire, May 1513. Residents of Skipton refuse to submit their income details for a new subsidy tax (→ 6/7/23).

Calais, France, 30 June 1513. Henry VIII of England lands with 35,000 men (→ 25/9).

Ireland, 3 September 1513. Gerald fitz Maurice FitzGerald [Gearoid Mor], the earl of Kildare, dies of gunshot wounds while campaigning against the O'Mores; he is succeeded by his son Gerald [Gearoid Og] (→ 26/11).

France, 22 October 1513. Henry VIII of England sets sail from Calais at the conclusion of his war with France (→ 7/8/14).

Ireland, 26 November 1513. Gerald FitzGerald [Gearoid Og], the earl of Kildare, is made deputy.

Extravagant 'gothic' style excites the eye

"Gothic" splendour: the roof of Henry VII's chapel, Westminster Abbey.

Westminster, 1512

The chapel of Henry VII, begun by him in 1503 and still unfinished when he died, is now complete. Although built onto the abbey here, it stands almost as a separate church – and one in a far more elaborate "gothic" style. The outer walls, adjoining the abbey's sanctuary, are covered with a dense grid of perpendicular panelling; they are supported with flying buttresses and onion-domed turrets. The overall effect, by the royal masons Robert and William Vertue, is mesmerizing – yet the interior of the chapel is even more lavish. The roof is an amazing network of fan vaults that hang down like cones of petrified lace. Down below them the unfinished tomb of Henry and his queen, Elizabeth of York, is being carved by the Florentine master sculptor Pietro Torrigiano, whose realistic style contrasts with the idealized effigies favoured in the past for kings and queens.

Fan-vaulting, the ultimate refinement of the gothic style, has also been used in St George's chapel, Windsor, the tower of Canterbury Cathedral, in the new abbey at Bath, and in the chapel of King's College, Cambridge.

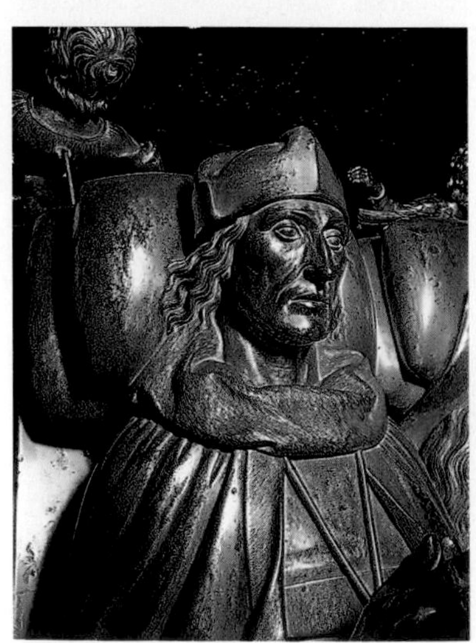

A realistic portrait: the late king's tomb, carved by Pietro Torrigiano.

The splendid fan-vaulted roof to King's College chapel, Cambridge.

Franco-Scots links renewed by James

Scotland, March 1512

James IV's diplomats have this month renewed the 1492 alliance between Scotland and France – essentially it is both an offensive and a defensive measure against England. Although James became the brother-in-law of Henry VIII of England when he married Margaret Tudor in 1503, he has refused to join Henry and the other members of the Holy League – the papacy, Venice and Aragon – against his old ally and supporter Louis XII of France.

James has already paid a spiritual price: on 21 February Pope Julius II excommunicated him for failing to back the League as it prepares for war with Louis. Yet there may be military and political gains; James could well be tempted into an attack on England while Henry is embroiled in a campaign across the Channel (→ 3/1313).

Mercers' guild will run St Paul's School

London, 15 June 1512

The scholar John Colet attended a meeting today of the court of a trade guild, the Company of Mercers, and formally read the proposed articles of governance of a new school, to be called St Paul's. The company readily accepted the articles, which make them trustees of St Paul's. Colet has been working towards this triumphant day ever since he inherited his father's substantial estate in 1505, when he resolved to use a large part of this fortune to found a school in the heart of his native London.

When it came to who should run the school, Colet preferred to have lay trustees and chose the Mercers, whom he knows well. St Paul's is by no means the first school to have lay trustees – the practice started at least a century ago. As for the curriculum, Colet wants to stress moral education more than strictly academic training. In contradiction to the current vogue for humanism, which looks favourably on the Greek and Latin classics, St Paul's will emphasize Christian values and avoid such "pagan" works (→ 1515).

Scots slaughtered at Flodden field

Northumberland, 9 Sept 1513
A field near the village of Flodden, 11 miles (18km) south-west of Berwick, was the scene today of what can only be described as a massacre. This evening the corpses of 10,000 Scots and 1,500 English soldiers lie scattered on the ground; among them is James IV of Scots.

On 29 August James crossed the Tweed in support of his ally Louis XII of France, who is himself at war with England. His army captured Norham Castle and then took up a defensive position on Flodden hill, while an English force under Thomas Howard, the earl of Surrey, hurried north from Pontefract. Collecting troops at Newcastle and Alnwick, Howard pitted 22,000 men against James's larger force and cut off the line of retreat.

James next made a fatal error by ordering his army down from its higher position in five large phalanxes armed with 6-metre (20-foot)-long pikes. The ground was uneven, the pikes were very heavy, and the phalanxes lost their close formation. At close quarters the English made mincemeat of them with their short halberds, or bills, which can slice through armour and smash pikestaffs.

In the grim slogging match at the foot of the hill James fell after he was struck with an arrow and gashed with a halberd. Killed with him were his 20-year-old bastard son Alexander (the archbishop of St Andrews), a bishop, two abbots, nine earls and 14 lords. The English took no prisoners. Every Scot who fell into their hands has been killed and stripped naked – including the king and his nobles (→ 21).

Scottish discussions before the battle, as imagined by a 19th-century artist.

A bloody rout: the English army took no prisoners at Flodden field.

English king leads Holy League army in fall of Tournai

Flanders, 25 September 1513
King Henry VIII of England has marched into Tournai two days after its surrender to the army of the Holy League and three months after he first crossed to Calais with 35,000 men. Today's success is in stark contrast to Henry's total failure last year to recover Aquitaine. Then his demoralized troops mutinied. But this year Thomas Wolsey made sure that they were better armed and equipped them with 12 heavy guns called "bumbardells".

Slogging through the rain and mud of Flanders, Henry's army found its first success in battle on 16 August at Thérouanne, when a cavalry action, which is being referred to as "the Battle of the Spurs", led directly to the town's surrender six days later. Holy Roman Emperor Maximilian, together with his German and Flemish troops, joined the English expeditionary force while it advanced. After a preliminary bombardment of Tournai, a two-day truce was declared to negotiate a surrender.

Tonight the English king, red-bearded and towering over the emperor at his side, entered the city in a torchlit procession to be presented with the keys and six casks of burgundy. The news of a great victory over the Scots at Flodden [*see report left*] has arrived to add to the mood of rejoicing (→ 22/10).

Scotland faces up to a bleak future in the aftermath of Flodden

Scotland, 21 September 1513
A month ago Scotland was in the capable hands of James IV, a man of great culture and military expertise. Then came the massacre of Flodden [*see report above*]. Now Scotland is in the tiny and quite incapable hands of an infant of 17 months: James, the sole heir to the late king. He was today crowned King James V at Stirling. A council of regency will run the country whilst the dowager queen, Margaret, acts as *tutrix* to her son. By one dreadful tactical blunder at Flodden, James IV threw away both his life and the political stability of his realm. There is considerable apprehension over what Henry VIII of England – Queen Margaret's brother – will do once the war with Louis XII of France is over [*see report above right*]. He may want to punish the Scots for invading England while, as it were, his back was turned. Rivalries within Scotland pose another danger. In what is effectively a power vacuum various factions will be bound to seek influence with the queen, who is not quite 24 years old. Then there could be rival claimants to the throne. One such might be John Stewart, the duke of Albany, a grandson of James III. Although Stewart has lived all his life in France, recent events in Scotland may persuade him to press his own claim to the crown.

French splendour: King Louis XII.

1514 - 1515

London, 2 February 1514. King Henry VIII creates four new peers: Thomas Howard is the new duke of Norfolk and his son, also Thomas Howard, becomes earl of Surrey; Charles Brandon becomes duke of Suffolk and Charles Somerset is the new earl of Worcester.

Greenwich, 13 June 1514. Henry VIII launches the *Henri Grâce à Dieu* supplanting the Scotland's *Michael*, launched in 1511, as the world's biggest warship (→ 20/7/45).

Scotland, 6 August 1514. Queen Margaret Tudor, the widow of King James IV, sister of Henry VIII of England and regent of Scotland, marries Archibald Douglas, the earl of Angus (→ 6/11).

England/France, 7 August 1514. An Anglo-French peace treaty, arranged by Thomas Wolsey, chief adviser to Henry VIII, is signed.→

York, 15 September 1514. Thomas Wolsey, the bishop of Lincoln, is consecrated as archbishop (→ 10/9/15).

Scotland, 6 November 1514. A rival parliament is set up in opposition to the regent, the English-born Queen Margaret, and her husband, Archibald, the earl of Angus (→ 12/7/15).

Paris, February 1515. Mary Tudor, the widow of Louis XII and the youngest sister of Henry VIII, secretly marries Charles Brandon, who was created duke of Suffolk a year ago.

Greenwich, London. 24 June 1515. Sir William Darcy tells Henry VIII that the Anglo-Irish lords' corrupt "coyne and livery" system is at the root of Ireland's administrative problems (→ 9/1515).

Scotland, 12 July 1515. John, the duke of Albany, a cousin of the young James V, is accepted as Scottish regent in place of Queen Margaret, James's mother (→ 8/10/16).

Rome, 10 September 1515. The archbishop of York, Thomas Wolsey, is made a cardinal (→ 24/12).

Westminster, 1515. The Florentine sculptor Pietro Torrigiano finishes work on the elaborate chapel in the abbey dedicated to Henry VII.

Manchester, 1515. The bishop of Exeter, Hugh Oldham, founds the first free grammar school here (→ 7/1517).

Betrothal brings harmony to kings

France, 7 August 1514
Instead of mounting another invasion of France this year, Henry VIII of England today signed a peace treaty at St Germain-en-Laye with Louis XII. The ailing 52-year-old French king is to marry Henry's younger sister Mary, who is 18, to seal the new friendship between England and France.

This news is causing ribald comment in the courts of Europe. People are jesting that if Louis consummates the marriage it will be the death of him. In all respects the treaty is favourable to Henry and his adviser, chaplain and almoner Thomas Wolsey, who managed the supplying of Henry's campaign in north-east France last year.

Tournai, the city which Henry captured, is ceded to England, and Tournai is to recognize Wolsey as its bishop in place of the French bishop-elect. In return for not enforcing his claim to the throne of France, Henry is to be paid one million francs over ten years.

The French king also agreed to pay Wolsey an annual pension of 1,000 gold *écus* as a reward for his part in negotiating the peace. And Henry has nominated Wolsey as archbishop of York and has written to the pope asking for him to be made a cardinal (→ 5/10/18).

Church accused of murdering prisoner

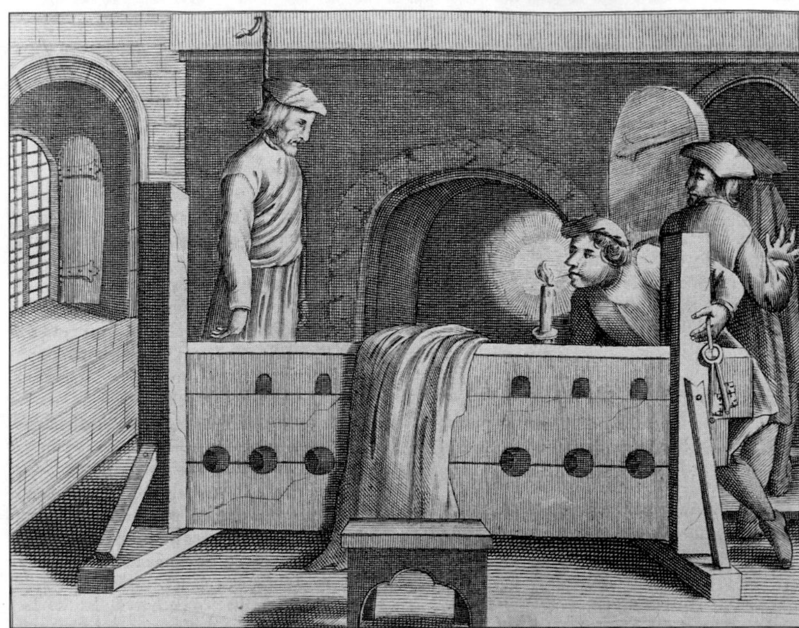

Richard Hunne's death, as seen in John Foxe's "Book of Martyrs" (1563).

London, 14 December 1514
Richard Hunne, a rich merchant-tailor renowned for his charities, was found hanged in the bishop's prison at St Paul's in the early hours of this morning. His friends claim that he was murdered, and one jailer is reported to have fled before the body was discovered. However, church officials contend that Hunne committed suicide.

Hunne was held captive in the Lollards' tower while awaiting trial for heresy. His quarrel with the church arose from his refusal to pay a burial fee to St Mary's Spital, Whitechapel, following the death of his infant son.

His case was that his son, being only a few weeks old, had no property. For him it was a matter of principle. He first challenged the church in the ecclesiastical court. When that failed he brought a further suit at the king's bench. His friends say that it was his challenge to church authority, not his beliefs, that provoked the heresy charge.

Role of England's hereditary constable is recognized but ignored

Buckingham: under suspicion.

Westminster, 1514
Edward Stafford, the duke of Buckingham, has been declared hereditary constable of England, but the king refuses to allow him to exercise the office. The duke's father was the greatest noble in England under King Richard III and was executed for treason; King Henry VIII and Archbishop Wolsey of York are most suspicious of the present duke's ambitions.

Under earlier baronial practice, there were three great hereditary offices in England: the high steward, the constable and the earl marshal. They had the right to "reform" evil counsellors and impose conditions on the king. In France the constable retains his powers, but the Tudor monarchy is determined to end such feudal relics. There is no place in England for a constable, or for any other hereditary office under the crown.

The duke of Buckingham had petitioned to have the office restored in 1510. He had previously exercised it for one day only, for the coronation of Henry VIII in 1509. Now the judges have ruled that the duke holds two manors in Gloucestershire by right, as hereditary constable, but they added prudently that the king might choose at his pleasure to invite the duke to exercise the office. The king has no intention of doing so. The duke is descended from Edward III and might lay claim to the throne if the king had no heirs. The king and Wolsey may consider him a man to be watched, as Richard III watched his father (→ 5/11/19).

Butcher's son is new lord chancellor

London, 24 December 1515
At Eltham Palace chapel, in the presence of Henry VIII, Thomas Wolsey was tonight sworn in as lord chancellor of England. The appointment is the most spectacular achievement so far of a man who began life some 40 years ago as the son of an Ipswich butcher.

An exceptional scholar, he graduated from the new Oxford college, Magdalen, at the age of 15. He later became the college bursar and hastened the work of building its tower beside the Isis. He sought preferment through the church and became chaplain to the archbishop of Canterbury, to the governor of Calais and then a royal chaplain at the court of Henry VII, where he was sent on diplomatic missions.

Wolsey accumulated wealth by holding several benefices at once, with papal leave of absence from all of them. He was the vicar of two parishes, dean of Lincoln and Hereford and almoner to the new king by the age of 36. Wolsey's persuasive tongue and his ability to work for 12 hours at a stretch are his strong assets. He offers to carry on all state business while the king devotes himself to hunting and his other pleasures. He has made himself indispensable and a very rich man. As archbishop of York he became a cardinal this year (→ 2/5/16).

King and chancellor: Henry with Wolsey, by Sir John Gilbert (d.1897).

Tyrannical Jersey governor cleared by royal whitewash

Jersey, September 1515
A royal commission sent from London has effectively cleared Sir Hugh Vaughan, the unpopular and tyrannical governor of Jersey, of serious misconduct. At the end of a two-day inquiry Sir Hugh has been rapped over the knuckles for a few comparatively unimportant offences and is left unquestioned master of this Channel Island.

Sir Hugh, Welsh and by trade a tailor, first caught the eye of Henry VII. He became a gentleman usher, was knighted and made high bailiff of Westminster and captain of Jersey in 1502. There have been persistent allegations of his involvement in the rape of young girls as well as violent assaults against islanders who stood in his way.

The inquiry is a skilful piece of whitewashing. Sir Hugh appears to have used his influence with the king's leading minister, Thomas Wolsey, to soften and reduce the charges against him. The commissioners – two English lawyers – and local jurors found that he had monopolized the export trade for profit, taken bribes from foreign merchants, illegally leased a mill and continued to levy an export tax on wheat instituted by the French.

Henry takes firm line against church pleas for legal immunity

London, November 1515
King Henry VIII has taken a firm line against clerical claims to independence from the common law – and, by implication, from his own power as king. Judges and councillors meeting here ruled that clergy had to show that the Roman canons under which they were appealing were based on divine law. Otherwise they had to get the express permission of the king before they could appeal.

Henry also made a further advance on the legislative front. The king was given permission to make new laws in parliament with Lords and Commons. He will be allowed to exclude the bishops under certain circumstances. The king has been following an astute policy of increasing his power over the control of church patronage and by raising church taxation. At Baynard's Castle, a royal palace in the city of London, he boasted: "By the ordinance and sufferance of God we are king of England, and the kings of England in time past have never had any superior but God alone."

Cardinal Wolsey, the archbishop of York and probably the cleric with most influence over the king, made a last-minute attempt to limit the damage to priestly power. He argued that the royal prerogative was not in question, but that the clergy were bound by the oath of their office to defend the liberties of the church. He knelt before Henry and prayed that the matter might be referred to the pope. The king was unmoved (→ 11/10/21).

The priest's words: the authority of church law is under challenge.

Wolsey turns blind eye to Irish woes

Dublin, September 1515
Gerald FitzGerald [Gearoid Og], the earl of Kildare, has been confirmed as deputy of Ireland only weeks after a damning report on its tribal chiefs: "Some call themselves kings, some princes, some dukes, some archdukes, that live only by the sword, and every one of them maketh war and peace without licence of the king." Gerald inherited the earldom in 1513 after the assassination of his father, whose ambition he seems also to have inherited. But Wolsey, on behalf of Henry VIII, takes little interest in Irish affairs and is leaving Kildare and other Anglo-Irish lords to run their protection rackets known as "coyne and livery" (→ 12/1/19).

1516 - 1519

Greenwich, London, 18 February 1516. Henry VIII's queen, Catherine of Aragon, gives birth to a daughter, Mary (→ 6/1525).

Borders, 8 October 1516. Alexander, Lord Home, is executed for defying the orders of the duke of Albany, who is the acting regent for King James V (→ 20/9/17).

Oxford, July 1517. Corpus Christi College, founded by Richard Fox, the bishop of Winchester, opens; it specializes in Greek and theology (→ 5/1518).

Borders, 20 September 1517. The French military commander in Scotland, Antony de la Bastie, is murdered near Dunbar by the Home family in revenge for the execution last year of Lord Home (→ 30/4/20).

London, 1517. King Henry VIII and his court leave London to escape an outbreak of plague in south-east England (→ 11/1520).

York, April 1518. Cardinal Wolsey, the archbishop of York, holds his first provincial synod in an attempt to improve the morals of the clergy (→ 17/5).

Rome, 17 May 1518. Cardinal Wolsey is appointed papal legate in England (→ 1/1522).

London, 12 January 1519. Gerald FitzGerald [Gearoid Og], the earl of Kildare and deputy of Ireland, is to appear before Henry VIII on charges of tyranny (→ 5/11).

Europe, 28 June 1519. Charles of Spain, the lord of the Netherlands and grandson of the late Holy Roman Emperor Maximilian, is elected emperor, taking the name Charles V. King Francis of France and King Henry VIII of England both offered themselves as candidates (→ 7/6/20).

London, July 1519. After Henry VIII's suppression of brothels earlier this year, Cardinal Wolsey leads a midnight raid on those in the city (→ 1546).

Ireland, 5 November 1519. The wardship of "Silken Thomas" FitzGerald, the son of Gerald FitzGerald [Gearoid Og]the earl of Kildare, is granted to Edward, the duke of Buckingham (→ 10/3/20).

London, 1519. Henry VIII's mistress, Elizabeth Blount, gives birth to a son, Henry Fitzroy (→ 18/6/25).

Chancellor plans radical law reforms

Westminster, 2 May 1516

The new lord chancellor, Cardinal Wolsey, is not only the king's chief minister and leader of the council but also chief judge in the courts of chancery and star chamber. He plans to reform the latter – officially "the king's council meeting in the Star Chamber at the palace of Westminster" – into a court which will enforce the rule of law impartially on the highest in the land. Today he spoke before the king and council of "enormities" and abuses of justice prevalent in the kingdom and sent the earl of Northumberland to prison for ravishing a royal ward. He threatens to try noblemen, councillors and JPs for corruption and defiance of the law.

He is extending the court's powers over perjury, libel, forgery and bribing or intimidation of juries in the common law courts. He will also punish contempt of court by bringing it before star chamber, where he sits several days a week.

Wolsey has made plain his belief that rich and poor alike have a right to justice. Anyone with a grievance against the courts can bring the case before him. On most mornings the cardinal sits in the court of chancery, resolving civil disputes and reviewing the verdicts of lesser courts (→ 4/1518).

Wolsey's elaborate palace at Hampton Court is fit for a king

A bold statement of Cardinal Wolsey's pre-eminence: a 20th-century view of the ornate palace at Hampton Court.

Middlesex, May 1516

For those who need outward signs of power and status, the new palace of Hampton Court that Thomas Wolsey has finished building this month announces that he is the greatest subject in the kingdom. The building, some 25 miles (40km) upstream from Westminster is, quite literally, fit for a king.

For others the confirmation of Wolsey's pre-eminence came last year when he received his cardinal's hat from the pope, to go with the positions of archbishop of York and lord chancellor. But by any measure Wolsey's power and wealth are unprecedented, especially for the son of an Ipswich butcher rather than an aristocrat.

The cardinal's taste for ostentatious display has not made him popular, but he is so important to Henry VIII, who at 25 is more inclined to hunting and dancing than chores of administration, that his position seems impregnable.

The huge new palace, built of brick in the ornate turreted style that the king's father, Henry VII, used downriver at Richmond Palace in Surrey, is an ideal setting for the feasting and gaiety that Henry enjoys. But it also serves Wolsey's purposes by showing so clearly who really is a power in the land (→ 1530).

London mobs launch vicious attacks on European immigrants

London, 1 May 1517

Foreigners and their properties were subjected to vicious attacks throughout the city last night by mobs convinced that the newcomers were stealing their livelihoods.

London merchants and craftsmen have for some time been alarmed at the growing influx of immigrants from France, Italy and the Netherlands who have set up here to compete with them. The riots were fomented by John Lincoln, a broker, who persuaded a cleric, Dr Bele, to preach against the foreigners, the merchandise they bring in from Europe and the products they make here.

In anticipation of trouble an evening curfew was imposed. The fighting flared when an alderman sought to arrest a curfew-breaker. The rioters dispersed several hours later after the lieutenant of the Tower of London ordered cannons to be fired into the city.

John Lincoln and Dr Bele will be tried for treason. They face execution for upsetting relations with Europe.

'Utopia' describes life in ideal society

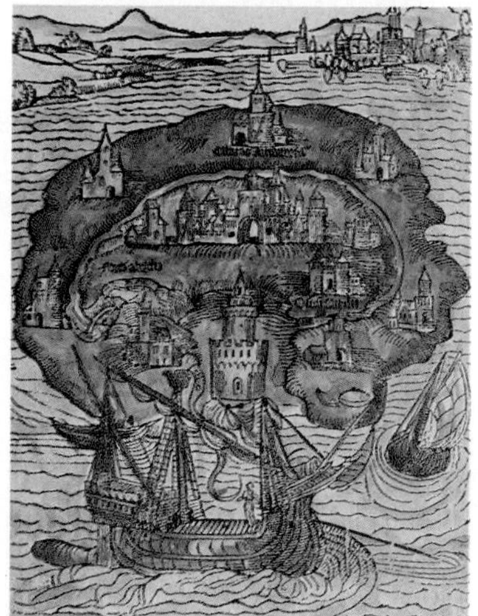

"No place": a page from "Utopia".

Flanders, December 1516
A new book, written by Sir Thomas More, one of England's leading lawyers and a member of parliament, has been published in Louvain. It is called *Utopia* (from the Greek meaning "no place") and is concerned with the search for a perfect form of government. In this "nowhere land" all are equal, men and women are educated together, all religions are tolerated, and satisfaction comes from mental, not material, satisfaction. The book takes the form of a series of voyages – an idea encouraged by the narrative of Vespucci's voyages which appeared in 1507 (→5/1521).

Treaty of London marks diplomatic coup

London, 5 October 1518
England and France have made peace and formed an alliance which also incorporates Christendom's major powers, including Pope Leo X, Holy Roman Emperor Maximilian and his grandson Charles, the ruler of Spain, the Netherlands and Burgundy. The Treaty of London, agreed three days ago, pledges its signatories to keep peace among themselves and to protect Europe from a Turkish invasion.

In a separate treaty signed today by Kings Henry VIII and Francis, the English have ceded the city of Tournai to France in return for 600,000 golden *écus*. The four-month-old *dauphin* [French royal heir] has been promised in marriage to Henry's daughter Mary, and in return for resigning as bishop of Tournai, Cardinal Wolsey is to receive an annual pension. Wolsey has pulled off a great coup in making London the centre of European diplomacy and has played his part in the festivities with great splendour. At royal banquets he shares the king's table, as if he were himself a prince, and he is being talked of as the real ruler of the kingdom.

When peace was proclaimed he officiated at the *Te Deum* in St Paul's, and he gave a sumptuous feast to mark the betrothal of the two-year-old Princess Mary at which 15 swans, four peacocks, six salmon, and dozens of larks were provided. Mary, in a black cap ablaze with jewels, was betrothed with a miniature ring (→28/6/19).

Landowner told to end field enclosures

Sir Nicholas Vaux: in court.

Westminster, 8 November 1518
Sir Nicholas Vaux appeared before Cardinal Wolsey in the court of chancery today charged with illegally erecting hedges to enclose 80 hectares (200 acres), and with destroying four houses on his land at Stantonbury, in Buckinghamshire

Sir Nicholas was bound over on recognizance of £100 to tear down the hedges and rebuild the houses. The case is one of a number to follow enquiries by the royal commission set up last year to determine the extent to which arable land is being converted to pasture, mainly for grazing sheep, at the expense of a sound rural economy (→30/3/34).

Royal College of Physicians is established

A doctor's work: treating the sick.

London, 23 September 1518
In an attempt to protect the public from quacks and charlatans who pass themselves off as medical experts, Henry VIII has granted a charter to establish the Royal College of Physicians here. Its president – Thomas Linacre will be the first – has the power to fine or even imprison anyone who tries to practise without proper qualifications. This is the first formal body to control medicine in England; barbers and surgeons are likely to follow soon (→1540).

In a move to reduce common civil injustices, Cardinal Thomas Wolsey has attacked the profiteering widespread among the nation's market traders. Wolsey has officially ordered the price of poultry to be fixed and is investigating a scarcity of beef, mutton and veal.

France and Scotland forge new alliance

Rouen, France, 26 August 1517
The "Auld Alliance" between Scotland and France was renewed today with a treaty sealed here by the duke of Albany, governor of Scotland during the minority of King James V. The boy king, now five years old, is to marry a daughter of the French king, assuming a princess is available. Albany, who was brought up in France, was invited to assume the role of regent by Scottish nobles who feared the influence of the king's mother, Margaret, a sister of England's King Henry VIII. The dowager queen has also lost favour by marrying the earl of Angus (→19/11/21).

'Trojans' challenge 'Greeks' at Oxford

Oxford, May 1518
King Henry VIII has intervened in a row between "Greeks" and "Trojans" at Oxford University over the correct approach to learning. The Trojans bitterly oppose the ideas of "humanists", who set store by the teaching of Greek as the gateway to a new enlightenment. The humanist movement is led by the Dutch-born scholar Erasmus, who has written a Greek version of the New Testament. When the king heard about the dispute, he declared that all who wished to should be welcome to study Greek – sealing a theoretical victory of Greeks over Trojans (→6/1525).

1520 - 1521

Ireland, 10 March 1520. Thomas Howard, the earl of Surrey, the newly appointed lieutenant, arrives with 1,100 men to take control of the rebellious Gaelic lords (→ 4/5).

Humberside, 29 April 1520. The tower of St Mary's church at Beverley collapses.

Edinburgh, 30 April 1520. Archibald Douglas, the earl of Angus, who is the estranged husband of Queen Margaret Tudor, the former regent of Scotland and mother of King James V, seizes control of the city in a bloody street battle (→ 26/7/24).

London, 4 May 1520. Gerald FitzGerald [Gearoid Og], the rebellious earl of Kildare, is detained (→ 11/6).

Calais, France, 11 June 1520. The earl of Kildare, under the watchful eye of Henry VIII of England, accompanies the entourage to the "Field of Cloth of Gold" peace talks (→ 1/10).

Rome, 19 June 1520. Pope Leo X issues a bull giving Scotland his complete protection.

Munster, 1 October 1520. The earl of Surrey gains the submission of MacCarthy of Desmond and MacCarthy Reagh (→ 16/9/21).

Dublin, November 1520. An outbreak of plague hits the city.

London, May 1521. Thomas More, the author of *Utopia*, which was published five years ago, and also a lawyer, who is currently master of requests, is knighted and appointed under-treasurer of the exchequer (→ 1524).

Low Countries, 25 August 1521. Henry VIII and Holy Roman Emperor Charles V sign a secret treaty at Bruges as allies in the event of war with France (→ 19/6/22).

Ireland, 16 September 1521. The earl of Surrey requests his recall after a mere 18 months in the lieutenancy (→ 21/12).

London, October 1521. King Henry VIII sends the livery of knighthood to Conn Bacach O'Neill of Tyrone, thereby conferring English status on an Irish lord (→ 15/8/22).

Scotland, 19 November 1521. The regent for King James V, John, the duke of Albany, returns to Scotland, having been detained in France since the 1517 Treaty of Rouen as a result of English diplomatic pressure (→ 13/6/22).

Kings meet at 'Field of Cloth of Gold'

Colourful finery at the kings' summit, as seen by Sir John Gilbert (d.1897).

Leaders seek to shape balance of power

Guines, France, 7 June 1520
Amidst the glittering splendour of the "Field of Cloth of Gold", as the site of the Anglo-French summit meeting has come to be known, the two monarchs, Henry VIII of England and Francis of France, have finally got down to serious political negotiations; they are accompanied in their discussions by only their closest advisers.

The summit is largely the work of Henry's lord chancellor, Cardinal Thomas Wolsey, who has been attempting to restore the balance of power in Europe, which was shaken last year when Charles of Spain succeeded to the Austrian inheritance and became Holy Roman Emperor Charles V, thus uniting the two thrones. In Wolsey's view *détente* with France has become a vital necessity. The private talks have been accompanied by much public talk of lasting friendship between the two countries, but it is doubtful whether anything substantial has in fact been achieved. A Venetian observer at the summit, which is being held at Guines, near Calais, claims that the two kings "hate each other cordially".

After his talks with the French, Henry has had a second meeting with the emperor, who is visiting his Netherlands possessions. This was meant as a demonstration of England's evenhandedness in relations with the two continental powers. Charles succeeded in drawing the English into a secret alliance against the French (→ 25/8/21).

Gold and jewels are exchanged as gifts

Guines, France, June 1520
An exchange of costly gifts between Henry VIII and Francis I and their retinues has marked the conclusion of the Anglo-French summit here. The two kings began by producing diamond and ruby rings and, after many magnificent *objets d'art* had changed hands, finished off the ceremony by exchanging horses.

Cardinal Wolsey presented the French queen mother with a cross of precious stones; other French notables received gifts such as gold vases, a gown of cloth of gold lined with sables and a salt cellar of gold studded with jewels. The queen mother gave Wolsey a jewelled crucifix which is thought to be worth some 6,000 crowns. Queen Catherine gave the French Queen Claude palfreys [light horses ridden by women] and received mules and pages adorned with cloth of gold.

Food fit for kings: no expense spared

Guines, France, June 1520
The diplomatic haggling of the Anglo-French summit at Guines, a few miles from Calais, is being accompanied by a series of vast banquets where Henry VIII and Francis, with their ministers, dine in one room, the ladies in another and the gentlemen in a third – all of them meeting afterwards to enjoy music and dancing.

A typical meal of three courses starts with soup, capon, cygnets, venison, pike, heron, pear pies, custard and fritters. Another soup begins the second course, followed by capon, wren, sturgeon, peacock, pigeon, quail, apples, venison, tarts and fritters. It is soup again to open the third course, followed by stork,

Royally entertained: at a banquet.

pheasant, egrets, chicken, gulls, "hagges of almayn" [bone marrow fried in butter], bream, oranges and more fritters.

Each course, carried on dishes with gold covers, is signalled by an overture on 24 trumpets; quieter instrumental music accompanies the eating, which lasts some four hours. As the third course gets under way, heralds arrive to distribute largesse on Henry's behalf.

The meal is washed down with choice wines from the Rhineland, Greece and Gascony, while specially erected fountains pour out French *vin ordinaire* for the general public. Venetian observers at the summit say that the English – especially the ladies – have a reputation for hard drinking.

Campaign launched against 'heresy'

Rome, 11 October 1521
Pope Leo X has today bestowed on King Henry VIII of England the title of *"Fidei Defensor* [Defender of the Faith]" for his forthright book denouncing the teachings of the German theologian Martin Luther. Henry's book, *The Assertion of the Seven Sacraments*, was published in England on 12 July and presented to the pope last week by the English ambassador to Rome, John Clerk.

The king's work, written with the help of a number of advisers, condemns Luther for setting his own views on man's relationship with God against the authority of the pope. The book represents the English establishment's second attack on the writings of Luther in six months. On 12 May the German's works were publicly burned in St Paul's churchyard in the presence of Cardinal Wolsey, the papal nuncio and a crowd of 30,000.

Luther's books have been smuggled into England from Germany, where his attacks on the church have caused a sensation. Beginning with a denunciation of the sale of papal indulgences, Luther has now challenged the church's right to come between man and his worship of God. His ideas first took hold at the university of Cambridge; Wolsey, dismissing the movement, failed to take account of a new technology – printing. Books are being read aloud in inns and at gatherings in private houses (→ 1523).

Martin Luther: attacking Rome.

Lollards also hunted in new heresy probe

Amersham, Bucks, 1521
The clash between Luther and papal authority is not the only source of religious conflict in England this year. John Longland, the new bishop of Lincoln, has begun a ruthless campaign to stamp out a distinctively English heresy – Lollardy. This has its roots in the late 14th-century teachings of John Wyclif; it rejects, among other vital tenets of the church, transubstantiation at the altar and challenges the worldly authority of priests. Successive rounds of persecution sapped the strength of Lollardy, but it has begun to enjoy a revival in the past 25 years.

Much of this renewed growth has occurred in the Thames valley where the new bishop of Lincoln's aides claim that they already have evidence against 400 Lollards in the Chiltern area alone. One Lollard heretic called John Scrivener has just been burnt at the stake, but whether more will follow is an open question. Among the Lollards are some of the wealthiest and most powerful men in the area (→ 11/10).

A heretic's end: burnt at the stake.

Buckingham executed for threat to king

London, 17 May 1521
Edward Stafford, the duke of Buckingham, was executed for treason on Tower Hill today. His alleged disloyalty began many years ago, but his arrest was decided when he asked permission to raise an army to collect his rents in Wales. Summoned to Greenwich Palace on 8 April, he was seized as he passed through London and convicted on the evidence of his servants. They said that he had told them that he would become king of England and had plans to stab the king to death. After the verdict, Buckingham was taken to the Tower by river. An executioner carried an axe with its blade turned towards the duke as a sign of his guilt.

Buckingham: plotting for power.

Earl of Surrey quits as Irish lieutenant

Ireland, 21 December 1521
Thomas, the earl of Surrey and lieutenant of Ireland, has been recalled at his own request after only 21 months in office. On his arrival last year he found the country in a state bordering on anarchy, and he told King Henry VIII so. He requested more men and more money to "pacify" the Irish. The king prefers, however, to adopt a more conciliatory approach. He told Surrey to deal with the Irish lords not by conquest but by "sober ways, politic drifts and amiable persuasions". Surrey has quit all the same, leaving a reputation for fairness unequalled amongst previous rulers (→ 9/1522).

Intellectual Major rewrites 'mythical' history of Scotland

France, 1521
A Scottish intellectual, John Major, has upset his compatriots this year by publishing a book here in which he dismisses as "mythical" the legendary origins of the Scottish nation. He even advocates the heresy of a united British monarchy.

John Major became the principal regent of Glasgow University three years ago, having been educated at Cambridge and in Paris. Now 54 years old, he was born at Gleghornie as the son of an East Lothian farmer. He has published several other books and articles, but none has aroused the controversy of his *History of Greater Britain*.

In this work Major throws out as invalid many of the early Scottish kings and brusquely dismisses the myth that the Scots are descendants of Scota, a daughter of a pharoah. But most provocatively of all, he advocates a common British monarchy. Coming just eight years after the battle at Flodden, and after so much Scottish blood has been spilt in battles against the English, this idea has already been attacked as unpatriotic. The duke of Albany, governor of Scotland during the minority of James V, has just returned from France to take up the cudgels against England.

Until his venture into history Major had been known as a conservative scholastic writer in the fields of theology and philosophy. Some of his countrymen may wish he had stayed that way (→ 1527).

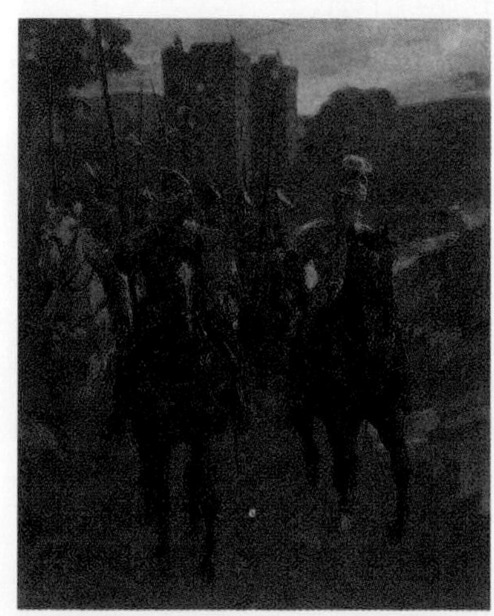

Defending Scotland: border raiders.

1522 - 1523

France/Scotland, 13 June 1522. King Francis of France ratifies the 1517 Treaty of Rouen with the Scots (→ 7/1522).

Windsor, 19 June 1522. Henry VIII and Holy Roman Emperor Charles V sign the Treaty of Windsor (→ 6/7/23).

Borders, July 1522. Scottish nobles, under the command of the regent, John, the duke of Albany, refuse to attack England without the support of the French (→ 17/9).

Co Tyrone, 15 August 1522. Aodh Dubh O'Donnell, the lord of Tyrconnell, defeats a confederation of Irish lords led by Con Bacach O'Neill at Knockavoe, near Strabane (→ 1/1/23).

Borders, 17 September 1522. An Anglo-Scots truce is agreed (→ 25/10).

Irish Sea, September 1522. English ships patrol after Henry VIII discovers that James Fitzmaurice FitzGerald, the earl of Desmond, is in secret negotiations with King Francis of France (→ 25/2/25).

France, 15 October 1522. An unsuccessful expedition into Picardy, led by Thomas Howard, the earl of Surrey, returns to Calais (→ 6/7/23).

Fife, 25 October 1522. The regent, John, the duke of Albany, embarks at Dumbarton for France in the hope of acquiring French military support against the English (→ 6/1523).

London, 1522. Gavin Douglas, the bishop of Dunkeld and celebrated Scottish poet, who translated Vergil's *Aeneid* into Scots as the *Eneados*, dies.

Ireland, 1 January 1523. Gerald FitzGerald, the earl of Kildare, returns after four years' detention in England (→ 5/1523).

Ulster, May 1523. The earl of Kildare defeats Aodh Buidhe O'Neill of Clandeboye and captures Belfast Castle and Carrickfergus (→ 12/1523).

Borders, June 1523. English troops burn Kelso Abbey on a border raid (→ 24/9).

Borders, 24 September 1523. Thomas Howard, the earl of Surrey, and his troops burn Jedburgh Abbey (→ 3/11).

Ireland, December 1523. Aodh Dubh O'Donnell, the lord of Tyrconnell, approaches the Scots in an attempt to make an alliance (→ 7/1524).

Poet turns satirical pen against Wolsey

John Skelton: a literary critic.

London, November 1522
Cardinal Wolsey, the king's chief minister and the architect of England's diplomatic manoeuvrings in Europe, has come under attack from a new and unlikely source. The pen of John Skelton, usually known for such allegorical poems as *Phyllyppe Sparrow* (1505) and *The Tunnyng of Elinour Rummyng* (1517), has been turned on the cardinal, attacking what the poet sees as Wolsey's abuse of his position and relentless self-promotion during his rise to ecclesiastical and political power.

Such piercing satires as *Collyn Clout* (a tramp's complaint against corrupt clergymen), *Speke Parrot* and *Why come ye nat to Court?* are all focused on Wolsey, pillorying him for his alleged megalomania and underlining the ill effects such a politician may bring upon on the country at large.

Nor is Skelton averse to attacking what he sees as the general corruption of both church and court. His first satire, *The Bowge of Court*, in which he mocked the excesses condoned by King Henry VII, appeared in 1498, long before Wolsey's rise to power.

For all this outspoken verse, Skelton has been honoured by those whom he attacks. He was created "poet laureate" by the universities of Oxford, Cambridge and Louvain, and tutored Henry VIII when he was still a prince. He enjoys a reputation for great learning and was admitted to holy orders in 1498. He was the rector of Diss, in Norfolk, before moving to Westminster in 1511 (→ 21/2/24).

Military reserves checked by survey

Westminster, September 1522
The first results of a national survey of England's financial capacity and military strength are now coming in. The inquiry – set up in March by Cardinal Wolsey – shows that, in 28 counties, there are 128,250 men available for conscripted service under their traditional obligation to serve in territorial militias led by the local nobility and gentry. A third of these are archers.

The survey is necessary to bring the force up to date in preparation for the invasion of France planned for next spring. But since the war will cost large sums of money, an assessment of people's means is also being made to enable the crown to demand a "loan" from the wealthy. Wolsey promises to refund the loan from the proceeds of the next subsidy raised by parliament. He hopes by this means to raise a very large sum – possibly £250,000.

Wolsey is thwarted in bid to be pope

Rome, January 1522
The apparently relentless rise of Cardinal Wolsey has met a setback. He has failed in his attempt to be elected pope here in Rome. Wolsey believed that he had the support of Holy Roman Emperor Charles V, and therefore of his cardinals in the conclave, but other cardinals opposed his candidacy, thinking him too young at 49. Wolsey received at best only 19 votes out of 39.

However, he is not without consolation in England. Last year he became abbot of St Albans, which is the third richest monastery in England. Not being a monk, Wolsey was not qualified to be an abbot, but he was granted a dispensation allowing him to hold the office in addition to being archbishop of York and bishop of Bath and Wells. He rarely visits any of his sees, from which he has been given leave of absence (→ 11/1522).

Pay your tithes or forgo communion, parishioners told

Rural tithes are easier to assess.

London, 1523
Robert Shoter, the curate of St Botolph's in Aldgate, has shocked his parishioners with an outburst against those who do not pay their tithes, or church dues. Describing the culprits as "naughty fellows and heretics", he has denied them Communion at Easter. Tithes and similar payments are now the leading source of friction between laity and clergy, especially in London; they are harder to calculate in cities than in rural communities, where they are one tenth of agricultural produce. Many clergy have sued their parishioners over tithes (→ 1525).

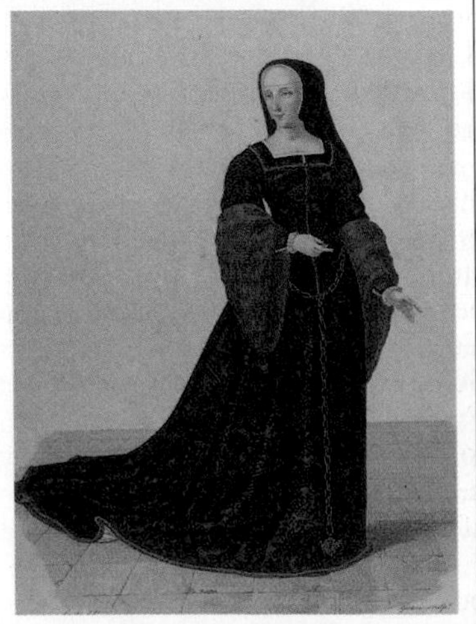

Elaborate style: ladies' fashion is for flowing robes with splendid decorated cuffs on the sleeve.

Wolsey wins more money for French war

Westminster, 6 July 1523
The House of Commons, after prolonged resistance, at last agreed today to grant the king part of the subsidy for the war with France that Wolsey has been demanding. The "loan" that Wolsey raised last year and promised to repay is still outstanding, so that when he summoned parliament in April and demanded a further £800,000 there was much opposition.

As lord chancellor Wolsey has no right to enter the House of Commons, but he went there from the Lords with an armed retinue and demanded admission. The speaker, Sir Thomas More (selected with the king's approval), persuaded the members to admit Wolsey, but the chancellor only succeeded in making them grant half of what he desired – a tax of two shillings [ten pence] in the pound on lands and goods, instead of four shillings.

Parliament was prorogued until July when the Commons again defeated the proposal, and More had to intervene to calm tempers in the house. The rates of tax finally agreed are only slightly better than those Wolsey previously refused.

Thomas Wolsey: lord chancellor.

The tax will be a subsidy, like that developed since 1512, in which the richest noblemen will have their income strictly assessed and pay 5 per cent of it in tax (→15/12).

Relief of Wark Castle is setback for Scots

Northumberland, 3 November 1523
The Franco-Scots army was today forced to retreat northwards when Thomas Howard, the earl of Surrey, relieved the besieged castle at Wark, in Northumberland. This is the latest setback for what has been a disappointing campaign for the Scots, who have been led by the regent, John, the duke of Albany.

During the past summer English raids have resulted in the burning of Kelso and Jedburgh in the Borders, but Albany's return from France with 4,000 infantry and more than 500 cavalry raised Scottish hopes for a counter-attack this autumn. But the lateness of the season, poor organization and tension between the Scots and the French have ensured another failure barely ten years after the fiasco at Flodden.

Neither the French nor the Scots seem particulary distressed that their joint expedition is over. The French suffered repeated criticism from their Scottish allies, who regarded them as haughty and said that they burnt too much winter fuel to keep warm (→20/5/24).

Free from siege: a 20th-century view of the castle at Wark, Northumberland.

Duke's army gives up attack on Paris

France, 15 December 1523
The duke of Suffolk and his army of 11,000 troops have been forced to abandon their march on Paris and retreat to Valenciennes with their Dutch allies. The failure of Charles, the duke of Bourbon and constable of France, to provide his promised support to overthrow King Francis resulted in a crushing failure for Suffolk only 50 miles from the French capital.

Despite a number of problems – inadequate transport, an outbreak of smallpox and disagreements over strategy – Suffolk's campaign had been full of promise: landing in Calais in August, he crossed the Somme and was a threat to Paris. Progress was so good that Wolsey told King Henry VIII "there shall never be such an opportunity hereafter for the attaining of France".

But Suffolk's men, without support, began to mutiny. The duke's plan to winter in northern France and launch a fresh attack in the spring was foiled by bitterly cold weather (→1524).

Author compares women with horses

England, 1523
A farmer should rely on the same criteria when choosing a wife as those he uses to select a horse. This is the considered advice of an author named Master Fitzherbert in his *Boke of Husbandrie*, which was written this year.

Desirable qualities in both woman and beast, says Fitzherbert, should include a good temper, a broad forehead and broad buttocks. The farmer's ideal woman should also be "well paced", good on a long journey, easy to jump on and strong under a man.

Master Fitzherbert goes on to list an exhausting number of "workes" that a good and attentive farmer's wife should undertake during her day. As well as thoroughly cleaning the house and preparing three large meals for her family and servants, he says that she should be able to make cheese and butter, tend the farm animals and crops, spin flax, make clothes, sheets and towels, and also take produce from the homestead to market.

Lady's French style is not without tears

Anne Boleyn: lady-in-waiting at the centre of a major row at court.

Hampton Court, spring 1523
Anne Boleyn, among the most stylish of Queen Catherine's ladies-in-waiting, is at the centre of a row involving Lord Henry Percy – a member of Thomas Wolsey's household and heir to the great Northumberland fortune – and the lord chancellor himself. Anne, chic after several years at the French court, has "all the puppy dogs of the court baying at her heels", according to one observer. Percy, the front-runner, was said to have won a promise of marriage despite the fact that he was betrothed to another. Apparently at the instigation of Henry VIII himself, Wolsey reprimanded Percy, who was told by his own father that he would "benefit little" from his father's will if he pursued the romance (→3/8/27).

1524 - 1525

Scotland, 20 May 1524. The regent, John, the duke of Albany, sails for France to discuss marriage proposals for the young James V to a French princess (→ 26/7).

Scotland, 26 July 1524. A palace coup returns Queen Margaret and her pro-English allies to power in the absence of John, the duke of Albany (→ 16/11).

Ireland, July 1524. Gerald FitzGerald [Gearoid Og], the earl of Kildare, and Piers Ruadh Butler, the earl of Ormond, agree to settle their differences, regulate their private armies and reduce the exactions of their "coyne and livery" protection rackets (→ 24/9/25).

Scotland, 16 November 1524. The regency of John, the duke of Albany, ends on his failure to return and reclaim power from Queen Margaret, the mother of James V (→ 3/1526).

London, 1524. Soap is manufactured in England for the first time.

England, 1524. Royal funds are greatly diminished because of the long, costly war with France; Cardinal Wolsey introduces the "Amicable Grant", a non-parliamentary tax, to raise money (→ 13/5/25).

Europe, 25 February 1525. Holy Roman Emperor Charles V defeats and captures King Francis of France at Pavia (→ 6/1525).

Southern England, 13 May 1525. Taxpayers refuse to pay the "Amicable Grant", and it is withdrawn (→ 14/4/36).

London, 18 June 1525. Henry Fitzroy, the bastard son of Henry VIII, is created duke of Richmond (→ 8/1325).

Europe, June 1525. Emperor Charles V repudiates the terms of the 1521 Treaty of Windsor; he refuses to marry Mary, the only daughter of Henry VIII (→ 7/1536).

Co Tyrone, 24 September 1525. The earl of Kildare allies with Conn Bacach O'Neill, the lord of Tyrone, against Aodh Dubh O'Donnell, the lord of Tyrconnell (→ 24/3/28).

Scotland, 1525. The Scottish parliament bans all heretical literature and discussion of Protestant ideas (→ 26/1/26).

Germany, 1525. Printing begins of an English translation of the Bible by William Tyndale, an English Lutheran (→ 1526).

Wolsey gets job for life

Westminster, 21 January 1524
Cardinal Wolsey has at last attained his wish to be made papal legate for life. Since 1518 he has been legate – the equivalent of the pope's special envoy – but only for a year at a time.

As legate, Wolsey is in a position to overrule the decisions and courts of the archbishop of Canterbury. Since he himself is archbishop of York, his writ runs throughout the land. His latest acquisition is the bishopric of Durham, instead of Bath and Wells, but he has never been able to displace William Warham as archbishop of Canterbury.

Wolsey has plans to reform the church, close some of the smaller and ill-run monasteries and create new dioceses to serve the changed patterns of population. But he is himself a glaring example of abuse of power, with his many bishoprics, which he never visits, his enormous income, estimated at £12,000 a year (twice that of anyone but King Henry VIII), and his notorious lack of celibacy. He has a son and a daughter by a Mistress Lark, the daughter of an innkeeper. The boy is known as "Thomas Winter, the cardinal's nephew".

His interference in other bishops' sees, his taking over of part of their revenues, the fees he exacts for probate of wills, his appointment of foreign absentee bishops and his despotic ways have made him hated by the clergy (→ 18/10/29).

The first lady behind the speaker's chair

The family of Sir Thomas More: Margaret rests an open book on her knee.

London, 1524
Margaret More, the eldest daughter of Sir Thomas, the eloquent speaker of the House of Commons, was born with a silver bookmark in her mouth. At 18 she has just published an excellent English translation from Latin of Erasmus's *Devout treatise upon the Pater Noster.*

Erasmus is a family friend, as are other humanists like Reginald Pole and John Veysey. "Erudition in women is a new thing and a reproach to the idleness of men" writes her father, so she has had an unusually full classical education, learning Greek, logic, philosophy, theology and mathematics. As a child she would write a letter to her father in Latin every day. She is his favourite, being the only one allowed to wash his hair-shirt.

Despite the education, her marriage at 15 was rumoured to be less enlightened. She first encountered her husband-to-be when her father brought him into a bedroom where she slept with her sister. He pulled back the sheets and chose the naked body he preferred (→ 25/10/29).

Royal children are named to head new councils of Marches

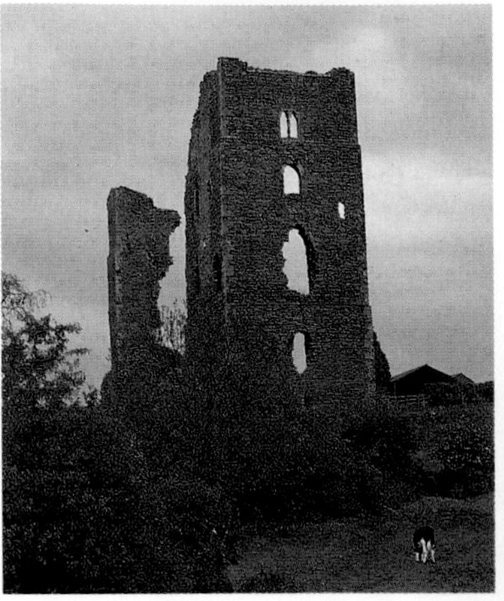

Duke's castle: Sheriff Hutton.

Westminster, August 1525
Henry VIII has appointed his bastard son, Henry Fitzroy, the duke of Richmond, warden-general of the northern Marches and lieutenant-general in the north of England. The king's daughter, Mary, has been given a council to administer Wales and the Welsh Marches.

The duke will take up residence at Sheriff Hutton, in Yorkshire, and the princess at Ludlow, in Shropshire. The two children will exercise no direct authority themselves – for the princess is nine, and the duke even younger. The councils which will rule in their name have been appointed by Cardinal Wolsey and are made up of priests, knights, lawyers and some members of the nobility.

At present the Marches are badly governed by a welter of lordships under no effective central control. The cardinal intends to remedy this situation and has hit upon the device of appointing the two royal children to these important positions while in fact keeping them under his own control and using "new men" for the task. He is likely to succeed more in Wales than in the north of England where the nobles remain very powerful.

Regular courts will be set up throughout the Marches. Commissions will be sent to each county to organize juries and inquiries into crimes. The council has been told to ensure that priority is given to the poorest litigants, who are to be provided with lawyers (→ 22/6/29).

Church lands are seized to fund colleges

Righteous anger: the deprived monks are led away against their will.

Oxford, June 1525
Cardinal Wolsey, whose palaces surpass those of King Henry VIII in splendour, is raising money to pay for planned new colleges at Oxford and Ipswich by suppressing small religious houses and taking over their assets. Some of these communities consist of only three people but own valuable goods and lands.

Wolsey is planning a new college at Oxford University to produce well-educated young men for the priesthood, and a new school at his birthplace, Ipswich, to get students ready for the university. The new Oxford college – to be named Cardinal's College in his honour – is intended as a place "where scholars shall be brought up in virtue and qualified for the priestly dignity". He is planning it on the grand scale, with imported stone, and large enough to take 500 students at a time. Last year he took possession of the monastery of St Frideswide in Oxford to make way for the new college. On this site, he is looking to incorporate the priory church into the complex as the chapel for the new college.

Wolsey's purge may be seen as one of the church's periodic attempts to impose a degree of discipline on its less respectable elements. Over the last year some 80 monks, canons and nuns of more than a dozen orders have been deprived of their homes. Some of these have been pensioned off, but many face an uncertain future and the threat of poverty (→ 19/12/46).

The finished building: Cardinal's College, Oxford, as drawn in 1566.

East Anglia rises against unpopular tax

Suffolk, 11 May 1525
A rebellion by the agricultural and clothing communities of Suffolk and other areas of East Anglia over another government fund-raising venture has been crushed without loss of life. After a confrontation outside Lavenham, a prosperous cloth town [*see below*], several thousand demonstrators asked for pardon and have been indicted for riot and unlawful assembly.

The uprising has followed a new attempt to raise money for Henry VIII's aggressive foreign policy by raising a levy of one-sixth on the goods of the laity and one-third on the goods of the clergy. Opposition to this so-called "Amicable Grant" has been widespread, despite talk of its being modified so that taxpayers would be sounded out about how much they could pay.

The trouble began after talks on the tax between the duke of Suffolk and rich clothiers, who told their workers that as a result some of them would have to be laid off. One report says that about 10,000 demonstrators led by a wizened little weaver from Long Melford, John Grene, surrendered to a force of 4,000 gentry and their tenantry headed by the dukes of Norfolk and Suffolk. But the Amicable Grant is now likely to be scrapped (→ 13).

Wool profits fund church improvements

Lavenham, Suffolk, 1525
The church of Saints Peter and Paul at Lavenham has attracted the envy of nearby parishes this year with the completion of a magnificent new tower and chapel. The chapel bears the name of the Springs, the local family of prosperous wool merchants which funded it, and which combined with the lord of the manor, the earl of Oxford, to pay for the tower.

The church at Lavenham.

The boom in Britain's wool and cloth industry has been particularly advantageous for local churches. In many of the most successful towns in East Anglia and the west country, lavish improvements have been funded by merchants keen to glorify and perpetuate their family names.

Masons and sculptors who have enjoyed the benefits of this patronage are contributing to a new style in church architecture. It is characterized by tall towers, ornate timbered roofs and richly decorated porches. The splendid timber roof at the church of St Mary at Woolpit, in Suffolk, distinctive on account of its beautifully embellished short horizontal beams (which are known as "hammerbeams"), was finished towards the end of the last century. St Wendreda's church, at March in Cambridgeshire, has a vast hammerbeam roof, adorned with 200 carved angels, which is widely renowned.

St Mary's, Woolpit: the roof.

1526 - 1528

Scotland, March 1526. Queen Margaret, the regent for her son James V, not yet divorced from Archibald Douglas, the earl of Angus, secretly marries Henry Stewart, the treasurer and lord chancellor (→ 4/9).

England, August 1526. Hans Holbein, a German painter, arrives at court (→ 5/1527).

Lothian, 4 September 1526. The earl of Angus, who refused to release James V from his custody, defeats and kills the earl of Lennox in his rescue bid.→

Ipswich, 1527. Thomas Bilney, a Lutheran preacher, is arrested and sent to the Tower of London (→ 1/1527).

England, January 1527. John Fisher, the bishop of Rochester, publishes *De veritate corporis et sanguinis Christi in Eucharista* in which he attacks the Lutheran movement (→ 29/2/28).

England/France, 30 April 1527. The signing of the Treaty of Westminster allies England and France against Holy Roman Emperor Charles V (→ 20/10/32).

England/France, July 1527. Henry VIII's decision to divorce his queen, Catherine of Aragon, halts plans for his daughter, Mary, to marry a French prince; her status after the divorce may be different (→ 3/1530).

Scotland, 1527. Hector Boece publishes *Histories of the Scots from the origin of the race*, rejecting the demythologizing of Scottish history by his former teacher, John Major, in favour of romantic nationalist traditions (→ 1534).

Ireland, 23 February 1528. Piers Ruadh Butler, until now earl of Ormond, is made earl of Ossory; Sir Thomas Boleyn, the earl of Wiltshire and father of Henry VIII's present mistress, Anne, is the new earl of Ormond (→ 24/3).

Ulster, 24 March 1528. Conn Bacach O'Neill, the earl of Tyrone, asks for free passage for his subjects throughout the Pale, which is in recession and hungry for cheap labour (→ 4/8).

Ireland, 4 August 1528. The earl of Ossory is made deputy (→ 11/11).

Spain, 11 November 1528. An agent of James fitz Maurice FitzGerald, the earl of Desmond, visits Toledo to negotiate with Holy Roman Emperor Charles V (→ 4/8/29).

Church faces 'Protestant' challenge

The new testament.

The gospell of S Mathew.
The gospell of S.Marke.
The gospell of S.Luke.
The gospell of S. Jhon.
The Actes of the Apostles

The epistles of S. Paul.

The epistle unto the Romaynes.
The first and seconde epistle to the Corinthians
The epistle to the Galathians.
The epistle to the Ephesians.
The epistle to the Philippians.
The epistle to the Colossians.
The first and secode epistle to the Tessalonians
The first and seconde epistle unto Tymothy.
The epistle unto Titus.
The epistle unto Philemon.
The first and seconde epistle of S. peter.
The thre epistles of S. Jhon.
The epistle unto the Hebrues.
The epistle of S. James.
The epistle of S. Jude.
The Revelacion of S. Jhon.

A title-page from William Tyndale's English translation of the Bible.

English edition of New Testament burnt

London, 1526
A new edition of the New Testament, translated from the Latin by William Tyndale, a leading scholar and an avowed "Protestant", has been burnt on orders of the bishops. Tyndale has thus gained the dubious honour of being the first Englishman ever to have a printed book burnt in his native country.

The bishops objected to what they called his "seditious" notes on the scriptures, and, after collecting every one of the 6,000 copies that appeared in England this March, they had all but one of them burnt outside St Paul's Cathedral.

Tyndale, who has dedicated his life to his vernacular version of the Bible, has always faced problems with the English hierarchy. He began work in 1522, but when his efforts were condemned as "pernicious merchandise" he went to Germany, where he visited the reformer Martin Luther and then settled in Cologne. Driven from Cologne, he finished and published the New Testament at Worms last year.

Once released in England the book proved very popular, bringing the scriptures to many whose education did not extend to Latin. This was seen as a threat by the authorities, and the bonfire at St Paul's was the outcome of their concern. Indeed, so worried are they by Tyndale's "sedition" that efforts are being made to hunt down copies circulating in Europe as well. Cardinal Wolsey has also ordered his agents to pursue Tyndale himself.

The author, safe in Germany, has no plans to abandon his work. He has now turned to the Old Testament and is currently working on the Pentateuch, the five books of Moses (→ 1527).

Lutheran heretics face death threats

London, 26 January 1526
Three German merchants were arrested today on the orders of Cardinal Wolsey and charged with importing heretical books. They were taken from the Steelyard, the headquarters of the Hanseatic League, by Sir Thomas More, the chancellor of the duchy of Lancaster, and a large bodyguard. The arrest is part of Wolsey's campaign against Lutheranism, the "Protestant" reform movement whose followers have been attacking both the orthodox Catholic Church and Wolsey as a symbol of its faults.

While the merchants are not accused of spreading the new faith, it is believed that their comings and goings between Germany, the cradle of Lutheranism, and England provide a perfect opportunity for smuggling prohibited texts, notably William Tyndale's translation of the New Testament. The flow of such texts has been increasing, and, as Sir Thomas More told the accused men, it has "been causing great error in the Christian faith amongst his majesty the king's subjects", errors which "first arose in the Steelyard". It appears that one merchant in particular is suspected of smuggling. He was not among those arrested, and his partners have been ordered to deliver him to the cardinal. They all must stay in England for 20 days (→ 1/1527).

George Gisze, a German merchant.

King seeks to end 20-year marriage

London, 22 June 1527
Henry VIII summoned his wife, Catherine of Aragon, to his presence today to tell her that they have been living in sin for 20 years – or so he claims. Cardinal Wolsey, both the king's chancellor and the papal envoy, has sent envoys to Rome to persuade the pope to annull the marriage on the grounds that Henry should not have married his elder brother's widow.

Whether the pope will agree is unlikely. Queen Catherine is the aunt of Holy Roman Emperor Charles V, whose troops are occupying Rome. The marriage was only allowed after an earlier papal dispensation, and the pope is unlikely to cancel that. Catherine is also resisting an end to the marriage, saying she was a virgin when she married Henry so that there is no question of an incestuous marriage as the king claimed. The queen is also concerned about the succession rights of their one surviving child, 11-year-old Princess Mary, who would be made illegitimate if the marriage were ended.

Despite eight pregnancies Catherine has produced only one surviving child, Mary, and Henry is anxious that Mary's marriage to a foreign bridegroom could damage English interests. Henry is desperate for a male heir and has elevated his illegitimate son, Henry Fitzroy, to the dukedom of Richmond. He is also entranced by a courtier, Anne Boleyn (→ 7/1527).

Henry and Catherine: locked in disagreement after 20 years of marriage.

Henry Fitzroy: now a duke.

Henry gives lavish gifts to new courtier

London, 3 August 1527
No one at the royal court now doubts that Henry VIII is totally, romantically and hopelessly in love. The king is showering expensive presents – rings, brooches, bracelets and a sparkling assortment of other jewellery including diamonds set in lovers' knots – on a 26-year-old courtier, Anne Boleyn.

Letters from the king make it abundantly clear that he regards himself as betrothed to Anne and plans to marry her as soon as his divorce has been arranged. Even before he decided to divorce his present wife he wanted Anne to be his mistress. Her sister, Mary, is said have enjoyed his affections, but court gossip insists that Anne has spiritedly withheld her favours. She hopes to be wife and queen rather than mistress.

Henry is infatuated. After telling Anne of his divorce plans last June, he wrote this week assuring his love that "henceforth my heart shall be dedicate to you alone ..." and enclosing her initials in a heart-shaped design. The king awaits, with some impatience, papal approval for his divorce (→ 14/7/31).

Teenage king held hostage by stepfather

Lothian, 4 September 1526
The earl of Lennox was killed today in an unsuccessful attempt to free Scotland's 14-year-old king, James V, from captivity. Victory in the battle went to the Douglas family, which is holding the king as a prisoner in Stirling Castle.

James should have been freed in June when Archibald Douglas, the earl of Angus, ended his tenure as custodian of the young king. But Angus refused to do this, prompting unavailing rescue attempts by Lennox, first near Abbotsford and then again today at Linlithgow. The way is now clear for the earl to strengthen his hold on the levers of government. Ironically, the king's captor is his stepfather. The earl married the king's mother, Margaret Tudor, in 1514, and this enabled him to boost the position of the Douglas family. A palace coup in 1524 effectively ended the regency of John, the duke of Albany, and affirmed the dominance of the pro-English faction centred upon the dowager Queen Margaret. This faction is now seeking power in its own right following Margaret's divorce from the earl of Angus and her remarriage this year to Henry Stewart, Lord Methven (→ 6/7/28).

Realism of German artist's portraits is the talk of society

London, May 1527
Hans Holbein, a German artist from Augsburg, has amazed London society with the astonishing realism of his new style of painting. He arrived in England last year from war-torn Switzerland and, like many other foreign artists, quickly found work in court circles. Among his first patrons was the lawyer and scholar Sir Thomas More, to whom he was recommended by the scholar Erasmus.

Holbein has just completed a group portrait of Sir Thomas and his family which is causing a sensation. From the texture of Sir Thomas's skin and the stubble of his beard to the fabrics of the clothes and curtains, Holbein conveys an intense realism as well as a mastery of oil painting. Another work has the astronomer Nicholas Kratzer surrounded by instruments – using the portrait medium to reflect a subject's life as well as his appearance. Holbein, who is in his late twenties, works at great speed, completing chalk and watercolour drawings that form the basis of his paintings in only three hours.

Holbein plans to return to Europe this year, but his court connections are so strong and his reputation so high that he expects to visit England again before long (→ 1538). ▷

The Holbein style, seen here in his portrait of a "lady with a squirrel".

Scottish Protestant burnt at the stake

Fife, 29 February 1528
The first Protestant martyr was burnt at the stake today at St Andrews. Patrick Hamilton, who was a young teacher at the local university, faced death with great courage, his agony having been intensified by slow-burning flames on a cold and damp day.

Hamilton had led the Protestants at St Andrews, heading the most active cell of Protestantism in Scotland – much to the embarrassment of Archbishop James Beaton, who is the university's chancellor. Elsewhere in Scotland Protestantism has made little headway, although anti-heresy legislation in 1525 and 1527 betrayed growing concern.

Hamilton, who was 24, was a graduate of Paris and had studied at Louvain before returning to St Andrews in 1523. Last year he was disciplined by Archbishop Beaton for encouraging Lutheran opinion in St Leonard's college. Hamilton, a relative of the archbishop, went abroad to Marburg where his Protestant ideas were confirmed. On his return he appeared to court martyrdom, refusing to flee abroad when alerted to possible arrest.

Damp conditions today made it difficult to start a fire, so gunpowder was added. This caused Hamilton to be badly scorched, but he remained unrepentant to the end, showing exemplary fortitude. Church leaders hope that this will deter other would-be heretics, but some fear that Protestants will be inspired by martyrdom (→ 10/1529).

Protestant martyr: the teacher Patrick Hamilton is burnt at the stake.

Irish rackets lead to emigration to Wales

Dyfed, 1528
Over this year a huge number of Irishmen – reckoned to be around 20,000 – have emigrated to Wales. They landed in Pembrokeshire and have spread throughout the county.

Their motive lies in the feud that has raged between the Butlers and the Geraldines – the FitzGerald family, which has its origins in Pembrokeshire. Last year James fitz Maurice FitzGerald, the earl of Desmond, launched a campaign against Piers Ruadh Butler, the then earl of Ormond; James Butler, Ormond's son, besieged FitzGerald at Dungarvan, in Co Waterford, but he escaped and took to the sea with some 40 men.

Many, if not most, emigrants are fleeing the burden of the "coin and livery" rackets, by which ordinary people are obliged to pay protection money to support the armies of feuding lords. In parts of Wales the Irish now greatly outnumber the natives. Many Irish ships are engaged in trade or piracy, with Desmond taking a share of the profits to finance his battles at home.

Teenage king leads an army into Scottish capital to assume control of his realm

Edinburgh, 6 July 1528
Scotland's teenage king, James V, today entered Edinburgh with an army of supporters to assert his right to rule his kingdom. He has been king since his father died at Flodden in 1513, but until this summer he has been a mere pawn in the power battles between leading Scottish families.

He was brought up nominally by his mother, the English-born Margaret Tudor. She married the earl of Angus, a leading member of the powerful Douglas family, and between them they saw off the regency of the duke of Albany, the French-based heir to the throne. But the earl refused to surrender James when his turn as the young king's custodian came to an end in 1526 and held James, in effect, a prisoner.

With the king captive and the chancellor, Archbishop Beaton, too weak to offer serious opposition, Angus developed a stranglehold on the government of Scotland, with key posts given to members of the Douglas family. It is said that James was not a total captive – he has already, at 16, gained a reputation as a womanizer from nightly excursions. However, on 27 May this year he escaped and fled to Stirling Castle where he rallied supporters. Now it is the turn of his stepfather, Angus, and other members of the Douglas family to flee as James moves to regain control of his kingdom (→ 11/5/34).

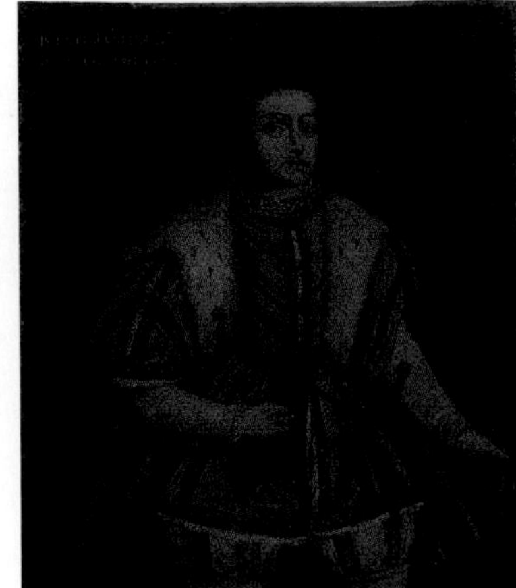

James V, the 16-year-old king of Scotland: a pawn in power battles.

Magic healer gives away herbal secrets

London, 11 November 1528
As growing numbers are unable to afford the services of orthodox medicinal men, and cling to their traditional faith and folklore in these questioning times, the services of the "magician", "sorcerer" and "wise woman" have rarely been more eagerly sought after.

Today one "sorcerer", Margaret Hunt, revealed her secrets to the bishop of London's commissary. The "secrets" turned out to be a combination of Latin prayers and natural herbs, an ancient formula, she claimed, passed down to her by an old Welsh witch, Mother Elmet. For the ague she prescibed herbs, for sores she prescribes herbs and honey, mixed with holy water, to be taken with prayers. Most of the herbs are in fact traditional folk remedies, used by the peasantry for hundreds of years.

The prayers are usually in Latin (to impress the sick client), or, if in the vernacular, couched in religious language. Hunt told her patients to recite eight *Paternosters*, eight *Aves* and four *Creeds*, "in the worship of Saint Spirit". In spite of the efforts of the church, these "holy healers" are gaining increasing popularity with their simple message that all you need is a little faith.

To some a "wise woman", to others a "witch" and an enemy of religion.

Dublin, 1 June 1529. John Alen, the archbishop of Dublin and newly appointed vice-legate of Ireland, begins to reclaim church land from Gerald FitzGerald, the earl of Kildare (→ 4/8).

Ireland, 22 June 1529. Henry Fitzroy, the duke of Richmond, Henry VIII's illegitimate son, is appointed lieutenant (→ 22/7/36).

England, June 1529. John Skelton, the poet who attacked the power of Wolsey, dies.

Ireland, 4 August 1529. A secret council headed by the archbishop of Dublin sacks Piers Butler, the earl of Ossory, from his position as deputy (→ 2/6/30).

London, 18 October 1529. Cardinal Wolsey is ordered by Henry VIII to surrender the great seal, the badge of office of the lord chancellor(→ 30).

London, 25 October 1529. Sir Thomas More, a lawyer and advocate of moderate church reform, is appointed lord chancellor (→ 16/5/32).

Waltham, Essex, 1529. Thomas Cranmer, a divinity lecturer, becomes royal chaplain and archdeacon of Taunton after Henry VIII consults him on his divorce proceedings (→ 1/1531).

Calais, 1529. Thomas Wyatt, a courtier and poet, is appointed high marshal.

Bologna, Italy, March 1530. Sir Thomas Boleyn, the earl of Ormond and father of Anne, Henry VIII's favourite, visits Pope Clement VII to persuade him to agree to the king's divorce (→ 8/4/30).

Oxford, 8 April 1530. The universities of Oxford and Cambridge vote in favour of a divorce for Henry (→ 9/1530).

Ireland, 2 June 1530. Sir William Skeffington replaces Lord Ossory as deputy (→ 1531).

Rome, September 1530. The pope politely ignores a letter signed by English nobles, under pressure from Henry VIII, trying to make him agree to the king's divorce (→ 1/1531).

Leicester, 24 November 1530. Cardinal Wolsey, arrested for treason earlier this month and being taken from York to the Tower of London, dies at Leicester Abbey (→ late 1530).

Hampton Court, late 1530. Henry VIII takes possession of the palace given to him by Wolsey in 1525 (→ c.1536).

1529-1530

Cardinal Wolsey is stripped of power

London, 30 October 1529
The ruin of Cardinal Wolsey was made final today when he pleaded guilty before the king's bench to the near-treasonable offence of "praemunire" – for which he was sentenced to imprisonment and the forfeiture of all his property to King Henry VIII. Two weeks ago he was ordered to give up the lord chancellor's great seal, and on 25 October Sir Thomas More was appointed lord chancellor in his place.

"Praemunire", an offence since 1353, is the usurping of the king's sovereign powers in his realm. Wolsey's exercise of his powers as papal legate in his own court was cited. But the underlying reason is the king's desire to break with Wolsey's other master, the pope, under the influence of Anne Boleyn who has made him promise not to give Wolsey a hearing in person.

The cardinal's humiliation: Wolsey is forced to give up his seal of office.

So the cardinal, who until a few weeks ago was the near-equal of the king, sitting in judgement on Henry's divorce, is brought low, to the delight of the courtiers who have long resented his pride, greed and ostentation and his hold over the king. Wolsey, who is 55, pleaded guilty on the understanding that the king would allow him to remain at liberty and keep his estates as archbishop of York, provided that he gave the king York Place. Wolsey has already surrendered Hampton Court; Henry is expected to make this a royal palace in name as well as style (→ 24/11/30).

Anti-church propaganda war escalates

Upholding the faith: a reconstruction of the sacristy at Cleeve Abbey, Glos.

London, 30 October 1529
With Cardinal Wolsey dismissed as lord chancellor, a powerful defender of the church against attacks has been removed, at a time when anti-church propaganda is growing.

Anti-clerical feeling has been given a powerful impetus by Martin Luther's denunciation of the Roman church. Seven years ago Luther outraged the papacy by publishing a German translation of the New Testament. William Tyndale's English translation was burnt by order of the bishops, but copies were still smuggled into England. One bishop admits that it is impossible to stop the anti-clerical books.

Many of the attacks are directed towards exposing corruption within the church and clerical extortions, with bishops denounced as "ravenous wolves" with too much wealth. These "idle, holy thieves", one writer alleges, will not let Tyndale's bible appear in case people should see that they serve not Christ but their own interests, and that the remission of sins is granted not by the pope but by Christ (→ 17/12).

MPs square up for challenge to church

London, 17 December 1529
After heated debates, members of parliament have voted to reform the church in England. The initiative was taken by the Mercers' Company in the City of London, which attacked the imposition of mortuary and probate fees as an abuse of church power. Further statutes forbid pluralism [the holding of several ecclesiastical offices] and non-residence [a priest receiving an income while never turning up to perform his duties].

The pluralism law is particularly controversial, since it places parliamentary law above dispensations from Rome and thus has a direct bearing on the repeated attempts by Henry VIII to divorce Queen Catherine and marry Anne Boleyn. Henry failed to persuade Pope Clement VII to annul the marriage. Pro-Catherine members denounced the pluralism measure; those pro-Boleyn were equally strong in support – and won. They believe that since parliament can reform the church it can direct the bishops to give Henry a divorce (→ 11/2/31).

1531 - 1532

Rome, 5 January 1531. Henry VIII is ordered by Pope Clement VII not to remarry until the divorce problem is solved.→

Windsor, 14 July 1531. Henry VIII gives up all pretence of a marriage to Catherine of Aragon; he moves to Woodstock with his mistress, Anne Boleyn (→ 1/9/32).

Ireland, 1531. Thomas fitz Thomas FitzGerald, the earl of Desmond, reconciles his differences with Sir William Skeffington, the deputy (→ 9/1531).

Dublin, September 1531. Parliament curtails the rights of Gerald FitzGerald, the earl of Kildare, to wastelands in Kildare and Leinster (→ 5/7/32).

Norwich, 1531. Thomas Bilney, a Lutheran preacher arrested in 1527, is executed as a heretic.

England, 1531. Sir Thomas Elyot, a diplomat and humanist scholar, dedicates his new work, *A Book Named the Governor*, to Henry VIII; in it he sets out the humanist ideal of the educated monarch.

Rome, 25 January 1532. The pope threatens Henry VIII with excommunication (→ 3/1532).

Edinburgh, May 1532. Following a financial deal with the pope, parliament decides to found a college of justice with salaried judges to preside over civil cases.

Ireland, 5 July 1532. The earl of Kildare is appointed deputy of Ireland following the dismissal of Sir William Skeffington (→ 9/1533).

Kent, 28 August 1532. The archbishop of Canterbury, William Warham, one of the strongest opponents to Henry VIII's divorce, dies (→ 9/1532).

England, 1 September 1532. Anne Boleyn is created marchioness of Pembroke (→ 25/1/33).

England, September 1532. *A Glass of the Truth*, commending Henry VIII's divorce, is published; it is written with the king's consent (→ 20/10).

Calais, 20 October 1532. Henry VIII meets King Francis of France in an effort to secure his support for his divorce (→ 10/4/33).

Bristol, 1532. Robert and Nicholas Thorne found the first grammar school here (→ 1557).

Boleyn supporters offer divorce plan

London, January 1531
As the factional battle over Henry VIII's proposed divorce from Catherine of Aragon intensifies, the king is preparing to take steps towards the creation of an English church independent of Rome.

Pope Clement VII has continued to frustrate Henry's attempt to annul his marriage to Catherine in order that he might marry Anne Boleyn. In July 1529 the pope revoked the powers of a legatine court sitting at Blackfriars to hear the king's appeal. Last September, however, Henry's case was boosted by a document that attempts to validate the king's claim to absolute spiritual sovereignty [*see below right*]. The manuscript, *Collectanea satis copiosa*, was compiled by Thomas Cranmer, formerly a lecturer in divinity at Cambridge, and Edward Fox.

After meeting at Waltham in Essex, Cranmer and Fox came up with a plan to resolve the royal dilemma. Cranmer suggested that, if the universities and canon-law experts should decide that Henry's marriage to his brother's widow was illegal, then the ordinary ecclesiastical courts could declare the marriage null and void, and there would be no cause for a further appeal to Rome (→ 11/2).

England flirts with Protestant alliance

Germany, 1531
Protestant German princes have invited England to join their alliance against the Catholic Holy Roman Emperor Charles V, the ruler of the Netherlands, Spain and parts of Germany and Italy. Henry VIII has responded tentatively, but negotiations are unlikely to succeed, partly because Martin Luther disapproves of the king's divorce.

Though Henry shares with the German Protestants their rejection of papal authority, he mistrusts their Lutheran radicalism. Besides, the king is anxious not to give Charles further cause for offence; Henry is seeking to divorce Queen Catherine, who is Charles's aunt, in order to marry Anne Boleyn.

King Henry declares himself 'supreme head of the English church and clergy'

Power play: Henry adopts a bold stance in this portrait by Hans Holbein.

London, 11 February 1531
Desperately short of funds for his war chest, Henry VIII has turned to the clergy for a repeat of a tax he levied eight years ago. This time, however, he has coupled with it a declaration describing himself as "sole protector and supreme head of the English church and clergy".

The convocation of Canterbury agreed to pay the tax but reacted with dismay to Henry's claim to combine royal and ecclesiastical power. Convocation has eventually given in, though only after adding the qualification "as far as Christ's law allows". Henry's power play is seen as yet another manoeuvre in his bid to divorce Catherine of Aragon and marry Anne Boleyn.

The Boleyn faction at court has presented the king with a lengthy manuscript putting the case for royal authority over the church, quoting from the Bible, traditional Catholic texts, Anglo-Saxon laws, the Roman Emperor Constantine and other authorities. The manuscript contends that the English church has always been subject to royal jurisdiction as a separate province of Christendom. This is what Henry wishes to hear. He believes it gives him the right to summon the bishops and direct them to issue a divorce decree (→ 25/1/32).

Clergy's payments to pope will cease

Westminster, March 1532
Thomas Cromwell, an increasingly influential adviser to Henry VIII in the king's quarrel with Rome, has skilfully exploited the anti-clerical feeling in the House of Commons to strike another blow at papal authority in England. He has persuaded the Commons to pass an act banning the payment of annates – a tax requiring clerics to remit their first year's income to the pope.

The tax, which gives the pope about £4,500 a year, is "impoverishing the realm and should cease", members say. However, Henry has said that the act will not come into operation until he has formally given it his endorsement.

Some observers have taken this as a gesture of appeasement to critics in the House of Lords, where a bishop protested that "Down with the church" has become the rallying cry in the House of Commons. Another view is that Henry is merely delaying his consent until Pope Clement VII has published the bull appointing the new archbishop of Canterbury, Thomas Cranmer – who is expected to annul Henry's marriage to Catherine.

The annates move will enhance Cromwell's power. A lawyer, he entered public service by working for Wolsey and is now a leading member of the king's council (→ 15/5).

Henry signals final break with papal power over church

Westminster, 15 May 1532
Henry VIII made a break with Rome virtually inevitable today when he bluntly put the bishops in the Canterbury convocation on notice that they must take orders from him and him alone. Convocation, he said, "always hath been and must be" assembled only by royal writ. Thus the church's independence of temporal authority has been extinguished.

The bishops had already been told that no new canons, or decrees, could be enacted without royal assent, and existing ones deemed prejudicial to the king's prerogative would be annulled. Under intense pressure convocation had sought a compromise, offering both to give up the right to enact any new legislation during Henry's reign and to submit existing ecclesiastical law to his "examination and judgement". Henry would have none of it. He had been enraged by an Easter day sermon preached in his presence by the chaplain to Princess Mary, his daughter by Catherine of Aragon. The chaplain denounced the king's attempts to divorce Catherine.

Today's action by Henry came as a climax to weeks of intrigue and manoeuvres in parliament and convocation by the king's supporters, orchestrated by Thomas Cromwell, and the rival factions supporting Catherine and Anne Boleyn. Sir Thomas More, the lord chancellor, is now certain to resign in protest at the clergy's submission (→ 28/8).

Thomas Cromwell: the king's ally.

Scots monastery rebuilt as grand palace

A spacious residence: a 20th-century view of Holyrood Palace, Edinburgh.

Edinburgh, 1532
The transformation into a royal palace of Holyrood Abbey, founded near Edinburgh by King David I in 1128, which has been going on since the beginning of this century, has been largely completed by King James V.

Since 1529 James had been building for himself and Mary of Guise, his queen-to-be, a tower-like residence which stands at the north-western corner of the palace and is now completed. He has plans to add a delightfully elegant range of more public rooms, built on a splendid scale and given a bright and spacious feeling by being lit by a row of vast windows.

Even before the present king began rebuilding to suit his own needs and those of his future queen, his father, King James IV, had already made substantial changes to the building in order to please his own queen, Margaret Tudor.

Between 1501 and 1505, James IV rebuilt and added to those parts of the abbey used as royal living quarters in accordance with the designs of the master mason Walter Merlioun, producing a spacious residence around three sides of the main abbey complex.

Suspected poisoner boiled in stockpot

London, 1532
In a grim tale of a punishment that truly fitted the crime, one Richard Rosse, the bishop of Rochester's cook, has been boiled alive in his own stockpot after a stew that he had made poisoned 17 people at dinner. Two of them died. According to Rosse, it was all a ghastly mistake. He had indeed added some laxative herbs to the stew – as a joke. Unfortunately it was one that fatally misfired. King Henry VIII himself chose Rosse's punishment and made parliament pass a special law to carry it out. It only added to the irony that the cook was executed at Smithfield, London's main meat market.

Sir Thomas More quits as lord chancellor

London, 16 May 1532
Sir Thomas More, arguably the most respected scholar in England, today resigned as lord chancellor. His departure had been regarded as inevitable after the convocations of Canterbury and York yesterday yielded to pressure from the king and voted to accept that royal authority superseded that of the pope. Sir Thomas, although a champion of reform in the church, opposes political manoeuvres to obtain the king's divorce. He has handed in the great seal of an office which he had been reluctant to accept in 1529 and now plans to retire from public life. The king retains an affection for Sir Thomas, but it is another Thomas – Cromwell – whose star is now rising (→ 17/4/34).

More: opposes divorce manoeuvres.

1533

Westminster, 14 March. Thomas Cromwell, who is rapidly rising in royal favour, introduces a bill to enable the settlement of King Henry VIII's divorce in England and cut the country off from papal jurisdiction (→ 4/1533).

Westminster, 30 March. Thomas Cranmer becomes archbishop of Canterbury; he takes the necessary oath of loyalty to the pope, insisting that he does so only for form's sake (→ 7/1539).

Westminster, March. The Act in Restraint of Appeals is passed by parliament; it abolishes appeals to Rome on a wide range of subjects, including those concerning matrimony (→ 8/1533).

Bedfordshire, 9 April. Catherine of Aragon is told at Ampthill that she is no longer to use the title of queen; she will be known as the dowager princess of Wales, as the widow of Henry's elder brother, Arthur (→ 10/4).

London, 10 April. Holy Roman Emperor Charles V's ambassador in England advises him to declare war on Henry VIII to avenge the treatment of his aunt, Catherine of Aragon (→ 23/5).

London, April. Thomas Cromwell is made chancellor of the exchequer (→ 4/1534).

Ireland, June/July. Thomas fitz Thomas FitzGerald, the earl of Desmond, entertains an agent of Charles V (→ 9/1533).

Rome, 11 July. Pope Clement VII gives Henry VIII until September to take back his first wife, Catherine of Aragon, or suffer the penalty of excommunication (→ 23/3/34).

England, August. Henry VIII confirms the Act in Conditional Restraint of Annates, which was introduced last year, ensuring that the flow of taxes to Rome is greatly reduced.→

Ireland, September. Gerald FitzGerald [Gearoid Og], the earl of Kildare, is summoned to appear before the English court in order to answer charges of maladministration (→ 2/1534).

London, 23 November. Elizabeth Barton, known as "the Holy Maid of Kent", who had prophesied that Henry VIII would cease to be king if he married Anne Boleyn, is declared guilty of treason and imprisoned in the Tower (→ 20/4/34).

King defies pope and weds mistress

A secret ceremony

London, 25 January
It was the most curious time for a wedding. An hour before dawn in a small room in Whitehall Palace, in front of a handful of witnesses, Henry VIII of England finally chose to defy Rome and marry his pregnant mistress, Anne Boleyn.

Few details have emerged of the wedding, which was held in almost complete secrecy. No one can agree on the identity of the celebrant. Some say that it was a priest called Rowland Lee, others that it was George Brown, the prior of the Augustinian Friars in London.

Although the king's marriage to Catherine of Aragon remains valid, Henry bluffed when it came to his licence to wed Anne. "I trust you have a licence," said the celebrant. "What else?" said the king. Henry believes the pope will accept this as a legal marriage, but had to imply papal consent to the priest (→ 14/3).

First royal marriage annulled by Cranmer

Cranmer: backing his monarch.

Dunstable, Bedfordshire, 23 May
In a move that is bound to infuriate the pope, Thomas Cranmer, the archbishop of Canterbury, has annulled Henry VIII's union with Catherine of Aragon and declared legal the king's marriage with Anne Boleyn, which took place in January [*see report left*].

It is over five years since Henry declared his intention to seek a divorce from Catherine – who is now 47 and has failed to produce a male heir – and marry Anne. Pope Clement VII has remained deaf to royal pleas, prompting Henry to defiance. However, on 30 March, Clement consecrated Cranmer, the king's nominee, as archbishop. Cranmer took his oath of allegiance to the pope insisting that he did so "for form's sake" and that no oath could bind him to act against his duty to the king.

Last month a split with Rome looked increasingly inevitable when two convocations of English bishops declared that the king's union with Catherine had violated a holy law that the pope could not dispense with (→ 1/6).

Anne Boleyn crowned queen of England with glittering pageantry

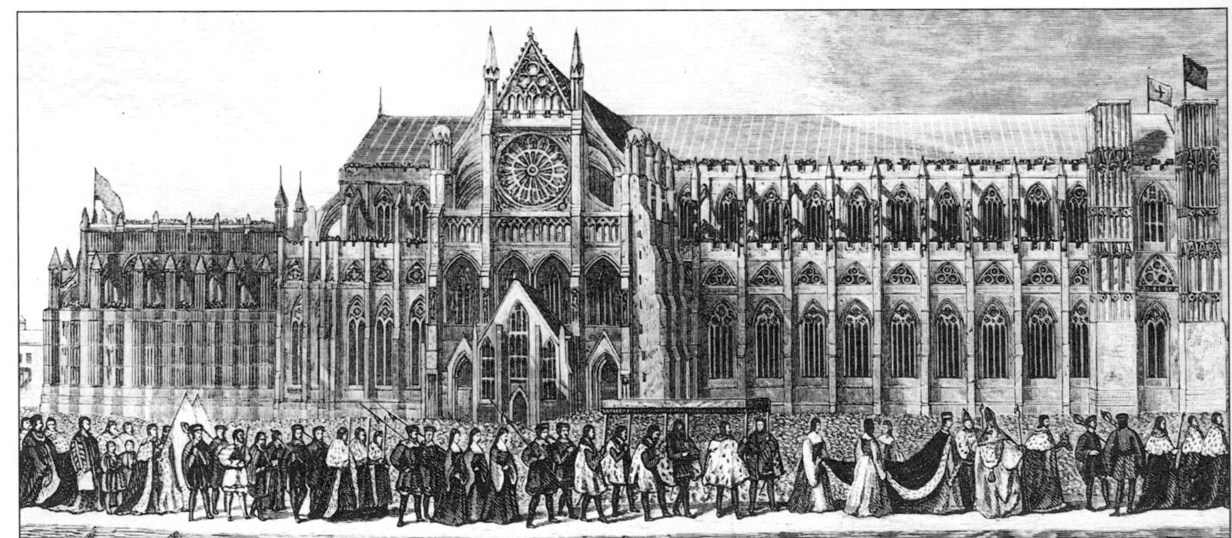

Glittering pageantry: Queen Anne Boleyn's splendid coronation procession as it makes its way past Westminster Abbey.

London, 1 June
After three days of pageantry and feasting, Anne Boleyn was crowned queen of England in Westminster Abbey today. A proud King Henry VIII was determined that the festivities on this Whit Sunday would outshine the coronation of Anne's predecessor, Catherine of Aragon, in both scale and colour. The celebrations began with 50 huge city livery barges, dressed overall with flags and bunting and hung with gold foil that glistened in the sun, making their way to bring the king from Greenwich to Westminster. They ended with a procession through the City where the new queen, accompanied by lords and knights, was greeted by the lord mayor bearing a gift of 1,000 gold marks. The crowds, though, were subdued. Catherine remains popular, and her successor's visibly advanced pregnancy did not help.

Although Anne was crowned by the archbishop of Canterbury, few failed to notice the empty pew reserved for the former chancellor, Sir Thomas More (→ 7/9).

English church makes dramatic split with Rome

King asserts right to head the clergy

London, August

Henry VIII's break with Rome has become an accomplished fact with the king's implicit rejection of an ultimatum from Pope Clement VII. Last month the pope condemned the king's separation from Catherine of Aragon and marriage to Anne Boleyn and gave Henry until September to take back his former wife – or suffer expulsion from the Roman church. The king has responded with a series of punitive measures designed to strengthen his control over the English church.

The schism represents a triumph for the shrewd archbishop of Canterbury, Thomas Cranmer, whose actions forced the pope's hand. Only a few weeks after taking his oath of allegiance, the archbishop openly flouted papal authority by annulling Henry's first marriage [*see report on page 412*]. When the news of Cranmer's perfidy reached Rome, an outraged Clement informed Henry that he was under threat of excommunication.

Several moves have already been made to enhance Henry's role as leader of the English church. He has ordered the diversion of all papal taxation to his royal coffers and also signalled his intention that in future all ecclesiastical licences should be issued by the archbishop of Canterbury. Although there is little sign of popular opposition to the split with Rome, Henry is determined both to give his rule legitimacy and to counter claims such as that from the so-called "Holy Maid of Kent", famous for her prophetic utterances, who has said that with his marriage to Anne Boleyn Henry ceased to be king in the eyes of God.

The woman for whose love the king of England precipitated the great schism in the church became queen in June. She has yet to win the affection of the people – some of whom call her "the goggle-eyed whore" (→ 7/9).

An allegorical print shows King Henry trampling Pope Clement underfoot.

Henry frustrated in wish for male heir

Greenwich, 7 September

To Henry VIII's disappointment, Queen Anne today gave birth to a daughter – leaving unfulfilled his desperate wish for a male heir. In this desire lie the origins of the saga that has culminated in the momentous split with Rome.

Henry's 24-year marriage with Catherine of Aragon produced six children, only one of whom, a sickly girl, survives. By the time Catherine was 40, in the mid 1520s, the king had convinced himself that his lack of a son was divine retribution for marrying the widow of his brother, Arthur. He ordered Cardinal Thomas Wolsey to open talks with Rome to have the marriage annulled – a move staunchly opposed by Catherine. Wolsey's failure brought about his dismissal as lord chancellor in 1529. Events were brought to a head by Henry's secret marriage to Anne Boleyn in January this year and Thomas Cranmer's appointment as archbishop of Canterbury [*see reports left*].

The king managed to obtain a divorce in England following parliament's endorsement in April of the Act in Restraint of Appeals. This abolished appeals to Rome in a wide variety of cases – particularly matrimonial ones (→ 29/1/36).

Devon tinners close ranks on privileges

Devon

Keen to uphold the influence of the tin industry, a special parliament has restated all the ancient rights and privileges of the tin-miners and had them printed on Devon's first printing press at Tavistock Abbey.

Tin has been mined in Devon for more than 2,000 years. It is now a vital source of wealth, particularly from exports, providing work for up to 5,000 people. By charters of 1201 and 1305 tinners could dig for tin anywhere without telling landowners. Such rights, and their exemption from ordinary taxes, have involved tinners in disputes, often leading to court. Now the tinners have decided to close ranks.

The labours required to mine tin.

Taste grows for expensive French wine

England

So great has the demand become in recent years for sweet wines to drink between courses that members of parliament are considering fixing the price at 12d [five pence] a gallon. Among sweet reds the two most widely drunk are Malmsey, originating in the Mediterranean island of Crete, and Romeyn, from the Balkans, which is treated with burnt lime. The most popular sweet whites include Muscadel and Campole. A new wine has lately become fashionable: Hippocras, made by straining and restraining through layers of spices. Some vintners are offloading bad wine by using spices to disguise its taste.

A glazed jug used for serving wine.

1534

Ireland, February. Gerald FitzGerald, the earl of Kildare, leaves for England, making his son, "Silken Thomas", Lord Offaly, his deputy (→11/6).

Rome, 23 March. The pope declares that Henry VIII's marriage to Catherine of Aragon is valid (→5/1534).

Westminster, 26 March. Parliament passes the Act of Succession commanding allegiance to Anne (→17/4).

London, 17 April. Sir Thomas More, the former lord chancellor, is sent to the Tower on his refusal to take the oath of succession (→21).

London, 21 April. John Fisher, the bishop of Rochester, is sent to the Tower for refusing to take the oath of succession.→

England/Scotland, 11 May. After two years of border raiding an Anglo-Scots peace treaty is signed.

Cambridgeshire, May. Catherine of Aragon, the former wife of Henry VIII, is under house arrest (→7/1/36).

Ireland, 11 June. "Silken Thomas", Lord Offaly, repudiates allegiance to Henry VIII (→29).

London, 29 June. The earl of Kildare is sent to the Tower (→28/7).

Dublin, 28 July. The English archbishop of Dublin, John Alen, is murdered on Clontarf beach by supporters of "Silken Thomas" (→2/9).

Edinburgh, 27 August. Norman Gourlay and David Stratoun are burnt as heretics.

London, 2 September. The earl of Kildare dies; his son, "Silken Thomas", succeeds him (→9/1534).

Dublin, September. The earl of Kildare besieges the city (→24/10).

Dublin, 24 October. Sir William Skeffington, the lord deputy, arrives to quell Kildare's rebellion.→

England. Polydore Vergil, an Italian, publishes *Anglica Historia*, a history and topography of England.

Ireland. The *Ordinances for the Government of Ireland* are published; the aim is to curtail the Anglo-Irish lords' protection rackets called "coin and livery" (→11/6).

London. A new coinage for Ireland, called the "coin of the harp", is struck (→9/1545).

King arrests opponents

London, 21 April

Sir Thomas More, the former lord chancellor, and John Fisher, the bishop of Rochester, have been arrested and sent to the Tower. Fisher today joined Sir Thomas, who was imprisoned four days ago. Both men refused to swear the oath to uphold the Act of Succession, which provides that King Henry VIII's children by Queen Anne shall succeed to the throne.

It is a revolutionary act because it both confirms the legality of the king's divorce and new marriage and rejects the pope's authority. Commissioners are to administer an oath to royal councillors, bishops, nobles, justices of the peace and to heads of households.

Bishop Fisher was one of Queen Catherine of Aragon's most outspoken supporters and was never likely to swear the oath. Sir Thomas is a lawyer, not a bishop, and has never opposed the divorce in public, though he worked against it privately when he was lord chancellor from 1529 until 1532. He managed to avoid taking the side of either the king or the pope until Cromwell devised the oath to force every man to declare himself. More was one of the first to be summoned to take the oath at Lambeth Palace before Archbishop Cranmer, Thomas Cromwell and Lord Chancellor Audley. He refused to swear.

More in prison: a romanticized view.

They argued with him, tried to persuade him, told him to wait and think on his refusal while others came in to take the oath. Still he refused and was sent to the Tower, to be joined today by Fisher.

By striking against a leading churchman such as Fisher, Henry risks aggravating the clash with the pope which could lead to his public excommunication. The king's advisers hope to persuade More to recant and plan to send his friends to see him. But he has steadfastly resisted pressure from family and friends to give his views on the king's divorce by refusing to incriminate himself (→17/11).

Thomas Cromwell consolidates his rapid rise to power

London, April

Thomas Cromwell, the chancellor of the exchequer and Henry VIII's chief minister, is continuing to consolidate his grasp on the offices of power in the king's household and government. Henry has now appointed him principal secretary as well as master of the king's jewels.

A former lawyer, merchant and moneylender, Cromwell was born in Putney, near London, in around 1485. He became an MP in 1523, but he began his rise in public life as a member of Cardinal Wolsey's household. He was involved in the dissolution of the small monasteries in the 1520s, and later he caught the king's eye by his adroit control of parliament. By 1530 he was a leading member of the king's council, and he has since made himself indispensable to Henry.

Cromwell: growing in power.

He has set himself the task of restructuring the government, making sure it runs efficiently from the centre and uniformly throughout the the far reaches of the kingdom. This is already bringing about reaction from the old nobility and the church because it involves getting rid of ancient privileges and making real the theoretical supremacy which Henry has achieved over the bishops.

This clever, energetic man is also determined to keep the reins of government in his own hands. If he is to keep his head, however, he must remember Wolsey's fate (→4/1540).

Sheep-farmers forced to cut size of flocks

East Anglia, 30 March

Large sheep-farmers across the country have been dealt a heavy blow today by a new law banning anyone from owning more than 2,000 sheep. Some farms here in East Anglia support ten times this number, and the Spencer family in Northamptonshire, for example, has about 30,000 sheep.

The legislation has been steered through parliament by Thomas Cromwell, the chancellor of the exchequer, in a bid to stop rural depopulation. Sheep-farming is enormously profitable – in recent years substantial areas of arable land have been converted to pasture to accommodate grazing sheep, and this requires a much smaller labour force (→1/6/48).

Sheep are a source of vast wealth.

English forces sent to crush Irish revolt

Gerald FitzGerald, the earl of Kildare: prevented from returning to Ireland.

Dublin, 19 December
A rebellion that broke out this summer under Lord Offaly, known as "Silken Thomas", has at last led to a truce. Trouble began earlier this year when King Henry told Thomas's father, Gerald FitzGerald, the earl of Kildare, and Piers Ruadh Butler, the earl of Ormond, that unless they gave up their "coin and livery" racket – for extorting protection money – he would publish the *Ordinances for the Government of Ireland*, detailing their abuses.

Kildare did not believe that Henry would do it, but when Ormond agreed to sign the ordinances and commit himself to reform, Kildare's bluff was called. He was summond to London, where he was put in the Tower on 29 June. When Thomas heard of this, he put into action a pre-arranged plan to besiege Dublin castle. It was more of a token show of defiance than a serious threat and when Sir William Skeffington – who replaced Kildare as lord deputy on 30 July – arrived here on 24 October, support for Thomas was already waning. Kildare died in the Tower on 2 September, but King Henry is worried that certain lords in England might be waiting to take a leaf out of Thomas's book (→23/3/35).

Gathering the harvest: a vision of the end of the world taken from the first edition of the Luther Bible, which was published in 1534.

'Holy Maid of Kent' executed at Tyburn

London, 20 April
A fiery young prophetess, who predicted that the king would die a villain's death if he married Anne Boleyn, has been hanged at Tyburn. Elizabeth Barton, known as "the Holy Maid of Kent" for her visions and prophecies, began to attack the royal divorce in 1527. She was taken up by a group of Canterbury divines, lead by her spiritual director Dr Edward Bocking, who saw her as a useful weapon to harass the king. The authorities, terrified by their visions of a popular uprising, arrested her, seizing all 700 copies of an inflamatory work about her called *The Nun's Book*. Bocking and three others were hanged with her.

Barton: punished for prophecies.

Act recognizes king as head of church

London, 17 November
The Act of Supremacy which has been passed this month makes Henry VIII the "supreme head" of the church of england. The break with Rome is irrevocable, and every cleric in England must now bend his knee to the king.

Henry has won wide-ranging powers, allowing him to control "all honours, dignities, privileges, immunities, profits and commodities" in a church which no longer owes allegiance to the pope. Indeed, the law of heresy has been changed to allow attacks on papal authority. Common-law safeguards, such as the two-witness rule and hearings in open court, are to be enforced in ecclesiastical trials. The road to reformation, espoused by the Boleyn faction, is wide open.

Using a combination of threats, bribery and punitive taxation, Henry has progressively bullied his bishops into submission from the moment that he chose to end his marriage to Catherine of Aragon and marry Anne Boleyn. A series of parliamentary acts followed, each enhancing the king's authority.

The king's marital problems are by no means the only reason for the break with Rome. Moves towards religious reformation have been taking place in England for more than 20 years as Protestants continued to make their mark all over Europe (→20/5/35).

English power increases in the Marches

Welsh Marches, May
The king has appointed Rowland Lee, the bishop of Coventry, to be president of the council of Wales. He has been ordered to restore order in the Marches and Wales, securing them against religious opposition and insurrection.

The council in Westminster has concluded that law enforcement in Wales, the Marches and the border counties of England has been dangerously lax. The national crisis involving the king's divorce and the split with Rome might provoke rebellion in Wales, Ireland and the north of England, and Thomas Cromwell is determined to avert it. Bishop Lee has a reputation for brutal efficiency. Traditionally, clergymen administrators have not imposed the death penalty on criminals, but he has obtained a special indulgence permitting him to do so. He will use whatever force is needed to bring the principality and the Marches as tightly under royal control as southern England.

The Welsh council has acquired powers to deal harshly with offenders and officials who have protected them. The powers of the Marcher lords will be curtailed, and English justices of the peace will be permitted to operate in Wales for the first time. This will introduce one element of the English shire system to Wales (→14/4/36).

1535 - 1536

Lothian, 21 February 1535. James V is invested with the Order of the Garter by an envoy from Henry VIII of England (→ 10/9/36).

England, April 1535. Thomas Cromwell, the king's secretary, orders the imprisonment of clergy preaching the pope's supremacy (→ 20/5).

Rome, 20 May 1535. Pope Paul III makes John Fisher, the bishop of Rochester who is imprisoned in the Tower, a cardinal (→ 22/5).

Tower Hill, 22 June 1535. Cardinal Fisher is executed for refusing to take the oath of supremacy (→ 6/7).

Ireland, August 1535. "Silken Thomas", the earl of Kildare, surrenders to Sir William Skeffington, the deputy; he will be taken to England by Lord Leonard Grey (→ 31/12).

Ireland, 31 December 1535. Sir William Skeffington dies (→ 23/2/36).

Cambridgeshire, 7 January 1536. Catherine of Aragon, the former wife of Henry VIII, who has been under house arrest at Kimbolton since 1534, dies.

Greenwich, 29 January 1536. Queen Anne miscarries a male child (→ 2/5).

Westminster, February 1536. Henry, desperate for a male heir, shows an interest in Jane Seymour, one of the queen's ladies-in-waiting (→ 30/5).

Ireland, 23 February 1536. Lord Leonard Grey is appointed deputy (→ 3/2/37).

Westminster, 10 May 1536. A grand jury indicts Anne Boleyn for high treason (→ 19).

London, 30 May 1536. Henry marries his third wife, Jane Seymour (→ 12/10/37).

London, 22 July 1536. Henry Fitzroy, the duke of Richmond, Henry's illegitimate son, dies of consumption at St James's Palace.

London, July 1536. A second Act of Succession declares the Princesses Mary and Elizabeth illegitimate (→ 5/12/53).

France, 10 September 1536. James V of Scots arrives in Dieppe to marry the daughter of the duke of Vendôme (→ 1/1/37).

Low Countries, 6 October 1536. William Tyndale, a leading Lutheran in exile, is executed by the local authorities.

Thomas More is beheaded for treason

A last farewell: Sir Thomas More is taken away by guards to be executed.

London, 6 July 1535
Sir Thomas More was beheaded on Tower Hill today, 14 days after Cardinal John Fisher. He had difficulty climbing the scaffold, and said to the lieutenant of the Tower "I pray you, Master Lieutenant, see me safe up, and for my coming down let me shift for myself."

He called on everyone there to pray for him, and to bear witness that he died for the holy Catholic Church, and then told the executioner: "Pluck up thy spirits, man, and be not afraid to do thine office; my neck is very short; take heed therefore thou strike not awry, for saving of thine honesty."

More and Fisher were convicted of treason for denying Henry VIII's new title, "Supreme Head of the Church in England", given by the Act of Supremacy last November. Fisher was tried after the pope made him a cardinal on 20 May, and executed on 22 June.

At his trial in Westminster Hall, More said he had never denied the king's supremacy; he had always refused to answer questions on the matter. Then the solicitor-general, Richard Rich, testified that in private conversation More had told him a man could not be bound by the act against his conscience.

More denounced the perjury, but after the verdict he admitted his guilt by telling the court that parliament had no power to end papal authority in the church, and that acts against the union of Christendom were capital sins (→ 18/5/36).

'Silken Thomas' is crushed in Kildare

Co Kildare, 23 March 1535
Last year's rebellion is over. December's truce between the rebel leader, "Silken Thomas", the earl of Kildare, and Sir William Skeffington, the deputy, broke down on 6 January. The king has chosen to make an example of Thomas to show lords in England that he will not tolerate defiance. Today Skeffington bombarded Thomas's men at Maynooth Castle with devastating results. The rebels were astonished at the overwhelming scale of Skeffington's "iron fist" response. Skeffington has had many of the defenders – though not Thomas – summarily executed (→ 8/1535).

Death duties due under new statute

Westminster, 14 April 1536
King Henry VIII has forced a new law through parliament obliging all heirs to land tenancies to pay death duties to the crown. Although the king is technically the overlord of all the major landowners in England, his tenants have been able to pass their tenancies on to their heirs without being taxed – by transferring "use" while trustees retained the tenancy. The Statute of Uses, passed today, closes that loophole and enshrines the right of the eldest son to succeed to his ancestor's estate to the exclusion of others, while also providing revenue for the crown (→ 7/1540).

Henry adds a great hall to the palace at Hampton Court

Hampton Court, c.1536
King Henry VIII has completed building the great hall at Hampton Court, the most magnificent of all country houses so far built in England during his reign. Started by Cardinal Wolsey, the house by the Thames west of London was given to the king by the cardinal to try to avert his fall. Since the death of Wolsey, Hampton Court has become Henry's favourite palace, but not content with his former chancellor's work he has ordered a lot of rebuilding of his own. Recently he has replaced Wolsey's relatively modest hall with a more spectacular version. Measuring 35 metres long and 22 metres wide (38 x 24 yards), it is a massive construction with a large central hearth. Towering 13 metres above the floor is a vast hammerbeam roof designed by the master carpenter James Nedeham. The roofing technique is in the "gothic" style, but the detail has lantern-shaped roof pendants, carved by Richard Rydge, and the coats of arms of Henry, Anne Boleyn and Jane Seymour carved on the spandrals above the braces.

The great hall at Hampton Court.

At the end of the hall a screen hides the servants' passage, and communication between the high table and the kitchen is via a stairway that also leads to the king's private rooms. The king can thus be served efficiently whether dining in public or in private (→ 8/1538).

Act of parliament dissolves monasteries and adds church funds to royal coffers

Government vandals: a monastery's considerable wealth is plundered.

Westminster, 18 March 1536

All religious houses worth less than £200 a year are to be dissolved under the Act of Suppression manoeuvred through parliament today by Thomas Cromwell, the king's chief minister. It is thought that some 372 houses in England and 27 in Wales will be closed down and their assets seized by the crown.

Cromwell prepared the ground carefully to make sure that his act was passed. Last year he organized a survey of monastic resources and sent out teams of "visitors" to assess the morale of religious houses. The visitors had another purpose, for their very appearance frightened a number of institutions into surrendering to the crown in return for pensions.

Cromwell's men also gathered incriminating evidence against various houses so that there was little opposition in parliament to the act. As master of the jewels Cromwell has control of the proceeds from the dissolution, which are being kept in chests in the king's bedroom at Whitehall (→ 31/5).

Wales joined to England

Westminster, 14 April 1536

King Henry VIII has given the royal assent to an act of parliament uniting Wales with England. Wales is to be administered by the English system of shire government, with sheriffs and justices of the peace. Welsh customs are abolished, along with the traditional powers of the Marcher lords.

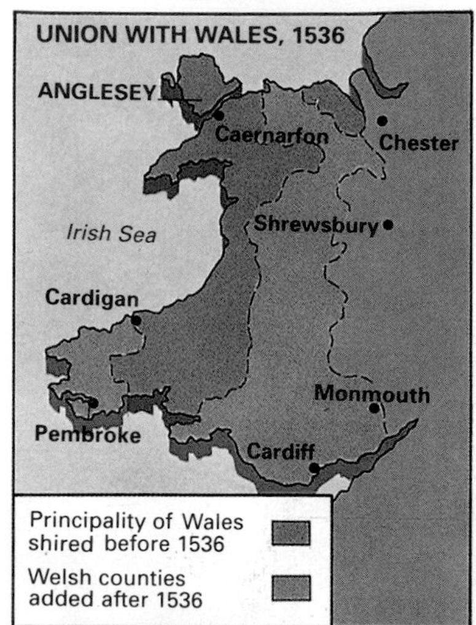

English power over Wales has been absolute since the defeat of Owain Glyndwr's rebellion in the early years of the last century. But it is only now, as part of the moves to quash any independent church power, that an English king has felt the need to extinguish the separate laws and customs that reflect the quasi-independence of Wales.

In recent years English rule has been exercised through a Welsh council headed by Rowland Lee, the bishop of Coventry. He has administered justice in Wales with some vigour, being said to have hanged 5,000 criminals. This rough justice did not pacify the country, however, so Thomas Cromwell will now try direct administration and turn over the courts to local JPs.

The act directs that law and administration will be conducted in English, and no one who speaks Welsh may hold office unless he is also able to speak English. The Marcher lordships – which have ruled most of Wales for centuries – are to be replaced by shires based on Brecon, Denbigh, Radnor, Monmouth and Montgomery. Each shire will elect one knight to parliament, apart from Monmouthshire, which will elect two, and each shire borough will elect one burgess, making 24 in all when added to the older principality shires like Caernarfonshire and Cardiganshire, also newly enfranchised (→ 1543).

Anne sent to the Tower to face charges of adultery – and death

London, 2 May 1536

Just over three years after her marriage to Henry VIII, Anne Boleyn is facing the executioner's block. The queen was arrested today and taken to the Tower of London where she faces charges of adultery brought by her husband. Her alleged lovers – including her brother, Lord Rochford, who denies the accusation – are almost certainly being tortured in another part of the Tower.

After a blissful start Anne's marriage to Henry became increasingly unhappy, despite the death in January of Catherine of Aragon. Anne is unpopular and remains a political liability to her husband because of Holy Roman Emperor Charles V's hostility to her and her daughter Elizabeth. She has also failed to produce a male heir; a miscarriage this year fuelled Henry's fears that this marriage, like that to Catherine, was against God's wishes. However, the king is also making no attempt to hide his affection for an attractive 27-year-old aristocrat, Jane Seymour.

Anne learns about Henry and Jane Seymour, by G Cruikshank (d.1878).

Conservative courtiers conspired to cause the queen's downfall. Henry was told that she had been unfaithful with a number of courtiers. More serious is talk of the king's impotence and Anne's involvement in the witchcraft that has caused it – and the claim that Elizabeth is not Henry's daughter (→ 10/5).

'Privy' council set up to advise king

Westminster, 1536

Important modifications have been made to the body of advisers that forms the "king's council". In the early years of Henry VIII's reign the council numbered more than 70 members, who were drawn from a wide spectrum of influential men. This has now been reduced to a so-called "privy" council of about 20, most of whom are experienced administrators.

Creation of this new body, membership of which confers great prestige, has much enhanced the potential power of central government, as has the transformation of the office of principal secretary. Exploiting his influence with the king, Thomas Cromwell has turned this once minor post into the chief executive instrument of both domestic and foreign policy.

Anne loses her head

The last moment: Anne waits in prayer for the swordsman's fatal stroke.

London, 19 May 1536
The executioner's sword glinted in the morning sun as Anne Boleyn was brought to the block today. Escorted by four ladies-in-waiting the queen, dressed in grey, climbed the scaffold and faced the French swordsman whose services she had specifically requested. The beheading, it is reported, was swift and efficient, requiring only one stroke of the sword.

The charge against the queen and Lord Rochford, her brother, was treason. They were accused of attempting to hasten Henry VIII's death by their incestuous liaison. Four other men have already lost their heads for alleged adultery with the queen. A tribunal headed by Anne's uncle, the duke of Norfolk, the lord high steward, found both guilty, and the sentences of death were passed.

Anne appeared resigned to her fate, even praising Henry to the last: "I pray God, save the king and send him long to reign over you, for a gentler, nor a more merciful prince was there never, and to me he was ever a good, a gentle and a sovereign lord" (→ 11/7).

Ireland adopts Henry VIII's reformation

Dublin, 1536
Catholicism as reformed by Henry VIII has become Ireland's official religion, and the king has been declared "the only supreme head on earth of the whole Church of Ireland called Hibernica Ecclesia".

This "reformation" parliament, as it has been called, which opened on 1 May, has passed an act forbidding appeals to Rome. Poynings' Law has been suspended, and "Silken Thomas", the earl of Kildare who led the rebellion of 1534/35, has also been attainted.

Parliament has shown itself to be made of stern stuff in its response to the proposed closure of the lesser monasteries. While they have now ceased to play a part in the spiritual lives of the population, the monasteries have become so richly endowed with land that influential landowners now sponsor their immediate relatives as heads of monasteries or appoint themselves as lay stewards to manage monastic property. They therefore balked at passing legislation that would deprive them of income.

After a delegation was sent to King Henry, assurances have been given that they will receive compensation when the monastic property is distributed, and they have withdrawn their opposition. Both the king and Thomas Cromwell have reason to be pleased with the increased revenue that will accrue to them (→ 5/5/38).

Henry VIII as head of the church agrees to adopt ten articles of Lutheran faith

Westminster, 11 July 1536
A new statement of doctrine has been issued by authority of Henry VIII as head of the church in England. Known as the Ten Articles, it denies the full doctrine of purgatory and contains hints of a shift towards the views of the radical German ex-monk, Martin Luther.

In the past the king has been seen as a conservative in theological matters; in 1521 he was accorded the title "defender of the faith" by a grateful Pope Leo X for a book attacking Lutheran theology. But the logic of Henry's quarrel with Rome is shifting him towards Protestantism, just as it escalated from an original plea for a divorce into a frontal assault on papal authority over the English clergy.

In a move away from Catholic orthodoxy, he has kept only three of the traditional seven sacraments – baptism, penance and the Eucharist (partaking of consecrated of bread and wine). The others – matrimony, confirmation, extreme unction and holy orders – are not mentioned in the document, approved by a cowed convocation.

Thomas Cromwell, now lord privy seal, has been given the task of enforcing the king's views on the clergy. Royal injunctions are being prepared by Cromwell to cause superstition to "vanish away", and the clergy are ordered not to "set forth or extol any images, relics or miracles for any lucre, nor allure the people by any enticements to the pilgrimage of any saint".

'Pilgrimage of Grace' brought to an end

Doncaster, 8 December 1536
The rebellion in Lincolnshire and the northern counties of England, which came to be known as the "Pilgrimage of Grace", ended today when its leaders accepted the offer of a general pardon from the duke of Norfolk, acting on behalf of King Henry VIII. However, Norfolk has promised the king that he has no intention of carrying out any pledges made to the rebels.

The uprising, which began in October, is seen as the expression of a general feeling of resentment at many of the policies being implemented on the king's behalf by his chief minister, Thomas Cromwell: the dissolution of the monasteries, new and unexpected taxes and the spread of Protestant doctrines. It was rumoured that taxes were to be levied on christenings, marriages and burials, and that people would not be allowed to eat white bread without paying dues to the king.

The gentry as well as commoners joined demonstrations centred on Lincoln and York, where its leader was Robert Aske, a landowner and lawyer, who spoke of a pilgrimage for the preservation of Christ's church. He attacked the suppression of monasteries but preached non-violence and proclaimed his loyalty to the king (→ 10/3/37).

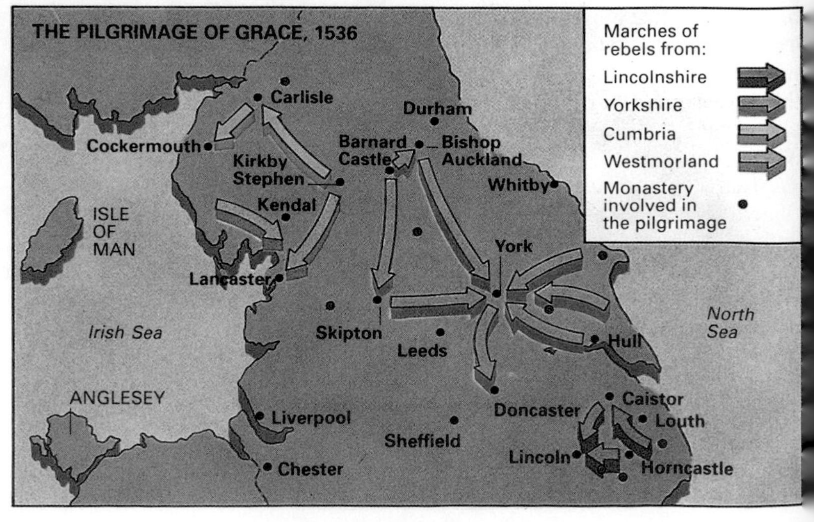

1537

Paris, 1 January. King James V of Scots marries Princess Madeleine, the frail daughter of King Francis of France (→ 7/7).

London, 3 February. "Silken Thomas" FitzGerald, the earl of Kildare, and his five uncles are executed for treason; his half-brother Gerald is the sole surviving male member of the house of Kildare (→ 5/7).

Westminster, 18 March. Thomas Wyatt, the poet, receives a knighthood.

Middlesex, 30 June. Henry Percy, the earl of Northumberland and the most powerful northern noble, dies; he bequeaths all his lands to the crown.

Ireland, 5 July. On the death of Aodh Dubh O'Donnell, the lord of Tyrconnell, he is succeeded by his son Manus (→ 8/9).

Edinburgh, 17 July. Jane Douglas, the sister of the earl of Angus, is burnt at the stake after being found guilty of conspiring to poison King James V (→ 10/6/38).

York, July. Robert Aske, the leader of the "Pilgrimage of Grace", who was sentenced to death in May, is executed (→ 19/12/38).

Ireland, 8 September. Anthony St Leger arrives to open a royal commission to investigate allegations of abuse in Ireland and charges of corruption against the Irish deputy, Lord Leonard Grey; he is also to provide a general survey of royal rents and revenues (→ 12/1537).

Northern England, September. The council of the north is reorganized in order to give more power to the central administration in London.

Hampton Court, 12 October. Jane Seymour gives birth to a boy, who will be called Edward. He is Henry VIII's son and heir (→ 12/11).

Hampton Court, 18 October. Edward Seymour, the brother of Jane Seymour, Henry VIII's third wife, is made earl of Hertford.

Windsor, 12 November. Jane Seymour, who died last month, is buried.

Dublin, December. New legislation in the Irish parliament requires that legal business be conducted in English and that all parish schools teach English (→ 6/1538).

Henry purges rebel clerics in fresh crackdown on the church

A group of monks is expelled.

Lancaster, 10 March
The execution of Abbot John Paslew of Whalley and several others is the latest episode in a purge of the clergy. King Henry VIII seems to be taking belated revenge for last year's "Pilgrimage of Grace", and his vengeance has taken its most brutal form in the northern counties. It appears that no prominent priest can consider himself safe.

Since the executions in 1535 of Sir Thomas More and Cardinal John Fisher for refusing to swear the oath of succession, churchmen have been anything but cowed. There were two significant revolts last year, in Yorkshire, where 40,000 men briefly confronted the king's army, and in Lincolnshire.

Leaders of what was dubbed "the Pilgrimage of Grace" protested their loyalty to the king, and were pardoned. But four canons of Barlings, six monks of Bardney and the abbot and three monks of Kirkstead, who supported the Lincolnshire rebels in the same cause, were subsequently arrested and executed four days ago.

Last month the duke of Norfolk had 74 rebels hanged – 12 on Carlisle's walls and 62 in surrounding villages. Throughout England between 220 and 250 people have been executed (→ 7/1537).

Carthusian monks are forced to surrender

London, June
The austere monks of the powerful Carthusian monastery known as the London Charterhouse, sited just outside the city near Smithfield, have finally been forced to surrender to the forces of Henry VIII's reformation of the church.

Thomas Cromwell's agents have waged a brutal campaign against these holy men who wear the hair shirts of penitents, keep almost total silence and eat no meat. When they refused to swear to the Act of Supremacy three of them were sentenced to death and, clad in their white habits, drawn across London to Tyburn on hurdles, hanged and then quartered.

Their continued refusal to close their doors and surrender their wealth to the crown led to ten of them being taken to Newgate prison, where they were chained to posts and then left to starve to death – only one survived. Now they can resist no longer. The king's men have occupied their monastery, which will be demolished or used as a royal storehouse. The Carthusians' wealth, accumulated over nearly two hundred years, will go to replenish the king's coffers.

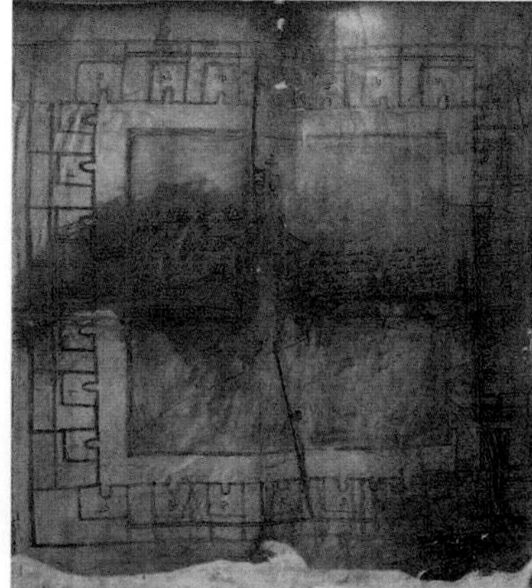

A map of Charterhouse monastery.

Scots mourn queen

Edinburgh, 7 July
The Scottish court is in mourning following the death today of Queen Madeleine, just two months after her arrival in Scotland. A daughter of the French king, Francis, she had been married to James V for just seven months. Although she was only 16 years old, Madeleine had a history of poor health. In choosing a wife James invoked the Treaty of Rouen, which entitled him to a daughter of the king of France. In spite of having lost his young queen, James retains her dowry of 100,000 *livres* (→ 17).

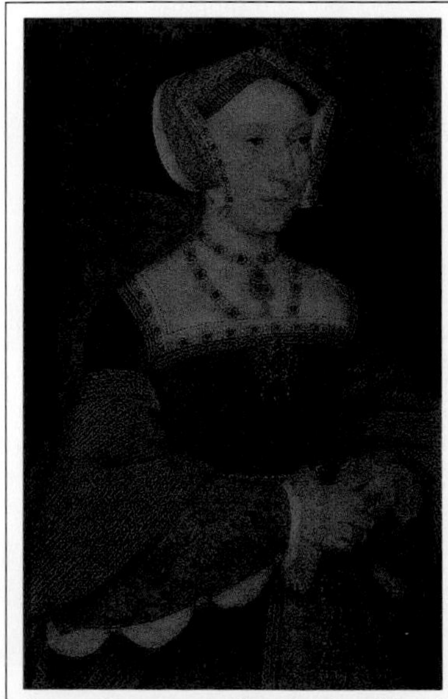

Jane Seymour, the third wife of Henry VIII, died on 24 October, 12 days after giving birth to a male heir to the English throne.

Bishops' book is too radical for Henry

London, December
Henry VIII has at last got down to examining the weighty theological treatise which he commissioned earlier this year – and he is not pleased with what he has found.

The treatise, which is known as the *Bishops' Book,* was compiled under the aegis of Henry's chief adviser, Thomas Cromwell, who, like Thomas Cranmer, the archbishop of Canterbury, has been shocked by the king's amendments. The First Commandment has been altered to say that a Christian can pray only to Christ, not to God the Father.

Henry, who keeps an astrologer, has exempted astrology from the bishops' list of prohibitions which also include "divination and palm-reading"; and only "uncleanly and wanton words" has survived the bishops' list of bad habits that included "tales, songs, sights, touchings, gay and wanton apparel and lascivious decking" (→ 5/1543).

1538

Dublin, 5 May. The city's clergy resist the attempt by Arcbishop George Browne to introduce liturgical reform.

Hampton Court, May. King Henry VIII is seriously ill; a blood clot moves from his leg to his lung, leaving him unable to speak and black in the face.

Fife, 10 June. Mary of Guise, originally one of the candidates for Henry VIII of England's fourth wife, arrives to join her husband James V of Scots, whom she married by proxy on 4 May (→ 22/5/40).

France, 18 June. France and the Holy Roman Empire sign the Treaty of Nice; their alliance has led England to fear an invasion (→ 27/12).

Hampton Court, August. The renovation of Cardinal Wolsey's palace is finished, at a cost of £46,000.

Rome, 17 December. Pope Paul III finally excommunicates King Henry VIII of England (→ 7/4/39).

Lincolnshire, 19 December. Henry VIII gives former church lands to Charles Brandon, the duke of Suffolk, in exchange for his lands in East Anglia; he will live in Lincolnshire in an attempt to prevent a recurrence of the unrest of 1536.

Rome, 20 December. David Beaton, the abbot of Arbroath, is created a cardinal, following French pressure. After several diplomatic visits to the French court, Beaton has won rights of citizenship in France and was made a bishop there by King Francis last year (→ 1538).

Rome, 27 December. Cardinal Reginald Pole, Henry's exiled cousin, sets out to rally the support of the Catholic kings of France and Spain against Henry (→ 6/1546).

Europe. Hans Holbein, England's official royal painter, enlisted in the search for a fourth wife for Henry VIII, visits the courts of Europe, making portraits of possible candidates (→ 1543).

Surrey. King Henry begins work on an elaborate new palace near Cheam, to be called Nonsuch (→ 1545).

St Andrews, Fife. Archbishop James Beaton founds St Mary's College for the teaching of theology (→ 14/2/39).

England. Sir Thomas Elyot, a diplomat and scholar, publishes a dictionary in Latin and English.

Government orders destruction of shrines

Canterbury, September

The shrine of the blessed St Thomas in Canterbury Cathedral has been torn down by men working for Thomas Cromwell, the king's chief minister. The men have taken away several cartloads of loot, which are presumed to be destined for the royal coffers.

It is part of a campaign by Cromwell's agents who, while preaching against idolatry, are searching for jewels and gold. At Winchester they crept into the cathedral in the early hours of the morning to smash the shrine and tomb of St Swithun. They then swept away the saint's bones in case people thought that "we came more for the treasure than for avoiding the abomination of idolatry".

Yet this officially sanctioned vandalism of holy relics and shrines has led to the destruction of irreplaceable works of art. In Gray's Inn chapel in London the stained-glass window depicting the martyrdom of St Thomas Becket has been smashed. Mediaeval metalwork has been melted down, Gothic buildings have been destroyed and libraries broken up with their books being sold or burnt (→ 3/12).

A glittering shrine to St Edmund.

Vendetta pursued against king's critics

London, 9 December

Two outspoken opponents of King Henry VIII were executed on Tower Hill today: Henry Courtenay, the marquis of Exeter, and Henry Pole, Lord Montagu. The two men been convicted of treason for backing Montagu's brother, the exiled churchman Reginald Pole. Henry's hatred of Pole – a former ally who went to Italy in 1532 after opposing the royal divorce – has steadily intensified. Made a cardinal two years ago, and sent as papal legate to the Low Countries, Pole now has a price on his head – set by the English king (→ 27/12).

Exiled critic of the king: Reginald Pole, created a cardinal in 1536.

Nobles plan to rise against the English

Ireland, June

The failed rebellion of "Silken Thomas" FitzGerald, the earl of Kildare, ended the supremacy of the Kildare Geraldines. In order to save the only remaining heir, Lady Eleanor, the widow of MacCarthy Reagh, Thomas's aunt, decided to make a very politic marriage to the great Ulster chief Manus O'Donnell, the lord of Tyrconnell.

The heir – 11-year old Gerald FitzGerald, Thomas's half-brother – was smuggled out of Co Kildare in a basket and taken to Cork to live with Lady Eleanor. She, meanwhile, had been planning a confederacy of Geraldine nobles to revive Kildare fortunes.

When Lady Eleanor was widowed, in 1531, she was courted by Manus O'Donnell, but she refused him and retired to Cork. Then she came to see the advantage of such a union, especially when Manus undertook to protect young Gerald.

This month Lady Eleanor and Gerald made their way safely to Donegal, proof of the devotion felt by the Irish people for the house of Kildare, whose interests were adopted by a coalition of all the great Gaelic lords. In particular – and much to the anxiety of the English – Manus has formed a temporary alliance with Conn Bacach O'Neill, the lord of Tyrone. A powerful Gaelic alliance in Ulster is the last thing that Lord Leonard Grey, the deputy, wants to see. Lady Eleanor, now married to O'Donnell, is preparing a new rebellion. The hope is to sweep the English into the sea and proclaim Gerald king on Tara Hill (→ 7/1539).

Church 'plough lights' are banned by government injunction

Westminster, September

Acting in his capacity as the king's "viceregent in spirituals", Thomas Cromwell has issued a set of injunctions ordering churches to scrap objects of "superstitious" worship and to cease rituals not justified by the scriptures. All parish clergy must make sure that English bibles are available in their churches for the laity to study, and keep registers of baptisms, marriages and burials. In most parish churches the candles kept burning before images of favourite saints will have to be snuffed out, while in the eastern agricultural regions the traditional "plough light" will no longer be lit.

These lights, thought to bring God's blessing on the spring ploughing, are paid for by a collection on the second Monday after Epiphany by the young men of the village going from door to door dragging a plough. The only lights now allowed in churches are those on the altar, in the rood loft and before the Easter sepulchre. Such changes will fundamentally affect rural religious life by breaking the links between folk rituals and formal religion.

There seems to be a general acceptance of the ban on plough lights if only because the people fear that if they resist they will also be forced to remove the images of their favourite saints. The Plough Monday collection may continue, but the proceeds will go to church funds.

Monastic wealth seized in savage royal attacks

All objects of worth are being confiscated from monastic buildings.

The remains of Rievaulx Abbey, which was stripped of its treasures in 1538.

Westminster, 3 December
The confiscated treasure of the monasteries is pouring into King Henry VIII's coffers as the great religious houses are suppressed, their wealth seized, their lands sold and their buildings torn down.

Abbots are often made to sign false confessions of wrongdoing in order to bring about their surrender to Cromwell's officials. Others are simply intimidated into giving up the struggle to keep their houses alive, and some, recognizing the impossibility of fighting against the implacable officials, make deals under which they surrender quietly in exchange for pensions.

Today it was the turn of 400-year-old Rievaulx Abbey, in North Yorkshire, when the abbot and 21 monks of this Cistercian monastery, one of the most beautiful of all the English religious houses, signed a deed of surrender. They have been granted pensions.

The abbey's future is bleak. If the normal procedure is followed plate and jewels which have escaped previous visitations will be sent direct to Henry's treasury, with selected books for the royal library.

Then everything of value in the abbey, down to the poor furnishings in the monks' cells, will be sold by auction on the spot. The buildings themselves will be sold or leased and the lands let for farming, but the new owner will only be allowed to turn part of the abbey into a private house or farm buildings. The rest will be pulled down. The leaden roof will be torn off and melted down into "pigs". The doors, locks and anything else recoverable will be sold. Then the building will be demolished or left as a shell exposed to wind and rain and the ravages of looters. There is a certain group of Italians, led by one Giovanni Portinari, which specializes in utterly destroying great churches, sometimes using gunpowder to bring them down right to their foundations.

Some new owners, granted monasteries on condition that they destroy them, cannot afford the cost of demolition. Having made the buildings uninhabitable, they allow the ruins to be used as quarries for building stone. The king himself is using the chapel of the Charterhouse near Smithfield as a store for his tents and garden furniture.

There is profit in these activities for many people, but none can approach the huge fortune made out of the sack of the monasteries by the king. It is estimated that he has already gathered in half a million pounds, and there remain some rich abbeys still untouched by the wave of government-inspired attacks.

While many are concerned with profit there are others, however, who deeply regret the destruction of some of the finest buildings in the land, buildings which have stood for centuries representing the triumph of God over Mammon. And now they are gone for ever (→ 17/12).

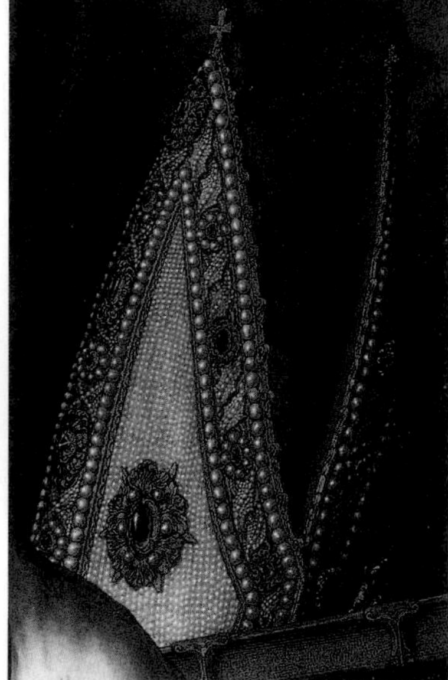
Valuables of the type now swelling the royal coffers: a cross and jewelled mitre belonging to William Warham, archbishop of Canterbury 1503-15.

Whitby Abbey, North Yorkshire: another victim of the royal attacks.

1539-1540

Fife, 14 February 1539. James Beaton, the archbishop of St Andrews, dies; his nephew, Cardinal David Beaton, succeeds him (→ 18/12/42).

Humberside, 26 February 1539. Friars at Beverley surrender to Bishop Richard Ingworth of Dover (→ 1/12).

Ireland, 7 April 1539. A royal commission organizes the surrendering and re-leasing of monastic lands (→ 16/6).

England, 1 July 1539. The recent Act of Six Articles forces the bishops of Salisbury and Worcester to resign.

Canterbury, July 1539. Archbishop Cranmer sends his wife to Germany, as the Act of Six Articles forbids clerical marriages (→ 4/1543).

Co Meath/Co Monaghan, July 1539. The deputy, Lord Leonard Grey, defeats the joint forces of O'Neill and O'Donnell at Bellahoe (→ 21/3/40).

France, 21 March 1540. Gerald FitzGerald, escaping from Ireland, reaches St Malo.

Waltham, Essex, 23 March 1540. The last abbey in England surrenders (→ 12/1546).

London, April 1540. Thomas Cromwell, the lord privy seal, is created earl of Essex and appointed lord great chamberlain (→ 28/7).

Scotland, 22 May 1540. Queen Mary gives birth to a son, James (→ 8/12/42).

Westminster, 19 June 1540. Thomas Cromwell is accused of treason in the House of Lords.

Lambeth, June 1540. King Henry VIII's new mistress is Catherine Howard, the niece of the duke of Norfolk (→ 12/7).

London, 12 July 1540. King Henry's marriage to Anne of Cleves is declared null and void by an act of parliament on the grounds of non-consummation (→ 28).

Surrey, 28 July 1540. Henry marries Catherine Howard at Oatlands (→ 14/11/41).

Ireland, 12 August 1540. Sir Anthony St Leger (knighted last year) is appointed deputy after the imprisonment of Grey in June (→ 18/6/41).

Edinburgh, 16 August 1540. Sir James Hamilton of Finnart, the master of the works and former favourite of James V, is executed after being accused of plotting against the king.

King backs moves to religious uniformity

Westminster, 16 June 1539
After his years of radical religious reform, Henry VIII, as head of the church in England, has spent the last six months reviving Catholic orthodoxy, and half a dozen key items of belief have now been included in an act of parliament to impose religious uniformity.

The Act of Six Articles "abolishing diversity in religious opinions" provides for harsh punishment of offenders. Repudiation of transubstantiation (the doctrine that the bread and wine change into the body and blood of Christ, when consecrated in the Eucharist) carries a mandatory death penalty as a heretic. Denial of the divine authority for clerical celibacy, vows of chastity, private Masses and the necessity for confession to a priest carry a possible death penalty.

Henry made many amendments to the draft act. In defining transubstantiation he emphasized his conservatism by introducing a reference to the Mother of God. He also included widowhood in those vows of chastity binding by divine law; any widow who breaks the vow is liable to be executed (→ 1/7).

King Henry in the House of Lords.

Change in land law is forced on crown

Westminster, July 1540
For the first time most of the upper classes in England have won a clear right to bequeath freehold land by will. The Statute of Wills, passed during the session of parliament that ended this month, gives the crown feudal rights over only one third of a tenant's land, freeing tenants to dispose of the other two thirds by will.

This new legislation reflects a change of heart by Henry VIII, who four years ago – in order to safeguard the crown's rights and boost its revenues – passed the Statute of Uses, which severely limited landholders' ability to bequeath land by will [*see page 416*]. While a great financial success, this move was bitterly unpopular, contributing to the 1536 "Pilgrimage of Grace". Now the king has been forced to relent (→ 12/1522).

New wave of attacks engulfs monasteries

England, 1 December 1539
Fears early this year of a Roman Catholic-inspired invasion of England by France and Spain meant that King Henry VIII was once again urgently in need of money to improve the country's defences. This, certainly in part, motivated him to complete the project that he initiated three years ago, the dissolution of the monasteries.

In 1536 it was generally just the smaller and more impoverished monasteries and nunneries which fell victim. Most of the inmates, especially nuns, chose to transfer to the larger houses. Now during the past few months the axe has fallen on these as well in increasing numbers. The monks and nuns are being forced to relinquish their cloistered lives and face the rigours of the world at large. Their only compensation is a tiny financial one. They are being awarded small annual pensions – some five pounds for monks, but only an average of three pounds for nuns (→ 23/3/40).

Powerless: the sisters look on as their nunnery is stripped of its valuables.

Satirical Scots poet exposes corruption

Linlithgow, Lothian, 1540
The Scots court has been shocked and amused by a new play attacking "the naughtiness in religion, the presumption of bishops". Written by the diplomat-poet David Lindsay, *A Satire of the Three Estates*, which exposes corruption in church and state, had its first showing before King James V and his council at Linlithgow this year.

A personal companion to James during the present king's infancy, Lindsay has since secured an influential position at court and been entrusted with crucial diplomatic missions – as well as writing popular poetry and drama dealing with vital contemporary issues, including the oppression of the poor. His new play examines the state of Scotland with humour and compassion, offering outspoken advice on how things might be improved.

At the end of the first performance the king is reputed to have told his bishops that if they did not act on the play's lessons he would despatch them to England, where his uncle Henry VIII had already taken harsh measures against the Catholic church.

Henry takes dislike to his fourth wife

A political union: Henry and Anne.

Greenwich, 6 January 1540
King Henry VIII finally married Anne of Cleves today after a delay of 48 hours, during which time he failed to find a reason for not going ahead. Despite Henry's reluctance, the marriage should secure an alliance with North Germany's Protestant princes against the influential Catholics, Francis of France and Holy Roman Emperor Charles V. The treaty between the king and Duke William of Cleves was signed in September. However, Henry is said to have been disappointed with Anne since he first saw her on New Year's Day. The new queen is 34 years old, tall, thin and slightly pockmarked. She is unable to speak any English (→ 12/7).

Practical style: solid-frame box chairs are increasingly popular.

Thomas Cromwell falls from power

London, 28 July 1540
Thomas Cromwell, for so long the most powerful man in England after the king, died on the scaffold at Tower Hill today. He was arrested last month at a meeting of the privy council after a group of nobles led by the duke of Norfolk convinced King Henry VIII that Cromwell was guilty of treason and heresy. Cromwell died protesting his innocence and, as the executioner's axe was blunt, in great agony.

The duke of Norfolk has thus emerged as the victor in an intense power battle within the government. As recently as April Cromwell appeared to enjoy the king's confidence. It was then that he was elevated to the peerage as lord great chamberlain of the royal household. He remained in charge of parliamentary business. But he had made many enemies in his rise to power, particularly among conservative nobles who resented being supplanted by a low-born lawyer.

These nobles have exploited the failure of Henry's marriage to Anne of Cleves. Cromwell had not been alone in advising the king to seek a wife who would seal a Protestant European alliance, but he was blamed for this marriage's failure. The royal eye has now turned towards Catherine Howard, the niece of the duke of Norfolk.

Thomas Cromwell: his time is up.

In the weeks before his arrest, Cromwell sought to bolster his position by ordering the arrests of leading conservative bishops and aristocrats, but the king's growing infatuation with Catherine seems to have made him more susceptible to being persuaded that Cromwell had plotted against him and usurped royal power. Cromwell went to his death still insisting upon his innocence. He said on the scaffold that "many have slandered me and reported that I have been a bearer of such as have maintained evil opinions, which is untrue".

His death ends a remarkable career at the heart of government in the dramatic changes of the 1530s: the breach with Rome, the assertion of royal supremacy through parliament, the imposition of English rule on Wales, the dissolution of the monasteries, the reforms of the law and finance. Cromwell's administrative skills made him an ideal lieutenant for the king after the fall of his original sponsor, Wolsey. There is no obvious successor, as Cromwell had made himself within a few years of Wolsey's fall.

Every parish church to have a new bible

London, 28 July 1540
In the months before he met his death [*see report above*] Thomas Cromwell oversaw the printing of an extra English 3,000 bibles. He also arranged for the return of 2,500 bibles which he had had printed last year in Paris, but which were seized by the French inquisitor-general. With the 3,000 bibles that he had printed in London last year Cromwell was in a position to impose his injunction of 1538 that a bible should be placed in every parish church in the country.

There are just over 8,000 parishes in England and Wales. In 1538 there were neither enough bibles in existence nor enough printers interested in printing them to meet the new demand, so Cromwell decided to go into the business himself. He obtained royal letters patent giving him a monopoly of the new translations for five years. His new "Great Bible" is essentially a revision by Miles Coverdale of William Tyndale's translation.

Barbers and surgeons unite to lift status

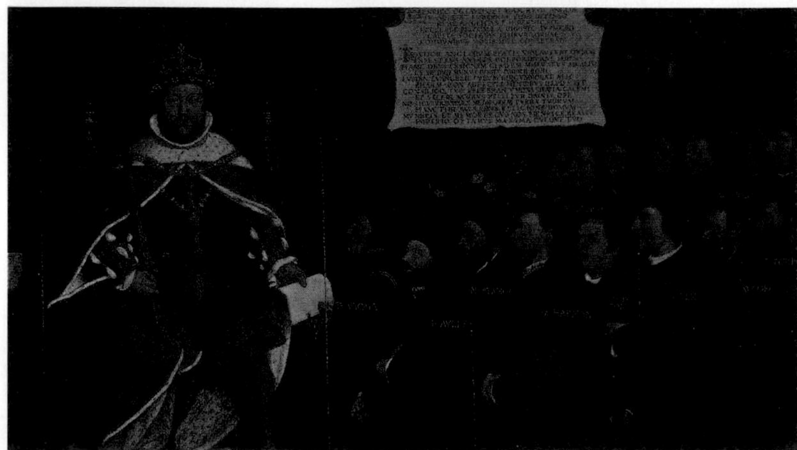

Henry presents a charter to the College of Barbers and Surgeons (Holbein).

London, 1540
Two English guilds have decided to unite this year. The Barbers' Company, incorporated by Edward IV in 1461, has joined forces with the Guild of Surgeons. The new organization represents an attempt by the surgeons to raise their status. At present they are regarded as little more than assistants to physicians, who formed their own college in 1518. Physicians, unlike surgeons, generally have university educations. But they use surgeons for treatments such as blood-letting, and surgeons hope to boost their skills and status by introducing a series of lectures to train their members. Physicians and surgeons have also long been anxious to bar charlatans and other untrained individuals who, they believe, give their emerging disciplines a bad name among the general public.

1541 - 1542

London, 28 July 1541. Lord Leonard Grey, the former deputy of Ireland, is executed for treason.

Ireland, 6 August 1541. Manus O'Donnell, the lord of Tyrconnell, submits to Sir Anthony St Leger, the deputy (→28/12).

Scotland, 18 October 1541. Margaret Tudor, the mother of James V and sister of Henry VIII of England, dies at Methven Castle.

Middlesex, 14 November 1541. Catherine Howard is confined to house arrest at Syon Abbey on charges of adultery (→10/12).

Co Tyrone, 28 December 1541. Conn O'Neill, the lord of Tyrone, submits to Sir Anthony St Leger (→1/4/46).

Dublin, 1541. Christ Church Cathedral is consecrated.

Ireland, 1541. The first Jesuits arrive.

Cambridge, April 1542. The lord chancellor, Thomas, Lord Audley of Walden, founds Magdalene college.

Borders, 24 August 1542. George Gordon, the earl of Huntly, defeats an English army at Haddon Rig.

Greenwich, London, 1 October 1542. Conn Bacach O'Neill is created earl of Tyrone; the succession will go to his illegitimate son, Matthew, created baron of Dungannon.

Cumbria, 24 November 1542. The English rout the Scots at Solway Moss (→14/12/42).

Lothian, 8 December 1542. Mary of Guise gives birth to a daughter, Mary, at Linlithgow Palace (→14).

Edinburgh, 18 December 1542. Cardinal Beaton is chosen as the chief ruler of the council, defeating James, the earl of Arran and heir to the throne (→27/1/43).

England, 29 December 1542. King Henry VIII frees Scottish nobles captured at Solway Moss on the condition that they work towards the marriage of Prince Edward and the infant Mary Queen of Scots.

Bristol, 1542. Henry creates the dioceses of Bristol and Oxford, having created those of Chester, Gloucester, Peterborough and Westminster over the last two years.

Britain, 1542. The "ruff", a new neck fashion, has arrived from France.

Henry heads north, but Scottish king snubs appointment

York, 29 September 1541

Relations between England and Scotland are now deteriorating following the collapse of King Henry VIII's plan to settle all quarrels and remove the northern part of his kingdom from the triple threat of Scotland, France and Spain. As Henry prepares to return to London it is now clear that he has been dramatically snubbed by his nephew, King James V. The Scottish king, advised by his councillors not to trust Henry, did not turn up.

In other respects, the stately "royal progress" north has served its purpose well enough. One thousand armed men and a train of artillery have been a salutary reminder to those of doubtful loyalty here who survived the retribution that followed the "Pilgrimage of Grace" uprising in 1536. And the magnificence of the royal court, housed in a grand lodging and some 200 tents just outside the city walls here, demonstrates that there is no power or wealth in England which can begin to rival the house of Tudor.

The decision to visit the north was made in April, but it was not until June that the royal retinue set out, including the king's new wife Catherine Howard. It is Henry's furthest venture north in his reign, but the gloss has been taken away by the snub by James (→24/11/42).

James with his first wife, Madeleine.

Catherine is executed

A queen disgraced: Catherine Howard is taken to the Tower of London.

London, 13 February 1542

Catherine Howard, the fifth wife of King Henry VIII, was beheaded in the Tower of London today. So was Lady Rochford, the head of her household, who played an important part in arranging the queen's meetings with Thomas Culpeper, one of two men with whom Catherine was alleged to have committed adultery [*see below*].

Henry married Catherine in July 1540. She was then 20, and the king is said still to grieve for his young wife despite her betrayal. He entrusted her trial and punishment to a commission so as to spare himself having to listen yet again to the "wicked facts of the case".

Equally unhappy is the former queen's uncle, the duke of Norfolk. Catherine was his second niece to marry the king, and like the first, Anne Boleyn, she has now been executed accused of adultery. As with Anne Boleyn, the duke's motive for dangling Catherine before the king was to advance his family's influence at court. His success helped to bring about the fall of Thomas Cromwell, but now that coup has turned sour.

Queen's lovers pay fatal price of adultery

London, 10 December 1541

Two elegant heads were struck from their gentlemanly shoulders today as Francis Dereham and Thomas Culpeper paid the inevitable price for consorting immodestly with a queen.

Adultery is a treasonable offence both for a king's consort – Catherine Howard, King Henry VIII's fifth wife, is now under house arrest – and her lovers. Dereham's offence, at least in so far as has been proved, took place before Catherine's marriage to Henry in July last year, and there is a rumour that they were pledged to each other before the vivacious Catherine caught the 49-year-old king's eye, and the English throne caught hers. However, her adultery with Culpeper was an open secret in the court, and they had conducted their affair with particular indiscretion during the recent royal progress to York. The king was the last to know, and it was Archbishop Cranmer whom the privy council finally sent to break the news.

Henry received it very badly, alternately raging and bursting into tears. He was naturally reluctant to believe that all the time he was parading his royal radiance to his subjects in the north he was being cuckolded semi-publicly by an audacious courtier. The failure of his fifth marriage leaves him still with only one legitimate male heir, four-year-old Edward (→13/2/42).

Henry is persuaded to assume the title of king of Ireland

Dublin, 18 June 1541
An act passed today at a parliament called by Sir Anthony St Leger, the lord deputy, makes Henry VIII of England also king of Ireland. From now on "the king's highness, his heirs and successors, kings of England, [shall] be always kings of this land of Ireland".

The country has long been divided between, on the one hand, the English Pale and the lands held by largely independent Anglo-Irish lords and, on the other, the areas ruled by Gaelic lords according to Irish custom, leading to a crude distinction between "loyal English" and "hostile Irish". By making Henry king of Ireland, and not just an English lord in Ireland, the act aims to abandon this divisive thinking and put everyone in Ireland on an equal footing. Ireland is no longer to be seen as "foreign".

St Leger is following a policy of assimilation through a conveyancing scheme called "surrender and regrant", whereby Gaelic lords first give up their lands to the crown and then get them back on English terms. He believes that Henry's assumption of the sovereignty will further that end (→6/8).

Spring fancy: a page for April from an illustrated calendar.

James V dies after Solway Moss rout

Fife, 14 December 1542
King James V died suddenly today, aged only 30, leaving the throne in the nominal hands of his sole surviving child – his daughter Mary, who is just six days old. She becomes Scotland's first queen. The king's premature death came in the wake of a series of personal and political blows which culminated in the humiliating defeat of a Scottish army last month at Solway Moss, west of Carlisle. Since then he had behaved like a broken man, retiring to Falkland Palace, where he died.

James himself came to the throne as an infant; he was just 17 months old when his father was killed at the Battle of Flodden in 1513. When he reached the age of 16 he asserted his right to rule his kingdom at a time when Scotland was riven by pro-English and pro-French factions.

Noted for his authoritarian style, James was keen on law enforcement and keener still on raising money. He ordered the construction of expensive new castles at Falkland, Stirling and Holyrood. New taxes were imposed on the church, but the king showed no inclination to imitate the break with Rome brought about by his uncle, Henry VIII, in England.

King James V: an untimely death.

James sought to maintain the "auld alliance" with France partly in order to raise money. He was married twice, each time to a Frenchwoman who brought him a generous dowry. His second wife, Mary of Guise, who survives him, bore him two sons as well as Mary. But both boys died in the spring of last year, throwing the king into bitter despair, and his health was also declining.

Last summer James summoned his nobles to join him in an attack on England but found few supporters. Many of the nobles were wary of repeating the disaster of Flodden and unconvinced by calls to fight Protestantism. Despite some success in skirmishes during the summer, a weak Scottish force – largely recruited by the clergy and led by a royal favourite, Oliver Sinclair – was routed by a smaller English army at Solway Moss on 24 November.

James, who was with another part of his army, returned to Fife suffering from nervous strain. On his daughter's birth he is reported to have said: "It came with a lass and it will pass with a lass" – a reference to the origins of the dynasty with Marjorie Bruce and to the new monarch, Mary Queen of Scots. James Hamilton, the earl of Arran, is likely to be appointed governor (→29/12).

House of Commons asserts its authority

Westminster, March 1542
George Ferrers, a member of parliament for Plymouth, has been freed from arrest after the House of Commons successfully asserted its power, as the highest court in the land, to overule the rights of lower courts. This demonstration of parliamentary privilege – backed by King Henry VIII – reflects the growing authority of parliament which has occurred during the Tudor years.

Ferrers, a member of "the Spears", the king's honorary bodyguard, had been arrested on allegations that he had failed to honour the surety he gave for a debt. Now not only has he been freed but also charges have been dropped after parliamentary privilege was invoked by the House of Commons. An unprecedented meeting of its leaders ruled that parliament, as the highest court in the land, had the right to enforce the freedom of its members from arrest in civil cases.

This follows other changes introduced in Henry's reign. In 1515 the Commons gained control over the attendance of its members, who have also grown steadily in number. In 1523 the right to free speech was urged by Sir Thomas More, then speaker, and accepted by the king. This right has not yet led to clashes with the crown because Henry has boosted parliamentary prestige by giving members a pivotal role in the reformation.

King Henry VIII with his council.

Henry seeks to win control of Scotland

London, 29 December 1542
King Henry VIII has freed Scottish nobles captured at the battle of Solway Moss last month on condition that they return north to promote English interests. They have been made to swear support for a marriage between Henry's son, Edward, and the infant Mary, Queen of Scots.

Henry also wants Mary to be brought up in England, not least because he fears that the influence of her French-born mother, Mary of Guise, may encourage links between Scotland and France at a time when he is planning a new attack on France next year. Henry's moves against France, which he has been discussing with Holy Roman Charles V for over a year, have been delayed by what the English king sees as new opportunities in Scotland. He has decided against an outright military assault, confident that diplomacy will win England a bloodless victory (→3/1/43).

1543 - 1544

Lothian, 3 January 1543. James Hamilton, the earl of Arran, is appointed governor, or regent, of Scotland.

Edinburgh, 27 January 1543. Arran calls for the arrest of Cardinal David Beaton, who opposed his appointment.

England, 11 February 1543. Henry VIII allies with Holy Roman Emperor Charles V, against France.

Edinburgh, March 1543. Parliament authorizes the reading of the Bible in the vernacular.

London, 19 April 1543. Henry VIII appoints George Dowdall to succeed George Cromer as archbishop of Armagh.

Greenwich, 1 July 1543. An Anglo-Scots treaty is signed by which the infant Mary Queen of Scots will marry King Henry's son and heir, Edward, as soon as she is ten years old.

Hampton Court, 12 July 1543. Henry VIII marries his sixth wife, Catherine Parr, a twice-married widow from Northamptonshire.

London, July 1543. Ulick Mac William Burke is created earl of Clanricard, and Murrough O'Brien earl of Thomond; the succession to Murrough is to go to his nephew Donough, who is created baron of Ibracken.

Stirling, 9 September 1543. After a reconciliation between governor, Arran, and Cardinal Beaton, Mary is crowned queen of Scotland.

Edinburgh, 3 May 1544. The earl of Hertford burns the city.

Westminster, 18 May 1544. Sir Anthony St Leger, the deputy of Ireland, is created a knight of the garter.

Stirling, 10 June 1544. Mary of Guise, the dowager queen, attempts to depose Arran.

England, 11 June 1544. By order of Henry VIII, English, not Latin, will be used in the church litany.

Calais, 14 July 1544. Henry VIII joins his army here.

France, 18 September 1544. Holy Roman Emperor, Charles V abandons Henry and makes peace with France at Crépy.

Lothian, 7 November 1544. The joint forces of the earl of Arran and Mary of Guise stand against the English.

Thomas Cranmer survives a 'heresy' plot

Whitehall, April 1543

In dramatic fashion Archbishop Cranmer has survived a plot to condemn him for heresy and has so turned the tables on his enemies that the faction which oppposes the reformers is in disarray. His victory, of course, depended on King Henry VIII's support, but the way in which the king chose to show it was wilful, even by the standards he himself has set in recent years.

The plot had begun when a group of conservatives on the council thought they had persuaded Henry that Cranmer was heretical to the point of endangering the state. He told them to summon Cranmer to this morning's council and there imprison him in the king's name.

But last night Henry himself saw the archbishop and told him of the conspiracy. However, when Cranmer announced his willingness for a full trial of the doctrines of reformation Henry became alarmed, either for Cranmer's own sake or because he foresaw endless trouble might come of it, and gave Cranmer a ring as a sign of full royal support.

Thomas Cranmer: a close escape.

This morning the confident plotters were dumbfounded when, after being kept waiting for nearly an hour, their victim silenced his accusers by showing the ring. They are now rehearsing their excuses for the king (→28/1/47)).

Bishops' book to be replaced by king's

London, May 1543

The *Bishops' Book*, of which King Henry VIII has been highly critical ever since he read it in 1537, is to be replaced. Not surprisingly the new book is to be called the *King's Book*. The king has had a major influence on its theology, making no fewer than 100 corrections to the *Bishops' Book* and even more to the *King's Book*.

The king stands between Archbishop Cranmer's Protestant enthusiasts and the conservatives. He is strongly in favour of transubstantiation and of priestly celibacy, but his views both on the authority of priests and extreme unction are closer to those of the radicals. But Henry is above all a pragmatist careful to maintain his own power. When it came to the view that all men, rich and poor, are equal in God's eyes, Henry added that equality existed "touching the soul" only (→11/6/44).

Hans Holbein, painter to the king and his courtiers, has died

England, 1543

The court painter Hans Holbein has died. He had become the greatest artist in the country where he had lived since 1532, a man whose lifesize portrait of Henry VIII in a wall-painting for Whitehall Palace was widely hailed as a masterpiece.

Hans Holbein the younger was born in Augsburg in 1497 and by 1515 was working in Basel. He painted the scholar Erasmus, who recommended him to Sir Thomas More. A group portrait of the More family was among the works completed by Holbein on his first visit to England in 1526/27. His realistic portraits won him a high reputation in court circles so that, although he returned briefly to Basel, he came back to settle in England. By 1537 he was painter to King Henry.

He portrayed a quarter of the peerage as well as several of the king's wives; his depiction of Anne of Cleves made the king agree to marry her, a decision he regretted when he saw her in the flesh. The Whitehall wall-painting was perhaps his finest, encompassing not only the king but also his queen (then Jane Seymour) and parents as a panoply of Tudor monarchy, and showing Henry as the embodiment of kingship. Such was the success of his portraits that Holbein had less time for the wider range of work he had undertaken before moving to England, but he also designed notable jewellery and household objects, including a painted cradle for Princess Elizabeth.

An engaging portrait: "The Ambassadors" shows a fine eye for detail.

All of Wales now subject to English law

Westminster, 1543
A new act of parliament this year completed the Act of Union between England and Wales passed in 1536. English law is now extended to all parts of Wales, with the old distinction between the principality and the Marches abolished.

England's lord chancellor now has the responsibility of appointing justices of the peace for Wales. Among the laws they will have to implement is a new act passed this year which reflects King Henry VIII's efforts to impose doctrinal uniformity upon his kingdom and to control both extreme Protestants and Catholics loyal to the pope.

The act forbids women (except noblewomen) and the lower classes to read the English Bible and sets severe penalties for illegal books, ballads, plays, songs, fantasies and unauthorized translations of the Bible. Tyndale's "crafty, false and untrue translation" of the Bible is forbidden.

Yet reading even the authorized English Bible is controlled since the act says that this misleads "the lower sort" and there have thereby "grown and increased in divers (people) naughty and erroneous opinions". The act says that "no women, nor artificers, prentices, journeymen, servingmen, yeomen, husbandmen or labourers" may read the Bible. Upper-class men may read it, and also noblewomen "to themselves alone".

Marriage treaty is denounced by Scots

Edinburgh, 11 December 1543
The Scottish parliament today denounced a peace agreement sealed at Greenwich on 1 July with King Henry VIII of England. The Treaty of Greenwich stipulated that the infant Mary Queen of Scots would marry the English king's son, Edward, when she was ten years old. However, Henry failed to persuade the Scots to agree to end their alliance with France.

Today's rejection of the deal follows a reconcilation between James Hamilton, the earl of Arran, and Cardinal David Beaton, respectively the regent and primate of Scotland. Arran had become regent in January, declaring that he did not recognize the pope. His appointment was contested by Beaton, the archbishop of St Andrews, who himself laid claim to the regency. However, Arran, who is next in line to the throne, has a powerful reason for keeping Scotland independent. In September, before Queen Mary's coronation at Stirling, he renounced his Protestant sympathies and joined forces with Beaton to thwart English ambitions.

The pro-English faction has now been defeated in the Scottish parliament, which today also annulled liberal religious legislation passed by Arran in March, including a law permitting the reading of the Bible in the vernacular (→ 10/6/44).

Scottish 'heretics' go to their deaths

A Protestant is burnt at the stake.

Perth, January 1544
The execution here of a number of "heretics" has shocked the small Scottish Protestant community. Disquiet was stirred by the case of Helen Stirk, who was put to death for refusing to call on the Virgin Mary during childbirth. The persecution was supervised by Cardinal Beaton, who seeks to regain church authority after the annulment of last year's liberal legislation [*see report left*]. Beaton was accompanied to Perth by the regent, Arran.

Henry leads his forces into Boulogne, but the invaders are split on the next moves

The king's men: Henry VIII's troops setting up the siege of Boulogne.

Boulogne, 18 September 1544
In what appear to be a rare moment of decisive action in his long-running campaigns of diplomatic and military manoeuvre against the French and the Scots, Henry VIII has besieged and taken Boulogne.

The action took place under his personal supervision, and the king entered the French port today in buoyant mood. The return to all-out war, some 30 years after his first military excursions in Europe, appears to have invigorated the king after years of indecisive raids into Scotland and inconclusive negotiations with Holy Roman Emperor Charles V for a war against France. Yet quite where Henry's success at Boulogne will lead is another matter. English forces landed at Calais in June, but since then the campaign has been hindered by uncertainty and division about what its objectives should be.

Some English generals favoured a march on Paris, others on Normandy. The role of the emperor has been equally unclear. Henry decided that Boulogne and Montreuil had to be taken if his forces were to be supplied on any advance further into France. Montreuil is still being besieged by forces under the command of the duke of Norfolk, but it is not clear what either the English army or the imperial forces under Charles V will do next (→ 15/7/45).

Protests are growing at the proliferation of English alehouses. In 1544 Coventry magistrates complained that "a great part of the inhabitants of this city be now become brewers or tipplers [alehouse-keepers]".

1545

Borders, 27 February. Archibald Douglas, the earl of Angus, defeats an English army at Ancrum Moor, avenging the English sacking of Jedburgh and Melrose Abbey (→ 9/9).

Rome, March. Pope Paul III appoints a second archbishop of Armagh, Robert Wauchop, in opposition to Henry VIII's appointment in 1543 of George Dowdall.

Le Havre, 15 July. The French fleet sets sail to attack England as a diversion from the English attempt to recapture Boulogne (→ 20/7).

Portsmouth, 5 August. The sails and yards of the sunken *Mary Rose* have been recovered by Italian salvage experts, but all attempts to refloat the ship have failed.

Guildford, Surrey, 22 August. Charles Brandon, the duke of Suffolk, a close friend and old jousting partner of King Henry VIII, dies after a short illness.

Ireland, 5 September. James Butler, the earl of Ormond and Ossory, is appointed general of the Irish forces in Scotland.

Normandy, early September. The lord admiral, John Dudley, Viscount Lisle, avenges French attacks on England by raiding the French coast (→ 1545).

Windsor, 27 September. Henry Howard, the earl of Surrey, the newly appointed governor of Boulogne, is warned by his father, the duke of Norfolk, and others not to urge the king to try to keep Boulogne, since its loss may be the only means of gaining peace with France (→ 1/1546).

Ireland, September. The English mint issues a debased coin for use in Ireland which increases inflation (→ 14/7/56).

Brussels, December. Holy Roman Emperor Charles V acts as mediator in peace talks between England and France; similar peace talks are being held in Calais (→ 1/1546).

London. Sir Thomas Elyot, the diplomat and scholar, publishes his latest work, *Defence of Good Women* (→ 1546).

England. John Taverner, the composer, dies, aged 50.

London. John Heywood, the dramatist, writes a highly entertaining short play or interlude which is called *The Four P's*.

Pride of fleet sinks

A tragic loss: the flagship "Mary Rose", now at the bottom of the Solent.

Portsmouth, 20 July
The *Mary Rose*, the pride of Henry VIII's fleet, lies at the bottom of the Solent after capsizing on the way out to sea to confront a suspected French invasion fleet. At least 500 soldiers are feared to have drowned with the ship, which sank before the eyes of the horrified king.

Reports that the French fleet had been sighted in the Channel arrived at Portsmouth just after dawn. As the harbour became the scene of frenzied activity, the *Mary Rose*, newly delivered from the builders' yard after extensive refurbishment, was prepared for action.

The armaments which the flagship carried were impressive. As well as a large number of small iron guns, the *Mary Rose* boasted 15 bronze pieces – including two cannons, two demi-cannons, two culverins, six demi-culverins, two sakers and a falcon. There were 600 troops aboard and 100 seamen.

Having inspected his troops, King Henry watched from Spithead as the great ship made her way towards the open sea. There was a stiff wind blowing from the Needles, but this caused little concern until the ship was suddenly seen to be listing to one side. Within moments the guns had broken loose and sent the *Mary Rose* into her death-roll. She sank within a minute. At this stage the reason for the sinking remains a mystery, but there are suspicions that portholes may have been left open, allowing water in (→ 5/8).

English court adopts fashions from Spain

London
New Spanish styles in dress have spread through the court. The look – wasp-shaped, with padded knees, padded shoulders and a tightly laced stomach – gives the aged king's court the appearance of a luxurious hornets' nest. Padding, or bombast, exaggerates the contours of the male body, particularly around the codpiece. The latest fashion is for short Spanish cloaks, and feathers are also popular. Two new types of garment have appeared, the ruff (a rich man's conceit since it goes limp after a few days) and knitted stockings, unknown in England until a few years ago.

Flamboyant feathers: all the rage.

How the English navy won control of the Channel

Portsmouth
Despite the disastrous loss of the *Mary Rose*, the English navy has grown enormously in size, strength and efficiency since Henry VIII came to the throne. The fleet now includes 50 well-armed warships and effectively controls the Channel, ensuring that Boulogne can be constantly supplied, while the French king cannot consider any part of his coastline safe.

It is hugely expensive to maintain a fleet at sea for any length of time, so most of the king's ships are laid up in port for easy care and maintenance, ready to be mobilized for service in home waters. As the vessels are not designed for long periods at sea, only rudimentary victualling is usually required. Almost the entire capacity of warships is for weapons and men, who are expected to remain on board for no more than a day or two.

A naval architect at work designing ships for Henry's fleet.

Naval engagements are expected to be short and sharp. Guns and longbows are usually the decisive weapons, and in both these areas the English are well equipped. The king has taken a particular interest in the art of gunnery, and the English have developed a compact naval gun carriage, with stepped sides and four small wheels, which is more manoeuvrable.

Nonsuch Palace completed for Henry VIII

French style: a view of King Henry VIII's Nonsuch Palace when completed.

Surrey
Work is forging ahead on what has become King Henry VIII's favourite building scheme, the completion of his new palace at Nonsuch in 2,000 acres of Surrey parkland. The village of Cuddington, near Cheam and Ewell, was demolished to make way for a palace upon which the king has already spent some £23,000. The project is likely to cost a good deal more before it is all finished.

Henry has summoned some of the greatest artists in Europe to England to carry out the decorative work at Nonsuch. Many of the artists he has brought across the Channel have previously worked on the palace of the French king at Fontainebleau, south of Paris.

Building at Nonsuch was begun in 1538 with the idea of repeating in a permanent structure the extravagant, but temporary, splendour of the building and decorations erected at Guines for the meeting between Henry and King Francis of France at the Field of Cloth of Gold in 1520.

The construction is traditional, but the inside is embellished with naturalistic plaster garlands and strapwork, while on the outside the panels between the timbers are filled with a very hard plaster, known as "stucco-duro", and decorated in the French style.

English forces strike back in border war

Hermitage Castle: a Douglas family stronghold during the border wars.

Borders, 9 September
English forces under the command of Edward Seymour, the earl of Hertford, have launched a counterattack against Scots and French forces on the Anglo-Scottish border. Skirmishes have been going on for most of the year, as King Henry VIII fought on two fronts, against the Scots and against a threatened invasion by France.

The Treaty of Greenwich in 1543 was meant to have secured peace between England and Scotland. But the Scottish parliament renounced the treaty, moving closer to France, the birthplace of Mary of Guise, the queen's mother, just as Henry resumed hostilities with the French. Internal differences among Scots were forgotten as Mary of Guise, Cardinal Beaton and the earl of Arran, Scotland's governor, formed a united front against the English.

In February Archibald Douglas, the earl of Angus, led a successful attack on English forces at Ancrum Moor, and the collapse of Henry's alliance against France with Holy Roman Emperor Charles V this summer allowed France to send 5,000 troops to bolster the Scottish cause. Yet the Franco-Scottish raids have done little but antagonize people in the borders. Many Scots are therefore backing the English invasion today in the hope of securing Henry's protection.

Master of the revels appointed by Henry

London
A new post, that of *magister jocorum* or master of the revels, has been created this year by Henry VIII. His duties will be to supervise court entertainments, but his wider role will be to censor all theatrical performances. As head of the revels office he will report to the lord chamberlain.

What the master will be looking out for is any hint of sedition in the theatre. The king quite naturally sees the crown – as the church agrees – as above criticism. Thus any attack, even in a play, must be suppressed. It is hoped that the master will make sure of that.

A mystery play staged at Coventry: a possible target for the censor.

Religious unity called for by English king

Westminster, 24 December
In probably the finest speech of his reign, Henry VIII had members of parliament in tears today as he delivered a passionate plea for an end to religious division in England. The occasion was the end of the parliamentary session and Henry chose to speak himself rather than through the lord chancellor.

After thanking the speaker, Sir John Baker, for the expressions of loyalty by parliament, not to mention the grant of the subsidy, the king went on to deplore the "lack of love" in which "some are called Papists, some Pharesins, some Lutherians and some Anabaptists, names devised by the devill". He called on the bishops to help heal these divisions by affirming that there is but "one truth".

Although the speech was heartfelt, and movingly delivered, there were lighter moments too, as when he said: "Some be too stiff in their old Mumpsimus, others be too busy in their new Sumpsimus." This taunt at uneducated priests who get the word sumpsimus wrong in the Latin Mass, has become a popular phrase for church pedantry. Now it has the royal seal of approval. Henry then gave the royal assent to the session's laws, and parliament rose (→28/1/47).

1546

Boulogne, January. The governor of Boulogne, Henry Howard, earl of Surrey, is defeated by the French when he attacks part of their besieging army (→ 21/3).

Boulogne, 21 March. The earl of Surrey is superseded in command by his rivals the earl of Hertford and Viscount Lisle, whose recent military careers are more successful than his (→ 7/6).

Ireland, 1 April. Following the serious feud between James Butler, the earl of Ormond and Ossory, and the deputy, Sir Anthony St Leger, both are summoned to appear before King Henry VIII to explain their dispute (→ 31/12).

France, 7 June. England and France make peace after signing the Treaty of Ardres; England will retain control over Boulogne for the next eight years (→ 9/1546).

Trent, Italy. June. The exiled English moderate Cardinal Pole, a cousin of King Henry's, decides to withdraw from the pope's council being held here because of the general shift towards conservatism.

Boulogne, September. King Henry nearly restarts the war with France when he ignores his council's advice and secretly orders the soldiers garrisoned at Boulogne to destroy the construction of a French fort close by (→ 8/1549).

London, October. Sir Anthony Denny, a reformist and a political ally of Edward Seymour, the earl of Hertford, is appointed chief gentleman of the king's privy chamber, giving him considerable control over access to the king's apartments.

Surrey, 2 December. Stephen Gardiner, the bishop of Winchester, infuriates the king by refusing to exchange lands in his bishopric with some owned by the crown (→ 26/12).

Cambridge, 19 December. Henry VIII founds Trinity College.

Surrey, 26 December. Henry summons Hertford, Lisle and Denny to his bedside to witness alterations to his will; he removes Bishop Gardiner from the list of councillors prescribed for Prince Edward's minority (→ 5/1547).

Oxford. Henry VIII refounds Cardinal College, formerly founded by Cardinal Wolsey, as Christ Church (→ 19/12).

Irish lord dies in mystery poisoning after long-running feud with ambitious deputy

London, 31 December
Mystery surrounds the death this year of James Butler, the earl of Ormond and Ossory, one of the foremost Irish lords. Ormond came to London in April to settle a dispute before the privy council between himself and Sir Anthony St Leger, the deputy of Ireland. It was some while after the two men had made their cases and been reconciled that Ormond accepted an invitation to dine, with some 50 of his servants, at Limehouse. Everyone was taken ill after the meal, and Ormond was among 17 who died.

Suspicion rests, not surprisingly, on St Leger, who returned to Dublin on 16 December. He was at odds with Ormond from the time he arrived in Ireland, in September 1537, to inquire into the English administration of the country. St Leger had an ambitious programme to set up circuit courts in Munster, extend county organization beyond the Pale and create a system of presidencies to entrench English rule in Munster, Connacht and Ulster.

He made little progress and was accused by Ormond of running a wasteful and expensive administration. St Leger, meanwhile, claimed that Ormond was actively obstructing his proposed reforms and that his loyalty to King Henry VIII was questionable. Ormond was, however, not alone in finding St Leger difficult to deal with. The lord chancellor, Sir John Alen, grew impatient with St Leger's lack of success on any front. Eventually all parties agreed to refer the matter to the privy council in London. The whole affair has ended well for St Leger. His chief enemy is dead, while Alen has been sentenced to a spell in the Tower (→ 31/5/47).

London 'stews' face immediate shutdown

Dens of vice: King Henry has moved against the brothels of Southwark.

London, April
In his latest attack on the spread of vice within London, King Henry VIII has ordered the stews – the brothels of Bankside – to be shut down immediately. This has been done, though cynics believe that it will not be long before they are replaced by new establishments.

It is not Henry's first attempt to "clean up" London. In 1519 he authorized Cardinal Wolsey to suppress both brothels and gambling houses, while a later act declared that buggery, for centuries an offence judged by the religious courts, was now to come under civil law and be punishable by death.

The royal commands may seem admirable, but they have little long-term effect. The appetite of men for pleasure, however rigorously condemned, apparently outstrips all attempts at suppression.

Survey reveals how the church lost land

A title deed to an Essex manor.

Yorkshire, December
A survey of land ownership carried out this year in the West Riding of Yorkshire has shown dramatic changes over the last decade. The survey, which assessed land in terms of value rather than acreage, reveals that the proportion owned by the church slumped from 44 per cent in 1535 to just 17 per cent this year. By contrast, the crown's landholdings tripled from nine per cent to 27 per cent. The gentry have also prospered, with 47.5 per cent compared with 40 per cent in 1535, while land owned by the nobility is much the same. The changes here illustrate the national decline in land owned by the church – and therefore in its wealth – following the dissolution of the monasteries.

Wise educator dies

Carlton, Cambridgeshire
Sir Thomas Elyot, the diplomat, scholar and supporter of Thomas Cromwell who died this year, will be best remembered for his handbook on how educate the new breed of "inferior" governors, or magistrates as he called them, created by Cromwell's reforms. *The Book of the Governor*, published in 1531 supports the new idea from the continent that education is more than professional training. Rather, he says, it should involve the whole personality and give a firm grounding in the arts. A musical instrument, for instance, should be learnt but played "without wanton countenance and dissolute gesture".

Scots cardinal murdered

St Andrews, Fife, 29 May
Cardinal David Beaton, the archbishop of St Andrews, was killed today by a group of Protestant militants. He had paid dearly for sending a popular preacher, George Wishart, to the stake in March. One of the assassins urinated on the face of the cardinal as his mutilated body was paraded before the large crowd outside St Andrews Castle.

The killers gained easy access to the castle early this morning; either security was very lax or the guards had been bribed. The alarm was raised, however, before members of the gang reached the cardinal's chamber, which they found to be stoutly barricaded. Beaton or one of his servants opened the door when the assassins threatened to set the room ablaze. They rushed in and ran him through with their swords. The cardinal's dying words were: "I am a priest ... I am a priest. Fye, fye. All is gone."

Beaton was an obvious target for Protestant militants. His vigorous persecution of heretics culminated in his presiding at the heresy trial of Wishart, Scotland's most vocal opponent of the Catholic Church. The many enemies whom the cardinal made in sending the preacher to be burned at the stake were joined by others in Scotland who backed the Anglophile cause. A linchpin of Tudor security is the need to control Scotland. Beaton, as the leader of the country's French faction, had helped to overturn the Treaty of Greenwich and was a danger to Henry VIII in symbolizing a possible Catholic resurgence.

David Beaton is savagely murdered.

Radical gentlewoman burned as heretic

London, 16 July
She had been broken on the rack and was unable to walk, so today they carried her to the stake in a wooden chair. Still sitting, she was burnt alive at Smithfield in London for her heretical views.

The execution of Ann Askew has sparked furious controversy, particularly as she was a gentlewoman with connections at court. Her torture was authorized by two senior judicial officials, Richard Rich and Thomas Wriothesley, in the face of protests by the lieutenant of the Tower, who refused to torture her a second time.

Rich and Wriothesley are heading a conservative drive to stamp out religious radicals. The real target is Queen Catherine Parr, who is suspected to be a supporter of the "new" religion, but Askew died without implicating anyone.

Speculation rife as king's health fails

Guildford, Surrey, September 1546
King Henry VIII's health is again a political issue. Lord Wriothesley, the lord chancellor, claims that Henry only has a cold, but rumour says it is more serious. Speculation also abounds as to who would advise Prince Edward, although discussion of the king's death is strictly outlawed.

It cannot be long now, however. The king, now 55, is grossly fat and can barely walk; he is carried about in a pair of specially constructed chairs, called "trams", covered with quilted tawney velvet and embroidered with roses in Venice gold. To go upstairs he needs special machinery.

For nearly 20 years the king has been tormented by agonizing leg ulcers, possibly caused by drastic treatment for varicose veins. A cycle of serious illness, sparking succession disputes, followed by recovery has marked recent years. In 1538 Henry appeared close to death after a clot from his leg caused a blockage in his lungs; for several days he was speechless and black in the face. Three years later he had serious fever derived from his ulcer, and another in March 1544, and again in February this year.

Yet the king keeps on riding, despite intense pain and the fact that it keeps his ulcers from healing. The same fierce will that keeps him riding has kept him alive – so far. Henry has not decided who will act as regent during the minority of his son, Edward, who will be nine next month. One candidate is Edward Seymour, the earl of Hertford, but this would be resisted by the Howard family, headed by the duke of Norfolk (→28/1/47).

Earl faces death as Howard plot fails

London, 12 December
In what seem to be the last days of Henry VIII's reign, the power of the Howard family appears finally to have been broken and the ascendancy of the new men at court assured. After ten days of investigations Henry Howard, the earl of Surrey, faces execution for treason, and his father, the duke of Norfolk, has been placed under arrest.

The charges are complex, but it seems that William Paget, the royal secretary, has amassed enough evidence to show the king how high the Howards hoped to stand in the kingdom after Henry's death, when the young Edward's reign must necessarily be dominated by whoever controls the regency.

Henry Howard, the earl of Surrey.

Among the damaging revelations are a suggestion by Henry Howard that his sister, Mary of Richmond, should attempt to win influence over the king by becoming his mistress, and the way that Surrey had flaunted his own royal descent by incorporating the arms of Edward the Confessor into his own. Despite a lifetime of plots and ambition, his father is charged only with concealing Surrey's treasons.

Although the fall of the Howards will be seen as a victory for the party of religious reform, in reality it has been a conspiracy by efficient politicians against an arrogant and ambitious noble who never made a secret of his disdain for "these new erected men" (→21/1/47).

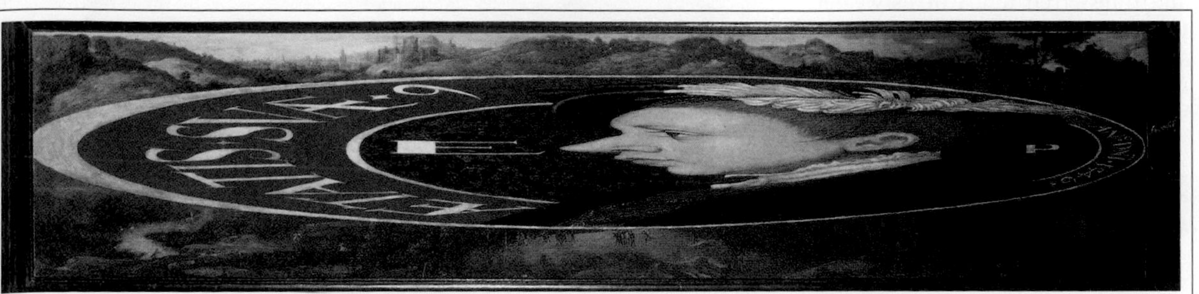

A distorted "anamorphic" portrait of Prince Edward: perspective has been altered in such a way that the work appears grotesquely misshapen, but the portrait appears from one angle to be in three dimensions. "The Ambassadors" on page 426 features a skull in the foreground which has been painted "anamorphically".

1547

London, 21 January. Henry Howard, the earl of Surrey, who was arrested with the duke of Norfolk, his father, for treason, is executed.

Westminster, 31 January. The king's council appoints Edward Seymour, the earl of Hertford, as lord protector of the young King Edward (→ 16/2).

Westminster, 7 February. The privy council supports the protestant insurrection at St Andrews, Lothian (→ 31/7).

London, 16 February. Edward Seymour, the earl of Hertford, is made duke of Somerset (→ 20/3/49).

St Andrews, Fife, 10 April. John Knox is made chaplain to the Protestant garrison in castle (→ 9/1555).

Ireland, 31 May. The deputy, Sir Anthony St Leger, is told by the English council that Sir Edward Bellingham and reinforcements will restore order here (→ 21/5/48).

Winchester, May. Bishop Gardiner of Winchester annoys the lord protector, the duke of Somerset, by his efforts to suppress the religious radicals in his bishopric (→ 25/9).

London, May. Despite disapproval from the council, Catherine Parr, the widow of Henry VIII, marries Thomas Seymour, the younger brother of the duke of Somerset (→ 7/9/48).

England, 31 July. The new *Book of Homilies* is published; it contains 12 sermons, some by Thomas Cranmer, the archbishop of Canterbury.

St Andrews, 31 July. The castle surrenders to the earl of Arran, the governor of Scotland, after bombardment by a French fleet (→ 10/9).

Tayside, 11 September. Mary Queen of Scots is sent to the remote island of Inchmahome on the Lake of Menteith after the defeat at Pinkie (→ 7/8/48).

London, 22 September. City authorities order a survey of all parish churches, to restrain the destruction of statues and stained glass by Protestants.

London, 25 September. Bishop Gardiner is put in Fleet prison for opposing the new *Book of Homilies* (→ 20/2/48).

Lincoln, September. Bishop Henry Holbeach has to give 20 of the bishopric's manors to the crown and nine to the lord protector, Somerset.

King Henry VIII slips into long sleep

A comfort in his old age: King Henry and his sixth wife, Catharine Parr.

Westminster, 28 January
King Henry VIII of England died early this morning. He was 55 and is survived by his sixth wife, Catherine Parr, and three legitimate children: Edward, the new king, Mary and Elizabeth. News of his death has not been officially announced, but it is clear that Edward Seymour, the earl of Hertford and uncle of nine-year-old Edward, enjoys great power.

The late king's will, revised several times during his last illness, provides for the country to be governed during Edward's minority by a 16-strong regency council appointed by Henry himself. A so-called "unfulfilled gifts clause", which allows the council to make awards in Henry's name after his death, on the grounds that he had intended to make them himself, is said to have been added to the will.

The regency council is empowered to take necessary action for the good of Edward and the realm as it sees fit. Using this clause, Hertford is tonight constructing an agreement which will make him lord protector (and, it is rumoured, duke of Somerset) by promising titles and lands to his supporters. He will then dominate the council.

The chief source of lands are the estates of the duke of Norfolk, who lies in the Tower condemned to die. It is not clear whether Henry's death will mean that he lives. His son, the earl of Surrey, was executed for treason earlier this month. During Henry's last illness, the king used his will to threaten and reward factions at court (→ 19/2).

How Henry changed the Church of England during his reign

London, 28 January
Henry VIII's death might seem to have left the religious affairs of England equally balanced between the conservatives and the Protestant reformers, with the balance perhaps tilted towards the latter by the fall of Norfolk in the last month of the king's life. However, that would be to misread the irreversible nature of the changes that came about as Henry grappled with his immediate problems of divorce, state security and finance.

The church in England is now irrevocably bound up in the process of government – not as a semi-independent estate of the realm but as an integral arm of the modern Tudor state.

The dissolution of the monasteries has impoverished the church and transferred much of its wealth to the nobility and gentry – who, as a result, have acquired a vested interest in preserving the present state of affairs.

Henry's politicking raised up (and brought low again) men who genuinely desired to see in England a reformed church free of the shackles of Rome. Thomas Cromwell may have been executed after organizing so much of the change, but in Thomas Cranmer England now has a Protestant primate who even eats meat on Fridays.

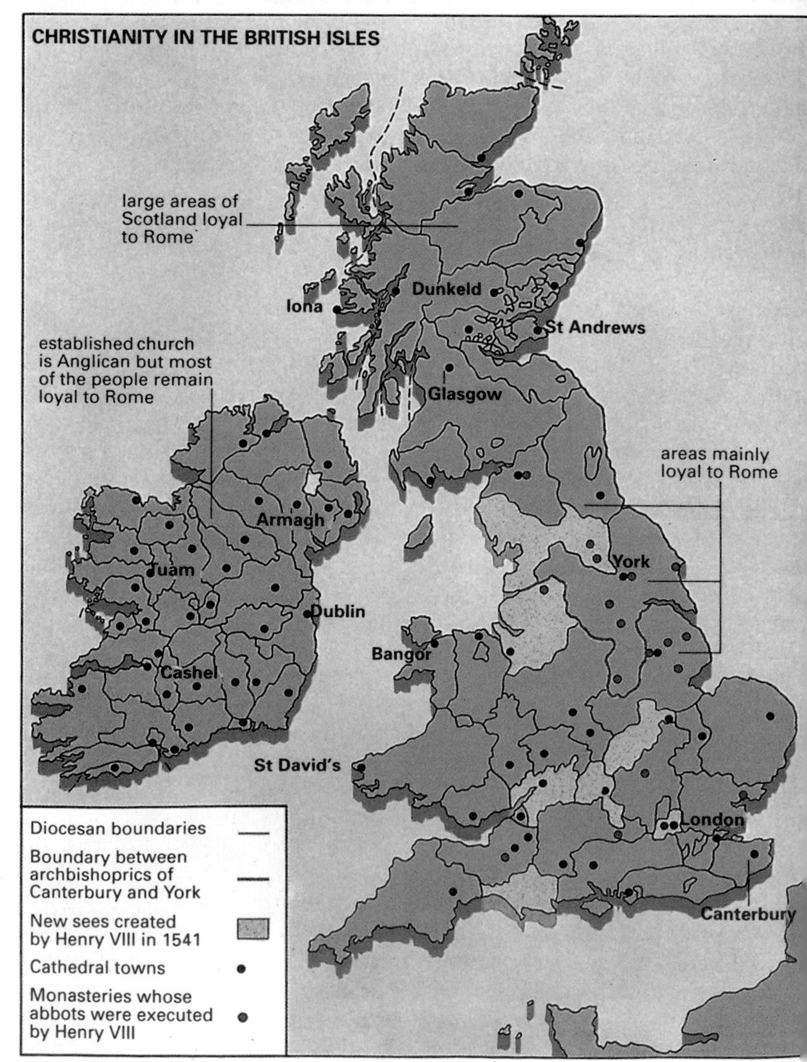

Pageants herald coronation of boy king

Winter honour: the young king's coronation parade through a snowy London.

London, 19 February
It has been a long day for Edward, the nine-year-old heir of Henry VIII. From the Tower of London to Westminster, the boy king has been made to ride in procession through a series of disorganized pageants, with costumes, singing, children, acrobats, wine fountains and endless speeches. His coronation will take place tomorrow.

Less than three weeks since Henry's death was announced, today's celebrations bore all the hallmarks of haste and improvisation. Much of the pageantry was devised by John Lydgate, who died 100 years ago, and hurriedly updated by a team of writers.

In Cornhill, two children greeted the king, a song was performed in his honour, and a fountain ran with wine. A giant awaited him at London Bridge, followed by a pageant of Nature, Grace and Fortune, the Seven Gifts of the Holy Ghost, and the Seven Gifts of Grace.

The conduit at Cheap offered a bewildering variety of tableaux, and Urson and Valentine, two obscure figures from Romantic literature, declaimed in his honour. Elsewhere the king did not have time to hear all the speeches but he was entertained by a high-wire artiste at St Paul's.

In Fleet Street, adorned with arras and banners, Edward was greeted by three children representing Truth, Faith and Justice. At a garishly decorated Temple Bar, more music wound up an event which the imperial ambassador described as "not very memorable".

Scots defeated at Pinkie

Lothian, 10 September 1547
Thousands of Scottish spearmen were killed in a fierce and bloody battle at Pinkie, near Musselburgh, against English forces led by the lord protector and duke of Somerset, Edward Seymour. The duke, whose army marched north to enforce Henry VIII's deathbed wish for Scotland to observe a marriage treaty, is England's virtual ruler and will now try to make peace with the Scots.

But this was a terrible defeat for the larger Scottish army headed by the governor, Arran, and it came after it looked as though the English had lost. Better discipline and tactics turned the tide, however. After the schiltrons – the circles of spearmen pointing outwards – had been broken, the English moved in among their panic-stricken enemy and inflicted a huge number of casualties. There were also many prisoners taken.

It is likely that Arran will face a challenge to his shaky authority. He will be under pressure from the rival Scottish factions to deal with England or to seek more military assistance from Henry II of France. As for Somerset he now has to exploit his victory at Pinkie by achieving his war aim, and thereby secure his own domestic position (→11/9).

Seymour's triumph: the duke's English cavalry routs the Scots at Pinkie.

Vagabonds to be branded and enslaved

London, 19 December
A law passed today provides for vagabonds to be whipped and, if they fail to return to their parishes and find honest work, to be branded with a "V". If they still fail to knuckle under, they may be enslaved for two years. This new measure repeals a law of 1535 which prescribed death for long-term offenders, and it draws a sharp distinction between the deserving and the undeserving poor. Most vagabonds are dispossessed peasants – victims of the forced enclosure of land – but the number of "sturdy beggars" is so vast that it threatens the social fabric of the nation.

Facing persecution: the homeless.

England set to lose cherished institutions

Westminster, December
Institutions which have been part of the daily social scene in England for centuries are set to disappear under a new act of parliament dissolving the chantries. Chantries – of which there are more than 2,000 across the country – are chapels endowed for the singing of Masses for the souls of the dead.

Justification for the abolition of chantries rests on the stated aim to rid the church of superstition, and to divert resources into strengthening universities, founding grammar schools and making "better provision for the poor and needy". More importantly perhaps, the seizure of chantry lands will give government funds a much needed boost. In 1545 Henry VIII tried to dissolve the chantries, asserting that the money produced was needed to pay for the French and Scottish wars.

The towns of King's Lynn and Coventry have been exempted from the legislation after their MPs mounted strong protests. But the dissolution will severely affect large sections of the population whose hopes and fears have long been dependent on the chantries. Moreover, the realization that the government plans to seize religious endowments to meet secular needs may give rise to social unrest.

1548 - 1549

Southwark, 20 February 1548. Bishop Stephen Gardiner of Winchester is freed after persuading the council that he will implement the new religious policies (→ 29/6).

Oxford, March 1548. Pietro Martire Vermigli, an exiled Italian Protestant, is made regius professor of divinity to teach Protestant theology.

Ireland, 21 May 1548. Sir Edward Bellingham is appointed deputy after the recall of Sir Anthony St Leger (→ 12/1548).

London, 29 June 1548. Gardiner is sent to the Tower after preaching to Edward VI and failing to persuade the council that he will change.

Leith, Lothian, June 1548. Over 6,000 French troops reinforce the lowlands to stop the lord protector of England gaining control.

Co Laois, June 1548. Fort Protector, the first major English garrison in the midlands, is established.

Gloucestershire, 7 September 1548. Catherine Parr, now married to Thomas, Lord Seymour of Sudeley, dies at Sudeley Castle eight days after giving birth to a baby girl.

Ireland, December 1548. The O'Connors and O'Mores, who rebelled last year, submit and are sent to England (→ 10/9/50).

London, December 1548. Foreign Protestant exiles in London are to set up a church.

London, 1548. Thomas Gresham founds seven professorships in the city.

London, 25 February 1549. Thomas, Lord Seymour of Sudeley, is charged with high treason for attempting to win support for Edward VI against the lord protector, Somerset, his brother (→ 14/10).

England, May 1549. Riots against enclosures break out in Somerset, Wiltshire, Kent, Hampshire, Sussex and Essex (→ 1557).

England, June 1549. Riots directed against the new Prayer Book break out in Devon and Cornwall.→

Boulogne, August 1549. The French besiege the city as Henry II of France declares war on England (→ 24/3/50).

London, 10 September 1549. Edmund Bonner, the bishop of London, is deprived of his bishopric for opposing the new Prayer Book (→ 10/1549).

Religious statues ordered to be destroyed

A satire of Edward's attitude to the pope and the upsurge in iconoclasm.

London, 22 February 1548
Official orders have been issued today that all religious images throughout the realm are to be destroyed. With King Edward VI still only ten years old, the orders have come from the privy council, acting under the king's uncle and protector, the duke of Somerset. The archbishop of Canterbury, Thomas Cranmer, has set about converting the schismatic but still largely Catholic church in England left by Henry VIII, into a fully Protestant organisation.

This has unleashed tensions which have found an outlet in a wave of iconoclasm that has resulted in mob violence and the smashing of statues, crucifixes and religious images. Now the government has pre-empted further destruction by ordering the statues to be taken down (→ 6/1549).

Preacher sets up pulpit in king's garden

A radical sermon: Dr Latimer preaching before King Edward (in the window).

Westminster, 7 March 1548
Dr Hugh Latimer, who was only released from jail a year ago and for the last seven years has been banned from preaching what were considered his overly radical Protestant sermons, has returned to the pulpit – in the king's own garden. Invited by King Edward VI, Latimer set up his pulpit in the privy garden at Westminster and, as a large crowd listened, preached on the duty of restoring stolen goods. The sermon had an immediate effect – some £520 in conscience money was returned anonymously.

Poetic priest writes of social problems

England and Wales, 1548
Although the poor are bearing the burdens of inflation, high rents, unemployment and landlessness, few consciences are troubled in these grasping times. But some hark back to what they see as the security of the feudal and Catholic systems, while others claim that man is his brother's keeper. One voice which stands out for its compassion is that of William Forrest, a priest:

The worlde is chaunged from
that it hathe beene,
Not for the bettre, but for the
warsse farre:
More for a penye wee have
before seene
Then nowe for fowre pense,
whoe liste to compare.
This suethe the game called
makinge or marre.
Unto the riche it makethe a
great deale,
But muche it marrethe to the
Commune weale.

Forrest, from a rural parish, writes from experience. He has seen parishioners driven from the land by enclosures, selling their cows to pay the rent and forced to beg; he has ridden through empty villages whose people had once provided the backbone of the English army. Now peasants are destitute, beggars plague the roads, and England relies on mercenaries to fight its wars.

Queen of Scots sails to safety in France

Strathclyde, 7 August 1548
Mary Queen of Scots left Dumbarton today for France. The five-year-old Scottish queen is leaving to avoid capture by the English forces led by the duke of Somerset, lord protector during the minority of Edward VI. Somerset, having defeated the Scots at Pinkie last year, now controls much of lowland Scotland. Mary, who had been betrothed to Edward under the 1543 Treaty of Greenwich, is now promised to the French *dauphin* [royal heir] Francis, in a treaty agreed last month under which France will guarantee the liberties of Scotland. She will live with the family of her mother, Mary of Guise.

King's uncle charged with high treason

Thomas Seymour: brought to ruin.

London, 20 March 1549
Thomas Seymour, Edward VI's uncle and the brother of the lord protector, was executed today at the Tower of London, guilty of high treason. It was the marriage of his sister, Jane Seymour, to Henry VIII that opened influential doors for him in his youth, leading to knighthood in 1537 and appointment in 1547 as lord high admiral of England. Despite his brother Edward's aid and indulgence, he was jealous of his pre-eminence in affairs of state and planned his downfall. Seymour even bribed the young king with pocket money.

Investigations revealed evidence amounting to 33 formal articles of accusation, including the use of his estate at Sudeley to hoard military supplies and making secret pacts with piratical leaders. Worse still, he tried to manipulate the succession by seeking to marry Princess Elizabeth without first consulting the council for permission.

The Bill of Attainder declaring Thomas to be "adjudged and attainted of high treason" was introduced on 25 February in the Lords and passed on 4 March. The council asked that it might "proceed to justice ... in this heavy case" without troubling the protector. After the execution, Princess Elizabeth was said to have murmured: "This day has perished a man of much wit and ... little judgement" (→14/10).

New Prayer Book is sanctioned by Lords

Westminster, 15 January 1549
By a huge majority, the House of Lords today passed the Act of Uniformity which makes the Book of Common Prayer the prescribed liturgy throughout England. Only two of the temporal peers voted against, and the bishops split ten in favour and eight against.

Although it is not intended as a statement of doctrine, this is clearly a success for Protestantism and for Thomas Cranmer, the archbishop of Canterbury, who is primarily responsible for the work. From now on God will be worshipped every Sunday throughout the realm using the same form of words in the native tongue of the English. And even though the words are in a language not used for religious services before, everyone acknowledges that Cranmer has given them a grace and beauty that matches their solemn use.

Members of the House of Lords.

But this has also been a great political occasion. The measure is an act of parliament in a real sense, not as in the past when the king's will has been either automatically agreed to or more or less thwarted. Since 17 December there has been dignified debate leading up to the vote. And the result, although not unexpected, will be more easily implemented because of the way it was reached (→6/1549).

Enclosure of arable land to be probed

Country life: under investigation.

London, 1 June 1548
A new commission charged with probing land enclosure and related issues started work today. Its operations are confined to seven counties in the English midlands. Similar commissions are planned to cover other parts of the country.

The commission's purpose is to collect evidence that, it is hoped, can be used to give teeth to the present ineffective agrarian laws, and to help in drafting new laws to curb landowners who are converting arable land into pasture, which is causing decay of towns, villages and the farmhouses around them. The government is concerned that those enclosures which lead to the decline of tillage are a danger to internal security and military capacity. "The realm must be defended with force of men ... not with flocks of sheep," said the proclamation on the commission.

The government feels that the decline of arable farming is causing depopulation, inflation and poverty, which will be leading ultimately to the "utter undoing and decay of the realm".

Although the new commission has no powers itself to reform the countryside's ills, its existence may give some comfort to disaffected peasants alarmed at the encroaching pastures; and it will at least pose a threat to encloser landlords, skilled at placing impediments in the way of the law (→5/1549).

Summer fruit and veg enrich family diets

Surrounded by plenty: vegetables are abundant in the English summer.

England, 1548
The arrival of spring and summer brings some welcome, juicy variety to bear on the everyday English diet, which tends to be rather dull during the winter months. While the trees and fields are bare, the average household's menu consists mainly of bread, cheese, smoked bacon and salted beef. With the advent of longer days, apples, pears, plums, strawberries and cherries find their way onto English tables of all classes.

So to do a range of vegetables, including peas, beans, carrots and onions. Salad herbs are gathered from hedgerows. Citrus fruits are exotic rarities, however, available only to the rich.

Religious and economic woes fuel popular unrest

Exeter besieged by Prayer Book rebels

Exeter, 2 July 1549
Exeter, the main city both of the county of Devon and in the west of England, has come under siege today by rebels who have recently taken up arms in protest at the use of the new Book of Common Prayer in church services. Trouble had been brewing for some time in the west, but it boiled over about a month ago when angry parishioners began to resist the introduction of the new vernacular liturgy of the Book of Common Prayer demanded by the Act of Uniformity, which had been passed by parliament at Westminster.

The rebellion has spread to Devon from Cornwall, where Cornish speakers added to their list of grievances the decree that services must now be in English, a language which they understand less than the church Latin, with which they were at least familiar. The rebels have surrounded Exeter, cut its food and water supplies and mounted guns on the nearby hillsides, from where they can shoot into the city with great accuracy.

The city's defence is being hampered by the fact that there is a good deal of sympathy for the rebels among both the city's leaders and its ordinary citizens, and there is no shortage of plots to open the gates to the rebels (→23).

The radical landowner: Robert Ket hears the grievances of the rebels.

Norwich captured by agrarian protesters

Norwich, 23 July 1549
Rebels under Robert Ket, a local tanner and landowner, have taken Norwich after a rising that has grown so swiftly it has taken everyone by surprise. The rebels were driven by resentment about enclosures, high rents and the overstocking of common land by the gentry.

Trouble began only a month ago when villagers at Attleborough in Norfolk threw down hedges in protest at enclosure. When they visited Ket's estate he surprised them all by saying that he agreed with their aims and offering to lead them. Rebellion then flared throughout East Anglia, in places as far apart as Ipswich in the south and Castle Rising in the north, spreading as far as Cambridge, although there the authorities have managed to bring it under control.

Ket arrived at Norwich on 10 July, and his following soon grew to an estimated 16,000, but serious fighting did not begin until three days ago. Then Ket's men brought up cannon but their bombardment had little effect, and they asked for a truce. When this was refused they stormed the city, which fell easily as most of the defenders were sympathetic to the rebels (→18/8).

Royal troops fight back beating rebels

Devon, 18 August 1549
The Cornish and western rebels have suffered a stunning and bloody defeat at the village of Sampford Courtenay, near Okehampton, today. Hundreds of them are dead, and the end of the rebellion cannot now be far away.

Royal troops under John, Lord Russell, have advanced steadily against them since the beginning of the month. They defeated and killed almost two thousand in a battle near the Devon village of Clyst St Mary, which the rebels had heavily fortified, and defeated them again shortly afterwards at nearby Clyst Heath. But Russell's advance has been slow, and his tactics have been dictated by the desire to avoid defeat by the rebels, who have greatly outnumbered him. After Clyst Heath he raised the siege of Exeter, but the rebel strength remained formidable.

Hearing that they had gathered at Sampford Courtenay, Russell marched from Exeter two days ago. In the fighting today the royal troops came close to being defeated by the Cornish, the most courageous and able of the rebels – who were spurred on by their priests, who fought alongside them. In the end hundreds died, and the rebel leaders are either dead or fled back into Cornwall (→10/9).

Top officials accused of complicity in Bristol royal mint fraud

Bristol, February 1549
A network of fraud involving top officials has been uncovered at the Bristol royal mint. At the centre of the scandal is the mintmaster, Sir William Sharington, whose conversion of the former abbey at Lacock into a beautiful house has largely been paid for of his illicit profits. The plotters defrauded the realm of some £4,000 by manufacturing coins that were two-thirds alloy, illegally using waste bits of coin, and destroying as well as falsifying records. The lord high admiral, Thomas Seymour, is among those linked to the conspiracy.

The fruit of dishonesty: Sir William's grand house at Lacock, Wiltshire.

Scottish church bids to promote reforms

Fife, 1549
Attempts have been made at a meeting of the council of the Scottish church this year to introduce internal reforms without precipitating an outright break with Rome, as has occurred in England. John Hamilton, the archbishop of St Andrews, chaired the council as it considered such abuses as plural religious holdings, absentee priests and uneducated preachers. The larger abbeys have been ordered to send students to the universities and to promote good preaching.

Government reinstates censorship laws

The printing press: a radical tool, now subject once again to state censorship.

London, August 1549

State censorship, introduced by Henry VIII in 1538 when he ordered that no publication might appear without a royal licence, has been reinstated by his son Edward VI only two years after the new regime had allowed it to lapse. It is a direct response to the flood of literature, much it written by radical Protestant reformers, that has appeared since Edward came to the throne.

Led by Edward Seymour, the king's uncle, a Protestant faction gained great influence at court and relaxed Henry's censorship, permitting many hitherto censored works. For the first time in Tudor history, no one was executed for heresy.

But such radicalism was seen as undermining the throne, and, with religious and social divisions deepening, the extremists came under attack. By a series of proclamations state censorship, conducted by the privy council, has begun once more to check and license publications that threaten the status quo.

Lord protector ousted and taken to Tower

Edward Seymour when in power.

London, 14 October 1549

The duke of Somerset was arrested today and taken to the Tower along with many of his family. Twenty-nine charges have been laid against him, ranging from ruling without the assent of other councillors to encouraging rebels. The earl of Warwick has taken over the reins of government. Warwick and his faction have been working to undermine Somerset since the spring, and the rebellions in the west country and East Anglia finally discredited his regime. However, as he was the king's uncle and protector, it was difficult to unseat him until he fled to Windsor with the king, enabling Warwick to present his coup as a "rescue" of Edward (→21/2/50).

Protestant reformers and conservatives look to Warwick (and God) for support

The agonizing choice: a noblewoman considers joining a convent.

England, October 1549

Religious reformers and their conservative opponents are both putting in extra hours on their knees this month in the hope that the earl of Warwick, Somerset's successor as leading councillor during Edward VI's minority, will give them his support.

So far the reformers have been making the running. On Henry's death they quickly took control; conservatives like Gardiner and Bonner were left off the council, and persecution of Protestants ended with the abolition of the Act of Six Articles. There were outbursts of iconoclasm in London, scurrilous Protestant propaganda appeared, and England attracted continental reformers. Conservative bishops like Gardiner were outraged when the council declared that the new king had the right to re-appoint all the bishops – logically Henry VIII's Act of Supremacy rendered them all royal officials.

The abolition of chantries pleased reformers and brought support from the gentry who acquired the lands. Further moves towards the protestant camp were the English Order of Communion, Book of Common Prayer and Act of Uniformity. But the Cornish riots against the new Prayer Book have shown that a bedrock of conservative support remains (→1/1550).

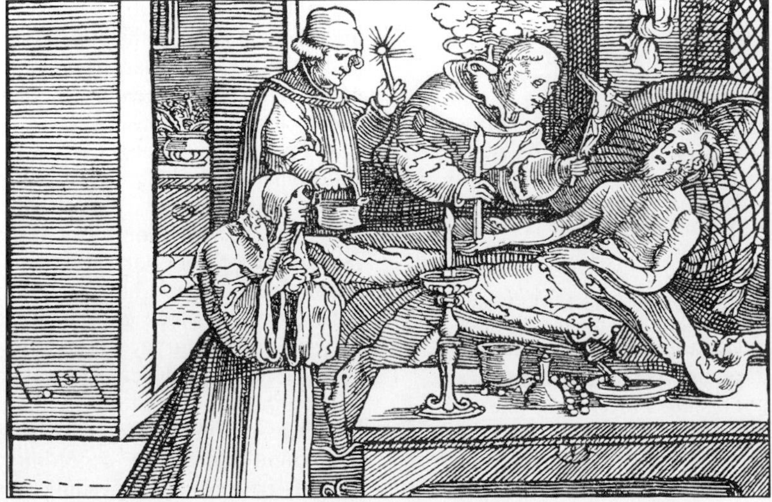

Bringing comfort: a monk administers the last rites to a dying man.

England, January 1550. The destruction of Catholic religious objects continues; stiff penalties are imposed on anyone hiding holy relics (→23/11).

Ireland, February 1550. Secret negotiations are held between French agents and Manus O'Donnell, the lord of Tyrconnell.

Boulogne, 24 March 1550. England signs the Treaty of Boulogne, agreeing to abandon the city to the French and withdraw troops from Scotland (→9/9).

Dublin, 27 June 1550. A mint is established by order of the English council (→7/6/52).

Ireland, 10 September 1550. Sir Anthony St Leger is reappointed lord deputy; he is ordered to enforce regulations against Catholic worship (→29/6/54).

England, 23 November 1550. Nicholas Ridley, the bishop of London, orders that all church altars be replaced with Communion tables (→3/3/51).

London, 25 December 1550. Edward VI rebukes his sister Mary for her adherence to the Catholic faith (→18/3/51).

London, February 1551. The earl of Warwick creates the *gendarmes*, a mounted guard of 850 cavalry (→10/1552).

London, 3 March 1551. The privy council orders that nearly all church plate be removed from places of worship (→1/11/52).

Essex, 18 March 1551. The rift between Edward VI and Princess Mary worsens; she rejects the new Prayer Book and continues to hold Mass in her own home.

England, 10 June 1551. An Anglo-Scots treaty is signed (→24/9/52).

Angers, France, 19 July 1551. A marriage alliance is made for Edward VI and the daughter of King Henry II.

London, 11 October 1551. John Dudley, the earl of Warwick, is made duke of Northumberland; he is now the most powerful man in England (→22/1/52).

England, autumn 1551. The harvest is bad for the third year running.

Dublin, 1551. The *Book of Common Prayer* is the first book to be published in Ireland (→2/7/57).

Earl of Warwick secures supreme power

The ambitious earl of Warwick.

Arundel: banished from court.

London, 21 February 1550
John Dudley, the earl of Warwick, has taken power in a palace coup, with the 12-year-old king, Edward VI, as his puppet. Warwick's four-month intrigue, which began last October with the arrest of the lord protector, Somerset, reached a climax today with his appointment as lord president of the council and master of the king's household.

Warwick had long disliked Somerset's autocracy, and his tactics to bring down the protector were subtle and ruthless. First he made use of the Catholic party at court, led by the earls of Southampton and Arundel, who had hoped to establish a conservative regency under Edward's half-sister Mary. Then, after they had served his purpose and put Somerset in the Tower, Warwick discarded them in favour of the Protestant party under Archbishop Cranmer, exiling the earls of Southampton and Arundel from court. He rules now unopposed, adept at persuading the boy king of the wisdom of decisions which he has already taken (→5/9).

Traveller loses his wits after great survey

London, 1550
John Leland, an ardent antiquarian who has spent 18 years preparing a great survey of England and Wales, has "by a most piteous occasion fallen besides his wits" – according to John Bale, the Protestant pamphleteer, who has decided to edit Leland's "moth-eaten, mouldy and rotten" pages into a book.

A Protestant radical, Leland became chaplain to Henry VIII and then "king's antiquary", charged with visiting every monastery in the realm in search of books and manuscripts for the king's library. It was these journeys which gave him the material for his survey.

John Leland: obsessive antiquarian.

Nothing escaped him. He watched men panning for tin on the river Dart, saw puffins on the Scilly Isles, and found Minehead "exceedingly full of Irishmen". Travelling the length and breadth of the country, he made notes on everything from "the hospital for poor folk" at Winchester and the leper cemetery at Worcester to the work of the Flemish weavers in Manchester and of the smiths and cutlers in Birmingham. "I trust so to open this window [on the country]," he wrote, "that light shall be seen by the space of a whole thousand years."

Cloth exports hit by sharp downturn

England, 1551
A sharp downturn in English cloth exports to the Dutch port of Antwerp, following three bad harvests, eight years of almost continuous conflict with Scotland and an ill-advised revaluation of the currency, suggest that England may be heading for its worst recession for half a century. The country's economy is almost entirely reliant on a single export, cloth – England's "golden fleece", as it has been described. Last year 150,000 cloths were sold to Antwerp (which takes in nine-tenths of England's cloth exports), flooding the market; this year only 100,000 were sold (→1557).

Sheep-shearing: an early stage in the manufacture of woollen cloth.

William Cecil made secretary of state

London, 5 September 1550
William Cecil, the brother-in-law of John Cheke, King Edward VI's staunchly Protestant tutor, has been made secretary of state and a member of the privy council. Originally Cecil was protégé of the duke of Somerset (spending two months in the Tower with him after his fall); his administrative abilities brought him to the attention of the earl of Warwick, and he was quick to join Warwick's camp. He plans to open up trade and abolish monopolies (→11/10/51).

France 'liberates' Scots

Normandy, 9 September 1550
King Henry II of France presided over a spectacular ceremony at Rouen today to celebrate his defeat of the English in Scotland. For the past two years the French have been supporting the Scots against the English onslaught, and banners of castles liberated from the enemy – those of Haddington, Dunglass, Broughty, Roxburgh and Lauder – were carried like trophies through the streets.

Fighting was halted in March when, following successful French attacks on English-held Boulogne, England signed a treaty agreeing to abandon the city and withdraw from Scotland. The Treaty of Boulogne brought to an end some eight years of hostilities between England and Scotland, which began with the border skirmishes during Henry VIII's reign [*see page 429*] and virtually bankrupted England.

Henry II's guest of honour today was Mary of Guise, visiting from Scotland, who was reunited with her seven-year-old daughter, Mary Queen of Scots, after a long separation. The younger Mary was sent to France in 1548 for her own safety. By a deal agreed that year to cement an alliance with France, Scotland's queen was betrothed to the French king's eldest son and heir, the *dauphin* Francis, who is now six years old.

England's fallen lord protector, the earl of Somerset – who vigorously prosecuted the campaign against the Scots – would have been sore at heart to witness today's festivities at Rouen. They appear finally to have put paid to his dream of bringing about a union between England and Scotland (→10/6/51).

Henry II of France: revelling in his defeat of the English in Scotland.

DWARDVS
sextus dei gratia Angliae Franciae et Hiberniae Rex. fidei defensor, ac in terra
ecclesiae Anglicanae et Hibernicae supremu
Caput. OMNIBVS et singul
ad quos presentes litterae pervenerint salu
CVM CERTVS TRACTATV
pacis inter predilectos et fideles consiliarios nostros Iohannem Com-
tem de Bedford privati nostri sigilli custodem. Gulielmum
Paget Dominum Paget de Beaudesert Ducatus Lancastrie
Cancellarium, ordinis nostri garterij equites auratos. Gulielmum Petre primarium secretarium nostrum. et Iohannem
Mason secretarium nostrum pro lingua gallica equites aura
tes ac in privato consilio nostro consiliarios. oratores. commis
sarios. procuratores et ambassiatores nostros speciales ex una
et egregios magnificos ac nobiles viros Franciscum de Mont
morancy Dominum de la Rochepot, insule Franciae prore
gem, atque gubernatorem, nomine christianissimi Regis fratris
consanguinei et perpetui confederati nostri, in Picardia locum
tenentem generalem. Gaspardum de Colligny Dominum de
Chastillon in comitatu Belonensi gallorum peditum prefe
ctum, ab insignium Michaelis equites auratos. Andream
Guillart Dominum de Mortier equitem auratum, eiusdem
Christianissimi Regis consiliarium in suo sanctiore et priva
to consilio, et Gulielmum Bochetel Dominum de Sassy
eiusdem christianissimi regis consiliarium et status regni a
secretis, ac etiam ordinis sancti Michaelis ab aliis sui grapha
rium, ac eius oratores commissarios, procuratores, ambassiato

A page from the Treaty of Boulogne.

Death toll from feared 'sweating sickness' stirs up social and religious differences

England, December 1551
The fatal "sweating sickness" has struck with a vengeance this year, killing many thousands of people throughout the country. The disease, which progresses with great speed, is characterized by profuse sweating, high fever, dizziness and pains in the head and abdomen. This outbreak – the fifth since 1485 – began in Shrewsbury, where almost a thousand people died within a week. People have fled the towns for the perceived safety of the countryside, but the disease can strike anywhere.

Protestants have interpreted the epidemic – coupled with bad harvests and high prices – as divine retribution for the delay in implementing religious reforms. Fear of consequent public unrest may have bolstered the hardline Protestant attitude adopted by the former earl of Warwick (who became duke of Northumberland in October). This has been particularly evident in his role in a dispute between King Edward VI and his Catholic sister Mary. Backed by Northumberland, the king has sent a series of stern letters to Mary insisting that she conform to the Protestant religion. Mary remains defiant (→12/6/52).

Sickness fills the hospital wards.

Arden falls victim to a crime of passion

Canterbury, 1551
Alice Arden, the wife of the London merchant Thomas Arden of Faversham, has been burnt to death for the murder of her husband – sharing the fate of all women found guilty of such a crime. The dead man was noted as a leader of Protestantism in their home town of Faversham, in Kent.

Alice Arden had fallen in love with Mosbye, one of her father's servants, and she wanted to be rid of her husband. Although Arden had tolerated the affair because of Alice's father's good connections – he controlled much former monastic land – his wife felt that she could no longer wait. Mosbye had declined to undertake the killing, and a hired assassin, called Black Will, was brought in to do the deed. The criminals were caught, however – after depositing the body in a churchyard – by the shape of their footprints in the snow. Mosbye has been hanged for his role in this crime of passion.

Former lord protector sentenced to death

London, 1 December 1551
Edward Seymour, the duke of Somerset and former lord protector of England, has been found guilty of felony on a trumped-up charge and sentenced to death.

Somerset, the brother of King Henry VIII's third wife, Jane Seymour, and a convinced Protestant, was the most powerful figure in England for the first two years of his nephew Edward VI's reign, defeating a Scottish army at Pinkie in 1547 and amassing a fortune, which he spent recklessly and ostentatiously on such projects as the rebuilding of Somerset House. But his arrogance made him enemies at both ends of the political and religious spectrum, and when the earl of Warwick took power in a palace coup [*see report on page 438*], Somerset discovered that he had few friends (→22/1/52).

The imagined scene at the murder of Thomas Arden by his wife's hired killers.

1552 - 1553

London, 22 January 1552. Edward Seymour, the duke of Somerset and former lord protector, is executed, ending a threat to the new protector, John Dudley, the duke of Northumberland (→ 10/1552).

Westminster, 15 April 1552. Parliament passes an act making it illegal to charge interest on loans (→ 12/1552).

Ireland, 7 June 1552. King Edward VI of England devalues the Irish currency to reduce inflation.

Borders, 24 September 1552. Following 16 months of negotiations, the Anglo-Scottish border is settled.

Westminster, October 1552. Economic cuts force the duke of Northumberland to disband his new palace guard, the *gendarmes* (→ 22/8/53).

England/Wales, 1552. Taverns and alehouses are licensed to sell alcohol (→ 31/3/53).

England, January 1553. Government commissioners strip all churches of their wealth to boost government finances (→ 14/9).

Ireland, 2 February 1553. John Bale, an English Protestant, is consecrated bishop of Ossory (→ 8/1553).

London, 31 March 1553. Parliament limits licensed alehouses here to 40 (→ 12/6).

London, 12 June 1553. Edward VI makes a will, on his sick-bed at Greenwich, formally naming Lady Jane Grey, his cousin, as his successor to the throne (→ 21).

Westminster, 21 June 1553. A royal patent declares the royal sisters Mary and Elizabeth to be illegitimate and denies them the right to succeed to the throne (→ 6/7).

Greenwich, 6 July 1553. Edward VI dies (→ 10/7).

London, 10 July 1553. Lady Jane Grey is proclaimed queen at the Tower (→ 3/8).

Ireland, August 1553. Catholic demonstrations against the Reformation force Bishop John Bale to flee the country.

London, 14 September 1553. Mary orders the arrest of Archbishop Cranmer (→ 5/12).

London, 1 October 1553. Mary is crowned queen (→ 5/12).

Whitehall, December 1553. Bowing to papal authority, Mary relinquishes her title of "Supreme Head of the English Church" (→ 28/11/54).

Cranmer publishes new Prayer Book

London, 1 November 1552

A new official Prayer Book has been issued, the second since the break with Rome. Created by Archbishop Cranmer, the *Second Book of Common Prayer* firmly commits England to Protestantism. Many regard it as Cranmer's reward for backing the duke of Northumberland against the duke of Somerset. The old Mass has been abolished and replaced with a Communion service. Altars are to disappear in favour of Communion tables. Gorgeous vestments will be discarded, and the new Communion service will be celebrated by clergy clothed in simple surplices. How the people will react is unclear. The last time that they had a Prayer Book imposed on them, in 1549, many in the west country rebelled (→ 1/1553).

Cranmer: issued first Prayer Book.

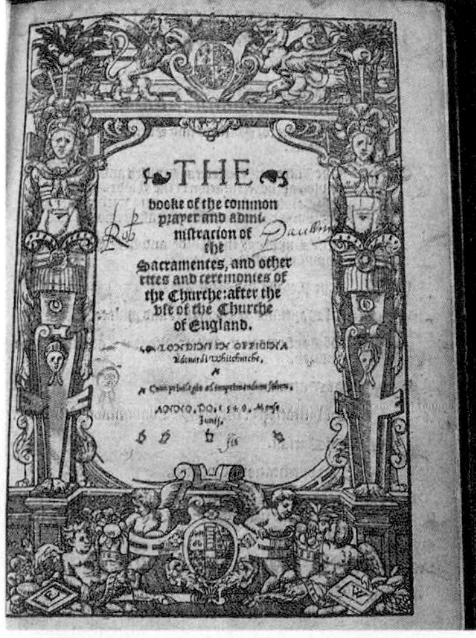

THE booke of the common prayer and administracion of the Sacramentes, and other rites and ceremonies of the Churche: after the use of the Churche of England.

The first Prayer Book of Edward VI.

Fiscal policy links courts and taxes

London, December 1552

A royal commission, set up only nine months ago by the duke of Northumberland to investigate the royal finances and the revenue courts, recommends drastic reform.

The detailed mastery of the subject, and the speed of the commission's investigations, are largely attributable to the involvement of Sir Walter Mildmay, one of the best legal minds in the country. The commissioners conclude that either the present byzantine system of revenue courts be streamlined (leaving only two, one responsible for revenue from crown lands, the other for the remaining revenues), or that all revenue courts be merged with the exchequer.

The report is just one aspect of the general reform of the administration which the duke of Northumberland and his allies on the privy council, such as Sir William Cecil, have undertaken to strengthen the royal finances, build up a centralized civil service and establish England as a modern state.

King Edward founds 'blue-coat' school for London's orphans

London, 1553

In an attempt to reduce the ever growing number of orphans living rough on the teeming streets of London, Edward VI has founded a new school, to be called Christ's Hospital, on premises once used by the Grey Friars in Newgate Street. Here more than 700 boys will learn the arts of spinning and weaving and will be dressed in a distinctive uniform of a blue coat and yellow stockings. They will also be taught how to read and write.

England has long lagged behind the remainder of Europe in the field of education – two-thirds of the nation is said to be illiterate – and the king is determined to change the situation. Christ's Hospital is part of an ambitious scheme involving several foundations to tackle poverty in London. Edward has also refounded what are known as "grammar schools", but the harsh economic climate causes many students to "drop out" (→ 1557).

King Edward VI presenting a charter to Christ's Hospital, whose aim is to take orphans off the streets.

Mary triumphs in struggle for throne

Queen Mary, attended by Princess Elizabeth, is greeted on arrival in London.

London, 3 August 1553
Mary Tudor arrived in London today flanked by 10,000 supporters to be acclaimed as England's first "queen regnant", succeeding her 15-year-old half-brother Edward VI, who died on 6 July of tuberculosis. Mary, who is 37, had seen off a challenge by Lady Jane Grey, aged 15, who is descended from Henry VIII's sister Mary. Lady Jane was proclaimed queen on 10 July by the duke of Northumberland but is now in the Tower.

Northumberland was acting in accordance with a declaration accepted by the ailing Edward that Mary and Elizabeth, the daughters of Henry VIII, were illegitimate. He had reckoned without public opinion, however [*see report below left*]. As he marched towards Suffolk, where Mary had installed herself in Framlingham Castle, his army began to desert in large numbers, while support for Mary swiftly mounted (→ 1/10).

Northumberland is executed for treason

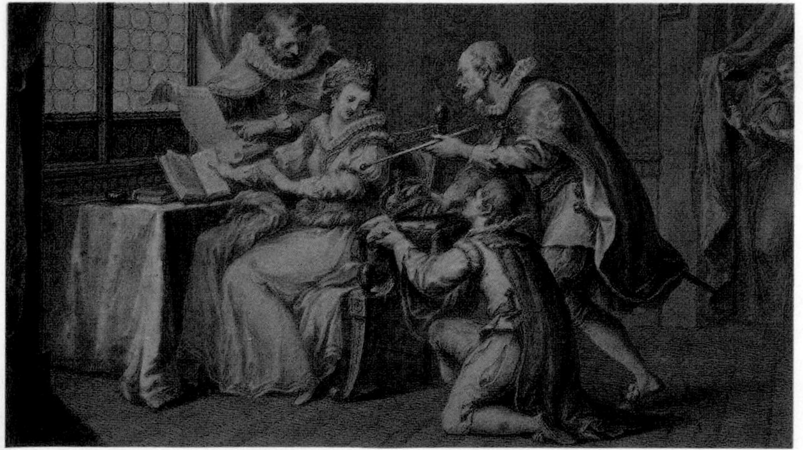

Northumberland and Suffolk begging Lady Jane Grey to accept the crown.

London, 22 August 1553
As bells rang out over Tower Green today, John Dudley, the once proud duke of Northumberland, was beheaded for treason. Lady Jane Grey, his daughter-in-law, watched this last act from a window of her Tower cell. Mounting the scaffold, the duke made a bold speech to the crowd. Begging for mercy, he pledged allegiance to Queen Mary, renounced Protestantism and confessed his sins: "I have done wickedly all the days of my life and, most of all, against the queen's highness, of whom I here ask forgiveness."

Northumberland, who controlled Edward VI during the latter years of his reign, had tried to manipulate the succession in favour of Lady Jane Grey, a great-niece of Henry VIII. The exploit ended in disaster because of hatred of him in the country; he stirred up further resentment by keeping Edward's death a secret while he mustered his forces against Mary (→ 12/2/54).

English queen is to wed Catholic cousin

London, 16 November 1553
Weeks of rumour that Queen Mary intends to marry her cousin Philip of Spain today brought a delegation from the House of Commons to petition the 37-year-old queen to marry someone in her own realm. But Mary seems determined to reject the advice; she has said that she is already "half in love" with Philip after seeing his portrait.

Desperate for an heir who will sustain her Catholic principles, Mary has taken the decision in the face of widespread opposition in England. Her council believes that Philip, the son and heir of Holy Roman Emperor Charles V, will treat England as little more than a distant colony. The public also seems opposed; anti-Spanish ballads and broadsheets are circulating in London. However, Mary intends to love and obey Philip, to whom she will have given herself "following divine commandment", while insisting that if he should wish to encroach on the government of the kingdom she would be "unable to permit it" (→ 1/1554).

Bishops arrested as church reforms are swept away

England, 5 December 1553
Queen Mary dissolved her first parliament today after repealing most of Edward VI's religious legislation and passing an act declaring the marriage of her parents, Henry VIII and Catherine of Aragon, to have been legal – thereby ending her own illegitimacy. Even though Mary conceded that her half-brother's burial, in August, should be performed in accordance with Protestant rites, Protestant services will soon cease to be legal, and the queen's council has accepted her proposed Catholic marriage. England may be seething with religious turmoil but the country seems firmly set on the road to reconciliation with Rome.

Edward VI: Protestant burial.

In other respects, the new queen has lost no time in demonstrating her desire to eradicate Protestantism. Since her accession in July, her agents have been rounding up leading churchmen and confining them in the Tower on charges of treason or sedition.

The best known among these is Thomas Cranmer, the archbishop of Canterbury and architect of the controversial Prayer Books of 1549 and 1552. Others include three bishops – Nicholas Ridley, John Hooper and Hugh Latimer (→ 12/1553).

1554 - 1555

Kent, January 1554. A plot to is uncovered to prevent Queen Mary's marriage to Philip of Spain, the son of Holy Roman Emperor Charles V (→ 6/3).

London, 7 February 1554. Sir Thomas Wyatt is arrested on the failure of his rebellion in Kent against the marriage of Mary to Philip (→ 11/4).

London, 6 March 1554. Mary is officially betrothed to Philip (→ 25/7).

Ireland, 14 April 1554. George Dowdall, the archbishop of Armagh, is ordered by Pope Julius III to deprive all married clergy of their positions (→ 29/6).

Ireland, 13 May 1554. Gerald FitzGerald is restored to the earldom of Kildare (→ 6/1555).

London, 22 May 1554. Mary frees her sister Elizabeth from the Tower, having failed to prove her part in the Wyatt conspiracy (→ 17/11/58).

Co Meath, 29 June 1554. Bishop Edward Staples of Meath is deprived of his diocese for being married.

Westminster, 28 November 1554. Parliament permits Cardinal Pole to reconcile the English church to Roman Catholicism (→ 16/10/55).

Ireland, June 1555. Sir William Fitzwilliam is appointed head of a commission to inquire into corruption in the English administration (→ 28/4/56).

London, 8 September 1555. Hugh Curwin, nominated by Queen Mary, is consecrated archbishop of Dublin, replacing Archbishop Browne.

Scotland, September 1555. The Protestant reformer John Knox returns from exile (→ 10/1557).

Winchester, 16 October 1555. Stephen Gardiner, the bishop of Winchester, dies.

Europe, 25 October 1555. Emperor Charles V hands over the government of the Netherlands to his son, Philip of Spain (→ 16/1/56).

Canterbury, 13 November 1555. Thomas Cranmer loses the archbishopric of Canterbury (→ 12/1555).

London, December 1555. Cardinal Reginald Pole is appointed archbishop of Canterbury (→ 21/3/56).

Oxford, 1555. Sir Thomas Pope and Sir Thomas White found Trinity and St John's Colleges.

Lady Jane requests a quick execution

Lady Jane Grey: a hapless victim.

London, 12 February 1554

A hapless victim of this month's Wyatt rebellion [*see report below*], 16-year-old Lady Jane Grey met her death today with courage and dignity, hours after being forced to see the bleeding corpse of her husband, Lord Guildford Dudley. Queen for nine days last year, Lady Jane had been captive in the Tower ever since Mary Tudor successfully claimed the crown. Saying that she died a "true Christian woman", she forgave her executioner but begged him to dispatch her quickly (→ 11/4).

Wyatt is beheaded after failed rebellion

London, 11 April 1554

Opponents of Queen Mary's plans to marry Philip of Spain were taught their lesson anew today, when Sir Thomas Wyatt finally lost his head on Tower Green.

In the wake of the revolt raised three months ago by Wyatt, of Allington in Kent, there have been savage reprisals, with some 90 of his followers executed. Among the victims have been Lady Jane Grey and her husband, even though they took no part in the uprising. The bloody trail looks set to continue, such is the fervour of feeling. Wyatt had no difficulty gathering support in the Kentish towns, and as he marched north-westwards to enter Southwark on 3 February more and more rushed to join him. A passionate appeal by the queen to Londoners was almost certainly responsible for saving her crown as the 4,000 rebels tried to attack the city. Held off by royal supporters, they managed to cross the Thames at Kingston and marched east. After several skirmishes, Wyatt was captured and brought to Whitehall.

A fanciful view of an encounter between the rebels and Mary's supporters.

Elizabeth arrested for alleged conspiracy

Tudor sisters: Catholic Mary (l) suspects Protestant Elizabeth of conspiracy.

London, 12 February 1554

Queen Mary today arrested her Protestant sister Elizabeth – next in line to the throne – and gave orders that she should be held in the Tower until the rebellions led by Sir Thomas Wyatt and others around the country are quelled. The secret manoeuvrings of such men as Edward Courtenay, the earl of Devon, who has been named as a possible husband for Elizabeth, have left Mary in no doubt that there is a conspiracy afoot to unseat her. Many of her subjects dislike the queen's Catholicism and fear her proposed marriage to Philip of Spain. Mary is determined to go ahead with the marriage, however, and produce a Catholic heir (→ 22/5).

Mary of Guise is regent of Scotland

Falkland, Fife, 12 April 1554

The dowager queen, Mary of Guise, has been appointed regent, replacing the unpredictable earl of Arran, who has been in command of Scotland since the death of Mary's husband, James V, in 1542.

The appointment will fuel fears of growing French influence in Scotland. Scots are resentful of the presence here of 7,000 French troops, who were brought over several years ago to fight the English and show no signs of departing. Protestants in particular are fearful that Mary of Guise's regency will see a return of Catholicism. One of her brothers is a cardinal, the other commands the French army. Her daughter, Mary Queen of Scots, is betrothed to the *dauphin* [French royal heir] (→ 2/5/56).

Mary marries Philip

Philip: poised to dominate Europe.

Winchester, 25 July 1554
In a day marked by magnificent celebrations, the queen has married her cousin Philip of Spain. People have been thronging the streets, lighting up the skies with bonfires. Opponents to the match, however, made their objections clear.

After his storm-tossed crossing of the English Channel, the widower Philip – the son of Holy Roman Emperor Charles V and destined to become the most powerful man in Europe – made little effort to speak English. The queen, who has no Spanish, in spite of being the daughter of Catherine of Aragon, felt at a loss. His only words in English were to dismiss Mary's courtiers as he led his new wife to the bedchamber: "Good night, my lords all." Mary's hopes are now pinned on producing a son and heir for England (→26/8/55).

Wish for heir brings on phantom pregnancy

London, 26 August 1555
Philip of Spain sailed from Greenwich today after taking leave of his grief-stricken wife. His departure follows fast on the revelation that, despite months of confinement and preparations for a birth, Mary is not pregnant. Misled by her imaginings, the queen had kindled keen anticipation among Catholics; bonfires were lit when false news of a birth leaked out, only to be doused when the truth emerged. Hopes for an heir faded further as Philip set out to assume control of the Netherlands, which have been granted to him by his father, Holy Roman Emperor Charles V (→30/3/58).

New company opens trade with Russia

A Russian merchant: new markets.

London, 1555
The Muscovy Company, formed by Richard Chancellor, has won royal charters from both Queen Mary of England and Ivan IV of Russia to open trade between the countries.

Two years ago Chancellor, backed by a consortium of 200 merchants, set out to bypass Spanish and Portuguese possessions and find a new route to the Far East. In spite of losing two ships (whose crews were found frozen in ice last spring), he landed at Archangel, a place where the sun never sets, and from there travelled by sledge to Moscow – the first Englishman to visit the city. It was an epic journey, and though Chancellor failed to find a new route to China he has opened up new and profitable markets for English merchants.

Prominent Protestants burnt at the stake

A table describing the burning of the bishops Ridley and Latimer at Oxford.

Oxford, 16 October 1555
Two of England's most senior clerics, Nicholas Ridley, the bishop of London, and Hugh Latimer, the former bishop of Worcester, have been burnt for heresy. Their deaths mark the latest stage in Queen Mary's campaign to silence all opposition, both real and imagined.

Ridley had been chaplain to Henry VIII and bishop of Rochester before succeeding the conservative Bishop Bonner in the see of London, and on the death of Edward VI he supported Lady Jane Grey, Mary's short-lived rival. Mary sent him to the Tower, and his bishopric was returned to Bonner. Latimer, a former chaplain to Henry's second wife, Anne Boleyn, had devoted his last 20 years to furthering the Protestant cause. He was twice imprisoned by Henry for his uncompromising stand.

Imprisoned by Mary, Ridley and Latimer were tried by a commission appointed by Cardinal Pole, as legate, and found guilty of heresy. After 18 months in prison, and a second show trial for Ridley, the two men were burnt this morning outside Balliol College (→12/1555).

The heraldic red griffin and white hound flank the coat-of-arms of Henry VIII: on 18 July 1555 Queen Mary granted a building in London to the College of Heralds, reflecting growing popular interest in heraldry.

1556 - 1557

Europe, 16 January 1556. Holy Roman Emperor Charles V abdicates; his son, Philip II, now rules Spain and the Netherlands, and Charles's brother Ferdinand succeeds him as emperor (→9/1556).

England, 18 March 1556. Queen Mary orders the arrest of leading nobles on the discovery of a plot, led by the exiled Sir Henry Dudley, to put Elizabeth on the throne.

Canterbury, 22 March 1556. Cardinal Pole is consecrated archbishop (→6/1557).

Ireland, 28 April 1556. The English begin the confiscation and "plantation" of Co Laois and Co Offaly (→26/5).

Ireland, 26 May 1556. Sir Anthony St Leger, the lord deputy of Ireland, is recalled to England in disgrace; he is replaced by Thomas Radcliffe, Lord Fitzwalter (→7/1556).

Whitehall, 14 July 1556. Mary considers a recoinage of the English currency (→9/12/60).

Ulster, July 1556. Lord Fitzwalter campaigns against the Scots in Ulster (→17/2/57).

Europe, September 1556. Mary's relationship with Rome deteriorates when her husband, Philip II of Spain, is provoked into a war against Pope Paul IV (→20/3/57).

London, 1556. The Stationers' Company of London is granted a monopoly of printing in England (→29/6/66).

London, 17 February 1557. Lord Fitzwalter is created earl of Sussex (→6/1557).

Greenwich, 20 March 1557. Philip II, bankrupt, returns to England in search of financial help (→7/6).

Dublin, 2 July 1557. The Irish parliament closes with a repeal of all Reformation legislation (→12/1/60).

Co Offaly, 10 July 1557. The earl of Sussex begins a campaign against the O'Connors (→27/10).

Armagh City, 27 October 1557. The earl of Sussex destroys the city during his campaign against Shane O'Neill (→27/4/58).

London, 1557. Thomas Tusser publishes *A Hundred Points of Good Husbandry*, which in doggerel verse gives advice for organizing homes and farms; it is an instant bestseller.

Derbyshire, 1557. A new boys' school is founded at Repton.

Cranmer burnt at Oxford

An engraving of the dramatic scene at the martyrdom of Thomas Cranmer.

Oxford, 21 March 1556
Thomas Cranmer, archbishop of Canterbury in the reigns of Henry VIII and Edward VI, was burnt at the stake in front of Balliol College, in The Broad, here today.

Since the executions of Latimer and Ridley five months ago, which he witnessed from his jail, Cranmer had signed seven recantations, but on hearing this morning that he would still be burnt, he retracted them. Taken out to the stake, he put his right hand into the flames, crying: "This hath offended! Oh this unworthy hand!"

Queen Mary was set on seeing the death of Cranmer. A willing conformist to all of Henry's turnabouts, he had not only declared her illegitimate, pronouncing her mother's marriage null and void, but he had also been the main force promoting Protestantism in her late father's and brother's turbulent reigns (→22).

Scots protest at tax increases to pay for war

Edinburgh, 2 May 1556
The failure of Mary of Guise's government to secure a permanent tax to pay both for defensive measures against the English and for the French army still in Scotland has decisively altered the balance of power in Scotland.

Mary's regency is only two years old. It started well – a committee was established to fix uniform weights and measures, the shortage of livestock was abated by orders forbidding the killing of lambs, and forests were replanted. But in spite of her practical successes, the Scots remain profoundly suspicious of her pro-French policies, and they cannot forget that she belongs to the second most powerful family in France, where their child queen, Mary, lives, betrothed to the *dauphin* [royal heir].

Smouldering resentment has been fanned by a ruling that makes it illegal to "speak evil against the queen's grace and of Frenchmen".

French cavalry: irksome to Scots.

Fearing that Scotland may become a French satellite, nationalists and Protestants have united against the regent. There is a sense of crisis in the air (→24/4/58).

Famine and illness claim thousands of lives as prices rise

England, 1557
Famine again stalks the land. The harvest has failed for a third year running, and the death rate has risen rapidly this year. Last year's harvest was reckoned the worst this century, and the outlook is grim. As well as starvation, thousands are dying from new scourges. "What diseases and sicknesses everywhere prevail," notes one observer. "The like whereof has never been known before. Hot burning fevers and other strange diseases." To make matters worse prices have been rising sharply, and last year grain cost double what it did in 1553. This is a disaster for the 60 per cent of the population who live at subsistence level, especially wage earners who reckon to spend 80 to 90 per cent of their income on food.

Harvesters (detail from a painting by Pieter Breughel the Younger).

Many believe that enclosures – fencing off common land – are responsible for the price rises, and violent denunciations of the practice has had an effect on government policy. Others point to yet another crisis: the collapse of the cloth trade. Exports are believed to be down by as much as 30 per cent from five years ago.

It is widely believed these troubles are a sign of God's anger at the government, but as yet there have been no serious uprisings.

Laois and Offaly targeted for 'plantation'

An Irish chief inspects his lordship [lands] accompanied by his attendants.

Lord deputy: the earl of Sussex.

Ireland, June 1557
Led by the lord deputy, the earl of Sussex, the English are trying to extend the Pale and subdue some of the most troublesome Irish by confiscating and "planting" two midland counties – Laois and Offaly. By moving in settlers from England with sound farming experience, they hope to have their garrisons fed, thus reducing the cost of maintenance while at the same time making them more secure. The Dublin parliament this month decided to re-name the two counties Queen's County and King's County, and the English system of local organization and law enforcement is to be established there (→2/7).

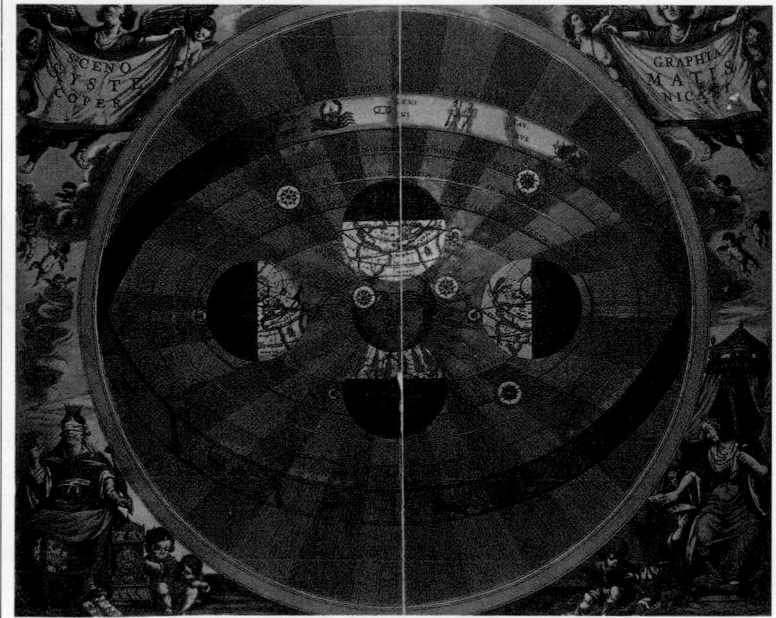
In 1556 the mathematician John Dee stirred up interest in England in the "system" of the Polish astronomer Copernicus (illustrated above). In 1543 Copernicus challenged the idea that the earth is the centre of the universe by arguing that it and the other planets revolve around the sun.

English declare war against the French

London, 7 June 1557
Queen Mary has agreed to join her husband, Philip II of Spain, in his war against France, which is in league with the pope. Although most people in England – fearing loss of trade and further taxes – are opposed to fighting the French, a formal declaration has been sent today to Henry II of France.

Trouble erupted in April with a raid on Scarborough Castle by a disaffected aristocrat, Thomas Stafford, who had fled to France in 1554. Believing that he had a claim on the English throne, Stafford arrived at Scarborough with a small French force. He was captured and has been executed, but the incident spurred Mary into action (→1/1/58).

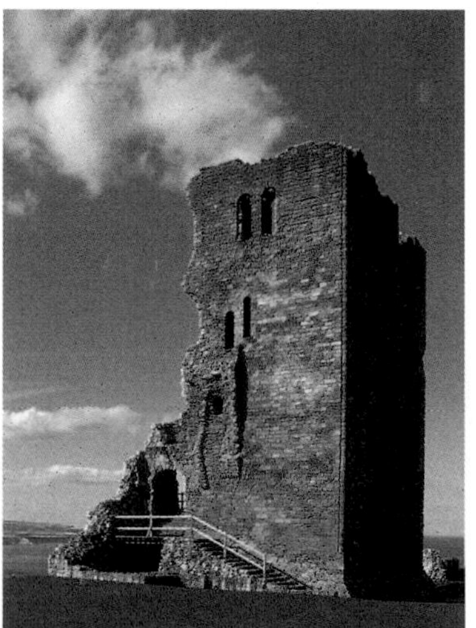
The keep of Scarborough Castle, attacked by Thomas Stafford.

Scots sign covenant

Edinburgh, 3 December 1557
A "Covenant with God" aimed at lighting the fire of Protestantism in Scotland has attracted only a few signatures. Led by the earl of Argyll, five nobles have pledged themselves to "forsake and renounce the Congregation of Satan with all the superstition, abomination and idolatry thereof". The lack of support derives not from the weakness of Protestantism, which is growing in importance among the landowning and urban classes, but from the presence in Scotland of a 7,000-strong French force maintained by the regent, Mary of Guise (→1/9/58).

Pole row puts Mary at odds with Rome

England, June 1557
Cardinal Reginald Pole, the new archbishop of Canterbury, has been recalled to Rome by Pope Paul IV to answer heresy charges. Pole, who left England before Henry VIII's break with Rome, became a cardinal in 1536 and returned to his native land as papal legate three years ago. He has reconciled the church of England to Rome. The pope is now allied with France in its war against Spain and England, however, and regards Pole's position as untenable. But Queen Mary is refusing to let Pole go to Rome or to recognize the replacement nominated by the pope, Friar William Peto – a sad irony for this devout Catholic queen (→17/11/58).

Dartford nuns back after two decades

Dartford, Kent, 8 September 1557
A group of Dominican nuns returned to the nunnery here today to resume a life broken off two decades ago when King Henry VIII dissolved the monasteries. This development is the latest in a small number of refoundations of monastic houses during the present reign, most of which have been undertaken with the encouragement of Queen Mary. The greatest restoration has been that of the royal Benedictine abbey at Westminster, which took place last year.

Nuns take their place in the choir.

1558

Calais, 1 January. The English, led by Thomas, Lord Wentworth, attempt to rebuff French attacks to gain control of Calais (→ 7).

London, 30 March. Queen Mary, once again believing herself to be pregnant, makes out her will in case she dies in childbirth; the will provides that only her children can succeed to the throne.

Ireland, 27 April. Thomas Radcliffe, the earl of Sussex and lord deputy, returns to his post (→ 15/9).

Strathclyde, 15 September. The earl of Sussex sets out from Kintyre to campaign against the Scots in the isles (→ 8/11).

Dublin, 8 November. The earl of Sussex returns after a successful campaign against the Scots and also, on his way back here, against the Scots in Antrim (→ 30/8/59).

Canterbury, 10 November. Despite Queen Mary's illness, the persecution of the Protestants continues; five are burnt at the stake (→ 17/11).

Scotland, 11 November. The Scottish parliament agrees to offer the French *dauphin*, Mary Queen of Scots' husband, the crown matrimonial, making him king of Scotland if Mary dies first (→ 30/6/59).

London, 17 November. Queen Mary dies, at St James's Palace, aged 42; her half-sister Elizabeth, aged 25, succeeds her as queen.→

Hatfield, 17 November. Queen Elizabeth establishes her household and chooses her advisers, reinstating several prominent Protestants dismissed during the reign of Queen Mary; Sir William Cecil is re-appointed chief secretary of state (→ 28).

London, 28 November. Queen Elizabeth makes a triumphal entry into the city (→ 15/1/59).

Co Tyrone, winter. Shane O'Neill has Matthew, the baron of Dungannon, assassinated; he was a possible rival for the earldom of Tyrone held by O'Neill's father, Conn Bachach (→ 14/5/59).

Geneva. John Knox, the exiled Scottish Calvinist preacher, follows his *First blast of the trumpet against the monstrous regiment [rule] of women* with the *Appellation to the nobility and estates of Scotland*, urging the people of Scotland to revolt against the regent, Mary of Guise (→ 1/9).

England surrenders Calais to the French

A medal marking the Calais battle.

Calais, 7 January
The main English garrison at Calais has fallen to the French. The onslaught that began on New Year's Day has come as a great shock to the English people, who saw Calais – an English possession for more than 200 years – as impregnable.

No one had expected the French to attack during winter, and the garrison at Calais had been reduced to its peacetime strength of some 600 men, against a potential invading force of 27,000, led by the duke of Guise. Frozen marshes allowed the French to seize a fortress between the harbour and the coast. Then, as the English commander, Thomas, Lord Wentworth, appealed for reinforcements, the French artillery swept in, fighting off the English fleet, bombarding the main fort and forcing its abandonment (→ 2/4/59).

Militia is reformed by new legislation

Westminster, 3 March
An important act has been passed today to improve England's defence forces. The bill was discussed at great length in parliament where many members have had experience of raising forces. The long overdue reform obliges all sections of society to provide men, horses and equipment, and those who try to evade the act will be penalized.

Since more people will be needed to organize the increased forces, a shift of leadership from the exclusive control of the aristocracy to the wider group of the gentry seems to be inevitable.

Scottish queen marries French 'dauphin'

Paris, 24 April
At a glittering ceremony in Nôtre-Dame Cathedral today 15-year-old Mary Queen of Scots married the French *dauphin* [royal heir] Francis, sealing an alliance which England has dreaded.

The bride's procession was headed by Swiss guards, followed by musicians in yellow and red with trumpets, flageolets and violins. Mary herself – who has lived in exile in France for almost a decade – was resplendent in a lily-white robe of sumptuous silk, defying the French tradition that white is the colour of mourning. The rubies, pearls and sapphires in her gold crown surrounded one great diamond, said to be worth 500,000 crowns. The 14-year-old *dauphin*, who is regarded as ugly, was virtually ignored.

Marriage now links England's old enemy with a leading claimant to the English crown. Queen Mary of England remains childless, and, although her half-sister Elizabeth looks most likely to succeed, Mary Queen of Scots has a strong claim as the granddaughter of Henry VIII's sister Margaret (→ 11/11).

Mary and new husband, Francis.

Edinburgh is rocked by Protestant riots

Mary of Guise: upset by covenant.

The priest Walter Myln is burnt.

Edinburgh, 1 September
Serious rioting has broken out on the streets of Edinburgh in response to French persecution of Protestants, with priests brazenly defying the Catholic government of Scotland's regent, Mary of Guise. Feelings have been running high ever since the death earlier this year of 80-year-old Walter Myln, a parish priest from Lunan, near Montrose, who was sent to the stake at St Andrews. Mary of Guise is clearly disturbed by the events of last year.

Five high-ranking Scottish Protestants, known as "the lords of the congregation", then drew up a covenant promising to "maintain, set forward and establish the word of God and his congregation". Above all, the lords were driven by the concern that France intends to make Scotland simply a French province (→ 24/7/59).

Tragic 'Bloody Mary' dies with Calais in her heart

Reign of England's first queen cut short

England, 17 November
The death this morning of 42-year-old Mary Tudor ends the inglorious reign of England's first "queen regnant". Her marriage to Philip II of Spain was not popular, even though it carried on England's traditional foreign alliance, and the success of her restoration of the "old religion" depended on her having enough time to make it secure. Her ill-health meant that time was short.

Mary's persecution of Protestants led to the deaths of more than 300 men and women, including the martyrdom of Bishops Ridley and Latimer and Archbishop Cranmer. The policy earned her popular contempt and the nickname "Bloody Mary". The loss of Calais earlier this year was the final blow. Before her death the queen was reported to have said: "When I am dead and opened they shall find Calais engraved in my heart" (→14/12).

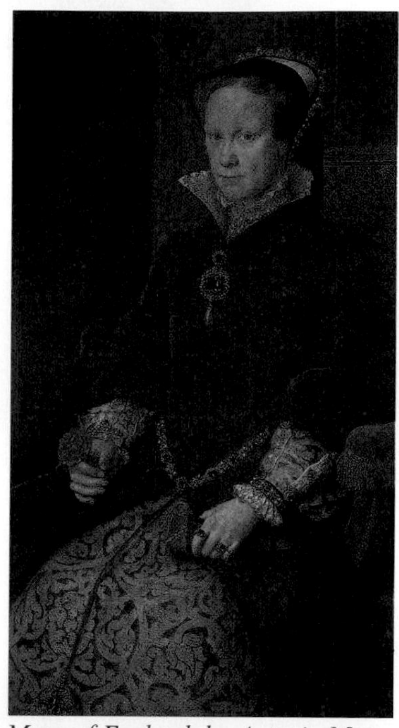

Mary of England, by Antonio Mor.

Cardinal Pole dies within hours of Mary

England, 17 November
Within hours of Mary's death, her closest adviser, Reginald Pole, the archbishop of Canterbury, has also died – an unhappy man who failed to realize his youthful potential. Born in Staffordshire in 1500, Pole won the favour of Henry VIII, but their relationship was destroyed by the break with Rome. Pole left the country and was made a cardinal by Pope Paul III. As papal legate in England under Mary he reconciled the English church to Rome and backed the queen in her persecution of Protestants. But he fell out with Pope Paul IV, who stripped him of his authority.

Funeral speech warns of Geneva 'wolves'

Westminster, 14 December
Queen Mary's burial took place at Westminster Abbey today with full Catholic rites. In a funeral oration, Bishop John White of Winchester referred to the European Reformation movement, warning that "the wolves be coming out of Geneva and other places ... and have sent their books before them, full of pestilent doctrines, blasphemy and heresy to infect the people".

Today's funeral ceremony was overshadowed by the tragedy of an unfulfilled life. The daughter of Henry VIII and Catherine of Aragon, Mary was declared illegitimate after the English church's break with Rome. She remained a devout Catholic all her life, vowing – with disastrous results – to bring England back to the "old religion" [*see report left*]. Deserted by her husband, Philip II of Spain, who spent much of their marriage attending to affairs of state on the continent, Mary's hopes of producing an heir were not to be. She died sick and disappointed, unloved and alone – and obliged to accept that her Protestant half-sister Elizabeth would succeed (→31).

A group of Geneva "wolves", dominated by John Calvin (centre left).

Famine and disease add to unrest (Breughel's "Seven Acts of Mercy").

Turmoil intensified by natural disasters

England, 31 December
The reign of Mary Tudor was marked not only by intense religious turmoil but also by a series of natural disasters that had serious economic consequences for the ordinary people. Famine and disease have had a devastating effect. Twice as many died from famine caused by bad harvests this year than did so two years ago. Thousands also continue to die from the epidemic [of influenza] that began then. Particularly lethal to the elderly, the epidemic struck hard at Mary's closest circle in politics and the church, undermining her leadership just as it faced the succession of a Protestant. There were, for example, five bishoprics vacant at the time of Mary's death; Pole's death left a sixth, and four more bishops have since died.

Since her accession Elizabeth has been swift to reorganize the royal household. With the assistance of William Cecil, her chief secretary of state, England's new queen is engaged in appointing a new circle of advisers. The privy council is dominated by Cecil's friends and includes his brother-in-law Nicholas Bacon.

1559

England, 10 January. King Philip II of Spain, the husband of the late Queen Mary, proposes marriage to Queen Elizabeth (→ 10/2).

Scotland, January. Friars are ordered by parliament to vacate their premises for the use of the sick and the poor.

Westminster, 10 February. Queen Elizabeth tells parliament that at present she has no intention or desire to marry (→ 5/6).

Edinburgh, 26 March. The regent, Mary of Guise, makes known her determination to stamp out Protestantism in Scotland (→ 24/7).

France, 2 April. The Treaty of Cateau-Cambrésis brings peace between France and England; by the treaty the French will control Calais for the next eight years (→ 11/4/64).

Ulster, 14 May. Shane O'Neill captures Calvagh O'Donnell (→ 17/7).

Strathclyde, 21 May. The Catholic Mass is outlawed by the burgh of Ayr.

France, 30 June. Henry II dies in a jousting accident; his 15-year-old son, Francis, with his young wife, Mary Queen of Scots, succeeds to the French throne (→ 5/12/60).

Co Tyrone, 17 July. Conn Bacach O'Neill, the earl of Tyrone, dies; his son, Shane, claims the earldom (→ 8/6/61).

Edinburgh, 24 July. The regent, Mary of Guise, and the Protestant "lords of the Congregation" agree to a truce (→ 21/10).

Ireland, 30 August. Thomas Radcliffe, the earl of Sussex, is reappointed lord deputy (→ 12/1/60).

Leith, Lothian, 24 September. Protestants appeal to Elizabeth of England for aid against the French forces of Mary of Guise garrisoned in Scotland (→ 21/10).

Edinburgh, 6 November. The Catholic Mass is reinstated by Mary of Guise after the Protestant "army of the Congregation" fails in its assault on French troops garrisoned at Leith (→ 12/1559).

Canterbury, 17 December. Matthew Parker is consecrated archbishop of Canterbury.→

Fife, December. French troops force the Protestant army to retreat westwards and occupy Fife.→

Elizabeth crowned with great pomp

Powerful pageantry: the coronation procession to Westminster Abbey.

A Protestant queen wears the crown.

London, 15 January
Elizabeth Tudor, the daughter of Henry VIII and Anne Boleyn, was crowned queen of England at Westminster Abbey today – in a ceremony that left no one in doubt about the nature of her future religious intentions. Although the coronation itself had all the traditional splendour, the Gospel and the Epistle were said in English as well as Latin – a sign of further Protestant changes to come. The service was performed by the bishop of Carlisle, since Archbishop Heath of York had refused to make the modifications that Elizabeth had insisted he should include.

The Protestant pageantry during the state drive from the Tower and the procession through the City of London yesterday, together with the lack of Catholic ritual, emphasized the shape of things to come.

It is not surprising therefore that Queen Elizabeth is already being referred to as Deborah – the female judge in ancient Israel – a term that is a favourite description of her among Protestants (→ 29/4).

Papal authority in England is renounced under new legislation

Westminster, 29 April
Parliament today passed Acts of Supremacy and Uniformity which renounce all papal jurisdiction over England. The Uniformity measure only scraped through the House of Lords; had three leading churchmen not been absent (two of them in prison), it would have failed.

Although this settlement is vital to the future of the English church, it did not receive a positive vote from any churchman entitled to sit in the Lords. Nor did the church's assemblies influence its drafting.

The settlement restores the religious situation to how it stood at the death of Edward VI in 1553 but makes some concessions to conservative opinion. One such is that the queen's title is supreme governor, rather than supreme head of the church. The Prayer Book of 1552 is restored, while questions of church ornament and vestments are left to the queen's discretion. The most significant concession is one concerning the Communion service and it allows religious conservatives to regard the bread and wine as containing the real presence of Christ's body and blood. It has also been decided that the few monasteries and chantries which were refounded under Queen Mary should be dissolved and their property returned to the crown (→ 2/1563).

An allegorical satire representing Elizabeth's rejection of papal authority.

Knox ignites rebellion among Scots

Perth, 29 May
After nearly three weeks of violent confrontation between supporters of the Protestant preacher John Knox and the forces of the Catholic regent Mary of Guise, the two factions have agreed a truce.

Knox arrived at Leith on 2 May from exile in Geneva. He came by ship, having been refused permission to travel through England because of his *First blast of the trumpet against the monstrous regiment [rule] of women* – a published attack on women rulers which offended Queen Elizabeth.

On 11 May Knox preached an inflammatory sermon at Perth in support of Protestant preachers who had defied a summons to appear before the regent, and a riot ensued. The monasteries of the Black Friars, Grey Friars and Carthusians were razed, and the rebels seized control of the town. With Protestant support bolstered by the arrival of the earl of Glencairn and forces from the west, the regent agreed to an armistice (→7/7).

A stained-glass window shows Knox preaching one of his controversial sermons.

English queen faces pressure to marry

Westminster, 5 June
Queen Elizabeth today wrote to Holy Roman Emperor Ferdinand, rejecting a proposal that she should marry his Catholic son Charles, the archduke of Austria, and saying that she had no desire to give up her solitude.

Elizabeth is undoubtedly the best matrimonial prize in Europe. Since she became queen many royal ambassadors have courted her favour and she has already turned down offers of marriage from her late sister's husband, Philip II of Spain, and Prince Eric of Sweden.

Elizabeth's marriage plans are of burning interest to her government. On 4 February the House of Commons urged her to marry for the sake of the succession. The queen insisted that she would be happy to live and die a virgin. However, she assured parliament however that, if she changed her mind, she would choose a husband as committed as herself to the security and prosperity of the realm (→8/9/60).

Victorious Protestants occupy Edinburgh

Edinburgh, 7 July
The fiery Protestant preacher John Knox was today appointed minister of St Giles's, following the occupation of the town by his supporters. Over the past two months Knox has stoked a powerful rebellion against the French Catholic regent Mary of Guise, the widow of James V of Scotland.

While Knox continues to urge attacks on the "idols" of Catholicism, the regent's support has been eroded after her breach of the armistice agreed in May and Protestant propaganda against French domination of the country (→24).

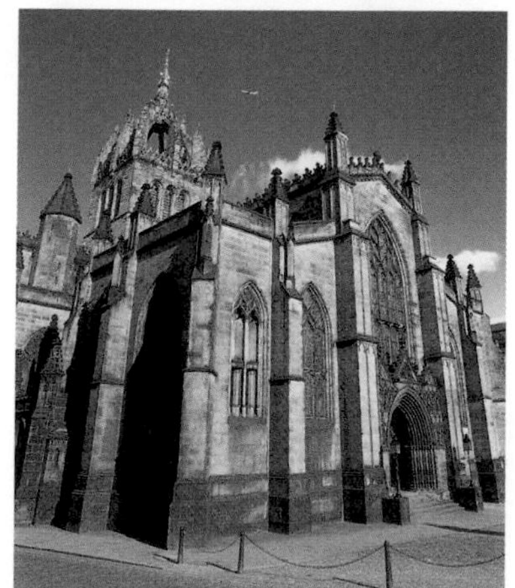
St Giles's: Knox is now minister.

Mary of Guise suspended from regency

Edinburgh, 21 October
Mary of Guise has been suspended from the Scots regency by the Protestant "lords of the Congregation". Mary heard the news at Leith, the last Scottish enclave still under her command, having fled Edinburgh before the Protestants arrived six days ago. For six months Scotland has been at war with itself. Mary, her French army and a diminishing band of Catholic loyalists have steadily lost control of the country, while the rebels, led by the earl of Arran (now known as the duke of Châtelherault) and backed by England, have grown in confidence until victory looks certain (→6/11).

Protestants flee as French forces take control of Stirling

Scotland, December
The clash of religious passions in Scotland has finally come to a head, with thousands of Protestants fleeing the advancing French forces, which now have occupied Stirling and are pressing on into Fife. The Catholic government of Mary of Guise is once more asserting its supremacy over the rebel "Lords of the Congregation" – who were stirred into action by the return of John Knox [*see reports left*].

There has been a French military presence in Scotland since Henry VIII of England first renewed hostilities with the Scots in the 1540s. The depleted army was reinforced last August by the arrival of more troops from France, who began building a major fortification at Leith. The Protestants appealed to Elizabeth of England for help.

Wary of being seen to have encouraged the rebellion, Elizabeth agreed to provide clandestine aid in the form of money and munitions. (In April she had signed a peace treaty with the French, confirming England's loss of Calais.) However, a Protestant assault on the French at Leith last month ended in failure, and the "army of the Congregation" had to retreat to Stirling. Meanwhile, the Mass was restored in Edinburgh. With the fall of Stirling to the French, the Protestant rebels are in disarray (→23/1/60).

Matthew Parker, the Norwich-born churchman: he became the second Protestant archbishop of Canterbury in December 1559.

1560 - 1561

Dublin, 12 January 1560. Parliament meets to pass the English Act of Uniformity, imposing the use of the *Book of Common Prayer* and royal supremacy (→ 10/1564).

Fife, 23 January 1560. The French abandon the area on the arrival of an English fleet led by Admiral Winter (→ 22/2).

Northumberland, 22 February 1560. Scottish Protestants and Queen Elizabeth sign the Treaty of Berwick, by which England agrees to send the Protestants military aid against the French (→ 6/7).

Ireland, 6 May 1560. The earl of Sussex is sworn in as lord lieutenant (→ 7/1561).

Edinburgh, 6 July 1560. The Treaty of Edinburgh ends the war in Scotland.→

France, 5 December 1560. Francis II dies; his widow, Mary Queen of Scots, is pushed aside by his mother, the regent of France, Catherine de' Medici (→ 13/7/61).

London, 9 December 1560. Legal formalities for the recoinage of the currency are completed (→ 24/8/62).

Lothian, 20 December 1560. The Church of Scotland holds its first general assembly (→ 27/1/61).

Scotland, 27 January 1561. The Church of Scotland approves the *First Book of Discipline*, a plan for the future of the church (→ 6/1563).

Ireland, 8 June 1561. Shane O'Neill is proclaimed a traitor by the earl of Sussex (→ 11/1562).

England, 13 July 1561. Mary Queen of Scots is forbidden by Elizabeth to return to Scotland via England on her failure to ratify the Treaty of Edinburgh and recognize Elizabeth as queen (→ 19/8).

Armagh City, July 1561. English troops are garrisoned at the cathedral (→ 11/1562).

Westminster, 26 December 1561. Elizabeth creates Lord Ambrose Dudley, the elder brother of Lord Robert, earl of Warwick (→ 28/7/63).

London, December 1561. *Gorboduc*, by Thomas Norton and Thomas Sackville, the earl of Dorset, the first English tragedy in blank verse, is performed at court.

London, 1561. Silk stockings are the latest fashion craze (→ 1564).

English and French to leave Scotland

Edinburgh, 6 July 1560

A treaty was signed here today ending the war in Scotland. England and France are to withdraw their troops and let the Scots settle their own religious future. However, the Protestant party will be able to set up a provisional government. Mary Queen of Scots – who is still living in exile in France and has yet to ratify the treaty – will cease to use the English arms, signifying her recognition of Elizabeth as queen of England. (Mary has a claim on the English throne through her grandmother, Henry VIII's sister.)

The end of the war follows the death last month of Mary of Guise, the former regent of Scotland and scourge of the Protestant rebels. The daughter of the most powerful noble in France, Mary of Guise married James V of Scotland in 1538. Their daughter, Mary, became queen when she was only six days old and was sent to France for her own protection at the age of five. Suspended from the regency last October, Mary of Guise made a comeback, but her power was greatly reduced (→ 13/7/61).

Scotland breaks with Rome and abolishes Mass as religious revolution is completed

Edinburgh, 24 August 1560

Parliament has broken with the pope, banned the Latin Mass and adopted a reformed faith. The religion of the young Mary Queen of Scots, still in France, is irrelevant. Scotland has opted for Protestantism in the Geneva mould. The revolution was carried through in the face of strong opposition; its success depended on Protestant propaganda that managed to present the fight against the regent, Mary of Guise, as a war of national liberation against French occupation.

No man sees this as a greater vindication of his life's work than John Knox. In 1545, a disillusioned notary, he met the radical George Wishart and was converted to reformist zeal. Captured by French troops in the Protestant stronghold of St Andrews, he spent 18 months in the galleys before being freed on English intervention. In England he became chaplain to Edward VI before fleeing to Geneva, where he stayed for five years. He returned to Scotland in 1559 in triumph, universally acclaimed as the spiritual leader of the Protestant rebels.

A memorial statue of John Knox.

With the regent's death and the defeat of the French army [*see report left*], Scotland's revolution is uncompromising – although the Protestant minority remains concentrated in a few localities such as Ayrshire, Fife and Perth (→ 20/12).

Elizabeth advances claims on Ireland

Ireland, 1 February 1560

In an effort to impose Queen Elizabeth's Protestantism on Ireland, an Act of Supremacy has been passed that restores the spiritual supremacy of the English crown here and demands from all church leaders and judges an oath of recognition. An Act of Uniformity makes attendance at church compulsory, on pain of a fine of 12 pence, and provides for the use of the *Book of Common Prayer*. From now on priests are to be called ministers. The queen's title to the crown of Ireland has also been recognized.

Clearly it is hoped that these measures will counteract the growing influence of Catholicism in Ireland, which has given rise to complaints from the Protestant bishops. But the success of Catholic missionaries is probably due more to resentment of the English than to strong religious belief (→ 6/5).

Rumours link queen to mysterious death

Lord Robert Dudley, Elizabeth's favourite, and his wife Amy Robsart.

Oxfordshire, 8 September 1560

The court is buzzing with rumours that the wife of one of Elizabeth's favourite courtiers has been killed so that the courtier can marry the queen. Amy Robsart, married to Lord Robert Dudley, on whom the queen has showered gifts and privileges, has been found dead after falling from a "pair of stairs". She had been living in relative seclusion near Oxford for the past two years, fuelling rumours that Dudley, the son of the late duke of Northumberland, was keeping her out of the way. Dudley is particularly unpopular with the queen's chief secretary, Sir William Cecil (→ 3/1564).

Idea to teach girls breaks new ground

England, 1560

Ridiculing the theory that girls are fit only for domestic training, the Protestant cleric Thomas Becon has advocated establishing schools specifically for the female sex. This controversial idea is put forward in Becon's immensely popular *Catechism*, a manual for teaching religion at home, published this year.

Few women apart from those at the very top of society are able to write, although it is thought that many more can read. The education of women is held to be a waste of time, partly because all the professions are closed to them. Women are excluded from the universities, from the professional law schools and the inns of court, as well as from the grammar schools which have become the centrepiece of English education. There are no institutional schools for women – only individual tuition for certain members of the aristocracy. There are some signs of change, however. Apart from Becon, the Spanish humanist scholar Juan Luis Vives, who was at Henry VIII's court in the 1520s, and the English writer Sir Thomas Elyot have spoken up for the education of women.

Those who have been well educated have included Lady Jane Grey, Queen Mary and the present queen, Elizabeth, who converses with foreign ambassadors in fluent Latin.

Young Scottish queen returns home

A romanticized 19th-century view of Mary Stuart's sad farewell to France.

Mary depicted in confrontation with her bitter adversary John Knox.

Leith, Lothian, 19 August 1561

A 13-year exile ended today when a sad and beautiful young queen arrived here with a magnificent retinue of princes, musicians, poets and a large quantity of the French crown jewels. After five days sailing from the splendours of the French court, Mary Stuart came to claim her throne in a country which she only dimly remembers and whose language she barely knows.

The 18-year-old queen is credited with prudence and wisdom as well as charm and courtesy – and she will need them all. She might never even have arrived had it not been for thick fog. Rumour has it that a group of English ships, commanded by her half-brother, James Stewart, the earl of Moray, was lying in wait to seize her. The prospect of an unmarried Catholic queen, who is also an heir to the English throne and a friend of France, ruling in Scotland, deeply alarms Queen Elizabeth.

The situation in Scotland, however, does not promise tranquillity. Mary is a Catholic monarch in a country under Protestant control, following last year's religious revolution and the ejection of French troops under the Treaty of Edinburgh [*see reports on page 450*]. The dour figure of the Protestant radical John Knox, who has trumpeted against all female rulers, awaits her in Edinburgh (→20/9/62).

The south view of St Paul's Cathedral, London, whose steeple – renewed in 1315, when needle-spires were popular – was destroyed by fire on 4 June 1561. There has been a church on this site since the seventh century.

Exiled Protestants publish new Bible

Geneva, April 1560

A new translation of the Bible into English has been completed and published by English and Scottish exiles here, with a dedication to Queen Elizabeth and a preface by the uncompromising Protestant reformer John Calvin.

The translators, led by William Whittingham of Oxford, have printed it in easily legible Roman type and numbered each verse for easy quotation; their notes are strongly Calvinist in theology. The unusual translation of Genesis III,7 has given rise to comment: "They sewed fig-leaves together and made themselves breeches" (→1568).

Claimant to throne sent to the Tower

London, August 1561

A younger sister of the ill-fated Lady Jane Grey – who was queen for only nine days in 1553 before she surrendered to Mary Tudor – has been arrested and placed in the Tower. As a Protestant claimant to the throne, Lady Catherine Grey – a great-niece of Henry VIII – is a major embarrassment to Queen Elizabeth. Her position requires her to obtain the queen's permission before getting married, so when her secret marriage to Edward, the earl of Hertford and son of the former lord protector, Somerset, came to light with the birth of a son, Elizabeth feared a plot (→8/1565).

1562 - 1563

Edinburgh, January 1562. Mary Queen of Scots agrees to compromise on the financing of the Protestant Church of Scotland (28/10).

London, 20 September 1562. Elizabeth signs a treaty giving aid to French Protestants; in return, the English hold Le Havre as a pledge for the recovery of Calais (→ 19/3/63).

Plymouth, October 1562. John Hawkins sets sail for the West Indies to break the Spanish trade monopoly (→ 9/1563).

Grampian, 2 November 1562. Mary Queen of Scots collapses at the execution of Sir John Gordon, the son of the earl of Huntly, one of the failed rebel leaders (→ 6/10/65).

Co Fermanagh, November 1562. Shane O'Neill lays waste to the county, ruled by the Maguire family (→ 12/1562).

Lincoln, February 1563. William Byrd is appointed cathedral organist.

France, 19 March 1563. The French civil war between Catholics and Protestants worsens, putting England in a difficult position (→ 28/7/63).

Ireland, March 1563. An inquiry begins into the abuses of the earl of Sussex's troops here (→ 4/1563).

Fife, 11 April 1563. John Hamilton, the archbishop of St Andrews, is imprisoned after presiding over Mass at Maybole, in Ayrshire.

Westminster, April 1563. Parliament orders the Bible and *Book of Common Prayer* to be translated into Welsh.

Ireland, April 1563. The lord lieutenant, the earl of Sussex, campaigns against Shane O'Neill (→ 11/9).

Edinburgh, June 1563. As requested by the church, parliament makes adultery and witchcraft capital offences.

Le Havre, 28 July 1563. Ambrose Dudley, the earl of Warwick, is forced to surrender his troops to the French after the signing of the Treaty of Amboise (→ 11/4/64).

Ireland, 11 September 1563. Shane O'Neill submits to the earl of Sussex (→ 25/5/64).

London, 1563. Elizabeth bans the selling of any unauthorized portraits of herself.

England, 1563. Over 20,000 people are thought to have died in this year's plague epidemic.

Irish earl repudiates deal with England

Ireland, December 1562
Shane O'Neill has gone back on a deal with Queen Elizabeth of England by campaigning to extend his dominion in Ulster.

At present English rule here is effectively confined to a coastal strip known as the Pale, centred on Dublin, and a few pockets in Leinster and Munster, although England claims overlordship of the whole country. The English are especially keen to control Ulster, thought vulnerable to Scottish invasion. On the advice of the earl of Sussex, the lord lieutenant, efforts were made to subdue O'Neill, who claims the earldom of Tyrone once held by his father, Conn Bachach. Conn had named another son, Matthew, the baron of Dungannon, as his heir, but Shane had him killed.

Shane visited Queen Elizabeth in London earlier this year. His negotiating position was strengthened after Sussex tried, and failed, to have him poisoned. Elizabeth accepted O'Neill as captain of Tyrone, provided that he yielded to her nominal overlordship. This interim agreement has now been violated by O'Neill (→ 3/1563).

Total recoinage restores foreign confidence

Artisans at work at the royal mint, producing the coinage of the realm.

London, 24 August 1562
Foreign confidence in England's money has been restored by a total recoinage, completed today. When Henry VIII came to the throne England had the finest coinage in Europe. But he, like Edward and Mary later, was seduced by the profits of debasement – minting coins with metal worth less than their face value. It was a dangerous short-term policy, causing damage to trade. Plans for recoinage were drawn up in Edward's and Mary's reigns but only partly implemented. Now all base coins have been withdrawn and new coins issued that are worth their weight in silver.

Smallpox gives fuel to succession fears

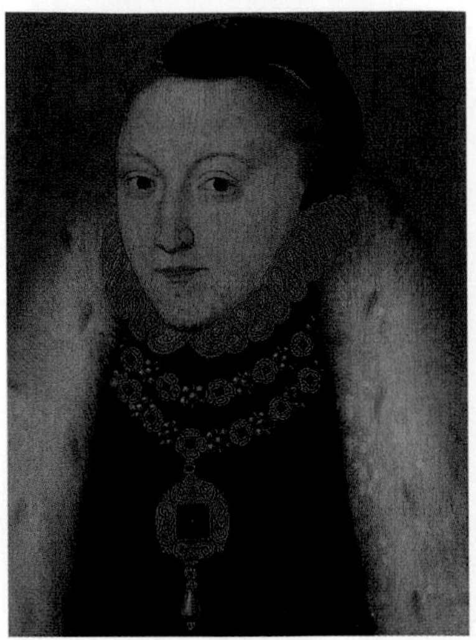

Elizabeth: preparations for death.

Hampton Court, 31 October 1562
Concern about the English succession has been fuelled by the queen's recent brush with death. Earlier this month Elizabeth – who remains unmarried and childless – had been feeling unwell. Walking in the palace gardens, she noticed tiredness and a high temperature. Dr Burcot, who was called, diagnosed smallpox. The signs are itching skin, pain in the face and throat, and a hoarse voice. But the queen distrusted Burcot's diagnosis as she had no red marks on her skin.

Four days later Elizabeth was so ill that her servants, fearing that the end was near, sent for her councillors. She insisted that they appoint Lord Robert Dudley protector of the realm. She was making other provisions for her death when Burcot was induced to return. Following a 14th-century cure, he wrapped her body in a scarlet cloth and laid her in front of the fire. The queen now seems to be recovering, her skin unblemished (→ 28/9/64).

Mary Queen of Scots' army victorious against rebellious earl

Grampian, 28 October 1562
Troops loyal to Mary Queen of Scots have won a victory at Corrichie in Aberdeenshire over the Catholic leader George Gordon, the earl of Huntly. Huntly – commonly regarded as the greatest magnate in Scotland and nicknamed "cock of the north" – died of a heart attack after the battle. Among Mary's prisoners is Huntly's son Sir John Gordon, a former suitor of hers, who now awaits the executioner's axe.

The queen's forces were lead by her illegitimate half-brother James Stewart, the earl of Moray, a Protestant ambitious to displace the Gordons from their control of the north-east and a strong influence on the 19-year-old Mary. Scottish Catholics are now even more confused by the policies of their queen, who fiercely defends her own private devotion to Rome while favouring Protestants and destroying the man best equipped to carry out a counter-reformation. But they admire her courage as she rides all day with her troops (→ 2/11).

Industry and agriculture face shake-up as parliament seeks to boost economy

Workers pay their dues on rent day; now they fear lower living standards.

England, April 1563
Agriculture and industry are facing a shake-up as a consequence of important legislation passed this year. The Statute of Artificers regulates wages and conditions of employment; it aims to make all males aged between 12 and 60 work for their living and so "banish idleness, advance husbandry and yield unto the hired person ... convenient proportion of wages".

Workers fear that it will reduce living standards. Earlier acts have tried to fix wages, but this is the first to fix hours of work too. In agriculture these are to be from 5am to 7pm or 8pm in summer, dawn to sunset in winter, with two and a half hours off for meals. Justices of the peace have the power to set wages, taking current conditions into account, but workers can be fined for missing work. A daily wage of sixpence is not unusual.

The statute also attempts to regulate industry, detailing a system of apprenticeships lasting up to seven years in various industries. The apprenticeships are for men aged between ten and 24, with conditions varying not only between industries but also between town and country.

Help for the fishing industry is also in prospect through legislation passed this year making Wednesdays, as well as Fridays, Saturdays and Lent, meat-less days.

A handsome catch: William Cecil, the queen's secretary, aims to restore demand for fish to the level it was at before the dissolution of the monasteries.

Hawkins's slave trade makes huge profit

Plymouth, September 1563
Captain John Hawkins has arrived back here after a profitable venture that involved the export of negroes from West Africa and their sale to Spanish settlers on the Caribbean island of Hispaniola in return for hides, sugar, ginger and pearls.

Hawkins has been trading with the Canary Islands for nine years, but only on this last voyage has he discovered the profits arising from human cargoes, and although the Spanish in Seville confiscated half his ships and their loads, and declared Hawkins a pirate, he has still made a gigantic profit (→8/1564).

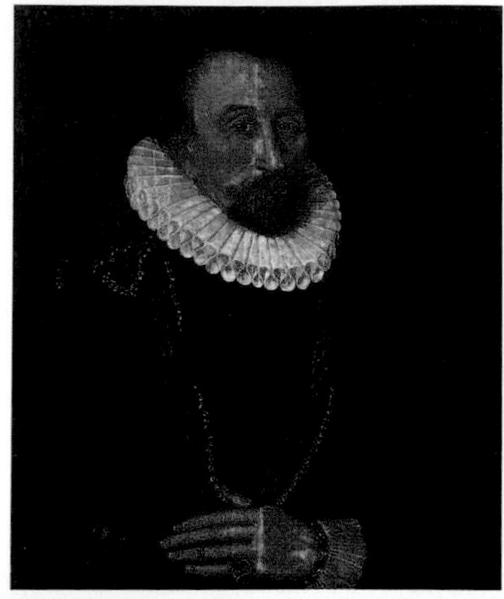

"Pirate": Captain John Hawkins.

French poet loses his head over verse

Fife, 22 February 1563
Another admirer of the beautiful Queen Mary has been beheaded. The handsome French courtier and poet Pierre de Châtelard confused literature with life. Encouraged by her appreciation of his romantic verse he hid under Mary's bed, so she banished him from court. Interpreting this as a test of his devotion he followed her to St Andrews where he broke into her rooms and attempted passionate consummation. Mary cried for help, and her half-brother, the earl of Moray, arrested the poet. Romantic to the last, de Châtelard recited Ronsard's *Hymn to Death* on the scaffold.

Protestant doctrine backed by church

London, February 1563
The convocation of the Church of England has agreed on a statement of doctrine consisting of 39 "Articles" to which all clergy are obliged to assent. They reflect the Protestant theology of the majority. An attempt to make the worship of the church far more radically puritan was narrowly defeated. A further six articles were proposed, involving abolition of saints' days, clerical vestments other than the surplice, the signing of the cross on a baby's head at baptism, kneeling to receive Communion and the use of organ music at services. These were lost by a single vote (→9/12/65).

Edmund Bonner, who was deposed as bishop of London in 1559, flogging Protestants in his garden: from John Foxe's "Acts and Monuments of the Church", or "Book of Martyrs", first published in English in 1563.

1564 - 1565

Armagh, 22 March 1564. Richard Creagh is appointed archbishop (→ 10/1564).

Scotland, March 1564. Lord Robert Dudley, an English nobleman and a cousin of Mary Queen of Scots, is put forward by Elizabeth as a possible husband for the young queen (→ 28/9).

Strathclyde, March 1564. The marriage of John Knox, the Calvinist preacher, who is almost 60 years old, to a teenager, Margaret Stewart, causes surprise.

Ireland, 25 May 1564. Thomas Radcliffe, the earl of Sussex and lord lieutenant, is recalled to England (→ 2/5/65).

London, 6 August 1564. The Spanish ambassador in London is ordered by Philip II of Spain to break off negotiations with Irish Catholics.

Plymouth, 18 October 1564. John Hawkins, the slave-trader, embarks on his second expedition to the New World (→ 1565).

Ireland, October 1564. A court of high commission is to be established to enforce religious conformity (→ 22/2/65).

England, 1564. A new form of transport is introduced from the Netherlands: the horse-drawn coach.

England, 1564. Fashions are revolutionized by the introduction from the Netherlands of starch.

Ireland, 1564. Revolts against the English scheme for plantations occur in Co Laois and Co Offaly (→ 10/1565).

Fife, 17 February 1565. Henry Stuart, Lord Darnley, meets Mary Queen of Scots (→ 7/1565).

London, 22 February 1565. Archbishop Creagh of Armagh is arrested by Elizabeth and put in the Tower.

Co Antrim, 2 May 1565. Shane O'Neill defeats the MacDonnells at Glenshesk (→ 10/1565).

Scotland, July 1565. King Henry begins to resent the close friendship between the Italian royal secretary, David Riccio, and Henry's wife, Mary Queen of Scots (→ 29).

Plymouth, 1565. John Hawkins brings sweet potatoes and tobacco back from his New World voyage.

Canterbury, 1565. The archbishop's palace is rebuilt.

Irretrievable loss of Calais confirmed by treaty with France

France, 11 April 1564

The signing today of the Treaty of Troyes has finally brought an end to England's humiliating war with France. What Mary had begun in 1557, Elizabeth renewed in 1562. But despite the queen's best efforts, Calais – which had been an English possession for more than 200 years – is irretrievably lost.

Fighting effectively ended last year when, weakened by plague, the English garrison at Le Havre, led by Robert Dudley's brother, the earl of Warwick, surrendered on 29 July after months of siege.

The English presence in the town had arisen from a bargain between Elizabeth and the French Huguenots [Protestants]. In exchange for help in their civil war against the Catholics, the Huguenots had surrendered Le Havre to the English, saying that they could keep it until France restored Calais to England. In recompense Elizabeth paid the Huguenots a subsidy and sent an army to occupy Le Havre in 1562.

When the French civil war ended early last year, the Catholics and Huguenots united in a common front against the English. Determined to regain Calais, Elizabeth decided to fight on. But the plague claimed thousands of English lives at Le Havre, forcing the garrison there to admit defeat.

Dudley is created earl and given estates

Kenilworth Castle, Warwickshire, during Elizabeth's reign: a reconstruction.

England, 28 September 1564

Queen Elizabeth has given the widowed Lord Robert Dudley the title of earl of Leicester and made him a lavish grant of lands that includes Kenilworth Castle.

Since 1562, when the queen was brought close to death by smallpox, speculation about her successor has been rife, with parliament urging her to marry in order to provide a Protestant heir. By bestowing these honours on Dudley and suggesting that he should marry Mary Queen of Scots, Elizabeth is reassuring the concerned members of parliament that she has no designs on Dudley herself and intends to continue to "rule and die a virgin" (→ 9/1570).

Dudley, Elizabeth's "favourite".

Long freeze brings starvation to Scots

Aberdeen, 20 January 1564

Tens of thousands of highlanders are perishing in the worst winter that Scotland has known in living memory. Sheep, cattle and fowl are freezing to death, virtually ensuring that this cold spell will be followed by a livestock famine. Forests are being denuded of wood in spite of all efforts by the authorities and landowners to prevent this. Entire valleys are also being depopulated. Most people die in their hovels, too weak even to search for food. The disaster comes after a series of bad harvests, resulting in food shortages and price rises.

England seeks alternative trading outlets

A merchant bargaining his wares.

London, August 1564

Part of England's vital wool trade may soon be flowing through the small Dutch port of Emden rather than through its traditional outlet, Spanish-controlled Antwerp. Last year the Spanish, furious at attacks by English privateers on their ships in the Channel, used the pretext of a plague in southern England to ban English imports to Antwerp.

The recent Emden deal is part of a long-term strategy to reduce England's dependence on Antwerp and to find new outlets – hence the Muscovy company, trading with Russia since 1553, and John Hawkins's West Africa/West Indies voyage last year (→ 18/10).

Sidney is appointed Irish lord deputy

Ireland, October 1565
Sir Henry Sidney has taken up the post of lord deputy of Ireland following the resignation as lord lieutenant of Thomas Radcliffe, the earl of Sussex. Sidney is already familiar with the country, and on his return to Dublin he has found the administration in disarray, with the authorities suspected of widespread corruption and unable to control mounting expenditure. Sidney is expected to bring a forceful personality to English affairs here. He will also have to take on Shane O'Neill, the would-be earl of Tyrone, who, again at loggerheads with the English, may ask France to send an army to Ulster (→ 1566).

Sir Henry Sidney: new lord deputy.

Mary marries young cousin, Lord Darnley

A love duet: Mary Queen of Scots and her second husband, Lord Darnley.

Edinburgh, 29 July 1565
Holyrood Palace was the scene today of the second marriage of the 22-year-old Mary Queen of Scots. Her husband, who becomes king of Scots, is 19-year-old Henry Stuart, Lord Darnley; his mother, Margaret, and Mary's father, James V, were half-siblings, children of the English Margaret Tudor from her first two marriages. Not only are they both cousins and Catholics, but also, as great-grandchildren of Henry VII of England, both have claims to the English throne. Not surprisingly, their cousin Queen Elizabeth disapproves strongly, seeing the match as a threat.

But Mary, infatuated with Darnley since February, is deaf to warnings of the political consequences and blind to his faults. For although handsome, elegant and accomplished, Darnley is also weak-willed, spoilt and vain. In addition he has made himself very unpopular by his arrogant behaviour. As one diplomat remarked: "He can have no long life among these people" (→ 6/10).

Scottish uprising against Mary fails

Borders, 6 October 1565
The leaders of a rebellion against Mary Queen of Scots have today fled across the border into England, a triumph for Mary that effectively destroys the Anglophiles, weakens the Protestants and dents the credibility of her interfering English cousin, Queen Elizabeth.

This latest challenge to Mary was led by her half-brother James, the earl of Moray, a Protestant but one-time supporter, who had put down the revolt by the Catholic lords three years ago. He resented his loss of influence following the queen's marriage to Darnley.

Others had been driven to revolt either by Mary marrying a Catholic or by her husband's insufferable behaviour. The rebels were promised aid by Elizabeth, but it never arrived as Mary's Catholic allies were seen as too powerful.

The French had warned Elizabeth to keep her hands off Scotland, and her major fear was of boosting the Franco-Scottish connection. Philip of Spain had also showed his support for Mary by sending a small subsidy. Elizabeth feared bringing in the Catholic League against England. By contrast Mary rallied her subjects, restored the exiled Catholic earls of Huntly and Bothwell, and hunted Moray and the rebels from one town to the next – already it is called "the Chaseabout Raid" (→ 9/3/66).

Lady Mary Grey's marriage exposed

London, August 1565
In a shocking repeat of her sister Catherine's fate, young Lady Mary Grey has been exposed as having secretly married one of the queen's men, the tall and handsome Thomas Keys. Just as Lady Catherine, who secretly wed Lord Hertford, is ending her days in the Tower, so it appears will Mary. The Greys – whose eldest sister, Jane, was executed in 1554 – are seen to pose a threat to England's "virgin queen". As the granddaughters of Mary, Henry VIII's sister, they are in the line of succession while Elizabeth remains without an heir (→ 22/1/68).

Elizabeth warned about growing strength of hard-line 'puritans'

The chapel at King's College, Cambridge, visited by Elizabeth last year.

Westminster, 9 December 1565
Queen Elizabeth was warned today about the activities of a new group of religious hardliners, known as "puritans", based at Cambridge University. The group is criticizing her for not moving swiftly enough against "popery". Elizabeth has ordered her chief minister, Cecil, "to use all severity expedient" to make sure that it causes no trouble.

The new movement, centred on St John's College, is influenced by the radical Protestantism of John Calvin and rejects anything which, in its eyes, smacks of Rome or the pope. The liturgy, it says, is still too much like the Mass, and vestments are "popish trumpery" (→ 3/1566).

1566

Ireland, early 1566. Ignoring his oath of loyalty to Queen Elizabeth of England, Shane O'Neill, the would-be earl of Tyrone, launches a campaign to bring the whole of Ulster under his control (→ 4/1566).

Edinburgh, 9 March. Mary Queen of Scots is taken prisoner at Holyrood Palace, just outside Edinburgh, after the brutal murder of one of her favourites, the royal secretary David Riccio.→

Lothian, 12 March. King Henry is persuaded by his wife, Mary Queen of Scots, to flee to Dunbar to escape the killers of Riccio (→ 20).

London, March. At the instigation of Archbishop Matthew Parker of Canterbury and Bishop Edmund Grindal of London, 37 members of the clergy are suspended in punishment for their refusal to wear clerical dress (→ 12/1566).

Ireland, April. Shane O'Neill appeals to King Charles IX of France for aid against the English (→ 3/8).

Armagh City, 3 August. Shane O'Neill, who appealed throughout Ireland for support against the English, burns the cathedral and is proclaimed a traitor; a reward is offered in return for his capture, dead or alive (→ 6/9).

Bristol, 6 September. An expeditionary force of 1,000 men, led by Colonel Edward Randolph, sails for Ireland to help the government to deal with the worsening situation there (→ 11/1566).

Borders, 25 October. Mary Queen of Scots fights back from death's door at Roxburgh, where she had been taken ill; only the persistence of her doctors revived her after she appeared to have died (→ 20/11).

Lothian, 20 November. Mary Queen of Scots holds a conference at Craigmillar Castle to discuss what to do about her husband, King Henry (→ 20/12).

Scotland, 20 December. Mary Queen of Scots, in anticipation of church approval of her decision to divorce her husband, makes a generous donation of £10,000 to the church (→ 24).

Scotland, 24 December. Mary Queen of Scots forgives the men responsible for the murder of her Italian secretary, David Riccio (→ 20/1/67).

Queen's private secretary butchered

Mary held captive after fatal stabbing

Edinburgh, 9 March
Queen Mary is captive in her own Holyrood Palace tonight after a bloody coup led by her husband. She was having supper with friends, including her Italian secretary David Riccio, when her husband, Henry, burst in, followed by the gaunt and disease-stricken figure of Lord Ruthven in full armour.

The queen, who is six months pregnant, was roughly handled but not hurt as Riccio, clinging to her skirts, was dragged from the room crying "Save me, lady, save me" in French. Later 60 dagger wounds were counted on his lifeless body.

But the coup was only partly to remove Riccio, a musician who had got close to the queen and so earned the hatred of the lords – for being Italian and for being arrogant – as well as Henry's jealousy. It also aims to force the queen to make Henry king in his own right, while the involvement of militant Protestants such as Lord Ruthven, and the recent murder of a Dominican friar, suggest an attempt to halt the queen's pro-Catholic policies. It certainly looks as though the exiled Protestant lords such as the earl of Moray, who were due to lose their lands on Tuesday, will now keep them (→ 12).

The scene at the stabbing of David Riccio, as painted by John Opie.

Royal control restored as conspirators flee

Edinburgh, 20 March
Queen Mary is back in control of the country after a remarkable escape from the rebel lords who murdered her secretary, David Riccio, eleven days ago. Immediately after the killing she was furious with her husband but fooled the conspirators with her reasonable manner and promises of a pardon.

Yet within 48 hours, with the help of some loyal nobles, notably Lord Bothwell, she had talked her husband back onto her side and escaped from the palace through underground passages in the chapel of the royal tombs. Then, despite being six months pregnant, she rode for five hours through the night to reach Dunbar 20 miles (32km) away. There she sent out a call to arms while the plotters fled to England. A week later she returned, triumphant, to Edinburgh (→ 16/6).

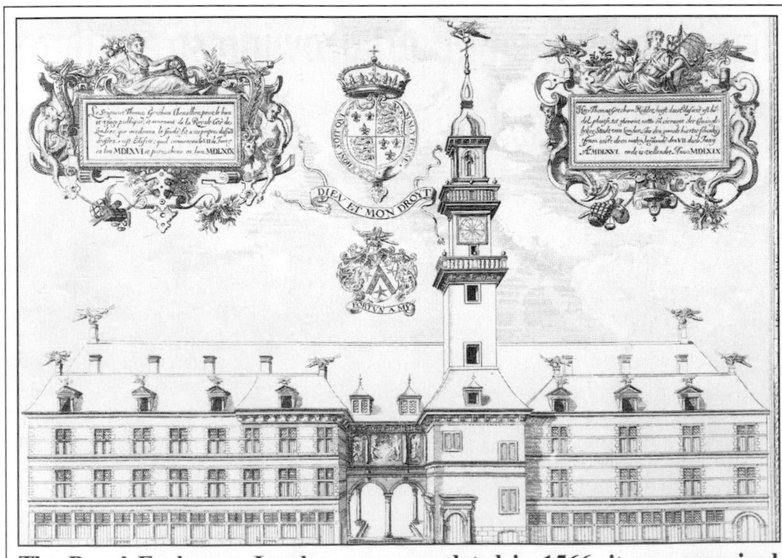

The Royal Exchange, London, was completed in 1566; it was conceived by the business tycoon Sir Thomas Gresham to attract foreign trade.

New Scots heir has a claim on England

Edinburgh, 16 June
Three months after foiling an attempted coup [*see reports above*], the 23-year-old queen of Scots has given birth to a son, James, at Edinburgh Castle. The birth is an event of major significance, for the baby – a great-great-grandson of Henry VII of England – is heir not only to the throne of Scotland but also, while Queen Elizabeth remains childless, to that of England as well. Furthermore, the existence of an heir strengthens Mary's own claim to the English crown; her relations with her cousin Elizabeth seem unlikely to improve (→ 25/10).

Royal 'progress' used for political ends

Oxford, 4 September
During her first state visit to Oxford, Queen Elizabeth attended this evening a play performed in her honour in Christ Church College hall. The play – *Palamon and Arcite*, by Richard Edwards – was a welcome diversion for the queen, who has spent most of her time here listening to sermons and university disputations in Latin.

The trip to Oxford, where the queen arrived after visiting Stamford, in Lincolnshire, and Woodstock, is part of this year's "summer progress" – an event that is assuming increasing importance during the present reign. A progress gives Elizabeth a chance not only to meet her people and bask in their adulation but also to advance the crown's political ends. Part of the queen's purpose on this occasion, for example, has been to root out religious dissenters at Oxford and to ensure that the university and the city recognize her as head of the English church. The visit was also intended to honour Robert Dudley, the earl of Leicester, who was appointed chancellor of the university in September 1564 (→ 1575).

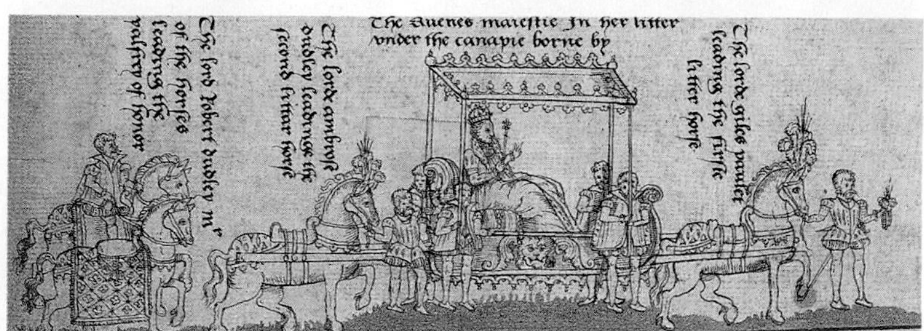

Queen Elizabeth's procession during one of her summer "progresses".

Stationers now control English printing

London, 29 June
The Stationers' Company today became the sole arbiter of printing and publishing in England. Their monopoly, granted under Queen Mary in 1557, was confirmed by the privy council. "Stationers" – booksellers as well as printers and publishers – get their name from the "stations" or stalls that they set up in cathedral precincts. In London their trade is centred on St Paul's Cathedral's walls and churchyard. Every title a stationer publishes must be entered in advance in the company's register, and no other member is allowed to publish the same book. Any book ruled illegal by the bishop of London is burnt in the kitchens of Stationers' Hall. No edition can exceed 1,250 copies, after which the type must be re-set to provide work for printers. Books are therefore very expensive.

A 16th-century printing works: English printing is now a monopoly business.

Sidney launches campaign in Ireland to thwart rebellious lord once and for all

Shane O'Neill – who remains at large – imagined submitting to Sidney.

Ireland, November
Sir Henry Sidney, the English lord deputy in Ireland, has mounted a campaign to defeat Shane O'Neill, the rebellious would-be earl of Tyrone, once and for all. Sidney was spurred into action by the knowledge that O'Neill – who aims to secure control of Ulster – had written to the French court asking for military help to expel the English. Then, afraid that the English would try to occupy Armagh Cathedral as a military post, O'Neill burnt it and resumed negotiations with his Scottish friends.

Sidney marched north from Dublin in early autumn, living off the harvest and destroying what his men could not eat. His advance was backed up by a large-scale amphibious expedition from England: 1,000 men, led by Colonel Edward Randolph, came by sea from Bristol to Lough Foyle and established themselves at Derry.

Sidney made a triumphal progress to Tyrconnell – where he restored to power Calvagh O'Donnell, who had been deposed by O'Neill – and then returned to Dublin through Boyle and Athlone. But, angered by this show of arrogance on the part of the English, O'Neill has now attacked Derry, leaving English influence in the north of Ireland still looking decidedly weak (→ 3/1567).

'Puritans' embroiled in row over clothing

England, December
Queen Elizabeth is losing patience with high-minded Protestants who are seeking to interfere with reforms in the Church of England by insisting on a greater level of purity in doctrinal matters. In defiance of royal injunctions, these so-called "puritans" refuse to wear the surplice ("the livery of Antichrist"), to make the sign of the cross in baptisms or to kneel to receive Communion. Defiance has persisted in spite of the publication this year of a *Book of Advertisements* by Archbishop Parker laying down rules for the conduct of services. The controversy deepened when some 40 members of the London clergy were deprived of their benefices for wearing incorrect dress (→ 1568).

Queen Elizabeth at her devotions.

1567

Strathclyde, 20 January. Mary Queen of Scots persuades her estranged husband, Henry, to return to the Edinburgh court despite his syphilis attack (→ 10/2).

Dublin, March. The unruly earl of Desmond, Gerald fitz James FitzGerald, is put in the castle by Sir Henry Sidney, the lord deputy, after being arrested at Kilmallock, Co Limerick (→ 2/7).

Edinburgh, 12 April. James Hepburn, the earl of Bothwell, is cleared of the murder of King Henry; the earl of Lennox, Henry's father, was unable to press charges owing to the presence of Bothwell's armed men surrounding the courtroom (→ 24/4).

Lothian, 24 April. Mary Queen of Scots is abducted by James Hepburn, the earl of Bothwell, on her return to Edinburgh; she is held prisoner at Dunbar Castle, where the earl allegedly rapes her (→ 15/5).

Edinburgh, April. The first book printed in Gaelic is published: *Foirm na nvrrnvidheadh*, a translation, by Bishop John Carswell of the Isles, of the *Book of Common Order*.

Lothian, 15 June. Scottish nobles opposed to Mary's marriage to the Protestant earl of Bothwell achieve a bloodless victory at Carberry Hill, outside Edinburgh; Bothwell and his army flee north, and Mary is taken prisoner (→ 20).

Rome, 2 July. Pope Pius V severs all communication with Mary Queen of Scots after the recent scandals.

Scotland, 29 July. The infant Prince James is proclaimed King James VI (→ 2/5/68).

Plymouth, 2 October. John Hawkins embarks on his third expedition to the West Indies (→ 21/9/68).

Ireland, 9 October. Sir Henry Sidney is recalled to London for discussions on further reform (→ 12/1567).

Ireland, December. The earl of Desmond is sent as a prisoner to London (→ 1/3/68).

Rugby. A new boys' school is founded by Laurence Sheriff (→ 1568).

Wales. The *Book of Common Prayer* and the New Testament are published in Welsh translations by the scholar William Salesbury and Bishop William Davis (→ 1568).

Royal consort murdered in Edinburgh

Edinburgh, 10 February 1567
Shock has given way to wild speculation in Edinburgh following the assassination this morning of King Henry. A massive explosion woke the city at 2am when Kirk o'Field House, where Queen Mary's second husband had been staying, was reduced to rubble. But Henry was not killed by the bomb. He and his servant were discovered dead in the grounds, apparently strangled.

Informed sources have suggested that the house must have been mined, and that Henry, when he became aware of this, tried to escape but was intercepted by the assassins. His body was clothed only in his nightgown; beside it was a chair, a dagger, a furred cloak and some rope.

The list of suspects is headed by James Hepburn, the fourth earl of Bothwell, a long-standing rival of King Henry and, according to some, the queen's lover. Bothwell's complicity might suggest that Mary herself was involved.

Rumour has named several other possible culprits, however. Henry had many enemies, including James Douglas, the earl of Morton, whom he double-crossed after the killing of David Riccio last year.

It is also known that the royal marriage was a disaster. A week ago Queen Mary persuaded her husband to come from Glasgow to Kirk o'Field House, since when domestic peace had reigned – until Mary left Henry last night to attend a wedding party (→ 12/4).

Conspirators meet to plot the murder of Queen Mary's husband, Henry.

Mary marries her Protestant 'lover'

Edinburgh, 15 May 1567
Little more than three months after she became a widow, Queen Mary has married James Hepburn, the Protestant earl of Bothwell, at Holyrood Palace. Some people have claimed that Bothwell abducted and raped Mary, but few believe it. Last month a court in Edinburgh cleared Bothwell of the murder of Mary's previous husband, Henry, but only after Bothwell's men had prevented the victim's father, Matthew Stewart, the earl of Lennox, from testifying (→ 15/6).

Defeated Mary imprisoned after scandal

Edinburgh, 20 June 1567
Letters have been discovered in a casket that may implicate Mary Queen of Scots in the murder of her second husband, Henry. Mary was taken prisoner five days ago after noblemen opposed to her recent marriage to the earl of Bothwell defeated the royal forces at Carberry Hill. She now languishes in the island castle of Lochleven, near Kinross, while the provisional government weighs up the evidence against her.

The so-called "Casket Letters" are thought to include eight letters from Mary to Bothwell, a long sonnet expressing her love and two marriage contracts. But the authorities seem reluctant to reveal precisely what it is that proves her complicity in the murder.

Queen Mary has alienated most of the nobles on whom any Scottish monarch must to some extent rely. But she is the rightful queen, and it is rumoured that she is once again with child. While the nobles bicker and vacillate under pressure from England, her humbler subjects have no doubt of Mary's deserved fate. In Edinburgh three days ago the crowds were shouting "Burn the whore!" (→ 2/7).

Lochleven Castle, the remote island fortress where Mary awaits her fate.

Ulster chieftain O'Neill, seeking refuge with Scots settlers, dies in drunken brawl

Ulster, 2 June 1567
Shane O'Neill, who fought the lord deputy, Sir Henry Sidney, for control of Ulster, has been murdered. Their rivalry came to a head when O'Neill led an attack on the English garrison at Derry last November, during which Colonel Edward Randolph was killed. Then, on 21 April this year, an accidental powder explosion destroyed the camp there. The survivors withdrew to Carrickfergus. Emboldened by success, Shane moved against a rival, Sir Hugh O'Donnell, on 8 May but was defeated. He then marched swiftly to Cushendun in Co Antrim, where he hoped that the Scots would protect him. But a hostile reception awaited him, a drunken quarrel broke out, and he was hacked to death. The English, who were negotiating for the services of the Scots against Shane, secured his head. It was pickled in a barrel and sent to Dublin where it was then impaled on a spike on the castle wall. Shane's mantle has now been taken up by Turlough Luineach O'Neill (→9/10).

Shane O'Neill is brutally slain by Scottish settlers in Cushendun, Co Antrim.

Scots queen abdicates

Mary Queen of Scots, a prisoner, is forced to abdicate her throne.

Lochleven Castle, 24 July 1567
Declaring that she is "worn out by long, irksome and tedious travail", Mary Queen of Scots has renounced the Scottish throne "in favour of our most dear son [James]", who is just over a year old. Her half-brother, James Stewart, the earl of Moray, will act as regent until the infant James is 17. Yet some are saying that the queen is ill and was talked into abdicating by Lord Lindsay, Moray's brother-in-law.

Since Mary's imprisonment last month Sir Nicholas Throckmorton, the ambassador of Queen Elizabeth of England, has been campaigning for better treatment for her. His efforts seemed successful, when, two days ago, the Scottish lords wrote to Elizabeth and made no mention of the "Casket Letters", implicating Mary in the murder of her second husband, Henry. Instead they blamed her present husband, James Hepburn, the earl of Bothwell. Others are less generous. The Protestant minister John Knox has denounced Mary, comparing her to Jezebel and Delilah (→29).

Small armies of beggars crowd the outskirts of English towns

England, 1567
Beggars, criminals and tramps are now so numerous that on the outskirts of many English towns they form small armies. A book published this year by Thomas Harman, *A Caveat or Warning for Common Cursetors vulgarly called Vagabonds*, lists all the categories of this underclass, about whom there is a popular rhyme: "Hark, hark, the dogs do bark; the beggars are coming to town!"

Harman identifies "rufflers", former soldiers who have turned to armed robbery, "grantners", who put soap in their mouths and pretend to be mad, "dummerers", who feign dumbness, "priggers" or horse-thieves, and "caperdudgeons", who set out to look filthy and ill. One caperdudgeon, Nicholas Gennings, is known to have smeared himself with sheep's blood. After he was revealed to be a well-born and healthy man, he was whipped and pilloried from one end of London to the other. Among the most notorious gangs is the so-called "Beggars' Brotherhood" of Whitefriars. Many end up in the Bridewell, a beggars' prison established in 1557 (→30/6/72).

Onlookers watch as a beggar is tied and whipped through the streets.

Earl of Moray made regent for James VI

Edinburgh, 22 August 1567
James Stewart, the earl of Moray, has been proclaimed regent of Scotland following the abdication of his half-sister, Mary [*see report above*]. Although the appointment – sanctioned by Mary from her prison in Lochleven Castle – offers the promise of much needed stability, there is no mood of rejoicing in the country. With the throne nominally held by Mary's one-year-old son James, who was crowned at Stirling on 29 July, there is still much unseemly jostling for power.

Moray apparently spent several hours berating his half-sister for her faults and misjudgements before persuading her to grant him the regency. Mary, meanwhile, is gravely ill; pustules have erupted all over her body (→23/1/70).

1568 - 1569

Yoxford, Suffolk, 22 January 1568. Lady Catherine Grey, a distant cousin of Queen Elizabeth and possible successor to her throne, dies; Elizabeth sent her to the Tower in 1561 for marrying the earl of Hertford without royal consent (→ 23/9/91).

Co Tyrone, 1 March 1568. Hugh O'Neill receives royal recognition as baron of Dungannon (→ 20/10).

Fife, 2 May 1568. Mary Queen of Scots escapes from Lochleven Castle and joins her supporters in southern Scotland (→ 16).

Mexico, 21 September 1568. Anglo-Spanish relations deteriorate following a clash between John Hawkins's English fleet and Spanish ships off San Juan de Ulloa on the Mexican coast (→ 12/1568).

Ireland, 20 October 1568. Sir Henry Sidney, resuming the post of deputy, returns from England to implement government reforms (→ 2/1569).

Canterbury, 1568. Matthew Parker, the scholarly archbishop of Canterbury, promotes the publication of a new version of the Bible, the *Bishops' Bible* (→ 14/11/69).

London, 1568. Alexander Nowell, the dean of St Paul's, begins bottling beer.

London, 1568. The company of London Bricklayers and Tylers is incorporated.

Netherlands [now France], 1568. William Allen, an Oxford don who was exiled for teaching Catholicism, founds a college at Douai offering a Catholic education for young English scholars (→ 1571).

England, 10 January 1569. Elizabeth refuses to condemn her cousin Mary Queen of Scots; she does give a limited amount of financial aid to the Scottish regent, James Stewart, the earl of Moray (→ 1/11).

Plymouth, January 1569. John Hawkins and his fleet return to England (→ 14/8/74).

Ireland, February 1569. James Fitzmaurice FitzGerald proposes asking Philip II of Spain for help against English rule (→ 9/1569).

Durham City, 14 November 1569. The Catholic Mass is reinstated at the cathedral.

London, 1569. A public lottery is held to finance repairs to the port.

Scots queen flees to safety in England

Mary escapes from her island prison and sets sail for England and safety.

Cumbria, 16 May 1568
Mary, the former queen of Scotland, has fled to England. Today she arrived at Workington after her defeat three days ago at Langside, south-west of Glasgow, by her half-brother, James Stewart, the earl of Moray and regent of Scotland. After Mary's escape on 2 May from prison on Lochleven, a number of earls, bishops and lairds declared for her. But as 5,000 of Mary's supporters skirted Glasgow on the way to Dumbarton, they engaged Moray's smaller army, only to be soundly defeated.

The Hamilton family, Mary's strongest allies, bore the heaviest losses at Langside – lost through the incompetence of Archibald Campbell, the earl of Argyll, who commanded the royal army. After the battle Mary decided to flee to England instead of France, the obvious option. It seems she intends to throw herself on the mercy of Queen Elizabeth – a potentially risky course (→ 10/1/69).

Welsh keep poetic traditions alive at Caerwys eisteddfod

Clwyd, 1568
For the first time since 1528 an *eisteddfod* [session] was held last year at Caerwys. The meeting – the first since the Reformation – was held under a commission from Queen Elizabeth, which augurs well for the acceptance of the bardic tradition in this Protestant age. The *eisteddfod*'s aim was to tighten the controls that keep bards up to scratch. The guardians of Welsh high culture want to prevent mere rhymesters incapable or just plain ignorant of the complexities of true bardic verse from ruining the art. The gentry, however, pay bards to boost the prestige of their families in *pur Fryttaniaeth*, "the pure British [Welsh] language".

Welsh is still the mother tongue of 90 per cent of the people. The Church of England has, reluctantly, come to recognize this. In 1547 Sir John Pryce of Brecon published the first book in Welsh, *Yn y llyvyr hwn*, containing the ten commandments, the creed and the Lord's Prayer. The Epistles and Gospels read in services appeared in 1551, and only last year the complete New Testament was published.

Anglo-Spanish relations worsen as English seize treasure fleet

Southern England, December 1568
Five Biscayan ships laden with wool and 450,000 ducats' worth of Spanish bullion have been seized at Plymouth and Southampton on the orders of William Cecil, the queen's chief minister. This apparently foolhardy move was prompted by England's serious financial problems – caused by fraud among exchequer officials. Technically, the treasure did not yet belong to Spain, but after John Hawkins's privateering at Spanish expense in the Indies such an action has increased the risk of a European war.

Hawkins is at present licking his wounds off the coast of Spain, having returned from a third, disastrous voyage to the Indies. At San Juan de Ulloa, in Mexico, he exchanged hostages with the Spanish, who then turned on his men, killing many of them (→ 1/1569).

The Spanish take their revenge on John Hawkins at San Juan de Ulloa.

Plans to impose English government in southern Ireland spark fruitless rebellion

Munster, September 1569
Queen Elizabeth's agents are gradually establishing English government in Munster. The process has, however, met with determined resistance, and in June of this year both Munster and south Leinster rebelled.

Local feeling had been running high since December 1567, when Gerald fitz James FitzGerald, the earl of Desmond and one of the biggest landowners in the province, was sent to the Tower of London. His people feared that the entire Geraldine lordship, on which Munster is dependent, was being undermined. Then, in December 1568, an English adventurer called Sir Peter Carew was granted the barony of Idrone in Co Carlow on the basis of ancient Anglo-Norman laws, setting an ominous precedent for future confiscations of Gaelic Irish land. The Butler earls were particularly outraged that land claimed by them of old had gone to an English newcomer.

Fighting began when Desmond's cousin, James Fitzmaurice, the "captain" of the Desmond FitzGeralds, persuaded Sir Edmund Butler to join him. Fitzmaurice is still at large, but it is clear that Sir Henry Sidney, the lord deputy, has crushed the rebellion (→ 2/1570).

Edinburgh hit by outbreak of plague

Another plague victim is diagnosed.

Edinburgh, February 1569
A plague which has raged in the city since last September has killed 2,500 people, one in four of the inhabitants. It is thought to have been introduced by James Dalglish, a merchant. The burgh magistrates have taken draconian measures to isolate the plague, which seems at last to be abating. Infected individuals have been obliged to leave the city, and are living in shanty huts on the outskirts, visited by friends and relatives only at certain times, on pain of death. Bailies of the muir, in grey cloaks with the white cross of St Andrew, supervise house inspections and the boiling of infected clothes (→ 8/1579).

Writer hits out at art of star-gazing

England, 1569
The pamphleteer Nicholas Allen is attacking almanacs – popular books that say what the movements of the stars predict for coming the year. *The Astronomer's Game* compares three sets of predictions in order to expose astrology to ridicule. Most educated people, however, would agree with the mathematician Robert Recorde who said: "No dearth and penury, no death and mortality, but God by the signs of heaven did premonish men thereof." The "game" is highly regarded; the astrologer and mathematician John Dee was asked to choose the best day for Queen Elizabeth's coronation (→ 1574).

The sorcerer: an object of scorn.

Catholic earls flee after Elizabeth crushes their anti-Protestant rebellion in the north

Northumberland and Westmorland plot their course of action with Ridolfi.

Highland, 20 December 1569
The Catholic earls of northern England, who rebelled last month, have fled across the border to Liddesdale in Scotland. As the royal army under Thomas Radcliffe, the earl of Sussex, moves north, the rebels' only hope is to find safety here.

This – the gravest challenge yet to face Queen Elizabeth – began when Thomas Howard, the duke of Norfolk, tried last spring to undermine William Cecil, her chief adviser, at court. This, combined with Norfolk's support for Mary Stuart, attracted suspicion about his plans. In September an unnerved Norfolk protested his loyalty, but his allies, Thomas Percy, the earl of Northumberland, and Charles Neville, the earl of Westmorland (Norfolk's brother-in-law), rebelled. Northumberland raised an army, seized Durham and marched south in the direction of Tutbury, where Mary was being held. But then the rebels lost their nerve, and they fled before the royal army could catch up with them (→ 1/1570).

Duke is arrested after marriage intrigue

Norfolk, 1 November 1569
After fleeing the court in panic, the duke of Norfolk has been arrested at Kenninghall and is on his way back to London. Speculation has been mounting about the possibility of his marriage to Mary Queen of Scots, which would create a potent Catholic alliance and an obvious threat to Elizabeth's throne. Cecil, who remains the English queen's closest adviser, now wants Norfolk married, quickly, to someone else.

Thomas Howard, the fourth duke of Norfolk, is England's premier nobleman, a likeable man whose position is bound to be the focus of intrigue. Anguished by the deaths of three wives in childbirth, torn between loyalty to the crown and the rebellious plotting of his kinsmen in both East Anglia and the north, he seems to have lost his political judgement (→ 3/8/70).

Norfolk, who is accused of treason.

1570 - 1571

Northern England, January 1570. Some 450 of those who took part in the Catholic revolt are executed (→ 8/7).

Ireland, February 1570. Piers and Sir Edmund Butler, the earl of Ormond's brothers, surrender to Sir Henry Sidney, the lord deputy; Conor O'Brien, the earl of Thomond, rebels against the inclusion of Thomond in the jurisdiction of Connacht (→ 21/12).

Strathclyde, July 1570. A sea monster with two crowns on its head, seen in Loch Fyne, is interpreted as an omen of troubled times.

London, 3 August 1570. William Cecil, the chief secretary of state, persuades Queen Elizabeth to free Thomas Howard, the duke of Norfolk, into house arrest; he was arrested on suspicion of support for last year's northern rebellion (→ 3/9/71).

England, September 1570. Marriage negotiations reopen between Elizabeth and the Habsburg Archduke Charles; Elizabeth is also considering an alliance with Henry, the duke of Anjou, the Catholic heir to the French throne (→ 6/1572).

Ireland, 21 December 1570. The earl of Thomond surrenders and is pardoned (→ 25/3/71).

Ireland, 25 March 1571. Sir Henry Sidney is recalled in disgrace to England (→ 8/1572).

Co Limerick, March 1571. James Fitzmaurice FitzGerald burns the town of Kilmallock.

Stirling, April 1571. John Hamilton, the archbishop of St Andrews, is hanged after supporters of the regent, Matthew Stewart, the earl of Lennox, attack Dumbarton Castle (→ 3/9).

Dublin, June 1571. John Kearney's *Aibidil Gaoidheilge & Caiticiosma [Gaelic Alphabet and Catechism]* is the first Irish book printed in Ireland.

Stirling, 3 September 1571. Supporters of Mary Queen of Scots kill the earl of Lennox (→ 28/10/72).

Harrow, 1571. John Lyon, a local yeoman, founds a school for local village boys.→

Oxford, 1571. Dr Hugh Price founds Jesus College.→

England, 1571. The mathematician Leonard Digges invents the theodolite, an instrument for measuring angles.

Scottish regent assassinated while riding

Scotland's ambitious regent, Moray, is shot dead by an unknown assassin.

Lothian, 23 January 1570
James Stewart, the earl of Moray and regent of Scotland, has been shot dead while out riding in the main street of Linlithgow. The man who gunned him down is believed to be an assassin in the pay of the Hamilton family, which has long been in rivalry with Moray.

Scotland had been controlled by Moray for the past three years: Mary Queen of Scots' son, James, in whose favour she abdicated, is only three and a half years old. Moray had sought in this short time to build a firm alliance of noblemen – a ruling élite for Scotland – but failed to impress his peers. They suspected that he, as Mary's half-brother, had his own eye on the throne. Clearly someone among the Hamiltons decided that the time was ripe to kill his ambitions – and him (→ 12/7).

Civil war looms over new Scottish regent

The earl of Lennox is sworn in as regent for his four-year-old grandson.

Edinburgh, 12 July 1570
Scotland's new regent is Matthew Stewart, the earl of Lennox and grandfather of James VI. The country has verged on rebellion since the killing of the former regent, James Stewart, the earl of Moray (no relation) [*see above*]. The standard of Mary Queen of Scots was raised again; this time her backers were joined by rebels from the north of England. Thomas Radcliffe, the earl of Sussex, made a short, sharp border raid in April, but Queen Elizabeth has now chosen a more diplomatic approach. Lennox is her nominee and so, like Moray, will back her against Mary (→ 4/1571).

Unrest over foreign workers in Norwich

Norwich, June 1570
Unrest in East Anglia, partly resulting from the influx of Huguenot refugees from the continent and partly fomented by backers of the disgraced duke of Norfolk, has led to a crackdown by local authorities in Norwich and elsewhere. The ringleaders have been calling for the expulsion of Flemish weavers, resented for bringing changes to the cloth-making industry and for setting up their own churches. With the trouble-makers locked up, however, the Huguenots seem to be here to stay. Imitation of their more labour-intensive style of working could alleviate unemployment.

The cloth trade: a source of trouble.

'Book of Martyrs' is second to the Bible

England, 1571
John Foxe's *Book of Martyrs*, covering Christian martyrs since the 11th century, has been ordered to be set up in every cathedral and collegiate church. Formally named *Acts and Monuments of the Church*, it focuses on recent English Protestant martyrs such as Cranmer, Ridley and Latimer. Drawing on eye-witness reports of executions, Foxe details speeches made at the stake, along with vivid illustrations. He also identifies the pope with the Antichrist. Since its first English edition in 1563, the work has become one of the most widely read books in England after the Bible.

Queen excommunicated

Pope Pius V hands out the papal bull officially excommunicating Elizabeth.

London, 8 July 1570
The bull from Pope Pius V excommunicating Queen Elizabeth and releasing her subjects from their allegiance has led to the death of one of them. John Felton, a wealthy Catholic, fixed a copy of the bull – apparently obtained from the Spanish ambassador – to the gate of the bishop of London's palace. Despite torture he refused to acknowledge Elizabeth as queen and was executed today. The pope's aim was, it seems, to take advantage of recent civil strife in the north of the Protestant queen's country.

Felton's treatment is typical of recent state policy of keeping up pressure on Catholics to conform. Government propaganda stresses that all Catholics are potential rebels ready to welcome a foreign invasion. Yet most English Catholics seem intensely loyal to the queen, however much the papacy tries to bring her down (→ 17/5/75).

Many new schools and colleges founded

England, 1571
Growing demand for education has led in recent years to the founding of many schools, colleges and inns of court. In 1560 Westminster School was detached from the abbey as a separate foundation by Queen Elizabeth. There followed the school of the Merchant Taylors' livery company (1561) and Rugby, founded by Lawrence Sheriff in 1567. This year John Lyon set up Harrow School. They were preceded under Edward VI and Mary by Shrewsbury, Christ's Hospital, Tonbridge, Gresham's and Repton. The universities are also expanding. At Oxford, Trinity and St John's Colleges were set up during Mary's reign, and Jesus was founded this year.

The scholar and his pupil.

Teaching methods have been hotly debated since last year's publication of *The Schoolmaster* by the late Roger Ascham, a tutor to both Queen Elizabeth and Lady Jane Grey. An opponent of corporal punishment, he contended that "children are sooner allured by love than driven by beating to attain good learning", and that "there is no such whetstone to sharpen a good wit as is praise" (→ 14/4/82).

Norfolk arrested in plot to kill Elizabeth

London, 3 September 1571
Thomas Howard, the duke of Norfolk, a popular figure at court and in the country, was back in the Tower today, having been arrested on suspicion of taking part in a plot to bring down Queen Elizabeth and replace her with Mary Queen of Scots. England's sole remaining duke, he had been let out of the Tower only a year ago after being sent there for allegedly intriguing to marry Mary in 1569.

Norfolk is now being interrogated, but the government has been aware for some time that he was part of a plot hatched by a Florentine banker, Roberto Ridolfi. The plotters, said to include the duke of Alva, the Spanish military commander, the pope and Philip II of Spain, as well as Mary, aimed to land a force of 6,000 men at Harwich who would march on London.

Norfolk was to rise in revolt, seize Elizabeth and hold her hostage for Mary's safety. The Catholic faith was then to be restored, with Mary and Norfolk – who had hopes of exchanging a ducal crown for a matrimonial one – ruling in both England and Scotland.

The plot came unstuck because Ridolfi could not keep his mouth shut, but also because of some good intelligence work. Spies employed by Lord Burghley tailed Ridolfi and intercepted his messengers. When they found some letters and managed to break the cipher, Norfolk was done for (→ 16/1/72).

Traditional Gaelic clothing is banned

Irish clothing is to be anglicized.

Munster, December 1571
Sir John Perrot, the new president of Munster, who arrived in Waterford from England on 27 February, has introduced clothing restrictions on the Gaelic Irish population. He has decreed that townspeople are forbidden to wear cloaks, shorts, Irish coats or great shirts. They must not have long hair or beards, and no young women are to wear linen cloth on their heads but must instead put on hats, caps or French hoods. Anyone found wearing traditional Irish clothing will be fined £100. These restrictions are part of Perrot's larger purpose – to impose English law in the land.

Bards, an essential part of Gaelic Irish society, are to stop singing songs glorifying the past, since they represent an un-English and "barbaric" tradition (→ 21).

Elizabeth rewards Cecil with a peerage

A portrait of Lord Burghley.

London, 25 February 1571
William Cecil, the principal adviser and minister of Queen Elizabeth, was today raised to the peerage as Lord Burghley. Cecil has been at the queen's side since the start of her reign as chief secretary of state and he has shown extraordinary expertise in directing her financial and religious policies.

Cecil was largely reponsible for the decision to tackle the country's defencelessness and bankruptcy by buying desperately needed arms and munitions from abroad and by restoring the purity and strength of the currency.

1572 - 1573

Westminster, 16 January 1572. Thomas Howard, the duke of Norfolk, is found guilty of treason in the Ridolfi plot (→21).

London, 21 January 1572. Queen Elizabeth defers the execution of the duke of Norfolk (→2/6).

Southern England, 1 March 1572. Elizabeth expels Dutch refugees, known as the "sea beggars"; they seize the Spanish-controlled port of Brill in the Netherlands.

Blois, France, 21 April 1572. An Anglo-French treaty is signed, providing for mutual military aid if either country is attacked by a third power and a joint effort to pacify Scotland (→27/8).

West Indies, 29 August 1572. Francis Drake, left Plymouth on 24 May, lands at Nombre de Dios and seizes Spanish treasure (→9/8/73).

Ireland, August 1572. Around a hundred English colonists, led by Thomas Smith, land at Strangford Lough (→3/1573).

Scotland, 28 October 1572. The regent, John Erskine, the earl of Mar, who replaced the murdered earl of Lennox last year, has died; he is replaced by James Douglas, the earl of Morton (→23/2/73).

London, 1572. Archbishop Parker of Canterbury publishes a history of his predecessors, *De Antiquitate Britannicae Ecclesiae*.

London, 1572. The Society of Antiquaries is founded.

Perth, 23 February 1573. The regent, the earl of Morton, and supporters of Mary Queen of Scots come to an agreement, ending resistance to James VI; only Edinburgh still defies the king (→28/5).

Munster, July 1573. Sir John Perrot, the president, leaves for England on grounds of ill health (→10/1573).

London, 9 July 1573. Elizabeth gives Walter Devereux, the earl of Essex, colonization rights over Co Antrim (→7/1573).

Ireland, October 1573. The earl of Essex, aided by Hugh O'Neill, of Dungannon, clashes with Brian O'Neill of Clandeboye (→11/11).

Dublin, 11 November 1573. Gerald fitz James FitzGerald, the earl of Desmond, escapes from captivity in the castle (→8/5/74).

Parliament gives the poor a better deal

London, 30 June 1572
Queen Elizabeth's England totals some five million people, and it is growing in wealth and strength, but the country is beset by widespread unemployment and vagrancy. The queen and her ministers are now poised to get to grips with the problems. A bill passed today in parliament, which in effect provides statutory relief for the poor, could be the first of its kind in Europe.

The new Poor Law makes the parish [an area with its own church and parson] the unit of relief, dividing those in need of assistance into two classes. For those ready, willing and able for work but unable to find it, a job, tools and other working materials must be found by the parish. The aged and handicapped who cannot work will now be supported in their own homes.

But the Poor Law is tough on the work-shy. As in the past they will be branded as "idle rogues and vagabonds", whipped and sent back to their own parishes. Houses of correction will be set up where they could work "as a true man should do". The bill had a painful passage through the House of Commons, where the member for Liverpool suggested that the rich should employ more servants to reduce unemployment (→1596).

Maundy money is given to the poor.

England shocked by Protestant massacre

Rye, East Sussex, 27 August 1572
A number of Huguenots [French Protestants] have arrived here in search of asylum after a massacre of their fellows in Paris on St Bartholomew's day (24 August). The news is destined to sour relations with France, greatly improved since the Treaty of Blois in April.

The Huguenots had gathered for the wedding on 19 August of the young Protestant Henry of Navarre to Margaret, the Catholic daughter of the regent, Catherine de' Medici. It seems that the massacre, in which up to 40,000 people died, was provoked by Catherine, who alleged that the Huguenots were plotting to kill the royal family. The bloodbath is bound to be regarded here as a sign that, whatever they may say, the French are pursuing a literally murderous anti-Protestant policy (→7/5/74).

Thousands flee after the senseless slaughter of St Bartholomew's day.

Pressure mounts for birth of royal heir

London, June 1572
Queen Elizabeth's name is being linked with that of Francis, the duke of Alençon, the youngest brother of King Charles IX of France and 20 years her junior. Only last year the queen mother, Catherine de' Medici, put forward – in vain – the name of another of her sons, Henry, the duke of Anjou.

There is great pressure on Elizabeth to produce an heir, but the treaty signed at Blois in April is likely to satisfy her policies better than any marriage. Yet time is marching on: Elizabeth is 38 years old, and the chances of her bearing a child lessen with each year that passes. It seems that she is content to use her eligibility as a powerful political tactic (→1575).

Catherine de' Medici: a portrait.

Norfolk is executed on treason charge

London, 2 June 1572
The duke of Norfolk today became the first noble of Queen Elizabeth's reign to perish on the scaffold. His head was removed with one blow of the executioner's axe at a spot near the Tower, where he had been since January after being found guilty of treason. Although his complicity in the Ridolfi plot to bring back Mary Queen of Scots was proven [*see page 463*], Elizabeth had to be persuaded by parliament to proceed with the execution. Parliament is now calling for Mary's head (→4/4/78).

Regent seizes Edinburgh

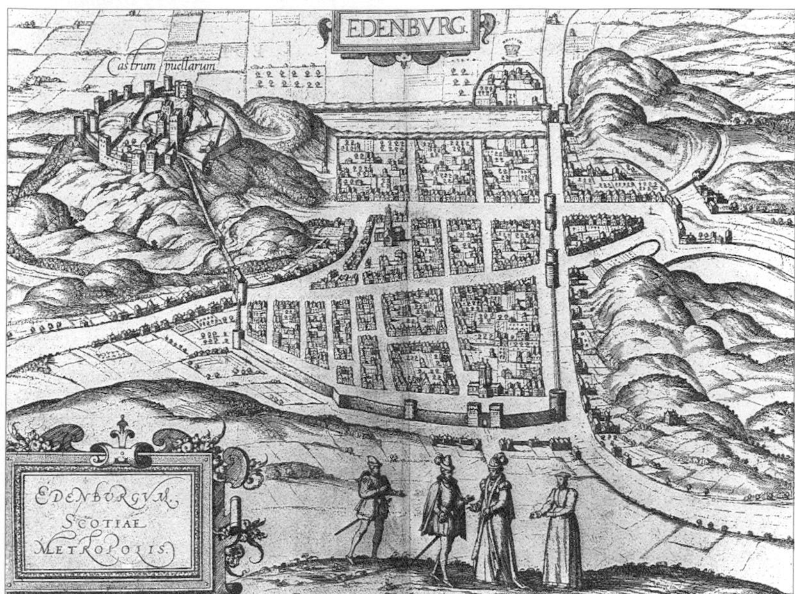

Edinburgh: the earl of Morton has seized control of the Castle.

Edinburgh, 28 May 1573
The flag of surrender flies from Edinburgh Castle today: the pro-Mary garrison has been ousted by the regent, James Douglas, the earl of Morton, a sworn enemy of the queen. For Mary, imprisoned in England, and her backers (the so-called "queen's lords"), the loss is a crushing blow. For the Anglophile party surrounding the six-year-old King James VI it is, however, a great victory, ending the civil war that began after James Stewart, the earl of Moray, was killed three years ago [*see report on page 462*].

Defections from the queen's party allowed Morton's men to occupy Edinburgh last autumn, but they failed to take the strongly fortified castle until an English army was summoned. Heavy cannon were brought by sea to Leith, enabling Morton's combined Scots and English army to begin a bombardment lasting 11 days. Mary's cause is now finished (→ 4/3/78).

Scottish scourge of Catholic church dies

Edinburgh, 24 November 1572
No man has done more to convert the people of Scotland to Protestant Christianity than John Knox, the fiery preacher and pamphleteer who died at his home here today. Knox's legacy is an austere kirk in which spontaneous prayer has replaced the liturgy, and unaccompanied singing is the norm.

A farmer's son, Knox graduated from St Andrews University and became a minister in the English church. But during the six years or so that he spent in Geneva he was won over to the radical views of John Calvin. He returned here to conduct an evangelistic tour and in 1559 played a major role in the anti-Catholic revolution.

Irish Catholic rebel submits to English

Dublin, March 1573
Gerald fitz James FitzGerald, the earl of Desmond, returned this month to Ireland from prison in England, only to be arrested and imprisoned once more – this time in Dublin. It was Desmond's original arrest in December 1567 that sparked a revolt in Munster by his supporters in June 1569 [*see report on page 461*]. Last month one of the rebel leaders, James Fitzmaurice FitzGerald, at last submitted to the English president of Munster, Sir John Perrot. Desmond was freed because the English realized that it was the only way to secure a lasting peace in Munster. Yet it seems that some still consider him a threat to English interests here (→ 9/7).

Drake returns from dramatic expedition

Plymouth, 9 August 1573
Francis Drake, a daring young sea-captain, and his tiny company of seamen sailed into Plymouth harbour today laden with treasure after an extraordinary expedition to the Caribbean. When news got about that Drake was back after more than a year away everyone rushed to the waterside to greet him.

Francis Drake: the daring captain.

Drake left for the Darien Isthmus in central America with two small ships on a crusade against Spain. He came close to taking the fortified West Indian city of Nombre de Dios, where he was wounded, before spending months attacking and plundering ships plying the Spanish Main [the northern coast of Latin and Central America].

Once, while planning an attack on the far side of the isthmus, Drake set eyes on the Pacific Ocean, the first Englishman to do so. By then the 73 men who had left Plymouth had been reduced to 31 and Drake decided to come home. Typically, on 1 February he paid a final visit to Cartagena, where he indulged his taste for arson on the grand scale by putting all the Spanish shipping there to the torch.

The treasure seized from Spanish ships and mule-trains equals almost a sixth of the crown's annual revenue. But Queen Elizabeth is not pleased – she has been trying to negotiate a new alliance with Philip II of Spain (→ 13/12/77).

Drake's dial, an essential navigational aid at sea: a compass and sundial.

Policy change as Walsingham appointed

London, December 1573
Sir Francis Walsingham has been appointed a secretary of state in a move that could have important implications for Queen Elizabeth's foreign policy. Sir Francis, a fanatical Protestant and former ambassador to Paris, has been a protégé of Lord Burghley, the man closest to the queen. An expert in diplomacy and espionage, he will now have a greater say in running England. A second new secretary will be Sir Thomas Smith, who has had an up-and-down career as a scholar and civil servant. At one time he spent a few months' imprisonment in the Tower, and he has retired from public life more than once.

Sir Thomas is considered to be upright and honest and intensely patriotic. Both his knowledge and his experience will prove invaluable to the queen (→ 14/8/74).

1574 - 1575

London, 7 May 1574. Queen Elizabeth gives a royal licence to James Burbage, a servant of Robert Dudley, the earl of Leicester, to open a theatre (→ 8/1577).

Ireland, 8 May 1574. Brian O'Neill of Clandeboye submits to Walter Devereux, the earl of Essex (→ 2/9).

Bristol, 14 August 1574. Anglo-Spanish relations improve with the arrival of Bernardino de Mendoza, the Spanish ambassador; England and Spain agree to the Convention of Bristol, which settles the disagreements that sprang from the English seizure of Genoese gold in 1568 (→ 12/1577).

Scotland, August 1574. Food prices increase following a poor harvest (→ 2/1575).

Ireland, 2 September 1574. Gerald fitz James FitzGerald, the earl of Desmond, whose castle of Derrinlaur was seized in August, submits to Sir William Fitzwilliam, the vice-deputy (→ 11/1574).

Dublin, November 1574. After capturing Brian O'Neill in Belfast earlier this month the earl of Essex orders his execution, precipitating a rebellion (→ 3/1575).

Scotland, February 1575. Basic foods are in short supply because of last summer's bad harvest (→ 1581).

Ireland, March 1575. James FitzMaurice FitzGerald sails for France to seek Catholic support against Queen Elizabeth (→ 22/5).

London, 22 May 1575. Elizabeth tells the earl of Essex that she will no longer support his colonization plans in Ulster (→ 26/7).

Borders, 7 July 1575. An Anglo-Scots row erupts following the capture of the English warden of the region when fighting broke up a meeting between officials from the two kingdoms.

Co Antrim, 26 July 1575. The earl of Essex's troops take Rathlin Island and massacre the inhabitants (→ 18/9).

England, October 1575. The earl of Leicester commissions Federico Zuccaro, an Italian artist, to paint two portraits, of Elizabeth and himself.

England, 1575. Christopher Saxton begins to publish the first large-scale maps of England and Wales, by county (→ 1576).

Scots introduce law to control beggars

Edinburgh, March 1574
More and more peasants are fleeing the poverty wrought by recent bad harvests. So many have moved to the towns – seeking work, begging or turning to crime – that parliament has introduced a law, modelled on the English legislation of 1572, to control these "sturdy beggars" and offer some relief. Whole families have to sleep in the streets as places in the few hospitals founded for the poor are hard to come by. The new law follows last year's move to force gypsies to find work and settle down or face more penalties. It allows magistrates to impose forced labour in the coal and salt works outside the towns, but it also allows for organized distribution of alms and provision of begging licences (→ 8/1574).

Bright star points to heavenly chaos

London, 1574
The astronomer Thomas Digges has published a book on a bright star seen two years ago that has since been the subject of intense deliberation. In *Alae seu scalae mathematicae* Digges concludes from his observations that the heavens, far from being ordered, are – like the earth – a region of chaos. Like other English scientists, such as John Dee, he follows the Polish astronomer Copernicus, who taught that the earth revolves around the sun, not vice versa (→ 9/1583).

English impose new land tax on Ireland

Sir Henry Sidney, reappointed lord deputy of Ireland, is back in Dublin.

Ireland, 18 September 1575
Sir Henry Sidney was sworn in today as lord deputy, having been absent from Ireland since March 1571. He wants a fundamental reform of the country and to turn Irish lordships into English shires. To do this, Sidney has first to eliminate the "coyne and livery" protection rackets, by which lords extort money and goods from tenants.

Sidney's plan is to replace coyne and livery with a land tax called the "composition", whose payment is to be supervised by government soldiers. Common folk should be happy, since the new tax will be lower than their present rents. Landlords will save money, meanwhile, by disbanding the private armies needed to gather coyne and livery, offsetting the lower incomes that they will receive. But those in the Pale and Anglo-Irish areas generally are suspicious of what seems to them an unparliamentary tax (→ 1576).

Diplomatic Elizabeth plays a double role

London, 7 May 1574
Queen Elizabeth has today renewed the defensive alliance signed between England and France two years ago, the Treaty of Blois. Her actions show how finely morality and expediency must be weighed in international politics. Moral outrage after the St Bartholomew's day massacre of Huguenots [*see report on page 464*] dictates that Protestant England spurn Catholic France – especially as the new French king, Henry III, the former duke of Anjou, is a fanatical Catholic. Yet England needs a strong ally against Spain, and so while Elizabeth has granted some money to the Huguenots she is staying on good terms with France (→ 14/8).

Moderate archbishop, who suffered attacks from all sides, dies

Canterbury, 17 May 1575
Matthew Parker, the archbishop of Canterbury, has died a disappointed man. Chosen by Queen Elizabeth for his moderation and integrity, this quiet, scholarly man was attacked from all sides during the 15 years of his office. In his struggle with the puritans he never felt that he had the queen's full support. Influential courtiers such as Robert Dudley, the earl of Leicester, opposed him, while the Catholics disliked him although he tried to limit their persecution (→ 15/3/76).

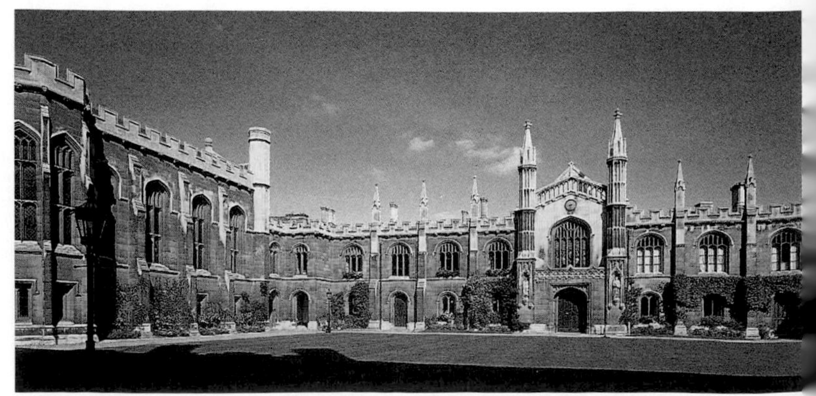
Corpus Christi College, Cambridge, which inherits Parker's book collection.

Flowering of court music honoured by new 'Sacred Songs'

London, 1575
Thomas Tallis and his pupil William Byrd have published jointly a collection of *Sacred Songs* in honour of royal patronage of their music. Tallis was one of the great composers of church music during Henry VIII's time and was organist at Waltham Abbey until its dissolution. He published a famous *Canon* in a psalter of 1560, when he was organist at the Chapel Royal. Byrd was trained there as a chorister and became organist at Lincoln Cathedral before returning to London to share the duties at the Chapel Royal with Tallis, who is now 70.

Tallis, the master (top), and Byrd.

Although both have written music for the Catholic Mass, and Byrd is a Catholic recusant, they enjoy the Queen's favour to the extent that she has granted them a monopoly of all music printing for 21 years. Their licence prohibits the importation into England of "any song made and printed in foreign country to sell or put to sale, upon pain of our high displeasure". This means that they have a lucrative and exclusive right as sole song publishers in a musical society.

Both Byrd and Tallis are extremely versatile composers, masters of a range of styles, from church music to secular songs, madrigals and music for strings.

Lavish entertainments of hunting, dancing and feasting greet Queen Elizabeth on her 'summer progress' across the country

Musical performances play a central part in the entertainment.

Elizabeth dancing with Robert Dudley, the earl of Leicester, who laid on lavish entertainment for the queen at Kenilworth Castle this year.

England, 1575
In contrast with her two predecessors, Queen Elizabeth likes to see and be seen, and so every summer she and her court set out on a "progress", or procession, to various towns across the realm. Many nobles are eager to entertain the queen in order to curry royal favour, even though the expense is huge. Progresses allow Elizabeth to exploit her superb skill in pleasing the crowds. As the mayor of Coventry said during the queen's visit there in 1565, she had won "the hearts of all [her] loving subjects".

The queen's visits to Warwick in 1572 and Bristol in 1574 were recent high points. Her destinations this year have included Worcester, Lichfield, Reading, Woodstock and Windsor, but nothing rivals her visit in July to Kenilworth Castle near Coventry, where Robert Dudley, the earl of Leicester, entertained on a grand scale – all to induce the queen to marry him. The myriad diversions here included poetry and masques by the noted writer George Gascoigne. A sibyl prophesying "long prosperity" met the queen, and a young man in the guise of Hercules presented her with the keys to the castle. The following three weeks saw a spectacular succession of plays, fireworks, bear-baiting, hunting, music, dancing and sumptuous banquets. Yet at the end Elizabeth rode away, Leicester's plea unheeded (→6/1578).

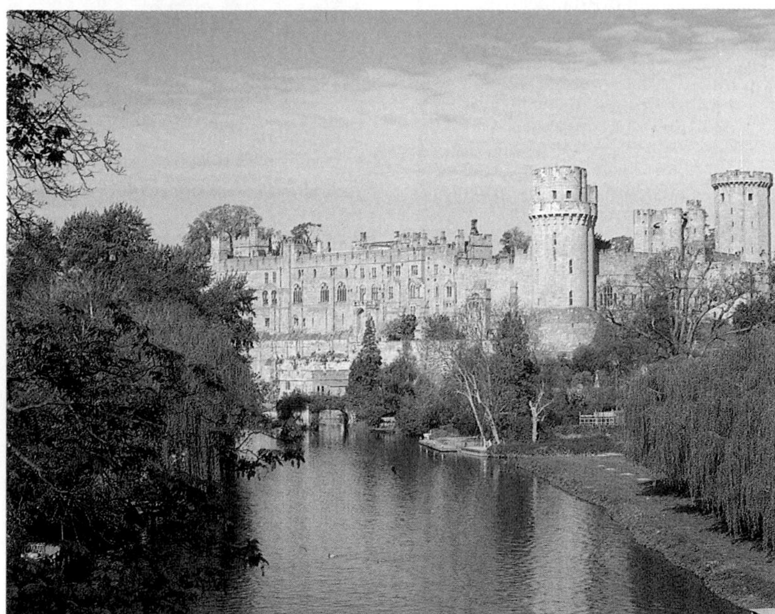
Warwick Castle, the home of Ambrose Dudley, the earl of Warwick, where a mock battle was enacted with fireworks during Elizabeth's visit in 1572.

Poet George Gascoigne presents the queen with one of his works.

The palace at Woodstock: once the queen's prison, now revisited.

1576 - 1577

Europe, 1576. James Fitzmaurice FitzGerald, the earl of Clancare and leader of the Munster Confederacy, who sailed for France last year, is gathering Catholic support for a rebellion against English rule in Ireland (→ 9/3).

Ireland, 9 March 1576. Walter Devereux, the earl of Essex, is appointed marshal (→ 22/9).

England, spring 1576. Humphrey Gilbert, the navigator, publishes his *Discourse to Prove a North-west Passage* (→ 11/6/78).

London, 7 June 1576. Martin Frobisher sets sail from Blackwall to try to discover the north-west passage which leads to Asia (→ 2/10).

Dublin, 22 September 1576. Avenging the death in 1574 of Brian O'Neill of Clandeboye, his supporters poison and kill the earl of Essex (→ 12/9/78).

Lambeth, 20 December 1576. Edmund Grindal, the archbishop of Canterbury, writes defiantly to Queen Elizabeth refusing to follow her order to put an end to the popular "prophesyings" or preaching exercises for the clergy (→ 24/3/77).

London, 24 March 1577. Elizabeth appoints John Aylmer, at present archdeacon of Lincoln, who is a strong opponent of puritanism, bishop of London (→ 5/1577).

London, August 1577. The Curtain theatre is opened in Shoreditch as a rival to James Burbage's playhouse; both are situated outside the city because of the restrictive censorship laws (→ 1583).

Dyfed, 23 September 1577. Martin Frobisher returns to Milford Haven from a second journey to find the north-west passage (→ 10/1578).

Worcester, 23 September 1577. John Whitgift, the dean of Lincoln, who is an opponent of puritanism, is appointed bishop of Worcester (→ 6/7/83).

London, 11 November 1577. Christopher Hatton is knighted and becomes vice-chamberlain of the privy council.

Plymouth, 13 December 1577. Francis Drake sets out in the *Pelican* to sail around the world (→ 7/1579).

London, 31 December 1577. John Hawkins, the slave-trader, succeeds his father-in-law, Benjamin Gonson, as treasurer of the navy.

Outspoken puritan sent to Tower after antics in parliament

Elizabeth presides over parliament.

London, 15 March 1576
A dramatic session of parliament ends today, with one member having been sent to the Tower after he infuriated not only fellow members but also Queen Elizabeth.

The culprit was Peter Wentworth, the staunch puritan who represents Barnstaple and places great importance on the independence of parliament. On 8 February he complained in the House of Commons that free speech was threatened by constant rumours there that certain matters could never be raised because the queen would not like it. He wished that such rumours "were buried in hell". When Wentworth went on to suggest that members were "time-servers" he was ejected. Not long afterwards he returned to the house to bow to its judgement – and was ordered to the Tower for a month.

Wentworth's concern is the exact relationship between monarch and parliament. It is by no means a new debate. Five years ago another member was barred from the house after proposing a bill to reform the Anglican Book of Common Prayer. The queen argued that, as head of the Church of England, any such proposal was her prerogative. Then, as in this session, parliament knuckled under to her (→ 20/12).

Frobisher returns safely from expedition

Harwich, Essex, 2 October 1576
An expedition to find the north-west passage – a route to China and India by going round the northern tip of America – has come home with a native who was taken prisoner and "black earth" which is rumoured to contain gold.

Led by Martin Frobisher, aged 40, and sponsored by the queen and a number of prominent lords, the expedition left in June. It sailed past "monstrous great islands of ice", nearly sank "in the rage of an extreme storm which cast the ship flat on her side", and lost five men to hostile natives. From the top of a high mountain on one of the islands, however, the explorers believe that they saw the "West Sea" – the route to China.

Interest in the new route has been spurred by the publication this year of *Discourse to Prove a North-west Passage*, written by the navigator Humphrey Gilbert. Gilbert collected information on ocean currents and winds and examined ancient geographical works and chronicles to back up his belief "that there lies a great sea between [America], Cathaia [China] and Greenland" through which English traders might pass to the varied markets of the east (→ 23/9/77).

The dangers that faced Frobisher in his quest for the north-west passage.

Local history book puts Kent on map

Kent, 1576
The first guidebook to an English county, published this year, has been accused of giving away too much information to a potential enemy. *Perambulation of Kent*, by William Lambarde, contains a map showing the sites of the beacons – the chain of fires to be lit if invasion threatens. Countering this, the author says that the map will help defenders to operate the system more effectively. Otherwise the book paints a lush portrait of the county: "The soil is for the most part bountiful ... as for orchards of apples and gardens of cherries, and those of the most exquisite and delicious kinds, no part of the realm has them, either in such quantity or number or with such art and industry set and planted" (→ 1577).

Football is fast becoming a popular pastime in Scotland; in 1576 George Gordon, the earl of Huntly, one of the former leading opponents of Mary Queen of Scots, dropped dead after an energetic football match.

'Black Assizes' men hit by a fatal fever

Oxford, 6 August 1577
An extraordinary epidemic that only affects men has hit Oxford. So far it has claimed nearly 300 lives, but none of the victims has been a woman or a child. The infection seems to have started in the courthouse, since nearly everyone who attended there on the 4, 5 and 6 July has been affected, including all the jurors and Robert Bell, the lord chief baron.

Some are saying that these "Black Assizes" result from a Catholic plot while one poet has given Death's view: "Think you on the solemn 'sizes past/How suddenly in Oxfordshire/I came and made the judges all aghast." Others, more worldly, have already written to ask for the jobs of the deceased.

Judges wearing their robes of office.

Strange 'black dog' kills two in storm

Suffolk, 4 August 1577
Something terrible – a black dog, some claim – rushed into the church at Bungay during the Sunday morning service today, seized two people by the throat, killed them and bit a third on the back so that he "shrivelled up like a piece of leather". Outside, the shaken parishioners found the church door "marvellously rent and torn", with marks that might have been made by claws; furthermore, the wires and wheels of the church clock were twisted and broken.

Archbishop placed under house arrest

London, May 1577
Queen Elizabeth has ordered the archbishop of Canterbury, Edmund Grindal, to be put under house arrest in Lambeth. She is furious with him for defying her. At the end of last year he wrote her a letter in which he boldly declared: "I choose rather to offend your earthly majesty than to offend the heavenly majesty of God."

The offence was his refusal to condemn the regular bible-study classes, common in the south-east, where clergymen practise their preaching skills. The queen, who is no respecter of sermons, ordered Grindal to have these "prophesyings", as they are called, stopped, probably because she sees them as a veiled attempt by radicals to carry out further illegal church reforms.

Grindal made investigations and became convinced that, far from being harmful, the "prophesyings" were vital for the health of the entire church and explained why in a 6,000-word memorandum. He sees himself in the tradition of great clerics who have rebuked princes, such as the fourth-century bishop of Milan, Ambrose, who upbraided Emperor Theodosius (→23/9).

England agrees to treaty of alliance with Dutch rebels to join forces against Spain

Elizabeth agrees to help the Dutch against relentless Spanish persecution.

Netherlands, December 1577
Queen Elizabeth has finally signed a treaty with the Dutch rebels after months of confusion. In September a loan of £100,000 was agreed, plus a force of 6,000 men to counter the threat of a French invasion. But the rebels are split between Catholics and Protestants; while both want the money, the Catholics are wary of Protestant English soldiers and in November turned down the offer of their help. Now, however, they say that the English can come if France invades.

The queen has sent Sir Thomas Wilkes to Spain to persuade Philip II to agree to a settlement in the Netherlands. She is also supporting a round-the-world expedition by Francis Drake which is likely to disrupt Spanish shipping (→1580).

'Chronicles' published in England despite cries of disloyalty

London, 1577
Accusations of "disloyalty" from Queen Elizabeth have greeted the publication of Raphael Holinshed's "Chronicles of England, Scotland and Ireland". The queen was angered by parts of the Irish section and wants them cut. The offending passages are, however, not by Holinshed but by, among others, Richard Stanyhurst and Edward Campion. The Scottish section, meanwhile, is a translation of Hector Boece's Latin work *Scotorum historiae*.

Holinshed was assistant to the London printer Reginald Wolfe, whose researches for a universal history he took over on Wolfe's death in 1573. Holinshed invited several contributors to help him complete the present book. One section, "A Description of England", by the clergyman William Harrison, deals with today. He observes how much wealthier the country is – houses of "brick or hard stone" replacing those of "strong timber". More chimneys can be seen, and sleeping conditions have improved: people have pillows instead of "a good round log under their heads". But wealth, he complains, has led to an unhealthy interest in fashion: "Except it were a dog in a doublet you shall not see any so disguised as are my countrymen of England" (→1579).

An engraving of King Macbeth of Scotland (1040-57) and the three witches.

1578-1579

Stirling, 4 April 1578. In a second coup, allies of the deposed regent James Douglas, the earl of Morton, regain control of King James VI (→30/9/79).

New World, 11 June 1578. The charter for colonizing Newfoundland is granted to the navigator Sir Humphrey Gilbert (→9/9/83).

England, June 1578. Queen Elizabeth reconsiders marriage to the French Catholic duke of Anjou (→3/11/79).

Ireland, 12 September 1578. Sir Henry Sidney resigns as lord deputy (→10/7/79).

Harwich, Essex, October 1578. Martin Frobisher returns from a third attempt to find a north-west passage.

Scotland, 1578. The general assembly of the Church of Scotland approves the *Second Book of Discipline*; it outlines plans for the church (→1584).

London, 1578. A prefabricated building called Nonsuch House – "No-other-such-house" – is brought from the Netherlands and rebuilt on London Bridge (→1580).

Co Kerry, 18 July 1579. James Fitzmaurice FitzGerald lands at Smerwick and builds a fortress (→24).

Co Kerry, 24 July 1579. Sir Humphrey Gilbert attacks Fitzmaurice and the Munster rebels (→1/8).

Ireland, 1 August 1579. Sir James and Sir John FitzGerald, brothers of the earl of Desmond, Gerald fitz James, murder the English negotiator in his bed (→16).

Ireland, 16 August 1579. Sir John Perrot becomes admiral of the English fleet; he is to prevent European aid from reaching Fitzmaurice (→18).

Co Limerick, 18 August 1579. James Fitzmaurice FitzGerald dies in a fight with the Burkes of Castleconnell (→2/11).

Edinburgh, 30 September 1579. James VI makes his state entry (→31/12/80).

Ireland, 2 November 1579. The earl of Desmond is declared a traitor (→15/7/80).

Glasgow, 1579. The cathedral is saved from demolition by craftsmen who threaten to riot if it is destroyed.

London, 1579. William Clowes, a surgeon at St Bartholomew's hospital, publishes the first text in English on syphilis.

Scots government taken over by James VI

Stirling, 4 March 1578
The highland earls of Atholl and Argyll, John Stewart and Archibald Campbell, have persuaded King James VI to dismiss his regent, James Douglas, the earl of Morton, and to assume the administration of Scotland despite his youth. The king has agreed, although no one believes that an 11-year-old can cope with the confusion that reigns in Scotland.

James has relied entirely upon the stern and often brutal tyrant who had so far succeeded in maintaining good relations with Elizabeth of England while not succumbing to her policies. Under Morton the country has remained Protestant, although the regent has taken a firm line with the more outspoken ministers of the church.

Morton made the mistake of depriving the king of money, and Atholl and Argyll used this as a pretext for petitioning James here at Stirling to call his noblemen to judge between them and Morton. Morton, in turn, sent word from Edinburgh that he was prepared to resign if the king accepted the word of the rebels. In so doing he played into his enemies' hands. The fearful king had little choice but to agree to the resignation (→4/4).

James VI takes control as king.

Royal visit brings plague to Norwich

Norwich, August 1579
Royal progresses – processions – are an expensive business for the gentry, what with masques, feasts and daily hunts [*see report on page 467*]. The ordinary people of Norwich, however, are paying for last year's progress in the dearest currency that there is – their lives.

Queen Elizabeth's progress to their town last August was, ironically, eagerly welcomed. A progress can put a town on the map, and Norwich was delighted that its ailing cloth industry might be given a boost. Alerted to the queen's proposed visit in June, the aldermen had the town spruced up and also organized masques and pageants for Elizabeth's week-long stay.

Tragically, the royal baggage-train brought plague to the town. It has raged there ever since and still shows no sign of abating. Far from securing prosperity, thousands of townsfolk have achieved only a premature death (→1592).

The figure of death haunts Norwich.

Earl of Bothwell dies in mad exile

Dragsholm, Denmark, 4 April 1578
James Hepburn, the fourth earl of Bothwell and third husband of Mary Queen of Scots, died in a dungeon here tonight, chained to a wall and hopelessly insane after five years in jail. After the defeat at Carberry Hill in 1567 he fled to Scandinavia, but he was arrested and held in first Norway and then Denmark, where he was denounced by a discarded mistress. Before he died Bothwell apparently made a confession exonerating Mary from the murder of King Henry, her second husband (→11/1583).

James Hepburn, earl of Bothwell.

French coin-maker hanged for forgery

Norwich, June 1578
Eloye Mestrell, the famous French coin-engraver, has been hanged – for forging coins. Usually forgers are punished by either the chopping off of a hand or emasculation. What so outraged the authorities (and ensured his death sentence) was that Mestrell was formerly a most trusted employee of the royal mint. Indeed, 18 years ago he was responsible for inventing the first machine for minting coins in England. It was the discovery of Mestrell's second, unauthorized, machine that led to his downfall.

Queen takes firm line with puritan critic

London, 3 November 1579
John Stubbe, a Protestant pamphleteer, has had his right hand cut off for criticizing the queen's proposed marriage to Francis, the duke of Anjou [formerly of Alençon] and brother of Henry III of France.

Most of England was horrified when news of the projected marriage spread. Protestants objected because Anjou is a Catholic, even though the 46-year-old queen is presumed too old to bear children. Catholics objected because he supports the Dutch rebels against Catholic Spain. Sensing the opposition, and humiliated by the news of her favourite Leicester's secret marriage to Lettice Knollys, the queen renounced the engagement last month, breaking down in tears in front of her council (→2/11/81).

Prince's tutor writes 'History of Scotland'

Scotland, 1579
George Buchanan, Scotland's leading poet, teacher and man of learning, has abandoned politics in his old age to concentrate on his Latin *History of Scotland*. Formerly a member of the court of Mary Queen of Scots, Buchanan acted as tutor to her son, the young King James VI. Like Mary, he spent most of his early years in France, after escaping imprisonment in the castle at St Andrews for a poem he wrote satirizing the Franciscan friars. Buchanan became a professor at Bordeaux, and among his pupils was the essayist Michel Eyquem de Montaigne. In Portugal he was arrested as a heretic and, while in prison there, wrote a Latin paraphrase of the Book of Psalms.

Buchanan and Queen Mary used to study the Roman historian Livy together, and he wrote a poem to mark the birth of her son, James. But after King Henry's murder and her abdication he wrote a tract attacking her, the *Detectio Mariae reginae*, and has followed it this year with *De jure regni apud Scotos*, on the right of kingship among the Scots. In this he argues that in Scotland unacceptable kings can be deposed and even killed by private subjects, since they should rule only by the will and for the good of the people. As a Latin verse writer he has no equal (→ 1580).

Elizabeth faces Catholic revolt in Ireland

The pope and Philip II of Spain back plans for a Catholic revolt in Ireland.

Ireland, 18 July 1579
Queen Elizabeth of England is facing a Catholic revolt led by James Fitzmaurice FitzGerald, a cousin of the earl of Desmond. James had been forced to flee to the continent but has now landed at Smerwick with a force of 700 well-armed men, to preach a crusade against the "heretic" queen and seek support from disgruntled political leaders in Ireland. His moves are backed by Pope Gregory XIII and Philip II of Spain.

The rebels have been irritated by the critical attitude towards all things Irish shown by the English officials who are serving in the central and provincial administrations set up under the rule of the lord deputy, Sir Henry Sidney. But, until now, they have been reluctant to take any action which could be seen as disloyalty to the crown.

Now all is changed, and Fitzmaurice, who hopes to involve the earl of Desmond in his campaign, has already won wide support in Munster and the English Pale. While some in the English establishment think that Sidney should be recalled from England, where he has been since last September, others think that an iron-fist policy is needed and that Arthur, Lord Grey de Wilton, is the right man (→ 18).

Drake reaches the coast of California

San Francisco Bay, July 1579
Having sailed around Cape Horn in the south Atlantic, Francis Drake has made his way up the Pacific coast of America, raiding Spanish settlements on the way, and landed here to repair his ship, the *Golden Hind*. The natives are friendly, the climate is temperate, and the soil rich with deposits of gold and silver. Drake has decided to call the land New Albion, because of its white cliffs and morning fogs. He will not be returning to England the way he came, however, for fear of Spanish ambushes. Instead he has a bolder plan – to circumnavigate the globe (→ 26/9/80).

Drake: welcomed to the west coast.

In 1579, reflecting a growing interest in geography, the cartographer Christopher Saxton issued an atlas of the first large-scale maps of England and Wales, which he began to produce four years ago. His work includes the countries in their entirety (l) and individual counties, such as Cornwall (r).

1580 - 1581

London, 6 April 1580. An earthquake damages St Paul's Cathedral (→ 23/7/97).

Dover, June 1580. The first Jesuit missionaries, the friars Edmund Campion and Robert Parsons, arrive; they aim to re-establish Roman Catholicism (→ 18/3/81).

Ireland, 15 July 1580. Arthur, Lord Grey de Wilton, is appointed lord deputy (→ 25/8).

Co Wicklow, 25 August 1580. Grey is defeated by Munster rebels at Glenmalure, and many of his senior officers are killed (→ 3/10).

England, 26 September 1580. Francis Drake returns from a round-the-world trip laden with treasure for Queen Elizabeth (→ 4/4/81).

Ireland, 3 October 1580. Sir James FitzGerald, the brother of Gerald fitz James, the earl of Desmond, is executed by Lord Grey (→ 10/11).

Edinburgh, 31 December 1580. James Douglas, the earl of Morton and former Scottish regent, is arrested for treason (→ 2/6/81).

London, 1580. An Anglo-Ottoman treaty gives England a new outlet for trade and an ally against Spain (→ 7/1584).

London, 1580. John Stow compiles and publishes *The Chronicles*, a collection of earlier narratives of English history (→ 2/5/86).

Ireland, 1580. Edmund Spenser, a poet, is appointed secretary to Lord Grey.

London, 18 March 1581. Parliament is dissolved after passing a new law making it treasonable to convert anyone to Catholicism (→ 17/7).

Munster, March 1581. Rebellion is general throughout the province (→ 3/1/82).

Edinburgh, 5 August 1581. The Frenchman Esmé Stuart, as part of his rise to power following the fall of James Douglas, the earl of Morton, is promoted from earl to duke of Lennox (→ 8/1582).

London, 2 November 1581. Francis, the Catholic duke of Anjou and heir to the French throne, arrives to finalize negotiations for his marriage to Elizabeth (→ 2/1582).

London, 1 December 1581. The Jesuit Edmund Campion is executed.

England, 1581. The population is estimated to be 3.5 million.

Irish rebellion crushed with great ferocity

The earl of Desmond mercilessly murders an aide of the English deputy.

Ireland, 10 November 1580
The revolt set off last year by James Fitzmaurice FitzGerald has been crushed by English forces, and today Lord Grey has massacred all those in Fitzmaurice's Smerwick fort. Fitzmaurice himself was killed in a skirmish in August last year; his cousin, the earl of Desmond, was then drawn into the revolt. Its failure was largely due to the efforts of Sir Nicholas Malby; fresh from conquering Connacht, he had been made temporary governor of Munster and showed his mettle by beating 2,000 men fighting under the papal banner, a new symbol in Irish warfare. No favour has been shown to the leaders. Those in the Pale have had their property seized and then been hanged, drawn and quartered. Munster has been devastated. Never has Ireland seen such systematic slaughter (→ 3/1581).

Splendid house is completed at Longleat

Warminster, Wiltshire, 1580
After 30 years Longleat House is finished. Its boldly modern design does away with the traditional inner courtyard; instead the house looks out onto the world. Purists are shocked and bewail Longleat's "inhuman" proportions. The owner and designer, Sir John Thynne – the brother-in-law of Sir Thomas Gresham – purchased the former Augustinian priory from King Henry VIII for £53, but he died before work was completed. Meanwhile Robert Smythson has begun Wollaton Hall, near Nottingham, to be built in the same blend of "gothic" and classical styles (→ 1587).

Longleat House, with its blatantly modern design, is finally finished.

Outspoken Melville moves to new post

Edinburgh, 1580
Andrew Melville, a theologian and educationalist, has been appointed principal of St Mary's College, St Andrews, where he studied before teaching in Paris and Poitiers. As principal of the University of Glasgow from 1574, Melville succeeded in transforming this institution by the introduction of greater specialization in teaching. His international reputation as a linguist also played a major part in improving the university's status. Melville is at the forefront of those demanding the complete independence of the church from state control.

Sidney writes his defence of poetry

Sir Philip Sidney: romantic poet.

Wiltshire, 1580
Philip Sidney, formerly an ambassador of the queen but now out of favour at court, has retired to Wilton, the home of his sister Mary, the countess of Pembroke, to write. His latest work is *A Defence of Poesie*, intended as a reply to a puritan pamphlet abusing the art.

He defends poetry as "the poor pipe which can show the misery of the people, under hard lords and ravening soldiers". The poet comes forth "with a tale which holdeth children from play and old men from the chimney corner". Sidney leads the vogue among courtiers for writing sonnets and songs and is at present working on *Arcadia*, a long pastoral romance (→ 1586).

A knighthood for Drake

London, 4 April 1581
Back at Deptford after two and a half years spent circumnavigating the globe, Captain Francis Drake has been knighted on the deck of his ship, the *Golden Hind*, by Queen Elizabeth.

For Drake and his crew it has been an epic voyage. Sailing first down the American Atlantic coast, and then up the American Pacific coast, he raided Spanish ships and settlements all the way. Then he crossed the Pacific, and sailing via the Moluccas and Java rounded the Cape of Good Hope. He later landed at Guinea, where he saw three elephants, before returning to Deptford. The Spanish ambassador is furious at the honour bestowed on a "pirate" and regards it as a deliberate royal snub (→ 7/9/85).

Sir Francis receives his knighthood.

Former regent of Scotland beheaded

Edinburgh, 2 June 1581
When the former regent, James Douglas, the earl of Morton, introduced the "maiden" [a type of guillotine] to Scotland, he could hardly have imagined that it would be used to sever his own head. But that is just what happened today, when 65-year-old Morton was executed in Edinburgh for complicity in the murder of King Henry, the king's father, in 1567. His accuser was James Stewart, the earl of Arran, a close associate of the Frenchman Esmé Stuart, the earl of Lennox, who is suspected of opposing Morton's staunch Protestantism and policy of friendship with England. Harsh rule had made Morton unpopular during his six-year regency, which ended in 1578 (→ 5/8).

Jesuit Campion is accused of treason

Lyford, Berkshire, 17 July 1581
The biggest man-hunt for a decade is over. Edmund Campion, an alleged papal spy, has been arrested by the priest-hunter George Eliot. He was found hiding above the stairwell in Lyford Grange with two other priests.

Campion is credited with one of the most brilliant minds of his generation. A graduate of St John's, Oxford, and later a tutor, he escaped to France and joined the Jesuits, becoming professor of rhetoric at Prague University before returning to England 13 months ago. With the arrest of Campion and the two priests, the hunt is now on for a fourth man, the former Oxford professor and professed Jesuit Robert Parsons (→ 1/12).

Scotland focuses attention on the economy

Scotland, 1581
In spite of continuing political uncertainty, the coming of more peaceful times has focused attention on the expansion and consolidation of manufacturing and trade. The first silk factory was opened in Perth this year, for example, and in 1579 parliament banned the import of English cloth in order to protect Scottish jobs.

Linen, along with skins, hides, fish and coal – products of an essentially rural economy – is one of the key exports to northern Europe, with which Scotland enjoys strong trading links. For this small, relatively poor country on the fringe of the continent, vital imports include industrial raw materials such as iron and wood and, in years of poor harvest, supplies of grain.

However economic enterprise remains rare in some of the small towns, where the merchant guilds are often preoccupied with preserving their privileges at the expense of advancing commerce and industry. In the countryside, development of natural resources is the responsibility of the landowners, who control the materials and labour force, and most income still derives from the land itself.

An engraving from John Derricke's recently published book "The Image of Ireland": a varied collection of poems, woodcuts and engravings which vividly depicts the customary way of life in Ireland in the 16th century.

Better academic tuition urged for women

Lady Sidney and her daughters: all hoping for a better education.

London, 1581
A woman's place is in the home – even if she is educated. "I know it to be a principal commendation in a woman: to be able to govern and direct her household, to look after her house and family, to provide and keep necessities, and to know the force of her kitchen," writes Richard Mulcaster in a treatise advocating education for women.

There is nothing new in this. Erasmus and Sir Thomas More wanted women to enjoy a broad, humanist education, and Queen Elizabeth was herself educated according to such ideas.

Since then literacy has improved amongst both middle- and upper-class women. Girls already attend parish schools, women are managing households, and in some parts of London they are even managing the accounts of their shopkeeper husbands – although this particular intrusion into the male world is not greeted quite so enthusiastically by Mulcaster (→ 1589).

1582 - 1583

Co Cork, 3 January 1582. Sir John FitzGerald, a brother of the earl of Desmond, is killed near Castle Lyons (→31/8).

Sandwich, Kent, February 1582. Francis, the duke of Anjou, leaves for the Low Countries; his proposed marriage to Queen Elizabeth will not take place, and instead England will aid him against the Dutch (→1600).

Ireland, 6 April 1582. Nicholas Nugent, the chief justice of the court of common pleas, is executed on a fabricated charge of treason.

Edinburgh, 14 April 1582. A new university is founded and given a royal charter (→3/3/91).

Dublin, 31 August 1582. Lord Grey de Wilton, the lord deputy, is recalled to England because of his savage policies (→2/1583).

Scotland, 28 September 1582. George Buchanan, a renowned scholar and former tutor to King James VI, dies.

Ireland, February 1583. Gerald fitz James FitzGerald, the earl of Desmond, seeks refuge in Sliabh Luachra [west of Cork and east of Kerry] (→11/11).

Fife, 27 June 1583. James VI escapes to St Andrews after ten months in captivity near Perth (→2/5/84).

Lambeth, 6 July 1583. Archbishop Edmund Grindal of Canterbury, under house arrest since 1577 for displeasing the queen, dies (→23/9).

Atlantic Ocean, 9 September 1583. Sir Humphrey Gilbert, who took formal possession of Newfoundland last month, is drowned at sea.→

Canterbury, 23 September 1583. John Whitgift, formerly bishop of Worcester, is consecrated archbishop (→11/1589).

London, November 1583. Francis Throckmorton, a Catholic conspirator, confesses under torture to a plot to put Mary Queen of Scots on the throne of England (→1/1584).

Scotland, 1583. King James VI establishes the Castilian Band, a group of poets at his court.

London, 1583. Sir Edmund Tilney, the master of the revels, forms "the Queen's Players" (→1587).

London, 1583. The Venice company is formed for Anglo-Italian trade.

Scots king kidnapped

Ruthven Castle, where Protestant nobles imprisoned the young King James.

Perth, August 1582

The 16-year-old king of Scotland was lured into Ruthven Castle near here today and held captive by Protestant conspirators. James VI had been hunting when he was persuaded to spend the night at the castle. In the morning, dressed for a further day's sport, he found the master of Glamis barring his exit. The king was furious, vowing dire punishment on his captors, and finally burst into tears.

Seeing him weep, the master told him: "It is no matter of his tears, better that bairns should weep than bearded men." The king was told that he would remain a prisoner until he signed a proclamation condemning his close friend and favourite, Esmé, the duke of Lennox. Still tearful, the king remains a prisoner and refuses to sign, knowing that Lennox will be killed or exiled.

Despite a pledge by the king that he would never marry a Catholic, the conspirators – the earls of Gowrie, Mar and Angus and Lord Lindsay – feared that Lennox was seeking to convert James to the Catholic faith by force. They also suspected that Lennox was plotting to invade England (→27/6/83).

City of London gets new water system

London, 1582

A Dutchman has initiated a major improvement in London's water supply. Water is normally taken from the Thames by "carriers", but Pieter Morice, a servant employed by Sir Christopher Hatton, a courtier and favourite of Queen Elizabeth, has devised a method of pumping it from the river to the city by the use of a water-wheel on the north side of London Bridge. Despite opposition from the carriers, the plan won approval when Morice showed officials he could direct a jet of water over a churchtower.

A 16th-century water-pump system.

English 'abuses' are condemned by fiery puritan commentator

England, 1583

A second edition of Philip Stubbes' controversial book *The Anatomy of Abuses* – a fiery denunciation of the manners, fashions and customs of the time – is published today, four months after it first appeared. However, his original preface, an attempt to qualify the extremism of his views, is no longer included.

In the book he condemns football for being a "bloody and murdering practice rather than a fellowly sport or pastime" and blames it for the growth of "malice, rancour, hatred and envy". A bowling alley is a waste of "wit, time and money"; a Maypole is a "stinking idol" around which "heathens leap and dance"; and plays, he says, induce "whoredom and uncleanness".

Stubbes casts a jaundiced eye on festivities such as this fête at Bermondsey.

England stakes its claim in New World

Atlantic Ocean, 9 September 1583
Sir Humphrey Gilbert, the English navigator, has died at sea off the Azores, going down with his frigate *Squirrel* on the voyage home. Last month, on 5 August, he landed in Newfoundland, planted the English flag and took possession of the territory for Queen Elizabeth.

Born in Devon in 1539, and the step-brother of Sir Walter Raleigh, Gilbert was educated at Eton and Oxford. Yet another Devonian to take to the sea, he was a champion advocate of the north-west passage explorations during the 1570s.

He left Plymouth in June this year with five ships and the queen's blessing to occupy "heathen lands not actually possessed of any Christian prince or people as should seem good to him ...".

Astronomer's house is destroyed by mob

Surrey, September 1583
The Mortlake home of John Dee, one of England's foremost astrologers, has been ransacked during his absence by a mob, angry and suspicious about his scientific activities. Much of his furniture, as well as instruments and books, has been destroyed.

Dee, at present in Europe with the astrologer, medium and necromancer Edward Kelley, is no stranger to controversy. In 1553 he was imprisoned, suspected of using sorcery to bring about the death of Queen Mary Tudor – although she pardoned him three years later. He gained the reputation of being a magician after staging at Cambridge Aristophanes' *Peace*, in which an actor appeared to levitate, to the audience's astonishment.

Irish rebel leader killed

The rebel earl of Desmond is brutally murdered by Daniel Kelly in Tralee.

Ireland, 11 November 1583
The leading figure in the Munster rebellion against the English, Gerald fitz James FitzGerald, the earl of Desmond, has been killed by a servant of a rival clan while hiding in a cave in Co Kerry. He was proclaimed a traitor by the English, and his death is being seen as marking the end of the rebellion.

Following the arrival of Thomas Dubh Butler, the earl of Ormond, who replaced Malby as governor-general of Munster, Desmond abandoned his castles and took to the hills. He pillaged Youghal, where he pulled down the royal arms from the courthouse, claiming that he was defending the Catholic faith. But his opponents swept through the countryside, seizing cattle, burning the harvest, killing all who stood in their way and producing widespread famine as a result of this scorched-earth policy.

Despite the success of the government forces, efforts to find the earl and kill him proved fruitless. Queen Elizabeth, anxious to curtail expense, decided to pardon all but the leaders of the revolt. Desmond was hunted relentlessly. With his death the dying embers of the Munster rebellion have been stamped out, but famine remains rife across the country (→ 7/1/89).

Four social groups defined in survey

England, 1583
Elizabethan society outside the nobility is divided into four distinct groups, according to *De Republica Anglorum*, a social survey published this year. The book was written in 1565 by Sir Thomas Smith, the Greek scholar and statesman who died in 1577.

At the top, rubbing shoulders with the nobility, is the gentleman, defined as he who "studies the laws of the realm, has been to university, is versed in the liberal sciences and, to be brief, can live idly without the need to do manual work". Any man with these qualities, and with the bearing and countenance of a gentleman, should "be called master".

The next level is that of citizens and burgesses – men who are free within the cities and have substance enough to hold positions of authority. The third group is composed of yeomen, English-born freeholders of land with a revenue to the value of 40s [£2]. The fourth and final group comprises the great majority of the population – from the relatively well off to the poor and destitute. Smith categorizes these as "having no voice nor authority but are there to be ruled – the lower orders" in society.

Dee: alchemist and astronomer.

Three executed for vilifying the queen

Suffolk, July 1583
Three separatists have been executed at Bury St Edmunds for their parts in painting an inscription around the royal arms at St Mary's, vilifying Queen Elizabeth. The text, taken from the Bible, was used to imply that she is a Jezebel who causes her servants to "fornicate and eat meat sacrified to idols".

The incident highlights growing disputes between followers of the established church and Protestant separatists determined to found a "pure" church.

The Sunday pursuit of activities such as bear-baiting raised a controversy after deaths resulted from the collapse of a spectators' gallery at London's Paris Gardens, a major baiting centre, on 13 January 1583 – a Sunday.

1584-1585

Ireland, 7 January 1584. Sir John Perrot, a former admiral of the fleet and president of Munster, is made lord deputy (→ 11/1584).

Fife, March 1584. Andrew Melville, the principal of St Andrews University and an academic reformer, flees to England after a confrontation with the government.

Scotland, 2 May 1584. William Ruthven, the earl of Gowrie, is executed after the failed coup in April to overthrow the government of James Stewart, the earl of Arran, in Stirling (→ 27/7/85).

France, 10 June 1584. Francis, the duke of Anjou, a former suitor of Queen Elizabeth, dies; the heir to the throne is Henry of Navarre, a Protestant.

Dublin, 20 June 1584. Dermot O'Hurley, the archbishop of Cashel, is executed for alleged complicity in the Munster rebellion (→ 21/8).

London, 10 July 1584. Francis Throckmorton is executed at Tyburn for plotting to replace Elizabeth with Mary Queen of Scots (→ 20/9/86).

Europe, July 1584. The assassination at Delft on 10 July of William of Orange, the leader of the Protestant Dutch revolt against the Spanish, deepens English concern over the power of the Catholic Habsburg family (→ 5/1585).

Dublin, 21 August 1584. The archbishop and Protestant clergy oppose a plan by the lord deputy, Sir John Perrot, to convert St Patrick's Cathedral into a university.

Cambridge, 1584. Sir Walter Mildmay founds Emmanuel College for the training of puritan ministers.

Plymouth, 9 April 1585. Sir Richard Grenville sets sail to establish a colony in America (→ 18/10).

Borders, 27 July 1585. Sir Francis Russell, is killed by the Scots, giving Elizabeth an excuse to plot against the earl of Arran (→ 2/11).

Plymouth, 7 September 1585. Sir Francis Drake sails for Spanish America (→ 1/1/86).

Perth, 21 October 1585. The Scots mint is moved here from Dundee to escape the plague.

Stirling, 2 November 1585. An English-backed coup topples the government (→ 17/4/89).

Spanish envoy expelled

The ambassador is expelled from England for his part in a Catholic plot.

London, January 1584
Bernadino de Mendoza, the Spanish ambassador, has been expelled from England following revelations by Francis Throckmorton of his complicity in a plot to overthrow Queen Elizabeth and put Mary Stuart on the English throne. By cultivating the sympathies of disenchanted English Catholics and winning Throckmorton's support, Mendoza had allegedly planned to liberate the Scottish queen.

Throckmorton's confession was extracted under torture, to reveal that the French duke of Guise was preparing to lead an invasion in the south of England, financed by the king of Spain and the pope.

A zealous Catholic throughout his life, Throckmorton became embroiled in Catholic plotting while living on the continent. He came back to London last year and took a house beside the Thames from where he organized a communications network between Paris and the Spanish ambassador. Throckmorton is to be executed for his treason (→ 10/7).

Controversial 'black acts' puts Scots king at head of church

Edinburgh, May 1584
Parliament has declared James VI to be the head of the Scottish church, ending the presbyterian system and giving the king and his council jurisdiction over ecclesiastical cases. The courts and assemblies of the kirk have been dissolved; bishops will be appointed, and no longer will the affairs of state be discussed from the pulpit.

The Presbyterians are furious at what they have termed "the black acts". But the earl of Arran – the chancellor and a close adviser to James – has threatened dissidents that he will "shave their heads, pare their nails and make examples of all who rebel".

James, 18 next month, has begun to make his mark in public life. He is highly educated and has a firm grasp of theology and languages. Although a Protestant, he is emerging as a political and religious conservative. In England, Elizabeth – fearing a move to Catholicism – is keeping a suspicious eye on events in Scotland (→ 7/1587).

Tension builds in Anglo-Spanish relations

England, May 1585
An overt act of aggression by Philip II of Spain has brought England dangerously close to the brink of a war that seems increasingly inevitable. By his seizure of English shipping and goods in Atlantic ports, Philip's plan to intimidate England's Queen Elizabeth into breaking off negotiations with the Dutch Protestants has backfired.

Diplomatic relations between the two nations have deteriorated as a result of the Spanish annexation of Portugal and the conquest of the Azores – leaving the Atlantic seaboard free for Philip to launch an invasion of England.

The European balance of power has been shifting over the past few years, largely as a consequence of the growing influence of Catholicism. With the authority of the French government in decline, the spectre of Spain's success in the conquest of the Netherlands looks ominous to England.

In spite of three plots against the queen's life in the past two years – one of them backed by the pope – Elizabeth has rejected the advice of her ministers, who favour a preemptive strike against Spain. But Philip's latest aggression seems likely to force her hand (→ 10/8).

Philip II of Spain: the aggressor.

Colonists establish base in 'Virginia'

Plymouth, 18 October 1585
Sir Richard Grenville has returned from Virginia, where he established a colony on Roanoke Island. It is a rich and beautiful place, which was first reconnoitred last year by an expedition sponsored by Sir Walter Raleigh, who conceived the plan for the colony and has named it after the virgin queen, Elizabeth.

This first colony, with a hundred men, has built a fort and houses and planted vegetables. The Indians are most friendly and helpful, and the expedition's artist, John White, has painted many pictures of them.

They have a medicinal herb called tobacco whose dried leaves may be smoked in a clay pipe. The smoke opens the body's pores and purges phlegms and bad humours. The colony might make a great traffic in tobacco to England and profit by it. Grenville will return with supplies next year (→ 5/1586).

Plantation scheme is planned for Ulster

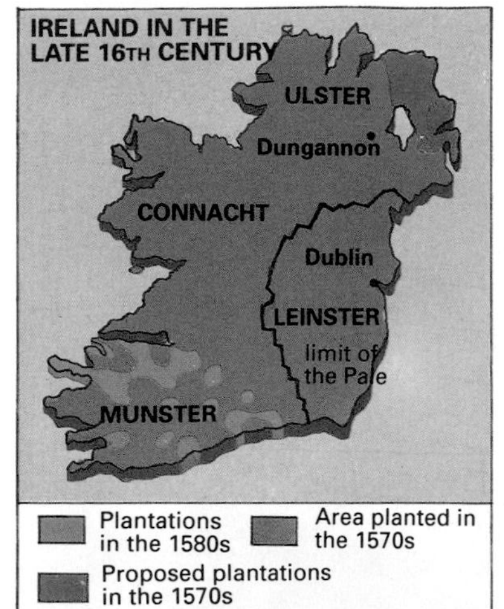

Ireland, November 1584
Having subdued Munster, Sir John Perrot, the lord deputy, is turning his attention to Ulster. He has always seen it as dangerous, with its numerous independent lordships and its proximity to Scotland. Perrot regards the Scots, whom he is determined to oust, as being England's prime enemy. He is of course aware that some of the native lords depend upon their Scottish mercenaries to maintain power.

As well as imposing military might on Ulster, Perrot hopes to extend there the plantation scheme which has been used in Desmond lands in Munster. Native landowners who do not subscribe to the oath of supremacy – to a Protestant monarch – are dispossessed of their property, and their lands are given to English settlers.

Perrot also means to impose the "composition" land tax throughout the country, and especially in the Pale and Ulster, where Sir Henry Sidney failed to make it stick [*see report on page 466*]. It has been decided that the huge territory owned by the O'Neill dynasty in Ulster shall be divided into segments, one of which has been assigned to the ambitious Hugh O'Neill, the baron of Dungannon. Perrot plans to have O'Neill created earl of Dungannon as a reward for complying with his plans (→ 18/6/86).

Tough anti-Catholic legislation, designed to protect Elizabeth, comes into effect

London, February 1585
Parliament has passed a new bill which gives legal force to a proposal drafted by Lord Burghley and Sir Francis Walsingham last October, designed to protect Queen Elizabeth from her enemies – especially Mary Queen of Scots. This proposal was called the "Bond of Association"; people could sign it (and thousands have) to pledge themselves to prevent anyone who overthrew the queen from taking power, and to pursue all plotters to the death.

The bill ushers in ruthless measures against Catholic priests. Seminary priests, Jesuits and any who have joined the Catholic priesthood since 1559 will have to leave the country within forty days and risk charges of treason if they return. Englishmen who have entered a Catholic seminary abroad must return within six months or be guilty of treason. Members of parliament uneasy about the bond's legality fear that if Elizabeth's life is threatened and, as the bond allows, Mary is killed, then the life of James VI, even if he is innocent, might be in danger (→ 23/3/87).

New legislation threatens James.

General election dominated by archbishop

Puritans are ordered by John Whitgift to observe the Three Articles.

England, November 1584
The parliamentary election would appear to have been one of the most fiercely fought this century, with John Whitgift, the archbishop of Canterbury, dominating the event with his characteristic assault on religious dissenters.

Last year, Whitgift's first major sermon as archbishop was a sign of his uncompromising nature when he demanded full observance of the Three Articles, provoking furious reactions from many of his clergy, as well as papists and puritans.

His hardline approach alarmed Lord Burghley, who likened it to the Spanish inquisition, and nearly precipitated a landslide of elected puritan members (→ 29/2/85).

England gives support to Dutch Protestants

Surrey, 10 August 1585
A treaty of alliance has today been agreed at Nonsuch Palace between England and the United Provinces [Netherlands]. England is now to back the Protestant Dutch in their revolt against the Catholic Spanish, whose campaign in the Netherlands has proved highly successful – especially since the assassination last year of the Dutch leader, William of Orange. The treaty comes after a heated debate in the privy council between "interventionists", believing war with Spain inevitable, and "neutralists", anxious to avoid any involvement in Europe.

The earl of Leicester will lead a force of over 7,000 men, whose upkeep will cost £126,000 annually. But it is money spent in the national interest: Spain could invade England from the Netherlands. Jubilant puritan gentry are flocking to take part in this "crusade" against the Spanish (→ 14/6/86).

On 2 November 1585 the earl of Arran's government fell following an English-backed coup at Stirling (above) by a broad coalition of noblemen.

1586

West Indies, 1 January. Sir Francis Drake captures the island of Santo Domingo from the Spanish (→ 2/1586).

Low Countries, February. Robert Dudley, the earl of Leicester, infuriates Queen Elizabeth by accepting the office of governor-general of the United Provinces without first gaining her permission (→ 2/1587).

South America, February. Drake ransoms the city of Cartagena for 110,000 ducats after overwhelming its defences with a combined land and sea attack (→ 2/4/87).

Virginia, May. Ralph Lane, the English military leader, defeats an attack on the colony by native Indians (→ 6/1586).

Co Antrim, 18 June. Sir John Perrot, the lord deputy, abandons his plan to expel the Scots of Antrim and signs a treaty with Sorley Boy MacDonnell, recognizing the Protestant settlements (→ 27/6).

Munster, 27 June. Queen Elizabeth consents to a plantation scheme for English immigrants (→ 10/5/87).

Virginia, June. Supply ships arrive to provision the first colonists, only to discover that they have returned to England with Sir Francis Drake (→ 12/12).

Plymouth, 21 July. Thomas Cavendish, an Ipswich-born navigator, sets off to circumnavigate the world; he has three ships and 123 men.

Dartmouth, Devon, October. John Davis returns from his second unsuccessful voyage to find the north-west passage.

England, October. Sir John Hawkins, the slave-trader, returns after a two-month scouting voyage to Spain; his prisoners confirm rumours of a planned Spanish invasion (→ 10/1587).

Suffolk, 29 November. Most of the town of Beccles is burnt to the ground after a chimney is accidentally set on fire.

England. The harvest is severely damaged by bad weather, leaving a shortage of corn.

England. William Webbe publishes *A Discourse of English Poetrie* (→ 1590).

Westminster. Parliament orders Kent to provide 1,500 men, 9,000lb of gunpowder, 900lb of lead and six guns for the defence of its coasts against the feared Spanish invasion.

Philip of Spain plans war with England

King Philip II of Spain is seen goading the European leaders into war.

Madrid, 14 June
Philip II of Spain's plans to invade England are being put into final shape by Don Juan de Zuniga, his senior adviser. The king, the leader of the world's greatest Catholic power, has known for 15 years that he would eventually have to deal with Protestant England.

He regards Queen Elizabeth, whose hand he once sought for a political marriage, as an illegitimate heretic. Her support for the Dutch Protestants rebelling against Spanish rule in the Netherlands has only deepened his enmity. It was, however, the warlike impudence of Francis Drake which finally forced him to take action.

Drake, with a contribution of £10,000 from the queen, mounted a swashbuckling expedition against the Spaniards last September. He took the port of Vigo in north-west Spain and had the audacity to use it to fit out his ships. He then raised havoc in the Cape Verde islands before sailing to raid Spain's possessions in the West Indies. Philip decided to prevaricate no longer. He is gathering a huge fleet to bring England to heel (→ 10/1586).

Historian publishes enthralling view of Britain and Ireland

London, 2 May
A new and brilliant account of the history and geography of England, Wales, Scotland and Ireland has just been published by the antiquarian William Camden. In *Britannia* he describes in Latin every county in the three kingdoms – its antiquities, people and nobility.

This is all part of the modern interest in history and geography. Camden has visited and studied every county, and he says in his preface: "I will show who were the ancient inhabitants, what was the reason for the name, what are the bounds of the country, the nature of the soil, the places of greatest antiquity, and of greatest eminence at present, and lastly, who have been dukes or earls of each, since the Norman Conquest."

Britannia is full of fascinating detail, whether it is discussing the rise of certain towns, such as the spa resort at Buxton, or the people who inhabit the land. Camden describes, for example, those who live in the Cambridgeshire fens: like the place, they are "of brutish, uncivilized tempers ... walking aloft upon a sort of stilts they all keep to the business of grazing, fishing and fowling". He pictures London's wharves, filled with masted ships, as a "wooded grove" (→ 1589).

Colonists are driven out of Virginia by threat of starvation

Bideford, Devon, 12 December
Sir Richard Grenville's squadron of seven ships has arrived here after a fruitless voyage to relieve the English colony set up in Virginia in July 1584. The colony is the project of Sir Walter Raleigh, who appointed Arthur Barlow and Philip Amadas to lead the first expedition. A second party of 108 colonists, led by Grenville, arrived at Roanoke Island in July 1585. Poorly supplied, they faced starvation, and so, when Francis Drake passed in June this year, they eagerly took passage.

A supply ship sent by Grenville – who was unaware of Drake's actions – turned up just days later, to find only the bodies of a native and an Englishman (→ 17/8/90).

Sir Francis Drake and his expedition collect the starving colonists.

Anglo-Scots league agrees to share aid

Britain, 7 July
With Catholic conspirators still active and Spain threatening invasion, Elizabeth of England has signed a mutual defence treaty with James VI of Scotland, which also grants James a pension of £4,000 a year. He has accepted reluctantly – he wanted £5,000 a year, together with an English dukedom and the return of his father's lands.

The English parliament has meanwhile ratified the "Bond of Association", chiefly aimed at Mary Queen of Scots and barring anyone who has plotted against Elizabeth from succeeding to the English throne [*see page 477*].

Soldier-poet dies from battle wound

Sidney lies fatally wounded.

Zutphen, Flanders, 17 October
England's greatest poet and most chivalrous knight, Sir Philip Sidney, died here today of a wound to the thigh. Sidney received the fatal wound in an attack on a Spanish convoy. He showed great courage during 26 days of suffering. As he lay dying, he passed a cup of water to another wounded man, saying: "Thy necessity is greater than mine." Although they were never published, Sidney's works range from sonnets and a prose romance called *Arcadia* to literary criticism in *Apologie for Poetrie*.

Mary Queen of Scots goes on trial

Brutal execution of Babington plotters

London, 20 September
All the bells of London rang out today as citizens merrily made their way to watch the execution of Anthony Babington and six of his co-conspirators against the life of Queen Elizabeth. Drums and tabors echoed through the streets as the men were placed on hurdles and dragged from Tower Hill to St Giles's Fields where a scaffold had been erected and a pair of gallows – of "extraordinary height" to ensure that all could see – built.

The grisly business of hanging, drawing and quartering began, with the executioners showing such hideous cruelty that the queen has ordered that at tomorrow's executions – of seven more conspirators – the victims should at least be hanged until they are dead before the mutilation begins.

There was never any doubt about the guilt of Babington and the others. Letters delivered covertly by a brewer's drayman to Queen Mary from Babington were intercepted by spies employed by the zealous Protestant Sir Francis Walsingham. They spelt out clearly the plotters' intent to kill Elizabeth and rescue Mary from imprisonment at Chartley while a foreign force invaded the country (→11/10).

Mary Queen of Scots, Queen Elizabeth's cousin, stands accused of treason.

Queen Mary found guilty of treason

Fotheringhay, 11 October
Dressed entirely in black velvet, Mary Queen of Scots today faced her accusers in the great hall of Fotheringhay Castle in Northamptonshire, knowing that her chance of acquittal on a charge of treason is slender. Crippled by rheumatism and her once slender figure thickened after 17 years' imprisonment in England (nearly all of it in Sheffield Castle), Mary has none the less been defiant. "I am queen by right of birth and my place should be there," she declared, pointing to a throne bearing the English coat of arms. She was directed instead to a chair covered in crimson velvet and sat quietly as the lord chancellor outlined the case against her.

Mary vehemently denies that she plotted with Anthony Babington to kill Queen Elizabeth. "Can I be responsible for the criminal projects of a few desperate men, which they planned without my knowledge or participation?" she demanded. Mary told the commissioners of the illness that has kept her bedridden for much of her imprisonment. "I have only two or three years to live and I do not aspire to any public position," she insisted (→4/12).

Elizabeth is reluctant to sign her Scottish cousin's death warrant

The queen hesitates, pen in hand.

London, 4 December
The privy council has publicized its decision to pass the death sentence on Mary Queen of Scots in an attempt to push Queen Elizabeth of England into action. Even though Elizabeth has no love for her Scottish cousin, who was found guilty of treason on 14 October, it would still be tremendously hard for her to sign Mary's death warrant. [*See report above.*]

This reluctance does not spring from any sentimentality on Elizabeth's part. She is, after all, under no illusions that Mary and her co-conspirators in the Babington plot wanted her dead and the country turned Catholic. Elizabeth's reason for hesitating is the fear that by executing a fellow monarch she may create a dangerous precedent, with all the serious repercussions from abroad that might ensue. It has even been rumoured that Elizabeth has mooted assassination as a convenient way out of her predicament.

Never one to make a decision until forced into it, Elizabeth will probably ignore the actions of the privy council for now. Mary, for her part, remains under lock and key at Fotheringhay Castle, where she spends her days sewing and trying to cheer her household, in the bleak knowledge that her ordeal will soon end (→1/2/87).

1587

London, 1 February. Queen Elizabeth, pressurized by parliament, signs a warrant ordering the execution of Mary Queen of Scots (→ 8).

Low Countries, February. Robert Dudley, the earl of Leicester, is humiliated when his troops, garrisoned at Deventer, are forced to surrender to the duke of Parma (→ 25/7).

Dumfries/Galloway, 26 March. King James VI quells a planned Catholic revolt.

Plymouth, 2 April. Sir Francis Drake sails for Spain to destroy the Spanish fleet and hinder Philip II's invasion plans for England (→ 21/4).

London, April. Sir Christopher Hatton, a favourite of the queen's, is appointed lord chancellor.

Plymouth, 8 May. Sir Walter Raleigh sets sail on a second expedition to establish a New World colony (→ 7/8/92).

Ulster, 10 May. Hugh O'Neill, the baron of Dungannon, is created earl of Tyrone (→ 22/9).

Spain, 2 July. Sir Francis Drake sails for the Azores is to divert the Spanish fleet in order (→ 10/87).

Low Countries, 25 July. The duke of Parma captures the English garrison at Sluys (→ 12/1587).

Co Donegal, 22 September. Hugh Roe O'Donnell of Tyrone, who opposes the "composition" land tax, is kidnapped at Rathmullen by agents of Sir John Perrot (→ 17/2/88).

Dartmouth, Devon, September. John Davis returns from a third expedition to find the north-west passage; new ground is charted in his exploration of the North Pole.

Spain, October. The Spanish fleet needs repairs after a wild-goose chase to the Azores, delaying Philip II's planned invasion (→ 2/1588).

Low Countries, 24 December. The disgraced earl of Leicester is replaced as commander by Peregrine, Lord Willoughby (→ 9/1589).

Southwark. Philip Henslowe builds the Rose theatre, the first on the south bank of the Thames (→ c.1590).

Cambridgeshire. William Cecil, Lord Burghley, completes the building of his new home, Burghley House.→

Dignified Mary goes to the scaffold

Northamptonshire, 8 February
The queen of Scots took the news of her sentence calmly last night and put her hand on a new testament, swearing that she was innocent of any crime. She asked when she was to die, and the earl of Shrewsbury, broken-voiced, told her that the execution would take place today at Fotheringhay Castle.

Mary lay fully clothed on her bed all night as one of her maids read to her from the Bible. She rose at six and prayed before walking in procession to the great hall, led by her groom holding a large crucifix. The queen was wearing a black dress over a red petticoat, a transparent veil hanging from her shoulders. No one noticed one of her little dogs trotting under her skirts.

Three hundred people watched as Mary entered the great hall and climbed the scaffold. She endured a lengthy theological harangue from the dean of Peterborough demanding she should forswear her Catholic faith. "I have lived in this religion, and am resolved to die in this religion," she told him firmly.

Mary kissed the crucifix before her maids began to help her remove her outer garments. She smiled when the two executioners helped the distraught servants, who were weeping copiously. Mary knelt on a cushion and recited a final psalm before she groped for the block and leaned forward, her hands held by the second executioner. It took three strokes of the axe to remove her head. The dog fought to stay with its dead mistress (→ 14/2).

After a tragic life, Mary moves with dignity to the executioner's block.

Queen Mary (second from right), with some of the major figures in her life.

Elizabeth grief-stricken and hysterical at the death of Mary

James hears of his mother's death.

Greenwich, London, 14 February
Considering that it was she who signed the warrant for the execution of Mary Queen of Scots, Queen Elizabeth is putting on a great show of grief at her cousin's death. While Londoners celebrate the execution with bells and bonfires, the queen is in ostentatious mourning. Everyone is being blamed for the execution – except herself.

The queen's fury has fallen on her secretary, William Davison, who drew up the death warrant. He has been brought before the star chamber and thrown into prison. Elizabeth claims that she signed the warrant only for "safety's sake" and has accused her privy council of "criminal" activities.

Lord Burghley, the secretary of state, is trying to persuade Elizabeth that her dramatic recriminations are unlikely to convince those who knew too well about her hatred for Mary. Mary's son, the 20-year-old James VI, seems less than distraught. Although some say that he retired to bed without supper after hearing the news, others report that he said to those nearby "I am now sole king."

Drake 'singes the King of Spain's beard'

Cadiz, Spain, 21 April
Sir Francis Drake has destroyed part of the Spanish fleet that was preparing to invade England. He sank 30 large ships and scores of small ones and burnt thousands of tons of supplies. "I have singed the king of Spain's beard," he said.

He had sailed with four of the queen's warships and 23 merchant ships. They reached Cadiz on 19 April, and Drake at once sailed through the narrows and into the harbour, ignoring the forts and their guns. The English ships then set about attacking the Spanish.

Enemy galleys rowed out to meet them, but their guns were no match for Drake's. The battle lasted for two days, with the English systematically sinking the Spanish warships and supply ships and galleys. At two o'clock this morning, Drake sailed safely out of the harbour. The great Spanish invasion fleet will not sail this year (→ 2/7).

Tourists get first guide for 'grand tour'

Travel is becoming increasingly easier and more available to the rich.

London
Travel has become an essential requirement for today's rich young man, but many are abusing it, according to Albert Meier's *Methodus Describendi Regiones*, just published. "Some, by passing the seas, change climates but not minds, returning nothing quickened by the varieties of the world". In spite of the Spanish wars, young foreigners continue to flock to England for the London/Cambridge/Oxford tour, and English gentlemen regard a year in France and Italy as rounding off their education.

Not all take it as seriously as Meier would wish. A new kind of book, a polyglot phrasebook, published in Liège, tells young men how to seduce a chambermaid in seven different languages.

Scots lawmakers pass reformist measures

Edinburgh, July
Parliament has passed a package of bold and important legislation. The Act of Annexation empowers the state to appropriate a certain acreage of former church lands. The ranks of parliament itself have been increased through the Shire Election Act, which provides for the representation of shire commissioners. A number of statutes have also been passed to improve the criminal justice system. Parliament has, controversially, approved usury – lending money at interest, previously forbidden to Christians. The maximum interest rate is set at 10 per cent (→ 5/1592).

Provocative church reform bill dropped

A traditional church service.

Westminster, 23 March
The puritans have abandoned their attempt to abolish the Church of England and replace it with a presbyterian system. A bill with this intention, introduced to parliament by Anthony Cope – which also sought to repeal all laws governing the church – has been dropped.

Cope's bill was presented on February 27, and Queen Elizabeth at once forbade any further discussion. Puritan members probably never expected anything so radical to pass; they merely wanted to debate church reform. When Peter Wentworth protested at the limit on parliamentary debate he was promptly sent to the Tower, and Cope soon followed him. The house then all agreed that now was no time for reform (→ 10/1588).

Disgraced Leicester resigns his post

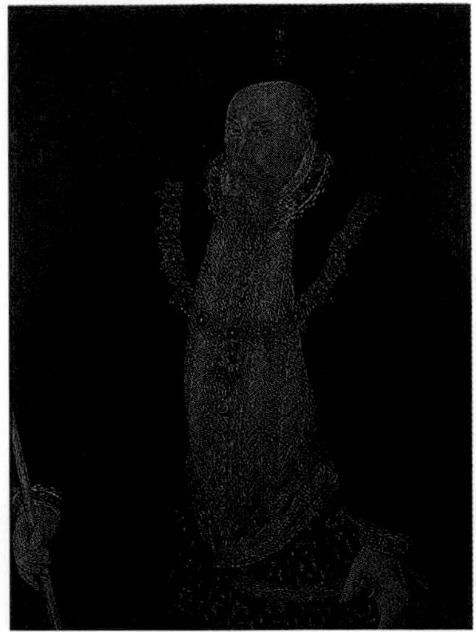
Disgraced: the earl of Leicester.

London, December
The earl of Leicester, Robert Dudley, has resigned as governor-general of the Protestant United Provinces in the Netherlands and returned in disgrace. Two years of fighting against Spanish rule here and lavish expenditure of crown funds have barely slowed the Spanish down; in fact, open war with Spain is now much closer.

Leicester arrived in Flushing exactly two years ago to coordinate Protestant Dutch resistance but infuriated Queen Elizabeth when, in February 1586, he made himself governor-general. Far from showing he merited this self-promotion, Leicester lost the key garrison of Sluys last July. Two months later he resigned his position, but the damage had been done (→ 24/12).

A 20th-century view of Burghley House, near Stamford in Lincolnshire, the magnificent residence of the lord high treasurer, Lord Burghley. Built of local stone, it was completed in 1587 after more than 30 years' work.

1588

Ireland, 17 February. Sir William Fitzwilliam is appointed lord deputy.→

Low Countries, 27 February. Anglo-Spanish peace talks begin at Ostend (→20/5).

London, March. John Field, a leading Presbyterian clergyman, dies.

Lisbon, 20 May. The Spanish Armada is finally at sea en route for England.→

Ireland, 30 June. Sir William Fitzwilliam is sworn in as lord deputy (→5/1589).

Dumfries/Galloway, June. King James VI crushes a Catholic rebellion.

Scilly Isles, 19 July. The Spanish Armada is first sighted (→23).

London, 23 July. Queen Elizabeth orders the reinforcement of the earl of Leicester's headquarters at Tilbury in Essex (→25).

Low Countries, 25 July. Anglo-Spanish peace talks disintegrate at Bourbourg (→3/8).

Oxfordshire, 4 September. Robert Dudley, the earl of Leicester and former favourite of Elizabeth, who fell from favour after a disastrous campaign in the Netherlands, dies suddenly at his home at Cornbury; Elizabeth is grief-stricken.

Plymouth, 10 September. Thomas Cavendish, who returns from his round-the-world voyage, is knighted by Elizabeth for his success.→

Ireland, 11 September. A violent storm wrecks at least 25 Spanish ships (→4/11).

Co Antrim, 18 October. The *Girona* from Scotland is shipwrecked at Dunluce.

Ireland, 4 November. Sir William Fitzwilliam begins a thorough search for Spanish castaways (→24).

London, 24 November. Elizabeth holds a grand service in St Paul's Cathedral to celebrate and give thanks for the English victory (→6/12).

Wales, November. William Morgan completes his Welsh translation of the Bible.

London. Timothy Bright, a clergyman, publishes *Characterie*, the first system of shorthand in England.

London. William Byrd, the composer, publishes *Psalmes, Sonnets and Songs*.

'Enterprise of England' is launched

Fleet is commanded by a reluctant Sidonia

Madrid, February
The duke of Medina Sidonia has been appointed commander of the Armada, or invasion fleet, as a replacement for the marquis of Santa Cruz, a recent victim of the typhus epidemic now ravaging the Spanish fleet. He is a highly efficient administrator who won King Philip II's gratitude by saving Cadiz from Sir Francis Drake when he set out to "singe the king of Spain's beard" last year [*see report on page 481*]. Medina Sidonia is, however, reluctant to take command. He wrote to the king begging to be excused, pleading lack of naval experience.

When Philip refused, he wrote again, arguing that the expedition was ill-conceived. This letter was intercepted by the king's advisers who then blackmailed the duke by threatening to leak his letter and make him appear a coward (→27).

Lord Howard of Effingham.

English navy ready to take on Spanish

Plymouth, February
Sir Francis Drake has persuaded Lord Howard of Effingham, the lord admiral, to concentrate the fleet at Plymouth. He will then be able to strike out against the Spanish Armada, or invasion fleet, and harry it as it sails up the Channel, rather than wait for it off the Flemish ports, where the Spanish are planning to embark the battle-hardened soldiers of the duke of Parma.

A running battle will suit the English ships. Although outnumbered by the Spanish, they are well designed fighting ships, fast and heavily armed. Their crews, all seamen, have been trained to work their guns in broadsides, while the Spanish, mostly soldiers, fire their cannon only once before preparing to board. The English intend to hammer their enemies at close range and then slip away before they can be boarded (→26/6).

Despite confusion Armada sets sail

Lisbon, 20 May
The Spanish Armada sailed down the river Tagus today under the leadership of the duke of Medina Sidonia in the great flagship *San Martin de Portugal*. The 132 ships of the Armada, carrying 30,000 men, are a motley collection of warships, hulks, armed merchantmen, grain ships and oared galleys. They are now heading north to rendezvous with Alexander Farnese, the duke of Parma, off the Netherlands. Philip II's "Enterprise of England" is under way at last.

Medina Sidonia has done an extraordinary job in sorting out the fleet's logistics. He has restored morale, ensured that each ship has charts and pilotage instructions, seen to the proper stowage of provisions and attempted to standardize guns and ammunition. Yet problems remain: he cannot transport enough food, and his ships find it hard to keep station (→25/7).

Sir Francis Drake.

The duke of Medina Sidonia.

Reserve army to be based near London

London, 26 June
Hasty preparations are being made by the government to resist the Spaniards if they manage to land on the Channel coast. County militias are to deploy one third of their men to oppose a landing on the beaches and another third to attack them as they march inland, with the rest being sent to join a reserve army based south of London. The capital has been ordered to arm 10,000 men, but although the men are willing they do not have adequate modern arms to be sure of defending the city against well-equipped, well-trained Spanish regulars who are renowned throughout Europe.

If the Armada evaded the English ships and landed its soldiers, the English army would be hard pressed to stop them capturing London, and Queen Elizabeth would be in great danger (→19/7).

Alexander Farnese of Parma.

Devastating defeat is inflicted on Spanish Armada

The Spanish are forced to flee in a desperate bid to reach safety after the English fireships attacked and destroyed much of the enemy fleet.

Armada is smashed by English fireships

Channel, 3 August
The Armada, still 100 ships strong, is being driven up the North Sea by strong south-westerly winds with English ships snapping at its heels as they have done ever since the Armada was first sighted off the Lizard in all its awesome power.

The English ships, led by Lord Howard of Effingham in the *Ark Royal*, were ordered out of Plymouth to "pluck the feathers" of the Spaniards as they advanced in a close-packed crescent array up the Channel to rendezvous with the duke of Parma and his Flanders army for the assault on England.

This tactic had little success, and as the Armada approached the vulnerable Isle of Wight, Lord Howard divided the English fleet into four squadrons led by himself, Sir Francis Drake, John Hawkins and Martin Frobisher. While three of the squadrons denied the Spaniards entry into the Solent, Drake unleashed a furious attack on the crescent's right wing. It was a decisive move, forcing the Armada further along the Channel. The English fleet, short of powder and shot, followed the Spaniards for the next three days while Medina Sidonia tried to make contact with the duke of Parma, but Parma's small transports had no escorts, and he was not prepared to put to sea until the English had been beaten.

Frustrated, Medina Sidonia lay at anchor off Calais. It was now that the English unleashed their most dreaded weapon, sending fireships in among the close-packed Spanish ships. The Spaniards panicked as the blazing ships, filled with pitch and with their guns double-shotted to explode in the flames, bore down on them. They cut their anchor cables and fled.

Medina Sidonia strove valiantly to bring order to his scattered fleet, but it was driven further to the east, and a fierce eight-hour battle was fought along the Flemish coast, off Gravelines. Then the wind began to blow, and, despite its admiral's efforts, the mighty Spanish Armada had been defeated (→9).

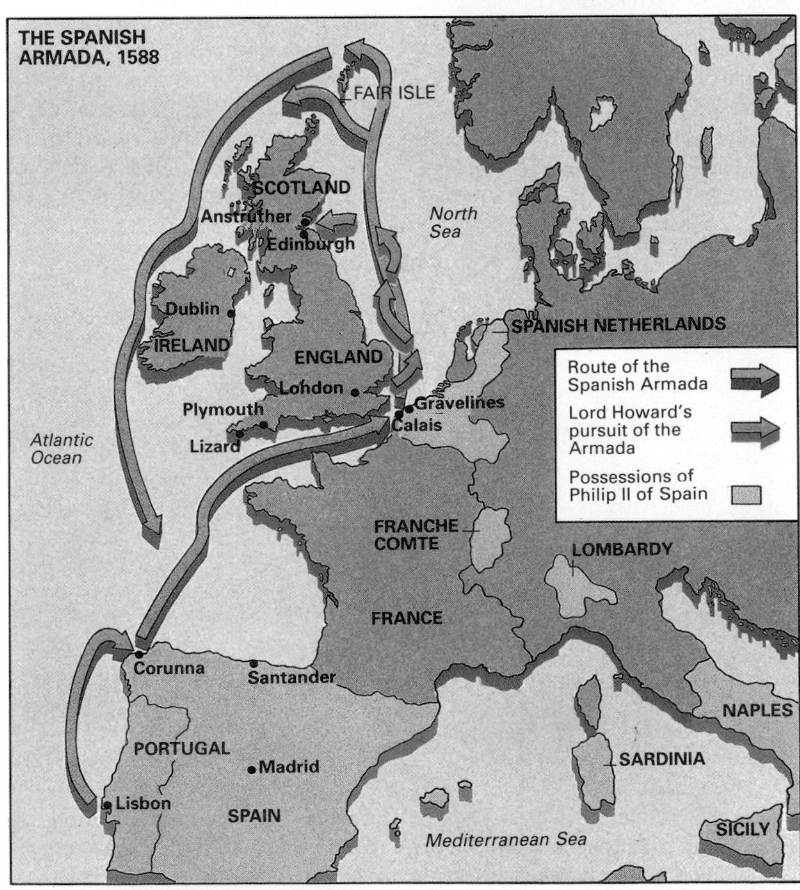

The Armada was engaged three times before the final action off Gravelines.

Ireland's 'rash' lord deputy is recalled

Ireland, 17 February
Sir John Perrot, the lord deputy, has been dismissed and recalled to London. A man of fierce temper, he was accused by Queen Elizabeth of "rash, unadvised journeys" into Ulster. Perrot, who considers himself an illegitimate child of the queen's own father, Henry VIII, once called her a "base bastard piss-kitchen" in front of the privy council. Perrot has failed in his aim to impose the "composition" land tax, part of his plan entirely to reform Ireland. He alienated everyone – Catholics, over the oath of supremacy, and Protestants, over his wish to turn St Patrick's Cathedral into a university (→30/6).

Elizabeth inspires troops at Tilbury

Elizabeth boosts the troops' morale.

Tilbury, Essex, 9 August
The first round in the war against the Spanish Armada may have gone to England, but the duke of Parma is still loading his army onto invasion barges, and England's captains fear that the Armada could put into Norwegian ports to refit and return to the fight. Queen Elizabeth therefore delivered a rallying cry today to the 20,000 men waiting here under the earl of Leicester to take on the Spanish.

She said: "I know I have the body of a weak and feeble woman, but I have the heart and stomach of a king, and of a king of England too, and think foul scorn that Parma or Spain or any prince of Europe should dare invade the borders of my realm, to which, rather than any dishonour shall grow by me, I myself will take up arms ... By your valour in the field, we shall shortly have a famous victory over these enemies of my God, of my kingdom and of my people."

Closely guarded against attempted assassination by Catholic fanatics, the queen had sailed down the Thames yesterday and dined with the earl of Leicester in his pavilion. This morning, riding a grey horse and carrying a marshal's baton, she rode through the ranks of pikemen and musketeers assembled on a flat expanse of ground beneath their fortified ridge to deliver the emotional and stirring rallying-cry to her troops (→11/9).

Anglicans infuriated by puritan's scorn

London, October
Churchmen are furious over some scurrilous pamphlets, signed by one "Martin Marprelate", which attack clergy of the Church of England – especially the bishops (whence the name of "mar-prelate"). It is, apparently, the irreverent, mocking style that has provoked clerical apoplexy as much as the content.

Martin Marprelate, whose pro-puritan tracts started to appear last year, eschews mere dry ecclesiastical debate. His *Epistle to the Terrible Priests* is, for example, a lively and personal assault on John Bridges, the dean of Salisbury and a supporter of Archbishop Whitgift. "Master Bridges was a very patch and a dunce while he was in Cambridge," writes Marprelate.

The government is torturing people to find out who the author is. But the tracts have also upset puritan leaders. One, Thomas Cartwright, fears that they will lead to puritans being branded as dangerous troublemakers (→2/1589).

The Suffolk-born explorer Thomas Cavendish arrives at the Ladrones, a group of islands in the western Pacific. On 10 September 1588 he returned to Plymouth after a two-year circumnavigation of the world (→5/1592).

Despite defeat Spain vows to continue war

Beset by storms, and battle weary, the valiant Spanish attempt to fight on.

North Sea, 6 December 1588
The inhabitants of Anstruther, in Fife, are hosts today to some 260 Spanish sailors from the Armada flagship *El Gran Grifon*, which ran aground on Fair Isle in September. The sailors, described as "for the most part young beardless men", are being given food and shelter while their repatriation is negotiated. Their experience, although grim, could have been worse.

Of the 132 proud ships that set out only 60 have returned to Spain, their crews dying of thirst and hunger. More than 11,000 men have perished. Stragglers are being generously treated on the orders of Philip II, in marked contrast to the treatment of sick and wounded English seamen left to rot by Elizabeth's celebrating courtiers.

Yet Philip means to continue the war, while Elizabeth plans to send Sir Francis Drake to destroy the remnant of the Armada. He will not find many surviving vessels. The great storm that struck the fleet as it rounded Scotland and headed home past Ireland wrecked more ships than the English fleet destroyed (→8/4/89).

1589

London, February. The Anglican cleric Richard Bancroft causes a stir with a sermon at St Paul's declaring that bishops govern the church by a divine right (→ 9/1589).

Plymouth, 8 April. Sir Francis Drake and Sir John Norris set sail with 150 ships and 15,000 men; their intention is to distress the Spanish and if possible to put the pretender Don Antonio on the Portuguese throne (→ 7/1589).

Grampian, 17 April. King James VI subdues Catholic rebels at the river Dee outside Aberdeen (→ 27/12/91).

Ireland, May. Investigations begin into the progress of the Munster plantation scheme (→ 23/12).

France, 22 July. Henry of Navarre, the Protestant heir to the French throne, is proclaimed king by his troops following the murder of the Catholic Henry III (→ 12/1589).

Lancashire, September. The secret printing press of Martin Marprelate, the writer whose recent satirical propaganda lampoons bishops specifically and the Church of England generally, is found when the cart transporting it is involved in an accident (→ 13/5/91).

Connacht, 23 December. Sir William Fitzwilliam, the lord deputy, begins a campaign to try to restore order (→ 14/3/90).

Netherlands, December. Sir Francis Vere, who succeeded Peregrine, Lord Willoughby, as commander-in-chief, inflicts a major defeat on a 3,000-strong Italo-Spanish force (→ 1/1590).

London. William Davison, Queen Elizabeth's former secretary of state, is released after two years in the Tower.

Bath. Sir John Harington, a godson of the queen, instals the first flushing lavatory in his home at Kelston (→ 1596).

England. Jane Anger publishes *A Protection for Women*, a pamphlet defending the honesty and integrity of women (→ c.1590).

Nottingham. The Reverend William Lee, a fellow of King's College, Cambridge, who was refused the patronage of the queen and the London city merchants for the development of his hosiery-knitting machine, opens a stocking factory in Calverton.

London. William Byrd, the composer, publishes *Cantiones Sacrae* [*Sacred Vocal Music*].

Drake returns from Portuguese fiasco

Plymouth, July

Sir Francis Drake's battered ships have returned with news of total failure. Nearly half the 15,000 men have been killed or died. The main aim, to wipe out the remains of the Spanish fleet, was not even attempted. Instead Drake attempted a coup in Portugal to make Don Antonio king. His attack on Lisbon failed. He then sailed for the Azores, but gales stopped him getting plunder. Queen Elizabeth, who herself put up £20,000 and some ships, is not amused (→ 9/1589).

Melancholy mood is the latest fashion

London

Over the last ten years or so Queen Elizabeth's courtiers have been eagerly adopting the latest fashion from Italy – melancholy. They are to be introspective and depressed and utter deep sighs of unrequited ardour. Italy has long fascinated the English. Many have been delighted, for instance, by Baldassare Castiglione's *Il Cortegiano* [*The Courtier*], translated in 1561. Castiglione lists the skills and virtues that the man about court needs and proposes a radical new idea: that people can create personalities for themselves.

Melancholy young man (Hilliard).

Scots king marries Anne of Denmark

James VI: an ardent suitor.

Princess Anne: now a queen.

Oslo, 23 November

Scandinavia has been thrilled by the romantic dash with which the 23-year-old James VI of Scotland has wooed and married Princess Anne, the younger daughter of Frederick II of Denmark.

When Anne was stranded here by winter weather, while on her journey to Scotland, James braved the terrible North Sea and crossed to join her. Writing passionate, if rather unmemorable, poetry during the voyage, the Scottish king rushed from the quayside into the Norwegian palace "boots and all" to meet his 14-year-old bride.

Overwhelmed by her beauty, he decided to marry at once. The ceremony in the hall of the old bishop's palace in Oslo was marred only by the fate of four negroes hired to dance artistically in the snow: all died of pneumonia (→ 1/5/90).

England gives support to Huguenot king

London, September

Now that victory over the Spanish Armada has established English control of the seas, Queen Elizabeth is concentrating all her attention on the land war in Europe.

Although the Huguenot [Protestant] Henry of Navarre succeeded to the French throne last July, his position is far from secure. Civil war is raging in France, with Philip II of Spain and the Catholic League giving powerful support to the Catholics. Lord Willoughby is gathering 4,000 men to fight in Picardy, Normandy and Brittany, where the Catholics are very strong.

Elizabeth is also planning to aid the Dutch, to help them to fight off Philip's Army of Flanders. Above all she wants to keep the Channel ports in friendly hands (→ 1/1590).

Mapmaker recalls world-wide voyages

London

The English love to read stories of exploration and voyages to the new worlds, and one of the best of such books has just been published, the *Principal Navigations, Voyages and Discoveries of the English Nation*. It is by Richard Hakluyt, who studied navigation and map-making at Oxford and has compiled and edited these *Voyages* from mariners' descriptions and ships' logs. He is already at work enlarging it to three volumes. Most of his adventures are recorded at first hand (→ 1602).

Women hanged at Chelmsford, Essex, in 1589 for witchcraft – an increasing focus for concern.

1590 - 1591

England, January 1590. Lord Willoughby returns from campaigning for Henry IV of France (→ 3/1591).

Ireland, 14 March 1590. The lord deputy, Sir William Fitzwilliam, campaigns against Brian O'Rourke, the lord of Leitrim (→ 3/8/91).

Leith, Lothian, 1 May 1590. King James VI returns from Norway with his new wife, formerly Princess Anne of Denmark (→ 15/4/91).

London, 1590. Sir Philip Sidney's pastoral romance *Arcadia* is published four years after his death (→ 1593).

London, 1590. Edmund Spenser publishes the first three volumes of *The Faerie Queen*, an allegorical poem containing many contemporary references (→ 1593).

Dieppe, March 1591. Sir Roger Williams leads 600 men to aid Henry IV of France (→ 3/8).

Westminster, 13 May 1591. A group of puritan ministers, identified in the search for the "Marprelate" tracts, is accused of sedition by the star chamber (→ 29/5/93).

Whitehall, 20 May 1591. Robert Cecil, the son of William Cecil, Lord Burghley, is knighted (→ 8/1591).

Plymouth, May 1591. Lord Thomas Howard and Sir Richard Grenville set out to intercept Spanish treasure fleets in the Azores (→ 9/1591).

Edinburgh, 21 June 1591. Francis Hepburn, the earl of Bothwell, escapes from his imprisonment in the castle (→ 27/12).

Dieppe, 3 August 1591. Robert Devereux, the earl of Essex, lands with 3,400 men to aid Henry IV of France (→ 1/1592).

Ireland, 3 August 1591. In order to ally himself with an English military family, Hugh O'Neill, the earl of Tyrone elopes with and marries Mabel, the daughter of Nicholas Bagenal, the commissioner for Ulster (→ 3/11).

London, August 1591. Sir Robert Cecil joins the privy council.

London, 3 November 1591. Brian O'Rourke is executed at Tyburn; he sought refuge in Tyrconnell and then Scotland but was handed over to Queen Elizabeth (→ 26/12).

London, 20 November 1591. Sir Christopher Hatton, the lord chancellor, dies.

Charity fund set up for injured sailors

Chatham, Kent, 1590

Admirals Howard, Hawkins and Drake have set up a new fund for "poor sailors maimed in the navy". A small deduction is to be made from seamen's wages and deposited in a large locked chest at Chatham dockyard. It will provide pensions and compensation for the injured.

Howard has been fighting a long campaign for government help. Last September he pointed to the hundreds dying on crowded ships: "It would grieve any man's heart to see them that had served so valiantly die so miserably." So far the government has provided £180.

Drake's men battle for their lives.

Pioneer settlers disappear in New World

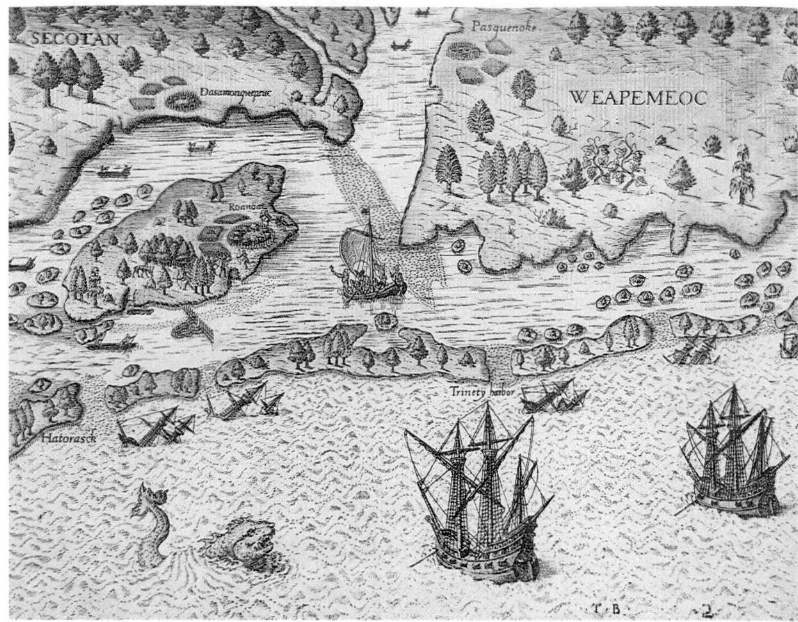

John White, the governor, sails into the harbour at Roanoke Island.

Virginia, 17 August 1590

John White, the governor of Roanoke Island, arrived today at the spot where he left 100 settlers, among them his baby granddaughter Virginia, three years ago. The high wooden palisade of the settlement, founded in 1584, still stands, but all the houses and cottages inside have been dismantled. There were no signs of life.

Some iron bars and pigs of lead were found, as well as, buried in a ditch, five chests containing framed pictures, maps and armour. The only clue to the mystery is the word "Croatoan" carved on a post at the entrance. White says that the settlers were thinking of moving, and he expected them to leave such a clue. Croatoan is an Indian village some 50 miles (80km) away.

It is possible that the settlers were led there by Indians under their chief Manteo, whose home village it is; perhaps it was thought to be safer for them. White will have to wait before finding out, however; bad weather is likely to stop him moving until spring (→ 2/1607).

Queen's spymaster dies deeply in debt

Surrey, 6 April 1590

The most important achievements of Sir Francis Walsingham – who died at Barnes, near Richmond Palace, today – are shrouded in mystery. As secretary of state to Queen Elizabeth for 17 years he quietly built up an impressive secret service comprising over 50 spies in Europe and at home, as well as hundreds of informal contacts. His particular skill was in turning Catholic spies to work for Protestant interests.

He began by using his own money, but recently the thrifty queen had given £2,000 a year to help – a sure sign of how much she valued his work. None the less his estate is said to be deep in debt.

Nobleman 'catalogues' his art collection

Lumley Castle, Durham, 1590

For the first time in England a nobleman's art collection has been catalogued during his lifetime, and the pictures labelled with their titles and artists' names. Lord Lumley got the idea in Florence, where he was sent in 1566 to recover money lent to the Medici family by Henry VIII. He was greatly impressed by the Medici art collections and statuary. Since then he has commissioned portraits of his past family and notable contemporaries. He had the first equestrian statue in England made, a painted wooden carving of Edward III which stands in the great hall of the castle. He also has paintings by Hans Holbein. All are listed in a sumptuous inventory, the *Red Velvet Book*.

King Edward III on horseback: the first equestrian statue in England.

Sensational evidence in witchcraft trial

Lothian, 15 April 1591
Evidence put before a trial has accused Francis Stewart Hepburn – the earl of Bothwell and one of the country's greatest magnates – of summoning the powers of darkness against King James VI. This astonishing claim comes from Richie Graham, identified as a wizard of a coven active in North Berwick.

Graham claims that in May last year the earl took part in a "black mass" on the shore at North Berwick – part of Bothwell's lands – while the king was sailing home from Denmark with his new bride, the 14-year-old Princess Anne of Denmark. Near the Bass Rock, off North Berwick, James's ships were caught in a ferocious storm, during which James claims that he saw witches in the guise of hares bobbing about on sieves. To the king's mind, the storm was raised by the witches. After arriving in Leith, he had anyone in the area suspected of witchcraft arrested. Some named Bothwell as a fellow occultist.

As a result of this the king and several of his men went down to North Berwick and waited secretly at the church of St Andrew, where Bothwell and his coven were said to meet. There they witnessed 94 bare-breasted witches and six wizards dancing and cavorting around in the church and kissing the exposed backside of their leader – whom James took to be Bothwell. But when the king's men swooped on the satanists, the leader – whoever he was – managed to escape.

Bothwell, who is denying everything, has been ordered to give himself up and face charges. Although he has attracted suspicion through his study of esoteric science while in Italy , there are political reasons for hunting him down. He was involved in the Catholic rebellion of 1589 and is a sworn enemy of the chancellor, Maitland (→21/6).

The trial hears how the devil lured Bothwell and others to a "black mass".

'Wizard' earl in murder attempt on king

Edinburgh, 27 December 1591
King James VI narrowly escaped death when Francis Hepburn, the earl of Bothwell, cornered him at Holyrood Palace today.

Bothwell was jailed in Edinburgh Castle earlier this year following charges of witchcraft against him [*see report above*], but in June he escaped and has nearly turned the tables on James. With a band of followers he burst into Holyrood and chased James into one of the palace towers. Not to be thwarted, Bothwell set fire to the door, which his men battered with hammers for good measure. The chancellor, Maitland, also caught unawares, had the same treatment meted out to him. Luckily for both, a crowd rushed up from the city and forced Bothwell to flee (→7/2/92).

High drama becomes a popular spectator sport amid the lowlife of south London

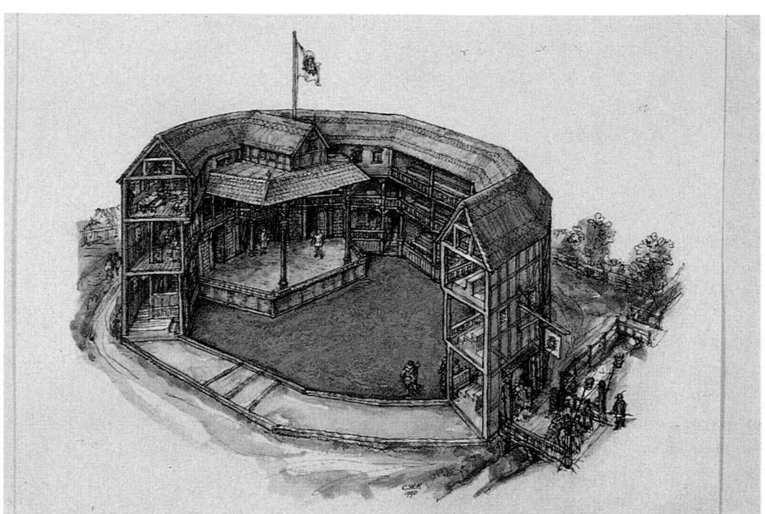

The Rose theatre in London: drama amid the bear-pits and brothels.

London, c.1590
Some 20 years ago actors were regarded by law as in the same class as "rogues, vagabonds and sturdy beggars". Since 1572, however, when legislation was passed requiring groups of players to be licensed, a new breed of professional has emerged and play-going has become the rage.

The drama on stage unfolds.

At first, dramas were staged in the courtyards of inns, but London now has three theatres. In 1576 James Burbage acquired land at Shoreditch to construct a wooden polygonal auditorium with galleries and a stage thrust into the central open-air space for standing spectators. He called it, simply, the Theatre. Another, the Curtain, went up next door. In 1586 they were joined by the Rose, built among Bankside's bear-baiting pits and brothels, as the City of London bans performances within its walls.

The companies of players all have noblemen as patrons, such as the earls of Pembroke or Worcester. The leading playwrights include 26-year-old Christopher Marlowe, who has recently finished two dramatic epics, *Tamburlaine the Great* and *The Jew of Malta*. Among the most promising young actors is Edward Alleyn, who is associated with "the Lord Admiral's Men", a company named after its patron Lord Howard of Effingham, the lord high admiral.

A player: no longer a vagabond.

Earl of Hertford is back in favour after his hospitality on Elizabeth's royal 'progress'

Cowdray Castle, where the queen and the earl were reconciled: a later picture.

Hampshire, 23 September 1591
The second of this summer's progresses, or royal journeys (the first was to Cowdray Castle in Sussex), has marked Elizabeth's reconciliation with Edward Seymour, the earl of Hertford. The queen once imprisoned him for secretly marrying Catherine, the sister of the executed usurper Lady Jane Grey. Yet three days ago, when Elizabeth arrived at Hertford's home at Odiham, near Elvetham, all that seemed forgotten. While musicians played a *pavane* by Thomas Morley the earl escorted the royal party to the magnificent ivy-roofed palace of wood built for the occasion. Three days of feasts, pageants, fireworks and music followed. As the queen left today a choir sang "Come Again, faire Nature's Treasure".

Elizabeth enjoys the gracious hospitality of her host, the earl of Hertford.

Howard's fleet returns from the Azores

Plymouth, September 1591
Lord Thomas Howard has returned home greatly chastened after a brush with Spanish men-of-war in the Azores – but with a story of great heroism by Sir Richard Grenville and his crew on board the *Revenge*. Howard was hoping to plunder Spanish treasure ships but withdrew when told of the men-of-war. He and Grenville were separated, and the *Revenge*, with 150 men, engaged 15 Spanish ships and some 5,000 men in hand-to-hand combat lasting 15 hours. Grenville was captured and taken aboard the Spanish flagship, the *San Pablo*, where he later died (→ 9/1/96).

The last brave fight of the "Revenge", from a painting by Charles de Lacy.

O'Donnell escapes from Dublin Castle

Ireland, 26 December 1591
Hugh Roe O'Donnell, the son of Hugh O'Donnell, the lord of Tyrconnell, has escaped from Dublin Castle where he had been a prisoner since 1587. It is rumoured that Sir William Fitzwilliam, the lord deputy, was bribed to let him escape. O'Donnell is expected to return home and succeed his father, who wants to retire from public life. This will annoy the English, who hoped that an unstable O'Donnell lordship would weaken the clan's position in Connacht (→ 2/1592).

Tough measures to deal with puritans

London, 28 July 1591
Ten puritan clergymen hauled before the court of star chamber today and accused of treason are victims of Archbishop John Whitgift's determination to impose ecclesiastical uniformity. The veteran Thomas Cartwright is accused of renouncing ordination by bishops, of establishing a presbyterian church while chaplain to the Merchant Adventurers abroad, and of preaching without a licence.

Cartwright and the others have been meeting in small groups – taken as proof that they seek a church governed by presbyters, or lay elders. It is bad luck for them that two over-enthusiastic admirers, Edmund Copinger and Henry Arthington, decided to parade in Cheapside, hailing William Hackett, an illiterate simpleton, as the new messiah and saying that Queen Elizabeth had been deposed. This absurdity confirmed the church authorities' worst suspicions. Hackett has been executed; doubtless others will follow (→ 6/4/93).

Fewer working women are marrying as hard times start to bite

England, c.1590
For most women, marriage is unavoidable. Honoria Denny, when about to marry James, Lord Hay, was told: "All the time of your life you have been gathering for this day." But one out of ten adult women never marry, a figure that is increasing amongst the poor, who now face hard times and low wages. For the upper classes, marriages are mostly decided by parents on property and money grounds, and girls marry young. As Joan Hayward, the daughter of a lord mayor of London, said when she was married at the age of 16: "I do put my trust in God and in my good father." Working women may have more choice. Many do not marry until their late twenties, when they have some savings. Although they too may be influenced by families and friends, they can ignore them. One Rosa Clarke, for instance, bluntly told her fiancé after friends had opposed their union: "You are the man I make choice of and therefore I do not care for their goodwills or consent" (→ 10/1599).

1592

England, January. Queen Elizabeth recalls Robert Devereux, the earl of Essex, from his position of commander of English forces in Rouen (→ 2/1592).

Co Donegal, February. Hugh Roe O'Donnell expels Captain Humphrey Willis, the English sheriff of Fermanagh (→ 3/5).

Rouen, February. Reinforcements of 1,600 men arrive from England (→ 2/1593).

Dublin, 3 March. A royal charter founds the College of the Holy and Undivided Trinity.→

Connacht, 3 May. Hugh Roe O'Donnell is inaugurated as lord of Tyrconnell and chief of the O'Donnells on the resignation of his father, Hugh (→ 3/8).

Atlantic Ocean, May. Thomas Cavendish, the navigator, dies on his disastrous second round-the-world trip.

Fife, 28 June. Francis Hepburn, the earl of Bothwell, attacks Falkland Palace but is unsuccessful in his attempt to capture King James VI (→ 1/1/93).

Dundalk, Co Louth, 3 August. Hugh Roe O'Donnell, the lord of Tyrconnell, submits to the lord deputy, Sir William Fitzwilliam (→ 4/1593).

London, 7 August. Sir Walter Raleigh, a former favourite of Queen Elizabeth, is imprisoned in the Tower after seducing and breaking a marriage promise to Bess Throckmorton, one of the queen's maids in waiting (→ 9/1592).

Oxford, 28 September. Elizabeth makes a visit to the university.

Ireland, December. Catholic bishops hold a synod in Tyrconnell arranged by Hugh Roe O'Donnell, the lord of Tyrconnell.

London. Robert Greene, a dramatist and pamphleteer, one of "the University Wits", dies; earlier this year he published a semi-fictional autobiography called *Greene's Groatsworth of Wit bought with a Million of Repentance*.

London. Thomas Nashe, a colleague of Robert Greene, publishes *Pierce Pennilesse His Supplication to the Devil*, a satirical pamphlet.

London. The plague kills an estimated 15,000 people this year (→ 20/5/1601).

Moray murdered by a Catholic enemy

Edinburgh, 7 February

Extraordinary news of the killing of James Stewart, the earl of Moray, by the Catholic earl of Huntly has sent the city into a ferment. Rumours from the north say that another Huntly foe, John Campbell of Cawdor, has also been murdered. Moray had been outlawed in December for helping the rebel earl of Bothwell, but he was at his castle at Donibristle on the Firth of Forth ready to make his peace with King James VI. Someone – and many suspect the king – told Huntly, who attacked the castle and murdered Moray (→ 28/6).

'Trinity' college to be set up in Dublin

Dublin, 3 March 1592

A royal charter has established a university in Dublin, to be known as the "College of the Holy and Undivided Trinity". It will provide "for the education, formation, and instruction of youths and students in the arts and faculties". Its principal function, however, will be to train an indigenous Protestant clergy, since it is thought that the best way to make converts to the established church is by using native preachers. The lord mayor and corporation have chosen All Hallows, an Augustinian monastery granted to the city by Henry VIII, as the site of the university (→ 1594).

Raleigh ordered to recapture treasure

Walter Raleigh: a royal release.

Dartmouth, Devon, September

Sir Walter Raleigh, imprisoned in the Tower last month, has been freed by Queen Elizabeth and sent here with the task of recovering the valuables looted from the Spanish treasure ship *Madre de Dios*, which was seized by English privateers who were backed by Elizabeth. By the time the ship arrived most of the cargo, estimated to be worth about £800,000, had vanished into the pockets of the crew.

The seamen ran amok when another of the venture's backers, the earl of Cumberland, tried to recover the loot. The queen then sent for Raleigh, whom she had imprisoned for seducing Bess Throckmorton, one of her maids of honour. The seamen gave him a rousing welcome but held on to most of the treasure (→ 6/2/95).

Financial success for Lord Burghley

Westminster, 24 October

Queen Elizabeth's chief minister, William Cecil, Lord Burghley, has skilfully resolved a long-running dispute with the counties over purveyance, the supply of foodstuffs to the royal household. The officers making the purchases, the purveyors, drive a hard bargain, often offering only half of the goods' market value. Burghley, with a committee of privy councillors, proposed that each county should make a comprehensive agreement each year to cover all the goods to be supplied. The counties sent delegates to Westminster to endorse the deal. Only Norfolk has objected; the gentry were ready to cooperate, but local puritans mistrust central government.

Bakers of York supply the queen.

Elizabeth recalls Essex from unsuccessful campaign in Rouen

Henry IV of France leads the charge in his fight with the Catholic League.

London, February

The impetuous 24-year-old earl of Essex has finally returned home with the remnants of an expedition force which lost ten men through sickness for every one in battle. Only after persistent pleading from Essex had Queen Elizabeth allowed him to take 3,400 men to join other English troops helping the Protestant Henry IV in his struggles with the Catholic League. They were supposed to besiege Rouen, but there was little action; yet Essex rewarded 24 of his officers with knighthoods. A furious Elizabeth ordered him to return (→ 2/1593).

1593 - 1594

London, 25 February 1593. Robert Devereux, the earl of Essex, joins the privy council.

Aberdeen, February 1593. King James VI marches on the city (→ 24/7).

Brittany, February 1593. Twelve hundred English troops arrive to aid Henry IV of France (→ 7/1593).

London, 6 April 1593. The Protestant activists Henry Barrow and John Greenwood are hanged for sedition (→ 29/5).

Ireland, April 1593. Hugh Roe O'Donnell, the lord of Tyrconnell, sends the Catholic Archbishop James O'Hely of Tuam to treat with Philip II of Spain (→ 2/2/94).

London, April 1593. William Shakespeare, a poet and playwright, publishes his poem *Venus and Adonis*, dedicated to his patron, the earl of Southampton (→ 5/1594).

London, 29 May 1593. John Penry, the radical Protestant, is hanged for his connections with the "Marprelate" tracts.→

England, July 1593. Queen Elizabeth is relieved when Henry IV of France converts to Catholicism; it will save on defence and give England an ally against Spain (→ 7/1601).

Aberdeen, 1593. George Keith, the earl marischal, founds Marischal College.

London, 1593. George Gifford, an Essex minister, publishes a *Dialogue concerning Witches* (→ 7/1597).

Co Fermanagh, 2 February 1594. The English, led by John Dowdall and George Bingham, capture Enniskillen (→ 16/5).

Lothian, 19 February 1594. Queen Anne gives birth to a son and heir, Henry.

Edinburgh, 3 April 1594. Francis Hepburn, the earl of Bothwell, fails to seize the city (→ 3/10).

Ireland, 16 May 1594. Sir William Russell is appointed lord deputy (→ 6/1594).

Co Fermanagh, June 1594. Hugh Roe O'Donnell, the lord of Tyrconnell, besieges Enniskillen (→ 30/8).

Grampian, 3 October 1594. Catholic rebels led by the earl of Huntly defeat the earl of Argyll, the king's lieutenant, at Glenlivet (→ 4/1595).

Low Countries, 1594. The College of St Patrick is founded by Irish Catholics at Douai (→ 1602).

Scots Catholics in plot to oust king

Scotland, 1 January 1593
Tortured, the Scottish Catholic George Ker has confessed to a plot that seems to implicate the Catholic earl of Huntly and two other earls, Errol and Angus, in a plot to incite a Spanish invasion of Scotland and overthrow the king. Ker was arrested as he boarded a ship for Spain, but he was found to be carrying nothing more incriminating than several blank sheets of paper signed by Huntly, Errol and Angus. Now he has confessed that these were to be filled in with the details and terms that the earls demanded for aiding the invasion (→ 2/1593).

Government's puritan critic is executed

Elizabeth: a powerful force.

Westminster, 29 May 1593
One of the government's most troublesome opponents, the puritan John Penry, has been hanged after a trial on the doubtful charge of writing with intent to cause rebellion. Penry's pamphlets, printed on presses that were constantly kept on the move, claimed to expose rampant evils in the Church of England. Puritans in parliament have also been causing trouble with complaints of repression; after the most recent debate Queen Elizabeth sent for the speaker and forbade further discussion. Members went on to upset the queen still more by holding up taxes for war. She has now dissolved parliament (→ 12/1595).

Playwright stabbed to death in pub brawl

Deptford, London, 30 May 1593
England's top playwright, Christopher Marlowe, met a violent death here tonight during a mysterious quarrel at a tavern. He was stabbed above the right eye with his own dagger by Ingram Frizar, who took hold of the weapon after Marlowe had allegedly attacked his companions, wounding one of them. Marlowe died cursing and blaspheming. He had been a government spy for Sir Francis Walsingham, and his assailants had secret service links. His death is seen as a fitting end to a life of atheism. He was under arrest and due to appear before the privy council. At 23 he revolutionized English drama with his blank verse epic *Tamburlaine the Great* and followed it with *Dr Faustus* and *Edward II*. He was only 29.

Mary Herbert publishes Sidney's 'Arcadia'

Wilton, Wiltshire, 1593
Mary Herbert, the countess of Pembroke and one of England's great patrons of literature, has published a revised version of *Arcadia* by Sir Philip Sidney, her late brother. This elaborate story of lovers, which first appeared in 1590, was dedicated to Mary and in fact written at her house, Wilton, for her and her circle to enjoy. It includes songs and sonnets that the lover, Astrophel, addresses to his Stella, such as this one on true love:

My true love hath my heart
and I have his,
By just exchange one for
another giv'n;
I hold his dear and mine he
cannot miss,
There never was a better
bargain driv'n.

Literary patron: Mary Herbert.

Mary Herbert's influence on the literary scene is enormous. Her circle includes, for instance, Edmund Spenser, whose as yet incomplete poem *The Faerie Queene* was published in 1590. Spenser has dedicated to Mary Herbert his *Ruins of Time*, and he has included her, as "Clorinda", in his elegiac poem for Sidney, *Astrophel* (→ 1595).

Royal anniversary is marked by tilts

Cumberland: a tilting contestant.

Windsor, 1 November 1593
Because of the outbreak of plague in London, Queen Elizabeth and her court are to remain at Windsor for the contests to mark the 35th anniversary of her accession to the throne. The tilts, as the contests are called, give courtiers the chance to win the queen's favour with elaborate and intriguing disguises. The earl of Essex once appeared as a sorrowing knight in black – an appeal to Elizabeth to forgive him for his secret marriage to Frances, the daughter of her late spymaster, Sir Francis Walsingham, and widow of Sir Philip Sidney.

Bothwell takes over at Holyrood Palace

Edinburgh, 24 July 1593
At the third attempt the earl of Bothwell has succeeded in carrying out a coup against King James VI at Holyrood Palace. Bothwell has been accused of witchcraft against the king, and James, obsessed with witches, fears him more than any man in the world and refuses to hear his pleas of innocence.

In order to get a hearing Bothwell has twice tried to take over the court. Today he succeeded, assisted by a large party of armed men and sympathetic courtiers. When James saw Bothwell enter his rooms he panicked, convinced that he would be killed, but later Bothwell agreed to withdraw from court provided that the charges against him are dismissed (→ 3/4/94).

Ulster stronghold falls to the English

Co Fermanagh, 30 August 1594
Sir William Russell, the lord deputy, has raised the siege of English forces at Enniskillen Castle, a key site in the struggle with the Ulster lords. Trouble flared last year when Hugh Maguire – the lord of Fermanagh and son-in-law of Hugh O'Neill, the earl of Tyrone – campaigned against the English, who were aiming to displace him.

Maguire took Enniskillen and rebuffed an attempt in October to win it back. In February the English recaptured Enniskillen, only to be besieged by Maguire and Hugh Roe O'Donnell, the lord of Tyrconnell, in June. On 7 August they destroyed an English supply force at the "Ford of the Biscuits" on the Arny river but have been unable to exploit that success (→ 23/8/95).

Enniskillen Castle: finally captured after being besieged by land and sea.

Earl and queen row over post for Bacon

London, 26 March 1594
In spite of his success in achieving "domestical greatness", as he puts it, the earl of Essex has found himself frustrated in his efforts to secure remunerative appointments for his admirers. The earl, a privy councillor at the age of 25, pushed Francis Bacon for the attorney-generalship but was stopped by the Cecil family. He tried to get Bacon made solicitor-general, but Elizabeth blocked the appointment. She was offended by a speech by Bacon in parliament.

Essex: frustrated by Elizabeth.

Jewish doctor tortured to death for alleged plot to kill queen

Dr Lopez caught in a conspiracy to poison and kill Queen Elizabeth.

London, February 1594
The earl of Essex has scored an unsavoury triumph by making a false accusation against Queen Elizabeth's physician, the Jewish Dr Roderigo Lopez, of plotting to poison her, and then having him castrated, disembowelled and hanged before a mob howling anti-Semitic insults. Numerous interrogations of Portuguese and Spanish agents had failed to establish Lopez's guilt; the queen had angrily rebuked Essex and dismissed him with a wave of her hand. The humiliated earl had locked himself away and sulked for two days before resolving to torture witnesses into giving evidence against Lopez.

William Shakespeare adds poems to his burgeoning reputation

London, May 1594
The publication of *The Rape of Lucrece*, following that of another long poem, *Venus and Adonis*, last year, has put the name of William Shakespeare among the foremost poets of the day. "Age I do abhor thee, youth I do adore thee," runs a line from the poem, echoing its dedication to Henry Wriothesley, the earl of Southampton, who is 20. Shakespeare has also had success with plays like *Titus Andronicus* and *The Comedy of Errors* (→ 1599).

A rare illustration to one of Shakespeare's early plays, "Titus Andronicus".

1595 - 1596

Plymouth, 6 February 1595. Sir Walter Raleigh sails to find "El Dorado" (→ 8/1595).

Scotland, April 1595. Francis Hepburn, the earl of Bothwell, flees into French exile (→ 1598).

Co Fermanagh, 15 May 1595. Hugh Maguire, the lord of Fermanagh, and Hugh Roe O'Donnell, the lord of Tyrconnell, recapture Enniskillen (→ 1/7).

Armagh City, 1 July 1595. Sir William Russell, the lord deputy, converts the cathedral into a garrison (→ 23/8).

Ireland, 23 August 1595. Tyrone and Tyrconnell offer the crown of Ireland to the Habsburg Archduke Albert, the governor of the Spanish Netherlands (→ 10/1595).

Plymouth, 28 August 1595. Sir Francis Drake and Sir John Hawkins sail for the West Indies (→ 29/1/96).

Atlantic Ocean, October 1595. A Spanish fleet en route for Ireland is lost at sea (→ 18).

Dublin, 18 October 1595. Tyrone and Tyrconnell seek peace with the Dublin government (→ 12/5/96).

London, 19 November 1595. Philip Howard, the earl of Arundel, imprisoned in the Tower since 1585 for Catholic beliefs, dies.

Puerto Rico, 1595. Sir John Hawkins is buried at sea.

England, 1595. Philip Sidney's *Apologie for Poetrie* is published (→ 1596).

London, 1595. Francis Langley, a goldsmith, builds the Swan theatre in the Paris Gardens, Bankside (→ 5/2/96).

London, 5 February 1596. The actor James Burbage is to turn an alehouse into a theatre at Blackfriars (→ summer 1599).

Scotland, February 1596. King James VI and his government attempt financial reform.

Munster, 6 July 1596. Tyrone calls for war against the English (→ 18/10).

London, July 1596. Sir Robert Cecil, the son of Lord Burghley, becomes principal royal secretary (→ 4/8/98).

Spain, 18 October 1596. A second Spanish fleet for an invasion of Ireland is wrecked in a storm off Finisterre (→ 11/1596).

Armagh City, November 1596. Tyrone attacks the English garrison (→ 7/1597).

Raleigh's expedition to Guyana returns

Raleigh seizes Trinidad from Spanish control in his search for "El Dorado".

Plymouth, August 1595
Sir Walter Raleigh has returned from a six-month voyage to South America in search of the legendary city of gold, "El Dorado", with little to show for his efforts. He sailed along the coast of Trinidad, raiding Spanish settlements, before entering the Orinoco river on the mainland. Friendly Indians advised him that because of the imminent rainy season it was better not to press on into Guyana.

Raleigh is no stranger to adventure. He has fought in both France (1569) and Ireland (1580), while in 1584 he sponsored the Virginian colony on Roanoke Island. Yet sceptics are suggesting that Raleigh, far from seeking El Dorado, spent the time hiding in Cornwall. His quartz specimens contain traces of gold, but again some doubt if they are truly from South America. Raleigh, undeterred, is planning to engage in some shameless self-publicity with a book about his voyage: *The Discovery of the Large, Rich and Beautiful Empire of Guiana*. He is, after all, as much a man of letters as of action, and has a modest reputation as a poet (→ 5/1603).

Queen makes bid to stop Cambridge row

Lambeth, London, December 1595
A theological row at Cambridge University has led Queen Elizabeth to ban publication of the so-called Lambeth Articles, approved by the archbishop of Canterbury, John Whitgift. The controversy began in April with a sermon at the university by William Barrett attacking the doctrine of predestination, which holds that God has marked out some people for salvation and the rest for damnation. Barrett, the chaplain of Gonville and Caius College, appealed to Canterbury after the university had disciplined him. Whitgift's Articles, which support belief in predestination, alarmed the queen, who said that discussion of the subject was "dangerous to weak, ignorant minds" (→ 14/12).

Adventurous life of Drake ends at sea

Panama, 29 January 1596
The navigator and adventurer Sir Francis Drake, who died this morning, has been buried at sea. It was perhaps a fitting end for the first Englishman to sail around the world. He was in his mid-50s.

Drake's final voyage, against Spanish possessions in the Americas, was meant to repeat the success of the 1577-1580 expedition, which yielded immense riches. But by the time he tried to march overland from Nombre de Dios to Panama, the Spanish had already secured their treasure. The English put to sea again, with supplies and morale running low. Sir John Hawkins, Drake's kinsman, had already died; Drake himself caught dysentery and died at 7am today (→ 4/7).

Northern Catholics lose a staunch foe

York, 14 December 1595
Henry Hastings, the fiercely puritan earl of Huntingdon and lord president of the council of the north since 1572, has died at the age of 60. After the Catholic uprising of 1569, when an attempt was made to free Mary Queen of Scots from captivity in England, he was made Mary's joint custodian. As lord president Hastings pursued a vigorous policy against Catholics in the north of England. Many are under pressure to conform to the Church of England. Puritans – seen as politically if not theologically sound – receive more lenient treatment in the north of England than in the south.

Hastings, the earl of Huntingdon.

The newest fashion is for breasts to be exposed and flaunted. It originated with the late French regent Catherine de' Medici.

Irish rebel leader gets royal pardon

Hugh O'Neill, the earl of Tyrone.

Ireland, 12 May 1596
Hugh O'Neill, the earl of Tyrone, has received a royal pardon. Declared a traitor in June of last year for leading an attack against Sir Henry Bagenal, whose forces were bringing supplies to Monaghan, he has now agreed to break off his negotiations with Spain and to abandon his efforts to establish his authority east of the river Bann.

Evidence of the earl's complicity in a widespread rebellion has been growing. The government has been aware that the Ulster lords are in touch with King Philip II of Spain, with a view to securing his support against Queen Elizabeth. It has asked for a force of 3,000 men to be sent to help it (→6/7).

King at odds with clergy in Scotland

Edinburgh, 17 December 1596
Members of the congregation of St Giles's church rushed into the streets today to demand arms to defend both their king and their church against the "papists". It is just the latest in a series of incidents in which the common people have been roused to action by inflammatory sermons and is intended as a demonstration to King James VI of the power of the clergy.

The clergy are annoyed at the king's sympathy for Catholics, and in a recent row a leading minister, Dr Andrew Melville, grabbed the king's sleeve and called him "God's sillie [weak] vassall". James was infuriated, and this and other disrespectful acts, in addition to today's demonstration, have induced him to move his capital to Linlithgow tomorrow.

Royal water closets flush with success

London, 1596
Since men of culture are expected to excel in all things, no one is surprised that Sir John Harington, a courtier, poet and translator, turns out to be a good plumber too. This year he published *The Metamorphosis of Ajax*, a humorous work with diagrams on how to build a water closet. (The title punningly refers to this – a "jacks" is a lavatory.) One such, complete with a unique flushing mechanism, is now installed at his godmother Queen Elizabeth's Richmond Palace.

English torch Cadiz

The wealthiest port in Spain falls to the combined English and Dutch fleet.

Cadiz, Spain, 4 July 1596
A combined English and Dutch fleet has dealt a heavy blow to Spain. Cadiz, perhaps the country's wealthiest port, is a smoking ruin after a fortnight of looting. The attack on the town on 20 June, led by Robert Devereux, the earl of Essex, achieved total surprise. Denied the time to escape, the Spanish had to scuttle the outward bound Indies fleet – complete with its cargo of 12 million ducats. Essex wanted to stay and keep the attention of the Spanish away from Calais, which they seized just three months ago, renewing fears in England of invasion. Yet, with supplies low and many of his men eager to return, Essex set sail today (→26/10/97).

Romantic poem praises 'Faerie Queene'

London, 1596
Edmund Spenser has become the toast of literary London following the publication of the final three volumes of his verse romance *The Faerie Queene*. No poem of such length and richness has appeared in English before. It was actually written at Kilcolman Castle, Co Cork, which the poet was granted after serving as secretary to Lord Grey de Wilton, the lord deputy of Ireland. In 1589 his friend Sir Walter Raleigh persuaded him to return to London. Spenser brought back with him the first three volumes, which he ceremoniously laid at the feet of Queen Elizabeth. The books were published the following year, to immediate acclaim.

"The Faerie Queene": a woodcut.

This long allegorical poem celebrates the chivalric virtues that culminated in King Arthur. It also glorifies the "virgin queen", "Gloriana", as the Protestant empress and saviour of the English church, reformed from the errors of Rome. Yet Spenser has said that, fundamentally, the poem shows how to "fashion a gentleman or noble person". Spenser owes this idea – that it is possible to forge one's own identity – to the Italian author Baldassare Castiglione (→1610).

Living standards for workers plummet

England and Scotland, 1596
Social unrest has risen this year in the wake of one of the worst harvests this century. It follows two previous bad harvests and is fuelling the spiralling rate of inflation – food prices have risen some 35 per cent in recent years. In November men from Enslow Hill, in Oxfordshire, toured local villages to enlist support for a march on London. The rebels were protesting against enclosures as much as at the general economic crisis. The authorities learnt of their movements, however, and arrested them.

Kent has experienced food riots at Canterbury and Hernhill, although these had no revolutionary overtones. Here the people have also been hit by the plague, which has taken a heavy toll since 1592.

The troubles have not been confined to England, however. Last winter the people of Scotland also suffered galloping inflation and a gruelling famine after heavy rains wiped out their harvest (→1598).

1597 - 1598

Borders, January 1597. An Anglo-Scottish border commission is established.

Ireland, 6 February 1597. Spanish-Irish trade is prohibited (→ 5/3).

Ireland, 5 March 1597. Thomas, Lord Burgh, replaces Sir William Russell as lord deputy (→ 7/1597).

Scotland, 23 July 1597. An earthquake hits the country (→ 29/3/1606).

Co Armagh, July 1597. Lord Burgh, the lord deputy, marches against Hugh O'Neill, the earl of Tyrone (→ 10/1597).

Bay of Biscay, October 1597. A Spanish fleet, bound for Ireland, is wrecked (→ 13).

Co Down, 13 October 1597. Lord Burgh dies suddenly of typhus at Newry (→ 29).

Plymouth, 26 October 1597. Robert Devereux, the earl of Essex, returns home after his disastrous expedition to intercept Spanish treasure ships (→ 12/1597).

Ireland, 29 October 1597. Thomas Dubh Butler, the earl of Ormond, is appointed lieutenant-general of Queen Elizabeth's army (→ 22/12).

Ireland, 22 December 1597. Having lost hope of Spanish aid, Tyrone submits to Ormond (→ 25/6/98).

London, December 1597. Queen Elizabeth makes Essex, who retired from court in October, earl marshal (→ 10/1598).

Highland, December 1597. Chiefs are summoned before the privy council to prove their right to their estates. New burghs are to be established at Kintyre, Lochaber and Lewis to "civilize" them (→ 10/1599).

Westminster, 1597. An act of parliament allows for criminals to be transported to the colonies.

Leinster, 25 June 1598. Ormond campaigns against Tyrone (→ 14/8).

London, October 1598. The earl of Essex apologizes to Elizabeth for their fierce quarrel last year (→ 12/3/99).

Dublin, November 1598. Tyrone is joined by Edmund Butler, Viscount Mountgarret, and Thomas Butler, Lord Cahir, in carrying out raids on the city (→ 12/3/99).

England, 1598. A severe famine hits the north-west (→ 11/1601).

Healing properties are to be found in all herbs and plants

London, 1 December 1597
One of the best known gardeners of the time, John Gerard, has published a *Herball* which gives much prominence to the medicinal qualities of herbs, as well as to the new vegetables which have lately been introduced into England from the Americas. Gerard has a garden in Holborn and is also in charge of Lord Burghley's garden at Cecil House in the Strand. He studied medicine and calls his book an aid to "That excellent art of Simpling, a studie for the wisest".

He devotes a whole chapter to the potato, which he claims he got from Virginia, and describes as "round as a ball, greene at first and blacke when it is ripe". He does not state how he got those which "grow and prosper in my garden". Kitchen gardens have come into fashion at great houses to grow new delicacies, such as tomatoes, apricots and artichokes. Tomatoes (introduced last year) are cultivated, says Gerard, as a curiosity. They are thought to be dangerous and aphrodisiac and are called "love apples", although in Spain they are eaten "as sauce to their meat, even as we do mustard". Rhubarb is grown as a medicinal crop, as a purgative. Most fruit is cooked long with sugar and spices before being eaten, as it is suspected of causing fever.

Witch-hunting hysteria engulfs Scotland

Women accused of witchcraft as Scotland is gripped by witch-hunting hysteria.

Scotland, July 1597
The publication by King James VI of *Demonologie*, a book on witchcraft that he has written himself, has fuelled a steadily growing witch scare that now threatens to plunge the country into hysteria. Witch hunts and trials are happening all over Scotland, with numerous accounts of confessions which were obtained under torture.

Testimonies beaten and tortured out of men, women and children contain claims of night-flying, diabolical assemblies, sex with demons and sermons preached by the devil himself. This is the second wave of a witch hunt that began in 1591. Then the king attended some of the torture sessions, in the belief that there was a demonic pact against the Lord's anointed, by which he meant himself.

The mixture of demons, witches and a plot against the king has brought urgency and a hard political edge to what might otherwise have been a fairly low-key move against people suspected of un-Christian practices (→ 1612).

Two contrasting experiments in architecture brought to fruition

The symbolic Triangular Lodge.

English Midlands, 1597
Two architectural adventures have been brought to fruition this year: Sir Thomas Tresham's Triangular Lodge and the stunning Hardwick Hall in Derbyshire. The lodge, at Tresham's Rushton Hall estate in Northamptonshire, is three storeys high and in the shape of a triangle with sides 10 metres (33 feet) long, built to mark his conversion to Catholicism. Its shape and decorative features symbolize the Holy Trinity. Hardwick Hall – built for Elizabeth, the countess of Shrewsbury – was designed by Robert Smythson, as were Longleat in Wiltshire and Wollaton in Nottinghamshire (→ 1601).

Hardwick Hall: the east front.

Rural poverty stirs up fears of unrest

Westminster, 9 February 1598
Two laws were passed today to try to stem rising rural poverty and the depopulation of the countryside. They come in the wake of the 1596 Oxfordshire "revolt", whose instigators threatened to break down enclosures and murder the gentry. The plot, which never involved more than 20 men, was betrayed, and the leaders were arrested. But the local gentry were very alarmed because of the talk of revolution.

From today all land which has been tilled for 12 consecutive years and converted to pasture during this reign must revert to tillage. The second law notes that the destruction of towns, parishes and houses of husbandry has caused many poor people to become "wanderers, idle and loose". Houses so destroyed must now be rebuilt.

Irish fight the Battle of Yellow Ford

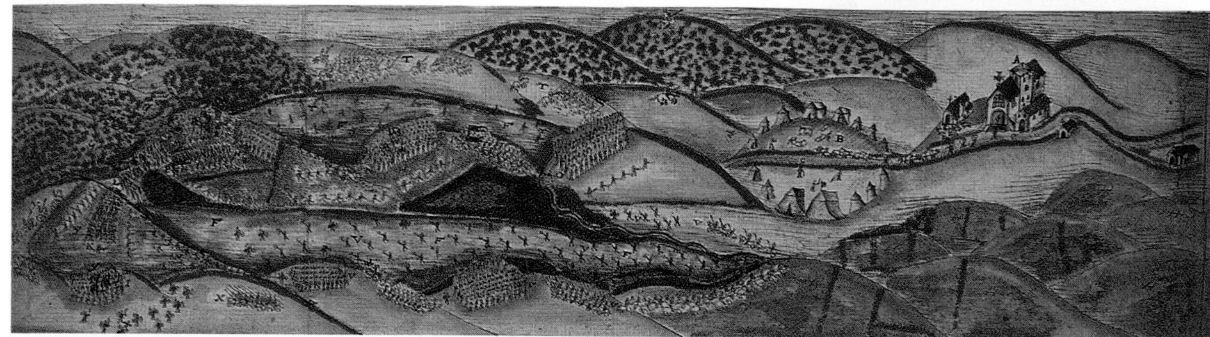

Ulster battleground: the map shows how the Irish planned their strategy for the Battle of Yellow Ford.

Ulster, 14 August 1598
Hugh O'Neill, the earl of Tyrone, together with Hugh Roe O'Donnell, the lord of Tyrconnell, and Hugh Maguire, the lord of Fermanagh, has decisively defeated the English forces of Sir Henry Bagenal at what is being called the Battle of the Yellow Ford. It represents a bloody culmination to strenuous attempts by the English to invade Ulster. They made a disastrous mistake, however, in placing a garrison to protect the ford over the river Blackwater. Promptly blockaded by Tyrone, the Blackwater garrison was being starved out.

The English were not sure whether they should try to relieve the garrison or do nothing. Sir Henry Bagenal then offered to lead a relief expedition of 4,000 men, but Tyrone attacked and heavily defeated them at the Yellow Ford between Armagh and the Blackwater. Bagenal is among those killed in the action, which may well inspire rebellion throughout the country – especially in those areas being planted, like Munster (→ 11/1598).

Local justices charged with keeping peace

Administering justice: a suspected offender pleads his case in court.

England, 1598
As fears mount of growing lawlessness in the countryside [*see report above*] there has been a marked expansion in the powers and duties of local government in England, with the aim of boosting stability. In the counties the post of sheriff has gradually been subordinated to that of lieutenant – a relatively recent creation. Lieutenants, or their deputies, take responsibility for raising the county militias – a vital task, in view of the invasion threats of recent years.

Central to effective local government are the justices of the peace; there are now about 40 or 50, usually from prominent local families, in every county. They have to enforce over 300 statutes, some 75 of them enacted during Elizabeth's reign, and settle all kinds of criminal and civil cases, ranging from witchcraft and murder to failure to attend church (→ 9/2/98).

Wise king enlivens culture in Scotland

Scotland, 1598
It is being said that no country in Europe has a more learned king upon its throne than Scotland has in James VI. This year, at the age of 32, he has produced two books which set forth his views on kingship. They are *Trew Law of Free Monarchies* and *Basilikon Doron*, which latter work contains his instructions to Prince Henry, his heir. Both books claim divine right for kings. Kings existed before parliaments and they are the makers of laws, not laws the makers of kings. He tells his son: "God hath made you a little God to sit on his throne and rule over other men." He adds that God will punish the faults of kings most severely. "The highest bench is sliddriest to sit upon."

James's accomplishments have been celebrated since his youth. At the age of eight "he could read a chapter of the Bible out of Latin into French and out of French into English". Last year he published *Demonologie* [*see report opposite*]; he has also translated the Psalms of David. In 1583 he encouraged the foundation of Edinburgh University, and he has a group of poets around him at court (→ 5/8/1600).

Queen mourns loss of her chief adviser

London, 4 August 1598
Lord Burghley died today at his house on the Strand. For 40 years he had been Queen Elizabeth's most valued adviser, maintaining his position while so many other favourites came and went. As Sir William Cecil he was close to her before she came to the throne. In a rare maternal gesture the queen visited him on his sickbed and fed him with a spoon, like "a dutiful nurse", he wrote to his son (→ 5/1599).

William Cecil, Baron Burghley.

1599 - 1600

Dublin, 12 March 1599. Robert Devereux, the earl of Essex, is the new lord lieutenant (→ 29/5).

Co Wicklow, 29 May 1599. Essex is routed by guerrillas at Deputy's Pass (→ 8/1559).

Westminster, May 1599. Thomas Sackville, Lord Buckhurst, is appointed lord treasurer, and Sir Robert Cecil is appointed master of the court of wards (→ 6/1601).

London, summer 1599. A new theatre, the Globe, opens on the south bank of the Thames (→ 1603).

Brittany, August 1599. A third fleet sent by Philip III of Spain to the Irish is wrecked (→ 7/9).

Ulster, 7 September 1599. Essex and Tyrone meet on the Louth-Monaghan border to discuss a truce (→ 24).

Ireland, 24 September 1599. Essex returns to England without Queen Elizabeth's permission (→ 2/12).

Scotland, October 1599. The Gentlemen Adventurers of Fife begin a lowland settlement of the Western Isles in a new policy to civilize the region.

Scotland, 17 December 1599. The calendar is to be brought into line with that on the continent; the new year will begin on 1 January and not 25 March.

Nottingham, 1599. The Reverend William Lee, who developed the first hosiery-knitting machine, develops a silk-knitting machine.

London, 1599. The first performance of *Julius Ceasar* by William Shakespeare takes place (→ 2/1602).

Munster, May-August 1600. Sir George Carew, the provincial president, mounts a massive scorched-earth campaign against rebels supporting Tyrone (→ 13/6).

Westminster, 5 June 1600. Essex is partly reprieved by the queen (→ 30/10).

Ireland, 13 June 1600. The earl of Ormond, kidnapped by the O'Mores in April, is released but his credibility is badly dented (→ 10/1600).

Ulster, October 1600. Lord Mountjoy a path cuts through the Moyry Pass from the Pale into Tyrone's Ulster lands (→ 9/1601).

London, 1600. Ben Jonson publishes his first play, *Every Man Out of his Humour*.

Essex charged after Irish campaign fails

London, 2 December 1599
The queen's one-time favourite, the earl of Essex, weak and sick from a month in prison, is disgraced. On the orders of the star chamber his household has been dispersed and his 160 servants dismissed.

A packed hearing four days ago heard of his disastrous and costly Irish expedition which left the nationalist leader Tyrone triumphant, and his disobedience in deserting his post and returning home.

He had gambled that he could work his old magic on Queen Elizabeth and rode hard to Nonsuch Palace in Surrey to be first with the news, bursting into her bedchamber to find her unadorned. She greeted him kindly but was offended by his behaviour. No man alive has seen her even in a nightgown. When she was fully dressed the queen called a council which placed Essex under house arrest while examining his conduct in Ireland. He had taken 16,000 men to Ireland last March but failed to attack Tyrone in Ulster as ordered. He had then agreed a truce with him before precipitately returning home (→ 5/1600).

Disgraced: the earl of Essex.

Organ-builder ends Turkish adventures

London, May 1600
The adventures of Thomas Dallam and his astonishing organ are the talk of the town. Over a year ago the organ-builder left for Constantinople to take his creation as a gift from Queen Elizabeth to the sultan, Mohamed III. It was 4 metres (13 feet) high, had a 24-hour clock and a figure of the queen in precious stones surrounded by eight mechanical figures – armed men that struck bells, cocks that crowed – and could play four or five songs without anyone touching the keys, non-stop, for up to six hours.

The sultan was understandably delighted; Dallam was amazed by his entourage, which included "a 100 dumb men in gold with hawkes on their wrist" and 100 dwarves with scimitars. He was nearly forced to stay but escaped.

Essex faces financial ruin without wine

London, 30 October 1600
The earl of Essex faces total ruin. After months of delay Queen Elizabeth has finally decided not to renew his right to customs duties on sweet wines which, since it was granted ten years ago, has been his main source of income. His immediate debts total £5,000, and there is no way that he can repay them.

Essex's increasingly desperate letters – "my soul cried out unto your Majesty for ... an end to this exile" – had no effect, and the one-time favourite is just another, very scared, courtier (→ 8/2/1601).

East India company gets royal charter

London, 1600
To regulate trade between England and the Far East, Queen Elizabeth has this year granted a charter to the East India company. Like the Muscovy company, established in 1555 to trade with Russia, the new company will be a joint-stock organization, with investors sharing in the profits of voyages in proportion to capital invested. It will challenge the thriving Dutch trade with India and the Spice Islands.

Prison and hell make a woman's paradise

London, October 1599
"The women-folk of England, who have mostly blue-grey eyes and are fair and pretty, have far more liberty than in other lands" is how a 25-year-old German visitor, Thomas Platter, writes about them. One place in which they practise this unusual freedom is in the pub: "Women as well as the men, in fact more often than they, will frequent the taverns or ale houses for enjoyment ... if one women only is invited she will bring three or four other women along and they gaily toast each other."

While the men have to like it or lump it, women "often stroll out in gorgeous clothes – they lay great store by ruffs and starch them blue – and the men must put up with such ways and may not punish them for it, indeed the good wives often beat their men". A proverb sums it up: "England is a woman's paradise, a servant's prison, because mistresses ... are very severe, and a horse's hell because they are ridden hard" (→ 1616).

The women-folk of England.

In February 1600 the comic actor Will Kemp completed the first "sponsored" morris dance, from London to Norwich, in nine days.

Gowrie conspiracy fails

Perth, 5 August 1600
King James VI has survived what appears to have been an assassination attempt in which two of his most bitter enemies have been killed. The detals of what happened at Gowrie House in Perth are shrouded in mystery, and the versions from the two sides conflict greatly. The only facts beyond dispute are that James rode to the house of the earl of Gowrie and his brother, and that James is alive and the Gowries are both dead.

James says that he received a message inviting him to view a pot of gold found by the Gowries. When he arrived he was entertained to supper and then led through a series of rooms to where the gold was supposed to lie. Instead, he found himself locked in a tower where the younger Gowrie tried to kill him. Only the intervention of his servants saved him.

The Gowries had good cause to want James out of the way; he executed their father, and their grandfather Lord Ruthven had held a knife to Mary Queen of Scots' belly while she was pregnant with him. But their surviving relatives say that the king arrived unannounced at Gowrie House and then used a false accusation of treason to have them murdered (→6/1601).

Gowrie and his plotters are foiled in their attempt to assassinate James VI.

Ambitious lord deputy arrives in Ireland

Ireland, May 1600
The dawn of the new century has coincided with the arrival in Ireland of a new lord deputy, Charles Blount, Lord Mountjoy. He represents a new breed of deputy, both a soldier and an administrator, and it is no secret that his ultimate purpose is the destruction of the earl of Tyrone's power, the recovery of Ulster and the completion of the English conquest of Ireland.

He intends to achieve his plans by destroying Tyrone's financial resources, setting up permanent garrisons in Ulster and utilizing English sea-power to support land operations. Ireland is still perceived by Englishmen as a small isolated colony on the western periphery of Europe, and, despite the declining power of the old Irish chiefs, the cultural, social and economic life of the country remain far removed from that of England.

The English, therefore, see it as essential that they should introduce a process of "civilization" and "anglicization", aimed at decreasing political instability and reducing the possibility of Ireland being used by the Spanish as a strategic base for an attack on England. The Spanish threat, of course, remains very real. King Philip III continues to support Tyrone with both arms and the possibility of sending a military expedition to Ireland (→5-8/1600).

'Gloriana cult' takes hold as images of queen become more and more popular

Queen Elizabeth: the image she portrayed of a beautiful proud queen.

Richmond Palace, Surrey, 1600
At 66 Queen Elizabeth has lost neither her vanity nor her awareness of a regal image. Portraits of her are used at home and abroad as propaganda to present an image of beauty and strength. Unofficial portraits were barred in 1563, but many official ones hang in grand houses as symbols of loyalty or appear on metal medallions. The youthful beauty captured by Federico Zuccero has inevitably faded, despite the queen's search for an alchemical elixir of youth. But courtiers still play on her vanity by pandering to the cult which represents her as "Gloriana" (→24/3/03).

The young Elizabeth, from a crayon drawing by Zuccaro.

An exquisite miniature of the queen by Nicholas Hilliard.

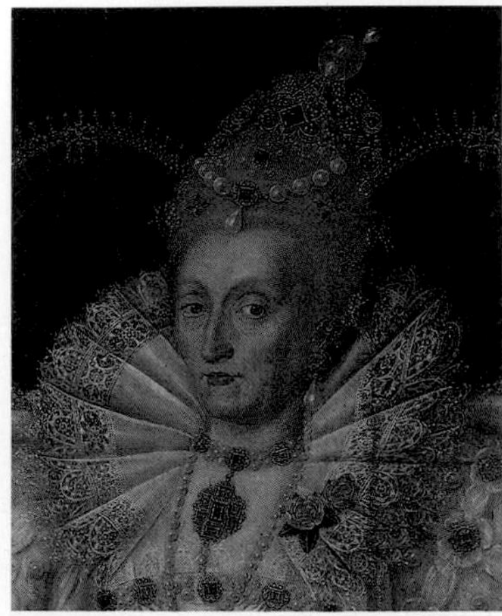

Elizabeth: an old woman, never seen without her face made up.

London, 8 February 1601. Freed from house arrest, Robert Devereux, the earl of Essex, once Queen Elizabeth's favourite, launches a coup (→ 25/2).

Scotland, 20 May 1601. A day of thanksgiving marks the end of the plague which has raged through the winter (→ 12/1603).

Low Countries, July 1601. An Anglo-Dutch force fends off an attack by the Spanish on Ostend (→ 8/1604).

Co Cork, September 1601. A Spanish fleet lands at Kinsale to support the Irish, led by Hugh O'Neill, the earl of Tyrone, and Hugh O'Donnell, the earl of Tyrconnell, in their fight against England (→ 26/10).

Co Cork, 26 October 1601. Mountjoy, the lord deputy 1600, arrives with 10,000 troops (→ 7/11).

Co Cork, 7 November 1601. Sir George Carew, the president of Munster, joins Mountjoy in besieging Kinsale (→ 24/12).

Westminster, November 1601. Parliament passes a new act for the care of the poor.

Co Cork, 27 December 1601. Following a disastrous defeat Tyrone withdraws to Ulster, and Tyrconnell flees to Spain (→ 2/1/02).

London, 1601. Thomas Nashe, the pamphleteer and playwright, dies.

Co Cork, 2 January 1602. The Spanish commander surrenders to Lord Mountjoy (→ 25/3).

London, February 1602. William Shakespeare publishes *The Merry Wives of Windsor* (→ 1603).

Ireland, 25 March 1602. The English seize Ballyshannon Castle (→ 17/2/03).

Dublin, 1602. The New Testament is translated into Gaelic.

London, 1602. Richard Carew publishes a lively *Survey of Cornwall* (→ 1610).

Oxford, 1602. Sir Thomas Bodley returns from the continent to start building up the university's library.

Strathclyde, 9 February 1603. The MacGregors massacre their rivals, the Colquhouns, in a raid on Glenfruin (→ 20/1/04).

Ireland, 17 February 1603. Mountjoy is authorized by Elizabeth to grant a royal pardon to the earl of Tyrone if he surrenders (→ 30/3/).

Proud Essex is executed

London, 25 February 1601
The earl of Essex was beheaded today at the Tower of London. Unusually, he was granted a private execution within the walls of the Tower rather than having to face a public death. Once a man with a golden future, destined perhaps to rule the country under Queen Elizabeth, he was led by his overweening arrogance into a plot to take over the court by force and compel the queen to do his bidding.

The plot was a complete failure, and at his trial the queen's chief minister, Sir Robert Cecil, roundly condemned him: "The difference between me and you is great. For wit I give you pre-eminence. For nobility I also give you place. I am no swordsman: there also you have the odds. But I have innocence, conscience, truth and honesty to defend me ... and in this court I stand as an upright man, and your lordship as a delinquent."

With those words ringing in his ears Essex was sentenced to death.

A private execution for Essex.

At first he believed that it was the plots of his enemies which had brought about his fall, but eventually he came to realize that he was the author of his own destruction and repented of his actions.

Negotiations begin for James to succeed

London, June 1601
A secret correspondence has been in progress during the past three months between Queen Elizabeth's chief minister, Robert Cecil, and the king of Scotland, James VI. It is clear that the queen cannot live for much longer, and the only real contender for the throne is James. Robert Cecil and a number of other leading English politicians and lords are anxious to make themselves as useful as possible to their future king, if for no other reason than the desire to keep their high offices at court (→ 5/1603).

Bess of Hardwick fashions a great new hall

Bess, the countess of Shrewsbury.

Derbyshire, 1601
The construction of a great new hall at Hardwick, near Chesterfield, is nearing completion. Only a few yards from the equally lavish Old Hall, it is the work of Elizabeth Talbot, the countess of Shrewsbury. Four times widowed and enormously rich, "Bess of Hardwick", as she is known, has incorporated many new design features in the hall, including windows so big that they appear to be walls of glass. Shrewsbury, her last husband, was the jailer of Mary Queen of Scots, and Bess spent many hours making tapestries and embroideries with the late queen, which she intends to use to decorate the new hall (→ 1616).

Queen seeks to calm parliament's fears with 'golden speech'

Westminster, 30 November 1601
Queen Elizabeth has tried to calm growing fears in parliament about the abuse of "monopolies" – royal grants bestowing the sole right to make or sell specific commodities. Members have complained that the creation of sole traders has led to higher prices because there is no alternative supply. Salt has doubled in price, and so many goods are now monopolies that some fear even bread will be added to the list.

In reaction to these complaints the queen sent for a delegation of about 160 members to come from parliament to the Palace of Westminster. There she made what is being called her "golden speech", in which she sought to calm their fears and assured them that she was no "greedy scraping grasper". She went on to say that she would not tolerate monopolies to be "made grievous to my people" but reminded them that to "be a king and wear a crown is a thing more glorious to them that see it than it is pleasant to them that bear it". Then, after thanking them for bringing the problem to her attention, the queen assured them in a memorable passage: "Though you have had and may have many mightier and wiser princes yet ye never had, nor never shall, have any that will love you better." (→ 24/3/03).

Queen Elizabeth in parliament.

Mountjoy routs Tyrone at Kinsale

Ireland, 24 December 1601
After months of bloody fighting, and terrible devastation of cattle and crops, Lord Mountjoy, the deputy, has defeated the earl of Tyrone at Kinsale in a short engagement lasting merely three hours.

The expedition sent by King Philip III of Spain proved ineffective. There was confusion about where the 4,500 men should land. Their leader, Juan del Aguila, chose Donegal but was persuaded that the Cork coast would be better. The Irish force marched rapidly to Kinsale but was attacked by Mountjoy before it could present a united front with its Spanish allies. With its largest division broken and having suffered heavy losses, Tyrone admitted defeat. With the collapse of the Ulster resistance the Tudor conquest is complete (→27).

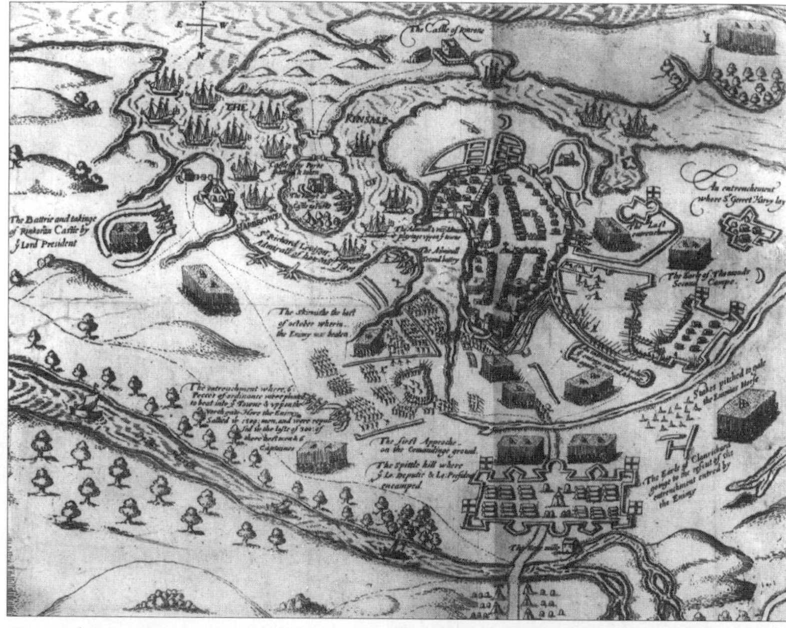

Spanish troops are besieged by Lord Mountjoy in the town of Kinsale.

The queen is dead after 45-year reign

Richmond Palace, 24 March 1603
Royal messengers are being dispatched from here with the momentous news that Elizabeth Tudor, queen of England for almost 45 years, is dead. Some are heading north to tell King James VI of Scotland that what his mother, Mary Queen of Scots, failed to take by force is now freely given to him – the English throne. Elizabeth died between two and three o'clock this morning. Before she lost the power of speech Elizabeth said that she would "have none but [James]". The question of the succession that had dogged her reign was therefore settled at almost literally the last moment. Her skilful procrastinations over marriage are perhaps the greatest testimony to what was an extremely astute mind.

Death of 'virgin queen' ends era of Tudor dynasty

British Isles, 24 March 1603
An era has ended. Not just the Elizabethan era but the Tudor dynasty has been eclipsed by the death today of England's "virgin queen". In the reign of Elizabeth the country became a major force in the world. The Spanish were vanquished, new colonies were established. Yet it was at home that the greatest changes were wrought.

The "Memorial Picture of Sir Henry Unton" illuminates contrasting scenes from the life of a Tudor gentleman.

Perhaps the most striking feat of Elizabeth's reign was the preservation of the peace during a period when religious ferment was tearing apart France and the Netherlands. Herself a Protestant, she had neither sympathy for the more extreme puritans nor hatred for English Catholics who could demonstrate loyalty. She fostered a patriotism which maintained peace and enabled England to prosper.

The signs of success are clear: new trading links, the expansion of the cloth industry, an increase in agricultural yields as the result of land enclosure, growing numbers of schools and universities and a stimulating cultural life. Yet these national achievements mask the troubles of the great mass of the English people whose standard of living declined during the Elizabethan era.

England's population has increased from about 2.25 million in 1500 to four million today. Food prices have also risen, improving the incomes of landowners but causing widespread hardship. Real wages have fallen by something like 60 per cent over the last century. Growth in the numbers of beggars and paupers resulted in the introduction of Poor Laws to protect labourers and their families. Only a few could find work in the new luxury industries (furniture, glass, draperies, woollens) created by the increased spending power of other sectors of English society.

Wales, where the Tudor dynasty originated, has also seen a rise in wealth, although it is less marked than in England. The Protestant Reformation is now accepted, and the translation of the Bible into Welsh in 1588 has done much to encourage an upsurge in Welsh literature.

In Scotland the saga of Mary Queen of Scots led to political weakness, but the local nature of government exercised by the great lords lessened the problem. New taxation was introduced in 1581; although the country is not rich there are many well-off merchants, and James VI is leading a cultural renaissance.

In Ireland Hugh O'Neill, the earl of Tyrone, has led the only recent Gaelic rebellion to have stood a chance of success. Over the last century the English have extended their rule over much of Ireland, destroying local rulers and customs. Much of the country has been wasted by war and English domination, but it remains potentially rich (→28/4).

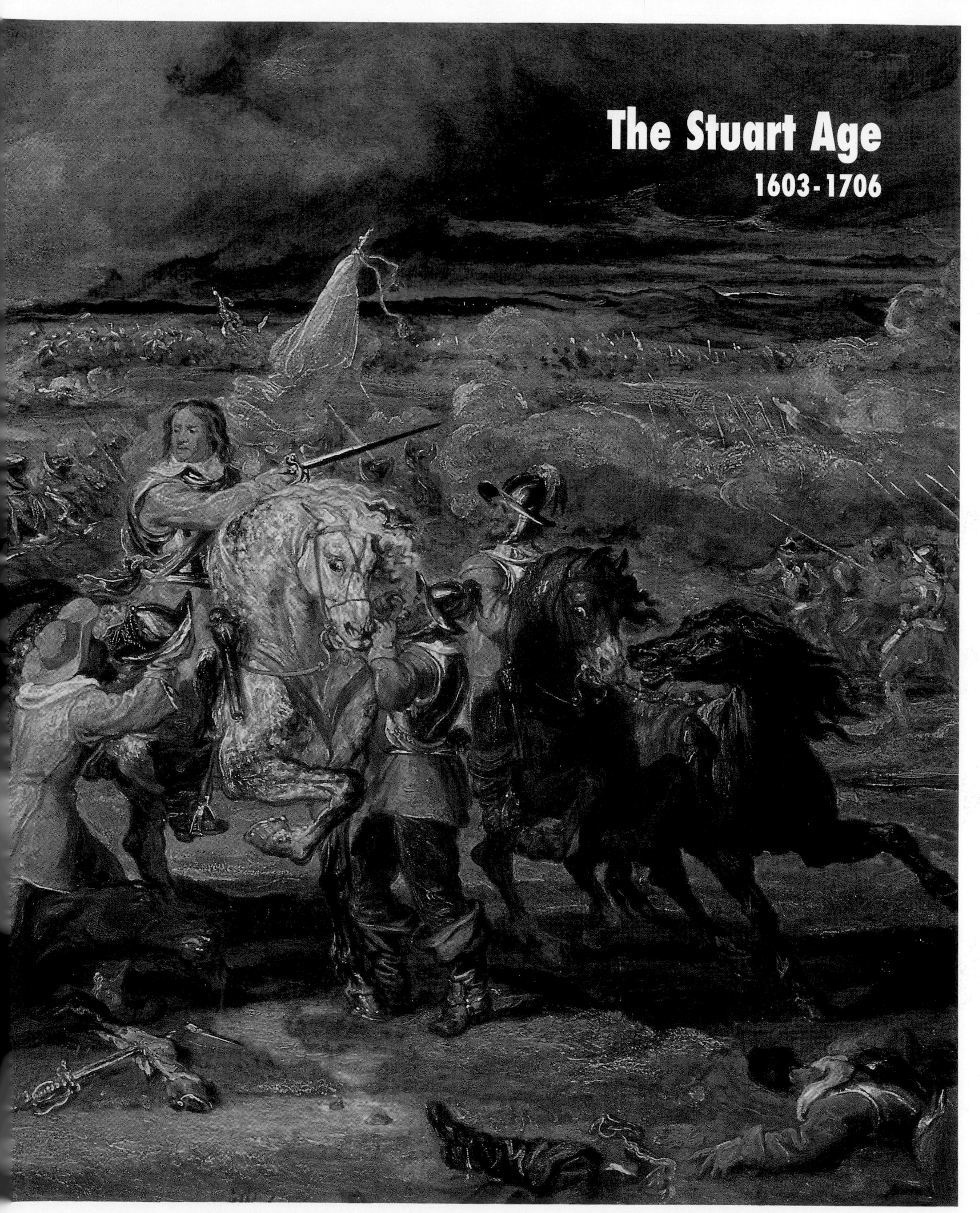

The Stuart Age

1603-1706

1603

Edinburgh, 26 March. Sixty hours after Queen Elizabeth's death, Sir Robert Carey arrives to break the news to King James VI of Scotland that he has now also become king of England (→5/4).

Dublin, 5 April. King James of Scotland and England is proclaimed king in Ireland (→6).

Ireland, April. The Catholic form of Christianity is restored in southern towns such as Kilkenny, Wexford and Munster (→13/11/05).

Westminster, 13 May. Sir Robert Cecil is made Baron Cecil of Essendon by King James (→20/8/04).

Ireland, 30 May. Sir George Carey is appointed lord deputy in succession to Lord Mountjoy (→31).

Ireland, 31 May. Charles Blount, Lord Mountjoy, the former lord deputy, departs for England, accompanied by Hugh O'Neill, the earl of Tyrone (→6/1603).

London, May. Sir Walter Raleigh is dismissed as captain of the guard; he supports the war with Spain which James hopes to end (→10/12).

Greenwich, London, June. The defeated earl of Tyrone, Hugh O'Neill, is received at court by James; his title is officially confirmed (→12/9).

London, 12 September. A royal pardon is issued to the earl of Tyrone (→10/1604).

London, 17 September. King James authorizes the striking of a new coinage for Ireland.

London, September. The Spanish ambassador negotiates the opening of peace talks with James after two decades of war (→8/1604).

Winchester, 29 November. William Clark and William Watson, two Catholic priests, are executed for their suspected involvement in a conspiracy to depose James in favour of his cousin Lady Arabella Stuart of Hardwick (→10/12).

Scotland. Sir Thomas Craig publishes *Jus Feudale*, a huge treatise on Scottish feudal law.

London. William Shakespeare's company performs *Sejanus*, a tragedy by Ben Jonson, at the Globe theatre (→1608).

London. King James gives William Shakespeare's theatre company his royal patronage – its members are now to be known as "the King's Men".

Earl surrenders to end nine-year war

Co Louth, 30 March

The earl of Tyrone, Hugh O'Neill, has surrendered to the lord deputy, Lord Mountjoy, at Mellifont, and a treaty has been signed to bring an end to the nine-year war. O'Neill's 10,000-strong army fought fearlessly against Mountjoy's forces, which employed a "scorched-earth" policy. O'Neill was finally defeated at Kinsale in 1601. Today's surrender is a major blow to the Gaelic lords, although O'Neill has been treated generously: the treaty allows him to keep all his lands and feudal rights (→30/5).

Crowds mourn for 'good Queen Bess'

Westminster, 28 April

Queen Elizabeth has been buried at Westminster Abbey after an elaborate funeral procession through the City of London. Ever since she died last month crowds have been mourning "Good Queen Bess". She had reigned for almost 45 years, and her death also signalled the end of a dynasty: the house of Tudor is to be replaced by that of Stuart.

The new king will be Scotland's King James [*see report opposite*], and he is now heading to claim the kingdom which Elizabeth said on her deathbed should be his. Robert Cecil, her chief minister, had been writing secretly to James to prepare the way for his accession. Both Elizabeth and James trace their ancestry back to Henry VII.

James inherits a kingdom which is far wealthier and more powerful than Scotland. It is said that he talks of England as "a land flowing with milk and honey". One king will now reign over two countries which have repeatedly been locked in conflict over the centuries. The union of the crowns should prolong the current peace, but there are no plans to create a single government. James may face problems similar to those troubling the king of Spain, who rules over both Spain and the Spanish Netherlands (→5/1603).

Bubonic plague kills a quarter of the population of London

Death stalks the land as one in four Londoners die in an outbreak of plague.

London, December

Some 30,000 Londoners – almost a quarter of the city's entire population – are believed to have died this year in the latest outbreak of bubonic plague. Having taken root in the poor quarters on the outskirts, the plague swept through central areas, its spread hastened by overcrowding. All the best horses have been stolen by people desperate to flee the city.

Children have been the first to succumb, and more men have died than women. Entire families die one after another, although their neighbours may remain untouched. Norwich and Bristol have suffered similar epidemics (→24/11/24).

Women riot over plans to drain fens

East Anglia

Women at Deeping Fen, in Lincolnshire, have vandalized a ditch and threatened to burn houses in the latest protest against attempts to drain the fens. The high price of agricultural produce has persuaded enterprising capitalists to embark on drainage schemes that will bring more fields into cultivation. But these schemes threaten the way of life of many of the inhabitants of East Anglia. Known as "slodgers", these people live in wattle huts at the mosquito-infested waterside and eke out a living by snaring, fishing and cutting reeds.

A drawing from a recent book on magnetic theory by William Gilbert, the president of the College of Physicians, who died on 30 November 1603.

Scotland and England united by House of Stuart

London, May
King James, who has been king of Scotland since 1567, has arrived in London after a triumphal journey south to be crowned king of England. He has already knighted some 300 people recommended either by Scottish nobles or by English lords who were gaining influence with him even before he left Edinburgh.

On crossing the border [*see report below*] James was so carried away that he rode 40 miles (60km) in under four hours, his entourage straining to keep up. In York and other northern cities he was greeted with great pomp, and he conferred with his English councillors who had hurried north to meet him. He hunted as he went, live hares being released from baskets. At Newark-on-Trent he had a thief hanged without trial. Near Burghley he fell from his horse with a suspected broken collar-bone.

The weight of expectation on the new king is formidable; some Protestants have welcomed him to London with a petition to end bishops' privileges, restrict music and bowing in church and make other controversial reforms (→1/1604).

King James VI of Scotland enters London in triumph on his way to be crowned King James of England.

Scots have mixed feelings at loss of king

Henry VII 1485–1509 = Elizabeth of York

- Arthur
- **Henry VIII** 1509–47
  - **Mary I** 1553–58
  - **Elizabeth I** 1558–1603
  - **Edward VI** 1547–53
- Margaret = **James IV of Scots** 1488–1513
  - **James V of Scots** 1513–42 =(2) Mary of Guise
    - **Mary, Queen of Scots** 1542–67 =(2) Henry, Lord Darnley
      - **James VI of Scots and I of England** 1567–[1603]–1625

Dates = reigns

Berwick-Upon-Tweed, 6 April
Almost a century after a Scottish king last stepped onto English soil, James VI crossed the border here today to widespread jubilation. For many Scots, the accession to the English throne of James – a great-grandson of Henry VIII's sister Margaret [*see family tree*] – is a form of conquest. Others are not so happy, fearing that it could result in Scots having less control over their own affairs. James has promised to return every three years, but this is little consolation for a people losing their king and court. Although he is not a popular king, he is widely respected. His lofty views of monarchy are well known, but these are offset by a relaxed style, willingness to compromise and open access to suitors (→22/3/04).

Raleigh wins a reprieve on the scaffold

Winchester, 10 December
To the apparent disappointment of a large crowd, Sir Walter Raleigh, Sir Griffin Markham and Lords Grey and Cobham have been reprieved on the scaffold. Convicted of high treason, the four were supposed to have shared the fate of two Catholic priests and Cobham's brother George Brooke, all executed within the past two weeks. As Raleigh watched from a window, each of his "co-conspirators" had his execution postponed until the sheriff announced that the king had granted them all their lives.

At last month's trial, Raleigh, notorious for his anti-Spanish privateering, was convicted of being in the pay of Spain, and of plotting to put Lady Arabella Stuart on the throne, although there was no evidence of any links between them. Since then Raleigh's pleas for his life have been almost as unedifying as the king's last-minute scaffold reprieve (→3/1616).

Arabella Stuart, the king's cousin.

1604 - 1605

Edinburgh, 20 January 1604. The laird of Macgregor and 18 of his kinsmen are hanged in punishment for their massacre of the Colquhoun clan during a raid on Glenfruin last year (→ summer 1610).

Middlesex, January 1604. At the Hampton Court conference King James authorizes a new translation of the Bible.→

Canterbury, February 1604. Archbishop John Whitgift dies (→ 7/1604).

Westminster, 22 March 1604. At his first English parliament King James outlines plans for a union of Scotland and England under the name of "Great Britain" (→ 20/10).

Derry City, 11 July 1604. The city is incorporated.

Westminster, July 1604. James passes a measure against "recusants" [Catholics who refuse to attend Church of England services] (→ 4/12).

London, 20 August 1604. Robert Cecil, Baron Cecil of Essendon, becomes Viscount Cranborne (→ 4/5/05).

Ireland, October 1604. Sir Arthur Chichester is appointed lord deputy (→ 22/6/06).

England/Scotland, 16 November 1604. It is decided that a common currency is to be introduced and customs tariffs abolished between the two countries (→ 12/4/06).

Canterbury, 4 December 1604. Bishop Richard Bancroft of London is created archbishop of Canterbury (→ 5/2/05).

England, 4 May 1605. Robert Cecil, Viscount Cranborne, becomes earl of Salisbury (→ 25/5/07).

London, July 1605. James calls for 29 ministers who have summoned a general assembly without royal permission to be investigated (→ 8/6/10).

Dublin, 13 November 1605. The lord deputy, Chichester, issues mandates compelling Catholics to attend services of the established church (→ 6/12).

Dublin, 6 December 1605. The promoters of a petition calling for religious toleration and resistance to Chichester's mandates are jailed. The petition was supported by Dubliners and gentry of the Pale from the Old English community (→ 25/4/15).

England/Scotland, 1605. The new Anglo-Scots border commission executes 104 people for border offences.

Holy row debated at Hampton Court

Middlesex, January 1604
In a bid to clarify the differences between his bishops and the growing puritan movement, King James has brought both sides to a conference at Hampton Court. He made the decision after the puritans, seeking a simpler, Calvinistic form of worship, presented him with the "Millenary Petition" in which they sought to end certain church rituals and the wearing of many of the clergy's traditional vestments. The also wanted to stop such practices as the use of the wedding ring in marriage services and the signing of the cross at baptism.

By accepting the petition, and by calling this conference, the king upset the bishops, but he sought to assuage their fears by showing his disapproval of the puritan movement, which he says is "unlawful, and do savour of tumult, sedition and violence". Many of the puritans' less contentious requests have been met, however, in the cause of church unity (→ 2/1604).

Title 'king of Great Britain' is adopted

Westminster, 20 October 1604
In anticipation of the union of England and Scotland, James has today taken the title "king of Great Britain, France and Ireland". His attitude to union is clear: "What God has conjoined, let no man separate. I am the husband and my whole isle is my lawful wife." In April, commissioners for the English and Scottish parliaments were named to consider the issue. They are now in London to discuss a treaty for the union of the parliaments, laws and economies.

However, certain members of the English parliament have attempted to place restraints on James's actions by asserting parliamentary supremacy. Having formally rejected the king's contention that the Commons "derived all matters of privilege from him and by his grant", they went on to publish an *Apology and Satisfaction* in which they insisted: "Our privileges and liberties are our right and due inheritance" (→ 16/11).

Peace treaty ends 20-year Spanish war

The peace conference: Robert Cecil (r) leads the English delegates; to his right are the earls of Northampton, Devonshire, Nottingham and Dorset.

London, August 1604
King James has agreed a peace treaty with Spain this month which ends nearly 20 years of war. Negotiations have continued for much of the summer, with Robert Cecil heading the English delegation to the talks. But the decision to pursue peace was made by the king who, being Scottish, does not share the widespread animosity amongst the English towards their Spanish foes. He saw no reason to prolong a state of war now that the threat of invasion had been vanquished. James rejected pressure from the Dutch – England's allies against Spain – and France to maintain a common front against Philip III.

However, James refused either to denounce the Dutch as rebels, as Spain had demanded, or to break off trade with them. He was also able to win trading rights for English companies in all Spanish possessions except those in the New World. Cecil had hoped to secure freedom of the seas for all English traders, but Spain refuses to accept this for the West Indies.

Royal book warns of smoking dangers

Smoking has become fashionable.

London, 17 October 1604
As they filled their clay pipes in the smoke-filled alehouses of Britain today thousands of smokers were contemplating a fierce condemnation of the tobacco habit written by none other than King James himself. The king dislikes smoking, and in *Counterblast to Tobacco* he derides the belief that smoking is beneficial to health.

It is, he says, a "custom loathsome to the eye, hateful to the nose, harmful to the brain, dangerous to the lungs, and in the black stinking fume thereof nearest resembles the horrible Stygian smoke of the pit that is bottomless". James did not stop there: today he imposed a huge duty on tobacco imported into Britain from the New World.

Customs system is given an overhaul

London, 1604
After months of complex negotiation, England has a unified customs system which will be operated by private financiers. A great "farm" [a form of franchise in which a fee is paid for the right to exact dues] covers every port in the country and guarantees revenue to the crown and wealth to investors. The system does not apply to Scotland.

The existing farm system had been discredited – with merchants denouncing the inefficiency, bribery and extortion of the "customers". It was not until King James signed a new "book of rates" that the plan for a general farm covering the whole country was mooted.

The principal secretary, Robert Cecil, Viscount Cranborne, sought tenders, but as none received were satisfactory he himself decided to tender. In a dubious transaction he secured large investments and retired, having sold the rights – and clearly having had no intention of being a customs farmer (→ 5/1608).

Catholic bomb plot is discovered

The "gunpowder plotters" gather to discuss their plan to blow up parliament.

Guy Fawkes goes to light the fuse.

Westminster, 5 November 1605
A conspiracy involving the opening of parliament today by King James had been suspected. Orders were given to search both houses, and it was just before midnight when a cellar door was opened to expose an ex-mercenary, Guy Fawkes, guarding 20 barrels of gunpowder hidden under a pile of coal and faggots. Fawkes had no choice but to admit that he had intended to blow up both king and parliament. He was bound hand and foot and then carried off, no doubt to face the death penalty for treason.

It was an anonymous letter to Lord Monteagle, a Catholic peer, warning him against attending parliament, that alerted the government. Led by a devout Catholic, Robert Catesby, a group of six men, fearful of an apparent increase in persecution of their church, had planned the outrage. Fawkes's co-conspirators are already in flight, racing from London to the midlands where Catesby had invited Catholic nobles to a hunting party – hoping that they would support him in an uprising triggered by the king's death (→ 31/1/06).

Archbishop wages war on nonconformists

Archbishop Richard Bancroft.

Canterbury, 5 February 1605
Richard Bancroft, consecrated as archbishop of Canterbury in December, has lost no time in attempting to stamp out nonconformity in the church. His campaign is particularly aimed at the suppression of puritans. In a circular letter to his bishops he has ordered that, on pain of dismissal, all curates and lecturers must accept the king's supremacy as head of the church; declare that the Prayer Book is the true word of God; and agree to abide by each of the 39 Articles of the Church of England.

Bancroft has been more lenient towards the beneficed clergy [those who enjoy church livings]. Those refusing to conform will be deposed immediately, but those who are prepared to conform – even if they do not do so at present – will be left in peace. So far at least 300 clergymen have been ejected for refusing to comply with the demands, and King James is urging the worried bishops to keep up the pressure against puritanism.

The king is also said to be furious with a petition presented to him by four Northamptonshire knights on behalf of deprived clergy. The petition suggests that thousands of the king's subjects will be discontented if James denies the suit. The king sees this as a threat, and his council has been told to act (→ 11/1610).

Bacon writes 'Advancement of Learning'

London, 1605
Sir Francis Bacon, whose name appeared among the 600 knights to be created by King James during his first year's reign, has published a remarkable discourse, *The Advancement of Learning*, in which he argues that knowledge can only be derived from experience, and that scientists should experiment "to the benefit and use of men". The book is a plea for the reorganization of scientific method. Bacon was at one time a close friend of the earl of Essex, although he was later one of the counsel who prosecuted him for treason. He now seems likely to thrive under James (→ 1613).

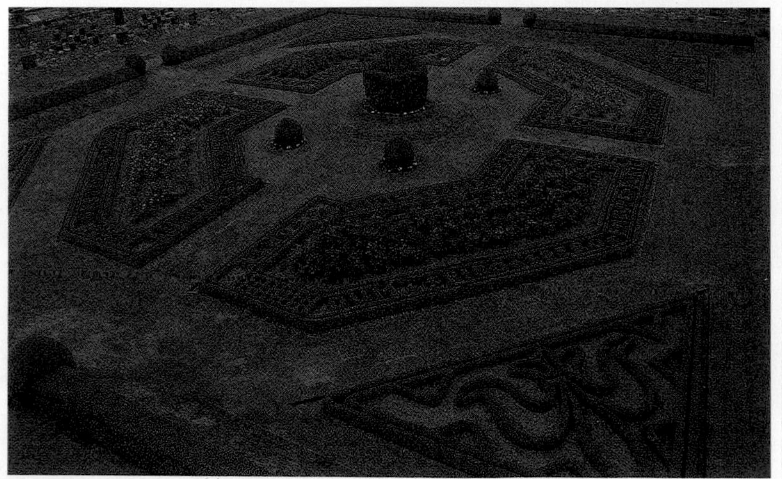
Formal gardens, such as this one at Edzell Castle, on Tayside, are becoming increasingly popular among the wealthy and upper classes.

1606 - 1607

Scotland, 29 March 1606. Severe storms cause widespread damage (→ 1607).

Britain, 12 April 1606. King James orders a "union" flag, combining the crosses of St Andrew and St George, to be adopted by both Scottish and English shipping (→ 1607).

London, 3 May 1606. Henry Garnett, a Jesuit and a conspirator in the "gunpowder plot", is executed.

Ireland, 22 July 1606. A commission is set up to enquire into "defective titles" to land (→ 16/7/07).

Perth, July 1606. On James's orders the "red parliament" – all the nobles and officials wear red cloaks – meets and grants the first major tax to the king.

Oxford, 1606. Edmund Gunter, a mathematician and astronomer of Christ Church College, invents the surveying chain (→ 1607).

London, 1606. John Lyly, the dramatist and romantic poet, dies.

London, 1606. Thomas Dekker, the pamphleteer, publishes *The seven deadly sinnes of London.*

Hertfordshire, 22 May 1607. Robert Cecil, the earl of Salisbury, gives his country mansion, Theobalds, to King James; Salibury now plans to rebuild Hatfield House, the former residence of Queen Elizabeth, for himself (→ 5/1612).

Ireland, 16 July 1607. Hugh O'Neill, the earl of Tyrone, is summoned to London (→ 4/9).

London, 7 September 1607. Sir Arthur Chichester, the lord deputy of Ireland, declares that the native Irish of Co Donegal and Co Tyrone will keep their lands if they behave as dutiful subjects (→ 1/1608).

Scotland, November 1607. Severe frost sweeps the country; in some places the river Forth freezes over.

Westminster, 23 December 1607. The king's new favourite, Robert Carr, a gentleman of the bedchamber and the youngest son of the Ferniherst family, is knighted (→ 9/1/09).

Somerset, 1607. Torrential rains cause great damage (→ 8/11/08).

England, 1607. John Norden, the topographer, publishes *The Surveyors' Dialogue*, a manual of surveying.

'Gunpowder plotters' meet gruesome end

Guy Fawkes and the "gunpowder plotters" are dragged to their executions.

London, 31 January 1606
A group of five men involved in the November conspiracy to blow up the Houses of Parliament were executed today. Among them was Guy Fawkes – the Yorkshireman who had served with the Spanish in the Netherlands after converting to Catholicism. Tortured until he confessed, Fawkes was brought from the Tower with three other plotters. Another four were executed yesterday in St Paul's churchyard. They were hanged, drawn and quartered, and their heads were set on poles as a warning to others. All Catholics, they apparently died believing that they were martyrs to God's cause.

The plot had involved planting 20 barrels of gunpowder in cellars at Westminster – to blow up when King James, the Lords and Commons had assembled for the opening of parliament. A Catholic peer tipped off to stay away warned the king's chief minister (→ 3/5).

English settlers put down roots in Virginia

The first English settlers come ashore to found "Jamestown" in Virginia.

Virginia, February 1607
More than a hundred people have arrived from England to create a settlement controlled by a colonial council. They are building a new town which will be given the king's name – Jamestown – and have also called two peaks at the mouth of the Chesapeake river after the two English princes, Henry and Charles. Three ships sailed to Virginia last year under a charter granted by James. The ships were fitted out by merchants and gentlemen of a London company, but the settlers are very largely drawn from the west country. The king is able to veto any legislation (→ 1/1608).

Leading Scots cleric refuses to conform

London, 30 November 1606
A determined attempt to browbeat Dr Andrew Melville, a top Scottish cleric, into conforming with King James's religious views ended in a furious row today with the English privy council. For the second time Melville refused to be overawed by the English clergy. He not only refused to kneel but also insisted on lecturing the shocked councillors.

Melville and other Presbyterian ministers were invited to London in August for talks with James. The king lost his temper at that meeting and has since been using leading English clergy to try to persuade the Presbyterians to acknowledge royal supremacy in the church and the efficacy of bishops (→ 2/1609).

Andrew Melville defies King James.

Danish king royally amused by revels

Hertfordshire, July 1606
King James, who is fond of revelry, has been royally entertaining his brother-in-law, King Christian IV of Denmark. The two kings have been staying at Theobalds, Lord Salisbury's Hertfordshire home. According to the court wit Sir John Harington, there have been round-the-clock "shows, sights and banquetings" which the women have also enjoyed. He says that one girl was so drunk that she fell on the Danish king, and when he got up to dance he himself fell over and had to be carried off and put to bed.

English midlands rebel over land grabs

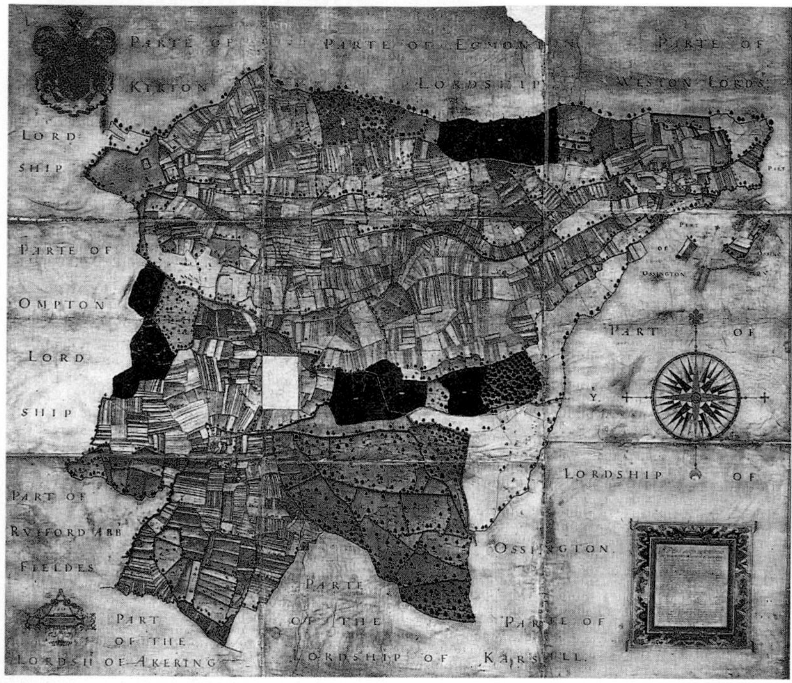

A map of a midlands estate showing strip cultivation after enclosure.

Rugby, May 1607
Angry agricultural workers in the counties of Northamptonshire, Leicestershire and Warwickshire have risen in revolt against land enclosure. Five villages, none more than 20 miles (32km) from any other and where the practice of enclosing open fields has made swift strides, are the worst affected. But the English midlands are suddenly ablaze with tumult and rumours of worse to come. A shortage of grain which has raised prices in the midlands is the immediate cause of the trouble.

Hunger and threats of starvation have driven peasants to vent their anger on the enclosing farmers, some of whom are merchants from London who are doing well out of converting land to cattle and sheep pasture. A gallows has been erected in Leicester, where training of the militia has begun.

Irish earls flee into exile on the continent, leaving Ulster to the mercy of the English

Ulster, 4 September 1607
After four resentful years of subjection to the English crown, the earls of Tyrone and Tyrconnell, Hugh O'Neill and Rory O'Donnell, together with 90 of their followers, have left Ireland and gone into voluntary exile on the continent. The so-called "flight of the earls" has left Ulster leaderless – and the English government greatly relieved.

Both O'Neill and O'Donnell had been frustrated in their attempts to have an influence in administrative and political matters, such as the appointment of local officials. They had also been hostile to the recent commission for "defective titles". This is in theory a chance for people who lost valid titles to their lands when English property law was imposed to secure firm titles. In effect Catholic landholders are losing their rights, while Protestant ones are having their own confirmed.

Irish Catholics are losing more of their lands by this method than through plantation, although that is still being pursued. Substantial groups of settlers have been "planted" in Laois, Offaly and Munster despite considerable local opposition. Their numbers are likely to increase as the English argue that the best way to avoid rebellion is to dispossess the native Irish (→ 7).

Images of the different classes of native Irish in the early 17th century.

Since King James's accession to the English throne, the Scottish game of "golf" has been taken up with enthusiasm in England.

Mutual suspicion marks plans for union of Scots and English

Britain, 1607
The English and Scottish parliaments have been equally hostile this year to proposals put forward by King James for an act to cement the union between England and Scotland. Neither kingdom is keen to pursue the idea of uniting the two parliaments, laws and economies.

At Westminster, country squires have attacked Scots in general and warned of dangers if too many of them decide to come and live in England. Abusive remarks by English members about Scots as "beggars, rebels and traitors" were later seized upon by their Scottish counterparts to intensify fears that union would lead to Scotland being exploited by the arrogant English.

Scotland's parliament eventually agreed to repeal anti-English legislation and to accept a union treaty – as long as England reciprocated. The Scots are confident that the English rejection of union means that such a proposal will never be implemented. But for King James, who has been the principal advocate of a united "Great Britain", this double defeat in his parliaments represents a major embarrassment from which he will find it difficult to recover (→ 1608).

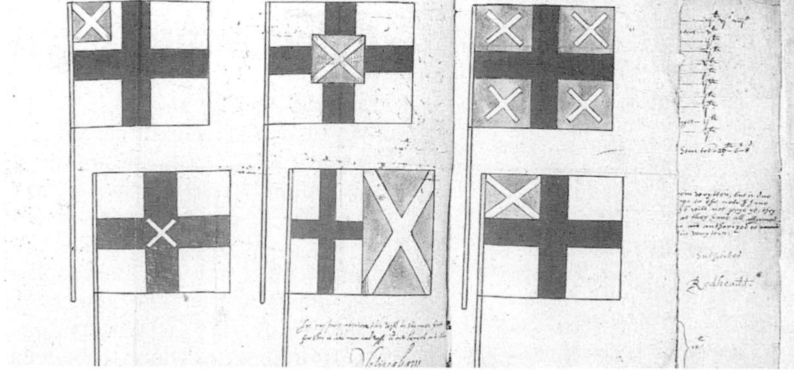

Designs for a new flag combining the crosses of St Andrew and St George.

1608 - 1609

Ireland, January 1608. The traditional inheritance system, "tanistry", is banned (→ 29/4).

England, 19 April 1608. Thomas Sackville, the earl of Dorset, lord treasurer since 1599 and a poet, dies. He worked with Thomas Norton to produce the first tragedy in blank verse, *Gorboduc*, which was acted before Queen Elizabeth in 1562.

Rome, 29 April 1608. Hugh O'Neill, the earl of Tyrone, and Rory O'Donnell, the earl of Tyrconnell, who fled from Ireland last September, arrive seeking refuge (→ 28/7).

England, June 1608. King James agrees a treaty of mutual defence with the Dutch United Provinces.

Rome, 28 July 1608. The earl of Tyrconnell dies after contracting a fever (→ 6/9).

Ulster, 6 September 1608. A survey of six counties in Ulster – Armagh, Cavan, Donegal, Coleraine, Fermanagh and Tyrone – finds that nearly all the area should be made over to King James (→ 7/1609).

Aberdeen, 8 November 1608. An earthquake rocks the city (→ 6/1612).

London, 1608. Captain John Smith, one of the first settlers in the colony of Virginia, publishes *A true relation of such occurrences and accidents of note as hath happened in Virginia since the first planting of that colony*, the first book on colonial life (→ 1/1608).

Dublin, 1608. William O'Donnell completes a Gaelic translation of the *Book of Common Prayer*.

Britain, 1608. Dual nationality is to be given to all Scots and Englishmen born after King James's accession to the throne of England (→ 1/1/11).

London, 1608. William Shakespeare completes his latest play, *King Lear*, some four years after the appearance of another powerful tragedy, *Hamlet* (→ 1609).

Blackheath, London, 1608. King James founds the Royal Blackheath Golf Club.

London, 2 June 1609. King James grants a royal charter to the Virginia Company (→ 1612).

North America, 13 September 1609. Henry Hudson, the English navigator, sails north from New Amsterdam [New York] to find a passage to the Orient (→ 8/1610).

Plan to impose rates angers merchants

King James presides over parliament, but trouble is brewing over finance.

England, May 1608
The effects of the new "book of rates", which comes into operation today, are – as anticipated – drawing angry protests from merchants. It is the first major revision of the country's customs duties since the marquis of Winchester's reforms of the 1550s, and it should bring to the exchequer a projected annual income of between £60,000 and £70,000.

Until today, the levy imposed on merchants was introduced as a way of regulating trade. But following the outcome of the John Bate case in 1606, when he was found guilty of refusing to pay an "imposition" of 5s 6d [27.5p] on every hundredweight [51kg] of currants, it was decided to levy import duties as an extra source of revenue.

The new rates, which will affect 1,400 items, are likely to become a constitutional issue, since they contravene the old fundamental right of parliament "that no such charges should ever be laid upon the people without their common consent". It would appear that finance is about to usurp religion as the major issue of the day (→ 17/7/1610).

Native princess saves New World settler

England, January 1608
Reports have reached England that Captain John Smith, the leader of the Jamestown settlers in Virginia, has been saved from death by an Indian princess called Pocahontas. In December last year Smith and a few others had left the settlement, where many were facing starvation, to try trading with local tribesmen for corn. He was alone in a forest when warriors seized him and took him before their chief. If Pocahontas, a girl of about ten years old, had not rushed forward when she did, to lay her head upon Smith's, the chief would have had the settler butchered (→ 2/6/09).

Smith takes on a Virginian native.

Chief justice at odds with James over the issue of divine right

London, February 1609
The lord chief justice, Sir Edward Coke, was involved in an astonishing scene at Whitehall today following a heated exchange with King James. A discussion between them finished with the king clenching his fists in anger as if he were about to hit Coke, who fell to the ground grovelling for mercy.

Differences between them arose out of the king's belief that he has the divine right to interfere with the jurisdiction of ecclesiastical courts. Disturbed by growing prohibitions, ecclesiastical lawyers, fearing that their professional status and living were at stake, sought the help of Archbishop Richard Bancroft.

Although sympathetic, and just as anxious to strengthen the power of the church courts, Bancroft was cautious. He believed that the king was more likely to dispense justice in favour of the poor than were members of parliament or judges associated with them, and therefore he was a valuable mediator.

Chief justice: Sir Edward Coke.

Bancroft also held that since jury members were most often drawn from the ranks of the gentry, the king's influence would enhance the cause of justice. However, the king was petitioned, and several judges, including the chief justice, were summoned to Whitehall. It was Coke's forceful manner, urging the king to respect the common law of the land, that so inflamed the monarch (→ 1611).

Scottish secretary to be put to death

St Andrews, 10 March 1609
James Elphinstone, Lord Balmerino, King James's Scottish secretary, has been sentenced to death for treason. Elphinstone confessed to obtaining the king's signature on a letter to the pope ten years ago. The letter, implying that James was open to conversion, was aired by Cardinal Ballarmine in order to triumph in a pamphlet war which he was waging with James. But although the king had never planned to become a Catholic, evidence of dealing with Rome could damage his reputation with Protestants – hence the sacrifice of Balmerino.

James rewards his special young men

London, 9 January 1609
King James is living up to his reputation as a man of alarming extravagance, showering his favourites with gifts. In the course of the past two years he has settled the debts of Viscount Haddington, the earl of Montgomery and Lord Hay to the tune of £44,000.

His latest act of benevolence is to give the Sherborne estate, in Dorset – the last remaining property owned by the disgraced Sir Walter Raleigh – to his current favourite, Robert Carr. Many at court are concerned at both the king's unnatural profligacy and the damage that he is perceived to be causing the exchequer (→3/1611).

Robert Carr, the royal favourite.

Alien 'plantation' planned in Ulster

Ireland, July 1609
A rebellion last year by Sir Cahir O'Doherty – who seized Culmore and Derry before being killed – has induced King James's government to "plant" Ulster: land is to be taken from its Catholic owners and given to English and Scottish settlers. At the risk of provoking violence, the aim is to cut resistance to English rule and create a strong Protestant community. Land has already been seized in Armagh, Cavan, Donegal, Coleraine, Tyrone and Fermanagh, and is being given to immigrants, who must let it only to Protestant tenants (→5/1610).

An Irish soldier (l): conflict with his Scots counterpart (r) may threaten.

New curb proposed for Scottish crime

Scotland, June 1609
A number of commissioners of the peace are to be introduced into the country as a means of controlling the increase in crime. They will have authority to deal with minor disturbances as well as to monitor beggars and vagabonds and be involved with the provision of extra jails. In addition the commissioners will control the repair of roads and administration of ale houses, supervise markets, regulate weights and measures and fix wage levels. Their wide-ranging powers, modelled on the English example, will extend to the introduction of whatever measures are necessary to prevent the spread of diseases.

Highland chiefs accept bishop's reforms

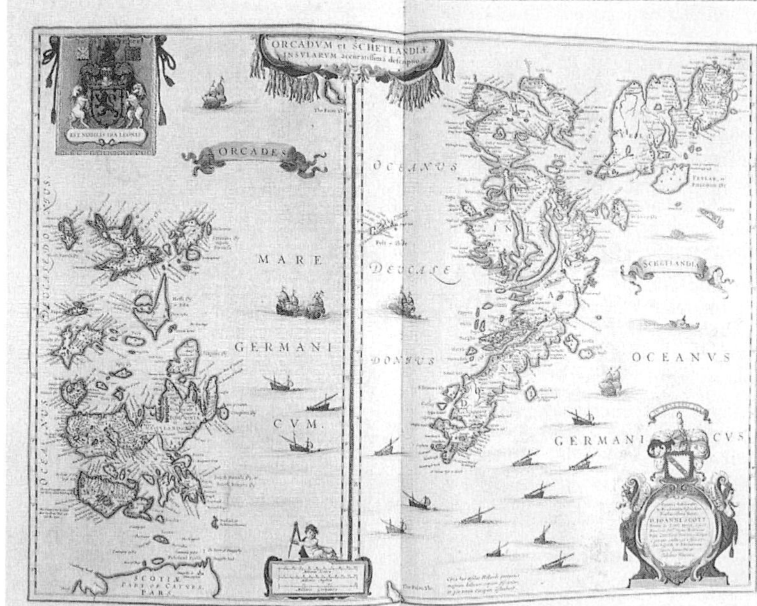

The Western Isles in the 17th century: now subject to the "Statutes of Iona".

Iona, Strathclyde, August 1609
At a meeting with Andrew Knox, the bishop of the Isles and King James's representative, the chiefs of the Scottish western isles and seaboard have accepted a series of crucial reforms. The "Statutes of Iona" represent a victory for those who have argued that the crown should deal directly with the chiefs to seek their cooperation, instead of relying on the intervention of ambitious magnates such as the earl of Argyll.

The Iona pact means the end of schemes to colonize the highlands with lowlanders. In addition, there are clauses that bind the chiefs to support the church and to send their sons to the lowlands for their education. The chiefs have agreed to follow laws being enforced elsewhere in the country by law commissioners [*see report below left*] and to control the production of alcohol. They are to reduce the power of their retinues as well as preventing the carrying of arms. They have further agreed to be responsible for their men and meet before the privy council every year.

Will Shakespeare publishes sonnets

England, 1609
William Shakespeare's *Sonnets* are at last in print, published by Thomas Thorpe and available in the London bookshops of William Aspley and John Wright. Begun some time around 1594, when the plague had closed the theatres, the poet's "sugared" sonnets have been circulating among his closest friends.

Shakespeare, already celebrated as a playwright, has been a member of Richard Burbage's company at the Globe theatre in London for the past ten years, during which time he has appeared in many of his own plays, including *Henry V*, *Hamlet*, *Macbeth*, *King Lear* and *Antony and Cleopatra* (→29/6/13).

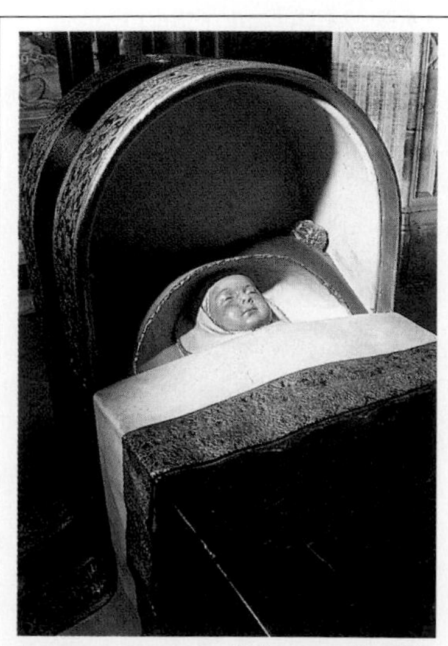
A monument to Princess Sophia – King James's daughter, who died soon after birth in 1606 – by Maximilian Colt, made master sculptor to the crown in 1608.

1610

Rome, 15 April. Robert Parsons, the leader of the Jesuit movement in England, dies.

England, May. Lady Arabella Stuart, a cousin of King James and possible heir to the throne, secretly marries William Seymour, the earl of Hertford, a grandson of Lady Catherine Grey and possible successor to the throne (→ 9/7).

Ireland, May. Immigrants from England and Scotland known as "undertakers" are assigned land in the Ulster plantation (→ 12/1610).

Glasgow, 8 June. The general assembly approves the restoration of the diocesan episcopacy in Scotland.

London, 9 July. King James imprisons his cousin Arabella and her husband, William Seymour, following the discovery of their secret marriage (→ 6/1611).

North America, August. Henry Hudson, an English navigator, discovers what will be called the Hudson river and Delaware Bay (→ 12/1611).

Central [Scotland], summer. The privy council orders the extermination of the Macgregor clan; all men are to be killed, women are to be branded on the face and children detained.

Lambeth, November. Richard Bancroft, the archbishop of Canterbury who pursued a hard line against those refusing to conform to the established church, dies. He is replaced by George Abbott (→ 4/1618).

Fife, 24 December. Sir George Hay is granted a patent to establish a facility for glassmaking at Wemyss.

Bristol. John Guy, a merchant, is appointed the first governor of Newfoundland in the New World.

London. Ben Jonson's new play, *The Alchemist*, receives its first performance (→ 11/9/11).

England. John Donne, the poet, is writing a series of intense love poems that combine spiritual imagery with sensuality (→ 1615).

Oxford. It is decreed that the Bodleian library should be given a copy of every book published by the Stationers' Company in London.

Oxford. Nicholas and Dorothy Wadham found Wadham College (→ 1611).

Prince Henry, heir to the throne of England and Scotland, becomes prince of Wales

Queen Anne dressed for a masque.

Prince Henry as "soldier of God".

London, 6 January
The highlight of today's investiture of Prince Henry as prince of Wales was the spectacular masque – a costume drama with both songs and dances – written by Ben Jonson and produced by Inigo Jones. The 15-year-old prince played the star role of Moeliades, an anagram of *miles a Deo*, or soldier of God. His mother, Anne, is also fond of such diversion. Jonson skilfully wrote his script to create an amusing entertainment and at the same time pay homage to the king's well-known mystical views on the monarchy. James appears as a pagan god and Anne as a classical queen. There was no doubt about the political message: the God-given right of James's son to succeed to the English and Scottish thrones.

The youthful Henry shows more interest in reason than in mysticism and is starting a new royal trend by his patronage of scientists.

James insists that he is accountable to nobody but God

London, 21 March
King James was criticized again today after a highflown speech on divine right. "Kings are justly called gods," he said, because they exercise "divine power on earth". He claimed: "For kings are not only God's lieutenants upon earth, and sit upon God's throne, but even by God himself they are called gods."

What worried parliament was the insistence that kings, like gods, have absolute powers and are "yet accountable to none but God only". This includes the power of life and death and being judges of all their subjects. The king went on: "They have power to exalt low things, and abase high things, and make of their subjects like men at chess – a pawn to take a bishop or a knight ..."

Those close to the king say that he gets carried away when making theoretical points of this kind. They suggest that a speech which his minister, Robert Cecil, now earl of Salisbury, made on his behalf two weeks ago is a better guide to his policies. The earl said: "It was dangerous to submit the power of the king to a definition." But Salisbury stressed that "he is a king by the common law of the land" and acknowledged that James "had no power to make laws of himself without the consent of his three estates" (→ 19/12/21).

Millers safeguard commercial success of river Wandle in Surrey

There has been a big increase in the number of water-mills for grinding corn.

Wandsworth, London, 14 February
Millers on the river Wandle, which joins the Thames here west of London, have succeeded in stopping attempts to divert one-tenth of the river water to London for domestic water. Mills have existed on the river since Norman times, and the millers have been ingenious in making the most of the small drop of 37 metres (124 feet) over its 9-mile length. They have built ponds for water storage. There are now 24 corn mills on the river, which produce one-third of Surrey's supply of corn to London. The Wandle is the most important river in Surrey for water-wheels. It supports an increasing number of industrial mills for grinding dyestuffs.

Royal cash deal agreed

Westminster, 17 July
Months of wrangling ended today when the English parliament and King James reached agreement on royal finances. The "Great Contract" is the result of hard bargaining worthy of small shopkeepers. Parliament has persuaded the king to give up his feudal tenures and wardships in return for compensation of £200,000 a year. The king wanted £220,000, and parliament did not want to stick at £180,000.

But the king's financial worries persist. He is negotiating a short-term loan of £100,000 from the City of London to tide him over while he looks for new sources of revenue. The "book of rates", introduced by his minister Robert Cecil, the earl of Salisbury, is the most promising of these. It levies import duties on 1,400 items.

The mercantile interests in parliament are even more worried about the new rates than about the old feudal levies. They have long allowed the king to levy duties to regulate trade. But when he does it to raise revenue, it seems to them as if he is taking money from their pockets to put it into his own (→9/11).

Robert Cecil: finding new revenues.

Telescopes magnify scientific discoveries

London, 31 December
Thomas Harriott and his pupil Sir William Lower are making discoveries with their new telescopes that rival those of the Italian Galileo. Harriott, who was formerly mathematical tutor to Sir Walter Raleigh, has made well over one hundred observations of sunspots this month which have enabled him to measure the sun's axial rotation. Many of the findings here confirm those of Galileo – for instance, the Englishmen have found much the same pattern of new satellite planets around Jupiter – but there are some conflicts of interpretation.

Galileo is convinced that he can see mountains on the moon. Lower has seen a spot, "which represents unto me the man in the moon (but without a head)".

Aided by telescopes, English scientists make discoveries that rival Galileo's.

Salisbury's 'Great Contract' disintegrates

Westminster, 9 November
The "Great Contract", so ingeniously devised by Robert Cecil, the earl of Salisbury, has collapsed. The Commons decided today not to proceed with it. In July Cecil was ready to concede that parliament should have the power to veto the import duties imposed by King James. He is now reluctant to do so because there is no sign that it is going to find the money to make good the shortfall in the king's finances. A land tax alone could not raise the necessary £200,000. Cecil believes that he has reached his limit in meeting parliament's price for abolishing feudal dues (→9/2/11).

A weird creature from "History of the Four-Footed Beasts", a scientific investigation published by Edward Topsell in 1610.

Irish face expulsion by Ulster 'planters'

Ulster, December
The London Salters' Company has this year built two plantation villages near Lough Neagh, Magherafelt and Salterstown. This follows the City of London's agreement with the English privy council for the plantation of the city of Derry and the county of Coleraine, and the assigning of other lands in Ulster to English and Scottish "undertakers". Protestant newcomers are fostering a different way of life from that of the native Irish. They have set up markets and local industries and built churches, schools and amenities. Most Irish in planted areas face expulsion (→6/1611).

Artistic maps provide a national portrait

London
John Speed is planning to publish his exquisite maps of England and Wales in a single work to be called *Theatre of the Empire of Great Britain*. He has already published 54 maps separately over the last four years which have won widespread admiration. Speed began his working life as a tailor and was admitted to the Merchant Taylors' Company in 1580. But his passions are map-making and history. Thanks to the patronage of the poet Sir Fulke Greville, he has been able to devote himself full-time to this work for several years. He also plans a *History of Great Britain* (→23/11/16).

John Speed's map of London and surrounding areas is one of 54 regional maps which are to be combined into one volume on England and Wales.

1611 - 1612

Scotland, 1 January 1611. A new book of customs rates is introduced on English imports; all steps for economic union have halted (→ 27/3/25).

Westminster, 9 February 1611. King James dissolves his first English parliament; he is angry over members' refusal to pay attention to his financial needs (→ 7/6/14).

England, March 1611. Robert Carr is created Viscount Rochester (→ 15/9/13).

Ireland, June 1611. Lord Carew is appointed to inquire into governmental problems here (→ 1612).

England, 11 September 1611. Simon Forman, the astrologer, dies; he was the inspiration for Ben Jonson's *The Alchemist*.

Orkney Islands, 1611. The privy council enforces Scottish law here, abolishing the long established Norse law.

London, 1611. Charterhouse School for boys is opened (→ 13/7/13).

Oxford, 28 January 1612. Sir Thomas Bodley, the founder of the Bodleian library, dies.

Dublin, 1 February 1612. Cornelius O'Devany, the Catholic bishop of Down and Connor, who was convicted of treason last month, is hanged (→ 29/3/13).

Britain/Europe, May 1612. Negotiations are completed for the marriage of Elizabeth, James's eldest daughter, to Frederick V, the Elector Palatine (→ 14/3/13).

London, 29 June 1612. A Scottish nobleman, Robert Crichton, Lord Sanquhar, is hanged for ordering the murder of a fencing master who struck out one of his eyes; the affair raises Anglo-Scottish tensions at court.

Scotland, June 1612. Fires caused by drought damage crops and fruits (→ 12/10/21).

England, 1612. Captain John Smith, the explorer and navigator, publishes a map of the Virginia colony (→ 22/3/22).

Ireland, 1612. Sir John Davies publishes his *Discovery of the true causes why Ireland was never entirely subdued until the beginning of his majesty's happy reign*, an official history from the English viewpoint.

London, 1612. The composer Orlando Gibbons publishes a selection of madrigals including *The Silver Swan* (→ 1619).

Mutinous crew sets Hudson adrift at sea

Henry Hudson cast adrift to die.

London, December 1611

A leading explorer and his teenage son have almost certainly died in an open rowing boat in the Arctic after being set adrift. This is the story being told by the exhausted survivors of a disastrous expedition, led by Henry Hudson, to find a north-west passage; they have recently returned to England and are now in prison for mutiny.

Hudson sailed from London in the *Discovery* in April last year and found a great bay which he mapped for three months, but then the ice set in, and the expedition had to winter on land. Hudson could not control the tensions created by bitter cold, little food and no work, until in June, amid allegations of favouritism, the men mutinied.

Authorized version of the Bible published

London, 1611

A new version of the Bible, authorized by the king, has been praised for the majesty and music of its language – especially remarkable in that it was written by a committee. The project began seven years ago when James resolved to replace the popular Geneva Bible, which he believed was seditious.

Fifty-four scholars produced a new translation from the original Hebrew and Greek; this was then reviewed by a committee of 12, and finally Thomas Bilson and Miles Smith went over it all again. The result is a wonderful unity of style. It was printed by Robert Barker, the king's printer (→ 4/8/17).

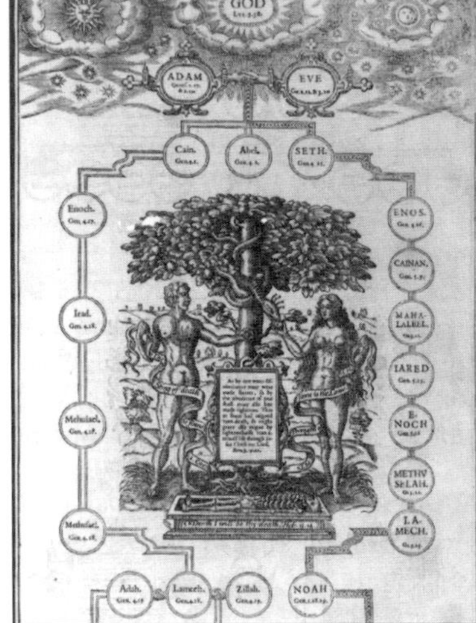

The family tree from the new Bible.

Brand new titles are offered for sale

London, 1611

You, too, could become a member of the aristocracy. All you need to take advantage of the once-in-a-lifetime opportunity which has been announced this year by King James is £1,095 cash, lands worth £1,000 and a coat of arms going back three generations. Then, if you are one of the lucky candidates – you will have to swear an oath that you did not bribe a courtier to be nominated – you could buy one of the newly created titles of hereditary baronet. This offer is strictly limited to 100 applicants.

King loses trusted Scottish secretary

London, 30 January 1611

King James's Scottish treasurer, George Home, the earl of Dunbar, has died suddenly in Whitehall. Dunbar has been one of the most powerful men in Scotland since the union of the crowns led to the prolonged absence of its king in England. In 1605 he pushed through the unpopular and rigged trial of the rebellious Scots ministers who had infuriated James by disobeying him. James has not been to Scotland since 1603, despite his promise to do so, leaving Dunbar and others to run the government.

New book tells of the exotic crimes of 'the Pendle witches'

Three witches of Pendle ride out on a pig to perform their evil deeds.

Lancaster, 1612

An astonishing tale of witchcraft has been revealed in *The Wonderful Discovery of Witches in the County of Lancashire*. This book, by one Thomas Potts, describes the trial and execution of two men and seven women after years in which two rival witch clans, headed by formidable matriarchs known as Old Chattox and Old Demdike, had flourished in Pendle. They allegedly sold protection against evil powers and charms to heal the sick. But then a zealous justice of the peace, Roger Nowell, launched an inquiry which uncovered crimes such as necromancy and the plotting of acts like blowing up Lancaster jail.

Royal claimants make bid for freedom

Dover, June 1611
A young cousin of King James who married in defiance of him and then escaped from custody has been recaptured within sight of Calais as her boat waited for her husband. Lady Arabella Stuart, a claimant to the throne, had fallen in love with William Seymour, the earl of Hertford – also a claimant through Lady Catherine Grey, his grandmother, who was imprisoned with *her* husband by Queen Elizabeth for marrying. James was as alarmed as Elizabeth, and history repeated itself. Seymour also escaped, but the couple missed a rendezvous on the Essex coast. Seymour reached Ostend, but he is unlikely ever to see Arabella again (→9/1615).

Chief minister dies abandoned by king

Hatfield House in Hertfordshire: the home of the unhappy Robert Cecil.

Marlborough, Wiltshire, May 1612
King James's chief minister, Robert Cecil, the earl of Salisbury, has died an unhappy man, virtually abandoned by the king who not only owed him his throne but whom he served as loyally as he had Elizabeth. While the king hunted, Salisbury virtually ran the administration, trying to control the finances of a king who has spent more than £55,000 on 13 royal houses alone.

Once the king would call him "my little beagle" – a nickname he detested, but it did show affection. Recently Salisbury had been given the blame for the king's conflicts with the last parliament, and the new favourite, Sir Robert Carr, had turned the king against him.

Prince of Wales is dead

London, 7 November 1612
The unexpected death of the 18-year-old prince of Wales has been greeted with shock throughout the country. The handsome, athletic heir to the throne, who died of typhoid fever yesterday evening, had come to personify the ideals of a Protestant knight: courageous in spirit and learned in culture. "Our rising sun is set ere scarce he has shone and all our glory lies buried," writes the earl of Dorset.

Prince Henry in the hunting field.

Henry was invested as prince of Wales in January 1610. In contrast to the cultivation of a circle of favourites practised by his father, King James, the prince proved himself to be a serious young man, with an independent outlook, who despised what he saw as the unseemly manners at court. Henry was religious but had a flair for public life. He supported science and the arts, especially the new "masques", as well as being keen on military skills and interested in the navy. His 11-year-old brother Charles, the new heir, will have a hard time following in his footsteps (→1614).

'Old English' Catholics defy 'New English'

Ireland, 1612
The English administration in Ireland has been forced to confront a large and influential group who term themselves the "Old English". These people – English by descent but Catholic in confession – own one third of the land and are loyal to the crown. Yet they believe that England, assuming all Catholics to be disloyal, no longer values their allegiance; they also fear that they will lose their lands if there ceases to be a distinction between them and the native, Gaelic Irish. Their discontent has been heightened by the activities of the "New English" – freebooting *parvenus* who are exploiting the government's policy on "defective titles" to get land from the crown on favourable terms [*see report on page 507*] (→1/2).

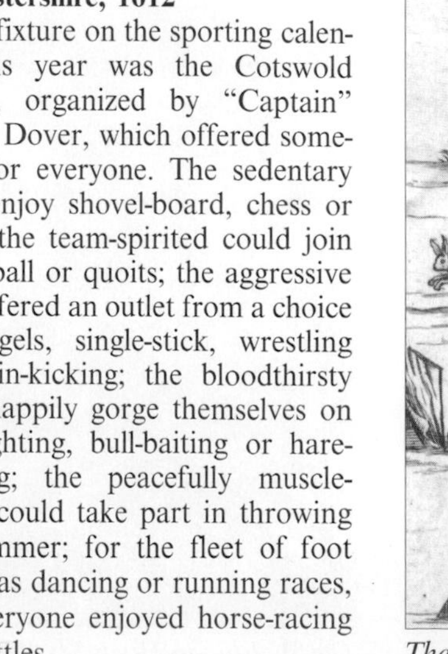

Hemlines are getting shorter – provoking Protestant criticism.

Games festival in Cotswolds provides something for everyone

Gloucestershire, 1612
A new fixture on the sporting calendar this year was the Cotswold Games, organized by "Captain" Robert Dover, which offered something for everyone. The sedentary could enjoy shovel-board, chess or bowls; the team-spirited could join in football or quoits; the aggressive were offered an outlet from a choice of cudgels, single-stick, wrestling and shin-kicking; the bloodthirsty could happily gorge themselves on cock-fighting, bull-baiting or hare-coursing; the peacefully muscle-bound could take part in throwing the hammer; for the fleet of foot there was dancing or running races, and everyone enjoyed horse-racing and skittles.

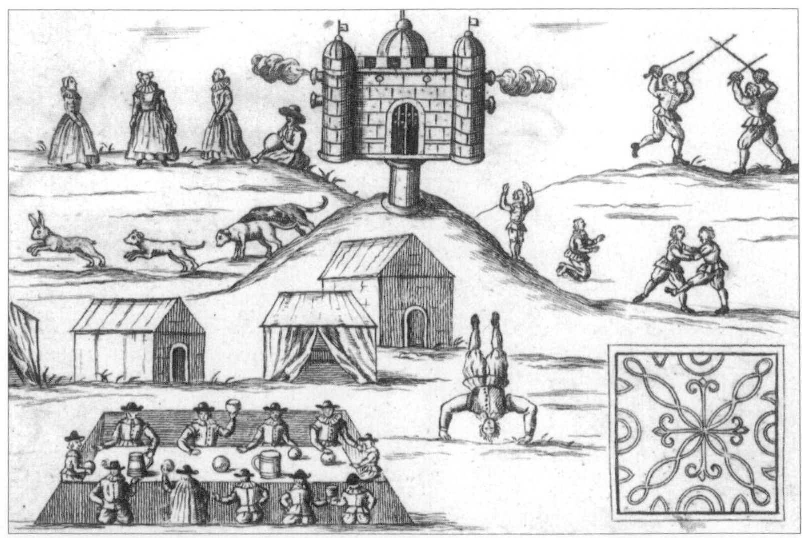

The Cotswold Games: a festival that boasts a wide range of attractions.

1613-1614

Derry, 29 March 1613. A royal charter incorporates Derry as the city of Londonderry and creates the county of Londonderry; the city's administration passes to the London corporations which came to Ireland with the plantation (→18/5).

Dublin, 18 May 1613. King James opens his first Irish parliament; Catholic members remain loyal after a row over the election of a Protestant English speaker for the House of Commons (→1613).

London, May 1613. Diego Sarmiento de Acuna takes up his post as Spanish ambassador (→26/5/21).

London, 29 June 1613. The Globe theatre burns down during the first performance of *Henry VIII*, a play by William Shakespeare (→23/4/16).

London, 15 September 1613. Sir Thomas Overbury, a close friend of Viscount Rochester, dies in the Tower (→25/9).

London, 25 September 1613. James intervenes to obtain a divorce for Frances, the countess of Essex, the lover of Viscount Rochester (→26/12).

London, 26 December 1613. The earl of Somerset (the former Viscount Rochester) marries Frances, the countess of Essex (→12/10/15).

London, 1613. The playwright John Webster follows his success of last year, *The White Devil*, with a tragedy called *The Duchess of Malfi*.

London, 1613. Sir Francis Bacon becomes solicitor-general (→6/1616).

Belfast, 1613. A charter incorporates the city (→7/8/14).

England, 26 January 1614. King James bans duelling.

Westminster, July 1614. Thomas Howard, the earl of Suffolk, is appointed lord treasurer; the earl of Somerset succeeds him as lord chamberlain (→7/1615).

Ireland, 7 August 1614. James dismisses Catholic allegations of corruption in elections to parliament (→4/1615).

Strathclyde, September 1614. The MacDonald clan rebels on the island of Islay.

London, 1614. Negotiations open for the marriage of the king's son, Charles, to the *infanta*, Maria Anna, the Catholic daughter of Philip III of Spain (→11/1616).

Princess Elizabeth weds German elector

Part of the fireworks display for the lavish wedding of Princess Elizabeth.

London, 14 March 1613

Amid lavish and costly celebrations that her father, King James, can hardly afford, Princess Elizabeth has married the Elector Palatine, Frederick. There had been political moves to stop the wedding, which carries diplomatic implications by linking the throne of England so closely with the fate of the Protestant princes of Germany. The expense apart, James is pleased with the marriage. He plans to use it to build closer links with Protestants in both Germany and the United Provinces, thus elevating himself to the role of the champion of Protestant Europe (→1618).

Laird fails to get away with murder

Edinburgh, 21 May 1613

For the first time a peer of the realm has been put to death for a common criminal offence. In this case the offence was murder, but nonetheless most lords are shocked that King James should insist on the execution of Lord Maxwell for the killing of John Johnstone, the laird of Johnstone. Lords expect to get away with murder, even of each other, and do not usually expect to pay with their lives for any crime short of treason; and often they are forgiven even for that.

But King James is determined to take a tough line with his lords, particularly the Scottish ones, who have given him nothing but trouble since his childhood. Lord Maxwell's crime was particularly obnoxious in that he called Johnstone to a peace conference to end a feud between their two families, which in 1608 had cost the lives of both men's fathers. But when Johnstone turned up, Maxwell shot him. For this, and other outrageous crimes, the king has had him beheaded.

Oxford college built by Somerset couple

Oxford, 13 July 1613

The opening of hundreds of schools in England during the reign of Queen Elizabeth has led to a steady increase in literacy throughout the country and among people of all classes. As a result there has been a greater demand for university education, a demand that cannot be satisfied by the present facilities.

At Oxford it is hoped that the new Wadham College will help to deal with the press of new students. The college has been endowed by Nicholas Wadham and his wife Dorothy, a rich landowning couple from Merifield in Somerset.

It is unusual among university colleges in that it has been started and completed in a short space of time, rather than over a period of many years, sometimes centuries. Begun in 1610, it has just been finished, and its design is particularly notable for the regularity of its windows, which are spaced according to a strict plan (→10/12/16).

'New River' brings fresh water to London

London, 29 September 1613

It seemed as if all London flocked to Clerkenwell in Islington today to witness the opening of the New River, which has brought the first ever supply of fresh, clean water to the city. Already seen as a huge benefit to public health, the "river" is really a conduit dug for nearly 40 miles (64km) to bring water from pure chalk springs near Ware in Hertfordshire. The inauguration is a triumph for Hugh Myddelton, a Welsh-speaking Welshman from Denbigh, who has pushed the project through despite all opposition.

The Welshman Hugh Myddelton brings London its first fresh-water supply.

'Addled parliament' out

Northampton: conservative earl.

Suffolk: soon to be treasurer.

London, 7 June 1614
Parliament has been dissolved after sitting since April and achieving nothing. It was called because King James is desperate for money, and dubbed the "addled parliament" when it failed to produce any. The attorney-general, Sir Francis Bacon, had induced James to summon members against the advice of the court faction led by Henry Howard, the earl of Northampton.

Bacon hoped that the parliament would not only approve funds but also bridge the divide between king and Commons. As it was, the gulf widened, with members refusing to grant extra money without being allowed to air their grievances over the king's pro-Spanish foreign policy and his toleration of pro-Catholic courtiers such as Howard. A disgruntled king therefore sent them home and later grumbled to Sarmiento, the Spanish ambassador: "I am surprised that my ancestors should have permitted such an institution to come into being."

James plans to appoint Thomas Howard, the earl of Suffolk, as the new lord treasurer, with his favourite, Robert Carr, the earl of Somerset, taking over from Suffolk as lord chamberlain (→ 7/1614).

Cockayne proposes to ban the export of all unfinished cloth to northern Europe

London, December 1614
Wool merchants have devised a plan to squeeze more profit from their trade by getting King James to ban the export of cloth that has not been dyed and dressed in England. Dyeing is the most profitable part of cloth manufacture, and the merchants are annoyed that in large parts of the continent they cannot sell dyed English cloth at any price. They believe that this is prejudice against English goods, and they claim that continental merchants deliberately stretch their cloth to cover the greatest number of metres. This treatment results in its wearing badly, a fault for which the English are blamed.

Weavers hope for bigger profits.

The continentals say that the English are simply bad dyers and that their wares are not up to standard. None the less, a group of rich merchants, led by Alderman Cockayne, has persuaded James that dyeing done at home will provide more jobs for Englishmen and enhance profits that the financially hard-pressed king can share (→ 1617).

Numerical calculations easier with logs

Edinburgh, 1614
Tired of the massive and complicated calculations required in higher mathematics, the Scottish mathematician John Napier has spent nearly 25 years researching an easier way of doing them. The result of his work has been the invention of logarithms, a device which he has now announced with the publication of his book *Descriptio*. Logarithms are particularly useful to map-makers, surveyors and navigators. They reduce the calculation of a position by trigonometry from a long, difficult sum, using multiplication, division, square and cubic extractions, to a matter of addition and subtraction using logarithmic tables. Napier himself, in the foreword to his book, says that he wanted to avoid the tedious expenditure of time and the "slippery errors" of the old system (→ 1617).

Old rituals move from church to alehouse

England, 1614
There is growing concern among the ruling class about the influence of alehouses, whose popularity is steadily rising. This is not least because the alehouse provides an alternative meeting place to the church – which has been made uncomfortably rigid by puritans and is also a means by which the élite try to police the working classes.

An attack on old rituals by the puritans has moved them from the church, with the result that dancing at Candlemas, football at Shrovetide, mummers at New Year and other such events now centre on alehouses. Common-law marriages are often contracted in the bars, while ceremonies for funerals and christenings now tend to start, and finish, in the alehouse.

The élite have also been using the church to keep an eye on the workers by the introduction of compulsory attendance, the registration of births, marriages and deaths, and hierarchical seating arrangements which leave labourers standing at the back. The response of many is to go for a drink rather than to church.

The goings-on in alehouses are attracting growing attention from the authorities, concerned that they lure too many away from church.

1615 - 1616

Edinburgh, 6 February 1615. Patrick Stewart, the earl of Orkney and a cousin of King James, is executed following a rebellion, led by his son, to overthrow James.

Glasgow, 28 February 1615. John Ogilvy, a Jesuit, is hanged for saying Mass (→ 1/8/18).

Ireland, 25 April 1615. The convocation of the Church of Ireland adopts the 104 basic articles of religion (→ 17/10/17).

London, April 1615. James knights his new favourite, the young courtier George Villiers, making him a gentleman of the bedchamber (→ 4/1616).

England, July 1615. James is reconciled with his former favourite, the earl of Somerset, who fell after scandalous rumours at court (→ 12/10).

Strathclyde, September 1615. Archibald Campbell, the earl of Argyll, ends the MacDonald rebellion in Islay.

London, September 1615. Lady Arabella Stuart, James's cousin, who was jailed on her marriage in 1610 to William Seymour, the earl of Hertford, and again after escaping in 1611, dies in the Tower.

London, 12 October 1615. The earl of Somerset and his wife, Lady Frances Howard, are charged with the murder of Sir Thomas Overbury in 1613; he opposed Lady Frances's controversial divorce from Robert Devereux, the earl of Essex (→ 5/1616).

England, 1615. The poet John Donne is appointed royal chaplain (→ 1625).

London, March 1616. Sir Walter Raleigh is freed after 13 years' imprisonment in the Tower (→ 12/6/17).

Scotland, 22 May 1616. The privy council bans tobacco, for health reasons.

London, May 1616. The earl and countess of Somerset are found guilty of murder (→ 13/7).

Westminster, June 1616. Sir Francis Bacon joins the privy council (→ 7/3/17).

Rome, 10 July 1616. Hugh O'Neill, the earl of Tyrone, dies (→ 23/1/18).

London, November 1616. Prince Charles, aged 16, is invested as prince of Wales (→ 3/1622).

Edinburgh, 10 December 1616. An act is passed providing for a school in every parish.

Plot to kill Ulster settlers discovered

An Irish spearman rides to attack.

Ulster, April 1615
A plot to massacre Protestant settlers in Ulster has been uncovered. The leader of the conspiracy, Rory Oge 'Cahan, has been arrested together with six other men. The killing was to start at Coleraine and spread from there to all the English settlements. Some claim, however, that the lord deputy, Chichester, is exaggerating the danger in order to give legitimacy to tougher action against the native Irish.

Resentment against English policy is high. A "fixed" parliament – with a built-in Protestant majority – has been dismissed for not being pliable enough, while English settlements multiply on lands confiscated from the rebel earls of Tyrconnell and Tyrone (→ 10/7/16).

Famous chronicler of exploration dies

London, 23 November 1616
Richard Hakluyt – a man whose name is at the forefront of discovery and exploration – has died. He never once ventured further afield than Paris. Born 64 years ago, Hakluyt lectured in geography at Oxford University and it was he who introduced the globe into English schools. But it is as the chronicler of Elizabethan explorers that he is famous, and his *Principal Navigations, Voyages and Discoveries of the English Nation* is the most detailed record published of the voyages of John and Sebastian Cabot, Francis Drake and John Hawkins.

Countess wins royal reprieve for murder

London, 13 July 1616
Frances Howard, the beautiful but wilful countess of Somerset, has been pardoned for murder. She and her husband, King James's former favourite Robert Carr, now earl of Somerset, were found guilty of conspiring to murder Carr's secretary, Sir Thomas Overbury, but will escape the axeman. The couple will be confined in the Tower of London, where the alleged poisoning of Overbury took place.

The guilt of the countess is unquestionable. The same is not true of her husband. He arranged to lock up Overbury in the Tower, but that was because Overbury knew too much about Frances, who had sought a controversial divorce to marry the earl. There is no firm evidence that Somerset was mixed up in murder, but the guilt of his wife damned him by association. The trial opened on 25 May before a court of peers chosen by the lord high steward, one of Somerset's bitterest enemies. Sir Edward Coke, prosecuting, was relentless, and the earl was saved from death only by the king's intervention.

Frances Howard: guilty of murder.

Misogynist publishes his views on women

A misogynist's view of society, featuring "Fill Gut and Pinch Belly": "One being fat with eating good men, the other lean for want of good women."

London, 1616
A new book has provoked scorn and contempt from the growing number of educated women in England – but it has proved so popular amongst the nation's men that it is being reprinted.

Joseph Swetman, the author of *An Arraignment of Lewd, Idle, Forward and Inconstant Women*, contends that "women spring from the Devil, whose heads, hands, hearts and minds are evil". Women, he goes on, are born not only to be subordinate to men but to be ruled by them, and he strongly advocates regular bouts of wife-beating to maintain patriarchal order.

The last half-century has seen a remarkable expansion of women's education, and the advance by women into areas previously deemed to have been exclusively reserved for the male sex. Swetman's *Arraignment* is the most aggressive assertion yet promulgated of man's supposed divine right over women – and a passionate answer to Jane Anger's recently published tract *A Protection for Women*, which provoked the fury of misogynists all over the country.

Viscountcy given to new royal favourite

Woodstock, Oxon, June 1616
George Villiers, King James's new favourite, has just received the title of Viscount Buckingham. The king is reported to have performed the ceremony "with the greatest alacrity and princely cheerfulness". Villiers has risen in the king's favour with a speed matched only by that of the earl of Somerset's fall. From the night that James first set eyes upon him at Apethorpe House, two years ago, he developed an obsession with his "dear, sweet Steenie". The new favourite – who, unlike Somerset, possesses intelligence – flirts shamelessly with his gout-ridden king (→5/1/17).

George Villiers: the new favourite.

Catholic schools for girls are under fire

France, 1616
Mary Ward, an English Catholic who has set up schools for women here, is facing criticism for over-educating her pupils. Ward seeks to teach young Catholics who "in the sadly afflicted case of England can undertake something more than ordinary". Since 1609 she and her lay community have built up her school at St Omer, making dangerous journeys to England to recruit students. This year she opened a second school at Liège. Greek, Latin, French, mathematics and astronomy are offered, far more than a girl at a English school would learn.

Aristocrats indulge themselves in vast mansions as peace and prosperity offer opportunites for flamboyant displays of wealth

The magnificent west front of Audley End, the home of the earl of Suffolk, near the river Cam.

England and Scotland, 1616
The sense of security after long years of peace has led to a flamboyant display of wealth by the aristocracy in England – and nowhere is this more apparent than in their vast mansions. Among the finest is Audley End, near Saffron Walden in Essex, finished this year by Thomas Howard, the earl of Suffolk and lord treasurer, at a cost of 200,000.

It is the largest and grandest house built by a king's subject, rising on the banks of the river Cam. The house, of pale grey Ketton stone, is not "modern"; the references to ancient Rome and Greece seen in contemporary continental buildings are absent. Rather, its "gothic" influences display a concern with romantic conservatism, similar to that seen at Hatfield House in Hertfordshire, rebuilt by Robert Cecil, the earl of Salisbury, and completed in 1612. Elsewhere, the designer Inigo Jones is planning an extravagant new house for Queen Anne, this time in a modern style, at Greenwich.

The long period of peace has also had its effect on Scottish architecture. As need for sturdy defences has waned, the traditional tower has given way to more ambitious castellated mansions. One of the most spectacular new buildings is the palace at Kirkwall built by King James's cousin Patrick Stewart, the earl of Orkney, who has also created an imposing castle at Scalloway in Shetland (→1619).

The Queen's House at Greenwich, designed by Inigo Jones for Queen Anne.

The staircase at Hatfield House has gates to stop dogs going up.

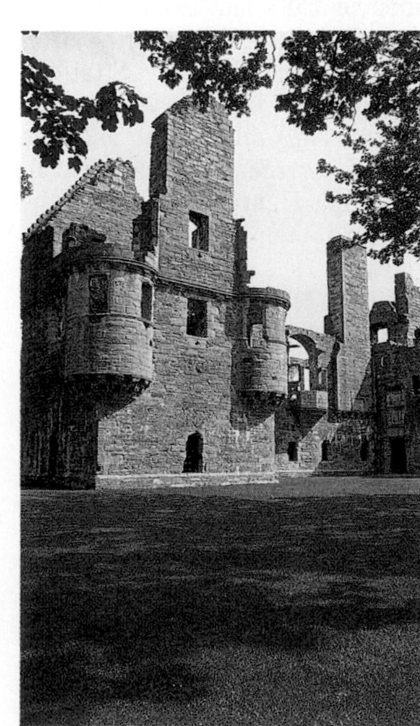
Remains of the palace built by the earl of Orkney at Kirkwall.

Shakespeare bequeaths matchless literary legacy

Stratford, 23 April 1616
William Shakespeare died today at his house, New Place, in Stratford-upon-Avon, where he was born and spent his last five years. It was his 52nd birthday. He is to be buried in the chancel of Holy Trinity church. He was the author of 36 plays, 18 of them published; his fame exceeds that of any living author.

He was a handsome, well-shaped man whose "honest, open and free nature" impressed all who met him. He was called "mellifluous and honey-tongued". Ben Jonson, his friend, who was with him shortly before his death, says that he had "small Latin and less Greek", for he lacked university education, but that "his wit flowed with such facility that sometimes it was necessary he should be stopped".

It is a wonder that a country-bred man making his way as an actor could acquire such knowledge of humanity that he could create kings, queens, nobles, soldiers, yokels, taproom wags, rogues, fools and harlots, fops and philosophers, women innocent or devious, gay, shrewish, witty or rebellious. But it was his genius that he could inhabit the soul of any fellow being, knowing the doubts of Hamlet, the superstition of Macbeth, the madness of Lear, the mischief of Falstaff, finally the capacity to build fantasy and magical illusion out of words – the gift of Prospero, with whom he took his leave of us.

William Shakespeare, the dramatist, who died at his birthplace of Stratford.

Yeoman's son has first views of stage

Early years: Shakespeare's first experiences of the stage were the visits to Stratford made by "the Earl of Leicester's Men". His father, John, had been a yeoman and town bailiff but later got into serious debt. His mother, Mary, came from a farming family. William was educated at Stratford grammar school. At 18 he married Anne Hathaway of Shottery, who bore their daughter Susannah in 1583 and twins, Hamnet and Judith, in 1585. Shortly afterwards Shakespeare left Stratford for London. His early narrative poems, *Venus and Adonis* and *The Rape of Lucrece*, were dedicated to his patron, Henry Wriothesley, the earl of Southampton.

Patron: the earl of Southampton.

Developing dramatist learns how to act and 'fit up' old plays

Richard Burbage: leading actor.

The Globe theatre at Southwark, where Shakespeare wrote and acted.

1592-1600: When Shakespeare got to London, the theatre was dominated by a group of writer-actors known as "the University Wits". Thomas Kyd, Robert Greene and George Peele were Oxford men, and Christopher Marlowe, a shoemaker's son, went to Cambridge. Untutored, Shakespeare learned to act and to "fit up" old plays by rewriting them for Richard Burbage's company. In 1592 Greene wrote to his fellow wits about actors, including one who "supposes he is as well able to bombast out a blank verse as the best of you ... and is in his own conceit the only Shake-scene in the country". By this time Shakespeare is believed to have written the three parts of *Henry VI*, *Two Gentlemen of Verona*, *The Comedy of Errors* and the horror-play *Titus Andronicus*. In 1593/4 plague closed the theatres, and he turned to poetry, notably sonnets.

In 1594 Burbage formed a new company, "the Lord Chamberlain's Men". For them the poet poured forth comedies such as *A Midsummer Night's Dream*, tragedy – *Romeo and Juliet* – and histories such as *Richard II* and *Richard III*. Their Shoreditch theatre was torn down and its planks transported across London Bridge to the south bank, where it was re-erected and reopened in 1599 as the Globe. Burbage made Shakespeare a shareholder in the enterprise. The public paid a penny to stand or 2d for a seat in the covered galleries. The opening plays included *Henry V*.

What a piece of work is man, how noble in reason, how infinite in faculties; in form and moving how express and admirable, in action how like an angel, in apprehension how like a god: the beauty of the world, the paragon of animals! And yet to me what is this quintessence of dust?

Hamlet II, ii.

Life's but a walking shadow,
a poor player,
That struts and frets his hour
upon the stage,
And then is heard no more.

Macbeth V, iii.

... We are such stuff
As dreams are made on ...

The Tempest IV, i.

The actor-turned-playwright grows rich

1600-08: During the 1590s there had been many performances of a play called *Hamlet*. In 1602 Shakespeare's rewritten version of the story was registered as *The Revenge of Hamlet, Prince of Denmark*, and after more rewriting it became his company's leading attraction, with Richard Burbage playing the title role and Shakespeare the Ghost. Plots of bloody revenge were popular with Elizabethan audiences. Shakespeare followed this with further tragic roles for Burbage as Othello, King Lear, Macbeth and Antony by 1608.

Queen Elizabeth had admired his work and was so fond of Falstaff in *Henry IV* that she asked for another play showing him in love – which Shakespeare supplied in *The Merry Wives of Windsor*. In 1603 King James licensed Burbage's company to play "comedies, tragedies, histories, interludes ... for our solace and pleasure". By this time the playwright, with a share in the company profits, was a rich man. By 1608 he had given up acting and written his final tragedy, *Coriolanus*. That year his daughter Susannah gave him a grandchild, Elizabeth.

An actor of Shakespeare's time.

Blackfriars and the return to Stratford

The comfortable interior of the Blackfriars theatre: a later reconstruction.

1608-16: In 1608 Burbage took over the indoor theatre at Blackfriars for winter seasons instead of the Globe. It was more intimate and comfortable, and cost more to attend. Lit by candles, it lent itself to more elaborate scenic effects, and Shakespeare wrote a new kind of play for it, the romances *Cymbeline*, *The Winter's Tale* and in 1611 *The Tempest*. By 1610 he had left London for New Place, the house he had bought at Stratford in 1597. He still kept in contact with his fellow-playwrights. One of them, John Fletcher, sought his help with a play, *Henry VIII*, which they co-wrote for the season of 1613. On 2 July that year a stage cannon set fire to the thatched roof, and the Globe was burnt to the ground. So ended his career as a playwright.

Genius of Shakespeare's contemporaries ushers in golden age of English drama

London, 1616

Shakespeare was at the head of an unprecedented outpouring of drama. By 1600 there were five theatres regularly needing new plays and no lack of writers to fill them with blood, horror, tragedy and comedy. Shakespeare himself began writing just as the London stage lost Christopher Marlowe, whose greatest plays *Tamburlaine the Great* and *Dr Faustus* were written in the few years before his death in 1593.

Among Shakespeare's contemporaries the biggest draw is Ben Jonson, whose *Every Man in his Humour* (1598) began a series of mordant comedies about rogues, tricksters and their dupes. *Volpone* (1605) and *The Alchemist* (1610) were performed by "the King's Men", and *Bartholomew Fair* came in 1614. In 1600/01 Jonson and John Marston waged a "war of the poets", pillorying one another as lightly disguised characters in their plays. Then they co-wrote *Eastward Ho!*, which landed them both in jail for caricaturing the king's Scots courtiers. John Fletcher, who co-wrote with Shakespeare, now writes with Francis Beaumont. *The Knight of the Burning Pestle* is one of their most popular comedies (→ 1623).

Marlowe was greatly admired.

Ben Jonson: won in "poets' war".

A scene from Ben Jonson's highly successful play "The Alchemist".

1617 - 1618

Westminster, 5 January 1617. Sir George Villiers, King James's favourite, is created earl of Buckingham (→ 1/1/18).

Westminster, 7 March 1617. Sir Francis Bacon is appointed lord keeper of the great seal, replacing Sir Thomas Egerton, Lord Ellesmere, who resigned on 3 March (→ 7/1/18).

Plymouth, 12 June 1617. Sir Walter Raleigh sets sail on his second voyage to Guyana (→ 29/10/18).

Edinburgh, June 1617. Parliament introduces a register to record transactions of landed property.

Ireland, 17 October 1617. A royal proclamation orders the banishment of all priests educated abroad (→ 2/1624).

Fife, November 1617. The general assembly at St Andrews rejects the controversial Five Articles which the king wishes the church to adopt (→ 1/8/18).

London, 1617. James appoints Ben Jonson poet laureate.

Edinburgh, 1617. John Napier, the mathematician who this year published *Rabdologieae*, a mechanical calculating device, dies (→ 1624).

London, 1617. The Society of Apothecaries is founded.

London, 1617. Fynes Moryson publishes his *Itinerary*.

Westminster, 1 January 1618. George Villiers is promoted from earl to marquis of Buckingham (→ 7/1618).

London, 7 January 1618. Sir Francis Bacon is appointed lord chancellor (→ 1620).

Ireland, 23 January 1618. The Waterford charter is revoked after nonconformists are elected to parliament (→ 1/10).

London, April 1618. The clergy are furious over a new book published last year by John Selden, *History of Tithes*; in it he denies that the payment of tithes is sanctioned by a divine right.

Perth, 1 August 1618. The general assembly of the Church of Scotland, browbeaten by the king, finally passes the Five Articles.→

Ulster, 1 October 1618. Native Irish are ordered to leave the lands owned by British "undertakers" by 1 May 1619 or pay a fine (→ 20/1/21).

England, 1618. David Ramsay and Thomas Wildgoose develop a ploughing machine.

King James pays visit to his homeland

James at Houghton Tower, Lancashire, on his way to visit Scotland. It was his first visit since being crowned king of England and was not a success.

Berwick, 4 August 1617
King James has ended his three-month tour of Scotland without achieving his objective, which was to pressure the Scots into adopting Anglican forms of worship. He scandalized Presbyterians by producing choristers and surplices for a service at Holyrood Palace, and then at a gathering of clergy at St Andrews he proposed that Communion be received in a kneeling position, that private Communion and private baptism be allowed, that bishops should administer confirmation and that all church festivals should be observed. The clergy protested that such matters could only be settled by a general assembly of the Scottish church.

It was the king's first visit since he left Scotland 14 years ago to receive the English crown. Despite the stag-hunts and the banquets arranged for him by the nobility, he alienated many people. The Scots, who remain overwhelmingly loyal to the kirk and opposed to episcopal authority, believe James has become too anglicized (→ 11/1617).

Howard family eclipsed by Buckingham

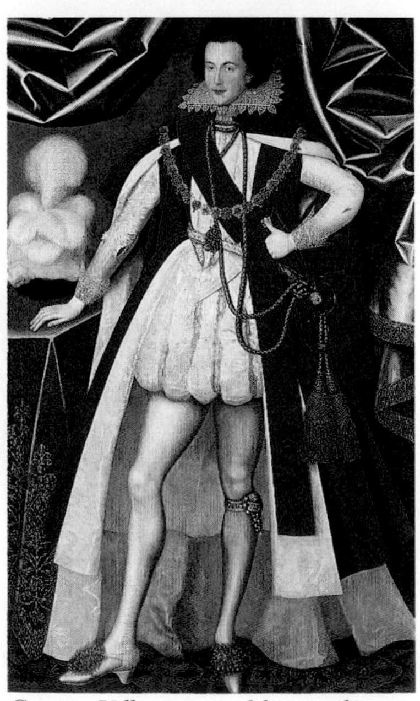

George Villiers ousted his rivals.

London, July 1618
A struggle for King James's favour between George Villiers, the marquis of Buckingham, and Thomas Howard, the earl of Suffolk, has ended with Suffolk and his wife being accused of embezzlement and heavily fined.

Buckingham introduced James to Sir Lionel Cranfield, a former cloth merchant turned financier. He was of great help to the king, who was trying to economize, but the Howards despised both this upstart and his sponsor. Observing that the king had a fancy for stroking Buckingham's face and hair, the Howards brought to court several handsome young men whose posturings caused discreet titterings. James saw what was happening and banished the boys. The Suffolks' downfall followed (→ 1/1619).

Cockayne's export plan for dyed cloth collapses in chaos

England, 1617
King James has been forced to drop the scheme devised by Alderman Cockayne to increase the value of English woollens by exporting only dyed cloth, following a decline of one-third in sales over three years. Dyeing enhances the value of woollen cloth by nearly 50 per cent, and Cockayne and some of his fellow merchants wanted to ensure that exports, particularly to the Dutch, were all of dyed wool.

But the merchants had reckoned without the determination of the Dutch to fight back against cloth whose dyes they consider greatly inferior to their own. First the Dutch banned imports of dyed cloth from England; then they began setting up their own weaving industry, even offering a bounty for each new loom that was established in their country. Cockayne had underestimated the speed with which he could expand the dyeing industry, which meant that there was not have enough dyed cloth for export, even if the Dutch had wanted it.

English wool was sold to Europe.

The consequence was that unemployment in England, especially in the western counties, soared – while the profit from the wool trade slumped, badly hitting the king's revenues as well as that of the merchants. Convinced at last that the scheme could not be made to work, James has ended the ban on undyed exports.

Outcry at James's religious policies

Puritans conciliated by 'Book of Sports'

London, 1 August 1618
King James has stirred up a hornets' nest with his effort to find a middle course between the puritans, who want Sunday to be observed by complete abstention from work and amusements of all kinds, and the rest of the people, who want to enjoy themselves after church service.

He has issued a *Book of Sports* allowing that puritans can hold to their beliefs but must not seek to coerce others, who can indulge in "dancing, archery, leaping, vaulting, or any other harmless recreation". But bear- and bull-baiting and bowling are banned.

James gave orders for his declaration to be read in church; clergy up and down the country have risen in protest. Strict Calvinists say that they will refuse to read the declaration; others intend to read it and then, from the same pulpit, preach a sermon against it (→ 5/1619).

From a private box, King James listens to a sermon at St Paul's Cathedral.

King imposes his 'popish' policies on Presbyterian Scotland

Perth, 1 August 1618
The royal will has prevailed – on paper. A browbeaten general assembly has endorsed the Five Articles for a "decent and comelie" church service, which were bitterly resisted by the Presbyterian kirk when James raised them during his visit to Scotland last year. The kirk will now be expected to observe such festivals as Christmas and Easter and cease to teach that the weekly Sabbath is God's main holy day. In the view of the kirk, other articles – including private Communion for someone about to die and confirmation by bishops of children aged eight – are papist practices revived. Most offensive of all is the article requiring Communion to be received in a kneeling position, a reminder of the Catholic doctrine that the bread and wine are transformed into the body and blood of Christ.

Despite the assembly's vote, the articles are certain to be widely ignored; the kirk is too firmly established in the hearts and minds of the Scottish people (→ 5/1619).

Fludd tells how universe was constructed

London, 1617
A hugely ambitious attempt to explain how the universe was constructed is being published by a wealthy London physician and dedicated to God and King James. Dr Robert Fludd has travelled extensively in Europe, where he became interested in the theories of the Swiss physician and alchemist Paracelsus; he has also defended the medical-mystical Rosicrucians.

Fludd contends that all human knowledge should be founded on scripture and nature, and that spiritual truths and physical truths are identical. He regards the sun as the symbol of the supreme deity, but he does not follow the 16th-century astronomer Nicolaus Copernicus, who taught that the earth and the other planets rotate around it. Fludd believes in an alchemical and mystical explanation for the creation, and his cosmology depends on mathematical arguments which are based on musical harmonies. The book has numerous illustrations showing how the universe emerged from the "great darkness" (→ 1623).

The work of alchemists promises much but delivers very little. As a result it is cruelly lampooned.

Raleigh beheaded for his part in plot

London, 29 October 1618
After he had placed his head upon the block, Sir Walter Raleigh saw that the headsman was reluctant to act and urged him to strike. In two blows the head was severed.

A last voyage in a vain pursuit of gold and a clash with the Spanish in South America have led directly to the gallows. King Philip demanded Raleigh's head, and King James yielded. After legal wrangling the 66-year-old adventurer has died, not for what he did in South America but for his alleged part in a plot to overthrow James in 1603. It was argued that he could not be sentenced to death twice.

Sir Walter Raleigh: executed today.

James dithers over European alliances

London, 1618
King James is undecided about opposing the offer of the crown of Bohemia [Czechoslovakia] to his son-in-law, Frederick V, the Elector Palatine, by the Protestant *diet* [parliament] in Prague. James is fearful of being dragged into a Protestant war when he is seeking an alliance with Catholic Spain by marrying his son Charles to the *infanta* [king's daughter]. Without English support Frederick has little hope; his troops are badly led and lack supplies. If the Catholic Holy Roman Emperor Ferdinand II invades, Frederick is not expected to survive (→ 9/1619).

1619 - 1620

London, January 1619. George Villiers, the marquis of Buckingham, is appointed lord high admiral (→ 13/2).

Edinburgh, 4 March 1619. The privy council orders the city to clean up its streets which are strewn with sewage, offal and rubbish.

Europe, September 1619. Frederick, the Elector Palatine, King James's son-in-law, accepts the crown of Bohemia [Czechoslovakia], much to the king's dismay (→ autumn 1620).

Lothian, October 1619. Nathaniel Udward, an English merchant, sets up a pioneering soap-making business at Leith in the hope that Scotland will not need to import soap.

Somerset, October 1619. Samuel Daniel, the poet, best known for his eight-book work *A History of the Civil Wars between York and Lancaster*, dies.

Dulwich, London, 1619. Edward Alleyn, the actor, founds Dulwich College.

London, 1619. William Harvey, a physician at St Bartholomew's hospital, outlines his discovery of the way in which blood circulates in a series of lectures.

London, 1619. Inigo Jones, the architect, begins work on a new banqueting hall for Whitehall Palace (→ 1622).

London, 1619. Richard Burbage, the celebrated actor and theatre-builder, dies.

London, 1619. James appoints Orlando Gibbons as a virginals player at court (→ 5/6/25).

Scotland, 1620. English leather-workers, forced north by the growing economic depression in the cloth industry, introduce the process of tanning leather.

Plymouth, September 1620. "The Pilgrim Fathers", a group of puritans, set sail in the *Mayflower* to make a new life in the New World (→ 25/12).

England, autumn 1620. Volunteers leave to join the army of Frederick, the Elector Palatine, in Bohemia (→ 8/11).

Westminster, December 1620. Sir Henry Montague is appointed lord treasurer.

London, 1620. Cornelius Jacobzoon Drebbel, a Dutch physicist, begins work on an underwaterboat – a wooden craft covered in leather and smeared with tallow to render it watertight.

Dropsy kills king's estranged queen

London, 2 March 1619
Queen Anne, the frivolous but good-hearted consort of King James, died of dropsy at her home, Denmark House, today. She and the king had lived apart since 1606, but he visited her often during her illness although he attended neither her death nor her funeral. One of the reasons for their estrangement was her conversion to Catholicism, but she played no part in political life. A patron of Inigo Jones, she was interested more in masques and fine buildings than the affairs of state. Two of her six children survive her. She was 45.

Queen Anne, who died of dropsy.

James backs denunciation of 'free will'

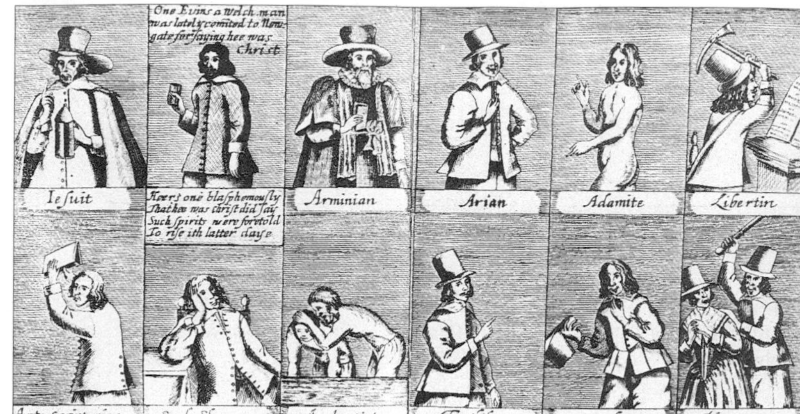

A satirical view of varieties of religious belief from a pamphlet of the time.

London, May 1619
King James, who is fascinated by religious doctrine and spends hours discussing theology with his clergy, has backed the decisions of the Synod of Dort, held to arbitrate between the Protestant factions of Calvinism and Arminianism in the Dutch United Provinces.

The synod has decided in favour of the Calvinists, who believe that human destiny is preordained by God, and has denounced the "free will" theology of the Arminians, who want a return to some of the early church's doctrine and worship and support a revival of ceremonial practices. The Arminians now face heavy penalties; they are to be denied church services, and their leaders are banished. James heartily approves (→ 4/8/21).

Secretary of state dismissed in scandal

London, 13 February 1619
Sir Thomas Lake, the secretary of state, has been dismissed after being found guilty in the star chamber of complicity in making false charges against the countess of Exeter. The countess was accused by Sir Thomas's daughter, Lady Roos, of attempting to poison her, and a complicated web of evidence involving forged letters was concocted by Lady Roos. King James himself played a vital role in disproving the evidence, and he read out the sentence ordering Sir Thomas, his wife and daughter to be detained during his pleasure.

Lake's resignation, demanded at once, is not only a personal disgrace but also marks the end of the influence of his patrons, the Howards, and confirms the ascendancy of the king's favourite, the marquis of Buckingham (→ 16/6/21).

Death of royal miniaturist painter, Hilliard, marks end of era

London, 7 January 1619
Nicholas Hilliard, court painter to Queen Elizabeth and King James, has died at the age of 72. Acclaimed for the brilliance of his miniatures, he painted in the tradition of Holbein the Younger and François Clouet and was England's first true limner, or miniaturist. When cutbacks in the royal art budget forced him out of the court ten years ago he set up shop off Fleet Street and sold portaits at 40 shillings a time. One of his most noted pupils, Isaac Oliver, a talented miniaturist in his own right, died in 1617.

This Nicholas Hilliard self-portrait is a fine example of his style.

An Isaac Oliver miniature of a child – probably intended as a gift.

Indian trade links forged by explorer

Overdressed traders visit India.

London, September 1619
Sir Thomas Roe, a member of parliament, an explorer, and England's first ambassador to the court of Jahangir, the Moghul emperor of India, has returned after an eventful mission lasting nearly five years.

Only two of the gifts he carried pleased the emperor: a crate of alcohol and some English miniatures. Jahangir was displeased by a globe of the world which revealed that his empire was smaller than he believed. Nevertheless Roe, a man of charm and solid judgement, won from him important trading, travel and naval concessions.

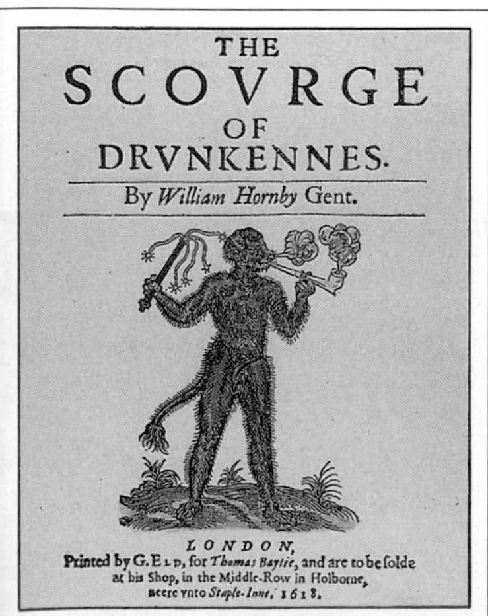
THE
SCOVRGE
OF
DRVNKENNES.
By *William Hornby* Gent.

LONDON,
Printed by G. ELD, for *Thomas Baylie*, and are to be solde at his Shop, in the Middle-Row in Holborne, neere vnto *Staple-Inne*, 1618.

Drunkenness of all kinds is under fire from social reformers and pamphleteers; a new target is the devil of tobacco "drinking".

Catholic win upsets 'peacemaker' king

Prague, 8 November 1620
The battle at the White Mountain, fought today to decide who is going to rule Bohemia [Czechoslovakia], has resulted in a decisive victory for the Catholic forces of Holy Roman Emperor Ferdinand II over the Protestant army of King James's son-in-law, Frederick V, the Elector Palatine of the Rhine.

It has been an extraordinary affair. The Bohemians first elected Ferdinand to their throne, then, alarmed by his fervent Catholicism, changed their minds and offered it to Frederick, who was comfortably settled on his own throne and had no need of Bohemia. James wisely warned him against accepting this poisoned chalice, but he pressed on, and Ferdinand then took the field against him in the Catholic cause.

Now Frederick and his wife, Elizabeth, are fleeing, in danger of losing the Palatinate as well as Bohemia, and James, who sees himself as the peacemaker of Europe, is desperately embarrassed (→13/6/23).

'Pilgrim Fathers' settle in New World

"The Pilgrim Fathers" gratefully set foot on American soil for the first time.

New World, 25 December 1620
The settlers who arrived here last month on board the *Mayflower* – both puritans and the less strict "Strangers" – have decided to create a settlement on a bay offering a calm anchorage, good water and fertile soil. They will call it Plymouth Bay. The settlers have suffered desperate hardships, battered by storms, since they first sighted land, but they spent today felling trees and cutting logs for their cabins. The settlers, known as "the Pilgrim Fathers", have elected John Carver as their first governor to head their sober, industrious efforts to build a new life (→spring 1621).

Bacon calls for revolutionary new approach to scientific inquiry

London, 1620
Sir Francis Bacon – lord chancellor, philosopher and courtier – has finished the second part of his massive work *Instauratio Magna* [*The Great Renewal*]. Entitled *Novum Organum* [*The New Instrument*], it argues that a total reformation of science is needed, involving the rejection of old "idols" which have to be cleared away so that man can see nature as it really is.

Bacon sets out a programme for achieving this new knowledge by taking a series of logical steps "to discover the forms of simple natures". He plans to use instruments, communication, criticism and the questioning of established philosophical systems to establish this new method of thought.

The book is undoubtedly brilliant, and its demand for scientific thinking is welcome at a time when new discoveries are outrunning the old philosophies. It is, however, heavy going, and, while it may be fashionable to refer to it in a knowing way, it is unlikely to be widely read; it is doubtful if those that venture into it will get far, except for the most learned of scholars.

The anatomy lesson. Bacon believes scientific inquiry leads to the truth.

Nevertheless the book contains many provocative thoughts. For example: "The fabric of human reason for enquiry into nature ... is a magnificent building with no foundation" ... Aristotle's natural philosophy was "in bondage to his logic", and he did not "consult experience" ... The ancient Greeks "knew nothing of the world outside the Mediterranean but now we know the New World" (→5/1621).

1621

Dublin, 20 January. Plantation grants are given for parts of Leitrim, King's County, Queen's County and Westmeath (→ 20/3/22).

Westminster, 26 March. Parliament revives the ancient procedure of impeachment (→ 16/6).

North America, spring. John Carver is appointed the first governor of the colony that has been recently established at Plymouth (→ 6/1630).

Westminster, May. Lionel Cranfield is appointed lord treasurer.

London, June. Sir Francis Bacon, the lord chancellor, who has been held in the Tower after being convicted of accepting bribes, is released after a few nights (→ 1622).

Westminster, 16 June. George Villiers, the marquis of Buckingham, facing the threat of impeachment as a monopoly holder, orders the arrest of the earls of Oxford and Southampton in order to stave off the parliamentary challenge (→ 10/7).

Westminster, 10 July. James issues a royal proclamation cancelling 18 monopolies and announces his intention to review many others to mitigate parliamentary opposition to them (→ 18/5/23).

Perth, 12 October. Heavy flooding on the river Tay sweeps away the new bridge and floods the city (→ 1623).

Borders, 1 November. The special border commission is disbanded as part of a process of normalizing the "middle shires".

Surrey. William Outred, the rector of Albury, invents a slide rule.

Dyfed. William Laud, the dean of Gloucester, is made bishop of St David's.

Lisbon. Philip O'Sullivan Beare publishes *Historiae catholicae Iberniae compendium*, a Catholic response to Sir John Davies's history of Ireland which appeared in 1612.

London. John Williams, the bishop of Lincoln, becomes lord keeper of the privy seal.

London. John Barclay, the Scots writer, publishes *Argenis*, an allegorical political novel.

London. John Fletcher's new play, *The Wild Goose Chase*, opens.

Lord chancellor falls

Francis Bacon: accepted bribes.

London, May

Sir Francis Bacon, the lord chancellor, has been severely punished after confessing to accepting substantial bribes during the exercise of his great office. The Lords fined him £40,000, sentenced him to be imprisoned at King James's pleasure, and disbarred him from holding any office of state or from sitting in parliament. He retains his peerage as Viscount St Albans.

The fine and imprisonment are more symbolic than real and will almost certainly be remitted by the king. In mitigation, scant evidence was produced to show that the chancellor was ever persuaded by bribes to alter his judgements.

Bacon made no attempt to deny the charges. He wrote a penitent letter of confession to be read out in the House of Lords from his sickbed (→ 6/1621).

Scots dream of new home across ocean

London, 10 September

The dream of a Scots laird, of founding a new Scotland in the New World, was fulfilled today when King James appointed Sir William Alexander titular lord proprietor of territory which he intends to call Nova Scotia.

Sir William, a member of Prince Charles's household in London and his former tutor, felt that a Scottish colony across the ocean would provide a fruitful outlet for many of the needy Scots who want their sovereign to find them important jobs in England. He was also fired by last year's founding by London and Plymouth merchants of "New England" across the Atlantic.

He will name one half of his province Caledonia and the other Alexandria. Colonists may not easily be found.

Spanish envoy is a target for insults

London, 26 May

As public antipathy towards Spain mounts, the influential Spanish envoy successfully appealed today to King James for justice after a youth called him "the devil in a dungcart" as he rode down Fenchurch Street in his litter. Diego Sarmiento, now Count Gondomar, at first appealed to the lord mayor, who sentenced the boy and his friends to whipping. Onlookers, livid that boys should be flogged for insulting a Spaniard, rescued the youths. James ordered the sentence to be carried out.

Gondomar: influence over James.

Trade crisis worsens as recession bites

Billingsgate market in London: among those affected by the recession.

Britain, 1621

Worry about the deeply depressed state of trade has provoked a wide public debate about the root cause of the problem. Is it the consequence of bad farming, of plague, of the follies of merchants? Or does the blame lie largely across the Channel? Although domestic disasters and conflicts have doubtless played their part, it is clear that German and East European princes are major culprits.

English foreign trade is still highly dependent on exports of unfinished woollen goods. It is now collapsing at an alarming rate, mainly because European currencies are being manipulated for quick profit. The recession is also affecting Scotland.

Import prices in Europe have risen, damaging home markets. Moreover, since prices of local goods have fallen in the countries concerned, European traders have been encouraged to export more to Britain at reduced prices. To make matters worse, English merchants have been exporting bullion to Europe in exchange for goods which are then brought here for sale. The net result is a burgeoning deficit in the balance of trade.

Scots give religious moves a rough ride

Scotland, 4 August
A stormy session of parliament has enacted religious changes known as the Five Articles of Perth by 86 votes to 59. The closeness of the vote, coming after overwhelming crown management and bribery, and the extent of public opposition make it unlikely that the articles will be enforced.

The articles call for observation of Christmas, Good Friday, New Year and other holidays regarded by Scots as Catholic festivals. Private baptism and Communion are to be recognized and episcopal blessing of children is to be encouraged. Most controversial is kneeling at Communion, which appears to imply a worship of the sacraments. During the debate there was a flash of lightning followed by darkness and heavy rain – seen by Presbyterians as evidence of God's wrath. The passage of the articles through parliament was made harder by a bill imposing a £1.2 million tax on Scots over the next four years.

Commons challenge royal power

London, 19 December
Parliament adjourned today after recording in its journal a spirited affirmation of its role and privileges that, in tone and content, will inevitably incense King James.

The protestation followed the receipt by the speaker of a letter from the monarch instructing the Commons not to meddle in matters of foreign policy. This was sent in spite of James's earlier written pledge that he "never meant to deny them [the Commons] any lawful promises that were ever enjoyed in our predecessors' time".

James is now angry because the Commons had urged him to lead a Protestant alliance in an offensive against Spain; they are strongly opposed to his efforts to engineer a marriage between his surviving son, Prince Charles, and the *infanta* [Spanish king's daughter].

The protestation declared that parliament's privileges and jurisdiction are the "undoubted birthright and inheritance of the subjects of England". It went on to argue that urgent affairs concerning the king, state and defence of the realm and of the Church of England are proper subjects for debate in parliament. Some members had demanded that the protestation be laid directly before the king but this proposal was rejected. In spite of this, James's reaction is expected to be swift and drastic.

The Commons were angered by James's warning on foreign affairs.

Archbishop accidentally bags a keeper

Bramshill Park, Hants, 24 July
George Abbott, the archbishop of Canterbury, accidentally killed a gamekeeper with a shot from a bow while hunting deer today on Lord Zouch's estate near here.

News of the tragedy was immediately relayed to King James, who said: "No one but a fool or a knave would think the worse of him. It might be any man's case."

William Laud, an anti-puritan who is soon to be consecrated bishop, may now not attend the ceremony if it is conducted by the Calvinist Abbott.

t was on a hunt like this that the archbishop fatally shot a gamekeeper.

Melancholy blamed on imaginative failure

Oxford
A work of extraordinary scholarship called *The Anatomy of Melancholy*, which examines disturbed mental states ranging from brief unhappiness to actual insanity, has been published here to wide academic and also popular acclaim.

The author, Robert Burton, an Oxford clergyman, says that he wrote of melancholy to assuage his own melancholy, an "inbred malady in man". The encyclopaedic book ("all mine, none mine," he confesses in the introduction) is the fruit of immense reading. Burton bolsters his arguments with extensive quotations from both Latin and Greek writers, the Bible, the early Christian fathers and many European writers.

The resultant storehouse of erudition sets out to define melancholy, examine its causes, identify its symptoms and put forward possible cures. Burton believes that melancholy originates in a failure of imagination which then affects the power of reason. He warns against solitude and idleness.

A melancholic type: a detail from the frontispiece of Burton's work.

1622 - 1623

Spain, March 1622. John Digby, the earl of Bristol, visits Madrid to finalize negotiations for the proposed marriage between Charles, the prince of Wales, and the *infanta*, Maria Anna (→ 17/2/23).

Scotland, August 1622. Scottish wool merchants are outraged at plans to restrict the sale of surplus Scottish wool to England.

Ireland, 18 September 1622. Viscount Falkland is sworn in as lord deputy (→ 23/12).

Ireland, September 1622. James Ussher, the bishop of Meath, calls for severe measures to be taken against Catholics here (→ 2/1624).

Dublin, 23 December 1622. The country's first court of wards and liveries is established in an attempt to combat corruption and tax evasion (→ 24/9/24).

London, 1622. King James orders all the landed gentry in London to leave the capital and return to their duties on their estates.

France, 1622. Andrew Melville, the Scottish Presbyterian, who has been working at the University of Sedan since his release from prison and exile in 1611, dies aged 77.

London, 1622. Inigo Jones completes the Banqueting Hall in Whitehall (→ 1625).

London, 1622. Sir Francis Bacon publishes a *History of Henry VII* (→ 9/4/26).

Dover, 17 February 1623. Prince Charles and George Villiers, the marquis of Buckingham, his close friend, set out incognito for Madrid with the intention of bringing Charles's bride-to-be, Maria Anna, to England (→ 6/10).

Westminster, 18 May 1623. George Villiers is created earl of Coventry and duke of Buckingham (→ 15/6/26).

Scotland, May 1623. A committee for grievances is set up to examine the effects of patents and monopolies.

Essex, 4 July 1623. The Lincoln-born composer William Byrd dies aged 80.

Scotland, 1623. Thousands of people die as the result of a dreadful famine.

Westminster, 1623. Parliament passes the Patents Law to protect inventors and their inventions.

Hundreds killed in Indian attack on Virginian settlement

Settlers massacred: a later view.

Virginia, 22 March 1622
An eight-year peace was shattered today by an Indian attack in the James river area which has left 347 English colonialists dead in their homes and fields. The massacre was carried out by Indians under Chief Opechencanough who had recently signed a peace treaty with the settlers. Trusting his word, they had taken the Indians into their homes and went about unarmed. Inhabitants of Jamestown, the main settlement, were spared by the warning of Chanco, an Indian converted to Christianity who had been living on a settler's farm. The disaster will add to concern in London about the future of the Virginia company, headed by Sir Edwin Sandys.

The history of the Virginia settlement, established in 1607, has been blighted by tragedies, including the failure by settlers to grow their own food despite fertile soil and a good climate. The immigrants have been forced to buy or extort grain from the Indians. The Virginia company was set up to trade in the one successful crop – tobacco – which in 1618 earned £50,000. Even this business has suffered, however, following King James's denunciation of smoking. Worse, the easy profit to be had from tobacco has led to further neglect of basic foodstuffs. Pressure on local Indians to supply corn on unfair terms provoked today's massacre (→ 6/1624).

Investigation opens into Irish corruption

Ireland, 20 March 1622
A full-scale inquiry into the civil and ecclesiastical condition of Ireland has been ordered by the English government, and a commission that comprises officials from both countries has been appointed to conduct it.

King James's financial situation has reached a crisis point and attempts are being made to cut costs and improve revenue. Clearly, it is hoped to relieve the English exchequer of its annual subvention of £20,000 towards the costs of governing Ireland. However, the Irish government's debt has reached an alarming size, and arrears outstanding to the army alone are greater than the annual revenue. It is believed that the real problem is not the inadequacy of the revenue but the laxity and dishonesty of the administration. Both the state of Ireland and the government clearly require attention. Officials are expected to be called to account for the sums of money they have handled; a ruthlessly pared administration is in prospect (→ 18/9).

Scotland loses long-reigning chancellor

Lothian, 16 May 1622
Alexander Seton, Scotland's chancellor for the last 18 years, has died at his seat at Pinkie House, near Musselburgh, at the age of 67. Seton, who was created earl of Dunfermline in 1606, has effectively dominated the administration in Scotland since 1611 through a masterly knowledge of the law and a strongly independent judgement.

Seton was educated at the College of Jesuits in Rome (and remained a closet Catholic throughout his life) before taking up law to become an advocate. Popular with both King James and the ordinary Scottish people, he was also made a member of the English privy council.

Alexander Seton, chancellor of Scotland for the past 18 years.

Fludd and Kepler in astronomical row

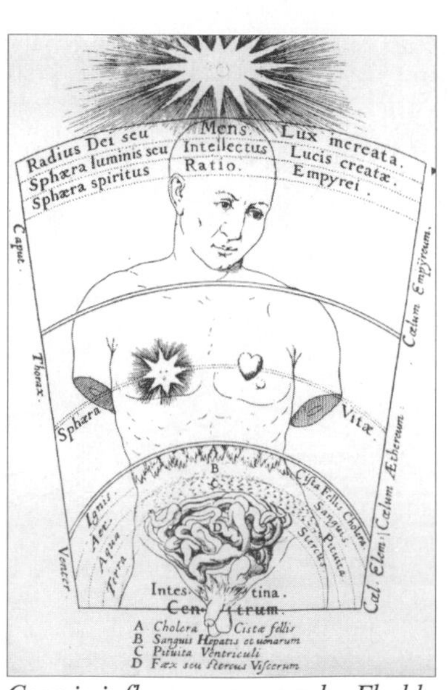

Cosmic influences as seen by Fludd.

London, 1623
A long and intense argument about astronomy between Germany's Johannes Kepler and England's Robert Fludd appears to be coming to an end, with both men still unable to see each other's point of view. Four years of correspondence and wordy volumes have merely underlined that the astronomers have different philosophies.

Kepler has applied the principles of geometry to the movements of the planets, in particular to Mars: this is already being referred to as Kepler's Law. Fludd got the debate under way with his account of the universe's construction. He interpreted the motion of the planets in terms of mathematical harmonies and "magical" analogies.

England faces growing foreign tensions

James's daughter Elizabeth and her husband, who are now living in exile.

Germany, 13 June 1623
As England's foreign policy worries grow, King James's exiled son-in-law Frederick was today dethroned as Elector Palatine. Ten years ago Frederick, whose Protestantism is popular in England, married the king's daughter Elizabeth; he later accepted the Bohemian crown. The couple fled to The Hague after their defeat by Catholics in 1620. While keen to keep England out of the European war, James faces intense pressure to intervene.

Charles and Buckingham fail in mission to Spain to woo and win king's sister

London, 6 October 1623
Extraordinary scenes today greeted the return of King James's son and heir, Prince Charles, after his mission to Madrid to woo and win the *infanta* Maria Anna, the young sister of King Philip IV. People lined the streets, church bells rang out, and a cartload of felons on their way to be hanged were pardoned to mark the safe return of the heir to the throne.

Charles, who is 22, and the king's favourite, the marquis (now duke) of Buckingham, slipped out of the country in February, disguised and armed. By the time they reached Madrid three weeks later the secret was out. It caused widespread surprise, although James has wanted to marry his son to Catholic Spain for some time. But the *infanta*, manipulated by her brother and his advisers, was reluctant.

In hospitable Madrid, Charles and Buckingham became locked in months of negotiations about the marriage contract while James kept imploring his son to come home.

Prince Charles: a spurned suitor.

The money ran out. Spain imposed more and more conditions for a marriage, and in August Charles decided to give up. He returned home without a bride and angered at Spanish perfidy (→3/1624).

Trade war leads to a savage massacre

South-east Asia, 1623
Anglo-Dutch rivalry over the spice trade of south-east Asia has intensified with the deaths of members of the small English community at Amboyna, the centre of the spice trade in the Spice Islands, or Moluccas, west of New Guinea. Twenty men running a factory outside the Dutch castle there were seized and tortured until they "confessed" to a plot to drive out the Dutch; ten were beheaded.

The incident is deplored by London trade circles as "a massacre". The Dutch are under fire for breaking the 1619 treaty calling for disputes between the two sides to be referred to a mixed council of defence or discussed by the two governments. Moreover the alliance with the United Provinces is a cornerstone of English foreign policy. Given the untold wealth to be tapped in the area, the rivalry between European adventurers and traders could become more hostile.

Jacobean audiences show relish for bloodthirsty horror stories

London, 1623
The publication this year, for the first time, of the texts of plays by William Shakespeare is another milestone in this astonishingly rich period for English drama. In his dedicatory poem Ben Jonson calls Shakespeare, who died in 1616, "Sweet Swan of Avon, the wonder of our stage!". But today's playwrights are continuing to provide a feast for audiences, who display a relish for bloodthirsty tragedies full of horrors such as poisoned skulls or potions, rapes and dismembered bodies.

John Webster offered all that they could desire in *The White Devil* and *The Duchess of Malfi* (1612/13), as did Thomas Middleton and William Rowley in *The Changeling*. In another collaboration, Middleton and Rowley wrote *A Fair Quarrel* (1617), and Middleton alone has been responsible for *Women Beware Women* and comedies such as *A Chaste Maid in Cheapside*. Ben Jonson thinks his tragedies superior to his comedies, but had little success with *Sejanus*. Other notable dramatists are John Marston (*The Malcontent*) and Cyril Tourneur (*The Atheist's Tragedy*). Last year saw the appearance of an expanded version of *The Maid's Tragedy* by Francis Beaumont and John Fletcher, first written in 1620.

"The Maid's Tragedy": a typically bloodthirsty play about revenge.

1624

Ireland, February. A proclamation issued on 21 January, ordering all Catholic clergy to leave Ireland within 40 days, is suspended (→ 13/9/29).

Westminster, March. Parliament reduces the legal interest rate on loans from 10 to 8 per cent.

Fife, 25 May. Dunfermline, the birthplace of Prince Charles, is gutted by fire.

Co Londonderry, 24 September. In the wake of his government's failure to find sufficient English settlers, King James approves the reform of the plantation here (→ 27/3/25).

Edinburgh, 24 November. The city is hit by an epidemic of plague, believed to have been brought by a Danish merchant ship (→ 6/1625).

Britain/France, November. Following the failure of the Anglo-Spanish marriage alliance, an Anglo-French marriage treaty is agreed for Prince Charles and Princess Henrietta Maria, the youngest daughter of Henry IV and Marie de' Medici of France (→ 1/5/25).

Edinburgh. George Heriot, a goldsmith, who amassed great wealth as goldsmith to both King James and Queen Anne, bequeaths a large part of his fortune to found a hospital for the poor here in his birthplace.

Oxford. Henry Briggs, a professor of astronomy and former colleague of the late John Napier, the mathematician, publishes *Arithmetica Logarithmica*; it introduces the use of a decimal base in logarithms (→ 1631).

Oxford. Pembroke College is founded by Thomas Teesdale and Richard Wightwick.

West Indies. The first English colony in the Caribbean is founded by Captain Thomas Warner at St Christopher [St Kitts].

England. Edward Herbert, a poet, philosopher and diplomat, publishes *De veritate*, a philosophical look at religion.

London. Thomas Middleton's *A Game at Chess*, a political satire on the king's failure to marry his son to a Spanish princess, has a successful run at the Globe theatre until performances are stopped at the request of the Spanish ambassador.

Parliament says 'Yes' to war with Spain

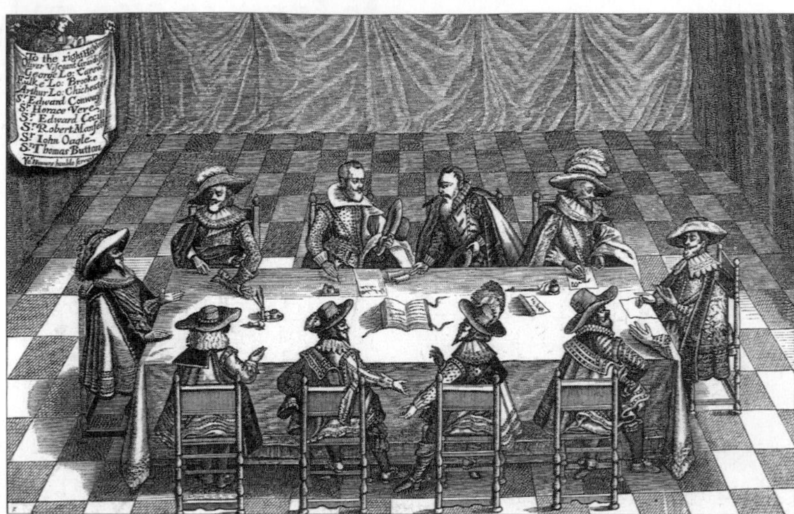

A council of war meets to discuss the opening of hostilities with Spain.

Westminster, March
Parliament has given its backing to the growing support for war with Spain, though voting a grant of only £300,000. The duke of Buckingham and Prince Charles joined the "war" party after their trip to Madrid; the puritans want to make war on popery; and the City of London hopes for booty from the Indies. King James has opposed wars since he came to England but is now too old to resist his "darling boys", Charles and the duke. Spain has also seized his son-in-law's electorate in Germany and helped Holy Roman Emperor Ferdinand II expel him from Bohemia. A French alliance, and a French princess for Charles, seems likely (→ 11/1624).

Treasurer fired for 'bribery and deceit'

Westminster, May
Impeached by parliament, Lionel Cranfield, the lord treasurer, has been dismissed for alleged "bribery, extortion, oppression, wrong and deceits". But the real reason for his downfall may lie elsewhere – in his opposition on financial grounds to war with Spain, and in the enmity of Buckingham, who had looked to him for monetary gain but been disappointed.

Cranfield, a London merchant, had been made earl of Middlesex for his brave but vain attempts to make sense of the royal accounts. "The more I look into the king's finances," he wrote, "the greater cause I have to be troubled."

Cranfield: tried to end corruption.

Virginia company faces total collapse

London, June
The Virginia company has been dissolved, and its investors have lost all their money. The colony has been grossly mismanaged, and the directors in London have shown themselves quite unfit to rule it. All hopes of finding gold there have failed, although it is exporting good tobacco to Britain. The government will now take over. Over 4,000 settlers have moved to Virginia since 1619, and only 1,200 are still alive. Most died of disease, but more than 300 were killed in the Indian massacre in 1622 [*see report on page 526*], including many black servants who were brought from Africa.

James gives his support to moves against prostitution

Inside a Jacobean brothel: gambling and drink went with the women, but the king's attempts to stamp out such goings-on met with little success.

London
King James has issued a stern ordinance against disorderly houses in London, particularly those in Turnmill Street, Clerkenwell – where "many lewd persons keep common brothel houses and harbour divers impudent queens". Another parish, Farringdon, "hath been pestered with divers immodest and shameless women, common whores, who sit usually at the doors and shamefully allure such as pass by". Raids have pulled in hundreds of whores to send to the Bridewell prison and have led to the arrest of at least one murderer.

Hertfordshire, 5 March. King James falls ill after a hunt in Theobald Park (→27/3).

Armagh, 21 March. James Ussher, the bishop of Meath, an academic and antiquarian, is consecrated archbishop of Armagh.

France, 1 May. George Villiers, the duke of Buckingham, represents King Charles at his marriage by proxy to Princess Henrietta Maria; he will accompany the king's wife back to England (→1/5).

Westminster, 5 May. King James's funeral takes place at the abbey after a magnificent procession through the City of London; the occasion is marred by the refusal of the archbishop of St Andrews to take part, following the orders of King Charles that English vestments must be worn.

Canterbury, 5 June. Orlando Gibbons, one of the most celebrated composers of sacred music, dies aged 42; one of his best known compositions is *Hosanna to the Son of David*.

Dover, 11 June. King Charles meets his young wife, Henrietta Maria, for the first time before their official wedding ceremony in Canterbury (→19/11).

London, mid June. The numbers of those dying of the plague has reached a weekly figure of 165 (→1/8).

London, 19 November. King Charles celebrates his 25th birthday (→7/1626).

London, autumn. John Fletcher, the poet and dramatist, dies in the plague epidemic sweeping London.

London. Captain Bailey, a retired sea captain, introduces for transport hire the use of four Hackney horse-drawn coaches.

London. Inigo Jones, the architect, begins work on a church in Covent Garden.→

London. King Charles appoints Daniel Mytens, the Flemish-born artist, as his official court painter.

London. Ben Jonson, the poet and dramatist, writes a new comedy, *The Staple of News*.

England. Horse-drawn fire engines are introduced as a fire-fighting aid.

London. William Camden's *Annals of the Reign of Elizabeth* are published posthumously.

'The wisest fool in Christendom' dies

Hertfordshire, 27 March
King James of Scotland and England died today, of a violent fever and dysentery, at his favourite home of Theobalds in Hertfordshire. He was 58 and had reigned in both kingdoms for 22 years, having been James VI of Scotland since he was one year old. A man of paradoxes, he was learned in theology and the sciences, a skilled politician who mastered the brutal factions in Scotland and the nobility and puritans in England, but he was also lazy, profligate, vain and a prey to his corrupt favourites.

There were rumours that James was homosexual, and he certainly showed great love for his favourites. His court was very informal, quite unlike Queen Elizabeth's, and very corrupt. Yet he enjoyed learned disputes with theologians and wrote a manual on kingship, as well as a famous attack on tobacco. The French statesman Sully called him "the wisest fool in Christendom".

James: a learned but lazy monarch.

Mixed legacy inherited by English subjects

London, 27 March
King James's reign will be remembered as a time of peace. He ended the war with Spain in 1604 and avoided all wars afterwards, though the country is now clamouring to fight Spain again. The king also kept the peace between the puritans and the Church of England and moderated Catholic persecution.

The reign saw the first permanent colonies in America – in Virginia and New England – a new translation of the Bible and the expansion of the East India company. Literature, theatre and music enjoyed a golden age.

On the other side of the coin the king failed to resolve the problem of financing the government, and his relationship with parliament deteriorated. He raised money by selling monopolies to his courtiers for enormous sums, and increased import duties without consulting parliament. The country, which prospered in the early part of the reign, is now suffering from a loss of exports as a consequence of the wars in Europe (→7/5).

James died here at his favourite home, Theobalds in Hertfordshire. His son Charles was proclaimed king immediately by men shouting from the gate.

Desire for union of kingdoms thwarted

Edinburgh, 27 March
It was a great triumph for the Scots when their king came to the throne of England, after all the wars and invasions and James IV's death on Flodden Field. However, the union of the crowns has not brought the two countries any closer. The old enmities persist.

This was King James's greatest disappointment. He had hoped to unite the kingdoms and was thwarted by English hostility. He managed to repeal English laws that harmed Scotland, and reduced raiding across the border, but that was all. The king returned to Scotland only once, in 1617, to introduce further reforms into the church. It was all part of his long campaign to restore royal authority in ecclesiastical matters and control the assembly and the Presbyterians.

The king encouraged literature as well as mathematics, medicine, map-making and other sciences in Scotland. In the 1590s he launched a nationwide hunt for witches, in the belief that witches had plotted against him; hundreds of deluded women and a few men were burnt during his reign (→12/10).

King's policy hated by most in Ireland

Dublin, 27 March
James leaves a bitter legacy among the Gaelic majority in Ireland, having presided over their piecemeal dispossession. A motley collection of "New English" freebooters, such as Richard Boyle, the earl of Cork, has exploited legal loopholes in his policy of "defective titles" to wrest land from both Gaelic and Anglo-Irish communities [*see report on page 507*]. This has been more effective than the plantations in dispossessing the native majority. In Co Antrim and Co Down, however, an independent Scottish plantation under Hugh, Viscount Montgomery, has proved very successful, unlike the failed English plantation in mid-Ulster (→22/9/26).

New king marries a Catholic princess

Henrietta Maria: the new queen.

Paris, 1 May
The new king of England and Scotland, Charles, was married today to Henrietta Maria, the sister of King Louis XIII of France. The splendid ceremony took place in Nôtre-Dame, with the duke of Buckingham standing proxy for Charles. The bride is 15 years old, vivacious, devoutly Catholic and of strong opinions. Charles has promised that she may take priests to London so that she and her court may practise her religion openly.

The new king is 24, a serious and shy young man who grew up in the shadow of his elder brother, Henry, who died of typhoid in 1612. He has acquired a great love of music and art, which promises to make the new court one of some splendour. Charles also acquired his father's belief in the dignity and divine right of kings. The latter belief, allied to his queen's religion could pose problems (→ 11/6).

King Charles: married by proxy.

Charles confronts hostile parliament

Westminster, July
There is now a worse crisis between king and parliament than England has suffered for many years. Only one month after the meeting of Charles's first parliament, he is in bitter disagreement with it over religion and money, and there are signs that members are preparing to impeach the duke of Buckingham.

The Commons voted the king a subsidy of £140,000, not nearly enough to pay for the reconquest of the Palatinate and the proposed war with Spain. He was also voted tonnage and poundage customs revenue for one year, instead of for life, like all his predecessors.

Charles and his advisers may be somewhat to blame for this disaster. He opened parliament with a short speech, which was a relief from his father's verbosity, but it contained no explanation of his policies, and ministers refused to explain why they needed the very large subsidies that they were demanding. Parliament saw an opening and voted a derisory sum.

The king was even more enraged when the Commons demanded that the recusancy laws against Catholics be enforced and attacked the king's new chaplain, Richard Montague. He is a high church, or Arminian, preacher who rejects the official Calvinism of the Church of England (→ 12/10).

King Charles's reign begins in a bitter row with parliament over money.

Parliament flees to Oxford to escape plague, but rows continue

Oxford, 1 August
Parliament has reassembled at Oxford after fleeing London to escape the plague. Thousands have died, far more than in 1603, including Orlando Gibbons, England's finest composer. It is thought to be the most serious outbreak of plague since the Black Death 300 years ago. Even here there have already been many deaths, as the epidemic spreads through the country. When people part at night, they do not say "Good night" but "God send us a joyful resurrection".

King Charles's disputes with parliament over money and religion are as sharp as ever, and the Commons are in no mood to bow to his demands, even if it means that parliament will be dissolved (→ 3/1630).

Lord have mercy! Plague rages through London, killing thousands a week.

Revocation received badly in Scotland

Edinburgh, 12 October
Property owners in Scotland are furious at King Charles's plan to revoke all grants of crown lands that have been made since 1540, including land confiscated from the church. Usually Scottish kings reclaim lands given away during their minorities, but Charles acceded to the throne as an adult, unlike all Scottish monarchs for the past 220 years, so the revocation may not be legal. It has to be enacted before his 25th birthday next month. The revocation would produce a sweeping rationalization of the landholding system, increase crown revenues and reduce the powers of the feudal lords. It would also give the king greater influence over the church. The proposal was bound to be unpopular, and the fact that it is being handled secretively has aroused further animosity.

Charles was born in Scotland, but his Scottish subjects are beginning to fear that he might now be more English than Scottish. They are particularly offended at his increasing Arminianism (→1/1626).

Great English poet publishes his sermons

London
John Donne, the dean of St Paul's, is England's finest preacher and also one of its best poets. His *Devotions*, published last year, and a volume of sermons, which has appeared recently, reveal prose writings in English that match anything produced in the past century.

Donne was born in 1572 and brought up as a Catholic. He was attached to the earl of Essex and went on his expedition to Cadiz in 1596. In his youth he wrote much love poetry, which he now deplores, before turning to religious subjects. He was ordained as an Anglican priest in 1616 (→1631).

John Donne, preacher and poet.

War with Spain starts badly after naval expedition by Buckingham ends in fiasco

The flagship makes a brave sight, but the attack on Spain was a disaster.

London, 16 November
The great naval expedition to Spain has ended in fiasco. The 10,000 soldiers on the fleet failed to capture Cadiz, and the blockade failed to secure the Spanish treasure fleet. Now they are returning in disgrace.

The soldiers were untrained, ill-equipped and undisciplined. They were set ashore without provisions and drank themselves insensible on wine captured on the march. Then they were returned to the ships. The fleet did not seize the Spanish ships at Cadiz, and the colliers and merchant ships that been brought along refused to fight. The fleet had been supplied with rotten food and filthy water, the ships were old and leaking, and at least one set of sails had served against the 1588 Armada.

After their failure at Cadiz the English tried to intercept the Spanish treasure fleet from the Indies, but it slipped into Cadiz without difficulty. King Charles and Buckingham's war with Spain has begun badly (→9/1626).

The costumes for "The Fortunate Isles" (right), a masque by Ben Jonson first shown in 1625, were designed by Inigo Jones, who introduced the proscenium arch and movable scenery to the English stage. Extensively influenced by the work of the Italian architect Palladio, Jones has also made a lasting mark on English architecture. Three years ago he completed the Banqueting Hall in Whitehall (above). He has also designed the Queen's House at Greenwich and the Queen's Chapel at St James's Palace.

1626-1627

London, January 1626. A deputation of Scots nobles fails to persuade King Charles to abandon the revocation; he plans to revoke all grants made since 1540 in a rationalization of the landholding system to increase crown revenue and boost church resources (→ 23/3).

London, 26 February 1626. The funeral takes place of the composer John Dowland.

Scotland, 23 March 1626. Charles's unpopularity grows when he ends James's system of government and purges the privy council (→ 18/6/33).

Westminster, 27 March 1626. Sir John Eliot tells the Commons that the royal collection of jewellery and treasures, obtained mostly from the dissolution of the monasteries, has been pawned abroad to raise money for the king (→ 6/1626).

Westminster, June 1626. Parliament complains to Charles over what it calls his unauthorized collection of tonnage and poundage (→ 15).

London, June 1626. King Charles appoints William Laud, an Arminian, as bishop of Bath and Wells (→ 1627).

Westminster, September 1626. King Charles plans to collect a forced loan to finance the war with Spain (→ 11/1627).

Dublin, 15 November 1626. Irish notables meet to discuss the concessions that King Charles has proposed (→ 26).

Dublin, 26 November 1626. Protestant bishops join in condemning the proposed toleration of Catholics in Ireland (→ 19/4/27).

Scotland, February 1627. Charles sets up a tithe commission on properties; the increased revenue will raise clerical salaries and his own income and allow landowners to buy out their feudal superiors (→ 11/1627).

Westminster, April 1627. King Charles appoints Bishop Laud to the privy council (→ 4/7/28).

Dublin, 19 April 1627. King Charles's proposals for Ireland are rejected (→ 26/6).

Ireland, 26 June 1627. The lord deputy, Viscount Falkland, gives the go-ahead for an unofficial parliament of Old English county gentlemen when he gives provincial conventions the power to nominate delegates to meet the king (→ 1/1628).

Second parliament dissolved to block attack against duke

London, 15 June 1626

King Charles today dissolved his second parliament in order to block the impeachment by the Commons of his close friend and adviser, George Villiers, the duke of Buckingham. Summoned to meet only a few months ago, the Commons have been locked in a series of rows with the king over his prerogatives and Buckingham's influence in several areas of policy, including religion [*see report below right*].

Charles had mistakenly thought that the failure of last year's parliament was due to the actions of a few trouble-makers, so he weeded some of them out of the new assembly. But one member, Sir John Eliot, called for a Commons inquiry into the kingdom's ills. This led to the formation of a "committee for evils, causes and remedies".

The committee has been looking at state expenditures and summoning members of the council of war to appear before the Commons. But its real target has been the duke of Buckingham, who is believed to be the main cause of the country's problems. Attacks on Buckingham by the Commons angered the king so much that he had two members sent to the Tower. When parliament insisted on the removal of Buckingham, he closed it (→ 2/1627).

George Villiers, the members' target.

Concessions offered to Irish Catholics

Falkland: lord deputy of Ireland.

Ireland, 22 September 1626

King Charles has offered 26 concessions or "graces" to the "Old English" here – Catholics who are English by descent. They include minor measures applicable to all, but some are aimed specifically at Catholics, such as the suspension of fines for recusancy [failure to attend Anglican church services] and the abolition of religious tests for inheritance and appointment to legal office. In return, the king and Viscount Falkland, the lord deputy, hope to receive substantial funds to help finance the war against Spain. The "graces" are being seen as a substitute for the militia which the Old English wished to set up within the Pale, and also as a recognition of their special position and their loyalty to the crown (→ 15/11).

Charles and his queen row over religion

London, July 1626

The royal marriage appears to be in trouble, with Charles and Henrietta Maria arguing over religion, money and other matters – such as if it is raining or not. He blames his wife's French servants for some of the marital problems and is thinking of packing them off home. She has angered him by making a visit to Tyburn to pray for the souls of executed Catholic martyrs.

The king has struck back against his wife's Catholicism by stationing officers outside the chapel of the French ambassador to London to take the names of English subjects attending Mass. And it was the ambassador who was called in to settle a row between the royal couple over the weather (→ 29/3/30).

The queen rows with Charles over everything, including the weather.

Buckingham chairs theological debate

London, February 1626

Growing concern among Protestant subjects about the alleged Catholic inclinations of King Charles has prompted the duke of Buckingham to hold a conference at his London home. The duke, who is the king's leading adviser, is aiming to resolve some of the disputes over religion which are beginning to make the king unpopular with some of his subjects and inflaming his problems with parliament. Buckingham himself is now coming under mounting criticism from the Commons, and his conference is not expected to achieve much.

He has had links with Richard Montagu, whose writings appeared to belittle the European reformed churches and to be too sympathetic to Rome. Buckingham is also under fire for refusing to dissociate himself from the Arminians, a high-church group, whom he defended to the Commons.

War opens between England and France

France, 8 November 1627
Propelled by the machinations of George Villiers, the duke of Buckingham, England and France are now at war. Scotland, too, has been dragged into the war and is to supply a regiment. Yet already an expedition to relieve the besieged Huguenots in the fortress of La Rochelle on the coast south of Brittany has come unstuck, and the duke's support for the war is beginning to cause an outcry at home.

Buckingham's attempt to redeem a fading reputation by embarking on a military expedition to France to back the Protestant Huguenots against their Catholic king has been supported by King Charles. A list of the causes of friction between the two countries includes the king expelling his wife's French maids and seizures by the English fleet of ships owned by Calais merchants.

But Buckingham, who assembled some 6,000 men in Portsmouth, is claiming that his expedition is bent on defending English trade, asserting English supremacy at sea along the French coast and interrupting Spanish trade between Flanders and the West Indies. Although the duke took personal command at the assault on La Rochelle and led his men with courage, the force was not equal to the task.

The unpopular duke of Buckingham leads an attack upon France.

Eminent philosopher and scientist dies

London, 9 April 1626
Francis Bacon, England's leading philosopher and a prominent statesman, died today, aged 56, of a cold caught while stuffing a fowl with snow to observe the effects of cold in the preservation of meat. He pursued an experimental approach to solving scientific problems, and was a prolific writer.

Bacon's principal works were *The Advancement of Learning* and the *Novum Organum* [*The New Instrument*] – part of a planned six-volume work entitled *Instauratio Magna* [*The Great Renewal*] surveying methods and theories of experimental science. He also wrote the short and Utopian *New Atlantis* and *Sylva Sylvarum*, as well as witty and original essays.

Bacon argued that most previous claims to knowledge were untrustworthy. He argued that his philosophical predecessors had made hasty generalizations which only served to prevent the acquisition of knowledge. But he also thought that the mind could discover truth, and that humanity could thereby gain power over nature.

Bacon: victim of his own curiosity.

Bacon went to Trinity College, Cambridge, and held several high government posts, including that of lord chancellor, before being convicted of taking bribes.

Charles orders arrest of five knights who refused to pay compulsory state loans

The judges ruled that the king's "special command" could imprison anyone.

Westminster, November 1627
Strenuous efforts by King Charles to finance his policies have caused a major row and led to the imprisonment of five knights who refused to contribute to a forced loan. A test case brought by four of the jailed "refusers" resulted in the decision that prisoners so committed could not be bailed by habeas corpus.

Charles turned to the forced loan after demanding "free gifts" from selected citizens, commandeering ships and having to sell much of his plate. It has led to numerous arrests as well as the dismissal of judges. There have been riots in parishes in London, and other protests by taxpayers. Some of the nobility have also expressed their indignation.

The five knights arrested had demanded to be brought to trial or given bail. Their move called into question the king's right to lock up his subjects in this fashion, but technically he was right in claiming this power. No writ ran against the king, and he did not have to show cause why offenders had displeased him in any way.

The judges ruled that the king's "special command" was cause for imprisonment in this case only, but it is feared that Charles may interpret the ruling as a general right to imprison without trial (→4/1628).

Top churchman falls foul of government

London, 1627
King Charles has suspended from office George Abbot, archbishop of Canterbury for the last 14 years, whose criticisms of Spain, Roman Catholics and high-church Arminians have long irritated him. Abbot's powers have have been taken over by a commission headed by Bishop William Laud.

Four years ago, while hunting, the archbishop shot a gamekeeper, and the episode clouded his career. But he has been suspended for refusing to allow a sermon to be published supporting compliance to the king's financial demands (→4/1627).

London stage loses leading playwright

England, 1627
Thomas Middleton, one of the most notable and sometimes controversial of English playwrights, has died, aged 47. He was probably best known for *Women Beware Women* and *The Changeling* (one of his collaborations with William Rowley). His most notorious play was *A Game of Chess*, which depicted the return of the then Prince Charles from Spain without a wife. Performances were stopped after nine days by the privy council. Middleton's satires of London life pleased audiences but not puritans, who condemn the stage for decadence.

1628 - 1629

London, January 1628. Old English delegates from the Irish counties arrive (→ 20/3).

Cambridgeshire, February 1628. Oliver Cromwell is elected member of parliament for Huntingdon.

Low Countries, 13 March 1628. The English composer John Bull, aged 65, exiled for adultery in 1623, dies at Antwerp.

London, 20 March 1628. Irish delegates offer King Charles financial aid in return for greater concessions to Irish Catholics (→ 24/5).

London, 24 May 1628. Charles offers the Irish delegates 51 "graces" in return for a subsidy of £40,000 a year for three years (→ 26/12/29).

Westminster, 7 June 1628. Charles agrees to the Petition of Right (→ 12/1628).

London, 4 July 1628. William Laud is consecrated bishop of London (→ 4/1630).

Westminster, July 1628. Richard, Lord Weston, is the new lord treasurer; to restore financial stability he advocates withdrawal from the war.

France, October 1628. La Rochelle falls to Louis XIII.

London, 28 November 1628. John Felton, who killed the duke of Buckingham, is hanged.

London, 17 January 1629. Charles suppresses an anti-puritan pamphlet, *Apollo Caesarem*, by Richard Montagu, the bishop of Chichester.

Westminster, 10 March 1629. Charles dissolves parliament after imprisoning the leaders of the Commons demonstration of 2 March (→ 8/1630).

Scotland, 1629. The war with France devastates trade.

Ireland, 13 September 1629. William Bedell becomes bishop of Kilmore and Ardagh.

Dublin, 26 December 1629. The lord justiciars, Viscount Loftus and Richard Boyle, the earl of Cork, order the suppression of Irish Catholic religious houses; the mayor is instructed to attack all such houses in the city (→ 1/1632).

London, 1629. Charles grants the Spectacle Makers' Guild a royal charter.

London, 1629. John Ford, the dramatist, writes a new play, *The Lover's Melancholy*.

Parliament set for row with king over royal power curbs

Westminster, April 1628

King Charles and his parliament are on a collision course as the king contemplates the prospect of a Petition of Right supported by the overwhelming majority of his influential subjects. Parliament wants an end to arbitrary imprisonment, forced employment abroad, forced loans and the billeting of soldiers without the consent of the householder. The king wants to retain the right to disregard parliament at his absolute discretion.

The billeting of troops is probably the single greatest grievance against the king. In Sussex in particular several hundred soldiers, including demoralized remnants of last year's disastrous French expedition, have been unwelcome guests for six months – doubly unwelcome as almost no householder has been paid for his involuntary hospitality. The soldiers are also blamed for importing the plague.

Coke will lead the attack on Charles.

Sir John Eliot, an eloquent thorn in the king's side, led parliament's protest by blaming Catholics for many of the depredations. But the most significant voice is that of Thomas Wentworth who, while stressing his belief in the union between king and parliament, has come out in support of all the demands in the Petition of Right. Sir Edward Coke will handle the wording of the Petition. He was responsible last month for a bill preventing imprisonment without trial for more than two months (→ 7/6).

Turncoat peer heads Council of the North

Thomas Wentworth (l), parliament's man who switched sides to join the king.

Westminster, December 1628

Thomas Wentworth, a rich Yorkshire landowner who was at the forefront of parliamentary opposition to King Charles, has been made a viscount and appointed president of the Council of the North – making him the crown's principal agent north of the river Trent. Wentworth had been given a barony in July after changing sides.

An austere, devout and authoritarian figure, Wentworth has never been popular. Now he will have alienated all his former colleagues in parliament. Born in London, but brought up mostly in Yorkshire, he came to court at 18 and inherited his father's lands in 1614, at the age of 21, when he was elected to parliament. He made influential friends but criticized royal policy, and he was made sheriff of Yorkshire in 1626 to keep him out of the House of Commons. In 1627 he refused to pay the forced loan and was briefly imprisoned. He believes in an Elizabethan ideal of the monarchy and has never sided with extreme anti-royalists (→ 2/3/29).

Quack doctor killed for links with duke

London, 14 June 1628

Dr Lambe, an astrologer and quack doctor, died early this morning from injuries which he suffered last night at the hands of a murderous mob. While rumour had it that the doctor led a bizarre and immoral life, it was his friendship with the duke of Buckingham that was his undoing. With the duke being denounced in ditties and ballads everywhere, it was his associate's misfortune to be spotted leaving the theatre. The mob grew louder and more violent as Dr Lambe sought shelter in one tavern after another. Eventually four constables were brushed aside, and he was beaten senseless on the pavement.

Pardon and reward for royal chaplain

London, 6 July 1628

King Charles has pardoned his chaplain, Dr Roger Manwaring, three weeks after the controversial cleric was fined and imprisoned by order of Commons, and his speeches were ordered to be burnt. In a clear snub to parliament, the king has also awarded Manwaring the rectory of Stanford Rivers – having promoted the equally unpopular Richard Montague from that office to be bishop of Chichester. Backed by the king, Manwaring had insisted in his sermons that the authority of parliament was subordinate to "that which unto kings doth appertain by natural and orginal law and justice".

Hated courtier stabbed

The duke of Buckingham, as seen by Rubens, in a typically vainglorious pose.

Portsmouth, 23 August 1628
The duke of Buckingham was killed this morning by a single stab wound to the chest. His assassin, John Felton, is vengeful soldier from Suffolk who served in Buckingham's last expedition to France and was denied promotion. He walked all the way from London to kill his enemy. King Charles will mourn his closest friend, but the crowds are already toasting Felton as the man who rid them of the preening, boastful courtier who wasted men's lives and the people's money pursuing his dreams of glory. Buckingham was on his way to Brittany to make a second attempt to recover La Rochelle, and had just finished breakfast at the Greyhound Inn when his attacker struck. As he fell dying, his wife and sister-in-law screamed from the gallery.

John Felton's knife has accomplished what parliament never could. The Commons repeatedly – and in vain – called on the king to dismiss Buckingham, most recently in June in a move which grievously affronted Charles (→28/11).

William Harvey unlocks secret of blood

Frankfurt, Germany, 1628
William Harvey, a Cambridge-educated physician from Folkestone, has proposed that it is the heart that makes blood circulate around the body. The evidence is assembled in Harvey's book *De motu cordis* [*On the motion of the heart*], published here. Working largely through experiments on animals, Harvey has shown that the heart acts as a pump, contracting as it expels blood into the arteries. Blood passes from the right ventricle through the lungs into the left ventricle; then it travels through the arteries to the veins, which carry it back to the right ventricle. Harvey, aged 50, is treasurer of the Royal College of Physicians and was made physician extraordinary by King James in 1618 (→1632).

Politicians come to blows at Westminster as radicals mount challenge to royal power

John Eliot ruined his big moment.

The speaker is forced to his chair.

Westminster, 2 March 1629
Sir John Finch, the speaker of the House of Commons, was held down in his chair amid uproar today as members defied King Charles's authority. With Black Rod, the royal messenger, barred from the chamber, members shouted and argued while Finch protested that it was his duty to carry out Charles's wishes and adjourn the session.

Three motions were passed before the eventual adjournment, two insisting on parliamentary approval for all taxes and one outlawing "popery and Arminianism". It now seems inconceivable that parliament and king can be reconciled. Charles's fondness for the high-church doctrines of William Laud and Richard Montague, the bishops of London and Chichester, is probably even more emotive than the constitutional issue.

Set on blocking debate of the subject, Charles had ordered Finch to rise and adjourn immediately. But the rebel members were ready, and Denzil Holles and Benjamin Valentine pinned the speaker to his seat. When John Eliot, the leader of the rebels, alienated some of his own supporters with accusations of treason, he threw his draft motion into the fire, and it was left to Holles to voice the house's defiance (→10).

In April 1629, as war continued to devastate much of Europe, England – facing acute financial problems – signed the Treaty of Susa, ending its 18-month conflict with France after a series of humiliating reverses.

1630 - 1631

London, March 1630. Plague breaks out (→10/1665).

Oxford, April 1630. William Laud, the bishop of London, is appointed chancellor of the university (→1631).

Suffolk, April 1630. John Winthrop, a royal official and puritan dismayed by King Charles's support of Arminianism, sails for the New World to seek religious freedom.

England, September 1630. Bread prices soar after the severe drought and bad harvest of this summer (→1/1631).

England/Spain, November 1630. The Treaty of Madrid ends the Anglo-Spanish war.

England, 1630. Richard Delamain, a former pupil of William Oughtred, the mathematical clergyman from Surrey, develops a circular slide rule (→1631).

Westminster, 3 March 1631. King Charles knights Peter Paul Rubens, the Flemish painter and diplomat.

London, 14 May 1631. Lord Castlehaven is executed for sexual crimes.

Co Cork, 20 June 1631. Barbary pirates sack Baltimore.

Germany, August 1631. James, the marquis of Hamilton, leads an Anglo-Scots force of over 7,000 volunteers to help the king of Sweden recover the Rhine Palatinate.

London, 4 November 1631. Queen Henrietta Maria gives birth to a daughter, Mary; she is to be known by the new title of "the princess royal" (→14/10/33).

Scotland, 1631. The crown issues cheap copper coins in a monopoly fraud; it makes huge profits for Sir William Alexander, the Scottish secretary, but causes poor people great hardship.

London, 1631. Sir John Eliot, imprisoned in the Tower since 1629 for defying the king, publishes *Monarchy of Man* in which he stresses the powers of the monarch (→27/11/32).

London, 1631. King Charles and William Laud, the bishop of London, launch a campaign to raise money for renovating St Paul's Cathedral (→6/8/33).

Guildford, 1631. William Oughtred publishes *Clavis Mathematica*, in which he proposes the symbol "X" for use in multiplication.

Barons give go-ahead for tax on land

Westminster, August 1630
The barons of the exchequer have ruled that the courts may fine gentlemen if they have failed to accept knighthoods. The rule applies to men whose income is over £40 a year, and the lord treasurer, Weston, has revived an earlier law stating that such men owe the duty of knighthood to the king, along with the customary fees.

The fines imposed are usually £10 but may go as high as £70. This is the latest of King Charles's schemes for raising money without the consent of parliament. Weston and the chancellor, Cottington, are trying to cut royal expenses while increasing revenues. Customs duties, tonnage and poundage and the increased fines on Catholics are raising very large sums, but even with the foreign wars ended there is in sufficient revenue for Charles's government, and not nearly enough for a standing army.

The gentlemen of England pay their fines, and merchants pay the customs duties, but the split between county and court is steadily widening. Justices of the peace, appointed by the king, find it most onerous to enforce fines on their neighbours (→9/1632).

Critic of bishops is fined and whipped

London, November 1630
Alexander Leighton, a Presbyterian preacher, has suffered a frightful penalty for attacking bishops. In 1628 he wrote a pamphlet, *Sion's Plea against the Prelacy*, in which he called them "caterpillars, moths and cankerworms". The court of star chamber defrocked him, fined him £10,000 and jailed him for life. Now he has been whipped at the pillory, had his ears cut off and his nose slit and has been branded on both cheeks with "SS" – "Sower of Sedition".

Birth of an heir cements the reconciliation of Charles and Henrietta

A baby prince: the birth of an heir has brought royal couple together.

Westminster, 29 May 1630
King, queen and court are rejoicing today at the birth of an heir to the throne. He is to be named Charles, and King Charles rode in state to St Paul's for a formal thanksgiving. The birth not only strengthens the Stuart dynasty but also marks a crucial stage in the restored affections of the king and queen.

For the first three years of their marriage the pair were practically estranged. The queen depended on her French Catholic servants, and the king clung to the duke of Buckingham. In 1626 the king expelled the queen's French courtiers. Then the duke was killed, and Charles and Henrietta Maria – both now bereft of close allies – were reconciled; their union has since become a love match. They lost their first son at birth last year (→4/11/31).

New World settlers

North America, June 1630
A fleet of 11 ships carrying over a thousand puritans has arrived to establish a colony in the Massachusetts Bay area, after sailing from Southampton in April. There have been many such attempts in the past decade; only a small group of puritan fanatics, "the Pilgrim Fathers", has succeeded, in Plymouth.

The new colonists are led by John Winthrop, who intends to found a "city upon a hill", far from the sins of old England. "The Lord will make our name a praise and glory," he announced.

In 1631 Richard Braithwaite published "The English Gentlewoman", a primer for young ladies on the etiquette of the day; he advocates modesty, chastity and obedience as the true virtues of the good gentlewoman.

Divine poet Donne breathes his last

London, 1631
England has lost its great poet, divine and preacher, John Donne, the dean of St Paul's. He wrote erotic love poetry in his youth, but later he turned to devotional works, sermons and religious poetry. Few of his poems have been published, but they have been widely circulated in manuscript form.

He had an adventurous life. He sailed to Cadiz and the Azores with the earl of Essex in 1597/8 before becoming secretary to Sir Thomas Egerton, the keeper of the great seal. But he fell out of favour in 1601 after eloping with Anne More, Egerton's niece, and was reduced to flattering his patrons and writing odes to famous ladies.

He wrote polemics against Roman Catholics, although he himself was brought up as one, and hesitated for ten years before taking orders in 1615. After that he became one of the great men of London, being quickly promoted to become dean of St Paul's in 1621 (→1633).

Earl abandons plan to drain the fens

Lincolnshire, 1631
An ambitious scheme to drain 30,000 acres of the fens between Deeping and Spalding was abandoned this year by the earl of Exeter. He had begun his plan to drain this stretch of low-lying fenland as long ago as 1610 after an act of parliament of 1600 had given landowners greater power to overcome common-law rights.

However, Exeter's plans have been thwarted by a combination of high tides, causing flooding, and local opposition. Some locals argue that drainage simply moves flooding to other areas, while others fear that lack of regular flooding will make their land less fertile.

Despite this setback, it is expected that other landowners will seek to "reclaim" the watery landscape of the fens for more intensive farming. They will not be the first to make this attempt: the first drainage canals and river diversions in this area were built hundreds of years ago by the Romans.

Council acts to stem rise in poverty

After a period of good harvests from 1626-28, the serious failures of 1629 and 1630 provoked social unrest.

Westminster, January 1631
The spectre of famine and disorder aroused by the disastrous harvests of 1629 and 1630 and troubles in the cloth trade has prompted the privy council – now dominated by Richard Weston, the lord treasurer, and Francis Cottington, the chancellor of the exchequer – to take decisive action. A *Book of Orders* has been issued setting out local magistrates' duties to relieve hardship, and "commissioners for the poor" have been appointed to supervise the work.

Prosperous parishes are to help those in distress; the consumption of grain is to be restricted and its export prevented; the number of alehouses is to be reduced, and beer is to be diluted, to save grain; cloth manufacturers are to maintain employment; and justices of the peace are to report regularly on progress. High sheriffs are to compile quarterly reports from the justices and forward them to the assize courts. The commissioners will oversee the system closely, with decrees regularly sent out from London.

While local gentry and justices of the peace support the aims of the policy, they dislike crown interference in local affairs – part of a trend towards the centralization of power that originated in the last century. But in times of famine court and country unite to prevent vagabondage and disorder. There were food riots in the west country last year, in addition to great discontent in the cloth towns there and in East Anglia. All agree that this must be controlled (→20/6/32).

Francis Cottington, the chancellor of the exchequer since 1629.

Increasing poverty across the country and fear of widespread famine led the authorities to take action.

1632 - 1633

London, January 1632. King Charles appoints Thomas, Viscount Wentworth, lord deputy of Ireland (→23/7/33).

London, 20 June 1632. Charles issues a proclamation ordering all gentry to leave London and return to their country estates to perform their duties as justices of the peace.

Yorkshire, September 1632. Thomas, Viscount Wentworth, suppresses all opposition to the introduction of knighthood fines (→1633).

Edinburgh, 1632. Work begins on a new parliament house.

England, 1632. Sir William Harvey is appointed royal physician.

London, 1632. Thomas Dekker, the dramatist, dies; among his best-known works are *The Witch of Edmonton* and *The Honest Whore*.

London, February 1633. William Prynne, a puritan pamphleteer, is imprisoned for his *Historiomastix: A Scourge of Stage Players*, which attacks the theatre as immoral and libels Queen Henrietta Maria, who participates frequently in masques (→11/5/34).

Surrey, 4 August 1633. George Abbot, the archbishop of Canterbury, dies at Croydon.

Edinburgh, 11 October 1633. Charles designates the city as a new bishopric.

London, 14 October 1633. Queen Henrietta Maria gives birth to her third son, James (→29/12/35).

London, December 1633. Following an outcry over the grant of the state soap monopoly to a syndicate with Catholic links, an officially sponsored demonstration by two washerwomen fails to convince onlookers that "papist soap" is as good as an unidentified second brand.

Co Londonderry, 1633. The construction of a Protestant cathedral here is completed.

Southwark, 1633. The first Baptist church opens in the city.

England, 1633. Puritans are outraged by the reissue of King James's *Book of Sports*.

London, 1633. Sir David Foulis, who was punished by Wentworth for non-payment of knighthood fines, is found guilty by the star chamber and imprisoned (→10/1634).

Hopes end for Scots colony in New World

Edinburgh, July 1632
Only the name "Nova Scotia" and a clutch of specially created Scottish baronets have survived the failure of an attempt to found the colony of New Scotland on the models of New England and New France in North America.

William Alexander, a grammar-school boy and classical scholar, enjoyed royal favour when he outlined his plan. King James made him titular lord proprietor of land adjacent to the French settlement at Quebec; the king also agreed to sell baronetcies and land grants to wealthy Scots who would promote emigration. Alexander's son, William, sailed with 70 men and two women to join the settlement.

Alexander's vision was brought to naught after Charles came to the throne. A disastrous war against France left the king desperately short of money; he begged the French to release unpaid instalments of his French wife's dowry. The French agreed – provided that the Scottish colony in North America was given up. A humiliated Charles surrendered, leaving Alexander deeply in debt.

The proud arms of Nova Scotia.

Sir John Eliot dies, a prisoner in Tower

London, 27 November 1632
Sir John Eliot, who has died at the age of 40, spent the last three years of his life in the Tower because of his opposition to King Charles's authoritarian style of government. He was a stout defender of the House of Commons, but he also firmly believed that the monarchy had a role in constitutional government; however, the king must rule for the good of his subjects, not for his private advantage. In 1629, when Charles ordered the adjournment of parliament, members held the speaker in his chair while Eliot read a protest against illegal taxes and "innovations" in religion. He became ill earlier this year and begged to be allowed to go into the country, promising to return to the Tower when he had recovered. The king refused, saying that the request was not sufficiently humble.

King grants charter for a Catholic colony

London, 1632
A new colony offering refuge for Catholics from England is to be founded in the Chesapeake Bay region of North America, adjacent to Virginia.

King Charles has this year granted a charter to George Calvert, Lord Baltimore, who served as secretary of state before resigning and declaring himself a Catholic. The colony will be named Maryland in honour of the king's French consort, Henrietta Maria.

New artist at court

London, 1632
King Charles has appointed the Flemish-born artist Anthony van Dyck as his official court painter. He receives a house in Blackfriars, London, and an annual pension of £200. He has also been knighted.

Van Dyck, born in 1599, began his working life in his hometown of Antwerp, then spent a productive period in Italy from 1621 to 1628, before returning home. He was once assistant to Sir Peter Paul Rubens, knighted last year.

Posthumous poetry puts feelings in verse

John Donne: an effigy in St Paul's.

London, 1633
The collected poems of John Donne and George Herbert have appeared in separate editions this year, both posthumously and both exhibiting the intense feeling that the two men injected into English verse.

Donne, brought up as a Catholic, converted to Anglicanism at about 30, and as dean of St Paul's for ten years until his death in 1631 [*see page 537*] he was a famous preacher. Just two of his verse works – commemorative poems for patrons – were published in his lifetime, but his other poetry was well known in manuscript versions.

Donne's early love poems are both more erotic and more spiritual than Elizabethan sonnets, which were addressed to beautiful but unattainable mistresses. He writes of love in metaphors that are complex and mystical, as in his *Holy Sonnets* which reflect on the transitoriness of earthly delights compared with the immortal longings of the soul.

His friend George Herbert renounced society to be a country rector, dedicating himself to a life of humility. His *Sacred Poems* include "The God of Love my Shepherd is" and "Let all the World in Every Corner Sing".

Coronation upsets Scots

A map of Charles's Scottish kingdom, flanked by some of his ancestors.

Edinburgh, 18 June 1633
King Charles has caused great offence to the Presbyterian faithful in Scotland by having himself crowned in the palace of Holyrood with all the trappings linked with popery – elaborate episcopal vestments, music and anthems, and anointing oil. He had already incurred ill-will by remaining in England and delaying his Scottish coronation for eight years after succeeding to the crown.

Many Scots are convinced that Charles has become thoroughly anglicized and is determined to impose on them the hated Church of England forms of worship. Even Scots who support the episcopalian role introduced into the kirk are unhappy at the king's plans for replacing the Calvinist Prayer Book with one much like that used in the English church (→28).

Charles: badly upset the Scots.

Scottish parliament ends after just 11 days

Edinburgh, 28 June 1633
King Charles's first Scottish parliament, formally opened after his coronation, has ended after only 11 days. The king's reputation – already damaged by the Anglican ritual he adopted for the coronation ceremony – suffered another blow when he forced through parliament contentious tax laws and Anglican-style religious measures. He stifled debate, exploited crown patronage, manipulated questionable proxy votes and pointedly took down the names of members who voiced their opposition to him. The king will return to London having achieved his legislative programme at the cost of forfeiting Scottish loyalty.

Talk is growing here of resisting the policies of the king by extra-parliamentary means. Local government is collapsing because of the revocation and anger at royal interference. There are plans to form a rebel army of clansmen (→3/1635).

Bishop of London is new Anglican head

London, 6 August 1633
William Laud, aged 60, a firm disciplinarian in religious matters and King Charles's most loyal supporter in the Church of England, has been appointed to the see of Canterbury. The new archbishop, with his well known dislike of puritanism, is expected to exert considerable influence on the 32-year-old king.

Laud was bishop of St David's in Dyfed when Charles came to the throne in 1625; in three succesive years he became bishop of Bath and Wells and then was appointed to the privy council before becoming bishop of London.

In his services Laud puts the emphasis on Communion administered at the high altar, and he has adopted the rich vestments and elaborate ceremonial of the past. His aspiration is to banish all nonconformist preaching in England and Scotland.

To the king's Protestant subjects all this smacks of popery. But Laud is a complex figure. He rejects the predestination of the Calvinists, but he also sees the Church of England as the only true Catholic church, free from the excesses of Rome. He has adopted the doctrine of free will expounded by the Dutch theologian Jacobus Arminius, who argues that this is not incompatible with belief in the grace of God. He is said to have warned Charles of dangers posed by the queen's large retinue of Jesuits and priests (→30/6/37).

Laud: a strong dislike of puritans.

Wentworth to take the helm in Ireland

Ireland, 23 July 1633
Thomas Wentworth has today been sworn in as Ireland's new lord deputy. His appointment is a departure from precedent in that he has had no previous connection with the country or indeed any experience of Irish affairs. Yet he has shown considerable administrative ability and an unswerving devotion to the English king. It seems likely that King Charles is hoping that this loyal and efficient servant might make Ireland a source of security and profit to the crown, instead of a burden and a liability.

In a bid to reassure the Old English community, Wentworth insists that he is opposed to the plantations. Doubts remain about his sincerity, however (→11/1634).

Wentworth: the new lord deputy.

Pretender to Scots throne faces probe

Edinburgh, 1 May 1633
A little-known member of the royal house of Stuart is in trouble with the king because he is suspected of claiming to have a better right to the throne of Scotland than King Charles. The earl of Menteith is said to be tracing his descent from a grandson of King Robert I Bruce. When reports of this reached the king in London, he at once dismissed the earl from his appointment as lord president of Scotland's privy council, sent him back to his country estate and ordered the college of justice to investigate.

1634 - 1635

Co Londonderry, 26 May 1634. John Bramhall is consecrated bishop of Derry.

Ireland, 29 June 1634. A commission for remedying "defective" land titles is re-established (→ 14/7).

Dublin, 14 July 1634. King Charles holds his first Irish parliament (→ 11/1634).

England, 20 October 1634. The maritime counties are forced by Charles to pay "ship money" to subsidize the cost of the navy (→ 5/1635).

Ireland, November 1634. Viscount Wentworth, the lord deputy, withdraws the commission to introduce the most controversial of the "graces" promised by the king in 1628 (→ 16/8/35).

Scotland, December 1634. The appointment of John Spottiswood, the archbishop of St Andrews, as chancellor increases fears of clerical dominance within the privy council here.

London, 1634. Covent Garden market opens.

London, 28 February 1635. The star chamber fines the City of London and the Irish Society £70,000 and confiscates the Society's Londonderry charter for mismanaging the plantation.

England, May 1635. To raise money for the crown, a depopulation commission will fine owners of lands which were once cultivated but are now left fallow (→ 6/1635).

Ireland, 30 June 1635. The manufacture of linen cloth is regulated by a royal proclamation.

England/Scotland, 31 July 1635. The first national postal service between London and Edinburgh is established.

Co Galway, 16 August 1635. A Galway jury declares invalid all titles to lands in Connacht – including the king's titles – granted in the composition settlement (→ 12/1636).

London, 29 December 1635. Queen Henrietta Maria gives birth to a second daughter, Elizabeth (→ 29/6/39).

London, 1635. Hackney coaches are limited to 3mph (4.8km/h).

Greenwich, London, 1635. Inigo Jones, the architect, completes the Queen's House, begun originally for Queen Anne and finished to the design of Henrietta Maria.

Libellous author faces savage penalties

A contemporary satirist shows Archbishop Laud feasting on Prynne's ears.

London, 11 May 1634
A puritan lawyer has been sent to the pillory and had both his ears cut off because his published denunciation of vulgarity and immorality on the stage has been taken as an attack on King Charles and Queen Henrietta Maria. William Prynne objected to the custom of boys playing female roles on stage; he also denounced actresses as "whores" and declared dancing to be a scandalous pastime. Since the queen is known to be fond of dancing and has appeared in masques at court, Prynne was prosecuted for libel. The court of star chamber fined him £5,000 and ordered him to be imprisoned for life and mutilated. His fellow lawyers expelled him from Lincoln's Inn, and copies of his book were burnt under the pillory in which he was locked by the neck and wrists.

A masque costume for the queen.

Forest laws to raise taxes from the land

Westminster, October 1634
In his search for ways of raising money without seeking the approval of parliament, King Charles has turned up a law, long fallen into disuse, which allows the king to fine any landowner who is held to have encroached on royal forest land. This summer Charles ordered the sheriff of Essex to make a survey of all encroachments since the reign of Henry III in the 13th century.

Landlords of the county, led by the earl of Warwick, produced evidence of their titles, taken from archives in the Tower. The king brushed the documents aside and demanded payment (→ 20).

Keating tries to put Irish record straight

Ireland, 1634
The famous Gaelic writer Geoffrey Keating has published his *Foras Feasa ar Eirinn* [*The Basis of Knowledge Concerning Ireland*]. Meant as a comprehensive reply to English historians such as Edmund Spenser and Richard Stanihurst, the work attempts to clear the ancient Irish of charges including cannibalism and sexual irregularity. Fearful that Irish folklore may be forgotten, many poets and priests are collating it in book form.

Play by poet John Milton is the high point of Welsh celebration

Ludlow, Shropshire, 1634
A masque by John Milton has been performed at Ludlow Castle for the earl of Bridgewater, who has been appointed lord president of Wales and the Marches. Comus, who gives the masque its title, is a pagan god who waylays travellers and tempts them with a magic potion which changes their faces into those of wild beasts. A girl and her two brothers (played by the earl's children) become lost in a forest. Comus presses the drink upon the girl, whose purity stiffens her resistance. The masque, with music by Henry Lawes, closes with Sabrina, a goddess from the river Severn, coming to the rescue, accompanied by water-nymphs (→ 1643).

Marcher stronghold: Ludlow Castle, in Shropshire, as it appeared in 1634.

'Ship money' extended

Charles's "Sovereign of the Seas": now inland areas must fund such vessels.

Westminster, June 1635
King Charles and his financial advisers have devised a controversial new expedient for raising money without parliamentary approval. "Ship money", traditionally levied on ports and coastal towns to pay for warships when the country is under threat, is to be extended to inland areas immediately. England is not at war, nor is there a threat of war, but the king has declared a national emergency – because of pirates in the Channel.

In the six years since Charles dissolved parliament and decided to rule as absolute monarch his agents have repeatedly increased customs dues, revived long-forgotten taxes and extracted arbitrary fines from landowners. Even so, his financial situation has continued to deteriorate. Almost half the king's annual income is spent on the royal household, which, as a source of patronage, is stubbornly resistant to economies. Charles has been driven to borrowing money on the security of future revenues. This has worsened his problems; as interest and repayments are bound to grow year by year, he is left with an ever-decreasing supply of ready money for current expenditure (→ 9/10/36).

Royal couple enjoy Derbyshire hospitality

Derbyshire, 30 July 1634
A royal visit to Bolsover Castle, the earl of Newcastle's home, has been marked by the completion of the long gallery – a spectacular addition to the fine building begun by the earl's father, Charles Cavendish, a son of Bess of Hardwick [*see page 498*]. It is the second successive year that the earl has entertained Charles and Henrietta Maria; last year they visited Welbeck, his Nottinghamshire abbey. This time Ben Jonson's masque *Love's Welcome to Bolsover* was shown. The king and queen were greeted by two lovers, Eros and Anteros, who were equipped with bows and quivers, breeches, buskins and periwigs.

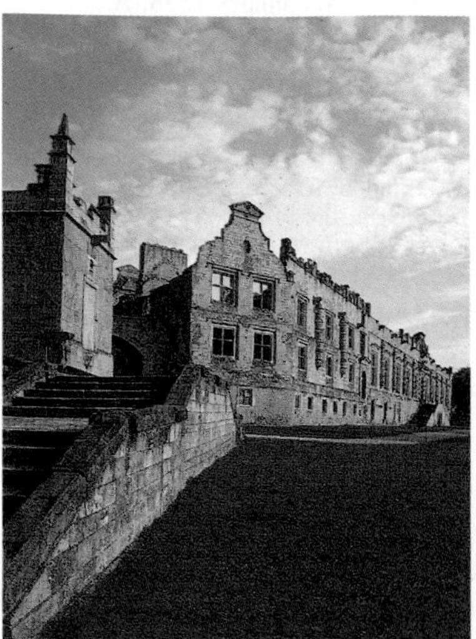

Bolsover Castle: the long gallery.

Anti-royalist is found guilty of treason

Edinburgh, March 1635
A two-year-old document setting out objections to King Charles's religious and taxation policies in Scotland has led to John Elphinstone, Lord Balmerino, being faced with a death sentence after conviction on a charge of treason. Archbishop John Spottiswood of St Andrews, who had pushed Charles's religious measures through the general assembly of the kirk at Perth, gave a copy of the document to the king. At his trial Balmerino was found not guilty on all counts except that of failing to identify the author of the document. On this, the assize [jury] voted seven for and seven against conviction. The accused's fate was sealed by the casting vote of the king's lord treasurer, the earl of Traquair (→ 18/10/36).

"Sir Thomas Aston at the deathbed of his wife" by John Souch: an allegory of the transition from birth to death, imbued with deep foreboding.

Authors join the literary 'tribe of Ben'

Sir John Suckling, a poet of "The Tribe of Ben", followers of Jonson.

London, 1635
Ben Jonson, the grand old man of the London literary scene, now 63, has gathered about him a group of keen young disciples who style themselves "the tribe of Ben". Fond of meeting at taverns such as the Devil in Fleet Street to seek advice from the master, the circle includes the playwright Richard Brome and the poets Sir John Suckling and Thomas Carew, noted for his elegy on the death of John Donne. Another enthusiast, the poet Robert Herrick, who is now a vicar at Dean Prior, near Ashburton in Devon, comments on Jonson in a description of the tribe's feasts: "And yet each verse of thine out-did the meat, out-did the frolic wine."

1636 - 1638

Scotland, January 1636. A new *Book of Canons* is published for the Church of Scotland, reaffirming episcopal government and elements of Anglican ritual.

London, March 1636. William Juxon, the bishop of London, is appointed lord treasurer, the first cleric to hold this office.

Low Countries, 10 August 1636. Irish scholars at Louvain, under the direction of Michael O'Clery, complete a national history, the *Annala rioghachta Eireann* [*Annals of the kingdom of Ireland*].

England, 9 October 1636. The third writ of "ship money" is issued (→ 12/1637).

Scotland, 18 October 1636. King Charles orders the new English Prayer Book to be used here (→ 23/7/37).

Co Galway, December 1636. The Galway jurors who refused to recognize King Charles's land titles in Connacht, and were heavily fined and imprisoned, submit and are released (→ 21/5/39).

Humberside, 1636. Dutch drainage experts begin work on an area of 60,000 acres in the Isle of Axholme (→ 5/7/38).

Edinburgh, 18 October 1637. A supplication is delivered to remove bishops from the privy council (→ 15/11).

Edinburgh, 15 November 1637. Supplicants who have delivered over 20 petitions to the government this autumn organize a "provisional government" with representatives from the nobility, gentry, presbyteries and burghs (→ 27/2/38).

Westminster, December 1637. John Hampden, a member of parliament who refused to pay the "ship money" tax, faces trial by the court of the exchequer (→ 12/6/38).

Nantwich, Cheshire, 1637. A coach service begins between Birmingham and Holywell.

Dublin, 1637. The city's first theatre opens in Werburgh Street.

Scotland, June 1638. The marquis of Hamilton, the king's commissioner, arrives to negotiate with the "covenanters" (→ 10/9).

London, 10 September 1638. Charles permits Hamilton to hold a general assembly and Scottish parliament, and also suspends the Prayer Book and *Book of Canons* (→ 28/11).

Court comes down hard on puritans

London, 30 June 1637
A large and demonstrative crowd gathered in Palace Yard, Westminster, today to witness the violent punishment of the pamphleteers John Bastwick, Henry Burton and William Prynne.

The three men were sentenced earlier this month in the high court for their vicious attacks on the bishops, and on Sabbath frivolity, after William Laud, the archbishop of Canterbury, had condemned them as "great incendiaries in the state".

Each man preached eloquently from the pillory before the executioner approached to cut off his ears, and in the case of Prynne (already cropped once after a previous indictment) to brand his face with the initials "SL", standing for "Seditious Libeller". Prynne bitterly joked that the letters really meant "Sign of Laud" (→ 5/1640).

Fears widespread of Roman Catholic plot

Threading rosaries: apprehension is generated by such popish practices.

London, September 1638
The arrival of Henrietta Maria's mother, Marie de' Medici, for an extended visit adds fuel to popular belief that the court is becoming a nest of secret popish sympathizers. Recalling the queen's earlier dealings with papal agents, the rumourmongers now criticize the luxury in which Charles's Catholic mother-in-law and her 600 retainers are entertained at public expense while his Protestant sister, Elizabeth, the exiled queen of Bohemia, is forced to live in relative poverty abroad.

Prayer book sparks riot

Violence erupts in St Giles's Cathedral at the reading of the new Prayer Book.

Edinburgh, 23 July 1637
A riot broke out in St Giles's Cathedral here today and rapidly spilt into the streets. The cause of the disturbance was the introduction of the new Prayer Book, which King Charles insisted should be used in all Scottish churches. Efforts by the bishops to remove any hint of popery or Anglican influences have failed to sway the public.

The foisting of the book on the church by royal prerogative has proved extremely unpopular. And by announcing months in advance that the Prayer Book would be used for the first time today, the government played into the hands of the Presbyterians, who had time to plan a protest. An apparently spontaneous action by women in the congregation, who threw stools at the dean of St Giles, was probably premeditated; some people are even saying that the women were apprentices in disguise.

Behind the protest were leading dissident noblemen – the earl of Rothes, Lord Balmerino and Lord Loudon – and the Presbyterian Church. It gathered its own momentum as the people of Edinburgh gave vent to their deep-rooted grievances against a government unpopular for its economic as well as its religious policies (→ 18/10).

Dancing, feasts and extravagant continental influences on fashion are ripe targets for puritan attack. In 1638 "Truth of the Times", a broadside by Henry Peacham, castigated France as "the magazine of our fooleries".

Scots defy king and sign 'covenant'

Edinburgh, 27 February 1638
Scotland has moved closer to open revolt against King Charles with the signing today at Greyfriars, by leading noblemen and gentry, of the "National Covenant". Frustrated by Charles's refusal to listen to their requests for a reversal of his religious policies, the supplicants have united to challenge royal authority.

The National Covenant has been compiled by Alexander Henderson, the minister at Leuchars, and Archibald Johnston, a brilliant young lawyer who has been acting as clerk to the "Tables", a provisional government formed last November. With the aristocratic leaders of the movement – Rothes, Balmerino and Loudon – they have produced a document intended to appeal to a wide public.

The covenant is virulently anti-Catholic, attacks innovations in the church over the last 20 years, and binds the signatories to a common defence of the king, church and one another. The intention is to take the form of loyal opposition while attacking the bishops and appealing to a popular hatred of popish practices. The covenant is a logical extension of the protests which began over the Prayer Book in Edinburgh last July and continued with a series of petitions through the autumn.

Although Presbyterian clergy are increasingly strident, religion is not the only reason for the strength of support for the covenant, especially among the nobility taking this action. The government's fiscal policies are also unpopular, as are its use of the royal prerogative, the role of bishops in government and the refusal to tolerate dissent. What Charles can do to quell the revolt is unclear; his government in Scotland is falling apart, and using English forces would only strengthen the "covenanters" (→6/1638).

Signing the "National Covenant" in Greyfriars' churchyard in Edinburgh.

'Ship money' tax wins legal sanction

London, 12 June 1638
Sir John Finch, the chief justice, today gave judgement that King Charles was in the right when he demanded "ship money" from the country's property-owners, even when they resided in an inland county. With this decision the case for non-payment, brought last year by a Buckinghamshire member of parliament John Hampden, was lost by seven votes to five.

On behalf of Hampden, who has extensive estates and business interests, his counsel, Oliver St John, had argued that even for defence the king could only raise money with the consent of parliament.

Among the seven judges who rejected this view, the most forthright was Robert Berkeley, who held that no conflict was possible between king and law. "Rex is lex," he said, "a living, speaking, acting law". But although Hampden has lost, resistance to ship money is growing. Receipts so far this year have dropped by two-thirds (→12/1639).

'Covenanters' plan to abolish bishops

Glasgow, 28 November 1638
A week after the opening of the first general assembly of the Church of Scotland to have been held for 20 years, the marquis of Hamilton, King Charles's commissioner, has walked out of the assembly.

The breakdown came when the assembly decided to go ahead and pass judgement on the bishops. Faced with a likely defeat, Hamilton demanded that the moderator, Alexander Henderson, dissolve the assembly. When this was refused, Hamilton withdrew. However the assembly has continued to sit, with many "covenanters" pleased that they can now get on with their programme of annulling the liturgy and abolishing the bishops.

The latter made no appearance at the assembly, and there have been accusations that the Presbyterians have rigged local elections to ensure a majority. The introduction of powerful lay members has given control to the nobility and its new Presbyterian allies (→27/3/39).

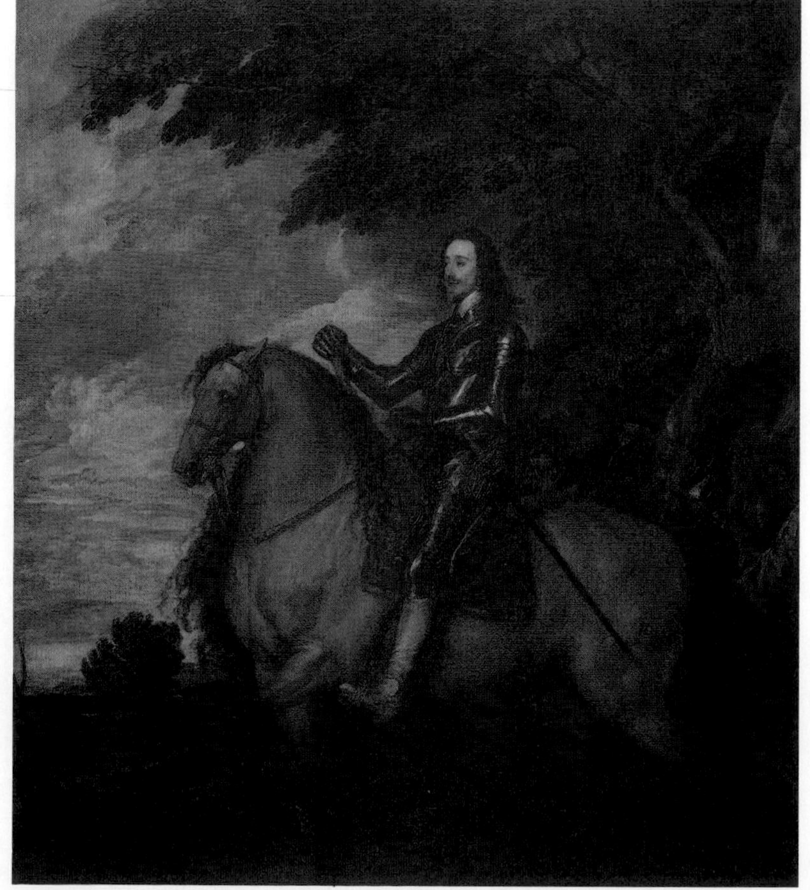

King Charles rides into a storm gathering on both sides of the border.

Fens protest set off by 'football' crowd

Isle of Ely, Cambs, 5 July 1638
A mob of 200 men gathered in the fenlands today, on the pretext of attending a football match, and began to destroy the drainage works constructed by the duke of Bedford and the Dutch engineer Cornelius Vermuyden. Many arrests followed and the angry crowds was dispersed before serious damage could be caused. Heavy overnight rain had also discouraged many would-be demonstrators.

This is the latest of many violent protests by the local fishermen and willow-cutters, who are angry that they will be deprived of their traditional common-land rights if the fens are converted to agricultural use. King Charles intends to take over the project personally, and this may resolve the trouble. As one ringleader said: "I will obey God and the king, and no one else." Only these, he shouted as he was dragged away, would "do the poor good and help them to their commons again".

1639

London, 27 March. King Charles leaves London and heads for York to raise an army against the Scottish "covenanters" (→ 14/5).

Aberdeen, 14 May. Royalist forces drive out the covenanters after a clash at the Trot of Turriff (→ 19/6).

Ulster, 21 May. Thomas, Viscount Wentworth, the lord deputy, enforces the "black oath", requiring all Scots here to swear loyalty to King Charles (→ 1/1640).

Aberdeen, 19 June. James Graham, the earl of Montrose, recaptures the city from the royalists.→

Whitehall Palace, 29 June. Queen Henrietta Maria gives birth to her seventh child, Catherine, who dies soon after her birth (→ 8/7/40).

Ireland, 27 July. King Charles summons Viscount Wentworth to England to be his chief minister and adviser (→ 22/9).

Edinburgh, August. The decisions made at the Glasgow assembly of the kirk are ratified, and bishops are condemned as contrary to the law of God; the assembly orders that subscribing to the "National Covenant" be mandatory (→ 14/11).

London, 22 September. Thomas, Viscount Wentworth, who has a reputation for ruthlessness and efficiency, arrives from Ireland.

Edinburgh, 14 November. Parliament, which has met and ratified the decisions of the general assembly, elects a standing committee to sit after its dissolution (→ 12/6/40).

London, December. King Charles, on the advice of Wentworth, summons parliament for the first time since 1629; he intends it to secure money to finance the war with Scotland (→ 13/4/40).

India. English settlers make their home in Madras after an agreement is reached between the English East India trading company and a local ruler on the Coromandel Coast; this first settlement is named Fort St George.

England. Thomas Carew, one of King Charles's "cavalier" poets, dies; he was best known for his elegy on the death of John Donne, published in 1633.

London. The Drury Lane theatre receives its first royal patent.

King forced into war over Scots bishops

Archbishop Laud, shown here as man and devil, seeks to rival God.

Berwick-Upon-Tweed, 19 June
King Charles has been forced into a humiliating treaty with the Scots "covenanters", who have been resisting his attempts to impose a high-church settlement on them.

His advisers realized that his poorly trained and equipped army – 30 per cent smaller than planned because of defections – was no match for the Scottish forces, poised to advance after defeating Scots royalists. Many of them were mercenaries and veterans of continental wars, but others were fired with religious fervour, especially against the power of bishops. The king had devised an ambitious plan involving a frontal border assault and simultaneous seaborne attacks from east and west. The reality was less impressive.

The war was unpopular with the English, who were reluctant to attack fellow Protestants opposed to religious reforms equally hated in England. It was underfunded, too; London financiers refused loans until a new English parliament was called, while the nobles resisted Charles's plan that they, not he, should pay for uniforms (→ 8/1639).

Fêted female artist arrives from Italy

London
The most fascinating new arrival at court is the Italian painter Artemisa Gentileschi. Since 1612, when she featured in a rape case in Rome brought by her artist father, Orazio, against her teacher Agostino Tassi – during which both of them were tortured – she has been as famous for her private life as for her paintings. Gentileschi's work, influenced by Caravaggio, combines dramatic realism with theatrical lighting and unusual perspectives. Her most striking work is *Judith Beheading Holofernes*. She will be helping her sick father to finish a ceiling in the Queen's House at Greenwich.

The London headquarters of the prospering East India company, which in 1639 won leave to erect a fortified trading post on the Coromandel Coast near Madras.

Deposed chancellor at centre of row in Scottish church dies

England, 26 November
Archbishop John Spottiswood of St Andrews, the former Scots chancellor who came here in exile last year, has died at the age of 74. He was the most senior of the churchmen who have had their political and religious worlds destroyed.

As a crown servant, Spottiswood received his highest reward in 1635, when he became chancellor; three years later, after failing to negotiate between the government and the rebel "covenanters", he was forced to resign by King Charles and retired to England, remarking: "All that we have been doing these 30 years past is thrown down at once." Since the Treaty of Berwick in June the changes which Spottiswood deplored have accelerated. A new assembly of the kirk has confirmed the abolition of the bishops and declared that no churchman is to hold civil power.

The archbishop, who died today.

This ruling removes the king's control over the estates [Scottish parliament] – which he had wielded through the bishops. The estates this summer consolidated its revolution by legislating for elections every three years and taking control of the key committee. Constitutionally Charles is now little more than a figurehead.

London, January. Thomas, Viscount Wentworth, is made earl of Strafford and lord lieutenant of Ireland (→16/3).

Dublin, 16 March. The earl of Strafford, back in Ireland, summons parliament and successfully raises a royalist army, by means of a grant of £120,000, to aid Charles's fight in the second "Bishops' War" (→3/4).

Ireland, 3 April. The earl of Strafford leaves Ireland; the new lord deputy is Christopher Wandesford (→7/11).

Westminster, 13 April. Parliament opens (→5/1640).

London, May. Four aldermen are imprisoned for refusing to give names of rich men to lend King Charles money for his cause against Scotland (→5).

Surrey, 8 July. Queen Henrietta Maria gives birth to her eighth child, Henry; he is to be given the title "duke of Gloucester" (→2/5/41).

England/Scotland, 20 August. The Scottish army crosses the border and routs the English at Newburn (→21).

North of England, 21 August. The earl of Strafford takes over as commander of the English army at Newburn (→29).

Newcastle upon Tyne, 29 August. The city falls to the Scots, who are now poised to take over the whole of northern England (→24/9).

York, 24 September. The council of the north refuses to cooperate with King Charles until he agrees to call a new parliament (→21/10).

Westminster, 7 November. In a desperate attempt to secure funds, Charles opens a new parliament.→

Dublin, 7 November. Parliament adopts a petition of remonstrance – complaints against the earl of Strafford – which delegates will take to England (→31/12).

Westminster, November. John Lilburne, a radical who was jailed for smuggling puritan pamphlets in 1638, is released after Oliver Cromwell, now the member for Cambridge, speaks on his behalf.

Ireland, 3 December. Christopher Wandesford, the lord deputy, dies (→9/6/41).

London. John Ford, the dramatist and poet, dies.

Edinburgh. The new parliament house is completed.

Financial crisis mounts

A furious King Charles dismissed his parliament after only three weeks.

London, 5 May

The first parliament in England for ten years has been dissolved after three bad-tempered weeks. King Charles called it because he had no other way to raise the £300,000 needed for a fresh war against the rebellious Scots "covenanters". But the Commons were not prepared to agree to the subsidy bill proposed by the king without prizing concessions out of him on such grievances as religious policy, "ship money" [*see report on page 541*] and the jailing of members after the last session. Charles offered to drop the hated ship money in return for a reduced number of subsidies, but the Commons then sought abolition of the new charges for funding the military, which amounted to more than three times as much as before.

Furious at the organized opposition, and against the advice of the earl of Strafford – who thought that a deal was still possible – Charles has dissolved parliament. However, he has not got his money, and his opponents are more united than ever (→24/9).

King's divine right set out by bishops

London, May

The convocation of bishops has fully supported Archbishop Laud's unpopular high-church reforms. In session at Westminster, protected by armed guards since the mob's recent attack on the archbishop's palace, it clearly set out the doctrine of the divine right of kings and ruled that all members of the professions will have to swear that they will never subvert "the government of this church by archbishops, bishops, deans and archdeacons, etc".

Furious puritans are claiming that behind that faceless "etc" lurks the Mass, the pope and Rome. More legal-minded critics point out that the convocation is illegal since it usually only meets while parliament is sitting (→31/12).

Scottish parliament boosts its powers

Edinburgh, 12 June

There has been a peaceful revolution in Scotland which poses a direct challenge to King Charles. Over the past ten days, meeting without royal approval, parliament has passed a number of radical acts which transform its powers. There is to be an election every three years; free debate is guaranteed; the gentry's share of the vote is increased, and a committee of lords, used by Charles to control parliament, has been emasculated.

The king's own double-dealing has played into the radicals' hands; these changes mean that he will not be able to use parliament to overturn any concessions he is forced to make. Only force can reverse the "covenanting" revolution (→20/8).

'Cumbernauld Bond' signals split in the ranks of 'covenanters'

Edinburgh, August

A serious split threatens the "covenanters". One of their leaders, the earl of Montrose, this month signed a document known as the Cumbernauld Bond, whose signatories bind themselves to back the public aims of the "National Covenant" but not the alleged private ambitions of some "covenanting" leaders.

The bond – said to be aimed at the earl of Argyll – follows a proposal put recently to the leaders that Scotland should be divided north and south of the Forth, the north to be under Argyll and the south under the marquis of Hamilton, King Charles's commander in Scotland. It was rapidly rejected, but suspicions have grown about what the bond calls the "particular and indirect practising of a few".

Tension between Montrose and Argyll surfaced two months ago when Argyll went to neutralize the Ogilvys, thought to support the king. Montrose had already put troops in Airlie Castle, but Argyll still burnt it, evicting the pregnant Lady Ogilvy.

Defeat leads to recall of parliament

Charles humiliated in 'Bishops' War'

Ripon, N Yorkshire, 21 October
Today, in yet another climbdown, King Charles has signed a treaty ending the second "Bishops' War". The Scots will keep Newcastle and occupy six northern counties, and their army will be paid £850 a day while it stays on English soil. In order to secure such sums, the king will be forced to recall parliament.

Both sides had been preparing for war since last year's Treaty of Berwick [*see report on page 544*]. Charles ordered the public burning of the "covenanters'" version of - that treaty; Berwick was refortified, swords were turned out at the rate of 1,000 a month, and military aid was sought from Spain. Meanwhile the Scots were obtaining arms from the Dutch, and their parliament passed a series of laws reducing Charles to a virtual figurehead.

The war was deeply unpopular in England; there were frequent mutinies, and the gentry were hostile. When the earl of Strafford took command in August he wrote privately: "Never came a man to so lost a business." On 20 August the Scots crossed the border. Eight days later they routed the English at Newburn and then marched into Newcastle. "Never so many ran from so few," remarked one Englishman. On 15 September Edinburgh Castle, held by the royalist Lord Ruthven, capitulated (→ 7/11).

Scottish soldiers: victorious over the English in the battle at Newburn.

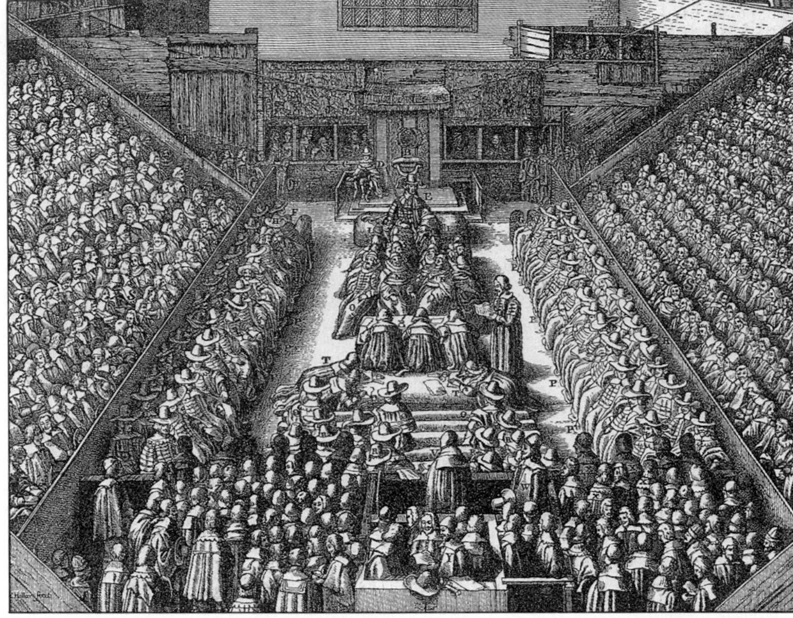
The earl of Strafford, the king's closest adviser, on trial for his life.

Archbishop and king's adviser impeached

London, 31 December
It has been an extraordinary two months since parliament opened. Two of King Charles's most unpopular advisers, Archbishop William Laud and Thomas Wentworth, the earl of Strafford, are in the Tower, having been impeached, while two other senior ministers, the secretary of state, Sir Francis Windebanke, and the lord keeper, Sir John Finch, have fled the country after being denounced in the House of Commons. The king has done nothing to save them. Strafford, described as "that grand apostate to the commonwealth", will be hard to convict legally. Arrogant he may be, but he is brave and well versed in the law. John Pym, the leader of the anti-court party, will have to move carefully to avoid a failed impeachment which would be disastrous for parliament. Laud, denounced as "the centre from whence our miseries flow", is far weaker (→ 10/4/41).

Ireland's members speak in England's House of Commons

Ireland, 7 November
For the first time ever delegates from the Irish House of Commons have spoken in the English House of Commons. An even more significant event is the return to England of Thomas, Viscount Wentworth, now earl of Strafford.

While lord deputy, Strafford failed in his aim "to make every Irishman a loyal and prosperous English citizen", yet his influence has been felt in every sphere of Irish life. Now that he is gone, the Irish parliament is making him responsible for all manner of grievances. Strafford's mistake was to ignore the political effect of his actions, with the result that he alienated every influential group in the country. He also undertook many private speculations in native Irish land and in trade monopolies here, all of which were costly failures.

Strafford backed William Laud, the archbishop of Canterbury, and so sought to bring the Church of Ireland into line with that of England by purging it of puritanism. Yet he failed to conciliate the native Irish, and his refusal to confirm the "graces" promised in 1628 alienated the Old English. His most dubious achievement is to have united bitter enemies, the native Irish and the settlers, through their hatred of him (→ 3/12).

'Root and Branch' petition raises pressure for bishops' abolition

London, 11 December
"Abolish the bishops" is the radical demand of a petition with 15,000 signatures presented to parliament today by Alderman Isaac Pennington. It begins: "Whereas the government of archbishops and lord bishops ... have proved ... a main cause of many foul evils ... we most humbly pray [it] with all its roots and branches may be abolished" and goes on to blame the bishops for evils like "idle and unprofitable books", monopolies and patents and the "increase of whoredoms".

John Pym has sent it to committee to avoid a divisive vote so that he can concentrate his fire on Archbishop Laud himself.

An angry mob of protesters attacks the archbishop's palace at Lambeth.

Local government in state of collapse

England, December
During the year local government in England has been in a state of near-collapse as the result of a taxpayers' "strike". It began last year in protest at the tax known as "ship money" [*see report on page 541*] – about 80 per cent of which remains uncollected. The need to pay for an unpopular war against the Scots has compounded public anger. The administrative problems of collecting ship money and the tax's perceived unfairness have put a great burden on local officials. The number of violent assaults on tax collectors has grown; in one incident at Whatcroft in Cheshire a man "drew out his knife and threatened the constable to whet it in his guts". Meanwhile, the gentry across the country is increasingly upset at the disruptive effects of royal policies on peace and order in local society.

Bishop believes in flying to the moon

London
It may be possible to fly to the moon. This is the conclusion of a book – *The Discovery Of A New World, With A Discourse Concerning The Possibility Of A Passage Thither* – reissued this year by the clergyman John Wilkins.

When it was first published two years ago it put forward arguments for the moon being another world, with seas and mountains and inhabitants; this edition has a new chapter which discusses getting there.

The addition was inspired by a recent book by another clergyman, Francis Godwin, which describes the voyage of a Spanish noble to the moon in a "engine" pulled by 25 wild swans. Forty-five miles up he became weightless and watched the earth rotating. He took 12 days to reach the moon, where he found friendly people 28 feet high.

Women take the lead in religious changes

Female influence on religion: a puritan woman holds forth at a public meeting.

England
Many women are as worried as men about the religious aspects of the current conflict – especially since it is women, Protestant or Catholic, who most actively promote family worship through prayer at home. A wife often organizes her household's entire day around prayer and devotion, and worship occupies a great deal of time; one Staffordshire woman, Mary Gifford, is said to have worn holes in the knees of her dress after spending so many hours praying. Catholic families – forbidden to pray in public places – devote the greatest amount of time to worship in the home, and several Catholic women have been executed for sheltering priests. Some Protestant women, who take part in public worship, are educating their children to a fierce commitment to puritan beliefs.

Royal agents scour Europe for fine works to add to king's magnificent art collection

A tapestry based on one of Charles's collection of Raphael cartoons.

A typical work of van Dyck.

The Banqueting Hall: interior.

Whitehall Palace
Sir Peter Paul Rubens calls King Charles "the greatest amateur of painting among the princes of the world", and of the royal collection he says: "I have never seen such a large number of fine pictures in one place." Charles's agents scour Europe for renaissance and contemporary works of art for him. One of his biggest purchases was the collection of the dukes of Mantua, including a set of huge wall panels, *The Triumphs of Caesar*, by Mantegna and another set of Raphael cartoons for tapestries.

In 20 years the king has acquired 1,500 works, and his surveyor of pictures, the Dutch expert Abraham van der Doort, has just completed an inventory of his wealth of Titians, Rubens, Raphaels, Correggios and portraits by Holbein, Dürer and Rembrandt. Charles inherited his connoisseur's taste from his mother, Queen Anne. He commissioned the ceiling panels for the new Banqueting Hall in Whitehall from Rubens, whom he knighted. He did the same for Rubens's chief assistant, Anthony van Dyck, who has been Charles's court painter since 1632. Inigo Jones, who designed the Banqueting Hall in 1622, has also finished the Queen's House at Greenwich. This was begun for Queen Anne but completed to designs by Henrietta Maria.

1641

Westminster, 10 April. The trial for high treason of the earl of Strafford, which opened on 22 March, collapses (→ 21).

Westminster, 21 April. The Commons pass a bill of attainder against the eral of Strafford (→ 23).

London, 23 April. King Charles tells Strafford that he cannot help him, despite his earlier promises (→ 10/5).

England/United Provinces, 2 May. Charles arranges the marriage of his eldest daughter, Mary, aged nine, to Prince William of Orange, aged 15 (→ 17/6/44).

Westminster, 10 May. An act is passed denying Charles's right to dissolve parliament without its consent (→ 12).

Dublin, 9 June. Patrick Darcy, a member of the Old English community, argues for the legislative autonomy of the Irish parliament, which can at present be overruled by Westminster (→ 10/1641).

Scotland, 11 June. James Graham, the earl of Montrose, is imprisoned when letters to from him to the king are found.

Westminster, 22 June. Charles agrees to the Tonnage and Poundage Act, declaring illegal customs duties levied without parliament's consent (→ 24).

Westminster, 5 July. The king agrees to abolish the court of star chamber (→ 17).

Westminster, 17 July. Parliament refuses to allow the queen to leave the country; it is feared that she would sell the crown jewels to raise support abroad (→ 12/8).

London, 28 July. Charles makes Robert Devereux, the earl of Essex, commander-in-chief of the army in southern England (→ 12/7/42).

London, 12 August. Charles signs the Treaty of London, recognizing the demands of the Scottish covenanters (→ 14).

Scotland, 14 August. Charles tries to obtain support from the covenanters (→ 12/10).

Co Meath, 21 November. A force of Ulster rebels besieges Drogheda (→ 3/12).

Ireland, November. Over 80 Protestants die when rebels attack Portadown Bridge.

Co Meath, 3 December. The Ulster Irish and Anglo-Irish, meeting at Knockcrofty, form a defensive alliance (→ 19/3/42).

'Black Tom' is executed

A huge crowd gathers on Tower Hill to watch the execution of Strafford.

London, 12 May

As the executioner brought down the axe and raised the severed head, a huge crowd on Tower Hill roared approval. Thomas Wentworth, the earl of Strafford, known as "Black Tom Tyrant" to his foes, was dead. Strafford's fate was sealed after parliament's recall last November. The parliamentary leaders could not afford to let the strong, autocratic earl – King Charles's ablest minister – live. Strafford was arrested, along with Archbishop William Laud, and the Commons compiled charges against him. Much useful material for his impeachment came from the Irish parliament, united in its hatred of him.

With the Scots pressing for his execution the earl was impeached, accused of conspiring to bring an army from Ireland in order to enforce an absolute monarchy. Strafford ably defended himself, and so, when it became clear that impeachment was going to fail, the Commons passed a bill of attainder which declared him guilty without the need for a trial.

Matters came to a head ten days ago when a dramatic attempt to rescue Strafford from the Tower failed. A force of 60 monarchists under Captain Billingsley, a mercenary adventurer, arrived at the Tower and demanded entry but was refused. Reports of the incident quickly spread and developed into wild rumours of a royal coup and a popish plot. On 5 May, John Pym informed the Commons that troops from France were sailing towards Portsmouth to support the king. After a highly charged debate, the Bill of Attainder was passed by the Lords on 10 May. Two days later Charles agreed to sign the death warrant of the man whom he had promised to save (→ 22/6).

The fall of the bishops: a favourite dream of those who fear popery.

King offered list of 'ten proposals' by parliament

London, 24 June

The two houses of parliament today passed ten new proposals that are so revolutionary as to render impossible any compromise between King Charles and parliament. The proposals, put forward by the parliamentary leader John Pym, bring the appointment of royal advisers and the control of the army under parliamentary authority. Even more offensive for a king who believes passionately in the concept of absolute monarchy, the proposals insist that appointments to the queen's household can only be made with the consent of parliament – thus isolating her from her Catholic priests and royalist supporters.

Like all Pym's assaults on the monarchy during the past six months, this one was well timed. Since the earl of Strafford's execution there has been an ebbing of support for the parliamentary cause, and he has had to spin out his "revelations" of a popish plot – involving the queen, the army in Ireland and a French invasion force – to hold on to waverers. A month ago a Commons bill to deprive bishops of seats in the House of Lords was thrown out by the upper house. Many see Pym's "ten proposals" as deliberate provocation.

He and his fellow parliamentary leaders – John Hampden, Denzil Holles, Lord Mandeville and Lord Saye and Sele – are determined to continue their campaign to reduce the power of the monarchy. They do not see themselves as revolutionaries, rather as constitutionalists set on winning back for the people rights rooted in the *Magna Carta* of 1215. The king's supporters see themselves as equally legitimate, intent on maintaining the rights of the crown in the face of demagogues. Rumours of coups and plots abound, and news that the king is preparing to visit Scotland – where he may raise an army – adds to the sense of crisis (→ 5/7).

Rumours of royalist plot mar Charles's visit to Scotland

Edinburgh, 12 October
King Charles's visit to Scotland, to drum up support against the English parliament, has turned into a disaster. The king is accused of plotting to kidnap the covenanting leader, the earl of Argyll. The army of the Covenant has been pushed from neutrality to enmity.

The royal visit had begun well. Charles flattered the covenanters, ignoring his own supporters and doing nothing to secure the release from prison of his most hot-headed champion, the earl of Montrose.

Charles studies a map of Scotland.

But while the king was on his best behaviour with the covenanters, his groom of the bedchamber, Will Murray, was conspiring to turn two Scottish regiments over to Charles and, with the help of the earl of Crawford, a former mercenary, kidnap the earl of Argyll from the king's own chambers in Holyrood.

Charles denies all knowledge of the conspiracy. But coming within weeks of the so-called "papal plot" – and bearing in mind the king's covert methods of raising troops by keeping the army of Ireland in being and recruiting mercenaries supposedly to assist his nephew, the Protestant Elector Palatine – he has become deeply compromised (→23/11).

Hundreds die as Irish gentry rebel

Sir Phelim O'Neill led the rebels.

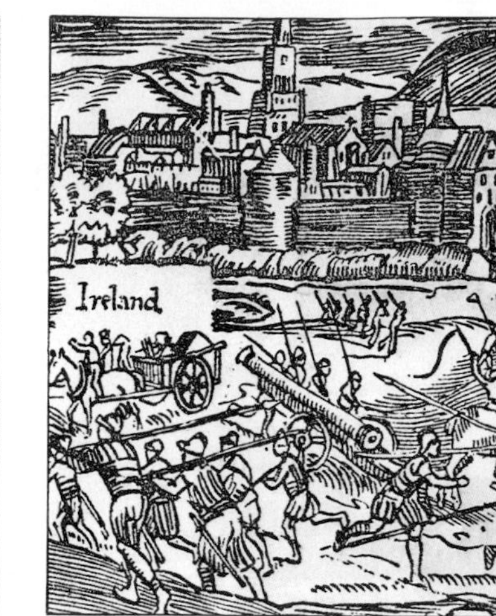

Catholic Irish forces attack a Protestant town during the Ulster revolt.

Ulster, October
Several hundred people, most of them Protestants, have been murdered in an insurrection that broke out here on 22 October. The rebel leaders are, surprisingly, not the dispossessed native majority, embittered by their desperate living conditions, but the Catholic Ulster gentry, of Irish origin and still owning land but under increasingly tough economic pressures.

These leaders – Rory O'More, Lord Maguire and Sir Phelim O'Neill – claim to be fighting for religious freedom and to save their land but stress their loyalty to King Charles. They are afraid that if Westminster acts against him there will be no one to protect them from the demands of the New English. They were bolstered in their belief that they were not acting disloyally by rumours that Charles had asked the earl of Ormond to reassemble and strengthen the army raised last year by the earl of Strafford. This was part of a plan to form a military alliance with the Irish Catholics against the English parliament, but it came to nothing.

Meanwhile mobs have swooped on Protestant settler homes and murdered the occupants. Some reports are, however, exaggerated, and in many cases the rebel leaders are able to enforce restraint on the men who follow them (→16/11).

James Butler, the earl of Ormond.

King faces new worry at news of Catholic rebellion in Ireland

A propagandist's view of rebel acts.

London, 16 November
The news of the Ulster rebellion has shocked the Commons, and both King Charles and the members of parliament have been told that Ireland could be lost and its entire Protestant population destroyed. Propaganda stories of massacres are having the desired effect of mobilizing energies towards suppressing the revolt: James Butler, the earl of Ormond [*see above*], will be the leader of the royalist forces in Ireland. A force of 5,000 will be sent to support him. Meanwhile reports continue of Protestant men, women and children being marched naked through the bitter nights. These are symbolic punishments – the Catholics are stripping those who dispossessed them (→21).

The Protestant version of the revolt.

Royal power challenged

John Pym led the attack on the king.

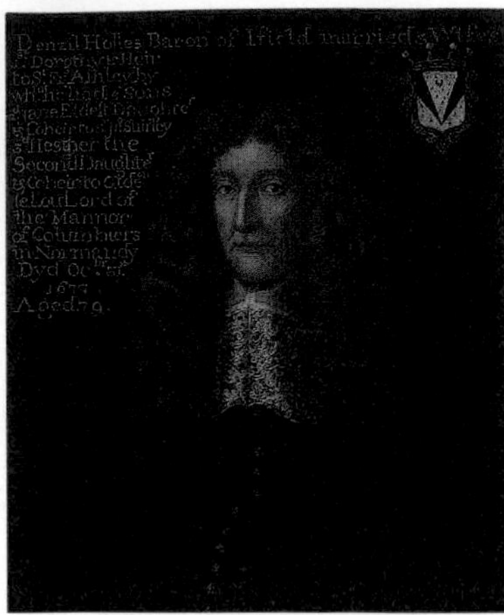
Denzil Holles ably assisted Pym.

Westminster, 23 November
A "Grand Remonstrance" against King Charles was carried in the House of Commons in the early hours of this morning. It was a close vote, with members divided 148 against and 159 in favour. Organized by John Pym, the member for Tavistock, the Grand Remonstrance is a major attack on what are perceived to be Charles's numerous abuses of power. Other members who played a leading role in the action include Denzil Holles and John Hampden.

The remonstrance aims to undermine royal authority and force the king to accept advisers appointed by parliament – an unprecedented restraint. It also implies that members should have the right to appoint military commanders. Such a development would remove the mainstay of royal power – the right to raise and control armed forces and to make war – and King Charles is bound to resist.

Pym was able to get the remonstrance through against the background of the revolt in Ireland, for which troops will have to be raised. Parliament and many ordinary people are worried about the influence at court of Roman Catholics, particularly those who serve the Catholic queen, Henrietta Maria. Given that the king has threatened to use Irish soldiers in offensive actions against the Scots, there is suspicion that an army raised to fight Irish rebels could just as easily be used against English Protestants.

But the fact that even a master organizer of parliamentary business such as Pym can conjure up only a wafer-thin majority for such an important bill is indicative of how deep the splits in English society are becoming and how bitterly they are felt (→ 1/12).

Two members for Kent who support Charles: Sir Edward Dering ...

... and Sir John Colepeper, who is highly esteemed by the king.

Whitehall clashes escalate the conflict of the 'cavaliers' and the 'roundheads'

London, 30 December
After three days of growing violence there was a serious outbreak of fighting last night between riotous apprentices and officers who had just come from dining with King Charles in Whitehall. The conflict spread to a number of locations, and while no one was killed about 60 apprentices and citizens were hurt and two officers injured, neither seriously.

Eight or ten officers emerged from dinner to find a mob of about a hundred armed with clubs and swords, who accused them of being papists. The angry officers retaliated by calling the apprentices "roundheads", on account of their closely cropped hair. Stones were thrown, and then the officers climbed the railings around the palace; swords were drawn on both sides, and the officers attacked.

As the apprentice boys ran off, leaving behind several wounded colleagues and a few prisoners, they taunted the officers with chants of "*cavaliero, cavaliero*" – an insulting reference to the heavily armed Spanish troopers who are seen as the national enemy and brutal oppressors of good Protestants everywhere. Taken up and corrupted to "cavalier", this cry was soon being heard everywhere (→ 11/1/42).

A heavily armed "roundhead".

A gentleman cavalier steps out.

The terms of the 'Grand Remonstrance'

Westminster, 1 December
The Grand Remonstrance [*see report above left*] – which has been formally proclaimed today – describes members of parliament as King Charles's "most humble and faithful subjects", but it then goes on to insist that those members consider it to be their compelling duty to condemn the "evils under which we have now many years suffered". The text then identifies the people regarded as responsible for "subverting the fundamental laws and principles of government upon which the religion and justice of this kingdom are firmly established". These are as follows:

"1. The Jesuited papists, who hate the laws.

"2. The bishops and the corrupt part of the clergy, who cherish formality and superstition.

"3. Such councillors and courtiers as for private ends have engaged themselves to further the interests of foreign princes ... [who maintain] continual differences and discontents between the king and his people."

The document also says that unless the king appoints councillors in whom parliament can confide "we cannot give his majesty such supplies for support of his own estate ... as is desired" (→ 30).

1642

Westminster, 13 February. The Bishops' Exclusion Act prevents clergy from holding secular offices without royal consent.

Westminster, 5 March. The Militia Ordinance allows parliament to raise an army; it becomes law even though the royal assent is refused (→23/4).

Westminster, 19 March. The Adventurers' Act offers Irish rebels' confiscated lands to those who give money for Cromwell's army (→4/1642).

Ulster, April. Scottish troops under Robert Monro arrive to quell rebels after an Anglo-Scots agreement (→10/5).

Co Antrim, 10 June. The first formal Presbyterian church in Ireland meets at Carrickfergus.

England, 2 July. The navy accepts Robert Rich, the earl of Warwick, as lord high admiral of the fleet: he was parliament's candidate in preference to Sir John Pennington, a royalist.

Co Donegal, 8 July. Owen Roe O'Neill, a nephew of the late Hugh O'Neill of Tyrone, returns from military service on the ontinent to lead the Ulster rebels (→15/9/43).

Westminster, 9 July. Robert Devereux, the earl of Essex, who was Charles's commander-in-chief of the army in southern England, accepts the same position with parliament's army (→8/1642).

Westminster, 11 August. The Commons stand firm against the king despite his offer of a pardon to Essex and his rebels (→22).

Westminster, 2 September. Parliament orders the closure of all theatres.

Nottingham, 13 September. Charles leaves for Shrewsbury to raise an army (→23).

Worcester, 23 September. The royalists ("cavaliers") defeat the parliamentarians ("roundheads") at Powick Bridge (→23/10).

Middlesex, 12 November. Royalist troops under Prince Rupert win a battle at Brentford (→12/1642).

Westminster, November. Parliament asks the Scots for their support against the king.

Humberside, December. New sluice gates are opened, flooding large drained areas on the Isle of Axholme to prevent royalist troops from passing through.

King takes flight as royal coup fails

London, 11 January

King Charles and Queen Henrietta Maria left London today after the king's failed coup against parliament on 4 January, when he tried to arrest five members of the House of Commons. His action followed moves to impeach the queen, whom he loves dearly, on charges of high treason – a conviction for which carries the death penalty.

Charles arrived at the house, escorted by troops, to find that the members – John Pym, John Hampden, Sir Arthur Haslerig, Denzil Holles and William Strode – had fled. Had he succeeded, it would have been a demonstration of royal power, but his failure only underlined the weakness of the crown.

Pym, forewarned of Charles's intentions, may have baited the trap, with himself and his friends staying until the last moment to be certain that the king was coming to arrest them. The thinking was that, in this way, Charles would be tempted into an act of violence against parliament which he could never later deny; the Commons could always say that Charles had struck the first blow.

A dangerous mistake: King Charles finds that all his birds have flown.

In response to the incident, Londoners rose in an angry swarm to defend parliament, with apprentices, mariners, tradesmen and all kinds of citizens offering their services. As it is clear that he can no longer rule in London, the king has left by coach for Hampton Court this morning, accompanied by his wife and children (→23/2).

Queen escapes with crown jewels to seek military aid abroad

Queen Henrietta Maria leaves for France: a highly romanticized view.

Dover, 23 February

There was a painful parting between King Charles and Queen Henrietta Maria today on the deck of the king's warship *Lion*. The queen is going abroad to seek military aid and money for the conflict with parliament that now seems inevitable. In her luggage are the crown jewels, which the royal pair are prepared to pawn in return for help. Although their public parting had of necessity to be somewhat stiff and formal, both their faces were seen to be streaming with tears. While it is thought that the queen has frequently given the king bad advice, and that her careless tongue is partly to blame for his present troubles, he clearly remains deeply devoted to her. Rupert, the king's nephew, had volunteered to travel with the queen to the continent, but Charles decided that he would be of more use in England.

The squadron of five ships assembled to take the queen to the United Provinces are under the command of Captain John Mennes, a dedicated royalist and an experienced seaman whose loyalty is beyond question. The sight of the ships may have given the king renewed confidence, but others believe that – Mennes's men excepted – most ships' crews prefer the parliamentary side. After the *Lion* sailed, King Charles followed her course, riding alone along the clifftops, waving until she finally disappeared from view (→5/3).

Clergy give backing to the Irish rebellion

In Ireland, the bitter war has spread from its original Ulster flashpoint.

Kilkenny, 10 May
In line with a proposal made at the Synod of Kells last March, a national congregation of clergy and laymen is meeting at Kilkenny to set up a provisional government under a "supreme council". The meeting, which will go on for three days, represents church approval of the war that has now spread from Ulster to the rest of the country. From now on the insurgents, who are fighting the Protestant New English, are to call themselves "the Confederate Catholics of Ireland". Ironically the rebels are meeting in the principal seat of the house of Ormond – the present earl, James Butler, is the principal defender of the crown in Ireland.

The Confederation is a union of the native Irish Catholic rebels with their co-religionists among the Old English. But ethnic divisions are less important than religious conflicts here (→ 8/7).

City of Hull comes out on parliament's side

Kingston upon Hull, 23 April
A well-laid plan by King Charles to take control of the vital port of Hull has misfired. With the queen in the United Provinces buying arms, the royalists need a major east coast port in which to unload them. They also need the control which that port would give them of North Sea shipping, together with the lucrative customs revenue that comes from ordinary port business.

The governor of Hull is Sir John Hotham, who has already declared for parliament. He was unprepared for the sudden arrival yesterday of the eight-year-old duke of York, the king's younger son, with a small group of attendants. Although suspicious, Hotham decided to allow them in – under pressure from the royalist mayor.

Today Charles arrived with little warning, but with a troop of horse, and sought entry. With the duke already inside, Hotham was in an awkward position. But he realized that the king would take possession of the castle, port and magazine, so he refused and expelled the duke and his party – leaving Charles angry but impotent (→ 2/7).

Hull refuses to admit King Charles.

Charles raises standard

Nottingham, 22 August
King Charles has raised the royal standard at Nottingham and issued a proclamation calling on his supporters to rally to him. This is a formal and traditional declaration of war by a king, and, barring a miracle, fighting cannot now be far away. There has already been a skirmish at Coventry, when the town said that it would allow Charles to enter alone, but not his soldiers. The king tried to force an entry, and the local defenders sallied out and drove off his men, killing a few. Charles is no more popular in Nottingham than he is in Coventry, but he has ignored advice to rally his men in a part of the country where he has strong support, preferably a town closer to London.

The royal standard was carried from Nottingham Castle by the knight-marshal, Sir Edmund Verney, and erected to cries of "God save the king and hang all roundheads" from a small band of loyal supporters (→ 13/9).

Charles raises his standard at Nottingham: it blew down within a week.

Cromwell gathers troops in Cambridge

Cambridge, August
The city's member of parliament, Oliver Cromwell, has been gathering and training troops in the area with the aid of his brother-in-law Valentine Walton. Two companies of volunteers have been gathered just in time to stop a huge shipment of silver plate, estimated to be worth £21,000, being sent to King Charles by the university colleges.

Charles had wanted the plate to boost his flagging finances, but Cromwell outmanoeuvred him by marching his men to King's College with drums beating and flags flying. Hearing that the king's men were coming to collect the treasure, Cromwell lined the nearby lanes with his musketeers and held them off. He has been warmly congratulated by parliament (→ 11).

Oliver Cromwell: a later portrait.

Struggle for power divides England in civil war

Edgehill sees first major clash of war

Warwickshire, 23 October
The first big battle of the civil war was fought today at Edgehill, near Banbury. The result was a draw, with neither side able to obtain a significant advantage. However, on balance, the parliamentary troops under the earl of Essex looked better organized and were in a slightly stronger position when nightfall forced a halt.

This could be because of King Charles's decision to take personal control of his army, which caused considerable confusion. The king is not a professional soldier and so has no military experience worth talking about, yet he decided to place himself at the head of his men and take control away from his veteran general, the earl of Lindsey.

The result was that while Charles behaved with great bravery he exercised little influence over the battle. Prince Rupert's cavalry attacked the enemy horses but then went off looting, accompanied by the king's mounted bodyguard. Without cavalry the infantry was reluctant to advance, and without experience Charles was unable to lead it. The late return of Rupert's horses restored the balance, but it was a near thing (→ 12/11).

Prince Rupert charges at Edgehill. His men often lacked good discipline.

Eastern counties join up against king

East Anglia, 20 December
Parliamentary opponents of King Charles in five counties have banded together to form an "Eastern Association". Lord Grey of Warke heads the association, which was formed today by parliamentarians from Norfolk, Suffolk, Essex, Hertfordshire and Cambridgeshire.

The group's aim is to overcome the danger of local rivalries – known as "localism" – preventing the development of a coherent national military strategy. It is early days yet in the civil war, but there are fears among parliament's leaders that their volunteer forces will be willing to fight only to defend their own territories.

Other county associations are being formed, but the Eastern Association is a step towards a broader strategy. Oliver Cromwell, who represents Cambridge and last August used the forces which he had raised locally to stop royalist troops collecting college silver for the king, is one of its members (→ 1/1648).

Two armies dig in for a long struggle

England, December
The close of the year has brought the chilling realization that the war is not going to be over quickly. Both sides embarked on hostilities under the illusion that the other would give in pretty quickly once it realized that it had a fight on its hands. Now neither side shows any signs of quitting, and veterans of the war which has been raging in Europe since 1618, who have found both camps eager to hire them, are saying that, with any luck, they could have employment in England until they retire.

During the year King Charles has lost his fleet, which defected to parliament, but has raised an army that managed an honourable draw at Edgehill, in Warwickshire, in the only big battle so far. The king has been unable to regain London, which means that parliament, with its access to the London money market and loans from merchants, is in the stronger financial position. Yet Charles enjoys strong support, his coffers are reasonably full, and the queen is abroad pawning the crown jewels to buy arms. In all, things are fairly evenly balanced, with the king in perhaps the slightly better military position (→ 20).

A musketeer of the period.

How the two main sides shaped up for war

England, September
King Charles has raised his standard at Nottingham, while parliament's forces have assembled at Northampton under the earl of Essex. On paper the two sides look fairly matched: Charles has some 13,500 men, while Essex has about 15,000. Both have infantry, cavalry and dragoons – mounted infantry – and a few guns, but neither army has men who have been more than partially trained.

The king has appointed himself commander-in-chief of his forces, although he has no personal military experience, and his deputy, the 69-year-old earl of Lindsey, is perhaps too old to last long in the field. But the king does have at his side his dashing 23-year-old nephew, Prince Rupert of the Rhine. Rupert *is* experienced, having seen action in several wars on the continent, and he is being put in command of the cavalry. The earl of Essex has also fought before, in the Low Countries, and is a sound, if an uninspiring, soldier.

Both sides are seeking Scottish support, but the parliamentarians have two major advantages: they are being backed by the merchants, so that they have more money and support from the ports and ships; and they hold London. However, an early decisive victory for either side is unlikely (→ 13).

A cavalier officer with a pike.

1643

Scotland, January. Nobles sympathetic to Charles sign "the Cross Petition" in the hope of peace in England (→ 28).

Cheshire, 28 January. Roundheads led by Sir William Brereton seize Nantwich (→ 14/4).

Oxford, 14 April. Peace talks between King Charles and parliament fail (→ 23).

Ireland, 23 April. Charles authorizes James Butler, the earl of Ormond, to negotiate with the confederates (→ 27).

Lincolnshire, 13 May. Royalist troops are defeated at Grantham by Oliver Cromwell and the roundheads (→ 23).

Westminster, 23 May. The Commons vote to impeach the queen for selling the crown jewels (→ 24/6).

Yorkshire, 30 June. The royalists win a battle at Adwalton Moor and control most of the county (→ 7/1643).

Westminster, June. The Commons invite the Scots to join an assembly to decide a post-war religious settlement.

Oxford, 13 July. Henrietta Maria, who in February landed at Bridlington with arms and money from abroad, arrives from York (→ 14).

London, 14 July. Parliament offers to double the forfeited Irish land available to those who add 25 per cent to their war contributions (→ 28).

Lincolnshire, 28 July. William Cavendish, the earl of Newcastle, seizes Gainsborough after a clash with Cromwell (→ 8/1643).

Humberside, August. The earl of Newcastle forces Sir Thomas Fairfax's forces to retreat at Beverley (→ 7).

Lothian, 7 August. Commissioners appointed by the English parliament arrive to discuss an alliance (→ 17/8).

Exeter, 4 September. The city surrenders to Prince Maurice, the younger brother of Rupert and a nephew of Charles (→ 25).

Lincoln, 20 October. The city surrenders to parliament (→ 18/11).

Clwyd, 18 November. Troops from Ireland land to join Charles (→ 16/12).

Oxford, 16 December. Charles orders the arrest of the duke of Hamilton, his old ally, for siding with the covenanters while negotiating for him (→ 18).

Royalists surrender garrison at Reading

Reading, 27 April

The royalist garrison marched out of the town here today and handed it over to the roundheads. It is a coup for the parliamentary forces under the overall command of the earl of Essex, but the royalists regard it as a shoddy episode reeking of treachery and insufficient determination to resist.

Reading's royalist commander, Sir Arthur Ashton, was a Catholic who complained that his men refused to obey him. Ashton was wounded and replaced by Colonel Feilding, whose kinsman the earl of Denbigh fights for parliament. He then surrendered the town when King Charles's relieving force was almost in sight (→ 13/5).

The earl of Essex, the commander-in-chief of the parliamentary forces.

Roundhead leader dies after a battle

Thame, Oxfordshire, 24 June

John Hampden, one of the boldest of the parliamentary leaders and one of their best brains, died here today of wounds received six days ago during a clash with Prince Rupert's cavalry. Rupert had been raiding south from Oxford in the hope of capturing a parliamentary convoy carrying £21,000. He missed his prey, but at Chalgrove Field, near Chiselhampton, he was challenged by a small force which included Hampden. In the short fight that followed Rupert had the better of it, and Hampden was fatally wounded, possibly by the explosion of his own pistol (→ 30).

Londoners flock to build capital defences

London

The poet John Milton, an extreme puritan and ardent supporter of parliament against King Charles, has helped build substantial new defences for London. One hundred thousand Londoners were pressed into service to construct them, and puritans like Milton even agreed to work on Sundays, erecting forts and digging ditches.

Engineers have been imported from the United Provinces, and servants, and even children, have been ordered into the workforce that has now completed 18 miles of ramparts around the capital. In places the earth ditches that form the main defence are almost 3 metres wide and 6 metres high (9 by 18 feet). Forts housing thousands of soldiers have been built at strategic points, and 212 cannons have been mounted along the earthen battlements. It all makes a formidable and impressive array. Nevertheless, Milton prefers to rely on his own method of defence; he has nailed a poem to his door begging attackers to spare his house (→ 24/11/44).

Londoners muster their forces, build defences and destroy "popish" symbols.

John Hampden dies of his wounds.

War of words being won by royal paper

Oxford, May

The propaganda war has been won so far by the royalists, whose newspaper *Mercurius Aulicus* is a far better production than anything that the parliamentary side can manage. King Charles is well aware of the value of the printed word in war and has taken personal trouble to see that printing presses are set up around the country to carry his case to the people. *Mercurius Aulicus* appears once a week, usually on Mondays, and is read avidly by both sides because of its reputation for accuracy.

Reforms to public finance pay for war

London, July
The heavy financial burden of the civil war has force parliament to introduce the kind of "absolutist" taxes that it went to war to prevent. King Charles had toyed with the idea of bringing in an excise tax in the 1630s, but he had backed down in the face of bitter parliamentary opposition.

Excise is a common form of tax on the continent, where it is popular with absolute monarchies and has therefore come to be linked with the kind of arbitrary government that parliament is warring against. Now it has been forced to introduce the tax on a wide range of foodstuffs, such as meat, butter, salt and beer, a move which has hit the poor particularly hard. The tax is so unpopular that a special commission with wide powers of arrest has been set up to enforce it.

A 'divine assembly' holds first meeting

Westminster, July
A newly formed "Westminster Assembly of Divines", comprising 119 members of the English clergy, 20 members of parliament, ten peers and eight Scottish representatives, has held its first meeting with the intention of advising parliament on a new form of church government and liturgy to replace that established in 1559. But, even allowing for the enormous complexity of the work involved, it is expected to make progress only slowly.

One of the main purposes of the assembly is to aid the military negotiations now under way between parliament and the Scots and thus bolster hopes of an Anglo-Scottish alliance against King Charles. Scotland's military support for the English parliament would be a heavy blow for the king, especially in the northern counties of England.

THE ENGLISH CIVIL WAR: 1642/43

Land held by the king at end of 1643
Land held by parliament at end of 1643

Carlisle
Durham
North Sea
Adwalton Moor
York
Hull
Liverpool
Gainsborough
Flint
Chester
Lincoln
Winceby
Hopton Heath
Nottingham
Shrewsbury
Coventry
Powick Bridge
Edgehill
Cambridge
Gloucester
Oxford
Turnham Green
Pembroke
Lansdown
Reading
London
Atlantic Ocean
Roundway Down
Newbury
Brentford
Stratton
Lyme Regis
Poole
Braddock Down
Plymouth
English Channel

Royalist army claims winning streak

England, July
King Charles appears to hold the military advantage in the war in England. Although he has so far been unable to capitalize on his advances sufficiently to bring an end to the fighting, his army has recently notched up an impressive series of victories over the parliamentary forces. In the west Sir Ralph Hopton trounced the earl of Stamford at Stratton, so that Devon and Cornwall are now in the king's hands. This defeat compelled Sir William Waller to abandon the successful parliamentary campaign in the midlands, allowing Prince Rupert to raid almost to London. In the north, Sir James Fairfax has lost all of Yorkshire except Hull to Queen Henrietta Maria. Unless Scottish support tilts the balance towards parliament, the queen's army is set to strike south (→ 14).

Royalists secure victory at the Battle of Hopton Heath, near Stafford.

Fifteen months of war leave both sides deadlocked in battle to control England

England, December
After 15 months of civil war it is difficult to say which side is winning – if indeed anyone is winning at all. Both sides are riven with guilt that their quarrel has come to war, and both sides have put out feelers for peace and then withdrawn them. Both sides have assumed the dominance in certain areas of the country, but it has often been transient.

At the start of the war both sides enjoyed a good deal of popular support, and, although neither of them possessed an army, both had roughly equal numbers of fully trained professional officers who had all fought in continental wars and knew their business. These officers were put to training armies of volunteers as quickly as possible – but, as always with amateur armies, the results have been variable, to say the least.

Some units are tough and dependable, while others are hardly worth their pay – not that they are likely to receive much pay, or many rations, for neither camp has managed to organize its supply side properly, and troops are often unpaid and badly fed, twin ills that quickly lead to ill discipline. The only big battle so far has been the one at Edgehill last year, and that, despite some fierce fighting, was a draw. Both sides claimed victory, but eventually the parliamentary forces, under the veteran earl of Essex, retreated on London, fearful that King Charles would march on the capital.

The king hesitated, and when he did at last move it was too late. Essex arrived first and rallied the troops. Charles and his forces advanced as far as Turnham Green where he found Essex's army, backed up by thousands of citizens and apprentices, standing blocking his path. Both sides eyed each other nervously all day; then, without a single shot having been fired, the king – his forces outnumbered two to one – gave his men the order to retreat to Oxford, which he has made his new capital.

Scottish and English parliaments agree a 'covenant' over religion against king

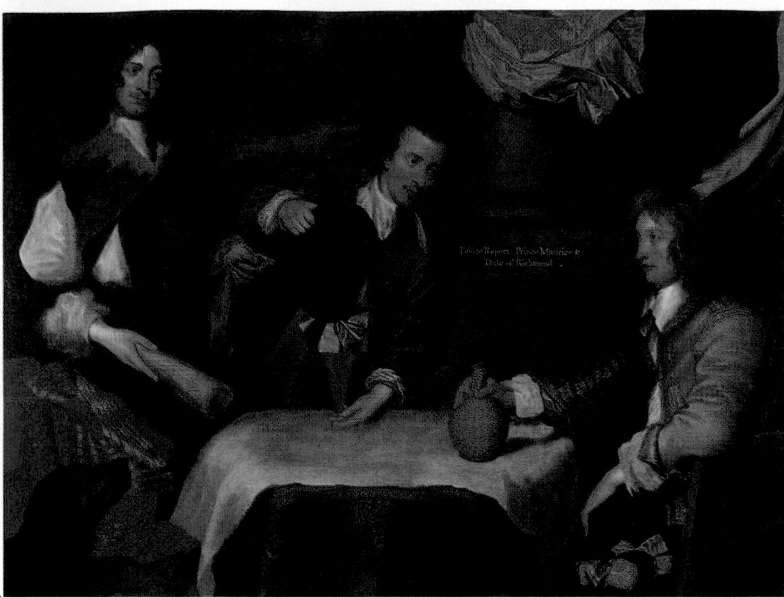

Prince Rupert, Prince Maurice and the duke of Richmond talk tactics.

Edinburgh, 17 August
The recent royalist successes in the civil war ravaging England have led the parliamentarians to form an alliance with the Scots against King Charles. By what is known as "the Solemn League and Covenant", the Scots will provide an army in return for a monthly payment of £30,000. The victory in the Scots parliament of the pro-war party led by Archibald Campbell, now the marquis of Argyll, over a quasi-royalist party allowed talks to proceed. Despite the reservations of some parliamentarians, the English have conceded the enforcement of a Presbyterian church throughout Britain, enhancing popular support for the treaty in Scotland (→4/9).

Women march on Westminster Hall

Westminster, August
Parliament has been blockaded for an afternoon by a riotous assembly of women demanding an end to the civil war. Shouting "peace and our king", the women forced their way into the yard of Westminster Hall and began attacking members – particularly puritans, who were conspicuous by their short hair. There have been reports that up to 6,000 women took part in the protest, but two to three hundred is probably a more accurate estimate.

The women are angry that peace proposals have been rejected by parliament, so they occupied the yard, refusing to move until they received a satisfactory response. Bands of militia were called up to persuade them to move, but the protesters stood firm, and the trained bands, all Londoners, were not inclined to use force against them.

Eventually Sir William Waller's cavalry was called in, and these seasoned troops rode into the yard and chased the women out, inflicting a good deal of violence. Two or three of the women were killed, and most of the rest have been rounded up and sent to Bridewell prison for punishment (→12/1644).

Parliament loses mastermind of its campaign strategy

John Pym: leader who died today.

London, 8 December
Parliament has been dealt a huge blow today by the death of John Pym, at the age of 59. Pym was the foremost of King Charles's enemies and the mastermind behind the parliamentary campaign; without him members might have submitted to Charles's unbending attitude and agreed to a compromise.

Born at Brymore, near Bridgwater in Somerset, Pym had spent most of his life as a minor royal administrator, and in the parliaments of the 1620s he spoke up for increased royal revenues. He came to work closely with a group of peers critical of the king's government, notably the earl of Warwick and Viscount Saye and Sele, and embarked on a forthright challenge to royal authority.

Pym insisted that the appointment of army commanders and royal counsellors and ministers should be subject to the approval of parliament, and he campaigned to destroy the ancient system of ecclesiastical government.

When it was clear that the king would fight, Pym's genius in "managing" parliament saved the day for the rebels. He introduced each unpalatable measure at just the right moment: the raising of troops for the earl of Essex, taxation without the king's consent, the covenant with the Scots. Thus he began the war and kept it going (→2/1/44).

English parliament ratifies covenant

London, 25 September
The treaty agreed with the Scots last month has today been ratified by the English parliament, but it is clear that "the Solemn League and Covenant" means different things to its two signatories.

In Scotland the aim of forcing the English to accept Presbyterianism is seen as not only a religious crusade but also the best means of preserving the Scots own independence and identity within Britain. In England there are reservations about Presbyterian uniformity and particularly the lack of political control over the Scottish church, but John Pym persuaded parliament to accept the covenant because of its military merits. The Scots' reputation as warriors has soared since their victories in the two Bishops' Wars (→20/10).

Irish rebels enlist to the royalist cause

Irish soldiers of the kind who fought with O'Neill against the English.

Ireland, 15 September
A year's truce has been agreed at Sigginstown, Co Kildare, between the Confederates and the earl of Ormond, Ireland's new lord lieutenant. Hostilities are to cease, and the Confederates are to pay King Charles £30,000. The Dublin government's military position will be weakened by the expected dispatch of 2,500 troops to England to fight the king's cause, but the truce will give Owen Roe O'Neill a chance to consolidate his army. A nephew of the earl of Tyrone, and long regarded by the Ulster Irish as their natural leader, he has come from Spain to help them (→24/3/44).

Oxford, 2 January. King Charles calls a royalist parliament (→ 8).

Scotland, 8 January. Parliament introduces an excise tax to finance the war (→ 9).

Borders, 19 January. Alexander Leslie, the earl of Leven, invades England with 21,000 covenanters in support of parliament (→ 24).

Scotland/England, January. The parliamentarians and the covenanters form a committee to coordinate the war effort.

Scotland, 13 February. James Graham, the earl of Montrose, becomes lieutenant-general of the king's forces (→ 21/3).

Nottinghamshire, 21 March. Prince Rupert, Charles's nephew, relieves Newark (→ 11/4).

Oxford, 24 March. Irish Confederates negotiate with Charles (→ 17/4).

Leeds, March. The city is ravaged by plague.

York, 11 April. Roundheads besiege the city (→ 5/1644).

Oxford, 17 April. An Irish Protestant delegation arrives (→ 24/10).

Dumfries, April. Montrose and the royalist army are forced to retreat (→ 4/1644).

Aberdeen, May. A royalist rising is crushed by the marquis of Argyll (→ 5/6).

Liverpool, 5 June. Prince Rupert, who captured Stockport and Bolton last month, besieges the city (→ 27).

Waterford City, 27 June. Irish royalist troops, led by Alaster McDonnell, sail to join James Graham, now marquis of Montrose, in Scotland (→ 29).

York, 16 July. Royalists surrender the city to the parliamentarians (→ 27).

Cornwall, 27 July. Robert Devereux, the earl of Essex, enters Cornwall (→ 1/9).

Tayside, 1 September. Montrose occupies Perth after defeating a covenanting army at Tippermuir (→ 2).

Newcastle upon Tyne, 19 October. The covenanters seize the city (→ 27).

Westminster, 24 October. Any Irishman taken in arms against parliament may be executed (→ 25/8/45).

England. Christmas day is abolished by the puritans.

A cohesive military force is established in eastern counties

Cambridge, 31 January
After a shaky start, the Eastern Association of counties, led by the earl of Manchester and his lieutenant-general, Oliver Cromwell, is transforming itself into a cohesive military force. The association now covers Norfolk, Suffolk, Essex, Hertfordshire, Cambridgeshire, Lincolnshire, the Isle of Ely and Huntingdonshire, and in 1642 it was given the task of raising an army.

The association's first military commander, Lord Grey of Warke, found it hard to raise troops – and many of those who were recruited deserted when attempts were made to march them away from their home territory. A shortage of funds meant that the troops were poorly paid and fed, while most of the money available went to the earl of Essex's army.

But now the southward march of King Charles's forces has brought the eastern counties under a direct threat of invasion. This, in addition to the advent of Manchester and Cromwell, and the fact that Essex is out of favour, has transformed the association's fortunes. In August last year it was empowered to impress an army of 20,000 men. Then, on 20 January, it was given permission to raise money within its territory to support this army. These twin reforms have allowed Manchester and Cromwell to raise and maintain troops and train them to the highest standards (→ 13/2).

Crushing defeat for royalists at Nantwich

Melting ice divided the royalist army and led to inevitable defeat.

Nantwich, Cheshire, 24 January
A tactical error by Lord Byron has resulted in King Charles losing the long promised Irish infantry after it had been in England for only a few weeks. The country has been in the grip of a great frost, with the result that military movement has been almost impossible.

However, Lord Byron turned the inclement weather to his advantage by besieging Nantwich from both sides of the frozen river Weaver. Unfortunately, Sir Thomas Fairfax and a thaw arrived at the same moment, and the divided army had to surrender. To add insult to injury, most of the Irish have now agreed to fight for parliament (→ 31).

Princess born in besieged city of Exeter

Exeter, 17 June
Queen Henrietta Maria has given birth to a daughter here, where she fled to find refuge from the earl of Essex and his parliamentary troops after parting from King Charles at Abingdon. The child will be named Henriette-Anne.

A midwife and a physician called Mayerne attended the birth, but the queen's health is giving cause for concern. Fears for both her own life and that of the king are worsening the after-effects of her pregnancy. She has lost all feeling in one arm and the sight in one eye. Mayerne declares that these symptoms are hysterical, but friends are very worried. The queen has begged Essex for safe conduct from Exeter. Believing her a threat, he has refused.

Henrietta Maria: although ill, she has been denied safe conduct.

Strict kirk rules behind rising discontent in Scottish highlands

Lord's day observance: the kirk uses Sunday to burn a sports book.

Scotland, January
The rigid policies that have been adopted by the Scottish kirk are not so universally popular as some in the country would like to believe. Minor offences, such as watering the vegetable patch on a Sunday, lead to harsh public humiliation. Many resent the exacting standards that the kirk imposes. The centre of opposition to the covenanters is to be found in the highlands, where ancient Gaelic customs and the Roman Catholic religion still stand firm against the onslaught of the government in Edinburgh.

Parliament's troops suffer casualties in southern skirmish

Oxfordshire, 29 June
King Charles's cavaliers inflicted a sharp defeat on Sir William Waller's parliamentary army in confused fighting at Cropredy Bridge east of Banbury today. The two armies spent the morning marching parallel to one another along the banks of the Cherwell until the royalist forces became separated.

Waller then crossed Cropredy Bridge and, leaving a small force to guard it, went in pursuit of the royalist vanguard, which promptly barricaded the road and held him off with musket fire. Meanwhile Lord Cleveland, commanding the king's cavalry, galloped up to the bridge and trapped Waller.

Fighting swirled along the river banks and around the bridge all afternoon. Waller would have been utterly defeated if Colonel Birch, a stalwart soldier, had not held the bridge itself. Waller was eventually able to get his battered force to safety across the river, and the two armies are now binding their wounds and glowering at one another through the willows.

Waller has suffered heavy casualties and lost all his light artillery, but he is claiming to have won by stopping Charles marching north to join Prince Rupert. The king now intends to march west to deal with the rebel earl of Essex (→ 2/7).

Royalists crushed at Marston Moor

Their first clear victory: Oliver Cromwell leads his tired, but victorious, "Ironsides" back from Marston Moor.

Marston Moor, N Yorks, 2 July
The royal army commanded by the dashing Prince Rupert of the Rhine has been crushed here today by the combined forces of the English and Scottish parliaments in a battle which has left King Charles's power in the north in ruins.

Rupert had outmanoeuvred the parliamentary army yesterday by relieving nearby York, besieged by the Scots. He wanted to attack the retreating parliamentarians at first light, but by the time that both armies were drawn up there was only an hour of daylight left. Rupert, thinking that it was too late to give battle, allowed his men to break ranks and eat. But Oliver Cromwell, at the head of his formidable cavalry, "the Ironsides", saw what was happening and charged, breaking the cavaliers' first line. Rupert counter-attacked, causing the parliamentary right wing to collapse. The Scottish infantry held the centre, however, and on the left Cromwell's cavalry and David Leslie's Scottish horse routed the royalists before turning on the centre.

The fighting swayed to and fro by the light of the rising moon until by midnight the roundheads had prevailed. Over 3,000 royalists are now lying dead on the field of battle. "God made them as stubble to our swords," said Cromwell, who is acclaimed by the English (if not the Scots) as the hero of the hour (→ 16).

Essex's infantry surrender in Cornwall

Cornwall, 2 September
King Charles's fortunes, at a low ebb after Marston Moor, have been revived by the surrender at Lostwithiel today of the parliamentary army commanded by the earl of Essex. The king, marching west, had cut off Essex, forcing him out of Devon into Cornwall and then into the narrow Fowey peninsula.

Adverse winds meant that no help reached Essex from the parliamentary fleet commanded by his cousin, the earl of Warwick. By the time the wind changed, the royalists had occupied positions above Fowey harbour. The noose tightened. Charles's cavalry occupied the outlying villages of St Blazey and St Austell on 26 August, and Essex's position became hopeless.

Before dawn yesterday he allowed two thousand horsemen to break out. They outwitted the besiegers and slipped away while he abandoned his army and was rowed out to one of Warwick's ships. The rest surrendered today to the king. Six thousand men with 5,000 muskets and pistols and 42 artillery pieces have fallen into his hands. He has kept the arms but freed the men.

The victory has restored the cavaliers' morale, but the king's army is exhausted and short of cavalry. Much depends now on the help which Queen Henrietta Maria is trying to raise in France.

Women meet varied demands of civil war

England, December
Jane Ingleby's name will be one to remember: she has fought in disguise as a man alongside the cavalry at Marston Moor [*see report above*]. Jane, a Yorkshire yeoman's daughter, is thought to have escaped home wounded. Jane's adventures are of the sort which inspired a ballad that is currently popular: "Her husband was a soldier, and to the wars did go/And she would be his comrade, the truth of all is so/She put on men's apparel, and bore him company/As many in the army for truth can testify."

Many other women are helping in the war effort. Several work as camp-followers, nurses and cooks. Last year Cromwell rode with a troop of women from Norwich, known as "the Maiden Troops", using them as auxiliaries "for stirring up the youth, to cast in their mite". These women did not fight.

On both sides women are being called on to defend their homes while their husbands and sons are absent. In July and August 1643, Brilliana, Lady Harley, held besieging royalist troops at bay for six weeks at Brampton Bryan in Herefordshire, while her husband Sir Robert was away. She survived the ordeal, and the troops departed; but shortly afterwards she died – of exhaustion, it is said – when her home was again besieged (→ 13).

Scottish city sacked by royalist troops

Aberdeen, 13 September
The marquis of Montrose with his army of fierce Scots and Irish clansmen today defeated a strong force of covenanters drawn up outside Aberdeen. He fought the battle with his usual *élan*, his musketeers driving off the covenanter cavalry and his foot soldiers, armed with dirks and claymores, cutting their way into the city with a wild charge. Montrose, enraged by the killing of a drummer boy who had accompanied his envoy to the city before the fighting started, has unleashed his soldiers, and tonight they are looting every house even though many of the Aberdonians are unwilling covenanters. The Irish Macdonalds are loaded down with plunder. "The riches of that town," said one officer, "hath made all our soldiers cavaliers."

The marquis, who cannot bear to watch, has remained outside the walls. He plans to march into the highlands, living off the land and drawing his enemies after him, before coming down to slash at another city (→ 19/10).

The powerful armies of the covenant march to the singing of psalms.

Milton publishes plea for press freedom

London, 24 November
John Milton, the poet and ardent parliamentarian, has today published a stirring call for the freedom of the press. His pamphlet, *Areopagitica*, is an answer both to those members of parliament demanding censorship and to a recent ordinance regulating publication. It is named after the Areopagus, the democratic assembly of ancient Athens. "Give me the liberty to know, to utter and to argue freely according to conscience, above all liberties," Milton demands. "Who kills a man kills a reasonable creature; but he who destroys a good book, kills reason itself ... A good book is the precious life-blood of a master spirit."

This pamphlet follows his others against episcopacy and for divorce reform. It is five years since he published his last poem, *Lycidas*. *Comus* was performed as a masque at Ludlow Castle in 1634 (→ 5/1660).

Major division in parliamentary party as Cromwell faces criticism from Manchester

Oliver Cromwell: struck first.

The earl of Manchester: hit back.

Westminster, 2 December
The quarrel which broke out between Oliver Cromwell and the earl of Manchester over the failure of the parliamentary forces to win the second Battle of Newbury [*see report below*] has become a major political issue. Cromwell struck first a week ago when he gave his version of events in the House of Commons and placed all the blame on Manchester's "backwardness to all action, his averseness to engagement ... and declining to pursue advantages upon the enemy". Manchester retaliated today in the House of Lords with a written statement in which he described Cromwell as a defiant subordinate and a man of dangerous ideas. Cromwell, wrote Manchester, had said that he hoped "to live to see never a nobleman in England".

The dispute is now so bitter that either Manchester, backed by the parliamentary nobility, or Cromwell, the leader of "common men", must go. Cromwell has also been attacked by the Scots as an "incendiary" stirring up trouble (→ 2/2/45).

Both sides struggle in vain at Newbury

Newbury, Berkshire, 27 October
The opposing forces of parliament and King Charles met here for the second time today, and again the result was bloody but inconclusive. Charles should have been defeated, for he was betrayed by the turncoat Sir John Hurry, who revealed that 1,500 cavalier horsemen had gone to the relief of Banbury. The earl of Manchester and Oliver Cromwell planned to attack on both flanks, but the attack was mismanaged, and the royalists, protected by the cannon of Donnington Castle, put up a staunch defence. Charles withdrew towards Oxford at nightfall, and Manchester, instead of giving chase, has gone to bed (→ 2/12).

A Campbell of Glernorchy family tree by the famed Scots artist George Jameson (died 1644).

1645

London, 10 January. William Laud, the archbishop of Canterbury, imprisoned since 1640, is beheaded.

Strathclyde, 2 February. James Graham, the marquis of Montrose, defeats the marquis of Argyll and his Campbell clan at Inverlochy (→11).

Edinburgh, 11 February. Montrose is declared a traitor by parliament (→17).

Shrewsbury, 22 February. The royalist garrison falls to the roundheads (→9/5).

England, April. John Lilburne, the radical pamphleteer, resigns his army position rather than accept the Scots' covenant (→14/3/46).

Faversham, Kent, April. Three women, Joane Willford, Joan Carride and Jane Holt, are executed as witches (→1647).

Grampian, 9 May. Over 2,000 die when Montrose has yet another victory over the covenanters, at Auldearn (→31).

Leicester, 31 May. Prince Rupert's royalist troops sack the city (→14/6).

Oxford, May. Oliver Cromwell clashes with royalist forces.

Grampian, 2 July. Montrose defeats the covenanters again, at Alford (→8).

Sligo City, 8 July. A parliamentary force, led by Sir Charles Coote, seizes the city from the Confederates (→31).

Strathclyde, 15 August. Montrose is ready to reclaim Scotland for King Charles after his sixth victory this year, at Kilsyth (→18).

Ireland, 25 August. The earl of Glamorgan signs a secret treaty with the Confederates to raise troops to serve for Charles in England (→20/12).

Cheshire, 24 September. After a defeat at Rowton Heath, Charles is unable to reach his Scottish supporters (→2/1646).

Ireland, 20 December. Archbishop Giovanni Rinuccini, the papal envoy to the Confederates, dictates a complete revision of August's Glamorgan treaty (→26).

Dublin, 26 December. The earl of Glamorgan is arrested by James Butler, now marquis of Ormond (→5/6/46).

Suffolk. John Lowes, the vicar of Brandeston, is executed for witchcraft.

Halifax, West Yorkshire. Plague breaks out in the town.

Traditional Prayer Book is replaced by new code of worship

Westminster, 4 January
Today, in a move towards establishing Presbyterianism as the uniform national church, parliament abolished the *Book of Common Prayer* with its "unprofitable and burdensome ceremonies" and replaced it with a *Directory of Worship* compiled by the divines of the Westminster assembly.

The new directory presents a simplified code of services and goes some way to accommodating the puritans' belief in extempore prayers. It remains, however, firmly based on the parish system and makes no concessions to the "dissenting brethren" who want to worship within congregations of their own choice and not those imposed on them by parish boundaries.

The dissenters form only a small minority in parliament but are vociferous in their opposition to the directory. They have produced a list of objections, but it is so long that the Commons have ordered that no more than 300 of their complaints should be printed. For the moment, at least, the Presbyterians are the victors (→4/1645).

'Model Army' is planned

Westminster, 17 February
Parliament today passed the New Model Army Ordinance, by which the army will be reorganized along the lines of Cromwell's "Ironsides". The old regiments personally raised by parliamentary nobles are to be broken up and their officers and men incorporated in new regiments with professional rather than aristocratic officers. Cromwell argues: "I had rather have a plain russet-coated captain that knows what he fights for, and loves what he knows, than what you call a gentleman and nothing else." The new army will consist of 11 cavalry regiments, each 600 strong, 12 foot regiments, 1,200 strong, and 1,000 dragoons, giving a total strength of 22,000.

It is hoped that most of the men will be volunteers who will be better paid, and therefore better disciplined and more willing, than other armies. It is also planned that the army will pay for its quarters instead of living off the country and antagonizing the populace.

What remains to be decided is who will be put in command of this new army. The Lords have stayed loyal to the earls of Manchester and Essex, but the terms of the "self-denying ordinance" – which was proposed to settle the quarrel between Cromwell and Manchester – mean that no member of either house can be given command. The nobles would therefore seem to be out of the game (→19).

A soldier of the New Model Army.

English pre-history fascinates Charles

Oxford, April
King Charles is finding life pleasant enough here in this university city where, among the preparations for war at his headquarters, he finds time to discuss art and literature with the learned men of the colleges. His patronage of artists such as Rubens and van Dyck is well known, but his interests are spread through many fields.

He has, for example, a fascination with the monuments of England's pre-Roman history, and he commissioned the antiquary John Aubrey to prepare a discourse for him on Stonehenge. Aubrey, a Wiltshireman, has also brought the great henge monument at Avebury in north Wiltshire to the king's attention. Alas, he can visit these sites only on the march from one battle to another.

New army's commander-in-chief named

Fairfax takes over the army.

Westminster, 19 February
Sir Thomas Fairfax was approved by the Commons today as commander-in-chief of the parliamentary army. His task will be to whip the New Model Army into shape and lead it to victory against King Charles. A brave professional soldier who is unobtrusive in both politics and worship, he is ideally suited for the task. He made an excellent impression in the House of Commons when he appeared with his recently wounded arm in a sling but refused to sit down out of respect for parliament.

The Commons also appointed the admirable Philip Skippon as major-general of the new army. It was Skippon who negotiated honourable terms with the king after the earl of Essex had abandoned his army at Fowey.

The choice of these two men is in accordance with the "self-denying ordinance" which excludes members of parliament from command. The earls of Manchester and Essex have effectively been sidelined; it remains to be seen if the ordinance will also apply to Cromwell (→22).

King flees after defeat

Naseby, Northants, 14 June
King Charles is in flight tonight, heading for the safety of Hereford after suffering a heavy defeat at the hands of Sir Thomas Fairfax and his New Model Army. The parliamentary forces, with Oliver Cromwell commanding the cavalry and Philip Skippon leading the infantry, outnumbered the royalists, but at first the roundhead cavalry which was opposing Prince Rupert's cavaliers was swept aside.

The weight of numbers soon began to tell, however, and Cromwell's "Ironsides" broke the royalist cavalry on the far side of the battlefield and then charged the king's untried Welsh infantry. Seeing them falter Charles urged his horse forward, but one of his attendants, fearing that he would be killed, seized his bridle and turned him away from danger. The soldiers misunderstood this; fear swept through their ranks, and they broke. Rupert's cavalry covered the king's retreat, but while he has his life he has lost his infantry, his guns and, almost certainly, the war (→ 20).

Troops of the New Model Army cheer Cromwell after victory at Naseby.

Cromwell in the ascendant as royalists retreat before parliamentarian attacks

Westminster, 31 July
The war is going well for parliament. Oliver Cromwell and his disciplined troopers have destroyed the army of Lord Goring at Langport in Somerset; Bridgwater, full of royalist guns and supplies, has surrendered to Sir Thomas Fairfax, and communications between King Charles's proposed headquarters at Bristol and his forces in Devon and Cornwall have been cut.

It is the same story in the north, where the Scottish army of the covenant has been so effective; royalist strongholds such as Carlisle and Scarborough have fallen. Only Montrose's brilliant victories in the Scottish highlands provide the king with good news.

An added threat to both sides in England is the emergence of so-called "clubmen", bands of country people tired of the depradations of war who have joined together to harry stragglers and ambush small parties travelling the country lanes.

Meanwhile, the king has begun clutching at straws. He has attempted to raise new levies of foot soldiers in Wales but has discovered that the men there are unwilling to serve him. He has sent the earl of Glamorgan to Dublin on a secret mission to bring an Irish army to his rescue. In exchange he has promised to adopt a more tolerant approach to Roman Catholics, but the Irish are demanding to be allowed to preach their faith openly and to keep hold of any churches that they may capture.

Charles also hopes that disagreements between the Scottish covenanters and parliament will lead to the covenanters making common cause with him and Montrose, but this would involve his being prepared to tolerate Presbyterianism.

The king has now made up his mind to join Montrose in Scotland – a move strongly opposed by Prince Rupert, who has told his uncle that he "hath now no way left to preserve his posterity, kingdom and nobility, but by a treaty. I believe it a more prudent way to retain something than to lose all." But Charles refuses to "abandon God's cause" (→ 15/8).

Cromwell appeals to Commons for liberty

Westminster, 20 June
Oliver Cromwell's triumphant report to the Commons on the victory at Naseby has caused an uproar, for he ended it with a plea for religious liberty on behalf of the "Independents". "Honest men served you faithfully in this action," he wrote, "I beseech you in the name of God not to discourage them ... He that ventures his life for the liberty of his country, I wish he trust God for the liberty of his conscience, and you for the liberty he fights for." The Commons printed his report but censored his plea. It slipped out, however, through the Lords and has added more fuel to the religious quarrels which are so troubling parliament (→ 7/1645).

King's letters put royal cause at risk

Westminster, July
Great harm is being done to King Charles's cause by the publication of letters found in his cabinet, captured after his defeat at Naseby. The letters, mainly his correspondence with the queen over the last two years, demonstrate beyond dispute that he intended to bring an Irish army to England and to abolish laws against the Catholics.

The letters also show how he tried to get men and money from the king of France, the king of Denmark, the prince of Orange and the duke of Lorraine. Londoners rushed to buy printed copies of the letters, and there is a public outcry against the king at a time when he faces military disater (→ 2).

Royalist army of highlanders and Irish wins series of victories over covenanters

Montrose: won stunning victories.

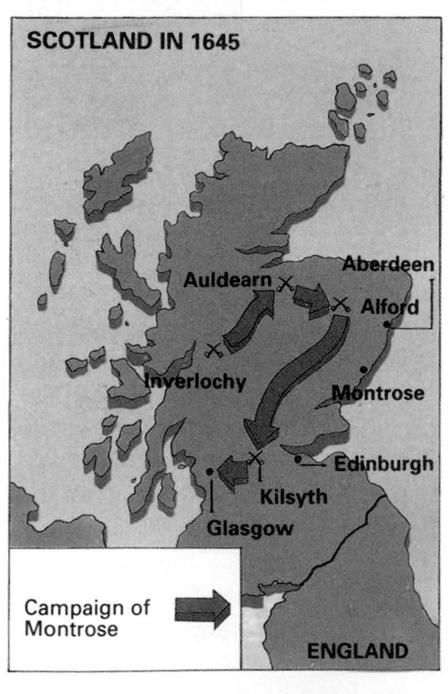

Glasgow, 18 August
In direct contrast to the plight of King Charles in England, the marquis of Montrose has led his highlanders and Irishmen to victory after victory in Scotland in the king's cause. Three days ago his men, stripped to their shirts in the sweltering heat, caught the covenanting army at Kilsyth on rough ground, where it was unable to manoeuvre, and drove it from the battlefield.

There is now no army in Scotland to oppose Montrose. Edinburgh, racked by plague and fearful of being sacked, has given in to his threats and released his friends from prison. Today he entered Glasgow in triumph to be feasted by the citizens and to issue a proclamation in the name of the king summoning a new parliament.

All this has been accomplished by lightly armed men who live off the country, sleeping in the heather and foraging for food, drawing their heavily armed opponents into the hills and then turning on them with wild claymore charges and disabling their horses with dirks.

Montrose's success has forced the covenanters to appeal to Westminster for help and has greatly encouraged Charles as he attempts to make his way north. There is talk of Montrose marching south, gathering recruits in the lowlands and invading England to join the king. But his highlanders are unenthusiastic, with many keen to return north to their homes (→ 14/9).

Civilian anti-war movement gets started

Wiltshire, December
A dramatic plea for an end to the fighting, on both sides, has come from the Wiltshire Clubmen Association. Although some people assume that these popular groups must take sides, theirs is definitely an anti-war platform.

These associations have grown out of villages and local counties, from people who are tired of soldiers, whether they be royalist or parliamentarian, plundering crops, destroying homes and demanding money or provisions for their troops. A grassroots movement is growing for an end to the war and a return to old-fashioned methods of local government.

The Clubmen are demanding an end, too, to the conflict between the state and church, and to the ban on the Prayer Book. They want to go back to "the pure religion of Queen Elizabeth and King James".

The most common complaint heard from the Clubmen is that the nation is "bleeding under the devouring sword". In Wiltshire law and order have disappeared, while violence among the armies and the people has grown out of proportion. Yet no one wants to see anarchy take over.

New blows for Charles

Prince Rupert reviews his defences; he was always in the thick of battle.

Bristol, 14 September
In two days the royalist cause has suffered two grievous blows. Yesterday the marquis of Montrose, King Charles's champion in Scotland, was routed in the borders. Today Prince Rupert has surrendered Bristol to the forces of Sir Thomas Fairfax. The furious king has stripped Rupert of his commission.

At Bristol a storm made the ground too slippery for the horses, and Fairfax was able to bring up his siege guns to breach the walls. As Oliver Cromwell's cavalry rushed in, Rupert's position became hopeless. He asked for terms to save his men and marched away to Oxford.

The defeat of Montrose came within a month of his success in occupying Glasgow. Most of his highland troops refused to follow him south, and his depleted army was caught by a surprise dawn attack by David Leslie's forces at Philiphaugh. Montrose escaped capture, but all of his Irish soldiers were executed, along with 300 camp-followers, at the instigation of the Presbyterian clergy (→ 24).

'Leveller' wants to have annual parliaments

John Lilburne: a thorn in all sides.

London, 15 October
John Lilburne, known as "Freeborn John" for his championing of liberty of conscience and the press, has just emerged from prison to publish, anonymously, *England's Birthright Justified*, which calls for free speech, annual parliaments and the rule of law. It also denounces monopolies, tithes and excise tax.

Lilburne was put in Newgate for two months by the Commons, to whom he read *Magna Carta* when members came to examine him. He and other radicals like William Walwyn and Richard Overton have been dubbed "Levellers". His dissident career began in 1638 when he defied the star chamber and refused to swear the oath. For this he was whipped from the Fleet to Westminster, where he was put in the pillory. Shackled to the wall in prison, he still turned out pamphlets demanding his release (→ 28/3/49).

1646

Scotland, 2 February. The covenanters pass the Schools Act, restricting financial provision for parish education.

Chester, 3 February. The besieged royalists surrender to the roundheads (→ 5/5).

Westminster, 14 March. Parliament orders the setting up of a Presbyterian church system in England.

Scilly Isles, 31 March. Charles, the prince of Wales, who arrived here earlier in the month, has set sail for the Channel Islands. He intends to join his mother, Queen Henrietta Maria, in France.

Nottinghamshire, 9 May. King Charles, who on 5 May gave himself up to the Scots at Newark and ordered his garrison there to surrender to them, is taken to Newcastle upon Tyne (→ 24/6).

Co Armagh, 5 June. The Ulster Irish army under Owen Roe O'Neill defeats the Scots at Benburb (→ 30/7).

Oxford, 24 June. The royalists surrender (→ 7/1646).

Westminster, June. Parliament bans the Prayer Book (→ 5/9).

Dublin, 30 July. James Butler, the marquis of Ormond, proclaims peace in Ireland (→ 3/8).

Kilkenny City, 3 August. The supreme council of the Confederates proclaims the peace negotiated with Ormond in March (→ 1/9).

Gwent, 19 August. Royalists at Raglan Castle, led by Henry Somerset, the earl of Worcester, surrender to Sir Thomas Fairfax, parliament's commander-in-chief (→ 20/12).

Fife, 19 August. Alexander Henderson, the minister of Leuchars and one of the architects of the "National Covenant", dies, depriving moderate Presbyterians of their most accomplished spokesman.

Co Waterford, 1 September. The papal envoy to the Confederates, Archbishop Rinuccini, persuades the Waterford synod to reject the Ormond peace (→ 16).

England, 16 September. Robert Devereux, the earl of Essex and a staunch parliamentary leader, dies.

London, November. John Lilburne publishes anonymously *London's Liberty in Chains*, demanding more political, legal and economic reforms from parliament.

Lady Bankes cedes Corfe Castle to the parliamentarians

Dorset, February

After a long and bitter struggle, Mary, Lady Bankes, has had to lay down her weapons and cede Corfe Castle to the parliamentary troops. The valiant Lady Bankes has held on to her home since her husband's death in December 1644, hoping that her son would inherit the title and property.

This lady's stout heart and determination will live on after these days of battle are over. When the castle was first besieged by Sir Walter Erle, whilst her husband was with King Charles at Oxford, the stubborn lady defended the upper ward herself with the help only of her daughters, the waiting women and just five soldiers.

Lady Bankes, who defended Corfe.

Although Erle was not noted for his strength or ferocity, the fighting was in fact very fierce. However, the besiegers fled on hearing the rumour that the king was shortly to arrive with his troops. For the following two years Lady Bankes hung on to the castle, but after the defeat of King Charles at the Battle of Naseby it was again besieged. She was finally betrayed by one of her own lieutenants, one Pitman, who, growing weary of siege conditions, let some of the enemy onto the castle walls. The troops rushed the defences; Corfe was lost (→ 3).

Charles flees north disguised as servant

Charles: a 1644 "Oxford pound".

The prince of Wales's armour, 1643.

Nottinghamshire, 5 May

His hair shorn, and wearing a false beard and dark suit, King Charles rode into the courtyard of the Saracen's Head at Southwell tonight and made contact with the Scottish headquarters nearby. It is eight days since he fled Oxford disguised as a servant of his two companions: a chaplain, Dr Hudson, and a groom of his bedchamber.

Oxford is under siege, and Colonel Rainsborough's army was attacking Woodstock. An appeal to the colonel to take the king under his protection was not answered, and Charles believed that his only hope was to treat with the Scots.

Maintaining the servant's role, the king travelled first towards London and turned north at Hillingdon, in Middlesex. Hudson was dispatched to the Scottish camp as Charles continued towards King's Lynn, prepared to flee the country if the Scots refused to accept him.

Charles, the 15-year-old prince of Wales, who was at his father's side earlier in the campaign, has meanwhile fled to Jersey, in the Channel Islands; his mother, Henrietta Maria, is in France (→ 13).

Religious sects are targeted for attack

London

The debate on religious tolerance rages. This year has seen the popular appeal of *Gangraena*, by Thomas Edwards, a report of religious heresies, blasphemies and pernicious practices. The 700-page tome is by a Presbyterian minister who, although he believes in religious uniformity, was himself criticized by Archbishop Laud. Edwards sees the movement towards independent forms of worship leading to the breakdown of society, citing women and boy preachers, drunkenness, fornication and swearing. He says that rebellion, anarchy and atheism must follow.

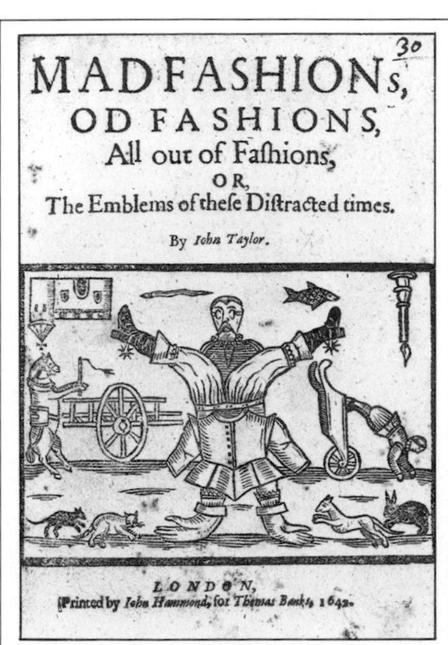

30

MAD FASHIONS,
OD FASHIONS,
All out of Fashions,
OR,
The Emblems of these Distracted times.
By John Taylor.

LONDON,
Printed by John Hammond, for Thomas Banks, 1642.

The country changed so much during the war that people had trouble making sense of it, as this contemporary cartoon shows.

Disillusioned troops launch mutinies in England and Wales

Cheshire, July
In the aftermath of the civil war, parliamentarian troops, idle, rarely paid, often hungry, ill-clad and bitter at their treatment, are threatening the peace which they gained. Reports of mutinies have been received from 22 counties in England and several in Wales. Parliament, already saddled with massive debts to the City of London, the Scots and other creditors, is hard pressed to meet arrears in pay of at least two and a half million pounds and is looking to royalist funds and local taxation to pay the army. An offer of three months' money has been rejected, and local committees are meeting the full fury of the discontented soldiery.

A parliamentary agent, William Ball, recently sent a report from Newbury in Berkshire describing "soldiers having almost starved the people where they quarter and are half starved themselves and for want of pay are becoming very desperate, ranging about the country and robbing houses and driving away sheep and other cattle before the owners' faces".

Similar incidents are taking place nationwide, often with officers joining the mutineers, hoping to minimize the violence. Here in Cheshire whole regiments are threatening to disband and at Nantwich 500 soldiers marched from the garrison and threw the sequestration committee into the local jail, forcing the local justices to flee (→ 19/8).

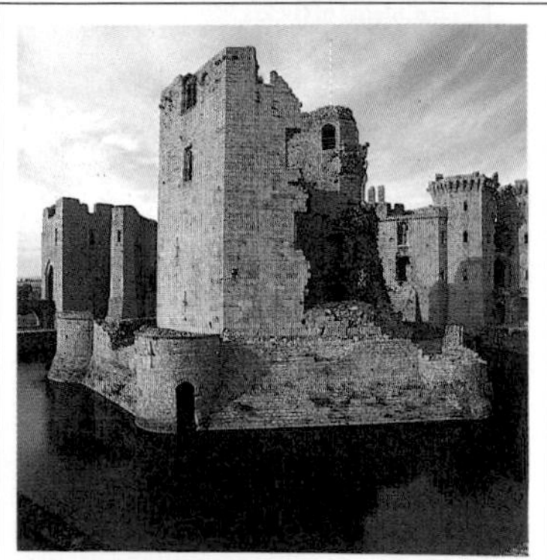

The royalist garrison of Raglan Castle, in Gwent, survived a siege of two months before surrendering on 19 August 1646.

Radical new moves rock establishment

Westminster, 5 September
The entire establishment of the Church of England was rocked today by an act of parliament which abolishes the offices of both Archbishop of Canterbury and bishops throughout the country. The act is seen by many as another step in the campaign to introduce Presbyterianism as the official form of worship. Despite parliamentary approval of the move, a large minority of members has become increasingly vocal in its opposition to this and other Calvinist measures passed since 1643, including the abolition of the *Book of Common Prayer* and the substitution of the Presbyterian *Directory of Worship* last year. A move towards the Scottish system in which the church, not the state, appoints its elders was rejected.

In another radical move, parliament has this year abolished the court of wards and liveries, along with all feudal tenures. This court, established to enforce the crown's feudal rights, was given statutory powers by King Henry VIII more than a century ago.

The court of wards and liveries in session: a casualty of radical reforms.

Gaelic rebellion culminates at Benburb

Co Armagh, 16 September
Owen Roe O'Neill, the leader of the Catholic Confederates in Ulster, has failed to consolidate the victory that he won last June at Benburb. Robert Monro, the Protestant commander, let himself be drawn into an unfavourable position at Benburb, just outside Armagh. O'Neill seized the advantage, and Monro lost half his infantry.

Although Benburb was thought a great victory, O'Neill failed to rout the Scots, who later regrouped. Instead he marched in support of Archbishop Rinuccini, the papal envoy to the Confederates, who, reinforced by O'Neill's army, has now entered Kilkenny, imprisoned the supreme council and set up a new one, with himself as president.

The Confederates have had some success and are forging a more cohesive unity. Yet this unity is very much under threat, since Rinuccini wants to reject the peace terms put forward by the royalist marquis of Ormond, James Butler (→ 27/5/48).

O'Neill did not follow up victory.

Refusing to accept parliament's plan, king plays for time

King Charles was harangued daily.

Newcastle, 20 December 1646
For the past seven months a whole army of Scottish clerics has been employed in an attempt to persuade King Charles to accept Presbyterianism. The royal prisoner, now without his English companions, has been cajoled, harangued, flattered and hectored, his only relaxation found on the golf course and his beloved chessboard.

The king, though calm, continues to vacillate, refusing to abandon the Anglican form of worship, yet prepared to accept Presbyterianism for a three-year period – although he would use the time to "lay a ground for a perfect recovery".

Charles is also procrastinating over his response to the English parliament's proposals – known as the "Propositions of Newcastle" – which would seriously curtail his royal authority. These include command of the army by parliament for 20 years, the punishment of the king's leading supporters, swearing to the covenant and a reformation of religion. While not directly refusing, the king is playing for time and hoping that his opponents will fall out with each other.

His Scottish hosts are growing impatient, knowing that their continued occupation of northern England is unpopular. Negotiations are now under way for a deal in which they will hand him over in return for money owed for their services in the civil war (→ 2/1647).

Borders, February. The Scottish army returns over the border to end four years of occupation in northern England after receiving half of the £400,000 owing to it.→

Westminster, 18 February 1647. The Commons vote to cut the army drastically (→21/3).

London, 21 March 1647. The army demands full payment of wages in arrears before it demobilizes (→4/1647).

London, April 1647. The Commons find that the army pay demand is treasonable (→27/5).

Westminster, 27 May 1647. The Commons again vote to disband the army (→14/6).

Westminster, 20 August 1647. The army cancels all recent government decisions (→8/11).

Hampton Court, 11 November 1647. King Charles escapes from house arrest and flees to the Isle of Wight (→26/12).

Westminster, 3 January 1648. Parliament ends talks on discovering Charles's secret deal with the Scots (→21/4).

London, 21 April 1648. Charles's younger son, James, the duke of York, escapes to the United Provinces (→12/6).

Ireland, 27 May 1648. Archbishop Rinuccini, the papal envoy to the Confederates, excommunicates all those supporting a truce made a week ago with the parliamentarian Murrough O'Brien, Lord Inchiquin (→17/1/49).

Strathclyde, 12 June 1648. An "engager" army which supports Charles defeats the covenanter forces (→8/1648).

Staffordshire, 25 August 1648. After their defeat at Preston the duke of Hamilton and his army surrender to Oliver Cromwell at Uttoxeter (→22/9).

Edinburgh, 4 October 1648. Cromwell reinstates the radical Covenanters in power (→15/11).

Westminster, 15 November 1648. Parliament votes to allow Charles to return to London (→16).

Westminster, 16 November 1648. Henry Ireton calls for the king to stand trial (→1/12).

London, 2 December 1648. The army occupies the city (→6).

Windsor, 17 December 1648. Charles is moved to the castle under guard (→2/1/49).

Cheers greet Charles as he heads south

When Charles refused to accept Presbyterianism, the Scots gave him back.

Northamptonshire, February 1647
This was no solemn, secretive journey: it was a triumphal entry by King Charles of England after his release by the Scots, and thousands of his subjects ensured that he was given a rapturous welcome. Church bells rang, and the roads were lined with cheering, rejoicing subjects wherever the king appeared. The king touched for "the king's evil" at Ripon; at Leeds he was greeted by two miles of well-wishers.

At Nottingham his old adversary, Sir Thomas Fairfax, rode out to meet him and kiss his hand; and even in puritan Northamptonshire – where guns were fired in his honour – the local gentry turned out in their hundreds to escort him to Holmby Hall, where he is to be housed while awaiting news of the will of Westminster.

Such a rapturous welcome has given Charles new hope. He knows that his people are tired of war and high taxation and the rigid teachings of the Calvinists and long for the old order that he, their rightful king, alone personifies (→18).

Witch-hunting stepped up in East Anglia

Suffolk, 1647
In many parts of Britain the past few years have seen a rapid rise in the number of witchcraft cases brought to court and ending in convictions. But by far the most zealous witch-finder has been Matthew Hopkins, the son of a Suffolk minister, whose work has identified some two hundred alleged witches and led to several hangings.

Hopkins travels the countryside of East Anglia, accompanied by a male assistant and a female searcher, charging a fee wherever he finds a witch. Suspects are stripped and searched for the supposed secret third nipple. They are accused of fornicating with the devil.

Hopkins with two alleged witches.

Most of those implicated in witchcraft in England are elderly women, often living alone. With the exception of cases like Hopkins's, prosecutions are initiated by neighbours rather than magistrates or church authorities. The women are usually charged with causing harm to their accusers or their accusers' children, relatives or animals.

Parliament and the army on the brink of another civil war

Hertfordshire, 14 June 1647
Parliament's attempt to reduce the New Model Army has failed. Thousands of troops are marching on London, issuing a series of proclamations as they go and insisting that they will not disband until their grievances are met.

Here at St Albans, Oliver Cromwell, Henry Ireton and John Lambert have drafted a *Representation* of the army arguing that they, unlike their comrades in continental armies, do not lead "a mercenary army hired to serve any arbitrary power of a state". They were, they said, determined to protect their own and the people's "just rights and liberties".

Ireton: leading army negotiator.

It was a powerful conservative faction in the Commons, led by Denzil Holles and Philip Stapleton, that voted to disband the New Model Army's infantry regiments with no more than eight weeks' pay and establish a smaller force led only by Presbyterian officers. Petitions by the army at its treatment have been dismissed as seditious. Few doubt that the Holles faction is seeking a settlement with King Charles, and there are rumours that Cromwell has ordered 500 cavalrymen to ride to Northamptonshire and bring him to London (→6/8). ▷

Army revolt leaves country in chaos

City of London put under martial law

London, 6 August 1647
London is virtually under martial law today, with General Cromwell occupying the Tower and the city ringed by troops of the New Model Army. Angered by riots fomented by their parliamentary opponents, the army council gave the order to march on London where they are demanding that the army's pay should no longer be witheld.

London has been in a state of high tension since 26 July when a noisy, violent mob burst in on the Commons protesting against the re-establishment of the parliamentary committee of militia. The Commons held out for four hours before they acceded under duress.

With the "Independent" members now withdrawn from the house, the Presbyterians were clearly in control of an illegal parliament and were beginning to prepare London for a siege. Their leaders attempted to begin negotiations with King Charles, who is delighted at the enmity between parliament and the army and, devious as ever, is refusing to agree a set of proposals put to him by Sir Thomas Fairfax.

Anarchy was near in the streets, and parliament was discredited. Fairfax gave the order for 18,000 troops to march with Cromwell, threatening to "purge and purge and purge" the Commons (→ 20).

London was virtually under military rule as anarchy threatened the state.

'Levellers' produce a radical manifesto

London, 19 October 1647
The radical group known as "the Levellers" has called for a new constitutional framework by which, after a wide extension of the franchise, ordinary individuals would elect a representative parliament answerable only to the people. *The Agreement of the People* was jointly drafted by civilian and army Levellers. It follows another Leveller manifesto, *The Case of the Army Truly Stated*, issued earlier this month, calling for swift action to settle soldiers' grievances (→ 8/11).

'Grandees' try to defuse 'Leveller' threat

Putney, 8 November 1647
The army leaders today announced that the debates in the army council which have been in progress since 28 October in Putney church will end in a week's time. The debates have been characterized by growing animosity between "the Grandees" – the army commanders – and radical elements among the officers and NCOs, as well as the "Levellers" [*see report left*], who have been active recently in London.

The Levellers have made no secret of their discontent; in March this year their "Large Petition" complained of religious oppression by the Presbyterian clergy, a lack of promised reforms and the continued existence of tithes and monopolies. The petition was burnt by parliamentary order, but this only served to fuel the Levellers' discontent. Their cause has gained in strength in the weeks since the army's occupation of London, during which they have joined forces with radical elements within it.

The "Leveller" idea that all should be equal was considered dangerous.

Matters came to a head when it was learnt that the Grandees were still negotiating with King Charles on the *Heads of the Army Proposals*, the New Model Army's peace proposals first presented to him on 23 July this year. Fearing that these talks would lead to a sell-out settlement being made with the king, the radicals produced their blueprint for a democratic constitution, *The Agreement of the People*, and here at Putney the last week has seen remarkable discussions on the issues of religious and civil liberty contained in the *Agreement*. Leveller and army representatives have made impassioned pleas for a one-man, one-vote system.

Alarmed by such radical arguments, the Grandees have intervened; they have now issued an order that all soldiers should report back to their regiments within one week (→ 11).

Charles signs secret deal with the Scots

Isle of Wight, 26 December 1647
After his escapes from Oxford and Hampton Court, no one has ever doubted the ability of Charles Stuart to survive. But few would have believed that he could rescue the royalist cause and once again pose a threat to his parliament.

Yet he has done just that in a secret agreement with Scottish noblemen led by the duke of Hamilton. In an engagement, buried tonight in lead in the grounds of Carisbrooke Castle, Charles has won the promise of military support from Scotland. In return he has promised to confirm the "Solemn League and Covenant" in the English parliament, although he will not take it himself. The Solemn League and Covenant – pledging to enforce the Presbyterian Church throughout England and Ireland – was signed in August 1643 by the Scottish and English parliaments [*see page 556*], and today's deal arises from concern among members of Scotland's covenanter government that English members have not kept their promise.

Charles has also agreed to a three-year trial of the Presbyterian system in England, to observe the constitutional reforms imposed in 1641 [*see pages 548-50*] and to back the covenanters' plans for closer links between England and Scotland. Hamilton is sure to face some opposition over the engagement in Scotland, where some may see it as just a royalist ploy (→ 3/1/48).

Cavalier poet: the frontispiece to the works of Robert Herrick, published this year. Herrick lost his living as a clergyman in 1647 because he was a royalist.

Cromwell crushes Scots at Preston

Preston, 20 August 1648
General Oliver Cromwell's army has annihilated the invading Scots and ensured that King Charles now has no hope of turning the scales against parliament. After a four-day fight, the duke of Hamilton's raw and untrained troops are surrendering in droves.

Hamilton has escaped, no doubt to ponder on what he must see as his bad luck. He failed to persuade the army of the covenant to join him; he faced political opposition from the covenanters of the south-west that delayed him. But it was ultimately bad weather and Cromwell's generalship that defeated the army of the north (→25).

New Model Army: defeated Scots.

Engager regime in Scotland collapse

Scotland, 22 September 1648
The duke of Hamilton's "engager" government – founded on his engagement treaty of 1647 with King Charles [*see page 566*] – has collapsed. Today the new committee of estates has agreed with Cromwell, whose army has entered southern Scotland, that all "engagers" will be driven from office.

The engager government lost its grip on power earlier this month when disaffected supporters of the "Solemn League and Covenant" took advantage of the confusion and even panic which followed the crushing defeat of Hamilton's armies at Preston on 20 August [*see report left*]. These covenanters – or "whigs" (derived from the word *whiggam*, to spur on a horse) – rode down to Edinburgh and seized the government.

In the face of this coup, the engagers gathered forces and appealed to the army in Ireland for help. But the approach of Cromwell's army saved the new regime. The covenanters, with little liking for the English army, had no choice but to accept its aid.

With the fall of Hamilton, King Charles has lost his last real ally in Scotland. Whether the new government will remain thus aligned if Charles Stuart, himself a Scot, is treated harshly by the English parliament remains to be seen (→4/10).

Parliament under attack

Colonel Pride arrested 140 members and gave the army control of parliament.

Westminster, 6 December 1648
Brandishing a list, Colonel Thomas Pride stood outside the House of Commons today with a force of musketeers, giving each member a courteous salute before placing 140 of them under arrest. In a carefully organised coup the army has taken control of the government, leaving a "rump" of 60 members who can be relied on to prepare legal steps against King Charles.

What is already being called "Pride's Purge" became inevitable when the army learned that not only had parliament been negotiating with the king but a treaty with him was imminent. This followed members' rejection of the *Remonstrance of the Army*, a document holding the king responsible for starting the civil war and arguing that he should be tried for treason, which General Henry Ireton, Cromwell's son-in-law, laid before the Commons on 20 November.

On 2 December, the day after troops moved King Charles to a new prison in Hampshire [*see report below*], the army occupied London. Ireton wanted to dissolve parliament, but he was ordered by the army's general council merely to purge it and so create a radical body which would back moves to try the king (→17).

Three months of siege ends when Essex rebels surrender

Colchester, Essex, August 1648
After three months of siege, with the civilian population forced to eat cats and dogs, the royalist garrison finally surrendered the town of Colchester to the army of General Sir Thomas Fairfax today. News had arrived of Oliver Cromwell's great victory in the north, and further resistance was pointless.

The leaders might have expected to be treated as honourable prisoners, but Fairfax, angered at the slaughter of his troops, chose otherwise. Sir Charles Lucas and Sir George Lisle were taken to the keep of the castle and shot. Lord Capel has been sent to the Tower for execution, and several other officers have been sent to the galleys (→20).

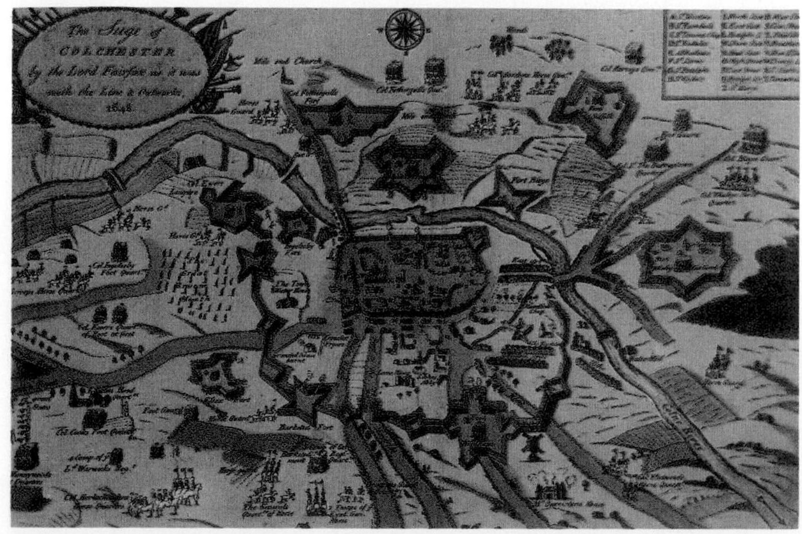
Colchester's stubborn resistance ended with its commanders being shot.

King under house arrest in Hampshire

Hampshire, 1 December 1648
An army guard has today forcibly moved King Charles from the relative comfort of Carisbrooke Castle to imprisonment in the bleak and dank Hurst Castle, situated on a Hampshire sandspit opposite the Isle of Wight. His new quarters are a small dark room with a slit for a window from which he can can watch ships in the Solent near the Needles. General Sir Thomas Fairfax has ordered that the king should be treated well. He is allowed 12 servants, including two gentlemen of the bedchamber, a carver, a cupbearer and three cooks. Local villagers often watch him dine (→2).

1649

Westminster, 2 January. Parliament appoints a high court to try King Charles for treason (→ 23).

Kilkenny City, 17 January. James Butler, the marquis of Ormond, Charles's lieutenant in Ireland, agrees a peace treaty with the Catholic Confederate army (→ 23/2).

Edinburgh, 23 January. Parliament is purged of all those who supported the "engager" movement (→ 27).

Westminster, 29 January. The "Rump" parliament issues Charles's death warrant (→ 30).

Windsor, 8 February. The body of King Charles is secretly buried (→ 9/3).

Ireland, 23 February. Archbishop Rinuccini, the papal envoy to the Confederates, leaves for Rome (→ 30/3).

Edinburgh, 1 March. Parliament passes a new Poor Law; each parish is to list its poor and raise a local tax for their upkeep.

London, 9 March. James, the duke of Hamilton and leader of the "engager" party, is executed (→ 22).

Edinburgh, 22 March. The covenanters execute the royalist marquis of Huntly (→ 28).

Co Galway, July. Plague arrives from the continent and spreads rapidly inland.

Dublin, 15 August. Oliver Cromwell, who was appointed commander-in-chief of Ireland on 30 March, arrives (→ 11/9).

Wexford City, 11 October. Following the massacre at Drogheda last month, Cromwellian troops storm the garrison, killing at least 2,000 soldiers and civilians (→ 19).

Ireland, 19 October. Cromwell bans Mass (→ 6/11).

Co Cavan, 6 November. Owen Roe O'Neill dies at Cloughoughter (→ 3/2/50).

Westminster. Parliament orders the sale of King Charles's art collection.

Scotland. Witch-hunting hysteria sweeps the country.

England. Building begins of a frigate, the *Constant Warwick*.

England. Richard Crawshaw publishes *Steps to the Temple*, a collection of religious poems.

Hawthornden, Lothian. The poet William Drummond dies.

King Charles is beheaded for treason

The final solution: Cromwell saw no end to war while King Charles lived.

Dignity marks last minutes on scaffold

London, 30 January

Charles Stuart has met his judgement day. In a moving ceremony, the king was beheaded this afternoon outside the Banqueting Hall in Whitehall. True to character, Charles remained dignified and unafraid of death. Wearing two shirts – to protect him against the cold weather, so that he should not appear to tremble from fear – he laid his neck resolutely on the block.

The king was proud to the end, proclaiming his Christian faith, emphasizing his loyalty to the Church of England and forgiving those responsible for his death. "I go from a corruptible crown to an incorruptible crown," he said, "where no disturbance can be, no disturbance in the world." As the executioner severed Charles's head with a single blow, a howl rose from the crowd – prompted more by horror at the act of regicide than by grief at the king's death.

Conspicuously absent from the proceedings was Oliver Cromwell, who was busy rushing through parliament an act to stop Charles's eldest son succeeding him (→ 5/2).

Parliament condemns the king to death

London, 27 January

In a dramatic scene at Westminster Hall, Charles Stuart was today condemned to death. Fifty-nine men, mostly soldiers led by Oliver Cromwell, have been induced to sign the king's death warrant, although General Sir Thomas Fairfax declined.

Eight days ago the king was brought to London from Windsor. In bitterly cold weather there were few people to watch him being taken by closed sedan chair to Whitehall, thence by barge to Westminster. Heavily guarded at all times, the king never lost his pride.

Entering court dressed in black, he refused to remove his tall hat, as he would not recognize the court of law. He also refused to answer questions put to him by John Bradshaw, the president of the court. When he was condemned as "a tyrant, traitor, murderer and a public enemy", Lady Fairfax cried out in his defence. But the king will die (→ 29).

Scots support royal heir – at a price

Edinburgh, 5 February

Angry that King Charles has been executed without reference to opinion in Scotland, parliament today declared his eldest son, Charles, to be his lawful successor. The government is at present dominated by Archibald Campbell, the marquis of Argyll, who heads the powerful kirk party. Argyll seeks an alliance with the new "king" to bolster the position of his party, which has the largest representation in parliament, but he insists that Charles must adhere to the "Solemn League and Covenant" of 1643 [*see page 556*] and promise to establish Presbyterianism in both England and Scotland. Talks are under way with Charles at The Hague, where he is living in exile (→ 7).

Monarchy and Lords abolished by 'Rump'

A satirical view of the "Rump".

London, 7 February

The "Rump" parliament has voted to abolish the monarchy, arguing that "the office of a king in this nation ... is unnecessary, burdensome, and dangerous to the liberty, safety and public interest of the people". Today's vote follows a similar resolution yesterday to abolish the House of Lords.

The Rump consists of a radical core of fewer than a hundred members who have continued to sit in the House of Commons since last December's "Pride's Purge". The purge removed some 370 of the Commons, either forcibly or on their own initiative, making possible the events of last month which culminated in the execution of King Charles. An unrepresentative minority has now begun an overhaul of England's constitution (→ 8).

Government moves to quell dissent

Troops at Arundel: "Leveller" support is strong among the army rank and file.

Radical agitators are dispatched to Tower

London, 28 March
The radical leader John Lilburne has been arrested for the fourth time and sent to the Tower, along with his fellow pamphleteers and "Levellers" Richard Overton and William Walwyn.

Lilburne, who fought on parliament's side during the first civil war, has emerged as the champion of freedom of conscience during the current unrest. The ideas of the Levellers, popular among ordinary soldiers, have been gaining ground over the past two years, particularly in London, where their activities are centred. Arguing that all people should be equal before the law, the Levellers have issued many pamphlets and won the support of thousands for their petitions demanding liberty of conscience and the press, the disestablishment of the church and the abolition of compulsory tithes. They have come into increasing conflict with army leaders. An opponent of King Charles's execution, Lilburne recently appeared before the "Rump" parliament with a petition entitled *England's New Chains Discovered*; the government today took its revenge (→4/1649).

Women 'Levellers' make their voices heard

"Levellers" are campaigning for a greater equality between the sexes.

London, April
Female "Levellers" have presented to parliament a petition calling for the release of their jailed colleagues [*see report above*]. Over the past two years these women have taken part in protests in London, and recently they defended their right to speak to parliament, saying: "Since we are assured of our creation in the image of God, and of an interest in Christ equal unto men ... [we also have] a proportionate share in the freedom of this commonwealth."

Most notable among this group is Elizabeth Lilburne, the wife of John. Leveller goals include greater equality between men and women, including freedom under the law and better education (→14/5).

Mutinous soldiers crushed at Burford

Oxfordshire, 14 May
Mutinous troops have been crushed and their ringleaders summarily executed by firing squad outside Burford church. The mutineers – some 1,200 men – had been pursued by Sir Thomas Fairfax and Oliver Cromwell, who led troops far outnumbering their quarry.

There has been speculation linking the army rebels with civilian London "Leveller" radicals such as John Lilburne, but rebel statements make no mention of this. Instead they list as their grievances military matters like court martials and arrears of wages.

Cromwell recently addressed his men in London, telling them that any who wished to leave the army were free to do so, and that they would receive all payment due to them. Amid general dissatisfaction fuelled by wage arrears and the mobilization of troops to fight in Ireland, army mutinies broke out last month at places such as Banbury and Salisbury. The authorities acted swiftly, with Fairfax's army cutting off the mutineers at Burford. Yesterday Cromwell's troops moved in, taking the rebels unawares. After an exchange of gunfire hundreds surrendered, leading to today's executions (→19).

THE
Declaration and Standard
Of the *Levellers* of *England*;
Delivered in a Speech to his Excellency the Lord Gen. *Fairfax*, on *Friday* last at White-Hall, by Mr. *Everard*, a late Member of the Army, and his Prophesie in reference thereunto; shewing what will befall the Nobility and Gentry of this Nation, by their submitting to community; With their invitation and promise unto the people, and their proceedings in *Windsor* Park, *Oatlands* park, and severall other places; also, the Examination and confession of the said Mr. *Everard* before his Excellency, the manner of his deportment with his Hat on, and his severall speeches and expressions, when he was commanded to put it off. Together with a List of the severall Regiments of Horse and Foot that have cast Lots to go for *Ireland*.
Imprinted at *London*, for *G. Laurenson*, *Aprill* 23. 1649.

Fairfax receives a radical petition.

England is declared a republican state

London, 19 May
Following the formal abolition two months ago of both the office of king and the House of Lords, the "Rump" parliament has today passed an act declaring that, for the first time in its history, England is a republican state.

According to the wording of the act: "The people of England and of all the dominions and territories thereunto belonging, are and shall be, and are hereby constituted, made, established and confirmed to be a Commonwealth and Free State." The country will from now on be governed "by the supreme authority of this nation, the representatives of the people in parliament ... and that without any king or House of Lords".

In spite of its protestations, however, the Rump parliament does not appear to represent popular opinion in England; it is more accurately characterized as the effective voice of a revolutionary army which has set itself up as the supreme power in the state (→20/9).

'Diggers' set up a commune in Surrey

Surrey, April
A group of radicals led by Gerard Winstanley has begun to dig up common land on St George's Hill at Walton-on-Thames with the intention of establishing here a new settlement devoted to "communist" principles. "The Diggers", or "True Levellers" as they call themselves, want all land to be held in common and seek equality of the sexes. To men like Winstanley, the son of a Wigan mercer, Cromwell's revolution merely follows society's traditional patterns. Winstanley believes in a return to a golden age before the Norman Conquest, when people lived free and equal under the law, and the earth was "a common treasury of mankind". The Diggers are more radical than groups such as "Levellers", "Fifth Monarchists", "Ranters" and "Quakers", whose demands include religious freedom, separation of church and state and free education for both men and women (→7/1650).

Irish civilians massacred by Cromwell

Cromwell storms Drogheda, as the best army in Europe sets about crushing military resistance in Ireland.

Co Louth, 11 September
Oliver Cromwell, the leader of the victorious parliamentarians in England, has arrived in Ireland to put down the Catholic rebellion that has raged since 1641. He has besieged Drogheda and killed most of the garrison as well as townsfolk and recusant clergymen [those who refused the oath of supremacy]. About 2,600 people have died in this explosion of brutality. Cromwell has a three-point programme for Ireland: to crush military resistance, to remove all priests and landowners implicated in the rebellion, and to bring the entire population to Protestantism.

He has met a confused situation. The Old English, maintaining their support for the crown, have refused to concede military leadership to Owen Roe O'Neill. O'Neill has also been denied the means to defeat the Scottish covenanter army in Ulster. In the meantime, the marquis of Ormond, who had been hoping to take Dublin with his royalist forces, had only reached Rathmines on the city's outskirts when, on 2 August, he was attacked by the Irish rebel army. He was forced to flee to Kilkenny. Two weeks later Cromwell with 3,000 "Ironsides" reached Dublin determined to take revenge for massacres of Protestants. By a grim irony Drogheda had actually stayed loyal when the rebellion began (→11/10).

Oliver Cromwell, the parliamentary servant who rules England

Oliver Cromwell rides out.

England
There is no question that Oliver Cromwell is the most powerful man in the country; yet he is a servant of parliament. An enigmatic man, a forceful character who sometimes takes months to make up his mind, he believes that everything he does is the will of God.

Born at Huntingdon in 1599, he became a farmer of comfortable, rather than wealthy, means. He served as a member of parliament for Huntingdon without distinction and spent the first 40 years of his life in obscurity.

Cromwell's opportunity came with the civil war, when he knew exactly where he stood on a great issue. Raising troops early in the war, he made his position clear, telling his men that he personally was prepared to shoot King Charles, and anyone who was not had better stay at home.

Cromwell fought at Edgehill in 1642, but his reputation as the greatest cavalry commander that English history has yet seen was forged in 1643, when his "Ironsides" cleared the eastern counties of royalist troops in a series of quick campaigns. At Marston Moor he outfought the forces of Prince Rupert and helped to make possible the parliamentary victory.

Printing and press restricted by harsh new censorship law

London, 20 September
The government has finally clamped down on the newsbooks and pamphlets that have been flooding the market. The Printing Act, passed today by parliament, is an emergency measure to suppress "the ignorance and assured boldness of the weekly pamphleteers".

Royalist propagandists have, until today, been able to put across their ideas in these privately printed works, but now their "secret" presses will be actively sought by Thomas Scot, a prominent republican on the council of state. He will be assisted by the energetic Elizabeth Alkin, also known by the nickname of "Parliament Joan".

Officially sponsored newsbooks will shortly appear; *The Brief Relation*, edited by Gualter Forst, a council of state member, will be the journal of government affairs, followed by a daily journal of parliamentary business.

The well-known journalist and writer Marchamont Needham, who only a few months ago was arrested for editing the royalist publication *Mercurius Pragmaticus*, is to oversee a new weekly journal, *Mercurius Politicus*, which is planned to become the popular mouthpiece of the new republic (→2/1/50).

Censor's target: royalist newsletter.

1650

Westminster, 2 January. The "Rump" parliament orders all men over 18 to swear allegiance to the "commonwealth" (→21/5).

Co Tipperary, 3 February. In return for supplies for his army, Oliver Cromwell excludes the town of Fethard from all present and future penal [anti-Catholic] legislation (→27/3).

Kilkenny, 27 March. The city yields to Cromwell (→26/5).

Ireland, 26 May. Henry Ireton, Cromwell's son-in-law, replaces Cromwell as lord deputy; Cromwell returns to London (→4/6).

Co Donegal, 21 June. Resistance to the Scots in Ulster ends as Sir Charles Coote, the earl of Mountrath, defeats the Ulster Irish army at Scarrifhollis (→15/8).

Grampian, 24 June. King Charles II lands at Garmouth to claim his throne; he swears an oath of loyalty to the covenanters (→16/8).

Westminster, 26 June. Cromwell is made commander-in-chief of all commonwealth forces (→22/7).

Borders, 22 July. Cromwell crosses the river Tweed into Scotland (→3/9).

Ireland, 15 August. James Butler, the marquis of Ormond and a staunch royalist, is repudiated by the Catholic bishops at Jamestown (→15/9).

Fife, 16 August. Charles II, at Dumfermline, repudiates the "bloody Irish rebels" (→3/9).

Scotland, 3 September. Charles II, unable to fulfil his promises to the covenanters, writes to William II of Orange, his uncle, and plans his flight to Europe (→5/10).

Ireland, 15 September. Catholic bishops excommunicate Ormond and his supporters (→11/12).

Strathclyde, 17 October. The more extreme covenanters, who distrust Charles II, draw up the "Western Remonstrances" (→1/1/51).

Westminster, October. The "Rump" decrees that all court proceedings are to be written in English rather than Latin.

Ireland, 11 December. Ormond and his supporters leave for exile in France (→27/10/51).

Edinburgh, 24 December. The castle surrenders to Cromwell's men (→20/7/51).

Montrose is executed

Montrose's remarkable career is ended on the gibbet in Edinburgh.

Edinburgh, 21 May
James Graham, the marquis of Montrose, was hanged today on a 9-metre (30-foot) gallows. The execution of this charismatic and feared royalist aroused great interest, with even his enemies impressed by his courage. He was captured in Assynt on 30 April, three days after his defeat at Carbisdale.

Tied to a horse, Montrose was brought to Edinburgh and sentenced to death. He went to the scaffold spotlessly groomed, joking as he combed his hair "my head is yet my own". Montrose made no scaffold speech but submitted himself to God, forgiving his enemies and declaring the late King Charles a martyr. Three hours later his body was cut down, beheaded and quartered; his head is now fixed to a spike on Edinburgh tolbooth.

To the covenanters Montrose was a traitor to the "National Covenant" which he had signed: a warmonger responsible for the slaughter of thousands of his fellow Scots. To his friends he was a moderate who backed that covenant but hated the "Solemn League and Covenant": a brave soldier prepared to sacrifice everything in the cause of his God and his king (→26/6).

Despite the war people went on investing in luxury. This sumptuous room at Wilton House, Wiltshire, designed by Inigo Jones, attempts perfection.

Cromwell is given hero's welcome on return from Ireland

London, 4 June
Oliver Cromwell has returned from Ireland to a hero's welcome after spending most of the last year bringing that country to submission by force of arms. Ireland was a thorn in the English side during the entire civil war, and though Cromwell's success in his enterprise is undoubted, whether it will be sufficient to keep the rebellious Irish in check has still to be seen.

The violence of Cromwell's actions, though execrated in Ireland, is generally approved of in England and has not been excessive by the standards of European armies when dealing with their own people, let alone foreigners. But the Irish have already begun embroidering the reports of his activities, and many of the atrocities attributed to Cromwell are alleged to have happened in places where he has never been.

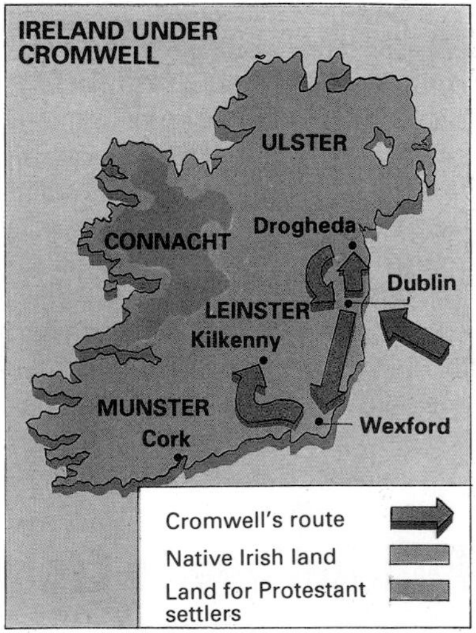

Parliament has declared a day of public thanksgiving for the return of its hero. The poet Andrew Marvell has written: "Tis madness to resist or blame/The force of angry heaven's flame." And the speaker of the House of Commons, William Lenthall, has delivered a soaring oration describing Cromwell as an instrument of God.

While it is true that imposing peace on Ireland is something of a miracle – allowing the "planting" of immigrant settlers to continue – Irish aspirations to throw off the English yoke are not dead (→21). ▷

Parliament passes the Blasphemy Act to restrain growth of new extremist cults

Controversial: sinner's punishment.

Westminster, July
Parliament is alarmed at the growing popularity of such cults as the "Levellers", "Diggers", "Ranters" and "Quakers" – which challenge accepted ideas about God, sin and society. They are causing such concern in a closely ordered society that parliament has been stirred to activity and passed the Blasphemy Act. It is aimed chiefly at the Ranters [*see below*], who claim that sin is a good thing because it was made by God. They see nothing wrong with sexual promiscuity, drunkenness and immoral behaviour of all kinds, a doctrine that adds greatly to their popularity (→9/1650).

'Ranters' claim that sin is non-existent

England, September
The "Ranter" movement is causing growing concern among the more conservative sections of society. The Ranters hold extreme opinions on most subjects, but most alarming are their views on free love and sin. They declare that, as sin was created by God, there can be no sin in the sense in which it is ordinarily interpreted. In short, it is good to sin, a view that strikes at the heart of established belief and is thought to threaten social order. One of the Ranter leaders, Laurence Clarkson, has written: "There is no such act as drunkenness, adultery and theft in God. Sin hath its conception only in the imagination.

"Whatsoever is done in light and love is light and lovely, though it be that act called adultery. No matter what scripture, saints or churches say, if that within thee do not condemn thee, thou shalt not be condemned."

The Ranters' appeal is to the urban poor, which worries the ruling classes, but the extent of their following is hard to assess (→12/1654).

Scots royalists crushed

Cromwell before the battle at Dunbar – the closest he came to defeat.

Dunbar, Lothian, 3 September
Oliver Cromwell has won a stunning victory over the Scots today, just as defeat and capture looked certain at the end of a campaign both difficult and disappointing. Faced with Cromwell's invasion the canny and experienced Scots commander David Leslie, refused to fight, and Cromwell spent six frustrating weeks trailing round Scotland in the rain, hunting an enemy who melted into the mist.

Casualties from both hunger and sickness mounted until Cromwell turned for home, by which time his progress had begun to resemble a retreat. He had 11,000 men left, most at the end of their strength, when Leslie cornered him at Dunbar with an army of more than 23,000. It should have been the end, but command of the Scots army had shifted to a committee of ministers and politicians who ordered their men to abandon an impregnable position ready to attack the next day. Capitalizing on this mistake, Cromwell launched a surprise assault at 4am and routed them, killing 4,000 Scots and capturing 200 colours and 10,000 men (→4).

Political ode to Cromwell by Marvell raises some eyebrows

London, July
Andrew Marvell's *Horatian Ode upon Cromwell's Return from Ireland* leaves the reader wondering which side this young tutor to General Sir Thomas Fairfax's daughter is on. The poem praises Cromwell's ruthlessness and triumphs:

'Tis madness to resist or blame
The face of angry heaven's flame;
And if we would speak true,
Much to the man is due.

But when it comes to the execution of King Charles a note of frank admiration and regret is sounded:

He nothing common did or mean
Upon that memorable scene ...
But bowed his comely head
Down as upon a bed ...
While round the armed bands
Did clap their bloody hands.

Marvell is a schoolmaster's son from Hull who is already known for his love lyrics. *To His Coy Mistress* argues against sexual reticence:

But at my back I always hear
Time's wingéd chariot
hurrying near.

His *Thoughts in a Garden* relish the beauty of fruits and trees and "delicious solitude" where the mind can "annihilate all that's made/to a green thought in a green shade".

Henry Vaughan, a Breconshire doctor, is another poet who writes about nature in a manner both religious and mystical. *Silex Scintillans*, the title of his new collection, means "the flashing flint"; on the title page a hand from the clouds is shown striking fire from a heart-shaped flintstone.

Andrew Marvell, the lyrical poet.

Radical reforms are sought by Cromwell

Dunbar, Lothian, 4 September
Cromwell's victory on the battlefield here yesterday has led him to call for parliamentary reforms. As often in the past, he sees his success as a sign of God's blessing on his and the army's cause. Straight after the battle he wrote to the speaker of the English House of Commons urging members to "relieve the oppressed, hear the groans of poor prisoners in England ... be pleased to reform the abuses of all professions". His letter also attacks "anyone that makes many poor to make a few rich", but it is thought that most members are too conservative to heed such demands for sweeping and radical reforms (→24/12).

Fugitive Charles is seized at Glen Cova

Tayside, 5 October
Young King Charles II was recaptured today at Glen Cova after an abortive attempt to escape from the Presbyterian faction in Scotland which has kept him a virtual prisoner since he came to the country to be proclaimed king. The young man has had to listen to endless sermons, some of them running on for hours, during which every ill that has befallen Scotland is laid at the door of himself and his family – including his executed father – for not repenting sufficiently of their sins. Finally, while at Perth, Charles made a run for it but was stopped after only 40 miles (→17).

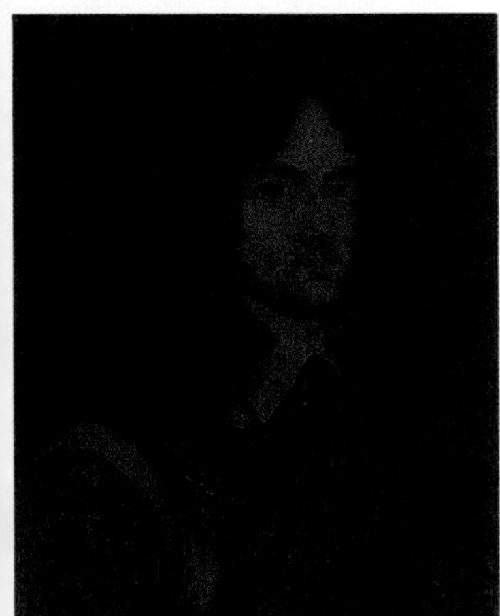

Charles: blamed for Scotland's ills.

Royalist squadron smashed by Blake

Mediterranean Sea
The land war may be over, but the war at sea goes on between two outstanding commanders, Admiral Robert Blake and Prince Rupert of the Rhine. Both of them are land generals who have never held any sort of command at sea before. Nevertheless, they are both proving to be exceptionally able.

Rupert had been practising profitable piracy against English ships until the admiral was sent to hunt him down. After preliminary clashes in the English Channel, Blake followed him to Portugal and then into the Mediterranean, where he is reported to have intercepted and destroyed Rupert's squadron.

London grows to become the largest city in western Europe, its population swollen by mass immigration from the provinces

By 1650 London was the most populous city in Europe and 20 times bigger than any other city in Britain.

England
London has grown so fast that since the year 1500 its population has increased from 50,000 to 400,000. It is now 20 times larger than the next largest cities in the country, Norwich and Bristol, and is the biggest city in western Europe. Only Constantinople in the east has more people. The secret of this massive growth – twice as fast as that of the population in general – is large-scale and continuous immigration from the provinces.

In the absence of this immigration the population would quickly fall, because living conditions in London are so unhealthy that the death-rate is far higher than the birth-rate. Even so, many people are willing to move from the country for the superior opportunities available here. Great wealth is now being produced in this quickly expanding city, and even though conditions can be awful, the chances of striking it rich and of regular employment are more attractive than labouring on the farm.

Yet even the farmers are getting richer. The city needs ever greater supplies of food and pays handsomely for them.

Scotland's recently booming economy now on verge of collapse

Scotland
The disastrous toll exacted by disease and famine, in addition to the heavy cost of the recent war, has brought the Scottish economy to the brink of collapse.

Just 20 years ago the country was enjoying a boom in trade. While nine out of ten people still live in the countryside on small farms and crofts, the population of the towns began steadily growing in the early part of the century, as did the wealth of merchants as Scottish ships traded further afield. Coal, skins, wool and fish, for example, were exported to France, Scandinavia and the Baltic countries, while imports included wine, cloth and luxury goods.

The population of Edinburgh – a city remarkable both for its towering tenements and for its spectacular wide high street – rose to more than 30,000, and that of Glasgow to about 13,000. However, the huge financial burden of the recent war has brought about the ruin of many merchants, and an epidemic of plague is estimated to have killed about 20,000 people in the course of the past five years – or one town-dweller in five.

Towering: Edinburgh tenement.

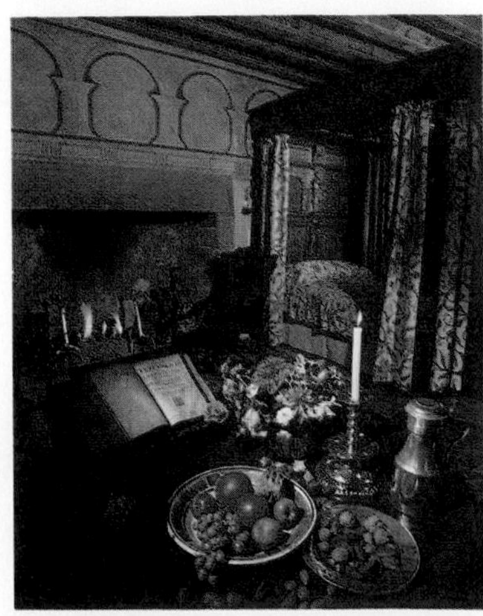

The interior of a wealthy home.

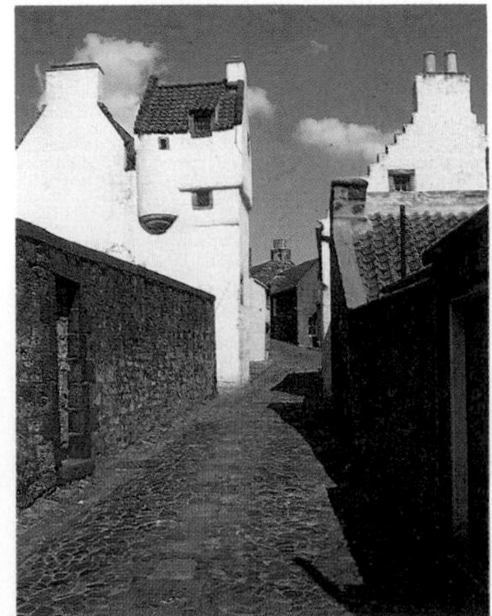

Culross, Fife: a growing town.

1651 - 1652

Tayside, 1 January 1651. Archibald Campbell, the marquis of Argyll, crowns Charles II king of England, Scotland, Ireland and France at Scone (→ 8/1651).

Fife, 20 July 1651. Oliver Cromwell defeats a royalist army at Inverkeithing (→ 3/9).

Borders, August 1651. Charles II enters England (→ 3/9).

Dundee, 1 September 1651. English troops, led by General George Monck, sack the city.

Worcester, 3 September 1651. Charles II, defeated by Cromwell, fails to reclaim his crown (→ 14/10).

Bolton, 15 October 1651. James Stanley, the royalist earl of Derby, is executed (→ 24/5/52).

Limerick, 27 October 1651. The city surrenders to the English after a five-month siege (→ 7/11).

Ireland, 7 November 1651. Edmund Ludlow becomes lord deputy on the sudden death of Henry Ireton (→ 12/4/52).

Westminster, 24 December 1651. The "Rump" parliament states that Scotland will be incorporated into England (→ 24/2/52).

Westminster, 24 February 1652. The "Rump" pardons all royalists (→ 13/8/52).

Galway, 12 April, 1652. The city surrenders to the English (→ 9/7).

Grampian, 24 May 1652. Dunnottar Castle, the last royalist stronghold, surrenders (→ 12/8).

England, 8 July 1652. War on the Dutch is declared (→ 30/11).

Ireland, 9 July 1652. Cromwell appoints Charles Fleetwood, his son-in-law, commander-in-chief of the army (→ 12/8).

Strathclyde, 12 August 1652. The marquis of Argyll surrenders; the English conquest is complete (→ 6/1653).

South Coast, 30 November 1652. The English fleet, led by Admiral Blake, is defeated by the Dutch (→ 31/7/53).

Westminster, 17 December 1652. A new act makes the estates of royalists subject to forfeit (→ 20/4/53).

Glasgow, 1652. The city is severely damaged in a fire.

London, 1652. "Pasqua Rosee", a coffee house named after its Greek owner, opens.

England challenges supremacy of Dutch in overseas trade

Westminster, 9 October 1651

A new trading measure passed by parliament today poses a direct challenge to the Dutch, who dominate mercantile interests in Europe and the Far East and reign supreme in the carrying trade. The Navigation Act envisages the building of a merchant fleet that will provide English warships with a reserve of trained men, and aims to bring England and its New World colonies into a unified economic and defensive system. Imported goods and goods travelling from one colony to another must be carried on English ships, and no merchandise will be allowed into England that has already passed through another country – a thinly veiled attack on the Dutch.

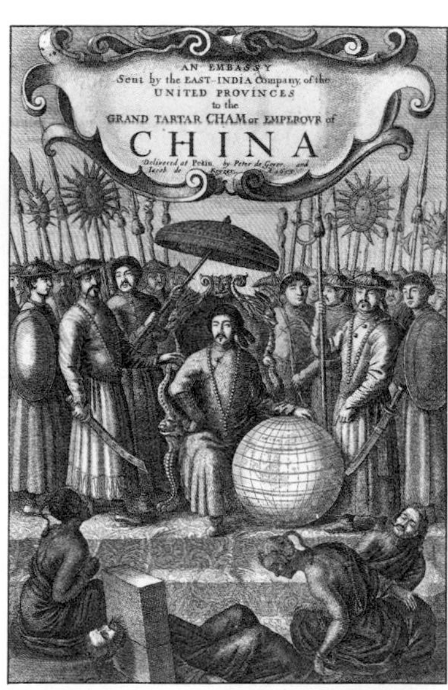

An event during a visit to China by the Dutch, supreme in foreign trade.

This is a spectacular about-turn in English policy. The Plantagenets, Tudors (even Elizabeth) and Stuarts saw England primarily as a continental power. Parliament, on the other hand, sees England as a maritime power whose interests are best served by avoiding continental entanglements and enriching itself through trade with its colonies and beyond. Members hope that this dose of protectionism will boost the economy, now deeply depressed after three years of plagues and harvest failures as well as a decade of political instability (→ 16/5/52).

Defeated Charles flees

Charles II looks out from Boscobel Oak as troops search for him below.

West Sussex, 14 October 1651

Charles II has set sail for France after six perilous weeks on the run. Since Oliver Cromwell crushed his army at Worcester the king, with a £1,000 price on his head, has been hunted by parliamentary troops.

In early August, as Cromwell occupied Perth, Charles led a 14,000-strong force of Scots and royalists over the border into England. But he had fallen into a trap. General Monck occupied Stirling to prevent a retreat, while Cromwell set off in pursuit of the king.

Failing to win the support that he had hoped for in the north, Charles made for London to reclaim his throne, with Cromwell shadowing his left flank. The king headed west, and battle was joined at Worcester on 3 September. Cromwell routed Charles's army and cut off his escape route to Wales; the king fled from the town in a desperate cavalry charge down the high street.

Charles then disguised himself, blacking his face and donning a worn suit. After finding that the ferry across the river Severn was guarded he turned back, intending to take shelter in woods near Boscobel House. Warned that the woods were being searched, he hid with another Worcester fugitive in the branches of a lone oak tree in an open field. Then, disguised as the servant of Jane Lane, the sister of one of his colonels, Charles made the hazardous trek southwards. He is now sailing across the Channel in a coal-brig called *Surprise* (→ 15).

New light cast on reproduction of animals

Harvey: revolutionary new theory.

London, 1651

William Harvey, the former royal physician who discovered the way in which blood circulates, has come up with a new theory about the development of embryos. In his book *De generatione animalium* [*On the generation of animals*], published this year, he writes: "An egg is a body, the fluids serving both the matter and the nourishment of the foetus." Harvey's claim is that, contrary to earlier belief, it is not semen and menstrual blood that produce an embryo, but rather an egg in the female, which also contains nourishment for the foetus (→ 3/6/57).

New World accepts parliamentary rule

North America, 29 March 1652
Maryland – the last of the New World colonies to refuse to recognize the English revolution – has finally submitted. Protestant Newfoundland and New England have long sympathized with the cause of the radicals, but Virginia, Maryland and the West Indian colonies had remained staunchly royalist until the arrival of Admiral Asycue's squadron off the island of Barbados last October. From there Asycue embarked on a stately progress north, accepting the submission of one colony after another, until his arrival in Maryland.

'Law of Freedom'

Surrey, 20 February 1652
One of the most articulate and passionate of the ultra-revolutionary leaders who emerged after the civil war, Gerard Winstanley, has committed his ideas to paper. In *The Law of Freedom* the leader of the group known as the "Diggers", which has been digging up and cultivating common land in Surrey, emerges as a Utopian visionary, working to build a community of equals uncorrupted by private property – a community not very different from the communism of the early Christians.

Radical solution for Ireland is prepared

Ireland, 12 August 1652
Although Oliver Cromwell is back in England, the regime he has left behind is rigorously enforcing the law. Military opposition has been crushed, and terrible atrocities have occurred. The English administration is now planning a vast reorganization of the whole country. The population will be categorized into three groups: rebels, accomplices of rebels, and those innocent of rebellion. Defeated rebels will be "transplanted", or forcibly transferred, from Munster to Leinster, while Scots settlers are to be moved from Ulster to Munster (→ 10/3/53).

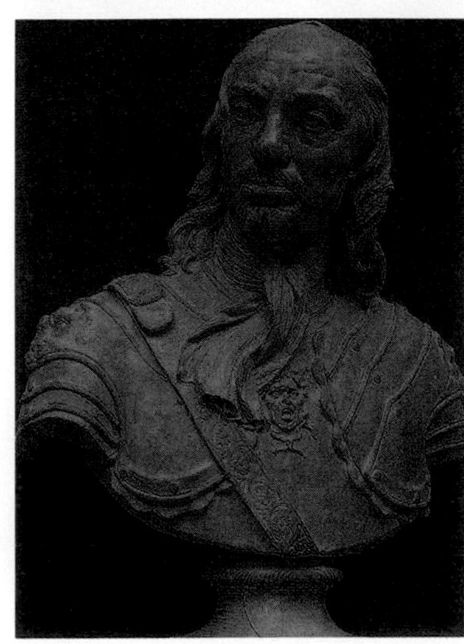

Cromwell: harsh regime in Ireland.

Sea battle over Anglo-Dutch trade war

The English and Dutch fleets battle it out in the English Channel.

Dover, 16 May 1652
An inconclusive battle in the English Channel between Admiral Robert Blake's naval squadron and Admiral Maarten Tromp's Dutch fleet this afternoon will almost inevitably lead to war between the two Protestant republics. The conflict stems from the refusal of the United Provinces to allow English naval ships to search Dutch ships for goods destined for France. In spite of Dutch maritime dominance, the strategic advantage is expected to be with England, which lies astride the Dutch trade routes (→ 8/7).

Hobbes publishes radical views on politics

Paris, April 1651
Thomas Hobbes, the exiled King Charles II's tutor, has brought out a startling new book, *Leviathan*. Hobbes writes that as "the life of man is solitary, poor, nasty, brutish and short" his self-interest causes him to surrender his freedoms to a state to ensure his survival. Although royalists should be pleased by what at first appears to be a justification for monarchy, Hobbes makes no moral distinction between monarchy and republic.

Hobbes also says that the contract between man and the state is binding only as long as the state has the power to enforce it – which many in England see as justification for accepting parliamentary rule. Indeed, *Leviathan* is being greeted more favourably in republican England than among the author's fellow exiles.

'Rump' faces criticism over slow reform

The "Rump": lampooned as dregs.

London, 13 August 1652
A petition signed by almost every leading officer of the army except Oliver Cromwell himself was presented to the "Rump" parliament today. It follows a passionate all-day debate by army officers on 2 August and calls for the abolition of tithes, law reforms, a work programme for the unemployed, an investigation into the abuse of monopolies, and – most radical of all – the dissolution of parliament and new elections.

Cromwell is believed to be generally in favour of these demands. The only reason that he has not signed the petition is to be in a position to determine some suitable compromise acceptable to both the army and parliament (→ 17/12).

"Leviathan" rising: the book comforts both monarchists and republicans.

Dublin, 10 March 1653. The Ulster rebel Sir Phelim O'Neill is executed for high treason (→27/4).

Co Cavan, 27 April 1653. Cloughoughter, the last rebel stronghold, surrenders (→23/5).

Ulster, 23 May 1653. Orders are given for Presbyterians to be "transplanted" to Munster (→22/6).

Ireland, 22 June 1653. Sir William Petty orders an ordnance survey (→26/9).

Scotland, June 1653. William Cunningham, the earl of Glencairn, is appointed commander-in-chief of royalist rebels here (→12/4/54).

Edinburgh, 20 July 1653. English forces break up a meeting of the general assembly; future ecclesiastical gatherings are banned.

Westminster, 26 September 1653. The Act of Satisfaction lays down plans for granting lands confiscated from Irish rebels to speculators and soldiers while preparing Connacht for the transplantation there of Old English Confederates (→12/1653).

Co Kerry, December 1653. The Gaelic poet Piaras Feiriteir is hanged as a rebel at Killarney (→7/1654).

England, 1653. John Taylor, "the Water Poet", dies.

Strathclyde, 1653. "Quakers" begin meetings in East Kilbride, Glassford and Kirkintilloch (→26/2/55).

Westminster, 12 April 1654. A formal ordinance of union incorporating England and Scotland is passed (→22).

Lothian, 22 April 1654. General George Monck arrives at Dalkeith to take over as commander-in-chief of the occupying army (→19/7).

Westminster, April 1654. England and the United Provinces sign a treaty (→21/4/64).

Ireland, July 1654. Charles Fleetwood, Cromwell's son-in-law and the commander-in-chief of the army here, is appointed lord deputy (→30/11).

Westminster, 12 September 1654. Cromwell demands that parliament should not change the constitution.→

Ireland, 30 November 1654. All transplantations are ordered to be effected by March 1655.→

Parliamentary tensions reach climax

Cromwell dissolves the defiant 'Rump'

Westminster, 20 April 1653
Oliver Cromwell led a file of musketeers to Westminster today and promptly dissolved the "Rump" of the "Long parliament", which had sat for the past twelve and a half years. The tension between parliament and army, growing steadily since 1649, finally came to a head this week over the question of fresh elections. Cromwell decided to act as members tried to rush through a "perpetual bill" which would have guaranteed that all of them retained their seats.

Just before the vote he arrived at the house, listened briefly and then rose to denounce the proceedings. After he had bitterly condemned the gathering for its corruption and dishonesty, he cried out: "In the name of God, go!" and called in the soldiers waiting outside. Seeing that the mace remained in its place, although the speaker, Lenthall, had already fled, he commanded the men to "take away that bauble" and empty the chamber. He later formally suspended the council of state and ordered the army officers to support him (→4/7).

Cromwell brings in troops to dismiss the discredited "Rump" parliament.

New parliament said to be 'called by God'

Westminster, 4 July 1653
The derisively named "Barebones parliament", meeting for the first time today, has been welcomed by Cromwell with the words: "Truly you are called by God to rule with him, and for him." The members of this new body, created to replace the "Rump", which was dissolved in April, have been nominated rather than elected. Hoping to get a compliant legislature, the army leaders and Cromwell wrote to churches in each county asking for nominations. They then opted for those whom they thought would be politically reliable. The parliament, which has 129 English members, five Scottish and six Irish, is named after one of its more colourful figures, the Anabaptist extremist Praisegod Barebones (→12/12).

'Compleat Angler' evokes riverbank joys

London, 1653
Izaak Walton – the Stafford-born writer most widely known as an amiable and learned biographer, with lives of the poets John Donne and Henry Wotton to his credit – has now turned his hand to the subject of fishing. His new book, *The Compleat Angler, or the Contemplative Man's Recreation*, is much slighter in style and content than his more weighty earlier works; yet in its own way it offers much satisfaction, with its affable mixture of technical instruction, culinary ingenuity, reflections upon nature and philosophy, humorous anecdote and even the occasional excursion into popular song.

The book will appeal to those who desire a quiet life in the country away from the heady political events taking place in London.

Walton fishes beside the river Lea.

'Barebones' hands power to Cromwell

London, 12 December 1653
The "Barebones parliament" [*see report above*] has voted to dissolve itself and hand power to Cromwell. This is the outcome of a coup by General John Lambert, who wants Cromwell to adopt a constitution drawn up by himself and several officers. Known as the "Instrument of Government", it is the first written constitution in English history.

Though it carried controversial measures such as the abolition of the court of chancery, the Barebones parliament failed because many of its nominees were religious zealots with no administrative experience. Its attack on church patronage and tithes prompted the moderates, encouraged by Lambert, to secure today's vote (→16).

Dutch are defeated in battle at Texel

Admiral Blake attacks the Dutch.

Dover, 31 July 1653

The English fleet scored a crushing victory today in its struggle with the Dutch for control of trade and fishing in the Channel and the North Sea. Hostilities broke out last year as a result of the 1651 Navigation Act, which was intended to boost English trade at the expense of the Dutch. Since their defeat off the North Foreland in June, the naval forces of the United Provinces, under their famous admiral, Maarten Tromp, have been bottled up in the shallow waters close to the island of Texel.

Early this morning Tromp came close to achieving a breakout, but then 18 fresh English vessels, under Admiral Blake, arrived from the Thames and swiftly turned the tide. By nightfall the Dutch had lost 30 men-of-war, and Tromp himself was dead, shot through the heart. Oliver Cromwell is trying to secure a negotiated peace (→ 4/1654).

Cromwell installed as lord protector

London, 16 December 1653

Oliver Cromwell, who has spurned many invitations to become king, was today proclaimed lord protector, with wide-ranging (but not unfettered) powers. At the installation ceremony he swore to rule "upon such a basis and foundation as by the blessing of God might be lasting, secure property, and answer those great ends of religion and liberty so long contended for".

Moderate members of the "Barebones parliament", led by General Lambert, met four days ago and won support for the hand-over and for their own dissolution [*see opposite page*]. Their intentions, and those of the army, have now been incorporated in a far-reaching document, the "Instrument of Government", which will be the legal constitution for the protectorate which replaces the now-moribund commonwealth.

A satirical suggestion that Cromwell would ignore the advice of an angel.

Under its provisions the authority of the lord protector, though extensive, will be restricted by the council of state – whose members will be appointed for life and thus free from any intimidation. Parliament will meet every three years, for at least five months, and the distribution of constituencies will be radically changed. The proportion of members from urban boroughs, which was formerly three-quarters, will now come down to one-third (with northern manufacturing centres such as Manchester, Leeds and Halifax being represented for the first time), while the rural counties get two-thirds of the seats.

Voting rights are to be sharply reduced. The property qualification is now £200 (against a previous 40 shillings [£2]). The effect of these changes will be to put control of parliament firmly in the hands of the gentry (→ 12/9/54).

Scots resistance forces face disastrous military defeat by English

Tayside, 19 July 1654

Scottish resistance forces suffered a potentially crippling setback tonight at Dalnaspidal when they were comprehensively defeated in a late-evening encounter with General George Monck's English troops.

Human casualties were slight on both sides, but the Scots lost many of their already scarce horses. Deprived of his cavalry, their leader, John Middleton (who himself was among the few wounded), will be forced to restrict his operations to the highlands and curtail his far-ranging guerrilla attacks. Hitherto these have been panicking local garrisons and threatening the English presence as far south as the border country. During the winter and spring it has been touch and go for Monck's occupation forces.

Only dissension among the Scottish leaders, and an acute local shortage of military equipment, have enabled Monck to avoid a humiliating evacuation. But now, strengthened by victory, he is expected to mount a major offensive to re-establish control (→ 4/1655).

Royalist executed for plot to kill Cromwell

London, 10 July 1654

Two murderous conspirators, John Gerard and Peter Vowell, were executed today for their leading parts in an abortive attempt to assassinate Oliver Cromwell. Three of their companions are already on their way to the slave island of Barbados, after being sentenced to transportation.

Their plan, which was discovered in advance by government agents, had been to fall on the lord protector, with his escort of 30 mounted troopers, on 13 May, as he travelled to Hampton Court. Thanks to the prior warning, however, the party went by water instead, and the attack was frustrated.

The plotters were arrested on 21 May, the day that they had chosen for a second attempt, involving a surprise assault on Whitehall chapel. Under interrogation they revealed that their ultimate aim was a Stuart restoration (→ 12/4/55).

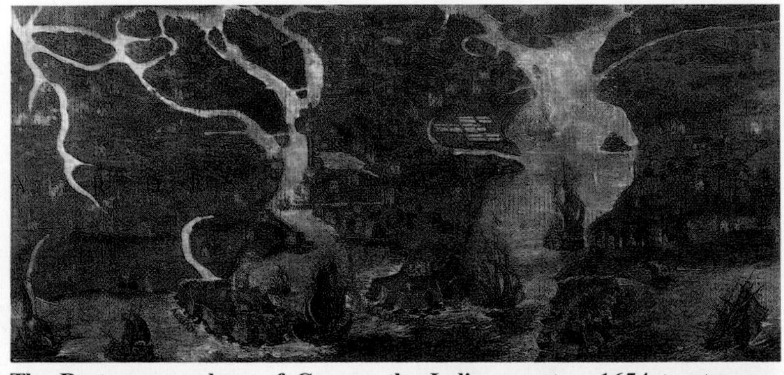

The Portuguese colony of Goa on the Indian coast: a 1654 treaty gave England trading rights in the Portuguese colonies in Asia and Africa.

Cromwell calls for war against Spain

London, 20 July 1654
Despite strong objections by General John Lambert, Cromwell has made clear his intention of going to war with Spain. In a debate in the council of state, the lord protector insisted that peace with Roman Catholic Spain was out of the question while commerce was denied to English Protestants.

Lambert argued that the cost of an expedition to Spain would be excessive; the country could not afford it, especially with the expense of keeping an army of occupation in Ireland.

The protector insisted that if this were the case the operation would be put off for ever. Apart from that "providence seems to lead us, having 160 ships swimming". A committee has been set up to inquire into the whole state of the English treasury (→ 25/4/55).

Catholic landowners relocate in Connacht

Ireland, 30 November 1654
Under the re-allocation of land decided by the Cromwellians, only Protestants may own estates in Leinster, Munster and Ulster. The Catholics, who will be given small parcels of land west of the Shannon, are to be cut off from foreign contact by a colony of soldier settlers.

This complex (and controversial) "transplantation" policy has been made possible by Sir William Petty, the forces' physician general. As a result of his comprehensive survey of land ownership, which was completed in record time, Ireland is now the most accurately surveyed and mapped country in Europe.

The work of dispossession seems to be proceeding rapidly, despite major obstacles. Catholics are sent across the Shannon to take whatever land they can find in the poorest part of the country (→ 3/1/55).

Lord protector's plea for move towards 'healing and settling' falls on deaf ears

Westminster, 12 September 1654
Despite a plea by Oliver Cromwell for "healing and settling", the lord protector's first parliament is threatening to break up in chaos. Cromwell has been attacked viciously by political enemies and former allies alike, and about a hundred members have withdrawn, rather than sign a document agreeing to the principle of government by a single person and parliament.

Cromwell is politically isolated and seems unable to manipulate parliament. Changes in electoral laws and constituency boundaries have produced a more independently minded Commons than before, with substantial representation by the landed gentry. The protector himself has failed to spell out his reform programme adequately.

Many members are attacking the present system of government, insisting that parliament alone must be the supreme authority. However Cromwell is convinced that he rules with God's blessing and is pressing reforms: that parliament should not be permanent; that there must be liberty of conscience in religion; and that control of the army must be shared between him and parliament (→ 26/6/56).

Cromwell depicted as the devil.

Leading physician and astronomer dies

This astrologer's print of 1651 may have foretold the Great Fire.

Apothecaries prepare medicine.

London, 20 January 1654
Few members of the determinedly exclusive medical profession will mourn the death today of one of the best-known physicians in London, Nicholas Culpeper, who was 38. It was Culpeper, an astrologer and herbalist, who took much of the mystique out of medicine when he translated the Latin *Pharmacopaeia* into English. His book *A Physical Directory, or a translation of the London Dispensatory* infuriated doctors but brought its author great and lasting fame.

Culpeper, who was the son of a Sussex clergyman and a staunch parliamentarian, established himself in practice in 1640, in Red Lion Street, Spitalfields, east London, using astrology as his principal means of diagnosis. His first book was entitled *An Astrological Judgement of Diseases ... wherein is laid down the way and manner of finding out the cause, change and end of disease.*

Culpeper's opponents frequently indulged in unrestrained attacks on his competence and methods. One broadside, published in a pamphlet, accused him of "... bringing into obloquy the famous societies of apothecaries and surgeons".

Religious freedom attacked by Commons

The lure of cults like "the Ranters" took people away from the churches.

Westminster, December 1654
To the dismay of the lord protector, Oliver Cromwell, who favours religious freedom, parliament voted today to suppress "atheism, damnable heresies, popery, prelacy, licentiousness and profaneness". The decision follows a petition from the Presbyterian City of London seeking religious uniformity in the wake of an orchestrated press campaign directed at minority sects such as "Ranters" and "Quakers". Committees will approve the appointment of ministers, and "ejectors" can dismiss ministers thought to be unfit to hold office. In August similar powers to vet clerical appointments were given to Scottish Presbyterians (→ 26/2/55).

England, 3 January. Vincent Gookin, the pamphleteer, publishes *The great case of transplantation in Ireland*, outlining the disadvantages of uprooting Irish Catholics (→ 26).

Dublin, 26 January. Oliver Cromwell, the lord protector, orders the governor to ship all Roman Catholic priests in his custody not found guilty of murder to the colony of Barbados (→ 9/7).

England, February. The lord protector sends an English envoy, Prideaux, on a state visit to Russia.

West Indies, 25 April. The English expeditionary force led by Admiral William Penn and General Robert Venables is defeated at Santo Domingo and Hispaniola by Spanish troops (→ 17/5).

Highland, April. After hiding in the western highlands and islands throughout the winter, refusing to surrender to General Monck, General Middleton escapes by sea to the continent (→ 9/1655).

West Indies, 17 May. Admiral Penn takes Jamaica (→ 9/1655).

Dublin, 9 July. Cromwell's youngest son, Henry, is appointed commander-in-chief of the army in Ireland (→ 6/9).

Westminster, 31 July. The lord protector proclaims that local militias will be raised and the size of the standing army reduced (→ 8/1655).

Westminster, August. Cromwell promotes 11 officers to the rank of major-general to command the new local militias (→ 1656).

Ireland, 6 September. Charles Fleetwood, the lord deputy, returns to England, leaving Henry Cromwell in command (→ 17/11/57).

Edinburgh, September. A council of state, composed largely of Englishmen and under the presidency of Lord Broghill, is established by Oliver Cromwell (→ 5/10).

Edinburgh, 5 October. Ministers here and in the neighbouring presbyteries yield to the resident English government and stop praying for King Charles II (→ 8/1656).

Scotland. *The History of the Church of Scotland*, by the late John Spottiswood, a former archbishop of St Andrews, is published.

England. The 1,000-tonne battleship *Naseby* is launched.

Leader of 'Quakers' meets the protector

George Fox: impressed Cromwell.

London, 26 February
After drafting what many see as a charter for religious tolerance the lord protector, Oliver Cromwell, invited the founder of the "Quaker" movement, George Fox, to a face-to-face meeting today – though by all accounts it was the vociferous Fox who did most of the talking.

Cromwell is curious about the movement that is attracting so many of his countrymen and asked Fox – who was being held for sedition – why the Quakers were so hostile to the established church. Fox explained that he and his fellow Quakers had nothing but contempt for ministers who preached for money. Cromwell was so impressed with Fox that he ordered his release – and gave him permission to address meetings anywhere in the commonwealth. In his proclamation, Cromwell allowed for freedom of belief but condemned "Ranters" and Quakers and others who are given to interrupting the worship of others (→ 12/1656).

Royalist rebellion in Wiltshire crushed

South-west England, 12 April
An abortive attempt at insurrection in the west of England came to a swift and savage end today with the beheading of its two ringleaders and the hanging of six more insurgents after the Exeter assize.

It was less than a month ago that 120 horsemen, led by Colonel John Penruddock and a fellow Wiltshireman, Hugh Grove, rode into the unsuspecting city of Salisbury before dawn and arrested two judges and the high sheriff, James Dove. The jail was unlocked, and the call went out for recruits, although few were forthcoming. Having beaten the sheriff for refusing to proclaim Charles II as the rightful king, the insurgents rode on to Blandford, in Dorset, where the town crier was equally obstinate, leaving Penruddock to proclaim the king.

Government supporters rallied in their thousands in the west country, but it was a small army unit, 60 strong, under the command of Captain Unton Croke which chased the insurgents and surrounded them at South Molton in Devon.

Colonel Penruddock's rising fails.

Explorers jailed for Caribbean disaster

A rare success against Spain.

London, September
Cromwell's "western design", an expedition to bring godliness – and trade – to the West Indies, has ended in disaster. Its two leaders have returned to England to be detained in the Tower. Heartbroken, Cromwell has shut himself in his room, refusing to speak.

The full story emerged when the naval commander, William Penn, and Colonel Robert Venables, who led the 8,000 soldiers in an abortive attack on Hispaniola, sailed home separately. Trouble had begun soon after the army was augmented by volunteers, according to Venables "... the most profane, debauched persons we ever saw ... cowardly, as not to be made to fight ...".

Short of food and water and led by ineffective officers, the army began the march to Santo Domingo in a mutinous mood after an order forbidding pillage. Before long dysentery and fever took their toll, and men started to die.

Nothing went right for Venables, who put his trust in a captured Irish guide and was enticed into a lethal ambush by Spanish settlers. Then the rainy season set in and, with hundreds of his men lying helplessly ill in the mud, Venables – himself crippled by fever – was jeered when he chose to be nursed by his wife on the flagship. At least on their return Venables and Penn were able to report the occupation of Jamaica, potentially a far greater prize; but nothing will console the lord protector (→ 4/1656).

Unofficial return of Jewish community

London, 12 December
For the first time since the 13th century Jews are to be permitted to live, trade and practise their religion in England without fear of persecution. The decision is unofficial, but it was the lord protector, Cromwell himself, who fostered the move after pleas by Manassah Ben Israel, a rabbi newly arrived from Amsterdam. In his "Humble Addresses" the rabbi argued that the re-admission of Jews would be the signal for the coming of the Messiah. The council prefers to believe that re-admission will bring economic benefits. Cromwell's aims are biblical; he believes that converting the Jews to Christianity will take England nearer to the promised land.

1656 - 1657

Atlantic Ocean, April 1656. Admiral Blake fails in an attempt to intercept a Spanish treasure fleet which was returning to Spain from the Caribbean (→2).

Spanish Netherlands, 2 April 1656. Charles Stuart, who was proclaimed Charles II in Scotland, forms an alliance with the Spanish, who are openly at war with England and Scotland (→9/9).

Westminster, 26 June 1656. As the cost of war with Spain rises dramatically Oliver Cromwell, the lord protector, calls a new parliament (→17/9).

Scotland, August 1656. Of the 30 members returned to parliament, 16 are English, mostly army officers and civil officials (→10/1656).

Atlantic, 9 September 1656. The navy intercepts a Spanish treasure fleet off the coast of Spain (→20/4/57).

Westminster, 17 September 1656. The second protectorate parliament meets for the first time (→8/5/57).

London, 26 September 1656. Sir William D'Avenant, the poet, stages the first opera at Rutland House, *The Siege of Rhodes*.

Scotland, October 1656. Fears of a Spanish-backed royalist rising lead to a widespread round-up of suspects.

England, 1656. Thomas Wharton publishes *Adenographia*, a description of his discoveries about the glands in the human body.

Armagh City, 16 April 1657. Edmund O'Reilly is appointed Catholic archbishop of Armagh.

Surrey, 3 June 1657. William Harvey, the former royal physician and pioneer of research into the circulation of the blood, dies.

Whitehall, 26 June 1657. Oliver Cromwell is inaugurated as lord protector for the second time (→4/2/58).

England, 30 August 1657. John Lilburne, nicknamed "Freeborn John" and a campaigner for political and religious liberties for the poor, dies.

Ireland, 17 November 1657. Henry Cromwell is appointed lord deputy (→7/6/59).

Cheshire, 1657. A coach service begins running three times a week between London and Chester.

Opposition grows to provincial 'clean-up'

The government feared that alehouses were dens for royalist plotters.

England and Wales, 1656
The country people of England and Wales are grumbling at the rule of the 11 major-generals, appointed by Cromwell in the summer of 1655 to clean up the provinces in the wake of the Penruddock rising [*see report on page 579*]. The lord protector's aim appears to be to stifle the activities of royalist plotters and criminals who gather in alehouses, at cockfights, race-meetings, bear-baitings and theatres. But the closing down of these places of recreation has done nothing to improve the government's popularity.

The zeal of the major-generals varies. Whalley not only allows but supports racing at Lincoln, whereas Worsley in Lancashire is proud of having banned racing and closed 200 alehouses. Policing is by local militias, financed by a decimation tax on moneyed royalists.

'Oceana' envisages a republican state

London, 1656
The Commonwealth of Oceana, by James Harrington, proposes a republican state, with a vital limitation on landowners. No one should own land worth more than £2,000 a year, and dowries should be limited to £1,500. Harrington's theory is that stability can only be achieved through a balance between political and economic power. He envisages government in the hands of an elected senate, to propose laws, and an assembly, to vote on them by secret ballot. At the head of the executive is the "Olphaeus Megaletor", clearly Oliver Cromwell, to whom the book is dedicated.

James Harrington is an aristocrat who travelled through Italy as a young man and admired the Venetian constitution. Although a republican, he attended King Charles I in his captivity. Harrington does not believe in extending the franchise to poor people, or to servants, but his land regulations would stop powerful landowners controlling parliament. He proposes free, compulsory education for all boys from the ages of nine to 15.

Collection of poems written by royal spy

London, 1656
The poet Abraham Cowley, who went into exile in Paris with Queen Henrietta Maria and acted as a secret courier of messages to King Charles, was arrested on his return to England last year but freed on bail of £1,000. He is now at Oxford studying medicine and has published a verse collection, *Miscellanies*. It includes an epic on the biblical history of King David and a series of odes on the model of the Greek Pindar, one of which focuses on Richard Crawshaw, his fellow-poet who died in 1649. Cowley has celebrated scientific advance in, for example, his elegy on William Harvey. He started writing poems as a schoolboy at Westminster at the age of 15. Much of his epic about David was written at Trinity College, Cambridge, from which he was ejected during the civil war. So he went to royalist Oxford (→1667).

Top Quaker is punished for blasphemy

James Nayler is whipped and his tongue bored through with a hot iron.

Westminster, December 1656
James Nayler, a Quaker whose followers treat him as a latter-day Christ, has been convicted by the Commons of "horrid blasphemies" – although he has not broken any exisiting law. He will be whipped through the streets of London and Bristol, pilloried, branded and have his tongue bored through. Nayler's case is the first occasion on which the Commons have sat as a judicial chamber – a role taken the Lords until their abolition in 1649. There is public opposition to Nayler, but there is almost equal outrage at the arbitrary powers assumed by the Commons (→30/6/59).

English victorious in battle at Santa Cruz

Canary Islands, 20 April 1657
An English fleet, led by Admiral Blake, has inflicted a resounding defeat on the Spanish in the Bay of Santa Cruz, at Tenerife. Since the beginning of winter Blake's ships have maintained a blockade of the Spanish coast, and when they received news of a Spanish treasure fleet in the Canaries they moved quickly to intercept. So swift and devastating was the attack that every Spanish galleon was destroyed, as were the shore batteries. The treasure remains stranded on Tenerife, as Blake will not overload his ships for the journey home.

This victory, which gives the English mastery of the seas, is the belated result of Spain's refusal to give religious toleration to Englishmen in Spain and to allow English trade with Spanish colonies. Three years ago Cromwell was contemplating allying with Spain but chose the French instead. Last September Captain Stayner intercepted and destroyed a Spanish treasure fleet off Cadiz. Now it seems like the Armada all over again, as England celebrates another victory over the smoking remains of once-splendid Spanish galleons (→ 4/6/58).

The English admiral Robert Blake.

A medal struck for Blake's victory.

Cromwell rejects crown

London, 8 May 1657
After prolonged agonizing, Oliver Cromwell, the lord protector, has rejected the crown. Urged by a two-to-one majority of the House of Commons to accept the title of "King of England, Scotland and Ireland", Cromwell was clearly attracted by much in the "Humble Petition and Advice". In the end he may have been swayed by a combination of loyalty to his old army colleagues, who were against his acceptance, and his own belief in providence. Only three weeks ago he said: "I would not seek to set up that that providence hath destroyed and laid in the dust, and I would not build Jericho again."

The Humble Petition provided for a limited, hereditary monarchy, with a second chamber act as a brake on the zeal of the puritans in the House of Commons. The arguments of Thurloe and others about the people's ingrained reverence for the crown were not lost on Cromwell. On the other hand, he certainly thought that an allowance of £1,300,000 a year was some way short of what a king might need. In spite of occasional jests about the crown being "but a feather in a man's cap", he has brooded morosely for several weeks. As influential as any was Captain William Bradford, who reminded him that "you are but a man, and men of high degree are vanity" (→ 26/6).

A satirical view of "King" Oliver.

College of learning planned at Durham

Durham City, 1657
Oliver Cromwell, the lord protector, has approved the founding of an educational establishment at Durham "for the better advancement of learning and religion in those parts". The committee to set up the new college includes government figures such as the speaker, Sir Thomas Widdrington, as well as Walter Strickland, John Lambert and Sir Christopher Packe, and academics such as Robert Wood and Samuel Hartlib, a disciple of Comenius.

A centre of learning springing from the appropriated lands and money of Durham's dean and chapter may endear the government to the people of the north. Cromwell is equally attracted by its potential as a source of future ministers. But this mingling of church and state both appals the "Quakers" and alarms the universities.

Cromwell ally retires after refusing loyalty oath to protectorate

London, 16 July 1657
John Lambert, one of Cromwell's best soldiers and staunchest allies, has been forced to retire from public life after refusing to take the oath of loyalty to the protectorate. Whether from personal ambition or republican conviction, he could not accept the hereditary provisions of the new constitution into which Cromwell had been so solemnly and grandly inducted three weeks ago. The enthronement of the lord protector beneath the cloth of state in the presence of foreign ambassadors and heralds, was a pageant fit for a king.

Lambert's retirement marks the end of a distinguished career. He fought at Marston Moor, became a major-general at 28 and showed outstanding leadership in the Preston campaign and at Dunbar, Inverkeithing and Worcester. Never a religious zealot, he was respected even by royalists. He helped Ireton draft the *Heads of the Army Proposals* in 1647, engineered the dissolution of the "Barebones" parliament in 1653 and has been Cromwell's effective deputy ever since.

When Lambert made known his objections to the protectorate, he and Cromwell had an emotional meeting. The upshot was that Lambert surrendered his commissions, and told the clerk of the council that "I desire nothing more than a retired life in my own house". Cromwell has granted him a yearly pension of £2,000.

Oliver Cromwell and his close friend John Lambert in better times.

1658 - 1659

Westminster, 4 February 1658. Oliver Cromwell, the lord protector, dissolves parliament (→ 3/9).

England, March 1658. A new treaty prolongs the Anglo-French alliance (→ 4/6).

Edinburgh, 10 September 1658. Richard Cromwell is proclaimed lord protector (→ 23/11).

London, 23 November 1658. An elaborate funeral procession marches from Somerset House to Westminster Abbey for Oliver Cromwell, who was buried two weeks ago (→ 2/4/59).

England, 1658. Richard Lovelace, the poet who wrote *Lucasta* in 1649, dies.

London, 2 April 1659. A general army council meets to petition parliament on its grievances (→ 18).

London, 18 April 1659. Parliament attempts to regain control of the army; it forbids the meeting of the general council and claims that it will comply with its demands (→ 22).

Westminster, 6 May 1659. The "Rump" reassembles (→ 7).

Westminster, 24 May 1659. Richard Cromwell resigns after the army coup; England is again a commonwealth (→ 5/10).

Westminster, 7 June 1659. The "Rump" selects commissioners to administer Ireland and replace Henry Cromwell, the lord deputy (→ 14/12).

Cheshire, 19 August 1659. John Lambert and his troops crush a royalist revolt (→ 16/9).

Derby, 16 September 1659. John Lambert draws up the "Derby Petition"; it demands parliamentary reforms and a structure in the army (→ 5/10).

Westminster, 5 October 1659. A second army petition is delivered to parliament (→ 20).

Scotland, 20 October 1659. General Monck denounces the coup, declaring his support for the "Rump"; the army is divided (→ 27).

Newcastle upon Tyne, 23 November 1659. John Lambert commands forces preparing to advance into Scotland against Monck (→ 6/2/60).

London, 13 December 1659. The navy declares for the "Rump".

Ireland, 14 December 1659. Cromwellian army officers declare support for the Restoration (→ 24/4/60).

Anglo-French troops win battle in dunes

The battle in the dunes was a victory for the new Anglo-French alliance.

Dunkirk, France, 4 June 1658
Oliver Cromwell's expansionist foreign policy won a fresh triumph today when the combined Anglo-French army which was besieging the Spaniards occupying Dunkirk defeated a powerful Spanish relief force in the sand dunes around the port. Tonight Dunkirk is in the hands of the Anglo-French force and, under the terms of the treaty of alliance signed three months ago, is to be ceded to England.

Six thousand veteran English soldiers fought in the battle under the command of Marshal Turennes while English warships patrolled the coast in a demonstration of England's growing naval power.

The battle was welcomed by the English soldiers who, used to a war of movement, were heartily sick of the siege and, bored, were just as inclined to fight the French as the Spanish. Their victory has changed all that. The English say the French cavalry is "very loving and civil", while the English have surprised the French generals with their martial prowess.

Lord protector dies; his son takes over

London, 3 September 1658
Oliver Cromwell, the lord protector of England, died at Whitehall Palace today, the anniversary of his victories at Dunbar and Worcester. He was 59. Ill for some time, he had been shattered by the death last month of his daughter Bettie. Yet even as death approached many felt that God would not let him die because England would be lost without him. Too weak to speak, he nodded when asked if his eldest surviving son Richard – two others had died – should succeed him. The new lord protector, a politically inexperienced country gentleman, faces an unenviable task (→ 10).

The unknown protector: Richard.

Notorious robber Moll Cutpurse is dead

London, 1659
Moll Cutpurse, the notorious highwaywoman, has died at the age of 75. Always armed, and dressed as a man, she made a fortune from her "money or your life" activities and had the audacity to open a shop in Fleet Street where her outraged victims were able to buy back their stolen possessions.

She was jailed only once and that was for robbing that redoubtable soldier, General Sir Thomas Fairfax, on Hounslow Heath; even then she escaped by paying a £2,000 bribe. It is said that she has left a full account of her criminal life, telling how she changed from being Mary Frith, the cobbler's daughter, to Moll, the cutpurse.

Moll Cutpurse disguised as a man.

Troops defect after an army coup fails

London, 22 April 1659
Richard Cromwell, "Tumbledown Dick" to his enemies, has lost his trial of strength with the army, which is determined to preserve its independent power rather than be brought under the authority of the civil power. While the radical regiments massed in St James's, the hapless lord protector was deserted even by his personal guard. Led by General Lambert, the radicals have forced the humiliated Richard to dissolve parliament. In return the army's grandees have allowed him to remain in office without power, but even this is opposed by the radical troops (→ 6/5).

'Rump' restored as sole governing body

The "Rump" assembles: but outside apprentices shout "kiss my parliament".

Westminster, 7 May 1659
In spite of the power of its swords, the army has found it impossible to rule England without the sanction of a civil authority, and its grandees have decided upon the expedient of summoning the survivors of the "Rump" parliament, which was dismissed so contemptuously by Oliver Cromwell in 1653.

Declaring that the members of that parliament had been "champions of the good old cause and had been throughout favoured with God's assistance", a delegation yesterday visited the former speaker, Lenthall, and invited him and his surviving colleagues to renew the exercise of their powers.

Forty-two of them – making an even smaller Rump than existed before – came to Whitehall today to resume the seats from which Cromwell had evicted them. A council of state is to be formed comprising the three republican leaders Vane, Haslerig and Scott, 18 other members and eight generals. Meanwhile there is a growing threat of royalist uprisings (→ 24).

Fourth civil war is looming after eruption of dissent between army and parliament

London, 27 October 1659
A fourth civil war looms following clashes between the army and the recalled "Rump" parliament. Two weeks ago regiments loyal to General John Lambert blockaded parliament and refused entry to members. Even the speaker, Lenthall, was repulsed; when, outraged, he asked if they did not know him, the troopers replied that they had not noticed him at Winnington Bridge, where on 19 August they had defeated a resurgent royalist army.

The immediate cause of the friction was Lambert's arrogance after the fight at Winnington Bridge. He returned to London set on intervening in political affairs. Some members wanted him put in the Tower, and on 12 October the Rump acted, abolishing the post of commander-in-chief and dismissing Lambert and eight other senior officers. The next day Lambert and his men retaliated. Parliament called "loyal" troops to its defence, but they refused to attack comrades.

Parliament has been humiliated, Lambert overshadows his nominal commander, Charles Fleetwood, Richard Cromwell is out of the picture, and there is talk of Lambert restoring the monarchy with himself as the power behind the throne. Meanwhile, a letter arrived today from General Monck in Scotland declaring himself and his troops to be on the Rump's side. The army is divided against itself (→ 23/11).

General George Monck: he has sent a letter of support for parliament.

John Lambert is powerful and arrogant enough to defy the "Rump".

The "Quakers" were persecuted and mocked for their belief in free will.

'Rump' worried at fears of 'Quaker' revolt

England, 30 June 1659
The ageing veterans of the recalled "Rump" parliament are becoming increasingly perturbed by reports that "the Quakers", a vocal puritan sect, are making preparations to stage a *coup d'état*.

The politicians are justified in fearing a challenge to their power, for there is a spirit of anarchy abroad in a country beset by a succession of disappointing harvests and growing economic hardships. These fears are focused on the Quakers, a sect which originated a few years ago in Lancashire and Cumberland and is now gaining supporters all over the country. The Rump sees them as a menace to society.

Quakers have been implicated in incidents where violence has been used against church ministers. They also oppose tithes and refuse to take off their hats in front of magistrates, addressing them by the familiar forms of "thee" and "thou". Many Quakers have joined the army, in which disaffection with parliament over wage arrears is growing rapidly. The current agitation is strengthening demands for the reintroduction of religious uniformity and the return of strong government (→ 1/1661).

1660

Westminster, 6 February. General George Monck, who crossed the border from Scotland on 1 January, addresses the "Rump" and calls for a free parliament (→ 9).

Westminster, 9 February. The "Rump" orders Monck to reduce the city's defences and demolish the city gates (→ 11).

London, 11 February. Monck places his men in the city; he calls for the "Rump" to dissolve itself by 6 May (→ 21).

London, 9 April. John Lambert, a former Cromwellian general and an opponent of Monck, is put in the Tower (→ 1/5).

Dublin, 24 April 1660. A convention to prepare the restoration of the Irish parliament, ushers in the first poll tax in Ireland (→ 8/5/61).

Westminster, 1 May. Both houses of parliament formally read out the Declaration of Breda for the restoration of the monarchy (→ 14).

United Provinces, 14 May. Charles II meets parliamentary delegates to plan his return to England.

Scotland/Ireland, 14 May. Charles II is proclaimed king (→ 25).

Dover, 25 May. King Charles II returns (→ 29).

Westminster, 28 August. Parliament agrees to a general pardon in accordance with the Declaration of Breda (→ 3/9).

London, 3 September. The bodies of Oliver Cromwell, Henry Ireton and John Bradshaw are exhumed, strung up and beheaded (→ 20/10).

England, 13 September. Charles II's younger brother, Henry, the duke of Gloucester, dies.

London, 25 October. Charles II issues the Worcester House Declaration to reconcile himself with the Presbyterians (→ 17/5/61).

London, 30 November. Charles II confirms the titles of all Cromwellian soldiers and others awarded land by the Adventurers' Act, but Catholics who can prove consistent loyalty to the crown are to get their lands back (→ 24/12).

Westminster, 24 December. The "convention parliament", which restored the monarchy to England, is dissolved (→ 24/4/61).

'Rump' parliament re-admits formerly excluded members

Westminster, 21 February
George Monck, the commander of the army in Scotland, has returned to London in triumph to dissolve the "Rump" parliament and establish a free one, re-admitting members who were excluded from the Commons by "Pride's Purge" in 1648 – largely Presbyterians, but many with royalist sympathies.

Monck's decision – that it was time for a free parliament – sprang partly from overtures made to him by advisors of all political persuasions. But during his march south the people of the towns and cities he passed through had left him in no doubt that they, too, longed for a return to a settled constitution.

The day ended with church bells ringing throughout the city and the streets glowing with bonfires as the excited Londoners drank toasts to the start of a new era. The first act of the reformed parliament was to make Monck commander-in-chief of all forces. The next will no doubt be a vote for the restoration of the monarchy and a call for Charles II to return to England and Scotland to take the thrones (→ 4/4).

Contrite king tries to 'heal the wounds'

Charles II issues the Declaration of Breda before setting out for England.

[Dutch] United Provinces, 4 April
Before returning to England from exile to reclaim the throne, King Charles II has today issued a declaration at Breda in order to "heal the wounds". In response to parliament's invitation, the king begins by announcing that he is anxious to restore peace to the kingdom. He then lists four main promises.

First, a general pardon will be granted to all the king's subjects except those for whom parliament decrees otherwise. Second, there will be freedom of worship for those who have "tender consciences" in matters of religion that do not disrupt the peace of the kingdom. Third, the army will be paid and soldiers accepted into the king's service on the same terms as before. Fourth, all matters relating to grants and forced sales of land will be settled by parliament (→ 9).

Coffee-housing is new fashion in London

London, January
Rota, the republican club founded by James Harrington, is now meeting regularly at the Turk's Head coffee house in New Palace Yard. Harrington, a political theorist, was a great favourite of Charles I, with whom he often argued in favour of a commonwealth. Coffee-housing is a new fashion in London. The first house opened eight years ago, and others have since sprung up all over the city. Some encourage an exclusive clientele; others are less reputable establishments, acting as focal points for rogues of all sorts.

The coffee house: a new meeting-place for all sorts of groups in London.

'Fanatical' tract is condemned to fire

England, May
Obstructours of Justice, the book by the puritan minister and author John Goodwin, is to be burnt. It was published 11 years ago and is a defence for the execution of King Charles I. During his trial, at which he was not present, Goodwin was accused of being the leader of the fanatical group calling itself "the Fifth Monarchists".

However, it is widely understood that his real crime, in the eyes of the present monarchy, was to have lent his support to the heinous offence of regicide. Goodwin's work joins two other books condemned under the Restoration – John Milton's *Eikonoklastes* and *Defensio Populi Anglicani*, both of which were burned at the assizes last year for their anti-monarchical views concerning Charles I (→ 1667).

Britain rejoices at the restoration of the monarchy

King's return met by wild celebrations

London, 29 May
After nine years' exile King Charles II entered London today – an historic event that marks the restoration of the monarchy and a return to parliamentary government.

Returning from the Dutch coast, where 100,000 people had gathered to bid him farewell, he landed at Dover four days ago to a welcome from a large assembly of nobles and gentry. The royal party then travelled to London by easy stages. The roads were lined from start to finish with cheering crowds, rejoicing in a state of wild excitement, some seen to be weeping uncontrollably.

At Blackheath Charles was met by the lord mayor and 120,000 people waiting to escort him on the last stage of his journey back to Whitehall Palace. The city's streets were strewn with flowers and hung with tapestries, and the bells were rung throughout his progress.

According to a new conception of royalty, the king will be allowed to uphold a belief in divine right but denied absolute power. This means that he can no longer levy taxes without the consent of parliament. The king is to be granted revenues for the rest of his life which, with his hereditary properties, should yield him about £1,200,00 (→28/8).

The entry of Charles II into London caused wild celebrations; Samuel Pepys became so drunk that he fell over.

Regicides go with courage to scaffold

London, 20 October
Ten of the 11 regicides sentenced to death this month have been hanged, drawn and quartered at Tyburn. The regicides – some 50 men involved in the trial and execution of Charles I – are excluded from the general pardon. The condemned men died bravely; one soldier, still alive while being disembowelled, managed to sit up and hit his executioner. According to the admiralty official Samuel Pepys, who saw the executions, one of Cromwell's officers, General Harrison, went to the scaffold "as cheerful as any man could in that condition" (→30/11).

Scots regain control as occupation ends

Edinburgh, 23 August
The committee of estates has resumed the government of Scotland, returning power to the Scots after nine years of military occupation by the English. While a skeleton English garrison remains in the country, this is the most conspicuous sign yet that Scottish independence will be restored.

The imposed union with England has been in doubt since the fall of the protectorate last year, and there is little doubt that the Scots are relieved to see it laid to rest. The Scots have been subject to martial government, intense policing and constant surveillance, as well as heavy taxation required to pay for the English army's presence.

The earl of Middleton, who was in exile with Charles during the interregnum, is to be royal commissioner in the future parliament, the earl of Glencairn will preside over the committee of estates, and the earl of Lauderdale will be secretary of state (→1/1/61).

With the Restoration the king's brother James, the duke of York, pictured here with Anne Hyde, his wife, becomes a possible successor to the throne.

Women given right to perform on stage

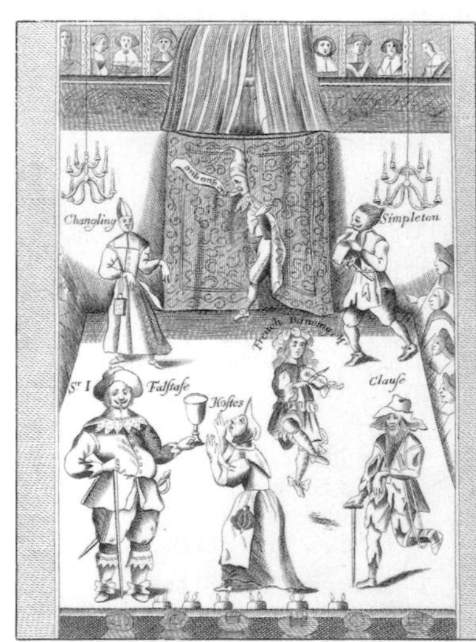

The stage of a typical playhouse.

England, 22 August
A royal warrant has been issued to allow women to appear on the English stage for the first time. The new attitude is justified by the claim that plays could be "useful and instructive representations of human life" instead of the "harmless delights" they are at present. The use of actresses, as opposed to youths playing women's roles, augurs a revival in the fortunes of the theatre – one result of the time that Charles II and his court have spent in exile on the continent (→25/4/62).

1661 - 1662

Edinburgh, 1 January 1661. Parliament meets for the first time since 1651 (→ 28/3).

Dublin, 27 January 1661. The Church of Ireland is restored, with the consecration of 12 bishops at St Patrick's Cathedral (→ 20/8/63).

Westminster, 24 April 1661. Charles II is crowned (→ 8/5).

Westminster, 8 May 1661. The first Restoration parliament meets; largely royalist, it is dubbed the "cavalier parliament" (→ 7/1662).

Dublin, 8 May 1661. Charles II's first Irish parliament meets (→ 21/2/62).

Westminster, 17 May 1661. The "Solemn League and Covenant" is destroyed and bishops are restored to the House of Lords (→ 25/7).

Lothian, 1 June 1661. James Guthrie, the radical minister of Stirling, is executed.

Scotland, 14 November 1661. James Sharp, a Presbyterian minister, becomes archbishop of St Andrews (→ 27/5/62).

West Africa, 1661. English forces capture Fort James.

Edinburgh, 1661. Thomas Sydserf produces the first Scottish-based newspaper, *Mercurius Caledonius*.

Ireland, 21 February 1662. James Butler, elevated to the dukedom of Ormond last March, is appointed lord lieutenant (→ 31/7).

London, 25 April 1662. Sir William D'Avenant opens Lincoln's Inn theatre with a production of Shakespeare's *Hamlet* (→ 10/1662).

Westminster, 22 May 1662. Charles II marries a Portuguese princess, Catherine of Braganza (→ 1669).

Edinburgh, 27 May 1662. Parliament restores the episcopacy (→ 10/1663).

Dublin, 31 July 1662. An Act of Settlement enforces Charles II's declaration of 30 November 1660 concerning land titles (→ 20/9).

Dublin, 20 September 1662. A court opens to decide land claims arising from the Act of Settlement (→ 21/5/63).

Dublin, October 1662. John Ogilby opens a new theatre, in Smock Alley (→ 7/5/63).

England, 26 December 1662. Charles II says that he will allow some religious toleration within the church (→ 6/5/64).

Power bid by 'Fifth Monarchists' ends in a bloody failure

London, January 1661

The English government is in a state of panic over an apparent armed rebellion by some 50 men, led by a cooper, Thomas Venner, aimed at seizing the capital and setting up a "fifth monarchy", or reign of Jesus Christ on earth. In the four-day crackdown by the militia and royal guards, former army officers as well as the rebel ringleaders have been arrested. Fourteen men have been executed and their heads placed upon London Bridge.

Venner was the leader of a small extremist church, and his abortive uprising is being seen as "proof" that all dissenters are politically dangerous. The news of Venner's rising has spread from London to alarm the provinces, and it has been closely followed by a royal proclamation banning unauthorized meetings for any reason. Armed gentry have joined in the general round-up of sectarian churches and "Quakers", and some 5,000 people are behind bars (→ 24/8/62).

Thomas Venner: religious fanatic.

Argyll goes to scaffold

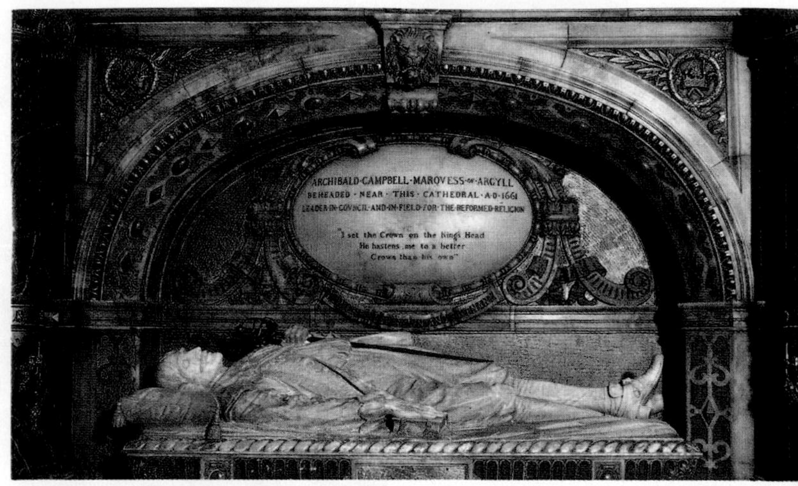

The tomb of the marquis of Argyll, who was executed for aiding Cromwell.

Edinburgh, 27 May 1661

The execution took place today of Archibald Campbell, the 54-year-old marquis of Argyll. The great highland chief and patriotic Scotsman, called MacCailen Mor by his Gaelic supporters, had been convicted of treason. His head has been placed on a spike on the Edinburgh tolbooth [town hall]. A cautious convert to the "National Covenant", Argyll rose to become leader of the movement which overturned Charles I's Scottish government. Defeats by the marquis of Montrose destroyed his military reputation, and, while cooperating with both Charles II and Oliver Cromwell, he retired from active politics in 1651.

Last year he moved south to welcome his returning monarch, only to be arrested and sent back to Scotland, where he was condemned for working with Cromwell (→ 23/7/63).

Scots parliament turns clock back 28 years

Edinburgh, 28 March 1661

Parliament today wiped the slate clean of all parliamentary measures enacted since 1633. A far-reaching "recissory" act has, at a stroke, effectively ended both the abortive "covenanted union" with England, introduced in 1643, and the recent nine years of militarily imposed union. Thus the constitutional revolution imposed by Cromwell has been reversed, and the king can once again enjoy a monopoly of power in appointing officers of state and privy councillors. Parliament can also again be managed through the "lords of the articles", abolished in 1641. The act also removes parliament's guarantee of support for the Presbyterian Church and makes likely the return of bishops.

Scotland has been exhausted by civil warfare and impoverished by high taxation, and it is ready for a return to old-fashioned monarchy. Moreover the nobility are to be less heavily taxed and will no longer come under local justices (→ 27/5).

Savoy conference fails to mend religious rifts of the church

London, 25 July 1661

After weeks of debate, representatives of Episcopalian and Presbyterian clergy have failed to agree on how the *Book of Common Prayer* could be added to and revised. The "Savoy conference", meeting under royal commission at the bishop of Lincoln's lodgings in the Strand, was hopelessly deadlocked. Long before it was due to end today, the conference was brought to grief by politics and personalities.

Bishop Gilbert Sheldon of London assumed the leadership of the Episcopalian clergy, who hampered work by insisting that exchanges were written down. The Presbyterian case for a formula providing for clergy to conform to the church was articulated by Richard Baxter, whose proposals would have given the clergy the option to omit certain objectionable ceremonies as well as to use a directory in place of the Prayer Book. The bishops saw that this could result in a substantial reduction of their authority. So goodwill and fraternity swiftly ran into the sands (→ 24/8/62).

'Cavaliers' overturn Cromwell's laws

Charles II rides towards a new relationship between king and parliament.

Every household now faces a tax of two shillings for each hearth and stove.

London, July 1662
Charles II and his so-called "cavalier parliament" have set out to rid the country of some of the consequences of the Cromwellian regime and obliterate most of the legislation of the past 20 years. Members of the House of Commons, which is now strongly royalist, have given orders for the public burning of certain documents including that enshrining the "Solemn League and Covenant", the Anglo-Scots alliance agreed in 1643.

The parliament wants the king to govern, but it also wants him to do so efficiently. At the same time it is worried about the shortfall in royal revenue and has introduced a crude system of direct taxation by levying two shillings [10p] on each stove and hearth in a dwelling. But this attempt to replace surviving feudal dues could prove unpopular.

Support for Roman Catholicism is not the key to Charles's policies, but, in the belief that Catholics have long been harshly treated, he favours repealing the more draconian laws against them. This has put his chief adviser, Edward Hyde, the earl of Clarendon, in an awkward position, as he opposes favouring Catholics too openly.

Parliament will back measures that are designed to help Charles contain disruptive forces. But it will not sanction the rebuilding of a dictatorial regime of the type seen in the 1630s (→8/2/67).

Nonconformists are driven out of jobs

London, 24 August 1662
Today, St Bartholomew's day, is the deadline by which all clergy must swear allegiance to the new state church – or be deprived of their livings. Under the new Act of Uniformity, clergy must also take an oath of non-resistance and declare the "Solemn League and Covenant" invalid. The act enforces the use of the revised *Book of Common Prayer*, accepted by parliament in April but hated by many dissenters. So far, almost 2,000 clergy are believed to lost their livings for refusing to conform (→26/12).

The Prayer Book: title page.

Royal charter won by scientific society

London, 1662
King Charles II has given a royal charter to a group of scientists and philosophers who have dedicated themselves to the pursuit of learning. His imprimatur for what will now be known as the Royal Society formalizes cooperation between the various strands of scientific inquiry, such as those of Cambridge University biologists and physicists from Oxford. The granting of the charter is also expected to accelerate the fashionable and thriving amateur interest in science among the landowning classes. The king himself is building a laboratory in Whitehall.

"Two Ladies of the Lake Family" by the Dutch-born artist Peter Lely, appointed court painter in 1661; the painting bears witness to the current fashion for exposed shoulders and breasts, which has infuriated puritans.

Satire of 'Hudibras' is popular reading

London, December 1662
A new satire on the puritans, tersely written in verse and called *Hudibras*, is swiftly going the rounds of London literary circles. Its author, Samuel Butler, is supposed to have based his would-be reformer, Hudibras, on Sir Samuel Luke of Bedfordshire, a puritan firebrand. In the poem he is shown as a busybody and know-all: "For every why he had a wherefore." The poem ridicules puritans who

Compound for sins they are inclin'd to
By damning those they have no mind to.

1663-1664

Dublin, 26 May 1663. Charles II orders Phoenix Park to be enclosed and stocked with deer.

Lambeth, London, June 1663. William Juxon, the archbishop of Canterbury, dies; Gilbert Sheldon, the bishop of London, is nominated as his successor.

Edinburgh, 23 July 1663. Archibald Johnston of Wariston, a former covenanter, extradited from Rouen in France, is executed (→23/9).

Westminster, 27 July 1663. The second Navigation Act is passed, restricting Irish trade with the colonies and cattle exports to England.

Dublin, 21 August 1663. The court of claims closes, leaving most Catholic claims unheard (→23/12/65).

Ireland, 20 August 1663. James Margetson, the archbishop of Dublin, is appointed archbishop of Armagh (→18/6/66).

Edinburgh, 23 September 1663. Parliament empowers Charles II to levy an army of 22,000 Scots (→7/12/66).

Glasgow, 2 November 1663. Alexander Burnet is appointed archbishop of Glasgow; his new see is one of the most sensitive religious areas in Scotland.

Edinburgh, 16 January 1664. The court of high commission is re-established in Scotland with powers to try all ecclesiastical cases.

England, March 1664. Charles II grants his brother, James, the duke of York, control of the New Netherlands [New York State].

Westminster, 21 April 1664. The Commons back war with the Dutch United Provinces (→6/1664).

London, June 1664. Charles II borrows £200,000 to prepare for a Dutch war (→26/8).

London, 28 October 1664. The Royal Marine Regiment is established.

Gibraltar, December 1664. A Dutch convoy from Turkey is attacked by a British fleet (→22/2/65).

Ireland, 1664. The renowned antiquarian Sir James Ware publishes a compilation of Irish annals, *Rerum Hibernicarum Annales*.

Westminster, 1664. Christopher Gibbons, the musician, is appointed master of the choristers at the abbey.

Theatre opening marks dramatic revival

Westminster, 7 May 1663
The opening of the Theatre Royal in Drury Lane tonight puts the seal of royal patronage on the revival of drama with the Restoration. One of King Charles II's first acts on his return was to grant exclusive rights to put on theatrical performances in the city of Westminster to two of his favourites who had shared his exile in Paris, Thomas Killigrew and Sir William D'Avenant. The new theatre is the first to be built under the royal patent.

In 1642 all theatres were closed by the puritans and stripped of their furnishings. Actors were arrested for performing in secret. Those who survived were divided into two companies in 1660: "the King's Players", run by Killigrew, and "the Duke's Players", which included the leading actor Thomas Betterton, run by D'Avenant. D'Avenant claims to be Shakespeare's natural son – his parents kept the Crown inn at Oxford, where the poet stayed on his journeys to London. He is presenting Betterton in *Hamlet*, using scenery for the first time at his theatre in Lincoln's Inn Fields. The new Theatre Royal has a proscenium arch and elaborate scenic effects. In both theatres actresses are now allowed to play in public.

The theatre at Lincoln's Inn Fields.

Colonel Blood fails in Irish power bid

Dublin, 21 May 1663
A group of army officers led by Colonel Thomas Blood has failed in an attempt to seize Dublin Castle and murder James Butler, the lord lieutenant and duke of Ormond. The plot was betrayed, and Blood, who fought for parliament in the Civil War, is on the run.

Cromwellians such as Blood fear that they are being undermined by the Act of Settlement, which allows claims for repossession of land previously owned by Catholics to be considered. If the estate is now held by a Cromwellian planter, he is supposed to be compensated with land of equal value, but the planters fear that they will not be compensated. Ormond himself is feared as well: of Anglo-Irish stock, he has many Catholic relatives (→21/8).

Colonel Blood: Irish adventurer.

King's friend punished for obscene libel

Covent Garden, June 1663
Scandalous doings off the Strand brought three young bloods, including the poet Sir Charles Sedley, a friend of King Charles II, before the lord chief justice today. It was alleged that, at the Cock tavern in Bow Street, the three – "being inflamed with strong liquor" – had gone out onto the balcony, pulled down their breeches and "excrementized" into the street. Sedley then stripped naked and preached blasphemy to the assembled crowd, which pelted them indoors. Sedley was tried for obscene libel – his speech – and fined £500. Hearing his sentence he remarked that he must be the first man to have paid for shitting. Sedley had hoped that the king would get him off but he was forced to pay the fine in full.

Ancient stone circles are investigated by curious antiquarian

John Aubrey has an idea that Stonehenge might be connected with the Druids.

Wiltshire, 1663
The first man to take an interest in the archaeology of Britain is John Aubrey, the antiquarian, who is surveying the ancient stone circles at Stonehenge and Avebury. He is a man of immense curiosity about many topics, astronomy, astrology and the supernatural among them; he also keeps notes on the lives of his contemporaries and amasses anecdotes about the great. Aubrey collects knowledge in a haphazard fashion. Some of his theories, such as the belief that the stone circles were once temples of Druid worship, have aroused controversy.

Dissenters' rising is scotched in north

West Yorkshire, October 1663
The latest in a series of dissenters' plots against the government has been scotched in Yorkshire. Alerted by insistent talk of a "northern rising", the privy council ordered the militia to muster at Ferrybridge and put many dissenters under arrest, while musketeers were placed on guard in the larger towns.

A group of northern Presbyterians and Anabaptists were behind the so-called Derwentdale plot, by which Edmund Ludlow – a man involved in the execution of Charles I – was to return from exile in Switzerland to hold Wales with 10,000 men. General Sir Thomas Fairfax and the earl of Manchester are said to have been ready to take part, although they deny it.

There is substantial support in the north for the aim of the rising: to seize Whitehall and force King Charles II to honour his promise of liberty of religious conscience made at Breda in 1660. The rebels also planned to restore a "gospel ministry" and abolish excise tax. The ringleaders were seized in advance and will be executed (→ 16/1/64).

Captured Dutch colony in North America given name 'New York' by the English

New Amsterdam: now captured by the English and renamed New York.

North America, 26 August 1664
A small English fleet easily took possession of the Dutch colony of New Amsterdam today. The town is to be renamed "New York", after King Charles II's brother, James, the duke of York. James obtained a royal grant and charter that confer on him absolute power in his personal territory, with the proviso that the laws enacted conform to English law. The man chosen to become governor, Captain Richard Nicholls, assured the Dutch settlers that they would have all the rights and liberty of conscience of English subjects. New York will be governed as a municipal corporation with a mayor and aldermen.

The duke's patent includes Long Island and Nantucket, which are occupied not by Dutch but by English settlers. The land between the rivers Hudson and Delaware is to be called New Jersey – its new owner, Sir George Carteret, was formerly a governor of Jersey, in the Channel Islands (→ 12/1664).

Breakaway prayer meetings outlawed by 'Clarendon Code'

Westminster, 6 May 1664
Religious gatherings of more than five people (except for the purpose of family worship) have been banned by a new law passed today. The Conventicle Act aims to stop nonconformist clergy deprived of their livings by the 1662 Act of Uniformity [*see page 587*] from forming congregations of their own outside the established church. It is part of what is being called the "Clarendon Code" – although the chief minister, the earl of Clarendon is half-hearted about these policies.

Similar measures have already been introduced in Scotland. The imposition of episcopacy has been deeply unpopular among the large population of Presbyterians in the south of Scotland, and by the end of last year 268 dissenting clergymen, a quarter of the country's total, had been deprived of their livings. Many deposed ministers formed – now illegal – conventicles.

Parliament has passed all these measures in spite of the promises of religious toleration made at the Restoration. Meanwhile, backed by the archbishop of Canterbury, Gilbert Sheldon, pamphleteers have stoked up anxiety about nonconformism by emphasizing its anti-monarchical nature. Numerous rumours of real or imagined counter-Restoration plots have added to the atmosphere of fear (→ 10/1665).

Long wigs such as this, worn by London's lord mayor, Sir John Robinson, are in vogue. Charles II adopted the fashion in 1664.

Adventurous gardener publishes survey of native British trees

London, February 1664
John Evelyn has presented the Royal Society with a book called *Sylva*, or *A discourse of forest trees and the propagation of timber in His Majesty's dominions*. It was begun two years ago after a discussion at one of the society's meetings on how to ensure that the navy's future needs for timber could be met. Evelyn's treatise is a massive folio volume which is quickly selling out. It comprehensively surveys all native British trees and their planting and conservation, together with recipes for medicinal use: for instance, oak leaves decocted in wine are recommended as a gargle, and powdered woodlice for curing jaundice and scurvy or improving eyesight.

But Evelyn is better known as a gardener. He has laid out his house, Sayes Court, at Deptford, with elm groves, box hedges and a garden following the contours of the land on the open continental pattern. His *Gardener's Almanac* is a popular guide, arranged by the month to give guidance on planting, staking, pruning, sowing flowers and harvesting fruit and vegetables, including orange trees, lemons, melons, mulberries, blue plums and cluster grapes. His knowledge of vegetables and how to cook them is extensive, and he has so arranged his garden that a green salad can be put on the table every day of the year. His favourite ingredient is the new vegetable from Italy, celery – "for its high and grateful taste".

The diarist John Evelyn's book on gardening quickly became a bestseller.

1665 - 1666

England, 22 February 1665. England declares war on the Dutch United Provinces (→3/6).

Atlantic, August 1665. The English fail in an attack on a Dutch fleet returning from the West Indies (→4/6/66).

Oxford, October 1665. The English parliament moves here in an attempt to escape the plague (→12/1665).

England, 1665. Isaac Newton, the scientist, begins experiments on the earth's gravitation (→1666).

Bedford, 1665. John Bunyan, a Baptist preacher who has been jailed for preaching in places other than a parish church, writes *The Holy City* (→1678).

England, 1665. Robert Hooke, the scientist, discovers that plants breathe and contain living cells (→10/10/67).

Ireland, 4 January 1666. The second court of claims opens; Irish Catholics may try to regain lands lost under Oliver Cromwell (→18/1/71).

France, January 1666. War is declared on Britain (→4/1666).

Germany, April 1666. The bishop of Munster, England's only ally, defects to side with the French (→1/1668).

Co Antrim, May 1666. Troops mutiny at Carrickfergus.

Dublin, 18 June 1666. The Act of Uniformity is passed; it entails the use of the revised *Book of Common Prayer* and the episcopal ordination of the clergy and bans schoolteachers from teaching without a special licence (→25).

Dublin, 25 June 1666. A convention of Catholic clergy proclaims loyalty to King Charles II but leaves the question of the pope's authority open (→9/5/69).

North Sea, 25 July 1666. Prince Rupert, a cousin of Charles II, defeats a Dutch fleet in a battle at Orfordness, off the Suffolk coast (→1/1667).

Lothian, 7 December 1666. Ten covenanters are hanged; their right hands will be sent to Lanark and their heads displayed around the country (→6/7/67).

England, 1666. Isaac Newton measures the moon's orbit (→1668).

England, 1666. James Shirley, a dramatist, has died; his best known works were *The Traitor*, *The Cardinal* and *The Lady of Pleasure*.

War with Dutch worsens in North Sea

The English fleet inflicts a telling defeat on the Dutch off the Suffolk coast.

North Sea, 3 June 1665
The duke of York has won a great victory over the Dutch off the coast of Lowestoft. The guns could be heard miles away on shore, and in the evening the enemy ships fled for home. They were not pursued.

The Dutch lost 16 ships sunk and nine captured, and 2,000 men killed, including Admiral Opdam. The war began in March, provoked by British envy of Dutch trade and British attacks on Dutch possessions in West Africa and America. New Amsterdam was captured in 1664 and renamed New York. Parliament voted £2.5 million for the war, which will be a naval conflict for commercial gain. The fleet is led by James, the duke of York, Prince Rupert of the Rhine, and the duke of Albemarle (→8/1665).

Irish lands restored to rightful owners

Ireland, 23 December 1665
A controversial new law, the Act of Explanation, has been passed to deal with the vexed question of land ownership. It provides that Cromwellians here should give up one third of their holdings to Roman Catholic "innocents" – those who can prove consistent loyalty to the crown and from whom land was previously confiscated. To mitigate the severe blow to Protestants who will have to give up land, extensive grants are to be made to influential people. These beneficiaries include the English secretary of state, the earl of Arlington, and Roger Boyle, the earl of Orrery (→4/1/66).

Henry Bennet, the earl of Arlington.

Roger Boyle, the earl of Orrery.

Five-mile limit put on nonconformists

Oxford, October 1665
Nonconformist ministers have been banned from living within 5 miles (8km) of any major town unless they swear to repudiate armed opposition to Charles II and any alteration in church or state government. The law was proposed by Lord Clarendon, who accused nonconformists of being scorpions in the nation's bosom who might sting it to death. Parliament is here to escape the plague [*see opposite*], and many Church of England clergy have also fled London, leaving dissenters to replace them (→12/4/60).

Aches and pains cured by Valentine

Valentine Greatrakes, the healer.

England, 1666
Sick people from all over the country are flocking to Valentine Greatrakes, the Irish miracle-worker, who has performed a long series of remarkable cures for "the king's evil" [scrofula], eczema, asthma, aches in the head and back, constipation, paralysis, and internal bleeding. He has shown his powers before King Charles II and many learned men, one of whom writes that "the thing is wonderful, and stupendous, and astonishing, and makes us as men in a dream".

Others believe that Greatrakes is a fraud, a republican and a danger to the state. He effects his cures by vigorously massaging his patients, sometimes for days together.

Plague kills up to 100,000 Londoners

London, December 1665
The plague has at last subsided in London after having killed between 70,000 and 100,000 people, up to one in five of the population. The worst month was September, when over a thousand died every day, by official count. In fact the toll was much higher. King Charles II, the court and parliament all fled the city, as did leading clergymen, lawyers and doctors. The poor living in crowded and insanitary parts of the city were worst afflicted [*see diary by Samuel Pepys, right*].

By government order each house in which plague was found was shut up with its residents inside. Entire familes were left to die in infected houses. These were marked with red crosses, and every day men with carts passed through the streets, crying "Bring out your dead!", and took away the bodies for burial in plague-pits. Public meetings were banned, fairs were cancelled, and bonfires were set in the streets to purge the air. Church bells tolled, funerals passed through the city at all times, and men and women were in constant fear of catching the disease from their neighbours. Plague is thought to come from a miasma emanating from the earth. There is no known cure nor any means of prevention. There have been many outbreaks in the past century, but this was by far the worst.

The procession of death is aptly demonstrated by this contemporary print. People flee the plague by land and water to avoid the gaping burial pit.

LONDON DEATHS, 15/22.8.1665: OFFICIAL FIGURES

Aged	54	Plague	3,880
Cancer	2	Pleurisy	1
Childbed	23	Quinsy	6
Colic	1	Rickets	23
Consumption	174	Rupture	2
Convulsion	88	Sciatica	1
Dropsy	40	Scurvy	1
Drowned	2	Spotted fever	190
Fever	353	Stillborn	8
Flox and smallpox	10	Stone	2
Flux	2	Stopping of the stomach	16
Gangrene	1	Suddenly	1
Gout	1	Surfeit	87
Griping in the guts	74	Teeth	113
Jaundice	3	Thrush	3
Infants	21	Ulcer	2
King's evil	10	Vomiting	7
Palsy	2	Wind	8
		Worms	18

Parishes clear of plague = 34
Parishes with plague = 96

Parish records: plague far outstrips all other causes of death in London.

Burying plague victims at dead of night in the fields of St Paul's.

Opposition mounts to leading minister

London, January 1666
The opposition to Lord Clarendon is gathering strength. He has been King Charles II's chief minister since the Restoration, as he was his chief adviser in exile, but the king himself and the court are bored with his moralizing and stuffiness as well as of his ministerial incompetence. The fact that his daughter, Anne, married the duke of York has not increased his popularity. He has failed to build up support for himself in parliament and thus depends wholly on King Charles. Clarendon failed to prevent the Dutch war and now has to find the money to pay for it (→27/11/67).

Diarist bewails 'so many sick' in city

Samuel Pepys: a later portrait.

London, 16 October 1665
A 32-year-old clerk in the navy office called Samuel Pepys, who has been keeping a diary for the past five years, wrote today: "But Lord, how empty the [city] streets are, and melancholy, so many poor sick people in the streets, full of sores, and so many sad stories overheard as I walk, everybody talking of this dead, and that man sick, and so many in this place, and so many in this place, and so many in that. They tell me that in Westminster there is never a physician, and but one apothecary left, all being dead" (→6/9/66).

Great fire sweeps across capital city

Thousands are homeless as the great fire turns night to day: in the distance the flames destroy St Paul's Cathedral.

London, 6 September 1666
The splendid Norman cathedral of St Paul is today a gaunt skeleton. Its roof has collapsed into a heap of stones mantled by the tonnes of lead that formed a torrent of molten metal at the height of the fire that has raged here for five days. The inferno has ravaged 160 hectares (400 acres) of London, razed 97 parish churches and 13,000 houses and killed at least nine people.

Early on Sunday morning smoke was seen pouring from a bakery in Pudding Lane. The parish watchman roused the lord mayor, Sir Thomas Bloodworth, who dismissed the fire as trivial and went back to bed. A spark from the bakery ignited hay in an inn yard. The inn was soon ablaze, and flames swept into adjoining warehouses stacked with tallow, oil and spirits. By daybreak on Monday half a mile of riverfront was burning.

In Whitehall, King Charles II gave orders for buildings to be torn down to provide firebreaks. The hitherto complacent lord mayor was now in a panic. "Lord, what can I do? I am spent. People will not obey me." The king put his brother, James, the duke of York, in charge of operations and he formed firefighting teams and brought in naval gunpowder crews to blow up whole streets. By yesterday midnight the fire had been checked. Charles has promised food and shelter for the thousands of homeless camped outside the city.

Many escaped the blaze by water.

Fire engines were hardly efficient.

'Pigeons burnt their wings and fell down'

London, 6 September 1666
The diarist Samuel Pepys [*see report on page 591*] was awoken by a maid at about 3am last Sunday. From the window of his house, next to his office near London's cornmarket, he noticed that some buildings were on fire, but he decided to go back to bed. The following day he noted that his heart was "full of trouble" as he saw fires raging out of control: "Everybody endeavouring to remove their goods and flinging them into the river ... the poor pigeons ... hovered about windows and balconies till they burnt their wings and fell down."

Pepys loaded his belongings, including diaries, wines and Parmesan cheeses, into a cart and drove to Bethnal Green – where he buried them in a friend's garden.

Yesterday, as the fires continued to spread, he packed his iron chests and bags of gold and, wearing only his nightshirt, drove to Woolwich with his wife. Returning to London, and judging his home to be safe, he "lay down and slept a good night about midnight" (→ 11/1673).

Heavy losses in Anglo-Dutch war

Sheerness, Kent, 4 June 1666
In four days of running battles with the Dutch in the North Sea, the English have lost 20 ships and 8,000 men killed, wounded or captured. The Dutch, it is reported, have lost seven ships and 2,000 men. Some of the English corpses seen in the water at the mouth of the Thames were in their best Sunday clothes, evidence that they had been press-ganged into service at the church door. The English had allowed their fleet to be divided. A squadron commanded by Prince Rupert of the Rhine, the grandson of King James, was at Portsmouth, while the duke of Albermarle's main force of 60 ships went into battle against 83 Dutch ships (→ 25/7).

Presbyterian rebels routed in Scotland

Edinburgh, 28 November 1666
A ragtag and bobtail force of rebels from south-west Scotland has been put to flight by dragoons commanded by the royalist general Thomas Dalyell, whose military career includes service with the Russian czar. The rebels, numbering about 1,000, were pledged to defend their Presbyterian faith – as are most Scots – but these men failed to gain popular support; they were short of weapons and lacked military training. Some 80 prisoners brought to Edinburgh by Dalyell face death by hanging (→ 11/7/68).

Covenanters with bibles and guns.

1667

Westminster, 18 January. Parliament prohibits the importing of Irish cattle in an attempt to keep prices high in England.

Westminster, January. King Charles II begins to negotiate a peace treaty with the Dutch (→3/1667).

Westminster, 8 February. Parliament questions Charles II about his finances (→5/1667).

United Provinces, March. The Dutch agree to open peace talks at Breda (→5/1667).

London, May. The royal treasury begins systematic record-keeping of all financial transactions.

United Provinces, May. A French invasion of Flanders increases pressure on England to reach peace terms with the Dutch (→10/6).

Sheerness, Kent, 10 June. A Dutch fleet of 51 men o'war, 14 fire ships and three frigates seizes the coastal town and bombards the fort at the mouth of the Medway (→11).

Kent, 11 June. The Dutch fleet sails up the Medway estuary to destroy the anchored English fleet (→14).

Scotland, 6 July. A study of army activities in the south-west of Scotland reveals extensive corruption and extortion (→8/1667).

Dublin, 8 August. A royal charter incorporates the College of Physicians.

Edinburgh, August. The privy council resorts to traditional means of checking the now endemic cattle-raiding in the highlands by empowering a number of magnates to police the region.

Scotland, August. Charles II agrees to disband the standing army and to rely instead on the militia (→11/1668).

England. Abraham Cowley, a poet and royalist, has died; he was best known for his love poem *The Mistress*.

England. John Milton publishes his epic poem *Paradise Lost* (→1671).

Edinburgh. Parliament appoints commissioners to assess the recently-introduced land tax.

England. George Wither, the satirical poet, has died; he was jailed several times for his published works, and his later ones were written in the belief that he was God's prophet.

Clarendon forced to flee

Clarendon leaves Whitehall Palace after his last interview with the king.

London, 27 November
Edward Hyde, the 58-year-old earl of Clarendon, who played a key role in the restoration of the monarchy, has been sacrificed by King Charles II in an attempt to appease the government's many critics. Clarendon recently saw the completion of a splendid new mansion in Piccadilly, which took seven years to build – but it seems unlikely that he will ever live in it.

For 30 years Clarendon had proved himself an ardent royalist, sharing exile with the prince who was to be restored to the throne as Charles II. Now Charles has threatened to put him on trial for treason unless he leaves the country.

Clarendon has been blamed for the disasters of the Dutch war; he has been denounced for measures to penalize religious dissenters and for preventing the king from hearing the advice of others. Charles's animosity was aroused some months ago when one of his mistresses eloped with the duke of Richmond and Lennox; a furious king blamed Clarendon for this (→20/8/70).

Dutch shock English in battle on Medway

English ships are captured and burnt as the Dutch maraud in the Medway.

Chatham, Kent, 14 June
A daring foray by Dutch men-of-war against the English fleet in the Medway has caused despondency at court and a panic-stricken run on the London banks. The government is preparing a proclamation guaranteeing prompt payment of its debts. The Dutch sailed up the Thames and into the Medway, attacking English ships before retiring today on the ebb tide with the duke of York's flagship, the *Royal Charles* (→21/12/70).

Scientists make big strides to improve 'natural knowledge'

London, 10 October
In what must surely be the medical marvel of the century a young woman judged to be dead has been brought back to life. Ann Green had been hanged for infanticide when she was examined by William Petty, a lecturer in anatomy at Oxford. With the help of a colleague he applied artificial respiration based on an experiment carried out by the scientist Robert Hooke.

Hooke had earlier told a meeting of the Royal Society that he had operated on a dog, attaching its windpipe to a pair of bellows to demonstrate that it is not the independent motion of the lungs that sustains life by driving blood round the body, but the regular filling of the lungs with air.

Hooke's experiment was inspired by the work of the chemist Robert Boyle, who had found that an animal sealed in a glass receiver would pant and eventually be "just ready to die", but would revive when the seal was removed. "There is some use of the air which we do not yet so well understand," he reported. Boyle, Hooke and Petty are among the distinguished band of scientists and philosophers who have made the present era outstanding for its contribution towards "improving natural knowledge", in the words of the Royal Society's charter, granted five years ago.

In the early years of the century the physician William Harvey, who had studied medicine in Italy, described how the action of the heart made blood circulate around the body. Isaac Newton, the farmer's son who graduated in mathmatics at Cambridge, is working on what he terms "fluxions", a calculus for analysing the slopes of curves. Edmund Halley, another mathematician, is planning a visit to St Helena to catalogue the stars of the southern hemisphere.

This has been an era in which the physical sciences, based on observation and experiment, have broken dramatic new ground. In Europe interest in measurement and calculation has led to the invention of the thermometer, the barometer and the pendulum clock.

1668 - 1670

Europe, January 1668. England, Sweden and the United Provinces form a triple alliance against France (→ 19/9).

London, 3 March 1668. The *Charles*, the navy's latest warship, is launched at Deptford.

Europe, April 1668. The Treaty of Aachen ends the war between France and Spain.

Britain, November 1668. Negotiations for an Anglo-Scottish union begin.

Scotland, 1668. The royal regiment of the Scots Dragoons (Royal Scots Greys) is founded.

Cambridge, 1668. Isaac Newton develops a reflecting telescope (→ 1669).

Low Countries, 9 May 1669. Peter Talbot is consecrated as Catholic archbishop of Dublin at Antwerp (→ 1/12).

Westminster, 16 November 1669. The Act of Supremacy passed by the English parliament brings the Scottish church under the control of King Charles II (→ 24/12).

Low Countries, 1 December 1669. Oliver Plunkett is consecrated as Catholic archbishop of Armagh at Ghent (→ 27/10/73).

Glasgow, 24 December 1669. Archbishop Burnet is forced to resign for objecting to the Act of Supremacy (→ 8/1670).

Cambridge, 1669. Isaac Newton becomes professor of mathematics on the resignation of his tutor, Isaac Barlow.

Europe, January 1670. The Triple Alliance agrees to assist Spain if the French continue their attacks (→ 21/12).

Spain, 18 July 1670. The Spanish recognize British ownership of land in the West Indies by the signing of the Treaty of Madrid.

England, 20 August 1670. Anne Hyde, the duchess of York and daughter of the disgraced earl of Clarendon, says that she has converted to Catholicism (→ 31/3/71).

Scotland, August 1670. Laws are passed against Presbyterian dissenters; the Clanking Act imposes fines and prison sentences for attendance at conventicles (→ 3/9/72).

Dublin, 26 December 1670. Several people are killed when the galleries of the Smock Alley theatre collapse during a performance (→ 1/1672).

Rioters hit brothels and bawdy houses

London, March 1668
Mobs rampaged through the city over the Easter period, sacking a number of brothels in a serious outburst of rioting that went beyond the high-spirited attacks on bawdy houses that often take place as a prelude to Lenten penance. This year's riots appear to have been a political protest against the licentiousness of the court and the continuing policy of religious persecution. The troublemakers threatened to sack Whitehall if their request to be allowed to exercise "liberty of conscience" were refused.

Scottish archbishop has a lucky escape

Edinburgh, 11 July 1668
James Sharp, the archbishop of St Andrews, was fortunate to escape with his life today after being shot at while boarding a coach. Andrew Honeyman, the bishop of Orkney, who was with him at the time, was wounded by the bullet. Sharp was made archbishop in 1661, following the restoration of episcopal government in the church of Scotland – since when he has been a target of Presbyterian venom. His would-be assassin, believed to be one James Mitchell, has eluded capture by the authorities (→ 16/11/69).

French ambassador proposes alliance

London, 19 September 1668
Charles Albert de Croissy, the ambassador of King Louis XIV of France, arrived here today on a mission to secure an Anglo-French alliance. The brother of Louis's famous minister Colbert, de Croissy intends to seek King Charles II's support for Louis's projected drive into the Low Countries; to achieve success, the venture needs English participation or, at least, neutrality. In spite of his recent flirtation with the United Provinces and Sweden, Charles's inclinations are to agree to the proposed alliance (→ 1/1670).

All the king's ladies: sensual Charles and his lovely mistresses

Lady Castlemaine was a mistress ...

London, 1669
King Charles II, a prodigious sensualist, has enjoyed the favours of countless mistresses, but only three have so far appeared to play an important part in his life. Lucy Walter, a squire's daughter, was the first woman Charles loved with abandon. He was aged 18 when they first met. Twenty years ago she bore him a son, who is now the duke of Monmouth. One of Lucy's successors was Barbara Villiers, a demanding mistress and powerful influence over the king. She is now countess of Castlemaine. Growing tired of her tantrums, he turned two years ago to a petite actress, Nell Gwynn (→ 10/10/71).

... and Nell Gwynn was another.

Buckingham duels with cuckolded earl

London, January 1668
The earl of Shrewsbury, the premier earl of England, has been killed in a duel by King Charles II's companion, the duke of Buckingham. The countess of Shrewsbury, Buckingham's mistress and the pretext for the duel, is said to have watched the fight disguised as a page. Courtiers said that Buckingham later took the widow to bed wearing his bloody shirt as a trophy.

Shrewsbury, the challenger, had agreed to a three-man-a-side contest. All the combatants were injured, and one of Buckingham's seconds was killed.

Oxford's Sheldonian theatre, built by Christopher Wren, opened in 1669.

Secret Anglo-French treaty made public

King Charles II in all his glory points to his growing sea power.

Paris, 21 December 1670
An Anglo-French agreement was signed here today committing the two countries to war against the Dutch and making provision for England to receive French subsidies of £225,000 per year during the fighting.

However, the agreement merely repeats most of the contents of the top-secret Treaty of Dover which was signed last May between King Charles II and King Louis XIV and known at the time to only four ministers. But omitted from today's accord was any reference to Charles's rash undertaking at Dover that he would convert to the Roman Catholic faith as soon as might be convenient.

Both parties agreed that the war should begin no later than May 1672. England is now unlikely to receive the £150,000 which it was agreed at Dover that Charles could use to offset domestic troubles likely to follow any declaration of his conversion to Catholicism. He may have committed himself simply to get the war subsidies (→ 13/3/72).

Strict act passed against nonconformists

London, 12 April 1670
A second Conventicle Act, designed to exercise stricter control over religious nonconformists, became law today. It was promptly described as the "quintessence of arbitrary malice" by the poet and politician Andrew Marvell.

The first Conventicle Act [*see report on page 589*] placed the burden of enforcement on the local gentry, many of whom were themselves nonconformists – a fact that raised serious obstacles to the effective implementation of the legislation. The new act increases the penalties available to deal with nonconformist ministers and imposes a £100 fine on justices of the peace who fail to prosecute them. Scotland plans to take even more draconian steps to resolve the problem (→ 14/3/72).

Creation of New World company is latest milestone in expansion of overseas trade

London, 1670
England's growing overseas trade and its burgeoning power and prestige in the world have been reinforced this year by the formation of the Hudson's Bay company. The company of Merchant Adventurers, which has risked substantial capital in opening up this area of North America, has been granted a charter by King Charles II which guarantees it sole authority over all the land in the New World with water draining into Hudson's Bay.

Meanwhile, English colonization of the New World continues apace, with the establishment this year of a new colony in the Carolinas, following that of the colonies of New York and New Jersey in 1664. While the volume of English trade with Europe continues to expand, commercial links with America, Africa and the Far East – in particular India and China – are commanding growing attention. The exchange of woollen cloth for other commodities and for manufactured goods remains the mainstay of England's overseas trade. But its importance is being challenged by the re-export to Europe of imported goods such as tobacco and sugar from the colonies and calico and tea from India. The thriving East India company won Bombay as a major base under the 1661 marriage settlement between Charles II and his queen, Catherine of Braganza. England's involvement in the slave trade from West Africa to the Caribbean is also proving lucrative.

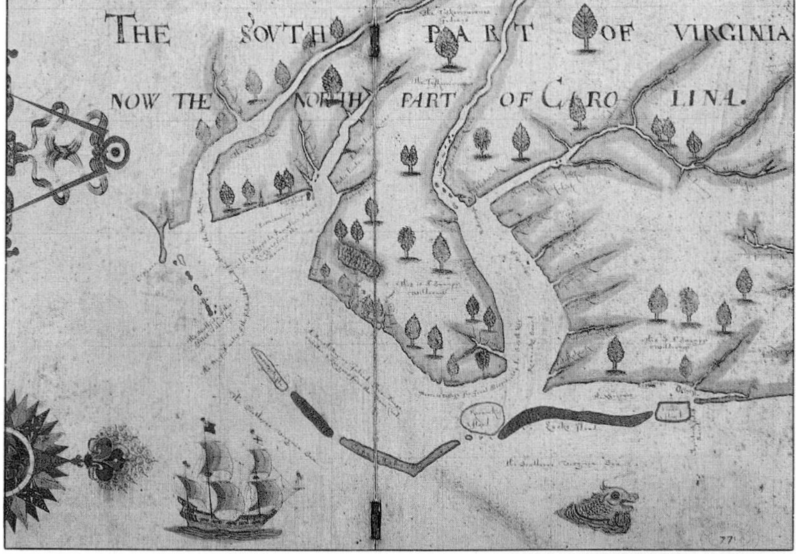

Trade with the New World: part of the new colony of the Carolinas.

A representative of the East India company trades with merchants in Delhi.

1671 - 1672

Westminster, 18 January 1671. Richard Talbot, an Irish courtier close to James, the duke of York, petitions King Charles II on behalf of the Irish Roman Catholic nobility; Talbot is himself from an Old English family (→22/9/75).

Scotland, February 1671. The court of justiciary is created.

London, 31 March 1671. Anne Hyde, the duchess of York and sister-in-law of Charles II, dies, aged 34; she gave birth to her eighth child, a daughter, earlier this year (→19/12/74).

Westminster, 22 April 1671. A Navigation Act, banning direct imports from the colonies to Irish ports, is passed by parliament.

England, September 1671. The crown takes control of customs administration.

Dublin, 5 December 1671. A royal charter is granted to King's Hospital, the Bluecoat charity school for poor Protestants.

England, 1671. Edmund Blood, a textile worker, develops a machine for carding and spinning silk.

London, January 1672. Fire destroys the Theatre Royal, Drury Lane.

Britain, 13 March 1672. Britain declares war on the Dutch (→28/5).

United Provinces, 23 June 1672. Louis XIV of France invades and begins negotiations with the Dutch (→4/11/73).

Ireland, 5 August 1672. Arthur Capell, the earl of Essex, is sworn in as lord lieutenant.

Scotland, 3 September 1672. A second "indulgence" raises the number of conforming ministers to 136 (→12/3/75).

Scotland, 4 September 1672. A new Poor Law permits parishes to levy assessments on landowners and tenants to supplement the poor.

London, 27 September 1672. The Royal African company is granted a royal charter and a monopoly on slave-trading from Morocco to the Cape of Good Hope.

Westminster, November 1672. Thomas Clifford is appointed lord high treasurer (→7/1673).

Oxford, 1672. An official printing house for the university is founded.

Dublin, 1672. Sir William Petty writes his *Political anatomy of Ireland*.

Milton returns to paradise theme in latest publication

London, 1671
The blind poet John Milton has published another epic masterpiece, *Paradise Regained*, about Christ's victory over Satan's temptations. Milton – whose blindness is seen by some as divine retribution for his defence of the men who executed Charles I – has been a wanted man since the Restoration. In 1660 he lost the position of "secretary of foreign tongues", which he had held during the commonwealth, and went into hiding, while two of his controversial books were suppressed and burnt. He was imprisoned for a month but then freed on payment of £150.

"Paradise Lost": the frontispiece.

Milton abandoned politics for poetry and in 1667 published *Paradise Lost*, an epic poem about the fall of first Satan and then Adam. Written "to justify God's ways to man", it was greeted with admiration by such poets as Andrew Marvell and John Dryden. Both of them had served as his assistants in the commonwealth period, during which time his eyesight failed.

After the majestic blank verse of *Paradise Lost*, which sold out its first edition of 1,300 copies in two years, he dictated further editions, together with sonnets on his blindness and to his second wife, who died in childbirth (→1674).

Mystery plot to steal crown jewels fails

London, 29 August 1671
In an apparent travesty of justice, Captain Thomas Blood, who was caught trying to steal the English crown jewels three months ago but never brought to trial, has been given a full pardon and a grant of lands in Ireland worth £500 a year.

The truth may never appear, but Blood certainly had friends in high places. A week after he was arrested he was, astoundingly, granted a private interview with Charles II. Some say that he was working for the king's favourite, Buckingham, others that Charles himself ordered the robbery to raise money by selling the jewels secretly.

Aged about 53, and an Irish Protestant, Blood is probably a double agent. Despite his known involvement in several uprisings, and there being a £1,000 reward on his head for attempting to kidnap the duke of Ormond last year, he has never been arrested. It is believed that he was saved by his unrivalled knowledge of dissident groups at a time of growing tension with the Dutch.

For the Tower burglary Blood disguised himself as a parson and over several weeks became friendly with Talbot Edwards, the guardian of the jewels. A marriage between the two families was agreed. On 9 May Blood and five friends arrived for the "wedding", but instead, with several "unkind knocks on the head", they overpowered Edwards and made off with the jewels. However, the alarm was raised, and they were quickly caught.

Captain Blood steals the crown.

French maid-of-honour is new mistress

Suffolk, October 1671
King Charles II has a new mistress. After several months of resistance, the beautiful Louise de Kéroualle, one of Queen Catherine's ladies-in-waiting, has finally succumbed. The diarist John Evelyn, who was with the royal party at Lord Arlington's house near Newmarket, described what happened: "The fair lady was bedded one of these nights and the stocking flung after the manner of a married bride ... she was for the most part in her undress all day and there was fondness and toying with that young wanton."

New mistress: Louise de Kéroualle.

The court has breathed a sigh of relief. Louise, it was felt, had been holding out for too long, and Lady Arlington had to explain to her what was expected. Louis XIV of France is especially pleased, as he had sent Louise over to help the king to recover from the recent death of his sister, Henriette-Anne ("Minette"), and to cement the current treaty talks. Not so delighted are Charles's other mistresses, Lady Castlemaine, who has been out of favour because of her rages and her avarice, and the witty Nell Gwynn, who makes fun of Louise's aristocratic airs (→9/8/75).

Debt and interest payments frozen

London, 2 January 1672

All government debt repayments and interest due on loans are to be frozen. This drastic move, which King Charles II announced today, is the latest in a series of money-raising schemes in preparation for the coming war with the Dutch.

Experts say that the freeze could save the government up to half a million pounds this year but at the cost of severely alienating the bankers and badly damaging the government's financial reputation.

There has been controversy over who is responsible for the scheme. Some say that it is the work of the chancellor of the exchequer, Anthony Ashley Cooper, but the evidence seems to point instead to the treasurer of the household, Sir Thomas Clifford, who is reported to have said that the exchequer "will soon be open again and everybody satisfied". Critics point out that "soon" may be too long for the widows and orphans who hold government bonds and for whom a stop on their income is likely to mean ruin (→7/1673).

Penalties against Catholics and dissenters suspended by 'Declaration of Indulgence'

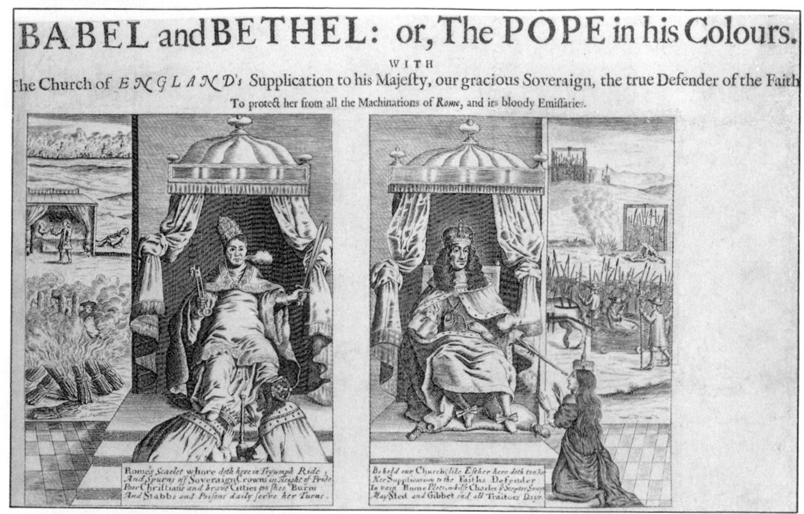

An appeal to Charles to uphold laws against supporters of the pope.

London, 14 March 1672

In a surprise move, Charles II has suspended all penal laws against Catholics and Protestant dissenters. A "Declaration of Indulgence" has been issued, claiming that "the sad experience of 12 years [is] that there is very little fruit of all those forcible courses". It is a demonstration to King Louis XIV of France of Charles's Catholic leanings and an attempt to pacify the dissenters in advance of war with the Dutch. Its likely effect, however, will be to antagonize everyone. The Anglican Church sees the dissenters as direct competition, while being soft on Catholicism is very unpopular. Parliament is asking what other laws the king might choose to suspend.

Anti-Catholic fears stoked by leniency

London, 14 March 1672

King Charles has taken a huge gamble in suspending laws against Catholics [*see report left*]. Hatred of the papacy runs deep: every schoolboy knows Foxe's *Acts and Monuments* describing the burning of 300 Protestants during the reign of Mary Tudor. Anti-Catholic feeling is also intensifying as rumours grow of an imminent Catholic rebellion in Ireland. Henry Care has given lurid expression to such fears: "Your daughters ravished by goatish monks, your smaller children tossed upon pikes ... while you have your bowels ripped out ... and holy candles made of your grease." Others draw on the biblical Book of Revelation to paint Rome as the Antichrist and England as the "elect nation" chosen by God to fight the "whore of Babylon".

Together with Charles's rumoured conversion to Catholicism and his alliance with aggressively Catholic France against the Protestant Dutch, today's legislation could spark off a wave of anti-Catholic sentiment (→8/3/73).

Anglo-French fleet surprised off Southwold

The Anglo-French fleet, surprised by the Dutch, suffered heavy damage.

North Sea, 28 May 1672

Anglo-French forces have been defeated by the Dutch in Southwold Bay off the Suffolk coast, and the admiral, Lord Sandwich, has been killed. The fleet, which had been hunting in vain for a lightly defended Dutch convoy from Smyrna, in Turkey, was surprised while taking aboard stores. Hundreds of wounded men and prisoners have come ashore and been taken to Ipswich. This unpopular war, declared just over two months ago, is officially about disputes over sovereignty in the Indies, but critics claim that this is just a cover for English commercial expansion (→23/6).

'Freemason' Ashmole writes Garter story

London, July 1672

Elias Ashmole, the Lichfield-born antiquarian and astrologer, has this month published a major history of England's oldest chivalric brotherhood, the Order of the Garter, which was inaugurated in 1348. Ashmole, whose interests also include botany and alchemy, is increasingly consulted by influential people in England about the most propitious times to take certain actions. In 1646 Ashmole was initiated at Warrington as a member of an obscure and secretive society known as "the freemasons".

"Crucifixion" by the young sculptor Grinling Gibbons, who was discovered at Deptford in 1671 by the diarist John Evelyn and introduced to the king.

1673 - 1674

Westminster, 11 March 1673. King Charles II gives assent to the Test Act, excluding non-Anglicans from public office (→ 2/6/75).

England, April 1673. James, the duke of York, refuses to take the Anglican sacraments in public, fuelling rumours that he is a convert to Roman Catholicism (→ 6/1673).

Westminster, July 1673. Thomas Clifford is replaced as lord high treasurer by Sir Thomas Osborne (→ 9/1673).

England/Italy, 30 September 1673. The duke of York marries by proxy Mary d'Este, the 15-year-old Catholic daughter of Alfonso IV, the duke of Modena (→ 18/8/76).

England, September 1673. Thomas Clifford, unable to cope with his dismissal earlier this year, dies a broken man.

Ireland, 27 October 1673. Parliament calls for the banishment of all Catholic bishops and priests from Ireland (→ 22/9/75).

London, 1673. Christopher Wren, the architect, is knighted (→ 26/3/74).

Glasgow, 1673. Colonel Walter Whiteford opens the city's first coffee house (→ 1677).

Westminster, January 1674. Having faced stiff opposition in the Scottish parliament, the duke of Lauderdale comes under fire for his absolutist policies in Scotland (→ 20/8/82).

Westminster, February 1674. Parliament insists that George Villiers, the duke of Buckingham, and Maitland John, the duke of Lauderdale, be sacked for their part in the Cabal (→ 7/1677).

London, 26 March 1674. Drury Lane theatre, rebuilt by Sir Christopher Wren, is officially reopened (→ 10/8/75).

London, June 1674. King Charles makes Thomas Osborne, the lord treasurer, earl of Danby (→ 2/1677).

North America, November 1674. All Dutch-held areas of New York are returned to English control in accordance with the Treaty of Westminster (→ 1676).

France, 19 December 1674. Edward Hyde, the earl of Clarendon and former lord chancellor, who went into exile in 1667, dies at Rouen.

England, 1674. John Milton, the blind poet best known for his epic *Paradise Lost*, dies.

Anti-Catholic laws reimposed by king

Westminster, 8 March 1673

Just a year after issuing his "Declaration of Indulgence" suspending penal laws against Roman Catholics and Protestant dissenters, King Charles II has been forced to cancel it. He was obliged to recall parliament in order to obtain funds for his Dutch war; but members made the declaration their first business and called on the king to cancel it before they voted three years' war supplies. The declaration was presented as a gesture of toleration, but many suspect Charles of promoting Catholicism and of having secretly promised to convert to it in return for French subsidies (→ 11).

Charles's brother converts to Catholicism

The wolf in priest's clothing: a widespread view of the Catholic threat.

London, June 1673

The conversion to Roman Catholicism of King Charles II's brother, James, the duke of York, has at last been forced into the open, and he has resigned as lord high admiral of the navy. At the Easter day service last March James failed to take the Anglican form of Communion with the king for the second year in succession, an omission that caused "exceeding grief and scandal", according to the diarist John Evelyn, who was present. Matters were brought to a head when the Commons, deeply suspicious of Catholic influence in court circles, passed the Test Act, which requires holders of public office to take communion according to Church of England usage (→ 7/1673).

James twice refused Communion.

Royalty looks to the stars for guidance

Seeking knowledge from the stars.

London, July 1673

Charles II's younger brother, James, the duke of York, has provoked a political storm by admitting his conversion to Catholicism [*see report above right*] and marrying an Italian Catholic, Mary of Modena. The angry reaction of the Commons has shaken Charles so badly that he has taken to consulting astrologers for guidance on handling relations with members. A readiness to consult both astrologers and soothsayers in general is not confined to royalty; there is an eager market for such books as *The Wonderful History of Mother Shipton*, telling of her prophecies over the centuries (→ 30/9).

Dutch pamphlet stokes anti-French fire

Westminster, 4 November 1673

A frustrated Charles II abruptly prorogued parliament today after members had delivered a succession of attacks on the Dutch war and the king's alliance with Louis XIV. Much of the opposition to Charles's policies has been fuelled by propaganda promoted by the Dutch *stadholder* [viceroy], William of Orange. One of his agents, the Huguenot Peter du Moulin, has issued a pamphlet which presents the French alliance and the war as a Roman Catholic plot against the Protestant form of worship and English liberty. Royal ministers are accused of betraying the country's vital interests. The pamphlet was circulating in the summer, when it seemed that the French were allowing the English to bear the brunt of the fighting and suffer the losses. After that, members began working with du Moulin in the propaganda battle (→ 9/2/74).

Shaftesbury sacked as lord chancellor

Westminster, 9 November 1673
Anthony Ashley Cooper, the earl of Shaftesbury, who was appointed lord chancellor last year, has been summarily dismissed by Charles II for his opposition to the king's pro-French, pro-Roman Catholic policies. Shaftesbury played a leading role with General Monck in the restoration of the monarchy in 1660 and was then appointed chancellor of the exchequer. He became disillusioned with the king after learning that Charles had given Louis XIV a secret pledge to convert to Catholicism in return for French subsidies (→ 6/1675).

Playwright duchess of Newcastle dies

London, 7 January 1674
Many will be saddened to hear of the death today of Margaret, the extravagant, flamboyant duchess of Newcastle. Known for her plays and other writings, the duchess often attracted criticism for her outlandish style of dress and natural arrogance. Margaret, née Lucas, the daughter of an Essex gentleman, married William Cavendish – then marquis of Newcastle – at court in Paris. She conducted a love-hate relationship with court life, turning out many a witty aphorism on the topic. Best known for plays such as *Love's Adventures*, she refuted cynics who claim that women cannot write drama.

The flamboyant duchess's family.

Rakish duke under fire

The duke's riotous private life soon became a matter of public concern.

Westminster, 14 January 1574
Waiving his privilege as a peer, George Villiers, the second duke of Buckingham, has appeared before the Commons to defend himself against a string of charges levelled against him by members. The duke, known as the "Restoration rake", is accused of treating serious matters with frivolity, promoting popery, speaking against King Charles II and having an adulterous affair with the countess of Shrewsbury, whose husband died after duelling with Buckingham. The duke did not deny his affair with the countess, but insisted that Shrewsbury did not die of his duelling wounds. He denied the other charges. Unconvinced, the Commons called on the king to dismiss Buckingham. This move seems to be part of an effort to break up Charles's close circle of advisers (→ 2/1674).

Treaty of Westminster ends Dutch war

Westminster, 9 February 1674
In the face of mounting demands from parliament for an end to the Dutch war, Charles II has given in and made peace. Under the Treaty of Westminster, signed today, the English have gained almost nothing from a two-year conflict in which their navy, under the command of Prince Rupert of the Rhine, proved no match for the Dutch.

Politically, the war delivered a fatal blow to Charles's alliance with Louis XIV of France. In the public mind France represents popery and absolutism, and members of both houses of parliament were soon calling for the repudiation of the alliance. The war, which brought higher taxes, trade restrictions and the closure of the Baltic to English shipping, has also depressed the English economy (→ 8/1675).

Prince Rupert: led navy in war.

Samuel Pepys, a navy man with a passion for books

London, November 1673
Samuel Pepys, a tailor's son who was schooled at St Paul's and Cambridge, has risen high in the service of the navy, being made secretary to the admiralty and now a member of parliament. The protégé of the earl of Sandwich, he is on easy terms with both King Charles II and the duke of York.

His friend Humphrey Wanly declares: "Tis never a drudgery to wait on Mr Pepys, whose conversation is more nearly akin to what we hope for in heaven than that of anybody else I know." Pepys is a man of business, who runs the navy efficiently, but also a man of taste and pleasure.

A pedlar and "ballad-monger".

He is passionate about music, dabbles in writing, and enjoys playgoing – to admire actresses. He collects popular books and ballads, as well as "penny merriments" such as *The Adventures of Tom Stitch the Tailor* or *The Unfortunate Welshman*. Many deal with weather lore, predictions, amorous misfortunes, riddles and potions. Besides these, Pepys has a fine library. He is a lively *bon viveur*, whose great sorrow was the death in 1669 of his French wife, Elizabeth. He also finds time to keep a daily diary (→ 1690).

1675

Glasgow, 12 March. The privy council sends in troops to encourage city magistrates to take action against unauthorized prayer meetings (→3/1676).

London, June. Anthony Ashley Cooper, the earl of Shaftesbury and a former minister, is a founder member of the Green Ribbon Club, a political group formed in opposition to King Charles II's government (→2/1677).

London, 9 August. Three-year-old Charles Lennox, the illegitimate son of Charles II and Louise de Kéroüalle, the duchess of Portsmouth, is created baron of Settrington, earl of March and duke of Richmond (→1675).

Britain/France, August. King Charles II and Louis XIV of France agree to continue their alliance (→2/1676).

Connacht, 22 September. King Charles orders a commission to look into claims from Roman Catholics who say that they were unjustly transplanted here (→8/10/78).

England. William Woolcott develops a water filtration system to provide cleaner water.

England. George Ravenscroft, a glass manufacturer, succeeds in making crystal-clear flint glass.

Jamaica. Sir Henry Morgan, the pirate and buccaneer, who was knighted by Charles II earlier this year, takes up his new role as governor.

London. William Wycherley, a dramatist well known for his biting wit and cynicism, publishes his latest play, *The Country Wife*.

London. King Charles II's mistress, Louise de Kéroüalle, who was created duchess of Portsmouth in 1673, receives an annuity from the crown of £10,000.

London. Textile workers riot against an influx of immigrant French silk workers; they destroy looms and burn mills to stop the French cornering the silk market.

London. Charles II takes a new mistress, Hortense Mancini, the duchess of Mazarin.

Northampton. Much of the town is destroyed in a conflagration believed to have been started by a woman who left her pot of washing on the fire for too long.

Political and religious freedom in danger

Westminster, 2 June
A new Test Act that will impose a one-party political system on England has been passed by the Lords despite vigorous protests from 15 peers, who objected that the measure was an invasion of privileges acquired by birth.

The measure was introduced by Thomas Osborne, the earl of Danby, who as lord high treasurer gained King Charles II's confidence by his success in increasing the royal revenues. Danby, an old royalist and Anglican, proposed that all office-holders, including members of parliament, should be required to take an oath declaring resistance to the king unlawful and seeking no alteration of the government in church and state.

The effect of such a measure would be to stifle all political criticism, since such criticism could be interpreted as violation of a sacred oath. Anthony Ashley Cooper, the earl of Shaftesbury, a former favourite of King Charles, is spearheading opposition to the measure. He is manoeuvring to bring about a prorogation of parliament before the measure can come before the Commons (→1676).

Thomas Osborne, the earl of Danby.

Anti-Catholic fears aroused by role of the royal confessor

London, November
The sensational story of a French priest who converted to Protestantism and fled to London has put the confessor of the Roman Catholic duchess of York in an unfavourable light. The priest, de Luzancy, wrote to two Protestant parliamentarians, Lord Holles and Lord Russell, appealing for protection because, he said, the Jesuit St Germain, the duchess's confessor, was threatening to have him kidnapped and then taken to France.

The affair has been raised in the House of Commons, with members denouncing the scandal, as they see it, of "popish" machinations being given royal protection. St Germain has now fled to Paris, and the story of de Luzancy's career in the Catholic Church reveals him as a distinctly unsavoury character. But St Germain, writing to Edward Coleman, the duchess's secretary, has not denied threatening de Luzancy.

Anti-Catholic feeling has been running high, with attempts being made to deport priests and to prevent Mass from being celebrated anywhere in the realm except in foreign embassies and royal chapels. Last May the Commons passed another bill "to prevent the growth of popery", but it has yet to be approved by the Lords.

Book puts Britain's major roads on the map

London
John Ogilby, a cartographer, has published a book containing strip maps of every major road in England, Scotland and Wales. There are also details of the geographical features on the routes, the distance in miles from one town or village to the next, and – most important of all – the exact definition of the English mile. For the first time ever a stranger can travel from Land's End to John o' Groats without need of a guide. Ogilby is calling this remarkable new book *English Itinerary: A Book of Roads*.

Talking violins and London pollution inspire diarist's writings

London, December
A fondness for amateur music-making is the latest trend to catch the ear of the diarist John Evelyn, a noted observer of the fashions and preoccupations of London society. Evelyn records a recent musical evening at which a violinist made his instrument "speak like the voice of man". On another occasion he went with his friend Samuel Pepys to hear an Italian eunuch, deemed the best in Europe, but found his singing "effeminate and childish".

Another of Evelyn's current concerns is the smoke that poisons London's air – "that hellish and dismal cloud of seacoal perpetually overhead". His pamphlet *Fumifugium* offers remedies for it (→1690).

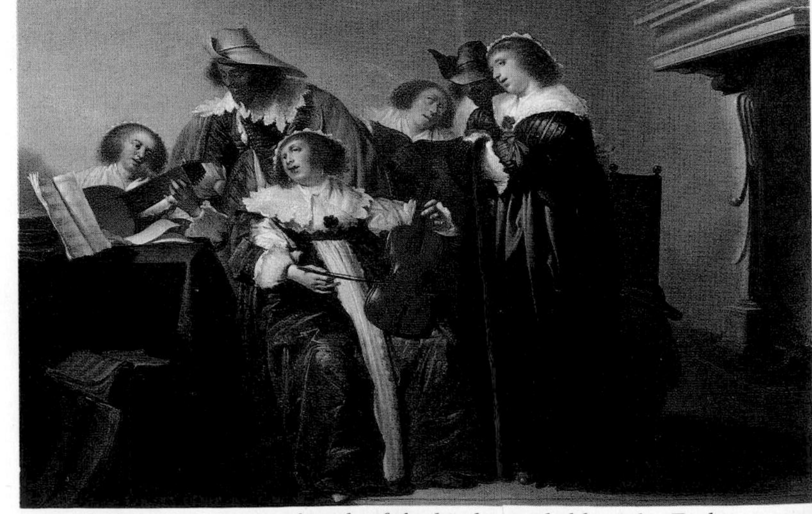
A musical evening among friends of the kind attended by John Evelyn.

Coffee and gossip face a clampdown

London, 29 December
An official proclamation has been issued ordering the closing down of all coffee houses in London. But it is unlikely to be put into effect, since it is known that they have their uses for the government. During the Dutch wars the diarist Samuel Pepys was asked to visit them and put about stories of Dutch ill-treatment of English seamen. Generally, however, coffee houses are seen by officialdom as meeting-places for political malcontents. In some houses, customers who purchase a dish of coffee for a penny are provided with newsletters containing the latest political gossip and commentaries.

Royal Observatory begun at Greenwich

Greenwich: appliance of science.

Greenwich, London, 10 August
At precisely 3.14pm today John Flamsteed laid the foundation stone for the Royal Observatory ordered by Charles II to be "built upon the highest ground". The building has been designed by Sir Christopher Wren, himself a professor of astronomy although better known as the architect who is rebuilding much of London after the great fire [*see report right*]. Flamsteed, as the first astronomer royal, will compile a catalogue of the stars and establish lines of longitude and latitude on the earth's surface.

New plan for London is rejected, but the city benefits from wider streets and safer buildings, stone replacing wood after the fire

King Charles has made his Whitehall Palace (l) the subject of major extensions and refurbishments.

London
A new, improved City of London has risen from the 160 hectares (400 acres) destroyed in the great fire of 1666. Nothing could symbolize this better than the start of construction work on the new St Paul's Cathedral, directed by Sir Christopher Wren, in June this year. Meanwhile, King Charles II has been making substantial additions and alterations to his Whitehall Palace.

Several architects and planners, including Wren, produced ambitious schemes to build a new city from scratch; but lack of money, time and, above all, enthusiasm for a total rebuilding has meant that very little change has been made to the old shape. But new building regulations designed to prevent another tragic fire have made a big difference to the city's appearance. The newly built houses are in brick and stone, rather than wood; the new streets are of three different widths, and houses are of four, three or two storeys according to the street width.

The city has spent £75,000 on widening streets and straightening frontages to allow coaches through. Drainage pipes have replaced the old water spouts, the choked Fleet river has now been dredged, and the Guildhall and Royal Exchange have both been rebuilt. About 50 new churches are planned (→ 1681).

The rebuilt Guildhall, the headquarters of the city's administration.

One of Wren's many designs for a cathedral to replace the old St Paul's.

1676 - 1677

England, February 1676. In return for financial subsidies, King Charles II agrees secretly to continue his alliance with France (→28/5/77).

Edinburgh, March 1676. Parliament imposes fines on anyone not attending Church of Scotland services (→21/1/78).

London, 18 August 1676. Mary of Modena, the Catholic wife of James, the duke of York and brother of King Charles, gives birth to a second daughter, Isabella. Her first died as a baby (→10/6/88).

Westminster, 24 October 1676. Christopher Gibbons, the celebrated organist of Westminster, the chapel royal and Winchester, dies.

New England, 1676. King Charles gives his support to the colonies in America in their struggle against the native Indians (→10/1677).

London, 1676. The results of a recent census on religion by Sir Henry Compton, the bishop of London, show that the majority of the population conform to the established church (→1677).

London, 1676. Richard Wiseman, the royal surgeon, publishes *Severall Chirurgicall Treatises*, a work describing surgical operations including amputations and trepanning.

Westminster, 28 May 1677. King Charles II prorogues parliament on its insistence that he abandon his alliance with France (→17/5/78).

London, July 1677. George Villiers, the duke of Buckingham, who was arrested earlier this year, is released from prison.

Ireland, 24 August 1677. James Butler, the duke of Ormond, is sworn in as lord lieutenant (→20/3).

England, October 1677. In an attempt to improve Anglo-Dutch relations, Charles II agrees to the marriage of Mary, the duke of York's eldest daughter, to Prince William III of Orange (→4/11).

Strathclyde, October 1677. Landowners refuse to enforce the laws against covenanters.

London, 9 November 1677. Gilbert Sheldon, the archbishop of Canterbury, dies; he is succeeded by the dean of St Paul's, William Sancroft (→2/1690).

Edinburgh, 1677. The first coffee house is opened.

City radical thrown into jail for asking for new parliament

London, June 1676

Francis Jenks, a linen-draper and city councillor for the Cornhill district, has clashed with King Charles II and been thrown into prison for making a bold and unusual speech about the right of representation. He is refusing to petition the crown for his release following his speech at a meeting of London's Common Hall to elect new sheriffs.

Jenks identified various grievances and played on his audience's fears about French competition, linking these with doubts about the security of Protestantism. But then he went further and suggested that the lord mayor call a meeting so that the corporation of London might petition the crown for a new parliament. Jenks's audacity, and the support he got from other liverymen, led to his being summoned to appear before the king. After he declined to confirm suspicions that he was backed by some members of parliament, he was imprisoned.

The episode reflects the radical character of political opposition in the City of London. By his stand Jenks has promoted the cause of petitioning, as well as highlighting both the rights of the individual and the London corporation's popular authority.

Natural history of Oxfordshire written

Oxford, 1677

An unusual natural history book, complete with maps and coloured plates and dedicated to Charles II, has been published here. Written by Robert Plot, an Oxford scholar and antiquary, it is called *The Natural History of Oxfordshire: Being an Essay towards the Natural History of England*.

Plot is already being hailed as a leading authority on rare plants. He describes his new book as dealing with "animals, plants and the universal furniture of the world; secondly, nature's extravagancies and defects; and as she is restrained, forced, fashioned, or determined by artificial operations".

Parliament hit by crisis

Private indiscretion and public dissent led Buckingham to the cells.

The earl of Shaftesbury: also jailed.

London, February 1677

Several leading peers and members of parliament have been sent to the Tower for daring to challenge the decision to reassemble parliament after its 15 months of prorogation. Among the peers were Shaftesbury, Buckingham and Salisbury. They were all committed by the Lords and received little sympathy from the Commons.

The members' "crime" was to insist that parliament had in fact been dissolved, because of a statute of Edward III declaring that a prorogation of more than a year was illegal. This was not accepted by their fellows, and they were taken away to languish in the Tower.

At the centre of the controversy is Thomas, the earl of Danby, the king's treasurer and chief adviser, who has been trying to develop the art of parliamentary management. He is also doing his best to persuade Charles that it is in his interest to adopt policies appealing to the prejudices of Anglican members.

Despite his efforts Danby has failed to overcome the Commons' deep suspicions of the king's pro-French and Catholic leanings. They have pointed to agreements reached with France whereby King Louis XIV is paying Charles a subsidy of £112,000. Danby has been unable to get the king to drop Louis and deal with the Dutch (→15/5/79).

In 1676 the court painter Peter Lely painted this nude of Nell Gwynn, a mistress of Charles II. Born at Hereford of humble parentage, Nell became an actress at Drury Lane theatre but retired in 1669, aged 19.

Census results are blow to religious bills

English Protestant bishops make their demands known to King Charles.

Westminster, 1677
Both houses of parliament have rejected anti-Catholic bills designed to secure Protestantism's leading position in English life. The introduction of the bills follows the results of last year's national census on religious affiliation.

The census demonstrated that nonconformists made up less than 5 per cent of the population, and Catholics constituted less than 1 per cent. The census also confirmed that the "profane and unstable", the irreligious and apathetic, were a growing party in the nation and a long-term threat to the Church of England. In addition it showed that many churchgoers did not even receive the sacrament.

The government bill put forward in the House of Commons called for more effective conviction as well as prosecution of "popish recusants". In the House of Lords another bill was introduced with the purpose of securing Protestantism in the event of the accession of a Catholic monarch. It provided for the children of such a monarch to be brought up as Protestants. The bills were given short shrift.

William of Orange weds king's niece

London, 4 November 1677
In a ceremony which is seen to have strengthened his claim to the English throne, a Dutch prince, William of Orange, today married Mary, a niece of Charles II. Mary, aged 15, wept before and during the ceremony. William is 27, 10cm (4 inches) shorter than she is, slightly hunched and humourless. This is a political marriage as it puts the seal on Anglo-Dutch rapprochement. But Charles is said to think the arrangement a huge joke (→3/1678).

William: closer to English throne.

Pamphlet spreads anti-Catholic alarm

London, 31 December 1677
The appearance of an anonymous pamphlet, *The Growth of Popery and Arbitrary Government in England*, has spread alarm by suggesting that Rome plans to "change the lawful government of England into an absolute tyranny and convert the Protestant religion into downright popery". It goes on to claim that "the firing of London" in 1666 was part of a Catholic plot. "There are those amongst ourselves that are leading us into a fair way of reconciliation with the pope," it alleges.

Suspected authors include the poet Andrew Marvell, recently involved in a row with Archdeacon Samuel Parker. Parker condemned religious toleration in his *Discourse of Ecclesiastical Politie*, and then Marvell lampooned the churchman in a satire, *The Rehearsal Transpos'd*, which was based on the duke of Buckingham's well-known farce *The Rehearsal*, performed in 1672. Parker replied, calling him "Rat-Divine – thou hast not the wit and learning of a mouse!", but Marvell argued that King Charles merited more trust than an unscrupulous, scaremongering churchman seeking preferment (→1678).

Heretics no longer face death by fire

London, 1677
The penalty for heresy in England has been reduced from death by public burning to excommunication. Parliament has repealed the act of 1401 known as *De heretico comburendo* [*On the burning of heretics*] as well as all "punishment by death in pursuance of any ecclesiastical censures".

The measure was introduced to combat the Lollards [*see report on page 339*]. Suspected heretics were arrested and tried by the diocesan courts and, if found guilty, were handed over to the local sheriff or mayor for burning. But no heretic appears to have been put to death by burning in England since the time of Shakespeare. Since the civil war a reputation as a troublemaker in religious matters has no longer endangered a man's life or freedom.

Bawdy comedies and lively sex farces pack reborn London theatre

London, 1677
Since the theatres here reopened in November 1666, having been shut because of the plague, comedy has been all the rage. John Dryden has been a leader of the trend, producing a comedy of manners, *Marriage a la Mode*, in 1673. He says in his *Essay of Dramatick Poesie*: "Gentlemen will be entertained with the follies of each other."

Sir George Etherege, an ambassador who also writes plays, exposes French affectations in his play *The Man of Mode* with Sir Fopling Flutter, an "English blockhead" who, like many courtiers, returns from Paris swooning over French fashion, dances and expressions. William Wycherley satirizes the sexual free-for-all of London society in *The Country Wife*, whose leading character's husband vainly attempts to keep her away from all male company. Aphra Behn, a widow who writes prolifically, had a success with the scandalous *The Town Fop* last year and follows it with *The Rover*, a story of cavalier sexual adventurers. But Dryden's verse tragedy *All For Love* is this year's top draw. The two patent theatres at Drury Lane and Dorset Garden are both designed by Christopher Wren (→1678).

A scene from a play by Etherege.

The Dorset Garden theatre.

1678

Strathclyde, 21 January. The government orders in the "highland host", or militia, to stamp out unauthorized prayer meetings (→ 13/5/79).

England, March. An alliance is finally sealed with the Dutch (→ 4/1688).

Westminster, 13 May. Parliament adjourns after voting to disband the army.

North America, 10 July. The colony of New Hampshire is claimed for the English crown (→ 1682).

London, 13 August. King Charles II orders Thomas Osborne, the earl of Danby, to investigate rumours of a plot to take his life (→ 6/9).

London, 6 September. Titus Oates, a Jesuit, is summoned before a magistrate, Sir Edmund Berry Godfrey, to swear to the truth of his information on the "popish plot" to kill the king (→ 28).

Newgate, London, 1 October. Edward Coleman, a former secretary of James, the duke of York, is jailed in connection with the "popish plot" (→ 17).

Dublin, 8 October. Peter Talbot, the Roman Catholic archbishop of Dublin, is arrested (→ 15/11/80).

Ireland, 16 October. The 1673 proclamation for the banishment of Catholic bishops and priests from the country is renewed (→ 27/2/79).

London, 20 October. £500 is offered for information on the murder of Sir Edmund Berry Godfrey (→ 1/11).

London, 1 November. Parliament orders all popish recusants to depart beyond a 10-mile (16-km) radius of the city (→ 12/78).

Westminster, 4 November. Parliament proposes that the duke of York be barred from the court (→ 20).

Westminster, 20 November. The Test Act is given royal assent, with a proviso exempting the duke of York; it excludes all Catholics from public office (→ 3/79).

England. Henry Purcell, the composer, writes music for William Shakespeare's *Timon of Athens* (→ 21/11/95).

England. *All for Love* is published by John Dryden, the poet laureate (→ 11/1681).

England. Andrew Marvell, the poet, satirist and member of parliament, dies.

Suspicion grows about king's intentions

London, 15 July

As parliament breaks up today after a six-month session, suspicions are growing among many members about the nature of King Charles II's relationship with Louis XIV of France [*see report below*] and about the imminent establishment of popery. Events during the session have given grounds for belief that the court is planning a military coup.

Charles has certainly maintained the alliance with France, despite attempts by Thomas Osborne, the earl of Danby – his chief minister – to persuade him not to. Many members have become aware of the king's latest round of talks with Louis, over a further French subsidy which would be in exchange for disbanding the army as well proroguing parliament.

This has intensified the distrust of the Commons for both the court and Danby – whom pamphleteers portray as a devious puppet-master exerting control over a weak king and corrupt officers, peers and members. There were widespread fears that the army being raised supposedly to fight the French – who had seemed to be about to take all of the Spanish Netherlands – would be used instead against parliament. Since the Dutch-French armistice the army has not been disbanded (→ 1/4/81).

Louis XIV: influence distrusted.

Earl of Pembroke is cleared of murder

England, April

Violence is growing in England and the aristocracy seems to be getting away with brutal crimes. A case this month involved Philip Herbert, the earl of Pembroke, who had been found guilty of manslaughter by the court of the lord high steward. A man with a criminal record – in the coffee houses they say that his sword has run through a great many men – Pembroke was freed because as a peer he enjoys certain legal privileges.

There are other cases indicating that legal suits against a peer can rarely be contested successfully by a commoner, at a time when lawless behaviour is widespread among the nobility. Meanwhile, although never as fashionable as on the continent, duelling has become popular in England and especially in London. By contrast duelling remains rare in Scotland, where the government continues to crack down on anyone who even issues a challenge.

Charles signs secret deal with France

London, 17 May

England may or may not be facing a threat from Catholic France, but Charles II is energetically pursuing two entirely contradictory policies – one public, one secret – towards Louis XIV and his government. This has caused a deepening sense of confusion among his subjects. Publicly Charles is threatening to square up to the French. He has secured an alliance with the Dutch, who are struggling to beat off the French and avoid occupation. He persuaded parliament to budget for an army of 30,000 men and a fleet, and an advance force was sent to save Ostend.

At the same time the king today negotiated a secret agreement with Louis, promising the disbanding of the army, neutrality and parliament's prorogation in return for a subsidy. He is apparently not aware that Louis is already subsidizing Charles's most bitter opponents in the Commons, encouraging them to obstruct all royal policies – including French funding (→ 15/7).

Betting and boozing are relaxing hobbies

The lord of the manor entertains his tenants and keeps them happy.

Halifax, West Yorkshire

A series of foot-races, organized by local alehouse-keepers and held near their premises, has been drawing crowds to Halifax drinking spots this year. Such events – a crucial aspect of which is heavy betting – exploit the growing passion for gambling and spectator sports in England and reflect a trend towards the commercialization of leisure. While alehouses remain a vital focus for the community, another important influence on social life since the Restoration has been the growth in paternalism by the ruling classes, which have sought to bring popular gatherings and rituals back within the control of church and manor. To maintain goodwill and ensure the smooth running of their estates, landowners are often willing to support traditional local festivities; some themselves provide entertainment for tenants and their families (→ 1680).

Persistent preacher finishes 'Pilgrim's Progress' in prison

Bunyan: allegorical vision of life.

Bedford
John Bunyan, a tinker's son famed for his preaching in nonconformist communities in Bedfordshire, spent 12 years in Bedford jail for refusing to stop preaching after 1660. Soon after his release in 1672 under the "Declaration of Indulgence" he was arrested under the Conventicle Act and jailed again for six months. It was then that he wrote the first part of *The Pilgrim's Progress*, just published and widely read for the simple dignity of its prose.

Bunyan's allegory is a vision of life as a journey of pilgrimage to the River of Death and the Heavenly City which lies beyond it. On his way Christian meets many obstacles: the Slough of Despond, the Valley of Humiliation, and the ridicule he receives from the citizens of Vanity Fair and Doubting Castle, where he meets Giant Despair. His companions include Mr Worldly Wiseman, Mr Greatheart and Mr Valiant-For-Truth, for whom "all the trumpets sounded on the other side". Bunyan continues to preach unaffected by his fame. Congratulated by friends on his "sweet sermon" one day, he said: "Aye, the devil told me of it before I was out of the pulpit." (→ 1682).

Titus Oates warns of a 'popish plot'

Allegations provoke a widespread panic

London, 28 September
The country is in the grip of anti-Catholic hysteria following the discovery of an alleged "popish plot" involving the murder of Charles II, the burning of London, the massacre of Protestants and the raising of a Catholic army. Details of the plot were "revealed" today before the privy council by the informers Titus Oates and Israel Tonge.

Oates is a disgraced clergyman who lived on Jesuit charity while feigning conversion. Tonge can be described as a crazy visionary. Also involved in the "plot" are several men with bogus military titles, and dissatisfied and discarded servants of Catholic nobles. But their stories have the country buzzing with fear.

Charles is sceptical about the so-called revelations because Oates has been shown to be a liar. He is treating the plot as no more than a threat against his life and dismissing the wider implications. But as well as denouncing priests who had befriended him, Oates has named as the main conspirator one Edward Coleman, a former secretary to James, the duke of York, and well known at Westminster as a Catholic lobbyist. Oates also swore his information before Sir Edmund Berry Godfrey, a magistrate who has since disappeared (→ 1/10).

Oates discloses the plot to Charles.

Assassins shown pursuing Godfrey.

Murdered judge is discovered in a ditch

London, 17 October
The body of Sir Edmund Berry Godfrey, the missing Westminster magistrate and Charing Cross coal-merchant, was found in a ditch on Primrose Hill, north of London, today. The dead man had a sword through him, and his neck had been broken. The discovery has sparked off panic and fanned anti-Catholic prejudice. He is being mourned as the first victim of the papists.

Godfrey disappeared three weeks ago after taking evidence about the "popish plot" from Titus Oates, one of the principal informants. Oates showed Godfrey documents which Oates claimed proved that there was a plot to murder King Charles II and put James, the Catholic duke of York, on the throne.

The coffee houses have throbbed with speculation about Godfrey's disappearance because it was widely thought that he had come to possess some explosive information. There are rumours of an imminent French invasion which have led to the positioning of cannons around Whitehall Palace (→ 20).

Reprisals are taken against Catholics in wake of 'revelations'

Edward Coleman is drawn through the streets on his way to execution.

London, December
The heads of those said to have been involved in the now notorious "popish plot" are beginning to fall. The first man to be executed for allegedly plotting the murder of King Charles II was Edward Coleman [*see report above left*]. Now three Jesuits incriminated by Titus Oates have been sentenced to death, and five Catholic peers who have been sent to the Tower are about to be impeached. As a result of the plot a score of Catholic peers have been deprived of their seats in the House of Lords and the king is under pressure to stop Catholics sitting in either house (→ 29/12/80).

1679 - 1680

Ireland, 27 February 1679. Michael Boyle, the Protestant archbishop of Dublin, becomes archbishop of Armagh (→6/12).

Westminster, 26 March 1679. Laurence Hyde, the son of the late earl of Clarendon, joins the treasury (→1/4/81).

London, March 1679. King Charles II sends his brother James, the duke of York, into exile (→21/4).

London, 10 April 1679. Thomas Osborne, the earl of Danby, is arrested.

Westminster, 21 April 1679. Charles II's appointment of the earl of Shaftesbury as president of his privy council appeases the "Whigs", who hope to exclude the duke of York from the succession (→27).

Westminster, 4 May 1679. Parliament calls for impeachment of the duke of York (→27).

Strathclyde, 29 May 1679. The covenanters publish the Rutherglen Declaration; it denounces the episcopal church, the royal supremacy and the abandonment of the covenant (→22/7).

Scotland, 29 June 1679. A third "indulgence" is offered to dissenting clergy to reduce the growing religious tensions (→22/7/80).

London, August 1679. The king's illness prompts the recall from exile of the duke of York (→6/1680).

Ireland, 6 December 1679. The Roman Catholic primate, Archbishop Oliver Plunkett, is arrested for allegedly plotting against the crown (→30/10/80).

Middlesex, June 1680. The earl of Shaftesbury makes moves to try the duke of York as a recusant (→16/11).

London, 30 October 1680. Archbishop Plunkett, whose trial in July at Dundalk ended without indictment, is sent to Newgate prison (→3/5/81).

Dublin, 15 November 1680. Peter Talbot, the Roman Catholic archbishop, dies a prisoner in the castle.

Westminster, 16 November 1680. George Saville, the earl of Halifax, proposes that the duke of York should be exiled again (→21/3/81).

London, 29 December 1680. William Howard, the earl of Stafford, who was imprisoned after the "popish plot", is executed (→5/1685).

Catholic duke of York targeted for attack

London, 27 April 1679

Accusations that the duke of York had encouraged the "popish plot", as outlined by Titus Oates, have brought grave problems not only for James and his brother King Charles II personally but also for the succession. Parliament, unwilling to have James as Charles's successor because of his clearly pro-Catholic position, favours James's daughter Mary.

Parliament fears that the plotters could be moving towards an absolutist monarchy which, if the monarch happened to be James, might attempt to impose Catholicism on the nation. But there is another factor, namely that Lord Shaftesbury, who has already clashed with the king [*see report on page 602*], believes that he can now bully Charles into agreeing that his brother can be excluded from the throne.

Shaftesbury has made the exclusion of the duke of York from the succession the main plank of his policy of opposition to the court party, although this spring's election has somewhat altered the character of the Commons, which could make for slow progress. However, the attack on the duke has at least obliged the king to make a stand and demonstrate his willingness to restrain the powers of any papist successor (→4/5).

James: dancing at the French court.

Bid to stop Catholic accession is blocked

Westminster, 27 May 1679

King Charles II has killed off the Exclusion Bill that would have prevented his Roman Catholic brother James, the duke of York, from ever succeeding to the throne. The basis of the bill is that James has so antagonized the fiercely Protestant people that they are not prepared to be ruled by him. This may be true, but when the bill looked certain to be passed by the Commons, Charles prorogued parliament, effectively killing it off.

In reality the king had little choice, because while he is aware of the widespread ill feeling against his brother, he can hardly let the Commons choose his successor. The members wanted Mary – the duke's Protestant daughter – but to allow them to have their way would have reduced the monarchy to an elective position and removed the right of kings to pass the throne to either their children or named successors (→8/1679).

Mock processions of the pope helped to stoke up anti-Catholic sentiment.

English traveller throws light on Ireland

Ireland, 1680

The English antiquarian Thomas Dineley has recorded his recent tour of Ireland in a well-illustrated journal which provides valuable insights into the architecture and social life of the country.

He travelled mainly in the south, drawing spirited sketches of towns, castles and houses, and he paid particular attention to Limerick and Youghal, now a thriving centre for trade because of its sheltered harbour. He found Waterford and Carlow to be prosperous towns and thought that Kilkenny was the most delightful town of all.

Dineley's sketches of country houses are especially interesting. Unlike England, which has recently seen the building of many grand stately homes, the fortified house is still a common sight here – the witness to continuing troubles.

The antiquarian is upset by the deterioration of the Irish language, which is now incomprehensible to many, but he notes approvingly that English is spoken better here than in most places in England.

'Whigs' in political battle with 'Tories'

England, 1679

New names for old faces can now be heard mentioned in the houses of parliament with the advent of tags for adherents of different political philosophies. "Whigs" and "Tories" – both terms of abuse – denote government supporters and opponents. Broadly, the Tories form the court party; they back the established church and the monarchy, and their instincts are conservative. The Whigs are broadly anti-government and against the Roman Catholic duke of York.

The word "Tory" was originally used to describe a particularly unpleasant type of Irish robber. A "Whig", on the other hand, is a Scottish outlaw, covenanter and sanctimonious prig.

Political commentators go further. "A Tory is a creature with a large forehead, prodigious mouth and no brains," says one pamphleteer. A Whig "has principles like chaos" and "prays for the king with more reservations than an honest man," says another.

Scots archbishop killed

Fife, 13 May 1679
Trouble in Scotland has culminated in the murder of Archbishop James Sharp as he travelled home to St Andrews with his daughter. He was crossing Magus Moor, only a few miles from his destination, when his coach was fired upon and stopped by a party of armed men. The archbishop, who had already been grazed by a bullet, was pulled from his seat and slashed to death by nine men armed with swords.

All the killers appear to be local men. More to the point, they are all believed to be covenanters, the extreme defenders of Scottish Presbyterianism. Sharp, a former covenanter himself, had been a marked man since 1661, when he was entrusted with presenting the Presbyterian position to King Charles II but changed sides and accepted the archbishopric instead. The move earned him the undying contempt of his former colleagues.

Last year James Mitchell was executed in Edinburgh for an assassination attempt on the archbishop ten years earlier, in 1668. But Mitchell had been in prison since 1674, and the evidence against him was dubious. The part played by the archbishop in Mitchell's execution, and his approval of highland troops being brought in to keep peace in the lowlands, had made him a deeply hated man (→29).

Archbishop Sharp was murdered.

Duke of Monmouth routs rebellious Scots

Glasgow, 22 July 1679
The duke of Monmouth decisively defeated a rebel covenanting army of about 4,000 today at Bothwell Brig, a few kilometres from Glasgow. The rebels had been in control of the city since 3 June, two days after their defeat of government troops under John Graham of Claverhouse at Drumclog in Ayrshire. Monmouth, the illegitimate son of King Charles II, brought up a force of 10,000 against 4,000 ill-armed and ill-organized covenanters, who were already demoralized by their failure to attract support. The fight around the bridge was short and casualties were light, but pursuing cavalry killed 400 covenanters as they fled. However, the duke has won great popularity by sparing most of the rest (→22/7/80).

Claverhouse is defeated by the covenanters at Drumclog, in Ayrshire.

Satirical libertine is victim of his excess

Woodstock, Oxon, 26 July 1680
John Wilmot, the earl of Rochester, satirist, love poet and ranger of Woodstock Park, has died here at the age of 33 worn out by debauchery. He was put in the Tower for making off with a young heiress and banished from court for calling the king "a merry monarch, scandalous and poor". His quatrain on Charles II was celebrated:

We have a pritty witty king
Whose word no man relies on;
He never says a foolish thing
Nor ever does a wise one.

This was written on the door of the king's bedchamber, and Charles replied: "True, for my words are my own. My deeds are my ministers'."

The debauchee: "worn out at 33".

Zealous covenanter dies in a skirmish

Strathclyde, 22 July 1680
An extremist covenanter leader, Richard Cameron, was killed today during a skirmish with royal troops at Aird's Moss, near Kilmarnock. Last month Cameron, a powerful preacher who recently returned from exile in the United Provinces, and 20 other radicals drew up the "Sanquhar Declaration". In this document they claimed to represent the true covenanted Presbyterian church, disclaimed Charles II as the king who had broken the covenant and declared war on him.

King's illegitimate son wins popularity

Monmouth: the Protestant duke.

England, autumn 1680
The duke of Monmouth's popularity as a potential heir to the throne of Charles II has been greatly enhanced by a series of semi-royal progresses which he has undertaken to show himself around the country. The "Protestant duke," as he is known, is greatly preferred by the common people to the rightful heir, Charles's brother James, the Roman Catholic duke of York.

Monmouth, who is Charles's illegitimate son by Lucy Walter, is handsome and popular. But he is neither a strong character nor particularly clever. These qualities recommend him to certain politicians who want a candidate for the throne whom they can manipulate for their own ends (→21/3/81).

Grub Street is home of new Farting Club

London, 1680
With the restoration of the monarchy under Charles II, there has been much greater tolerance in society. This has been demonstrated in one way by the church being reluctant to repress heretical ideas. On a social level a good deal of bawdy behaviour is now tolerated in public, a typical example of which is the Farting Club, founded in Grub Street. Its members meet at a public house in Cripplegate and compete with each other to produce the loudest and longest farts.

1681

Westminster, 4 January. The Lords claim that there was a Catholic plot in Ireland to massacre the English.

Westminster, 18 January. The 1671 Navigation Act expires, allowing direct trade from the colonies to Ireland to resume.

Edinburgh, 27 January. To encourage manufacturing in Scotland, the privy council sets up a committee of trade.

London, 4 March. William Penn, a Quaker, acquires a royal grant in honour of his father, Admiral Penn, to buy a tract of land in North America (→ 13/5/83).

Oxford, 21 March. The "Whigs" try to exclude James, the duke of York, from the succession in favour of James, the duke of Monmouth, Charles II's illegitimate Protestant son (→ 28).

London, March. Robert Murray, a former government clerk, sets up a penny-postage system in the city.

Ulster, 25 April. Redmond O'Hanlon, a leading *toraidhe* [tory], or bandit, in Armagh, dies of exhaustion.

London, 3 May. Oliver Plunkett, the Roman Catholic archbishop of Armagh, stands trial for high treason (→ 1/7).

London, 2 July. The earl of Shaftesbury is arrested for treason (→ 24/11).

Edinburgh, 13 August. Parliament passes an act of succession ensuring that James, the duke of York, will succeed his brother, Charles (→ 8/3/85).

Edinburgh, 2 November. Sir Robert Sibbald founds the Royal College of Physicians.

Scotland. James Dalrymple of Stair, the lord president of the court of session, publishes *The Institutions of the Laws of Scotland*.

England. Thomas Burnett, a theologian, causes a stir with the publication of *Sacred History of the Earth*, in which he expresses ideas on the evolution of man.

London. A hospital for wounded soldiers is founded in Chelsea.

England. Aphra Behn, the writer, publishes part two of *The Rover*, a satirical play loosely based on the late earl of Rochester.

London. Sir Christopher Wren is elected president of the Royal Society (→ 1711).

Charles makes bid for lasting power

Oxford, 28 March

To the utter confusion of the "Whig" majority, King Charles II has dissolved parliament, quashing yet again any prospect of an act that would exclude Catholics from the succession. Charles's well-planned move is the latest manoeuvre in a continuing battle for lasting political power. This time the pendulum may have swung the king's way. The elections of last month saw an unprecedented polarization between the Whigs, inclined to puritanism, and the "Tory" landed gentry. The Whigs lost a handful of seats, but they also lost the initiative when Charles summoned parliament to Oxford, away from their radical supporters. He then promised to consider any arrangement that might safeguard the Church of England while preserving the proper order of royal succession. With the Whigs intransigent, fears are growing of another civil war.

But now the king has offered to establish a regency under which James would be king in name only, the government safe in the Protestant hands of James's daughter Mary and her husband William of Orange. This, too, has been rejected, making the Whigs, in the public's eyes, equally responsible for the dissolution (→ 13/8).

Parliament was dissolved against a ferment of anti-Catholic feeling generated by the alleged "popish plot".

Clandestine treaty sealed with France

London, 1 April

Charles II of England and Louis XIV of France have concluded a secret peace treaty, but nothing is written down. Final details were negotiated in the queen's bedroom in the presence of the French ambassador. Charles has assured Louis that if war develops over French encroachments into the Spanish Netherlands, England will not join the Spanish war effort, regardless of any Anglo-Spanish treaty commitments. In return, Louis has promised £385,000 over three years.

The secret treaty is inextricable from Charles's domestic difficulties with the Whigs, who back alliance with the Protestant Dutch. Charles has little time for his nephew, Prince William, and going to war on his behalf is the last thing that he wishes to do when he has just dissolved parliament and must rely on the tight financial regime imposed on him by the first lord of the treasury, Laurence Hyde.

King Charles has privately promised Louis that he will not allow parliament to meet in case members should raise the matter. But he has no intention of recalling it anyway.

Astrologer who published predictions dies

Hersham, Surrey

William Lilly, one of the leading astrologers in Britain, has died at the age of 79. His case-books, which show that he handled nearly 2,000 cases a year, testify to the remarkable popularity of astrology.

Most of Lilly's clients were rich people who consulted him in person or via a messenger. From 1644 until his death he published an annual volume of his predictions entitled *Merlinus Anglicus, Junior*. Born at Diseworth, in Leicestershire, of yeoman stock, Lilly got his first job as a servant in a rich man's house. When his master died Lilly married his widow, learnt astrology and began to make money. He showed similar astuteness in attaching himself to the winning side in the civil war and was subsequently rewarded with a pension. When the monarchy was restored, however, Lilly was briefly imprisoned. He was jailed again in 1666, following accusations that he knew the cause of the great fire of London.

Finding meaning in the heavens: astrologers study a new star in 1660.

Poet mocks 'Whigs' in satirical verse

John Dryden: the poet laureate.

London, November
John Dryden, made the first "poet laureate" in 1668, has paid his debt to his royal patron by writing a satiric poem at the expense of the "Whigs", who support the succession of the duke of Monmouth and the exclusion of James, Charles II's Catholic brother. The poem is called *Absalom and Achitophel*, but the leading characters represent Monmouth and the earl of Shaftesbury ("great wits are sure to madness near allied") and others, like Buckingham: "Stiff in opinions, always in the wrong,/Was everything by starts and nothing long:/But in the course of one revolving moon,/was chemist, fiddler, statesman, and buffoon." (→ 1699).

Oxford expels Locke

Oxford, August
The "Tory" antagonism towards Shaftesbury has caught up with his friend, the philosopher John Locke, who has been expelled by Oxford University. Locke, who has been close to Shaftesbury since he became his personal physician in 1667, is working on a philosophical treatise which not only challenges the divine right of kings but also sets out the grounds for rebellion against an arbitrary monarch. The Christ Church college librarian had been spying on him on the government's behalf (→ 1690).

Armagh bishop executed for treason

London, 1 July
Oliver Plunkett, the Roman Catholic archbishop of Armagh, has been executed at Tyburn for allegedly conspiring to bring a French army to Ireland to defeat the English. He has been the victim of a supposed "popish plot", rumours of which first surfaced in England, where anti-Catholicism has been inspired by reports of atrocities inflicted by the Irish on the English during the recent rebellion.

James Butler, the duke of Ormond and lord lieutenant, has done his best to persuade Protestants that they have little to fear from their Catholic neighbours. But the earl of Shaftesbury persisted in his belief that Ireland was in grave danger. Under such pressure Ormond did his best. He put the army on alert and ordered all Catholics to hand over their arms. He was criticized for not going further, but he resolutely refused to impose harsher measures, such as arresting all dispossessed Catholic landowners, for fear that they might indeed foment rebellion.

His efforts could not, however, prevent Archbishop Plunkett from being arrested in May last year or his transferral to London to stand trial on a trumped-up charge. Although he was aware of the man's innocence, King Charles II did nothing to save him.

Plunkett: victim of a "popish plot".

Ex-lord chancellor on trial for treason

Middlesex, 24 November
A jury has acquitted the earl of Shaftesbury, the former lord chancellor, of treason. In spite of several months of preparation, Charles II's "Tory" allies never succeeded in constructing a strong enough case to convince a jury elected by the "Whig" sheriffs of Middlesex. It is unlikely that Shaftesbury will now be able to resurrect his political career, but the dismissal of the case against him shows the limits of the king's power.

Shaftesbury's prosecution was part of a concerted effort against the Whigs, which led to Stephen College, one of their leading propagandists, being tried at Oxford and executed in August. But Shaftesbury's alleged crimes were committed in Middlesex, where he had to be tried. The indictment said that Shaftesbury had sought the use of force if the king refused to pass the Exclusion Bill. Prosecution witnesses included the same Irishmen whom Shaftesbury had induced to perjure themselves in the course of setting up the "popish plot". The judge would not allow the jury to know whether any of these witnesses was indicted. The duke of Ormond said that the "MacShams", as they were known, had left Ireland "with bad English and worse clothes" and had "returned well-bred gentlemen" (→ 9/1682).

Scots earl flees to escape death sentence

Argyll, condemned for refusing to recognize James as heir, with his wife.

Lothian, 31 December
The earl of Argyll has escaped from jail and fled to the Dutch United Provinces. He was condemned to death by a Scots court for refusing to take the Test Oath, recognizing James, King Charles II's brother, as heir to the throne of Scotland.

Furious, James sent his great ally Charles, the earl of Middleton, to argue for the confiscation of the earl's estates. But Halifax and Lauderdale opposed such draconian action, and the king, who turned a blind eye while Argyll escaped from London, has chosen a compromise. The death sentence remains, and Argyll's jurisdictions will be shared among highland chiefs, but his son will inherit the Campbell estate. When Charles appointed James as commissioner to the Scottish parliament, most Scottish nobles responded loyally and voted the army funds that he wanted. But the Test Act caused problems.

James Dalrymple of Stair, the lord president of the council, fled abroad rather than take the oath, and four other nobles hesitated for several months before signing. The act requires adherence to the 1560 Protestant confession of faith and acknowledgement of the supreme spiritual and temporal authority of the king. Eighty ministers may be obliged to forfeit their churches for refusing to sign (→ 18/6/85).

1682 - 1684

Scotland, August 1682. The crown issues stricter laws to combat the increase in cattle-raiding and lawlessness in the highlands.

London, November 1682. The earl of Shaftesbury flees into exile following the abandonment of a planned revolt by James, the duke of Monmouth (→ 2/1/83).

Edinburgh, 1682. Sir George Mackenzie of Rosehaugh founds the Advocates' Library.

England, 1682. John Bunyan publishes *The Holy War* (→ 31/8/87).

United Provinces, 21 January 1683. The earl of Shaftesbury dies.

North America, 13 May 1683. William Penn, the Quaker, writes an account of his successful founding of a community (→ 1687).

London, 21 July 1683. William, Lord Russell, is beheaded for his involvement in the Rye House plot (→ 7/12).

London, 28 July 1683. Princess Anne, the younger daughter of James, the duke of York, marries the Protestant Prince George of Denmark (→ 19/2/92).

Oxford, 17 September 1683. An earthquake shakes the city.

England, 21 November 1683. The duke of Monmouth flees into exile after being implicated in the Rye House plot (→ 11/6/85).

London, 7 December 1683. Algernon Sidney is executed for his part in the Rye House plot (→ 6/2/84).

London, 25 December 1683. The river Thames freezes over (→ 4/2).

Dublin, 1683. William Molyneux founds the Dublin Philosophical Society, which aims to advance studies in the arts and the sciences (→ 4/98).

London, 6 February 1684. John Hampden goes on trial for his part in the Rye House plot.

Scotland, June 1684. George Gordon, the earl of Aberdeen, is ousted as lord chancellor by James Drummond, the earl of Perth, whose brother, John, is appointed secretary of state.

Edinburgh, 1684. A Dutch painter, Jacob de Wet, is commissioned to paint over a hundred portraits of King Charles II's ancestors, to be displayed in Holyrood Palace.

Shaftesbury urges Monmouth to rebel

Cheshire, September 1682
James, the duke of Monmouth and bastard son of King Charles II, is playing a dangerous game. He has just completed a tour of north-western England which gathered in large crowds of enthusiastic supporters. The earl of Shaftesbury, the former lord chancellor turned arch-plotter, has taken this as evidence of popular support for a full-scale revolt against King Charles. Monmouth and top "Whigs" like Russell and Essex, do not seem so convinced.

Shaftesbury argued Monmouth's case in 1670 when members of parliament first addressed the thorny problem of the succession, and ever since there has been a strong pro-Monmouth lobby amongst not only the leading Whigs but also all who fear a return to Roman Catholicism. The young duke won praise for his defeat of the Scots covenanters at Bothwell Brig in 1679 and for his clemency with prisoners against the king's wishes [*see page 607*].

That clash prefaced more serious conflicts at court. When Monmouth congratulated Shaftesbury on his acquittal last year, Charles stripped him of his offices. When the duke of York returned to court Monmouth vowed never to submit to him, prompting his father not only to forbid other courtiers to speak to him but also to remind him of his illegitimacy (→ 11/1682).

Maitland, former Scots minister, dies

Maitland: a long serving minister.

Kent, 20 August 1682
King Charles II has lost his longest serving minister. John Maitland, the duke of Lauderdale, has died at Tunbridge Wells, two years after being incapacitated by a stroke. He was appointed Scottish secretary in 1660, after which his rule became gradually more repressive. A clever but coarse man, Lauderdale was an unusual combination of royalist and Presbyterian. Having negotiated the "engagement" with Charles I in 1647, he was imprisoned from 1651 to 1660. After the Pentland rising of 1666 he persuaded the king to conciliate Scots dissenters. When two "indulgences" failed, however, he used the iron fist.

Crown controls all civic appointments

London, 18 June 1683
The City of London's municipal independence has disappeared with the removal of its charter. From now on the king's approval will be required for the appointment of lord mayors, sheriffs and all major office holders. This is the culmination of a major judicial inquiry begun in December 1681. It is also a watershed in the government's systematic campaign to use the courts to remove all potential obstacles to royal power. Other boroughs are now offering to surrender their charters before they are forfeited.

For months, Charles II and the privy council have been calling for courts to punish dissenters, and responsive judges have been rewarded. Gradually, local autonomy is being eroded. Last year, where charters allowed, the government refused to accept the appointment of "Whig" officials, and courts began to amend charters. The king was granted a series of new rights: first to approve aldermen, then to remove them, then to remove stewards, clerks or magistrates. This year whole charters have been disappearing. The earl of Bath, for instance, is eliminating opposition and winning favour by securing the wholesale surrender of charters in Devon and Cornwall.

The lord mayor and aldermen.

Frenchman puts pressure on in the kitchen

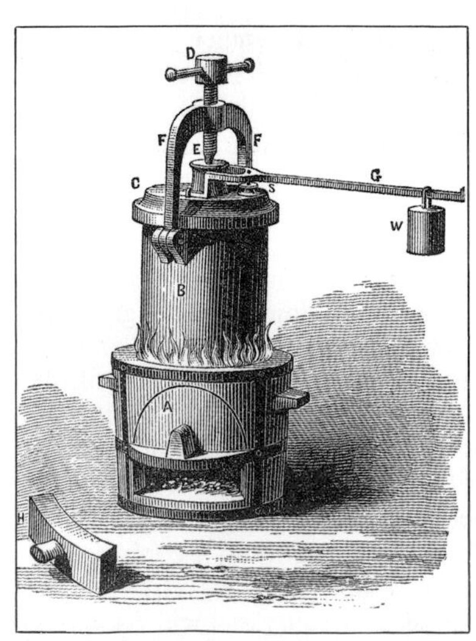

Papin's design for a pressure cooker.

London, 12 April 1682
Members of the Royal Society were entertained this afternoon by Denys Papin, a French doctor, who produced a sumptuous feast with his extraordinary equipment for cooking food under steam pressure. This method of cooking has never been seen before in Britain.

John Evelyn, the diarist, was one of the guests who were served fish, beef, mutton and pigeons. Papin's cookers use a low heat to cook food in its own juices, without any additional liquid. According to Evelyn, this process "made the hardest bones as soft as cheese". The pressure cookers are particularly good for preserving fruit.

Ringleader faces death sentence as Rye House conspiracy to kill king is uncovered

Lord Russell faces the judges for his part in the Rye House Plot.

London, 14 July 1683
Lord Russell, one of the leading conspirators in the Rye House plot, was sentenced to death today. His fate was sealed yesterday when his fellow defendant the earl of Essex was found dead in the Tower. His throat had been cut with a razor, and the assumption is that he committed suicide because of his guilt. Several others remain to be tried amid a fever of intrigue.

The plot was revealed by Josiah Keeling, an Anabaptist, who spoke to George Legge, Lord Dartmouth. Two men whose names were mentioned, Rumsey and West, told of overlapping plots. One was to kill Charles II, either in the playhouse, or by running down his barge on the Thames, or by ambushing him on his way to Newmarket as he passed Rye House, a farm in Hertfordshire. The other was to start a revolt leading to the removal of the duke of York and the earls of Halifax and Rochester, and the enthronement of Princess Anne.

Some fanciful evidence has been given at the trial, recalling the fabrications of the 1678 "popish plot". One thing beyond doubt is that a group of "Whig" supporters of the duke of Monmouth did exist, but their plans seem to have lacked direction since the earl of Shaftesbury's flight to the Dutch United Provinces last November. One of the group, Lord Howard, gave evidence against his co-plotters. Set against a background of increasing repression of dissent, aimed at "Quakers" and other sects, a fair trial is hard to imagine (→21).

Oxford dons criticize Milton and Hobbes

Oxford, 21 July 1683
The convocation of the university of Oxford passed a decree today condemning certain propositions in books by John Milton and Thomas Hobbes as "damnable doctrines" and ordered its members not to read them and the books to be publicly burnt. Condemned extracts include one from Milton's *Defensio*: "King Charles the First was lawfully put to death and his murderers were the blessed instruments of God's glory in their generation." And from Hobbes's *Leviathan*: "A domestic rebel acquires by his rebellion the same rights over the life of his prince as the prince for the most heinous crimes has over the life of his own subjects." (→21/10/87).

The frozen Thames becomes a fairground

The "frost fair" brings cold comfort to Londoners on the frozen Thames.

London, 4 February 1684
For more than a month the Thames has been frozen over, creating an open space in London that every trader and entertainer has hurried to exploit. Among the diversions offered by this continuous carnival on ice are sword-swallowing, puppet plays, horse races, bear-baiting, dancing and even fox-hunting. The most popular booths include one containing a printing press, where individuals can have their names printed on cards. But the cold has also caused hardship, and a week ago the Company of Watermen distributed £200 to poor watermen and widows.

Cocoa, a commodity exploited by the English, being made in America.

Colonial trade takes off in the New World

Caribbean, 1682
The New World across the Atlantic is providing many profitable outlets for trade among England's colonies – trade that is dependent on the work of black slaves. Most important among English territories in the West Indies is the island of Jamaica, captured from Spain in 1655 by Venables and Admiral Penn and offering plentiful supplies of sugar, coffee, ginger, pepper and cinchona bark, cattle and horses. More than 15,000 people have settled here, cultivating large areas and building sugar refineries, indigo works and cocoa walks.

King Charles II has made a grant of Surinam and the Windward and Leeward Islands to Francis, Lord Willoughby. Chief among these is the well-fortified island of Barbados, where a thriving trade keeps 10,000 tonnes of shipping occupied. Sugar has superseded tobacco as the main crop but is now falling in price. Bermuda, another island, is run by an English company and exports provisions, tobacco and cedar wood.

1685

England, 6 February. The Catholic duke of York accedes to the throne as James II.→

York, 3 March. King James II calls a general election (→24/3).

Ireland, 7 March. Richard Talbot and Justin MacCarthy, Roman Catholic soldiers, take command of English regiments based here (→20).

Ireland, 20 March. James Butler, the duke of Ormond and lord lieutenant, returns to England (→20/6).

Scotland, 8 May. Parliament imposes the death penalty for preaching at or attending a conventicle service (→24).

Grampian, 24 May. Over 150 covenanters are imprisoned in appalling conditions in Dunnottar Castle (→1/1886).

Dorset, 11 June. James, the duke of Monmouth, the illegitimate son of the late Charles II, lands at Lyme Regis with an army to stake his Protestant claim to the throne (→6/7).

Ireland, 20 June. Richard Talbot, from a minor family of the Old English Catholic gentry, is created earl of Tyrconnell by James II (→9/1/86).

Westminster, 2 July. Parliament prohibits direct trade from the colonies to Ireland (→5/4/1697).

Dublin, August. The first issue of the *Dublin News-Letter* is published by Joseph Ray.

France, October. Louis XIV revokes the Edict of Nantes and exiles thousands of Huguenots [Protestants], many of whom seek refuge in England (→25/4/86).

Westminster, 20 November. James II closes parliament after saying that he wants the Test and Corporation Acts and all penal laws against Roman Catholics repealed (→23).

Westminster, 23 November. James II issues dispensations to Catholics allowing them to hold public office despite the Test Act (→12/1685).

England, December. James II dismisses Henry Compton, the bishop of London, from the privy council for opposing Catholic toleration (→6/9/86).

London. Thomas Tenison, the rector of St Martin-in-the-Fields, founds a grammar school, and London's first library, in Leicester Square.

Conflict greets devout Catholic king

Charles II dies after reign of 25 years

London, 6 February

Charles II died today after a short, painful illness. He was 54 years old, and had reigned for 25 years. Four days ago he collapsed with a apoplectic fit, and despite a brief rally he failed to recover. His 51-year-old brother, the duke of York, succeeds to the throne as James II.

Last night the king sent away the Church of England bishops waiting to administer Holy Communion and confirmed what many of his subjects had long suspected: his intention to die a Roman Catholic. His old friend Father John Hudlestone, had helped him to escape after the Battle of Worcester in 1651, was admitted by the back stairs to administer the last rites. Shortly before the end, Charles requested that the curtains be drawn back so that he might see the light of day. Then, handing over the keys of office, he asked his brother to look after his children, and sought the queen's forgiveness (→3/3).

Charles II's last Sunday at court: surrounded by friends and revellers.

Sacrament omitted from coronation service

London, 23 April

The coronation of James II took place today with the usual splendour. But one important break with tradition was widely noted: as the new king is not an Anglican the customary sacrament was omitted from the order of service.

So far the new king has tried to defuse worries that he will return England to Roman Catholicism. He has told the privy council that he will "maintain the government of church and state as by law established", but Anglicans are concerned by his warning to the archbishop of Canterbury that if he is thwarted in his policies he will "readily find the means of attaining my ends without your help" (→20/11).

Despite serious misgivings, particularly about his religion, King James II was crowned with full ceremonial.

Two women martyrs drown determined to stick to their religion

Dumfries and Galloway, 11 May

Horrified crowds, held back by troops, watched as two local women were forcibly drowned today on the steeply sloping beach at Wigtown. Their "martyrdom" can only intensify the religious divisions that have gripped Scotland. Margaret McLauchlan, who was described as "elderly and in her sixties", and 18-year-old Margaret Wilson had been sentenced by the courts to this rare form of punishment for the crime of refusing to forsake their religious beliefs. They were tied to stakes and guarded by dragoons as the tide inexorably rose, until it finally covered them. McLauchlan had been placed closer to the sea in the hope that her fate would persuade the younger girl to recant. But she held steadfast, and in the end her head was forced below the waves by a soldier's halberd.

Duke of Monmouth's rebellion fails

Defeated duke flees battle at Sedgemoor

Somerset, 6 July
The ragged army assembled by the duke of Monmouth tried to break out last night from Bridgwater, in Somerset, where it had been pinned down by James II's loyal troops. Monmouth's 5,000 ill-trained supporters, armed with little more than scythes and pitchforks, were systematically cut to pieces as they attempted a desperate night attack across the desolate Sedgemoor marshes east of the town. Their commander escaped in the confusion, but he is now being hunted across the southern counties. His capture is expected soon.

This comprehensive victory effectively puts an end to the revolt which began in early June when the duke, an illegitimate son of Charles II, landed at Lyme Regis, in Dorset, and claimed the throne. Any serious chance of success evaporated when all his imported weapons were seized before they could even be distributed (→15/7).

The duke of Monmouth: utterly defeated in the battle at Sedgemoor.

Scots rebellion by earl of Argyll fails

Glasgow, 18 June
Archibald Campbell, the earl of Argyll, has been caught by English forces trying to cross the river Cart in Renfrewshire after failing in his plan to raise the covenanting banner in his Argyllshire homeland and along the Scottish borders.

He is now on his way to Edinburgh to face execution under a sentence imposed four years ago, when he refused to take the Test Oath. With his arrest the attempt to raise a Scottish rebellion, in parallel with the duke of Monmouth's English invasion, has totally collapsed.

Its chances never looked good. When Argyll landed at Kintyre in May his family estates were already occupied by the loyal marquis of Atholl, and few people were fired to support him by his hardline pro-Presbyterian slogans. Atholl's men, backed by English warships, quickly had the earl trapped (→6/7).

Protestant duke is executed for treason

London, 15 July
James, the duke of Monmouth, found barely a week ago huddled in a ditch, walked out today to his execution at the Tower. As well-wishers and admirers crowded even the nearby roofs and chimney pots, the duke mounted the scaffold with a firm, dignified bearing and announced to the hushed audience: "I come here, not to speak, but to die. I die a Protestant of the Church of England."

He then tested the edge of the axe, expressed some doubts about its sharpness and ordered his servants to pay the official headsman, Jack Ketch, six gold guineas to do a swift, clean job. But as he had rightly feared, the operation was badly bungled.

In the end it took Ketch no fewer than five desperate strokes to dispatch his victim, and even then the body was seen to be twitching. To the sound of yells of rage and horror from the onlookers he threw down the axe, saying: "I cannot do it. My heart fails me." Finally the sheriff ordered that a knife be used to separate the duke's head from his shoulders (→9/1685).

Monmouth's execution was badly botched, and the headsman lost his nerve.

Culprits punished by 'Bloody Assizes'

Bristol, September
The series of trials involving those who took part in the Battle of Sedgemoor or supported the Monmouth rebellion, known as "the Bloody Assizes", is now nearing its climax. Judge Jeffreys and his judicial colleagues, who have already given judgement in Winchester, Salisbury, Dorchester, Exeter, Wells and Taunton, are about to start their final hearings here in Bristol. So far they have sentenced about three hundred people to death (including 70-year-old Alice, Lady Lisle, who was condemned to be burnt for harbouring two rebels) and hundreds more to either transportation or flogging through all the market towns in their county.

Judge George Jeffreys: handed out stiff penalties at "Bloody Assizes".

Titus Oates found guilty of perjury

London, May
Justice has finally caught up with Titus Oates, the infamous perjurer. Judge Jeffries has ordered that he be sent to prison for life after first being subjected to a scourging through the streets of the capital, first from Aldgate to Newgate and then from Newgate to Tyburn.

The charges went back to 1678 when Oates's "discovery" of a Roman Catholic plot to murder the then king, Charles II, start a second great fire of London and instal a papist dictatorship set off a nationwide panic.

1686 - 1687

Ireland, 9 January 1686. Henry Hyde, the earl of Clarendon, is appointed lord lieutenant (→ 5/6).

Edinburgh, January 1686. King James II's decision to reintroduce the Roman Catholic Mass in Scotland provokes riots (→ 6/1886).

Ireland, 5 June 1686. Richard Talbot, the earl of Tyrconnell, takes command of the Irish army (→ 12/2/87).

Edinburgh, June 1686. Parliament refuses to grant toleration to Catholics (→ 12/2/87).

England, 26 October 1686. An Irish Catholic lawyer, Richard Nagle, writes an open letter asking the earl of Tyrconnell to redress injustices against Catholics that have arisen as a result of the Cromwellian "transplantations".

England, November 1686. James II makes an attempt to appease dissenters by granting them the right to buy dispensation from penal legislation (→ 14/4/87).

Scotland, 1686. James II is delighted when three of his most influential Scottish ministers, Lord Perth, the chancellor, and the secretaries Lords Melfort and Moray, announce their conversion to Catholicism.

Ireland, 10 February 1687. The guilds of barbers and surgeons and of apothecaries are reincorporated by royal charter.

Ireland, 12 February 1687. The earl of Tyrconnell is sworn in as lord lieutenant (→ 8/1687).

Scotland, 12 February 1687. James II proclaims religious toleration for Catholics and "Quakers" (→ 6/87).

Oxford, April 1687. James campaigns to force Magdalen College to accept a Catholic president (→ 25/10).

Scotland, June 1687. Religious toleration is extended to Presbyterians.

Chester, August 1687. The earl of Tyrconnell meets James II to discuss future plans for Ireland (→ 21/2/88).

Ireland, 1687. Thomas Wharton writes *Lillibulero*, a song satirizing the lord lieutenant, the earl of Tyrconnell; it becomes popular both here and in England.

Bishop of London is suspended by new church commission

London, 6 September 1686
The ecclesiastical commission, set up by King James II to "suppress zealous preachers", today claimed its most august victim so far when the influential bishop of London, Henry Compton, was suspended from office "during his majesty's pleasure" for his alleged contempt and disobedience.

The controversial proceedings, which were bitterly contested by both lawyers and churchmen, centred round the question of whether James could require his subjects, in this case the commissioners, to act unlawfully – by suspending a clergyman without giving him the benefit of a formal judicial hearing.

The commissioners themselves were divided, and one of them, the archbishop of Canterbury, William Sancroft, refused to attend the initial hearings. As a result he has now lost his place on the privy council and will attend no longer at court.

Predictably, the king's principal minister, Robert Spencer, the earl of Sunderland, who is the head of the commission, admits no such doubts about the validity of its actions. In his view the overriding objective must be "to regulate the licence of the Protestant ministers and to curb the audacity of the bishops". This outweighs all other considerations (→ 11/1686).

Secrets of gravity unlocked by Newton

Isaac Newton: mathematician with a new theory about gravitation.

The telescope Newton used to check star positions against his theories.

London, 1687
The effect of the force of gravity on the earth has been revealed. Isaac Newton, the Cambridge professor, mathematician and physicist, has finally released details of the scientific evidence in his newly published opus *Principia Mathematica*. Newton links his exposition of gravity with an explanation of movement among the sun, moon and stars and the planets.

However, a controversy has now broken out as to the original ownership of these ideas. Newton's old colleague Robert Hooke, the curator of the Royal Society, claims that he was first to discover the "inverse square" law in the heavens.

The normally reticent Newton has been forced to speak out. His ideas began to take root in the 18-month period in 1665/66 when, during the great plague, he retired to his family home farm at Woolsthorpe Manor, near Grantham in Lincolnshire, to pursue the experiments. There Newton tested his theories of gravity – that every piece of matter, whether a star, a piece of coal or a feather – will travel in unimpeded motion in a straight line and exert a force on every other particle. He delayed publication because he did not have full mathematical evidence.

With the publication of the *Principia*, Newton has now been able to provide the necessary back-up. The bachelor professor stands firmly by his findings (→ 16/2/1704).

English church begins to raise money for French Protestants

London, 25 April 1686
In spite of official discouragement and sustained opposition from the French ambassador, churches today asked their congregations to give money for the relief of the French Huguenots. According to one minister, these Protestant citizens had been "cruelly, barbarously and inhumanly oppressed". However, Englishmen are finding it increasingly difficult even to discover what is happening to co-religionists across the Channel. The *London Gazette* has been forbidden to publish any reports, and there have been rumours that a book describing various well-documented massacres is about to be burnt.

King Louis XIV is said to have "cruelly oppressed" the Huguenots.

William Penn fails to gain Dutch help

London, spring 1687
William Penn, the leader of the Quakers, has returned from the United Provinces with disappointing news of his mission to William of Orange and his wife Mary, the daughter King James II.

He had hoped, on behalf of his friend the king, to win Dutch backing for the royal campaign to establish more toleration for England's Roman Catholics, and particularly for the repeal of the Test and Corporation Acts which bar them from high office in government, education and the armed forces. But although William of Orange showed sympathy for these objectives, he considered them far too politically unpopular to embrace openly. He was therefore unwilling to endorse James's programme.

The likely result will be an increase in efforts to circumvent the penal laws and promote Catholic influence in public life. The first steps have already been taken with the launch of what is likely to be a long-drawn-out campaign to impose a Catholic president on Magdalen College, Oxford, which is a stronghold of Anglican intellectual orthodoxy.

King wants the church to be more Catholic

King James II is widely portrayed as being an oppressor of Protestants.

London, 14 April 1687
James II today published his long-expected "Declaration of Indulgence". This grants full liberty of worship (though only in public places) and includes a general suspension of the tests brought in to bar non-members of the Anglican Church (including both Catholics and Protestant nonconformists) from various types of office. The proposals were formally welcomed by spokesmen for the groups mainly affected. But it is already clear that there will be considerable difficulty in getting them endorsed by parliament (at present prorogued, and widely expected to be soon dissolved) unless there are significant changes in its membership. Vigorous steps are likely to be taken by royal advisers to make possible the election of more compliant members next year (→ 4/1687).

Catholics gain from repeal of penal laws

London, September 1687
Magistrates across the country are being required to answer the "three questions" posed by King James II to establish their support for his repeal of the Penal Laws and the Test Acts. Those who refuse to comply face the loss of their offices and replacement by more amenable justices of the peace, most of whom will inevitably be Catholics.

By April, when the "Declaration of Indulgence" was issued, some 290 Catholic justices had been appointed, and the number has grown during the summer since new rules were issued making it unnecessary for magistrates to take any religious test. Now the process is expected to accelerate (→ 4/5/88).

The king: devout in his religion.

Outspoken author urges a royal hospital and trained midwives

London, 1687
A new publication demanding the skilled training of midwives has sparked off a furore. *A Scheme for the Foundation of a Royal Hospital* seeks to "raise a revenue of £5,000 or £6,000 a year, for the maintenance of a corporation of skilled midwives". The author, Elizabeth Cellier, is a Roman Catholic convert who was recently held in Newgate prison before being tried for and acquitted of complicity in "the meal-tub plot". Accused of being involved in the release of a man who had been conspiring to murder the then king, Charles II, Cellier was alleged to have concealed plans in a meal tub at her house.

Cellier emerged from Newgate to launch an exposé of the terrible conditions she had experienced there. She was tried for libel, sentenced to the pillory and fined £1,000. Now she is determined to tackle the shortcomings of her own area of expertise: midwifery.

Training for midwives is needed to cut infant and maternal mortality.

A sustantially female occupation, midwifery lags behind other areas of medicine; it has neither a royal charter nor professional status. Horrified by the level of infant and maternal mortality, Elizabeth Cellier has set out a plan to replace the system of church licensing of midwives by one of proper training.

Fellows expelled

Oxford, 21 October 1687
King James II's impatience with the recalcitrant Fellows of Magdalen College reached breaking point today. After they refused to beg pardon for their resistance to his wishes, or to admit the legality of his chosen method for packing the college with Catholic appointees, he deprived them all of their positions. He also barred them from accepting any church preferment, and thus made it difficult, if not impossible, for them to earn any kind of a living.

1688

United Provinces, April. William of Orange, King James II's nephew and son-in-law, informs Admiral Edward Russell of plans to invade England (→ 30/9).

England, 4 May. James II orders the "Declaration of Indulgence" to be read out in churches (→ 18).

Ireland, 21 July. James Butler, the duke of Ormond, dies; he is succeeded by his grandson, also James (→ 22/2/89).

England, 31 August. John Bunyan, the preacher and author of *The Pilgrim's Progress*, dies.

United Provinces, 30 September. William issues a "Declaration of Reasons", a manifesto for a Protestant nation (→ 9/1688).

Germany, September. The French attack the Palatinate, leaving William free to invade England (→ 21/10).

London, 15 October. The prince of Wales, James Francis Edward, is baptized in a Catholic ceremony (→ 10/12).

English Channel, 21 October. Bad weather forces William and his invasion fleet to turn back (→ 9/11).

Westminster, 27 October. Robert Spencer, the earl of Sunderland and former head of James II's recently disbanded ecclesiastical commission, is dismissed; he flees to the United Provinces.

Wiltshire, 23 November. James II leaves for London when the army abandons him at Salisbury (→ 27).

London, 27 November. James's advisers urge him to call a free parliament, issue a general pardon, ban all Catholics from office and send a commission to meet William (→ 8/12).

Berkshire, 8 December. The marquis of Halifax, Lord Godolphin and the earl of Nottingham, representing the king, meet William at Hungerford to open negotiations (→ 24).

England, 9 December. Queen Mary and the prince of Wales flee to France (→ 6/9/1701).

Edinburgh, 10 December. The royal government collapses as the chancellor, Perth, flees.

London. The playwright Aphra Behn publishes a novel, *Oroonoko, or the History of the Royal Slave*. She is the first woman to publish under her own name and to earn a living by writing.

King faces conflict with defiant church

Lambeth, London, 18 May

The Church of England defiantly took a stand today against James II and his relentless drive to establish the Roman Catholic Church on the same footing as itself. Across the country Anglican clergy refused to obey the king's command that they read out from the every pulpit his "Declaration of Indulgence".

The Declaration, first issued last year, was the fervently Catholic king's ostensible act of reconciliation with his Protestant subjects. It was at the time received with mistrust, and James has since been steadily trying to undermine the Anglican Church and packing the privy council and many other important bodies with Catholics.

In another move, four bishops appointed by Rome to govern English Catholics announced to their flock that divine providence and royal piety had restored to them episcopal authority. This came as a shock to the Church of England – hence the last ditch stand over the reissuing of the Declaration.

The London clergy have been in the forefront of the latest struggle against the king's attempt to cow churchmen. Six bishops went from Lambeth Palace to see James with a final petition warning him that the Declaration would not be read. In the event it was read in Westminster Abbey and in only about 400 other churches (→ 30/6).

Seven bishops who defied the king are acquitted and freed to popular acclaim

The seven bishops: the country exploded with delight at their acquittal.

London, 30 June

In cities, towns and villages across the land tonight the people are celebrating, for seven Anglican bishops on trial on serious charges brought against them by King James II were found not guilty and freed. This is a victory for the Church of England in its struggle to keep England a Protestant country.

The bishops were committed to the Tower by the king after the publication of a petition to him about his "Declaration of Indulgence". But they outmanoeuvred him at every stage. They were visited by clergy, and an impressive array of gentlemen and nobility offered to stand surety for them. At their trial they were charged with publishing a false, malicious and seditious libel. From the start the prosecution were sidetracked into debating the issue of whether the crown really did enjoy a suspending power in ecclesiastical causes. When Sir Roger Langley, the foreman of the jury, brought in a verdict of "not guilty" there were shouts of approval, and a roar went up which some said shook the building.

The verdict had an extraordinary effect on the people of London. The cheering was taken up by watermen on the Thames, and the noise rolled up and down the river and was spread by people in the streets. Bonfires were lit across the country.

Queen gives birth to Catholic heir, much to Protestants' alarm

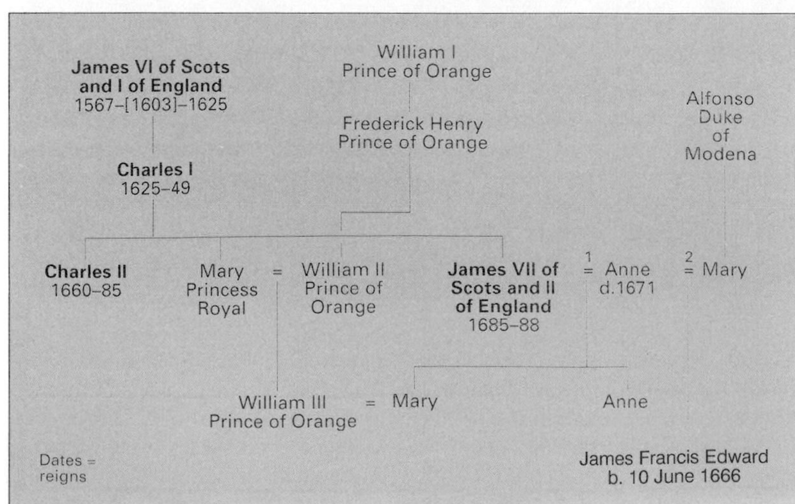

The birth threatens the claim on the succession of James II's daughter Mary.

London, 10 June

Bells rang out and guns fired salutes today to mark the birth of a son to Queen Mary Beatrice. James II now has a son to succeed him, and one whom he might bring up as a Catholic. There is a mounting expectation that this will encourage the Protestant William of Orange, the husband of the king's daughter Mary, to try to take over the English crown. Widespread concern at the birth among Protestants is reflected in the circulation of a story that the infant was a "supposed child" smuggled into the queen's bed in a warming-pan. The birth follows 15 years of infant deaths and miscarriages (→ 15/10).

William of Orange invades England

Devon, 9 November
William of Orange has embarked on his long-expected invasion of England. The Protestant prince rode into Exeter today at the head of a 15,000-strong army of French Huguenots, Swiss, Dutch, Germans and Swedes. The news that his son-in-law has landed in the west with an army at his back – reminiscent of the Monmouth rebellion – has dismayed James II.

William landed at Brixham four days ago, having overcome logistical problems by taking advantage of the prevailing winds which kept the English navy helplessly at anchor. But the groundwork had been carefully laid. He has long been in touch with opposition leaders in England and has kept himself well informed about public opinion.

"Whig" and "Tory" magnates in the west country are already defecting to his side, an illustration of the extent to which James's Catholic policies have united the Protestant nation against him. There has been a series of provincial risings and demonstrations, with major towns declaring in William's favour.

It is far from certain at this stage that either he, or most of his supporters, are aiming to depose James. William has issued a declaration which speaks only of halting the king's policy of returning the country to Roman Catholicism (→23).

The revolution begins: William of Orange enters Exeter with his army.

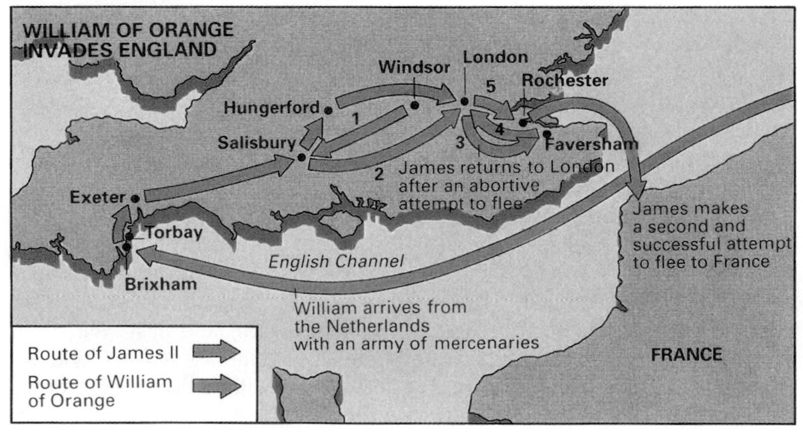

James, deserted by his army, flees to France without a fight

James's wife flees with her baby son.

London, 24 December
James II, England's king for less than four years, has fled to France without a fight, opening the way for William of Orange to take power. His ignominious exit has left England and Scotland with a ruler who knows little about the countries he appears destined to govern, but who will promote the Protestant cause and restore civil liberties.

James's cherished army began to fall apart within a week of William's invasion. Having created a "modern army" he had set about employing it for absolutist ends, and when he went down to Salisbury to lead it against William he learned of defections to the other camp, and it was clear that it had become demoralized. A fortnight ago James sent Queen Mary to France with their baby son. He had disbanded the army and created a governmental vacuum. The next day he tried to get away to France himself, throwing the great seal into the Thames en route, but was intercepted by Kentish fishermen and attacked. Only last night did he successfully make his escape.

James's collapse of nerve will ensure that when William reaches London he will have the support of all leading "Whigs" and "Tories". He is likely to want to make peace with the army, which James had transformed into a political machine. One-third of its officers may join James, and another third be retired, but the rest should be the backbone of a future army (→31).

Protestants look to a Dutch prince for their salvation

London, 31 December
William of Orange, a 38-year-old Dutch Protestant, has led a successful invasion of England. Yet he has not had to seize power – it was handed to him by alarmed Protestants who asked him to take over the country, and by King James II, whose high-handed imposition of Roman Catholicism became increasingly resented and who has now fled [*see report below left*].

William's main aim has been to prevent an aggressive expansionist France under Louis XIV from engulfing his homeland, but for many years he has been unable to organize an effective European coalition to halt and reverse the French gains. He has never made clear his motives for invading England, but one is likely to be his plans to bring it out of its isolation and into an impending war with France.

William picked the moment to invade for other reasons. The odds against success were great until September when the problem of Dutch security was removed by the full-scale attack by the French on the Palatinate. And William learnt that James was not only expanding his army but also intended to remodel it during the winter. There was William's English wife, Mary, too; her right of succession to the throne had been threatened by the birth of James's son.

William: power given to him.

1689

Westminster, 28 January. The Commons declare the English throne vacant after James II's flight into exile (→ 6/2).

Westminster, 6 February. The House of Commons offers the throne jointly to William and Mary (→ 12/2).

Westminster, 12 February. Parliament agrees to terms of the "Declaration of Rights" (→ 11/4).

Ireland, 22 February. William issues a declaration for Irish Jacobites to submit by 10 April (→ 14/3).

Co Down, 14 March. Jacobites under Richard Hamilton rout Protestants under the earl of Mountalexander (→ 17/4).

Tayside, 13 April. John Graham of Claverhouse, Viscount Dundee, raises James II's standard on Dundee Law, announcing his intention to fight (→ 27/7).

Derry City, 17 April. James II, supported by Richard Talbot, the new duke of Tyrconnell, besieges the city (→ 4/5).

Dublin, 4 May. James II is proclaimed king (→ 7).

Co Fermanagh, 7 May. Enniskillen Protestants defeat Jacobite forces in a battle at Belleek (→ 13/6).

London, 11 May. William and Mary take the Scottish coronation oath at Whitehall Palace (→ 13).

Britain, 13 May. William III declares war on France (→ 26/7/90).

Derry City, 13 June. William III's fleet arrives in Lough Foyle (→ 25/7).

Ireland, 18 June. A royal proclamation is made for the introduction of "brass money" – debased coinage.

Dublin, 25 July. William King, the dean of St Patrick's, is jailed by Tyrconnell (→ 31).

Co Down, 13 August. Marshal Schomberg and his Williamite forces land at Bangor Bay (→ 12/3/90).

Tayside, 21 August. The Cameronian regiment halts advance of the Jacobites, at Dunkeld (→ 1/5/90).

Devonport, Devon. William III builds new naval dockyards.

Dublin. A Catholic priest, Michael Moore, is appointed provost of Trinity College by James II, although the fellows did not elect him; he is the first Catholic to hold the post.

Thrones of England and Scotland given to William and Mary

Westminster, 11 April

William of Orange and his wife Mary, the daughter of the deposed James II, were crowned king and queen of England in Westminster Abbey today. This is the first time in English history that two people have been crowned to reign equally.

In another development, the ceremony combined the traditional pomp and pageantry of a coronation with the oaths demanded of a constitutional monarchy. William and Mary were required to swear that they would govern according to the "statutes of parliament" and maintain "the Protestant reformed religion established by law".

The new king and queen have also been proclaimed joint sovereigns in Scotland. At the same time the convention of estates has passed the "Claim of Right", a statement of constitutional principles. Among its demands are that the Scottish succession be limited to Protestants; no Catholics are to hold office; the royal prerogative is to be subject to the rule of law; the use of torture is to be strictly defined, and prelacy is condemned.

This Claim of Right is far more revolutionary than the English Declaration of Rights. It is to be carried to London by a delegation which will offer William and Mary the Scottish crown on the implicit understanding that they will accept its provisions (→ 11/5).

Queen Mary: daughter of James II.

'Patriot parliament' is opened in Dublin

The Dublin parliament sits to consider James's urgent request for money.

Dublin, 7 May

The so-called "patriot parliament", representing the dispossessed Roman Catholic majority, held its first sitting today in Dublin. Of its 224 members, only six are Protestants. The opening ceremony was performed by the deposed James II, wearing his royal robes and a newly made crown.

James set sail two months ago from France, where he had sought refuge after William of Orange's invasion of England last year. He landed at Kinsale, in Co Cork, on 12 March with a fleet of 22 ships. The first English king to visit Ireland for almost 300 years, James had arrived with the aim of winning Catholic support for his attempt to regain the crown and defeat William III. He went immediately to Cork, where he presented the lord lieutenant, Richard Talbot, the earl of Tyrconnell, with a dukedom before proceeding to Dublin. Most of Ireland has since rallied to the Catholic king, with the exception of Derry, whose Protestant garrison has been under siege from James's troops since 18 April.

James's supporters hope to repeal anti-Catholic laws and reverse the iniquities of the land settlement, so setting the seal on what they see as the Catholic revival. But there is a major practical problem that they have to overcome: local government is in the hands of Protestant sheriffs and justices of the peace. The "patriot parliament" is not in touch with real power (→ 13/6).

East End terrified by violent murders

London

Fear stalks the mean streets of the East End of London after a series of gruesome murders which have claimed the lives of Queen Catharine of Braganza's butler, his mistress, Sarah Hodges, the madam of a notorious brothel, and two of her girls. The murders took place in the slums of Tower Hamlets, infamous for whoring and drunkenness. Decent citizens, appalled at the disorder and the spread of venereal disease, are banding together to fight the criminal gangs.

April 16: Aphra Behn, the first Englishwoman to be a professional playwright, dies aged 49.

Siege of Derry is lifted

Derry City, 31 July
The siege of Derry has been lifted, and the Jacobite army has fled. For the defenders it has been a triumph of persistence and faith. There has been terrible suffering. Thousands have died, and the city is in ruins. Throughout the countryside farms have been burnt and crops destroyed, but the city walls remain standing. Protestant grit and endurance have been rewarded, and a firm base in Ulster has been secured for King William III.

King James II had arrived in Derry on 18 April, expecting its immediate surrender. But the townspeople threw out the royal governor, Robert Lundy, and defied the king. As the siege continued, Ulster Protestants adopted a "scorched-earth" policy which left besiegers and besieged equally short of supplies. The Jacobites kept up a continuous artillery bombardment.

In June, after a failed attempt to storm the walls, a boom was thrown across the river Foyle to block the sea route into the city. Later a flotilla from England with ample supplies and a troop contingent led by Percy Kirke anchored in Lough Foyle. Kirke was content to play a waiting game, unwilling to run the gauntlet of the narrow river between the loch and the sea.

Finally, on 28 July King William's commander-in-chief, Marshal Schomberg, ordered Kirke to break the boom. Arms and food flowed into the city, and the siege was over, after 105 days (→13/8).

The siege of Derry City has been lifted after 105 days of defiance.

Royalist highlanders defeat the redcoats

Tayside, 27 July
A rebel army of highlanders loyal to King James II defeated a government force of 3,000 "redcoats" here today. The highlanders broke the redcoat line with a wild charge and drove them into the narrow gorge of Killiecrankie, north of Pitlochry, where they were slaughtered.

At the moment of victory the rebel leader, Viscount Dundee, was mortally wounded. As he fell he asked: "How goes the day?" His aide replied: "Well for King James, but I am sorry for your lordship." "If it is well for him," said Dundee, "it matters the less for me" – and died. His leadership will be sorely missed by the rebels (→21/8).

Lord Dundee: victorious in death.

Divine right of monarchs replaced by 'Bill of Rights' in a 'glorious revolution'

William and Mary are formally presented with the "Bill of Rights".

Westminster, 16 December
The recent sequence of events that has resulted in the overthrow of the Roman Catholic King James II and the accession of the Protestant William and Mary has been dubbed by some "the glorious revolution". Others have described it more pointedly as "the bloodless revolution". In England the revolution has indeed been bloodless, for William has a dislike of revenge, and most members of parliament now desire to forget and forgive. No one has so far been executed for showing loyalty to James.

Jacobite support in Scotland, however, has turned out to be more tenacious – and the actions of the Jacobites have produced a bloodier outcome. Following a victory over a Williamite army commanded by General Hugh Mackay at Killiecrankie [*see report left*] – which saw the deaths of more than half of Mackay's 4,000-strong army – the Jacobites were defeated in a vicious street battle at Dunkeld by the devout Cameronian regiment and are now retreating northwards. William and Mary had formally accepted the Scottish throne on 11 May, and soon afterwards Edinburgh Castle was surrendered to their supporters.

The revolution has brought an end to the belief in the divine right of kings, substituting constitutional rule enshrined in a "Bill of Rights", based on the earlier "Declaration of Rights", which was passed by the Westminster parliament today. The bill – in effect a social contract between monarch and people – seeks above all to restrain royal power and establish parliament as the supreme law-making body. It stipulates that only parliament can raise taxes or wage wars; it protects judges from political pressures; and it bars all Catholics from succeeding to the throne.

Many of the provisions in the Bill of Rights are a pragmatic response to what are regarded as the anti-parliamentary excesses of James and earlier Stuart kings. Scotland's more radical "Claim of Right" [*see report on page 618*] was implicitly accepted by William and Mary when they agreed to take the Scottish crown.

The Scottish Presbyterians are now preparing to press home their demand for the Church of Scotland to abandon episcopacy. Meanwhile, the Church of England has been affected by the Toleration Act, which bans the persecution of religious dissenters.

Many people believe that the new measures are only the start of a far-reaching programme of reform that will touch every aspect of life. "The Bill of Rights is to be as long as we are a nation," said Sir John Tredenham in the House of Commons. Some are now arguing for an extension of the rights of the nation's subjects.

1690 - 1691

England, February 1690. William Sancroft, the archbishop of Canterbury, who refused the oath of allegiance to William III, is deprived of his position (→ 31/5/91).

Cork City, 12 March 1690. French troops arrive to support James II (→ 14/6).

Highland, 1 May 1690. The remnant of the Jacobite army is defeated at Cromdale in Strathspey (→ 7/6).

Scotland, 7 June 1690. The crown agrees to Presbyterian government in the Church of Scotland (→ 11/1690).

Co Antrim, 14 June 1690. William III and his troops land at Carrickfergus (→ 1/7).

Co Limerick, 11 August 1690. Jacobites under Patrick Sarsfield destroy a Williamite baggage train at Ballyneety (→ 5/9).

Ireland, 5 September 1690. William III returns to England (→ 12).

Ireland, 12 September 1690. Richard Talbot, the duke of Tyrconnell, and the French army sail for France (→ 28).

Cork City, 28 September 1690. Having landed near here five days ago, John Churchill, the earl of Marlborough, and his British troops force Cork to surrender (→ 12/7/91).

Scotland, November 1690. The Church of Scotland general assembly holds its first meeting since 1653 (→ 6/1691).

Westminster, 5 January 1691. William III concedes to parliament the right to settle the distribution of estates forfeited by Irish Jacobites.

England, 13 January 1691. George Fox, who founded the Society of Friends – "the Quakers" – dies.

London, 31 May 1691. John Tillotson is made archbishop of Canterbury (→ 22/11/94).

Strathclyde, June 1691. Acting for William, John Campbell, the earl of Breadalbane, negotiates terms with the Jacobites at Achallader.

Co Galway, 12 July 1691. William III's Dutch general, Baron von Ginkel, defeats the Jacobites at Aughrim (→ 14/8).

Limerick City, 14 August 1691. Tyrconnell, who returned here on 14 January, dies (→ 3/10).

Ireland, 22 December. Patrick Sarsfield leaves for exile in France.

James defeated at the river Boyne

Drogheda, Co Louth, 1 July 1690
In what is being seen as an important triumph for the Grand Alliance against France, William III has defeated James II in battle at the river Boyne. The drama of two kings fighting at an Irish river for an English throne has had a sensational impact. Casualities have been light, and many Jacobite troops have retreated west of the Shannon, while James has fled to France.

William had landed near Carrickfergus in Co Antrim on 14 June [*see map on page 621*]. He brought with him 15,000 troops, a train of Dutch artillery and an eagerly awaited £200,000 in cash. His arrival created enormous confidence amongst Ulster Protestants. Belfast Lough resembled a wood with the masts of hundreds of ships laden with provisions and ammunition.

On 29 June James's army crossed the Boyne in two columns, and the next day William's much larger army appeared on the northern heights above it. Although William was advised to cross the river at once, superstition prevented him from taking action on a Monday – yesterday. He took the risk, however, of riding out in full view of James's army. A one-kilogram (two-pound) ball hit him on the right shoulder, drawing blood and causing an excited rumour in James's camp that he was dead.

Today William returned to lead a frontal assault across the river. The sheer weight of numbers forced the Jacobites to retreat (→ 11/8).

King William III leading his cavalry to victory across the river Boyne.

The defeated King James II flees for his life, back to France and safety.

'Tories' return to government to establish moderate regime

King William III presiding over proceedings in the House of Lords.

Westminster, summer 1690
After some fierce "political" jockeying earlier this year, the "Tories" are back in government. The elections in February and March followed William III's dissolution of parliament after he lost patience with the "Whigs", to whom – ironically – he owes much of his success. The Tories, led by Thomas Osborne, the earl of Danby, are promising William steady parliamentary support. Their job should not be hard: the new parliament is far less combative than the previous one, with a number of members not rigidly attached to either party.

French fleet attacks English south coast

Ships clash in the English Channel.

Channel, 26 July 1690
The French navy followed up its devastating defeat of the combined English and Dutch fleets off Beachy Head earlier this month by bombarding the Devonshire fishing village of Teignmouth today. The French now seem able to rove the Channel as they will, and there is consternation in London amid fears of a French invasion to restore James II to the throne. Letters have been sent to William III in Ireland, urging him to return before French ships block the Irish Channel. William's victory at the Battle of the Boyne, however, has ruined James's ambitions (→ 19/5/92).

Two diarists record foibles of the age

London, 1690
Two friends, John Evelyn and Samuel Pepys, are both members of the Royal Society, each having served as president or vice-president, and each is an assiduous writer of a daily diary, recording vivid impressions of contemporary public life and social foibles.

Pepys, now retired, has written his *Memoirs Relating to the State of the Royal Navy* up to 1688. This year he read Evelyn his paper on the "ignorance and incompetency" of its present administration. He dined with Evelyn after being released from the Tower, where he had been held for five days on suspicion of being a supporter of King James II.

Pepys frequently visits Evelyn at his house at Deptford, where Evelyn reads him poems and plays which he has written. In the opinion of Pepys, they are "very good, but not as he conceits them, I think, to be. A most excellent person he is and must be allowed for a little conceitedness, being a man so much above others."

At one dinner at Greenwich "Mr Evelyn did make us all die almost with laughing ... we sat in this humour till about 10 at night. I never met with so merry a two hours." Yet neither man knows that the other is keeping a record of their meetings in his secret diary.

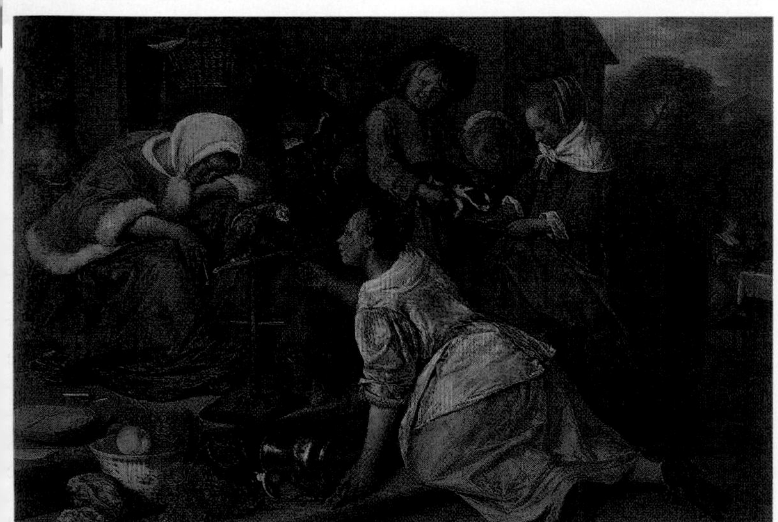

A new morality is emerging in England, where societies for the reformation of manners have appeared; this moralistic painting, "The Effects of Intemperance" by the Dutch artist Jan Steen, attacks moral decay.

Limerick surrenders to King William, as he secures stronger control over Ireland

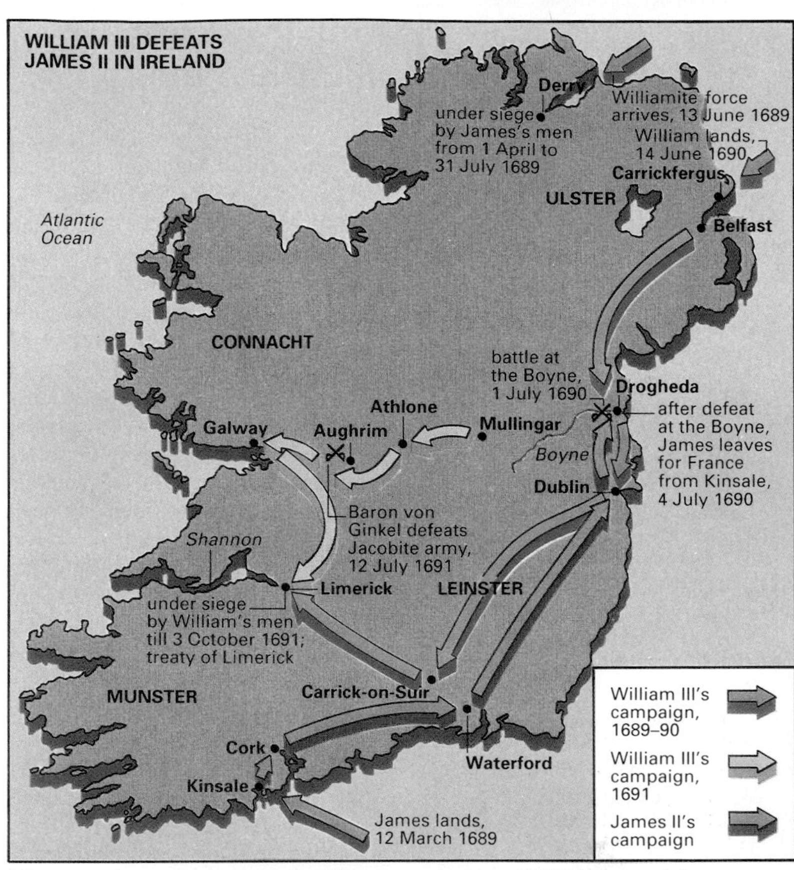

The map shows the principal military movements of William and James.

Limerick City, 3 October 1691
Limerick has surrendered to King William III, and the lords justices of Ireland have signed the treaty negotiated by Godert von Ginkel, William's commander, and Patrick Sarsfield, James's general.

The Williamites have won several important victories this year, most notably at Cork, Kinsale, Athlone and Galway. Their first attempt to take Limerick, where 14,000 Irish troops were based, failed last August, and the Williamites suffered heavy casualities. But the fact that Limerick was the only city of consequence left, after months of fighting, along with the failure of promised help from France, depressed Irish morale. The idea of prolonging resistance into the winter simply in order to suit French long-term strategy had little appeal for the Irish. The treaty includes toleration for Catholics and a pardon for Irish soliders who take the oath of allegiance. There are also guarantees for property rights. Yet there is a strong feeling that the English parliament and Irish Protestants will not support these generous terms (→ 5/10/92).

Human understanding expounded by Locke

London, 1690
John Locke, who was once the earl of Shaftesbury's physician and his children's tutor, has published a work of philosophy that is achieving international fame. *An Essay Concerning Human Understanding* asserts that "all knowledge is founded on and derived from sense or sensation". Unlike the French philosopher René Descartes, Locke holds that all ideas derive either from the senses, when the mind perceives external objects, or from reflection on the mind's workings. He also wrote two *Treatises on Government* last year. In them he denies theories of divine right, arguing that political power proceeds from natural morality (→ 28/10/04).

1692 - 1694

London, 7 January 1692. The funeral of the chemist and physicist Robert Boyle takes place. Thirty years ago he formulated "Boyle's Law", which states that the pressure and volume of a gas are inversely proportional.

London, January 1692. On suspicion of plotting against King William III and Queen Mary II, John Churchill, the earl of Marlborough, is dismissed as commander of the English forces in the United Provinces; his wife, Sarah, remains a close friend of Princess Anne (→5/5).

London, 19 February 1692. Princess Anne and her family move out of the royal apartments in Whitehall Palace (→2/1695).

London, 5 May 1692. John Churchill, the earl of Marlborough, is arrested on suspicion of treason (→24/3/02).

France, 19 May 1692. William III's combined Anglo-Dutch fleet defeats the French at La Hogue (→24/5).

United Provinces, 24 July 1692. The French defeat the British at Steenkerke (→7/1693).

Dublin, 5 October 1692. William III opens his first Irish parliament (→27/8/95).

Dublin, 15 December 1692. A new charter reconstitutes the College of Physicians as the King and Queen's College of Physicians.

Westminster, January 1693. The Million Loan Act originates a "national debt"; parliament underwrites the king's debts.

United Provinces, 19 July 1693. Patrick Sarsfield, the Irish Jacobite who joined up with the French, is mortally wounded in a battle at Landen (Neerwinden).

Britain/France, July 1693. Representatives of William III open peace negotiations with Louis XIV of France.

London, 25 October 1694. Queen Mary founds the Greenwich hospital for wounded sailors; Sir Christopher Wren is the architect.

London, 22 November 1694. Dr John Tillotson, the archbishop of Canterbury, dies at Lambeth (→1/1695).

London, 20 December 1694. Queen Mary falls ill with smallpox at Kensington Palace (→28).

Macdonald clan massacred at Glencoe

Highlanders suffer merciless butchery

Scotland, 13 February 1692
On this bitter highland morning, soldiers of the Argyll regiment rose before dawn at Glencoe and began the systematic butchery of the Macdonalds, their hosts for the past 12 days. They shot, stabbed and clubbed men, women and children to death in cold blood.

Their commander, Robert Campbell of Glenlyon, had seven prisoners lined up and shot them one after another, finishing them off with his bayonet. Another officer was seen to shoot a 13-year-old boy. The chief of the Macdonald clan, the elderly Alisdair McIain, was shot in the back as he pulled on his trews; his wife was stripped and turned out into the freezing cold.

The soldiers killed indiscriminately and smeared dung on their victims' corpses. A man dying of fever was stabbed to death along with his five-year-old son. Their bodies were hurled into the river.

Many Macdonalds, warned of the treachery, fled to safety; but in the first grey light, 35 men and an unknown number of women and children lay dead among the smouldering ruins of their homes.

The river and forbidding pass of Glencoe, where the massacre took place.

Recriminations begin over mass killings

London, February 1692
The full horror of the Glencoe massacre has reached London, but the man who wrote the order to put the Macdonald clan to the sword, Sir John Dalrymple, is showing no remorse. King William III signed the order – allegedly unaware of the awesome consequences – and he is said to be deeply shocked.

Dalrymple, the Scottish secretary, is justifying the killings on the grounds that Alisdair McIain, the Macdonald chief, had failed to take an oath of loyalty to King William before a deadline of 1 January. McIain had, indeed, ridden to Fort William to take the oath, only to be told that he should be at Inverary, 60 miles (96km) away. Riding through heavy snowstorms, he eventually swore the oath on 6 January. Although aware of this, Dalrymple, a lowlander, ordered that all Macdonalds under the age of 70 should be "extirpated".

Irish dismayed by passing of new act

Ireland, 3 November 1692
Catholic suspicions that the Protestant establishment will ignore the Treaty of Limerick [*see report on page 621*] seem confirmed by new legislation that was enacted today. The act is for the "encouragement of Protestant strangers to settle in this kingdom of Ireland", and it also allows them freedom of worship. The "Protestant strangers" in question are Huguenot settlers. This act follows another measure, passed on 24 December last year, enforcing a new and strongly anti-Catholic oath of allegiance to William III. It bars Catholics from membership of parliament and public office in Ireland, overturning the Limerick treaty.

The Royal Chelsea hospital for veteran soldiers represents a new attempt to provide care for those men who have fought bravely and well in the service of their country; the first pensioners were admitted to the hospital in 1692.

France abandons its plans for invasion

Normandy, 24 May 1692
The threatened French invasion of England has been abandoned following a massive defeat of Admiral Tourville's fleet off La Hogue on the Normandy coast. Still smarting from their own defeat off Beachy Head two years ago, the English navy, this time combined with its Dutch allies, sank 15 ships of the French line in the deep waters off La Hogue in a battle lasting six days. With English forces heavily committed in Ireland and Flanders, all had seemed set fair for the French and the exiled James II.

Thousands of troops had been stationed on the Cotentin peninsula, with the French Mediterranean fleet racing up from Toulon to lend support. Sadly for King Louis XIV and his protégé, gales delayed the reinforcements, and Admiral Tourville found his 44-strong fleet off Barfleur pitched against 99 allied ships (→ 24/7).

The combined English and Dutch fleets destroy the French off La Hogue.

Triennial Bill gets William's approval

Westminster, 14 March 1694
Despite two previous royal rejections, William III has finally yielded to parliament's insistence that it must meet at least once in every three years. The Triennial Bill, which was given the royal assent today, also calls for the dissolution of parliament after a three-year term, to be followed by a general election for a new parliament.

Previous triennial acts had succeeded in reducing the king's power to summon parliament, but this one limits his power of dissolution. Two factors appear to have changed William's mind. He was made aware of a groundswell of public discontent if he continued to challenge the power of the government; and the "Tory" leader Robert Harley told the Commons that they could withhold money essential for the war in the United Provinces.

Wales loses its last bard, Sian Daffyd

Nannau, Gwynedd, 1694
With the death this year of Sian Dafydd, itinerant Welsh bards have almost become a thing of the past. He was the last bard resident in the houses of his patrons, a dozen noble families of north Wales, in the ancient tradition.

Bards have always had patrons for whom they sing and declaim their poetry. They serve a long apprenticeship, learning the elaborate rules of rhyme and metre that they have to master – there are 24 strict and different metres. Then they earn the rank of *pencerdd*, which entitles them to travel from one great house to the next. Most of the poems are in the form of the *cywydd*, rhymed couplets with seven syllables, often written in praise of the bard's patron and his Welsh national pride. Yet the apprenticeships have of late fallen into disuse.

Bank of England opens its accounts

The bank: set up to lend money.

London, 21 June 1694
London is set to oust Amsterdam as the financial capital of Europe with the opening today in Lincoln's Inn Fields of the Bank of England. Under the Tonnage Act passed earlier this year, duty on beer, ale and tobacco has been set aside to service a loan of £1,200,000. King William III has incorporated the subscribers as a bank and given his consent for their dealing in bullion and bills of exchange. Governments have always relied on the business community to pay for wars. This government has created a political infrastructure for today's exceptionally heavy borrowing.

William mourns the death of his queen

London, 28 December 1694
King William III seems beyond all consolation in his mourning for his wife, Queen Mary II, who died today at the age of 32. Mary will lie in state in Whitehall Palace while London prepares to hold a magnificent funeral for her, at a cost that is estimated to exceed £50,000.

William may not attend the funeral. His agony began when doctors told him that Mary was suffering from smallpox. He moved a campbed into her room and cried so much that he upset his dying wife.

The heartbroken king, both of whose parents died of smallpox, was called to Mary's bedside yesterday to say farewell after she had taken the sacraments for the last time. She eventually passed away at one o'clock this morning, a popular and much loved queen (→ 5/3/95).

Queen Mary II lies in state.

Ashmolean given Aubrey's 'Brief Lives'

Aubrey: "Brief Lives" took 20 years.

Oxford, 1694
John Aubrey, the antiquarian who surveyed Stonehenge, has given the manuscripts of his *Brief Lives*, which he has been compiling for 20 years, to the Ashmolean, the university's collection of rarities, donated by Elias Ashmole. Aubrey collected them for a planned history of Oxford. Some concern Elizabethans such as the earl of Oxford who, bowing low to the queen, happened to let out a fart, at which he was so abashed that he went travelling for seven years. On his return the queen welcomed him, saying: "My lord, we have forgot the fart."

1695-1696

Canterbury, January 1695. Thomas Tenison, the bishop of London, is consecrated archbishop of Canterbury (→14/12/15).

London, 5 March 1695. Queen Mary II is buried.

London, 10 June 1695. Drunken Jacobites are arrested after causing an uproar at a reunion to celebrate the birthday of James II's son, James, the former prince of Wales.

Scotland, 26 June 1695. The Company of Scotland is founded with the purpose of trading with Africa and the Indies; the company has a monopoly on all Scottish trade with North America, Asia and Africa (→10/1698).

Dublin, 27 August 1695. King William III is present at the opening of his second Irish parliament (→7/9).

London, 21 November 1695. Henry Purcell, the composer and organist at Westminster Abbey, dies.→

Westminster, December 1695. William III establishes a council of trade, avoiding demands for a council nominated by parliament and overseeing the appointment of its members himself.

Highland, 1695. The threat of severe famine following last year's atrocious harvest results in a wave of migration to Ulster (→1696).

Bristol, 1695. William Bonny sets up the first printing press in the city.

London, 1695. William Congreve, the dramatist, publishes a comedy, *Love for Love* (→1700).

Westminster, January 1696. William III gives his assent to the Treason Trials Act.

London, 15 February 1696. A Jacobite plot to kill William III is discovered (→27/4).

Edinburgh, 9 October 1696. Parliament passes the Education Act; schools are to be set up in every parish, and the teachers will be paid by the parish landowners.

Scotland, 1696. Famine, which has been prevalent in the highlands since 1692, reaches the lowlands, as a consequence of last year's bad harvest.

London, 1696. Edward Lloyd, of Lloyd's coffee house, publishes a thrice-weekly newspaper, *Lloyd's News*.

William recognizes Anne as his heir

Westminster, February 1695
Although relations between them remain frosty, King William III has relented and recognized Princess Anne, his sister-in-law, as his heir. William has accepted that her five-year-old son, William, the duke of Gloucester, is the only hope for a Stuart succession to the throne, sickly though he is.

Anne is to move from the gloom of Windsor Castle to London, where she and her husband, Prince George of Denmark, will occupy St James's Palace. The move is unlikely to improve her health, however. Apart from being almost crippled by rheumatism, she is apparently suffering a phantom pregnancy; her doctors say that it is "nothing but the vapours" (→30/7/1700).

Anne with her young son, William.

Water is put on tap in city of Oxford

Oxford, 6 July 1695
Much to the surprise – and possible inconvenience – of academics and burghers alike, workmen are digging up the streets of this university city to lay water mains. Sixty-centimetre (2-foot) trenches have been dug from Carfax to Northgate, and the water will pass through bored-out elm trunks.

Work began today on connecting All Souls and Queen's Colleges, with further digging under way in Cat Street. The water will be pumped from a water house at Welcom's Folly next month.

Severe penal laws introduced in Ireland

A Protestant view of the atrocities of which rebellious Catholics were capable.

Ireland, 7 September 1695
Eager for their support, King William III has agreed to the demands of Irish Protestants for new penal laws against Roman Catholics. Parliament in Dublin is being presented with two measures calculated to please Protestant opinion: a bill to disarm all Catholics and prevent them from owning horses worth more than £5, and another to prevent their children from being sent abroad to be educated. By enacting the so-called "popery code", the Irish parliament is hoping to keep Catholics in a state of permanent subjection and eventually to eradicate them. Ireland will now have the doubtful privilege of being the only country in Europe where the persecuted actually form the majority of the population (→4/3/04).

Licensing and censorship of press ended

England, April 1695
Press censorship has been brought to an end by the lapsing of the 1662 Licensing Act. The measure was introduced to stop publication of "heretical, seditious, schismatical or offensive books or pamphlets" or anything considered to be "contrary to good life or good manners". Unlicensed printing was banned, officials had powers of search and seizure, and the number of master printers was limited to 20. The act has been allowed to lapse because the licensing system, as administered by the Stationers' company, had become corrupt and ineffective, mainly because the book trade has outgrown all attempts to control it.

The capture of Namur on 1 September 1695 by English and Dutch forces burst like a thunderclap on King Louis XIV of France; the siege, which went on for some three months, was financed by the Bank of England.

Henry Purcell plays his final melody

London, 21 November 1695
Henry Purcell has died of consumption, at the age of 37. He was, according to John Evelyn, "esteemed the best composer of any Englishman hitherto". The son of a gentleman of the Chapel Royal, he spent his life there, as choirboy, organist, composer in ordinary and keeper of the instruments, for which he was paid £60 a year, and at Westminster Abbey. Apart from his church and coronation music he wrote birthday odes for Queen Mary, the last being *Come, Ye Sons of Art*. He also wrote music for *God Save the King*, in 1685. Purcell will be buried in the abbey, when the musicians will play the same music as was used for the funeral of Queen Mary just eight months ago.

Henry Purcell, by John Closterman.

Christianity is no mystery says Toland

London, 1696
As part of the current rationalist debate on "revelation" in the Bible, a sensation has been caused by the appearance of *Christianity Not Mysterious, or A treatise showing that there is nothing in the gospel contrary to reason, nor above it*. The author, an Irish writer from Derry called John Toland, quotes Archbishop Tillotson: "We desire not better evidence that any man is in the wrong than for him to declare against reason." John Locke's *Reasonableness of Christianity* came out last year (→ 11/9/97).

'Whig Junto' takes politics by storm

Westminster, November 1695
England is reeling from monetary reforms introduced by a forthright group of "Whig" grandees calling itself "the Junto". This group, led by Charles Talbot, Lord Shrewsbury, includes John, Baron Somers, Thomas, Lord Wharton, and the financial expert Charles Montagu, the commissioner of the treasury and chancellor of the exchequer. It was Montagu who proposed, soon after the election of the new government this month, that the existing coinage – much of which is "clipped" or forged faulty silver – should be replaced with new coins. The effect has been a loss of money in circulation, creating unemployment, disruption in the retail trade and shortage of credit for industry and commerce, with many unable to pay debts or taxes.

Despite widespread discontent the Junto is unmoved, even though its monetary policy makes fighting the war harder. There are new taxes on salt, leather, windows and water-borne coal, with additional duties imposed on wine – but to little effect.

New law passed after failed assassination

Fenwick: noted enemy of the king.

London, 27 April 1695
If he had any doubt about the sudden upsurge in his popularity, King William III need only have walked through the streets of London to find thousands of his citizens sporting bright red ribbons bearing the slogan "General Association for King William". It is now considered almost unpatriotic *not* to wear one of them.

The change in the public's attitude follows what is seen as a failed assassination attempt on William by Jacobites – who are vehemently denying any such threat. An Act of Association has today been passed requiring office-holders to take an oath "that his majesty is the rightful and lawful king".

A shocked parliament was told that the plot was hatched at the French court by Sir George Barclay who, earlier this year, had arrived in England in an attempt to raise an army of insurrection. He made contact with Sir John Fenwick, a noted opponent of King William. The duke of Berwick, the son of the exiled James II, is also involved.

Several informers agreed that the king would be attacked in Richmond Park on 15 February after a day's hunting. Some 50 men on horseback, led by a Jacobite brigadier, would attack his guards, after which 12 men led by Barclay would kill the king's horses and shoot through the windows of the royal coach. William, who at first refused to believe the story, was finally pursuaded to hunt in Kensington Park instead. An alternative assassination plan to kill the king as he returned from church to St James's was foiled when 14 plotters were arrested in London.

English social survey shows wide disparity between rich and poor

England, 1696
A statistician, Gregory King, has produced some startling figures about the disparity of wealth in England. He has carried out calculations over the past two years which show that, for example, 63 per cent of the population have incomes below the poverty level, which King puts at £40 a year.

According to King's figures, families classed as "cottagers and paupers" are among the poorest in society; making up 29.4 per cent of the population, they earn on average just £6 10s. [£6.50] a year. A shopkeeper might earn £45, and a "lesser trader" £198 annually. King estimates that peers' families net about £2,800. In reality they probably receive twice as much.

However, great changes have been under way in England since the civil war, with the emergence of a more prosperous "middle" class between the peasants and the landed gentry. The economy is expanding, as traders look beyond Europe to the wider world of the colonies. Old-fashioned farming methods are giving way to new agricultural techniques, and crop rotation and profits from produce are on the increase. The new methods on the farms require fewer labourers, and as a result more people are now drifting to the towns and to London, where there is not enough work to go round.

A peasant woman in a kitchen: 63 per cent of people are living in poverty.

1697 - 1698

Westminster, 5 April 1697. Parliament bans the export of Irish woollen goods (→ 25/9).

Europe, May 1697. Peace talks are held to end the nine-year war on the continent (→ 20/9).

Dublin, 11 September 1697. Parliament orders the burning of *Christianity not Mysterious* by John Toland, an atheist.

Dublin, 25 September 1697. The Banishment Act requires all Catholic clergy to leave Ireland by next May (→ 4/1698).

Ireland, 27 October 1697. Arbitration begins for land claims under the Treaties of Galway and Limerick (→ 11/4/1700).

Scotland, 1697. The general assembly passes the Barrier Act; any future legislation passed by the assembly must be approved by a majority of presbyteries before being returned to the assembly for ratification.

Ireland, January 1698. The poet Daibhidh O Bruadair dies.

Westminster, 27 June 1698. Parliament declares William Molyneux's tract *The case of Ireland's being bound by acts of parliament in England stated* "dangerous" to the crown and the people of England (→ 26/1/99).

Central America, October 1698. Three ships sent by the Company of Scotland from Edinburgh to build a colony at Darien, on the Panamanian isthmus, arrive in a sheltered inlet (→ spring 1699).

Europe, October 1698. King William III and Louis XIV of France sign a partition treaty to try to solve the Spanish succession question (→ 3/1700).

London, December 1698. George Farquhar's play *Love and a Bottle* opens at the Drury Lane theatre (→ 4/1709).

Westminster, 1698. By a new arrangement called the "civil list", William III is granted £700,000 a year for life, in effect making him dependent on parliament (→ 1/2/99).

London, 1698. *The Provok'd Wife*, by the architect and dramatist Sir John Vanbrugh, is performed (→ 26/3/26).

London, 1698. The Reverend Jeremy Collier publishes *A Short View of the Immorality and Profaneness of the English Stage*; Vanbrugh is one of the dramatists attacked in the pamphlet.

'Tories' anxious about threat to church

Royalty looks on as the pope's nose is pressed to the Protestant grindstone.

London, November 1697
The increasing popularity of the dissenting churches at the expense of Anglicanism has led to cries of "the church in danger" and calls by high "Tories" for a recall of convocation – the Anglican synod – to ensure the predominance of the established church.

The Tories have not forgiven the "Whigs" for the Toleration Act of 1689, on which they are casting most of the blame for the present state of religious affairs in England. Moreover they see King William III's government as dangerously lax in its interpretation of religious conformity. The lapsing of the Licensing Act in 1695 has made the situation even worse, in their eyes, opening the floodgates to outpourings against the established church which threaten not only it but also society itself (→ 24/11/99).

Scottish student executed for blasphemy

Edinburgh, 8 January 1697
Thomas Aikenhead, a 19-year-old student who repeatedly mocked the Christian religion, has been executed for blasphemy. The son of an apothecary, Aikenhead referred to Christianity as a "rhapsody of feined and ill-invented nonsense", denounced Christ as an impostor and predicted that Christianity would disappear by 1800, and that the human race would be happier as a result. To Scotland's Presbyterian clerics this was satanic prose, and fearing that the country would be engulfed by free-thinking anarchy they pressed for prosecution.

It is an indication of their power and ruthlessness that they were able to force the court to impose the death sentence on Aikenhead, even though he made no attempt to defend his views, pleading only the folly of youth.

Continental war is ended by signing of Peace of Ryswick

Europe, 20 September 1697
William III's nine-year war with France has ground to a halt. The treaty signed today at Ryswick in the Dutch United Provinces is the result of months of secret negotiations. France's conquests prior to 1678 are to be recognized, but it is to withdraw from territories occupied after that date; William is recognized as the rightful king of England (a blow to the exiled James II); and the Dutch are to garrison the Spanish Netherlands.

The immediate cause of the war was the French invasion of the lower Palatinate (in Germany) in 1688. William – whose aim was to contain Louis XIV's France – assembled a coalition, joining the power of Britain to that of Austria (in the Holy Roman Empire), the United Provinces, Spain and the German princes. The war was waged as far afield as Catalonia, Italy and Ireland, as well as on the Rhine and the Danube, and in the English Channel and the Mediterranean. At one time the French were allied to the Turks, and at another William found himself allied to the *bey* [ruler] of Algiers.

In the first six years William was outwitted by the French commander, the duke of Luxembourg. Both the fall of Namur in the Spanish Netherlands – the most fortified city in Europe – in 1694, and Luxembourg's death a few months later helped William's position, but it was war-weariness that finally led to today's agreement (→ 10/1698).

Royal art treasures pulled from blaze as fire destroys Whitehall

London, 4 January 1698
Whitehall Palace, built by Cardinal Wolsey 177 years ago, has burnt to the ground. Although much of the contents was rescued, only Inigo Jones's banqueting hall still stands. The fire was started inadvertently by a Dutch laundress who left some clothes to dry too near a brazier; she perished in the blaze. King William III, who so disliked the smoggy air at Whitehall that he moved to Kensington Palace some years ago, is unlikely to regret the loss.

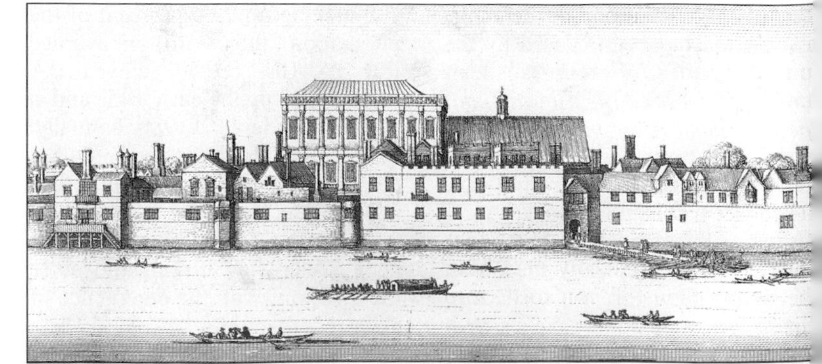
The palace of Whitehall before a careless laundress burnt it down.

Molyneux puts the 'case for Ireland'

Dublin, April 1698
William Molyneux, a member of the Irish House of Commons, has published a pamphlet entitled *The case of Ireland's being bound by acts of parliament in England stated*, in which he contends that the English parliament should have no right to override that of Ireland.

Westminster has condemned the pamphlet and stressed Ireland's dependence on England. Members there have presented an address to King William III, urging him to discourage woollen manufacturing in Ireland and encourage linen production instead (→27/6).

Full steam ahead for Cornish mines

Savery's pump uses steam pressure to force water out of mine shafts.

St Austell, Cornwall, 1698
Thomas Savery, a military engineer, has patented a device for pumping water out of mine shafts. It is powered by steam funnelled from a tank of water heated to boiling point. Major Savery is calling his new invention a "fire engine".

There is little likelihood of the invention making Savery's fortune. Cornwall's tin mines are going through a severe recession. According to *The Tinners' Grievances*, published last year, the average miner's wage was £10 per year, perilously close to starvation level.

Lone woman traveller makes grand tour of England and Wales

Midlands and East Anglia traversed

Newcastle-under-Lyme, 1698
Celia Fiennes, the granddaughter of Lord Saye and Sele, one of the parliamentary leaders during the civil war period, has arrived at her uncle's house here in Staffordshire, having completed the first stage of a figure-of-eight journey through England and Wales.

Her travels have so far taken her through Colchester, Ipswich, Norwich, Ely and Leicester. She was impressed by Colchester: "The whole town is employed in spinning, weaving, washing, drying and dressing their baize." But she shuddered at "proud and slothful" Ipswich and dismissed Norwich Cathedral as "nothing remarkable". Ely was "the dirtiest place I ever saw", while its inhabitants, the Fen Slodgers, who still use stilts when herding their cattle, were "a lazy sort of people, afraid to do too much". From the houses in Leicestershire where cow dung is plastered onto the walls, to the roadside knitters in East Anglia, nothing escaped her observant eye.

The inhabitants of the villages that Fiennes passed through appear to have been as astonished by her as she was by them. She is a most aristocratic dissenter and an imperious traveller, journeying in the company of only a maidservant. While her family worries that she may fall foul of highwaymen, one look at the dauntless Miss Fiennes would reassure the casual observer that no highwayman would find her easy prey.

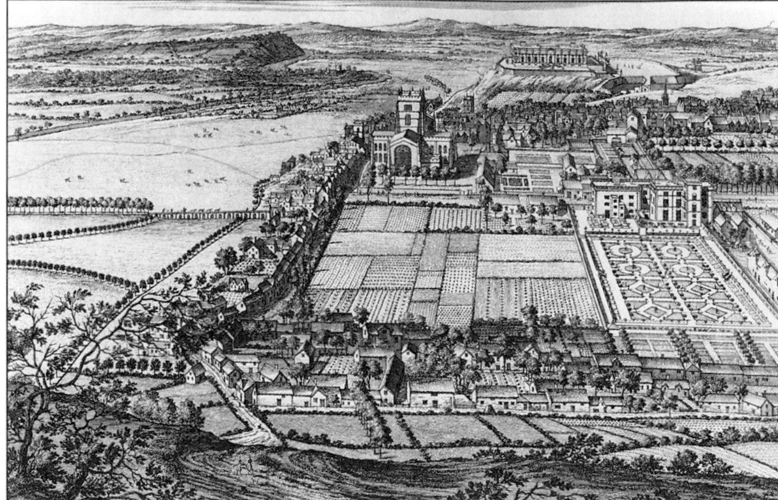
Nottingham at the time when Celia Fiennes made her eventful journey.

'Sulphur' taints air in northern regions

Newcastle upon Tyne, 1698
From a hill two miles (3.2km) from this town in north-east England Celia Fiennes looked down on the biggest coalfield in Britain: "The country all about is full of this coal, the sulphur of it taints the air, and it smells strongly to strangers."

In her travels around England Miss Fiennes had left the midlands and ridden to Liverpool, said by some to be England's most modern city and "London in miniature as much as I ever saw anything". She continued across the mountains and lakes of Cumberland and Westmorland, where she at first mistook the "sad little huts made up of dry walls" that the natives live in for barns. After Carlisle she turned east along Hadrian's wall and came to Newcastle.

Liverpool was "London in miniature", the intrepid traveller concluded.

Fiennes goes west into cider country

St Austell, Cornwall, 1698
The intrepid Celia Fiennes has had her first taste of Cornish cream: "They scald their cream and milk so it is a sort of clotted cream as we call it, with a little sugar, put on top of the apple pie." She was less captivated, however, by the Cornish fondness for smoking. "Men, women and children all have pipes of tobacco in their mouths, which was not a delight to me when I went down to talk to my landlady for information of any matter or customs amongst them."

Since leaving Newcastle upon Tyne she has travelled more than 600 miles (960km). She decided to avoid Halifax on principle – on account of the town's notorious execution machine, while at Shrewsbury she managed to escape from two highwaymen who had attempted to hold her up. Bristol she found packed with slave ships; Bath she knew well, having frequented the hot baths in her younger days; in Wookey Hole the stalagmites reminded her of candy; and in Somerset she berated the cider-pressers for wastefully pulping good and bad apples indiscriminately.

Miss Fiennes now plans a short trip to Land's End, then she will return to London by way of Exeter and Salisbury. By the end of her journey she will have covered some 1,500 miles (→8/1726).

1699

Dublin, 26 January. Parliament passes an act preventing all "papists" from becoming solicitors (→ 1/2).

Westminster, 1 February. Parliament orders that foreign troops in Ireland should be disbanded and sets a limit of 12,000 on the royal (standing) army (→ 4/5).

England, 7 May. All lotteries, apart from one benefiting the newly opened Greenwich hospital, will be banned after this Christmas; it is felt that they cheat the public.

England, May. Edward Russell, the earl of Orford, who defeated the French fleet in the Battle of La Hogue of 1692, is dismissed from the post of first lord of the admiralty.

London, 10 June. A great fire at Rotherhithe burns over 300 houses and many ships.

Ireland, early August. Edward Lhuyd, a Welsh antiquary, begins a tour (→ 5/1707).

Wales, August. Bishop Watson of St David's is deprived of his living following accusations that he exploited his position for financial gain.

Edinburgh, September. The Company of Scotland hears that the colony it has sponsored at Darién, in the Panamanian isthmus, has been abandoned; unfortunately a second expedition set sail to join it last month (→ 11/1699).

Central America, November. The second expedition to Darién arrives to find the colony deserted (→ 15/2/1700).

Westminster, December. John, Baron Somers, remains lord chancellor despite charges that he bears responsibility for the activities of Captain William Kidd, who turned pirate after being sent to the Indian Ocean to protect East India company merchants (→ 23/5/1701).

London. The poet laureate John Dryden publishes *Fables Ancient and Modern*, a collection of translations from Homer, Ovid, Boccaccio and Chaucer (→ 1/5/1700).

Scotland. Jacobites [supporters of James VII of Scots and II of England] claim that the terrible famine which is killing thousands in the country is an act of God; they blame King William III for usurping the throne from James.

London. A fish market opens at Billingsgate.

Export bans batter Ireland's economy

Westminster, 4 May

An act passed today prohibits the export of woollen goods from Ireland to any country except England. It follows an act passed by William III's Irish parliament on 26 January imposing duties on woollen exports from Ireland.

These measures are sure to have serious effects on the Irish economy, which has recently been doing well. Helped by good harvests at a time when harvest failure has been general in much of Europe, Irish farmers have had large surpluses to sell at high prices. The economic boom has been strongest, however, in the steadily growing woollen industry. This has aroused the jealousy of English manufacturers, who are finding themselves undersold by Irish goods on the continental market and are concerned that skilled workmen are moving from England to Ireland where the cost of living is lower.

The woollen industry is largely owned by Protestants, so it is they who will suffer most from this setback. There is anger that an Irish industry should be curtailed in England's interests. There is also fear that any Irish undertaking that appears to threaten England may get similar treatment (→ 14/2/1700).

Commons vote for savage defence cuts

Fewer men will be taking "the king's shilling" under the Disbanding Bill.

Westminster, 1 February

Parliament has again rebuffed King William III and voted to disband all military forces in England which contain over 7,000 men. Reluctantly, he has acquiesced and given his assent to the Disbanding Bill passed by the Commons. The bill also provides for severe penalities to be imposed on foreign troops left in the realm after March.

The struggle between king and Commons over the strength of the armed forces has been going on for months. At first certain members demanded that the army of some 15,000 men in England and 16,000 in Ireland be cut to the strength of 20 years ago.

William strongly argued the case for keeping a large standing army in peacetime; he was also dismayed by the proposal that his Dutch guard was to be removed from service along with all other foreign officers and men. At one time he was so close to despair that he hinted that he would withdraw from the conduct of government, retire to the United Provinces and abdicate. William is convinced that "the nation is left too much exposed".

'Time for tea' says Orvington in his essay on latest popular fad

An English family sits down for tea: Chinese-style cups are the fashion.

Britain

All the best people are doing it these days – drinking tea. So fashionable has it become in the last ten years, with the East India company importing tea directly from China, that John Orvington has written an essay extolling the beverage's virtues entitled *The Nature and Qualities of Tea*.

Tea is usually drunk after dinner, the hostess brewing it up and ceremonially serving it to guests, and there are several brands of it. Most often it is served black, with sugar, and there is nothing wrong with drinking it from the saucer. The East India company, aware that it has struck a seam of gold, is also encouraging an interest in the use of genuine china teacups and teapots. Kettles are increasingly being used instead of copper urns (→ 1706).

Scots leave witches and spells in peace

Edinburgh
Hunting witches in Scotland these days is not what it was. Two years ago a spate of accusations led to renewed interest in tracking down alleged witches, but that is now petering out. Alarmed that the secular powers have lost interest in the whole matter, the church's general assembly here has put up ideas of its own on controlling witches, but it is getting little response.

Witch-hunting in Scotland has had its ups and downs over the last 100 years. Fishing villages on the east coast have been good areas for witch-hunts, chiefly because of the alleged link between witchcraft and sea disasters. Yet although witchcraft has been held responsible for vague general conditions, such as an increase in sin, riots and even storm-raising, it is rarely blamed for large-scale disasters, such as the current famine, for which the cause is of course natural. While the general assembly is unlikely to give up on witches just yet, the public's appetite for hounding old women to death is on the wane (→1700).

Improvements in morals and law-abiding behaviour promised by Christian society

London, 24 November
A revival of moral puritanism is under way in England and Wales, symbolized by the Society for Promoting Christian Knowledge. The SPCK is an Anglican organization founded today by Dr Thomas Bray, who plans to provide schools in London where children can learn the catechism. The aim is also to print improving literature for the poor and promote Christianity in the American plantations.

The organization has its origin in Anglican alarm at the growth in crime and irreligion. There has recently been an unprecedented number of robberies and murders, and societies for the reformation of manners – some of which date back to the 1500s – are busy as never before, enforcing laws against prostitution, blasphemy, drunkenness and sabbath-breaking.

Already, in London, these societies have been responsible for hundreds of prosecutions. They have aroused resentment by using paid informers. The SPCK also faces problems in Wales, where Anglicans have been reluctant to provide Welsh-speaking schools in areas where Welsh is spoken. In some Welsh counties, parents are also reportedly unwilling to send children to school because they need them to beg for food (→1701).

A Smithfield execution: the number of robberies and murders is soaring.

New political party formed by a 'Tory'

London
The English political scene is changing shape with the formation this year of a new "Country" party, which intends to provide opposition to the "Whig" ministry and its policies. The party has been formed by Robert Harley, a "Tory" member who was once a Whig and who comes from a gentry family with a background in dissent. Harley and his backers, many of whom are also Tories, adopt the traditional "country" attitude of suspicion towards the court and foreigners, and vigorously attack "placemen" and corruption in parliament (→24/1/1708).

Doctor claims apes are man's cousins

London
Edward Tyson, an English doctor and enthusiastic anatomist, has dissected an African chimpanzee and concluded that it is man's closest relative among the animals. In a copiously illustrated report entitled *Homo sylvestris or the anatomy of a pygmie*, Tyson lists 48 physical similarities, such as hair, the heart and the brain, and 34 differences between man and ape. It is doubtful whether many people will find the comparison flattering.

The simian "man of the woods".

Scottish colony established in New World

Central America, spring
Ships carrying eager Scots arrived last October at Darien, on the Panamanian isthmus, where they are trying to set up a colony. The expedition has been long in the planning and has cost its sponsor, the Company of Scotland, huge sums, but it is badly equipped and already short of supplies. Moreover, of the 1,200 who sailed from Edinburgh, 200 died during the voyage. The survivors have called their tropical home New Caledonia and begun building a capital, New Edinburgh. Yet fever and starvation are taking a grim toll, and some settlers are thinking of pulling out (→9/1699).

The restored and lavender-filled "parterre" – a level space in a garden occupied by flower-beds – of Ham House in Surrey is a typical example of the late 17th-century vogue in England for Dutch garden designs.

Churches back plan for Welsh schools

Wales
A religious outreach of sorts is being planned for Wales, with church leaders and reformers placing a priority on education and literacy as a way to spread the gospel. A pioneer Welsh Trust has been established to found and organize schools in the principality. Its work is supported by leading churchmen and dissenters and is to be carried further by the new Society for Promoting Christian Knowledge [*see report above*].

Dissenters in Wales are still united against the deliberate harassment meted out to them by the Anglican authorities and the justices of the peace. Their churches are denied licences, and they themselves are refused burial in parish cemeteries. Welsh dissenters – who tend to be men of substance rather than affluence – are usually drawn from the ranks of artisans, traders and the minor gentry.

1700

Ireland, 14 February. A warrant requires the lord justices to pay a subsidy to Louis Crommelin "for establishing a linen manufacture in Ireland" (→ 4/3/04).

Central America, 15 February. Scottish colonists at Darién defeat an attack by Spanish troops, themselves the target of an earlier attack by the colonists (→ 1/4).

Central America, 1 April. The Scottish colonists at Darién, who surrendered to the Spanish in March in return for their freedom, abandon Darién because of sickness and lack of food and shelter (→ 5/1700).

Westminster, 11 April. Parliament rescinds re-grants of land in Ireland made by King William III.

Westminster, 11 April. William III prorogues parliament after it requests that he remove all foreign advisers (including his Dutch compatriots) from court (→ 17).

Westminster, 17 April. John, Baron Somers, is dismissed as lord chancellor (→ 5/1700).

London, 1 May. John Dryden, poet laureate since 1668, dies; his last work, published earlier this year, was the *Preface to the Fables*.

Edinburgh, May. Parliament, which blames William III for the Darién colony fiasco, threatens to withhold funds from the king (→ 10/1700).

Birmingham. A recent census shows that the town has 30 streets, 100 courts and alleys, 2,504 houses and 15,032 inhabitants.

London. A barrister, John Asgill, is jailed for publishing a pamphlet claiming that "man may be translated from hence into that eternal life without passing through death"; the pamphlet is burnt.

London. John Blow is appointed official composer to the chapel royal (→ 1/10/08).

London. Whig men of letters form the Kit-Kat Club (→ 12/1703).

Norfolk. Dutch engineers assist an attempt to drain the fens.

St Albans, Hertfordshire. A mob hounds a woman accused of witchcraft to death.

Westmorland. M Beaumont, a Frenchman, finishes the topiary garden at Levens Hall, one of the finest of its kind in the country.

Restoration comedy loses some sparkle

John Dryden: biting satirical wit.

Actors in "The Provok'd Wife".

London
William Congreve's latest play, *The Way of the World*, has not met with his accustomed acclaim this season, despite the sparkling dialogue. Congreve had great success three years ago with his comedy *Love For Love* and his tragedy *The Mourning Bride*, from which everyone quotes the line: "Hell hath no fury like a woman scorned."

Yet satirical wits such as the Irish-born Congreve and his fellow playwrights John Dryden, who died this year, and Sir John Vanbrugh have been under attack ever since the Reverend Jeremy Collier published his pamphlet *A Short View of the Immorality and Profaneness of the English Stage* in 1698. "Cursing, swearing and the abuse of religion" was one of his charges. "As for swearing, 'tis used by all persons and upon all occasions: 'tis all the rhetoric some people are masters of," he wrote, instancing the plays of Congreve and Vanbrugh as "particularly rampant and scandalous".

Congreve, who is 30, is talking of giving up the stage, and Vanbrugh, whose plays *The Relapse* and *The Provok'd Wife* were singled out by Collier, is busy designing Castle Howard. He has waspishly quipped, however, that Collier's mind has been corrupted by reading too many bawdy plays.

Royal succession in doubt as child dies

Windsor, 30 July
The death took place early this morning of William, the duke of Gloucester and sole surviving child of Princess Anne, the heir to the throne. As he was the only native-born candidate for the throne, the succession seems certain to go to the Hanoverians – descendants of Charles I's sister Elizabeth, who married Frederick V, the Elector Palatine. William celebrated his 11th birthday only six days ago; afterwards he complained of a chill and a sore throat. He was confined to bed, but his illness, either smallpox or scarlet fever, worsened, and he died (→ 1705).

William, the young duke, who died.

King signs pact without Commons' consent

London, March
King William III's independent foreign policy is causing alarm at Westminster. The king, being a Dutchman, sees Britain in the context of Europe and understands that there can be no security for the country until there is a settlement with the continental powers over the Spanish succession. This month William has reached a second agreement with Louis XIV of France to partition Spanish possessions – without consulting parliament. His thinking is that such moves will eventually limit French expansion. Whether or not they agree, members are angry at being left out of negotiations (→ 11/4).

Louis XIV: William III's partner.

Commons demand ban on 'foreigners'

Westminster, 10 April
Moves are afoot in parliament for yet another attack on the royal prerogative. Both Lords and Commons are infuriated by King William III's conclusion of two treaties with the French on the partition of Spanish lands, without bothering to inform them. The first was in October 1698, but it has since been nullified; the second was put together just last month [*see report left*]. Convinced that the king is being misled by the fellow Dutchmen advising him, parliament wants to ban "foreign" – that is, Dutch – advisers from his council (→ 4/5/02).

Scottish colony collapses amid fiasco

Edinburgh, October
Confirmation has just been received of the utter disaster that has befallen the Company of Scotland's attempt to found a colony overseas, at Darién on the Panamanian isthmus in Central America. The first expedition of about 1,200 people – of whom some 200 had died on their way from Scotland – arrived in October 1698 but abandoned the colony within months after many died of fever and starvation. The survivors sent word to Edinburgh of the impossible conditions in Darién, but the warning arrived just 12 days too late to stop the departure of a second expedition, in August 1699, of 1,300 more colonists inspired by false tales of easy riches.

The latest news is that almost everyone on the second expedition is dead, chiefly of fever. Most of the few hundreds who abandoned the colony were drowned when their three ships were wrecked as they sailed for New York. The expedition has cost vast sums, for which there is nothing to show but a crowded graveyard and a few empty huts on a fever-infested coast.

Disease, rations that turned out to be rotten, Spanish threats and a refusal by the governors of English colonies in the West Indies to help for fear of upsetting the Spanish all contributed to thwart the first colonists in the land which they named New Caledonia. When the survivors went to the English in Jamaica for help early in 1699, they found that strict orders not to assist had been sent from London. Of the original 1,200 settlers, only 300 lived to see Scotland again.

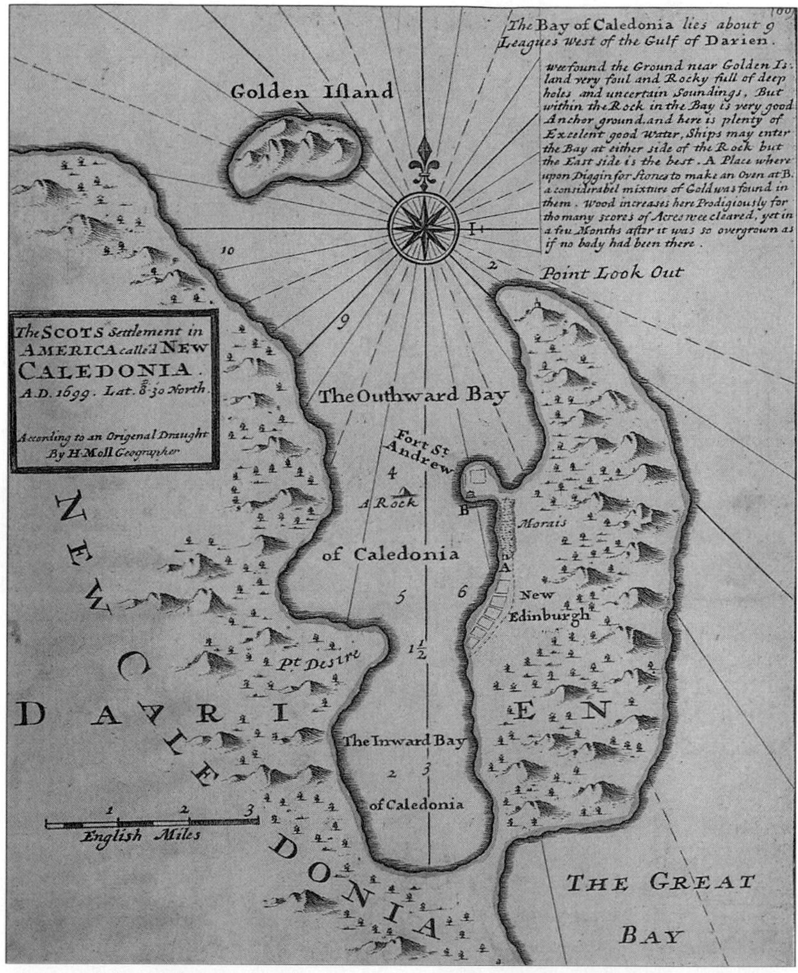

A map of the Caledonia settlement in the Central American isthmus of Darien.

The second expedition arrived in November 1699 to face similar difficulties, this time compounded by active Spanish aggression. The settlers, unaware of the grim fate of their forerunners, were horrified to find that New Edinburgh, the colony's capital, was nothing but a cluster of abandoned and decaying huts. Worse, they had not brought enough saws or axes to rebuild it; there was an attempted mutiny, and early this year the Spanish attacked them. The Scots fought back well, but with 600 sick from fever, ammunition running low and the Spanish gathering for the kill, the colonists chose on 1 April to abandon Darién. Again, the English refused help. One Scottish ship was wrecked off Cuba, and as the other two made for New York they were overwhelmed by a hurricane and lost with all hands.

Economy of England is revolutionized by colonial trade boom

England
The foundation of colonies in North America, the Caribbean and India is providing huge benefits and profits for England, which has become the major re-exporter of the goods shipped in from these places. In an extraordinarily short time such goods have moved from being thought of as luxuries to being considered necessities.

Until about 1650 most English overseas trade consisted of the export of wool, or wool cloth, which was exchanged for luxury goods such as wine and foods, including grain. Now sugar, tobacco and Indian calicoes make up about 30 per cent of English exports, while wool has dropped to 47 per cent. Although many of these goods from the colonies are re-exported at great profit, an increasing amount is retained for sale at home.

The change is evident in the revenues of the East India company. Between 1600 and 1640 the total value of its trade only twice exceeded £100,000 per year. By the 1680s it grew to as much as £600,000 annually, but this year it reached £703,497. The result is an increase in wealth as the value of English exports begins to outstrip the cost of imports. At the same time the number of colonists in the Americas is growing rapidly, from 48,000 in 1640 to 440,000 by this year, partly by natural increase and partly as a result of emigration (→ 1709).

Indian cottons are greatly prized.

Scotland's desire to establish a stake in empire led to disaster

Scotland, October
The bungled attempt to establish a Scottish colony in Central America grew out of the anger that Scotland feels at being denied access to the growing English empire in the West Indies, North America, Africa and India. The alleged double-dealing of King William III has already led to the Glencoe Massacre [*see report on page 622*] and involvement in a continental war that is ruining Scotland's trade. The Scots therefore set out to establish their own colony in Darién, and while William did nothing to stop it he used his influence to stop money being raised in London or abroad. Consequently huge amounts of Scots money was poured into the project, without anyone apparently questioning if the manufacture of wigs, woollen hose and plaid was really suitable for a colony in the tropics. The expeditions were badly equipped and supplied, but what really finished off the Scots were the hot climate and tropical diseases, for which they were utterly unprepared. Hundreds died before they ever reached Darién, and when they turned to the English for assistance they found that William had given strict instructions to his colonial governors that the Scots were to be left to live or die unaided.

1701 - 1702

Dublin, 1 July 1701. Grinling Gibbons's statue of William III is unveiled on College Green.

Norwich, 1701. The *Norwich Post*, Britain's first provincial newspaper, appears (→ 11/3/02).

Dublin, 1701. Ireland's first public library, founded by Archbishop Narcissus Marsh, opens.

Oxfordshire, 1701. Jethro Tull, a lawyer turned farmer who runs Howberry Farm, near Wallingford, invents a machine drill for sowing seeds in precise rows (→ 1714).

England, 1701. The Society for the Propagation of the Gospel in Foreign Parts is founded to evangelize English workers in colonial plantations (→ 1702).

London, 8 March 1702. King William III dies at Kensington Palace after a riding accident in Richmond Park; he was 51 years old (→ 23/4/02).

London, 11 March 1702. England's first daily newspaper, the *Daily Courant*, is printed (→ 1704).

Europe, 24 March 1702. John Churchill, the earl of Marlborough, is made commander-in-chief of British forces (→ 17/12).

Europe, 4 May 1702. England, the United Provinces and the Austrians declare war on France over the question of the Spanish succession (→ 12/1702).

Britain, 18 November 1702. Queen Anne insists on talks for a union between England and Scotland (→ 1702).

London, 17 December 1702. The earl of Marlborough is made a duke for his war services (→ 2/8/04).

Edinburgh, 1702. George Mackenzie of Rosehaugh's Advocates' Library is moved from the Faculty of Advocates to Parliament Hall.

London, 1702. John Sheffield, the duke of Buckingham, has Buckingham House built to designs by William Talman and a Dutch architect, William Winde.

London, 1702. Sarah Trimmer publishes *The Sacred History*, an expurgated Bible for young people (→ 6/2/04).

Scotland, 1702. George Ridpath writes a *Discourse upon the union of England and Scotland*, attacking the present regal union and seeking guarantees for the protection of Scottish interests (→ 8/3/03).

Scots privateer Kidd is hanged for piracy

London, 23 May 1701
After being found guilty at the Old Bailey on charges of piracy and murder, the Greenock-born Captain William Kidd was hanged today. He had been arrested in the American colonies after complaints reached London that instead of making war on enemy pirates he had been attacking and plundering ships on his own account.

Kidd's defence was that the ships had been sailing under the French flag and were legal prizes according to a special contract he had secured with members of the government. Kidd is rumoured to have hidden a huge horde of treasure – the fruits of his piracy – on an island.

Kidd's corpse goes on display.

Apprentices sign up

London, 1702
Business is booming in London, thanks to the hundreds of young people coming from all over the country to sign up here as apprentices and learn a trade. The system calls for a seven- or eight-year apprenticeship – an attractive proposition to the masters, who demand substantial premiums.

There are growing complaints that the laws and regulations governing apprenticeship are not tough enough. It is said that people are setting up in business without going through proper apprenticeships and are not being prosecuted.

Succession battle erupts

Allegorical figures of England, Ireland and Scotland surround William III.

Westminster, 12 June 1701
Roman Catholics were barred from the British throne today when the Act of Settlement received the royal assent. Although it made smooth progress through the Commons, in Scotland the act has caused uproar.

The Scots parliament – which has not been consulted – is protesting that the act can legally apply only to England. It accuses Westminster of arrogantly assuming that it can legislate for all three British kingdoms. The act was largely prompted by the death last year of the duke of Gloucester, the son of Princess Anne, the wife of Prince George of Denmark and heir to the throne, and aims to complete the work of the 1689 Bill of Rights.

Any successor must be an Anglican; anyone who converts to Rome or marries a Roman Catholic will be declared "incapacitated". The succession after William and Anne goes to Electress Sophia of Hanover, the granddaughter of James I. Yet the Scots are making it clear that they will refuse to ratify the Hanoverian succession (→ 6/9).

Silversmiths such as those above are part of Britain's growing economy.

France hails son of James II as Britain's monarch after his father's death in exile

France, 6 September 1701
After more than a decade in exile the former James VII of Scots and II of England died at St Germain today at the age of 68. His host, Louis XIV, has lost no time in publicly recognizing James's 13-year-old son as James VIII and III.

James succeeded Charles II, his elder brother, in 1685 but reigned for only three years. Unfortunately for England and Scotland he lacked the ability of Charles to dissemble about his Roman Catholicism. Less than ten years after the Restoration he was hearing Mass every day in London and was bent on bringing England back to Catholicism. It proved to be his undoing; William of Orange was asked to invade as a champion of Protestantism with a claim to the throne.

James fled England to spend his time in France planning invasions and devoting himself to religious observances. He coveted other men's wives just as much as his brother did, but he lacked the warmth as well as the humour that Charles often showed. There is no evidence that he ever told or enjoyed a joke; Nell Gwynn, one of Charles's mistresses, dubbed him "Dismal Jimmy" (→2/1702).

James II died an exile in France.

James III inherits a dubious title.

Plain princess to rule English and Scots

London, 23 April 1702
Anne, the daughter of James II, has been crowned queen at Westminster Abbey. She had earlier taken the Scottish coronation oath in the presence of her ministers at Whitehall. At the coronation banquet a mounted knight in armour entered Westminster Hall to challenge to combat anyone who denied the new queen's title to the crown.

Queen Anne succeeds William III, whose 13-year reign saw the creation of a modern government in England. In Scotland, however, he was highly unpopular owing to his role in the Glencoe Massacre and the Darién affair. William died on 8 March after a fall from his horse, which stumbled on a molehill.

Anne is reputedly dull, obstinate and unattractive. She has been pregnant 18 times, but only five of her babies were born alive, and they are all now dead. She is devoted to Protestantism – probably even more than she was to her Roman Catholic father, James II.

Anne will have to master politics: Tories and Whigs will both be trying to win her over. Her personal advisers, the earl of Marlborough and Lord Godolphin, are standing apart from both. Her highest political ambition is an Anglo-Scottish union, to break the deadlock over the royal succession – Scotland opposes the Hanoverian succession – and to block the Jacobites (→18/11).

Plain Anne: the Protestant queen.

Godolphin: staying above the fray.

Stuart 'pretender' barred from throne

Westminster, February 1702
The decision of France's Louis XIV to recognize James, the son of James II and VII, as the king of England and Scotland [*see report above*] has resulted in the passing of the Abjuration Act.

This Tory-sponsored legislation repudiates James, now dubbed "the pretender", and requires all office holders to recognize William III as the "lawful and rightful" monarch. Louis's declaration may be simply a chivalrous act, characteristic of his generosity to a luckless dynasty, but it has angered many people on this side of the Channel because it implies that the choice of their king rests with Versailles (→23/4).

Jacobites make big strides in elections

Edinburgh, autumn 1702
The elections have seen big gains by the Country Party and the Jacobites, who back James Stuart's claim to the throne of England and Scotland [the name comes from *Jacobus*, the Latin for James]. The election, the first in 13 years, was called after parliament was boycotted by the Country Party, angered that the privy council had declared war on France without consulting parliament. English Tories pressed for the election believing that the Episcopalians would win seats from the Presbyterian Court Party. Parliament here now has 100 Court supporters, 70 Jacobites and 60 Country members (→27/2/03).

War breaks out over Spanish succession

London, December 1702
A war for the Spanish succession is under way. Since 4 May England and, since 30 May, Scotland have been involved in a conflict in Europe, and on an unprecedented scale. On the one side is the Grand Alliance forged by England, Scotland, the United Provinces, Prussia, Austria and most of the other states of the Holy Roman Empire; on the other are France and Spain.

The death of Charles II of Spain in 1700 triggered the war. All Europe was interested in the succession, and, childless, Charles left a will giving the crown to France's Prince Philip of Anjou, the grandson of Louis XIV. Philip became king of Spain, but, with French power already feared in Europe, alarm grew that France might annex the Spanish empire. France is stronger now than it was when England declared war on Louis in 1689 after James II fled there.

A vast empire controlled from Versailles is feasible. Yet patriotic Englishmen, who know something about Europe and are convinced of England's importance there, are not afraid of a fight.

The England of Charles II was neither a major player on the European scene nor a military power; but now things are changing, and the English are getting caught in the meshes of European power politics. There is, crucially, a formidable English navy, and the army was turned by William into a great fighting force (→23/7/04).

1703 - 1704

Westminster, 27 February 1703. The English parliament demands that public office holders in Ireland abjure Jacobitism (→ 14/3/08).

Britain, 8 March 1703. Queen Anne prorogues Anglo-Scots union negotiations (→ 22/6).

Germany, 3 May 1703. John Churchill, the duke of Marlborough, seizes Cologne.

England, 26 May 1703. Samuel Pepys, the former secretary to the admiralty and president of the Royal Society, dies.

Scotland, 22 June 1703. Andrew Fletcher, the laird of Saltoun, proposes putting a limit on the powers of the monarchy (→ 13/8).

Edinburgh, 16 September 1703. James Douglas, the duke of Queensberry and government leader, adjourns parliament following a series of disastrous ministerial defeats (→ 1704).

England, 27 November 1703. A two-day storm has left 17,000 trees uprooted in Kent; thousands have drowned in flooding of the Thames and the Severn, as well as at sea; the Eddystone lighthouse has been destroyed. The bishop of Bath and Wells, Richard Kidder, was killed when part of his house collapsed.

London, December 1703. Rumours of a "Scotch plot" involving the duke of Queensberry are rife.

Westminster, 1703. The Commons are petitioned over the rise in salt prices, as this is "a grievance to the poorer sort of people who mostly feed on salted provisions".

Spain, 23 July 1704. The English, led by Sir George Rooke, capture Gibraltar (→ 2/8).

Essex, 28 October 1704. John Locke, the Whig philosopher, dies.

Scotland, December 1704. The Bank of Scotland suspends all payments.

Bath, 1704. The first pump room here opens.

Bristol, 1704. A local newspaper, *The Bristol Postboy*, begins publication.

London, 1704. Daniel Defoe publishes *The Review*, a weekly political paper (→ 1706).

Gwynedd, 1704. Ellis Wynne, a clergyman, publishes a satirical work idolizing Queen Anne, *Gweledigaethau y bardd cwsc* [*Visions of the sleeping bard*].

Scottish parliament rebels over union with England and Hanoverian succession

At Parliament House in Edinburgh Scots are fighting union with England.

Edinburgh, 13 August 1703
The recently elected parliament is intensifying efforts to nullify the proposed union with England. The Act of Security, passed today to widespread acclamation, insists on Scotland's right to be ruled by a monarch who, except in the most tightly defined circumstances, will not be the same as the one who sits on the English throne. The new act is designed to thwart the English court, which wants the Scots to knuckle under and accept the Hanoverian succession. This is the latest in a series of legislative developments designed to divide the prospective partners. Unity negotiations broke down on 8 March.

Already this year the Scots have passed an act that gives them the right to begin and end any hostilities involving their troops, as well as two other measures concerning the wine and wool trades, which are bound to have an adverse effect on England's ability to exert economic pressure on France. The resulting mutual exasperation is reaching a high pitch and bringing the two sides closer to armed conflict (→ 28).

Defoe pilloried for ironic attack on dissent

When the Tories did not see the joke it was no laughing matter for Defoe.

London, May 1703
"He is a middle-sized, spare man, about 40 years old, of a dark complexion and dark brown hair, but he wears a wig. A hooked nose, sharp chin, grey eyes and a large mole near his mouth; he was born in London and for many years was a hose-factor in Cornhill and is now owner of a brickworks near Tilbury Fort, Essex." So ran the notice offering a £50 reward for the capture of the journalist Daniel Defoe. His offence was writing a pamphlet entitled *The Shortest Way with Dissenters*, in which he suggested exterminating them all. It was meant ironically, but the Tories missed the joke. Defoe has been pilloried for three days and fined (→ 1704).

Choose your drink and your politics

London, December 1703
The polemics of the wine bottle, which have raised many a gentleman's temper during recent election campaigns, received new spice this month when Lord Methuen, a Whig, successfully negotiated his commercial treaty with the Portuguese. Under its terms Queen Anne has agreed that the port wine which comes from the Douro – and has long been extolled by those of the Whig persuasion – shall never be subjected to excise duty at more than two-thirds of the level imposed on the claret of Bordeaux, which is so much preferred by Tories and those who support the claims of the house of Stuart.

Taxing employment: wine-sellers.

'Royal touch' used to cure 'king's evil'

London, 1703
The ancient ceremony of "the royal touch", prescribed as a certain remedy for scrofula, the skin disease traditionally known as "the king's evil", has been enthusiastically revived by Queen Anne.

Ever since the reign of Edward the Confessor, in the 11th century, English sovereigns have regularly called together groups of sufferers to go through this healing ritual (and so underline the divine origins of their own office). The practice was discontinued by William III, who did not believe in it. But this year the queen has on several occasions ministered to groups of up to 300 sufferers, after solemnly preparing herself for the occasion with a 24-hour fast.

Penal laws passed against Irish Catholics

The pope is often seen as urging all Catholics to betray their country.

Ireland, 4 March 1704
The severe penal laws introduced in 1695 against Catholics – the great majority of the population – have been strengthened by a bill that has just received the royal assent.

Under the new legislation Roman Catholics may not acquire land other than by a lease for a period of at most 31 years. They cannot inherit land from a Protestant or acquire it through marriage. On their deaths, their land must be divided amongst all their sons, but if the eldest conforms to the established [Protestant] church he may inherit the whole estate. These harsh measures aim at the gradual decline of the Catholic gentry.

Under more general restrictions, Catholics may not have their children educated abroad, and before voting in elections or holding any public office they must take the oath of allegiance – to a Protestant monarch. These new rules are clearly designed to keep Catholics in a position of social, economic and political inferiority. Members of the Dublin parliament, meeting for the first time for five years, aim to improve the position of Protestants and keep Catholics out of political power (→ 14/3/05).

A great storm in November 1703, resulting in some 8,000 fatalities, destroyed Eddystone lighthouse (above), in Plymouth Sound.

Clarendon records events of rebellion

London, 1704
The *True Historical Narrative of the Rebellion and the Civil Wars in England* by Edward Hyde, the earl of Clarendon, has been published in three volumes exactly thirty years after his death in exile. Clarendon began it in 1646 as a counter to the history commissioned by parliament. He intended it for King Charles I's eyes only and hoped to publish it "when the passion, rage and fury of this time shall be forgotten". Oliver Cromwell's victory sent Clarendon into exile. He returned to become Charles II's lord chancellor but was exiled again and completed the work as a history of his own time. His sons authorized publication, and it looks set to become a bestseller.

Queen's bounty set up for poor clergy

Windsor, 6 February 1704
Queen Anne has celebrated her 39th birthday here by confirming a new bounty – initially set at £16,500 per annum – which she is dedicating to help to support the poorer members of the clergy, many of whose impoverished livings are currently worth barely £10 a year.

The archbishop of York, John Sharp, thanked Anne for "this surprising instance of your kindness to the church", which had "outdone all your predecessors since the Reformation". The bounty represents a redistribution of minor church taxes, such as "tenths" and "first-fruits", which previously went to selected royal pensioners (→ 1709).

Scottish parliament fights Hanoverians

Edinburgh, 28 August 1704
Rejecting all compromise, parliament ended another tumultuous session today by reaffirming its determination to block any possibility of a Hanoverian succession to the throne of Scotland.

The New Party, also called the *Squadrone Volante* and led by John Hay, the marquis of Tweeddale, since Queen Anne sacked the duke of Queensberry, is jealous of Scottish interests but not opposed to union. It failed to split the opposition and has, for the moment, conceded defeat. In desperate need of finance, Tweeddale has agreed to barter acceptance of the controversial Act of Security for six months' tax receipts (→ 16/9).

Isaac Newton leads scientific advances

Scholars listen attentively to a lecture in geography and astronomy.

Cambridge, 16 February 1704
The formal publication today of Isaac Newton's great work *Opticks* suitably marks the culmination of a remarkable half-century of scientific achievement. These past few decades of war, revolution and social upheaval have also seen an explosive expansion in man's understanding of the natural universe, and British scholars and experimenters have led the way.

Many of these achievements are described in a new encyclopaedia, the *Lexicon Technicum*, which has been prepared by John Harris, the administrator of the Royal Society, whose members have made a formidable contribution to this growth of knowledge. He catalogues and explains such pioneering investigations as those of Edmund Halley in astronomy and Robert Boyle on the behaviour of gases, as well as Newton's own extensive studies in mathematics, mechanics and the formation of light.

It is these last speculations, previously available only in manuscript, that are now selling well even in the most fashionable bookshops (→ 20/3/27).

British win at Blenheim

A 19th-century view of the 16th Regiment of Foot in action at Blenheim.

Germany, 2 August 1704
John Churchill, the duke of Marlborough, today roundly defeated the forces of France and Bavaria at the village of Blenheim on the Danube, routing the proud French cavalry, cutting the infantry to pieces and capturing Marshal Tallard, the French commander.

The victory stemmed from Marlborough's brilliance as a daring master of the art of manoeuvre. He marched his allied regiments from the North Sea coast deep into the heart of Germany. Moving swiftly, his redcoats crossed the Rhine on a pontoon bridge and joined up with his ally, Prince Eugène of Savoy.

When the armies clashed this morning the French advantage in numbers and guns meant that the issue was in the balance for several hours. Then, after attacking both wings to draw men from the French centre, Marlborough hurled an overwhelming force of cavalry supported by guns and infantry against the centre. The French broke, thousands drowned in the Danube, and tonight Marlborough has sent a message to his wife celebrating "a glorious victory" (→14/10/05).

Furious Scotsman argues against union

Edinburgh, 1704
Andrew Fletcher, the laird of Saltoun in East Lothian, has been a member of parliament for only a year, but he has already made a name for himself as a passionate defender of Scottish independence in the face of mounting pressures for union with England.

In his pamphlet *An Account of a Conversation* he argues that it would be against the interests of England to allow Scotland to grow rich as a separate state, for fear that its wealth would be used to the prejudice of England. Soon after his election, Fletcher told fellow members that Scotland should have a separate monarchy or else power should be transferred to parliament. He carried through an Act of Security which seeks to guarantee Scottish sovereignty and keep the conduct of religion and trade free from English interference.

Fletcher supported James II's overthrow in 1688 and came over with William of Orange, hoping that Scotland would be given a better deal by him. But he soon realized that William was preoccupied with England (→5/2/05).

The jealously guarded kingdom: John Speed's 1662 map of Scotland.

Marlborough, the man behind the army

Blenheim, 3 August 1704
The soldier who destroyed the French army here yesterday, John Churchill, is the son of a country gentleman, Sir Winston Churchill. Fifty-four years old, he is a handsome man skilled in both warfare and politics. He was taken into the court of Charles II, and he served James II loyally, playing a decisive role in the defeat of the duke of Monmouth at Sedgemoor. William III did not entirely trust him but, aware of his military skill, made him commander-in-chief. His progress has been helped by his witty and beautiful wife, Sarah, who was appointed a lady of the bedchamber to Princess Anne. Now that Anne is queen, Sarah wields great influence at court (→12/5/06).

Churchill became a duke in 1702.

Swift satirizes religion in 'A Tale of a Tub'

London, 1704
Jonathan Swift, a Church of England priest who was born in Dublin, has spared no one in his attack on the narrow conventional thinking of most of his fellow clergymen. His *A Tale of a Tub* is a brilliant satire directed at the religious attitudes of Catholics and Presbyterians as well as of his brothers in the Anglican Church. It will be resented by those in the establishment who have been made to feel uncomfortable by his strictures. It will also do little to remove the stops put on his career outside the church by his youthful acceptance of holy orders at Trinity College, Dublin. He wanted to go to Oxford but says that he was prevented by the "ill-treatment of my nearest relations" (→27/11/11).

Tub tales hit at narrow thinkers.

1705 - 1706

Westminster, 5 February 1705. Parliament passes the Alien Act, which threatens to treat all Scots in England as aliens unless the Scottish parliament agrees to the Hanoverian succession or opens union talks by 25 December (→ 28/6).

Westminster, 14 March 1705. Parliament allows the export of Irish linen to the American colonies (→ 24/10/07).

Edinburgh, 1 September 1705. The Scottish ministry secures control of the commission discussing union with England after a dramatic about-turn by the duke of Hamilton, the leader of the opposition Country Party (→ 15/11).

Spain, 14 October 1705. The English navy, led by Charles Mordaunt, the earl of Peterborough, captures Barcelona (→ 12/5/06).

Westminster, 15 November 1705. Parliament repeals the hostile clauses in the Alien Act after the Scots agree to negotiate union (→ 16/4/06).

Lisbon, 31 December 1705. Catherine of Braganza, the widow of Charles II, dies.

England, 1705. George Louis and George Augustus, respectively the son and grandson of Sophia, the electress of Brunswick-Lüneburg and heir to Queen Anne, become naturalized British subjects (→ 12/01/06).

London, 1705. Her Majesty's theatre in the Haymarket, England's first opera house, opens.

York, 12 April 1706. A regular stage-coach service to London begins.

London, 16 April 1706. Talks for Anglo-Scottish union begin in earnest (→ 22/7).

Spain, 27 June 1706. Alliance forces led by Henri de Ruvigny, the earl of Galway, occupy Madrid (→ 14/4/07).

London, 22 July 1706. A union treaty is drafted (→ 3/10).

Edinburgh, 4 November 1706. Parliament agrees by a majority of 32 to the first article of union (→ 7).

Glasgow, 7 November 1706. Anti-unionists riot (→ 16/1/07).

England, 1706. John Evelyn, the diarist, dies.

London, 1706. The nation's first evening paper, the *Evening Post*, is published (→ 12/4/09).

Dublin, 1706. Tailors' Hall, Back Lane, is completed.

Scottish parliament raises the spectre of a Jacobite coup

Edinburgh, 28 June 1705

The increasing assertiveness of parliament, fuelled by the "Patriot", or Country, Party, has given new urgency to the issue of union with England. The English parliament believed that by its Act of Settlement in 1701 it had made certain a Protestant succession after the eventual death of Queen Anne. Now the Scottish parliament, by refusing to be bound by the English act, has raised the spectre of a Jacobite [pro-Stuart] coup in Scotland. Certain noblemen, such as the duke of Hamilton, are suspected of favouring such an intervention. In order to avoid this, the commissioner – or leader – of the new parliamentary session that opens today is the pro-union duke of Argyll, John Campbell.

James, the duke of Hamilton.

Scotland has become more and more anglicized in the past century, with Scottish peers being drawn to London by the prospect of royal patronage. Resentment against this process has led to the emergence of the so-called "cavaliers" group of Jacobite members of parliament, fiercely opposed to union and the Protestant succession. Allied to the Country Party, they may try to dominate parliament (→ 1/9).

'Standard English' fails to silence dialects

Scots gentry speak the court language of Queen Anne, here in parliament.

Edinburgh, c.1705

When King James VI of Scotland travelled south to become England's James I, Londoners ridiculed his accent, assuming that he was an uncouth provincial speaking a degraded form of their own language. In fact, both English and James's Lowland Scots are derived from sister dialects of Germanic origin brought to Britain by invaders in the sixth century.

When King Edwin of Northumbria carried his conquests up to the Firth of Forth in the seventh century he took with him the dialect of the Angles, and this gradually displaced Gaelic as the language of the Scottish lowlands. But Scandinavian and Celtic contacts have also added to the vocabulary of Scots.

For example, *kirk*, the distinctive Scots for church, comes from the Old Norse *kirkja* but has been adapted for English-style compounds such as *kirkyaird*, "churchyard" or "cemetery". The second element is from the Old English *geard* – the first letter pronounced like a "y" – rather than Old Norse *garthr*.

With the accession of the Stuarts to the throne of England a century ago, a form of standard English began to be adopted as the literary language in Edinburgh. But *literati*, aristocrats and gentry all continue to speak Lowland Scots just as their forefathers did.

The Royal Naval Hospital, designed by Sir Christopher Wren, opened at Greenwich in 1705; weekly allowances for pensioners [ex-sailors] include 3kg (7lbs) of bread, 1.5kg (3lbs) of beef and 16 litres (28 pints) of beer.

Halley predicts that comet will reappear

London, 1705
After massive calculations over at least ten years, the mathematician and astronomer Edmund Halley has predicted that a comet last seen in 1682 will reappear in 1758. He believes that this comet is the one on record as having been sighted in 1531 and 1607. For his calculations Halley needed information from an old adversary, the astronomer royal John Flamsteed, and he was obliged to appeal to his friend Isaac Newton: "He will not deny it you, though I know he will me." (→ 1717).

Edmund Halley: predicts a comet.

Marlborough is victorious at Ramillies

The victory at Ramillies was celebrated by a thanksgiving at St Paul's.

Spanish Netherlands, 12 May 1706
John Churchill, the duke of Marlborough, led his cavalry to drive the French from the field and win another victory here at Ramillies, south-east of Brussels. The charge almost ended in tragedy when the duke was unhorsed and ridden over by the French cavalry. Then, when his equerry, Colonel Bingfield, was helping him to remount, a cannonball took off Bingfield's head.

Marlborough recovered and directed his infantry at the village of Ramillies, while his cavalry rampaged through the rear of the French lines. The battle was fought between armies of equal strength, quality and determination. What triumphed was Marlborough's tactical genius. The whole of the Spanish Netherlands now lies open to the British and their Dutch and Danish allies.

However, while Marlborough's success is celebrated, it should not be forgotten that his army could not be maintained without the support of the lord treasurer, Sidney, Lord Godolphin (→ 27/6).

New scientific ideas put to Royal Society

London, 13 November 1706
Francis Hauxbee, the curator of experiments at the Royal Society, caused a sensation at the society's meeting today when he showed how light could be created in a glass vacuum tube. When he rotated the tube against a cloth attached to a brass spring light appeared in the tube, but it disappeared when air was let in.

The discoveries have their roots in Hauxbee's study of the "Torricelli effect", the mercurial phosphorescence that takes place in barometer tubes. The barometer's inventor, Evangelista Torricelli, was Galileo's secretary in Florence. Hauxbee's electrical experiments have reminded Isaac Newton of his discovery that chafing the top of a telescope could cause "electrical vapour" to issue from the bottom.

Hauxbee is unable to offer a theory to explain the phenomenon of light appearing in the tube, although he calls it electricity, from a Greek word meaning "amber-like". It was William Gilbert, the physician and scientist, who first used the word a century ago.

Provisions made for council of regency

Westminster, 12 January 1706
Queen Anne and her parliament have skirted around a prickly question of protocol with the Regency Act, by which a regency council will be set up on the queen's death. The Act of Succession, passed in 1701 to ensure a Protestant monarch, puts the German house of Hanover in line for the English throne. But Anne, although backing the Protestant succession, has no wish to see members of the Hanoverian family living in England while she is alive. The Regency Act, therefore, bestows sovereign power on a regency council until such time as the Hanoverian successor arrives in England. In addition, the Act of Naturalization gives all Protestant Hanoverians the status of English subjects (→ 3/3/14).

Daily life of shopkeepers revolves around coffee-house society

London, 1706
A striking portrait of a typical London shopkeeper appears in a lengthy poem by Ned Ward, who used to keep a tavern. From modest beginnings as the son of either a yeoman or a parish priest, this shopkeeper has acquired a fortune of £10,0000 by middle age.

After giving his apprentices their tasks for the day, the shopkeeper visits the local coffee house to gossip about the latest news. He never treats his friends to more than a dish of coffee and has been known to wrangle over a farthing. Dinner at noon is followed by a nap till one o'clock; then it is down to Lloyd's coffee house to make deals. In the late afternoon he visits his club for a half-pint of beer. He indulges in another dish of coffee on his way home to dinner and is in bed before nine, after listening to one of his apprentices read a chapter from the Bible. Yet not all shopkeepers are as prosperous as Ned Ward's. A recent survey of 29 London shopkeepers has revealed that two died insolvent, another left only £20 and ten others less than £1,000. Only three left over £10,000. By far the commonest type of shopkeeper in London nowadays, apart from food and drink vendors, is the haberdasher. A haberdasher deals chiefly in sewing-threads, ribbons and other articles for dressmaking but may also sell other goods such as paper, playing cards and jewellery (→ 1710).

Coffee houses of the sort where Ned Ward would argue over a farthing.

Union talks reopen Scottish parliament

Edinburgh, 3 October 1706

The city is buzzing with rumours of money, titles and royal favours being heaped on members of parliament as the debate on the Articles of Union with England opens. James Douglas, the duke of Queensberry, who has the task of getting the articles approved, is said to have brought huge sums from England. A group of members belonging to the New Party, or *Squadrone Volante*, committed to a Protestant succession in Scotland, supports union with England and will also welcome any cash hand-out on offer, having lost heavily when the Company of Scotland, set up by parliament to promote a trading settlement at Darién, was forced out by the Spanish, with English connivance [*see report on page 631*].

In the face of London's highly organized campaign for union, the opposition has accepted the prospect of defeat but will fight a stiff rearguard action to delay approval for many weeks. Full details of the 25 Articles of Union are not yet available, but it seems likely that some concessions will be made, notably one to guarantee the role of the Presbyterian Church in Scotland and the preservation of a separate Scottish legal system (→ 23).

Queensberry: bribery and union.

Powerful duke and his wife put pressure on queen to get relative into top job

London, 10 December 1706

Much against her better judgement, Queen Anne has succumbed to pressure from the duke of Marlborough and his wife, Sarah, to include their son-in-law, Charles Spencer, the earl of Sunderland, in her government. When his appointment as a secretary of state in the foreign office was first suggested, Anne rejected it out of hand. She has disliked Sunderland ever since he took a prominent role in opposing the grant of an income to her husband, Prince George of Denmark.

Yet Sarah and then Marlborough himself told the queen that Sunderland's appointment was necessary to retain Whig support in parliament for the war with France. Despite the Marlboroughs' success in pressing the Whig cause, there are signs that the duchess's years of influence over the queen are drawing to a close. Anne was dismayed by Sarah's recent comment that: "It looks like infatuation [when the queen] who has sense in all other things should be so blinded by the word "Tory"." (→ 9/1707.)

Sarah: losing the queen's favour.

Violent demonstrations in Edinburgh as passionate debate on union continues

Edinburgh, 23 October 1706

As parliament enters the fourth week of its debate on the controversial Articles of Union with England, the capital city has become the scene of violent demonstrations. In spite of both the cold and the lashing rain, a hostile crowd surrounds Parliament House each day, jeering and shouting at known supporters of union.

The home of Sir Patrick Johnson, one of the court-appointed commissioners responsible for negotiating the articles, has been sacked by the mob of protesters, and the privy council has responded by bringing troops into the city. There are concerns that the English are making preparations to move troops up to the border.

Opposition in parliament is being coordinated by Andrew Fletcher, the laird of Saltoun. "The Scots deserve no pity," he says, "if they voluntarily surrender their united and separate interests to the mercy of a united parliament, where the English shall have so vast a majority."

The government has ignored demands from the opposition that an election should be held on the issue of union, as the government would almost certainly be defeated. A third of Scotland's parliamentary constituencies have submitted addresses opposing union, and none has been in favour.

The London government has dispatched the pamphleteer and novelist Daniel Defoe to Edinburgh to spearhead the campaign for union. His arguments, combined with the prospect of future royal favours for unionists, seem be gaining ground: the opposition has rallied no more than 83 members of parliament against the government's 116. For many members the most persuasive argument in favour of union is the promise of unfettered access to English and colonial markets for Scottish products.

In some respects, though, the change will simply be a matter of legality, especially for the port of Glasgow, which at present is notorious as a base for large-scale smuggling across the Atlantic to North America (→ 4/11).

Glasgow is a major smuggling port for goods from North America.

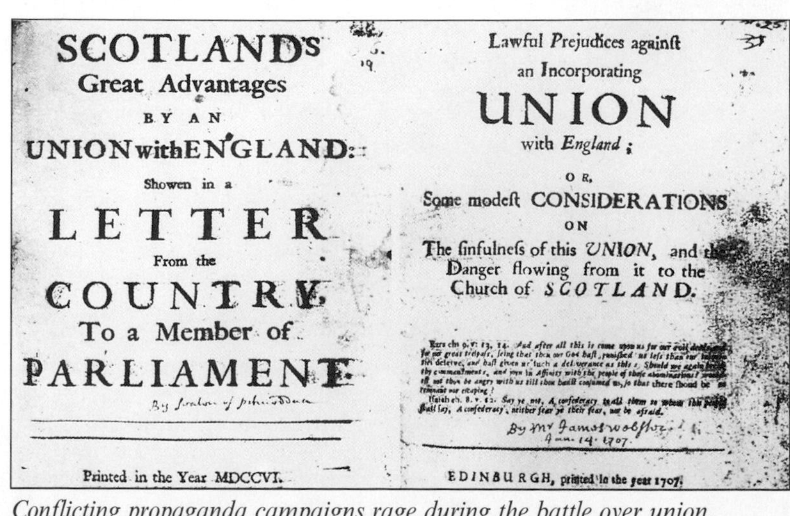

SCOTLAND'S
Great Advantages
BY AN
UNION with ENGLAND:
Showen in a
LETTER
From the
COUNTRY,
To a Member of
PARLIAMENT.

Printed in the Year MDCCVI.

Lawful Prejudices againſt
an Incorporating
UNION
with *England*;
OR,
Some modeſt CONSIDERATIONS
ON
The ſinfulneſs of this *UNION*, and the
Danger flowing from it to the
Church of *SCOTLAND*.

EDINBURGH, printed in the year 1707.

Conflicting propaganda campaigns rage during the battle over union.

Genesis of a Great Power

1707-1800

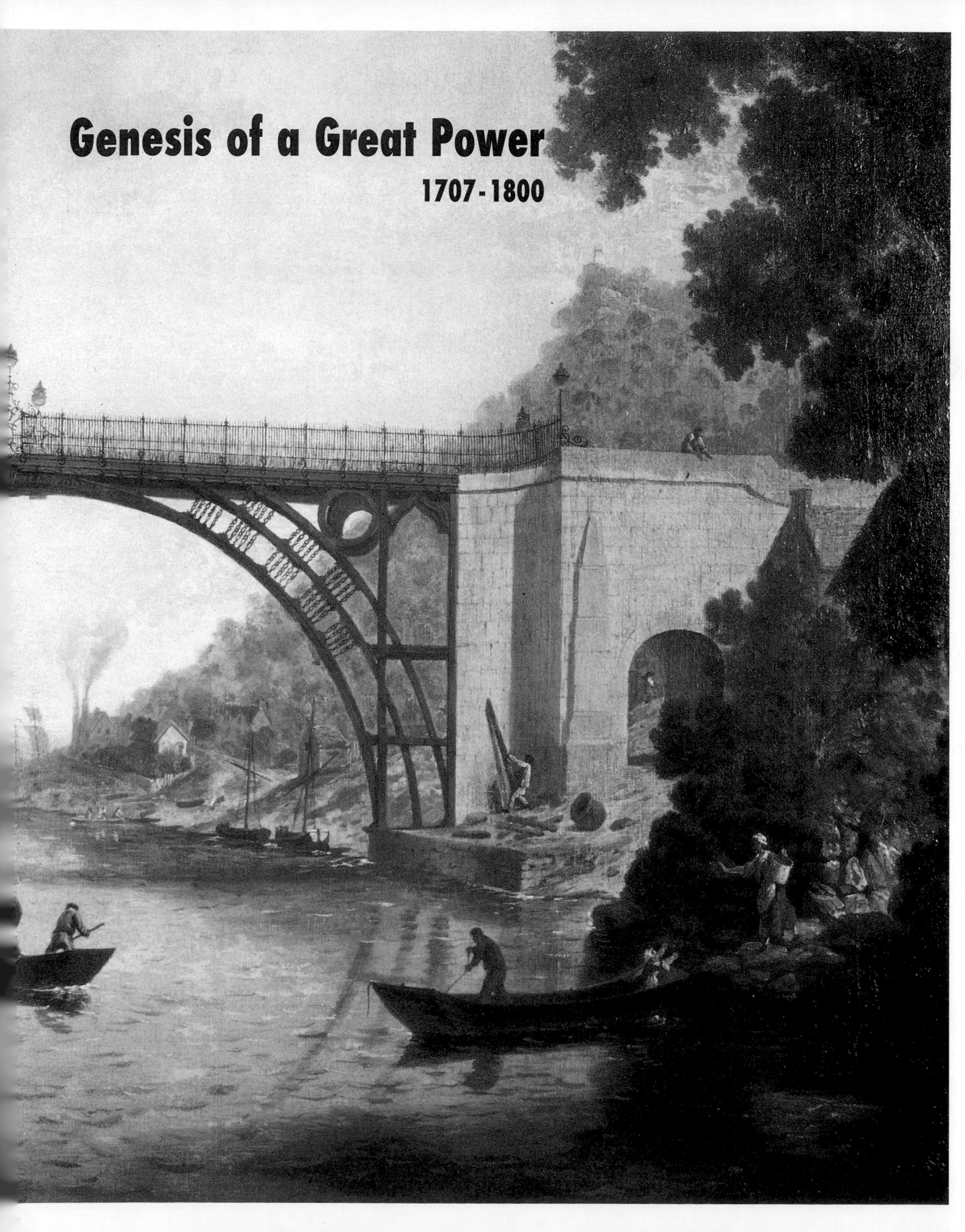

1707

Edinburgh, 16 January. The terms for the treaty of union are passed by parliament, with only 69 votes against (→ 28/2).

Westminster, 28 February. The Commons pass the treaty of union with a majority of 158 votes (→ 6/3).

London, 6 March. The Act of Union receives royal assent.→

Spain, 14 April. James Fitz James, the duke of Berwick and the eldest illegitimate son of the exiled James II, defeats the allies in battle at Almanza (→ 14/3/08).

Scotland, 28 April. Parliament is formally dissolved, and the chancellor, James Ogilvy, the earl of Seafield, remarks: "There's an end to an auld sang." The new parliament of Great Britain will meet on 1 May (→ 1/5).

Wales, May. The antiquary Edward Lhuyd publishes *Archaeologica Britannica*; he argues that Welsh is a Celtic language, and that the Welsh can thus claim literary and cultural descent from the Gauls and Britons described by Julius Caesar.

Dublin, 24 June. Thomas Herbert, the earl of Pembroke, is sworn in as lord lieutenant.

London, September. Sarah Churchill, the duchess of Marlborough, once a close friend of the queen, sees her influence at court fade as Anne chooses to confide in Abigail Masham, a cousin of Robert Harley, the Tory secretary of state for the north (→ 8/2/08).

Dublin, 24 October. Queen Anne's first Irish parliament reorganizes customs and excise on an official basis and sets up a harbour board (→ 28/8/10).

Westminster, 18 December. Queen Anne agrees to annual finance bills and all-party government.

Edinburgh. James, the lunatic son of the duke of Queensberry, murders a kitchen boy in Holyrood Palace, roasts him on a spit and eats his flesh.

London. Sir John Floyer, a physician, publishes *The Physician's Pulse*, in which he explains the usefulness of pulse-rate counting.

London. A homosexual brothel – one of 20 such in the capital – has been raided; 40 men, including respected City merchants, have been charged with buggery, a capital offence, or with the lesser offence of "attempted buggery".

Irish dramatist dies after great stage hit

A scene from Farquhar's witty and popular "The Beaux' Stratagem".

London, April

The noted Irish playwright George Farquhar has died in straitened circumstances only a month after his play *The Beaux' Stratagem* opened and set audiences roaring with delight at its wit and novelty. He wrote it during his last illness, which has removed him at the tragically early age of 29. Farquhar brought a freshness and naturalism to the stage after the artifice of Restoration comedy. He excelled at putting ordinary people on the stage, such as the raffish army types of *The Recruiting Officer* at large among the citizens of Shrewsbury. His character Sir Harry Wildair, in *The Constant Couple*, is notable for being played by an actress, such as his own mistress Anne Oldfield.

Bawdy writers cleared of obscene libel

Engravings such as this, and others more explicit, provide titillation.

London

In what may well prove a landmark case, the publishers James Read and Angell Carter have been acquitted on charges of obscene libel after a court found that, while they were indeed guilty, no law existed under which they might be sentenced.

Read and Carter were charged with publishing a pornographic French novel, *Fifteen Plagues of a Maidenhead*, by the pseudonymous author "Madame B–le". While they were definitely guilty, they escaped sentencing when the court of queen's bench, which tried the case, was forced to admit that its jurisdiction did not cover such material. In the words of Mr Justice Powell, "the book is bawdy stuff, but there is no law to punish it". The two men went free, although the book has been burnt.

This problem, which must soon be remedied, stems from the fact that hitherto church rather than civil courts have dealt with obscene material. Church courts are largely obsolete now, but no new laws exist to replace their powers.

Queen Anne gives her blessing to the Anglo-Scots union

London, 6 March

The Articles of Union have now received the royal assent from Queen Anne, seven weeks after going through parliament in Edinburgh, where the debate lasted ten weeks. In London the articles were approved by both houses in under six weeks. The determined Whig "Junto" forced the bill through the committee stage in the House of Commons at a single sitting against bitter opposition from "High Tories", who complained that Presbyterianism was being enshrined as the established Church of Scotland.

In Scotland the dukes of Queensberry and Argyll managed to round up an army of fellow peers who voted two to one in favour of the union. The overall vote was 110 to 69, but even Sir John Clerk, one of the government's commissioners, admitted that the articles had been carried "contrary to the inclinations of at least three-fourths of the kingdom". He nevertheless went on to describe the union as "the best expedient to preserve the honour and liberties of Scotland" from the threat of an English invasion, which would have followed if union had been rejected. Andrew Fletcher, the laird of Saltoun, who has spearheaded the opposition, strode out of parliament saying that Scotland was "fit only for the slaves who have sold it" (→ 28/4).

The Heaven Room at Burghley House, Lincs: its Italian painter, Antonio Verro, died in 1707.

United Kingdom of Great Britain comes into being

Surrounded by her ladies, lords and bishops, Queen Anne receives the Act of Union, which has aroused fierce debate on both sides of the border.

London, 1 May
Wearing the English Order of the Garter and the Scottish Order of the Thistle to symbolize the historic union of the two peoples, Queen Anne rode in state today to St Paul's Cathedral for a service to mark the creation of the United Kingdom of Great Britain. The central feature of the Act of Union that brings England and Scotland together is its denial of a separate Scottish – and possibly Jacobite and Roman Catholic – succession on the death of the queen. In other words, it guarantees the Protestant succession already enshrined in English legislation. Specifically, it guarantees the Hanoverian succession, until now bitterly contested by the Scots.

The long road to union has been marked by acrimony and misunderstanding. An Act of Union was first proposed by James VI of Scotland when he became James I of England in 1603. Neither the English nor the Scots had much liking for it. Queen Anne, who has spent only a few months in Scotland, when she was a girl of 16 in 1681, probably reflected the attitude of many English people when she spoke of her Scottish subjects as both "unreasonable" and "strange".

Yet when Anne ascended the throne five years ago, and after it became apparent that she would die childless – since her marriage in 1683 she had suffered a series of yearly miscarriages – the question of the royal succession became urgent. Consequently she appointed a commission to negotiate a union treaty. At this time the Scots were reluctant to consider being incorporated into a political union with a dominant England. They preferred to discuss free trade within some kind of economic union. But the English merchant class, which had seen Scotland shift its export market from the United Provinces to England, were opposed.

The Scottish parliament reacted to English intransigence by declaring that Scotland should not automatically be committed to wars mounted by the English. The English parliament then passed the Alien Act, which threatened to treat all Scots living in England as aliens. In Scotland, anti-English feeling boiled over.

The Whig ministry in London sent John Campbell, the duke of Argyll, who has an English mother and an English wife, to Edinburgh to mount a pro-union offensive. In parliament, James Douglas, the duke of Hamilton, who had been against union with England, suddenly proposed that nominations to a commission on union should be made by the queen alone. The proposal was carried by a mere four votes, but it made sure that the Scottish commission would, like the English one, favour union. In subsequent negotiations an outline treaty was agreed within ten days, and the 25 Articles of Union were settled within three months.

When she gave the royal assent to the union treaty – by tradition in French – Queen Anne said: "I desire and expect from all my subjects of both nations that from henceforth they act with all possible respect and kindness to one another, that so it may appear to all the world they have hearts disposed to become one people. This will be a great pleasure to me" (→ 1/5/08).

Terms that seal union of two countries

London, 1 May
According to the terms of the 25 Articles of Union the parliaments of England and Scotland are to be dissolved, and a parliament of Great Britain will be established, consisting of 16 peers and 45 elected members from Scotland, and 190 peers and 513 members from England and Wales. (Ireland has its own parliament.) To avoid a rebuff at the polls the government has decided that Scottish members in the first parliament will be co-opted rather than elected. Scotland keeps its own (Presbyterian) church in addition to its own legal and educational systems.

England will grant to Scotland £400,000 to clear public and private debts, but Scots are resentful that most of this will go to civil servants and judges instead of to people who lost money in the ill-fated Company of Scotland project at Darién in Central America. Some Scottish industries will be receiving subsidies.

1708 - 1709

Westminster, 19 January 1708. Robert Harley, the Tory secretary of state for the north, loses support when his clerk is found guilty of selling official papers to the French (→ 24).

London, 24 January 1708. Robert Harley tells Queen Anne that he wishes to form a government excluding Sidney, Lord Godolphin (→ 8/2).

Kensington Palace, 8 February 1708. Godolphin and the duke and duchess of Marlborough threaten to resign if Harley is not dismissed (→ 11).

Westminster, 11 February 1708. Harley resigns (→ 30/6).

France, 7 April 1708. James Stuart's failed invasion fleet limps into Dunkirk.

Belfast, 27 April 1708. The castle is destroyed by fire.

Spanish Netherlands, 30 June 1708. Marlborough defeats the French at Oudenarde (→ 5/1709).

Westminster, 1 October 1708. William Croft is made composer at the chapel royal on the death of John Blow.

Bristol, 1708. Edward Colston, a philanthropist, establishes a hospital and free school.

Bath, 1708. A theatre and an assembly room are opened.

Deal, Kent, 1708. The mayor is re-elected after campaigning against drunkenness and prostitution in the town.

Leeds, 1708. A stage-coach service to London begins.

Co Durham, 1708. A pit explosion at Chester-Le-Street kills a hundred miners.

London, 12 April 1709. Sir Richard Steele begins publication of the *Tatler*, a thrice-weekly magazine (→ 1710).

Dublin, September 1709. About 800 Palatine families fleeing persecution arrive from Germany (→ 3/1713).

Connacht, December 1709. Agrarian outrages begin as impoverished tenantry maim their landlords' cattle.

Liverpool, 1709. Negro slave-trading from here starts (→ 26/3/13).

Scotland, 1709. The severe English law on treason is introduced.

Scotland, 1709. The Society in Scotland for Propagating Christian Knowledge is founded to promote religious education in schools (→ 1710).

Resignation stokes fear of party strife

Westminster, 24 February 1708
The resignation of the Tory secretary of state for the north, Robert Harley, after treachery charges, has led Bishop Burnet of Salisbury to say today that party strife might come "in some critical time or other, at the death of a prince, or on an invasion, to have terrible effects". After last year's defeat of an allied army at Almanza in the war of the Spanish succession, Harley admitted that of the 29,000 men provided by parliament only 8,600 fought in the battle. Then in January it was learnt that his secretary had leaked secrets to the French. Without the confidence of the other members of the ruling "triumvirate", the duke of Marlborough and Lord Godolphin, Harley had to go (→ 9/8/10).

French-backed plan to hand Britain over to James Stuart runs into deep waters

North Sea, 14 March 1708
James Stuart, the only legitimate son of James VII of Scots and II of England, has turned back from the Firth of Forth, after failing to keep a planned rendezvous with Jacobite supporters on shore. Still shadowed by Admiral Byng's superior fleet, James's French-led convoy is abandoning its efforts to help him to regain the throne. Queen Anne is mightily relieved, as are the Whigs.

Dubbed by some the "warming-pan baby", after suggestions that he was smuggled into the royal bed in 1688, James has been dogged by ill luck. This expedition, backed by Louis XIV of France, was delayed when James developed measles. In recent days even the weather has been against him (→ 7/4).

James: measles delayed invasion.

Whigs enjoy great victory in election

Westminster, 1 May 1708
The first elections for the parliament of Great Britain, comprising England, Scotland and Wales, have resulted in a sweeping victory for the Whigs. The statesman Charles Spencer, the earl of Sunderland, has hailed this as "the most Whig parliament there has been since the revolution".

The explanation for the Whigs' success springs partly from the abortive invasion launched by James Stuart in March [*see report above right*], during which certain Tory financiers managed to orchestrate a run on the Bank of England. They have gained about 30 seats in England and Wales, while the majority of the 45 new Scottish members (who have been co-opted rather than elected) are expected to vote with the Whigs.

Queen mourns husband's sudden death

Anne's husband, Prince George.

London, 28 October 1708
Prince George of Denmark, the husband of Queen Anne and her comforter through the loss of all their children, has himself died, aged 55, at Kensington Palace. His death follows several asthma attacks, which began last month. The queen, who married him in 1683, is desolate. In spite of at least 18 pregnancies, she has given birth to only five live children, all of whom have since died.

George will not be widely mourned, especially by the Whigs, who have threatened to withhold supplies partly because of mismanagement of the admiralty, of which he was nominal head. Despite his incompetence in such areas, he was valued by Tories like Lord Westmorland for protecting Anne from "whisperers and sycophants". His death will make it very hard for the queen to resist Whig demands for government appointments. In addition it can only worsen her relations with the lord treasurer, Sidney, Lord Godolphin, and his close allies John Churchill, the duke of Marlborough, and Marlborough's forceful wife, Sarah.

Scots angry over abolition of their privy council by Westminster

Scotland, 1 May 1708
In a major shake-up of the constitution, Scotland's privy council has been abolished. Justices of the peace are to have their powers extended and will be commissioned by English councillors, including the archbishop of Canterbury. The once influential "masters", the eldest sons of peers, are now barred from sitting for shires and burghs, and even from voting at elections.

The Scots are understandably aggrieved at the manner in which their traditional systems of government are being subsumed by the English. Popular resentment over heavy Scottish losses in the duke of Marlborough's continental campaigns in the war over the Spanish succession is also being fuelled by taxes levied on the people by the new parliament that is now sitting in London (→ 20/12/12).

Whig grandees to keep Britain at war

The Hague, May 1709
With France's rejection of peace demands by the Grand Alliance in the dispute over the Spanish succession, the "Junto", Britain's ruling group of Whig grandees, is bent on continuing the war. Louis XIV had been asked to order his grandson, Philip of Anjou, to withdraw his claim to the Spanish throne in favour of Archduke Charles, the son of the late Holy Roman Emperor Leopold, or join the alliance against Philip. But Louis has offered to surrender claims in Spain, the Indies, Italy and the Low Countries, to recognize Britain's Protestant succession and to ask James Stuart to leave France (→ 31/8).

Evictions reveal the failure of Poor Law

The poor are to be kept busy.

Nottingham, June 1709
A widow's plight has highlighted the problems of today's poor. Mrs Hood and her two children have been thrown out of various towns six times this month by authorities eager to keep them off the poor rates. Starting in London, her travels have ended here – for now. Paupers like Mrs Hood can lawfully be ejected from any parish. To curb such "undesirables", an act of 1697 required the consent of parish officers and the approval of two justices before people could seek work or housing outside their own parish.

Carnage at Malplaquet

In the thick of it: Marlborough thought Malplaquet a "bloody battle".

France, 31 August 1709
The duke of Marlborough has won another great victory over the French, but the casualties are so high that war-weary Europe will be horrified by the carnage. Marlborough had hoped not to go to war again, but when peace talks broke down the enemies set themselves to fight a decisive battle.

Marlborough manoeuvred his forces with his customary skill and speed. This morning he launched 110,000 men at 90,000 Frenchmen defending positions around Malplaquet, south-east of Lille. He used much the same tactics as he did at Blenheim, five years ago, first attacking the wings and then setting 30,000 horsemen, led by the great fighting horses of the Scots Greys, at the centre.

The Dutch suffered heavy losses, but finally the French were beaten. Marlborough has, as usual, written to his wife, but there is little joy in his letter: "I am so tired that I have but strength enough to tell you that we have had this day a very bloody battle; the first part of the day we beat their foot, and afterwards their horse. God Almighty be praised, it is now in our powers to have what peace we please" (→ 11/4/1713).

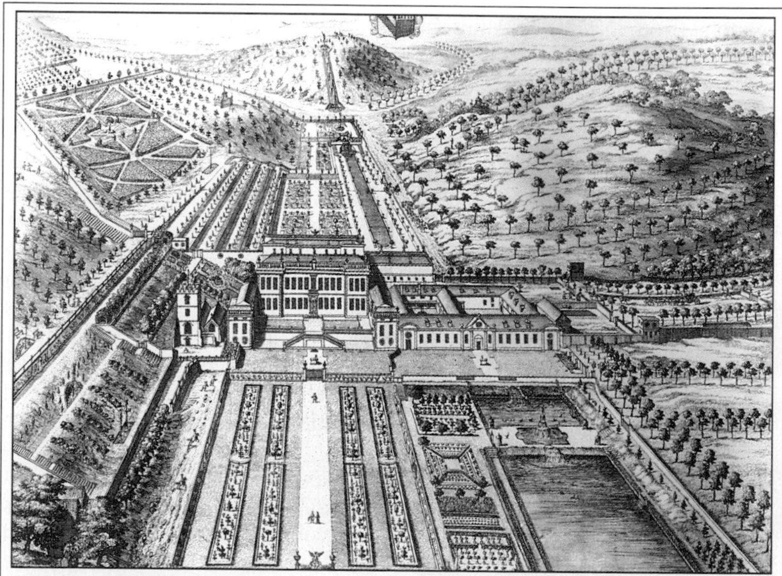

William Blathwait's estate at Dyrham Park, Avon, from Leonard Knyff and Johannes Kip's "Britannia Illustrata" (1707/08); to have their estates included landowners gave money towards the publishing cost.

Preacher is charged with malicious libel

Westminster, 13 December 1709
A high-church Oxford cleric, Dr Henry Sacheverell, faces impeachment for a "malicious, scandalous libel". The Commons voted today to proceed against him for a sermon that he gave in St Paul's Cathedral on 5 November. The tenor of his remarks – denouncing the threat to church and state from dissent and reasserting the doctrine of passive obedience to the crown – was familiar. But his onslaught against the political principles of the Whig "Junto" was the cause of great offence. A reference to the "crafty insidiousness of such wily Volpones [foxes]" was intended for Sidney, Lord Godolphin (→ 1/3/10).

Sacheverell: faces charges of libel.

Jacobite lord to die for killing teacher

Scotland, 29 November 1709
Robert, Lord Balfour of Burleigh, has been condemned to death by a court of law. His crime was to kill a rival for the affections of a girl whom Balfour wanted for himself. His jealousy got out of control when the girl in question married the rival, a schoolmaster called Henry Stenhouse from Inverkeithing, near Dunfermline. Balfour was subsequently arrested and went on trial for the murder on 4 August. The date for his execution has been set for 6 January next year. Balfour, who is the only son and heir of the previous Lord Balfour, is unlikely to receive mercy: he is known to be a Jacobite sympathizer (→ 6/1/10).

1710

Scotland, 6 January. Lord Balfour, sentenced to death last November for the murder of a schoolmaster, escapes both his warders and his execution, set for today, by exchanging clothes with his sister.

London, 1 March. Crowds run riot at the opening of the trial of Dr Henry Sacheverell, who was arrested last year after an outspoken sermon that he had delivered at St Paul's Cathedral (→20).

Westminster, 5 April. Parliament is prorogued by Queen Anne (→6).

Westminster, 14 April. Queen Anne dismisses Henry Grey, the earl of Kent, as lord chamberlain; he is replaced by Charles Talbot, the earl of Shrewsbury (→14/6).

Westminster, 14 June. The leading Whig politician Charles Spencer, the earl of Sunderland and secretary of state for the south, is dismissed (→8/8).

Dublin, 14 June. The board of Trinity College assigns land for the construction of a medical school.

Westminster, 8 August. Another leading Whig politician, Sidney, Lord Godolphin, the lord treasurer, is dismissed (→9/1710).

Westminster, 9 August. Robert Harley takes over as head of a new Tory administration (→9).

Dublin, 28 August. Queen Anne establishes a board of trustees for the manufacture of Irish linen (→9/1710).

Dublin, September. Parliament makes an attempt to crush the outbreak of cattle maiming, known as "houghing", in Connacht by imposing collective fines.

London, September. Four Bank of England directors, deeply worried by the recent dramatic dismissals in the government, refuse to advance any further loans to finance Britain's part in the war over the Spanish succession.→

London, September. Following the dissolution of parliament this month, Robert Harley persuades Tory financiers to replace Bank of England war loans (→25/11).

London. The German-born composer George Frederick Handel arrives (→1713).

London. The first issue of *The Examiner*, a literary periodical, is printed (→1712).

'Ranting parson' is tried

London, 20 March

At the end of his three-week trial in the House of Lords, Dr Henry Sacheverell, "the ranting parson", has been found guilty and sentenced. His impeachment and trial have rocked the nation and provoked mob riots in London.

Queen Anne, attended by her ladies, has sat through every session. Many great names, including Sarah Churchill, the duchess of Marlborough, have been observed at dawn engaged in an undignified scramble for seats in Westminster Hall. The queen fears the depth of feelings aroused in both Whigs and Tories by Sacheverell's sermon [*see page 645*], so it must be a relief that his sentence is light. Despite being found guilty by 69 votes to 52, he has received just three years' suspension from the pulpit.

An angry mob destroys a church.

Sacheverell's sermon last November at St Paul's Cathedral had revealed him to be a "concealed Jacobite". He attacked both the "glorious revolution" of 1688 and religious toleration of dissenters. His arguments go to the roots of the division between the political parties. Sacheverell asks whether civil government should be religious or secular, and whether the Church of England can be secure in an age of religious dissent. The mobs which have wrecked dissenting chapels from Drury Lane to Blackfriars have already made up their minds.

Sexual slurs lead to fierce row at palace

London, 6 April

In a tempestuous meeting this afternoon at Kensington Palace, Queen Anne severed her 30-year friendship with Sarah Churchill, the duchess of Marlborough. Anxious to rid herself of the "tyranny" of the Marlboroughs, Anne accused Sarah of lies and financial deceit. Sarah broke down in tears and protested her innocence, but the queen remained unmoved.

Sarah's Whig supporters are putting the blame for her fall from grace on Abigail Masham, who has replaced her as the queen's closest confidante. Two years ago Sarah attacked Abigail's friendship with the queen, accusing the two women of lesbianism. She now threatens to publish Anne's letters (→14).

Abigail Masham: accused of supplanting Sarah Churchill.

Queen Anne meets Iroquois Indian chiefs

London, April

Queen Anne's court has been cheered by the colourful spectacle of a visit by four Indian kings of the Iroquois tribe in North America. When they first arrived in London the kings wore their traditional warpaint, blankets and beribboned boots. Their striking appearance was completed by the gilt-edged scarlet mantles with which they had been provided.

One of the queen's Indian guests.

For their audience with Queen Anne, however, the kings were obliged to follow protocol and wear black, since the court remains in mourning for Prince George of Denmark, the queen's husband, who died last October.

Through an interpreter, Queen Anne learnt that the kings came as representatives of the peoples inhabiting the wilderness between the French lands and the New England colonies further south. "We have made," they said, "a long and dangerous journey ... to see our great queen." The Indians brought gifts of *wampum* [strings of beads] and shell necklaces. In return, they were given 200 guineas, a portrait of the queen, looking-glasses, a magic lantern, scissors, knives, guns and swords.

Durham pit tragedy kills over 80 men

Co Durham, 1710

In an alarming repeat of the tragedy ago at Chester-Le-Street two years ago, a coal-mine explosion at Bensham has led to 80 deaths. Chester-Le-Street, where over a hundred miners lost their lives, was the worse of the two incidents.

These explosions are caused by the depth of contemporary mines and the build-up of fire-damp, or methane, a gas that is explosive when mixed with air. The number of men employed in the mines seems to be outpacing the owners' ability to guarantee safety.

Parliament suspended to halt Whigs

The House of Commons in session in 1710, just before the dissolution.

London, September
In a remarkable reversal of Whig fortunes Queen Anne has dissolved parliament and called a general election. The queen's "backstairs adviser", Robert Harley, a leading Tory, engineered the changes, exploiting pro-Tory public opinion following the Sacheverell impeachment [*see reports on pages 645/46*].

The Whigs are now out of favour with Anne, who shares her subjects' apprehension about dangers to the Church of England and their alarm at high casualties among British forces led by the Whig duke of Marlborough in the continuing war over the Spanish succession.

The Whig ministry has fallen. Recent weeks have seen the dismissal of, among others, Charles Spencer, the earl of Sunderland, replaced as secretary of state for the south by the Tory George Legge, Lord Dartmouth. And last month Lord Godolphin, another Whig, was dismissed as lord treasurer – against the wishes of the Bank of England.→

Tories have majority of seats as new parliament assembles

Britain, 25 November
The general election has left the House of Commons with a landslide majority of 151 Tory members. Voters have thus backed the Tory policies of supporting Dr Sacheverell and ending the war on the continent. Whig electoral casualties include John Churchill, the duke of Marlborough.

Tory leaders are promising a restoration of harmony and cooperation between an honest, frugal administration and a "country" majority in the Commons. Talk is of integration of church and state, an end to the war, and renewed stabilization of Britain's finances.

Robert Harley, a short man whose slovenly speech belies his political skill, heads the new government as chancellor of the exchequer. He manipulated the changes leading to the dissolution of parliament two months ago in a masterly way that impressed Queen Anne but would not have surprised anyone who knows him. In political circles the 48-year-old Harley is known as "Robin the Trickster", a nickname earned by his love of intrigue and the use of backstairs manoeuvres.

Harley: Britain's new chancellor.

Churchill: a Whig electoral casualty.

The most critical problem his administration faces is how to create peace with France and Spain. The mounting debt from war taxation and borrowing has to be ended. Bankers are nervous, meanwhile, of the impact of the dissolution of parliament and the change in party majority (→8/3/11).

'Polite' behaviour is adopted as cult by English high society

English gentlemen at their leisure.

England
English high society is taking on airs and graces. Gentlemen, the professional classes and businessmen now take it upon themselves to set moral standards in what has become a "polite" society.

Although it is unusual to do so on the continent, in England different classes – the leisured gentry, merchants and professionals – live in congenial coexistence. Fashionable squares, built around common gardens or paved areas, are popular not only in London but also in Bath, Bristol, Manchester and Birmingham.

Coffee houses play a vital role in this new way of life, bringing together people from all occupations to meet, conduct business and discuss politics. The Whig and Tory divide, as strong in fashion as it is at the hustings, means that while Whigs patronize London's Kit-Kat Club, Tories prefer to pass the time of day at the Society of Brothers or Ouzinda's chocolate house in St James's Street.

Periodicals such as Richard Steele's *Tatler*, also reflect changing beliefs in the moral standards of daily life. Many women in particular are reading and enjoying the *Tatler's* comic portrayal of social vices. Civility and politeness are these days considered the mark of a well-read populace.→

Mood of change runs through British way of life

Church: dissenters advance in strength

Britain
Since the passing in 1689 of the Toleration Act, which exempted Protestants dissenting from the Church of England from the penalties of certain laws, dissenters have been increasingly integrated into British society. Their numbers in London have been estimated by a parliamentary committee to be in the region of 101,500, which includes French, Dutch and German Calvinist refugees, Presbyterians, Baptists, Quakers and Unitarians.

The recent Treaty of Union has also enshrined the ideal of religious pluralism. The Church of Scotland, rooted in Calvinism, is presbyterian in organization, in contrast to the episcopalian Church of England. Consequently Britain now has two very different established churches. Religious toleration does not exist, however, in Scotland.

High-church Anglicans, politically Tories, are arguing that their church is in danger. One such, Francis Atterbury, the dean of Oxford, wants to restore the authority of the church courts and give bishops the power to license all schools. The proposed bill for the Building of Fifty New Churches should, if passed, help overcrowded Anglican parishes (→12/1711).

A variety of ploughs and implements is available to till the fields.

Economy: high corn prices cause concern

Britain
A revolution in economic forces is under way as country gentlemen, traditionally Tory "landed interests" who have the vote, feel the squeeze. The landowning classes complain that war taxation has been levied solely on their rental income. At four shillings [20 pence] in the pound, they have been paying 20 per cent tax. Whig "moneyed interests", the city bankers, pay no tax. The Scots are not complaining either, since they enjoy levels of taxation that are much lower than those which are imposed on their English counterparts.

None the less, with corn prices kept artifically high, some doubt whether the Tory landowners have a real grievance. Indeed, now that trade with the Baltic is threatened by an outbreak of plague, the Dutch are turning to England for their corn supplies – which will push prices to even higher levels.

Education: on offer to widening number

Britain
Scotland's education system is among the best in Europe. The 1696 Education Act confirmed the Church of Scotland's determination to establish a school in every parish, paid for by landowners and open to all. As for higher education, the university of Edinburgh was drastically reformed two years ago when the latest method of specialized teaching was introduced from the Dutch United Provinces.

Education in England also aims to be free or at a rate affordable by most. The gentry send their sons to local grammar schools – where they will sit beside yeomen's or shopkeepers' sons. Schooling need not be costly. For example, Robert Molesworth, a Yorkshire squire, pays only £20 a year to educate each of his sons – not much on a rental income of £2,000. Aristocrats still send their children to major schools such as Eton, Winchester or Westminster. Girls are taught to read, write and manage the household by their mothers.

Poorer children receive their education through Anglican charity schools. The Anglican Church set up the schools to control the spread of nonconformity and instil respect for the established church.

Quakers in earnest discussion.

Society: summer seasons are the fashion

Bath
The summer season in Bath has quickly become a "must" for the English or Welsh lady and gentleman of fashion. This cult of fashionable life has been set up by the Welsh-born Richard "Beau" Nash.

Nash, whose expensive lifestyle depends on gambling, moved here from London as an already well known arbiter of fashion and good taste. He established the Assembly Rooms, forbade duelling and set down a code of behaviour and dress that he himself enforces.

Once established in the city, both the master and the lady of a fashionable household spend the early hours of the morning at one of the five baths, where a pleasant hour or so is passed in companionable relaxation. The ladies come in closed chairs, already dressed in their bathing clothes.

After they have bathed, people retire to the pump rooms to indulge in gossip with other visitors. Men then withdraw to coffee houses to discuss the news; ladies can retire to their own such houses. Breakfast is often taken in public, while afternoons are passed in walks along the parade, cultivating the art of seeing and being seen. In the evening people may dine privately *en famille* or in public, and make arrangements to play cards, visit the theatre or enjoy dancing (→1713).

Girls may learn only at home.

1711 - 1712

London, 8 March 1711. Robert Harley, the lord chancellor, is wounded with a knife by a French spy being interrogated by the privy council (→ 1/5).

Dublin, 15 April 1711. Fire destroys the surveyor-general's office and many of the state papers kept there.

London, 1 May 1711. The South Sea company is formed to trade with South America and finance war debts (→ 23).

London, 23 May 1711. Robert Harley becomes earl of Oxford (→ 7/7/12).

Ireland, 3 July 1711. James Butler, the duke of Ormond, is made lord lieutenant (→ 1/1/12).

Berkshire, 11 August 1711. A horse-race meeting is held at Ascot for the first time.

Dublin, 16 August 1711. Ireland's first medical school opens, at Trinity College.

London, 6 November 1711. James Douglas, the duke of Queensberry, nicknamed "the Union Duke", dies aged 49.

London, 27 November 1711. Jonathan Swift publishes *The Conduct of the Allies*, a Tory pamphlet advocating peace in the war over the Spanish succession.

Britain, December 1711. The Act of Occasional Conformity bars dissenters from qualifying for civic office by attending Anglican services either once or occasionally (→ 5/1714).

London, 1711. Sir Godfrey Kneller, the royal portraitist, opens England's first painting academy, in Great Queen Street (→ 19/10/1723).

London, 1 January 1712. The duke of Ormond replaces the duke of Marlborough, dismissed last December, as commander-in-chief of the armed forces (→ 1/8/14).

Dublin, 12 May 1712. The foundation stone of Trinity College library is laid.

Westminster, 7 July 1712. Henry St John, the Tory secretary of state for the north, becomes Viscount Bolingbroke (→ 9/1713).

London, 8 July 1712. Robert Walpole is released from the Tower (→ 10/1714).

Dublin, 4 November 1712. At a performance of Nicholas Rowe's *Tamerlane* the audience riots, seeing the play as an attack on William III.

England, 1712. Parliament introduces the Stamp Act.

Young Tories thirst for bribery reforms

London, April 1711

The Bell tavern in King Street, in Westminster, has become the home of the October Club, a group comprised of some 150 radical young Tories. Buoyed by their election success last November and convinced that the future belongs to them, these new members are demanding a clean sweep of all Whigs from central and local government.

The October Club believes that it was only corruption and manipulation that kept the Whigs in power. Consequently they are calling for an investigation into £35 million allegedly missing from treasury accounts, as well as the introduction of parliamentary bills to end corruption in elections. The Tory leader and chancellor, Robert Harley, is worried that if they succeed in setting the agenda then his own influence will be reduced.

Robert Walpole expelled and imprisoned

London, 17 January 1712

Robert Walpole, the most aggressive of the young Whigs, has been charged with corruption, expelled from the House of Commons and jailed in the Tower. He is widely seen as being another victim of the relentless drive for peace by Queen Anne and her Tory ministers.

The Lords' Whig majority had been able to block a peace treaty with France. But on New Year's Eve the Tory leader, the earl of Oxford, who became lord treasurer last May, delivered an audacious double attack. He persuaded Queen Anne to create 12 new peers, overturning the Whig majority, and to dismiss the duke of Marlborough as commander-in-chief of the army on charges of corruption.

There was an immediate outcry. The new lords, branded "Oxford's packed jury", were sneeringly asked if they intended to vote individually or by their foreman, while the dismissal of Britain's finest general was said to have followed a "frivolous and groundless complaint". Yet Oxford, the wiliest of politicians, had done it again. Old scores were settled, and the British delegation has just set off for treaty negotiations in Utrecht (→ 8/7).

Robert Walpole: put in the Tower.

Goldsmiths undercut by foreign workers

London's goldsmiths, undercut by Huguenot workers, are pleading poverty.

London, 1711

Cheap immigrant workers "whose desperate fortunes oblige them to work at miserable rates" are undercutting English craftsmen, says the Worshipful Company of Goldsmiths. The company complains, perhaps unwisely, that its members have been forced to "bestow much more time and labour ... than [they did] when prices of workmanship were much greater". The "necessitous strangers" attacked in the petition are the Huguenot silversmiths whose simple and beautiful designs are certainly cheaper than and, some believe, superior to the English product. Meanwhile the government is worried that silver plate sales are too high for the good of the economy, and so it has substantially increased the amount of pure silver that each piece of plate must legally contain 108 grams. Nevertheless, so far customers seem content to pay more.

Scots furious over power of the Lords

Westminster, 20 December 1712

James Douglas, the duke of Hamilton, was today refused his seat in the House of Lords, an action that is sure to fuel growing Scottish anger over the Act of Union.

Hamilton was created duke of Brandon, an English title, on 10 September last year. Yet the Lords have now decided that no Scottish peer may join them by virtue of an English title granted after the Union (1707). To Scottish minds this is not a unique affront; the Treason Act of 1709 is also resented because, although it abolishes torture, it brings to Scotland the draconian penalties of English law.

In March last year the Lords interfered in the kirk. James Greenshields, an Episcopal clergyman who had clashed with Scottish civil and church authorities, got the Lords to overturn the decision of the court of session in Edinburgh, which had denied him redress. The Lords can, in fact, exercise jurisdiction in Scotland, whereas many Scots believed that they were among the "courts sitting in Westminster Hall" barred from so doing by the Act of Union (→ 1712). ▷

Wren sees completion of his crowning achievement

Completed at last, the great dome of the cathedral looms over London.

Architect: Sir Christopher Wren.

The interior of St Andrew's church in London, also designed by Wren.

St Paul's: the glorious chancel.

Tom Quad at Christ Church, Oxford: the tower was added by Wren.

Wren built Greenwich observatory.

Marvellous dome of St Paul's is finished

London, 1711
The new St Paul's Cathedral has been declared complete by parliament, 36 years after the foundation stone was laid. Its architect, Sir Christopher Wren, who was 34 when the old cathedral burnt down in the great fire, is now 79.

On his Saturday inspections Wren has been winched up in a basket to check the interior of the dome. He left it to his son, Christopher, to lay the final coping stone on top of the lantern. After St Peter's in Rome, St Paul's has the largest dome in the world. In fact it consists of two domes, an outer one of lead and a smaller inner one, with a brick cone separating them as unseen support for the lantern. It is 111.25m (365 feet) to the top of the surmounting cross, and the weight of the dome and lantern is 65,024 tonnes (64,000 tons) – a feat unparalleled in England.

The building has been a saga of frustrations for Wren. His first two designs were rejected, and the third has been much altered in construction. Parliament voted to withhold half of his annual salary of £200 in 1697 until completion, as an incentive to speed, and he had to petition for the arrears in January this year. The total cost stands at more than £721,550, raised by a tax on coal coming into London's port.

Born at East Knoyle in Wiltshire in 1632, Wren first made his mark as a scientist, becoming a professor of astronomy at London's Gresham College in 1657; four years later he helped found the Royal Society. He won his first architectural commissions in 1663, for a chapel at Pembroke College, Cambridge, and the Sheldonian theatre at Oxford. He was appointed surveyor-general by Charles II and chosen to design the new St Paul's and more than 50 other churches to replace those destroyed by the fire. Among his other spectacular achievements are the Greenwich observatory, the library at Trinity College, Cambridge, and additions to Hampton Court Palace and Christ Church, Oxford. He was knighted in 1672 (→1716).

Pope publishes his 'Rape of the Lock'

Little big man: Alexander Pope.

London, 1712
Alexander Pope, the poet whose small stature (4 feet 6 inches) and hunchbacked form have been the targets of mockery, has completed an epic satire, *The Rape of the Lock*. Based on a real-life quarrel between two noble families, caused by Lord Petre cutting off a lock of hair belonging to Arabella Fermor, Pope's story unfolds in heroic couplets which lend to this trivial offence the proportions of the Trojan War in Homer's *Iliad* (→ 1713).

Scots kirk is under fire from new laws

Scotland, 1712
Anti-English feeling is running high in the wake of three acts passed this year by the Tory-dominated parliament at Westminster. First there is the Yule Vacance Act. This reinstates for the law courts the Christmas holiday abolished in 1690 because the Presbyterian kirk regarded it as a popish festival. The Toleration Act, making it obligatory for all clergymen to take an oath of allegiance to the monarch, is viewed with even more distaste. It means that, in effect, Presbyterians are being asked to pledge allegiance to the head of the Church of England – which is Episcopalian in character.

Thirdly, the Patronage Act re-establishes the right of Scottish nobles – in other words, laymen – to appoint ministers to vacant parishes on their land. This constitutes an open breach of the Act for the Security of the Scottish Church. To the elders of the kirk all three acts represent a betrayal of the 1690 settlement and the Act of Union of 1707, which promised them control of the national church. Their fear now is that episcopacy will be foisted on them (→ 1/6/13).

Hyde Park duel results in a double death

How to get even: an illustration from an instruction book for duellists.

London, 15 November 1712
Party politics took a deadly turn today when a Whig and a Tory lord slew each other in a duel at Hyde Park. A fanatical duellist and a Whig, Charles, Lord Mohun, "who gave the affront and yet sent the challenge", was killed by the Tory James Douglas, the duke of Hamilton, who was then dispatched by his opponent's second. Hamilton, Scotland's premier duke, was due to leave for France tomorrow as the new ambassador overseeing the peace treaty. Queen Anne is "stupefied with grief".

New daily paper 'The Spectator' prospers with elegant writing and hint of scandal

Addison: a gentleman journalist.

A London newspaper vendor.

London, 1712
When Richard Steele and Joseph Addison's daily, *The Spectator*, an elegant coffee-house periodical for "gentlefolk", made its début in March last year, not even its publisher, Samuel Buckley, dared hope that it would be such a remarkable success. (Buckley is the editor of the *Daily Courant*, the world's first daily newspaper, founded in 1702.)

Modelled on Steele's *Tatler*, which had contributions by Joseph Addison and appeared three times a week from 1709 until last year, the *Spectator* is supposedly written by members of a club representative of the English middle classes: a lovable Tory squire, Sir Roger de Coverley (country gentry); a gallant ex-Coldstream Guardsman, Captain Sentry (military); a self-made City merchant, Sir Andrew Freeport (trade); an ageing womanizer, Will Honeycomb (town); and Mr Spectator himself (an independent gentleman).

According to Mr Spectator, "we clubmen have always preferred to put out views rather than news to our readers". He has also explained that his principal intention is "to bring philosophy out of the closets and libraries, schools and colleges, to dwell in clubs and assemblies, at tea-tables and in all coffee houses". It has thus been possible for the two editors to provide readers with an excellent daily commentary on the manners, morals and literature of the day.

From its first arrival in a bookshop off Ludgate Hill, the *Spectator* has been well received. However, it only began to sell really briskly when one edition used, satirically, an economist's dream together with a tale of sexual temptation, ensuring a complete sell-out before noon. Yet for various reasons the periodical is being suspended for the foreseeable future (→ 1713).

Richard Steele: coffee-house wit.

1713

Ireland, 23 May. Edward Tyrell, the notorious priest-hunter, is executed for polygamy.

Dublin, 13 June. Jonathan Swift is installed as dean of St Patrick's Cathedral.

Westminster, 18 June. A bill to ratify a Franco-British trade treaty is defeated by nine votes when Tories desert the government line, fearing that the pro-French policies of a fellow Tory, Viscount Bolingbroke, might benefit the "Pretender" James Stuart (→ 30).

Westminster, 30 June. The Commons petitions Queen Anne to press for the removal of James Stuart from Lorraine and from any country friendly to Britain (→ 24/6/14).

Ireland, 27 October. Charles Talbot, the duke of Shrewsbury, is appointed lord lieutenant.

Ireland, October. James Kirkpatrick publishes anonymously his *Historical essay upon the loyalty of Presbyterians*.

London, 24 December. Queen Anne falls seriously ill at Kensington Palace (→ 31).

London, 31 December. The queen's sudden illness causes panic in the City.

England, 1713. The mathematician Roger Cotes revises Isaac Newton's *Principia Mathematica*.

Ireland, 1713. George Berkeley, the bishop of Cloyne, publishes a philosophical work, the *Three Dialogues between Hylas and Philonous*.

London, 1713. Alexander Pope, the poet, publishes *Windsor Forest*, the last line of which is nearly identical with the first line of his *Pastorals*, published in 1709.

London, 1713. George Frederick Handel composes the *Utrecht Te Deum* (→ 17/7/17).

London, 1713. Joseph Addison, the Whig poet and essayist, publishes *Cato*, a classical tragedy (→ 1713).

London, 1713. The Scriblerus Club, which aims to satirize politics through the memoirs of the fictitious Martinus Scriblerus, is formed by Alexander Pope, Jonathan Swift and others (→ 20/12/14).

Kent, 1713. Francis Atterbury, the dean of Oxford, becomes bishop of Rochester (→ 19/4/22).

Work and pleasure recorded in account by Liverpool squire

Crosby Hall, Liverpool
Hunting, shooting and fishing may be considered the traditional pursuits of country squires, but, as the daily diary kept by one such gentleman reveals, concern to bring about agricultural improvements is also a major preoccupation.

Nicholas Blundell, the master of Crosby Hall, near Liverpool, notes in his *Great Diurnal* that the demands of land ownership are unceasing. Like any prudent farmer, Blundell has had a detailed map of his holdings made, with every field, pit and watercourse clearly marked. Even the trees are numbered. It is from this that he organizes his daily labours.

Blundell, who opts for traditional methods, is open to novelty. Typically he employs marl [limey clay] to improve crop yields and, not wanting to waste an opportunity, fills the then empty marl-pit with carp. Not that pleasure is ignored. Before the pit was filled it was used this year for a celebration, with sword-dancers and bull-baiting.

Blundell also runs both kitchen- and market-gardens. And, like many a patriotic Englishman's, his flowerbeds give pride of place to tulips, a species associated with the Dutch homeland of William III.

Peace signed at Utrecht

Europe gathers to end 13 years of war and sign the Treaty of Utrecht.

United Provinces, 11 April
Eleven years of pan-European bloodshed, known as the War of the Spanish Succession, ended today as three main rivals – Britain, the United Provinces and France – signed the Treaty of Utrecht. Only Holy Roman Emperor Charles VI still covets the Spanish throne. As Archduke Charles he helped to precipitate the war [*see page 633*].

The treaty strikes a new balance of power in Europe and is especially beneficial to Britain, which retains the strategically vital naval bases of Gibraltar and Minorca as well as gaining sovereignty over much of French North America. It also confirms the Hanoverian succession to the British throne. The loser is Spain, whose empire has been pared to the bone. Britain's rivals may scorn the country as "Perfidious Albion", but its government and people have good cause to celebrate. French power has been severely curtailed, while Britain is stronger than ever before (→ 19/11/16).

German refugees in Ireland driven out

Ireland, March
Of the 800 or so German Protestant families who fled to Ireland from the war-torn Palatinate four years ago, only 260 remain. Those who came – all of them peasants – were settled on the estates of landlords who drew lots for them, allowing the Germans to lease land at reasonable rates, mainly in Co Limerick and Co Kerry. A commission composed of judges, bishops and landowners was set up to supervise their settlement.

Although the colonies flourished at first, with the Germans growing flax and hemp, rents have now been increased; many are emigrating to England or North America.

Britain to supply South America with slaves

Britain enters the slave trade.

London, 26 March
As a direct result of the negotiations at Utrecht, due to be signed next month, Britain's South Sea company has gained access to the lucrative trade in African slaves. Henceforth the company will be permitted to take some 4,800 slaves to South America every year. The agreement will last until 1743.

The company thus joins those other traders who enjoy the *asiento de negros*, the official slaving contracts granted by the Spanish government to a variety of foreign merchants. The first *asiento* was granted in 1517. Under its provisions a number of merchants are licensed to transport slaves, paying a price per head to Spain and profiting from their sales (→ 7/1718).

Scottish attempt to repeal union fails

Westminster, 1 June
A motion to dissolve the Act of Union has been defeated in the House of Lords by just four votes. It was put forward by the earl of Findlater – ironically, one of those responsible for masterminding the union negotiations. He denounced the abolition of the Scottish privy council, the introduction of the English Treason Act, slights to Scottish peers in the Lords, the new malt tax, and the ruin of Scottish trade from English competition. Many English peers supported him, believing that the union profits England little and is unnecessary now that the military threat from France has faded (→14/5/17).

Civil service born

London
England's government is changing, and not simply in terms of policy. For the first time there is evolving a new class of professional bureaucrats – "civil servants" – whose entire careers are dedicated to the business of administration. The days of cronyism and placemen are not, of course, completely over, but as government becomes ever more complex the need for such administrators, free of the old political ties and responsibilities, becomes ever more apparent.

Tories jubilant over second election win

London, September
For the second time in two years the Tories, led by Robert Harley, the earl of Oxford, and his deputy, Henry St John, Viscount Bolingbroke, have won a crushing victory over their Whig opponents in the general election. But their rivals have gained some ground in Scotland, while the Tories' deep divisions over the succession are far from healed.

Three years of Tory power have seen the successful overcoming, in 1711, of a national financial crisis, and continuing attacks on dissenters through the Occasional Conformity Act (1711). The outstanding success was the negotiation of this year's Treaty of Utrecht, which has left Britain in an unprecedentedly powerful position.

Yet for all that, the party has been under increasing pressure both from the Whigs and from internal arguments, notably between Oxford and Bolingbroke, whose enmity is all too obvious. Even more divisive is the succession.

While the Whigs are united in their support of the Hanoverians, the Tories are split three ways: some for Electress Sophia of Hanover, others for a return to the Stuarts, while many are simply undecided. That Queen Anne herself grows ever less fond of Oxford only adds to Tory problems (→3/3/14).

Lloyd, founder of marine insurance, dies

Safety at sea: the latest version of Plymouth's Eddystone lighthouse.

London
Edward Lloyd, the founder of London's trade in marine insurance, has died. His greatest achievement, the coffee house that bears his name, is likely to outlive its founder by many years.

For all his success Lloyd remains a shadowy figure; he first appeared in the City with the foundation of his original coffee house in Tower Street – one of the main streets of the docklands area – in early 1688. Lloyd's was not the first coffee house to focus on marine trading, but it soon proved to be the most successful, and in 1691 Lloyd relocated to new premises at 16 Lombard Street.

By 1710 Lloyd's had become the city's chief commercial saleroom of both ships and their cargoes, and Lloyd had added a new interest: marine insurance. He began publishing *Lloyd's News* – specializing in shipping-related information – but this was shut down after complaints about its inaccuracies.

Grand style to reflect a "polite" age: a silver kettle with burner.

A beautiful walnut settee of the period complete with elaborately carved legs and richly embroidered upholstery (now kept at Clandon Park, Surrey).

A green lacquer "secretaire" in the state bedroom at Clandon.

1714

London, March. Richard Steele, the newly elected Whig member for Stockton and editor of the *Spectator*, declares the Protestant succession to be in danger; he is expelled from the House of Commons.

Westminster, May. Parliament passes the Schism Act, making the separate education of dissenters illegal (→ 27/7).

Hanover, 8 June. Sophia, the electress of Brunswick-Lüneburg, the heir to the British throne, dies, aged 84; her son George, aged 54, is now the heir (→ 1/8).

Westminster, 24 June. £100,000 is offered for the capture of James Stuart, the pretender, believed to be in Britain (→ 23/6/15).

Westminster, 27 July. Queen Anne prorogues parliament, dismissing Robert Harley, the earl of Oxford, as lord treasurer (→ 30).

Westminster, 30 July. The earl of Shrewsbury becomes lord treasurer (→ 21/6/15).

Dover, 1 August. John Churchill, the duke of Marlborough, and his wife, Sarah, return from self-imposed exile in France, where they fled in November 1712 (→ 1719).

Westminster, 1 August. Parliament proclaims the accession to the British throne of Prince George of Brunswick-Lüneburg, the elector of Hanover, a second cousin of and the Protestant successor to Queen Anne, who died today.→

Hanover, 6 August. King George reinstates the duke of Marlborough as captain-general of the armed forces (→ 22/9).

Westminster, 22 September. King George invests his son, George Augustus, who became duke of Cornwall and Rothesay on his father's accession, as prince of Wales (→ 20/10).

London, 20 December. The *Spectator*, re-launched earlier this year following its demise in 1712, closes once more (→ 1/2/15).

London. Newgate prison bans inmates from keeping pigs within the prison walls; they may still keep domestic pets.

Wiltshire. Jethro Tull, the inventor of the machine seed drill, introduces the horse hoe.

Oxford. Sir Thomas Cokes founds Gloucester College.

Parliament rocked by crisis over the succession to Anne

Westminster, 3 March
Parliament and government are in crisis over the royal succession. Queen Anne is slowly dying of dropsy in Kensington Palace and is not expected to live much longer. Her Roman Catholic half-brother, James Stuart, and the Protestant Sophia of Brunswick-Lüneburg, the electress of Hanover, are the chief claimants to the crown.

The Tory government is split. The lord treasurer, the earl of Oxford, is a tepid Jacobite who will accept the Hanoverians. But Viscount Bolingbroke is plotting to put James on the throne – if he renounces Catholicism. The Whigs are committed to the Hanoverian succession. When the queen dismissed the Whig government in 1710 and brought in the Tories to make peace with France she seemed to prefer her half-brother's claims, but she failed to pack the government with Jacobites.

The country would never support a Roman Catholic king, however little enthusiasm there may be for a German. Bolingbroke has meanwhile sent secret envoys to James Stuart in Paris, to persuade him to change to Anglicanism, but they have met with no success. He is also trying to pack the council of regency with pro-Stuart ministers, but he can only succeed if Queen Anne dismisses Oxford and lives long enough to confirm Bolingbroke's policies (→ 8/6).

Oxford depicted as puppet-master.

Queen's death draws Stuart era to a close

Queen Anne's cortège makes its way towards her last resting-place.

Kensington, 1 August
Queen Anne died today in Kensington Palace, at the age of 49, bringing to an end a reign that has seen Britain rise to become the dominant power in Europe. British armies under the duke of Marlborough defeated all the power of King Louis XIV of France in the most spectacular military victories since Agincourt almost 300 years ago, and the British navy is now the undisputed master of the seas. The political union of England and Scotland was finally enacted in 1707, and constitutional cabinet government was also established during Anne's reign. At the same time literature, architecture and science have all flourished, while Britain has also become Europe's leading commercial nation (→ 6).

Village greens are graced by a new sport

Cricket has become an important game, often played for high stakes.

England
All kinds of sports have become popular in England during Queen Anne's reign, from peaceful bowls and cricket to bear-baiting and cock-fighting. Men gather in bear-pits and cock-pits to bet recklessly on how animals will perform, wagering which cock will kill the other or how long a bear will hold off a pack of dogs.

Bowling is always popular on village greens, and cricket matches are now regular occasions for rural amusement. Old-style puritans deplore sport on Sundays, but modern England cares nothing for their disapproval.

Hanoverian dynasty succeeds to the British crown

Jacobites fail to halt coronation of George

Westminster, 20 October
George of Hanover has become King George of Great Britain. Cannon roared and bells pealed today as Londoners cheered the new king, whose coronation ceremony was held in Latin, since George speaks little English.

Yet not all the British are rejoicing at the succession of the elector of Hanover. Jacobites have been demonstrating in London and in many other parts of the country, proclaiming "James III" – James Stuart – king and attacking dissenting chapels and Whig property – their owners being associated with the Hanoverian succession. The defeated Tories, who had pinned all their hopes on the restoration of the Stuarts, drink openly to the health of "the king over the water" (James is in France). Parts of Scotland and the north of England are ripe for rebellion.

George is 54, and although his heart remains in Hanover he has already immersed himself in British politics. He is, after all, no stranger to this country, having visited London back in 1680. During that visit Charles II suggested that George marry his (George's) second cousin, the then Princess Anne. She was only 15 at the time and took a dislike to George, which may explain her lack of enthusiasm for the Hanoverian succession. King George may not be popular, but his safe establishment on the throne means that the uncertainties of the past have been removed (→ 12/11/15).

King George in equestrian mood.

Old hands lead first parliament of reign

Westminster, October
King George, who arrived in England on 18 September, has appointed his first goverment and, as expected, drawn his ministers from the Whigs. The post of lord treasurer has been allowed to lapse, and the government will be headed by James, Earl Stanhope, and Charles, Viscount Townshend. John Campbell, the duke of Argyll, has been put in charge of Scotland.

Stanhope and Townshend are both tough-minded officials who should work better together than the earl of Oxford and Viscount Bolingbroke did in the last years of Queen Anne's reign. Among the allies that Townsend has brought into the government is his own brother-in-law, Robert Walpole, the new paymaster of the forces.

Dissenters all over the country are saying prayers of thanks for George and his new government. The Schism Act, passed by the Tories last year to outlaw all separate dissenting education, has been allowed to lapse, as has the Occasional Conformity Act, which punished dissenters who attended Church of England services on an occasional basis simply to qualify for civic office. A new era of toleration has now opened for them, although it does not extend to Roman Catholics. The Whigs, meanwhile, are triumphant. In the last years of Queen Anne they staked everything on the Hanoverian succession and are now reaping their reward. The Tories, who either backed the Stuart pretender or else equivocated, are now dispersed and ruined. Bolingbroke, James Stuart's chief English supporter, is out of government and may soon be prosecuted by his enemies (→ 11/10/15).

Townshend: a tough bargainer.

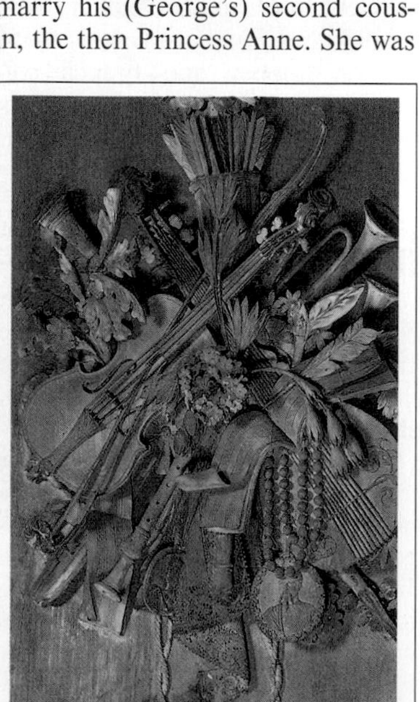

A limewood carving of musical instruments, flowers and lace by Grinling Gibbons, who was made master carver to the king in 1714.

Hanover's Protestantism regarded as most crucial consideration

Westminster
King George reigns by act of parliament. The "divine right of kings" proclaimed by the Stuart kings has been abolished in Britain, thanks to the "glorious revolution" of 1688 and the Act of Succession which provided for the Protestant succession to the throne. The act was passed in the reign of William III, when it was apparent that he would die childless, as also did Queen Anne.

Many have a better hereditary claim to the crown than George – starting with James Stuart, the son of James II. Others include the royal family of Savoy, descended from the daughter of King Charles I, Henriette-Anne. Yet they are all Catholics. Britain deposed James II, its last Catholic king, in 1688 and will not tolerate another. The house of Hanover is Protestant, and that is more important than anything else. George is the grandson of James I's daughter Elizabeth, who married Frederick V, the Elector Palatine. Their daughter, Sophia, married Ernest Augustus, the elector of Hanover, and was heir to the throne until she died shortly before Queen Anne.

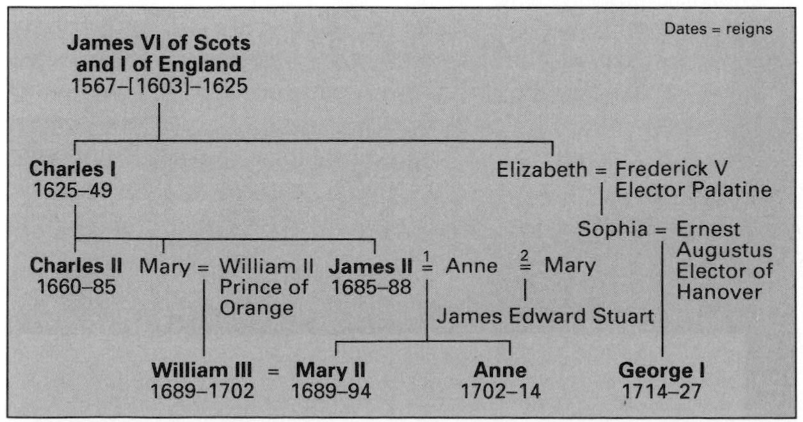

A family tree showing King George's position in the hereditary scheme.

1715

Cork City, 1 February. The *Idler*, the first Irish newspaper to be published outside Dublin, appears (→14/11).

Westminster, 21 June. James Butler, the duke of Ormond, is impeached for treason (→23).

Manchester, 23 June. Dragoon guards restore order after a month of Jacobite riots (→1/8).

London, 1 August. King George snubs the earl of Mar, whom he suspects of Jacobite dealings; Mar resolves to flee to Scotland (→7/8).

Grampian, 27 August. During a deer hunt the earl of Mar plans a rebellion with fellow Jacobites (→30).

Scotland, 30 August. The Act for Encouraging Loyalty in Scotland pushes many wavering Tories into the Jacobite camp, as they fear persecution (→6/9).

Edinburgh, 8 September. A Jacobite attempt to take the castle is foiled (→20).

Aberdeen, 20 September. James VIII is proclaimed king by the earl marischal (→6/10).

Westminster, 11 October. Robert Walpole, the Whig member of parliament, is appointed chancellor of the exchequer and first lord of the treasury (→1715).

Lancashire, 9 November. Jacobites enter Preston and seize control when the militia flees (→13).

Dublin, 12 November. King George opens his first Irish parliament; William Conolly is elected speaker of the House of Commons (→6/1716).

Preston, 13 November. Government troops, led by Generals Carpenter and Wills, surround the town and besiege the Jacobites.→

Glasgow, 14 November. The *Glasgow Courant*, a thrice-weekly newspaper, appears (→1719).

Preston, 14 November. James Forster, the leader of the English Jacobites, surrenders (→22/12).

Canterbury, 14 December. Archbishop Thomas Tenison dies (→1/1716).

Westminster, December. Parliament passes the Riot Act to curb recent unrest (→6/1/16).

Britain, 1715. The national debt now stands at £40 million, with an annual interest charge of £2 million; many fear national bankruptcy.

Tories purged from army and politics

Recruiting officers prefer Whigs.

Westminster, March

The first session of parliament since the Whigs won the general election, has opened. The Whig majority of 150 represented a spectacular victory that, for the time being, has thrown the Tories into the political wilderness.

The Tories' mistake, if it can be called that, was to allow themselves to be so closely identified with the cause of James Stuart, the pretender. Britain's new monarch, King George, is deeply distrustful of the Tories and has been determined to be rid of them. In fact he sacked all Tory ministers – except for two known to be sympathetic to his cause – shortly after coming to the throne, even though the Tories had at that time a majority in the House of Commons.

The king has not been shy about letting people know which way he expected them to vote. In January, when he dissolved parliament and called the election, George openly stated that electors should vote only for candidates who were strongly in favour of a Protestant succession – in other words, candidates who wanted George, and not the Catholic James, for king.

Tories are being purged from their political and military posts, and there is even a move to impeach some party leaders. The prime targets for legal action are the earl of Oxford and Viscount Bolingbroke, against whom charges of treason may be levelled (→2/1716).

Pretender joined in Paris by Irish duke

Paris, 7 August

James Butler, the duke of Ormond, fleeing from impeachment by parliament, has joined the Jacobite court here and intends to play a major role in the military attempts to restore the Stuarts to the throne of Britain. He claims that he has men ready to seize the arsenals in Bristol, Exeter and Plymouth.

An Irish grandee, he has considerable military experience and was made captain-general of British forces by Queen Anne after her dismissal of the duke of Marlborough. He is not, however, regarded as a soldier of genius, and this latest move of his could prove to be highly ill advised (→27).

The duke of Ormond gets ready.

Earl of Mar raises Jacobite standard

Grampian, 6 September

John Erskine, the earl of Mar, has raised the Jacobite standard at Braemar and proclaimed the exiled pretender, James Stuart, the rightful king of Britain. As he unfurled the flag the gilt ball on top of the flagpole fell off, but the significance of this mishap was lost on Mar, who spoke of the uprising expected in England and the money and soldiers which he hopes will arrive from France with the future James VIII of Scots and III of England.

Mar, who used to be Queen Anne's secretary of state for Scotland, wisely did not point out that he played a role in shaping the Act of Union, hated in Scotland, and that he had fervently expressed his support for the accession of King George. He is, in fact, so notorious for changing his allegiance that he is known as "Bobbing John".

Yet he has gained the support of a number of Jacobite nobles, mostly from the Episcopalian north-east, and highland chieftains. Among them are the marquises of Tullibardine and of Huntly and the clan leaders Gordon of Auchintoul and Campbell of Glendaruel.

Much depends on how effectively Mar can strike at the weak government forces in Scotland and how soon James Stuart can arrive with cannon, money and French soldiers. Only a decisive early success will persuade the waverers to go on fighting (→8).

Jacobite revolt erupts in north of England

Northumberland, 6 October

A Jacobite rising here in the north-east of England has been declared by Thomas Forster, a member of parliament who fled from London when about to be arrested for his rebel sympathies. He has accepted the military command turned down by James Ratcliffe, the dashing earl of Derwentwater, who has brought a group of northern gentry down from Scotland. They have joined a party of Jacobite borderers led by Lord Kenmure to form an army of 2,000 foot and 600 horse.

Derwentwater has refused the military command of this force because he is a Roman Catholic and fears that this will prejudice the cause. The rebels may regret this decision, as so far Forster has shown little military skill.

There is much rumour of other uprisings in England, where the new king, "German George", is generally disliked. Yet the English Jacobites seem unwilling to make a move until James Stuart arrives with a French army. Hopes for French support are, however, rapidly waning following the death on 8 September of Louis XIV. Jacobite circles both in London and Paris are also riddled with government spies. James must look to Scotland to win his crown (→9/11).

Royal army halts Stuart rebellion at Sheriffmuir

Stirling, 13 November
The Jacobite rebellion has experienced a serious setback in a drawn battle fought at Sheriffmuir, near Stirling, between the earl of Mar's 12,000 men and the duke of Argyll's army of just 3,000. Although the battle is being reckoned a strategic, rather than a tactical, defeat – the Jacobite army is still intact and remains a threat – Mar should have gained a decisive victory. However, he conducted his part of the battle with the lack of foresight that has plagued the rebellion from its start.

Remarkably, Mar waited for several weeks at Perth, which fell to the Jacobites on 14 September, before making his move. Despite his huge numerical advantage over Argyll's forces, he feared risking his men in an engagement. It now appears that he should have marched south and denied Argyll the chance to occupy Stirling; then he could have joined up with rebels in the south-west of Scotland and north of England. Instead, Argyll was able to take Stirling, effectively barring the rebels from getting any further south. All that Argyll has to do now is sit tight and wait for Hanoverian reinforcements, already on their way from England.

The rebellion was begun two months ago by Mar, who returned from London to Scotland to find a country deeply resentful of the Hanoverian succession [*see report on page 657*]. His most ardent supporters have been the Episcopalian nobility of the north-east, whose priests seek a Stuart restoration.

The rebellion raised in the north-east of England by the pretender's cousin, the earl of Derwentwater, has also suffered a serious blow. Derwentwater's Anglo-Scots force, which was incompetently led by Thomas Forster, was defeated yesterday by General Wills at Preston. Like Mar's campaign in Scotland, the English uprising has been poorly directed. With the recent failure of the duke of Ormond's seaborne expedition against Plymouth, the Jacobite cause is facing the prospect of disaster (→ 14).

The duke of Argyll – "Red John of the Battles" – stops the Jacobite earl of Mar at Sheriffmuir, near Stirling.

Mar: an incapable commander.

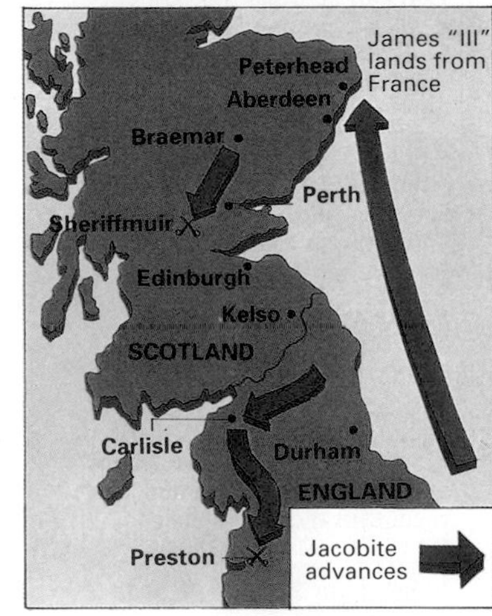

James's progress south is checked.

Pretender sets foot on British soil in order to claim the throne

Grampian, 22 December
James Stuart, the pretender, has landed at Peterhead in the hope of leading a victorious army to London to claim the throne from which his father was ousted. Delayed by bad weather and avoiding the watchful British navy, he arrived disguised as an ordinary sailor, seasick and so weak from the ague that he had to be carried ashore. He has no guns, no soldiers and has lost most of his treasury in a shipwreck. Despite all this, Jacobite leaders still trust that they will turn the tide if James can inspire his army – which, although checked, has not been utterly defeated (→ 12/1715).

Hanoverian propaganda: the devil is casting both the pope and captured Jacobite rebel leaders onto a blazing fire in this contemporary woodcut.

Scottish divine dies

Edinburgh, 28 December
William Carstares, the principal of Edinburgh University, has died of apoplexy, aged 66. A strong Presbyterian, Carstares was a towering figure in church affairs and oversaw the Presbyterian settlement of 1690. He came into conflict with Charles II in 1674, when he was imprisoned for five years, and after the Argyll plot of 1683 he was tortured. He finally fled to the United Provinces, where he became chaplain to William of Orange, whom he later accompanied to England as a keen supporter of the "glorious revolution". A moderate, he was gracious to his Episcopalian rivals.

1716

Dundee, 6 January. The Jacobite army is given an enthusiastic reception (→ 8).

Scone, Tayside, 8 January. The pretender arrives to claim his throne as James VIII (→ 21).

Perth, 21 January. The pretender flees when John Campbell, the duke of Argyll, marches on Perth (→ 4/2).

Canterbury, January. William Wake, the bishop of Lincoln, is appointed archbishop.

Westminster, 7 May. Parliament passes the Septennial Act; general elections will take place every seven years instead of every three (→ 14/6).

Westminster, 14 June. Robert Walpole, who became chancellor of the exchequer last October, accuses the exiled Tories Henry St John, Viscount Bolingbroke, and James Butler, the duke of Ormond, of Jacobitism (→ 20).

London, 20 June. Parliament deals a crippling blow to the house of Ormond by confiscating the dukes's estates in Munster and Leinster (→ 9/4/17).

Munster, 20 June. Drainage schemes to make the river Shannon navigable are started by royal order.

London, June. The rift between King George and his son, George, the prince of Wales, worsens as plans go ahead for the king's visit to Hanover; his son will act only as "guardian of the realm", not regent, in the king's absence (→ 17/7).

London, June. King George dismisses the duke of Argyll for being too gentle with the Jacobites, after he fails to capture the pretender, and for siding with the prince of Wales (→ 1717).

Hanover, July. King George visits his homeland (→ 1717).

Bristol. The first bank outside London opens.

London. The restoration of St Paul's Cathedral is completed with the addition of a bell to the bell tower.

England. William Wycherley, the dramatist, best known for his last two plays, *The Country Wife* and *The Plain Dealer*, dies.

Virginia. The first company of English actors to visit America appears in Williamsburg.

Britain. The Royal Regiment of Artillery is founded.

Scots uprising collapses

In the wake of the pretender's defeat the highlanders retreat from Perth.

Montrose, Tayside, 4 February
The dejected clansmen of Scotland are going home. Their uprising has failed, and the clan chiefs are lining up to submit to King George. The rebel leaders, James Stuart and John Erskine, the earl of Mar, have today taken to their ships – without telling their army.

It was Mar who raised the Stuart banner at Braemar last September. The pretender knew nothing of the uprising then, but he sailed to Scotland from his French exile sure that he would receive massive French support – which failed to appear following the sudden death last year of Louis XIV. The eastern rising went well at first: Perth fell, and James was proclaimed king both in Aberdeen and Inverness. But the tide turned at Sheriffmuir after the duke of Argyll's men held off Mar's army – which was three times bigger – and a western uprising collapsed (→ 1717).

'Sinking fund' set up to pay nation's debt

Westminster
In a determined attempt to tackle the national debt, the chancellor of the exchequer, Robert Walpole, has created a "sinking fund" to which increased taxes are to be devoted annually, in the hope that the debt will eventually be discharged. Walpole has consolidated debts totalling £54 million – mostly created by the long war with France – into one big national debt paying a common rate of interest (→ 2/1716).

The national debt is weighed up.

Agricultural and rural hardship get worse as enclosures begin

Stockport, Cheshire
Ignoring both peasant and parliament, John Warren, the lord of the manor of Stockport, has taken the law into his own hands and sold off common land in order to build factories and houses. Ominously for those peasants who depend on grazing land for their livings, Warren has earmarked one plot to build a workhouse for 170 people. The only patch of land left as common is, equally ominously, being set aside for a jail.

With common land and smallholdings gradually disappearing under enclosure in favour of larger, more productive farms, these are hard times for thousands of rural workers. Many rely on grazing a pig or keeping a few hens on the common to eke out their meagre farm wages and see them through winters. Common land is vital for small "strip" farmers who are being forced to sell up in great numbers. Worst hit are the "squatters", living in shacks on commons with no legal right of occupancy. A new homeless class has been born in rural England: no wonder that Warren is planning a workhouse. Meanwhile, as farms grow ever larger and more efficient under enclosure, the landowning class becomes ever wealthier and more powerful.

A new regimentation is creeping in as farming becomes more efficient.

Tories with Jacobite sympathies purged

Westminster, February
Robert Walpole and his fellow Whigs are purging Jacobite sympathizers among the Tory opposition. Following the recent Stuart uprising – the danger of which is being exaggerated by the Whigs – Tories who survived earlier purges are being removed from government and many public offices.

Tory justices of the peace are being thrown out, together with lords lieutenants and their deputies. Officers of the duchy of Cornwall have been sacked, and promotions to senior positions in the Church of England, the law, the diplomatic service and the court are now largely restricted to Whigs.

The government still fears that there could be a new revolt. While some Jacobite supporters, such as Viscount Bolingbroke and the duke of Ormond, have fled to France, others, such as Thomas Forster (who led the Northumberland rebels) and the earls of Nithsdale and Winton, have escaped from prison and are at large.

On 24 February two rebel leaders who failed to escape, the earl of Derwentwater and Viscount Kenmure, were beheaded at the Tower of London. It seems that the government wanted to make an example of them. While they can hope to escape with their lives, many Scottish nobles who were involved are certain to forfeit their estates and be driven into exile (→ 7/5).

Bolingbroke: a political refugee.

Papists and Jacobites are feared.

'Patriot' who stood up for Scotland dies

London, September
He was neither a great soldier nor a distinguished politician, yet Andrew Fletcher, the laird of Saltoun, who died far from his homeland today, will be mourned greatly by all Scots who cherish the dream of independence. He was a scholar, a linguist and a defiant opponent of the English government at a time when many were only too happy to be bribed into submission. Dubbed "the patriot", Fletcher believed that Scotland would take its rightful place in a united Europe. His last words were: "Lord have mercy on my poor country, that is so barbarously oppressed."

Britain slow to sign a European treaty

The Hague, 19 November
An impatient King George is urging his ministers here to hasten the signature of a treaty of alliance between Britain, the United Provinces and France. What is worrying the king is the possibility of a Baltic alliance between Sweden and Czar Peter of Russia that could threaten Hanover. Although delays in signing this triple alliance are partly a consequence of communication problems, with diplomatic messengers scurrying between European capitals, a more significant factor is British ministers' anxiety that France will become the most powerful of the allies (→ 1/1717).

Wives are denied access to contraception

Women remain largely tied to a never-ending round of domestic duties.

Britain
The fate of many women in today's society is exemplified by Elizabeth, the second wife of John Hervey, Lord Bristol. This year has seen the birth of her 20th child. She has in fact given birth on average once a year since her first child was delivered in 1696, the year following her marriage at the age of 19. Not all of her pregnancies have had a happy outcome. In 1701 she miscarried triplets, and three years after she produced a stillborn son.

This constant round of childbearing and its attendant domestic duties take a heavy toll of a woman's health, ageing her before her time, but for many it is inescapable. Few have access to contraception. Condoms are on sale in London, but they are usually used by men anxious to avoid catching venereal disease from prostitutes rather than by husbands wishing to spare their wives another pregnancy.

Denied the use of contraceptive devices, women have to resort to other means to stay off the treadmill of annual childbirths. Some try to prevent further conception by breastfeeding a previous baby. Others practise *coitus interruptus* or simply refuse to have sex with their husbands. In the last resort some can do nothing but feign illness.

'Natural' architecture is now the vogue

St George's church in Wapping, designed by Nicholas Hawksmoor.

London
A group of architects led by Colin Campbell and Lord Burlington has launched a movement to "purify" British architecture of baroque extravagance and return to the classical styles of Andrea Palladio and Inigo Jones. Two new books – a translation of Palladio's *I Quattro Libri dell'Architettura* (published this year) and Campbell's own *Vitruvius Britannicus* (published last year) – have ushered in the new movement, favoured by Whig politicians opposed to Stuart "romanticism". Campbell's austere design for Wanstead House here contrasts sharply with baroque Blenheim Palace, designed by Sir John Vanbrugh and Nicholas Hawksmoor.

1717 - 1718

Europe, January 1717. Britain, France and the United Provinces form a "triple alliance" to uphold the Treaty of Utrecht of 1713 (→ 11/17).

Sardinia, November 1717. Philip V of Spain occupies Austrian-ruled Sardinia, jeopardizing both the Treaty of Utrecht and British foreign policy (→ 1/6/18).

London, 1717. Edmund Halley, the astronomer and mathematician, invents a diving bell (→ 1719).

Westminster, 1717. The Act of Grace pardons many Jacobites who rebelled in 1715 (→ 7/3/19).

London, 21 May 1718. John Price, a hangman, is himself executed at Bunhill Row, for murder.

England, 1 June 1718. Admiral George Byng sails for the Mediterranean to seek to dissuade Philip V from breaching the Treaty of Utrecht (→ 7/1718).

Ulster, July 1718. Severe famine and unemployment force a mass emigration of Ulster Scots to the American colonies.

Sicily, July 1718. Philip V invades, contravening the Treaty of Utrecht (→ 8/1718).

Europe, August 1718. A quadruple alliance of Britain, France, the United Provinces and the Holy Roman Empire is formed to try to avoid a war with Spain (→ 1).

Dublin, 28 October 1718. Jewish citizens lease land for a cemetery at Ballybough.

Britain, 17 December 1718. Britain declares war on Spain (→ 10/1719).

Westminster, December 1718. The Whig Robert Walpole, who left the government last year, enters into a tactical alliance with Tories and other rebel Whigs to overthrow the government's policies (→ 1719).

Dublin, 1718. The first modern charity hospital in either Ireland or Great Britain opens in Cook Street.

Gloucestershire, 1718. A mineral spring is discovered at Cheltenham.

Liverpool, 1718. Paupers are ordered to wear special badges so that outdoor relief is not given twice to the same person.

Dyfed, 1718. Isaac Carter sets up the first Welsh printing press, at Trefhedyn, near Newcastle Emlyn.

King George dismisses secretary of state

London, 9 April 1717

King George has sacked one of his chief ministers, Charles, Viscount Townshend. With his brother-in-law Robert Walpole, Townshend ran the government last year in the absence of the king, who was visiting his native Hanover.

The row is over Britain's policy in the Baltic. George is worried that Russia, Sweden and Prussia will sign an accord to dominate the area, so he has been urging an alliance with France to offset this threat. Yet the reluctance of Walpole and Townshend to negotiate with the French has driven the king to distraction. Townshend is a blunt, sometimes coarse man whose outlook is fundamentally English rather than European. To make matters worse, the king is also convinced that Townshend is an ally of his detested son, the prince of Wales. Walpole has resigned in protest at the dismissal (→ 12/1718).

Charles, Viscount Townshend, who has fallen out of favour with the king.

Welsh bishop wants state to rule church

London, 31 March 1717

The continuing argument between church and state over which is to rule the other reached new heights today after Benjamin Hoadly, the bishop of Bangor – who is known to be a Whig activist – preached before King George. Hoadly's sermon, which set the state above the church, and relegated its bishops strictly to spiritual matters, has outraged traditionalists, who see the church as ideally the supreme authority in the land.

It is not the bishop's first foray into the controversy. His pamphlet *A Preservative against the Principles and Practices of Nonjurors*, supporting the state's power to discipline nonjurors – those who would not swear loyalty to William and Mary in 1688 – emphasizes his backing of the secular power against the spiritual (→ 2/11/19).

Blazing row divides royal father and son

King George with the prince and princess in a rare moment of peace.

London, 1717

Relations between King George and his son reached a new low this autumn when the king placed his son and daughter-in-law under arrest in Kensington Palace, denied them access to their children, and threatened to jail them in the Tower. The prince and princess of Wales now live at Leicester House, in the less than salubrious West End of London, where they hold what is in effect a rival court. The row climaxed over the christening of the prince's son, George William, born on 2 November.

The king wanted the duke of Newcastle to be godfather; the prince refused. When the prince argued with Newcastle, his heavy accent led the duke to believe that he was being challenged to a duel. The king then banished the royal couple from the palace (→ 2/11/26).

Church 'soft' on sin

Edinburgh, 14 May 1717

The Church of Scotland's Calvinist evangelicals are furious at what they see as soft treatment of an alleged heretic. Professor John Simson of the university of Glasgow has been merely reprimanded by the church's general assembly. The Calvinists are dismayed because Simson's Arminian views of salvation for all believers rather than just an elect few are shared by their rivals, the less numerous but more influential moderate wing (→ 1720).

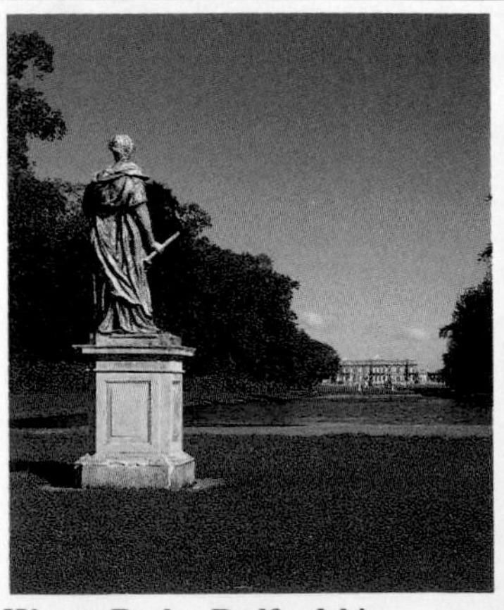

Wrest Park, Bedfordshire, completed in 1718: fine vistas are typical of great-house design.

Handel's 'Water Musick' played on river

The view up the Thames past Westminster Bridge, painted by Canaletto.

London, 17 July 1717
This evening at eight o'clock King George took the royal barge from Whitehall to supper at Chelsea with a flotilla of other boats. The oars were rested, and the boats drifted upstream with the incoming tide as music written for the occasion by George Frederick Handel was played by 50 musicians in a barge alongside the royal one. George liked the *Water Musick* suite so much that he had it played again at supper in a Chelsea garden and a third time as the boats drifted home in the small hours. Handel and his orchestra were paid £150 by Baron von Kielmannsegge, the husband of the king's half-sister, who had arranged the entertainment (→ 1719).

Captain Blackbeard, terror of the American coast, is pursued and killed by Royal Navy

Virginia, 22 November 1718
Edward Teach, better known as "Blackbeard" and perhaps the most notorious of the pirates who prey on shipping off the American coast, will thieve no more. Pursued up the James river by Lieutenant Maynard of the Royal Navy, Blackbeard was forced to stand and fight. Allegedly he took a last glass of rum and declared: "Damnation take my soul if I give up or take any quarter!" before he turned to face the foe. Of the 25 wounds found on his dead body, five were inflicted by Maynard and his men.

Blackbeard will go roving no more.

Blackbeard, in the words of the writer Daniel Defoe, "has frightened America more than any comet". He took his name from his massive beard, into which he would stick lighted gunners' matches, spluttering like some hellish fire. Obsessed with violence, he was a psychotic and impulsive sadist who offered pain and punishment to friends and enemies both, with neither rhyme nor reason. His origins, some said, were quite respectable – he was possibly of Bristol merchant stock – but he traded on his terrifying image to conduct a bloody career, filled with atrocities, that lasted unabated for two years.

Freemasons open 'grand lodge' in London

London, 4 June 1717
The secretive society of freemasons, which claims its origins in the biblical temple of King Solomon, has set up a headquarters in London. The Craft, as freemasonry terms itself, is to be run from a "grand lodge" at the Goose and Gridiron tavern in Covent Garden. Members – the majority of whom are professional men rather than real masons – meet here to engage in elaborate rituals, swap arcane handclasps and, like men in any other club, use their friendships to advance their social and professional interests.

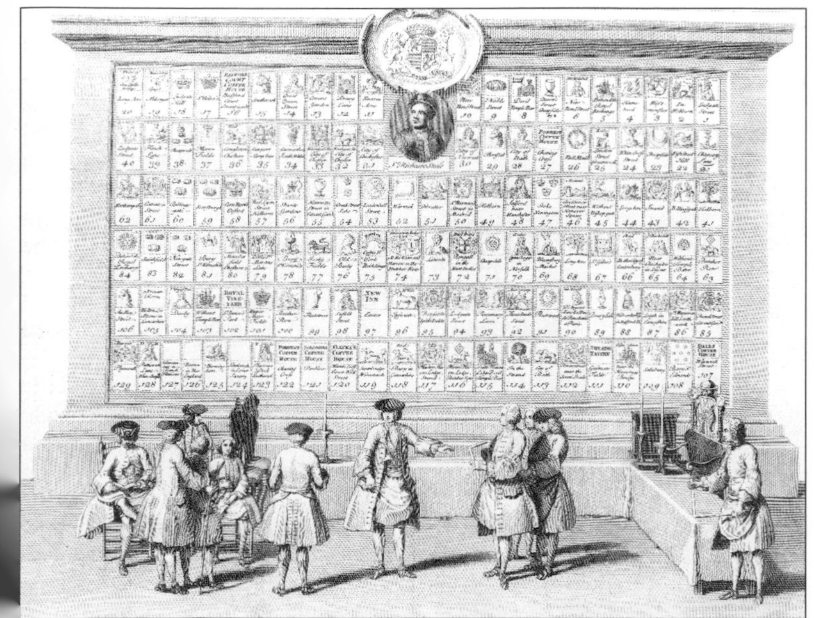

A later engraving showing London lodges; Covent Garden is number 13.

British face pirates in battle at Passaro

A contemporary view of Admiral Byng's fleet in the Straits of Messina, Sicily.

Sicily, 1 August 1718
A British fleet under Admiral Byng has smashed Spanish ambitions in the Mediterranean. Byng has destroyed a Spanish squadron of 18 ships of the line at Cape Passaro, off the coast of Sicily. Eight ships have been annihilated and the rest captured. The Spanish made successful attacks on both Sardinia, last November, and Sicily, last month, but this comprehensive defeat will surely put a stop to such raids.

Despite the battle, Spain and England are not actually at war; indeed the crux of Lord Stanhope's foreign policy has been to reconcile Spain with its main rival, Austria (part of the Holy Roman Empire). But such efforts have proved vain. Philip V of Spain has been determined to wrest Italy from Austrian influence, and in the end the members of the Triple Alliance, including Britain, equally determined to maintain the balance of power achieved by the Treaty of Utrecht, have opted for Austria's side. Now Emperor Charles VI has been offered partnership in the alliance (→ 17/12/18).

1719 - 1720

Spain, 7 March 1719. James Butler, the duke of Ormond and captain-general of the Spanish troops, sails for Britain to put the pretender, James Stuart, on the throne (→28).

Spain, 28 March 1719. James Stuart arrives from Rome to lead the Jacobite invasion of Britain (→9/5).

Italy, 9 May 1719. James Stuart marries by proxy the 17-year-old Princess Maria Clementina Sobieska, the wealthy granddaughter of King John III of Poland (→10/6).

Dublin, 25 August 1719. The Lords amend an anti-popery bill calling for Roman Catholic clergy in Ireland to be branded on the cheek; the Lords want the penalty to be castration, but the British privy council, to which the legislation must be sent, is likely to reject this suggestion (→2/11).

Sicily, October 1719. The British fleet under Admiral George Byng raids this Spanish-held island off the Italian coast (→9/1725).

London, 1719. Daniel Defoe, the journalist, publishes a novel, *The Life and Strange Surprising Adventures of Robinson Crusoe of York, Mariner*, followed immediately by *Further Adventures of Robinson Crusoe* (→1720).

Derby, 1719. Thomas Lombe founds the first English silk factory.

London, 1719. Joseph Addison, the journalist who worked on both the *Tatler* and the *Spectator* with Richard Steele, dies.

London, 1719. King George donates £1,000 for the foundation of the Royal Academy of Music; the German composer George Frederick Handel is to be its director (→13/2/26).

Greenwich, London, 1719. John Flamsteed, created the first astronomer royal in 1675, dies at the age of 73 (→9/2/21).

Westminster, February 1720. The South Sea Company Act is passed (→11/6/20).

Derbyshire, 1720. The first issue of a new local paper, the *Derby Post*, appears (→1720).

Edinburgh, 1720. Divisions within the Church of Scotland deepen as the general assembly denounces *The Marrow of Modern Divinity*, a 17th-century English Calvinist classic which was republished in 1718 (→15/10/28).

Jacobite rebels face defeat at Glenshiel

Jacobite highlanders bravely fight in a doomed battle at Glenshiel.

Grampian, 10 June 1719

An incipient Jacobite rising in the highlands has been crushed in a battle at Glenshiel. Those highland chieftains who returned from exile to raise their clans for "James III" have fled, as have their Spanish mercenaries, and the Hanoverians are now supreme.

The Jacobites were commanded by George Keith, the earl marischal, who also had the support of "Rob Roy's" MacGregors. Their aim was to make a diversionary attack on government forces while a Spanish invasion of south-western England took place, but this plan began to fall apart after a storm prevented the Spanish ships from landing. Meanwhile another force of 500 Spaniards had already joined the highland Jacobites in March.

News of the failed invasion in the south left the highland Jacobites utterly at a loss. Before they could decide what to do General Wightman marched his troops out of the government garrison at Inverness to meet the rebels. The armies were of about the same size – 1,200 men – but the Jacobites fled after being subjected to mortar fire and infantry attack. Casualties were light on both sides (→31/12/20).

Toleration measure fails to dispose of test of conformity

Dublin, 2 November 1719

A Toleration Bill has been passed in the Irish House of Commons which extends freedom of worship to dissenters but leaves the controversial sacramental test untouched.

This test, which became law in 1704, has meant that all dissenters, including members of the Presbyterian Church, must conform to the established church if they wish to hold public office. While it has done little to worsen the position of Roman Catholics, who are already heavily discriminated against as a result of the penal laws, the test has rankled with Presbyterians, who have persistently attempted to have it repealed.

In England the Commons eventually drew up the heads of a bill that included the suspension of the test for the army and the militia. But members of the House of Lords disagreed and had all reference to the test excised. The Irish privy council then submitted a compromise bill which, though passed by Westminster, failed to get through the Irish House of Commons. Now, under pressure from England, the Toleration Bill has finally been passed (→7/4/20).

'Friendly society' is formed by workers

Newcastle upon Tyne, 1719

The shoemakers of this town have formed what they call a "friendly society", which aims to protect its members against the misfortunes of illness and unemployment, and to succour widows and orphans. It is a rare movement among workers to unite for their mutual benefit.

The authorities generally repress all attempts by workers to improve their position. The ruling classes believe firmly that low wages and high prices keep workers busy and contented. It is thought that if a worker had more than the bare financial necessity, he would spend it on gin. In fact, there are frequent riots against the rigours of life in towns and in the country, but they are usually put down.

Highwayman foiled at Hampstead Heath

Highwaymen robbing two women.

London, 19 December 1719

A highwayman who tried to hold up an old army officer at the foot of Hampstead hill this evening was driven off by the officer's skill and courage. The robber had called on the man to stand and deliver as he was returning to his lodgings in Pond Street, but he was told that he would have to fight for the money. The two men exchanged pistol shots, and the robber fled, wounded in the arm.

Although romanticized by some as "gentlemen of the road", highwaymen are more usually seen as a curse. They attack not only out on lonely country roads but even in the parks within London. Unless adequately armed – like today's near-victim – or well horsed, people have no choice but to hand over their valuables.

Whigs repeal the nonconformist acts

Westminster, 1719
The Whig government has repealed the Occasional Conformity and Schism Acts, measures of Tory bigotry designed to repress religious dissent. James, Lord Stanhope, the secretary of state for the north, has long wanted to abolish these injustices, and by this year at last felt strong enough to do so.

The Test and Corporation Acts remain, but Stanhope has issued an indemnity waiving their provisions for a year. He also hoped to relieve some of the burdens on Roman Catholics, but even the most tolerant dissenters draw the line at that.

Commons say no to the Peerage Bill

Westminster, 1719
The Commons have voted down the Peerage Bill by which Lords Sunderland and Stanhope hoped to thwart their rival, Robert Walpole. It proposed the creation of 31 new peers, all to be supporters of Sunderland. The peerage was then to be almost closed, giving Sunderland a built-in majority in the Lords. Walpole is the prince of Wales's chief adviser, and Sunderland hoped that the bill would stop the prince creating peers loyal to himself when he becomes king. Sunderland's defeat indicates Walpole's strength in the House of Commons (→2/1720).

Military hero's prize palace takes shape

The splendid north front of Blenheim Palace as seen from across the lake.

Woodstock, Oxfordshire, 1719
The duke of Marlborough's gigantic house here is taking shape in a park stretching over a mile to a hilltop on which a statue of the duke is to be placed. When finished, Blenheim Palace will be one of the most splendid residences in England. Royalty, bishops and archbishops have palaces, and now so does John Churchill, the duke, alone among English noblemen.

Blenheim is on the site of a former royal palace, Woodstock. It was presented to the duke by Queen Anne for his greatest victory, after which the building is named. She promised to pay for it, but in the event the duke has had to pay for most of it himself. Fortunately, his services to the crown have made him an extremely wealthy man.

The palace has been designed by Sir John Vanbrugh, the playwright. Its façade is covered with trophies carved by Grinling Gibbons showing the duke's victories over Louis XIV. The duke and duchess have matching suites of private apartments in the east wing, and the west wing is given over to a gallery for the duke's superlative art collection. The centre of the house is devoted to a series of enormous state rooms (→1722).

The saloon at Blenheim Palace.

London weavers riot over Indian imports

The backbone of England's trade: wool-weavers, drawn by Hogarth.

London, 1719
Spitalfields weavers have been rioting in protest at the widespread use of printed cotton cloth which is imported from the East Indies. The act of 1700 prohibiting the wearing of printed calicoes has been largely ignored, and woollen-cloth weavers now fear that they will lose their markets. To prevent this they want a new, more stringent law.

Weaving is the greatest of England's industries and also provides its largest export. English cloth is sold everywhere in the world except Asia. The silk industry has also developed much in the past decade, helped by the smuggling of machinery from Italy, and now cotton manufacture is starting in Lancashire. Cotton is imported from India, where it is also woven into calicoes or fustian, a mixture of cotton and linen. British exports of cotton goods are now becoming important, and the American colonies are a particularly good market.

Manufacturing is now developing rapidly in the English midlands and north, far from the old traditional centres in areas such as Norfolk and Essex. Even London has lost some of the industry as manufacturers move to places where labour is cheaper and the guilds are less restrictive (→1726).

'Cato' makes rallying-cry for free speech

London, 1720
An anonymous pamphlet has appeared attacking the government and the various laws on seditious libel that sharply limit the freedom of the British press. The pamphlet is signed "Cato", after the Roman philosopher; there is much speculation as to its author's identity.

Cato says that instead of prosecuting libels, people should "laugh at them, despise them". He writes that "without freedom of thought, there can be no such thing as wisdom; and no such thing as public liberty without freedom of speech". He warns that royal absolutism is spreading over Europe and that it is developing here also. Cato denounces the standing army, wild speculation in stocks, and government corruption. He is particularly incensed against Robert Walpole, the paymaster of the forces, who uses the seditious libel laws to gag government critics (→24/11/22).

Dublin parliament on collision course with Westminster over who has the last say

Dublin, 7 April 1720
The Declaratory Act passed today by Westminster, asserting its right to legislate for Ireland and denying appeal to the Irish House of Lords, is sure to provoke indignation here. The problem is an old one: ever since the establishment of the kingdom of Ireland in 1541 the autonomy of the Dublin parliament has been vigorously defended by men such as Patrick Darcy (in 1641) and William Molyneux (in 1698).

The act has arisen out of a lawsuit over ownership of an estate in Co Kildare. One of the parties was granted possession by the Irish House of Lords. The other party then appealed to the British House of Lords, which reversed the original decision and ordered the Irish courts to give possession to *their* appellant. But the county sheriff refused to comply and was fined for contempt. The Irish Lords backed the sheriff and imprisoned the court officials, asserting Dublin's right of jurisdiction in Ireland. Britain rejected compromise and has answered with the new act (→24/6/21).

Birth of a Stuart heir raises Jacobite hopes

James Stuart, the pretender, places the wedding ring on his bride's finger.

Rome, 31 December 1720
The hopes of the Jacobites have been raised by the birth of a son to the exiled James Stuart. The child, who will be christened Charles Edward, was born to the Polish Princess Maria Clementina Sobieska today at their Palazzo Muti home, a wedding gift to Clementina from her godfather, Pope Clement XI. The birth is a welcome boost to the sad band of exiles gathered round the man who styles himself "King James VIII of Scotland and III of England". He holds court with his "queen", Clementina, but nothing can hide the fact that every attempt to return him to the throne has failed. At least the arrival of a son gives hope for the future (→8/1724).

Scotsman leads France to financial ruin

France, 27 May 1720
John Law, a 49-year-old Scot who has been head of French finances since January, has been sacked. The son of an Edinburgh goldsmith, Law was the protégé of the duke of Orleans, who backed his project to found a bank of France in 1716 and a West India company a year later. As France's comptroller-general, Law experimented with his pet project of paper money, but it has led to a ruinous speculation boom. Perhaps the duke was ill advised to hire a man addicted, as Law is, to the gambling table (→1729).

Walpole and Whigs return to royal favour

Robert Walpole: rising politician.

Westminster, 11 June 1720
The one-time party rebel Robert Walpole and his friends have been accepted back among fellow Whigs led by James, Lord Stanhope. Even better, from Walpole's viewpoint, is the fact that the quarrel between King George and the prince of Wales is over – enabling Walpole to clamber back into government as paymaster general, the job which he took up today.

Until recently Walpole led "the prince's party", an opposition group, and so the king would not allow him into the government. The truce means that Walpole now enjoys enough royal favour to hold office, although as he was previously chancellor of the exchequer he still has much ground to recover.

The change is due largely to Walpole's defeat of an attempt to set a permanent limit to the number of peers in the House of Lords [*see report on page 663*]. This would have limited the power of the Commons, but Walpole defeated the bill on the grounds that it also meant that, since no more peers were to be created, no member of the House of Commons could become a lord. This caused many ambitious members to vote against it (→9/1720).

Defoe's desert island hero is a literary hit

London, 1720
Encouraged by the success last year of his first novel, *The Life and Strange Surprising Adventures of Robinson Crusoe of York, Mariner*, the London-born businessman and journalist Daniel Defoe has this year brought out two new novels entitled *The Life and Adventures of Mr Duncan Campbell* and *Captain Singleton*. Last year he also completed *Further Adventures of Robinson Crusoe*. The first Crusoe book was considered by many to be a true story; it was indeed based on one – that of a Scots sailor, Alexander Selkirk, who was put ashore on the island of Juan Fernandez after a quarrel and left there for four years. Crusoe is marooned for 20 years, finding "Man Friday" after 15 of them. He eventually escapes on a ship. In the second volume he revisits mutineers whom he had left behind and voyages on to China, returning across Siberia (→1722).

Robinson Crusoe's island adventures are capturing the public imagination.

Misery for thousands as South Sea 'bubble' bursts

Investors face ruin as share prices fall to catastrophic low

London, September 1720
After an extraordinary run that saw its shares rise from a face value of £100 to a peak of £1,000 between Christmas and June, the South Sea company has collapsed, bringing ruin to thousands of investors both large and small and in almost all classes of society. It is a financial disaster without parallel, and even King George has lost £100,000.

The stock rose so fast that it was possible for a man to be poor on a Monday and rich by Friday. In a famous exchange, a lady asked an exquisitely tailored young man how long he had been a gentleman. "Only a week, madam," came the honest reply. The businessman and journalist Daniel Defoe reported that so many new coaches, coats and gold watches were being ordered that London tradesmen were quite worn out by their efforts to keep up. Unfortunately, the vast rise in the price of South Sea company shares was based on little truth and much fraud.

In theory the company had exclusive rights to trade with South America under a new treaty with Spain. In reality the Spanish have allowed only one trade ship a year but, by spreading rumours of vast opportunities to trade woollens for gold and gems, bribing the king and his court with free gifts of shares and offering to take over the national debt, the company was able to inflate the value of its shares.

The few people who sold out before the crash have done well. The duke of Marlborough has made £100,000 profit, and Sir Thomas Guy more than £180,000 – he is said to be founding a hospital with the money – but most people have lost huge sums, if not everything they own. In August it was believed that the share price would reach £1,500, and many bought in at the top of the market, or failed to realize profits in the expectation of more. But within weeks the stock crashed back to £126 a share, and now the hunt is on for scapegoats.

Panic ensues as the "bubble" bursts and investors try to sell off shares.

A sad sight greets a "Canting Miser" in a contemporary broadsheet: he stares into the "Bubbler's Mirrour" and sees reflected his own greed.

The greedy and the gullible both fall for crazy investments

London, September 1720
There is no secret as to why so many invested all they had in the South Sea "bubble". The lure of easy money can make mad even the sanest of people. As the madness took a grip, quite ordinary people sold everything they had, borrowed even more money and then invested every penny in the rising stock of the South Sea company.

London has been awash with country gentry come down to mortgage their estates and invest the money in the full expectation of returning home in a carriage and six. In the wake of the South Sea company dozens of other companies sprang up, offering shares that also soared in value. Some of them were genuine businesses, but others varied from the bizarre to the downright fraudulent.

There were schemes to breed silkworms in Chelsea Park; to construct a perpetual motion wheel; and one to make great profit "but no one to know what it is". The proposer of the latter simply disappeared with investors' money. At first the shares in all these schemes rose, but the crash has brought them all to an end, ruining thousands of people (→ 1/3/21).

One of the many ruined by the "bubble" now begs for his bread.

1721 - 1722

Greenwich, 9 February 1721. Edmund Halley is appointed astronomer royal (→ 1725).

Westminster, 10 February 1721. Charles, Viscount Townshend, Robert Walpole's brother-in-law, becomes secretary of state on the death of James, Lord Stanhope (→ 1721).

Westminster, 1 March 1721. The Commons pass ten resolutions condemning the South Sea company for gross breach of trust (→ 3/4).

Ireland, 24 June 1721. Charles Butler, the earl of Arran, is allowed to buy forfeit lands originally belonging to his brother James, the duke of Ormond (→ 28/8).

Ireland, 28 August 1721. Charles Fitzroy, the duke of Grafton, is sworn in as lord lieutenant (→ 9/12).

Dublin, 9 December 1721. The Commons rejects a proposal to establish a national bank of Ireland (→ 1722).

Dublin, 1721. A reservoir is built by the engineer Thomas Burgh to improve the city's water supply.

Scotland, 1721. Robert Walpole is forced to turn the running of Scotland over to the duke of Argyll, who delegates business to his younger brother Archibald, the earl of Islay.

Westminster, 1721. Robert Walpole, having opposed the 1719 Peerage Bill, refuses the peerage that King George offers him (→ 30/4).

London, 30 April 1722. Charles Spencer, Lord Sunderland, a great rival of Robert Walpole, dies of pleurisy during the election campaign (→ 5/1722).

Oxfordshire, spring 1722. Blenheim Palace, belonging to John Churchill, the duke of Marlborough, is finished after 13 years' work (→ 16/6).

London, 24 August. Bishop Atterbury of Rochester is arrested (→ 29/6/23).

London, 24 November 1722. The *British Journal* newspaper calls for government reform in Ireland (→ 27/3/25).

Edinburgh, 1722. The Signet library is founded.

London, 1722. Daniel Defoe publishes another novel, *Moll Flanders* (→ 1726).

London, 1722. Sir Thomas Guy, a wealthy bookseller, gives £300,000 for a hospital.

King mourns loss of a 'bubble' victim

London, 5 February 1721

King George has good reason to mourn the death of his secretary of state, James, Lord Stanhope, who has become an accidental victim of the South Sea "bubble". Stanhope was largely blameless for the financial disaster, but became so irate while rebutting charges against himself in the House of Lords that he suffered a stroke and died. He was a good servant of the Hanoverians, whose arrival in England might have gone worse but for his guidance. Now the king will have to rely on Roberrt Walpole, whom he cordially detests (→ 10/2/21).

George faces threat of 'bubble' scandal

London, 3 April 1721

Robert Walpole has been appointed first lord of the treasury and chancellor of the exchequer – in effect, "prime minister" – by a parliament desperate to sort out the crisis left by the South Sea "bubble" [*see reports on page 665*]. King George in particular will need Walpole's help. His ministers and friends received between them about £1.5 million of shares as "gifts" from the South Sea company. These were thinly disguised bribes, and the court is deeply implicated (→ 1721).

Post arrives faster in provincial towns

Bath, 1721

Ralph Allen, the energetic postmaster here, has devised a new system of posts that will greatly speed the delivery of letters throughout the country. Until now all post has first gone to London, where it has to be redirected and put aboard the appropriate coach for its destination. This is clearly a slow and expensive way of going about things, and Allen has devised a series of "cross-posts" that establish direct links between provincial towns. This system will be both faster and cheaper than the present system, and Allen is expecting to make £12,000 a year from his idea.

Bishop is chief suspect as a Jacobite plot to seize power in London is uncovered

A medal commemorates the plot.

Atterbury: pro-Catholic subversive.

London, 19 April 1722

A Jacobite plot incriminating Francis Atterbury, the bishop of Rochester, has been uncovered, much to Robert Walpole's delight. Walpole, Britain's "prime minister", has long been obsessed with the idea that Jacobites, who support James Stuart, the pretender, lurk round every corner, waiting for the right moment to murder King George and return the country to Roman Catholicism.

While it is true that plots have existed, few have been serious, and Walpole's obsession has sometimes gone beyond the bounds of reason. But on this occasion there appear to be genuine grounds for alarm. The chief suspect, Atterbury, is a high-churchman disliked for his rudeness and appointed to Rochester to keep him out of the way. He has connections among extreme Tories who would be all too ready to aid the return of James Stuart, the 34-year-old son of James II, already proclaimed "James III" by Pope Innocent XIII. The plot seems to have been to murder King George as he travelled to Hanover this summer and then to capture the Royal Exchange, the Bank of England, the Tower and St James's Palace in a grand coup.

Ironically, Walpole once tried to get this Tory cleric onto the side of the Whigs by offering him the see of Winchester, together with a good job at the treasury for his son-in-law. When Atterbury rejected the offer, Walpole suspected that it was because the bishop had ambitions of his own (→ 1/5).

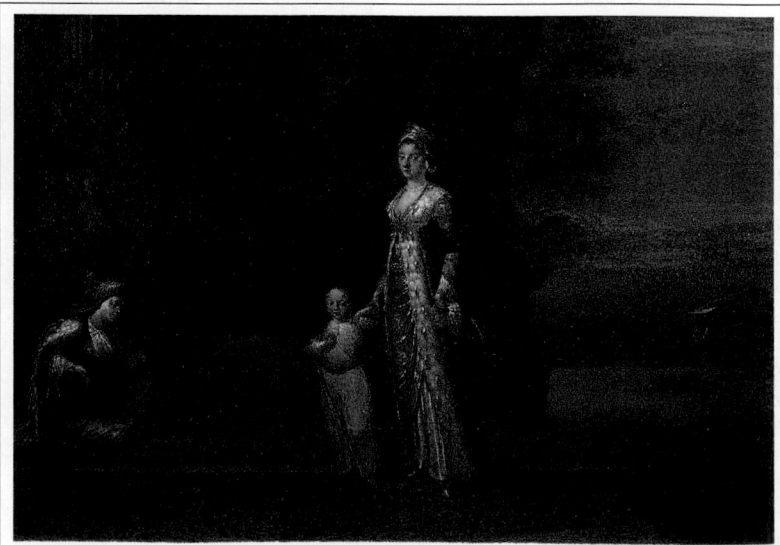
Lady Mary Wortley Montagu, seen here with her son and attendants, is the wife of the British ambassador to the Ottoman Empire; in 1721 she introduced to Britain a serum for inoculation against smallpox (→ 1/7/96).

Fears of rebellion bring troops to city

London, 1 May 1722
Thousands of troops have been brought into the capital in the wake of the discovery of a Jacobite plot involving Francis Atterbury, the high-church bishop of Rochester [*see report on page 666*]. Watched by hundreds of curious spectators, a large military camp has been set up in Hyde Park, and the soldiers look as if they are prepared for a long stay.

The arrival of so many troops has obviously raised tension in London, particularly since Robert Walpole has so far elected not to make the plot public knowledge until he has gathered more evidence. This has led to endless rumours about the purpose of the troops, but a few people have now got wind of some kind of plot against King George and his government.

Bishop Atterbury's secretary, George Kelly, has been sent to the Tower of London – a risky move, as the bishop is popular with sections of the London mob, some of whom followed Kelly's carriage to the Tower gates. Atterbury himself may also be arrested. At least – from Walpole's point of view – it takes people's minds off the South Sea "bubble" disaster (→ 24/8).

Country backs Walpole

Walpole in the House of Commons.

London, May 1722
This month's general election is a resounding victory for the Whig government, and it confirms the growing fortunes of Robert Walpole. He has been a member of parliament (for King's Lynn) for 20 years, apart from a short period when he was imprisoned in the Tower for corruption. Appointed prime minister just last year [*see report on page 666*], he has benefited from the death on 30 April of Charles Spencer, Lord Sunderland – his great political rival. The untimely death of Spencer, who led a rival faction to Walpole's within the Whigs, has removed any challenge to him within the party.

Walpole seems to do well out of other people's misfortunes: his promotion last year owed a lot to the South Sea "bubble" crisis [*see report on page 665*]. Out of government at the crucial time when the "bubble" began to rise, he is one of the few politicians seen as blameless for the disaster that followed.

Although King George and many of Walpole's fellow Whigs dislike and distrust him, this overweight, 46-year-old Norfolk squire has played his cards well. The king and many of his friends and ministers were deeply involved in the corruption surrounding the South Sea company, but Walpole has acted swiftly to protect them and as a result has made them politically indebted to him.

To stabilize the financial situation he has transferred what remains of South Sea company stock to the Bank of England, begun a parliamentary inquiry into the collapse, rejected demands that the company's directors be hanged and insisted that those who owe the company money pay their debts. All this has restored confidence and calmed the nation (→ 6/1723).

Marlborough, hero of the nation, dies

The duke's death: a French view.

Windsor, 16 June 1722
The death today at Cranbourne Lodge of the duke of Marlborough, aged nearly 72, marks the end of an era. The duke, born John Churchill, owed his formidable success to his military genius and gift for politics and diplomacy.

His desertion of James II in favour of William of Orange won him an earldom. His shrewd wife, Sarah, enjoyed a close friendship with William's successor, Queen Anne. The dukedom was granted in gratitude for the crushing defeat of the French at Blenheim in 1704. By means of this and other victories Marlborough has assured himself a lasting reputation as one of Britain's greatest commanders.

Welsh religion castigated for cowardly bishops and poor curates

Wales, 1722
A desperate state of church affairs in Wales is described in the recently published *View of the State of Religion in the Diocese of St David's* by Erasmus Saunders. Casting his eye much further than the diocese of his book's title, Saunders describes poor Welsh curates holding perfunctory church services, with most people's religious knowledge virtually non-existent. In addition to this spiritual sleep, Saunders says, Roman Catholic and even pagan practices can be found.

The situation is at its worst in the south, he says, where there are many rapacious peers, such as Pembroke, as well as "cowardly, time-serving" bishops such as Kitchen of Llandaff, who have almost given away their rich episcopal lands to appease powerful lords. Saunders, like many others, fears the resurgence of Roman Catholicism in Wales. Although Catholics are a small minority here, they exist in local pockets, in Monmouthshire and elsewhere, which make up for their size by an intense activism that fuels Protestant imaginations. The English authorities are especially anxious about Catholicism in Wales because of its long and vulnerable coastline – as well as its proximity to Ireland.

Part of a troubled church: Caebach chapel, Llandrindod Wells (1715).

Brass farthings for Irish coin system

Ireland, 1722
Anglo-Irish relations are again under strain over the affair known as "Wood's halfpence". A patent, originally granted to King George's mistress, the duchess of Kendal, was sold by her to an English ironmaster, William Wood. He has been authorized to coin halfpence and farthings for Ireland to the value of £100,800. This has caused outrage; the true value of the coinage is thought to be too low while the amount to be coined is, on the other hand, excessive (→ 10/1727).

1723 - 1725

London, 29 June 1723. Francis Atterbury, the former bishop of Rochester, is exiled for his part in last year's Jacobite plot.

London, 19 October 1723. Sir Godfrey Kneller, the royal portrait painter, dies; he is succeeded by Charles Jervas.

Rome, August 1724. James Stuart, the pretender, dismisses the earl of Mar, who has been betraying him to the English for years (→1726).

Ireland, 22 October 1724. John, Lord Carteret, is sworn in as lord lieutenant.

Dublin, October 1724. A fourth anonymous letter to appear this year attacking William Wood's copper coinage has been published; called the *Drapier Letters*, the four are rumoured to be by Jonathan Swift, the dean of St Patrick's Cathedral (→21/9/25).

Dublin, 1724. Turlough Carolan publishes *A Collection of the Most Celebrated Irish Tunes*, the first collection of Irish secular music.

London, 1724. Longman's publishing house is founded.

Dublin, 27 March 1725. The first edition of *Faulkner's Dublin Journal* appears (→21/8/29).

Glasgow, 9 July 1725. General Wade's army occupies the city; the new lord advocate, Duncan Forbes, is now to open a judicial investigation into last month's riots (→1726).

Westminster, 27 July 1725. Robert Walpole is knighted by King George (→9/1725).

Dublin, 21 September 1725. William Wood's coinage patent is withdrawn (→8/3/26).

Westminster, September 1725. King George pardons Henry St John, Viscount Bolingbroke, a leading Jacobite (→26/5/26).

Europe, September 1725. Britain, France and Prussia sign the Treaty of Hanover against Spain and Austria (→9/11/29).

London, 1725. The Scots architect Colen Campbell completes a collection of some 300 architectural illustrations, *Vitruvius Britannicus*, that began publication in 1712.

London, 1725. Sir Richard Grosvenor completes the building of estates in Mayfair, Belgravia and Pimlico.

Wales, 1725. John Rhydderch publishes his *English and Welsh Dictionary*.

Leading statesmen jockey for position

London, June 1723

King George has been drawn into an unseemly squabble about the great office of state left vacant by the duke of Marlborough's death [*see report on page 667*]. William, Earl Cadogan, a friend of Lord Carteret – one of the chief rivals of the prime minister, Robert Walpole – has assumed Marlborough's mantle, including the title "captain-general". Heedless of the cost, he has ordered the mustering of troops for six months instead of the three which had been agreed between Walpole and King George.

Cadogan's actions annoyed the Guards regiments, whose complaints were eagerly taken up by Walpole, who then persuaded the lords justices to refuse permission for Cadogan's move. Charles, Viscount Townshend – the prime minister's brother-in-law – has been obliged to mediate. The king, meanwhile, is backing Walpole to the hilt. Dismissing protestations from Carteret in support of Cadogan, the king insists that Walpole has acted solely on his orders, while Cadogan has jumped the gun. This trivial spat shows how desperately tense the struggle for power in the court is becoming (→4/1724).

In 1723, in an attempt to stamp out poaching, the death penalty was introduced for the offence.

Walpole strengthens grip on government

Robert Walpole reigns supreme over the cabinet, king and government.

Westminster, April 1724

After two years' dogged rivalry with the remnants of the late earl of Sunderland's faction at court, Robert Walpole is now unquestionably in charge. All the major offices of state are controlled by his men. The preferment of his friend the duke of Newcastle over William Pulteney as secretary of state, and the elevation of Henry Pelham, the duke's brother, to secretary-at-war leave the Commons docile. Equally vital has been the success of Walpole's ally Charles, Viscount Townshend, in outmanoeuvring John, Lord Carteret, over foreign policy.

Townshend maintains that his cautious policy towards Russia has been responsible for avoiding war in the Baltic. Prussia is also now an important ally courted by Townshend. The king's appointment of Walpole's brother, Horatio, as ambassador to Paris proves that he too has been won over (→27/7/25).

Ancient Welsh links with Druids claimed

Anglesey, Gwynedd, 1723

Bards and Druids – pre-Christian Celtic priests – were active here long before they were seen worshipping in Gaul [France] by Julius Caesar, according to Henry Rowlands in his *Mona Antiqua Restaurata [Ancient Remains on Anglesey]*, published this year.

Druidical remains can also be found in Brittany, he says, in the form of "mounts, pillars, heaps, altars and other appurtenances of their sun and moon worship". But Stonehenge and other stone circles in Britain and Europe are thought to predate Celtic culture.

A romanticized view of a Druid.

Crop-farmers kill cattle in land riots

Dumfries and Galloway, June 1724
Several hundred arable farmers are roaming the Galloway countryside, maiming or killing cattle and destroying enclosures. Bound by a covenant and calling themselves "Levellers", these are men whose livelihoods are under great threat from the expanding cattle trade with England. Bigger farmers and the gentry – the leaders of the trade – are coming down hard on these crop-growers, who are way behind with rents after a run of poor harvests. Now such men, many of whose farms have been enclosed to make room for cattle-raising, are fighting back.

This month the Levellers have killed 53 cattle which belonged to the laird of Baldoon. Six troops of dragoons have now arrived in the area wih instructions to restore order. Local magistrates are hoping, however, that the soldiers will exercise minimum force.

Glasgow hit by tax riots

Glasgow, 25 June 1725
Eight people have been killed and 18 wounded, some seriously, after troops opened fire on crowds protesting at the imposition of new taxes on malt, ale and beer. But the violence has not deterred the angry crowds, and the soldiers have retreated to Dumbarton. The rioters began yesterday by looting and burning the house of the local Whig member of parliament, Donald Campbell of Shawfield. Now they control all Glasgow.

The trouble stems from the malt tax, which has stood at 3d [1.5p] a barrel since 1713. It was inefficiently collected and raised little money. The government's decision to increase it by 6d a barrel, and apply it to ale and beer as well, produced a rash of petitions. The offer by the prime minister, Robert Walpole, to reduce the malt tax to a level half of that paid in England has done nothing to stifle Scottish fury. In Edinburgh the brewers are on strike, backed by judges and politicians of the *Squadrone* faction.

Troops open fire on the rioters.

General Wade must act quickly to quell this of civil unrest. Since he was appointed commander in Scotland this year, he has set about garrisoning the principal towns (→9/7).

Bookseller charged with obscene libel

London, November 1725
Edmund Curll, a London bookseller and pamphleteer, has been charged with obscene libel after the publication of an erotic book entitled *Venus in the Cloister, or the Nun in her Smock*. When he heard of the ire which had been aroused by his book, Curll printed a "humble representation" begging forgiveness. But he was arrested in March, and the question now is whether he will be tried under common or ecclesiastical law.

The book is a translation of a 17th-century pornographic work, and Curll claims that it is merely a reprint of a 50-year-old edition. No stranger to controversy, he upset Alexander Pope by publishing his poetry without permission in 1716, and two years later Daniel Defoe called for his "abominable catalogue" to be suppressed. Rumour has it that he is also a government spy for Sir Robert Walpole.

Lifetime's work of astronomer published

There is a growing interest in astronomy, thanks to Flamsteed and others.

England, 1725
The star catalogue of the former astronomer royal, John Flamsteed, has been published, six years after his death. A landmark in astronomy, it is based on extensive use for the first time of the telescope. Appointed by King Charles II, Flamsteed spent £2,000 of his own money to build the necessary instruments at Greenwich, near London. His painstaking work, in which he made 20,000 outstandingly accurate observations over 12 years, was undermined by the jealous Sir Isaac Newton. When Flamsteed was reluctant to publish his findings prematurely, Newton insisted on publishing them himself. Flamsteed had a long struggle to reclaim his work, which has now been published by friends.

Thief and thief-taker meets his maker

London, 25 April 1725
Jonathan Wild, "the great thief-taker" who doubled as "the great thief", met his desserts today when, watched by a crowd of underworld characters who revelled in his demise, he was hanged at Tyburn. Ironically, the man who had sent some 57 villains, including the great Jack Sheppard, to the gallows for a variety of serious crimes stumbled over a relatively minor affair – the "fencing" [*see below*] of some £40 worth of lace.

Yet this last crime, for which he was arrested when he attempted to sell the lace back to its owner, having bought it from the thief, typified the means of his success. A former valet and a veteran of debtors' prisons, Wild set himself up as a specialist in receiving stolen goods – fencing – then selling them back to their owners. He split the profits 50/50 with the thief. The opportunities for blackmail that his "purchases" gave him made Wild a master of the underworld.

Yet to the public Wild was just "the thief-catcher general". Claiming a bounty of £40 for each conviction, he lived in style, mocking the law even as he pretended to uphold it. Yet the law got him in the end: in 1718 a new act outlawed the receiving of stolen goods. Using middlemen Wild sidestepped it for a time, but today, after 15 years at the top, the great thief-taker finally went to the gallows.

Wild goes through his accounts.

1726

Dublin, 8 March. Parliament passes an act preventing Catholic priests or degraded clergy from taking the marriage services of Protestants (→6/1726).

Ireland, 9 April. Eoghan O'Caoimh, the Irish poet and scribe, dies.

Westminster, 26 May. Sir Robert Walpole is made a Knight of the Garter by King George; he is the first commoner for generations to receive the honour (→12/1727).

England, May. The leader of a male brothel, run by Frenchmen and called an *école et bordel de sodomie*, is burnt alive; other male prostitutes are given three- to six-month prison sentences (→1726).

Co Tyrone, June. The Presbyterian Church, meeting in general synod at Dungannon, splits (→4/1727).

Ireland, August. Bad weather destroys the harvest.

London. François Marie Arouet, the celebrated French writer and philosopher better known as "Voltaire", arrives in exile (→5/1727).

Dublin. Caleb Threlkeld writes *Synopsis Stirpium Hibernicarum*, the first catalogue of Irish flora.

Edinburgh. Allan Ramsay establishes the first circulating library.

Scotland. General George Wade starts a programme for building over 250 miles of military roads in the highlands.

London. Renovations to the church of St Martin-in-the-Fields are completed by the Scots architect James Gibbs.

London. Margaret Clap is prosecuted for keeping a "molly house" – a house of male prostitutes.

London. Daniel Defoe publishes his latest novel, *The Four Voyages of Captain George Roberts* (→8/1726).

London. John Harrison, a clockmaker, invents a gridiron pendulum for clocks.

London. King George takes a new mistress, Ann Brett.

Newbury, Berkshire. A great flood destroys the new arch of the wooden bridge over the river.

South-western England. The woollen industry is hit by widespread stoppages and riots over continuing wage disputes.

Handel is granted British citizenship

London, 13 February
George Frederick Handel, widely regarded as the greatest living composer in Europe, is now British. King George signed a bill making him a British subject today. Handel, like the king, speaks poor English, but his rousing music has won the hearts of the British people.

Handel, who has been in England for 16 years, decided to be naturalized only after his great rival, the Italian musician Marc Antonio Bononcini, a son of the late composer Giovanni Bononcini, began spreading scurrilous remarks about him. Handel thought it politic to declare his allegiance to the king (→spring 1734).

Woman burnt alive

London, 9 May
In an execution that some people are calling judicial murder, a woman who was sentenced to die for the savage murder of her husband has been literally burnt to death at Tyburn. Catherine Hayes, who conspired with her lovers Thomas Wood and Thomas Billings to murder and then butcher her husband John, was condemned to die at the stake. It was agreed that to spare her undue pain she should be garrotted first, but the flames were lit too soon, and they prevented the executioner from strangling her. She died in extreme agony.

Royal architect and playwright is dead

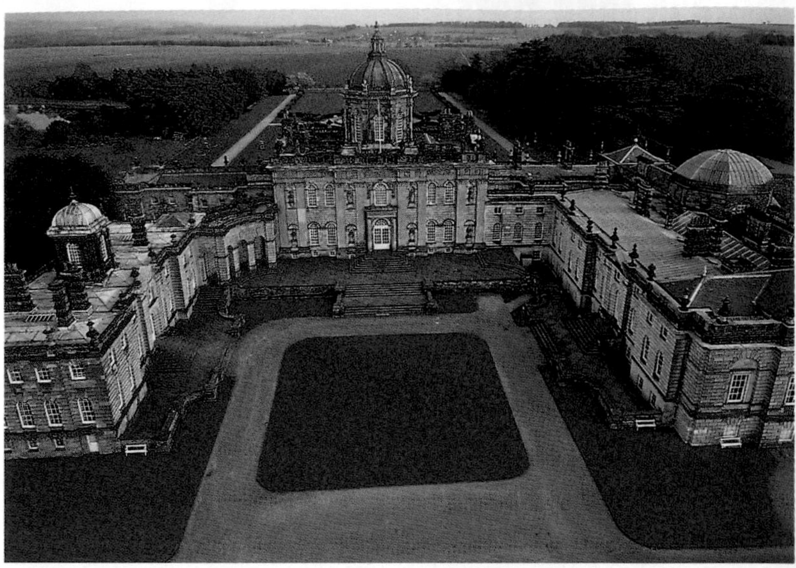

Castle Howard in Yorkshire: part of Vanbrugh's magnificent legacy.

Greenwich, London, 26 March
The death occurred today of Sir John Vanbrugh, soldier, architect and dramatist. While imprisoned in the Bastille as a spy, Vanbrugh wrote a précis draft of *The Provok'd Wife*, creating one of his great comedy characters, Sir John Brute, rivalled only by Lord Foppington of *The Relapse*. As an architect he designed Castle Howard, Seaton Delaval and Blenheim Palace. He was dismissed as controller of the board of works after quarrels with the duchess of Marlborough over payment for Blenheim. He built Castle Vanbrugh at Greenwich for himself and wanted this to be his epitaph:

Lie heavy on him, earth, for he
Laid many a heavy load on thee.

Sir John: master of all trades.

King's surgeon in scandal: woman claims she gave birth to rabbits

Mary Tofts's claim to have given birth to rabbits fooled a lot of people.

London, 7 December
After a ten-day examination Sir Thomas Clarges, a justice of the peace, has exposed a woman from Guildford who claimed to have given birth to a litter of rabbits. In the process he has made a laughing stock of M St André, the surgeon and anatomist to King George, who had believed that she really *was* pregnant with rabbits.

Mary Tofts had already duped her local surgeon. But Sir Thomas got an admission from a porter, Thomas Howard, that she had employed him to procure a rabbit. Her sister Lucy has also admitted to being an accomplice in the fraud.

Irish Quakers open a boarding school

Co Kildare, 1 March
A Quaker boarding school has been opened in Ballitore by Abraham Shackleton, a leading member of the local community of Quakers. The founding of such a school emphasizes their wish to retain their separate ethos.

Quakers first came to Ireland with the Cromwellian soldiers and settlers around 1650. Their numbers have grown to some 3,000, with more than 50 communities scattered throughout the country. Most live in either Dublin or Co Laoise, while a few have settled in Ulster. Quakers are typically merchants, specializing in textiles and milling, but some are landowners and farmers. They are highly respected by the Irish for their honesty and their moral principles in all their business dealings.

Their path has not, however, been entirely smooth, and they have come into conflict with the authorities over their refusal to serve in the army, take oaths or pay tithes to support the clergy. The military issue was solved by an act in 1716 that exempted them from service provided they pledged their loyalty to the king and denied the claims of the pope. Tithes continue to be a grievance, as with other nonconformists, and the Quakers are still liable to have their property confiscated or be imprisoned for non-payment of rates.

Joshua Morris's Soho (London) workshop held a sale on 1 December of tapestries such as this.

Rob Roy is imprisoned

Rob Roy: hero or criminal?

London
Rob Roy MacGregor, one of the most wanted men in Scotland, has this year been sent to Newgate prison, where he is awaiting deportation. Rob, or Red, Roy is the younger son of Donald MacGregor of Glengyle, who was a lieutenant-colonel in the army. Although he received a conventional education, Rob soon became a bandit, like many of his kinsmen, and he had his own gang of freebooters by the time that he was 20 years old.

He supported James VII and II in the "glorious revolution" in 1688 but later sought the protection of the duke of Argyll. From around 1700 to 1711 he was a respected cattle dealer – but then came a year of severe economic depression and, bankrupted, he ran off to the Western Isles with £1,000 belonging to his customers, including the duke of Montrose. From that time on he became the sworn enemy of the duke and lived a bandit's life, extracting protection money from cattle-owners.

In 1714 Rob declared for James Stuart, the pretender, but he was absent from the Battle of Sheriffmuir a year later. He was active later in the campaign for the Jacobites, fighting Hanoverian forces as far south and east as Falkland and Fife. In 1717 Montrose succeeded in capturing him, but Rob escaped and turned up two years later in the Jacobite ranks at the Battle of Glenshiel. It was then that his luck ran out: captured once again, he was brought south to London and his present confinement (→1/1727).

King's former wife dies alone in castle

Celle, Germany, 2 November
King George's former wife died here today after 30 years of isolation in the castle of Ahlden. Sophia Dorothea was divorced in 1694, long before George became king of Britain and Ireland. In 1689 she had fallen in love with a handsome count, Philip Christopher von Königsmarck. The infatuation became an open scandal, and the count was murdered while on his way to meet Sophia by officers allegedly acting on George's orders (→3/6/27).

Sophia: isolated for 30 years.

Jonathan Swift writes 'Gulliver's Travels'

London, November
The runaway success of the book called *Gulliver's Travels* is almost unparalleled. Since it was published on 28 October, 10,000 copies have been sold. Translations are being rushed out in French and Dutch. Although the identity of the author behind "Capt Lemuel Gulliver" is not given, it is known by many to be Jonathan Swift, the dean of St Patrick's Cathedral in Dublin.

His friend Alexander Pope has written to him: "From the highest to the lowest it is universally read, from the cabinet council to the nursery ... the whole town, men, women and children are full of it." Swift is delighted by the reaction of an Irish bishop who said: "For my part I hardly believe a word of it." As a satire on mankind and the politics of today, it has no rival for severity and sarcasm (→29/10/29).

Giant: Gulliver towers over Lilliput.

Country parson has animal laboratory

Middlesex, December
A parson called Stephen Hales has found a way of measuring the blood pressure of animals. "I caused a mare to be tied down alive on her back," he said. Then he inserted a brass pipe in an artery and fitted a glass tube onto it. The blood rose to a height of 2.51 metres (8 feet 3 inches) in the tube. Hales discovered that the blood rose and fell in line with the horse's pulse rate.

His parsonage at Teddington, west of London, is a virtual animal laboratory. He experiments on cows, dogs, oxen, deer and even frogs. Hales has shown that the bigger an animal is, the higher is its blood pressure. The pulse rate, however, varies in inverse proportion to size: the smaller the animal, the faster its pulse (→1727).

'Crusoe' author completes grand tour of Britain

Tunbridge Wells: for "those ... who have nothing to do anywhere else".

Southern England: castles and commuters

London, August
The third and final volume of Daniel Defoe's *Tour Through the Whole Island of Great Britain* is now out. The first volume appeared two years ago. Defoe, whose fictional *Robinson Crusoe* was set on an exotic island, has described his native land in this work.

The first volume was based on a journey through East Anglia, begun on 3 April 1722. Ipswich saddened him: "The great ships go to sea no more, but lie by, the ships are unrigged, the sails carried ashore, the top masts struck." But Norfolk impressed him: "The very children after four or five years of age could every one earn their own bread." He crossed the fens, "the sink of 13 counties", passed Ely, "wrapped up in blankets" of mist, and returned to London via Cambridge.

Defoe's second circuit was based on earlier journeys through southern England. He crossed the Medway to Rochester, where the naval dockyard was "like a well-ordered city". Canterbury seemed full of Huguenots, Dover Castle was "old [and] useless" and Winchester "the skeleton of an ancient city". Visiting Tunbridge Wells, Brighton and Southampton ("dying with age"), he returned to London, noting how at Epsom businessmen travel by horse to the city each day, returning to their families in the evening.

On familiar ground in the south-west

Plymouth, August
Defoe's first volume ends and his second begins with a tour of England's west country. It is familiar territory to him: 41 years ago he fought in the west country with Monmouth's rebels – a "cause I never doubted".

Passing west through "venerable" Winchester, Defoe came to Old Sarum, a ghost town that none the less returns two members to parliament: "Who those members can justly say they represent, would be hard for them to answer." He noted with disgust how three rivers, polluted by dyers and clothiers, run through the streets of Salisbury, leaving them "always dirty, full of wet and filth, and weeds". By way of recompense, Salisbury Plain "excelled the plains of Mecca".

After Stonehenge, whose construction Defoe reckoned a "mystery", he went on to Penzance and Land's End, where he took off his boots and dangled his toes in the sea. Cornwall was "fruitful and pleasant", but the walls of Launceston depressed him, "seen now only in their old clothes, and ... all in ruins". Then, passing through the "deep and frightful chasm" of Cheddar Gorge, he returned via Windsor Castle to London.

Welsh are 'civil, hospitable and kind ... especially to strangers'

Bristol docks, showing the increased prosperity brought by the slave trade.

Ludlow Castle was built against the Welsh, but Defoe found them friendly.

Coventry, August
Defoe's first stop on his tour of the west midlands and Wales was Oxford, "the greatest university of the island, and perhaps the most flourishing at this time in the world". He journeyed on through Cirencester, "full of clothiers and driving a great trade in wool", to the fashionable spa of Bath, now "the resort of the sound rather than the sick", and then Bristol – wealthy, but, to Defoe's mind, overcrowded.

From Bristol he wandered up the river Severn, visiting Gloucester, Worcester ("not a very well-built city") and Ludlow, and eventually coming to Wales. He found the Welsh "civil, hospitable and kind ... especially to strangers. They believe their country to be the pleasantest and most agreeable in the world, so that you cannot oblige them more than to make them think you believe so too."

Leaving Wales, Defoe rode east, passing through Lichfield, "a place of good conversation and good company", to Coventry, where "the timber-built houses [projected] forwards and towards one another, till in the narrow streets they were ready to touch one other at the top". He journeyed on to Lincoln, "an ancient, ragged, decayed and still decaying city", and so back again to London.

Defoe seeks to stir Scots from 'lethargic dream'

Finding new ground in the north and across the border

Although prized by some, Scarborough's spa waters tasted to Defoe "of vitriol, alum, iron, and perhaps sulphur".

Gentry stroll at their leisure in the fields outside Carlisle, which Defoe found to be "a small but well-furnished city".

Defoe admired Edinburgh Castle.

Glasgow was "the cleanest, beautifullest and best built city in Britain".

Edinburgh, August
Defoe's account of his trips to Scotland is organized into two fictional journeys, one along the east coast to Edinburgh, the other along the west coast into the highlands. Defoe knows Scotland well. He was sent there in 1706 by the Tory minister Lord Harley as a secret agent to promote the union. His views are colonialist, and he sees England's role as reawakening Scotland "from thy long lethargic dream".

For his east coast trip he came to Scotland via Scarborough and Newcastle, which was black with coal dust and "not the pleasantest place in the world to live in". Its river, the Tyne, was crowded with colliers. Across the border he travelled for mile upon mile over bleak moorland, but everywhere he passed he was made welcome. The Scottish gentry, he decided, are the most civilized in Europe.

Keeping to the coast road he came to Haddington, "an old half ruined, yet remaining town, which shows the marks of decayed beauty", where the local weavers, undercut by English competition, quietly starved. He rode on to Leith, and inspected a bottle-making factory, then crossed the "spacious, rich and pleasant plain" to Edinburgh.

He liked Edinburgh, and called its main street, Canongate, "perhaps the largest, longest and finest street for buildings and numbers of inhabitants, not only in Britain but in the whole world". It was overcrowded and stank, but he defended it: "I believe that in no city in the world so many people live in so little room."

His second tour – to the highlands – began by calling at Liverpool and Manchester. Liverpool he had visited three times, and it had doubled in size between each visit. "What it may grow to in time, I do not know." Manchester, with its 50,000 inhabitants and not one member of parliament to represent them, he dubbed "the greatest mere village in England". Passing then through Carlisle he entered Scotland at Gretna Green. The union, he reckoned, had brought prosperity to some and poverty to others; in Dumfries "the benefits of commerce obtained by Scotland with the union appear visible", but further on Kirkcudbright revealed "a harbour without ships, a port without trade, a fishery without nets, a people without business". Glasgow he called "a very fine city"; its "four principal streets are the fairest for breadth and the finest built that I have seen in one city together". Glasgow's main business is with the New World, importing cotton, sugar and tobacco, and exporting servants, "and these they have in greater plenty and upon better terms than the English, the poor people offering themselves fast enough, and thinking it their advantage to go".

North lay the highlands, "the true and real Caledonia". Defoe hated the area – "a frightful country", where there was no law but tribal law, men walked armed and lived in poverty, and children walked barefoot – just the sort of place where England should be imposing "benevolent" colonialism.

1727

London, January. Rob Roy MacGregor, the Jacobite bandit, is granted a pardon by King George (→ 1/1728).

London, 11 February. The *Daily Courant* reports that a feast at St James's Palace for the City, hosted by King George, broke up amongst scenes of wild and drunken debauchery.

Westminster, 28 March. Sir Isaac Newton is buried in Westminster Abbey.

Limerick City, April. A Roman Catholic priest is executed for infringing a law passed last year preventing Catholic priests from marrying Protestant couples (→ 6/5/28).

London, May. Voltaire, the exiled French philosopher and writer, dedicates his epic poem on Henry IV, *La Henriade*, to King George.

Greenwich, London, 3 June. George sets out for Hanover after ensuring that the prince of Wales has no more power in his father's absence than at any other time (→ 11).

Osnabrück, Germany, 11 June. King George suffers a cerebral haemorrhage brought on by a serious stomach disorder; he dies at the castle, aged 67.→

Westminster, 27 June. King George II opens the first parliament of his reign (→ 7/1727).

Paris, July. Horatio Walpole, the brother of the British prime minister, Sir Robert Walpole, and ambassador here, receives the reassurance of Cardinal Fleury, the chief minister of Louis XV, that the French will give their full support to King George II rather than to James Stuart, the pretender (→ 11/10).

Bath, 14 August. William Croft, one of the first British composers to use the baroque style, dies aged 49.

Gravesend, Kent, 24 August. A great part of the town is destroyed by fire.

Dublin, 28 November. King George II opens his first Irish parliament (→ 1728).

Cornwall. Riots break out owing to the shortage of food and high prices.

Twickenham, Middlesex. Stephen Hales, a clergyman, publishes *Vegetable Staticks*; it is concerned with the motion of fluid in plants.

Britain. The first horse-racing calendar is printed.

King George is dead

George's reign was solid rather than heavenly, despite the efforts of artists.

Osnabrück, Germany, 11 June
King George, who had been visiting Hanover, yesterday suffered a violent attack of diarrhoea which left his face distorted and his right arm hanging limply. He collapsed, and died at 1.30 this morning.

He was the elector of Hanover when he ascended the British throne in 1714, at the age of 54, his claim coming through his grandmother, Elizabeth of Bohemia, the daughter of James VI of Scots and I of England. George was a dull and uninspiring monarch, but in Stanhope and Walpole he was fortunate in his choice of ministers.

He was not so lucky in family matters; he divorced his wife in 1694 over her adultery and never remarried. His chief mistress was Melusine, later the duchess of Kendal. His relationship with his son was one of mutual detestation (→ 27).

Eminent scientist Sir Isaac Newton dies

London, 20 March
England's greatest scientist, Sir Isaac Newton, has died. His greatest work, *Principia Mathematica*, has revolutionized the way philosophers think about the movement of the planets and of ordinary objects. Newton's idea that everything in the universe attracts everything else by a force called gravity has captured scholarly imagination.

Born near Grantham in 1642, Newton was an aloof man who rarely smiled. Beside his scientific inquiries, he was also interested in alchemy and unorthodox theology. He is to be buried in Westminster Abbey (→ 28).

Unloved monarch leaves legacy of peace and wealth

London, June
Rarely can a reign have begun so unpromisingly as when George arrived in Britain 13 years ago from his native Hanover. An uncharismatic figure, he spoke virtually no English and made his preference for Hanover clear. The only positive thing most of his subjects had to say about him was that at least he was not a Roman Catholic.

He came to rule a country that had alienated its European allies – including Hanover – with unilateral deals over the Treaty of Utrecht, faced possible civil war fuelled by support for his Jacobite rival to the throne, James Stuart, and had a £54 million national debt. George dies respected, if not loved: the Jacobites have been rendered impotent (although still a useful bogey at election time); trade is booming; and Britain has led Europe in creating an edifice of interlocking treaties that have prevented large-scale war.

His legacy is one of peace and prosperity. Not only has the spectre of civil war faded but the struggle between Anglican and dissenter has also been softened by greater toleration. The Tories have been excluded from government ever since the bloodless Whig coup at the beginning of the reign, but they have been mollified by being left to rule in the countryside.

The mood of the country is personified by George's prime minister, Sir Robert Walpole, a genial dispenser of patronage who does not believe in fixing things if they do not need mending. His economic genius has also created a boom.

George's most lasting and bitter conflict was with his son, George Augustus, the prince of Wales, but even that brought unexpected benefits. When dissenting Whig politicians gathered round the prince in 1717 they were obviously still loyal to the dynasty while attacking the government of the day.

Second Hanoverian accedes to throne

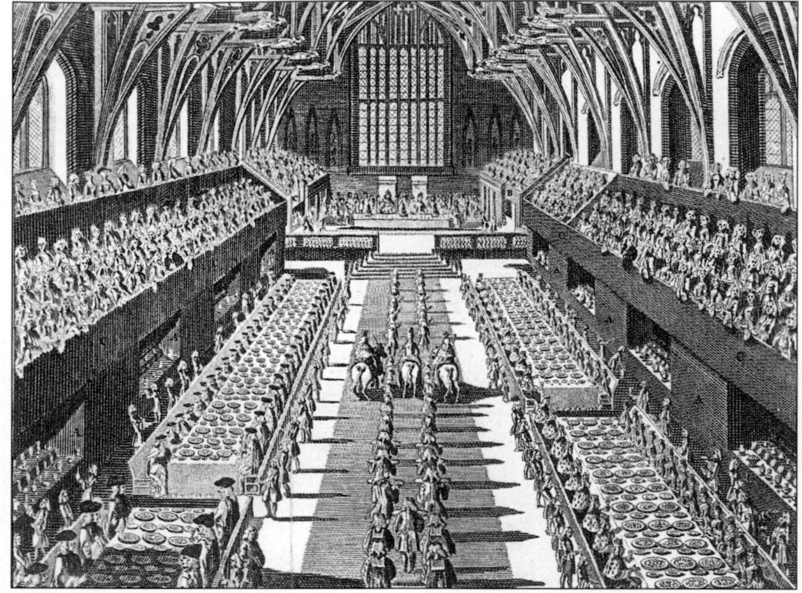
The nobility gathers in Westminster Hall for the coronation banquet.

London, 11 October
In a lavish velvet robe – floor length, but showing off his feet, of which he is inordinately proud, and with white fur shoulders – George Augustus was crowned George II today at Westminster.

He is 43 years old, a small man of delicate build and prominent blue eyes who has been described by his critics, of whom his father was the fiercest, as a humourless, choleric, conceited bore and womanizer. Although he has kept a mistress, Mrs Henrietta Howard, for the last ten years, George's greatest asset is his wife, the intelligent Caroline of Brandenburg-Ansbach. In spite of his mistress, the king clearly dotes on Caroline, by whom he has had nine children – four boys and five girls.

Coronation planned down to last detail

Westminster, 11 October
Instructions for today's coronation were explicit. A baroness's mantle could trail a yard on the ground, but that of a viscountess had to be "a yard and a quarter" [*see conversion table*]. Even the ladies' underwear conformed: petticoats were to be "cloth of silver, or any other white stuff, either laced or embroidered". Jewellers were ordered to keep the pearls on barons' coronets flat, not raised on spikes – or answer "to their perils". Peers had to be in the House of Lords at 8am sharp for the royal couple's arrival at 9am, while at noon precisely everyone was to move to the abbey for the crowning, and then back to Westminster Hall for the banquet (→28/11).

Irish Huguenots go from rags to riches

Co Antrim, July 1727
Samuel-Louis Crommelin, the Huguenot refugee who founded linen manufacturing in Lisburn, has died. His commercial success was typical of his community.

The Huguenots came to Ireland at the beginning of this century and have been successful ever since in various trades. They established the silk and poplin industries in Dublin, whilst in Waterford and Cork they introduced glove-and lace-making and silk-weaving. They are especially interested in horticulture, and the Dublin Huguenots have formed a "florists' club". They import French seeds and bulbs, and some even drink toasts to individual flowers.

New queen backs Walpole's government

London, December
Sir Robert Walpole is firmly back in royal favour after a short-lived attempt by George II to replace him. When Walpole broke the news of his father's death, the new king replied: "Go to Chiswick and take your directions from Sir Spencer Compton." George has only now forgiven Walpole for reconciling him – as the prince of Wales – to his father in 1720 and then transferring his loyalty to the king. Sir Spencer, the speaker of the House of Commons and the prince's treasurer, was not up to leading a government and even asked Walpole's help in drawing up a Commons address. Walpole's trump is his friendship with the new queen, Caroline, who is by far the more impressive half of the royal couple (→16/5/30).

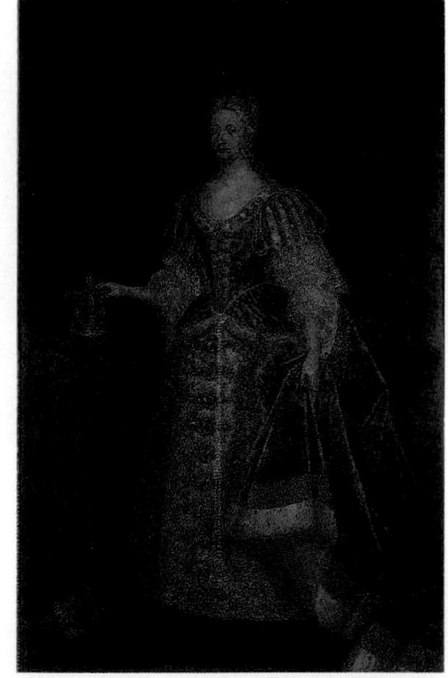
Queen Caroline, Walpole's ally.

The Royal Bank of Scotland is open

Edinburgh
The foundation of the Royal Bank of Scotland this year is the government's latest attempt to breathe new life into the Scottish economy. Many Scots were sold the union of 1707 on promises of wealth from free trade with England, but few of those promises have come true. While the cattle trade is indeed booming, formerly protected industries such as coal, salt and woollens have all suffered badly from English competition. The Royal Bank, which ends the Bank of Scotland's monopoly, will help administer part of the financial settlement of 1707. It will also finance the newly established board of trustees for fisheries and manufactures.

A mock royal elegy

London
A mock elegy for George I, called *Robin's Pathetick Tale*, has been published, in which Robin – alias Sir Robert Walpole – mourns his royal patron, now a "lifeless lump". George's timing was poor:

What greater curse could envious fortune give
Than just to die, when I began to live!

Races, such as this one at Newmarket, are becoming popular; this year the first racing calendar appeared.

1728

Dublin, 11 January. A parliamentary select committee is appointed to consider the erection of a new parliament house.

Rome, January. James Stuart, the pretender, returns here after an unsuccessful visit to France seeking aid for an invasion of Britain (→ 18/1/35).

Dublin, 14 March. John Gay's *The Beggar's Opera* is performed at the Smock Alley theatre (→ 4/12/32).

Dublin, May. The Corn and Husbandry Act requires all occupiers of 100 acres of land or more to put 5 per cent under the plough.

Dublin, May. The Dublin Poor Relief Act is passed to provide money for the care of foundlings [orphans and abandoned children].

Edinburgh, 15 October. John Glas, a minister from Tealing, is deposed by the Church of Scotland for criticizing it; he is expected to set up an independent church with his old congregation (→ 1729).

Dublin, 14 November. The Linen Hall opens on a site near North King Street.

St James's Palace, December. Frederick, the prince of Wales, the eldest son of King George II and Queen Caroline and heir to Hanover and Britain, arrives in London from Hanover (→ 26/4/36).

Dublin. Charles Brooking publishes a *Map of Dublin*.

Ireland. Matthew Dubourg is appointed master of state music.

Ireland. The poet and scribe Aodhagan O'Rathaille dies.

London. George II pays £1,200 to Charles Howard, the husband of his mistress, Henrietta; he is to be paid until he inherits his brother's earldom of Suffolk, if he leaves his wife in peace (→ 26/4/36).

Wales. The nonjuror [refused the loyalty oath in 1688] and one-time Cambridge don William Law publishes *A Serious Call to a Devout and Holy Life*, following his 1726 *Treatise on Christian Perfection*; the new book instructs ordinary believers on Christ-like living.

Wales. John Rhydderch publishes *Gramadeg Cymraeg*, a book on Welsh grammar which also contains a summary of bardic rules on rhyme and metre.

Beggars take starring role in new opera

A scene from the controversial "Beggar's Opera", painted by Hogarth.

London, 30 January

John Gay showed his musical play about the highwaymen and whores of Newgate prison, *The Beggar's Opera*, to Jonathan Swift, who first suggested it, and to Alexander Pope and William Congreve before it opened last night at the Lincoln's Inn Fields theatre. None of them thought that it would succeed. They were wrong. It ended with clamorous applause, and the songs – *Youth's the season made for joys* and *How happy could I be with either, were t'other dear charmer away* – were relished. It has taken the town by storm and looks set to put Italian opera out of fashion.

In the scramble for tickets people are saying that it will make Gay rich and Rich (the theatre owner) gay. Gay, a Tory, has written what is in fact a political satire on the court and the government – in particular the Whig prime minister, Sir Robert Walpole, represented by the rogue Peachum. Walpole is coming to see the play (→ 14/3).

Pope publishes latest poem, 'Dunciad'

London

The city's *literati* are agog at the anonymous publication this year of an three-volume poem entitled *The Dunciad*, whose hero is a scholar named Lewis Theobald. Equipped with a full textual apparatus, as though it were an edition of some literary classic, the poem fires off insults at various unnamed poets and scribblers for their alleged mediocrity. London writers are anxiously combing its pages to see if they can recognize themselves or their friends in these attacks.

It is strongly suspected that the author is in fact Alexander Pope, the 40-year-old writer who in 1725 published a scholarly edition of Shakespeare which was pulled to pieces the following year by a critic – Lewis Theobald.

Pope: the satirist is satirized.

Catholics are told bluntly: 'You have no right to vote'

Dublin, 6 May 1728

A new act of parliament passed today baldly states that Roman Catholics are not allowed to vote – making explicit for the first time what has always implicitly been the case here. It reinforces the wish of the Protestant establishment to deprive Catholics of significant status in the community. Laws against ownership or inheritance of property ensure that power remains in the hands of the ruling class.

The Catholic Irish are on the whole a defeated and leaderless people. Strongly attached to their church, which supplies continuity with their past, they see the clergy as a substitute for political leadership. In the west of Ireland the Dublin government has little authority. The old order survives there amidst nostalgia for a vanishing Gaelic society. Irish poetry reflects this with its emphasis on long-dead chieftains and ancient battles. Most people still speak Irish here, and interpreters sometimes have to be used in the assize courts.

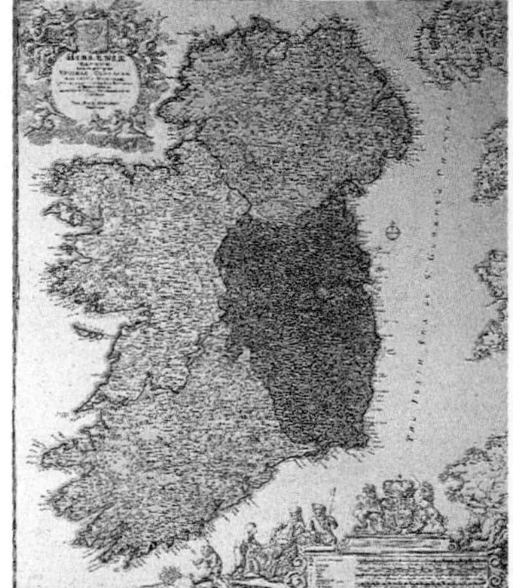

The four provinces of Ireland.

Certain Catholic families, however, have kept their economic positions by securing generous leases – they are not, of course, allowed to own property – from complaisant Protestant landlords. The heads of some families have circumvented the anti-Catholic legislation by becoming nominal converts to the established church while the other members of their families remain Catholics (→ 11/1731).

Classical columns and facades adorn buildings

British Isles

If Inigo Jones were alive, he would rejoice to know that the style of architecture which he brought from Italy a century ago is popular again. "Palladianism" is slowly changing the face of grand public buildings with a display of well defined classical details.

Interest was reawakened in 1712, when the Scottish architect Colen Campbell began issuing his three-volume *Vitruvius Britannicus*, an illustrated review of architectural work, including his own. Among Campbell's works are the exquisite Ebberston Lodge in Yorkshire, for Sir William Thompson, a member of parliament, and Stourhead mansion in Wiltshire. Full of Palladian designs, Campbell's book is a personal manifesto in which he argues against "affected and licentious" baroque in favour of a more restrained "antique simplicity".

In 1716 Lord Burlington had just returned from Italy, where he had studied the work of the great 16th-century architect Andrea di Pietro, better known as Palladio, when an English translation of Palladio's *I quattro libri dell'architettura* was published. It was this, together with Campbell's theories, that fired Burlington's enthusiasm and led him to commission Campbell to remodel his home in London's Piccadilly.

Since then Burlington has not only made the new style fashionable among the Whig aristocracy – Tories prefer baroque – but has also designed a number of buildings for himself and his friends. His villa at Chiswick, which is nearing completion, is already being regarded as a masterpiece. The villa, and Campbell's Mereworth Castle in Kent, pay conscious homage to Palladio's Villa Rotunda.

Henry Herbert, the earl of Pembroke, is also fluent in the new style – as is clear from the house that he built three years ago at Marble Hill, Twickenham, for Henrietta Howard, the countess of Suffolk, King George II's mistress. William Kent, the artist, interior designer and protégé of Burlington, who worked on the interior of the villa, has recently edited the *Designs of Inigo Jones*. There is also interest across the Irish Sea, where Alessandro Galilei has built a huge Palladian house at Castletown, Co Kildare, for William Conolly, the speaker of the Dublin House of Commons.

Major architects not won over to Palladianism include James Gibbs, whose St Martin-in-the-Fields in London boasts a Gothic spire combined with antique elements, and Nicholas Hawksmoor, who prefers to mix gothic with baroque styles, as in his church of St Anne, in London's Limehouse district.

The classical portico of Stourhead.

Palladian houses in Hanover Square, developed by the earl of Scarborough.

The Scottish architect James Gibbs renovated St Martin-in-the-Fields.

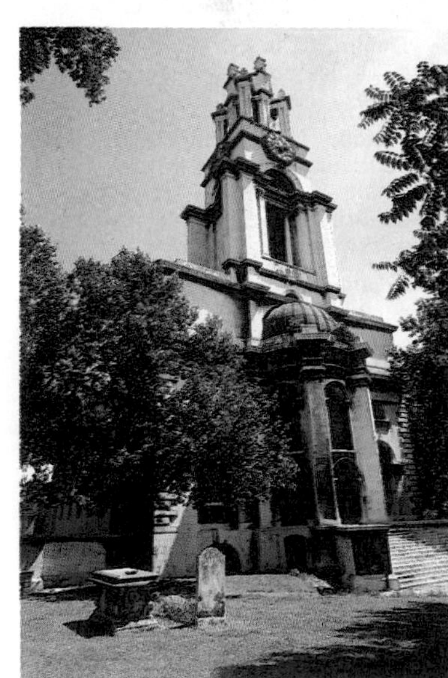

Nicholas Hawksmoor's St Anne's, Limehouse, was built 1712-14.

Castletown House, Co Kildare, showing its clean lines and classic columns.

Lord Burlington's Chiswick House and gardens were early masterpieces.

1729 - 1731

Dublin, 3 February 1729. The architect Edward Lovet Pearce lays the foundation stone of the new parliament building in College Green (→ 16/1/31).

Edinburgh, 13 May 1729. The Church of Scotland sets up riding committees to impose ministers on congregations which refuse them (→ 6/12/33).

Waterford City, 21 August 1729. The first issue of the *Waterford Post* appears (→ 1730).

Europe, 9 November 1729. Britain and Spain sign a treaty at Seville; Spain renounces claims to Gibraltar (→ 9/4/31).

Ulster, 1729. More Scots emigrate to America.

Bristol, 1730. Walter Churchman is granted a royal patent to make chocolate.

Dublin, 1730. George Rye publishes *Considerations on Agriculture*, a manual (→ 1734).

London, 1730. John Hadley, a mathematician, invents an "octant"; known as "Hadley's quadrant", it estimates positions at sea.

London, 1730. The first performance of *Tom Thumb*, by Henry Fielding, is staged.

Edinburgh, 1730. The Royal Infirmary is founded (→ 1736).

London, 1730. The first issue of the *Grub Street Journal*, taking its name from a London street frequented by journalists, is printed.

Ireland, 16 January 1731. Edward Lovet Pearce is appointed surveyor-general and knighted.

London, 6 March 1731. Edward Cave launches *The Gentleman's Magazine*, giving advice to all who style themselves gentlemen (→ 1732).

London, 9 April 1731. Rumours abound of a Spanish attack on a British ship in the Caribbean, in which Captain Jenkins of the *Rebecca* claims to have lost an ear (→ 5/1731).

Ireland, 7 May 1731. A revision of the (British) Navigation Act allows the import of certain goods directly from the American colonies.

Europe, May 1731. Britain and Austria sign the Treaty of Vienna, marking the end of the Anglo-French alliance (→ 1733).

Dublin, 25 June 1731. The Dublin Society for Improving Husbandry and Manufacturing is founded.

Strict religious society founded by Wesley

John Wesley leading "the Holy Club", an Oxford University religious society.

Oxford, 1729
Undergraduates at Oxford University's Lincoln College have been struck by the earnest spirituality of a group of students who have formed a religious society there. These young men, led by a college fellow called John Wesley – ordained an Anglican priest just last year – are nicknamed "the Enthusiasts", "the Bible Moths" or "the Holy Club". Most people call them "the Methodists", after their methodical way of life. The group, which includes Wesley's younger brother Charles, looks inwards to personal holiness rather than outwards to the needs of the world (→ 1732).

'Modest Proposal' published by Swift

Dublin, 29 October 1729
Jonathan Swift, the political wit, controversial dean of St Patrick's Cathedral and author of *Gulliver's Travels*, has published a pamphlet with the title *A Modest Proposal*. Beneath the unassuming title, this savage satire suggests that poverty in Ireland be alleviated by the simple expedient of getting the poor to fatten their children so that the rich may eat them. Swift is already seen as a national hero and was given the freedom of Dublin last February. The publication of his *Drapier Letters* in 1724 played a large part in ending the patent granted to William Wood in the "Wood's halfpence" affair [*see reports on pages 667 and 668*] (→ 1739).

Jonathan Swift as a young man.

Controversial Scots professor suspended

Glasgow, 1729
The Church of Scotland's general assembly has decided that it is "not fit or safe" for John Simson, the professor of divinity at Glasgow University, to go on teaching. In a re-run of the fourth-century Arian heresy, Simson argues that since Christ is the son of God, He had a beginning and so belongs to the created order; He does not, that is, share the deity of God. The controversial professor, who has outraged the church's evangelical wing for the past 15 years, is suspended on full pay (→ 13/5).

Death in Venice for Scottish gambler and speculator John Law

Venice, Italy, 1729
John Law, the Scots-born financier who singlehandedly ruined the finances of France [*see story on page 664*], has been found dead in his bed in Venice. The extraordinary story of this son of an Edinburgh goldsmith, who became one of the most noted financial names in Europe, is sure to live beyond his days.

Despite being discredited nine years ago by the French, and fired from his position as comptroller-general on the failure of the Banque Royale, Law's name will always be associated with paper bank notes (based on gold currency held by the bank), and with the word "millionaire" – a status that he himself achieved by means of bold property speculation in America.

Gambling is a national passion, but most do not go to the lengths of Law.

Squalid living conditions in debtors' jails are focus of investigation by parliament

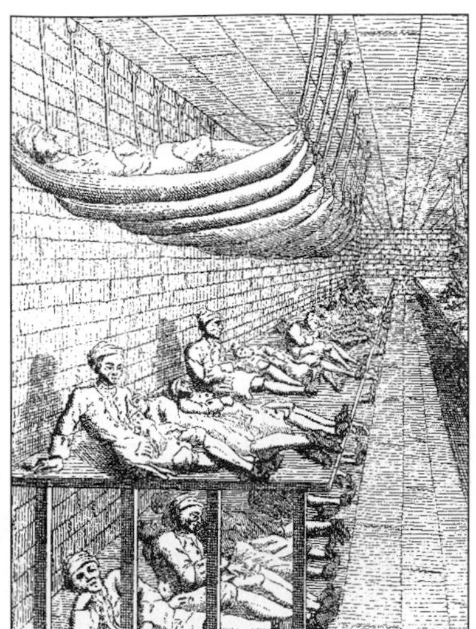
Awful conditions in the Marshalsea.

Prisoner restraint proves effective.

London, 1729
James Oglethorpe, the member of parliament, battle hero and friend of the Wesley brothers, has persuaded parliament to do something about the scandalous conditions of debtors held in London's Fleet and Marshalsea prisons.

A parliamentary committee is now to be set up, although few hold out much hope for real change. Most people are not even aware that men, and often their whole families, are kept behind bars for several long years, in the dirtiest of conditions, for running into debt. Prisons are not used in this country to improve culprits. Serious criminals are hanged or transported to the New World. Only debtors are kept languishing in jail.

Jailers demand money, called "garnish", from prisoners in their charge both as a bribe for good treatment and to cover their expenses for food and heat. Therefore debtors, who arrive in prison with little or no money, end their days in even greater debt – to the jailers. The Wesley brothers, John and Charles, the founders of Oxford University's "Holy Club", visit the prisons to see if the situation can be improved (→ 1732).

Prime minister is rid of awkward relative

London, 16 May 1730
Charles, Viscount Townshend, has resigned from the Whig government as secretary of state for the north, the post he has held for the last ten years. The prime minister – and Townshend's brother-in-law – Sir Robert Walpole has accepted the decision. Most of their colleagues in parliament have been been expecting something like this, since both are incapable of even a smile in each other's direction. Walpole, it is believed, has just been waiting to get rid of Townshend.

Although both from Norfolk, they are very different men. Townshend is austere where Walpole loves to spend lavishly and over-indulge all his appetites. Their relationship became especially difficult after the death on 29 March 1726 of Dorothy, Walpole's sister and Townshend's wife.

Arguments have flared before, and they once came to blows. When the Treaty of Seville with Spain was drawn up last November by William Stanhope, Lord Harrington, the seal was set. Stanhope is to replace Townshend, who will retire to his Norfolk estates (→ 10/1732).

King George II opening parliament.

Irish penal laws prove to be ineffective

Co Galway, November 1731
The authorities have carried out a number of raids in an attempt to find Augustinian friars, but without success; the friars were tipped off in advance. The raids are in accordance with an order made on 20 October by the mayor and magistrates of Galway authorizing sheriffs to arrest Catholic clergy and suppress religious orders in Galway town. The penal laws discriminating against Roman Catholicism that lie behind this order are – as in the present case – largely ineffective. Those excluding Catholics from the vote and land tenure are, by contrast, highly successful (→ 29/4/34).

Women are trapped by lack of education

British Isles, c.1730
An anonymous female writer has recently said: "Men, by thinking us incapable of improving our intellects, have entirely thrown us out of the advantages of education, and thereby contributed as much as possible to make us the senseless creatures they imagine us." Indeed, when it is possible for even a woman who has married well to be reduced to poverty – through widowhood – the question arises as to why women are not being educated for work that would provide them with more secure livelihoods.

Lower down the scale, women in farming families can no longer make the sort of "pin money" which they used to earn. Unfortunately, enclosure and loss of common land have now cut the incomes that farmers' wives used to enjoy from the sale of eggs or dairy products. Increasingly, women of all classes seem to prefer the "genteel" middle-class life. However, earning even a small income gave farmers' wives a certain independence which was completely unknown to their middle-class peers.

Even if women work in mines or factories, their rate of pay is far lower than that given to any man. Both spinning and lace-making bring in very low incomes. A woman might earn tenpence or a shilling [five pence], and girls even less – just fourpence or sixpence – for a full day's work.

Women's work remains largely restricted to poorly paid chores.

1732

London, 4 December. John Gay, the poet and dramatist best known for *The Beggar's Opera*, dies.

London, 7 December. Covent Garden theatre opens; all seats are on special offer for five shillings [25p].

London. King George II gives No 10 Downing Street to the government to be used as the official residence of the prime minister.

Edinburgh. Michael Menzies invents a threshing machine; it is driven by a water-wheel.

Westminster. Parliament prohibits the import of hats from America; this is designed to protect British hat-makers.

Stockport, Cheshire. The first silk mill, using a water-powered silk-throwing machine patented by Thomas Lombe of Derby, opens.

America. James Oglethorpe, a Tory philanthropist, is granted a charter by King George II to found a new colony in America; he plans to found the colony with debtors from London's prisons and give them a new start (→13/1/33).

Liverpool. The city opens a new workhouse to cope with the increase in poor people.

Oxford. George Whitefield joins John Wesley, the "Methodist" preacher, in his "Holy Club" (→6/2/36).

London. Jonathan Tyers publishes the first edition of the *London Magazine*, a rival to *The Gentleman's Magazine*.

London. Speculation is rife after the christening of Cornwall Fitz-Frederick Vane, the illegitimate son of Anne Vane and, supposedly, the prince of Wales; Lords Hervey and Harrington also claim paternity.

Britain. George Berkeley, the Irish-born philosopher and clergyman, publishes *Alciphron, or the Minute Philosopher*, a defence of Christian orthodoxy.

London. The Academy of Ancient Music is founded.

London. Only 44 churches now offer daily services; in 1714 there were 72.

New York. A London theatrical company performs for the first time in New York.

Paris. Two Irish writers, Conor Begley and Hugh MacCurtin, publish an *English/Irish Dictionary*.

Walpole causes political fury with salt tax

Westminster, October
The widely resented decision of the Whig government to reimpose the salt tax has finally been forced through parliament. The legislation has generated enormous opposition, both inside and outside the House of Commons, and at its final reading it was passed by just 29 votes, the smallest government majority for many years.

When the prime minister, Sir Robert Walpole, abolished this long established but much hated tax two years ago, the move won him enormous acclaim, especially among the poor, so his proposal to bring it back was predictably greeted by a wave of furious protest. The pamphleteers and scurrilous cartoonists have had a field day.

The Craftsman, which is at present Britain's leading political newspaper, has been a vociferous critic. Its editors accuse Walpole not only of ruthlessly forcing through his unpopular policies by means of corruption but also of extending excise duties to cover all the goods that make up Britain's fast-growing import and export business. This suspicion is vehemently denied, but it is no secret that Walpole's officials have been looking hard at the tobacco and wine trades, where the tax yield could be considerable and the scale of smuggling is certainly immense (→23/4/33).

The salt tax will hit the poor hard.

Financial scandals rock the Whig Party

London
Two fresh financial scandals this year have intensified the whiff of corruption that surrounds the government and many of its leading Whig supporters. The sale of the £200,000 estate forfeited by the earl of Derwentwater because of his role in the Jacobite rising in 1715 has now been annulled after the discovery that the commissioners involved (two members of parliament and an associate of the prime minister, Sir Robert Walpole, in the City of London) had fraudulently sold it to friends for just £1,060.

This comes in the wake of the unsavoury affair of the charitable corporation, where funds set aside to help poor traders were diverted for the benefit of the publicly appointed trustees. Walpole brushes aside the significance of such incidents, merely repeating his notorious statement that he is "no saint, no spartan, no reformer".

London's night life is brightest at Vauxhall pleasure gardens

Vauxhall's new pleasure gardens offer townsfolk an escape from the city.

London
Londoners are flocking regularly to Vauxhall, on the south bank of the Thames, to visit the New Spring Garden. Jonathan Tyers, its proprietor since 1728, has enlarged the original gardens, and this year he had the privilege of entertaining Frederick, the prince of Wales, at a fancy-dress ball here. It costs one shilling [five pence] to enter this veritable wonderland, where the walks, each with its own vista, are spanned by triumphal arches; cold suppers are served in the crescent-shaped Chinese pavilions and everywhere there is music.

Riots break out during campaign for by-election at Chester

Chester, October
Polling to replace the late Sir Richard Grosvenor as Chester's member of parliament is taking place here against a background of sustained bloodshed and violence. In spite of Herculean efforts on the part of the government party, the Whigs, the embattled Tories are now expected to retain the seat. The trouble started with rumours that the Tories planned to "steal" the vote overnight by secretly appointing 300 new freemen.

A Whig mob, including many believed to have been brought in from outside by the local leaders, Thomas Brereton and Lord Malpas, the son-in-law of the prime minister, Sir Robert Walpole, then marched to the town hall, expelled the aldermen and destroyed the building. The next day the Welsh Tory magnate Watkin Williams Wynn sent 1,000 of his tenants into Chester, armed with clubs, to "beat the Whiggish rascals". They rampaged their way through the city and went on to ensure that a member of the Grosvenor faction was installed as mayor. This is regarded as virtually certain to ensure their parliamentary victory too.

London, 7 March 1733. Sarah Malcolm, a laundress who killed a customer and two of her servants, is hanged; her skeleton is to be displayed at the Botanical Gardens, Cambridge.

London, April 1733. *Lloyd's List*, consisting largely of shipping news, begins publication.

Dublin, 2 July 1733. Dr Stevens's hospital is opened.

Dublin, 24 October 1733. The Society for the Promotion of English Protestant Schools is incorporated.

London, November 1733. Anne, the princess royal, the eldest daughter of King George II, is betrothed to Prince William of Orange (→ spring 1734).

Britain, 1733. The use of Latin in the law courts is abolished.

London, 1733. The new lake in Hyde Park, the Serpentine, started in 1730, is completed.

Westminster, 1733. The Bastardy Act obliges every woman with an illegitimate child to name the father.

Colchester, Essex, 1733. John Kay, the son of a woollen-mill owner, develops the "flying shuttle", a device to speed up the work of the handloom weaver.

London, spring 1734. George Frederick Handel, the royal composer, writes *Parnasso in Festa* for the marriage of the princess royal to William of Orange (→ 18/11/41).

Dublin, 29 April 1734. Converts to the established church with Catholic wives are banned from bringing up their children as Catholics (→ 1739).

England, 4 May 1734. The artist Sir James Thornhill dies.

Co Cork, 19 May 1734. The philosopher George Berkeley is consecrated bishop of Cloyne.

Dublin, 17 August 1734. Mercer's hospital is opened.

Dublin, November 1734. George Faulkner, a printer, publishes the first three volumes of Jonathan Swift's collected works.

Central, 28 December 1734. Robert MacGregor, better known as "Rob Roy", dies at his home in Balquhidder; in his last years he converted to Roman Catholicism.

Bristol, 1734. The Royal Infirmary is opened.

Excise Bill stirs furore

A pamphlet shows rejoicing in the City as the Excise Bill is postponed.

Westminster, 23 April 1733
In the first serious setback of his long political career, Sir Robert Walpole, the prime minister, has abandoned the cherished Excise Bill that he has spent most of the past year trying to impose on a reluctant parliament. His plan was to reduce smuggling and increase government revenue by taxing imported wine, brandy and tobacco, but on 9 April he had to admit defeat.

Feeling over the bill has run high. William Pulteney, the leader of the opposition in the House of Commons, denounced "that monster, the excise, that plan of arbitrary power". Walpole gave as good as he got but, despite a brilliant fighting speech to his supporters, in which he denounced the excise crisis as a malicious Tory plot, he has been subjected to dwindling majorities in divisions in the House of Commons. He faced defeat in the House of Lords and gave in.

Today, however, he has won some satisfaction. King George II has, at Walpole's request, sacked those members of the royal household who voted against the bill. A coterie of men such as Lords Chesterfield, Stair and Burlington has been seeking to use the excise furore to discredit Walpole. The prime minister has, however, had the support of Queen Caroline. When Lord Stair told her that he opposed the excise out of conscience she rebuked him: "My lord, speak not to me of conscience. You make me feel faint" (→ 1734).

British troops to stay out of foreign war

London, 1733
French and Spanish troops have attacked Austrian possessions in Lorraine and northern Italy. They are backing the claims of Stanislaus Leszczynski, the father-in-law of the French king, Louis XV, to the throne of Poland, vacant following the death this year of Augustus II.

This is in opposition to Frederick Augustus II, the elector of Saxony, who is the candidate of Emperor Charles VI. Although Britain is bound by treaty to support Austria (part of the Holy Roman Empire), Sir Robert Walpole has no intention of committing British troops to actione. Both King George II and Queen Caroline are urging him to go to war, but he is adamant that Britain would not accept this prior to next year's election (→ 8/10/39).

Britain increases its colonial power in North America

Georgia, 13 January 1733
Colonel James Oglethorpe, the noted parliamentarian, philanthropist and social reformer, landed today at Charleston, on the south-east coast of North America, with a shipload of settlers. Many of them are men rescued from London's packed and inhumane debtors' prisons to start a fresh, Christian life overseas. They are to be the first citizens of a new state that he has named "Georgia" in honour of his patron, King George II. It will be Britain's 13th American colony and confer the strategic advantage of barring any further northward advance by Spanish adventurers in Florida.

The colonel, who received his royal warrant last June, has secured wide public backing for his schemes. On an earlier visit to the territory he befriended a local Indian chieftains, Tomo-Chichi, and invited him to London, where he quickly became the toast of the salons. As a result Oglethorpe has had little difficulty in attracting support and subscriptions. The initial funding has reached £18,000, with £600 donated by the king.

There are 130 people in the pioneering group. They include not only many of "the industrious and deserving poor", but also a significant group of German and Swiss Protestants fleeing from religious persecution in Europe. The intention now is to allocate them land south of the Savannah river. Slave-owning is to be forbidden.

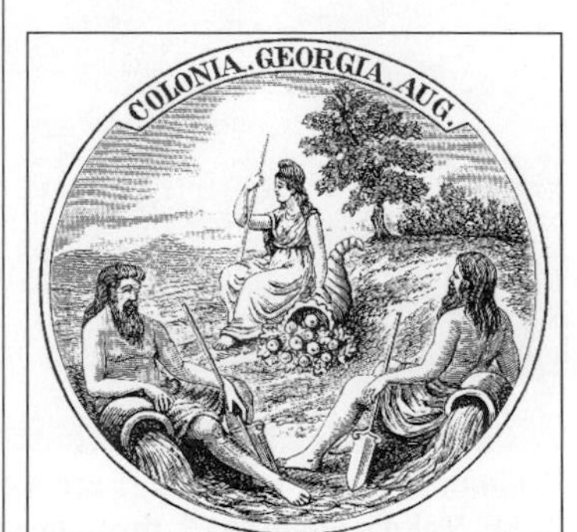

The seal of the Georgia colony.

▷

Irish economy is hit by a bank collapse

Dublin, 25 June 1733
News of the failure of Burton & Falkiner's bank has been greeted with alarm and dismay by Dublin's business community. It is regarded as the inevitable result of low agricultural prices which, in turn, have led to a scarcity of money and a general decline in confidence.

The three bad harvests of the years 1726-8, resulting in increased imports of grain and rising food prices, have been followed by years of good harvests and low prices, which have caused problems for this poor and indebted community. It is becoming evident that one of Ireland's major problems is the lack of sufficient external markets to stimulate the economy.

Church of Scotland divided in dispute

Stirling, 6 December 1733
Angered by patronage laws barring the election of ministers in the Church of Scotland, a Stirling minister, Ebenezer Erskine, has formed an "Associate Presbytery" and seceded from the established, Presbyterian, church. He has preached and written against the church's law allowing the elders of a parish to "call" a minister to his kirk.

Erskine and his followers see this system as a betrayal because it reflects a form of the patronage which is imposed by the British parliament – a system opposed by the church. The church is taking a lenient view of the seceders, and there is no question of their being deposed – for the time being.

Walpole is victorious in general election

Westminster, 1734
After a fiercely fought election marked by corruption, violence and unbridled libel, the prime minister, Sir Robert Walpole, has retained his Whig majority and is busily purging enemies in his own government. Whether this is politically wise remains to be seen: his foes are powerful men such as the duke of Bolton and the earl of Chesterfield, friends of the prince of Wales. Both could seize power if an opportunity should arise.

Many thought that Walpole had little chance after being forced to withdraw his hated Excise Bill [*see report on page 681*]. Vitriolic newspapers such as *The Craftsman* brought the mob onto the streets; Walpole's coach was once attacked outside Westminster (→ 1737).

William Hogarth's paintings are a commentary on the times: here he charts "The Rake's Progress" through an orgy of drink, gambling and sex, in which he is taken advantage of by women, who even steal his watch.

Princess Royal marries William of Orange

Princess Anne and William: George II had plans for their wedding night.

London, spring 1734
It is clear that King George II does not have much time for his new son-in-law, Prince William of Orange. William's physical deformities – he is small in stature and humpbacked – mean that he is a less than glamorous addition to the already unloved Hanoverian family. But his bride, Anne, the king's eldest daughter, is content with the match since it sets her free from her father's constant boasting – particularly of his sexual conquests – and his foul temper.

The lecherous George even planned to secrete himself behind a curtain in the marital bedchamber, but he was persuaded not to do so by his courtiers. Two things in William's favour are his Protestantism and his Whig politics.

Farming manifesto launched by Jethro Tull

The latest farm technology: a drill plough with seed and manure hopper.

Wallingford, Berkshire, 1734
Jethro Tull, whose horse-drawn drilling machine is proving popular with his neighbouring farmers here in the Thames valley, has published *The Horse-Hoing Husbandry* – a series of essays in which he outlines his revolutionary approach to farming technology.

It was early in the century when the university-educated Tull devised the machine seed drill, which plants seeds in a straight line at regular intervals and depths before covering them with earth. Tull hopes that his drill will replace the wasteful method of haphazard scattering. He has also invented a mechanical hoe to weed between the lines of crops, although this has not proved so popular.

Tull's invention has boosted crop yields wherever it has been used – as has the four-course rotation system devised by Charles, Viscount "Turnip" Townshend, the former Whig politician, on his Norfolk estate. Townshend's system involves a four-year sequence of crops – clover, wheat, turnips and barley – eliminating the fallow field. His nickname is from his use of turnips as winter feed for cattle that would otherwise be slaughtered (→ 1738).

1735 - 1737

Rome, 18 January 1735. Maria Clementina Sobieska, the wife of James Stuart, dies (→ 2/2/44).

Westminster, 15 June 1735. The Copyright Act is passed to stop engravers pirating artists' work.

London, October 1735. William Hogarth founds the St Martin's Lane academy for painters (→ 25/6/40).

Dublin, December 1735. Bishop Berkeley publishes the *Querist*, an analysis of Ireland's financial problems.

Bristol, 1735. *The Gentleman's Magazine* reports that a crowd, thwarted of a good hanging, exhumed the wife-murderer James Newth (he poisoned himself before he could be hanged) and "dragged his guts about the highway, poked his eyes out, and broke almost all his bones".

Edinburgh, 1735. The Edinburgh Burgess Golf Club is founded.

London, 1735. A convivial club for gentlemen, the Sublime Society of Beefsteaks, is founded, dedicated simply to the eating of beefsteaks.

Georgia, 6 February 1736. John Wesley, the "Methodist" preacher, arrives (→ 1737).

London, 1736. James Barclay, a Quaker, founds Barclay's bank.

Edinburgh, 1736. The Royal Infirmary is incorporated.

Britain, 1736. Legislation against witchcraft is repealed.

Canterbury, 28 February 1737. John Potter, the bishop of Oxford, is the new archbishop after the death last month of Archbishop William Wake.

Edinburgh, 21 June 1737. Following last year's Porteous riot, a Bill of Pains and Penalties is passed; the city is fined and the lord provost barred from public office.

Ireland, 7 September 1737. William Cavendish, the duke of Devonshire, is sworn in as lord lieutenant.

London, September 1737. King George II expels the prince of Wales from court (→ 20/11/37).

England, 1737. Elizabeth Cooper publishes the first general anthology of English poetry, in her *Muses' Library*.

Y Wern, Powys, 1737. Howell Harris founds the first Methodist Society in Wales (→ 1/2/38).

Loathed prince of Wales gets married

London, 26 April 1736
A glowering King George II saw his despised son, Frederick, the prince of Wales, married today to a tall, awkward German girl who speaks no English. This is indeed no love match: 17-year-old Princess Augusta of Saxe-Gotha was chosen because George wants an alliance with Prussia, and parliament wants an heir to the throne. The bride could hardly have imagined what a complicated domestic situation is waiting to engulf her.

George, his queen and daughters have hated the 29-year-old prince ever since he arrived from Hanover, where he spent his first 20 years. Despite his appearance and behaviour (he is short, pop-eyed and lecherous), Frederick is more popular than his father and is courted by politicians opposed to Sir Robert Walpole, the king's favourite. The royal family does not hide its contempt. "Popularity always makes me feel sick, but Fritz's popularity makes me vomit," the queen has said. He is "the greatest villain that was ever born," declared the king. To his sister he is "a nauseous beast [who] cares for nobody but his own nauseous self" (→ 2/1737).

Riots shake Edinburgh

The mob breaks into prison and drags out Captain Porteous to lynch him.

Edinburgh, 7 September 1736
An angry mob broke into the Tolbooth prison here tonight, dragged out a prisoner and lynched him in the street. The victim, Captain John Porteous, had been sentenced to death for ordering his soldiers to fire on a crowd at the hanging, on 14 April, of a convicted smuggler. Six people died in the incident. Porteous was granted a six-week respite by Queen Caroline so that an appeal might be lodged. The incident arose from a recent tax on imported tea, wines and brandy that has given rise to a massive smuggling industry. The government has responded by creating customs officers, two of whom brought the smuggler – and an accomplice who escaped – to Edinburgh for trial (→ 21/6/37).

Marriages are arranged in order to secure 'interest or gain'

The marriage contract has become an agreement similar to horse-trading, with just as many pitfalls and doubtless just as many expensive mistakes.

London, March 1735
Sir William Temple once remarked of marriages that "they are made, just like other common bargains or sales, by the mere consideration of interest or gain, without any love or esteem". Fathers now have to dangle handsome dowries as bait to catch a well-connected husband for their daughters. Sometimes the newspaper advertisements dealing with such bargain-hunting seem to be no more than mere horse-trading. Among the betrothals announced in this month's papers are the following: a John Parry, Esq, is to marry Walter Lloyd Esq's daughter – for £8,000. A lord bishop is to wed a Miss Orell, for £30,000. Then a 26-year-old vicar is to marry a woman "upwards of eighty", who will pay £8,000 in cash, in addition to providing £300 a year income and a coach-and-four "during her life only". ▷

Gin Act sparks outrage

London, 1736
Drunken crowds have taken to roaming the city's streets, breaking windows and stoning coaches in protest at a tax that threatens to deprive them of their favourite tipple. With a host of gin shops blatantly inviting customers to get "drunk for a penny, dead drunk for twopence", parliament has imposed a swingeing duty of 20 shillings [£1] on every gallon of gin, home-made or imported, and raised retailers' licences to £50.

Addiction to gin has become a serious problem. One factor is the over-production of cheap grain easily distilled into cheap gin; another is the use of the excise duty to contribute to King George II's civil list. The third is the drab life of thousands who can drown their misery in alcohol flavoured with juniper, often brewed in back-street basements from dubious materials. In addition to home brewing, chandlers are an excellent source of alcohol used "for medicinal purposes". There are over 8,600 spirits shops here – one for every 11 houses.

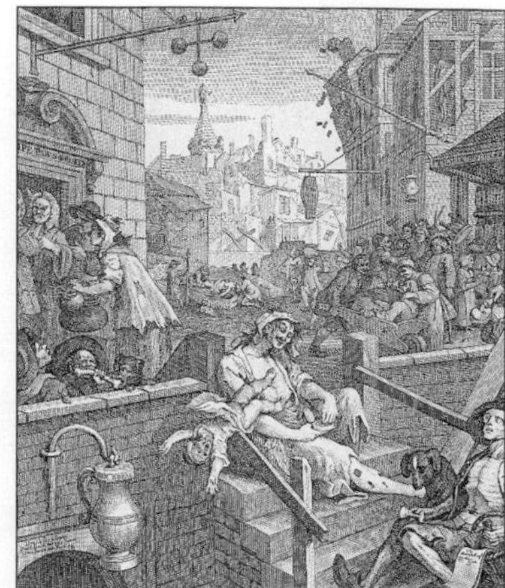

"Gin Lane" by William Hogarth.

Theatre comes under government power

The new law lies on stage reminding players to watch how they act.

London, 1737
Britain's unpopular prime minister, Sir Robert Walpole, has reacted to a series of playwrights' verbal attacks on him by insisting that all plays and players be licensed by the lord chamberlain. Under the Stage Licensing Act all theatres except the two "patent" ones in Drury Lane and Covent Garden are to be closed; nothing can be staged without prior approval. *Polly*, John Gay's sequel to *The Beggar's Opera*, is already banned. Since 1730 Henry Fielding has put on a series of plays lampooning politicians and the royal family at the Haymarket theatre which he manages, culminating in *The Historical Register for the Year 1736*, accusing Walpole of corruption. His theatre will now be closed (→ 13/2/41).

Row over civil-list cash for the prince

London, February 1737
London society is agog with the blistering row that has set King George II and Queen Caroline even further against their son Frederick, the prince of Wales. Strong words are echoing along the corridors of Hampton Court, with George, who is suffering badly from piles, branding his son as "the lowest stinking coward in the world".

The prince's allowance is at the centre of the row. Frederick has demanded £100,000 a year from the civil list. An offer of £50,000 by Sir Robert Walpole, the prime minister, was rejected out of hand; it was this that infuriated the king and queen. Meanwhile, parliament has refused to double the prince's allowance (→ 9/1737).

Bishop publishes religious analogy

London, 1736
A new theological work, *Analogy of the Christian Religion*, asserts that there is an analogy between the religious revelations of Christianity and the natural order. It is this that makes it "reasonable" for people to hold to the Christian faith. The author, Joseph Butler, the bishop of Bristol, is typical of the church establishment in wishing to substitute reason for "enthusiasm" – by which is meant fanaticism – in religious matters.

King mourns loss of much loved queen

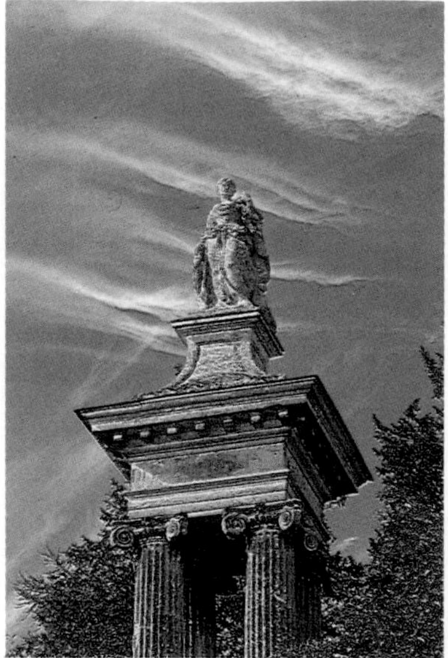

A monument to Caroline at Stowe.

London, 20 November 1737
Just 11 days after she collapsed with stomach pains and nausea, Queen Caroline has died in St James's Palace. Doctors tried all the known treatments – including lancing and bleeding – but infection from an old umbilical rupture continued to spread. King George II is said to be deeply distressed, although, even during his wife's last illness, he still complained that her movement in bed was keeping him awake. He was considerate enough, however, not to allow Frederick, the estranged prince of Wales, to see his dying mother; Caroline hated her son ("this monster") to her very last breath (→ 4/6/38).

The garden at Claremont, near Esher, in Surrey, landscaped to a design by William Kent, who in 1735, through the patronage of Lord Burlington, was appointed to the post of royal master mason and deputy surveyor.

Deal, Kent, 1 February 1738. The "Methodist" John Wesley returns from his preaching tour of America (→ 24/5).

Co Roscommon, 25 March 1738. Turlough Carolan, the poet and musician, dies.

London, 24 May 1738. At a church service in Aldersgate Street, John Wesley, feeling his heart "strangely warmed", undergoes a conversion (→ 1739).

London, 4 June 1738. The princess of Wales gives birth to a son, George William Frederick (→ 2/1742).

Norfolk, 21 June 1738. Charles, Viscount "Turnip" Townshend, dies at East Raynham, aged 63.

London, 1 January 1739. John Wesley forms the United Society, an Anglican religious body, in Fetter Lane (→ 2/4).

Europe, January 1739. Britain signs the Convention of Pardo over trade differences with the Spanish West Indies (→ 8/10).

Bristol, 12 May 1739. John Wesley, who began open-air preaching here on 2 April, lays the foundation stone of the first "Methodist" chapel (→ 1/6).

Ireland, August 1739. The grain harvest is very poor (→ 12/1739).

Ireland, 26 September 1739. Roman Catholic aristocrats petition King George II for longer land leases under the penal laws (→ 31/3/40).

Europe, 8 October 1739. Britain declares war on Spain over the freedom of navigation in the Caribbean (→ 22/11).

Westminster, November 1739. The earl of Winchilsea assures the Lords that "the Jacobite party is entirely broke".

Ireland, December 1739. Severe frost brings famine (→ 2/6/40).

Britain, 1739. Dean Swift publishes *Verses on the Death of Doctor Swift* (→ 19/10/45).

England, 1739. Elizabeth Carter translates Algarotti's *Sir Isaac Newton's Philosophy for the Use of Ladies*, to make the new science available to women.

London, 1739. The architect George Dance builds the Mansion House.

Scotland, 1739. The Association of Highland Gentlemen is formed to plot for a Stuart restoration.

Highland, 1739. The Black Watch regiment is formed.

Turpin goes to gallows

Dick Turpin escapes pursuers armed with pitchforks by jumping a tollgate.

York, 10 April 1739
The notorious highwayman, smuggler and horse-thief Dick Turpin has been hanged here for murdering an Essex gamekeeper. Turpin was caught after having accidentally shot and killed his partner in crime, Tom King, whom he was actually trying to save from arrest. It was the dying King who provided the clues that led to Turpin.

The son of an innkeeper, Turpin was born at Hempstead in Essex 33 years ago. Apprenticed to a butcher, he soon saw more profit in stealing rather than in cutting up cattle. He tried his hand at most criminal trades, and his ability to escape the law soon made him into something of a "folk hero" in his native East Anglian county.

The most famous tale told about him is that he galloped his horse, Black Bess, all the way from Essex to York in record time in order to establish an alibi. It is, alas, untrue. There was nothing romantic about the man who died on the scaffold today: he was guilty of a number of brutal crimes.

Anglo-Spanish relations worsen over ear

Westminster, 17 March 1738
There was uproar in the House of Commons today when Captain Robert Jenkins, a shipmaster trading in the West Indies, showed members what he alleged to be his severed ear, cut off by Spanish coastguards seven years ago. He said that the Spaniards had pillaged his ship and tortured his crew while he was engaged in legitimate trade.

It seems, in fact, that Jenkins was engaged in smuggling in contravention of the terms of the Treaty of Utrecht, which restrict British merchants to the *Asiento*, a contract to supply slaves to the Spanish colonies, and the right to send one ship a year directly to the colonies.

Jenkins holds up his severed ear.

However, Jenkins's claim that when the Spaniards attacked him he "committed his soul to God and his cause to his country" has inflamed public opinion and given the opposition a powerful weapon to use against the prime minister, who is anxious to secure a peaceful settlement to the problem of Spain's interference with British trade to its colonies. Walpole may, however, be forced to go to war by an increasingly bellicose nation (→ 8/10/39).

'Methodist' preacher Wesley accused of sedition by Nash

Bath, 1 June 1739
There has been a remarkable encounter here between the preacher John Wesley, who believes in salvation through inner discipline, and Richard "Beau" Nash, the arbiter of social life in Bath. Wesley, an Anglican priest, was addressing a large audience on his disciplined, "Methodist" approach to religion when Nash stood up and accused him of sedition.

Wesley denied this charge, insisting that he had the right to preach "by the authority of Jesus Christ, conveyed to me by the archbishop of Canterbury when he laid hands on me and said: "Take thou authority to preach the Gospel"." Nash argued: "I say it is [seditious]; and besides, your preaching frightens people out of their wits." The argument continued for some time, with the congregation increasingly restive at Nash's arrogance, so that when he asked: "Sir, I desire to know what these people come here for?" an old woman spoke up. "You, Mr Nash, take care of your body; we take care of our souls; and it is for the food of our souls that we come here." Nash, who is renowned for his love of luxury, said nothing more, turning and walking away. Although Nash was worsted in this argument, weightier minds than his are also troubled by Wesley's methods, which seem alien to the traditions of the Anglican Church (→ 1740).

Wesley: clashed with Beau Nash.

Politician turned farmer leaves an inventive legacy

Norfolk, 1738
Charles, Viscount Townshend, who died this year, eight years after retiring from political life to his Raynham Hall estate, made a new career for himself as a revolutionary agriculturalist – "Turnip" Townshend.

He adopted Dutch methods of cultivating turnips for animal feed, enabling cattle to be kept alive during the winter. Previously most of the stock on farms was killed off just before Christmas and salted down for winter eating, leaving only the draught

"Turnip" Townshend: a pioneer of new methods of agriculture.

animals and breeding stock. Using Townshend's methods of feeding turnips to the cattle, whole herds can now be sustained throughout the year, giving a continuous supply of both fresh meat and milk.

This is part of an agricultural revolution involving further enclosures of fields (which is giving the English countryside the appearance of a patchwork quilt), crop rotation, the dressing of land with marl, and the growing of clover and rye grass. In Norfolk Townshend pioneered four-field crop rotation, whereby each year a different crop is sown in each field, avoiding the need to leave fields fallow. This maximizes fertility and allows the soil to be restored more quickly.

Lady writer speaks out against Lords

London, 1738
The Lords have tried to exclude a group of women – who wanted to listen to the political debates – from the gallery of the house, reports the author and reformer Lady Mary Wortley Montagu.

Lady Mary, the daughter of the duke of Kingston, is no stranger to controversy. She first shocked society when she eloped with Edward Wortley Montagu. When he became ambassador to the Ottoman Empire, it was Lady Mary who brought inoculation against smallpox from Istanbul to this country.

But Lady Mary is best known as a literary figure, with published volumes of letters about her travels and friends. Yet, as a self-styled "bluestocking", even the formidable Lady Mary has been heard to advise her daughter to keep her learning to herself: to parade it would "only draw on her the envy and the most inveterate hatred of fools". Lady Mary would like to see education opened up for women. She is unlikely to see her dream realized in the immediate future.

'Methodist' preaches gospel in America

George Whitefield's preaching is winning him acclaim in America.

Pennsylvania, 1739
George Whitefield, an Anglican colleague of the Wesley brothers and their "Methodist" movement, is having much success in Philadelphia in the "Great Awakening" among the east coast colonies. He has considerable histrionic gifts, and people at open-air meetings are spellbound by his preaching. Whitefield, who gained his education as a servant at Pembroke College, Oxford, having begun his working life as a tapster at the Bell inn in Gloucester, hopes to build an orphanage in Bethesda, Maryland. He is not without his detractors, partly because of the unconventional nature of his meetings, but also because of his attacks on "unconverted ministers" whom he blames for the religious failings of the people (→ 1/1).

Strategic road network laid across Scotland to keep clans quiet

Edinburgh, 1738
The government's commander-in-chief in Scotland for the past 14 years, General George Wade, is returning to England. He has completed a remarkable campaign of military road-building, opening up the inaccessible highlands with 250 miles (400km) of roads and 42 stone bridges, including a splendid five-arched crossing of the Tay at Aberfeldy. The system is designed to create a *cordon sanitaire* against the highland clans, based along the line of the Great Glen. It is protected by forts, and a naval galley capable of carrying 60 soldiers is based on Loch Ness.

Wade came to Scotland in 1724 to deal with the clans and the Jacobites as the result of a memorandum drawn up by Simon Fraser, Lord Lovat. A convicted rapist and an erstwhile Jacobite, Lovat painted a picture of clan lawlessness and Jacobite plotting. It was designed to prove his newfound trustworthiness and so promote his own territorial influence. Fortunately for him the memorandum matched the fears of the government in London, and Wade, a soldier of greater organizational than fighting skills, was sent north. He organized his "highwaymen" in work parties of 500 soldiers to make the roads, paying them an extra sixpence [2.5 pence] a day. They have done a superb job, and the army can now move swiftly around Scotland.

This beautiful bridge over the river Fechlin at Inverness was built by Wade.

British capture Spanish treasure depot

Panama, 22 November 1739
Admiral Edward Vernon has won the first victory of the "War of Jenkins' Ear" by capturing the powerful Spanish-held treasure depot of Porto Bello. It was strongly fortified, but Vernon, who has always insisted that Spain is weak, took in his six ships in a bold, well planned attack, and Porto Bello has fallen after only two days' fighting.

Vernon is one of the most enlightened of the navy's commanders, and the success at Porto Bello owes far more to him than to the government, which has allowed the navy to fall into disrepair. Many ships are undermanned and poorly equipped. The lords of the admiralty are little help, being old in years and lightweight in mind.

The victory at Porto Bello will no doubt increase Britain's thirst for war, but Sir Robert Walpole seems not to have his customary strong grip on events. It is a situation in which errors can so easily be made. Vernon's advice is to rest content with keeping a powerful fleet in West Indian waters, "by which means, let he who will possess the country, our royal master may command the wealth of it". He advises against costly land campaigns in a tropical climate, but Whitehall may choose not to heed him (→ 18/9/40).

Admiral Vernon's fleet was in good shape and took Porto Bello speedily.

Edinburgh leads world in medicine

Edinburgh, 1738
Scotland's capital is fast becoming established as the world's leading medical centre. The city's keen commitment to health care has been underlined this year with the Royal Infirmary, founded eight years ago and granted a royal charter just two years ago, moving into a new, purpose-built site. Medicine has flourished here since the foundation of the Royal College of Physicians in 1681. Four years later Edinburgh University had its first medical chair, and since then further chairs have been established in various branches of medicine. Only 12 years ago a new faculty of medicine was opened – the first of its kind in Britain.

Foundling hospital is set up in London

London, 1739
Something is at last being done to ease the plight of the unwanted children of the poor. Often they are left to die by the roadside or put in the charge of gin-soaked parish nurses, who sometimes maim them so that they excite pity when begging. Now Captain Thomas Coram, a shipwright and master mariner who could not bear to see "young children exposed, sometimes alive, sometimes dead and sometimes dying", has been given a royal charter to build a foundling hospital. He has powerful patrons: Handel and Hogarth have promised help, and subscriptions are pouring in to build what will be Britain's first such institution (→ 25/3/41).

Catholics in Ireland are pushed further and further to the margins of public life

Parliament House, Dublin: constitutional bastion of Protestant privilege.

Ireland, 1739
Despite the fact that Catholics form 70 per cent of the Irish population of roughly three million, the penal laws have effectively ensured that they now own only 5 per cent of the land. The remaining 95 per cent belongs to the small but privileged Protestant élite, which was created by the land redistribution of the last century and adheres to the established Church of Ireland.

Roman Catholic freeholders were conclusively deprived of the vote 11 years ago, and the Dublin parliament, which meets in the large and imposing Parliament House on College Green, represents solely Protestant opinion and interests. There is, however, much disparity of wealth amongst Protestants. A few – the ascendant élite – own huge estates, while others are impoverished peers living on government charity. Most get by on middling to low incomes. Nor are all Protestants equal before the law: Ulster Presbyterians are burdened with similar restrictions to those imposed on Catholics.

Many rich Protestant landlords own land in England. Their sons, who are often educated also in England, sometimes make the "grand tour" of Europe and marry into English aristocratic families. The absenteeism of many Irish landlords remains a bone of contention. A pamphlet listing their names has recently been published, and there is a strong demand that they should be taxed (→ 26/9).

The élite of Protestant society attend a state ball at Dublin Castle.

1740

Ireland, 31 March. King George II reinforces laws forbidding Catholics from keeping arms (→4/1743).

Dublin, 2 June. Riots erupt over the price and shortage of bread (→8/1740).

London, June. William Hogarth finishes a full-length portrait of Captain Coram, who has set up a foundling hospital here (→28/2/45).

Britain, 21 August. Admiral Edward Vernon, called "Old Grog" for the grogram fabric of his boat-cloak, orders sailors' rum to be diluted; it is nicknamed "grog".

Ireland, August. A cold, dry summer results in a poor harvest for the second successive year (→12/1740).

Austria, 20 October. Holy Roman Emperor Charles VI dies; he is succeeded as ruler of the Habsburg dominions by his daughter Maria Theresa (→16/12).

Central Europe, 16 December. Frederick II of Prussia, a nephew of King George II, who succeeded to the throne of Prussia earlier this year, invades Silesia [in Poland] in protest against the succession of Maria Theresa (→10/1741).

Ireland, December. Famine and an epidemic of dysentery break out (→1741).

London. Thomas Arne's *Alfred*, a great musical extravaganza of patriotic music that includes *Rule Britannia* and is based on the life of King Alfred the Great, opens.

Co Mayo. A steam engine is installed – the first of its kind in Ireland – in Doonane colliery, at Shrule.

Newcastle upon Tyne. The guildhall is destroyed during food riots.

Sussex. Benjamin Martin, an instrument-maker, develops a pocket microscope.

Dublin. Walter Harris publishes his *Topographical and Chorographical Survey of the County of Down*, the first Irish county history.

Britain. John Snetzler, a German-born organist and organ builder, settles here.

Britain. An inventor, Benjamin Huntsman, improves the "crucible" process of smelting steel.

Kent. The river Medway is partly canalized by the building of a series of locks.

Scots thinker attacks man's basic beliefs

London
This year saw the completion of a new book of philosophy called *A Treatise of Human Nature* by a young Edinburgh thinker, David Hume, who claims to set out the principles of human knowledge on a strictly empirical basis. He is a sceptic who holds that there are no such things as innate ideas. The most fundamental beliefs of mankind, such as the immortality of the soul, cannot be supported by reason. Even the law of cause and effect cannot be proved, and our expectation that it will hold good is derived only from habit. He holds that "nothing can be in the intellect which was not first in the senses" – all perceptions come from outside.

Apart from direct sensations, there are ideas, from memory or imagination, that copy previous sensations. Hume denies the existence of the self because no single perception corresponds to "myself". He concludes that human beings "are nothing but a bundle or collection of different perceptions, which succeed each other with inconceivable rapidity in perpetual flux and movement" (→1741).

Popular 'Pamela' warns of virtue in danger

Richardson: moralistic author.

London
A novel written in letter form, *Pamela, or Virtue Rewarded*, has appeared this year. It tells of a country maid whom the squire of the household, Mr B, tries to seduce. She resists all his temptations until he sees fit to make her his wife. The author is Samuel Richardson, a printer in Salisbury Court who, while writing the work, read extracts of it each evening at his suburban villa to a circle of admiring ladies – who breathlessly awaited the next instalment of the perils of Pamela and her virginal virtue. Richardson says that her story is based on a true case and that he wrote it "to cultivate the principles of virtue and religion" (→1748).

British fleet sails to challenge Spain

A later portrait of George Anson.

Portsmouth, 18 September
In the wake of last year's outbreak of war with Spain over trade in Spanish American waters, a British force of six vessels set sail today for Cape Horn. It is commanded by Captain George Anson, aged 43, who has already attained a formidable reputation in Britain's navy.

Anson's task is to challenge the Spanish fleet around the colonies in Chile and Peru, picking up any galleons or other treasure-ships he can find, and if possible to circumnavigate the globe. He and his men could be away from Britain for as long as four years (→20/6/43).

Welsh firebrand makes his mark

Wales
Religious fervour has been growing here this year, stimulated by a 26-year-old evangelical, Howell Harris. In Monmouth a riot erupted after the fiery preacher attacked the nobility's vices. Harris, from Trevecca, in Breconshire, is a friend of the Methodist leaders John Wesley and George Whitefield, preferring the latter's narrow Calvinism to Wesley's universalist Arminianism, and has been at the forefront of a great religious awakening that began in 1735. The brand of Methodism preached by Whitefield and Harris has struck a chord with the Welsh people (→1742).

The Thames froze solid in January, giving people the chance to hold a "frost fair"; Londoners flocked onto the ice, and tents were hastily put up by traders – there was dancing, skating and even an ox-roast.

1741 - 1742

Westminster, 13 February 1741. An attempt in the House of Commons to force the dismissal of Sir Robert Walpole is defeated by 184 votes (→ 4/1741).

London, 25 March 1741. Captain Thomas Coram's foundling hospital in Bloomsbury is formally opened (→ 1742).

London, 30 April 1741. A royal military academy is founded in Woolwich.

Westminster, summer 1741. Sir Robert Walpole loses his majority in the parliamentary elections owing to the support of Frederick, the prince of Wales, and John Campbell, the duke of Argyll, for the opposition.

Dublin, 2 October 1741. The new Music Hall is opened in Fishamble Street.

Dublin, 18 November 1741. George Frederick Handel, the royal composer, visits the city (→ 13/4/42).

Scotland, 1741. David Hume, the philosopher, publishes *Essays Moral and Political*, a comment on contemporary society.

Cumbria, 1741. Dr William Brownrigg, a chemist, invents fizzy mineral water.

England, 1741. Sheep-stealing becomes a capital offence.

London, 25 January 1742. Sir Edmond Halley, the astronomer royal, who gave his name to Halley's Comet, dies at Greenwich (→ 12/1748).

London, February 1742. Despite their feud, Frederick, the prince of Wales, visits the court to see his father, King George II, for the first time in many months (→ 1751).

Westminster, July 1742. Parliament agrees to move troops to Europe to support Austria against France (→ 12/1742).

Westminster, December 1742. Parliament agrees to fund 16,000 of King George II's Hanoverian troops (→ 11/1743).

London, 1742. The first indoor swimming pool, the "bagno", opens in Lemon Street.

London, 1742. The magistrate and writer Henry Fielding, who published *Shamela* last year, publishes *Joseph Andrews*.

Mid-Glamorgan, 1742. Wales's first Methodist chapel is built at Groes-Wen, near Caerphilly (→ 11/7).

Walpole suffers severe losses in election

Hogarth's view of some of the rituals that take place at elections.

London, April 1741
Sir Robert Walpole, for nearly 20 years the most influential politician in Britain, is losing his grip on parliament and his popularity with the electorate. A group of young members calling themselves "Patriots" have played a major part in causing Walpole's first serious setback at the polls. This month's general election has seen his majority fall to little more than a dozen.

Walpole's problems have steadily mounted over the last few years with the opposition sniping at him at every opportunity over alleged corruption in his government and his handling of foreign affairs. The war with Spain that began in 1739 has not helped his cause.

The origins of the war lay in a claim by Captain Robert Jenkins, a trader in the West Indies, that Spanish sailors had pillaged his ship and cut off his ear with a cutlass [*see report on page 685*]. The opposition supported his case and stirred up feelings in the country, forcing Walpole to declare war. But the war has not gone well, because Britain suffers from a shortage of ships and men (→ 11/2/42).

Leading Tory faces corruption charges

Denbigh, Clwyd, 1741
Disqualified by the returning officer after winning handsomely in a parliamentary election here, Sir Watkin Williams Wynn, a Jacobite and leading member of the High Tory group at Westminster, has been officially accused of bribery and corruption. But the proud head of the Wynn family has countercharged the sheriff with corruptly accepting bribes from the Walpole administration. Having won the seat of Denbighshire after spending all of £5,000, Sir Watkyn is prepared to spend up to £20,000 to correct what he says is the "injustice" that has been perpetrated.

Britain anxious to avoid Austrian war

London, October 1741
Anxious to stop the war on the continent over who should succeed to the Habsburg dominions, Sir Robert Walpole's government is pressing Empress Maria Theresa of Austria to climb down. Walpole wants the empress to cede Silesia to Frederick II of Prussia, who invaded this part of her lands last December. The war began after Maria Theresa succeeded her father, Holy Roman Emperor Charles VI, as ruler of the Habsburg dominions. This succession is contested by Prussia, Bavaria, Spain and Poland. The British are worried that fighting could endanger King George II's Hanoverian lands (→ 7/1742).

Empress Maria Theresa of Austria.

Methodists, followers of the revivalist Anglican priest John Wesley, lay the cornerstone of their first chapel in Bristol on 12 May 1739; the chapel officially opened in 1741 as "the New Room in the Horsefair".

Irish famine kills nearly 400,000

Children easily fall prey to famine.

Ireland, 1741
This year will be remembered as "the year of the slaughter". Famine is rampant throughout Ireland, and everywhere dead and dying people are to be seen. While bodies are being buried in fields and ditches, survivors make do with a diet of leaves and nettles.

An unusually wet summer and autumn two years ago was followed by a long and severe frost. The corn could not be ground, and fuel prices rose sharply. Amid widespread distress, cattle died of cold and starvation while unemployment rose sharply, but worse was to follow. A late spring and a cold summer last year reduced the yield of the grain and potato harvests, and famine has now resulted, accompanied by typhus and dysentery. The final death toll could reach 400,000, out of a total population of some 3,000,000, with Munster suffering the greatest losses, while the northern counties appear to be escaping comparatively lightly. George Berkeley, the bishop of Cloyne, who reports that whole villages have been wiped out in Co Limerick, has said: "The nation will probably not recover this loss in a century."

The famine and its devastating effects serve as a sharp reminder that policy on Irish agriculture has to be changed. Parliament has already shown concern at the extension of pastureland and intends to encourage the cultivation of corn, arousing worries in England, where farmers fear competition (→ 1742).

Handel's 'Messiah' rapturously greeted at Dublin première

Handel in informal pose, wigless.

Dublin, 13 April 1742
The first performance of an oratorio called *Messiah*, by George Frederick Handel, given for "the relief of prisoners in the [city's] several gaols", was sung to an enraptured audience at the new Music Hall in Fishamble Street tonight. The *Hallelujah Chorus* moved to tears many in the audience, who had been advised not to come wearing hoop petticoats, if women, or swords, if men, to leave room for more people to sit. Handel arrived here last November to give a series of oratorio concerts and, over three and a half weeks, wrote this new work to conclude the season. He turned to oratorio after John Gay's *The Beggar's Opera* in 1728 ended the fashion for his Italianate operas, which it parodied (→ 1743).

The Music Hall, Fishamble Street.

Thousands of Irish migrate to North America to seek better life

Ireland, 1742
Ireland's population has been so badly affected by emigration in recent years that the government has become concerned. Thousands of Protestants have sailed from Belfast to New England and Nova Scotia, while many Presbyterians have travelled to other American colonies or to the West Indies. The recruiting of Catholic men into the French and Spanish armies has been another drain on the population, and several thousand convicts, mainly Catholics, have been transported to North America. These developments are taking place against a background of grinding poverty and recurring famine (→ 10/1744).

Creating a new life in the New World: the construction of a settlement.

Outburst of religious fervour in Strathclyde

Strathclyde, 11 July 1742
In an extraordinary outburst of religious fervour, over 20,000 people gathered today at Cambuslang, a parish just outside Glasgow, to hear George Whitefield, thought by many to be the most enthralling preacher in Britain. Whitefield, an Anglican priest who is spearheading the Methodist movement along with the Wesley brothers, is here at the invitation of the local Church of Scotland minister, William McCulloch. As Whitefield preached in his usual flamboyant and scintillating style, some of his listeners started speaking in tongues and even fainting. The religious revival at Cambuslang is taking place during the "holy fairs" that have marked Scottish devotional life for some 120 years. These take place out of doors and lead up to the receiving of Communion – not a regular feature of Presbyterian worship. Before Communion there are days of preaching and prayer to bring the faithful to repentance, and during them emotions run high, as today's events show (→ 25/6/44).

Dr Oliver opens a hospital in Bath

Bath, 1742
Four years after the foundation stone was laid, the Mineral Water hospital has been opened here. The plan to build a hospital in the city was dreamt up in 1716 by Richard "Beau" Nash and the physician Dr Oliver, both local men. Beau Nash used his influence among the gentry to raise funds: he even won £200 from King George II. There is room for 110 patients, drawn from the city's poor (→ 1745).

Prime minister wants to call it a day

Westminster, 11 February 1742
Sir Robert Walpole, the 65-year-old Norfolk squire who has been first lord of the treasury, or prime minister, for more than 20 successive years, has resigned. The immediate cause of his fall was his defeat by just one vote in the House of Commons which he had dominated for so long through his debating skills, political management and constant attendance.

Born on 26 August 1676 into a landed country family, Walpole became the member of parliament for Castle Rising, in Norfolk, in 1701, and for King's Lynn the following year, and attached himself to a group of Whig noblemen. In 1721 he became first lord of the treasury and chancellor of the exchequer as the South Sea "bubble" burst, seizing the chance presented by the scandal to boost his political influence. He ran the country according to a policy of sound finances and freedom from war on the continent. Walpole knew that in war even the victors lose, but as the pressure on him in recent years grew for a vigorous war with Spain, so his hold on the Commons declined.

Then, on 2 February, came his defeat over a petition contesting an election at Chippenham in Wiltshire. Although Walpole lost by a single vote, the defeat symbolized his loss of support in the House of Commons. When, on the same day, he told George II that he intended to resign, the king put his arms around his prime minister, wept and begged him to come and see him often. As consolation Walpole was made, on 9 February, earl of Orford. The House of Commons has been deprived of one of its most colourful characters. Walpole liked to affect the manners of an ordinary country squire, and he used to sustain his corpulent frame with small Norfolk apples as he gave his parliamentary speeches (→4/1742).

The House of Commons will never be quite the same without Sir Robert.

New government rejects plans for reform programme

Westminster, April 1742
Britain's post-Walpole government has rejected a reform programme, including a bill that aimed to stop office-holders from being members of the House of Commons. The rejection by the Lords of the Place Bill has enraged much of the opposition, comprised of the Tories and some Whigs, such as the outspoken and dynamic William Pitt.

Pitt, who fiercely criticized Walpole and had persuaded parliament to investigate the former prime minister's past actions, has been excluded from the new government appointed by King George II. This is not surprising, as the member for Old Sarum has not flinched from attacking the king for any moves that could be interpreted as putting the interests of Hanover above those of Britain.

The king has quickly filled the void left by Walpole's resignation. The post of first lord of the treasury – prime minister – has gone to Spencer Compton, the earl of Wilmington. Thomas Pelham-Holles, the duke of Newcastle, remains secretary of state for the south, while John, Baron Carteret, is secretary of state for the north. Carteret, who is popular with the king, leads with William Pulteney a parliamentary group sometimes referred to as the "New Whigs" (→2/7/43).

Newcastle: a political survivor.

Changing face of politics under leadership of Robert Walpole

The bottom line for patronage.

London, 1742
With the downfall of Sir Robert Walpole, for so long the dominant politician in Britain, an era has come to an end. Walpole sponsored no memorable legislation and did little to improve the tarnished reputation of government, but he brilliantly demonstrated how to manipulate business in the House of Commons in order to achieve his aims. Moreover, one result of his holding power year after year for two decades is that a genuine parliamentary opposition has gradually come into being.

Walpole's power ultimately rested upon the crown. He never formed a whole ministry of his own, but he managed to gain a position of superiority that is new to British politics. In fact, his control and use of patronage put him above his colleagues, and so did his mastery of the business of government. Walpole recognized the importance of the House of Commons. Before his time in power, principal ministers had customarily sat in the House of Lords, leaving the government's policy to be defended before the Commons by less important members of the ministry.

Walpole's pre-eminence was not secured without a struggle. He was obliged to win public support, and he also had to eliminate potential threats from rival ministers. The outcome, which left him in a more influential position, has had a significant effect on the development of the cabinet system.

1743 - 1744

Pacific Ocean, 20 June 1743. Captain George Anson seizes a Spanish treasure ship (→15/6/44).

London, 2 July 1743. Spencer Compton, the prime minister and earl of Wilmington, dies; he was 69 (→25/8).

Westminster, 25 August 1743. Henry Pelham, the Whig member of parliament, becomes prime minister (→23/11/44).

London, 1743. To mark the victory at Dettingen of 16 June, George Frederick Handel composes the *Dettingen Te Deum* (→4/4/59).

Northampton, 1743. The city hospital is opened.

Cheshire, 1743. The first silk mill in Macclesfield is opened, built by Charles Roe.

London, 1743. Drury Lane theatre is wrecked by rioters.

London, 2 February 1744. Fears of a French-backed Jacobite invasion, led by Charles Edward Stuart, grow as news arrives that Charles is travelling to France from Rome and that the French fleet has already left port (→24).

English Channel, 24 February 1744. The French fleet abandons its planned invasion of Britain because of bad weather off Dungeness (→23/7/45).

France, 15 March 1744. France declares war on Britain.

Dublin, 14 April 1744. The Physico-historical Society is formed in order to preserve "manuscripts ... and natural curiosities relating to Ireland".

Dublin, 23 May 1744. The Hospital for the Incurables opens.

London, 18 October 1744. John, Baron Carteret, the secretary of state for the north, becomes Earl Granville and Viscount Carteret.

Ireland, October 1744. Wet and cold weather destroys much of the staple potato crop (→1745).

Staffordshire, 1744. The Worthington family founds a brewery at Burton upon Trent.

Britain, 1744. Edward Moore publishes *Fables for the female sex*, offering advice to women on how to attract men.

London, 1744. John Sotheby and his bookseller uncle Samuel Baker found an auctioneering firm.

Tactician who saw off Jacobites dies

Edinburgh, 4 October 1743
John Campbell, the duke of Argyll and commander-in-chief of the British Army, has died. A highly influential Whig politician, he was also a skilful military tactician, trained by John Churchill, the duke of Marlborough. It was Argyll who crushed the Jacobites in battle at Sheriffmuir [*see report on page 657*].

Argyll agreed to accept the union of England and Scotland in return for the dukedom of Greenwich, a major-generalship and a financial inducement. His fierce opposition to Walpole in the 1741 election contributed to Walpole's defeat but lost him the chance of gaining a seat in the government.

John Campbell, the duke of Argyll.

George makes a triumphant return home after his victory in battle at Dettingen

The king appears as a tiny figure on the far right of this battle scene.

London, November 1743
King George II has returned to London a hero after his successful campaign against the French (the latest stage in the war over the Austrian succession), which culminated in a battle at Dettingen in Germany. Although there have been criticisms of the way the king handled the army after the victory, in particular for having failed to press home his advantage, his reception by people here has been ecstatic.

The 60-year-old king assumed command of the 40,000-strong Hanoverian, Hessian, Austrian and British infantry, bringing with him a personal baggage train of 13 carriages, 54 carts, 35 wagons and 662 horses. Despite these creature comforts, he and his son William, the duke of Cumberland, displayed heroic courage throughout the conflict. At one time during the battle, which took place on 16 June, the king's horse bolted when the French cavalry charged. Sword in hand, George dismounted and led the allies into action on foot, directing the fire against the enemy. Although outnumbered two to one, the British won the day.

Elated with victory, the king revived the ancient practice of conferring knighthoods for valour on the field of battle – the first went to Lord Stair and the last to a trooper, Thomas Brown (→11/5/45).

If it is not played by the rules the game just is not cricket

Moorgate, London, 1744
A game of cricket played at the Artillery Ground near Moorgate between sides representing All-England and Kent has been hailed as "the greatest cricket match ever known". A large crowd of spectators included the prince of Wales and the duke of Cumberland.

All-England almost snatched a last minute victory when Kent, in need of three runs but with their last two batsmen at the crease, hit a possible catch. It was dropped, and Kent won. This year the laws of the game have been established, prescribing a 22-yard-long pitch, two stumps, underarm bowling, and four balls to an over.

The laws of cricket: nothing underhand, but bowling must be underarm.

Lucas calls for civil rights in Ireland

Dublin, April 1743
Dr Charles Lucas, a Dublin apothecary and an influential journalist, has published a pamphlet called *A remonstrance against certain infringements of the rights and liberties of the commons and citizens of Dublin*. A supporter of Dean Swift and cast in the same vituperative mould, Lucas insists on Irish constitutional rights. He resents Westminster's legislating for Ireland and restrictions decided there on Irish trade. He is now attacking the electoral system in Dublin, parliament and the judiciary (→ 16/10/49).

Britain and France square up in India

Britain, 1743
An uneasy truce between Britain and France is in danger of collapsing as the two countries prepare to fight for commercial supremacy in India. Fleets from both nations are already in the vicinity. Until now, rival trading companies have maintained an agreement for the area to stay neutral, but with Britain and France at war over the Austrian succession this commercial neutrality may crumble.

Despite their late arrival in India the French have prospered and at times have seemed close to overtaking British interests. Both sides are keen therefore to strengthen their alliances with influential Indian princes (→ 5/11/51).

Methodists hold their first 'conference'

John Wesley addressing the first Methodist Conference, held in London.

London, 25 June 1744
The Methodists, an Anglican movement led by the priest John Wesley, have held their first "conference" – a gathering of clerical supporters and preachers at what is planned to be an annual event to discuss their activities for the forthcoming year. It was held at their chapel in the Foundry, Moorfields. Since 1739 Wesley has travelled up and down the country, preaching to thousands at open-air meetings. His interests are by no means confined to Methodists, however. As a man who claims that the whole world is his parish, he has been active in trying to improve the lot of prisoners of war as well as jail conditions in general. His recently published *Thoughts Upon Slavery* is a reasoned attack on that trade (→ 4/7/45).

Welsh argue over aims of charity schools

Wales, 1743
Piety is the aim and end of all instruction in the new Welsh charity schools, according to Griffith Jones, the founder of more than 60 religious schools over the past 25 years. But this claim is denied by Howell Harris, the radical revivalist from Breconshire, who insists that they are primarily intended to defend the Anglican Church from all dissenters and Jacobites, and to instil deference into the hearts and minds of all poor children. In turn Jones accepts that the Welsh language is still the popular tongue, but in his recently published book *Welch [sic] Piety* he rejects the claim that charity schools are for "conditioning" poor people.

'Broad bottom' rule set up by Pelham

London, 23 November 1744
John Carteret, Earl Granville, has been ousted from government by the prime minister, Henry Pelham, and Pelham's brother, the duke of Newcastle, who want to form a broader coalition government.

Although Granville, who was until today secretary of state for the north, is an intimate of King George II, sharing the king's desire to play a greater role in imperial politics, his arrogance and mishandling of foreign affairs have won him few friends. The king has reluctantly been obliged to accept his resignation. Pelham is putting together a new ministry composed of men of all political persuasions, including even the Jacobite Sir John Hynde Cotton. It has already been dubbed the "broad bottom" administration (→ 18/3/45).

Earl Granville: looking for a job.

Anson returns from round-the-world trip

Hampshire, 15 June 1744
George Anson has returned to Spithead, having circumnavigated the globe in three years and nine months. When he sailed from England in 1740, shortly after the outbreak of war with Spain, he commanded six ships and 510 men [*see report on page 688*]. He returns with only one ship and 130 men, but a huge amount of Spanish treasure.

The loss of so many sailors was largely due to the prevalence of scurvy, a disease that poses serious problem on extended voyages. After a month or so at sea, sailors become weak and develop ulcers and bleeding gums. Scurvy invariably leads to infection, often with fatal consequences.

Some two centuries ago Sir John Hawkins gave his crew oranges and lemons to combat the illness, which he put down to a lack of fresh fruit and green vegetables. In spite of Hawkins's success, the navy has no plans to follow his example. Seamen continue to be provisioned with rancid meat, mouldy biscuit and bad water.

Anson made his fortune with the capture of this Spanish treasure ship (l).

1745 - 1746

Birmingham, 28 May 1745. A two-day "Flying Coach" service to London begins.

Hebrides, 23 July 1745. Charles Stuart, who landed at Eriskay from France two days ago with seven companions, crosses to the mainland at Loch nah Uagh (→ 19/8).

Ireland, 31 August 1745. The earl of Chesterfield, Philip Dormer, is sworn in as the new lord lieutenant.

Tayside, 4 September 1745. Charles Stuart enters Perth (→ 17).

London, 5 September 1745. All Catholics are ordered to leave.

Edinburgh, 17 September 1745. Charles Stuart enters the city (→ 21).

Dublin, 19 October 1745. Jonathan Swift, the dean of St Patrick's Cathedral and author, dies.

Britain, autumn 1745. Thomas Arne and Dr Charles Burney popularize an anti-Jacobite song, *God Save the King*.

Cumbria, 8 November 1745. The Jacobite army crosses the river Esk into England (→ 18).

Cambridge, 9 November 1745. The *Cambridge Journal* calls for a reprint of Foxe's *Book of Martyrs*, outlining the perils of Roman Catholic rule.

Scotland, 20 December 1745. The Jacobite army crosses the Esk back into Scotland (→ 1/1746).

Dublin, 1745. The landscapist Joseph Tudor publishes six line engravings of the city.

London, 1745. Surgeons, until now thought inferior to physicians, break away from the Barber-Surgeon company.

Scotland, January 1746. The rebel crisis forces the secretary of state, the marquis of Tweeddale, to resign (→ 16/4).

Ireland, April 1746. An act annuls future marriages celebrated by a Catholic priest between two Protestants or a Protestant and a Catholic.

Dublin, 8 August 1746. St Patrick's hospital is founded to provide care for the insane.

Scotland, 12 August 1746. Highland dress is banned for all but serving soldiers.

London, 1746. The Locke hospital for venereal disease opens.

Scotland, 1746. The British Linen company is founded.

Artist exposes modern vices at work

Self-portrait of artist and friend.

The moralist shows the danger of drink: "A midnight modern conversation".

London, 28 February 1745

William Hogarth, the painter and engraver of "modern moral subjects", as he calls them – dramatized series examining current follies and vices – held a sale today at his house in Leicester Square. He will be disappointed that buyers did not pay higher prices – £22 was typical – for the oil paintings behind *The Harlot's Progress* and *The Rake's Progress* which, as engravings, reach a wide public and have made him famous.

Hogarth is widely admired for his skill in composing crowd scenes and capturing dramatic moments. "My picture is my stage and men and women my players," he has said. Hogarth is unusual in that he draws inspiration from across the whole range of social classes. He has also painted a number of conventional portraits (→ 26/6/57).

The rake's downward progress leads him at last to the Bedlam madhouse.

Politics loses a consummate manipulator

Walpole: survived political dogfights.

London, 18 March 1745

The man whom his critics regarded as a supreme manipulator of parliament and political organizer, the earl of Orford – better known as Sir Robert Walpole – has died at the age of 69. Walpole weathered political dogfights to become Britain's first prime minister after saving both government and crown in the wake of the South Sea "bubble" disaster of 1720. He restored the country's finances and kept it at peace for two decades. Most importantly, he helped to secure the Hanoverian succession against the Jacobites (→ 3/1754).

Famine faces Irish after crop failure

Ireland, 1745

Famine has returned once more to Ireland, and although it is not so serious as in 1741, when Munster was badly hit, this time the north is severely affected. Many cattle have died, and the oats and potato crops have been seriously reduced.

The decline in tillage is now so great that Ireland is importing more grain than it exports. In the north, where the poorer people depend on oatmeal as much as on potatoes, this is resulting in severe distress (→ 4/1756).

Mixed fortunes in war with France

French batter allied forces into retreat

Fontenoy, France, 11 May 1745
A British force under the 24-year-old duke of Cumberland was defeated here today by the French, but at least it put up a brave show. It marched under withering fire towards a French force that was well dug in and nearly twice its size, led by the brilliant General Saxe. Then Lord Hay, waving a brandy flask, declared: "We are the English guards and hope you will stand till we come quite up to you."

It was not enough. After four hours of attacks and a final charge by the Irish Brigade – French allies and supporters of the Jacobite pretender, Charles Stuart – Cumberland's men had to retreat.

The British force, which formed part of a "pragmatic army" including Hanoverian, Dutch, Hessian and Austrian troops, was trying to stop a French invasion of the Netherlands, controlled by Britain's Austrian allies. The country now looks sure to be overrun (→ 3/5/47).

British forces from New England make their landing at Cape Breton Island.

Royal Navy triumphant at Cape Breton

Nova Scotia, 16 June 1745
As the fight with France for dominance in North America continues, British forces, having fired 9,000 cannonballs into the French-held Fort Louisbourg on Cape Breton Island, today received the fort's surrender. Some see this as fatal to French control of the maritime provinces. The task force comprised ships from the New England colonies – whose poorly trained crews included students from Harvard college – as well as a Royal Navy squadron from the West Indies. Commodore Peter Warren, the task force commander, is to be made governor of the island (→ 13/7/55).

Methodist preacher escapes lynching

Cornwall, 4 July 1745
A lone preacher faced down a mob at Falmouth today after it burst into a house he was visiting. John Wesley, a leading figure among the Methodists, says that a crowd surrounded the house shouting "Bring out the *Canorum*" (a Cornish term for Methodist). When sailors from a privateer broke down the door, Wesley faced the crowd, asking: "Neighbours, countrymen! Do you desire to hear me speak?" After hearing Wesley out they all drifted away. Attacks on Methodists are not uncommon; some say they are incited by local gentry who fear Wesley's ideas (→ 1748).

Wide powers given to justices of peace

England, 1746
"Hannah Carrington of Corsham, spinster, for stealing one shift value 5 shillings, pleads not guilty, jury guilty, whipt and imprisoned for 3 months." This case from Devizes is typical of those heard by justices of the peace, the workhorses of local government.

Appointed by the lord lieutenant of the county, justices have wide-ranging powers. They fix prices and wages, regulate apprentices, order highway maintenance, assess county rates and license – or ban – fairs and amusements.

A justice is reminded of his duty.

Bath is threatened by the severe restrictions of Public Gaming Act

Bath, 1745
It is not only the betting men who are anxious in the elegant gambling rooms here these days but also the city's master of ceremonies for the last 41 years, Richard "Beau" Nash. He sees lucrative revenues threatened by this year's Public Gaming Act, which aims to restrict gambling and gambling houses.

Nash, now aged 71, has transformed Bath into the most fashionable town in England. His splendid public balls have become legendary, with visitors flocking to the stylish Pump Room and Assembly Room, where they come chiefly to gamble but also to rub shoulders with the cream of society. Enhancing these centres is a sparkling new series of terraces and crescents built in classical style by Nash and the architect John Wood.

The key to Nash's success has been to make pleasure not only respectable but also good for people. Smoking and swords are banned, "whisperings of lies and scandals" are vetoed, and ladies are not allowed to appear in aprons. The hot springs, meanwhile, are proclaimed a cure for fainting, sweating and the disorders that come from eating fruit. Yet not everyone finds Bath's rigorously genteel atmosphere to their taste. "The only thing one can do one day one did not do the day before," a lady visitor has ironically commented, "is to die."

The prince of Wales (second on the left) favours games such as "hazard".

'Bonnie Prince Charlie' leads Jacobites in rebellion

Stuart standard is raised in Scotland

Highland, 19 August 1745
Charles Edward Stuart, the elder son of the Stuart pretender, James, has raised his rebel standard here at Glenfinnan after spending weeks quietly gathering support. The fight is now on to oust the Hanoverians from the British throne. "Bonnie Prince Charlie" (who is known to his highland followers as "Tearlach", pronounced "Charles") has been waiting aboard his ship in Loch nah Uagh since 25 July, but he is now ready to move.

Even though clan chiefs and their men have been steadily coming in to join Charles, government troops in Fort William have not been alerted. In fact, they are so completely ignorant of his presence that his men have been able to buy supplies from the fort. Having arrived with just a handful of men – a ship carrying 700 rebels was turned back to France by a British warship – Charles has now assembled an army of many hundreds (→4/9).

Highlanders send royal army packing

Lothian, 21 September 1745
The government's forces have been routed in their first encounter with Prince Charles's highland army, and their commander, General Sir John Cope, has been forced to flee. The "battle" at Prestonpans – some are calling it more a scuffle – was decided in just four minutes when the highlanders charged and Cope's men took to their heels.

There followed several minutes more in which government troops who had not escaped were either killed or captured. Prince Charles took little part in the fighting but ran across the battlefield afterwards begging his men to spare lives. About 300 government troops are dead and 1,500 captured; the highlanders' losses are negligible. Cope attributes his rout to the speed of the Scots attack and the rawness of his troops – yet the prince's men are just as raw (→18/11).

"Bonnie Prince Charlie" lands in Scotland for the first time, at Eriskay.

"The Young Pretender" is warmly welcomed on his arrival in Edinburgh.

The highlanders' deadly broadswords strike terror into the English troops.

Carlisle surrenders to Jacobite forces

Carlisle, 18 November 1745
"Bonnie Prince Charlie", who invaded England ten days ago, has captured Carlisle. It was not much of a victory, as the city was defended by only a few ageing militiamen, who locked themselves up in the dilapidated castle. Yet it has gone a long way towards showing up certain tensions that exist within the Scots army, whose strength is now put at about 5,000.

The prince wanted to besiege the castle and ordered trenches to be dug. As a result, 10 per cent of his army deserted because the highland troops thought trench-digging beneath their dignity. The siege turned out to be unnecessary in any case, since the militiamen inside were just waiting to surrender. Charles blundered again by sending the Roman Catholic duke of Perth to negotiate, causing his army commander, Lord George Murray, to resign. When Murray was reinstated, the duke resigned (→6/12).

Jacobite rebels are forced to turn back

Derby, 6 December 1745
The rebel Jacobite army has begun to retreat. Prince Charles had hoped to find widespread support in England, but apart from 200 volunteers from Manchester he has not drawn a following. The country people do all they can to hinder him by destroying bridges and withholding supplies.

The decision to retreat was taken at an acrimonious breakfast meeting in Derby yesterday, during which Charles, who wants to march on London, accused his generals of betrayal. But the generals know that, to escape alive, they must get back to Scotland. At present their army numbers about 5,500; London is defended by some 4,000 soldiers and large numbers of volunteers. General Wade is heading a force of 6,000 men, and William, the duke of Cumberland, is to provide about 13,000 (→20).

Culloden slaughter puts an end to Jacobite dream

Cumberland's men smash rebel army

Scotland, 16 April 1746
The flower of the highlands has been laid low, and the great Jacobite dream of taking power is over. In 40 minutes of fighting on Culloden moor, near Inverness, the vastly superior army of Prince William, the duke of Cumberland, has cut to ribbons the half-starved clansmen of Tearlach MacSheumais – or Charles, the son of James Stuart. Prince Charles, who was reported to have been drinking before the battle, took no part in it.

He was taken away when cannon fire began, but this time even his closest supporters had had enough. As he left, the chief of his bodyguard, Lord Elcho, cursed him for a "damned Italian coward!". With the prince gone there was no one to give orders, and the clansmen had to withstand a 20-minute bombardment before they attacked. They advanced, said a government soldier, "like wildcats", tearing and slicing at the ranks. But the highland army, reduced to some 2,000, was outnumbered nine to one, and the slaughter was fearful. Above the noise of battle the chief of the MacDonalds of Keppoch could be heard yelling in Gaelic: "Has it come to this, that the children of my clan have forsaken me!" In fact most had perished – as have two thirds of the prince's army (→ 23/8).

The defeat at Culloden may break the power of the highland clans forever and bring an end to Jacobite hopes.

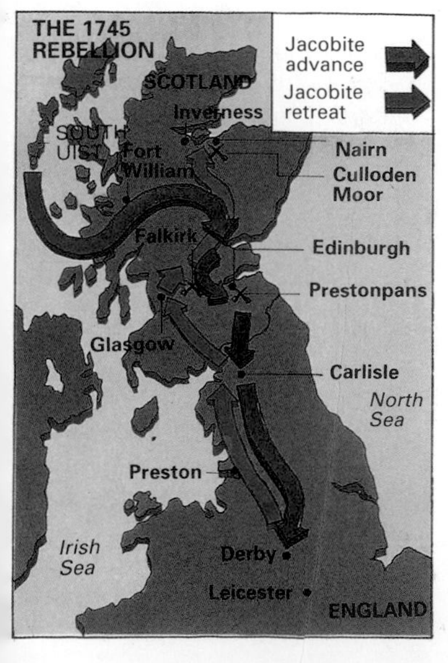

Highland rebels executed by royal troops

Crowds watch rebel Jacobite lords beheaded on Tower Hill in London.

Scotland, 23 August 1746
William, the duke of Cumberland, has been replaced as commander-in-chief in Scotland by the earl of Albemarle. Cumberland, the obese second son of King George II, has won the nickname of "Butcher" for his ferocious reprisals against the highlanders. As early as February, while pursuing the retreating Jacobites, Cumberland's men were busy ravaging the estates of known rebels and their sympathizers.

Since Culloden, when Cumberland ordered no quarter to be given and hundreds of clansmen were massacred, systematic destruction of whole communities has begun. Homes have been looted and burnt, livestock driven away and rebels transported to the West Indies or simply strung up. Certain rebel noblemen are to suffer the fate of Lord Balmerino and the earl of Kilmarnock, who were executed five days ago in London.

The government forces are extremely zealous. Captain John Fergussone, for instance, has ravaged Eigg, burned houses throughout Arisaig and Morar – and captured the elderly Lord Lovat (→ 20/9).

Pretender flees to France in disguise

Highland, 20 September 1746
After months of hardship, hiding and marching through the highlands, "Bonnie Prince Charlie" has escaped to France on board a French ship. Whatever else can be said of the prince – and little of it is flattering – the physical stamina and toughness which he has displayed during five months on the run have been truly astonishing.

After fleeing the defeat at Culloden he crisscrossed Scotland and the Outer Hebrides. Sleeping rough and traversing mountains, glens and sea in all weathers, he covered hundreds of miles on foot and sometimes avoided capture only by minutes. Despite the £30,000 on his head, the poverty of the highlanders and government reprisals, no one has betrayed him.

On South Uist Charles was disguised as a sewing maid by a local woman, Flora MacDonald. When she objected to his hiding a pistol under his skirts, he quipped: "If they search that far up, they'll know I'm no spinning-maid." His health has declined: he has suffered dysentery and scurvy, added to which he has been drinking a bottle of brandy a day. Today's rescue from Loch nah Uagh, west of Fort William on the shores of Moidart, comes just in time (→ 9/4/47).

1747 - 1749

Bay of Biscay, 3 May 1747. Admiral George Anson defeats the French off Cape Finisterre in the war over the Austrian succession (→ 14/10).

London, May 1747. Antonio Canale, the Italian artist known as "Il Canaletto", exhibits paintings of London.

Ireland, 13 September 1747. William Stanhope, the earl of Harrington, is sworn in as lord lieutenant.

Bay of Biscay, 14 October 1747. Admiral Sir Edward Hawke defeats a French convoy in a second battle off Cape Finisterre (→ 18/10/48).

Canterbury, 1747. Thomas Herring, the bishop of York, succeeds John Potter as archbishop.

Scotland, 25 March 1748. The Heritable Jurisdictions Act abolishes the hereditary right of many noblemen to judge legal disputes, a last vestige of feudalism here.

Britain, 13 April 1748. Uniforms are introduced for naval officers.

France, 18 October 1748. The Treaty of Aix-la-Chapelle ends the war over the Austrian succession; the French retreat from the Low Countries but regain Louisbourg, the gateway to North America (→ 27/4/49).

Bath, 1748. John Wesley founds Kingswood school.

Dublin, 1748. Walter Harris publishes *Hibernica*, a collection of rare tracts and documents relating to Irish history.

London, 1748. London Bridge is completed.

Scotland, 1748. William Adam, the architect of Edinburgh's Royal Infirmary, dies.

Dublin, 16 October 1749. Parliament declares Charles Lucas, who published *Censor*, an enemy to his country.

London, 1749. Henry Fielding founds the "Bow Street Runners" (→ 18/2).

London, 1749. Dr William Smellie opens the first lying-in hospital for pregnant women (→ 1751).

Scotland, 1749. A stage-coach service between Edinburgh and Glasgow opens; the trip takes 12 hours each way.

Aberdeen, 1749. The first bank outside Edinburgh, the Aberdeen banking company, is founded.

Rebel leader Lord Lovat is executed

London, 9 April 1747
Simon, Lord Lovat, the chief of Clan Fraser, was led onto the scaffold at Tower Hill today and beheaded for his part in last year's highland uprising. The 80-year-old Jacobite who brought his clan into action at the last moment – on the promise by Charles Stuart of a dukedom – kept his wry sense of humour even in the shadow of the axe. So huge was the crowd at the Tower that a stand collapsed as Lovat was being brought to the place of execution, killing several spectators. "The more the mischief, the better the sport," the old warrior said (→ 15/5/52).

Lord Lovat, painted by Hogarth.

London opens war on Scottish culture

Scotland, 17 April 1747
A sullen silence has descended on the glens. By order of parliament in the distant south, even bagpipes are banned as "instruments of war". In an attempt to destroy the clan system, severe penalties have been imposed for carrying or possessing weapons, and for wearing the kilt, plaid or any tartan garment. The patriarchal role of the clan chiefs is diminishing daily. Meanwhile, the kirk is being encouraged to expand into the highlands in order to "civilize" the people there.

Disaster hits celebratory firework display

Another firework display is held in May to celebrate the end of the war.

London, 27 April 1749
Fireworks had been ordered – but neither King George II nor several thousand of his loyal citizens expected quite such a spectacle as the one that laid waste to Green Park tonight. Three spectators lie dead; hundreds are nursing burns and other injuries; George is furious; and few can recall the *Music for the Royal Fireworks* written for the occasion by George Frederick Handel, the king's favourite composer.

A great firework display was commissioned to mark last year's Treaty of Aix-la-Chapelle, which ended the war over the Austrian succession. An elaborate rococo temple of peace, complete with built-in fireworks and cannons, was erected in the centre of the park, and all looked set for a great show – until a rocket misfired and prematurely ignited the other 10,650 rockets housed in the temple. As 100 musicians fled from the blaze, the comptroller of the royal fireworks exchanged blows with the temple's Italian architect, while a drunken cobbler threw himself into the pond, and a burning girl was stripped to her stays.

Surgeons practise their skill on real bodies

London, 1748
Hundreds of eager medical students are queuing daily at a house in London's Windmill Street to attend lectures and watch dissections by a Scots surgeon, William Hunter, whose advertised course offers every student a chance to dissect a corpse. How the bodies are obtained remains mysterious – the legal number of hanged murderers' bodies alloted to the Company of Surgeons is only four a year.

Hunter's younger brother, John, is proving to be an equally gifted surgeon whose anatomical work involves a comparative study of how animals' bodies function.

It is two years since the government recognized the difference between the dubious skills of barbers (who are allowed to shave people and pull teeth) and trained surgeons, who are making rapid advances in medical practice, thanks in particular to the knowledge gained by the great anatomist John Munro and his son in Edinburgh.

Hogarth sees dissection as cruel.

Novel style of writing achieves wide popularity

Fielding's comic epic, 'The History of Tom Jones', causes a stir

London, 18 February 1749
The publication of Henry Fielding's *The History of Tom Jones* has provoked a great stir, with many people complaining that its events and its hero's rumbustious life offend both morals and propriety. Others prefer it to Samuel Richardson's *Clarissa* [*see report below*] because it does not moralize but paints life in the raw.

Fielding was well known as a writer of stage satires and burlesques until the Theatre Licensing Act, brought in by Walpole in 1737 as a response to them, put paid to his career as a dramatist. He was then called to the bar and is now a justice of the peace for Middlesex and Westminster as well as chairman of the quarter sessions.

Fielding's first novels were satires on Richardson's *Pamela*, published over 1740/41. After a spoof called *Shamela* (1741) he wrote *Joseph Andrews* (1742), whose hero is Pamela's brother, a virtuous footman who repulses the advances of Lady Booby, just as Pamela did those of Mr B, her nephew. But Tom Jones is quite unlike these unbelievable paragons. He attains his heart's desire – Sophia, the daughter of Squire Western – via the arms of many another. For him, "life was a constant struggle between honour and inclination". The fact that Tom Jones wins his Sophia despite his faults outrages many readers. Sophia is based on Fielding's own wife, who died five years ago; he has since married her maid. His wide knowledge of low life as seen from the bench enables him to fill his novel with a gallery of rascals of all classes (→1750).

A scene from the bawdy doings of "Tom Jones", which has become a hit.

Richardson writes a classic history of a young lady, 'Clarissa'

London, 1748
The seventh, and final, volume of *Clarissa* is out. The eponymous heroine, whose tragic death is now revealed, is first punished for not marrying the man whom her family have chosen for her. Then a handsome rake, Lovelace, entices Clarissa to come to London, where he installs her in a brothel. Eventually he drugs and rapes her – an experience that kills her. The author, 59-year-old Samuel Richardson, seeks to portray a spiritual integrity that refuses to be corrupted.

Richardson, who is a successful printer, turned novelist at the age of 50 when he began *Pamela, or Virtue Rewarded* [*see report on page 688*]. Inspired by its huge success, particularly among women readers, he went on to produce this million-word epic. As in *Pamela*, he narrates the novel not in the third person but in letters of huge length supposedly written by the characters themselves. "All the letters are written while the hearts of the writers must be supposed to be wholly engaged," he says. "Much more lively and affecting must be the style of those who write in the height of a present distress, tortured by pangs of uncertainty, than the dry, unanimated style of a person relating dangers surmounted can be." Translations are bringing the novel to readers in Europe such as the French novelist and philosopher Denis Diderot (→1761).

Pamela, the heroine of Richardson's first novel, with her children.

Smollett's hero is Roderick Random

London, 1748
A new name to challenge those of Fielding and Richardson as authors of the novel is that of Tobias Smollett, a Scotsman who began life in the navy as a surgeon's mate at the age of 20. He then set up as a surgeon in London and now, aged 27, has published *Roderick Random*, which Fielding has attacked in the *Covent Garden Journal*. It is modelled on *Gil Blas* the famous French novel of a wandering hero's comical adventures, by Alain Lesage.

Like Smollett himself, Roderick Random is a Scottish doctor who enters the navy after being press-ganged and sails on an expedition to Cartagena in Spain. He is shipwrecked, takes service as a footman, falls in love, is kidnapped, imprisoned for debt, rescued by his uncle Tom Bowling and discovers his own father, disguised as a rich Spanish grandee. "Picaresque" misadventures of a comic hero (like Gil Blas or Don Quixote) are the rage, with a whole gallery of rich characters. Smollett creates caricatures in words similar to those created in drawings by William Hogarth. He aims at "that generous indignation which ought to animate the reader against the sordid and vicious disposition of the world" (→1751).

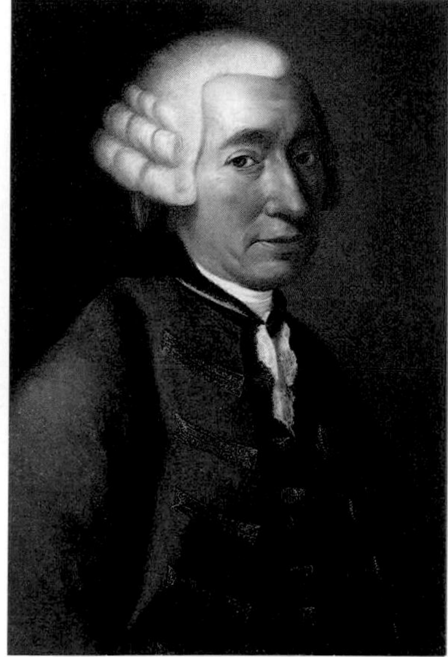
Tobias Smollett, painted later in life.

1750 - 1751

London, 17 November 1750. Westminster Bridge is opened.

Derby, 1750. Porcelain is being manufactured at St Mary's Bridge.

Margate, Kent, 1750. Benjamin Beale invents a bathing machine on wheels; it can be pulled in and out of the sea, providing privacy. Less elaborate machines have been popular at Scarborough, Brighton and other seaside resorts over the past 15 years.

Britain, 1750. Dr Richard Russell publishes *A dissertation on the use of sea water in the diseases of the glands*, promoting the new craze for seabathing and taking spa waters for health.

London, 1750. Peter Dollond, an optical specialist, opens a workshop near the Strand.

London, 1750. Samuel Whitbread founds a brewery in Chiswell Street.

London, 1750. St Luke's lunatic asylum opens.

Kent, 1750. Work begins on a new harbour at Ramsgate.

Rome, January 1751. Now that the secular British rulers are taking a more lenient line towards Irish Catholic clergy, the papal authorities issue regulations to make sure that they are orthodox.

Britain, 1 July 1751. A royal warrant requires that regiments be numbered instead of named after colonels.

Ireland, 19 September 1751. Lionel Cranfield Sackville, the duke of Dorset, is sworn in as lord lieutenant.

Bath, 1751. A new playhouse opens.

Westminster, 1751. After the death of the prince of Wales a Regency Act is passed; in the event of King George II's death, Augusta, the princess dowager of Wales, will be regent until her 13-year-old son George comes of age.

Britain, 1751. Tobias Smollett publishes his second novel, *The Adventures of Peregrine Pickle* (→ 1767).

London, 1751. John Stuart, the earl of Bute, a former lord of the bedchamber, is appointed "groom of the stole" to George, the new prince of Wales (→ 27/10/60).

London, 1751. Welsh gentry and clergy living here found the Cymmrodorion Society to promote the Welsh language and culture.

Earthquake warnings terrify Londoners

London, 7 April 1750

Thousands fled from London yesterday after a warning that the city was about to be devastated by a powerful earthquake – but they returned sheepishly today to find the city intact.

London has indeed been hit by earthquake tremors this year – on 8 February and again on 8 March. Following the second tremor a soldier gave a warning about the catastrophe that was supposed to take place yesterday. People's fears were then heightened by Thomas Sherlock, the bishop of London, who rushed out a pamphlet called *A letter from the Lord Bishop ... on occasion of the late earthquakes*, warning of God's wrath if Londoners did not heed the message.

London vice: targeted by bishop.

Sherlock listed several vices that, he says, have so angered God that he wants to pulverize London, but chose homosexuality as that which most angered the deity, describing it as "the unnatural lewdness, of which we have heard so much of late", as well as threatening divine vengeance "and the destruction of *Sodom* by fire from heaven".

The bishop's tract sold 10,000 copies, but returning Londoners are being greeted with a pamphlet ironically describing the "dreadful and melancholy earthquake" that did not take place. The soldier is now an inmate of a lunatic asylum.

Force of 'thief-takers' is set up in London

Convicted men and women are led off, chained by the neck and the hands.

London, 1750

The imaginative Bow Street magistrate Henry Fielding has adopted an innovative system of enforcing the law in this city, where crime continues to increase. Fielding, who is also a popular novelist, has created a force of "thief-takers", who are proving to be more successful – perhaps on account of their intimate and dubious criminal associations – than ill-paid, incompetent parish constables. London today is a dangerous city, as Fielding's fellow writer Horace Walpole – who was held up and robbed by highwaymen in Hyde Park only last year – has lamented: "One is forced to travel, even at noon, as if one is going to battle."

Despite the death penalty – which applies even to the theft from a house of goods worth more than 40 shillings and countless other minor offences – crime continues to increase, according to Fielding. Fifty-six people have been hanged in London alone this year (→ 1754).

'Bluestocking' club for learned women

Newbury, Berkshire, 1750

There is nothing quite like the wit and wisdom heard in Mrs Elizabeth Montagu's salon at Greenham Priory. What makes conversation here so unusual is that it is almost exclusively between women of the middle classes, many of them – daughters of lawyers, doctors and prosperous merchants – with scholarly interests.

One man who attends these literary parties is Benjamin Stillingfleet, whose habit of wearing blue worsted stockings has given these ladies the somewhat disparaging title of "bluestockings".

Doctor publishes essay on midwifery

London, 1751

Unlike his fashionable societ, colleagues, Dr William Smellie is said to be "uncouth, rough-mannered, with hands big enough to stretch boots" – and yet this Scots-born doctor is making remarkable advances in the practice of midwifery.

Smellie teaches midwifery partly by attendance on poor women in their own homes and also by demonstrations on a dummy of his own making at his Gerrard Street practice. Although Smellie bases much of his technique on nature, his leather-covered metal forceps have been used with great success in difficult confinements. So, too, has his technique of reviving babies by inflating the lungs by means of a silver catheter (→ 1752).

Iron Act is passed

Westminster, 1750

Worried by trading problems with Sweden – the source of much of Britain's iron ore – parliament has passed the Iron Act, which is meant to encourage imports from other sources, principally the Americas. The act allows the import of iron from the colonies there duty free, under certain conditions. Britain's ironmasters have insisted, however, on clauses that ban the building of new steel furnaces and finishing mills in the colonies (→ 1759).

Churchyard inspires Gray to write elegy

London, 1751
The *Elegy Written in a Country Churchyard*, a poem published this year by Thomas Gray, is being admired for its felicitous expression of otherwise conventional thoughts on life and death. Gray went to Eton and Cambridge before making the "grand tour" of Italy with his schoolfriend Horace Walpole; yet it was the village churchyard at Stoke Poges, in Buckinghamshire, that inspired him. There the "rude forefathers of the hamlet sleep", their humble and obscure lives over; "Far from the madding crowd's ignoble strife,/Their sober wishes never learn'd to stray." Rather than scorning such folk, those who account themselves great should recall that "The paths of glory lead but to the grave."

A meditative setting for the poem.

Frederick, the prince of Wales and heir to the throne, dies suddenly, aged only 44

Prince Frederick, here stag-hunting, was himself the prey of politicians.

London, 20 March 1751
He was a rake and a womanizer in the true Hanoverian mode, and he delighted in intrigue against his hated father, King George II, and Sir Robert Walpole's government. Yet Frederick, the prince of Wales, who died today aged 44, was far more popular with the British people than the 69-year-old king.

Frederick contracted a chill in his gardens at Kew, but it was a burst abdominal ulcer – which had been growing since he was hit by a tennis ball three years ago – that killed him. His 12-year-old son, George William Frederick, becomes the heir to the throne. From the moment that Frederick arrived in England from Hanover at the age of 20, his parents made it clear that they had no love for him and that there was no place for him in government. There were frequent and bellicose family rows, mostly involving Frederick's allowance, and the prince and his wife were banished to Kew Palace in 1737 following the birth of their first child.

It was inevitable that "poor Fred" should become the centre of opposition politics. Indeed his other home, Leicester House, in the west end of London, came to be seen almost as an alternative court by politicians, including the ambitious William Pitt, now a minister in the Whig government (→4/6/55).

Clive triumphs over the French in India

Arcot, India, 5 November 1751
Eight years ago Robert Clive, then a clerk in the East India company, twice tried to shoot himself, and twice failed because the pistol misfired. That made him decide "I am destined for something. I will live." He lived – and destiny reached out to him today. In the continuing struggle between French and British trading interests here, Clive – now a lieutenant in the East India company's army – has defeated a superior French force trying to relieve Arcot, a town which he seized from them on 12 September. The capital of the Carnatic in the south-east of India, Arcot is strategically vital to both sides. By today's action Clive, who is 26, and his British and Indian troops have survived a 53-day French siege (→7/1752).

Robert Clive, by Gainsborough.

From 1741 to 1751 Lancelot "Capability" Brown was head gardener at Stowe House, Buckinghamshire, the grounds of which are shown here.

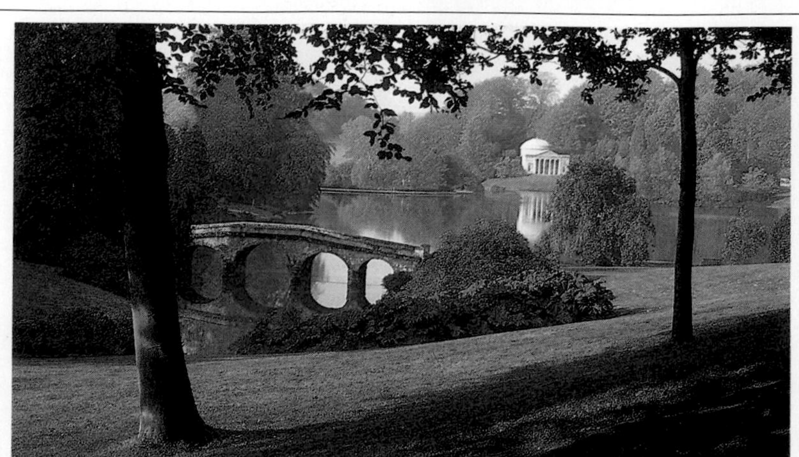
A picturesque Greek temple by an artificial lake adorns the gardens of Stourhead, Wiltshire, planned from 1744 onwards by Henry Hoare.

Extravagant styles stimulated by foreign contacts

Opulent new styles in fashion and interiors are emerging as prosperous Britons enjoy a growing sense of security and, encouraged by the popularity of the European "grand tour", exploit a wide range of influences from the outside world. Many rich young men favour the most extreme Italian and French styles, including glittering gold and silver buttons, elaborate buckles and ruffles, embroidered waistcoats open to reveal fine linen shirts, and flamboyantly cocked hats. A huge variety of wigs pass in and out of vogue. Women, meanwhile, are wearing tall and extravagantly decorated head-dresses, and many still sport enormous hoop petticoats of the type introduced some 40 years ago. The expansion of foreign trade, and cheaper imports, has affected social interests and behaviour, giving a particular boost to the new preoccupation with tea-drinking.

The Italian-inspired classical revival in architecture and interiors, which was spearheaded in the early part of the century by Richard Boyle, the earl of Burlington, is gradually giving way to light-hearted rococo decorative forms. The new name in furniture is Thomas Chippendale, who prefers to work in mahogany rather than the more common walnut or pine; his elegantly curved designs contrast with the heavy, rich, baroque style favoured by his predecessor William Kent. In another move away from classicism, the writer and member of parliament Horace Walpole has recently purchased a small coachman's cottage at Twickenham, in Middlesex, which he has begun to transform into an architectural masterpiece in the "gothic" tradition. It is to be renamed Strawberry Hill.

The magnificent clothing of this family group is the mark of their wealth.

A lady in a fashionable hat.

A boy-gentleman in his dress coat.

A sumptuously dressed young girl.

A stylish man poses, without wig.

A decorative silver coffee pot.

Silverware and china adorn the table at which an elegant family takes tea.

A tea kettle in high rococo style.

Rococo and 'gothic' compete with classical revival

An ornate rococo gilt mirror.

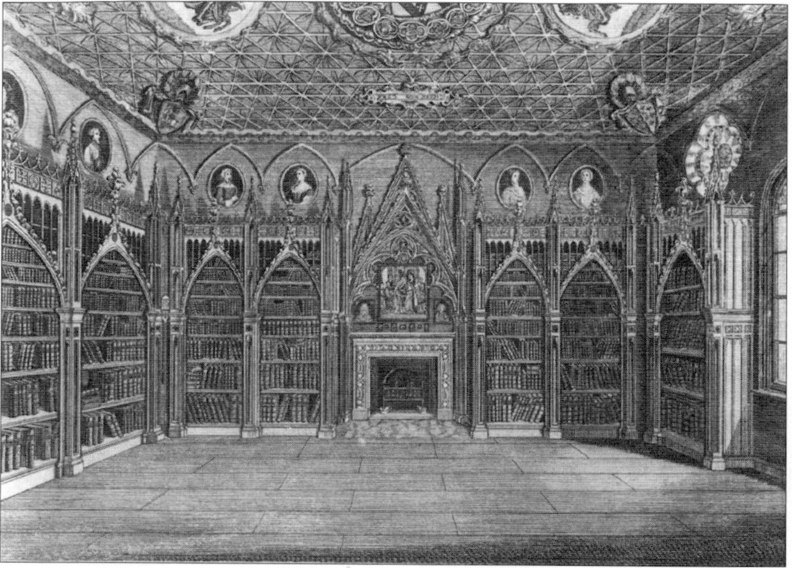
The "gothic" library of the writer Horace Walpole at Strawberry Hill.

Stedcombe Manor fireplace, Devon.

Robert Adam and Thomas Chippendale built this marble-topped table.

Chippendale mahogany chairs with interlaced backs and chamfered legs.

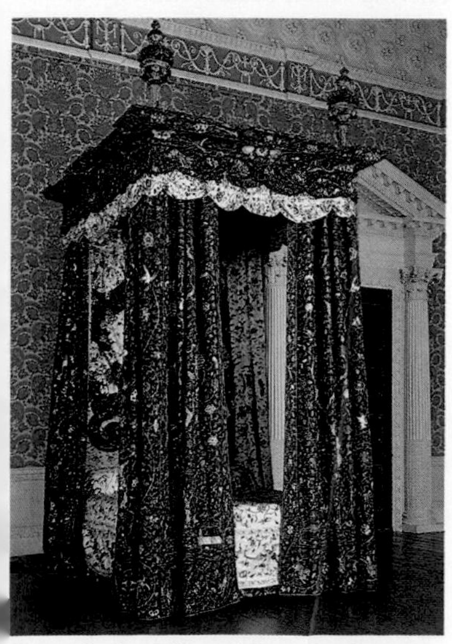
State bed: Calke Abbey, Derbys.

A punchbowl for gentlemen of the turf given as a racing trophy in Ireland.

Two exquisite glass goblets.

1752 - 1754

Dublin, July 1752. The first Methodist chapel here opens (→1753).

Scotland, 7 November 1752. Despite his protests of innocence, James Stewart of the Glen is hanged in Appin for the murder last May of Colin Campbell of Glenmure (→2/10/60).

London, 1752. St George's hospital is founded.

Britain, 1752. Dr William Smellie publishes his *Treatise on Midwifery* (→1760).

Liverpool, 1752. The Seaman's hospital is founded.

Westminster, 1752. The Murder Act allows a convict's corpse to be hung in chains or handed over to a surgeon for anatomical use.

Manchester, 1752. The Royal Infirmary is founded.

London, April 1753. Parliament pays £20,000 for the private library of Sir Hans Sloane.

Dublin, April 1753. St Nicholas's hospital opens.

Dublin, 22 December 1753. Parliament gives permission for the river Lagan to be made navigable and for a passage by water to be built between Lough Neagh and Belfast.

Britain, 1753. John Wesley issues *Twelve Rules of a Helper*, intended for Methodist lay preachers (→1760).

Dublin, 1753. Charles O'Conor publishes his *Dissertations on the ancient history of Ireland*, reflecting new interest in Irish Celtic antiquities (→6/1755).

Liverpool, 1753. Molly Bushell makes toffee commercially at her cottage in Everton.

Liverpool, 1753. The Salthouse docks are built.

Westminster, 1753. The Commons reject a bill for a national census as an "attack on liberty".

Britain, 1754. Henry Fielding, the novelist, dies.

Edinburgh, 1754. Allan Ramsay, the portraitist, founds the Select Society, which includes leading intellectuals such as David Hume.

Fife, 1754. The Golfing Society is founded at St Andrews.

London, 1754. Thomas Chippendale, the cabinet maker, publishes *The Gentleman and the Cabinet Maker's Directory*, a portfolio of his work available for sale.

British New Year to start on 1 January

Britain, 14 September 1752
Yesterday was 2 September, but today is not 3 September. Despite popular protest, Britain is falling into line with the rest of Europe and adapting to the Gregorian rather than the Julian calendar. The change is a relief for diplomats such as Lord Chesterfield, who was chiefly responsible for the decision, made in May last year. Now, when he flits between London and Paris, the dates match. The benefits are less clear to people who must recalculate rents, leases, debts and wages, as well as adjusting to new saints' days. Hence the popular cry: "Give us back our 11 days!"

The Julian calendar, devised by Julius Caesar, applied throughout Europe until the 16th century but has gradually moved out of phase with the solar year. Pope Gregory XIII introduced ten extra days in 1582, but Protestant countries were slow to respond. A leap year has since widened the gap by another day. The new year, which used to start on 25 March, will now begin on 1 January.

All married couples to register by law

Celebrations for a wedding of the type that the new law is designed to prevent.

Britain, June 1753
Hardwicke's Marriage Act, named after the lord chancellor who has framed it, forbids marriage under 21 without parental consent, and requires a church ceremony, with the publishing of banns, recorded in a parish register. The new act, from which only Jews and Quakers are exempted, derives largely from the desire of aristocratic families to control their children's choice of spouses. It should prevent secret marriages, occasionally involving prostitutes or confidence tricksters, ratified by crooked clergymen.

The act was opposed by some members of parliament, such as Henry Fox, who himself secretly married the eldest daughter of the duke of Richmond. Fox says that it will enable parents to impose loveless marriages on their children, entrench an oligarchy in ownership of property and discourage the poor from marrying.

Scots commissioner shot in eviction feud

Highland, 15 May 1752
Colin Campbell of Glenmure, who was a commissioner in charge of confiscating the forfeited estates of Jacobite rebels, has been shot dead near Ballachulish, in the Appin district. His assailant, who escaped, is thought to be one of the Stewarts of Ardsheil, whose estates Campbell had been supposed to administer. Today's murder took place as the victim was on his way to carry out evictions of suspected supporters of the Jacobite cause.

The Vesting Act of 1747 entitled the crown to manage and receive income from the estates formerly held by rebel families. This year's Annexing Act provided for rents from 14 specified estates, including the large domains of Lovat, Keppoch, Cromarty, and Lochiel, to be used to promote the Protestant faith, good government, industry, and loyalty to King George II.

The 28 commissioners, most of them Scots, have already tried to improve industrial conditions in the lowlands. Their task looks harder here, where tenants remain loyal to their exiled chiefs to the point of voluntarily sending them rent. Paying rent again, to the agents of the crown, would be insupportable for many of them (→7/11).

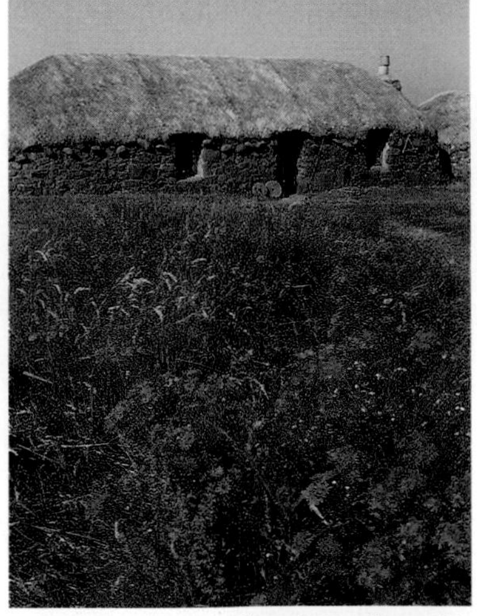

Jacobite tenants of crofts such as this one are facing the threat of eviction.

Clive forces French to flee Trichinopoly

Southern India, July 1752
French forces have been driven out of the Carnatic, a region in southeast India, by Anglo-Indian troops led by Lieutenant Robert Clive. Having taken the capital city of Arcot last year, Clive has now expelled the French from Trichinopoly, another important town in the Carnatic [*see report on page 701*]. Mohammed Ali, an ally of the English, will be restored as governor of the region, a position from which he had been ousted by the French.

Since the collapse of the 1748 Treaty of Aix-la-Chapelle, France and England have been at war, with their respective East India companies staging the conflict. The French governor, Joseph Dupleix, had won control of the entire Deccan plain until the arrival of Clive. This young adventurer has found the excitement he craved when, five years ago, he enlisted in the East India company's tiny army (→21/6/56).

Newcastle forms new government after the sudden death of his cautious brother

Westminster, 31 March 1754
Thomas Pelham-Holles, the duke of Newcastle and secretary of state for the north for the past six years, has been made prime minister. His elevation follows the sudden death, on 6 March, of his brother, Henry Pelham, who had held the position since August 1743. Henry Fox remains as secretary-at-war and William Pitt paymaster of the forces.

Henry Pelham broadly followed the policies of Robert Walpole: fiscal restraint and a cautious approach to foreign policy. He also avoided controversial legislation and left alone the Church of England – whose upper echelons are solidly pro-Whig. Pelham benefited from the relatively peaceful situation that has existed in Europe since the war over the Austrian succession ended in 1748. But King George II is convinced that the future will be less settled. He received the news of Pelham's death with the comment: "Now I shall have no more peace" (→11/1756).

Henry Pelham, who died aged 59.

Franklin calls for union of British colonies

New York, 10 July 1754
Benjamin Franklin, the scientist and statesman, has a plan to unite the American colonies which seems to have won the support of both the native Indian tribes and the white settlers. The government of the union will consist of a general council drawn from colonial assemblies, with a president appointed by the crown. The government will regulate Indian trade, buy Indian land, build forts and raise troops.

The idea of a union came from the British government, which offered many gifts and promises to the Indians. But the Iroquois chiefs have become sceptical about the white man's intentions since the removal of William Johnson, a crown agent who spoke several Indian languages and a trusted ally of theirs. The new arrangements may not be universally accepted. Benjamin Franklin is the delegate from Pennsylvania and has recently been appointed postmaster general for the colonies. He has become famous for his view that slavery is poor economic policy. Yet he seems less enlightened where Indians are concerned, saying that they are wild by heritage and predilection and cannot be educated.

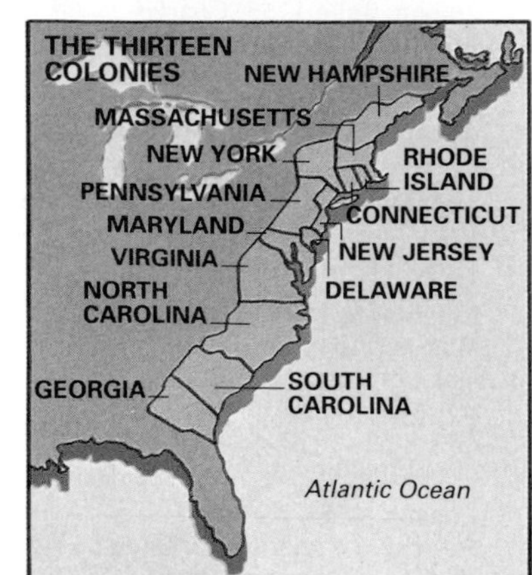

Move to naturalize Jews under threat

London, May 1753
A new act to give British citizenship to Jews may soon have to be repealed, such is the fury that it has caused. Jews from central and eastern Europe have been entering England since Cromwell's time, and now number about 5,000. A synagogue was built at Aldgate in 1722. But the mob comes down hard on not only Jews but all minorities, such as Methodists, Catholics, witches, homosexuals, Scots, Irish and French. And politicians respect the prejudices of the mob.

Weir destroyed by women in Taunton

Somerset, 25 June 1753
The so-called French Weir, close to the grist mills at Taunton, has been demolished by several hundred women to prevent any corn from being ground. The women are furious with the mill manager, whom they accuse of selling their flour elsewhere in the country, inflating local prices so that many people can no longer afford bread. The women want the corn to be sold locally or not produced at all. Their drastic action is typical of popular protest against rising food prices.

John Kay, the inventor of the flying shuttle, fled to France in 1753 when an angry mob stormed his house; his invention has enabled hand weavers to double their output but raises fears of mass unemployment.

Statesman wins medal for scientific work

In this parlour game iron rods are rubbed to produce small electric charges.

London, 30 November 1753
The Royal Society has bestowed its highest award, the Copley Medal, on the scientist Benjamin Franklin. Franklin, who is from the American colonies, caused particular excitement last year with a series of experiments with lightning conductors. He was the first scientist to consider lightning as an electrical phenomenon, and the earl of Macclesfield said today that Franklin had proved electricity to have "a most surprising share in the power of nature". Franklin studied the theories of Watson and the properties of the Leyden jar. He has explained the generation of positive and negative "charges" by seeing electricity as a single fluid with two contrary states. All matter contains electricity, he says, and electrical particles are mutually repellent, yet are attracted to other matter.

1755 - 1756

Dublin, June 1755. Charles O'Conor publishes *The Case of the Roman Catholics in Ireland*, arguing for the repeal of penal legislation.

North America, 8 September 1755. British forces defeat the French at Lake George (→ 30/11).

Edinburgh, 1755. Alexander Webster, the minister of the Tolbooth church, publishes his *Account of the Number of People in Scotland*, estimating the population at 1,265,380.

London, 1755. Rioting audiences wreck Drury Lane theatre for the third time in 12 years.

London, 1755. Figures released this year show that of 2,339 children received into London workhouses since 1750, only 168 remain alive.

Westminster, 16 January 1756. King George II and his nephew, Frederick of Prussia, sign a treaty to secure the neutrality of German states in the Anglo-French conflict (→ 17/5).

Ireland, April 1756. The shortage of corn and potatoes worsens (→ 1763).

Europe, 17 May 1756. Britain declares war on France.

Calcutta, 21 June 1756. An Indian force under Surajah Dowlah, the *nawab* [governor] of Bengal, yesterday took the East India company's garrison; of 146 British prisoners put in a tiny prison cell overnight only 23 have survived (→ 2/1/57).

Minorca, June 1756. Admiral John Byng fails to recapture the island from the French (→ 28/12).

Westminster, November 1756. William Cavendish, the duke of Devonshire, takes over from the duke of Newcastle, a fellow Whig, as prime minister (→ 29/6/57).

Edinburgh, 14 December 1756. A performance of *The Douglas*, a play by John Home, the minister of Athelstaneford, causes outrage. A "moderate", Home believes in the need to reconcile the church and the new "enlightened" ideas.

England, 28 December 1756. Admiral Byng is court-martialled for neglecting his duty during the attack on Minorca (→ 14/3/57).

Glasgow, 1756. Joseph Black, a Glasgow University chemist, discovers carbon dioxide.

Johnson finishes 'painful' dictionary of English language

London, 15 April 1755
Dr Samuel Johnson has published his magnum opus – a two-volume *Dictionary of the English Language*. Johnson describes the work rather bleakly as "a long and painful voyage around the world of the English language". It has taken him seven years to amass the 41,000 entries, even with the assistance of six clerks. According to one visitor, his Gough Square attic was "decked out like a counting house". Halfway through the work Johnson's wife, Tetty, died of drink and opium. At times he was so poor that he feared the milkman would arrest him for debt. Yet, considering that the new French dictionary took 40 academicians 40 years, Johnson's is a stupendous achievement. He is perhaps the most prolific writer in London, the author of half of every issue of *The Gentleman's Magazine*. Ten weeks ago he handed the final pages of the dictionary to his printer, Andrew Millar, who simply said: "Thank God I have done with him."

Johnson: "a harmless drudge".

Some definitions, such as "a hateful tax" for *excise* and "a faction" for *Whig* will annoy certain readers. But Johnson's humility makes wounding criticism hard to deliver. Asked by a lady why he had called a *pastern* the knee (instead of the foot) of a horse, he retorted: "Ignorance, madam, pure ignorance." A *lexicographer*, meanwhile, is "a harmless drudge" (→ 15/5/63).

Washington takes control of colonial army

A satirical view of the current Anglo-French struggle in North America.

North America, 13 July 1755
A 1,500-strong British column has been routed on its way to attack the French garrison at Fort Duquesne, which guards the Ohio valley and was won by the French last year.

The troops were ambushed at the Monongahela river four days ago. They had little chance against a French and Indian force, which compensated for its lack of numbers by using guerrilla tactics. Ordered to stand and fight, one British soldier replied: "We would, if we could see anyone to fight with." About a thousand British troops were killed or wounded, including the column commander, Major-General Edward Braddock, who died of his wounds today.

It was only the action of 23-year-old Colonel George Washington, General Braddock's *aide-de-camp*, that prevented total disaster. Although he twice had a horse shot from under him, and received four bullet holes in his jacket, Washington took command of the survivors and supervised the withdrawal of the broken Virginians (→ 8/9).

British expel French colonists in America

Acadians are dragged protesting down to the shoreline by British soldiers.

Maryland, 30 November 1755
The first 900 of the expected 7,000 French settlers, expelled by the British from their homesteads on the Atlantic coast of North America, have arrived here by ship from Acadia – or Nova Scotia [New Scotland], as the British call it. Two earlier shiploads of expelled settlers drowned when their ships sank in a storm. The French colony of Acadia, stretching from Cape Breton Island to the lower Hudson river, was ceded to Britain in 1713 by the Treaty of Utrecht. For 42 years the French were tolerated, but with the onset of war between Britain and France that has changed (→ 5/1/57).

Evangelicals decry 'moderate' opinion

Edinburgh, 1755
Evangelicals and "moderates" in the Scottish church are again locked in dispute. The evangelical minister John Bonar has accused David Hume, the philosopher, of heresy for his *Analysis of the moral and religious sentiments ... in the writings of Sopho and David Hume Esq.* (Sopho is Hume's friend Lord Kames.) Bonar condemns Hume for calling religion "prejudicial to mankind". Hume, who regards the Scottish reformation as a new "dark age", is unperturbed; he has many allies among the moderates. Others are concerned that, if the evangelicals get their way, there is the danger of a "witch-hunt" against any person with "unorthodox" opinions.

Britain's future king comes of age

Bute: prince's political adviser.

London, 4 June 1755
Celebrations are under way at Leicester House, the residence of George, the prince of Wales. Today is his 17th birthday and the start of his legal majority, four years after the unexpected death of his father, Frederick. The young prince may not have a long wait to inherit the throne of Britain: King George II, his grandfather, is 72. The prince is heavily influenced by his tutor, John Stuart, the earl of Bute. Stuart opposes the king and has, with the prince's mother, Augusta, made Leicester House a centre for political opposition to him (→25/10/60).

Hospitals grow in number and scope as new methods transform treatment of patients and medicine is recognized as a science

Thomas Guy, satirized here as a miser, founded Guy's hospital.

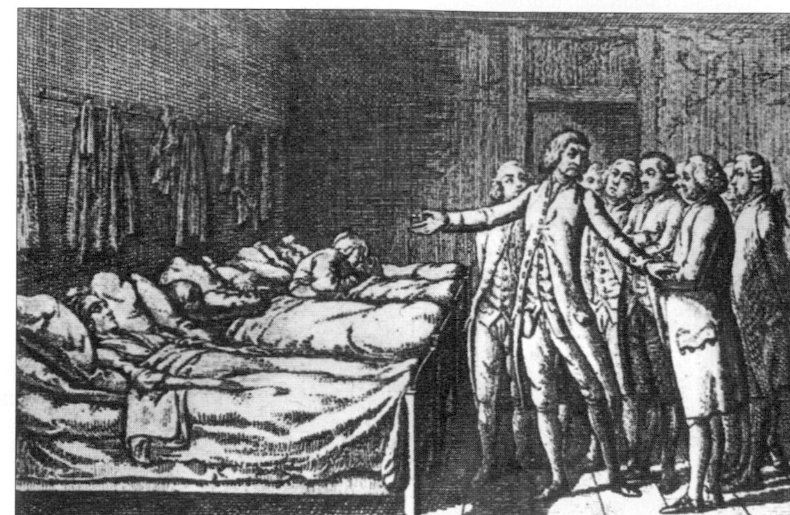
The sickroom of a typical hospital is generally crowded and dark, but at least the patients in it are being cared for, and the treatment is free.

Manchester, April 1755
With the completion this month of the first buildings of the Manchester Royal Infirmary, every major provincial city in Britain now has its own hospital. The Manchester block will be able to provide facilities for 40 patients, and there are plans to make substantial extensions to it.

Since 1720, 12 new hospitals, providing free treatment, have opened in London, Edinburgh, Bristol, Aberdeen, Winchester, York, Liverpool and Exeter. Five are in London: Guy's, St George's, the Westminster, the Middlesex and the London. Not all hospitals are for the physically ill. There are homes for the insane, such as London's Bethlehem hospital in Moorfields, and a refuge for abandoned children at the Foundling hospital.

There has also been a revolution in medical practice. Dr William Smellie has established new techniques in midwifery; in 1743 Dr William Hunter, a fellow Scot, began his lectures on anatomy, while his brother, John, pioneered methods that are saving thousands of lives every year. In 1745 the Company of Surgeons was formed, and members of the profession ceased to be known as "barber-surgeons". Medicine and surgery, once seen as trades, have now been recognized as sciences.

St Mary's of Bethlehem hospital (alias Bedlam) in London's Moorfields; fashionable visitors can pay a penny admission to taunt the inmates.

When other treatments fail, the final option available is radical surgery.

Captain Thomas Coram, who built the Foundling hospital.

1757

India, 2 January. Lieutenant-Colonel Robert Clive and Admiral Watson recapture Calcutta (→ 23/6).

Scotland, 5 January. Simon Fraser, the son of the executed Lord Lovat, raises a regiment from his clan to fight the French in Canada (→ 8/7/58).

England, April. Matthew Hutton, the bishop of York, succeeds Thomas Herring, who died last month, as the archbishop of Canterbury.

London, 6 June. William Hogarth is appointed serjeant-painter to King George II. His father-in-law, James Thornhill, was a former holder of the same post (→ 1764).

Edinburgh, 4 July. A test case to determine the legality of slavery in Scotland is brought to a dramatic halt when the man at the centre of the row – a negro bought in Virginia and brought by his master to Scotland – dies before the matter can be resolved.

Germany, 26 July. Hanoverian troops under William, the duke of Cumberland, are crushingly defeated at Hastenbeck by the French (→ 30/9/57).

Ireland, 25 September. John Russell, the duke of Bedford, is sworn in as lord lieutenant.

Dublin, 8 December. Dr Bartholomew Mosse opens the Rotunda, a maternity hospital; the architect is Richard Castle.

Dublin. Garret Wesley founds the Dublin Academy of Music.

Liverpool. The Sankey Brook Navigation canal is completed, providing the means by which coal can be transported from the St Helens coalfield.

Liverpool. The city opens a library.

London. The *London Chronicle* newspaper publishes its first issue.

London. George II donates the royal collection of books and manuscripts to the British Museum (→ 1759).

London. Houses on London Bridge are demolished in order to allow more traffic to cross the Thames (→ 1760).

London. William Boyce is sworn in as "master of the king's musick".

London. Women are given basic midwifery training with the start of the Lying-in Charity for pregnant poor women.

Admiral is executed for neglect of duty

Byng lets fall a handkerchief as a signal for the firing squad to shoot.

Portsmouth, 14 March
After a good deal of shuffling and trimming by King George II and the politicians, Admiral John Byng was taken on board a ship at Portsmouth today and executed by a firing squad of marines.

Last year Byng was commanding a poorly equipped squadron when he was order to relieve the British garrison on the Mediterranean island of Minorca, then blockaded by the French. The vanguard of the British force was severely mauled, and the rear, under Byng, became disorganized and sailed back to Gibraltar. Brought to England and court-martialled, Byng was acquitted of cowardice and treachery but found guilty of neglect of duty.

William Pitt was among those who wanted Byng pardoned, and he urged the king to take account of the views of members of parliament as well as of the court martial's recommendation of mercy. But the king tartly reminded Pitt that in the past he had been lectured by politicians to listen to public opinion. What the public thinks is not in doubt: effigies of Byng are being burnt in towns throughout the land. It was believed that Byng had to die as an example to others.

Pitt and Newcastle form new government

London, 29 June
For almost a month Britain, locked in a land and sea war against France, has been virtually without a government. The interregnum, brought about by the resignation of the prime minister, the duke of Devonshire, ended today when William Pitt, the secretary of state for the south, agreed to form a ministry with Thomas Pelham-Holles, the duke of Newcastle, whom he had earlier judged to be incompetent in prosecuting the war. Although Newcastle will be prime minister it is Pitt who will be running the war and, no doubt, dominating the cabinet.

Pitt tried unsuccessfully to form a ministry himself last November. He then alienated King George II by opposing the execution of Admiral Byng [*see report above*]. In April the king curtly sacked Pitt, but only last month he was allowed to return to office. Whatever the king's personal feelings, the political reality is that the backing of the "great commoner", as Pitt is nicknamed, is necessary to ensure that any ministry will be able to hold together in a coherent form.

Pitt: back in the seat of power.

Philosopher muses on art and nature

London, 21 April
Edmund Burke, the Dublin-born son of a Protestant father and a Catholic mother, has published a new work, *A Philosophical Enquiry into the Sublime and Beautiful.* In it he emphasizes the awe that art and nature can inspire.

The notion of the sublime as something boundless and immeasurable, and infused with a divine fire, dates back to classical times, but for Burke the sublime inspires deep veneration, as in the contemplation of wild and rugged landscapes. Immensity and brooding darkness characterize the sublime. Burke distinguishes it from the beautiful, which is characterized by smallness and smoothness, producing in the observer a sense of peace and happiness.

Burke: philosophical enquirer.

Militia Act rioting

London, 1757
William Pitt's efforts to raise a militia by ballot for home defence, and to rid the country of its dependence on Hanoverian soldiers, have taken shape as the Militia Act. But as the act went through parliament and counties prepared to register men for training, traditional public hostility to the idea of a standing army has led to rioting. Pitt is appealing to the patriotism of the people by reminding them that the threat of a French invasion is a real one, and that it is better to defend onself than to rely on Hanoverians.

Clive wins at Plassey

Robert Clive receives the surrender of Bengali forces at Plassey.

Calcutta, 23 June
Robert Clive, a one-time clerk with the East India company, has scored a stunning victory over a Bengali army and French auxiliaries at Plassey, north of here. Today the company is master of the rich provinces of Bengal, Bihar and Orissa, and the *nawab* [governor] of Bengal, Surajah Dowlah, notorious for a massacre last year of British prisoners in the "black hole" of Calcutta, is to be executed.

Clive, now 31 years old, was only 18 when he arrived in India to work for the East India company. In 1747, four years later, he became an ensign and soon afterwards a lieutenant, fighting at Pondicherry and Devikota. In 1751 he succeeded in taking Arcot [*see report on page 701*], but two years later he returned to England, where from 1754 to 1755 he served as a Whig member of parliament. The following year he was back in India as a lieutenant-colonel and was subsequently made lieutenant-governor of Fort St David, near Pondicherry.

At Plassey, Clive's force of 3,200 men, a third of them British, faced a joint French and Bengali army of 50,000 foot and 18,000 horse. But Clive had bribed one of the nawab's relatives, Mir Jaffier, to keep his troops out of the battle. A cannonade from Clive's forces settled the issue. The *nawab* and his men fled in panic. Clive has rewarded Mir Jaffier by making him *nawab* of Bengal in place of Surajah Dowlah. The East India company is now the effective ruler of a population twice that of England (→ 1758).

CLIVE IN INDIA
Agra [British 1602]
BENGAL
Plassey [British 1757]
Ahmedabad [British 1612]
BIHAR
Chandernagore [French 1673]
Surat [British 1618]
Calcutta [British 1690]
Bombay [British 1661]
ORISSA
INDIA
Yanaon [French 1725]
Bhatkal [British 1638]
Madras [British 1639]
Mahé [French c.1725]
Pondicherry [French 1699]
Karikál [French 1738]
CEYLON [Dutch 1644]
Towns = European trading posts with date of acquisition

India at the time of Plassey.

Dowlah, the doomed "nawab".

George humiliated by Hanoverian treaty

London, 30 September
After July's crushing defeat at Hastenbeck of Prince William, the "butcher" duke of Cumberland at the hands of the French, King George II – as elector of Hanover – hoped to make a unilateral peace with France that would have kept his Hanoverian lands safe. This would have meant abandoning his nephew and ally, Frederick the Great of Prussia. But, as George wrote to his son, Cumberland, the main concern was "to extricate yourself, me, my brave army and my dearly beloved subjects out of the misery and slavery they groan under".

The French would have none of it. When Cumberland went into negotiations at Klosterzeven, north of Bremen, the final treaty, signed on 8 September, required his troops to be immobilized, those of his allies to be sent home to Hesse-Cassel and Brunswick, and Hanover itself to be opened to military occupation – and, no doubt, plunder. When George heard the news he wept for shame, cursing Cumberland as his "rascally son". After the duke arrived at court here he was rebuffed by the king who, without looking up from his card table, said: "Here is my son, who has ruined me and disgraced himself" (→ 8/1758).

Cumberland, the "rascally" duke.

Scottish economy enjoys new prosperity

Eighteenth-century Edinburgh: at the centre of a new economic boom.

Scotland, 1757
Fifty years after the union with England, Scotland is steadily growing more prosperous – largely as a result of a quiet revolution under way in agriculture. At the end of the last century bad climatic conditions plunged the economy into depression, causing extensive famine from which thousands died. Since then, however, agricultural improvements pioneered by such men as Sir John Cockburn of Ormiston and Sir John Clerk of Penicuik have born rich fruit.

In some areas, the traditional "run-rig" method of strip farming has been abolished and replaced by consolidated farms held by tenants on long leases. Tenants have been obliged to carry out improvements such as enclosures, drainage, liming and new crop rotations. Organizations like the Society of Improvers, created in 1723, have done much to propagate ideas first tried out in England and Holland. In a country where the struggle to raise farming above subsistence level has always been hard, the success of the new methods has been shown in recent years when poor weather caused food shortages but no famine. Greater credit facilities through expanded banking services centred on Edinburgh have also helped.

1758 - 1759

London, 11 May 1758. Richard Vaughan is hanged for forging Bank of England notes; he is the first person known to have attempted this.

North America, 8 July 1758. French troops rebuff a British attack on Ticonderoga (→26).

Canada, 26 July 1758. British troops led by General James Wolfe capture Louisbourg from the French (→8/1758).

Canada, August 1758. The British capture Fort Frontenac from the French (→25/11).

France, August 1758. The port of Cherbourg is destroyed by a British raiding party (→1/8/59).

Senegal, December 1758. A British fleet seizes the island of Goree.

England, 1758. John Hutton, the archbishop of Canterbury, dies; he is succeeded by Thomas Secker, the dean of St Paul's Cathedral.

Dublin, 1758. The first volume of Abbé James MacGeoghegan's *Histoire de l'Irlande* is published.

India, 1758. Robert Clive is made governor of the East India company's possessions (→1760).

Quebec, 12 January 1759. General Wolfe is appointed commander-in-chief of British troops (→19/7).

West Indies, May 1759. The British seize Guadeloupe and Basse-Terre from the French.

North America, 19 July 1759. John Prideaux is killed leading the British victory at Fort Niagara (→13/9).

Germany, 1 August 1759. An Anglo-Hanoverian force defeats the French at Minden (→18).

Portugal, 18 August 1759. Admiral Boscawen defeats the French, thwarting their plans to invade England (→20/11).

London, 20 November 1759. General Wolfe, who died in the battle for Quebec in September, is buried at Greenwich.

Dublin, 1759. The west front of Trinity College is completed.

Manchester, 1759. James Brindley begins work on a canal to transport the duke of Bridgewater's coal from Worsley to Manchester.

Staffordshire, 1759. Josiah Wedgwood opens a pottery at Burslem.

British troops recapture Fort Duquesne

An earlier and vital success: British troops capture Louisbourg on 26 July.

North America, 25 November 1758

A force of combined British and colonial troops under the command of General John Forbes has seized the French stronghold of Fort Duquesne and broken France's hold on the Ohio valley, opening the way north to Lake Erie. The fort is to be renamed after the British politician William Pitt and will serve as an ideal base for the expansion of British America.

Today's victory follows the capture in July of the strategically important fortress of Louisbourg, on Cape Breton Island, Nova Scotia. Louisbourg surrendered to the British Generals Jeffrey Amherst and James Wolfe after a siege and fierce fighting.

The French have been put on the defensive everywhere in North America. The Royal Navy has cut communications between France and America, allowing the British to capture French positions one after another. Fort Frontenac, near Lake Ontario, was taken in August.

The attack on Duquesne was a bold move by General Forbes, who sent 6,500 men through the Pennsylvania wilderness under the command of his Colonels George Washington, John Armstrong and Henry Bouquet. Washington and others had opposed the general's plan, but Forbes insisted. They overcame every difficulty, and the French garrison, which was hopelessly outnumbered, blew up the fort and abandoned it as the enemy approached.

William Pitt aims to keep France busy in Europe by subsidizing Frederick the Great of Prussia while using British naval superiority to capture French colonies and bases in North America, the West Indies and India. The victory at Fort Duquesne – or rather, Fort Pitt [Pittsburgh] – shows that the plan is working (→12/1/59).

'Halley's comet' appears in the night sky

British Isles, December 1758

A great comet has appeared in the sky, just as Edmund Halley predicted in 1705. He claimed that the comets observed in 1531, 1607 and 1682 were all the same object, which circles the sun in an elliptical orbit every 77 years and six months. He based his calculations on Newton's *Principia*, which allowed him to work out his comet's movements. This proof of Halley's theory confirms that all comets follow a regular orbit. They are not sudden, surprise visitors, let alone the harbingers of disaster that superstitious ancients believed. A comet is just another heavenly body.

London-based Welshmen launch a cultural revival

Wales, 1758

Welshmen living in London are trying to launch a revival of Welsh culture in an effort to infuse some new life into and respect for the Welsh language.

Lewis Morris, born in Anglesey but now working in London for the customs service and as a steward of crown lands in Wales, has persuaded his exclusive London literary and philosophical society, the Cymmrodorion, to finance a book of "great gems of Welsh literature", including the 6th-century poem the *Goddodin*, for presentation to Dr Samuel Johnson.

Discovered only recently by Morris while searching for ancient Welsh poetry and music in some privately owned libraries in Cardigan, this "exceptionally beautiful and strikingly original poem" is to be compared, he says, "to the very best of Homer or Milton". Unfortunately, its exceptional beauty may not be able to survive translation into the more formal English that is commonly spoken nowadays by fashionable members of the London gentry.

The development of a Welsh-language press, with a whole range of type in Welsh, as well as wood-blocks and line engravings, is also being organized from London by Thomas Jones of Corwen, who is becoming renowned as a pioneer of Welsh journalism. He has just moved to Shrewsbury to supervise his agents in several towns in Wales and the Marches in their selling of his books and almanacs in Welsh and English.

It is also reported that Lewis Morris has sought to emulate in Welsh the high-quality English literary journals, and to exploit the current interest in antiquarianism made fashionable by Edward Lluyd, the Welsh assistant to the keeper of Oxford's Ashmolean museum. Lluyd's original proposals for a Welsh studies course were published privately in London last year.

Crusade under way to save prostitutes

Whores entice a sailor on leave.

London, 1758
A moral crusade to reclaim the souls of prostitutes is under way at the new Magdalen House, a hospital dedicated to their care. The women are brought to repentance here and then restored to society. The hospital has been founded by Charles Dingley, who argues that it is possible to reform prostitutes and save them from "disease, death and eternal destruction, [suffered] not through choice but necessity".

The hospital chaplain is Dr William Dodd. He preaches that these women are sinners and must first hate their past lives before they can be redeemed. "Reflect upon yourselves," he says, "abhorred by the thinking and the virtuous, despised and hated even by the most abject and vicious." Members of his respectable congregations are encouraged to visit Magdalen House to admire the work in progress.

King mourns loss of favourite composer

London, 4 April 1759
George Frederick Handel has died at the age of 74. He will be buried in Westminster Abbey with all the honours due to the country's greatest composer.

Handel was born in Germany in 1685, the same year as Johann Sebastian Bach and Giuseppe Domenico Scarlatti. He first visited England in 1710 and decided to settle here, employed to begin with by aristocratic patrons. In 1726 he became a British subject. During the 1720s he wrote Italianate operas for London's Royal Academy of Music, but by the end of the decade the academy was foundering, while the success of John Gay's parody *The Beggar's Opera* in 1728 showed that the public was bored with high opera. Handel turned to oratorio, with great success. His output includes 46 operas, 32 oratorios and numerous instrumental pieces.

Handel died loved and honoured.

British Museum opens doors to public

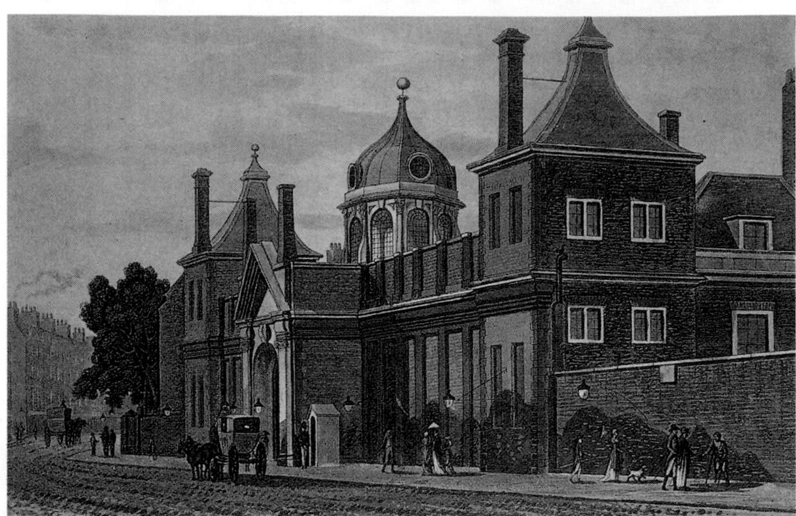
A slightly later view of Montagu House, complete with sentry-box.

London, 1759
The British Museum has been opened to the public as the first national "repository for all arts and sciences". It is housed in Montagu House, in Great Russell Street, Bloomsbury; its principal collections of antiquities were assembled by the late Sir Hans Sloane and by the first and second earls of Oxford. Robert Harley, the first earl, was Queen Anne's chief minister and formed a superb collection, including many valuable books and manuscripts. Sloane was a distinguished physician and botanist – he founded the Chelsea botanical gardens. The museum was planned after his death in 1753.

Parliament approved a British Museum lottery, which raised £300,000 to buy the Sloane and Oxford collections and to buy and enlarge Montagu House to hold them. King George II has donated to the museum the royal library, consisting of thousands of books accumulated over the centuries.

Latest telescope gives clearer view of stars

London, 1758
John Dollond has been awarded the Copley medal for inventing an achromatic telescope – one that transmits light without breaking it up. This permits a far clearer view of the stars. Dollond first worked as a silk weaver, but both he and his son Peter are now opticians. Astronomy is making great strides, helped by inventions such as Dollond's as well as by the navy's search for accurate means of navigation.

The nature and vastness of the universe are now becoming apparent, just as medicine, chemistry, botany and mathematics are also showing dramatic advances.

Peasants riot over latest land reforms

England, 1758
The enclosure movement, by which common land is sold off to farmers, has provoked riots in various parts of the country. Poor peasants who used to hunt or gather firewood on public wastelands are no longer allowed to do so. The loss of such an important source of food and fuel has led to the protests.

Most farmers, not surprisingly, support the enclosures, which are regulated by commissioners appointed by parliament and are also supposed to be approved by the majority of people in the area concerned. The rise in the price of grain has meant that the traditional practice of dividing a village's land into three open fields, two for grain, one to lie fallow, has become inadequate. Farmers can now own strips in each of the open fields. Enclosed farms are usually far more productive, because they are more suitable for modern crops and methods.

Georgian pride in town planning is epitomized at Bath, where the Circus, which was begun in 1754 by John Wood, was completed by his son in 1767.

Wolfe is felled in battle for Quebec

Quebec City, 13 September 1759
Five days after a British convoy slipped past French sentries and took General James Wolfe's troops to a safe landfall, the city of Quebec has fallen and the way to New France lies open. But the victory has come at a price: Wolfe has died of wounds received today. He was 32 years old.

The battle was, ironically, almost fought by default. Forced to delay when the French captured his plans, Wolfe had become depressed, his morale growing ever lower as the two sides jockeyed for advantage. Yet it was his indecision that helped win the battle, since Montcalm was unable to forecast the direction of the attack.

Montcalm thought that he had Wolfe trapped, believing that no army could scale the cliffs outside Quebec – the Heights of Abraham – where Wolfe's troops stood. But he was wrong. Late last night Wolfe sailed downriver, sneaking his men ashore above Quebec and scaling the cliffs under cover of darkness. Both sides paused, until at 10am today the French charged. The British waited and then, at 35 metres (115 feet), fired volley after volley into the attackers. Minutes later it was all over. Some 650 Frenchmen were dead, but only 60 British troops. If Montreal now falls, New France will be Britain's (→8/9/60).

Wolfe's men scale the Heights of Abraham to fight the French for Quebec.

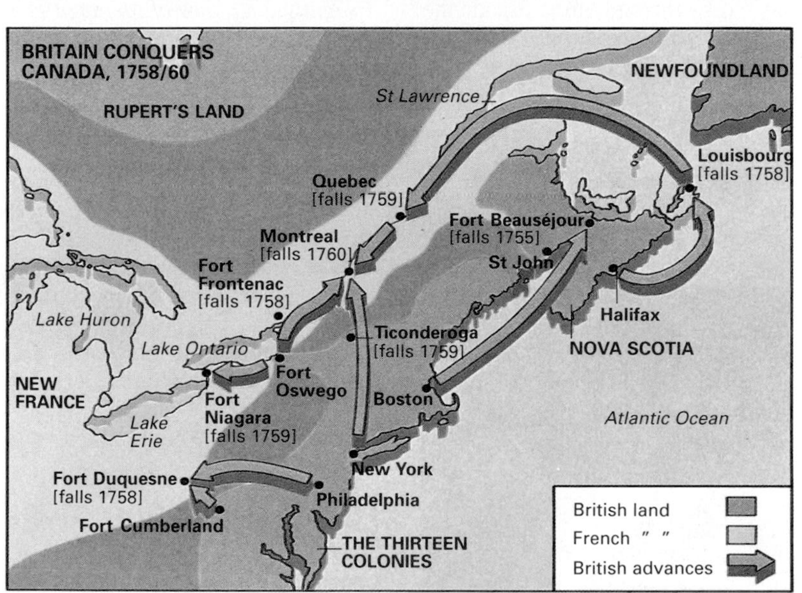

British finally crush French at Quiberon

Brittany, 20 November 1759
Another chapter in the struggle with France is closed: Admiral Hawke has destroyed the French fleet at Quiberon Bay on the Brittany coast. Admiral Conflans had his flagship burnt from under him, and of his 25 other ships four were destroyed and most of the rest badly damaged. The French fleet had been gathered to ferry an invasion force across the Channel. There will be no invasion now.

The plan to invade England was France's greatest gamble. Forced onto the defensive in both the West Indies and North America, the duke of Choiseul believed that such an invasion would reverse the situation. If nothing else, it would tie down British forces. Bearing in mind Britain's recent successes, the need for a victory had become ever more urgent.

Two fleets were mustered – one at Toulon, the other at Brest. The former was destroyed when it tried to slip unnoticed through the Straits of Gibraltar. The other, holding France's last chance of success, managed to evade the British patrols, but its plans became known. Admiral Hawke tracked Conflans to Quiberon, with the result that the French master strategy has turned into yet another military disaster (→31/7/60).

Race is on to complete Wentworth houses

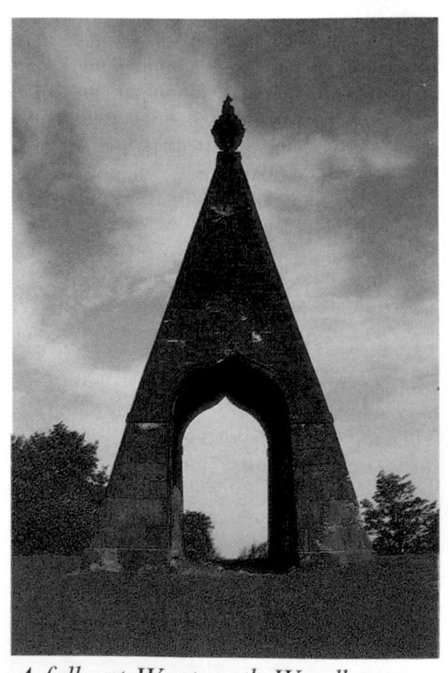
A folly at Wentworth Woodhouse.

South Yorkshire, 1759
In a bizarre example of conspicuous consumption married to political rivalry, two cousins – one Whig, one Tory – from the Wentworth family have been indulging in what can only be termed "a house-building race". The winner, at least to date, in a competition that has been thriving since both parties laid their foundation stones in 1708 is the Whig, whose massive mansion, Wentworth Woodhouse, has just been finished. Wentworth Woodhouse, with its 182.9-metre (600-foot) Palladian frontage, is the largest house in England. Although it also boasts a Palladian frontage, Wentworth Castle, erected north of Sheffield by the Tory cousin, is much less distinguished.

Dublin, 1759: a lease is granted to Arthur Guinness to establish a brewery at St James's Gate.

Carron Ironworks is set up near Falkirk

Central [Scotland], 1759
A consortium of Scottish and English businessmen has come together this year to establish a facility near Falkirk for working iron. The site of what is to be known as the Carron Ironworks has been carefully chosen for its proximity to coal and ironstone deposits, and to river transport. The founding of a similar centre at Dowlais in South Wales suggests a revival in the fortunes of Britain's rudimentary iron industry. Early this century the industry was badly hit by a dearth of wood for charcoal, but in recent years new methods of using coke for smelting have made possible furnaces on a much larger scale.

1760

Dublin, 31 March. A meeting of Catholics at the Elephant tavern in Essex Street leads to the formation of the first "Catholic committee".

Dublin, 15 April. The House of Commons votes that recent bank failures should be examined by a committee of inquiry.

Dublin, May. The Public Lighting Act gives city authorities the right to levy a lighting tax.

Germany, 31 July. The marquis of Granby decisively defeats the French at Warburg in the continuing continental war (→ 8/6/61).

Netherlands, 2 October. Lord George Murray, the former lieutenant-general of Prince Charles Stuart's Jacobite army, dies in exile at Medenbik (→ 1/1/66).

Westminster, 25 October. King George III accedes to the throne of Great Britain and Ireland.→

London, 27 October. John Stuart, the earl of Bute, a close friend of Augusta, the dowager princess of Wales, and one-time tutor to the young king, is appointed to the cabinet (→ 28/5/62).

West Yorkshire. The first bank opens in Bradford.

Bristol. John Wesley moves to stop the Methodists from breaking away from the Church of England (→ 1768).

Britain. The self-taught midwife Elizabeth Nihell publishes a *Treatise on the Art of Midwifery*; she attacks the celebrated gynaecologist Dr William Smellie for his use of forceps during childbirth.

Edinburgh. Thomas Braidwood opens the first school here for deaf and dumb children.

India. Robert Clive resigns as governor of the East India company and returns to England (→ 15/1/61).

England. The Irish-born clergyman Laurence Sterne publishes the first two volumes of an eccentric novel, *Tristram Shandy* (→ 1764).

London. The Society of Arts holds its first exhibition of contemporary art.

London. London Bridge across the river Thames is demolished.

London. A botanical garden opens at Kew.

Fall of Montreal is triumph for Britain

Montreal, 8 September

Montreal, the capital of New France, has surrendered to British troops under General Jeffery Amherst. The governor, General Pierre de Rigaud de Vaudreuil de Cavagnial, realized that his 2,000 soldiers had no chance against 17,000 British troops and accepted defeat. Under Amherst's surrender terms all civil and religious rights are to be maintained. The fall of Montreal brings to an end the New World phase of an Anglo-French conflict that has lasted since 1754; the war in Europe has still to be concluded. The conquest of New France has taken a long time, but few expected any other conclusion; French isolation from reinforcements made the outcome inevitable.

Heart attack kills king

London, 25 October

King George II died at 6am today of a massive heart attack, just five days before his 77th birthday. In a fulsome tribute Horace Walpole has declared the king's an enviable death "in perfect tranquillity", and even William Pitt, never known as a particular intimate, has spoken of George's "manly virtues".

Such tributes reflect less on the king than on the successes of the country he ruled. Indeed, his reign has typified the continuing reduction of royal power and the creation of a "constitutional monarchy", with the monarch essentially a figurehead for parliamentary government. Yet George achieved one thing that few recent kings have managed: in 1743 he actually led his troops in battle (→ 8/9/61).

George brought stable monarchy.

Scots lead the way in higher education

Tayside

The opening this year of Perth academy will even further improve Scotland's education system, already renowned for its high quality. The academy aims to offer further education in accounting and other commercial subjects for those unable or unwilling to go to university. Funding will be by private subscription – and there is no lack of middle-class parents prepared to pay for their sons to get a head start in a business career.

Scottish education as a whole is expanding and diversifying. The number of teaching staff at the universities – at St Andrews, Glasgow, Aberdeen and Edinburgh – is increasing, and more subjects are being offered than the traditional ones preparing ministers for the church. Medicine, chemistry and history are especially popular.

There are nowadays more students, too, and from a wider range of social backgrounds than would be found in England's two universities of Oxford and Cambridge. At Glasgow, for instance, three in four students are from non-aristocratic families. Universities are likely to face increasingly stiff competition from academies in the battle to attract would-be students.

Interest grows in science and technology

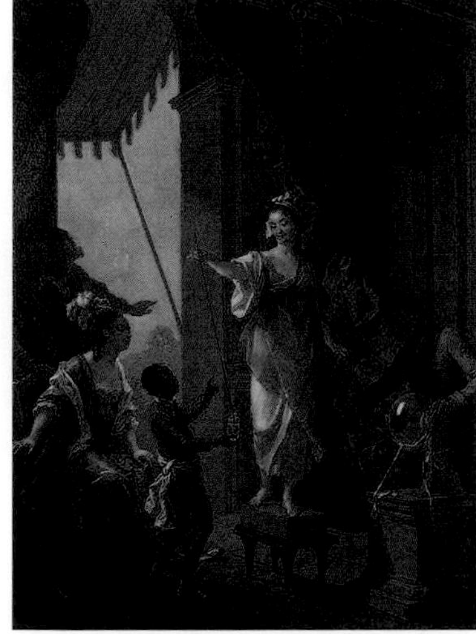

An early electrical experiment.

Britain

Typified by last year's opening of the British Museum, the country is enjoying a burst of interest in "natural philosophy" – the twin topics of science and technology. Popularized by such travelling showmen as the lecturer and instrument maker Benjamin Martin, who began touring the country in 1743, science has moved from being the rarefied pursuit of a few into a mass interest. The experts may resent it, but science is in vogue. Experiments with electricity are thought especially fascinating, and their spectacular effects persuade many people to make their own ventures into this revolutionary area.

At Tyburn on 5 May Lord Ferrers, who murdered a steward, became the first nobleman to be hanged, rather than beheaded, for 200 years.

Town and country prosper in mid-century Britain

The square, hedged fields that follow enclosure are obvious from this picture of harvesters at work cutting corn.

Agriculture is revolutionized by enclosures and new methods

Nottinghamshire

The transformation of the English countryside, already noticeable in many of the midland regions, is expected to speed up even more in the coming years. Some 20 enclosure bills are set down for hearing in this year's session of parliament, and dozens more are believed to be on the way. They will bring a large amount of undercultivated land into more productive use.

The process is well illustrated by events here in Nottinghamshire. For example, the land in the village of Flintham included 450 acres 182 hectares (450 acres) of unfenced common, which were always heavily overstocked with the cows and pigs of the cottagers. It has just been consolidated into one large unit; enterprising local farmers now expect to push up yields and profits by over 50 per cent as they apply the innovations in livestock-breeding, crop rotation, development of tools and scientific manuring pioneered almost 30 years ago by Jethro Tull, with his seed drill, and Lord "Turnip" Townshend.

Tobacco profits line Scotland's coffers

Glasgow

Clydeside is currently enjoying a great wave of prosperity, thanks mainly to its success in cornering a large and profitable part of the North American tobacco trade. Great new finance houses have arisen, such as the Glasgow Arms bank and the Glasgow Ship bank, and fortunes are being made by the "tobacco lords" whose ships and agents now dominate the business. Their fine houses, offices and quayside warehouses are beginning to transform Glasgow into one of Europe's finest modern commercial cities. But to the regret of many, this boom has not been shared by Scotland's biggest local industry, fishing. Some 135 Dutch boats were busy lifting herring this summer, while Fraserburgh and Peterhead could barely muster 17.

New towns grow up around workplaces

Lancashire

Preparations are almost complete for a great project devised by Francis Egerton, the duke of Bridgewater. He plans to construct a deepwater canal linking the fast-growing industrial and commercial centres of Liverpool and Manchester to improve their advantages as magnets for labour and trade.

Thanks to the growth in popularity of cotton as a fashion material, the population of cotton-producing Lancashire is expanding at a huge rate; the county is second only to Middlesex in activity and wealth. The cotton-workers' houses are being transformed into small factories as their villages expand into towns beside the Pennine streams. Similar developments are reported in the English midlands, where the demand for ironware in Birmingham and Josiah Wedgwood's pottery around Stoke rapidly creating an urban-based economy.

Industry of all kinds is expanding: these men are making gunpowder.

Transport improves with turnpike roads

The turnpikes are about to be challenged by the growth of the canals.

Westminster

The spate of turnpike bills at present going through parliament signals a further drive to improve the many deficiencies of Britain's roads. All over the country property owners are tabling plans to upgrade stretches of public highway that cross their estates. In return they seek the right to erect tollgates and charge fees, in order to cover their capital investment and in time generate a small profit.

Typical fees are one penny for a horse, threepence for a coach, fourpence or sixpence for a heavily loaded cart, and sixpence or a shilling [5p] for a wagon. Cattle and sheep, which are often driven immense distances to market, are charged by the score [20] or by the head.

Although these payments are individually modest, they can mount up substantially over a long journey. Yet most travellers are happy to pay whatever is asked if it allows them to avoid such regular hazards as mud, dust, deep rutting and exposure to the murderous attentions of highwaymen.

Ireland wins renown for elegance and good sport

Forests disappear as farming improves

Ireland
Despite the efforts of the Dublin Society, founded in 1740, to encourage the planting of trees by awarding premiums and medals, much of the countryside still looks bleak and bare. Deforestation, which began in earnest towards the end of the 16th century, has by now all but destroyed the forests of oak, ash, hazel, yew and juniper. Fields are divided by bare earthen banks or stone walls, and while these may be popular with those who love hunting, both landlords and tenants are being encouraged to plant hawthorn hedges and the newly introduced hardwoods such as sycamore, beech and horse chestnut.

The drive to improve estates, introduce enclosures and encourage cottage industries has put the landscape into a state of transition. Density of population and differing degrees of prosperity are other factors affecting the appearance of the countryside. The fertile grasslands of the counties of Tipperary and Limerick contrast sharply with the rough sheep country of Galway or Sligo. While Tyrone is regarded as bleak and boggy with little appeal for visitors, the area between Monaghan and Carrickfergus is highly appealing, with its orchards and well planned gardens.

The wild beauty of Bantry Bay.

A plan for Dublin's new customs house: its building will reflect the city's growing commercial importance.

Grand public and private buildings adorn city and countryside

Dublin
With the accession this year of George III, underlining the stability of the Hanoverian dynasty and, by extension, life generally in the British Isles, Dublin has embarked upon a period of urban expansion greatly helped by the appointment of a commission to widen and improve the city's narrow and congested streets.

Dublin Castle is being remodelled and fine residences such as that for the provost of Trinity College and Kildare House add greatly to the elegance of the city, as well as enhancing its social life, regarded by visitors as more splendid than anything in England. A new customs house is planned to deal with growing foreign trade. As prosperity increases, many landowners have improved their properties or built magnificent mansions, such as Powerscourt in Co Wicklow or Westport in Co Mayo. The architect Richard Castle and stucco workers such as Paul and Philip Francini are much in demand.

This pleasure-orientated society also has a social conscience, however, and functions to raise money for charity are usually well attended. Among other medical foundations, Dr Bartholomew Mosse has opened the Rotunda maternity hospital for women from the inner city, an area of poor housing, poverty and deprivation.

Horses and hounds provide popular diversions for the landed rich

Ireland
Thomas Conolly, who lives in Castletown, in Co Kildare, one of the loveliest houses in the country, has become the first Irish member of the English Jockey Club and has been prominent in developing a racecourse at the Curragh in Co Kildare. "Pounding matches" are popular in Munster and Connacht, where a group of riders jumps across country until only the winner remains. In a famous race ten years ago in Co Cork, two gentlemen raced from Buttevant church to the spire of St Leger church, four miles (6.4km) away, thereby coining the term "a steeplechase".

There are racecourses all over Ireland. Meetings often last a week, interspersed with entertainments such as fox-, hare- and doe-hunts, and grand balls are held most nights. Hunting is an increasingly favoured pastime with leading landowners, who keep their own packs of hounds. Although all of these pursuits are chiefly the preserve of a leisured and wealthy few, drunkenness is becoming such a serious problem among poorer people on race nights that Lord Kenmare has suppressed the Killarney races and compensated the publicans by reducing their rents. The female members of high society enjoy altogether gentler amusements. They arrange picnics, visit spas, play cards, collect shells and hold musical evenings.

A comfortable life for the rich: driving in Glenarm Castle park, Co Antrim.

1761 - 1762

India, 15 January 1761. Comte de Lally, the French leader, surrenders to the British at Pondicherry (→22).

France, 8 June 1761. The British seize Belle Ile, off the coast, as Anglo-French peace talks collapse (→8/1761).

Edinburgh, July 1761. The Irish actor Thomas Sheridan lectures members of polite society on how to pronounce English correctly.

Europe, August 1761. Spain allies with France against Britain (→5/10).

London, 8 September 1761. King George III marries Charlotte, the daughter of Duke Charles of Mecklenburg-Strelitz (→22).

Munster, October 1761. Violence breaks out between Protestant artisans and land-hungry Catholics, "the whiteboys" (→15/3/66).

Britain, 1761. Samuel Richardson, the writer, best known for his novels *Pamela* and *Clarissa*, dies.

Manchester, 1761. The Bridgewater canal, built for Francis Egerton, the duke of Bridgewater, to transport coal from his mines at Worsley to Manchester, opens.

Britain, 4 January 1762. War on Spain is declared.

Edinburgh, 26 January 1762. A committee is formed to agitate for a Scottish militia.

Ireland, 1 February 1762. Irish Catholics offer their armed services to George III.

Caribbean, 16 February 1762. British troops seize the French island of Martinique (→12/1762).

London, 12 August 1762. Queen Charlotte gives birth to George Augustus Frederick, the first son and heir of George III (→4/1765).

Westminster, November 1762. In an attempt to keep John Stuart, the unpopular earl of Bute, in power, the king appoints Henry Fox, the paymaster-general, as leader of the Commons (→8/4/63).

Portugal, December 1762. British troops support the Portuguese to repel a Franco-Spanish invasion (→10/2/63).

London, 1762. John Montagu, the earl of Sandwich, during a 24-hour gaming session, creates a filled snack made with slices of bread: the "sandwich".

British in control in India after Afghans smash Hindu forces

Panipat, India, 22 January 1761
As many as 200,000 Marathan warriors lie dead on the battlefield here after an eight-hour battle which may well have decided the fate of India. Ahmed Shah Durrani's Afghan army is victorious, though its losses have also been heavy. The real victor is the East India company, which has taken advantage of the conflict between the Hindu Marathas and the Moslem Afghans since the 1740s. Today's terrible losses mean that there is no longer an effective Indian army to challenge Robert Clive's army, with its field guns and other sophisticated western weapons.

Durrani challenged the Marathas, the principal allies of India's Moghul emperors, to battle last October, and the Marathas built a fortified position here, confident of holding off any siege. It was a bad decision: the Marathas, numbering 300,000 with their camp-followers, were running out of food when they chose to give battle, although they had the advantage until Durrani's cavalry made a sudden and near-suicidal charge in which they wounded the Maratha leader's son, Viswas Rao.

An eye-witness described the scene thus: "As if by enchantment, the whole Marathan army turned their backs and fled at full speed, leaving the battlefield covered with heaps of dead" (→1767).

Scots church splits

Dunfermline, Fife, 1761
Another group of dissenters has this year seceded from the established church in Scotland. Led by Thomas Gillespie, the minister of Carnock, the "Relief Church" is attracting new members in droves.

The debate over patronage – should lay patrons or the congregations appoint ministers? – remains a bone of contention. Ebenezer Erskine's "Secession Church" has split into "Burghers", led by Erskine, and "Anti-Burghers" led by Adam Gib; now it is further divided into "Old Light Burghers" and "New Light Anti-Burghers".

George III crowned king

George: monarch at the age of 23.

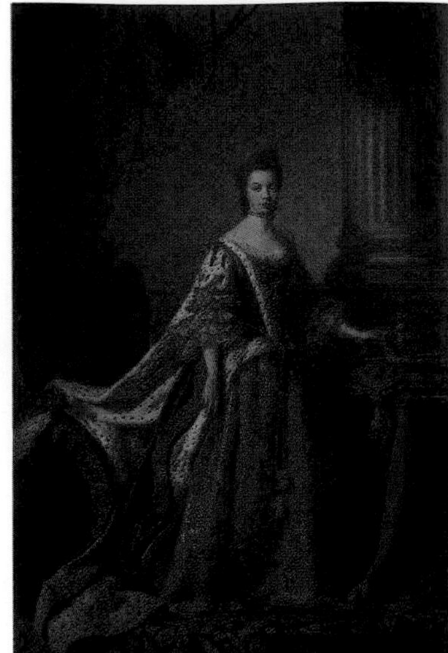

Charlotte: speaks no English.

Westminster, 22 September 1761
Watched by thousands – many of whom had paid small fortunes to secure the best vantage points – King George III and his queen were carried from St James's in sedan chairs to their coronation here today. The 23-year-old George, the first Hanoverian monarch to be born in Britain, gave a unique demonstration of his piety by removing the crown before taking the sacrament, an act that greatly impressed many in the congregation.

Despite his immaturity, young George has already shown a strong sense of responsibility. He had been deeply in love with 15-year-old Lady Sarah Lennox, but he agreed with his mentor, the earl of Bute, that marriage to her would be unsuitable, and – "contrary to my passions" – he sought a review of eligible Germany princesses. Within a week of his accession he issued a proclamation encouraging "piety and virtue" and punishing "vice, profaneness and immorality".

His queen, the homely Charlotte of Mecklenburg-Strelitz, arrived here 13 days ago, speaking no English and meeting her husband and his family for the first time on the wedding day.

George reigns over a country that is developing a great empire and controls half the world's trade. Many are worried, however, by his reliance on advice from the erratic Lord Bute (→12/8/62).

The "quack" doctor is a figure of fun, often lampooned on stage, but he can make quite a name for himself. Joshua Ward, who died on 21 November , became a favourite of King George II after fixing the king's dislocated thumb. He made a fortune and left four London houses.

Secretary of state William Pitt is forced to resign when his war strategy is rejected

London, 5 October 1761
Britain's political scene was thrown into chaos today by the resignation – "in disgust" – of William Pitt, the minister whose brilliant use of sea power and mastery of world-wide strategy has made Britain one of the strongest countries in the world. King George III, who dislikes Pitt's domineering manner, has accepted the resignation with delight, although he has granted Pitt an annual pension of £3,000 and a peerage for his wife. Pitt stormed out of the government after a dispute with his arch-rivals the duke of Newcastle and the earl of Bute over his conduct of the war. Pitt is convinced that the French are intriguing to bring Spain into the war as an ally, and he argued for a pre-emptive attack on the Spanish treasure fleet sailing from the New World together with an offensive in Europe, where Prussia is about to fall to the Russians.

Newcastle resisted this policy on grounds of cost – although he accepted the need for more assistance to beleaguered Hanover (→ 1762).

Lord Bute, in a kilt, and Newcastle plot as Pitt kneels before the king.

Argyll, 'father of Scottish nation', is dead

London, 15 April 1761
The man regarded by many Scots as the father of the nation, Archibald Campbell, the third duke of Argyll, died quietly at his London home this afternoon at the age of 77. Argyll has presided over Scottish politics for most of the last 36 years, firstly as agent for his brother, the second duke of Argyll, and then – from 1746 – for himself.

Born at Ham, in Surrey, in 1682, he went to the university of Glasgow in 1699 before going on to study law at Utrecht. After a brief spell in the army he turned in 1705 to politics, and under the patronage of his elder brother John, the second duke and a successful soldier, Archibald succeeded to a number of political offices and was created earl of Islay.

In 1725, when John gained a dominant position in Scottish politics, he sent Archibald to pacify the country in the wake of the Shawfield riots. Increasingly, however, Archibald took responsibility for Scottish affairs, and when John split with Sir Robert Walpole over the Porteous riot, Archibald parted company with his brother. John died in 1743, and Archibald succeeded him; within three years he had regained a dominant position in Scottish politics.

He followed his brother's policy of keeping English ministers out of Scottish affairs, and operated a vast patronage network which entered into every aspect of secular and religious administration. There were few people in public life who did not owe a favour to Argyll.

Britain seizes control of Spanish colonies

The British fleet, commanded by Lord Hervey, sails in to St Lucia.

West Indies, 1762
Faced by the formidable alliance of France and Spain, Britain has taken the initiative in the west with an expedition seizing French and Spanish colonies in the West Indies and Canada. Within days of the declaration of war on Spain, troops took the French island of Martinique and followed this victory up by taking Grenada, the Grenadines, St Lucia, St Vincent and Tobago.

St John's, Newfoundland was captured by the French in June, but it was promptly recaptured, and in August Havana was taken from the Spanish. The war reached to the Far East in October when an expedition fitted out in Madras forced the Spanish garrison at Manila, in the Philippines, to surrender.

The course of the European war changed rapidly early in the year following the death of Czarina Elizabeth of Russia. Her son, Peter III, a German enthusiast, stopped all hostilities against Prussia in February, but now he has been overthrown by his wife, Catherine, leaving the issue in doubt.

Walpole puts painter's notes into print

Strawberry Hill, Middlesex, 1762
Horace Walpole, who has installed a private press at this "gothic" imitation castle beside the Thames, has begun publication of his book *Anecdotes of Painting in England*, which is the first history of native art. The basis of his anecdotes are the notebooks which the engraver George Vertue compiled on his contemporaries and predecessors and left unfinished at his death, when Walpole bought them. Walpole is known for his concise style and sharp tongue. He said of Joshua Reynolds: "All his own geese are swans and the swans of others are geese." He writes that Lely's portraits show his sitters as nymphs "trailing embroidery through purling streams in a sort of fantastic nightgown ... a ladies' painter".

In an age of elegance even the stable block was a wonder to behold. This one, at Chatsworth House in Derbyshire, was designed by James Paine.

'Moderate' leader appointed to head Scots university

Robertson: diplomatic leader.

Edinburgh, 1762
Following hard on the great success of his *History of Scotland 1542-1603*, published in 1759, the enlightened thinker William Robertson has this year been appointed principal of Edinburgh University. Born at Borthwick in Midlothian in 1721, Robertson has recently become both a royal chaplain and a joint minister of Greyfriars. For the past decade he has played a prominent role in the turbulent general assembly of the Scottish church, now controlled by the group of "Moderates" of which he is leader.

Believing in an order founded on heightened moral awareness, the Moderates have tried to reassert discipline in church government and to raise the social standing of the clergy. But their worldliness has raised eyebrows in some quarters. The Moderate minister of Inveresk, Alexander Carlyle, who is fond of pastimes such as dancing and card-playing, provoked a furore a few years ago by openly attending the performance of a tragic play.

As leader of the Moderates Robertson has proved himself to be a man of exemplary integrity and diplomacy. Nor is he afraid of controversy, having openly supported Catholic emancipation.

Earl of Bute takes leading political role

London, 28 May 1762
John Stuart, the third earl of Bute, has been appointed first lord of the treasury and prime minister. Bute's political career began with a rain storm. This forced the cancellation of a cricket match in which Frederick, the prince of Wales, was due to play. With nothing else to do the prince asked to play cards, and Bute made up a fourth.

Bute and the prince became firm friends, and when Frederick died Bute became an intimate adviser of the widowed princess and tutor to their young son George, the heir to the throne. Bute managed to place himself at the head of a group of Scottish members and lords in parliament, and now that George has succeeded to the throne as George III he has placed his mentor at the head of his government (→11/1762).

Bute: the new prime minister.

Wilkes produces first issue of 'North Briton'

London, 5 June 1762
A new weekly newspaper called the *North Briton* appeared today. This in itself would not be surprising, but just seven days ago another new newspaper called *The Briton* appeared. *The Briton* is a tool of the new prime minister, the earl of Bute, and intended to peddle his policies. The *North Briton*, however, does just the reverse.

The brainchild of the parliamentarian and agitator John Wilkes, the *North Briton*, which by its very title satirizes Bute's Scottishness, is an unrestrained attack on the prime minister and his works. Wilkes, no mean penman himself, has called in the satirical poets Charles Churchill and Robert Lloyd to help, and the result is devastating. In this first issue Wilkes marks out his ground by saying that "a free press is the terror of all bad ministers". There is no doubt that Lord Bute has been warned (→23/4/63).

Composer fosters a busy musical scene in his Dublin exile

Dublin, 17 September 1762
The composer Francesco Geminiani, Italian-born but a frequent visitor to Ireland, died here today. A pupil of the great Corelli, he wrote many treatises on the practice of baroque performance and assumed an active role in establishing the high standard of instrumental playing which George Frederick Handel commented on so favourably during his visit to Dublin.

Musical entertainment has long been an important aspect of social life in the capital, and performances have often raised substantial sums for charity. The Rotunda maternity hospital, inspired by Dr Bartholomew Mosse and opened five years ago, was funded in this way.

Mercer's hospital is another charitable institution noted for promoting musical events, and it was responsible for inviting Handel to Dublin when his now famous oratorio, *Messiah*, had its première in Fishamble Street in 1742. On that occasion ladies were asked not to wear hoops and gentlemen left their swords at home, so that a maximum audience of 700 could be accommodated inside the new Music Hall. The performance was greeted with tumultuous applause – and Handel generously donated the proceeds to charity.

Button factory brings industry to the coalfields of the Midlands

Boulton's Soho Works was a pioneer of industry in the Birmingham area.

Birmingham, 1762
Matthew Boulton has established his Soho Manufactory in Birmingham to make buttons, buckles and similar goods, from iron. There are no other factories in the area, and Boulton has been able to move here only because of advances made in the iron-smelting industry.

Until about ten years ago most English iron works were small and used charcoal to smelt their iron which meant that they had to be near forests. But now it has become more usual for iron to be smelted by coke, in the manner invented by Abraham Darby in Shropshire. This means that ironworks can now come out of the forest and onto the midlands coalfields.

1763 - 1764

Prussia, 15 February 1763. Prussia, Austria and Saxony conclude the Treaty of Hubertusburg, bringing an end to the German wars.

Westminster, 15 April 1763. George Grenville is appointed prime minister following the resignation of John Stuart, the earl of Bute, over an unpopular cider tax (→ 13/7/65).

London, 23 April 1763. John Wilkes, the member of parliament for Aylesbury and editor of the *North Briton*, a satirical periodical, causes a furore with the publication of issue number 45, in which he criticizes the recently signed Treaty of Paris and accuses King George III and Lord Bute, prime minister at the time of signing, of telling untruths (→ 30).

London, 15 May 1763. Samuel Johnson, the critic, poet and essayist, meets James Boswell, a diarist and pamphleteer; Boswell hopes to write a biography of Johnson (→ 1764).

London, December 1763. An obscene poem entitled *Essay on Woman*, written by "Pego Borewell", otherwise known as John Wilkes, is published; on its publication Wilkes travels to France, escaping a summons for seditious libel (→ 20/1/64).

London, 1763. John Spilsbury, an engraver, invents a "map dissector in wood" [jigsaw puzzle] to help in the teaching of geography.

London, 1763. A printed cheque is used in Hoare's bank.

Staffordshire, 1763. Josiah Wedgwood, the master potter, designs a new porcelain and calls it "Queen's ware".

Co Meath, 1763. Construction begins of a five-storeyed flour-mill, the first major industrial building in Ireland.

Lothian, 1763. James Small, from Dalkeith, patents a new plough which requires only one pair of horses and one man instead of the team of eight or more oxen and a number of men which has been customary in Scotland.

Dublin, February 1764. The Society of Artists is founded.

Dublin, 1764. The Rotunda concert hall is founded.

Leicestershire, 1764. The "Flying Machine", a stage-coach, makes the journey from Leicester to London in a single day.

Britain is all-powerful in the colonies

Quarrel over peace sparks war at home

London, 10 February 1763
The Treaty of Paris has ended the seven years of war with France, but the war among the British politicians has been no less fiercely fought and no less deadly. The row over the peace terms has cost a number of politicians their places, and at one time King George III and his prime minister, Lord Bute, found themselves in opposition to the entire cabinet.

The long-serving duke of Newcastle, who had been in the cabinet for most of the last 40 years, departed in the preliminary skirmishes. Others followed, and when Newcastle tried to influence the duke of Devonshire to oppose the war settlement the king snubbed Devonshire, and Devonshire resigned. The king then called in his other ministers for talks at which he soundly berated them for not supporting him – a drubbing of which they took little notice.

However, when matters were put to the vote in parliament, the peace terms were accepted by a large majority of members. This is partly because the terms are good for Britain and confirm its mastery of many colonies across the world, but also because war-weariness has set in, and people know a decent settlement when they see one.

The treaty is celebrated by a huge firework display in London's Green Park.

Strategic lands secured around the globe

Paris, 10 February 1763
Britain has gained a great deal from the peace treaty to end the seven years of war between it and France which was signed here today. In effect Britain has won all of Canada and all French America, gained a free hand in India and acquired a string of strategic islands and colonies across the globe.

In North America Britain acquired Canada, Cape Breton and all the islands in the St Lawrence river, Louisiana and all French lands in America east of the Mississippi river. In the West Indies it gained Tobago, Dominica, St Vincent and the Grenadine islands. In Africa it retained control of Senegal, and in India the French agreed to recognize Britain's leading position and conquests. Finally, Britain has received both Florida and Minorca from Spain.

Politicians in London may argue – and they have – that an even better deal could have been won from the position of Britain's military superiority. They are also annoyed that islands captured from the French, like Martinique and St Lucia, are being returned. But over all there has been an overwhelming gain of influence and power.

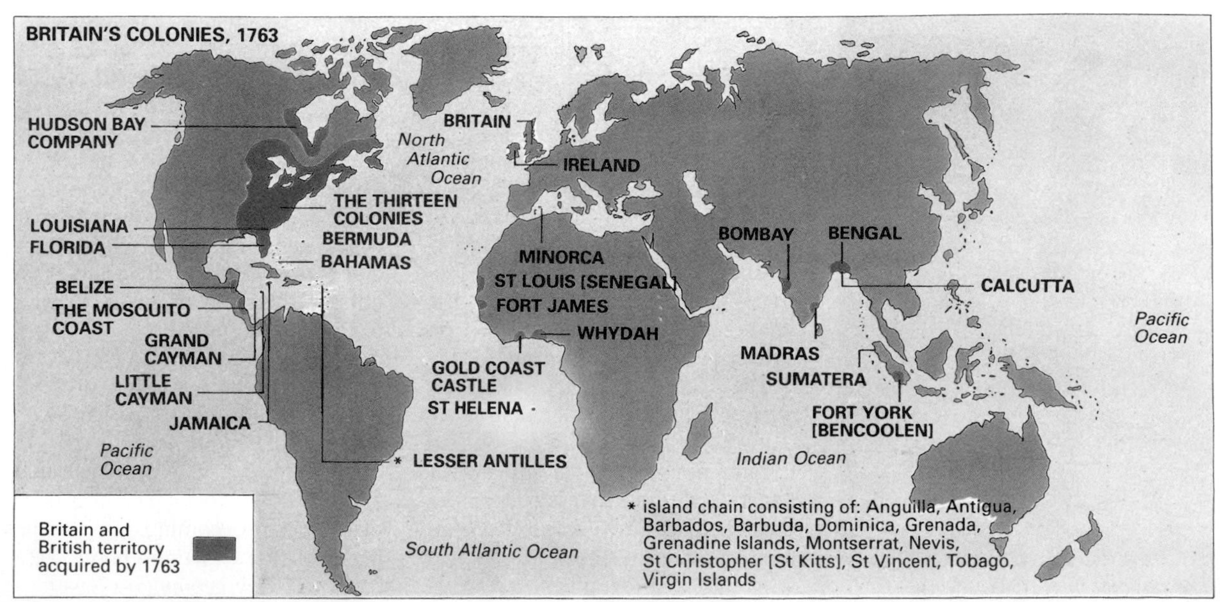

Prime minister quits over cider tax

Westminster, 8 April 1763
To general astonishment, John Stuart, the earl of Bute, has resigned as prime minister only four months after a victory in the House of Commons which confirmed his ascendancy over his rivals. His departure comes in the wake of public outcry over the imposition of a tax on cider. But the crucial votes had been won, the riots and petitions weathered. The real reason seems to be that Bute, whose health is now poor, has simply lost his nerve.

Last December's Commons vote of 319 for peace against 65 for war brought problems – notably the urgent need to raise taxes to finance the war debt. Direct taxes were out of the question; but beer was already subject to excise duty, so why not cider too? One problem was that whereas beer could be taxed at the maltings or breweries, a cider excise involved the investigation of every apple-grower. This led to additional intrusion from inspectors and the prospect of smallholders being dragged through the courts.

The unpopular Bute will not be missed. "The northern thane" – or "Sir Pertinax MacSycophant" – is the target of widespread innuendo in the press. Some hope that his incompetent chancellor, Dashwood, will follow him (→ 15).

Bute – satirized as Jack Boot – seemed to have won the battles ...

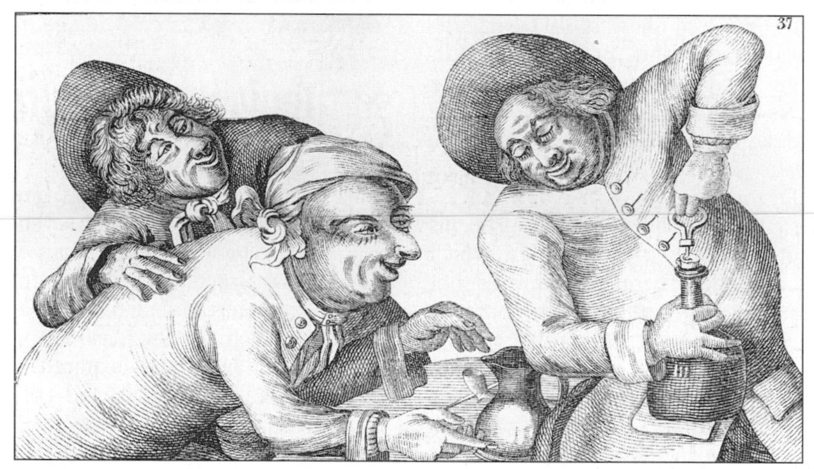

... but desire for cheap drink, in this case cider, brought him down.

Farm army protests at poverty in Ulster

Ulster, 1763
After a fierce pitched battle near Newtownstewart in Co Tyrone, the military have dispersed a group of militant farmers. Widespread rural unrest resulting from bad harvests and economic hardship has inspired the formation of an agrarian army in Ulster. Known variously as "the Oakboys", "the Greenboys" or "the Hearts of Oak", they have won support throughout the province with their protests against rates (known as the "county cess") and the unfair burden of tithes which are paid to Church of Ireland clergymen (→ 4/1765).

Smart praises world in 'Song to David'

Bethnal Green, London, 1763
Christopher Smart languishes in a private mental asylum in here while academic and clerical circles acclaim his latest poetry. *A Song to David* has echoes of Milton and is a passionate affirmation of the beauty of creation and the glory of God. Smart is a classical scholar who has twice won the Seatonian prize from Cambridge for his poetry. He married in secret and has now declined from indebtedness into insanity. His poems, however, satisfy a widespread yearning for faith.

A portrait of his wife, Margaret Lindsay, by the highly original Scottish painter Allan Ramsay, who recently settled in London.

Luxurious gardens landscaped at Kew

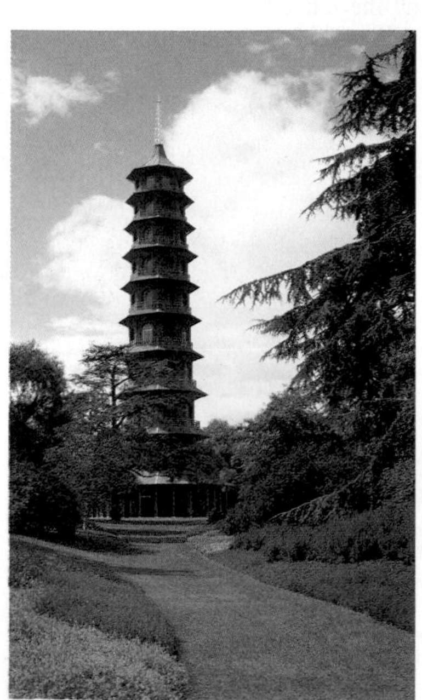

The pagoda in Kew Gardens.

Kew, Surrey, 1763
Sir William Chambers, a pioneer of garden design, has put many of his most exotic ideas into practice in the gardens which he has laid out here, near the Thames to the west of London. He has created a wilderness garden, entered through a ruined arch. A path leads via a Moorish alhambra, which is based on a design by Muntz, to a Turkish mosque, then to a 48-metre (160-foot)-high Chinese pagoda – not an accurate reproduction, but an exuberant rococo invention.

The accent in gardens like Kew is on architecture rather than horticulture. Architects who are obliged to build houses in the dominant Italianate style find that gardens offer greater imaginative scope. Kew has many temples, a Greek theatre and a "gothic" cathedral.

French silk imports spark London riots

Spitalfields, London, 1763
Weavers from the east of the City have taken to the streets to protest at the threat to their livelihoods posed by imported French silks. The immediate cause of the problem is the reopening of the market in silks following the end of the war with France, and the rioters are quick to blame the politicians, notably the duke of Bedford, who negotiated the peace.

Weavers are not the only workers facing hardship at the present. Demobilization of troops has swollen unemployment, and a slump in exports to the colonies has only made matters worse. The effects of this recession, coming hot on the heels of the wartime boom, are being felt very keenly (→ 1765).

'Gaelic poems' said to be modern fraud

London, May 1763
A young Scotsman who claims to have discovered the 1,000-year-old poems of the legendary Celtic hero Ossian has been condemned as a fraud. James Macpherson says that he has deposited with his publishers, Beckett and de Hondt, original manuscripts on which his translations are based. If enough subscribers come forward, he will publish the material in its entirety.

This literary row is exacerbated by the fact that Macpherson's patron is Lord Bute, the former prime minister. Scots are convinced that attempts to denigrate the discovery are pure partisanship on the part of the English. There has been great interest in the poems unearthed by Macpherson, at least some of which seem to be genuinely authentic.

A later view of Ossian's "Dream".

British face defeat by Indian chief

Pontiac urges war on the British.

Canada, August 1763
An Indian revolt against British forces in North America has gathered momentum with a surprise victory that now threatens the garrison at Detroit. Angry with the British for fortifying and settling Indian lands, Chief Pontiac of the Ottawa Indians has embarked on a campaign to harass and kill white settlers as far south as Maryland and Virginia. When Captain James Dalyell led 250 troops out of Fort Detroit to subdue the Indians, his force was ambushed, and he and 19 of his men were killed at the Battle of Bloody Run. Pontiac and his braves have seized all but one of the British forts in the Upper Great Lakes. The British worry is that with French support, Pontiac could take Detroit.

Radical author is seized

London, 30 April 1763
The radical member of parliament John Wilkes and 48 others have been arrested for their involvement in the 45th issue of the *North Briton*. The newspaper launched a scathing attack on King George III's speech at the opening of parliament, denouncing it as "the most abandoned instance of ministerial effrontery". The king was most offended, and the general warrant accuses the 49 of publishing "a seditious and treasonable paper". Wilkes is the son of a Clerkenwell distiller. A lucrative marriage gave him the chance to play the gentleman, and he has quickly won a reputation for wit and rakishness. The earl of Bute has been the butt of Wilkes's sharpest gibes (→ 12/1763).

Wilkes, proving the power of the pen.

Exiled Wilkes is expelled from parliament

London, 20 January 1764
John Wilkes, who fled to exile in France last December, failed to appear in court here today on a charge of seditious libel. In his absence he received a suspended 22-month sentence and was expelled from the House of Commons.

Following his arrest last April [*see above*], Wilkes was released on 6 May after pleading that as a member of parliament he was immune from arrest on any charge save that of treason. In December he was indicted in the House of Lords over his "scandalous, impious and obscene" *Essay on Woman*. He had a row in the House of Commons with Samuel Martin, the treasury solicitor, and Martin challenged him to a duel, during which the solicitor wounded Wilkes in the groin. Wilkes is currently staying with his daughter, Polly, in Paris and recovering from the wound.

Since the popular cry of "Wilkes and liberty" went up after the *North Briton* arrests, the establishment has been set on bringing Wilkes down. Wilkes's chief mistake was to offend King George III, whom he accused in a letter of "hypocrisy, meanness, ignorance and insolence" (→ 25/2/68).

Chattering classes form select new club

London, 1764
The political, literary and artistic figures of the day have gathered to form *The Club*, of which the leading light is unquestionably Samuel Johnson. Every fortnight when parliament is in session the members meet over food and wine at the "Turk's Head" in Soho, to sharpen their wits, argue and set the world to rights.

It was Johnson's friend Joshua Reynolds who had the idea of forming the club as the pair sat over a winter fire late last year. They decided that the club should contain only people who could pass a pleasant evening as a pair, and would not need more company to have an agreeable time, and drew up a list of just seven of their friends whom they thought acceptable. Among these founding members were Oliver Goldsmith and Edmund Burke.

The club is proving a uniquely stimulating forum, and, for Dr Johnson, the perfect environment in which to indulge his greatest pleasure: conversation. Debates on politics often become heated, however, and Johnson is at present not on speaking terms with Burke on account of the latter's allegiance to the Rockingham party (→ 1765).

Hogarth's 'Progress' comes to conclusion

London, 1764
William Hogarth, the highly original painter and engraver who examined the moral health of the English through dramatized series such as *The Harlot's Progress* and *Marriage à la mode*, has died. He leaves a fascinating body of work in which the lives of the whole range of the English people are reflected, as well as a penetrating set of portraits.

Born in 1697, the son of a London schoolmaster, he tasted the raw side of life in his youth when his father was imprisoned for debt – an experience which stayed with the artist until he died. He was apprenticed as an engraver and then studied painting under Sir James Thornhill, with whose daughter he eloped in 1729.

Throughout the 1730s and early 1740s, Hogarth developed the "modern moral subjects" for which he is most famous [*see page 694*]. In the following years, in works such as the *Industry and Idleness* series [1747] and *Gin Lane* [1751], he concentrated particularly on the life and vices of the poor of London. He also took on politicians, with a cartoon of Wilkes, Pitt and Temple as warmongers in 1762 and a series in 1755 examining the election.

1765

Armagh City, 8 February. Richard Robinson, the bishop of Kildare, is appointed archbishop of Armagh.

Westminster, 24 March. Parliament passes the Quartering Act which requires Britain's colonies to provide food and shelter for British soldiers and their horses.

Ireland, April. The country is hit by drought (→ 8/1766).

Chatham, Kent, 7 May. The Royal Navy launches HMS *Victory* from the dockyards.

London, 31 October. Shortly after his promotion to the position of prime minister, the duke of Cumberland, George III's brother, dies aged 44.

North America, 31 October. Some 200 merchants in New York join the non-importation movement, pledging not to buy British goods until the Stamp and Sugar Acts are repealed (→ 17/12).

Westminster, 17 December. George III favours a repeal of the Stamp Act (→ 1/1766).

Birmingham. Samson Lloyd and John Taylor, both successful businessmen, join forces to form Lloyds bank.

Manchester. In an attempt to halt the increase in crime, the town obtains a cleaning and lighting act.

London. Laurence Sterne, the Irish-born clergyman, publishes volumes VII and VIII of his epic novel *Tristram Shandy* (→ 1767).

Westminster. Parliament passes the Prohibitory Act, which prevents the use of imported French silk, in an attempt to stop the unrest of weavers in Spitalfields.

Isle of Man. The British government acquires fiscal rights.

London. Dr Samuel Johnson publishes a collection of Shakespeare's plays (→ 2/1767).

London. Major Robert Rogers writes to King George III proposing an expedition in search of a north-west passage around North America.

Lincolnshire. The Black Sluice Drainage Board drains the area between Boston and Bourne.

London. Johann Christian Bach and Carl Friedrich Abel launch a concert series in which the latest music from Europe is played alongside their own pieces.

Black blows hot and cold in science lab

Glasgow
Water freezes below 0 degrees celsius (32 degrees fahrenheit), and above that ice melts. Every educated person knows that. Well, up to a point. The top scientist Joseph Black has been doing some experiments on heat which show that it is not so simple. For a start he has found something called latent heat which is there although it may not be detected by a thermometer. This is why snow does not melt at once on a warm day.

Black is now putting this finding to practical use in a series of experiments with James Watt, a 19-year-old apprentice instrument-maker, who has developed an experimental steam engine called a "condenser".

Black found that cold could be hot.

British colony set up on Falkland Islands

Falkland Islands
A British expedition to the South Atlantic has landed on one of the western islands of the Malvinas [Falkland Islands] and set up a base called Port Egmont.

These remote and infertile islands, already claimed by Spain, have a marginal value in their safe harbours, but the spur to this settlement was France's founding of Port Louis last year on one of the most easterly islands. A British settlement had been planned in 1748, but although a Spanish protest had been rejected, the expedition never sailed (→ 1770).

Stamp Act likely to enrage New England

Troops escort the stamped paper to City Hall, New York: a later view.

London, March
The government could be on a collision course with the touchy colonists of New England following the passing of the Stamp Act, which is intended to cover the costs of defending the colony against both the native Indians and the French.

The colonists' leaders in London, such as Benjamin Franklin, accept the principle of paying for their defence but want to raise the money themselves. However, over the past year they have been unable to produce acceptable schemes. Already there is great hostility in New England to last year's Sugar Act, which was designed to raise revenue. Although it actually reduced the tax on molasses, it was combined with a determination by the government to crack down on widespread smuggling. A committee of the Massachusetts house of representatives has claimed that it was an infringement of the right of British subjects to assess their own taxes. The Stamp Act, which is the first *direct* tax on the colony, can only inflame feelings further (→ 31/10).

'Model' Inveraray is near to completion

Inveraray was intended as a model town, but it took a long time to build.

Strathclyde
The "model" town of Inveraray, built over the course of the past 20 years by Archibald Campbell, the third duke of Argyll, is almost finished. The duke died four years ago [*see page 717*] and so unfortunately did not see the completion of either the town or the great new castle which he was putting up for himself nearby. The new town was designed by John Adam of the great architectural family. It is laid out beside Loch Fyne and replaces an earlier town that lay between the remains of the old castle and the river Aray

Mysterious disease strikes King George

London, April
King George III is recovering from the mystery illness that has forced cuts in the royal schedule for the past three months. Since the middle of January his pulse has been fast and his voice hoarse, he has complained of sharp pains in the chest and has had violent coughing fits. The doctors do not know what it is, but George suffered from a similar ailment about three years ago. The prime minister, George Grenville, has dismissed the problem as no more than a cold, but others point out that the king has been feeling harassed and depressed, complaining that ministers no longer make proposals to him but expect him to obey their orders. His illness has scared him so much that he is talking of setting up a council to rule in the event of his death (→ 13/5).

Regency Bill sparks fierce political row

London, 13 May
The bill to set up a regency council has been passed, but King George III feels humiliated. He wanted a council after his illness, but its composition quickly became an issue.

Ministers such as Grenville and Halifax were desperate to keep the king's mother – the princess dowager of Wales – off the council, fearing a revival of the scandal that had destroyed Lord Bute. George reluctantly agreed, but he was made to look an ungrateful son by a Commons motion demanding that she be on it (→ 1/11/71).

London amazed by Mozart prodigies

The young Mozart and his family.

London, 8 May
It was announced today that two musical child prodigies would give a concert next week. Wolfgang and Anna Mozart from Salzburg are the children of a violin teacher named Leopold. Wolfgang, aged nine, will be playing his own composition.

The family, which arrived last year and amazed George III and Queen Charlotte with its skill, is staying in Thrift [Frith] Street in Soho. Daily, between noon and 2pm, visitors are welcome to put Wolfgang's "talents to more particular proof by giving him anything to play at sight".

Music-lovers also have on offer a concert series by J C Bach and C F Abel, where they play the newest European works.

Weaving is changed by 'spinning jenny'

Lancashire
A carpenter from Blackburn, 35-year-old James Hargreaves, claims to have invented a machine called the "spinning jenny" that allows eight threads to be spun at once.

However "jenny's" welcome in Lancashire is unlikely to be friendly. This is the fastest growing area of the country, and its wealth is based on textiles, much of it produced by families working at home. In 1753 John Kay, the inventor of the flying shuttle that doubled the speed of a handloom, was driven out of his home by a furious mob claiming that it had lost them their jobs.

But the large profits make it unlikely that this example of English skill in "the contrivance of mechanic powers", as Josiah Tucker put it, will not be put to work. They also make it likely that most people will continue to ignore the fact that the entire industry depends, in Horace Walpole's words, on "that horrid traffic of selling negroes". The negro slaves provide the cheap cotton and then form a market for the finished cloth (→ 10/5/68).

Rockingham ministry lacks Pitt power

London, 13 July
After two months of behind-the-scenes deals George Grenville is out of office, and Charles Watson-Wentworth, the second marquis of Rockingham, is the new first minister to George III. Although Grenville had few allies, and lost the king's support during the Regency Bill fiasco, there is little enthusiasm for Rockingham. He is affable and leads a group of Whigs; but he entered politics only out of a sense of duty and has rarely spoken in the House of Lords. His real interests are centred on his vast estates in Yorkshire and horse-racing.

The obvious man for the job was William Pitt, the most respected orator in the House of Commons. The duke of Cumberland, negotiating for the king to set up a new ministry, twice approached Pitt. But the talks came to nothing when Pitt's brother-in-law, Lord Temple – whom Pitt wanted to serve in office alongside him – tried to do his own deal with Grenville. In the end Pitt said no, pleading his gout. Many ambitious politicians have refused to serve in what they see as a short-lived administration beset by problems; quite apart from fractious Americans and Pitt in opposition, the harvest is poor and silk weavers are rioting (→ 7/1766).

Cumberland negotiated for king.

Lord and Lady Bangor could not agree on style when they were designing their residence at Castle Ward, Co Down, so they came to an unusual compromise: the entrance front (left) is in the Palladian style which he prefers, while the garden front (right) is in the "gothic" style which she likes.

1766 - 1767

London, January 1766. Widespread riots against the proposed Stamp Act for the colonies break out (→ 3/1766).

London, 27 March 1766. The writer Oliver Goldsmith publishes his latest novel, *The Vicar of Wakefield* (→ 29/1/68).

Westminster, March 1766. The Stamp Act is repealed by parliament (→ 6/1767).

Ireland, 7 June 1766. Parliament passes the Tumultuous Risings Act in an attempt to curb the violent outbreaks against the "whiteboys" (→ 4/4/76).

Ireland, August 1766. Widespread rioting breaks out because of serious shortages and increasingly high prices of food.

Bristol, 1766. The Theatre Royal opens.

Westminster, 1766. London's first paved footpath is laid.

Newbury, Berkshire, 1766. The high price of bread causes violent rioting in the town.

Britain, 1766. Henry Cavendish, the chemist, discovers that the gas hydrogen is less dense than air.

Britain, 1766. George Stubbs, the artist, publishes a series of plates entitled *Anatomy of the Horse*.→

Westminster, June 1767. Charles Townshend, the chancellor of the exchequer, imposes duties on certain goods exported to North America to pay for defence and administration of the colonies.→

Ireland, 14 October 1767. George, Viscount Townshend is sworn in as lord lieutenant of Ireland (→ 2/5/68).

Boston, Mass, 28 October 1767. Boston boycotts all British goods in protest at the Stamp Act (→ 9/1768).

India, 1767. Robert Clive finishes his second term as governor-general and leaves the country, which is in absolute chaos (→ 1773).

Manchester, 1767. The Manchester-to-Liverpool canal link is completed.

London, 1767. Allan Ramsay is appointed royal painter to King George III.

Highland, 1767. A Gaelic translation of the New Testament is published.

Edinburgh, 1767. Construction of the New Town begins.

Jacobites mourn loss of 'Old Pretender'

Britain, 1 January 1766
The death of James Stuart, the son of James II and VII and known as "the Old Pretender", has brought to an end the life of an unfortunate prince who spent the last 50 of his 77 years in exile, a broken and melancholic man. Despite his loyal supporters, James's hopes of gaining the throne of Britain were never to be realized after the failure of the 1745 uprising.

Even his desire to be reunited with his son, "dearest Caluccio" – Charles Edward Stuart – was not to be, since Charles had sworn that he would not visit his father until the pope recognized him as the true heir to the British throne (→ 1777).

"The Old Pretender" is dead.

Irish Catholic priest faces executioner

Co Tipperary, 15 March 1766
Father Nicholas Sheehy, the parish priest of Clogheen, has been found guilty of murder and executed at Clonmel. His parish had been a centre of activity for the "whiteboys" since their secret society was formed five years ago, and he was regarded as supporting many of their aims, which sometimes took the form of reprisal house-burnings and cutting off victims' ears. They are bent on challenging landlords' rights and have protested against the payment of fees demanded from Roman Catholics on behalf of the Church of Ireland. Father Sheehy was accused of inciting the whiteboys to murder a so-called "informer", although no body was ever discovered. He died protesting his innocence (→ 7/6).

Eminent scientists join Lunar Society

Boulton: co-founder of the society.

Britain, 1766
The Lunar Society of Birmingham, founded earlier this year by three men with an interest in science and technology, has gained a fourth: Richard Edgeworth, said to be a member of the notorious Hell-Fire Club in Buckinghamshire. The original members are Erasmus Darwin, a physician from Lichfield, Matthew Boulton, a metal manufacturer, and Dr William Small, a physician from Birmingham.

They meet in each others' houses once a month, at full moon, in order to have light enough to travel home safely – a common enough precaution nowadays, when travel on the roads is so dangerous. Topics discussed at meetings range over a broad spectrum of interests, from transportation to technological and scientific experiments, as well as recent scientific books, botany, medicine and education.

Often, in their correspondence, they refer to themselves as "the insane" or "the lunatics", with puns referring to devilry or conjuring up the powers of darkness. However, it is all light-hearted stuff and in no way relates to devil worship or anything sinister.

Pitt back in power after five-year gap

England, July 1766
William Pitt, who has been out of office since his resignation in 1761, has been invited by King George III to form an administration, with the freedom to choose his own ministers and to assume control of home and foreign affairs once more. In forming a new ministry, Pitt has chosen for himself the near sinecure office of privy seal, with a seat in the House of Lords as Viscount Pitt and earl of Chatham.

Doubts are already being voiced at the wisdom of Pitt accepting a peerage, when his absence from the Commons will mean the loss of his oratorical influence. The duke of Grafton, Augustus Henry Fitzroy, is the first lord of the treasury, and Charles Townshend is the chancellor of the exchequer and leader of the Commons (→ 12/10/68).

Pitt in his robes as Lord Chatham.

Riots break out as price of wheat soars

England, June 1766
Outbreaks of violence have occurred once again as a result of the ever-increasing cost of food, this time in the south of England. At the market at Barnstaple, in Devon, the price of wheat has risen so much that the poor have joined together in protest, hoping to compel farmers to lower their prices. Some of the farmers, conscious of the distressed situations of housewives, have responded to the pressure and done so.

Rival authors make 'sentimental' trips to France and Italy

London, 1767
The Rev Laurence Sterne, the Irish-born author of the whimsical novel *Tristram Shandy*, has almost completed his latest work, *A Sentimental Journey through France and Italy*. Half fiction, half fact, the book sets out to ridicule the caustic commentary provided by the Scottish novelist Tobias Smollett in his *Travels through France and Italy*, which was published last year.

In his *Travels*, Smollett detests (and relishes detesting) the food and customs of these lands, although no more than he does those of London, which he describes as nothing but bad air, bad smells, bad water, bad food and horrid noise. Sterne begins his journey with the declaration that "they order this matter better in France". He lampoons Smollett as "the learned Doctor Smelfungus".

The two books reflect the enduring popularity of the "grand tour", the custom of members of the nobility travelling through Europe to study the architecture, art and manners of the French and Italians. The "tourist" heads first for the highly fashionable city of Paris – where, Smollet noted, he cannot appear until his appearance "has undergone a total metamorphosis" at the hands of tailors – and then on through Provence to the Riviera. He is likely to proceed either by boat or over an alpine pass into Italy (→ 1768).

Colonel William Gordon poses in Rome during his "grand tour".

New act taxes everyday items in colonies

Americans saw taxes as a threat to the comforts that they enjoyed in life.

Britain, June 1767
Charles Townshend, the chancellor of the exchequer, has persuaded parliament to adopt his way of raising taxes in the colonies – the American Import Duties Act. The act will impose duties on a number of small items such as lead, glass, paper, paints and tea. His theory is that since these are "external taxes" – a way of regulating trade which colonists have agreed – Americans would not find them unacceptable. It was cuts in the land tax made last November during riots over the price of grain which deprived the crown of about £500,000 of annual revenue and forced the chancellor to consider other ways of raising money. Although the new act was grudgingly passed by parliament, it remains to be seen how it will be received by members of the New York assembly (→ 28/10).

Dr Johnson meets the king in library

London, February 1767
Dr Samuel Johnson, the celebrated author of the *Dictionary of the English Language*, has had a private audience with King George III. The king had heard that Johnson made periodic visits to the royal library, which the lexicographer had helped to establish, and asked to see him when next he called.

Led by the librarian carrying a candle, George entered the library to find the author "in a profound study" by the fire. Asked what he was now writing, Johnson replied that he had no work in hand and thought that he had done his part as a writer. "I should have thought so too," said the king, "if you had not written so well." The meeting left Johnson "glowing with satisfaction" (→ 9/11/73).

Woman hanged for sadistic murders

London, 14 September 1767
The sadistic murderess Elizabeth Brownrigg went to the gallows today, with a howling mob accompanying her death cart from Newgate prison to Tyburn tree.

Brownrigg was the leading spirit in a family seemingly dedicated to the sadistic torture of a series of girls taken from the foundling hospital and employed as servants under conditions of extreme cruelty. Girls were kept in filthy conditions, whipped constantly and even forced to work naked. They slept on rotting straw, ate scraps and suffered every indignity. Only when one girl escaped, and the parish officers found another on the point of death, did the torture cease and Elizabeth Brownrigg, cruellest of mistresses, receive her just desserts.

Agricultural expert makes grand tour of southern Counties

Salisbury, Wiltshire, July 1767
Farmers throughout southern England and Wales are being visited by an agrarian enthusiast who is keen to chronicle the beginnings of a revolution in agriculture. Arthur Young is noting every change in farming practices – such as intensive cultivation, rotation of crops and the use of manure – with great approval. He plans to write a book after he has completed his six-week tour.

From East Anglia he travelled through Essex, passing Billericay, where he found the country "very rich, woody and pleasant", then headed across the south midlands to the Cotswolds. In the fields around High Wycombe in Buckinghamshire – abundant in turnips, barley, clover and wheat – he found farmers making use of crop rotation. In the Cotswolds he saw the horse pulling the plough giving way to the more efficient ox.

Wales was a disappointment, its farmers being too conservative to change. But Salisbury amazes him. "The flocks of sheep they keep on the plain are the greatest in England", he says (→ 12/1768).

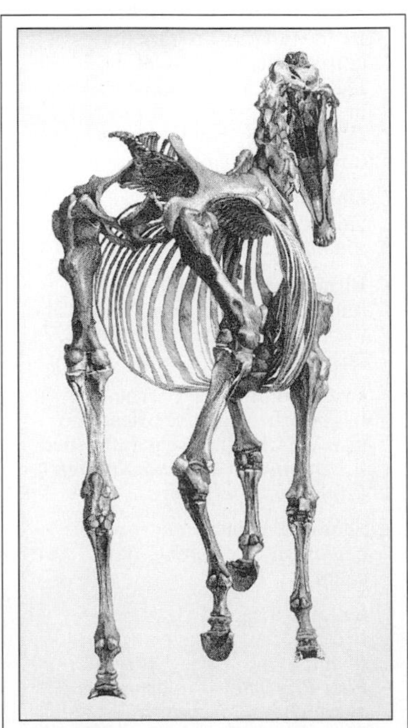

Fascinated by horses, the artist George Stubbs produced a book of their anatomy and skeletons.

1768

London, 29 January. Covent Garden theatre stages the first performance of Oliver Goldsmith's latest play, *The Good-natured Man* (→1770).

London, 16 February. Parliament passes the Octennial Act; this limits the duration of English and Irish parliaments to eight years.

Ireland, 18 February. Frederick Hervey, the bishop of Cloyne, is appointed bishop of Derry.

Westminster, 25 February. John Wilkes, who was expelled from government after the publication of issue number 45 of the *North Briton*, announces that he will stand as a candidate in the forthcoming general election (→10/5).

Ireland, March. King George III gives his approval to an increase in the number of boats in service between Dublin and Holyhead.

Lancashire, spring. Rioting and destruction of new machinery spreads to Blackburn.

Dublin, 2 May. The House of Commons refuses the request by Viscount Townshend, the lord lieutenant, to increase numbers in the army from 12,000 to 15,235 (→27/2/71).

Plymouth, 25 August. Captain James Cook sets sail with his crew in HMS *Endeavour* on an expedition to find a southern continent (→10/4/69).

Boston, Mass, September. British infantry regiments commanded by Lt-Col Dalrymple set up quarters here in an attempt to restore order to the colony following recent unrest (→7/11/69).

Dublin. The Poolbeg lighthouse at the entrance to the harbour is completed.

Birmingham. The city hosts a music festival to raise funds for the newly founded general hospital.

Britain. Laurence Sterne, the Irish-born Anglican priest and novelist who this year published *A Sentimental Journey through France and Italy*, dies.

Scotland. Construction work begins on the Forth/Clyde canal.

Britain. Joseph Priestley, a Presbyterian minister and scientist, publishes *Essay on the First Principles of Government* in which he advocates happiness for the majority (→17/8/71).

Riots in London mar general election

Parliament shocked at Wilkes's victory

England, 10 May
Just ten days after being cleared of charges of outlawry, John Wilkes, the member of parliament for Middlesex, has been sentenced to 22 months in prison and fined £1,000 for libel – on the charges first made in 1764 of publishing the *North Briton* newspaper and the *Essay on Woman*.

Since Wilkes returned from exile in Europe earlier this year to seek public office, he has been a thorn in the side of both parliament and George III. His victories in four elections, despite being expelled from the House of Commons for being "incapable" as a member, have won him public sympathy.

Attempts by the government to prevent Wilkes from taking his seat have led to the rallying cry in the streets of "Wilkes and no king!". Supporters have paid the fine, and they plan to sweeten Wilkes's imprisonment with every manner of luxury, from wine and women, to food and money (→2/1769).

Attempts to silence Wilkes were futile, and the mob rioted in his favour.

Royal troops fire into demonstrating mob

London, 10 May
Troops are being used to quell riots in St George's Fields, Southwark, following the imprisonment of John Wilkes. Mobs have been roaming the streets, chanting: "Damn the king, damn the government and damn the justice." Six rioters have been shot dead and 15 wounded. A woman assaulted a policeman after being arrested for shouting "Wilkes and liberty". Merchants travelling by coach to address King George III at St James's Palace have also been targets of attack, and the windows of the Mansion House have been smashed.

The Wilkes riots have coincided with outbreaks of violent disturbances elsewhere in London, arising from high prices, low wages, and workers protesting at conditions.

New machinery destroyed by weavers who fear huge job losses

Spinning is important to the home economy; now it is under threat.

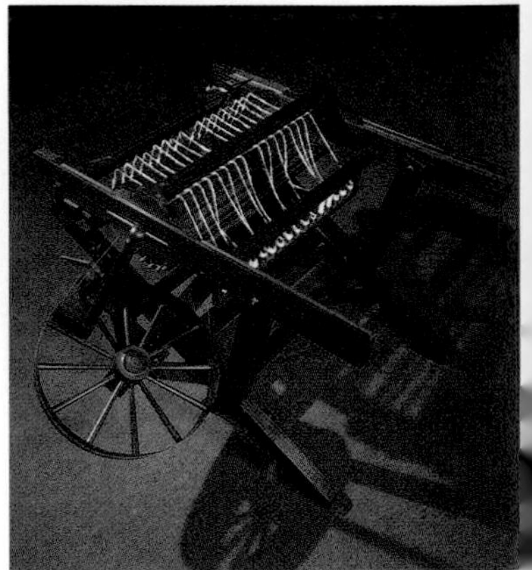
Hargreaves's "spinning jenny".

England, 10 May
The use of new machinery in the textile industry is provoking increasing resentment and violence from weavers in fear of losing their livelihood and independence. What were once isolated attacks on the machines are now becoming more commonplace. The first sign of things to come, and of likely redundancies for those working at home in the weaving industry, appeared four years ago, when James Hargreaves invented the "spinning jenny" – the result of an accident. When a spinning wheel was knocked over and continued to revolve, he calculated that a single wheel could drive a line of spindles. He has since perfected the idea and built machines for sale.

But this month hand spinners and weavers broke into his home and smashed all his machines. Hargreaves has plans to move to Nottinghamshire and set up a business partnership there (→1769).

Poor health forces Chatham to resign

Westminster, 12 October
Ill-health has finally defeated William Pitt, the earl of Chatham, who has resigned from the administration which he formed just two years ago. Sickness has plagued Pitt throughout his political life, and this last administration – noted for its weakness and the mismanagement of the Wilkes affair – has taken its toll, especially since he lost his popularity with the people by taking a peerage. With the duke of Grafton prime minister, the unpopular earl of Shelburne – no longer able to rely on Pitt's protection – has pre-empted his imminent dismissal and resigned (→ 28/1/70).

Countess to found Methodist college

Selina, countess of Huntingdon.

Wales
Women are making their mark in the new Methodist Church. After the expulsion of six Calvinistic Methodists from St Edmund's Hall, Oxford, a new college is now to be set up in the town of Trevecca by Selina, the countess of Huntingdon. The countess, who experienced her own conversion some 30 years ago in the strictest form of Methodism, is a well-known and respected figure. A wealthy lady, she endows the cause with her money and also her connections. Whether women make suitable leaders of the church will soon be revealed. Some people see it as the end of traditional marriage (→ 1/4/77).

King backs creation of new art academy

This painting of the Royal Academy, by Wheatley, is in the grand style.

London, 10 December
The Royal Academy came into being today when King George III signed its instrument of foundation and declared himself to be "patron, protector and supporter" of the 50 academicians. Joshua Reynolds, a Devon man, has been elected its first president. He studied in Rome, and as a portrait painter he began the taste for the "grand style", incorporating classical allusions, antique sculpture and an historical manner. He is to deliver discourses on art to students of the Academy schools to be established in Somerset House. The Academy will hold annual exhibitions in its premises in Pall Mall. Among its founders is Thomas Gainsborough, Reynolds's chief rival as a society portrait painter. Ladies often prefer to be painted by Gainsborough in ballgowns rather than in the plain "night-gowns" on which Reynolds insists as being more "classical". Gainsborough likes to pose his subjects in the country with their mansions and parks about them. Reynolds founded "The Club" with his friends Dr Johnson, David Garrick, Edmund Burke and Oliver Goldsmith [*see page 721*]. He has made Johnson the Academy's professor of ancient literature, a purely nominal honour (→ 21/7/69).

Liverpool becomes slave-trading port

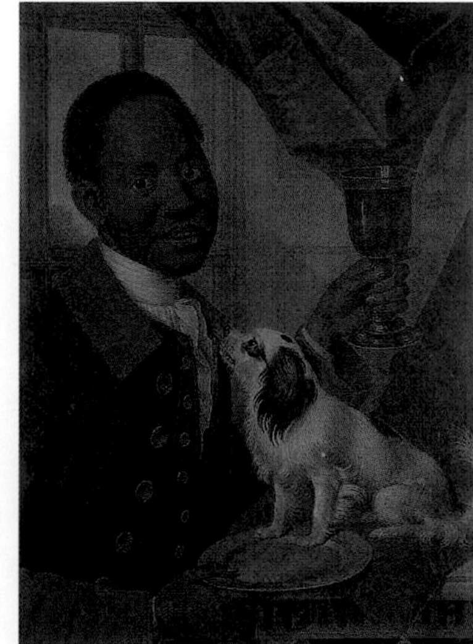

Black children are forced into service as part of the slave trade.

Liverpool, 15 December
Liverpool is fast becoming a major slave-trading port, operating in conjunction with the Lancashire cotton industry. Cargoes of finished goods are shipped to Africa and traded for negroes, who are transported across the Atlantic and exchanged as slaves for the raw materials needed in the industry, as well as for sugar and tobacco.

As abolitionists attempt to bring an end to this inhumane commerce – a trade that is also practised by the French, Dutch and Portuguese – an advertisement published in today's *Liverpool Chronicle* offers a 12-year-old black child for sale. It says that he is "of a sober, tractable and humane disposition ... and can dress hair in a tolerable way".

Variety of thriving industries is found in northern towns

Manchester, December
Arthur Young, the author of a survey of farming in southern England and Wales in 1767, set off on a new trip this year – in search of the agricultural revolution in the north of England. But he found an industrial revolution instead.

In Rotherham he visited iron and coal mines employing almost 500 miners, as well as foundries forging boilers and ploughshares. In Sheffield he observed plate works and steel and iron mills, and was particularly impressed by the tilting mill, "an immense hammer in constant motion on an anvil, worked by waterwheels, and by the same power the bellows of a forge adjoining kept regularly blown".

In Newcastle upon Tyne's coal mines he saw a road of rails: "The coal waggon roads, from the pits to the water, are great works of nine or ten miles. The tracks of the wheels are marked with pieces of timber let into the road, for the wheels of the waggon to run on."

Nearby were Crawley's iron works, thought to be "the greatest manufactory of the kind in Europe". Crossing the neck of Britain, he then made his way to Manchester. On the way he paid a visit to a pin factory in Warrington employing two to three hundred children.

Manchester is the biggest cotton city in the country. "Large families in this place are no encumbrance, all are set to work," Young enthuses. Cotton is not Manchester's only boast, he discovered. The city is the terminus of the most modern waterway in the world, the duke of Bridgewater's canal. It runs from the duke's coal mines near Worsley right into the city, where it ends in a subterranean quay beneath an area containing yards and warehouses. An extension – to Liverpool – is being built and has reached as far as Altrincham, 20 miles (32km) southwest of Manchester (→ 1769).

1769 - 1770

Westminster, February 1769. Parliament votes to expel John Wilkes, the jailed member for Middlesex, for his criticism of its part in the deaths of 11 people last year outside King's Bench prison (→ 8/10/74).

Ireland, 5 April 1769. Peadar O'Doirnin, the poet, dies.

Tahiti, 10 April 1769. Captain James Cook arrives on his voyage to find a southern continent (→ 7/10).

London, 21 July 1769. Joshua Reynolds, the artist who was one of the founding members of the Royal Academy, is knighted (→ 23/2/92).

Ulster, July 1769. Rioting breaks out when "steelboys" rebel (→ 12/1770).

New Zealand, 7 October 1769. Captain James Cook discovers the islands (→ 19/4/70).

Britain, 1769. General Pasquale Paoli, the Corsican freedom fighter, escapes here in the wake of the defeat of his nationalist forces by the French, who purchased Corsica from Genoa in 1768.

New York, 19 January 1770. A group of New Yorkers, "the sons of liberty", attack British troops here (→ 3/1770).

Westminster, March 1770. Parliament repeals the act imposing a duty on glass, paper and paint exported to the American colonies, but the duty on tea remains; the duties were imposed by Charles Townshend, the then chancellor of the exchequer, in 1767 (→ 5).

Australia, 19 April 1770. Captain Cook and his crew believe that they have found a southern continent (→ 6/5).

Blackburn, 12 July 1770. James Hargreaves patents the "spinning jenny" which he invented in 1764 (→ 1771).

Britain, 30 September 1770. George Whitefield, the preacher and former companion of John Wesley, dies.

South Atlantic, 1770. Spain expels British settlers from the Falkland Islands; a British colony was founded here in 1765 (→ 1/1771).

Leeds, 1770. Work is begun on the Leeds/Liverpool canal.

Leicestershire, 1770. Robert Bakewell, a local farmer, makes the first advances in the science of breeding with "New Leicester sheep" and "Dishley long-horn cattle".

Full steam ahead for new inventions

"The water frame" for spinning.

The Scots scientist James Watt has seen the potential of steam power.

London, 1769
What is being called an "industrial revolution" is sweeping the country, and nowhere is it more typified than in the development of three inventions all central to the great changes in manufacturing, especially of textiles. They are as varied as James Watt's harnessing of steam to drive engines in the "condenser" which he has patented this year, and James Hargreaves's so-called "spinning jenny", a device that enables one operator to control multiple spindles. Another significant advance is represented by the water-powered loom designed by Richard Arkwright and known as "the water frame".

The steam engine first appeared in the early years of this century, developed by Thomas Savery and Thomas Newcomen. The device introduced by Watt makes it more economical by condensing the steam compressed in the engine's cylinder in a separate chamber; the cylinder stays hot and does not need to be reheated on each stroke. Arkwright's water frame – which can also be driven by steam power or by a horse – enables weavers to spin a yarn strong enough to produce an all-cotton cloth for the first time; previously cotton has been mixed with linen (→ 12/7/70).

Colonies join forces in British trade ban

North Carolina, 7 November 1769
South Carolina joined Virginia and New England today in a ban on trade with Britain until the Townshend Act taxes are repealed, and underlined the determination of the colonies to stand firm against what they see as unacceptable taxation. Instead, domestic manufacturers are to be encouraged, and lists of goods not to be purchased, notably "luxurious and enervating tea", are being circulated.

This opposition, which puts paid to any ideas Britain might have had of gaining an easy and substantial revenue from the colonists, is open and even actively hostile. Not only are goods left unsold but also customs officers are manhandled, and troops, the only effective police force, are harassed and obstructed with impunity (→ 19/1/70).

Lord North takes over as prime minister

Lord North: ugly but charming.

London, 28 January 1770
Britain has a new prime minister. The duke of Grafton has been replaced by Lord North, a former playmate of King George III, a classical scholar and, as a member of both the Grenville and Chatham governments and a former chancellor of the exchequer, a man of formidable political experience.

Despite his grotesquely ugly appearance, Lord North has a charm and wit that endear him to his many supporters. Add to these a skill in debate and prudent understanding of financial affairs, and he appears to be an admirable choice for prime minister.

In foreign affairs he intends to keep Britain out of Europe's quarrels and promises a policy of "quiet firmness" for the colonies. Whether North America will accept his decision to maintain the detested tea duty remains to be seen (→ 21/6/79).

Ottawa Indian chief found murdered

North America, 20 April 1769
The Ottowa chief Pontiac was murdered today in an incident that poses a serious threat to the stability of Indian-British relations. The leader of the revolt against Britain in 1763, Pontiac had finally signed a peace treaty, but of late he appeared to have turned against his old enemy once again.

Witnesses say that they saw an Indian named Black Dog strike Pontiac from behind, at the trading post of Cahokia, and then stab him. Black Dog escaped after the attack, and his motive is unknown; many are claiming that he was hired by the British to assassinate the troublesome Ottawa chief.

Potter is expanding

Stoke-on-Trent, 1769
The master potter Josiah Wedgwood has underlined his domination of the Staffordshire potteries with the opening of his latest works, Etruria, in open country west of Hanley, near Stoke-on-Trent. A purpose-built village to house the workforce stands alongside the new factory.

Wedgwood, whose first factory opened ten years ago in nearby Burslem, has based his success on the ability to provide every class in society with first-rate porcelain ware.

British troops open fire on demonstrating colonists in Boston, claiming five lives

Boston "massacre": British troops take aim and fire into the rioting crowd.

Boston, Mass, 5 March 1770
Three colonists died today, and eight others were serious wounded, when British troops opened fire on a riotous mob which had gathered to protest at the alleged attack by a sentry of the 29th Regiment on a young barber, Edward Garrick.

Captain Thomas Preston mustered a small patrol and found himself confronted by a shouting crowd led by a mulatto, one Crispus Attucks. Sticks and stones rained down on the soldiers, as did shouts of abuse and defiance. Whether Preston gave an order is unknown, but firing broke out, and Attucks and two others were killed. The colonists are enraged, but in an atmosphere of increasing hostility the only surprise is that the "massacre" has not happened before (→10/6/72).

Burke airs views on his discontentment

London, April 1770
Fired by the controversy surrounding the Wilkes affair, the political commentator Edmund Burke has published a controversial pamphlet, *Thoughts on the Present Discontents*. In it he sets out the idea of a "party", which he defines as "a body of men united for promoting ... the national interest upon some particular principle upon which they are all agreed", against that of "the king's friends", seen as a clique united not by principle but only by self-interest. Such theories favour Lord Rockingham but are unlikely to please King George III, whose influence on government it undermines yet further.

Edmund Burke has radical ideas.

Talented young poet Thomas Chatterton takes his own life

"The Death of Chatterton": a romanticized Victorian view by Henry Wallis.

London, 25 August 1770
The body of the precocious poet Thomas Chatterton was found at his lodgings this morning; he had died of arsenic poisoning. It is not clear if he took his life deliberately or died of the arsenic cure that he was taking for syphilis. Only 18, he was already famous for his ability to turn out poems in every style. Dr Johnson said: "It is wonderful how the whelp has written such things." Horace Walpole was thrilled by the mediaeval manuscript poems that Chatterton sent him, said to have been found in a church at Bristol, his home town. Chatterton claimed that they were by a monk called Rowley, but Walpole later decided that he wrote them himself.

Thomas Gainsborough painted one of his most famous pictures, "The Blue Boy", in 1770.

Cook claims Australia for Britain

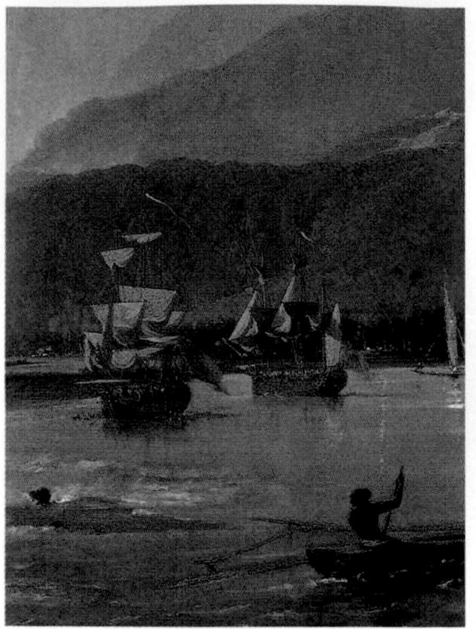
Cook's ships arrive at Tahiti.

After an epic voyage Captain Cook raised the Union flag in Australia.

Australia, 6 May 1770
Contemplating the profusion of plants and trees from their ship, the *Endeavour*, Captain James Cook and his expedition promptly named the place Botany Bay. They then noticed a party of natives cooking over a fire and ignoring the pale-faced strangers. But when Cook attempted to land they threatened him with strange, curved throw-sticks which returned to the thrower after striking a target. Cook eventually effected a landing some distance from the hostile natives and hoisted the Union flag to claim the territory for the British crown. Cook, the son of a labourer, served aboard North Sea colliers after starting his working life in a haberdasher's shop. He taught himself mathematics before joining the Royal Navy. The admiralty made him commander of this expedition over the heads of well-connected aristocrats. Cook reached Tahiti via Cape Horn and, sailing south-west, discovered New Zealand.

Following a three-week voyage he sighted land once more – Australia, a name first used over 70 years ago for the fabled lands of the South Seas (→ 12/7/71).

'Steelboys' attack Belfast barracks

Belfast, December 1770
In one of the worst incidents to be recorded since the formation of the "steelboys" movement in the south of Co Antrim, more than a thousand farmers, who are protesting against evictions in their area, have marched on Belfast barracks to release one of their colleagues who had been arrested for maiming cattle. Five were killed when the Belfast military opened fire.

The steelboys' organization is a sophisticated one. It has recruited its members from amongst the Presbyterian population, and they are mainly agitating against land being given to Catholics who are prepared to pay high rents. They also support the notion of fair rent levels and the regulation of meal and potato prices.

They are being seen as part of a potentially political rural underground movement which is quickly learning how to achieve its aims through intimidation. Rich landowners are now being forced to barricade their houses against possible attacks (→ 28/3/72).

Marquis of Granby, popular general, dies

North Yorkshire, 18 October 1770
John Manners, the marquis of Granby, idolized by his troops in the Seven Years' War with France, died today at Scarborough, aged 49.

In 1760, at the head of his cheering squadrons of cavalry, Granby stormed Warburg in Westphalia, capturing 1,500 men. Returning to England, he was acclaimed by the public but dismissed by Walpole as "the mob's hero". He lavished £60,000 on his troops, and many of them, demobilized with his payoffs, set up as publicans and named their public houses after him.

Blackfriars Bridge in London, designed by the Scotsman Robert Mylne, opened in 1769. This view of its construction was engraved in 1763.

Goldsmith attacks the evils of enclosures

London, 1770
Oliver Goldsmith, the Irish poet, has spoken out against the evils of enclosures of common land in England by large landowners in a poem entitled *The Deserted Village*. It recreates a vision of "Auburn", the poet's beloved birthplace, which he revisits to find only decay and dereliction because the villagers have moved on, many to miserable poverty in the towns.

He conjures up an idyllic memory of his boyhood when the village had a preacher whose persuasive powers won respect, and a schoolmaster, a man "severe and stern to view", was a source of rustic pride:

And still they gazed, and still
the wonder grew
That one small head could
carry all he knew.

The life he recalls had dignity and has been sacrificed for greed:

Ill fares the land, to hastening
ills a prey,
Where wealth accumulates
and men decay.

Villagers leaving for a new life.

Goldsmith first established his literary reputation as a novelist in 1766 with *The Vicar of Wakefield*. Both this novella and his poem exhibit his warm and simplehearted human sympathy (→ 16/3/73).

1771

Dublin, 27 February. George, Viscount Townshend, the lord lieutenant of Ireland, who has been attempting to increase the size of Britain's army in Ireland, is forced to use military strength to quell an outbreak of violent rioting (→30/11/72).

Portsmouth, 12 July. Captain James Cook and his crew aboard the *Endeavour* return to England after a successful expedition to discover a southern continent (→13/7/72).

Leeds, July. The Tate Wilkinson theatre is opened.

Belfast, 1 August. The foundation stone of the new Poor House and Infirmary is laid.

Birmingham, 17 August. Joseph Priestley, the scientist, discovers that growing plants release a gas (→1774).

Italy, 17 September. Tobias Smollett, the Scottish novelist, best known for his picaresque novels *The Adventures of Roderick Random* and *The Adventures of Peregrine Pickle*, dies at Leghorn [Livorno].

England, 1 November. King George III is furious when he discovers that his younger brother, Henry, the duke of Cumberland, has secretly married a widowed commoner, Ann Horton, the daughter of the earl of Carhampton, an Irish politician (→8/2/72).

Cumbria, 17 November. Sollom Moss, near Longtown, erupts, destroying many houses with mud and moss.

Dumfries. Troops from Edinburgh are sent to quell bread riots.

India. Warren Hastings, a council member in Calcutta and Madras, is appointed British governor of Bengal (→2/1772).

Britain. John Hunter, a Scottish physiologist and surgeon, publishes *The Natural History of Human Teeth*, the first study of dental anatomy.

Liverpool. Bidston lighthouse is built by the borough corporation to meet the growing needs of the port.

London. To hinder the increase of forged coins, coining copper is made a felony.

London. Dr Charles Burney, a musicologist, publishes his findings in his survey *The present state of music in Italy and France* (→1773).

Falklands accepted as British by Spain

South Atlantic, January

The Spanish government has, reluctantly, agreed to restore the British garrison on West Falkland island in the South Atlantic Ocean, some 250 miles (400km) from the South American mainland.

The two countries came to the brink of war last year after a Spanish raiding expedition from Buenos Aires ejected the small British force from Port Egmont in West Falkland. West Falkland and its sister island, East Falkland, have been disputed territory since they were discovered, by a navigator in an English fleet, in 1592.

Botanical research centre set up at Kew

Kew, Surrey

Joseph Banks, the 27-year-old naturalist who has returned to England after his voyage round the world with Captain James Cook, has been presented to George III. He told the king of the breadfruit tree, mango and other exotic plants he had collected during the voyage.

The king was enthusiastic when Banks suggested that a royal park should be set aside to preserve his plant collection, and he chose Kew Gardens near Richmond, west of London, which was developed by his mother, Augusta, the dowager princess of Wales.

Enquire within on arts and science

Edinburgh

Three young Scots completed a labour of love this year with the publication of the third and final volume of their dictionary of the arts and sciences, the *Encyclopaedia Britannica*. The book was conceived by Andrew Bell and Colin Macfarquhar and edited by William Smellie. It was initially published as a periodical, with the first parts appearing in December 1768; the first bound volume was completed in 1769, the second last year. The price of the full set, which consists of 2659 pages, is £12.

Arkwright builds a water-powered mill

Arkwright's mill at Cromford, housing his remarkable new "water frame".

Derbyshire

Richard Arkwright has set up a mill at Cromford, near Matlock, to accommodate his innovative water-powered cotton-spinning frame [*see page 728*]. Traditional home-based textile workers, who use the spinning wheel, are incensed, saying that his invention will put them out of work. Arkwright's frame, using bobbins and rollers, spins flax into 20 to 30 threads with no more labour than was previously needed to spin a single one, and they have a strength and fineness never before achieved (→1779).

Thomas Gray finds final resting place

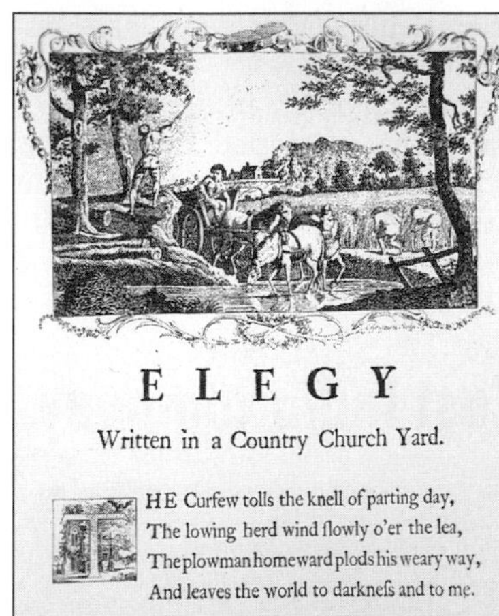

The "Elegy": an illustrated page.

Cambridge, 30 July

Thomas Gray, the leading poet of the day, died today at Cambridge, where he spent the last 30 years of his life and was professor of history. He is to be buried in the churchyard at Stoke Poges, in Buckinghamshire, about which he wrote his *Elegy* – beside his mother and "the rude forefathers of the hamlet". He aimed to be "concise, pure and musical".

Tobacco cash funds boom in Glasgow

Glasgow

Imports of tobacco through Glasgow this year have risen to a phenomenal 46 million pounds' weight [more than 20 million kilograms], underlining the dominance that the city has won over the Atlantic trade. The profits from this trade are funding a boom in the city.

The "tobacco lords" – as the merchants are known – have invested their wealth in the west of Scotland, where the economy has also been boosted by the export of goods such as linen to North America. In Glasgow the population is rising fast, and industries are springing up to supply the growing export market. The lords have brought a new level of wealth to the city, funding building programmes and cultural activities.

Since the early part of this century, when Scottish trade with North America and the West Indies was carried on illicitly, Glasgow merchants have exploited their proximity to the New World. As long ago as 1740 the city controlled 40 per cent of the tobacco trade.

1772

London, 8 February. Augusta, the dowager princess of Wales, and mother of King George III, dies aged 52 (→ 13).

London, 13 February. Rioting mars the funeral of the king's mother as her funeral procession is mobbed (→ 24/3).

India, February. Warren Hastings, the new governor of Bengal, arrives to take up his position.

Ulster, 28 March. Parliament imposes severe restrictions on "steelboys" to repress the outbreaks of violence in the area.

North America, 10 June. American patriots, led by Abraham Whipple, attack a British customs ship, the *Gaspee*, which has run aground near Providence, Rhode Island; the ship is destroyed and the young commander, Lieutenant Dudington, is wounded (→ 6/1773).

Southampton, 13 July. Captain James Cook, who discovered and claimed the new British colony of Australia, sets out on his second voyage of discovery to the southern continent (→ 16/1/73).

Windsor, 13 September. William Henry, the duke of Gloucester and younger brother of George III, informs his brother of his secret marriage six years ago to Maria, the dowager Lady Waldegrave (→ 1777).

Dublin, 30 November. Simon, Earl Harcourt, is appointed as lord lieutenant of Ireland after the recall of George, Viscount Townshend.

Britain. Daniel Rutherford, a Scottish scientist, publishes a report on his discovery of a new gas, nitrogen.

London. The building of the Pantheon in London's Oxford Street is finally finished; it has cost £60,000.

Britain. "Pressing" is abolished in prisons. This was a cruel form of torture inflicted on those who refused to stand trial; the victim was placed face down on the floor and weighted down by heavy stones until all life was finally "pressed" out of him.

Britain. The novel *The Man of Feeling*, by the Scottish author Henry Mackenzie, is published anonymously; when a Bath clergyman, Mr Eccles, claims to be the author, Mackenzie's publishers are forced to reveal his name.

King wins right to veto royal marriages

Westminster, 24 March
Despite the fierce opposition of the liberal politician Charles Fox, the Royal Marriages Act has easily won the support of both houses of parliament. Fox tried to portray the issue as an abuse of the royal prerogative, but the majority saw it as a sensible attempt by King George III to bring his wayward relations to heel.

The king was furious when he learnt recently that his brother, Henry, the duke of Cumberland, had secretly married a commoner named Ann Horton. The new act requires royals under the age of 25 to have the monarch's consent before marrying (→ 13/9).

Gloucester: marriage angered king.

Scots in financial crisis as bank fails

Ayr, 24 June
More than a million pounds may be lost in the crash today of the Ayr bank. The collapse of the London bank of Neale, James Fordyce and Downe two weeks ago triggered a demand by London financiers for repayment of £600,000. Ayr cannot meet this, nor can it pay creditors £300,000, and notes worth £200,000 are unlikely to be honoured. The Ayr bank had thrived since its opening in 1769, because of the mean lending policies of the main Scottish banks, but became overambitious, opening branches and making high-risk loans.

Author of scandal-mongering 'Junius' letters keeps anonymity

London
A stream of pseudonymous letters that has caused fury in government circles for the past five years seems to have dried up. The scandal-mongering and invective-laden letters appeared in the *Public Advertiser* under the pen-name "Junius". They heaped scorn on King George III and members of the government, which was condemned for incompetence, corruption and disregard of the law.

Speculation about the identity of Junius has suggested such men as Edmund Burke, John Wilkes and Edward Gibbon. But the favourite is Sir Philip Francis, a clerk in the war office.

Edmund Burke (l) was among the leading suspects in the letter-writing saga.

East India company in financial trouble

India: are the good times ending?

London, July
The East India company is on the verge of bankruptcy. So grave is the financial situation that the directors have asked the government to defer the payment of £203,000 now due to the customs for excise duties.

On top of the collapse of commercial confidence following the slump in Europe, the company has grave problems of its own: revenues have slumped on account of the famine in Bengal, while costs have soared because of the expense of fighting Indian princes. The directors brought trouble on themselves by optimistically putting up the dividend to 12.5 per cent (→ 1773).

Irish land laws on Catholics relaxed

Ireland, 2 June
The passing of the Bogland Act will allow Catholics to take 61-year leases for bog reclamation and is seen as the beginning of the relaxation of Irish Land Laws penalizing Catholics. As a result of the penal laws their share of profitable land has fallen dramatically, from 22 per cent in 1688 to around 5 per cent today. This legislation will be seen as a victory for the Catholic Committee, founded in 1760 by the scholar Charles O'Conor to persuade the government to introduce some relief from the penal laws.

1773

Dublin, 5 January. Art mac Cubhthaigh, the poet, dies.

Antarctic Ocean, 16 January. Captain James Cook and his crew cross the Antarctic Circle on their second voyage south to Australia (→30/7/75).

London, June. The crown disbands the commission appointed to hunt down the gang who destroyed the cutter *Gaspee* (→9/1773).

London, September. Benjamin Franklin, an American politician enraged at proposals to tax all tea imported into the colonies, publishes *Rules by which a great empire may be reduced to a small one* in several English newspapers (→10/1773).

London, early October. The Tea Act is passed to aid the failing finances of the East India company; it allows the direct export of 500,000 pounds of tea from India to the American colonies (→13).

Philadelphia, Pa, 13 October. At a mass meeting, colonists protest at the tax on tea and the monopoly given to the East India company (→30/11).

Boston, Mass, 30 November. An angry crowd demands that the cargo ship *Dartmouth*, which has been anchored off the harbour for the last two days, be sent back to Britain still laden with its cargo of tea; the *Dartmouth* is the first of three ships bound for Boston to arrive (→16/12).

Shropshire. Work begins on the building of the first cast-iron bridge, at Coalbrookdale (→1779).

Britain. Dr Charles Burney, the musicologist, publishes his findings on the *Present state of music in Germany, the Netherlands, and the United Provinces (→1776).*

Scotland. John Erskine, a lawyer, publishes *Institutes of the law in Scotland.*

London. Jonathan's coffee house becomes known as the London Stock Exchange; stock-brokers began to come here when they were ejected from the Royal Exchange.

Cornwall. Local tinners, hit by low returns and high grain prices, riot and seize stocks of grain; troops are sent in to deal with the crisis.

Bradford. The Piece Hall opens for the sale of cloth made by handloom weavers at their homes in the nearby hills.

Charges are dropped against Clive

London
Robert Clive, the hero of many wars in India, has survived the vicious attack on him by the Burgoyne committee. Its report was scathing about the the East India company's rule: "Oppression in every shape has ground the faces of the poor defenceless natives; and tyranny in her bloodless form has stalked abroad."

Clive hit back, saying that he was "astonished at his own moderation" in taking so little for himself. The Commons ruled that though he had pocketed £234,000 he had performed "great ... services to the state". Many others have enriched themselves in India, but few have done so much as Clive for Britain's glory overseas (→22/11/74).

Robert Clive talks terms with native rulers after his victories in India.

Adam's neo-classical lines shape design

The neo-classical exteriors ...

... and interiors of the Adams.

Britain
The genius of Robert Adam, and his innovative neo-classical designs in building and decorative work, are having a marked influence on the style of architecture both here and abroad. Some of his later commissions – Syon House, Luton Hoo and Kenwood – are already regarded as masterpieces of interior design by his peers.

Robert Adam and his brothers, John, James and William, are the sons of the late William Adam – the leading architect of his day in Scotland. All four of his sons were trained in his Edinburgh office and have since established flourishing practices in London. They plan to develop a large riverside estate which they have acquired in the Strand, called "The Adelphi".

Robert is the most famous of the brothers. His "grand tour" in 1750-54 was mostly spent in Rome, where he studied Pompeiian and Etruscan ruins. The experience encouraged him to develop his now familiar neo-classical style, embodying lightness, elegance and colour to soften the academic severity of Palladian architecture.

New act will curb East India excesses

London
The government has now moved to control the East India company through the Regulating Act, in the face of mismanagement and financial irregularities in the company's activities. The company has no choice but to fall into line because it needs a government loan to stave off bankruptcy.

Under the new legislation the company has agreed to limit the dividend. More importantly, it has accepted a new supreme council in Bengal, whose members will be government nominees.

Tobacco was a money-spinner. Smoking clubs sprang up to consume America's main export.

Irish Protestant is cleared of murder

Cork City, 4 September
In a judgement which has surprised and angered many Roman Catholics, Abraham Morris, a rich Protestant, has been acquitted of the murder of Arthur Leary, a Catholic and a colonel in the Austrian army.

The incident arose over the sale of Leary's famous racing mare, for which Morris offered the statutory £5. (Under the law, Catholics are not permitted to own a horse of greater value than this.) Outraged by the offer, Leary hit Morris. Morris refused to fight back, believing it to be beneath his dignity to strike a Catholic; instead he had Leary outlawed. This led to the fatal shooting of Leary by soldiers in Co Cork last May.

His wife, Eileen, who has threatened to avenge his death, has written a poem in Irish entitled *The Lament for Arthur Leary*, widely regarded as one of the finest examples of this genre.

Boston rebels defy British Tea Act

A tax man is tarred and feathered.

Crowds of cheering onlookers play their part in "the Boston Tea Party".

Boston, Mass, 16 December
Local patriots struck a cheeky blow today against the British government and the power of the East India company. They went aboard three tea ships in the harbour and dumped the contents of 340 tea chests into the sea. By low tide huge piles of tea were visible all along the shore. Many of the raiders were disguised as Red Indians. They were armed with axes and pistols, and shouted blood-curdling war cries as they boarded, but they were careful not to injure the sailors, nor to damage any cargo other than tea. This was a political protest over Lord North's Tea Act. North wanted to boost the declining finances of the East India company and to punish tea smugglers. The colonists have shown how much they resent what they see as arbitrary rule from Britain (→4/1774).

Bristol citizens acquire new library society

Bristol
Bristol, like Leeds, now has its own library. The Bristol Library Society will operate on much the same lines as the one started in Leeds five years ago. Members will pay a guinea a year, and in return for that they will be able to borrow from a stock of more than five hundred works. The emphasis will be on travel books, histories, and novels, like those of Sterne and Fielding, which are increasingly popular with readers. However, more studious lenders will be able to borrow scientific and theological books.

City of London financiers meet at Jonathan's coffee house in Change Alley. A group of brokers set up a club here in 1722, two years after the South Sea Bubble disaster; in 1773 it was renamed the Stock Exchange.

Goldsmith's play 'stoops to conquer'

Goldsmith's play is an attempt to revive the 17th-century comedy of manners.

London, 16 March
She Stoops to Conquer, a new comedy by Oliver Goldsmith, was given its first performance last night, and "the theatre was filled with the loudest acclamations that ever rung within its walls", according to the *Morning Advertiser*. Dr Goldsmith avers that its plot – in which the young hero Marlow mistakes the house of his future father-in-law for an inn and behaves accordingly – came to him in his boyhood in Ireland, when he asked to be directed to "the best house in the village" and treated the local squire like an innkeeper.

The author relies on his friends to help him out of financial crises. When Goldsmith was arrested for not paying his rent, Dr Johnson took his newly finished *The Vicar of Wakefield* to a bookseller and sold it for publication (→4/5/74).

Increase in transport makes travel easier

Britain
Glasgow can now be reached direct by turnpike road from London, and the Scots will be able to share in the transport revolution that has produced more than 300 new turnpikes in 20 years. York and Gloucester can be reached from London in a day and Chester in two – in 1740 the London-to-Chester journey took six days.

This vast increase in speed is only available to the rich, however. The new "flyers" use 70 horses in two days, whereas the old stage-coach needed only 18. For the poor, too often the only way of getting to another town is to walk. Of greater benefit to the poor are the barges moving sedately along the new canals.

A few canals have been in existence in Britain since Roman times, but recent industrial expansion has created a demand for improved transport routes to move goods. The British Isles' first modern canal opened in Ireland in 1742, covering 18 miles from the East Tyrone coalfield to the port of Newry; it was followed by the Sankey canal in Lancashire, linking St Helens to the river Mersey, which opened in 1757. But it was the duke of Bridgewater's canal, running from the duke's coalmines in Worsley to Manchester, with its imposing 183-metre (600-foot) aqueduct carrying the waterway over the river Irwell, that really convinced people of the possibilities of this new means of transport [*see report on page 727*]. The canal, which opened in 1761, was surveyed and built by James Brindley, a Derbyshire farmer's son who trained initially as a millwright. Brindley is now working on the even more ambitious Grand Union canal, designed to link the Trent and Mersey rivers. The project is already more than half completed. By lowering transport costs, the new canals ensure cheaper coal and food prices for all.

Growing numbers of people are making use of the new means of transport.

Female negro slave publishes poetry

London, 1 September
Poems on Various Subjects, Religious and Moral, published today, has astonished the reading public. The reason is that it was written by a former negro girl slave, Phillis Wheatley. She is 20 years old and comes from Boston, Massachusetts, where she is a maid in the household of John and Susannah Wheatley, whose name she was given when she was delivered from a slave ship from Africa at the age of seven. Phillis Wheatley started composing poetry at the age of 12, and she came came to the notice of readers in the colonies two years ago with her elegy for an evangelist from Britain. In June she came to Britain for a poetry-reading tour. Her collected poems were rejected by the Boston publishing houses, but Archibald Bell, a London publisher and printer, is taking a risk on the little-known author and hopes to have a bestseller on his hands. Curiosity, at least, is likely to bring sales to the black servant-girl poet.

Dr Johnson and Boswell journey north for tour of Scotland and the Hebrides

Edinburgh, 9 November 1773
Dr Samuel Johnson has returned here after his tour of the highlands and islands. His sycophantic friend James Boswell, best known for having written an anonymous book and dedicated it to himself, accompanied him.

Johnson and Flora MacDonald.

Why the doctor, 64 years old and "unwieldy from corpulency", made the journey is a mystery. Until his arrival in Edinburgh on 14 August the kindest thing that he had ever said about the Scots was that there were too many of them in London. From Edinburgh, which he hated for its smells and provincialism, he travelled up to Inverness, picking up the freedom of the city of Aberdeen on the way. Then he cut across "the bosom of the highlands" to the west coast.

These were the "last shelters of national distress". Few people spoke English, and some, according to Boswell, "were as black and wild as any American savage". On 2 September they crossed to Skye, where Johnson met Flora MacDonald, who had helped "the Young Pretender" to escape 28 years ago. There was hardly a middle-aged man who had not been out in 1745. "Where here was formerly an insurrection, there is now a wilderness."

On Skye Johnson also saw an old woman grinding oats with a quern – a practice familiar to the ancient Romans had done. He noted that "their winter overtakes their summer, and their harvest lies on the ground drenched with rain". October was spent "hopping" around the Hebrides, the doctor's moods as changeable as the weather.

Johnson and Boswell journeyed on to Mull (by way of Coll) and also visited Iona, which made a profound impression on both men. Johnson remarked: "The island, which was once the metropolis of learning and piety, has now no school of education, nor temple of worship, only two inhabitants can speak English, and not one that can read or write. Perhaps, in the revolutions of the world, Iona may be sometime again the instructress of the western regions" (→ 1779).

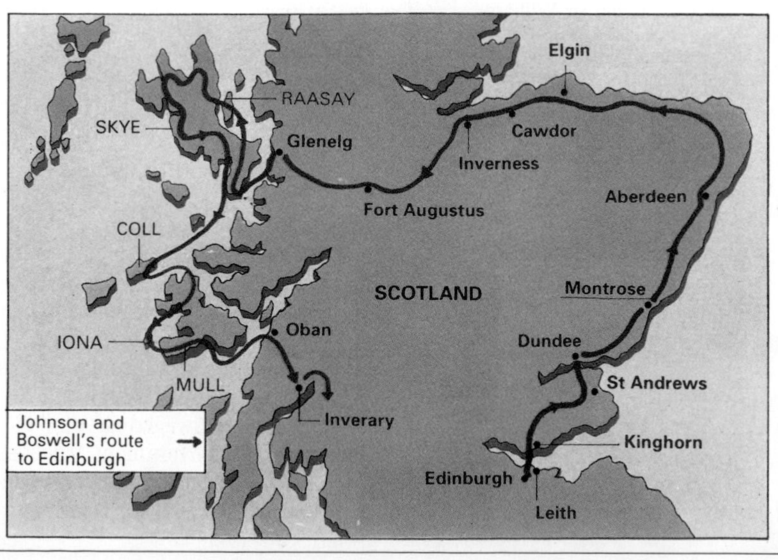

1774-1775

Westminster, April 1774. Parliament repeals the Tea Act (→20/5).

Britain, 4 May 1774. Oliver Goldsmith, the Irish-born poet and playwright, dies.

Westminster, 20 May 1774. Parliament passes the Coercive Act; this closes the port of Boston and reduces the legislative powers of the Massachusetts assembly (→2/6).

North America, 2 June 1774. The Quartering Act is revived; colonists must house British troops in America (→1/12).

Canada, 22 June 1774. The Quebec Act brings religious freedom to Roman Catholics.

Edinburgh, 16 October 1774. Robert Fergusson, a poet, commits suicide, aged 24.

Westminster, 29 November 1774. John Wilkes, the lord mayor of London, is elected as the member of parliament for Middlesex (→26/12/97).

Virginia, 1 December 1774. George Washington signs the Fairfax Resolve which bars the importation of slaves and halts colonial exports (→14).

North America, 14 December 1774. American militias seize control of Fort William and Mary (→22/3).

Bath, 1774. John Wood, the architect, completes the Royal Crescent, begun in 1767.

London, 22 March 1775. Edmund Burke, the member of parliament for Bristol, calls for conciliation with the Americans (→4/1775).

North Carolina, 20 May 1775. Mecklenburg County declares its independence from Britain (→25).

Boston, Mass, 25 May 1775. Reinforcements from Britain, under Generals Sir William Howe, Sir Henry Clinton and John Burgoyne, arrive (→15/6).

Boston, 15 June 1775. George Washington takes over as commander-in-chief of the American rebels (→17).

Boston, 17 June 1775. The British claim victory in a battle at Bunker Hill, despite serious losses (→23/8).

Plymouth, 30 July 1775. Captain Cook returns from his second voyage to the southern hemisphere (→25/6/76).

London, 23 August 1775. George III rejects the "Olive Branch Petition", the colonies' offer of peace (→3/2/76).

Quaker pushes for drastic prison reform

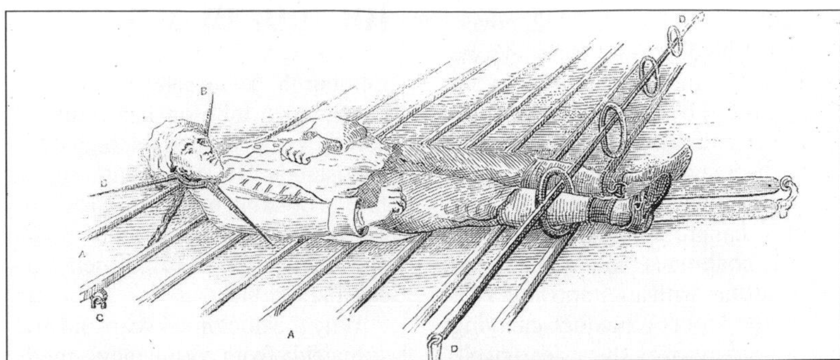

A prisoner in a spiked collar is chained to the floor in Lincoln prison.

London, 1774
A campaign for prison reform by John Howard gained momentum with acts of parliament enforcing cleanliness in the country's prisons and providing for regular salaries to be paid to jailers. English prisons are a national disgrace, and there have been cases where those in charge of them have tortured prisoners to death in order to extract fees. Howard, a Quaker and also the high sheriff for Bedfordshire, has been touring Britain investigating conditions in prisons. He says that many people are being held in prison untried, or even after they have been found innocent, until they or their friends have paid certain fees to the jailers (→1777).

Clive, hero of India, takes his own life

London, 22 November 1774
Robert Clive, who won the victories in India which put Bengal under the rule of the East India company, has died by his own hand. Aged 49, and with his reputation as a great British soldier and administrator fully restored, Clive had been ill and suffering from depression.

Clive went to India as a clerk with the company before becoming a soldier. He proved to be a fine leader and defeated the French at Arcot and elsewhere before returning to England a wealthy man. During Clive's second spell in India, Bengal became virtually a British province. Clive tried to reform the company and tackle corruption; by doing so he aroused hatreds and was the subject of a parliamentary inquiry (→6/1780).

Wilkes is new lord mayor of London

Wilkes and liberty: an old team.

London, 8 October 1774
London's new lord mayor is John Wilkes, who achieved notoriety as an early champion of reform after his arrest for criticizing George III. Wilkes claimed immunity as a member of parliament but was expelled. He has waged several battles with the government, such as the right to report parliamentary debates. Wilkes stands for freedom in politics (→29/11).

Priestley discovers 'dephlogisticated air'

London, 1774
A series of experiments involving the burning of substances has been carried out by Joseph Priestley, and he believes that he has discovered a new gas. Priestley, who has been working for his patron, the earl of Shelburne, is a natural philosopher with an interest in electricity and chemistry. In laboratories in London and at Calne, in Wiltshire, Priestley burned substances almost at random and tested the various airs emitted. One of them he is now describing as "dephlogisticated air" [oxygen]. In France the chemist and physicist Antoine Lavoisier is working on similiar experiments and is studying Priestley's results with great interest (→1790).

Extreme hair fashions have spread to Ireland; witness the shock of this country farmer on his daughter's return from a trip to Dublin.

America revolts against British rule

King George III: under attack.

London, April 1775
Britain's 13 Atlantic coast colonies in America are in a state of revolt against rule from London, and both sides now are preparing for war. General Thomas Gage, in charge of British troops, has been told to use force to maintain law and order and to halt any military build-up by the colonists. But it is known that many independent companies of militiamen are being raised and trained – and armed.

Behind the looming conflict are the British moves to reorganize the vastly expanded North American possessions, and the tax demands, and trade controls, that have been imposed on the colonists. There has been widespread unrest, and in 1773 colonists boarded British ships at Boston and dumped a tea cargo overboard as a protest.

Last year representatives of the colonies met in Philadelphia and condemned British actions. They also drafted a petition insisting that there should be no taxation without representation. There was little talk of independence, but King George III, and his prime minister, Lord North, have been treating the actions of this congress as rebellion. Lord North has now extended the New England Restraining Act to several of the colonies. This forbids them to trade with any country other than Britain or Ireland (→ 19).

David Garrick stars as London theatres grow in popularity

London, 1775
Theatregoing has greatly increased in London in proportion to the greater decency of the plays put on and the less rowdy behaviour of the now largely middle-class audiences. Drury Lane and Covent Garden theatres seat 2,000 and play to 12,000 patrons weekly. In addition there are six unlicensed theatres, at one of which, Goodman's Fields in the East End, David Garrick made his astonishing début in 1741 as King Richard III. Four years before he had walked to London from Lichfield with Dr Johnson, his tutor, and three halfpence in his pocket. He was soon at Drury Lane earning 500 guineas a year.

Garrick's innovations have transformed staging. First he insisted that no playgoers were to sit on the stage or in boxes behind the proscenium. He used realistic scenery in place of formal backdrops, and he now employs the Alsatian scene-painter Philippe Jacques de Loutherbourg and uses stage lighting, mainly by means of "floats" or footlights – lighted wicks floating in tallow at the edge of the forestage.

Theatre audiences are increasing.

He cuts Shakespeare's texts, altering the ending of *Hamlet* and turning *The Tempest* into opera. "We that live to please must please to live," he has said. There are still riots, and an orange was thrown at one of the actors in Sheridan's *The Rivals* when it opened this year. But at least no more duels are fought in the auditorium (→ 10/6/76).

Britain takes tough line with colonists

Westminster, 19 April 1775
Britain's parliament today rejected a motion to repeal the controversial duty on tea and thus to head off the threatened confrontation with the increasingly rebellious colonists in America. During the Commons's debate several members made a case for the Americans and warned that in the event of war they would put up a stiff fight. But neither King George III nor his ministers, neither the Lords nor the Commons, were disposed to listen, and so the motion was rejected.

The crackdown on the colonists is being opposed by several Whig politicians, including Charles Fox and Edmund Burke who have been arguing that a British victory is not a foregone conclusion. They point to serious logistical problems – an Atlantic crossing never takes less than a month – and warn that a great deal of time can elapse between orders leaving London and their reaching British forces.

But there is general support for George III and his government, both in parliament and in the country. The king finds the concept of rebellion and independence so outrageous that he is convinced that only a few Americans are against Britain. He has also been told that the colonists lack rifles and supplies, and that the revolt he is facing will soon be over (→ 20/5).

First shots of revolt ring out in Lexington

Boston, Mass, 19 April 1775
British redcoats and Massachusetts militia – known as minutemen – clashed on the common at Lexington near here today, signalling the start of open rebellion against the crown. The redcoats later marched on to Concord, where there was more fighting as they searched for rebel supplies. The many months of shouting between London and the 13 colonies is over; war has begun.

Some 2,000 redcoats are straggling back to Boston, having been surprised by the response of the minutemen. There is some dispute about who fired the first shot, but in two skirmishes the British lost 73 dead and 200 wounded or missing, while American losses were 49 killed and 39 wounded. The redcoats' mission had been to destroy the colonists' armaments and supplies, stored on a farm at Concord. But before they arrived American patriots – including a local silversmith, Paul Revere, who made an brave midnight ride from Boston in an attempt to reach Concord – had spread the word of their advance. The British were met in Lexington by a small contingent of minutemen, who were dispersing when a shot was fired, and both sides opened fire.

British losses were much heavier at Concord when, after destroying what stores the rebels had been unable to remove, the redcoats were ambushed by snipers (→ 20/5).

A romanticized vision of the fighting at Lexington, painted much later.

1776

London, 3 February. Parliament issues an embargo on Irish exports in an attempt to secure extra provisions for British forces fighting in North America (→26/3).

Boston, Mass, 26 March. British troops led by General Sir William Howe evacuate the city to take refuge in Halifax, Nova Scotia (→2/5).

France, 2 May. King Louis XVI of France offers his aid to the American colonies in their struggle to break free of British rule (→7/6).

Quebec, 7 June. British troops maintain their hold on Quebec, forcing a total retreat of all American forces (→28).

Deptford, London, 25 June. Captain James Cook sets off on his third voyage to the Pacific (→24/12/77).

Philadelphia, Pa, 28 June. Thomas Jefferson presents a draft of the declaration of independence, to separate the American colonies from Britain, to the second continental congress (→29).

New York, 29 June. British troops begin their planned invasion of New York City.→

Virginia, 29 June. Virginia declares itself to be an independent state (→4/7).

New York, 10 July. Soldiers pull down the statue of King George III (→2/8).

Edinburgh, 25 July. An observatory is founded on Calton Hill.

Philadelphia, 2 August. The congress signs the Declaration of Independence (→30).

North America, 30 August. General Howe leads the British troops to victory in a battle at Long Island (→9/9).

Philadelphia, 9 September. The United Colonies officially change their name to the United States (→28/10).

New York, 28 October. British troops led by General Howe make American forces, under the command of General Sir George Washington, retreat from White Plains (→26/12).

Dublin, 29 October. King George III grants a salary of £100 per annum to employ language professors at Trinity College.

New Jersey, 26 December. American forces defeat a force of Hessian auxiliaries fighting for Britain, at Trenton.→

David Garrick gives farewell performance

Garrick between the muses of Comedy and Tragedy, by Joshua Reynolds.

London, 10 June

The Theatre Royal, Drury Lane, was packed with admirers of David Garrick tonight to see his last performance and farewell speech from the stage. And so, in a play called *The Wonder*, ended 30 years of Garrick as manager and star actor in the theatre of which he became the owner. It has made him rich, and he retires to his riverside house at Hampton having sold his share of the theatre to Richard Brinsley Sheridan for £10,000.

Garrick's acting was so natural that he could adapt himself to any kind of play – Shakespearean tragedy, comedy or farce – with equal effectiveness. In a scene in her novel *Evelina* Fanny Burney's heroine goes to see him in a modern comedy and is dazzled: "Such ease, such vivacity in his manner, such grace in his motions, such fire and meaning in his eyes! Every word seemed spoke from the impulse of the moment. His voice so clear, so melodious, yet so wonderfully various ... Every look speaks!"

And his friend Oliver Goldsmith paid him an ironic tribute in a mock epitaph:

On the stage he was natural,
simple, affecting,
'Twas only that when he was off
he was acting (→21/1/79).

Irish restrained by new public order act

Dublin, 4 April

In an attempt to curb the influence of "the whiteboys" in Munster, the Irish parliament has passed an act "to prevent tumultuous risings", decreeing the death penalty for several whiteboy activities and increasing the power of magistrates.

This legislation will be largely ineffective since most of the local population are either sympathetic to the aims of the whiteboys or else afraid to give information against them. As things stand at present, anyone breaking the law has a good chance of not being caught. But for anyone breaking the whiteboy regulations, punishment is swift and severe. Threats of excommunication have done nothing to ease the situation (→19/1/90).

'History of Music' published by Burney

London

Dr Charles Burney, who is well known as a musician and traveller, has brought out the first volume of his authoritative *General History of Music*. Burney studied music under the guidance of Dr Thomas Arne, the composer of *Rule Britannia*, and travelled through France, Austria, Germany and Italy to collect material for his history.

His friend Dr Samuel Johnson, whose musical ear is not of the best, has written in the dedication that music "may with justice be considered as the art that unites corporal and intellectual pleasure without weakening reason".

Charles Burney: musical history.

Shipping flourishes as trade expands

Ships queue to unload in London.

Britain

British power in the world depends on trade and shipping, and even country gentlemen living far from the sea support naval expenditure and the laws that encourage British shipbuilding and sailing. Ships are built on the Thames, and also in Massachusetts, and used in the three-way transatlantic trade and in trade with India and the Baltic. Britain exports woollen goods, tin, metal goods and cured fish, and re-exports goods from the colonies. The trade needs ships and sailors, and these are also essential for the wars with France.

America declares its independence

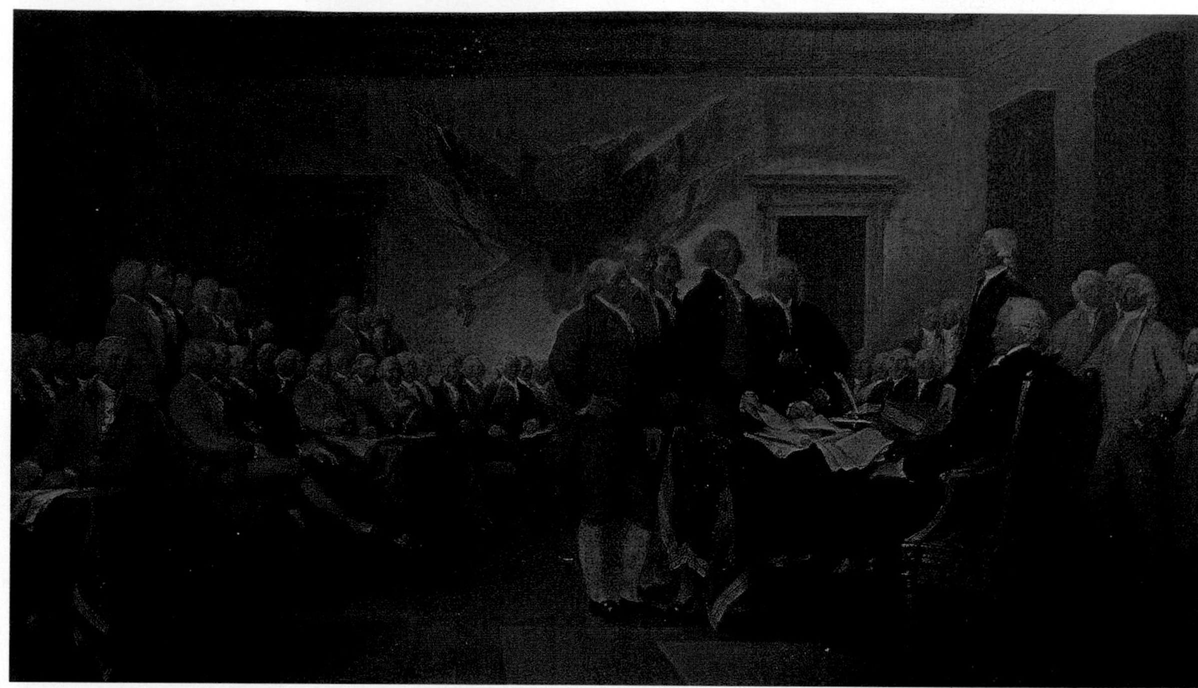

Signing the American Declaration of Independence in Philadelphia: all colonies except New York voted for it.

Philadelphia, USA, 4 July
The American colonies have declared themselves independent, renounced allegiance to the crown and dissolved all political connection between them and Britain. Of the 13 colonies, 12 voted for the declaration, New York abstaining.

The principle of independence had already been approved in the state assemblies. The debate in the continental congress here concerned its terms. The congress entrusted the writing of the declaration to Benjamin Franklin, John Adams and Thomas Jefferson, but the first two ceded their pens to Jefferson's eloquence.

He proclaimed America's commitment to the principle that all governments depend for their authority on the consent of the governed. He declared that King George III has forfeited his American subjects' loyalty, and that they are therefore absolved from obedience. He asserted, and the congress accepted, the revolutionary doctrine that all men are created equal.

The colonies have been in revolt for over a year. They have driven the British from Boston but failed to conquer Canada, and the British in New York now threaten Philadelphia. This Declaration of Independence [*see right*] is a final burning of bridges. The colonies must now win independence, or face submission (→10).

Washington claims a victory at Trenton

New York, USA, 26 December
General George Washington has won a dramatic victory over the Hessian mercenaries at Trenton, in New Jersey. He crossed the Delaware with 2,400 ill-equipped soldiers and attacked the 1,200 Hessians at night, as they were sleeping off the Christmas festivities.

Two weeks ago he was driven out of New Jersey by superior British forces under General Lord Cornwallis. This first colonial success shows that the British will not have an easy victory. Washington exhibited great qualities of leadership in bringing his men through sleet and rain, half frozen, their feet wrapped in rags. The colonial militia is now an army (→17/6/77).

General George Washington.

Paine puts the case for independence

Philadelphia, USA
Thomas (Tom) Paine, a recent immigrant from England, has published a blazing attack on Britain and a demand for the full independence of the American colonies. His pamphlet is called *Common Sense*, and it excoriates not only the British but also everyone who continues loyal to the crown as a man "with the heart of a coward and the spirit of a sycophant".

Common Sense is a simple and crude polemic, very different from the subtle arguments of John Adams and Thomas Jefferson, and also much more effective at stirring up the multitude (→3/1791).

The terms of the Declaration of Independence

Philadelphia, USA, 4 July
The declaration opens with the words: "We hold these truths to be self-evident, that all men are created equal, that they are endowed by their Creator with certain unalienable rights, that among these are life, liberty, and the pursuit of happiness. That to secure these rights, governments are instituted among men, deriving their just powers from the consent of the governed. That, whenever any form of government becomes destructive of these ends, it is the right of the people to alter or abolish it, and to institute new government, laying its foundation on such principles, and organizing its power in such form, as to them shall seem most likely to effect

Down with the king: George's statue is toppled in New York.

their safety and happiness." It then denounces George III for "a history of repeated injuries and usurpations, all having in direct object the establishment of an absolute tyranny over these states".

The declaration ends: "Appealing to the Supreme Judge of the world for the rectitude of our intentions, [we] do, in the name, and by the authority of the good people of these colonies, solemnly publish and declare, that these United Colonies are, and of right ought to be, free and independent states."

Scotland's glittering cultural life dazzles Europe

Adam Smith publishes 'Wealth of Nations'

London, 9 March
Yet another Scot looks set to become a worldwide name with the publication today of Adam Smith's grand opus entitled *An Inquiry into the Nature and Causes of the Wealth of Nations.*

For true wealth in today's industrial world, argues Smith, all government controls, regulations of trade and monopolies have to be withdrawn. Only by allowing individuals freedom to accrue personal wealth will we release the innate competitiveness of mankind and see its fruits come to our nations.

Smith, now 53 and ever the bachelor, was born at Kirkcaldy, in Fife. A good friend of other Scots intellectuals such as the philosopher David Hume and the biographer James Boswell, he has taught at both Glasgow and Oxford Universities, where he has lectured on moral philosophy and economics. Well travelled, Smith gave up academic life ten years ago, first to guide the duke of Buccleuch on his travels and then to write this book. In Paris he mixed with economists such as Quesnay and Turgot and the writer Voltaire. Although arguing for individual liberty, Smith takes a moral stance: any wealth that people make should also help society as a whole (→ 17/7/90).

Portrait of a city in the "age of enlightenment": Parliament Close, in Edinburgh, showing many of its leading figures in the late 18th century.

Scots mourn the loss of philosopher and scientist David Hume

Hume: transformed philosophy.

Edinburgh
The passing of David Hume, the philosopher and man of letters, must be felt all over Europe, but nowhere so strongly as in Scotland. He was his country's leading light at a time when Scotland took its place firmly at the centre of the intellectual map of Europe.

The 1740 publication of Hume's much discussed volume *A Treatise of Human Nature* was not followed by the long and difficult work being widely read; nevertheless, its ideas exerted a wide influence both on Scottish scientists and on the Edinburgh *literati*. The basis of Hume's philosophy was a profound religious scepticism which led him not only to study the ways in which fact and fantasy are differentiated in thought but also to develop a more scientific approach than was then common to the analysis of human behaviour and history.

Hume was no solitary thinker but rather a leading public figure, a sociable man who played an enthusiastic part in Edinburgh life. He published books of popular essays as well as a six-volume history of Britain.

Universities home to brilliant generation of Scottish scientists

Scotland
The universities of Glasgow and Edinburgh have fostered a golden age in Scottish science. With men such as Joseph Black, the chemist who discovered "latent heat" in 1764 and is professor of chemistry and anatomy at Glasgow, his fellow chemist William Cullen, who teaches in Edinburgh, and the geologist James Hutton, who is engaged in fascinating research at Edinburgh, the two establishments are home to a remarkable trio.

There is a close link between the researchers in the universities and those involved in practical work. James Watt, the designer of the first commercial steam engine launched this year, used some of Black's ideas in his early experiments. Watt was employed at that time as "mathematical instrument maker to the university" and benefited greatly from the stimulating company of men such as Black, and John Robison, now professor of natural philosophy in Edinburgh.

Scotland also boasts a number of the leading figures in contemporary medical life with Alexander Monro – the professor of anatomy at the Edinburgh medical school, which was founded by his father, also Alexander – and the surgeon brothers William and John Hunter.

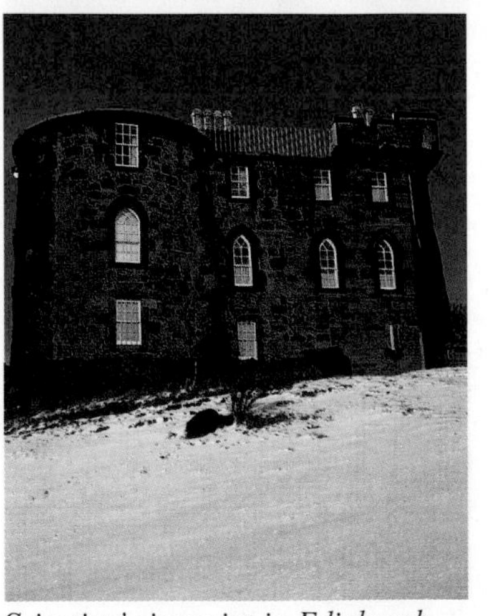

Scientists' viewpoint in Edinburgh.

Scottish writing and arts win acclaim

Scotland
Scotland is witnessing a remarkable flowering of talent in the fields of art, architecture and literature. In Edinburgh the New Town is being built to the north of the Royal Mile to the plans of the architect James Craig. Meanwhile, the city's Register House was begun two years ago to designs by Robert Adam, the eldest of four Kirkcaldy-born brothers who were childhood friends of Adam Smith [*see above left*] and who have established themselves as among Britain's leading architects.

This year sees the publication of *The Gentleman Farmer* by Lord Kames, the judge and philosopher, an attempt to apply rational ideas to estate management; other notable members of an astonishing crop of philosophical writers include Adam Ferguson, who published an *Essay on Civil Society* in 1766, and the historian William Robertson whose *History of Scotland 1542-1603* (1759) was very successful. In literature there is Henry Mackenzie, who published *The Man of Feeling* anonymously in 1772; the promising poet Robert Fergusson committed suicide, aged 24, in 1774. In London the Scottish artist Allan Ramsay is meeting with great success, as is his compatriot Gavin Hamilton in Rome.

1777

Ireland, 25 January. John Hobart, the earl of Buckinghamshire, is sworn in as lord lieutenant.

London, 1 April. The Methodists found City Road chapel, one of their first London chapels (→ 1779).

Canada, 17 June. General John Burgoyne and the British head south along the Hudson valley, planning to join up with the British led by General Sir William Howe (→ 7/7).

New York State, 7 July. American troops surrender Fort Ticonderoga, on Lake Champlain, to the British (→ 27).

Pennsylvania, 27 July. General Sir William Howe opens a major offensive against the American troops in Philadelphia (→ 26/9).

Philadelphia, 26 September. General Sir William Howe defeats General George Washington to seize the city of Philadelphia (→ 4/10).

Pennsylvania, 4 October. George Washington is defeated when he attacks General Howe's army at Germantown (→ 17).

Indian Ocean, 24 December. Captain James Cook, the explorer, discovers a group of islands, which he names the Christmas Islands (→ 21/2/79).

London. The heads of Jacobite rebels executed for treason after the rebellion of 1745 are finally removed from spikes at Temple Bar (→ 4/5/84).

York. The city opens a lunatic asylum for the poor and mentally ill.

Edinburgh. A penny-post service begins; Peter Williamson, a bookseller, offers to deliver letters and parcels to any address within one mile of the city's mercat cross for one penny.

Britain. John Howard, the prison reformer, causes a sensation with the publication of his book *The State of Prisons*, in which he reveals the dreadful truth of conditions in jail.

Westminster. Parliament agrees to a civil-list settlement on King George III's children; on his death, each of his sons will receive £10,000 and his daughters £6,000 (→ 1778).

Central [Scotland]. The Carron Ironworks near Falkirk begins delivery of a superb new gun, the "carronade", to the Royal Navy.

British Army defeated

Without supplies and let down by his own side, Burgoyne surrenders.

New York State, 17 October
General John Burgoyne has surrendered his army to the Americans at Saratoga in the Hudson valley. The British plan to cut off New England from the rest of the rebellious colonies has thus utterly failed, and British arms have suffered a catastrophic defeat.

Burgoyne advanced south from Canada, expecting General Sir William Howe to march north from New York to meet him. But British irresolution, confusion and incompetence thwarted the plan. Howe, instead of helping Burgoyne, marched off to Philadelphia. Burgoyne, meanwhile, won a string of victories on his way south. He came down Lake Champlain and took Fort Ticonderoga in July. Harassed by "the Green Mountain Boys" from Vermont, he pressed ahead until confronted by the Americans under General Horatio Gates on the heights above Saratoga.

By then Burgoyne had run out of supplies, was cut off from his base and could expect no help from Howe in New York. He had lost 1,400 men in his advance; he could see no possibility of escape and therefore surrendered his force of 6,000 men to Gates (→ 6/2/78).

Highland troops recruited for colonial war

Highland troops won back the kilt.

Scotland
Recruiters are scouring the highlands to find men to take "the king's shilling" and fight in North America. Highland regiments have fought in British wars since the last century, and they did particularly well in America during the Seven Years' War; the government is counting on them to repeat that success. The oldest regiment, the Earl of Crawford's, known as the Black Watch, served in Europe and in Canada. Others were disbanded at the end of each war; the British distrust standing armies. Now London hopes to raise 16 regiments to send to America. The soldiers will wear kilts, their own tartans and highland bonnets – clothes forbidden to civilians (→ 8/1778).

'School for Scandal' is another hit for youthful Sheridan

London, 8 May
The Theatre Royal, Drury Lane, had one of its most brilliant first nights this evening with the opening of *The School for Scandal*, a new play by Richard Brinsley Sheridan. Members of the audience, including the duchess of Devonshire and many other fashionable beauties, were agog to see themselves depicted on the stage by the popular author of *The Rivals* and the comic opera *The Duenna*. Sheridan, who is 25, has had three successes in a row. He will be glad of this since he is now the owner of the theatre and has many debts to pay.

The play is an attack on the cant of "sentiment" as well as on scandal-mongering – both vices now typical of London society. Joseph Surface is always ready with a moral aphorism to cover his immoral designs, while his brother Charles, though a hard-drinking profligate, has far more honesty and generosity. The discovery of Lady Teazle in Joseph's house by the fall of the screen when her husband, Sir Peter, calls proved a sensation. Sheridan remarked before putting pen to paper "My comedy is finished; I have nothing now to do but to write it." But it was only just ready for the opening night, having been carried from his lodging one sheet at a time to the actors who were rehearsing it.

Social commentators continue to rail against the perils of drink, particularly gin, seen in this case as the destroyer of marriages.

1778

France/USA, 6 February. France and the United States sign a treaty to form a trade alliance (→ 16/3).

Westminster, 16 March. Parliament agrees to Lord North's plan to form a British peace commission, offering major concessions to colonists in the hope of forestalling further American alliances with France (→ 22/4).

Ireland, 6 April. Banking is hit by a series of failures.

Pennsylvania, 22 April. Congress declares that all who deal with the British peace commission should be branded as traitors (→ 18/6).

Westminster, 7 April. William Pitt, the earl of Chatham, collapses while speaking in the House of Lords (→ 11/5).

Dublin, 11 June. Parliament gives its consent to the construction of a circular road around the city.

France, 17 June. France declares war on Britain (→ 27/7).

Philadelphia, Pa, 18 June. British troops led by General Henry Clinton evacuate the city and march north to New York (→ 28).

New Jersey, 28 June. The British flee after defeat by General Washington in a battle at Monmouth (→ 27/10).

Dublin, June. Parliament incorporates the Charitable Music Society.

Edinburgh, August. The newly raised Seaforth Highlanders mutiny and dig in on the hill Arthur's Seat until their demands are met.

New York, 27 October. Lord North's peace commission sails for Britain after failing to prevent the Franco-American alliance (→ 4/11).

Ireland, 4 November. The *Hibernian Journal* publishes a letter from Benjamin Franklin, claiming that the cause of the United States is that of Ireland (→ 29/12).

Georgia, 29 December. British troops seize the capital Savannah (→ 25/2/79).

Windsor. King George III takes up residence at Windsor Castle (→ 2/8/87).

Britain. Joseph Bramah patents his invention of a ball cock for use in water closets.

Lothian. Scotland's first cotton mill to be powered by a water wheel is built at Peniciuk.

Britain and France at war over colonies

Anglo-French relations had reached a new low even before the war started.

London, 27 July
A British fleet botched an action today to destroy French warships off the island of Ushant, 27 miles (43km) north-west of Brest. Disciplinary action is likely to follow.

The bungled duel, which followed France's entry into the war over the colonies, prompted an immediate row between Admiral Augustus Keppel, the British commander, and the commander at the rear of the fleet, Sir Hugh Palliser, an old friend of his.

Keppel charged that Palliser had disobeyed vital signals. The latter counter-charged with a critique of the admiral's conduct of the battle. Both face court-martials, but naval observers say that political considerations make it unlikely that either man will be blamed.

Chatham dies after collapsing in Lords

Peers rush to aid the earl of Chatham as he collapses in the House of Lords.

London, 11 May
William Pitt, the first earl of Chatham and a great statesman, died at his home today just over a month after collapsing in the House of Lords while making a very vigorous speech opposing the recognition of American independence. He was crippled with gout, and his final attempt to save the empire that he had helped to create proved too much for the frail 70-year-old. He will be buried in Westminster Abbey. Pitt was renowned throughout the kingdom as both an outstanding leader and a pungent parliamentary orator with a well deserved reputation for integrity (→ 21/6/79).

Irish Catholics get relief from new act

Dublin, 14 August
After long and acrimonious debates the Catholic Relief Act has been forcibly pushed through parliament here against strong Protestant opposition. The act enables Roman Catholics to take leases for 999 years and to inherit land on the same terms as members of other Christian denominations.

With rumours spreading of a French invasion, the British government decided to force the issue of Catholic relief on the grounds that wartime strategy and the security of the empire demanded it. But the more cynical suspect that it is motivated by the need for Catholic recruits for the army (→ 1/1779).

New female novelist publishes 'Evelina'

Fanny Burney was a sensation.

London
A new author who will delight women readers has been catapulted onto the literary scene. Fanny Burney's father is well acquainted with *literati* such as Samuel Johnson, David Garrick and Sir Joshua Reynolds. Miss Burney's first novel, *Evelina*, written at the age of a mere 26, is a triumph of the new literary form used first by Samuel Richardson – the novel as a series of letters. Evelina, who marries Lord Orville, is introduced to society, and lively social observation accompanies her travels through it.

1779

London, 21 January. David Garrick, the actor and former manager of the Drury Lane theatre, dies aged 61.

London, 7 February. William Boyce, an eminent composer and Master of the King's Musick since 1757, dies.

Hawaii, 21 February. The body of Captain James Cook is buried at sea following his brutal murder last month by natives on the island (→1780).

Illinois, 25 February. American troops led by George Rogers Clark successfully recapture the fort at Vincennes after the British governor, Henry Hamilton, surrenders (→21/9).

Belfast, 19 May. The Belfast Charitable Society agrees to proposals by Robert Joy and Thomas McCabe to begin the manufacture of cotton in the city's poorhouse.

Britain/Spain, 16 June. Spain declares war on Britain and besieges the island of Gibraltar (→21/9).

Dublin, June. The first boat begins operating on the Grand canal, travelling between Dublin and Ballyhealy in Co Kildare.

Britain, 19 July. The Royal Navy orders that fruit juices be supplied on board its ships to prevent the disease of scurvy.

Louisiana, 21 September. The Spanish seize control of Baton Rouge from the British (→23).

Georgia, 28 October. The French fail to wrest Savannah from British hands (→24/2/80).

London, 29 November. Fire destroys the ancient waterworks at London Bridge.

Lothian. A new fort is built at Leith as a defence against possible attacks by the Scottish-born American naval commander John Paul Jones.

Britain. George Cussons, a Methodist preacher, founds the Army and Navy Bible Society (→28/2/84).

London. Dr Samuel Johnson, the essayist, critic and compiler of a *Dictionary* brought out in 1755, publishes his *Lives of the Poets* (→1784).

Britain. Samuel Crompton combines the principles of James Hargreaves's "spinning jenny" and Richard Arkwright's "rollers" to produce the "spinning mule", a device which dramatically speeds up the process (→9/10).

World's first iron bridge is completed

Shropshire

A bridge entirely engineered in cast iron, the first such structure anywhere in the world, has just been completed across the river Severn one mile downstream from Coalbrookdale, an area which is becoming a centre of English industry.

The bridge was built by Abraham Darby, the ironmaster whose Coalbrookdale company has been smelting iron here since 1707. It spans 37 metres (120 feet), with the most slender and elegant cold-blast iron structural members. The unprecedented use of cast iron in this bridge has been made possible by a new technique developed by Darby which allows the metal to be fashioned without fracturing.

The iron bridge symbolizes the changes under way in industry, many of which have been pioneered at Coalbrookdale. When the first Abraham Darby was made ironmaster of a small blast furnace here, the location offered woodland for making charcoal, and deposits of iron, clay and coal, plus the river for transport. Darby revolutionized iron manufacture by experimenting with coke from local coal to smelt the iron ore and thereby overcome an increasing shortage of charcoal. Coke has now replaced charcoal here. In 1755 Darby's son built the new and larger Horsehay ironworks nearby, and now his grandson has constructed the historic iron bridge across the Severn.

A watercolour of the remarkable Coalbrookdale bridge painted in 1790.

Glasgow riots over Catholic Relief Act

Glasgow, January

Presbyterian mobs have rampaged through through the streets here in an orgy of destruction to protest at the Catholic Relief Act which recently had an easy passage through parliament. Government ministers have decided that, for the time being, the legislation will not be applied in Scotland.

The act frees Roman Catholics from the many penal restrictions and regulations which they have suffered since the Reformation. Under the old ordinances, the saying of Mass was made a felony for a foreigner and high treason for a native; Catholics were not permitted to buy land; and persons educated in the Roman faith were deemed to be incapable of inheriting property.

The new freedoms apply to those Catholics prepared to take an oath of allegiance, renounce the pope's temporal jurisdiction in Britain and sever all connection with heretics. Catholics are still denied full political rights (→29/5/80).

'Blue stockings' impress in London salons

London

Learned or literary women lead very unusual lives these days. Now the darlings of fashionable "salon" life in London, they have been nicknamed "bluestockings" after the group which met at Greenham in the 1750s [*see report on page 700*].

Alongside well-known figures such as Dr Samuel Johnson, Sir Joshua Reynolds and Dr Burney (father of Fanny) one might meet Elizabeth Montagu, Catherine Talbot or Mary Monckton. As much as any man, these women delight in the salonière's art of informal, learned conversation. They also finance each others' projects – Elizabeth Carter's translations from Greek philosophy are a prime example.

The female muses of Britain: a contemporary view of the "bluestockings".

▷

George III urges firmer cabinet leadership as the crisis over America becomes worse

George: threatens to take control.

London, 21 June
Faced in a year of intolerable strain with a divided and incompetent government lacking direction in the pursuit of the war abroad or affairs at home, King George III took the unusual step today of summoning the cabinet to the Queen's House. With his chief minister, Lord North, seemingly on the verge of a nervous breakdown, the king's message was stark: firm leadership must be promptly asserted, or he himself would be forced to drive the nation on.

Avoiding possible charges that he was seeking to reimpose the full powers of the crown, George proclaimed that he would always act within, and in defence of, "the beauty, excellence and perfection of the British constitution ... I have never harboured a thought of injuring the constitution or abridging the people's liberties," he said.

To the suggestion that the base of the administration be enlarged, George agreed, but with the proviso that it must offer him "firmness and support" and pledge itself to keep the empire intact. Charles Fox said that he was willing to join the government provided that North resigned. The marquis of Rockingham and the duke of Grafton, however, laid down terms which the king finds unacceptable (→2/1780).

Armed volunteers march in Dublin city

The Dublin Volunteers assemble for inspection on the city's College Green.

Dublin, 4 November
The Volunteers, a Protestant force which was formed last year during the American War of Independence to defend Ireland against a French invasion, have demonstrated their military strength in an armed parade through the streets of Dublin, watched by thousands.

Having gathered on St Stephen's Green, and led by the duke of Leinster and Captain Gardiner, they marched with drums beating and colours flying to College Green, accompanied all the way by cheers from the enthusiastic crowds.

The Volunteers have captured the imagination of the people with their patriotic fervour and are regarded as "the guardians of our freedom". Although they came into existence to repel the French, the oppression of England by Ireland is high on their agenda, and they are seen as a strong force prepared to fight for their rights.

Defiant American privateer shocks British navy in North sea battle

England, 23 September
The Scots-born Captain John Paul Jones is today the first great hero of the American navy after scoring a singular victory against a superior British force off Flamborough Head, on the north-east coast of England. To the demand from Captain Pearson, the British commander, that he should strike his colours, Jones replied defiantly: "I have not yet begun to fight."

The American was in command of three ships led by the *Bonhomme Richard*, an old French vessel. Pearson's great and unrivalled firepower came from the newly built *Serapis*, a double-decker with 54 guns. Pearson had encountered the Americans while convoying a fleet of merchantmen.

Although he was so heavily outgunned, Jones closed for battle and managed to grapple with the *Serapis*. The two ships fought for most of the night. The duel ended when the *Serapis* surrendered with the loss of 49 dead and 68 wounded.

Jones beat the "Serapis", but his own ship was badly damaged and sank.

The American losses were greater – 150 killed or wounded from a crew of 300. The *Bonhomme Richard* was so badly damaged that she had to be abandoned. Jones, the son of a Scots labourer, was born at Kirkcudbright in 1747. In 1764 he shipped as a mate on a slaver and made several voyages to America. He later settled in Virginia and was commissioned in the American navy when war broke out (→28/10).

Riot mob smashes Arkwright factory

Lancashire, 9 October
Richard Arkwright's revolutionary water-powered spinning factory near Chorley was destroyed today by a rioting mob. The works, at Birkacre, was England's first water-powered spinning mill when it was opened by Arkwright, the inventor of the "spinning jenny", in 1771. The local weavers, however, came to see it as a symbol of the unsatisfactory and often oppressive new working conditions.

It has been a year of unrest in the textile industry, with workers who are squeezed by the rising cost of living and lower wages taking the law into their own hands. The violence, however, is often the last resort of people who have previously tried more reasoned protests. This year framework knitters in the Nottingham area rioted, but only after their campaign demanding an act to regulate their wages had been defeated in parliament (→1783).

1780

West Indies, 16 January. Sir George Rodney defeats a Spanish squadron off the coast of Cape St Vincent.

England, 26 March. The first issues of the *British Gazette* and the *Sunday Monitor* make their first appearance.

London, March. John Wyvill, the Yorkshire reformer, heads a reform meeting.

Dublin, 19 April. Henry Grattan, an Irish politician, puts forward his motion for legislative independence of Ireland from Britain.

London, April. The Society for Constitutional Reform is established; its main aim is to press for radical reform.

Dublin, 2 May. The Irish parliament abolishes the sacramental test; this allows Presbyterians to hold official offices.→

South Carolina, 12 May. The town of Charleston and over 5,000 American rebels surrender to British troops.→

Westminster, 29 May. Lord George Gordon presents parliament with a petition from the Protestant Association which demands an immediate repeal of the Catholic Relief Act (→6/6).

India, June. Hyder Ali of Mysore invades British territory in the Carnatic (→9/1780).

South Carolina, 16 August. General Lord Cornwallis leads the British to victory over the Americans in a battle at Camden (→17/1/81).

Britain, 20 November. Anglo-Dutch relations collapse and war breaks out on the discovery that the Dutch have been supplying French and Spanish arms to the American rebels through the Dutch Caribbean.

Dublin, 23 December. Frederick Howard, the earl of Carlisle, is sworn in as lord lieutenant of Ireland.

London. Martin Maden, the first chaplain of the Lock hospital for venereal diseases, is forced to resign his position after publishing a book advocating polygamy.

Scotland. Following the remarkable management feats of Henry Dundas, lord advocate since 1775, the government wins 41 of 45 seats in the general election; of these, 12 are held personally by Dundas.

Intrepid explorer's ship 'Resolution' returns home without Captain Cook

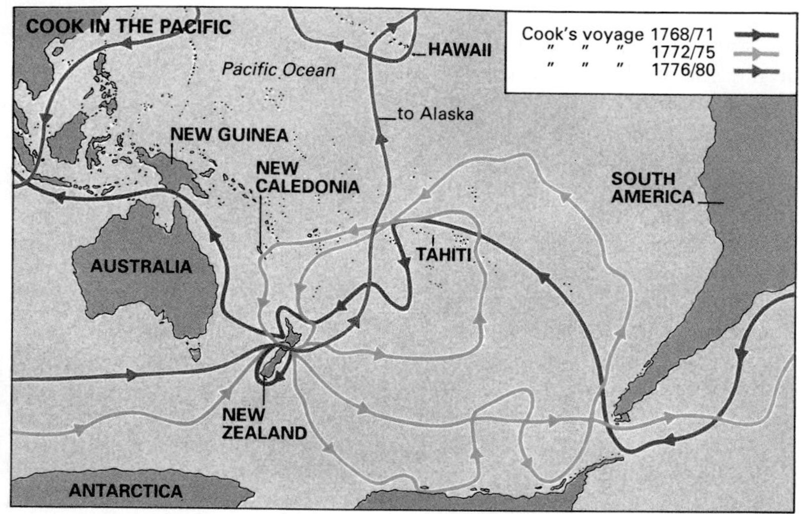

London
The exploration ship *Resolution*, which set off with high hopes of discovering a north-west passage between the Pacific and the Atlantic, has finally returned to England, where the nation is still mourning the death last year of her legendary commander, Captain James Cook.

The man who, on earlier epic voyages, had reached Tahiti, charted the coasts of New Zealand and eastern Australia and sailed deep into the Antarctic regions, where he discovered the land mass of New Caledonia, was ultimately killed, quite pointlessly, in a skirmish with a group of Hawaiian natives.

After circumnavigating Alaska as far as the Arctic ice pack and establishing that there was no sea lane linking the two oceans, he sailed south to Hawaii. There, while trying to resolve a quarrel with a local chieftain over a stolen cutter, he was fatally wounded. Cook was a self-taught Yorkshireman; he began his sea-going career as captain of a humble North Sea collier. But his curiosity and navigational skills have added an entire hemisphere to the world's geographical and scientific knowledge (→13/5/87).

Cook was a self-educated man.

In the cold of the Arctic, Captain Cook's crew hunted walrus for food.

British troops seize city of Charleston

South Carolina, 12 May
Five thousand Americans led by General Benjamin Lincoln surrendered here today after suffering the heaviest defeat inflicted by British troops on the colonial insurgents since the start of the revolutionary war. General Sir Henry Clinton, who started his spring campaign in February with a successful assault on Fort Moultrie in Charleston harbour, completed today's victory by sinking four American warships and seizing a huge supply of vital munitions. His own relatively light casualties amounted to fewer than 260 men out of the 8,000 under his command (→16/8).

Irish free to export cloth to colonies

Dublin, 24 February
In what is being seen as an important relaxation of the trade embargoes, legislation forbidding the export of wool and glass from Ireland has been repealed, and an act has been passed allowing the Irish to trade with British settlements in Africa and North America on the condition that the Irish parliament imposes the same duties as the British one already has.

These concessions towards free trade have been greeted with delight and a sense of triumph that the English have been compelled to surrender to Irish demands. The Volunteers [*see report page 744*] are now determined to go further and win parliamentary independence for Ireland (→12/5).

Religious changes

Ireland, 2 May
The removal of the sacramental test imposed on Presbyterians and dissenters in 1704 and preventing them from holding public office has done very little to ease their resentment. The dominant position of the Church of Ireland as the established church, together with the fact that the Irish parliament is controlled by Church of Ireland landlords, has left Presbyterians largely at that church's mercy. ▷

Business booms in the Scottish linen industry

Edinburgh
The yarn and the fabric that are spun and woven from the flax plant have become the basis for one of Scotland's thriving industries. Since the 1707 Act of Union removed all significant trade barriers, it has grown to a point where it now employs 40,000 men and over 180,000 women in the counties round the Clyde and Tay rivers.

It is this activity, even more than tobacco and cattle-droving which have enjoyed similar booms, that has brought prosperity to the Scots. As flax is not a profitable crop for farmers, most linen production, particularly in weaving, has moved to a group of villages which have developed this speciality, or to industrial suburbs of large towns, like the Calton district of Glasgow. The raw material is mainly imported from Russia and Poland via the ports of Leith, Dundee and Aberdeen.

A Scottish weaver's stamp.

To supply capital and provide marketing services, the British Linen Association was founded in 1746 by the duke of Argyll and other subscribers. It has now ceased trading and developed into an investment bank.

Yorkshire petitions for complete reform

York, February
The great protest meeting held here at the end of December has succeeded in focusing a nationwide movement in favour of parliamentary reform. The anger of Yorkshire's landowning gentry over the cost of wasteful administration and the extension of royal influence over public affairs is now being reflected in a flood of petitions from other equally disaffected counties.

They all demand the establishment of policy-making "committees", which their authors claim would be more representative than Westminster of the interests of "the people" (by which is meant "the freeholders"). Although this is recognized as a serious, possibly even a revolutionary, challenge to the nation's established institutions, it is getting a good deal of support from political leaders like Charles James Fox and Edmund Burke.

They see the "petition" movement as a useful weapon to put pressure on Lord North, King George III's much disliked prime minister, and at the same time to take advantage of the country's growing antipathy towards the North American war (→ 27/3/82).

British defeat threat to Indian territories

Peace talks with Hyder Ali failed, but his army was finally defeated.

Madras, India, September
Warren Hastings, the governor-general of India, has successfully defused a threat by the French, in alliance with various hostile local rulers, to eject the East India company from its extensive and valuable territories in the southern half of the subcontinent.

Earlier this year Hyder Ali, the rajah of Mysore, invaded the Carnatic, which occupies the south-east tip of India, and ravaged vast areas of countryside, up to the walls of Madras. There he was joined by a French seaborne army, while further north the Marathan chieftains of central India launched a major assualt on south-western Bengal.

Hastings countered this with a combined diplomatic and military thrust. He negotiated peace with the Marathas while sending a hastily assembled but highly effective British army to confront and shatter Hyder Ali. Madras was saved, and France's colonial ambitions were thwarted (→ 1/7/81).

Increased demand and new technology fuel boom in coal-mining

Newcastle upon Tyne
Coal-mining, still only a tiny, very localized industry at the start of this century, is now undergoing into a period of dramatic growth. Here in north-eastern England, as in Scotland, South Yorkshire, Lancashire, Derbyshire, Nottinghamshire, the midlands and as far south as Bristol and the Forest of Dean, a combination of soaring demand – caused by the widespread use of steam engines – and improved technology has already quadrupled output. Investors anticipate even faster growth once James Watt's new, improved steam engines, which are currently under test, become generally available for pumping out the deeper workings.

Coal mines are springing up all over the country to feed the rise in demand.

Water is one of the most intractable of the hazards facing the mine-owners. Flooding has both caused widespread fatalities and made many promising deposits virtually unworkable. So far it has mainly been tackled by the use of Thomas Newcomen's atmospheric steam pumps, developed for the Cornish tin mines, but these are inefficient and hugely expensive. Once these are replaced, the ingenuity of the industry's inventors will have to deal with other problems, like fire-damp, poisonous air, collapsing tunnels and lack of underground haulage.

Rioters storm Newgate prison

London, 6 June
Newgate prison was sacked today, and all its inmates were released, on the fifth and most violent day of the riots provoked by Lord George Gordon in protest at parliament's proposed extension of the Catholic Relief Act of 1778. The escaped convicts then eagerly joined in the widespread looting.

Earlier the mob had burnt down the house of Sir John Fielding, the Middlesex magistrate who had attempted to restrain its fury, and from there proceeded to blow up the gin distilleries in Holborn. The City authorities are still refusing to sanction the use of armed troops. The lord mayor, Kennett, said yesterday, while houses and chapels were being indiscriminately sacked: "There are very great people at the bottom of the riot."

Trouble started on 2 June when a crowd of 60,000 people accompanied Gordon to the House of Commons to support his petition for the relief measure to be repealed. Their mood grew ugly as they were packed in tight all around the parliament building, and then Gordon interrupted his speech inside the chamber to harangue them from the steps. Finally they embarked on the orgy of destruction (→8).

George Gordon's supporters carry their petition to the House of Commons.

Troops confront the rioters at the height of the violence in London.

Children to be told Bible stories at a 'Sunday school'

Gloucester
The new "Sunday school", founded here earlier this year by Raymond Raikes, the owner of the *Gloucester Journal*, is proving very popular with the city's ragamuffin children, who previously had nowhere but the streets to go when they were not working or begging, and no useful or improving occupation for the Lord's day.

Raikes's hope is that through his philanthropy they will learn to read, recite the catechism and listen to stories from the Bible. He has agreed to pay a teacher 1s 6d [7.5 pence] for the day.

His first insistence was that the children, all aged between six and 14, should be clean and tidy before being allowed to attend. But he now recognizes that many of the most needy are orphaned or abandoned by their parents and far too destitute for proper cleanliness. "If you have no clean shirt," he says, "come in what you have on."

The only stipulation now is that they behave while in class and desist from their habit of swearing "in a manner so horrid as to convey to any serious mind an idea of hell".

The aristocrat who instigated the riots

London, 8 June
Troops were finally called out yesterday to quell the anti-Roman Catholic riots which had reduced large parts of the city to rubble over the past week. Some 235 people are reported to have been killed, 173 wounded and 139 arrested, including Lord George Gordon, who first instigated the violence. He will be charged with high treason.

Born the younger son of Cosmo, the third duke of Gordon, he was educated at Eton, became a lieutenant in the Royal Navy and in 1774 was elected a member of parliament, where he quickly established himself as a virulent critic of both major parties. As president of a leading Protestant association he was incensed by the Catholic Relief Act of 1778 (though this measure was only brought in as a way to attract extra recruits for the armed forces), and his opposition quickly became an obsession. At his trial, counsel will try to demonstrate his well known eccentricity in the hope that he will be acquitted of responsibility for the riots.

Gordon was held in the Tower.

Rioting ringleaders to pay the penalty

London
As expected, Lord George Gordon was acquitted when the ringleaders of the riots to which he has given his name were brought to trial at the high court. But all the other 25 accused were found guilty and sentenced to be hanged.

After hearing lengthy evidence, the judges agreed that there was no clear proof that either Gordon or the Protestant association that he headed had deliberately planned the outbreak of violence, or any of its specific episodes.

These included, among many other outrages, some 500 deaths, the destruction of more than a hundred private buildings (most of them owned by either Catholics, sympathizers or magistrates) and an assault on the Bank of England.

Fertility and bliss for married couples

London
Dr James Graham, whose temple of health in Pall Mall has become a place of pilgrimage for childless couples and those in search of the "elixir of life", is clearly finding increasing difficulty in attracting the more free-spending type of customer. The fee for using the "great celestial bed", with its "guaranteed" cure for infertility, has recently been dropped from £100 a night to a mere 20 guineas [£21].

Similarly, the "elixir", which at the peak of Dr Graham's fame was on offer to the hopeful purchaser at £1,000 for a life-enhancing bottle, has now been quietly withdrawn. And the temple's once exclusive wonders can be viewed by the curious passer-by for just one shilling [five pence] a head (→23/6/94).

1781 - 1782

South Carolina, 17 January 1781. The British under Sir Banastre Tarleton are defeated by Daniel Morgan at Cowpens (→ 15/3).

Bath, 13 March 1781. William Herschel, the German-born astronomer, discovers a new planet; it is named Georgium Sidum, after the king (→ 1782).

North Carolina, 15 March 1781. General Lord Cornwallis leads his troops to victory over the Americans at Guildford despite heavy losses (→ 25/4).

South Carolina, 25 April 1781. British troops led by Lord Rawdon regain South Carolina, defeating General Nathanael Greene at Hobkirk's Hill (→ 9/5).

Florida, 9 May 1781. Pensacola, the last British base in western Florida, falls to the Spanish (→ 5/9).

India, 1 July 1781. General Eyre Coote leads the British to victory over Hyder Ali, the sultan of Mysore, at Porto Novo (→ 7/1784).

North America, 5 September 1781. Admiral Thomas Graves is defeated by the French under Admiral de Grasse in Chesapeake Bay (→ 19/10).

London, 21 January 1782. George III refuses to accept the independence of the Thirteen Colonies (→ 28/2).

Ulster, 15 February 1782. The Ulster Volunteers agree to legislative and judicial independence from Britain (→ 16/4).

Westminster, 28 February 1782. The day after parliament voted to halt the American war, Lord North introduces a bill to make peace with the colonies (→ 4/2/83).

Westminster, 16 April 1782. Henry Grattan, an Irish MP, proposes the Irish declaration of rights to parliament for a third time (→ 7/7).

Britain/France, 7 May 1782. Anglo-French peace talks begin (→ 11/10).

London, 13 July 1782. The earl of Shelburne becomes prime minister (→ 4/4/83).

Dublin, 15 September 1782. George Grenville, Earl Temple, is sworn in as lord lieutenant of Ireland.

Edinburgh, December 1782. Thomas McGrugar, a burgess, publishes his *Letters of Zeno*, denouncing the system by which just 25 men elect the city's member of parliament.

British troops surrender

A later depiction of the Americans storming the ramparts at Yorktown.

Yorktown, Va, 19 October 1781
A British army did the unthinkable today: it surrendered to the forces of the American George Washington. This defeat may mark the end of one of the most inglorious campaigns in British military history. A crucial role was played by the French navy, which restricted the movement of British forces.

When the defeat took place the 30,000-strong main army under General Sir Henry Clinton was in New York. This left General Lord Cornwallis and his ill-supplied army, including German mercenaries, surrounded in Virginia. When Washington saw that he could not defeat Clinton, he outmanoeuvred him and rushed to Virginia. Here, Cornwallis was obliged to retreat.

The Americans and French moved into former British posts, dug trenches and began to bombard the Yorktown garrison with artillery and mortar. A night assault by French troops, followed by Americans, made the British position untenable. While the surrender was being signed, the band played, aptly enough, *The World Turned Upside Down* (→ 21/1/82).

German organist is king's astronomer

England, 1782
William Herschel, a German organist and mathematician, has been appointed astronomer royal. Herschel, who settled in England in 1757 at the age of 19, is an expert at building giant reflecting telescopes. With his sister Caroline he has built the largest telescope yet assembled, and he has made some important discoveries.

Last year he found Uranus, a large planet beyond Saturn. In his "review of the heavens" Herschel has noted 269 pairs of stars revolving round one another, suggesting gravity at work outside the solar system. No one has yet investigated these systems (→ 8/1789).

Herschel and one of his telescopes.

Artist leaves Britain for Italian landscape

London, 1781
England's loss is Italy's gain. Angelica Kauffmann, the acclaimed Swiss painter who has lived in London since 1766, is to move to Italy to join her new husband, the Venetian painter Antonio Zucchi.

During her time in England, Kauffman, who is 40, has become famous for her portraits and for her historical and mythological paintings. Some of them decorate notable buildings in the capital, such as the Royal Academy, of which she was a founder member.

She is well known in London artistic circles not only for her painting but also for her wit and intellect; her company will be missed.

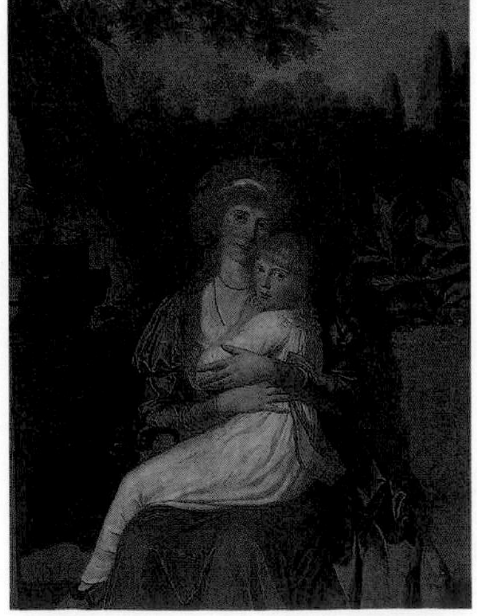

Kauffmann's view of Lady Hervey.

British strengthen hold on West Indies

West Indies, 12 April 1782
Admiral Rodney has avenged the catastrophe of Yorktown. In a bloody battle in the Saints passage, a reinforced British fleet of 36 ships today attacked a 34-strong French fleet under Admiral de Grasse, destroyed nine of them and secured the surrender of the flagship *Ville de Paris*. Control of the seas, which Britain crucially lost in the build-up to Yorktown, has been regained. The victory has also removed the threat to the West Indies which, combined with the loss of the Thirteen Colonies, could have destroyed Britain's economy (→ 7/5).

North resigns as first lord of the treasury

North: victim of the American war.

Westminster, 27 March 1782
Wounded by the failures of British policy in America, and deserted by its former supporters among the country gentlemen, Lord North's administration collapsed today. North announced his resignation before Lord Surrey could put the motion for his removal. The king is devastated, and the Commons were surprised, having expected a long debate. On a cold, snowy evening, only Lord North had kept his coachman waiting outside the house. "You see the advantage of being in the secret," he said as he took leave of his colleagues.

The government has led a precarious existence since 1778, when Lord North was so unnerved by the capitulation at Saratoga that he asked the king to let him resign. As the war in America continued to go badly, discontent grew in Ireland, and the national debt rose towards £170 million. The growth of the petitioning movement added to the impression of a beleaguered administration lacking in confidence. The defeat at Yorktown began a terminal decline. Although King George III has so far refused to contemplate American independence, North realized its inevitability after the calamity of Yorktown.

Viscount Sackville, the minister for the American colonies, was replaced on 31 January, whilst the navy's failures led to demands for the earl of Sandwich, the first lord of the admiralty, to go. On 27 February the anti-war lobby finally achieved a voting majority. Rockingham waits to take over (→ 13/7).

Gibraltar garrison holds off huge onslaught

The British fleet turns back a previous attack on the island in April.

Gibraltar, 11 October 1782
A massive Franco-Spanish attack on Gibraltar has been repulsed. Floating batteries were launched against the British garrison, but the navy managed to get supplies and reinforcements through the enemy blockade, enabling General Elliot to win a famous victory. It is an isolated success in a period of uncertainty for Britain abroad. The garrison at Minorca surrendered in February, and King George III has privately reconciled himself to the loss of such costly outposts.

George recently described Gibraltar as "the source of another war or at least of a constant lurking enmity". The new government formed by the earl of Shelburne on 13 July lacks clear foreign policy aims (→ 20/1/83).

British parliament gives more freedom to the Irish, increasing Catholics' rights

Grattan's power base and debating arena: the Irish House of Commons.

Ireland, 7 July 1782
Under the leadership of Henry Grattan, the parliamentarian and orator and one of the founders of the Volunteers, legislative independence has been won for Ireland. In what is being called "the constitution of 1782", Barry Yelverton's act has completely altered the operation of Poynings' Law. This law, which has been a constant source of grievance since it was passed almost 300 years ago, in 1494, effectively meant that laws introduced in Ireland could be suppressed or altered by the English privy council.

Under the new act, bills sent to England and approved by the king are to be returned unaltered, although – in theory – the king retains the power of veto. During the parliamentary debate some members proposed the repeal of Poynings' Law, and others wished the power of veto to be removed. However, it was generally accepted that the crown must be left with an effective veto over Irish legislation, as over British legislation.

Other legislation includes the replacement of the Perpetual Mutiny Act by a limited one which will regulate the raising of the Irish Army. Irish judges are to be granted the same tenure as their English colleagues, and the final jurisdiction of the Irish courts has been specifically established.

It remains to be seen how independence will affect the government of the country, since administration is still in the hands of the lord lieutenant, who is responsible to British ministers (→ 17/4/83).

Westminster's 16 Scottish peers abandon their trousers after the ban on the wearing of the kilt, which was imposed after the 1745 rebellion, is lifted.

1783

Kilkenny City, 13 January. The first Catholic academy for education opens here.

Paris, 20 January. Preliminary articles of peace are signed; this brings an end to Anglo-Spanish and Anglo-French hostilities (→ 9/1786).

Dublin, 22 January. Henry Ussher is appointed the first professor of astronomy at Trinity College.

Westminster, 4 February. Parliament proclaims an end to all hostilities in North America (→ 15/4).

Dublin, 10 February. The chamber of commerce is founded in Dublin.

London, 19 March. Frederick Cornwallis, who succeeded Thomas Secker as archbishop of Canterbury, dies (→ 26/4).

North America, 15 April. Britain relinquishes its hold on all land east of the Mississippi, excluding Florida, allowing the state of Alabama to join the United States (→ 3/9).

Westminster, 17 April. Parliament passes the Renunciation Act; this acknowledges the exclusive right of the Irish parliament to legislate for Ireland (→ 10/11).

Canterbury, 26 April. John Moore, the bishop of Bangor, is appointed the new archbishop of Canterbury.

Dublin, 3 June. Robert Henley, the earl of Northington, is sworn in as lord lieutenant of Ireland.

Scotland, August. Henry Dundas is replaced as lord advocate and head of the administration in Scotland by Henry Erskine.

Dublin, 10 November. The Ulster Volunteers hold their second provincial reform convention; the first was at Dungannon on 8 September (→ 29).

New York, 25 November. The last British troops leave from the harbour (→ 1/6/85).

Dublin, 29 November. Parliament refuses to accept the Ulster Volunteers' parliamentary reform bill (→ 21/3/84).

Waterford City. A glass factory is opened.

London. The "Eclectic Society" – an offshoot of the "Clapham sect" of prominent evangelicals – is formed; its members believe in politeness and moral behaviour.

United States gains its independence

Colonies are freed by Treaty of Paris

Paris, 3 September
Britain made peace with America and all its other enemies today. The independence of the United States, which was accepted last November, has now been recognized. Britain cedes the positions it still holds, including New York, Charleston, Savannah and all the western territories, to the new nation.

The treaty is very advantageous to the Americans, thanks to the diplomacy of John Jay and John Adams, two of the American diplomats in Paris, who refused to be bamboozled by the French. The British were utterly tired of the war and quite ready to renounce their former colonies, but France wanted the west, from the Alleghenies to the Mississippi, for its ally Spain. The Americans prevailed. In a separate treaty, Spain has recovered Florida, which it lost in 1763, but does not get Gibraltar, which withstood a prolonged siege in the war.

France has won little from the war, apart from the gratitude of the United States. The French crown is now burdened with crippling debts.

George III insists that the loss of the United States is no fault of his, and that "knavery seems to be so much the striking feature of its inhabitants that it may not in the end be an evil that they become aliens to this kingdom" (→ 25/11).

America scourges George III and his advisers in this contemporary cartoon.

Britain keeps a hold on Quebec and India

Paris, 3 September
The British have kept Quebec, which they won in the Seven Years War, and remain the dominant power in India, despite their defeats in the American war. The Royal Navy came back from disaster when Admiral Rodney destroyed the French fleet under de Grasse in the Battle of the Saints last year and restored British supremacy in the Atlantic. France was left with only St Pierre and Miquelon, two small islands off Newfoundland, of all its North American empire.

The population of what was formerly New France has accepted British rule because its laws, language and church are protected, but it is angry that the Ohio valley has been ceded to the United States. Large numbers of loyalist refugees have settled in British North America and Newfoundland. The treaty provides that congress will "earnestly recommend" the states that they restore their property, but that is a vain hope.

The Royal Navy has again protected British possessions in India, including Bengal, Madras and much of the east coast. The French were unable to take advantage of Britain's difficulties by sending an army, and the British were able to hold all Clive's conquests. The few small French outposts in India pose no danger to Britain.

New economic confidence results in creation of Bank of Ireland

Ireland, 25 June
The establishment of the Bank of Ireland in Dublin, which opened today, is seen as further evidence of confidence in the economy. With the development of industrial and capital investment, financial arrangements have become more refined, and since the 1720s cash supply has increased tenfold.

Irish banking has been mainly initiated by merchants, who are key figures in the Irish economy. Private banks can provide large returns on capital, although there is a high risk and frequency of financial failure.

The new bank's splendid building is a fine addition to Dublin's architecture.

Presbyterians move to Belfast venue

Belfast, 1 June
The Presbyterians have opened a new meeting house in Belfast. This reflects their sturdy independence, their growing prosperity in the linen trade and their determination to assert their position throughout Ulster, where they are much stronger than in the south.

Presbyterians in Ireland have been politically disadvantaged and socially overshadowed for most of this century. The discriminatory legislation against them has often caused bitter resentment, but the situation has now improved somewhat. The validity of their marriages has been recognized, and they are allowed to teach in schools and to have their own places of worship.

Water harnessed to power cloth factory

Arkwright's new Masson mill.

Derbyshire
Richard Arkwright, the inventor of the water-powered spinning frame, has completed construction of the handsome Masson mill on the river Derwent. It is just a short distance up the valley from Arkwright's first water-powered mill at Cromford, near Matlock, which opened 12 years ago [*see page 731*]. Arkwright also built the village of Cromford to house his workforce (→ 4/4/85).

Political crisis causes Commons chaos

Have Fox's supporters been deceived? Are they geese, doomed to slaughter?

Fox and North join forces to form coalition

Westminster, 4 April
King George III has appointed a new government under Lord North and Charles James Fox, two political enemies who have been fighting for 20 years. It is an unprecedented coalition. The king calls it "the most daring and unprincipled act that the annals of this kingdom ever produced". Fox is determined to reduce royal power.

When Lord Shelburne resigned in February the king asked the 23-year-old William Pitt to form a government, but he declined. Shelburne was defeated by Fox, the leader of the opposition Whigs, and North, the former prime minister, on the question of peace with America. Although they both demanded peace, Fox and North led their allies to vote against the terms proposed. Now they are in power, they will have to accept them.

Fox, the younger son of Lord Holland, is detested by the king partly because of his radical views and partly because he has befriended the prince of Wales. The king and his heir, in true Hanoverian tradition, espouse different politics. North turned against the king after being sacked when his policies lost the American colonies (→ 19/12).

William Pitt, 24, is new prime minister

Westminster, 19 December
King George III has dismissed the government and appointed William Pitt prime minister. He is 24, and Charles James Fox, now once more leader of the opposition, prophesies that this will be a "mince-pie government". He means that it will not last beyond Christmas.

The coalition government of Fox and Lord North was defeated in the Lords over the India Bill, introduced by Edmund Burke to reform the East India company. The king let it be known that any peer who voted for the bill would be considered his enemy. By then the government had been much weakened by quarrels between ministers. The king saw his chance to get rid of ministers he detested.

Pitt is the second son of Lord Chatham, who led the country to victory in the Seven Years War and was then dismissed by George III. The younger Pitt was chancellor of the exchequer in Shelburne's last ministry. He is eloquent, very able and determined to impose himself on the Commons, even though his supporters are in a minority. Fox bitterly resents Pitt's sudden accession and promises a vigorous opposition. Fox is charming, sociable and has innumerable friends; the rather cold and aloof Pitt is much admired, but little loved (→ 6/1784).

Scots are by far the best-educated Britons

Scotland
Scottish education is gaining the reputation of being among the best in the world. Visitors often comment that ordinary folk are better educated than in England or on the continent; the late Tobias Smollett, the Scots novelist, said that in Scotland "every peasant is a scholar".

Behind this success lies a long church campaign to ensure that every parish had its own school, and thus to create godly communities where every member was able to read the Bible. As long ago as the turn of the century, Scots were already among the better-educated peoples of Europe; the 1696 Education Act, which aimed to encourage landowners to finance local schools, helped further.

Standards vary widely, but education is available to most families. Schooling is voluntary, and girls are less likely to attend than boys. Recent estimates suggest that, in towns, nine out of ten men are literate, whilst in country areas two-thirds of men can sign their names.

Fox depicted as an Indian tyrant.

1784

Dublin, 11 February. The Royal College of Surgeons in Ireland is incorporated.

London, 28 February. John Wesley, the Anglican preacher, issues a Deed of Declaration for the Methodist movement (→29/3/89).

Dublin, 21 March. The Ulster Volunteers' parliamentary reform bill is defeated on its second reading.

Edinburgh, March. Agitators hold a meeting to discuss reform of the corrupt electoral system in Scottish towns; representatives of half of Scotland's 66 royal burghs attend (→18/4/92).

London, 2 May. Britain declares Cape Breton Island, an official part of Nova Scotia for the last 20 years and previously a French possession, a British colony (→18/6).

Ireland, 14 May. The Post Office is established by official statute.

Belfast, 30 May. St Mary's Roman Catholic chapel is officially opened.

Canada, 18 June. King George III creates New Brunswick, a new province in Canada, to cope with the influx of loyalist British settlers from the United States (→19/5/90).

Bristol, 2 August. John Palmer, the postmaster, introduces the first mail coach, which will travel between Bristol and London.

London, 15 September. The first balloon ascent in England is made by Vincent Lunardi, an Italian (→4/1/85).

Yorkshire. Joseph Bramah, a lame mechanic, invents a burglar-proof barrel-shaped combination lock, with over 494 million combinations; such is his confidence in the invention that he offers 200 guineas as a prize to anyone who can pick the lock (→1785).

London. Samuel Johnson, the poet, critic and essayist, dies at his home off Fleet Street; he is best known for his publication of a *Dictionary of the English Language* (→1791).

Hampshire. Henry Cort, the ironmaster of Funtley, has invented "puddling", a new process for manufacturing wrought iron which, it is believed, could revolutionize the iron industry.→

Scotland. Allan Ramsay, the portrait painter, dies.

Estates forfeited by Jacobites restored to rightful owners

Edinburgh, 4 May

The large estates forfeited by highland chiefs who supported "Bonnie Prince Charlie" in 1745 have been restored to their former owners, or their heirs. Once before, after the 1715 rebellion, Jacobite estates were confiscated and sold; there were many innocent sufferers, but the Act of Indemnity in 1717 set out to remedy the injustices. After 1745 the repression was even more severe: highlanders not only lost their lands but were also forbidden to carry arms or play the bagpipes, and the wearing of the kilt was banned until two years ago.

In the highlands especially, possession of land is seen as the basis of political and social influence; the right to vote and eligibility for public appointments come with landed status. The old Jacobite families can now be expected to join other landowners who have encouraged settlement on their estates as a source of extra income.

Some landowners have used the money for landscaping, the building of dykes and hedges to fix the boundaries of new tenancies, new farmhouses and even new villages. It may not be long before highlanders begin to follow the lowland proprietors who have been attracted to the power and social prestige of London (→31/1/88).

Pitt budgets to assist financial reform

Pitt's political opponent, Fox, on the hustings during this year's election.

Westminster, June

William Pitt, his position as prime minister strengthened by a sweeping victory for his supporters in the general election which was held in April and May, could become the most ingenious tax-gatherer of all time. During the American War of Independence, the national debt soared to a staggering £238 million; interest on this is £9 million a year, which is nine times the cost of running the civil government.

Pitt, who is also chancellor, has imposed taxes on horses, hackney coaches, bricks, hats, ribbons, candles, linen, cotton – and windows. He is also seeking to undercut the smuggling that became widespread during the war by reducing some taxes. Tea duties will be lowered from 119 to 25 per cent *ad valorem*.

Pitt is also creating a treasury consolidated fund, into which all imposts will be paid as they are collected. This will replace the 105 separate revenue accounts, which have caused confusion and losses. Government contracts are to be put out to competitive public tender.

Pitt reckons his new taxes will raise an extra £930,000 in the first year. But householders have started bricking up their windows because of the tax, and many glaziers fear for their livelihoods (→4/1785).

Foreign investors fund rapid growth of iron industry in Wales

Swansea

English capital is pouring into Wales to finance an industrial revolution generated by steam power and a variety of other new technologies. In six years four major ironworks have been built: at Ebbw Vale, Beaufort, Sirhowy and Penydarren. Anthony Bacon, a Maryland merchant who emigrated to England, founded the ironmaking industry at Merthyr Tydfil and made a vast fortune from government contracts for the manufacture of cannon. Wars with France have been a major stimulus to Welsh industry. In three years Robert Morgan's Carmarthen forges cast over 700 guns.

These ironworks on the banks of the Severn forge cannon for the military.

India Act controls trading activities

Westminster, July
Under Pitt's India Reform Bill, the East India company will cease to be the ruling power in the subcontinent. Ultimate authority passes to a newly created ministry of the British government; political, military and financial powers on the spot will be exercised by a governor-general, answerable to London. The company retains its trading monopoly, including the valuable tea trade with China. A bill introduced last year by Edmund Burke suggested handing over management of the company's possessions to commissioners appointed by the government. This blatant political patronage caused an uproar which brought down the government and led to Pitt's appointment as prime minister (→ 1/1785).

Ulster erupts in more religious violence

Ulster, July
The formation this month of "the Peep O'Day Boys", a Protestant agrarian movement, has resulted in sectarian incidents throughout Co Armagh. Claiming that they are merely enforcing the penal laws in the absence of action by the gentry, members of this blatantly sectarian group have terrorized many Roman Catholics by their administration of rough justice.

The authorities appear to be incapable of disciplining them, and the only solution seems to be to enrol the more discontented elements into the Volunteers. Living standards amongst the weaving community are dropping, and it is feared that, as a result, Protestant aggression will become increasingly articulated (→ 9/1795).

Scot floats in balloon

Up, up and away: James Tytler soars aloft in his hot-air balloon.

Edinburgh, 17 August
James Tytler, the Scottish academic who contributed the scientific articles to the second edition of the *Encyclopaedia Britannica* last year, has become the first man in Britain to make an ascent in a hot-air balloon. The balloon, which was of Tytler's own construction, rose from Comely Gardens, Edinburgh, today, and descended shortly afterwards about half a mile away on the road to Restalrig.

Tytler has beaten by a few weeks the attempt by Vincent Lunardi, an attaché at the Neapolitan embassy, to make a balloon ascent over London. He planned to ascend from the grounds of Chelsea hospital, but permission was refused after a mob ran riot and destroyed another balloon belonging to a Frenchman. Lunardi will now make his ascent from the Honourable Artillery Company's grounds at Moorfields.

Lunardi's balloon will be filled with hydrogen produced under the supervision of Dr George Fordyce, a chemistry lecturer at St Thomas's hospital. The first balloon ascents were made in France last year, when Jean François Pilâtre de Rozier ascended in a fire-balloon from the Bois de Boulogne, in Paris. Jacques Charles, the physicist, ascended from the Tuileries in a hydrogen balloon and made a two-hour, 27-mile flight (→ 15/9).

Irish linen industry is growing in Belfast

Linen is a business for the whole family – seen here preparing flax for weaving.

Ireland, September
The dramatic expansion in the linen industry in the north is reflected in the opening of the White Linen Hall in Belfast this month. The healthy condition of the linen trade has been facilitated by free access to British markets, whilst imports from the continent have to face a tariff barrier. Exports have risen from 305,000 yards in 1700 to 18,700,000 yards in 1780, 98 per cent of which goes to Britain. Belfast is rapidly replacing Dublin as a port for shipment of cloths. However, the booming linen industry has also created sectarian rivalry in densely populated areas.

Protestant weavers consider it essential to have a plot of land to fall back on in hard times. Intense competition for land between Protestant and Catholic weavers has brought conflict. Protestant gangs, such as "the Nappach Fleet" and "the Peep O'Day Boys", have been formed to victimize Catholics and stir up sectarian violence.

The Bath mail-coach on its way to the west of England; the introduction of the mail-coach system this year could revolutionize transport.

1785

London, 1 January. John Walter publishes the first issue of *The Daily Universal Register* (→ 1/1/88).

Birmingham, 4 January. A balloon ascent is made from the tennis courts on Coleshill Street (→ 7).

London, 5 January. George, the prince of Wales amasses huge gambling debts, estimated to amount to at least £150,000 (→ 15/12).

Dublin, 19 January. Richard Crosbie makes the first balloon ascent from Irish soil at Ranelagh, near Dublin (→ 19/7).

Westminster, 24 March. Parliament allows grocers licensed by law to sell alcohol for consumption off the premises.

England, 4 April. Edmund Cartwright patents the power loom which he has invented (→ 1789).

Westminster, April. William Pitt, the prime minister, proposes a limited parliamentary reform bill; it is defeated by 248 votes to 174.→

London, 1 June. King George III receives the first American ambassador to Britain, John Adams (→ 28/2/86).

Dublin, June. The Irish Academy begins a collection of manuscripts with the acquisition of the *Book of Ballymote*.

Irish Sea, 19 July. Richard Crosbie, the Irish aeronaut, is rescued by the barge *Captain Walmitt* when his attempted balloon crossing of the Irish Sea is ruined by a storm.

London. Joseph Bramah, the mechanic who invented the combination lock, designs a beer-pump handle.

England. Josiah Wedgwood sets up the General Chamber of Manufacturers of Great Britain, bringing together a number of small associations; it is hoped that the larger body will be better able to influence parliament (→ 1790).

Scotland. James Hutton, the geologist, publishes his *Theory of the Earth*.

Westminster. William Pitt reduces the duty on tea in an attempt to take the profit out of smuggling.

Warwickshire. The Reverend James Wilmot claims that the plays of William Shakespeare were actually written by Francis Bacon, Viscount St Albans.

Balloon makes first Channel crossing

Northern France, 7 January
Two intrepid flyers today landed in a clearing in the Forêt de Felmones, 12 miles from the coast, after the first aerial crossing of the English Channel in a hydrogen balloon. Dr John Jeffries, an exiled physician from Boston, Massachussetts, had put up the money; his partner, the Frenchman Jean Pierre Blanchard, is a professional balloonist.

Flying English and French flags, Blanchard and Jeffries beat several rivals. The flight from Dover, in Kent, took two and a half hours.

Since a Montgolfier balloon flew in front of the king of France two years ago, ballooning has become a huge craze. Flights of 150 miles and 3,510 metres [11,700 feet] have already been achieved; the Channel was the next challenge (→ 19).

The balloon approaches France.

Sarah Siddons a hit as Lady Macbeth

London
Audiences at the Theatre Royal have seen Sarah Siddons give a terrifying performance as Lady Macbeth. The 30-year-old actress took the city by storm three years ago in *The Fatal Marriage* with her magnificent suffering.

Siddons makes audiences weep, and even faint, with emotion. Her large eyes reflect every nuance of feeling, and she "conjures up the ghost of her character", living the part. Lady Macbeth's sleepwalking scene inspires real terror. "I smelt blood!" said Sheridan Knowles.

Sarah Siddons: in rehearsal.

Poisonous plant used to combat disease

London
One of the most effective but also the most dangerous drugs in the physician's armoury now has an authoritative handbook. Dr William Withering was worried about the widespread and careless use of the plant foxglove, which can be very useful against dropsy but can also cause vomiting, convulsions and death. *An Account of the Foxglove* is a clear and honest account of his use of digitalis "proper or improper, successful or otherwise" in 163 cases. It stresses the importance of giving a standard dose, using the leaves in an infusion. Adults take one to four grains of powdered leaves a day in an "ounce of any spiritous water". Withering claims that "in proper doses ... it is mild in its operation and gives less disturbances to the system ... than almost any other active medicine".

Cowper evokes nature in popular comic ballad 'John Gilpin'

Cowper's creation John Gilpin, on horseback, just keeps on going ...

London
William Cowper, the poet who suffers from bouts of melancholy, has this year published a long, mock-heroic poem, *The Task*. It begins in light-hearted tones, with an address to his sofa, then evokes a country park. It contains many fine descriptions of rural life.

Born the son of a rector in 1731, Cowper trained to be a lawyer but suffered a mental collapse in 1763, since when he has lived in rural retirement. Although he has suffered tremendous mental distress, his friends have seen a lighter side in his letters. He is known for his hymns – including *God moves in a mysterious way, / His wonders to perform* – and also for the ballad *John Gilpin* about the exploits of a London train-band captain (→ 1800).

'Sinking Fund' may be the only way to rescue dire finances

London, April

The greatest task facing the new government is the national debt, which has been swollen by £100 million to a gargantuan £243 million by the American War. The annual interest alone on it now runs at nearly £9.5 million – over half the total budget.

Even some of those who have profited hugely from government stock are worried that the debt makes the country vulnerable to foreign manipulation, since the Dutch hold nearly 50 per cent of it.

The reformer James Burgh has warned of complete social collapse, beginning with a run on stocks, if the debt gets much larger. There are several schemes for tackling it, most of which involve more taxation, since the current shortfall in the budget is about £2 million.

Wiiliam Pitt, the new prime minister, is said to be keen on the ideas of the dissenting minister Dr Richard Price, who has advocated a "sinking fund", of the sort set up over 60 years ago by Walpole, to reduce the debt gradually.

There are worries about imposing yet more taxes. Already everything from glass and silver plate to male servants, newspapers and dice is taxed (→15/6/92).

Hastings resigns as governor of India

Hastings coughs up his ill-gotten gains – into the care of a judge.

India, January

Warren Hastings, the beleaguered governor-general of India, has resigned and will return to face his critics in London. He is well aware of the fate of his predecessor, Sir Robert Clive, driven to suicide in 1774 by similar corruption charges.

For years Hastings was engaged in a fierce bureaucratic struggle with a London-appointed, three-man council designed to curb his powers. But in 1780 he seemed to have won. Two members of the council had died and the third, Philip Francis, went home after being wounded in a duel with Hastings, so bitter had their dispute become. But despite Hastings's triumphs – in 1781 he defeated an attack by two Indian princes and the French – the Whigs have made India a hot political issue.

East India company agents have long been regarded as corrupt, devoted to lining their own pockets; there is also a widespread belief that Hastings' treatment of the Indians has been at times high-handed and cruel, and the issue of who runs India, the crown or the company, has never been resolved. Unfortunately Hastings's arrogant manner earns him few friends (→12/9/86).

Prince of Wales is secretly married to Maria Fitzherbert

London, 15 December

The prince of Wales has jeopardized his future and risked a constitutional crisis by getting married in secret – to a Catholic. He and his bride, Maria Fitzherbert, were married in her house by a young curate whom George had got out of prison by paying his £500 debt.

The bride is attractive, twice widowed and exactly the prince's type: older than him (she is 29 and he is 23) and amply proportioned. The problem has been her refusal to become his mistress, since under the Royal Marriages Acts of 1772 members of the royal family under 25 cannot marry without the king's consent, which George III would certainly have withheld. It is also illegal for anyone married to a Catholic to succeed to the throne.

The prince has pursued Maria for a year, once even faking suicide. When she went to the continent to cool things off, he became desperate. Charles Fox described how he "cried by the hour, rolling on the floor ... swearing he would abandon the country, forgo the crown and ... fly with [her] to America". The prince's problems include debts of nearly £150,000 – mainly spent on lavish improvements to his London home, Carlton House – which parliament will be asked to clear. This marriage will not make it easy to win that vote (→30/4/87).

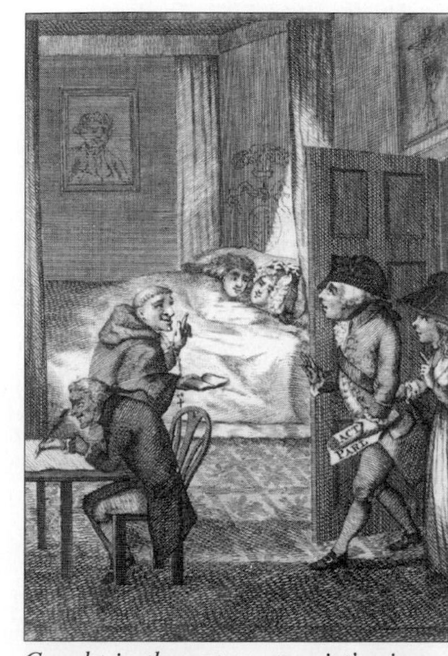

Caught in the act: cartoonist's view.

Glasgow banker to open 'caring' mill as cotton industry booms

New Lanark cotton mill: a model factory set in beautiful surroundings.

New Lanark, Strathclyde

A revolutionary cotton-mill village being built here, which promises to provide the best working conditions in Britain, is nearly finished. It is designed by the Glasgow banker David Dale. Its 1,300 employees will work from 6am to 7pm with two breaks. Child-workers, aged six upwards, will get free clothes, proper food and two hours' schooling.

A sudden drop in the price of West Indian cotton several years ago, combined with the flying shuttle which doubled production, has triggered a cotton boom here; the first mill was built at Penicuik in 1778, and there are now about 15. Most of the workers come from the highlands or Ireland, and 75 per cent of them are under 21.

1786 - 1787

London, 28 February 1786. The United States ambassador, John Adams, is told by the British government that British settlers will not leave American bases until all debts are cleared (→ 30/4/89).

Belfast, 1 May 1786. The Belfast Academy is officially opened.

Dublin, 3 May 1786. The city establishes an official police force.

India, 12 September 1786. Lord Cornwallis, one of the leading British commanders in the American revolution, is appointed governor-general of India (→ 13/2/88).

Dublin, 3 December 1786. John Thomas Troy, the Catholic bishop of Ossory, is consecrated as archbishop of Dublin.

London, 1786. The British Fisheries Society is founded, with a remit to improve fishing in the Scottish highlands as a means of halting emigration from the region.

England, 1786. George Hepplewhite, the master cabinet-maker, dies.

Westminster, 30 April 1787. Charles Fox assures parliament that the prince of Wales is not married to the Roman Catholic Mrs Maria Fitzherbert (→ 5/1787).

Portsmouth, 13 May 1787. The first convict ship sets sail for Botany Bay (→ 26/1/88).

London, June 1787. King George III issues a proclamation against vice and immorality after William Wilberforce, a Yorkshire member, lobbies parliament (→ 11/1787).

Dublin, June 1787. The last performance at the Smock Alley theatre takes place.

Brighton, 6 July 1787. The prince of Wales takes refuge in his new seaside home following the settling of his debts (→ 1788).

Birmingham, 24 July 1787. John Wilkinson's 70-foot iron barge *Trial* sails on the canal.

London, 9 October 1787. Lieutenant William Bligh and his crew set sail from Deptford on HMS *Bounty* (→ 28/4/89).

Dublin, 12 November 1787. Bad weather floods the river Liffey, causing much damage.

Darlington, 1787. Kendrew, an optician, and Porthouse, a clockmaker, combine their skills and invent a flax-spinning machine.

Scots dialect poems by young Ayr farmer are hailed by Edinburgh's intellectuals

Edinburgh, 9 December 1786
A review in *The Lounger* out today hails as a "heaven-taught ploughman" the author of a recent collection of *Poems Chiefly in the Scottish Dialect*. He is Robert Burns, from Ayrshire. He was born in a lowly clay cottage in Alloway, near the town of Ayr, 27 years ago, and from the age of 15 was the chief labourer on his father's farm. His education was chiefly through his own reading in such English and French literature as could be obtained. He composed his first poem at the age of just 17 – to "Handsome Nell", a fellow-labourer in the fields.

His friends encouraged him to print his poems by subscribing for 350 copies, and they were brought out by a Kilmarnock printer last July. His fame soon spread farther afield, and on 28 November he arrived in Edinburgh on a borrowed pony to a warm welcome from the literary lights of the capital. They are struck by his honest simplicity and the force of his conversation. His eyes, those who have met him say, are "like coals of living fire". The poems are notable for their power, insight and bold use of Scots, the spoken language of lowland Scotland. The *Address to the Deil*, *Jolly Beggars* and *Address to a Mouse* – lines to a mouse whose nest he had ploughed up – show its remarkable force (→ 21/7/96).

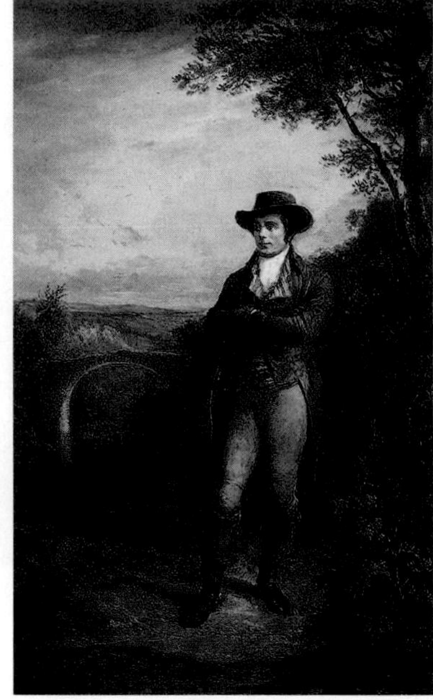

The poetic labourer Robert Burns.

Royal charter given to Irish Academy

Ireland, 1786
The Royal Irish Academy has been incorporated under royal patronage as a society for "promoting the study of science, polite literature and antiquities", with King George III as its patron. The academy is to have a president (Lord Charlemont), treasurer and secretary and a council of 21.

One of the leading lights behind the formation of the academy is Thomas Barnard, the bishop of Killaloe, famous for his sociability and wit, who is anxious that the academy should be governed "as much as possible on aristocratick principles".

The idea for the academy grew out of the Medico-Philosophical Society, which was founded in 1756. It was inspired by Charles Smith, who has done valuable work in preparing county surveys of Cork and Waterford; he drew attention to the important role played in European intellectual life by societies which are devoted to "the pursuit of truth and the sound method of reasoning first introduced by [Francis] Bacon".

Thomas Lord founds London cricket club

The sound of leather on willow is heard at the new Marylebone Cricket Club.

London, 1787
The Yorkshire sportsman Thomas Lord has opened a new cricket club at Marylebone, on the city's northern outskirts. Before this, he superintended the ground at Islington on behalf of the earl of Winchilsea – one of the founder members of the White Conduit Cricket Club. Country players are free to wear what clothes they wish, but white top hats with black bands are to be encouraged for gentlemen players.

There is still resistance to the idea of wearing gloves and pads, despite the fact that most of the blood spilt on the field is from injuries to the fingers (→ 1788).

Prince of Wales in row over huge debts

London, May 1787
The prince of Wales and his father George III are at loggerheads over the heir to the throne's extravagance and his mounting debts. By the end of last year, these had soared to £270,000, more than a quarter of the annual expenditure of the realm. The prince of Wales has been overspending at the rate of £80,000 a year.

Parliament has agreed to provide £161,000 towards the settlement of the prince's debts and to increase his annual grant by £10,000. He will also receive £60,000 towards the completion of Carlton House. Three years ago George Hotham, the prince's treasurer, revealed that work had been commissioned on Carlton House without any regard to cost. Considerable sums are owed to both the builder and the upholsterer, as well as to the prince's jeweller and tailor (→ 6/7).

Anglo-French trade treaty is good news for British exports

Britain, September 1786
There are clear prospects for better Anglo-French trading relations with the signing this month of the Eden Treaty. It takes its name from Britain's skilled negotiator, William Eden, a senior government trade official.

The French have been pushing for a trade deal, promised by both sides in the 1783 Treaty of Paris, for some time. The agreement is intended to end each nation's longstanding policy of trying to damage the economy of the other by doing as little trade with it as possible, and to suppress smuggling in order to favour national revenues. To discourage smuggling Britain and France have agreed to impose moderate duties (of ten to 15 per cent) on each other's products. This will benefit French wine producers by bringing British import duties on their products down, but lower French duties are sure to be of greater long-term benefit to Britain's burgeoning heavy industries, particularly cotton, which exports most of its output.

A ban on all Anglo-French trade in silk goods will protect the British silk industry from its stronger French counterpart. Each country will also now grant favourable terms to visiting ships and resident traders of the other (→13/12/92).

George Romney's painting of Cassandra, as portrayed by one of his favourite models, the lovely Emma, Lady Hamilton.

Knife assault on king

One of the king's guards foils Margaret Nicholson's assassination attempt.

London, 2 August 1787
An attempt to kill King George III was foiled today when members of the public rushed forward to stop the would-be assassin. The king had just arrived at St James's Palace for a reception when one Margaret Nicholson rushed forward clutching a knife and attempted to stab him. The king remained calm and collected throughout the incident as his guards surrounded him, and Nicholson was seized by onlookers before doing any harm.

George shouted to the crowd: "The poor creature is mad! Do not hurt her, she has not hurt me!" and pushed forward to show himself to be unhurt and safe. He then gave strict orders that Nicholson should be taken care of and proceeded into the palace (→7/1788).

British alliance hits Dutch Patriot rebels

Britain, September 1787
William V of Orange is in power once more in the United Provinces following a British-backed Prussian invasion. The "revolution" which was fermented in the country by the democratic and middle-class Patriot party, representing French influence and opposed to patrician families, has collapsed.

The present crisis was brought about when the princess of Orange, William's wife and the sister of the Prussian King Frederick William II, was arrested by the Patriots while on a secret journey to rally support for her husband. Frederick William demanded redress for this insult to his sister and her husband's reinstatement in power. Pitt's cabinet, seeing the chance to act against the pro-French interest, promised the Prussians military aid and raised a small naval force.

Confident in the knowledge that Britain would back them up if necessary, the Prussians intervened to help William regain command of the army that he was deprived of by the Patriots last year.

'Proclamation Society' attacks pornography and loose morals

England, November 1787
During the past six months, since the founding of the Proclamation Society in June this year, churchmen of all ranks have been touring the country campaigning against the evils of loose living and "the grand corrupter" of youth: pornography. The Proclamation Society aims, among other condemnations of immoral excesses, to suppress "all loose and licentious publications, books and prints dispersing poison to ... the young and unwary, and to punish the publishers and vendors thereof".

It was William Wilberforce, a social reformer and evangelical philanthropist, who, with the backing of King George III, launched the society in an attempt to revive the aims of Methodism. "God has set before me as my object the reformation of manners," he said, and he has gained the enthusiastic support of the archbishops of Canterbury and York, 17 bishops, six dukes and 11 other peers. The Proclamation Society has already instituted a number of prosecutions for libel, indicting pornographic classics such as *The Memoirs of a Woman of Pleasure* and *The School of Venus* (*L'Escholle des Filles*). Writs have also been issued against *The Rambler's Magazine* and various other pornographic periodicals currently in circulation.

Love in a gutter: an illustrator's view of England's declining morals.

1788

London, 26 February. James Edward Smith founds the Linnean Society, the first specialized scientific society concerned with the study of botany and zoology.

Belfast, 13 May. The Belfast Reading Society is formed.

Gloucestershire, July. King George III takes the waters at Cheltenham Spa after a bilious attack (→20/11).

London, 2 August. Thomas Gainsborough, the celebrated portrait and landscape painter, dies at the age of 61.

Europe, 13 August. The Triple Alliance is agreed between Britain, Prussia and the Netherlands, as a counterweight to the combined coalition of France, the Holy Roman Empire and Russia.

London, 17 October. John Brown, a Scottish physician who advocated the treatment of opium or whisky to cure many ailments, dies at the age of 53.

Edinburgh, 16 November. The first stone of Edinburgh University is laid.

Kew, Surrey, December. Francis Willis, who runs a private asylum in Lincolnshire, has been called to Windsor to give his advice on King George III's mental and physical condition. With no medical qualifications and deeply mistrusted by the royal doctors, Willis has promised a cure for the king's mysterious illness (→15/1/89).

Britain. Hannah More, an eminent "bluestocking" and social reformer, publishes *Thoughts on the Importance of the Manners of the Great to General Society* (→1789).

Edinburgh. William "Deacon" Brodie, a burgh councillor and cabinetmaker, who fled to the Netherlands when his secret life as leader of a gang of robbers was uncovered, is traced, tried and hanged.

Britain/Africa. The African Association is founded to promote legitimate trade to replace slavery.

Co Roscommon. Ironworks are opened at Arigna; this is the first time that local coal and iron ore has been used for smelting in Ireland.

London. The Marylebone Cricket Club (MCC), founded last year by Thomas Lord, codifies the rules and regulations of cricket (→7/1814).

'Young Pretender' dies in Rome exile

Rome, 31 January

Charles Stuart died here today, aged 68, on the 139th anniversary of the execution of King Charles I, his great-grandfather. Though still lauded in Scotland as "Bonnie Prince Charlie", in memory of his valiant attempt to win back the British throne in the 1745 rebellion, he had become a sad and lonely figure. Only his courtiers recognized him as King Charles III, and for many years he remained in the Palazzo Muti, drinking six bottles of wine a day to drown his sorrows.

He even failed to produce an heir. He married a 19-year-old princess but she found him "the most insupportable man that ever existed" and took a poet for a lover.

The Stuart "Young Pretender".

Prince's horse wins Epsom Derby

Epsom, Surrey

George III can feel well satisfied with his sons this year. They have found a way to the hearts of the British people. Both the prince of Wales and the duke of York maintain racing stables, and they have helped to make horse-racing a national sport. The prince's victory in the Derby this year boosted both his own popularity and the sport's.

The king makes regular visits to Epsom and Ascot to see his sons' horses perform. The queen, however, dislikes the sport and the betting that goes with it (→11/1791).

Hastings is impeached

Not a seat to spare as Warren Hastings faces politicians in Westminster Hall.

Westminster, 13 February

Warren Hastings, aged 53, the man chosen by the government to be the first Indian governor-general, today found himself in the dock in Westminster Hall. Ranged against him were three of the most powerful parliamentarians in Britain, Edmund Burke, Charles Fox and Richard Sheridan. Hastings was appointed to end the corruption surrounding the East India company. He resigned three years ago and returned home expecting to convince the public of what he had achieved.

It has not turned out that way. He has faced attacks in parliament and now impeachment. One charge is that he forced native rulers in the Ganges area to give funds to pay company dividends. Sir Philip Francis, a friend of Burke, has branded Hastings a villain. Francis was once a councillor in India, where he was shot by Hastings in a duel. He wants revenge (→21/3/90).

Convicts build their new lives 'down under'

Sydney Cove, near Botany Bay, where Phillip built the first penal settlement.

Botany Bay, Australia, 26 January

British convicts have found an ideal place to make a new life in the New World. Arthur Phillip, the commander of six transports carrying 736 convicts, describes it as "the finest harbour in the world".

Phillip is an unusually caring man to be doing such a tough job. He is carrying convicts because he refuses to take slaves. He had made many improvements in the men's living quarters, so that only 48 died on the 36-week voyage, a much smaller number than usual. He spent six days sailing around the Australian coast until he found somewhere that he felt was a fit place in which human beings could make a fresh start (→26/11/91).

Gibbon finishes his 'Decline and Fall'

London, 27 April
The epic labours of Edward Gibbon are at an end with the completion of his *The Decline and Fall of the Roman Empire*, a history whose grand sweep is echoed in the cool dignity of its style, however lurid the subject-matter. For history, he writes, "is little more than the register of the crimes, follies and misfortunes of mankind".

It was while visiting Rome on a "grand tour" in 1764 that the idea of writing the book came to him, "as I sat musing amidst the ruins of the Capitol while the barefoot friars were singing Vespers in the Temple of Jupiter". This seemed symbolic to Gibbon, who attributes the fall of the empire very largely to the rise of Christianity. His great panorama begins in AD180 and ends with the extinction in 1453 of Byzantium and the Eastern Empire which, he writes, had existed for 1058 years "in a state of premature and perpetual decay". Gibbon laid down his pen in Lausanne after 15 years' work, saddened by the thought that "I had taken leave of an old and agreeable companion" (→ 1794).

Britain concerned by king's illness

A cartoonist draws on the regency crisis caused by the king's ongoing illness.

Windsor, 20 November
This morning's official bulletin will do nothing to alleviate the public anxiety about George III's health that has been sweeping the capital for several weeks now. The bland official language reports: "His majesty has had a more undisturbed night than the former, but the fever has not quite left him." Those who have been seeing the king regularly put it quite differently and much more plainly in conversation. They fear that the king has gone mad.

His "fever", they report, involves delirious ramblings, sudden bursts of anger alternating with benign saintliness, combined with sleeplessness, sweating, a fast pulse and hoarseness. According to one story going around, the king even got out of his carriage in the great park here and greeted an oak tree as the king of Prussia. A few weeks ago he began to talk incessantly at concerts he usually listens to with rapt attention. According to Lady Harcourt, the queen says his eyes "compare to nothing but black-currant jelly". Lady Harcourt goes on: "The veins in his face are swelled, the sound of his voice is dreadful, he often speaks till he is exhausted ... foam runs out of his mouth."

The six or seven doctors attending him here are mystified by his condition. They first thought he was suffering from a recurrence of the bilious attacks and gout that caused him to take the waters at Cheltenham last July. But in the last few days, while his physical condition has improved, his mental state has become far worse.

The king himself reports his eyesight is blurred and his memory confused. He cannot concentrate to read his dispatches. The prime minister is reluctantly considering the appointment of a regent. The opposition leader, Charles Fox, is urging the immediate declaration of a regency under the prince of Wales, Fox's close friend (→ 12/1788).

'The Times': a new name for old paper

London, 1 January
Further evidence of rising competition for the pennies of newspaper readers comes with this morning's name change for one of the newer entrants in the field. *The Daily Universal Register*, which began just three years ago, has abandoned its rather ponderous title. Henceforth it will be known as *The Times*. It will be competing with The *Morning Chronicle*, whose editor William Woodfall has won widespread acclaim for the excellence of his parliamentary reports. "Memory Woodfall" has been known to write as much as sixteen columns without even a note to aid his memory.

The front of today's *Times* is full of advertisements. Musicians can buy new scores such as Mozart's "Haydn" quartets, while Kemble and Siddons are recommended in *Julia, or the Italian Lover* at the Theatre Royal (→ 13/10/1808).

Wildlife observations by Gilbert White

A memorial to White at Selborne.

Selborne, Hampshire, December
The vicar of Selborne is putting the final touches to his book *Natural History and Antiquities of Selborne*, which should prove a delight to scientists and poets alike. The Reverend Gilbert White has devoted his days to observing the plant, animal and bird life in his locality. He writes about it with an eloquence that reveals his love of the nature poetry of William Cowper, William Collins and Oliver Goldsmith.

A native of Selborne, White learnt his science at Oxford, becoming a fellow of Oriel College. He then became a country curate, a job which gave him an ideal opportunity for his wildlife observations. His work was inspired by Newtonian science and by the growing interest in the detailed observation and recording of natural life. His present work was helped by his correspondence since 1767 with two fellow naturalists, Thomas Pennant and Daines Barrington (→ 1789).

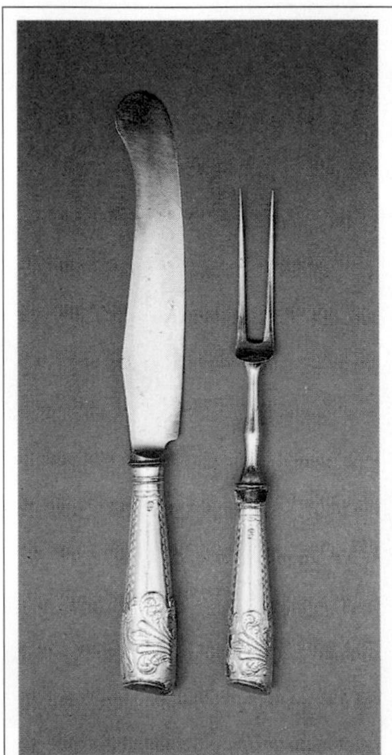
Fine examples of Sheffield plate remain as memorials to Thomas Boulsover, the inventor of the plating process, who died this year.

1789

Kew, Surrey, 15 January. George III is reported to be improving slightly (→2/1789).

London, 10 March. George is fully recovered (→23/4).

Dublin, 29 March. John Wesley, the Anglican preacher, visits Ireland (→2/3/91).

France, March. King Louis XVI is presented with a list of grievances and complaints from the Estates-General; the legislative assembly meets for the first time since 1614.

Tahiti, 28 April. Lieutenant William Bligh and 18 of his crew are set adrift from HMS *Bounty* after a mutiny provoked by his cruel treatment of his men (→14/8).

New York, 30 April. George Washington is sworn in as the first president of the United States of America.

Dublin, 26 June. The Whig Club is founded in Dublin.

Europe, August. Europe is astounded by the outbreak of revolution in France (→11/1789).

Dorset, September. King George III continues his convalescence at Weymouth, on the coast (→21/1/90).

Dublin, 24 October. The Royal canal company is incorporated, and plans go ahead to build a canal linking Dublin and the Shannon river.

United States, 6 November. John Carroll, of Irish descent, is appointed bishop of Baltimore, the first Roman Catholic bishop in the US.

Londonderry. Lemuel Cox, an engineer, begins the construction of a bridge over the river Foyle.

London. Hannah More, the "bluestocking" and social reformer, opens her first Sunday school (→1799).

Selborne, Hampshire. Gilbert White, a clergyman, publishes the *Natural History of Selborne*, a series of observations of natural history recorded in his family home.

Manchester. The first steam-driven cotton factory opens.→

Glasgow. John Austin invents the steam-engined power loom, a variation on Edmund Cartwright's invention (→1790).

Oxfordshire. John Elwes dies at Marcham; he built large parts of the Marylebone area of London, including Portland Place and Portman Square.

Pitt backs controversial Regency Bill

The king's son: a chance to rule?

Westminster, February
Rarely has there been such political manoeuvring here as there has been since last November, when King George III showed the first signs of madness. All were preoccupied by one question: who would be regent if the insanity became permanent?

The prince of Wales was one clear constitutional choice, and he was heavily backed by his friend Charles Fox, who argued for a 12-month regency. William Pitt, the prime minister, seeing his power base threatened, brought in a bill under which the queen and prince would share the regency. The prince now has to explain his conduct to the king, who has regained his sanity (→10/3).

William Pitt: diminished power?

Country rejoices over king's recovery from his mysterious illness

London, 23 April
This great city was ablaze with light tonight as its citizens rejoiced at the news that George III has recovered his sanity. Candles glowed in every window in a brilliant display of national loyalty. Banners proclaimed "God save the king", and great crowds lined the streets to cheer the king as he rode to a thanksgiving service at St Paul's Cathedral.

No one has greater cause to rejoice at his recovery than George himself. His supposed madness showed itself first in November. His voice became hoarse and his speech voluble; he sweated freely, and his violent behaviour terrified the queen [*see report on page 759*].

One story – told by a dismissed royal page who plans to publish a pamphlet of royal gossip – alleged that he was seen talking to an oak tree in Windsor Great Park. But it was not until the king began to have hallucinations, giving orders to imaginary servants, that he was put under the medical care of Francis Willis, whom many doctors regarded as a quack.

Willis used harsh treatment. The king was hectored, mocked, placed in a straitjacket, gagged and even beaten by Willis's assistants. Other doctors saw the illness as a medical disorder and tried blistering his legs with mustard plasters. Small wonder that the king's recovery is seen as "miraculous" (→9/1789).

St Paul's Cathedral is the setting for a service of thanksgiving for the king.

Musicians accompany George III as he is assisted in taking a royal dip.

Bloody Paris revolution stuns Britain

Bentham advocates huge law reforms

London
Moves by a young radical lawyer and philosopher for sweeping change in the approach to law are attracting the attention of Britain's more liberal elements. In *Principles of Morals and Legislation*, Jeremy Bentham argues the case for what he calls Utilitarianism, a doctrine that holds that the best action is the one that will result in the greatest happiness and the least pain for the greatest number of people.

Bentham, whose background is middle class, studied at Oxford and Lincoln's Inn before he was 15. He has been active in the causes of both prison reform and the revolution in France (→1802).

Herschel telescope brings stars closer

England, August
William Herschel, the astronomer royal, is celebrating the completion of a magnificent 48-inch mirror telescope at his observatory, financed by the king. George III is delighted with Herschel's work. In 1781 he discovered a new planet, which he named Georgium Sidum for the king and which European scientists are calling Uranus. Two years ago he found two satellites circling this planet and named them Oberon and Titania.

Turmoil in France sparks keen debate

Rye, East Sussex, July
It was not until the first French refugee émigrés sailed into this harbour in open boats that the real horror of the revolution in France [*see report below right*] struck home in Britain. But since the first news filtered across the Channel, events in Paris have been eagerly followed by the British.

In London, intellectuals and politicians are arguing fiercely about the revolution and its implications. Some, like William Blake – who is sporting a red cap of liberty in his walks about the city – and Charles James Fox have welcomed the revolution. Fox believes that it is "the greatest event that ever happened in the world". Edmund Burke, however, is less enthusiastic and argues in favour of restraint. William Pitt, the prime minister, is remaining quiet on the subject. But he is not blind to the effect which these events are likely to have on France's ability to wage war in Europe.

In Scotland the revolution has been widely welcomed by many people including the poet Robert Burns. Reaction in Ireland, which has religious and family connections with France, as well as intellectual and commercial links, is even more enthusiastic (→14).

Irate citizens storm the Bastille in Paris, previously believed impregnable.

Rebellious crowd storms Bastille prison

Paris, 14 July
The grim Bastille prison, the very symbol of tyranny in the centre of Paris, fell to an angry mob today after a short and bloody siege. The crowd had held back for hours as its leaders negotiated with the Bastille's governor, the marquis de Launay. The storming began when he refused to surrender or to hand over the 250 barrels of gunpowder stored in the vaults.

Many believed that the building, with cannons in each of its eight towers and manned by more than a hundred soldiers, was impregnable, but a group of youths succeeded in climbing onto a roof and dropping the drawbridge. Shots were fired as the mob raced into the courtyard. Fighting went on throughout the afternoon until five cannons, dragged through the streets, were deployed by the insurgents. De Launay was forced to surrender and face the wrath of the besiegers, many of them woodworkers who fought with the tools of their trade. The governor was executed, and his head was paraded through the city on a pole with those of other "enemies of the people" (→8/1789).

Official investigation begins into mutiny aboard HMS 'Bounty'

Portsmouth, 14 August
The admiralty has ordered a Royal Navy frigate to sail "with all dispatch" to the South Seas to arrest the crew of HMS *Bounty*, which mutinied on 28 April and cast the captain, William Bligh, and 18 loyal seamen adrift. The crew, demoralized during a long mission to carry bread-fruit plants from Tahiti to the West Indies, rose against Bligh's strict discipline.

On 14 June Bligh reached Timor, having endured great hardship on an epic 3,618-mile voyage with no chart and few provisions. The whereabouts of his rebellious crew, including First Lieutenant Fletcher Christian, are unknown (→12/8/92).

The mutineers watch as William Bligh and some of his crew are set adrift.

New revolutionary society is formed

London, November
Inspired by events in France, "revolutionary" societies are mushrooming in Britain, their leaders welcoming the new French constitution. The most influential of them, the Revolutionary Society – founded last year to celebrate the 1688 revolution in England – has sent congratulations to the French; and Charles Grey, a young Whig aristocrat, has founded a Society of the Friends of the People. The elderly dissident and preacher Richard Price has welcomed the revolution, thanking God that the French were "starting from sleep" (→21/6/91).

1790

Dublin, 5 January. John Fane, earl of Westmoreland, is sworn in as lord lieutenant of Ireland.

London, 21 January. King George III's coach is attacked by a man while en route to the opening of parliament (→ 18/9).

Belfast, 28 February. The Northern Whig Club is inaugurated.

Dublin, 15 March. The Society for the Relief of Sick and Indigent Room-Keepers of All Religious Persuasions is founded.

India, 21 March. Lord Cornwallis, the governor-general, invades Mysore and seizes its capital, Bangalore (→ 3/1792).

Canada, 19 May. Canadian Indians surrender land south of Lake St Clare and La Tranche, down to the north-western shore of Lake Erie, to King George III (→ 19/6/91).

Ireland, 5 July. The first mail-coaches come into operation.

Edinburgh, 17 July. The great philosopher and economist Adam Smith dies, aged 67. His work *An Inquiry into the Nature and Causes of the Wealth of Nations* (1776) is generally acclaimed as the greatest study of political economics of the age.

London, 18 September. Henry Frederick, the duke of Cumberland and a younger brother of King George III, dies, aged 44; he leaves behind huge debts (→ 29/10/95).

Britain/Spain, 28 October. Britain and Spain sign the Nootka Sound Convention, in which they agree over their claims on the north-west coast of North America.

Faversham, Kent. The first steam engines are being used at Shepherd's Brewery.

London. Pentonville prison is completed.

London. James Bruce, the Scottish explorer, publishes *Travels to Discover the Sources of the Nile, 1768-1773*; his account is greeted sceptically and he is accused of fabricating many of the stories.

London. Thomas Saint, a cabinet maker, invents a boot-sewing machine.

Britain. Edmund Cartwright, the Leicestershire clergyman who invented a steam-powered loom, has designed a wool-combing machine (→ 1792).

Wedgwood produces his finest vase yet

Both practical and decorative works are made at Wedgwood's Etruria factory.

Stoke-on-Trent
Josiah Wedgwood, the potter who dominates the world's china trade with his remarkable skill and energy, has just completed his finest technical achievement – a copy in jasperware of the Portland Vase, which was originally made 1,800 years ago in Alexandria.

The delicate process, perfected after years of experimentation in Wedgwood's Etruria factory at Hanley, in Staffordshire, requires opaque quartz to be fired until it is glass-like and slightly transparent. Fifty copies of the vase will be made for sale at 30 guineas each.

Although this Portland vase is clearly aimed at the top of the market, Wedgwood, a humanitarian, has built his markets at home and abroad by catering for all classes. His products range from what he terms the "useful" to the "ornamental". He made exquisite table china for the royal family and the czarina of Russia, but has also produced earthenware plates and vessels that have ousted unhygienic pewter from most ordinary households. He has built houses for his workers and has promoted canals to cut transport costs (→ 3/1/95).

Wedgwood's Portland vase.

Soldier's slavery tales fuel abolition drive

London
A first-hand account of slavery published this year seems likely to fuel the campaign for its abolition within Britain's empire. It appears in a journal written by a Scottish-Dutch soldier, John Stedman, who spent five years as a mercenary fighting against rebel slaves in Dutch Guyana [Surinam].

Stedman is not against slavery as such, although he is critical of what he calls the excesses of whites who abuse the system. He describes how "overgrown widows, stale beauties and over-aged maids" sometimes torture young slave women to death for reasons of sexual jealousy. The physical punishment of slaves for minor misdemeanours is also catalogued in the book.

He pays tribute to the skill and courage of blacks as jungle fighters, commenting sardonically that it is only the "slaves in red coats" – the soldiers – who ensure that white rule survives in colonies which have black majorities. Stedman's detailed journal is certain to be used by anti-slavery campaigners (→ 6/1804).

Irish Catholics want penal law reforms

Ireland, 19 January
The Catholic Committee, which has been formed by a group of politically radical Dublin businessmen, has decided to press for the removal of the remaining penal laws against Roman Catholics. Encouraged by the emphasis on religious equality in the United States, the removal of religious privilege in France and the successful efforts of English Catholics in achieving their rights, the committee intends to seek a number of concessions.

It wants Catholics to be admitted to both branches of the legal profession, to be allowed to sit on juries, and to be given the vote in Irish general elections (→ 14/10/91).

Scientific answers are found in the air

London
Scientists have isolated an important element, "oxygen". Credit for the discovery must be shared between Joseph Priestley of Britain, Carl Scheele of Sweden and Antoine Lavoisier of France. Priestley discovered the element in 1774 but did not see its significance. Scheele subsequently confirmed the discovery, and Lavoisier has now proved the crucial role of oxygen in respiration, combustion and combining with metals (→ 6/2/1804).

A cartoonist's view of Priestley.

New canal links Irish and North Seas

'Canal mania' set to gain momentum

Scotland
Scotland's first canal, the Forth/Clyde waterway linking the North Sea with the Irish Sea, has finally opened to navigation 21 years after the massive development started. It is emblematic of a "canal mania" which seems certain to gather still greater momentum.

The Forth/Clyde project has been completed in the face of formidable challenges. Laws allowing a canal to be built between Edinburgh and Glasgow were passed as long ago as 1768, but progress was slow because of enormously high costs. Part of the route, linking Grangemouth, close to the mouth of the river Carron in the east, and Stockingfield, just north of the river Kelvin near Glasgow, was working by 1777 and quickly proved itself to be a sound investment. Among the engineers consulted about the programme were John Smeaton, James Watt and James Brindley.

Now that the canal is fully operational, long and hazardous sea trips around Scotland will be replaced by safe and relatively speedy transit across country for goods and materials – coal, slate, stone, brick, timber and iron products. Work is also underway to link the Forth/Clyde canal with the unfinished Monklands canal, a 12-mile waterway which will bring the important Lanarkshire coalfields within easy reach of Glasgow.

Almost 4,000 miles of inland waterways have been completed in Britain during the last 30 years. Canals date back to Roman times, but the current boom was inspired by the waterways developed by the duke of Bridgewater in the Manchester area. This year alone the Mersey, Thames and Trent have been linked to manufacturing areas so that goods can be moved more cheaply, though more slowly, than by road. Trade has boomed – up 20 per cent a year since 1786 on the canal from Wigan to Liverpool, for instance. There is every sign of expansion in the future, with canals to link London and the midlands and even to cross the Pennines (→1801).

Built over two decades, the Forth/Clyde canal links east and west Scotland.

Burke publishes his reactions to the French Revolution

London, 1 November
Edmund Burke, the Irish-born political philosopher who defended the cause of the rebellion of the American colonists in 1775, has no such sympathy with the revolution in Paris. His *Reflections on the Revolution in France*, just published, is written not only to condemn the theories of the French but also to uphold the English revolution of 1688 and to warn Britons against emulating the French.

His book was provoked by a sermon in praise of the happenings in Paris by a nonconformist typical of the rationalist supporters of the revolution. Burke declares that the "Glorious Revolution" in England did not overturn the social order but restored a just balance in the country's historic constitution. This has grown and been adapted over the centuries to fit the nature of English society. Under it Englishmen hold their liberties as an "entailed inheritance".

The French national assembly, by contrast, has torn up the constitution in favour of a doctrine of "natural rights", which Burke claims is morally false: "The real rights of man apply only in a civil society ruled by law from which man obtains his right to justice, property, inheritance and to the fruits of his industry." He claims that democratic anarchy in France will give way to military dictatorship (→9/7/97).

A satirist's view of Burke.

Poet Blake dissects troubled human soul

London
William Blake, who illustrates his poems, such as *Songs of Innocence*, is now at work on a revolutionary prose work entitled *The Marriage of Heaven and Hell* in which he sets forth beliefs that contradict Christian doctrines. He aims to abolish the dichotomy between soul and body, an error inscribed in "all Bibles or sacred codes", with evil identified as proceeding from the body. "Man has no body distinct from his soul ... Energy is the only life and is from the body. Energy is eternal delight." The new book also contains a startling set of "Proverbs of Hell": "The road of excess leads to the palace of wisdom ... The tigers of wrath are wiser than the horses of instruction ... Damn braces. Bless relaxes" (→12/8/1827).

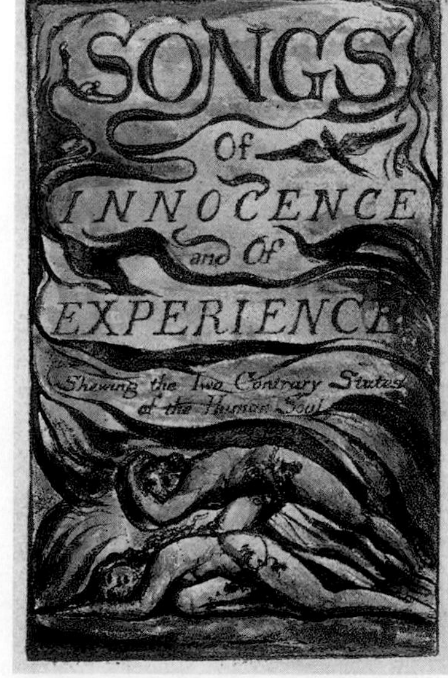

Blake examines states of mind.

Bid by Spanish to take outpost fails

North-west America
Spain has failed in an attempt to seize British-held Nootka Sound [off Vancouver Island] which it made to assert its claim to the north-western coast of America. Britain contests Spain's claim to all territory on the Pacific coast as far north as 60 degrees latitude.

Three ships sailed into the settlement unopposed, and the Spaniards immediately set about building warehouses so that their ships could be unloaded. The occupation was shortlived. Spain appealed to the French revolutionary government, which promised support, but in the face of overwhelming British strength the invaders were forced to withdraw (→28/10).

1791

London, 7 January. Captain George Vancouver on HMS *Discovery* sets sail from Deptford for Canada's Pacific coast to search for a north-west passage (→ 1798).

Co Louth, 28 January. The "Defenders", a Catholic mob, attack Alexander Barclay, a Protestant schoolmaster, and his family at Dundalk (→ 1810).

London, 2 March. John Wesley, the Anglican preacher who founded the Methodist movement, dies.

Dublin, 5 March. James Gandon, the architect, lays the foundation stone of the Carlisle Bridge.

Dublin, 10 May. Dr Richard Kirwan founds the Dublin Library Society.

Varennes, France, 21 June. Louis XVI and his family are captured by the revolutionaries while attempting to escape in disguise (→ 14/7).

Ireland, 14 July. In Dublin and Belfast demonstrations commemorate the fall of the Bastille in Paris (→ 15).

France, 21 July. The national assembly disbands the Irish Brigade based in Paris.

Nova Scotia, September. Some 1,300 Scottish emigrants arrive in Pictou on board a small fleet of four ships; most of them are extremely poor.

Dublin, 9 November. The first meeting of the Dublin Society of United Irishmen takes place (→ 4/1/92).

London, 19 November. Prince Frederick, the duke of York, returns to Britain with his new wife, Princess Frederica of Prussia (→ 1795).

New South Wales, 26 November. The first Irish convicts arrive to begin a new life (→ 1792).

Newmarket, Suffolk, November. Rumours are rife that the prince of Wales is implicated in the fixing of horse-races (→ 31/5/92).

London. The *Observer* becomes Britain's second Sunday newspaper.

Dartford, Kent. The powder mill is destroyed in a massive explosion.

Nuneaton, Warwickshire. John Barber patents his invention of a gas turbine.

Scotland. John Sinclair publishes the first part of his *Statistical Account of Scotland.*

New act gives equal rights to Canadians

Quebec City, 19 June

French and English settlers are to have equal rights, according to the new Constitution Act signed by King George III today in London. Canada, previously governed by French laws, is to be split in two. Upper Canada, on the Great Lakes and facing west, will be English-speaking and under English laws. Lower Canada, facing the Atlantic, will remain French in laws and language. Each province will have its elected assembly, the electorate limited by a small property qualification. Roman Catholics are to have full civil rights (→ 9/1791).

Composer Haydn is honoured at Oxford

Popular music: Joseph Haydn.

Oxford, July

Joseph Haydn, the great Austrian composer whose current visit to London is such a success, has been made a doctor of music by the university. "I felt very silly in my gown," he said of the ceremony, but he is very flattered by the accolade. At a concert afterwards he conducted a recent symphony, which was instantly dubbed the "Oxford".

Meanwhile, for his London concerts in the Hanover Square rooms, he is writing a series of new symphonies. "Dr Haydn" thinks the noise of London "intolerable" compared with Vienna, but its musical life is better organized, with broader, paying audiences (→ 18/2/92).

Thomas Paine publishes 'Rights of Man'

London, March

The most outspoken reply in print to Edmund Burke's attack on the revolution in France is Thomas Paine's *The Rights of Man.* Paine comes from Thetford, in Norfolk, but made his name in North America as a journalist; his pamphlet *Common Sense* helped to inspire the Declaration of Independence in 1776, and he returned to England in 1787 after helping to found the republic. He is "astonished and disappointed" at Burke's attack, after his support of the American revolutionaries, "as if he were afraid that England and France would cease to be enemies". Paine dedicates his book to President Washington.

Tom Paine: man of principle.

Paine's tract is in huge demand. In it he sets out his belief that all men have equal rights in nature and therefore the right to equal representation. It follows that hereditary government and privilege are illegitimate. Man's rights are to liberty, property, security and resistance of oppression. The French Declaration of the Rights of Man was based on these principles, as first stated in the US. Paine scorns Burke's defence of the French court and of Marie Antoinette, of whose plight he said: "The age of chivalry is gone." Burke "pitied the plumage but forgot the dying bird", writes Paine, who had great difficulty in getting his text published. The printer withdrew for fear of prosecution by the government (→ 19/9/92).

Irish Protestants unite to help Catholics

Ireland, 14 October

A group of Belfast liberals has founded an organization called the Belfast Society of United Irishmen. It has been joined by a young Protestant barrister from Dublin, Theobald Wolfe Tone, and a Dublin branch of the society is expected to follow shortly.

Tone recently attracted attention with his pamphlet *An Argument on Behalf of the Catholics of Ireland*, in which he argued that the only way to counteract British influence on Irish affairs was by parliamentary reform. He suggested that this could be achieved by Irish Catholics and Protestant radicals co-operating on a joint programme of Catholic emancipation and parliamentary reform. His views greatly impressed the Belfast liberals, who invited him to join their new association (→ 9/11).

November 7: The architect James Gandon's imposing Custom House, which opened today, gives a new grandeur to Dublin's waterfront.

Anti-French mob runs riot in Birmingham

Mob rule: the streets of Birmingham are in the hands of a rioting crowd.

Birmingham, 15 July
Britain's largest industrial centre is in a state of anarchy following two nights and a day of rioting by "church and king" mobs. Drunken looters roam the streets, radicals and dissenters hide in fear of their lives, and the magistrates have temporarily abandoned responsibility.

The rioting started when a mob led by 30 ringleaders, apparently directed by the authorities, broke up a banquet to celebrate the anniversary of the revolution in France. Among those attending was Joseph Priestley, the well-known scientist and dissenter. Whig radicals and religious dissenters have been more sympathetic to the French revolutionaries than any other groups – a fact not lost on the rioters, who burnt down one Baptist and two Unitarian meeting-houses and also sacked the house of Dr Priestley, destroying his library and laboratory. After that they opened the town prison.

The rioters' own political allegiances are somewhat confusing. Some shout "church and king", others "no popery"; most seem only concerned with redistributing the wealth of their victims – in a most revolutionary fashion.

Cabinet maker publishes trade secrets

London
The style of furniture which is popular with the wealthy is now called "Sheraton" after Thomas Sheraton, who has published *The Cabinet Maker's Drawing Book*, a catalogue of neo-classical designs. Sheraton's touch is light and refined, with feminine curves, thin, tapered legs and neat and restrained ornamentation. It contrasts with the more robust lines of Thomas Chippendale, who in 1754 published a *Gentleman and Cabinet Maker's Directory* which had great influence on his fellow craftsmen.

Chippendale's work is being carried on by his son, whilst Sheraton has taken over leadership in the trade centred in St Martin's Lane.

The Sheraton style defined.

'Life of Samuel Johnson' is completed by James Boswell after almost 30 years' work

London
The long-awaited *Life of Samuel Johnson* by his Scottish companion James Boswell has been published, and such is its popularity that its author is already preparing a new edition. Boswell, the son of a Scottish judge, met the great doctor in 1763, when he was 22 and Johnson 54. He then made it his chief task to observe and record the conversation of "vigour and vivacity" to which Johnson devoted his energies.

The biography abounds in pithy sayings: "The full tide of human existence is at Charing Cross ... When a man is tired of London, he is tired of life ... A man should keep his friendship in constant repair ... He who does not mind his belly will hardly mind anything else ... There is nothing contrived by man by which so much happiness is produced as by a good tavern or inn ... The noblest prospect a Scotchman ever sees is the high road that leads him to England." Despite his jibes at Scotland, Dr Johnson was taken on a tour to the Hebrides by Boswell, who wrote an entertaining account of it which gave a foretaste of the *Life*, a unique complete portrait, warts and all (→ 19/5/95).

Johnson's biographer, Boswell.

Long-time companions: Samuel Johnson and his biographer James Boswell.

Anglo-Russian relations strained by war

Westminster, April
William Pitt's government has very nearly fallen as a result of his attempt to take Britain into a war against Russia. In the current war between Russia and the Ottoman Empire, the Russians have captured territory around the Black Sea and annexed the Turkish fortress of Ochakov. Pitt, fearing Russian ambitions to gain access to the Mediterranean, wants to force the Russians to give back the fortress, which Czarina Catherine II resolutely refuses to do. The party of Charles James Fox and Edmund Burke, with popular backing, opposed war. Now Pitt has backed down, and his foreign secretary, the duke of Leeds, has had to resign.

1792

Belfast, 4 January. The first issue of the *Northern Star*, the paper of the United Irishmen, is printed (→ 25/7).

Dublin, 14 February. John Field, a pianist-composer, makes his first public performance at the Rotunda.

London, 18 February. Joseph Haydn opens his second London season with a new symphony (→ 4/5/95).

India, March. General Cornwallis, the governor-general, who has been besieging Seringapatam for the last month, makes peace with Tipu Sahib, the Indian leader (→ 10/1793).

London, 18 April. Parliament rejects a motion for burgh reform in Scotland forwarded by Richard Sheridan, the politician and former playwright, and refuses even to consider the need for it (→ 11/12/92).

Europe, 20 April. France declares war on Austria.

Westminster, 31 May. The prince of Wales makes his maiden speech in the House of Lords nine years after taking his seat, supporting the government proclamation suppressing seditious publications (→ 8/4/95).

Westminster, 15 June. William Pitt, the prime minister, has consolidated his position and power by forcing George III to ask for the resignation of one of his oldest and closest ministers, Lord Thurlow, the lord chancellor (→ 11/1797).

Belfast, 7 July. The *Hibernia* is the first vessel to be launched from William Ritchie's shipyard.

Portsmouth, 12 August. Ten of the mutineers from HMS *Bounty* go on trial for mutiny and treason.

France, 19 September. Thomas Paine seeks refuge in France on being charged with treason in Britain for his book *The Rights of Man* (→ 12/2/93).

Dublin, 5 December. A Catholic convention presses for more reforms of the Catholic Relief Act (→ 2/1/93).

Westminster, 13 December. Parliament votes to support William Pitt, the prime minister, with preparations for war with France (→ 21/1/93).

Edinburgh. The Edinburgh Goldsmiths' Hall Association is formed to counter the activities of the reforming movements.

Feminist writer calls for equality of sexes

London

In *A Vindication of the Rights of Woman*, the feminist author and radical Mary Wollstonecraft has taken up the gauntlet from Tom Paine's *The Rights of Man*. Now women must be treated as men's equals, she argues.

In France recently, she proposed that the revolutionary government should introduce free education for both sexes. She argues the need for the law to help secure women's rights. Otherwise, women will continue to be in low paid, unskilled work, suitable only to be wives and mothers, she argues. The daughter of an Irish drunkard and wifebeater, Miss Wollstonecraft herself has been forced to make a living as a companion, seamstress and teacher.

Women's champion: Wollstonecraft.

Artisans combine to discuss equal rights

London, January

In public houses and taverns around Britain groups of working men, artisans and small traders are eagerly meeting to discuss politics, reform and new pamphlets. The latest group, formed this month and already growing, is the London Corresponding Society. This is the brainchild of a shoemaker, Thomas Hardy, and originally boasted just eight members, meeting at a pub in Covent Garden; now its membership is linked with societies in other British cities and could well run into thousands. Its appeal lies in being based on Thomas Paine's *The Rights of Man*; also it charges just one penny a week and is open to any working man.

Irish music festival of mediaeval harps

Belfast, 14 July

The first Belfast Harp Festival ended today and has been hailed as a success. The organisers' main aim was to record the music, poetry and oral traditions of Ireland from the old harpers who have been holding their own festivals for the past four years at Granard, in Co Longford. The 18-year-old organist Edward Bunting was engaged to take down the music from the ten harpers, most of whom are over 70, and six of whom are blind. The star of the festival was the oldest living harper, Denis Hempson, who is 96.

The growing sense of national consciousness has renewed interest in the now declining Irish rural musical tradition. The most famous harper/composer of recent times was Turlough Carolan, who died in 1738. His patroness, Mary MacDermott Roe, recognized his musical talent, and after he went blind from smallpox she paid for him to be trained by a harper. When he was 21 she gave him a horse, a guide and some money and sent him off on a successful career as an itinerant harper. He played in Dublin's most fashionable drawing rooms and was friendly with Swift.

Joshua Reynolds, artist and founder of the Royal Academy, dies

The duchess of Devonshire and her daughter as Reynolds wished to see them.

London, 23 February

The Royal Academy is mourning its first president, Sir Joshua Reynolds, who died today aged 68. He is to be buried in St Paul's, a fitting place for one who greatly raised the standing of his profession.

Reynolds and Dr Johnson founded the Literary Club in 1763. Other friends included Boswell and Goldsmith, who wrote wryly of him:

A flattering painter who made it his care,
To draw men as they ought to be, not as they are.

He took a lot of snuff, which often made his sitters sneeze and lose their pose. Reynolds was in great demand and used to charge 200 guineas a portrait; late in life he asked as much as 3,000 guineas for a triple portrait. He became partly deaf through copying Raphael's work in the Vatican in a draught, and his sight failed three years ago.

Wolfe Tone joins the Catholic Committee

Ireland, 25 July

Theobald Wolfe Tone has joined the Catholic Committee as assistant secretary. The committee, led by some energetic Dublin businessmen, has achieved some success as a pressure group in petitioning the Irish parliament for a further relaxation of the penal laws, but its claim to represent the Catholics of Ireland has been challenged during parliamentary debates.

By engaging the Protestant Tone the committee is demonstrating tolerance, and plans are being laid for a major convention in December for Catholic delegates from the whole of Ireland (→5/12).

Theobald Wolfe Tone.

Scots radicalism grows

Fear of mob rule is expressed in this lurid cartoon of revolutionaries at work.

Edinburgh, 11 December

Thomas Paine's *The Rights of Man* has set off an explosion of popular revolt. Scotland leads the way in the reform movement, attempting to keep up pressure on the government. A general convention of the Friends of the People Society, which was formed in July to unite reform societies throughout Scotland, met today in Edinburgh. Some 160 delegates attended from all over Scotland, mostly middle-class professionals – lawyers, merchants and some landowners – annoyed at London's refusal even to discuss reform of the burghs.

Agitation has been smouldering here for the past six years, since many wealthy businessmen were disenfranchised by the present system of electing members of parliament to the House of Commons.

This year has seen mob riots in both Glasgow and Edinburgh; in Perth, crowds burned an effigy of Henry Dundas, the home secretary, and in Dundee troops were brought in to disperse riots of two weeks' length. Societies for reform have been springing up around Britain. But the reform movement is unnerved by popular revolt and the example from France. Already a number of its supporters have withdrawn support from the Friends of the People Society for fear of being associated with mob rule (→2/1/93).

Worried handloom weavers burn factory

Manchester, March

The latest reaction to the increased mechanization of the weaving industry has come from angry groups of weavers who have attacked and burnt down Grimshaw's factory here. Following the introduction of Samuel Crompton's spinning mule, Edmund Cartwright's invention of a horse-driven power loom for weaving – and then a loom powered by steam engine – enraged the handloom weavers. Worried for their jobs, they destroyed the mechanized factory in which Cartwright had invested with Grimshaw.

Such revolts just might prove a powerful threat to the weaving industry, where workers tend to be skilled men able to organize.

Phillip, founder of Sydney, is home

London

Four years after establishing the first penal colony in Australia, Captain Arthur Phillip has returned home. He landed at Botany Bay but built a settlement in a nearby cove, which he named after Viscount Sydney, the home secretary [*see page 758*]. Since then he has explored the interior and discovered the Hawkesbury river. He cites food and supply shortages and conflicts between settlers and aborigines as major problems (→5/3/1804).

Scotland's finest architect, Robert Adam, died this year, shortly after Culzean Castle, in Strathclyde (left), was completed for the earl of Cassilis; at the remarkable Osterley Park, London (right, 1763-80), he modernized the existing red-brick house by adding a superb decorated double portico.

1793

Westminster, 2 January. Irish Catholic delegates present their petition for reform of the Catholic Relief Act to King George III (→11).

Edinburgh, 2 January. Thomas Muir of Huntershill, the leader of the radical wing of the reform movement in Scotland, is arrested (→9/1793).

Dublin, 11 January. The Dublin Society of United Irishmen prepares a plan for parliamentary reform (→4/1793).

France, 21 January. Britain and Europe are shocked by today's execution of King Louis XVI of France (→1/2).

France/Britain, January. Anglo-French relations deteriorate following the execution of Louis XVI.

France, 1 February. Revolutionary France declares war on Britain and the Netherlands.→

Birmingham, 12 February. An effigy of Thomas Paine, the author of *The Rights of Man*, is burnt in the streets (→1795).

Britain, 22 February. *The Times* newspaper lays the blame for the recent Irish disturbances on the revolution in France.

Ireland, 9 April. The Militia Act is passed; independent volunteers are replaced by government militia.

Ireland, April. Violence worsens as Catholic "Defenders" continue attacks on the British; over 60 "Defenders" have been executed in the last two months (→9).

India, 14 June. A British squadron blockades French-controlled Pondicherry (→23/8).

Westminster, July. William, the duke of Clarence, makes an embarrassing speech in the House of Lords in favour of making peace with France.

Carlow City, 1 October. St Patrick's College, the first Catholic college for higher education, opens.

Birmingham, 24 October. The city erupts in rioting after attempts to collect rates to pay for the riots of 1791.

Edinburgh, November. A British reform convention meets in Edinburgh.

London. Henry Dundas, the Scottish lord advocate, is appointed to the new post of president of the board of control for India (→1794).

Revolutionary France declares war

Paris, 1 February
Having executed their king, Louis XVI, in an act of defiance against all monarchical regimes, the leaders of France have declared war on Britain and appealed to British republicans to help them. This move has jolted the Pitt government, which has only recently begun to grasp that what is going on in France can only result in a basic clash of national interests and create problems of both war and internal security.

The French are spoiling for a fight and have ordered total mobilization. They plan to raise an army of 700,000 men (→5/1793).

The prime minister, William Pitt, addresses a crowded House of Commons.

New war with France sparks bitter political battles at Westminster

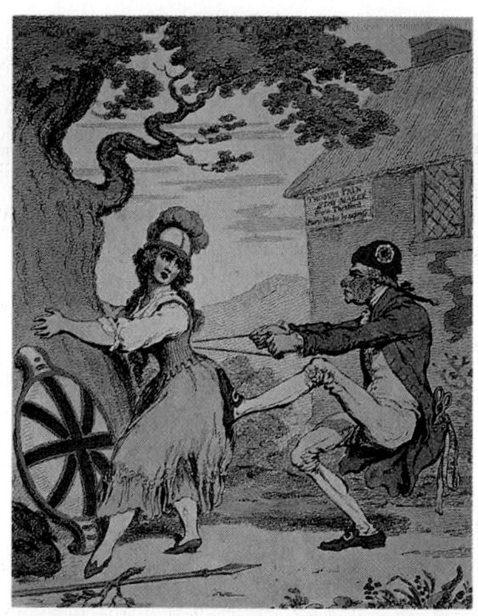

Some think that French "reforms" would restrict Britain's constitution.

London, February
Once again Britain is at war with France. The government must now come to terms not only with the revolution there but also with the threat to the balance of power in general and British interests in the Low Countries in particular. Britain's leader and war minister William Pitt is determined to win what he says will be a "short war" of one or two campaigns.

But the onset of war looks set to have a major impact on British politics. A call by Pitt for unity to fight the war and tackle problems of internal security has led to a split within the ranks of the Whig opposition. The independently minded and effective leader of the Whigs, Charles James Fox, persists in his claim that George III poses a greater threat to the British constitution than do the French. Pitt's proclamation establishing the militia as a precaution against insurrection has already enraged Fox, who has said he will oppose anything and everything Pitt puts before parliament.

This attitude has led to defections to the Tories, whilst other leading Whigs say that they will act as a body in support of war policy. Among these is Edmund Burke, who is opposed to the revolution in France because, he argues, it has destroyed historically established institutions in the country.

British seize initiative in the West Indies

West Indies, May
British forces here have captured a number of the French-controlled islands in a triumphant campaign. General Grey's small army of 7,000 men has extended its hold over Martinique – first captured in March – as well as St Lucia and Guadeloupe. Tobago was captured on 14 April. There is no doubt that France is being humbled in the West Indies in accordance with William Pitt's policy.

The battle fleet under Admiral Jervis was instrumental in the initial capture of Martinique two months ago, and Britain's naval build-up over the last eight years has played a major part in all these successes. The Royal Navy has been much strengthened since setbacks connected with the American war, with over 30 ships of the line being built since 1779. Reforms of the management of dockyards have ensured that there are sufficient supplies to fit out vessels quickly prior to active service.

At the same time, the French fleet has been weakened by discipline problems in the wake of the revolution. The success in the West Indies is all the more satisfying because, owing to Britain's commitments in Europe, only a weak force could be sent to the area (→23/8).

British take French settlement in India

India, 23 August
The important French base of Pondicherry in south-eastern India has fallen to British troops today after a siege that lasted nearly two months. The surrender follows the failure of French troops to reinforce the town. The British marched in to a great cheer and shouts of "Long live Louis XVI!". It turned out that the residents have only just learnt of the execution of their king and were distressed by it. Under the act of surrender the colony will be in British hands until order is restored in France (→17/5/94).

Jubilant Irish Catholics win right to vote

Dublin, 9 April
In what is being seen as a breakthrough for Catholic emancipation, the Catholic Relief Act, its terms virtually dictated by England, has been passed by parliament here. Under the terms of the act, most of the discriminations endured by Catholics have been removed and they now have the same rights as Protestants to vote in Irish parliamentary and municipal elections.

Catholics can carry arms, act as grand jurors, take degrees at Trinity College, Dublin, and become members of corporations. But they are still excluded from parliament, the judiciary and the higher offices of state. A paid home-defence force – the militia – is to be formed under government control, and the Convention Act is to be passed forbidding assemblies that claim to represent a large section of Irish opinion.

Although Roman Catholics are profuse in their gratitude for their improved position, the act will not add much to their political power. But the British government, now at war with France, is anxious to conciliate Irish opinion and to subdue rural unrest. The introduction of the Catholic Relief Act seems to have achieved this. By a mixture of concession and repression, the authorities are hoping to weather this time of crisis (→ 15/2/94).

Riots break out over Irish conscription

Ireland, June
The new Militia Act – aimed at enlisting 16,000 men for home defence – has met with universal resistance, and anti-militia riots are raging in almost every county. The regular troops cannot restore order, and even the priests and gentry who have tried to intervene have been attacked by angry crowds.

Since the declaration of war between Britain and France many regular soldiers have already gone away to fight. The riots are seen as a response to a measure that threatens to remove many more families' breadwinners.

Thomas Muir goes on trial in Scotland

Muir: leader of the Scottish radicals.

Edinburgh, September
After a trial widely seen as a test case in the struggle between the Tory government and its critics, a court has sentenced Thomas Muir, a prominent radical and lawyer, to 14 years' transportation to Botany Bay in Australia. Muir was found guilty of sedition after the presentation of a weak crown case. Muir used the courtroom as a platform to make political speeches.

Muir has been a passionate advocate of parliamentary reform and has devoted his life to the cause of the Scottish working class. He has helped to organize the radical clubs that have sprung up in western Scotland and has addressed meetings of workers (→ 1796).

Man who strengthened British position in India heads home

Lord Cornwallis hosting a reception at Calcutta's Old Government House.

Calcutta, October
After a remarkable and reformist seven-year stint in British India, Charles, Lord Cornwallis, has left for home. As governor-general he has extended British control from Bengal to most of the subcontinent and provided scope for Britain's industrial expansion.

He continued reforms begun by Warren Hastings, and bribery is no longer normal practice. But he has caused some resentment by saying that "every native in India, I verily believe, is corrupt" and by a campaign of "Europeanization" of the civil service. A system of land taxation is also unpopular with the overburdened peasantry (→ 23/4/95).

Keen farmers form board of agriculture

Paying the haymaker.

Britain
The boom in British agriculture has led to the formation this year of a new body, the board of agriculture. It has been set up by supporters of the "new agriculture" such as Sir John Sinclair, a member of parliament, and Arthur Young, respectively the board's first president and secretary. They believe that there is money to be made through new methods of drainage and husbandry, as well as crop rotation and the use of fertilizers, and are organizing a wide-ranging survey of British farming. The board is supported partly by public funds and partly by private subscription.

October: Lord Macartney, the leader of a British mission, meets the Chinese emperor, Qianlong, to ask the Chinese to lift restrictions on British merchants trading with Canton. Qianlong refuses to negotiate.

1794

Britain, 16 January. Edward Gibbon, the historian and author of *The Decline and Fall of the Roman Empire*, dies.

Dublin, 15 February. The *Dublin Evening Post* publishes the United Irishmen's plans for parliamentary reform (→ 2/5).

Dublin, 1 March. Trinity College amends its statutes in accordance with last year's Catholic Relief Act to allow Catholics to sit degree examinations.

Dublin, 28 April. The Reverend William Jackson, an agent of the French revolutionary government, is charged with high treason (→ 30/4/95).

Indian Ocean, 17 May. British troops seize control of Mahé, formerly a French-controlled island (→ 1/6).

Britain, 22 May. Habeas corpus is suspended.

Dublin, 23 May. Police raid a meeting of the Dublin Society of United Irishmen (→ 24/1/95).

France, 1 June. A British fleet led by Admiral Howe defeats the French at Ushant(→ 3).

West Indies, 4 June. British troops take Port-au-Prince, the French administrative headquarters on the isle of Santo Domingo (→ 7).

Guadeloupe, 7 June. French forces led by Victor Hugues recapture the island, to regain control from the British (→ 21/8).

London, 23 June. James Graham, the quack doctor who opened the "Temple of Health" promising health and fertility to all those who believed, dies.

Corsica, 21 August. The British, commanded by Captain Horatio Nelson, bombard parts of the island forcing the French to surrender (→ 5/1796).

Edinburgh, August. Robert Watt, a former government spy, is found guilty of treason in the so-called "Pike plot", following the discovery of a store of weapons in the city, and is sentenced to death.

Westminster, 17 October. William Pitt, the prime minister, cuts all finances for Prussian troops; he blames Prussia for recent losses against the French.

London. The new Drury Lane theatre is reopened and for the first time uses a safety curtain, nicknamed "the Iron".

Irish rebel escapes and flees to France

James Gillray's vision of the United Irishmen raiding a farm for supplies.

Dublin, 2 May

Archibald Hamilton Rowan, a prominent member of the United Irishmen and an Ulster aristocrat, has escaped from Newgate prison and fled to France. At the beginning of the year Rowan was found guilty of distributing the address of the Dublin Society of United Irishmen to the Volunteers. As the address was considered to be seditious libel, he was sentenced to two years in prison.

At about the same time the authorities seized the Reverend William Jackson, a preacher and journalist. He was suspected of being a French agent and of conspiring with Theobald Wolfe Tone and Rowan. Rowan, realizing that he was dangerously compromised, made his escape. But Tone has stood his ground. He has given the government a statement that provides evidence against himself alone, and the government, thankful to be rid of such an able organizer and publicist for the United Irishmen, is allowing him to leave the country.

Rowan represents a small but important landowning element of the society, which is mainly drawn from the business and professional sectors (→ 23).

'The Mysteries of Udolpho' published

London

A new kind of fiction, the "gothic" novel, has enjoyed great vogue since the publication of Walpole's *The Castle of Otranto* in 1764. This year has seen the appearance of *The Mysteries of Udolpho* by Mrs Ann Radcliffe, for which she was handsomely paid £500 on publication. Like her three previous books, this is a tale of "a terror purely sublime that leads us to seek even the object from which we shrink". Her heroine, Emily, is plunged into a world of ruined castles with dungeons, sinister monks, forests, bandits and supernatural events (→ 2/3/97).

A horror story illustrated.

Communications improve in Ireland as bridges are completed

Ireland, May

The construction of a bridge over the river Suir at Waterford is seen as a further important advance in communications structures here. These have much improved over the last 20 years, with a shift from horseback to wheeled vehicles. The first mail-coach came into operation in 1790.

An oak bridge over the river Foyle at Derry was begun in 1789 and completed in 1791. The engineer was an American, Lemuel Cox, and he has also worked on the Waterford bridge. In Dublin the Carlisle Bridge over the Liffey, begun in 1791, is nearing completion. Until now rivers have mainly had to be crossed by ferries which were often old, leaky and dangerous.

Improved transport links: an elegant bridge spans the river Suir at Waterford.

British victory at Ushant

Shipwrecked sailors cling to their lifeboats as the sea battle rages on.

Britain, 3 June
Bonfires have been burning and church bells ringing the length and breadth of the land for the past two days, to celebrate Admiral Lord Howe's defeat of the French off Ushant. The triumph has already been dubbed "The Glorious First of June" and is being hailed as one of the greatest victories in the annals of sea warfare.

The English sailors acquitted themselves magnificently and succeeded in capturing almost one third of the French vessels engaged in the action. However, a few critics have pointed out that the main object of the exercise was not in fact achieved. The French warships were engaged in escorting a huge grain convoy, bringing essential food supplies from the US to relieve the besieged port of Brest. While the battle was raging the civilian vessels managed to limp through and land their vital cargo (→4).

'Zoonomia' discusses animal evolution

London
Dr Erasmus Darwin, whose long biologically-based poem *The Loves of the Plants* recently generated much interest and some scandal (because of its many explicit references to sex), has now published the first volume of a more serious scientific work, *Zoonomia, or The Laws of Organic Life*, which argues that all life forms "evolved" from one single source.

Darwin, who is a well-known (though often controversial) physician and radical freethinker, puts forward the argument that all progress and development in nature stems from competition and the need to adapt to changing circumstances. Different species, he suggests, acquire their distinctive characteristics first through the need to survive, and then by the selective inheritance of those qualities that have proved most resilient and effective for this purpose. The doctor's critics point out that he has, so far, advanced no convincing proof for this thesis. But they willingly recognize that Darwin's ideas are interesting (→1802).

Darwin: no proof as yet.

Dundas appointed as secretary of war

Edinburgh
This year has seen yet further advancement for the man who has come to be known, by friends and enemies alike, as "the uncrowned king of Scotland". Henry Dundas, who has steadily risen in power and influence since he became solicitor-general for Scotland in 1766, was already home secretary and president of the board of control for India in William Pitt's government, and he has now been asked to take on further heavy responsibilities as secretary for war.

Dundas, who first trained as an Edinburgh advocate (and recently piloted through the act setting up the new Edinburgh University), has built up a formidable political power base. Shrewdly deploying the patronage that was available to him in a variety of posts, he has surrounded himself with loyal Scottish supporters and nowadays virtually controls all parliamentary representation north of the border.

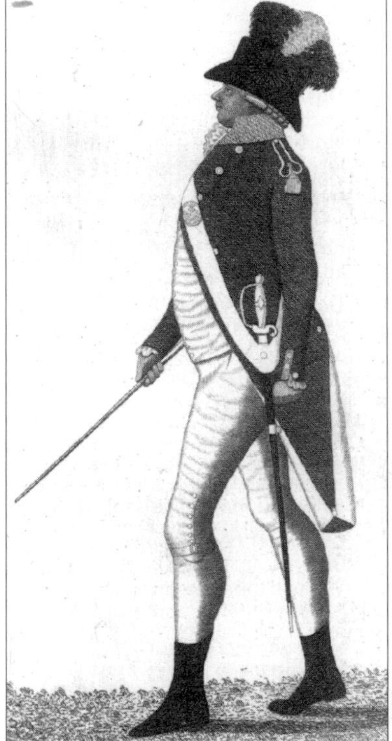

The rapidly rising Dundas.

How the armed forces line up for action

Britain
Admiral Lord Howe's recent victory over the French fleet off Ushant [*see report above left*] shows that the quality of the French navy has suffered from the Jacobins' purges. But the convoy of US grain, which triggered the battle, succeeded in getting through to Brest, so that Howe's blockade of the Atlantic coast will have to be strengthened. In the Mediterranean, however, Admiral Hood has the main French base at Toulon well blockaded, and the French fleet is unable to get out.

The army's main focus of interest remains the Low Countries, where the duke of York, with his Austrian and German allies, is maintaining his efforts to destroy the French forces. The French have recently been reinforced, and there are signs that the tide is turning in their favour. The quality of some of the duke's troops is in doubt, and lack of professionalism among some officers is a weakness.

The other theatre of war is the West Indies. British troops, helped by the Royal Navy, have captured the islands of Martinique, St Lucia and Guadeloupe, but they are now faced with a revolt by slaves. Fever continues to be the main enemy in this campaign, however.

At home the army is undergoing a massive expansion, and several new regiments are being raised. Apart from those in the highlands, where clan loyalty is uppermost, there are doubts over the quality of many of the new regiments. The army is in urgent need of reform before it can be a truly effective fighting force.

The army's raw material.

1795

Stoke-on-Trent, 3 January. Josiah Wedgwood, the master potter who built up a huge business empire, dies aged 64.

Dublin, 4 January. William, Earl Fitzwilliam of Norborough, is sworn in as lord lieutenant of Ireland (→ 24).

Belfast, 24 January. Protestants petition parliament for a repeal of all statutes against Catholics (→ 25/2).

Dublin, 31 March. Edward Noel, Earl Camden, is sworn in as lord lieutenant of Ireland, replacing the dismissed Earl Fitzwilliam.

Belfast, 10 May. The United Irishmen of Ulster meet secretly and adopt a new constitution (→ 13/6).

London, 19 May. James Boswell, the biographer of Dr Samuel Johnson and a popular figure in literary circles, dies.

Westminster, 30 May. Parliament makes a large contribution to the debts of the bankrupt prince of Wales following his marriage to Princess Caroline of Brunswick.

Belfast, 13 June. Theobald Wolfe Tone embarks for the United States (→ 2/2/96).

London, 19 June. Demonstrators protest the continuing war with France and demand annual parliaments and manhood suffrage.

Armagh City, September. Catholics and Protestants clash in the worst sectarian violence for many years; over 30 people are killed (→ 12/7/96).

Co Kildare, 1 October. The Royal College of St Patrick, a Catholic seminary, is opened at Maynooth.

Westminster, November. After the recent attack on King George III's coach, and amid growing fears of a pro-French Jacobite invasion, parliament extends the treason laws and introduces a law prohibiting mass meetings (→ 15/5/1800).

London. George III appoints Frederick, the duke of York, his second son, to the new post of commander-in-chief of the army.

Britain. The issuing of lime juice on board Royal Navy ships is made compulsory, as a means of fighting scurvy.

Ireland. Protestants form the Orange Order, a secret society to defend their interests.

Lord lieutenant of Ireland dismissed

Dublin, 25 February

Earl Fitzwilliam has been dismissed as lord lieutenant of Ireland after only 50 days in office. From the moment of his arrival he seemed to have a constitutionally unprecedented notion of the scope of his powers. He immediately dismissed many heads of departments who had been in office for over 20 years in a purge that dismayed the British government.

He then presented a plan for Catholic emancipation, which was too premature but was eagerly adopted by Henry Grattan, who promptly introduced a bill into parliament. Before it could be debated, however, the English government became seriously alarmed and recalled Fitzwilliam (→ 10/5).

Warren Hastings acquitted of all charges

Warren Hastings: innocent at last.

London, 23 April

After seven interminable years of hearings and political posturing, Warren Hastings, the former governor-general of Bengal, has been acquitted of all the corruption charges brought against him on his return from India.

Initially the prosecution was supported by the prime minister, William Pitt, and eloquently pursued by Edmund Burke. But it soon became clear that the case rested on little more than the enmity of Hastings's former colleague and rival Philip Francis. The trial at Westminster Hall initially drew packed audiences, like a theatrical first night, but soon degenerated into a long-running bore. Now it has collapsed, but not before completing the ruin of one of England's ablest overseas administrators (→ 3/2/99).

Christians outraged at 'Age of Reason'

Tom Paine: book prohibited.

London

Thomas Paine, once the idol of British sympathizers with the French revolution, has lost many friends with his new work, *The Age of Reason*, a frontal assault on all Christian beliefs other than the bald statement: "I believe in one God and no more." He rejects the Biblical accounts of the creation, the bloodthirstiness of Jehovah and the Virgin Birth ("hearsay upon hearsay") and pleads for tolerance – "there is a morning of reason rising on the world". Even dissenters are horrified. The book is banned and is being publicly burnt (→ 6/1809).

French agent commits suicide in court

Dublin, 30 April

The Reverend William Jackson, a French agent, poisoned himself in court today before sentence could be passed on him. He was arrested almost exactly a year ago and later found guilty by a Dublin court.

Jackson, Irish-born but ordained in the Church of England, was an idealist who drifted to Paris attracted by the bohemian way of life. He then came to Dublin to assess British and Irish opinion for the French government. He assured the French that any invasion would be supported by the Irish. But then, as a result of information supplied to the British government by his supposed friend John Cockayne, Jackson's letters were intercepted, and he was arrested. In the wake of this, police raided a meeting of the radical Dublin Society of United Irishmen on 23 May last year, seizing papers and frightening the society into stopping its meetings.

The "grand old" duke of York (r), the new commander-in-chief, is an able and highly trained soldier. A failed Flanders campaign in 1793, lampooned here by Gillray, unjustly damaged his professional reputation.

Prince of Wales is forced to marry

The prince's unwanted bride.

London, 8 April
The prince of Wales gave in to official pressure today and married Princess Caroline of Brunswick, his 26-year-old cousin. But he did not do it with good grace; he was so drunk that he had to be supported by his best man, and he asked his brother to tell Mrs Fitzherbert, the Catholic whom he "married" secretly and unofficially ten years ago, that "she is the only woman I shall ever love". The prince has been forced into this union by his father George III, who is desperate for an heir to ensure the succession; he only agreed to it when promised that his huge debts would be paid by parliament (→30/5).

Cape Town seized by British troops

Cape Town, 16 September
British troops landed here today and, after a brief struggle, wrested control of Cape Colony from the Boer settlers who had declared it, and several of the surrounding regions, to be "revolutionary republics". The Dutch farmers have been steadily expanding northwards, under the French slogan of "liberty, equality, fraternity", and attacking and killing any native Africans who resist their advance.

The "revolutionary stance" has little ideological content. It was only adopted when officials arrived from the Netherlands with orders to halt the land seizures.

The Union flag is raised.

Mob anger aims at king

Despite the close range the shot misses, and the king's carriage proceeds.

London, 29 October
A shot was fired at King George III's coach today as the king drove through the city to the state opening of parliament. Fortunately the attacker's aim was poor: the bullet went wide, inflicting no serious damage or casualties.

Later an angry crowd hurled stones, clods and lumps of ordure at the royal procession as it passed down Whitehall. The windows of the prime minister's house in Downing Street were broken, whilst the mob kept up a sullen chant of "No war! No famine! No Pitt! No king!". A cold, wet summer, followed by a poor harvest, has reinforced the public's general mood of hostility to the government and to its costly and so far ineffectual campaign against France.

The suspension of the Habeas Corpus Act earlier this year, the decision to detain political dissenters without trial, the trebling of the taxes on windows, carriages and servants, and new details of the prince of Wales's extravagant lifestyle have all helped to swell the countrywide chorus of disenchantment. Already, this autumn has seen bread riots in Nottingham, Coventry and Sussex (→11/1795).

Haydn takes leave of grateful public

London, 4 May
Joseph Haydn, the Austrian composer who is coming to the end of a highly successful second visit to London, took an astonishing £400 tonight from tickets to an orchestral concert at which he was conducting. "Such a thing is possible only in England" he said, and he is right: in many other countries such musical evenings are the preserve of the aristocracy, and there are few, if any, paying concerts. Haydn's first visit to England in 1791-3 [*see page 764*] was such a hit that he returned last year. This spring he has premièred three new symphonies in London to wide acclaim.

Poor Rates subsidy will save Speenhamland poor from starvation

Newbury, Berkshire
The county magistrates here, after studying the disastrous onset of rural poverty in the area, have embarked on a remarkable social experiment. They have given authority for the wages of impoverished farmworkers in the nearby parish of Speenhamland to be subsidized from the Poor Rates, so that every family has sufficient to buy a minimum ration of bread every week.

Taking the cost of a standard loaf as one shilling [5p], they calculate that every man needs 3s for himself and 1s 6d for each member of his family to survive. When weekly pay falls below these figures the difference will be made up from public funds.

Poverty-stricken farmworkers will now receive subsidies for their labours.

1796 - 1797

London, 23 January 1796. The cartoonist James Gillray is arrested on publication of his work *The Presentation* which satirizes royalty.

France, 2 February 1796. Theobald Wolfe Tone, the leader of the United Irishmen, arrives to muster French aid for an Irish uprising (→ 17/10).

Britain/France, May 1796. Britain refuses to make peace with France (→ 9/8).

Mediterranean, 9 August 1796. The British, led by Captain Horatio Nelson, seize Elba (→ 27/12).

Westminster, 17 October 1796. Parliament rejects Henry Grattan's proposal that Roman Catholics be admitted into the government (→ 12/3/98).

Margate, 1796. The Royal Sea Bathing Hospital is founded; John Coakley Lettsom claims sea air is good for pulmonary conditions such as tuberculosis.

Glasgow, 1796. The Royal Technical College is founded.

France, 1796. Thomas Muir, the Scottish radical, arrives in France after being rescued by American supporters from the British ship transporting him to Australia (→ 11/1797).

London, 20 February 1797. Horatio Nelson is knighted and promoted to rear-admiral (→ 14).

Spithead, 18 April 1797. The navy mutinies over poor pay and conditions (→ 1/5).

Spithead, 1 May 1797. The admiralty brings the mutineers under control (→ 8).

Westminster, 8 May 1797. Parliament passes the Sailors' Bill to improve conditions for sailors (→ 12).

The Nore, 12 May 1797. The British North Sea fleet anchored in the river Thames mutinies (→ 13/6).

England, 9 July 1797. Edmund Burke, the Irish-born statesman-philosopher, dies.

Canary Islands, 25 July 1797. Rear-Admiral Nelson loses his right arm raiding Santa Cruz (→ 1/8/98).

London, 26 December 1797. John Wilkes, a former mayor of London and radical member of parliament, dies.

Lothian, 1797. Troops carry out an unprovoked attack in Tranent on civilians protesting against the forced militia draft; 11 people die, including a 13-year-old boy.

Quakers open York lunatic asylum

A lunatic in chains.

York, 1796

A new kind of asylum for the mad opened this year. It is called York Retreat, and it is run by Quakers. York Retreat is unlike any other lunatic asylum. It stands in rural surroundings, and there are no cells, no chains, no cold baths and no beatings. Patients are treated with dignity and are at liberty to move about. Considering that it is only 20 years since lunatics in Bedlam provided Londoners with entertainment, the treatment of the mad has made enormous strides.

Scots mourn a great poet

Dumfries, 21 July 1796

Scotland is in mourning today for Robert Burns, who died of rheumatic fever brought on by falling asleep at the roadside while returning from a drinking session. His wife, Jean Armour, is due to have a child at any moment. Burns had taken the lease of a farm outside Dumfries and obtained an appointment as an excise officer. He gave up the farm for the excise, which required him to ride 200 miles a week and left little time for poetry. He always refused money for his poems. "I'll be damned if I ever write for money," he said. He and his wife already had three sons; there were a number of other children from his many liaisons.

Scotland's loss: Robert Burns.

Burns and his contribution to literature

Scotland, 21 July 1796

Scottish readers are realizing what a loss the tragically early death of Robert Burns at the age of 36 is to their literature. He had already been recognized as the national bard who had preserved the heritage of Scots folksong from olden times. He collaborated with James Johnson in collecting five volumes of *The Scots Musical Museum*, and later with George Thomson in *Select Scottish Airs*. Burns took down old songs and half-forgotten fragments and completed or rewrote them to old Scottish airs.

Songs owed to his patriotic labours include *Auld Lang Syne, My Bonnie Mary* and *O My Luve is Like a Red Red Rose*. Others such as *Scots Wha Hae Wi' Wallace Bled* were entirely his own, as were the many songs written to celebrate his loves, such as *The Highland Lassie* (Mary Campbell) and *Ae Fond Kiss and then We Sever*. The long poem *Tam O'Shanter* tells of the witches who accost and chase tipsy Tam.

Smallpox can be kept away by Edward Jenner's new inoculation

An unwilling Phipps is "vaccinated", a term derived from the Latin for cow.

Gloucestershire, 1 July 1796

A 47-year-old doctor at Berkeley, Edward Jenner, appears to have inoculated an eight-year-old boy against smallpox, which ranks with cholera as Britain's biggest child-killer. If confirmed, Jenner's discovery will be one of the medical breakthroughs of the century.

Jenner, who studied medicine under the great John Hunter, was determined to test the old country lore that those who had had the cattle disease cowpox, such as most dairymaids, did not catch smallpox. On 14 May he scratched cowpox fluid into the arm of James Phipps, who was infected at once. Since then, despite contact with children suffering from smallpox, the boy has not caught it (→ 6/1798).

Orangemen fill the streets of Armagh

Co Armagh, 12 July 1796
Members of the newly formed Protestant organization "the Orange Order" held their first orderly public demonstrations in towns in Co Armagh today. They are being seen as the inevitable response to "the Defenders", the federated secret Catholic society formed some years ago to protect Catholics from the outrages of "the Peep O'Day boys".

Last September a fierce clash, dubbed "the Battle of the Diamond", took place between the Defenders and the Peep O'Day boys at a crossroads in Loughgall. This concentrated the minds of Protestants on the need for an organization to represent them at all levels, and so the Orange Order was formed, complete with secret meetings and initiation ceremonies at which armed members take an oath to maintain allegiance to the king, as long as he upholds the Protestant Ascendancy (→10/1/1800).

French invasion of Ireland fails totally

Co Cork, 27 December 1796
France's attempted invasion of Ireland has ended in disaster. The fleet has been scattered, and none of the ships that have managed to reach Bantry Bay in Co Cork have been able to land.

The French had been considering an invasion of the British Isles since the beginning of the war, with Ireland an obvious point of entry. They were reassured by Theobald Wolfe Tone's promise that they would have a friendly reception from the Irish. Once the French controlled the Irish ports, British trade would be seriously affected.

But the French fleet delayed its start, and, on 15 December, in the teeth of winter storms, it set sail from Brest, in Brittany with 43 ships and 14,000 men, under the command of General Hoche. He was accompanied by Tone. Now all the battered fleet can do is limp back to France (→20/2/97).

Holland builds Southill Park for brewer

Builders labour on to turn Henry Holland's imposing design into reality.

Bedford, June 1796
Henry Holland, who is vying with James Wyatt as the most fashionable architect of the decade, has been asked by the brewery magnate Samuel Whitbread to build a spectacular neo-classical mansion at Southill Park.

Since 1776, when Holland, the son-in-law and pupil of "Capability" Brown, was commissioned to build Brooks's club, he has been the favourite architect of the Whig aristocracy. In 1783 the prince of Wales employed him to embellish his home, Carlton House, in London's Pall Mall. It cost a fortune, but Horace Walpole called its interior "the most perfect in Europe".

Since then Holland has worked on Althorp House in Northamptonshire, Broadlands in Hampshire and Woburn Abbey in Bedfordshire – as well as making a fortune out of his London developments around Sloane Square.

Death of Horace Walpole emphasizes the growing cult of the 'gothic' horror novel

Middlesex, 2 March 1797
The death of Horace Walpole at his "gothic" castle called Strawberry Hill, near Twickenham, has stopped the pen of the most prolific correspondent of the times. The youngest son of Sir Robert Walpole, Horace was a dilettante and snob, an author and artist, who put his wit into his letters, which number several thousand, describing the politics and social life of the past 50 years. His gothic design for his home helped to alter classical taste, and he began the fashion for the gothic novel by writing *The Castle of Otranto* in 1764.

Horace Walpole: wit and writer.

This mediaeval romance, set in a castle he dreamt of, so thrilled the public with its ghosts and knightly fantasy that it inspired a whole school of gothic novelists, such as Ann Radcliffe [*see page 770*] and William Beckford. Beckford wrote *Vathek*, the orgiastic tale of a prince who has five pavilions in which to gratify each of the senses and is damned for the wild excesses of his behaviour – suffering "the punishment of unrestrained passions and atrocious deeds".

"Vathek", tale of "gothic" vice.

Perhaps the ultimate in horror is *The Monk* by Matthew Lewis, whose heroine is shut in a vault with rotting corpses while the villain, the monk, rapes and kills his own sister before being hurled to his doom by the devil.

A fireside tale transports listeners into a world of fantasy and horror.

Nelson is hero of Cape St Vincent victory

The British navy wins a great victory at Cape St Vincent: by Richard Paton.

Portugal, 14 February 1797
A British fleet under Admiral Jervis has defeated a Spanish convoy twice its size off Cape St Vincent. The hero of the battle was a young commodore, Horatio Nelson, who divided the Spaniards by breaking from the line and sailing his ship through the middle of them.

The victory is a boost to sagging British morale. Napoleon's victories in Italy, together with Spain's declaration of war last October, had combined to drive Britain out of the Mediterranean with the loss of Corsica and Elba. Then in December British forces had become stretched so far that there were no ships to meet a French invasion of Ireland at Bantry Bay. Only bad weather and poor seamanship had thwarted the French (→25/7).

Anti-militia riots erupt across Scotland

Lothian, August 1797
A 13-year-old boy was among the 11 people who died at Tranent when the cavalry charged a group of locals protesting against the hated militia draft. The victims were ridden down as if they were foreign enemies and butchered in the corn fields "like partridges".

Among the many badly wounded was another schoolboy, Adam Blair, who was struck twice with a sabre and left for dead. Witnesses tell of troops running wild and looting nearby houses.

This is only the worst of many incidents sparked off by the Militia Act. The act, passed this year, makes conscription by ballot compulsory for all men aged between 18 and 23. Its passage shows how worried the government is about invasion; in the past Westminster parliaments have resisted militias, fearing that noblemen could use them for local Jacobite activity.

Resistance has been stiffened by the fact that militiamen can be drafted overseas – all fear the disease-ridden West Indies – and by the unfairness that enables the wealthy to avoid it by hiring substitutes. Schoolmasters, who have had to draw up the ballot lists, have had their homes ransacked.

The forced draft has sparked rioting.

Resistance has been particularly fierce in Tranent, especially among the colliers, although there are rumours that men from the radical group "the United Scotsmen", were also involved. Locals believe that a cover-up is already under way and that no one is likely to be tried for this atrocity.

Financial crisis faces Pitt's administration as war costs mount

Westminster, November 1797
A patriotic proposal by the speaker of the House of Commons, Henry Addington, has enlivened the budget debate in which members have been wrestling with a terrifying £19 million deficit. His suggestion of "voluntary contributions", starting with £2,000 from himself, has been well received.

However, it does not begin to deal with the financial crisis that has already forced William Pitt, the prime minister, to suspend cash payments by the Bank of England. Spending on the war has so far largely been met by borrowing, which is up from £11 million in 1794 to £32 million this year. As a result inflation is rising sharply, and wages are not keeping pace.

Bank in crisis: "The Old Lady of Threadneedle Street in Danger!" by Gilray.

The solution is to raise taxes, but rather than raise indirect taxes, that are harder on the poor, Pitt is proposing trebling taxes on things like windows, carriages and servants and introducing a differential rate of payment so that, for example, four carriages are taxed more than four times one. The new taxes should raise £7 million towards the deficit; the other £12 million will be met by more borrowing. It is also believed that Pitt is planning a tax on income. As a first step the old land tax is being phased out in this year's budget (→4/1799).

Sound of the harp boosts Irish music

Ireland, November 1797
The distinguished young organist Edward Bunting has produced the first volume of his *A General Collection of the Ancient Music of Ireland*, including 66 airs not previously published which came from the first Belfast harp festival, held in 1792 [*see report on page 766*]. At that festival Bunting was on hand to take down the melodies played by Ireland's oldest living harpists, including Denis Hempson, the eldest one, who is now 101.

A number of harp societies have been founded with the specific aim of reviving the native music and poetry of Ireland. The publication of the melodies that Bunting noted down looks like marking the beginning of a serious interest in the music of Irish oral tradition. Bunting himself is certainly determined to devote the rest of his life to its preservation.

Scots working-class hero flees to France

Paris, November 1797
A Scottish revolutionary has been warmly welcomed here after amazing adventures. He escaped from an Australian penal colony, was captured by the Spanish and wounded in an attack by a British warship.

Thomas Muir, a 32-year-old lawyer, was a leading figure in the Scottish campaign for radical reform of parliament. He was a founder of the Edinburgh Society of the Friends of the People in July 1792 and advocated an alliance with the Irish radicals. He was arrested but allowed to go on an extraordinary mission to France to try to save King Louis XVI's life. On his return he was tried and sentenced to seven years' transportation (→ 10/10/1802).

Why women should help each other out

London, 1797
A women's friendly society to offer mutual support to working-class women has been proposed this year. The idea comes from Sir Frederick Eden, whose book *The State of the Poor* examines the fate of working women. The wife of a tenant farmer may earn nothing, being so preoccupied with child-bearing. Even if she earns a few shillings a year from spinning or weeding, Eden says her husband can take that money for drink.

Fan-maker: one job open to women.

Naval mutineers surrender after months of protest about conditions of service

The leaders of the mutiny state their case while government members hide.

Thames estuary, 13 June 1797
The mutiny by Britain's North Sea fleet anchored at the Nore in the Thames estuary is over. The mutineers were forced to surrender when a captain took a boat out at night and destroyed navigation markers in the estuary. Unable to sail in such treacherous waters, the rebel ships hauled down their red flags.

The naval mutiny began in April at Spithead when the Channel fleet, led by better educated civilians recruited for the war, refused to put to sea in protest at appalling conditions. Wages had not risen for over a hundred years, the food was inedible and discipline brutal.

In May the fleet at the Nore came out in support. It had just sent a number of the most violent officers ashore when the Spithead fleet went back to work with the promise of pardons and a sailors' bill to improve service conditions. The more political Nore mutineers stayed out, however, and now face sterner treatment (→ 12/1797).

Royal Navy bottles up enemy fleets

English Channel, December 1797
The Royal Navy, having recovered from the trauma of this year's mutinies [*see report left*], is ending the year by reasserting its strength over its European enemies.

On 11 October the North Sea fleet foiled an attempted Dutch invasion of Ireland. During the mutinies Admiral Duncan had fooled the Dutch into thinking that he was still blockading them at Texel when, in fact, he had just three loyal ships. When the Dutch under Admiral Jan de Winter did break out they made a feint at the Clyde to lure British troops from Ireland – the main focus of their mission. But Duncan was waiting, and much of the Dutch fleet was destroyed in the Battle of Camperdown.

By then the Channel fleet had ended its mutiny at Spithead and returned to patrolling the coast of Brittany. The mutineers had won support during their protest by saying that they would put to sea if the enemy appeared. Promises of better conditions put the sailors in good heart, and the Royal Navy has now confined the enemy fleets to their ports in the Low Countries, Brest, Cherbourg, Cadiz and Toulon. Invasion seems unlikely, at least for some time.

Scots explorer returns home after successful Niger expedition

Scotland, 22 December 1797
Christmas will be especially merry for members of the Park family of Foulshiels, near Selkirk, this year as they welcome their son Mungo back after two and a half years exploring the jungles of Africa.

At the age of 26, he is already assured of a place in the history books. He describes that day on 20 July last year when he became the first European to see the Niger river: "I saw with infinite pleasure the great object of my mission ... glittering in the morning sun, broad as the Thames at Westminster and flowing slowly to the eastwards."

The explorer Mungo Park gets his first glimpse of the Niger: a later picture.

Park travelled with only two African servants, living off the land. At one point he was imprisoned by the Moors, and later, after trekking for 11 months to the coast, he was reduced to selling the buttons off his rags to buy food. Park trained as a surgeon and became a protégé of Sir Joseph Banks, the president of the Royal Society, who got him a position on an East India company ship to Sumatra in 1793. The trip gave him a taste for travel, so when the African Association selected him for an expedition in 1795 he accepted the offer readily (→ 1805).

1798

Scotland, January. Robert and James Haldane found the Society for Propagating the Gospel at Home in an effort to evangelize the Scottish working classes.

Dublin, 12 March. Police acting on the information of an informant, Thomas Reynolds, arrest 12 leaders of the Leinster directory of United Irishmen (→30).

Westminster, 30 March. The privy council declares Ireland to be in a state of rebellion (→23/5).

Caribbean, 2 May. The French force the British to evacuate the port of Santo Domingo.

Leinster, 23/24 May. A United Irish rebellion begins (→4/6).

Dublin, 4 June. Lord Edward FitzGerald, the leader of the United Irishmen, who was wounded during his arrest on 19 May, dies of his wound (→6).

Ulster, 6 June. Rebellion breaks out as Henry Joy McCracken calls the United Irish to arms (→21).

Britain, June. Edward Jenner publishes his observations on smallpox inoculations (→1802).

France, 6 August. Unaware that the Irish rebellion has failed, a force sets sail for Ireland (→22).

Co Mayo, 22 August. General Jean Humbert and 1,000 French troops land to aid the Irish against the British (→8/9).

Co Longford, 8 September After defeating several British contingents, General Humbert and his troops are forced to surrender Ballinamuck to British troops led by General Cornwallis (→6/10).

Dublin, 6 October. Henry Grattan is removed from the privy council for being a sworn member of the United Irishmen (→11/1789).

Minorca, 15 November. The British fleet captures the island (→29/12).

Bradford. The first steam-powered spinning mill opens here (→21/1/1806).

London. The Thames police office is established to patrol the riverside districts.

Norfolk. Captain George Vancouver, the explorer who successfully mapped the Pacific coast of Canada and gave his name to several places along it, dies.

'United Irish' rebel at Vinegar Hill

Ireland, 21 June
The rebellion led by the United Irishmen was finally defeated today in a battle at Vinegar Hill. The episode is already being described as one of the bloodiest in Irish history. Terrible atrocities have been carried out by both the militia and the insurgents. Property has been destroyed, and innocent people have been executed merely on suspicion of having harboured rebel fugitives.

It had been evident for some time that the United Irishmen, now closely linked with the militant Catholic group "the Defenders", were committed to rebellion. They were hoping that a French invasion might be imminent and reckoned that they could count on 280,000 armed men in Ulster, Munster and Leinster. The government's policy of military repression only spurred on the leaders of the rebellion to act more swiftly.

The government, however, used its spy system to the best advantage, and in March most of the principal conspirators were arrested in Dublin and their papers seized. This threw the central organization of the United Irishmen into confusion, and the introduction of martial law threatened to paralyse the movement.

In May it suffered a further blow with the arrest and imprisonment of the most charismatic of its leaders, Lord Edward FitzGerald. Badly wounded during his capture, FitzGerald died later in prison. Despite these serious setbacks, the insurrection broke out on 23 May. It made little headway in the Dublin area or in Ulster, where the troops quickly contained the insurgents, but in Wexford, where the rebels were led by Father John Murphy, they managed to defeat a body of the North Cork militia. After this, almost the whole county was in their hands. However, their defeat at New Ross, after 12 hours of savage fighting and enormous losses, proved to be the turning-point of the war, and now that their main stronghold at Vinegar Hill has been taken the rebellion may peter out (→6/8).

Members of the rebel army reduce Enniscorthy church to a mound of rubble.

Thirsty for revenge: a crowd of rebels executes prisoners on Wexford Bridge.

Economist warns of population explosion

London
The greatest threat to humanity, if the economist and Anglican minister Thomas Malthus is to be believed, is neither war nor pestilence but the simple fact of the world's ever-increasing population.

Medical advance and social reforms have combined to boost population, but the supply of food, which is vital to feed that human tide, increases at a far slower rate. If the trend continues, with the birth-rate far outstripping improvements in food production, all human survival is at risk.

Malthus's theories are propounded in his newly published *Essay on the Principle of Population.* In it he lays out what he sees as the threat, and as a remedy he suggests that, rather than attempting to help society's failures by economic welfare, Poor Laws should be repealed and individuals be educated and encouraged to save money and work for their betterment, rather than depend on the state.

Doctors like 'soda'

London
Schweppe's mineral waters, which have been available since 1792 from Jacob Schweppe's shop at 141 Drury Lane, are now recommended by the medical profession. Dr Tiberius Carvallo, FRS, has stated that "soda water" is an ideal treatment for nephritis, and that with its unrivalled percentage of carbonic acid gas, Schweppe's variety surpasses every rival. It is also beneficial for treating fever, indigestion and nervous illness, he says.

Nelson routs French fleet in a battle on Nile at Aboukir Bay

Mediterranean, 1 August
Rear-Admiral Horatio Nelson has scored yet another victory against the French, leading his fleet in a devastating attack on their squadron at Aboukir Bay at the mouth of the river Nile. In today's battle five French ships were sunk with their crews – a loss of 4,000 men. For Britain, the only setback was that the admiral himself was wounded.

The victory means the end of French power in the Mediterranean and leaves General Napoleon Bonaparte trapped with his army in that country. He remains master of Egypt, but his armies are displaying signs of internal disarray. Any ideas that Bonaparte may have harboured of recapturing France's eastern possessions seem to be as good as dead.

The battle is the culmination of a sustained cat-and-mouse game in which Nelson has been pursuing Bonaparte since he took Malta in May. Fearing that the strategic port of Naples, vital for Britain's alliance with Austria, would be the next to fall, Nelson moved his ships into the eastern Mediterranean to find the French. At first he was unable to make contact and returned to Naples, but a second patrol discovered them at Aboukir Bay (→15/11).

The importing of classical statues has become a highly fashionable pastime among the well-to-do. Here Charles Townley, the painter, displays his collection to a group of friends in his gallery.

French invasion of Ireland a fiasco

Irish rebels falter as French aid fails

Ireland, November
The aspirations of the United Irishmen, which were based on the expectation of French help, have been dashed by the failure of two new expeditions. Preparations went ahead so slowly that the rebellion had been crushed before the first expedition, under the command of General Humbert, reached Killala in Co Mayo on 22 August.

Disappointed by the lack of effective support from the Irish, Humbert nevertheless fought a brave campaign and defeated a vastly superior force under General Lake at Castlebar before finally surrendering. The rebels went on with the struggle, but with the recapture of Killala the uprising in Connacht came to an end.

Meanwhile another expedition with Theobald Wolfe Tone and 3,000 French troops sailed from Brest. It was intercepted off the coast of Donegal by a British naval force. Tone has been arrested and is to be sent to Dublin to stand trial.

Far from being a struggle by Irishmen of all religious denominations against the British, as Tone wished, the insurrection has failed to unite Irishmen of different religious backgrounds (→19).

French invaders face a hostile reception as they try to land at Bantry Bay.

Imprisoned Irish leader takes his own life

Ireland, 19 November
Theobald Wolfe Tone, the leader of the United Irishmen, has died in prison eight days after cutting his throat in a suicide bid on the day of his public execution. He had been court-martialled and sentenced to death for his part in the French invasion to help the revolt.

When he was discovered lying in a pool of blood in his cell, three surgeons were called to stitch his wound, and he was placed in a straitjacket to prevent further suicide attempts. His execution was postponed, pending his recovery, but the wound became infected, and he died today. He is expected to be buried in the family plot at Bodenstown in Co Kildare. He is regarded by some as a hero but by others as a revolutionary who was instrumental in causing the deaths of over 30,000 people. Tone himself always claimed that his main object in life was Ireland's independence from Britain, and that he had endeavoured by every means in his power to break that connection by uniting Catholics and Protestants. In a speech at his trial he said: "For a fair and open war I was prepared; if that has degenerated into a system of assassination, massacre and plunder I do most sincerely lament it" (→31/1/99).

European powers unite with Britain in alliance against France

Europe, 29 December
Faced by Napoleon Bonaparte's ambitions, which threaten to make him dominant in Europe, several interested powers today declared themselves united in an alliance against France, determined to halt its expansionism.

Russia is to join the Anglo-Austrian alliance, and as well as sending troops against France's puppet states in Italy it will invade the Batavian Republic [Netherlands]. In return, Britain will pay £225,000 down as well as a further £75,000 a month to the costs of the war. The Ottoman Empire, Portugal and the kingdom of Naples and Sicily have also announced that they will join the alliance (→7/3/99).

A costly enterprise: Pitt "feeds" various European allies with British gold.

1799

Dublin, 17/19 January. Roman Catholic bishops meeting in secret agree to adopt resolutions in favour of state remuneration of clergy and to veto the government's nomination of bishops.

Westminster, 31 January. William Pitt, the prime minister, makes a speech to parliament in favour of union with Ireland (→ 26/3).

Canada, 2 February. St John Island is renamed Prince Edward Island in honour of King George III's son, Prince Edward, the duke of Kent.

India, 3 February. British troops storm into Mysore in an attempt to prevent Napoleon Bonaparte from establishing Franco-Indian relations (→ 4/5).

Glasgow, 15 February. The city erupts in violent demonstrations over the scarcity and high price of bread.

Palestine, 7 March. Bonaparte and the French army capture Jaffa; the soldiers massacre over 2,000 Albanian prisoners (→ 25/7).

Highland, 26 March. Irish rebel prisoners, including Thomas Addis Emmet, Thomas Russell and other leading United Irishmen, arrive to be interned at Fort St George (→ 22/6).

Dublin, 1 July. Thomas Bray, the Catholic archbishop of Cashel, assures Archbishop Troy that he will cooperate and try to persuade Irish Catholics to support the union of Ireland and Britain (→ 13/1/1800).

Egypt, 25 July. Bonaparte and his army retake Aboukir, control of which was seized on 17 July by Ottoman forces using British ships (→ 9/10).

Germany, 29 September. Irish political prisoners are handed over to the British authorities in Hamburg.

France, 9 October. Bonaparte returns to France and is hailed as a hero (→ 10/11).

Paris, 10 November. Following a *coup d'état* Bonaparte seizes power as "first consul" of France (→ 12/1799).

London. Hannah More, the conservative Christian feminist and writer, who became involved in the founding of both Sunday and day schools, publishes *Modern Female Education*, in which she expresses her views on educating women (→ 1809).

Pitt plans 'income tax' to fund the war

John Bull is terrified by an overgrown and ugly new predator: income tax.

London, April

The war against France may be the source of military glory, but victories do not come cheap; indeed the campaigns are so costly that William Pitt, the prime minister, is imposing a new "income tax".

The tax will be levied on anyone whose income exceeds £60 a year, and it will start at twopence in the pound. Higher rates will be levied according to income, with a top rate of two shillings in the pound for those worth more than £200 a year. Given the profits that so many wealthier merchants have gleaned from Britain's expanding trade, Pitt hopes that the tax, while likely to be unpopular, will not be seen as overly unfair (→ 3/2/1801).

Workers restrained by Combination Acts

London, 20 July

Workers who aim to improve their working conditions by coming together in "combinations" or "trade unions" will find themselves in serious legal trouble after today's passage of the Combination Acts, which now outlaw such groupings.

Trade unions – associations of workers of every craft – have existed throughout the past century, but usually they have been short lived, ineffectual and bogged down by elaborate, irrelevant ceremonial. But some, notably those of the coopers, silkweavers, tailors and goldbeaters, have gained genuine power – and that power has frightened both the employers and the government.

It was to curb just such a union, the millwrights', that group of owners petitioned parliament in April. Response was swift and, inevitably, wholly in the employers' favour. Unions are to be banned.

Under the acts any worker combining with another faces three months' jail or two months' hard labour. Appeals are allowed, but the cost is beyond most men.

Indian ruler, Tipu Sahib, dies as British besiege Mysore capital

British troops overcome desperate defenders to storm Seringapatam. The city-fortress is the headquarters of Tipu Sahib, the sultan of Mysore.

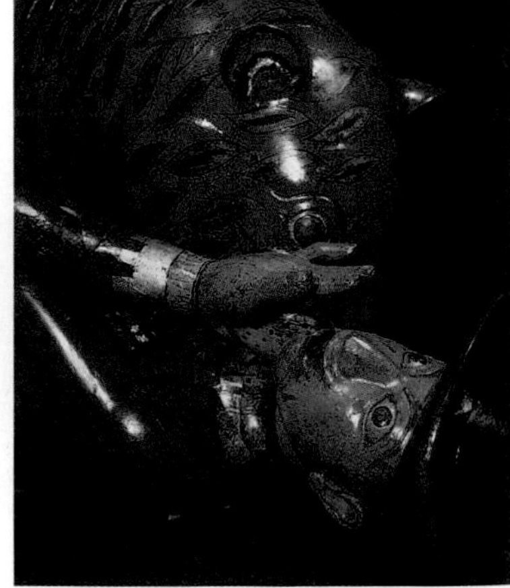

Tipu's tiger: a carved wooden torture device from Mysore, c.1790.

Southern India, 4 May

Tipu Sahib, the sultan of Mysore, who for the past decade has been one of the most irritating thorns in the side of British rule in India, is dead. He died as British forces under Col Arthur Wellesley took his fortress capital, Seringapatam. Tipu, a notably corrupt and covetous ruler, had already been defeated in 1792, when his attack on the Carnatic had been thrown back by Lord Cornwallis. But, mindful of the liberal India Act, he was neither deposed nor deprived of his territories. British tolerance ended in 1797 when Tipu befriended the French, requesting aid and promising a campaign that would expel Britain from India. In 1798 Wellesley arrived in India, determined to destroy any possibility of Tipu supporting Napoleon Bonaparte. Despite some worries, his plan worked perfectly. Tipu's capital was taken, and during the fighting the sultan was killed (→ 10/1802).

Irish vote 'No' to union with Britain

The Irish parliament: Lord Clare is in the left foreground holding a paper.

Dublin, 22 June
After a turbulent sitting of parliament, the Irish government has lost the first round of its fight to form a union with Britain. A majority of members have voted No.

William Pitt, the British prime minister, has been anxious for some time to achieve both union with Ireland and Catholic emancipation. Yet he met with opposition, especially from Lord Clare, the lord chancellor, who regards union as a bulwark of Protestant privilege. Clare's influence is so strong that it was decided that union be suggested on a Protestant basis without Catholic emancipation. Despite some opposition the chief secretary, Lord Castlereagh, felt confident that parliament would favour union after a debate had been held on the best way of achieving it. But opposition members first forced the issue by voting on a resolution that was anti-union; they won this by a mere two votes. Emboldened by success they then moved the deletion from the viceroy's address of the paragraph relating to union. This was supported by a majority of five votes (→ 1/7).

"Three witches", by Henry Fuseli. This year saw the opening of his Milton Gallery – paintings inspired by the poet John Milton. His works also appeared in John Boydell's Shakespeare Gallery, which opened in 1786.

Bonaparte's peace moves are spurned

Westminster, December
Overtures of peace from Napoleon Bonaparte, who seized power in France last month, have received a hostile response from the British cabinet. Although William Pitt, the prime minister, favours a settlement of the seven-year-long war, doubts about Bonaparte's authority and hopes of military success next year persuaded the government to reject the peace moves.

The nations allied against France now hold most of Italy, and the Royal Navy is dominant at sea. However, an Anglo-Russian expedition to the Dutch Batavian Republic was withdrawn last October without having ejected France from Dutch soil (→ 4/1800).

Scottish miners to lose their serfdom

Scotland
The last serfs in Scotland have been freed, following the passing of the Emancipation Act which frees colliers from working in coal-mines. Until now coal-miners and their families have been bound to the mines, which are owned by coal-masters. The purpose was to make sure of labour in unpleasant and unhealthy work. Coal-masters had pointed to the relatively high wages which they paid and to the hostility of colliers to jobs going to people from outside their communities. But since the first coal serfs were freed in 1778, most coal-masters had accepted that serfdom – scrapped elsewhere 400 years ago – was neither justifiable nor necessary.

Scientific Royal Institution is founded

Scientific instruction: inspecting an orrery (a model of the solar system).

London
An expatriate American Tory, who was forced to flee the revolution in the colonies, has established a centre for the scientific instruction of artisans. Benjamin Thompson's creation is to be known as the Royal Institution, and it will be devoted to improving, through science, the lot of the poor. But it is clear that the Institution will work less to benefit the poor than to teach them how best to benefit their betters. The theory is that if the workers know how to use scientific methods their work will improve, and as profitably employed men they will be less likely to ponder revolution (→ 1800).

Practical applications for science.

1800

Ulster, 10 January. The Grand Orange Lodge [Irish Protestants] adopts a new set of rules including ten secret articles (→3/1800).

Dublin, 13 January. Daniel O'Connell, a Roman Catholic Irish lawyer, makes his first speech at a Catholic meeting protesting against the proposed union with Britain (→6/2).

London, January. Maria Edgeworth, an Irish-born novelist, publishes *Castle Rackrent*, a "gothic" novel; the book instantly becomes a bestseller.

Westminster, 6 February. Parliament approves the proposals for union with Ireland by 158 votes to 115 (→2/7).

Brest, France, 17 March. Royal Navy mutineers aboard HMS *Danaë* hand the ship over to the French in the port here.

Ulster, March. The Grand Orange Lodge opposes Irish union with Britain (→12/7/13).

Norfolk, 25 April. William Cowper, the poet and writer of hymns, dies in East Dereham.

Egypt, April. British troops begin to disperse the French based here (→14/6).

London, 15 May. The première of Mozart's opera *Le Nozze di Figaro* is interrupted by an attempt on King George III's life by a member of the audience, James Hadfield.→

Westminster, 2 July. Parliament passes the British Act of Union (→1/8).

Dublin, 1 August. Parliament passes the Irish Act of Union; this creates the United Kingdom of Great Britain.→

Dublin, 2 August. The last Irish parliament, which began its session in January 1799, is ended (→1/1/01).

London. The Company of Surgeons becomes the Royal College of Surgeons.

Westminster. Parliament makes Good Friday a public holiday.

Birmingham. Thomas Gryll, a Cornish-born ironmonger working here, invents a screw-down tap.

London. Benjamin Outram, a civil engineer, begins work on the first iron tram-tracks; the route will be from Croydon to Wandsworth.

Ireland. Thousands die as famine strikes.

King survives shooting

Hadfield disrupts "The Marriage of Figaro" by taking a pot shot at the king.

London, 15 May
A second assassination attempt on George III failed today when a man tried to shoot him during a performance of *Le Nozze di Figaro* [*The Marriage of Figaro*] at the Drury Lane theatre. James Hadfield's bullet was close enough to pierce one of the pillars in the royal box. After the shot, George's reaction was to step forwards to the front of the box and calmly look around.

Richard Brinsley Sheridan, the playwright, was in the audience, and he responded by improvising an extra verse to *God Save the King* which the singer Michael Kelly performed to loud applause:

From every latent foe,
From the assassin's blow,
God save the king!
O'er him thine arm extend,
For Britain's sake defend,
Our father, prince and friend,
God save the king!

The performance then continued, and the king, apparently unperturbed, dozed peacefully during a later interval. Michael Kelly said afterwards: "Never shall I forget his majesty's coolness – the audience was in an uproar." In August 1786 George III reacted to another attempt on his life with equal self-assurance when a woman tried to stab him (→11/3/01).

Bonaparte victorious at Marengo battle

Marengo, Italy, 14 June
Napoleon Bonaparte has beaten the Imperial Austrian army at Marengo in northern Italy, snatching a surprise victory when it seemed that the French were doomed. Believing the Austrians to be at Turin, his army was advancing widely separated when at Marengo, near Alessandria, he encountered the entire enemy force. With 10,000 men against twice that number, he tried to hang on until the scattered French corps could come to his aid. Defeat seemed certain until General Desaix and two divisions arrived. The Austrians were then driven from the battlefield (→12/1800).

Bonaparte: survived a close call.

Work of Swedish botanist causes uproar

Britain, c.1800
More than 20 years after his death, the Swedish scientist Carolus Linnaeus continues to embarrass botanists by his system of classifying plants according to their sexual characteristics. Even the Reverend Samuel Goodenough, a botanist and the vice-president of the Royal Linnaean Society in London, is said to be disturbed at "the gross prurience of Linnaeus's mind".

But Linnaeus's development of a "binominal" system which gives a plant two names, the first relating to its **genus**, and the second to its **species** within the genus, is contributing to the creation of a much needed international language of classification and is already widely adopted in Europe.

Linnaeus's anatomy of a sunflower.

Davy discovers that laughter kills pain

Bristol, 9 April
Humphry Davy, a chemist at the Pneumatic Institute at Clifton, has discovered a gas which when inhaled produced a euphoric effect that had him "laughing and stamping". He has been experimenting throughout the past year on the physiological effects of different gases, primarily nitrous oxide.

During one test the pain that he was suffering from a wisdom tooth was eased – "for a few minutes swallowed up in pleasure". Davy's conclusions are that if nitrous oxide is able to destroy pain, it may "be used to advantage during surgical operations in which no great effusion of blood takes place".

Welshman heads showpiece Scottish town

Strathclyde, 1 January
A Welsh businessman and social reformer, George Owen, today became manager of New Lanark – the model industrial community justly celebrated for both the quality of its cotton and its enlightened social conditions and advanced system of education.

It was founded in 1783 by David Dale, and the mills were built and spinning within three years. Since then New Lanark has flourished, employing a workforce of 1,300 employees who enjoy some of the best living and working conditions in Britain. Child apprentices receive free food and clothing and are given two hours' education every day. Owen, who is Dale's son-in-law, intends to pursue this ideal, establishing a community of all social classes living together in complete harmony.

Model community: the growing mill-town of New Lanark, near Glasgow.

Female food rioter goes to the gallows

Manchester, June
Hannah Smith has been given the death sentence at Lancaster assizes for the crime of highway robbery, an unexpectedly harsh punishment for the theft of food. During the Manchester food riots, earlier in the year, she was seen by witnesses to be urging a group of 100 people to steal vegetables from a potato cart.

Later that same day she was seen leading a larger mob of rioters in a raid against a cart bringing milk and butter into the town. Smith offered to pay the owners reduced prices for their produce, warning them that otherwise they would be taken for nothing. She was eventually caught selling stolen butter to the crowds.

Judge Thompson, who sentenced her to be hanged, said that she had been "guilty of robbery on the highway", and that this proved that she was one of the most "determined enemies to good order". He added that her "sex is not entitled to any mitigation of punishment".

Elegant town planning is giving a facelift to the centre of Scotland's capital city

Grand houses in a private development: the newly finished Charlotte Square.

Edinburgh
A further stage in the redevelopment of Scotland's capital has been marked by the completion of Charlotte Square, in the heart of the city. The square is the heart of a major exercise in town planning which has been undertaken here in recent years. Unfortunately the principal figure behind the redevelopment did not live to see its completion – Robert Adam, the architect, died in 1792. Other designs of his here include the General Register and the new university college.

The square combines elegance and ambition – an entire street composed of huge, lofty detached houses, all having stuccoed and pedimented façades and doorways beneath steeply-pitched roofs. The houses are flanked by pavilions, and there are wrought-iron gates to secure the wealthy residents from intruders. Plans are proposed for similar streets of grand houses to be built in other parts of the city.

The Adam family – not only Robert's father but also his three brothers were architects too – has contributed much to the current revival of Scottish architecture, continuing the tradition of styles based on classical antiquity that were first introduced by Sir William Bruce in the 17th century.

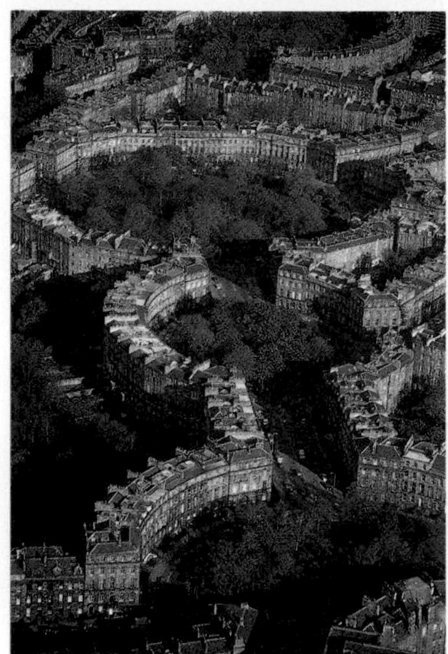

Edinburgh's elegant New Town.

Oxford tests written

Oxford, England, c.1800
Written examinations have been introduced at Oxford University, to bring it in line with the custom already in force at Cambridge. Until now examinations have been conducted on the basis of students giving written answers to oral questions in moral philosophy, mathematics and logic over a four-day period. The reform comes at a time when applications for a place at universities are on the increase.

Emigration grows as highlanders seek a new life in south

Scotland, c.1800
The migration to the south by highlanders continues, despite efforts by landlords to prevent it. Although potatoes, cattle and kelp make farming in the highlands profitable, it cannot support a large population. Many of the emigrants seek work in lowland farms, but an increasing number have been drifting south to towns and cities in search of work in the textile industry or as domestic servants. Some see the move as simply a temporary expedient; many more are leaving for good.

In Edinburgh the city guard now has so many Gaelic-speaking highlanders that one resident says: "Few of the citizens understand or are understood by them." Ambitious plans for the redevelopment of the capital [*see report above*] drew large numbers of highlanders to Edinburgh with offers of work in rebuilding the streets, while others have completely taken over the city's sedan-chair trade.

In most of the lowland towns and cities there are now enough resident highlanders to justify Gaelic chapels. And even in England the Highland Society of London works for the preservation of the Gaelic language – and the relief of distressed highlanders.

▷

French give up Malta after naval blockade

Malta, 16 December
Malta has been captured by the British, just two years after the French invaded and took it from the mediaeval order of the Knights of St John. Napoleon Bonaparte had seized the island on his way to Egypt to use as a staging post for his intended capture of India.

That plan having been scotched by Rear-Admiral Nelson's destruction of the French fleet at Aboukir Bay, the island garrison came under an increasing British blockade and has now surrendered. Bonaparte's attack had one unforeseen result, however. The czar of Russia was so incensed by the affront to the Knights of St John that he joined Britain against France (→ 9/2/01).

Island defender: a knight of Malta.

Britain is isolated as French power grows

Britain, December
These are dark days for Britain as the situation on the continent noticeably worsens. Victories by Napoleon Bonaparte have shattered the alliance of states which the prime minister, William Pitt, painstakingly put together to oppose him.

Only a few months ago it all looked so much brighter. The destruction by Rear-Admiral Nelson of the French fleet at the Battle of the Nile forced Bonaparte to abandon his Egyptian army and return to France. This gave Pitt the prestige to make a second coalition against him, bringing together Russia, Naples, Portugal and the Holy Roman and Ottoman Empires.

But the new allies quickly began to fall out. The czar quarrelled with Emperor Francis II and left in October 1799. Then Napoleon went on the offensive and this year inflicted two defeats on the Imperial Austrian troops at Marengo and Hohenlinden. This caused both empires and Naples to sue for peace, and Portugal was defeated by Spain, which was still a French ally (→ 16).

"The Exhibition Stare Case": a satire on the British art public by Thomas Rowlandson.

Royal Society given new theory on light

London
The Royal Society has been treated to a lecture by a young doctor named Thomas Young, who believes that he has found the answer to the mystery of how light travels. He suggests that it must travel in waves, rather like sound; but no one is terribly interested.

Young himself is a prodigy who learnt to read at the age of two, and by the time that he was six he had read the Bible twice and was studying Latin. Lacking a tutor, at the age of 13 he took up independent study of Hebrew, Chaldean, Syriac, Samaritan, Arabic, Persian, Turkish and "Ethiopic", while continuing with his Latin and Greek.

Wordsworth waxes lyrical on Romanticism

Cumbria
A second collection of poems called *Lyrical Ballads*, first printed anonymously two years ago, contains a preface by William Wordsworth, the author of most of them, which sets out new aims for poetry in this so-called "romantic age". In his "manifesto" he states: "Poetry is the spontaneous overflow of powerful feelings; it takes its origin from emotion recollected in tranquillity. I have chosen subjects from common life and endeavoured to bring my language near to the real language of men in a state of vivid sensation. The reader will find no personifications of abstract ideas and little of what is usually called poetic diction."

Wordsworth's aim of banishing 18th-century poetic artificiality is borne out by his simple poems about rustic life and humble people. His *Lines Above Tintern Abbey* treat nature as the source of near-religious illumination. The longest poem in the book, *The Rime of the Ancient Mariner*, is by Wordsworth's close friend and neighbour in the Lake District, Samuel Taylor Coleridge. It is a tale of guilt, doom, horrors and marvels that will not let the listening wedding guest (or reader) go. Coleridge has also written, but not yet published, an extraordinary unfinished poem, *Kubla Khan*. His dream of this visionary palace in Xanadu was induced by opium and written down on waking – until he was interrupted (→ 1820).

Wordsworth: a philosophical poet.

Radical attitudes to French Revolution

Godwin: a radical philosopher.

London
The enthusiasm with which English writers, thinkers and poets greeted the French Revolution has waned fast since the Terror and the advent of Bonaparte. Among the strongest supporters of Tom Paine at the time when he published *The Rights of Man* were the philosopher William Godwin and Mary Wollstonecraft, the pioneer feminist. Though both opposed marriage, she became his wife in 1797 when pregnant. While Paine's tract was banned as "seditious", Godwin's *Inquiry Concerning Political Justice*, published in 1793, was not because at three guineas [£3.15] it was too costly to influence the mob.

Godwin believes in the perfectability of man, the scrapping of evil institutions and the education to act for the common good. Reason, not law, would maintain order and government would be reduced to a minimum. These notions inspired Coleridge and Robert Southey to plan an ideal community in America, but they never sailed. Now both poets, and William Wordsworth, who went to revolutionary Paris at the age of 21 and fathered a daughter there, are disillusioned with the French experiment. But Wordsworth writes: "Bliss was it in that dawn to be alive,/But to be young was very heaven!"

Great Britain and Ireland united by Act of Union

Ireland, 1 August
The Act of Union between Great Britain and Ireland has received the royal assent. On 7 June the Bill for Union passed both the House of Commons and the House of Lords. Thus the Irish parliament enacted its own dissolution, having been in existence for 500 years.

The country has gone through troubled times since the suppression of the rising in 1798. Agrarian crime has become so widespread and so violent that witnesses and jurymen live in constant terror of reprisals, and the courts are almost powerless. Martial law has been introduced, backed up by reinforcements of British troops. Reports of a new French invasion are rife, and bad harvests have increased the general discontent.

Against this background William Pitt, the British prime minister, determined to press ahead with his plans for union. Support for it was to be imposed on every candidate who wished to hold government office, thus enabling Lord Cornwallis, the lord lieutenant, to build up a parliamentary majority.

The anti-union struggle continued for some months, supported by barristers, Orangemen and the country gentry. But the spirit of 1798 seemed to have been replaced by one of apathy, and the union was finally accepted (→2).

James Gillray takes a jaundiced view of those celebrating the new union.

How Britain has changed in the century since England and Scotland were united

Britain
Almost a century after union, England and Scotland are still ruled by the monarch and a small group of peers. Most of the land remains in the hands of these lords, but all around them great changes are occurring. The population of England and Wales has grown from five million to some nine million, and in Scotland numbers are up from one million to 1.6 million. Enclosure Acts since 1720 have all but eliminated open-field systems, changing the landscape and making agriculture more efficient. Scotland, for instance, is now self-sufficient.

Steam power is luring industry from areas where rivers had offered water power to coalfields in England and Scotland. Factories are small, with most industrial production being carried out at home. In Scotland the largest employer is Andrew Milne of Aberdeen; his workforce of between 3,000 and 4,000 is scattered through villages for many miles around. Child labour is widespread.

Industrialization has stimulated a demand for goods, with Yorkshire, Lancashire and Lanarkshire among the areas to have prospered. Roads have been improved by turnpiking, so that the journey from London to Shrewsbury, which took four days in 1753, now takes only a day. Canals allow heavy goods and raw materials to be transported quickly and cheaply. Ports have also been improved, and foreign trade has boomed. There has been a big migration from the countryside to the towns; London now has a population of one million, and one-third of the population of England is urban. In Scotland only Glasgow and Edinburgh have populations above 50,000, but both are growing faster than any other cities in Europe.

The material advances of the past century have been matched by an explosion of artistic creativity and scientific inquiry into the natural world. Scotland has seen a great ferment of intellectual ideas, symbolized by the work of David Hume and Adam Smith [*see report on page 740*]. Ireland has produced such influential figures as the satirist Jonathan Swift, the philosopher Edmund Burke and the dramatist Oliver Goldsmith. Burke and Goldsmith were leading members of the Literary Club [*see page 721*] which, as the greatest of many such groups formed in the second half of the century, came to dominate intellectual life in London. "The Club" was founded in 1763 by the scholar Samuel Johnson and the painter Sir Joshua Reynolds, who invited their friends to join.

Industrialized landscape: a view of Coalbrookdale, Shropshire, in 1777.

At a party hosted by Sir Joshua Reynolds the guests include (left to right) Boswell, Johnson, (Reynolds), Garrick, Burke and (far right) Goldsmith.

Industrial and Imperial Supremacy

1801 - 1900

1801

Britain/Ireland, 1 January. King George III is proclaimed king of Great Britain and Ireland on the passing of the Union Act.→

Westminster, 3 February. Following a disagreement with George III over Roman Catholic emancipation, William Pitt, the prime minister, offers the king his resignation (→14/3).

France, 9 February. Austria and France sign the Peace of Lunéville; this brings an end to the Franco-Austrian war, leaving Britain without an ally against France (→8/3).

Egypt, 8 March. British troops land in the country, which is currently in the hands of the French (→28).

London, 11 March. George III is recovering after a month-long attack of his debilitating illness, which takes the form of nausea, mental confusion and hoarseness (→2/11/10).

Italy, 28 March. Italy and France sign the Treaty of Florence; the ports of Italy are closed to Britain, and, to enforce this, the French fleet blockades the Adriatic coast (→2/4).

Denmark, 2 April. The British fleet bombards Copenhagen; this action hastens the break-up of the League of Armed Neutrality, formed by Russia, Sweden, Denmark and Prussia on 16 December last year to resist British rights of search.→

London, 22 May. Rear-Admiral Horatio Nelson is created a viscount in reward for his heroic services to Britain (→28/6).

Cairo, 28 June. The British seize control of the city, forcing French troops to move out (→30/8).

Westminster, 2 July. Parliament passes the Copyright Act in an attempt to stamp out illegal pirating of British-published books in Ireland; it requires that one copy of every book which is published in Britain should be placed in the libraries of Trinity College and King's Inns in Dublin.

Egypt, 30 August. French troops under the command of General Menou begin to leave after losing control of Alexandria to the British forces (→25/3/02).

London. A new newspaper, *Bell's Weekly Messenger*, prints its first issue.

Act of Union confirmed with new flag

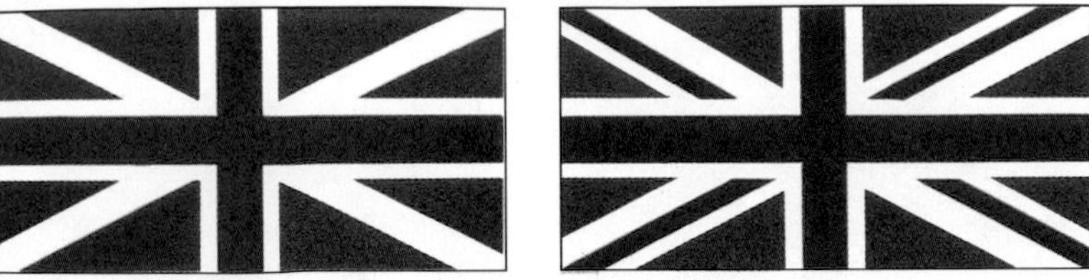

The flag before (left) and after (right) the addition of the new cross.

Ireland, 1 January

The Act of Union between Britain and Ireland has been confirmed with the unfurling of a new flag on the Bedford Tower of Dublin Castle. There is a rumour going about, however, that the Irish section of the Union Jack – the cross of St Patrick – is not, in fact, the saint's cross at all but the hastily incorporated cross of the Knights of St Patrick. The Knights were established in 1783 to affirm loyalty to England and to emphasize lack of sympathy with the Volunteer movement. It is being claimed that their flag was the armorial device of the FitzGerald family, perhaps to flatter the duke of Leinster, himself a FitzGerald (→30/6/02).

Canal is final link in English network

Manchester

This year's completion of a trans-Pennine canal linking the Humber and Mersey navigation systems provides England's industrial cities with access to a complete, nationwide, waterborne transport network. This virtually completes a development that has transformed the economy. Farmers can profitably supply distant markets; barges carry lime to improve the soil and stone to upgrade the once impassable roads. And factories, in turn, can send their goods to distant towns or ports for export (→1803).

Linen Hall houses the Belfast library

Belfast, 10 November

The Belfast Society for Promoting Knowledge has established permanent premises in the Linen Hall for its library. Previously known as the Belfast Reading Society, it was part of a movement to set up subscription libraries to encourage the spread of literacy in large commercial towns.

The society has publicly favoured rights for Roman Catholics, and two of its early members were Henry Joy McCracken, one of the leaders of the United Irishmen, and his sister Mary Ann.

First census shows population of over ten million people

British Isles

For the first time in the long history of the British Isles a census has been held this year to establish an accurate figure for the total population of these islands. It shows that, to the nearest thousand, there are 9,061,000 men, women and children living in England and Wales, 1,625,000 in Scotland and a further 5,216,000 in Ireland. In each part of the United Kingdom women are in the majority.

John Rickman, who prepared the census report, has calculated that a century ago England and Wales had 5,175,000 inhabitants, so that there has been an increase of more than 77 per cent in the past 100 years. The rise appears to have been most rapid in mid-century, but birth-rates have generally risen while the death-rate has fallen. But perhaps more significant is the greater number of children surviving into adulthood, which in turn produces more women of childbearing age. One reason for the lower death-rate is a better supply of food. Improvements in agriculture have enabled an increasingly urban population to be fed. One in three of the population in England and Wales now live in towns – one in six in Scotland. Although few people actually die of starvation nowadays, disease remains a big killer.

More help for the poor needed as bread prices hit new record

Charity goods are distributed to the poor of Durham in the late 18th century.

London

The ever rising cost of Poor Relief has dominated domestic politics this year as war and another poor harvest pushed the price of bread to the highest levels ever recorded.

Wheat, which was selling at 47 shillings a quarter [£2.35 for 13kg] ten years ago, now stands at an unprecedented 110 shillings, leaving many parishes stretched to provide adequate subsistence even for their orphans and widows, let alone for the increasing numbers of able-bodied men who are unable to find work or afford the spiralling prices. The Poor Rates have almost trebled in the last decade, and there is growing resistance from taxpayers.

Pitt resigns on principle

Westminster, 14 March
William Pitt resigned today after 18 continuous years as prime minister. King George III has invited the speaker of the House of Commons, Henry Addington, to head the new government [*see below*].

The departure followed a head-on confrontation with the king over the issue of Catholic emancipation. In order to win Irish support for the recently ratified Act of Union between Great Britain and Ireland, Pitt had allowed informal assurances to circulate in Dublin that he would back moves to guarantee improved treatment for the Roman Catholic majority there, in both civil and religious affairs.

He failed, however, to convince either the bulk of his party, or a number of leading members of his cabinet, of the need for such sweeping concessions. And when the king heard what was proposed and declared his irreconcilable opposition, Pitt felt that, in honour, he had no alternative but to go. The surprise in political circles is that such a shrewd and experienced leader should have pushed so hard on a matter which was bound to be contentious. Many suspect it may only have been a ploy to win a respite from the cares of office and the war with France, and that Pitt will soon be back in Downing Street.

Pitt: resigned over Catholics' rights.

Boyhood friend succeeds as premier

London, 14 March
Henry Addington, who today becomes King George III's surprising choice to succeed William Pitt, is an almost total contrast to the brilliant predecessor who has been both patron and friend for most of the new prime minister's somewhat less than incandescent career. They have known each other since boyhood, when Addington's father was family physician to the earl of Chatham, Pitt's father. But Addington made little mark when he entered parliament as member for Devizes – in fact he spoke only twice in his first three years – and it was only when Pitt chose him to become speaker in 1789 that he began to rise in public esteem (→ 1803).

Danish fleet under attack from Nelson

Copenhagen, 2 April
British warships under the command of the intrepid Vice-Admiral Horatio Nelson today smashed the Danish fleet near here after surprising it at anchor. The English commanders are now threatening to bombard the city if the government does not accept London's surrender terms. As a result, Denmark is expected to abandon its support for "the armed neutrality of the north" and allow Britain to include the crucial Russian grain trade through the Baltic in its increasingly effective French blockade. A story is circulating that at one point Nelson was ordered to withdraw by his superior, Sir Hyde Parker, but clapped his telescope to his blind eye and ignored the signal before pressing home his attack (→ 22/5).

Nelson: in control at Copenhagen.

Science made fun by Humphry Davy

Humphry Davy: science popularizer.

London, 1801.
Humphry Davy, a young Cornishman who has just been appointed lecturer in chemistry at the Royal Institution, is already showing a remarkable talent for popularizing developments in science.

Audiences of several hundred people, including a number of fashionable – and fascinated – ladies, have been flocking to hear him expound the latest thinking on the mysteries of heat and light, and the exciting new work being done by himself and other researchers in the field of "electricity". Under its founder Benjamin Thompson (now Count Rumford) the Institution had already established a formidable reputation, but now, with Davy, it is "electrifying" the capital's intellectual life (→ 1802).

A new face to the land: stone enclosure walls at Chelmorton, Derbyshire.

New act boosts enclosures of commons

Westminster
One of the most important measures passed by parliament this year may well turn out to have been the General Enclosure Act. This is designed to simplify and speed up even further the process of fencing in and consolidating commons, open fields and wastelands, and encouraging the spread of large-scale farming.

Even in the short period since 1760 there have been 1,600 such pieces of legislation, and in many sessions MPs seem to have concerned themselves with very little else. But these acts were all individually promoted; now they can be dealt with in batches.

The effects of enclosure are already transforming both the appearance of the landscape and the structure of the rural economy. In large parts of England, Wales and Scotland the smallholder has virtually disappeared. Poverty, on the other hand, has sharply increased, with a dramatic surge in the number of labourers forced to work for very low wages (→ 1808).

1802

London, 10 February. King George III knights the Scottish-born explorer Alexander Mackenzie; he was the first white man to reach the Pacific coast of North America, on 22 June 1793.

Westminster, 3 April. Thomas Douglas, the earl of Selkirk, proposes a programme of emigration to the sparsely populated reaches of north-western Canada as a way of coping with Britain's population and economic problems.

France, 2 August. Napoleon Bonaparte is elected "first consul" for life.

Edinburgh, 10 October. A new radical publication, the *Edinburgh Review*, is launched.

India, October. As Anglo-French relations deteriorate parliament in Britain orders that the formal restitution of Pondicherry to the French be delayed until the situation is clearer (→31/12).

Cumbria, 15 November. George Romney, the portrait painter, dies at his home in Kendal.

India, 31 December. The Marathan Peshwa Baji Rao signs the Treaty of Bassein with Lord Wellesley, giving the British control of central India (→4/1804).

West Sussex. Charles Lennox, the duke of Richmond, introduces horse-racing at Goodwood.

London. Humphry Davy, the scientist, and Thomas Wedgwood, the son of the renowned English potter Josiah, succeed in copying paintings onto glass (→1815).

Britain. Thomas Young produces a scientific paper, *On the theory of light and colours*.

Bechuanaland [Botswana]. Two Britons, John Trüter and William Somerville, have successfully reached Lake Ngami.

Britain. Erasmus Darwin, the botanist and poet who wrote *Zoonomia*, which introduced the idea of evolution in organic life, has died.

Britain. John Dalton, a scientist, introduces the "atomic theory" into chemistry with his table of atomic weights.

Sunderland. Henry Greathead launches the *Zetland*, the lifeboat for the town of Redcar, in Cleveland.

Anglo-French peace treaty signed

Amiens, France, 25 March

The nine-year-long war between Britain and France ended today, and the constant threat of an invasion of England is removed. But several of the British team are displeased by the Treaty of Amiens signed here by Lord Cornwallis. They feel that he has been worsted by the French led by Joseph Bonaparte, the brother of the wily general, Napoleon, who now rules France as its "first consul".

France gains far more from the peace than Britain. All the overseas possessions won by British naval power are handed back, with the exception of Trinidad and Ceylon. Egypt and the Cape of Good Hope are given up, and Malta is returned to the Knights of St John.

The terms are worse than the preliminary ones signed in London six months ago: the Cape was then to have been a free port. Bonaparte has conceded nothing on trade. He can exclude the English from the Cape and other overseas possessions. London merchants also cannot hope for a revival of their European trade; no country can stand up to Bonaparte, and the Low Countries are under his sway. But something has been gained from Nelson's Mediterranean victories: the French are to give up Naples. Yet as Bonaparte has made a truce with the pope, French influence in Italy is unchecked (→20/3/03).

Bringing peace home: the coach bearing news of today's treaty with France.

European exile for 19 United Irishmen

Highland, 30 June

As a result of the Treaty of Amiens signed in March [*see above*], 19 United Irishmen leaders who have been imprisoned in Fort George, near Inverness, since shortly after the failure of their rebellion in 1798 have been released on condition that they go into exile. They have been refused leave to organize their affairs in Ireland before their permanent banishment and are being shipped direct to Hamburg.

The Irish state prisoners have been a headache for both the British and the Irish governments, and the excuse of Amiens to release them on condition of permanent exile was welcome. Glaring shortfalls in security legislation have been highlighted by their detention, and the prospect of their unconditional release when the Habeas Corpus Suspension Act expired last year caused panic in London.

Wary of possible failures of security in Dublin, the British authorities transferred the 19 prisoners to Fort George three years ago, in 1799 (→27/7/03).

Military reforms gain royal imprimatur

London, April

The establishment this year of the Royal Military College will give the duke of York the backing of a growing group of young officers for his sweeping reforms of the army. In the closing years of the war with France the duke instilled a new spirit of professionalism into the army.

He seeks to maintain discipline by leadership instead of flogging, insisting on drill and exercises, along with lectures for officers. The duke has installed a regular reporting system to a new central office, and he urges that uniforms be chosen to conceal men from the enemy instead of for pomp. And the troops now get a government issue of greatcoats instead of having to rely on the clothes supplied by their colonels. The reforms are transforming Britain's biggest-ever army of 130,000 men. It may soon be active again – despite the Treaty of Amiens [*see above left*] Napoleon Bonaparte is building up his army (→1803).

The "Charlotte Dundas", designed by William Symington, is the first working steamship. She is seen here shortly after her launch on the Clyde.

'Bride of the Lamb' is popular prophet

London, October 1
A Devonshire prophetess who calls herself "the Lamb's bride" is convinced that she is destined to produce the second Christ. Joanna Southcott, a farmer's daughter, is already 52, but she expects to give birth to a spiritual man whom she calls "Shiloh". She first began to give prophecies ten years ago when she attended the Exeter Methodist meeting. Last year three London clergymen were convinced of her powers and brought her to Paddington, where she now has thousands of followers (→ 27/12/14).

Joanna Southcott: religious seer?

New legislation regulates child labour

Children, the engine of the industrial machine, at work in a rope factory.

Westminster
A Lancashire mill-owner and member of parliament, Sir Robert Peel, is making the first effort to control the growing use of child labour in the textile mills. He has piloted through the Health and Morals of Apprentices Act to enforce certain minimum standards on the cotton-mill owners. Many of the children start work at the age of six or seven and eat, and work, live and sleep at the mill.

Most of them are orphans or the children of local paupers who have become a charge on the parish. The new act is an attempt to cope with the problems posed by industrialization within the Poor-Law system. Just how badly children are treated can be gleaned from the provisions of the new act: their working day is to be limited to 12 hours; there must be enough windows to ensure fresh air; the walls and floor must be washed regularly; there must be separate bedrooms for the two sexes and no more than two children in one bed; two suits of clothing are to be provided for each child, one new each year.

For at least the first four years of apprenticeship the children must be instructed in reading, writing and arithmetic. Every Sunday there has to be at least an hour's teaching of the Christian religion, with tests conducted by the local vicar. Fines on owners breaking the new laws range between £2 and £5 (→ 1804).

Bentham examines civil and penal law

London
Jeremy Bentham, the 54-year-old writer on law, ethics and penal reform, is winning the recognition in France that he has been denied at home. Though he is no lover of the revolution his ideas are finding favour with the French, whose government he has been advising.

Bentham has been driven to the brink of bankruptcy by the failure of British public figures to make good their promises to him. For more than ten years he has been pouring his own money into plans for his "Panopticon" – a new kind of prison. Although an act of parliament authorized it in 1794, neither land nor government money have been supplied. The Panopticon is a huge circular building where the governor in the middle can see the prisoners in their cells around him. The prison will pay its way through the work of the prisoners. Years ago Bentham had been shocked by the conditions which he saw in convict hulks on the Thames, but he did not have this idea until he saw a similar building being built as an inspection house for Prince Potemkin in Russia.

Bentham was allotted land, first by Lord Spencer, in Wimbledon, and then by the dean of Westminster, in Tothill Fields. But when it came to the point neither wanted prisoners as neighbours. Bentham should not have been surprised, as he believes that men inevitably pursue pleasure and avoid pain (→ 1824).

Bentham: philosopher and reformer.

Smallpox vaccine gets financial backing for further research

London
Edward Jenner, who found that inoculating with cowpox serum prevented smallpox, has been awarded a grant of £10,000 to carry on with his work. A milkmaid in Gloucestershire first told him of the ancient belief that people who had had cowpox could not get smallpox. Jenner tested this scientifically and proved it [*see report on page 791*].

When he published his work in 1798 he was criticized by doctors, attacked by clergy and made fun of by cartoonists. None of them liked the idea of humans being given an animal disease. Within a year, however, 70 leading doctors came out in his favour. Since then over 100,000 people have had the vaccine in Britain, although a good deal of popular suspicion remains (→ 14/1/04).

Many are fearful that inoculation will multiply disease rather than fight it.

1803

Ireland, January. Thousands die when an epidemic of influenza sweeps across the country.

France, 20 March. Napoleon Bonaparte declares that Britain has breached the terms of the Treaty of Amiens (→ 5/1803).

Paris, May. Lord Charles Whitworth, the British ambassador, is recalled to London as Anglo-French relations break down (→ 18).

Westminster, 17 May. Parliament, with the backing of King George III, declares war on France and its ruler, Bonaparte.→

Dublin, 23 July. Nationalists under Robert Emmet kill Lord Kilwarden, the lord chief justice, and attack the castle (→ 27).

Maidstone, Kent, 2 August. Residents hold a meeting to discuss the possibility of a French invasion and what action they should take about it (→ 5/1804).

India, 14 September. General Lake and his British troops, having defeated the Marathas, take control of Delhi (→ 23).

India, 23 September. Major-General Arthur Wellesley leads the British troops to victory over the Marathas in a battle at Assaye.

Co Down, 21 October. Thomas Russell, a former leader of the United Irishmen, is executed at Downpatrick after being found guilty of high treason.

West Indies. British troops reoccupy St Lucia, Tobago, Demerara and Essequibo following the outbreak of war with France.

Scotland. Construction work begins on the Caledonian canal which, it is planned, will link east and west Scotland.→

London. The first issue of *The Globe* newspaper is printed.

London. J M W Turner, the 28-year-old English painter, who has just completed his latest work, *Calais Pier*, is elected to the Royal Academy; he is the youngest painter to be accepted by it.→

Britain. The army adopts the use of Henry Shrapnel's shell which he invented in 1794.

Edinburgh. Henry Raeburn, the celebrated Scottish portrait painter, completes *The MacNab*, one of his rugged masculine-style portraits.

Bonaparte violates all peace treaty terms and Britain then declares war on France

Bonaparte, about to make a meal of Britain, sees the writing on the wall.

Britain, 17 May

Britain has declared war on France, shattering the Treaty of Amiens signed last year. Renewed fighting was inevitable as the treaty's terms, heavily weighted from the start in France's favour, have been constantly violated by Napoleon Bonaparte in the last few months.

Piedmont and Elba have been annexed, Switzerland occupied, and Dutch ports closed to British trade. Although the prime minister, Lord Addington, was vilified at home for conceding too much in the treaty, it is now clear that he never regarded it as a final solution but only as a truce to gain time.

In the meantime he has placed a war-weary nation in a stronger position by building up stores and timber to remobilize the Royal Navy, and the regular army and militia are better disciplined and more efficient following reforms introduced by the duke of York. Addington will be attempting to blockade France, smash its commerce at sea and retake colonies recently returned to it (→ 2/8).

MPs are divided as Britain goes to war

Westminster, May

As Britain embarks on a war, parliament is seriously divided. Even in peace Lord Addington, the prime minister, had been under fire. Now that war has been declared there are two camps in opposition to the prime minister: some MPs favour attempting to prolong the peace, and others urge an all-out war, unlike the defensive campaign envisaged by Addington. There is also the former prime minister, William Pitt, who would like to be running the war himself and with whom Addington finds himself at odds over finance (→ 10/5/04).

Addington defends his position.

Over 3,000 volunteer for active war service under new army act

Put your best foot forward: Gillray's view of "John Bull going to the wars".

Britain

Thirty thousand men have volunteered to serve as soldiers this year following the introduction of the Army of Reserve Act by the prime minister, Lord Addington, who is concerned about the shortfall in army recruitment in the face of a possible invasion by the French. More than half of the new volunteers quickly accepted transfer to the regular army.

Addington was attempting to remedy mistakes made by the earlier revival of the Volunteers, independent bodies operating outside the militia or the regular army. Many volunteered then, but their companies were provided with no proper arms or instructors, and expense allowances were minimal.

Income tax returns under 'war budget'

Westminster
Income tax has been reintroduced this year as part of a "war budget" designed to raise funds. The tax, first introduced by William Pitt in 1799, was dropped last year as part of other financial reforms. But now the tax is back at one shilling [12d – 5p] in the pound on incomes above £150 a year – compared with 2d in the pound on those above £60 a year previously. Simpler methods of collection are expected to raise £4.5 million a year, compared with £6 million at the previous levels (→ 5/1803).

Telford plots new links for highlands

Scotland
Following an exhaustive survey of communications in the highlands by Thomas Telford, the government has announced plans to make far-reaching improvements. Commissioners for roads are to be established with funds allocated to major capital projects, including a canal from Inverness to Fort William. Telford is to be chief engineer for the commission. He was born in Dumfriesshire in 1757 and began work as a stone-mason. He built canals in England and Wales before returning to Scotland with a reputation as Britain's leading engineer.

Rebel rouser Emmet leads Irish revolt

'United Irishmen' attack Dublin Castle

Dublin, 27 July
Robert Emmet, the brother of Thomas Emmet, one of the leaders of the 1798 rebellion, has attempted to stage another rising and to issue a proclamation of a "provisional government of the Irish Republic". His attempt has ended in ignominious failure. Emmet has gone into hiding, and his confused and frightened followers have murdered Lord Kilwarden and his son-in-law.

The ill-judged rising arose out of a belief that, once again, help would be forthcoming from France. Encouraged by the optimism of the United Irishmen returning from France, Emmet and his followers decided first to capture Dublin Castle and hope that the rest of the country would follow.

But the arrangements and instructions for the distribution of arms and for the management of the rising were ineffective. Carriages failed to arrive to bring the leaders to the gates of Dublin Castle, and they were forced to march there on foot through Thomas Street. Troops were alerted, the castle gates closed, and there were brief skirmishes in the streets. The rising quickly petered out, and Emmet is believed to be hiding in the hills of Co Wicklow (→ 20/9).

Emmet briefs his followers as they make preparations for the coming conflict.

Rebel leader hanged after rebellion fails

Ireland, 20 September
Robert Emmet, the leader of last July's rising, has been convicted of treason. After an eloquent speech from the dock he was today hanged and decapitated. He was 25. His love affair with Sarah Curran, the daughter of the liberal barrister John Philpot Curran, caught the public imagination, and he is seen as a romantic visionary who has sacrificed himself for Irish freedom. Some 21 other rebel leaders have also been executed, most notably Thomas Russell, the charismatic "man from God-knows-where".

Emmet set out to restore the dignity which Irish republicanism had lost in the 1798 rebellion. While preparations were going ahead he wrote to his brother Thomas (exiled in Paris) that he wanted to give the attempt in Dublin "the respectability of insurrection". To this end he surrounded it with a theatrical sense of drama. The leaders wore elaborate uniforms, the weapons included sophisticated rockets and combustible planks designed to hamper troop movement, and the rebels were ordered to take prisoners and not to kill anyone.

The timing of the outbreak was ill-judged, but even the authorities have conceded that the idea of a surprise attack on the nerve-centre of British rule in Ireland showed both talent and judgement (→ 21/10).

Duke of Bridgewater, canal pioneer, dies

Pioneer of a new means of transport.

Manchester
The duke of Bridgewater, regarded as the "father" of inland waterways, has died at his home near here. His pioneering work in canal-building has played a prominent part in giving Britain the finest transport network in Europe.

Bridgewater's death comes at the same time as the first cuts made for an ambitious new canal through the counties of Inverness and Argyll – the Caledonian, which will link the North and Irish Seas via a chain of lakes. The enthusiasm for canal-building in the last 40 years follows Bridgewater's linking in 1761 of his coal mines at Worsley with Manchester (→ 1804).

"Calais Pier", the new work by the British painter J M W Turner. This year he has been elected to the Royal Academy at the age of just 28.

1804

Dublin, 14 January. The Cow-pock Institution, using Edward Jenner's newly discovered vaccine for smallpox, opens (→26/1/23).

Pennsylvania, 6 February. Joseph Priestley, the British scientist and discoverer of the gas oxygen, who was forced to emigrate to escape religious and political persecution, dies in Northumberland, aged 71.

New South Wales, 5 March. Colonists and convicts run riot at Castle Hill (→1824).

London, 7 March. The British and Foreign Bible Society is formed.

India, April. War breaks out between the East India company and the Marathan leader, Holdar (→1805).

Westminster, 10 May. William Pitt returns to office as prime minister after Henry Addington's government falls.→

Paris, 18 May. Napoleon Bonaparte is proclaimed emperor by the French senate and tribunate (→2/12).

Kent, 20 August. Prince Frederick, the duke of York, reviews over 10,000 troops garrisoned at Coxheath ready to face a French invasion of the south coast (→17/3/05).

Dublin, 4 September. The Royal College of Surgeons appoints Abraham Colles as professor of anatomy, physiology and surgery.

Atlantic Ocean, October. Captain Moore's *Indefatigable* and three other British frigates attack and seize a Spanish treasure convoy bound for Cadiz from the Americas (→12/1804).

Paris, 2 December. Napoleon is consecrated emperor by Pope Pius VII.

Spain, December. Anglo-Spanish relations deteriorate following British attacks on Spanish shipping; Spain declares war on Britain.

Kent/East Sussex. Construction work begins on the Royal Military Canal; it will stretch from Hythe westwards to Pett as part of the defence system against invasion (→1822).

London. The first savings bank in Britain opens in Tottenham.

London. George Morland, the English painter who was best known for his rustic paintings and bouts of heavy drinking, has died.

Episcopalian Church unites after hundred years of separation

Edinburgh

After more than a hundred years of division, the two main factions in the Episcopalian Church of Scotland have been reunited. The Jacobite "high" church – whose congregations exist mostly north of the river Tay – is to share the same form of worship as the "qualified" Episcopal Church which uses the English Prayer Book.

The move ends years of persecution of the "nonjurors" – so called because of their refusal to take the oath to the reigning sovereigns – who backed the Jacobite rising in 1745. Until the death of Charles Stuart ("the Young Pretender") in 1788, when they abandoned Jacobitism and prayed for the Hanoverian king, their congregations were limited to no more than four people. The proscription on them was lifted in 1792, and the two churches slowly began to move together as the population drifted southwards.

Although the "qualified" church survived under Queen Anne's Toleration Act, its congregations were forced to "import" ministers from England and Ireland because Scottish bishops continued to support the exiled Stuarts. Based mainly in central Scotland and the borders, and especially strong among the Edinburgh middle classes, the "qualified" congregations were collectively known as the "English Congregation".

Fears of French invasion of Britain grow

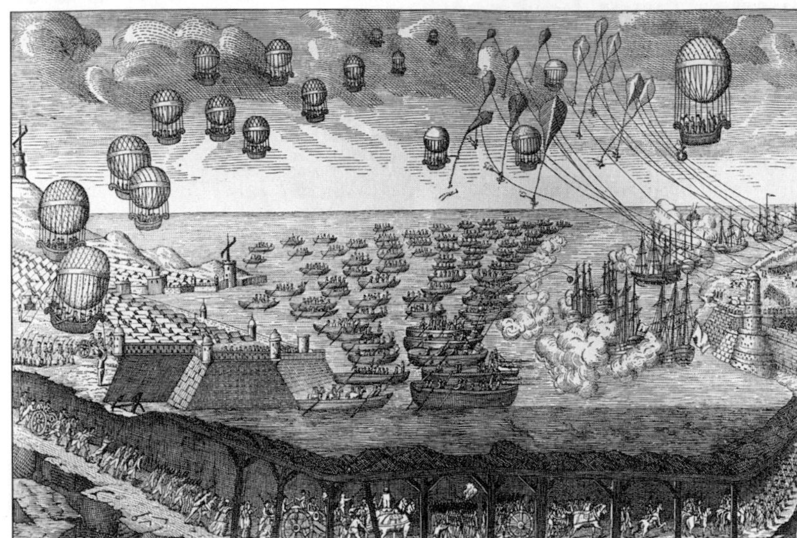

Some Britons feared that French invasion plans included a Channel tunnel.

Dover, May

An army of more than 100,000 seasoned French troops is preparing to invade England. The white tents of Napoleon's army are clearly visible from the white cliffs of Dover, and 2,000 landing craft are ready for an assault on southern England.

With the British Army cut to 52,000 men by government economies, a part-time volunteer force, 350,000 strong but untrained and armed mostly with pikes, is braced for combat. Martello towers are under hasty construction along the Kent and Sussex coast, and a defensive canal is being dug from Hythe to Pett. A chain of semaphores has been set up on hilltops to pass messages from Dover to London in two minutes. King George III, who has recently recovered from madness, is determined to lead his defending army; the queen will be sent to Worcester with the crown jewels. Napoleon is relying on the escape of his blockaded fleets from Brest and Toulon. Everything depends on the Royal Navy (→20/8).

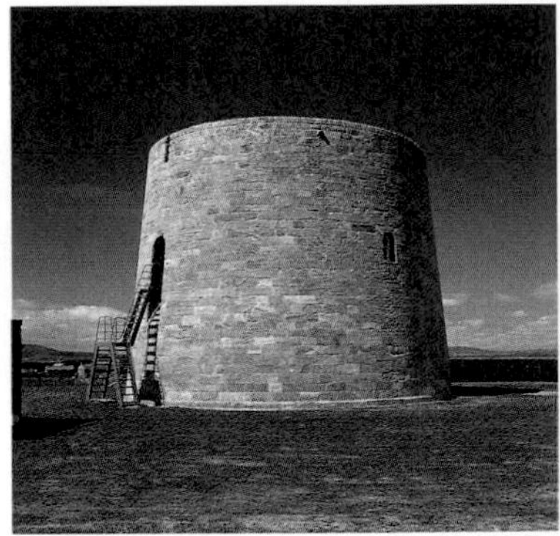

A defensive Martello tower.

Trevithick develops steam locomotive to haul goods on railway

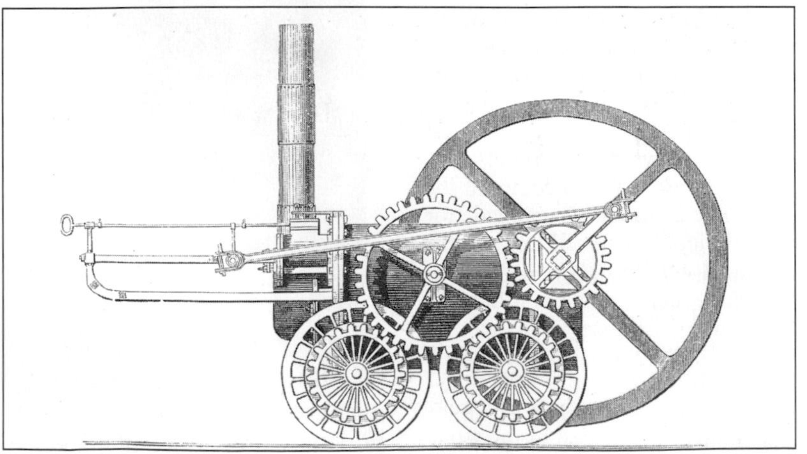

Transport breakthrough: Richard Trevithick's design for a steam locomotive.

South Wales, 21 February

History has been made by "Captain Dick's puffer", as 32-year-old Richard Trevithick's steam locomotive is known in his native Cornwall. Today it became the first steam locomotive to be employed on a permanent track railway. It carried ten tonnes of iron, 70 men, and five oak wagons some 9.5 miles (15km) at a rate of nearly five miles an hour. Trevithick is working as an engineer at Merthyr Tydfil's Pen-y-darran ironworks and is buoyed by his success. "We have also tried the carriage with 25 tons of iron," he says (→1810).

William Pitt forms new ministry after fall of Addington

Westminster, 10 May
William Pitt is prime minister again following the fall of Henry Addington, his childhood friend and the son of one of his father's doctors. Addington took office after Pitt resigned three years ago in response to George III's insistent refusal to accept Catholic emancipation [*see page 789*] – which the king regards as in conflict with his coronation oath to uphold the rights and privileges of the church of England.

The most important event during Henry Addington's administration was the conclusion of the Treaty of Amiens in 1802. Among Addington's personal services to the king was the suggestion that he should use a hop pillow during his recent attack of dementia, which gave George his first night's sleep since the start of the bout.

Pitt supported Addington for a time but refused to rejoin the government in any capacity other than prime minister. He has now returned to office on the understanding that he will abandon his campaign on behalf of Roman Catholics. In view of the resumption of the war with France, and the fear of invasion, Pitt intends to combine the most eminent men of all parties in his new ministry, including, perhaps, Charles James Fox (→ 1805).

An illumination to the poem "Jerusalem" by the prophetic writer and engraver William Blake, which appeared in 1804.

New law bans imports of foreign corn

London's Corn Exchange, where trade will be slowed by the new restrictions.

Westminster
The price of bread is certain to rise following the introduction of the latest Corn Law, which effectively bans the import of cheap grain from abroad. The government has raised the ceiling at which foreign corn can be brought in, in order that farmers can cope with the heavy taxes caused by the war. The price of home-produced wheat must now rise from the price, which was fixed in 1791, of 50 shillings a quarter [£2.50 for 12.6 kilos] to 66 shillings. The effect of this has been to raise the price of a four-pound loaf from eightpence to about a shilling, a rise likely to cause considerable hardship among the poorer classes. High corn prices have also caused a marked increase in land enclosure, with large estates prospering as the small "strip" farmers are forced to sell out at low prices.

Concern grows over child labour abuse

Manchester
Reforming politicians are becoming very concerned at the growing abuse of women and children in Lancashire cotton mills. Children of seven or even younger are expected to work as long as 18 hours a day; women work the same long hours as men – with overseers maintaining harsh discipline.

The textile industry is booming. Fortunes are being made – the inventor Richard Arkwright has earned more than £200,000 – with cotton and wool ranking as Britain's second biggest industry after agriculture. But the conditions in which many employees are forced to work – noisy, hot and damp mills, with fines for lateness, even for talking at work – are threatening serious unrest.

Two years ago parliament passed a bill which supposedly limited to 12 hours the working day of the hundreds of pauper children sent from parishes throughout Britain to provide cheap labour in the cotton mills. But no system of inspection exists (→ 1819).

Anti-slavery lobby scenting a victory

Westminster, June
Despite the rejection by the Lords of his bill to abolish the slave trade – already passed by the Commons – William Wilberforce is confident that he is close to success and that Britain will lead the world in ending this lucrative trade. With Hannah More, a fellow evangelical, Wilberforce, a convinced Tory, has fought against slavery for nearly 20 years, basing his argument on his religious belief that all God's creatures must be free.

Opponents in the powerful slave-masters' lobby contend that slaves are happy and better off than free men, and that other nations would take over British trade. The evangelicals have also been attacked by radicals who have described their campaign on behalf of slaves in other lands as "blatant hypocrisy" – when measured against what they see as the repressive policies within Britain itself (→ 13/9/05).

Four-year-olds 'work as chimney sweeps'

Westminster
Parliamentary concern is growing over the use of children as young as four, five or six years old as chimney sweeps. Last year the Society for Superseding Climbing Boys was formed to press for reform, and now parliament has before it a bill to register and license apprentices.

Yet the abuses continue. Although no child should be employed under nine years old – or for longer than eight hours a day – master chimney sweeps still seek the smallest boys to climb the tiniest flues, maybe just 17.5cm (seven inches) square. As few boys want to climb up suffocating, dark and dangerous flues, they are forced to do so by a variety of threats: beatings, having pins stuck in their feet, or by straw being set on fire at the foot of the chimney.

The boys' knees and elbows are ripped sore in the first months as, say their masters, "they learn their business". Boys have died trapped in narrow flues; they may suffer serious burns, be suffocated by soot, or catch serious diseases such as cancer. They lead inhuman lives, not even taking baths. Some of the boys are paupers. Others have been sold by their own parents, who lie about their ages (→ 1819).

Climbing boys: cruelly exploited.

1805

London, 18 January. John Moore, the archbishop of Canterbury, dies; he is to be succeeded by Charles Manners Sutton, the dean of Windsor.

London, 20 January. London docks are officially opened.

Italy, 17 March. Emperor Napoleon of France seizes Italy and proclaims himself king (→4/1805).

Europe, April. The Anglo-Russian alliance demands that Napoleon withdraw all French troops from Germany (→11).

Britain/Russia, 11 April. Britain and Russia ally against Napoleon under the Treaty of St Petersburg (→9/8).

Edinburgh, 27 May. The evangelicals in the Church of Scotland win a crucial victory over their moderate rivals in the appointment of a new professor of mathematics at Edinburgh University.

London, 4 June. The Horse Guards at Buckingham Palace troop the colour for the first time.

Europe, 9 August. The Austrian Empire joins the Anglo-Russian alliance against Napoleon (→21/10).

Prussia, 3 November. Coerced by Russia, Prussia signs the Treaty of Potsdam to join the Anglo-Russian-Austrian coalition against Napoleon (→14).

Vienna, 14 November. Napoleon and his troops enter the city (→2/12).

Portsmouth, 4 December. HMS *Victory* arrives with the body of Vice-Admiral Horatio Nelson (→26).

Austria, 26 December. The Austrian Empire, defeated at the Battle of Austerlitz, signs the Treaty of Pressburg with France, destroying the Anglo-Russian-Austrian alliance.→

Westminster. William Pitt, the prime minister, increases income tax by threepence to cover the cost of financing the wars in Europe (→23/1/06).

India. Lord Wellesley, the governor-general of Bengal, who successfully made India part of Britain's empire, is recalled (→11/1814).

Africa. The Scottish explorer and surgeon Mungo Park sets off on an expedition to the river Niger.

London. The British Institute for the Development of Fine Art is founded.

Gaelic poet praises full life for women

Ireland, May 1805
Brian Merriman, the author of a remarkable 1,000-line poem in Gaelic, *The Midnight Court*, has died in Limerick at the age of 65. His poem, whose principal glory is its vigorous use of the spoken Irish of Co Clare, has already made his reputation among lovers of Gaelic. But he has lived without recognition from his peers writing in the English tradition.

Merriman's poem is a remarkable attack on puritanism in Irish society, employing erotic imagery and arguing for the right of women to fulfil their sexual desires and to have children. The work is a classic of its kind, assuring Merriman of a permanent place in European literature. The poet, who is a teacher by profession, came from humble origins in Co Clare.

Dundas quits over navy corruption charge

Melville: now fallen from power.

London, May
Henry Dundas, Viscount Melville, for nearly 30 years the most powerful figure in Scotland, has been forced to resign pending an investigation into alleged corruption in the navy. He had become first lord of the admiralty when William Pitt returned to power last year.

Melville, who is 63, has held most of the great offices of state, but he now faces the possibility of impeachment. His career is threatened by an inquiry which revealed that he had apparently connived in speculation, using Royal Navy funds undertaken by Alexander Trotter, a fellow Scot who was the navy's paymaster.

Melville was condemned in a vote in the House of Commons and forced to resign while an investigation took place. In Scotland his fall has been greeted with disbelief. He has dominated Scottish affairs as the right-hand man of William Pitt and a ruthless manipulator of patronage. So successful were his methods that in the 1796 election his supporters were returned in 44 out of 45 seats (→29/04/06).

Clamp-down by William Pitt on slave-trading in West Indies

Slaves at work in a juice-processing plant on Antigua: a later view.

London, 13 September
The importation of slaves into the former French and Spanish colonies of the Caribbean has been abolished by an order in council. The order, by William Pitt, the prime minister, comes a year after the failure of the abolitionists to secure the passage of a parliamentary bill banning the trade.

Though dismissed by some in the anti-slavery lobby as a mere half-measure, it is expected to do irreparable damage to slave-owning interests and is seen as a major victory for William Wilberforce's 18-year campaign to end the cargo in human flesh (→25/3/07).

'Hackney monster'

Hackney, London, 28 April
William Cooper, known as "the Hackney Monster", who terrorized the women of Hackney for a year by indecently exposing himself to them, has been sentenced to two years' imprisonment in Cold Bath Fields. Cooper, a respectable married man with three children, was caught by the local gravedigger in Church Well on 11 March and put in the watch house, where his victims identified him.

The new London docks, begun in June 1802, were opened on 20 January. The whole complex, which has spacious warehouses for storing tobacco and vaults for brandy and wine, covers some 18 hectares (45 acres).

Nelson dies victorious at Trafalgar

Nelson lies stricken on the busy deck of the "Victory" after being shot by a French sniper during the battle at Trafalgar.

Trafalgar, Spain, 21 October
Vice-Admiral Lord Nelson won a crushing victory over the combined French and Spanish battle fleet off Cape Trafalgar today but was mortally wounded in the hour of victory. Calmly pacing his quarter-deck in the fury of the battle, he was easily recognized by the decorations which he insisted on wearing and was shot down by a sniper in a mast of the French battleship *Redoubtable*. Nelson, who had chased Admiral Villeneuve to the West Indies and back, finally caught up with him after he had emerged from Cadiz. As the fleets drew together Nelson made a signal from his flagship *Victory*: "England expects that every man will do his duty." The British ships, with their bands playing *Hearts of Oak*, followed Nelson's revolutionary tactics of splitting into two squadrons and sailing through the French line. The French fell into confusion, a pell-mell battle ensued, and superior British seamanship and gunnery won the day. Eighteen enemy ships have been taken, and Napoleon's sea power is destroyed, but many sailors feel that Nelson's death was too great a price to pay (→ 11/1805).

Nation mourns the loss of heroic sailor

Britain, November
The nation has been plunged into mourning by the death of Horatio, Lord Nelson. Few men have captured the popular imagination more than this slight, battle-scarred son of a Norfolk vicar. He was seasick at the start of every voyage but was an incomparable fighting sailor who won the hearts of his captains and men with his "Nelson touch". Despite the loss of an eye and an arm in battle he was immensely attractive to women and became the lover of Lady Hamilton, by whom he had a daughter, Horatia. As he died he commended them as a legacy to the country (→ 3).

Lord Nelson: a popular hero.

Napoleon claims a victory at Austerlitz

Austerlitz [Czech], 2 December
Napoleon has inflicted a shattering defeat on the Russian and Austrian armies here today. Watched by Czar Alexander and Emperor Francis, the allies were feeling confident of victory, but Napoleon and his marshals conducted the battle with consummate skill and routed them. Many drowned as they fled across frozen marshes when the ice broke under French bombardment. It seems tonight that Russia and the Austrian Empire will be driven out of the war, leaving Britain to face France alone once again (→ 4).

Round one of war brings disaster, triumph and fear

Westminster, 26 December
The year and the first stage of what threatens to be a long war against Napoleon are ending amid disaster on land and triumph at sea. The Royal Navy rules the waves following Trafalgar, and Napoleon's invasion force has marched away from its camp at Boulogne. However, the French army rules Europe following a series of brilliant battles culminating in the crushing defeat of the Russian and Austrian armies at Austerlitz.

The collapse of the Third Coalition, so carefully constructed by William Pitt, was confirmed today when Emperor Francis signed the Treaty of Pressburg surrendering the Austrian Empire's possessions in Germany and Italy and withdrawing from the war. The Russians have retired to lick their wounds, and Pitt's hopes have been wrecked.

Pitt's speeches, like bad sherry.

Elsewhere Britain is consolidating the victories won in India by a young major-general, Sir Arthur Wellesley, and has reoccupied the Cape of Good Hope. There is trouble with the US over Britain's insistence on stopping ships on the high seas to search for contraband. At home, Pitt, worn out by his endeavours, is becoming increasingly ill and may not be able to remain in office (→ 15/1/06).

1806

London, 9 January. The funeral of Vice-Admiral Lord Nelson takes place.

London, 15 January. Britain declares war on Prussia after a Franco-Prussian treaty is signed in Paris (→22/4).

Portsmouth, 1 February. The Naval Academy is renamed the Royal Naval College.

Dublin, 17 March. The foundation stone of the Royal College of Surgeons is laid.

Devon, 20 March. The foundation stone of a prison on Dartmoor is laid.

France, 22 April. Admiral Villeneuve, the commander of the fleet, dies from self-inflicted stab wounds after his release from British captivity (→16/5).

Westminster, 29 April. Henry Dundas, Viscount Melville, who was impeached last year, is cleared of charges of corruption by his peers.→

Westminster, 16 May. The cabinet orders the blockade of all European ports from Brest to the Low Countries (→4/7).

South America, June. British forces capture Buenos Aires in an unauthorized expedition following the flight of the Spanish viceroy.

Germany, 6 August. Holy Roman Emperor Francis II accepts Napoleon's ultimatum and is forced to abdicate, breaking up that empire.

Edinburgh, 11 August. Francis Jeffrey, the editor of the *Edinburgh Review*, fights a duel with a poet who was unhappy with a critical review.

London, 7 October. Ralph Wedgwood takes out a patent for "carbon paper" – it duplicates writing.

English Channel, 8 October. The Royal Navy uses rockets for the first time, to bombard Boulogne.

Britain, 22 October. Thomas Sheraton, the cabinet maker and author, dies.

Dublin, 10 November. The Hibernian Bible Society is formed.

Berlin, 21 November. Napoleon issues the Berlin Decree; the British Isles are declared to be in a state of blockade, all British goods are to be confiscated and any British subjects imprisoned, and all French ports are closed to British ships (→7/1/07).

French are ousted by British at Maida

British discipline took advantage of French impetuosity in the battle at Maida.

Southern Italy, 4 July
A British expeditionary force under Admiral Sir Sidney Smith, the victor of the siege of Acre in 1799, and General Sir John Stuart attacked and decisively defeated a numerically superior French force at Maida today. Disciplined British troops used bayonets to withstand impetuous French charges until the French were driven from the field. The objective of the expedition, which was mounted from Sicily, is to restore the queen of Naples to the possessions from which she has been driven by Napoleon's brother Joseph. Today's victory is an encouraging example of what well-trained troops can do against the all-conquering French, and it will encourage the local peasantry to rise against the invaders. However, with only 4,800 men General Stuart would not be able to withstand a serious attack by a major force of the enemy (→21/11).

Irish giants star in English fairgrounds

Ireland
Patrick Cotter (alias O'Brien), the tallest Irishman whose height has been officially recorded, has died. Measuring 2.35 metres (7 feet 10 inches), Cotter was born in Kinsale and worked as a stone-mason who could plaster the ceilings of rooms without ladders. His father sold him for £30 to a showman, who took him to England and exhibited him, calling him O'Brien and pretending that he was a descendant of Brian Boruma, the Irish high king [*see report on page 162*].

Irish giants are common enough at fairs and exhibitions, often teaming up with midgets in a double act. Their bodies are eagerly sought by anatomy schools; £500, said to be the highest figure ever paid, was given for the body of Charles Byrne, who died in 1783.

Ireland's most famous giant was Corney MacGrath, an orphan who was employed by Bishop Berkeley. The bishop, who dabbled in quack medicine, is reported to have experimented on MacGrath to see if he could increase his size. He was so successful that, at 16, the orphan was 7 feet tall.

New steam loom in Manchester revolutionizes life in factories

Manchester, 21 January
An advertisement for the sale of steam-driven powerlooms appears in the *Manchester Mercury* today. Enthusiasts for the machine say that it will revolutionize not just the cotton industry but all industry. Its detractors say that with handloom weavers' wages so low there is little incentive for manufacturers to invest in new machinery, and it will soon be forgotten.

Cotton manufacturing is now the country's biggest industry, growing at a rate of 5 per cent a year and affording "the means of subsistence of nearly a tenth part of the population of the island", according to the loom's manufacturers in Glasgow. Half the produce is exported, mostly to Europe and the Americas.

Much of the industry has already been mechanized. Cotton spinning has been utterly transformed by the invention of the water-frame, the "spinning jenny" and the "mule", although cotton weaving remained unmechanized until the Reverend Edmund Cartwright patented a steam-powered loom in 1785.

But this was only able to produce the movements of weaving; it did not do anything to mechanize the time-consuming preparations of dressing the yarn and feeding it into the loom. These problems were not solved until William Radcliffe developed a feeding machine and a dressing machine, powered from the loom, two years ago (→1811).

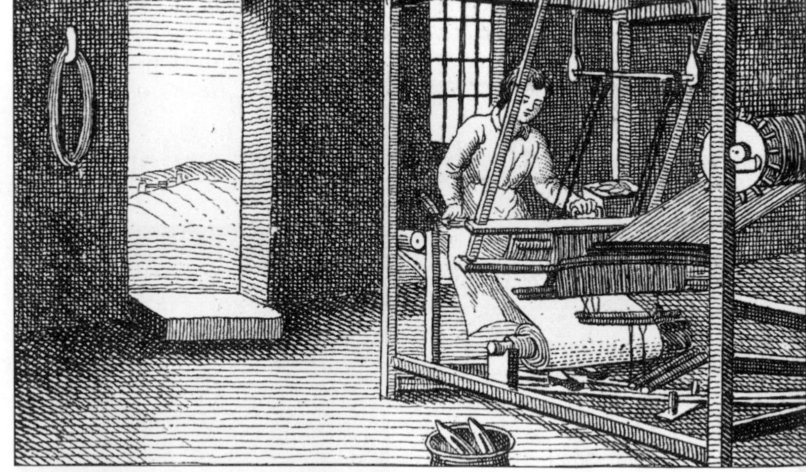

A weaver at a manual loom: but mechanization is spreading fast.

'Ministry of all talents' takes office

Grenville forms a coalition cabinet

London, 30 January
Lord Grenville has been appointed prime minister, barely a week after the death of his cousin William Pitt [*see report below*]. Grenville's government will be a coalition – a "ministry of all the talents", as it is being called – although the supporters of Pitt, who are now in opposition, are already calling it a "ministry of no talents".

The best positions go to the Foxites, with Fox himself as foreign secretary, charged with concluding peace with France, Spencer Perceval at the home office and William Windham at the war office. But Grenville controls the purse-strings, with supporters in the treasury and board of trade.

How successful the "ministry of all the talents" will be is questionable. Grenville is hardly a charismatic figure. In 1803 he wrote: "I can hardly keep wondering at my own folly in leaving my books and garden for one day in the House of Lords." Though he possesses more experience of government than anyone else, his preference, as he put it, to "rather follow than lead" suggests that it will be Fox who dominates the cabinet (→ 13/9).

Doing what he did best: Fox, the great debater, in the House of Commons.

Charles Fox, 'the greatest debater', dies

Chiswick, London, 13 September
Charles James Fox, called by Edmund Burke "the greatest debater the world ever saw", has died. Born in 1749, the son of an aristocrat, he entered parliament at the age of 19, before he was old enough to vote.

It was the American war that turned Fox into a radical. His spectacular speeches led to the downfall of Lord North in 1782, but the following year he formed a coalition with North until the rejection of the East India Bill led to his fall. Pitt took power, and so began one of the most dramatic political contests that the House of Commons has witnessed. It lasted for 23 years, 18 of them with Pitt as premier, ending last January with Pitt's death [*see below*]. Fox, wrecked by drinking and gambling, returned to office but died before concluding his two ambitions: peace with revolutionary France, and the end of the slave trade (→ 24/3/07).

Princess's private life is investigated

London, September
Caroline, the estranged wife of the prince of Wales, has *not* given birth to an illegitimate son, government commissioners have concluded. William Austin, who lives in her house at Blackheath, is her adopted rather than her natural son.

The "delicate investigation" began after Lady Douglas, one of the princess of Wales's entourage, accused her of having had a baby and of saying: "I have a bedfellow whenever I like." Though she has been acquitted of maternity, Caroline's honour is hardly intact. George III refuses to receive her.

Caroline, with daughter Charlotte.

Pitt, who held the purse-strings of Britain for many years, dies

Napoleon helps himself to Europe as he and Pitt carve the "plum pudding".

Putney, London, 23 January
William Pitt, prime minister at the age of 24 and holder of that office for 18 years, died today, broken by Napoleon's victory at Austerlitz. His last words were: "Oh, my country! How I leave my country!"

Sometimes brilliant but always arrogant, he improved criminal administration, supported (ultimately) William Wilberforce's campaign against slavery, worked towards the Act of Union with Ireland and led Britain through eight years of war with France. Yet that war showed his darker side, and the suspension of Habeas Corpus and his Seditious Meetings Act provoked the accusation from his opponents, particularly Charles Fox, that he was overly repressive (→ 30).

Dundas cleared of corruption charges

London, 29 April
Henry Dundas, Viscount Melville, has been cleared by his peers after his impeachment on corruption charges. However, the once powerful Scot has little future. Aged 64, tainted by the corruption charges and without the support of his friend William Pitt, who died in January, Melville is no longer the man he once was. He was forced to resign as first lord of the admiralty last year for allegedly conniving at the use of naval funds for speculation. In fact no money was lost, and Melville made nothing from the speculation. He has been cleared of corruption but seems unlikely to regain any influence (→ 28/5/11).

1807

London, 7 January. In response to Napoleon's Berlin Decree, made last year, the British government issues an order banning sea-borne trade to and from French-controlled ports (→ 7/7).

Dublin, 19 January. The Gaelic Society holds its first meeting.

Westminster, 26 February. Lancashire cotton workers present to parliament a petition in support of the minimum working wage.

Cork City, 20 March. The Institution for Promoting Science and Agriculture is incorporated.

Egypt, March. British troops occupy Alexandria.

Russia, 7 July. Czar Alexander, who was defeated by Napoleon at Friedland last month, signs the Treaty of Tilsit and ends Franco-Russian hostilities; this further isolates Britain and strengthens the blockade on British shipping and trade (→ 5/9).

London, 25 September. George Cayley publishes a paper on hot-air engines and the use of internal combustion engines for flight (→ 12/1809).

Denmark, 30 October. Following a British bombardment of Copenhagen in September, Denmark forms an alliance with France (→ 11/1807).

Britain, 11 November. Britain extends its port blockade in Europe to encompass Russian coastal waters (→ 22/12).

Ireland, 20 November. Two transport ships are lost off the east coast when severe gales sweep across the country, leaving many dead.

Washington, 22 December. Congress passes the Embargo Act banning all import to and export from the United States; this is in response to the French and British port blockades. Congress is enraged by an attack on the USS *Chesapeake* in which 21 people died when a Royal Navy ship, HMS *Leopard*, opened fire after the *Chesapeake* refused an order to stop (→ 4/1808).

Scotland. Clearances begin on the highland estates of the countess of Sutherland.

Ascot, Berkshire. The first Gold Cup horse-race is held.

West Africa. Sierra Leone and the Gambia become a joint British crown colony.

Slave-trading abolished

Cramped and thirsty, victims of the slave trade resign themselves to their fate.

Westminster, 25 March
Britain at last made the slave trade illegal today with the passage of the Abolition Bill despite the opposition of the West India merchants and the belief held by King George III and many Tories that slavery is a natural condition. A number of attempts to abolish the trade have been made in the past 20 years, but until today they had foundered in the House of Lords. The measure is the result of the work of a number of dedicated men.

These include Charles James Fox, who died before he could introduce the bill; Thomas Clarkson, whose revelations of the cruelty of the trade shocked the nation; and, above all, William Wilberforce, the former man of society, who devoted his political life to the abolitionist cause after his conversion to evangelical Christianity (→ 1814).

Commons opens its doors to radicals

Westminster, 26 June
Sir Francis Burdett and Thomas Cochrane take their seats in the House of Commons today in what is seen as a triumph for middle-class Radicalism. They won their seats at the general election for the Westminster constituency, which, with all its ratepayers having the vote, has moved nearer to representative democracy than most.

At first sight neither of the two men seems to have genuine revolutionary tendencies. Burdett, while the leader of the Radical movement, is an enormously rich landowner, recently wounded in a duel with another Radical candidate; Cochrane, a dashing naval officer, is heir to the earl of Dundonald.

Of the two, Cochrane is more likely to cause trouble in the house. Naturally rebellious, he intends to campaign for naval reform, blaming the admiralty for the loss of unseaworthy ships pressed into service to maintain the blockade of Europe. He plans to use the debate on King George III's speech to denounce the political corruption of both Tories and Whigs.

Portland becomes new PM as 'ministry of all the talents' falls

Westminster, 24 March
The duke of Portland has been summoned by King George III to form a new government following the collapse of Lord Grenville's "ministry of all the talents". Grenville's government, a coalition formed to prosecute the war against French following the death of Pitt, fell because of Grenville's attempts to remove some of the anomalies in the legal disabilities still placed on Roman Catholics.

At a time when the nation needs to be united to face Napoleon, it seems ridiculous to many that Catholics are permitted to hold the rank of colonel in the Irish army but cannot keep that rank when they come to England. The king agreed to ease this restriction, but when it was further proposed that all ranks in the army and navy should be open to Catholics, he refused and demanded from his ministers a written assurance that they would never again raise the matter of concessions to the Catholics. It was, of course, constitutionally impossible for ministers to give such a pledge, and so the "talents" resigned. In the meantime Portland had made it known that he was willing to serve according to the king's wishes. He is to form an entirely Tory government, and the Whigs will be in the wilderness. Portland is a dull, sick man who must sit in the House of Lords, and Spencer Perceval will lead the government in the House of Commons (→ 6/1809).

Lord Grenville's multi-talented "Broad Bottomites" are finally unseated.

Many spectators at execution crushed

London, 23 February
Thirty-two spectators were crushed to death and hundreds were injured when a crowd 45,000 strong gathered outside Newgate to watch the executions of John Holloway and Owen Haggerty panicked.

Increasing numbers, particularly in the middle classes, find public executions, with their carnival atmosphere, distasteful, and this disaster will strengthen their case. But a majority agree with the late Dr Johnson: "Executions are intended to draw spectators. If they don't, they don't answer their purpose."

'Faction fight' in Co Tipperary kills 20

Clonmel, Co Tipperary, May
In one of the worst incidents of agrarian violence, 20 people have been killed at a "faction fight" involving "Shanavests" and "Caravats" at a fair in Golden, Co Tipperary. There has been a revival of rural protest movements since the turn of the century, especially in Munster. And while they are all loosely termed "whiteboys", they are categorized, often according to locality, as "Threshers" or "Ribbonmen", Shanavests or Caravats. There are believed to be several thousand activists spread across several counties in Munster. Protesting against rents and tithes, they impose a reign of terror, often mutilating animals as well as people.

With hats trimmed with ribands and ostrich plumes, two ladies of fashion enjoy a morning ride.

British fleet strikes back

English Channel, November
The "Continental System", Napoleon's blockade of British goods, is causing such damage to Britain's export trade that the government has decided to reply in kind. Until now the navy has intercepted contraband goods destined for enemy ports and disrupted coastal traffic between those ports. Now far more stringent measures are to be adopted under an order in council passed this month.

The order states that all harbours from which British ships are barred will be in a state of blockade; neutral traffic with these harbours will have to pass through specified British ports and pay transit duties; any direct French or French-allied trade with American or French colonial destinations is prohibited.

The purpose of these measures is to create shortages and force up prices, especially of goods such as sugar which are produced in the colonies, thus fomenting discontent with Napoleon's rule. There is no reason why this plan should not work, but there are dangers; American shipping interests will resent losing direct access to Europe and will object to the navy searching American ships on the high seas, and it will be difficult for the navy, already hard-pressed, to find the men and vessels to maintain a ring of warships round Europe (→11).

Militia Transfer Bill increases army size

London, April
Lord Castlereagh, reappointed as secretary for war under the new Portland administration, has taken swift measures to increase the strength of the British army. He has secured the passage of the Militia Transfer Bill by which militiamen may volunteer for transfers to regular regiments for a bounty of £10. This has provided nearly 30,000 extra men for the army but virtually destroyed the militia – not so serious a matter as it might have been before Napoleon's threat to invade was itself destroyed at Trafalgar.

Copenhagen under fire from British

Copenhagen, 5 September
After three days of bombardment, the governor of Copenhagen surrendered tonight to Admiral James Gambier, commanding the British expeditionary force. Gambier had ordered the Danes to hand over their fleet, to prevent it from falling into Napoleon's hands. When the Danes refused, the bombardment began. British sailors are now preparing 18 Danish battleships and filling 90 transports with naval stores to sail to England (→30/10).

Reinforcements are sent to trouble spots in the Mediterranean

London, August
The increase in size of the British army, brought about by encouraging militiamen to join regiments of the line [*see top right*], has enabled a striking force for overseas operations to be raised. Reinforcements have been sent to bolster the garrison of Sicily, and Sir John Moore has been ordered to Gibraltar with 7,000 men, who are intended to constitute a mobile reserve.

Following his military experience in the American War of Independence, Sir John has raised and trained the Light Division, unique for its combination of discipline and initiative. It is expected that adequate replacements for home defence will be found from Lord Castlereagh's recent reforms of the Volunteers.

The Rock of Gibraltar: one of two overseas bases for British strike forces.

1808 - 1809

France, April 1808. The British raid French ships near Rochefort, destroying four and damaging seven (→5/1808).

London, May 1808. Spanish envoys seek British aid against Napoleon's plan to put his brother on the throne (→20/7).

Spain, 20 July 1808. British troops land in Corunna to support the newly made Anglo-Spanish alliance (→1/8).

Lisbon, 1 August 1808. British troops, led by Sir Arthur Wellesley, arrive (→21).

London, 20 September 1808. Covent Garden theatre is destroyed in a fire.

London, 26 January 1809. Frederick, the duke of York and commander of the British Army, goes on trial on a corruption charge involving army funds (→18/3).

Belfast, 7 March 1809. The Belfast Harp Society is founded to teach blind children to play the harp.

Persia [Iran], 12 March 1809. An Anglo-Persian treaty forces the French to withdraw from the country(→22/4).

Portugal, 22 April 1809. Wellesley returns as commander-in-chief of the British Army after the duke of York's resignation (→12/5).

India, April 1809. Britain signs the Treaty of Amritsar; Britain will control east India, and Ranjit Singh, the Sikh ruler, will control the west.

Portugal, 12 May 1809. Wellesley defeats the French at Oporto (→28/7).

Glasgow, June 1809. A General Association of Operative Weavers is formed to campaign for better wages.

Dodecanese, September 1809. British troops occupy the islands to safeguard Turkey from French attack (→22/12).

Ireland, November 1809. The Sunday School Society is formed.

Low Countries, 22 December 1809. British troops evacuate Walcheren island; a landing had been staged as a diversion, but the defeat of the Austrians at Wagram in July left the British isolated (→5/2/10).

North Yorkshire, 31 December 1809. George Cayley, an aeronautical researcher, builds and test flies an unmanned full-size glider at Scarborough (→1/1/34).

Irish MP fails to win royal veto on church

Westminster, 25 May 1808
A proposal guaranteeing King George III a veto on the appointment of Roman Catholic bishops in Ireland was presented to the House of Commons today by Henry Grattan, the member of parliament for Dublin. It was part of an attempt to win the support of the British government for wider rights for Irish Catholics. But although the measure was suppoorted by the bulk of the Irish members of parliament in Westminster, and was widely backed by members of the opposition, it was heavily defeated.

The veto scheme – first proposed in 1800 – is supported by leading members of the Catholic Association but is the source of some controversy in Ireland.

The statesman Henry Grattan.

Huge areas of land enclosed in Wales

Wales, 1808
Soaring food prices arising from a run of bad harvests have prompted a large-scale enclosure movement all over England and Wales, but especially in Wales. Strip-farming, widespread here until this year, has virtually disappeared, and the gathering up of arable land into a very few Anglo-Welsh hands is proceeding apace. Even before the outbreak of war in 1793, which stopped all imports, home production of corn was barely sufficient for the ever-growing demand. But poor harvests almost every year since 1795 have given the government reason to fear that there will always be unavoidable starvation.

Dalton elaborates chemical philosophy

Manchester, May 1808
The Cumberland-born son of a Quaker weaver, John Dalton, who has become one of Britain's leading scientists, has revived the "atomic theory of matter" known to the ancient Greeks and used it to devise a novel table of atomic weights.

In his new book, *New System of Chemical Philosophy*, Dalton says: "Chemical analysis and synthesis go no further than the separation of particles from one another and their reunion." No new creation or destruction of matter is possible. Dalton explains how the relative weights of different particles, and combinations of particles, can be ascertained. His book includes a table of elements, from hydrogen, through oxygen, soda, iron and gold, to mercury, each identified by a symbol.

Dalton's own inability to see the colour red led him to investigate the nature of colour-blindness. He lectured in Manchester in 1794, when he was 28 years old, on "Extraordinary Facts Relating to the Vision of Colours, with Observations".

British forces move into Macao colony

South China, 1808
Napoleon's take-over of Spain, and then, at the end of last year, his move into Portugal, have given the British the chance to deliver another blow at the French economy. The Royal Navy has occupied the Portuguese colony of Macao, which is the chief centre for Chinese trade with Europe. The navy's task is to enforce a world-wide embargo on trade with both France and French-occupied Europe.

Navy ships enforce slave-trading laws

Freetown, Sierra Leone, 1808
The Royal Navy has deployed a squadron of six ships to patrol 3,000 miles (4,800km) of the West African coastline and seize ships carrying Negro slaves to the Americas. An act of parliament which came into effect last year prohibits British citizens from slave-trading. Freed slaves are brought to Freetown and given small plots of land to cultivate. The settlement was pioneered by Granville Sharp, the grandson of an archbishop of York, who saw it as a haven for the 15,000 Negroes living in poverty in London after being brought by their masters from the Americas.

With all aboard for the round trip, the train moves off at Richard Trevithick's Euston Square railroad, as illustrated by Thomas Rowlandson.

Cotton workers ask for higher wages

Feeling fleeced by France's war?

Westminster, 19 February 1808
A petition signed by 100,000 cotton weavers in Lancashire has been presented in the House of Commons in a bid to persuade the government to impose statutory minimum wage levels on the industry, which has been badly hit by Napoleon's trade war. Spencer Perceval, the chancellor of the exchequer, is sympathetic but says that parliament can legislate only if there is broad agreement among employers. This seems unlikely; a minimum wage, they argue, would drive many small firms out of business.

First newspaper war reporter appointed

Corunna, Spain, 13 October 1808
The first war correspondent of *The Times*, and the first ever appointed by any newspaper, Henry Crabb Robinson – "Old Crabby" to his colleagues – arrived in Corunna a few weeks ago and was on hand today to report the arrival of a British expeditionary force commanded by Sir David Baird. Baird's orders are to join up with Sir John Moore coming up from Lisbon. But Old Crabby is not impressed. He reports grimly on "the utter want of all preparation for promoting the march of the army", and he notes great waste, mismanagement and dishonesty (→25/8/19).

Britain embroiled in Peninsular War

Wellesley storms to victory at Vimeiro

Lisbon, 21 August 1808
In his first battle since landing here in Portugal, Sir Arthur Wellesley, known as "the sepoy general" for his India campaigns, for which he was knighted in 1804, has destroyed the Napoleonic myth of invincibility by crushing a French force commanded by General Junot. But Wellesley's triumph has been short-lived; two bumbling senior generals, Sir Harry Burrard and Sir Hew Dalrymple, cronies of the duke of York, the commander of the British Army, have arrived and agreed that the vanquished French can withdraw [*see right*].

British ships have been making use of Portuguese ports to defeat the French trade war. Intervention in the Iberian peninsula became imperative when Napoleon occupied Spain and then Portugal. Wellesley landed his 12,000 men near Coimbra and, having been joined by another 5,000 from Andalusia, moved south towards Lisbon. At Vimeiro the redcoats sighted the uniforms of the French and, holding their fire until the last moment, suddenly let fly with grapeshot and muskets, crying "there goes another of Boney's invincibles". The French lost a quarter of their 13,000 men (→30).

Wellesley: "the sepoy general".

Portugal freed, but French repatriated

Portugal, 30 August 1808
France has given up the fight in Portugal, but under the Convention of Cintra agreed today the French forces are to be allowed to return home – complete with their equipment. The terms of the armistice seem certain to provoke opposition in England, coming just days after the British forces under Sir Arthur Wellesley had inflicted a crushing defeat on France at Vimeiro.

It was the scale of losses at Vimeiro that forced General Junot, the French commander, to seek today's settlement. But Wellesley had already been replaced as commander by Sir Harry Burrard who, within 24 hours, was himself superseded by Sir Hew Dalrymple, previously commander at Gibraltar. These changes weakened the command structure and precipitated the decision to allow the repatriation of French forces (→17/1/09).

Commander killed as British forces stage fighting withdrawal

Corunna, Spain, 17 January 1809
After a gruelling 250-mile (400-km) retreat over the rocks and snows of Galicia, General Sir John Moore rallied his bedraggled and demoralized forces and delivered a stunning blow at their French pursuers. Marshal Soult's troops, exhausted by their long chase and broken by an unexpected battle, withdrew in disarray. Moore was hit by grapeshot while urging his men into action, and he died later this evening while 24,000 of his 30,000 troops were busily embarking for England.

Moore had begun his campaign last October by driving north-east out of Portugal to help the Spanish to save Madrid and southern Spain from French occupation. But three Spanish armies lying between him and the French collapsed in rapid succession, and Moore received intelligence that Napoleon had arrived from France and was advancing with a force of 250,000.

It was time, Moore decided, "to make a run for it", and he turned north-west towards Corunna. Napoleon, reckoning on annihilating Moore's army with a massive pincer movement, took 42,000 men himself and entrusted a similar number to Soult. Moore, driving his men on marches of 17 hours a day, escaped, though he lost some 6,000 troops on the way. Corunna, a victory-in-defeat for the British, has put paid to Napoleon's plans to conquer the whole Iberian peninsula, and the frustrated emperor has now returned to Paris (→24/2).

Victorious in defeat, the weary British troops retreat to Corunna.

Duke of York quits as army chief after scandal is revealed

Westminster, 18 March 1809
Frederick, the duke of York and second son of King George III, has resigned as commander-in-chief of the army, a position that he has held since 1798, after a scandal that has shocked the nation.

His departure follows a parliamentary inquiry into allegations that his former mistress, the actress Mrs Mary Anne Clarke, had used her position to take money from people who wished to buy army commissions and promotions. The affair was exposed by the radical member of parliament for Okehampton, Colonel Gwylym Lloyd Wardle. Last month, in the House of Commons, Wardle demanded an investigation into rumours that Mrs Clarke had accepted money from officers, and that the duke not only knew of her activities, and agreed her list of promotions, but also shared in the proceeds.

Mrs Clarke: favours for friends.

Mrs Clarke, who was discarded by her royal lover two years ago, proved a vengeful witness at the inquiry, telling members how she used to remind the duke of her transactions by pinning notes to their bed-curtains.

By 278 votes to 196, parliament decided that the duke was not guilty of corruption, but York was so compromised that his resignation became inevitable. The affair has damaged not only him but also the king and the government.

French cede their control of Martinique

Royal Fusiliers of the 7th Foot Regiment charge French troops on Martinique.

Fort-de-France, 24 February 1809
The British returned again today to the French West Indian island of Martinique, and this time they are prepared to stay until Napoleon has been defeated in Europe. The island, which lies between the British colonies of St Lucia and Dominica, was first seized by Admiral Rodney in 1762 and given up the following year, only to be retaken in 1793 after the French Revolution erupted. It became French again when a peace treaty seemed likely. Despite its strategic significance, the island is better known as the birthplace of the Creole Empress Josephine, who married Napoleon after her husband, Viscount Beauharnais, was guillotined in 1794 (→12/3).

Covent Garden theatregoers run riot

London, 16 June 1809
When the rebuilt Covent Garden theatre opened today, the queuing crowd stormed into the auditorium, ripped out the newly installed seats and demanded the restoration of the old pit. The protesters' fury appeared to be aimed at the decision of Charles Kemble, the theatre's actor-manager, to raise the ticket price from 3/6 to 4/- [17.5 pence to 20 pence]. Yet since most people cannot afford even 3/6, the new price is not really an issue. In fact, audiences are often let in free of charge for the second half of a play's performance. What the demonstrators really want is a return to the rowdy and unruly atmosphere of the pit.

The audience expresses its displeasure with the new interior decoration.

Parliament throws out Reform Bill

Westminster, June 1809
After a desultory debate attended by fewer than one hundred MPs the Commons have thrown out a bill for parliamentary reform; the voting was 15 for it, 74 against. A leading sponsor of the bill was John Cartwright, who resigned his commission in the navy because he would not fight the American colonists. The bill called for annual parliaments, constituencies of equal size and a franchise embracing all freeholders, householders and taxpayers, with polling to take place on a single day.

The reform movement has been given impetus by the growth of the middle class. The 1807 election returned a handful of reforming politicians, some of them with City of London backing. Earlier this year a bill outlawing the sale of parliamentary seats was passed with government cooperation. Many of its supporters believed that it would reduce pressure for wider parliamentary reform (→26/9).

Lord Byron satirizes his contemporaries

London, 1809
George Gordon, the son of an eccentric captain who deserted his Scottish mother, succeeded to his great-uncle's title of Baron Byron at the age of ten. He went to Harrow and then to Cambridge, where he published a collection of juvenile verse, *Hours of Idleness*, which was savaged by critics, especially in the *Edinburgh Review*, last year. Now aged 21, Lord Byron has made a promising début as a satirist with his reply, a long poem called *English Bards and Scotch Reviewers*.

He attacks critics as men whose minds are "skilled to find, or forge a fault, with just enough of learning to misquote". Byron also condescends to his elders: "simple Wordsworth, framer of a lay as soft as evening in his favourite May" and Coleridge, Southey and Scott. He far prefers the 18th-century wit of Pope and Sheridan. The young lord, noted for his dissipation, club foot and sexual gluttony, has now left for the "grand tour" (→1817).

Wellesley adds to his war honours

Lisbon, 28 July 1809
Less than three months after his return to the Iberian Peninsula with fewer than 25,000 troops, Sir Arthur Wellesley has driven the French from Portugal and scored a second stunning victory at Talavera, on the road to Madrid, despite the incompetence and cowardice of his Spanish allies.

Wellesley, advancing north from Lisbon at the beginning of May, found that Marshal Soult had retreated across the river Douro, blown the only bridge and taken all the boats. An English captain found a Portuguese barber who led them to a fleet of barges; the British were across the river and had fortified themselves in a convent before Soult discovered what was happening, and then the French were soon in disorderly retreat. That evening, in his requisitioned villa, Wellesley sat down to the excellent meal with vintage wines that had been prepared for Soult.

A month later Wellesley was at Talavera, his men half-starved by the failure of the Spanish to keep their promise to bring up supplies. The Spanish commander, Don Gregorio de la Cuesta, who was so decrepit that he had to be held on his horse by pages, disagreed with everything that Wellesley suggested, and his troops panicked at the sound of their own gunfire. But Wellesley, with only 16,000 men and 36 guns, broke every attack by 28,000 French troops with 80 guns. In one encounter the French lost 1,300 men in 40 minutes (→9/1809).

Under Wellesley's leadership, the British won a stirring victory at Talavera.

Wellesley becomes Viscount Wellington

London, 20 August 1809
In a letter of fulsome praise written after news of the victories at Douro and Talavera last month, Lord Liverpool, the home secretary, likens Wellesley's achievements to those of the duke of Marlborough a century ago. "You have raised the British military character in the eyes of all Europe," he says, before adding: "I have just had the satisfaction of receiving directions to prepare the warrant for your creation as a viscount and a baron."

So Sir Arthur Wellesley, the fifth son of an Irish peer and known to his troops as "the long-nosed bugger", becomes, at the age of 40, Baron Douro and Viscount Wellington of Talavera.

Radical Paine dies in the United States

New York, June 1809
The radical political theorist Tom Paine has died here at the age of 72, alone and in dire poverty. He was buried at his farm at New Rochelle on the outskirts of the city; there were no dignitaries and no eulogies.

Born to a former Quaker family at Thetford in Norfolk, Paine provided the popular radical movement with both a programme and an intellectual bite that made him loved by the reformers but feared by men of property. Hounded out of England in 1774 for publicly voicing his aversion to monarchy, he fled to Philadelphia and urged the aggrieved colonists to break with Britain. "These are the times that try men's souls," he told them, and his words had a great effect.

In 1787 he returned to England where he wrote and published *The Rights of Man*, which led to his flight to France in 1792. When he returned to the United States in 1802 he was practically ostracized for his so-called atheism.

'Honest little fellow' to become premier

Westminster, 26 September 1809
Spencer Perceval – described by his friends as an "honest little fellow" – is to be the next prime minister following the collapse of the present premier, the duke of Portland, and the recent resignation of two other possible contenders, Lord Castlereagh and George Canning. Perceval, the younger son of the earl of Egmont, had won a reputation as a skilled barrister before he entered parliament for Northampton in 1796, aged 34. He was a confident speaker to a brief in court, earning 5,000 guineas a year, but at first he broke down stuttering in the House of Commons when fellow members barracked him. Nevertheless he became solicitor-general, then attorney-general and, most recently, chancellor of the exchequer. He has won the support of King George III for his intention to build a government of national unity and for his fanatical opposition to Catholic emancipation. He was a supporter of Wilberforce's anti-slavery campaign.

Lord Castlereagh, the war secretary, and George Canning, the foreign secretary, resigned this week after fighting a duel over Canning's intrigues to secure his rival's dismissal from the government. Canning was wounded in the thigh, and Castlereagh had a button shot off his lapel (→11/5/12).

Prime minister elect: Perceval.

Hannah describes the perfect wife

London, 1809
The writer Hannah More's latest novel, with the strange title *Coelebs in Search of a Wife*, has gone straight into its 12th edition, selling like hot cakes to less wealthy women. Her old-fashioned story has a renewed appeal among lower-class readers. Mrs More, once called St Hannah by Horace Walpole, upholds the traditional womanly virtues: to be devout, modest, chaste and subservient. Her ideal woman serves husband, family, church and the poor (→1833).

The saintly Hannah More.

1810

Caribbean, 5 February. A British fleet led by Lieutenant-General Sir George Beckwith and Vice-Admiral Sir Alexander Cochrane captures the island of Guadeloupe from the French (→ 9/7).

Britain, 14 February. Henry Cavendish, the scientist who discovered the properties of hydrogen and other gases, dies.

Dublin, 10 June. A commission is established to look into the state of bogs and the possibility of reclaiming land in Ireland.

Netherlands, 9 July. Napoleon incurs the wrath of the European powers with the annexation of all Dutch territories to France following the abdication of his brother, Louis Napoleon, as ruler (→ 8/1810).

Manchester, August. Napoleon's trade restrictions begin to take effect; five major businesses are declared bankrupt.

Lisbon, August. Lord Wellington is forced to retreat behind defence lines at Torres Vedras after a severe attack by French troops under Marshal Masséna (→ 10/1810).

London, 25 October. King George III celebrates the golden jubilee of his reign.

France, October. Napoleon orders the destruction of all British goods found in any European port under his control (→ 18).

London, 2 November. George III is devastated by the sudden death of his youngest and favourite daughter, Princess Amelia, at the age of just 27; the bad news causes a recurrence of the symptoms of his alarming mental and physical illness (→ 3).

Sweden, 17 November. Sweden declares war on Britain.

Indian Ocean, 3 December. Britain seizes the islands of Réunion and Mauritius from French control.

Westminster, 20 December. In view of the king's declining health and mental state, Spencer Perceval, the prime minister, introduces the Regency Bill; he bases it on the bill originally devised by William Pitt in 1788 during the king's first attack (→ 2/1811).

Strathclyde. The first railway in Scotland is opened, operating between Kilmarnock and Troon (→ 27/9/25).

Riots follow imprisonment of Radical MP

London, April

Riots have broken out, and there is widespread clamour for reform, following the imprisonment of the Radical MP Sir Francis Burdett. In an article published in William Cobbett's *Weekly Register*, Burdett protested at the Commons' action against the organizer of a Covent Garden debating society, John Gale Jones, who was jailed for contempt for daring to question the house's exclusion of strangers. The popular cry now is for both men to be released and systems of representation to be reformed.

Sir Francis is the most popular politician of the moment. Educated at Westminster and Oxford, he married Sophia Coutts, of the banking family, and became an MP in 1796. Since then he has opposed the war with France and advocated reform of parliament and of prisons, Roman Catholic emancipation and freedom of speech. Last June he made a speech urging annual parliaments, equal constituencies and a franchise embracing all freeholders, householders and taxpayers. Like John Wilkes nearly 40 years ago, Sir Francis provoked the state to penal measures and then fortified his house and arranged with the City authorities to arrest anyone who tried to lay a hand on him. But the authorities failed to stop soldiers taking him away even as his son was studying *Magna Carta*.

A rioter dies at point-blank range.

Primitive Methodists get more supporters

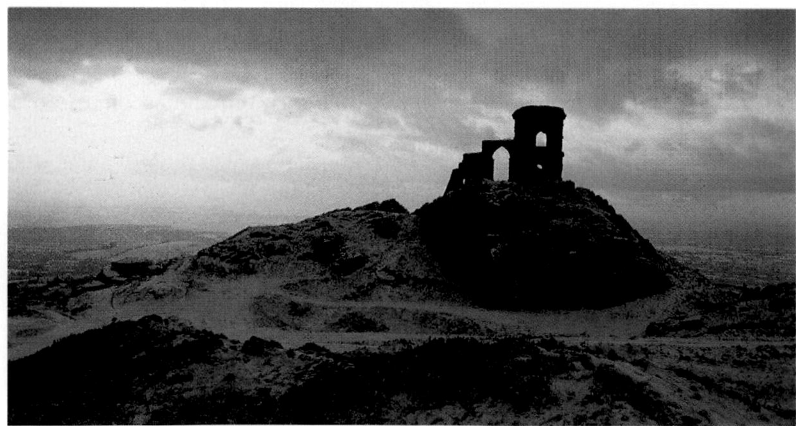

Mow Cop in Cheshire, the site of the first Primitive Methodist meeting.

English midlands

As Wesleyan Methodism becomes ever more respectable, the more evangelical members of the faith have split to form the Primitive Methodists. There have been minor splits before, like the New Connexion of 1797, but this may be more serious.

The catalyst appears to have been the arrival in Liverpool five years ago of an Irish-American revivalist called Lorenzo Dow, whose meetings proved to be hugely popular. American-style "camp meetings", which took place out of doors and lasted for a day and a half, were introduced to England by Hugh Bourne, a preacher from Stoke-on-Trent, with a meeting held on Mow Cop on 31 May 1807. The Methodist conference would have no truck with such potential subversion, and the meetings were forbidden. Bourne was expelled, followed by William Clowes with whom he has founded the Society of Primitive Methodists(→ 1811).

Scottish sheriff is a bestseller with his 'Lady of the Lake'

Edinburgh

Since he published *The Lay of the Last Minstrel* in 1805, Walter Scott has been accounted the leading poet in not only Scotland but also Britain. This "gothic" tale recited by an aged minstrel swept readers along, and some lines of it have passed into common currency:

Breathes there the man with soul so dead,
Who never to himself hath said,
This is my own, my native land!

Since then Scott, who is an advocate in Edinburgh and the sheriff of Selkirkshire, has produced more long poems, which have sold in their thousands of copies. *Marmion* is an adventure story about a scoundrel nobleman and a knight called Young Lochinvar, and it ends in the Scottish defeat at Flodden Field. Interwoven amongst the narrative are short lyrics such as:

O Woman! in our hours of ease,
Uncertain, coy and hard to please
And variable as the shade
By the light quivering aspen made;
When pain and anguish wring the brow,
A ministering angel thou!

His latest poem, *The Lady of the Lake*, has surpassed both of these in popularity, selling 20,000 copies within a year of publication. Amid descriptions of the scenery of Loch Katrine it depicts a gathering of the clans and a stag hunt (→ 7/7/14).

Walter Scott's Lady of the Lake.

Wellington's troops hold lines at Torres Vedras to stall French attack on Lisbon

Seemingly unbeatable, Wellington's troops are well dug in at Torres Vedras.

Portugal, 18 October
The combined efforts of British officers, Portugese soldiers and local militias appear to have stopped the French in their tracks. Apart from a brief engagement at the Sierra Busaco, Wellington has retreated steadily from the advancing French troops led by Marshal Masséna, scorching the land after him. But local knowledge enabled him to get to Lisbon well before the French, and at Torres Vedras his army is solidly entrenched. The outlook for Masséna is bleak. Because of the need to deploy 100,000 troops to secure supply lines, he has only 90,000 to attack Lisbon.

Numerically the two armies are well matched, but Wellington's defensive position looks impregnable. Stone walls have been built across valleys and the lines of approach flooded. The French face three defensive lines that cordon off the peninsula (→ 12/1810).

King's illness is grave

Windsor, 3 November
King George III's illness has worsened dramatically following the death yesterday of his daughter Princess Amelia. His doctors hold out so little hope of complete recovery that the political world is preparing for a regency and a possible change of government.

Even before the death of Amelia at the age of 27, Sir Henry Halford, the royal physician and friend, was so despairing of the king's condition that he called in Dr Simmons, whom George hates. Since Amelia's death the king, utterly traumatized and losing his sight, has been held in a straitjacket.

George III: held in a strait-jacket.

George III has been prone to illness since 1762, a mere two years after his accession to the throne. In the early years it was chest pains, but in 1788 the first specialist in mental illness was called in, and for a while the prince of Wales acted as regent. There was a recurrence in 1801, but this is the most serious outbreak so far, and, at 72, the king seems unlikely to recover sufficiently to resume his royal duties.

Spencer Perceval's Tory administration has been living on a knife-edge for months. After success last year at Talavera British armies have suffered reverses in both the Low Countries and Spain. Now, when at last they might be bolstered by Wellington's apparent success in Portugal [*see report left*], they have been plunged into uncertainty once more. The king has been a resolute supporter of the war, but a regency seems inevitable. The prince of Wales's friends are Whigs, who oppose the war (→ 20/12).

England resists the Napoleonic empire

Europe, December
As winter falls, the French forces encamped outside Lisbon remain blocked by the forces marshalled by Wellington [*see report above*]. Long supply lines through a devastated countryside are causing great hardship for the French army, but elsewhere in Europe the power of Napoleon has never been greater.

This year has seen the annexation of the papal states and also of Dutch lands. The emperor's codes and laws are being implemented with increasing force. France's European empire has never been more extensive, with problems only on the flanks from Russia and Britain. In addition to thwarting the French drive on Lisbon, Britain has also had some success at sea. The islands of Guadeloupe and, this month, Ceylon have been recaptured, while a naval blockade of French ports continues (→ 3).

Rural poverty intensifies as Ireland's population grows larger

Ireland
Rural Ireland is currently facing a serious economic crisis, resulting from a rapid increase in population. From about five million at the time of the union, ten years ago, it has steadily risen by almost one million. Some people have drifted to towns in search of work, but opportunities for employment in manufacturing industries are contracting. Most people still live on the land, and most also exist in conditions of dire poverty caused principally by the endless subdivision of their land.

Holdings, already too small, are continuously divided so that sons, on marriage, can have a scrap of land on which to build a mud cabin and plant potatoes. While casual labour and seasonal work at harvest time (often in England) may pay the rent and bring in a little money with which to buy food during the winter months, the potato patch remains an essential lifeline for thousands of people. Even the better-off tenants, with enough land to grow corn and raise cattle, still depend on seasonal labour to make ends meet. Many believe that the only solution to the problem lies in consolidating holdings to create viable farms, but this would involve large-scale evictions. Some landlords, meanwhile, are actively encouraging emigration to the United States or Canada as a solution to these problems.

Refugees from rural poverty find only urban chaos here in Dublin.

1811

Westminster, 10 January. Parliament is forced to introduce paper money as an economic crisis grips the country.

Spain, March. A British force, led by General Graham stops the French advance at Estramadura, near Barossa (→4/1811).

Gloucester, 5 April. Robert Raikes, the philanthropist and founder of the Sunday school movement, dies.

Portugal, April. Lord Wellington lays siege to the fortress of Almeida, the last French stronghold, and prevents Marshal Masséna, the French commander, from regaining control (→8/5).

Portugal, 8 May. Wellington defeats the French at Fuentes d'Oñoro (→6/1811).

Edinburgh, 28 May. Henry Dundas, Viscount Melville, the Scottish politician who ran his country's affairs for over three decades until his resignation in 1806, dies.

Portugal, June. The British, led by Wellington and Beresford, are forced to abandon their three-month siege of Badajoz on the arrival of French reinforcements (→8/1811).

Portugal, August. Wellington makes his plans for the British attack on Ciudad Rodrigo; British troops are positioned between the rivers Coa and Aguedao, curbing French activities on both sides (→6/4/12).

London, 6 October. The first women's county cricket match, Hampshire versus Surrey, finishes after three days' play; Hampshire are the winners (→7/1814).

Lothian, 27 November. Andrew Meikle, the Scottish agricultural engineer who invented the threshing machine in 1786, dies at his home in Dunbar.

London. *Sense and Sensibility*, a novel of two sisters with contrasting temperaments is published anonymously (→29/1/13).

London. John Nash, the architect, begins designing Regent Street (→1818).

London. John Rennie begins building Waterloo Bridge over the river Thames.

Britain. James Gillray, the renowned cartoonist, suffers a mental breakdown.

Prince becomes regent

Westminster, February
George III's insanity has prompted the government to appoint the flamboyant prince of Wales as prince regent – effectively the king of England. But under the Regency Act – which has had to be approved by a special commission because of the king's mental illness – the powers of the 49-year-old prince are severely limited.

For the next year the regent can make no long-lasting changes that George might object to if he somehow managed to recover from his illness. So the regent is restrained from granting peerages, except in reward for military services, or bestowing pensions, and he is unable to deal in the king's property.

The care of the king has been entrusted to Queen Charlotte, and her powers of appointment are to be limited to those officers who are in immediate attendance on him. The king will resume active power once the queen notifies the privy council of his recovery, but this appears to be a remote possibility.

The 73-year-old monarch, who lost his sight last year, has a history of mental illness which intensified last year after the death of his favourite child, Amelia. The Prince Regent is the complete opposite of his father. He is a man of taste and tantrums, a womanizer, and moves in Whig political circles (→20/1/17).

George: regent but restricted.

Methodist 'schism' is widened by bill

Westminster
The "great schism" between the Methodists and their fellow Anglicans has been deepened this year by the publication of a parliamentary bill to impose qualification standards for Methodist preachers. All of them, both itinerant and local, in England and Wales, would be covered by the terms of the bill, which was first tabled by the home secretary, Viscount Sidmouth, in May.

At first the bill seemed to do no more than raise the intellectual level of all preachers outside the established church. But it now looks as though the exceptionally high qualifications suggested in the bill have been designed specifically to admit respectable middle-class nonconformists into the profession while barring radical, working-class Methodists (such as Primitive Methodists) who, it is thought, are never likely to reach the same high academic standards.

Fear of open rebellion is thought to have been behind the measure, but in fact it has only boosted the growth of the independent Methodist movement (→1813).

Educational reforms made throughout the United Kingdom

British Isles
The continued development of the new industrial society in much of Britain has put the organization of education on the agenda. Vigorous attempts are now being made, particularly by the churches, to lift the clouds of ignorance from the minds of the poor. Some staunch conservatives are also in favour of new and cheap forms of teaching – as a prophylactic against revolution.

Among those pointing the way is Joseph Lancaster, who a decade ago formed an association to provide a general educational system in all parts of the country in place of the previous intermittent private efforts. He has devised a "monitorial" method by which half-trained children under the controlling eye of a master drill even younger children in the rudiments of reading, writing and arithmetic.

This system, which allows large numbers to be taught at one time and at low cost, is also being used by the Church of England's new body, the National Society. The movement to promote literacy is echoed in Scotland, although far more people there already have access to education at school or university level. In addition, "anglicization" has continued apace in Scotland. Even the Society for the Support of Gaelic Schools sees Gaelic as a stepping-stone to English, the language of industry and the lowland churches. Peasants are also learning English in rural Ireland.

A charity school teacher tries to provide even the poor with some education.

O'Connell stands up for Catholics

Dublin
A new committee called the Catholic Board has been set up to promote Irish Roman Catholic interests. Considered to be more widely representative than any of its predecessors, it is partly the inspiration of Daniel O'Connell, a rising barrister from Co Kerry.

Totally opposed to the union, O'Connell is a former member of the Catholic Committee and is a tough and aggressive campaigner. The new board is essentially a middle-class body, dominated by the progressive wing of the emancipation movement and totally opposed to the idea of a royal veto on episcopal appointments.

However, even the supporters of emancipation at Westminster still feel it wise to retain the principle of the veto (→24/5/13).

O'Connell: an advocate of reform.

Wellington poised to advance in Spain

The British Army is making relentless progress towards achieving its war aims.

Lisbon
Britain is underlining its determination to oppose French domination of continental Europe and is now locked in a major offensive to clear the Spanish peninsula of the armies of Napoleon. British troops under Wellington have cleared Portugal – although not secured it – and are now poised to begin challenging the French forces in Spain.

Wellington has shown great skill over the last two years in tying down the vastly superior French forces. He was always prepared to withdraw behind defences when it was necessary and rely on being supplied by sea by the Royal Navy. Wellington has also made use of intelligence gathered by his allies.

The French army of some 90,000 men which had forced its way into central Portugal last year began to withdraw in March, harassed by an Anglo-Portuguese force. Fighting since then has been for control of the frontier fortresses. Napoleon is referring to the Peninsular War as "the Spanish ulcer" – it is a constant irritant to him (→3/1811).

Booming population tops 12.5 million

Britain
The second official national census has shown that the population is rising at a prodigious rate. The total population of England, Wales, and Scotland is 12,552,144. In England there are 4,555,257 males and some 4,944,000 females. The population of Wales is 600,000, while that of Scotland totals 1,804,000. The first official census was held in 1801, and censuses will now take place on a regular basis, every ten years.

Towns are growing fast, especially in the new industrial areas, as factories increase in size and numbers. There is also clear evidence of a sharp decrease in infant mortality despite the attendant evils of the new factory system.

'Luddites' attack textile machinery

Nottingham
Unrest is sweeping across the midlands and the north, with rioters protesting against low wages and unemployment attributed to the use of new textile-making machinery. Those involved in destroying new machines which are displacing the old handicraft methods are called "Luddites" – followers of the mysterious and probably mythical Ned Ludd of Sherwood Forest.

The machine-wrecking is being carried out by framework knitters in the Nottinghamshire hosiery industry, by cotton weavers of south Lancashire and by cloth workers in Yorkshire. Public opinion appears to be on their side, but the Luddites have caused so much alarm that troops are being used to hunt them down, and it is now a capital offence to smash machines (→4/1812).

A "Luddite" in womanly guise.

New turnpikes give boost to road travel

Britain
With major improvements in the techniques of road-building, new highways are being built to replace the country's old horse tracks. These are making passenger transport faster and much more pleasant. At the same time the cheap, high capacity canal network is helping to fuel the new industrial system. There is also talk about the possibilities of railways moving coal from the pithead to the ports and the industrial centres. Many of the pioneer road engineers work for the turnpike trusts which control highways linking the larger towns.

Among these engineers are men such as Thomas Telford and John Macadam, the inventor of a road surface composed of a mixture of broken stones, sand and water. Telford is also being hailed for his bridges. Mail-coaches are linking the big towns at high speed. They charge twice as much as stagecoaches – but then they are going twice as fast.

Renowned for his bridges, Thomas Telford is transforming transportation.

1812

Scotland, January. Henry Bell's *Comet* is launched on the river Clyde; weighing 25 tonnes, she is the first steam-propelled ship intended for commercial use on a navigable river in Europe (→17/3/16).

Portugal, 6 April. Lord Wellington, who seized Ciudad Rodrigo from French control, takes Badajoz (→6/1812).

Sheffield, April. "Luddites", the machine-wreckers, run riot as prices and scarcity of food increase (→30/10/23).

Westminster, 8 June. Lord Liverpool resumes office as prime minister after resigning last month following a vote of no confidence.

United States, 19 June. The United States declares war on Britain (→16/8).

Spain, June. Wellington reaches Salamanca with over 40,000 troops (→24).

Europe, 24 June. Napoleon and his troops cross the river Niemen and enter Russian territory en route for Moscow (→18/7).

London, 29 June. Sarah Siddons, the celebrated actress, makes her farewell performance, as Lady Macbeth, at the Covent Garden theatre.

Lancashire, June. Four of the eight food rioters arrested last month are sentenced to death; the others are acquitted.

Europe, 18 July. Britain makes peace with Sweden and Russia by the Treaty of Orebro (→12/8).

Michigan, 16 August. British troops, led by General Isaac Brock, capture Fort Detroit (→13/10).

London, 10 October. Drury Lane theatre, which was destroyed by fire, is reopened after a massive renovation.

Canada, 13 October. American troops fail in their bid to seize Queenstown; General Brock again leads his troops to victory.→

London, 16 November. John Walter, the founder of *The Times* newspaper, dies.

Britain. The Baptist Union of Great Britain is formed.

London. Bryan Donkin establishes Britain's first canned-food factory, in Bermondsey; iron cans are coated with tin and are found to preserve the life of foods such as meat.

Premier assassinated

Stunned faces surround Perceval as he dies from an assassin's bullet.

Westminster, 11 May
The prime minister was shot dead today in the lobby of the House of Commons. Spencer Perceval was on his way to take part in a committee designed to look into the recession, when he was shot by a man who had fallen into debt. Ironically, the assassin, John Bellingham, was not in debt because of Perceval's custody of the country, but owing to his being imprisoned in Russia. Unfortunately Bellingham was an obsessive type, perhaps even a little mad, and returned from Russia convinced that the British government should make good his losses. When he failed to convince ministers, he put a pistol in his pocket and lay in wait for the unfortunate Perceval, who becomes the first British premier to be assassinated (→8/6).

London glows in a new gas-lamp haze

Evening perambulations in Pall Mall, now illuminated by the new gas lights.

London
London has become the first city in the world to have a street lit by gas lamps, and now the scheme is to be greatly extended. The first 13 lights were erected on the south side of Pall Mall, near Carlton House, in 1807. The gas came from a carbonizing iron furnace set up in two nearby houses by a German-born enthusiast, Frederick Winsor, and piped through iron pipes laid to the lamps. Now a company has been formed which plans to install gaslights in Piccadilly, Coventry Street and part of Prince's Street.

Poor feel the pinch as bread prices rise

Britain
The war, population growth and unplanned industrial development have led to a rise in food prices, particularly in the price of such basics as bread and potatoes. The result has been a series of food riots, during which mobs have attacked shops and looted them, which have have broken out all over the country. In Sheffield six men and one woman were arrested for stealing butter, in Carlisle 40 people, mostly girls, were held, and in Manchester there was rioting over the price of potatoes. The cost of corn has risen to record levels, and the situation is causing concern.

Glasgow halted by striking weavers

Strathclyde, March
A strike of weavers in Lanarkshire has highlighted a problem that has been dogging British industry for some time. Wages are fixed by local magistrates, after submissions from employers and workers, but some are set above the rate that small employers can afford. The present strike has been caused by Lanarkshire men wanting wages fixed for the entire Glasgow area, which their employers claim that they cannot afford (→3/1813).

In step with current fashion a couple take to the floor for the latest dance, known as "the waltz".

Major powers battle for supremacy in Europe

Wellington's troops seize city of Madrid

Spain, 12 August

After a year of trials, the tide of war in the Iberian Peninsula is at last swinging in favour of the British expeditionary force. Arthur Wellesley, now earl of Wellington, entered Madrid today at the head of nearly 30,000 troops. The army was greeted with wild enthusiasm by Spaniards anxious to throw off the yoke of Joseph Bonaparte, who was appointed king of Spain by his brother Napoleon.

The breakthrough came at Salamanca last month when the British engaged 40,000 French troops and beat them in only 40 minutes. Wellington said of his extraordinary victory: "Everything went as it should. There never was an army so beaten in so short a time." The result has been to put fresh heart into the Spanish guerrillas, who are operating everywhere, and to still growing criticism at home of the slow progress which had so far been made in Spain (→ 10/1812).

Wellington scores success in Spain

Spain, October

After a slow start Arthur Wellesley, now marquis of Wellington, has built up a position of enormous strength and looks certain to drive the French out of Spain altogether. His main tactic has been to tie the French down and force them to fight for a long period in one place. French armies rely on foraging for supplies, but now, unable to move, they are short of everything, including food and ammunition.

Wellington first built himself an impregnable position in Portugal by occupying Lisbon and protecting it behind fortifications known as the lines of Torres Vedras. Secure in this base, he tied down large numbers of French troops and occasionally broke out on lightning summer raids. At first his army was not good, but with fighting and training he built it into a very effective force (→ 15/6/13).

British troops storm Badajoz: another victory in the Peninsular campaign.

Napoleon faces Jack Frost's icy fingers as his troops struggle across Russia.

Grateful Spaniards cheer Wellington as he leads his troops into Madrid.

War-weary French abandon Moscow

Russia, winter

The remnants of the French Grand Army are struggling home across the frozen wastes of Russia and are already in a disastrous condition, with little food, shelter or warmth. All around them bands of mounted Cossacks rove like ravening wolves, making it impossible for a man to wander for more than 100 metres from the line of march without falling prey to them.

This means that the 100,000-strong army, encumbered by its sick, its loot and its artillery, is unable to forage for food, as its own cavalry horses have long ago been killed and eaten. Marshal Ney, in charge of the rearguard, has 800 men left out of 8,000, and more drop out by the hour. It is so cold that men frequently set fire to buildings which could have sheltered them, just for the chance to feel some warmth. Sometimes they stand so close that their clothes catch light, and they burn to death.

British forces race to Canadian victory

Canada, 13 October

British troops threw the Americans off Queenstown Heights in Upper Canada today, after they had been occupied in preparation for an attack on Fort Niagara. The British commander, Sir Isaac Brock, raced a small body of troops over eight miles and launched an immediate attack but was killed leading his men up the escarpment. His second in command, General Roger Hale Sheaffe, then arrived with the main body of troops and completed the victory that Brock had begun.

It was the third military reverse suffered by the Americans in as many months: Detroit was surrendered by Governor William Hull of Michigan without a shot being fired, and the powerful Wyandot (or Huron) Indian allies have defected to the British. This latest loss has serious implications for the Americans (→ 24/2/13).

1813

London, 29 January. *Pride and Prejudice*, believed to be written by the author of *Sense and Sensibility*, is published to great acclaim (→ 1814).

South America, 24 February. American troops sink the British ship *Peacock* off the coast of Guyana (→ 27/4).

London, February. John Hunt, the editor of the *Examiner*, and his brother, Leigh, are jailed for two years and fined £500 for libelling the Regent, whom they called "a corpulent gentleman of 50" (→ 1815).

Ohio, 9 May. American troops force the British siege of Fort Meigs to collapse (→ 27).

Ontario, 27 May. American troops take control of Lake Ontario after dislodging British troops from three forts around the lake (→ 10/9).

Europe, 15 June. The Treaty of Reichenbach seals the Anglo-Russian-Prussian alliance against Napoleon (→ 12/8).

Belfast, 12 July. Riots break out as Catholic/ Protestant tension worsens (→ 14/12/22).

Westminster, 12 August. Parliament gives a subsidy of £1,000,000 to the Austrian Empire on its decision to declare war on Napoleon (→ 10/1813).

North America, 10 September. A British fleet is sunk on Lake Erie by the US Navy (→ 25/7/14).

Britain/Austria, October. An Anglo-Austrian alliance is signed; the Austrians, in exchange for a financial subsidy, will supply 150,000 men to fight Napoleon.→

Dublin, 29 November. John Magee, the proprietor of the *Dublin Evening Post*, is jailed for two years and fined £500 for libelling the lord lieutenant of Ireland.

Europe, December. Viscount Castlereagh, the foreign secretary, negotiates within the Anglo-Prussian-Russian-Austrian alliance to ensure that any deals will not leave Britain standing alone against Napoleon (→ 12/3/14).

Britain. Augustus Frederick, the duke of Sussex, and Edward, the duke of Kent, are installed as grand masters respectively of the Premier Grand Lodge and Antients Grand Lodge; the two lodges plan to merge as the United Grand Lodge (→ 1815).

British forces are driven out of Toronto

Today's victory was one of several US successes on the Great Lakes this year, culminating in the naval triumph on Lake Erie on 10 September, shown here.

Upper Canada, 27 April
British forces have been driven out of York – or Toronto, as it is known by the Indians – but not before claiming hundreds of American casualties. As the victorious Americans under General Dearborn moved into the Upper Canadian capital, on the shores of Lake Ontario, the fort, which was still flying the British flag, blew up. As one witness described it, "the sky rained boulders", and many were killed or wounded.

The British also burnt the naval storehouse and a half-built warship, determined that no supplies or ammunition should fall into the hands of an increasingly potent American fleet (→ 9/5).

American pirates sail up the Channel

London, 14 August
The American sloop *Argus*, having captured 27 ships in a campaign of terror and piracy around the coast of Britain, has finally met its match. Confronted in the English Channel by the 18-gun sloop *Pelican*, the 16-gun *Argus* could have outrun her rival but opted to fight. Her guncrews were not equal to the task, however, and the engagement had an ignominious ending when the American ship made a vain attempt at disguise by striking her colours before she was boarded. Captain William Henry Allen, the commander of the *Argus*, had his leg shot off at the height of the battle, and he has been taken to London. He is not expected to live.

Court decisions can no longer fix wages

Westminster
The repeal of the Statute of Artificers, after 250 years, brings to an end the practice whereby wage rates are fixed by justices of the peace. The legislation was framed in 1563 alongside an obligation to work, fixed conditions of labour and apprenticeship rules – all aimed at keeping the working population in order, while safeguarding their basic welfare. The statute has declined in use, and its repeal reflects the prevailing belief in laissez-faire economics rather than any appetite for social reform.

Parliamentary veto ends Catholic Bill

Westminster, 24 May
The Catholic Relief Bill introduced by Henry Grattan has been defeated in the House of Commons by four votes, and Ireland's new chief secretary, Sir Robert Peel, is facing parliamentary confrontation on the issue of Catholic emancipation.

Grattan had put down a motion in February for a committee to consider the Catholic question, and a draft bill followed. But while members approved the idea of relief in principle, an amendment deleting the rights of Catholics to sit in parliament was passed, and Grattan withdrew the bill (→ 13/5/20).

Weavers are outmanoeuvred in legal battle to boost wage rates

Glasgow, March
Attempts by weavers here to use the law against their employers have failed. Weavers were once among the best-paid workers in the country, but wages have slumped by half since 1800. Last year a group of weavers sought to use a 1661 act enabling magistrates to set fair wages. But employers appealed to the higher courts, prompting a strike which was crushed. Now the government plans to repeal the 1661 act, making clear its own political sympathies (→ 15/9/18).

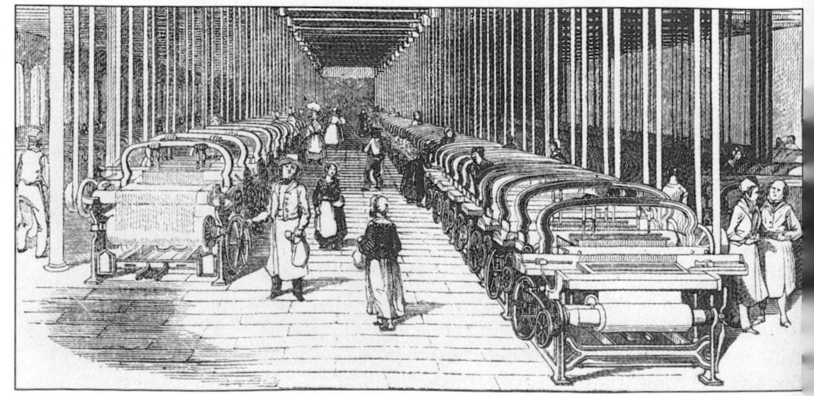

Defeated in their bid for fair pay, the Glasgow weavers return to work.

Napoleon's war-weary soldiers finally face defeat

French troops forced to retreat in Spain

Spain, July: Wellington crosses the Pyrenees to step up the Peninsular war.

Northern Spain, 8 October
The news that the French have been virtually driven from Spain has given new heart to the anti-Napoleon alliance. In St Petersburg Cathedral a *Te Deum* has even been sung for the first time in praise of a foreign army. It was celebrating two victories. At Vittoria, Wellington cornered the main French army and routed it, also capturing about five million dollars intended for the troops' wages; at Pamplona the French garrison surrendered to General Don Carlos d'Espana. The turning of the tide in Spain is the culmination of a brilliant military campaign, aided by French difficulties in maintaining supplies and communications.

Since April the French had been harassed by a 40,000-strong guerrilla army, while 50,000 Spanish troops boosted allied numbers to around 200,000. In May, Wellington set about encircling the retreating French army. A feint sent 30,000 troops in one direction while the main force of 60,000 men was moved into the mountains north of the Douro. Their escape cut off, the French had to fight (→12/1813).

Allied army blocks withdrawal to Rhine

Leipzig, October: an Austrian soldier under attack from French forces.

Germany, October
Napoleon is retreating towards the Rhine, undefeated but blocked by a growing allied army. For three days the two massive armies, whose combined strength approaches 300,000 men, have sporadically collided, with heavy casualties on both sides.

The so-called "Battle of the Nations" may have been militarily indecisive, but Napoleon has lost 40,000 men and countless deserters. His hold on Germany slipping, he may now be losing his troops' loyalty. But the allies have not had things all their own way. Russia and Prussia are uneasy allies, and Austria did its best to keep out of the war until Napoleon's aggression forced it into hostilities in August. Sweden is also on the allies' side.

In an attempt to drive the French out of Silesia and back across the Elbe, the allies met Napoleon's full force at Dresden and retreated to Bohemia. But by the middle of this month, with an army of 150,000 Austrians committed in support, the allies had forced the French back to the Elbe, while Prussia's Marshal Blücher and Sweden's Bernadotte reclaimed Silesia (→8).

Owen outlines new vision of society

Strathclyde
The community of New Lanark is the living example of the ideas outlined this year by Robert Owen in his *New View of Society*. Owen, a saddler's son from Wales, took over the management of the mill-town from his father-in-law in 1800. In New Lanark, and in his book, he espouses good labour relations which extend beyond fair wages to providing schools and houses for the welfare of his workforce. Owen argues for a well-educated society in which all strive for the common good, and no one goes hungry (→18/3/23).

Change to Toleration Act spurs spread of missionary societies

Methodist ritual: a "love feast".

Britain
The Wesleyan Methodists have become the latest denomination to set up its own missionary society. The growth in evangelical fervour has seen Baptists, Congregationalists and Anglicans all setting up such organizations. The amendment of the Toleration Act has given confidence to all religious groups to go out and spread the gospel. The Anglican Clapham Sect set up the Church Missionary Society last year, while the Scottish Unitarian Society has been founded this year.

The Baptists began the spread of missionary activity through their County Associations, the first of which was set up in Northampton in 1764. In 1792 that flourishing body sent William Carey to India to make converts. Five years later a society was started in London to spread the word to outlying villages, and this year the Baptists have created a General Union of Baptist Ministers and Churches.

Evangelical zeal has made remarkable progress, particularly in the growing industrial towns, with Sunday schools spreading all kinds of religious teaching. The Sunday School Society, founded in 1785, the Religious Tract Society (1799), the British and Foreign Bible Society (1804) and the Sunday School Union (1812) all invite Christians to work together.

1814

France, 12 March. On the abdication of Napoleon, the allies, led by the marquis of Wellington, seize Bordeaux, and ensure the restoration of the Bourbon monarchy (→28).

Paris, 28 March. Allied leaders drink a toast to King Louis XVIII of France (→20/4).

Dover, 23 April. King Louis XVIII, who has been exiled in Britain, sets sail for France to reclaim his throne (→30/5).

Edinburgh, 7 July. *Waverly*, a novel set against the background of the 1745 rising, is published anonymously to great public acclaim (→1823).

Ontario, 25 July. British and American forces clash at Lundy's Lane in one of the bloodiest battles of the war (→24/8).

Washington DC, 24 August. British troops led by General Ross storm Washington (→5/11).

Ontario, 5 November. American troops, having abandoned all attempts to seize the Niagara frontier, depart, blowing up Fort Erie (→7).

Florida, 7 November. British troops are driven out of Pensacola by American troops led by General Andrew Jackson (→23/12).

Nepal, November. Sir Francis Hastings, the governor-general of India, begins campaigning against the Gurkhas, who refuse to cede to British control (→1816).

S Carolina, 23 December. General Jackson halts a British advance on the city of New Orleans (→24).

Staffordshire. Charles Talbot, the earl of Shrewsbury, begins landscaping large private gardens at Alton Towers.

Edinburgh. A huge public meeting takes place to protest against West Indian slavery (→29/7/33).

London. Gas street lighting is installed in Piccadilly, Coventry Street and Princes Street, and in St Margaret's parish.

London. An anonymous novel, *Mansfield Park*, believed to be by the author of *Pride and Prejudice*, has a great success (→18/7/17).

New Zealand. British missionaries establish relations with the Maori natives.

London. Britain's first public art gallery opens at Dulwich.

Celebrated prophet and poet, 'the bride of the lamb', dies

London, 27 December
The religious visionary Joanna Southcott had died of brain disease following a phantom pregnancy at the age of 64. The uneducated daughter of a Devonshire farmer, she spent her early life in domestic service but in 1792 began to write prophecies in a mixture of rambling prose and rhyming doggerel.

Southcott gradually built up a following, and after the publication of her first book, *The Strange Effects of Faith*, she moved to London and in 1805 opened a chapel in Southwark where her "revelations" attracted many adherents. She declared herself to be "the bride of the lamb", and in her *Third Book of Wonders*, published in 1813, she announced that she was about to bring into the world a spiritual man, "the second Shiloh".

A cartoonist's view of the prophet.

She took to her bed last March, and six of the nine doctors who examined her said that her symptoms would indicate pregnancy in a younger woman. This news thrilled her followers and they began costly preparations for the birth, but last month she announced that she was dying and returned the gifts which had been prepared for "Shiloh". She has left a locked box which she has directed should be opened in the presence of all the bishops at some time of national crisis.

Treaty of Ghent ends Anglo-American war

British troops burn the White House during their attack on Washington.

Low Countries, 24 December
The war between Great Britain and the United States, which started in 1812 as the result of Britain's blockade of trade with Napoleon, ended at Ghent today with the signing of a treaty by which neither side gains an advantage, and which reflects the realities of the military situation.

The United States had failed in its attempt to take Canada and, despite some dashing victories by its frigates, was suffering from Britain's naval superiority which culminated in the burning of the White House. Britain, unable to enforce a complete victory and facing the threat of further hostilities in Europe, was also anxious for peace. Under the terms of the Treaty of Ghent the existing boundaries between the United States and Canada are accepted, with minor changes being referred to special commissioners. Both parties pledge to use their best endeavours to abolish the slave trade.

What is curious about the treaty is that it does not mention a single one of the original causes of the war. With the ending of the war in Europe, Britain has lifted its blockade and America's right to trade is no longer an issue. Even the question of press-ganging British seamen from American ships is not mentioned (→8/1/15).

A new steam locomotive which is the first to run with a smooth wheel on a smooth rail is now working in Wylam colliery, on Tyneside. Known as "Puffing Billy", it was designed last year by William Hedley.

Flags fly as French war finally ends

Relief as Napoleon is exiled to Elba

Paris, 20 April
Napoleon Bonaparte, once the master of Europe and commander of a fearsome military machine, today said an emotional farewell to his Guards at Fontainebleau Palace. He kissed their standard and left to board HMS *Inconstant*, bound for Elba in the Mediterranean. There he will rule 86 square miles (223 square kilometres), with just one battalion of the Imperial Guard.

His downfall has caused rejoicing throughout Europe, weary of 22 years of war. The Bourbons have been welcomed back to the throne of France, and Paris is the scene of glittering receptions. Wellington's army, having crossed into France and fought one last bloody battle to take Toulouse, is on its way home, the infantry by sea and the cavalry, to save the horses a long sea passage, by easy stages overland.

Napoleon's abdication came only after his military situation became hopeless, despite a brilliant defensive campaign against and overwhelming alliance of Britain, Austria, Russia and Prussia forged by the British foreign secretary, Viscount Castlereagh, under the Treaty of Chaumont. The end came on 31 March when the allies stormed Montmartre and occupied Paris. Napoleon refused to admit defeat but Marshal Ney, "bravest of the brave", told him: "The army will not fight." On 6 April he abdicated, and the celebrations began (→23).

How a cartoonist sees Napoleon.

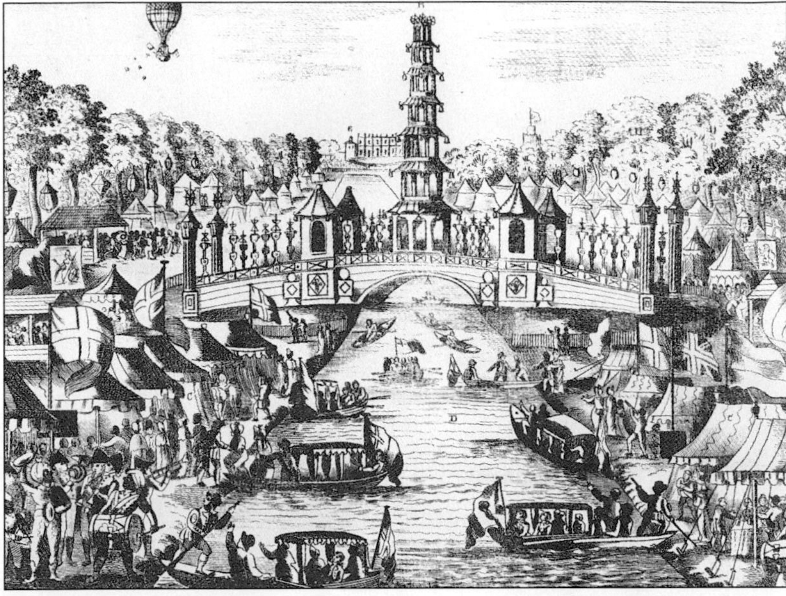

Hailing the peace: St James's Park is the focus of London's celebrations.

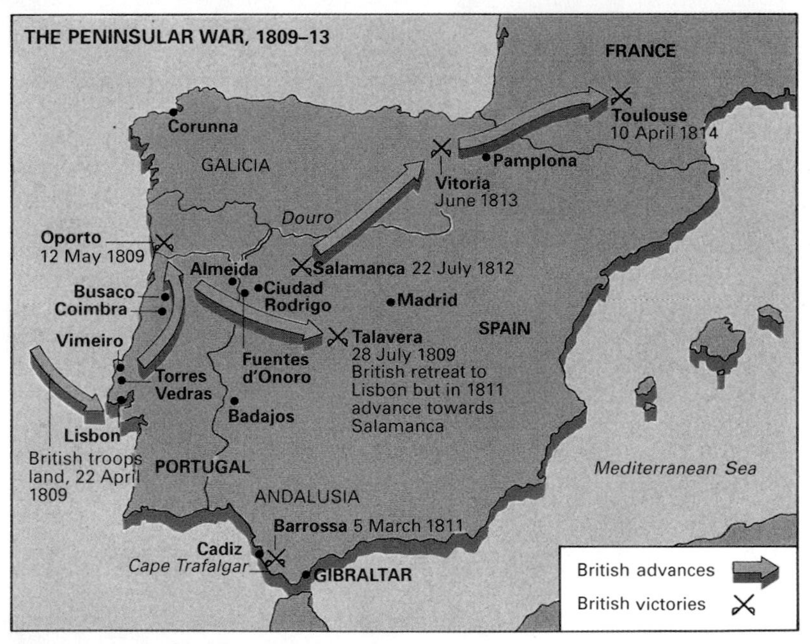

Britain signs treaty of 'perpetual peace'

Paris, 30 May
The victorious signatories of the Treaty of Chaumont, which bound Britain, Russia, Austria and Prussia into the military alliance that defeated Napoleon, have today signed the Treaty of Paris to bring "perpetual peace and friendship" between themselves and France.

The treaty is a triumph for the diplomatic skills of Talleyrand, the French foreign minister, who has not only won the return of all the French colonies captured by Britain, except for Tobago, St Lucia and Mauritius, but also placed France on equal footing with the victors as one of the arbiters of settling the boundaries of Europe.

It is proposed that this will take place at a grand congress in Vienna where all the nations of Europe will be represented. There is criticism in Britain that France is getting off lightly, but the foreign secretary, Viscount Castlereagh, believes the only lasting settlement is one seen by the French to be just (→31/12).

Three-way alliance at Vienna congress

Vienna, 31 December
The intricate diplomatic manoeuvrings at the congress here have led to a surprising triple alliance between Britain, Austria and France. The alliance arose from Castlereagh's fear that the rival territorial claims of Austria and Prussia would upset the balance of power. Talleyrand, seeing the opportunity to re-establish France's position, suggested the alliance. Castlereagh, the British foreign secretary, was hesitant, but when Prussia hinted that it would go to war with Austria over Saxony, he agreed (→3/1/15).

Thomas Lord finds new home for MCC

London, July
The Marylebone Cricket Club (MCC) is moving to a new ground just north of London in St John's Wood, where its founder, Thomas Lord, has relaid his turf. This is the third move for Lord since he opened his ground on what is now Dorset Square in 1787 and, backed by Lord Winchilsea and Charles Lennox, formed the MCC. The club has become the principal authority of a rapidly growing game, supplanting the Hambledon club in Hampshire whose Broadhalfpenny Down ground is regarded as the birthplace of the modern game (→1825).

Jesuit monks open first Irish college

Co Kildare, May
Father Peter Kenney, a Jesuit, has bought Castle Browne, a large house here, and intends to open a school to be called Clongowes Wood College. Since their first mission to Ireland in 1542 the Jesuits have had a long history of involvement in education in Ireland, and at one time they established a temporary university in Dublin.

Children of wealthy Catholics have traditionally had to travel abroad to be educated, so the idea of a good classical education being offered at home is likely to be widely welcomed.

1815

Europe, 3 January. Britain signs a defensive alliance with France and Austria against any plans Russia and Prussia may have for Poland and Saxony (→ 25/3).

Calais, France, 15 January. Emma, Lady Hamilton, the mistress of Vice-Admiral Lord Nelson, dies in poverty.→

Westminster, 16 February. A bill to enable Scottish courts to extend trial by jury to civil cases is introduced by the lord chancellor, Lord Eldon.

London, 6 March. Soldiers rescue Lord Eldon and his family when his house is attacked by a mob protesting against the Corn Bill (→ 23).

Westminster, 23 March. Parliament passes the Corn Law; it will protect grain farmers.→

Europe, 25 March. Britain, Austria, Prussia and Russia, sign a quadruple alliance against Napoleon (→ 25/5).

Dublin, 28 March. The *Thames*, a paddle steamer, becomes the first steamship to make the crossing to London carrying passengers and cargo.

Westminster, 25 May. Henry Grattan, the Irish politician, calls for the immediate resumption of war on the news of Napoleon's escape from the isle of Elba (→ 6/1815).

Westminster, 29 June. Viscount Castlereagh, the foreign secretary, proposes a public monument be erected to commemorate the Battle of Waterloo (→ 15/7).

France, 15 July. Napoleon surrenders to Captain Maitland (→ 31).

Scotland, July. An English radical, Major Cartwright, conducts a tour and stimulates interest in Hampden Clubs to agitate for political reform.

Europe, 20 November. Britain, Russia, Prussia and Austria renew their quadruple alliance (→ 15/11/18).

London. Humphry Davy, the scientist, develops the Davy Lamp, a safety lamp for miners (→ 29/5/29).

Westminster. Largely owing to the extravagance of the Prince Regent, the civil list has increased greatly this year and now amounts to £1.5 million (→ 2/5/16).

Britain. The United Grand Lodge of the freemasons issues a new *Book of Constitution* for discussion (→ 1816).

Triumphant British win at Waterloo

Wellington rallies his troops during the battle at Waterloo; it was "hard pounding" but finally a decisive victory.

Brussels, 18 June
Napoleon's army has been smashed in one of the bloodiest battles ever fought, and tonight its shattered remnants are in full flight, pursued by Marshal Blücher's Prussians, while Napoleon, his carriage captured, rides for his life.

The news of Napoleon's advance on Brussels arrived while the duke of Wellington's officers were dancing at a ball given by the duchess of Richmond on 15 June. Next day the French drove Blücher back at Ligny, splitting the allies. Marshal Ney attacked the British at Quatre Bras, and Wellington withdrew to a ridge across the Brussels road near the village of Waterloo.

It was there this morning that Napoleon and Wellington at last faced each other on the battlefield. Napoleon attacked while Wellington held the line, waiting for Blücher. Waves of French cavalry swept down on the British infantry squares. The carnage was appalling on both sides. One British regiment, the 27th of foot, lies dead in its square. "Hard pounding, gentlemen", said Wellington. It went on all day. Then Napoleon sent in the Imperial Guard; they were halted by a wall of shot and the French, horrified, cried: "La Garde recule!" At last Blücher arrived and the French broke. It was, said Wellington, "the nearest run thing you ever saw in your life" (→ 29).

Rioters rampage in London to protest against higher corn prices

Crowds protest against the Corn Law, fearing it will mean costlier bread.

Westminster, 23 March
Mobs rampaged across London today as parliament passed the controversial Corn Law prohibiting foreign imports until the home price reaches £4 for 13 kg (28lbs). The homes of several ministers came under attack. Lord Palmerston, the war minister, ordered his servants to "pepper the faces of the mob" with shot. At the home of Frederick Robinson, the sponsor of the bill in the House of Commons and the vice-president of the board of trade, three soldiers and a butler fired on the crowd, killing several people. Landlords and farmers say that imports are forcing down corn prices (→ 1838).

Jackson leads US to New Orleans victory

Louisiana, 8 January
With a ragbag force of militiamen, civilians, pirates and a few regulars, General Andrew Jackson, "Old Hickory" to his men, today smashed an attempt by 8,000 British troops to capture New Orleans. The Americans took up positions with the Mississippi on their left flank and a cypress swamp on the right, and cut down the British with a storm of musket and artillery fire. The British lost 2,000 dead and the Americans 13. In fact, the battle was unnecessary: a treaty ending the war had been signed on Christmas eve, but neither side had heard the news (→20/10/18).

O'Connell wins duel

Dublin, 1 February
Daniel O'Connell, a leading champion of Roman Catholic emancipation, has killed John D'Esterre, a Protestant and a member of Dublin corporation, in a duel. The victory has been celebrated with bonfires in the streets of Dublin.

O'Connell had criticized the corporation as being "beggarly". D'Esterre, on the verge of bankruptcy, took this a personal criticism which had to be avenged.

A new type of lamp, invented by Humphry Davy, is in use in British mines; as well as giving light, it warns of dangerous gases.

European boundaries fixed in Vienna

Vienna, June
While the foreign ministers and diplomats of the great powers have been redrawing the map of Europe, the families of the *ancien régime*, now reinstated by the defeat of Napoleon, have celebrated with an endless round of balls, banquets and romantic intrigues. After nine months of bargaining, the Congress of Vienna has agreed on a "final act" intended to secure peace in Europe for a generation and more.

The congress has been dominated by Lord Castlereagh, the British foreign secretary, and Prince Metternich of Austria, who were determined to curb the appetites of the Prussians and to keep Russia out of central Europe. They agreed that France must never again be allowed to dominate Europe; but neither must it be humiliated.

Prussia's demands for Alsace and Lorraine have been rejected, and the allied army of occupation will be restricted to north-eastern France. To create a bulwark against both France and Prussia, German states have been assembled in the Confederation of the Rhine under Austrian suzerainty.

Under the new arrangements, Prussia has gained parts of Saxony, some Rhineland provinces and a piece of Poland. Russia has kept the grand duchy of Warsaw and taken Finland from Sweden, which has been compensated by being given Norway. Castlereagh has rejected Russia's proposal to create a "holy alliance" of Christian kings (→18).

Diplomats and soldiers slice up the map of Europe at the Vienna congress.

Napoleon exiled for life to lonely island

Plymouth, 31 July
When HMS *Bellerophon* sailed into Plymouth carrying Napoleon today, the British under-secretary of state Sir Henry Bunbury, went aboard and, addressing the exiled emperor as General Bonaparte, told him that he was being removed forthwith to the remote island of St Helena in the south Atlantic; he could take with him four aides, 12 domestics and Dr O'Meara, an Irish naval surgeon, all with their wives and children. Napoleon was relieved of £4,000 in cash before being put aboard HMS *Northumberland* for the voyage (→20/11).

Napoleon on the "Bellerophon".

Nelson's mistress, Lady Hamilton, dies

Calais, France, 15 January
The beauty which captivated Lord Nelson (among others) is no more. Emma, Lady Hamilton, mistress to the naval hero and mother of his daughter, has died here, where she fled last year to avoid debts. Born in Cheshire, she had several liaisons before marrying Sir William Hamilton in 1791. Two years later she met Nelson, who defied scandal to make her his mistress. She bore Nelson's child in 1801. "My own dear wife, in my eyes and the face of heaven," wrote Nelson.

1816

Strathclyde, 1 January. Robert Owen, now sole owner of the mills at New Lanark, opens an infant school for the children of his employees.

Le Havre, France, 17 March. The *Elsie*, a 38-tonne steamboat, becomes the first steam passenger ship to cross the English Channel (→1817).

London, 2 May. Princess Charlotte, the Prince Regent's only daughter and the future heir to the throne, marries Prince Leopold of Saxe-Coburg-Saalfeld (→23/7).

Ireland, 18 May. The National Institute for the Education of Deaf and Dumb Children is founded.

London, 4 June. Vauxhall Bridge over the river Thames is opened.

London, 7 July. Richard Brinsley Sheridan, the playwright who wrote *The Rivals* and *The School for Scandal*, dies in poverty.

London, 23 July. Princess Mary, a younger and favourite sister of the Prince Regent, marries her cousin, Prince William Frederick, the duke of Gloucester.

South Atlantic, 16 August. British troops annexe and settle on Tristan da Cunha, a group of four islands.

China, 29 August. Lord Amherst, the ambassador to China, fails to negotiate a trade treaty after refusing to *kowtow* – kneel three times and knock his head on the floor as a mark of respect – to the Chinese officials.

Ireland, August. The failure of this year's potato crop, owing to excessive rain, is already causing a serious famine problem (→1817).

Ireland, 30 September. The Horticultural Society of Ireland is founded.

Ireland, October. For the last month a typhus epidemic has been spreading rapidly across the country.

Ireland, 1 November. Arthur O'Neill, the celebrated Irish harpist, has died.

Britain. The Grand Lodge of Masons agrees to a new ritual devised by the Lodge of Reconciliation (→1818).

London. *The Times* reports on an "obscene" new dance, the waltz, which was danced at Carlton House at the Prince Regent's request.

Education for the poor to be studied

Westminster, May
Thanks to the lobbying of Henry Brougham, a Scottish lawyer and Whig MP, the government is to set up a select committee on the education of the poor in London. Brougham argues that charitable funds are misapplied, and that money is not reaching the people who really need it. His concerns are with many other forms of welfare as well as education, and he believes that if something is not done quickly to help the poor there will be a revolution in the city.

Highland clearance endorsed by court

Highland, 23 April
Patrick Sellar, a worker on the huge Sutherland estates in northern Scotland, has been cleared of charges in connection with the brutal eviction of tenants. Homes in Strathnaver were burnt and two tenants of the countess of Sutherland died subsequently. But a jury of landowners took just 15 minutes to decide that Sellar was not guilty, accepting the defence's case that the causes of improvement and property rights were at stake.

Evictions or "clearances" take place because landlords want to turn tenants' land over to sheep farms (→1828).

Poverty intensifies in aftermath of war

Bringing in the harvest: the whole family works together to make a living.

Britain, 2 December
Reports from rural areas all over the country reveal that agriculture is in a far worse position than it was before the war. Many small farmers have gone bankrupt, particularly those who bought their land at high prices during the war. The new Corn Law, designed to help farming profits by restricting foreign imports, has not worked in practice.

But if the lot of the farmers leaves room for sympathy, that of the agricultural labourers is far worse. The population has risen, and thousands are starving, while hundreds of thousands are hovering near starvation levels. Wages are low even for those who have work; the price of bread is often so high that they cannot afford it.

The labourers have been hard hit by the abolition of income tax and its replacement by high taxes on staples like soap, candles, paper, sugar, beer and tobacco. Poor Law relief rates have been drastically cut. Despite this the amount paid out in poor relief this year is nearly £7 million, against some £2 million before the war. There are now calls for the reform of the Elizabethan Poor Law for parish-based relief of poverty.

Elgin's Parthenon marbles to be housed at the British Museum

London
Friezes from the Parthenon are to go on permanent display at the British Museum, despite controversy over their removal from Athens. They were brought here by Lord Elgin, a former British ambassador to the Ottoman Empire. He maintains that he had permission from the sultan to dismantle parts of the antiquities, although he originally sought permission simply to take plaster casts. A select committee of the Commons has now recommended that these Elgin "marbles" be bought for the nation at a price of £35,000, a relatively low price that reflects criticisms of Elgin for removing the treasures.

A detail of a Parthenon frieze which is destined for the British Museum.

Wales in chaos over iron industry cuts

South Wales, 28 October
Drastically reduced wage packets for more than 35,000 workers in the iron industry here have provoked mass strikes from Merthyr Tydfil to Llanelli, with violent unrest spreading over the region as far east as Newport. Troops from Brecon have been dispatched to protect the shopkeepers of Merthyr and Tredegar from rioters and looters. Falling demand for iron to make cannon, plus ever-increasing wheat prices, have brought starvation to many along the coast.

Two poets catch the public's attention

Shelley: a shining poetic star.

London, December
This year has seen the publication of work by two much talked about poets. One is Samuel Taylor Coleridge, whose long delayed fragment *Kubla Khan* and long but unfinished poem *Christabel*, begun nearly 20 years ago, have appeared. After his *Ode to Dejection* in 1802 he fell silent, though he writes as a journalist, lectures on Shakespeare and talks for hours at a time. He has long been enslaved by opium.

The second poet is Percy Bysshe Shelley, whose first major works, *Alastor* and *Queen Mab*, proved so radical that they were prosecuted. The 24-year-old poet, sent down from Oxford for a pamphlet on atheism, eloped with Mary Godwin, who bore him a son this year, while his forsaken wife Harriet drowned herself in the Serpentine.

Reform rally erupts in mob violence

Rousing the masses: a cartoon view of the calls for reform, and the confusion, at the Spa Fields protest meeting.

London, 2 December
A large protest meeting in Spa Fields, Islington, today erupted into violence. The angry crowd surged down to Clerkenwell where it broke into a gunsmith's shop. It marched on to the City, but the looting had hardly started when a force assembled by the lord mayor dispersed it. A few of the rioters were carrying the tricolour flag and a revolutionary cap on top of a pike, but most of the crowd seemed more bent on looting. At the meeting in Spa Fields, too, there was a confusion of aims.

The meeting was called by the followers of Thomas Spence, who advocates radical land reforms. The main speaker was that fiery orator, Henry Hunt. But he refused to talk about land reform and instead put the case for lower taxes and parliamentary reform. A rival meeting then started, with speakers putting Spence's views, and some hotheads shouted revolutionary slogans. Few were bent on revolution, but there is widespread discontent. It runs through London's relatively well-off artisans and extends to industrial workers all over the country. Anger with high taxes, cuts in Poor Law payments, the Corn Law and the factory system is rising.

One clear sign of the discontent is the success of *The Political Register*, published by the radical William Cobbett. Cobbett brought out a cheap twopenny edition this year, and it has already sold no fewer than 60,000 copies (→28/1/17).

Lord Exmouth meets Omar Pasha in August to discuss the activities of pirates operating from the North African, or Barbary, coast.

British troops end the Gurkha war

Kathmandu
British forces under Sir David Ochterlony have finally crushed the Gurkhas in a fierce battle in the Kathmandu valley. It has taken nearly three years to defeat these mountain fighters. They had been terrorizing Indian villages from Darjeeling to Simla and taking East India company revenues. Police forts were set up at strategic points in the country, but it took four divisions, moving simultaneously through four mountain passes, to force the first Gurkha surrender last year. Sir David has now defeated the main army (→2/6/18).

1817

Windsor, 20 January. King George III's mental and physical health has not improved as hoped; he now fails to recognize his wife, Queen Charlotte (→ 29/1/20).

Scotland, January. The first issue of *The Scotsman*, a daily newspaper which will give a voice to the Whigs, is published.

Westminster, 1 March. Parliament suspends *habeas corpus* as fears grow of unrest and riotous behaviour across the country (→ 10).

Manchester, 10 March. A delegation of spinners and weavers sets off to march to London to present its grievances to the Prince Regent (→ 11).

Edinburgh, 1 April. William Blackwood, the antiquarian and bookseller, begins publication of his *Magazine*, a Tory periodical in opposition to the Whig *Edinburgh Review*.

London, 18 June. Waterloo Bridge over the river Thames is opened on the anniversary of the Battle of Waterloo.

Britain, 5 July. Gold sovereigns are issued as coins.

Westminster, 11 July. Parliament passes an act to provide for the establishment of asylums for the lunatic poor in Ireland.

Co Cork, July. The first total abstinence society is formed, in Skibbereen, by Jeffrey Sedwards.

Esher, Surrey, 5 November. Princess Charlotte gives birth to a stillborn son, after a painful 50-hour labour (→ 6).

Cheshire. The *Etna* becomes the first steam ferryboat to go into service between Tranmere and Liverpool; the journey takes ten minutes (→ 20/6/19).

Britain. The romantic poet John Keats publishes his first anthology of poems (→ 1818).

London. James Parkinson, a surgeon, gives his name to the nervous disorder more commonly known as "the shaking palsy".

Britain. Lord Byron publishes his poem *Manfred* (→ 17/4/24).

London. Brixton prison is the first to use the treadmill punishment machine devised by William Cubitt of Ipswich.

Britain. Samuel Taylor Coleridge, the poet, publishes a book of autobiography and literary criticism, *Biographica Literaria*.

Attack on Prince Regent in his coach

London, 28 January
Nationwide discontent came to a violent climax today when a demonstrator threw a stone at the Prince Regent as he made his way to parliament. The prince was unhurt, but the cabinet immediately went into emergency session, with some members, mindful of recent events in France, demanding draconian laws to stamp on any working-class uprising.

The incident followed months of protest and rioting in almost every English county against the high price of bread – which has brought thousands close to starvation, particularly in northern and eastern counties. The post-war boom was short-lived, and now the country is in recession after a dramatic fall in textile exports. The growing number of unemployed has been swollen by 400,000 demobilized servicemen, and even those in work have had their wages cut by nearly a half.

Faced by small forces of special constables or local yeomanry, protesters are turning to rick-burning and the breaking of machines – under the constant threat of hanging or transportation (→ 1/3).

'Bribe' charge ends Scots sedition trials

Edinburgh, 19 July
The government and the judiciary in Scotland have been made to look both foolish and corrupt following a series of trials which resulted from allegations of a conspiracy in Glasgow. The claims were made in February by Alexander Maconochie, the lord advocate, and helped to trigger the suspension of *habeas corpus*. Trials of the alleged conspirators, who were said to have taken blood-curdling oaths of sedition, began in March.

The first case resulted in two convictions, but lenient sentences were seen as an embarrassment for the government. Other cases resulted not only in acquittals but also in the revelation that one prosecution witness had been offered a bribe by the lord advocate in order to give evidence, causing the latest case to collapse today.

Strict laws passed against public disorder

Liberty Suspended: a hard-hitting 1817 illustration by George Cruikshank.

Westminster, 11 March
The government has wasted no time in implementing the stern measures passed last month to quell alleged revolutionary movements. These followed claims by Alexander Maconochie, the Scottish lord advocate, of a radical conspiracy in Glasgow and similar allegations by paid informers. As a result the Commons have voted to suspend *Habeas Corpus* and have passed acts, rushed through parliament in a week, against holding seditious meetings or attempting to weaken the loyalty of troops.

Even peaceful demonstrations can now be stopped by troops, as the authorities have made clear. One group of spinners and weavers, known as the "blanketeers" because of the blankets that they carried, set out to march to London to petition the Prince Regent but was stopped by troops at Stockport today, and the leaders were arrested (→ 1818).

Corpulent Prince Regent is little loved

London
In the six years since he became regent, George Augustus Frederick has done little to endear himself to the British public; on the contrary, his low level of morality has made him something of a laughing stock with middle-class society, and his self-indulgence – at a time when thousands are close to starvation – has angered radicals.

At the age of 56, the prince is indeed the "corpulent gentleman" described by Leigh Hunt, who served two years in prison for libelling George and became a literary hero in the process. The prince's dissipated lifestyle and affairs, his secret marriage to Mrs Fitzherbert and his disastrous official marriage to Caroline of Brunswick have all taken their physical toll. But George is also an intelligent and cultured man who has been a patron of the arts and sciences, supporting the composer Haydn, the architects Holland and Nash, the novelists Austen and Scott and the scientists Davy and Herschel (→ 5/11).

The prince – by James Gillray.

Author of 'Pride and Prejudice' dies at the age of 42

Winchester, 18 July
Jane Austen, whose sparing output has made her a novelist esteemed by the connoisseur, died today of Addison's Disease at the early age of 42. Her work has been published anonymously to date, beginning with *Sense and Sensibility* in 1812.

She saw herself as a miniaturist who worked on "a little bit (two inches wide) of ivory with so fine a brush as produces little effect after much labour". In this she underestimated herself for her admirers included the Prince Regent, who asked for a dedication, and Sir Walter Scott, who praised *Emma* for presenting "instead of an imaginary world, a striking representation of that which is daily taking place around the reader".

Jane Austen: miniaturist in prose.

Miss Austen, the daughter of a Hampshire country parson, travelled no farther afield than to Bath, which she disliked as noisy. She never married. But these were not limitations, for she declared that "three or four families in a country village is the very thing to work on". It is her observation of human frailty, which she treats with irony and delicate sarcasm, that delights her readers. *Pride and Prejudice* made her name in 1813, though it was rejected when first written years earlier. *Mansfield Park* came out in 1814, *Emma* in 1815, and it is understood that she left two more novels completed (→ 1818).

Large-scale emigration from Ireland as potato famine kills thousands of people

A familiar sight in Ireland: a funeral in a land racked by famine.

Ireland
Poverty and food shortages caused by two bad harvests, resulting in near-famine conditions, have led to a steady rise in Irish emigration. Ireland did well during the Napoleonic Wars by providing large-scale labour-intensive grain tillage, requiring a large workforce. But with the war over and agricultural prices dropping, it is becoming more profitable to keep livestock. The increasing population – up from just over 5 million at the turn of the century to around 6.5 million today – now faces decreasing job opportunities. Traditionally the Irish have gone to North America, although numbers have been low. By 1795 there were only 44,000 Irish-born people living in the United States.

Shipowners have been quick to « take advantage of the trend, offering lower prices and passages to places like Quebec and New Brunswick where the Irish can go for a mere £5, as opposed to £10 for the United States. Many emigrants are opting for England or Scotland, however, since even the poorest can raise the few shillings for the fare. Most of those who go are labourers or servants, although many textile workers are also being forced to leave as a result of the decline in their trade. It is noted that the emigrants tend to give their ages in round numbers, thus calling their literacy into question (→ 7/6/19).

Succession crisis on death of Charlotte

London, 6 November
The Prince Regent collapsed into the arms of his brother the duke of York tonight at the news that his only daughter, Princess Charlotte, had died in childbirth at the age of 21. She had spent 50 hours in labour at Claremont, near Esher, in Surrey. She died at midnight after giving birth to an abnormally large boy – sadly still born. She had complained of feeling cold and failed to respond to stimulants.

With the long-term succession uncertain, the death of Princess Charlotte, who was second in line to the throne, may create a constitutional crisis (→ 11/1819).

Charlotte: died in childbirth at 21.

William Hone is an unlikely new hero

London
Radicals have found an unlikely hero in William Hone, a mild mannered bookseller who has successfully fought off three consecutive actions for criminal libel brought by the Tory government. Such is Hone's popularity that a public subscription raised more than £3,000 to pay his costs and cover some of his losses. He also writes on social welfare causes and parliamentary reform. It was a series of parodies on religious texts in his broadsheet *The Reformists' Register* that infuriated the government, which accused him of "impious and seditious libels".

George Rennie, the Scots engineer, begins work on a much needed new harbour in Dun Laoghaire, outside Dublin. This was first proposed in 1811, in a pamphlet believed to have been written by a Norwegian, Captain Richard Toutcher, entitled "Considerations on the Necessity and Importance of an Asylum Port in the Bay of Dublin" (→ 3/9/21).

1818

Westminster, 30 May. Parliament provides for the establishment of fever hospitals in Ireland.

India, 2 June. The Marathas are conquered by the British Army, and their empire is annexed (→ 22/8).

North Sea, 14 June. The *Rob Roy* makes her first crossing from Belfast to the Clyde.

Worcestershire, 22 August. Warren Hastings, the first British governor-general of India, dies aged 85 (→ 2/1826).

Lancashire, 7 September. The leaders of the cotton weavers and spinners, who have been striking against starvation wages, are arrested (→ 15).

Europe, 15 November. Britain renews its quadruple alliance with Russia, Prussia and Austria as a precaution against any possible recurrence of war with France (→ 21).

France, 21 November. The allies withdraw their troops from France (→ 26/1/26).

London. Thomas Love Peacock publishes *Nightmare Abbey*, a satirical novel poking fun at the romantic "gothic" thriller novels which are favoured at the moment.

Britain. Augustus Frederick, the duke of Sussex, the grand master of the premier Grand Lodge of Masons, receives a patent from France to form the Supreme Council of the Ancient and Accepted Rite of Masons (→ 1819).

London. Dr James Blundell of Guy's hospital completes the first human blood transfusion.

Britain. The Institute of Civil Engineers is founded.

London. *Northanger Abbey* and *Persuasion*, written by the novelist Jane Austen, are published posthumously.

Portsmouth. Jeremiah Chubb, an ironmonger, invents a type of lock which is so secure that even a professional lockpicker is unable to crack it.

London. John Keats, the poet, publishes *Endymion*, an allegory which is greatly criticized in both the *Quarterly Review* and *Blackwood's Magazine* for its uneven quality (→ 1820).

Westminster. Some 14,000 Londoners present a petition to the House of Commons complaining at the high price and poor quality of alcoholic drinks sold in the capital.

Politicians alarmed at election violence

London

The shadow of the French Revolution continues to hang over the British political scene, with conservative politicians objecting to every proposed reform on the grounds that any concession will lead to further demands. With no regular nationwide police force to contain frequent demonstrations, the ruling classes are permanently uneasy.

After a Westminster mob got out of hand at an election this year, Charles Greville, the duke of York's old Etonian racing manager, noted in his diary that it "displayed the savage ferocity which marked the mobs of Paris in the worst times". Significantly, one of the candidates in that London election, Henry Hunt, a noted reformer, gained no more than 84 votes. Hunt is a close friend of William Cobbett, a fellow radical, who has fled to the United States to avoid prosecution for seditious libel. Like many radicals, Hunt and Cobbett have fuelled conservative fears by wearing revolutionary emblems – including red caps – and producing anti-clerical and even atheistic propaganda (→ 7/1819).

Young woman creates monster horror tale

London

Mary Shelley, 20, the daughter of the feminist Mary Wollstonecraft and the radical philosopher William Godwin, has amazed the reading public with a "gothic" horror story called *Frankenstein*. The monster which is brought to life by its creator, Dr Frankenstein, is abominated by everyone and finally turns against the doctor and destroys him. The book was written when Mary was 18, when she and her lover, the poet Percy Shelley, and their friend Lord Byron were in Switzerland. Kept indoors by bad weather they passed the time by writing horror tales. Only hers was completed. She and Shelley later married, after his first wife killed herself (→ 1/2/51).

A terror-stricken Frankenstein flees as his own creation comes to life

Bowdler cleans up Shakespeare plays

London

A sign of the increasing prudery of popular taste is the appearance of *The Family Shakespeare*, edited by Thomas Bowdler from Bath. He has cut many passages from the plays, explaining that "those words and expressions are omitted which cannot with propriety be read aloud in a family". Ten years ago readers were spared the trouble of reading the plays at all. The essayist Charles Lamb and his sister Mary compiled their famous *Tales from Shakespeare* which give the stories of the plays in easy narrative form and have proved extremely popular.

Workers form new 'friendly societies'

A society membership certificate.

Manchester

With more than 500 unlicensed pawnbrokers flourishing in London alone, life remains unremittingly hard for Britain's poorer working class. More affluent workers and their families are able to provide against loss of earnings through sickness or unemployment by joining so-called "friendly" societies which collect weekly subscriptions.

An estimated 8.5 per cent of the population belong to these societies – equalling the number of reported paupers in the country. To ensure financial stability, several societies here have joined together to form the "Manchester Unity" – although the "Ancient Order of Foresters" is rapidly becoming the biggest of the societies.

Captain John Ross and his ship land at icy Prince Regent's Bay in northern Canada. Accompanied by Lieutenant Edward Parry, Ross left England this year on an expedition to Baffin Bay in the hope of discovering a north-west passage from the Atlantic to the Pacific Oceans.

Cotton mills go on strike for more pay

Manchester, 15 September
The cotton mills here are silent. The clatter of the looms has stopped as spinners and weavers unite in a strike which few thought possible until recently. After years of recession the textile industry is booming, and workers are demanding the restoration of the 20 per cent cut in their wages of 1815.

Despite the Combination Acts – designed to prevent workers from uniting – both trades succeeded in calling meetings of delegates from the main textile towns. Some delegates have travelled to London where an attempt is being made to bring every worker into what is being called a "general union of trades". The textile strike is unlikely to succeed. Already the spinners' leaders have been jailed for conspiracy; hunger will do the rest.

Britain agrees new north border of US

London, 20 October
Lengthy negotiations between London and Washington – originally about fishing rights on the Great Lakes – have resulted in an agreement between the two nations on the Canadian-American border. This will run west from the Lake of the Woods to the Rockies along the 49th parallel.

The Americans wanted the line extended to the Pacific, but Britain, with the fur trade in mind, proposed the Columbia river as the boundary. With no possibility of either side being able to colonize the Oregon territory, negotiators have settled on dual occupation for another ten years at least. They agreed that neither country will maintain armed naval forces on the Great Lakes – except for the prevention of smuggling (→ 3/3/38).

Elizabeth Fry campaigns to reform prisons

A later (and idealized) vision of Elizabeth Fry in Newgate prison.

London, March
Women held in Newgate prison are cooped up in filthy rooms and their children are often kept with them. Some are in fetters so that they cannot escape, yet their crimes may be no more serious than petty theft or forgery. Others await the death sentence or being sent to Australia.

This description of jail life comes from Elizabeth Fry, the wife of a London merchant and a well-known reformer, whose first charitable act was to open a school for the poor. A devout Quaker, Mrs Fry set out originally to bring the Bible inside prison walls. A year ago she formed a ladies' association for female prisoners in Newgate.

She has since given evidence to parliament that women prisoners need proper beds, good food and clothes, and also religion. She denounced flogging, hanging and the practice of taking women across town chained together in open carriages, to be jeered at by people in the streets (→ 1840).

John Nash changes the face of London

Part of the eastern side of Regent Street, named after Nash's patron.

England
The highly original work of John Nash, the Prince Regent's architect and surveyor-general, is spreading throughout London. His ambitious scheme for a wealthy garden suburb is taking shape with the building of Regent Street, a broad thoroughfare running from the prince's residence in Pall Mall, Carlton House, to the Regent's Park, formerly Marylebone Park, on the capital's northern edge.

A redesigned Royal Pavilion.

Nash's plan for the splendid new park includes a programme of substantial planting, with grassed open spaces, trees, lakes, and villas, as well as a new canal. Fronting the parkside will be rows of grand terraced houses, complete with ornate stuccoed façades and classical features designed to give each terrace the appearance of a single monumental palace.

In Brighton, a facelift by Nash of the Royal Pavilion which was designed by Henry Holland in 1786 is nearing completion. The Chinese-style interior remains untouched, but the façade has been transformed by the addition of a bizarre mixture of Indian, "gothic" and Chinese details (→ 1827).

Inside the Royal Pavilion.

Houses such as Attingham Park, in Shropshire, made Nash's name.

1819

Maidstone, Kent, 8 March. One hundred and forty-one prisoners are transferred to the newly completed prison.

London, 24 March. Southwark Bridge over the river Thames is opened.

London, 25 May. The duchess of Kent gives birth to her first child, a daughter named Alexandrina Victoria (→ 23/1/20).

Westminster, 7 June. The second and final report of the House of Commons select committee publishes its findings on the condition of the poor of Ireland (→ 12/2/20).

Liverpool, 20 June. The steamship *Savannah*, built by Francis Fickett and Stephen Vail, which departed from Savannah, Georgia, only 26 days ago, arrives in Liverpool after making the first transatlantic crossing powered entirely by steam (→ 27/8/22).

Liverpool, 26 June. The first detachment of Irish and English soldiers sets sail to join Simon Bolivar's troops in the South American wars of independence.

Birmingham, July. In an attempt to push for parliamentary reform, radicals elect an attorney to represent the city at a self-styled parliamentary convention (→ 17/8).

Birmingham, 19 August. James Watt, the Scottish inventor who patented the invention of the steam engine, dies.→

London, September. Henry Hunt, known as "Orator Hunt", a Radical advocate of parliamentary reform and repeal of the corn laws, is released on bail after the "Peterloo" massacre and makes a triumphant entry into the city (→ 11/1819).

Italy, September. Percy Bysshe Shelley, the poet, writes *The Mask of Anarchy* after hearing of the Peterloo massacre in Manchester; the poem is a satirical ballad attacking contemporary politicians (→ 22/7/22).

Scotland. The industrialists Charles Macintosh and Thomas Hancock perfect a process for manufacturing waterproof fabric.

Wales. The *eisteddfod*, a cultural and musical festival of Welsh music and language, takes place at Carmarthen.

London. The Burlington Arcade is opened in Piccadilly.

Eleven killed in 'Peterloo' massacre

Manchester, 17 August

There has been public outrage at yesterday's massacre at St Peter's Field, when a troop of yeomanry charged a peaceful mass meeting, killing 11 and wounding over 500. The incident has already been ironically called "Peterloo".

Most of the crowd of 80,000 were weavers who had come to hear the Radical Henry Hunt speak. Their banners proclaimed: "Universal Suffrage" and "Election by Ballot". In the crowd was the weaver-poet Samuel Bamford, who wrote down what he saw: "Sabres were plied to hew a way through naked held-up hands and defenceless heads; and then chopped limbs and wound-gaping skulls were seen and groans and cries were mingled with the din of that horrid confusion."

Soldiers charge into the crowd, scattering and cutting down demonstrators.

The government's line is to blame Hunt as the "odious instigator of the day's calamity". It laments "some fatalities" but declares that the "revolutionary attempts of this base junto" could "no longer to be tolerated". The government shows great concern, though, for one yeoman, whose injuries are described as "heart rending". Hunt's poster calling the meeting warned: "Our enemies will seek every opportunity by the means of their sanguinary agents to excite a riot that they may have the pretence for spilling our blood." In fact, they did not bother to pretend (→ 9/1819).

Editor of 'The Times' faces the cabinet

London, 25 August

Thomas Barnes, the editor of *The Times*, was summoned before the cabinet council in Whitehall today to explain his motives for giving "outstanding" publicity to an angry reader's letter which insisted on a ministerial apology regarding the so-called "Peterloo" massacre [*see report above*].

Barnes says that he was received most courteously and detained only briefly after answering several searching questions. The interview was evidently intended to warn the 33-year-old editor that he must watch his step in future. "But if that was its object," Barnes said afterwards, "it has failed utterly. We intend to devote as much space as we can to reports of the inquests on the 500 victims of "Peterloo"."

The editor said that he would also campaign against two of the proposed "Six Acts" which are aimed at the newspapers in the wake of the bloodshed in Manchester. The letter which so upset the ministers was signed by Sir Francis Burdett, the Radical MP for Westminster.

Macadam outlines secret of good roads

The Colossus of Roads: how contemporaries see the Scot John Macadam.

Bristol

Bumpy coach journeys may be a thing of the past if the advice of a new book is taken. John Macadam, the surveyor-general of Bristol's roads, has just published *A Practical Essay On The Scientific Repair and Preservation of Public Roads.*

Macadam was born in Ayr but lived in New York from the age of 14. He became interested in roads after returning to Scotland to purchase an estate at Sauchie in Ayrshire. He has now developed his own method of road-building. It involves putting down on a drained surface a layer of small stones, which then bond together under pressure. This process, called by some "macadamizing" the streets, has greatly improved the quality of road surfaces (→ 26/11/36).

'Six Acts of Repression' give magistrates wide powers to restore law and order

Westminster, November
Determined to show their support for magistrates in the wake of the "Peterloo" massacre, the government has rushed through a batch of tough law and order measures. The Six Acts give magistrates even greater powers against the radicals than they received under the Gagging Acts two years ago. It is now easier to convict political suspects summarily, and magistrates can search almost anywhere, prevent arms training and ban any meeting that they do not like.

The acts are also directly aimed at radical journals like Cobbett's *Weekly Register* or Wooler's *Black Dwarf*, which face stiffer penalties for blasphemy and sedition as well as new taxes [*see report right*]. Critics argue that much of the disorder is of the government's own making. Peterloo was an unprovoked attack on peaceful women and children, while the activities of so-called revolutionaries often turn out to have been inspired by government spies and *agents provocateurs*. Not that there are no deep grievances. The Corn Law of 1815 and the current depression have caused widespread hardship, and many feel that parliament is badly in need of reform. But the government, still haunted by the spectre of the French Revolution, believes that all change must be resisted (→23/2/20).

A hostile view of the "Six Acts".

Factories Act limits a child's working day

London
Mill-owners can no longer employ children under nine in textile factories, and children under 16 can only work for 12 hours a day, under the Factories Act. The act was introduced by Robert Peel, whose father, Sir Robert, had proposed the 1802 act limiting the working hours of poor-law children. Moves to extend controls to all children were opposed by peers extolling the virtues of "free labourers" or objecting to any measure which "interfered with a manufacture of such importance". Lord Stanley complained that conditions in other industries were not controlled.

A key figure in setting the new limits was the idealistic mill-owner Robert Owen. He has shown that a mill-owner can make profits without employing children. He told a parliamentary committee that as a result of child labour "limbs were generally deformed and growth was stunted" (→7/1833).

Recession blamed for rise in crime

Britain
The crime rate has soared since the end of the war. In three years the number of committals for indictable offences in England and Wales has almost doubled, from 7,818 in 1816 to 14,254 this year. Some say that this is due to depression and unemployment as demobbed soldiers and sailors come home; others point to the decline of hanging – only a third of those guilty of the 200 hanging offences are actually executed, a drop of 30 per cent on 70 years ago.

Particularly worrying is the rise of organized crime in the towns, much of which seems to involve children and petty thieving; half the crime in the country is committed by youngsters between 15 and 24. The police, who have only about 27 men patrolling London in the day, are squeezed between the working classes which hate them, and property owners, who resent them as a burden on the rates.

Independent press faces cash curbs

Westminster, November
Two of the Six Acts devised this autumn by the home secretary, Lord Sidmouth, to curb public criticism of the government have been aimed directly at independent newspapers. Both the Blasphemous and Seditious Libel Act and the Stamp Duty on Newspapers Act make it obligatory for newspaper proprietors to pay more tax on individual newspapers – first, by increased stamp duty, and second, by having to deposit a large sum of money as security for any fines which might be inflicted. The aim is to prevent the publication of any newspaper selling at less than sixpence [2.5p], exclusive of duty.

Watt steams out

Birmingham, 19 August
The man whose genius trebled the efficiency of the steam engine has died at the aged of 83. James Watt was born in Greenock and was considered dull at school. He set up a workshop in Glasgow in 1757 and worked on heat with Professor Joseph Black. Around 1763 he repaired a Newcomen steam engine and his subsequent improvements led, in 1774, to a business here with Matthew Boulton. Watt's engines are used all over Britain, transforming the profitability of mines and factories.

Caroline plans to return as queen

Caroline: eyes on the throne.

London, November
A rebel MP, Henry Brougham, has taken up the case of Princess Caroline, the all too robust ghost at the royal feast. A large vulgar woman, once condemned by an enquiry for her "levity of conduct", she was separated from the Prince Regent, shortly after their marriage in 1795 and lives in Italy. The 81-year-old King George III cannot last long, and when the regent inherits Caroline has a good claim to be queen. Brougham, as her adviser, now says that she will renounce her title in return for a pay rise from £35,000 to £50,000. The regent is unpopular, and Caroline can be sure of Whig support (→31/1/20).

The steamship "Savannah" arrives in Liverpool after completing the first Atlantic crossing by steamboat – in 26 days from Savannah in America.

1820

Newbury, 12 January. Francis Baily, an eminent astronomer, is one of 14 founders of the Astronomical Society.

Sidmouth, Devon, 23 January. Edward, the duke of Kent, next in line to the throne after the Prince Regent, dies.

London, 11 February. King George IV begins divorce proceedings against his estranged wife, Queen Caroline (→17/8).

Cork City, 12 February. The *East Indian* and the *Fanny* set sail for Cape Colony with over 350 Irish emigrants (→11/1821).

London, 23 February. A plot to murder the cabinet is thwarted when troops and Bow Street officers raid a loft in Cato Street where the plotters are gathered (→1/5).

Glasgow, 1 April. Radical posters call for the Scots to support a provisional government in Scotland.

Dublin, 13 May. The politician Henry Grattan receives a Catholic deputation which urges him to go to London to press again for Catholic emancipation (→11/2/23).

Cork City, 25 May. The economic crisis worsens as two major banks, Roche and Leslie, fail.

London, 17 August. The inquiry opens into Queen Caroline's conduct, which will determine whether or not George IV has grounds for divorce.

Britain, August. Women petition parliament in protest at the queen's shoddy treatment by George IV.

South Africa, 1 December. The Reverend Patrick Scully establishes the first Irish Catholic mission at the Cape of Good Hope (→10/11).

Edinburgh, 16 December. A large crowd protests at the king's treatment of Queen Caroline; this provides Whig leaders with the ideal cover to organize their campaign against the government (→1/1821).

Britain. Charles Cameron develops a method of carbonating water to make "soda water".

London. John Keats publishes *Lamia and Other Poems*, a collection of odes and ballads which is hailed as a landmark in English poetry; the poems include *Ode to a Nightingale*, *The Eve of St Agnes* and *On a Grecian Urn* (→23/2/21).

George III finds peace

Windsor, 29 January

George III, Britain's king during a most critical period in the country's history, died this evening at the age of 82. He had been king for 60 years, although his mental instability had rendered him incapable of ruling since 1811 when his son, the prince of Wales, was appointed regent. He had reigned longer than any previous sovereign.

George died at Windsor Castle, where he had passed the last years of his life blind, deaf and mad. But his beard had been allowed to grow, and he had been glimpsed staring with sightless eyes from a window. He was oblivious of the death of his granddaughter, of the marriages of his three sons, and even of the death of the queen.

Since he came to the throne in 1760 several revolutions had modified every aspect of British life. The French Revolution threatened the country's stability; the American war led to the loss of those colonies, although some new territories have been acquired; and now an industrial revolution is beginning to change society radically. The monarchy's power and influence was much reduced during his reign, although he took a greater part in governing Britain than did George I or George II. He was more popular than his Hanoverian predecessors, and his interest in agriculture won him the nickname of "Farmer George", which pleased him. He was a hard worker, and was proud of being British (→31).

The ailing king in his old age.

Prince Regent is, at long last, king

London, 31 January

George IV was proclaimed king today after the death of his father [*see report left*]. Troops drawn up outside Carlton House cheered as George, aged 57, succeeded to the throne after nine years as regent.

The new king is unlikely to win cheers from the public as readily as those from his soldiers today. He has acquired two reputations. On the one hand there is the educated man, a patron of science and the arts, the darling of high fashion. On the other is the extravagant and dissolute libertine, overweight and self-indulgent. Politically George has been close to Whigs, but as regent he has cooperated well enough with the present Tory administration.

King George IV has one particular and pressing problem: what to do about his estranged wife, Caroline. She has been living abroad since 1814 but is now expected to return to take up her position as queen. Their marriage was a disaster, and their only child, Charlotte, died in 1817 (→11/12).

Wordsworth's Lake District guide popularizes area for visitors

Tranquil Grasmere: the lake overlooked by two of Wordsworth's homes.

Dove Cottage, also the poet's home.

Grasmere, Cumbria

A guidebook to the Lake District by the poet William Wordsworth looks set to become a best seller. The work, *A Topographical Description of the Country of the Lakes*, is an expansion of an introduction which Wordsworth wrote for a collection of drawings of the Lakes in 1810, and appeared this year as an appendix to a book of his poems. It is so successful it is to be republished as a separate volume.

The Lake District first became popular at the end of the last century and its bohemian image – the poets Coleridge and Southey have lived there as well as Wordsworth – has served to enhance its popularity. It now attracts scores of visitors in search of the "picturesque". Guidebooks on the area already exist. The first, by Thomas West, appeared in 1778. But none have caught caught the public's imagination as Wordsworth's has – though he has mixed feelings about it. One enthusiast, a clergyman, asked him if he had ever written anything else (→4/1843).

Conspirators executed

London, 1 May
The government's determination to suppress discontent was underlined today with the beheading for treason of five of the men at the centre of the Cato Street conspiracy. The last to die was the leader of the gang, Arthur Thistlewood, aged 50, one of those imprisoned after the Spa Fields riot. The episode shows the government's readiness to use spies and tough measures against the whole reform movement.

Thistlewood and 13 other men had met in a stable loft in Cato Street, off the Edgware Road, to plan the murder of cabinet members during a dinner in Grosvenor Square. They then intended to seize key buildings in London and declare a revolutionary republic.

One of the group, however, was a police informer. Armed soldiers and Bow Street officers raided the loft and seized firearms on 23 February, the very night of the dinner. Thistlewood ran one officer through before being captured with other conspirators. Eleven plotters escaped across the rooftops.

How an artist saw the rooftop escape of the Cato Street conspirators.

Public inquiry clears Caroline's reputation

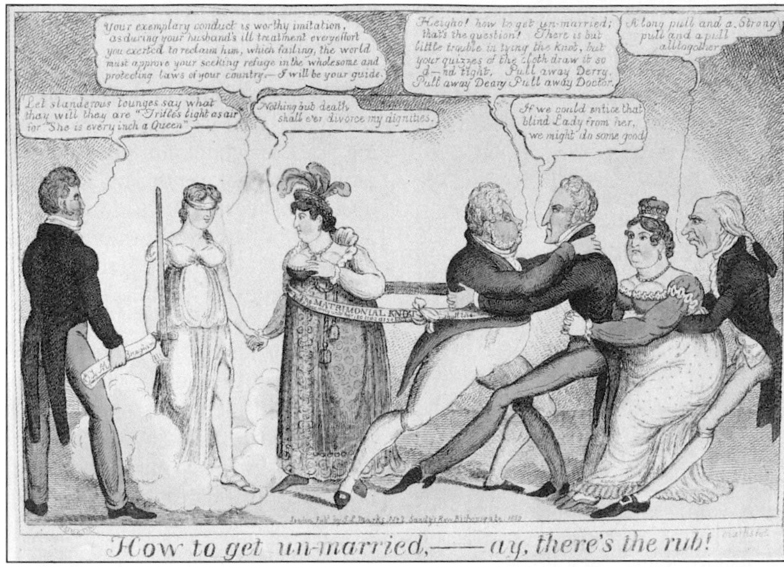

The portly and unloving royal couple delighted contemporary caricaturists.

London, 10 November
Bonfires and bells in London and many other cities are celebrating the victory of Queen Caroline over her husband, George IV, who has vilified, persecuted and humiliated her for many years. After an 11-week "trial" inquiring into her conduct and effectively designed to deprive her of her title, Caroline has emerged triumphant.

The case had been heard in the House of Lords where evidence was introduced by the prosecution to show that there had been an adulterous liaison between the queen and an Italian gentleman. A bill to dissolve Caroline's marriage and deny her the title of queen was passed by the Lords by just nine votes. Given such a small margin, however, government ministers decided not to proceed with the bill in the House of Commons.

The London public has been on the queen's side, and caricaturists have profited from the turmoil, running off sheets of scurrilous cartoons against George. Radical agitators have threatened the carriages of any royal ministers who dared to appear on the streets. Caroline attended many sessions of the case, while George remained at Windsor comforted by his latest mistress, Lady Conyngham (→ 16/12).

Troops crush abortive radical insurrection

Falkirk, Central, 5 April
An uprising at Bonnymuir, close to here, has been crushed by troops. Hussars reinforced by local volunteers dispersed a band of radicals supposedly on their way to seize the munitions at the Carron iron works. Four of the radicals were wounded and many rounded up, possibly to face trial for treason. Trouble has been brewing in the west of Scotland since the state trials of 1817 [*see report on page 820*]. Mass meetings have been held in Glasgow and surrounding towns, inciting workers to agitate in the face of falling wages and rising unemployment. As many as 60,000 workers are estimated to have joined strikes in the area. However, a close watch has been kept on radical organizations by government spies, and in February all 27 members of the Glasgow radical committee were arrested.

In response the radical groups, now without their leaders, stumbled into a poorly planned insurrection. On 1 April notices were posted in Glasgow calling upon workers to support a provisional government that would soon take charge. Today some 50 radicals marched from Glasgow towards Carron, where they were joined by others from Stirling. A third group had set out from Strathaven, south of Glasgow, but all of them were easily dispersed by troops before they could unite.

Edmund Kean is dominating the London stage, winning renown for his great performances in Shakespearean tragedies.

Benbow stands trial for satirizing king

London
The government and two new anti-obscenity groups have got together in an attempt to silence William Benbow, the outspoken artist and illustrator. But when Benbow went on trial for two cartoons deemed as unacceptable attacks on George IV, a jury refused to convict him.

Benbow's "offensive" cartoons were captioned *The Brightest Star in the State, or, a Peep Out of a Royal Window* and *The Royal Cock and Chickens, or, the Father of His People*. Benbow has been a target of the government for the help that he has given to William Cobbett, the radical journalist.

1821

Gold Coast [Ghana], 15 January. British troops annex the area (→ 22/1/24).

Dublin, 18 January. The Theatre Royal opens.

London, January. Queen Caroline accepts £50,000 and a house as part of her settlement after the inquiry into her private life (→ 19/7).

Westminster, 17 April. William Conyngham Plunket's bill for Roman Catholic emancipation is defeated in the House of Lords.→

Ireland, 28 May. The results of the census show that the population has risen to 6,801,827.

Ireland, 1 June. The Bank of Ireland resumes payments in gold.

Belfast, 5 June. The Belfast Natural History Society is founded.

Westminster, 19 July. King George IV is crowned in a lavish ceremony from which Queen Caroline is barred, despite the fact that she had demanded to be crowned alongside her husband (→ 7/8).

Co Dublin, 3 September. As George IV leaves from Dun Laoghaire after his three-week visit to Ireland, it is renamed Kingstown to commemorate both the visit and the completion of the east pier.→

Britain, October. Thomas de Quincey publishes *Confessions of an English Opium Eater.*

Ireland, November. The potato crop fails (→ 24/5/22).

Ireland, 29 December. Marquis Wellesley, the elder brother of the duke of Wellington, is sworn in as lord lieutenant.

London. Michael Faraday, a scientist, has developed an electric motor to show that electricity will produce a rotary motion.

London. The monumental new building for the Bank of England is completed by the architect Sir John Soane.→

London. The Suffolk-born painter John Constable exhibits an important new work, *The Haywain*, at the Royal Academy (→ 10/1/29).

London. John Galt, a Scottish writer, has just published *Annals of the Parish*, a sequel to the first and popular *The Ayrshire Legatees*; both vividly portray village life in Scotland.

Results published of British census

Britain

The results of the national census conducted this year reveal fascinating statistics concerning population growth in Britain during the last decade. The new figure of some 20,893,584 shows an increase of nearly three million since 1811, with just under two million of those in England and Wales.

The balance of the sexes favours women, with just under half a million more of them than of men. The figures also reveal that women are living longer than men, with 191 women aged 100 or more compared with 91 men who are "centurions".

The main reasons for the steady expansion in population over the last 50 years are the reduction in infant mortality and the better clothing and food enjoyed by people during their early years and middle age. Town populations are on the increase, although most people still live in the country, and nearly a quarter of families earn their living from the land.

Uncrowned, unhappy Queen Caroline dies

Caroline: "the injured queen".

London, 7 August

After a long night of pain, Queen Caroline died today at her house in Hammersmith, to the west of London. She was 53. She fell ill three weeks ago, while at the theatre on the evening of the coronation. Her physician, Henry Holland, had diagnosed "acute inflammation of the bowels" and after bleeding her had administered enough calomel and castor oil "in a quantity ... to have turned the stomach of a horse". She rallied enough to sign her will.

Caroline of Brunswick married the then prince of Wales in April 1795, a few days after their first meeting and despite an instant dislike of one another. Within a year, after the birth of their only child, Charlotte they lived apart. Caroline was limited to seeing Charlotte at infrequent intervals. As a result of her husband's indifference, she won wide public sympathy.

She ran an orphanage for children in Blackheath where, in 1806, allegations were made that she had had an illegitimate child; but a "delicate investigation" cleared the princess. She then spent six years abroad, and further rumours of sexual impropriety were used by parliament, at the urging of King George, to try to rob her of the throne. She was excluded from her husband's coronation and asked that her coffin should bear the inscription "Caroline of Brunswick, the injured queen of England" (→ 3/9).

'Manchester Guardian' gives manufacturers a voice in the press

THE SCOTSMAN,

OR

EDINBURGH POLITICAL AND LITERARY JOURNAL.

This is not the cause of faction, or of party, or of any individual, but the common interest of every man in Britain.——Junius.

NO. 1. SATURDAY, JANUARY 25. 1817. Price 10d.

First edition: the masthead of the Edinburgh newspaper launched in 1817.

Manchester, 5 May

Reformers in Manchester are not expecting too much of *The Manchester Guardian and British Volunteer*, a new, independent liberal weekly which was born today in a sparsely furnished room above a shop at 29 Market Street. The reason for this cautious, wait-and-see attitude is an awareness that John Edward Taylor, the Salford-born businessman who has created the joint-stock company that is responsible for the new weekly, is only a very moderate reformer. He has said many times recently that he must respect the political views of the dozen other merchants and businessmen who have invested £100 each in the venture.

"We are the enemies of slander," he declares in a prominent leading article, "and we strongly believe that it will be by industry and careful attention, rather than on any other terms, that we will be able to support those who are aiming so hard at public improvement."

The birth of the *Manchester Guardian* reflects not only the spread of newspapers beyond London – *The Scotsman* was launched in Edinburgh in 1817, for instance – but also ownership by manufacturing interests seeking better representation in parliament. The *Leeds Mercury* is another example of a robust provincial culture.

"Read all about it": newsvendors.

First royal visit to Ireland since 1690

George acknowledges the cheers.

Ireland, 3 September
The visit of King George IV ended today with his departure from Dun Laoghaire, now to be renamed Kingstown in his honour. Spectators lined the shore, some of them following the royal barge until they were up to their necks in water.

The first royal visit since 1690 has been a tremendous success, despite its somewhat inauspicious start. The king arrived on 12 August, his 59th birthday, upset by the death of his estranged wife, Caroline, five days earlier. His unsteady condition when he left the boat at Howth, in Co Dublin, caused a good deal of amusement, and the alcoholic excesses which have accompanied the tour have been the subject of scandalized comment and have already passed into popular legend.

But nothing could dim George's rapturous reception. His public entry into Dublin along Sackville Street was attended by a mile-long procession of carriages, and he was loudly cheered wherever he went.

While the visit has no outward political significance, many people are trying to estimate whether or not there has been a change in the new king's declared opposition to Catholic emancipation. The Catholic bishops presented him with a loyal address, which was graciously received, and in a gesture of goodwill George later installed the earl of Fingall, Ireland's leading Catholic layman, as a knight of the Order of Saint Patrick (→ 1824).

Romantic poet dies of consumption

Rome, 23 February
"A thing of beauty is a joy for ever," wrote John Keats, and that will surely be true of the small but voluptuous body of poetry left behind after his death today of consumption, at the age of just 25, here in his lodgings above the Spanish Steps. He was originally apprenticed to an apothecary, and his first poetry was savaged by reviewers. One wrote: "Better be a starved apothecary than a starved poet so back to the shop, Mr John, back to plasters and pills." Since 1818, when he fell in love with Fanny Brawne, he had produced *Lamia*, *The Eve of St Agnes* and his odes, whose sensuous imagery is worthy of Shakespeare: to a Nightingale, to Autumn, on a Grecian urn, and on Melancholy. The epitaph he chose is "Here lies one whose name was writ in water".

Keats: cut down in his prime.

Relief bill rejected

Westminster, 17 April
A bill for Catholic relief, introduced by William Conyngham Plunket, has passed through the House of Commons but has been defeated in the House of Lords.

Although Catholics have won important concessions and are now entitled to vote in parliamentary elections, they are still excluded from high public office and, most significantly, are forbidden from becoming members of parliament, judges or generals.

Bank of England building is completed

The new Bank building in Threadneedle Street in the City of London.

London
Much of the rebuilding work on the Bank of England, started in 1791 by Sir John Soane, is nearing completion, although some further developments of the site are expected to continue within the next decade. Soane was appointed architect in 1788 with a complex brief involving the piecemeal reconstruction of existing buildings, governed by exacting conditions. The needs of security meant that the bank had to be surrounded by a windowless wall, with many of the interiors lit from above, and be fireproof.

Soane's way of solving the problem, with domed halls and an austere simplicity, aroused controversy among some of his peers, largely due to the style of ornamentation used, consisting of incised lines and grooves instead of the more conventional classical features.

Prison reformers open the 'farm school'

Redhill, Surrey
Prisons are squalid, overcrowded places where children as young as eight mix with hardened criminals, the insane and the sick. Unsurprisingly, there are calls for change on behalf of child prisoners.

Following the opening of new model prisons for adults such as that on London's Millbank, reformers have this year achieved what could be an important first landmark. The Reform Institution of Bermondsey, a squalid area of south London, has founded a so-called "farm school" at this country town south of the capital. The institution believes that a child can be saved from a life of crime if it is removed to morally and physically healthier surroundings and given a religious education (→ 1823).

The "London Engineer" arrives at Margate from London. Trips by steam-boat down the Thames are booming, with twice as many passengers as eight years ago. Return fares start at five shillings.

1822

London, 15 January. His Majesty's Coast Guard is founded.

Fife, 27 March. Sir Alexander Boswell, the essayist son of James Boswell, dies of injuries received in a duel yesterday with James Stuart, another writer, over a literary disagreement.

Westminster, 24 May. The Poor Employment Act provides £50,000 for the building of new roads in Ireland (→6/1822).

Western Ireland, June. Fever spreads rapidly through the families already weakened by famine (→1836).

Westminster, 5 July. King George IV abolishes the Irish tax which imposes taxes on the number of windows and hearths in a house.

Westminster, 22 July. An act sponsored by Richard Martin, known as "Humanity Dick", to prevent the cruel and improper treatment of cattle, becomes law (→16/6/24).

London, 25 August. Sir William Herschel, the astronomer royal, dies aged 84.

Ireland, 1 August. Parliament orders the establishment of a police force for each county; local magistrates will direct, but central government will fund, the forces.

Cork City, 27 August. The *Duke of Lancaster*, a passenger and cargo steamship, begins a Cork/Bristol ferry service (→4/1838).

Westminster, 9 September. George IV, despite reservations, appoints George Canning, a former favourite of Queen Caroline and rival of the late Castlereagh, as foreign secretary.→

Italy, September. The duke of Wellington replaces Castlereagh as the British representative at the Congress of Verona (→20/10).

Dublin, 5 November. Loreto Abbey is founded by Frances Ball, a member of the Institute of the Blessed Virgin Mary; the nuns begin educational work in Ireland.

London, 20 December. The *Sunday Times* newspaper is first published.

Edinburgh. The first Highland and Agricultural Show is held.

Edinburgh. Henry Raeburn, 66, becomes the first Scottish artist to be knighted since the union.

Castlereagh, autocratic and distinguished foreign secretary, dies by his own hand

Kent, 12 August

Robert Stewart, Viscount Castlereagh, the foreign secretary, committed suicide today at his Kent seat, Foots Cray, with overwork being cited as the reason for his death. Throughout the summer his friends had been aware of his deteriorating condition and of a strange persecution mania that sinister forces were attempting to ruin him with suggestions of homosexual conduct.

The duke of Wellington, his comrade during the Peninsular War, told him: "I am bound to warn you that you cannot be in your right mind." Castlereagh responded by covering his face with his hands, saying: "Since you say so, I fear it must be so." Today he cut his throat with a penknife which he had somehow managed to obtain unnoticed by his attendants.

Although Castlereagh was autocratic by temperament and hostile to popular radical movements, his role as foreign secretary, when he led the coalition against Napoleon in 1813-14, won him international esteem. Ironically, his political rival George Canning, with whom he fought a duel in 1809 on Putney Heath, is tipped to succeed him as foreign secretary (→9/9).

Lord Castlereagh in his prime.

Robert Peel takes over at home office

Westminster, January

Robert Peel, who has been out of office for the past four years, has been made home secretary by the prime minister, Lord Liverpool, who is anxious to bring a more liberal tone to the cabinet. He replaces Viscount Sidmouth, who remains in the cabinet without portfolio.

Peel plans to abolish the death penalty for more than a hundred offences and to lessen the penalties for a number of minor ones. He also intends to tackle the appalling condition of British prisons and to compel judges to submit quarterly reports to the home office (→1823).

Robert Peel: rejoining the cabinet.

Canning recalled in Tories' hour of need

Westminster, 9 September

George Canning has been recalled to the cabinet to be foreign secretary in succession to Lord Castlereagh, who died last month [*see above*]. Canning will also become the government's leader in the House of Commons – a startling comeback for a man about to abandon British politics to become India's governor-general. He had resigned as president of the board of commerce in 1820 in protest at the government's treatment of Queen Caroline. But now Lord Liverpool, the prime minister, needs the support of Canning, whose views on Catholic emancipation and trade reforms promise to give the government a more liberal edge.

Romantic poet meets a watery grave in sailing accident off Italy

Sorrow on an Italian beach: the funeral of Shelley, by L E Fournier.

Viareggio, Italy, 22 July

The bodies of the poet Percy Bysshe Shelley and a friend, drowned when a squall upset their sailing boat off the coast near here, have been washed up and burnt on the shore near Lerici in the presence of Lord Byron. In Shelley's pocket was a volume by Keats, whose death he elegized in *Adonais*. He was 30. *The Mask of Anarchy*, his outraged response to the "Peterloo" massacre, bade his countrymen to "Rise like Lions after slumber/In unvanquishable number". His best-known odes have all been written in Italy in the past four years.

King and kilt pay royal visit to Scotland

A contemporary view of the king's royal progress north of the border.

Edinburgh, 29 August
Although George IV's visit here started with wet, windy and foggy conditions, he was greeted by thousands of citizens. Looking at them from the battlements of Edinburgh Castle, he said: "Good God! What a fine sight! I had no conception there was such a scene in the world ... the people are as beautiful and extraordinary as the scene."

The king brought £1,354 worth of highland dress with him for the tour and wore a kilt for the levée at Holyrood Palace – an act that has won over many Scots. The visit has focused attention on several outstanding Scots. Sir Walter Scott, the novelist, arranged a procession up the Royal Mile from Holyrood to the castle; Henry Raeburn, a miniaturist and portrait painter, was knighted; and David Wilkie, another noted artist, returned after nearly 20 years in London to paint the king at Holyrood.

European tension is discussed in Verona

Italy, 20 October
The worsening of the Spanish situation and the weakness of Ferdinand VII, who is asking for help to fight democratic extremists, is hanging like a cloud over the Congress at Verona, where the duke of Wellington is Britain's representative.

France wanted assurances that if it needed to withdraw its minister from Spain, the rest of the allied powers would follow suit, and that if it then went to war with Spain, it would receive assistance. Continental allies have agreed to withdraw their ministers, if necessary, and to give France any help it needs.

Czar Alexander has an army of 150,000 ready to be mobilized to help maintain the balance of power in Europe and is eager to intervene. Wellington, however, has protested at this offer of "moral support" and refused to sign an agreement to this effect (→ 1823).

'Attempt on life' of lord lieutenant

Dublin, 14 December
Marquis Wellesley, elder brother of the duke of Wellington and Ireland's new lord lieutenant, has been hissed by the audience at a performance in the New Theatre Royal in Dublin. A bottle and part of a watchman's rattle were thrown at the viceregal box.

Wellesley's support for Roman Catholic emancipation has been welcomed by Catholics. But his attempt to interfere with the ceremonies carried out at the statue of William III on College Green has brought him into open conflict with Protestants. The statue was due to be decorated on 4 November, and the "Orangemen" assembled in defiance of Wellesley's ban, only to be dispersed by troops and police. Outrage at this interference resulted in the theatre incident, which the lord lieutenant is claiming as a serious attempt on his life (→ 15/9/28).

Caledonian canal adds another link to Britain's network of inland waterways

The Caledonian canal has opened to traffic this year, although it is still not complete. Work began in 1804 on the canal (shown in the lower photograph), which bisects Scotland by linking lochs and rivers from Inverness to Fort William. Thomas Telford has supervised this major contribution to the nationwide network of canals which has been built in the last 60 years (see map). The Regent's canal (top photograph) was completed in 1820, linking London's docks to the Grand Junction canal and the midlands. Canals have transformed the economy by providing cheap transport – roughly one-third of the price of road transport – of raw materials for factories and finished goods (→ 1836).

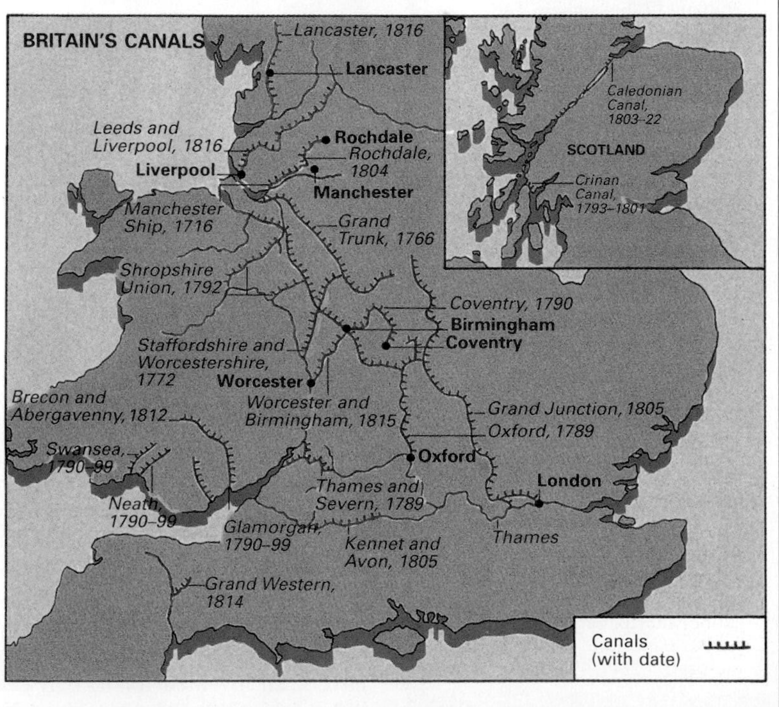

1823

Gloucestershire, 26 January. Edward Jenner, the physician and pioneer of the smallpox vaccine, dies in his home village of Berkeley (→1853).

London, January. King George IV gives the British Museum his father's vast collection of over 65,000 books.

Co Dublin, 11 February. Henry White, the pro-emancipation candidate, defeats Sir Compton Domville in the by-election by 994 votes to 849 (→12/5).

Dublin, 18 March. Robert Owen addresses the first of a series of meetings on social reform (→27/8/26).

Dublin, 11 May. Daniel Murray becomes the Catholic archbishop on the death of Archbishop Troy.

Co Londonderry, 12 May. Violent rioting resulting in several deaths breaks out between Catholics and Protestants at a local fair in Maghera.→

Edinburgh, 8 July. Sir Henry Raeburn, the celebrated Scottish portrait painter, dies.

London, 14 July. King Kamehameha II and Queen Kamamalu of the Hawaiian Islands both die after contracting measles on their first visit to Britain.

East Sussex, 30 October. Edmund Cartwright, the inventor of the power loom and the wool-combing machine, dies at Hastings, aged 80 (→7/1826).

Dublin, 17 November. The Committee of Catholic Association recommends the formation of a burial committee to purchase land for Catholic burials after a priest was prevented from carrying out a burial service.

Edinburgh. The Bannatyne Club is founded, with Sir Walter Scott as its president; it is dedicated to the publication of Scottish history and literature sources (→23/2/27).

Britain. The *Lancet*, a medical journal, is founded by Thomas Wakley, a surgeon and political radical.

Oxford. The Oxford Union Society is founded.

Manchester. Charles Macintosh, a Glaswegian chemist, who patented a formula for making waterproof rubber fabric, begins making rubber capes and hoods in his factory (→25/7/43).

Science lectures for studious workforce

London

Dr George Birkbeck has founded a Mechanics' Institute, following the example of Glasgow. It offers lectures on science and mechanics to skilled workers and artisans. Its middle-class supporters hope that the workers will be diverted from public houses and become more docile members of society. The workers themselves want to better their own conditions.

There have been many improving societies over the years. In 1800 Dr Birkbeck started a series of very successful lectures at Anderson's Institution in Glasgow, where he was the first professor of natural philosophy. The lectures continued when he moved to London in 1804 to practice medicine and ultimately led to this year's foundation.

Catholics launch campaign for full rights

Ireland, 12 May

The chief spokesmen for Catholics on both sides of the debate over the right to veto Irish episcopal appointments, Daniel O'Connell and Richard Lalor Shiel, have buried their differences. They have set up a Catholic Association with the aim "to adopt all such legal and constitutional measures as may be most useful to obtain Catholic emancipation". Support for the association has been overwhelming in Munster and Leinster. It is to be funded through a subscription from members of a penny a month, called "Catholic rent". In return, the association intends to work for tenants, for the church and for the whole Catholic community.

By enlisting the support of the masses, emancipation has become a popular cause, with O'Connell its undisputed leader (→1824).

O'Connell: Catholic champion.

Royal Hibernian Academy gets charter giving boost to Irish art

Sackville Street, Dublin: the location for the Royal Hibernian Academy.

Ireland, 5 August

After much delay the painters and sculptors of Ireland have been granted a royal charter for the foundation of the Royal Hibernian Academy. Under its terms the academy will consist of 14 members and ten associates, with William Ashford, the distinguished landscape artist, as its first president.

For almost a century Irish painters, sculptors, architects and engravers have formed and re-formed themselves into societies and associations which, almost without exception, have come to grief. With the coming together of the best artistic talent in the country, the RHA may flourish.

Anyone for rugby?

Rugby, Warwickshire

Rugby school has invented a new form of football. During a game this year a boy called William Webb Ellis took up the ball and ran with it, "with a fine disregard for the rules of football". The other boys pursued him, and now whenever they play football they carry the ball as often as they kick it. The new game is so popular that rules have been invented for it. It is called "rugby football".

Brighton may have lost its most famous resident now that the Prince Regent is king, but this year the Sussex resort gained a new chain pier.

Excise Act helps to improve whisky

Scotland
The new Excise Act has had a revolutionary effect on distilling in Scotland. Illicit distilleries all over the highlands are disappearing and are being replaced by legal ones, and production as well as quality are rising rapidly. The smugglers are out of work, and increased production and profits mean great improvements in efficiency.

Distilling whisky has been a major industry for at least two centuries. The government has always tried to control it, imposing strict regulations and heavy excise taxes, but there was always a large illicit industry in the highlands.

The big lowland distilleries became the largest factories in Scotland. One of them, in the 1780s, was the first in Scotland to use a steam engine. Whisky competed with gin in England as a cheap alternative to brandy, and the English distillers fought to impose heavy duties on Scotch whisky. They finally gave up the struggle last year when legal distinctions between English and Scottish distillers were ended.

With lower taxes and a secure legal base of operations, lowland distillers will be able to improve the quality by blending and maturing the liquor in casks for three or more years. Highlanders will be able to concentrate on their own distinct varieties of whisky.

Death sentence axed for 100 offences as Peel ushers in wave of prison reforms

Penal times: women prisoners are worked to exhaustion on a treadmill.

Westminster
If a man can be hanged as easily for a sheep as a lamb, why should he care if he steals the whole flock? Overnight Robert Peel, appointed home secretary last year, has used his pen to end the death sentence on about a hundred offences.

Until now, a man could be hanged for stealing five shillings [25 pence] from a shop, or for theft on a navigable river, for taking forty shillings from a dwelling house or even for impersonating a Greenwich pensioner. With sentences so harsh, many a jury had acquitted offenders rather than see them hanged. One hundred and thirty statutes concerned with petty larceny are now reduced to one act. Prisons are to be funded from the rates, administered by local magistrates. Jailers will finally be paid salaries, not made to take fees from the prisoners. Wealthy prisoners have long been able to buy privileges from prison keepers, while the poor suffered harsh treatment. Peel has also set up prison welfare reforms: medical care, better diet, schooling, religious instruction and even jobs for prisoners (→26/9/29).

Britain aims for a balance of power

Westminster
The British government is intent on a policy of neutrality in the war between the Greeks and the Turks of the Ottoman Empire. George Canning, the foreign secretary, wants to ensure that the war does not affect the balance of power between the major nations. This balance of power, and naval supremacy, are seen as the two arms of British foreign policy.

Britain supports Austria, Prussia and Russia, to keep France in its place; it supports Austria, France and Russia, to prevent Prussia from dominating Germany; and it supports the Ottomans against threats from Russia. Lord Palmerston, a junior minister, says: "We have no eternal allies and no permanent enemies. Our interests are eternal."

Greece struggles for independence.

Britain is also backing American demands that European powers should not intervene in Spain's American colonies, which have revolted. The Royal Navy is to guarantee the policy of non-interference in the western hemisphere expounded this month by James Monroe, the president of the United States.

The Graeco-Turkish war poses more of a problem for Canning. Protecting the route to India is increasingly important and was the main reason for supporting the Turks. But public opinion here supports the Greek revolt, and this autumn Lord Byron has joined the fight. Neutrality is seen as the best way to ensure that the conflict does not spread (→4/4/26).

Covered cabs bring new level of comfort for London's travellers

London, 23 April
Londoners have grown used to the speed and convenience of the French *cabriolet*, or "cab", a two-wheeled, one-horse vehicle which carries one passenger seated alongside the driver. These vehicles first arrived here at the turn of the century and quickly gained in popularity, being much faster than the hackney carriages which were the main alternative. From today, however, travellers in the city can enjoy a new level of comfort, with the arrival in service of a design of cab capable of carrying two passengers under a hood, away from crowds, noise and inclement weather. The driver rides outside, on the right.

One of the old-style "cabs": passenger and driver faced danger together.

1824

Britain, 4 March. The Royal Naval Lifeboat Institution is founded by Sir William Hilary.

London, 15 March. Work begins on repairing fire damage to London Bridge.

London, 9 April. *Memoirs of Captain Rock* is published anonymously; it is thought to be by Thomas Moore, the Dublin-born poet, lawyer and a close friend of the late Lord Byron.

Burma, 11 May. British naval forces under the command of Sir Archibald Campbell seize the city of Rangoon (→ 12/1825).

London, 2 June. The Guildhall officially opens its new library.

Westminster, 6 June. Parliament passes a law recognizing the right of workers to go on strike (→ 1825).

London, 7 August. Gas street lighting is installed throughout Greenwich.

Yorkshire, 21 October. Joseph Aspdin patents Portland Cement – a new product that is impervious to water and as durable as material used by the Romans.

Dublin, 29 October. The first issue of the *Morning Register* is printed.

Edinburgh, 5 November. A major fire destroys the steeple of Tron church, the east side of Parliament Square and many other buildings.

London. The National Gallery opens in Pall Mall.

London. Jeremy Bentham, a philosophical radical, publishes the first issue of the *Westminster Review*; it was founded as an alternative to the Whig *Edinburgh Review* and the Tory *Quarterly* (→ 1832).

Queensland, Australia. The first penal colony in Brisbane is opened (→ 1829).

London. The last unfinished satirical cantos of *Don Juan* by George Gordon, Lord Byron, the poet who died tragically earlier this year, are published.

Vienna. Ludwig van Beethoven's ninth symphony, the *Choral*, which was commissioned by the Philharmonic Society of London, is first performed (→ 1825).

Windsor. At the behest of Kng George IV, the architect Jeffry Wyatville begins the restoration of Windsor Castle (→ 26/6/30).

A new breed of conservatives spearheads sweeping reforms of trade restrictions

Westminster, 12 April

Britain's import duties on raw materials, its Navigation Laws and its long-standing statutes of economic protectionism will be modified, simplified and in some cases abolished, William Huskisson, the president of the board of trade, said in the House of Commons today.

The reforms are a great victory for the "new" conservatives who have gathered around Huskisson, Robert Peel and George Canning. They believe that it is essential for the Tory Party to discard its die-hard aristocratic image and embrace moderate reforms and so win over the industrial interests and the middle-class vote and they dominate the cabinet.

Huskisson: wooing industrialists.

An ending of trade restrictions, the renegotiations of trade treaties with the United States (Britain's largest trading partner) and many smaller countries, and an easing of the burden of taxation on the industrial interests are not the only changes that the government is making – to the fury of the Whig opposition, which accuses the Tories of stealing its reformist clothes.

Canning, at the foreign office, has not only cold-shouldered the reactionary Holy Alliance of Austria, Prussia and Russia but also, by his speedy recognition of the new South American republics, has now opened up new markets to British goods and trade.

Gold Coast defeat for British forces

Gold Coast [Ghana], 22 January

An Asante army has wiped out a British force. The British commander, Sir Charles MacCarthy, has paid the price for underestimating an enemy and has taken his own life. Convinced that the Asante are the major slave-traders of West Africa, the British supported the coastal Fante tribe's resistance to Asante hegemony. It proved an expensive mistake: the only major defeat that Britain has suffered from an indigenous African army.

War trophy: an Asante breastplate.

New society will prevent cruelty to animals

Unequal battle: a lion and two dogs set to fight in Warwick in the 1820s.

London, 16 June

A philanthropic pressure group has been formed after a meeting at the Old Slaughter Coffee House in St Martin's Lane: the Society for the Prevention of Cruelty to Animals. Amongst those attending was William Wilberforce, the campaigner against slavery. The meeting follows the passing two years ago of the first parliamentary bill to outlaw the cruel treatment of horses and cattle.

The man behind the society is the eccentric Irish landowner, wit and duellist Colonel Richard Martin MP, an advocate of Catholic emancipation and of penal reform, nicknamed "Humanity Dick" by the late King George III.

'Penny a month' boosts O'Connell

Ireland

Daniel O'Connell's Dublin-based, middle-class Catholic Association has already raised £16,000 from the "penny a month" subscription scheme, and the movement is still gaining strength throughout the country. By contrast, the "Rockite" movement is suffering a decline in popularity. Taking their name from the mythical hero of Thomas Moore's satire *Memoirs of Captain Rock*, the Rockites have been involved in stirring agrarian unrest.

They have been greatly helped by the "Pastorini" cult which has gained credence in many country areas. Based on a prophecy by an English Catholic bishop, Charles Walmesley, it predicts the annihilation of Protestantism in 1825.

"Pastorini" has been an embarrassment to the leaders of the Catholic Association, who wish to avoid sectarian tensions, and they welcome the increased support for O'Connell (→ 2/1825).

Trade-union activity flourishes in Britain

Brickmakers are among the many who may benefit from trades unions.

Manchester
With the repeal of the Combination Acts, processions of trade unionists have filled the streets, marching behind their embroidered banners with all the pomp and circumstance of army regiments marching behind newly blessed flags.

There had been unions of craftsmen before William Pitt brought in the acts, which outlawed unions of both employers and employees but in practice were used only against employees [*see page 780*]. They continued a shadowy existence, some under cover of clubs and mutual benefit societies, others, like the Society of Iron Founders, meeting on hillsides on dark nights. "Very few prosecutions have been made under the Combination Acts," said Gravener Henson, the leader of the framework-knitters, but they still constituted "a tremendous millstone" around the neck of the artisan. The motto of his union was *Taisez-Vous* [Keep Quiet].

The repeal, argue the Radicals Francis Place and Joseph Hume, who piloted the act through parliament, will diminish the militancy of the unions by bringing them into the open. Men like Henson see a different future (→6/6).

'The Ettrick Shepherd' creates literary stir

James Hogg: shepherd and poet.

Edinburgh
The Private Memoirs and Confessions of a Justified Sinner is the unlikely title of a book making a controversial stir in Edinburgh literary circles. It is by James Hogg, who already has a reputation as a poet and balladeer from Ettrick, in the borders. A shepherd's son, he taught himself to read and write while shepherding. His first poems were published in 1800, and he gave up farming ten years later when Edinburgh society took him up as "the Ettrick Shepherd", a sort of noble savage and heir to Robert Burns. He achieved his first major success with *The Queen's Wake* in 1813. The *Justified Sinner* is a macabre story of a Calvinist who falls in with an evil stranger (the devil?) and becomes a split personality who commits murder (→1835).

Poet-hero dies a martyr for Greece

Missolonghi, Greece, 17 April
Lord Byron, who has died of fever in the midst of his campaign to help the Greeks liberate themselves from Turkish rule, is more famous abroad than he is infamous at home. He "woke up to find himself famous" on the morning that he published *Childe Harold's Pilgrimage* in 1812, when he was 24. This and his other travelogue adventures are not real romantic verse, but Byron himself became the very essence of the romantic poet-hero, sighed for by women everywhere.

He was married (for only a year), sexually omnivorous, fêted then expelled by London society and a restless traveller in brooding exile, mainly in Italy; his best work is the witty verse of *Don Juan*: "Man's love is of man's life a thing apart, /'tis woman's whole existence."

Lord Byron: a brooding exile.

Vagrancy Act sets out indecency law

Street scene: a beggar seeks help.

Westminster
Parliament has passed a Vagrancy Act – a revised version of one passed in 1822 – which is an attempt to consolidate the many laws for punishing "idle and disorderly persons and rogues and vagabonds". There is a new emphasis in the act, however. The law now prohibits "every person wilfully exposing to view ... any obscene print, picture or other indecent exhibition".

This is partially a result of the lobbying of William Wilberforce's Society for the Suppression of Vice (known as the Vice Society). But what has really prompted the government's action is the wave of scurrilous cartoons celebrating the late Queen Caroline's complicated domestic arrangements.

Norfolk life: "Mousehold Heath – Boy Tending Sheep" by Norwich artist John Crome, the leading light of a flourishing "Norwich school" of artists. John Sell Cotman is another important member of the group.

1825

Westminster, February. Daniel O'Connell, the Irish Radical MP, lobbies against Henry Goulburn's proposed bill which will prohibit political societies in Ireland (→ 18/3).

Ireland, 18 March. The Catholic Association formally dissolves to conform with the requirements of the Unlawful Societies Act; it forbids the existence of any political society in Ireland for longer than 14 days (→ 7/7/26).

Westminster, 25 March. Sir Francis Burdett proposes a revision of the Catholic Relief Bill (→ 27/4).

Westminster, 27 April. Frederick, the duke of York, speaks out against the Catholic Relief Bill which has successfully passed three readings in the House of Commons (→ 17/5).

Westminster, 17 May. The Catholic Relief Bill is defeated in the House of Lords by 40 votes (→ 28/5/28).

Ireland, 30 May. The commissioners inquiring into the state of education in Ireland submit their first report.

Westminster, 27 June. The Currency Act assimilates the Irish currency into the British; it will take effect from next year (→ 5/1/26).

Bradford, June. Woolcombers go on strike, bringing all trade to a standstill.

Dublin, 13 July. A new Catholic Association is founded.

Dublin, 5 October. The city is lit by gas light for the first time.

Dublin, 14 November. The Catholic Metropolitan Chapel is opened.

Wiltshire, 21 December. Fonthill Abbey is destroyed when the great tower collapses.

Scotland. The Clydesdale bank is established.

London. A year after its Viennese first performance, Beethoven's monumental ninth symphony, the *Choral*, is given its British première by London's Philharmonic Society, which originally commissioned it.

London. Bookmakers are barred from Thomas Lord's cricket ground, the home of the Marylebone Cricket Club, after games played there had attracted heavy gambling (→ 22/8/45).

First passenger steam railway opens

Full steam ahead: "Locomotion No 1" pulls the world's first steam train from Stockton to Darlington and into history.

Co Durham, 27 September
Crowds erupted into wild cheers at Darlington today as the world's first commercial passenger steam railway opened for business, and *Locomotion No 1*, the locomotive designed by a local engineer, George Stephenson, triumphantly completed its inaugural journey from Stockton. There has been a long wait, and many important policy changes, since parliament first approved the scheme in 1821. But patience was well rewarded.

Stephenson himself not only forced through the decision to accept steam as the motive power but also exerted a decisive influence on the construction of the tracks. His engine weighs almost eight tonnes and travels at speeds of between 12 and 16 miles (19-25 kilometres) an hour. But it was discovered that up to half its pulling power would be lost unless it could run on virtually level rails. So Stephenson made an inch-by-inch survey of the route, and incidentally established the superiority of malleable iron over the crude cast iron used for tramways. Designed primarily for minerals, the railway is the first to carry passengers (→ 1826).

Scandalous memoirs make good reading

London
The book-publishing sensation of the year is undoubtedly *The Memoirs of Harriette Wilson*. It is already in its 30th edition and fourth volume, as fashionable London eagerly pays to learn whose names feature in the reminiscences of the notorious Mayfair courtesan.

Miss Wilson, who appears to have been mistress to half the aristocracy, frankly admits that she writes only for money. She went into print purely because one of her "liaisons", the Honourable Frederick Lamb, tried to cheat her out of a promised annuity. She would have kept quiet if he, and the other men in her life, had paid up more generously. Many did – but not the duke of Wellington, who told her: "Publish and be damned!"

Lacing the stays of Miss Wilson.

Southern Ireland is a land of fairy tales

Ireland, April
Thomas Crofton Croker has been praised by the German writer Wilhelm Grimm and the Irish novelist Maria Edgeworth for his *Fairy Legends and Traditions of the South of Ireland*, which has been an immediate popular success. Regarded as a pioneering collector of Irish folklore, Croker was born in Cork and travelled extensively in the south of Ireland to sketch and study the traditions of the countryside.

His recent book is a collection of stories about strange creatures like Banshees and Phookas. He does not merely take the fairy tales down verbatim but arranges them into effective narrative structures using rich, terse prose.

Strikes increase as unions speak out

Britain
A great wave of strikes and withdrawals of labour is sweeping the country as fresh groups of workers, in industry after industry, press for higher wages. Conservative politicians blame last year's repeal of the Combination Acts, which made possible, for the first time, the establishment of effective trade unions. Other observers attribute it more to the soaring cost of living and the natural urge of the labouring classes to share some of the rewards arising from the current commercial and stock market booms.

Law Society formed

London
A new body has been formed to represent and advance the interests of those members of the legal profession who describe themselves as "attorneys, solicitors, proctors and others not being barristers". By creating a formal Law Society this group hopes to raise the status and improve the training and qualifications of the many minor specialists who work around the courts.

Samuel Pepys' diary is put into print

London
A first selection has been published this year from an extraordinarily frank and vivid diary kept between 1659 and 1669 by Samuel Pepys, who achieved high office as secretary to the Royal Navy under King Charles II [*see page 591-2*]. His notebooks, which contain brilliant first-hand accounts of such events as the Restoration, the plague and the great fire of London, as well as many colourful details of daily life, were kept in an early type of coded shorthand, and have lain unread for well over a century in the library of Magdalene College, Cambridge.

They have been exhumed thanks to the efforts of the master's brother, Lord Braybrooke, and an undergraduate, John Smith, who did the actual transcription. The first extracts suggest that they are a unique historical treasure trove.

Britain extends its empire into Burma

British troops storm a Burmese fort in the attack on Rangoon in 1824.

Burma, December
British forces have defeated an attempt by the king of Ava, in Burma, to extend his territory into British-held India. Burmese forces had driven a British garrison from the island of Shahpuri near Chittagong and invaded the mainland last year, forcing Lord Amherst, the governor-general, to declare war. Rangoon was taken in May 1824, but the British forces became trapped by the rains. Nine out of ten British soldiers succumbed to disease before the attack resumed this year. Again, the monsoon made progress slow, but the Burmese suffered a heavy defeat last month, and as the British closed on Ava its king sought peace terms. He renounced all claims to Assam and ceded to Britain all territory along the coast from Chittagong to the Irrawaddy (→ 2/1826).

Ideal homes are far from the grim reality

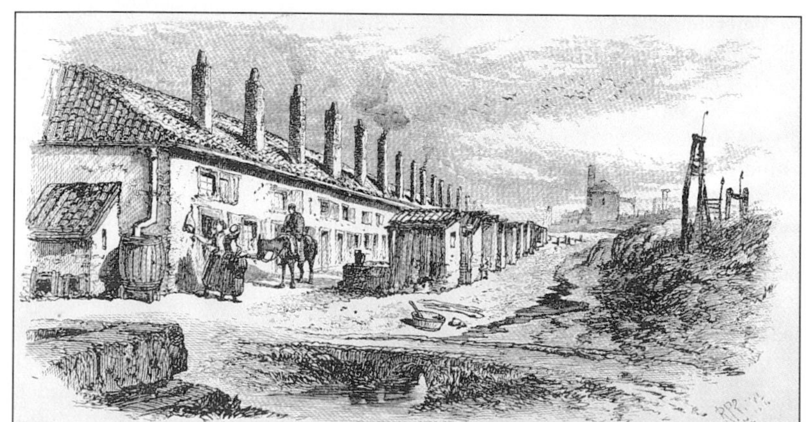

Miners' cottages on Tyneside, in a long line close to the dirt of the pits.

Britain
Houses with hot water are the preserve of the upper classes in Britain, but not for much longer if John Hall has his way. Hall, the secretary of the Society for Improving the Condition of the Labouring Classes, has outlined ambitious plans for improving the quality of housing in a book published this year. The model houses in *Designs for Cottages and Schools* all have running water – in stark contrast to the reality. Although water mains now take sewage away from some town streets, housing conditions remain bad, with dirt, stench and disease widespread.

Financial ruin and crisis in Britain as 60 banks collapse

London, 30 December
Staff and senior officials worked right through Christmas as the Bank of England continued its round-the-clock battle to contain the national credit crisis which has already caused the failure of 60 country banks and six major London financial houses. Beds were moved into its offices in Threadneedle Street when the storm first broke, and bank counters have stayed open for business beyond midnight.

Trouble was widely foreseen earlier in the year. The biggest stock market and commodity boom since the end of the Napoleonic wars was already many months old. Over 600 new companies had been floated, and there had been a flood of foreign loans (mainly South American). Much of the rampant speculation which followed was funded by advances from small provincial banks with neither experience nor gold reserves.

When the bubble started to burst, in early November, the first reaction from both government and Bank was to let the speculators stew. But all that changed after 27 November, when the partners in several of London's biggest and strongest financial establishments were urgently called from church to supply gold to their increasingly desperate customers.

As the news grew steadily worse, the military were called out to disperse one mob attacking a bank that had closed its doors. The Bank saved the partners on that occasion with an unsecured loan of £50,000, but many others went away empty-handed. By mid-December the Bank's own gold stocks, which stood at a healthy £12 million in 1824, were down to under £1 million and dropping fast. In the end the wealthy Rothschilds saved the day, buying bullion wherever they could find it, almost at any price. There will be an intensive enquiry to find out what went so wrong.

1826

Ireland, 5 January. The Irish currency is assimilated into the British currency system.

Britain, 26 January. Anglo-French relations improve with the signing of a Treaty of Navigation.

India, February. Britain and India sign the Treaty of Yandaboo, bringing an end to the Burmese war which has raged since 1824 (→4/7/28).

London, spring. Sir Stamford Raffles, the founder of the colony of Singapore, founds the London Zoological Society (→5/7).

Ireland, May. A *Life of Theobald Wolfe Tone*, the Irish nationalist, is published.

London, 5 June. The German composer Carl Maria von Weber dies of consumption, aged 39.

Ireland, 7 July. The Catholic Association reinstitutes the "Catholic Rent"; this brings a supply of funds into the movement (→30/8).

Dublin, 9 July. Over 200 weavers march in protest at increasing unemployment in the textile industry.→

Ireland, July. Dublin, Cork and Belfast are hit by an epidemic of fever.

Liverpool. A new customs house is built and the old dock is closed.

Edinburgh. The Royal Scottish Academy is founded.

London. Spitalfields silk weavers are enraged by the abolition of tariffs and the admission of cheaper French silks into Britain.

Stockton-on-Tees, Cleveland. John Walker, a chemist, invents the friction match; it is made of cardboard and coated with a mixture of potash and antimony (→7/4/27).

Britain. Elizabeth Barrett, a poet, publishes *Essay on Mind, With Other Poems* (→12/9/46).

Northampton. James Sharp installs the first domestic gas stove in his home.

London. The clock dial on St Bride's church, Fleet Street, is illuminated by twelve gas burners.

Lancashire. The first rail tunnel on the Manchester/ Liverpool line is built (→10/1829).

Canada. A promotion to encourage Scottish highlanders to emigrate to Canada is launched.

Menai suspension bridge is completed

The island of Anglesey is linked by road to Wales by Telford's genius.

Gwynedd, 30 January
There will be celebrations in the Welsh valleys and hills today, with the completion of Thomas Telford's dramatic suspension bridge across the Menai Strait between Anglesey and North Wales.

It is the first iron suspension bridge ever to be built on such a scale and will certainly bring Telford's name to the fore as one of the greatest civil engineers of the time. Links between Wales, England and Scotland are becoming ever easier, swifter and at last far more economical, improving trade, the postal service and normal communications; the impact on trade and industry is likely to be unparalleled.

Telford, who was born to a Scots shepherd, had previously rebuilt the turnpike road from Shrewsbury to Bangor and Holyhead; he has also been involved in the Caledonian canal and over 1,000 bridges as well as being a builder of roads.

Russia backs plan to end Greek war

St Petersburg, 4 April
The duke of Wellington completed a great diplomatic coup here today when Nesselrode, the Russian foreign minister, signed an agreement committing Britain and Russia to mediate – and, if necessary, intervene – in the Greek revolt against Turkish rule. France is expected to back the agreement, which will give Greece a degree of independence within the Ottoman Empire.

Many Britons feel great sympathy for the Greeks in their struggle against their overlords. When Lord Byron died at Missolonghi in 1824, he was seen as a martyr to their cause. But Russia has been an ever present threat, eager to extend its frontiers further south. George Canning, the British foreign secretary, has now achieved an agreement which checks Russian aggrandizement, sustains the Ottoman Empire and gives Greece semi-independent status (→6/7/27).

Profit-taking ends co-operative dream

Strathclyde, 27 August
Robert Owen's idealistic visions suffered a setback today with the closure of the 15-month-old Orbiston community at Motherwell. To Owen, the driving force behind the model mill town of New Lanark where workers enjoy excellent working and living conditions, Orbiston was to be the first of a network of villages run on the principles of profit and production sharing as a means to relieve poverty. But before the project could get under way, Owen had turned his attention to the United States, and it was left to his followers to push ahead. A range of crafts was established, but it proved difficult to persuade the more profitable sectors of the community, such as the iron foundry, to share their profits with others. The death of its manager, Abram Coombe, was the final blow. Community members have now decided to abandon the project (→1827).

British troops sent to thwart Spanish moves in Portugal

Westminster
A naval fleet and 4,000 British troops have been sent to Portugal to thwart moves by Spain to exploit a civil war within its Iberian neighbour. George Canning, the foreign secretary, has backed the moves by citing treaty obligations rather than supporting one particular cause.

The Portuguese problem arose after the death this year of King John VI. His younger son, Miguel, challenged his brother, Pedro for the succession and their dispute acquired constitutional significance when Pedro promised parliamentary government. Miguel and army deserters challenged the "constitutionalists" and won Spanish backing. The constitutionalists sought British help under the Anglo-Portuguese treaty, and Canning saw no reason to refuse. He believed that Pedro, as a legitimate sovereign, had every right to grant a constitution, and, in any case, the treaty was a "pledge of national faith". Canning added: "Let us fly to the aid of Portugal by whomsoever attacked, because it is our duty to do so; and let us cease our interference where that duty ends. We go to Portugal, not to rule, not to dictate, not to prescribe constitutions, but to defend and to preserve the independence of an ally."

Canning: new foreign vision.

Industrial unrest gathers momentum

Colliers lose strike battle in Glasgow

Glasgow, May
A strike of colliers which began here last month has ended in defeat. The Colliers' Association had sought to mobilize support in Scottish mines against wage reductions, but it encountered fierce opposition from the coalmasters. In addition to employing strike-break workers, the coalmasters used force to beat the union. At least one colliery resembled a fortified camp, being protected by guards armed with pistols. Despite the failure of the strike, it reflects an increasing militancy among workers and a readiness to take industrial action.

Power-loom weaving in the cotton industry: targets for jobless weavers.

A girl collier in eastern Scotland.

Handloom workers destroy new machines

Lancashire, July
Unrest among the industrial workforce is growing, and as the strikes grow violent, so does the reaction of owners. Where machines have been introduced, pushing men out, there has been a dramatic increase in poverty. The traditional system of poor relief on the rates is insufficient, with some jobless workers close to starvation.

The handloom weaving industry has been badly hit: there has been an explosion of machine-breaking among the handloom weavers in Blackburn and Bury. In three days, more than a thousand of the new power looms were destroyed. The trouble then spread to Manchester, where 46,000 men are unemployed out of a total population of 203,000.

Arms were distributed to the factory owners for self-defence. Many arrests were made; ten workers received sentences of transportation to Australia. In Scotland, coalmasters took up arms to defeat the strike of Glasgow colliers coming out against wage reductions. The Colliers' Association was defeated, and blackleg labour was hired at lower wages to continue mining. The colliery was a fortified camp with armed guards for weeks (→ 12/1829).

Dublin weavers faced with rising unemployment stage protest

Dublin, 9 July
Two hundred Dublin weavers have marched to the Royal Exchange here in protest against rising unemployment in the textile industry. With the rapid decline in cotton manufacture, the weavers' earnings have tumbled. Calico output that earned £1.6s [£1.30] in 1796 now earns just six shillings, and the south of Ireland has been very badly hit, resulting in hardship and emigration. The short-lived prosperity of cotton is thought to have resulted from parliamentary grants and tariff protection, and it has not certainly been helped by changing fashions and the availability of cheap new substitutes.

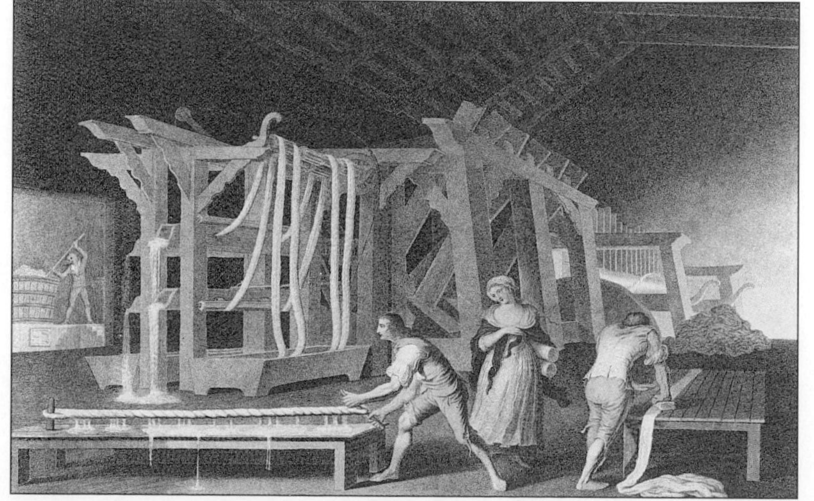

Hard at work in a Dublin bleach mill: washing, rubbing and glazing the cloth.

Pro-Catholics cause Irish election upset

Ireland, 30 July
There have been two shock results in the general election here, with victories for supporters of the Catholic Association in all four counties it contested. In Co Waterford Lord George Beresford, whose family had held undisputed control for generations, came third behind Richard Power, a pro-Catholic emancipation candidate, and Henry Villiers Stuart, a staunch ally of Daniel O'Connell, the Catholic Association's leader. In Co Louth the pro-emancipation candidate, Alexander Dawson, owed his surprise victory to the support of the Catholic clergy (→ 5/7/28).

Founder of colonial Singapore dies

Raffles: an enterprising naturalist.

London, 5 July
The death was announced today of Sir Thomas Stamford Raffles, the founder of the successful colony of Singapore and a great naturalist. He was 45.

Once a prosperous commercial centre, the islands of Singapore were in fact uninhabited in 1819 when Raffles extended the operations of the British East India company there. In 1811, when sent on the expedition to Java, he became fascinated by the Malaysian peninsula, but two years ago ill-health brought him home. Sir Stamford was also founder-president of the London Zoo.

1827

London, 5 January. Frederick, the "grand old duke of York" of the nursery rhyme and brother of King George IV, dies aged 64.

Britain, 7 April. Friction matches – known as "Lucifers" – are now on sale in packs of one hundred.

Westminster, 12 April. George Canning becomes prime minister, but the duke of Wellington, Robert Peel and five other members of the old cabinet resign (→ 8/8).

Bolton, 26 June. Samuel Crompton, who invented the "spinning mule" in 1779 for spinning fine yarn, dies at the age of 74.

Europe, 6 July. Britain, France and Russia sign the Treaty of London, agreeing to use force if the Ottoman Empire will not end the war with Greece (→ 27/10).

Britain, 16 July. Josiah Spode, the English potter and creator of the type of bone china that bears his name, dies aged 73.

Liverpool, 10 August. The *Liverpool Mercury* reports what is believed to be the first death during railway construction.

Dublin, 11 November. The Carmelite Church in Whitefriar Street is consecrated.

Bristol, 31 December. George Pocock demonstrates the "kite-carriage" – a kite-powered vehicle – which in a test run travels faster than the Bristol mail coach.

Plymouth. John Darby secedes from the Church of England to help form a fundamentalist denomination called "the Plymouth Brethren".

England. John Dalton, the chemist, publishes *New System of Chemical Philosophy* in which he presents the first ideas on atomic theory.

London. The *Evening Standard* newspaper is published for the first time.

United States. The commune of "New Harmony" begun by Robert Owen, the philanthropic Welshman who came from Scotland to the US to create an idealistic community, collapses from internal disputes (→ 1/1834).

London. John Nash, the king's favourite architect, who last year redesigned Buckingham Palace, begins work on Carlton House Terrace, to replace Carlton House (→ 13/5/35).

Premier suffers a stroke

Westminster, 17 February
Lord Liverpool suffered an incapacitating stroke today at the age of 58, after serving uninterruptedly as Britain's prime minister for the past 15 years. George Canning, the foreign secretary, is likely to be the new premier, but his foreign policy and attitude to Catholic emancipation have earned him the distrust of Tories as diverse as the duke of Wellington and Robert Peel.

Liverpool's tenure in office began with the successful conclusion of the Napoleonic wars. His political energies were then mainly devoted to controlling the wave of dissension that came with the onset of peace. His policy was essentially one of cautious advance, balancing order against progress (→ 12/4).

Liverpool: 15 years as premier.

Goderich replaces Canning as premier after four months

Westminster, 8 August
The post of prime minister became vacant for the second time in six months today. George Canning, who was already ill when he accepted the office, having never fully recovered from the chill that he caught at the duke of York's funeral earlier this year, finally died after five days of intense pain.

King George IV has chosen Lord Goderich, the former speaker, to replace him in office, but this is not expected to be a very long lasting appointment. The new head of the government is seen as too lightweight and susceptible to outside influence to survive the present situation of political turmoil easily.

Canning's own brief tenure was less than happy – Wellington, Peel and five others from the Liverpool administration resigned – and leaves many serious issues unresolved. His policy proposals came under vicious attack from fellow Tories, while the Whigs, after agreeing to support him, grumbled at the unimportant ministries they were allotted. This left Catholic emancipation, parliamentary reform and the Corn Laws all festering for a future cabinet (→ 22/1/28).

York's prestige as a home of learning grows

York
The enterprising and intellectually stimulating city of York has lately acquired yet another institution designed to promote popular learning and municipal welfare. The Institute of Popular Science and Literature joins a distinguished line which already includes a subscription library, a savings bank, and most recently a philosophical society (though with regard to the latter Leeds was the first Yorkshire city to found such a society). The chief promoter of these and many other valuable local causes is Charles Wellbeloved, a Unitarian minister, who crossed the Pennines from Manchester, where he had been tutor at that busy town's academy, and gave Yorkshire the benefit of his energy and vision.

New theology college gives boost to Welsh-speaking clergymen

St David's College, Lampeter: fresh hope for Welsh-speaking clergymen.

Lampeter, Dyfed, 12 September
Welsh-speaking clergy will find it easier to become curates in the Anglican Church as a result of the opening of the new St David's college of theology here. Speakers from the established church paid fulsome tribute to the man who has found most of the money for the college, Thomas Burgess, the former bishop of St David's.

Not only licensed but also financed by Bishop Burgess, Lampeter is proud to be the first all-Welsh-speaking divinity school. Its subsidized facilities will initially be made available only to poor incumbents from Welsh-speaking parishes. But when the first graduates begin to emerge, they will be directed to serve the church throughout Wales.

Bishop Burgess, who was transferred from St David's to Salisbury earlier this year, journeyed to Wales in his distinctive ceremonial coach for the opening. In his short address he told everyone that he would be leaving "a substantial legacy" to the college when he died and would continue to support it as long as he lived.

A college to raise the educational standards of Welsh clergy had been Burgess's dream since 1810. He had tithed his own income, and by 1820, when the foundation stone was laid, he had raised £11,000. He then obtained grants from George IV, and the rest, he said, is history.

Romantic poet and visionary Blake dies

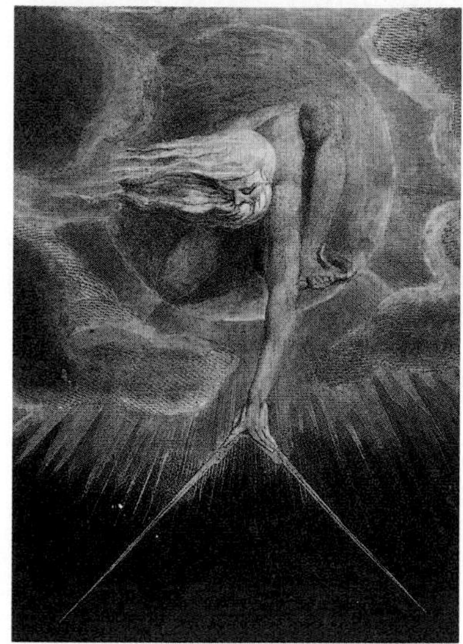

Blake's vision of the earth's creation.

London, 12 August
William Blake, one of the most remarkable poets in an age of poets, died today in his native London as he lived, in obscurity and poverty. He was 69 and hard at work on a set of illustrations for Dante's *Divine Comedy*. Like his illustrations to the *Book of Job*, done in 1826, they were commissioned by a painter, John Linnell, one of his few patrons. Both sets are masterly, quite unlike anyone else's vision. The Bible, Milton and Dante were his strongest inspiration.

His drawings were renderings of the visions that he saw all his life. "I am under the direction of messengers from heaven," he claimed. He saw angels who came down from treetops to speak to him, and once he asked: "Did you ever see a fairy's funeral?" and described one. For him the creative imagination was divine. His religious beliefs were his own, and his books expounding them are obscure. But in a few poems of great simplicity he showed his mystical insight. The "tyger" burning bright, the robin redbreast in a cage, the vision of a Jerusalem in England's green and pleasant land are unforgettable.

Scott admits he wrote 'Waverley' novels

The reading public is totally mesmerized by the gripping novels of Scott.

Edinburgh, 23 February
The "mystery" of the authorship of the Waverley novels was finally laid to rest today when Sir Walter Scott, Scotland's leading poet, confessed to being its most popular novelist as well. In his introduction to *Chronicles of the Canongate*, Scott admits that he is "the sole and unaided author of these novels of Waverley" which began with *Waverley* itself in 1814. At that time he said that he was not sure people would approve of an advocate writing novels.

Ever since then he has kept up the pretence of not knowing who wrote the series, which includes *Guy Mannering, The Antiquary, Old Mortality, Rob Roy, The Heart of Midlothian* and *The Bride of Lammermoor*. Yet it was an open secret. The resemblances between the novels and Scott's romances in verse were obvious (→21/9/32).

British, French and Russian fleet sails to controversial victory in Navarino battle

The battle at Navarino Bay: a "splendid victory" for Britain and its allies.

Athens, 27 October
A combined British, Russian and French naval force under the command of Admiral Sir Edward Codrington last week engaged and destroyed the cream of the Turkish and Egyptian navies in the bay of Navarino during what has been hailed, in some circles, as a "splendid victory".

That is certainly the view of Britain's lord high admiral, the duke of Clarence, who has already promoted a bevy of Codrington's senior officers and recommended to his brother, George IV, that the admiral himself should be rewarded with the Grand Cross of the Order of the Bath. But there are clear signs that this enthusiasm is not shared by the prime minister (who has let it be known that he found the congratulations premature and embarrassing) or even by the admiralty. Senior naval officials, when approached for comment about the battle, are reported to have been "cold and close", while cabinet ministers have been heard in private describing Navarino as an "untoward event". Meanwhile the duke had to fight hard to persuade even his own council to endorse the promotions. Rumours are starting to circulate that, far from being honoured, Codrington may soon be recalled and face dismissal from the Royal Navy (→3/2/30).

Terraces overlooking Regent's Park in London have now been completed by the architect John Nash: the latest stage in his plans for the capital.

1828

London, 2 January. *The Athenaeum*, a literary weekly, is founded by the reformer James Silk Buckingham.

London, 29 February. The newly renovated roof of the Brunswick theatre collapses, killing and injuring many people.

India, 4 July. Lord William Bentinck, the well known utilitarian, assumes office as governor-general of Bengal (→ 1830).

London, 21 July. Charles Manners-Sutton, the archbishop of Canterbury, dies at Lambeth Palace; his successor is to be William Howley, the bishop of London.

London, 14 August. William, the duke of Clarence, quits as lord high admiral of the fleet after disputes with both King George IV and parliament.

London, 23 August. Charles James Blomfield, an outspoken and reforming clergyman, is translated to Southwark as the new bishop of London.

Co Galway, 4 September. Anthony Raftery composes a lament, *Anach Cuain*, following the deaths of nine people in a boating accident on Lough Corrib.

Ireland, 15 September. Following the lapse of the Unlawful Societies Act the Orange movement in Ireland is formally revived by Eustace Chetwoode, the grand secretary (→ 14/4/36).

Edinburgh, 24 December. The trial begins of William Burke, who is accused of murdering 16 people in order to sell their corpses to doctors and medical students for use in practice dissections (→ 28/1/29).

Glasgow. Dr John Dunlop founds the Total Abstinence Society.

Britain. The first issue of the *Spectator*, a weekly periodical, is printed.

Britain. Thomas Carlyle publishes *An Essay on Goethe*, (→ 1838).

London. Richard Walker, a builder, invents "corrugated iron".

Britain. The romantic painter Richard P Bonington dies.

Rugby. Thomas Arnold, who was appointed as the headmaster of Rugby school this year, begins a reform programme to widen the curriculum and improve discipline (→ 12/6/42).

Duke of Wellington is new prime minister

Westminster, 22 January

King George IV has finally broken the political paralysis that followed Lord Liverpool's stroke, George Canning's death and the autumn interregnum presided over by the ineffectual Lord Goderich (who left office in a flood of tears) by inviting the duke of Wellington to form the next government. Despite many personal reservations, the hero of Waterloo has reluctantly agreed. The vacuum left by the refusal of both Whig and Tory party leaders to take office will be only partially relieved by this move. The Whigs are still remaining resolutely aloof, and only William Huskisson, Robert Peel and a handful of former "Canningites" have agreed to serve in the new ministry.

The duke is not alone in seriously doubting whether he is the best man to navigate his way through the storms that will doubtless be raised by such issues as Catholic emancipation and electoral reform. No one questions Wellington's many sterling qualities, but it is fair to say that they do not, on the evidence of his career so far, include a talent for compromise and delicate coalition-building. Such subtle abilities will probably be required in the months of constitutional crisis that are now looming (→ 5/1828).

Wellington: the man and the boot.

Government split by row over reform of 'corrupt boroughs'

Westminster, May

William Huskisson, the secretary for war and the colonies and a key member of the Wellington cabinet, has resigned. He leaves office accompanied by four sympathizers: Lords Palmerston and Dudley, William Lamb and Charles Grant.

His abrupt departure leaves unresolved several important matters initiated by Huskisson during his reforming spell at the board of trade until last year, including an amendment to the Corn Laws designed to protect British farmers while still giving consumers some access to the benefits of cheaper imported wheat. But this will probably go forward, as the high cost of bread is fuelling popular protest.

The split was caused by the issue of two disenfranchised corrupt boroughs, of East Retford (Nottinghamshire) and Penryn (Cornwall). Huskisson and his followers wanted to give the seats to under-represented towns, while high Tories wanted to see them simply absorbed into neighbouring county constituencies. A compromise was proposed, giving Penryn to Manchester and dissolving East Retford.

But the Lords voted against a new Manchester seat, so Huskisson opposed the East Retford Bill in retaliation. As he had voted against his government, he suggested resigning. Somewhat to his surprise, Wellington agreed (→ 16/11/30).

London students to get a new 'university'

London

Despite sustained opposition from Oxford and Cambridge, London has at last acquired a "university" of its own. The necessary money has been raised through the formation of a public utility company, supported by a group of eminent scholars including the economist James Mill, the historian Thomas Babington Macaulay and the poet Thomas Campbell.

At the moment the project consists only of a single college. But its ambitions embrace the extension of non-sectarian and scientific education to all students barred by the religious requirements and narrow curricula of the traditional centres of higher learning.

A blast of hot air changes industry

Glasgow, September

A major breakthrough in iron-smelting technology has been made here by the 36-year-old manager of the Glasgow Gas Works, James Beaumont Neilson. His newly patented "hot blast" furnace offers sharp cost reductions and quality improvements compared with today's unsatisfactory "cold blast" methods. By making it possible to use Lanarkshire's cheap black-band ironstone as a raw material, it is expected to give Scotland world leadership in the industry.

Enormous bonnets are the latest fashion craze. Large and over-trimmed, they serve to make amply clear the wearer's true position in society.

Catholic O'Connell barred from seat

Co Clare, 5 July
Daniel O'Connell has contested a parliamentary seat in Co Clare and has defeated Vesey Fitzgerald, one of the country's most popular landlords and a supporter of emancipation. O'Connell's refusal to take the oath of supremacy means that he cannot take his seat in parliament. He is hoping that, as a consequence, the question that has been agitating the country for so long will finally be resolved.

His victory has delighted Catholics, while the demonstrations that have been held throughout the country have greatly alarmed the government (→ 13/4/29).

O'Connell: barred at Westminster.

Repeal of Test and Corporation Acts gives non-Anglican Protestants more freedom

A meeting of Quakers, one of the Protestant sects affected by the repeals.

Westminster, 28 May
The repeal of the Test and Corporation Acts, dating from the reign of King Charles II, marks another small but important step in removing the disabilities that for the last century and a half have prevented Protestant dissenters from holding any but the most trivial forms of public office.

The repeal, which was proposed by Lord John Russell and tacitly supported by Robert Peel and the duke of Wellington, amounts to little more than a piece of legislative spring-cleaning, as Acts of Indemnity had been passed annually in recent years to exempt dissenters from the theoretical penalties of the statutes. But it has a greater political significance as it clears the way for the more contentious reform of laws restricting the rights of Roman Catholics. It is expected that a Catholic Emancipation Bill will be introduced next year.

Even the most cautious sceptics, like the duke of Wellington, appear to have been convinced by the continuing disturbances in Ireland, and by the ever-growing popularity of Daniel O'Connell's Catholic Association, that emancipation is now inevitable (→ 13/4/29).

Highlanders face slave conditions on Atlantic ships

Glasgow
Parliament has passed an act attempting once again to regulate the minimum amount of space that can be allotted on transatlantic emigrant ships to the pitiful swarm of Scottish landworkers who have been forced to desert their traditional lands to make room for the more profitable sheep.

After half a century of these "clearances", highlanders and their families are currently still leaving for Canada and the US at the rate of 30,000 a year. Conditions on board the transit ships in general remain unspeakable. When the brig *James* reached Halifax from the Clyde in 1826 everyone had typhus. The application of even the basic regulations covering the African slave trade to these voyages would cut abuses by at least 50 per cent. Yet captains see little reason to follow rules that they know will not be enforced, and few of their desperate passengers can afford to complain.

While the most notorious of the depopulation drives, such as those practised on the duchess of Sutherland's vast, remote estates, came to an end some years ago, the ruthless search for profit goes on, whatever the cost to human lives. Recently, in Easter Ross, the young laird of Novar, Hugh Monro, declared his intention of "placing the land under sheep" and called in 500 soldiers with three field guns to clear the glen. None of the former 700 tenants remains.

The streets of Glasgow, Greenock and Fort William are full of victims seeking the 30 shillings needed to buy three square feet (0.28 sq m) on the lower deck of a disease-infested ship sailing to Nova Scotia or North Carolina. Even when they have the deposit they may have to wait weeks or months before the ship to which they are contracted is full. The highway to Ullapool, from which many sail, is known as "destitution road".

Dream leads to arrest and hanging of brutal 'Red Barn' killer

Suffolk, August
Ten thousand people gathered at Bury St Edmunds to witness the hanging of William Corder for what is notorious throughout the country as "the murder in the Red Barn". After the execution, the rope was auctioned for a guinea an inch. The body of a young woman, Maria Marten, was found in April under the floor of the barn in the Suffolk village of Polstead. She had been shot through the head and stabbed to the heart. For months Corder, her fiancé, pretended she was still alive and well. But her corpse was found after her mother dreamt she had never left the barn.

Retribution looms for Corder as he and Maria go to bury their illegitimate baby. He had poisoned the child; he killed Maria when she grew suspicious.

1829

London, 10 February. After ten years as an associate of the Royal Academy, the painter John Constable is finally elected to full membership.→

United States, 4 March. Andrew Jackson, the son of Irish immigrants from Ulster, is inaugurated as president.

Westminster, 5 March. Parliament passes an act to suppress dangerous assemblies in Ireland.

London, 22 March. At an ambassadorial conference of Britain, France and Russia, an agreement is reached on the new boundaries of an independent Greece.

London, 13 April. The Catholic Emancipation Act becomes law.→

Westminster, 15 May. Daniel O'Connell, the elected Catholic MP for Co Clare, presents himself at the House of Commons; he is ordered to withdraw on his refusal to take the oath of supremacy (→30/7).

Switzerland, 29 May. Sir Humphry Davy, the inventor of the miner's safety lamp in 1815, dies in Geneva.

Italy, 27 June. James Smithson, the British scientist who left a bequest to fund a research institution in Washington, dies in Genoa.

Co Clare, 30 July. Daniel O'Connell is re-elected, unopposed, as MP (→4/2/30).

Ireland, August. The Reverend George Cart, an independent clergyman, is among those who begin an anti-spirits movement; he forms a society against spirit-drinking in New Ross, Co Wexford (→24/9).

Belfast, 24 September. Dr John Edgar, a Presbyterian minister, founds the Ulster Temperance Society (→6/1835).

London, December. *The Times* reports that customers are flocking to Thompson and Fearon's gin shop on Holborn Hill – at the rate of 360 every hour.

India. British rule in India has forbidden the practice of *suttee* by which a widow burns herself to death on her husband's funeral pyre.

Birmingham. The Birmingham Political Union is founded.

London. Dr Blundell, the surgeon who developed the procedure of the blood transfusion, successfully puts his theory into practice and saves a woman's life.

Full rights for Catholics

Daniel O'Connell raised high on the shoulders of jubilant Irish Catholics.

Westminster, 13 April

An "Act for the relief of His Majesty's Roman Catholic subjects" has received the royal assent, and Roman Catholic emancipation has finally been achieved. Catholics may enter parliament by taking a new oath by which they are bound to accept the Protestant succession and are asked to deny the pope's temporal jurisdiction.

However, an attempt to limit the practical implications of the admission of Catholics to full civil rights is contained in a separate bill, passed at the same time, which raises the property qualification for franchise from 40 shillings [£2] to £10. This effectively reduces the Irish electorate from 216,000 to 37,000 and disenfranchises the small freeholders who have been the most fervant supporters of Roman Catholic emancipation.

The passage of the Catholic Relief Act ends a controversy which has dominated British and Irish politics for over 20 years. But hostility between Catholics and Protestants remains dangerously high. Agrarian crime is once more on the increase, and Daniel O'Connell, the leader of the Catholic Association, intends to launch a campaign for the repeal of the Act of Union between Britain and Ireland(→15/5).

Story of murdering squire throws light on rural Irish life

Ireland

The novelist Gerald Griffin has captured the public imagination with the publication of his latest novel, *The Collegians*, regarded by many as his masterpiece. It is actually a fictionalized account of the true-life story of Ellen Hanly, who was murdered in July 1819. Hanly was poor, virtuous and beautiful, and married the local squire. The romantic love match turned sour: he later murdered her in what became a *cause célèbre*.

The squire was tried and found guilty. Daniel O'Connell, the champion of Roman Catholic emancipation who acted as defence counsel at the trial, is among those who have praised the novel.

But the novel is also a powerful parable of life in provincial Ireland as it is today, with a realistic mix of whip-cracking squires, farmers, peasants and servants from the big houses, as well as schoolmasters and cattle-dealers.

The Collegians is a profound and moving study of passion, murder, ambition and conscience. Griffin, who is already popular with British audiences, seems assured of success with his latest work, which may also enlighten readers "across the water" about the nature of life in rural Irish society.

Duke of Wellington in duel of honour with the earl of Winchilsea

London, 21 March

In an event unusual even by the standards of today's turbulent politics, the prime minister this morning fought a duel with one of his most flagrantly insulting arch-Tory critics, the earl of Winchilsea, who has always vehemently opposed even the most tentative moves towards Catholic relief.

The duke of Wellington issued his challenge after another letter had accused him of treachery and alliance with the Antichrist. The two men met at Battersea, but intentions, on both sides, were always more formal than lethal. The shots went wide, no one was even close to being injured, and honour was regarded as satisfied.

How caricaturists saw the duel between two pillars of the aristocracy.

Burke, convicted of trading in corpses, goes to the gallows

Edinburgh, 28 January
William Burke, who sold the bodies of his many murder victims to the doctors of Edinburgh so that they could practise their dissection and surgery, was hanged today in the Lawnmarket before a screaming crowd. "Burke him! Burke him!" yelled the mob, before his own corpse was delivered to the medical school, where students fought to watch the autopsy.

Burke, aged 38, was convicted mainly on the evidence of his fellow-criminals William and Margaret Hare, who testified to taking part with him in no fewer than 16 killings. Their collaboration was rewarded with blanket immunity on all charges.

Crowds witness Burke's execution.

They had started their grisly trail of death after selling the corpse of a man who had died at their lodging-house to Robert Knox, a surgeon. Seeing how easily money could be raised, Hare suggested to Burke that they prey on the city's vagrants. Depending on the age of their victims, they received sums ranging from eight to 14 pounds from Knox, who thought that at worst they were grave-robbers. Then on 31 October last year they killed Marjory Campbell, an old Irishwoman at Margaret Hare's lodging-house. Police were alerted after neighbours became suspicious, and they found the corpse in Knox's cellar.

Robert Peel sets up the first police force

One of London's new policemen gives a young suspect a hard time.

London, 26 September
After 72 years of libertarian resistance to the idea of a uniformed constabulary, Britain has an organized police force at last. A thousand men, mostly ex-soldiers, paraded today in their deliberately civilian-style top hats and blue frock coats. Despite derisive cries from the onlookers, they showed impressive discipline as they marched together for the first time, with their wooden truncheons, in Bloomsbury.

The home secretary, Sir Robert Peel, finally swept away fears that such a development might threaten individual freedom when he told parliament: "I want to teach that liberty does not consist of having your house robbed by organized gangs of thieves" (→ 12/1834).

Crime and violence increase in London

London
Robert Peel's new and controversial police force – nicknamed "the Peelers" – will have no shortage of work to do. In recent years parts of the capital, such as Lambeth and Southwark, south of the river, and Spitalfields and Seven Dials, within a stone's throw of the West End, have become little more than criminal dormitories where small armies of pickpockets, burglars and prostitutes are able to find safe haven. It is thought that there are now tens of thousands of Londoners living wholly or partly by crime. Many of them are ragged, often orphaned children, left to roam the city in search of money and food (→ 1839).

Constable wins a belated honour

London, 10 February
The latest Royal Academician to be elected is the landscape painter John Constable. In stark contrast to his fellow-student of the academy schools, J M W Turner, who was elected RA in 1803 at the age of 28 [*see page 793*], Constable has had to wait until he is 52 to receive the honour.

Constable is a miller's son from the Stour valley in Suffolk; success has come to him late because of his devotion to natural landscape, which is not regarded as highly as historical scene-painting or the dramatic seascapes at which Turner excels. He has made hundreds of sketches of the Stour valley which he works up into six-foot canvases to exhibit at the academy, but they seldom sell.

He is better known abroad than at home. His large painting of *The Haywain* was exhibited in 1821 with little impact in London, but in 1824 it was shown at the Paris Salon, where it caused a sensation and won the king's gold medal. An English critic wrote: "He has none of the poetry of nature like Mr Turner but more of her portraiture." However a French critic at the Salon reacted by saying "Look at these English pictures – the very dew is on the ground" (→ 1837).

Majestic Salisbury Cathedral in its rural setting, as seen by Constable.

"The Haywain" is quintessential Constable: a scene in the Stour valley.

Stephenson's 'Rocket' wins steam prize

"Rocket" leads its rivals in the Rainhill trials to win first prize.

Lancashire, October
The railway passed a new milestone this month when trials for the best steam engine at Rainhill, near Liverpool, were won by the aptly named *Rocket*, which was designed by George and Robert Stephenson. It was George Stephenson whose *Locomotion* pioneered steam travel on the Stockton-to-Darlington railway. The Rainhill trial was arranged to test whether steam locomotives could cope with the steep gradients on a line planned between Liverpool and Manchester. *Rocket* passed the test with flying colours to win the £500 prize. It is the first engine to incorporate a multitubular boiler with diagonal pistons on the side (→3/5/30).

Britain claims sovereignty 'down under'

Australia
Faced by renewed threats from the French to establish their own colony in the region – a scheme much beloved of the late Emperor Napoleon – Britain has this year proclaimed its sovereignty over the whole of Australia.

This vast southern land is among the latest of Britain's imperial acquisitions; indeed, the name itself was only settled in 1814, and alternatives, such as Jeremy Bentham's "Felicitania", are not without supporters. Nor did it have a very auspicious beginning. Discovered by Captain James Cook, this inhospitable land was deemed suitable only for penal settlements. The first of these, New South Wales, was founded in 1788, but its population is still barely 25,000, and other parts of the continent are even more sparsely settled (→1853).

Not everyone in Britain sees the potential of the new Australian colony.

Musical genius of Mendelssohn astounds and delights audiences

London
A new musical genius is thrilling the city's music lovers: the German pianist Felix Mendelssohn, on his first visit to England, has filled every concert hall where he has performed. Indeed, his remarkable performances have heightened musical appreciation throughout the country. The popularity of music has both altered and expanded over the last thirty years. While the last century provided a mainly aristocratic audience which enjoyed Italian operas and chamber music, recent decades have seen the expansion of that audience into the middle classes, whose tastes embrace mainly Germanic music, especially that of Handel, Haydn and Mozart, with a little Bach and Beethoven too. Choral music, beloved of the nonconformist chapels, is equally widespread.

Universities meet in Thames boat race

Oxfordshire, 10 June
Britain's two senior universities, usually embroiled in contests of an intellectual kind, took to the water today for a more muscular confrontation. The occasion was a competition to establish, if only for a year's interval, the superiority of one to the other – in rowing. A boat race, between eight-strong crews from Oxford and Cambridge, was held on the Thames at Henley. Oxford won today's hotly contested race, but Cambridge plan to challenge again next year.

July 4: the first "omnibus" service in Britain began today when George Shillibeer opened a route between Paddington and the Bank of England.

Six-month cotton strike is broken

Lancashire, December
The six-month strike by the Lancashire cotton spinners, led by John Doherty, the leading trade unionist from Ulster, is over at last. But while the strikers have been forced to accept defeat this time, their undaunted morale signifies that they may yet win the greater war.

Trade unionism, which suffered such savage repression earlier in the century, has been reborn since the economic crisis of 1825, when several years of prosperity came to an abrupt halt. As trade has picked up, so have the workers begun once more to flex their muscles. Unlike their predecessors, they refuse to hide their activities, openly admitting their campaigns for better wages and working conditions.

Their cause is further helped by a new, albeit brittle, liberalism in government. The current view of those in power is that it is better to have trade unions than hardcore radicalism (→1830).

1830

London, 7 January. Sir Thomas Lawrence, the president of the Royal Academy and a leading portrait painter, dies.

London, 3 February. Britain, France and Russia agree to guarantee the independence of Greece.

Liverpool, 1 March. The first light is shown from the Blackrock lighthouse.

Canterbury, 3 May. The Canterbury and Whitstable Railway, the first locomotive passenger railway in the world, is officially opened (→15/9).

Dublin, 10 May. The Zoological Society of Dublin is founded.

Windsor, 15 July. The funeral of the late King George IV takes place (→21/8).

Windsor, 21 August. King William IV celebrates his birthday with a banquet for the poor of the town (→8/9/31).

Europe, 4 October. All the powers are shocked when the provisional Dutch government declares Belgium to be independent (→4/11).

London, 4 November. A conference of European powers meets to settle the Belgian question.

Westminster, 16 November. The duke of Wellington is forced to resign as prime minister, bringing an end to over half a century of Tory government.→

Oregon, 13 December. Captain Black, a Royal Navy officer, lands at Fort Astoria and raises the Union flag.

Scotland. Francis Jeffrey, one of the founders of the *Edinburgh Review* and a critic of the Tory government, is appointed lord advocate.

Gloucester. Edwin Beard Budding, a textile engineer, develops the lawn mower.

Belfast. Thomas and Andrew Mulholland open a mill for wet-spinning of flax by steam power.

Scotland. The botanist Robert Brown discovers a cell nucleus in plant life.

London. The Royal Geographic Society is founded.

India. Troops bring the Mysore region under British rule (→1833).

Britain. Alfred Tennyson publishes *Poems, Chiefly Lyrical* (→1842).

O'Connell allowed to take his seat

O'Connell (c) meets leading Whigs.

Westminster, 4 February
At the age of 55, Daniel O'Connell, the hero of Catholic emancipation, has become the first Catholic in modern times to take his seat in the House of Commons. For 25 years he has been an agitator outside the walls of the legitimate political system. He is regarded with deep suspicion by British politicians, who see him as a rabble rouser, as personifying the force which threatens their hereditary domination, and as an intruder into a company of gentlemen. How he will deal with all this remains to be seen (→18/1/31).

William IV succeeds flamboyant George

Hampton Court, 26 June
King George IV is dead, the victim of a long and painful illness. He will be succeeded by his brother, William, the duke of Clarence. After the flamboyant George, William IV, who has promised to curb royal extravagance in both public and private life, will be a far quieter figure, and as such a far more popular one with his people.

He has, it is said, the "common touch", and his pleasures – peaceful walks and quiet conversation – will contrast, much to his credit, with the drinking, womanizing and immature behaviour of his brother.

That said, his bluntness, in some eyes, goes too far. For instance, when at 6am he was woken with the news of his brother's death he did no more than shake his informer by the hand and return promptly to bed, joking that he had "always wanted to sleep with a queen". A few hours later he reappeared with only a small piece of black crepe in his hat as merely token mourning, before riding to Windsor.

There are other areas in which this new monarch is not without problems. Aged 64, he only became heir to the throne when his elder brother, the duke of York, died in 1827. A bluff former sailor, with little experience of the graver burdens of kingship, William may find the realities of rule, especially at a time when major political and constitutional reforms are in the air, beyond his abilities.

William IV: the sailor king.

On top of this, he too has no male heir. All his legitimate children, of his marriage to Adelaide of Saxe-Meiningen, have died, and his ten illegitimate offspring, all born to the actress Dorothea Jordan, his mistress for 21 years, are naturally ineligible (→15/7).

Gentlemen find luxury, gambling and status in London's clubs

London
"Kindly remove the general", runs the popular joke, "he's been dead for three days." A little extreme, perhaps, but there is no doubt that for London's gentlemen the burgeoning world of "Clubland" offers a luxurious home from home where, untroubled by the mundane demands of the outer world, one may while away one's time – and, for that apocryphal elderly soldier, one's whole life.

Descendants of the last century's celebrated coffee houses, where such figures as Dr Johnson and his faithful Boswell might regularly be found, and of gambling houses such as Almack's and Brooks's (still thriving for high stakes), the clubs are enjoying a boom.

The first of them was the United Services, founded in 1815 by Lord Lynedoch for military men; its designer, Sir Robert Smirke, was himself a member of the militia. Smirke's splendid building, relying heavily on the Palladian style, set the standard for a number of other clubs, many of them sited along Pall Mall. These include the University Club, Crockford's and, most splendid of all, the Athenaeum, the London home of academics and clergymen.

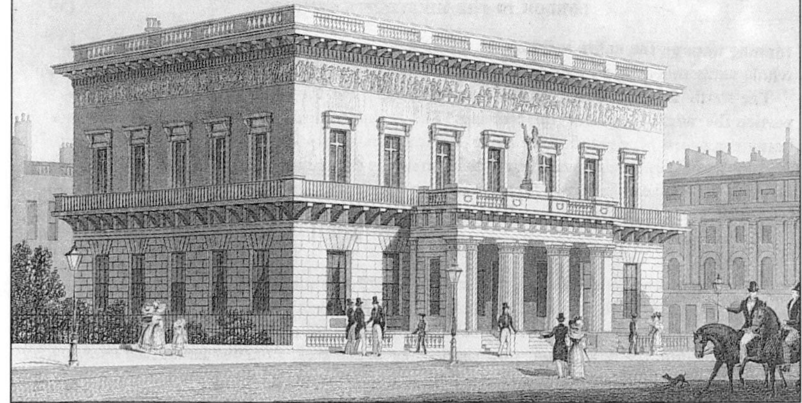

The new Athenaeum, said to be the most splendid of all London's clubs.

▷

Liverpool-Manchester railway opens

The railway tunnel at Edge Hill, near Liverpool, under construction.

Huskisson: accidental death.

Liverpool, 15 September
The epoch-making railway built to link Liverpool and Manchester opened for business today, but the celebration was marred by tragedy. William Huskisson, the former cabinet minister and a Liverpool MP, was killed by an oncoming train as he crossed the tracks to greet the duke of Wellington.

Huge crowds had turned out to see the most ambitious railway yet completed. Railways had begun in the early years of this century, mostly as a means of carrying coal. By 1821 parliament had approved 19 railway acts, but the greatest boost came with the 1825 opening of the railway between Stockton and Darlington. Even so, horse-drawn carriages on tramways were still favoured by some until last year's Rainhill trials demonstrated that steam locomotives could cope with a variety of gradients and operating conditions.

The winner of the Rainhill trials, *Rocket*, the engine designed by George and Robert Stephenson, has been adapted for use on the railway which opened today. It is the first in the world to operate a timetable for passenger and goods service. Despite safety fears, plans exist for a network of lines between Britain's major cities (→7/1831).

Two of the passenger trains hauled by steam engines (not "Rocket") on the pioneering Liverpool-Manchester railway.

William Hazlitt, pioneer of drama criticism, dies a happy man

London
William Hazlitt, the foremost critic of the age, died believing that he had "had a happy life". He summed up his achievements modestly: "I have loitered my life away reading books, looking at pictures, hearing, thinking, writing what pleased me best." The son of a dissenting minister, he studied theology and for a time earned a living as an itinerant portrait painter. Meeting Coleridge when he was 20 and hearing him talk opened his eyes to his own critical abilities. "I was dumb, inarticulate," he recalled, "but now my ideas floated on winged words."

He was the first regular drama critic of distinction, and his essays, originally lectures, are on the characters of Shakespeare's plays, the Elizabethan drama, and the English poets and comic writers; in addition there are his collected *Table Talk, Plain Speaker* and *The Spirit of the Age*. He quarrelled with his wives and loves and with most of his friends, such as Wordsworth, but never with his fellow essayist Charles Lamb. He had taste, style and a withering irony. "If I am ever damned, I should like to be damned by him," said Keats.

Lancashire cotton spinners in union

Lancashire
The Lancashire cotton spinners, whose six-month strike last year ended in failure, are once more spearheading the struggle for better wages and improved working conditions. Under their leader John Doherty, a steadfast supporter of Robert Owen, they have launched the National Association for the Protection of Labour.

This organization is designed to create a nationwide union, thus providing a much stronger force when it comes to bargaining, and making it harder for employers to break strikes by importing "blackleg", or non-union, labour.

Cloth workers press for a ten-hour shift

Yorkshire
For those in more leisured occupations it may still seem brutally long, but for the textile workers of Yorkshire the dream of a ten-hour working day is the driving force of a campaign designed to improve a basic aspect of working life.

Most workers, whatever their age, face a 12-hour day in the factory; but now, under the leadership of John Wood, a rich manufacturer, and Richard Oastler, a veteran campaigner for workers' rights whose inflammatory journalism has done so much to advance their cause, the textile workers may at last be able to reduce this.

Coals from Cardiff light London fires

South Wales, 12 November
The Welsh coal mines, already taking a major role in the production of iron, are to adopt a new, domestic role after the first ever shipment from Cardiff arrived in London today. The coal, some 400 tonnes, was sent by ship from the Abercanaid mine by the agent, George Insole. The mine, opened two years ago by the late Robert Thomas, produces first-class smokeless fuel, ideal for burning in the hearths of the nation's capital.

Agricultural workers riot in the south-east

"Captain Swing", the rick-burner.

Kent and East Sussex
They want no more than a living wage and have no overall plan and no particular leaders. They are hungry, and they are desperate – they are the agricultural workers of south-eastern England, who have staged violent protests this year. The uprising, which has yet to touch the north and which focuses on the poorest of all labourers, the farmworkers, has been nicknamed "the Swing riots" after the mysterious, pseudonymous "Captain Swing", supposedly the inspiration for the widespread rick-burning in Kent. Yet "Swing" himself is unlikely to exist – instead "he" is most probably a useful nickname, taken by anyone who wishes to play on the fear of such events.

Despite dire predictions by the authorities and landowners of a collapse of rural order, it does appear that these protests, and the burnings and the attacks on particularly exploitative and unsympathetic farmers that accompany them, are not part of some sinister plot; they are quite simply the spontaneous gestures of men too long deprived of what they see as the barest essentials of life for themselves and their families.

Pressure is increasing for electoral reform

London
Agitation for political reform is continuing to grow, and it seems increasingly certain that, however determined the opposition, both electoral and parliamentary reform must arrive. If nothing else, sheer weight of numbers will carry the day. On the one side, the Tory side, are ranged the traditional power-holders, the landed gentry. On the other is a wide-ranging group, which includes the Whig opposition (also landowners), William Attwood's Birmingham Political Union, the newly rich merchants and manufacturers (keen to transform wealth into political power), and the trade unions and radical artisans, who seek a greater say in the way in which the money they help create is spent.

Beer is on tap, if you have a licence

London
A new law has been passed which, while hardly as momentous as the much argued reform of the electoral procedure, will affect almost as many people. The Beer Act, coming in response to several decades of agitation for a change in the 200-year-old Licensing Acts, is set to change the way in which the British public enjoys its drink. Tied houses, owned by the big brewers, will now face stiff competition; from now on any householder who obtains the necessary licence is entitled to sell beer. It is even hoped that the quality of the drink itself may improve.

Pawnbrokers' boom: London now has over 5,000 unlicensed pawnbrokers but only 342 who are legitimate traders.

Wellington gets the boot

Under fire: Wellington is accused of blindness to the needs of the poor.

Westminster, 16 November
It is one thing to stand firm in battle, but in politics a man may be too unyielding – hence the fate of Britain's greatest soldier, the duke of Wellington, whose refusal to modify his absolute opposition to any form of electoral reform has today cost him his job as prime minister.

Two weeks ago, facing increasing agitation for reform, he declared that as far as changes went, "as long as I hold any station in the government ... I shall always feel it my duty to resist such measures".

It was a fatal blunder. The mob appeared in the streets, and a grand dinner was cancelled when the cabinet members feared appearing without armed guards. Yesterday the government was defeated in a vote on the civil list. This time even Wellington was forced to bend, and today he resigned (→22/4/31).

Earl Grey to lead Whig administration

Westminster, 16 November
Following the duke of Wellington's resignation [*see report above*] a new cabinet has been formed by Earl Grey. Lord Melbourne is home secretary and Viscount Palmerston is to be foreign secretary. Lord Brougham is lord chancellor.

Although critics see no more than the replacement of one set of aristocrats by another, Grey's cabinet brings the Whigs back to power after long years in opposition. That in itself is a real change, although few of the cabinet have any great reputations. Grey himself is a prudent grandee, a nature-lover, far happier in the country, who has little taste for the hurly-burly of political life, like the chancellor of the exchequer, Viscount Althorp.

The one star is Brougham, an acknowledged genius, albeit a wayward one, who stands way above his colleagues as an intellectual and an orator. His undoubted abilities, however, are undermined by emotional instability and an unrestrained vanity that teeters on the edge of madness. He has been condemned as "dirty, cynical and coarse", but the voters adore him, and his presence is indispensable to any Whig administration. ▷

Lord Grey leads the "Whigs".

Cobbett completes his travels with 'Rural Rides'

Boyhood: Cobbett grew up at a country pub in Farnham, Surrey.

Radical journalist tours the British Isles

London
William Cobbett, the most influential observer of British life since Daniel Defoe [*see pages 672-3*] and the self-proclaimed leader of the Radical cause, has published his *Rural Rides* in book form. The *Rides*, which have previously appeared in *Cobbett's Political Register*, are by far his most successful journalistic venture.

He is 67 years old, over six feet tall and "just the weight of a four-bushel sack of good wheat". He was the youngest sergeant-major in the British Army, but ruined his military career in an ill-thought-out attempt to expose corruption. He then went to the US, not as a republican but as a Tory pamphleteer, and continued as a Tory back in England in 1800, establishing the *Register* with Tory support. It was in 1808 that he became "the people's friend". His *Rides* are a report on the state of both the nation and himself. They show a fascination with the people of Britain, none of whom appears to interest him more than himself (→ 1832).

Youth: Cobbett volunteered to fight for the French revolutionary cause.

A nostalgic vision of life on British farms

Farnham, Surrey
Though the *Rural Rides* may at times tell the reader more about William Cobbett than about the countryside while he is passing through, the author would hardly see that as a criticism. Cobbett – born at the *Jolly Farmer* public house here in Farnham – sees himself as a countryman, a descendant of farming stock. To Cobbett, countryside and Cobbett merge into one.

He calls himself a Radical, indeed, the leader of the country's Radicals, but his *Rural Rides* – constantly harking back to a better yesterday – suggest a man of deep conservatism. Time and again he recalls the days when farmers and labourers sat and ate beef and drank beer from the same table, and there were no enclosures. His own efforts at farming have been disasters. He sank thousands into "improvements", losing most of the money he made out of writing. His seed nursery in Kensington went bankrupt, and his farm at Botley, in Hampshire, tottered for years on the edge of insolvency.

Yet in spite of his blindness to his own failings (he published his *Advice to Young Men and Women* two years after his wife tried to commit suicide), there is something endearing about him. He is, as his opponents admit, the most extraordinary living Englishman.

Country life: farmworkers toil in the fields near Rochester, Kent.

Southern counties are taken at a gallop

The confluence of Avon and Severn in Cobbett's favourite southern county.

Gloucestershire
Cobbett is at his best writing about southern England, where he grew up. He has his likes and his dislikes – he likes goldfinches singing, fertile farms, orchards and "puffing clouds" – but they are the long pondered thoughts of a man who grew up among these things.

His favourite southern county is Gloucestershire. Here "the girls at work in the fields (always my standard) are not in rags, with bits of shoes tied on their feet and rags tied around their ankles, as they had in Wiltshire". As for the city of Gloucester, it "is a fine, clean, beautiful place; and which is of a vast deal more importance, the labourers' dwellings, as I came along, looked good, and the labourers themselves pretty well as to dress and healthiness". His only complaint about Gloucestershire is that the county grows no turnips.

But there is a sadness and an anger in Cobbett's *Rides* through the southern counties. Small farms have been swallowed up by large ones. Landless labourers are forced to swell the ranks of the industrial workers, emigrate or surrender to the workhouse. Humble farmers are robbed of their profits by interest rates. And, most painful of all, the rural society in which Cobbett grew up is dissolving as Britain becomes industrialized.

Radical views on the industrial north

Sheffield, 31 January
William Cobbett's fame as the author of the *Rural Rides* in *Cobbett's Political Register* has ensured him an enthusiastic welcome on his travels. He has now arrived here on what is becoming a triumphant northern tour. All along the way, he says, "great numbers assembled to see me, to shake me by the hand, and to request me to stop". Tonight he spoke to a packed audience in Sheffield's largest music hall. In his speech he praised industrialization, praised the cause of reform – and praised himself.

Cobbett would appear to have mixed feelings about Britain's industrialization. In his earlier *Rides* he hated it. He pitied factory hands for being forced to abandon their rural birthright, and despised the factory owners for their greed and inhumanity. Now, having actually seen it, he glorifies it. But then Cobbett has never regarded intellectual consistency as a virtue.

"All along the way from Leeds to Sheffield, it is coal and iron, and iron and coal," he writes. "It was dark before we reached Sheffield; so that we saw the iron furnaces, in all the horrifying splendour of their everlasting blaze. Nothing can be conceived more grand or more terrific than the yellow waves of flame that incessantly issue from the top of these furnaces."

Cobbett's "arcadia" is no longer purely agrarian, he has announced. Industry and agriculture will marry in a new partnership to further the cause of reform.

Lincoln, with the great city dominated by its magnificent cathedral.

Newcastle-upon-Tyne, one of the industrial ports forged by the coal trade.

"Rural rider": William Cobbett.

How a countryman became a populist

London
Cobbett's Radicalism came to him slowly, as one would expect of a man who makes a public career of being a countryman. It was a long journey, taking him to Canada as an NCO, to the US as a Tory, and back to London as a Tory pamphleteer. His dislike of the arrogance of Pitt led him gradually towards Radicalism, but it was not until militiamen in Ely were flogged by German mercenaries for protesting against pay stoppages that Cobbett proclaimed his new opinions. The courts interpreted them as sedition, and he spent two years in Newgate prison. The once High Tory had been entirely transformed – into "the people's friend".

The man is unstoppable. In 1817 the cabinet offered him £10,000 to retire from politics; he refused and fearing arrest fled to the US, returning in 1819 with the bones of Tom Paine. In 1820 his defence of Queen Caroline made him more popular than Caroline herself. And in 1826, when he stood for parliament in Preston, he turned a humiliating defeat into a triumphant indictment of an unreformed parliament.

The new radicals: Cobbett and his contemporaries

London
Whatever venom Cobbett has for "the Thing" (the government), and "the Great Wen" (London), he always keeps sufficient in reserve for his fellow Radicals: Major John Cartwright, the old Jacobin; Henry Hunt, the orator; Sir Francis Burdett, the Radicals' tribune in the Commons; Francis Place, the scourge of the Combination Acts; and Lord Cochrane, the rebel peer.

Of all of them, Cartwright's views are closest to Cobbett's, looking back to an old Saxon England, where every man had land and liberties. Hunt is the most hot-tempered of the Radicals, and a speech occasioned by the "Peterloo" massacre earned him three years in jail. Burdett combines great wealth (he is married to a Coutts) with revolutionary fervour, much to the resentment of Cobbett, and in 1827, during a dinner in honour of the Westminster MPs Burdett and John Hobhouse, Cobbett and the two MPs ended up fighting on the table.

Francis Place still sees himself as the leader of the Radical cause – much to Cobbett's irritation. As for Lord Cochrane, a naval hero, MP and one-time leader of South American revolutionaries, even Cobbett cannot compete with him for glamour.

Hunt: hot-headed "Orator".

1831

Dublin, 18 January. Daniel O'Connell, the MP for County Clare, is arrested on a charge of conspiracy (→ 11/1833).

Ireland, 3 March. Police seize cattle in payment of tithes on the Kilkenny/Carlow border.

Tyne and Wear, 5 April. The Pitmen's Union strikes over low wages, tied cottages and a yearly bond (→ 6/1831).

Dublin, 1 May. The first issue of the *Comet*, the O'Connell weekly paper, is printed.

Westminster, May. The Whigs triumph in the general election (→ 29/10).

Arctic, 1 June. Commander James Clark Ross plants the Union flag at the north pole.

Tyne and Wear, June. The Pitmen's Union calls off its two-month strike.

Lothian, July. The Edinburgh/Dalkeith railway opens (→ 19/5/36).

Dublin, 1 September. The zoological gardens in Phoenix Park are officially opened to the public.

Westminster, 8 September. The coronation of William IV takes place; his niece and the heir to the throne, Princess Victoria, is absent owing to a dispute between her mother, the duchess of Kent, and the king (→ 17/5/37).

Bristol, 29 October. Riots break out after the rejection of the Reform Bill (→ 31).

Sunderland, October. The port is hit by an epidemic of cholera, believed to have spread from Russia and Europe (→ 6/2/32).

Portsmouth, 27 December. Charles Darwin, the naturalist, sets sail on a five-year expedition to South America, New Zealand and Australia (→ 1836).

Leicestershire. Edward Adcock of Melton Mowbray begins selling his home-made pork pies.

London. Sarah Siddons, the famous actress, dies.

Strathclyde. The Glasgow/Garnkirk railway is opened.

London. The first steam-powered omnibus, devised by Walter Hancock, goes into service between the city centre and Stratford in the east.

York. The British Association for the Advancement of Science is founded.

Welsh rioters shot dead

Powys, 3 June

Troops opened fire on protesting miners in Merthyr Tydfil today, killing at least 20 and seriously injuring many more. Earlier, a crowd of several thousand miners had attempted to seize the weapons of the soldiers sent from Brecon to disperse them. After failing to persuade the soldiers to turn on their officers and kill them, a young miner named Richard Lewis led the crowd into a battle with the troops. Enraged by the shootings, they became a terrifying force and were able to force some 450 armed soldiers to flee to safety until cavalry reinforcements from Swansea can reach them tomorrow (→ 16/1/32).

Merthyr rioters allegedly bathe their hands in the blood of a calf.

Population figures continue to soar

British Isles

The United Kingdom's population growth, which began to take off in the middle of the last century, is continuing at an accelerating rate, according to the latest census figures. The official census has been a regular event every ten years since 1801, when the population of England and Wales was just over ten million; it is now almost 14 million. Scotland's population has risen more slowly, from 1,600,000 to 2,400,000. Ireland has registered an astonishing leap, from five million to almost eight million. The figures are gathered by Poor Law officers and schoolmasters visiting homes.

Blacksmith's son Michael Faraday discovers secrets of electricity

The trappings of science: a scene from Michael Faraday's laboratory.

London, October

Michael Faraday, the self-educated blacksmith's son who is now director of the Royal Institution, has demonstrated how electric currents can be produced by means of magnetism. He has been experimenting with magnetic forces for some years, and last August he produced an electromagnet, an iron ring with two separate windings of insulated wire, and showed how an electrical "current" could be induced by another "current". Now he has built a machine which converts mechanical force into electrical force. A copper disc rotated between the poles of a permanent magnet produces an electrical current running from the centre of the disc through a wire to the edge (→ 25/8/67).

Churchgoers form a 'Lord's Day' society

London

The high-minded evangelicals of the Church of England, in their cutaway tail coats and high collars, are bent on imposing a strict austerity on Sunday with their newly founded Lord's Day Observance Society. They want to ban horse-racing and close public houses on Sundays, and in a bid to "rescue" the labouring classes they have set up a number of missions in slums, docks and army camps.

A new London Bridge is opened. Designed by the Scottish engineer John Rennie, it has fewer arches than its predecessor – and no houses or shops.

Parliament split as Reform Bill controversy rages

Crisis warning as third bill is introduced

Westminster, 12 December
Since the Whig government took office under Earl Grey a year ago, three bills have been presented to parliament in an attempt to reform the electoral system. Rotten boroughs such as Old Sarum, which is the site of an Iron Age fort, have two MPs, while flourishing towns such as Manchester have none.

The first Reform Bill was introduced in the House of Commons last March by the duke of Bedford's younger son, Lord John Russell [*see below right*]. He was jeered as he proposed disenfranchising 60 boroughs of fewer than 2,000 inhabitants and taking away the second MP from 47 boroughs of up to 4,000 inhabitants. These seats would be given to the new industrial towns, and the franchise would also be extended.

In the early hours of 23 March the bill won its second reading by a single vote, but it was later defeated by the Tories in committee stage. Parliament was dissolved [*see below left*], and the Whig reformers increased their majority in the subsequent election. A second bill, in essence the same as its predecessor but extending the vote to £50-a-year tenants in the counties, was rejected by the Lords on 8 October. Riots followed [*see below*], and Lord John today introduced the third Reform Bill with a warning that opposition would create a constitutional crisis (→ 7/6/32).

The great debate: one of the meetings campaigning for electoral reform.

King intervenes to force new election

Westminster, 22 April
Violent uproar broke out in both houses today when King William IV arrived in person to dissolve parliament. The king is no enthusiast for the reforms, but after initial hesitation he backed the constitutional right of the prime minister, Earl Grey, to call an election after the Reform Bill was defeated in committee two days ago.

When he heard that Tory lords were trying to force through a resolution against dissolution, William's resolve hardened. Angered by this challenge to a king's role, he dashed to Westminster, put on his crown and announced that parliament was dissolved immediately. His arrival caused a sensation in both houses. Whig MPs cheered when the firing of a cannon signalled the approach of the king, while in the House of Lords, Tory peers shook their fists under the noses of Whig dukes.

The dissolution paves the way for a general election on the single issue of reform. The Whigs are confident that they will win and plan to reintroduce the Reform Bill. The king still fears a clash between the Whig-controlled House of Commons and the Tory-dominated House of Lords (→ 5/1831).

Widespread riots follow 'No' vote by Lords

Flames engulf Bristol following riots over the defeat of the Reform Bill.

Bristol, 31 October
A cavalry charge today restored some order to this city after two days of violence which resulted in the Mansion House being sacked and a bishop's palace and other buildings being burnt. The violence is the most dramatic evidence yet of public anger over the rejection by the Lords earlier this month of the second Reform Bill.

Riots have also occurred in Derby, Nottingham and Worcester. Huge public meetings have taken place all over the country as the public vents its anger. In London newspapers appeared in mourning, and in Birmingham church bells were muffled and tolled. The public reaction is far greater than in the spring when the bill was lost in the House of Commons and there was the prospect of a general election.

Opponents of reform have been singled out for attack, as in the burning of the bishop's palace here yesterday – 21 bishops voted against the bill in the House of Lords, where it was defeated by 199 votes to 158. Many windows of the duke of Wellington's London home were smashed (→ 12/12).

The key reformers: Grey and Russell

Westminster
Despite the generation gap and the differences of background and temperament, Charles, Earl Grey, the prime minister, and Lord John Russell, his paymaster-general, have found a common purpose in their determination to drive the Reform Bill through a reluctant parliament.

The 67-year-old Grey is an aristocrat who prefers the peace of the countryside and his library. After Eton and King's College, Cambridge, he became MP for Northumberland when he was 22. An early advocate of electoral reform, he presented his first petition to parliament almost 40 years ago. The 39-year-old Lord John's early education was neglected because of his weak health; he later spent three years at Edinburgh University before travelling in Spain and Portugal. At 21 he became MP for Tavistock and he was initially more radical than Grey.

The prime minister told William IV last May that "it is the spirit of the age which is triumphing and that to resist it is certain destruction". But both he and Russell see the reforms as final touches for the constitution rather than the beginnings of more radical changes.

1832

Westminster, 19 January. A bill for Irish parliamentary reform is presented for its second reading in the House of Commons.

London, 6 February. People in the City are asked to fast to prevent the spread of cholera (→ 15/3).

Ireland, 15 March. The cholera epidemic reaches the ports of Belfast and Dublin (→ 27).

Dublin, 27 March. A Central Board of Health is appointed to contain the growing cholera epidemic (→ 6/1832).

Westminster, 8 June. Great rejoicing greets the passage of the Reform Bill.

Dublin, 30 June. The first issue of the *Dublin Penny Journal* is printed.

Westminster, 16 August. The Party Processions Act is passed to curb sectarian conflict and outbreaks of rioting in Ireland.

London. Jeremy Bentham, the radical political writer and originator of utilitarianism, dies aged 84; he has bequeathed his body to the university of London.

Manchester. Dr James Kay publishes *The Moral and Physical Condition of the Working Classes*, a study of the poor diet and appalling living conditions of the Manchester cotton workers.→

Westminster. The Warburton Act is passed, legalizing the sale of dead bodies for medical dissection and bringing an end to the practice of body-snatching.

Dublin. Aeneas Coffey, a distiller, opens the Dublin Dock Distillery.

Durham City. Durham University, one of the first provincial universities, is founded; over 90 per cent of the students will study to take holy orders.

Manchester. The city is granted parliamentary representation for the first time as part of the Reform Bill.

London. The Colosseum, a rotunda designed for panoramic shows by the architect Decimus Burton and begun in 1824, is finally finished.→

Lancashire. William Cobbett, the author of *Rural Rides*, published in 1830, is elected as the member of parliament for Oldham (→ 1835).

Britain ravaged by cholera epidemic

"King Cholera": unscrupulous quacks exploit the widespread fear of the disease in this 1832 cartoon. The epidemic travelled from Asia via Russia.

British Isles, June

Controversial quarantine laws imposed last year in a bid to ward off the killer disease cholera have been abandoned after the government's team of advisers admitted that they had proved ineffective. The first cases were reported in Sunderland last October; by February it had spread to London. The disease strikes with frightening suddenness; a victim suffers violent sickness and stomach pains, sometimes dying within hours of the first signs of illness. Until a few years ago cholera was confined to India, but since 1817 it has spread along trade routes and army movements westwards across Europe.

By last year the British government was sufficiently alarmed by the advance of the disease to send two doctors to St Petersburg, from where the current outbreak has spread, to see how the Russians were tackling it. A board of health had existed since 1804 to supervise quarantine measures at ports, and last autumn this was supplemented by the creation of local boards of health. The Cholera Prevention Act has made local boards compulsory, and several hundred now exist with powers to demand – but not enforce – sanitary measures.

Yet the efforts have stopped neither the disease's arrival nor its spread. It is estimated that over 20,000 have died, with doctors still divided over its cause (→ 5/1848).

Doctor portrays grim life of crowded Manchester cotton workers

Manchester

A 28-year old physician practising in a poor neighbourhood here has caused a sensation with his pamphlet *The Moral and Physical Condition of the Working Classes in the Cotton Manufacture in Manchester.* Dr Kay presents a grim picture of congested back-to-back houses without privies, and of slaughter-houses throwing refuse into unsewered alleys. Half of the children die before the age of five.

During the recent cholera epidemic, Kay noted that the disease struck most virulently among the poor. He recalls a night scene on the banks of the Irwell, where "60 of the most wretched of the population lived" – 27 died before morning. He argues that moral and physical evils must be tackled, with better homes and factory conditions and schools for the poor.

Welsh rioters win important concessions

Wales, 16 January

Trade unionism has won its first major victory in Wales as a result of last year's Merthyr riots in which more than 30 lives were lost – an act forbidding "truck", which is the payment of wages in goods instead of money. However the act, which comes into effect today, does not completely abolish truck. Nor does it prevent the over pricing of goods in company shops and the opportunities for blackmail which that gives to the more unscrupulous employers, who can threaten: "Pay up or lose your job."

Most Welsh miners seem to welcome the act, but those meeting in Cyfartha last week still decided to petition their anti-truck employer to open a "fair" or subsidized shop. They are convinced that they are being cheated outrageously by the ordinary local tradesmen of Merthyr and need some kind of protection from market forces.

Some "union clubs" in the less militant mining communities have said that they are prepared to dissolve themselves by agreement with employers. They expect, in return, to be exempted from all food price rises during the remainder of this year. Few imagine that this will be acceptable to many employers, or that support for a trade-union movement will cease to be strong in these areas.

The panorama of London, as seen in the city's new Colosseum rotunda, completed this year.

Sir Walter Scott, poet and romantic novelist, is no more

Scott: lawyer turned novelist.

Borders, 21 September
Sir Walter Scott, Scotland's premier poet and novelist, died today at his laird's estate, Abbotsford, which he purchased out of the rewards of his verse-writing and embellished expensively in baronial style with the profits of his historical novels. These made him as famous abroad as at home. He was renowned throughout Europe as the spearhead of the Romantic movement in fiction, "the magician of the north", described like Byron as "the wonder of the age".

Scott's historical novel sequence began with *Waverley*, in 1814. The books poured from his pen with amazing fecundity, based at first, in the borders or the highlands, on anecdotes and narratives which he had heard as a boy of the uprising by the Jacobites in 1745 or of the covenanters in 1685. In *The Bride of Lammermoor* he created a "gothic" masterpiece. The novel was dictated when he was in agony with gallstones.

With *Ivanhoe* he shifted into the Middle Ages; later he portrayed James VI and I arriving in London as king in *The Fortunes of Nigel*. *Quentin Durward* plunged into the history of Louis XI's France and in *Redgauntlet* Scott returned to Scotland and "the Young Pretender". In 1825 he fell into debt through the failure of his publishing venture and wrote himself almost literally to death to pay his creditors.

Parliament finally passes Reform Act

Westminster, 7 June
The stubbornly reactionary Lords have finally passed the Reform Bill. King William IV, under the threat of resignation by his prime minister, Earl Grey, had agreed to create at least 50 new peers if necessary to push the bill through, but in the end such a drastic measure was not needed. Before making the demand, Grey had agonized over the mass creation of peers, speaking of it as "a certain evil, dangerous as a precedent", but the resistance of the Tory majority in the House of Lords left him no other course.

It looked as though the crisis had been resolved last April when the Lords passed the bill by a majority of nine – 184 votes to 175. But then a Tory peer succeeded in pushing through, by 151 votes to 116, a wrecking amendment, which delayed consideration of clauses in the bill. Now even waverers in Grey's cabinet were resolved that the king must be presented with an ultimatum. William had been resisting, and had looked to the duke of Wellington to form a new government.

A banquet in the Guildhall, London, celebrates the passing of the act.

Within a week the duke had to throw in the towel.

It was a chastened William who once again sent for Grey – the reports of mass demonstrations had persuaded him that the country was on the brink of a "convulsion" – but he made the royal displeasure evident by keeping Grey standing during the interview. Three days ago, rather than be swamped by Whig peers, the Lords passed the Bill by 106 votes to 22. Today the bill received the royal assent (→8).

How the Reform Act will transform the shape of British politics

Westminster
The Reform Act brings sweeping changes to a system that has roots in the Middle Ages. Boroughs in the pockets of landowners, who simply appoint an MP, and those with a few electors, who sell their votes to the highest bidder, are to go, although calls for a secret ballot failed to win sufficient support.

In all, 143 seats have been taken from unrepresentative boroughs and allocated to counties and the new industrial towns, where the voting qualification will be a £10 household. But the proportion of houses of an annual value of £10 is greater in southern England than in the north, where houses of less than £8 are common so the artisan classes are still virtually debarred. In the counties, £2 freeholders, £10 copyholders and £50 leaseholders now have the vote.

Southern agricultural counties in England, with a quarter of the population, will have one-third of the 658 MPs. The electorate has been increased by about 50 per cent to

Attacking the rotten trees: a satirical comment on the reform debate.

around 810,000, or one-thirtieth of the total population. In England and Wales one in five adult males will have the vote (652,000); in Scotland and Ireland, which have separate reform acts, one in eight (64,000) and one in 20 (93,000) respectively. The Scottish electorate will increase tenfold in perhaps the most corrupt area of the system. The number of seats, static since 1707, goes up from 45 to 53, with more MPs for burghs such as Aberdeen, Dundee and Perth.

1833

Westminster, 1 January. Britain proclaims sovereignty over the Falkland Islands.

Dublin, 5 January. The first issue of *Dublin University Magazine* is printed.

Surrey, 15 May. Edmund Kean, one of the most celebrated actors of the time, dies at his home in Richmond aged 46.→

Leeds, May. Female workers in the woollen industry strike against low wages.

Berkshire, 3 July. Hungerford market is opened.

Westminster, July. Parliament passes an act ensuring the appointment of factory inspectors to enforce laws on child employment and working conditions (→8/1833).

London, 29 August. In a further move to prevent small bank failures the Bank Charter Act allows the creation of joint-stock banks for the issue of banknotes of not less than £5 within a 65-mile (104-km) radius of London; they have been allowed outside this radius since 1826, following a wave of failures.

Manchester, 2 September. The Statistical Society is founded.

Westminster, November. Parliament, despite opposition from King William IV, passes the Irish Coercion Bill and the Irish Church Bill; the king opposes the reform of the Irish church (→18/2/35).

London, autumn. William IV clashes with Lord Palmerston, the foreign secretary, over his response to Austria's opposition to liberalization within German states such as Hanover, of which William is also king.

Birmingham. Building work on the town hall is completed.

England. Charles Babbage, a mathematician and scientist, has completed his "Difference Engine", a small machine designed to calculate mathematical functions and compile tables of statistics.

Britain. Hannah More, an eminent feminist writer and evangelical who pushed for reforms for women, dies aged 88.

Dublin. Philip Dixon Hardy, a printer, installs the first steam-powered printing machine in Ireland.

London. Robert Browning publishes his latest poem, *Pauline*.

Scots local councils get new powers

Scotland
Three measures aimed at giving Scotland more popularly elected municipalities have reached the statute book in recent months. The first permitted Scots burghs to establish police authorities which, it was hoped, would limit the corruption of vested interests nominating members to suit themselves.

The other two extended the franchise in rural burghs to leaseholders as well as landowners, and granted the vote in the town burghs to men who occupy, either as owners or tenants, buildings valued at £10 annually. Scots representation in the House of Commons has now risen from 45 to 53; the electorate now stands at 60,000.

Trevithick, 'puffing devil' pioneer, dies

Trevithick: painted in c.1816.

Cornwall, 22 April
Richard Trevithick, the Cornish-born engineer and pioneer creator of steam engines, died today. His first steam "carriage", built in 1801 and known as the "puffing devil", ran between Camborne amd Tuckingmill, Cornwall, at between four and nine miles an hour. A second model followed in 1803, but rough roads defeated the engineering. In the following year Trevithick completed a steam locomotive that ran on tracks at five miles an hour pulling 10 tonnes of iron, 70 men and five wagons. The engine was a success – but the tracks collapsed.

Slavery is abolished

The slave deck of the "Albaroz", typical of conditions aboard slave ships.

Westminster, 29 July
Slavery throughout Britain's empire was officially abolished today. The enabling act of parliament, introduced by the colonial secretary, Lord Stanley, was the climax of a campaign first mooted by the younger Pitt in 1787 and pursued since by numerous ardent social reformers, in particular the Quakers and the evangelical Christian politician William Wilberforce – whose personal campaign against slavery has now seen final victory after over 40 years – and his friends.

Trading in slaves, outlawed by Britain in 1807 but thriving clandestinely, was created to meet British planters' needs in the West Indies and the former American colonies. Africans were shipped across the Atlantic in appalling conditions via the trade's headquarters, Liverpool, in return for cargoes of sugar, rum, cotton and coffee. The new act is rare example of legislation running counter to Britain's economic and financial interests. Commodities will be dearer; taxpayers must find £20 million to compensate slave-owners.

Wilberforce, who is now in his 70s.

Survey highlights working-class poverty

Manchester
Cholera, which struck here last year, has highlighted the appalling conditions in which this boom town's working classes exist. A survey by the Manchester Statistical Society, formed this year, has revealed a grossly underpaid, undernourished and overworked labour force in the local cotton mills, mines and factories. Living conditions are as grim as those at work, with people living in overcrowded and damp slums – often ten to a room – beneath an ever-present pall of smoke.

With virtually no drainage and only neglected privies or cesspools, sewage is swept into the nearest river. Typhus, typhoid and smallpox are rife. Diet is poor: potatoes with lard or butter and perhaps bacon are staple fare for people working 12 hours a day.

Factory Act improves child employment

Westminster, August
A social milestone was passed this month with the introduction of legislation limiting children's daily working hours in textile mills to no more than nine hours for those aged between nine and 13 and to 12 hours for those aged from 13 to 18.

The new Factory Act also reaffirms the ban on under-nines working, and prohibits under-18s from working at night. An hour and a half must now be allowed for daily meal breaks. Children under the age of 13 will be given two hours schooling a day. Championing the act was the philanthropist Lord Ashley, the son of the earl of Shaftesbury (→6/1844).

Child labour: new curbs on hours.

East India company loses its monopoly

Westminster
The East India company's monopoly of trading activities in British India has been ended by the government after mounting demands that the territory be thrown open to all British merchants. The India Act orders the company to close down its commercial operations as soon as possible in return for an annuity of £630,000. The company, granted its charter by Queen Elizabeth in 1600 [*see page 496*], rose to the position of a ruling power and greatly prospered from the abundance in India of natural resources such as tea and sugar (→8/1843).

Edmund Kean takes his final curtain

Kean: in his pomp and prime.

Richmond, 15 May 1833
Edmund Kean died today, two months after collapsing on stage in *Othello* at Covent Garden. In 1814, aged 27, he electrified Drury Lane as Shylock, discarding the traditional comic red wig and burning with a fury that made onlookers cringe. "For voice, eye, action and expression," wrote Hazlitt, "no actor equals him." His performances as *Richard III*, *Hamlet* and *Macbeth* took the town. "I wish I had a talent for drama; I would write a tragedy now," said Byron. Coleridge said: "To see him act is like reading Shakespeare by flashes of lightning." Drinking and arrogance spoilt his reputation before the end.

Consumption of beer and ale goes up as beer shops boom

England and Wales
An astonishing 35,000 new public houses have opened in England and Wales in the last three years, selling home-brewed beers in competition with the established producers. The boom follows the 1830 Beer Act which was passed both to appease the free-trade lobby and to provide an alternative to the adulterated beer, often further tampered with by publicans, being made by the breweries.

The act permitted any ratepayer to be granted a licence for £2 to brew and sell beer on his premises. With "gin palaces" abounding, many temperance workers see beer shops as a major evil.

A man's world: the interior of one of the many "pubs" which have opened.

Oxford academics stir religious ferment

John Keble: backing reform.

Oxford
A theological movement which is seen by many churchmen as raising the spectre of popery, has been established here this year by four fellows of Oriel College – John Henry Newman, Edward Pusey, John Keble and Richard Hurrell Froude. They have formed the Association of Friends of the Church and issued a number of tracts proclaiming that contemporary Protestantism is blighted by worldliness and incapable of halting the spiritual decay of the nation. The group believes that a return to the Catholic doctrine of the apostolic succession, and a reassertion of the church's role as a divine society with infallible and unquestioned authority, are necessary for rousing the clergy to action.

One of the tracts, most of which are addressed directly to the clergy, accused parliament of a "direct disavowal of the sovereignty of God" and denounced its members as apostates. For Newman, the outstanding intellectual of the group, the problem had started with the Reformation. The Oxford movement may give some sense of vocation to the clergy, but the "broad church" is unimpressed.

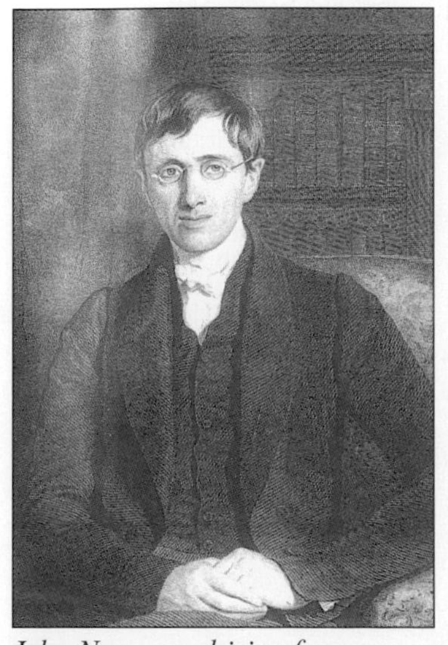
John Newman: driving force.

1834

London, 1 January. The European Aeronautical Society opens in Soho; it is selling passengers tickets to travel by balloon (→ 7/11/36).

Dublin, 23 January. St Vincent's hospital is opened by the Sisters of Charity; it is the first female-run hospital.→

Britain, January. The Grand National Consolidated Trades Union (GNCTU) is created by Robert Owen and covers all trades (→ 2/1834).

Hythe, Kent, 16 February. John Lionel Lukin, the inventor of the lifeboat, dies.

Europe, 22 April. Britain, France, Portugal and Spain negotiate the Quadruple Alliance to contain any instability on the Iberian peninsula.

London, 14 July. The Lyceum theatre, formerly the Opera House, which was totally destroyed by fire, is reopened.

Britain, 25 July. Samuel Taylor Coleridge, the well known poet, dies.

London, 10 September. The funeral of Thomas Telford, the Scottish-born engineer, road, bridge and canal builder, who died on 2 September, takes place.

Britain, October. The GNCTU, which was formed earlier this year, begins to break up (→ 1858).

Westminster, 17 November. The duke of Wellington is appointed as temporary prime minister after the resignation of Lord Melbourne (→ 12/1834).

Dublin, 17 December. The Dublin to Kingstown railway, the first steam-powered passenger train in Ireland, is opened.

Britain, 23 December. Joseph Hansom, an architect, patents his design for the Hansom cab.

Edmonton. Charles Lamb, the essayist and critic who wrote *Essays of Elia*, has died.

London. The London Statistical Society is founded to compile information on living conditions in the city.

Dundee. James Chalmers, a bookseller and newspaper publisher, invents an adhesive postage stamp.

Scotland. The Church of Scotland, dominated by evangelicals, passes the Veto Act, which gives congregations the right to object to ministers chosen for them by patrons.

'Tolpuddle martyrs' found guilty and all deported to British colony of Australia

Trade unionists protest at the "Tolpuddle martyrs'" fate and petition the king.

Dorchester, Dorset, March

In a controversial verdict, six farm labourers from the village of Tolpuddle, have been found guilty and sentenced to deportation to the colony of Australia, where they must labour for seven years.

The severity of the sentence reflects a fear among the property-owning classes of the emerging power of trade unions. Last year some 40 Tolpuddle villagers formed a branch or "lodge" of the Friendly Society of Agricultural Labourers, intending to join up with Robert Owen's Grand National Consolidated Trades Union (GNCTU). The Dorset authorities, mostly the agricultural men's employers, set out to crush the lodge with the tacit approval of Viscount Melbourne, the home secretary.

The fact that these men had taken an oath of loyalty to the newly founded union was the legal excuse. Dorset magistrates made much of this fact to charge the men with taking secret and unlawful oaths – contravening an act of 1797, passed to deal at the time with unlawful naval mutinies.

The Tolpuddle men have been made martyrs to a growing struggle between working men and their capitalist employers. There seems no doubt among ordinary men and women that their sentence far exceeds any supposed crime.

Robert Owen forms a National Union

London, February

Robert Owen, the pioneer of factory reform, has just formed the Grand National Consolidated Trades Union (GNCTU). The aim is to bring all occupations into one big union which will revolutionize society by running industry and commerce along cooperative lines. As many as 500,000 members from every sort of trade are claimed to be potential members.

Where other unions have failed Owen's may stand a greater chance of success. A true visionary, yet a successful businessman, he has already set up a model community based around his New Lanark cotton mills, near Glasgow. The impetus for the new union was a strike organized in support of Derby tradesmen who were "locked out" by their employers (→ 10/1834).

Robert Owen: a visionary reformer.

Tribal wars erupt in southern Africa

Cape Colony

Tribal wars have broken out here, threatening the security of British settlers who rely heavily on slave labour. The wars have intensified the problems facing Sir Benjamin D'Urban, the new governor of the colony, as he struggles with frontier problems. Tribes to the north and east of the borders of Cape Colony have been carving up territory for their own uses. King Chaka of the Zulus has devastated huge areas of land and broken tribal life in Natal, Nyasaland and the Kalahari desert.

Londoners can now mingle with the famous as never before. Lifelike waxworks – models of kings, statesmen and others – are the "stars" of a new exhibition opened in the capital this year by Madame Tussaud.

Melbourne takes over as new PM

Earl Grey, who is stepping down.

Westminster, July
The new prime minister, succeeding Earl Grey who has decided to stand down, is the 55-year-old home secretary William Lamb, the second Viscount Melbourne. It remains to be seen whether he will be strong enough to lead a divided government. Although a Whig, and a senior member of the cabinet which pushed through the Reform Act, he is no instinctive reformer. Somewhat snobbish in his disdain of the vulgar, he brings an arrogance to government, believing himself "entirely free to choose both the principles upon which, and the men with whom, I will consent to engage in government or opposition" (→17/11).

New law to help poor

England and Wales, March
A new Poor Law is to be introduced to alleviate some of the problems faced by both the poor and the parishes forced to support them. Setting aside the Elizabethan Poor Law of 1601, the new act will radically alter the situation in which people can turn to poor relief from the rates.

The growth in population and depression in agriculture have opened the floodgates of the poor turning to hard-stretched parishes for relief. Even back in 1818, the cost of poor relief was put at £8 million. Conservatives fear that handing out such money leads to a reduction in the daily rate of labourers' wages and encourages the poor both to have more children and to lose the desire to work.

The new law will restrict outdoor relief to the aged and the sick. In future, the able-bodied who seek poor relief must enter a "workhouse", whose conditions will be spartan, in order to discourage applicants. These so-called *bastilles* are controversial. Families will be split by age and sex, with little food. The policy will be to separate the deserving poor from the undeserving, to deter the latter and make the workhouse an incentive to self-help (→13/2/38).

A refuge for the poor: a "male ward" in an institution for poor relief.

Peel in power after an unsettled year

Peel: a Tory back in office.

Westminster, December
Sir Robert Peel is to be the fourth prime minister this year. Last month William IV accepted the resignation of Viscount Melbourne, who succeeded Earl Grey in July. The duke of Wellington acted as prime minister (and in other posts) until this month's appointment of Peel as the new Tory premier.

The Melbourne cabinet had been seriously divided, and last month Viscount Althorp, the chancellor and leader of the Commons, succeeded his father as Earl Spencer and went to the Lords. Without the able Althorp to defend the government in the Commons, Melbourne offered his resignation to King William IV, who accepted (→4/1835).

Dublin hospital is first run by women

Dublin, 23 January
St Vincent's hospital, the first hospital in the United Kingdom to be run by women, has been opened here by the Sisters of Charity. The founder of the order is Mary Aikenhead. Raised a Protestant, she became a Roman Catholic and was asked to establish a congregation of the Sisters of Charity in Dublin.

Following the granting of emancipation, the involvement of members of Catholic religious orders in health care and education is gradually increasing, and there has also been a resurgence in the building of Catholic chapels as well as Presbyterian meeting houses.

Fire destroys House of Commons, but Westminster Hall saved

London, 16 October
The night sky was lit by an incredible range of oranges and reds tonight as crowds gathered to watch (and cheer) the Palace of Westminster being gutted by fire. Much of both the houses, Commons and Lords, has been destroyed, including the chapel of St Stephen.

The fire was started by workmen burning long-discontinued wooden tallies. The flames raced through the old building. In the absence of any fire brigade, three regiments of the Guards and a detachment of cavalry were brought in to help. Westminster Hall itself was saved by taking fire engines inside and shooting water up at the ancient hammerbeam roof.

Flames sweep through the Palace of Westminster, causing massive damage.

1835

Dublin, 1 January. *Ancient Ireland*, the first issue of a new periodical intended to revive the Irish language, is published.

London, 18 February. Daniel O'Connell, the Irish Catholic MP for County Clare, meets Whig and Radical leaders at Lichfield House (→ 29/4).

London, March. The parish of Clerkenwell has established an infant school for children between the ages of two and six for the sum of twopence a day; this leaves mothers free to do other tasks.

Ireland, 29 April. Michael O'Loghlen is appointed solicitor-general; he is the first Catholic since the reign of James II of England to be appointed to a legal office (→ 11/1841).

London, April. The *Lancet*, a medical journal, publishes notice of a new cure for cancer; it is an old Indian remedy used for countering the venom from poisonous arrows.

Co Tyrone, June. John Finch, an English teetotaller, founds a total abstinence society at Strabane (→ 2/1836).

Westminster, 31 July. The government introduces an Irish municipal reform bill.

Dublin, 15 August. The British Association for the Advancement of Science holds its annual conference.

London, 31 December. Count Lennox demonstrates his dirigible *The Eagle*.

Britain. William Cobbett, the author of *Rural Rides*, a series of journeys through the British countryside, dies.

Britain. Journalistic pieces by a young writer, Charles Dickens appear in the *Evening Chronicle* (→ 2/4/36).

Scotland. James Hogg, the poet, known as "The Ettrick Shepherd" has died.

Wiltshire. William Henry Fox Talbot experiments with photography at Lacock Abbey and takes the first successful negative photographs in Britain (→ 31/1/39).

Cornwall. A schoolmaster issues the following advertisement: "every boarder must be provided with a bible and prayer book, a knife and fork and a silver dessert spoon; all of which, except the books, become the proprietor's perquisites on the pupil's quitting the school".

Melbourne returns on Peel's resignation

London, April

King William IV has given in. The Whig leader, Lord Melbourne, has formed a government. After five months of trying to govern without a majority in the House of Commons, Sir Robert Peel's Conservative ministry has resigned.

The king who has a deep distrust of reform, accepted Lord Melbourne's offer to go last November. Lord Althorp, whom he trusted, had gone to the House of Lords and Lord John Russell, whom he distrusted, was the natural successor as leader in the Commons. The king was delighted to be rid of the Whigs and at first asked the duke of Wellington to form a ministry. But the duke refused, saying that a modern prime minister had to be in the House of Commons. He stood until Peel returned from a continental tour to form his first ministry, albeit without a Commons majority.

A general election failed to give the Tories a majority in the House of Commons, and although one parliamentary defeat followed another Peel soldiered on for three months, urged on by the king. In the end, impotent without a majority, Peel was pleading with William to relieve him of office.

Lord Melbourne in his youth.

The constitutional lesson is clear. The 1832 Reform Act has altered the balance of power. Only a party with a Commons majority can now govern. The monarch's own preferences are irrelevant (→ 10/5/39).

Illicit home brewing increasing in Ireland

Illicit drinking is on the increase in Ireland as taxes hit the liquor trade.

Ireland

Since 1823 the legal distilleries in Belfast, Dublin and Cork have doubled their output. This has inspired a desperate attempt this year to raise revenue by taxing spirits and introducing draconian measures against illicit distilling.

But these official measures to collect increased taxation are proving difficult to enforce owing to inadequate resources. The situation is further complicated by the fact that in large areas of Connacht and the south-west, cash earnings from illicit distilling are a vital part of the local economy.

The revenue police appear to be badly trained and poorly educated, but an attempt is now being made to reorganize them with a better denominational mix.

City mission takes gospel to workers

London, 16 May

A new evangelical society has been founded to work amongst the urban poor: the London City Mission. Its sole premises is a work man's cottage in Hoxton and its sole missionary is a young Scot, David Nasmith, so poor that supporters had to pay for his fare to London.

Nasmith has vowed to take the gospel to those parts of London which the conventional churches cannot reach – the slums, whorehouses and workhouses – and he sees his first task as establishing a "ragged school" in a disused stable in Westminster.

Royal builder Nash leaves noble legacy

Isle of Wight, 13 May

The architect Sir John Nash, that "clever, odd, amusing man with a face like a monkey's" (according to the duke of Wellington's friend Mrs Arbuthnot) has died. He was the favourite architect of George IV, who was rumoured to be the father of Nash's five children – Mrs Nash was one of George's favourite mistresses. Nash's fine legacy includes Carlton House Terrace, Regent Street, Regent's Park and the remodelled Buckingham Palace with its Marble Arch in London, as well as the bizarre Royal Pavilion at Brighton.

Nash – and "Nashional Taste".

Elected borough councils run towns

Westminster, 9 September
New municipal corporations, all elected, are to take over the functions of local government in urban areas from the increasingly corrupt and inefficient old corporations and improvement commissions. Over two million people will be affected by the change.

Essentially the Municipal Corporations Act, which passed its third reading in parliament today, will transfer the property, powers *and* debts of the old municipalities to the new bodies. Justices of the peace are also to lose their highway duties to the urban corporations, but they will still retain their judicial and licensing powers.

The act gives new powers to towns such as Shrewsbury, shown here.

Prison inmates to have single cells

Westminster
Prisons are to have a state inspectorate, and prisoners are to have their own cells, a parliamentary committee has recommended. But following the disastrous experiments in solitary confinement in the United States, they are to be permitted to associate with other prisoners at work and on exercise. Where productive work is not available for prisoners, the treadmill is to be introduced.

The government has accepted the recommendations. The long campaign for penal reform, which was begun as long ago as 1773 by John Howard, and continued by the Quaker Elizabeth Fry and the philosopher James Mill, has won an important victory (→1856).

Cold Bath prison in London.

Road users pay a toll to improve the condition of the highways

A tollgate marks the entrance to Tottenham Court Road in London.

London
A new Highways Act has been passed – the latest attempt to regulate Britain's appalling roads, which are a nuisance to travellers and an obstacle to economic growth.

The *Corvée* [forced labour] has been abolished, and parish roads are to be financed by the rates and trust roads by tolls. But critics of the bill point out that no single authority has been given overall responsibility, and there is still much confusion about which roads are parish roads and which ones are toll roads, while the increasing frequency of toll gates is making long distance travel both expensive and time-consuming.

Edinburgh hailed as 'northern Athens'

Scotland
The transformation of Scotland's capital into a neo-classical city is complete. North of the Royal Mile, which runs from the Castle to Holyroodhouse, a New Town, Athenian in style, fans out from the old city to the estuary of the Forth and the hills of Fife beyond.

Two generations ago Edinburgh was an overcrowded ribbon of tall stone buildings perched precariously on volcanic rock. Unable to expand outwards, it expanded upwards, until the Royal Mile resembled a canyon with windows. Polluted by smoke and human excreta (there were no sewage arrangements), it was known as *Auld Reekie*. In 1766 James Craig was commissioned to lay out a New Town. Its style was Greek Revival, and it continued to expand north from Princes Street for nearly 70 years. But the city has paid a price for being "the Athens of the North". In Old Edinburgh rich and poor lived in the same tenements; now the rich have moved to the New Town, the classes have been segregated, and the old town has become a slum.

The High Street in Edinburgh, part of the celebrated "Royal Mile".

Belfast, February. A total abstinence society is formed (→ 1842).

Worcester, 2 March. The first point-to-point horse-racing meeting is held by the Worcester Hunt, on the Madresfield estate.

Chelsea, 2 April. Charles Dickens, the young writer, is married (→ 1837).

Ireland, 14 April. The Grand Orange Lodge decides to dissolve itself.

Westminster, 19 May. Parliament gives permission for a railway line from Belfast to Armagh (→ 12/1836).

Liverpool, 8 September. The Liverpool and Victoria dockyards are officially opened.

Britain, 15 September. The stamp duty on newspapers is reduced from fourpence to a penny.

Cornwall, 2 October. Charles Darwin, a naturalist, lands at Falmouth aboard HMS *Beagle* at the end of a world trip of almost five years.

Germany, 7 November. Charles Green and Monck Mason leave London in the *Royal Vauxhall* balloon, cross the Channel and land in Nassau (→ 24/7/37).

London, 14 December. The first section of the Greenwich railway is completed and opened; it runs from London Bridge to Deptford (→ 4/7/37).

Gravesend, Kent. The town hall is completed.

London. John Frederic Daniell, the first chemistry professor at King's College, invents the "Daniell Cell", the first battery capable of producing a steady current for a long period of time.

London. Lord George Bentinck, a race-horse owner, commissions the first horse-box, a means of transporting horses comfortably by road; it is built by Messrs Herring, coachbuilders, of Long Acre, Covent Garden.

Westminster. Parliament passes the Locomotive Act limiting the speed of all trains to five miles per hour, with a person carrying a red flag walking in front of the steam engine (→ 14/12).

London. The government pays the United States £1.2 million to keep 3,601 slaves who fought on the British side in the war of 1812-14.

Northern English towns act like magnets to draw in thousands hungry for work

The Lancashire town of Oldham: mills are magnets for country-dwellers.

Lancashire
The new towns of the English north and midlands are proving magnets for both the poor and moderately well-off artisans and tradespeople. In Manchester and its smaller neighbours, such as Oldham, the cotton industry has led to the proliferation of mills and textile factories. This has brought a huge influx of workers to service the new industries.

Banks are prospering, and there is a whole new professional class of solicitors, clerks and commercial travellers. There is a boom in demand for skilled workers, like saddlers, to meet the needs of the rising numbers who can afford horses – and a huge increase in domestic servants. Here, the magnet has pulled in some from as far away as Ireland. Birmingham is attracting many from the rural parts of Wales, where work is more scarce.

This massive shift in populations has already made last year's Municipal Corporations Act look very out of date. Neither Manchester nor Birmingham were included in the towns to be given the new powers. As a result of that, town councils were to be elected by all ratepayers in 178 boroughs. Manchester and Birmingham are already much bigger than most of those and are growing faster.

The port of Liverpool is thriving as industry grows in nearby towns.

Association formed for working men

London, 16 June
A Radical group called the "London Working Men's Association for Benefiting Politically, Socially and Morally the Useful Classes" was established today. Despite the ponderous name – it will be referred to as the London Working Men's Association (LWMA) – the group has a very hard-hitting manifesto. It wants the vote for all adult males, annual parliaments, vote by secret ballot, pay for MPs and constituencies of equal size.

The LMWA points out that 331 MPs, a majority of the House of Commons, are elected by 151,492 voters out of a population of six million adult males. No fewer than 205 MPs, the group claims, are related to peers of the realm. The new association grew out of a meeting held last February at the Crown and Anchor Tavern in the Strand. Its leaders are mainly skilled craftsmen like William Lovett and Henry Hetherington. Many, including Hetherington, are printers.

Potato blight hits highland crops hard

Glasgow
Relief committees here say that they are now confident that the threat of mass starvation in the Scottish highlands has been averted. Thousands of lives have been saved by charitable committees that sprang up in towns as soon as it became clear that blight was going to wipe out virtually the whole of the west-coast potato crop. Money was quickly raised, and parcels of basic foodstuffs were shipped up to the highlands.

Many highland areas are poorer than they were at the end of the Napoleonic wars. Lairds and sheep farmers have grabbed much of the fertile land, leaving the crofters dependent on a limited range of crops. Many poor Highlanders exist on a diet of potatoes and herring. Around Inverness the labourers normally eat about four kilos (nine pounds) of potatoes a day, as well as 230 grams (half a pound) of oatmeal and a litre (1.75 pints) of milk – and fish when they can get it.

Boer farmers break free of British control

Cape Town
Boer farmers, the descendants of the Dutch settlers, are leaving Cape Colony in large numbers to colonize new lands in the high *veldt* to the north-east. Discontent with British rule has escalated in recent years. The abolition of the slave trade hit the Boers, who had relied on black labour. And the British policy of trying to be fair to all races has led to blacks being given land which the Boers regarded as theirs.

The Boers became increasingly frustrated. They set up republics after the French Revolution, but these were crushed by British soldiers. Now they are moving out in their ox-drawn wagons, guarded by teams of armed horsemen. They are ready to fight the blacks in order to establish new settlements out of reach of the British (→ 1/1852).

Boer families begin the great trek.

Anglican clergymen face new controls

Westminster
Anglican clergymen will no longer be allowed to hold more than two livings. This is among a number of reforms which have followed a commission into the established church. Its first report last year recommended the creation of new sees at Ripon and Manchester plus reforms of the finances of many of the richer existing sees. A second report published this year proposed curbs on the number of clergymen attached to cathedrals and more help for poorer parishes. Tithe collection is also to be reformed.

Commission urges anti-poverty drive

Ireland
A grim picture of poverty here is revealed in the final report this year of a royal commission established in 1833. The commission was chaired by Richard Whateley, the Protestant archbishop of Dublin. The archbishop has a lifelong interest in social reform and conducted a detailed investigation of Irish social conditions. The commission discovered that there are no arrangements for public relief outside the capital, Dublin, and it urges government action to deal decisively with poverty in Ireland (→ 2/1837).

Charles Darwin is back from world trip

London
Charles Darwin, a 27-year-old naturalist, has returned from a five-year-long voyage around South America and in the Pacific with an amazing collection of animals, birds and plants. He is already talking excitedly about how much scientists can learn from detailed study of these different species.

Darwin showed great enterprise. He persuaded the captain of HMS *Beagle*, a ten-gun brig of 235 tons, to take him on board and asked for his food but no pay; he was looking for a chance to study. He has a deep interest in how life developed on earth. Hence on his voyage he has also become an expert geologist, collecting fossils with as much enthusiasm as live specimens. They show what plant and animal life was like centuries ago (→ 1839).

Darwin: voyage of discovery.

Macadam comes to the end of the road

Macadam: the road revolutionary.

Dumfries & Galloway, 26 Nov
The man who gave his name to the most effective road surface [*see report on page 809*], John Macadam, died today at the age of 80. "Macadamizing" is the process that he perfected. It involves raising the surface of the road by building in layers of graded small gravel bonded together. Drains are then built on each side of the road.

Macadam first began to experiment in Ayrshire, where he was a deputy county lieutenant and road trustee. In 1798, as agent for the navy in Falmouth, he developed his roads there to help to get goods to the ports. He became surveyor-general of Bristol roads in 1815, and in 1827 for the whole country. Parliament adopted his system in towns and it has made today's rapid mailcoach travel possible.

Passenger traffic brings new lease of life to Forth-Clyde canal

Passenger traffic will soon join the busy stream of vessels on the canal.

Glasgow
Scotland's oldest canal is enjoying a new boom. The Forth-Clyde canal was started in 1769 and completed in 1790. It is vital for carrying coal, building materials, iron and other heavy goods and enables Glasgow merchants to trade with Europe. Passengers have also taken to the water. Nearly 200,000 have used the canal this year, over four times the number in 1812. And the introduction of fast passenger boats on the Paisley-Glasgow route attracted a phenomenal 363,000.

Pitman invents a new form of writing

Bath
A local school teacher, Isaac Pitman, has invented a new form of writing which he hopes will make it possible for speech to be taken down at speed. Already he can write over 50 words a minute with his "Stenographic Sound Hand". It is based on the sound of vowels and consonants rather than conventional spelling. These are written as a mixture of straight lines, shallow curves, dots and dashes (→ 12/1/97).

1837

Glasgow, 11 January. Sir Robert Peel is installed as lord rector of the University.

Moscow, 23 January. John Field, the Irish pianist and composer who emigrated to Russia in 1803, dies aged 55.

England, 31 March. The painter John Constable dies aged 61.

Dublin, April. Dr William Stokes publishes *A treatise on the diagnosis and treatment of diseases of the chest.*

Windsor, 17 May. King William IV collapses on returning from a horse tournament (→ 20).

London, 20 May. Princess Victoria, under pressure from her mother, the duchess of Kent, is forced to decline the offer of a private income from her uncle, William IV (→ 24).

London, 24 May. Victoria comes of age; William IV increases the rift existing between her and her mother when he offers Victoria an independent household (→ 20/6).

Hanover, 20 June. Prince Ernest Augustus, the duke of Cumberland, becomes king of Hanover on the death of his brother, William IV.→

Westminster, 8 July. King William IV is buried with great pomp and ceremony.→

Bristol, 19 July. Isambard Kingdom Brunel launches his steam ship, the *Great Western.*

London, 24 July. Robert Cocking makes a daring jump from a balloon, the *Great Nassau*, over Blackheath, using an "inverted parachute"; his jump fails, and he falls from 180 metres (600ft) to his death (→ 4/4/40).

Leeds, 18 November. Feargus O'Connor publishes the first issue of his radical newspaper *Northern Star.*

Strathclyde. An underground explosion at Blantyre colliery kills 207 miners.

Cumbria. Twenty-seven men drown in a Workington coal-mine when the sea breaks in.

Scotland. Five cotton spinners are sentenced to transportation for seven years following their role in a strike against wage cuts and job losses.→

London. Official registration of all British births, marriages and deaths begins; records will be kept at Somerset House, in the Strand.

Victoria is queen at 18

Celebrations later in the year mark Queen Victoria's visit to Brighton.

Kensington Palace, 20 June
Victoria, the daughter of the late duke of Kent, was wakened at five this morning to be told that she was now queen of Great Britain and Ireland. Still in her dressing gown, the 18-year-old princess heard from the archbishop of Canterbury and the lord chamberlain that King William IV had died at Windsor.

William, who was 71, had been seriously ill with asthma for a month. His health had been in decline since April when his much-loved daughter, Sophia, died. He had not expected to be king and reigned for a few days less than seven years. During this time he had restored some stability to the monarchy after the excesses of his brother, King George IV.

William died without a legitimate direct heir – four children born to his wife Adelaide were either stillborn or died in infancy, although ten illegitimate children resulted from his 20-year liaison with the actress Dorothea Jordan. The crown therefore passes to his niece, Victoria.

The little princess – she is under 1.5 metres (5 feet) in height – is just 18. She is the youngest monarch since Edward VI in the 16th century, but she is old enough not to require a regent. William had distrusted the influence of Victoria's mother, the duchess of Kent and Sir John Conroy, her confidant. The new queen is not notably beautiful and is without experience of public affairs, but she is said to have a strong, determined character and is clearly aware of her duty to the country. She is also physically strong: a good horsewoman, a fine dancer and very fond of outdoor games and fresh air – which many hope that she will bring to court (→ 8/7).

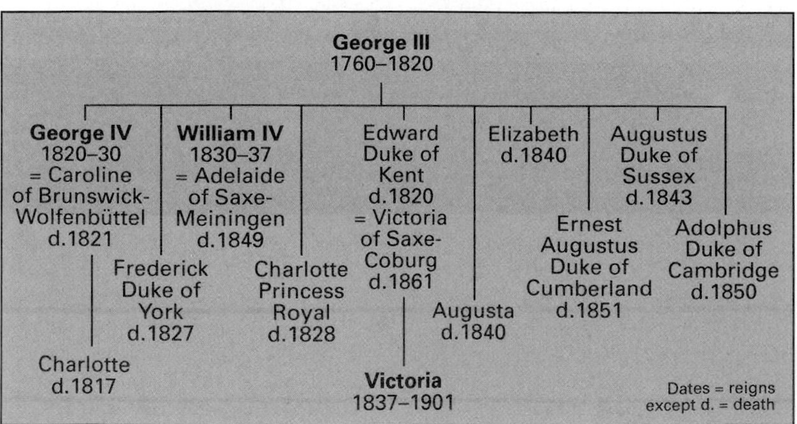

Reputation of the monarchy is low as Hanover link ends

Windsor, 8 July
The burial of King William IV here today closes an unhappy era in which Victoria's Hanoverian uncles brought the institution of monarchy into considerable disrepute.

George III was not unpopular, but his health declined so dramatically towards the end of his 60-year reign that he became incapable of exercising any role in the affairs of state. His eldest son was appointed Prince Regent, and although a man of considerable culture, he was better known for his excesses – in sexual matters as well as in the gluttony that gave him a corpulent figure and in the extravagance that ran up debts. Scathing obituary notices showed how little George IV had done to restore his (or the crown's) reputation during his ten-year reign. As George's only legitimate child had died in 1817, the succession went to his brother William, the bluff sea-going duke of Clarence. He was more widely liked, and fulfilled his role as constitutional monarch during the storms over the 1832 Reform Act. But he won no great respect.

Victoria: the new young queen.

Victoria, however, starts with one great advantage over her predecessors: Hanover's laws preclude a female succession, and it therefore passes to her uncle, the duke of Cumberland. She thus inherits a single, economically thriving and united kingdom (→ 10/2/40).

Passengers flock to admire the first main railway terminus to be opened in London

The "working" part of the station from where the trains actually depart.

London, 4 July
The capital's first main line railway terminus, Euston, opened today with services to Birmingham and north-western England. The station is attracting great interest, but this will certainly increase further next year when a massive Doric arch, designed to be its entrance, is completed. The arch will lead to a romanesque hall reaching almost 19 metres (62 feet) from floor to roof. Inspired by Robert Stephenson and designed by his protégés, Philip Hardwick and his son Philip, Euston is being made deliberately sensational to convince critics that railways are neither noisy or dangerous – indeed, the trains come as something of an anti-climax as they wait in sheds at the far end of the station (→ 17/9/38).

English Poor Law extended to Ireland

Westminster, February
Lord John Russell has introduced a bill to extend the new English Poor Law to Ireland. After the government had rejected the recommendations of the Whateley commission, Russell dispatched George Nicholls, one of the three newly appointed Poor Law commissioners, on a fact-finding mission to Ireland. Nicholls did a whirlwind tour and presented his report in November last year.

He recommended the English Poor Law system for Ireland and favoured the setting up of large workhouses (housing 800 inmates each). There is to be no outdoor relief, and conditions in the workhouses must be inferior to the labourers' living conditions outside. Given the deplorable squalor and poverty in which labourers live (children and parents sleeping together on filthy straw), this would be hard to achieve.

Nicholls believes in a minimum form of state intervention, and he rejects any scheme that would provide employment and improve living conditions. This he prefers to leave to private enterprise.

Irish poverty: many people live in hovels like this Connemara "cabin".

Parliamentary correspondent Charles Dickens wins literary fame

London
The new name on the lips of the readers of fiction published in monthly parts, who constitute an ever-growing reading public, is Charles Dickens. He was first noticed for his *Sketches by Boz*, published in the *Evening Chronicle* and collected in 1836 as a book with illustrations by George Cruikshank for which the author received £150. A second series appeared this year, along with the first number of *The Posthumous Papers of the Pickwick Club*. For this the 25-year-old Dickens provides the text to accompany a set of comic prints. They relate the misadventures of Samuel Pickwick and friends, illustrated by "Phiz" (Hablot Browne).

Meanwhile *Bentley's Miscellany* has begun to issue the parts of his tale *Oliver Twist*, a novel of crime and terror which is said to mirror parts of the author's own childhood, as harrowing as *Pickwick* is genial. The son of a clerk who was imprisoned in the Marshalsea for debt, as a boy Dickens had to fend for himself at a bottle-blacking factory. He had little formal schooling and was articled to a solicitor, then learnt shorthand to become a reporter in courts and parliament for the *Morning Chronicle* (→ 1838).

"Oliver Twist": asking for more.

"Mr Pickwick": instant success.

Judge comes down hard on workers

Glasgow
Allegations of murder, secret oaths, arson and intimidation of "nobs" – workers refusing to join strikes – were heard at the high court of justiciary when five cotton spinners were arraigned on various charges. The men, all of them members of a workers' "association", were sentenced to seven years' transportation after the jury heard dubious evidence given by paid informers.

Twelve charges were laid against the defendants. They included forming a secret committee; molesting spinners who had been working for less than the fixed wage; setting fire to cotton mills; sending threatening letters to non-strikers; and hiring one of the prisoners to murder a spinner.

1838

London, 21 January. The river Thames freezes over.

West Yorkshire, 13 February. The women of Elland press for an immediate repeal of the Poor Laws.

Canada, 3 March. A combined British and Canadian force repels an American attempt to expand into Canadian territory at Pelee Island (→ 9/8/42).

Edinburgh, March. The court of session decides in favour of the Reverend Robert Young in a case which asserts that the Church of Scotland is subject to the state.

London, 9 April. The National Gallery in Trafalgar Square is officially opened.

Quebec City, 29 May. John George Lambton, Lord Durham, the newly appointed governor-general of British North America, arrives to deal with the tense political situation between Lower and Upper Canada (→ 28/6).

London, 30 May. Queen Victoria grants an extension to the trading monopoly of the Hudson's Bay company in Canada.

Canada, 28 June. Lord Durham exiles the *patriote* rebel leaders to Bermuda rather than pass a death sentence (→ 1/11).

Portsmouth, 8 July. The Royal Naval College, which was closed last year, is re-established.

Westminster, 31 July. Parliament extends the Poor Relief Act to cover Ireland.

Ireland, 15 August. By the Tithe Act tithes become rent, and the amounts payable are to be scaled down.

Birmingham, 17 September. The London to Birmingham railway line is opened.→

Quebec City, 1 November. Lord Durham, the governor-general of Canada, who recently resigned his position after the British government repudiated his decision to exile rebels, leaves for Britain (→ 1839).

Dublin, 10 November. The Dublin Pathological Society holds its first meeting.

London. The first railway line in the city, linking London Bridge to Greenwich, is completed.

London. Charles Dickens publishes his latest novel, *Nicholas Nickleby*, in serial form (→ 31/12/43).

First steamships cross the Atlantic

New York, April

The safe arrival in New York harbour, within days of each other, of the two British ships, the *Great Western* and the *Sirius*, heralds the beginning of a transatlantic passenger and freight service.

Crowds flocked to the hills overlooking the American harbour to welcome these ships, powered by steam under screw propulsion – and their British passengers – after the 15-day trips.

The *Great Western* is a wooden paddle vessel, some 69 metres long and 10.5 metres wide (236x35 feet), far bigger than any previous steamship, such as those that have plied the seas between Aberdeen and London. Built by Paterson of Bristol, she is the brainchild of the great civil engineer Isambard Kingdom Brunel, who is currently building the Great Western Railway to run between London and Bristol; she is a vision of the future for transatlantic travel.

The *Sirius*, by contrast, was built for service in the Irish Sea. Chartered by the British and American Steam Navigation Company, she sailed to New York via Cork with 40 passengers aboard. Determined on steam propulsion throughout the voyage, her captain finally resorted to feeding spars into the furnace to avoid using sail. Although steam driven, by wood-burning furnaces, both ships have sails. They averaged around 10 knots per hour. Engineers are developing means to convert from wood-burning furnaces to those fired by coal, and new ships will be built of iron rather than wood. New shipbuilding yards are growing in the north, by the rivers Tyne, Mersey and Clyde, where iron and coal are available. The fruits of the industrial revolution are finally coming together.

The "Great Western": a vision of the future designed by Brunel.

The "Sirius": the first steamship to cross the ocean without using sail.

Public records to be the stuff of history

London

An act of parliament has established that all public records are to be permanently preserved in a new Public Records Office, under the master of the rolls, in Chancery Lane. The national depository of government papers, selected archives and legal documents will be put on a formal basis. Until now government papers have been kept in damp storerooms, rotting away.

The office of master of the rolls goes back to 1290, when charters, patents and deeds, entered on parchment rolls in chancery, were stored in a chapel called the Rolls. This year they will finally be removed to the new Public Records Office.

June 28: crowds fill the streets of London to cheer the 19-year-old Queen Victoria in the first coronation procession since George III's in 1761.

Working classes demand political reform and greater equality in 'People's Charter'

London, 21 May
The battle-cry of the impoverished working classes has been published today in a People's Charter. The demands run to six points: annual parliaments, universal male suffrage, equal electoral districts, the removal of the property qualification for MPs, a secret ballot, and payment for MPs.

The charter has given the name of "Chartists" to a group that has come to prominence since the demise of Robert Owen's Grand National Union. The men behind this new working-class movement are William Lovett, a Cornish cabinet-maker, and Henry Hetherington – both were founders of the London Working Men's Association – and Thomas Atwood of Birmingham's Political Union, which has middle-class members. Francis Place, the radical MP, helped to draw up the demands in the form of a parliamentary bill.

Francis Place: backing the people.

The Chartists' aim is to present a national petition to parliament in the hope it will accept the reformist terms of the Charter. It is fired by the bitterness of ordinary men and women who are going hungry in the present economic depression, by fears of job losses due to the introduction of machinery, by anger with the new Poor Law, and by a feeling of betrayal over the 1832 Reform Act (→4/2/39).

Carlyle publishes his philosophy of life

London
Thomas Carlyle, the Scottish social theorist – who moved to London four years ago with his wife Jane and lives in Cheyne Row, in Chelsea – has finally published in book form his highly unusual work of philosophy and moral views on life called *Sartor Resartus* [*Tailor Dispatched*]. In what really amounts to a thinly disguised spiritual autobiography, Carlyle confronts his own tendencies towards intellectual scepticism and spiritual denial; he dedicates himself rather to spiritual affirmation.

Carlyle: a distinctive voice.

The son of a religious-minded mason from the village of Ecclefechan, in Dumfriesshire, the young Carlyle attended parish school before going on to Edinburgh University. He read law, has always loved history, and worked previously as a tutor and writer, translating and reviewing German literature such as the works of Goethe and Schiller. In this new work Carlyle has adopted a singular and thoroughly individual style, which is nevertheless powerful. He takes an uncompromising stance, criticizing the mechanistic philosophy he sees underlying contemporary industrial society; he disowns spiritual mediocrity, material prosperity and moral lassitude (→1881).

Grace is nation's darling after rescue bid

Farne Islands, September
The name of Grace Darling is on everyone's lips. The 23-year-old daughter of a lighthouse keeper, who made a dramatic bid to save the lives of five survivors from the wreck of the steamboat *Forfarshire*, has become a national heroine. Countless letters find their way out to the remote lighthouse, asking for locks of her hair or a picture.

In almost impossible seas, father and daughter rowed out to the stricken ship and found the five men clinging to a rock in the wild ocean; they then managed to bring them onto the lifeboat.

The simple fact that this young woman, the seventh of nine children, born at Bamburgh, in Northumberland, was prepared to risk her own life for these unknown seamen has touched many hearts. For all her youth and beauty, Grace was brought up with strict religious beliefs. Father and daughter are to receive gold medals from the Humane Society. Money amounting to a handsome £1,700 has come in to create a reward fund (→20/10/42).

How an artist imagined the heroics of Grace Darling and her father.

Turkey opens markets to British traders

London
The *sultan* [ruler] of Turkey has agreed to open up the Ottoman Empire to British merchants by abolishing the monopolies that have been a barrier to overseas traders. These moves were among the concessions granted by Mahmud II in a commercial treaty signed this year with Britain. Lord Palmerston, the foreign secretary, sees the treaty as a way of bolstering the Turks and thus deterring predators.

Palmerston has spent much of his eight years at the foreign office endeavouring to secure stability in the volatile areas where European powers meet those of Asia. He has been particularly anxious to ensure that Russia does not exploit the weakness of the Ottoman Empire by extending its territory towards the Mediterranean. More recently there have been threats to Turkey from Mehemet Ali, the *pasha* [ruler] of Egypt, who sees the Syrian lands of the sultan as protection for his own kingdom. Palmerston is hoping that the treaty will strengthen Britain's influence with the Turks while helping his own country economically (→2/1853).

Support grows for Corn Law reforms

Manchester
A tide of anger against fixed corn prices is producing growing support for the reform movement launched by businessmen who favour free trade. An anti-corn law association has been formed here, headed by two northern manufacturers, Richard Cobden and John Bright. They argue that the corn laws harm not only the poor but also the entire economy. Bad harvests at a time of growing population have added to the groundswell of discontent. As the price of corn (and thus bread) continues to rise, mass starvation looms unless corn imports are increased without incurring high duties. Other cities are also planning to set up their own anti-corn law groups (→ 20/3/39).

Britain is to back former Afghan king

British troops marching to Kabul.

India
The new governor-general of India, Lord Auckland, following Palmerston's anti-Russian policy, has decided to take action against the growing unrest in Afghanistan. Fearing that disturbances might leave the way open for Russia and Persia, through Afghanistan, to threaten the Indian frontier, Auckland's plan is to support the deposed King Shah Suja in his claim on the throne. Afghanistan's former king has been under British protection in exile for 30 years (→ 7/8/39).

The first train reaches Birmingham from London as railway boom gathers steam with plans to link Britain's major cities

The entrance to Watford tunnel.

Speculators rush to promote new lines as "railway mania" takes hold.

Birmingham, 17 September
The Grand Junction Railway company's 112-mile (179-km) railway line from London to Birmingham opened today, the first train from London arriving here to the cheers of thousands of onlookers.

Five hours earlier the train had steamed out of London's Euston station, helped up the sharp gradient to Camden Town by a winding cable powered by a 60-horsepower stationary steam engine. As the train crossed the Regent's canal, Philip Hardwick's Doric arch, the highest building in London, erected in celebration of the railway at its London terminus, disappeared behind, lost in the billowing smoke and steam.

With the completion of the new Birmingham-to-Warrington link to the Liverpool & Manchester Railway, it is possible to travel all the way from London to Liverpool by train. Soon it may be possible to travel from one end of the country to the other on rails. Already the amount of railway track in the country exceeds 500 miles. In the last two years alone, 44 railway companies have promoted bills that – if they can raise the finance – will create another 1,498 miles.

The boom in railway building has been encouraged by the economic climate. Two raw materials, copper and iron, have been steadily falling in price, capital is available at low rates of interest, and there is political calm. Certainly the earliest railway investors did well. Shareholders in the Stockton & Darlington Railway saw their dividends increase from 6 per cent in 1831 to 14 per cent last year. Most of the new railway companies are paying much smaller dividends, but local industrialists, who can appreciate the inherent long-term benefits for transporting their products, continue to invest in them.

Already a spider's web of lines stretches out from London: a local one to Greenwich, a completed one to Birmingham, and two half-completed lines to Southampton and Bristol (→ 12/8/39).

1839

Ireland, 7 January. Violent windstorms sweep across the country causing much damage to land and property.

London, 4 February. The Chartist Convention, a movement pressing for reform, is founded (→14/6).

Liverpool, 26 February. The first official Grand National Steeplechase is run at Aintree racecourse; the winner is Jewn Mason on Lottery.

Westminster, 7 May. Lord Melbourne resigns after the Jamaica Bill is passed by the Commons by only five votes (→10).

Dublin, 29 May. The Irish Medical Association is founded.

Oxfordshire, 14 June. A regatta is held on the river Thames at Henley.

Westminster, 14 June. The Chartists present their petition with 1,280,000 signatures to parliament (→6/7).

Glasgow, 6 July. The *Scottish Patriot*, a Chartist newspaper, makes its first appearance (→12).

Westminster, 12 July. Parliament rejects the Chartist petition by 235 votes to 46 (→17).

Birmingham, 17 July. Chartists run riot after the rejection of their petition (→3/11).

Belfast, 12 August. The Belfast-to-Lisburn section of the Ulster railway line is opened (→1841).

Ireland, 19 August. The Act to Improve the Navigation of the river Shannon is passed at Westminster.

Westminster, 24 August. Parliament passes the Unlawful Oaths Act, directed against secret societies in Ireland using secret signs and passwords, or societies formed for the purpose of obtaining arms.

Gwent, 4 November. Troops fire into a crowd of Chartist demonstrators at Newport, killing several and dispersing the crowd.→

Ascot, Berkshire. Queen Victoria, who last year founded the Gold Vase horse race, orders the building of a grandstand at Royal Ascot.

Harpenden, Hertfordshire. John Bennett Lawes creates an artificial fertilizer for turnips.

Aberdeen. The first Aberdeen clipper ship is launched by Alexander Hall and Company.

Sir Robert Peel is defeated in battle for influence over ladies of the bedchamber

The young queen rides with Lord Melbourne (l) and Lord John Russell.

London, 10 May
The Tory attempt to form a government is on the verge of collapse. Lord Melbourne had offered his resignation as prime minister after his Commons majority was cut to only five votes. Sir Robert Peel prepared to take over, but his attempt to form an administration foundered on Queen Victoria's refusal to make changes in her household.

Last night Melbourne rallied Whig rebels by reading from a letter written by Victoria suggesting that Peel asked her to replace *all* her ladies of the bedchamber. Wags are calling it the "bedchamber plot", but it is more a tale of muddle and misunderstanding arising from the queen's youth and liking for Melbourne. She was distraught when he told her he must resign following his defeat over the Jamaica Bill. In tears she refused her dinner and wrote bitterly in her diary: "All my happiness gone! That happy peaceful life destroyed, that dearest kind Lord Melbourne no more my minister!"

Peel, faced with the prospect of forming a minority government, wanted changes in *some* of the queen's ladies, who are mostly married to Whigs, as a sign of Victoria's support. The queen had found him coldly formal in his 20-minute audience and is delighted to get more of Melbourne (→6/1841).

Messages can be sent by using wires

London
Two British inventors have moved in on the race to develop an electric telegraph system. William Fothergill Cooke and Professor Charles Wheatstone of King's College, London, have been granted a royal patent for their system of "writing at a distance". It works through five wires connected with five needles. Any two wires represent a letter.

In 1839 an American, Samuel Morse, developed a method based on a buzzer. Each letter is represented by a mix of short and long blasts on the buzzer. The railways and the army are watching to see which system is best (→20/8/58).

Cooke and Wheatstone's telegraph machine for "writing at a distance".

Rural areas given powers to set up own police forces

England and Wales
Rural areas will now be able to set up their own police forces, thanks to the County Police Act. The new act reflects a great deal of public worry about law-and-order issues. Whether crime is actually increasing is more difficult to judge.

The figures for committals show a doubling to 14,000 a year in the four years after the end of the Napoleonic wars, and a steady rise since then to around 24,000 a year. The first rise is usual after a war, when servicemen are discharged and unemployment increases. The second is partly due to extra new laws like the Vagrancy Act of 1824 and more efficient policing. Until Sir Robert Peel set up the Metropolitan Police in 1829 law enforcement was decentralized and poorly coordinated.

A London policeman on patrol.

The 1835 Municipal Corporations Act gave the newly created towns the power to appoint their own police forces. Now the counties can do the same. Formerly the local yeomanry was used for crowd control and political riots, but after the infamous "Peterloo" massacre of 1819 this became unacceptable. In recent years the Metropolitan Police have been sent out into adjoining towns to put down political agitation. Now the government is enthusiastic about setting up local police forces to deal with such emergencies as well as with petty crime (→1856).

Fox Talbot prints his first photographs: black-and-white pictures on paper

A summer's afternoon at Lacock: an early photograph by Fox Talbot.

London, 31 January
William Henry Fox Talbot held an audience of eminent scientists enthralled today at the Royal Society. The paper he was giving, *The Art of Photogenic Drawing*, explained a method of making pictures that enables anyone, even with no artistic talent at all, to produce a likeness of a person or a scene. Talbot, aged 38, is a man of many talents. Not only has he a formidable reputation as a translator from Assyrian, he has also made major discoveries in mathematics concerning elliptic integrals. Today's discoveries arise, ironically, from his lack of talent for art.

Self-portrait: Fox Talbot.

In 1823 he began to experiment with the camera obscura because he was so disappointed with his efforts to sketch Italian scenery. More recently, in the ancestral home at Lacock Abbey in Wiltshire, he has been using optics and chemistry to make pictures in boxes.

Talbot has found that exposure to a light source darkens silver nitrate spread on a plate. This produces a negative image which he reverses to make any number of positives. Recently Louis Daguerre announced in Paris a rival method of making negatives (→ 17/9/77).

New docks make Cardiff a major port

Cardiff
Coal exports from the city of Cardiff, small at present, are expected to reach phenomenal growth levels when the new, heavy capacity loading dock, Bute West, opens for business shortly. Built by Cardiff's principal resident, the marquis of Bute, at a cost of £350,000, the enterprise is thought to be the first major engineering venture undertaken anywhere in the world by one man at his own expense.

Exports first started in 1830, when coal from Abercanaid, near Merthyr Tydfil, was sent by ship to London from Cardiff. Trade is expected to grow tenfold next year.

Wales is at bottom of literacy league

England and Wales
Figures produced this year by the registrar-general show that two-thirds of the men and one half of the women in England and Wales can at least write their own name. London, where 88 per cent of men can write, heads the table, with four northern counties close behind. Newcastle upon Tyne has become a thriving book centre, and schools run by local women are increasing. Children pay a penny or twopence a week to learn to read, and threepence or fourpence if they attend writing classes. Wales is bottom of the league, with just 52 per cent of men and 30 per cent of women able to write. As most people there talk Welsh as their first language, they find it difficult to read books written in English.

Movement formed to fight corn laws

London, 20 March
Delegates from all over the country voted today to form the Anti-Corn Law League. The initiative started in Manchester, where an anti-corn law association was formed last year. Delegates to the association met earlier this year and adjourned to the capital, where the new league has been formed. Prominent among its spokesmen are two northern manufacturers, John Bright and Richard Cobden. Some delegates condemned what they see as the immorality of making the rich even richer while the poor cannot afford bread. Others argued that Britain cannot maintain industrial supremacy without free trade, and that the cost of importing cheap foreign corn would be offset by increased exports (→ 1/1840).

Trade war looms as opium cargo seized

Chinese artillerymen: no answer to the threat of British gunboats.

Canton [Guangzou], 30 March
Lin Zexu, the Chinese imperial commissioner, today ordered the seizure of all the opium in British ships and warehouses here. The opium trade has boomed since the monopoly of the East India company was abolished six years ago. Local traders say that around 20,000 chests worth 12 million dollars are at risk.

The Chinese emperor is worried that opium, which he calls a "dreadful calamity", utterly ruins the minds and the morals of the people. He is also concerned because most of the profits are going to British and other foreign merchants.

British merchants and ship owners are furious. They plan to put pressure on the foreign secretary, Lord Palmerston, to take military action. The Chinese have nothing to compare in fire-power with the British navy's gunboats. The merchants hope that Palmerston will send them in to force the emperor to change his mind (→ 26/1/41).

Soldiers fire on Chartist supporters

Newport, Gwent, 4 November
An armed march by thousands of Welsh miners and ironworkers was routed here tonight. The authorities had been tipped off about the revolt and troops hidden in the Westgate hotel fired into the march as it passed by. Several people were killed, while the rest fled.

The march was organized in protest at the arrest of the enormously popular Monmouth Chartist leader Henry Vincent. It was to have been a much larger affair, drawing on three forces assembling in the hills. Tonight's fierce storms, however, dampened the ardour of many marchers. Only the contingent led by John Frost, the draper and ex-mayor, made it to Newport.

Tonight's revolt reflects the increasing frustration of Chartists in many parts of England and Wales. Last July the Commons voted by a large majority not to debate the Chartist petition. This led to riots in Birmingham, where William Lovett and other Chartist leaders were thrown into jail. The Welsh leaders decided that an armed struggle was necessary. Others, like the London lawyer John Cobbett, eschew the use of violence.

Women are taking an important role in the Chartist movement. This has led to suggestions of new forms of political action. Julian Harney of Newcastle suggests that Chartist women should only grant favours to their sweethearts if they agree to support Chartism. "Soon the young men will be most uproarious democrats," said Harney, "and soon the young women will have sweethearts enough." Events have proved him over optimistic (→ 7/1840).

Troops hiding in the Westgate hotel fire on the Welsh Chartist marchers.

Canadian union is proposed in report

London
Lord Durham has proposed a union of Upper and Lower Canada in his long awaited report. Durham was sent to Canada as governor-general in May last year to deal with the disturbances of the previous year. He made an unhappy start, deporting to Bermuda eight of the men imprisoned for rioting. This angered both British and French settlers, and he was forced to resign. His report, however, promises a way forward. His proposed union will give the British in Upper Canada a built-in majority. On the other hand, the increased powers for the Canadian parliament will go some way towards satisfying the demands of the French Canadians in Lower Canada for more settler power. Durham recommends severely limiting the powers of the governor appointed from London, who should only be able to challenge legislation when it involves strictly British interests.

Scientist looks into links between species

London
Charles Darwin, the secretary of the Geological Society, has published an account of the wildlife that he encountered during a five-year voyage to the southern hemisphere on the naval brig HMS *Beagle*. In his account, *The Zoology of the Voyage of the Beagle*, Darwin describes many of the living creatures he observed during the trip, which ended in 1836. He was particularly struck by the interdependence of wildlife. His journal is essentially a description of the fossils and animals that he encountered, such as the Galapagos birds, but he believes that his observations have implications for current thinking about links between species (→ 24/11/59).

British troops capture city of Kabul

Kabul, 7 August
Shah Suja returned here today as ruler of Afghanistan, 30 years after his expulsion. Dost Mahomed, who has much more local support, fled as soon as he heard that the British Army was approaching the capital. The army of Indian and Sikh troops under Sir William Macnaghten has already captured Kandahar and Ghazni. The victory may prove a costly one, however. Shah Suja is no more popular here than he was 30 years ago, and the British colonial authorities have found themselves drawn into a complex web of Sikh and Afghan rivalries. But they may have succeeded in keeping Russia out of Afghanistan and India (→ 13/1/42).

Horses and riders tackle the Brook fence and stream in the new "Grand National" steeplechase, run for the first time this year.

Afghan rebels surrender to Sir William Macnaghten outside Kabul.

1840

Britain, 6 January. Fanny Burney, the novelist and diarist, has died aged 87.

Manchester, January. The Free Trade Hall is built to house the anti-corn law meetings (→20/12/45).

London, 10 February. Queen Victoria marries her cousin, Prince Albert of Saxe-Coburg-Gotha, at St James's Palace.→

Armagh City, 17 March. The foundation stone of the Catholic cathedral is laid.

Belfast, 26 March. The Belfast Music Hall is officially opened (→14/8).

London, 4 April. Charles Green, an aviator, announces a plan to cross the Atlantic in a balloon (→1/1/49).

Dublin, 24 April. The first union workhouse is opened.

London, 10 June. An 18-year-old youth, Edward Oxford, fires shots at Victoria (→21/11).

London, 23 June. Francis William Caulfeild, the earl of Charlemont, hosts a preliminary meeting of the Ulster Constitutional Association (→14/8).

Ireland, 10 July. The general synod of Ulster and the secession synod combine to form the general assembly of the Presbyterian Church in Ireland.

Ireland, 13 July. The National Association of Ireland, formed in April and keen to repeal the Act of Union of Ireland and Britain, renames itself the Loyal National Repeal Association (→15/10/42).

Belfast, 14 August. The first official meeting of the Ulster Constitutional Association is held in the new Music Hall.

Windsor, 21 November. Queen Victoria gives birth to a daughter, Victoria Adelaide Mary Louisa (→9/11/41).

Ireland, December. The Hungarian composer and musician Franz Liszt tours.

London. The Schweppes company adds quinine and sugar to its original soda-water recipe and creates tonic water.

Berkshire. Cox's Pippin, an apple developed by a farmer, Richard Cox, bears fruit for the first time.

London. James Pimm, a restaurateur, creates a new drink, Pimm's Number One.

New Zealand annexed

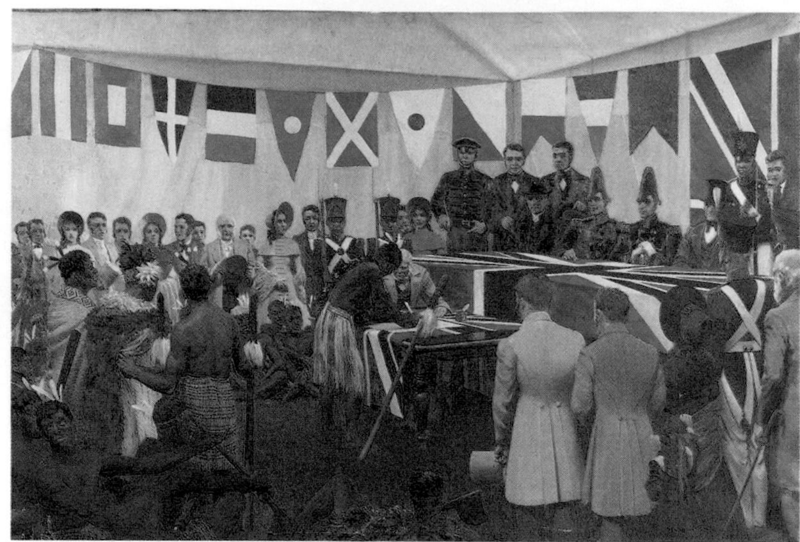

New Zealand is annexed to Britain in the Treaty of Waitangi.

London, 2 June

Britain, acting with what it termed "extreme reluctance", today gained sovereignty over the islands of New Zealand. Captain Hobson, the senior British naval officer in the region, concluded the Treaty of Waitangi with the native Maoris, a cultured warrior race.

In instructing Hobson, the government said that circumstances beyond its control forced it to act, although it hesitated because the Maoris had "indisputable" title to the islands. Britain, unwilling for some time to extend its territorial obligations, acted out of mixed motives. Adventurers, including escaped convicts from Australia, have been causing serious problems to both Maoris and British missionaries; but, above all, the government was aware that France was contemplating annexation of the islands. The Maoris will retain title to their lands (→1860).

Elizabeth Fry forms nursing institution

London

The remarkable Elizabeth Fry, now 60 years old and just returned from Germany, has set up a nurses' training home in London. The organization, called the Nursing Sisters, is being launched by Queen Victoria's mother the queen dowager, the duchess of Kent, as its patroness. Working on a non-sectarian basis, Mrs Fry will surely organize hospital nursing care as efficiently as she sorted out the prisons.

Twenty women from the lower middle classes have been selected for the training. They will work for a probationary period in one of the larger, better hospitals before being admitted as sisters. They live in the training home, wear simple uniforms and receive salaries. They may also "live in" with patients or visit on a daily basis. The service is free to the poor; the better-off pay one guinea a week.

Fry: from prisons to hospitals.

Growth of British Empire increases with new colonies

London

The annexation of New Zealand [*see report left*] is part of a new phase of expansion for Britain's empire following a period when many political leaders saw it merely as a burden on taxpayers. The lead has come from a group of reformers, including Lord Durham, who believe that it is in Britain's economic and strategic interests for the colonies to be knitted together with their own governments, to be modelled on the Westminster parliament. Development will be encouraged through emigration.

A start has been made in Canada, where the upper and lower regions have this year been formed into one province which will be empowered to create its own government responsible to the province's legislature. It is hoped that, in the process, the French settlers in lower Canada will become "anglicized".

Australia, with its divided coastal settlements, will be similarly unified, and immigration will be encouraged to bolster the present 130,000 white inhabitants. Convicts will eventually no longer be shipped there.

In New Zealand, land is being bought from the native Maori people for use by settlers; some disputes over ownership are likely in the short term. British immigrants in Cape Colony, which was taken over from the Dutch during the Napoleonic wars for a £6 million indemnity, are striving to control Boer farmers and are expected to declare Natal a British colony.

Britain is likely to become the dominant power on the west coast of Africa, at Sierra Leone and the Gold Coast [Ghana]. Missionary societies there are demanding a full British presence to combat illicit slave-trading. In the Far East, the island of Singapore is being developed into a major port. And improved administration of British India goes hand in hand with territorial gains.

Iron industry is booming in Wales

Industry transforms the Welsh landscape: the ironworks at Nant-y-Glo.

South Wales
Steampower, the newest and noisiest of the improved technologies, is transforming the iron and coal industries of South Wales. It has also created many more jobs of all kinds and led to massive industrial expansion over the entire region. Steam-heated air, added experimentally a few months ago to coke ovens, has greatly improved production by speeding up the separation process. Pig-iron output in the Merthyr-Dowlais foundries has doubled, and the new methods are rapidly becoming normal practice in most of the other 200 furnaces in the region. In all, some 35,000 workers have been affected by the Welsh iron boom.

Steam-driven pumps adapted to cope with large amounts of flood water have also encouraged deep-level coal mining for the first time in the area. This has meant that coal output, too, is soaring.

Victoria interrupts work to marry Albert

Windsor, 10 February
In a brief interruption to affairs of state, Queen Victoria and her new husband, Albert of Saxe-Coburg-Gotha, have arrived here for a short stay after their wedding at St James's Palace this morning. The ceremony went well, and it was followed by a magnificent wedding breakfast at Buckingham Palace.

After all the family arguments, and parliament's refusal to vote Albert more than £30,000 a year, Victoria was overjoyed when her fiancé finally arrived two days ago. The prince wanted a longer honeymoon, but the queen felt that she could not be away from her work for more than two days (→ 10/6).

Victoria weds her German prince.

Chartists renew their demands for reform

Manchester, July
The Chartist movement is regrouping after last year's disappointments and drama when parliament rejected its million-strong petition, and many leaders were arrested. A National Charter Association has been formed here this month, and there are plans for many branches. The emphasis is now on constitutional action. Newspapers and local groups are maintaining the pressure for electoral reform, but underlying divisions over ends and means still threaten the Chartists' strength.

William Lovett, who helped to draw up the People's Charter, believes that persuasion will work. Others, more extreme, still call for physical action (→ 11/10/41).

Post for a penny

Penny Black: a postal revolution.

London, 6 May
The Penny Post is here: all literate people can now correspond (not just the well-off) paying for letters on delivery. Rowland Hill of the Post Office had the idea that if letters were prepaid and had adhesive stamps affixed, costs could be cut. The world's first adhesive stamp is black, with a picture of Victoria.

Grammar schools get go-ahead to improve education syllabus

The grammar school at Abingdon, Oxfordshire: studies will be more modern, but teaching stays formal.

Westminster
Grammar schools will now teach a more all-embracing modern-style curriculum under new legislation which expands and clarifies their role in a rapidly developing industrial society. Their traditional function, to teach the classics free of charge to the poor, has in recent times been increasingly questioned as being too narrow in intent and not in the best interests of many of the young or indeed of the nation.

A number of grammar schools have responded by teaching elementary subjects as well as the classics, but new schools have now been created to provide an elementary education for many of the poor. The new Grammar School Act bolsters the field of secondary education by enabling grammar schools to teach not only the classics but also other advanced subjects up to university entrance standard.

The new curriculum is considered to be more in line with that now taught at the ancient "great" foundations, such as those at Winchester and Eton.

1841

Hong Kong, 26 January. The British and the Chinese end long negotiations over territory in the opium wars; China agrees to pay indemnites and to cede the island of Hong Kong to Britain (→ 8/1842).

Ireland, March. The Agricultural Improvement Society is founded.

Leicestershire, 5 July. Thomas Cook, a staunch member of the temperance movement, arranges with the Midland Railway for a special coach to bring people from Leicester to Loughborough to attend a temperance meeting.

Swindon, Wiltshire, August. Lack of catering facilities on trains leads Isambard Kingdom Brunel, the railway engineer, builder and inventor, to design a circular bar on the station platform for the sale of coffee; by special arrangement trains will stop for ten minutes to allow passengers to purchase refreshments (→ 21/9).

London, 21 September. The London-to-Brighton railway line is opened (→ 15/10).

Glasgow, 11 October. A Chartist demonstration at Glasgow Green is addressed by Fergus O'Conner (→ 12/1841).

Yorkshire, 15 October. The Leeds-to-Manchester railway line opens (→ 18/2/42).

London, 9 November. Queen Victoria gives birth to a son and heir, Prince Albert Edward (→ 25/12).

London, 25 December. Prince Albert introduces an old German custom to England: the "Christmas tree" a cut-down fir tree which is decorated with candles (→ 13/6/42).

Britain, December. The National Charter Association, created earlier this year to press for the demands of the People's Charter through peaceful means, has established 282 branches across the country (→ 9/1842).

Reading. Two Quakers, Thomas Huntley and George Palmer, begin making and selling "Superior Reading Biscuits".

London. The London Library is officially opened.

British Isles. The Miners' Association of Great Britain and Ireland is founded.

Scotland. Irish-born immigrants now constitute five per cent of the population.

All aboard the Great Western Railway

Box Hill railway tunnel, near Bath.

Western terminus: the new railway station at Bristol Temple Meads.

Paddington, London, 30 June
A gaily decorated train pulled out of London's new railway station at Paddington this morning and arrived at Bristol four hours later. Isambard Kingdom Brunel's 118-mile (189-km) Great Western route has finally opened, six years after plans were first discussed. The last section of the £6,500,000 project, completed earlier this month, was the 2-mile tunnel, lined with 20 million bricks, at Box Hill between Chippenham and Bath.

Brunel provoked controversy by designing a 7-foot- (2.13-metre)-wide track, arguing that this would enable trains to go faster and in greater safety. The standard gauge, about a third narrower, is based on the width of the coal-wagon track at Tyneside that George Stephenson adopted for his early railways.

After the first section, Paddington to Maidenhead, opened, Brunel had trouble with the carriages, which had been built by craftsmen of the stage-coach era; Brunel insisted on the work being taken over by engineers (→ 8/1841).

Steam engines get on the tracks in Wales

Smoke from a train joins that from chimney-pots in the Welsh countryside.

Mid-Glamorgan
A crucial and long-sought new link between Cardiff and Merthyr Tydfil has been achieved with the opening this year of the first railway in Wales, the Taff Vale Railway. It follows an old road and canal through the narrow Tongwynlais gap and has been constructed in record time by one of Britain's greatest engineers, Isambard Kingdom Brunel [*see right*]. The railway is regarded as an exceptional feat of engineering and will open the coal valleys of south Wales to the markets of the world. The new Bute West dock in Cardiff will be one of the chief beneficiaries (→ 30/6).

Brunel: the great railway engineer

London
Isambard Kingdom Brunel, the 35-year-old engineer, was a familiar figure along the turnpike when his Great Western Railway was under construction. Travelling in his horse-drawn covered wagon, in which he would sleep and work, he oversaw every mile of the project, for which he insisted on taking sole responsibility. He is the son of Sir Marc Isambard Brunel, a Normandy farmer who left France after the Revolution and, settling in England, became a public works contractor. The younger Brunel joined his father in the business, and together they planned the Thames tunnel. While working on the Great Western line, Brunel junior has continued to plan a suspension bridge at Clifton, in Bristol, docks at Sunderland and Bristol, and a suspension bridge across the Thames. He was 29 when he began work on the Great Western for the grand salary of £2,000 a year (→ 3/1843).

O'Connell elected as Dublin's mayor

Dublin, November 1841
Daniel O'Connell has been elected lord mayor, the first Roman Catholic to hold this office since 1688. This is seen as an important victory for O'Connell, whose political fortunes have been in decline since the departure of the Whigs from office and his subsequent inability to co-operate with Peel, the new British prime minister [*see right*].

Determined to display high standards, O'Connell saw the election as a trial run for Irish self-government and, while he based his campaign on his Repeal organization, he has declared that he will hold himself aloof from both partisanship and the Repeal Party during his term of office. His hand has been greatly strengthened by the fact that his Repealers won 47 out of 60 seats on the new corporation.

As a further endorsement of O'Connell's present stance, prominent Catholic clerics have supported his call for repeal (→ 11/7/46).

O'Connell: now a statesman.

Peel succeeds Melbourne as premier

Westminster, September
Faced with 368 Tories, or Conservatives as they now call themselves, in the new House of Commons, and only 292 Whigs, or Liberals, Queen Victoria has resigned herself to accepting Sir Robert Peel as her prime minister.

It is two years since Victoria had her first acrimonious encounter with Peel, and that came two years after she had ascended the throne and received her political education from the fatherly Lord Melbourne. "That dearest kind Lord Melbourne no more my minister," she wrote in her diary when he lost his Commons majority. She was also shocked when Peel demanded that she replace some ladies of the bedchamber suspected of being Whigs.

It was another two years before she was persuaded by Melbourne and Prince Albert to face political realities. She agreed to get rid of the controversial ladies if Peel would agree not to demand their dismissal. Peel will now set about tackling problems that Melbourne avoided – balancing the budget, helping economic recovery, reorganizing the banking system and ending the Opium War with China (→ 1842).

Peel: grudgingly accepted.

Magazine for punchy satire is launched

London, 17 July
A new weekly comic magazine has been launched by two London writers: Mark Lemon, who is best known for his stage farces, and Henry Mayhew, a solicitor's son who turned to popular journalism. The new magazine, *Punch, or the London Charivari*, was inspired by the Paris *Charivari*, which took its name from the word used to describe a mock serenade to newlyweds produced with pans, kettles, trays and buckets. Contributors to *Punch* include the lawyer and leader writer for *The Times* Gilbert Beckett, and Douglas Jerrold, who is writing social and political satires over the signature "Q".

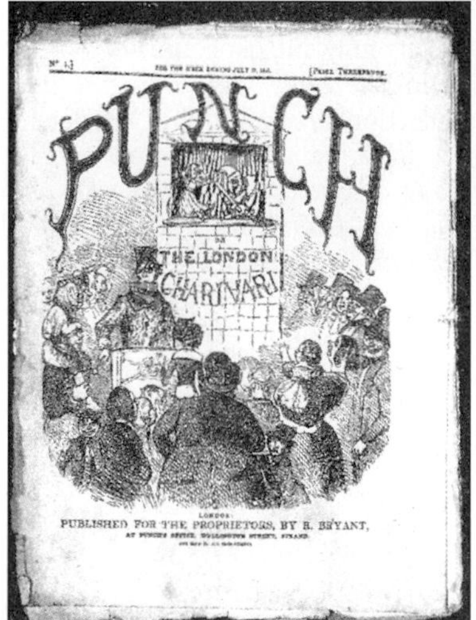
PUNCH
OR
THE LONDON CHARIVARI
LONDON:
PUBLISHED FOR THE PROPRIETORS, BY R. BRYANT,

Enter Mr Punch: issue number one.

National census reveals massive growth of urban life in Britain

British Isles
Though there are still well over one million agricultural workers, their numbers have been decisively overtaken by the two million men and 550,000 women employed in various manufacturing and trade occupations, according to this year's national census. Towns have simply kept on growing, with Sheffield now the sixth English town outside London to top 100,000. The population of Manchester has shot up by 53,000 over the last decade to reach 235,000, while Birmingham's has grown from 144,00 to 183,000.

Overall, the population of England and Wales is just under 16 million – an increase of around two million since 1831. The Scottish total of 2.6 million (up 250,000) masks significant trends, with the highlands being depopulated by emigration and the new industries based on Glasgow attracting substantial Irish immigration.

The scale of that Irish immigration – 5 per cent of Scotland's population was born in Ireland – can be seen in the census returns for Ireland itself. These show a fall in total population from just over eight million to 6,552,000.

Sugar row ends 11 years of office for Palmerston

Westminster, September
After 11 years as the foreign secretary who made British power felt around the globe, Lord Palmerston is out of office. He plans to spend his time travelling, hunting, racing his horses and playing games of billiards. Lord Melbourne's Whig government was brought down after clashes in the House of Commons over proposed lower tariffs on "slave sugar" from Brazil. Palmerston spent his last weeks in office working on a treaty to suppress the slave trade by giving rights of mutual search to ships of the great powers. But France is denying him his triumph by delaying signing of the treaty.

Palmerston had moved to the foreign office at the age of 46, having previously served as secretary at the war office. His prejudices as much as his patriotism have come to personify Britain in the diplomatic counsels of Europe. Yet beneath the bombastic manner was a diligent minister motivated by the principle that Britain backs "non-interference by force of arms in the affairs of any other country". He expected other countries to follow the same principle and strove to keep a balance of power through a succession of diplomatic crises. He was always especially wary of French and Russian ambitions for aggrandizement.

Palmerston: voice of Britain.

1842

Afghanistan, 13 January. Over 15,000 British soldiers under the command of Lord Auckland, and many civilians are massacred as they begin to retreat from Kabul.

Edinburgh, 18 February. The Edinburgh-to-Glasgow railway line is opened to the public (→ 12/9).

Cork City, 28 March. Daniel O'Connell, the lord mayor of Dublin, takes part in the Cork temperance procession.

London, 14 May. Herbert Ingram publishes the first issue of the *London Illustrated News*.

Belfast, 10 June. The first issue of James MacKnight's *Banner of Ulster* is published.

London, 13 June. Queen Victoria, with Prince Albert, makes the rail journey from Slough to Paddington, becoming the first British monarch to travel by rail (→ 3/7).

Ireland, 18 June. The death penalty for a number of crimes is abolished by parliament.

Washington, 9 August. The United States and Britain sign the Webster-Ashburton Treaty fixing the US-Canadian border.

Nanking, August. A treaty ends the Opium War, with China agreeing to open more ports to Britain and to cede Hong Kong "in perpetuity".

Co Down, 12 September. The Lisburn-to-Portadown section of the Ulster railway is opened (→ 1844).

Liverpool, 25 September. A terrible fire sweeps through the city, causing serious damage.

Dublin, 15 October. The first issue of the *Nation*, edited by Charles Gavan Duffy, is published; this weekly organ expresses the ideas of a group of young men whose political philosophy encourages a hatred of England and support for the repeal of the Act of Union (→ 2/3/43).

Britain, 20 October. Grace Darling, the heroine who saved the shipwrecked crew of the *Forfarshire* in 1838, dies.

Scotland. Queen Victoria makes her first visit.

Scotland. The government's refusal to accept the "claim of right" on the independence of the Church of Scotland is making a church-state clash inevitable.

Romantic Tennyson hits popular note

Tennyson: popular acclaim.

London
The publication of *Poems in Two Volumes* has consolidated the reputation of Alfred Tennyson as the most important and widely popular poet to emerge since Wordsworth. He is the son of a Lincolnshire clergyman; his early lyrics show the luxuriant language and mood of melancholy introspection of Keats, as in *The Lotos Eaters*. In the new collection are a number of poems set in King Arthur's time – *The Lady of Shalott, Sir Launcelot and Queen Guinevere* and *Morte d'Arthur* – which are parts of a planned epic, *Idylls of the King*. The revival of intense interest in the Middle Ages and the Arthurian legends has made Tennyson's romantic mysticism popular (→ 11/1850).

School pioneer dies

Rugby, Warwickshire, 12 June
Thomas Arnold, the headmaster of Rugby school, who was both loved and feared for his reforming zeal, died suddenly today of angina; he was 47. When Arnold arrived at Rugby in 1828 he found that the prefects, far from setting an example to the younger boys, incited school rebellions. He set out to gain their confidence and taught them discipline and self-respect. Arnold introduced French and maths as regular subjects and sought to stimulate free inquiry among the boys he taught by asking questions in addition to expounding.

Peel proposes to bring back income tax

Westminster
After reminding MPs of the succession of budget deficits totalling £7.5 million over the past five years, with further deficits in prospect, Sir Robert Peel, the prime minister, announced that he was proposing to reintroduce the controversial income tax that was imposed as an emergency measure during the Napoleonic wars only to be dropped when peace returned. Public spending has remained high in recent years, not least because of military operations in China, India and Afghanistan. The prime minister rejected "the miserable device" of funding the deficits by borrowing. He set the new income tax at sevenpence [three pence] in the pound on incomes over £150 a year. This would produce an estimated budget surplus in the region of £1.8 million, which would be used to encourage economic recovery by reducing duties on some 750 articles. In a gesture to the anti-corn-law lobby, Peel made a small reduction in the duties levied on imported corn.

Women and children banned from mines

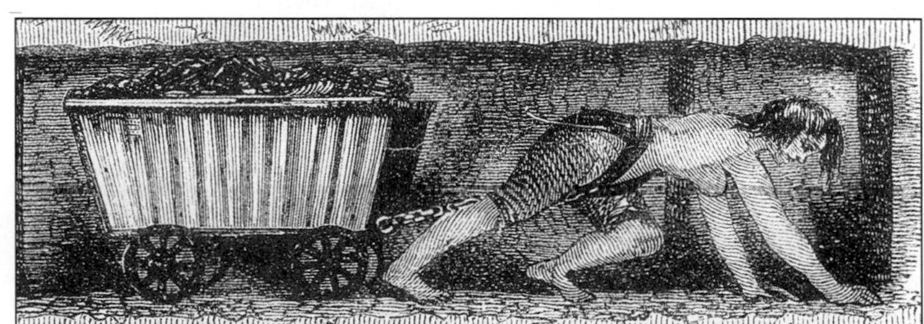

A woman or girl "hurrier" hauls a coal tub: soon there will be controls.

Westminster, July
Sweeping reforms in working conditions in the country's coal mines are foreshadowed in an act of parliament that has just received the royal assent. The employment of women and girls, and of boys below the age of ten years, is prohibited, and mine inspectors are to be employed to enforce the law. The new measures follow the publication of a report by a House of Lords select committee revealing that the employment of children of six or seven is common, and that in some mines children of four years are working below ground. The report said that married women, "and women with child", work almost naked alongside the men. Serious accidents are frequent and are attributed to the neglect of safety measures by the overwhelming majority of mine-owners (→ 6/1844).

The distinctive outline of Edinburgh Castle overlooks the construction of the Glasgow-to-Edinburgh railway line, which opened on 18 February.

Chartist revolt collapses in disarray

London, September
The recent wave of strikes and riots instigated by militant Chartists, which swept across the industrial north and the midlands and into Scotland, has ended in humiliating defeat after the leaders quarrelled over the use of force to overthrow the government.

The strikes were set off by the rejection by parliament in May of a second petition for the adoption of a Charter of Rights with six points: universal male suffrage, equal electoral districts, annual parliaments, payment of MPs, secret ballots and no property qualification for MPs. The petition had 3,317,702 signatures – three times as many as that presented in 1839 – and was six miles long. But MPs dismissed it by 287 votes to 49.

The first strike came at Ashton-under-Lyne; then workers in Manchester came out, and a Chartist activist, seeing the smokeless chimneys, cried: "Not a single mill at work! Something must come of this!" Strikers marched from town to town, pulling the plugs from boilers to close the mills and force reluctant workers to come out.

Yet the momentum of revolt had slackened by this autumn, just as it had three years ago when parliament rejected the first petition. Towards the end of last year the movement began to revive with a National Charter Association, which claimed a membership of 40,000 by the beginning of this year. A second national convention was held, resulting in the new petition, but the rejection of it in May polarized the supporters of constitutional and direct action for the Chartist causes. Feargus O'Connor, a powerful Irish orator and one-time MP who had played a leading role in the earlier campaign as one of the most extreme advocates of direct action, denounced the strikes, saying that they would fail (→10/4/48).

High hopes: the Chartist petition goes in procession to parliament.

Angry reaction: riots flare across Britain – here at a Salford mill.

Abstinence crusade a success in Ireland

Ireland
Father Theobald Mathew's temperance crusade is attracting thousands of supporters, and even Daniel O'Connell himself has taken the "pledge" never to drink again. Father Mathew, who is a Capuchin priest, joined the Cork Total Abstinence Society in 1839, declaring that alcohol was unnecessary to "anyone in good health".

Since then the movement has gathered astonishing momentum, with temperance medals – symbols of a growing belief in Father Mathew's miraculous powers – worn by thousands (→30/6/43).

Father Mathew: crusader.

Assassin is arrested after failed attempt to murder the queen

London, 3 July
A deformed youth with a "piteous expression" fired at Queen Victoria as she was out riding today. Luckily the pistol, wielded by John William Bean, was loaded – bizarrely – with more paper and tobacco than gunpowder. Victoria was unhurt. This is the third attack on the queen in less than two months. She was riding in the Mall with Prince Albert when a man described by the prince as a "swarthy, ill-looking rascal" came out of the crowd and pointed a pistol: it misfired. The next day, 30 May, near the same spot, the man fired again. Although the gun was unloaded, the assailant, John Francis, was sentenced to death; he was reprieved just two days ago (→28/12/48).

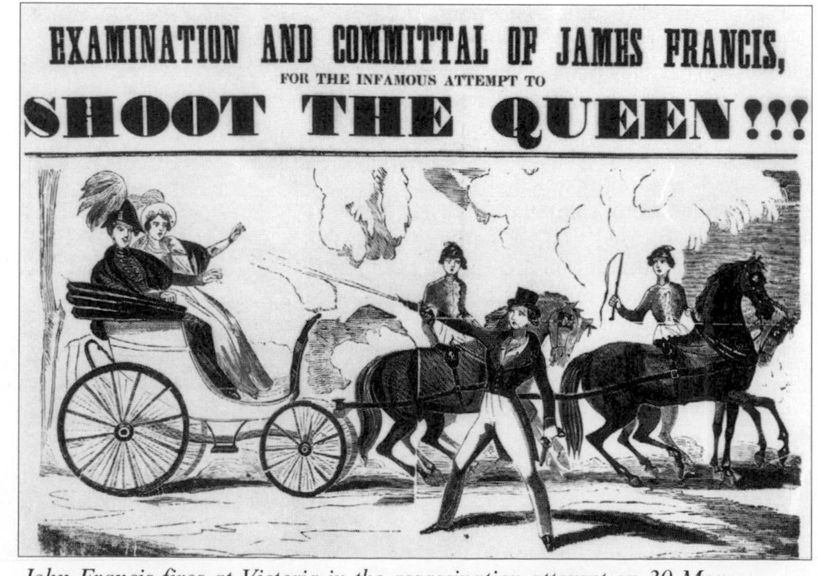

EXAMINATION AND COMMITTAL OF JAMES FRANCIS,
FOR THE INFAMOUS ATTEMPT TO
SHOOT THE QUEEN!!!

John Francis fires at Victoria in the assassination attempt on 30 May.

Glasgow slums 'the filthiest in Britain'

Scotland
A desperate picture of appalling poverty among the largely highland and Irish migrants who flocked to Scottish cities has been revealed this year. Edwin Chadwick's *Reports on the Sanitary Condition of the Labouring Population* describes Glasgow as "possibly the filthiest and unhealthiest of all British towns". It says that passageways and courtyards which link the tenements are little more than open sewers, and infant mortality is the highest in Britain – something like half of all children die before the age of five. Edinburgh is little better with filthy, overcrowded and badly ventilated one-room dwellings.

1843

London, 1 January. The English inventor and aviator George Cayley makes the first scale drawing of a helicopter-aeroplane in the *Mechanic's Review*.

Dublin, 2 March. The corporation debates Daniel O'Connell's motion for a petition to parliament for a repeal of the Act of Union (→ 15/8).

Dyfed, 25 April. The royal yacht *Victoria and Albert* is launched at Pembroke.

Edinburgh, 29 May. Seceders from the Church of Scotland decide to call themselves the Free Protesting Church of Scotland.

Cork City, 30 June. The Reverend Theobald Mathew sails for England on a total abstinence propaganda tour.

Bristol, 19 July. Prince Albert launches the *Great Britain*; designed by the engineer Isambard Kingdom Brunel; 96 metres (315 feet) long, she is the first propeller-driven ocean-going all-metal ship (→ 1/5/45).

Scotland, 25 July. Charles Macintosh, the Scottish chemist who developed and patented waterproof fabric in 1823, dies.

Cork City, 16 August. The British Association for the Advancement of Science meets.

Westminster, 22 August. Sir Robert Peel's government passes the Arms Act; this restricts the importation, manufacture and sale of arms in Ireland. Peel also drafts British troops to Ireland to disperse any further ideas of repealing the Act of Union (→ 8/10).

Co Dublin, 7 October. Daniel O'Connell is forced to cancel his "monster meeting" planned for tomorrow in support of the repeal of the Union, at Clontarf, after a parliamentary proclamation bans it (→ 16).

Dublin, 16 October. O'Connell and eight other Repealers are called to appear in the high court to face charges of conspiracy (→ 10/2/44).

London, 4 November. The huge column monument to Horatio, Viscount Nelson, raised in Trafalgar Square, is completed; the square received its present name 13 years ago when the site was redeveloped.

London. The *News of the World*, a Sunday newspaper, is founded.

Wordsworth to be new poet laureate

Grasmere, Cumbria, April
William Wordsworth, who lives at Rydal Mount, now aged 73, reluctantly succeeded Robert Southey as poet laureate this month. He refused until Sir Robert Peel, the prime minister, assured him that no duties were expected of him. His best work dates back to his two volumes of 1807, which included *Intimations of Immortality* and his sonnets, such as *Upon Westminster Bridge*. His enthusiasm for the French Revolution has long been a memory; he accepted a government stipend in 1813 and campaigned for the Tories – to the dismay of poet friends (→ 23/4/50).

William and Mary Wordsworth.

Scottish church splits

The Free Church of Scotland holds its first general assembly meeting.

Edinburgh, 18 May
Some 470 ministers, a third of the clergy of the Church of Scotland, have walked out of the general assembly. Dr Welsh, the retiring moderator, began the protest, followed by the Reverend Thomas Chalmers, the best known of the evangelical leaders. Huge crowds cheered the ministers as they left the Assembly Halls and made their way down the hill to Tanfield Hall.

The protest marks the formal breach between church and state that has been brewing for the last decade. It is expected that many teachers and missionaries, as well as thousands of lay members, will join their leaders in seceding. Yet what was intended as a demonstration of evangelical strength has resulted in a minority secession. Moderates who support the principle of keeping the church out of state affairs have been alienated by the willingness of some evangelical leaders to risk confrontation.

None the less the minority that staged what is being called today's "disruption" include many of the most talented of the church's leaders. Now they face the problem of creating a new church while the Poor Law and education, both run by the church, have been plunged into uncertainty (→ 29).

First tunnel under a navigable river completed at Rotherhithe

London, March
Despite great difficulties and dangers, the first tunnel built under a navigable river has been opened at Rotherhithe, in south-east London, to link the north and south banks of the River Thames. The opening was accompanied by a great celebration, although not everyone is pleased. The Thames watermen fear that it will rob them of a living and have hung out black flags. Designed by the French-born Sir Marc Brunel and his engineer son Isambard, the tunnel runs as little as six feet beneath the river bed, and the water has twice broken through. Unfortunately the Brunels have run out of money, and the tunnel, which was intended for road traffic, will now have to be for foot passengers only (→ 19/7).

The entrance to the tunnel seen here from the northern bank of the Thames.

'Rebecca' rioters fight for Welsh reform

Carmarthen, Dyfed, 19 June
In one of the largest and most serious "Rebecca riots" in Wales since they first erupted five years ago, the central workhouse in Carmarthen was destroyed today. A group of women were in a large crowd, including several hundred black-faced men dressed as women, who attacked the workhouse.

The part played by the women was mainly inspirational and symbolic. They represented the "Blessed Rebecca", the steadfast Old Testament mother, who was supposed to have used ritualized mass action to enforce community standards and secure natural justice for poor people. "Rebecca Riots" have occurred in west Wales since 1838, with men wearing women's clothes in attacks on toll-gates and other targets in protest at the Poor Law, tithes and tolls. Today's attack was unusual in so far as it involved women directly.

One of the women was Frances Evans, the daughter of a dissenting preacher, who led protesters up the workhouse stairs carrying a banner demanding (in Welsh) "better food, free tools and liberty". She was one of two people arrested when soldiers arrived, but this failed to halt the demolition of the workhouse. Hugh Williams, a leading Chartist, is arranging legal representation for those arrested.

"Rebecca and her daughters": a contemporary cartoon in "Punch".

British fear war in Ireland over union

O'Connell campaigning at Trim.

Co Meath, 15 August
Daniel O'Connell has addressed a huge meeting on the Hill of Tara, a place always associated with the high kings of Ireland. In what has been named by O'Connell as the "year of repeal", this has been the largest meeting to date.

Sir Robert Peel's cabinet has dismissed the Repeal movement as being of little importance. Peel himself has called it a "failing concern", but he has introduced a stringent arms bill and has expanded the Irish military establishment in case of trouble. O'Connell's speeches are becoming more flamboyant and aggressive – and, speaking at Mallow last June, he implied that, if the government attempted to stop his campaign, war might follow (→22).

Empire grows with annexation of Sind

Sind, India, August
Sir Charles Napier has completed the conquest of the enormous Indian province of Sind and greatly added to the boundaries of Britain's Indian empire. Napier acted to head off trouble from the local *amirs* [rulers] in the province, who he was convinced would make war on British India sooner or later.

Napier is a strong character with an aggressive streak. He combats the fierce Indian sun by wearing dark spectacles, which he rarely removes, and a large solar topee perched on his head. He has a beard that reaches almost to his waist, and an enormous aquiline nose.

The political agent in Sind, Sir James Outram, was sympathetic towards the native rulers and was convinced that peace with the amirs could be maintained. But Napier did not believe him, confiding in his diary: "We have no right to seize Sind, but we shall do so, and a very advantageous, useful, humane piece of rascality it will be." This attitude outraged Outram, who condemned Napier as "most tyrannical".

Napier marched into Sind with an army of just 3,000, largely made up of native Sepoy troops, and was met by the amirs with a combined force of 20,000 at Miani. There was almost a disaster when Napier misjudged his enemy, but he was saved by his own sepoys who refused – fortunately – to obey his faulty orders. This enabled him to recover and win the battle that has settled Sind's fate (→29/1/46).

Christmas past: Marley's ghost.

Dickens publishes Christmas bestseller

London, 31 December
Charles Dickens's first book to be published complete and not in monthly parts, *A Christmas Carol*, is a Christmas bestseller at the cost of five shillings [25p]. By Christmas eve it had sold 6,000 copies and is still in keen demand. In it Dickens calls up the memories of his own childhood – the Cratchit family live in similarly straitened circumstances. The character of Scrooge sums up the money-mindedness and lack of human generosity that Dickens sees all around him in commercial society. Scrooge's visions and final reformation represent the author's hopes for a new spirit – the spirit of Christmas, which is merely a one-day holiday with no celebration other than the giving of presents to those children whose parents can afford it.

Dickens himself has money problems, with a large family in constant need. Despite the success of *Nicholas Nickleby* and *The Old Curiosity Shop*, his current serial, *Martin Chuzzlewit*, is selling poorly (→31/1/46).

Dickens: a Christmas present.

1844

Dublin, 10 February. Daniel O'Connell, the lord mayor, and eight others are found guilty of conspiracy (→30/5).

Tweedmouth, 14 April. The remains of James Stuart, the would-be successor to the British crown, are buried in the churchyard. Over a thousand people attend the service.

Dublin, 30 May. Daniel O'Connell is given a 12-month prison sentence and fined £2,000 (→4/9).

London, 1 June. Czar Nicholas of Russia visits Queen Victoria unannounced to discuss an Anglo-Russian alliance against French intervention in the crumbling Ottoman Empire.

Britain, 27 July. John Dalton, the scientist who pioneered the study of meteorology and atomic theory, has died.

Westminster, 9 August. The act to abolish imprisonment for debts below £20 is given the royal assent (→3/1845).

Co Durham, 28 August. Thomas Dundas, the earl of Zetland, lays the foundation stone of a monument to Lord Durham, the former governor-general of Canada, at the top of Penshaw Hill.

Westminster, 4 September. The Lords revoke the judgement against O'Connell and his fellow supporters.→

London, 29 October. Crowds cheer as Queen Victoria opens the Royal Exchange.

Canterbury. St Augustine's Abbey is converted for use as an Anglican college for missionaries.

Manchester. The borough council, in an attempt to improve the living conditions of working people, forbids the building of back-to-back houses and insists on the installation of lavatories and ashpits to improve sanitation.

Scotland. Thomas Campbell, a poet, best known for *Ye mariners of England* and *The pleasures of hope*, has died.

Britain. The Young Men's Christian Aid (YMCA) is founded to rescue young men chiefly of the lower middle classes from the evils of the music halls and other vices; its motto is "Amusements are not necessary to your happiness, religion is".

London. Euston railway station, built by Philip Hardwick, is completed.

Workers join forces in Rochdale to form 'cooperative' shop

Rochdale, Lancashire
Unemployed workers in this Lancashire mill-town have got together and opened a new kind of shop – and at the same time found a way of helping others while helping themselves. A group calling itself the Rochdale Pioneers, with a membership of 50, has opened for business in Toad Lane.

Present stocks at the small shop are limited to a few essentials such as flour, and items are sold at regular market prices. But those who buy at the shop and become a member of the Pioneers' Society for a fee of one shilling [five pence] receive a share, or dividend, of the profits.

There have been earlier attempts to form a cooperative enterprise in Rochdale. The Pioneers have evolved from a socialist group based on the thinking of Robert Owen, a Welsh-born, self-made mill-owner whose humane treatment of his workers has made him a noted reformer. Ironically, one of the reasons behind the Pioneers' decision to open a shop was their disappointment with Owen's cooperative community, Harmony Hall, set up on an estate in Hampshire. The existence of two classes of settlers – the well-off, who paid their way but did no manual work, and the working-class Owenites – led to some discontent.

Parliament clamps down on factories and limits women and children's working day

Women work (and a man "supervises") in a Manchester cotton mill.

Westminster, June
The government is beginning to get to grips with a major abuse of the industrial revolution – the exploitation of child and female labour with long hours, low wages and wretched conditions. Increasing humanitarian concern has led to the passing of a series of acts to protect them.

The latest legislation approved in the House of Commons prohibits the employment underground of females, and of boys under the age of ten. Lord Shaftesbury's Mines Act has followed an investigation into conditions in coal mines and the publication of a "blue book" (so-called because of the colour of its cover) with illustrations of women and children working like beasts.

Many children have had to start working in the mines before they are seven years old. Some have worked as trappers, sitting all day in darkness to open doors. Others have dragged loaded trucks along narrow passages. The "blue book" also revealed that women and girls are working up to 16 hours a day in some mines and are paid two shillings [10p] a day or less. There are perhaps 6,000 so employed, mostly in the worst mines (→6/1847).

Government steps in to bring order to rampant 'railway mania'

Britain
"Railway mania" is sweeping the country. With the dramatic rise in the number of schemes for the "iron road" to criss-cross Britain, parliament has set up a select committee to regularize the new railways and approve their routes, for everyone wants a share of the high profits to be made from the early lines.

One regulation passed this year insists on the new companies running at least one daily train each way for which fares are no more than a penny a mile. Seats have to be provided for passengers in carriages protected from the weather. The speed of trains must not be less than 12 miles an hour (→3/1844).

All aboard please: railway travel may offer speed, but not always comfort.

Bank of England to take leading role

London, July
With industrial expansion quickening, the government has decided that the country needs a more elaborate banking system. Sir Robert Peel, the prime minister, has therefore introduced the Bank Charter Acts, which will secure the role of the Bank of England as the central note-issuing authority and guarantor of the rest of the banking system. The measure should promote financial stability and assist commerce and industry. The Bank was opened in 1694, as one of the first commercial banking ventures in the country, and was incorporated to lend the government £1,200,000 [*see report on page 623*]. It established the National Debt as a way of financing England's involvement in wars on the continent. Under the prime minister's new legislation it will issue notes in relation to the gold supply. Meanwhile the "joint-stock banks" are taking over more and more from the rather less reliable "country" banks.

Dividend day at the Bank of England: a quarterly pay-out on bank stock.

Dublin-to-Drogheda railway line opens

Dublin, 24 May
To mark the inauguration of the Dublin-to-Drogheda railway line, a special train has travelled to Drogheda with 565 passengers on board, including Earl de Grey, the lord lieutenant.

The railway, originally the idea of a Drogheda landowner, has had a troubled history. There was conflict over whether the route should run along the coastline or go inland. The engineer, William Cubitt, was asked to mediate, and he opted for the coastal route. No sooner had work begun in 1838 than a royal commission came out in favour of the inland route, and a new bill had to be shepherded through parliament by Daniel O'Connell. The railway has been built by William Dargan, the contractor and philanthropist who built the first railway in Ireland, between Dublin and Kingstown, in 1831 (→7/1845).

Steps taken to cut cost of road travel

Britain, July
Britons are paying out more than £1,500,000 a year in tolls to travel on roads, but it is looking as if the days of the turnpike trusts taking the money are numbered. These trusts, established a century ago by merchants, landowners and farmers interested in improving communications, now number about a thousand and cover some 20,000 miles. But the coming of the canals has taken away a great deal of the long distance freight from the roads. At the same time railways are making an ever greater impact on the way in which people make long journeys. Road transport is often less a matter of taking stagecoaches from London to Bath than of taking cabs to Paddington. Riots have taken place in some parts of Wales to expose abuses of the turnpike system. Under a new law, tolls are to be simplified.

Lords decide to overturn sentence on Irishman prosecuted by the government

"Punch" magazine satirizes Daniel O'Connell as "king" of Ireland.

Dublin, 4 September
Daniel O'Connell's imprisonment in Richmond jail has been ended by the Lords' reversal of the judgement by the court in Dublin, and thousands of admirers have called to congratulate him and shake his hand as he leaves.

His confrontation with the government came last autumn when he was planning his last great meeting of the year at Clontarf, outside Dublin, the scene of Brian Boruma's famous victory over the Danes in 1014 [*see report on page 171*]. As people were converging on the capital from all over the country the government declared the meeting illegal. Having always stated that he would behave constitutionally, O'Connell immediately cancelled it, enraging his supporters by what they saw as his tame surrender.

The government promptly prosecuted O'Connell and his associates on charges of conspiring to excite disaffection, and they were sentenced to a year's imprisonment. The trial was the sensation of the season. The friends were escorted to the Four Courts by the corporation of Dublin, in full regalia, and it was widely felt that O'Connell's only "conspiracy" had been if anything to prevent a revolution.

He has spent his months of imprisonment in considerable comfort in the private house of the governor of Richmond bridewell [jail], surrounded by his family (→6/1845).

Penrhyn Castle in Gwynedd, designed by Thomas Hopper as a Norman castle for the local slate king, J H Dawkes Pennant, is completed this year.

1845

Co Offaly, February. An amateur astronomer, William Parsons, the earl of Rosse, completes a 180-cm (72-inch) telescope, perhaps the world's largest, at Birr Castle.→

London, March. The Fleet prison is to be demolished; the abolition of imprisonment for debt has made it redundant.

Westminster, 3 April. Sir Robert Peel, the prime minister, introduces the Maynooth College Bill; he proposes to increase the annual grant to the Catholic college by £30,000 (→ 6/1845).

London, 1 May. Hungerford Suspension Bridge, designed by Isambard Kingdom Brunel, is opened to the public (→ 30/8).

Westminster, 30 June. The Maynooth College Bill is passed (→ 15/5/47).

Ireland, 31 July. The Colleges Act provides for the foundation of new colleges of higher education.

Cambridge, July. The London-to-Cambridge railway opens (→ 25/9).

Ireland, 8 August. Parliament orders asylums for the criminally insane to be built.

London, 22 August. Surrey County Cricket Club is founded (→ 8/1/63).

Dublin, 9 September. The *Dublin Evening Post* reports a potato blight in Ireland.

Cork City, 25 September. Construction work begins on the Cork-to-Bandon railway (→ 18/6/46).

Westminster, 31 October. Sir Robert Peel appoints a scientific commission, the Mansion House Committee, to investigate the failure of the Irish potato crop (→ 11/1845).

Westminster, 10 November. Peel orders the purchase of £100,000 of American corn for shipment to Ireland (→ 15).

Ireland, 15 November. Lyon Playfair and John Lindley issue a report on the state of the Irish potato crop (→ 3/1846).

London, 6 December. Sir Robert Peel tenders his resignation as prime minister to Queen Victoria (→ 20).

London, 20 December. Victoria refuses to accept Peel's resignation. →

Britain. William George Armstrong, an inventor and a solicitor, invents the hydraulic crane.

Scots amend Poor Law after church split

Poverty in Scotland's capital, with the Burns Monument in the background.

Edinburgh
Divisions in the Church of Scotland have led to it being less able than ever to carry out its old welfare and educational functions. As a result a royal commission has studied the operation of the old Poor Law in Scotland and proposed bringing in a new one. Its report is a sketch of the social problems in Scotland. The Poor Law Act retains the parish as an administrative unit but sets up parochial boards with some elected ratepayers.

A board of supervision will be based in Edinburgh and be representative of the regions of Scotland. It will establish minimum standards of care and hear complaints and appeals.

Great port of Liverpool opens new dock

The Albert Dock is opened officially (in 1846) by Prince Albert.

Liverpool
The dockland of Liverpool, the key exporting centre of north-western England, handling goods to the growing empire market, has been extended. Eight years of work – and controversy – have led to the construction of the Albert Dock, a remarkable example of dock architecture. The construction project was the idea of Jesse Hartley, who began his working life building bridges and has been using granite instead of sandstone, even though it is far more costly. The dock has five-storey warehouses on its four sides, with the ground floors being open in a Doric colonnade.

Row brews up over government grant to Catholic college

Co Kildare, June
The parliamentary grant to Maynooth College, a Roman Catholic seminary in Co Kildare, has now been made permanent through the passing of an act, and Protestants throughout the United Kingdom are loudly objecting.

The support for Maynooth College is being seen as an attempt by the government to divide the Irish Catholic clergy from the laity, long-supporters of Daniel O'Connell and the Repeal movement. The bishops had privately looked for financial help for the college in the past but had always been refused. Now their grant has been trebled and made permanent.

REPEAL
THE GREEDY BOY WHO CRIED FOR THE MOON.

How "Punch" sees O'Connell.

The government may be hoping that a better endowed college would turn out priests who are more anglophile than hitherto. Proposals are also under way to open colleges in Cork, Belfast and Galway to provide third-level education for Catholics and Presbyterians, who have previously had to attend Trinity College, Dublin. The idea is to give young men training for the priesthood a more general education. While some of the Catholic bishops are happy with this, those who support O'Connell may look for separate sectarian endowments. Already there are suspicious murmurings that these new institutions may turn out to be "Godless colleges" (→ 30).

Engels studies life of working classes

Manchester
Friedrich Engels, a highly unlikely combination of German businessman and socialist philosopher, has published an extraordinary account of the life and hard times of British workers this year. In his book *The Condition of the Working Class in England* he argues that the whole society of the country has been altered with the invention of the steam engine and of machinery for working cotton.

Engels writes about Manchester, where his business is based and where the population has rocketed from 75,000 to 250,000 this century alone. Owing to the lay-out of the town, he says, it is possible for people living there, and visitors, never to see the slums or working-class areas. Engels writes that Manchester's upper classes enjoy healthy country air while living in comfortable dwellings linked to the centre by regular omnibuses. The workers live in misery and filth in cottages built "60 at a time" (→6/1847).

Leading Anglican intellectual stuns the Church of England by converting to Rome

Oxford, October
John Henry Newman, the intellectual leader of the Oxford movement (for church reform), has this month joined the Roman Catholic Church. The movement has waged war on the established church since 1833 through a series of tracts, but even so Newman's decision has caused a sensation.

Newman and his friends began their series of tracts when he was the vicar of St Mary's church here and most of the rest of the group were fellows at Oriel College. They began by attacking the role of the state in Anglican affairs, but increasingly Newman appeared to be urging a return to some historical traditions of Catholicism. In 1841, for instance, he argued in *Tract 90* that the doctrinal basis of the Anglican Church was not incompatible with Catholicism.

What began as theological debate became more personal when the university authorities turned upon Newman's friends. Edward Pusey was accused of heresy and forbidden to preach for two years; W G Ward was deprived of his degree. As Oxford is a centre of theological studies, Newman felt that all the things he believed in were being rejected, and so he has now actively opted for Catholicism (→1864).

John Henry Newman: converted.

More common land is to be enclosed

Britain
With another act on the enclosure of common land being approved by parliament, the rural landscape of lowland Britain is looking very much like a chequerboard pattern of squarish and hedged fields. The General Enclosure Act is expected to complete the enclosure of all the best agricultural land and encourage still further large-scale and more productive farming.

Enclosure, or the practice of fencing off land formerly subject to common rights under the open field system, has been taking place since the end of the mediaeval period. The process has been accelerated over the last hundred years, with open fields, commons and meadows, as well as wastes, being affected. Large landowners are benefiting from enclosure. So are larger tenant farmers, as the greater productivity of an enclosed farm is usually more than sufficient to meet increases in rent. The small farmer, cottager and squatter are the losers.

Royal commission investigates Irish land

Ireland, February
The Devon Commission, appointed by the prime minister, Sir Robert Peel, in 1843, to investigate relations between landlords and tenants, the cultivation of land and the conditions and habits of farm labourers, has made its first report.

The commission has heard 1,000 witnesses and has acknowledged the need to alleviate the distress and poor living conditions suffered by farm labourers. It is also concerned at the prevalence of a mercenary landlord class that takes little interest in the running of its estates and often evicts its tenants. This is the first time in the United Kingdom that the landed system has faced real reform.

The world's largest telescope has been completed by William Parsons, the earl of Rosse; it is almost as large as his home, Birr Castle, Co Offaly.

'Great Britain' sets off on maiden voyage

The "Great Britain" when she was launched at Bristol on 19 July 1843.

Liverpool, 30 August
After her trials around the Bristol Channel and the English coast, the remarkable passenger ship *Great Britain* has set off on her first transatlantic voyage to New York. Isambard Kingdom Brunel believes he is on to a winner by building the most powerful ship afloat to break the American monopoly of traffic from Europe to the New World. The ship has demonstrated the possibilities not only of a large iron hull but also of the screw propeller as a means of efficient propulsion. Built at Bristol, where a new dry dock had to be specially built and others widened, *The Great Britain* is more than 100 metres (328 feet) long and has cost £118,000, plus another £53,000 for the dry dock. She can carry 252 people with berths and another 92 without berths, as well as a cargo of almost 1,200 tonnes.

Potato blight destroys crops in Ireland

Ireland, November
Over half the Irish potato crop has failed after being struck by potato blight, and while partial potato failure is not uncommon, this looks like being extremely serious. Remedies for staying the progress of the disease have ranged from drying the potatoes in lime or salt to treating them with chlorine gas. The most widely publicized remedies have been offered by a scientific commission appointed by the prime minister, Sir Robert Peel. But even these are conflicting, ranging from ventilating the potatoes in pits to keep them dry to soaking them in bogwater to keep them wet.

As the true extent of the disease becomes apparent, gloom and panic are beginning to set in as the threat of famine draws nearer (→10).

Starving families are driven by desperation to attack a potato store.

Disraeli's novel dissects our 'two nations'

London
The Tory rebel Benjamin Disraeli is having more success with the novel-reading public than with his fellow MPs, who shouted down his maiden speech. At 22 he became the talk of the town as the author of *Vivian Grey*, which financed a grand tour of Europe for him. His flamboyant manner and dandified appearance handicap him as a politician, but his books show wit and intelligence. Having married a rich widow he has become one of the Buckinghamshire landed gentry, but *Sybil*, his latest novel, claims to identify with the underprivileged.

Sybil, its heroine, is the daughter of a Chartist leader – Disraeli supported the Chartists – who is loved by Egremont, a young aristocrat. "I was told that the privileged and the people form two nations," she says. The two nations of Britain, rich and poor, are symbolized by the squalour of Mobray town and the splendour of its castle. Disraeli criticizes both Whigs and Tories for ignoring the people's wrongs and calls on the aristocracy to take responsibility. These are the romantic views of the "Young England" group of Tories.

Disraeli: the literary politician.

PM to abolish corn laws

PAPA COBDEN TAKING MASTER ROBERT A FREE TRADE WALK.

Richard Cobden leads Robert Peel towards repeal of the corn laws.

Westminster, 20 December
Sir Robert Peel is back in Downing Street and poised to bring in a bill to abolish the corn laws. He has been recalled by Queen Victoria after resigning as prime minister 15 days ago when his unexpected conversion to corn-law reform had split the Tory cabinet.

Peel had become increasingly persuaded by arguments against the corn laws – restrictions placed on both imports and exports of grain – put forward by Richard Cobden of the Anti-Corn Law League. But change was still bitterly resisted by the landed interests within the Tory Party. Events came to a head this autumn with the disastrous failure of the second Irish potato crop.

Poor harvests in England meant that there was no corn to be sent to Ireland, raising the prospect of widespread famine. Although relief measures were proposed for Ireland, Peel decided that reform of the corn laws could be delayed no longer. The Irish tragedy was a warning of potential disaster elsewhere in the United Kingdom if the poor were encouraged, because of high bread prices, to grow potatoes.

On 6 November Peel proposed that corn duties be reduced immediately by statutory order and a bill be introduced for more fundamental reforms. Only three members of the cabinet supported him. Further attempts at persuasion won him some support, but it was not enough and on 5 December he resigned. Lord John Russell, also a convert to corn-law reform, was invited to form a minority government but found little enthusiasm in his party for the inevitable battles with the Lords. So Peel is back, now with the support of most of his cabinet but still facing fierce conflict within his own party when he introduces the repeal legislation next year (→6/1846).

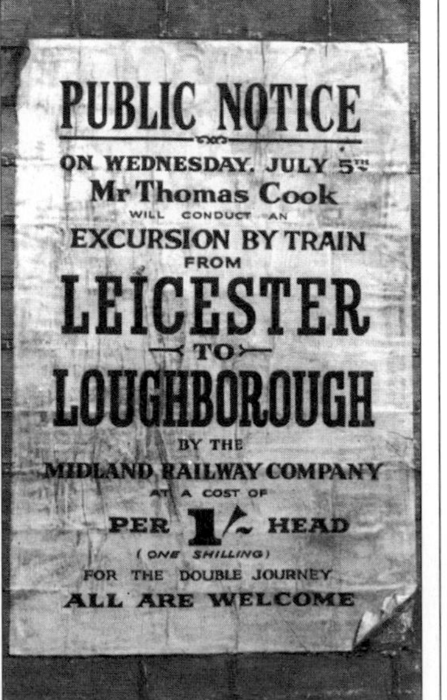

PUBLIC NOTICE
ON WEDNESDAY, JULY 5TH
Mr Thomas Cook
WILL CONDUCT AN
EXCURSION BY TRAIN
FROM
LEICESTER
TO
LOUGHBOROUGH
BY THE
MIDLAND RAILWAY COMPANY
AT A COST OF
PER 1/- HEAD
(ONE SHILLING)
FOR THE DOUBLE JOURNEY
ALL ARE WELCOME

Thomas Cook is establishing a new business offering trips by railway in the midlands; the first (above) was undertaken in 1841.

Spinster poet gives new life to cooking

London, August
Eliza Acton, the daughter of a Hastings brewer and an accomplished poet, with several volumes published, has produced a culinary tome, *Modern Cookery*, which aims to put today's cooks on their mettle.

The middle-aged spinster, who was once engaged to a French officer, lives at Tonbridge, in Kent, looking after her elderly mother. Her book recognizes that in many households it is the wife and mother who does most of the everyday cooking. The days are going when servants could be relied on to provide the meals.

Modern Cookery provides recipes for the standard fare that people enjoy eating. It looks like being a bestseller – perhaps a classic.

1846

India, 29 January. British troops defeat Indian Sikhs at Aliwal (→ 10/2).

London, 31 January. The *Daily News* is founded; Charles Dickens, the novelist, is its editor (→ 1849).

India, 10 February. The British defeat the Sikhs at Sobraon (→ 3/1846).

London, 27 May. Louis Napoleon, a nephew of Napoleon Bonaparte and a former claimant to the French throne, who has been imprisoned in France for the last six years, escapes and seeks refuge here.

Ireland, May. Widespread famine sweeps across the country after the failure of the potato crop last year (→ 7/1846).

Edinburgh, 18 June. The North British Railway Line is opened (→ 4/8).

Britain, 22 June. Benjamin Haydon, a portrait painter well respected for his art teaching and writings, commits suicide.

Manchester, 26 June. A public holiday is called to mark the repeal of the corn laws (→ 23/1/60).

Dublin, 11 July. John William Ponsonby, the earl of Bessborough, is sworn in as lord lieutenant of Ireland; Thomas Nicholas Redington is appointed as his under-secretary, the first Roman Catholic to hold this position.

Ireland, July. Fears are growing that this year's potato crop has fallen prey to blight. →

Dublin, 4 August. The Great Southern and Western Railway, between Dublin and Carlow, is opened (→ 8/1848).

Berlin, 23 September. A new planet, named Neptune, has been sighted in the solar system; its discovery is credited to John Couch Adams, a Cambridge scholar, Urbain Le Verrier, a French astronomer, and Johann Gottfied Galle, a German astronomer.

Scotland, 15 November. The North British Railway ends its Sunday service between Glasgow and Edinburgh after religious pressure to observe the Sabbath.

Britain/France, September. Anglo-French relations are strained after the marriage of the Duke of Montpensier, the son of King Louis Philippe of France, to Princess Louisa of Spain.

Treaty of Lahore ends British war in India

A delegation of Sikh leaders ceremonially surrender to the British.

India, March
After more than six years of conflict the Sikhs have come to terms with their British conquerors. The Sikh army has given up its claims to land on the left bank of the Sutlej, and to the Jalandhar Doab between the Sutlej and the Bias. It has also promised to pay an indemnity of £500,000, and to surrender Kashmir to the rule of the *raja* [ruler] of Jammu. The death of Ranjit Singh in 1839 left the Sikhs in turmoil, and in 1843 Maharaja Sher Singh, who was friendly with the Indian government, was murdered.

In the past few months the Sikhs have suffered a series of defeats at the hands of the British. Now they will be ruled by Henry Lawrence, a British agent with a garrison at Lahore [now Pakistan] (→ 12/1/48).

Health care crisis in Ireland deepens

Ireland, March
In a bid to provide more hospitals to cope with the huge numbers of people suffering from famine fever, Sir Robert Peel's administration has passed the Temporary Fever Act in parliament. Under this act, two of the five unpaid commissioners of health can require a board of guardians to set up a temporary hospital. Yet since they cannot be compelled to do so, it is believed that these measures will not solve the problem.

Fever has spread like wildfire through the overpopulated workhouses of Connacht and Munster, and efforts to deal with it have so far proved totally inadequate. The Poor Law commissioners have been warning boards of guardians for some time to prepare for the epidemic and to separate the diseased from the healthy, but this is impossible since almost everyone admitted is already sick. Typhus is rampant and thousands now have relapsing fever, dysentery or even scurvy, which has never been common here owing to the high consumption of potatoes (→ 5/1846).

Chadwick's report reveals the appalling poverty of city life

Dinner at a cheap lodging-house in London: diet and hygiene are poor.

Edwin Chadwick: social reformer.

Westminster
A terrible picture of the deprivation that has accompanied industrial expansion has been presented to parliament. Members are considering a wide-ranging report into poverty by Edwin Chadwick of the Poor Law commission. Most worrying to the ruling classes must be the report's findings about public health. Chadwick has shown how the rush of people into Britain's industrial centres has polluted water supplies and created waste, increasing the spread of cholera.

The rapid growth of industrial towns in Lancashire has produced some of the worst overcrowding, poverty and disease. In Liverpool some 40,000 people are living in cramped, unventilated cellars, with Irish immigrants daily adding to the overcrowding. Manchester is no better, and London has many of the same problems. The evidence of acute and increasing poverty makes reform difficult to resist (→ 1847). ▷

Corn-law repeal defeats government

Peel resigns after splitting Tory party

Westminster, 29 June
Sir Robert Peel, prime minister for the past five years and leader of the Tory or Conservative Party since 1832, has resigned, leaving his party in utter disarray. His departure comes just four days after the corn laws were repealed following five months of acrimonious debate in parliament. His downfall was precipitated by an Irish coercion bill, defeated by 73 votes when Tory protectionists joined Whigs to force his resignation.

Last December Peel had resigned as premier, having failed to persuade the cabinet of the need for reform of the corn laws. Within 15 days he was back, with the cabinet mostly behind him but opposed by a vocal group of protectionist MPs in the Commons – articulately led by Benjamin Disraeli – and the landed interests in the Lords. But the reforms passed the Commons in May and the Lords on 25 June.

As a result the duties on maize are abolished at once, and those on wheat, oats and barley are to be reduced to a nominal shilling a quarter until full repeal in 1849. In pushing through these reforms Peel believes that he will meet the need to import large quantities of grain to feed a growing population. Britain is therefore abandoning the aim of self-sufficiency in food and is going instead to rely on building up its industrial power at the expense of agriculture. Not surprisingly, Peel has paid a heavy price for reform. Shire Tories blocked moves by his supporters, such as William Gladstone, to find seats, and now his rebel MPs have forced him out of office (→ 7/1846).

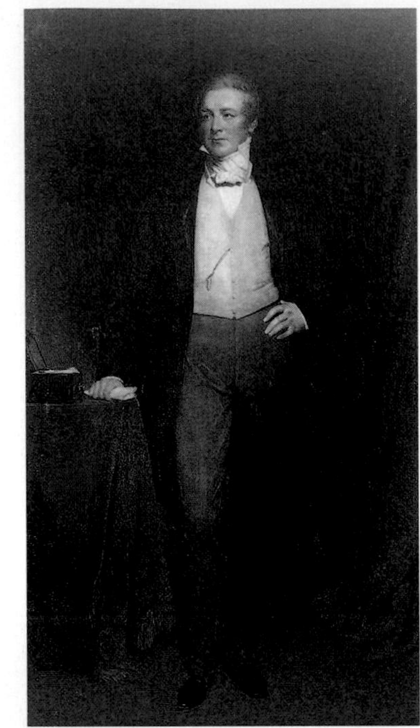

Peel: leaves his party riven.

What reform of the corn laws will mean

Britain, June
The repeal of the corn laws is a triumph for the campaign waged since 1838 by the free traders of the Anti-Corn Law League. In the Lancashire towns where its support originated, the league has proved more popular than Chartism, despite its middle-class character. In Wales it has won the backing of nonconformists. And Peel's last speech before his resignation contained a fulsome tribute to Richard Cobden, one of its leading lights.

The Anti-Corn Law League was started by a group of merchants meeting in Manchester. Funded by cotton manufacturers, it tapped popular distrust of Tory landowners and found two persuasive advocates in Richard Cobden, a calico manufacturer, and John Bright, a mill-owner from Rochdale, both of whom are now MPs. Cobden wants to see power move from the landed classes to the "intelligent middle and industrious classes". Bright is a Quaker with a puritanical commitment to free trade.

The repeal of the corn laws may or may not bring about any great change in the condition of the people. But to the consternation of shire Tories and radical Chartists alike, it has proved that the middle classes are the most potent social and political force in Britain (→ 26).

CARRYING THE CORN; OR, THE FREE-TRADE HARVEST-HOME.

Free traders celebrate their victory.

John Russell elected as successor to Peel

Russell: picking up the pieces.

Westminster, July
Lord John Russell, the leader of the Whigs in parliament, is the new prime minister, at the age of 54. Ironically, he must rely on the support of Sir Robert Peel, the man whom he replaces. Russell was MP for Tavistock, in Devon, from 1813 until in 1841 he moved to represent the City. A tireless reformer, he became paymaster for the forces in Lord Grey's ministry of 1830; he was then home secretary in Melbourne's 1835 administration. Russell became a convert to repeal of the corn laws last year and might have become prime minister six months sooner if only Lord Grey had not refused to serve with Palmerston (→ 6/1847).

Religious ferment explodes across the whole country

Britain
The people of Britain have not lost religious faith in the wake of industrialization. Instead they have found new forms of worship, as Catholics, Baptists, Methodists, Quakers, Congregationalists, Unitarians, and Presbyterians all compete to attract worshippers. It is a truly religious age, as people go to their chosen churches not out of loyalty to the state or even fear of persecution but out of personal conviction.

The repeal of the Test and Corporation Acts in 1828 and 1829 broke the monopoly held by the Anglican Church. Old divisions of Tory and Whig, church and dissent, were cast aside when Sir Robert Peel adopted a Whig proposal for a commission on the established church. A civil register freed dissenters in England from the obligation to marry in Anglican churches. But the latent tension between church and state has resurfaced.

Government efforts to suppress bishoprics in Ireland, meanwhile, spurred John Keble to a sermon that launched the Oxford Movement. A group of similarly minded high-churchmen then published a series of *Tracts for the Times*, stressing the unbroken historical tradition of the Roman Catholic Church. They brought back to Anglican worship surpliced choirs, incense, candles and turning to the east for the creed. In *Tract 90* John Newman went so far as to argue that the 39 Articles were compatible with Roman Catholicism. Last year he was received into the Church of Rome.

Yet it is the low-church evangelical form of worship that has a more potent hold on daily life. In the towns, working-class congregations are growing in the chapels, from which spring many civic leaders and a predominantly Liberal pressure for reform. In Scotland the Free Church, founded three years ago, is prospering (→ 1851).

Poet defies father to elope with lover

London, 12 September
Elizabeth Barrett, the poetess, eloped today at the age of 40 with a poet who is six years younger, Robert Browning, in defiance of her father's ban on marriage. She slipped out of no 50 Wimpole Street to a nearby church.

Barrett's poems include *The Cry of the Children*, a protest against the exploitation of children in factories. Most of her life has been as an invalid: she injured her spine in a riding accident. Robert Browning is best known for *The Pied Piper of Hamelin* and *Pippa Passes*. The couple are making for Italy (→ 1850).

The poets after arriving in Italy.

Scots and Irish devastated by famine

Scotland and Ireland, July
This year's potato crop in Ireland and the Scottish highlands has been destroyed by blight. Irish smallholders and labourers used up all their reserves during last year's crisis, and the outlook there is very bleak. In Scotland some 150,000 people on the west coast – whose diet is confined to oatmeal gruel, potatoes and the occasional herring – are threatened by starvation. Sir Edward Pine Coffin has been put in charge of relief operations, and food is on its way to the region.

Anxiety is felt in Ireland at the departure of Sir Robert Peel from office. He was firm and decisive in providing famine relief, and it is feared that his successor, Lord John Russell, will not be so sympathetic to Ireland's plight. There is also dismay that the abundant oat crop is being depleted through exports, which the government refuses to halt. As a result food prices have risen sharply. Late last year the government secretly bought cheap Indian meal in the United States which is now arriving here. Called "Peel's brimstone", it will be distributed through special food depots. Food will be sold rather than given away, and relief works have been set up, employing some 140,000 people. Yet not all of them are destitute, so the genuine poor continue to suffer (→ 1/1/47).

Starving peasants clamour for food at the gatehouse of an Irish workhouse.

Poverty in rural Ireland, without even workhouses, is growing more acute.

Mysterious author publishes collection of 'Nonsense' limericks

London, December
The "limerick" is sweeping through society following the publication of *A Book of Nonsense*, composed of these whimsical five-line stanzas. A typical example:

There was an Old Man who said
"Hush!
I perceive a young bird in this bush!"
When they said - "Is it small?"
He replied, "Not at all!
It is four times as big as the bush!"

Each of the limericks is illustrated with a spiky drawing of the eccentric people described – the Old Man of Thermopylae who never did anything properly, the Old Man of Peru who watched his wife making a stew (and ended up in it), or the Old Man on whose nose all the birds of the air could repose. They appeal to children, who are usually offered only "improving" verses – but also to their parents.

The *Nonsense* author's name is unknown; he describes himself on the title page with another limerick about an "old Derry-down-Derry, who loved to see little folks merry". He is said to be the water-colourist Edward Lear, employed by the earl of Derby, who invented the limerick to amuse the earl's children.

The Old Man who said Hush: an illustration from "Nonsense Poems".

Manchester shows a pride in itself

Manchester
Civic pride has taken root in many provincial towns as the industrial revolution has brought booming populations and, for some, wealth. Nowhere is this more evident than in Manchester, where three public parks have been opened this year. The middle classes enjoy physical activities such as cricket, where their ranks are occasionally swelled by paid artisans. The town's first rowing regatta was held in 1842, but games and gymnastic exercises for the common people in public parks are a genuine breakthrough. They are also a positive response to the separation of classes noted recently by Friedrich Engels.

1847

Dublin, 1 January. John MacDonnell becomes the first surgeon in Ireland to operate using anaesthesia; he amputates a young girl's arm at Richmond hospital (→11/1847).

Westminster, 1 January. The British Association for the Relief of Extreme Distress in the Remote Parishes of Ireland and Scotland is founded (→25).

Westminster, 25 January. Lord John Russell, the prime minister, proposes to substitute soup kitchens for public works to relieve the famine in Ireland (→26/5).

Westminster, 26 February. Parliament passes the Destitute Poor (Ireland) Act. (→4/1847)

Dublin, 5 April. Alexis Soyer opens the first soup kitchen.

Ireland, 10 April. The fever epidemic worsens.

London, 29 April. The Royal Navy adds canned meat to its provisions for sea journeys.

Dublin, 4 May. Attempts to reunite the Loyal National Repeal Association and the Irish Confederation fail.

Genoa, Italy, 15 May. Daniel O'Connell, the Irish radical politician who fought to repeal the Act of Union, dies (→4/8).

Edinburgh, 4 June. Half the city's population attends the funeral of Thomas Chalmers, the leader of the Free Church of Scotland, who died on 30 May, aged 67.

London, June. The Communist League is founded by Karl Marx, Friedrich Engels and Stefan Born (→1848).

Faversham, Kent, 14 July. Over 40 people die in an explosion at the Marsh Powder Works.

Ireland, July. Irish farmers reap a small potato crop (→9/1848).

Dublin, 4 August. The funeral of Daniel O'Connell takes place (→15/3/48).

Birmingham, 16 September. The corn exchange is opened.

Ireland, 1 October. Government soup kitchens cease to distribute food.

Scotland. The Educational Institute of Scotland is founded.

Westminster. Parliament passes the Juvenile Offenders Act; this raises the minimum age for adult criminality to 14 years (→1849).

Factory Act tackles 'abuse' of children

Westminster, June
John Fielden's Ten Hours Act provides that from 1 July no woman or child under the age of 18 shall work more than 11 hours a day, 63 hours a week, to be reduced from 1 May next year to ten hours a day, 58 hours a week. The act is the fruit of a campaign begun 17 years ago by the Tory evangelical Michael Sadler, who lost his seat in 1832, and carried on by Lord Ashley until he lost his seat last year. Despite the appalling abuse of child labour, this modest measure only passed when the protectionists supported it to spite free trader Sir Robert Peel.

Children winding cotton, c.1820.

Presbyterians form new United Church

Scotland
The "United Presbyterian Church" is a misnomer for this recently formed body. The truth is that the church in Scotland, solidly Calvinist for almost three centuries, has split apart. The United Presbyterian Church is the fusion of the Relief Church and the Secession Church, splinter groups from the Church of Scotland. A more important split occurred four years ago when evangelicals walked out of the Church of Scotland's general assembly in fury at the British state's role in terms of patronage and its right to interfere in church affairs. Of 1,200 ministers, 470 seceded to form the Free Church, which is now competing for congregations all over Scotland.

Emigration on 'coffin ships' is the only hope left for thousands of starving Irish

The central soup depot in Cork dispenses food during the famine of 1847.

Ireland, April 1847
The terrible winter, with gales and thick snow, has led to thousands of starving people in a pitiable condition streaming into the towns in search of food, with many suffering from "famine fever". Anyone in a fit condition to travel is seized by panic to get out of Ireland: in January 6,000 emigrants sailed from Liverpool alone. It is feared that almost a million people will have emigrated by the end of this year. So great is the demand that direct sailings are now being introduced from Ireland. Leavng mainly from the smaller ports, the vessels used are so old and in such bad condition that they are called "coffin ships".

As the crisis reaches new heights the administration of public works has come up against insuperable difficulties. The potato crop has almost totally failed while food prices have risen sharply. Labourers and small farmers have left the land in search of relief work, and this spring the total number thus employed reached an all-time high of 750,000. The problems are compounded by the fact that relief works are widely scattered, many of them in remote areas with new and inexperienced administrative staff.

Many landlords have dispatched their tenants to the public works in the hope that they will earn enough to pay their rent. Many who are under normal conditions incapable of doing heavy work are also turning to relief schemes in desperation. As the situation worsens and many men fall sick, their places are taken by women and children who labour on the public roads, dressed in rags, breaking stones and wheeling heavy barrows.

Realizing that the public works scheme is unable to cope with the crisis, the British prime minister, Lord John Russell, has decided to abandon it in favour of outdoor relief – bringing food to people in their own homes (→7/1847).

Looking for a new life: a family sets out for London and then the US.

Government to reform care of the poor

Westminster
The government has created a Poor Law board, replacing the Poor Law commission with an arm of government presided over by a member of the cabinet. The new board will supervise the activities of local boards of guardians, which have come in for much criticism. While some regard it as a success that the amount of public money given to the relief of poverty has been reduced, reformers believe that this is only because the conditions of the workhouses are so desperate as to deter many who really need help. As Sir George Grey explained in the House of Commons on 3 May, the new board will be "a general superintending authority immediately responsible to parliament".

It should have a better opportunity of eliminating any abuses that might have arisen from the fact that the Poor Law commissioners were not obliged to justify themselves publicly. The new board, by confronting its accusers in the house, should be able to vindicate its actions and decisions.

The men's dormitory in the St Martin's workhouse in central London.

Chloroform to numb pain of operations

Edinburgh, November
James Young Simpson, the professor of midwifery at the university of Edinburgh, has successfully conducted a public demonstration at the royal infirmary here of the use of chloroform in making a patient unconscious during an operation. As a result the patient is insensible to pain.

Professor Simpson, aged 36, first became interested in anaesthetics following experiments in the United States where sulphuric ether was used to deaden pain. He hoped that it would help relieve the pain of labour. Then, on 4 November, he and two assistants inhaled chloroform gas and became unconscious, providing themselves with the evidence for what might be a huge step forwards in medicine. Unlike ether, chloroform can be used in small amounts. There are however already some who are denouncing the experiments as dangerous to health, morals and religion (→ 12/1867).

Repercussions after Peel's resignation

Britain, June
A year after Sir Robert Peel's resignation as prime minister he still dominates the political scene not only at Westminster, where he is either the confidant of the Whig government or the mediator between contending factions, but also throughout public life. For most people his achievement was to raise politics from the narrow pursuit of sectional interest to the fulfilment of public duty. His own commitment to hard work, anathema to his privileged predecessors, is imitated in town halls all over the country.

The paradox is that though it was Peel – helped by F R Bonham at the Carlton Club – who made the Conservative Party into the formidable force it is today, it was the party that ruined him, politically. It remains to be seen which view will prevail: his own conviction that statesmen should be above parties, or Disraeli's that the party must come first (→ 2/7/50).

Moorland passion and immoral heroines provide contrasting literary highlights

Thackeray: the panoramic author of "Vanity Fair".

Mrs Rawdon leaving Paris: a scene from "Vanity Fair".

London, December
It has been a year of new departures in the English novel. *Vanity Fair*, by William Makepeace Thackeray, has been appearing in monthly parts. The popularity it is attracting has promoted its author's standing to rival that of Charles Dickens, whose recent *Martin Chuzzlewit* sold poorly by his standards.

Vanity Fair – a title that came to Thackeray in a dream – is a new departure in technique, with the author exhibiting his characters in the manner of an indulgent puppet-master. When Becky Sharp declares that "revenge may be wicked, but it's natural. I'm no angel", the author comments: "To say the truth she certainly was not." Every month he offers to "walk with you through the Fair". The work is a panorama of the upper and middle classes of society from about the time of Waterloo onwards, "where you can light on the strangest contrasts, laughable and tearful, you can be gentle and pathetic or savage and cynical with perfect propriety".

Mrs Gamp proposes a toast in Dickens's "Martin Chuzzlewit".

There could hardly be two more vividly contrasting heroines than the immoral Becky Sharp and Jane Eyre, the good, plain governess who refuses to be Mr Rochester's mistress but conquers him by sheer force of character and marries him after he is blinded. Yet this sensational novel by the mysterious Currer Bell is dedicated to Thackeray because, says the author in a preface to its second edition inside a year, "I regard him as the first social regenerator of the day, who would restore to rectitude the warped system of things".

The originality of *Jane Eyre* lies in its development of a female character of positive force and passion, equal to any man's, whereas Rochester is a more conventional Byronic hero, "proud, sardonic, harsh, moody too". A very different couple, Catherine Earnshaw and Heathcliff, inhabit *Wuthering Heights*, whose elemental passions are set on wild moorlands with a tragic intensity that is both unique and deeply poetic. Reviewers have been shocked by the book – "a gnarled and painful story", "dwelling on physical acts of cruelty", "a tale set against granite", say some. The relationship of Ellis Bell, its author, to Currer and to Acton Bell, the author of *Agnes Grey*, is a mystery (→ 7/7/48).

1848

India, 12 January. James Andrew Ramsay, the earl of Dalhousie, is appointed governor-general (→ 13/1/49).

London, 11 February. William Howley, the archbishop of Canterbury, dies at Lambeth Palace; his successor is John Bird Sumner, the bishop of Chester.

Ireland, 12 February. John Mitchel, a patriot, prints the first issue of *United Irishman* (→ 27/5).

Dublin, 15 March. The Irish Confederation is urged by William Smith O'Brien and Thomas Francis Meagher to use physical force (→ 3/4).

Surrey, March. Louis Philippe, the deposed king of France, seeks refuge for his family with Queen Victoria.

Dover, 3 April. Work on Admiralty Pier begins.

Paris, 3 April. William Smith O'Brien presents the provisional French government with a fraternal address of support from the Irish Confederation (→ 12/6).

London, 10 April. The Chartist movement, led by Feargus O'Connor, holds a march from Kennington to Westminster.

Scotland, April. A crowd of almost 100,000 meets on Glasgow Green to support the Chartists (→ 10).

Dublin, 27 May. John Mitchel, who was arrested earlier this month, is found guilty on charges under the Treason Felony Act; he is sentenced to 14 years' transportation.

Ireland, 12 June. The Loyal National Repeal Association and the Irish Confederation from the Irish League (→ 29/7).

London, 1 August. A regular mail service begins between London and Ireland.

Co Tipperary, 5 August. William Smith O'Brien is arrested for treason (→ 9/10).

Ireland, September. The potato crop fails again (→ 5/1849).

Dublin, 9 October. O'Brien is found guilty of high treason and sentenced to be hanged, drawn and quartered (→ 5/6/49).

Hertfordshire, 24 November. Lord Melbourne, the former prime minister and close friend of Queen Victoria, has died at his home in Welwyn.

Scotland/Ireland. A cholera epidemic breaks out (→ 5/1848).

Macaulay publishes 'History of England'

London
Although it is liberally sprinkled with inaccuracies and extremely prejudiced, Thomas Babington Macaulay's monumental *History of England* – the first volumes of which were published this year – tells more about the country's progress and achievements than any other book that has hitherto appeared in English.

Macaulay, for years a leading advocate of reform, the abolition of slavery and religious toleration, was a member of the supreme council in India, where he played a major part in drafting a legal code for the subcontinent. He began the *History* on his return to England.

Macaulay shows how Britain has advanced since the "glorious revolution" of 1688. "The history of our own country in the last one hundred and sixty years is eminently the history of physical, moral and intellectual improvement," he writes. He sees an even more glowing future, and his optimism is reflected in huge sales. No apology is offered for factual errors. "I shall cheerfully bear the reproach of having descended below the dignity of history," he says (→ 28/12/59).

Public Health Act follows cholera epidemic

Facing a clean-up: Father Thames is very dirty as well as very old.

Westminster, May
With the recent cholera epidemic still fresh in mind, and another sweeping across Europe, the latest statistics show that more than 20 per cent of deaths are caused by typhus fever, diarrhoea and other contagious diseases. Today's Public Health Act calls for the appointment of medical officers in every major city and borough.

Open sewers still flow through the centre of many towns, and the act gives boroughs – where such deaths exceed on average 23 to a thousand of the population – the right to petition for local boards of health. Within three days of the act, 62 towns and parishes have asked for inspectors. Birkenhead complained of "an extensive open ditch ... a very great nuisance". There are so many demands that the national board of health has confessed that it cannot possibly hope to satisfy all of them (→ 11/1849).

Publisher shocked to find that author of 'Jane Eyre' is a woman

London, 7 July
A London publisher, George Smith of Smith, Elder and Co, was taken aback today when he received a visit from the author of his current best-selling novel, *Jane Eyre*. A woman of 32, dressed in black, announced that she was "Currer Bell", the author of the story of the plain governess who falls in love with her employer, Mr Rochester, which has caused such a sensation that a third edition is already in print. William Makepeace Thackeray hailed it as "a fine book, the man and woman capital, the style very generous and upright".

The visitor explained that she was Charlotte Brontë, the daughter of a parson in Haworth on the Yorkshire moors. She was accompanied by her sister Anne, who publishes novels as "Acton Bell". A third sister, Emily, published *Wuthering Heights* as "Ellis Bell" (→ 1849).

From left: Anne, Emily and Charlotte Brontë, painted by brother Branwell.

Stephenson, father of railways, dies

Derbyshire, August
George Stephenson, the "father" of the railway which has so dramatically revolutionized travel in Britain, has died at his country home near Chesterfield. Stephenson, who began his working life as a colliery fireman, studied at night school before building his first locomotive, *My Lord,* for use on the tram tracks at Killingworth Colliery. His greatest steam locomotive was *Rocket*, which reached 30mph in competition with others in October 1829.

In 1821 the inventor was made engineer of the Stockton and Darlington railway, and he later built the Manchester-to-Liverpool line, which opened in 1830 (→1849).

Stephenson, family and "Rocket".

Queen's College, London, founded

London
Women have at last won the opportunity of a university education with the opening in Bloomsbury of Queen's College, where the principal, John Maurice, is training girls in such subjects as mathematics, classics and sport.

The college is funded by the combined efforts of the Governesses' Benevolent Association and Miss Murray, one of Queen Victoria's maids-of-honour. Two of its principal students are Frances Buss, who also teaches at her mother's school in north London, and Dorothea Beale (→1854).

Death toll rises in Highlands famine

Scottish settlers in North America: a new life can bring old problems.

Highland
Not only the Irish have suffered from the failure of the potato crop. Here in the highlands, where families depend equally on the potato, thousands are without food, although – unlike the situation in Ireland – the Scottish famine is being treated as a major crisis by charities, church, landlords and the central government. More than £250,000 has been raised, allowing a central board to distribute meal and seed corn. Even so, many families have been reduced to a diet of shellfish. Typhus is rampant in many villages, and hundreds have died from a variety of diseases associated with malnutrition.

As rent arrears accumulate and the lairds begin to run out of funds, the prospect of mass migration is looming. The duke of Argyll has already assisted 500 people on Mull and Tiree to leave for Canada, and thousands more will follow.

Successful women in world of science

London
Typical of so many parents, Admiral Fairfax was furious when he learned that his daughter, Mary, preferred mathematics to embroidery. He forbade her to read her brothers' Euclid and even refused her a candle in case she used it to study secretly at night. Mary got round this by memorizing problems and then working them out in her head in the darkness.

What her late father would have made of the gold medal that has been awarded to Mary, now Mary Somerville, by the Royal Geographic Society is hard to guess – but her book *Physical Geography* has gone into seven editions.

Other women who are making their marks in the world of science include Jane Marcet, whose *Conversations on Chemistry* and other books on political economy, natural philosophy and vegetable physiology have sold more than 160,000 copies in the United States and are found in every British classroom. Harriet Martineau, who is an expert on politics and economics, has published 25 volumes of her immensely popular *Illustrations of Political Economy*.

Professional actors make royal début performance for queen

Windsor, 28 December
Queen Victoria broke with tradition – and gave the much abused British theatrical profession a substantial boost – by inviting professional actors to join the Christmas festivities at Windsor Castle today. The theatre's dubious reputation, dating perhaps from the days of Nell Gwynn, is kept alive by rowdy music-halls and even cruder forms of entertainment.

With the queen and Prince Albert making regular visits to the theatre as well as the opera, things are clearly looking up for serious producers and players. At Sadlers Wells, Samuel Phelps and Mrs Warner are producing plays of high quality; while Charles Kean and his wife, who are preparing a season of Shakespeare for the Princess's theatre in London, today performed *The Merchant of Venice* at Windsor Castle. It is hoped that royal patronage will attract the wealthy middle classes.

The queen and Prince Albert watch Charles Kean as Shylock at Windsor.

Theatres are becoming more comfortable, with higher standards of scenery and costume. The rougher elements are left to the music-halls. The publication of cheap scores is also creating a growing public interest in music, with popular concerts planned for London and the provinces, and brass bands flourishing in the north (→19/5/49).

Britain stands alone as revolution rocks Europe

Rebellion explodes across power bases

Europe, May
With the suddenness and violence of a storm, the thrones of Europe have been rocked, shaken and toppled by violent revolution that has travelled across the continent with the speed of a lightening bolt. The trouble began without any warning at all in February, when the French king, Louis Philippe, was driven from his throne by a popular Paris uprising, ending in the proclamation of a republic.

Within weeks much of Europe was in revolutionary turmoil. On 13 March Prince Metternich, Austrian chancellor since 1821, was driven from office by rioters. On 21 March, after a week of serious disturbances in Berlin, the king of Prussia granted a free press, a constitution and general reform. Many small German states followed suit, while in Italy the Milanese drove out Austrian troops. This month the Austrian emperor has fled, and Hungary had been granted an autonomous constitution (→17).

Manning the barricades in Vienna after the Austrian emperor fled in May.

Louis Napoleon is elected in France

Paris, 11 December
The year that began with the overthrow of the monarchy has ended with the election of Louis Napoleon Bonaparte, the nephew of the former Emperor Napoleon, as president of France. In an astonishing electoral victory he polled two-and-a-half times as many votes as all his opponents put together.

It is quite an about-turn for a man who once invaded his country, accompanied by a handful of men and a vulture. The vulture, like the entire enterprise, was something of a mistake. Louis Napoleon had intended to land at Boulogne in the company of an imperial eagle, but when no such bird could be found the vulture had to do.

Sentenced to life imprisonment for this escapade, he wrote a popular book setting out his vision for the future of France, before escaping to England. It appears that the voters like his vision, or at least the security of the name Bonaparte, and have flocked to him in droves.

Austrian emperor is forced to flee

Vienna, 17 May
Despite granting huge concessions, the Austrian Emperor Ferdinand has been forced to flee to Innsbrück. Although he has done all he can to placate the revolutionary forces unleashed in the country, it may not be enough, and he may yet have to abdicate in favour of his 18-year-old nephew Franz Josef.

Since the fall just two months ago of Prince Metternich, his arch-conservative chancellor, Ferdinand has agreed to give more power to the people than any of his ancestors did. He has promised a constitution, freedom of the press and the formation of a council of ministers, given Hungary a constitution and published a draft one for Austria. On top of this, all Austrian citizens have been given the vote. Sadly for Ferdinand, no one appears to be particularly grateful (→11/12).

Mill, Marx and Engels use words to fan the flames of revolt

Karl Marx: communist apostle.

England
New voices are being raised to challenge the rich and powerful on behalf of the poor. In England John Stuart Mill has unleashed a forceful attack on the propertied classes, in which he critizes the defects of the capitalist economy. In a nation whose ruling class holds property to be sacred Mill's is fighting talk: this class has most to fear from the kind of political instability now raging throughout Europe.

Mill certainly pulls no punches in his *Principles of Political Economy*, published this year. A more just society, he argues, requires cooperation among working people and society in order to reduce social, political and economic inequalities.

In Belgium the exiled German, Karl Marx, in cooperation with compatriot Friedrich Engels, the radical son of a textile manufacturer, has just published a pamphlet that will alarm the rich even further. The *Communist Manifesto* proclaims: "All history has hitherto been a history of class struggles." Yet now, say the authors, the time has come for the workers to take control themselves and smash the old class system. They also accuse the churches of using religion as a means of social control.

The pamphlet has been written for a society of exiled German workers, the League of the Just, which Marx and Engels joined last year. Engels is now settled in England, where he has attracted attention for his exposé of urban poverty called *The Condition of the Working Class in England*. Published in 1844, this book has helped to mobilize support for both economic and political reform.

Now, with Marx, Engels is turning from reporter to propagandist. "Workers of the world unite!" the two say. "You have nothing to lose but your chains" (→5/8/95).

Revolution fizzles out in the rain

Attempts to march on Westminster fail

Westminster, 10 April
A giant petition, said to contain 5,706,000 signatures urging political reform, was handed to parliament today, but without the display of Chartist strength that the movement's leaders had forecast. The petition finally went to the House of Commons in three cabs.

This follows a rally called by Chartists for today at Kennington Common in south London. The revolutionary events across the Channel had both inspired the Chartists to relaunch their campaign for political reform and alarmed the authorities.

Queen Victoria left London on the advice of ministers, while the elderly duke of Wellington, now 78, brought troops into the capital and enrolled 170,000 special constables. The authorities in northern cities took similar precautions, but as it turned out numbers attending today's Kennington rally were far lower than anticipated: reports vary from 25,000 to 125,000. Heavy rain also cooled any revolutionary ardour, so there was no challenge to a ban on marching to Westminster.

The revolution that never was: Chartists rally at Kennington Common.

Parliament rejects latest Chartist petition

Westminster, April
For the third time parliament has rejected a Chartist petition for reform and, on this occasion at least, with some justification. Instead of the 5,706,000 signatures the leaders boasted about, it has been found to contain only two million, and many of those are faked.

No one seriously believes that "Queen Victoria" and "the duke of Wellington" have really signed the petition, still less "Wat Tyler" and "Bread and Cheese". So instead of being the bomb that the radicals hoped, the reform petition has turned out to be a damp squib.

It was delivered to Westminster by cab rather than by a dramatic march of the people, as envisaged by the leaders of the Chartist movement, including Feargus O'Connor, the only Chartist MP [*see report left*]. A new convention is to discuss the rejection of the petition, but the fake signatures have seriously undermined the credibility of the Chartist cause.

William Smith O'Brien leads an unsuccessful Irish revolt

Co Tipperary, 29 July
William Smith O'Brien, the MP, has attempted and failed to carry out what is being called the "Young Ireland" rising. O'Brien, a former follower of the late Daniel O'Connell, and his friends, disillusioned by the failure of O'Connell's constitutional methods to achieve repeal of the union, decided to liberate Ireland by themselves.

Without a clear plan, they wandered around Tipperary where their entourage attracted a hungry mob. At Ballingarry, O'Brien went to the aid of a widow whose house had been occupied by the police, who were hoping to arrest him. During the ensuing fracas the police killed two insurgents and wounded several others. O'Brien and some of his friends escaped, but their arrests are expected soon (→5/8).

William Smith O'Brien is arrested after the failure of the insurrection.

British and Irish fail to follow the way of revolution

British Isles
As revolution spread across Europe at great speed, toppling statesmen and monarchs like ninepins, the British authorities became more and more alarmed that the revolutionary fever could spread across the English Channel. In fact danger seems to have diminished, with the only genuinely revolutionary organization, the Chartists, in decline.

Quite why the British monarch should keep her throne, as all about her are losing theirs, is not entirely clear. The secret appears to lie in the fact that the British government is more tolerant, more willing to listen to grievances and try to address them, than its far more severe continental counterparts. As Macaulay has put it: "We had obtained concessions of inestimable value ... not by tearing up the pavement, not by running to the gunsmith's shop for arms, but by mere force of reason and public opinion." Not that the year has been entirely peaceful.

A Chartist arming for the fight.

There was an attempted armed rising by Chartists in Wales, and in the north of England similar risings were planned but did not come off. In Ireland a rebellion by the "Young Ireland" movement, under William Smith O'Brien, fizzled out in a few skirmishes in Tipperary.

1849

North Yorkshire, 1 January. Sir George Cayley, the aeronaut, designs and builds a triple winged glider, the first full-sized heavier than air aircraft (→1853).

India, 13 January. British troops defeat the Sikhs at Chilianwala (→21/2).

London, 15 February. Sixty-five people die when fire destroys the Theatre Royal.

India, 21 February. The Sikh forces are decisively defeated by the British in a battle at Gujrat (→3/1849).

London, 15 March. Dr Thomas Addison discovers and publishes a report in the *London Medical Gazette* on "Addison's Anaemia", a blood disorder.

India, March. The governor-general, the earl of Dalhousie, annexes the Punjab region to British rule.

London, 19 May. William Hamilton, an Irishman, fires blank shots at Queen Victoria as she is driven down Constitution Hill (→28/9/53).

West Yorkshire. Charlotte Brontë, the novelist, writes *Shirley* (→28/5).

North Yorkshire, 28 May. Anne Brontë, the novelist who under the pseudonym of "Acton Bell" wrote *The Tenant of Wildfell Hall* and *Agnes Grey*, has died aged 29 at Scarborough (→31/3/55).

Dublin, 5 June. The sentences of William Smith O'Brien and other members of the Irish Confederation are commuted to transportation for life (→1/1856).

Co Down, 12 July. Violence breaks out between Protestants and Roman Catholics at Dolly's Brae, near Castlewellan.

Ireland, October. Queen's Colleges at Belfast, Cork, and Galway are opened to students.

London, December. Dr John Snow discovers that cholera is carried in polluted water (→1854).

Dorset. Portland prison is completed.

London. Charles Dickens publishes his latest novel, *David Copperfield* (→1852).

British conquest of Punjab completed

Punjab, India, March
The Punjab and the Sikh nation have fallen to the British after a fiercely fought battle at Gujrat, north-east of Amritsar. Despite this success – two other battles at Ramnagar and Chillianwalla had ended in severe maulings for General Gough's army – Britain has now lost this buffer state between India and Afghanistan.

War become inevitable soon after the arrival in India of the new governor-general, the youthful earl of Dalhousie, an expert on railway trains but no warrior. Within three months of his taking up office in Calcutta, two British officers were murdered at Multan. The governor of that province, Mulraj, proclaimed a holy war and called on all Sikhs to join him.

After his two failures, Gough was about to be replaced but was finally persuaded to use his artillery to soften up the entrenchments at Gujrat. Mulraj has been taken prisoner, and now the whole Sikh army has surrendered.

The question now is: what to do with the Punjab? One course is annexation, bringing the Indian frontier to the borders of Afghanistan. Dalhousie favours this course, although the cabinet is contemplating the support of a titular *maharaja* [ruler]. The on-the-spot governor is likely to win and has asked Henry and John Lawrence to act as administrators (→1851).

British troops battle at Ramnagar.

Parliament repeals the navigation laws

Westminster, 26 June
Britain has finally conceded that the navigation laws are no longer necessary to sustain its position as ruler of the seas. Parliament today repealed the legislation that proved to be so effective against foreign shipping when first introduced in the 14th century.

Originally designed to restrict the import of Bordeaux wines to British ships with British crews, and later as an attempt to replace Antwerp as the world's cloth centre, the laws were never wholly enforceable – although they became more effective as Britain gained colonies and began the import of tobacco, sugar and cotton.

The laws became discredited with the secession of the United States, and, more recently, with the government's decision to remove trade embargoes with many countries. The laws were suspended during the Irish potato famine of the 1840s to allow home consumption of imported foodstuffs, but now repeal applies to all foreign trade.

Bridge over Menai Strait is constructed

A tubular span of the Menai bridge is about to be lifted into place.

Gwynedd
The new tubular bridge over the Menai Strait, designed by Robert Stevenson to carry the Irish mails all the way from London to Holyhead by rail, is nearing completion after almost five years of arduous trial and error. Although it will not be opened to traffic until next year, the bridge is already being spoken of as one of the great railway achievements of British engineering. However, the new railway is yet another east-west link being built to converge on London rather than to unite the various parts of Wales itself. The lack of a well planned railway system has been leading to a serious decline for small industry in North Wales.

Criminal law age now raised to 16

Westminster
The minimum age at which a person can be charged with a criminal offence has been raised this year from 14 to 16 years. This takes further a process of reform covering criminal law and the need to protect children that has been gathering momentum in recent years.

When the century began there were a large number of offences carrying the death penalty. Yet earlier reforms were scarcely less onerous: the death penalty for picking pockets was replaced, for instance, by transportation. Other crimes that are no more to be deemed capital offences include housebreaking and sheep-stealing. Although the Lords rejected moves to abolish the death penalty for forgery, in practice no individual has been hanged for anything except murder or attempted murder since 1838. Transportation is also being replaced by imprisonment within British prisons.

Irish appeals for famine aid go unheeded

Ireland, May
The potato crop has failed yet again, and a cholera epidemic has broken out. Families threatened by starvation are crowding into workhouses, and many unions (boards that administer the Poor Law System) are facing bankruptcy, since many farmers can no longer afford to pay their rates, while others have sold their stock and emigrated. Appeals to the British treasury for financial help have been to no avail. The only reponse has been a decision that a levy of 6d [2.5 pence] in the £ should be placed on the rates in the more prosperous Irish unions, thus producing £100,000 that could be transferred to more distressed unions.

A priest blesses a family of Irish emigrants as it prepares to leave home.

Irish Estate Act gives help to landlords

Ireland
An act has been passed allowing the sale of Irish estates that have been mortgaged and whose owners, because of hardship caused by the famine, have been unable to meet their repayments.

An encumbered estates court has been established, with authority to sell such estates on the application of the owner or encumbrancer [anyone with a claim on the estate].

After the sale, the court will distribute the money amongst the creditors and give clear title to the new owners. Tenants, however, remain unprotected by legislation. The estates are expected to be bought by speculators, and the numbers may run into thousands.

Queen Victoria and Prince Albert visit an infant school for girls in Dublin during a tour of Ireland which, despite kidnap plots, was a great success.

Cholera epidemic peaks

A court for King Cholera: a "Punch" cartoon of how disease spreads.

British Isles, November
The cholera epidemic that has ravaged the British Isles for the past year, taking as many as 2,000 lives a week, has reached a terrible peak. In London alone the disease has killed 12,847 in the past three months and shows no sign of abating. The general board of health has assumed draconian powers to clean up the country, ordering medical officers and borough surveyors to ensure the removal of "filth, ordure and nuisance" from the streets and to compel many citizens to "cleanse, whitewash or otherwise purify" their homes.

Despite advances in engineering and transport, Britain's sewage systems remain primitive, with water closets the property of the rich and open sewers flowing into rivers. As cholera spreads across Europe, 54 London slumdwellers appealed to *The Times*. "We live in muck and filth," they wrote. "We ain't got no privez, no dust bins, no water splies and no drain or suer in the whole place ... if the Colera comes Lord help us" (→12/1849).

Drogheda/Dundalk railway line opens

Co Louth
As a further extension of the railway system, recommended by the Drummond Commission in its report of 1836, a railway line has now been officially opened between Drogheda and Dundalk.

Although the Drummond Commission had advised government aid for railway construction, only 70 miles (112km) of track are currently in operation. Several imposing station buildings have however been built, most notably Amiens Street, in Dublin. Its architect, William Deane Butler, has designed a striking building of Italianate style, which is much admired (→1851).

Plans for massive exhibition go ahead

London
Prince Albert and members of the Society of Arts were almost in despair after looking at 245 proposed designs for the great exhibition planned for Hyde Park in 1851. Then Joseph Paxton, the duke of Devonshire's friend and gardener, came up with a true gardener's solution – a vast glass house, thrice the size of St Paul's, covering 13.6 hectares (19 acres) and able to contain nearly two miles of exhibits. While the official title is "The Great Exhibition of the Works of Industry of All Nations", *Punch* magazine has dubbed Paxton's design "the Crystal Palace" (→1/5/51).

1850 - 1851

Westminster, 12 March 1850. Parliament passes the Party Processions Act; it allows for the confiscation of the emblems and arms of rival Orange and Catholic parties in Ireland (→ 14/7/51).

Gwynedd, 18 March 1850. Robert Stevenson's Britannia railway bridge over the Menai Strait is opened to traffic.

Cumbria, 23 April 1850. William Wordsworth, the poet laureate, dies aged 80 (→ 11/1850).

London, 2 July 1850. Sir Robert Peel, the former prime minister, who was injured falling from his horse, has died aged 62.

Edinburgh, 30 August 1850. Prince Albert lays the foundation stone of William Playfair's Scottish National Gallery.

Rome, 29 September 1850. Pope Pius IX issues a papal brief to re-establish a Roman Catholic hierarchy in England and Wales (→ 4/11).

Westminster, 4 November 1850. Lord John Russell, the prime minister, announces in parliament that the papal brief is "insolent and insidious" (→ 1/8/51).

Dartmoor, Devon, 1850. A prison is built on the moor.

London, 1850. Elizabeth Barrett Browning, the poet and wife of Robert Browning, publishes *Sonnets from the Portuguese* (→ 1855).

England, 1 February 1851. Mary Shelley, the novelist, best known for her novel *Frankenstein*, dies.

Liverpool, 14 July 1851. Riots break out during a march of Orangemen through the city.

Westminster, 1 August 1851. Parliament passes the Ecclesiastical Titles Act against the papal brief issued last year; it prohibits Catholic clergy from assuming territorial titles (→ 19).

Dublin, 19 August 1851. The Catholic Defence Association of Great Britain and Ireland is formed in opposition to the Ecclesiastical Titles Act.

Manchester, October 1851. Owen's College, founded by the philanthropic merchant John Owen, is opened to local boys.

London, 1851. Reuter's news agency is established.

London, 1851. William Cubitt designs and builds King's Cross railway station.

Safety rules aim to cut deaths in mines

Westminster, 1850

A series of mining disasters has led to new safety laws being introduced this year. The Coal Mines Inspection Act lays down lighting and ventilation standards which, along with regular inspections, are intended to curb the heavy loss of life. The appalling conditions in many mines have been described vividly by Friedrich Engels: "The underground passages ... are so narrow that the workers have to crawl on their hands and knees. Most of the miners were ... bandylegged or knock-kneed or had some spinal or other deformity."

Hacking for coal underground.

Diplomatic row leaves Greece blockaded

Palmerston portrayed as a mischievous boy sorting out the Greek problem.

London, 29 June 1850

"The Roman in the days of old held himself free from indignity when he could say *"Civis Romanus Sum"* [I am a Roman citizen], so also a British subject, in whatever land he may be, shall feel confident that the watchful eye and the strong arm of England will protect him against injustice and wrong." With these ringing words the British foreign secretary, Lord Palmerston, won the support of parliament today after an extraordinary four-day debate on the affair of Don Pacifico.

Don Pacifico, a Jewish Portuguese moneylender but a British subject, since he was born in Gibraltar, had his house burnt down by the mob in Athens in 1847 and his suspiciously large claim for compensation refused by the Greek government. Palmerston took up the case and eventually blockaded Athens to force payment, outraging both the French, who had already arranged a deal, and the Russians, who were co-guarantors of Greek independence.

Palmerston's high-handed style also infuriates Queen Victoria, and even Lord John Russell, the prime minister, has admitted: "Palmerston's personal quarrels with foreign countries [are] doing serious injury to the country." Yet he has huge popular support, and for now he is invulnerable (→ 14/11/63).

Alfred Tennyson is new poet laureate

London, November 1850

Alfred Tennyson has been appointed poet laureate in succession to William Wordsworth, who died last April. Tennyson won admiration for his poem *In Memoriam*, published this year after 17 years' work. Concerned with the loss of love and faith, it is dedicated to the memory of the great friend of his youth, Arthur Hallam, who was engaged to Tennyson's sister. Personal and spiritual deprivation are strong themes: "Tis better to have loved and lost/ Than never to have loved at all ... He seems so near and yet so far" (→ 1855).

Local lending libraries bring books to all

Culture cart: a mobile library of the Warrington Mechanics' Institution.

Manchester, 1851

This year's Public Libraries Act marks another step in boosting the reading public. In Manchester, meanwhile, there are plans for a new "public library", to be funded out of the rates and housed in a building bought by the lord of the manor, Sir Oswald Mosley, following last year's Free Libraries Act, allowing up to a halfpenny rate to be spent on library services.

Existing libraries are either dear, at about £1 for membership, or stock trash, like the circulating libraries, or religious tracts, like the parish libraries. Reformers argue that libraries are cheap insurance against social unrest (→ 2/9/52).

Hopeful British join Australian gold rush

New South Wales, 1851
Britons are among the thousands with picks on their shoulders and dreams of riches in their eyes flocking to the tiny settlements of Bathurst, Ballarat and Bendingo in New South Wales in search of gold.

The first strike this year was by Edward Hargraves, a veteran of the California gold rush of 1848, who noticed that the rocks at Bathurst were like those in California. The authorities have known about the gold for years – the first man to find it, a convict, was flogged on the grounds that he must have stolen it – but have kept it secret to protect the wool trade.

New union is born

Britain, 1851
Fellow engineers William Allan and William Newton – who was once a publican – have founded the Amalgamated Society of Engineers, which combines the Journeymen Steam Engine Makers with machinists, smiths and millwrights. Members pay a weekly subscription of one shilling [five pence].

The new breed of unions, facing large employers ready to cooperate with one another, are increasingly ignoring the political battles of the last decade and concentrating on achieving "the greatest amount of benefit for ourselves".

Attempts to re-establish 'popery' fail

John Bull is torn between patriotism and popery in the Catholic debate.

London, November 1850
The state is again at loggerheads with the papacy. The prime minister, Lord John Russell, has warned of a "pretension of supremacy over the realm of England", and there have even been riots. The controversy arises from Pope Pius IX's moves last month to restore the Roman Catholic hierarchy in Britain by making Bishop Wiseman a cardinal and by appointing bishops to dioceses in terms which critics claim suggested papal rights over these territories.

When the cardinal returned from Rome on 5 November, his effigy was burnt to shouts of "No popery" and the sound of windows in Catholic churches being smashed. Journalists resorted to ancient propaganda – "mummeries of superstition", "foreign yoke" – to play on deep Protestant fears.

Although only about two per cent of the English population is Catholic, distrust of papal ambition has been intensified by the secession in recent years of such leading Anglicans as John Henry Newman to the Catholic Church. Cardinal Wiseman has sought to reassure the public (and politicians) by publishing a response that thanks the "brave and generous and noble-hearted people of England" for not hunting down "your unoffending fellow citizens".

Palmerston sacked from foreign office

London, 17 December 1851
The dismissal today of her foreign secretary, Lord Palmerston, was the best Christmas present that Queen Victoria could have had. For five years he has embarrassed her by supporting liberal causes, failing to tell her what he was doing or ignoring her express wishes.

The final straw came with his support for the coup by Louis Napoleon in France this month. The queen had been outraged by the coup and wanted the government to be "entirely passive". Palmerston's habit of speaking without consultation finally lost him the confidence of Lord John Russell, the prime minister, who dismissed him for "violations of prudence and decorum".

Palmerston: not a royal favourite.

Turner, the 'greatest painter', is dead

"The Fighting Temeraire towed to her last berth", by J M W Turner.

London, 19 December 1851
Joseph Mallord William Turner died today in his Thames-side cottage in Chelsea, where he lived with his mistress, Mrs Booth, and where he was known as "Captain Booth". He was 76. The originality of his later paintings led many critics to call him mad: he abandoned conventional landscape for the essentials of nature at fleeting moments – rising dawn mists, sunsets behind clouds, snowstorms at sea. The results were dismissed by some as "soapsuds and whitewash", but Hazlitt wrote discerningly: "They are pictures of the elements of air, earth and water." The critic John Ruskin pronounced him "beyond doubt the greatest painter and poet of the day".

Turner was a barber's son, born in Covent Garden, and began exhibiting at the Royal Academy, where he was taught, from the age of 15. He became famous for his sketching tours of the rivers and coasts of England and Wales, and then of Euope. His yearly exhibits at the Royal Academy reported events of the day – the burning of the Houses of Parliament, the last voyage of the wooden warship *The Fighting Temeraire*, and an early experience of train travel, *Rain, Steam and Speed*.

Great Exhibition is showcase of economic strength

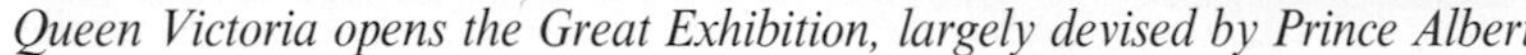

Queen Victoria opens the Great Exhibition, largely devised by Prince Albert.

"The Crystal Palace" erected in Hyde Park has itself become an attraction.

'Crystal Palace' is home of exhibition

London, 1 May 1851

Queen Victoria came today to Hyde Park to open the world's most remarkable demonstration of human ingenuity and resourcefulness. The Great Exhibition – devised by Prince Albert, planned by a specially created royal commision and housed in a fairytale structure of iron and glass, "the Crystal Palace", itself one of the most striking artefacts on show – is expected, during its five-month existence, to attract at least six million visitors.

Most will be brought by the railways that have done so much to promote Britain's industrial supremacy. Beneath the 63,000-square-metre (76,000-square-yard) roof of Joseph Paxton's giant greenhouse they will find proudly displayed the offerings of no fewer than 14,000 separate exhibitors, each bent on demonstrating the finest achievements so far attained in his own branch of engineering, manufacture or fine art.

The show offers a unique panorama of technological excellence, ranging from Nasmyth's steam hammer and the giant hydraulic presses used to form the Menai Bridge supports to the most delicate products of the Wedgwood pottery and the London watchmakers. Foreigners, too, are welcome, and there are breathtaking displays from every country in Europe.

Technical ingenuity boosts new industries

London, 1851

Britain smelted two million tonnes of iron last year, more than was made in the rest of the world put together. Half of it was exported, to all the other countries eager to develop their own transport systems and centres of heavy industrial production, in imitation of the runaway British success in these fields. But the other half remained at home to satisfy a continually growing domestic demand: for railway equipment, gas and water pipes, and above all for machinery.

It is largely thanks to the development of ingenious labour-saving devices – and the willingness to invest in them – that this country has moved, in trade after trade (including pig-iron itself), from the cumbrous, high-cost, low-volume producer it was a century ago to today's achiever of unparalleled levels of efficiency. Small wonder that Britain is happy to be called the "workshop of the world".

Many of the more spectacular end-products are on show in Hyde Park, from great locomotives such as the 31-tonne *Lord of the Isles* to de la Rue's new paper-folding machine, which can turn out 2,700 envelopes an hour. But observers recognize that the "intermediate machines", never seen by the public, may be even more important.

Without elaborate belt systems to harness the steam engine's power, without precision machine tools such as Maudesley's all-metal lathe, and indeed without the textile makers' variety of mechanical aids, it is doubtful whether Lancashire and Birmingham could have won global dominance.

The world of work goes on display at the Great Exhibition in London.

Finance and trade dominate economy

London, 1851

Trade is the great engine of Britain's present prosperity. New products, from improved bootscrapers to ever more elegant cutlery, ensure the regular expansion of domestic consumer demand. Abroad, the sheer cheapness of English goods, from Lancashire calico to Birmingham tin trays, promotes a continually rising export trade. In the capital goods sector, the regular improvements achieved by the machinery makers virtually guarantee their future order books.

Much of this activity is underpinned by important innovations in finance. Large-scale enterprises such as railways, gasworks, waterworks, insurance companies and some banks are already heavily reliant on the concept of joint-stock capital. Yet, for the present, such funding requires either a special act of parliament or – even rarer – a grant of privilege under the Companies Acts. Few ordinary manufacturers would qualify, and in any case the majority of them prefer to keep control under their own hands without having to consult outside shareholders.

Growth is therefore largely paid for out of reinvested profits. There is little interest yet in the new French credit institutions that have recently been set up expressly to harness public savings to industrial development.

Britain's empire expands as a great world power

British influence grows as revolutions sap strength of rivals

Britain, 1851
After the defeat of Napoleon, the only nations that really counted in world affairs were the five European "Great Powers": Britain, Russia, France, the Austrian Empire and Prussia. All but the first, however, have been significantly weakened by the continent-wide revolutions of 1848, and at mid-century the British foreign secretary (currently Lord Palmerston) has little difficulty in preserving the balance of national advantage.

The most threatening potential rival, the rapidly strengthening United States, still confines its diplomatic interests almost entirely to its own hemisphere. The latter is of little concern to Europe, whose chancelleries are content to leave any transatlantic opportunities to American businessmen and traders.

That apart, the most pressing sources of international friction are to be found in the Near East. A disintegrating Ottoman Empire and various simmering conflicts between Moscow and London (over such issues as control of the eastern Mediterranean and India's northern frontiers) combine to present a perennial threat of confrontation. But so far Britain's economic strength (and the Royal Navy's awesome reputation) have deterred any serious challenge. With free trade encouraging prosperity at home and peace abroad, Britain is at the centre of the world economy.

Part of the Indian display at the Great Exhibition in "the Crystal Palace".

Territories across the seas increasing

Britain, 1851
It was in 1828 that William Huskisson, the long-serving president of the board of trade, pronounced that "Britain cannot afford to be little". Since then the business of acquiring colonies, dependencies, strategic naval bases and access to distant markets has proceeded at a steady pace. New settlements have been established in Australia and South Africa. New Zealand has been annexed and the government of Canada revised. Singapore and Hong Kong have been added to an already global chain of trading outposts, and territorial control greatly extended in both India and Burma.

Officially, any charge of systematic empire-building is denied. Yet sceptical diplomats claim to detect an even bigger "informal empire" being constructed as commercial links proliferate.

Army sees India as main focus of activity

Delhi, 1851
With no serious fighting in Europe for the past 35 years, India has become the main focus of the British soldier's life. Almost every officer and enlisted man can expect to serve there for a large part of his military career. Its frontier skirmishes, heroic cavalry charges and closely fought engagements, such as the recently concluded Second Sikh War, provide the army with most of its activity and almost all of its modern battle honours.

By contrast, the home-based forces have been subjected to steady attrition. Treasury parsimony and widespread public fear of "continental-style" militarism have combined to cut regiments to the bone. With only 50,856 men under arms and almost no central organization, there is little muscle to back European policy initiatives (→1856).

Royal Navy roves the seas of the world

London, 1851
At mid-century, the Royal Navy finds itself stretched, like a thin blue line, to the ends of the earth. Some 129 vessels are on distant station: 31 in the Mediterranean, 25 guarding the newly acquired treaty ports in China or hunting pirates in the East Indies, 57 engaged in stamping out the Atlantic slave trade, while the rest is off South America or in the far Pacific. *Pax* Britannica [the British peace] is a reality across the world's oceans, and there are few places washed by the sea where Lord Palmerston's brand of gunboat diplomacy cannot readily be brought to bear.

Yet his supremacy has been bought largely at the expense of the home fleet. With only 35 warships within rapid sailing distance of a British port, many doubt their usefulness if European peace ended.

Battle honours: the British Army is more active in India than in Europe.

Britain's thin blue line: steam warships of the Royal Navy on patrol.

Population soars as industrial revolution booms

Cities grow at the expense of country

British Isles, 1851
The national census completed this year shows that for the first time a majority of the population of England no longer lives in rural areas. Ten years ago 51.7 per cent lived in the countryside; now the figure is only 46.3 per cent. Elsewhere in the United Kingdom the proportion is higher, but there is still a drift of population to the towns – one in three Scots now live in towns.

The overall population of the British Isles is 20.8 million, of whom 17.9 million live in England – evidence of the rise in population that has been a hallmark of this century, with the total figure up by approximately 25 per cent over the last 20 years. In Ireland, however, the ravages of the potato famine and consequential mass emigration have taken their toll. Here the population stands at 6.8 million, 200,000 fewer than it was in 1821.

London remains by far the largest city, having doubled in size this century to reach 2.7 million. Yet other cities have grown even more dramatically: Glasgow, Manchester and Liverpool have all quadrupled, or more, this century.

Textiles close gap on farm workers

British Isles, 1851
More people are employed on the land than in any other single form of employment. This year's national census shows 1,460,000 people involved in some form of agricultural work. But the runners-up in the occupational league table are the 1,100,000 workers involved in various textile trades – far more than for any other urban trade.

In other large-scale industries there are 220,000 miners and 80,000 ironworkers. The number of industrial workers is growing rapidly – as is the average size of factories – but they are still left dwarfed by such traditional occupations as bootmakers (275,000) and domestic servants (1,040,000).

Visitors pour into London, Britain's biggest city, for the Great Exhibition.

Stockport: a railway viaduct and factory chimneys change the townscape.

Leeds, where chimneys are now more prominent than church spires.

Religions revealed by national census

England and Wales, 1851
On Sunday 30 March this year a record was kept of how many folk attended church, in the first-ever religious census. Attendances at morning, afternoon and evening services were logged in denominations from the Church of England (4,939,514 worshippers) to Seventh Day Baptists (83 worshippers). A separate survey of church buildings has also been undertaken.

Church leaders have been dismayed by one finding of the survey – that over five million people did not attend church at all on that March Sunday. Otherwise what is most remarkable about the surveys – which were confined to England and Wales – is the diversity of churches and the strength of the denominations outside the national Anglican Church.

The figures below are an aggregate of attendance at morning, afternoon and evening services; it is possible that some may have attended more than one service. Figures may also combine totals from several internal sects. The total for Wesleyan Methodists, for instance, has seven distinct sub-sects, from the Original Connexion and Primitive Methodists to Bible Christians and Independent Methodists.

Church of England	**4,939,514**
Wesleyan Methodists	**2,370,460**
Congregationalists	**1,191,978**
Baptists	**910,082**
Roman Catholics	**365,430**
Calvinistic Methodists	**306,106**
Scottish Presbyterians	**79,064**
Unitarians	**47,628**
Mormons	**34,182**
Society of Friends	**21,933**
Brethren	**17,326**
United Brethren	**10,195**
New Church	**9,938**
Apostolic Church	**7,306**
Sandemanians	**3,604**
Other foreign churches	**2,661**
Isolated congregations	**98,267**

These worshippers attended services in 34,467 buildings designated as places of worship. Morning services were the most popular.

Railways change the life and landscape of Britain

All aboard: all social classes gather at the railway station, although each class has its own coaches for travel.

Trains even inspire popular music.

British Isles, 1851
Over 7,000 miles (1,120km) of railway track will be in use next year, with a further 3,000 miles sanctioned by parliament. In a quarter of a century, the railway has ceased to be a novelty and become a catalyst for economic and social change. Opposition from canal and turnpike companies was brushed aside as "railway mania" gripped boardrooms and parliament. Lines now link the main cities of the kingdom.

There have been times when the work of parliament seemed in danger of being submerged by an avalanche of proposals for new lines and new companies. In 1846 alone, at the height of the railway mania, committees sat for 867 days just on railway bills. Over 200 railway companies have now been incorporated, and many have found themselves in fierce competition for key routes. Attempts have been made to promote cooperation, notably in London, but the Great Western is still using a broader gauge than other major companies.

The plethora of individual (and competing) lines has inevitably led to some amalgamations and new procedures for regulation. Railway commissioners were abolished this year, for instance, with their responsibilities passing to the board of trade. Some entrepreneurs have over-reached themselves, and none more dramatically than George Hudson, the self-styled "railway king" of the North Midland Railway, whose career collapsed in bankruptcy in 1849. Parliament has not been ready to leave the railways to develop entirely as a free market.

Since 1844 each company has had to operate at least one train a day, with fares at no more than a penny a mile. This has made railways accessible to everyone, with potentially as profound an impact on towns as the mammoth cuttings and embankments have had on the landscape. Nor is this impact confined to spectacular stations and viaducts, or to the less welcome soot and grime.

Some workmen are travelling to work by train, enabling communities with railway stations to grow more rapidly than others. Seaside resorts with railways also seem likely to benefit from the growth of pleasure trips by train. The first day trip from London to Brighton took place in 1844, while in the English midlands Thomas Cook has organized large numbers of trips to London for this year's Great Exhibition. There are also towns that owe virtually their entire existence to the railway – key junctions in the network, such as Crewe (which was not even recorded in the 1841 census). Other railway towns such as Swindon and Derby have expanded hugely.

Most of the railway lines now in existence are in England, with London the focal point. In Scotland no main line has yet reached further north than Glasgow or Edinburgh, while in Wales the lines are essentially links to London and the ports. In Ireland some 400 miles of track are now in use (→10/6/52).

1852

Southern Africa, January. The British recognize the independence of the Transvaal Boers by the Sand River Convention (→ 23/2/54).

London, 2 February. The first public flushing lavatory for gentlemen is opened, on Fleet Street.

Burma, 14 April. British troops seize Rangoon (→ 4/6).

British Isles, 1 June. The first submarine telegraph cable is laid between Holyhead and Howth, linking Britain and Ireland.

Burma, 4 June. British troops take Pegu (→ summer).

Belfast, 10 June. The Portadown-to-Dundalk railway is opened; apart from the crossing of the river Boyne at Drogheda, Belfast is now linked with Dublin (→ 22/6/53).

Cork City, 10 June. The National Exhibition opens.

Belfast, 1 September. The British Association for the Advancement of Science begins a week's meetings.

Manchester, 2 September. The Free Library, a lending library, is opened to the public.

Kent, 14 September. Arthur Wellesley, the duke of Wellington, an heroic soldier and former prime minister, dies at Walmer Castle (→ autumn/1852).

Ramsgate, Kent, 14 September. Augustus Pugin, the architect and co-designer with Sir Charles Barry of the new Houses of Parliament, has died.

London, autumn. Alfred Tennyson, the poet laureate, writes *Ode on the Death of the Duke of Wellington* (→ 18/11).

Channel Islands, 23 November. The postal service introduces the use of "pillar boxes" for posting letters; the first are used in St Helier on Jersey.

Liverpool, 26 December. The *Marco Polo* returns from a round trip to the Australian goldfields in a record time of only five months and 21 days.

London. Isambard Kingdom Brunel and Sir Matthew Digby Wyatt begin designing a new Paddington railway station (→ 9/1859).

London. Charles Dickens publishes *Bleak House* (→ 1854).

Scotland. The Highlands and Islands Emigration Society is founded to promote the welfare of emigrants.

Derby succeeds failed Russell as PM

Westminster, February
Following Lord John Russell's resignation, the earl of Derby is the new prime minister, leading a Tory minority government and appointing Benjamin Disraeli as chancellor of the exchequer and Lord Malmesbury as foreign secretary. This means that the cabinet has only two members who have held office before – a clear indication of the government's lack of experience.

Russell's resignation was forced on him by Lord Palmerston's proposed amendment to the Militia Bill this month. When Palmerston openly acknowledged Louis Napoleon as emperor of France last December, Queen Victoria insisted that Russell dismiss him from the foreign office. Palmerston has gleefully boasted: "I have had my "tit-for-tat" with John Russell and turned him out ..."

Educated at Eton and Oxford, where he excelled as a classical scholar, Derby entered parliament in 1820 as a Whig, serving under Canning, Lord Goderich and Earl Grey. In 1835 he became a Conservative under Peel and in 1841 began a five-year stint as colonial secretary. Lord Derby has since been serving in opposition to Russell's Whig ministry (→ 12/1852).

Lord Derby: the new Tory premier.

Nation mourns loss of heroic 'iron duke'

The funeral of a hero: Wellington's cortège leaves his house for St Paul's.

London, 18 November
The nation was plunged into mourning today for the state funeral of the duke of Wellington, statesman, diplomat and commander-in-chief of the British Army. For more than two hours, tens of thousands lined the route to St Paul's Cathedral to see "the iron duke's" cortège pass by – a ceremony made all the more moving by the respectful silence of the crowds. Arthur Wellesley, the 5th son of an Irish peer, transformed the British army from, in his own words, "the scum of the earth" into "worthy fellows".

As prime minister in 1828, he avoided revolution in Ireland by conceding Roman Catholic emancipation – the right of Catholics to sit in parliament. He died in his 84th year.

Scots leave their homeland to seek new life overseas

Scotland
An increasing number of Scots are abandoning their homeland for the warmer climes of the southern hemisphere, settling down to new lives in Australia and New Zealand. For the unskilled immigrant there is an abundance of work just waiting, from sheep-farming and mining to engineering and manufacturing, while skilled middle-class emigrants with money and business acumen are playing a large role in Australian investment and farming enterprises.

Although North America remains the most important destination, a great many Scots are settling in New Zealand, where they are making a significant contribution to the nation's educational and political development. Otago in the South Island is a particular favourite among Scottish settlers, owing to its vigorous promotion by agents in Scotland, as well as its Presbyterian background.

James MacAndrew, who emigrated from his native Aberdeen three years ago, has established trading links with California and Australia. He was also elected this year as a member of the newly-created Otago provincial council. Scottish emigrants are also beginning to exert an influence on other British colonies, chiefly in Canada.

Emigrants who seek a new life.

Threat of a strike leads to 'lock-out'

Britain
Less than a year after its formation, the Amalgamated Society of Engineers is at loggerheads with the Masters' Association after advising its members to withdraw their labour until the "the abolition of overtime and piecework" is agreed.

The MA's reponse was to close its workshops "against all productive labour, hoping this starvation method will accomplish that which could not be attained by the use of nobler weapons ..." such as arbitration, fair discussion and an "appeal to the enlightened feelings of the British public". The lock-out has affected 36 firms and left 10,000 skilled operatives dependent upon others' charity.

Burma is added to Britain's empire

Burma, summer
Following the fall of Rangoon in April, Bassein in May and, finally, Pegu, the governor-general of India, Lord Dalhousie, has annexed the whole province. There has been no formal acknowledgment of surrender or any apparent desire to continue fighting, and the province is being organized peacefully.

The Lawrence brothers, Henry and John, who have been administering the Punjab since 1849 with considerable success, disagree over ways of treating local chiefs. Dalhousie is to leave John in sole command and give Henry an alternative post. The brothers' successes are evident in the loyalty which they have inspired in the Sikhs.

Hundreds drown as troopship hits rock

Disaster hits the troopship HMS "Birkenhead", as seen by a later artist.

Southern Africa, 26 February
HMS *Birkenhead*, at sea in her role as a troopship, hit an uncharted rock 50 miles (80km) off the Cape Town coast at 1.50am today and sank with a loss of 445 men and £240,000 of gold bullion. Among the 638 persons on board there were 56 women and children and 130 crew – the rest were officers and men drafted to reinforce troops fighting the Eighth Kaffir War.

The night sky was clear and the sea calm when the tragedy occurred. Captain Robert Salmond ordered a bow anchor to be dropped to try to prevent the *Birkenhead* from drifting off into deeper water. But the ship holed again, rapidly flooding the engine-room and the crowded lower troopdeck. Everyone below was drowned.

It took just 25 minutes from the time that the *Birkenhead* hit the rock for her to break in two and sink. Only three of the ship's eight lifeboats could be launched in time, and they were dangerously overloaded. The schooner *Lioness* rescued 40 men, but many of those left were attacked by sharks. All the women and children survived.

Lord Aberdeen to head coalition ministry

Gladstone (r) leads the attack on the budget of Disraeli (seated left).

Westminster, December
With the collapse of Lord Derby's ministry, following the defeat of his chancellor's budget, Queen Victoria sent for the earl of Aberdeen, urging him to form a Peelite ministry. Contrary to her wish, Aberdeen is now to lead a coalition of Liberal-Conservatives, with Lords Palmerston and John Russell from the Whigs and William Gladstone from the Peelite Tories. Last month the queen had talks with Lord Derby to find ways of strengthening his faltering government, primarily by forging a link with the Peelites. But they were not prepared to serve under Benjamin Disraeli as leader of the house. So Palmerston is to be home secretary, Gladstone is chancellor of the exchequer, and Russell – despite his protestations of ill health – has agreed, for now, to take the foreign office (→ 12/1854).

Children's hospital treats first two patients

London, 16 February
The Hospital for Sick Children – the first of its kind in the United Kingdom – which has opened at 49 Great Ormond Street with ten beds has today received its first two patients. The founder of the hospital is Dr Charles West, an eminent physician who has worked amongst the poor in their homes. He believes that the hospital will become "a means of moral as well as of physical good" and be another link in the "golden chain of benevolence and gratitude which should bind together all classes of society".

This year Queen Victoria opened the rebuilt Houses of Parliament.

1853

Kent, 15 February. James Andrew Ramsay, the marquis of Dalhousie and a former governor-general of India, is appointed lord warden of the Cinque Ports.

Russia, February. Russia proposes to Britain that the two countries share out what remains of the Ottoman Empire (→ 2/6).

England and Wales, 1 April. Earth tremors are felt by many as a minor earthquake hits southern and western regions.

Dublin, 12 May. Queen Victoria opens the Art-Industry Exhibition; it aims to promote the industry and arts of Ireland.

Drogheda, Co Louth, 22 June. A temporary wooden bridge is built over the river Boyne, completing the railroad link between Belfast and Dublin (→ 11/7/54).

Moldavia, 3 July. Russian troops cross over into Moldavia.

Van Diemen's Land, [Tasmania], 19 July. John Mitchel, the Irish patriot and journalist, who was sentenced to life imprisonment here, escapes and heads for the United States (→ 1854).

Mediterranean, 23 September. The British fleet is ordered to Istanbul (→ 4/10).

Grampian, 28 September. Prince Albert orders the renovation and enlargement of Balmoral Castle, a favourite haunt of the royal family (→ 1855).

Istanbul, 4 October. The Ottoman Empire declares war on Russia after rejecting the terms of the "Vienna Note" drafted at a conference held earlier in July at Vienna (→ 30/11).

Europe, 5 December. Britain, France, Austria and Prussia successfully reach an agreement to re-establish peace between Russia and the Ottoman Empire (→ 3/1/54).

Scotland. The Edinburgh Trades Council is established.

Scotland. The Association for the Vindication of Scottish Rights is formed in order to campaign for more Scottish MPs and a secretary of state for Scotland.

Scotland. The Public Libraries (Scotland) Act levies a penny rate to fund libraries, along the lines of legislation passed for England and Wales in 1851.

Royal Navy dispatched to Dardanelles

Westminster, 2 June
The cabinet has ordered a British fleet to sail to Besika Bay, outside the Dardanelles, where it will be joined by a French squadron as a warning to the Russians not to attack the Ottoman Empire, "the sick man of Europe".

The composition of the fleet reflects the great technical changes that have taken place since Trafalgar. Of the ten line-of-battle ships, seven have steam-driven propellers. There are steam-driven frigates and corvettes, and steam tugs for towing transports. It is feared, however, that the commanders have not kept pace with their ships. The navy has, after all, not fought a major war since 1815 (→ 7/1853).

Russian Bear threatens Turkey.

Patronage in civil service faces axe

Britain, 23 November
A report by Sir Stafford Northcote and Sir Charles Trevelyan, published today, calls for sweeping reforms in the civil service. The service is criticized for attracting "the unambitious ... the indolent or incapable ... those whose abilities do not warrant" success in open professions. In order to attract more efficient staff the report recommends a competitive entry system to end the present system of patronage. Candidates would sit an examination, followed by a period of probation. There should also be prior inquiries into the "age, health and moral fitness of candidates" (→ 1855).

Scots temperance movement scores victory over heavy drinkers

An illicit whisky still in the highlands: boosted by new licensing laws.

Scotland
The Public House Act, also known as the Forbes-Mackenzie Act after its principal supporters, has come into force to control drinking habits. The new law orders the closing down of public houses between 11pm and 8am and all day on Sundays. The growing temperance movement hopes that the act will help to tackle the massive alcohol problems here. Scots over the age of 15 consume an average of one pint of whisky a week – excluding consumption from illegal distilleries. The police say that the licensing laws have cut drunken behaviour on Sundays but have boosted illicit trafficking in spirits (→ 1854).

'Uncle Tom' is tops

London, April
Uncle Tom's Cabin, a novel about a slave who is beaten to death by his master, is breaking sales records in the United Kingdom and the United States. About 1.5 million copies have been sold over the past year. The anti-slavery theme is partly responsible, but there is also the appeal of the book's pathos: "Do you know who made you?" a black child is asked, and replies with a laugh, "Nobody, as I knows on. I 'spect I grow'd". The author, Mrs Harriet Beecher Stowe of Maine, says of it: "I feel as if I had written some of it with my heart's blood."

April 7: Queen Victoria used chloroform to lessen labour pains today before the birth of Prince Leopold; Dr John Snow was the anaesthetist. The queen is seen here following the birth of her first child, Victoria.

Vaccination to be made compulsory

British Isles
The government has this year introduced obligatory vaccination for all infants within four months of their births as part of the fight to control epidemics of smallpox. A great many children in towns have been treated already, and significant reductions in the number of fatalities from the disease, due to inoculation, can be discerned.

It was nearly 50 years ago that Edward Jenner first demonstrated the efficacy of this treatment, for which he was severely criticized at the time by the church, the press and his professional peers. Fortunately, in recent years prejudice has declined, with several distinguished doctors giving the practice of inoculation their support (→ 1869).

A doctor performs an inoculation.

Glider takes off

North Yorkshire, c.1853
The eccentric aeronautical engineer Sir George Cayley, aged 84, who has long been experimenting with various kinds of flying machines, has achieved the first manned – but not piloted – glider flight. The "new flyer" was manned by Cayley's reluctant coachman, crossing a dale at Brompton.

Mrs Thompson, Cayley's granddaughter, who saw the flight, said that after the crossing the coachman climbed from the glider and called: "Please, Sir George, I wish to give notice. I was hired to drive, not to fly" (→ 15/12/57).

Near East turmoil draws in Britain

Great powers seek solution in Vienna

Vienna, July
A last-minute attempt is being made here by the Austrian Empire, France, Prussia and Britain to prevent a war over the quarrel between Russia and the Ottoman Empire. The row has its ostensible beginnings in the rivalry between the French Catholic and Greek Orthodox monks for the right to guard the holy places in Jerusalem.

Russian claims in support of the Orthodox priests have developed into a demand by Czar Nicholas to be recognized as the protector of all Orthodox Christians in the Ottoman Empire. This demand has alarmed the European powers because it would give Russia the right to interfere in Turkish affairs.

A compromise is being negotiated by means of a "Note" proposing that the Turks would promise not to change the position of their Christian subjects without consulting Russia and France. Peace depends on its acceptance (→ 23/9).

The rival fleets open fire off Sinope, on the southern Black Sea coast.

Russian sea power breaks Ottoman navy

Black Sea, 30 November
Nearly two months after the declaration of war, Turkey and Russia have clashed. In the battle today between the Ottoman and Russian fleets at Sinope the Turks had their navy effectively destroyed.

The "Vienna Note", which was designed to ensure peace, did not work [*see left*]. Czar Nicholas argued that the note recognized Russia as the protector of the 12 million Christian subjects of the Ottoman Empire, but the Turks, supported by the British, said that they were to exercise that protection.

The Czar could not afford a public humiliation, and the British prime minister, Lord Aberdeen, felt pushed by Palmerston's war party into opposing Russia's plan to dominate the Ottoman Empire (→ 5/12).

Australia refuses to take any more convicts as immigrants

British Isles, c.1853
The transportation of criminals to Australia is to stop, following the refusal by Sydney and Melbourne to accept any more convicts. As a result, the British government is to introduce the Penal Servitude Act as a substitute for transportation. Criminals will receive longer prison sentences with hard labour.

In 1776 the hulks of redundant warships were moored in the upper reaches of the Thames, originally intended to house prisoners awaiting transportation. Although soon afterwards they became prisons in their own right, providing convict labour for public works in and around the area, they have since deteriorated, proving to be totally inadequate – badly organized, overcrowded and disease-ridden.

"Model" prisons were introduced more than 30 years ago, at Pentonville and Millbank penitentiaries in London, while new prisons followed at Portland (1849), Dartmoor (1850) and Portsmouth (1852), with Brixton built this year for women. Yet opinions still differ among experts regarding appropriate penal policy. Conditions at Millbank are bad, discipline is weak and the health of inmates poor. At Pentonville, however, the attempt to reform prisoners before transportation by solitary confinement and religious instruction did seem to be making some progress (→ 1856).

Bad old days: convicts forced to walk 30 miles (48km) with heavy weights.

1854

Black Sea, 3 January. British and French fleets enter the Black Sea to protect the Ottoman Empire's coastline (→26/3).

New York, 7 January. John Mitchel, the Irish patriot who last year escaped from Van Diemen's Land [Tasmania], publishes the first issue of *Citizen*.

Southern Africa, 23 February. By the Bloemfontein Convention the British government recognizes the independence of the Orange Free State.

Europe, 28 March. Britain and France, which formed an alliance with the Ottoman Empire on 12 March, declare war on Russia (→26/5).

Greece, 26 May. Anglo-French forces occupy the port of Piraeus to prevent the Greek fleet from aiding Russia (→20/9).

Preston, May. The cotton strike that began last October is brought to an end.

Co Kerry, 11 July. Ireland's first railway hotel is opened, at Killarney, by the Killarney Junction Railway Company (→9/1862).

Crimea, 17 October. Allied forces besiege Sevastopol (→25/10).

Crimea, 7 November. A team of British nurses, led by Florence Nightingale, arrives in Scutari to cope with the numerous wounded and diseased allied soldiers (→11/9/55).

Scotland. The Scottish Institute of Chartered Accountants is founded by A W Robertson and 14 other accountants.

London. Charles Dickens publishes *Hard Times* (→1861).

Britain. The British Medical Association is founded.

Cheltenham. Cheltenham ladies' college is founded; it is the first boarding school for daughters of the wealthy gentry (→1863).

England. Barbara Leigh Smith publishes a *Brief Summary, in Plain Language, of the Most Important Laws of England cocerning Women.*

Westminster. New licensing laws restrict the opening of public houses in Britain; Sunday opening hours are to be 12.30pm to 2.30pm and 6pm to 10pm (→1872).

Britain at war in Crimea

Crowds cheer as British forces leave Southampton for the Crimea.

Westminster, 26 March

Britain and France, as the allies of the Ottoman Empire, have declared war on Russia. It is a war for which public opinion is baying but which the prime minister, Lord Aberdeen, had wished to avoid. He recently wrote to Lord Clarendon, the foreign secretary: "I still say that war is not inevitable unless, indeed, we are determined to have it; which, for all I know, may be the case." Some troops have already been sent to Malta in preparation for operations in support of the Turks, and Lord Raglan, who lost an arm at Waterloo, is to be commander-in-chief. Apart, however, from preventing the Russians from taking Istanbul, the expedition's aims remain unclear, although there is talk of an attack on Sevastopol (→28).

Irishman in exile writes 'Jail Journal'

New York

The large Irish community here has been excited by the publication of John Mitchel's *Jail Journal*. It is being regarded as one of the most remarkable Irish autobiographies ever written.

Mitchel, who had been transported (along with William Smith O'Brien, the leader of the "Young Ireland" Rising), to Van Diemen's Land [Tasmania] for 14 years, succeeded in escaping last December and reached New York where he resumed his journalistic career. *Jail Journal* begins with his transportation and ends with his escape five years later, after he had gone round the world as a convict and fugitive. His harsh nature was reinforced by the tragedy of the famine and the rhetoric of Thomas Carlyle.

Mitchell's apocalyptic writings reflect the wounds inflicted on Ireland by the famine diaspora, and his reappearance is likely to irritate the British authorities (→7/1).

Ancient and bawdy fair is banned to preserve public morality

London

The City authorities have closed Bartholomew Fair, the last of the great mediaeval fairs in London, alleging that it led to drinking, whoring, rowdiness and crime. The May Fair was closed half a century ago, and the district where it took place is now a fashionable quarter; the big country fairs have also mostly shut down. For two weeks every summer there were all kinds of puppet and theatrical shows, games of chance, freak shows, dog-fights, bear-baiting, wrestling and any amount of eating and drinking. The London poor have little enough to amuse themselves, and for them the fair was a valued annual entertainment. Yet it could indeed be squalid and a mecca for pickpockets. London wants to become more respectable, and the fair did not sit well with the pretensions of the new age.

Built at Laxey in the Isle of Man, the Lady Isabella is Britain's largest water wheel: it has a massive diameter of 21.85 metres (71.7 feet).

Doctor links cholera and the water supply

London

The physician Dr John Snow has stopped an outbreak of cholera in Soho by removing the handle from a public pump. He observed that most people who died in the outbreak drank from the same pump. When the handle was removed people could no longer drink from that source, and there were no more fatalities.

Not everyone accepts Snow's thesis that cholera is spread by contaminated water. It has spread from the Orient in the past decade, killing tens of thousands in the British Isles and Europe (→1855).

Success and disaster in the Crimean battlefields

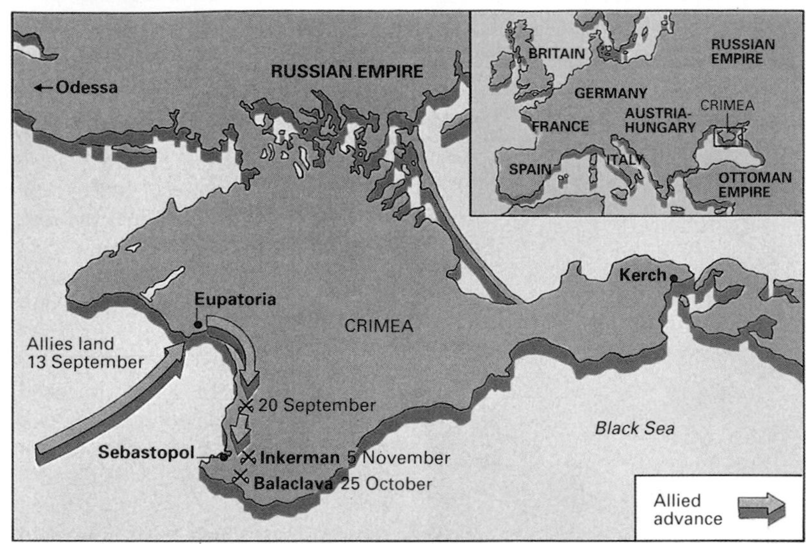

The map above shows the advance of British and French troops.

The Charge of the Light Brigade: riding into a valley of death.

Allied fleet bombards port of Sevastopol

Crimea, 20 September
The first battle of the war in the Crimea has been fought and won by the British and French here on the banks of the river Alma, when the Russians, with 40,000 men under Prince Menshikov, tried to block their advance on Sevastopol from the invasion beaches in the Bay of Eupatoria. The battle lasted all day and was hard-fought, ending only when the Brigade of Guards drove the enemy off the field with rifles and bayonets. The objective of occupying the heights above the Alma was accomplished, but when Lord Raglan, the British commander, proposed to advance on Sevastopol the French commander, Marshal St Aubyn, refused.

It is feared that a great opportunity has been missed. The victorious allies could have destroyed the Russian field army and taken the north side of Sevastopol. Ominously, cholera is raging in the ranks (→17/10).

British forces come under fresh attack

Crimea, 5 November
The Russians launched a furious attack on the British lines outside Sevastopol today, close to the ruins of Inkerman. The grey-coated Russians, almost invisible in the fog that shrouded the plateau, came on at a great pace, determined to drive the allies from the field.

The rough ground and the fog prevented any organized moves, and it soon became "a soldiers' battle", with British soldiers, their ammunition gone, using bayonets against equally determined Russians. For three long hours 8,500 British held off four times that number. Then the French Zouaves arrived at the *pas de charge*, and the Russians fled (→6/1855).

War failings rock government policy

Westminster, December
The government of Lord Aberdeen, split by rivalries and discontent at the conduct of the war, is growing steadily weaker. Not all its problems are of its own making; an unusually harsh winter in the Crimea, combined with a hurricane that blew away the troops' tents and sank two ships laden with ammunition and winter clothing, has brought hardship to the men.

Yet the organization of the war is shambolic. Transport and medical services are woefully inadequate. These problems have been made public by the correspondent for *The Times*, William Howard Russell, despite attempts by army chiefs to silence him (→29/1/55).

Light Brigade is cut down at Balaclava

Crimea, 25 October
Today has seen some astonishing feats of arms by the British Army. It started with the sudden appearance of a strong force of Russian infantry, cavalry and guns intending to drive the British from their base at Balaclava while the main allied force was engaged in the siege of Sevastopol some six miles away.

The first honours of the day went to the 93rd Highlanders under Sir Colin Campbell. Standing firm in a thin red line, they destroyed a Russian cavalry charge with disciplined rifle fire. Then it was the turn of Brigadier-General Scarlett and his Heavy Brigade. The Scots Greys and the Enniskillens, followed by the Royal Irish, the Dragoon Guards and the Royal Dragoons, hurled themselves, sabres slashing, at 3,000 Russian cavalry to drive them from the field. There followed a most extraordinary event.

Lord Raglan sent orders to Lord Lucan, the divisional commander, to prevent the Russians from carrying off some captured guns. The orders were not clear, and Lucan mistakenly ordered Lord Cardigan, commanding the Light Brigade, to attack well-defended Russian guns at the end of a long valley.

The Light Brigade set off as if it were in review, riding into a maelstrom of shot and shell fired at it from all sides. It reached the guns, sabred the gunners and then fought its way out. Of the 673 men who took part in this murderous encounter only 426 returned unhurt. General Boisquet watched in awe and said: "*C'est magnifique, mais ce n'est pas la guerre* [Magnificent, but not war]" (→5/11).

"The thin red line": the 93rd Highlanders stand firm at Balaclava.

1855

Westminster, 10 February. Lord Palmerston, a Whig, forms a government after the collapse of the Aberdeen administration (→ 3/1857).

West Yorkshire, 31 March. The novelist Charlotte Brontë, whose work includes *Jane Eyre* and *Shirley*, dies.

Dover, 16 April. Napoleon III (formerly Louis Napoleon) and Empress Eugénie arrive at Dover to begin their state visit to Britain.

London, 29 June. The first issue of the *Daily Telegraph* is printed.

Crimea, June. Allied troops attack Sevastopol but fail to capture the port (→ 28).

Co Kerry, 22 August. The Catholic cathedral at Killarney, designed by the late Augustus Pugin, is consecrated.

Crimea, 10 September. Sevastopol, besieged by allied troops for almost a year, surrenders (→ 14).

Dublin, 2 November. The Cecilia Street School of Medicine is opened as part of the Catholic University of Ireland.

Southern Africa, 17 November. David Livingstone, the explorer and missionary, discovers a massive waterfall during an expedition; he names it Victoria Falls after Queen Victoria.→

Manchester. Elizabeth Gaskell publishes her latest novel, *North and South* (→ 1865).

Grampian. Renovation work on Balmoral Castle is finally completed (→ 1/1856).

London. The sewers are to be modernized in an attempt to prevent the spread of another epidemic of cholera (→ 9/1866).

London. Alfred Tennyson, the poet laureate, publishes *Maud*, a poem that evokes a mentally deranged state (→ 1884).

London. Anthony Trollope publishes a novel, *The Warden* (→ 1857).

Ireland. George Petrie publishes *Ancient Music of Ireland*, sponsored by the Society for the Preservation and Publication of the Melodies of Ireland.

Scotland. Religious tests for university entrants are repealed.

Cardiff. New docks are being built to deal with the rapidly expanding coal business.

Aberdeen's coalition government falls

Westminster, 29 January
The government has been defeated in the House of Commons over the scandalous conditions facing the troops in the Crimea. The earl of Aberdeen has resigned as prime minister, and the search is now on for his successor.

Aberdeen has fallen victim to both Miss Florence Nightingale and *The Times*. The paper's war correspondent, William Russell, is reporting in detail on the frightful conditions in the military hospitals and on the incompetence of generals such as Lord Raglan. Meanwhile Miss Nightingale was sent to the hospital in Scutari, only to find every worst report true. The opposition has demanded a board of inquiry on the issue (→ 5/2).

Lord Aberdeen: victim of the war.

Exams hurdle set for civil servants

Westminster
A rearguard action to thwart civil service reforms proposed two years ago has failed to prevent changes from being introduced this year. Three commissioners have now been appointed to conduct the first examinations for entry to the civil service. No civil servant appointed after 1859 will qualify for a pension without first getting a certificate from the commissioners.

Critics of the 1853 report argued that governments needed the power of patronage, and also that examinations could not test "character". Public opinion, however, backed the reforms, which have now been approved by parliament.

Bessemer patents revolutionary new steel-making process

Inside a foundry: how Bessemer steel-converters are manufactured.

England
An English metallurgist, Henry Bessemer, has patented a new method of making steel by blowing air through molten pig-iron in a converter. The process is not yet perfect, but it is the most promising so far attempted. Steel is iron with a high carbon content. It can be cast or else shaped like wrought iron. When tempered it is far stronger than either. This is the latest of a series of inventions that are revolutionizing the iron industry and making the Black Country [in the English midlands] the marvel of the industrial world.

Newspapers to be spared stamp duty

London
The one-penny stamp duty on newspapers costing 6d or more has been lifted this year. Ministers want to suppress the "vile tyranny of *The Times*" as Lord John Russell put it, and radicals want to encourage the provincial press. *The Times*, at 5d, sells 60,000 a day, four times all its serious rivals put together; it has angered the government by its reporting in the Crimea. Since the stamp duty ended, the weekly *Manchester Guardian* has been made a daily, and the *Daily Telegraph* has been launched in London at 1d.

November 17: David Livingstone, the Scottish missionary, discovers a massive waterfall in southern Africa and names it after Queen Victoria.

Browning publishes new poetry collection 'Men and Women'

Florence, Italy
Robert Browning, hitherto best known as the man who eloped with Elizabeth Barrett, has increased his stature as a poet with two volumes entitled *Men and Women*. There are 50 pieces, mainly set in dramatic monologue, showing acute insight into his imaginary characters, among them the "faultless painter", Andrea del Sarto, of whom he says:

Ah, but a man's reach should exceed his grasp,
Or what's a heaven for?

The Brownings have settled at the Palazzo Guido in Florence, where Elizabeth bore a son, Robert, in 1849. Since then she has published her *Sonnets from the Portuguese*, written to her husband during their courtship. These love poems, recalling Shakespeare's sonnets in their measured language, are not translations: "my little Portuguese" was Robert Browning's pet name for Elizabeth at the time. Her possessive father has never forgiven her for leaving home, although as a result she is no longer an invalid. She writes in her sonnets:

How do I love thee? Let me count the ways ...
I saw in gradual vision through my tears
The sweet, sad years, the melancholy years,
Those of my own life who by turns had flung
A shadow across me (→1861).

Robert Browning: poetic vision.

Allies seize port of Sevastopol

Crimea, 9 September
The allies are today in possession of Sevastopol, the arsenal and port described as "the eyetooth of the bear". The end came after two days of bombardment and attacks on the strongpoints of the Redan and the Malakoff. The French scored a brilliant success at the Malakoff, taking the Russians by surprise and holding the fort against ferocious counter-attacks. At the Redan, however, the British attackers were slaughtered by well entrenched Russians. Another attack was to be launched this morning, but during the night the Russians blew up their own magazines, set fire to the city and marched away (→10).

The library is set ablaze by Russians evacuating besieged Sevastopol.

Royal Navy less than inspiring in campaign against Russians

Crimea, 14 September
The Russian Black Sea fleet lies scuttled on the bottom of Sevastopol Harbour, its fate summing up the lacklustre role of the Royal Navy in this war. This is not all the navy's fault, since the Russians refused to come out to fight, and the navy certainly carried out its task of safely escorting the troop transports to the Crimea; but there has been a lack of the "Nelson touch" among its commanders.

The only noteworthy actions were two expeditions to the Baltic and the White Seas and a combined operation to seize the Russian base of Kerch, 150 miles (240km) east of Balaclava. The northern forays captured the lightly held fortress of Bomarsund in the Baltic and bombarded Sveaborg on the coast of Finland. Fearing Russian mines, Admiral Sir Richard Dundas contented himself with shelling Sveaborg, "the Gibraltar of the north", at long range. In the Kerch attack the Straits of Kerch were forced, and the Sea of Azov was swept clean of Russian vessels (→16/1/56).

Lord Raglan dies a hero at Sevastopol

Crimea, 28 June
Lord Raglan, the commander of the British forces in the Crimea, has died at his headquarters outside Sevastopol. Worn out by the responsibilities of the campaign, he succumbed, like so many of his men, to cholera. He was not a great general and had not been to war since he lost his arm at Waterloo. He was, however, a brave and dignified man who was ill-served by the politicians at home.

Raglan was respected by the French and won for the British Army more influence than its numbers perhaps warranted. As the news of his death spread through the camp, the French and Sardinian commanders joined in mourning his passing. His successor is General James Simpson, an unwilling candidate who doubts his own ability to command the army (→9/9).

Florence Nightingale tends wounded men

The lady with the lamp: Florence Nightingale in the Scutari hospital.

Scutari, Crimea, 11 September
Florence Nightingale, highly revered among British troops as "the lady with the lamp", has performed great deeds since she arrived here last October with a team of 38 nurses to tend the wounded of the Crimean battles.

She found men dying like flies, not only of their wounds but also of cholera, dysentery and typhus. The sanition was appalling; even slightly wounded men were dying of infections. A strict disciplinarian, she set to work to introduce hygienic reforms and bullied the government into providing medical supplies. Many men owe her their lives. Sadly, it is feared that her own health has been broken (→1860).

1856

Russia, 16 January. Russia accepts the Austrian ultimatum for peace, and the Crimean War ends (→30/3).

London, 29 January. Queen Victoria institutes the Victoria Cross, an award for courage and bravery, for all ranks of the armed services (→26/6/57).

London, January. *The Times* newspaper leaks the news of the forthcoming engagement of Victoria, the princess royal, Queen Victoria's eldest daughter, to Frederick, the crown prince of Prussia (→25/6/57).

Dublin, January. James Stephens, a former associate of William Smith O'Brien, one of the leaders of the disbanded Irish Confederation, returns from exile in Paris (→17/3/58).

Dublin, January. The Irish Academy of Music is founded.

Tipperary City, 13 February. The Bank of Tipperary collapses.

London, 5 March. Covent Garden theatre is destroyed by fire.

Dublin, 1 May. John Hungerford Pollen, an architect, completes the building of the university church on St Stephen's Green.

South Wales, 15 July. A gas explosion at the Cymmer colliery kills 114 miners and seriously injures 42 others.

Southern Africa, 12 July. Natal is made a British colony.

China, October. Chinese troops board the British ship *Arrow* in the port of Canton [Guangzhou] and arrest the crew on suspicion of piracy (→25).

London, 1 November. In response to a Persian invasion of Afghanistan, Britain – which allied with the Afghans last year – declares war on Persia (→1/1857).

Highland, 2 December. Hugh Miller, a geologist and journalist who edited *Witness*, the journal of the evangelical wing in the Church of Scotland, shoots himself.

Co Cork. The Phoenix National and Literary Society is founded at Skibbereen by Jeremiah O'Donovan.

India. The British annex the kingdom of Awadh in northern India; this is added to the other states already annexed – Satara, Jhansi and Nagpur (→5/1857).

Allies victorious as Crimean war ends

War is concluded with Treaty of Paris

France, 30 March
The Crimean War is over. Following the loss of Sevastopol and an ultimatum from Austria, the Russians were forced to the conference table last month, and today the powers of the "Concert of Europe" signed the Treaty of Paris. The soldiers, who have not fired a shot for several weeks, can go home.

The treaty has four main provisions: 1. The Black Sea is to be neutralized, closed to all warships, and no fortifications will be allowed on its shores. 2. The Danubian provinces of Moldavia and Wallachia are to be independent under nominal Ottoman sovereignty. 3. The Danube is to come under international control and be dredged. 4. The Ottoman Empire's integrity is to be guaranteed by the powers, and Russia is to abandon its claim to protect the Christians within it; in return the *sultan* [ruler] has promised better treatment for his Christian subjects.

The war may be over but the underlying problems remain. The Empire continues to be the "Sick Man of Europe", and Russia can hardly abandon its military presence in the Black Sea (→4/1856).

Fireworks in London's Green Park celebrate victory in the Crimea.

The Victoria Cross: instituted this year "For Valour" among all ranks.

Military chiefs learn lessons of the war

London, April
The Crimean War, for all its horror, is proving beneficial to the men of the army and the navy. In the 40 years between Waterloo and the Alma little had been done for them. Now, thanks to Florence Nightingale, who reduced the death-rate at Scutari from 42 per hundred to 22 per thousand, the army medical service is to be overhauled.

Army chiefs might disagree, but thanks are also due to William Howard Russell, the war correspondent of *The Times*, who made the public graphically aware of conditions in the Crimea. His reports helped to bring reforms, the downfall of a government – and the introduction of censorship.

Soldiers' terms of service are to be improved, as are their uniforms, training and musketry practice. The institution of the Victoria Cross, a decoration "For Valour" open to all ranks, has done much to raise the standing of the previously despised ordinary soldier.

The Royal Navy is also undergoing drastic reform. The steam engine has revolutionized naval warfare, enabling ships to manoeuvre independent of the wind. There is talk of building armoured, steam-driven capital ships that will make all ships built before the Crimean War obsolete. Sailors also qualify for the Victoria Cross.

William Howard Russell: he made people aware of the horrors of war.

The effect of science on war and politics may be seen in the use of the telegraph. The submarine cable laid from Istanbul to the Crimea last year enabled Napoleon III to give orders directly to his generals in the field – much to their disgust. It also transmitted the despatches of correspondents. The effect of such reports on civilians could become a new factor in warfare (→30/7).

Australia to enjoy greater freedoms

Australia
Britain's largest, and still relatively unexplored, colony of Australia has moved this year towards the qualified independence enjoyed by the longer established Canada. New constitutions have come into effect this year that give the colonies considerable powers over their own affairs, with more limitations on the Westminster parliament to impose its authority. Each colony is to be separate, as distances are so great that talk of a single assembly for the whole continent have come to nothing, at least for now.

Australia is booming, with gold rushes in Victoria and New South Wales. The population is now nearly one million, and the country has acquired its first railway and university. Immigration is now voluntary – and growing (→6/9/70).

Towns and boroughs get police forces

London policemen prepare themselves to go on patrol, c.1850.

Britain
Every borough and county in the kingdom must now set up a local police force, under a new act of parliament. Many have been most reluctant to do so.

When people lived in villages and everyone knew his or her neighbour, crime seemed a less urgent problem; things are different in cities. London led the way with the Bow Street Runners in 1748 and the Metropolitan Police in 1829. Other cities have slowly followed London's example, and now the police principle is to be extended. Local authorities must now provide professional forces, and there is to be an inspector of constabulary to preserve and raise standards.

British fleet opens fire on civilians

Hong Kong, 25 October
British gunboats commanded by Admiral Sir Michael Seymour have captured Chinese forts guarding Canton [Guangzhou] and shelled the city itself. The incident arose out of the seizure by Governor Yeh of the *Arrow*, a vessel owned by a Chinaman living in Hong Kong. Yeh said that the crew included a pirate and arrested them. Sir John Bowring, the governor of Hong Kong, demanded their release and an apology for the "insult" to the British flag. When Yeh refused, Seymour attacked the forts, whereupon Yeh freed his prisoners but refused to apologize; so Seymour shelled the city. Yeh has now ordered the destruction of British shipping and is offering a reward for British heads. Britain and China are effectively at war (→24/2/47).

New-style prisons spread to provinces

Britain
The prison reform movement has now spread to the provinces, with new model prisons rising in many cities. Ever since Australia refused to take any more convicts in 1853 it has been necessary for Britain to house its own long-term prisoners, and the old, squalid, 18th-century jails were quite unsuited. So were the prison hulks – ancient wooden ships moored in various harbours, that have been used as prisons since the Napoleonic wars. The first modern prison was Pentonville, in London, where the treadmill and other ancient punishments were abolished. Prisoners were kept in solitary confinement and given religious instruction.

The Penal Servitude Act for the first time provided prison terms as the normal sentence for crimes previously punished with transportation. Now the provincial authorities, like those in London, have to provide the buildings to house criminals permanently.

The new prison of St Mary's in Chatham, Kent, completed this year.

Oxbridge now free of religious test bar

Brasenose chapel, Oxford: church attendance was once compulsory.

Cambridge
Cambridge University has now followed Oxford's example and will admit dissenters and Catholics as undergraduates, though not yet to higher degrees or to university offices. It is all part of the sweeping reforms of the two ancient universities, which are being challenged by London University and colleges established in the provinces.

A few years ago Oxford and Cambridge were still small, mediocre institutions producing clergymen of the Church of England. Standards and teaching had declined during the 18th century. That is changing as colleges break away from teaching principally classics and divinity, although fellows of colleges, except masters, must still be celibate.

Reformers hope that Oxford and Cambridge will educate future generations of the ruling class to govern Britain and its empire, and they are planning to develop a curriculum for that purpose. Strangely, their policy leaves little room for science.

1857

Persia [Iran], January. British troops seize the port of Bushire on the Persian Gulf.

London, 6 February. The British Portrait Gallery is founded in Westminster.

Europe, 3 March. Britain and France declare war on China (→31/3/58).

Manchester, 5 May. Local manufacturers and businessmen finance an exhibition of fine arts in a splendid wrought-iron building at Old Trafford.

India, 11 May. Indian soldiers in the Bengal army based at Meerut in northern India, having mutinied yesterday against British officers, seize Delhi.

London, 25 June. Albert, the husband of Queen Victoria, is made Prince Consort (→21/8/61).

London, 26 June. The first investiture of Victoria Cross medals takes place in Hyde Park in the presence of Queen Victoria.

Westminster, July. William Gladstone, a Peelite Tory MP, opposes the proposed divorce reforms (→1873).

India, July. Over 200 Britons are massacred in Cawnpore by Indian mutineers (→20/9).

Belfast, 6 September. Religious riots break out in the city.

India, 20 September. British troops recapture Delhi (→25).

Britain, 7 October. A national day of fasting is called to support the Indian mutiny crisis (→8/1858).

Birmingham, 12 October. The National Association for the Improvement of Social Science meets for the first time.

North Yorkshire, 15 December. Sir George Cayley, the pioneering aeronaut, dies at his home in Brompton (→5/9/62).

London. Anthony Trollope publishes his latest novel, *Barchester Towers* (→1867).

Scotland. The Western bank collapses amid a financial scandal.

London. David Livingstone, the explorer and missionary who discovered the Victoria Falls, returns (→15/12).

Kent. Kent County Constabulary is formed.

Manchester. Charles Hallé founds the Hallé orchestra.

'Painted pantaloon' wins general election

Palmerston shows Russell the way ahead in this contemporary cartoon.

British Isles, March
Lord Palmerston, once described by Benjamin Disraeli as "an old, painted pantaloon", has proved that despite such attacks he remains a star political performer. Defeated earlier this month in the House of Commons over the war with China, he called an election and promptly won it.

For Palmerston, who became prime minister two years ago when the earl of Aberdeen resigned, it has been a very personal victory. As Lord Shaftesbury put it: "There was no measure, no principle, no cry ... simply were you, or were you not for Palmerston." In the event 370 candidates successfully were, although observers suggest that self- rather than party interest is all that unites them.

Despite his aristocratic background, Palmerston is unopposed to reform in principle, even though he does little about it in practice. Indolence, rather than ideology, appears to be his basic attitiude. Only in foreign affairs, his real interest, does Palmerston act.

Gunboat diplomacy comes under fire

Westminster, 24 February
The war with China continues, with fresh bombardments from the British squadron. It has also spread to Westminster where the prime minister, Lord Palmerston, is coming under fierce attack from both the Lords and the Commons for his robust "gunboat diplomacy" towards the Chinese.

Lord Derby has proposed a motion condemning the government in the House of Lords, and Richard Cobden is demanding a Commons select committee into relations with China. He is supported by Disraeli and Gladstone, but Palmerston, confident after his Crimean victory, spurns their attacks (→3/3).

Dirty books banned

Westminster
The first ever legislation designed to bar the trade in pornographic materials has been passed by parliament. Under the Obscene Publications Act the authorities may now enter suspected premises and seize allegedly obscene articles. It is then up to their owner or seller to prove why the material should not be destroyed. The act is aimed at the "dirty book trade", but its critics fear that prudes will use it to target not filth but genuine, if controversial, works of literature.

British Museum's reading room offers a home for every book

London
The British Museum's new reading room is complete. The room, which fills the central courtyard, has been built by Sydney Smirke to cope with the requirement of the 1851 Copyright Act that a copy of every book published in Britain be deposited in the museum. This had left the old library brimming over.

The reading room's circular design, with cast-iron shelves for a million books, was proposed by Antonio Panizzi, a penniless Italian revolutionary who rose to become the keeper of printed books. "I want the poor student to have the same means of indulging his learned curiosity as the richest man in the kingdom," he said.

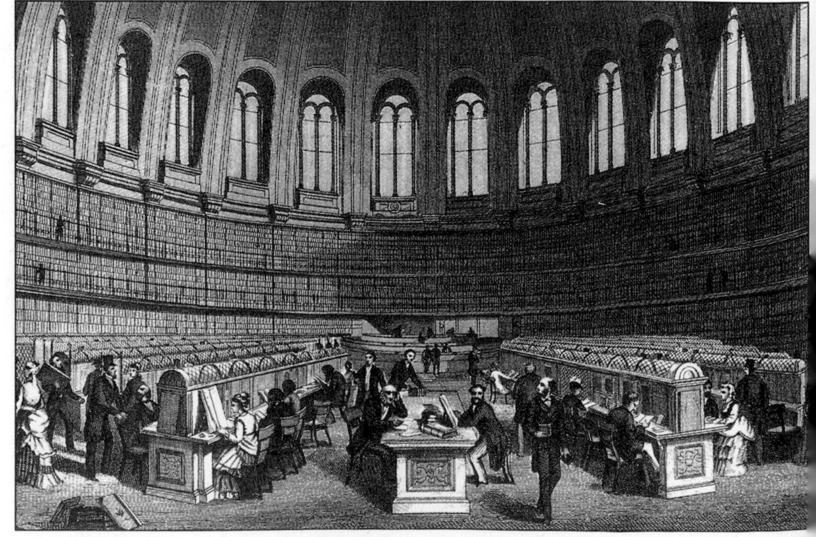

Silent study: the new circular reading room of the British Museum.

Indians rebel against British rule

Religion seen as cause of rebellion

Calcutta, May
A bloody uprising is sweeping India as native soldiers mutiny against their British officers. Women and children, as well as British soldiers, have been massacred. Delhi has fallen to the mutineers, and several British garrisons are under siege.

Trouble flared on 10 May when the sepoys [Indian soldiers in European service] at Meerut mutinied while their British officers were at church. Indian prisoners were set free and three regiments of sepoys marched south to Delhi. Another regiment was sent to restore order, but it joined the mutineers inside Delhi. By then the mutiny was spreading widely among Indian troops, who number 230,000, as against the 40,000 Britons in the Indian Army. Lucknow and Cawnpore are among the garrisons now under siege as Lord Canning, the governor-general in Calcutta, seeks to contain the rising.

Religion sparked the revolt, with British attempts to control Hinduism inflaming Moslem troops as well. Underlying this is a groundswell of dislike of colonial rule: the Indians regard charges of "mutiny" coming from the British as more than a shade ironic (→ 10).

British and loyal Indian troops recapture Delhi, 20 September 1857.

British authorities clamp down in India

Lucknow, 25 September
The beleaguered British garrison here was reinforced today, but the siege by Indian troops has not been broken. It is led by Nana Sahib, a prince who is being blamed by the British for the worst atrocities of the uprising to date.

These occurred three months ago at Cawnpore, where the garrison had been under siege. On 26 June Nana Sahib had agreed to permit the wounded and, the women and children to leave in safety; but his soldiers fired on their boats, killing the men and imprisoning the rest. Then on 15 July, as Sir Henry Havelock's loyal troops neared Cawnpore, Nana Sahib ordered the massacre of his prisoners: 200 died, hacked to pieces and their bodies tossed into a well.

Despite this, the British authorities are beginning to regain the initiative. Delhi has been recaptured, and British troops are exacting a bloody revenge for the killings at Cawnpore and elsewhere. The siege at Lucknow, however, has yet to end (→ 7/10).

Divorce courts for unhappy couples

Britain
Till death us do part, say the marriage vows, but such fidelity does not rule every nuptial bed. Now, for those who cannot live together, a new law should make it easier to part – the Matrimonial Causes Act, under which divorce courts are to be set up. The new act enshrines a double standard, however: while a man need prove only his wife's adultery, a woman has to show evidence of cruelty or desertion too (→ 7/1857).

Hero's welcome for David Livingstone

London, 15 December
David Livingstone, the Scottish missionary who discovered what he named the Victoria Falls in Africa, was honoured at a meeting of the Royal Geographic Society today. He was presented with a gold medal in recognition of his many discoveries in the interior of Africa over the past 13 years. Dr Livingstone went to Africa under the aegis of the London Missionary Society. Now 43 years old, he intends to write an account of his travels. He is the first white man to have seen many of Africa's lakes and rivers, as well as the waterfall that he named after the queen (→ 13/11/71).

Sailors in Royal Navy are to have uniforms to go with job

Royal Navy seamen show off their new uniforms alongside army redcoats.

London
Jack Tar, once resplendent in his blue jacket and bell-bottomed trousers, is finally to have a proper uniform. The commission of manning, which also plans for a new career structure, higher pensions and increased pay, has determined to re-outfit not just the Royal Navy's ships but its seamen too.

The blue jacket will stay, and the trousers are to be white; in addition the sailor will have drill and serge frocks [blouses], black canvas and straw hats, a pea jacket and a silk scarf. Yet the new uniform may not please everyone. Men like their own clothes, and the cry "Hands Make and Mend" is not quite history yet.

A scene from "Tom Brown's Schooldays", a novel published this year to popular acclaim.

1858 - 1859

London, January 1858. The city is split into ten postal districts.

Dublin, 17 March 1858. A secret organization, the Irish Republican Brotherhood, is founded by James Stephens, a former member of the Irish Confederation (→ 1859).

China, 31 March 1858. The Chinese agree to negotiate with the British and the French (→ 20/5).

China, 20 May 1858. British and French forces attack the Dagu forts in northern China to force a peace deal (→ 6/1858).

London, 22 May 1858. The new Theatre Royal, designed by Charles Barry, opens.

London, 7 August 1858. Queen Victoria chooses Ottawa as the capital of Canada.

Co Kerry, 20 August 1858. The first transatlantic message is received at Valentia; it has travelled from Trinity Bay, Newfoundland, via the newly laid cable (→ 2/9).

Belfast, September 1858. Presbyterian clergy form the Irish Temperance League.

Westminster, November 1858. William Gladstone is made high commissioner of the Ionian Islands (→ 20/6/59).

Westminster, 1858. Lionel de Rothschild is the first Jewish MP in the House of Commons.

Edinburgh, 21 March 1859. The National Gallery opens.

Dublin, 29 March 1859. The first issue of the *Irish Times* is printed.

London, April 1859. The Stock Exchange is thrown into chaos by the Franco-Russian alliance against Austria.

Westminster, 20 June 1859. William Gladstone becomes chancellor of the exchequer in Lord Palmerston's government.

China, June 1859. The British and French unsuccessfully raid the Dagu forts (→ 19/8/60).

Glasgow, 14 October 1859. Queen Victoria opens Loch Katrine, built to supply Glasgow with 50 million gallons of water a day.

Derbyshire, 1859. At the Rutland Arms in Bakewell the first Bakewell tart is baked.

England, 28 December 1859. Thomas Macaulay, a historian, poet and Whig, who regularly wrote for the Whig paper the *Edinburgh Review*, dies.

Lord Derby follows Palmerston as PM

Westminster, February 1858
An extraordinary chain of events has installed Lord Derby as prime minister once more, in place of Lord Palmerston. After years of patriotic pursuit of British interests abroad, Palmerston submitted to French pressure for action to prevent repetition of an assassination attempt on Napoleon III by an Italian revolutionary, Felice Orsini, who obtained his bomb in England. But Palmerston's initiative, a bill amending the law of conspiracy, was defeated by 234 votes to 215, with John Bright and others accusing the government of "truckling to France". Palmerston then resigned rather than risk facing a vote of no confidence (→ 6/1859).

Derby: back in Downing Street.

Treaty brings end to Chinese conflict

Tientsin, June 1858
After the capture by British forces of the Dagu forts at the mouth of the Peiko river, the Chinese have agreed to British demands, including a diplomatic mission in Beijing. But distrust between the two sides is so acute that it may only prove to be a lull in hostilities. The present tension between Britain and China arises from an incident in October 1856 when the Chinese boarded a British-registered ship in Canton and imprisoned 12 crewmen. The prisoners were returned, but the Chinese did not apologize, suspecting British involvement in piracy and smuggling (→ 6/1859).

Music festival marks the completion of new town hall in Leeds

Leeds, 1858
A music festival has been held here to round off a proud year for the people of Leeds. Queen Victoria was welcomed by no fewer than 32,110 Sunday-school children when she came to open the new town hall, designed by the Hull architect Cuthbert Broderick. Leeds has become the commercial capital of Yorkshire, employing many thousands in the woollen and worsted industries, and thousands more in the making of flax. Metal-working and engineering are growing industries, while tanneries and skinworks proliferate. Leeds has overtaken Wakefield in leather production. The council is clearing slums, widening roads and building squares and fine public buildings.

Civic pride: the new town hall in Leeds reflects new-found prosperity.

Horsepower gets London to work – with the help of omnibuses

Three horsepower: no room on top (or below) on this omnibus.

London, 1858
The London Omnibus Company has been founded, with nearly 600 buses, and 6,000 horses. Horse-drawn buses are an increasingly popular way of getting to work. They take most of the 27,000 daily rail travellers from their termini into the City of London, and they also carry many of the 250,000 others who commute from outer London. Despite their name, the omnibuses are not yet for all, being beyond the pocket of the average manual worker.

Robert Owen, who taught thrift and good order, dies

Newport, Gwent, 1858
Robert Owen, the father of socialism, has died in the town of his birth. He will be remembered not only for his social and economic theories but also for the fact that he put them into practice in model communities. His outstanding monument is New Lanark, in Scotland, but in recent years he established a village of about 2,000 inhabitants at New Harmony, Indiana, where he and his sons went to live.

His most ambitious project was unsuccessful: the Grand National Consolidated Trade Union, which was founded in 1834, quickly attracted 500,000 members, but just as quickly collapsed, although it influenced the Chartist movement. Yet New Lanark is living proof of Owen's belief that people can be educated to work towards the common good, rather than individual gain. Owen was a powerful personality whose integrity was never questioned. His judgement was another matter. By stressing communal goals at the expense of family and religious belief, Owen went too far for most people. New Lanark works because the mill dominates the lives of its people. More mixed communities proved less successful, and most have disintegrated amid fierce bickering.

A clock tower, nicknamed "Big Ben", is completed in 1858 for the new Houses of Parliament.

Peace in India as mutiny is put down

Last battle won by the British forces

Delhi, 1 November 1858
Queen Victoria rules once again throughout India. This message was proclaimed today by the viceroy, formerly governor-general, Lord "Clemency" Canning, whose nickname reflects a calmer British attitude after the months of savagery that followed last year's mutiny. Terrible massacres by Indian mutineers and equally bloody reprisals by British troops made the mutiny seem momentous. In fact, three-quarters of the Indian soldiery stayed loyal to the crown, and the revolt was never a serious threat to British rule.

Years of insensitive administration, including attempts to impose army discipline regardless of the caste system, lay behind the explosion of anger in May 1857. And sheer racial hatred fuelled the massacres and reprisals that followed. But since the enforced exile of the aged king of Delhi, the revolt has lacked purpose. For the past few months, sporadic fighting has continued in various parts of India, with the last pockets of resistance in Central Province.

At Lucknow, however, the British garrison had to survive a long siege. Sir Colin Campbell, the new commander-in-chief of the army, relieved the British contingent last November, but then had to move on to deal with a threat to Cawnpore. The garrison held out until reinforcements arrived, and the siege was finally lifted in March. Nana Sahib, who was blamed for the worst atrocities at Cawnpore, has disappeared (→8/2/72).

British forces charge against the mutineers at Lucknow in March 1858.

East India Company passes to the crown

India, August 1858
The East India Company has been abolished, and India is to be ruled by the British government. The governor-general, appointed by the crown, will be known as the viceroy, and will be supported by a 15-member council of India. It is a nominal change, as the company has been an effective arm of government since the India Act of 1833 ordered it to close its commercial business. The Indian civil service was opened to public competition five years ago.

More significantly for the people of India, the new act promises religious toleration. British attempts to impose Christian ethics have backfired for decades. The Brahmo Samaj, a reforming Hindu group, has increasingly lost influence as Indians have returned to their religious roots (→1/11).

End of an era: ships like this near Calcutta were the company's lifeline.

'Gray's Anatomy' published as manual for doctors and surgeons

London, 1 September 1858
A manual has been published for all aspiring doctors. *Gray's Anatomy* is the work of Henry Gray, a lecturer at St George's hospital, in Tooting. Its 750 pages contain 363 magnificent illustrations by Henry Carter, one of Gray's colleagues at the hospital. Black and white woodcuts are coloured with blue and red to represent veins and arteries. Edited by the surgeon-anatomist Timothy Holmes, the book aims to provide the student with all he needs to pass examinations and practise as either physician or surgeon.

Henry Gray is 31, the son of a court messenger. He enrolled as a medical student in 1845, won a prize from the Royal College of Surgeons in 1848 and, at 25, was elected a Fellow of the Royal Society. For a dissertation on the spleen, he was awarded the Astley Cooper prize of 300 guineas in 1853. His duties as lecturer and demonstrator on anatomy, and as curator of the museum at St George's, gave him the experience he needed to write his book. ▷

Odious or earnest? The Pre-Raphaelite Brotherhood divides the artistic world

"Pegwell Bay" by William Dyce, a disciple of the Pre-Raphaelites.

Rossetti: "The Annunciation".

London, 1858
The mysterious initials P R B first appeared in 1849 after the signature of the artist Dante Gabriel Rossetti. He was one of the founders of the Pre Raphaelite Brotherhood with fellow-painters John Millais and William Holman Hunt.

Once the meaning of the initials was revealed, the group was attacked for setting itself up as better than Raphael. The critic John Ruskin defended them in *The Times* for choosing to "draw what they see irrespective of any conventional rules of picture making, as artists did before Raphael's time ... there has been nothing in art so earnest as these pictures since Dürer". But Charles Dickens has denounced Millais' *Christ in the House of His Parents* as "mean, odious, revolting and repulsive".

"Christ in the House of His Parents" by Millais, which upset Dickens.

Darwin publishes 'The Origin of Species'

Britain, 24 November 1859
The 1,250 copies of *The Origin of Species*, by Charles Darwin, published today by John Murray, have sold out in advance to booksellers. Scientists and intellectuals believe Darwin's work constitutes probably the most coherent theory of evolution yet developed, but conservative clerics are worried that it contradicts the Book of Genesis, and undermines religious belief. Since Darwin himself is an intensely private man with complicated religious views, these arguments seem certain to rage on.

Darwin: intellectual bestseller.

Charles Darwin, aged 50, trained as a clergyman at Cambridge where he read Paley and became fascinated with natural history. His interest was sharpened by a voyage of exploration aboard the *Beagle*, and by reading Malthus's *Essay on Population*, and Lyell's *Principles of Geology*. His most radical idea is that species did not arise independently, but developed through a process he calls "natural selection". A keen pigeon-fancier, he cites pigeon breeding as evidence that species are not immutable (→1860).

Transatlantic telegraph cable breaks down

Making the international telegraph cables at a factory in Sunderland.

London, 2 September 1858
The new telegraphic link between Britain and the United States has been broken. Only 28 days ago a 3,000-mile (4,800-km) cable was laid via Newfoundland from New York to London, and the transatlantic telegraph was hailed as a technological breakthrough. Now there seems to be a rupture somewhere beneath the ocean, and no one knows if it can be repaired.

The cable was the work of Cyrus W Field, an American financier. Field, who is 48, made his fortune in the paper business. His passion for electronic communication led to the foundation of the New York, Newfoundland and London Telegraph Company, first in the United States, and now in England. Both American and British ships were involved in the laying of the cable, which Field insists can be repaired. His company has a charter giving it exclusive rights to lay telegraph cables on the coast of Newfoundland, and he promises that if repairs fail, his company will simply lay another cable (→26/7/66).

Conservatives are toppled from power

Westminster, June 1859
Lord Palmerston has returned as prime minister, following the collapse of Lord Derby's Conservative government. A shared sympathy for Italian nationalism has made allies of Palmerston and earl Russell, who becomes foreign secretary. Gladstone is chancellor of the exchequer. A vote on 31 March on electoral reform was the beginning of the end for Derby's government, with the non-Tory majority demanding a lower borough property qualification. The Tories won a few more seats at the general election, but on 10 June lost a vote of confidence. Queen Victoria asked Lord Granville to form a government, but he could not (→18/10/65).

Drinking fountain to help fight disease

London, April 1859
The first public fountain erected by an association formed to provide pure drinking water was unveiled today. The fountain outside the Old Bailey against the wall of St Sepulchre-without-Newgate is the work of the Metropolitan Free Drinking Fountain Association, which was founded by Samuel Gurney, the MP.

With polluted water supplies fostering cholera and typhoid in London and other cities, it has long been safer for people to drink gin or beer. Free, pure water will indeed, as the association claims, be "a boon to all classes".

Family fare at the first fountain.

If you want to get on, help yourself

London, 1859
Swift success has greeted a book called *Self-Help* this year. Its author, Samuel Smiles, combines maxims, such as "Heaven helps those who help themselves" with homilies: "Help from without is often enfeebling in its effects. Whatever is done *for* men takes away the stimulus of doing for themselves ... National progress is the sum of individual industry, energy and uprightness as national decay is of individual idleness, selfishness and vice ... This spirit of self-help has in all times been a feature of the English character and the measure of our power as a nation."

Smiles, one of 11 children, became a doctor, then a journalist and wrote a life of George Stephenson and other engineers. *Self-Help* has already sold 20,000 copies this year and has been translated into 17 languages; the case for *laissez-faire* has never been put better.

Fenian Brotherhood seeks free Ireland

Dublin, 1859
Irishmen dedicated to the forcible overthrow of the British government and the establishment of an independent Ireland are joining a secret society known as the Fenian Brotherhood. The name is derived from Fianna, an armed force led by a warrior of Celtic legend. It was chosen by John O'Mahony, a Gaelic scholar who was involved in the 1848 uprising and is now based in New York, recruiting sympathetic Irish Americans.

In Ireland, the Fenians are led by James Stephens, who mingled for a time with political exiles in Paris. Stephens was pardoned in 1856, and returned to Ireland where he set out on a 3,000-mile (4,800-km) recruiting tour. He now heads a revolutionary guerrilla group, comprising circles in which, to thwart informers, no member now knows more than one member of another circle (→8/1863).

Brunel, the greatest of British engineers, leaves a brilliant legacy on land and sea

Brunel's "Great Eastern": five times larger than any passenger ship afloat.

Britain, September 1859
Isambard Kingdom Brunel, the most versatile engineer in British history, has died aged 53. His last project – the Saltash bridge across the Tamar – is close to completion. The bridge, which takes the Great Western Railway into Cornwall, has two spans high enough for shipping to pass underneath.

Brunel, the master engineer.

Brunel worked with his father, Sir Marc Brunel, on the Thames Tunnel, which was started in 1825 and completed in 1843. But the son soon eclipsed his father's achievements with designs for railways, bridges and great ships.

In 1828, after three years working as resident engineer on the Thames Tunnel, Brunel was made engineer at Bristol docks. He designed docks at Monkwearmouth, Milford Haven, Brentford and Plymouth before becoming chief engineer to the Great Western Railway in 1833, for which he designed stations, such as Paddington in London, tunnels and bridges. His most spectacular bridge is the uncompleted Clifton suspension bridge. From his pioneering work on the railways, where he championed the broad gauge track, Brunel moved on to design ships such as the *Great Western* (1838), the *Great Britain* (1845) and the massive *Great Eastern* (1858), which carries 4,000 passengers, and is five times the size of the previous largest vessel afloat. He revolutionized iron-clad construction, screw-propulsion, and the use of steam power (→17/6/60).

The bridge taking the railway high over the Tamar into Cornwall.

1860

Shrewsbury, 18 January. A statue to commemorate Lord Clive, the founder of the British empire in India, is unveiled in his home town.

Britain/France, 23 January. Richard Cobden, a campaigner for the repeal of the Corn Laws, negotiates a commercial treaty with France to reduce customs duties on over 40 goods.

England, 12 May. Charles Barry, the architect of the new Theatre Royal in Covent Garden, dies.

Atlantic, 17 June. The *Great Eastern*, the largest ship afloat at 213 metres (692 feet) long, designed and built by the late Isambard Kingdom Brunel, begins its first transatlantic voyage to New York (→ 12/1864).

Plymouth, 10 July. Prince Albert Edward, the prince of Wales, sets sail for Canada and the US, where he will act as Queen Victoria's representative on a state visit (→ 1/9).

China, 19 August. Anglo-French forces defeat Chinese troops outside Shanghai (→ 21).

China, 21 August. Anglo-French troops seize the Dagu forts in northern China (→ 10/1860).

Canada, 1 September. The prince of Wales lays the foundation stone of the new parliament buildings in Ottawa (→ 16/11/61).

China, 6 October. Anglo-French troops seize the summer palace in the city of Beijing as the Chinese surrender (→ 24).

China, 24 October. The Treaty of Beijing is signed by the British, French and Chinese, bringing an end to the "Opium Wars".

Scotland. Aberdeen University is founded by the amalgamation of King's College and Marischal College.

Britain. Jeremiah Smith, a publisher based near Oxford, invents the self-adhesive envelope.

Britain. Mary Ann Evans, under the pseudonym of George Eliot, publishes *The Mill on the Floss*; it follows the success of her first novel, *Adam Bede* (→ 1872).

London. Blackheath rugby club is founded.

Britain. Wilkie Collins publishes his first novel, *The Woman in White* (→ 1868).

Launch of Royal Navy's iron ship turns traditional warships into museum pieces

The ironclad HMS "Warrior": what the first iron warship will look like.

London, 29 December
Today's launch of the remarkable HMS *Warrior* at Blackwall on the Thames signals a new era in the history of the warship. Unlike her predecessors, *Warrior's* hull is made of not just wood, but iron as well. It consists of 18-inch-thick (45.7-cm) teak, with 4.5-inch-thick iron plates bolted on it.

The Allied fleets in the Crimean War discovered that unprotected wooden warships could not stand up to the modern high explosive shell, but it was the French who took the lead. Two years ago they launched the "ironclad" frigate *Gloire* and laid down four more similar vessels. This forced the admiralty, which until then was only lukewarm, into action.

Warrior differs from the French ships in that she is not just protected by iron, but her complete frame is made of it, thereby making her the first true "iron ship". She is classified as a steam frigate, displaces about 9,200 tonnes, and is 65 metres (210 feet) long. She is expected to be completed next autumn. Her sister ship *Black Prince* will be launched in two months' time. The Royal Navy's "wooden walls", which have guarded Britain's shores and her communications across the oceans for so many centuries, look set to be consigned to the museums.

Prestwick hosts first golf championship

Prestwick, Ayrshire, October
The Prestwick golf club, founded only recently but already intent on making a lasting mark on this ancient game, has set up the first "open" championship. An attractive silver-buckled belt is the trophy. The contest, thrown open to all professional golfers, was won by William Park Senior, who narrowly defeated Tom Morris by 174 to 176 over the 12-hole course.

Leading amateur players have protested that, as they were excluded from playing, the championship could not be considered truly "open". The club has said that they can play in future (→ 1864).

Competitors at the first "Open".

Maori war flares over land claims

New Zealand
Britain and the Maoris are at war over land rights. Fighting began after the colonial government tactlessly passed a measure granting private ownership to settlers. This contravenes the terms of the 20-year-old Treaty of Waitangi, guaranteeing ultimate title to the Maoris [*see page 872*]. They have sold huge areas of land to settlers on the assumption they were disposing only of occupancy rights. Most settlers assumed that they were buying the land outright. The bishop of New Zealand is opposing the government measure (→ 19/3/61).

The first tram, or street railway, in England has opened in Birkenhead with horses pulling carriages of 60-70 people along a two-mile route.

Europe welcomes end of Chinese war

French and British troops take Beijing

China, October
Beijing has this month fallen to an Anglo-French expeditionary force, ending hostilities that have flared up intermittently over the last 20 years as China strove to exclude the "barbarian" Europeans from its soil. Britain, determined to extend its trading activities, first took up arms against China in the first of the so-called "Opium Wars", which lasted from 1839 to 1842. The latest fighting started after British and French envoys were last year unexpectedly attacked on the Peiho river and forced to withdraw with heavy casualties. Both allied governments were also intent on thwarting Russian ambitions in China; and Britain wanted to force China to respect the two-year-old Treaty of Tientsin.

The emperor's summer palace was razed to the ground after the murder of officers who had been sent forward with a flag of truce.

Anglo-French troops occupy the summer palace in Beijing to end the war.

Ports open as treaty confirms end of strife

China, October
Britain's commercial penetration of China is set to deepen following the ending of hostilities between the two countries. With Beijing now in Anglo-French hands, the Chinese have been compelled to ratify the two-year-old Treaty of Tientsin, which they had previously refused to honour. Diplomatic representatives will now be exchanged and five Chinese "treaty ports" – Canton, Shanghai, Amoy, Fu-chou and Ning-po – will be thrown open to British traders.

Previously confined to the outskirts of Canton, the traders will now be able to reside in any of the five towns and their interests will be protected by consuls (→6).

Bishop leads attack on evolution theory

Oxford
Churchmen have attacked the theory of evolution propounded by Charles Darwin in his book *The Origin of Species* last year. In a debate staged here by the British Association, Samuel Wilberforce, the bishop of Oxford, renewed the attack on Darwin that he had first made in the *Quarterly Review*.

Wilberforce's attack on Darwin's "atheistic" principle prompted a spirited defence by Thomas Henry Huxley, a scientist noted for his study of morphology and marine organisms. Huxley pointed to the years of detailed study that had preceded Darwin's book and contrasted these with the lack of evidence offered by the bishop to sustain his critique. Bishop Wilberforce, undaunted by the criticisms, sought to mock the evolutionary view by asking Huxley whether he was descended from a monkey on his grandmother's or on his grandfather's side. The clash has polarized opinion between science and religion in a way that many moderates regret (→1868).

Nightingale opens her school for nurses

London
The ignorant, mostly illiterate and sometimes drunken nurses staffing British hospitals are about to be swept away. Florence Nightingale, a national heroine since her selfless work tending the wounded during the Crimean War, has set up at St Thomas's hospital the nation's first training school for nurses. The public has contributed £55,000.

Miss Nightingale, who comes from a well-to-do family and trained as a nurse in Germany, will now strive to alter the traditional British belief that nursing is unsuitable for ladies and fit for only low-grade domestics. She is laying down strict rules in the school: nurses must be fully literate, sober, honest, orderly, clean and neat. She will mark their notebooks once a month.

Dedicated to hospital reform and now an adviser to the government, Miss Nightingale says her work will extend beyond training nurses. She completely reorganized the military hospital at Scutari, Turkey, during the war, saving many lives not only by skilled nursing but also by improving sanitation and hygiene. Most hospitals in Britain are still bleak and very unhealthy institutions. Many patients die from cross-infections. Even mortuaries are unsealed (→29/11/1907).

Nightingale: on the home front.

London to have first underground railway

London
Work has started in London on building the world's first underground railway. Called the Metropolitan Railway, it will run for four miles (6.4km), linking Paddington, Euston and King's Cross stations with a terminus at Farringdon near Smithfield. To avoid demolishing buildings, the railway will be built mainly underneath existing roads. Using the "cut and cover" method, a trench up to 18 metres (59 feet) deep will be dug. The sides will then be bricked in, roofed over and the road surface replaced (→10/1/63).

Building work at King's Cross for the capital's new Metropolitan Railway.

1861

United States, 15 January. Terence McManus, a founder member of the Young Irelanders, dies in San Francisco (→ 10/11).

Oxford, 5 February. Fire damages Blenheim Palace.

Southern England, 21 February. Severe gales destroy part of Crystal Palace and bring down the steeple of Chichester cathedral.

New Zealand, 19 March. A temporary truce brings an end to the fighting between Maoris and British troops over a land purchase at the Waitari river (→ 5/1863).

Birmingham, 4 April. The Birmingham Free Library opens.

United States, 12 April. A civil war breaks out between the northern and southern states; Confederate soldiers make an attack on Charleston in South Carolina (→ 13/5).

Sydenham, 1 June. Charles Blondin, the famous tightrope walker who walked across Niagara Falls, gives his first performance of daredevil stunts in England, at Crystal Palace.

Ireland, 21 August. Queen Victoria and Prince Albert make a state visit to Ireland (→ 15/12).

York, 27 September. Five people are killed when an iron bridge under construction at Lendal collapses.

Australia, 19 October. News reaches England of a terrible massacre of English colonists by Aborigines in Queensland.

Dublin, 10 November. The funeral takes place of Terence McManus, who died in America earlier this year.

Dublin, 16 November. A scandal erupts over the prince of Wales's involvement with a young actress, Nellie Clifden (→ 10/3/63).

Florence, Italy. Elizabeth Barrett Browning, the poet and wife of Robert Browning, who is best known for her collection of poems entitled *Sonnets from the Portuguese*, dies (→ 1862).

London. Charles Dickens, the popular novelist, publishes the first episodes of his latest novel, *Great Expectations*, in the periodical *All the Year Round* (→ 9/6/70).

London. The Aerated Bread Company (ABC) opens the first teashop on the Strand.

Fleet Street faces a revolution as hopes for popular press are boosted by tax cuts

Libraries, as here in Manchester, offer expensive newspapers free.

Britain, 1 October

Newspapers for the millions and not just for the privileged few is the prospect now that the last of the "taxes on knowledge", the duty on paper, has been abolished. With effect from today, all newspaper prices are expected to fall, even that of *The Times*, and all circulations will probably rise.

It was in 1853 that the duty on advertisements was abolished; this was followed two years later by the abolition of the stamp duty on newspapers. This led to the first penny national, the *Daily Telegraph*, and turned the *Manchester Guardian*, the *Liverpool Daily Post* and *The Scotsman* from sickly weeklies into lusty dailies. This was not, however, to the liking of everybody in Fleet Street, because it also seemed to herald the end of a supposedly intelligent, socially superior press – and the beginning of a popular, less cultivated one.

This great social change, whether it is welcome or not, would now seem to be inevitable, as there appears to be a popular demand for such a press. There is a real prospect of a national daily newspaper being produced for as little as one half-pence per copy.

Cassell hits target again with 'Quiver'

London

John Cassell, the publisher and philanthropist, has founded yet another popular magazine: the *Quiver*. Since 1850 when Cassell published the *Working Man's Friend and Popular Instructor*, followed two years later by *Cassell's Popular Educator*, the former carpenter and reformed alcoholic has sold nearly 250 million copies of his penny publications.

With subscriptions to private libraries too expensive for working men and public libraries confined to the big cities, evangelical tracts and newspapers were all there were for the poor to read until Cassell began his penny publications.

William Morris, seen here at work on a loom, founded his own company this year to design and produce textiles and wallpaper.

Philosopher-genius publishes call for electoral reform

London

England's leading philosopher, John Stuart Mill, brought out two challenging new works this year: his treatises on *Utilitarianism* and *Considerations on Representative Government*. Mill, a genius who learnt Greek at the age of three, was schooled by his father in the theory of Jeremy Bentham that "the greatest happiness of the greatest number is the foundation of morals and legislation". Bentham held that humans seek pleasure and avoid pain and that this is the principle of utility underlying all actions; but Mill distinguishes different levels of pleasure or happiness. He writes: "It is better to be Socrates dissatisfied than a fool satisfied."

Mill: champion of freedom.

Besides criticizing the inhuman materialism of Bentham, he argues in *Representative Government* that free institutions are superior to even the most benevolent despotism, and proposes a system of proportional representation. Here he is following up the principles laid down in his essay *On Liberty* of two years ago.

These include the argument that an individual can only be restrained against his will in order to prevent harm to others – "his own good, physical or moral, is not sufficient warrant". Mill, who provides liberalism with intellectual bite, believes that the suppression of an opinion is never justified, even if we could be sure that it was false (→ 1867).

Britain is neutral in American civil war

London, 13 May
As a civil war divides the United States between north and south, Earl Russell, the foreign secretary, has announced that Britain will follow a policy of neutrality.

The Russell proclamation comes just 11 days after the Washington government announced a blockade of the southern ports. Lord Russell's proclamation, which carefully describes the southern states as "the states styling themselves the Confederate States of America", recognizes the South's right to belligerency without recognizing its right to independence. In addition it forbids British subjects from enlisting on either side. "We have not been involved in any way in that contest by any act or giving any advice in the matter," Russell said, "and for God's sake, let us if possible keep out of it."

British sympathies are against slavery (*Uncle Tom's Cabin* sold more copies here than in the US), but since President Lincoln said he would not interfere in slavery, opinion has shifted towards the "rebel" states, partly through fear of what Lincoln's blockade may do to our cotton industry (→5/1862).

Mrs Beeton shares her cooking know-how

A mouth-watering, waistline-stretching array of Mrs Beeton's desserts.

London
"As with the commander of an army, or the leader of any enterprise, so it is with the mistress of a house." The opening words of Isabella Beeton's *Book of Household Management*, published this year, put the work of the married woman and housewife into a proper context. Anyone who ever thought a woman's work easy and her days idle should read some of the 1,000 plus pages, or the 3,000 recipes. At the age of 25, Mrs Beeton, the wife of a publisher, has achieved a remarkable feat, having taken four years to write and edit her book.

An invaluable guide to the domestic services women provide, Mrs Beeton deals with every task: organizing the servants, shopping for and cooking meals, running an orderly home, care of children and a woman's role as doctor. The book is proving very popular, which will please many husbands.

Prince Albert dies, the consort who became a minister

London, 15 December
The bells of St Paul's have been tolling since midnight to announce the death of the Prince Consort. He died late yesterday evening of typhoid, at the age of just 42. Queen Victoria is distraught.

A German prince, Albert recognized from the day of his betrothal to Victoria in 1839 that "my future position will have its dark sides". Unpopular at first, mocked by *Punch* for his interest in uniforms and treated with suspicion by a parliament jealous of its rights, he won the nation's respect – though rarely its love – for his relentless and worthy hard work. In addition to being in effect the queen's private secretary, he threw himself into such causes as Army modernization, working-class housing, the choice of frescoes for the new Houses of Parliament, the reform of the university of Cambridge and the establishment of a second Irish university.

Prince Albert: he won respect.

His greatest work, however, was his encouragement of arts and industry, and if the 1851 Great Exhibition was his triumph, the new buildings in South Kensington – museums, colleges and art galleries – are his monument. "He was really a minister," said Florence Nightingale. "This very few knew. He neither liked nor was liked, but what he has done for this country no one knows" (→29/3/71).

Government to help workers save money

London, 8 February
New savings banks for low-paid working men are to be established in every post office in the land, the chancellor, William Gladstone, announced to the Commons today.

Savings banks do exist for the small investor, but there are only 600 in the country – and 15 counties have none at all. Besides, many of the saving banks are owned by local employers, and employees fear that their wages will be cut if their employers discover they are able to save from their wages. By using post offices to deposit and withdraw money, people in 3,000 towns and villages will have their own bank. The bill has been welcomed in the House. "The state provides beer shops for working men to spend their money," said one MP, "but has not been sufficiently forward in giving them the facilities for saving".

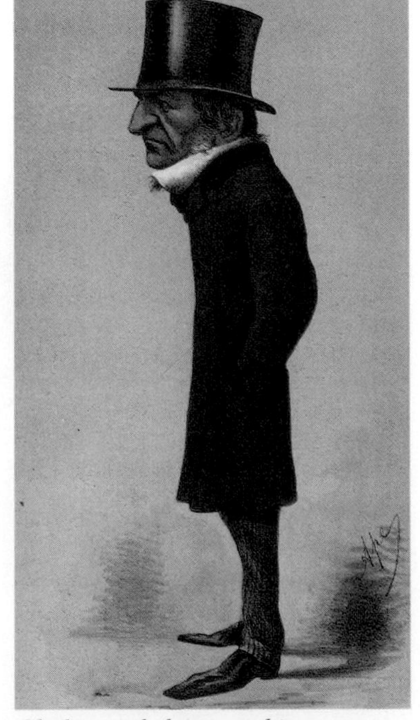

Gladstone: helping working men.

Payment by results plan for education

Westminster
A parliamentary commission into education has reported this year that 19 out of 20 children under the age of 11 are receiving some education. However, most leave school at 11 and many attend for fewer than 100 days a year. The commission, which was chaired by the duke of Newcastle, was not convinced that the quality of education was particularly good: they found little supervision and mostly untrained staff.

The report says that state funds should be allocated by results, in the hope that by pinning cash to targets standards will be raised. This suggestion seems more likely to be accepted by the government than a proposal by the commission for local boards of education, which ministers fear would start interdenominational rows.

1862

London, 1 May. The International Exhibition, a world trade fair, opens.

Westminster, 21 May. The new Westminster Bridge opens.

Liverpool, May. The *Alabama* is launched and sets sail for the United States to support the Confederate cause (→22/9).

Isle of Wight, 1 July. Princess Alice marries Prince Louis of Hesse and the Rhine.

Essex, 1 September. George Faux, aged 62, fails in his attempt to fly from the roof of his pub in Chigwell.

Wolverhampton, 5 September. Henry Coxwell, the aeronaut, and James Glashier, a meteorologist, achieve a record height of 8,850 metres (29,000 feet) in a balloon flight (→27/6/66).

Surrey, 6 September. John Bird Sumner, the archbishop of Canterbury, dies at Addington (→20/10).

United States, 22 September. President Abraham Lincoln surprises the British government by announcing that all slaves in the rebel southern states will be free from next year; but Britain stays neutral in the American civil war (→13/12).

Canterbury, 20 October. Charles Langley, the archbishop of York, is consecrated as the new archbishop of Canterbury.

Dublin, 22 October. The Dublin United Trades' Association is provisionally formed.

United States, 13 December. The Irish Brigade, led by Thomas Francis Meagher, suffers heavy losses at Fredericksburg, fighting in the civil war.→

Bristol. Clifton College opens.

London. Gilbert Scott designs a memorial to Prince Albert. This will stand opposite the Albert Hall, which is at present under construction.

London. Ebenezer Stevens, a baker of Cheapside, develops a bread-making machine.

London. *Last Poems*, by Elizabeth Barrett Browning, who died last year, is published posthumously (→1864).

London. Christina Rossetti, a deeply religious Anglo-Catholic poet, publishes her first collection of poems, *Goblin Market and other Poems*, to great acclaim.

Magazines flourish in literate society

Britain

Never has a higher proportion of the population been literate – and never have society's moral guardians been more worried about what the newly literate are reading.

The official definition of literacy is the ability to sign your own name. As the Registrar General of Births, Marriages and Deaths wrote last year: "If a man can write his own name, it may be presumed that he can read it when *written* by another; still more that he will recognize that and other familiar words when he sees them in print."

Magazines have multiplied to supply the new market. *The Illustrated London News* sells a quarter of a million copies each issue. *All The Year Round*, which started off two years ago serializing Charles Dickens's *A Tale of Two Cities*, sells 300,000 copies a week.

Their readership is mostly middle class. The working-class market is dominated by *Lloyd's* and *Reynold's*, with their weekly diet of murders, scandals, political analysis and popular science. These, of course, are the very magazines that the moralists condemn.

Italian politics foment riots in the park

Fighting breaks out in Hyde Park, London, with the police powerless.

London, 5 October

Hyde Park was the scene of sectarian riots today for the third Sunday running – with some 80,000 taking part in the disturbances. Today's riot followed a familiar pattern. Gangs of Irish immigrants, displaying Roman Catholic insignia and home-made banners, assembled to attack supporters of the Working Men's Garibaldian Fund Committee, who come each week to protest in support of Garibaldi and against the French occupation of Rome. Strengthened by Protestants, mostly immigrants from Ulster (few of whom have any idea who Signor Garibaldi is), the two groups – Irish Catholics on one side and republicans and Protestants on the other – clashed violently.

Today's rioting raged through the afternoon, centring on a mound in the park, dubbed by the rioters "The Redan", which both sides fought to occupy. About 100 off-duty Grenadier Guardsmen joined in on the side of the "Garibaldians" and eventually took it by storm. The police, to the discomfort of the home secretary, were powerless against such numbers (→4/1864).

Sligo link extends spider's web of Irish railways to west coast

Sligo, September

With the opening of the Longford/Sligo rail-link, it is now possible to travel under steam from Dublin to the north-west coast. The ever-growing spider's web of railway lines stretching out from Dublin has reached the Atlantic.

Ireland's first railway line, from Dublin to Kingstown, opened 31 years ago. It was six miles (9.6km) long. Ireland now has 1,598 miles of railways – a rather small amount compared to over 15,000 railway miles in Britain.

Things could have been otherwise. In 1847 Lord Bentinck proposed a bill to provide employment in Ireland, whereby the government would provide £200 for every £100 raised for railway construction. The bill was thrown out.

By then a few lines had already been built: from Dublin to Belfast and Cork; from Cork to Blackrock; from Belfast to Ballymena; and from Londonderry to Strabane. Railway construction has steadily increased since Bentinck's ill-fated bill, but at a slower rate than in England; most of the developments are extensions of the original lines.

In the north-west several of the extensions, such as the lines from Londonderry to Coleraine and to Lough Swilly, were combined with drainage projects. The majority of the new development has been in the industrialized north of the country, and the map of Ireland's railways shows not one, but two spider's webs: one spreading out from Dublin to Cork, Galway and now Sligo; the other spreading out from Belfast to Coleraine, Armagh and Londonderry (→11/1/64).

A viaduct of the Dublin/Belfast railway crosses the Boyne near Drogheda.

Shareholders win protection under a new company law

London
Shareholders no longer need be liable for the debts of companies in which they invest, according to a new Companies Act, passed by parliament this year.

Until 1855 shareholders had unlimited liability. The collapse of a company in which they had bought shares could result in personal ruin. Joint stock companies could secure the privilege of limited liability, but forming one was a complicated procedure. The latest act simplifies the whole process.

The act is unlikely to make a great deal of difference to the economy in the short term. Most industrial enterprises are still financed by venturing industrialists from their own profits, and there is neither a shortage of markets for British industry, nor a lack of capital, now that the Californian and Australian gold mines have been opened up.

In the long run, however, the new law, will make the home market attractive to the investor, at a time when more and more private investment is going abroad. Joint stock companies are spreading, particularly in the large-scale industries such as iron, shipbuilding and railways – the very industries that need a high capital outlay. The new Companies Act law on limited liability will make it much easier for these companies to raise capital.

Peabody Trust formed to help poor

Dudley Street, near Seven Dials, is all too typical a London scene.

Peabody: largesse for the poor.

London, March
George Peabody, an American millionaire and philanthropist, has established a trust to build sound and sanitary dwellings for working-class families at a reasonable rent. The first – which should be ready in two years' time – are to be built in Commercial Road, Spitalfields.

Housing for the deserving poor is not the only area that has benefited from Peabody's largesse. The Peabody Institute in Baltimore, Harvard University, numerous natural history museums and even an Arctic expedition have been funded from his millions. The new Peabody Trust is particularly welcomed by sanitation reformers.

The population of London has risen from one million in 1801 to three million. Housing conditions in the capital could not be worse. "Every night 100,000 men know not where they will lay their heads," writes the Russian refugee Alexander Herzen about London, "and the police often find women and children dead from hunger."

Some of the worst housing is concentrated around Spitalfields. One house off Commercial Road holds 60 people in eight rooms, with only nine beds in the whole house.

Equally notorious are the areas around Whitechapel, Drury Lane and Seven Dials. These are the poor lodging-house districts, where tuppence will secure a bundle of rags and a space on a bunk, amid pickpockets, prostitutes, vagrants and drunks. Yet for those thousands sleeping in the streets even these lodging houses – "hotbeds of unnatural vice", as the Manchester-based businessman and socialist Friederich Engels calls them – are a step upwards (→29/2/64).

Wales gets more training colleges

Wales
Plans have been made this year for a federal university for Wales, with colleges in Aberystwyth, Bangor, Cardiff, Swansea and Lampeter. A committee has been formed which has suggested that Aberystwyth should be the first college site – perhaps because it is equally inconvenient for both north and south Wales. Details will be discussed at next year's eisteddfod. A non-denominational training college for teachers opened this year at Bangor, joining Anglican colleges at Caernarfon and Carmarthen.

"Hammersmith Bridge on Boat Race Day" is a painting exhibited this year that has attracted praise – not least because the artist, Walter Greaves, is only 16 and makes his living as a Chelsea boat-builder.

Irish Brigade hit by losses in US war

Fredericksburg, 13 December
The Irish Brigade, led by Thomas Francis Meagher, has sustained heavy losses in an engagement at Fredericksburg. Meagher, a lawyer and former supporter of William Smith O'Brien, was arrested after the failed "Young Ireland" insurrection of 1848 and sentenced to penal servitude for life. He later escaped to America, where he joined the New York Bar. When the civil war broke out he became the organizer and brigadier-general of the Irish Brigade fighting for the Union (→8/5/63).

1863

Sheffield, 8 January. Yorkshire County Cricket Club is founded after a meeting at the Adelphi hotel (→12/8).

Belfast, February. The first issue of the *Irish Temperance League* is published.

Windsor, 10 March. The prince of Wales marries Princess Alexandra, the 18-year-old daughter of Prince Christian of Denmark.→

Dublin, 8 April. The Royal Dublin Society is presented with a collection of over 23,000 books belonging to Dr Jasper Joly.

Westminster, 20 April. Parliament passes an act enforcing the registration of all births and deaths in Ireland.

Dublin, 28 April. The foundation stone is laid of the Christian Brothers' School.

United States, 8 May. Thomas Francis Meagher, the commander of the Irish Brigade, resigns his commission in the US army on the grounds of discrimination against his men.

New Zealand, May. Fighting breaks out between Maoris and British settlers in Taranaki (→2/9/65).

Westminster, 24 June. Parliament passes the Revenue Act; this encourages the consumption of beer rather than spirits in Britain.

Hereford, 30 June. In an extravagant ceremony the cathedral is reopened after extensive renovations.

Southampton, 12 August. Hampshire cricket club is founded (→2/2/64).

Ireland, August. Catholic bishops condemn the Brotherhood of St Patrick, an organization which they believe has come under the influence of the Fenians (→27/3/64).

Ionian Islands, 14 November. The British government cedes the Ionian Islands to Greece.

Dublin, 28 November. The first issue of the *Irish People* is printed; it is run by Jeremiah O'Donovan Rossa, John O'Mahony and Thomas Clarke Luby (→15/9/65).

Glasgow. Dr Henry Littlejohn is appointed the city's first medical health officer.

London. Charles Kingsley, a novelist and clergyman, publishes *The Water Babies*.→

London underground railway opens

London, 10 January

Londoners got their first taste of subterranean living today when the Metropolitan Railway, linking Paddington, Euston, St Pancras, King's Cross and Farringdon stations, was opened to the public. It is the world's first underground railway.

Three years ago the first shaft was sunk in Euston Square. Since then 1,000 slum homes been demolished to make way for the railway, displacing 12,000 people. Yesterday the new railway was formally opened. From 6.00am today, the platforms have been packed as the trains – pulled by locomotives displaying dozens of exhaust pipes that divert the smoke and steam into a tank behind the engine – disgorge one set of passengers and swallow up another (→1884).

VIPs, including William Gladstone, have a preview of the new railway.

Pressure grows on universities to let women into higher education

Cambridge

The campaign by women to enter university made some progress this year when Emily Davies persuaded the Cambridge Examination Board to let girls sit the local examinations privately. This modest success will not yet bring girl students to our universities, or qualify them to take degrees, but it will provide a certificate when women are looking for work as teachers or governesses.

The right of women to education has found determined champions in Frances Mary Buss, the head of the North London Collegiate School for Girls, and Dorothea Beale, the principal of Cheltenham Ladies' College. Their success has so far been limited in terms of numbers, but it has been sufficient to stimulate a demand for women to have access to higher levels of education. There were angry scenes last year when a woman was not allowed to sit London University's matriculation examinations. (→1864).

Broadmoor asylum for criminally insane opens in Berkshire

The "airing court" at the new Broadmoor asylum for criminally insane inmates from all over Britain.

Crowthorne, Berkshire

On a remote heath a few miles from this village, work has been completed on a gaunt building of brick and stone – designed to hold as many as 600 inmates, all of them declared criminally insane. Built by convicts from Woking prison, the building has been given the equally gaunt title of Broadmoor. With the care of Britain's mentally ill a matter of great confusion – many paupers are being placed in lunatic asylums, while many lunatics are housed in workhouses and many more in private madhouses – this new institution will take inmates from all over Britain. It was not until 1845 that the building of county asylums became compulsory, but even so many local guardians treat the poor and the insane as equals under the law. Despite attempts by a few to improve conditions, "treatment" of inmates is harsh, with the mentally ill subjected to cruelty rather than handled with compassion.

Prince puts scandal behind him to wed a Danish princess

Windsor, 10 March
The prince of Wales was married today to Princess Alexandra of Denmark, and for once won the approval of his mother. Queen Victoria has not always been pleased by the behaviour of her high-spirited elder son Bertie, who is heir to the British throne.

She remains bitter over a scandal that linked the prince to an Irish actress, Nellie Clifden, during his stay at the Curragh military camp near Dublin two years ago. News of the affair shocked his parents, and Victoria blames Bertie's fall from strict moral standards for causing the illness that led to the death of her beloved consort, Prince Albert.

The prince recouped some of his lost favour by acquitting himself well during a five-month tour of the Middle East and European cities last year. "There's more to him than I thought," said Canon Arthur Stanley, a clergyman who accompanied the prince. But Victoria has resisted suggestions that Bertie, now 21, might be given a greater role in public life at home.

Differences were, however, forgotten today. Alexandra, aged 18, has charmed the queen as well as the prince, who first met the princess in September 1861 (→4/1868).

An illustration from the novel, "The Water Babies", by Charles Kingsley, which was published with great success this year.

British boxer is winner

Tom King, the English fighter (l), is attacked by America's John Heenan.

Wadhurst, Sussex, December
Bleeding heavily, his face disfigured after 25 rounds of bare-fisted boxing, John Heenan, the American champion, failed to leave his corner here and his British opponent, Tom King, was declared champion and winner of a £2,000 purse. A special train had brought 800 spectators to the field where the ring was built. Police officers were waiting at the station in case of trouble.

With his superior reach and superb figure, Heenan – "the mighty gladiator" – started as favourite in the betting, although the young British sailor was more popular with the crowd, who greeted his victory with "unbounded acclamation", according to the local paper.

New association lays down football rules

Football, a game for gentlemen and players, gains a new set of rules.

London, 26 October
No longer can a footballer – unless he is the goalkeeper – pick up the ball and run with it. Nor can he punch or gouge the opposition, under a set of rules agreed today in a Holborn tavern by the newly formed Football Association. Football has been played in Britain for centuries, often in streets or fields between neighbouring parishes, but it has also become popular at universities and public schools. Unfortunately there has been no agreement on rules as basic as how many players a side and how big the goals should be. In 1848 a group of public schools drew up what has become known as the "Cambridge rules". The first football club was formed in Sheffield in 1854, adding to the impetus for reform (→30/11/72).

William Thackeray dies, the cynical moralist of an age

London, 24 December
With the death today of William Makepeace Thackeray at the age of 53, English fiction has lost one of its sharpest observers, especially of the female sex. After the completion of *Vanity Fair* in 1848 he rivalled Charles Dickens for popularity and was called the Henry Fielding of the age, even though his robust cynicism can give way to passages of sentiment and moralizing.

Thackeray began adult life as an idle young man-about-town. His family fortunes were lost in India, forcing him to work first as an unsuccessful painter, then as a journalist. He became well known for his sketches and parodies in *Punch*, especially *The Snobs of England*, which became *The Book of Snobs*. His marriage turned out tragically. After bearing three daughters, his wife became insane.

W M Thackeray: sharp observer.

Soon afterwards, he fell in love with Jane Brookfield ,the wife of a friend, but she offered him only friendship: Major Dobbin's unrequited passion for Amelia in *Vanity Fair* was written from this experience. *Henry Esmond*, his historical novel set in Queen Anne's time, is a self-portrait in an age that would have suited him better. *Pendennis* and *The Newcomes* added to his reputation but *Vanity Fair* and Becky Sharp, the amoral but nevertheless amiable social climber, are his enduring monument.

1864

London, 11 January. Charing Cross railway station opens (→ 1/9/66).

Dublin, 30 January. The National Gallery of Ireland opens.

London, 2 February. Middlesex County Cricket Club is founded after a meeting in the London Tavern, Bishopsgate (→ 3/3/65).

London, 29 February. The Peabody Trust, established in 1862 to provide housing and funds for the poor, opens its first housing for the poor, in Spitalfields.

Sheffield, 11 March. Over 250 people drown when a reservoir dam, belonging to the Sheffield Water Co, bursts.

Dublin, 27 March. Archbishop Cullen, who has appealed to Rome for a definitive ruling on Fenianism, issues a pastoral for St Patrick's Day denouncing Fenianism (→ 8/8).

Dublin, 8 August. The foundation stone of the memorial to Daniel O'Connell, the Irish radical politician, is laid (→ 12/1864).

Belfast, 8 August. Sectarian rioting breaks out.

Nottingham, 10 August. Richard T Parker, aged 29, is hanged in public for the murder of his mother.

London, 8 November. Southwark bridge over the river Thames is opened to traffic.

Humberside. The first bridge across the river Trent, at Keadby, is completed.

London. A Working Women's College is founded in Bloomsbury (→ 11/10/66).

London. Robert Browning, the poet, publishes *Dramatis Personae*, a collection of poems which express his grief at the death of his wife, Elizabeth (→ 1869).

London. In an attempt to reduce drunkenness in the city, public houses will close between the hours of one and four in the afternoon.

Scotland. The Church of Scotland authorizes the singing of hymns.

Cardiff. New docks are built for the coal trade.

Britain. John Henry Newman, the theologian, writes an *Apologia pro Vita Sua*, in which he defends his conversion to the Roman Catholic faith.

London puts out red carpet for Garibaldi

London, April

London has gone wild over the visit of the Italian patriot and guerrilla fighter Giuseppe Garibaldi. He has been acclaimed almost as a national hero. He is mobbed wherever he goes, a new biscuit has been named after him and he has been received in the grandest houses in the land. Even the prince of Wales has been to see him, much to the disapproval of Queen Victoria.

The queen is in a quandary over men such as Garibaldi: she acknowledges that he is "honest, disinterested and brave", but he is nevertheless a revolutionary and in her opinion crowned heads would do well to keep their distance.

Marx plays key role in workers' society

Marx: philosopher of revolution.

London

The First International, more properly known as the International Working Men's Association, has been founded in London, with its general council drawn largely from among British trade union leaders and foreign exiles. Prominent among the latter is Karl Marx, the exiled German philosopher, who has been asked to draft the International's first address.

The position of the British trade unionists is, as usual, equivocal. In an organization that is unashamedly revolutionary, they are quite happy to foment revolution abroad, but make it clear that they have no wish to see such a thing at home. Few of the exiles can understand their attitude (→ 14/9/67).

Golf finds new followers as first all-English club opens in Devon

Lining up a putt before an attentive audience of players and caddies.

Westward Ho!, Devon

The boom in sport has boosted interest in old games as well as new. Golf has been played in Scotland for centuries, but it was not played in England until the Scots king, James VI, inherited the throne of England in 1603 and built a course at Blackheath, south of London.

Unfortunately, the hand-made leather balls were expensive and it is only the arrival of the cheap ball, made from rubber gutta-percha, that has made golf affordable. Now its popularity is spreading. The first all-English club, the Royal North Devon Club, was founded at Westward Ho! this year (→ 1866).

Brunel's suspension bridge over the Avon is at last completed

Bristol, December

The spectacular Clifton suspension bridge, linking Somerset and Gloucestershire 75 metres (245 feet) above the river Avon, has finally opened, 28 years after building began. Its designer, Isambard Kingdom Brunel, who submitted his plan in 1831, died five years ago. The foundation stone was laid in 1836 yet in 1840, when little except the foundations were complete, the money ran out. Rebuilding began four years ago and now the bridge, with a span of 702ft 3in and ironwork weighing about 1,500 tonnes, is a wonder of the age.

Brunel's magnificent legacy: the Clifton suspension bridge in Bristol.

'Co-ops' go from success to success

Manchester
The success of the Co-operative movement has been so astonishing that it is moving from retailing into the profitable wholesale business: the first Co-operative Wholesale Society was formed in Manchester this year.

The very first co-op was founded only 20 years ago by 28 Lancashire working men, who established a small shop in Toad Lane, Rochdale. They were all radicals – six of them were Chartists and most of the rest trade unionists. The idea was to give back the profits of the shop to the shoppers. The idea caught on immediately and now there are hundreds of "co-ops".

Venereal disease is rife in armed forces

Westminster
Venereal disease is so sapping the strength of the British armed forces that the government has been forced to act. It has brought in the Contagious Diseases Act, aimed at controlling the prostitutes who mill around all garrison and army and navy towns. The situation is serious, with anything up to one third of hospital admissions among the troops being caused by gonorrhoea or syphilis. The new act provides for the compulsory hospitalization of suspected prostitutes in protected districts in major military towns and cities such as Aldershot and Salisbury. It is hoped that this will diminish infection (→ 1866).

Catholic bishops launch a campaign for agrarian reform to head off the Fenians

The new association is intended to head off Fenian unrest, such as the prolonged sectarian rioting that broke out in Belfast in August 1863.

Dublin, December
Dr Paul Cullen, Dublin's Roman Catholic archbishop, has launched the National Association of Ireland in the Rotunda here. The Roman Catholic bishops are hoping to provide a constitutional alternative to Fenianism, during the instability of the current period of severe economic depression. The aims of this clerical pressure group are to have the Anglican church in Ireland disestablished, to secure compensation for tenants' improvements in the area of land reform, and to promote denominational education.

Since his return from Rome in 1849, Cullen has emerged as the dominant Irish prelate, with considerable power and influence. His new association does not have the unanimous support of Ireland's bishops, however, owing to Cullen's political disagreement with Archbishop McHale of Tuam over the Fenian question.

Cullen, who is known to oppose Fenianism or indeed any other political movement that does not primarily promote the interests of his church, is unpopular with politicians. His imposition of Roman discipline on the Irish church has been described as the "Cullenization of Ireland", while his promotion of the Roman Catholic ethos has served to heighten sectarian tensions, already exacerbated by Protestant attempts at proselytizing among the poor (→ 15/9/65).

Peasant poet ends his days in madhouse

Northampton
John Clare, "the peasant poet", has died in the Northampton county asylum where he has been confined for 20 years. The son of a farm labourer, he was working in the fields before he was seven. A copy of Thomson's *Seasons* inspired him with a love of poetry and his own *Poems Descriptive of Rural Life* appeared in 1820. They were favourably received and he met Coleridge, Hazlitt, Lamb and other patrons who provided him with £45 a year. His later work was not so well liked and he endured great poverty with his family. He continued to write poignant poetry in the asylum.

John Clare: country poet.

London is turning into an urban sprawl

London
London has grown so fast that it is now scarcely recognizable from the city of 50 years ago. Although by 1801 it was the biggest city in Europe, it was still a leafy, pleasant town of fewer than one million people. Today there are almost three million and the population is expanding faster than the city can manage. Plans are afoot for more roads and sewage systems. A new major road opened this year, for instance, between Blackfriars and London Bridge. This year has also seen the completion of a housing block for the poor of Spitalfields paid for by the American philanthropist George Peabody [*see report on page 923*]. Railways, too, are changing the capital, enabling more people to travel in for work and turning villages into suburbs. Following the opening of Victoria station in 1860, other stations opened this year at Charing Cross and Ludgate Hill. The underground Metropolitan Railway has been extended with overground lines to Hammersmith, with plans for extensions eastwards and new underground services elsewhere in the city.

The new block for the urban poor of Spitalfields, funded by Peabody.

1865

Worcester, 3 March. Worcestershire County Cricket Club is founded (→ 14/1/76).

Dewsbury, Yorkshire, March. Spinners strike for better pay and working conditions.

Dublin, 9 May. The prince of Wales opens the International Exhibition.

London, 20 July. The foundation stone of Blackfriars bridge is laid.

London, 25 July. The death of Dr James Barry, a surgeon in the British army since 1811, causes a huge scandal; he is discovered to be a woman in disguise.

Glasgow, 28 July. Edward Pritchard, a philandering doctor, is hanged after a sensational trial in which he is convicted of killing his wife and his mother-in-law.

London, July. William Booth holds the first meeting of a militarist Christian evangelist movement known as the Christian Revival Association.

New Zealand, 2 September. Fighting stops between British settlers and Maori tribes.

Dublin, 15 September. Police raid the offices of the *Irish People*; they arrest Jeremiah O'Donovan Rossa, the Fenian publisher, and Fenian employees (→ 16).

Dublin, 16 September. The last issue of the *Irish People* is printed (→ 11/11).

Derry, 10 October. Magee College is formally opened.

Westminster, October. Parliament abolishes the practice of transporting criminals to the colonies.

Dublin, 11 November. James Stephens, the Fenian leader, is arrested before his planned uprising can take place (→ 24).

Dublin, 24 November. James Stephens escapes from Richmond jail and flees to France.→

Manchester. The city death rate reaches 39 in every 1,000 due to insanitary living conditions.

Scotland. A report on the sanitary condition of Edinburgh paints a picture of filth and degradation.

Hampshire. Elizabeth Gaskell, best known for her novels *Mary Barton*, *North and South* and *Cranford*, and her biography of the novelist Charlotte Bronte, dies.

Unionists found a league for reform of voting system

London
A group of prominent trade union leaders has given the electoral reform movement new impetus by launching a Reform League with plans for mass rallies in Hyde Park to press demands for parliamentary elections on the basis of one man, one vote.

"There are one million voters in Britain," says George Howell, the bricklayers' leader and the secretary of the league, "but only one in ten belongs to the working class." Howell says six million adult males who pay taxes are denied the vote. Howell and his fellow trade unionists are backed by Ernest Jones and other veterans of the Chartist movement, as well as by a few middle-class sympathizers. The reform movement is gaining support in northern industrial towns.

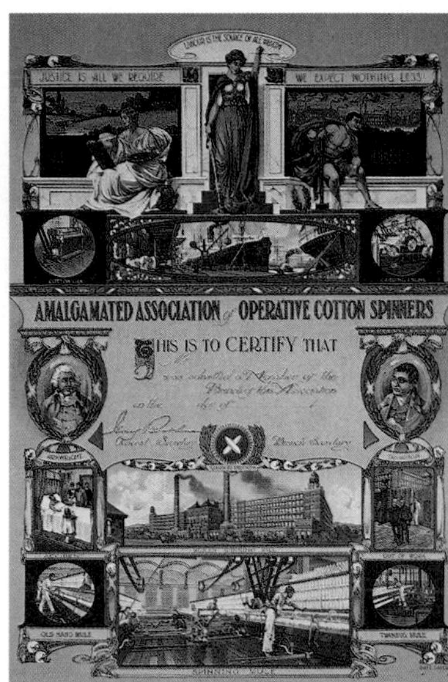

A cotton spinner's union certificate.

Last year a number of scattered groups, including the Leeds Working Men's Parliamentary Reform Committee and the Lancashire Reformers' Union, joined together to found the Reform Union in Manchester. Trade unions catering for skilled workers have been growing in size and influence in recent years; members of the prosperous Amalgamated Society of Engineers each contribute the unprecedentedly large amount of one shilling [5 pence] a week (→ 7/1866).

Colonial governor recalled over race riots

West Indians attack St Thomas's courthouse in Jamaica during the revolt.

London
Jamaica's colonial governor, Edward J Eyre, has been suspended and recalled to London to face an inquiry after he crushed a black uprising and, under a state of emergency, executed a mulatto preacher and member of the island's House of Assembly, whom he accused of instigating the revolt. The blacks were demanding the abolition of rent on their land. The affair has provoked furious controversy in Britain. John Stuart Mill, the philosopher and economist, has denounced Eyre as a tyrant, but the historian Thomas Carlyle, the poet Alfred Tennyson and the art critic and social reformer John Ruskin have all supported Eyre.

British mountaineers beat the Matterhorn

Zermatt, Switzerland, 15 July
The mighty Matterhorn has been conquered, but at heavy cost. Three of a party of four British climbers and one of four Alpine guides were killed while descending the 4,477-metre (14,688-foot) mountain on the Swiss/Italian border. The dead include the 18-year-old Lord Francis Douglas, the marquis of Queensberry's brother.

Edward Whymper: sole survivor.

The survivors, who came into Zermatt this morning, described how they reached the summit at noon yesterday and began their descent an hour later with Michael Croz, the senior guide, in the lead, followed by Robert Hadow. Hadow was seeking to secure his foothold when he slipped and fell on Croz; both went flying over a precipice, dragging with them the next two on the rope, the Reverend Charles Hudson and Lord Douglas. The three other guides and the sole British survivor, Edward Whymper, all braced themselves as the rope tightened and then broke. A search party found three of the bodies on a glacier 1,400 metres below the point where they went over the precipice. They were buried on the spot with a brief prayer. Lord Douglas's body is still missing.

Prison warders aid escape of Fenian

Dublin, 24 November
The Fenian leader James Stephens, who was arrested on 11 November, has made a sensational escape from Richmond jail, with the help of pro-Fenian warders. He is still in hiding and the episode has caused great embarrassment in government circles; rumours about an imminent Fenian rising have become almost a permanent feature of Irish life. Fenian recruits are busily drilling and are reported to have infiltrated the British army.

In an unusual development for a secret society, Stephens initiated a seditious newspaper, the *Irish People*, which advocated separation of church and state and preached a doctrine of physical force. He was arrested in a dawn raid on the newspaper's offices (→18/2/66).

James Stephens: flight to France.

Palmerston is succeeded by Russell

'Pam' dies after 40 years of power

London, 18 October
When news of Lord Palmerston's death reached the Stock Exchange today consuls fell by one quarter of a percentage point. Queen Victoria wrote in her diary: "Strange, and solemn, to think of that strong, determined man, with so much worldly ambition – gone." He had been staying with his wife in Hertfordshire when he caught a chill that developed into a violent fever. Vague with delirium, his mind turned to diplomacy and treaties. His last words were: "That's Article 98; now go on to the next." He died at 10.45 this morning, two weeks before his 81st birthday.

Palmerston was successively secretary for war and foreign secretary for more than 40 years, with only a brief spell in opposition; from 1855 until his death he was prime minister, again with only a brief spell out of office. "Pam", as he was known, was often accused of being a bully to the weak and a coward when faced by the strong. He did not see this as a reproach. He used England's power to further England's interests, but saw it as his duty to prevent England from becoming embroiled with powerful states that might gain the upper hand. He had no patience with "benevolence-mongers", or those who sought peace through pledges of goodwill. He argued that it was unreasonable to expect foreigners to be as trustworthy as the British.

Palmerston at the despatch box of the Commons as prime minister.

Champion of reform is the new premier

Russell: offended the queen.

Westminster, October
The new prime minister, John, Lord Russell, created Earl Russell four years ago, gained prominence for his support for electoral reform more than 40 years ago. He played a key role in framing the Reform Bill of 1832 and he plans to introduce a new bill next year. When he became foreign secretary he sought to keep England out of foreign disputes, standing back from the American civil war and Prussia's clash with Austria over Schleswig-Holstein. He offended Victoria by criticizing her opinions on foreign affairs and was obliged to apologize. He successfully opposed Palmerston's plan to use the navy to prevent Garibaldi conquering the kingdom of Naples (→12/3/66).

'Big Mac' to head national miners' union

Glasgow
Alexander "Big Mac" McDonald, who has become president of the recently formed National Miners' Union, must be the best-known trade union leader in Britain. It was McDonald's campaigning that led to the 1860 act of parliament permitting coalminers to elect checkweighmen to make sure miners are properly credited with the amount of coal they have hewn.

McDonald was eight when he first worked in the mines. He studied at evening classes and by the age of 25 he had saved enough money to go to Glasgow University. In many ways he is a typical Scottish trade union leader, a combination of personal respectability and public toughness. In his speeches he has urged his fellow workers to abjure drunkenness and vulgarity. His campaign to improve safety in mines brought him criticism from rankand-file miners when he accepted Lord Elcho, a Tory coal-owner from Fife, as an ally (→6/1868).

Richard Cobden, voice of free trade, dies

London, 2 April
Richard Cobden, who died today aged 60, was accepted as the true voice of the Manchester school of free trade and *laissez-faire*. In fact he was a Sussex man, born on a farm which had to be sold when his father died. Young Cobden became a clerk and then set up as a calico merchant before moving to Lancashire to run his calico-printing factory. He amassed a considerable fortune and in 1841 entered parliament. In the seven years he devoted to securing the repeal of the corn laws he neglected his business and faced ruin. Friends rallied round and raised £80,000 for him; he used part of the money to buy back his father's farmhouse at Dunford. Travelling widely in America and Europe, he worked for the promotion of peace and the reduction of armaments, which he saw as the logical extension of his free-trade policies. He mistrusted governments and turned down several offers of cabinet posts.

1866

Westminster, 18 February. Parliament suspends habeas corpus in Ireland in an attempt to halt further Fenian activity after the arrest of the leaders last year (→ 6/1866).

Westminster, 12 March. William Gladstone, the chancellor of the exchequer, introduces an electoral reform bill before the Commons (→ 25/6).

Edinburgh, 24 May. Prince Alfred is created the duke of Edinburgh.

Dublin, 22 June. Paul Cullen, the dynamic Catholic archbishop of Dublin, is created a cardinal, the first Irishman ever to achieve this rank.

Westminster, 25 June. Earl Russell resigns as prime minister, seven days after an Opposition amendment to the electoral reform bill was carried in the Commons (→ 7/1866).

London, 27 June. The first meeting of the newly formed Aeronautical Society of Great Britain is held (→ 1/1/68).

London, 23 July. A demonstration in favour of electoral reform ends in violence in Hyde Park (→ 8/1867).

London, 1 September. Canon Street railway station is opened (→ 1/4/76).

Dublin, 11 October. Alexandra College is opened for the education of young ladies (→ 12/1870).

Leeds, 17 November. More than 20 people have died over the last two days as torrential rain causes severe flooding.

Manchester, November. An association is founded to campaign for the closing of public houses on Sundays (→ 20/12).

Dublin, 20 December. The Irish Association is founded for the closing of public houses on Sundays.

England. Algernon Charles Swinburne publishes the first volume of *Poems and Ballads*.

Westminster. Parliament revises the Contagious Diseases Act; under the new terms, all prostitutes are to undergo three-monthly examinations (→ 1869).

St Andrews, Scotland. Tom Morris, the green-keeper of St Andrews golf club, wins the Open golf tournament for the fourth time in six years.

Fenian Army invades Canada from the US

Canada, June
Against his better judgement, one of the Fenian leaders in the United States, John O'Mahony, has been persuaded to invade Canada with the hope of defeating the British military forces there and then continuing to Ireland.

O'Mahony's first move, on 19 April, was an attempt to seize the island of Campo Bello off Maine, which is being disputed by Britain and the US. However, the engagement was shortlived because America's General Meade impounded the Fenian arms that had originally been sold to the Fenians by the American government.

O'Mahony's rivals, the Senate wing of the American Fenians, led by Colonel O'Neill, then took the initiative and crossed the Canadian border where they defeated 900 Canadian volunteers at the Battle of Ridgeway on 2 June, carrying a flag with the initials IRA (Irish Republican Army). British and American troops then cut off reinforcements. O'Neill was forced to retire, and was arrested. Another Fenian, General Speer, has stayed on with 1,000 troops but it seems the invasion is over (→ 11/2/67).

How the English see the Fenians.

Cholera epidemic savages Britain

London, September
For the fourth time in little more than 30 years cholera has struck in Britain. Though about 5,000 people have died within three weeks, the epidemic promises to be less severe than previous ones. In 1848-9 there were upwards of 70,000 deaths. At the time, John Snow, a doctor at St George's hospital, suggested cholera might be carried by water; he confirmed this in the 1854 epidemic when he traced the infection to a pump in the Broad Street area, where 600 people had died. In the present epidemic most of the deaths have been in the East End, which is not yet served by the new mains drainage system (→ 1872).

Public "disinfectors": unhygienic water supply carries the disease.

Economic crisis leads to a run on banks

London, August
The collapse of the reputable finance house of Overend and Gurney has caused panic in the City of London and led to a run on the banks. The government has given the Bank of England permission to step in and help firms in difficulties; in a single day the bank lent more than £4 million on the security of government stock. The bank rate has been raised to 10 per cent. Overend and Gurney had a high reputation as a discounting and billbroking house, but after two senior partners retired the firm moved into speculative dealings. When the firm turned itself into a limited liability company to raise more capital, its shares were snapped up by innocent investors; now these shares are worthless.

'Great Eastern' successfully lays transatlantic telegraph cable

Newfoundland, 26 July
Brunel's 12,000-tonne *Great Eastern* today steamed into Heart's Content Bay, Newfoundland, with the final length of a huge 2,300-mile (3,680-kilometre) underwater cable linking Britain and North America. Last year's attempt to lay the cable failed when it snapped while efforts were being made to raise it from 2,000 fathoms to repair a fault. The cable has been funded by governments on both sides of the Atlantic and by the American Cyrus Field, a one-time clerk who became a millionaire businessman. The first message, in Morse, will be transmitted tomorrow (→ 1870).

Transferring the Atlantic cable to the "Great Eastern" at Sheerness.

Riot pushes Lord Derby towards electoral reform

London, July

Electoral reform brought down the government of Earl Russell last month, but Lord Derby's minority Tory administration is preparing to produce its own reform proposals despite divisions in the cabinet.

The popular strength of feeling on electoral reform was dramatically illustrated on 23 July when the National Reform League defied a ban on meetings in Hyde Park. When a mass protest march in support of electoral reform reached the park, several thousand people broke away from the main procession, attacked police who had cordoned off Hyde Park and tore down railings. Order was restored only after Life Guards were deployed.

Gladstone out, Disraeli in: a change of fortunes for key political foes.

The will of the people: police efforts to turn back marchers calling for electoral reform led to a violent fracas on the borders of Hyde Park on 23 July.

The affray alarmed political leaders (and Queen Victoria) and gave new urgency to the issue, which has preoccupied parliament since the death of Palmerston last year. His successor, Lord Russell, backed by William Gladstone in the Commons, produced a bill extending the vote to householders in towns who pay £7 a year in rent and, in the counties, to those who pay £14 in rent. This ran into opposition from dissident Liberals and the Conservative opposition. Russell resigned after an Opposition amendment was carried last month, and Derby put together a Conservative government without a Commons majority. He and Benjamin Disraeli, who leads the Conservatives in the Commons, have concluded that reform is inevitable and are preparing to tackle the doubts of colleagues. In spite of substantial population movements, the distribution of seats is unchanged since 1832. Cornwall returns as many MPs as Middlesex and all the London boroughs north of the Thames. Over half the population has 34 MPs and the other half 300. Despite opposition, reform seems certain; the question is how far it will go (→23).

Working men and women form clubs

Britain, July

The clubs where working men can meet socially over a glass of beer have spread rapidly ever since the Reverend Henry Solly formed the Working Men's Club and Institute Union four years ago and set about soliciting donations from wealthy businessmen. Queen Victoria has herself responded by donating autographed copies of a book on the Prince Consort.

Solly saw the clubs as educational and beer was forbidden. But the working men who manage the clubs quietly restored the beer. The clubs are generally sparsely furnished, with few amenities, but for men accustomed to their dingy and cramped slum homes after long hours in the factory they offer comfort and even luxury.

"This is Henry Solly, my dear," a cabinet minister said, introducing the missionary clergyman to his wife, "who believes that Heaven consists of working men's clubs."

Improvements make Glasgow the 'second city of the Empire'

The private face: sordid slums.

The public face: the river Clyde at the heart of an expanding city.

Glasgow

The City Improvement Trust has been set up to carry out the systematic destruction of slum properties. It is only the latest of a number of reforms that have made Glasgow a by-word for enlightened local government.

The £1.5 million reservoir to bring water from Loch Katrine in the Trossachs, which was opened by Queen Victoria seven years ago, proved its value in the recent cholera epidemic: only 53 people died in Glasgow, while in the previous epidemic there were 4,000 deaths. Four years ago the corporation acquired powers to prevent overcrowding in working class homes. Then the city appointed its first Medical Officer of Health to tackle such health hazards as insanitary slaughterhouses.

Next year it intends to take over the city's gas supply and reckons it can cut prices.

1867

Chester, 11 February. Troops are sent to defend the city and the arms in Chester Castle from a 1,200-strong group of Fenians (→ 6/3).

Dublin, 6 March. Fenian violence breaks out (→ 17/8).

Westminster, 29 March. Parliament passes the British North America Act; the provinces of Nova Scotia, New Brunswick and Canada [Quebec and Ontario], are to be united into a self-governing nation known as the Dominion of Canada (→ 1/7).

Surrey, 14 July. Alfred Nobel, a Swedish inventor, demonstrates the use of a new substance, "dynamite", at Merstham quarry.

Manchester, 17 August. The Irish Republican Brotherhood convention appoints Colonel Thomas J Kelly, an Irish-American civil war veteran, to succeed James Stephens as leader (→ 18/9).

Glasgow, 9 September. Queen's Park football club, the first in Scotland, is founded.

Ireland, 12 September. The constabulary of Ireland is renamed the Royal Irish Constabulary (→ 9/8/70).

London, 14 September. Karl Marx, the exiled German who in 1848 wrote the *Communist Manifesto*, publishes the first part of a multi-volume work, *Das Kapital* (→ 14/3/83).

Manchester, 18 September. A mob of Fenians rescues Colonel Thomas J Kelly and Captain Timothy Deasy from a police van; in the struggle police sergeant Charles Brett is killed (→ 10/10).

Portland, 10 October. The *Hougoumont*, the only remaining convict ship, sails for Australia with 62 Fenian prisoners (→ 23/11).

Edinburgh, 6 November. The Scottish Women's Suffrage Society holds meets for the first time (→ 30/10/68).

Bradford. The wool exchange opens.

Westminster. In the first parliamentary debate on women's suffrage John Stuart Mill, MP and political writer, proposes an amendment to the reform bill, changing the word "man" to "person"; it is defeated (→ 1869).

East London. Thomas John Barnardo, a medical student, founds the East End Mission for Destitute Children (→ 1870).

Federation of Canada unites country

Ottawa, 1 July

The new Dominion of Canada came into existence today. From now on the four provinces of Quebec, New Brunswick, Nova Scotia and Ontario will form an almost completely self-governing federation. After many years of often bitter controversy, the British North America Act, which finally made this separation possible, was passed without debate. In fact many colonists complained that the British parliament showed little appreciation of the measure's importance. It went through, they claimed, like "a private bill uniting one or two English parishes".

Under its terms Queen Victoria and her successors remain titular monarchs, while responsibility for foreign affairs and the ultimate court of legal appeal will still rest in London. But otherwise the "Canadians" can look forward to virtually full independence. At some later stage it is expected they will be joined by the citizens of British Columbia and the North-West Territories – especially after the projected trans-continental railway has been built – but Newfoundland, on past form, will probably insist on going its own way.

The main question that has still to be settled is how decision-making will be shared between the individual provinces and the new federal capital in Ottawa. The act, say its critics, is long on principle but short on detail (→ 1/7/73).

Canadian representatives meet in London to forge the new federation.

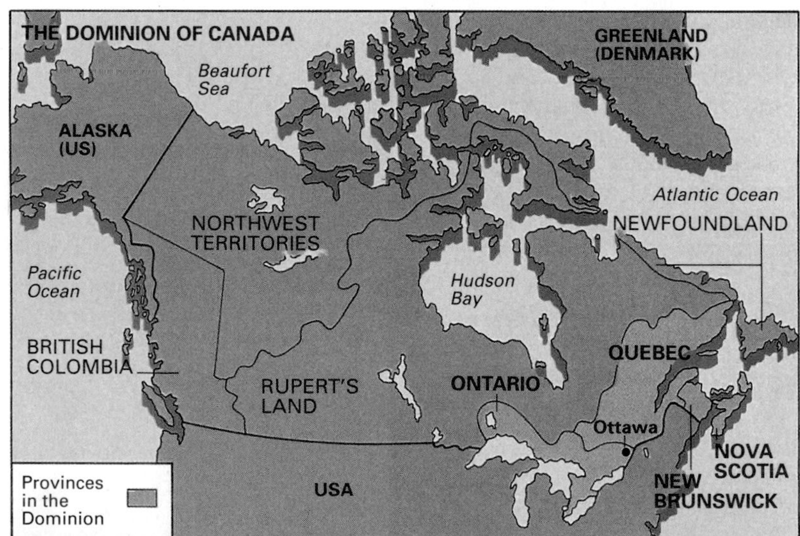

The map above shows the four provinces of the Dominion of Canada.

Dwarfed by his creations, the noted animal artist Sir Edwin Landseer sculpts the lions that are to appear at the foot of Nelson's Column in Trafalgar Square. The lions, started in 1857, were completed this year.

'Antiseptic' surgery is medical triumph

Edinburgh, December

New "antiseptic" surgical methods used by Dr Joseph Lister earlier this year to remove a cancerous growth from his sister's breast have proved a complete success. Isabella Pim spent a happy Christmas in excellent health, and her condition, which most medical specialists regarded as virtually inoperable, has not recurred.

Her case extends yet further Lister's triumphs, which he is reporting in the *Lancet*. Carbolic acid, he says, is insurance against gangrene and infection (→ 1869).

Parliament passes second Reform Act

Bagehot lays down the three rights of a modern monarch

London
It is a commonplace that Britain has an unwritten constitution, but a treatise published this year by a banker-journalist, Walter Bagehot, does much to explain its character and function. In *The British Constitution* Bagehot says parliament and the executive should not be separated on the American model. Cabinet government, he argues, is Britain's method of fusing them.

Bagehot does not believe the masses are "fit for an elective government", but sees society as evolving on Darwinian principles while held together by "the cake of custom" or conformity. The function of the monarchy is chiefly to provide this symbolic continuity and focus of national sentiment, rather than exercise any political power. He writes: "The sovereign has under a constitutional monarchy, such as ours, three rights: the right to be consulted, the right to encourage, the right to warn. And a king of great sense and sagacity would want no others."

Bagehot adds that "it is nice to trace how the actions of a retired widow and an unemployed youth (the prince of Wales) become of such importance". Maybe his cool analysis will improve the monarchy's present low public esteem.

Working men win the right to vote

Westminster, August
British working men are about to receive the right to vote, as parliament nears the end of its long debate on the second Reform Bill, which will shortly pass into law. At the bill's third reading, which has just been completed, the Conservative prime minister, Lord Derby, described the change as "a leap in the dark" but said that he had "the greatest confidence in the sound sense of my fellow-countrymen" and that he expected "the passing of the measure will tend to increase the loyalty and contentment of a great portion of her majesty's subjects".

The original draft was much less radical, but a string of amendments, most of them willingly conceded by the government as the price of getting the bill on the statute book, have progressively broadened its terms. The most important of these, extending the franchise to include not only full property owners but also lodgers and householders who pay rates indirectly as part of their rent, will between them transform the electoral rolls. Only John Stuart Mill's even more radical idea of introducing women's suffrage failed to win support (→15).

Disraeli: most eloquent supporter.

Derby "steals" reform as an issue.

Balance of power tilts to the cities

Britain, 15 August
The Reform Act, which became law today, effectively extends the right to vote to all adult males with an established place of residence. It is no longer necessary to be a significant property holder.

In future, to qualify for the franchise will require only continuous residence at the same address for at least a year, whether as lodger, tenant or owner-occupier. On this basis a city like Sheffield, with voters previously numbered in mere hundreds, will have virtually complete household suffrage. Protests that the reforms go too far were brushed aside by Benjamin Disraeli, the chancellor, who has been the bill's most eloquent supporter.

There have also been drastic changes in the allocation of parliamentary seats. Rural areas, which were over represented, will now see the balance of power tilted sharply in favour of populous urban districts and the big manufacturing cities. Liverpool, Manchester, Birmingham and Leeds will now have three MPs apiece. Separate but similar acts were passed for Scotland and Ireland. In Scotland the number of MPs is to be increased from 53 to 60 (→2/1868).

Faraday, the pioneer of electricity, dies

Hampton Court, 25 August
Michael Faraday, the man most clearly responsible for transforming electricity from scientific toy to potential power source, died here today, aged 75, in the house provided by an admiring Queen Victoria.

Although practically without formal education – he trained as a bookbinder – his experimental skills enabled him to establish the basic facts of electromagnetic induction (by which an electric current can be made to cause physical movement) and electrolysis (which is responsible for the phenomenon of electrochemical decomposition). As an immensely popular lecturer he introduced a whole generation to the joys of discovery and research.

Faraday: despite little education, he became a noted pioneer of science.

Popular Trollope completes Barset novels

London
The Last Chronicle of Barset is the sixth of the sequence of novels that Anthony Trollope has been writing since 1855. *Framley Parsonage* was written in six weeks for the launch of Thackeray's *Cornhill Magazine*. Trollope, who believes that a novelist is essentially a craftsman, writes 1,000 words an hour between 5.30 and 8.30am, before going to work as a surveyor for the Post Office. So believable are the characters of Barchester's Cathedral Close that one can hardly believe the author is not a clergyman. His creativity has also found expression at the Post Office, where he designed the red postboxes that are such an attractive feature of British streets (→1869).

Trollope: the fast-writing scribe of Barsetshire is turning to politics.

Arrests and betrayals in troubled Fenian revolt

Revolution in Ireland peters out following communication failures

Ireland, March
After repeated postponements, the long-awaited Fenian rising has failed, and sporadic outbreaks around the country have been easily subdued. Plans for the rising went seriously wrong last month when an ambitious scheme under Colonel John McCafferty was betrayed. He planned to seize the arsenal of Chester Castle, kidnap the mail train to Holyhead and then commandeer ships in the harbour to transport the arms to Dublin. Without arms the rising could not take place, but the Kerry Fenians did not get the message in time and rose under Colonel O'Connor. They captured the Kells coastguard station and then dispersed on hearing that the Chester plan had failed.

Meanwhile 1,000 Fenians assembled outside Dublin but were easily dispersed by the police, while a second detachment captured two police barracks. General Bourke's Tipperary Fenians were mostly unarmed and the military soon had them under control. Bourke has been taken into custody and will be tried for high treason. Troops have been dispatched to round up Fenians who are hiding in the hills despite miserable weather. Ordinary Irish people find recent events decidedly confusing, and seem to regard the Fenians as misguided enthusiasts (→6).

Police open fire on Fenian demonstrators at Tallaght, near Dublin.

'Manchester Martyrs' made to pay for embarrassing authorities

The Fenian prisoners are taken by armed escort to court in Manchester.

Irish eulogy for the "martyrs".

Manchester, 23 November
Three convicted Fenians, William Allen, Michael Larkin and Michael O'Brien, have been hanged at Salford jail; in Ireland they are being dubbed the "Manchester Martyrs". The three men were among those arrested following the sensational "springing" of Colonel Kelly and Captain Deasy from their prison van back in September, and were charged with the murder of Sergeant Brett.

Scores of other young Irishmen had also been taken into custody and were tried in an emotionally charged atmosphere. The continued court appearance of informers, such as the hated J J Corydon, on behalf of the state, raised anger in Ireland where strong doubts have been expressed about the fairness of the proceedings. During speeches from the dock, the accused men cried "God Save Ireland".

Priests in Ireland make the sacraments available to Fenians, and Archbishop McHale will officiate at a high mass in memory of the "Manchester Martyrs" (→12/1867).

Twelve die in major blast at London jail as plot goes wrong

London, December
In an attempt to rescue Fenian prisoners that has gone tragically wrong, 12 innocent people have been killed and almost 100 injured in an horrific explosion outside Clerkenwell detention centre.

Although the Fenian movement has reached a low ebb in Ireland, two active IRB units continue to operate in England, originally led by Colonel Thomas Kelly and Colonel Rickard O'Sullivan Burke, an ex-US Army engineer. O'Sullivan Burke was arrested and sent to Clerkenwell, and it was decided to rescue him by blowing down the wall of the prison by a gunpowder explosion, while he was exercising in the yard. It seems that O'Sullivan Burke masterminded Kelly's escape from a prison van last September, in which a prison officer was killed, and Kelly was returning the compliment.

Although an informer notified the authorities that there might be an explosion, they surprisingly ignored both the warning and the barrel propped against the prison wall, with the resultant loss of life. Irish public opinion has been outraged at the carnage, and heart-searching is believed to be going on in Fenian circles (→11/5/68).

The devastation at Clerkenwell.

1868

Sydenham, 1 January. John Stringfellow, an aeronautical designer, exhibits his steam-powered triplane, an untested prototype, at the first aeronautical show (→ 9/7/74).

London, 14 March. Elizabeth Lynn Linton, the first woman to be employed as a feature writer on an English newspaper, criticizes the modern young woman as "immodest, egotistical, self-assertive and unwomanly" in the *Saturday Review* (→ 1869).

Dublin, April. The prince and princess of Wales pay a state visit to Ireland (→ 1/8/71).

Yorkshire, 2 May. New public baths at Beverley are opened.

Lancashire, 11 May. Fenians riot at Ashton-under-Lyne (→ 26).

London, 26 May. The last public execution takes place at the Old Bailey; Michael Barratt is hanged for his part in the Fenian explosion in Clerkenwell last December (→ 12/11).

Dublin, 15 August. Irish teachers establish the Irish National Teachers Organization.

Surrey, 27 October. Charles Langley, the archbishop of Canterbury, dies at his home in Addington; his successor will be Campbell Tait, the bishop of London (→ 3/12/82).

Manchester, 30 October. The first meeting of the National Society for Women's Suffrage is held (→ 11/1868).

Dublin, 12 November. Isaac Butt, the political writer, presides over a meeting demanding an amnesty for all Fenian prisoners (→ 3/1869).

Westminster, 17 November. William Gladstone, the leader of the Liberals, defeats the Tory prime minister, Benjamin Disraeli, in the general election (→ 12/1868).

London, 1 December. Smithfield meat market is opened to members of the public.

London, 17 December. The London Association for the Prevention of Poverty and Crime is established.

Scotland. The Scottish Co-operative Wholesale Society is established.

London. Charles Darwin, the biologist, publishes *The Variation of Animals and Plants under Domestication* (→ 1871).

Disraeli climbs to 'top of the greasy pole'

Benjamin Disraeli addresses the Commons for the first time as premier.

Westminster, February

Britain's new prime minister is Benjamin Disraeli, the ambitious and wily parliamentary veteran who has revitalized the Conservatives with the passage of the Reform Act, which added more than one million voters to the electorate. He takes over from Lord Derby, who has resigned because of ill health.

Disraeli is quoted as saying about his new post: "Yes, I have climbed to the top of the greasy pole." But with a general election bound to follow the reforms enfranchizing most urban ratepayers, he may not be prime minister for long. William Gladstone, his Liberal rival, is trying to force the issue of an election by raising the Irish question. Disraeli, who is a favourite of Queen Victoria, has set out his idea of the perfect relationship between sovereign and minister in a letter to her – "on her part, perfect confidence, on his, perfect devotion" (→ 17/11).

Agency established for women's jobs

London

The most recent national census in 1861 showed 701,000 more women than men. With increasing numbers of middle-class women, unmarried and needing work to survive, Barbara Leigh Smith and Bessie Rayner Parkes this year opened a women's employment bureau here. The Association for the Promotion of the Employment of Women is intended to help guide such women into new types of work.

Women's work so far has encompassed nursing, teaching and the lowly paid, often poorly served, governesses. Now, women are urged to seek jobs as cooks, copyists of law papers, wood or ivory engravers, interior decorators, shoemakers, telegraphists, and printers' compositors. Some men may resent such moves (→ 1875).

Flogging in peace-time army banned

London

Much-needed reforms in the army are slowly being made. The latest is the ending of flogging in peace time. Hitherto flogging has been carried out for a limited number of offences, but it has been a common form of punishment. Up to 200 lashes can be imposed on a soldier found guilty at court martial.

Whole regiments are paraded to watch a flogging. When some 600 troops were ordered to witness a comrade being lashed at Aldershot recently, over 100 of the young soldiers fainted. Some of the officers present also left the scene to recover their composure (→ 17/8/71).

Outlawed: flogging in the army.

Revd Thomas Guthrie turns an Edinburgh church hall into a classroom for his "ragged school"; the new Liberal government elected this year has signalled its intention to promote major national education reforms.

▷

Pressure grows for radical reforms

First Trades Union Congress created as single organization

Manchester, June
With an eye to the expected battle with the government to win legal recognition, delegates from several trade unions in Britain have met and decided to set up a permanent organization. But at this first Trades Union Congress, divisions emerged over forming a common front against a forthcoming royal commission report that is expected to recommend only partial legalization of the unions.

Some delegates have argued for staying outside the law, and the powerful London Trades Council – which declined to hold the conference – wants to accept the royal commission's minority report. This document recommends legalizing unions and making their activities legal so long as they keep inside common law.

Over the last 30 years organized labour has been somewhat diverted from unionism by political causes like the Chartist movement which absorbed energies and resources. But many national craft unions are now emerging and they are putting the emphasis on friendly benefits, as well as on sick and unemployment pay. They are in favour of peaceful negotiations (→6/1871).

John Stuart Mill: philosophical champion of the female franchise.

Women's suffrage campaign goes public

London, November
Women are beginning to organize themselves in a campaign to be allowed to vote in general elections. They have taken the fight to the court of common pleas and were able to hire two top barristers to represent them. However, this test case, in which they argued that women were already legally enfranchised – because the word "person" was used in existing franchise laws – failed.

But those women in the flourishing suffrage societies are not downhearted. They are convinced that their campaign is unstoppable, and their case for equality with men is now being supported by politicians such as John Stuart Mill. The Commons have voted in principle in favour of female suffrage, but no government has given it serious consideration. The Liberal leadership believes that if women get the vote through household suffrage they will vote Conservative. Some Conservative leaders are in favour of votes for women, but their backbenchers are hostile (→1869).

Mr Punch, the policeman, proves powerless to stop union harassment.

Manchester, radical centre of England

Manchester
Manchester, the small market town that has become a great merchant and manufacturing city, is also the country's radical heart. This title was secured when Sam Nicholson, a local printer, initiated a meeting here this year of the first Trades Union Congress.

Earlier this century Manchester was also the home of the Anti-Corn Law League, led by local alderman Richard Cobden and textile manufacturer John Bright. Now Bright's brother Jacob is backing a campaign for women's suffrage launched here. It was in Manchester, too, that the Co-operative Wholesale Society was formed five years ago, in 1863.

The city began to expand a century ago when the Bridgewater canal – which runs right into the heart of Manchester – brought cheap coal. When it was extended, raw cotton was brought in and cotton mills multiplied. The arrival of the railway sparked still more commercial growth, attracting a vast increase in population – from some 75,000 in 1801 to 339,000 in the 1861 census – to work in factories and warehouses and, unfortunately, to live in slums.

Liberal government promises change

Westminster, December
With the Liberal Party's victory in the general election, William Ewart Gladstone has formed a ministry and become prime minister. He is promising a vast legislative programme of far-reaching reforms which will affect Ireland, the civil service, the army, education and the trades unions. Gladstone brings solid experience to the post. He is a master of parliamentary debate, and he has held many top posts in government (→1872).

Collins thrills public with mystery novel

Collins: success with a "thriller".

London
Wilkie Collins, a friend of Dickens and his collaborator on the magazines *Household Words* and *All the Year Round*, has brought out a new mystery novel, *The Moonstone*, which concerns a jewel stolen from an Indian idol. Collins is a master of suspense and sensational climax, as he showed in *The Woman in White*, a mystery crime novel of a new type, published in *Household Words* in 1860. In it the crime depends on the close resemblance of two women, one of whom turns out to be the illegitimate sister of the other. It is said that this "detective story" has influenced Dickens to emulate this sensational type of novel in his new work, *The Mystery of Edwin Drood* (→1889).

1869

London, 21 January. The lord chamberlain issues a warning to theatre managers over indecent dances and scanty dresses in their productions.

London, 31 March. Dockyards at Woolwich and Deptford are closed down.

Dublin, March. Following protest meetings, 49 Fenian prisoners are granted amnesty and released (→27/11).

Derry, 28 April. Religious rioting breaks out during the visit of Prince Arthur.

Westminster, July. William Gladstone, the Liberal prime minister, passes a bill which disestablishes the Anglican Church in Ireland.→

Liverpool, 28 October. The *Hibernian* sets sail for Canada with Maria Susan Rye and 68 children; she hopes to find homes and work for them with Canadian families.

Tipperary, 27 November. Jeremiah O'Donovan Rossa, the former editor of the Fenian periodical the *Irish People* who is serving a sentence on a treason-felony charge, is nominated and elected for the Tipperary vacancy in a by-election (→19/5/70).

London. Bedford College for women is opened (→12/1870).

London. John Stuart Mill, the political philosopher, publishes a controversial new book, *The Subjection of Women*; it demands emancipation for women and their equality with men (→8/5/73).

Westminster. Parliament passes the Municipal Franchise Bill which gives women ratepayers the right to vote in local elections (→1881).

Britain. Anthony Trollope, the novelist, publishes *Phineas Finn*.

Britain. Joseph Lister, the surgeon, introduces phenol as a form of disinfectant into his surgery; the higher standards of hygiene reduce the surgical death rate from 45 to 15 per cent.

Hertfordshire. A college for women which is linked with Cambridge University is founded, at Hitchin (→12/1870).

Stirling. After 13 years' work, the Wallace Monument is completed on the Abbey Craig.

London. Robert Browning publishes an epic poem *The Ring and the Book*; it is based on the story of a murder by an Italian aristocrat (→12/12/89).

Poet-critic hits out at religious decline in divided society

Arnold: moralist of society.

London

Culture and Anarchy is the title of a much-discussed book published this year, which trenchantly analyses the current age. It is by Matthew Arnold, the son of the famous Dr Arnold of Rugby. His spiritual home is Oxford, which he calls "sweet city with her dreaming spires" and "home of lost causes".

Arnold is a celebrated poet as well as serving as an inspector of schools. In 1865 he turned from poet to critic, leaving *The Scholar-Gipsy* and *Dover Beach*, a discomforting prophecy for an age that has lost its faith, as his major poetic works. In *Culture and Anarchy* he divides contemporary society into "barbarians, philistines and populace" – the three social classes.

The aristocrat "barbarians" and the brutalized "populace" are inaccessible to ideas while the middle-class "philistines" have "a stunted sense of beauty", a defective idea of religion and a materialism that "thinks it the highest pitch of civilization if railway trains run from Islington to Camberwell every quarter of an hour". Arnold places his hopes in the minority who seek after perfection – "the pursuit of perfection is the pursuit of sweetness and light ... to make reason and the will of God prevail". He dismisses the complacent self-satisfaction of contemporary England as spiritual anarchy.

Female emancipation campaign boosted by challenge to all-male medical course

Edinburgh

Sophia Jex-Blake is determined to shock the educational and medical establishments. Jex-Blake, who is 29, wants to become a doctor. And this year she became the first woman to be a medical student in Britain when, after initial resistance, the university here accepted her application.

Sophia Jex-Blake: putative doctor.

Jex-Blake has recently returned from America, where she worked in hospitals and where she met similar resistance at Harvard medical school. Her efforts recall the work of Emily Davies and Elizabeth Garrett in trying to open up the Oxford, Cambridge and London examination boards to women.

The current spate of magazine articles about the so-called "Girl of the Period" – based on last year's *Saturday Review* feature by Elizabeth Lynn Linton – makes academically minded young women angry. Linton, the first woman to hold a national feature-writing job, attacks the "bright young things" of today for having too much freedom and not enough of the traditional female virtues to make them attractive to men as wives.

Jex-Blake, Davies and Garrett do not object to husbands, but think there is more to women's fulfilment than marriage alone (→1872).

Beards in for sailors, moustaches out

London, June

Naval recruits are expected to sign up in their thousands, as a new dress code is announced – at the wishes of Queen Victoria. To make them stand out from soldiers, naval men and officers are to be clean-shaven or wear beards (but no moustaches) as soldiers favour hair on the upper lip. Following the uniform changes of 12 years ago – to the infamous "bluejackets", with their double-breasted monkey jackets of blue serge, bell-bottomed trousers and wide, straw-beribboned hats displaying the name of the ship – the latest uniforms are set to attract yet more eyes.

Races for bicycles (or velocipedes) were staged at Liverpool this year, drawing crowds to see competitors on machines first seen two years ago.

Douglas is new seat of Manx government

The parade at Douglas; the pretty port is now the capital of the Isle of Man.

Isle of Man
After a fierce battle, Douglas has ousted Castletown as the Manx capital: a state of affairs which the people of Castletown are finding it difficult to accept or forgive.

The rise of Douglas to pre-eminence among the individual communities on the Isle of Man is due to its deepwater harbour based directly on shale. Trade and industry are growing concerns.

Douglas has emerged as a fashionable town, with its Red Pier the source of pride. Government will be seated in the new capital, but civic affairs will still be controlled by smaller local authorities.

Church loses state link

Ireland, July
The Church of Ireland has been disestablished and from 1 January next year it will become a voluntary body. Despite opposition in England and Ireland, the act has passed the House of Lords and a major issue in last year's electoral policy of the prime minister, William Gladstone, has been resolved.

The act also provides for the disendowment of the church's landholdings, property and bequests, which are valued at £600,000 per annum. Apart from churches and churchyards, the rest of the holdings and property are to be vested in a body of Commissioners for Irish Church Temporalities. Compensation paid under the act will amount to £16 million, which represents about half of the value of the confiscated property. The remainder is to be used for the relief of poverty and as endowments for higher education. The land that the church is losing has been offered to tenants and some 6,000 are expected to avail themselves of the offer. Embodied in the legislation is a general disestablishment of all religion in Ireland. The existing grants to Maynooth College and to Presbyterian ministers have been abolished. Church of Ireland clergy will in future be paid by the Representative Church Body.

Gladstone (c) frees the Irish church.

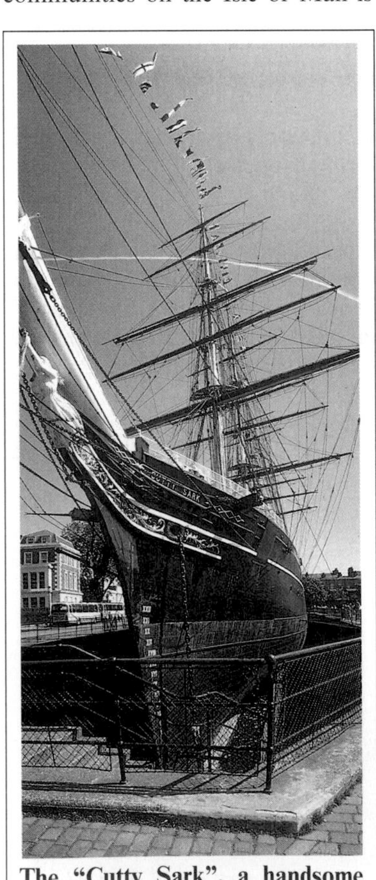
The "Cutty Sark", a handsome and speedy tea clipper, was built at Dumbarton this year.

Medical acts provoke fierce clash over government interference

Britain
Government acts calling for the preventative use of medicine are provoking angry public reaction. This year's Vaccination Act, which follows a previous act of 1853, is intended to protect public health in the wake of outbreaks of cholera and typhoid. But it is seen by many parents as an invasion of their rights. Some fear that their children might die as a result of vaccination and have formed an Anti-compulsory Vaccination League. This year has also seen a third Contagious Diseases Act, following two previous acts in 1864 and 1866, which has aroused a strong reaction. The acts are devised to prevent the spread of venereal disease in ports and army towns, and provide that anyone suspected of being a prostitute can be forcibly taken from the street and inspected for disease.

The campaign against the Contagious Diseases Acts is headed by Josephine Butler, the wife of a Liverpool college principal. Rallying against what she sees as a disregard of women's rights, she points out that the police can now forcibly investigate any or all women. Homeless girls are dragged away and painfully examined. One widow who was seen walking with soldiers committed suicide after investigation. Once cast as a prostitute, the only way out for a woman is to clear her name in the courts. Mrs Butler points the finger of blame at men. It is wrong to attack women as the carriers of venereal disease, she says, when it is men who seek prostitutes. Mrs Butler now leads the Ladies' Association for the Repeal of the Contagious Diseases Acts and has her own tract: *The Constitution Violated* (→15/4/86).

Mothers comfort children awaiting vaccination in London's East End.

1870

Westminster, January. Parliament passes the Tramway Act; local authorities can build municipal tramways.

Westminster, 10 February. The election as member of parliament for Tipperary of Jeremiah O'Donovan Rossa, the former editor of the *Irish People* who is serving a prison sentence on a treason-felony charge, is declared invalid by the Commons because he has been convicted as a felon (→ 19/5).

Europe, 19 July. France declares war on Prussia after the attempts by Prussia to place a junior member of the Prussian royal family on the Spanish throne (→ 4/9).

Britain, July. Britain declares its neutrality in the Franco-Prussian war despite the divided loyalties of the royal family; the princess of Wales is anti-Prussian while her husband believes the French are in the wrong.

Britain, 6 August. Lord Wantage founds the British Red Cross Society.

Westminster, 9 August. Parliament abolishes the city police force of Derry; the policing of the city will come under the control of the Royal Irish Constabulary.

Belfast, 27 August. The boat builders, Harland and Wolffe, launch *Oceanic*, the first White Star liner.

Dublin, 1 September. Isaac Butt's Home Government Association holds its first public meeting (→ 1/1871).

Paris, 4 September. France is declared a republic (→ 20).

Australia, 6 September. The last British troops serving in Australia are withdrawn.

Kent, 20 September. Empress Eugénie of France and her son, the Prince Imperial, settle at Chislehurst after escaping to safety on the capture of her husband, Napoleon III, by Prussian troops on 2 September (→ 8/10).

New York, September. The first issue of *Irish World* is printed by Patrick Ford.

Dublin, 8 October. Over 200 Irish volunteers set sail for Le Havre in France to assist the French in the Franco-Prussian war (→ 26/2/71).

Britain/India. The telegraph cable between Britain and India is opened (→ 3/6/71).

Irish 'home rule' movement is founded

Dublin, 19 May

Isaac Butt, a Protestant barrister and constitutional politician, today launched the Home Government Association to press for Irish home rule. He is president of the organization that protests about the treatment of Fenian prisoners in English and Irish jails, and is demanding an amnesty for political prisoners. While many Irish people consider the Fenian aims impractical, the plight of the imprisoned leaders has attracted considerable sympathy. For example, Jeremiah O'Donovan Rossa, the imprisoned editor of the *Irish People*, has had his hands handcuffed behind his back for 35 days continuously (→ 1/9).

Isaac Butt: Protestant home-ruler.

Act gives new rights to married women

Westminster, August

The much-vaunted Married Women's Property Act has become law, but some are calling it a "legislative abortion". Under the new law, women may retain money they have earned. With respect to property, however, they may only keep inherited property and money to the value of 200 guineas, together with savings and shares or other investments to the same amount.

The new law is not outstandingly generous, but it is being seen as a first step. Husbands no longer have right of ownership over their wives and all that belongs to them.

Doctor opens home to save abandoned boys from life on streets

Barnardo has taken pity on boys left to fend for themselves on the streets. In order to survive, many of them were forced to join gangs living by crime.

London

A great step forward in the fight against poverty was taken this year when Dr Thomas Barnardo, a Dublin-born physician who is already well known for his work in London's slums, opened a home for destitute boys at Stepney Causeway. The East End Juvenile Mission, based upon its founder's devout Christian principles, is designed to give the boys a chance to escape the streets, where poverty so often leads them into crime, and encourage a new sense of responsibility and discipline.

It is hoped that these "Barnardo boys", many of them orphans, and now freed of all the pressures of a degrading environment, will make a real contribution to society.

US yacht beats off stern British challenge in America's Cup race

New York City, August

The America's Cup, a yachting race between British and American vessels, was fought out along America's eastern seaboard this month, and the United States gained the victory. The first race, in 1851, took place around the Isle of Wight. America won then, and now the *Magic*, under Captain Osgood of the New York Yacht Club, has held off a new British challenger, the *Cumbria*. The winner takes a prize of 100 guineas and it is intended to make the competition a regular international event.

The "Cumbria" takes the race for the America's Cup across the Atlantic.

Charles Dickens dies, exhausted by fame

Dickens's dream: the author surrounded by characters from his novels.

Rochester, Kent, 9 June
Charles Dickens died suddenly tonight at the age of 58. His recent strenuous programme of public readings from his novels, here and in America, may well have contributed to his untimely death. He put into the readings all the energy that might have made him a great actor.

Dickens died at Gadshill, the house near Rochester that he had longed for as an impecunious youth and which he was able to buy in 1856. After *David Copperfield*, his favourite among his novels, written in 1850, a cornucopia of novels poured out: *Bleak House* (1853), *Hard Times* (1854), *Little Dorrit* (1857), *A Tale of Two Cities* (1859), *Great Expectations* (1861) and *Our Mutual Friend* (1865). When he died, he was still at work on *The Mystery of Edwin Drood.*

After his deprived childhood and the shortcomings of his education, Dickens made himself into a reporter and sketch writer before making his name with the *Pickwick Papers* at the age of 24. In 1858, he married Catherine Hogarth, the daughter of his editor, but his strongest affections were for her younger sister, Mary, who died suddenly in his arms at the age of 17. Her likeness is to be found in many of the sweet young girls in his novels.

Land act gives Irish tenants better deal as part of initiative to undermine unrest

An Irish tenant farmer, unable to pay his rent, is forcibly evicted.

Westminster, August
The 1870 Landlord and Tenant (Ireland) Act, which has been passed by Gladstone's government, is the first major piece of legislation to overturn the traditional relationship between landlord and tenant, which until now has favoured the landlord. Under the new act, a tenant may sell his right in his holding to anyone approved by the landlord; formerly, the landlord could recover the holding at the end of the lease. If a tenant surrenders his farm he has a right to compensation for improvements. And in future, landlords will only be permitted to evict for non-payment of rent – any other cause will now count as "disturbance", for which compensation must be paid.

On the insistence of John Bright, the member of parliament, what is being called the "Bright" clause has been added. This allows a tenant to purchase his holding by borrowing up to two-thirds of the price, repayable at the rate of five per cent over 35 years. The act, which follows from Gladstone's resolve to tackle the Irish problem, is being regarded with some scepticism. Landlords can still raise rents or refuse to renew leases, and the burden of purchase is thought to be too heavy for most tenants.

The Thames has gained a new north bank this year. Almost a decade of construction work has shifted the river's edge further south with the reclaimed land being used for new trunk sewers. In east London (right), work was under way by 1862 on the construction of new sewer outlets into the river Lea, which flows into the Thames near Blackwall. Further west, work on the embankment means that Somerset House (left) no longer has a river frontage.

Major Education Act means schools for all children

Local boards set up to manage schools

Westminster, 9 August
Parliament today passed the Education Act, designed by its proposer, William Forster "to supplement the present voluntary system ... to fill up the gaps at least cost of public money, with least loss of voluntary co-operation, and with most aid from the parents". The act allows churches to continue running their own schools and has increased their grants, but in school districts where the churches have failed to establish "efficient and suitable" schools, local school boards are to be established to build and run additional schools.

The school boards, to be elected by ratepayers, will have the power to require local authorities to raise a rate to help pay for the schools and will be able to enforce attendance. When Forster, who is the vice-president of the privy council's committee for education, first proposed the bill, it was well received; but it was later opposed by nonconformists who saw it as a means of preserving the Church of England's hold on education. William Gladstone, the prime minister, stood by the bill but accepted two amendments to meet the objections of the nonconformists. One makes religious instruction in the board schools non-denominational. The other, a "time-table" conscience clause, says that religious lessons must be held before or after the day's main lessons, thus enabling parents to withdraw their children more easily from religious lessons of which they do not approve.

THE THREE R'S; OR, BETTER LATE THAN NEVER.

William Forster (seated) tells children they will have an education ("Punch").

The slow progress to mass education

Westminster, 9 August
The Forster Education Act, which should ensure that every child in England and Wales receives an education, is the climax to a series of measures that started in 1833 when the government granted £20,000 to societies sponsored by the Church of England and nonconformists to build elementary schools. This was followed in 1856 by the establishment of a government education department and, two years later, by a royal commission to inquire into education in England. It recommended that there should be regular attendance, better teaching and a wider curriculum. These recommendations were incorporated in the revised code of 1862 under which grants were awarded to schools if their pupils could pass an examination in the "three Rs".

The act does not apply to Scotland, where mass education dates from 1560 and was given statutory backing in 1696 (→ 1872).

Universities bow to the tide of reform

Cambridge, December
Great developments are taking place in the ancient universities, with Oxford and Cambridge being dragged – albeit unwillingly – into the modern world. Nonconformists are already being admitted up to BA level and a bill is being prepared that will admit them to higher degrees, fellowships and the government of the universities.

The reformers are also seeking to change the system of admission to the colleges, throwing open to competition the scholarships and fellowships that are restricted to the founder's family or a particular school. Both universities, but especially Cambridge, are widening their curriculum to include science and mathematics. The next steps may be to allow the fellows to marry – a privilege at present reserved for heads of colleges – and to admit women as students.

How higher education has improved for middle-class women

Dorothea Beale and her staff at Cheltenham: fighting for women's rights.

The women's college at Hitchin, set up by untiring campaigner Emily Davies.

Cambridge, December
Middle-class women are gradually winning their battle to be given a higher education. Their latest success is to gain the right to sit the Cambridge Higher Examination. Leading the fight are Dorothea Beale, the principal of Cheltenham Ladies' College, and Frances Buss, who heads the North London Collegiate School for Ladies.

Another of the campaigners is Emily Davies, who has been in the forefront of efforts to open Cambridge university lectures and examinations to women. Last year she established a college at Hitchin that is linked with Cambridge. James Stuart, a young mathematics lecturer, is providing a great stimulus by giving open lectures at Cambridge. So many women attend his lectures that it has highlighted a need for safe accommodation; the campaigners hope that this will be the nucleus of Cambridge's first women's college (→ 1875).

1871

London, 25 January. The Royal Court Theatre opens.

Dublin, January. Thirty-three Fenian prisoners are granted an amnesty and released; among those released is Jeremiah O'Donovan Rossa, the former editor of the *Irish People* (→ 20/9).

London, 13 March. Britain, Russia, Germany, France, Austria, Turkey and Italy abrogate the 1856 Treaty of Paris, ending the Black Sea neutrality (→ 10/5).

Windsor, 21 March. Queen Victoria's fourth daughter, Princess Louise, marries John Campbell, Lord Lorne, the Liberal MP for Argyllshire and the heir to the duke of Argyll, in St George's Chapel.

London, 29 March. Queen Victoria opens the Royal Albert Hall (→ 29/2/72).

Germany, 10 May. France and Prussia sign a peace treaty in Frankfurt (→ 9/1/73).

London, 3 June. An underwater electric cable connecting Shanghai and London, via San Francisco, is opened (→ 9/5/1901).

London, 21 June. Queen Victoria opens St Thomas's hospital.

London, 29 June. The Metropolitan Board of Works purchases Hampstead Heath for £45,000.

Nottingham, 25 July. The Trent Bridge is officially opened to the public.

Dublin, 1 August. The prince of Wales opens the Royal Agricultural Exhibition (→ 26/12).

Westminster, 17 August. The Army Regulation Act, proposed by Edward Chadwell, the secretary of state for war, is passed; it abolishes the practice of purchasing a commission in the army.

Limerick, 20 September. Isaac Butt, the Protestant lawyer and founder of the Home Government Association, is elected MP for Limerick city in a by-election after six years outside parliament (→ 8/2/72).

Cork, 30 November. St Finnbarre's cathedral is consecrated.

Norfolk. Anna Sewell writes *Black Beauty*.

London. The Slade school of fine art is established, with funds donated by the art collector Felix Slade.

Union chiefs condemn law reform

Britain, June
The Trade Union Act, which has been steered through parliament by the home secretary, Henry Bruce, has aroused the hostility of many trade union leaders. Although it gives full legal status to the unions, and takes in some of the recent royal commission's recommendations, it also includes a clause relating to criminal law.

This is put forward as a restatement of the existing law. But to many unionists the clause creates a series of ambiguous offences that would effectively reduce the power of a trade union to picket. Since it is normal for employers to recruit alternative labour during a strike, the right to picket peacefully is seen as an essential weapon. It is the precise way in which the use of such words as "threats", "intimidation", "molestation", and "obstruction" will be interpreted in relation to picketing that is causing apprehension among trade unionists (→ 1872).

Iron and coal: as industries grow in size, so do their workers' demands.

Miners and pit owners clash in South Wales over the new laws

Wales, June
The passing of the Trade Union Act has strengthened the Amalgamated Association of Miners (AAM) by granting it legal recognition. This is a further victory for the AAM after a year which started with a depression in the Welsh coal trade and the pit owners giving notice of a five per cent reduction in wages. The AAM responded with a demand for a ten per cent rise, which led to a long and bitter trial of strength and a strike by 11,000 men from the Rhondda and Aberdare pits. After 12 weeks on strike, they returned to work pending arbitration, the result of which won the miners an increase in their wages.

The victory has, however, led to the closing of ranks among pit owners and induced them to form the Monmouthshire and South Wales Coal-Owners' Association.

'Bank holidays' to give four days off

Westminster
Sir John Lubbock, the Liberal MP for Maidstone, has sponsored an act that will provide the public with four extra "bank" holidays. These will fall on Boxing Day in England – New Year's Day in Scotland; on Easter Monday, except in Scotland; Whit Monday, but in Scotland the first Monday in May; and the first Monday in August.

The benefit of these extra days will be particularly significant to the lower middle classes – whose leisure hours are greatly restricted. Workers in industry have unpaid holidays each year when the works are closed for maintenance.

Alice travels 'Through the Looking Glass'

Alice and the Cheshire Cat.

London
The long-awaited sequel to *Alice's Adventures in Wonderland* has appeared. *Through the Looking Glass and What Alice Found There* continues her adventures among creatures from the world of chess and has the same dreamlike qualities that made Alice appeal to adults as much as to children. Lewis Carroll, the author, is the pen-name of Charles Dodgson, a mathematics lecturer at Christ Church, Oxford. He wrote the original story for Alice Liddell, the daughter of the college dean. His interest in riddles and "improving" rhymes in children's books, which he parodies, combine to give these books a unique quality with a remarkably wide appeal (→ 1898).

Darwin adds to his evolution theories

London
Twelve years after he first set the world arguing with his *Origin of Species*, Charles Darwin has published the major statement of his theories, *The Descent of Man*. In it he makes his definitive claim that man is descended by evolution from "some less highly organized form" and that "he who is not content to look, like a savage, at the phenomena of nature as disconnected, cannot any longer believe that man was a separate act of creation".

"Man is descended from a hairy, tailed quadruped, probably arboreal in its habits," he writes. Despite this Darwin believes that the development of human intellect and moral sense can be explained by selection, the success of superior individuals in propagating the species. "My conclusions will be denounced by some as highly irreligious," he writes (→ 9/4/82).

Cartoon of Darwin with an ape.

Explorer Stanley discovers Dr Livingstone

Central Africa, 13 November
Dr David Livingstone, the Scottish missionary and explorer, has been found alive at Ujiji on the edge of Lake Tanganyika, putting to rest fears that he had died four years ago. A *New York Herald* correspondent, the Welshman Henry Morton Stanley, had been sent by the paper to locate the whereabouts of Livingstone. When he finally found him, he saw "an old man" among some Arabs. Then Stanley lifted his hat and said: "Dr Livingstone, I presume?" to which he received the flat reply: "Yes". Stanley's words were the first Livingstone had heard spoken by a European in five years. They spent the next four months exploring together to the north and east. But when Stanley tried to persuade the frail and sickly doctor to return home with him, he refused, and continued in his quest to trace the source of the Nile (→ 1/5/73).

Stanley: journalist turned explorer.

German strength is test for diplomacy

London, 26 February
With a peace treaty signed today at Versailles following last year's German defeat of France, British diplomacy is bracing itself to tackle new and formidable problems. The old European order is now cracked, with a newly powerful Germany poised to send troops into Paris and demonstrate its mastery. An era of armed peace appears to have begun and the British government – long absorbed by home affairs and the empire – is starting to wake up to the existence of a German menace.

Britain did its best to mediate in the row between the Prussians and the French, only to become equally unpopular with both sides. Failures of British diplomacy led to London becoming an uncommitted, uneasy spectator in the struggle.

London is currently the setting for a conference of seven powers – Britain, Russia, Germany, France, Austria, Turkey and Italy – over Russia's repudiation of the Black Sea clauses of the 1856 Treaty of Paris which followed the Crimea war. Britain is attempting to uphold the principles of international law and a compromise is considered to be the likely outcome (→ 13/3).

Prince's recovery counters republican tide

Britain, 26 December
The crisis that has surrounded the future of the monarchy as republicanism grew has subsided since the prince of Wales's recovery from typhoid fever. Throughout his illness, Queen Victoria watched over him from behind a screen. On 14 December – the exact anniversary of the death of Prince Albert ten years ago from similar causes – he took a turn for the better.

Popular sympathy for the queen seems likely to sweep away the agitation which was aroused last month by the politician, Sir Charles Dilke. His speech at Newcastle criticizing Queen Victoria for not attending to her duties, and advocating that she be deposed and a republic set up, was widely publicized. Despite reactions of private and public hostility to his views, the government was clearly troubled, as republican feelings appear to have been gaining ground in working-class areas. Relations between the queen and the prime minister, William Gladstone, were further strained by his failure to admonish Dilke publicly. Gladstone did not wish to give Dilke any further publicity (→ 3/11/74).

The Royal Albert Hall: opened this year as a memorial to Prince Albert.

Rush for diamonds in southern Africa

Southern Africa, 27 October
Britain has annexed the diamond region of Griqualand West on the lower Vaal four years after the discovery of diamonds at Kimberley. This discovery sparked a diamond rush and precipitated frontier problems in some of the early mining settlements. The area was claimed both by the Transvaal, citing the Bloemfontein Convention, and the African Griqua, who argued they were entitled to British protection.

Independent arbitration found in favour of the Griqua to the exclusion of the Transvaal. Britain has now gone further and annexed the area, with a view to establishing it as a separate crown colony in the near future.

Thousands of prospectors have been streaming into the region ever since diamonds were first discovered. Many of them are veterans from the Californian and Australian gold rushes – men who call themselves "diggers" after the Australian term. But the term has little to do with what they do. Digging is done by the many thousands of blacks who have migrated to the mines in search of work. They form Africa's first industrial proletariat.

1872

Galway, 8 February. Captain John Philip Nolan, a supporter of Irish home rule, defeats William Le Poer Trench, a Conservative, in a by-election (→2/5).

London, 29 February. Arthur O'Connell, a young Irishman, is arrested following his attack on Queen Victoria with an unloaded pistol (→9/4).

West Africa, 6 April. The British seize the Dutch forts on the Gold Coast.

London, 9 April. Arthur O'Connell pleads guilty and is sentenced to flogging and imprisonment (→1/5/76).

Westminster, 2 May. William Gladstone, the prime minister, makes his first speech in the House of Commons for Irish home rule (→8/1/73).

Liverpool, 20 May. Prince Arthur opens Sefton Park to the public.

London, 19 June. The builders' strike, which began early this month, is brought to an end as both employers and employees agree to negotiate.

Belfast, 20 August. Sectarian rioting follows the Catholic Feast of the Assumption procession.

Belfast, 28 August. The first horse-drawn tramcars run (→1883).

London, September. An epidemic of smallpox sweeps through the city.

England, October. The League of the Cross, a Catholic abstinence society, is founded.

London, 5 November. Roundell Palmer, Lord Selborne, the lord chancellor, opens the new city library and museum at the Guildhall.

Scotland. A new Education Act makes school compulsory for children aged between five and 13; new school boards will run the system, with aid for poorer families, under a Scottish education department (→1876).

Warwickshire. Joseph Arch of Barford founds the National Agricultural Labourers' Union (→1875).

Britain. Samuel Butler, the satirist and scientific writer, publishes *Erewhon*, a Utopian satire on religious morals.

Glasgow. Rangers football club is formed.

London. The London School of Medicine for women is established (→11/8/76).

Lord Mayo, India's viceroy, assassinated

The moment of death for Mayo.

India, 8 February
The viceroy of India, Lord Mayo, has been murdered. He was visiting a penal colony in the Andaman Islands when he was stabbed by an Indian nationalist. Mayo was appointed in 1868 and pursued a conciliatory policy. He corrected the deficit caused by his predecessor's lavish public works by increasing the salt and income taxes, and he reformed local government. He sought peace with the Afghans, and settled Afghanistan's frontier with Russia on the Oxus.

He continued the reforms provoked by the 1857 mutiny. The princes are now conciliated and consulted, but they no longer enjoy their old authority. The army is firmly under British control and the protection of tenants' rights keeps the peasantry quiet. Railways have transformed the country, and a modern legal system has been installed. But these reforms have been in place for some time.

The current government is able, but remote from the people. Three universities, in Calcutta, Madras and Bombay, were founded at the time of the mutiny, and these now produce regular crops of educated young people. They play little part in government, however, and there are signs of growing disenchantment with British rule.

First tramcars take to the roads in Dublin

Trams must share Dublin's roads with a variety of forms of transport.

Dublin
Dublin's first street tramway was inaugurated earlier this year, beating the city of Cork to it by only a few months. Ireland's first permanent horse tramway company is operating services along a line from Hoggins Green [College Green] to Garville Avenue. It is proving very popular and will probably be extended to all parts of the city. Not only is the word "tram" of Irish origin, but the first horse street tramway system in the world, in New York City, was invented by an Irishman, John Stephenson, with financial backing from his fellow exiles. The first horse-drawn street tramway in Europe was at Birkenhead in 1860. It was developed by a colourful American, appropriately called George Train (→28/8).

The fight begins for football honours

Heading towards goal at Glasgow.

Glasgow, 30 November
The first "international" football match took place today at Queen's Park, Glasgow, between England and Scotland. It ended in a goalless draw. Teams and supporters can now travel by rail all over the country for matches, and the spread of the Saturday half-day has allowed the game to become the favourite entertainment of working men.

The Football Association, founded in 1863, set the rules of the game and started a competition last year. Only 15 teams, mostly from public schools, have entered for the cup, but that is sure to change. Many clubs in northern England have found football so popular that they can charge admission (→13/3/74).

Rival players tussle for the ball.

Voters gain privacy of polling-booth

Westminster
The government has passed the Ballot Act, after 50 years of pressure for change from reformers. Voters will now choose their members of parliament by marking a ballot paper in the secrecy of a voting-booth, instead of raising their hands in a public meeting or announcing their individual votes to the returning officer.

This is the latest of a long series of reforms introduced by William Gladstone, the Liberal prime minister. Reformers claim that voters were often intimidated by their bosses or landlords. If so, the act should help the Liberals.

How much intimidation exists is hard to establish, but it is widely felt at Westminster that it is worst in Ireland, where voters are often intimidated by their landlords. One Irish MP, Charles Stewart Parnell, says: "Now, something can be done, if full advantage will be taken of this Ballot Act." He thinks that "an independent Irish party, free from the touch of English influence, could be elected under the act". This is not what Gladstone has in mind (→ 2/1873).

Licensing Act tightened to curb drunks

A London pub scene: better England free than sober, says one bishop.

Westminster
The new Licensing Act has provoked riots and disturbances all over Britain and has made the Liberal government very unpopular. Every pub in the country is now a hotbed of Tory propaganda, with the Tory party presenting itself as the defender of the working man. The act has put all liquor retailers under magistrates' control and regulated opening hours, in an attempt to limit drunkeness. Thousands of beer shops have closed and the pubs have profited greatly. Pubs already play a key role in working-class life and now that role is being strengthened. The law is so unpopular because it is seen as as an attack on individual freedom. The bishop of Peterborough said: "Better England free than England sober."

Novel captures life of a provincial town

London
The appearance of *Middlemarch* has put the name of George Eliot high above most novelists of the day. Subtitled "A Study of Provincial Life", it contains some 50 characters who represent a Midlands society in a state of change. The spread of the railways, the state of medicine, political reform, the frustration of gifted women by custom – all these are themes the author draws into her wide net. "Her" net, because it is well known that the *nom de plume* conceals the name of Mary Ann Evans, a long-time companion of George Henry Lewes and the author of *Adam Bede* and *The Mill on the Floss* (→ 1876).

Mary Evans, alias "George Eliot".

University College opens in Aberystwyth

Once a hotel, now home to the first university students at Aberystwyth.

Aberystwyth
The first university college in Wales has opened here, with 25 students in a bankrupt railway hotel. A group of Welsh exiles in London started raising money for the college in 1863, and are counting on small donations to keep it going. The college is a sign of the growing national consciousness of the Welsh people and their pride in their history and traditions. There are already Welsh schools and teacher training colleges. Welsh nonconformists have long resisted the Church of England, which until recently had a monopoly of English higher education.

Act makes health officers compulsory

Westminster
This year's Sanitary Act has completed the reforms in public health begun last year with the creation of of the Local Government Board. The whole country is to be divided up into sanitary areas, each with its own medical officer of health and an inspector of nuisances.

The proposed reform met with strong opposition in many places. But the long epidemic of cholera has at last been brought under control by the provision of clean water and the proper treatment of sewage, and that success finally overcame the opposition to a national sanitary policy.

The new demand for cleanliness in public places has already changed the whole face of Britain's cities, which are no longer filled with filth, harbouring disease, as they were just a few years ago (→ 1875).

No sign of life on the 'Mary Celeste'

Atlantic Ocean, December
A British freighter has made an extraordinary discovery in the middle of the Atlantic ocean. The American brig *Mary Celeste*, sailing from New York to Genoa with a cargo of alcohol, was found abandoned and lifeless, her sails flapping in the wind, and no sign of her crew. The brig's boats were all missing, but the table in the saloon was set for tea. The cargo was intact, there were no signs of mutiny or piracy or any sort of violence. There had been no storms before she was found nor was she leaking or in any danger of sinking. The freighter searched for the missing boats for days. But it found nothing.

1873

Manchester, 8 January. Isaac Butt, the MP for Limerick and the founder of the Irish Home Rule Association, addresses a large meeting in the Free Trade Hall (→ 17/3).

Kent, 9 January. The deposed emperor, Louis Napoleon Bonaparte III of France, who has lived at Chislehurst in Kent since his deposition in 1870, dies.

Dublin, January. Patrick Weston Joyce publishes *Ancient Irish Music*.

Greenwich, 1 February. The Royal Naval College opens.

Westminster, early February. William Gladstone, the prime minister, proposes the Irish University Bill; radical reforms will amalgamate colleges and universities, and many annual grants will be cut or stopped (→ 8).

Ireland, 8 February. Irish Catholic bishops express disapproval of the University Bill, which will not provide them or a hoped-for Catholic university with state aid (→ 13/3).

Westminster, 13 March. Following the defeat of the Irish University Bill, Gladstone is forced to resign as prime minister (→ 19).

Dublin, 17 March. The convention of the Irish Republican Brotherhood adopts a new constitution, replacing the Irish Constitution of August 1869 (→ 21/11).

Westminster, 19 March. Gladstone returns to office as prime minister.→

Canada, 23 May. A police force is founded, they are to be known as the North West Mounted Police force.

Canada, 1 July. Prince Edward Island officially joins the Dominion of Canada.

Britain, September. An advance force under Sir Garnet Wolseley is despatched to Britain's Gold Coast colony [Ghana] where the Asante tribe under its king, Kofi Kari-kari ("King Coffee"), is threatening British interests; a support army of 2,400 men will follow (→ 12/1873).

Dublin, 21 November. The Home Rule League is founded after a successful three-day conference (→ 7/1874).

Scotland. A religious revival begins, inspired by two American evangelists, D L Moody and I D Sankey.

Irish Bill creates dilemma for Gladstone

Westminster, 19 March

William Gladstone is in a worse mess than ever over his defeat on the Irish University Bill on 12 March. Although Gladstone resigned, Benjamin Disraeli, the Conservative leader, refused to accept the premiership. Shrewdly, Disraeli realized that he had nothing to gain and much to lose in forming a minority government with weak and divided coalition partners. Moreover, Disraeli believes there is a growing tide of support in the country for his party.

Now Gladstone has to take office again at the head of a demoralized Liberal government. His University Bill was an attempt to meet the Catholic bishops' demand for their own university without upsetting opposing groups. The bill proposed a university with full examining powers, but excluded the teaching of theology, moral philosophy and history. The compromises pleased no one (→ 26/1/74).

Gladstone: reluctant premier.

Law reforms create a unified system

Westminster, March

The new Judicature Act will bring far-reaching changes in the legal system. Since the time of Edward I there have been two separate streams, common law and equity, each with their own separate courts. Now they are to be unified.

There are three main common law courts – the queen's bench, common pleas and exchequer. The court of chancery is the main court for equity law while there are three special courts, the high court of admiralty, the court of probate, and the court for divorce and matrimonial purposes.

All seven are to be brought together to form the supreme court of judicature with a high court and an appeal court. The changes were proposed by a royal commission in 1869 and have broad support, with some misgivings over the abolition of appeals to the House of Lords.

Teacher hanged for murder of stepson

Durham, 24 March

Mary Ann Cotton, a West Auckland Methodist Sunday School teacher, was hanged here today. It is the first hanging of a woman here for 74 years. She was found guilty of the murder of her seven-year-old stepson, Charles Edward Cotton. For several weeks newspapers have been running stories linking her with the deaths of 21 people.

According to the coroner, the boy died of gastro-enteritis, but the doctor found traces of arsenic poisoning. Mary Ann, who was once a nurse, knew all about poisons. She had bought a soft soap and arsenic mixture from the chemist "to remove bugs from the bed".

The deaths began with that of Mary's father when she was nine. According to the newspapers, most of the 21, including many children, ex-husbands and lovers, died of gastro-enteritis. She claimed that she was as "innocent as the child unborn". But many were swayed by the fact that she had collected insurance on all the deaths, including £8 on Charles Edward. Her surviving husband is uninsured.

Divorced women win right to claim children

London

A woman in dispute with her husband now has the right to claim custody of any of their children below the age of 16, under the Custody of Children Act.

Following the Divorce Act of 1857, which established the first divorce courts [*see page 913*], the new act is a further step towards recognizing women as separate from their menfolk under the law. In 18th- and early 19th-century law, a woman was treated as a piece of property, belonging first to her father and then to her husband. The man took control of all the woman's property and children. The act is an advance on the Infant Custody Act of 1839, which allowed mothers to claim control of only very young children (→ 1/6/86).

British naval officers and men. The Royal Naval College moved from Portsmouth during 1873 to four splendid blocks in Greenwich, London, designed by Wren and built in the grounds of the old Greenwich Palace.

Mill dies, praising wife in final book

Avignon, France, 8 May
John Stuart Mill, who died today, was regarded as one of the greatest intellects of his age. But in his *Autobiography* now to be published, he rated himself far below his wife Harriet. "A real majestic intellect, not to say moral nature like yours, I can only look up to and admire," he told her. They had to wait years until her first husband's death to marry, and she died only seven years later, in 1868. He dedicated *On Liberty* to her as "the inspirer of all that is best in my writings". His famous *The Subjection of Women* was a statement of her views. He lived on at Avignon with her daughter Helen after Harriet died there of tuberculosis.

Mill: writer on liberty.

British defend Gold Coast in Asante war

Members of the Fanti tribe perform a "fetish" dance to ward off the Asante.

West Africa, December
A British force led by Sir Garnet Wolseley is finalizing plans for a daring raid early next year into the tropical jungle behind the area known as the Gold Coast [Ghana]. Its target will be Kumasi, the palace headquarters of Kofi Kari-kari, king of the Asante people whose armies invaded British territories here last spring.

The Asante invasion came in response to Britain's attempts to stamp out slave-trading, one of Kofi Kari-kari's main sources of income. The prize was the coastal fort of Elmina, which Britain took over from the Dutch on 2 April 1872 following a treaty the previous year, and which the king sees as an ideal slave-trading port.

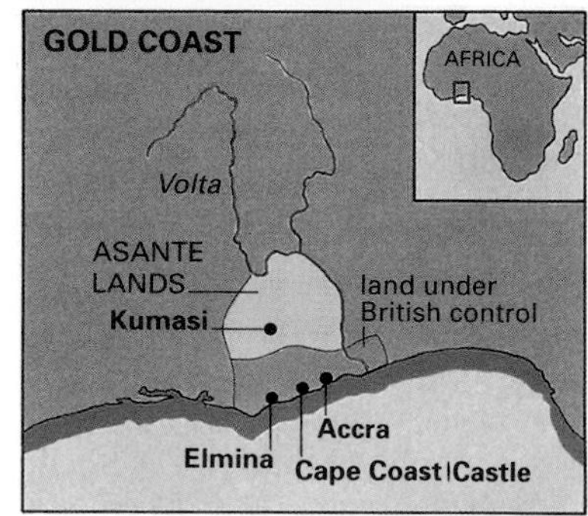

The Asante armies overran the Fanti people – friendly to the British – and got to within 12 miles (19 kilometres) of the British headquarters. In June, they attacked Elmina, but were repulsed. The British government, determined to teach them a lesson, despatched Wolseley in September. Wolseley knows that he has to act quickly. The rainy season comes in March, making military operations impossible (→ 14/3/74).

Livingstone reaches end of his 32-year African exploration

Central Africa, 1 May
David Livingstone, the Scottish missionary who dedicated his life to exploring and evangelizing Africa, has died aged 60. He was found dead by his servants today at Chitambo's village [in Zambia], kneeling in an attitude of prayer.

Born in Lanarkshire in 1813, Livingstone was sent to work in a mill at the age of ten, but was encouraged in his schooling and qualified as a doctor before being taken on by the London Missionary Society in 1838. He first arrived in Cape Town in March 1841.

He made three great exploratory trips into central Africa. On the first, between November 1853 and May 1856, he visited the extraordinary waterfalls called Mosi-oa-tunya ("smoke that thunders") [on the Zambia/Zimbabwe borders], and renamed them Victoria Falls in honour of the queen.

His second trip from March 1858 to July 1864 was at the head of an official, government-sponsored survey of central and eastern Africa. In March 1866, he set out on his final expedition, determined to realize his lifelong ambition – sadly now unfulfilled – to discover the source of the Nile.

Livingstone was a firm believer that missionaries should promote British civilization and trade alongside Christianity. In this he helped to shape current attitudes. The recent growth in British missionary work to Africa is opening up the continent to trade (→ 19/3/79).

Livingstone: spreading the word.

Scots football clubs form official body

Scotland, 13 March
Eight football clubs have formed the Scottish Football Association. They have agreed to compete for the first Scottish Cup next year.

The top club in Scottish football is Queen's Park, from Glasgow, which has not lost a single match since its formation in 1867. Last year, 11 Queen's Park players formed the Scottish team for the world's first international match, against England. It ended 0-0 (→ 1874).

Landseer, master of animal portraits, dies

Landseer's "Monarch of the Glen".

London, 1 October
Sir Edwin Landseer, who died here today, was the greatest British animal painter since George Stubbs, and the favourite painter of Queen Victoria, who knighted him in 1850. He once dissected a dead lion in order to master its anatomy, as is apparent from the magnificent lions he sculpted for the foot of Nelson's Column in 1869. He was a master of painting dogs and deer. *The Monarch of the Glen* and the two dogs, *Dignity and Impudence*, are his most loved pictures.

1874

Russia, 23 January. Despite Queen Victoria's disapproval, her son, Prince Alfred, the duke of Edinburgh, marries the Grand Duchess, Marie, the daughter of Czar Alexander.

Westminster, 26 January. William Gladstone, the prime minister, asks for a dissolution of parliament (→ 20/2).

West Africa, 14 March. After suffering a defeat by British forces in January, Kofi Karikari, the king of the Asante, signs a treaty with British officials, ending the Anglo-Asante war.

Westminster, May. Queen Victoria approves the Public Worship Bill in the hope that it will bring an end to "papist practices" which she fears may undermine the Church of England.

Westminster, 2 July. Isaac Butt, the MP for Limerick, proposes home rule for Ireland; the motion is debated in the House of Commons and defeated by 458 votes to 61 (→ 30).

London, 9 July. Vincent de Groof, a Belgian aviator nicknamed the "flying man", falls to his death when his balloon crashes into a Chelsea street (→ 31/7/94).

Westminster, 30 July. Joseph Biggar and other Irish home-rule supporters use "obstruction" tactics to delay the government's progress in an attempt to push for home rule (→ 16/2/75).

London, July. The Criterion theatre opens in Piccadilly.

Birmingham, 3 November. The prince of Wales meets the radical republican mayor of Birmingham, Joseph Chamberlain (→ 8/11/75).

Dublin, 14 December. The Irish Football Union is founded.

Scotland. The first Scottish Cup Final is won by Queen's Park in a 2-0 victory over Clydesdale.

London. Thomas Hardy, the novelist and poet, who sets his novels in the imaginary county of Wessex, publishes *Far From the Madding Crowd* (→ 1886).

Scotland. The Patronage Act, which has been the centre of much controversy in Scotland since 1712, is repealed.

London. The Midland Grand Hotel at St Pancras, designed by George Gilbert Scott, is completed.

Gladstone loses: Disraeli becomes PM

Tory administration plans social reforms

Westminster, 20 February

After the Conservative election victory, Benjamin Disraeli, at the ripe age of 70, has today become prime minister for the second time; he succeeds William Gladstone, who went to the country with a promise to abolish income tax.

Disraeli will not do that, but he has an extensive programme of social reforms lined up to improve the conditions of the labouring classes and now has an effective parliamentary majority with which to carry it out.

Local authorities are to be given powers to buy up and demolish slums and build new homes; the working week is to be cut from 60 hours to 56; public health is to be safeguarded by the appointment of medical officers, to whom infectious diseases must be reported, the use of harmful substances in food is to be prohibited under new laws and officials will monitor the pollution of rivers by industry. Abroad, Disraeli plans to develop the empire with Lord Salisbury as the secretary for India and Lord Derby as the foreign secretary (→ 13/1/75).

Spokesmen for the workers: Alexander McDonald (l) and Thomas Burt.

Two miners take their places in the House

Westminster, February

Two miners who campaigned on an independent labour platform, but with Liberal support, have been elected to the House of Commons. Alexander McDonald, leader of the National Miners' Association and the first working man to be elected, is MP for Stafford, and Thomas Burt, the Northumberland miners' leader, is MP for Morpeth.

In their manifestos they called for the repeal of laws making trade unions liable for criminal damages, and amendment of the Master and Servants Acts so that breach of contract ceases to be a criminal offence. They also want to limit the working day for women and children to nine hours, and want workmen or their families to be able to sue employers when death or injury results from accidents caused by negligence. Burt wants to tackle drunkenness giving local authorities powers to oversee alcohol sales.

Anyone for tennis? Formal rules are set down for popular game

"Tennis", by Horace Cauty, shows a game for ladies as well as gentlemen.

London, February

Walter Clopton Wingfield, known as "the sporting major", has devised and patented a "new and improved portable court for playing the ancient game of tennis". The major's version of the game is played on an hourglass-shaped court, and he calls it "*Sphairistike*", from the Greek for playing ball; the word "tennis" probably comes from the French *tenez!* [take it!].

The major first tried out his game at house parties last year, and its popularity encouraged him to draw up an elaborate set of rules this year. At the London suburb of Wimbledon, the All England Croquet Club, founded six years ago and still struggling to pay its way, has decided to add "Lawn Tennis" to its title and lay out several grass courts for the new sport (→ 9/7/77).

Irish home-rule MPs disrupt Parliament

Westminster, 30 July
The small group of Fenians who belong to the Irish parliamentary party, led by the lawyer and MP for Limerick, Isaac Butt, are becoming increasingly restless at the lack of progress towards their goal of home rule for Ireland. Joe Biggar, a member of the Irish Republican Brotherhood and a pork butcher from Belfast, today used a novel obstructionist tactic to draw attention to the issue. During a sitting in the House of Commons, he spoke for four hours against a new coercion bill, reading extracts from newspapers and other documents.

The movement for home rule is gathering force. Last November the Home Rule League was established in Dublin following a three-day conference on the subject. However, Butt's motion proposing Irish home rule was resoundingly defeated in the House of Commons earlier this month.

Trial of the 'baron from Wagga Wagga'

London, 28 February
After two lengthy trials estimated to have cost £200,000 in legal fees, Thomas Castro, a butcher from Wagga-Wagga, New South Wales, otherwise known as Arthur Orton, the son of a Wapping butcher, has been sentenced to 14 years' hard labour for perjury.

Orton turned up after the death of Sir Arthur Joseph Tichborne, eleventh baronet of an old Catholic family. Orton told Henrietta, the dowager Lady Tichborne, that he was Sir Arthur's brother and her long-lost son, Roger, who had been reported drowned off Rio de Janeiro 20 years ago.

Lady Tichborne had never been persuaded that Roger was dead and she had advertised widely in the hope of news of him. She heard that a man answering to Roger's description had been found in Australia and acknowledged him as her son, but other members of the family found evidence that he had been born in Wapping and had jumped ship in South America. He went to court three years ago to support his claim, but after 103 days his case collapsed. He was arrested and charged with perjury; the second trial, which ended today, lasted 188 days.

Arthur Orton: butcher or baron?

The magnificent Midland Railway hotel, designed by George Gilbert Scott, has now been completed adjoining St Pancras station in London.

Ten-hour day campaign succeeds at last

Hard labour: inside an engineering factory for the shipbuilding industry.

Westminster, August
Disraeli's reforming Conservative government has passed a new Factory Act to prevent the exploitation of workers in textile factories. No child below ten years of age can now be employed at all, and women and girls and adolescent boys will not be allowed to work for more than ten hours a day between 6am and 6pm. Men are permitted to work for ten and a half hours, but in practice they are expected to do no more than ten. The ten-hour campaign was begun 44 years ago when Richard Oastler, who worked as steward for a Huddersfield landowner, caused a sensation with a letter to the *Leeds Mercury*, headed "Yorkshire Slavery".

His vigorous campaigning led to several factory acts, which millmasters found ways of evading by working children and women in relays between 5.30am and 7.30pm. They served the machines operated by men, who were thus kept working 14 hours (→ 1875).

Medicine-man Boot opens his first shop

Nottingham
Jesse Boot is putting his own name above his mother's little shop in Goose Gate, Nottingham, whose shelves are crammed with pots and packages of herbal remedies and proprietary medicines. Jesse, the son of a farm labourer who earned extra coppers with home-made herbal mixtures, was ten when his father died in 1860 and he left school to help in the shop.

Jesse and his sister Jane spend many hours in the country collecting herbs to be brewed in the iron pot in the fireplace. His ambition is to sell quality products, especially drugs, at competitive prices in attractive packaging. His idea is to buy in bulk direct from manufacturers. He says other shops are overcharging the public.

Islands of Fiji are annexed by Britain

London, October
The Fiji islands in the Western Pacific have been annexed by Britain – at the request of the islanders. Fiji has had mixed fortunes since it was first visited by a European, Abel Tasman, in 1643. Early in this century a group of escaped convicts and sailors who had jumped ship arrived from Australia and took local wives. King Thakombau, a heathen in his youth, converted to Christianity and dismissed all his wives except one. When he was attacked by warriors from Tonga, the US consulate was accidentally burned down; he got a bill from Washington which he could not pay and asked for his islands to be annexed. He got no reply – the US had a civil war on its hands – so he turned to Britain.

1875

London, 23 January. Charles Kingsley, the author of *The Water Babies*, dies aged 55.

London, 1 February. Sir William Sterndale Bennett, the distinguished pianist and composer, dies aged 60.

Edinburgh, 6 February. The Royal theatre is destroyed by fire, which kills many people.

Ireland, 16 February. John Mitchel, an Irish patriot and convicted felon, is returned unopposed at the Tipperary by-election; he is not permitted to take his seat (→ 20/3).

Newry, Ireland, 20 March. John Mitchel, who earlier this month was returned for a second time as MP for Tipperary, dies at his home in Dromalane (→ 26/4).

Westminster, 26 April. Charles Stewart Parnell, the newly elected MP for Meath, makes his maiden speech in the House of Commons (→ 1/7/76).

London, 28 April. The prince of Wales is installed as Grand Master of the English Freemasons at the Albert Hall.

Westminster, 11 August. Parliament passes the Irish Pharmacy Act; it institutes and incorporates the Pharmaceutical Society of Ireland.

Bombay, 8 November. The prince of Wales begins his first state visit to India (→ 5/1877).

Britain. Emma Paterson, who organized the Women's Protective and Provident League in 1874, and Edith Simcox are the first women delegates to the Trades Union Congress (→ 17/5/87).

North London. Alexandra Palace, based on the elaborate Crystal Palace, is opened to the public.

Central Africa. The British explorer Verney Cameron is the first European to cross Africa from Zanzibar to Benguela in Angola.

London. The main sewerage system is completed.

London. The first roller-skating rink opens.

Edinburgh. The Institute of Bankers is founded to improve the qualifications and status of banking employees.

Histon, Cambridgeshire. Chivers opens a jam-making factory; fruit-farming has spread to this area from the west of England.

Morris backs crafts, not mass production

London

William Morris has designs on your drawing room. He wants to empty it of porcelain figures, papier-mâché boxes, models of Swiss chalets and embroidered bell pulls and fill it only with what you "know to be useful or believe to be beautiful".

Morris, a designer and craftsman, has just become sole proprietor of the decorating firm Morris, Marshall and Faulkner. He is a champion of medieval arts and crafts, which he believes have a beauty that been lost by today's mass production. Already noted for wallpapers, the company has begun experimenting with fabrics (→ 1891).

Daffodil chintz designed by Morris.

Welsh miners succumb after long strike

Miners' wives and children scramble for fuel on a tip during the strike.

Wales, May

Trade unionism suffered a serious blow this month when the Amalgamated Association of Miners (AAM) was forced into bankruptcy during one of the longest and most extensive pit strikes in the history of the south Wales coalfield.

The strike, which began so confidently but ended so ignominiously, involved more than 17,000 Welsh miners. They gathered in strength from every working pit in south Wales for several pitched battles with blackleg labour, brought into the region by the Employers' Federation, as well as for protest marches in every valley town, complete with big brass bands and elaborate and colourful silk banners. Initially, the miners were all receiving generous strike pay from the 42,000-strong AAM and the employers appeared anxious to negotiate a settlement. The pit owners have also been hit by a slump in the price of coal.

Unfortunately for the miners, there were many calls on the strike fund and once the union's financial problems were revealed, the resolve of the employers was greatly strengthened. Without union funds, many miners and their families were reported to be close to starvation.

The AAM had no choice but to accept a savage wage cut of 12.5 per cent per week for all its Welsh members (→ 19/8/89).

Gladstone gives up Liberal leadership

London, 13 January

There is a huge pair of shoes to fill at the Liberal Party HQ. William Gladstone today resigned as leader nearly a year after losing the last election to the Conservatives. He claimed last March that he needed a rest, but since then he has mounted a vigorous attack on a bill designed to curb the spread of Roman Catholic ritual in the church and has written a hugely popular pamphlet against the new doctrine of papal infallibility. His wife opposes his resignation, but it seems genuine. He talks of selling his London house and retiring to Hawarden [in Clwyd] to write (→ 11/1879).

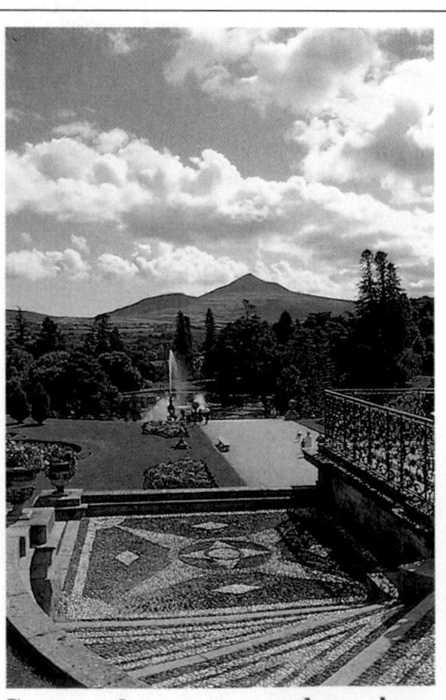

Spectacular new gardens have been completed this year at Powerscourt, Co Wicklow.

Colleges for women open in Cambridge

Cambridge

The dream of a full higher education for women is moving towards reality in Cambridge, where, as yet, women still cannot sit the same tripos as men. A college to prepare women for the new Higher Local Examination has just opened at nearby Newnham and last year a college founded by the firebrand campaigner Emily Davies to prepare girls for exams moved to Girton, two miles outside Cambridge, from its original base at Hitchin in Hertfordshire. The impetus for the college came from a group of Cambridge academics led by Professor and Mrs Henry Sidgwick (→ 1877).

English mariner is first to swim Channel

Calais, France, 25 August
After an extraordinary feat of courage and endurance Captain Matthew Webb waded ashore here at 10.40 this morning to become the first person to have swum the English Channel.

The 27-year-old master mariner from Dawley in Shropshire covered the 40 miles (64 kilometres) between Dover and Calais in 21 hours and 45 minutes, his body smeared with porpoise grease as protection against the cold. His supporters had fed him from boats through the night with cod-liver oil, beef tea, brandy, coffee and ale. Webb, who learnt to swim in a river when he was eight and saved his brother from drowning at nine, is already talking about taking up swimming as a profession (→ 24/7/83).

Captain Webb is helped ashore at Calais after completing his historic swim.

Disraeli negotiates control of Suez canal

London, 25 November
Disraeli has bought a controlling interest in the Suez canal for Britain for £4 million after a fortnight of high politics. It is a coup that secures the route to India, frustrates the French and delights the queen.

The khedive of Egypt needed the money to avoid bankruptcy, but the French were demanding exorbitant terms so Disraeli persuaded the cabinet to make an offer. Now he crows: "We have had all the gamblers, capitalists, financiers of the world ... arrayed against us ... and have baffled them all." The deal almost failed because parliament could not consent fast enough to raise the money but the Rothschilds saved the day (→ 29/10/89).

Disraeli buys the key to India: the Suez canal shipping route.

Boys may not be used as chimney sweeps

London
The evil of child chimney sweeps, some of whom are only five years old, has finally been outlawed by an act of parliament sponsored by Lord Shaftesbury. Two previous acts of 1840 and 1864 tried to control the practice, but were widely ignored. The children's plight was first revealed more than 100 years ago by Jonas Hanway and just over ten years ago the clergyman and reformer Charles Kingsley's heart-rending *The Water Babies* renewed public concern. "No one knows the cruelty they undergo in learning," said one sweep. "The flesh must be hardened; this is done by rubbing it, chiefly on the elbows and knees, with the strongest brine ... close by a hot fire. You must stand over them with a cane ..." (→ 1878).

Conspiracy Act ends ban on picketing

London
The Conservative government under Benjamin Disraeli has legalized collective bargaining and peaceful picketing – rights for which trade unionists have been campaigning for 50 years.

The Conspiracy and Protection of Property Bill follows a royal commission on trade societies, and virtually meets in full the demands of the parliamentary committee of the TUC. It was pushed through by Disraeli, who, despite cabinet opposition, felt secure enough to placate an important section of the electorate. The act comes as the recession whittles away union successes such as the nine-hour day won by engineers four years ago. Two years ago 70,000 iron workers lost a strike against a 10 per cent wage cut (→ 5/1875).

Laws impose tight public health controls to improve life in cities

London
Local councils' powers have been transformed by two acts sponsored by the Conservative government. The Public Health Act, reflecting Disraeli's concern with sanitation, enables councils to act against local "nuisances" or places "injurious to health", while the Artisans' and Labourers' Dwellings Improvement Act allows slum clearance and rebuilding on a massive scale, like that of the 50-acre (20-hectare) scheme planned by Birmingham's radical lord mayor, Joseph Chamberlain. Many believe action is vital. Many reports have described the appalling conditions in the cities, where the life expectancy of a labourer is 22: "rutted broken streets ... holes filled with refuse and excrement ... cottages cramped almost to suffocation", says one.

Others, such as a writer in the *Economist*, are sceptical: "Suffering and evil are nature's admonitions ... the impatient attempts of benevolence to banish them ... have always been more productive of evil than good" (→ 1883).

A train battles its way into Nottingham's Midland station in October during the city's worst floods for 80 years.

1876

Chelmsford, 14 January. Essex County Cricket Club is founded (→ 15/3/77).

Ireland, 1 April. The Great Northern Railway is established by the amalgamation of the Dublin, Drogheda and Belfast Junction and the Irish North-Western and Ulster Railways (→ 28/12/79).

Dublin, 24 April. The Church of Ireland general synod recommends the establishment of temperance societies (→ 14/6).

Westminster, 14 June. Parliament proposes the closure of public houses in Ireland on Sundays (→ 3/8).

Britain, 23 June. The *Daily News* publishes an account of the Turkish atrocities in Bulgaria which shocks the British public (→ 9/1876).

Westminster, 1 July. Isaac Butt's motion proposing home rule for Ireland is defeated in the House of Commons by 291 votes to 61 (→ 8/1877).

Westminster, 3 August. A bill to close public houses on Sundays in Ireland is withdrawn through lack of support.

Westminster, 11 August. Parliament passes the Medical Act; this permits the registration of women medical practitioners (→ 1877).

Strathclyde. Homes for orphans are founded by William Quarrier at Bridge of Weir.

Belfast, 15 August. Violent sectarian riots erupt.

Bristol, 10 September. The University College is opened.

Dublin, 29 December. The Society for the Preservation of the Irish Language is founded.

Westminster. Lord Sandon's Education Act is passed by parliament; it establishes a form of compulsory primary education and sets up committees to monitor school attendance (→ 1880).

Britain. Mary Ann Evans, the novelist who writes under the name of George Eliot, publishes her latest novel, *Daniel Deronda* (→ 22/12/80).

Westminster. Parliament passes the Rivers Pollution Act; it attacks the problem of pollution of rivers by industrial waste and sewage.

Scotland. David Bryce, the renowned Scottish architect, dies aged 73.

Radical Mayor Chamberlain becomes MP

Westminster
Joseph Chamberlain, the "constructively radical" lord mayor of Birmingham, who has already made his brand of "gas-and-water socialism" nationally famous, has joined the political mainstream as a newly elected MP. Few observers doubt that he will be a leading minister when a Liberal government next achieves power.

His by-election success in one of the safe Birmingham seats brings a sharp new flavour to Westminster, both ideologically and in terms of party organization, of which he is already, at 40, an acknowledged master. Two years ago he retired from the screw-cutting industry, having amassed a fortune, and he plans to devote his formidable energies to public life (→ 5/1877).

Chamberlain: a Birmingham lion roars onto the national stage.

'Plimsoll Line' bans overloaded ships

Westminster
Hundreds of seamen's lives are expected to be saved each year by the passing of the government's Merchant Shipping Bill. In future no British merchantman will be allowed to sail with an overweight cargo, as demonstrated by the submergence of a "load-line" painted on the side of its hull.

This simple but effective device is already known as "the Plimsoll Line" in honour of the Derby MP, Samuel Plimsoll, who forced it on to the statute book. Owners tried to silence his denunciations of "coffin ships" by issuing a series of potentially crippling libel writs, but withdrew after no fewer than 440 vessels were found unseaworthy last year.

Public outcry follows reports of Turkish 'atrocities' in Bulgaria

London, September
Graphic and horrifying newspaper reports of the ruthless massacres allegedly perpetrated by Turkish irregulars in Bulgaria have generated a vast surge of public anger here. This is expected to intensify now that William Gladstone, the former Liberal premier, has taken up the cause in a pamphlet, *The Bulgarian Horrors and the Question of the East*. More than 200,000 copies were sold in a week.

Politically the issue has opened up an enormous rift between the two major parties and among their individual members. The prime minister, Benjamin Disraeli, has attracted bitter criticism for his efforts to cast doubts on the size and significance of the death toll, while even some Liberals suspect that Gladstone may have somewhat exaggerated the figures (→ 24/4/77).

Alexander Graham Bell makes first telephone call a cry for help

Philadelphia, USA, March
Alexander Graham Bell's invention of what is already becoming popularly known as the "telephone" proved its extraordinary potential usefulness before it even left his workshop. Earlier this year, the Scottish-American pioneer of methods for teaching deaf children was about to test a new device for sending sounds down a length of wire when he spilt corrosive battery acid on his leg. So the first message on his "electric speech machine" was an urgent call to his assistant: "Watson, come here. I need you."

Later the system was demonstrated more formally at the Great Exhibition and generated enormous interest. Originally developed as a deaf-aid its crucial innovation is a vibrating diaghragm, which is then activated by the human voice. The resulting sounds are passed on to a receiver, which amplifies the message. On one memorable occasion, Bell himself used it to recite Hamlet's soliloquy "To be or not to be?" across 130 metres (150 yards) of wire to the emperor of Brazil, who excitedly shouted back "I hear, I hear!" Bell was born in Edinburgh and educated in London, before emigrating to Canada and then the USA. His discoveries have achieved worldwide recognition, and are already promising to spawn an entirely new industry (→ 15/1/80).

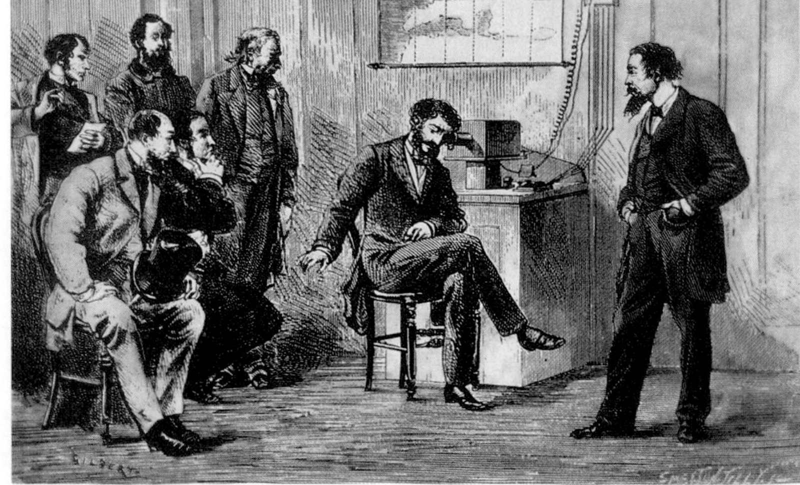

Thomas Watson, Bell's assistant, hears his master's voice on the telephone.

Victoria appointed empress of India

The raj celebrates the acquisition of an empress by gathering in splendour to mark the new royal title of Queen Victoria.

Westminster, 1 May
The Royal Titles Bill has today completed its tempestuous passage through parliament, and the queen will now be entitled to call herself the empress of India. She has indicated that in future she intends to sign herself as "Victoria R & I" (*Victoria Regina et Imperatrix*).

This extension to her already long list of honours represents the achievement of an ambition that she has nursed for several years. She is known to be irritated by the number of overseas royal families who are claiming imperial status. Czar Alexander II of Russia now insists that his daughter. Grand Duchess Marie, the wife of her own second son, Prince Alfred, must be addressed as "Her Imperial Highness" and the screw was twisted by the decision of the king of Prussia, William, to call himself emperor of Germany.

As Victoria's eldest daughter, Vicky is married to William's heir, Crown Prince Frederick, there was an increasingly intolerable likelihood that one day she would outrank her own mother. Now that danger has been averted.

In steering the bill through a surprisingly hostile Commons, the prime minister, Benjamin Disraeli, was at pains to underplay the dynastic question and emphasize the measure's importance for foreign policy. Russia in particular needed reminding, he declared, that Britain would not tolerate empire-building in Asia (→1/1/77).

Disraeli retires to calm of House of Lords

Westminster, 12 August
Few members realized last night as the prime minister once more passionately rejected the Opposition's charges of neglecting the Bulgarian atrocities that they were witnessing the last appearance of Benjamin Disraeli in the House of Commons that he has entertained, entranced and infuriated for the past 39 years.

Disraeli: leaving the Commons.

Today Queen Victoria announced that she has created him earl of Beaconsfield. So he will now lead the government from the House of Lords (where his wife, after some controversy, sits as a peeress after he requested this when declining a peerage in 1868).

Although this retreat from the hurly-burly of the House of Commons has probably been forced on him by a combination of administrative stress and failing health, his colleagues are expressing concern at the decision. They fear that if Gladstone carries out his threat of returning to active politics, the Tories will need all the debating fire and in-fighting skills they can muster. Without "Dizzy's" constant presence they are likely to look a lacklustre team.

The Albert Memorial to the late prince consort is completed this year – in Kensington Gardens opposite the Royal Albert Hall.

Benign imperialism draws to a close as new struggles loom

London, May
Imperialism is a relatively new word in the British political vocabulary. Other nations fret enviously about the proportion of the world's territory and trade that is effectively controlled from London but there has been little sustained discussion, even in parliament, about the way in which this dominance has been achieved and maintained. This may be about to change.

European countries' colonial expansion now embraces two-thirds of the world's land surface, after proceeding steadily since 1800 at the rate of about 216,000 square miles (560,000 square kilometres) a year. But so far it has generated remarkably little international friction. Apart from Russian penetration in Asia and the consolidation of the Dutch East Indies, most development has taken place in and around the long-established British territories in Canada, Australia, South Africa and India. The almost universal acceptance of free trade has diminished the importance of whose flag was flying above the local government house.

That benign period is probably at an end. The combination of global recession, the ambitions of Germany, Belgium and Italy and growing protectionism suggests there could soon be a struggle over such unexploited areas as Africa, East Asia and the Pacific (→4/1887).

Queen Victoria tries on the hat of empress of India and finds it fits.

1877

Windsor, 1 January. Queen Victoria is formally proclaimed Queen-Empress of India (→2/3/82).

South-east coast, 1 January. The coastal resorts of Dover, Hastings and Folkestone are badly damaged by severe rain and flooding.

Bristol, 24 February. The Avonmouth docks are opened.

London, February. The first issue of the *Daily Chronicle*, a Liberal newspaper, is printed.

Melbourne, 15 March. The Australian cricket team wins the first cricket test match against England, by 45 runs (→25/3/79).

Europe, 24 April. Britain declares its neutrality as Russia declares war on the Turkish empire (→15/2/78).

London, May. The prince of Wales has found a new mistress, the beautiful actress, Lillie Langtry (→22/2/84).

Wimbledon, 9 July. The All England Croquet and Lawn Tennis Club stages its first lawn tennis championships.→

Westminster, 1 August. The House of Commons is delayed by Irish obstructionists, led by Charles Parnell, the MP for Meath, for 24 hours in an attempt to force the issue of Irish home rule (→22/10/77).

Merseyside, 13 August. Birkenhead is made a borough with John Laird, a shipbuilder, as the first lord mayor.

Westminster, 23 August. Parliament passes the Merchandise Marks Act, which obliges all exporters to indicate the place of manufacture of their goods.

Liverpool, 6 September. The Walker Art Gallery, a gift of the mayor, Andrew Walker, is opened by Edward Stanley, the earl of Derby.

Wiltshire, 17 September. William Henry Fox Talbot, the British pioneer of photography, dies at Lacock Abbey aged 72 (→4/1/90).

Dublin, 7 November. William Gladstone, the former Liberal prime minister, is awarded the freedom of the city.

Glasgow. The Association for the Higher Education of Women in Glasgow and the West of Scotland is founded (→28/3/78).

Scotland. The Distillers Company Ltd is formed by the amalgamation of six firms.

Britain acts swiftly to seize Transvaal

Southern Africa, April

Britain has annexed the Boer republic of Transvaal in a hurried move that it sees as vital to protect its interests in southern Africa. Fighting between Boers and Zulus has bankrupted the Transvaal and now threatens to spread outside its territory into a bloodbath between whites and blacks. The Boer leaders had talked of calling in Germany if Britain did not act. In moving without waiting for the approval of the inhabitants, Britain risks future conflict with the Boers (→23/1/79).

Parnell leads Irish home rule campaign

Ireland, August

At the annual convention of the Home Rule Confederation of Great Britain, Charles Stewart Parnell has replaced Isaac Butt as the president and is now effectively the leader of the home rule campaign. His aggressive attitude and open contempt for English opinion has made a strong impression on the Irish in Britain. Parnell, who was elected to parliament two years ago, comes from a distinguished Anglo-Irish landlord family. His "obstructionist" tactics in the House of Commons have already earned him a high reputation.

Parnell: fighting for home rule.

Authorities close Cremorne pleasure gardens in Chelsea clean up

Cremorne gardens, modelled on the Vauxhall gardens of the last century.

London

Pickpockets and prostitutes have forced the closure of the Cremorne pleasure gardens in Chelsea with their pretty pagoda-shaped bandstand, lavender-scented amorous alcoves and theatre. Entertainments held here included firework displays, balloon ascents and circus performances. It was from the Cremorne gardens that Charles Green, the "intrepid aeronaut", made his famous ascent with a lady and a leopard, and "Madame Geneviève" crossed the Thames on a tightrope. The gardens' licence was revoked after they were dubbed a "nursery of every kind of vice."

Torpedo gives navy increased firepower

Lima, Peru, 30 May

The Brazilian pirate ship the *Huescar* today surrendered to Brazil's navy after an inconclusive action yesterday against two British warships, *Shah* and *Amethyst*. During it the *Shah* fired a Whitehead torpedo. Robert Whitehead developed his torpedo, the first to travel underwater, ten years ago, and a number of navies have bought it. The Royal Navy did so in 1871, and has begun to arm some of its ships with it, as well as to build special torpedo boats. Yesterday was the first time that it has been fired in anger. Although it missed its target it is expected to have a major influence on future warfare at sea.

London, 24 March: for the first time the university boat race ends in a dead heat; Oxford and Cambridge crews here at Hammersmith Bridge.

Voice of the people to be heard through Liberal federation

Birmingham, May
The Liberal Party has taken a major step towards making itself more representative of voters by establishing the National Liberal Federation with the aim of enabling the enlarged electorate to play a more prominent part in shaping national policy. The lead came from Joseph Chamberlain, the former Birmingham mayor and now an MP, who was contemptuous of the governing class in London which, he said, has made the party a "boneless, nerveless thing". Forty-seven English and Welsh borough associations immediately linked themselves with the federation, which will operate down to street level through ward leaders. Activists will campaign for social reform measures to be put before the national party as representative of the real voice of Liberal democracy.

Chamberlain: seeking supporters.

The Conservative Party, meanwhile, has used its National Union of Conservative and Constituency Associations more as a means to broaden its voting base than to shape policy. It is now seeking support not only in the shires but also increasingly in urban and suburban areas. It has derided the "factionalism" of the Liberal Party, and is presenting itself as the "natural and national" ruling party with supporters drawn from every strata of society. Its appeal seems gradually to be widening.

Reformer charged over birth control book

Challenging the authorities: Annie Besant and Charles Bradlaugh.

London, July 1877
A jury has returned an inconclusive verdict in the trial of Mrs Annie Besant, one of the most extraordinary women of the century, who was charged with having published a booklet said to advocate obscene and unnatural practices calculated to corrupt the young.

In a deliberate challenge to authority, Mrs Besant, social reformer and a one-time fervent Christian now turned atheist, and Charles Bradlaugh, her co-defendant, had re-issued a 40-year-old American work, *The Fruits of Philosophy, The Private Companion of Young Married People*, which called for the use of physical contraception. In a preface of their own, they said that it was more moral to prevent the conception of children than "murder them after birth by want of food, air and clothing", or by resorting to "revolting" abortion.

The prosecution contended that the real objective was to promote sex outside marriage. Mrs Besant retorted with scorn that she spoke not for herself but for those mothers worn out from child-bearing. The judge summed up in the defendants' favour. The jury's verdict was a compromise: the booklet was calculated to deprave but there was no intent to corrupt. The baffled judge interpreted that as guilty, but whatever the outcome, the trial has served to disseminate ideas about birth control.

Gore coasts to easy win in first tennis final at Wimbledon

London, 9 July
The world's first championship of the new game of lawn tennis has been played in the small London suburb of Wimbledon. Alerted by a small announcement in the magazine *The Field*, a crowd of some 200 made its way to the tournament by carriage, bicycle and the new railway service to see Spencer Gore handsomely defeat W C Marshall by 6-1, 6-2, 6-4.

The match was played on an hourglass-shaped court, the product of the self-styled inventor of the game, cavalryman Major Walter Clopton Wingfield, who has developed a variant of the ancient game of Real Tennis. The net, five feet tall at the wings and dipping to three feet three inches at the centre, is shorter than the baselines. The shrewd Gore, serving roundarm, saw that passing shots were virtually impossible with a net so high at either side. He dominated the rallies by moving to the net and volleying alternately to the forehand and the backhand sides.

The match was held at the All England Croquet and Lawn Tennis Club, founded in 1868. A member, Henry Jones, saw the possibilities of tennis and arranged for a court to be built. He was allocated £25 to buy equipment (→ 6/1884).

Ruskin attacks Whistler for 'flinging paint in public's face'

London, 2 July
The art critic John Ruskin today launched a stinging attack on the *Nocturnes* which James McNeill Whistler is exhibiting at the Grosvenor gallery in Bond Street. The paintings, in blue and silver or black and gold, are vague impressions of the Thames at twilight, of moonlight on water. Many people have found them incomprehensible and Ruskin, a noted defender of Turner when he was under fire, calls them "wilful imposture".

"I have seen and heard much of cockney impudence before now; but never expected to hear a coxcomb ask two hundred guineas for flinging a pot of paint in the public's face," he writes (→ 26/11/78).

Wilful imposture?: Whistler's delicate impression of a falling rocket.

John Ruskin (centre) with Dante Gabriel Rossetti and William Scott.

1878

Black Sea, 15 February. The British fleet arrives off the coast of Istanbul (→ 19).

Britain/Russia, 19 February. An Anglo-Russian agreement states that Russia will not occupy the Turkish city of Gallipoli if British troops do not land in Turkey in support of the Turkish empire (→ 3/3).

Westminster, 27 March. Edward Stanley, the earl of Derby and foreign secretary, resigns after the signing of the treaty of San Stefano (→ 4/6).

London, 28 March. The University of London is granted a charter allowing it to grant degrees to women students (→ 29/4/84).

Westminster, 2 April. Robert Arthur Talbot Gascoyne, the marquis of Salisbury, is appointed foreign secretary.

Europe, 4 June. Britain and Turkey sign a secret treaty allowing Britain to occupy Cyprus in return for British help against Russian advances (→ 7/1878).

Westminster, 30 July. William Gladstone criticizes the terms of the Berlin treaty in which Britain and the European powers reached agreement on the future of the Balkan states.

Wales, 11 September. A gas explosion in an Abercarn mine kills 268 miners.

London, 5 October. Waterloo Bridge is opened toll-free.

Dublin, 22 October. Charles Parnell is re-elected as the president of the Home Rule Confederation (→ 6/4/79).

London, 11 November. The Institute for the Advancement of Technical Education is founded.

Glasgow. The African Lakes Company is founded by local businessmen "to advance the kingdom of God by honest trade".

Zanzibar. William Mackinnon leases territory from the sultan and founds the British East Africa Company.

Scotland. The Roman Catholic hierarchy is re-established.

Britain. Arthur Sullivan and William S Gilbert combine their musical and literary talents to produce the light opera *HMS Pinafore* (→ 1880).

Scotland. The Glasgow School of Painters is formed by a group of artists reacting against the Edinburgh establishment.

War fears mount in Balkans crisis

Russian triumph is a threat to Britain

London, 3 March

Russia today imposed a punitive peace on the Turks at San Stefano, while the British fleet remains anchored 40 miles off Constantinople. Russia has freed most of the Balkans and set up Bulgaria as a client state stretching from Albania to the Black Sea and the Aegean. It is a great victory for the Czar and a defeat for the British who a few months ago were singing "We don't want to fight, but by jingo, if we do" and vowing to protect Turkey.

The war began when Turkey put down a revolt in Bosnia, and then repressed troubles in Bulgaria with great savagery. Russia intervened to protect the Bulgars, and British diplomatic efforts to prevent war failed. The fleet was sent to Constantinople in January, and though the Russians did not occupy the city they won everything else.

The earl of Beaconsfield, the prime minister, is unhappy with the treaty because it makes Russia master of the Balkans and threatens British power in the Mediterranean and the vital route to India. Austria, coveting Bosnia, and Germany, wanting to curb Russia, both back Britain (→ 27).

Disraeli's Turkish balancing act.

Salisbury: new foreign secretary.

Berlin Congress is a victory for diplomacy

Berlin, July

The Congress of Berlin has ended in a diplomatic victory for the earl of Beaconsfield, as Benjamin Disraeli is now known. The prime minister says he has won "peace with honour". Russia is to allow Turkey to recover most of its European provinces conceded in the Treaty of San Stefano in March. Austria has been given a protectorate over Bosnia and Britain has been given Cyprus. The congress was summoned by Bismarck, the German chancellor, to consider the consequences of the Balkan war, but the triumph was Beaconsfield's. Supported by Lord Salisbury, the foreign secretary, and by Austria and Germany, the British prime minister was determined to preserve Turkey and to keep Russia out of Constantinople. He has succeeded.

The ailing Ottoman empire has been preserved, although Serbia, Bulgaria, Romania and Greece, as well as Russia, are all dissatisfied with the result (→ 30).

Hundreds drowned as holed pleasure steamer sinks in Thames

An artist's reconstruction of the impact and tragedy on the river Thames.

London, 3 September

Over 600 people were drowned today when the pleasure steamer the *Princess Alice* sank in the Thames at Erith, below Woolwich. Boatmen tried frantically to rescue men, women and children floundering desperately in the murky waters of Galleons Reach, but very few were saved.

The London Steamboat Company paddle-steamer was returning from an excursion downriver when she was rammed by a collier, the *Bywell Castle*. She broke into three parts and sank immediately. There were between 600 and 700 people on board. The disaster is the worst the river has ever known, and shows how dangerous the very heavy traffic on the river can be.

Panic as City of Glasgow Bank collapses

Glasgow, October
The city's financial institutions have been shaken to their foundations by the collapse of the City of Glasgow Bank and the arrest of its directors. They are accused of stealing over £5 million. The losses will fall to the shareholders, many of whom are prominent members of the Free Church.

Glasgow is Scotland's principal industrial and commercial city, and boasts that it is the second richest in the empire. Scottish banks have supported the rapid development of Scottish industry over the past 50 years, particularly in linen, shipbuilding, mining and steelmaking. They have preserved their independence from London, and have often proved more imaginative than their English counterparts. News that one of Glasgow's main banks has failed through the corruption of its leading officers will be a severe blow to self-confidence (→ 1882).

Anxious crowds gather at the bank.

William Booth recruits for Salvation Army

London
The Christian Mission founded by William and Catherine Booth has changed its name. Now it will be known as the Salvation Army, with Mr Booth as General. It is already one of the most successful missionary societies in England, with centres all over London, and has now started setting up permanent missions in the provinces.

The Salvation Army is wholly devoted to rescuing the poorest and most miserable, and bringing them to Jesus. One of the general's children said of him: "the sins of London don't shock him, they seem to tear at his heart with claws that draw blood". His wife Catherine is equally important in the organization, and its rules make no distinction at all between men and women.

Dr Thomas Barnardo was a follower of General Booth until he left to set up orphanages for abandoned boys. The Salvation Army makes use of music and parades to lure people to its services and its anthem is *Onward, Christian Soldiers* by Arthur Sullivan. The organization provides food and shelter for the destitute (→ 4/5/80).

Booth: spreading God's word.

Women and children get more protection

Young women workers take a lunch break from the mills in Wigan.

London
The Conservative government has passed its second Factory and Workshop Act to improve working conditions for women and children. It extends protection to trades that were missed in the 1874 act, including sweatshops and small factories. This is one of a long series of laws designed to protect workers from the harsh conditions of the early industrial revolution. The two acts forbid the employment in most trades of children under ten, and none under 14 can be employed full-time. Women, girls and adolescent boys are limited to a 10-hour day. In practice, this also means a 10-hour day for men. The acts are the fruit of a long agitation, but male workers have been more concerned to protect their own jobs than to protect women from exploitation. Only last year, the TUC demanded that parliament restrict female employment (→ 1886).

Whistler sues Ruskin – and gets a farthing

London, 26 November
A High Court jury today decided that John Ruskin libelled the artist James McNeill Whistler by saying he asked 200 guineas for "flinging a pot of paint in the public's face" but awarded Whistler damages of just one farthing.

Several artists gave evidence, some declaring that Whistler's *Nocturnes* were true works of art, some giving evidence to the contrary, but public sympathy was with Ruskin. Whistler, admitting that one of the *Nocturnes* had been painted in two days, was asked: "And for that labour you ask 200 guineas?" He replied: "No, I ask it for the knowledge of a lifetime." He now has to face crippling costs.

Whistler, an American, earlier called his works by such titles as *Symphony in White* or *Arrangement in Grey and Black* – this was a portrait of his mother rejected by the Royal Academy (→ 2/1899).

Frederick Spofforth, the "demon bowler" of Australia, bowls in England during the first overseas tour by a team from Australia; an English team played a test match against Australia in Melbourne in March last year.

1879

London, 18 January. England beat Wales 2-1 in a football match played at Kennington Oval (→ 18/11/80).

Glasgow, 19 March. A statue of Dr David Livingstone, the explorer, is unveiled in George Square.

Leicestershire, 25 March. Leicestershire County Cricket Club is founded (→ 9/1880).

Dublin, 6 April. Michael Davitt and John Devoy, the leaders of the American Irish Republican Brotherhood, meet for the first time with Charles Parnell (→ 20).

Co Mayo, 20 April. Michael Davitt chairs a mass meeting of small farmers demanding massive agrarian reform at Irishtown (→ 5/5).

Warwickshire, 23 April. The Shakespeare Memorial Theatre is officially opened at Stratford-upon-Avon.

Ireland, 5 May. Isaac Butt, the Irish politician who founded the home rule movement, dies (→ 8/6).

Westport, Co Mayo, 8 June. Charles Parnell addresses a land reform meeting (→ 10/1879).

Chislehurst, Kent, 12 July. The funeral takes place of Prince Louis Napoleon, the son of the late emperor of France, Napoleon III, who was killed fighting with the British army in South Africa.

Co Mayo, 21 August. An apparition of the Virgin Mary is reported in Knock.

Dublin, 21 October. The Irish National Land League is founded; Parnell is the president (→ 19/11).

Liverpool, 27 October. The first issue of the *Liverpool Echo* newspaper is printed.

Dublin, 19 November. Michael Davitt and other Fenian supporters and members of the Irish National Land League are arrested on sedition charges (→ 11/3/80).

Humberside. The prince of Wales opens the renovated docks at Grimsby and renames them the Alexandra docks.

London. Henry James, an American novelist based in Britain, publishes his latest novel, *Daisy Miller* (→ 1881).

Birmingham. The Cadbury chocolate factory moves out of the city centre to Bournville.

London. The city's first telephone exchange opens.

Zulus launch bloody war in Africa

British troops are massacred at base

Southern Africa, 23 January
A British force sent to deal with the aggressive King Cetewayo of the Zulus met disaster yesterday when 20,000 Zulu warriors overwhelmed the advanced British base at Isandhlwana and "washed their spears" in the blood of the garrison.

The disaster was brought about both by a clever Zulu manoeuvre which drew Lord Chelmsford and his main force away from the camp and by the inept positioning of the garrison – a mixed force of South Wales Borderers, colonists and native levies – who were scattered over a large area.

The defenders fought until their ammunition ran out but were then slaughtered. The Zulus took no prisoners. Fifty white officers and 776 NCOs and men were killed along with 800 men of the black contingents. About 40 Europeans got away, some of whom rode to alert the 130-strong garrison, mainly South Wales Borderers, left behind at Rorke's Drift. These men threw up defences and when 4,000 of Cetewayo's warriors attacked, poured a hail of bullets into them. They held out for 12 hours until the Zulus retreated at dawn, leaving their dead behind (→ 4/7).

Saving the regimental colours.

King Cetewayo: fearsome soldier.

Mud hut capital hit by British firepower

Southern Africa, 4 July
King Cetewayo's brave and fearsome warriors have been crushed at his mud hut capital of Ulundi today. His men, ranged in their massed impis, and armed mainly with shield and assegai, were cut down by the ruthless firepower of Lord Chelmsford's punitive force. Defeat at Isandhlwana in January has been bloodily avenged, but it is no comfort to Chelmsford; he is to be replaced by Sir Garnet Wolseley.

Cetewayo is now a fugitive and the Zulu threat to the Transvaal has been lifted but this colonial war has been full of embarrassment for the British government. Shortly after the humiliation at Isandhlwana, the only son of Napoleon III, Prince Louis Napoleon, who was serving in the British army as a volunteer, lost his life in a skirmish.

There is also the threat of future trouble. The Boers acquiesced in the British annexation of the Transvaal two years ago because they needed the British army's protection against the Zulus, although few would admit it. But they are becoming increasingly resentful at the loss of their independence. With the Zulus crushed, that resentment seems certain to fester (→ 12/1880).

Joseph Swan demonstrates electric lighting 'bright as sunshine'

A lamp developed by Swan.

Newcastle-upon-Tyne, 3 February
Members of the Newcastle Chemical Society marvelled tonight at a glass bulb glowing – "with great splendour" – powered by electricity and invented by one of their members, Joseph Swan. His invention burns carbon in a bulb exhausted of air and gives off a light as "bright as sunshine". Swan appears to have won the race to produce light by means of electricity – at least three other inventors are striving in the same direction.

The carbon system has a short life, however, and in New York, Thomas Edison has devised an alternative system using metal filaments. Already, writs are being prepared by both men (→ 18/9).

Electric light admired in London.

Gladstone hits the hustings in Midlothian

Edinburgh, November
At the ripe old age of 70, William Ewart Gladstone, twice prime minister, has taken his campaign to the people here, determined to beat his arch-rival, the earl of Beaconsfield, formerly Benjamin Disraeli, and secure a third term as premier. No politician has ever stormed the hustings before in such a way: in the course of this campaign for the Midlothian constituency – where Gladstone is standing – he has addressed more than 85,000 people, many from his train at stations between London and Scotland.

Gladstone's campaign recognizes the importance of the huge number of new voters following the 1867 Reform Act – and the importance of newspaper reports of speeches. Queen Victoria and Beaconsfield are furious at these "unconstitutional" tactics – but Gladstone has beaten the Tory Lord Dalkeith for the Midlothian seat (→8/3/80).

Gladstone prepares to leave West Calder station to the cheers of the crowds.

Disaster at Tay Bridge

Divers prepare to search for the train lost when the bridge collapsed.

Dundee, 28 December
Britain's railway system suffered its worst-ever disaster tonight. The central section of the Tay Bridge collapsed, plunging the Edinburgh/Dundee train into the icy river and killing nearly 100 passengers and the crew. Hurricane-force winds had lashed the Tay into a mass of crested waves and spectators on the shore described seeing a sheet of flame and a hail of sparks as girders collapsed, sending the train crashing into the water some 27 metres (88 feet) below.

The bridge was the longest in the world. Before it was opened in May six locomotives, with a combined weight of some 430 tonnes, were run over the bridge at speeds of 40mph. The Board of Trade inspector, General Hutchinson, declared tests to be "very satisfactory", but imposed a 25mph speed limit and said he would like to do a test in high winds (→1883).

Farmers facing ruin after crop failures

Britain, September
Following a summer of "cloud and continuous rain", Britain is suffering the worst harvest for decades with thousands of farmers facing financial disaster. Grain prices have been hit by cheap American corn flooding the market thanks to low-cost transport by rail on the prairies, fierce competition by steamship companies and fast-developing agricultural technology. Cattle farmers have had an equally difficult year with the world monetary depression forcing down the price of meat and other produce. Millions of sheep have been lost in a huge outbreak of liver-rot.

Bankruptcies are multiplying, the value of land has plummeted, and countless farms are being left neglected as tenants seek work in the cities. Farmworkers are once again on reduced wages.

Parnell heads Irish National Land League for rights of tenants

Ireland, October
Michael Davitt has formed the Irish National Land League with Charles Parnell as president. The impact of agricultural depression on rural Ireland has been so severe that American Fenians (notably John Devoy) have suggested that the parliamentary party should campaign in support of the peasantry's struggle with the landlords. Thousands of tenant farmers are in arrears with their rent and the number of evictions has risen so sharply that the rural economy seems in danger of collapse.

Davitt has been quick to see the need for a national movement linked to the land question. At the age of four his family were evicted from their home in Mayo, leaving him with a lifelong hatred of the landlord system. He later joined the Fenians and spent seven years in an English prison. Now back in Ireland, he seems determined to bring the land question into the centre of Irish politics. During the summer he had informal discussions with Parnell and John Devoy, after which an informal alliance was established, known as "the new departure". Parnell sees his presidency of the Land League as an important step towards the leadership of the parliamentary party (now made even more possible by the death of Isaac Butt), and he is conscious that his influence is growing throughout the country (→21).

Reading the news: the proclamation of the Land League (Howard Helmick).

1880

London, 15 January. The London Telephone Company publishes the first telephone directory, with 255 names in it (→ 16/3/91).

London, 2 February. The first consignment of frozen meat arrives from Australia on the *SS Strathleven*.

Westminster, 8 March. The earl of Beaconsfield, the prime minister, requests a dissolution of parliament and calls a general election (→ 23/4).

United States, 11 March. Charles Parnell, the leader of the Irish National Land League, completes his American tour in New York with the launch of the Irish National Land League of the United States (→ 17/5).

Westminster, 21 April. The earl of Beaconsfield resigns.

Westminster, 23 April. William Gladstone is appointed prime minister.→

Liverpool, April. Liverpool is given city status (→ 9/1880).

Belfast, 4 May. Five women "soldiers" bring the Salvation Army to Ireland (→ 1890).

Dublin, 17 May. Charles Parnell is elected chairman of the Irish parliamentary party (→ 11/1880).

Aberdeen, 18 May. George Washington Wilson, a former artist, is appointed royal photographer to the queen.

Dublin, 18 September. The Trades Union Congress meets for the first time in Ireland.

Liverpool, October. University College is founded.

Ireland, 18 November. The Irish Football Association is founded (→ 22/3/88).

Dublin, 28 December. The trial of Charles Parnell and his fellow colleagues for conspiracy begins (→ 25/1/81).

Southern Africa, December. The Boers declare war on the British and drive them out of the Transvaal (→ 27/2/81).

Glasgow. The Scottish Football League is founded.

London. The Guildhall School of Music is founded.

Dunfermline, Scotland. Andrew Carnegie, the Scottish philanthropist and millionaire, donates a free library to his home town (→ 11/6/90).

Britain. Arthur Sullivan and W S Gilbert compose the operetta *The Pirates of Penzance* (→ 1885).

'Tit-Bits' aims for a new class of reader

London
A new illustrated weekly has appeared which is designed to appeal to a mass popular market. It is called *Tit-Bits* and contains short segments of prose with snappy headlines clearly designed for the new young reading public emerging from the recently created elementary schools.

Tit-Bits has been started by George Newnes, the former manager of a Manchester fancy goods business. He looks like having an instant success, cultivating an audience entirely separate to those who buy the traditional weeklies and daily papers with their dense layout, serious tone and middle-aged, middle-class readerships.

Gladstone is victorious in general election and takes over for Liberals once again

Westminster, 23 April
Much to the dismay of the queen, William Gladstone's Liberal Party has won a spectacular election victory and she has been forced to invite the man she dislikes to form a government again. A despairing Victoria turned to the Liberal leaders in the House of Lords, Hartington and Granville, but Gladstone's success in Midlothian made him the undisputed leader of his party.

The Liberal majority of 130 was assured by the economic situation, with high unemployment and a disastrous harvest causing a major depression. Irish home rulers have consolidated their position as the third party with 60 seats in the House of Commons (→ 19/4/81).

Gladstone, the cabinet-maker, seeks approval from a sceptical Victoria.

New MP causes uproar by refusing to swear oath of allegiance

Bradlaugh's stand led to his arrest on the floor of the House of Commons.

Westminster, April
Lord Randolph Churchill and his right-wing "ginger group" have been quick to take advantage of a radical MP's refusal to take the oath of office. Charles Bradlaugh, the member for Northampton, insisted on affirming his allegiance on the grounds that he was an atheist.

Although Bradlaugh agreed to take the oath after a committee voted against affirmation, Conservatives united with Irish and nonconformist MPs with shouts of "Bradlaugh and blasphemy". The new member will be forced to go back to his constituency in Northamptonshire to seek re-election if he wishes to fight on (→ 1/1886).

Mine blast kills 160

Co Durham, 10 September
At least 160 men are feared to have been killed today in an explosion at Seaham colliery. Thirty bodies have been brought to the surface and rescue workers are losing hope of finding anyone still alive. The rescuers are working amid the threat of further explosions. Naked lights have been banned in the area of the pit, where inspectors have already begun to investigate the cause of the disaster. Queen Victoria has sent a message of sympathy to families of the men who are missing.

The first telephone exchange opened in London last year, just three years after Alexander Graham Bell demonstrated his invention in the United States. The picture shows telephone operators at work in 1883.

'George Eliot' dies: the moralist who became a novelist

London, 22 December
The novelist George Eliot (born Mary Ann Evans) died at her home in Cheyne Walk, Chelsea, today, not eight months after her marriage to John Cross, a New York banker and friend who did much to comfort her after the death two years ago of G H Lewes with whom she lived for many years. She had met Lewes when she was assistant editor of the *Westminster Review*, for which he wrote as a critic.

It was after their liaison began in 1854 that she turned to fiction, bringing to the novel her moral earnestness and demonstrating how her characters' fate was controlled by their moral choice of actions. She drew memorable characters, such as Maggie Tulliver of *The Mill on the Floss*, the hero who gives his name to the novel *Silas Marner* and Gwendolen Harleth in the later *Daniel Deronda*. She also excelled at portraying whole societies in Coventry and rural Warwickshire.

George Eliot was very conscious of her thick-set, masculine features, which she always set off by a fashionable, oddly frivolous Paris hat. She liked to be addressed as "Madonna" and was proud, she said, of "being able to live without opium". Once an evangelical, she was converted to agnosticism as a young woman and belonged to a positivist circle which included Herbert Spencer, the philosopher.

Mary Ann Evans, or George Eliot.

Irish launch 'boycotting' campaign

Police protect cattle from the Erne estate as they are driven to market.

Captain Boycott: Irish target.

Co Mayo, November
Fifty Protestant Orangemen from Co Cavan have been drafted in to harvest the crops at Lord Erne's estate in Co Mayo. They were protected by 1,000 members of the Royal Irish Constabulary. A local man has described it as "the queerest menagerie that ever came into Connaught". Lord Erne's agent is Captain Boycott, whose offence was to bid for a farm from which a tenant had been evicted. As the first victim of the Land League's campaign of organized ostracism he has given his name to the activity of "boycotting" his estate.

An emergency measure designed by the government to protect tenants from being evicted without compensation, has been defeated in the House of Lords, causing an immediate increase in agrarian disturbance. The Land League has ordered rents to be withheld, evicted farms to be kept empty, and landlords to be excluded from all transactions within the community if they mistreat their tenants (→ 28/12).

W G Grace is undisputed star of England/Australia test match

Lord Harris, the England captain, saves a boundary in the first test match against Australia to be played in this country.

London, September
A year after obtaining his medical degree, Dr William Gilbert Grace strode to the wicket at the Oval ground and delighted the crowd of 20,000 with an innings of 152. The cricketing doctor's skilful batting gave England under Lord Harris a narrow win over Australia in the first test match played in England; one was played in Melbourne in March 1877. With his giant beard and bold contempt for the fastest bowler, "W G" has already become a legend. At the age of just 16 he was playing for Gloucester County and was selected for the Gentlemen against the Players. The Oval at Kennington, formerly a market garden, has been used for a variety of sports. It was the scene of the first football Cup Final in 1871, when the trophy was won by a team of public schoolboys, the Wanderers. The following year, it was also the arena for the world's first international rugby match (→ 9/1882). ▷

Busy port of Liverpool is made a city and is first to float itself on Stock Exchange

St Nicholas's church and the telegraph tower overlook the thriving docks.

Liverpool, September

This bustling seaport has marked its elevation to city status this year by becoming the first British city to achieve a successful stock flotation. Under an act of parliament £2 million was subscribed for Liverpool's consolidated municipal stock. Now other cities – most notably Birmingham, where the new president of the board of trade, Joseph Chamberlain, was mayor in the 1870s – are bound to follow suit as the need for urban finance increases and local government becomes more and more entrepreneurial.

Liverpool has led the country in "municipalization". Large sums of money have been invested in the docks and the municipality is about to begin a major programme of slum clearance. Its population has grown from 82,000 in 1801 to over 500,000 today. In addition to becoming a city this year, Liverpool has gained a bishopric.

The most obvious indication of municipal prosperity is to be seen in the monumental town halls which have risen in northern industrial cities. Manchester town hall, designed by Alfred Waterhouse and finished two years ago, is said to be unequalled for size among the municipal buildings of Europe; Bradford's vast Italianate building has inspired many a rococo copy among the chimney stacks of Yorkshire and Lancashire.

Glasgow is leading the way in municipal trading with its own water, gas, and electricity monopolies. London relies on private enterprise for its services – and already there is a rash of complaints about the quality of water.

Lime Street, Liverpool: now known as the terminus (r) of the railway.

The siege of Kandahar garrison is lifted

Kandahar, India, 31 August

General Sir Frederick Roberts VC forced his way into Kandahar today at the head of a 10,000-strong army after a forced march across the Afghan hills from Kabul, covering 313 miles (503km) in just 23 days to take the Afghan rebels under Ayub Khan by surprise.

The exploit, typical of "Bobs", who is idolized by his men, became necessary following the defeat last month of a British force under General Burrows at Maiwand. Burrows lost nearly 1,000 dead out of his force of 3,500; the survivors had to fall back on Kandahar and prepare for a desperate defence.

With the defeat of Ayub Khan, the son of Sher Ali, the deposed pro-Russian emir of Kabul, the way is now clear for Britain to lend its support to Abdur Rhaman, another member of the ruling family, in his claim to be emir. One condition of this support will be that he will enter into no independent relations with any foreign power. In return, Britain will not interfere with his administration (→ 31/1/84).

General Roberts sits at the centre of Afghans who support Britain's cause.

Law forces children to attend school

London

Education has become compulsory throughout Britain with every child between the age of five and 13 legally bound to attend school – although they can leave to work part-time if they have reached a sufficient standard of learning.

Since the Education Act came into force ten years ago, a major building programme has been under way with locally elected school boards – charged with bringing a basic education to working-class children – creating schools where there had been none before and waiving fees to poorer parents.

In Scotland, nearly 1,000 school boards took over existing schools after 1872 and ran them as a single national system. Unlike England and Wales, the Scottish churches have agreed on a common form of religious education and attendance has been compulsory for the past eight years (→ 12/1881).

National eisteddfod society for Wales

Wales

Welsh national consciousness, revitalized during the Llangollen eisteddfod of 1858, has been given a further boost of confidence, as well as financial security, by the formation of the National Eisteddfod Association led by Hugh Owen. From now on, there will be guaranteed funding for a national eisteddfod to be held annually. Prizes will be offered to encourage literary and musical prowess among the entire Welsh community.

Hugh Owen, elected to be the first life president of the association, is a native of Anglesey. He has been active in Welsh affairs since 1843. Based in the offices of the Poor Law Commission in London, he has been a leading figure in Welsh educational movements for nearly 40 years. The modern eisteddfod dates only from 1789. The prime mover in its historic revival was Thomas Jones of Corwen.

1881

Dublin, 25 January. Charles Parnell, the leader of the Irish National Land League, is indicted for conspiracy to prevent tenants paying rent; the trial ends in disagreement among the jury (→ 3/2).

Britain, January. A "great freeze" sweeps across the country, bringing everything to a halt.

London, 5 February. Thomas Carlyle, the Scottish-born historian, philosopher and critic, best known for historical works such as *The French Revolution*, *Oliver Cromwell* and *Frederick the Great*, dies aged 85.

Westminster, 7 April. The Irish National Land League, of which Parnell is the leader, is outlawed by parliament (→ 22).

London, 19 April. The earl of Beaconsfield, the former prime minister and Tory leader, dies aged 77.→

Dublin, 22 April. The Land League Convention considers the proposed Land Bill (→ 20/5).

Co Limerick, 20 May. The Revd Eugene Sheehy, the president of the Limerick Land League, is arrested (→ 13/8).

Dublin, 13 August. The first issue of *United Irish*, Parnell's weekly periodical, is printed by William O'Brien (→ 9/10).

Wexford, 9 October. Parnell makes a stirring reply to Gladstone's speech at Leeds on "resources of civilization" (→ 13).

London, 10 October. The Savoy theatre is opened.

Belfast, 29 October. The United Trades' Council is founded.

London, 31 December. Lillie Langtrey, the prince of Wales's mistress, makes her début as an actress at the Haymarket theatre.

Westminster. Parliament passes the Householders of Scotland Act; it gives some women a local vote (→ 18/2/1902).

Scotland. An observatory is built on Ben Nevis, the highest mountain in Britain.

Dundee. University College is established.

Britain. The Institute of Chartered Accountants is founded.

Britain. The army and navy abolish flogging as a punishment.

Irish troubles disrupt the Commons

Parnell among MPs suspended in clash

Westminster, 3 February
Charles Parnell and 35 of his Irish home rule supporters in the House of Commons have been suspended after the government forced through a motion limiting debate on its Coercion Bill. This bill suspends habeas corpus and gives the Irish authorities sweeping powers of arrest.

Parnell and his supporters had been fighting the bill, which was introduced on 24 January, by using the obstructionist tactics at which they have become adept. One sitting of the Commons lasted a continuous 41 hours. This was more than the speaker could bear. He suspended the time-honoured rules of the House and yesterday he forced a division on the first reading. Today William Gladstone, the prime minister, moved a closure resolution to restrict future debate and it was this that led to the suspension of 36 Irish members.

There is now a possibility that Parnell will consider withdrawing from Westminster to establish a self-styled national assembly in Ireland. But it is doubtful whether enough of his supporters would be willing to follow him (→ 2/3).

Armed soldiers enforce an eviction in the west of Ireland this year.

Coercion Act passed, habeas corpus ends

Westminster, 2 March
The Peace Preservation (Ireland) Act, more popularly known as the new Coercion Act, has been passed by parliament. It is unpalatable to many liberals and was stubbornly resisted to the last by Charles Parnell and his followers, but Gladstone, the prime minister, has forced it through despite opposition. The cabinet's Irish policy combines coercion and concession: a bill for the suspension of habeas corpus and a bill for the reform of the land system [*see below*]. The authorities have been alarmed by the growing power of the Land League and the success of its boycotting campaign, which has provided much greater protection for tenants than more violent methods.

Attempts to prosecute Parnell and Land League leaders for conspiracy failed, persuading Gladstone to back a call by W E Forster, the Irish secretary, for a strong measure of coercion to reassert the government's authority (→ 4/1881).

Tenants granted fair rents and greater protection from eviction

Westminster, April
A bill introduced by William Gladstone, the prime minister, has virtually conceded the basic demands of the Land League, popularly known as the "three F's":

* fair rent, to be assessed by arbitration;
* fixed tenure while rent is paid;
* freedom for the tenant to sell his right of occupancy at the best market price.

By these provisions, and by recognizing the permanent interest of the tenant in his holding, the bill establishes a system of dual ownership and has reduced the landlord to a mere receiver of rent. Gladstone expects the measures to be welcomed in Ireland, offsetting anger over the Coercion Act (→ 7).

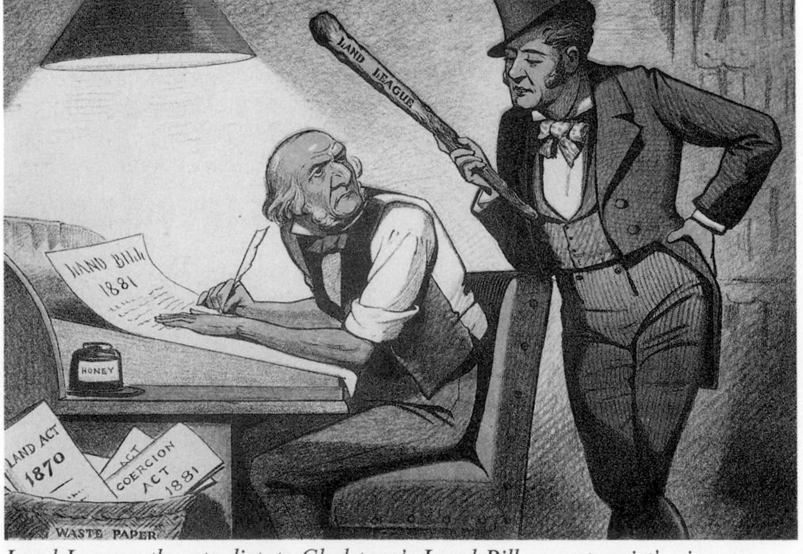

Land League threats dictate Gladstone's Land Bill: a cartoonist's view.

Salisbury to follow Beaconsfield as the leader of the Tories

London, 19 April
With the death today of Benjamin Disraeli, the earl of Beaconsfield, the leadership of the Conservatives devolves on Robert Cecil, the marquis of Salisbury. Calm, calculating and sardonic, Salisbury is the very antithesis of the flamboyant, passionate Disraeli. He is an aristocrat to his fingertips and welcomed his transition from the House of Commons to the House of Lords as a way of escaping the verbal fireworks of Disraeli and Gladstone in the lower chamber.

His upbringing has been typical of his class: Eton, which he hated, was followed by Oxford and then an adventurous two years of voyaging under sail to southern Africa, Australia and New Zealand. His main interest remains experimental chemistry and he has installed a telephone and electric lighting at his Hatfield House seat.

He entered parliament through an unopposed family constituency and in 1866 became the secretary for India, but later resigned to register his disapproval of Disraeli's Reform Bill. Believing implicitly in the established order of church and state, he remains sternly opposed to social reform.

He is, however, interested in foreign policy and served Disraeli well as foreign secretary. He will no doubt lead his party with calm intelligence, but it may be in a nation which is passing him by (→ 1884).

Salisbury: aristocratic leader.

Boers defeat British at Majuba Hill

British troops learn a bloody lesson as the Boers win the battle at Majuba.

Southern Africa, 27 February
The British army has suffered a humiliating and bloody defeat at the hands of sharpshooting Boer farmers on the rocky outcrop of Majuba Hill today. Sir George Colley, who led a force of 1,500 men into Transvaal to put down the rebellion, misjudged his enemies.

Despite suffering a serious reverse at Laing's Nek a month ago he still regarded the Boers as poor soldiers. Today they proved him wrong, their withering rifle fire cutting down the regular British soldiers as they scurried for cover on the bare hillside. More than 300 died. Sir George will not benefit from the lesson. A Boer marksman fired a bullet through his forehead, killing him (→ 2/8).

Pretoria Convention grants limited independence to the Transvaal

Pretoria, southern Africa, 2 August
Britain and the Boers have today signed the Pretoria Convention, which gives the Boers of the Transvaal complete independence within their own territory. Britain remains responsible for foreign relations and there is to be a British Resident in Pretoria, in recognition of British suzerainty.

This would appear to be the result of the defeat inflicted on the British at Majuba Hill in February, but the Gladstone government had already decided that the annexation of the Transvaal had been unjust and is now insisting that the defeat had no effect on the decision to give the Boers their independence. This does not sit well with a number of officers who wanted to avenge Majuba before making peace with the Boers (→ 29/12/95).

A group of heavily armed Boers photographed after the recent Zulu wars.

Census reveals growth of the professional and middle classes

Britain, August
This year's census of the population shows a steady growth in the size of the middle class as the ranks of the managerial, commercial and professional salary earners expand. This transition is largely due to the urbanization, increase in wealth, and development of communications brought by the industrial revolution over the past century. The middle class has in fact grown so large that it is almost impossible to define its limits. At the lower end, the clerk struggles to stay one rung above the working class, while at the upper end the rich manufacturer is often grander than the poor aristocrat. The majority are, however, developing their own code of "middle-class behaviour". As their wealth and influence grows, so does their political power; while they may wish to enjoy aristocratic society, they have no intention of allowing landowners to maintain their dominance of government.

Total populations revealed by the census were 25,974,000 people in England and Wales, 3,736,000 in Scotland and 5,175,000 in Ireland – an overall increase of 3.4 million over the past decade.

University education spreads to provinces

Nottingham's new University College symbolizes the growth of education.

Britain, December
This year has seen the opening of two more centres of higher education, the University College of Liverpool and the University College of Nottingham, which join the increasing number of provincial foundations designed to serve the needs of their local communities. These establishments are often far removed from the liberal arts of Oxford and Cambridge: they follow more practical lines and they stem from the concern of industrialists for the future of British industry and commerce in face of well-trained foreign competition.

An example was set by Henry Roscoe, Professor of Chemistry at Owen's College in Manchester. The college was founded in 1851 to provide a liberal education for young Mancunians but was not successful until Roscoe made it relevant to local needs and aspirations. Its success was recognized last year when it was given full university status as Victoria University.

Other recent establishments with roots in local industry are the Newcastle College of Physical Science (1871), the Yorkshire College of Science at Leeds (1874), Firth College in Sheffield (1874), University College in Bristol (1876) and the Mason College of Science, Birmingham (1880). These are moving towards becoming full universities. Oxford and Cambridge may sneer at their "intellectual narrowness" but they serve their purpose and their communities (→27/7/89).

Parnell is sent to prison

Dublin, 13 October
In a surprise move by the government Charles Parnell has been arrested and thrown into Kilmainham prison. John Dillon and other leaders of the Irish National Land League have also been jailed.

To the dismay of the government, neither Parnell nor the leaders of the Land League have supported Gladstone's Land Act. They complain that it does little or nothing for tenants. Enraged by this, W E Foster, the Irish chief secretary, accused Parnell of deliberately trying to wreck the act. Believing that if he was out of the way tenants would accept the measures, Forster ordered his arrest. The Land League has called on people to withhold all rents until their grievances have been righted (→2/5/82).

Parnell and Dillon come under the watchful scrutiny of their jailer.

James wins praise for 'Portrait of a Lady'

London
The most admired new name in English fiction is that of the American expatriate Henry James, who lives mainly in London and writes about Americans abroad in Europe. Already known for *Daisy Miller*, whose flirtatious heroine was called "a libel on American womanhood", he provides a more acute psychological study of his heroine in *Portrait of a Lady*.

Isabel Archer is a free, confident spirit who refuses marriage both to a rich American and an English aristocrat, only to fall under the spell of an American aesthete living in Florence, who marries her for her fortune. Like other Americans in Europe, she is an innocent who becomes a victim. "She had an infinite hope that she would never do anything wrong." Her principles, unhappily, work against her chance of finding happiness.

James, from a wealthy New York family, spent a rootless youth in many capitals. He keeps notebooks of the stories he hears while dining out in London society (→1897).

Welsh agree to ban drinking on Sunday

Wales
Public houses in Wales are to be closed on Sundays. A majority of Welsh churchgoers, voting in parish churches and nonconformist chapels, have been persuaded by the Society for the Suppression of Vice (founded in 1802) to back the forced closing of public houses on the Sabbath.

In Scotland, complete Sunday closing was enforced in 1853. In England it was achieved in 1854 and modified slightly in 1855. But it was not until this year that a majority of the Welsh fell into line.

Designer William Morris is expanding his products this year with a range of carpets and rugs (left). Morris is known for his wallpaper and furniture; the cabinet (right) was designed by Philip Webb and painted by Morris.

1882

London, February. The Royal College of Music is founded.

Windsor, 2 March. Roderick MacLean is arrested after attempting to shoot Queen Victoria (→ 19/4).

London, 9 April. Charles Darwin, the anthropologist and explorer who wrote the controversial *Origin of Species*, dies, aged 71.

Kent, 9 April. The artist and poet Dante Gabriel Rossetti dies, aged 54.

London, 19 April. Roderick MacLean, on trial for his attempt on the life of Queen Victoria, is acquitted as insane (→ 29/3/83).

Ireland, 2 May. Charles Parnell and other imprisoned Land League leaders are released from Kilmainham prison after a secret agreement to bring an end to the violence over the Land Act.→

Westminster, 19 May. The House of Commons votes 203 to 83 against the opening of museums and public galleries on a Sunday.

London, 16 June. The Council of the Society of Arts awards the Albert medal to the French scientist Louis Pasteur for his "researches in connection with fermentation".

Newcastle, 5 July. The city is given a formal royal charter.

Dublin, 17 October. The Irish National League is formed as a successor to the outlawed Land League (→ 26/1/83).

Glasgow, 2 November. Women celebrate the passing of the Married Women's Property Act: a married woman is entitled to own property in her own right; previously all property passed into the possession of her husband.

London, 18 November. The renovated Strand theatre is reopened.

Lambeth, 3 December. Archibald Campbell Tait, the archbishop of Canterbury, who succeeded Charles Langley in 1868, dies aged 70 (→ 1/1883).

London, 12 December. The City of London School on the Victoria Embankment opens.

Edinburgh, 18 December. The city is brought to a standstill by severe winter weather.

Glasgow. The directors of the City of Glasgow Bank, which collapsed in 1878 with debts of over £7 million are found guilty of fraud.

Trouble in Ireland over Coercion Act

Land Leaguers are freed in secret deal

Dublin, 2 May

As a result of a secret "Kilmainham treaty", Charles Parnell and other Irish National Land League leaders were released from prison today. William Gladstone, the prime minister, has told the Commons that W E Forster, the Irish chief secretary, and Lord Cowper, the viceroy, are resigning in protest at the terms of the treaty, which allows the Coercion Act to lapse and arrears of excessive rent owed by tenants to be settled.

In return, Parnell has agreed to use his influence to try to quell the disorder which has increased sharply since he and others were thrown into Kilmainham jail six months ago. There were 1,440 incidents of unrest during the first quarter of this year, although there were only 14 deaths.

Many of Parnell's allies are regarding the "Kilmainham treaty" as a selfish surrender to the British government. But Parnell is determined to quell agrarian disturbance and work for a peaceful solution to the real problems: conciliation and cooperation are to be tried in place of coercion (→ 6).

Bloodshed in the park: one view of the murder of Cavendish and Burke.

Minister and aide killed in Phoenix Park

Dublin, 6 May

Widespread horror has been expressed at the murder today in Dublin of the new Irish chief secretary, Lord Frederick Cavendish, and Thomas Burke, his under-secretary. They were stabbed to death as they walked in Phoenix Park. Later the assailants left black-edged cards at newspaper offices stating that the murders had been carried out by the hitherto unknown "Irish Invincibles". Charles Parnell, the leader of the Land League, is said to be devastated by the murders, which come just four days after he was released from prison under the "Kilmainham treaty" to work for peace. But his offer to resign his seat as an MP has been refused by William Gladstone, the prime minister, who does not wish to lose Parnell's restraining influence.

The effect of the double assassination on the English public is expected to be profound, however. The "Kilmainham treaty" is discredited and the decision by the former chief secretary, W E Forster, to resign is vindicated (→ 17/10).

The Church Army is founded to tackle the problems of the cities

London

The Reverend Wilson Carlile, an Anglican clergyman born in Buxton, has founded the Church Army, a body of lay evangelists who will be trained not only to spread the gospel but also to look after the day-to-day needs of the less fortunate. Its officers, who will be designated captains and sisters, are to work in prisons and with prisoners' families. They will also work with local authorities to provide shelter for the jobless and homeless.

The organization is an attempt to make the church more relevant to the needs of working people, whose presence in church is becoming rare. It is also an imitation of the Salvation Army, founded 12 years ago by the Methodists William and Catherine Booth.

A Church Army worker distributes the organization's newssheet, c.1890.

Wives now able to own their homes

Westminster, August
The second Married Women's Property Act gives married women the same rights over their property as unmarried women. According to *The Times*, this act, which becomes law in January, "probably portends indirect social effects much greater than the disposition of property, and may in the end pulverize some ideas which have been at the basis of English life".

One of those long-held ideas is that the married couple are one. Wives' earnings have legally belonged to their husbands – an injustice that has fuelled the growing campaign for women's rights. Some middle-class husbands can see advantages in the new law. Financial autonomy makes wives separately liable for debts (→2/11).

Musing on what the future holds.

'Champion of Islam' is trounced in Egypt

Egypt, 13 September
Sir Garnet Wolseley has shattered the forces of Colonel Ahmed Arabi in a battle at Tel el-Kebir today. Sir Garnet planned the battle with such precision and carried it out with such skill that "Arabi Pasha" was driven from the field for only 400 British dead and wounded.

The battle was the culmination of Arabi's revolt against the Khedive Tewfik, which led to the mob massacre of 50 Europeans in Alexandria on 11 June. A British fleet bombarded the Alexandria forts in retaliation, forcing Arabi to withdraw. The mob took over the city and the British government, fearing for the safety of the Suez canal, decided that it must act.

Sir Garnet was sent out with an expeditionary force but Arabi, proclaiming himself the champion of Islam, entrenched himself with an army at Tel el-Kebir. The military issue was settled today but Britain is now embroiled in the uncertain politics of Egypt (→11/1883).

'Ashes' of English defeat go to Australia

The Australian cricketers who shattered the mother country's invincibility.

London, September
Ivo Bligh, the captain of the England cricket team, has promised a "crusade to regain the Ashes" when he leads his men to Australia later this year. The term "Ashes" refer to an article in the *Sporting Times*, which greeted last month's first victory by Australia over England with a mock obituary notice: "In affectionate remembrance of English Cricket, which died at The Oval on 29th August, 1882. Deeply lamented by a large circle of sorrowing friends and acquaintances."

Cricket has long been played on village greens, but the first international match took place only five years ago between England and Australia in Melbourne. England won that and every subsequent game, until now (→9/1908).

Epping Forest made public property to save it from developers

Essex, 6 May
Queen Victoria was welcomed by huge crowds today as she travelled by train from Windsor to Epping to open the forest as a public park. Volunteers and troops lined the three-mile route from the station, as the queen and her daughters, accompanied by London's lord mayor, rode in the royal carriage, entering the forest through a lavishly decorated arch.

The lord mayor provided lunch for 10,000 people in a temporary building. The local recorder read an address to which the queen replied, prompting cheers. Among the audience were the inhabitants of some of the poorest streets of Essex and the East End of London. Epping Forest has now been saved from potential development as London grows and is intended as a recreation area for the people.

'Crofters' war' in the Scottish Highlands

Skye, 7 April
Violence has broken out here between local people and the police. Troops and gunboats are now to be sent to the island to ensure that disorder does not spread to neighbouring islands, where anger over Highland clearances is running high. The conflict is essentially over tenants' rights, which are being eroded by landlords like Lord Macdonald, who has tried to remove customary privileges. Tenants have responded by refusing to pay their rents and have resisted eviction orders. Officials of the sheriff were humiliated recently when a crowd of women and children forced them to burn their papers.

But Sheriff Ivory summoned 50 constables from Glasgow and at 6am today they arrived to carry out the evictions. Most of the younger men had already left to go fishing, but the remaining locals pelted the police with stones, and fierce hand-to-hand fighting followed. Large numbers were injured on both sides, but no-one was killed.

Since the mid-1850s, Skye has seen its number of inhabitants fall from 23,074 to 17,680 as landlords have encouraged their poorer tenants to leave (→2/1883).

More peaceful days: Highland hospitality inside a crofter's home.

1883

London, 18 January. The Prince of Wales theatre opens.

Belfast, 26 January. The Ulster Land Committee is formed as the central organization representing tenants' rights associations (→4/1883).

Canterbury, January. Edward White Benson, the bishop of Truro, is appointed archbishop of Canterbury (→11/10/96).

Highland, February. A royal commission is established by Lord Napier to investigate landholding in the region.

London, 14 March. Karl Marx, the revolutionary thinker who wrote *Das Kapital* and in collaboration with Friedrich Engels drew up the *Communist Manifesto*, dies, aged 67.

Windsor, 29 March. Queen Victoria is deeply distressed by the sudden death of her close friend and servant, John Brown (→21/6/87).

London, 5 April. The alleged "Dynamite Conspirators" are arrested for bombings in London and Birmingham (→14/6).

Suffolk, 14 June. Edward Fitzgerald, a poet and the translator into English of the *Rubaiyat of Omar Khayyam*, dies.

London, 14 June. The "Dynamite Conspirators", led by Henry Wilson, are found guilty and sentenced to life imprisonment.

United States, 24 July. Matthew Webb, the first man to swim the English Channel, in 1875, drowns while attempting to swim the rapids above the Niagara Falls.

Co Antrim, 28 September. Portrush is linked to Bushmills by the world's second electric railway (→6/3/93).

Glasgow. The Highland Land League is founded; it will campaign for security of tenure for the crofters (→11/1885).

Scotland. The Scottish Amateur Athletics Association is founded.

Liverpool. The first society for the prevention of cruelty to children is founded (→1884).

Leeds. The first steam tram service begins (→1885).

Huddersfield. Locals weavers go on strike for better working conditions.

Cardiff. The University College of South Wales opens.

'Treasure Island' is part of boom in novels for children

London

The appearance of *Treasure Island* in book form this year, after its serialization in *Young Folks*, reflects a new taste for boys' adventure stories. The author, Robert Louis Stevenson, wrote the first half in just a fortnight in a cottage at Braemar as an amusement for his young stepson. It began with a map of the island that Stevenson drew: "As I pored over my map the future characters of the book began to appear there visibly among imaginary woods; their brown faces and bright weapons peeped out upon me. ... It was to be a story for boys. Women were excluded."

The popularity of *Treasure Island* is due to Stevenson's gift for telling an exciting story about rascally but fascinating characters like Long John Silver, who was based on his friend W E Henley. Children's books free of moralizing are in demand. Stevenson was indebted to the seafaring yarns of Captain Frederick Marryat, the author of *Mr Midshipman Easy* and *Children of the New Forest*. Other novels for young readers in vogue are Mark Twain's *Tom Sawyer*, Louisa Alcott's *Little Women*, Charles Kingsley's *The Water Babies* and *Black Beauty* by Anna Sewell. Still popular is last year's *Vice Versa* by F Anstey, in which a father and son change places (→1889).

The villain: Long John Silver.

Pamphlet on the horror slums of London moves the queen and shakes politicians

Back-to-back housing beneath the noise and dirt of London's railways.

London

Queen Victoria and several of her ministers have been deeply moved by a pamphlet drawing attention to the plight of London's poor and homeless. *The Bitter Cry of Outcast London* is believed to be the work of nonconformist missionaries and in particular Andrew Mearns, the secretary of the London Congregational Union. Serious newspapers struggle to reconcile the wealth and glory of the British empire with the squalor and deprivation of the poor, while the popular *Daily News* runs a column by George Sims which describes in lurid detail the suffering of the "London heathen". Both highlight the growing separation of classes and the dangers to social and political cohesion.

Since the Public Health Act of 1875, there has been growing concern about housing. Two acts in 1879 stepped up slum clearance, and increased pressure on landlords to maintain their property. In London, the Metropolitan Board of Works has displaced and rehoused more than 20,000 people; but it relies on charities like the Peabody Trust to build houses (→1884).

'Invincibles' guilty of Irish park murders

Ireland, April

Five members of the "Invincibles", a secret society, have been tried and found guilty of the Phoenix Park murders last May [*see report on page 966*], and have been sentenced to death. Hunting down the killers was largely the responsibility of Superintendent Mallon, of the Dublin Metropolitan Police. There have been many twists to the story and one informer has been murdered.

Suspicion first fell on the Dublin Fenians and was then transferred to Patrick Egan, treasurer of the Land League. He was linked with James Mullett, a pub owner and Fenian, then in Kilmainham jail. Mallon offered to settle his debts and obtain his release in exchange for information, and Mullett supplied the names of a number of Invincibles, particularly James Carey.

As the trail grew warmer, two bloodstained knives and a rifle were found and suspicion once more fell on Carey. It was later proved that he had formed a Dublin branch of the Invincibles with 30 recruits, and Mullett as one of the leaders. Eventually an Invincible, Robert Farrell, realized that the game was up and betrayed his comrades. It was finally Carey's evidence that helped to convict the suspects, and solve the crime (→1/10/84).

Limits are imposed on election spending

Westminster, August
Parliamentary elections are to be made fairer under the Corrupt and Illegal Practices Prevention Act, which widens liability for prosecution, defines the role of agents, and limits expenses. Under the existing Corrupt Practices Prevention Act of 1854, the candidate alone could be punished for treating, threatening, bribery or personation. Now anyone acting on his behalf will be similarly liable.

The new act bans payment for election expenses, except by duly appointed agents. On or before the day of nomination, a person standing for parliament must nominate an agent and, depending on the size of the constituency, a number of deputies. These agents must record all payments of £2 or more, and keep receipts. Accounts must be submitted to the returning officer within 35 days of an election.

Candidates' personal expenses must not exceed £200, nor must miscellaneous expenses. The labour and legal costs are limited, in constituencies of 2,000 electors or less, to £350 in a borough, £650 in a county. In larger boroughs, the allowance is set at £380, plus £30 for every further 1,000 electors. Larger counties have their limits similarly upgraded. Allowances are slightly lower in Ireland.

"King Cash": election boss?

Electricity changes the British way of life

Britain, September
Electric trains, telegraphs and street lamps are revolutionizing Britain's transport, communications and public amenities. Since 1821, when Michael Faraday demonstrated electromagnetic induction, physicists and engineers have come up with ever more ingenious schemes for using electrical power. This year has seen the first electric railway in the British Isles open at Portrush in Ireland, followed by a miniature electric railway along the seafront at Brighton, designed by a German engineer, Magnus Volk. Trams may be next to go electric.

R E B Crompton introduced the first electrically powered public lighting scheme, at Godalming, Surrey, two years ago. Now the General Post Office in Glasgow, the Mansion House in London, and a growing number of railway stations are using similar systems. A generating station at Holborn Viaduct was opened last year by Joseph Swan and Thomas Edison, to provide current for street lighting.

The electric telegraph, so important in the development of the railways, is threatened only by the telephone, invented by the Scots-born American Alexander Graham Bell. Private companies are competing to emulate the first telephone exchange, opened in 1879 (→1889).

Turbines for the Portrush railway.

Army may leave Sudan after Mahdi's revolt

Hicks Pasha and his army on the march against the Mahdi in Sudan.

Sudan, November
The massacre of a British-led force in the Sudan suggests that the occupation of Egypt is turning into a disaster. After several outbursts of nationalist fervour against the inept government of the Khedive, a more serious threat has emerged in the shape of the Mahdi, or "expected one", a prophet who is leading an Islamic *jihad* against the unbelievers. The Mahdi overran Kordofan last year, and has just ambushed and wiped out an Egyptian army led by Hicks. He now threatens Khartoum. Sir Evelyn Wood, the commander of Britain's army in Egypt, has written advising Queen Victoria to evacuate the Sudan. He says Egypt is incapable of governing the area, and occupation is a drain on resources (→18/2/84).

Cheap Trains Act means workers pay less

London
The Cheap Trains Act requires all railway companies to offer a cheap workman's fare. Now the rest of the country may follow London, where a workman's fare has been available on the Metropolitan Railway for 19 years. Urbanization has created great demand for commuter transport. The first electric tramcar was introduced in Birkenhead in 1860 and since 1870 a number of tramcar companies have compulsorily purchased by local authorities. In London, however, the railways have been developed more imaginatively, with the Metropolitan Railway Company leading the way.

Within two years of the opening of the Metropolitan Railway in 1862, 259 projects had been presented for underground railways. There are now 110 such trains, carrying 25,000 workers a day. An inner circle line should be completed next year (→28/9).

An early morning workers' train arrives at Baker Street station in London.

Scottish towns flourish as heavy industry spreads

The Clyde: the main artery of Glasgow and its shipbuilding industry.

Smoke rises from the chimneys of Dundee's numerous jute mills.

Tragedy mars shipbuilding success story

Glasgow
Tragedy has hit the Clyde, in a year in which Scottish shipbuilding has scaled new peaks of success. The coaster *SS Daphne* was launched at Linthouse on 3 July, but rolled over and sank almost immediately, killing the 124 workmen aboard.

The disaster has focused attention on ship design, and Sir Edward Reed's commission of inquiry is expected to call for improvements. Mrs Isabella Elder, widow of the designer John Elder, has founded a chair of naval architecture at the university of Glasgow, and William Denny & Brothers of Dumbarton has opened the first ship model experimental tank for commercial use. The coming of the steam age has certainly given the Clyde a new lease of life.

John Elder's the *SS Brandon*, built in 1854, used steel to replace iron and carried the first engines to use the new technique known as "compounding" – using and re-using steam before it enters the condenser. This reduces fuel consumption by as much as 35 per cent and enables steamships to compete with sail on long ocean routes. The *SS Aberdeen*, launched two years ago, is fitted with the very latest "triple expansion" steam engine, and may sound the death knell of large iron bulk cargo sailing ships. The Clyde has championed steamships – a vital means of communication on Scotland's west coast.

The Trongate in Glasgow, now said to be the second city of the empire.

Dundee booms as 'jute capital of world'

Tayside
Dundee is a city like no other, dominated by a single industry. It is the jute capital of the world. At the beginning of this century flax and linen were the main industries of a town with 26,000 people. Today the population is 140,000.

The Crimean War and American Civil War accelerated demand for the cheapest form of sacking and canvas. With Dundee's whale fisheries supplying oil to soften the fibres, profits from jute have rocketed. But those profits have remained in the hands of a very few, and the classes are extraordinarily polarized. While the workers toil and cough beneath the belching chimneys of the jute mills, their bosses enjoy the sea air three miles away. Most of the workforce are women, who get lower wages. Trapped in overcrowded, disease-ridden tenement buildings, the poor turn to crime, and vice is rampant. From University College, founded two years ago, and the Dundee Social Union come the first stirrings of social conscience.

Boys' Brigade adds to church schooling

Glasgow, 4 October
The first meeting of the Boys' Brigade, a uniformed organization of teenage volunteers, was held today in the West End of the city. William Smith, the 29-year-old founder, is an evangelical Christian who has worked in Sunday schools and missions. Smith believes that boys of 14, many of whom are working alongside adults, need more than a Sunday-school education. He and his colleagues from the North Woodside Mission want to imbue these young people with Christian and citizenly values while keeping them active with sport and music. Bands and parades will be a feature of the Boys' Brigade.

Professor of Gaelic at Scots university

Edinburgh
The Gaelic language has achieved academic status with the establishment of a chair of Celtic at Edinburgh University. Although the English language dominates north of the border, many Scots treasure their inheritance from the Gaels, who landed from Ireland in the fourth century. Until 12 years ago, the duke of Argyll used to pay a woodsman on his estate to gather Gaelic tales. Pipe music is one of the most enduring features of Gaelic culture, practised in the Glasgow police. The new chair will encourage study of comparative Celtic philology, and ensure that professional men know the language.

1884

Afghanistan, 31 January. Britain is alarmed by the Russian invasion of Merv (→28/4/85).

Sudan, 18 February. General Gordon, who was sent to evacuate British troops, reaches Khartoum (→12/3).

Westminster, 22 February. The prince of Wales makes his first speech in the House of Lords, on the condition of the poor (→22/8).

London, 5 March. Anthony Ashley-Cooper, the earl of Shaftesbury, is granted the freedom of the city.

Sudan, 12 March. The Mahdi, the rebel leader, refuses to negotiate with General Gordon and besieges Omdurman (→1/1885).

Colchester, Essex, 22 April. An earthquake lasting a minute is felt up to 180 miles (300km) away; it causes damage to 1,200 buildings.

Oxford, 29 April. A statute is passed allowing women to sit examinations (→22/10).

Wimbledon, June. Women are allowed to compete in the lawn tennis championships for the first time (→1886).

Bangor, 18 August. The University College of North Wales opens.

Ireland, 1 October. Irish Catholic bishops formally recognize Charles Parnell and his party as representative of their interests (→24/1/85).

Dublin, 22 October. Nine women receive degrees at the Royal University of Ireland; they are the first women to graduate in Ireland (→1892).

Glasgow. A huge procession of over 100,000 people gathers on Glasgow Green to demand electoral reform.→

London. The Circle line on the underground railway system is completed (→1890).

Westminster. A royal commission on housing for the poor is established; it is headed by Sir Charles Dilke, the radical MP, and has the prince of Wales as a member (→4/1889).

Liverpool. The University College, founded in 1781, is amalgamated with the Victoria University of Manchester.

London. George Bernard Shaw, the Irish playwright, becomes a member of the newly formed and radical Fabian Society (→12/1889).

Socialist societies grow with public unrest

Sidney Webb, a member of the new Fabian Society, and his wife Beatrice.

Britain

Going almost unnoticed among the hurley-burley of everyday politics, there has been a steady growth in the popularity of socialist ideas – and not just among the poor. Some talented, wealthy individuals are exploring ideas that would once have been thought scandalous among the members of their class. Since the defeat of Chartism a generation ago, little has been heard of the sort of radical ideas which its adherents peddled. This was despite the presence in the country of the exiled Karl Marx and an influx of refugees from the defeated Paris Commune of the 1870s. But socialist ideas are now gaining currency.

The Social Democratic Federation was founded (as the Democratic Federation) in 1881 by former stockbroker H M Hyndman. It was joined by the poet and artist William Morris, who brought many artists into the movement. Morris left this year to found his own Socialist League, while in January Sidney Webb was among a group of young people who founded the Fabian Society, dedicated to promoting socialist views (→7/2/86).

Singer tries to stitch up market in sewing

Glasgow

The Singer sewing machine company has opened a giant new factory at Kilbowie, Clydebank. The company has been in Scotland since 1867, but the new factory is designed to produce 12,000 machines and could lead to Singer's complete domination of the British home market. This would indeed be a strange quirk of fate, because only five miles away is the base of the giant Coats Company, whose sewing thread is so successful it dominates the American market.

The first Singer sewing machine.

Society founded to protect children

England

Building on the work of others, a National Society for the Prevention of Cruelty to Children (NSPCC) has been formed in England. The plight of homeless and orphan children has been recognized for some time, and Dr Barnardo's first home in the East End of London was opened as early as 1867.

Since then other organizations have been formed, but the NSPCC is different in that it has been formed not to help children directly, but to attack cruelty through exposing abuse, demanding inspection of schools and children's homes and by working for new laws to protect the young (→14/6/89).

A new, and potentially deadly, form of gun has been invented this year by Hiram Maxim, an American engineer who moved to London in 1881. His "machine gun" fires bullets without being reloaded for each round.

Poet laureate wins a higher honour

Tennyson: now to be a lord.

Faringdon, Isle of Wight
Queen Victoria has bestowed a peerage on Alfred Tennyson, the poet laureate since 1850, in the year that he has completed his *Idylls of the King*, a cycle of poems of Arthurian romance which have been appearing since 1859. Tennyson's great popularity is due to *In Memoriam* and occasional poems such as the *Ode on the Death of the Duke of Wellington* and *The Charge of the Light Brigade*. His own favourite of his verse "monodramas" is *Maud*. He dedicates his *Idylls* to the memory of Prince Albert:
"Wearing the white flower of a blameless life,
In that fierce light that beats upon a throne" (→ 6/10/92).

Athletic Association is a hit in Ireland

Thurles, Co Tipperary
The Gaelic Athletic Association, founded this year in Co Tipperary by Michael Cusack, is reported to have swept the country "like a prairie fire". Cusack, originally a teacher, has risen from humble beginnings to run the extremely successful Civil Service Academy. He was a fine athlete in his youth and believes passionately in the value of physical exercise.

A nationalist, Cusack asserts that the English influence has destroyed native pastimes, that these must be revived, and that athletics should be available to the poor.

Parliament passes third Reform Act

Westminster
After a titanic struggle, the new reform bill has finally been passed by the House of Lords. Known technically as the Franchise Bill, it has given the vote to every householder with property worth more than £10 a year and will increase the electorate from three million to more than five million.

Householders in towns have been able to vote since 1867, but the new bill will extend this right to farmworkers, the last major group of people – women excepted – not to have the vote. This seems likely to change the balance of power in the countryside between workers and landowners and so the bill came in for fierce opposition from the House of Lords, which contains the biggest landowners.

Their lordships, led by the Tory leader Lord Salisbury who is almost fanatically opposed to the measure, embarked on a series of blocking measures after the bill had easily passed in the House of Commons. Their demand was for a Redistribution Bill, which would reduce the number of constituencies with more than one MP. But their hope was that argument over the redistribution of seats would sink both bills.

Instead they unleashed a storm of pent-up anger against the Lords, and the phrase "the peers against the people" became widely heard. Eventually direct negotiation took place between William Gladstone, the prime minister, for the Commons, and Salisbury, for the Lords. It was decided to pass both bills as agreed measures, with redistribution going ahead next year (→ 1885).

A Hyde Park rally protests against the Lords' rejection of the Reform Bill.

Prince has lucky escape during royal visit to Newcastle

A street scene in Newcastle.

Bridges carry road and railway across the river Tyne in Newcastle.

Newcastle-upon-Tyne, 22 August
A visit by the prince and princess of Wales to Newcastle almost ended in disaster today. The prince came close to being accidentally struck by a sword carried by the colonel in charge of the guard of honour, who had lost control of his horse. Fortunately, the prince ducked at the right moment and no harm was done. Newcastle is booming as a shipbuilding centre and coal port, and over the past two days the royal couple have visited many of the city's most important industrial sites. Yesterday, they sailed down the Tyne to Tynemouth, and en route the Prince opened the city's new Albert Edward dock, which was named in his honour. Earlier, he and the princess inspected the Armstrong shipbuilding works on the banks of the Tyne. The dredging of the river and the construction of new docks over the past 25 years have more than doubled the trade carried through the city, and last year over 6.25 million tonnes was transported on the river. The dredging ships clearing the bed of the Tyne shifted as much material as was removed when the Suez canal was built in Egypt (→ 4/1885).

1885

London, 24 January. The House of Commons and the Tower of London are damaged by Fenian bombs (→ 1/5).

Berlin, 26 January. Delegates from 15 nations, including Britain, have agreed terms for the partition of central and east Africa (→ 26/5/87).

Westminster, January. The cabinet is divided over the situation in Sudan (→ 26).

Britain, 13 March. A national day of mourning is called to honour General Gordon (→ 2/9/98).

Cork, April. Angry, booing crowds greet the prince and princess of Wales at the end of a tour of Ireland (→ 10/6/91).

Ireland, 1 May. The Irish Loyal and Patriotic Union is formed to defend the union of Great Britain and Ireland against the home rule movement (→ 17/11).

Westminster, 9 June. William Gladstone, the prime minister, resigns after the defeat of his budget by the Commons (→ 23).

Westminster, 23 June. Lord Salisbury is appointed caretaker prime minister (→ 24).

Munster, Ireland, 14 July. Munster Bank, which was established in 1879, suspends all payments.

England, 1 October. The earl of Shaftesbury, the philanthropist who led the factory reform movement, dies aged 84.

Westminster, 17 November. Gladstone declines to make any declaration on home rule for Ireland (→ 21).

Britain, 21 November. Charles Parnell calls upon the Irish in Britain to vote against Gladstone in the forthcoming general election; his secret discussions with the Conservatives had helped defeat Gladstone earlier in the year.→

Burma, November. British troops head towards Rangoon to halt French intervention in upper Burma (→ 1/1/86).

Scotland, November. Four of the six candidates of the Highland Land League are elected in the general election (→ 6/1886).

Bombay, 28 December. The Indian National Congress meets for the first time (→ 1892).

Lancashire. The first electrical tram service starts, in Blackpool (→ 16/5/93).

General Gordon killed at Khartoum

British troops bid family and friends farewell as they depart for the Sudan.

General Gordon's last stand.

Khartoum, Sudan, 26 January
General Charles Gordon – the embodiment of the "Christian soldier" – is dead. "Chinese Gordon", the man reputed to lead his troops into battle with a bible in one hand and a cane in the other, was shot today on the steps of the palace here with the Anglo-Egyptian relief force under Sir Garnet Wolseley within two days' travel of Khartoum. The city, on the confluence of the Blue and White Niles, has been besieged since April.

The army of Mohammed Ahmed (known as the Mahdi) broke into the city and encountered Gordon on the steps of the palace firing his revolver. At first wounded by a spear, he was then hit by a rifle shot which killed him. The Mahdi, who had wanted his fellow zealot alive, is so furious at the deed that the marksman has not owned up.

For 60 years the Sudan has been pillaged by slavers. Gordon, the hero of the anti-slave lobby, the scourge of the Taiping rebels in China and the former governor of the Sudan, was sent back when the Mahdi's revolt broke out with orders to evacuate the garrisons – by a government determined to avoid any colonial adventures. But when he arrived he refused to evacuate. A firm believer in his own judgement and in the inherent errors of the British government, he was convinced both that he could defeat the Mahdi alone and that Britain must commit an army to the Sudan.

Ministers in London delayed authorizing a relief expedition until last August and there were further delays when these troops met up with Gordon's steamboats a week ago. The delays seem certain to rebound on the popularity of William Gladstone, the prime minister, when news of Gordon's death becomes known in Britain (→ 13/3).

Young Wales group to back home rule

Wales
Home Rule for Wales, or *ymreolaeth*, is one of the main purposes behind the formation of the new Young Wales movement, Cymru Fydd, which started recently under the leadership of Thomas Edward Ellis. Supporters say it is in direct imitation of the Young Italy and Young Ireland movements and that it will be for the political use of Welsh at all levels of education. Others say it is not really political at all, although it owes allegiance to the Liberal Party.

The main insistence, however, is on Welsh national aspirations, and this has brought to the surface a conflict between Welsh and English Liberalism (→ 15/5/87).

Crisis in India over Russian expansion

Peshawar, India, 28 April
Britain and Russia stand on the edge of war, following the Russian seizure of Penjdeh in Afghanistan. For 30 years the proponents of the "forward policy" in both Russia and British India have steadily advanced their respective frontiers towards each other. Now only the mountains of Afghanistan stand between the two empires, and Herat lies open to the Russians. Yesterday William Gladstone, the prime minister, asked the Commons for £11 million to buy war supplies. But former Indian leaders refuse to panic. "In England they are fidgety about this border beyond all reason," Lord Dalhousie, a former viceroy, once said (→ 5/1887).

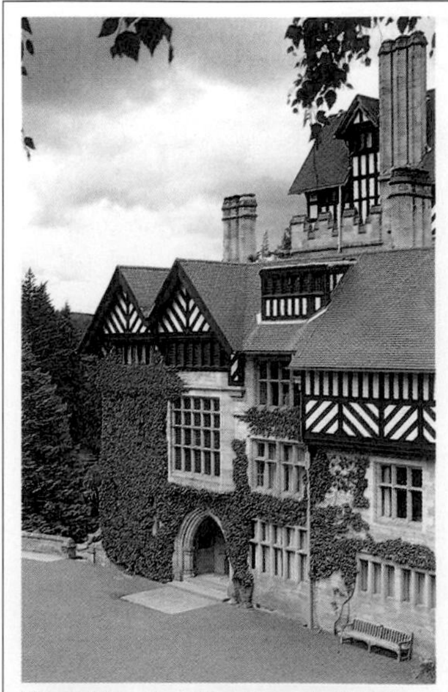

Cragside, in Northumberland: a nostalgic "Old English" design by Richard Norman Shaw, was completed this year.

▷

Tories look to gain as old constituency lines are redrawn

Westminster
Parliamentary constituencies are to be of approximately equal size under the terms of the Redistribution Act. The act, which will benefit the Conservatives by creating middle-class suburban seats, is intimately connected to last year's Franchise Act, which gave the vote to householders in rural areas, and which was originally bitterly opposed by the Tory-dominated Lords, who saw it as giving unfair advantage to the Liberals.

William Gladstone's new act will deprive towns of fewer than 15,000 people of their MPs and merge these constituencies with their rural neighbours. Some 36 boroughs with populations under 50,000, which previously returned two MPs, will now elect only one. Boroughs with populations between 50,000 and 165,000 will get two MPs and two constituencies. Cities are to be divided into a number of separate constituencies.

The beneficiaries will not only be the Conservatives, but also radicals. Liberal constituencies in industrial areas previously returning two MPs often elected one Liberal and one radical. With only one to elect, they are likely to return radicals (→9/6).

Irish MPs help topple Liberal government

Windsor, Berkshire, 24 June
Robert Cecil, the marquis of Salisbury and the Conservative leader, kissed the hand of the queen today and became prime minister. Earlier in the day William Gladstone returned to Queen Victoria the seals of office.

Since the death of General Gordon last January, Gladstone's government has become increasingly vulnerable. Last month two radical Liberals, Joseph Chamberlain and Sir Charles Dilke, resigned from the cabinet over Irish policy. Then, after Tory undertakings to Parnell, enough Irish MPs voted with the Tories to defeat the government on a budget amendment (→11/1885).

Salisbury addresses a party rally.

'Safety bicycle' is developed in Coventry

"SALVO" SAFETY
NEW ILLUSTRATED CATALOGUES POST FREE.
STARLEY BROS.,
St. JOHN'S WORKS, COVENTRY.

Dangerous?: the old style of bicycle.

Coventry
A new bicycle has been developed. Its designer is John K Starley, the nephew of James Starley, who died four years ago and has been described as the "father of the bicycle".

The new "safety bicycle" will be manufactured in Coventry, and is expected to be in the shops next year. Until now cycles, dubbed "penny-farthings", have been difficult to ride and dangerous. The new cheap-to-produce "safety bicycle" could make cycling available to everyone (→1888).

Newspaper editor is prosecuted for child prostitute exposure

London, September
Wiiliam Thomas Stead, the editor of the *Pall Mall Gazette*, has been found guilty after a trial at the Old Bailey in which he was accused of abducting a 13-year-old girl for £5 during the course of an inquiry into the white slave traffic for London brothels. This inquiry was published as *The Maiden Tribute of Modern Babylon*.

Stead was apparently indicted following information supplied to the authorities by two known enemies of Stead and the Salvation Army, which had helped in his enquiries. They are believed to have persuaded the parents of the child to bring the charge against him. Bramwell Booth, one of four social workers who were also accused, said: "Every blackguard in London was assembled in Bow Street to gloat upon our discomfiture. I was mobbed more than once, dragged out of a cab and maltreated, and only rescued with difficulty by a police inspector."

Stead said that he had taken the precaution of giving details of his inquiry to the archbishop of Canterbury and Cardinal Manning, the head of the Roman Catholic church in Britain. Despite their willingness to give evidence, the churchmen were not called upon during the trial, during which the attorney-general led for the prosecution.

Stead: seen after his conviction.

Gilbert and Sullivan score with 'Mikado'

A costume for "The Mikado".

London
The Mikado, the latest of William Gilbert and Arthur Sullivan's operettas, has been greeted as the greatest hit of the partnership to date. Its songs, *A Wandering Minstrel I*, *The Flowers that Bloom in the Spring*, *Tit Willow* and *Three Little Maids From School* are favourites in every drawing room. Gilbert and Sullivan began collaborating with *Trial By Jury* in 1875, followed by *H M S Pinafore* (1878), *The Pirates of Penzance* (1879), *Patience* (1881) and *Iolanthe* (1882).

The Savoy operas, as they are called, are now played at the newly built Savoy theatre under the direction of Richard D'Oyly Carte. A quarrel over the cost of its carpet led to a temporary rupture between D'Oyly Carte and the pair (→1889).

Scotland given own secretary of state

London
Scotland is to get its first secretary of state for 140 years. Scottish affairs will now be run by a Scottish Office in London under the new secretary of state.

Since 1745, when Scotland was punished for its rebellion by being deprived of its secretary of state, affairs have being in the hands of the lord advocate, a law officer. The vast tide of legislation passed in the past 40 years – on local government, education, public health – has overloaded the lord advocate's office, causing administrative confusion, since much of the new legislation is the responsibility of the home secretary. All will now come under the Scottish Office (→1888).

Secret deal lies behind Parnell/Tory pact

Making deals: Churchill (extreme left) and his less than rapt colleagues.

London, 21 November
Just two days before the general election, Charles Parnell, the Irish nationalist leader, has called on Irish voters in Britain to vote Conservative, and Irish voters in Ireland to vote against the Liberals.

A range of secret deals and political gambles lie behind Parnell's apparent conversion. Lord Randolph Churchill, the populist Conservative secretary for India, has spoken in favour of Irish home rule. The earl of Carnarvon, Ireland's viceroy, promised Parnell that he would avoid a coercion policy at a secret meeting on 1 August in London. Even before then, Tory promises to Parnell had resulted in the downfall of Gladstone's government [*see report opposite*]. Parnell's overtures to Gladstone later achieved no clear commitment from the Liberals, leading the Irish leader to launch his "vote Tory" manifesto.

Assuming Parnell's well-drilled supporters vote as their leader has told them, Liberals will lose their few remaining seats in Ireland to either nationalists or unionists, and over a dozen industrial seats in Britain with large Irish minorities.

If Parnell has guessed the electoral temperature correctly, his party will hold the balance of power in a House of Commons where the Liberals will have the largest number of seats by a whisker.

"Fish Sale on a Cornish Beach" by Stanhope Forbes attracted much interest at the Royal Academy this year. It established the Newlyn school of painters as a group representing a new French influence on art here.

Liberals win most seats in hung parliament but Salisbury has temporary grip on power

Westminster, November
The electors have returned a hung parliament. The Liberals won 335 seats, the Conservatives 249 and Irish nationalists 86 – giving government and opposition exactly 335 seats each. The marquis of Salisbury has remained in office while the parties jostle for position, but in the longer term Gladstone, as the leader of the largest party, looks set to be the prime minister again.

The mathematical consequences are that a combined vote of Conservatives and Irish nationalists could block any government bills, but a combined vote of Conservatives and right-wing Liberals (the old Whigs) could block any move to home rule. To govern, Gladstone must give the Irish what they want – but the Commons is most unlikely to let him do it. Deadlock looms.

Many Liberal MPs are so bitter at Parnell's advice to his supporters to vote Conservative that they would prefer to ally with the Conservatives than to make peace with the Irish. Radicals are even contemplating a Churchill/Chamberlain pact. In the election, the Liberals did well in rural areas, gaining the votes of newly enfranchised agricultural workers, though they lost many of the new urban seats to the Conservatives (→ 17/12).

Premier and the people: Gladstone travelling with members of the public.

Gladstone converts to Irish home rule

London, 17 December
The Liberal leader William Gladstone was reported in the press today to be in favour of home rule for Ireland. The news was leaked to newspaper editors by his son, Herbert, who acts as his secretary.

According to Herbert, the former premier became convinced of the need for home rule after last month's election, which suggested that Britain will never be able to carry out a consistent policy on Ireland while this policy rests on fragile parliamentary majorities, which allow Charles Parnell, the Irish leader, to disrupt all business and openly tout for his party's vote.

In the election Parnell advised his supporters to vote Conservative, after coming to an unspoken understanding with the Conservative, Lord Randolph Churchill. Similar but less successful negotiations were held with the Liberals.

There seems no doubt that Gladstone, the "Grand Old Man" of British politics, is sincere in his conversion to the cause of home rule. It has been exercising him for many months, even though he declined to make promises to Parnell before the general election. His problem now will be to convince his Liberal colleagues if, as seems likely, Lord Salisbury fails to win the support of parliament when it assembles early next year (→ 1/1/86).

1886

India, 1 January. Britain annexes upper Burma.→

Westminster, 1 January. The marquis of Salisbury's government rejects proposals by William Gladstone for a bipartisan settlement for Ireland (→22/2).

Westminster, 28 January. Salisbury resigns as prime minister after his government is defeated by 329 to 250 votes on the Queen's Speech (→1/2).

Westminster, 1 February. Gladstone begins his third term as prime minister (→25/7/86).

London, 21 February. Police break up a mass meeting in Hyde Park of the Social Democratic Federation.

Ulster, 22 February. Lord Randolph Churchill makes a militant speech against home rule at a meeting of the Ulster Conservatives (→19/3).

Belfast, 19 March. The Liberal Convention splits on the home rule question (→8/4).

Westminster, 8 April. Gladstone introduces the Home Rule Bill (→13).

Belfast, 13 April. Ulster Conservatives and dissident Liberals agree to resolutions on home rule (→24/5).

London, 24 May. The *Pall Mall Gazette* publishes a report that Charles Parnell is residing at the home of Mrs Kitty O'Shea in Kent; Mrs O'Shea is the wife of Captain William O'Shea, one of Parnell's supporters (→8/6).

Ulster, 4 June. The Ulster Liberal Unionist Committee is formally established.

Westminster, 8 June. The Home Rule Bill is defeated.→

Belfast, 10 June. Protestant mobs run riot (→9/1886).

London, 21 June. Prince Edward lays the foundation stone of Tower Bridge.

Scotland, June. The Crofters Act becomes law, giving crofters security of tenure.

Westminster, 25 July. Salisbury is appointed prime minister.→

Dublin, 25 October. The Guinness brewery in Dublin becomes a public liability company; shares worth £6 million are offered for subscription on the London Stock Exchange.

Scotland. The Scottish Home Rule Association is formed.→

Six-year wait pays off for Bradlaugh

Westminster, January

Charles Bradlaugh, the radical MP for Northampton, has finally been granted the right to take the oath of allegiance and thus take his seat in parliament. Six years ago, when he was first elected, his wish to affirm as an atheist rather than take the oath was rejected by the Speaker. Even though he later agreed to take the oath, the reaction of MPs was so hostile that he was not allowed to do so. Three times he was re-elected by his constituents, however. And now – thanks largely to a speech by Gladstone asking the Commons to exercise tolerance – Bradlaugh has at last been allowed to take his seat as an MP.

Bradlaugh: six-year campaign.

Young shop workers get an easier life

Britain

The passing of the Shop Hours Act, restricting the amount of time worked by young people in the retail trade, will be welcomed by both reformers and children. The act limits shop assistants under the age of 18 to a maximum of 74 hours work a week.

This means they will now work a 13-and-a-half-hour day during the week, with a six-and-a-half-hour day on Saturdays. This is the first time that the state has taken steps to prevent the abuse of child labour in the retail trade (→8/1897).

Social democratic rally breaks up in riots

Social Democratic leaders go on trial at Bow Street magistrates' court.

London, 7 February

A meeting of the Social Democratic Federation (SDF), organized by the leaders of the society and held in Trafalgar Square, broke up in disorder today when rioting started and spread to Pall Mall, where windows were broken. Police moved in and a number of people were arrested, including H M Hyndman, who in 1881 founded the organization (then the Democratic Federation), and John Burns, an early member known as an agitator.

Hyndman, an old Etonian and a Cambridge scholar who converted to socialism after reading Marx's *Das Kapital*, is a stockbroker. He is using his wealth and energy to promote the principles of class warfare and revolution. The federation he heads is the first modern English socialist organization.

Three years ago, the celebrated poet and artist-craftsman William Morris joined the federation and introduced a number of influential thinkers as well as his own Utopian ideas. A year later, disillusioned by the SDF's "political opportunism", he broke away to form the Socialist League. Hyndman, Burns and two leading members of the SDF have been prosecuted and are to stand trial at the Old Bailey for disturbing the peace (→21).

Workers pause during construction of one of the approaches to the new railway tunnel opened under the Severn estuary this year. The new line cuts one hour off the journey between south Wales and London.

Irish home rule dominates turbulent political year

Liberal rebels throw out Gladstone's bill

Westminster, 8 June
The Liberal government's Home Rule Bill was soundly defeated in the early hours of this morning with 93 Liberal MPs joining the Conservatives in the division lobby. The bill has split the Liberals, alienating old-style Whigs such as Lord Hartington and radicals such as Joseph Chamberlain, who resigned from the cabinet in April. William Gladstone is undaunted: he plans to seek a dissolution of parliament and give the electorate a chance to judge his policy in a general election.

The bill was debated for 16 days by the Commons with Gladstone speaking no fewer than five times. A leading Tory, Lord Randolph Churchill, said that home rule could encourage other nationalists in the empire to seek independence. Churchill laid great emphasis on the Protestants in the north of Ireland. "Ulster will fight," he said, "and Ulster will be right" (→ 10)

Gladstone launches the bill.

Salisbury looks after Ulster.

Riots break out in Belfast as Protestants rally against the Home Rule Bill.

Irish MPs meet to discuss their tactics in the controversy over home rule.

Tories sweep back to power in election

Westminster, 25 July
Seven months after his resignation, the marquis of Salisbury is again prime minister. The election called after the defeat of the Liberal government's Home Rule Bill last month has brought the Conservatives back to power with a clear majority. And Salisbury is now stronger, due to an alliance with the Liberal Unionists – Liberals opposed to Gladstone's Irish policy.

The Irish home rule controversy and Gladstone's compact with Parnell have aroused strong passions throughout the country. Gladstone has lost his gamble that electors would back his policy: the Liberals supporting home rule secured only 191 seats. Against them are ranged 316 Conservatives and 78 Liberal Unionists. Although there are also 85 Irish nationalist MPs, Salisbury has an effective working majority of 118. "We had a drubbing," Gladstone admits (→ 12/1886).

Belfast Protestants riot against change

Belfast, September
Serious and large-scale rioting has broken out in Belfast, instigated by Protestant mobs, and 39 people have died. Tension has been steadily rising amongst Ulster Protestants at the imminent prospect of home rule. Last December a prominent Orangeman hinted that the passing of Irish home rule could result in a civil war, and earlier this year a member of the Ulster loyalist anti-Repeal Union called for an appeal to Germany if its call to the British government in Westminster fell on deaf ears.

The conservative MP Lord Randolph Churchill has been the most vocal ally of the Ulster Protestants in parliament. In one of several outspoken statements of support Churchill said: "The Protestants of Ireland ... in a national crisis such as this, are the only nation which is known to the English people in Ireland" (→ 18/4/87).

Churchill quits over a trivial matter

Westminster, December
Lord Randolph Churchill, the leader of the House of Commons and chancellor of the exchequer, has resigned following a clash of wills with the prime minister, the marquis of Salisbury. Churchill's abilities had marked him out as a potential Tory leader, but his attitude over domestic and foreign policies had recently caused endless conflicts between him and most of his colleagues, largely due to his impatience, volatility and exceptional rudeness.

Churchill's scathing criticism of Salisbury's handling of the current crisis in the Balkans, and his own proposals for a radical programme of domestic reforms, brought them to a collision course over the army and navy estimates. Churchill's demands and overbearing manner led to a routine threat to resign – one that was promptly accepted by the prime minister (→ 13/7/88).

Hardy ends silence with 'Casterbridge'

London
Thomas Hardy has published his first work for four years. Called *The Mayor of Casterbridge*, it relates the tragic fate of its hero, Michael Henchard. The town of Casterbridge is a thin disguise for Dorchester, where Hardy lives. Hardy was born in a hamlet near Egdon Heath, a wild part of Dorset memorably described in his novel *The Return of the Native* (1878). The son of a master stone mason, he became an architect, but gave up his profession in 1874 in the wake of the success of his fourth novel, *Far from the Madding Crowd*. Other novels to date include *Under the Greenwood Tree* (1872), *The Trumpet-Major* (1880) and *Two on a Tower* (1882) (→ 1891).

Child custody alters

Westminster, June
Who cares for the children if there is a divorce? The Guardianship of Infants Bill, now going through parliament, states that the "welfare of the child" should be a consideration. The mother's role in child care is recognized, whereas in the past a father's absolute right to child custody was taken for granted and a mother proved to be adulterous was denied access to her children. Another measure allows maintenance if the husband deserts his family.

J E Millais's painting "Bubbles" is used for advertising by Pears, the big soap manufacturers.

The Raj expands east as Burma annexed

Burma's King Thibaw is escorted to British ships before being deported.

Burma, 1 January
Britain has added a new territory to the Indian empire with the annexation of the kingdom of Upper Burma. The deposition of Burma's King Thibaw removes a ruler who had aggressively asserted his independence against imperialist encroachment since coming to the Burmese throne eight years ago.

France had conquered Tongking in Indochina and was showing interest in Burma, when Thibaw confiscated the British Bombay-Burma Company and offered it to French rivals. After his refusal to arbitrate, Britain sent an ultimatum, followed a month later, in November last year, by 10,000 troops under General Prendergast. Thibaw was deposed and deported in an action which cost only a dozen casualties.

In his report to Queen Victoria, the viceroy of India, Lord Dufferin, claimed he had no alternative but to attack Burma.

Prison threat to suspect prostitutes lifted

London, 15 April
Josephine Butler, the tireless campaigner who led the movement to repeal the three Contagious Diseases Acts of the 1860s, has finally succeeded. Under the acts – intended to regulate prostitution – women suspected of being prostitutes who refused to undergo medical tests might be imprisoned. William Gladstone's government backed the repeal of the acts last month and today saw royal assent.

The history of public opinion about venereal disease, the social and medical horrors of syphilis and gonorrhoea, now waits to be written. It has finally been proved that the forcible investigation and incarceration of prostitutes – or women suspected of prostitution – did not solve the problem. The facts speak for themselves. In 1865, there were 260 cases of venereal disease per thousand in the armed forces. The figure remains the same today.

Social reformer: Josephine Butler.

Mrs Butler once said: "Men ... hypocritically cloaked their own sensuality in the outward garb of punishing the being whom they alone brought to shame. Men made prostitutes the scapegoat of their brutishness – of their animal passions unhallowed by affection."

Many women classed as prostitutes are forced into lives of misery, poverty and degradation.

Women take centre court at Wimbledon

London, summer
Maud Watson, the unbeaten champion of two years since the first ladies' championship was held at Wimbledon in 1884, will attempt a hat-trick by playing the up-and-coming player Blanche Bingley again this year. Bingley is certainly a player to watch. Soon to be married to Wimbledon club secretary Commander Hillyard, she has a powerful forehand stroke and could make a considerable impact on the women's game. Players like Bingley and Charlotte Dod are raising the profile of women's tennis. They have replaced the clumsy crinoline with a loose blouse and skirt and brought a new strength to the ladies' game (→ 7/1894).

Ladies warming up before a match.

Home rule moves

Scotland
Following agitation among Scots, protesting that the government has been giving Irish autonomy unlawful priority over Scotland's affairs, a Scottish Home Rule Association has been set up to campaign for further reform. Last year a Secretary for Scotland was appointed, but he is not a Secretary of State and lacks real power to initiate legislation. Although he is spokesman in parliament for the various Scottish boards, which will remain based in central London, the Scottish Secretary has only limited control.

1887

Oxford, February. The Pitt-Rivers museum is opened to house the collection of ancient artefacts belonging to General Pitt-Rivers, an English soldier and archaeologist.

Westminster, 7 March. The marquis of Salisbury, the prime minister, appoints Arthur James Balfour, the former secretary of Scotland, as the new chief secretary for Ireland.

Westminster, 31 March. The earl of Cadogan introduces the Irish Land Law Bill; it will give land courts the power to fix the rents of leaseholders and to revise rents (→23/8).

London, 18 April. Scandal follows the publication of *The Times* article *Parnellism and Crime: Mr Parnell and the Phoenix Park murders*; the article links Charles Parnell to the murders (→7/1887).

London, 26 May. The Imperial British East Africa Company is established to develop part of east Africa [Kenya and Uganda] (→1888).

Mediterranean, May. In an attempt to stabilize relations with Mediterranean countries and stop any French or Russian designs in the area, Britain signs treaties with Italy and Austria-Hungary, guaranteeing the regional status quo (→12/12).

London, 20 June. Queen Victoria meets Annie Oakley, the American markswoman, as part of the jubilee celebrations (→21).

Westminster, 19 August. The Irish National League is declared a dangerous association under the recently passed Criminal Law and Procedure Act (→9/9).

Westminster, 23 August. Parliament passes the Irish Land Law Act.

Britain, August. Severe drought sweeps across the country damaging the harvest.

India, 1 October. Britain declares northern Baluchistan, a region on the north-west frontier occupied since 1879, British territory (→12/2/1901).

London, 17 October. Terry's theatre on the Strand opens.

London, October. An epidemic of scarlet fever breaks out.

Co Tipperary, 9 November. The annual convention of the Gaelic Athletic Association at Thurles ends in a dispute between the Fenians and the Catholic priests.

Welsh farmers unite and protest against tithe taxes on land

Llangwm, Clwyd, 15 May
More than a dozen Welsh protesters were seriously injured and many more were trampled underfoot when mounted police charged a large crowd during an anti-English riot in the Vale of Clwyd at Llangwm, near Mold, today.

It began when over-strenuous attempts were made by some church officials to collect unpopular tithes from debtors in the area. Helping these officials were heavily armed auctioneers and valuers sent from London. Local farmers, who had formed an anti-tithe society to reimburse anyone whose property might be seized, arranged for horns to be blown to summon crowds to obstruct the officials. This was to prevent the sale of property from being rushed through.

The climax came just before dawn today when two cows were taken from a defaulting farmer in the nonconformist Vale of Clwyd. This was followed by an equally determined attempt to hold a public auction of seized property in the town square at Llangwm. Crowds gathered in silence to try to stop the proceedings by passive resistance, but scuffles broke out between the crowd and the police. Armed troops were immediately drafted into the area, exacerbating an already inflamed situation (→8/1892).

'The Times' publishes allegations linking Parnell to Phoenix Park assassinations

Parnell forced into a tight corner as "The Times" throws allegations about.

London, May
The Times newspaper has published a series of articles accusing Charles Parnell of complicity in the Phoenix Park murders [*see page 966*]. They seek to implicate Parnell and members of the Irish parliamentary party in criminal conspiracy and murder during the Land War of 1879-82. One of the articles contains the facsimile of a letter allegedly written by Parnell, dated 15 May 1882, condoning the murders. The articles are clearly designed to destroy Parnell and wreck the alliance between the Irish Nationalist party and the Liberals.

Some of these articles have been written by a Dublin-born civil servant, Robert Anderson, who was appointed to the secret service branch at the home office in 1867, where he has dealt with Irish affairs, advised on political crime and investigated the Fenian movement. He has boasted that they were published with the full consent of the home office, although this seems highly unlikely. He is now being labelled as the author of "Anderson's Fairy Tales". A former member of the Irish parliamentary party is suing *The Times* for libel, and the House of Commons has established a special parliamentary commission to investigate Parnell's career and that of his leading associates over the past ten years (→19/8).

Truro Cathedral, designed by John Loughborough Pearson, was begun in 1878 and consecrated this year. Pearson, who specializes in building or restoring churches, has worked on the restoration of Westminster Abbey.

Popular writer, Mrs Henry Wood, dies

London
Mrs Henry Wood, perhaps the best-selling of all modern novelists, has died at the age of 73. Her name will always be linked with *East Lynne*, published in 1861 and adapted for the stage, where it is hugely popular. The line "Dead! Dead – and never called me Mother!" has become something of a catchphrase.

Mrs Wood was born Ellen Price, the daughter of a glove manufacturer in Worcester, who married the head of a banking firm. Because of spinal curvature she wrote all her novels in a reclining chair, often at a rate of two a year. ▷

Victoria celebrates golden jubilee

London, 21 June
After an extraordinary day of great celebrations to mark her 50th year on the throne, Queen Victoria must now know she is one of the best-loved monarchs ever. All day the sun shone – people are calling it "queen's weather" – and the event was proud, gaudy and sentimental.

The queen passed in procession through the capital to Westminster Abbey for a jubilee thanksgiving service. The procession included 47 carriages bearing royalty from India and Europe and her numerous children, and a sovereign's escort of the Household Cavalry. Victoria herself preferred not to appear in her crown, full robes and state coach, choosing instead a white bonnet, simple black dress and open landau. At the abbey a choir of some 300 voices sang music by the late Prince Albert, and the illustrious congregation included bishops, professors and poets. The tiny monarch perched on the coronation chair heard the archbishop of Canterbury thank God for her long reign and beseech Him to "stay the growth of iniquity".

Across Britain a thousand bonfires were lit, fireworks blazed, and 30,000 children were fed buns and milk in Hyde Park. For a while the dimmer back streets of industrial Britain were lit up. In her diary Victoria has described her day as "heart-stirring", "marvellous" and "deeply touching" (→ 7/1888).

Victoria, a much-loved monarch, cheered on her way to Westminster Abbey.

A portrait of the queen in 1883.

The jubilee is celebrated in India.

London hosts first colonial conference

London, April
The government has organized a "colonial conference" attended by the prime ministers of all the self-governing colonies. They were already here for the celebrations to mark Queen Victoria's jubilee, but it is envisaged that similiar conferences will be held in the future.

The conference reflected the alarm felt by the colonial leaders at the overseas ambitions of other European countries. One of the most important tasks of the conference is to plan for self-defence. Britain has 120,000 troops in India, Egypt and other territories (→ 7/1887).

Empire unites in jubilee celebrations

London, July
More than a national rejoicing, Queen Victoria's golden jubilee is also a festival of empire. Her reign has seen her people fashion the furthest-flung empire in the history of the world. There have been several weeks of parades, presentations and parties, and not only in Britain. All over the empire the jubilee has been marked.

Australia had a public holiday with parades, fireworks, souvenir medals, church bells and children's parties. In Canada, Houses and businesses were decorated with flags and streamers. In Sind in India the authorities celebrated by opening a Queen Victoria Jubilee Burial and Burning Ground. Prisoners have been released in the monarch's honour. In Singapore extra rice has been given to hospital patients, including – by the queen-empress's command – lepers. In Burma, jubilee robes of saffron were presented to Buddhist monks.

From all parts of the world have come thousands of letters and telegrams of loyalty and affection. The jubilee jamboree has given the empire a new sense of cohesion. It now comprises about a quarter of the earth's land surface and nearly a quarter of its people. It ranges from the huge autonomous white colonies such as Canada to tiny protectorates and islands (→ 28/7/97).

Britain's position as top industrial power threatened

Britain
From being the very first industrial nation and workshop of the world, Britain is now one of several industrial nations. She is beginning to lose her leading position, with the United States and Germany poised to catch up, and other countries beginning to make their own goods. An era of prosperity and calm is giving way to uncertainty.

The economic growth that has taken place in the 50 years of Queen Victoria's reign has involved major changes in the country's economic structure. There has been a marked drift away from the land, which has diminished the importance of farming itself. The obverse of the decline has been the growth of industry and the service sector.

The rate of growth of industrial production, however, is slowing. Foreign manufacturers are supplying their own needs and are often protected by a wall of tariffs.

There has been a massive capital outflow from London. In the last 30 years overseas investment has risen from £235 million and now is approaching £2 billion. While Britain is losing its leading position as an industrial power, it is ahead in shipping, insurance and banking.

A satirical view of capitalism and Britain's industrial prosperity.

Britain signs triple maritime treaty

London, 12 December
Britain has secured a new – secret – alliance for security in the Mediterranean with Italy and Austria-Hungary. The agreement, signed today, is designed to secure the status quo not only in the Mediterranean but also in the Adriatic, Aegean and Black Seas.

Behind the new alliance is the concern of Lord Salisbury, the prime minister, about French and Russian hostility and expansion overseas. Britain's role under the treaty is to protect the Italian coastline from the French fleet.

Sherlock Holmes is new-fangled sleuth

Doyle: creator of Sherlock Holmes.

London
A new figure has joined the ranks of fictional detectives: Sherlock Holmes, of 221B Baker Street, London. In *A Study in Scarlet* he is introduced as a man of amazing powers of deduction by Dr Watson, late of the army, whom he greets with the observation: "You have been in Afghanistan, I perceive." Watson is astonished by Holmes's gifts for reading footprints and cigar ash. He is an advance on Wilkie Collins's Cuff and Edgar Allen Poe's Dupin. His creator, Arthur Conan Doyle, owes his deductive logic to Joseph Bell of Edinburgh, with whom he studied (→ 1891).

Violence erupts over Irish home rule

Police fire on mob in Mitchelstown riots

Cork, 9 September
Three people were killed and two were wounded at Mitchelstown, Co Cork, today when police opened fire on "plan of campaign" supporters being addressed by John Dillon MP.

The Land War continues, and eviction of tenants is on the increase. Last November, both John Dillon and William O'Brien (editor of the nationalist newspaper *United Ireland*), supported tenants on the Clanricard estate at Portumna, Co Galway, when they offered land agent rents due less 40 per cent on condition that evicted tenants were reinstated. This became the model of the National League (formerly the Land League) for the "plan of campaign". The following month Dillon, O'Brien and others were arrested for collecting rents for the "plan of campaign" and the British government denounced it as a criminal conspiracy. But protest meetings continue (→ 13/11).

Irish home-rule demonstrators clash with police in a bloody battle.

Rioters spark Trafalgar Square bloodbath

London, 13 November
Rioting erupted today at an open-air meeting in Trafalgar Square of British radicals and Irish nationalists protesting at the imprisonment in Cork of William O'Brien [*see report left*]. Such force was used by the police and military to suppress the rioters that there were over 100 casualties, and the day has been given the name "Bloody Sunday".

O'Brien has caught the public imagination with his insistence that he should be treated as a political prisoner. He refuses to associate with other prisoners, to clean out his cell or to wear prison dress.

The nationalist press, notably the *Freeman's Journal*, has kept the public abreast of developments, and much sympathy has been generated for the plight of O'Brien (→ 6/8/88).

Lancashire women miners march to London for the right to work

London, 17 May
Twenty-three Lancashire women, known as "pit-brow" workers, marched today to the Home Office to plead for their right to work above ground in the coal mines. Women, many argue, belong in the home. But the opposing argument is also strong: women need jobs and if work is available in the mines – maybe better paid than agricultural work – then why should the law stop them taking it?

"Pit-brow" women sorted the coal and performed a variety of jobs above ground. Many of them wore trousers; this fact alone offended men, to the point that last year's Coal Mines Regulation (Amendment) Act excluded women from any kind of pit work. Supported by suffragists and the growing fervour for women's rights, these women workers are confident (→ 17/7/88).

South African gems

Kimberley, southern Africa
After a bitter financial battle over control of the Kimberley diamond field, and thus the world's diamond market, victory has gone to Cecil Rhodes, the son of an East Anglian clergyman. Rhodes, a founder of the De Beers diamond company here in 1880, has seen off Barney Barnato's Central Company with money advanced from Rothschild's bank in London. Rhodes says profits from the Kimberley diamonds will finance a white man's homeland in southern Africa (→ 11/1893).

The Tay bridge on the Dundee to Edinburgh railway line, which collapsed in December 1879 killing over a hundred passengers, reopened this year.

1888

South-east Asia, 17 March. Britain establishes a protectorate over Sarawak in Borneo (→12/5).

Dublin, 1 May. *Poems and Ballads of Young Ireland*, by John O'Leary, T W Rolleston and W B Yeats, is published (→28/12/91).

Glasgow, 8 May. The International Exhibition of Art and Science opens.

South-east Asia, 12 May. Britain establishes a protectorate over North Borneo (→31/7/93).

Ireland, 14 May. A royal charter establishes the Institute of Chartered Accountants in Ireland.

Westminster, 13 July. The prime minister, Lord Salisbury, establishes a commission to investigate all allegations made against MPs (→2/10/91).

London, 6 August. *The Times* publishes a letter revealing secret negotiations between Charles Parnell, the leader of the Irish parliamentary party, and Joseph Chamberlain in 1884 and 1885 (→13).

London, 13 August. A commission begins investigating the charges made by *The Times* newspaper against Charles Parnell (→20/2/89).

London, 31 August. The body of Mary Ann Nichols is found in Whitechapel; she has been brutally murdered (→8/9).

London, 8 September. Another savagely mutilated body, that of Annie Chapman, is found in Whitechapel (→30/9).

London, 30 September. Two more victims of the Whitechapel killer, Elizabeth Stride and Catherine Eddowes, are found (→18/11).

Westminster. Under a new formula Scotland is guaranteed 13.75 per cent of any government spending in the United Kingdom.

East Africa. Sir William McKinnon's Imperial British East Africa Company gets a charter to develop the area between German East Africa [Tanzania] and Italian Somaliland [Somalia] (→1/7/90).

Glasgow. Celtic football club is founded by a Catholic priest, Brother Walfrid, the headmaster of the Sacred Heart School in the east of the city, to raise money for poor children.

Keir Hardie founds Scots Labour Party

Glasgow, 19 May
Today, at the Waterloo Rooms here in Glasgow, Keir Hardie, the socialist, pacifist and feminist, met with a group of fellow socialists to found the Scottish Labour Party. Its programme embraces causes as varied as Scottish home rule, land reform, the eight-hour day, national insurance, and a demand for the public ownership of the railways and mineral mining royalties.

Born in 1856, Hardie was down the Lanarkshire pits at the age of ten, a union militant at 23, and has since pursued the cause of social change and reform, rather than doctrinaire socialism (→3/8/92).

Keir Hardie: founder of the party.

Cycling latest craze

Britain
The popular craze for cycling, enjoyed by all classes of people, is about to enjoy a massive boost of interest following the recent invention of a pneumatic tyre by Belfast veterinary surgeon John Dunlop. He developed the idea of the tyre with rubber treads for his ten-year-old son, to make the boy's tricycle easier to ride. It was so successful, Dunlop is forming a commercial production company (→1895).

Matchgirls strike a blow for better pay

The strike committee calls off the matchgirls' strike after a pay settlement.

London, 17 July
A settlement has been reached to end the 12-day strike by an estimated 1,100 to 1,400 female workers at the Bryant & May match factory here. The strike was the unexpected outcome of an article in the press by Mrs Annie Besant, the radical political campaigner, in which she exposed the matchgirls' appalling conditions of work.

Hearing about the high dividends paid to shareholders and the low wages paid by the company, Mrs Besant discovered that employees started work each day at 6.30am in the summer, and 8am in the winter, finishing at 6pm. They had 30 minutes for breakfast, and an hour for lunch, and stood at a workbench for the whole of the day.

A typical 16-year-old was paid four shillings a week as a piece worker. Out of this she paid two shillings a week for the rent of a room, and ate only bread-and-butter and tea for breakfast and dinner. Wages were subject to a number of fines. For example, a shilling was forfeited if a burnt match was left on a bench, and two thirds of a day's pay was forfeited for being late.

Mrs Besant raised £400 to help win the girls' cause – a settlement which will bring them better pay and conditions (→1891).

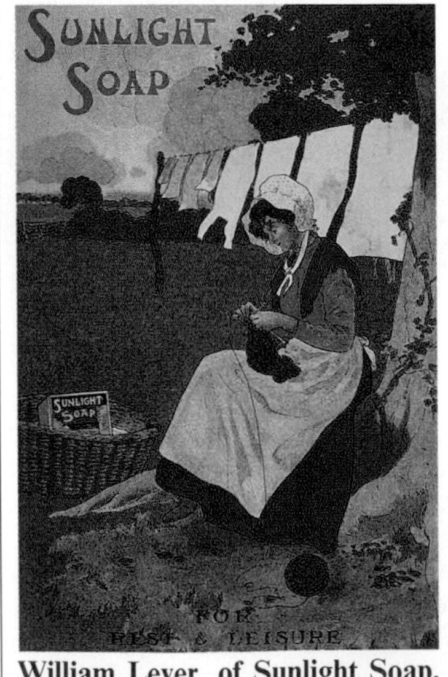

William Lever, of Sunlight Soap, builds Port Sunlight, a company village of subsidized housing for his workers in Merseyside.

Football clubs are to form a league

London, 22 March
Football clubs in the English north and midlands are to play under a new league system which will be independent of the game's governing body, the Football Association (FA). The aim is to generate greater interest in the sport and guarantee regular matches for the increasing number of professional players.

The 12 clubs involved will play each other twice during the season – once at each ground – and guarantee to field their best players, subject to the imposition of penalties. In order that key players can afford to take time off from work to train for big matches, clubs will pay them wages and expenses (→29/8/95).

County councils change face of local government

England and Wales, 9 August
A landmark in the development of local government was passed today when the Local Government Act became law. It establishes 62 new elected "county councils" as the basis of the administration of England and Wales. The councils replace the old system of rule through the justices of the peace (JPs), handing over their administrative functions to the new authorities. JPs retain judicial power in their capacity as magistrates. One new county – London – is created by the act.

Each county council will be responsible for all the county's administrative and financial affairs, and will be controlled by a chairman, aldermen and councillors. The only mandatory qualifications for someone to stand for election is that he must own property – either as a peer of the realm or as a parliamentary voter. Councillors will be elected for a term of three years, after which they must seek reelection. The number of county councillors for each district will be determined by the Local Government Board.

The financial powers of a county council will include assessing and charging the rates; appointing and fixing the salaries and fees of all paid officials, such as the county treasurer, county surveyor, coroner and public analysts; financing the police; and providing jails, shire halls, court houses, judges' lodgings, and county buildings.

County councils will also be responsible for licensing places of entertainment and providing asylums for the care of pauper lunatics and reformatory schools. They will also provide and maintain all roads and bridges in their county. And they will ensure that government acts relating to subjects from the control of contagious diseases and vermin to the conservation of fish and wild birds are enforced. Among other responsibilities are those on the control of weights and measures.

At election time, councils will divide the county into its polling districts, arrange where the election is held, and maintain the list of all those eligible to vote.

The new act applies only to England and Wales; plans for an overhaul of Scottish local government are being developed (→ 8/4/89).

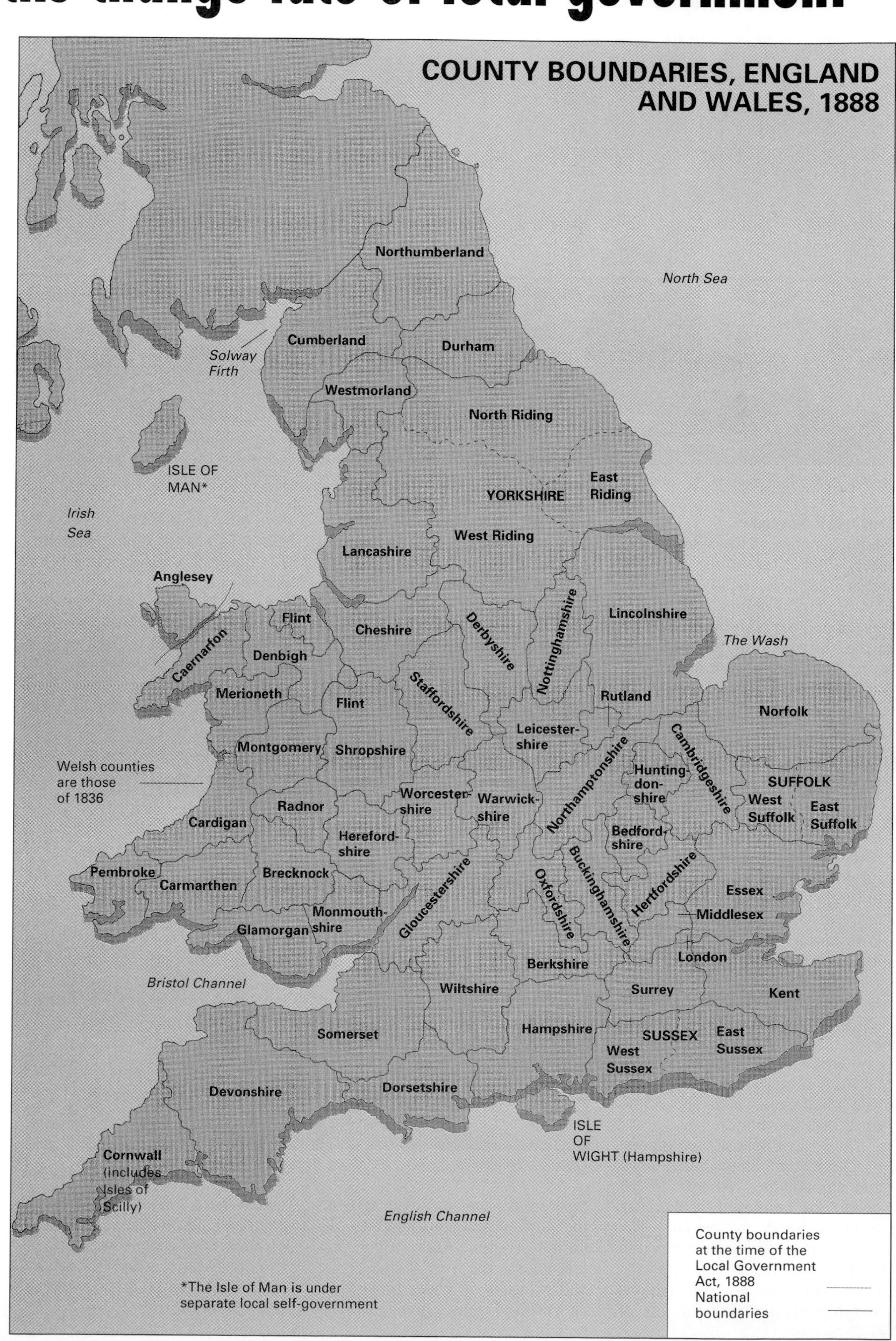

'Jack the Ripper' terrorizes London

Another victim is discovered by police in the darkened streets of the East End.

THE PENNY ILLUSTRATED PAPER AND ILLUSTRATED TIMES

KATE EDDOWES THE MITRE SQUARE VICTIM

SKETCH OF THE MAN WHO VISITED Mr LUSK

SKETCHES IN CONNECTION WITH THE WHITECHAPEL AND ALDGATE MURDERS.

The killings are front-page news.

London, 9 November

Another victim of the Whitechapel killer – the fifth in the past ten weeks – has been found dead in the East End of London. Her throat was cut and her body was mutilated in the same way as her predecessors', all of whom were prostitutes. This killing, of 25-year-old Marie Jeanette ("Mary Jane") Kelly, is reported to be the most violent to date. Parts of her dismembered body had been arranged symmetrically on her bedside table.

Over 600 plain-clothes police are hunting for the murderer, who has been dubbed "Jack the Ripper". The search is concentrated on the narrow streets and courts around where the murders have occurred. Theories are rife about the killer's identity: some think he is a Polish Jew, others a butcher, or a doctor with a hatred for immoral women. The queen has criticized the prime minister, Lord Salisbury, in a telegram on the police's handling of the case: "This new, most ghastly murder, one of a series by Jack the Ripper, shows the necessity for some very decided action ... our detectives [must be] improved for they are not what they should be."

Victoria's grandson succeeds to throne of German empire

Germany, July

Queen Victoria's grandson has succeeded to the German throne as Emperor William II, following the death of his father, Frederick III, at Potsdam on 15 June. Frederick had been suffering from throat cancer for several months, and was emperor for just 99 days.

The queen visited her dying son-in-law, husband of her eldest daughter Victoria, on his sickbed in April, on her way back from a visit to Berlin, and talked with his physician, Sir Morrell Mackenzie, who "seemed to think Fritz was better". The queen wrote to her grandson on receiving a telegram from him on his father's death: "I am broken-hearted. Help and do all you can for your poor dear mother and try to follow in your best, noblest, and kindest of father's footsteps."

The behaviour of the headstrong William since then is worrying the queen, who finds it "indecent" that he has not observed a period of mourning. "How sickening it is to see Willy, not two months after his father's death ... at banquets and reviews", she has said (→26/6/94).

Belfast prospers as big centre of engineering and shipbuilding

Belfast

Although Ulster society is largely rural, there are many flourishing towns in the province and Belfast has just been designated a city. With an increase in its population from just under 100,000 in 1851 to over one third of a million at present, it has grown faster than any other urban centre in the British Isles. The writer William Thackeray approvingly described it as "hearty, thriving and prosperous, as if it had money in its pocket and roast beef for dinner".

The base of Belfast's growth and prosperity are engineering, linen and shipbuilding. Almost 75,000 people are employed in manufacturing industry in the city. The Chambers Encyclopaedia noted in 1868 that Belfast exhibited all the trade and commerce of Glasgow and Manchester with far less of their smoke and dirt. The spirit of the city is well illustrated by the Grand Trades' Arch, which was erected for the visit of the prince and princess of Wales three years ago, with slogans extolling the virtues of hard work, trade, employment and temperance. The growth of Belfast and other towns has led to a significant increase in the prosperity and numbers of the northern Irish middle classes.

Queen's Bridge in Belfast: entrance to the bustling city and port.

Explorer publishes 'Arabian Nights'

England

The explorer and multi-linguist Sir Richard Burton has published a 16-volume unexpurgated translation of *The Arabian Nights*, with detailed annotations by him on such things as clitoral surgery, homosexuality and bestiality. Burton left Oxford without graduating and has been travelling extensively ever since in India, Arabia and Africa amassing facts about the habits, languages and sexual customs of the peoples he has met on the way.

A master of nearly 40 languages and dialects, Burton has published many other books, including translations of the Indian *The Kama Sutra* (1883) and the Arabian *The Perfumed Garden* (1886) – two erotic works which deal almost entirely with the intimate details of sexual mores.

1889

Edinburgh, 18 January. The city is hit by an earthquake.

Dublin, 4 May. The first Irish Federated Trade and Labour Union conference is held.

London, 8 May. Charles Parnell, the head of the Irish parliamentary party and leader of the home rule movement, gives evidence before the commission investigating the Pheonix Park affair in which, letters implicating him in a political murder were published in *The Times* (→ 20/7).

Ireland, 14 June. The Irish Society for the Prevention of Cruelty to Children is founded.

Edinburgh, 20 July. Charles Parnell is granted the freedom of the city (→ 24/12).

London, 19 August. The dock workers call an all-out strike (→ 16/9).

Southern Africa, 29 October. The British South Africa Company is chartered.

Europe, 29 October. Britain signs an agreement with all major powers in Europe declaring the Suez canal neutral and open to all shipping.

Britain, 12 December. Robert Browning, the poet and author who wrote, *The Pied Piper of Hamelin* and *The Ring and the Book*, dies.

London, 24 December. Captain William O'Shea files a petition for divorce on grounds of the adultery of his wife Katherine with Charles Parnell (→ 21/1/90).

Britain. William Wilkie Collins, the author of *The Woman in White*, a crime novel, dies aged 64.

Britain. The Royal Society for the Protection of Birds is founded in an attempt to protect birds from being killed for the millinery trade.

Britain. Robert Louis Stevenson, the Scots author who retired to Samoa this year, publishes *The Master of Ballantrae* (→ 12/1889).

Glasgow. New city chambers are opened.

Bradford. The new city council establishes a municipal electricity works and commences a public supply (→ 1890).

London. *The Gondoliers*, the latest operetta by William S Gilbert (words) and Arthur Sullivan (music), is premièred at the Savoy theatre.

Journalist admits forging letters to implicate Parnell

London, 20 February 1889

Richard Pigott, an Irish political journalist, has confessed to the special commission set up by the House of Commons to investigate nationalist activity that he forged the scandalous letters that appeared in *The Times* in 1887, implicating its alleged author Parnell in the Phoenix Park murders.

Pigott, who is notorious in Dublin for his involvement in shady enterprises, plotted his campaign to discredit Parnell in 1885 when he was short of money. He became involved with Edward Houston, formerly associated with *The Times* and now secretary of the most prominent unionist association in Ireland. Pigott lured Houston to Paris and handed him what he said were incriminating documents which had fallen into his hands. Houston paid out £605, returned to London and approached *The Times* with his evidence. So eager were they to discredit Parnell that the editor ignored warnings about the reliability of the letters, and they were duly published.

Pigott's treachery was unmasked before the commission through the simple expedient of a spelling test, which proved the letters to be false. As even the eminent judges collapsed with laughter, the hapless forger confessed his guilt (→ 8/5).

Piggott: unmasked as a forger.

Inquiry reveals that one in three live in abject poverty in the world's largest city

Women, children and chickens share the road in front of their squalid homes.

London, April

With a population of 5.5 million, London is the largest city in the western world and according to a new study – the first of its kind – one third of its citizens are living below the poverty line. In his *Life and Labour of the People in London*, the social investigator Charles Booth also says that almost half of the 900,000 inhabitants of London's East End are "poor".

Booth, who began his study in 1886, divided Londoners into eight classes. At the lowest level he found 11,000 "occasional labourers, loafers and semi-criminals"; just above them he placed 100,000 very poor people living on casual earnings. Then came 75,000 people with intermittent earnings, among them dockers and porters. They were also poor, along with the next class, of some 129,000, who had small regular earnings. The largest group of 377,000 people had regular standard earnings of 22 to 30 shillings [£1.10 to £1.50] a week.

Booth defined his poverty line as an income of between 18 and 21 shillings a week for a man, his wife and three children. He said outgoings of 9 shillings on food and 5 shillings 9 pence on rent, heating and lighting would absorb almost all of this income (→ 15/8/90).

The stove is cold, the pans are empty, where does the next meal come from?

Powerful Royal Navy still rules the waves

The Royal Navy: keeping abreast of change to remain supreme at sea.

Britain
While the British army keeps an uncertain peace on land around the globe, the Royal Navy links the far-flung empire, as well as preventing any invasion of the mother country.

Britain's naval programme is based on the "two-power standard" – having a fleet effectively greater than the strengths of the two next largest navies, those of France and Russia. The navy is changing rapidly; every few years sees the development of new guns, armour and ship designs. The old threedeckers have given way to steam-powered ships of the line, and heavy breech-loading guns have replaced the old muzzle-loading cannon. But even as the "Admiral" class battleships are being completed, a new pattern of big and more powerful guns is being designed. The Royal Navy currently consists of 90,000 well-trained men and 300 ships of different kinds (→1894.)

The 'workshop of Europe' enjoys a boom

Birmingham
For long a centre of religious nonconformity, of radical politics and of scientific research, Birmingham has this year officially become a city. The new city is home to a major industrial boom.

Birmingham's remarkably rapid expansion was initially due to transport. First there were canals, then railways boosted its position as the "workshop of Europe". Here was the great Soho factory where the first practical cylindrical steam engines were built for the market, attracting visits and admiration from manufacturers, statesmen and princes alike.

The city's population has soared from about 70,000 at the turn of the century to more than 800,000 today. The city is bent on improving public utilities such as street lighting and clean water.

The Exchange: home for many of Birmingham's new businesses.

County councils are formed in Scotland

Westminster, 8 April
A start is being made on tackling the muddled state of local government in Scotland. To deal with the chaos, the lord advocate today announced a series of measures aimed at replacing the old appointed commissioners of supply in the shires with new, elected county councils as in England and Wales. The commissioners had control over county police and joined with burgh magistrates on bodies such as boards of control over lunacy and prisons.

It is also proposed to replace the central board of supervision set up in 1845 at the time of the belated reform of the Scottish poor law. This has taken on the duties of a kind of central welfare office, but it has had only feeble powers.

A new act is designed to replace the board of supervision by a much more authoritative local government board. Plans are also being drawn up to end the system of dual responsibility between police magistrates and town magistrates in town government (→1/3/94).

Technical education gets more funding

Westminster, 27 July
The British government has at last realized that it is a long way behind its industrial competitors in the field of technical education. The Technical Instruction Bill, which is published today, is a first attempt to build up a national system of technical education.

Hitherto, technical education has been effectively an uncoordinated private enterprise. The existence of over 600 mechanics' institutes has, however, led to the development of national examination systems, with the South Kensington department of science and art paying government grants to schools for examination successes.

The government now concedes that countries such as the United States and Germany have excellent systems of industrial education for factory managers. The bill sets up local authorities with responsibility for stepping up technical education. The councils can levy a penny rate to expand it and raise money for new buildings (→23/4/91).

Success flows to 'Three Men in a Boat'

Jerome's three men in a boat making merry music with their passengers.

London
A young writer of 29 has set the public laughing at the whimsical adventures of three friends taking a boat on a leisurely trip up the river Thames from Kingston to Oxford. *Three Men in a Boat* is the work of Jerome K Jerome, who has led a casual life as a clerk, schoolmaster, actor and journalist. With his two friends George and Harris, the narrator sets set off on the voyage with no object but to idle away the long summer days pleasantly. "Work?" he says, "I like work: it fascinates me. I can sit and look at it for hours."

Jerome was born in Walsall but was brought up in London. This year he has also published *The Idle Thoughts of an Idle Fellow*, and following the success of *Three Men*, he is at work on a sequel, *Three Men on the Bummel.*

Socialist essays are published by Shaw

London, December
The surprise book of the month, snapped up like a fashionable novel despite its price of six shillings, is *Fabian Essays in Socialism*. Privately printed and distributed by the Fabian Society, it consists of lectures from meetings edited by George Bernard Shaw, who wrote two of the essays. The society, formed in 1884, is gaining new members daily. Shaw and Sidney Webb are the leading lights of Fabian socialism, which aims for a "revolution without violence", unlike William Morris's Socialist League (→1892).

Tough laws clamp down on obscenity

Westminster, July
A tough new law aimed at curbing "indecent or obscene" material will shortly be passed. The Indecent Advertisements Act will prohibit the display of any such material, on pain of a fine or imprisonment. It is seen as the most wide-ranging piece of censorship since the Obscene Publications Act of 1857.

Backed by the puritanical National Vigiliance Association, the measure is set to enforce that group's concept of "social purity". As well as barring all forms of allegedly indecent advertising, it prohibits the display of any material relating to venereal diseases.

Emma Cons is first female alderman

London
Emma Cons, an artist and housing reformer, has been made the first woman alderman on London County Council. An ardent feminist and an executive of the Women's Liberal Foundation, she has worked to bring some beauty to lives in the London slums. Born to a poor piano maker, at 14 she studied at the charitable Ladies' Guild of Arts. Already she has replaced pubs with "coffee palaces", introduced model housing schemes and taken on the lease of the Victoria theatre for her tenants (→1890).

All-out strike brings docks to a halt

Hundreds of dockers vote "Yes" to an all-out strike demanding more pay.

Ben Tillet: fighting for the dockers.

London, 16 September
London's dockers have won a great triumph. Their month-long strike ended today when the employers conceded their demands: pay of sixpence an hour – the "dockers' tanner" – and a hiring period of not less than four hours at a time.

The strike is a breakthrough for the pioneers of the growing British socialist movement and for the new unionism espoused by the dockers' leaders, such as Ben Tillett and John Burns. They persuaded the 10,000 dockers, who up until then had been unorganized, to come out on strike together and take part in some mass marches through the City of London.

The strike won massive public support. Just when the dockers' relief funds were running out, cash began to pour in from the public, even from as far afield as Australia. This allowed the men to draw strike pay, whilst the dock companies found it hard to recruit blackleg labour. This is a victory that has lifted the hearts of dockers – and of gasworkers, general labourers and unskilled building workers – and has boosted the cause of trade unionism (→25/4/90).

Writer Robert Louis Stevenson retires to his own treasure island

Robert Louis Stevenson and family celebrate on arrival at their new home.

Samoa, December
Robert Louis Stevenson, the restless traveller who wrote that "to travel hopefully is a better thing than to arrive", has settled here to build himself a house, Vailima, among the islanders who call him "Tusitala" – the "teller of tales". He and his wife Fanny have been wandering the South Seas in search of a climate better for his lungs than Switzerland or California.

After the runaway success of *Treasure Island*, followed by his second boys' adventure *Kidnapped*, Stevenson had an even bigger success with *The Strange Story of Dr Jekyll and Mr Hyde*, inspired by a nightmare, which has been staged in New York and London, where it had to be taken off prematurely because of its resemblance to the Jack the Ripper case. *The Master of Ballantrae*, published this year, is another study of evil (→1894).

1890

Cork, 21 January. The Irish Democratic Trade and Labour Federation, an association of agricultural labourers and town workers, is formed by Michael Davitt (→ 13/2).

South-west Ireland, 25 April. Employees on the Great Southern and Western Railway call a strike (→ 1893).

London, 17 May. *Comic Cuts*, the first comical newspaper, goes on sale.

London, 24 May. Queen Victoria invests her grandson, Prince Albert, the eldest son of the prince and princess of Wales, as duke of Clarence (→ 29/10).

Edinburgh, 11 June. The Free Public Library, founded by Andrew Carnegie, the Scottish-born millionaire, is opened to the public (→ 1898).

London, 21 September. The first issue of Michael Davitt's weekly newspaper, *Labour World*, is published.

Liverpool, 29 October. The duke of Clarence opens the new Royal Infirmary (→ 3/12/91).

London, 18 November. The *Pall Mall Gazette* calls for the retirement of Charles Parnell as leader of the Irish parliamentary party following his involvement in the O'Shea divorce (→ 12/1890).

London. The first electric power station is opened, at Deptford (→ 23/9/92).

London. *The Times* newspaper employs Flora Shaw Lugard as a foreign correspondent; she is the first female correspondent on a British newspaper.→

Cambridge. James Frazer, a Glasgow-born fellow at Trinity College, publishes *The Golden Bough*, a major new work of anthropology.

Scotland. William McGonagill, a Scottish-born poet, publishes *Poetic Gems*.

Manchester. The Withworth Institution of Art is opened.

London. William Booth, the founder of the Salvation Army, publishes *In Darkest England and the Way Out*; it is concerned with the problems of the poor in London and the mass migration of people from country areas to cities.

Birmingham. Antonin Dvorak, the Bohemian composer, premières his *Requiem Mass*, which was commissioned for the city's music festival.

'Graphic' is the first paper with pictures

London, 4 January

Britain's first illustrated daily newspaper, the *Daily Graphic*, was launched today by W L Thomas. It carries the first half-tone photographs ever to appear in a British newspaper. This marks a major step forward in press photography. Mr Thomas said: "We are hopeful of eventually reaching a larger circulation than any morning paper in the English language, once we have overcome the technical limitations of slow presses needed for half-tone reproduction." Clement Shorter, who is the editor of the *Daily Sketch* and a firm believer in the future of visual news, says "*The Graphic* is the first newspaper to publish real news pictures in order to help understanding and not just to satisfy curiosity".

DAILY GRAPHIC
An Illustrated Newspaper

The first edition of the new paper.

Irish library opens

Dublin, 29 August 1890

The National Library has opened in Kildare Street and a knighthood has been conferred on the architect, Thomas Deane. The origins of the library go back to the foundation of the Dublin Society in 1731, when a library was set up for members, with the emphasis on keeping scientific works. Then, in 1815, it moved to Leinster House, but its continued expansion, together with the gift by Dr Jasper Joly of his magnificent collection, necessitated a further move, to larger premises.

Working-class housing to be improved

Narrow alleys in a Glasgow slum.

Back-to-back misery in Yorkshire.

Westminster, 15 August

The latest Housing of the Working Classes Act offers little hope to workers suffering in the appalling conditions of Britain's urban slums. While it consolidates a number of existing measures, it does not provide the financial resources that hard-pressed local authorities need if they are not to fall foul of their ratepayers.

The property tax that is the basis of local government finance draws on a narrow band of people. It does not provide a broad enough base to fund large-scale house-building programmes, which are almost certain to lose money, given the poverty of the tenants.

The Public Health Act of 1875 – which gave the municipal authorities swingeing new powers over the supply of basic utilities – and a number of house clearance schemes set the process of improving workers' housing in motion, but real change has been slow. More urgent action followed the findings of a number of Commons committees, and reached a peak with Andrew Mearns's pamphlet, *The Bitter Cry of Outcast London*, a catalogue of misery that moved Queen Victoria and many politicians. In 1884 a royal commission on the housing of working people was set up. Its members included the prince of Wales and Cardinal Manning. This commission amassed the greatest body of evidence on housing collected this century. Its report in 1885 highlighted the problems of the poor.

It also noted that whilst many charities exist, they are keen to draw a line between the "deserving" and "undeserving" poor. Such bodies are often set against any form of public welfare, either local or national (→ 14/1/1902).

The Forth rail bridge, a monument to three pillars of the Victorian economy – coal, iron and railways – is finally completed after eight years.

Marshall publishes study of economics

Cambridge
Alfred Marshall, professor of political economy at the university here, has this year published a pioneering volume, *The Principles of Economics*, in which he goes further than any predecessor in establishing the discipline of economics as a major science. A number of further volumes are promised.

The *Principles* is a truly groundbreaking work, in which Professor Marshall introduces such hitherto unknown concepts as "elasticity" – the flexibility in supply and demand as dictated by the variations in other economic factors – and "time analysis".

An excellent mathematician, the professor became a fellow of St John's College in 1865, and after spells as the principal of University College, Bristol, and as a lecturer at Balliol College, Oxford, he returned to Cambridge university to take up the chair of political economy some five years ago.

British empire expands into Africa

Britain and Germany sign African treaty

London, 1 July
As European colonies continue to expand in Africa, Britain and Germany have underlined their mutual interests with the signature today of the Anglo-German Convention. Uganda and Zanzibar will now come under British rather than German control; in turn Germany will gain access to the Zambezi river through the Caprivi Trail and will gain the North Sea island of Heligoland. Queen Victoria objects to the latter move, fearing that the islanders have been handed over to an unscrupulous government, but popular opinion tends to that of the explorer Henry Stanley, who compared the territorial handovers to exchanging "a trouser button for a suit of clothes". Lord Salisbury, the prime minister, who engineered the treaty, takes the strategic view: without the agreement there would be no peace with Germany (→ 17).

Germany: ready to swoop on Africa.

Cecil Rhodes is new PM of Cape Colony

Southern Africa, 17 July
Cecil Rhodes, one of the world's richest men, has today capped his many achievements with a new appointment, quite outside the world of business, as prime minister of the Cape Colony. The appointment puts Rhodes in an excellent position to further his dedication to British imperial expansion.

Born just 37 years ago, Rhodes was sent to southern Africa to help his weak chest. After failing as a cotton-grower, he set off for the Kimberley diamond fields and won himself an enormous fortune. In 1880 he founded the De Beers diamond company and in 1887 moved into gold, boosting his millions even further after he set up Consolidated Goldfields (→ 14/11).

Cecil Rhodes: colonial master.

Anglo-Portuguese trade treaty concluded

Westminster, 14 November
As part of Britain's continuing efforts to rationalize her colonial empire in Africa, the government has followed up this summer's Anglo-German Convention [*see above*] with a new agreement signed this month with Portugal. Under it the territories of Mashonaland and Nyasaland will come under British imperial control.

The treaty effectively puts an end to Portuguese ambitions, and leaves it with two major African possessions – Angola to the west and Mozambique in the east. Portuguese east African expansion had already been cut off by Germany to the north; now Cecil Rhodes's push out of Cape Colony and into Matabeleland has effectively denied any opportunities for further incursions into the interior.

In a further treaty signed on 5 August, France ceded Britain Zanzibar in return for the British government's acceptance of French claims on Madagascar (→ 11/4/94).

Death ends tragedy of 'Elephant Man'

London, 11 April
One of the saddest and yet most fascinating stories of the age came to an end today with the death of Joseph Carey Merrick, better known to the public as "the Elephant Man". He was 27 years old.

Born to a slightly crippled but otherwise healthy mother, Merrick showed no signs of the disfigurement which gained him his popular name until the age of five. It was then that he began to show signs of acute neurofibromatosis, a rare and horribly disfiguring disease. His head swelled to three feet in circumference, large bags of brownish spongy skin hung from his face, his jaws were too deformed to allow speech, his right arm became distended, ending in a flipper. His legs were similarly afflicted.

He was confined to a workhouse, from whence he escaped to join a freakshow in 1883. Four years later he was rescued by Dr Frederick Treves, who placed him in the London Hospital. Here he was cared for until his death.

Trains are all electric on new London underground railway line

Passengers board the windowless carriages of London's new "tube" line.

London
The first underground railway to rely wholly on electric rather than steam power has opened this year. The world's first underground system, the Metropolitan Railway, began operating in 1863. But the new City and South London Railway, linking the Monument to Stockwell, is the first line to run deep underground through tunnels or "tubes" rather than using the "cut and cover" system (→ 10/9/96).

Women win social liberty, but not political advance

Britain
Two more barriers fell to the advance of women this year. Flora Shaw Lugard became the first woman to be appointed as a foreign correspondent for *The Times* while Philippa Fawcett outscored all male undergraduates in the senior maths tripos at Cambridge. Yet Fawcett's top marks have failed to win her a degree, since although women can attend lectures, they still cannot be awarded degrees.

The achievements of Lugard and Fawcett highlight a growing debate about the role of women in society. Political reforms in the last 20 years have extended the franchise to more men, but women have no comparable rights. Campaigns for female suffrage have begun, but so far have achieved neither national momentum nor the support of the major political parties.

Fawcett (top r): brilliant student.

Socially, at least, women seem to be enjoying more freedom. Clothing is less fussy. With the passing of the crinoline and the slow dying out of the bustle, women are adopting simpler skirts and looser blouses, and taking the bold step of using the cosmetics rouge and lipstick. Hair dyes are common. The bicycle has brought women another liberty: transport under their own steam. Around a third of all workers are women, of whom a quarter are married (→22/12/98).

Parnell triumph turns to political ruin

Prestige is at peak as claims disproved

London, 13 February
The report of a special commission has found that the letters published by *The Times* in 1887, accusing Parnell of complicity in the Phoenix Park murders, were forgeries. Parnell has been exonerated of all serious charges.

After the evidence given by Richard Pigott, the forger of the letters [*see page 985*], Parnell advised his solicitor to keep an eye on Pigott in case he fled abroad. It was a prophetic warning. By the time the commission met again, Pigott had left the country and sought refuge in Madrid. Here, as luck would have it, he was spotted by Captain William O'Shea, husband of Parnell's mistress, Katherine. When the police came to Pigott's hotel room, he seized a revolver out of a suitcase, placed the muzzle against his mouth and shot himself.

The accusation against Parnell, and his subsequent vindication after Pigott's appearance, received much publicity. Parnell reached a new level of political respectability in both Britain and America, and was given a standing ovation when he appeared in the House of Commons. The commission's official report will further enhance his reputation (→11/1890).

Charles Parnell: cleared of murder.

Affair spells doom for political career

Westminster, December
After a protracted debate over Parnell's suitability to lead the Irish parliamentary party after acknowledging his liaison with Katherine O'Shea [*see report below*], the party has split. Justin McCarthy, the vice-chairman, walked out, calling on those who agreed with him to leave the meeting; 43 members followed. Parnell, with 27 loyal supporters, remained behind.

Members of Gladstone's Liberal Party, appalled by Parnell's sexual indiscretion, demanded that their leader should repudiate his alliance with the Irish party so long as it was led by Parnell. Gladstone realized that he could do nothing to achieve home rule unless Parnell stepped down. The members of the Irish parliamentary party have had to choose between loyalty to the political principles taught them by their leader, and loyalty to the man himself. In the end their principles won, although Parnell is determined to fight the next election with a much-depleted party (→10/3/91).

Former supporter O'Shea cites Parnell in divorce proceedings

London, November
In a scandal which has stunned and shocked both Britain and Ireland, Captain William O'Shea has taken an action for divorce against his wife, Katherine, citing Parnell as co-respondent. Parnell offered no defence, and the verdict has been given against him. At a time when the prospects for home rule have never been brighter, Parnell's career is in ruins. It seems like the end of the man regarded by many as the uncrowned king of Ireland.

It now emerges that Parnell and Katherine have been lovers for some years and that she has at least two children by him. Two years ago, it was hinted in the *Pall Mall Gazette* that Parnell seemed to spend a lot of time in a suburban retreat at Eltham, outside London. This was Katherine's home and it may have been the publicity which goaded O'Shea (once a member of Parnell's party) into eventually suing for divorce (→18).

Parnell's political career is hit as he is cited as co-respondent in the controversial O'Shea divorce case.

1891

Motherwell, 5 January. Striking coal miners riot in protest at attempts by pit owners to evict them from their homes.

Dublin, 10 March. The Irish National Federation, an organization of anti-Parnellites, is formed (→ 2/4).

Ireland, 2 April. The anti-Parnell candidate, Bernard Collery, defeats the Parnell candidate, Valentine Dillon, in the North Sligo by-election (→ 1/6).

London, 21 April. The Grenadier Guards mutiny at Chelsea Barracks.

Scotland, 21 May. Dumbarton Football Club are the newly formed Scottish Football League's first champions.

Dublin, 1 June. An anonymous article, *Stop Thief!*, is published in the *National Press*, the anti-Parnell paper; it accuses Parnell of embezzling party funds (→ 25).

Sussex, 25 June. Charles Parnell, who is still intent on retrieving his career, marries divorcee Katherine O'Shea, his mistress of many years (→ 8/7).

Westminster, 29 June. Cardinal Vaughan lays the foundation stone of the Roman Catholic cathedral.

Ireland, 8 July. Parnell's supporters lose the Carlow by-election (→ 2/10).

Brighton, 2 October. Parnell collapses from exhaustion and rheumatism (→ 6).

Brighton, 6 October. Parnell dies at the age of 45 (→ 11).

Dublin, 11 October. Thousands turn out for the funeral of Parnell (→ 17/6/92).

London, 3 December. Prince Albert, the duke of Clarence, is engaged to Princess Mary ("May") of Teck, the daughter of Queen Victoria's first cousin, Princess Mary Adelaide (→ 14/1/92).

London, 28 December. William Butler Yeats, the Irish poet, forms the Irish Literary Society of London; the first meeting is held in his home (→ 1893).

London. Thomas Hardy's novel *Tess of the D'Urbervilles* is published.

London. Sir Arthur Conan Doyle publishes *The Adventures of Sherlock Holmes*, his popular detective, in the *Strand* magazine.

Education will be free under new act

Westminster, 23 April

The new Elementary Education Bill will make free education available for all families in England and Wales, however poor. There is to be a grant of ten shillings a year for all children between the ages of three and 15. This is more than the fees of most schools. Lord Salisbury, the prime minister, has not been a great fan of free education. He wrote that "the duty of sending your children to school is not a natural duty like that of feeding them – it is an artificial duty invented within the last 60 years". But he feared that the Liberals would make board schools free, hitting fee-paying church schools (→ 20/4/92).

Royal gambling scandal

The prince of Wales is caught in a scandal involving an illegal baccarat game.

London, 10 June

This morning's leading article in *The Times* makes a devastating attack on the prince of Wales. He is condemned for mixing in doubtful society and indulging in "questionable pleasures", thereby putting at risk the "monarchical principle".

The attack follows the nine-day trial of a slander case at which the prince has been present nearly every day and in which he has given evidence. The trial arose out of an incident at the Doncaster races during St Leger week last year. The prince was staying at the house of a wealthy shipowner, Arthur Wilson. He had brought his own baccarat counters and was the banker for the game. During its course Wilson's son accused a good friend of the prince, Sir William Gordon-Cummings, of cheating.

Five people supported the cheating charge and Sir William was then induced to sign a paper confessing his guilt. He promised never to touch cards again. He expected the matter to be hushed up, but it became part of London gossip so he sued for slander. Sir William lost the case. He has been expelled from the army and thrown out of all his clubs (→ 3/6/92).

Ever-young 'Dorian'

London

Oscar Wilde, aesthete and advocate of "art for art's sake" and butt of Gilbert and Sullivan's *Patience*, has published *The Picture of Dorian Gray*, whose hero remains untouched by age or debauchery so long as his portrait bears the consequences. W H Smith refuses to stock "this filthy book" but Wilde claims in the preface: "There is no such thing as a moral or an immoral book. Books are well written or badly written. That is all" (→ 20/4/93).

Hello, Paris, this is London calling, as telephones go overseas

London, 16 March

Those who have a telephone can now speak to their friends in Paris thanks to the submarine cable which has just been finished. Paris is the first overseas city to be linked up. It is only a year since London subscribers were able to talk to Birmingham and only seven years since they were linked to Brighton.

The telephone reached London in 1878 and the first exchange was opened the following year in Coleman Street in the City. There were only seven or eight subscribers, but now there are 20 exchanges in London alone. The individual telephone lines come into the roofs of the exchanges. Each exchange is linked to others by multi-core cables (→ 5/4/92).

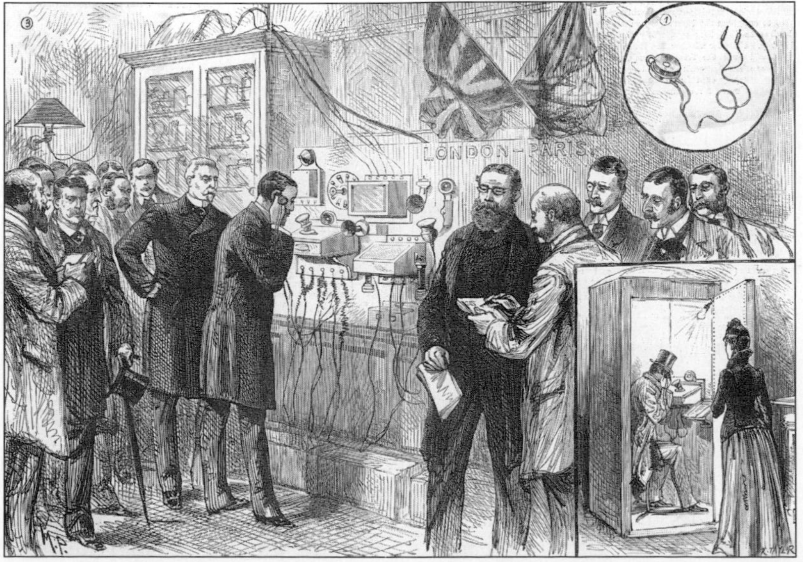

Onlookers wait with bated breath as the London/Paris telephone link is made.

'Service' jobs lure girls to the towns

Britain
More people than ever are living in towns and cities, according to this year's census. Nearly one third of the population now live in towns of more than 100,000 inhabitants, compared with just one in eight in France.

This urbanization is having a particularly important effect on the lives of women. Of the four million women workers, at least one and a quarter million are in "service". One estimate says that one in every three girls between the ages of 15 and 20 is a domestic servant.

Working-class parents are very ready to send their children into service. They believe it is preferable to factory work. But the domestic's life is often harsh. Many are seduced by the master or the son of the house and thereafter lose their jobs and "characters". The next biggest group of women workers are 1.1 million in dressmaking and textile manufacturing.

Radical manifesto splits the Liberals

Gladstone faces backlash over new policy

Newcastle, 2 October
The Liberal Party conference here has adopted a bold new set of policies called the "Newcastle programme". Gladstone hopes that it will rally the party and ensure the continuing support of Irish nationalist MPs. Top of the list is home rule for Ireland. This is the issue which has led to the loss of so many leading Liberals over the past two or three years. Nearly all the Liberal peers deserted Gladstone over this issue, together with Joseph Chamberlain, the powerful Birmingham Liberal leader.

The new policies are intended to pull in new voters and to encourage old ones. They propose a local veto on the sale of intoxicating liquors, triennial parliaments and "one man, one vote". Rural workers are wooed with the promise of land law reform. Trade unionists are promised an Employers Liability Bill and proposals to limit the hours of labour. Critics call the programme a ragbag of measures to catch votes. Its supporters say that each of the measures is based on consistent Liberal principles (→ 12/1891).

Rival roosters jostle for control.

Liberal Unionists led by Chamberlain

Birmingham, December
Joseph Chamberlain has taken advantage of the new radical Liberal Party programme by solidifying the base of his breakaway movement here. Manufacturers and professional classes in the Midlands are attracted by the Liberal Unionist policies sponsored by Chamberlain. They like the idea of seeking to combine good old-fashioned Liberal principles with the commercial benefits that come from a strong sense of empire.

Chamberlain, once regarded as a mob leader by the prime minister, Lord Salisbury, has moved a long way from the radicalism of his youth. Now the Conservatives are glad to have him on their side and find that many of his policies are closer to their own than to those of Gladstone's Liberals (→ 7/1892).

William Morris sets up press in Cotswolds

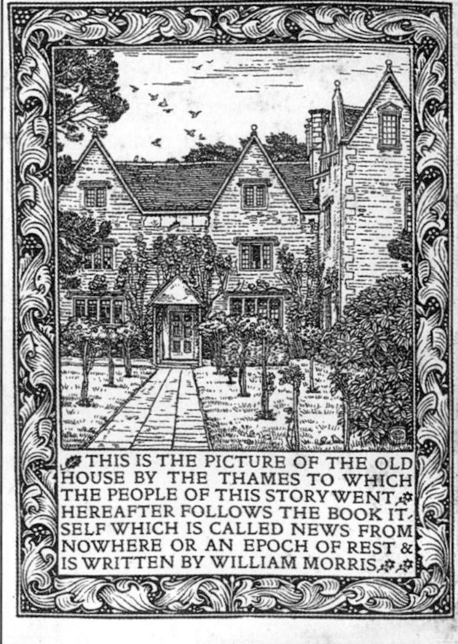

THIS IS THE PICTURE OF THE OLD HOUSE BY THE THAMES TO WHICH THE PEOPLE OF THIS STORY WENT. HEREAFTER FOLLOWS THE BOOK IT-SELF WHICH IS CALLED NEWS FROM NOWHERE OR AN EPOCH OF REST & IS WRITTEN BY WILLIAM MORRIS.

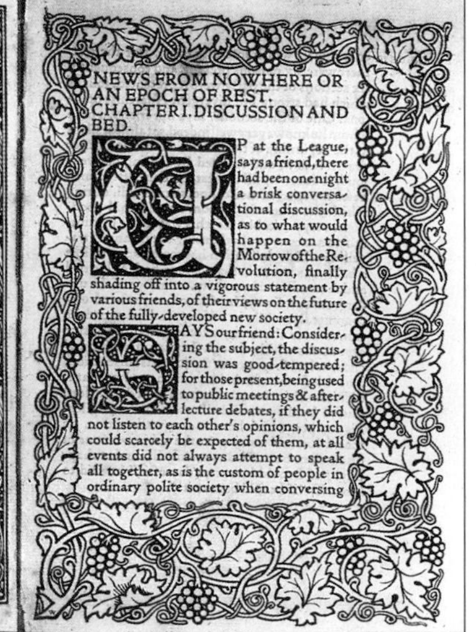

NEWS FROM NOWHERE OR AN EPOCH OF REST.
CHAPTER I. DISCUSSION AND BED.

UP at the League, says a friend, there had been one night a brisk conversational discussion, as to what would happen on the Morrow of the Revolution, finally shading off into a vigorous statement by various friends, of their views on the future of the fully-developed new society.

SAYS our friend: Considering the subject, the discussion was good-tempered; for those present, being used to public meetings & after-lecture debates, if they did not listen to each other's opinions, which could scarcely be expected of them, at all events did not always attempt to speak all together, as is the custom of people in ordinary polite society when conversing

Morris's utopian fantasy, "News from Nowhere", printed at Kelmscott.

London
William Morris, the socialist artist and disciple of Ruskin, who set up his own company to manufacture arts and crafts on the mediaeval model in 1861, has now added hand printing to the crafts he has revived. The Kelmscott Press, named after his Cotswolds manor house, produces illustrated editions of the classics. He also prints his own works including *News From Nowhere*, a utopian vision of a 20th-century Britain in which the slums have been cleared and people live in trim villages and country towns, happily working without the motive of personal profit (→ 3/10/96).

W H Smith, newsagent and politician, dies

London, 6 October
William Henry Smith, the first lord of the treasury and leader of the Commons, died today aged 66. But he will be remembered less for his distinguished political service – also as financial secretary to the treasury, first lord of the admiralty and secretary for war – than for turning the business he inherited into a household name. Henry Walton Smith opened a small newsagent's in London in 1792 and his son and grandson, both called William Henry, expanded the firm into the biggest in the country. W H Smith the younger became a partner in 1846 and won the right to sell books and papers at railway stations. He became a Conservative MP in 1868.

The original Smith's newsagents in central London, as it appeared in 1820.

1892

Northumberland, 2 January. Sir George Airy, the Astronomer Royal who modernized the Greenwich Observatory, dies aged 91.

Norfolk, 14 January. The duke of Clarence, the eldest son of the prince of Wales, dies of pneumonia at Sandringham House, aged 28.

Ireland, 5 April. Telephone links between Belfast and Dublin are established.

London, 18 April. Two women and six children are crushed to death in Easter Monday crowds descending the stairs into the railway station at Hampstead Heath.

Belfast, 17 June. Over 12,000 Unionists and Liberal Unionists attend an anti-home rule convention.→

Ireland, 27 June. Primary school education is to be free and compulsory for all (→ 1899).

Britain, July. Gladstone's Liberals and the Irish parliamentary party gain 354 seats in the general election, compared with 315 for the Conservatives and Liberal Unionists (→ 11/8).

Westminster, 11 August. Lord Salisbury is forced to resign as prime minister (→ 18).

London, 10 September. The Trafalgar theatre opens on St Martin's Lane.

Dublin, 23 September. The Dublin Corporation Electricity Works begins operating.

Belfast, 29 September. The Belfast Labour Party is formed (→ 13/1/93).

Westminster, 12 October. Alfred, Lord Tennyson, the poet laureate, is buried in Westminster Abbey; he died six days ago at the age of 83.

Dublin, 25 November. Douglas Hyde, the son of an Irish clergyman, talks to the National Literary Society of Ireland about "de-Anglicizing the Irish" (→ 31/7/93).

Leeds. Construction begins on an electricity power station.

North Wales. The river Vyrnwy is dammed to create a water supply for Liverpool.

London. George Bernard Shaw's latest play, *Mrs Warren's Profession*, is published (→ 1/11/1904).

Switzerland. Leading Anglicans meet nonconformist representatives at Grindelwald to discuss closer links.

Belfast venue for home rule protest

Belfast, 17 June

At what is the largest indoor political meeting ever held in Ireland, 12,000 Unionists and Liberal Unionists have gathered in a specially built pavilion in the Botanic Gardens to protest against home rule.

Protestant fears seem to have been greatly exaggerated, being founded on the belief that Britain will abdicate control over Ireland. Yet even though Gladstone's modest proposals fall short of full self-government, Protestants still see them as leading to grave internal conflict in Ireland (→ 13/2/93).

Keir Hardie is the first 'labour' MP

Westminster, 3 August

Keir Hardie today took his seat at Westminster as the MP for West Ham and the first independent labour member of the Commons. Hardie, who was born in Lanarkshire in 1856, was once sacked from the mines for his trade union activities. Since 1887 he has campaigned for a socialist party separate from the Liberals, and founded the Scottish Labour Party in the following year. Divisions within the West Ham Liberals are thought to have enabled him to win the seat in last month's general election (→ 29/9).

Indians to join the legislative councils

Indian elite: princes ready for action at a maharajah's tennis party.

London

Indians are to be given a limited role in overall British rule of the subcontinent. They will be eligible for election to provincial councils, some of which deal with legislation affecting the whole of India, under the India Councils Act now approved by parliament. Executive powers will be kept in British hands, however.

The purpose of the liberalization is to reinforce British interests and at the same time retain the acquiescence of Indians in British rule. The Indian National Congress (INC), founded seven years ago, is stepping up its agitation against Britain's domination of the economy and the civil service. Its members are drawn from a limited base, the educated middle class; but there is every possibility that the INC will develop into a mass nationalist movement.

The cost of administering India is increasingly burdensome because of higher administrative standards. To spread the tax net more widely and more effectively across the subcontinent, it has become necessary to foster Indian representation in the provincial regions (→ 26/12/94).

Thomas Cook, who revolutionized travel, makes his last journey

Leicester, 18 July

Thomas Cook, who combined morality with shrewd business instincts to build a worldwide travel agency, has died 51 years after organizing England's first railway excursion. The trip carried 500 passengers for a fare of one shilling return each from Leicester to Loughborough for a temperance meeting.

Ten years later, in 1851, 165,000 people booked Cook's tours to London to see the Great Exhibition, and in 1855 the Paris Exhibition prompted Cook to run his first circular tour of Europe, which was followed in 1872 by a world tour. A pillar of the temperance movement, Cook started work as a wood turner before becoming a printer.

Cook made a fortune from Britain's holidaymakers, here at play in Hastings. ▷

Women win entry to more colleges of higher education

Glasgow
Slowly but surely opportunities are opening up for women to pursue higher education. This year saw the establishment here of Queen Margaret College to house those taking the university higher local certificate for women. This course is run by the Association for the Higher Education of Women in Glasgow and the West of Scotland.

Since 1890 all Scottish universities have been able to accept women as students, but the situation is not so favourable south of the border, where questions are still asked as to whether or not women's brains are smaller than men's, or whether education at a university might destroy a woman's femininity or even her fertility.

A lady BA of London University.

Yet in England, too, there has been steady progress over the last 20 years. This year Dorothea Beale, the pioneering head of Cheltenham Ladies' College, announced plans for St Hilda's College to open next year. St Hilda's will join Lady Margaret Hall, Somerville and St Hugh's as Oxford colleges for women. Their Cambridge counterparts, Newnham and Girton, were established slightly earlier. Female students at Oxford and Cambridge are still prevented from becoming members of the university. This is not the case in London, where, as in Scotland, women are now admitted for full degrees.

Gladstone, at 83, prepares to form his cabinet for fourth term as prime minister

Confident campaigner: Gladstone.

Westminster, 18 August
William Gladstone, now 83 years old, today received from Queen Victoria a mandate to form a new government. It will be his fourth term as prime minister and almost certainly his last.

His Liberal Party's majority of only 40 in the recent general election disappointed the old man, who expected it to reach three figures. Even his own constituency, Midlothian, re-elected him by a slim margin, of only 700, a sharp drop on the 4,000 to 5,000 majorities he had gained in the past. Gladstone, who first became prime minister in 1868, is now frail and has failing sight, but he feels he must fulfil his promise to win home rule for Ireland (→ 1/3/94).

Popular diary is published by a 'Nobody'

London
Mr Charles Pooter, city clerk, of "The Laurels", Brickfield Terrace, Holloway, has attained the dignity of publication in a bound volume. His daily doings and reflections have been appearing for some time in *Punch* magazine but now they are collected and expanded as *The Diary of a Nobody*. Pooter prefaces his book with the words: "Why should I not publish my diary? I fail to see – because I do not happen to be a "Somebody" – why my diary should not be interesting." It is indeed interesting – not so much for his life of domestic mishaps, of misunderstandings with his "dear wife" Carrie and their wayward son Lupin or his friends Cummings and Gowing as for his sublime unawareness of the ridiculous but gentle figure he cuts. When Carrie says he is not important enough to be published, he replies grandly: "It's the diary that makes the man. Where would Pepys and Evelyn have been if it had not been for *their* diaries?" Author and illustrator are George and Weedon Grossmith.

Bowes museum at Barnard Castle: commissioned by John Bowes, the earl of Strathmore, in 1869 and completed after his death this year.

Wales in uproar over land reform

Wales, August
Angry demands for land reform and disestablishment of the Anglican church in Wales dominated the general election campaign here. It now looks likely that Wales will receive at least a full-scale land commission and a federal university charter now that Gladstone's Liberal Party has been re-elected [*see left*]. Gladstone has long sympathized with the Welsh over tithes and land tenure, but he is thought to be reluctant to back church disestablishment (→ 1899).

Thomson to be first scientist in Lords

Thomson: a lord among scientists.

Glasgow
William Thomson, Britain's foremost mathematical physicist, has become the first scientist to be elevated to the peerage. The new Lord Kelvin, whose working life has been spent at Glasgow University studying electricity, magnetism and heat, is no mere theoretician but believes in marrying his concepts to the real world of industry.

He invented the temperature scale based on an absolute zero of minus 273 degrees centigrade, a magnetic compass that was an instant success with the navy, and an apparatus that made long-distance telegraphy possible by producing recorded messages in Morse code. He played a key role in laying the first transatlantic cable.

1893

Armagh, 19 January. Michael Logue, the archbishop of Armagh, becomes a cardinal.

Westminster, 13 February. William Gladstone, the prime minister, introduces the second Home Rule Bill for Ireland (→ 2/3).

Belfast, 2 March. William Johnston, the MP for Ballykilbeg, carries a resolution in favour of passive resistance to the Home Rule Bill (→ 21/4).

Belfast, 21 April. Sectarian rioting breaks out after the second reading of the Home Rule Bill in Westminster (→ 1/9).

Dublin, 16 May. Electric trams begin a service from the city to the suburbs.

West Yorkshire, 4 July. Over 139 people die in a colliery disaster at Thornhill, Dewsbury.

London, 6 July. Prince George, the duke of York, marries his late brother's fiancée, Princess "May" of Teck, at St James's Palace.→

Dublin, 31 July. Douglas Hyde founds the Gaelic League, which aims to revive the Irish language and cultural identity.

Wimbledon, London, July. Charlotte (Lottie) Dod wins the All England Ladies' Singles Tennis Championships for the fifth time and third year running. The men's singles is won by Joshua Pim, an Irish doctor.

London, July. A debate arises over whether to admit women to the Royal Geographical Society.

Westminster, 1 September. The House of Commons passes the Home Rule Bill up to the House of Lords (→ 8).

Belfast, 5 September. The Trades Union Congress meets.

Manchester, 7 October. The new building for the Royal College of Music is officially opened.

Scotland. The Free Presbyterians split from the Free Church.

London. The idealist philosopher Francis Bradley publishes *Appearance and Reality*.

Leeds, West Yorkshire. Queen Victoria grants a royal charter to the borough, which becomes a city.

London. Alfred Gilbert's statue of Eros is unveiled in Piccadilly Circus.

Working-class joins battle for power

Independent Labour Party is founded

Bradford, 13 January
James Keir Hardie and the two other socialists elected as independents in last year's election formed an Independent Labour Party today. But Keir Hardie, as chairman, tried without success to retain the support of other socialist groups meeting here. The Fabian Society, whose delegation was led by George Bernard Shaw, left because the programme seemed too revolutionary. The leaders of the Social Democratic Federation refused to join the new party because it was not revolutionary enough.

Hardie, a former Lanarkshire coalminer, is determined to create a political party that specifically represents the interests of the working class. He has stressed the need to avoid the word "socialist" in the title because "the new party has to appeal to an electorate which has as yet no understanding of socialism". Nevertheless, the programme proposed was radical. The main object is "to secure collective ownership of all means of production, distribution and exchange" (→ 7/1895).

Socialist groups, like this one in Norwich, are springing up around Britain.

Employers set up a body to fight back

London
Employers have hit back against the growing militancy of the new trade unions. They have formed a new body called the National Free Labour Association. The inspiration came from the shipowners, whose Shipping Federation challenges union power; it compiles its own register of seamen and supplies blackleg labour if there is a strike.

The National Free Labour Association will do the same thing for a much wider range of industries. It will also engage in political lobbying to counter the propaganda of the unions. There was a tide of public sympathy for the unions at the time of the London dock strike in 1889. But the new body hopes to blame the unions for any strikes rather than employers (→ 17/11).

Strikes grow as unions flex their muscles

London, 17 November
The 15-week coal strike is at an end. William Gladstone, the prime minister, four days ago reluctantly invited the unions and the employers to a conference led by Lord Rosebery, the foreign secretary. A compromise has been reached and the men are to go back to work tomorrow. The strike has seen major developments in British unionism. It was called by the Miners' Federation and only affected the English Midlands, Lancashire and Yorkshire. But the strikers were determined to make the public notice their fight by causing a shortage of coal and sought to influence other areas. In South Wales, they encouraged a strike by the hauliers, using gangs who went from pit to pit trying to stop work. There was a pitched battle between one of these gangs and an army of South Wales miners, 2,000 strong, who did not want to join the strike.

Unionism has grown strongly since the 1889 London dock strike, particularly among miners and railwaymen, with an increase, too, in militancy. This year's strike figures are likely to be the worst ever, with anything up to 30 million days lost through disputes (→ 1895).

Mounted police try to control striking miners at Featherstone colliery.

Bill for home rule defeated again

Westminster, 8 September
William Gladstone's Home Rule Bill was resoundingly defeated on its second reading in the House of Lords tonight. There was a powerful speech in the closing stages by the marquis of Salisbury, the former prime minister, which rallied the Tory faithful to the cause.

Gladstone had had problems in getting the measure through the House of Commons. On the third reading he secured a majority of only 34 and this was after the bill had occupied no fewer than 85 sittings of the house. Gladstone himself held forth with great eloquence, but he had to face severe opposition from many former members of his own party as well as from the Conservatives. Joseph Chamberlain made a particularly effective attack and swung some of the waverers. The prime minister is now in a dilemma. He could dissolve parliament and go to the country to win support for home rule. But it is unlikely that his colleagues in the cabinet will want to take that risk.

The bill has never been very popular, even in Ireland. It excludes army, navy, customs, trade and foreign relations from the scope of the proposed Irish parliament, which does not please nationalists. The bill also does nothing to deal with the problem of Ulster Protestantism – and that alarms political leaders in Belfast (→ 7/11/95).

The House of Commons passes judgement on the second Home Rule Bill.

Balfour salutes as Belfast demonstrates strongly against home rule.

Franco-British row over Siam ends

London, 31 July
The earl of Rosebery, the foreign secretary, has managed to patch up the quarrel with the French and maintain British power in south-east Asia. Upper Burma is now safely part of the empire and Lord Rosebery hoped to use Siam as a buffer state between Burma and the French territories of Cambodia, Vietnam and Laos. Border fighting threatened the peace. However Siam's King Chulalongkorn, a shrewd political operator, has given full support for the British policy and thus keeps his country free of Western colonialism (→ 15/1/96).

University of Wales opens to students

Wales, 30 November
Students of the new federal University of Wales started their first year today. There have long been independent colleges at Lampeter (1827), Aberystwyth (1881), Cardiff (1883), and Bangor (1884). But not until today have they all been joined together, placed on an equal financial footing with each other, and given a special royal charter. This is intended to take Welsh scholarship out of Oxford and Cambridge, and put it back into Wales to be part of the national heritage.

Liverpool gets an overhead railway, dockers get an 'umbrella'

Lord Salisbury flicks a switch to open Liverpool's electric overhead railway.

Liverpool, 6 March
The new "Overhead Railway" here was opened to the public today, a little over a month after its official opening by Lord Salisbury on 4 February. It runs above the waterfront docks from Herculanean to Alexandra docks. This is one of the most congested parts of the Merseyside area. Horsedrawn buses, carts and carriages cause frequent jams.

The new railway, which uses electric traction, is proving a great tourist attraction as well as a business asset. Thousands of people are using it because they get a grandstand view of the world's ships loading and unloading their cargos. Locals are calling the railway the "dockers' umbrella" (→ 6/4/96).

London, 6 July. The duke of York weds Princess "May" of Teck, his late brother's former fiancée.

Rhodes extends control in southern Africa

British troops battle with guns and bullets against spears and shields.

Bulawayo, Zimbabwe, November
Cecil Rhodes and his British South Africa Company are steadily expanding their sphere of influence in southern Africa. Rhodes's agent in Mashonaland, Dr Leander Jameson, seized the opportunity presented by a raid on the Mashona by the Matabele chief, Lobengula, last July. The Matabele attacked the local white settlers. Jameson then sent British South African troops into the heart of Matabele country. The local warriors, armed with their traditional weapons, proved to be no match for the well-disciplined, well-armed company troops.

Rhodes now has effective control of all the country around here. The town of Bulawayo has been devastated, with most of the native houses burnt to the ground (→29/12/95).

Model village planned near Birmingham

Birmingham, November
George Cadbury has allocated a 502-acre plot of land near his chocolate factory here for the building of a model village. In the next year or so, some 200 houses are expected to be built. They are to be administered by the Bournville Village Trust, which will be entirely independent of the company.

George Cadbury: social reformer.

Strict regulations will ensure that the village never becomes overcrowded. No cottage may occupy more than one quarter of the site on which it stands. The roads are all to be 42 feet wide and they must be bordered with trees. One tenth of the area has been set aside as a minimum for parks and recreation.

The houses are expected to be occupied mainly by factory workers and skilled artisans. The cottages will be let on 999-year leases and for those with insufficient money to buy, mortgages will be granted at the rate of 2.5 to 3 per cent. Cadbury is anxious to make the best possible facilities available. Schools are to be built, ultimately accommodating 800 children and infants. There is to be a meeting-house capable of holding 400 people, sports grounds and swimming baths. Gardening tools are to be available for hire in the hope that each cottager will cultivate his plot (→22/3/99).

Wilde's new play is 'too clever by half'

London, 20 April
Oscar Wilde's new play, *A Woman of No Importance,* opened at the Haymarket theatre last night to warm applause but grudging notices for its "cynical epigrams" and for being "too clever by half". But William Archer, a leading critic, called it "the most virile and intelligent piece of dramatic writing of our day". Herbert Beerbohm-Tree, the actor-manager, plays Lord Illingworth, of whom Wilde admits "he is myself". It is he who calls the country gentleman hunting a fox "The unspeakable in full pursuit of the uneatable" (→14/2/95).

Irish tales revived in 'Celtic Twilight'

Dublin
The Irish literary revival has taken a further step with the publication of *The Celtic Twilight* by William Butler Yeats. It is a collection of Irish peasant legends and fairy tales imbued with an occult mysticism. The title is being adopted as symbolic of the aim of the movement to revive ancient Irish culture as part of national self-awareness.

Yeats, a Dublin-born Protestant, is the son of a well-known painter. He established a reputation with *The Wanderings of Oisin* in 1889. He is one of a coterie of poets, the Rhymers Club, in London.

Women tee off for first golf championship

Women golfers: putting on the 12th green at Westward Ho! club in Devon.

An advertiser exploits ladies' golf.

Surrey, July
Britain's first ladies' golf championship took place at Royal Lytham this month. It was won by Lady Margaret Scott, a leading figure in the recent formation of the Ladies' Golf Union in Britain. Lady Margaret's father, the earl of Eldon, and three brothers, Osmund, Denys and Michael, are all keen golfers, so for her participation must have seemed natural. Also, unlike most families, the Eldons have the luxury of their own private golf course in the grounds of the family home, Stowell Park in Wiltshire.

Women are not total newcomers to the sport: Mary, queen of Scots, was painted playing golf as long ago as the 16th century.

1894

Westminster, 1 March. William Gladstone makes his last speech as prime minister (→ 3).

East Africa, 11 April. Owing to the financial difficulties of the Imperial British East Africa Company, Uganda is brought under direct British rule as a protectorate (→ 14/6/98).

Dublin, 18 April. The Irish Agricultural Organization Society is founded by the Honorable Horace Plunkett.

Dublin, 27 April. The Irish Trades Union Congress meets for the first time.

London, 30 June. The prince of Wales opens Tower Bridge across the river Thames.

Kent, 31 July. Sir Hiram Maxim, an inventor, test-flies an aeroplane of his own design; unmanned and powered by two 180hp engines, it fails to fly (→ 2/10/99).

Wimbledon, London, July. Mrs Blanche Hillyard wins the All England Ladies' Singles Tennis championships; Joshua Pim wins the men's singles.

Lancashire, 18 September. The Blackpool Tower, a 500 foot (152-metre) replica of the Paris Eiffel Tower, is officially opened as another tourist attraction in the seaside resort of Blackpool.

Samoa, 3 December. Robert Louis Stevenson, the Scottish-born novelist and poet, who settled on the island of Samoa, has died aged 44; he is best known for his novels, including *The Strange Case of Dr Jekyll and Mr Hyde* and *Treasure Island*.

India, 26 December. Alfred Webb, the Irish MP for County Wexford, is elected president of the Indian National Congress.

Glasgow. Charles Rennie Mackintosh wins the competition to design the new Glasgow School of Art.

Scotland. The Scottish Grand Committee holds its first meeting.

London. The artist Aubrey Beardsley completes the illustrations for Oscar Wilde's play, *Salome*.

London. William Ramsey, a Scottish chemist at University College, London, who earlier this year discovered a new gas, helium, has, in tests with John Strutt, a physicist, discovered a second new gas, called argon.

'Grand old man' departs

Windsor, 3 March

In a move that has been increasingly expected in parliament, the prime minister, William Gladstone, today tendered his resignation in a brief, stiff audience with Queen Victoria. Thus ends his fourth ministry and a parliamentary career that has lasted 62 years and been central to every one of the century's great political struggles and achievements.

Gladstone's decision to go stemmed from the single issue which had become his passion and split the Liberal Party: Irish home rule. Back in power in 1892, Gladstone determined to push home rule through. He convinced the Commons, which passed the bill by 347 to 304 votes. But the Lords threw it out by 41 votes to 419. It was a devastating reverse. Four months later, in January, a new struggle – over the naval estimates – loomed. With his age at last telling on his abilities, Gladstone began planning his departure. He told the cabinet he was resigning on the morning of 1 March and in the afternoon made his last speech as premier, attacking the power of the Lords. For the "grand old man", it is the end of a career; for his country, it is the end of an era (→ 5).

The Grand Old Man, now aged 85.

Rosebery steps into shoes of Gladstone

Westminster, 5 March

Gladstone's successor as Liberal prime minister has been appointed. Gladstone is known to have preferred Lord Spencer and the Liberal rank and file Sir William Harcourt; but Queen Victoria has opted for Philip Archibald Primrose, the earl of Rosebery.

The Scottish-born Rosebery certainly has the right image – he is young, rich, eloquent and charming. For the last two years he has been foreign secretary and he played a crucial role in ending the 1893 coal strike. But critics wonder whether, especially after Gladstone, he possesses adequate political gravitas. He has no experience of life in the Commons, and while he has few rivals on a public platform, he has little parliamentary skill. Many liberal voters will find him too keen on imperialism. His aristocratic tastes are equally unlikely to appeal to the nonconformists, who so loved the puritanical Gladstone (→ 24/6/95).

Rosebery: young and fresh-faced.

Man-cub reared by wolves in 'Jungle Book'

Mowgli finds a friend in the wolf.

London

Rudyard Kipling began his writing career in India on the *Civil and Military Gazette* in Lahore. He came to London in 1889, not yet 25 but already famous for his stories of Indian life, *Plain Tales from the Hills* and his verses collected as *Barrack-Room Ballads*, including such favourites as *Mandalay*. Now, in the snows of Vermont with his American wife Caroline, he has written *The Jungle Book*, the story of the man-cub Mowgli, who is reared by wolves and taught jungle law by Baloo the bear, the panther Bagheera and Kaa the python.

'Parish Councils Act' will create a new tier of local government

Westminster, 1 March

Some 6,880 parish, rural and district councils are to be set up under the Local Government Act, which was passed today. While it may not bring the "village revolution" that some have promised, it is certain to make great changes in the way Britain is administered. It also increases the rights of women voters. Properly qualified single women have been able to vote for local councils since 1882, and now married women may do so too. In an equally important innovation, women may be elected to councils as well.

The new local authorities have been given substantial powers. But an opposition amendment, which limits their spending to the equivalent of a threepenny rate, may curb the useful exercise of many of those powers. Nonetheless the "Parish Councils Act", as the new legislation is also known, looks set to change the way in which the countryside is governed. The establishment of elected rural councils will bring in an unprecedented degree of local democracy (→ 12/8/98).

Budget makes it more expensive to die

The budget squeezes every last drop.

Westminster, 16 April
You cannot, as the saying goes, take it with you, but from now on, thanks to the budget of the chancellor, Sir William Harcourt, you cannot leave quite so much behind. The death duties he has introduced on all forms of estate mean that those expecting to inherit will have to turn over some of the parental wealth to the state.

Relatively few need fear the "death rate", but those affected, notably the great landowners whose estates come under direct threat, are unanimous in their opposition. Queen Victoria herself has written to the prime minister, Lord Rosebery, accusing Sir William of "spite". But the tax seems certain to be approved by parliament.

Government to fund development of navy

Westminster
Britain's army and navy, the twin bulwarks upon which the nation's defence depends, are to enjoy major investment and renovation, according to government plans published this year. The Royal Navy, under a programme devised by Lord Spencer, the first lord of the admiralty, is to be equipped with the latest in ships and armament, a move that comes in response to growing disquiet over allegedly obsolete vessels. The army faces pressure for a similar overhaul. This year a book by Spenser Wilkinson, *The Brain of an Army*, advocates the necessity for a coherent, intelligent military command structure (→ 1/3/1905).

Tea on the corner

London
Londoners keen to have a cup of tea and a cake without having to break off their shopping expedition are being offered a new venue: the teashops operated by the firm of J Lyons and Co. The first such teashop has opened at 123 Piccadilly, and more are scheduled soon. Lyons is named after its founder Joseph Lyons, but it is actually owned by the Salmon and Gluckstein families, who already operate a chain of successful tobacconists.

Jubilant queen is a great-grandmother

Four generations of royalty.

London, 26 June
Queen Victoria, already a formidable matriarch with connections to most of the royal households of Europe, saw a new generation added to her family tree today when a son was born to the duke and duchess of York. He is the queen's first great-grandchild and his birth means that for the first time there are now three heirs apparent in direct line to the reigning monarch, the others being the prince of Wales and the duke of York himself. But the queen is little concerned with such precedents; she is just delighted with the new baby (→ 5/8/95).

Manchester ship canal heads a year of impressive achievements by engineers

Working on Walton Locks, Warrington, to build the Manchester canal.

England, 21 May
Queen Victoria has opened the Manchester ship canal, completed 25 years after it was started – the year of the queen's first jubilee. The 36-mile-long waterway, which will enable sea-going ships to enter the heart of Manchester, runs from the Mersey estuary to inland docks on the outskirts of the city.

Four years ago, the project was close to foundering through a lack of funds; but Manchester Corporation saved the day by advancing 5 million on debenture. Liverpool showed no interest in the idea of a canal, and it only went ahead as a result of public subscription by the people of Manchester.

Two further engineering achievements have been completed this year: the Tower Bridge in London, and Blackpool Tower. The bridge, clad with granite and stone to match the nearby Tower of London, opens to allow large vessels into the Pool of London. It is operated by two 360hp steam engines housed in the two towers, and is opened and closed up to 50 times a day. The Blackpool Tower was built in just under four years and based on the Eiffel Tower in Paris. At 518 feet (158 metres) high – little more than half the height of the French original – it is the tallest structure in Britain.

Blackpool Tower: seen for miles.

The new Tower Bridge is the furthest downstream of all London's bridges.

1895

London, 14 February. Oscar Wilde's new play, the comedy *The Importance of Being Earnest*, is premiered at the Haymarket Theatre (→ 9/3).

London, 9 March. Oscar Wilde brings a libel action against John Sholto Douglas, the marquis of Queensberry, who had complained about Wilde's alleged homosexual association with his son, Lord Alfred Douglas (→ 5/4).

Ireland, 9 March. The Irish Agricultural Organization Society publishes the first issue of its weekly newspaper, the *Irish Homestead.*

London, 5 April. The marquis of Queensberry is acquitted of libelling Oscar Wilde (→ 22/5).

London, 22 May. Following the failure of his libel suit, Oscar Wilde goes on trial for homosexuality (→ 6/1895).

Britain, 29 June. T H Huxley, the biologist and staunch supporter of Darwin's theories, dies, aged 70.

Britain, July. All the Independent Labour Party candidates, including James Keir Hardie, one of the party leaders, fail to be elected in the general election (→ 27/2/1900).

London, 5 August. Kaiser William II pays an official visit to England (→ 23/9/96).

Westminster, 20 August. The House of Commons declares that John Daly, a convicted felon serving a prison sentence, is unable to take his seat as the newly elected MP for Limerick.

Belfast, 11 October. Men at the Harland and Wolff shipyard go on strike.

Ireland, 12 October. Frances Alexander, the Irish hymn-writer and composer of *All Things Bright and Beautiful*, inspired by the beauty of the Inishowen peninsula, dies.

London, 7 November. The executive of the Irish National League expels Timothy Healy and replaces him with Micheal Davitt (→ 13).

Dublin, 13 November. The Irish National Federation council meeting agrees to expel Timothy Healy from the executive (→ 2/2/96).

London. *The Time Machine*, a science fiction novel by H G Wells, is a huge success (→ 1897).

Birmingham. Wolseley Motors begins the manufacture of cars.

Critics hit Hardy as Irving is knighted

London
Men of literature and the theatre have been much in the news this year. Oscar Wilde's fall from grace [*see report right*] has stolen the headlines. Controversy also surrounded the latest novel by Thomas Hardy, *Jude the Obscure*, a tale of suffering which *The Pall Mall Gazette* denounced as "dirt, drivel and damnation". On a happier note, the knighthood bestowed on the great actor-manager Henry Irving has been applauded. He is the first man of the theatre to be so honoured.

Hardy: controversial novelist.

Oscar Wilde imprisoned

Wilde (l) and Lord Alfred Douglas.

Wilde's trial is front-page news.

London, June
Oscar Wilde's downfall from the pinnacle of theatrical and social success is complete. The disgraced writer is now undergoing a sentence of two years' hard labour in Reading jail after his conviction for homosexual practices. It was Wilde's second trial. At his first, the jury disagreed. At the second, the judge said when sentencing him: "It is the worst case I have ever tried. You, Wilde, have been the centre of a circle of extensive corruption of the most hideous kind." In January, Wilde's *An Ideal Husband* was produced, followed in February by *The Importance of Being Earnest*, which had extraordinary success. Then came the marquis of Queensberry's accusation that Wilde was a sodomite and Wilde's suit for libel, which he lost. He was advised to leave the country but instead awaited his inevitable arrest with composure at the Cadogan hotel.

Wilde's intimacy with Queensberry's son, Lord Alfred Douglas, whom the writer calls Bosie, was the cause of his fall (→ 2/1898).

Split in rugby football as some players opt to go professional

Huddersfield, 29 August
The ranks of rugby football split today when clubs which want to pay their members broke from the rigorously amateur Rugby Union and formed their own Rugby League after a meeting at the George hotel here. There will now be matches between professional rugby players, as there have been in football for years, though most players will keep their normal jobs and play for money only at weekends.

The dissidents are mostly in the north of England, where the sport has a large working-class following. In the south, it remains largely middle class. Football and cricket clubs make their profits by selling tickets to matches, and teams travel long distances to play. Rugby League will follow those examples.

"A dash on the goal line" during a game of rugby football, whose adherents have divided into two camps over the issue of payments for players.

Churchill dies after collapse of career

Westminster, 24 January
Lord Randolph Churchill died today, deranged from the effects of syphilis. He was 45. In the 1880s he was the most brilliant star in the Tory Party, apparently destined for the top, but he threw it all away.

Taking office in Lord Salisbury's government in 1886, he was the youngest chancellor of the exchequer since Pitt. He resigned in a dispute, hoping that his huge popularity would sweep him back to power. Instead, he was quickly forgotten. His health collapsed, and his death was a release. He leaves a widow, the American-born Jennie, and two sons, Winston and John.

New block-voting system for unions

Britain
The Trades Union Congress has introduced block voting, instead of voting by head. Now each union will decide its position, and then vote its whole strength. This system will give a boost to the big unions at the expense of the small ones. The TUC has also ruled that eligibility to attend its conferences will be restricted to delegates who work in the trades they represent. This will cut out middle-class supporters and representatives of trades councils, who are often socialists. The TUC thus becomes more united, more working class and also less politically radical (→26/3/97).

Rosebery's divided government falls and Salisbury leads the Tories back to power

Westminster, 24 June
Lord Salisbury has been returned to power after the resignation of the Liberal government over a dispute concerning the explosive material cordite. The war minister, Henry Campbell-Bannerman, was censured in the Commons on 21 June for failing to procure enough cordite for the army, and the prime minister, the earl of Rosebery, seized the opportunity to resign. Ironically, Campbell-Bannerman had on the same day announced a significant success: he had forced the retirement of the duke of Cambridge, the queen's cousin and a dogged opponent of change, as commander-in-chief of the army.

Cambridge: the ousted army chief.

The Liberals have been split and without clear direction since Gladstone retired last year. The party has been divided on social questions and on Ireland, and Rosebery has failed to impose the leadership it needed. Lord Salisbury has formed a strong government and plans an immediate general election [*see report below*]. Queen Victoria is said to be delighted (→12/8).

Latest craze for cycling dictates fashion

Mothers and daughters photographed on a summer excursion by bicycle.

Britain
The current craze of bicycle riding is catching on among women just as much as it is among men. The old hard tyre gave an uncomfortable ride, but pneumatic tyres – which have been produced commercially since 1889 – have greatly boosted the popularity of bicycling.

Some women workers ride to and from work along streets teeming with bicycles. The bicycle is also changing fashions. Those who thought women's "bloomers" too *outré*, or knickerbockers improper, now see sense in not wearing long skirts and petticoats, at least when riding a bicycle.

Inflatable tyres cushion the ride.

Conservatives sweep to victory in election

Britain, 12 August
The Tories have won a sweeping victory in the general election. They have 340 seats to the Liberals' 177, and will be joined by 71 Liberal Unionists in the new Commons meeting for the first time today. The Liberals are supported by 82 Irish nationalists.

The Tory-Liberal Unionist coalition will be much more radical than the last Tory government. Joseph Chamberlain, the former Liberal, is colonial secretary and will vigorously push imperial expansion in Africa, even if that means a clash with the Boers. As for Ireland, the government intends to "kill home rule with kindness" (→10/1896).

Salisbury, PM for the third time.

'Yellow Book' promotes 'art for art's sake'

London
A new and exotic quarterly journal has appeared, dealing with literature and the arts. It is known as the *Yellow Book*, because of its yellow cover, and because daring French novels are published on yellow paper. It is not pornographic, but its art editor is Aubrey Beardsley, whose drawings are exceedingly risqué. The movement for "art for art's sake" is very different from the improving traditions of recent decades. It thus stands in stark contrast to such projects as the *Dictionary of National Biography* and the *Oxford English Dictionary*.

Contributors to the *Yellow Book* include the famous novelists Henry James, H G Wells and Arnold Bennett as well as the painter Walter Sickert (→1898).

'National Trust' founded to save heritage

London
A new charitable organization to be known as the National Trust has been founded this year to protect historic buildings and open spaces in England and Wales. The principal figures behind the new organization are Octavia Hill, Sir Robert Hunter and Canon H D Rawnsley.

They fear that the spread of industry and the growth of the population will wipe out much of the countryside and important architecture. The trust will acquire land and buildings for the nation.

The new trust is a natural extension of earlier campaigns by the three to safeguard common land in London and the Lake District. From 1869, Sir Robert was a partner in the firm of solicitors which served the Commons Preservation Society, which had been founded in 1865. In this capacity, he helped save Hampstead Heath and Wimbledon Common for Londoners. Miss Hill is a disciple of John Ruskin, who in *Fors Clavigera* bemoaned the ruination of Miller's Dale in the Peak District by the construction of a mainline railway. In London, she led the fight to preserve Parliament Hill Fields.

Miss Hill: co-founder of the trust.

Transvaal raid launched

Southern Africa, 29 December
An invasion of the Transvaal was launched tonight with the apparent backing of Cecil Rhodes, the prime minister of Cape Colony. Led by Rhodes's chief assistant, Dr Leander Starr Jameson, 470 mounted police began a dash of 180 miles from the Bechuanaland frontier to Johannesburg in the Transvaal.

Rhodes has long coveted the Transvaal, a small Boer republic which has the richest goldfields in the world. British workers there, known as "Uitlanders", now outnumber the Boers, who refuse them all political power and tax them heavily. Rhodes may have supported the raid in the hope that it might encourage the Uitlanders to revolt; but although he claims that the raid is to protect the workers, his chief supporters are the mineowners.

Rhodes wants to expand British Africa all the way from the Cape to Cairo, and the Boers are in the way. The colonial secretary in London, Joseph Chamberlain, denies foreknowledge of the raid, which is a great embarrassment to Britain – not least because it seems unlikely to succeed (→3/1/96).

Jameson: leader of the attack.

Alfriston Clergy House, east Sussex: the first house acquired by the trust.

Gas adds light and heat to more homes

Britain
The use of gas for lighting and heating houses and for cooking is spreading rapidly in cities throughout the country. The invention of the incandescent gas mantle on the continent in 1885 revolutionized lighting in houses, and the invention of coin-operated meters has permitted landlords to install gas fires and stoves in the smallest flats. Electricity has been introduced in some places but cannot compete with the cheapness and popularity of gas. There are now networks of gas pipes under city streets everywhere and pipes are built into houses and office buildings, as well as lighting the streets. The gas fire has not yet replaced coal fires in houses but cooking is increasingly done on gas stoves.

Engels, the communist businessman, dies

London, 5 August
Friedrich Engels, the socialist capitalist pioneer, has died here at the age of 74. He was a German immigrant who ran a successful textile company in Manchester yet devoted his fortune to the propagation of communism.

He was closely associated with the late Karl Marx, another German immigrant theoretician, and helped him write such works as *The Communist Manifesto* and *Das Kapital.* Marx was the more remarkable intellectual, although Engels was a considerable theorist in his own right, as well as a prolific journalist and an expert on military strategy and doctrines. He also helped Marx financially. Communism has not had much success among British workers, although it has its intellectual supporters. Its tenets are more popular abroad.

December: the Belfast Opera House, designed and built by the celebrated theatre architect Frank Matcham, opens for its first performance.

1896

Southern Africa, 6 January. Cecil Rhodes resigns as prime minister of Cape Colony as a consequence of his apparent complicity in the recent Jameson raid (→24/3/99).

South-east Asia, 15 January. France and Britain guarantee the independence of Siam, and the French protectorate over Laos is recognized.

London, 25 January. Lord Frederic Leighton, the recently ennobled painter, sculptor and scholar and president of the Royal Academy, dies aged 65.

Dublin, 2 February. Justin McCarthy, the president of the anti-Parnell parliamentary party, resigns (→1900).

Dublin, 20 April. The first moving picture show is shown at the Olympia theatre.

Dublin, 29 May. The Irish Socialist Republican Party is formed.

Westminster, 5 September. A royal commission publishes its final report on the financial relations between Britain and Ireland.

Glasgow, 10 September. After six years work, the Glasgow underground railway system is finished (→1/1897).

Liverpool, 24 September. William Gladstone, the former prime minister, makes a speech condemning the massacre by Turks of 6,000 Armenians (→4/10/96).

Canterbury, 11 October. Edward White Benson, the archbishop of Canterbury, dies; he is to be buried in Canterbury Cathedral (→22/12).

Canterbury, 22 December. Frederick Temple, the bishop of London and former headmaster of Rugby school, is appointed archbishop of Canterbury.

London. State-owned museums and art galleries are allowed to open to the public on Sundays.

Wales. The Central Welsh Board is created to supervise all secondary schools in Wales.

Westminster. The National Portrait Gallery is moved from Bethnal Green to Westminster.

Worcester. Three years after the success of his *Serenade for Strings* and cantata *The Black Knight*, the composer Edward Elgar achieves further acclaim for the cantata *Scenes from the Life of King Olaf*, to words by Longfellow, and the oratorio *The Light of Life*.

Telegram raises tension in South Africa

Southern Africa, 3 January
A reckless attempt to seize the Boer republic of the Transvaal has been crushed by Boer commandos, to the embarrassment of the British government – especially that of the colonial secretary, Joseph Chamberlain. The invasion was led by Dr Leander Starr Jameson, the commissioner in Bechuanaland for the company headed by Cecil Rhodes, the prime minister of Cape Colony. Rhodes gave permission for the armed dash of 470 mounted police towards Johannesburg in the hope of inciting rebellion among British workers in the Transvaal.

But Jameson and his men never reached Johannesburg and they surrendered on 1 January. The British government, already facing charges of collusion with the raid, has been further embarrassed by a telegram sent today by the German kaiser to the Transvaal's President Paul Kruger, which has been seen as an insult to Queen Victoria. This congratulates the Boers, who without help from "friendly powers" had resisted "the armed hordes which ... broke into your country" and had "succeeded in re-establishing peace and maintaining the independence of your country" (→6).

Jameson surrenders as raid fails.

"Empire Makers", including Rhodes (centre) and Chamberlain (right).

First 'moving pictures' are seen in Britain

London, March
A public thirsty for entertainment is welcoming the arrival from the USA of the first "moving picture" shows. More appealing and realistic than the old magic lantern shows, or the zoetrope – whereby pictures were made to move in a revolving drum – the new Edison "Vitascope" shows dance routines, for example, a boxing match or waves breaking on the beach, as they appear in real life. These "flickers" are the consequence of almost simultaneous inventions on both sides of the Atlantic: by Thomas Edison in America and the brothers Louis and Auguste Lumière in France. Vaudeville theatres have been buying the pictures and machines to project the 16-frame-per-second film. The inventors are now said to be working on film with a simultaneous soundtrack, so that audiences can enjoy whole dramas or plays in "movie" form (→20/4).

Victoria notches up the longest reign

London, 23 September
Today Queen Victoria celebrates her crowning achievement, passing any previous record for the longest reign. Hers is longer than the record set by her grandfather, George III, who reigned for 59 years and 96 days, and longer than those of Edward III, who reigned for over 50 years, or James I and VI, who ruled Scotland for over 57 years (for 22 of which he was also king of England).

What is most remarkable is that, unlike George III, who spent his later years blind, mentally ill and incapable of governing, Queen Victoria is not only at the height of her powers but also still tremendously popular. She has asked that celebrations be restrained until she reaches her diamond jubilee (60 years on the throne) next year. In the meantime, congratulatory telegrams are pouring in (→22/6/97).

Prince of Wales's horse wins Derby

Epsom, Surrey, 3 June
The prince of Wales's horse Persimmon won the Derby today and the crowd roared with pleasure, with men throwing their hats in the air, gentlemen's toppers and policemen's helmets aloft together. It was a striking sign of the prince's popularity. He has been a leading breeder for many years, but this is his first victory in a classic race. Queen Victoria disapproves of his sporting proclivities, but that has only made him more popular (→23/1/1901).

Persimmon: a royal winner.

▷

Act aims to help farmers hit by slump

"Hard Times", by von Herkomer, reflects the agricultural workers' hard life.

Westminster, July
With the passing of the Agricultural Rates Act, landowners hope to see an improvement in farmers' conditions. Given the worst agricultural depression since the 1870s, Lord Salisbury's government – not known for reformism – has conceded that farmers should receive remittance on their rates.

A succession of bad winters and wet summers, with corn prices falling and cheap imports rising, has led many landowners to transfer land from corn production to cattle farming. Britain's wheat-growing acreage in recent years has dropped by 50 per cent. The main reason for the drop in corn prices has not been the climate, but rather the opening up of the British markets to US imports.

A number of factors has led to an influx of cheap American corn – among them the spread of the railways through the US wheatlands and improvements in steamship transport across the Atlantic. But there is a bright side to the crisis: Britain's farmers have been experimenting with different methods such as dairy farming and vegetable and fruit cultivation.

Critics of the new act are outspoken, alleging that it is not so much a progressive measure as a crude attempt to spend public money on Tory farmers.

'Daily Mail' proves instant popular hit

London, May
A new style of newspaper has been launched this month aimed at the newly educated masses. Called *The Daily Mail*, it is the brainchild of Alfred Harmsworth as proprietor and Kennedy Jones as editor. It sells at just a halfpenny and looks like being a runaway success: average sales during the first two weeks have been 202,000 daily.

"Brash and breezy" is how the paper is advertising itself and it is certainly different from its more staid rivals. Modelled on United States examples, the *Mail* has a greater variety of reports and snappier headlines on each page. Harmsworth, who is only 34, started in journalism on George Newnes's *Tit-Bits* magazine.

Harmsworth: newspaper genius.

Artist, designer and writer, Morris, dies

Morris: fresh ideas about design.

Oxfordshire, 3 October
William Morris, who died at his home at Kelmscott today aged 62, took English design away from the mass-produced manufacture of capitalism which he detested towards an idea of arts and crafts inspired by the mediaeval guilds. "Have nothing in your house that you do not know to be useful or believe to be beautiful" was his creed. He employed his friends Burne-Jones and Rossetti to help him design furniture, stained glass, tapestry and wallpaper. His long poem *The Earthly Paradise* was inspired by Chaucer. An ebullient all-rounder and pioneer socialist, he was known by friends as "Topsy".

The camera looks deep into the body with the new 'X-ray' photos

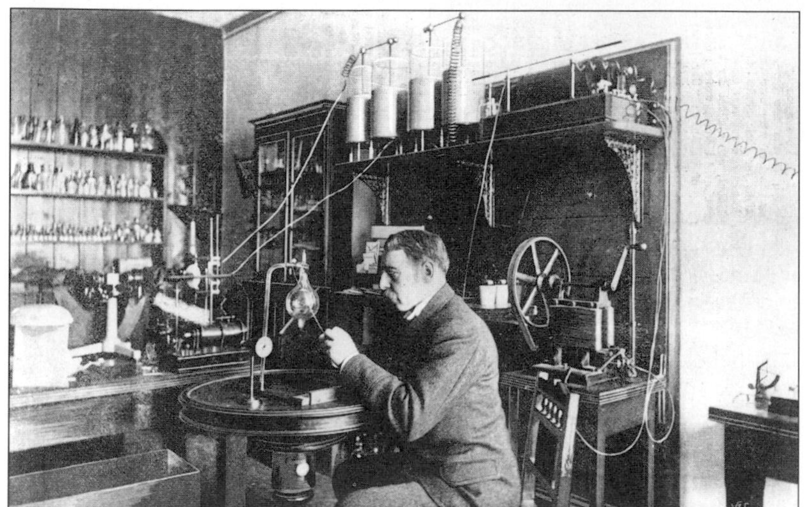

Gifford seen here experimenting with radiation beams to create an X-ray.

Glasgow
Doctors in Scotland are making medical history with the dramatic use of new "X-rays". These electromagnetic beams penetrate the skin and tissue to reveal inner organs. Following the pioneering work into X-rays by William Thomson, Lord Kelvin – a fellow of the Royal Society from the age of 27 – John Macintyre has this year achieved the "first X-ray cinematograph" at Glasgow's Royal Infirmary.

In England, scientists such as J W Gifford are also meeting with success in their experiments. Caution has been expressed by some, however, who point out that X-rays cause burns to skin.

Housman wistfully evokes Shropshire

London
A sudden burst of "continuous excitement" last spring produced the poems in *A Shropshire Lad*, according to their author, A E Housman, who is professor of Latin at University College, London. With crystal clarity and brevity they call up the loveliness of Shropshire and its "blue remembered hills" with grim fatalism – the melting cherry blossom, summertime on Bredon, the gale on Wenlock Edge ...

That is the land of lost content,
I see it shining plain,
The happy highways where I went
And cannot come again.

Tragedy strikes the Snowdon train line

Gwynedd, 6 April
Today's opening of the new mountain railway up Snowdon from Llanberis was marred when two trains went wildly out of control and collided at high speed, risking the lives of more than two hundred holidaymakers. The most seriously injured victim was Ellis Roberts, the landlord of the Padarn Villa Hotel in Llanberis. He jumped out of one of the trains and sustained severe injuries to his right leg, which had to be amputated. Many of the other passengers needed treatment for bruising and shock. Miraculously, nobody was killed.

Most people had managed to scramble out before the actual collision, which sent both driverless trains hurtling off the rails and over the Cymglas precipice to their destruction. The railway is a formidable feat of engineering, bringing Snowdon – at 3,560 feet, the highest mountain in England and Wales – within reach of everyone for the first time (→3/1899).

Speed limit goes up as red flag is waived

Charles Rolls driving at about 4mph behind a man with a red flag.

Britain
The repeal of the Red Flag Act this year may spur Britain into joining the great motor vehicle craze that is already sweeping through America and Europe. Few people, other than the rich or sporting, have invested in their own private motor cars. In Britain enthusiasts have been hampered by a 30-year-old law introduced to control steam-driven tractors on the roads. In those days the safety of sheep was more important.

Now the restriction requiring vehicles to be preceded by a man carrying a red flag has been lifted, and the speed limit has been raised from four mph to a more reasonable 20 mph [32kph] (→10/8/97).

Rosebery resigns as Liberal leader

Westminster, 4 October
Lord Rosebery resigned today as leader of the Liberals. In the two years since he succeeded Gladstone in the position, Rosebery has lived up to his own estimation of himself: "I am altogether unfitted for the post, as regards capacity and knowledge." A distinguished career politician, a rich and cultured aristocrat, he has long shown an oversensitivity to political change.

Ten days ago Gladstone, a former prime minister, made an epic speech in Liverpool, calling for an active British policy against Turkish interference in Armenia. Some 6,000 Armenians were massacred in the Turkish action, which has caused widespread revulsion. Now Rosebery has seen fit to resign after "some conflict of interest with Mr Gladstone". The "grand old man" of politics and now 86, Gladstone would not have intended his speech to have this effect. The move will disappoint the queen, who likes Rosebery (→19/5/98).

Art movement is started in Glasgow

Glasgow
Glasgow's artistic flowering has put Scotland in the forefront of art in Britain. The "Glasgow School", also known as the "Glasgow Boys", is a group of painters influenced by the French and by Whistler. John Lavery is the outstanding portrait painter, especially of women: his fine painting *The Tennis Party* was done just outside Glasgow. Other "boys" are James Guthrie, E A Walton, Arthur Melville and W Y Macgregor.

Glasgow's Art School has fostered the so-called "Glasgow style" of graphic work and design. One leading figure in the school is the 28-year-old designer and architect Charles Rennie Mackintosh, who has been commissioned to design a new school building. Mackintosh, Herbert MacNair and the Macdonald sisters, Frances and Margaret, are known as "the four" and exhibited this year at the Arts and Crafts exhibition in London.

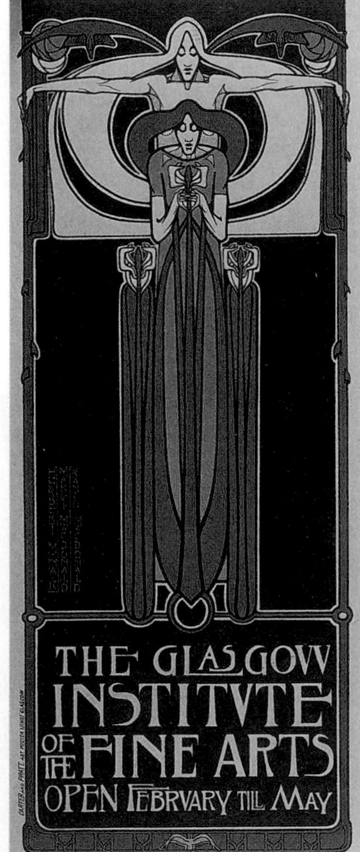

Glasgow's new style of art.

Sir John Lavery's "The Tennis Party" is a more traditional artist's view.

Sir William MacTaggart's "The Storm": chillingly realistic.

1897

Somerset, 12 January. Sir Isaac Pitman, who invented a phonetic shorthand system of writing in 1837, dies aged 84.

Argentina, 14 January. William Martin, Baron Conway of Allington, a British mountaineer, becomes the first climber to ascend Aconcagua, the highest peak in the western hemisphere.

Glasgow, January. The Glasgow District Subway underground railway is opened to the public.

Canada, 19 February. The Women's Institute organization is founded at Stoney Creek, Ontario.

Dublin, 17 May. The first Irish literary festival (Oireachtas) is held.

Dublin, 18 May. The first Irish music festival (Feis Ceoil) is held.

Ireland, May. Bram Stoker publishes a spine-chilling horror story, *Dracula*, about a vampire who lives on the blood of his victims.

Nottingham, 21 June. Queen Victoria grants a royal charter to Nottingham and it is made a city.

London, 1 July. The Tate Gallery, founded by the sugar manufacturer Sir Henry Tate and built on the site of the old Millbank prison, is officially opened.

Britain, 10 August. The Automobile Club of Great Britain is founded (→ 19).

London, 19 August. The first taximeter cabs begin operating in the City and West End of London (→ 10/9).

London, 10 September. George Smith, a London taxi-driver, is the first driver to be convicted of driving while drunk (→ 23).

London, 23 September. A nine-year-old boy is crushed to death by a taxi in Hackney; this is the first motoring fatality on a public highway (→ 1/9/1900).

Britain. H G Wells, one of the inventors of the science fiction novel, publishes *The Invisible Man* (→ 1898).

London. The American-born novelist Henry James publishes *What Maisie Knew*, which focuses on English society; his previous work has been about the clash between American and European cultures.

Humberside. Queen Victoria grants city status to Hull.

Victoria celebrates diamond jubilee

Lantern slide of a reflective queen.

Victoria and her royal procession reach St Paul's for a thanksgiving service.

London, 22 June
Throughout history there can hardly have been such a celebration as the diamond jubilee of Queen Victoria, which took place today in brilliant sunshine. The queen went in procession in an open carriage through the Cities of London and Westminster and on into the working-class areas of Southwark.

For 60 years she has provided the kind of stability which other countries can only dream about, and during her reign the empire has expanded to become the largest and richest the world has ever seen. Today, as she drove through her capital, she was greeted everywhere by wildly enthusiastic crowds. The empire is a source of unashamed pride for the British and its rise – and the reign of their queen and empress – has coincided with more changes than in any other era in world history. Since she ascended the throne the world has seen the advent of steam trains and steam ships, the coming of electricity, the bicycle, motor cars and motorbikes, the telegram, the telephone and an efficient post office. On top of this Victoria has given her name to an age in which almost all the world has at last been mapped, much of it satisfyingly coloured in the red of the British empire (→ 19/11/99).

The royal yacht "Victoria and Albert" (r) carries the queen at a naval review.

Scots TUC founded

Scotland, 26 March
The Scottish Trades Union Congress has been formed to give a better political platform to labour. It comes in the wake of a series of bitter strikes and lock outs that have characterized the trial of strength between Scottish owners and workers during the decade.

There have been three major strikes: on the railways in 1891, in the mines in 1894 and in engineering in 1897. Increased militancy is becoming a feature of Scottish trade unionism, backed by Keir Hardie's Independent Labour Party.

Cambridge students protest against the proposed admission of women.

Ill workers can now claim compensation

Westminster, August
The government has passed an act that for the first time entitles working people to claim compensation for injuries for which their employers are not directly responsible, as well as for those for which they can be held liable.

Traditionally employers have refused to take responsibility for injuries to employees, instead blaming workers' "carelessness". This has given rise to dangerous practices: lethal machinery is operated without safety devices and workers work without protective clothing.

Under the Conservative government's new Workmen's Compensation Act, workers will now be able to claim for industrial disease, as well as injury, against their employers. But some large groups of workers – notably seamen, agricultural workers and domestic servants – are not included (→ 1898).

Colonial conference is held in London

London, 28 July
With the leaders of 11 colonies in London for the celebration of Queen Victoria's diamond jubilee, it was a good moment to hold a conference on imperial matters and the problems of the colonies and their peoples. The main point at issue was how to "unite the empire", a vague idea with which all were in agreement, but which few had much idea of how to achieve.

The most likely path lay in political development, which meant devolving power from Westminster to a confederal body, in which the colonies had a say, with the right to make decisions governing the empire. But the idea failed because the colonies feared they would find themselves bossed about by a federation in which they had less individual influence than now. In any case, they still want the security of British military might (→ 1899).

Electricity gives boost to city transport

All aboard Liverpool's first electric tram at the Derby Square terminus.

Britain
The coming of electricity has given a great boost to public transport. The world's first electric underground railway was opened in London in 1890 and ran from the Monument (near London Bridge) to Stockwell. Liverpool opened its overhead electric railway, dubbed the "dockers' umbrella" in 1893. In Glasgow, developers chose cable power for the city's underground "District Subway" which reopened on 21 January this year, having been closed down after a disastrous first day's operations on 14 December 1896, when there was a breakdown and a collision. Electric tramways are also catching on in most major cities.

Retail stores tap new consumer market

Corner shops are thriving.

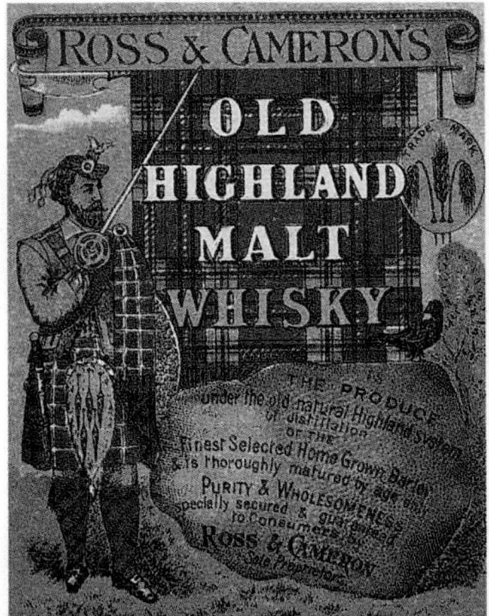

Whisky: pure and wholesome.

Britain
In spite of an economic depression, living standards have risen in the past three decades and there has been a big increase in consumer spending, which has transformed the lives of many ordinary workers. The growth in the number of shops reflects the fact that members of the public now have more money to spend.

While the growth of the country's heavy industry has slowed, the retail sector has blossomed. Big multiple stores such as Lipton's the grocers, Freeman, Hardy and Willis the shoeshops, Boot's the chemist, and Hepworths the tailors are expanding rapidly. There are now 11,000 multiple stores in Britain's high streets, against 1,500 in 1880. Advertising has come into its own with this growth in selling.

Hovis bread: for a healthier life.

The cats who want the cream should drink Nestlé's "Swiss Milk".

1898

Dublin, 8 January. The first issue of *Fainne an Lae*, (*Dawn*), the first Irish newspaper to carry domestic and foreign news in the Irish language, is printed.

Surrey, 14 January. Charles Lutwidge Dodgson, a mathematics lecturer at Oxford University, dies at Guildford aged 65. Better known by his pseudonym of Lewis Carroll, he wrote the children's classics *Alice in Wonderland* and *Alice Through the Looking Glass*.

Westport, Ireland, 23 January. William O'Brien founds the United Irish League; it is mainly formed by farmers.

Kew, London, 21 May. The palace gardens are opened to the public.

Nigeria, 14 June. Britain and France conclude the Niger Convention, settling one African dispute which is bringing them closer to war (→ 1899).

Westminster, 12 August. The House of Commons passes the Local Government Act for Ireland; it will provide for the election of county and district councils.→

Ireland, 22 December. Women are allowed to sit on district councils and town commissions (→ 26/6/99).

London, 25 December. The empire stamp rate comes into effect; a half-ounce letter can now be sent from Canada through much of the British empire for two cents.

Sutherland, Scotland. Andrew Carnegie, the Dunfermline-born American steel and railway billionaire, buys Skibo Castle (→ 1899).

London. Thomas Lipton, the Glasgow greengrocer who began with a shop in Finniston in 1870, and has since built up Liptons Ltd and acquired tea and rubber estates in the Far East, is knighted by Queen Victoria.

Liverpool. Sir Oliver Lodge, a professor of physics at University College, Liverpool, invents a "bellowing telephone" or loudspeaker.

China. Britain adds New Territories to Hong Kong under a 99-year lease from China, along with Wei-hai-wei [Weihaiwei] on the Shantung [Shandong] peninsula. France acquires Kwang-chau-wan [Guangzhouwan] in southern China under a similar lease arrangement.

Parliament repeals Vaccination Acts

Westminster, 9 August
The controversy over compulsory vaccination which centred on the conflict between two classic Victorian principles – personal liberty and the public good – has been resolved. Liberty has won the day with today's repeal by parliament of the two Vaccination Acts, which had been regarded as an important innovation in preventive medicine.

Behind the campaign to change the law was the Anti-compulsory Vaccination League. Stories were spread of children who had died after receiving vaccine. Some parents said they would rather go to prison than allow their children to be vaccinated.

Parliament has also repealed the Contagious Diseases Acts intended to prevent the spread of venereal disease in the armed forces. These gave the police powers to arrest any woman they suspected of being a prostitute, and subject her to physical examination.

Gladstone's death ends a political epoch

London, 19 May
William Ewart Gladstone, the towering statesman of the era of Queen Victoria, died today aged 87. His death is being felt as a national loss and he will be accorded England's highest honour for one of its dead – burial in Westminster Abbey.

Gladstone was first elected to the House of Commons in 1832 as a Conservative but during the bitter political row over the repeal of the Corn Laws he gradually switched parties. As Liberal chancellor he was noted for lowering income tax and abolishing import duties.

His first term as prime minister began in 1868 and saw many important acts, including one giving the country a system of elementary schools open to all children and another making it harder to evict Irish land tenants. During his second term Gladstone improved the property rights of married women and nearly doubled the electorate. His third and fourth terms were marked by his conversion to Irish home rule and foundered when home rule bills were defeated. Gladstone was no great imperialist and, despite his respect for her, was disliked by Queen Victoria. Unlike most politicians, he grew more radical as he got older, calling for curbs on the Lords' power in his very last speech as prime minister (→ 1899).

The Waleses (r) visit the Gladstones.

Wells's 'War of the Worlds' warns of earth invasion by Martians

A victim awaits his fate as strange creatures from another planet take over.

H G Wells: science fiction writer.

London
The War of the Worlds, the latest scientific fantasy from the pen of H G Wells, purports to describe an invasion of the earth by Martians. It is all too convincingly done and is creating a great stir. Wells has already won wide repute as a prophet of what science may one day bring to pass with his earlier books, *The Time Machine* (1895), *The Island of Dr Moreau* (1896) and *The Invisible Man* (1897).

Wells is the son of a housekeeper at a great country house, Uppark, and a small shopkeeper. He was brought up in poverty and apprenticed to a draper but attended T H Huxley's lectures at the Royal College of Science. With his scientific training he at first decided to become a teacher but his health broke down. He regards himself as a biologist and journalist rather than as a novelist. His writing promotes the theory that scientific progress can bring about the millennium if mankind can only act in a rational way. He has brought a new vision and tone to fiction.

Kitchener imposes order in the Sudan

Gordon avenged in battle at Omdurman

Sudan, 2 September
Britain's dream of recovering the Sudan and avenging the death of General Gordon [*see report on page 973*] was fulfilled today when a huge Sudanese army was destroyed at Omdurman. At least 10,000 Sudanese warriors were slaughtered by the Maxim guns of the Anglo-Egyptian force, for the loss of 28 on the British side.

The Sudan campaign has been meticulously prepared over many years by General Sir Herbert Kitchener, the commander-in-chief of the British-run Egyptian army. He designed his own gunboats for the passage up the Nile and commissioned his own railway to carry his armies to Khartoum.

Fighting began after the Sudanese, led by Khalifa Abdallahi, courageously and savagely attacked the Anglo-Egyptian encampment. Although they suffered terrible losses, they nearly won the day when they charged Kitchener's rear, only to be beaten off. The battle ended in a huge cloud of dust and a charge by the 21st Lancers. Kitchener sealed his victory with a requiem service at the shattered remains of Gordon's residency. The Union flag was triumphantly hoisted and three cheers were called for Queen Victoria. Kitchener was so overcome with emotion that he was unable to dismiss the parade (→ 11/1898).

Khalifa Abdallahi and his Sudanese forces fleeing after defeat at Omdurman.

War averted as French abandon Fashoda

General Kitchener: hero of the hour.

Southern Sudan, November
A French presence at the isolated fort of Fashoda on the upper Nile is about to be withdrawn after a firm British show of force. Several hundred Senegalese troops under six white officers, who had reached the area in order to establish French claims, have been imprisoned in the fort and have had enough.

General Kitchener himself headed the force that sailed southward from Omdurman to deal with the French. Determined to stop the headwaters of the Nile from being controlled by a rival power, he was backed by 2,600 men, field guns and Maxim guns. The affair had the makings of a major international incident until the French decision to withdraw (→ 21/3/99).

Sweeping changes are made to Irish local government

Ireland, 12 August
The Local Government Act which has just been passed is one of the most sweeping measures that has been introduced this century. Based on democratic principles which include female suffrage (women may now sit on district councils and be town commissioners, although they cannot be elected to county or borough councils), it has abolished the grand jury, destroying the power of the ascendancy and effectively handing control to nationalists.

Until now, local government has been based on counties, each of which was governed by a grand jury, mainly representing the interests of the Protestants. This grand jury financed local expenditure by raising a "cess", or levy, on the occupiers of the land that fell within its jurisdiction.

The new system rationalizes the existing web of authorities and boards. Four new authorities will be elected: county councils, borough corporations, urban district councils and rural district councils. Larger towns within each county will continue to be governed by town commissioners. The duties of the boards of guardians will now be restricted to poor relief. The county councils will take over responsibility for mental hospitals, fever hospitals and county infirmaries, thus reducing the plethora of boards who have run these institutions in the past (→ 1899).

MPs push for eight-hour working day

Westminster
The working week has been steadily reduced during the reign of Queen Victoria. Half a day off work on a Saturday has become an established practice. There are four statutory bank holidays a year. Now some MPs are campaigning for a maximum eight-hour working day.

In the forefront of the fight is the Liberal Party, but as with organized labour, it is divided on the question. There are some left-wingers in the labour movement like George Lansbury and Fabians such as Sidney Webb who are trying to commit the National Liberal Federation to an eight-hour day. But opposed to the idea are many influential Liberal employers.

In the Trades Union Congress, some members are in favour of a universal limitation on hours whilst others are against legislation and in favour of relying on collective bargaining. It is even the case that among miners there is no agreement since in some areas an eight-hour day has been improved upon already. Last year miners in Wales lost a long strike for a minimum wage independent of coal prices.

Harrods, the London store, woos shoppers with its new moving staircase.

▷

British artists take up sensuous 'nouveau' style

'Art nouveau' loses two leading lights within a single year

London
This year saw the deaths of two leading artists of the decade – Sir Edward Burne-Jones and Aubrey Beardsley – while the style that they both fostered, "art nouveau", continues to flourish.

Burne-Jones was apprenticed to Dante Gabriel Rossetti and became a close friend of William Morris at Oxford. Subsequently the trio collaborated in Morris's "arts and crafts" movement, Burne-Jones designing some of the finest stained glass and tapestries made by Morris and Co and doing woodcuts for the Kelmscott Press, especially the wonderful Kelmscott Chaucer. It was out of such designs that art nouveau developed in England.

As a painter Burne-Jones, like Rossetti in later years, was not so much a "pre-Raphaelite" as a mediaevalist and part of the "aesthetic" movement. His elongated, willowy females evoke a dreamy land of legend and chivalry, as in his best-known picture, *King Cophetua and the Beggar Maid*, and *The Sleeping Beauty*. The novelist Henry James described the Burne-Jones beauty as "pale, sickly and wan".

These are the very adjectives that would seem most fitting for the drawings of Aubrey Beardsley, who died of consumption aged just 26. He was notorious for the sinuous and erotic aestheticism of his line in the black and white illustrations to *Morte d'Arthur*, Wilde's *Salome* and the *Yellow Book*, the influential quarterly of the *fin de siècle* poets, for which he was art editor. He was the outstanding exponent of art nouveau in sophisticated black and white drawing and poster design. Sometimes, as in his drawings for *Lysistrata*, he overstepped the line between art and pornography. He died having been converted to Catholicism, begging his friends to destroy his "obscene" drawings.

Undulating draperies, tendrils, flower stems and heavy vegetation in flat, writhing patterns are characteristic of art nouveau. It derives from Japanese prints as well as from the pre-Raphaelitism favoured by Burne-Jones. It has spread across Europe, especially to Austria and Germany, where Beardsley's work, circulated in *The Studio* magazine, is greatly admired – more so than in England.

The Briar Rose Series 4: "The Sleeping Beauty" by Sir Edward Burne-Jones.

Burne-Jones hard at work.

Beardsley's decadent Salome.

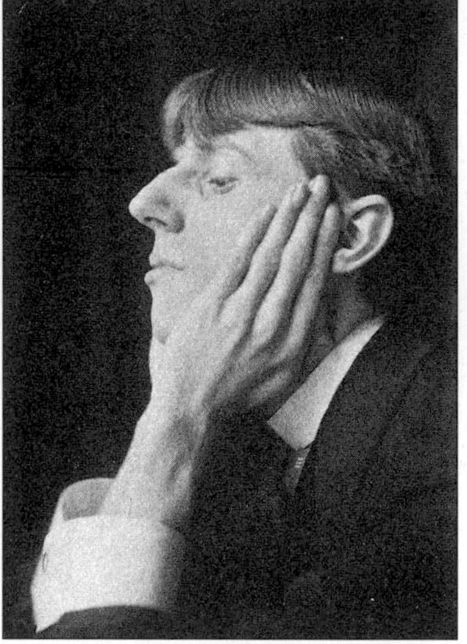

Aubrey Beardsley deep in thought.

Political art from Walter Crane.

"Heron and Fish", by art nouveau painter-illustrator Walter Crane.

Ceramicist William Morris was a leading member of the movement.

Wilde draws inspiration from jail torment

London, February
The Ballad of Reading Gaol is selling as no poem has sold for years. It has sold out its first three printings, which carry in place of the author's name, "C.3.3.". Everyone knows it is by Oscar Wilde, who has used his prison number, although the reviews do not mention his name. "Yet each man kills the thing he loves" is the theme of the poem. But another stanza comes closer to Wilde's own experience:

And the wild regrets and the bloody sweats
None knew so well as I:
For he who lives more lives than one
More deaths than one must die.

On his release from Reading jail in 1897, Wilde went into exile. He has been to Naples and now lives in Paris under the name "Sebastian Melmoth" (→30/11/1900).

1899

Sudan, 21 March. The British and French sign a convention ending the Fashoda crisis.

Southern Africa, 24 March. Queen Victoria is presented with a petition of grievances by British Uitlanders (foreigners) over their treatment by Boers in southern Africa (→5/6).

Westminster, 26 June. Lady Aberdeen presides over delegates from 28 nations at the first international women's congress.

Southern Africa, 27 September. After a summer of fruitless attempts at a settlement, the Orange Free State declares itself on the side of the Transvaal in its dispute with the British; the Boers now have 50,000 mounted troops compared with 15,000 British regulars (→9/10).

Southern Africa, 9 October. Britain and the Boers prepare ultimatums. The Boers issue theirs first: withdraw and end troop reinforcements or face war (→12).

Southern Africa, 12 October. War breaks out between Britain and the Boers (→15).

Southern Africa, 15 October. The Boers, who surrounded Mafeking in Bechuanaland two days ago, besiege Kimberley in Cape Colony (→30).

London, 24 October. The Garrick theatre opens.

Southern Africa, 30 October. John MacBride's Irish Brigade, fighting with the Boers, suffers heavy losses at Modderspruit.

Canada, 30 October. Over 1,000 Canadian troops set sail aboard the SS *Sardinia* for South Africa as reinforcements against the Boers (→2/11).

Southern Africa, 2 November. The Boers, led by Piers Joubert, besiege Ladysmith in Natal (→12/1899).

Portsmouth, 19 November. Kaiser William II and his family visit his grandmother, Queen Victoria, to celebrate her 80th birthday (→4/4/1900).

Southern Africa, 11 December. British troops are defeated at Magersfontein in Cape Colony by Piet Cronje's Boers (→15).

Southern Africa, 15 December. The British under Sir Redvers Buller are defeated by the Boers at Colenso in Natal (→28/2/1900).

London. Queen Victoria lays the foundation stone of the Victoria and Albert museum.

New trunk railway arrives in the capital

Plans to put the Great Central Railway through Lords were strongly opposed.

London, March
The latest, and possibly last, of Britain's mainline railways has arrived in London. Marylebone station was opened this month as the terminus for the Manchester, Sheffield and Lincoln railway, which from now on will be known as the Great Central Railway. It already seems that the great age of railway building is over, however, and many of the late arrivals are already finding it difficult to pay their way. Thus it remains to be seen whether the new main line can satisfactorily compete with Euston, St Pancras and King's Cross in attracting passengers and goods to and from the north.

Local government is reformed in London

Westminster
Only ten years after the first attempt to set up a local government to run London, so many problems have come to light that a second attempt has had to be made.

This year's London Government Act builds upon the act of 1888 that set up the London County Council (LCC). But it sweeps away the myriad small vestries and local boards responsible for minor matters, like street cleaning. Instead, there will be 28 metropolitan borough councils, which will share the administrative work and act as a counterweight to the social-reforming LCC.

College for workers

Oxford, February
Ruskin College, named after the great social critic John Ruskin, who was Slade professor of art at Oxford University, has been opened to enable working men and women to enjoy the benefits of studying in a great university city like Oxford.

The college is not actually part of the university, but that scarcely matters to those attending it, whose backgrounds would have made university entrance impossible. Its American backers, Walter Vrooman and Charles A Beard, see it as a practical demonstration of Ruskin's social ideas.

Elgar is acclaimed as musical 'genius'

London, summer
Hans Richter, the great Austrian conductor, has included a new British work in his London concerts this year: *Variations on an Original Theme – "Enigma"*, by Edward Elgar, a Catholic bandmaster and organist from Worcester known for his choral works for provincial choirs. The variations portray his wife and 12 of his friends, reaching a splendid climax with "Nimrod".

The work, premièred on 19 June, has established the largely self-taught Elgar, 42, as probably England's most important composer since Purcell. The German composer Richard Strauss summed it up neatly: "Hats off, gentlemen – a genius!" (→12/1908).

Edward Elgar: European fame.

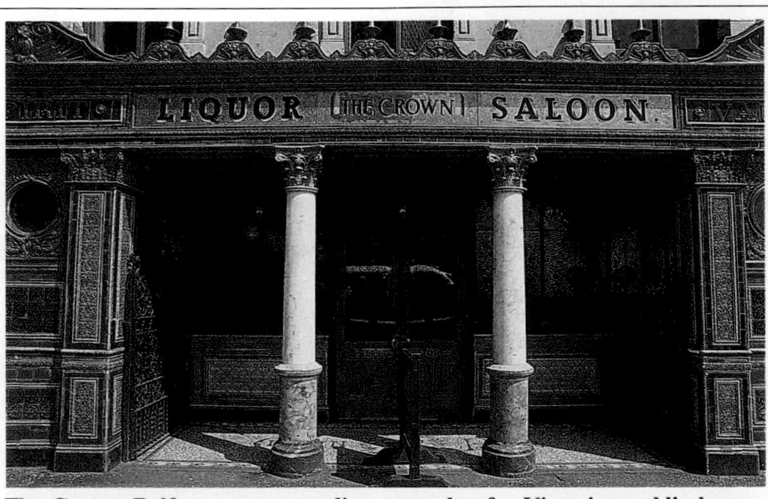

The Crown, Belfast: an outstanding example of a Victorian public house, complete with columns, an elaborate tiled frontage and patterned glass.

Education Board to cover art and science

The new board will provide these Wiltshire children with a better education.

England and Wales
The teaching of art and science has at last been put on a proper footing in England and Wales, with the constitution of the Education Board. For the first time this will bring under one body the old Department of Education and the Science and Art Department. Scientific and technical education in England and Wales has lagged badly behind that of continental rivals, because of the haphazard way in which the system has grown up.

State schools deliver little more than elementary education, whilst schools that take older pupils are often small and inefficient. But now proper grounding in science and art will be given (→ 22/3/1902).

British aviation pioneer dies after crash

Aviation pioneer Percy Pilcher taking off for his last, fateful flight.

Leicestershire, 2 October
Percy Pilcher, a pioneer of glider flight, has died from crash injuries. An adventurous pilot, Pilcher was flying his glider Hawk before a crowd at Stanford Hall in Market Harborough two days ago, when the tail broke off and he plunged 30 feet (9m) to the ground. He was knocked out by the fall and never regained consciousness. Like other glider pioneers, Pilcher hung from his machine and used his weight to guide it, rather like a cyclist leaning first one way, then another. However, his position beneath the wings made him extremely vulnerable in case of accident (→ 16/10/1908).

British hold talks with Boer leaders

Bloemfontein, 5 June
Talks between Paul Kruger, the president of the Transvaal, and the British high commissioner for southern Africa, Sir Alfred Milner, broke down today after six days of discussion in this small Orange Free State town. There had been hopes that the British and the Boers would reach a compromise over their differences, which centre on the rights of British workers or Uitlanders (foreigners) in the Transvaal. Kruger's intransigence over giving the Uitlanders the vote now makes this look unlikely.

Kruger seems prepared for war and has been arming his Transvaal state to the teeth for the last three years. Imports of war materials quadrupled to a value of some £256,291 a year between 1895 and 1897. Over £1.5 million has been spent on fortifying Johannesburg, heavy guns have been purchased and German artillery officers hired.

Asked why he wanted this enormous amount of armament, Kruger replied: "Oh, Kaffirs, Kaffirs – and such like objects." But the British government has not been fooled, particularly since discovering that Kruger is spending £70,000 a year on spies in areas of British-controlled southern Africa. War cannot now be far away (→ 27/9).

Liberals choose a new party leader

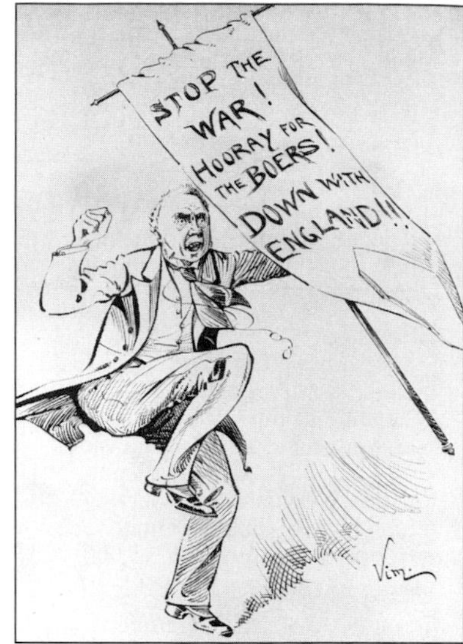

Campbell-Bannerman: taking over.

Westminster
Henry Campbell-Bannerman, war secretary in the last Liberal government, has been appointed Liberal leader following a series of resignations among leading politicians. In fact, the whips, who were in a position to make or break any leader, first offered the job to Herbert Asquith, a former home secretary, but he turned it down because he was unable to afford it. Asquith, a barrister, says he could not afford to be leader as it would mean giving up his bar practice (→ 17/10/1900).

Millionaire benefactor aims to die poor

Dunfermline
"What Benares is to the Hindu, Jerusalem to the Christian, all this is Dunfermline to me": so spoke Andrew Carnegie, one of the world's richest men and certainly the richest ever to come from the "auld grey toun".

Born the son of a poor Dunfermline weaver, Carnegie emigrated in poverty with his family to the United States in 1848, when he was 12 years old. A man of enormous talent and ability, he has built the huge Carnegie steel company and made himself a multi-millionaire. Now his main aim in life is to give his money away. After providing for his home town, he has already given $38 million to found 2,500 public libraries across the world and intends to die poor.

Scottish-born millionaire Carnegie.

Boers win first round as war erupts

British suffer heavy loss in early battles

Southern Africa, December
The simmering tension between the British and the Boer republics in southern Africa has finally flared into conflict – and the first weeks of fighting since war broke out in October have seen the Boers give the British a bloody nose. Superior in numbers, arms and tactics, the mounted and highly mobile Boer commandos have cut through the British lines and laid siege to Ladysmith, Kimberley and Mafeking.

With about 50,000 men at their disposal, against 15,000 British troops, they made rapid progress, killing some 2,000 British soldiers and capturing 12 heavy guns. The British then retired to await the reinforcements brought by their commander-in-chief, Sir Redvers Buller. But these fared no better.

Buller made the cardinal error of splitting his force into three and then committing his raw troops, piecemeal, against experienced and determined guerrillas. The result was a disaster and in one week from 10 to 15 December – the "Black Week" – each of the forces was defeated with heavy casualties.

Buller asked London for permission to surrender, but has been refused. Meanwhile, Britain has been rallied somewhat by the words of Queen Victoria, who said: "We are not interested in the possibilities of defeat. They do not exist."

Ready to face the Boers: British troops embarking in southern Africa.

Kitchener and Roberts lead counter-attack

Southern Africa, December
Lord Roberts, the commander-in-chief in India, has been sent to southern Africa with General Kitchener to try to restore the British position. This may be easier than at first thought because British army chiefs believe that the Boers have made serious strategic errors.

The Boers are superior so long as they move fast and concentrate their forces where the British are weak. But after their early successes they have been drawn into sieges at Ladysmith, Kimberley and Mafeking. The war has now been stood on its head and instead of small groups of Boers tying down thousands of British, small groups of British are tying down thousands of Boers. Kitchener and Roberts believe they have only to break the sieges and they will break the Boer army as well (→11).

British troops suffer setbacks at Colenso in December's "Black Week".

Lord Roberts: coming to help.

Wales finds a new champion in fiery MP, Lloyd George

Wales
Over the course of the past 20 years Welsh politicians have begun to realize that they must further Welsh interests and demands at Westminster if their country is to retain its identity.

The call for Welsh home rule is gaining popularity, and a Welsh word, *Ymreolaeth*, has been coined for it by the nationalist writer Emrys ap Iwan. The Liberal MPs of north and south Wales have banded together and with 25-30 votes at their disposal cannot now be ignored.

The Welsh Language Society was formed in 1885 and immediately set about righting the wrongs done to Welsh schoolchildren. Teaching is in English and children had been banned from speaking Welsh and punished for doing so. But within three years the society secured Welsh as a subject to be taught at school and is now pressing for equal status for the language.

A great agricultural depression has sat over the country since 1886, breaking up communities and forcing emigration overseas and to the coalfields. In these conditions the tithe demanded by the Church of England is resented not only because of economic hardship, but because 80 per cent of the farmers are nonconformists. This has provoked calls for the disestablishment of the church and a series of anti-tithe riots across the country from 1887, which continued until 1895.

At this critical time Wales has found a voice in the lawyer and MP David Lloyd George, who senses that, while the empire may not be eternal, Wales and its culture must be. In a typically thundering speech he has said: "When the last truckload of coal reaches Cardiff, when the last black diamond is dug out of the earth of Glamorgan, there will be men then digging gems of pure brilliance from the inexhaustible mines of the literature and language of Wales."

▷

Britain heads largest empire the world has known

British lands cover one-fifth of globe

Britain's empire is now the largest the world has ever known. It covers more than one-fifth of the land-mass of the globe and is continuing to expand. Vast numbers – one in every four human beings – live within its boundaries.

On top of this Britain rules a second empire, the empire of the seas. In spite of constant scares and challenges from other industrial nations, particularly Germany, the Royal Navy is unchallenged anywhere, and its mastery of the seas makes possible the expansion of the land empire and keeps it safe.

The British Empire is a relatively new creation. Its foundations were laid largely in the century between 1750 and 1850, but by the end of that period the idea of colonies was rapidly going out of fashion. Adam Smith, the theorist of free trade, demolished the economic theory that they brought wealth, and in 1852 Benjamin Disraeli spoke for many when he said: "The colonies are a millstone round our neck."

As late as 1870, with the exception of India, Britain held only Australia, Canada and New Zealand, which were sparsely populated, as was Cape Colony. Gibraltar, Hong Kong, British Guiana, British Honduras, various islands and a few colonies on the African coast made up the rest. How then has the empire grown to its present size? In the past 20 years, there has been a huge scramble for land in Africa among the European powers [*see opposite page*]. Britain emerged from this having only just failed to fulfil Cecil Rhodes's ambition to see unbroken British territory from the Cape to Cairo, and its power has expanded elsewhere, notably in Asia. The aim has been partly to secure resources and markets for British goods and investments, and partly to further what is now seen by many Britons as their country's civilizing mission to the rest of the world (→7/1902).

BRITAIN'S EMPIRE, 1899 †

Territory under British rule or control

CANADA
UNITED KINGDOM
North Atlantic Ocean
GIBRALTAR
BERMUDA
BAHAMAS
BRITISH HONDURAS
JAMAICA
CARIBBEAN ISLANDS *
TRINIDAD
BRITISH GUIANA
GAMBIA
SIERRA LEONE
GOLD COAST
NIGERIA
ASCENSION
ST HELENA
SOUTH AFRICA *
South Atlantic Ocean
TRISTAN DA CUNHA
FALKLAND ISLANDS
Pacific Ocean
MALTA
CYPRUS
EGYPT
ANGLO-EGYPTIAN SUDAN
KUWAIT
QATAR
ADEN
BRITISH SOMALILAND
BRITISH EAST AFRICA
INDIA
CEYLON
MALDIVES
SEYCHELLES
Indian Ocean
MAURITIUS
BURMA
FEDERATED MALAY STATES
HONG KONG
BRUNEI
BRITISH NORTH BORNEO
SARAWAK
CHRISTMAS ISLAND
BRITISH NEW GUINEA
AUSTRALIA
FIJI
NEW ZEALAND
Pacific Ocean

† not all the places listed on p.1015 appear on this map

* see maps below and opposite for more detailed views

Chamberlain in bid to help West Indies

Westminster, March

Worried about the dependence of the West Indies on the sugar trade, the colonial secretary Joseph Chamberlain is attempting to bolster their economies with grants of £20,000 a year for five years, and is seeking to expand the fruit trade.

He has arranged a direct mail, fruit and passenger service between Britain and Jamaica, set up a department of agriculture for the West Indies to encourage citrus fruit and banana growing, started inter-island ferry services, improved roads and settled peasant grievances on St Vincent and Dominica. Even so, the islands remain almost completely dependent on agricultural trade.

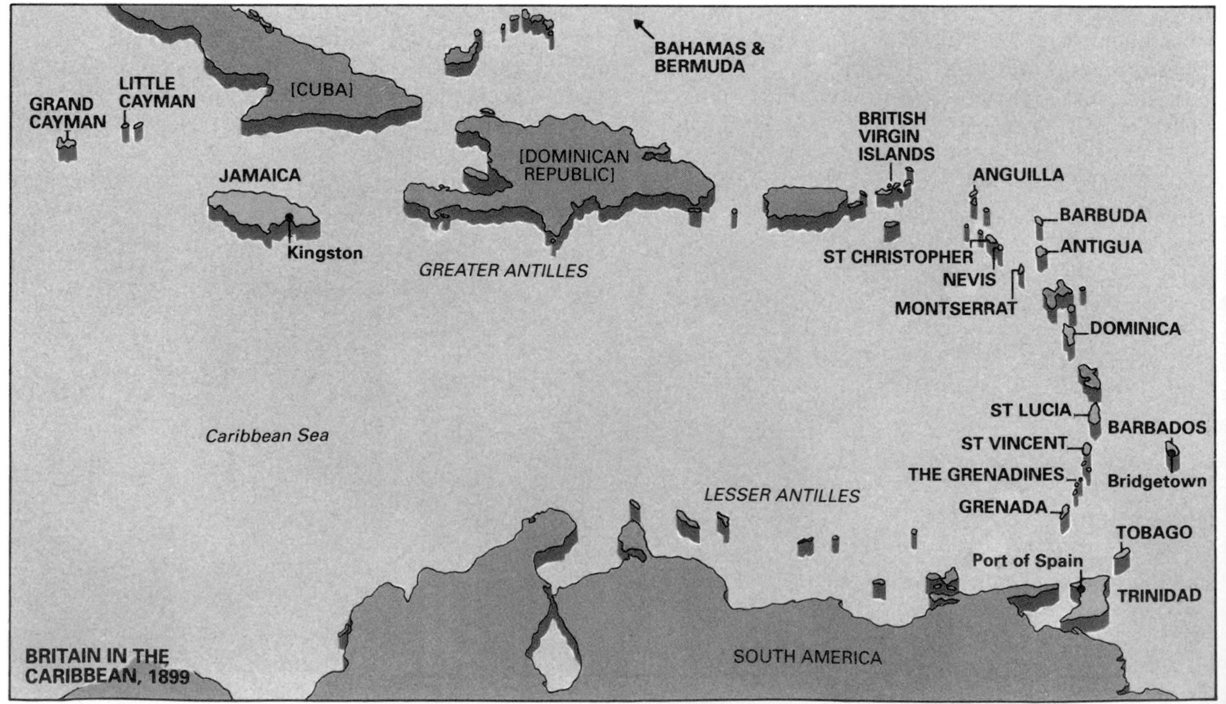

'Scramble for Africa' leaves few countries in the continent free of European control

Africa

The British Empire has grown so much that it is now becoming difficult to defend and administer. However, it has no choice but to continue to expand, otherwise it will face the rise of rival empires created by Germany and France.

With most of the world that could be colonized already brought under European influence, the only big area of expansion left was Africa, largely unknown to and unmapped by Europeans even 20 years ago. For some time the French had been trying to undermine British interests by expanding into central and west Africa and cutting off the British coastal colonies from their valuable hinterland. The Germans were anxious to expand into what the former "iron chancellor", Bismarck, called "a place in the sun", and the Belgian King Leopold, almost as a private venture, was securing large areas of the Congo. All this was a challenge to the British and before long the European powers were scrambling for territories in places of which they had never heard just a few years earlier. Often these places were, to them, little more than names and a few lines pencilled on a map in London, Paris or Berlin: the real reasons for taking the territory were often those of European politics. So Bismarck was able to buy off France's indignation over the loss of Alsace by giving it a free hand in Africa.

Any regard for indigenous African nations has rarely entered the question; the result is that, since 1880, of the 40 units into which Africa has now been divided only four are not governed by European states. Of these only Ethiopia, which beat off the Italians, and Liberia, backed by American money, can claim genuine independence.

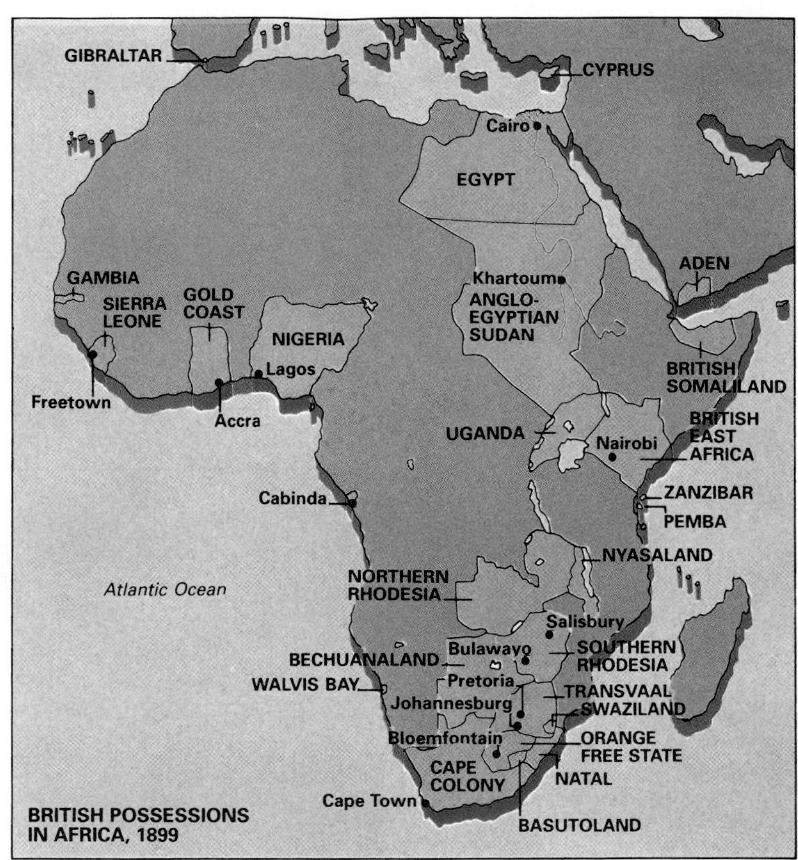

BRITISH POSSESSIONS IN AFRICA, 1899

The lands of the British Empire, excluding Britain and Ireland, at the end of the nineteenth century (see below right for key to abbreviations):

AFRICA: **Basutoland** [Lesotho] p.1868; **Bechuanaland** [Botswana] 1884, a.1885; **British East Africa** [Kenya and Uganda] 1886-95, p.1895; **British Somaliland** [now in Somalia] 1884-87, p.1887; **Uganda** 1888-95, p.1894; **Cape Colony** 1795-1815; **Egypt** occupied 1882, British-controlled 1883; **Gambia** 1631-1713, p.1894; **Gold Coast** [Ghana] 1871; **Natal** a.1843; **Nigeria** claimed 1885, p.1893; **Northern Rhodesia** [Zambia], 1889-90; **Nyasaland** [Malawi], p.1891; **Sierra Leone** p.1896; **Southern Rhodesia** [Zimbabwe] (formed from Matabeleland and Mashonaland in 1898), charter to British South Africa Company 1889; **Sudan**, Anglo-Egyptian condominium 1898; **Swaziland** p.1884; **Transvaal** a.1877; **Zanzibar and Pemba Island** [now part of Tanzania] p.1890.
ANTARCTICA: **British Antarctica** 1819-32.
ARABIAN SEA: **Laccadive Islands** sequestered 1877.
AUSTRALASIA: **New South Wales** 1788, crown c.1823, sg.1855; **New Zealand** 1840, sg.1852; **Queensland** 1859, sg.1859; **South Australia** 1834, sg.1855; **Tasmania** separate c.1812, acquired 1825, sg.1855; **Victoria** separate c.1801, acquired 1848, sg.1855; **Western Australia** 1829, sg.1890.
CANADA: **British Columbia** 1849, crown c.1858, sg.1871; **Manitoba** 1870; **New Brunswick** 1763, sg.1854; **Newfoundland** 1497-1713, sg.1855; **Nova Scotia** 1713-63, sg.1848; **Ontario** 1763, sg.1854; **Prince Edward Island** 1763, sg.1854; **Quebec** 1763, sg.1848; **Rupert's Land and North West Territory** 1670-1826, sg.1870; **Yukon** 1898. New Brunswick, Nova Scotia, Ontario and Quebec confederated 1867 by the British North America Act.
CARIBBEAN: **Anguilla** 1650; **Antigua** 1632, c.1663; **Bahama Islands** 1670, c.1783; **Barbados** 1627, c.1662; **Bermuda** 1609, c.1684; **British Honduras** [Belize], settled 1638, acquired 1786, crown c.1862; **British Virgin Islands** 1666; **Cayman Islands** 1655, ceded 1670; **Dominica** 1763; **Grenada** 1763, ceded 1783; **Jamaica** 1655, ceded 1670, crown c.1865; **Monserrat** 1632, c.1642; **Nevis** 1628; **Saint Christopher** [St Kitts] 1624; **Saint Lucia** captured from French 1803, acquired 1815; **St Vincent and the Grenadines** 1763, ceded 1783; **Tobago** 1763, linked to Trinidad 1888; **Trinidad** 1897.
GULF OF ADEN: **Aden** [South Yemen, now united with N Yemen] 1839.
INDIA: Queen Victoria made empress of India 1876. **Burma** a. to British India 1886; **Bengal** 1765; **Mysore** 1831; **Punjab** [Sikh Kingdom], a.1849; **Pegu** 1852; **Sind** a.1843.
INDIAN OCEAN: **Andaman Islands** 1858; **British Indian Ocean Territories** 1815; **Ceylon** [Sri Lanka] surrendered by Dutch 1795, c.1801, acquired 1815; **Chagos Islands** 1784; **Cocos Islands** 1857; **Maldive Islands** p.1887; **Mauritius** 1814; **Nicobar Islands** 1869; **Seychelles** possession 1794, administered as part of Mauritius.
MEDITERRANEAN: **Cyprus** p.1878; **Gibraltar** 1704-13; **Ionian Islands** 1815; **Malta** a.1800-14.
PERSIAN GULF: **Kuwait** p.1897; **Qatar** p.1868.
SOUTH ATLANTIC: **Ascension** 1815; **Falkland Islands** ceded by Spain 1771, a.from Argentina 1832, acquired 1833; **St Helena** 1569, direct British control 1834; **Tristan da Cunha** a.1816.
SOUTH CHINA SEA: **British North Borneo** p.1888; **Brunei** 1888, p.1888; **Federated Malay States** p.1874, Federated States 1896; **Hong Kong** occupied 1842, ceded to British by treaty of Nanking 1842; Kowloon acquired 1860, New Territories leased 1898 for 99 years; **Sarawak** 1842, p.1888, part of Federated Malay States 1896; **Singapore** 1819, part of Federated Malay States 1896.
SOUTH PACIFIC: **British New Guinea** p.1884; **Chatham Islands** a. to New Zealand 1842; **Christmas Island** a.1888; **Cook Islands** 1888; **Ellice Islands** [Tuvalu Islands] 1892; **Fanning Islands** 1888; **Fiji Islands** 1874; **Friendly Islands** 1899; **Gilbert Islands** [Kiribati] 1892; **Kermadec Islands** a. to New Zealand 1887; **Norfolk Island** claimed by New South Wales 1788, acquired 1853; **Palmyra** a.1889; **Pitcairn Island** 1838-87; **Phoenix Island** 1889; **Santa Cruz Islands** 1897; **Solomon Islands** p.1885; **Starbuck Island** 1866; **Tokelau Islands** p.1889.

Key: date only = acquired; a = annexed; p = protectorate; c = colony; sg = self-governing. Modern names in square brackets.

1900 - 1901

London, 9 January 1900. A nationwide influenza epidemic is taking 50 lives a day here alone (→ 17/2/05).

USA, 18 February 1900. The Briton Harry Vardon is the world golf champion.

South Africa, 28 Feb 1900. Ladysmith is relieved after 118 days of siege (→ 18/5).

Dublin, 4 April 1900. Strict security is in force as Queen Victoria begins a three-week visit to Ireland which will also take her to Cork and Galway (→ 19/1/01).

Brussels, 4 April 1900. The prince of Wales is shot at by a 15-year-old "anarchist".

Europe, 7 April 1900. Britain, France, Germany and the US warn China to suppress the Boxer rebellion or be invaded (→ 14/8).

South Africa, 28 May 1900. Britain annexes the Orange Free State (→ 25/10).

London, 22 June 1900. The Wallace collection of art is opened to the public.

England, 27 August 1900. The first weekly long-distance bus service in Britain begins; the journey between London and Leeds takes two days.

Britain, 31 August 1900. Coca-Cola goes on sale for the first time.

South Africa, 25 Oct 1900. Lord Roberts, the British commander-in-chief, claims that the Boer War is over as the Transvaal is formally annexed by Britain (→ 29).

Suffolk, September 1900. At Newmarket the prince of Wales's horse Diamond Jubilee adds the St Leger to victories in the 2,000 Guineas and Derby this year.

London, 24 October 1900. Members of the National Union of Women Workers hold a meeting about drunkenness and illness.

London, 29 October 1900. Huge crowds greet returning Boer War troops (→ 14/6/01).

Cumbria, 9 November 1900. The world's biggest battleship, the 15,150-ton Japanese *Mikasa*, is launched at Barrow-in-Furness.

Lancashire, 1 December 1900. Four people die and 2,000 are ill from drinking beer treated with arsenic.

Isle of Wight, 19 Jan 1901. Queen Victoria is gravely ill (→ 22/1).

Mafeking siege relieved in Boer War

The battle for Mafeking was long and hard; the joy of victory was intense.

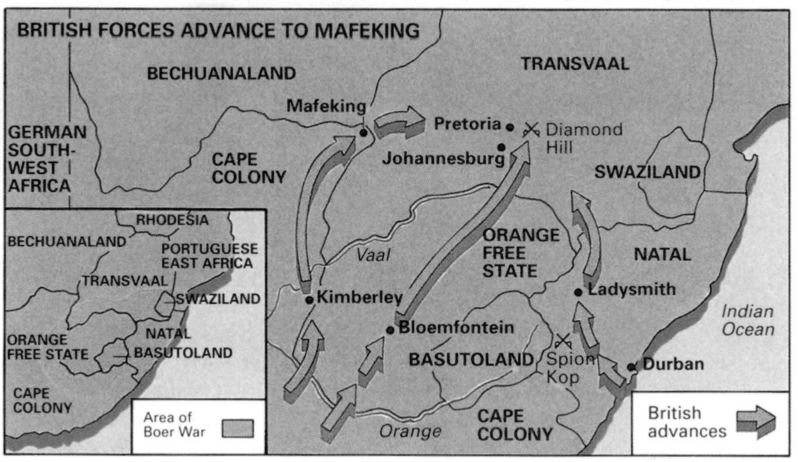

London, 18 May 1900
Mafeking has been relieved. The news that the seven-month-long siege was lifted two days ago was broken tonight by a Reuters news agency dispatch, and the whole of London is celebrating. Rarely has there been such a spontaneous outburst of joy. Even the government's reluctance to confirm the news has not disheartened crowds thronging the capital, singing patriotic songs. Special editions of the newspapers have been printed, and the prince of Wales led the festivities at Covent Garden opera house when the news was shouted from the gallery.

Viewed dispassionately the fervour is hard to understand, for the loss of Mafeking, an insignificant stop on the railway line to Rhodesia, would have had little effect on the outcome of the war. The siege has, in fact, cost the British 160 casualties and the Boers twice that number, a small bill to pay in the context of a war which has proved altogether more bloody than Britain had anticipated.

Yet, under the charismatic Colonel Baden-Powell, the defence of Mafeking has come to represent, in the words of *The Times*, "the fundamental grit of the breed". But the war is far from over; the Boers are turning to guerrilla tactics in their bid to resist the imperial ambitions of Britain in South Africa (→ 28).

A 'Labour Party' is created by unions

London, 27 February 1900
Trade union leaders meeting in London today resolved to abandon the old rather loose alliance with the Liberal Party and to sponsor their own candidates for the House of Commons. They set up a special action group, to be known as the Labour Representation Committee with James Ramsay MacDonald of the Independent Labour Party (ILP) as its secretary.

The move was opposed at first by the miners' union, whose strength has enabled it to force its candidates on the Liberals. But most union leaders had found the party unwilling to adopt working men as candidates. With the ILP making little headway outside the north of England, union leaders have looked enviously at the German socialists, who won 50 seats in the 1898 Reichstag elections.

Delegates representing over half a million trade unionists attended today's meeting in London, along with societies such as the Marxist-orientated Social Democratic Federation. However, socialist dogma took second place to practical politics. Moves to confine policy to "class war" issues and candidates to the working classes were rejected; a levy on union members to fund Labour candidates was accepted. James Keir Hardie, the ILP leader, said that the aim was to develop "a distinct Labour group in parliament" with freedom to shape its own policy. It poses a great challenge to existing parties (→ 3/9/02).

The friendship of actress Lillie Langtry with the heir to the throne shocked Britain. Now she is the talk of Washington as a dissolute heiress in a new drama.

An era ends as Queen Victoria dies

The British Empire mourns a great monarch; Victoria's reign began when royalty's popularity was at a low ebb.

Isle of Wight, 22 January 1901
Queen Victoria died peacefully today at Osborne House, her seaside home near Cowes. She was 81. Most of her large family were gathered at the bedside, among them the new monarch, King Edward VII. They each kissed her hand in farewell as the end approached, and the closing words of the blessing were pronounced by the bishop of Winchester: "The Lord lift up his countenance upon thee and give thee peace."

An extraordinary era in British history had ended. Victoria became queen at 18 and ruled for over 63 years, nearly 40 of them as a lonely widow following the death of her beloved husband, Prince Albert from the duchy of Saxe-Coburg-Gotha. He died of typhoid in 1861. The couple had nine children.

Victoria's reign started with the monarchy held in very low esteem; it ended, owing in large measure to her formidable character, with it as a revered institution. She presided over a burgeoning empire which she saw develop into the greatest in history; she lived through an industrial revolution at home that enabled Britain to become the world's pre-eminent producer of manufactured goods; and she oversaw reforms that made the country a model of constitutional government.

Her ministers at the heart of these great changes were never lacking in trenchant advice from their sovereign, who had a shrewd insight into government at home and abroad. In the last quarter of her reign Britain's strength was beginning to be challenged abroad, and at home there was much poverty. But it was then that her popularity reached its peak (→23).

Tories win power in the 'khaki election'

London, 17 October 1900
Lord Salisbury's Tories have been returned to power with an overwhelming House of Commons majority in what is being called the "khaki" election. With only one result still to come, the Tories and their Unionist allies have 402 MPs; the Liberals, Irish Nationalists and other opposition parties have 268.

The Liberals have been deeply divided by the Irish home rule issue, with MPs breaking away to join the Tories as Liberal Unionists. Tory popularity plummeted when the war in South Africa opened badly, but after the tide turned the government seized the opportunity to call a snap election attacking the Liberals as "unpatriotic" (26/2/02).

Wilde dies in exile and still in disgrace

Paris, 30 November 1900
The writer Oscar Wilde has died in Paris aged 44. Once the toast of London and renowned for his wit and humour as a dramatist, he was convicted of homosexual offences in 1895 and sentenced to two years' imprisonment with hard labour. He drew upon his experiences in *The Ballad of Reading Gaol* which was published anonymously. Since his release in 1897 he had lived in Paris under the name of Sebastian Melmoth. The cause of his death is thought to have been cerebral meningitis. None of his plays has been performed since his disgrace.

Oscar Wilde: a genius disgraced.

British forces lead Chinese rescue mission

Peking, 14 August 1900
British troops were in the forefront of an international force which today ended a 56-day siege of Europeans here in the Chinese capital. The allied column of 10,000 men had met fierce and determined resistance, but the so-called "Boxer rebellion" appears to be over; both the emperor and the empress dowager are reported to have fled the city. The Boxers are members of what started as a patriotic society devoted to martial arts. This grew into a popular movement against foreign influence generally; a German minister in Peking was murdered, and other foreign diplomats were besieged in their embassies. Diplomats and their families in the British embassy had less than a week's supply of food when their rescuers arrived. More than 1,500 foreigners elsewhere were killed.

Irish Nationalists in bid to heal the rifts

Ireland, 1900
The Irish Nationalist Party, which has been split since the scandal linking its former leader, Charles Parnell, to Mrs Katharine O'Shea, has been reunited into one party with John Redmond as chairman. New life has been injected by William O'Brien, the founder of the United Irish League (→5/3/01).

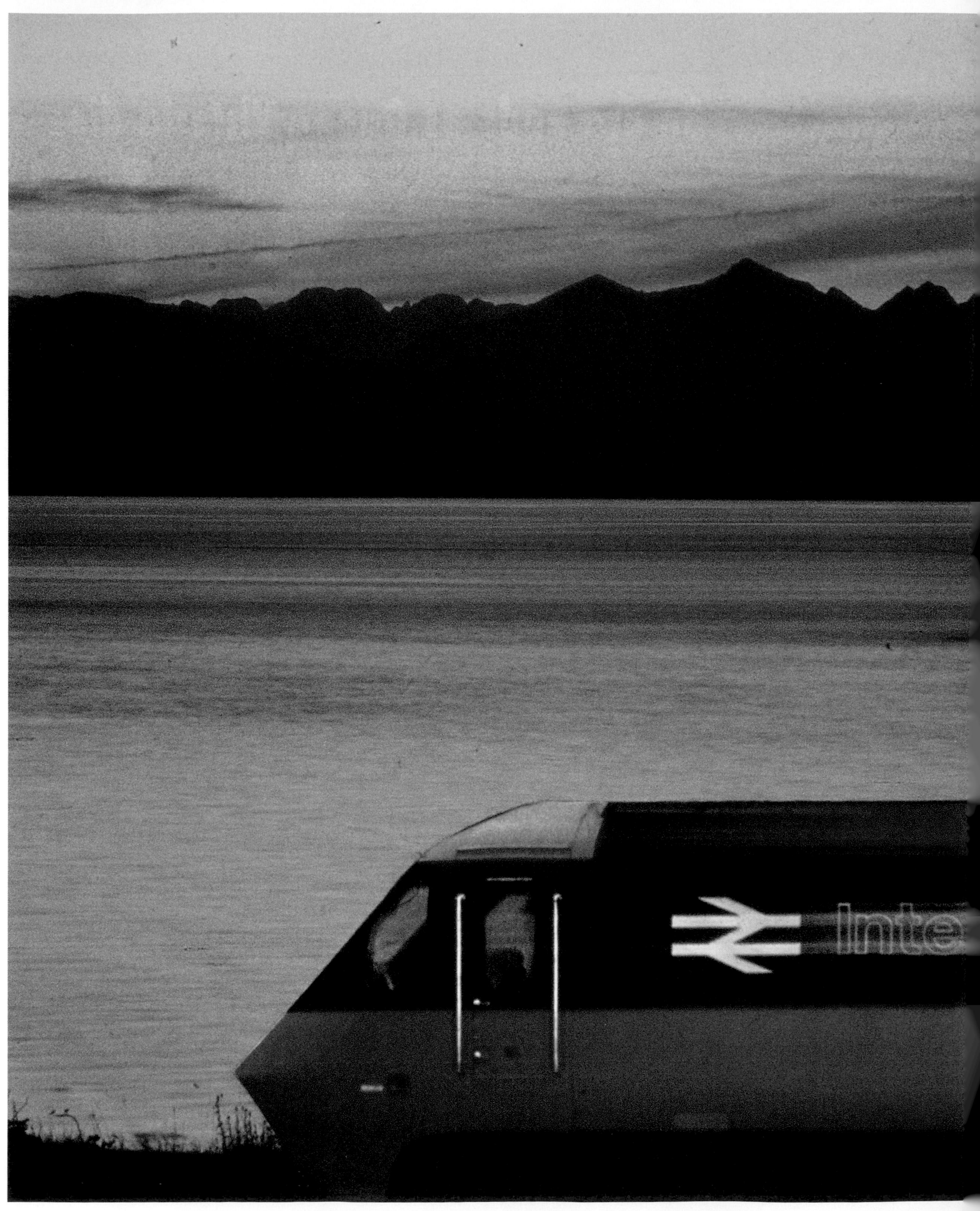
Inte

Towards a New Millennium

1901-1992

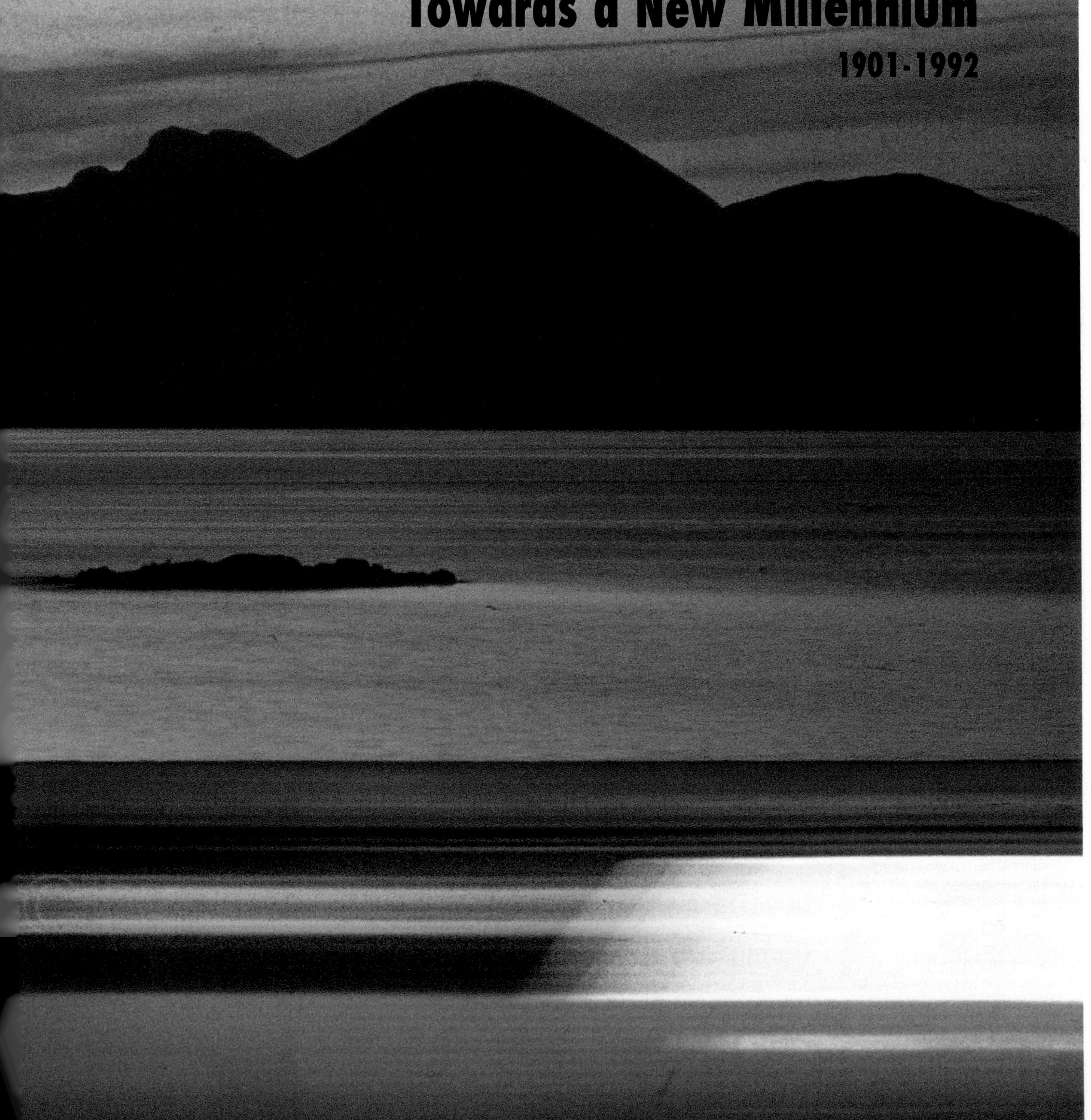

1901

London, 23 January. King Edward VII makes his accession speech at the age of 59 (→4/2).

London, 27 January. Edward gives Kaiser William of Germany, his nephew, the rank of field marshal in the British Army (→8/11/02).

Windsor, Berkshire, 4 Feb. Victoria is buried beside Albert, her beloved consort.→

Westminster, 5 March. Police eject Irish Nationalists from the House of Commons (→6/10).

London, 25 March. The first diesel motor goes on public display.

England, 27 April. Tottenham Hotspur, a non-league club, win the FA cup, beating Sheffield United 3-1 after a replay at Bolton; the first match, played at the Crystal Palace, ended in a 2-2 draw.

Britain, April. A game called "ping-pong", or table tennis, is growing rapidly in popularity.

London, 1 May. The miners' conference recommends a strike unless there is a cut in the coal export tax (→4/9).

South Africa, 9 May. Lord Kitchener introduces new tactics enabling the fast call-up of reinforcements by telegraph (→16/6).

Cowes, Isle of Wight, 22 May. The king has a narrow escape when the America's Cup yacht *Shamrock II* is damaged in a squall (→4/10).

Atlantic Ocean, 16 June. The liner *Lucania* is used for trials of wireless telegraphy at sea (→11/12).

Westminster, 17 June. The Liberal MP David Lloyd George attacks the government over the alarming death rate in South African "concentration camps" (→15/11).

Humberside, 18 September. Fifty-nine people die as the torpedo boat *Cobra* is wrecked off Grimsby.

New York, 4 October. The US yacht *Columbia* beats Britain's *Shamrock II* in the America's Cup.

South Africa, 15 November. Reports speak of goats' dung tea being served up in the "concentration camps" (→19/12).

Birmingham, 19 December. Lloyd George is forced to flee from a pro-Boer meeting as riots break out (→13/2/02).

Edward inherits a crown and empire

Windsor, Berkshire, 4 February
The queen who gave her name to an era was buried today as she had wished – "next to my dearly loved husband in the mausoleum". The mourners were led by her eldest son and successor, King Edward VII. He has inherited not only the crown but also the greatest empire that the world has ever seen.

Nearly one person in four lives under British rule in one form or another in an empire that now covers one-fifth of the world's surface. Edward is emperor of India as well as king of Great Britain, the symbol of a mother country to diverse peoples in every continent. Many of these peoples were represented at today's funeral. So, too, were the many royal families of Europe to which Britain's new king is related; among those attending is Edward's nephew, Kaiser William of Germany.

If today was an occasion to pay homage to the past, there are already signs that the new king intends to put his own distinctive stamp on the monarchy. For a start he chose the name of Edward VII, rather than Albert I as his mother had wanted. Later this month he plans to open the new session of parliament himself; the late queen had not done this since 1886. The new king intends to restore much of the pageantry which was abandoned during Queen Victoria's long years of mourning for Prince Albert. Edward also hopes to use his contacts in Europe to help the government to improve relations with Britain's continental neighbours. Already 59, the king will waste no time in making the most of his inheritance (→24/6/02).

A portrait of Queen Victoria on her deathbed in Osborne House.

King Edward VII leads the mourners at Queen Victoria's state funeral.

Curzon creates a new frontier for India

Calcutta, India, 12 February
The Indian empire is to be extended by the creation of a new frontier province in the north of the Punjab, bordering Afghanistan. The viceroy, Lord Curzon, said today in a communiqué that there had been so much fighting in the tribal areas of Peshawar, Khyber and Waziristan that they needed to come under the control of the central government. The proposed frontier will cover a tenth of the area of the Punjab and a twentieth of the people in a mountainous region where the warring tribes have been a constant source of difficulty for the imperial authorities. The northern frontier has always assumed great importance for the British because of the perceived need to keep the Russians from invading across Afghanistan into the jewel in Britain's imperial crown (→20/8/05).

Census reveals a population boom

London, 9 May
The population of Britain has reached a new peak of 41.5 million, according to this year's census. The total has now overtaken that of France. Ireland's total has fallen by 300,000 to 4.4 million, but elsewhere in the United Kingdom emigration and a lower birth rate were offset by a fall in the death rate.

Anger over British-run Boer prison camps

London, 14 June
The British policy of herding Boers into "concentration camps" came under fierce attack today by Sir Henry Campbell-Bannerman, the Liberal leader, who denounced "methods of barbarism in South Africa". His speech intensifies the pressure on the government, and parliament has been told that Sir Alfred Milner, the high commissioner for South Africa, is attending personally to improving conditions.

There is justice in the criticism, but the irony of the affair is that the camps were originally set up for humanitarian reasons – to feed and protect refugees whose farms had been destroyed in the war. Four months ago, however, General Kitchener decided to intern all families whose men were still fighting for the Boers in order to "limit the endurance of the guerrillas".

Since then the army has swept some 75,000 people, mostly women and children, into the camps, which cannot cope with such large numbers. The camp sites have been badly chosen, with little regard for hygiene or the need to supply food. The result is hunger and pestilence, with inmates dying of typhoid and measles. This is through inefficiency, but the charge of cruelty is ringing round the world (→ 17).

British brutality to Boer women – as seen by a German newspaper artist.

Unions hit by ruling on strike damages

Westminster, 4 September
Trade union leaders were outraged by today's decision in the House of Lords that employers can sue unions for damages arising from strike action. As a result the Amalgamated Society of Railway Servants will have to pay £32,000 in costs and damages to the Taff Vale Railway Company.

Today's decision confirms the ruling of Mr Justice Farwell in the high court, which was later overturned in the court of appeal. The Trades Union Congress promised that it would fight today's ruling, which provides a golden campaigning issue for the newly formed Labour Representation Committee, which aims to win Labour seats in the House of Commons (→ 8/9/05).

Temperance linked to Irish freedom

Dublin, 6 October
Father James Cullen, famous for his missionary zeal in promoting the virtues of temperance, has held the first annual general meeting of the Pioneer Association in Dublin, attended by 900 people.

Father Cullen is a staunch nationalist and believes that he has detected a deliberate attempt on the part of the English to keep Ireland submissive through drink. He is confident that the growth of national self-esteem will go hand in hand with the temperance movement and has adopted the motto "Ireland sober, Ireland free". He sees priests and children as being of major importance, with children raised on abstinence leading to the triumph of the movement (→ 10/1/02).

Above and below the waves, scientists transform the world of communications

On the sea: the newest craft for the fleet, the Holland nine-man submarine.

Cornwall, 11 December
At six o'clock this evening the three dots for the letter "S" in morse code were tapped on a machine here in Cornwall. The signals were heard, faintly but clearly, over 2,000 miles away in Newfoundland, opening a new era in global communications.

The transmission across the Atlantic Ocean was a triumph for Guglielmo Marconi, the Italian pioneer of wireless. In transport, too, there have been scientific breakthroughs this year, yet none was as dramatic as today's wireless transmission.

Marconi had begun his experiments in Italy, but lack of interest at home brought him to Britain where organizations as diverse as the Post Office and the Royal Navy soon took a keen interest in his work. Today, from an aerial 49 metres (164 feet) above the Lizard peninsula in southern Cornwall to an aerial on a kite above St John's, Newfoundland, they demonstrated that sound could be transmitted through the air.

The first British submarine, the *Holland I*, is a more local triumph, since the Americans have already tested vessels which go beneath the waves. Its nine-man crew breathe compressed air while it stays submerged for up to four hours. Another nautical first was the world's first steam-turbine powered passenger ship, the *King Edward*, launched at Dumbarton this year, while on land the king inaugurated London's first electric tramcar service.

Science has also been boosted by prizes to be awarded annually for achievements in various disciplines, funded from money left by the Swedish manufacturer Alfred Nobel. The first were presented in Oslo yesterday (→ 29/3/03).

Marconi, the pioneer of wireless telegraphy across the Atlantic Ocean.

1902

Westminster, 10 January. Irish MPs protest about interference at meetings and suppression of free speech (→ 10/7).

London, 14 January. Universal state pensions are supported by over 300 trade unions (→ 29/11/4).

London, 28 January. The population is 6,581,372, according to last year's census.

Australia, 4 February. England score 769 runs in a single test innings.

Westminster, 13 February. A German Boer relief committee wishing to visit "concentration camps" in South Africa is refused permission by the government (→ 1/6).

Westminster, 18 February. A petition demanding votes for women is presented to parliament by over 37,000 women textile workers (→ 22/4).

Dublin, 2 April. The first performance of W B Yeats's *Cathleen ni Houlihan* takes place.

Glasgow, 22 April. Magistrates require barmaids to be replaced by men (→ 12/5).

London, 29 May. The London School of Political and Economic Science opens.

London, 24 June. King Edward VII is operated on successfully for the appendicitis which has delayed his coronation (→ 9/8).

Westminster, 3 July. A ruling by the Lords restricts betting to the sites of sporting events.

Westminster, 10 July. Charges of jury packing are renewed by Irish Nationalists (→ 14/9).

Westminster, 9 August. Edward VII is crowned.→

Isle of Wight, 11 August. The king gives Osborne House, where Queen Victoria died, to the nation (→ 1/1/03).

London, 18 August. The shah of Persia begins a state visit.

Westminster, 10 September. A royal commission is to investigate British preparedness for the Boer War (→ 23/4/03).

Dublin, 14 September. An estimated 20,000 people demonstrate against strict law and order measures imposed by the government under a state of emergency (→ 14/8/03).

London, 8 November. In the hope of improving Anglo-German relations Kaiser William begins a 12-day visit (→ 8/4/04).

British Boer War victory

London, 1 June

The news that Britain has been waiting for with such expectancy broke tonight when a banner strung between the pillars of London's Mansion House announced "Peace Is Proclaimed". Nearly two years and eight months after the first shots were fired the Boer War is over.

The treaty was signed at Pretoria just before the midnight deadline yesterday after the Boer delegation reluctantly recognized that it could not continue the fight. After nine days of negotiation the Boers spent another two days arguing over whether to accept the British terms. Yesterday morning it seemed impossible that they could agree, but the respected General Christian de Wet suddenly changed his mind and voted for peace.

Jan Smuts and Judge Hertzog then drew up a statement agreeing to the terms, and the Boer leaders voted 54 to six to end the war. Lord Kitchener, who did so much to bring about the Boers' defeat, went among them, shaking their hands and saying: "We are all friends now." There is, however, bitterness among the Boers (→ 10/9).

Peace comes – with a bitter taste.

Schools to be taken over by councils

Westminster, 23 March

Major reforms of schools in England and Wales were outlined in an education bill today. County councils and the larger urban authorities are to take over responsibility for all secondary, elementary and technical schools in their areas, sweeping away the powers of several thousand school boards and the managers of voluntary schools.

For the first time public money will be made available for the education of children in all schools in an area. However, this reform, championed by the government as a means to improve educational standards, has encountered strong criticism from the nonconformist churches. They resent the use of taxes and rates to finance Anglican and Catholic schools, particularly when these schools will retain considerable autonomy from local authority control (→ 7/4/03).

Rosebery's return divides the Liberals

London, 26 February

Lord Rosebery, the former Liberal prime minister, re-entered the political arena today after an absence of five years to announce his break with the Liberal Party leadership and to trigger a battle between the party's imperialist and radical wings. He plans to head a new organization, to be called the Liberal League, to revitalize Liberal principles after years of internal squabbling over Irish home rule and foreign policy.

Rosebery is a supporter of the war in South Africa. He has the backing of Herbert Asquith and Sir Edward Grey but is opposed by more radical Liberals, such as David Lloyd George, who back the present party leader, Sir Henry Campbell-Bannerman (→ 12/7).

Colonies resist calls for imperial unity

London, July

The fourth colonial conference has met in London to discuss greater unity, only to find that the self-governing colonies – Australia, Canada, Cape Colony, Natal, New Zealand and Newfoundland – are increasingly asserting their own independence. The conference passed resolutions in favour of imperial preference to boost trade within the empire but made little progress in developing closer links over defence. This disappointed Britain's colonial secretary, Joseph Chamberlain, who wants a council of the empire to be created (→ 8/3/06).

Twenty die at international soccer match

Glasgow, 5 April

Twenty people died and at least 200 were injured today when terracing collapsed at the Ibrox Park stadium during a match between Scotland and England. More than 70,000 spectators were at the game when part of the wooden north-western terrace gave way. Some people plunged 15 metres (50 feet) to their deaths, but others died by being crushed as panicking fans sought safety on the pitch; their screams were lost in the cheers. The scale of the disaster was not at first apparent: play continued while mounted police rode into the area thinking that a disturbance had broken out.

Ibrox disaster: 20 fans are dead.

Major wins award

Stockholm, 10 December

A British Army major is one of the prize-winners in the second of the awards established under the will of a Swedish chemist, Alfred Nobel, for achievements in science. Major Ronald Ross is this year's laureate for medicine because of his work relating the causes of malaria to the bites of mosquitoes.

Balfour follows his uncle to be premier

London, 12 July
Arthur James Balfour, a Tory MP for almost 30 years, today succeeded his uncle, Lord Salisbury, as prime minister. He was leader of the outgoing government in the Commons as first lord of the treasury where he has been piloting the Education Bill through parliament. Another government change is the appointment of C T Ritchie, formerly the home secretary, as chancellor to replace Sir Michael Hicks-Beach, who goes to the Lords. The populist Joseph Chamberlain stays as colonial secretary (→ 22/8/03).

Balfour: 30 years an MP.

Edward VII crowned after postponement

A coronation feast for the poor.

Regal robes for a king: Edward VII.

London, 9 August
Edward VII was crowned today in Westminster Abbey. In his 61st year he has finally assumed the mantle of monarchy to which he was born, after spending a mainly hedonistic life waiting in the wings.

It was the first coronation in Britain in most people's lifetimes – 64 years – and the thousands lining a route bedecked with flags to the abbey were eager to cheer their new sovereign and his wife, Queen Alexandra, particularly as the king was still recuperating from an operation for near-fatal appendicitis which had delayed the ceremony by two months. In deference to the king's health the service was shortened, and Edward was spared the burden of carrying the heavy sword of state to the high altar. The king appeared, however, to be full of vigour.

The only hitch occurred when the king himself had to raise the frail archbishop of Canterbury, Frederick Temple, from his knees after he had sworn allegiance to his new sovereign on behalf of the church. Absent from the abbey were a number of the foreign heads of state who had returned home after coming to London in June when the coronation was originally to have been held (→ 11).

Unions back call to elect Labour MPs

London, 3 September
The Trades Union Congress voted in London today to back independent Labour candidates to win power at Westminster rather than to rely on local alliances with Liberals. The TUC plans to set up a central organization which will boost the Labour Representation Committee which it set up two years ago. Where possible, Labour candidates will fight constituencies independently.

One Liberal was given a hearing by the TUC, however. David Lloyd George, the Liberal MP for Carmarthen, urged support for quarrymen at Penrhyn who have been fighting for union recognition in a dispute lasting two years.

Automobiles tested

Folkestone, Kent, 1 September
Horse-drawn transport still rules the road, but not for long if the Automobile Club has its way. Today the club organized trials of motor cars designed to show the reliability of the internal combustion engine. The tests involved 63 cars, which were required to travel from the Crystal Palace in south London to Folkestone and back again. Most completed the 139-mile route without mishap, with club officials logging the performance of each car (→ 14/7/03).

Crucial alliance for Britain and Japan

London, 30 January
Britain and Japan today concluded a treaty of great mutual benefit which also ends an era of what has been called "splendid isolation" in British foreign policy. It aims to protect their parallel interests in China and Korea. Both countries guarantee not to make treaties with other nations without consultation. Each needs an ally in the area: following the Boxer rebellion, Britain considers its interests in China endangered by other European countries, notably Germany, while Japan is alarmed by Russian advances in Manchuria.

Barmaids win sex battle in Glasgow

Glasgow, 12 May
An appeal court ruled today that women can, if they so choose, be exposed to bad language, lewd suggestions and crude jests. These, it was said, were the hazards of working as a barmaid in a Glasgow pub. Last month magistrates here were sufficiently concerned by the threat to morality and public order that in effect they barred women from working in bars. Pubs employing women would not have their licences renewed. But today the appeal court reversed the decision, following protests by publicans, barmaids and public (→ 10/10/03).

Venezuela bombed by British gunboats

Caracas, 31 December
The British and German fleets have seized the Venezuelan navy and shelled a fort in Caracas this month to enforce demands for payment for property seized without compensation during the 1899 revolution. Venezuela, which denies all liability, has agreed to submit the dispute to the Hague tribunal. The two powers will continue to blockade Venezuela until their claims are met. The United States, invoking the Monroe Doctrine, has put pressure on them to end the blockade and refer the matter to the international court at the Hague.

A tiny book for children, "The Tale of Peter Rabbit", by Beatrix Potter – who also illustrates the text – is a popular bestseller.

1903

Delhi, 1 January. King Edward VII is proclaimed emperor of India (1/5).

East Africa, 4 January. British troops under General Manning land at Obbia to attack the forces of the "Mad Mullah", Mohammed bin Abdullah.

London, 27 January. Fifty-one people die in a fire at the Colney Hatch mental hospital.

London, 10 February. Two new streets are named Kingsway (after the king) and Aldwych.

Atlantic Ocean, 22 February. The first ship's newspaper is published on the liner *Etruria*.

Westminster, 26 February. A Commons debate calls for immigration restrictions.

Fife, 6 March. As the German navy grows, a huge new Royal Navy base is to be built in the Firth of Forth at Rosyth.

Dublin, 27 March. By the Bank Holiday (Ireland) Act, St Patrick's day (17 March) is to be a public holiday.

London/New York, 29 March. A regular news service using the Marconi wireless system begins (→ 28/12/04).

Westminster, 23 April. The government admits that the Boer and Boxer Wars cost a third of the national budget (→ 12/1903).

Paris, 1 May. Edward VII starts a goodwill visit (→ 1/8).

Belfast, 11 June. An independent Orange Order, more militantly Protestant than the main Orange organization, is formed.

Cork, 11 July. The Royal Cork Yacht Club stages the world's first power-boat race.

Westminster, 14 July. The government is to reject calls for penalties for drunken drivers, driving tests and vehicle inspection (→ 4/5/04).

Ireland, 1 August. At the end of a tour, the king expresses his hope that "a brighter day is dawning upon Ireland" (27/2/07).

Southern England, 10 Sept. A great storm causes widespread damage and deaths (→ 3/2/04).

London, 6 October. The duke of Devonshire resigns from the government.

London, 15 December. The Australian chamber of commerce here approves a UK preference in international trade.

Chamberlain quits over empire trade row

Westminster, 17 September
The House of Commons was rife today with speculation about the resignations of four of the most powerful members of the cabinet, including the colonial secretary, Joseph Chamberlain. For some months the cabinet and the party have been split over the issue of free trade versus imperial preference.

Chamberlain, the most passionate advocate of empire unity, has been arguing for preferential tariffs to foster empire trade. The duke of Devonshire, C T Ritchie, Lord Balfour of Burleigh and Lord George Hamilton have been pressing equally fervently for maintaining total commitment to free trade.

Whitehall insiders were saying today that the steely hand of the prime minister, Arthur Balfour, was behind the so-called resignations. According to them Chamberlain offered to resign over a week ago. Three days ago Balfour sacked Ritchie and Balfour without telling them about Chamberlain's offer. Both the duke of Devonshire and Lord George Hamilton resigned in protest. Balfour then accepted Chamberlain's resignation but managed to persuade the duke to stay before today's announcement of the four "resignations". Balfour is determined to find a compromise to heal the party split, but it seems unlikely that he will be able to retain Devonshire for long.

Joseph Chamberlain, the apostle of empire trade, juggles with bread.

For Chamberlain it is a bitter disappointment. Ever since the fourth colonial conference last summer he has been convinced that imperial preference is the only tangible policy upon which the new self-governing colonies can all agree. But he has failed to persuade his own prime minister and colleagues to give up free trade (→ 6/10).

Army criticized in Boer post-mortem

Whitehall, London, December
Wide-ranging reforms in the army and navy are likely to follow the reorganization this year of the committee of imperial defence. The committee had existed before the South African war, but it had been little more than a group of ministers: now it is to bring together the professional chiefs of the services with the most senior ministers under the chairmanship of the prime minister. There will also be a permanent secretariat, including army and navy officers.

The revamped committee is now considering the report of the royal commission into the Boer War. This has highlighted weaknesses in the army's organization and chain of command. The army never had a proper plan of campaign, regarding the war as a minor colonial skirmish, not a major affair against a well-organized enemy equipped with artillery, fighting in a style well suited to the terrain. The army's training and intelligene gathering were also criticized. One option is to abolish the post of commander-in-chief and create an army council similar to the admiralty board (→ 7/12/09).

Official inquiry is launched into London's traffic problem

A traffic jam at the Bank of England: can "twopenny tubes" be the answer?

London, 6 February
A new network of roads extending from the centre of London to the suburbs is among schemes to be considered by a royal commission set up today to examine the capital's rail and tramway systems. Street congestion has increased dramatically in recent years.

Proposals for electric-powered trams in the City and west end, such as those already working in cities such as Bristol and Manchester, would add to the pressure on the capital's roads. However, these would be quicker and cleaner than the horse-drawn vehicles which form the biggest part of the traffic on London roads. The commission will also look at plans for new underground railways, following the success of the "twopenny tube" Central Line which opened from Shepherd's Bush to the Bank three years ago (→ 12/3/04).

Irish tenants can now own freeholds

Ireland, 14 August
Irish tenant-farmers will be helped to purchase the freeholds of their lands under a land act which has now been approved by parliament in Westminster. George Wyndham, the Irish secretary, backed reform to try to remove some of the economic grievances which have fed past nationalist agitation. The new act will use public funds to help bridge the gap between what tenants can pay and what landlords are willing to accept.

These developments reflect increased prosperity. Cooperative creameries are being encouraged, agricultural wages are rising, and industry is benefiting from exports of linen-weaving and spinning, brewing and distilling (→ 2/1/04).

Rural economy: Irish tenant-farmers at the Carndonagh sheep fair.

Women suffragists prepare for action

Manchester, 10 October
A more militant campaign for women's suffrage was signalled tonight with the formation here of a new group under the leadership of Mrs Emmeline Pankhurst, the widow of a leading Manchester member of the Independent Labour Party. "Deeds, not words" is to be the motto of the Women's Social and Political Union. Until now women have sought to win the vote by trying to persuade sympathetic MPs to back electoral reform, but this has made no progress. Mrs Pankhurst favours a more active campaign. The new society, which met in her house, is to be confined to women and independent of all party affiliations (→ 12/5/05).

Company plans to build first 'garden city'

Hertfordshire, December
A company has been formed this year to turn the dream of "garden cities" into reality. Just under 1,600 hectares (4,000 acres) of land have been acquired by the company in Letchworth, north of London, and it is here that building will begin next year. The vision of creating a new environment, blending town and country, was first put forward by Ebenezer Howard in 1898. Republished last year as *Garden Cities for Tomorrow*, his work has been widely translated and inspired architects all over the country. The idea is to create new communities where industry and shopping zones will be separated from housing by open spaces. A belt of countryside will stop the city sprawling endlessly. Leafy streets, houses with gardens and open spaces will all contribute to the "garden" image.

Liberals in secret pact with Labour group

London, December
A secret electoral pact has been agreed by the Liberal chief whip in the Commons, Herbert Gladstone, and the secretary of the fledgeling Labour Representation Committee, James Ramsay MacDonald. They expect the Tories, deeply split by the tariff reform issue, to fall, and in the ensuing general election the Liberals will give Labour candidates a clear run in certain constituencies. Several branches of the socialist Independent Labour Party will be angered if told not to oppose Liberal candidates, but the pact offers the trade unions the prospect of quick results for their decision in 1900 to set up the Labour Representation Committee. Gladstone's enthusiasm for the pact stems from his concern at the growing strength of what is seen as an embryonic Labour Party (→ 5/12/05).

British explorers get closer to South Pole

Antarctica, March
Three British explorers, Lieutenant Ernest Shackleton, Captain Robert Scott and Dr Edward Wilson, have crossed the 80th parallel and have thereby travelled further towards the South Pole than any previous expedition. The epic journey began two years ago when the National Antarctic Expedition, led by Captain Scott, left McMurdo Bay in Victoria Land and headed south.

Since then the expedition's members have battled the elements and overcome a number of setbacks – notably the death of their dog-teams, after which they had to pull the sledges themselves – to achieve their goal. On the way they have discovered several new mountain ranges and gathered much valuable scientific information (→ 9/1/09).

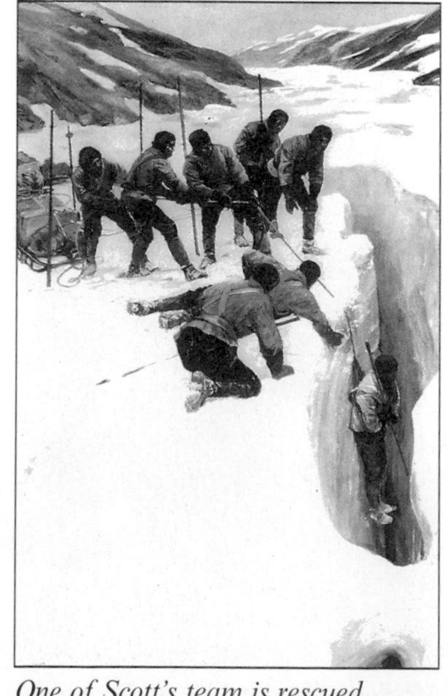

One of Scott's team is rescued.

Four times prime minister Salisbury dies

London, 22 August
Robert Arthur Talbot Gascoyne Cecil, the third marquis of Salisbury, four times Tory prime minister, died today aged 73. He is best known for his determination to preserve the union with Ireland, and for his mastery of foreign affairs amid growing imperial rivalries.

Lord Salisbury had suffered from a heart condition for some years; it was the deciding factor in his resignation from the premiership last year. His nephew and successor as prime minister, Arthur Balfour, was at his bedside when he passed away on the 50th anniversary of his first election to parliament. King Edward VII and other members of the royal family have expressed "profound sorrow" at Salisbury's death (→ 17/9).

Lord Salisbury: four-time premier.

1904

Dublin, 2 January. Arthur Griffith proposes that Ireland should separate from England but keep the same king (→3/2).

Somalia, 11 January. British troops kill 1,000 rebels under the command of the Islamic leader known as "the Mad Mullah".

Westminster, 3 February. The Irish Nationalist John Redmond renews the call for home rule (→12/1905).

Southern England, 3 February. A tidal wave devastates the Channel coast (→15/3/05).

Merseyside, 12 March. The first electric main-line train in the British Isles runs from Liverpool to Southport (→9/4).

Plymouth, Devon, 9 April. A train runs non-stop from here to London in less than four and a half hours – a record (→22/1/06).

Westminster, 22 April. The Commons approve a bill allowing "peaceful picketing".

London, 26 April. Tobacconists protest at a threepenny increase on the tobacco tax.

Co Cork, 4 July. The first summer school for training teachers of Irish opens at Ballingeary.

London, 5 July. Edward Elgar is knighted following the March festival of his music at Covent Garden (→12/1908).

London, 12 July. A five-year treaty between Britain and Germany, to resolve disputes through arbitration, is signed (24/7/05).

Liverpool, 17 July. A foundation stone is laid for a new Anglican cathedral.

British Isles, 17 August. Postcards increased in popularity by 25 per cent last year, according to a report by the postmaster-general.

Lhasa, 7 September. An Anglo-Tibetan treaty gives Britain trading posts in Tibet and a promise that the Dalai Lama will not cede territory to a foreign power such as Russia.

London, 1 November. George Bernard Shaw's play *John Bull's Other Island* has its première (→1/1/05).

London, 27 December. James Barrie's *Peter Pan* has its first performance.

London, 28 December. The first weather forecasts by radio telegraphy are published.

'Entente Cordiale' signed with France

London, 8 April

Britain has abandoned its "splendid isolation" in Europe to form an *Entente Cordiale* with France. This does not mean that Britain is allied with France against Germany, but the Germans will see it as a step in that direction.

France and Britain have signed agreements settling all their disputes. The most important concerns Morocco: Britain recognizes French primacy there. If the sultan's government collapses, France will take over. This means that Britain prefers France to Germany, which also covets Morocco. In exchange, France has at last accepted Britain's occupation of Egypt.

Another agreement settles a dispute over fishing rights off Newfoundland that goes back two centuries. France renounces some of its rights in exchange for minor colonial concessions in West Africa. A third agreement covers cooperation in the New Hebrides.

Britain's isolation was demonstrated during the Boer War, when it discovered just how unpopular it was everywhere. Relations with France had been strained since the Fashoda incident in 1898 when the countries had clashed over territorial rights in the Nile valley. But Germany's naval armaments programme is a greater menace, and the government was ready to listen when the French foreign minister, Théophile Delcasse, proposed a general settlement.

Hand in hand: London celebrates.

The improvement in relations was helped by both King Edward VII's visit to Paris last year and President Loubet's return visit. Edward charmed the French. He speaks the language well and signed himself "Edouard". The *entente* permits the Royal Navy to concentrate on the North Sea, leaving the Mediterranean to France (→12/7).

Dalai Lama flees as British seize Lhasa and war continues

Lhasa, Tibet, 3 August

Tibet's religious ruler, the Dalai Lama, has fled from Lhasa at the approach of the British mission led by Colonel Francis Younghusband. Lord Curzon, the viceroy in India, dispatched the mission in a bid to counter growing Russian influence over the rulers of Tibet on India's northern frontiers.

No real opposition has been offered to the British forces since a sharp engagement in the Karo Pass in May when 3,000 armed Tibetans positioned behind a wall connecting two stone forts poured a hail of fire on the advancing British, Sikh and Gurkha soldiers. The day was saved by the Gurkhas, who climbed a precipice to fire down on the Tibetans while the Sikhs outflanked the forts. The Tibetans fled, losing 400 dead, while the mission continued its arduous trek to the rooftop of the world. Colonel Younghusband is now camped outside the "forbidden city" of Lhasa. He has assured Tibetan officials that the mission will leave as soon as a treaty is signed between Britain and Tibet (→7/9).

Record-breaking Rolls signs agreement to make cars with Royce

Manchester, 4 May

One of the pioneers of motoring has signed an agreement with a leading Manchester engineer who has just produced his first automobile. The Hon Charles Rolls, who set a world land-speed record of 93mph last year at Phoenix Park, in Dublin, today agreed to sell cars produced by Henry Royce under their joint names – "Rolls-Royce".

Rolls was the overall winner of the Thousand-Mile Trial of 1900 which first popularized motoring in the British Isles. He runs a London company which sells and repairs cars. Royce is a self-made engineer who set up his electrical engineering company in Manchester. Last year Royce turned his attention to cars with his first model, a ten-horse-power vehicle being praised for its "excellent running". The two men's companies will not, as yet, merge completely (→29/6/05).

Mr Rolls (left) and Mr Royce: quality motor cars for people of quality.

Poverty is getting worse, says survey

Dinner time in a London workhouse.

Westminster, 29 November

Clear evidence of the extent of poverty was provided by new poor relief figures published today. Over 520,000 people in England and Wales are now on poor relief – more than at any time since 1888. A further 250,000 are in workhouses, 11 per cent up on last year. Low wages put a third of the total population near or below the poverty line. Half the population of Scotland and one-sixth of that of London live with more than two people per room. One result is poor health: two in five men who applied to enlist during the Boer War were rejected as medically unfit. The proportion was even higher from industrial areas (→ 14/3/06).

Hull trawlers are sunk by Russian ships

Hull, Humberside, 22 October

The Russian Baltic fleet, on the first stage of a voyage half-way round the world to give battle to the Japanese, opened fire on Britain's North Sea fishing fleet last night, sending its big shells crashing into the frail trawlers peacefully fishing the Dogger Bank. One of them was sunk, two of the Hull skippers were killed, and several fishermen were wounded.

It appears that the Russian commander, Admiral Rozhdestvensky, believed that the Japanese would attempt to repeat their devastating torpedo-boat attack on Russian warships at Port Arthur by sending ships under false colours to ambush him in European waters. As soon as he sailed from St Petersburg he posted extra lookouts and ordered his captains to be watchful for a surprise attack. It was in this trigger-happy atmosphere that the Russian ships suddenly found themselves surrounded by a flotilla of small ships in the dark of the night.

Without waiting to identify the "enemy" they opened fire. It was only after the first salvoes had fallen among the astonished trawlermen that the Russians realized what they done. Even then the admiral, still nervous at the possibility of a torpedo attack, did not stop to help but steamed off into the night.

The people of Hull were furious when the battle-scarred fishing fleet returned, and pressure is growing for the government to send the Royal Navy after the Russians to "teach them a lesson" (→ 9/3/05).

Dogger Bank aftermath: fishermen and their families survey the damage.

The Abbey is set to be national theatre

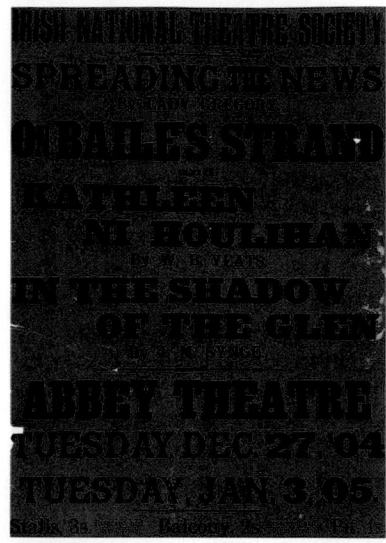

Curtain up at the Abbey theatre.

Dublin, 27 December

The Abbey theatre, Ireland's first national theatre, opened tonight in the former Mechanics' Institute in Abbey Street, Dublin. The lease was bought by an Englishwoman, Annie Horniman, the patron and friend of the poet W B Yeats.

Yeats, together with Lady Gregory and Edward Martyn, has been the guiding force behind the idea for a national theatre. It was appropriate, therefore that his play *On Baile's Strand* was chosen to inaugurate the theatre.

The Abbey, it is hoped, will become a focus for the national movement which incorporates literature and drama and also has a political dimension.

Eleven die as sub sinks in the Solent

Hampshire, 18 March

Eleven men died today when their submarine was hit by a liner in the Solent off Portsmouth. The submarine was one of six undergoing trials, and the accident happened just days after the Royal Navy had shown its confidence in the vessels by taking the prince of Wales – a former naval officer – on an underwater trip around Portsmouth harbour. All the men aboard the submarine today died in the accident which occured when she was manoeuvring in busy shipping lanes.

Fingerprints boost fight against crime

London, 23 September

The potency of a new weapon in the war against crime was shown again today when a fingerprint left by an alleged burglar was sufficient to commit the man for trial. The court at the Mansion House was told that Scotland Yard's fingerprint "bank" now exceeded more than 70,000 – and no two prints were identical. Magistrates have sent a 20-year-old clerk for trial after being told by police that his fingerprints had been found at the scene of a burglary in the Ludgate Circus area of London.

Wishing you were here: postcards are selling in their thousands as the new Edwardians travel further in search of sunshine and sandy beaches.

1905

South Yorkshire, 4 January. Seven people die in a rail crash near Barnsley.

Britain, 9 February. Greater thrift among children is called for by the board of education.

London, 17 February. A typhus outbreak is reported in the East End (→5/2/07).

London, 1 March. A 350 per cent increase in spending on the Royal Navy is announced (→28/2/07).

Britain, 9 March. Russia agrees to pay £65,000 compensation for the Dogger Bank incident last year.

South Wales, 10 March. Thirty-two miners die in a pit disaster.

Cornwall, 15 March. Fierce storms off Land's End cause 23 deaths as 100-mph gales lash the British Isles (→27/8).

London, 31 March. By public demand, Sir Arthur Conan Doyle's new book describes Sherlock Holmes's return – from death.

London, 9 April. A judge decides that the public have no right of way to Stonehenge (→21/9/15).

Plymouth, Devon, 8 June. Fourteen sailors drown when their submarine sinks.

Wimbledon, July. An American – May Sutton, aged 17 – is the first foreigner to win the ladies' singles championship.

Glamorgan, 11 July. An estimated 124 miners are feared to have died in a pit disaster.

Finland, 24 July. Kaiser William of Germany and Russia's Czar Nicholas sign a treaty of alliance after talks (→15/8/06).

Dover, Kent, 1 August. The founder of the Salvation Army, General William Booth, begins a 2,000-mile crusade around Britain.

Ireland, 27 August. Severe storms cause widespread flooding (→11/3/10).

Britain, 8 September. Figures show that 1,997,000 people belong to trade unions (→12/1906).

Britain, 30 October. Aspirin goes on sale for the first time.

London, 19 December. London county council announces plans for the first motorized ambulances (→14/8/13).

Women step up campaign for votes

MPs 'talk out' bill for suffrage reform

Westminster, 12 May
Moves to give women the vote were "talked out" in the House of Commons today. Under the rules of parliament a bill is automatically lost if MPs are still talking when the house is due to adjourn, as was the case today. Women have lobbied MPs to back their campaign for an extension to the franchise, but their parliamentary allies found too few friends in the house today. The debate was interrupted by constant laughter from MPs and one noisy interlude from the gallery. It is unlikely that today's setback will deter the women's suffrage movement.

For over 40 years women have been fighting for the right to vote. Nearly 100 different societies have been formed. One of these, the Women's Social and Political Union (WSPU) founded by Mrs Emmeline Pankhurst two years ago, has emerged as the champion of a more militant approach which can only be strengthened by the failure to persuade MPs by normal lobbying. Mrs Pankhurst rallied sympathetic MPs to plead the WPSU's cause, but the society has often been frustrated by parliament's refusal to debate the subject. Now, when a suffrage bill was finally proposed, it never even came to a vote.

This seems certain to plead the WSPU's cause who argue that women must fight to win the vote by adopting a more radical strategy, even breaking the law if necessary to shock the all-male parliament into action (→4/10).

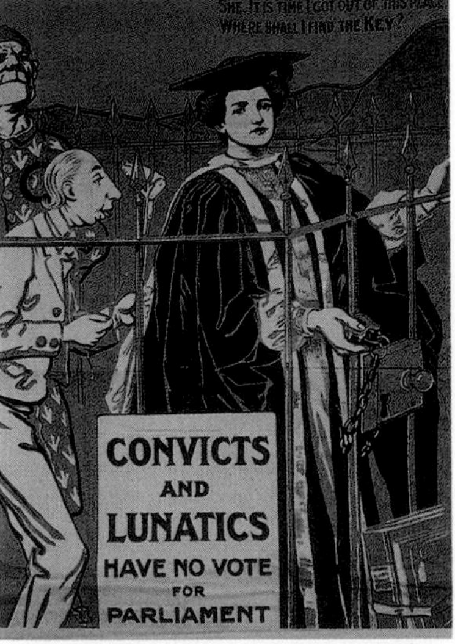

Irony: words – and chains – are the suffragettes' principal weapons.

Suffragettes choose jail instead of fines

Manchester, 4 October
The women's suffrage movement has revealed a new militancy today when, for the first time, two of its members elected to go to prison rather than pay fines. Christabel Pankhurst and her colleague Annie Kenney were arrested for assaulting police at the Free Trade Hall where a leading Liberal politician, Sir Edward Grey, was addressing a meeting. They were sentenced for up to seven days in prison.

It is two years since Mrs Emmeline Pankhurst, the mother of Christabel, founded the Women's Social and Political Union (WSPU) at her home in Manchester. She said then that its aims were to "secure for women the parliamentary vote as it is or may be granted to men; to use the power thus obtained to establish equality of rights and opportunities between the sexes and to promote the social and industrial well-being of the community".

"Deeds, not words" is the motto of the organization. Now the founder's daughter has shown that this is no empty slogan (→17/4/06).

Curzon quits over Indian Army changes

London, 20 August
Lord Curzon has resigned as viceroy of India in a dispute with Lord Kitchener, the army commander-in-chief, and the government. He will be succeeded by Lord Minto.

Lord Curzon has been viceroy since 1898 and has defended India's interests vigorously, claiming that it should be the key to imperial policy. He even had his own foreign policy, sending an army into Tibet last year. He also tried to control the army in India directly, against the wishes of the home government.

Lord Kitchener, the commander-in-chief in India, thought that he, not the viceroy, should exercise that control. The final, trivial dispute concerned the appointment of a military member of the viceroy's council. Kitchener and ministers in London opposed Curzon's nominee, so the viceroy resigned.

Lord Curzon: a viceroy steps down.

Motorists found a 'protection society'

London, 29 June
Fifty pioneer motorists met in London's Trocadero restaurant today to form an "Automobile Association" to counter what they see as popular prejudices and police hostility towards the motor car. The new association's objectives were defined at the meeting as "the protection and advancement of the legitimate interests of motorists and opposition to restriction on the use of the roads". Motorists complain particularly of speed-traps set by the police for anyone driving faster than 20mph, claiming that the stop-watches often used by policemen are inaccurate. For two guineas [£2.10] a year motorists now have an association to champion their cause in the country, if not in the courts (→19/12).

Liberal is new premier

London, 5 December
After 37 years as an MP Sir Henry Campbell-Bannerman, the Liberal leader, is to take over as prime minister at the age of 69 following the resignation yesterday of Arthur Balfour, whose Tory Party is in disarray over tariff reform. During his audience with the king Sir Henry said that it would take several days for him to form his cabinet, and Balfour is hoping that it might split before the next general election.

Indeed, the new premier's first task is to frustrate moves by more conservative Liberals to capture the top posts in his cabinet. He made many enemies in the party during the Boer War by his criticisms of British policy, and the conservative imperialist wing would have much preferred to see Herbert Asquith become prime minister. However, Campbell-Bannerman, for all his amiable easy-going ways, intends to ask the king to dissolve parliament for a snap general election which, if the Liberals won, would enhance his own authority.

Two powerful Liberal imperialists will need to be placated, though. Asquith is to become chancellor, and Richard Haldane will go to the war office with the task of reorganizing the army after the disasters in South Africa. He plans to set up an imperial general staff on the lines of the German army.

The new premier: history is made.

The new prime minister has already secured his place in constitutional history: he will be the first to hold the post as an office of state. In the past, the head of the British government has been obliged to take a post formally recognized by the constitution, usually that of first lord of the treasury, a sinecure. Now the king has promised a royal warrant creating the post of prime minister (→ 13/1/06).

New nationalist party, 'Sinn Féin', formed

Ireland, December
A new political party, Sinn Féin [We Ourselves], has been formed by a Dublin printer, Arthur Griffith, the founder of a weekly paper, the *United Irishman*, in which he preaches the doctrine which has now formed the basis of Sinn Féin. Griffith believes that Ireland must be politically free before it can be economically prosperous. In 1900 he organised a movement against the Boer War. Known as *Cumann na nGaedheal*, it has been seen as a broad front for cultural and economic nationalism.

With the formation of his new party he is urging a policy of non-cooperation. The Irish members would withdraw from the Westminster parliament and set up an Irish government which would be followed by the peaceful withdrawal of the British (→ 12/2/07).

Arthur Griffith, the mouthpiece for a new mood of Irish nationalism.

Dr Barnardo, champion of children, dies

Surbiton, Surrey, 19 September
A doctor who gave his name to homes for deprived children has died aged 60. Dr Thomas John Barnardo had meant to become a missionary after finishing his medical studies, but he was so shocked by the plight of homeless children in London's east end where he was studying that he found his vocation within the British Isles. He set up his first "home" in 1870 – a simple shelter and school in a former stable – and by the time his death was announced today there were 112 Barnardo homes.

No child was ever turned away, it was claimed, and many found new lives overseas. Some 17,000 children emigrated to Canada through the organization created by the Irish-born doctor.

Actors banned for indecency in Shaw play

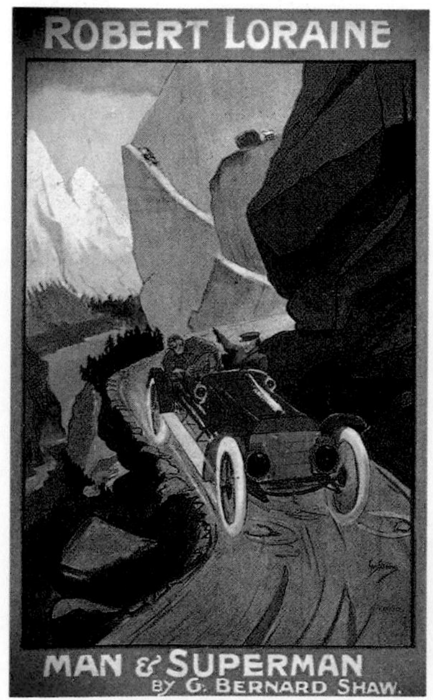

A poster for "Man and Superman": provocative philosophical comedy.

New York, 1 November
A controversial play by the Irish writer George Bernard Shaw about prostitution, *Mrs Warren's Profession*, got a brief showing here this week after being banned in London. But the play was promptly closed by the police who arrested the theatre manager, Arnold Daly, and his actors for offences against public decency. Chief Commissioner McAdoo testified that the play was "nauseating where it is not boring". Shaw spoke of his "pity for all those foolish people".

Shaw has other hits in London, too. *John Bull's Other Island* was seen by the king, who broke his chair laughing. *Man and Superman* followed, in which the superman was played by Harley Granville-Barker made up to look like Shaw. A third play, *Major Barbara*, opens later this month (→ 10/12/25).

Queen Alexandra visits the East End: loyalty is shown to royalty in the new Edwardian era, despite reports that millions live "in chronic poverty".

1906

Britain, 13 January. The former Tory prime minister Arthur Balfour loses his seat in the general election (→ 7/2).

Liverpool, 22 January. Thirty people die in a tram accident (→ 30/8).

London, 27 January. Oil on the surface of the Thames ignites, causing a fire on one stretch of the river.

Westminster, 12 February. Labour MPs in the Commons elect James Keir Hardie as their leader (→ 23/1/07).

London, 10 March. A "tube" line from Baker Street to Waterloo is opened (→ 15/12).

Westminster, 14 March. The principle of old age pensions is approved by parliament (→ 7/5/08).

London, 22 March. England win the first rugby international against France.

Britain, 17 April. Female emancipation is called for by the Independent Labour Party (→ 14/6).

Canada, 22 May. The last British troops leave the dominion (→ 10/9/07).

London, 12 June. Ellen Terry celebrates 50 years on the stage.

Westminster, 14 June. A bill proposes to ban women from dangerous sports following the death of a woman parachutist (→ 23).

London, 23 June. The prime minister sees a deputation representing 500,000 women who are pressing for the vote (→ 24/10).

Westminster, 15 July. MPs back the creation of a separate ministry for Wales.

Belfast, 1 August. The new city hall is opened.

Germany, 15 August. King Edward VII meets his nephew, Kaiser William, at Kronberg for talks (→ 31/10/08).

Cork, 30 August. An express rail service opens linking Cork and Waterford with London via the new ports of Rosslare and Fishguard (→ 15/12).

Wales, 25 September. The Liberal David Lloyd George tells Wesleyans that "the richest country under the sun [Britain]" has ten million living in chronic destitution.

London, 25 December. Suffragettes in Holloway prison refuse Christmas meals (→ 14/2/07).

Liberals sweep to landslide victory

FLATTENING HIM OUT, OR "BROADENING THE BASIS OF TAXATION."
TARIFF REFORM
IF YOU ARE TO GIVE A PREFERENCE TO THE COLONIES YOU MUST PUT A TAX ON FOOD.
MR J. CHAMBERLAIN
TAXATION
"MR BALFOUR AND THE TORY PARTY WANT TO "BROADEN THE BASIS OF TAXATION."
This simply means, and CAN ONLY MEAN, making the poor pay more in the way of taxation. As a Tory paper said some time ago, "to broaden the basis of taxation, OF COURSE, means to place A LARGER SHARE UPON THE MASSES."

War by posters: Liberals claim Chamberlain's high tariffs crush the workers.

Labour grows, but Tories flop at poll

London, 7 February

Sir Henry Campbell-Bannerman has led his Liberal Party to a landslide victory in the snap general election he called within weeks of becoming prime minister when the Conservative government resigned. There are now 400 Liberal MPs against 184 elected in 1900, with a majority of 130 over other parties.

The poll has been a disaster for the Tories, who held only 157 of their 402 seats – and even these are split between supporters of Balfour and of Chamberlain. The 83 Irish Nationalists appear to be a more cohesive group than has sometimes been the case in the past, but the most significant portent may be the success of the Labour candidates.

A secret pact with the Liberals gave Labour a free run against the Tories in key constituencies, and 29 of 50 candidates from the trade-union-backed Labour Representation Committee (LRC) have been elected. Another 24 MPs are Labour under various names, but not linked as yet to those from the LRC who intend to operate as an independent party. Labour's share of the total vote is still small at 4.8 per cent, but it has trebled since the 1900 election and threatens the two-party dominance of the Liberals and their Tory rivals (→ 12).

Government to enforce new welfare plans

Westminster, 7 February

Pressure for radical social changes has been intensified within the Liberal government by the success of Labour candidates in the general election. David Lloyd George, the 43-year-old president of the board of trade, is telling his cabinet colleagues that they must commit the government to a wide-ranging reform programme if they wish to stem the tide of socialism.

Lloyd George, a fiery champion of the radical Liberal wing, says that the traditional Liberal preoccupation with such nonconformist issues as education and teetotalism must give way to the notion of "positive liberty". This means a willingness to use the power of the state to give the "labouring classes" some form of help in time of need.

Sir Henry Campbell-Bannerman has dashed Tory hopes of a Liberal split first by succeeding in forming a government and now by winning a stunning election victory. However, he must keep his party together. The Liberal benches in the Commons are still largely occupied by men from the trading and manufacturing classes who have long been opposed to state intervention. Even more hostile to radicalism is the House of Lords, where the Conservative majority remains intact.→

Unions win battle over Taff Vale case

Westminster, December

A five-year campaign by trade unions to reverse a court ruling that gave strike damages to employers from union funds has ended in total victory. The Trades Disputes Bill was one of the first to be produced by the new Liberal government – and it has been approved untouched by the Tory-dominated House of Lords. The bill restores the protection to union funds which was generally thought to have existed before a 1901 case involving the Taff Vale Railway came before the law lords (→ 13/8/07).

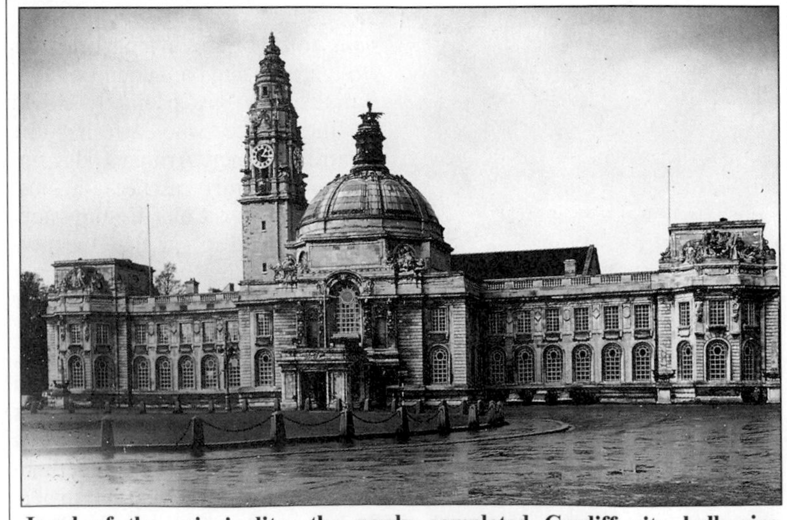

Jewel of the principality: the newly completed Cardiff city hall wins near-universal admiration as a triumph of Victorian-style architecture.

Britannia rules the waves with the launch of the world's most imposing battleship

HMS "Dreadnought": the supership will outgun and outpace any others.

England, 10 February
HMS *Dreadnought* was launched by King Edward VII today and immediately made every other battleship in the world obsolescent. The brainchild of the first sea lord, Admiral Sir "Jackie" Fisher, this revolutionary ship will mount ten 12-inch guns in five turrets. Eight of the guns will be able to fire salvoes of armour-piercing shells on either side of the ship, compared with the four guns of the present generation of battleships.

The *Dreadnought* is being equipped with steam turbines fuelled by oil, a system never tried before in a battleship. Much faster than previous ships, she will also be able to attack her enemy from a greater distance. Despite these overwhelming technical improvements, the *Dreadnought* programme aroused opposition within the admiralty. Some senior officers argued that making Britain's battlefleet obsolete destroyed the Royal Navy's numerical advantage over its rivals. But the blow to Germany will be even greater: the Kiel canal will have to be rebuilt if ships of this size are to pass through to the North Sea.

The need for such a warship was demonstrated, however, during the Russo-Japanese War when naval engagements were fought at long range. Naval strategists learnt that torpedo boats would have to be destroyed before they could get close enough to launch their deadly missiles, which have increased greatly in range and accuracy (→28/2/07).

More Londoners go down the 'tube'

London, 15 December
Another underground railway was inaugurated in London today, the second this year, running from Hammersmith to Finsbury Park. In March services began between Baker Street and Waterloo on what has been nicknamed the "Bakerloo" line. Both new lines, like the Central Line opened in 1900, run through circular tunnels (or tubes) at far greater depth than the older "cut and cover" Metropolitan and District Lines. A third new "tube", from Charing Cross to Golders Green, opens next year (→22/5/15).

'Man of Property': new style of novel

London, 31 December
John Galsworthy has come up with a new kind of novel this year which reflects changing society in succeeding generations of a single family. *The Man of Property*, its title, refers to Soames Forsyte, an Edwardian solicitor who values his houses, art collection and even his wife Irene as part of his social position. He is not a sympathetic character but is portrayed as typical of the upper-middle classes. Soames has doubts about the future, however, which would never have occurred to the Victorian ruling classes (→12/1913).

Eleven suffragettes jailed for their cause

London, 24 October
Women brought their campaign for the vote to Westminster yesterday in a rowdy demonstration at the Commons which saw several leading suffragettes arrested. Eleven of them – all members of the Women's Social and Political Union (WSPU) – were jailed today after refusing to pay fines of £10. Most of those arrested refused to acknowledge the court.

Sylvia Pankhurst: chose Holloway.

Among those beginning their sentences in Holloway prison tonight are Sylvia Pankhurst, a daughter of the WSPU's leader, and Emmeline Pethick Lawrence, the organization's treasurer. Mrs Pethick Lawrence said: "Women of England, we are going to prison for you and therefore we do it gladly. We call upon you to take up the standard and bear it on to victory."

This autumn has brought a new, violent chapter in the fight for women's suffrage. The WSPU take its task very seriously and uses its headquarters in Clement's Inn as a "battle headquarters". It favours a far more militant approach than the longer-established suffrage societies which generally prefer persuasion to protest (→25/12).

British Empire spans one-fifth of the globe

London, 8 March
It is official: Britain's empire now occupies one-fifth of the world's land surface. This and many other facts are published today in a 300-page government "blue book" drawing on data from the English local government board. The survey reveals that 400 million people now live under the British Empire. Its borders extend over 11.5 million square miles (29.79 million sq km), a third of which have been acquired in the last 25 years alone.

Just over a century ago Britain was still smarting at the loss of its American colonies. Now, by contrast, it has an empire on which the sun will never set – if only because, as someone has quipped, God would not trust an Englishman in the dark (→22/5).

Cornish tin miners make the most of "croust time", a break for pasties. Many children start working in the mines as early as the age of 12.

1907

Jamaica, 22 January. The island's British governor rejects an offer of medical and food aid from the US Navy after an earthquake.

Newcastle upon Tyne, 23 January. The Liberal David Lloyd George calls on the nation to defeat the power of the House of Lords (→ 12/4/08).

Ireland/Scotland, 5 February. Outbreaks of meningitis spread (→ 18/3/19).

Westminster, 12 February. The new parliamentary programme includes proposals for Irish home rule and better public housing (→ 10/12/09).

London, 14 February. A record number of suffragettes appear in court today after clashes with the police (→ 8/3).

London, 27 February. King Edward VII opens the new criminal courts at the Old Bailey (→ 9/6/08).

Britain, 28 February. Three more Dreadnought warships are to be ordered for the navy (→ 8/2/09).

Westminster, 8 March. A women's enfranchisement bill introduced by James Keir Hardie is defeated in the House of Commons (→ 22).

London, 22 March. More than 70 suffragettes are imprisoned for non-payment of fines (→ 16/11).

London, 24 April. Winston Churchill, the colonial under-secretary, is made a privy councillor (→ 15/8/08).

Westminster, 25 April. A Channel tunnel bill is defeated.

Belfast, 6 May. Dockers led by James Larkin go on strike (→ 13/8).

Dublin, 6 July. The Irish state jewels are discovered to have been stolen from the castle.

Poole, Dorset, 25 July. Twenty boys begin a "scouting" holiday on Brownsea Island organized by Sir Robert Baden-Powell (→ 16/1/08).

New Zealand, 10 September. The country gains autonomy as a dominion within the British Empire (→ 20/11/26).

London, 29 November. Florence Nightingale is appointed to the Order of Merit at the age of 87 (→ 20/8/10).

Middlesex, December. The English Rugby Union buys a site at Twickenham this year.

Suffragettes shout down cabinet minister

Warwickshire, 16 November
Militant suffragettes shouted down Herbert Asquith, the chancellor of the exchequer, at a meeting here today as part of their campaign to harass the government into support for a suffrage bill giving women the vote. The government has yet to throw its weight behind reform, and private bills have foundered, as did one introduced in March by James Keir Hardie, the Labour leader, for instance.

An act was passed this year to extend the right of women to sit as councillors, but they still lack a parliamentary vote. The failure to make progress has contributed to tensions within the suffrage movement. Some women are contemplating the formation of a new group, the Women's Freedom League, in protest against what they see as the domineering leadership of Mrs Emmeline Pankhurst, who heads the Women's Social and Political Union (WSPU). Yet internal divisions have not staunched the increasing militancy. Ministers are shouted down; women opt to be jailed rather than pay fines after being arrested; protests are staged in parliament (→ 30/1/08).

Suffragettes: now the fight hots up.

Concern grows over children's smoking

Exeter, Devon, 2 August
The king does it. Gentlemen and even some ladies do it. But doctors think too many children do it. Smoking amongst young people is increasing rapidly, and today at a meeting here of the British Medical Association doctors voiced their concern at this trend. Dr Herbert Tidswell, a Devon GP, attacked the habit as evil and claimed that it was damaging the health of the nation, causing, amongst other ailments, forms of cancer. He urged a campaign to stop children starting to smoke, although some other doctors said that the risks of moderate smoking had not been proved.

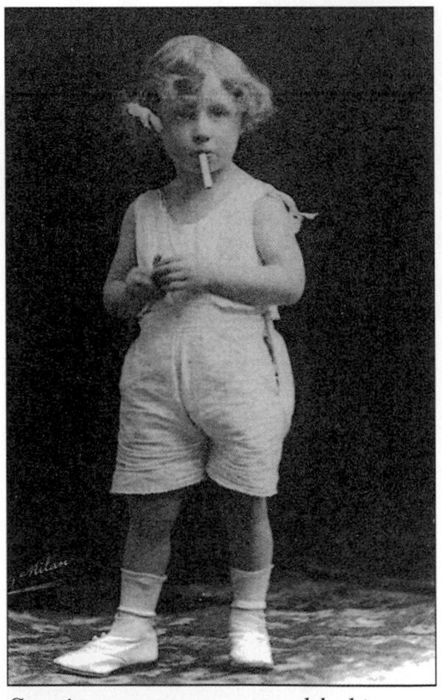
Starting young on a royal habit.

Riots in Dublin theatre over new play

Dublin, 28 January
Rioting in the Abbey theatre has broken up the first performances of *The Playboy of the Western World*, a new play by J M Synge set in the west of Ireland. The audience accused the author of misrepresenting peasant life in Ireland.

There was silence at the première until the third act, when fighting broke out. One of the theatre's founders, the writer W B Yeats, was sent a telegram in Scotland after the second act: "Play a great success." This was followed by a second telegram: "Audience broke up in disorder at the word shift [a woman's under-garment]." Police attended the second performance, but there was still uproar. The play focuses on a youth, Christy, who boasts that he has killed his father. Yeats plans to return from Scotland to defend the play.

Yeats defends "The Playboy of the Western World" from the Abbey stage.

War office unveils army reform plans

Whitehall, London, 13 January
Richard Haldane, the secretary of state for war, today announced far-reaching reforms in the administration and organization of the army. A general staff will head an army with an "expeditionary force" of six infantry divisions supported by a cavalry division plus artillery and logistical support to enable rapid mobilization. Support will also be provided by reorganizing the volunteer and militia detachments into a new "territorial force" organization of 14 divisions.

Two die as troops fire on strikers

Belfast, 13 August
A crippling three-month-old strike by dockers and unskilled workers in Belfast claimed its first victims when two civilians were shot dead yesterday by British soldiers protecting people still working in the Catholic Falls Road area of the city. One was a woman of 23, looking for her child, and the other was a man returning from his work.

A magistrate, Major Martin Thackeray, attempted to read the Riot Act to a crowd of 500 stone-throwers after four soldiers were injured but admitted that he was inaudible. James Larkin, the dockers' union leader, had urged mill workers to join the strike against low pay – often under 10 shillings [50p] a week – and the army decided to extend its protection to the Falls. By then both Protestant and Catholic workers were involved. Riots followed, becoming more serious until on 11 August a police van was ambushed on Grosvenor Road. The crowd grew to 2,000, and when a barracks was attacked the authorities sent in 2,600 soldiers, 80 cavalry and 500 police.

Belfast docks: bayonets are out as the Royal Irish Constabulary mobilizes.

Soldiers admitted to smashing windows and doors on the pretext of bayonet and cavalry charges. After the deaths yesterday the lord mayor responded to pleas by Catholic clergy and laity to withdraw the soldiers, who were originally deployed because some policemen were also on strike. Many Catholics feared attacks from neighbouring loyalist areas, but so far these have not materialized (→ 5/6/08).

English ship rules transatlantic waves

The SS "Lusitania": £2.6m to snatch the blue riband back from Germany.

New York, 11 October
Sirens resounded across New York harbour today to mark the arrival of the English ship *Lusitania* after a record-breaking crossing of the Atlantic. She had made the trip in just four days 19 hours and 52 minutes to beat the previous record by 11 hours and 46 minutes – at an average speed of just over 24 knots. This regains the "blue riband" for the fastest Atlantic crossing for Britain from Germany. The loss of the record had stung British pride and persuaded the government to give Cunard a loan of £2.6 million to build two new turbine vessels. Now the first, the *Lusitania*, has set a record without even trying, with the second, the *Mauretania*, due to make her maiden crossing next month (→ 13/5/15).

Stars go on strike in the music halls

London, 15 March
The show goes on again tonight as music halls reopen their doors after a pay dispute. Performers had gone on strike last month to back up their demand for more money, forcing several theatres to close or to use amateurs to provide entertainment for their customers. The strikes were by no means total, but no business was bad business for show business; after mediation the hall owners offered a deal which was accepted today.

Music halls draw far larger audiences than any other form of entertainment, with stars such as Marie Lloyd, Harry Lauder and George Robey known throughout the land. Most towns of any size have their own variety or music halls. So far music halls have not suffered unduly from the challenge of a new form of entertainment – cinema. However, the attraction of moving pictures is growing, which was another reason why the hall-owners wanted to end the pay dispute.

United Methodist Church holds first annual conference

London, 18 September
Nearly one thousand people were crammed into the City Road chapel of John Wesley in Islington today for the first conference of the United Methodist Church. It represents a three-way merger of the United Methodist Free Churches, the Methodist Connexion and the Bible Christians.

After the merger resolution was formally adopted the delegates rose and let themselves go in true Methodist fashion. The chapel rang to the sound of "Praise God, from whom all blessings flow". The newly elected president, the Rev Edward Boaden of Leamington, aged 80, then addressed the assembly. He said that the three groups "had met, not only because they thought union a good thing, but because they could not keep apart".

The new church has 184,000 members and 908 ministers. Other Methodist churches sent messages of support to the new church, and delegates were hopeful that it will lead to the union of all British Methodists. The strength of the movement as a whole can be gauged from the annual report of the Wesleyan Methodist Sunday School Union, which is just about to be issued. It will state that there are just over a million pupils in the 7,566 Methodist Sunday schools.

The "Nulli Secundus", Britain's first airship, rounds St Paul's after a flight from Farnborough. Strong winds later forced it to land at the Crystal Palace.

1908

London, 30 January. Nine suffragettes are arrested after incidents at the homes of cabinet ministers (→24/10).

Westminster, 27 February. A Licensing Bill which would cut drinking licences by a third is introduced (→26/9).

London, February. Lord Northcliffe, formerly Alfred Harmsworth, buys *The Times*.

Isle of Wight, 2 April. The destroyer HMS *Tiger* collides with the cruiser HMS *Berwick*; 35 sailors die.

Westminster, 7 May. The government proposes a weekly old age pension of 5/- [25p] for single people over 70, 7s 6d [37.5p] for a married couple (→24/9).

London, 19 May. A meeting calls for the establishment of a "national theatre".

Britain, 5 June. The Miners' Federation decides to affiliate to the Labour Representation Committee (→6/11).

Reval, Estonia, 9 June. King Edward VII meets the czar during the first visit by a reigning British monarch to Russia (→7/5/10).

London, 13 July. Controversy grows over why the Labour leader James Keir Hardie is not invited to the royal garden party for MPs.

Westminster, 1 August. The Irish Universities Act provides for two new universities in Ireland: one for Ulster, the other for the three southern provinces.

London, 15 August. Winston Churchill, the president of the board of trade, announces his engagement to Clementine Hosier (→23/10/11).

London, 26 September. An estimated 500,000 people demonstrate against the Licensing Bill in Hyde Park.

Britain, 31 October. Kaiser William of Germany causes an uproar by his anti-British remarks in an interview with the *Daily Telegraph* (→21/3/09).

Lancashire, 6 November. A cotton strike ends after seven weeks as workers agree to a wage cut (→28).

London, 28 November. The court of appeal rules that trade unions cannot use funds for political purposes (→2/9/10).

Stockholm, 10 December. Ernest Rutherford wins the Nobel prize for chemistry for his work on atoms.

Asquith steps up to be prime minister

Asquith: fondness for good life.

Churchill: expecting promotion.

Biarritz, France, 12 April
Herbert Asquith today became the first British prime minister to be appointed by kissing hands with his sovereign at a foreign hotel. He had travelled to Biarritz where King Edward VII is holidaying, following the resignation through ill health of Sir Henry Campbell-Bannerman. In fact Asquith has been acting premier for some time as Sir Henry's illness worsened.

There will be no dispute among Liberals about Asquith's right to succeed. He and Sir Henry had been rivals once, but he served loyally as chancellor of the exchequer and developed a high reputation as both a parliamentary performer and an administrator. He is a Yorkshireman, now aged 55, with a fondness for good living and, by his own admission, "clever and attractive women". He is not associated closely with the cause of social reform espoused by some of his more radical colleagues, but he is expected to promote the foremost of these, David Lloyd George, to be his own successor at the treasury. Two able junior ministers, Walter Runciman and Winston Churchill, can expect elevation to cabinet posts for trade and education (→24/4/09).

'Boy scouts' set up camp for first time

London, 16 January
The first edition of a new magazine, *Scouting for Boys*, is published today to encourage the growth of a new movement which is headed by Sir Robert Baden-Powell, the hero of Mafeking. He wrote a book on the idea in 1906 and last year took 20 boys from widely different backgrounds on an experimental camping holiday to Brownsea Island in Poole harbour. There they were introduced to what Sir Robert sees as the character-forming activities of army scouts living in the open, such as fire-making, woodcraft and life-saving. The first scout "troops" were formed last year (→4/9/09).

Baden-Powell: scouting hero.

'White City' marks Anglo-French entente

London, 14 May
Even a downpour could not dim the splendour of the Franco-British exhibition which was opened today by the Prince of Wales. More than 80 hectares (200 acres) of west London have been transformed by 25 palaces and halls, gardens and lakes to be a showcase for the two countries. The gleaming stone of many buildings has earned the exhibition the popular name of "White City". Also part of the site at Shepherd's Bush is a large sports stadium which will be used for the Olympic Games later this summer. As a symbol of Anglo-French accord four years after the *Entente Cordiale*, the White City seems certain to be a hugely popular success. Already a "tube" line has been extended to bring the crowds.

The "flip-flap" exhibition ride.

Cricket shocked by life without Grace

Gloucestershire, September
The most famous cricketer in the world has played his last first-class match. At the age of 60 Dr William Gilbert Grace (but better known by his initials "W G") played for the Gentlemen of England against Surrey this season but has said he will not play again. Thus ends a career which began in 1870 with Gloucestershire and included 22 caps for England. He was the first man to score a century for his country, the first to score 1,000 runs in May, the first to score 100 centuries and the first to perform the "double" of 1,000 runs and 100 wickets in a season. In all he scored 54,211 runs and took 2,808 wickets in first-class cricket (→8/5/23).

Court sends the Pankhursts to prison

London, 24 October
The leader of the most militant suffragette group, Mrs Emmeline Pankhurst, and one of her daughters, Christabel, were jailed today at the end of a sensational trial which saw two cabinet ministers summoned to appear as witnesses for their defence. The two women were found guilty of conduct likely to cause a breach of the peace by inciting members of the public to "rush" the House of Commons nine days ago.

Mrs Pankhurst, who heads the Women's Social and Political Union, startled the court by calling Herbert Gladstone, the home secretary, and David Lloyd George, the chancellor of the exchequer, as witnesses for her defence. The ministers had been reluctant to attend, but compelled to do so they attested to the orderliness of the demonstration on 13 October. So did other witnesses; one woman said that she had been jostled more at society weddings.

However, Mr Gladstone rejected Mrs Pankhurst's claim that she and her supporters should be treated as political prisoners. And the magistrates were equally unmoved by both the ministerial evidence and the spell-binding oratory of Mrs Pankhurst's tearful closing address. Five thousand police had been needed to keep order, and if the Pankhursts would not be bound over to keep the peace, or be willing to pay any fines levied by the court, they must go to jail (→12/10/09).

Solidarity: the Pankhursts in jail.

Old people sign up for first pensions

British Isles, 24 September
Old people queued today to register for the first pensions, payable in the New Year. The principle of old age pensions was announced in the budget last May. They were proclaimed by Herbert Asquith, the prime minister, as non-contributory pensions for everybody, but they only begin at the age of 70 and the money on offer is relatively modest: five shillings [25p] for an individual and – as though to penalize marriage vows – seven shillings and sixpence [37.5p] for a married couple. Those earning ten shillings [50p] or more a week are disqualified from the scheme. Payments will be made at post offices, with the first payday set for 1 January 1909 (→1/1/09).

Britain is the proud host to Olympics Games

Marathon man: Dorando is helped at the tape but later wins a gold cup.

London, July
An Italian runner who lost won the hearts of London at the Olympic Games this month. It was the first time that the Olympics have been staged in Britain, with no fewer than 21 different sports in what was the greatest sporting festival ever seen in this country. The centrepiece was the new stadium at White City in west London, and it was here that Dorando Pietri had his moments of glory – and agony. He had entered the stadium with a commanding lead in the 26-mile (42-km) marathon, only to stumble and stagger towards the finishing line. Well-meaning stewards picked him up so that, although he crossed the line first, he was later disqualified. The crowd's admiration for his courage was so great, however, that he later received a gold cup from Queen Alexandra.

Competitors from Britain offered the greatest challenge to the United States in the athletics events and dominated the rowing (staged at Henley), boxing, yachting, archery and cycling events.

Elgar's reputation soars to new heights

Manchester, December
It was here in the Free Trade Hall that the year's most notable musical première took place. Sir Edward Elgar's first symphony was an immediate popular success, so much so that it has already been performed nearly 100 times. But it has also confirmed Elgar's status as England's leading composer. The symphony, like his oratorio *The Dream of Gerontius* in 1900, is a work on the grand scale yet full of the melodies which appeal to the Edwardian public. The trio from the first of his four *Pomp and Circumstance Marches* was set to words in coronation year by A C Benson to become a rival national anthem as *Land of Hope and Glory* (→4/5/24).

Cowboy makes first flight in British Isles

Hampshire, 16 October
A former American cowboy in a French-engined aeroplane today became the first man to make a powered flight in the British Isles. He also became the first to crash. Samuel Cody was flying a plane financed by the war office at Farnborough in Hampshire. Helped by a strong tailwind the plane, *British Army Aeroplane No 1*, rose to 30 feet and continued for just over a quarter of a mile (400m) before Cody took too sharp a turn and crashed. Bleeding but undaunted, Cody emerged from the crash still wearing his Texas hat and apologized for the accident. He said, however, that he had "constructed a machine which flies". Britain has so far lagged behind the French and Americans in aviation (→19/3/09).

"British Army Airplane No 1" is wheeled out for trials at Farnborough.

1909

British Isles, 1 January. Thousands of people aged over 70 line up for their first old age pensions (→ 17/2).

Antarctica, 9 January. A British expedition has halted 111 miles (178km) from the South Pole – the closest yet to it (→ 1/6/10).

Britain, 8 February. The government says that the navy is to have six more Dreadnoughts (→ 9/3/11).

Brighton, 24 February. Colour films are screened in Britain for the first time (→ 20/12).

Britain, 12 March. British workers are better off than their counterparts in Germany or France, says a survey.

London, 15 March. Selfridge's department store opens with slogan "All your shopping under one roof".

London, 19 March. Britain's first international aircraft exhibition opens (→ 31/12).

Widnes, Cheshire, 9 April. The first closed-top double-decker buses in Britain begin service.

Westminster, 22 April. A bill is introduced in the House of Commons to abolish the censorship of plays (→ 20/8).

Dover, 25 July. The Frenchman Louis Blériot becomes the first man to fly across the Channel.

Westminster, 20 August. Two writers Bernard Shaw and Thomas Hardy appear before a Commons committee seeking freedom from stage censorship.

London, 4 September. Eleven thousand boy scouts attend their first national parade at the Crystal Palace (→ 31/5/10).

London, 7 September. Lord Northcliffe, the owner of *The Times*, claims that Germany is preparing for war (→ 8/1/10).

Westminster, 3 December. King Edward VII dissolves parliament, and because no budget has been passed taxes are lifted on beer, spirits, cigarettes and cars.

London, 10 December. Herbert Asquith, the prime minister, promises "self-government" for Ireland in a speech at the Royal Albert Hall (→ 11/1910).

Dublin, 20 December. The *Volta* cinema opens, the first in Ireland (→ 5/11/12).

Belfast, 31 December. Harry Ferguson makes the first aeroplane flight from Irish soil, at Hillsborough, near Belfast (→ 12/7/10).

Fears grow as arms race gathers speed

A new arm of the Royal Navy: submarines gather in Dover harbour.

Westminster, 21 March
There was dismay in the House of Commons today when Reginald McKenna, the first lord of the admiralty, told the house that the government had underestimated Admiral von Tirpitz's programme to rebuild the German navy.

Von Tirpitz intends to dispute Britain's naval supremacy and, according to Mr McKenna, may soon have more of the new Dreadnought-class battleships than the Royal Navy. The admiralty has been aware of this danger for some months and wanted to build six new Dreadnoughts. Some cabinet ministers feared that the cost of these more powerful and faster capital ships would torpedo the government's social reforms and so proposed a compromise: four ships this year and four more in the future. This has not appeased critics of the government. "We want eight and we won't wait" has become a popular slogan as pressure mounts on Asquith's government (→ 7/9).

Commission condemns workhouse laws

No more workhouses for children.

London, 17 February
No more children should live in workhouses, says a royal commission on Britain's poor laws. The commission split over the scale and speed of changes, but both majority and minority reports call for the boards of guardians who control poor law relief to be scrapped in favour of local government control.

Up to a third of people living in Britain's major cities and towns end their days in poor law institutions. These include children's homes, infirmaries and lunatic asylums as well as the workhouses themselves which have come to symbolize the poor law system. Old age pensions introduced this year are a modest attempt to ease poverty in the wider community as an alternative to institutional help. The commission backs this approach and wants children in particular to be helped outside the workhouse (→ 4/5/11).

White South Africa forms a new Union

London, 7 December
The Union of South Africa was proclaimed today, uniting the British Cape Colony and Natal with the Boer Transvaal and Orange River colonies. The act marks the fulfilment of a promise made at the end of the Boer War. All the white colonies in the British Empire are now self-governing.

The Afrikaners, having lost the war, have won the peace, although English settlers remain strong politically, economically and socially. Apart from the Coloureds in the Cape, the native people (plus Asiatics and people of mixed descent) have no vote.

General Botha, the Boer leader who has emerged as the most prominent advocate of reconciliation with the British, will be prime minister of the new dominion.

Hunger strike ends in 'force feeding'

Birmingham, 12 October
The high court today ordered an inquiry to be held at Winson Green prison in Birmingham after allegations by a suffragette that she was repeatedly force fed. Mrs Laura Ainsworth was imprisoned for obstructing the police and in jail adopted the new suffragette tactic of going on hunger strike. In an affidavit Mrs Ainsworth, who is now recovering in a nursing home, claims that after three days she was pinioned by wardresses while a prison doctor tried to force a cup through her teeth and a tube 60cm (2 feet) in length up her nostrils. Medical evidence to the court said that this entailed grave risks and should be investigated (→ 26/1/10).

Advertising a new detergent.

Budget stuns the Tories

Lloyd George raises taxes for pensions

Westminster, 24 April
David Lloyd George, the Liberals' radical chancellor of the exchequer, today stunned the Tory opposition with a "supertax" of sixpence [2.5p] in the pound on people earning over £5,000 a year. For people earning £2,000 a year the standard rate goes up to 1s 2d [6p].

There were other taxes, too, in his budget – new ones on petrol, car licences and land value, plus higher ones on tobacco and alcoholic drinks. These have all been imposed to pay for welfare schemes such as old age pensions and labour exchanges plus a major rearmament programme provoked by Germany's rapidly growing naval power. Money raised by taxes on motorists will also go into a special road fund to build new roads to accommodate the increasing number of motor cars. Altogether the new taxes make the budget the biggest in the nation's history.

One after another, Tory MPs denounced the budget as an attack on the propertied classes, who were described as the foundation of the nation's prosperity. The doubling of death duties, it was claimed, would lead to penny-pinching on large estates and harm local tradesmen and the labouring classes.

To the Tory-controlled House of Lords, the most provocative aspect of Lloyd George's budget is a scheme to be implemented later. All the land in the country is to be valued and a 20 per cent tax levied on "unearned increment". Yet Lloyd George has fashioned a politically astute package of measures, with many widely popular social reforms that have already led to the nickname "the people's budget".

Lloyd George: new taxes anger rich.

Lloyd George is unruffled by the Tory uproar; there is nothing he enjoys more than "dishing the dukes". Labour MPs view the budget with mixed feelings. They agree with many of its proposals, but are irritated that it has enabled the Liberals to seize the initiative on social reform (→30/11).

Mackintosh is the toast of Glasgow in a resurgence of British architectural style

Glasgow, December
Glasgow School of Art, a revolutionary building designed by a local architect, Charles Rennie Mackintosh, has been completed this year with the addition of its library wing. It is perhaps the highlight of a resurgent confidence among British architects.

Mackintosh won the competition to build the school of art when he was only 26. His style is spare and simple in outline, with tall projecting glass casements and light airy balustrades of ironwork for its only decoration. The interiors, also by him, have exposed structural beams of steel or timber. The overall plainness is relieved by the angular, yet subtly geometrical shapes of his tables and chairs. He is much admired abroad.

The competition to design Liverpool's Anglican cathedral was won in 1903 by Giles Gilbert Scott, who was then 22 and had built nothing. Work began in 1904, but Scott has changed his Gothic design to one with a huge central tower, baroque in spirit with Gothic details. Baroque is the fashion for public building, as in Aston Webb's work (the Victoria and Albert museum) and, also in London, the new county hall (Ralph Knott, 1907) and the Old Bailey (E W Mountford, 1907).

The solidity and pomp of the baroque style appeal to the Edwardian mind. A more individual style is being developed by Edwin Lutyens. So far this has been confined to country houses, such as Castle Drogo now being built in Devon, but it seems only a matter of time before he finds a more public stage.

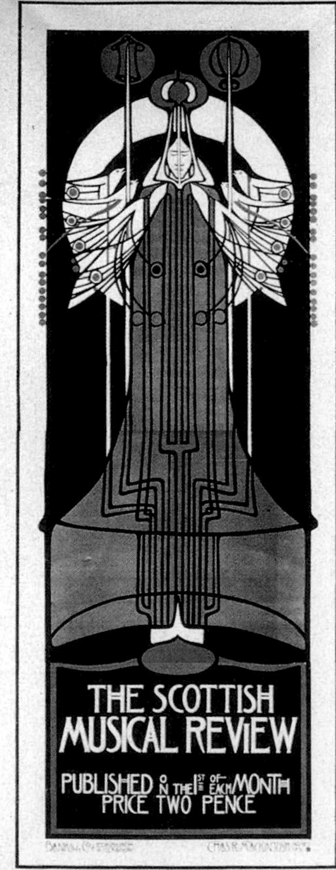

A poster design by Mackintosh.

'People's budget' thrown out by Lords

Westminster, 30 November
In the House of Lords tonight, with bejewelled peeresses looking on from the public galleries, the Tory-dominated peers overwhelmingly rejected Lloyd George's "people's budget", a controversial package of higher taxes and social reforms. The stage is now set for a major constitutional crisis which has been building up since the Liberals were returned to power in 1906 after years in the political wilderness.

Tory peers soon began rejecting bills sent up by the new government. A licensing bill to cut down the number of public houses was thrown out, as were other bills on education and Scotland. The Liberals did not react at the time, but it was a different matter when the Finance Bill implementing this year's budget proposals was attacked by the Lords.

For half a century it has been accepted that the non-elected Lords cannot reject a money bill from the Commons. But the Tories argued that the budget had too many non-money measures to be accepted as a finance bill. Faced with the peers' intransigence, the prime minister, Herbert Asquith, will call an election (→14/2/10).

Heathcote, a house at Ilkley designed by Edwin Lutyens in 1906.

1910

Britain, 8 January. Germany's military build-up becomes an election issue (→ 2/2).

London, 26 January. Police rescue the prime minister, Herbert Asquith, when he is mobbed by furious suffragettes (→ 17/6/11).

Britain, 1 February. The new labour exchanges are besieged by job-hunters.

Britain, 2 February. A report says that the country could face a serious shortage of horses should war break out (→ 22/7/12).

Westminster, 21 February. Sir Edward Carson is elected as leader of the Irish Unionist MPs (→ 23/9/11).

London, 22 February. Thomas Beecham conducts the first performance of Frederick Delius's opera *A Village Romeo and Juliet*.

London, 8 March. A royal commission is told that the cost of an undefended divorce is £81 and that of a defended one £121.

Wales, 11 March. In a dam-burst in the Rhondda valley 500 children are swept away; 494 are rescued (→ 26/8/11).

Westminster, 14 April. Asquith tells MPs that he has discussed with the king creating 300 new peers to approve the new Parliament Bill curbing the Lords (→ 16/6).

London, 6 May. Edward VII dies (→ 20).

Britain, 31 May. A sister organization to the Boy Scouts is formed, to be known as the Girl Guides.

London, 1 June. Captain Robert Scott sets out on a new attempt to reach the South Pole (→ 14/12/11).

London, 23 June. The king's eldest son, David, is created prince of Wales.

Bournemouth, 12 July. Charles Rolls, co-founder of the Rolls-Royce car company, dies in a flying accident (→ 13/4/12).

Britain, 2 September. Shipbuilders give 24 hours' notice of a lockout of 40,000 boilermakers (→ 9/11).

London, 23 November. Dr Crippen is hanged for his wife's murder.

Ireland, November. The first issue of *Irish Freedom*, the monthly publication of the Irish Republican Brotherhood, appears (→ 23/9/11).

Edward VII mourned by the nation

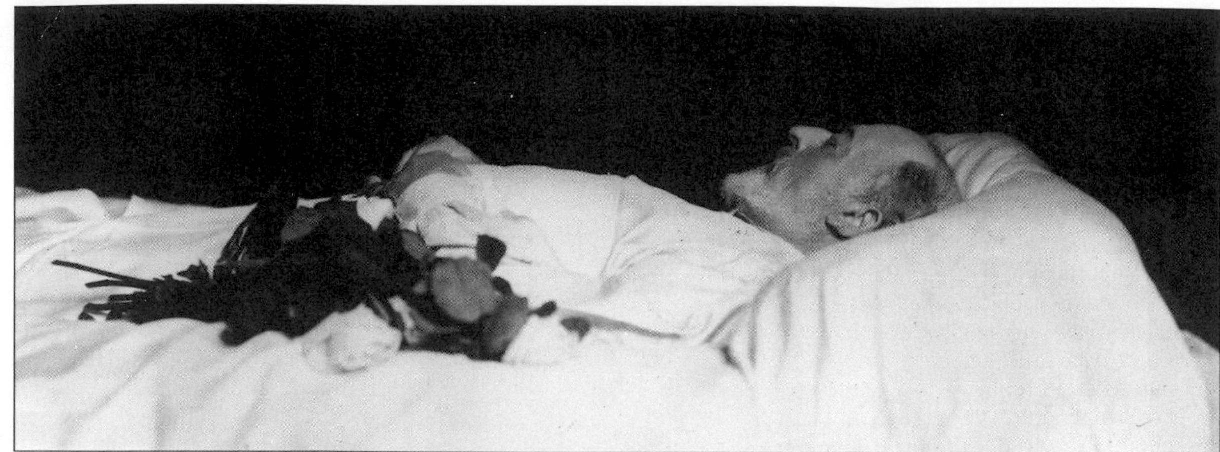

Edward VII lies in state: a beloved king who waited long in the wings. He shed his playboy image to work for peace.

Windsor, Berkshire, 20 May
The people of Britain were in deep mourning today for their beloved King Edward VII. The sovereign who had shed his playboy image to become a peacemaker was buried in the family vault in St George's chapel, Windsor Castle. He had died of bronchitis on 6 May barely a week after returning from what was intended to be partly a convalescent holiday in Biarritz. On 29 April he attended the opera at Covent Garden before spending the weekend at Sandringham. He returned to London with a chill but continued to work despite increasing difficulty breathing. The queen was in Corfu when he was taken ill and was only able to get home the day before the king died.

Edward was 59 when he finally came to the throne after a lifetime as prince of Wales which saw him embroiled more than once in scandal. He at once brought a sense of fun to court life, after the dour Victorian years; but he revealed a capacity for hard work and diplomacy that surprised many. Visits to France paved the way for the *Entente Cordiale* of 1904, and he was close to the rulers of other European countries, notably Germany and Russia. He is succeeded by his son, George (→ 1/2/11).

Radio link catches alleged killer at sea

Canada, 31 July
Transatlantic radio was used to arrest a suspected murderer today when Dr Hawley Harvey Crippen was taken into custody by police in Quebec. Police have been looking for Crippen and his mistress, Ethel le Neve, since they found the mutilated and dismembered body of his wife beneath the floorboards of his London house. Crippen and le Neve had posed as "Mr Robinson and son" on the SS *Montrose* from Antwerp to Canada, but the captain became suspicious. He radioed British police, who caught a faster ship to arrest the couple on their arrival in Canada (→ 23/11).

Crippen and le Neve are arrested.

Pit disaster kills 'up to 350 men'

Bolton, 22 December
The pit village of Westhoughton near Bolton is in mourning tonight after an explosion at the colliery which threatens to be Britain's second worst mining disaster. Up to 350 men are missing, and hope is fading. So far only one 16-year-old miner has been brought out alive, although rescue attempts continue. The cause of the blast, at a mine previously regarded as one of the safest and best-equipped in the county, is not yet known. If no more survivors are found, some 1,000 children will be orphans.

Nation pays tribute to Florence Nightingale, pioneer of nursing

London, 20 August
St Paul's Cathedral was packed today for a memorial service to Florence Nightingale, the great pioneer of nursing, who died last week at the age of 90. Later her coffin was drawn by two horses through the streets of London on its way to Waterloo and a family funeral in Hampshire. The coffin was covered by floral tributes – from Queen Alexandra, from London hospitals and from veterans of the Crimea. One of the wreathes was shaped like the army lantern she carried on her rounds in Scutari hospital during the Crimean War. She first made her name there, but she also left a lasting impression on the organization of nursing in hospitals at home.

King, peers and MPs split over who rules Britain

Labour props up Liberals after election

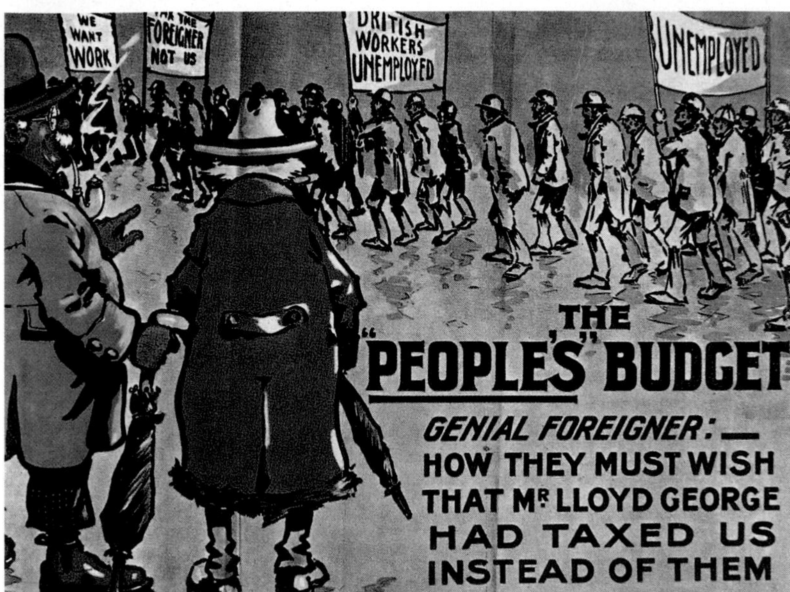

An election poster shows how strongly Tories feel about "the people's budget".

Westminster, 14 February
The general election has failed to give Herbert Asquith's government a "people's mandate" to push through last year's supertax budget against the opposition of the Lords. The chastened Liberals now have 273 MPs against 397 in the last parliament. The Tories also now have 273 MPs, Labour 42 and the Irish Nationalists 82. Asquith has returned to London from Cannes to find that his survival as prime minister depends on the support of Labour and the Nationalists. The Tories are being attacked because their defeat of the Finance Bill in the House of Lords has landed the treasury with a £10 million debt.

It is now expected that the combined Liberal-Labour-Nationalist majority in the Commons will resubmit the Finance Bill, and that the Lords will accept it. Then the real struggle will begin – to curb the powers of the peers. It is a battle which could embroil the crown in the party political fight (→ 14/4).

Commons backs moves to curb the Lords

London, 16 June
Leaders of the main parties met at Downing Street today for a constitutional conference first suggested by the new king, George V. He had come to the throne after the Commons had passed the Parliament Bill which enables measures passed by the Commons in three separate sessions to be given the royal assent without the consent of the Lords. A money bill would become law one month after passing the Commons.

If the Lords put up a fight, the prime minister, Herbert Asquith, intends to ask the king to create upwards of 300 new peers to swamp the hereditary Tory majority there. George hopes that talks will avoid this, but most politicians believe that a second election over "who rules Britain" is inevitable (→ 20/12).

The new king: seeking a truce between the Commons and the Lords.

Reluctant king backs plan to beat Lords

Westminster, 20 December
The second general election in 12 months over the constitutional clash with the has left the strength of the parties virtually unchanged. The Tories have 273 MPs, the Liberals 271, Labour 42 and the Irish Nationalists 84. But with Labour and Nationalist support the Liberal government can now push through the House of Commons its bill to curb the powers of the Lords. Herbert Asquith, the prime minister, will do so armed with the pledge given – albeit reluctantly – by King George V that he will create several hundred new peers to overwhelm any resistance by diehard peers. Even so some Tories plan to continue the fight which began when the Lords rejected the 1909 "people's budget" (→ 10/8/11).

Troops patrol Welsh streets after strikers clash with the police

Mid-Glamorgan, 9 November
A squadron of the 18th Hussars appeared on the streets of Tonypandy in south Wales today following clashes yesterday between strikers from the Cambrian collieries and police "specials" sent from London. The troops had been summoned after the strikers had stoned the police. Winston Churchill, the home secretary, ordered them to wait at Cardiff overnight, but the failure of a second police force to restore order brought the soldiers under General Macready. They found the strikers silent but orderly. "We might fight the police, but not regular soldiers with rifles," said one miner (→ 26/8/11).

Tonypandy: Metropolitan police arrive (with bedding) as strike spreads.

Nationalism stirs Scots and Welsh

Westminster, November
The confrontation between the Commons and the Lords has effectively sidelined discussion of greater independence from Westminster for Scotland and Wales. Until recently talk of "home rule" has focused solely on Ireland, but the model of a federation in Canada was raised at the constitutional conference set up at the behest of the king which ended without success this month. Home rule for Scotland is Liberal policy, but the government does not want to embark on another constitutional clash with the Tories, who oppose the idea.

1911

London, 18 January. An inquest returns verdicts of suffocation and justifiable homicide on two people killed during the Sidney Street siege.

London, 1 February. Edward Mylius, who accused King George V of bigamy, is sentenced to prison for criminal libel (→ 30/6).

Derby, 4 February. Rolls-Royce commissions a "Spirit of Ecstasy" mascot for the bonnets of its cars.

London, 9 March. Five more battleships are to be built, says the government.

Westminster, 31 March. The government's Shops Bill is proposing a 60-hour week for shopworkers, including half-day holidays.

London, 4 April. The duke of Marlborough and others oppose plans by Eton College to abolish the birch.

Westminster, 7 April. The Commons give a second reading to a bill giving copyright during authors' lifetimes and for 50 years after their deaths.

Belfast, 31 May. The White Star liner *Titanic* is launched (→ 15/4/12).

London, 17 June. Some 60,000 women march through London demanding the vote (→ 1/3/12).

London, 30 June. The king and queen hold a coronation fête for 100,000 children at the Crystal Palace (→ 10/12).

Westminster, 10 August. MPs' annual salaries are to be £400.

London, 26 August. At least 2,500 children are reported to have died in the recent heatwave (→ 26/8/12).

Wexford, 26 August. A lock-out begins of foundrymen who are demanding the right to join the Irish Transport and General Workers' Union (→ 29).

Wales, 29 August. An inquest returns verdicts of justifiable homicide on the strikers who were victims of the Llanelli shootings by troops (→ 31).

London, 23 October. Winston Churchill is appointed first lord of the admiralty (→ 6/11/24).

Antarctica, 14 December. The Norwegian Roald Amundsen beats Captain Robert Scott to the South Pole (→ 17/1/12).

Lancashire, 27 December. Some 300,000 cotton workers are idle after an employers' lockout (→ 15/6/12).

Two die as blaze ends 'anarchist' siege

Sidney Street: The home secretary, Winston Churchill, watches and waits.

London, 3 January
The siege of Sidney Street in the east end of London has ended with at least two members of an alleged "anarchist" gang being burnt to death in the house where they had been cornered by 1,000 soldiers and armed police. The gang's leader, known as "Peter the Painter", may have escaped. An unprecedented operation, personally supervised by Winston Churchill, the home secretary, was set in motion after three policemen had been murdered by the gang. Armed detectives arrived at 4am at 100 Sidney Street, just off the Mile End Road, to be met by a volley of pistol fire. One policeman was wounded.

Reinforcements included Scots Guards from the Tower of London, with a Maxim gun, and soldiers of the Royal Artillery with two 13-pounders. Pistol- and rifle-fire was poured into the house, while the anarchists replied with automatic weapons. Ten people were injured.

Smoke came from the chimney at 12.50pm, but Churchill forbade firemen to intervene. Within an hour the house was ablaze. Later two charred bodies were found (→ 18).

Tory peers bow to power of Commons

Westminster, 10 August
In the last hour before midnight, Tory peers shrank back from a last-ditch fight and, with most of them abstaining, allowed the controversial Parliament Bill to be passed by 131 votes to 114. The bill decrees that the Lords will have no legal power over money bills and will be able to hold up other measures passed by the Commons by no more than two years.

With the supremacy of the elected Commons now beyond question, MPs have agreed to reduce the maximum interval between elections from seven years to five. The Commons can thus effectively override the Lords only in the first years of a government's life, when it can claim a popular mandate.

The Tories were decisively influenced by the knowledge that, if they continued to fight, King George V would accept the list prepared by Herbert Asquith, the prime minister, and create upwards of 300 new peers who would vote for the bill.

Though much has been made of the fact that the Commons are an elected body, they are less than fully representative. There are around eight million voters in a population of over 42 million. Only six out of ten adult males have the vote, and women are still excluded from the franchise (→ 13/11).

Father and son crowned king and prince in year of pageantry

Royal occasions: King George V is crowned head of the world's greatest empire on 23 June. The following month his son, Edward Albert (known to the family as David), is invested as prince of Wales at Caernarfon Castle.

Troops and unions clash

Liverpool: 50,000 armed soldiers prepare to break riots in the north.

Liverpool, 31 August
A long hot summer of riots and strikes is ending, but only after bloody clashes between troops and trade unionists in what has been the hottest summer since 1868. Action by seamen in June sparked the wave of unrest. They won concessions which encouraged others, notably dockers who struck in several major ports. A settlement was reached in London, but the Liverpool dispute flared into serious rioting. Troops were sent, and on 15 August two men were shot dead in clashes. Two men were also killed by troops in Llanelli, where shops and a train were looted; five more died there in an explosion.

Industrial relations were equally explosive; the railway unions rejected the prime minister's plea and called their first national strike. With the country almost at a standstill David Lloyd George took over for the government and with Labour's James Ramsay MacDonald had talks with the railmen, reaching agreement on 19 August. Deals with the dockers followed and, as temperatures fell below 32C [90F], an uneasy peace ensued (→27/12).

King is crowned emperor of India

Delhi, 10 December
King George was today enthroned as emperor of India in a ceremony of great pageantry and splendour. The cabinet was unenthusiastic about the king's determination to attend today's *durbar*, but the monarch wanted to demonstrate the importance he accorded to his Indian empire. He also used the occasion to announce that the capital is to be transferred from Calcutta to Delhi, where the architect Sir Edwin Lutyens is to design imposing new buildings as symbols of British rule in what is by far the largest and most populous country in the empire (→30/3/15).

New leaders named

Westminster, 13 November
The Conservative Party today became the second party to change its leader this year. Andrew Bonar Law, aged 53, succeeds Arthur Balfour, who has resigned for health reasons. In February, James Ramsay Macdonald took over from James Keir Hardie as Labour leader. Both of the new leaders are Scots, although Bonar Law was born in Canada before being brought up in Glasgow (→25/5/15).

Art without taste finds champions in Camden Town

London, December
The newly formed "Camden Town Group" of 16 painters is holding an exhibition as a breakaway from the new English Art Club. Founded by Walter Sickert, a pupil of Whistler and an admirer of Degas, the group was much influenced by the Post-Impressionist exhibition of the works of Gauguin, van Gogh and Cézanne put on in London last year by the critic Roger Fry, which was met with a furore of incomprehension.

Sickert named the group after the working-class area of north London where he set up a studio to paint what are thought "sordid" subjects – prostitutes' bedrooms, music-hall galleries and cloth-capped passers-by "going to the pub". Taste, Sickert declares, is the death of a painter; he says: "The more our art is serious, the more it will tend to avoid the drawing room and stick to the kitchen." His associates, Harold Gimna, Spencer Gore, Charles Ginner and Robert Bevan, find their subjects in cheap eating-houses, railway stations and industrial landscape. In contrast the portrait work of Augustus John is firmly traditional, although his bohemian life-style is notorious. His sister Gwen's portraits of women are ultra-restrained.

"The Café Royal" by Charles Ginner, a member of the group.

Sickness insurance scheme is planned

Westminster, 4 May
A national insurance scheme to protect workers against sickness and unemployment was unveiled today by David Lloyd George, the chancellor of the exchequer, as the latest chapter of the Liberal government's social reforms. Old age pensions, labour exchanges and trade boards are now to be followed by a scheme in which employers, employees and the state all pay weekly premiums into a fund for sickness and unemployment benefits. The sickness scheme will cover 15 million workers with wages below £3 a week, but the unemployment insurance will cover only 2.25 million out of 19 million workers. Both schemes are intended to be self-financing (→13/1/13).

Carson addresses anti-home rule rally

Edward Carson: "Prepare to govern!"

Belfast, 23 September
The prospect of an Ulster Unionist backlash against home rule for Ireland came closer today with a defiant warning by Sir Edward Carson, the leader of the Irish Unionist MPs at Westminster. At a rally attended by 50,000 Ulster loyalists Sir Edward denounced home rule as "a tyranny to which we cannot submit". The Dublin-born lawyer, a former Irish solicitor-general, solemnly called on loyalists to defeat "the most nefarious conspiracy that has ever been hatched against a free people". He added: "We must be prepared ... ourselves to become responsible for the government of the Protestant province of Ulster." To cheers he said that Irish loyalists "should undertake the administration of the districts they are entitled to control" (→9/5/12).

1912

Britain, 1 January. The Post Office takes over the National Telephone Company.

London, 8 January. Producers must in future obtain licences from the lord chamberlain to stage music-hall plays.

Antarctica, 17 January. Captain Robert Scott reaches the South Pole (→10/2/13).

Westminster, 4 March. Police arrest 96 women after a suffragette raid on the House of Commons (→11/11).

Westminster, 27 March. The Commons pass the Coal Miners' Bill, giving miners a minimum wage.

London, 28 March. The university boat race is to be re-run after both boats sink.

Britain, 13 April. The Royal Flying Corps is formed (→2/10/13).

New York, 18 April. The liner *Carpathia* arrives carrying survivors from the *Titanic* (→24).

New York, 24 April. Officers from the *Titanic* say that hundreds drowned as the result of an inadequate supply of lifeboats (→2/5).

London, 2 May. The *Titanic* inquiry opens (→3/7).

Clonmel, Co Tipperary, 28 June. The Irish Labour Party is formed.

London, 2 July. Music-hall stars appear in the first Royal Variety Performance.

London, 3 July. Captain Smith of the *Titanic* – who went down with his ship – is found guilty of negligence.

Belfast, 12 July. More than 120,000 Ulstermen attend a rally against home rule for Ireland (→28/9).

Mediterranean, 22 July. Britain's fleet is ordered to move to the North Sea in order to counter the German naval build-up (→13/4/13).

England, 26 August. The worst August rainfall on record – six inches in 12 hours – cuts off Norwich and other towns.

London, 5 November. A British film censor is appointed (→26/3/27).

East London, 26 November. George Lansbury, the former Labour MP for Bow and Bromley who resigned to test public opinion on women's suffrage, is defeated in a by-election.

The 'unsinkable' sinks

The "unsinkable": last moments.

North Atlantic, 15 April
The pride of British shipping, the SS *Titanic*, sank in the early hours of this morning after hitting an iceberg on her maiden voyage. More than 1,500 of the 2,340 passengers and crew aboard a liner proclaimed as "unsinkable" are feared to have drowned. If so, it would be the highest-ever death toll in a shipping disaster.

The *Titanic* was regarded as unsinkable because of her 16 watertight compartments. But as the ship sped through the icy ocean in pursuit of the fastest-ever Atlantic crossing she hit an iceberg and sank within hours. The wireless operator, Harold Bride, was one of the survivors. He described the scene as he swam for his life: "The ship was tilting gradually onto her nose, like a duck going for a dive. The band was still playing. I guess all of them went down."

Several millionaires and the managing director of the White Star line got away in the first lifeboat. Others told of swimmers being pushed away from the lifeboats as the panic mounted, and passengers who sacrificed their lives helping women and children to safety. One question for an inquiry will be why there were so few lifeboats. Another will be whether any warnings about icebergs were ignored (→18).

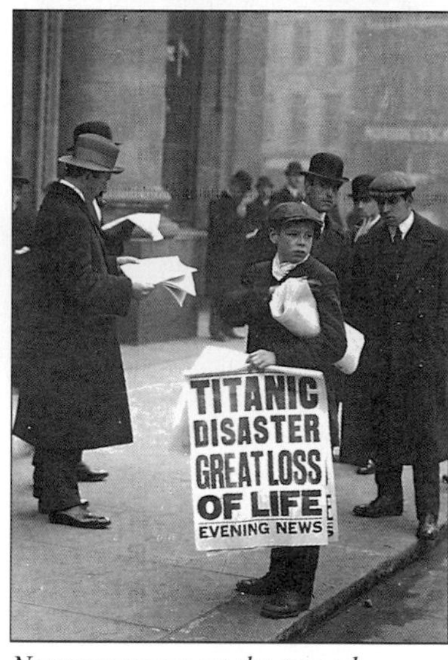

Newspapers report the tragedy.

Welsh Church Bill gets second chance

Westminster, 16 May
Despite protests by church leaders MPs have backed a bill that would disestablish the Church of England in Wales. Herbert Asquith, the prime minister, argued that the "clear and firm" precedent of Irish disestablishment gave parliament the right to legislate in this area. He said that the bill would remove the greatest obstacle to cooperation among Christians in Wales where nonconformist chapel membership is strong. If the Lords object, as is widely expected, the new powers of the Parliament Act could enable the bill to become law in three years if it is supported each year by the Commons.

Attempts to spread the dock strike flop

London, 15 June
Attempts to turn the London dock strike which began last month into a national dispute have collapsed. The fledgeling National Transport Workers' Federation today admitted that the national strike called five days ago had failed to win support outside the capital. The Sailors' Union, the biggest union in the new group, had withheld support as signs grew that even in London there was opposition to the strike. It began over one foreman working without a union card. Over 100,000 men went on strike, but the employers took a tough stand, refusing mediation and insisting on surrender (→26/8/13).

Shops are attacked as suffragettes try more violent style

London, 1 March
Suffragettes deployed new militant tactics today as they stepped up their campaign for the vote. More than 120 women were arrested, including the suffragette leader Mrs Emmeline Pankhurst, after a series of attacks on shops in London's west end. Women, many with stones and hammers hidden in their muffs, caused thousands of pounds' worth of damage by smashing windows as they rampaged through the streets. Two women also hurled stones at No 10 Downing Street.

The attacks appear to have been well-planned, as groups of women struck almost simultaneously. Within 20 minutes a trail of devastation stretched from Oxford Street to the Strand. Swan & Edgar's store at Piccadilly Circus was one of several famous shops to be attacked. Most of the women made no attempt to elude arrest after the attacks, which signal a new phase in the suffragette campaign reflecting the increasing influence of Christabel Pankhurst. Militancy has grown as suffragettes have seen the government grant concessions to railwaymen and miners after strikes had escalated into serious public disorder. By no means all suffragette leaders agree, but the militant wing of the movement hopes that it, too, can achieve its aims through disorder (→4).

REG CARTER
THE SUFFRAGETTES GET WILDER DAILY
& SMASH SHOP WINDOWS. OH! SO GAILY

Suffragettes: a smashing day out.

Tensions rise over Irish home rule

Ireland is promised its freedom by 1914

Westminster, 9 May
The Liberal government's attempt to meet Irish demands for home rule took a decisive step forward tonight when the Commons gave a second reading to the Home Rule Bill by 360 votes to 266. Tory MPs remained firmly opposed, and the government depended on Irish Nationalist and Labour MPs for its majority. If Tories in the Lords continue to oppose the bill, last year's Parliament Act ensures that it will still become law, and Ireland could have home rule in 1914.

The real threat to home rule lies elsewhere. The enmity between the Catholic majority in Ireland and the Protestants in Ulster has been sharpened by the prospect of home rule. In Belfast a flourishing shipbuilding industry has grown up in the past 50 years. It is now the biggest city in Ireland, and the merchants are at one with the workers in rejecting rule by Dublin.

Sir Edward Carson, a Dublin-born Protestant and former solicitor-general for Ireland, is planning to recruit some 80,000 armed volunteers who, he says, are ready to fight for Ulster's right to remain a province of the United Kingdom. But Herbert Asquith, the prime minister, says: "The British people, just and generous by nature, are not going to be frightened out of doing a just thing by the language of intimidation" (→ 12/7).

Ulster Day, Belfast. The signed covenant aims to stop the Home Rule Bill.

'Covenant' signed by Protestant loyalists

Belfast, 28 September
A ten-day speaking tour by Sir Edward Carson, the leader of the Ulster Unionists, reached its climax today when huge crowds queued for hours in Belfast to sign a "solemn covenant", swearing defiance against Irish home rule. In all, 471,414 signatures were collected as Ulster's self-styled "loyalists" declared their determination to stay part of the United Kingdom – some signing in their own blood.

In the words of the covenant, signatories declared that "being convinced in our consciences that home rule would be disastrous to the material well-being of Ulster, as well as the whole of Ireland" they pledged themselves as loyal subjects of the king to stand by one another in defending their equal citizenship in the United Kingdom.

The covenant threatens to use "all means which may be found necessary" to defeat home rule and, if a parliament is forced on Ulster, "to refuse to recognize its authority". Desks stretched for over 532 meters (580 yards) along the city hall corridors, allowing 540 people to sign simultaneously (→ 31/1/13).

Labour enters the newspaper battle

London, 15 April
First-day sales in excess of 200,000 copies were claimed in London alone today for a new national, socialist newspaper, the *Daily Herald*. Printed in London, Manchester and Glasgow, on cooperatively owned printing presses, the newspaper is edited by Charles Lapworth, who said: "We know there is a real need for a first-class socialist newspaper."

The *Herald* has a fight on its hands, however. The last 16 years have seen a revolution in popular journalism, spearheaded by Lord Northcliffe, who as Alfred Harmsworth in 1896 introduced the *Daily Mail* as the first halfpenny daily and then turned an ailing *Daily Mirror* (first published in 1903) into the first picture paper. He also bought *The Times* in 1908.

Daily Herald
THE LABOUR DAILY NEWSPAPER.
APRIL 15, 1912.

PRESIDENT TAFT'S DANGER
Fierce Struggle with an Armed Man.

IDEALS FOR WORKERS.
Mr. James Parker, M.P., on National Prosperity.

MOTOR ACCIDENT IN PORTUGAL.

"FORCIBLE FEEDING."
Miss Sylvia Pankhurst's Plea for Imprisoned Suffragists.
AN M.P. SHOUTED DOWN.

POISON SUSPECTED.
Mysterious Death of a Child near Preston.

COLOUR BLINDNESS.

"Daily Herald": Labour's voice.

London's central telephone exchange: now to be run by the Post Office.

Report calls for sexual equality in divorce

London, 11 November
A royal commission today offers some encouragement to women campaigning for greater rights. It says that men and women should be treated equally by divorce laws. At present, for instance, a husband can seek a divorce on the grounds of his wife's adultery, but the wife cannot petition on the grounds of a faithless husband; she must prove additional grounds for divorce if her petition is to be granted.

The 200-page report by the royal also urges that grounds for divorce be widened to include desertion for three years, cruelty, habitual drunkenness and insanity. The report, which says that divorce should no longer be the preserve of the rich, has been welcomed by women's groups, but there is some scepticism over whether the all-male Commons will back the proposed reforms. So far they have failed to pass suffrage bills even when those have been backed by the government, the most recent defeat being by 14 votes of a "Conciliation Bill" last March (→ 5/2/13).

1913

Britain, 13 January. The first payments are made under the National Insurance Act (→16/12).

Westminster, 31 January. The Lords reject the Home Rule for Ireland Bill by 326 votes to 69.→

Belfast, 31 January. The Ulster Volunteer Force is formed to resist home rule (→23/9).

London, 5 February. The imprisoned suffragette Sylvia Pankhurst threatens to begin a hunger strike (→24).

London, 24 February. Emmeline Pankhurst is arrested on a charge of being concerned in a bomb attack on the home of the chancellor, David Lloyd George (→2/3).

London, 2 March. Suffragettes in Hyde Park are attacked by mobs (→8/6).

London, 19 March. Leading ministers are cleared of illicit share dealing in a high court libel case (→13/6).

New York, 13 April. A £1 million war supplies loan for Britain is arranged (→4/8/14).

London, 8 June. The suffragette martyr Emily Davison dies from her Derby day injuries (→26/6).

Britain, 26 June. Emily Dawson is to be the country's first woman magistrate (→15/7).

Surrey, 15 July. A woman is arrested for wearing a split skirt in Richmond Park (→20/10).

Britain, 14 August. Street deaths involving motor buses are reported to have risen by 500 per cent since 1907 (→29/9/25).

Hendon, London, 2 October. An "aerobus" carries ten people, including its pilot (→31/12/17).

New York, 20 October. Emmeline Pankhurst is released as President Wilson reverses her deportation order (→4/12).

Dublin, 25 November. The Irish Volunteers are formed (→4/12).

Plymouth, Devon, 4 December. Emmeline Pankhurst is arrested on her return from the United States.→

Britain, 4 December. A royal proclamation bans the importing of arms and ammunitions into Ulster (→25/2/14).

Police play 'cat and mouse' with women

A martyr's death: Emily Davison is trampled by the king's horse, Anmer.

Plymouth, Devon, 4 December
Emmeline Pankhurst, the leader of the most militant suffragette group, was arrested here today on her return from the United States after a year of unprecedented violence by women campaigning for the vote. The last 12 months have seen:

* the death of a suffragette, Emily Davison, after she threw herself under the king's horse in the Derby at Epsom in June;

* physical attacks on the prime minister, Herbert Asquith, as he visited Scotland in August and November;

* widespread arson ranging from setting alight letters in pillar-boxes to fires at buildings including a railway station and Kew Gardens;

* the trial of Mrs Pankhurst after a bomb attack on the Surrey home of David Lloyd George, the chancellor, in February.

This new militancy followed another parliamentary rebuff when, in January, the speaker ruled a franchise bill out of order. But the recourse to more violent tactics had begun before then, largely orchestrated by one of Mrs Pankhurst's daughters, Christabel. The authorities hit back with a "Cat and Mouse" Act enabling the release of hunger-strikers so that they did not die in prison but leaving them liable to be rearrested (→3/1/14).

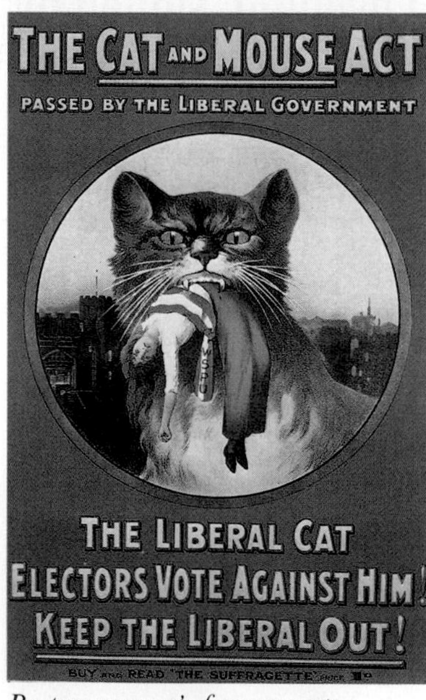

Poster: women's fury mounts.

The 'modern' novel adds class to the literary ingredients

Britain, December
The appearance of *Sons and Lovers* has thrust the name of David Herbert Lawrence to the front in a period already rich in literary brilliance. Lawrence is the son of a Nottinghamshire miner and a middle-class mother to whom he was abnormally close. Ill-assorted parents and mother/son conflicts are at the heart of this probing of painful adolescence.

The last decade has seen the birth of the "modern" novel. Henry James, a long-established master, achieved new psychological sophistication in *The Ambassadors* (1903) and *The Golden Bowl* (1904). The sea-faring Joseph Conrad, a man's writer with none of James's feminine intuition, wrote superb studies of male strength and moral weakness in *Lord Jim* (1900), *The Secret Agent* (1907) and this year's *Chance*. He is most blackly pessimistic in *Heart of Darkness* (1902).

The new realists deliberately went down the social scale for their characters. Arnold Bennett finds his among the lower middle class of his native Potteries, as in *The Old Wives' Tale* (1908) and *The Card*, a picaresque comic novel (1911). H G Wells, the son of a housekeeper and himself a draper's apprentice, put his good-humoured observation into *Kipps* (1905) and *The History of Mr Polly* (1910).

John Galsworthy is a chronicler of the moneyed and complacent middle class with the Forsyte family of *The Man of Property* (1906). E M Forster goes more subtly into their inhibitions in *A Room With A View* (1908) and *Howards End* (1910).

Ministers exonerated in share scandal

London, 13 June
Two leading government ministers who were involved in the so-called "Marconi scandal" have today been cleared of wrongdoing, but they have emerged with their reputations badly shaken.

Last year David Lloyd George, the chancellor of the exchequer, was persuaded by his friend Sir Rufus Isaacs, the attorney-general, to buy £1,000 worth of shares in the American Marconi radio corporation.

Shortly afterwards it became known that the British Post Office was negotiating a lucrative contract with the British Marconi company. The two companies are quite separate, and the ministers have been shown to have been unaware of the British negotiations.

Welsh pit disaster

Wales, 14 October
More than 400 miners are missing tonight after an explosion and fire ripped through a pit at Sengenhydd in the Aber valley. The blast was heard 11 miles away in Cardiff. Some 500 men escaped, but 21 bodies have been brought to the surface and a further 418 men are missing. Rescuers said tonight that there was no hope for them.

Scott of the Antarctic is found dead

Antarctica, 10 February
Captain Robert Falcon Scott and four companions have been been found dead, frozen to death just 11 miles from the safety of their camp. The five men had reached the South Pole on 17 January 1912.

Reaching the Pole was the climax of Scott's expedition, which had set off in October 1911, but even this triumph was marred when, after overcoming many difficulties, the team found that it had been beaten to its goal. A Norwegian expedition, under Roald Amundsen, had arrived one month earlier, and the Britons were greeted by evidence of their camp.

If the journey out had been hard, the return, with worsening weather, dwindling supplies, and the knowledge of being beaten, was worse. One by one Scott's men died: Petty Officer Evans on 17 February, Captain Oates a month later. Scott, Dr Wilson and Lt Bowers seem to have died together, around 29 March, when Scott wrote in his journal: "The end cannot be far. It seems a pity, but I do not think I can write any more."

CAPTAIN SCOTT MEMORIAL NUMBER 20 Pages

The Daily Mirror

THE MORNING JOURNAL WITH THE SECOND LARGEST NET SALE

CAPTAIN SCOTT'S FAVOURITE PORTRAIT OF HIMSELF: HIS LAST APPEAL TO THE PUBLIC.

The "Daily Mirror" breaks the news.

Rioting flares in Dublin after lock-out

Dublin, 26 August
A major industrial dispute has resulted in serious rioting. Earlier this year James Larkin of the Irish Transport Workers' Union had organised the Dublin tramwaymen and other poorly paid workers in the city to demand more wages. Strikes were followed by a lock-out by the employers, resulting in violent demonstrations and clashes with the police. The strikers and their supporters have claimed that the police acted in an aggressively brutal manner and have retaliated by forming the Irish Citizen Army for their own defence.

The army is led by J R White, an Ulster Protestant nationalist, and James Connolly who had been trying to convert the Belfast workers to socialism before being called to assist Larkin in Dublin. The spirit of the Citizen Army is seen as being close to that of revolutionary socialism (→30/8/18).

Ulster plots its defiance

Belfast, 23 September
The constitution of a provisional government for Ulster – to be implemented as soon as Irish home rule becomes law – was agreed today at a meeting of the Ulster Unionist Council. The standing committee of the council is to be the central authority, with Sir Edward Carson as its chairman. "We will scientifically, deliberately and carefully work out a plan which will make it impossible for a parliament in Dublin to govern this province," said Sir Edward.

The full panoply of an alterantive government is being planned. In addition to a military council there will be committees for areas such as finance, education, agriculture and the law. Sir Edward, the parliamentary leader of the Unionists, dismissed claims that the action being taken was seditious. Unionists had exhausted every means to bring the government to a real sense of the problems, he claimed, and if surrender was out of the question, what else could they do?

The council decided to raise a £1,000,000 indemnity guarantee fund for the Ulster Volunteer Force, the loyalist militia, to insure its members against loss or injury when acting on behalf of the provisional government. Ulster's resistance is alarming Irish Nationalists who fear that the province may be excluded from home rule legislation (→25/11).

Edward Carson: statesman or rabble rouser? It depends where you live.

Liverpool: emigrants head for Canada on the "Empress of Britain". More and more Britons are leaving for a new life in the dominions.

Emigration soars to reach new records

British Isles, December
Emigration has now reached record levels, with over half the people seeking a new life overseas now choosing the dominions of the empire. The average total of emigrants for the last three years has been 464,000, compared with an average of 284,000 in the first decade of the century.

Although the birth-rate is also falling it is sufficient, with some immigration from Europe, to ensure that the overall population is still growing, albeit more slowly. But the surge in emigration is having a marked effect on the average age of the people left behind. Most emigrants tend to be young, so that the boom of the last three years has exacerbated a trend towards an ageing society highlighted in the 1911 census report. This warned of the military and economic dangers of a falling proportion of "workers at the most economically efficient ages". In 1841 just under half the population was under 20; by 1911, less than a third was in this group (→8/4/25).

1914

London, 3 January. Sylvia Pankhurst is rearrested under the "Cat and Mouse" Act (→ 12/3).

London, 8 January. Successful treatment of cancer with radium is claimed by doctors at the Middlesex hospital.

Belfast, 25 February. There are now reported to be 100,000 armed men in the paramilitary Ulster Volunteer Force (→ 4/4).

London, 12 March. After damaging a Velazquez painting in the National Gallery the suffragette Mary Richardson receives a six months' prison sentence (→ 17/4).

London, 4 April. A rally in Hyde Park protests against the possible use of British troops against Ulster "loyalists" (→ 25).

London, 13 April. Shaw's *Pygmalion* causes a sensation at its first night by using the swear word "bloody".

Norfolk, 17 April. Great Yarmouth pier is destroyed by a suffragette bomb (→ 22/5).

Westminster, 4 May. Higher taxation is introduced in the budget; income tax now begins at 10 1/2d [4p] in the £ on £1,000 income.

London, 22 May. Emmeline Pankhurst is among 57 people arrested at Buckingham Palace when suffragettes try to present a petition.→

Britain, 4 August. War is declared on Germany (→ 17).

London, 10 August. Olympia becomes a detention centre for 300 German-born citizens under the wide emergency powers of the Defence of the Realm Act (DORA).

France, 17 August. Troops of the British Expeditionary Force land (→ 31).

London, 9 September. The government calls for a further 500,000 volunteer soldiers as the army grows from 386,000 to 825,000 men (→ 30).

Westminster, 18 September. The Home Rule Bill receives the royal assent but is suspended by another act passed today (→ 29/4/16).

London, 4 October. The city is hit by its first bomb (→ 31).

Sheerness, Kent, 26 November. HMS *Bulwark* blows up; 700 people die.

Dublin, 1 December. Anti-enlistment newspapers are suppressed by police.

Parties deadlocked over future of Ulster

London, 24 July

Leading British and Irish politicians have failed to agree on the future of Ireland at a conference held at Buckingham Palace with King George V in the chair. He has been criticised for intervening by Irish Nationalists but did so with the government's support. He told the party leaders: "For months we have watched with deep misgivings the course of events in Ireland. Today the cry of civil war is on the lips of my most responsible and sober-minded citizens."

However, the royal plea for "generous compromise" has failed to end the crisis. A home rule bill now before parliament would allow counties to vote on staying out of home rule for six years, until there had been two British general elections. Yet this has proved unpopular with both "loyalists" (who oppose the time limit) and nationalists (who oppose any exemptions).

The crisis has intensified over the last year as first Andrew Bonar Law, the Tory leader, threw his weight behind a plan to exempt Ulster from home rule, and then British Army officers had resisted moves to make them use force against Ulster. On 20 March, 57 out of 70 officers of the 3rd Cavalry Brigade based at the Curragh said that they would "prefer to accept dismissal if ordered north". Talks in London appeased them but infuriated supporters of home rule in Britain as well as Ireland. Then in April the Larne gun-running episode [*see below*] equipped the Ulster Volunteers as a fully armed force. With nationalists also arming, the stage was set for civil war (→ 18/9).

Women take their protests to palace

Palace arrest: Mrs Pankhurst held.

London, 22 May

Emmeline Pankhurst was among 57 women who were arrested today after clashing with police guarding Buckingham Palace. They were attempting to present a petition to the king in support of their campaign for the vote. Another franchise bill was defeated earlier this month as the protests by suffragettes continued unabated.

Some of this year's actions have alienated their own supporters, however. There have been attacks on paintings in the National Gallery and Royal Academy, bombs hurled at a London church and the pier at Great Yarmouth, arson attacks on private houses as well as public buildings. These tactics have been opposed by Emmeline Pethick Lawrence, one of the early leaders of the Women's Social and Political Union which was founded by Mrs Pankhurst (→ 24/2/15).

'Loyalists' unload gun cargo in Ulster

Larne, Co Antrim, 25 April

About 25,000 rifles and three million rounds of ammunition bound for the Ulster Volunteer Force (UVF) have been landed in at Larne to boost the campaign headed by Sir Edward Carson to keep Ulster free of Irish home rule.

The UVF took over the town for the night, severing communications and distributing the arms in 700 lorries and cars while the authorities looked on helplessly. The *Clydevalley*, a collier, also landed guns at Bangor and other Ulster ports. The gun-running coup was organized by a Boer War veteran, Col Fred Crawford. The guns, bought in Hamburg, were loaded on the 480-ton *Fanny* (described as "zinc plates") before being moved to the *Clydevalley* at sea (→ 24/7).

Sir Edward Carson presents colours to Unionist volunteers.

One Dubliner in five lives in tenements 'as squalid as Calcutta'

Dublin, 7 February

A major report on working-class housing in Dublin has revealed that 22 per cent of the population live in one-room tenement buildings in conditions of horrific squalor.

The Dublin housing inquiry began last year in the hope of improving the living conditions of the working class, and, later in the year, Dublin corporation set up a housing committee. The report has found that many houses are served by merely one tap in the yard. The basement rooms have little light or ventilation, and inspectors have found human excreta scattered about the yards and in the passages of houses. Some 118,000 people live in the Dublin tenements, and their conditions have been compared to those in Calcutta. The report acknowledges that the high Dublin mortality rate is a direct result of poor housing, and death from tuberculosis is the highest of any city in the United Kingdom. It is noted that when working-class girls are live-in servants their life expectancy improves considerably. Spasmodic attempts have been made to improve housing conditions in the city, but without success.

Britons go to war as Europe becomes a battlefield

Bloodshed at Mons dims the euphoria

France, 31 August
Cheering crowds greeted the declaration of war against Germany on 4 August, but the reality of war became apparent last week when the British Expeditionary Force (BEF) met the Germans at the Belgian town of Mons. The military skill of the British regulars held the Germans at first, but the weight of the German offensive drove back the French, leaving the British flank exposed. The BEF, forced to abandon its positions, is now retreating with the French to the Somme, where the allies plan to halt the German rush on Paris.

It was the German advance on France through Belgium that brought Britain into a war barely a month after the heir to the Austro-Hungarian empire was assassinated by a Serbian nationalist at Sarajevo. Austria delivered a tough ultimatum to Serbia, bringing in Russia as Serbia's ally. Germany backed Austria, France backed Russia, and Britain declared war on Germany for failing to respect the neutrality of the Belgians (→ 9/9).

Faces of war: British "Tommies" prepare for trench warfare in Flanders.

British troops help to rebuff Germans

France, 30 September
Paris can breathe again: the Germans have been stopped at the Marne and are retreating. It was a close-run thing, however. At one stage 600 Paris taxis were commandeered to rush troops to the front. One French general, Ferdinand Foch, under severe pressure, reported: "My centre is yielding, my right wing is giving way. An excellent situation. I attack tomorrow."

The BEF played a vital part in the battle, crossing the river into a gap between two German armies, threatening to outflank them and forcing them to abandon the battlefield. British losses have been heavy. Posters saying "Lord Kitchener wants you" posters are aimed at recruiting the 500,000 volunteers wanted by the war minister (→ 4/10).

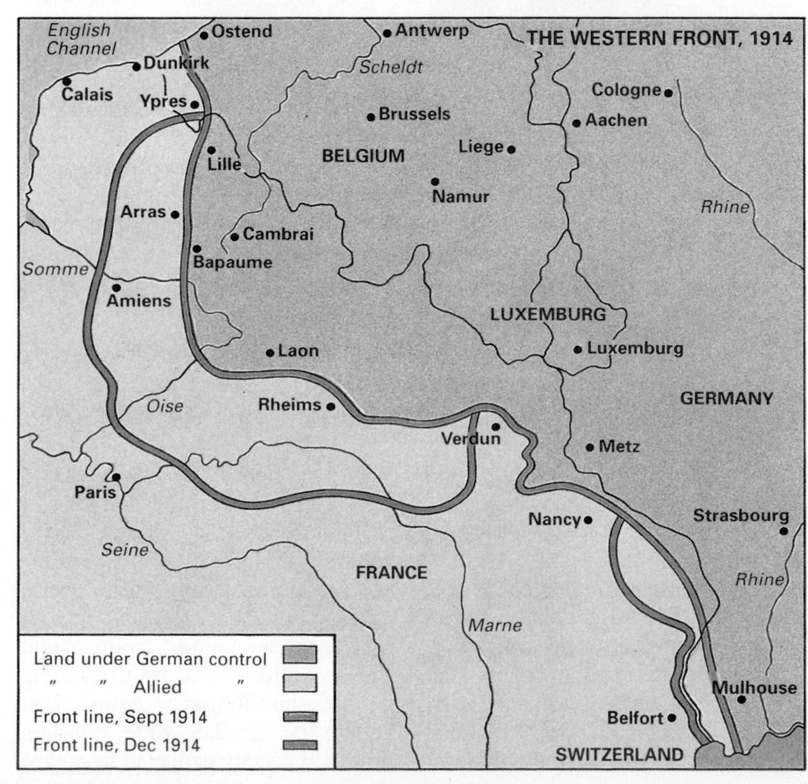

Front-line trenches dug across Europe

France, 31 October
The swirling battles of the rivers in northern France have given way to a new type of warfare, with lines of opposing trenches stretching from the sea to the Swiss border. Fierce struggles are going on for strong points along this line, with the BEF holding on to the Flanders town of Ypres. Aircraft, Zeppelins and submarines are also playing important roles. Paris has been bombed, and a U-boat has sunk three British cruisers. British airplanes have raided the Zeppelin sheds (→ 31/12).

Europe's war goes round the world

France, 30 November
While stalemate settles over the mud and barbed wire of the trenches in France the war is spreading to every part of the world. An Anglo-French fleet has bombarded the Dardanelles. The *Sydney*, an Australian cruiser, has sunk the German raider *Emden* off Sumatra. Britain has annexed Cyprus, and Russia has invaded Armenia. There is fighting also in Europe's empires. In East and West Africa British and German-led native troops have clashed, while loyal South Africans are moving against the German colony of South-west Africa (→ 31/12).

A Christmas truce, but no homecoming

France, 31 December
Soldiers who had expected to be "home for Christmas" have shocked their generals by holding a spontaneous truce in the front line, exchanging jam for cigars and playing football with the Germans before returning to their trenches. At sea the Royal Navy has won a great victory off the Falkland Islands, sinking Admiral von Spee's fleet. The German navy retaliated by shelling towns in eastern England, killing 100 people (→ 19/1/15).

Berkshire, 7 January. Severe floods hit the Thames valley and turn Windsor Castle into an island.

Norfolk, 19 January. A Zeppelin bombs Great Yarmouth and King's Lynn (→22/4).

France, 24 February. One thousand British suffragettes arrive for war work (→10/11).

London, 30 March. King George V offers to give up alcohol as example to munitions workers (→28/10).

Western front, 22 April. Germany introduces a new weapon – poison gas (→8/5).

Turkey, 26 April. On the day that Britain, France and Italy sign a secret war treaty, Allied troops land at Gallipoli (→20/12).

London, 13 May. Kaiser William is stripped of the Order of the Garter by his cousin, the king.

Britain, 13 May. Street violence against "suspect" aliens follows the sinking of the *Lusitania*.

Ghent, 8 June. Flight Sub-Lieutenant Reginald Warneford wins a Victoria Cross for bringing down a Zeppelin with bombs (→15/12).

London, 1 July. The "brides-in-the-bath" killer George Smith is to be hanged for the murders of three bigamous wives.

Wiltshire, 21 September. Prehistoric Stonehenge is auctioned for the knockdown price of £6,600.

Britain, 13 October. "Treating" – buying drinks for others – is banned to try to deter excessive drinking by industrial workers.

France, 28 October. King George is badly bruised by falling from his horse while inspecting troops,

London, 6 November. Police raid offices of *The Globe* newspaper after its false reports on Lord Kitchener, claiming he had resigned.

Britain, 10 November. A survey shows that women war workers have enabled factories to increase production by up to two and a half times (→31/12).

France, 15 December. Sir Douglas Haig replaces Sir John French as commander of British forces in Europe in a shake-up of Allied commands (→31/12).

War changes life on the home front

Women fill men's roles in the factories

Britain, 31 December

Women are playing an increasingly important part in the war effort, filling the gap left by the men at the front. As clerks, bus conductors, farm hands or industrial workers, over a million more women are now working full-time. Not only are women doing work they have never done before – most visibly in transport, most significantly in engineering factories – but they may be doing it better than men: a survey indicates that some munitions factories are now two-and-a-half times more productive with women workers. And they have been backed by the suffragettes. Christabel Pankhurst led a Whitehall march in July demanding women's "right to serve" and, for possibly the first time in her life, the authorities welcomed her presence (→1/1/16).

Home front: women take over.

Political parties in wartime coalition

Westminster, 25 May

The scandal of the shell shortage on the western front has today forced Herbert Asquith, the Liberal prime minister, to agree to a coalition cabinet in which 13 Liberals are joined by eight Tories and one Labour minister.

The grave situation facing British troops in France because of the lack of high-explosive shells was exposed by the *Daily Mail*. Copies of the paper were burned by scandalised stockbrokers in the City. But a shaken government has had to respond, and Lloyd George has been appointed to a new ministry of munitions. Lord Northcliffe, the *Mail's* owner, is being attacked by the Liberal press but says he welcomes the advertising (→7/12/16).

Germany threatens an unlimited naval blockade of Britain

"Lusitania" propaganda starts.

Queenstown, Co Cork, 8 May

The giant luxury liner *Lusitania* had just sighted land when two torpedoes struck. Twenty-one minutes later she reared up and slid under the waves, taking 1,200 passengers and crew, including women and children, with her. This was the latest move by Germany in its submarine blockade of Britain after Britain's unsuccessful attempt at a naval blockade of Germany.

The casualties included 128 Americans, among them the multi-millionaire Alfred Vanderbilt and several close friends of President Woodrow Wilson. Most of the survivors brought ashore at Kinsale were too exhausted to talk, although one Canadian journalist said that he had seen the U-boat's conning tower and a torpedo heading for the ship.

The savagery of this latest attack has brought universal condemnation of Germany in Britain and the United States. In Washington – where the German ambassador took newspaper space to warn Americans not to sail on the *Lusitania* last week – the former president Theodore Roosevelt condemned the sinking as an "act of piracy". The Wilson government's neutrality policy is certain to be reviewed.

In Liverpool, the ship's home port, serious rioting has broken out and no German shop is safe. Within hours of the news reaching London, well-dressed people crowded Cunard's offices in Cockspur Street for news of relatives (→8/6).

More than 200 soldiers die in Britain's worst-ever train crash

Dumfries and Galloway, 22 May

Over 200 officers and men of the 7th Royal Scots were killed today when a crowded troop train was one of five involved in a multiple collision at Quintinshill, near Gretna, ten miles (16km) north of Carlisle. Errors by signalmen are thought to have been responsible for the highest death toll in British railway history.

The southbound troop train crashed into a local train standing at Quintinshill shortly before 7am today. Its coaches were crushed, and as survivors struggled to escape it was hit by an express travelling north. Two other trains also waiting at Quintinshill were now entangled in the wreckage, which was swept by fire as the cylinders of the gas-lit troop train ignited. The final death toll is not known, but is feared to be 225 or more (→1/1/23).

Death and destruction as war encircles the globe

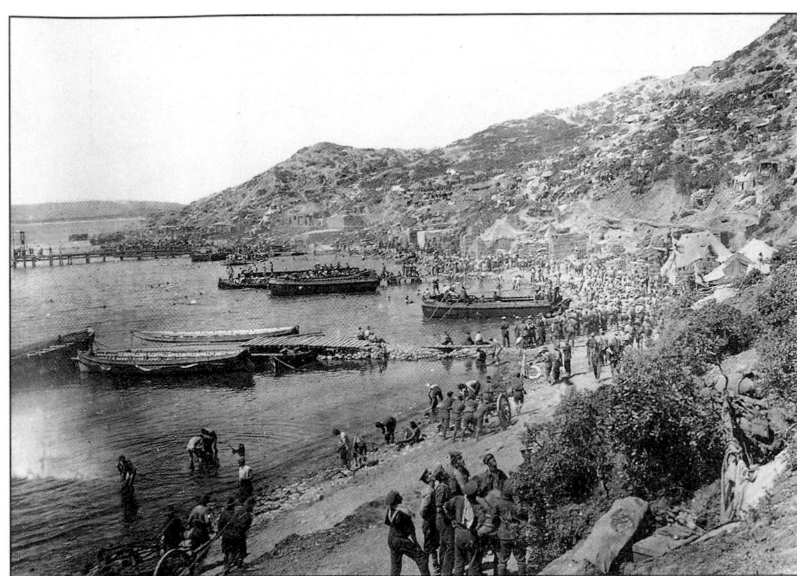

The beaches at Gallipoli: high hopes and then disaster for the Allies.

France: makeshift gas masks for French troops as a new weapon is born.

Gallipoli: Allies retreat from disaster

Gallipoli, 20 December
The Allies stole away from Suvla Bay and Anzac Cove on Gallipoli last night without losing a single man. The evacuation was carried out with great ingenuity. During the day the Turks could see reinforcements and stores being unloaded, but when darkness fell thousands of men, mules and guns were lifted off the beaches. They left behind rifles set to fire at intervals. At the last moment a destroyer trained its searchlight on the trenches, the Turks opened fire on the ship and, under the cover of their barrage, the allied rearguard finally slipped away.

It only remains for the men at Cape Helles to be evacuated for this whole sorry Gallipoli adventure to be ended. It is a story of bad luck, muddle, indecision – and the outstanding heroism of the soldiers on all sides of whom, for the Allies, a high proportion were Australians and New Zealanders.

The expedition was born out of a wish to circumvent the deadlock on the western front and to assist Russia by knocking Turkey out of the war and opening up a supply route across the Black Sea. At first it was thought that seapower alone could force the Dardanelles, but the loss of three battleships sunk and three crippled in the Turkish minefields ended that hope.

The expeditionary force landed on 25 April. On some beaches the men came ashore virtually unopposed, but at Sedd-el-Bahr the British soldiers walked into a wall of fire and died in their thousands. They hung on, their bravery matched only by the blunders of their commanders. Some generals have been sacked, and it seems impossible that Winston Churchill, judged responsible for the débâcle, can keep his post at the admiralty.

Europe: stalemate brings army changes

France, 31 December
Stalemate has settled over the frozen mud of the trenches which run from Ostend to the Swiss frontier. Their line has hardly changed despite the bloody fighting and appalling casualties which have marked this year.

The great offensives of September, with the British attacking at Loos in support of the French assault in Artois, which were brought to an end by bad weather in mid-October achieved little on the ground. The fighting cost the British 60,000 casualties to the Germans' 20,000, while the French lost 100,000 to 120,000.

Nowhere have the Allies made progress. The Gallipoli expedition has been abandoned [*see report left*]. General Townshend has been beaten back from Baghdad and shut up in Kut. The Italians, who entered the war on 24 May, failed in their offensives against the Austrians. The Russians have suffered a terrible defeat at the hands of General Falkenhayn at Gorlice. Serbia has been overrun.

The sense of failure at the lack of progress after 16 months of war is reflected in changes at the top of the Allied command. General Joffre was made commander-in-chief of the French army at the beginning of December, and Sir Douglas Haig replaced the ineffectual Sir John French as commander of the British forces on the western front. At the same time Haig's chief of staff and friend, Sir William Robertson, who rose from the ranks to become a general, has been made Chief of the Imperial General Staff.

These appointments reflect the disappointment felt in Whitehall at Lord Kitchener's conduct of the war, and his position as war secretary is at risk. More is expected of the new team (→6/1/16).

Victims of the war fought to end all wars

The British nurse Edith Cavell (l), accused of spying, died "bravely" in front of a German firing squad; the poet Rupert Brooke (r), the romantic symbol of his age, died of an infection while travelling to the Dardanelles.

1916

Britain, 1 January. Women's employment has increased by two million in a year (→27/6).

London, 23 January. The British museum and the Natural History museum are to close during the war.

London, 23 February. Well-off families are urged by the national organizing committee for war savings to release servants for "more useful purposes" (→10/3).

Southern England, 5 March. Zeppelin raids on eight counties kill 12 people (→25/4).

Westminster, 6 March. Only aliens with identity cards will be allowed into "prohibited areas", says the government.

London, 10 March. Less extravagance in women's dress is urged by the national committee for war savings (→21).

Britain, 21 March. While the war lasts there are to be no imports of spirits, pianos and motors (→21/5).

Westminster, 14 April. Following a report that ten per cent of the urban population is infected by venereal diseases, the government promises cash for diagnosis and treatment.

Westminster, 25 April. The terms of conscription are to be broadened by the government (→31/5).

Liverpool, 1 May. Four hundred Irish rebels arrive for internment in Britain (→12/5).

Britain, 21 May. Clocks are put forward by an hour under a daylight-saving scheme aimed at conserving coal (→29/9).

Orkney, 6 June. Lord Kitchener, the war minister, dies when his ship hits a mine (→15/9).

London, 27 June. King George V says that women can receive the Military Medal (→6/2/17).

London, 29 June. The former diplomat Sir Roger Casement is convicted of treason (→3/8).

Westminster, 29 September. A "meatless" day to cut food price rises is proposed by the government (→3/11).

Western front, 31 October. In the last three months British casualties are estimated to have been 350,000 (→15/11).

Britain, 23 December. Irishmen interned after the Easter Rising are freed (→11/7/17).

Nationalists stage an 'Easter Rising'

Hundreds die after republic is declared

Dublin, 29 April

An insurrection led by the Irish Republican Brotherhood has taken place in Dublin, leaving 450 dead and nearly 3,000 wounded. The main instigators of the rising five days ago on Easter Monday were Arthur Griffith, the founder of Sinn Féin; Thomas James Clarke, a leader of the Irish Republican Brotherhood; James Connolly, the founder of the Irish Citizen Army; and Patrick Pearse, a schoolmaster from the Gaelic League. Pearse has been influenced by the cult of violence which has spread through Europe in the past 20 years.

The insurgents were forced to use their meagre resources to the best effect, and plans were laid to get arms and ammunition from Germany, with the help of Sir Roger Casement, the Irish-born British diplomat. Although the British authorities suspected that a rebellion was imminent, the events of this Easter Rising seem to have taken them completely by surprise.

Unfortunately for the insurgents the ship bringing arms was captured and Casement taken prisoner on 21 April. Despite this setback, the Rising went ahead. The holiday crowds paid little attention to the columns of soldiers marching down O'Connell Street on Easter Monday morning. Without opposition they took possession of the General Post Office where they set up their headquarters.

From the steps in front of the building Pearse read a proclamation declaring the establishment of a republic and the constitution of a provisional government.

Many British officers had been given leave to attend a race meeting, and there were only 1,200 troops in the city. By the time that the authorities realized what was happening, the insurgents had captured almost the whole of the centre of Dublin and established a cordon of fortified posts in the suburbs. But as soon as reinforcements began to arrive, armed with heavy artillery, the hopelessness of the insurgents' position became apparent. The General Post Office caught fire and was evacuated, leaving many dead. After five days of bloodshed the rebellion effectively ended today when Pearse and Connolly offered their unconditional surrender. But harsh reprisals now seem certain to begin (→1/5).

British troops man a barricade in Talbot Street during the rebellion.

Roger Casement is hanged for treason

London, 3 August

Roger Casement, the Irish-born former British diplomat, was received into the Roman Catholic Church and hanged today in Pentonville prison. Regarded in Ireland as a patriot and humanitarian, he had sought aid for the Irish cause in Germany but had returned, disillusioned, in April to try to stop what he saw as a futile insurrection. However, he was arrested, found guilty of treason and sentenced to death. Intense efforts were made for his reprieve, but circulation of his "black diaries" by the prosecution (with the tacit approval of the cabinet) revealing his homosexuality damaged him further and made his reprieve impossible (→23/12).

Casement: guns for Sinn Féin.

Leaders of 'Easter Rising' executed

Dublin, 12 May

The British military authorities said today that James Connolly had been executed. This means that all seven men who signed the proclamation of an Irish republic are now dead. They were tried by courts martial set up by the military forces now running Ireland under martial law. Augustine Birrell, the chief secretary for Ireland, has resigned. Fifteen of the captured leaders of the insurgence have been shot by firing squads. Feelings against Britain are running high, even among many out of sympathy with the revolt, with the insurgents widely regarded as martyrs (→29/6).

Victory remains elusive as the bloodshed worsens

Single men will be conscripted for war

Westminster, 6 January
The Commons today gave their backing to the controversial Conscription Bill making armed service compulsory for single men between the age of 18 and 41, by 403 votes to 103. The Liberal Party was not as divided as Herbert Asquith, the prime minister, had feared, although Sir John Simon is resigning as home secretary.

Until now volunteers have been relied on to fill the ranks. In the early months of the war there was a fervent response to the recruiting posters of Kitchener's pointing finger and the appeal of the slogan "Your King and Country Need You!" Other registration and recruitment schemes followed, leading some 2.3 million men to enlist by the beginning of this year.

But there are still more men of military age outside the services, and numbers entering the army have fallen. Many civilians have failed medical tests, and some have been granted exemptions because of important war work at home. However, this has not necessarily spared them from abuse from the self-appointed "Order of the White Feather". Provision is to be made under the new bill for conscientious objectors to do noncombatant work such as driving ambulances (→5/3).

The great battle of the Dreadnoughts: HMS "Warspite" at Jutland.

Rival navies each claim victory at Jutland

North Sea, 31 May
A huge area of the North Sea was awash with hundreds of bodies of young British and German sailors tonight after what has been described as the "greatest sea battle in history". Both sides claim victory in the battle at Jutland: the Germans speak of the "destruction of the British Fleet", while the Royal Navy insists that it has routed the imperial German fleet.

The German commander, Grand Admiral Scheer, was determined to destroy at least part of the British fleet which was successfully blockading German ports. The British had the advantage of knowing the German codes, and Vice-Admiral David Beatty succeeded in luring the enemy into the gunsights of the rest of the British fleet commanded by Admiral Sir John Jellicoe.

German ships suffered more hits than the British – the guns of HMS *Queen Mary* and *Invincible* were still shooting with "commendable accuracy" when the ships blew up. Poor design and lack of magazine protection are blamed for the British losses. Britain is reported to have lost one battleship, one battle cruiser, five destroyers and 6,907 men. German losses include a battleship, a cruiser and a destroyer plus 2,545 men (→6/6).

War raises price of bread – and of sex

London, 3 November
Britain's bakers faced allegations of profiteering today after raising the price of bread to tenpence [4p] a loaf. The country's poorest families are complaining that the new price will deprive them of their staple diet at a time of particular hardship, and the government is also concerned about bakers increasing profits – knowing that prices are likely to be frozen by law following a report by a commission on wheat imports. Trade unionists have protested in their thousands in London's Hyde Park about increased food prices, and the government is proposing a meatless day once a week in the hope of reducing them.

While the price of food is arousing concern on the home front, the price of sexual promiscuity is alarming doctors after an apparent increase in syphilis, with over 50,000 cases reported among servicemen. Doctors are to help to provide diagnostic tests and drugs in the hope of combating disease, and a royal commission has been set up to examine the problem. Prostitutes "who haunt the camps of the men in training" are blamed by Dr Mary Scharlieb, a specialist in sexual diseases. Young men "overflowing with animal strengths and spirits" are easy prey, she adds (→2/5/17).

YOUR KING & COUNTRY NEED YOU
A WEE 'SCRAP O' PAPER' IS BRITAIN'S BOND
TO MAINTAIN THE HONOUR AND GLORY OF THE BRITISH EMPIRE

Sign up: a new recruiting poster.

'Tank' powers to success in its first foray on the battlefield

France, 15 September
A new weapon which could break open the deadlock of trench warfare was used today with startling results. Codenamed "the tank", this armoured monster rolled over the muddy battlefield of the Somme on its tracks, spitting bullets and spreading panic through the German lines. Some German soldiers fled shouting: "The Devil is coming." Within two hours the attacking British and Canadian troops had gained all their objectives and taken more than 2,000 prisoners. Open country was reached, but the reserves could not get up in time to exploit the tank's success (31/10).

British and German tanks clash in one of the first battles of machines.

Slaughter at the Somme: the army's worst days

By the end of day one, 19,000 were dead; four months later, 420,000 men were lost – and two miles were gained

The devastated Somme landscape: a muddy, bloody battlefield, and burial ground, in a war that seems endless.

The Somme, 15 November
The slaughter on the Somme is subsiding in the mud which drowns the wounded, makes attack impossible and has brought the exhausted soldiers to the very limit of endurance. The casualties are beyond belief. The British Army's dead and injured total 420,000 men; the French have lost 200,000, the Germans 450,000. At Verdun, where the French have withstood ten months of German attacks, both sides have lost some 400,000 men.

The German onslaught at Verdun drew French strength away from the Somme offensive, and, far from being the battering ram which would break through the German fortifications and bring victory to the Allies, it became a long-drawn-out battle of attrition.

The Germans were well aware that the "Big Push" was coming. They gathered huge stocks of ammunition and sat in their comfortable deep bunkers waiting for the storm to break over them. It came in the form of an artillery barrage which lasted for five days, thus destroying the last vestiges of surprise but not the German bunkers.

When the barrage lifted at breakfast time on 1 July, the Germans raced up ladders to their machine guns to greet the men of Haig's new army advancing in extended lines, their bayonets fixed, each man carrying his personal kit and weapons along with grenades and mortar bombs. The minimum load carried by any man that hot summer morning was 30 kilograms (66 pounds).

Thirteen divisions went "over the top". It is said that some men kicked footballs as they advanced. They were scythed down by the German machine guns playing along the lines as the Allies advanced. At the end of that first day 19,000 men lay dead and 57,000 were wounded – the greatest loss in a single day ever suffered by a British army.

The few gains that were made were mostly lost by bad communications and slowness in exploiting the success. On 3 July Haig reopened the attack, but the guns had little ammunition, the losses had weakened the attackers, and that night rain turned the battlefield into a quagmire, making advance impossible.

On 17 July General Rawlinson tried a new tactic, a night attack, and succeeded in punching a gap in the German line; but once again the success was not followed up. The same thing happened when tanks were introduced. Their breakthrough was not exploited.

So this bloody slogging match continued into the autumn. The British sacrifice saved the French at Verdun, but Haig's new army died on the Somme, and with it died the idealism of men who had marched so eagerly to war (→31/12).

Lloyd George to be new prime minister

Westminster, 7 December
After months of relentless criticism in the press and in parliament, and much behind-the-scenes intrigue, Herbert Asquith has resigned as prime minister and has been replaced tonight by David Lloyd George, the war secretary, with a commitment to wage all-out war against Germany. He takes over with strong support from hawks on the Tory back benches. Some Liberal colleagues of Lloyd George are persuaded that he has been conspiring with the Tories to oust Asquith. The new premier intends to replace the committee of 20 ministers which has been overseeing the war with a small action group of four or five ministers. He will work closely with the Tory leader, Andrew Bonar Law (→7/8/17).

Deadlock in west, Russia split in east

France, 31 December
The third Christmas of the war has passed without optimism. Nothing seems able to break the deadlock on the western front, where the slaughter continues, with both sides committed to a process of attrition.

The Russian army is riddled with revolutionaries. The czar's confidant, Rasputin, has been murdered, and there is fear that the army will collapse, freeing Germany's eastern army for service on the western front.

There is, however, a prospect of change. Three weeks ago the silver-tongued David Lloyd George was appointed, after much high-level intrigue, to succeed Herbert Asquith as prime minister. He has promised a more vigorous prosecution of the war (→4/1/17).

1917

Westminster, 4 January. Britain and Germany agree to exchange internees aged over 45 (→ 6/4).

Britain, 11 January. It is revealed that the war is costing £5.7 million a day.

London, 6 February. Neville Chamberlain, the director of national service, announces a non-military national service scheme for women (→ 13/2).

Westminster, 13 February. New regulations allow women to become taxi drivers (→ 29/3).

Atlantic Ocean, 20 March. A U-boat sinks a fully lit hospital ship.

Westminster, 29 March. Lloyd George says that the government plans to give the vote to married women over the age of 30 (→ 6/2/18).

Western front, 16 April. British, Canadian and Australian troops begin an Easter offensive near Arras (→ 26/5).

London, 2 May. King George V calls for national restraint on bread consumption (→ 10/7).

South-east England, 26 May. German planes bomb the coast, killing 76 people (→ 1/6).

London, 14 June. The Germans launch the first raid by aircraft: 100 die and 400 are injured in the east end (→ 20/8).

Westminster, 10 July. The government is to test "war bread" after complaints from the public (→ 15/10).

Co Clare, 11 July. The Sinn Féin candidate Eamon de Valera, imprisoned after the Easter Rising, wins the parliamentary by-election in East Clare (→ 30/9).

Western front, 31 July. Francis Ledwidge, the Irish poet, is killed at Ypres.

Westminster, 15 October. The board of trade calls for a cut in pleasure motoring (→ 31/12).

Ireland, 27 October. Eamon de Valera is elected president of the Irish Volunteers (→ 18/4/18).

Westminster, 9 November. Arthur Balfour, the foreign secretary, says that Britain will use its "best endeavours" to help the Jews to establish a homeland in Palestine (→ 9/12).

Westminster, 3 December. The government refuses to recognize Russia's new Bolshevik regime (→ 1/4/19).

U-boat attacks push America into war

Washington, DC, 6 April
The United States entered the war today as President Wilson signed the war resolution passed by large majorities in congress. He told them that this was a war "to make the world safe for democracy".

Ironically, Wilson was re-elected last year as the "man who kept us out of the war". It all changed on 1 February when Germany began unrestricted submarine warfare, causing heavy losses to US ships. A German telegram was also decoded revealing an attempt to persuade Mexico to attack the US to recover lost territory. America has already made a huge contribution by financing the Allies and manufacturing armaments, but its army will not be ready for months. Germany hopes to win the war first (→ 16).

August: newly arrived US troops dip their flags to the king and queen.

Air 'aces' give new dimension to warfare

France, 31 December
The war now being fought in the air has developed more rapidly than any previous form of warfare. Three years ago flimsy unarmed planes were used only for reconnaissance. Today daring aviators known as "aces", flying fighters equipped with twin machine guns, are popular heroes. Various types of aircraft spot for artillery, take photographs, bomb and "strafe" the trenches, take off from ships and drop torpedoes. Long-range bombers drop their deadly loads on munitions factories and marshalling yards. The air has become increasingly important for fighting wars. Bombing has also become a means of terrorizing nations, bringing the horror of war into the homes of civilians (→ 1/4/18).

War in the air: a German fighter finally downs Captain Albert Ball VC.

Convoys tackle the U-boat challenge

Western Approaches, 1 June
A large convoy of merchant ships protected by Royal Navy warships sailed into British waters today after an incident-free voyage from Gibraltar. Another convoy is due shortly from the United States. Naval experts believe that the convoy system is the answer to German submarines which have claimed thousands of tons of Allied shipping since the Battle of Jutland last year when Germany began trying to blockade Britain and France.

U-boats sank more than a hundred ships last month. Bitter rows have taken place in the war cabinet and the admiralty on how best to protect British ships. Royal Navy personnel wearing civilian clothing are taking a toll of U-boats as crews of "Q-ships" – merchantmen which lure U-boats to the surface before opening their gun-ports at the last possible moment (→ 14/6).

Irish hunger striker dies in Dublin jail

Dublin, 30 September
Around 40,000 Dubliners today defied the British government by turning out on the streets of the city to attend the funeral of Thomas Ashe, one of the leaders of the Irish Republican Brotherhood. He died five days ago in Mountjoy prison while on hunger strike, following an attempt by the prison authorities to feed him forcibly.

Many of the mourners followed the hearse to Glasnevin cemetery. They included a large contingent of Volunteers and members of the Irish Citizen Army led by Countess Markievicz, a member of a Protestant family, who had fought in the Rising. A volley of shots was fired over the grave, and Michael Collins, a militant leader of Sinn Féin, delivered an oration.

Ashe's arrest was one of a number carried out in an attempt to curb the increasing membership of Sinn Féin and the Volunteers. He led a campaign for prisoner-of-war status, and when this was refused he and 29 others went on hunger strike. The forcible feeding caused widespread revulsion (→ 27/10). ▷

British troops stuck in Flanders mud

Flanders, 20 August
Field Marshal Haig's great offensive, designed to break out of the Ypres salient, drive to the Belgian coast and then roll up the entire German front, is foundering in the mud of Flanders.

Haig's enthusiasm for this offensive, which he is convinced will win the war, wore down the doubters in the war cabinet, but when he launched the assault on 31 July it was proved once again that the essential initial breakthrough could not be made against German machine gunners in well-protected bunkers by the old way of bombardment followed by "over the top" attacks.

Rain lashed the battlefield, and the bombardment of over four million shells from 3,000 guns broke up the network of streams and dykes on which the Flanders drainage system depends.

The attackers struggled forward up to their waists in mud; men who fell off the duckboards which were laid across the morass drowned under the weight of their equipment. Guns and horses sank irretrievably; tanks could not be used.

At the British HQ Haig remains calmly optimistic and speaks of "successful operations by our troops" and "the capture of a series of strong points and fortified farms" but then concedes that the actual ground gained can be measured in "a few hundred yards".

The French, operating on the flank of the British offensive, are having far more success. They have learnt new methods of trench warfare and are moving forward in loose storming parties, taking advantage of the ground and shell-holes, unlike the British attempts at parade-ground precision. The soldiers also have a new enemy as well as the mud and machine guns – aeroplanes, having been used for reconnaissance, are now being used for the first time as flying artillery, swooping over the battlefield to bomb and machine-gun the enemy. Dogfights rise over the lines watched by soldiers envious of the pilots who, if they survive, fly back to good meals and clean sheets.

Down below, as the fighting builds towards a bloody climax in the morass around the Belgian village of Passchendaele, Haig is confident that the enemy may collapse "at any moment" (→13/4/18).

British troops struggle knee-deep in Flanders mud to save a comrade.

Government wields draconian powers

Britain, 31 December
The year is coming to a gloomy end tonight, with the war seemingly no closer to an end. Despite the success of the convoy system, food remains in short supply and strict rationing is in force. Never has a democratic British government taken such draconian powers. Individuals can be interned without trial; and now manpower is being conscripted – except, as yet, from Ireland – equally for war work at home or for fighting on the western front (→22/1/18).

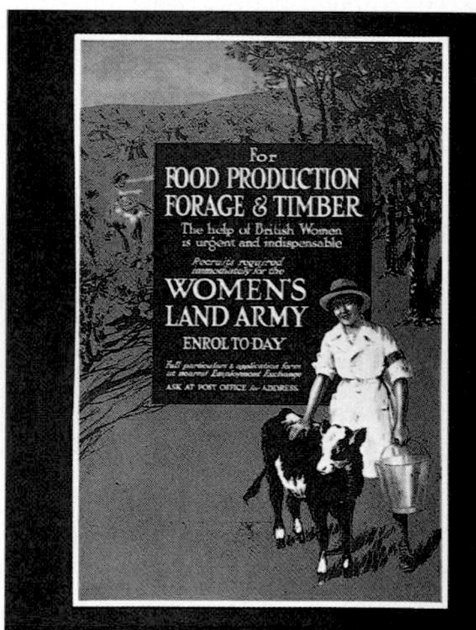

Land work is war work today.

British troops capture Jerusalem as Ottoman Empire crumbles

London, 9 December
Jerusalem was captured today by the British Army under the command of General Edmund Allenby. It was the climax of an offensive begun on 31 October with an attack on Gaza and Beersheba, and it reverses the defeat which Britain suffered at Gaza last spring.

The Turks have now withdrawn northwards. General Allenby expects to resume the attack in the spring, together with the Arab armies moving up to the east. Baghdad was captured last March, and the 600-year-old Ottoman Empire – from Turkey to Mesopotamia – is clearly on its last legs.

The British and French governments proposed a "national home for the Jews" in Palestine last month, and the capture of Jerusalem was a necessary first step in that direction (→25/4/20).

Men of the Hampshire Regiment march into Baghdad in triumph.

Lords debate the 'sale of honours'

Westminster, 7 August
A controversial king's birthday honours list, drawn up by the prime minister, David Lloyd George, provoked an indignant debate in the House of Lords today, with peers complaining that the many honours acquired simply by making donations to party funds had become a national scandal.

Lloyd George was not mentioned by name, though it is widely accepted that he is building up a secret fund in readiness for the general election after the war. The Earl of Selbourne, however, insisted that Tories as well as Liberals "are tarred with the same brush". He said that every recommendation for an honour should be accompanied by a declaration that no money or favour was involved (→28/12/18).

1918

Westminster, 22 January. The government orders two "meatless" days a week in restaurants (→ 25/2).

Firth of Forth, 31 January. Submarines collide in a night exercise; 103 sailors die.

Westminster, 6 February. Women over 30 and men over 21 gain the right to vote as the Representation of the People Act receives the royal assent (→ 19/9).

Britain, 25 February. The rationing of butter and margarine begins (→ 11/11).

Britain, 13 March. The minimum school-leaving age is to be raised to 14.

Dublin, 18 April. Sinn Féiners, Nationalists and Labour politicians combine to fight plans to extend conscription to Ireland (→ 23).

Westminster, 22 April. The penny post is abolished.

Dublin, 23 April. A one-day general strike in Ireland against conscription is widely supported, except in Ulster (→ 18/5).

London, 1 July. Dr Marie Stopes publishes *Married Love*, a controversial book about sex and marriage.

Britain, 19 September. A government commission investigates equal pay for women as women railway workers settle a dispute (→ 23/10).

Westminster, 23 October. The Commons vote 274-25 to allow women to become MPs (→ 7/10/20).

London, 26 October. Spanish flu has claimed the lives of 2,225 people in the capital alone this week.

Westminster, 19 November. The government says that total British war casualties were three million, including 767,000 dead (→ 2/12).

Britain, 2 December. One of the war cabinet's last acts is to demand Kaiser William's extradition (→ 31).

Britain, 24 December. An end to workhouses is recommended by a committeee on poor law (→ 6/1/26).

London, 27 December. King George V and Queen Mary greet President and Mrs Wilson of the United States.

London, 31 December. The war cabinet meets for the last time (→ 22/7/19).

Germans launch strong spring offensive

One last effort: the Germans launch a surprise spring offensive at Villers.

Lille, France, 13 April
Field Marshal Sir Douglas Haig has issued a personal call to all ranks of the British Army in the face of General von Ludendorff's offensive. It says: "Every position must be held to the last man: there must be no retirement. With our backs to the wall and believing in the justice of our cause, each one of us must fight on to the end."

The German commander, bolstered by 70 divisions released by the withdrawal of Russia from the war, launched his offensive against the junction of the British and French armies on the Somme on 21 March. His plan is to drive the Allies out of the war before the fresher American armies arrive.

Ludendorff used new tactics: there was a short "hurricane" bombardment, then small parties of shock troops probed the line for weak spots. Advancing under cover of fog, they left strong points to be dealt with later. The British line was deeply penetrated, and the Germans quickly advanced 40 miles (64km). Now his attack has been switched to Flanders; the Allies have their backs to the wall (→ 8/8).

Flying aces win an independent air force

Britain, 1 April
A third arm of the British armed forces was born today with the creation of the Royal Air Force. It has been formed by merging the Royal Flying Corps and the Royal Naval Air Service into a new body independent of both the army and the navy. An air ministry in London will be the equivalent of the war office and the admiralty, with Lord Rothermere, the newspaper tycoon, as its first head and Major-General Hugh Trenchard as the first RAF chief of staff.

Aviation has been transformed by the war. Initially used for reconnaissance, planes are now deployed to attack troops, supply lines and towns. In 1914 Britain had barely 100 planes; by the end of this year it will have more than 22,000. German raids on Britain aroused vociferous calls for revenge attacks. Last year this popular cry received high-powered backing in a report by Jan Smuts, the South African defence minister who joined the British war cabinet in June 1917. He argued that given enough aeroplanes air power alone could win the war. As the toll of casualties in the ground war mounted endlessly, the Smuts report was seized upon by politicians and paved the way for the birth of the RAF (→ 9/12/19).

Sinn Féin banned and leaders seized

Ireland, 18 May
In an attempt to curb the growing power of the Irish revolutionary movement, the British government has proclaimed Sinn Féin and the Volunteers to be illegal organizations and arrested many of their leaders, including Eamon de Valera and Arthur Griffith. All public meetings are also to be banned.

During the past year Sinn Féin, the political wing of the revolutionary movement, has been strengthened by many new members, mostly the internees and prisoners who had taken part in the 1916 Rising and who were released as a gesture of goodwill by Lloyd George. Sinn Féin candidates have been successful in two recent by-elections.

De Valera at a Sinn Féin rally.

The intention of the government to extend military conscription to Ireland has encountered fierce opposition across the political spectrum, but it is Sinn Féin, as the diehard opponent of British rule, which is benefiting most from the furore. De Valera is the best-known of the leaders arrested today. He fought in the Rising and was sentenced to death but later reprieved. As a Sinn Féin candidate he was returned for East Clare with a huge majority and later replaced Griffith as leader of Sinn Féin. He was also elected president of the Irish Volunteers and thus exercises authority over the movement's military and political wings (→ 20/6).

Allied counter-attack cuts deep into German lines

France, 8 August
The Allies today launched a great offensive against Ludendorff's army south-east of Amiens. Led by 420 fighting tanks and 120 supply tanks, and covered by swarms of RAF aircraft, British, Canadian, Australian, French and fresh US troops have inflicted a stunning defeat on the German army.

At last the lessons have been learnt. Surprise and secrecy were the watchwords. Low-flying aircraft drowned the noise of the tanks moving forward, and at first light they carried out pre-emptive attacks on German airfields.

The movement of the Canadians into the battle area was concealed by fake wireless traffic. A few tanks drove backwards and forwards to draw attention to the wrong area. Ammunition dumps were camouflaged, and the guns were registered without being fired.

The attack opened before dawn with 1,000 guns laying down a creeping barrage. Just 182 metres (200 yards) behind the shells came the tanks in groups of three, followed by small columns of infantry. The tanks crushed the wire; the infantry dealt with the pillboxes.

The Germans, worn out by the failure of their own spring offensive and demoralized by news of hunger, rioting and strikes at home, collapsed under the surprise and ferocity of the attack.

By midday, when the morning mist had burnt off, the battlefield had become a highway, with infantry, cavalry and field artillery going east and parties of prisoners moving west. The heavy guns have ceased firing because their targets have retreated out of range.

One Whippet tank wiped out a German battery and then caught a party of soldiers packing their kit. It then shot up many columns of retreating Germans before it was put out of action. The Canadians have destroyed two divisions; the Australians have virtually wiped out another. Tonight the Allies are in open country, eight miles in front of their start line. It remains to be seen if the breakthrough will be exploited, but there is no doubt that, in Ludendorff's words, this has been "a black day for the German army" (→11/11).

Disarmed German prisoners.

Lawrence leads the Arabs into Damascus

Lawrence: inspired the Arab revolt.

Cairo, 1 October
The Arab forces of Emir Feisal have entered Damascus. On horse and camel they poured into the city, like their ancestors in the days of the *caliphs*. Major T E Lawrence, who inspired and guided the Arab revolt, arrived in an armoured car.

They had fought their way up from Medina, where Shereef Hussein, Feisal's father, had proclaimed the revolt in June 1916. General Allenby won a crushing victory over the Turks in Palestine last month and is driving them in rout to Anatolia. They abandoned Damascus, and General Allenby allowed the Arabs the honour of liberating it. The British will now take over the city. The French, who have been promised a post-war mandate over Syria, were not consulted.

Guns fall silent on Armistice day

Compiègne, France, 11 November
After four years and three months, and upwards of ten million dead, the guns have fallen silent. Two German generals and a Catholic politician put their signatures to an armistice document shortly before dawn today in a railway carriage in the forest of Compiègne. Six hours later, at 11am on the eleventh day of the eleventh month, all fighting ceased on the battlefields.

The end came more swiftly than the Allies had expected. As late as the end of September the British, the French and the newly arrived Americans were planning a campaign in 1919. But General Erich von Ludendorff panicked when an Allied offensive, spearheaded by British troops, drove into the German lines. He collapsed foaming at the mouth and then begged Kaiser William to seek an armistice immediately.

Germany must hand over 5,000 heavy guns, 30,000 machine guns, 2,000 warplanes and all U-boats. The Germans must pay for Allied occupation of the Rhineland (→19).

Ireland reprieved from conscription

Dublin, 20 June
The government has bowed to widespread protests against plans to extend conscription to Ireland, but it also anounced today the postponement of home rule. Nationalist opinion in Ireland has swung towards the militant Sinn Féin, with the British relying increasingly on military force (→21/1/19).

U-boat sinks Irish mailboat: 587 die

Irish Sea, 10 October
The war ended early and horrifically for 587 passengers on the Irish mailboat *Leinster* today when she sank after being torpedoed by a U-boat off the Irish coast. Only four days ago two liners, one of them a US troopship, collided off the Scottish coast, killing 430 people, most of them servicemen.

Peace at last: members of the 6th Infantry celebrate the Armistice.

How the Great War transformed Britain

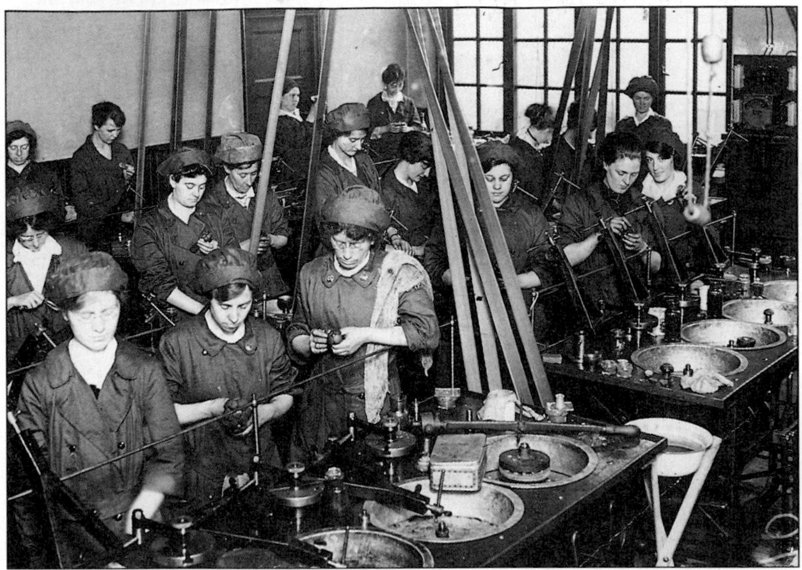

British women were fully employed backing the war effort. Many of them worked in factories, such as those seen here working in a lens factory.

Britain, 11 November
Church bells rang out at 11am today as war-weary Britain celebrated peace. The "Great War" was over, at last. Three-quarters of a million men from Britain – plus a further 200,000 from the empire – have been killed and 1.5 million seriously injured. The conflict has also transformed Britain, forging a sense of national identity out of adversity which is today erupting in a tidal wave of joy.

The authority of the state is now greater than ever, with emergency powers, state intervention in industry and controls over food and pub licensing hours. Trade unions and women's groups gained ground by backing the war effort. Labour politicians served in the coalition government and trade unions have joined "Whitley councils" to plan post-war industries. Women have worked in their millions and won the vote, at least for those over 30.

Rising prices and food shortages eroded some gains of higher wages ("meat every day" was one recruiting slogan), but overall it was a time of full employment and overtime bonuses. Gambling, smoking and movies boomed, with Charlie Chaplin the undisputed star.

Children to stay at school till 14

Westminster, December
A higher school-leaving age and new responsibilities for local authorities in child welfare are the first fruits of legislation designed to introduce social reforms after the war. The Education Act makes school compulsory under the age of 14 (compared with 13) and encourages local authorities to develop a system stretching from nursery schools to evening classes.

A further boost to the powers of local authorities, as long as they have the money, came with a Maternity and Child Welfare Act, also passed this year. This enables councils to expand provision of school meals, welfare clinics and ante-natal services. A ministry of health is likely to be formed next year.

Spanish flu takes its toll of Britons

Nov 20. Preparing to disinfect London's buses in the Spanish flu epidemic which has killed thousands – even returning troops.

London bobbies down their truncheons

August 30. London policemen went on strike for the first time today. Some prisoners were taken to court in taxis rather than Black Marias, but fears of a widespread crime wave have not yet materialized. Bus drivers helped to keep the traffic moving by doing point duty at busy junctions. More than 2,000 police officers marched to Tower Hill where a rally backed their claims for more money and the reinstatement of a man dismissed for his allegedly political activities. Underlying the dispute, though, is a demand for union recognition. Trade unions have grown significantly during the war – from 4,145,000 members in 1914 to 6,533,000 in 1918 – but this is the first time that working-class solidarity has shown itself in forces previously used to keep union disputes in order (→28/1/19).

Lloyd George wins the 'coupon election'

Westminster, 28 December
David Lloyd George has won his first general election as prime minister and the first in which women could vote after their years of often violent campaigning.

Lloyd George, the wartime coalition premier, has been returned in power with an overwhelming Commons majority. Within days, almost, of the war ending he called the election and asked the people to vote for those Liberal and Conservative candidates who received his letter – or "coupon" as Herbert Asquith, the former prime minister, called it – of endorsement.

It soon became known as the "coupon election", and now Lloyd George has the support of 478 MPs. The opposition has 229 MPs, of whom 63 are Labour. Asquith has lost his seat, as have two leading Labour figures, Arthur Henderson and James Ramsay MacDonald.

The first general election for eight years was also the first in which any women could vote. Years of war work by women finally won the vote where pre-war suffragette protests had failed. In addition to women over 30, all men over 21 were given the vote, almost trebling the size of the electorate. One women was elected: Countess Markievicz for a Dublin constituency. But as a Sinn Féin Nationalist she refuses to take the oath of allegiance to the king and will not take her seat in the house (→21/3/21).

Women vote at last – at least some do

The clerks seem more interested in the camera than the nurses at the ballot box as women over 30 are allowed to vote in an election for the first time.

1919

Co Sligo, 15 January. The municipal elections are the first in Britain or Ireland to use proportional representation.

Britain, 28 January. Over 200,000 workers are on strike in many industries, including coal-mining (→31).

Glasgow, 31 January. A sheriff is hit by a bottle as he reads the Riot Act during clashes between demonstrators and police; 40 people are seriously injured (→11/2).

London, 9 February. The first air service to Paris is inaugurated (→15/6).

Glasgow, 11 February. Strikers postpone their fight for a 40-hour week and return to work (→5/10).

Archangel, Russia, 1 April. British troops supporting the White Russians beat off a Bolshevik offensive (→22/11/21).

Dublin, 4 April. Dáil Eireann authorizes the issue of "republican bonds" (→5).

Dublin, 5 April. Sinn Féin elects Eamon de Valera as its president (→12/9).

Norwich, 15 May. The body of Nurse Edith Cavell, shot in Belgium as a spy, is reinterred.

Scapa Flow, Orkney, 21 June. German sailors scuttle 70 ships held captive by Britain.

Britain, 23 June. Nationalization of the mines is recommended by a government commission.

Co Galway, 15 June. A Vickers Vimy bomber piloted by Captain Alcock and Lt Brown lands near Clifden after the first non-stop flight across the Atlantic (→24/5/30).

London, 6 July. A service of thanksgiving for the Versailles Peace Treaty signed on 28 June is held in St Paul's Cathedral.

London, 3 November. In the capital's municipal elections Labour wins control of 14 out of 28 boroughs.

Ireland, 25 November. A proclamation is issued suppressing Sinn Féin, the Irish Volunteers, the Gaelic League and kindred bodies throughout Ireland (→19/12).

Dublin, 19 December. The Irish Republican Army (formerly the Irish Volunteers) makes an unsuccessful attempt on the life of Lord French, the lord lieutenant of Ireland (→2/1/20).

Divided Ireland moves closer to war

Sinn Féin rebels meet at the unofficial "Irish" parliament in Dublin.

Rebel parliament declares independence

Dublin, 21 January
Sinn Féin members who won seats in last month's British general election have ignored Westminster and met today in Dublin to proclaim themselves as the parliament of the Irish republic – Dáil Eireann. They reaffirmed the 1916 declaration of independence and adopted a provisional constitution. Delegates were chosen to attend the post-war peace conference in France.

Of the 69 members elected as MPs, only 25 were present at the rebel parliament in the Mansion House. Two are ill, seven absent on Sinn Féin business, one has been deported and 34 are in prison. Among the latter is Eamon de Valera, and in his absence Cathal Brugha, who also fought in the 1916 Rising, was elected as acting president. Despite efforts by the British authorities to quell the popularity of Sinn Féin, its success at the polls is enabling the party to claim that it now represents a majority of the Irish people.→

Dáil is banned, but Collins has escaped

Dublin, 12 September
Michael Collins, one of Ireland's most charismatic leaders, escaped through a skylight yesterday when police and troops surrounded the Mansion House where the Irish parliament was meeting. The parliament, or Dáil Eireann, was banned today, but the escape of Collins will only enhance his growing reputation within Ireland. Still only 28, he mobilizes irregular forces of around 30 men to carry out raids while also acting as finance minister. His aim is to create a state of disorder which will force Britain to withdraw. His intelligence network and military skill have put the British on the defensive; they now plan to bring in ex-soldiers to reinforce the police (→24/11).

Ministers hear plan to partition Ireland

Westminster, 24 November
Proposals to split Ireland in two were submitted to the British cabinet today. The Irish committee of the government is recommending that two parliaments, one for the Ulster counties and one for the rest of Ireland, be set up in Ireland, linked by a Council of Ireland. Both would remain subservient to the Westminster parliament in areas like foreign policy and defence. Each of the Irelands would continue to be represented at Westminster, should the committee's proposals be accepted. The concept of a partitioned Ireland will not be welcomed by Irish Nationalists. They oppose any dilution of "home rule", leading to a single independent parliament for Ireland (→25).

Republicans set to fight for freedom

Co Tipperary, 21 January
Irish Volunteers today ambushed a cart carrying gelignite at Soloheadbeg. The theft – on the very day that the rebel Irish parliament was proclaimed – symbolizes the readiness of a growing body in the Irish republican movement to use violence in the campaign to win freedom from British rule.

The more extremist Volunteers have formed themselves into a unit known as the Irish Republican Army, and they are increasing pressure on Sinn Féin to support their more confrontational tactics. These amount, essentially, to shooting policemen, on or off duty, on the grounds that the Royal Irish Constabulary represents an alien oppression. Some republicans hope that American influence may yet persuade Britain to give Ireland its freedom, but with British policy veering between ineffective repression and hopes of reconciliation Ireland appears to be perilously close to war.

Sinn Féin's political success has polarized the divisions within Ireland. The parliament set up today is expected to hold effective control over at least half the country. Many local authorities are also dominated by republicans, and arbitration courts have virtually superseded the courts of the crown. With two governments in existence, clashes seem inevitable (→4/4).

A Irish policeman at pistol practice.

Scientist shows how to 'split' the atom

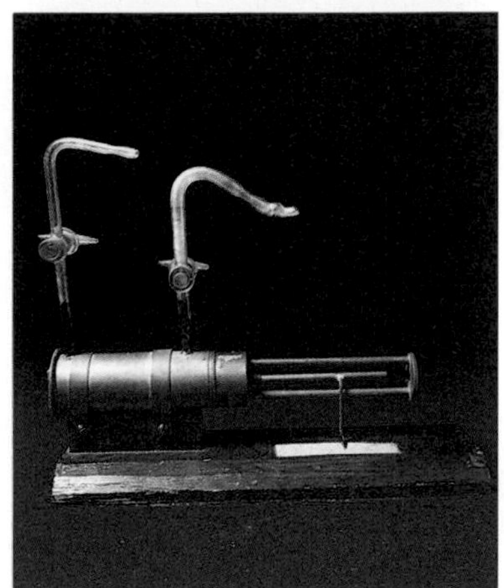

Apparatus for "splitting" the atom.

Manchester, 3 January
Atoms, the smallest particles of matter, are not indivisible, as was previously supposed for Professor Ernest Rutherford of Manchester university has succeeded in "splitting" the atom. And in doing so he transmuted atoms of one element, nitrogen, into those of oxygen.

What this first-ever artificial transmutation from one element to another – part of the alchemist's dream of old – portends is difficult to say, but scientists regard Professor Rutherford's achievement as a major breakthrough. As long ago as 1911 he outlined a theoretical model of atoms. Now he has demonstrated that atoms are not indivisible by using the alpha particles which are transmitted by some radioactive materials to bombard nitrogen atoms (→ 12/1932).

Rail strike settled as civil unrest grows

Britain, 5 October
A week-long rail strike was settled tonight, with victory for the unions, in a year marked by an explosion of civil unrest – a year when policemen went on strike and servicemen mutinied over their slow demobilization. Race riots in several ports led to three deaths in Cardiff and one in Liverpool, while another man was killed in Liverpool when troops opened fire to control looting during the police strike in August.

Over 30 million days have so far been lost through strikes this year compared with 5.8 million last year. Soaring prices, as wartime controls ended, were a principal cause of discontent, but many MPs believe that the militancy is fanned by Bolshevik agitators inspired by the 1917 Russian Revolution.

In Glasgow, the red flag was indeed hoisted over the city as workers struck in January for a 40-hour week to provide jobs for all workers. A sheriff read the Riot Act as police broke up a demonstration. Troops were also sent to "Red Clydeside", and, with some key unions refusing support, the strike failed. None the less it alarmed the government, as has the decision by railwaymen, miners and transport workers to reform their pre-war "triple alliance". Lloyd George was anxious to settle the rail dispute before it spread to other workers.

Forces of law and order close in on a union demonstrator in Glasgow.

Versailles treaty is approved by MPs

Westminster, 22 July
Lloyd George was praised for his role as a peacemaker when MPs today debated the treaty signed at Versailles last month. Only four MPs opposed the terms of the treaty – three of them Irish members objecting to the failure to grant home rule. The British prime minister has spent much of the last five months in Paris at the peace talks where he sought to counter French demands for punitive measures against Germany. More extreme proposals for partitioning Germany have been rejected, but some territory is to be yielded, the Rhineland demilitarized and high compensation payments, or "reparations", imposed. A league of nations, first proposed by the US president, Woodrow Wilson, is to be created to monitor the peace (→ 8/3/21).

Jazz is new sound down at the palais

London, December
A new type of music is being heard in Britain. It is known as "jazz" and was first brought here by American troops during the Great War. Although jazz music is associated with the black people of America, it was the all-white Original Dixieland Jazz Band which was the first to tour this year, playing at venues such as London's newly-opened Hammersmith Palais de Danse.

British massacre protesters at Amritsar

India, 13 April
British troops opened fire today on demonstrators in Amritsar, the Sikh holy city in the Punjab. There had been a series of riots following a call for a business strike by the radical Congress leader Mohandas Gandhi who advocates a policy of non-cooperation with the authorities. When a large crowd gathered on wasteland at Amritsar the local army commander, Brigadier Dyer, ordered his troops to fire without warning, killing 379 people and wounding 1,200. Many women and children are believed to be among the dead (→ 28/7/21).

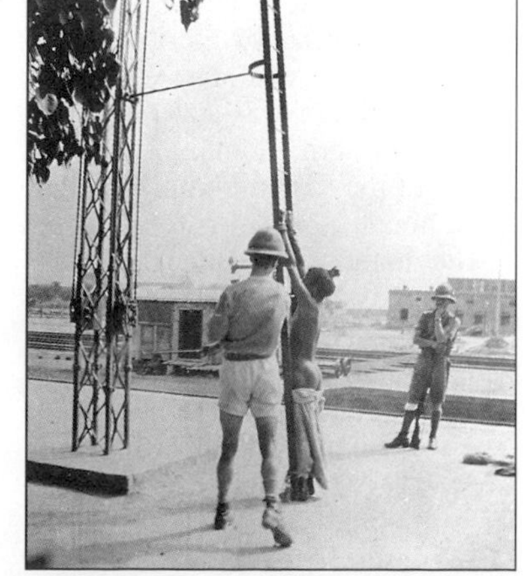

A flogging during the Amritsar riots.

Influenza epidemic has killed 150,000

Britain, 18 March
The outbreak of influenza known as "Spanish flu" has returned to strike again in the first three months of this year. Figures released today show that for the first time deaths exceeded births in the last quarter of 1918, largely as a result of the flu epidemic. Now, with the virus striking again, the death toll in England and Wales alone is forecast to be 150,000 since the first outbreak last year. The flu has spread around the world, causing more deaths than those in the Great War.

Dec 1. Nancy Astor becomes the first woman MP to take her seat.

1920

Dublin, 2 January. The Royal Irish Constabulary enrols its first British special constables, distinguished by their black-and-tan uniforms (→ 15/1).

London, 9 January. The government announces plans for the construction of 100,000 new houses in the coming year.

Ireland, 15 January. Sinn Féin, with Nationalists and Labour, wins control of 172 out of 206 seats at local council elections (→ 20/3).

London, 11 February. The council of the League of Nations, representing Britain, Belgium, Brazil, France, Greece, Italy, Japan and Spain, opens its first meeting.

Cork, 20 March. Tomas Mac Curtain, the lord mayor of Cork and head of the IRA's 1st Cork Brigade, is shot dead, allegedly by police (→ 26).

Dublin, 26 March. Alan Bell, a magistrate investigating Sinn Féin and Dàil funds, is taken from a tram and shot on the orders of Michael Collins, the Dàil finance minister and IRA intelligence chief (→ 24/7).

Ireland, 27 July. An auxiliary paramilitary force, recruited from former British Army officers, is inaugurated (→ 6/8).

London, 31 July. The Communist Party of Great Britain, a branch of the Third International, is formed (→ 25/11/25).

Belfast, 6 August. A boycott of Protestant-owned firms in the city begins, on the orders of the Dàil (→ 25/10).

Oxford, 7 October. The university, which gave women professors equal status with male colleagues on 18 May, admits the first 100 women to study for full degrees (→ 25/1/21).

London, 25 October. Terence MacSwiney, Mac Curtain's successor as lord mayor of Cork and a local IRA chief, dies on hunger strike in Brixton prison (→ 1/11).

Belfast, 1 November. Recruitment begins for part-time "B" category members of a special constabulary (→ 21).

London, 11 November. An unknown British soldier who fell in France is interred in Westminster Abbey.

Britain. The Medical Research Council is set up this year (→ 24/7/25).

Striking miners defy state of emergency

A poster justifies the British government's stance against the miners.

London, 18 October
Once again the miners are locked in a full-blooded confrontation with the government. Not a single mine is expected to open this morning. Over the weekend the government has declared a state of emergency to preserve coal stocks. Train services will be cut and all advertisement and display lighting is forbidden. The people are even being urged to economize on water consumption to save the fuel needed to operate pumps.

The miners are striking for more money, but underlying their action are political concerns. At present the mines are still under government control as they were during the war. But the owners want them to be returned to private enterprise. The miners, for their part, are using their new clout to call for nationalization.

They have formed an alliance with the transport workers and the railwaymen to get support. With trade union membership at a new peak of eight million and the recent by-election successes of Labour candidates, they think the time is ripe to press their claims (→ 15/4/21).

'Wee drams' cheer prohibition defeat

Edinburgh, 5 December
Thousands of Scots have enjoyed their amber-coloured fluid with extra relish tonight as they celebrated victory after a hard-fought campaign against prohibition. It was a battle between the "wee dram" supporters, backed by the distillery lobby, against the churches, particularly the strict Sabbatarian "wee frees".

The "wee frees" fought on economic grounds with the church, from the pulpit, stressing the high level of alcoholism in Scotland, particularly in city slums. The whisky lobby used more secular methods – like dropping "No Change" leaflets from aircraft.

British mandate in Palestine endorsed

San Remo, Italy, 25 April
The British mandate to control Palestine and Mesopotamia was confirmed here today by the League of Nations. There was hardly any discussion: Britain was given a new, Middle Eastern, domain from the debris of the Turkish empire in just three hours.

The mandate has delighted the Zionist movement because it incorporates the 1917 Balfour Declaration which promises the Jews a national home in Palestine. "Here we are, here we remain," said Dr Max Nordeau. The Arabs, however, are bitterly opposed and the Holy Land seems destined again to be the cockpit of intense rivalries (→ 25/8/29).

Dame Nellie loses Marconi its licence

Chelmsford, November
The Marconi company, which has transmitted experimental broadcasts by wireless from its factory at Writtle near Chelmsford, Essex, has had its licence withdrawn by the Post Office under pressure of people who disapprove of wireless telegraphy being used for mere entertainment. On 16 June the *Daily Mail* sponsored a Marconi broadcast by Dame Nellie Melba, the opera singer, which was picked up by listeners all over Europe, and even in faraway Newfoundland. Other radio manufacturers are now seeking air time. The armed services believe that broadcasting will interfere with aircraft signals. Commercial exploitation of the airwaves is rife in the US (→ 15/11/22).

Insurance extended

Westminster, December
Unemployment insurance is to be available to an additional nine million workers. The system of contributions and benefits introduced in 1911 was confined to building, engineering and shipbuilding. It was extended to munitions during the war and to ex-servicemen on a temporary basis after the war. Now it will cover virtually all people earning less than £5 a week.

Supporters chair a jubilant Albert Hill after his victory in the 1500 metres, his second gold medal of the Olympic Games at Antwerp.

Bloody war of independence ravages Ireland

Three Sinn Féiners lie dead as Black and Tans round up possible suspects.

'Bloody Sunday' reprisals leave 23 dead

Dublin, 21 November
In what is being regarded as a horrific climax to the reprisal killings which are prevalent throughout the country, the new police reinforcements, nicknamed the "Black and Tans" [*see below*] have fired into a football crowd causing 12 deaths, many people being crushed to death in the ensuing stampede.

Earlier in the day the IRA had shot and killed 11 unarmed British officers in Dublin on suspicion of their being intelligence operatives. The possibility of martial law is being considered, and it is felt that Sinn Féin will now be seen as waging a war against Britain, instead of merely targeting local policemen. Britain's refusal to recognize this "war" has meant reliance on the police and not the army.

As a result the army has been a less popular target for the IRA. To date, only 160 soldiers have been killed, compared with 400 policemen. Police resignations have now reached a critical level (→10/12).

Cork set ablaze in wake of martial law

Ireland, 12 December
The end of a year of terror and counter-terror in Ireland has been marked by the introduction of martial law in the south-west and the destruction of parts of Cork city by the Black and Tans and the "Auxies", an auxiliary division of the Royal Irish Constabulary. The City Hall and much of St Patrick Street in Cork were gutted yesterday in retaliation for the losses inflicted on police and soldiers by IRA flying columns in Co Cork.

In Ireland generally the combined force of police and military numbers around 40,000 at the moment. They face an estimated IRA force of 15,000 although only 3,000 can fight effectively. The IRA's greatest strength lies in the loyalty of the local people. When that fails, spies and informers are shot, and their bodies are left in the open.

The IRA has also resorted to use of the hunger-strike weapon. Back in October world attention was focused on the young lord mayor of Cork, Terence MacSwiney, who died in Brixton prison after 73 days on hunger strike. The British public, and some members of the government, are beginning to be disturbed by the savagery of the war being waged in Ireland (→23).

Cork: a city sacked and in ruins.

Belfast backlash over police murder

Belfast, 24 July
The murder by the IRA of Colonel Smyth, a Royal Irish Constabulary divisional commissioner, in Cork a week ago has created a violent backlash here. Thirteen people have so far died – seven Catholics and six Protestants – in three days of intensive rioting in east Belfast.

Trams carrying shipyard men home from work were attacked in the Catholic Short Strand area while Catholic workers came under attack at the Harland and Wolff shipyard. Some even jumped into the river Lagan and swam to safety. Loyalist groups are demanding that the government drive out Catholics and socialists from the yard (→27).

How 'Black and Tans' enforce British law

Dublin, 10 December
Martial law was declared today in south-west Ireland as the British authorities step up what has become an all-out war against Irish nationalists. At the forefront of this struggle has been a group of auxiliaries who have become hated by the Irish people. The "Black and Tans", as they have become known from their uniform, are theoretically linked to the Royal Irish Constabulary; but they are in reality an anti-terrorist cadre operating a shoot-to-kill policy that is alarming politicians in Westminster as well as in Dublin. Many Black and Tans are jobless war veterans who were enlisted through advertisements last year seeking men for "a rough and dangerous task" (→12).

Black and Tans present arms.

Westminster backs Ireland's partition

London, 23 December
King George today signed the act of parliament which partitions Ireland into two. The proposal, first floated a year ago, creates two Irish parliaments – one for 26 counties of Ireland in Dublin and the other for six counties of Ulster in Belfast. The Government of Ireland Act also envisages both parts of Ireland sending MPs to Westminster and creates an all-Ireland council to discuss unity. A year of bloodshed since partition was first mooted has all but destroyed its chances of success. Sinn Féin refuses to recognize the southern parliament while the Ulster Unionists reject the Council of Ireland (→4/1/21).

1921

Belfast, 4 February. Sir James Craig is elected leader of the Ulster Unionists (→4/5).

Oxford, 11 March. Queen Mary receives an honorary degree – the first full degree awarded to a woman by the university.

Africa, 15 March. Belgium cedes the small central African colony of Ruanda to Britain.

London, 21 March. Austen Chamberlain becomes Tory leader following the resignation of Andrew Bonar Law on 17 March, owing to ill health (→19/10/22).

Glasgow, 4 May. The Irish "troubles" spread to Britain when a police inspector is murdered by Sinn Féiners (→24).

Egypt, 23 May. British and Egyptian troops restore order during nationalist riots in Alexandria and Cairo (→24/11/24).

Ireland, 24 May. Sinn Féin wins 124 out of 128 seats in elections to the Southern Ireland parliament; in elections to the Northern Ireland parliament Unionists win 40 seats, Nationalists six and Sinn Féin six (→25).

Dublin, 25 May. The Custom House is destroyed in an IRA attack (→22/6).

Britain, 15 June. Two million workers are now involved in pay disputes as unemployment reaches 2.2 million.

Belfast, 22 June. King George opens the first Northern Ireland parliament in Belfast City Hall (→9/7).

Dublin, 9 July. A truce is signed between the British army in Ireland and the IRA (→22/7).

Bombay, India, 28 July. The All-India Congress Party votes to boycott a forthcoming visit by the prince of Wales and urges a boycott of imported cloth (→18/3/22).

London, 11 October. Anglo-Irish talks open (→6/12).

Kabul, 22 November. Britain signs a friendship treaty with Afghanistan, recognizing its independence in return for limits on the Soviet presence in the country (→24/5/27).

USA, 13 December. Britain, France, the US and Japan sign a treaty to control the size of their navies.

Britain. The Austin Seven motor car is introduced.

First birth control clinic opens in London

London, 17 March

Britain's first birth control clinic has opened today in the Holloway Road in north London. The clinic is the result of work by Dr Marie Stopes, a pioneer of birth control information, whose controversial best-selling books *Married Love* and *Wise Parenthood* appeared three years ago.

Dr Stopes, a fossil botanist rather than a physician, has long been established as a passionate advocate of a more open attitude to sexual matters in general, and of a commonsense discussion of birth control in particular. Above all she believes that family planning, for many people a taboo subject, is the basis of a truly fulfilled marriage.

Marie Stopes: women's best friend?

Allied troops to occupy Rhineland

Düsseldorf, Germany, 8 March

British, French and Belgian troops crossed the Rhine early this morning and are now on the streets here and in many other towns of the Ruhr. So far it has been a peaceful invasion. The Allies are hoping that the threat will be enough to impel Germany to pay war reparations.

Local opinion does not agree. Most Germans seem to think that the £6.5 million demanded is far beyond the country's ability to pay. Neither military threats nor taxes on German goods seems likely to work. The burden is just too heavy for an economy still ravaged by the war (→8/8/24).

Women jurors begin to hear divorce cases

London, 25 January

In a move that is guaranteed to shock legal traditionalists, six women were sworn in as jurors in the divorce court today – the first of their sex ever to serve in a case concerning marital breakdown.

The move is an example of the greater role women are playing in public life since the war and the logical extension of the 1919 Sex Disqualification (Removal) Act, giving women access to the professions. Although some feared that the details of cases might shock the ladies, none chose to stand down, although the possibility of exemption does exist.

Nonetheless, proprieties were scrupulously observed. When what were described as "abominable and beastly" letters were produced in evidence, it was agreed that their content would offend, even terrify, the female jurors. Accordingly the letters were read only by the six males; the ladies simply chose not to look.

Land sales boom

England, December

A quarter of England has changed hands since the end of the war, claims a report in the *Estates Times*. Land sales have boomed with between six and eight million acres changing hands since the beginning of 1918. This represents the most dramatic change since the dissolution of the monasteries in the 16th century. The agricultural depression, higher wartime taxes and death duties have led many landed families to sell their estates.

National strike called off as miners lose allies on 'Black Friday'

Wigan miners are urged to stand their ground despite dwindling support.

London, 15 April

The national strike called for ten o'clock tonight by the railway and transport workers in support of the miners, their allies in the "triple alliance" of key unions, has been called off. The miners have been locked out by the pit owners since 1 April in a pay dispute. The owners wanted lower wages and greater regional variations; the miners sought a "national pool" to equalize wages; the government urged both sides to talk. The pit owners suggested a pay standstill while there were negotiations over a national pool, but the miners' executive today rejected this by a majority of one. Its allies in the triple alliance backed off from a strike – on a day miners are calling a "Black Friday" of betrayal (→24/3/26).

Surprise peace treaty creates Irish Free State

London, 6 December
Following protracted negotiations between the British prime minister and a delegation from the self-styled Irish Republic an historic treaty was signed tonight in London. It confers dominion status (equivalent to that of Canada) on an Irish Free State, which will be made up of 26 southern counties – six of the nine counties in Ulster will remain part of the United Kingdom. The treaty concedes certain naval facilities to Britain. Members of the Free State parliament must take an oath of allegience to the king, but they will be allowed first to proclaim allegiance to the constitution of the Irish Free State.

A torrent of recrimination seems likely to engulf the signatories. But much criticism is also reserved for Eamon de Valera, the president of the Irish parliament or Dàil. Preoccupied with his wish for unity which he hoped to achieve through a subtle plan of "external association", he stayed at home and sent the finance minister and IRA military strategist Michael Collins as part of the negotiating team.

It can never be known whether de Valera could have gained time had he been in London by resisting Lloyd George's threat to end the summer truce. As it was, there was little consultation between the London delegation and the cabinet members who stayed at home. Four cabinet members are thought to be against the treaty (including de Valera) and three are for it on the grounds that it was the best available short of all-out war (→ 7/1/22).

Cease-fire declared after a year of terror in the Irish 'troubles'

Ireland, 22 July
A truce has been declared in the Anglo-Irish war which has continued now for two years. Known in Ireland euphemistically as the "troubles" it has seriously embittered Anglo-Irish relations. The truce has been brought about by strong public opinion in Britain following King George's dramatic appeal for conciliation at the opening of the Northern Irish parliament last month. The United States, too, has urged Britain to seek a solution. Eamon de Valera, the Irish leader, has made a financially successful, if politically controversial, tour of America.

Burning buildings have become a familiar sight to the people of Dublin.

The struggle has been characterized by guerrilla warfare, ambushes, raids on police barracks and planned assassinations on the one side, with reprisals, shootings and burning of towns on the other. During the past year the crown forces have lost 525 men with 1,000 wounded. At least 700 civilians have died already this year.

Greatly disturbed by what he found on his return from the United States, de Valera quickly realized that negotiations towards peace must get under way. It was a relief, therefore, when the British prime minister, David Lloyd George, followed the king's appeal by proposing a truce.

Poplar councillors jailed in rates row

London, 6 September
Five women councillors are facing prison sentences tonight after being arrested for their part in the refusal by Poplar borough council to levy a rate. A crowd of 3,000 people gathered outside Poplar town hall in the East End to protest, but one of the councillors, Susan Lawrence, said she and her colleagues were determined to go to prison like 25 male councillors who were jailed last week.

The dispute has arisen over protests by Labour-controlled Poplar council over a central rate equalization scheme which, it argues, means poor areas like Poplar paying more than richer areas. Poplar, led by George Lansbury, refused to set a rate with the result that councillors have been imprisoned for defying the law (→ 11/10).

Charlie Chaplin mobbed by fans as 'the Tramp' returns home

A hero's welcome: Chaplin reads in the "Daily Mail" of his triumphant return.

London, 9 September
Charlie Chaplin returned to Britain today and disappeared into the mob of thousands who waited at Waterloo to welcome him from the boat train. More surrounded the Ritz hotel in Piccadilly where he is staying – a long way socially from his native Lambeth. London cinemas are showing his classic films *Easy Street*, *The Immigrant* and his latest, *The Kid*. He explained how he chose his famous costume as the Tramp: "I wanted to create a satire on man – the cane for his dignity, the moustache for his vanity, the boots for the cares that weigh him down. That's how my character came about" (→ 26/3/27).

Women outnumber men by two million

Britain, 23 August
First results of this year's national census show an increase of almost two million in the total population of Britain since 1911 – despite the losses of the Great War. The preliminary total is put at 42,767,530 of whom some 7.4 million live in London. Wartime losses obviously affected the totals, but not so dramatically as might be imagined: more people emigrated in the prewar years than died annually during the war. There are now two million more women than men, but the ratio is much the same as it was before 1914.

1922

Dublin, 7 January. The Dàil votes 64 to 57 for the Anglo-Irish treaty (→12).

London, 12 January. The government declares an amnesty for Irish political prisoners (→17/2).

London, 26 February. Britain and France conclude a 20-year alliance.

London, 30 March. A peace pact is concluded at a conference on Ireland; signatories include Michael Collins for the Free State and Sir James Craig for Ulster (→14/4).

Dublin, 14 April. An anti-treaty IRA unit under Rory O'Connor seizes the Four Courts (→31/5).

London, 10 May. Dr Ivy Williams of Oxford is the first woman to become a barrister in England.

Belfast, 31 May. The Royal Ulster Constabulary is formed (→16/6).

Irish Free State, 16 June. In the first Free State general election, pro-treaty Sinn Féin wins 58 seats, anti-treaty Sinn Féin 36 and others 34 (→22).

London, 22 June. Field Marshal Sir Henry Wilson, former chief of the imperial general staff and an Irishman, is shot dead by Irish gunmen acting without IRA authority (→28).

Dublin, 25 August. William T Cosgrave becomes head of the provisional government of the Irish Free State, succeeding Arthur Griffith, who died of a cerebral haemorrhage on 12 August (→6/12).

London, 29 September. Britain warns Turkish forces at Chanak not to advance further in the Dardanelles.

London, 23 October. Bonar Law is re-elected Tory leader in succession to Austen Chamberlain and calls a general election (→16/11).

Britain, 16 November. Yesterday's election has given the Conservatives 345 seats, Labour – the main opposition party for the first time – 142 and the Liberals 117, a Tory majority of 77 (→21/5/23).

Egypt, 26 November. British archaeologists Howard Carter and the earl of Caernarvon discover the 3,000-year-old tomb of an Egyptian pharaoh, Tutankhamun.

Dublin, 17 December. The last British troops leave (→31/3/23).

Tory rebels oust PM

Westminster, 19 October
Lloyd George has fallen. The man who "won the war" and promised to win the peace resigned as prime minister this afternoon after Conservative MPs meeting at the Carlton Club deserted him and voted to fight the forthcoming general election as an independent party.

Lloyd George believed he could carry the wartime coalition into the peace. But first the newly confident Labour Party pulled out and then the Liberals' Asquith wing rejected his overtures. Since the 1918 election, Lloyd George has been sustained by the votes of 339 Tory MPs with only 134 Liberals remaining loyal to him.

The Tories, who have not formed a government since 1906, have been increasingly restless in the coalition harness; now power is within their grasp. At the Carlton Club meeting, Lloyd George, "the Welsh Wizard", was attacked as "a dynamic force ... a terrible thing" by Stanley Baldwin, a wealthy ironmaster who gave a fifth of his fortune to help reduce the national debt. As president of the board of trade, Baldwin has been only a minor political figure, but his words reflected the opinion of another political ironmaster, the Canadian-born Scot Andrew Bonar Law.

The new PM: Bonar Law.

After the meeting voted 185 to 88 to quit the coalition, Bonar Law became Tory leader; despite his poor health he expects to be prime minister next month (→23).

Sale of honours scandal causes a storm

Westminster, 30 June
The prime minister, David Lloyd George, has been forced by the House of Commons to hold an inquiry into the abuse of the honours system. For some time there has been disquiet at his wholesale handing out of titles and honours to many rich "profiteers" who qualified by making contributions to his personal political fund. The Lloyd George fund is rumoured to stand at over £3,000,000. Evidence was cited of people being approached by intermediaries such as the notorious Arthur Maundy Gregory and invited to contribute £80,000 to be a baron, £40-50,000 for lesser titles and around £12,000 for a knighthood. In the last 18 months 74 baronetcies and 294 knighthoods have been granted.

When the sun is out, the roof folds down: Austin's convertible Seven.

Daily broadcasting plans for wireless

London, 15 November
The British Broadcasting Company formed last month took over 2LO, Marconi's London station, yesterday and today opened stations in Birmingham and Manchester in a national service. The BBC is a consortium of radio manufacturers. Its general manager is John Reith, an engineer from Aberdeen. Since February the Marconi company has been transmitting weekly half-hour broadcasts from Chelmsford, and daily from 2LO, on top of Marconi House in the Strand. Most listeners with crystal sets are members of wireless societies (→1/5/23).

'Obscene' novel is published at last

Dublin-born James Joyce.

Paris, 2 February
James Joyce's eagerly awaited novel *Ulysses* has been published here in a limited edition of 1,000 copies. The book has already been the subject of legal action against its serial publication in the *Little Review* in New York, because of its alleged obscenity, and is considered too pornographic to be published in London. The author was born in Dublin but has lived abroad since 1904. He began writing *Ulysses* in 1914; it was championed by the international literary establishment and achieved notoriety well before its publication this week.

Twelve months in the bloody birth of free Ireland

MPs approve a Bill for Irish Free State

Ireland, 17 February
The terms of the historic treaty signed last December have been hotly discussed during parliament's Christmas recess. Since parliament reassembled, both sides have argued their case with conviction. Arthur Griffith and Michael Collins (both signatories of the treaty) saw it as a stepping stone on the way to full independence and a considerable achievement. Others, like Liam Mellows and Cathal Brugha, rejected the treaty, stating that "the honour of Ireland is too sacred a thing to make a bargain over".

Eamon de Valera, the president of the Irish Republic, believes his alternative to the treaty – "external association", a loose association between an independent Ireland and Britain – has been misrepresented and never discussed in the parliament as an alternative. This has led to de Valera's resignation as president, followed by the election of Griffith and the formation of a provisional government (→ 15).

Spiral of violence spreads to Ulster

Belfast, 15 February
Loyalists today hurled a bomb into a group of Catholic children in the north of the city, killing six, in revenge for the murder of four policemen in Clones, Co Monaghan. Winston Churchill, the colonial secretary, said it was "the worst thing that has happened in Ireland in the last three years". In all 31 people have died in four days of violence which the London *Star* called "a sort of Protestant pogrom against the Catholic minority".

The IRA launched a major offensive in January, but the spark for loyalist violence was an attack on a platoon of 16 policemen at Clones. The police shot dead the local IRA commandant, but an IRA guard killed four, wounded eight and took four prisoners. In Belfast, Catholics hit back by bombing trams bound for the shipyard (→ 30/3).

A ruined building provides Free State riflemen with a hidden gun post.

Wilson: assassinated in London.

Collins: the warrior politician.

Civil war breaks out over peace treaty

Dublin, 28 June
Violent repercussions have followed the signing of the treaty setting up the Irish Free State. Six days ago Field Marshal Sir Henry Wilson was gunned down in London. Now civil war is breaking out in Ireland itself over the peace treaty. The provisional government under its president, Arthur Griffith, is trying to take control but the anti-treaty faction within the IRA is defying the Free State army by occupying buildings here, notably the Four Courts, and by turning much of the city into a battlefield (→ 22/8).

Michael Collins is killed in ambush

Cork, 22 August
Michael Collins, one of the most admired and charismatic leaders in the fight for Irish independence, has been killed during an ambush at Bealnablath in his native Co Cork. Collins was one of the team which negotiated the Anglo-Irish Treaty in 1921. He is already recognized as having established new criteria for both urban and rural guerrilla warfare. He had also been the finance minister and at the time of his death was chairman of the provisional government and commander-in-chief of the army (→ 25).

Royalty proclaims Ireland's freedom

Ireland, 6 December
The Free State Constitution Act and the consequential Provisions Act have received the royal assent, and the Irish Free State today comes officially into existence. The king has also approved the appointment of veteran parliamentarian Timothy Healy as the Free State's first governor-general. He is to live in the former vice-regal lodge in Phoenix Park, Dublin, which Dubliners have already nicknamed "Uncle Tim's Cabin" (→ 17).

1923

Ireland, 23 January. A United Council of Christian Churches in Ireland meets for the first time, but the Catholic church is not represented.

London, 7 March. Neville Chamberlain becomes minister of health in succession to Sir Arthur Boscawen, who lost his seat two days ago (→27/8).

British Isles, 31 March. Customs barriers between the United Kingdom and the Irish Free State become effective (→10/4).

Waterford, 10 April. Liam Lynch, head of the anti-treaty IRA "Irregulars", dies in police custody after being wounded in fighting with Free State troops (→27).

London, 26 April. The duke of York marries Lady Elizabeth Bowes-Lyon in Westminster Abbey (→12/12/36).

London, 1 May. The BBC opens central London wireless studios at Savoy Hill; a new programme, "Woman's Hour", will be launched tomorrow (→23/4/24).

Bath, 8 May. The Surrey and England opening batsman Jack Hobbs scores 116 against Somerset to become only the third cricketer to achieve 100 centuries, after Dr W G Grace and Tom Hayward (→18/2/25).

London, 21 May. Stanley Baldwin becomes prime minister on the resignation of Andrew Bonar Law, who has incurable throat cancer; Baldwin remains chancellor of the exchequer for the time being (→21/11).

London, 13 July. Lady Astor's Liquor Bill, prohibiting the sale of alcohol to people under 18, is passed by the Commons.

London, 21 August. A seven-week-long dock strike ends.

London, 27 August. Neville Chamberlain succeeds Baldwin as chancellor of the exchequer; Sir William Joynson-Hicks takes over as minister of health.

Geneva, 10 September. The Irish Free State is admitted to the League of Nations (→10/5/24).

Africa, 1 October. Britain agrees to establish an autonomous government for Southern Rhodesia, which was ceded to direct crown control by the British South Africa Company on 12 September (→30/5/24).

De Valera calls off anti-treaty struggle

Ireland, 27 April

Peace of a sort has come to Ireland after its terrible civil war. Following the death this month of the IRA chief-of-staff, Liam Lynch, Eamon de Valera has called off his struggle against the treaty. He has sent a message to his republican followers ("Irregulars" and rebels in the eyes of the Free State's government) saying: "Further sacrifice of life would now be in vain. Military victory must be allowed to rest for the moment with those who have destroyed the republic."

Nearly 4,000 people have died, and the damage to property is estimated at £30 million. The bitter legacy of the past year will divide families for generations to come. The resistance of the anti-treaty minority has been broken by the determination and ruthlessness of the Free State government, together with lack of support from ordinary people. Over 12,000 people (amongst them 400 women) have been imprisoned under emergency powers, and a man can now be executed for having in his possession any plan or document prejudicial to the safety of the state.

The republican tactic has been to provoke destabilization by declaring the Free State government, courts and police illegal, and therefore legitimate targets. The policy of assassinating Dáil members and judges has produced strong reaction from the provisional government. During the blackest weeks of the civil war 77 executions without trial were carried out. De Valera, a former president of the Dáil, led the political opposition to the treaty.

President of the Irish Free State, William Cosgrave speaks his mind.

The conflict will leave deep scars for years, if not decades, to come. A deep divide has been established between revolutionary republicanism, which believes passionately in the unfinished business of uniting Ireland, north and south, and a strongly law-and-order administration which, under its president, William Cosgrave, has set a stamp of stern justice and inflexible authority on the running of the fledgling state (→10/9).

Sexual equality is reflected in divorce

London, 2 March

Until today a man could divorce a woman for adultery but a woman had to prove cruelty or desertion as well – and all but the fiercest backwoodsmen had come to recognize this as intolerable. Hence the cheers that greeted the passing of the Matrimonial Causes Bill, by 231 votes to 27, that evened matters up.

There have been numerous other victories for equality since Mrs Pankhurst raised the standard for women's suffrage 20 years ago. Besides the winning of the vote itself in 1918, triumphs include Nancy Astor as the first female MP to take her seat in 1919, Mrs Ada Summers the first JP in 1920, and Dr Ivy Williams, first woman to be called to the English bar in 1922. An estimated 4,000 women are now magistrates, mayors and councillors.

Much more noticeable is the contrast between Mrs Pankhurst's stiff Edwardian dresses and today's rising hemlines, short hair and lighter clothes; even she might have been shocked by the advertisements for "lingerie" and "undies" now seen in the newspapers. All are signs of the new freedom that allows a girl to go to the cinema with her boyfriend – unthinkable even ten years ago – and the numbers of divorces to rise from 823 per year in 1911 to 3,619 last year.

Mass disaster narrowly avoided at first Wembley football final

Astride a white horse, PC George Storey helps to clear the crowds at Wembley.

Wembley, 28 April

Mounted on a white horse, a lone policeman played a major part in averting disaster at the vast new Wembley Stadium today. The stadium, which will house much of next year's Empire Exhibition, is designed to hold a crowd of 100,000. But today's attendance was swollen to nearly double that by chaos at the turnstiles and by fans who climbed boundary walls to watch the FA Cup Final.

Fans spilled onto the pitch and organizers were about to cancel the match between Bolton Wanderers and West Ham – with the chance of a riot – when Constable George Storey quietly persuaded the invaders back on to the stands. Bolton won the cup 2-1.

Baldwin is rebuffed at snap election

Guests at the Savoy Hotel are kept informed of the latest election results.

Facing defeat: Stanley Baldwin.

Westminster, 21 November
Stanley Baldwin's decision to call a snap election only six months after becoming Conservative prime minister is being described today as a colossal misjudgement or, alternatively, a clever political tactic to dish the Liberals.

When Andrew Bonar Law resigned last May after doctors told him he was suffering from incurable throat cancer, King George sent for Baldwin rather than Lord Curzon, then foreign secretary, believing the premier should be in the Commons. Tory MPs duly made Baldwin their leader, though one speaker described him as "a person of the utmost insignificance". Baldwin likes to present himself as a simple country gentleman; in fact, in Lloyd George's words, he is "a formidable political antagonist".

The new prime minister revived an old controversy – tariff reform. Rising unemployment, he declared, could only be tackled by imposing tariffs on imports to protect the home market. He asked for a mandate from the voters. What he has received is a smart rebuff. In the new parliament Conservatives have 258 MPs, Labour 191 and the Liberals 159. It is the second time Labour has overtaken the Liberals.

Baldwin is certain to be defeated when the new House of Commons meets. Ramsay MacDonald, the Labour leader, will then expect to be asked to form a government, with the half-hearted support of the Liberals. Baldwin expects Labour and Liberals between them to make a mess of things and the voters to turn to him (→22/1/24).

Land Act holds out hope of new deal for Irish tenants

Dublin, 9 August
Under the 1923 Land Law Act introduced in the Irish parliament by Patrick Hogan, the agriculture minister, a land commission has been reconstituted to replace the Congested Districts Board and the Estates Commission.

The Hogan Act has made compulsory the sale to tenants of all land not yet dealt with. Rents fixed before 1911 have been reduced by 35 per cent, and those fixed later by 30 per cent. All rent arrears due up to 1920 have been forgiven and arrears after 1920 have been reduced by 25 per cent. Illegal sub-tenants are now recognized as tenants and sub-letting or sub-division of land is prohibited.

Given the importance attached to land legislation in Ireland, the Hogan Act is seen as a significant conclusion to a process which had begun in the last century when in 1870 the then British prime minister, William Gladstone, introduced the first major legislation.

From then on the landlord and tenant relationship began to change in favour of the tenant. Gladstone's legislation allowed tenants to be advanced two-thirds of the price of their farms to be repaid with interest over a 35-year period.

Reorganization of railway companies

Britain, 1 January
Britain's railways steamed into a new chapter of their history today when services began under the four new companies created by the Railway Act of 1921. The railways had been taken over by the government during the war, but the ambitious schemes for redevelopment and electrification were jettisoned two years ago in favour of a return to private ownership. But the pre-war companies have been reorganized into four regional groups, of which only the Great Western is similar to its predecessor. The others are the London and North Western, London and North Eastern, and the Southern Railway (→30/4/28).

Poetic voice of new Ireland wins prize

Dublin, 14 November
Ireland's most famous poet, William Butler Yeats, has been awarded the Nobel prize for literature. The award has created immediate controversy, coming as it does so soon after the creation of the Irish Free State.

Throughout the poet's career, in spite of his involvement in the Irish literary revival, he has been a member of the British literary establishment. But later he supported the 1916 Rising and wrote movingly about the relationship between literature and the acts of the rebels. This identified him clearly as the poetic voice of the new Ireland.

Puzzling those who were present, Edith Sitwell's latest poetic offering, "Façade", was delivered by the author via a megaphone behind a curtain.

1924

London, 1 February. The Labour government recognizes the USSR (→ 7/4).

Britain, 26 February. The Transport and General Workers' Union calls off a ten-day nationwide dock strike which has paralysed ports.

London, 7 April. The Labour government loses a vote on the Rent Restrictions Bill, its first parliamentary defeat (→ 7/10).

London, 4 May. The composer Sir Edward Elgar is appointed Master of the King's Musick (→ 23/2/34).

Southern Rhodesia, 30 May. The colony becomes self-governing as its assembly meets for the first time.

London, 5 June. The British government appoints a Northern Ireland representative to the border commission (→ 16/7).

London, 8 August. A ten-nation summit agrees to a plan drawn up by US banker Charles Dawes, designed to assist Germany's economy and its reparations payments (→ 30/1/26).

Belfast, 15 September. The BBC begins broadcasting from the city (→ 3/12/55).

Britain, 7 October. Labour bans Communists from becoming members of the party (→ 9/10).

London, 26 October. A letter, allegedly sent by a Soviet leader, Grigori Zinoviev, to British Communists instructing them to start a revolution, is published in the *Daily Mail* (→ 31).

Belfast, 1 November. Eamon de Valera is sentenced to one month in prison for entering Northern Ireland illegally (→ 8).

London, 6 November. Former Liberal cabinet minister Winston Churchill is chancellor in Baldwin's new cabinet (→ 26/1/31).

Dublin, 8 November. The Irish government offers an amnesty to those convicted in the civil war (→ 20/11/25).

London, 21 November. The new Tory government repudiates an Anglo-Soviet treaty negotiated by the Labour government (→ 17/2/25).

Cairo, 24 November. The Egyptian government resigns under British pressure following the murder five days ago of Major General Sir Lee Stack, governor-general of the Sudan (→ 6/8/29).

Labour comes to power for first time

Westminster, 22 January
The illegitimate son of a Scottish serving girl was today asked by the king to become prime minister of Britain's first Labour government. James Ramsay MacDonald hired court dress from Moss Bros for his visit to Buckingham Palace, where George V urged him to exercise prudence and sagacity.

The advice was hardly necessary. MacDonald's cabinet of 20 includes 11 with solid working-class backgrounds, two are Tories, one a Liberal and only one is left-wing. He is John Wheatley from Red Clydeside, a Roman Catholic born in poverty who became a successful businessman – but he, too, hired court dress and returned from the palace having charmed the king. MacDonald had decided to form a minority government before meeting his parliamentary party. He ridiculed leftwingers who wanted him to deliver a ringing socialist speech and then quit. That, he said, would be a betrayal of those who had voted for the party. Admitting that Labour was "in office but not in power", he said it had to show that the party was fit to govern.

In spite of MacDonald's resolute moderation, a Labour government represents a social revolution; for the first time the ruling elite of public school and Oxbridge are out.

Two ministers in particular will be worth watching: Wheatley at health plans a big public housing programme and Charles Trevelyan at education intends to provide working-class children with more than the three Rs (→ 1/2).

Ramsay MacDonald: Labour PM.

Wireless puts its stamp on empire show

Wembley, London, 23 April
Royalty became a little less remote today when millions of Britons, owners of the new wireless sets, heard their king's voice for the first time. The occasion was the opening of the British Empire Exhibition at the stadium here with hidden microphones on the royal dais carrying the king's message to listeners as far away as northern Scotland.

New technology was a feature of today's ceremony. The king sent a telegram to himself – routed via Canada, New Zealand, Australia, South Africa, India, Aden, Egypt and Gibraltar, and finally brought back to the king by a telegram boy, immaculate in blue suit and pillbox hat, a telegram pouch on his belt.

The exhibits here include a coal mine with real pit ponies, a Maori village, an effigy in butter of the prince of Wales and a working replica of Niagara Falls. There are vast exhibition halls and lakes, but with its fine scaled-down Chippendale and Queen Anne furniture and miniature watercolours by top artists, it was Queen Mary's dolls' house, designed by Sir Edwin Lutyens, that drew the largest crowds (→ 15/9).

Visitors flock to the British Empire Exhibition at Wembley, west London.

Storm looms over borders for Ulster

Ireland, 10 May
The government of Northern Ireland has refused a formal request from the British government to appoint a member to the proposed boundary commission. There are fears in Dublin and London that the governments there may fall on the issue.

The 1921 Anglo-Irish treaty allowed Northern Ireland to opt out of the Free State and remain part of the United Kingdom, in which case a boundary commission was to determine the boundaries of Northern Ireland. The Irish negotiators believed that the commission would give them at least three of the North's six counties and that an uneconomically viable Ulster would then be forced to join the Free State, thus ensuring longed-for unity. This swayed them to sign the treaty. Lloyd George, on the other hand, called the commission project "a slight readjustment".

Last July, the Free State government, which had been strongly criticized for inaction by the republican opposition, put the onus of responsibility on Britain by appointing its commissioner, Eoin MacNeill. The refusal of the Northern Ireland government to make its nomination is a serious complication (→ 5/6).

'Red Letter' scare topples Labour

Minority rule ends over sedition row

Westminster, 9 October
The life of the Labour government is in jeopardy tonight after Ramsay MacDonald lost a vote of confidence in the House of Commons by 364 votes to 198. The prime minister will advise the king to call a general election.

MacDonald took power as head of a minority government and was at pains to demonstrate its constitutional rather than revolutionary credentials. The Housing Act was probably its greatest domestic success, but it was over relations with communism that Labour came to grief.

Attempts to improve relations with the Bolsheviks had aroused vocal opposition even before the event which led to the government's downfall. This involved J R Campbell, editor of *The Worker's Weekly*, a communist magazine. Campbell, decorated in the war for bravery, had urged servicemen not to break strikes.

He was charged with incitement to mutiny, which outraged Labour MPs. The attorney-general then dropped the prosecution, outraging opposition MPs who claimed that improper political pressures had been exerted. It seems that it was more a muddle than anything, but the opposition scented blood – and the government fell (→26).

Zinoviev: was his letter forged?

Winston Churchill: Tory recruit?

Tories romp home; Liberals shattered

Westminster, 31 October
The Conservatives have romped to a general election victory in a campaign dominated by a "Red Letter" scare. Four days before the poll a letter, purportedly from a Soviet leader called Zinoviev to the tiny British Communist Party, was published by the *Daily Mail*. It gave instructions from the Soviet Union on how to start a revolution and was hailed by Tories and their supporters in the press as evidence that Labour was soft on communism.

Soviet diplomats claimed that the letter was a forgery, but the damage was fatal to a Labour Party already on the defensive over its handling of the Campbell affair [*see report left*]. The Conservatives won 419 seats compared to 258 in the last parliament while Labour has slumped from 191 to 151. The biggest losers, though, are the Liberals: the party of government less than a decade ago, they now have only 40 MPs as against 159 in the last parliament. Labour, in fact, gained one million more votes than a year ago. Among the Liberal casualties was Herbert Asquith, the former premier.

Stanley Baldwin will now return to Downing Street one year after he gambled on – and lost – a snap election. Winston Churchill is tipped to return to Tory ranks after 20 years as a Liberal (→21/11).

Two climbers lost within 1,000 feet of Everest summit

Mallory: presumed dead.

Khatmandu, June
With just a thousand feet between them and the elusive 29,028-foot summit of Mount Everest, British climbers George Leigh Mallory and Andrew Irvine were "going strong" in their latest attempt on the world's highest mountain. It was then that the support party below lost sight of the British climbers as a sudden snowstorm overwhelmed them. No trace has been found of the two men, who set off with high hopes that supplies of bottled oxygen would help them win. Asked on a US lecture tour last year why he was so obsessed with Everest, Mallory replied: "Because it is there."

Imperial Airways takes to the skies

Croydon, 1 April
Britain now has a national airline – Imperial Airways, an amalgamation of four of Britain's pioneering airlines: Handley Page Transport, Daimler Airway, Instone Airline and British Marine Air Navigation. Each of these private companies has had great problems in making profits. Just as their European rivals get strong financial support from their governments, so state ownership is seen as the only viable future for air travel on this side of the English Channel (→24/5/30).

De Valera ends 11 months in prison

Ireland, 16 July
The republican activist Eamon de Valera has been released after 11 months in prison, during which time he received a huge vote for Sinn Féin in the general election. Hundreds of men and some women continue to be detained, untried, and 146 men went on hunger strike for almost 40 days in Kilmainham gaol. Despite the ending of the civil war, Free State troops have continued to carry out raids and arrests amid an atmosphere of disunity and bitterness (→1/11).

Refusing to run in heats on Sunday, Scotland's Eric Liddell withdrew from the 100 metres, but snatched Olympic gold and a record in the 400 metres.

1925

Twickenham, 3 January. In a match against England Cyril Brownlie of New Zealand becomes the first rugby union player to be sent off for foul play in an international.

London, 17 February. Herbert Asquith, the former Liberal prime minister, takes his seat in the House of Lords as earl of Oxford and Asquith (→ 18/5).

Melbourne, 18 February. England win the fourth test by an innings and 29 runs – their first win against Australia since August 1913 (→ 18/8).

London, 13 March. MPs approve the Summer Time Bill, making annual daylight saving permanent.

Asia, 19 March. Plans are announced for a major Royal Navy base at Singapore.

London, 9 April. The government accepts guidelines on teachers' pay recommended in a report by Lord Burnham.

Cyprus, 1 May. The island, under British administration since 1878 and annexed from Turkey in 1914, becomes a crown colony.

Britain, 18 May. A report by the Trades Union Congress dismisses the "Zinoviev Letter" as a forgery (→ 14/10/26).

London, 30 May. King George opens the rebuilt Great West Road, hailed as a model for post-war development.

London, 24 July. Patricia Cheeseman, a patient at Guy's Hospital, is the first person to be successfully treated for diabetes with insulin (→ 24/1/27).

Britain, 19 August. Miners agree to cooperate in a government enquiry into their pay.

Shanghai, 7 September. Around 20,000 mainly student demonstrators stone British constables during protests against the British and other Western concessions (→ 31/1/27).

Britain, 29 September. White lines are to be painted on roads in a bid to reduce traffic accidents (→ 20/11).

Westminster, 20 November. MPs approve a £50 fine and four months in prison for people convicted of drunken driving (→ 29/3/27).

London, 25 November. Twelve leading communists arrested last month are jailed for sedition.

Britain returns to the gold standard

Westminster, 28 April
Britain has returned to the gold standard. The chancellor of the exchequer, Winston Churchill, made this announcement in his budget today. He told the Commons that he did not intend to renew the act of 1919 which suspended the standard.

Churchill hopes that this great symbolic act will boost the morale of his party and the confidence of the country. It suggests a return to prewar normality. It harks back to the Victorian age when the City of London was pre-eminent. The gold standard is the hallmark of stable money and a stable political society. A return will please businessmen and most academic economists.

There is only one major dissenting voice – that of the Cambridge economist John Maynard Keynes. Two years ago he published a devastating critique called *A Tract on Monetary Reform*. In it, he demonstrated that the United States was only pretending to maintain the gold standard.

According to Keynes the US does not ensure that the dollar matches the value of gold; it manipulates the price of gold at great expense to ensure that it stays level with the dollar. "This is the way by which a rich country is able to combine new wisdom with old prejudice," wrote Keynes. Britain by implementing the change makes itself the victim of a policy dictated by US power.

The Churchill budget also takes sixpence off income tax and brings in a new national pension scheme.

Hobbs's hundreds outscore W G Grace

Schoolboys surround their hero Hobbs, hoping for an autograph.

Taunton, 18 August
Cricket history was made today before a modest weekday crowd here at Somerset's county ground. Jack Hobbs scored his second hundred in two days for Surrey: his first equalled the record total of 126 first-class centuries set by W G Grace, the second surpassed that total. Today's effort was also the 14th century scored this season by the Surrey and England opening batsman – another record.

Hobbs is 42, but seems to be at the height of his powers, with no thought of retirement. He played his first match for Surrey in 1905 and within two years was capped by his country. He has taken wickets as a medium-pace bowler, but it is as a batsman that he has been acclaimed as one of the great players of all time. His elegance and his skill – especially on difficult wickets – have earned him worldwide recognition as "the Master". He has achieved particular success against England's greatest rivals, Australia. Last year Hobbs began a promising partnership with Yorkshire's 30-year-old opener, Herbert Sutcliffe (→ 18/8/26).

Cheap loans lure people to emigrate

Touting the delights of Canada.

London, 8 April
Plans were announced today to encourage 450,000 Britons to emigrate to Australia over the next ten years. Low-interest loans will be made available to the prospective settlers by a scheme to be funded jointly by the British and Australian governments. Although the figure seems high, it is in fact no more than the total average emigration from Britain in a single year during 1911-13. In the first decade of the century emigration averaged 284,000 a year, mostly to the United States and the dominions.

Legion is formed to tackle immorality

Ireland, 15 November
A new organization, the Legion of Mary, has been formed in Dublin to tackle what it says are widespread problems of drunkenness, prostitution, crime and disease. Its founder, Frank Duff, is a civil servant and a former active member of the Society of St Vincent de Paul.

In a city where open brothels operate on a scale scarcely paralleled in Europe and where drink always seems to be available, the Legion has taken the unprecedented step of opening a hostel for prostitutes willing to make a fresh start. Members go into the roughest parts of Dublin to offer help and advice to women living in conditions of poverty and degradation.

New party to back Welsh nationalism

Pwllheli, 5 August
When the first official meeting of the two clandestine Welsh nationalist groups, represented by Saunders Lewis and H R Jones, took place at the Maesgwyn temperance hotel, Pwllheli today, the event was hailed by the chairman as the first public meeting of Plaid Cymru, a "new" Welsh nationalist party. Dismissing supporters of Welsh home rule within the Labour Party, Saunders Lewis declared: "One cannot serve England and Wales." He stressed the need for unity and argued that persuasion by physical force should not now be necessary. His plan for a wholly Welsh-speaking summer school at Machynlleth in August 1926 was rapturously received.

A Nobel for Shaw

Stockholm, 10 December
George Bernard Shaw, regarded by many as the world's best-known living playwright, was awarded the Nobel Prize for Literature today. A non-believer in prizes, he declined to attend the award ceremony, however, and intends to use the prize money to create an Anglo-Swedish Literary Foundation. His plays include *Arms and the Man*, *Major Barbara* and the highly successful *St Joan* (→2/11/50).

Irish commissioner resigns in border row

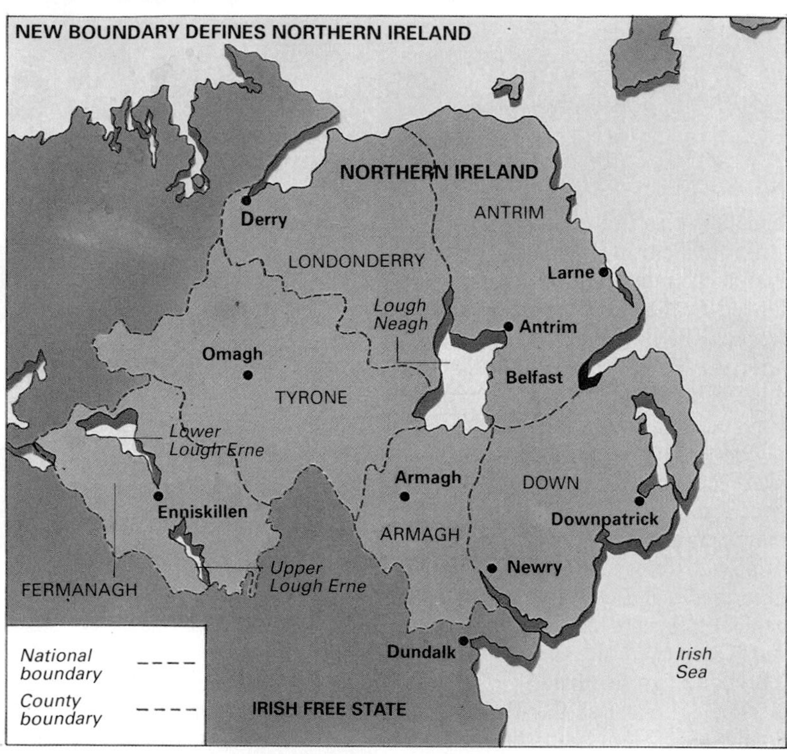

Dublin, 20 November
Eoin MacNeill has resigned from the boundary commission, set up under the Anglo-Irish Treaty of 1921 to determine the Irish border. This followed a crisis debate in the Dáil, after a leaked report, with map, in the *Morning Post* on 7 November predicted that there would be only minor adjustments.

The Free State was to gain parts of south Armagh, south-west Fermanagh and west Tyrone, while Northern Ireland was to acquire small portions of Donegal and Monaghan. It would have reduced the north's population by 1.8 per cent and its area by 3.7 per cent. Fearing defeat in the Dáil, Irish leaders sought a meeting in London to suppress the report. In debates on the treaty, members of the Dáil had assumed that the commission would bring major territorial gains, forcing the collapse of the Northern Ireland economy (→16/5/26).

Charleston gives a new kick to the Roaring Twenties

Britain, 31 December
This was the year the Charleston arrived from the US and carried away society high and low. Once the prince of Wales had done it, everybody was doing it. Dancing is the craze of Bright Young Things and the hit tune "I Want To Be Happy" is their guide. The foxtrot, tango, the Black Bottom and many more are performed nightly in smart hotels, known for their bands: Carroll Gibbons at the Savoy, Jack Hylton at the Piccadilly, Teddy Brown at the Café de Paris, Bert Ambrose at the Embassy Club.

The "flappers" are still waiting for the vote but not to shock their elders by smoking and applying lipstick in public, sipping cocktails, swearing, making life one long fancy dress party where morals are emancipated. Busts were banished in 1923; skirts grow shorter every year like hairstyles – from the bob to the shingle and this year's ultimate "Eton Crop".

Men have followed the prince into flapping Oxford bags, Fair Isle sweaters and caps. Their other model, Nöel Coward, who has three plays running in London at the age of 24, wrote for C B Cochran's new revue *On With the Dance* a song that asks "Cocktails and Laughter – but what comes after?"

Everybody's doing it.

Wireless broadcasts reach ten million people, claims the BBC

The magic of wireless is demonstrated in the Harrod's department store.

London, 3 December
The British Broadcasting Company can now reach 40 million people with its broadcasts and John Reith, its general manager, claimed today that it has an audience of over ten million listeners. The number of ten-shilling wireless licences issued is 1,654,000, so it is assumed that many listeners have not yet got round to buying the licence.

There has been a boom in sales of wireless sets – the BBC supplies crystal sets for £2 to £4 – but many people make their own. The BBC puts out 10,000 talks a year, classical concerts and live dance music from the Savoy hotel. Reith's plan is to lead public taste, not to follow it (→1/1/27).

1926

Britain, 6 January. The first widow's pensions are paid out at post offices (→ 12/1929).

London, 27 January. John Logie Baird demonstrates "television" – sending moving pictures by radio – at the Royal Institution (→ 30/4/34).

Germany, 30 January. The last British troops leave Cologne, ending the Allied occupation of the Rhineland (→ 1/5/33).

Tehran, 18 February. An Anglo-Persian treaty is signed, giving another 25-year oil exploitation contract to the Anglo-Persian Oil Company.

Stratford-upon-Avon, 6 March. The Shakespeare Memorial Theatre is destroyed by fire.

Britain, 24 March. The Miners' Federation rejects the report of a royal commission under Sir Herbert Samuel, which urges cutting the general level of miners' pay and scrapping a 1924 minimum pay agreement (→ 1/5).

Dublin, 13 April. The Coinage Act (Irish Free State) authorizes the issue of new silver, nickel and bronze coins.

Britain, 1 May. The miners strike; the TUC calls a general strike of essential services in sympathy (→ 3).

Britain, 3 May. The general strike begins at midnight tonight (→ 10).

Britain, 12 May. The TUC calls off the general strike (→ 20).

Manchester, 24 July. Britain's first greyhound racing track opens at Belle Vue.

London, 18 August. England beat Australia by 289 runs in the fifth test to win the Ashes for the first time in 14 years (→ 23/1/33).

Co Limerick, 5 September. Forty-nine die in a cinema fire at Drumcollogher.

London, 14 October. Lord Oxford, formerly Herbert Asquith, resigns as Liberal leader; Lloyd George takes over (→ 7/6/29).

Britain, 2 November. Imperial Chemical Industries (ICI) is formed.

London, 12 November. Miners agree to end the pit strike, accepting an eight-hour day and local rather than national wage settlements, in return for an independent wage tribunal for six months and no immediate pay cuts (→ 16/5).

TUC calls its first-ever general strike

Violence is avoided as class war erupts

Britain, 10 May

The first week of the first general strike in British history has accentuated class divisions but has not so far led to the violence which many feared. The strike began on 3 May after the TUC decided to back the miners in their strike against pay cuts and longer working hours.

Talks at Downing Street failed to avert the stoppage and broke down over a refusal by the TUC to repudiate action by printers at the *Daily Mail* who refused to print an anti-union editorial. A state of emergency has been declared and troops were deployed in south Wales, Yorkshire and Scotland.

The TUC stressed that foodstuffs would be exempt from the strike, which in heavy industry, building, railways, transport, gas, electricity and printing has been virtually 100 per cent effective. But the middle classes have been equally eager to offer their services free to stave off what they see as a threat. Students, ex-officers, retired managers and others have come forward in droves to drive lorries and buses or to act as special constables.

Winston Churchill is editing the *British Gazette* on behalf of the government, denouncing the working man as the enemy, but many others are trying to keep the temperature down. Apart from isolated incidents in Glasgow and Northumberland there has been little violence. In many areas police and strikers are combating the tedium by playing each other at football (→ 12).

Steel-helmeted troops man tanks leaving Wellington barracks in London.

A woman's work is never done: female volunteers assist at a post office.

Miners, bitter at desertion by TUC, continue the struggle

London, 20 May

Delegates at the miners' conference today showed their determination to fight on. They are still extremely bitter at the TUC's decision to call off the general strike a week ago, but they are in no mood to accept the latest terms of the prime minister, Stanley Baldwin, for settling the coal dispute. They intend to fight on alone. The TUC has opted for a compromise plan for a national wages board for coal. This would cut miners' wages, but only when the owners have agreed to adopt the Samuel commission proposals for the reorganization of the industry.

TUC leaders hoped that by calling off the strike public opinion would force the owners to a more moderate approach. The miners are sceptical. TUC leaders clearly have no stomach for the kind of revolutionary attempt to bring down the government of which their enemies accuse them. The emergency plans of the government also worked well. Essential supplies were getting through with the help of eager voluntary labour. As soon as workers saw this there was a gradual drift back to work on the railways and in other industries. With a choice between escalation into a constitutional crisis or surrender, the TUC chose surrender (→ 12/11).

Old empire to be new commonwealth

London, 20 November
The changing nature of the British Empire was acknowledged today when the Imperial conference here announced that Canada, Australia, New Zealand and South Africa will be self-governing dominions within the British Commonwealth. The declaration recognizes the independence of the dominions which will be equal in status to that of Britain "united by a common allegiance to the crown". Yet even the king's title is changed, for the Irish Free State, although also a dominion, does not recognize the monarch of Great Britain and Northern Ireland as its sovereign. But the king remains emperor of India, whose non-independent status is unchanged by the conference (→ 12/3/28).

De Valera to head 'soldiers of destiny'

Dublin, 16 May
Eamon de Valera, former president of Sinn Féin, has held an inaugural meeting in the La Scala theatre in Dublin to launch Fianna Fail (Soldiers of Destiny) as his new political party. In a rousing speech he told members that the main challenge facing them was the reunification of Ireland. No true republican, said de Valera, could accept the present division of the country, which stood in the way of the nation's advancement (→ 10/7/27).

National electricity grid planned for UK

Britain, 31 December
Millions will soon have electricity on tap to their homes thanks to the Electricity Supply Act. With many small competing power companies, progress has been slow and only about one in ten homes can run the new vacuum cleaners.

Now there is to be a Central Electricity Board which will enforce a uniform system and set up a National Grid. It will take some seven years to complete. By then about half the homes in the country will be wired up for electricity.

1927

Britain, 1 January. The BBC (formerly British Broadcasting Company, now Corporation) makes its first broadcasts as a company incorporated under royal charter (→ 15/3/32).

London, 24 January. The British Medical Association warns that deaths from cancer, particularly of the chest and tongue, have risen sharply in the past 20 years (→ 30/9/28).

Britain, 31 January. A 12,000-strong British Army division is ordered to China to defend British nationals in Shanghai, where the Chinese civil war is posing a threat to the Western enclaves.

Glamorgan, Wales, 1 March. Over 50 miners are feared dead in a firedamp explosion at Ebbw Vale; 150 are trapped.

London, 30 March. The Convocation of the Church of England approves changes to the Book of Common Prayer, including equal marriage vows for men and women (→ 15/12).

USA, 30 June. American golfers beat a team from Britain and Ireland to win a new trophy awarded by Samuel Ryder.

Dublin, 20 July. The Free State government introduces the Public Safety Bill giving it powers to deal more effectively with disorder (→ 11/8).

Dublin, 16 August. William Cosgrave, president of the Free State executive council, is opposed in a no confidence vote in the Dail by Eamon de Valera's new Fianna Fail party and wins only on the casting vote of the speaker (→ 20/9).

Edinburgh, 8 September. The TUC votes to cut ties with Soviet trade unions.

Irish Free State, 20 September. A general election gives Cosgrave 61 seats to Fianna Fail's 57; the government has an overall majority of six (→ 8/2/29).

Lancashire, 28 October. A great storm leaves a reported 50 dead and 400 homeless.

Westminster, 25 November. MPs approve the establishment of a commission to study the government of India, headed by Sir John Simon (→ 3/2/28).

London, 10 December. As greyhound racing booms, London's third track opens at Wembley, to join those at Harringay and White City; Britain's first track opened at Manchester last year.

Speed battle pushes record over 200mph

Malcolm Campbell prepares for a land speed record with BP's assistance.

Florida, 29 March
The rivalry between two Britons has taken the world land speed record to beyond 320 kilometres per hour (200mph) for the first time. The new record-holder is Major Henry Segrave who at the Daytona Beach racetrack in Florida today smashed the speed set only last month by Malcolm Campbell. In his *Mystery* car, Segrave reached 203.841mph – 30mph faster than the record set by Campbell along the Pendine Sands in South Wales on 4 February.

Campbell, a three-time record holder, had reached 174.224 mph in Wales and he was among the first to congratulate Major Segrave. He said it was an "excellent feat", but said that he was already practising in a faster car with which he was confident of regaining the record.

At a time when the motor car is growing dramatically in popularity, there is great enthusiasm for the efforts of pioneers like Campbell and Segrave. But there is also concern for their safety.

During a pit-stop to change the tyres on his 1,000hp car, Major Segrave said the wind pressure at such high speed had made steering virtually impossible. And when Campbell set his record, the wind blew off his goggles, temporarily blinding him. "It was most terrifying," Campbell said (→ 19/2/28).

Labour MPs livid at anti-union bill

Westminster, 16 May
Labour MPs lost their battle to talk out the Trade Disputes Bill today when the government used the guillotine. The bill makes any strike illegal that is "designed or calculated to coerce the government". It rules out actions like last year's general strike when other unions came out in sympathy with the miners.

The new bill also forbids civil service unions to affiliate to the TUC and hits at Labour Party finances by forbidding political levies unless members contract in.

Supplying groceries worldwide.

De Valera to take his seat in the Dáil

De Valera: in the Dáil at last.

Dublin, 11 August
Eamon de Valera has finally taken his seat in the Dáil. His Fianna Fáil party won 44 seats in the June general election, but were locked out of the Dáil chamber when they refused to take the oath of allegiance to the British crown which de Valera described as an acquiescence to a foreign power that made a nonsense of democracy. His attempt to have the matter resolved by a referendum was defeated.

Recognizing that his position was untenable, de Valera has satisfied his conscience by agreeing to take the oath having first removed the Bible which lay beside it, and then covering the oath with some papers before signing it (→16).

IRA assassinates Irish Free State minister

Dublin, 10 July
The Irish Minister for Justice, Kevin O'Higgins, has been assassinated by what is believed to be a dissident faction of the IRA as he walked home after Mass.

An able, energetic and fearless individual, O'Higgins was seen as the strong, if unpopular, arm of the government. His recent attempts to introduce an Intoxicating Liquor Bill were defeated by an outcry from 15,000 publicans. He was dedicated to rooting out militarism and stamping a civilian imprint on Irish government, and had actively pursued a policy (despite criticism) of replacing the 7,000 armed RIC men with 5,250 unarmed police. His death will be seen as a long-term loss for his party and for the country (→20).

O'Higgins: murdered after Mass.

Government expels all Soviet diplomats

London, 24 May
A series of espionage scandals led today to the severing of relations between Britain and the Soviet Union. Ordering all Russian diplomats and the Soviet trade mission to leave within ten days, Sir Austen Chamberlain, the foreign secretary, accused the USSR of spying and subversion throughout the British empire and said: "The limits to our patience are now reached."

The break followed a police raid on the Soviet trade organization, Arcos, in London. The security service had been tipped off that Arcos had acquired a document containing the RAF's plans for strategic bombing and recommended that it should be raided. The prime minister, Stanley Baldwin, gave permission and the raid was mounted at dawn 12 days ago.

When the police burst through a basement door they discovered two men and a women burning papers. The stolen document was not found but there was much evidence proving Arcos was a front for a campaign of espionage (→29/7/29).

New prayer book is called too 'popish'

Westminster, 15 December
The ability of the internal affairs of the Church of England to cause uproar in British political life was proved again today when the House of Commons rejected a revised prayer book which had been prepared by the Church Assembly and passed by the House of Lords. When the vote was read out hats and order papers were thrown into the air and wild cheering mingled with shouts of "No popery".

The revised book is anathema to low churchmen and their fears were voiced by Sir Thomas Inskip, the solicitor-general, who claimed the book goes too far towards Rome in its provisions for Anglo-Catholic practices such as those for the sacrament of Communion. Another major objection by the Commons, a bastion of male chauvinism, was to changes in the marriage service freeing brides from the obligation to "obey" their husbands.

The rejection of the revised book has, therefore, infuriated not only the bishops but also the feminists, a powerful combination. It has, moreover, raised the question of disestablishmentarianism, for the state is seen as preventing the church from conducting its domestic affairs as it wishes. A compromise is in the making, however, with bishops authorizing the use of certain sections of the revised book by their vicars (→27/7/28).

Support grows for British-made films

London, 26 March
Britain is to make serious efforts to make its own films, despite the lead that the war gave to Hollywood. Today saw the founding of the Gaumont-British Film Corporation, hot on the heels of British Incorporated Pictures. A new Cinematograph Films Act will oblige exhibitors to show a minimum quota of British films, beginning at 7.5 per cent and rising to 25 per cent. Last year only 5 per cent of the films shown in Britain were British-made and many talented actors, such as Charlie Chaplin, have gone to America (→17/3/30).

Baldwin refuses to meet Welsh miners

London, 22 November
Two hundred unemployed miners were snubbed by the prime minister today at the end of a 180-mile march from south Wales. They had walked from the Rhondda valley to draw attention to high levels of unemployment in mining areas following the failure of the pit strike last year. But Stanley Baldwin, the prime minister, refused to see a delegation of the miners. His decision angered the miners' leader, Arthur Cook, who told a rally that in the interests of the nation "the government will be compelled to take over the mining industry".

As an alternative to the established sport of horse racing, greyhound tracks are fast becoming popular, providing the punter with an opportunity to have a flutter as the dogs chase a hare around the track. Here at Dumpton Park in Kent, they are up and running, watched by a cheering crowd.

1928

London, 16 January. The novelist and poet Thomas Hardy, who died two days ago at the age of 87, is buried in Westminster Abbey.

Britain, 19 January. Figures show the birth rate last year was the lowest on record.

India, 3 February. Riots mark the arrival from Britain of the Simon Commission to report on the future government of India (→ 2/1/30).

Britain, 12 February. Eleven die as gales sweep the country (→ 5/12/29).

Oxford, 15 February. The Oxford English Dictionary is completed after 70 years' work.

Daytona, USA, 19 February. Malcolm Campbell's *Bluebird* reaches 332kmph [206.35mph], a new land speed record (→ 1/8).

London, 20 February. Britain, which has a League of Nations mandate for Palestine, recognizes the independence of Transjordan.

Malta, 12 March. The British colony becomes a dominion (→ 12/1931).

Britain, 30 April. The *Flying Scotsman* non-stop rail service is launched between London and Edinburgh; speeds of over 112 kmph (70mph) are reached during the 392-mile journey (→ 27/6).

London, 14 June. Veteran women's suffrage campaigner Mrs Emmeline Pankhurst dies at the age of 69 (→ 31/5/29).

Darlington, 27 June. A rail crash leaves 23 dead (→ 5/7/32).

Oxford, 1 August. The Morris Minor car is launched (→ 29/11).

Glasgow, 16 September. The P & O *Viceroy of India* is launched; it is the first liner to have oil-fired electric turbines.

Newcastle-upon-Tyne, 10 October. King George opens a new Tyne Bridge; it has Britain's biggest steel arch.

Britain, 22 November. The first £1 and ten shilling [50p] notes enter circulation.

London, 12 December. King George V, who fell dangerously ill with a chest infection on November 23, is reported much improved after a lung operation (→ 2/7/29).

London. Two sculptors, Henry Moore and Barbara Hepworth, each stage their first London exhibitions this year.

Private motoring booms, but so does the number of traffic accidents on the roads

Lane discipline is not apparent at Hyde Park Corner, where traffic is heavy.

Britain, 29 November
Figures released today show that traffic accidents have continued to soar this year. Last year's totals of 133,943 accidents and 5,329 deaths prompted demands for new laws to control the boom in private motoring. The number of private cars registered – just 200,000 in 1920 – is forecast to top a million by the end of the decade. Yet controls are few. Anyone over 17 can drive, subject only to an unsupported declaration of physical fitness. There is no driving test, although moves are beginning in parliament to press for one. Changes to the widely ignored 20 mph (32 kmph) speed limit have also been suggested. Motoring remains the preserve of the wealthy, but the Austin Seven car, introduced in 1921 at a price of £225, brought cars within reach of far more people (→ 16/6/29).

Germ-killing mould found by chance

London, 30 September
The blue mould spots that appear on stale bread may be able to cure disease. That anyway is the hope of Professor Alexander Fleming of St Mary's Hospital in London, who discovered that when the mould, *penicillium notatum* as it is known, comes into contact with the bacterium staphylococcus, which is responsible for many human infections, the bacterium is killed off.

He made the discovery when a dish of the bacteria was left out by mistake and became contaminated. *Penicillium* does not harm human white blood cells so it may be safe to use on humans. However extracting the active chemical is likely to be difficult (→ 3/2/41).

Flappers win vote

Britain, 7 May
Five million more women will be able to vote in the next general election thanks to an act of parliament which puts them on the electoral roll on an equal footing with men – the age comes down from 30 to 21. The act was introduced by the Tory government without any particular pressure, but many believe that the "flapper" vote will benefit Labour (→ 14/6).

Fourteen killed as Thames bursts banks

London, 7 January
The calamity that many have been predicting for years finally happened this month when the Thames burst its banks, flooding low-lying districts of London, drowning 14 people and causing millions of pounds worth of damage. Telephone lines were cut off as floodwaters rose and hundreds of people have been left with their homes uninhabitable.

A sudden thaw and strong winds combined with a high tide to wreak havoc along substantial tracts of the swollen river. Four young sisters – drowned in their basement home – were among the casualties. Twelve Landseer paintings were badly damaged at the Tate gallery, although the priceless Turner collection there was saved.

The pub will not be dry inside or out.

Floods engulfed the vaults of the palace of Westminster and water (and swans) returned to the moat of the Tower of London for the first time in many years (→ 12/2/28).

Dixie Dean scores a record 60 goals

Liverpool, 1 May
There is a double celebration in Liverpool tonight: Everton are the champions of the Football League and Dixie Dean, their centre forward, has hit a record 60 league goals in a season. He scored today in the final match of the season to help Everton clinch the title by two points from runners-up Huddersfield Town. Dean has achieved his record total from only 39 of his team's 42 league games. Not surprisingly Everton scored more than 100 goals this season, one of seven English and two Scottish sides to hit a century of goals. In Scotland's less competitive second division, Jimmy Smith of Ayr United even beat Dean's total with 66 goals. ▷

Archbishop resigns over new prayer book

London, 27 July
Randall Davidson, the archbishop of Canterbury, is to retire in November after 25 years as head of the Church of England. He is bitterly disappointed that the revised *Book of Common Prayer* was rejected for the second time by the House of Commons last month.

Yet his departure will not end the controversy as he is to be succeeded by Cosmo Lang, the chief advocate of the revised book and a powerful figure in the House of Lords. Sir William Joynson-Hicks, the home secretary and a leading opponent of the revisions, today called for Lang to "devote himself to the real call of the church – the evangelization of the people".

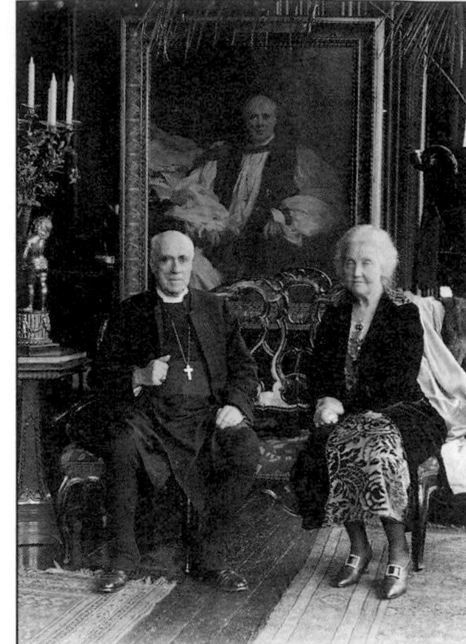

Dr Davidson and his wife.

Theatre in Galway aids Gaelic revival

Galway, 27 August
The Galway Gaelic theatre has opened with a production of *Diarmuid agus Grainne*, written and produced by Micheál MacLiammóir. The theatre has caused great excitement amongst Irish language enthusiasts as it represents another aspect of the Gaelic revival which began with the Gaelic League founded by Douglas Hyde 35 years ago. Its aims have been to renew interest in Irish culture, art and, most important of all, the Irish or Gaelic language.

Britain signs treaty to 'renounce war'

Paris, 27 August
Nearly ten years after the Armistice which ended the Great War, representatives of 15 countries today signed a pact here today renouncing war. Britain was among the signatories and the German foreign minister, Gustav Stresemann, was loudly cheered when he produced a large gold pen with which to add his name. The pact follows intense lobbying by the US secretary of state Frank Kellogg and Aristide Briand, his French counterpart. The pact bears both their names.

Britons are greatest cigarette smokers

Smoking: a burning desire.

Britain, 10 August
Britons are world leaders – in cigarette smoking. In 1924 we puffed our way through an astonishing 77,458,000 pounds of tobacco, up from 23,766,000 pounds in 1907, according to a report of the Imperial Economical Committee. Last year we burnt up an average of 3.4 pounds of tobacco per head.

All the increase has come from sales of cigarette, boosted by gimmicks such as give-away cards; cigar and pipe smoking have actually declined. The cigarette held between slim fingers has become one of the symbols of female emancipation, while lighting a girl's cigarette is fast becoming a romantic cliché.

1929

London, 4 February. Britain's first "green belt", a five-mile-long stretch of countryside near Hendon to be protected from development, is approved.

France, 12 February. Lillie Langtry, an actress who became a mistress of King Edward VII when he was prince of Wales, dies.

London, 15 April. The 325-year-old tea duty is abolished in Chancellor Winston Churchill's budget, knocking fourpence [2p] off the price of a pound of tea.

Karachi, India, 26 April. Twelve days after the first airmail flight from India to Britain, an RAF Fairey monoplane completes the first non-stop flight from Britain to India in 50 hours and 37 minutes (→ 24/5/30).

Britain, 31 May. The general election, in which six million more women voted, returns 13 women to the Commons, including Lloyd George's daughter Megan.

France, 16 June. Britain's Bentley team takes the first four places at this year's Le Mans 24-hour endurance race (→ 3/4/30).

London, 2 July. King George opens Parliament, delivering the first King's Speech for a Labour government (→ 25/12/32).

Dublin, 16 July. The Censorship of Publications Act comes into force; it provides for a board to censor or ban publications for obscenity or other reasons.

London, 29 July. The foreign secretary, Arthur Henderson, has talks with a Soviet representative on the restoration of Anglo-Soviet relations (→ 18/4/33).

London, 6 August. Britain agrees a draft treaty under which it will withdraw troops from the whole of Egypt except the Suez Canal.

Jerusalem, 25 August. The British declare martial law in a bid to quell clashes between Arabs and Jews which have left 60 dead (→ 19/10/38).

New York, 24 October. Shares crash on Wall Street.

Britain, 2 December. The first 22 public telephone boxes become operational.

Britain, 5 December. A 151 kmph [94mph] hurricane sweeps the country, causing 26 deaths.

'Chain stores' boom in the High Street

Britain, January
"Chain stores" have begun to change the British way of shopping during the present decade and none more so than those of the American-owned Woolworth's company. Its high street shops offer a wider range of mass-produced goods at lower prices than is available at traditional corner shops or individual department stores. A British company founded in Leeds called Marks and Spencer is also expanding around the country.

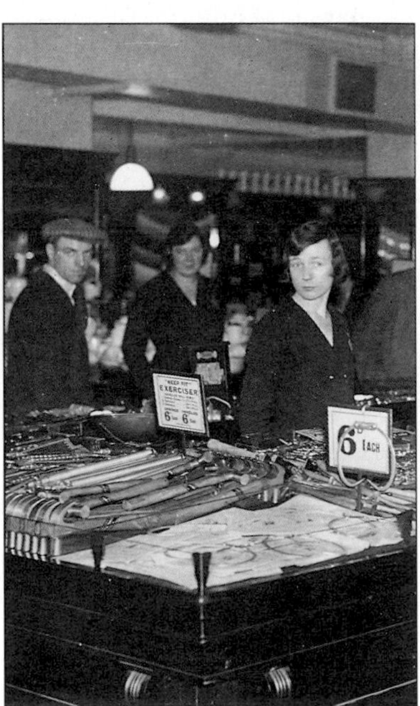

Woolworth's: a shopper's delight.

The river Shannon goes hydro-electric

Ireland, 21 October
A major initiative by the Irish government, the Shannon hydro-electric scheme, has begun commercial operations. Electricity is now to be generated by damming the river Shannon. The scheme is seen as a radical departure from the conservative policies of the prime minister, William Cosgrave. Until now all of the country's electricity has been provided by private generating operations, but only one-third of Dublin and a quarter of Cork has electrical power. The new scheme will dramatically increase the supply of electricity at a cost of around £5 million.

Labour returns to power

Labour's first cabinet, led by the prime minister, Ramsay MacDonald.

Westminster, 7 June
Ramsay MacDonald returned to No 10 Downing Street today with a pledge that his new Labour government will tackle the problem of unemployment, now passing the one million mark, almost 10 per cent of the workforce. Jimmy Thomas, the railwaymen's leader, is lord privy seal with the task of cutting the dole queues.

Any idea of giving socialism a trial is ruled out by the fact that once again Labour is without an overall Commons majority; last month's election gave Labour 288 seats, Tories 260 and Liberals 59. But the leadership anyway has little taste for left-wing nostrums.

The cabinet is resolutely respectable, with Philip Snowden as chancellor of the exchequer to keep firm control of public spending. The token left-winger is George Lansbury, the one-time East End councillor who scandalized Tories by paying high rates of poor relief not approved by government. One innovation is the appointment of Margaret Bondfield as minister of labour – the first woman cabinet minister (→ 20/5/30).

September 7. Britain wins the Schneider Cup and sets a new air speed record using this Supermarine S6, here being refuelled at Calshot, Hants.

Cinema blaze kills 69 Scottish children

Paisley, 31 December
Tragedy cast a terrible pall over the great Scottish festival of Hogmanay tonight as 69 children were found dead after a fire in a cinema here. Most of the dead, aged between 5 and 14, were crushed or suffocated as they fled in panic to escape the fumes, caused by a burning reel of film. A further 37 are badly injured, and the death toll may rise.

A special children's show had attracted an audience of 2,000 at the Glen cinema. Soon after the alarm sounded, there was a rush for the exits. Firemen who broke in found a pile of dead and dying children just ten steps from safety on a stairway. An 18-month-old child was on top of the pile.

Elsewhere, the corpses of children were found huddled together in the orchestra pit, beneath the seats, and beside the screen, which they had tried to climb to safety. Gas lights were broken in the chaos and some of the victims may have been asphyxiated. Fire doors had been ignored in the panic. This was the worst cinema fire in Britain, and might well have been avoided. The burning reel which started the fire was thrown out of a window before the panic started.

De Valera is arrested in Northern Ireland

De Valera: a month in jail.

Belfast, 8 February
Eamon de Valera has been arrested at the Northern Ireland border on his way to attend a function in Belfast hosted by the Gaelic League and the Gaelic Athletic Association. He was arrested on a previous occasion five years ago, ignoring warnings forbidding him to enter the six counties – despite the fact that he was an elected representative for Down, though he never attended the Belfast parliament.

This time he was taken from the train by the Royal Ulster Constabulary, brought to Belfast, where he was tried for contravening the exclusion order which had been issued against him five years ago, and sentenced to one month's imprisonment (→ 5/9/31).

Poor Law guardians to be swept away

Britain, December
The Poor Law guardians will soon be no more. Since 1834 they have administered the Poor Law, under which the starving and destitute could receive at least a bare minimum of subsistence help, but they are to be abolished next year. The move, embodied in this year's Local Government Act, is the culmination of a series of moves designed to reorganize the way the nation's poor are treated. Up to one and a half million people will be affected.

The 19th-century Poor Law has been seen as increasingly ineffective since 1909, when a royal commission suggested many of the changes which have now been achieved. The Poor Law unions and the guardians themselves have been swept away. Poor Law Hospitals have been turned over to local authorities as have the hated old workhouses (since 1913 known as Poor Law institutions). But the buildings will still be used to house the impoverished aged and infirm.

It is hoped that the new system will improve treatment for such unfortunates, up to a third of whom have still been dying in the workhouse, whatever its name, but some fear that a new authority will not mean the end to the old Victorian rigour (→ 12/2/32).

Arts and entertainment in the 'roaring twenties'

Everybody's going to 'the pictures'

The great new place to go for entertainment in the 1920s has been "the pictures". Every week people of all classes and ages go to sit before the silent screen accompanied by a pit pianist. The coming of "talkies" in 1927 increased the audiences, although many people predicted that sound was merely a passing fad, as Charlie Chaplin had declared it was. At least half the population are weekly cinemagoers. Glasgow had 96 cinemas by 1928.

Although our screens are totally dominated by Hollywood stars, such as Douglas Fairbanks and Mary Pickford, Chaplin and Buster Keaton, and now Mickey Mouse in place of Felix the Cat, the number of British films made jumped from a mere 34 in 1926 to 128 in 1927. The "quota" imposed by the Cinematograph Act will rise annually towards 20 per cent made in Britain.

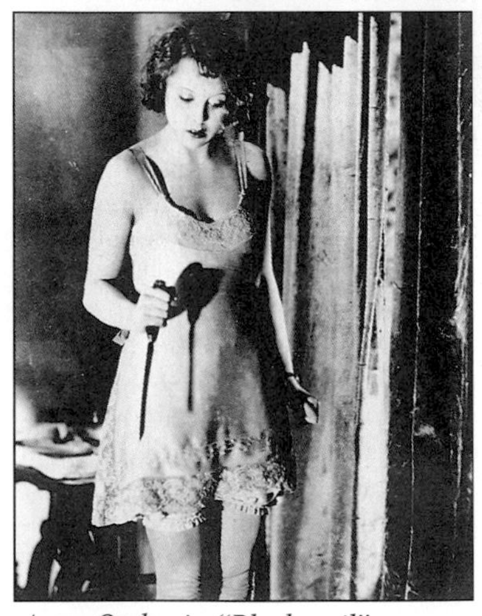

Anny Ondra in "Blackmail".

The two leading production companies are Gaumont-British and Gainsborough, with the Elstree studios of British International Pictures (BIP) described as Britain's Hollywood. Michael Balcon at Gainsborough has lost his tyro director, Alfred Hitchcock, to BIP where he directed *Blackmail*, the first British thriller talkie about a girl who stabs a man and is blackmailed. Her voice was "dubbed" by an actress standing just out of shot.

Singer Monti Ryan with Percival Mackey's dance band on the Savoy roof.

Jazz music puts its stamp on the decade

The American novelist Scott Fitzgerald dubbed the decade "the Jazz Age", and jazz bands were spearheads of the American invasion of British life. But "jazz" is a term for all kinds of sound – even Al Jolson counts as a "jazz singer".

The real thing was first heard in the Original Dixie Jazz Band's visits to London in 1919 and 1920, which brought audiences to their feet with *Tiger Rag*. They were followed by Paul Whiteman and his "jazz orchestra" which had given the première of George Gershwin's *Rhapsody in Blue*. Records of the jazz greats playing in Harlem or Chicago, of King Oliver, Louis Armstrong, Duke Ellington or Fats Waller, can only be obtained with difficulty in Britain.

British bands exist primarily for dancing. The BBC relays the Savoy Orpheans under Carroll Gibbons, Bert Ambrose from the Mayfair hotel and Jack Payne's BBC Dance Orchestra. They play *Yes, Sir, That's My Baby* or *I Can't Give You Anything But Love, Baby* – and that, baby, is "jazz".

Dance craze attracts millions to the Palais

The alternative to going to the pictures for a cheap night out has turned out to be going to the Palais. The craze for dancing – the foxtrot, the tango, the Black Bottom and of course, the Charleston – began as the war ended. The first "Palais de Danse", at Hammersmith in London, opened in 1919, and it has been copied in most other cities. Admission costs only a shilling [5p]. London hotels offer tea-dances and restaurants boast of their bands – one in the West End has them on all four floors. After hours there are the night clubs: the Embassy, with Ambrose's band and the prince of Wales's table always reserved, is the smartest.

Charleston: dance of the decade.

Literature explores modern wasteland

"Modernism" characterizes those writing in the Twenties. There has seldom been such a break with the past, led by two poets, Irish and American by birth. W B Yeats, the father of the Celtic twilight, has transformed his romantic style into a harsher one for brutal times in *Easter, 1916* and *Byzantium*, while T S Eliot, from Harvard, baffled but fascinated readers in 1922 with *The Waste Land*, which was ruthlessly edited by his fellow American Ezra Pound. Its bleak notes of despair and disgust echoed the traumatized post-war feelings of his young contemporaries.

In the same year James Joyce's epic *Ulysses* appeared, making Edwardian novelists such as Wells, Bennett and Galsworthy look obsolete, though they continued to write. Galsworthy completed his saga of the Forsytes in five sequels to *The Man of Property*. Like Joyce, D H Lawrence was banned and chose voluntary exile from Britain. *Women in Love*, a sequel to *The Rainbow*, did not find a publisher till 1921, and *Lady Chatterley's Lover*, published abroad, was accused of obscenity. Virginia Woolf experimented on Joycean lines with the "stream of consciousness" in *Mrs Dalloway* and *To The Lighthouse*, while E M Forster cut free from Edwardian domesticity in *A Passage to India*.

Wells: obsolete novelist?

Elgar falls silent so Holst picks up the musical mantle

After his 1919 cello concerto Sir Edward Elgar fell virtually silent, and British music was without its leading composer. The mantle fell first on Gustav Holst, whose suite *The Planets*, written during the Great War, was first performed in 1920, immediately becoming one of the most popular works in the repertoire. He followed it with a comic opera, *The Perfect Fool.*

New operas were not plentiful. One by Rutland Boughton, *The Immortal Hour*, with its well-known *Fairy Song*, ran for over 200 performances. Ralph Vaughan Williams's *Pastoral Symphony* was first performed in 1922. Then came his ballad opera *Hugh the Drover*, a ballet score, *Job*, and an opera based on Shakespeare's Falstaff, *Sir John in Love*. Frederick Delius provided the haunting score for the exotic play *Hassan* by James Elroy Flecker, a popular triumph in 1923. That was the year of the first public performance of poems by Edith Sitwell, *Façade*, declaimed through a megaphone to witty music by William Walton, a youth of 21 who was a protégé of the Sitwells. After showing his facility at parody of popular dance styles in *Façade*, he went on to produce an effective viola concerto in 1929, the year his friend Constant Lambert wrote the jazzy tone poem *The Rio Grande*.

Noël Coward is theatre's new shining star

Noël Coward (centre) stars in a scene from his own play "The Vortex".

The theatre has had two great playwrights and one entertainer of genius this decade, which is more than most decades can muster. The playwrights are George Bernard Shaw and Sean O'Casey, the entertainer is Noël Coward.

Shaw's decade got off to a slow start with *Heartbreak House*, produced in 1921. It was too long and too slow, and its run was short. One critic unkindly called it "Jawbreak House", but Shaw restored his reputation with *St Joan* in 1924. In it he created a heroine he was perfectly serious about and Sybil Thorndike was his perfect Joan. Sean O'Casey worked as a labourer in Dublin before writing three tragi-comedies about the troubles, which were mounted by the Abbey theatre. *The Shadow of a Gunman, Juno and the Paycock* and *The Plough and the Stars* (which was greeted by riots) won him a place beside Synge in the Irish pantheon.

Noël Coward's year of brilliance was 1925 when he was appearing as a drug addict in his play *The Vortex*, which scandalized, wrote a drunken scene for two ladies in *Fallen Angels* (more scandal) and then in three days turned out *Hay Fever*, in which actors humiliate weekend guests. And he was co-author of a revue still running in London.

How taboo topic of war has been ended in the arts

In 1920 the poems of Wilfred Owen appeared, made even more poignant by the fact that he was killed only a week before the Armistice. Poems such as his *Anthem for Doomed Youth* sounded a bitterly different note from the glory in war suggested by Rupert Brooke before he had seen any fighting. Owen's work was edited by his friend Siegfried Sassoon, whose own poems are full of scorching sarcasm at commanders' incompetence.

For nearly a decade of peace the subject of the war was taboo, but since 1928 the books have poured forth. First, from the German side, came *Im Westen Nichts Neues* – the ironic news bulletin tag, *All Quiet On The Western Front*, from Erich Maria Remarque. The English poet Edmund Blunden published *Undertones of War*, and this year brought the memoirs of Robert Graves, another war poet, *Goodbye to All That*, and Richard Aldington's *Death of a Hero*. All these are anti-war books attacking the false values put forward to justify it. Even more powerful is *Journey's End*, a play by R C Sherriff that tells the truth about trench warfare, which opened to critical acclaim this year. The only "clean" war that arouses enthusiasm is the *Revolt in the Desert* of T E Lawrence.

A scene from "Journey's End", one of this year's stage hits.

Abstract sculpture and bleak landscape set style in visual arts

The war artists who saw such destruction in Flanders found themselves without a war to portray. Paul Nash somehow makes his landscapes of England as bleakly empty as the western front; Stanley Spencer paints his memories of the ranks on the walls of Burghclere chapel, a private memorial, and sets his visions of the crucifixion and resurrection in the churchyard of his native Cookham. Elemental carving by Epstein now adorns the headquarters of London Underground. Similar massive simplicity is found in Henry Moore's carving of *Mother and Child* and *Reclining Figure*, and Barbara Hepworth's birds show a matching abstraction.

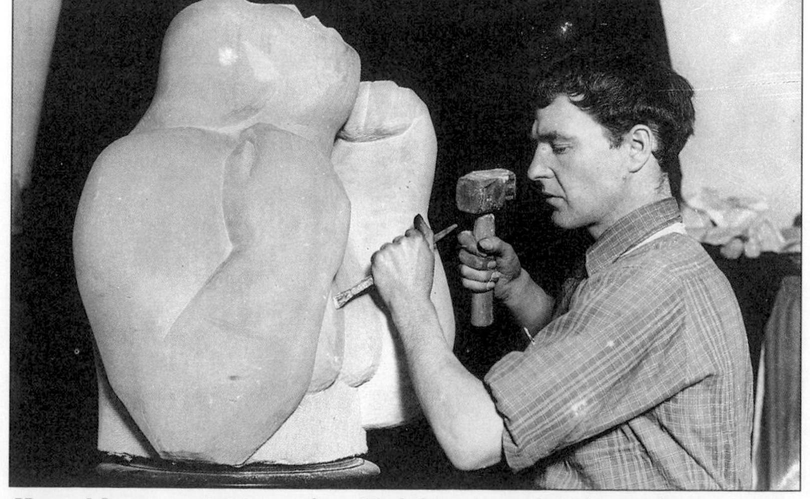

Henry Moore, a miner's son from Yorkshire, at work in his studio.

1930

Lahore, 2 January. The All-India National Congress calls for "complete independence" (→23/6).

London, 22 February. Lord Beaverbrook, the newspaper proprietor, launches the United Empire Party (→31/10).

London, 26 February. The TUC backs the idea of child benefit payments.

Britain, 17 March. The board of film censors reveals that cuts were made to 300 films last year, with "sordid themes" a particular problem (→30/9/36).

Britain, 1 April. Poor Law Guardians are abolished.

Britain, 3 April. The car firms of Rover, Lanchester and Standard are to merge (→7).

Britain, 7 April. The Automobile Association signs up its one millionth member (→15/12).

London, 21 April. A naval treaty is signed by Britain, the US, Japan, France and Italy limiting the size and number of warships and submarines.

Westminster, 20 May. Sir Oswald Mosley quits as a minister after his proposals to combat unemployment are rejected by the cabinet; he is to be replaced by Clement Attlee (→28/2/31).

Westminster, 22 May. Talks between Labour and Liberal leaders break down over electoral reform (→4/12).

London, 29 May. The BBC forms its own symphony orchestra under Adrian Boult.

Westminster, 5 June. The government rejects plans for a channel tunnel.

Westminster, 23 June. India should be a federation separate from Burma, says the statutory commission chaired by the Liberal, Sir John Simon.

London, 14 August. Cautious approval of birth control is announced in an encyclical letter from the archbishop of Canterbury.

London, 14 November. The imperial conference ends without agreement on measures to encourage trade.

Westminster, 4 December. Ramsay MacDonald, the prime minister, promises electoral reform to the Liberals.

Britain, 15 December. A draft Highway Code is issued (→1/1/31).

Novice is first to fly solo to Australia

Darwin, Australia, 24 May
Amy Johnson, a 26-year-old Englishwoman who won her pilot's licence just last year, has landed here at the end of an epic flight. Huge crowds turned out to welcome Johnson, the first woman to fly solo across the world.

Johnson – or "Johnnie" to her friends – took off on 6 May from Croydon in a second-hand de Havilland Gipsy Moth called *Jason*. It was a gruelling journey from the start. She nearly crashed into a mountain in Turkey and had to make an emergency landing in the Iraqi desert because of a sandstorm. Johnson sat the storm out in her cockpit, pistol at the ready in case of attack by wild dogs.

Johnson's arrival in Karachi on 10 May cut two days off the London-to-India record set by Bert Hinkler. The fact that she failed, however, to beat his record for the whole route has done nothing to dampen today's ecstatic welcome at Fanny Bay. She can now look forward to a well-earned rest before the return flight – courtesy of Imperial Airways (→5/10).

Airborne adventurer Amy Johnson.

Commission calls for Indian federation

Westminster, 23 June 1930
After three years of deliberations, a statutory commission on the future of India has rejected nationalist demands for independence. The commission, chaired by former Liberal minister Sir John Simon, proposes self-government at provincial level in a federation with the princely states, under a British viceroy at the head of the central government.

Gandhi, a peaceful protester.

The commission's findings are presented against a background of widespread civil disobedience instigated by nationalists led by a lawyer Mohandas Gandhi, who combines a saintly bearing with wily political skills. He embarrasses the authorities with calls for non-violent protests – which often lead to rioting.

When the commission visited India to gather evidence, it was greeted by noisy crowds waving "Simon Go Home" banners. In its report the commission highlights the bewildering diversity of the subcontinent's 319 million people, divided by race, religion, language and caste, and implies that British rule holds the country together.

Ramsay MacDonald, the prime minister, is planning a round-table conference in London to consider the proposals of the Simon commission. Gandhi, who has been in detention since May, is calling for a boycott.

Slum clearance is boosted by new act

Westminster, 21 April
A new Housing Act becomes law today, providing subsidies for slum clearance. Arthur Greenwood, the housing minister, believes the act will complete the postwar transformation of Britain's housing. Since Lloyd George launched the "homes fit for heroes" scheme in 1918, more than one million homes have been built. These dwellings are a mixture of council homes with controlled rents, and modest, often semi-detached private homes that cost about twice the annual salary of the average professional man. New building is concentrating on large estates on the fringes of the big cities.

Charities to profit in hospital lottery

Ireland, 4 June
Faced with the possible closure of hospitals owing to lack of finance, the government has reluctantly agreed to setting up the Irish Hospital Sweepstakes. The organizers are basing the gamble on English races such as the Grand National and the Derby, thus ensuring large fields and maximum publicity. As well as helping the hospitals, the "Sweep" is expected to employ large numbers of women, and to boost the economy.

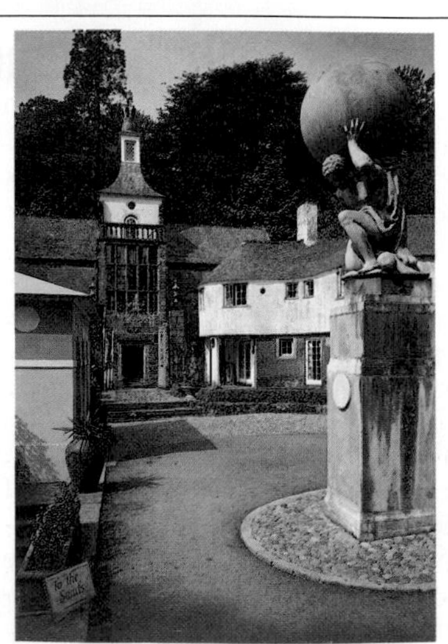

Portmeirion: an Italianate model village in Wales designed by Clough Williams-Ellis.

Two million out of work

Unemployed march along the Embankment to County Hall in Lambeth.

London, 7 August
Unemployment figures released today show that over two million are now out of work, the biggest number since 1921. The economic recovery of the last half of the 1920s was stopped in its tracks by last year's Wall Street crash. The collapse in US confidence has hit world trade generally and British exports and shipping.

So far the crisis has hit the older industrial areas, with coal, iron and steel, shipbuilding and textiles being the most severely affected. The Midlands, thanks to the motor car firms, and the south, which is more concerned with supplying domestic consumers, are more buoyant.

The financial crisis this year has added to the downward spiral. Falling food prices have hit developing countries which can no longer afford to buy British capital goods and shipping is facing its worst-ever slump. Even many of those not registered as unemployed are only working part of the year (→ 4/7/31).

R101 airship crashes over French fields

Beauvais, France, 5 October
Britain's secretary of state for air, Lord Thomson, and Major General Sir Sefton Brancker are among the 48 people who died when the R101 airship crashed in the early hours of this morning. There are only six survivors from what is believed to be British aviation's worst disaster.

The R101 took off yesterday from Cardington, Bedfordshire, on its way to India via Egypt but soon ran into trouble. Rain and a faulty engine forced it to fly low over the Channel and to keep low when it reached France. By that time the airship was also seen to be pitching and rolling.

Shortly before 2am over fields near the village of Beauvais the R101 suddenly dived. In a desperate attempt to gain height, water ballast was poured from the airship but it sank to the ground and burst into flames.

One witness said it looked "as if the whole world had exploded". Within seconds all that remained of the 237-metre (777-foot) R101 airship was a charred wreck (→ 5/3/36).

The burnt out skeleton of the R101 airship lies where it crashed near Beauvais.

Tory defeated by Beaverbrook's United Empire Party candidate

London, 31 October
A retired vice-admiral standing as an Empire Free Trade candidate in the South Paddington by-election has defeated the official Conservative candidate. Lord Beaverbrook, the press tycoon and strident advocate of the Empire policy, is exultant. "What a life!" he says. "A day to remember." The Tory leader, Stanley Baldwin, who regards Beaverbrook's free trade ideas as impractical, reacted to calls for his resignation by seeking a vote of confidence from Tory peers and MPs; the resolution was passed by 462 votes to 116. Beaverbrook said the 116 represent "the real spirit of the party". But critics say he is using his United Empire Party to increase the circulation of his Express newspapers (→ 17/3/31).

Lord Beaverbrook (third from right) rallies the United Empire Party's faithful.

Youth hostels give value to travellers

London, December
A new organization was formed this year to meet the growing demand for cheap accommodation in the countryside. Cycling and hiking are both increasing in popularity and a number of groups have provided cheap and basic accommodation in areas such as the Lake District and the Pennines. Now a new organization called the Youth Hostel Association (YHA) is being created along lines pioneered in Germany in 1914. The first permanent YHA hostel will be in Winchester with hundreds more planned throughout England and Wales. Separate YHA organizations are likely to be formed in Scotland, Ulster and Ireland.

1931

Britain, 1 January. The Road Traffic Act comes into force, making third party insurance compulsory (→ 12).

Westminster, 26 January. Winston Churchill quits the Tory shadow cabinet in protest over moves to give India greater freedom (→ 28/11/34).

Florida, 5 February. Malcolm Campbell sets a new world land speed record of 394kpmh [245mph].

London, 27 March. Lord Beaverbrook ends his empire crusade movement after his candidate lost to a Tory at a by-election this month.

Westminster, 20 April. A bill to allow cinemas to open on Sundays is given a second reading.

Britain, 4 June. Cuts in unemployment pay are urged by a royal commission as a means to avert an economic crisis (→ 31/7).

London, 1 July. Trolley buses begin regular services in the capital, 20 years after their introduction in Yorkshire.

Britain, 6 July. Census returns reveal a drift of population to the southern half of the country; London's population tops eight million, a growth of almost ten per cent since 1921.

Westminster, 31 July. Salary cuts and lower unemployment benefit are recommended in a report which threatens to split the Labour cabinet (→ 24/8).

Westminster, 28 August. Ramsay MacDonald is ousted as Labour leader to be replaced by Arthur Henderson (→ 20/9).

Ireland, 5 September. The first issue of *Irish Press*, the journal of Fianna Fail, is published (→ 20/10).

Britain, 7 September. The king decides to take a pay cut because of the economic crisis.

Dublin, 20 October. The IRA is among 12 groups banned as a tribunal is set up to punish "treasonable activities".

Westminster, 4 November. Herbert Samuel succeeds David Lloyd George as Liberal leader (→ 28/9/32).

London, 1 December. A round-table conference on India fails to reach agreement.

Britain, 15 December. Traffic lights are to be introduced throughout Britain, following their success in London (→ 8/1932).

Mosley breaks away from Labour Party

Mosley addresses a gathering in the hope of gaining support for his new party.

London, 28 February 1931
Sir Oswald Mosley, the wealthy Sandhurst-trained Tory who became a Labour MP in 1924, has stormed out of the party after having his radical plans for tackling unemployment decisively rejected. Since the minority Labour government took office in 1929, pledged to reduce unemployment, the dole queue has more than doubled to over two million. The prime minister, Ramsay MacDonald, seems resigned to impotence; capitalism is collapsing, he says.

Mosley's plans call for state direction of industry, a big increase in public spending and controls on imports. When the cabinet rejected his proposals, Mosley took them to the parliamentary party. His speech was loudly cheered by MPs, who then turned him down by 202 votes to 29. He appealed to the party conference and was again defeated.

So now he is launching his own movement, the New Party, which, he says, will be "a party of action" resolved to transform parliament "from a talk-shop to a workshop".

Mosley is promising "a mobilization of energy, vitality and manhood to save the nation". Four Labour MPs have followed him into his New Party; one of them is his wife Cynthia (→ 31/7).

Press lords likened to harlots by PM

Westminster, 17 March
Stanley Baldwin, the Conservative leader, has tonight rounded on the newspaper proprietors Lord Beaverbrook and Lord Rothermere. They have backed an Empire Free Trade candidate in a London by-election and are confident of beating the Tory candidate, as they did at another by-election last October. Baldwin tonight sought to rally anti-press opinion by denouncing the two lords for wanting power without responsibility. This, he said, was "the prerogative of the harlot throughout the ages" (→ 27).

The empire evolves – except in India

London, December
The great changes taking place in the British empire have been formally recognized. The Statute of Westminster over which Lord Balfour's committee has laboured for five years defines Great Britain and the dominions as "autonomous communities within the British empire, equal in status, in no way subordinate one to another in any aspect of their domestic or internal affairs, though united by a common allegiance to the Crown, and freely associated as members of the British Commonwealth of Nations".

The independence which the dominions enjoy in practice has thus been constitutionally confirmed. Only in India does the Raj continue unchanged.

Ford factory opens

Essex, December
The giant Ford Motor Company of America this year opened its biggest European plant on the banks of the Thames at Dagenham, east of London. Henry Ford set up his first European plant at Trafford Park in Manchester as long ago as 1910, but the Dagenham factory is much larger and it epitomizes the trend away from coach-building to production-line car manufacture. The new factory expects to be employing more than 7,000 men by the end of next year (→ 15).

Three Port of London Authority policemen put their trust in their new kapok-filled lifejackets as they take the plunge into the river Thames.

Economic crisis brings down Labour government

Ministers are split over economic cuts

Westminster, 24 August
The Labour government today fell after days of impassioned debate about how to tackle the economic crisis. Ramsay MacDonald, the Labour premier, will now head an all-party "National" government and has been denounced as a traitor by most Labour ministers and MPs.

MacDonald himself twice went to Buckingham Palace to resign, but was persuaded by King George to head a coalition government. The king also won backing for a National government from Stanley Baldwin and Sir Herbert Samuel, the Tory and Liberal leaders.

It was the run on the pound that brought the crisis to a head this month. The Labour cabinet had been rocked by a report in July calling for swingeing cuts in public spending to pull the country back from economic disaster. The report came from a committee of businessmen and trade unionists set up by the government in February and chaired by Sir George May, a former Prudential Assurance executive.

The report called for tax rises, pay cuts for police, teachers, civil servants and the armed forces, and a 20 per cent cut in the dole. Ministers were deeply divided, with a large minority threatening to resign over the dole cuts. The May report was taken by bankers as confirmation of their worst fears, intensifying withdrawals of funds from London and causing gold reserves to plummet. The Bank of England warned that national bankruptcy was near (→28).

Scuffles break out as police attempt to seize a red banner from protesters.

Ramsay MacDonald prepares to make a broadcast from the cabinet room.

Pay cuts provoke anger and a mutiny

London, 30 September
Philip Snowden's emergency budget of higher taxes and pay cuts has been followed by a month of demonstrations, clashes with the police and even a brief naval mutiny. In the House of Commons, Labour MPs have bitterly accused Ramsay MacDonald and Snowden, only last month comrades in the socialist cause, of betrayal and surrender to a "bankers' ramp".

But Snowden, the chancellor, stood firm and balanced his budget. Everybody paid by the state, from cabinet ministers and judges to the unemployed, has had to make sacrifices. Income tax has been raised to 5s [25p] in the pound.

The dole has been cut by 10 per cent, half the figure proposed in the controversial May report, but still enough to provoke cries of hardship. Outside Battersea town hall tonight some 5,000 unemployed staged a demonstration and in the West End postal workers brought traffic to a halt. Civil servants, too, have joined in protest marches.

The mutiny, by ratings at Invergordon, on Cromarty Firth, broke out on 15 September when word went round that their pay was to be cut by 25 per cent. The men defied their officers, held mass meetings and refused to take the fleet to sea. Discipline was restored after two days when the Admiralty promised a cut of only 10 per cent.

The mutiny has helped others. The teachers' 15 per cent cut has been reduced to 10 per cent. The police have done best with a cut of just five per cent (→28/10).

Run on the pound leads to devaluation

London, 20 September
Legislation is to be rushed through parliament tomorrow to do the very thing the Labour government was told only a month ago was impossible. The gold standard is being abandoned and sterling will be allowed to float. The National government acted under pressure from Sir Montagu Norman, governor of the Bank of England, who reported that reserves had been exhausted by speculation against the pound. This had intensified after the Invergordon mutiny five days ago. The pound's value against the dollar is expected to fall by a quarter to $3.40. Imports will be more expensive, but exports will be more competitive (→30).

Labour routed as coalition wins election

Westminster, 28 October
The Labour Party has been overwhelmed at the polls after an election campaign led by the man who was, until this summer, its admired leader, but is now seen as a traitor. Ramsay MacDonald is prime minister of a National government with the support of 554 MPs, 473 of them Tories, 68 Liberal and just 13 self-styled National Labour. MacDonald accused his old colleagues in the Labour cabinet of running away from the economic crisis and he appealed to voters to give his all-party government a doctor's mandate to restore foreign confidence in Britain. Voters have responded by returning just 52 regular Labour MPs (→4/11).

1932

Westminster, 12 February. A bill is introduced to ban the whipping of children aged under 14 (→ 1937).

Westminster, 29 February. The royal assent is given to a ten per cent tariff on imports, with concessions for the empire.

London, 15 March. The BBC makes its first transmission from Broadcasting House.

Dublin, 16 March. Eamon de Valera outlines government proposals, which include suspending the Public Safety Act, protective tariffs and abolishing the oath of allegiance (→ 30/4).

Stratford-upon-Avon, 23 April. The new Shakespeare Memorial Theatre is opened by the prince of Wales.

Dublin, 30 April. The Dáil votes to drop the oath of allegiance to the British king (→ 15/7).

Sussex, 5 July. The first main-line electric express train runs from London Bridge to Three Bridges in Sussex (→ 1/7/33).

Los Angeles, 2 August. Tommy Hampson of Britain wins the Olympic 800 metres in a world record time of 1 minute 49.8 seconds.

London, August. Three-letter car number plates are introduced; the first in London is AMY 1 (→ 3/1/34).

London, 8 October. The London Philharmonic Orchestra gives its first concert under its creator Sir Thomas Beecham.

Belfast, 13 October. Police clash with crowds after several days of strikes, marches and unemployment protests (→ 30).

Westminster, 25 October. George Lansbury is elected leader of the Labour Party.

London, 30 October. Police clash with jobless protesters after fighting in the streets (→ 12/1933).

Stockholm, 11 November. John Galsworthy is awarded the Nobel Prize for Literature.

Belfast, 16 November. The prince of Wales opens the Northern Ireland parliament buildings at Stormont.

Britain, 25 December. King George makes the first Christmas Day wireless broadcast to the empire.→

Britain. Instant coffee is first sold here this year.

De Valera topples Cosgrave to form a new government

Ireland, 9 March

Fianna Fáil today formed a new government with the support of the Labour Party. This follows the defeat in last month's election of William Cosgrave's party, Cumann na nGaedheal. The new prime minister, Eamon de Valera, has already given assurances that there will be no victimization of those who supported the 1921 treaty. As proof of this, his justice minister is a former Cumann na nGaedheal supporter. De Valera is taking the external affairs portfolio himself and Sean Lemass has been appointed minister for industry and commerce.

De Valera is widely seen as the embodiment of Irish national aspirations and inspires devotion in his followers. His party fought a well-organized campaign in which its leader appeared at many meetings throughout the country wearing a black cloak and riding a white horse. The new government is expected to introduce tough social and economic measures, as well as removing the oath of allegiance to the British king (→ 16).

Peak District hikers risk imprisonment

Ramblers gather in support of public rights of way across the countryside.

Edale, Derbyshire, 24 April

Five men were arrested today after a "mass trespass" involving thousands of hikers on the grouse moors of Kinder Scout above Edale. The men, who could face jail sentences, were arrested after clashes with gamekeepers who were seeking to keep the ramblers off private land.

Public access to the countryside has become increasingly contentious as cars, motor-cycles and bikes have brought once remote areas within reach of millions of town-dwellers. Hiking is booming as a recreation combining aesthetic appreciation of the countryside with the vogue for healthy outdoor fitness. The Peak District, close to Manchester, Sheffield and Derby, is in the forefront of the campaign for greater access: only 1,212 acres out of 150,000 acres of moorland are open to the public.

Dartmoor governor is saved by inmate

Princetown, Devon, 25 January

Troops with machine guns are ringing the bleak walls of Dartmoor prison tonight following a riot in which 70 inmates and six warders were injured. Police were rushed from Plymouth and other centres to join prison warders in a series of charges with truncheons on rampaging convicts armed with home-made spears.

The prison governor and a Home Office Commissioner owe their lives to George Donovan, serving a life sentence for murder, who put himself between them and ring-leaders of the mutiny. Donovan was reprieved an hour before he was due to hang.

Prisoners were complaining of poor and inadequate food, damp cells and the difficulties faced by relatives in reaching the remote granite prison on the moors.

Norfolk rector in sex case is defrocked

Norfolk, 21 October

The parish of Stiffkey is to have a new clergyman. A consistory court has today defrocked the Reverend Harold Francis Davidson after he had been found guilty earlier this year of behaviour causing "grave scandal to the Church".

Mr Davidson, which is how the former rector of Stiffkey must now be called, was brought before the consistory court last March. The rector's frequent visits to London and his alleged association with young girls kept the press happy, although he denied the charges.

The prosecution alleged that Davidson, aged 60, spent Sundays in his parish but weekdays in a bed-sitter in Shepherd's Bush, London. Waitresses from Lyons's and ABC tearooms complained that he had pestered them and a model told the court that he had set her up in lodgings. While the court deliberated, Davidson caused a scene in June by attempting to grab the bible of a clergyman deputizing for him at Stiffkey. But he was found guilty of associating with women of loose character and of accosting young women for immoral purposes.

The guilty rector leaves court.

Ramsay MacDonald isolated in cabinet as Liberal ministers quit government

Westminster, 28 September
Ramsay MacDonald's government is looking less and less National and more and more Tory since the abrupt resignation of four prominent cabinet ministers, three of them Liberals, the fourth, Philip, Viscount Snowden, the Labour veteran who became the "Iron Chancellor" in the first weeks of the National government. The resignations were provoked by agreements limiting tariffs on trade with the dominions and raising them on trade with foreign countries. Thirty back-bench Liberals have gone over to the opposition in protest at the government's repudiation of free trade principles (→3/1933).

Ramsay MacDonald: out of step.

Three Methodist churches agree to unite

Britain, 20 September
The Methodist churches will speak with one voice from today. After lengthy negotiations, the Primitive Methodists, the United Methodists and the Wesleyan Methodists have all agreed to transcend their differences and unite.

The Methodists are only the latest of the "low church" denominations to attempt to deal with the falling attendances and declining faith that some have attributed to the horrors of the Great War, by sinking their differences. In 1929 the United Free Church in Scotland, itself formed in 1900 from a union of the United Presbyterians and most of the Free Church, rejoined the Church of Scotland.

Certainly, in the face of competition on Sundays from motor cars and railway trips, the churches can no longer afford the attitude of one 19th-century Methodist preacher who said of another: "They say this dog barks well but he comes from a dirty kennel."

Land row starts Anglo-Irish trade war

Dublin, 15 July
True to its electoral pledge, Fianna Fáil has refused to pay land annuities to the British government. The annuities amount to around £5 million a year and Fianna Fáil believes there are economic, moral and legal reasons why they should no longer be paid. The British government, already smarting over Fianna Fáil's plan to drop the oath of allegiance to the crown, has responded to the challenge by imposing a 20 per cent duty on Irish agricultural exports. Eamon de Valera, the Irish premier, in turn is imposing duties on British coal.

De Valera does not intend to abolish the annuities but to halve them and retain the money for his government. But this would deprive farmers of 10 per cent of their net income, so feelings are running high. Cattle prices have dropped to 1914 levels, and farmers, recalling speeches by Fianna Fáil candidates, are refusing to pay their share of the annuities (→28/1/33).

Unemployment hits an all-time record

Britain, 30 September
Nearly three million workers are now out of work – one in four of the total British labour force. Yet the real situation is thought to be even worse. The official statistics exclude many agricultural workers, the self-employed and married women, who do not usually sign on the dole.

Many people have been driven below the poverty line. In Stockton-on-Tees, for instance, the average income for unemployed families is 20s [£1] a week against 51s 6d for those in work. However, those able to get unemployment relief are in some cases better off than workers in the lowest-paid jobs(→13/10).

King 'speaks from heart' at Christmas

Sandringham, 25 December
In a room under the stairs once used by his father's secretary, King George V today made his first Christmas broadcast to the nation and the empire. "I speak now from my home and from my heart to you all," the king said. His voice was first broadcast in 1924, when he opened the Empire Exhibition at Wembley. John Reith, general manager of the BBC, urged him to use the wireless again to speak directly to his subjects, but until today he has resisted. George was nervous – the broadcast was "live" – but it is thought likely that the royal message will become a Christmas tradition (→18/7/34).

Oswald Mosley to head new fascist movement in Britain

London, December
Sir Oswald Mosley, who left the Labour government two years ago over his radical solutions to unemployment, has formed a new party this year. Members of the British Union of Fascists will wear black shirts, like their Italian counterparts. Sir Oswald is apparently undaunted by the failure of the party he formed last year – the New Party, dedicated to mobilizing "energy vitality and manhood" – in the 1931 general election.

He advocates control of industry and massive state borrowing at a time when the new National government is cutting public spending. Many Conservatives, and newspaper tycoon Lord Rothermere, are said to support him (→22/8/33).

Mosley's new fascist party holds its first meeting in Trafalgar Square.

Atoms smashed in 'Brave New World'

Cambridge, December
Science made important strides this year at the Cavendish Laboratory in Cambridge. John Cockcroft and Ernest Walton, under the leadership of the Nobel prizewinner, Sir Ernest Rutherford, split the atom, as Rutherford had foreseen in 1919 could be done. Their atom smashing machine also transmuted lithium atoms into those of helium – the first artificial transformation. Also at Cambridge, James Chadwick discovered a new sub-atomic particle: the neutron. Not everyone is thrilled by science. Aldous Huxley, in *Brave New World* published this year, offers a bleak vision of people bred by test-tube.

1933

Dublin, 28 January. Eamon de Valera's Fianna Fáil wins an overall majority of only one in the general election held four days ago (→9/10).

Australia, 16 February. England win the Ashes at the end of the controversial "bodyline" tour (→25/2/35).

Oxford, February. Students at the university union shock their elders by voting 275-153 that they would not fight "for king and country".

Rome, March. Ramsay MacDonald upsets some MPs by meeting the Italian dictator Benito Mussolini to discuss disarmament (→23/2/34).

Westminster, 1 May. MPs back an Anglo-German trade pact; last month a bill banning Soviet imports became law (→24).

Britain, 24 May. The TUC calls for a boycott of Germany to protest against Hitler who came to power as chancellor on 30 January (→25/10).

London, 26 June. King George lays the foundation stone of the University of London's new Bloomsbury site.

London, 20 July. Over 50,000 Jews march in protest against Nazi anti-semitism.

France, 30 July. British tennis players win the Davis Cup, ending France's seven-year run of victories (→10/9).

London, 1 September. Kenneth Clark becomes director of the National Gallery at the age of 30.

USA, 10 September. Fred Perry becomes the first Briton to win the US open tennis championship since 1903.

Birmingham, 5 October. Compulsory powers will be applied to councils which fail to meet slum clearance targets, the government says.

Dublin, 9 October. Eamon de Valera introduces three bills to reduce further the jurisdiction of the British crown.→

London, 25 October. A Labour candidate opposed to rearmament wins the East Fulham by-election from the government (→29/11).

Britain, 28 November. New grounds are proposed for divorce, including cruelty, drunkenness and insanity.

Britain. The *Daily Express* becomes the first daily newspaper to top two million sales this year.

'Bodyline' rumpus threatens cricket tour

Woodfull is forced to take evasive action as Larwood delivers a thunderbolt.

Adelaide, Australia, 23 January
Cricket authorities in England and Australia have clashed bitterly off the field as their players fought out a bitter confrontation in the third test here at Adelaide. The dispute centres on what the Australians call "bodyline" and what the English captain, Douglas Jardine, calls "leg theory". By the time the test ended the Australian authorities had sent a telegram to the MCC in London protesting that the tactics, whatever they were called, were "unsportsmanlike" and should cease.

Jardine developed his controversial tactics as a ploy to counter the brilliance of Australia's batting hero, Don Bradman. It involves bowling fast deliveries on the line of the leg stump and batsman's body with a cordon of close fielders on the leg side. If bowlers are accurate, batsmen are forced to play, with any mishit likely to offer a catch.

Tempers flared when Australia's wicketkeeper Bert Oldfield was hit on the head by a ball from Larwood. After he was helped from the pitch, the home team's captain Bill Woodfull (who had been hit twice by bouncers) protested that there were two sides playing but "one was not playing cricket". The Australians fired off their telegram but, with a diplomatic row brewing, the MCC has declared its confidence in the English captain and deplored the accusation of "unsportsmanlike" behaviour (→16/2).

Fascist 'Blueshirts' banned in Ireland after IRA clashes

Dublin, 22 August
The Army Comrades Association, led by Eoin O'Duffy, a former chief of police, has turned itself into the "National Guard" aimed at the overthrow of communism. Known as the "Blueshirts", the Guard has clashed so frequently with the IRA that the Irish government led by Eamon de Valera has now banned the movement.

Fascism has grown on fertile ground in Ireland. Hardship and unemployment are everywhere and Irish exports dropped by half last year as a result of de Valera's trade war against Britain. The Army Comrades Association was established last year, declaring its aim to guarantee free speech by creating a "volunteer force". By the end of 1932 it claimed 30,000 active members. They wore blue shirts, drilling and saluting in the fascist manner – their leader admires Benito Mussolini, the Italian dictator, and wishes to see an end to parliamentary democracy.

Eamon de Valera's government has made several attempts to suppress the Blueshirts but to no avail. Their stern authoritarianism, seductive in these troubled times, has attracted public figures as diverse as the poet W B Yeats and the prominent Catholic churchman, John Charles McQuaid (→21/1/34).

British engineers are tried as spies

Moscow, 18 April
In one of Stalin's "show-trials" in which nothing is what it seems, two British engineers working for Metropolitan-Vickers have been imprisoned for "spying, wrecking and bribery". Three other Britons are to be deported and a sixth was acquitted. After being held for a month in the Lubyanka prison one of the defendants "confessed" but another protested that the case was "a frame-up, staged on the evidence of terrorized Russians". The Foreign Office deplored the sentences and Britain is expected to impose sanctions on Russia.

'Corner House' offers a food revolution

Tea for two, or three or four...

London, 23 October
Over 1,000 staff are poised to serve 2,000 customers in a huge new Lyons "Corner House" which is to open today claiming to offer a revolution in mass catering.

The revolution lies behind the kitchen doors. While the customers listen to background music, the waitresses will hurry down a "one-way" production-line system, passing over their orders at points signposted with notices like "fried fish" and "soups". The idea is that service should be as quick as possible.

Last year Lyons's smaller teashops won notoriety as places frequented by the defrocked rector of Stiffkey [*see report on page 1084*].

De Valera cuts links with British crown

Dublin, 9 October
The Irish parliament has jettisoned the oath of allegience to Britain by passing the Removal of the Oath Act, thus ending a long-standing Irish grievance. Together with the partition of the country and the continued British military control of the treaty ports, the oath has always been particularly objectionable to anti-treaty republicans since it appeared to affirm Britain's right to rule Ireland, and was in direct contrast to the long separatist tradition going back to Wolfe Tone and the 1798 rebellion.

Meanwhile the other major issue – the payment of land annuities to the British exchequer – remains unresolved. Eamon de Valera, the Irish prime minister, has been holding talks with members of the British cabinet and arbitration was being considered when, last July, the House of Commons passed a resolution to enable the British government to make good money lost by means of customs duties on imports from Ireland.

De Valera has sought further to reduce British influence with his request that the representative of the crown in Ireland – the governor-general – be removed from office. This was accepted and James McNeill, the present incumbent, was replaced by de Valera with Domhnall O Buachalla, a Fianna Fáil grocer from Co Kildare who has kept firmly out of the public eye ever since, thus dealing the office a death blow (→ 11/12/36).

Eamon de Valera, the Irish premier, presides over his Fianna Fáil cabinet.

New map launches reorganized 'Tube'

London, 1 July
Londoners travelled to work or pleasure today as customers of the world's largest transport organization. The new London Passenger Transport Board combines all the bus, tram, trolley and underground services that serve not only the capital but an area of some 2,000 square miles within a 20-30 mile radius of Charing Cross. Only the mainline railway companies are excluded from this new publicly owned organization which has been formed to coordinate services and promote expansion of the network. Symbolically, there is also a new diagrammatic map for the "Tube" designed by Harry Beck.

Britain reluctantly boosts its defences

Westminster, 29 November
Britain is to strengthen its armed forces to match those nations which refused to follow Britain's example of unilateral disarmament. Lord Londonderry, the air minister, told the Lords: "We cannot continue in our present inferiority. Our air force must be as strong as that of any other nation." In the Commons, the lord president, Stanley Baldwin, announcing measures to meet potential dangers, said that Britain could not continue to stand alone, half disarmed. He hoped, however, for international controls on arms spending and warned that increases in air force budgets would worsen relations with Germany (→ 25/6/34).

Economic improvement offers no cheer to industrial regions living on the 'dole'

Britain, December
Nearly three million people were registered as unemployed last winter – one in four of the insured working population. It now appears that this winter's figure will be lower, raising hopes that the worst of the depression is over. But more than two million people remain unemployed and this total excludes farm labourers, self-employed workers and married women. National figures also mask the continuing severity of the slump in some areas.

Ex-soldiers sing for their supper.

Although the depression hit all industries, its effects have been at their most savage and have lasted longer in regions dependent upon heavy industry. Unemployment in mining, shipbuilding and steel has been twice as high as the average for all industries; in cotton it has also been significantly higher. Last year, for instance, three in five shipbuilding workers were unemployed and two in five miners.

In many cases these industries were in decline even before the present slump, so the extent of long-term unemployment has been greater in the areas where these industries are concentrated – in particular, north-eastern England, south Wales, Northern Ireland and central parts of Scotland. With few alternative jobs men have often been out of work for years (some school leavers have never worked). With unemployment insurance benefits limited to 26 weeks, they have to apply for "transitional payments" which are subject to a much-hated means test. Life on the "dole", as the benefits are known, is hard and often humiliating. A glimpse into proletarian realities was movingly provided this year by *Love on the Dole*, a stage hit based on the novel by Walter Greenwood.

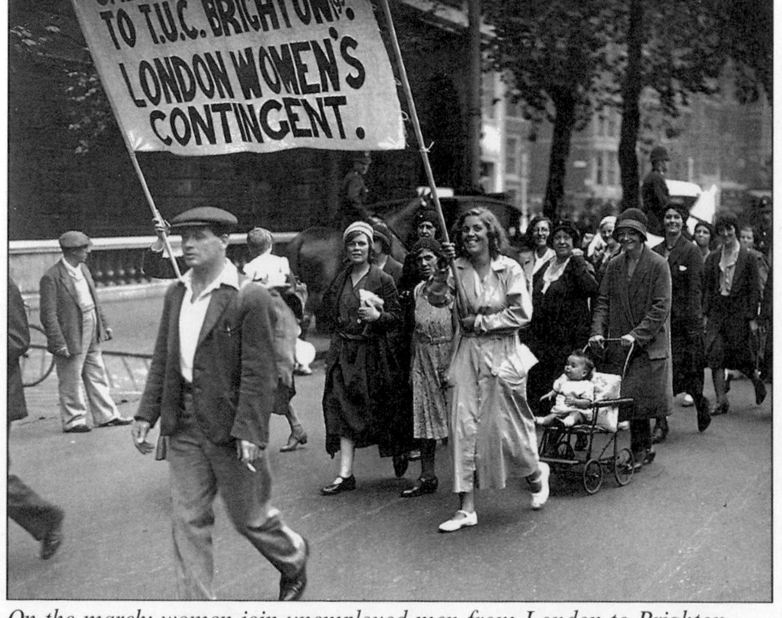

On the march: women join unemployed men from London to Brighton.

1934

Britain, 3 January. Road traffic signs are to be standardized (→ 28/3).

London, 23 February. Ramsay MacDonald refuses to see 500 "hunger marchers" after their trek from Glasgow (→ 7/6/35).

London, 8 March. Labour has won a clear majority on the London County Council for the first time.

Britain, 21 March. The slimming craze is blamed by the Fruit and Potato Trades Association for a decline in potato sales.

Westminster, 30 April. The government sets up a committee to examine the feasibility of a public television service (→ 21/8/36).

Dublin, 25 May. The Dail votes to abolish the Senate.

London, 8 June. Fierce fighting breaks out at Olympia during the latest rally staged by Sir Oswald Mosley's British Union of Fascists (→ 11/10/36).

London, 12 June. Pedestrian crossings are introduced to try to reduce road casualties (→ 18/3/35).

Britain, 25 June. A 20 per cent duty is imposed on German goods in retaliation for Germany's moratorium on loan repayments (→ 19/7).

Liverpool, 18 July. King George V opens the Mersey Tunnel, the longest underwater tunnel in the world (→ 6/5/35).

Westminster, 19 July. The RAF is to be boosted by 41 new squadrons, the government tells MPs (→ 28/11).

Glasgow, 26 September. The queen launches the Cunard-White Star liner, *Queen Mary*.

Britain, October. A Peace Pledge Union is launched against rearmament.

Britain, 20 November. Plans are announced for the introduction of numbered postal districts in major towns.

Oslo, 10 December. The Nobel peace prize is awarded to Arthur Henderson.

Dublin, 21 December. Agreement is reached over Britain buying Irish cattle and the Free State more British coal, thereby raising hopes of an end to the Anglo-Irish economic war.

East Sussex. A small opera house stages its first festival at a country house called Glyndebourne, near Lewes.

Mosley calls for fascist dictatorship

In characteristic black, Mosley outlines his plans for a government of action.

Birmingham, 21 January

A slim, upright figure in black shirt and slacks held by a wide leather belt, he raises his voice in well-rehearsed cadences as he calls on his audience of 10,000 to support his aim of a "modern dictatorship" to solve Britain's social and economic problems. This is Sir Oswald Mosley, whose chequered political career has taken him from the Tory Party into a Labour government and on to the British Union of Fascists, which he founded less than two years ago and modelled on the fascist and Nazi movements of Italy and Germany. Though Mosley is a wealthy man there is speculation that secret sympathizers are funding his movement.

In Birmingham tonight arms are upraised in the fascist salute as he steps forward to address his biggest ever rally. He promises that his fascist government, which he counts on coming to power after next year's election, will arm itself with emergency powers to "overcome the problems the people want to overcome".

Much of his speech articulates the impatience many people feel at the apparent impotence of democratic politicians faced with economic collapse and widespread unemployment. His mix of nationalism and socialist rhetoric goes down well. But there is a more sinister thread running through his strident denunciations of the old politicians at Westminster. There are sudden references to the malign influence of Jewish intrigues and Jewish money, which are enthusiastically applauded by at least a section of the audience, doubtless Mosley's own recruits. Anyone in the audience who tries to heckle or ask an awkward question is likely to be pounced upon by black-shirted stewards and roughed up before being thrown out of the hall.

This, by now, familiar feature of Mosley's meetings has lost him the support of right-wing Tories and of the press, though Lord Rothermere's *Daily Mail* continues to provide a platform for him (→ 8/6).

Suburbs boom as city houses sprawl

Britain, 6 April

Figures released today show that in the last ten years 1,900,000 houses have been built in Britain. State subsidies for slum clearances and for rented housing have helped local authorities build more houses; and mortgages averaging around 4.5 per cent interest rates have fuelled a boom in private housing. "Speculative" estates are creating new suburbs on the fringes of cities, offering semi-detached houses for prices as low as £450.

As many as 350,000 private houses are expected to be completed next year. With bathrooms, gardens and in some cases garages, these are a far cry from the overcrowded conditions still prevalent in major cities. But calls are growing for planning controls as suburbs spread into the countryside.

Double sporting win for British hosts

July. Britain has played host to two great sporting events and ended up winning both of them. Henry Cotton (left) drives off from the fourth tee on his way to victory at the Open Golf Championship at Sandwich, Kent, bringing the title back to Britain after 11 years abroad. Meanwhile at Wimbledon Fred Perry (right) strokes his way to victory in the men's final; Dorothy Round won the women's singles and the mixed doubles.

Tributes flow in to Sir Edward Elgar

Elgar: an unpompous man.

Worcester, 23 February
Sir Edward Elgar died at his home overlooking the Malvern Hills today and tributes came from the leaders of the musical world, Richard Strauss and Sibelius among them, to "the greatest English composer since Purcell".

One of his *Pomp and Circumstance* marches was given the words *Land of Hope and Glory*, but his genius was first shown in the *Enigma Variations* of 1899. His First Symphony (1908) was performed over 100 times within a year, but after the Great War he wrote only one major work, the cello concerto, first performed in 1919.

Novice motorists to face stiff driving test

London, 28 March
For the first time since men with red flags had to walk in front of motorized vehicles, new drivers will have to prove their ability in a test. Until today, the only requirement for drivers has been an unsupported declaration of physical fitness by anyone over the age of 17. A speed limit of 30mph (48kmph) will be imposed in built-up areas – defined by the number of street lights – and experiments with pedestrian crossings are to be made in London.

Although private cars have increased ninefold since 1918, the number of drivers charged with offences under the traffic acts has only doubled, with pedestrians being blamed for many accidents.

Under the Government's Road Traffic Bill published today, pedestrians, too, face fines for walking dangerously, and the use of horns by drivers will be subject to official scrutiny (→12/6).

Pedestrian crossings halt traffic.

Hope fades for 262 men after pit blast

Wrexham, 21 September
An explosion today at the Gresford colliery near here has resulted in one of the worst mining disasters of all time. The death toll now stands at 262 with hope abandoned of finding anyone alive. Three of those who have died were among the rescue teams which battled against flames and poisonous fumes. All day relatives waited in silence at the pit-head. As night fell, only 16 bodies had been brought to the surface leaving 243 entombed in the pit below ground. Few escaped the ferocity of the blast, although one man did inch to safety up a 200-feet vertical shaft just two feet wide. The chief inspector of mines, Sir Henry Walker, said the mine might have to be sealed and closed with the loss of 2,000 jobs.

Churchill warns of weak UK defences

Westminster, 28 November
Winston Churchill today continued his campaign for Britain to rearm in order to counter increased German strength. The former Tory and Liberal cabinet minister, now a backbencher, moved a Commons amendment declaring that "the strength of our national defences, and especially of our air defences, is no longer adequate to secure ... peace, safety and freedom".

He told a packed, attentive House that Germany's munitions factories were already working "under practically war conditions" and that even if there is "no acceleration on the part of Germany, and no slowing down on our part" the German military air force will have nearly double the strength of the RAF by 1937.

He warned that Britain's weak defences could lead to the nation being "tortured into absolute subjection", with no chance of ever recovering, in a war with Germany. Churchill said that while there was no reason to think Germany would attack, it was not pleasant to think that it could: "The time has come when the mists surrounding German armaments should be stripped away." His argument was rejected by fellow-Tory Stanley Baldwin, speaking for the government, who argued that Britain would retain a 50 per cent superiority over Germany (→4/3/35).

Telephones ring the exchanges in Britain

Every home should have one.

London, 1 January
There are now over two million telephone subscribers in Britain. The number of new installations has jumped to average 275,000 a year. Last year exchanges in London handled almost 800 million calls, the Post Office announced today. More than half of them were dialled through automatic exchanges and 637,000 were to countries overseas.

The roadside telephone kiosk, which first appeared in 1926 in a great variety of shapes and colours, has been redesigned by Sir Giles Gilbert Scott, architect of Liverpool Cathedral. His design, in prefabricated concrete painted red, won a Fine Arts Commission prize.

September 26. People hurry across fields at Glasgow to gain a riverside view and watch Queen Mary launch her namesake built by Cunard.

1935

Westminster, 16 January. Curbs on overcrowded housing are announced.

Britain, 10 February. A record film contract for a Briton is signed by Rochdale singer Gracie Fields; she will receive £150,000 for three films.

London, 25 February. Jack Hobbs announces his retirement from first-class cricket at the age of 53; he scored 197 centuries.

Dublin, 28 February. The Criminal Law Amendment Act prohibits the importation or sale of contraceptives in the Irish Free State.

England, 5 March. An LNER steam train reaches 173kpmh [108mph] between London to Newcastle-upon-Tyne.

Britain, 18 March. A 48kpmh [30mph] speed limit on vehicles is introduced in built-up areas (→ 29/4).

Britain, 29 April. Glass reflectors known as "Cat's Eyes" invented by Percy Shaw are used on British roads for the first time (→ 3/9).

London, 6 May. King George and Queen Mary celebrate their silver jubilee with a service at St Paul's Cathedral to mark their 25-year reign (→ 20/1/36).

Britain, 22 May. Plans are announced to treble the RAF in size over the next two years (→ 19/6).

Britain, 7 June. Stanley Baldwin becomes prime minister after Ramsay MacDonald resigns for health reasons (→ 8/10).

Britain, 19 June. An Anglo-German naval accord allowing the Nazis to build up their navy again upsets the French (→ 2/1/37).

London, 21 June. A Croydon telephonist wins a competition to find a voice for the "speaking clock".

Britain, 25 July. Arms sales to Italy and Abyssinia are to be banned by the government as war fears grow in Africa.

Westminster, 8 October. Clement Attlee is elected to succeed George Lansbury as Labour leader (→ 16/11).

London, October. A 90mph Jaguar costing £385 is the star of the Motor Show.

Westminster, 22 December. Anthony Eden takes over from Sir Samuel Hoare as foreign secretary.

'Lawrence of Arabia' dies after accident

Dorset, 19 May

One of the most romantic heroes of the Great War died today after five days in a coma, his skull fractured in a motorcycle accident.

Colonel T E Lawrence, or "Lawrence of Arabia", captured the imagination of Britain when, after years of desert warfare riding alongside his Arab allies, he helped to take Baghdad in 1918. His account of those times was told in his best-seller *Revolt in the Desert*. But the full story, including his capture and assault by the Turks, is contained in *The Seven Pillars of Wisdom* which he refused to publish in his lifetime.

He leaves behind two mysteries: the identity of "S A", to whom the book is dedicated, and the reason he joined the RAF to become Aircraftsman Shaw for 14 years. He left the RAF only two months ago and died when, riding his motorcycle from Bovington camp to his home, he swerved to avoid two boy cyclists.

The secretive Lawrence of Arabia.

Defence spending is set to increase

Westminster, 4 March

The government today produced a White Paper on defence which contains plans for a significant increase in the strength of all three services. The emphasis of the paper is largely on defence against attack from the air with more fighters for the RAF, new anti-aircraft defences and increased protection for ships against bombers.

Presenting the paper, which represents a considerable shift in the government's position, Stanley Baldwin said: "Our attempt to lead the world towards disarmament by unilateral example has failed." The fault, he argued, lay with Germany whose rearmament threatened to put peace at peril. The government hopes that Britain's determination will be made plain to the German chancellor, Adolf Hitler, through a meeting which is shortly to take place in Berlin (→ 22/5).

Thousands protest over 'means test'

South Wales, 18 March

Nearly 300,000 people took to the streets today in the biggest protest yet against the hated means test and regulations laid down by the new Unemployment Assistance Board (UAB). There were similar protests in Sheffield. Although these demonstrations were organized by the Communist-led National Unemployed Workers' Movement, they symbolize grievances that have festered for several years.

The spread of unemployment has made more and more families face the humiliation of being visited by their local public assistance committee, now replaced by the UAB. They have been obliged to reveal their personal lives, have their furniture valued and, in many cases, have their benefit reduced because of contributions from children or parents living with them.

The Unemployment Insurance Acts, introduced last year, were supposed to relieve hardship. But when details were published recently, relief scales in some areas were lower than those paid by the local authorities.

Use all your vigour to keep your figure

London, 8 October

Britain is fast becoming a nation of keep-fit fanatics. At least, that is what officials of the newly established Central Council of Recreative Physical Training are telling us. Women, young and old, are especially enthusiastic, flocking to the council's gymnasia with their slogan "Use your vigour to keep your figure", but men, boys and girls are not missing out. A spokesman declared: "A survey we have just completed shows that there are thousands of men, women and adolescents anxious to form keep-fit classes." Indeed, new gyms cannot open fast enough, and many classes are over-subscribed.

So widespread is the new fitness craze that no fewer than 130 organizations, each devoted to a form of physical activity, have set up a special conference in London.

Lunch-hour exercise classes keep office workers full of vim and vitality.

Tories surge to victory

Stanley Baldwin leads the Tories back into power with an increased majority.

Westminster, 16 November
Only a few National Liberal and National Labour remnants have survived the election to sit with the massed ranks of Tories to give the prime minister and Tory leader, Stanley Baldwin, the backing of 432 MPs. Ramsay MacDonald, who formed the National government in 1931 and retired as premier last June, was crushingly defeated in the Seaham mining constituency, picking up fewer than 18,000 votes against the 38,000-plus cast for his Labour opponent, the fiery Clydesider Emmanuel Shinwell. Labour has trebled its strength to 154 MPs; Liberals are down to 20.

Firmly on the election agenda were housing and unemployment, but the issue of rearmament was fudged. Baldwin, believing that the country has become pacifist, insisted in his speeches that "there will be no great armaments". But the election victory now gives him a solid parliamentary majority for rearmament (→ 28/5/37).

A formal portrait to mark the occasion of the Silver Jubilee of King George V and Queen Mary.

Allen Lane launches paperback books

London, July
The first ten paperback books, known as "Penguins" and selling at sixpence, have been published by Allen Lane to a chorus of disapproval. Lane had the idea on a station platform where there was nothing to buy for the journey but expensive novels or garish reprints. His aim is to sell well-produced reprints of top quality books. Woolworth's has ordered 10,000 copies of each title; these include Ernest Hemingway's *A Farewell to Arms* and two detective novels by Agatha Christie and Dorothy L Sayers.

Hoare quits over Abyssinian deal

Westminster, 18 December
Sir Samuel Hoare has been forced to resign as foreign secretary following his deal with France's premier, Pierre Laval, appeasing Mussolini over Abyssinia. The deal, which involved the recognition of Italy's right to keep the fertile areas she has occupied in her invasion of Abyssinia, has raised a storm of protest throughout Britain.

It brought the threat of resignation from Anthony Eden, minister for League of Nations affairs, unless Baldwin disowned the deal and Sir Samuel. With a Commons debate looming the prime minister gave his foreign secretary a choice: apologize or resign.

Sir Samuel has chosen to resign and the Hoare-Laval pact is dead but the world is faced with the danger that the League of Nations is impotent unless its members stand up to dictators.

Radio waves used to detect aircraft

Britain, December
Scientists under the direction of Robert Watson-Watt have this year patented a way of detecting aircraft by bouncing radio waves off them. The time that the waves take to return is also used to calculate the aircraft's distance from the transmitter.

In July researchers used the new method, called "radio direction finding", to track a Hawker Hart aeroplane as it flew to a distance of 34 miles (54.4km) over Suffolk. A formation of other aircraft was also successfully located and counted as blips on a cathode ray tube.

The new technology would enable Britain's air defences to detect aircraft over the horizon, and so has great military potential. Given the possible threat from Germany, it is ironic that it was a German scientist, Heinrich Hertz, who first discovered radio waves (→ 22).

Campbell breaks own land speed record

Sir Malcolm Campbell poses for photographers in front of his new "Bluebird".

Utah, 3 September
Speed hero Sir Malcolm Campbell narrowly escaped death today as he slowed down after beating his own world speed record on the Bonneville Salt Flats. Campbell, who has devoted much of his life to gaining records on land and sea, achieved an average speed of 485kmph (301mph) in his streamlined car *Bluebird* – even though he was temporarily blinded by a stream of salt whipped up by wind. Fifty-year-old Campbell's previous best speed was 442 kmph (276mph) set at Daytona beach last March. His sponsor, Esso, is making great play of the fact that the ethyl fluid used in *Bluebird* is also used in petrol sold from its pumps (→ 19/11/37).

1936

Sandringham, 20 January. King George V dies.→

Cheltenham, 12 March. Golden Miller wins the Gold Cup for the fifth successive year.

Dublin, 27 May. Aer Lingus makes its first commercial flight from here to Bristol.

Southampton, 27 May. The liner *Queen Mary* leaves on her maiden voyage to New York.

Britain, May. The Left Book Club is formed this month.

London, 3 June. Haile Selassie, emperor of Abyssinia, arrives in exile after defeat by Italy.

Wimbledon, 3 July. Fred Perry wins the singles title for the third successive year.

Yugoslavia, 10 August. King Edward VIII begins a cruise on the yacht *Nahlin* with Mrs Wallis Simpson (→27/10).

London, 21 August. The BBC makes its first television broadcast from Alexandra Palace (→2/11).

London, 26 August. A treaty gives Britain use of the Suez Canal for 20 years.

Buckinghamshire, September. New film studios are opened at Pinewood (→31/12/37).

London, 11 October. An estimated 100,000 people try to prevent fascist supporters of Sir Oswald Mosley marching through the East End (→10/11).

Ipswich, 27 October. Mrs Wallis Simpson wins a decree nisi from her second husband, Ernest (→16/11).

London, 16 November. The king tells the prime minister and his family that he intends to marry Mrs Simpson (→3/12).

Wales, 19 November. The king completes a tour of Wales in which he said "something must be done" about unemployment.

London, 30 November. Crystal Palace, designed for the 1851 Great Exhibition, burns down.

Britain, 3 December. British newspapers end their silence on the crisis over the king and Mrs Simpson (→10).

Windsor, 10 December. King Edward VIII signs the "instrument of abdication"; he is to be known as the duke of Windsor (→12).

Britain. John Maynard Keynes, a leading British economist, publishes a theory on how to combat (and prevent) recessions.

New powers to aid police against fascists

Police arrest a woman demonstrator during Mosley's East End march.

London, 10 November
Sir Oswald Mosley, the fascist leader, will need to rid himself of his black shirt and riding breeches if he wishes to lead political demonstrations in future. The thuggery which has become a familiar element in meetings organized by Mosley's British Union of Fascists finally persuaded the cabinet to take action.

A Public Order Bill, published today, will be rushed onto the statute book, banning the wearing of political uniforms and giving the police power to ban political demonstrations likely to cause disorder. Mosley's use of violence during meetings and marches is deliberately provocative; he then blames the subsequent disorder on Jews and communists – "Red agitators from the ghettos," he cries.

Three months ago, when he led 7,000 blackshirts into the Jewish neighbourhood of London's East End, 80 people, including 15 police, were injured. He hoped he could repeat the street battles between Nazis and communists that helped Hitler's rise to power (→1/1/37).

'Spitfire' prototype takes to the skies

Southampton, 5 March
The first flight took place today of the prototype of the Supermarine company's latest fighter – the Spitfire. "Don't touch anything," said an enthusiastic test pilot, "Mutt" Summers, after landing the plane at the Eastleigh aerodrome near here. The aircraft has striking, clean lines, but its future RAF pilots will probably be more impressed by its battery of eight machine guns mounted under the wings and the power of its Rolls-Royce PV-12 "Merlin" engine.

This engine is streamlined, with a small frontal area which offers less air resistance than similar engines and therefore greater speed and manoeuvrability (→27/5/36).

King George V dies

Sandringham, 20 January
King George V, monarch of Britain and her empire for the past 26 years, died today at the royal residence at Sandringham. He was 70. He is succeeded by his son, formerly the highly popular prince of Wales, now King Edward VIII. Thanks to the newly invented radio and the broadcasts he started making, King George was perhaps the best-known monarch in history.

Jarrow's crusade of unemployed workers fails to move Baldwin

Jarrow marchers leave a Bedfordshire village on their way to London.

Westminster, 11 November
The Jarrow crusade has failed to move the prime minister. Today Stanley Baldwin told the Commons that he would not meet the marchers: "This is the way that civil strife begins, and civil strife may not end until it is civil war."

It is a brutal snub for what has been one of the most peaceful of all the protest marches. Organized by the local council in a town where two-thirds are unemployed, it was supported by Labour and Conservatives and blessed by a bishop.

The 200 marchers bore a casket containing a petition with 11,572 signatures. On their walk south they gained favourable press comment, much public sympathy and the attention of the new cinema newsreels.

Edward VIII abdicates throne for love

Portsmouth, 12 December
The former king Edward is sailing for France and exile late tonight and for eventual reunion with Wallis Simpson, the American divorcee for whom he gave up his throne. Tonight he broadcast his decision to abdicate the throne – an act unprecedented in more than 1,000 years of British monarchy.

He said he found it impossible to carry the burden of kingship and discharge his duties "without the help and support of the woman I love". He said that the decision was his alone: "the other person most concerned has tried to persuade me to take a different course." King Edward VIII has reigned for only 11 months. He succeeded his father George V on 21 January.

It was soon apparent that he was bored by the duties of dealing with state papers and court functions; but he retained an ability to strike a chord with the public – which knew nothing of his romance with Mrs Simpson [*see below*] – as when he visited unemployed miners in South Wales last month, declaring "something must be done". But by then he had told the prime minister Stanley Baldwin and his family that he would renounce the throne rather than give up his plan to marry Mrs Simpson (→ 3/6/37).

Edward VIII: the final broadcast.

Sound and pictures broadcast by BBC

London, 2 November
The first public television service in the world was inaugurated by the BBC today from Alexandra Palace, north London. Transmissions were first made in August to the Radio Olympia exhibition, where sets costing about £110 were on view. Only 280 homes have sets. The Baird system with 240 lines on the screen is being used alternately with that of his rival, Isaac Shoenberg, for Marconi-EMI, which has 405 lines. The BBC has recruited two women announcers from 1,100 applicants, and one man, Leslie Mitchell.

Secret royal romance rocked the world

Wallis (second left) alongside the future king with friends on holiday.

London, December
The infatuation of the future King Edward with Mrs Wallis Simpson from Baltimore had begun in 1933, when he started going to dinner with her and her second husband, Englishman Ernest Simpson, who soon resented the prince's attentions to his wife. In 1934 Wallis alone joined his summer party at Biarritz and they took a cruise together. Thelma, Lady Furness, his long-standing mistress, was summarily dismissed. His complete subjugation to the striking American woman was the talk of high society. She had clearly captivated him.

On becoming king, Edward invited Mrs Simpson to see him proclaimed at St James's and in August the couple openly cruised the Adriatic and Aegean in the steam yacht *Nahlin*. Their relationship was plain to the watching crowds and widely reported in the press everywhere but in Britain. Even Simpson's arranged divorce by his wife (her second divorce) was reported merely routinely, at the king's request, through a sympathetic newspaper baron, Lord Beaverbrook.

It could not last – and when the bishop of Bradford said in a sermon the king should show more awareness of his Christian duty, the publicity broke and Mrs Simpson fled to France. From there she said she was willing to withdraw from an "unhappy and untenable" situation, but to the dismay of his family Edward was adamant he could not reign without her.

Shy Bertie becomes king as George VI

London, 12 December
Edward's younger brother Bertie, the duke of York, has been proclaimed king with the title of George VI and a natural reluctance to take on the burdens of the crown. His first act was to create the ex-king HRH the Duke of Windsor – but the courtesy title of "royal highness" is not to be extended to his brother's future wife.

The new king, who is 41, suffers from nerves and a stammer, which he has taken lessons to improve. During the crisis doubts were raised about whether he is competent to reign. His most popular act as duke of York was to marry a Scot, Elizabeth Bowes-Lyon, an extrovert wife. The couple have two daughters (→ 12/5/37).

George VI (l) at his father's funeral.

Irish bill removes deference to crown

Ireland, 11 December
With masterly timing, the Irish prime minister, Eamon de Valera, has taken advantage of the British government's preoccupation with the abdication crisis to launch his External Relations Bill. Instead of waiting for the completion of the new constitution, the new bill will remove all the references to the British crown and the governor-general. While the king no longer has any say in the internal affairs of the Free State, he will retain certain ceremonial functions in external affairs (→ 30/4/37).

Spending can cure crisis, says Keynes

London, December
One of the most talked-about books of the year has one of the dullest titles – *The General Theory of Employment, Interest and Money* – but it seems set to be highly influential. John Maynard Keynes, a former Treasury official and British economist, offers a way to combat (and prevent) economic depressions. These are caused, he says, by insufficient demand in the economy. Investment should be stimulated by spending on public works and by lowering interest rates, even if it unbalances the budget, in order to boost consumer demand.

1937

Britain, 1 January. The Public Order Act comes into force (→ 10/10).

Britain, 2 January. The RAF's target of trebling its strength in two years is achieved three months early (→ 16/11).

Mediterranean, 24 February. A British liner with 100 passengers on board is holed by a mine off Spain.

Spain, February. Volunteers from Britain and Ireland fight on both sides during the battle of Jarama this month.

London, 24 March. Oxford win the Boat Race, ending a run of 13 successive Cambridge victories.

Birkenhead, 13 April. The aircraft carrier HMS *Ark Royal* is launched.

Dublin, 30 April. Details are published of a new constitution which would rename the state "Eire" (→ 29/12).

London, 12 May. George VI is crowned at Westminster abbey (→ 3/5/38).

Tours, France, 3 June. The duke of Windsor marries Wallis Warfield (as Mrs Simpson is known after changing her name by deed poll) at the Château de Candé (→ 10/1937).

Skegness, 30 July. Harold Davidson, the ex-rector of Stiffkey, dies two days after being mauled by a lion at an amusement ground.

Liverpool, 10 October. Sir Oswald Mosley is knocked out by a stone as he prepares to address a rally (→ 31/5/40).

Germany, October. The duke and duchess of Windsor meet Adolf Hitler.

Utah, USA, 19 November. Briton George Eyston sets a new world land speed record of 501kmph [311mph].

Britain, 27 November. Steve Donoghue, many times champion jockey, retires.

Westminster, 22 December. Britain protests to Japan over attacks on Royal Navy ships on the Yangtse river.

Britain. A Factory Act cuts maximum working hours for young people and women to between 44 and 48 hours a week (→ 1/12/42).

Scotland. A new comic is published this year called *The Dandy*.

Skegness. Billy Butlin opens his first holiday camp.

Chamberlain succeeds Baldwin as PM

Westminster, 28 May
The man Lloyd George dismissed as "a pinhead" has taken over from Baldwin as prime minister: Neville Chamberlain, now aged 68, was a dismal failure as director of national service in 1917, but went on to initiate major reforms in local government, housing and public assistance before becoming chancellor of the exchequer. Now, however, he will be obliged to turn from domestic questions to foreign policy and the increasingly bellicose dictators in Europe.

Chamberlain is said to have little time for Sir Robert Vansittart, the foreign office permanent under-secretary, and his dire warnings about Nazi Germany echoed in the Commons by Winston Churchill.

Chamberlain, the new premier.

Conference urged on piracy in Med

London, 2 September
Foreign secretary Anthony Eden today demanded the setting up of an international conference to discuss "submarine piracy" in the Mediterranean following the sinking of merchant ships carrying supplies to the republican side in the civil war being waged in Spain. The submarines are said to belong to Spain's nationalist leader, General Franco, but there is little doubt that they belong to the Italian navy.

Eden, encouraged by Winston Churchill, intends to demand the establishment of patrols by French and British warships under orders to attack any "submarine pirates" they encounter.

'Green belts' may check London sprawl

London, 1 April
A "green belt" around London was proposed today in a bid to stop the capital's sprawl into the surrounding countryside. London County Council, which plans to spend up to £2 million buying land in the home counties, also sees "green belts" as offering recreation opportunities for its growing population.

Over eight million people now live in London, but the conurbation is much larger as suburbs have been spawned by new tube lines or as "ribbon developments" along new arterial roads. There has been a similar suburban sprawl around other major cities and it has been estimated that by the mid-1930s some 60,000 acres were being lost to agriculture each year. Some curbs were imposed on ribbon development in 1935, but groups such as the Council for the Preservation of Rural England want even greater controls and more "green belts".

Millionaires are growing in number

Britain, 3 March
Britons are getting wealthier and the taxman is reaping the benefit. An additional 50,000 people earned enough last year to pay income tax, according to figures released today. That makes 3,350,000 income tax payers, although new rules freed 250,000 from tax. There are now 824 millionaires and 85,449 people earning more than £2,000 a week.

Audiences flock to luxurious shrines of the cinema boom

London, 31 December
Cinemas and film audiences are booming in Britain, where 40 per cent of the adult population "go to the pictures" at least once a week. Cinema circuits began building in 1933 with the Odeons. Gaumonts, Granadas, Regals and Roxys now rise in Babylonian splendour, combining *art deco* style with rich trimmings of chrome and glazed, coloured tiles. Many seat 4,000 in escapist luxury. A ticket from as little as sixpence offers two features, a cartoon, a newsreel and serenading by a mighty Wurlitzer organ. Most films are also escapist. This year's British hits are Anna Neagle as *Victoria the Great* and Flora Robson as Queen Elizabeth in *Fire Over England* while *Oh! Mr Porter!* introduces Will Hay (→ 1/3/40).

In order to meet the increasing popularity of moving pictures, architects are designing ever more luxurious cinemas, monuments of the silver screen.

Crash in a Scottish snowstorm kills 35

Glasgow, 10 December
Thirty-five passengers were killed and 179 injured tonight when the Edinburgh to Glasgow express, hurtling through a snowstorm at 70mph, ploughed into a train standing at the small station of Castlecary near Glasgow.

The disaster followed a string of misunderstandings between signalmen. Despite the wintry weather the Pacific *Grand Parade* was almost at full speed when she hit the express from Dundee to Glasgow pulled by *Dandy Dinmont*.

Steel-built rolling stock saved many lives in the crash; and many passengers in the Edinburgh express stepped onto the platform unaware that a collision had taken place. Modern steel-built coaches are thought to have saved many lives in three serious train crashes in the past three years.

New constitution for Eire takes effect

De Valera (l) with Irish colleagues.

Dublin, 29 December
Eamon de Valera, leader of the ruling Fianna Fáil party, has introduced a new constitution for the Irish Free State which is now to be called Eire. It lays down a system of government which places authority in the prime minister, now to be known as the Taoiseach. The Senate has been restored and proportional representation is retained for election to the Dáil.

But this democratic approach is combined with an assumption that the Irish identity is Catholic, reflected in five articles defining "rights". Divorce is prohibited, the idea of working mothers is denounced and the Catholic Church is granted a special position "as the guardian of the faith professed by the great majority of citizens".

Despite this, the first articles of the constitution claim that Eire includes all 32 counties of Ireland and that subsequent provisions apply to the six of these counties in Northern Ireland pending "reintegration of the national territory". This may satisfy republicans, but it also confirms fears of Ulster Protestants that a united Ireland would be totally Catholic (→ 19/1/38).

Triumphant London debut for Fonteyn

Fonteyn in her debut as Giselle.

London, 19 January
The stage has a new ballerina who made a triumphant debut in the testing title role of *Giselle* last night at Sadler's Wells. She is only 17 and her stage name is Margot Fonteyn. She was trained at the Sadler's Wells school, founded by Ninette de Valois along with the ballet company in 1931.

After Alicia Markova left in 1935, Fonteyn was gradually given her roles and last year she helped to create a new ballet, *Apparitions* by Frederick Ashton, with her partner Robert Helpmann. He partnered her again in *Giselle* and they are to dance the Swan queen and prince in *Lac des Cygnes*. Fonteyn's real name is Peggy Hookham.

Orwell travels the 'Road to Wigan Pier'

London, March
Subscribers to the Left Book Club received a shock with this month's title, *The Road to Wigan Pier* by George Orwell. After passages of brilliant reportage of the poverty, squalor and hopelessness that the depression caused in the north, Orwell tackles the evils of snobbery – he himself went to Eton – and declares that "the lower classes smell. That was what we were taught. We were brought up to believe they were dirty ..." He claims that that is how the middle classes do feel. Repelled by the socialism advocated by vegetarian, sandal-wearing, bearded Marxist cranks whom he detests, he fears that the middle class will embrace fascism rather than abolish class distinction. The book's publisher Victor Gollancz writes a foreword apologizing to readers whom the book may offend. Its author is in Spain fighting for the republicans.

The duke and duchess of Windsor alongside the German chancellor, Adolf Hitler, during the couple's controversial visit to Germany in October.→

MPs back shelters as war fears grow

Westminster, 16 November
Plans to build air-raid shelters in Britain's towns and cities were backed by the House of Commons today as fears grow about the possibility of another war in Europe. This year has already seen increases in the defence budget which take spending on the Royal Navy, for instance, to the highest levels since the Great War. With war raging in Spain, piracy in the Mediterranean and bellicose noises from the fascist leaders of Italy and Germany, the international scene is more threatening than for many years.

Winston Churchill, the most vocal proponent of rearmament in the Commons, welcomed today's vote in favour of shelters, saying that they were "indispensable". He wants the RAF to be boosted, too, but said that well-organized precautions would mean that air attacks on Britain would not be worthwhile. Fears of air attacks have grown since the bombing of Guernica in Spain last April. This has given new menace to the warning of Stanley Baldwin, the former premier, that "the bomber will always get through" (→ 3/1/38).

The defrocked rector of Stiffkey met his maker after performing in the lion's den at Skegness.

1938

Britain, 3 January. All schoolchildren are to be issued with gas masks, the government says (→ 24/3).

London, 3 January. The BBC begins its first foreign language service – in Arabic.

London, 19 January. Eamon de Valera ends two days of talks with British leaders with prospects growing of a new Anglo-Irish agreement (→ 25/4).

Westminster, 21 February. Anthony Eden resigns as foreign secretary in protest over policies of appeasement towards Italy over its annexation of Abyssinia.

Westminster, 24 March. Neville Chamberlain pledges Britain to defend France and Belgium against attack in a statement ten days after German troops had occupied Austria (→ 29/4).

London, 31 March. Plans are unveiled for a national theatre to be designed by Sir Edwin Lutyens and to be built in South Kensington.

Britain, 7 April. All bicycles should be fitted with rear lights, the police say.

London, 29 April. Talks between the British and French governments end with a vague promise to defend Czechoslovakia against attack (→ 15/7).

Dublin, 25 June. Douglas Hyde is inaugurated as president of Eire after Fianna Fáil retains power in this month's general election (→ 11/7).

Britain, 15 July. The government orders 1,000 Spitfire fighters for the RAF as part of a general increase in strength of the armed forces (→ 30/9).

Paris, 19 July. King George and Queen Elizabeth receive an enthusiastic welcome at the start of a state visit (→ 8/6/39).

Glasgow, 27 September. The world's largest liner, the *Queen Elizabeth*, is launched.

Westminster, 19 October. The cabinet abandons plans to partition the mandated territory of Palestine.

Britain, 21 December. Plans are announced to spend £200,000 on air-raid shelters.

Britain. New publications this year include an illustrated weekly, *Picture Post*, and a comic, *Beano*.

Britain. The US-owned Gallup Opinion Polls forms a company in the United Kingdom.

Britain returns navy bases in Irish treaty

Dublin, 25 April

Eamon de Valera has scored the greatest political achievement of his career. The Irish prime minister has persuaded Britain to return the Irish ports which they had retained under the 1921 Treaty at Berehaven, Cobh, Lough Swilly, Haulbowline and Rathmullen.

Neville Chamberlain, the British premier, sees it as a gesture of appeasement – apparently believing that the ports could be made available again in time of war – but his backbench Tory critic Winston Churchill is said to be infuriated by the decision. De Valera believes that the return of the ports will make Eire's neutrality all the easier in the European war which he feels is imminent. Important trade concessions have also been agreed. The land annuities, so long a bone of contention between Britain and Ireland, have been cancelled in favour of a lump sum; trade duties and restrictions have been reduced on many items; and preference is allowed for some British goods.

Given that 96 per cent of all Irish exports go to British markets, the trade war between the two countries has affected all sections of the economy, and the balance of payments deficit has eaten into the government's reserves. De Valera has used the economic war to brilliant political effect on the home front, enhancing his reputation, and ensuring electoral support (→ 25/6).

King George opens Empire Exhibition

The king tours the exhibition.

Glasgow, 3 May

Mary Morrison flew from the island of Barra – "riding all the way in an aeroplane" – to meet the king and queen today at the opening here of the Empire Exhibition. The royal couple met Mary spinning wool and singing "Leaving Barra" outside a mock thatched cottage in a replica highland village.

This was the final stop in a five-hour royal tour of the huge exhibition, during which King George and Queen Elizabeth ascended the Tower of Empire in a lift travelling at 500 feet a minute. They were equally fascinated by the "Fitter Britain" display in the United Kingdom pavilion that used ping-pong balls to illustrate blood circulation in the human body (→ 19/7).

Football pools are 'menace to society'

London 25 April

Postal workers, tradesmen and Baptists have joined forces against the "menace" of football pools. As greyhound racing and other forms of gambling enjoy continuing popularity, ten million people are now thought to be filling in their pools coupons every week. While Baptists disapprove on moral grounds, sub-postmasters want extra cash for handling pools mail, which has grown enormously since the 1920s. And a Worthing butcher claims his customers are buying cheap foreign meat to save up for the pools.

Education reforms planned in Britain

London, 30 December

Free secondary education and raising of the school leaving age to 16 are advocated in a report sent to the Board of Education today by the Spens Committee. In the wake of the reorganization of most elementary schools, the report suggests expanding technical high schools, keeping "grammar" and "modern" schools. It favours progressive methods that encourage curiosity and do not allow examinations to dominate. It has been welcomed by teachers, but the government may not be so keen.

Workers go off to holiday camps with their first 'holiday pay'

Billy Butlin's camp at Clacton in Essex is full of happy holidaymakers.

Blackpool, 1 August

Bank Holiday crowds thronging the country's most popular holiday resort have more than usual to celebrate this summer. The Holidays with Pay Act passed this year will increase the number of people entitled to a paid holiday from the present three million to 11 million. In most cases, the holiday will be for a week. Resorts such as Blackpool have boomed in recent years anyway, with motor coaches (or "charabancs") and trains bringing in visitors. And last year a "holiday camp" was opened by Billy Butlin at Skegness, Lincolnshire, which proved an instant success.

Chamberlain bows to Hitler in Munich

Czechoslovak deal averts war threat

Munich, 30 September
Flying from London yesterday, the British prime minister Neville Chamberlain refused to discuss policy and tactics with his French counterpart, Edouard Daladier, but at once opened negotiations with the German leader, Adolf Hitler. At 1.45 this morning, after 12 hours of talks, Chamberlain and Hitler signed a paper which sets out the terms for settling the Czechoslovak question without a war. The Italian dictator, Mussolini, and Daladier also signed, but they had been onlookers. This is essentially a deal between Britain and Germany.

Chamberlain has accepted the demands he rejected in meetings with Hitler earlier this month. All Czechoslovak territory identified as being occupied by ethnic Germans is to be handed over to Germany. This territory, Sudetenland, strips Czechoslovakia of her frontier defences. In return, the truncated Czechoslovakia is given a four-power guarantee of its security.

It was Chamberlain's idea that Hitler should join him in putting his signature to a promise that Britain and Germany will "never go to war with one another again". In future, consultation not conflict will be the rule. The British prime minister is delighted (→6/10).

Chamberlain holds aloft the Anglo-German agreement he signed with Hitler.

MPs protest over appeasement of Hitler

Westminster, 6 October
After a three-day debate MPs have approved Chamberlain's agreement with Hitler at Munich, but the growing unease was reflected in the abstention of 30 Tories. The first lord of the admiralty, Alfred Duff Cooper, has resigned, saying that Britain should have gone to war, not to save Czechoslovakia, but to prevent one country (Germany) imposing its will "by brute force". He said the difference between himself and the prime minister was that Chamberlain believed in approaching Hitler with "sweet reasonableness", whereas "I have believed that he was more open to the language of the mailed fist."

Churchill was greeted with roars of protest when he said: "We have sustained a total and unmitigated defeat." He said Munich was only the beginning of a bitter reckoning.

Divisions are beginning to appear in the cabinet. Chamberlain returned from Munich saying: "I believe it is peace for our time." But most of his colleagues are saying that "our time" is merely a breathing space and that Britain should rearm fast (→9/2/39).

Hutton hits record test score of 364

London, August
A 22-year-old Yorkshireman set a new cricket record this month with a score of 364 in the final test against the Australians. It was the highest individual score in test history, eclipsing the 334 set by Don Bradman at Headingley in 1930. Hutton batted for 13 hours and 17 minutes to help his team towards other landmarks: their first innings total of 903 for seven wickets and their winning margin of an innings and 579 runs were also records. Len Hutton's triumph comes barely a year after an inauspicious test debut: 0 and 1. But a century followed in the next match to reward the selectors' faith in their new young opening batsman.

Last British troops withdraw from Eire

Cork, 11 July
The last British troops have handed over Spike Island to the Irish Army before finally leaving the country. It was a ceremony of military respect and political friendship between Britain's most fractious dominion and Ireland's oldest foe unparalleled in Anglo-Irish history. The Union flag was lowered and the green, white and orange tricolour of Eire was raised, as an Irish private, speaking the Irish language, took over the guard (→17/1/39).

The steam train now arriving is the record-breaking 'Mallard'

Leaving Kings Cross Station, "Mallard" heads for the record books.

Peterborough, 3 July
Mallard, a British locomotive of the Gresley A4 Pacific class, set a new world record speed for steam engines when, between London and Newcastle, it touched 203kmph (126 mph). Driver Duddington and Fireman Bray were joined on the footplate by Nigel Gresley, designer of the engine, as it attempted its record run. The locomotive, using the tracks of the London and North Eastern Railway, maintained a speed of over 120mph for more than five miles, easily surpassing the previous record, 182kmph (114 mph), achieved by *Coronation Scot* last year.

"The Beano", a companion to "The Dandy", makes its debut.

England, 17 January. Suspected IRA sympathizers are arrested by police after a series of bombs explode in London, Birmingham, Manchester and Alnwick (→25/8).

Westminster, 9 February. Plans are announced to provide free air-raid shelters for homes in cities judged most likely to be bombed (→30/9).

London, 27 February. The British government announces that it will recognize the new Spanish regime headed by General Franco.

Westminster, 26 April. The Commons back a bill for limited conscription.

Britain, 3 May. Farmers are urged by the government to plough up grazing land to produce more food at home (→25/12).

Washington, DC, 8 June. King George VI and Queen Elizabeth arrive in the US capital for the first visit to the country by a reigning British monarch (→25/12).

Moscow, 23 August. The signing of the Nazi-Soviet non-aggression pact shocks British leaders, who reaffirm, with France, their pledge to defend Poland.

London, 31 August. Forces are mobilized, reserves called up and children are being evacuated from major cities (→1/9).

Poland, 1 September. German troops and aircraft attack at 04.45 hours GMT (→3).

France, 11 September. Four British Army divisions have crossed the English Channel to be deployed alongside their French allies (→30).

Orkney, 13 October. The battleship *Royal Oak* is sunk in a daring raid by a German U-boat on the Royal Navy base at Scapa Flow (→17/12).

France, 12 November. The first concert is given to troops by the Entertainment National Service Association (ENSA).

North Sea, 20 November. British ships are being sunk by new magnetic mines (→19/12).

Britain, 19 December. Royal Navy scientists discover a way to counter the menace of magnetic mines.

London, 25 December. In his Christmas broadcast King George VI thanks the empire for its support to the "mother country" since war began.

Fears of war intensify

London, 31 March
The clouds of war gathering over Europe grew more ominous today when the prime minister, Neville Chamberlain, informed a crowded, cheering House of Commons that, if any action threatened Polish independence and the Poles felt it vital to resist, Britain and France would come to their aid. Chamberlain has written to Colonel Beck, the Polish foreign minister, making this offer, and it is reported that Beck accepted "between two flicks of the ash off his cigarette".

This hardening of the British and French position towards any further Nazi encroachments comes at the end of a tumultuous month. On 15 March Hitler made a triumphal entry into Prague and slept in Hradcany Castle, the former palace of the Bohemian kings. On 23 March he forced Lithuania, under threat of air attack, to surrender Memel. Now he is demanding Danzig from Poland, and tonight there are rumours that German troops are moving towards the Polish border.

It is apparent that, despite all the attempts to appease Hitler, he remains determined to plant his jackboots all over Europe. War seems inevitable. There is a scramble to re-arm. Plans have been made to evacuate children from cities vulnerable to air attack. Even Neville Chamberlain, who declared "peace for our time" after Munich, seems determined to fight (→31/8).

Bomb kills five in Coventry: IRA blamed

A man receives first aid amid the debris caused by the explosion.

Coventry, 25 August
Five people were killed today and nearly 50 injured when a bomb exploded without warning in the main street of Coventry. Police believe that the bomb was planted by the Irish Republican Army. If that theory is confirmed, this would be the most deadly episode yet in the campaign of violence launched by the IRA on the British mainland last January.

A series of blasts in London, Manchester and Birmingham signalled the start of the campaign by Irish republicans dissatisfied with last year's Anglo-Irish agreement. The IRA wants a united Ireland with no British presence. So does Eamon de Valera, the Eire leader, but two months ago he banned the IRA after bombs had exploded at London tube stations and in letter boxes around Britain; hundreds of suspected IRA sympathizers were rounded up by the police.

Today's bomb appears to have been left in a tradesman's bicycle. Exploding at 2.30pm, it shattered shopfronts, overturned cars and left Broadgate, the main street of this Midlands city, resembling a bloody battlefield. Coming at a time when war seems imminent in Europe, the outrage seems sure to foster anti-Irish opinion (→17/9).

Mighty 'voice of Ireland' is silenced

Yeats: a Nobel laureate.

France, 28 January
William Butler Yeats, Ireland's most famous poet and playwright, has died in France, aged 74. Born in Dublin of Irish Protestant stock, he was educated in London, and he later settled there, moving in aesthetic, literary and spiritualistic circles. Later, with the help and encouragement of his patron, Lady Gregory, he established the Abbey theatre in Dublin and was very much part of the revival of Irish literature this century.

He was awarded the Nobel prize for literature in 1923 and was an Irish Free State senator from 1922 to 1928. Together with George Bernard Shaw and George Russell he founded the Irish Academy of Letters in 1932. He reached the peak of poetic achievement with *The Tower* and *The Winding Stair*.

Seventy die in sub

Liverpool, 4 June
More than 70 men have died in the submarine *Thetis* after three days of rescue attempts failed. The new submarine sank just off Liverpool, but her stern was visible above the surface. Crewmen were heard tapping morse messages. Four escaped through a hatch, but it could not be closed and seeping water caused the sub to sink. Salvage vessels brought it to the surface. Six more men emerged, but the cables snapped sending the vessel back below the waves too late for further rescue.

PM: 'This country is now at war with Germany'

London, 3 September
At 11.15 this morning, 15 minutes after the deadline for Germany to stop all aggressive action against Poland and begin to withdraw from Polish territory, the prime minister, Neville Chamberlain, declared that "no such undertaking has been received and consequently this country is at war with Germany".

The country fell silent as families gathered round their wireless sets this sunny Sunday to hear the sombre voice of Chamberlain taking Britain into war with Germany for the second time in 25 years. Almost immediately their worst fears of a devastating aerial bombardment appeared about to be realized as air-raid sirens wailed over London, sending people scurrying to the shelters. It was a false alarm, but a fearful indication of destruction which might yet come.

The French ultimatum to Germany expired at five this evening, and despite the last-minute hopes of Georges Bonnet, France's foreign minister, that Mussolini might be able to avert war by persuading Hitler to attend a "big powers" conference, the French too are at war with their old enemies.

The British armed forces have already mobilized, and parliament today passed the National Service (Armed Forces) Act making all men aged between 18 and 41, other than those in reserved occupations, liable to be called to the colours. One old warrior who has joined the fray is Winston Churchill, who has been appointed first lord of the admiralty in the new war cabinet. While the Allies prepare to take the field, the news from Poland is grim. Hitler's tanks, supported by dive-bombers used as flying artillery, are carving their way through the Polish army which has been fatally concentrated along the border.

Polish lancers are bravely, but futilely, charging the panzer tanks, and the Luftwaffe's modern Messerschmitt fighters are hacking the obsolete Polish aircraft out of the sky. Warsaw has been heavily bombed, and the roads are now clogged with refugees who are being mercilessly attacked from the air (→11).

Children evacuated from major cities

London, 30 September
All this month parties of schoolchildren with labels on their coats and homemade knapsacks on their backs have been gathering at railway stations to be evacuated from cities believed to be in danger from German bombers. Leaving weeping mothers, they have steamed away, often for unknown destinations.

In the first three days of this mass movement nearly 1,500,000 "evacuees" were carried to safety; 827,000 were schoolchildren and 535,000 were women who are pregnant or have children under school age. Some made long journeys from London to small villages in Devon and Cornwall. One party of children from Dagenham went by pleasure steamer to Yarmouth.

On arrival the children have been taken to reception centres to be allocated to "billeters" who are being paid 10/6 [52.5 pence] a week to feed and look after one child and 8/6 a week for each extra child. The money will no doubt be welcome in many homes, but both evacuees and billeters are having to make considerable adjustments.

Some of the youngsters, especially those from London's East End, have never seen the countryside before. Some are also finding it hard to cope with an unusual, though healthy, diet. Their billeters are similarly finding it a challenge to cope with city habits and language. Evacuation may save many lives; it may also have profound sociological effects (→16/8/40).

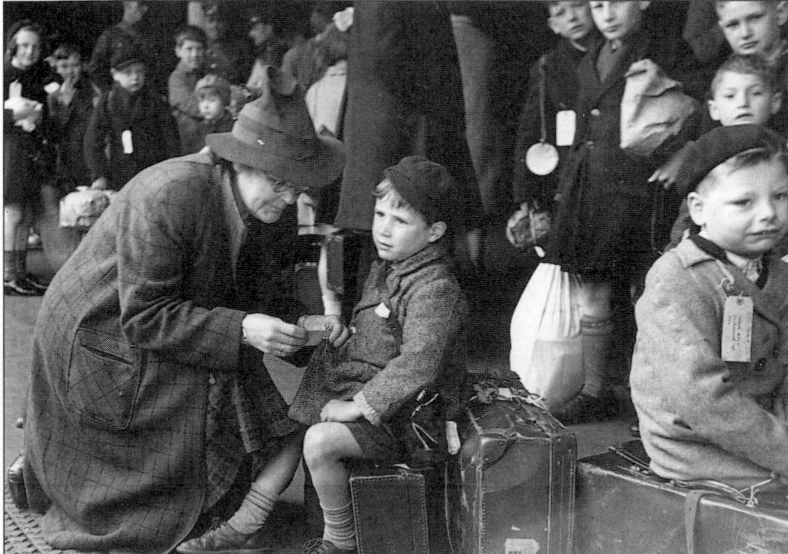

Tearful farewells as helpers check labels of children awaiting evacuation.

Anxious crowds read newspapers while they wait in Downing Street.

First British troops set out for France

Western front, 30 September
The British Expeditionary Force (BEF) has crossed safely to France and taken up position alongside the French army. The movement of four divisions – 158,000 men with 25,000 vehicles – along with their weapons, ammunition, fuel and supplies took place under conditions of great secrecy.

Regiments from all parts of Britain were carried by troop trains and lorries to ports in the south of England where ferries and transports escorted by destroyers took them across the Channel. There was no interference from U-boats or the German air force.

The men passed through towns their fathers knew well in the Great War as they moved up to the Belgian border. They are billeted in barns and stables and are living rough but like true Tommies are keeping their sense of humour. General Lord Gort, VC, a fighting soldier from the Great War who was previously chief of the imperial general staff, leads the BEF, but he comes under the overall command of General Gamelin, the French supreme commander.

There are no doubts about the fighting qualities of the regular British soldiers, but there remain serious deficiencies in their equipment. Of the 352 anti-aircraft guns assigned to the BEF only 152 have been delivered. There are also misgivings about the quantity and quality of the equipment of the RAF squadrons in France (→31/12).

Nations take sides as first shots of war are fired

Eire stays neutral, but empire rallies

London, 17 September
Eamon de Valera, the Irish prime minister, has made it plain that Eire, although still a member of the broader commonwealth, will not join the war against Hitler. If he maintains this policy it could cause problems for Britain because the navy would be unable to use Irish ports against a U-boat campaign.

Other members of the British Empire have come to Britain's aid without hesitation. The Australian prime minister, Robert Menzies, committed his country to the war only an hour after Neville Chamberlain. "There can be no doubt," he said, "that where Britain stands, there stand the people of the entire British world."

New Zealand's prime minister, Michael Savage, agreed: "Where Britain goes, we go; where she stands, we stand." The Canadian parliament debated the issue for three days before agreeing, with one vote against, to join the war. In South Africa the prime minister, General Hertzog, who wanted to stay out of the war, was forced to resign and was replaced by the pro-British General Smuts who immediately declared war (→ 3/1/40).

The final moments of the "Graf Spee" before she sinks below the waves.

'Graf Spee' scuttled as sea war hots up

Uruguay, 17 December
The war at sea, being fought in fierce contrast to the inactivity in western Europe (see report right), reached a blazing climax today when the German pocket battleship *Graf Spee* was scuttled at the mouth of the river Plate in the mistaken belief that an overwhelming force of British ships was waiting for her to put to sea. The *Graf Spee* had sunk ten merchant ships totalling 50,000 tons in the South Atlantic and Indian oceans.

Found by the cruisers *Exeter*, *Ajax* and *Achilles*, Captain Hans Langsdorff severely damaged the *Exeter*, but he was also hard hit and took refuge in Montevideo. Hitler told him: fight or scuttle. Explosions which ripped through the ship gave his answer: Langsdorff chose to scuttle rather than take his crew to their deaths (→ 8/4/40).

'Phoney war' drags on, except at sea

France, 31 December 1939
The year's end has brought no change to the "phoney war" or "sitskrieg" in France. Apart from a few patrols between the opposing Maginot and Siegfried line fortifications, there has been little activity and the cold, bored troops dig trenches and wait for a war which shows little signs of arriving.

After the brutal, lightning occupation of Poland, it had been expected that fighting would swiftly open on the western front but neither the Allies, unprepared for war, nor Hitler, quarrelling with his generals about the best route for attack, have made a decisive move before the onset of winter.

There is a similar lack of activity in the air. After a flurry of daylight raids on German shipping in which RAF bombers suffered heavy casualties, most of their work is restricted to night-time leaflet raids and chasing the occasional German on reconnaissance over Britain.

The "phoney war" mentality has led to many evacuees returning to the cities and schools have reopened. Only at sea, where the Germans are using U-boats and magnetic mines to challenge the Royal Navy's supremacy and harass merchant shipping, has the real battle begun (→ 3/5/40).

Belts tighten on home front as petrol and food rationing loom

A woman hands over her ration coupons at a petrol station in London.

Britain, 25 December
Most Britons were able to enjoy their traditional Christmas dinners today despite shortages of luxuries such as sweets and sugar, and also inadequacies in the food distribution system which have produced gluts and shortages of the same foodstuffs in different districts. Some shopkeepers will only serve their regular customers.

These anomalies are expected to disappear when food rationing is introduced. Preparation for the fair distribution of food to everyone has been under way for several months, with the ministry of food drawing on the experience of the last war. Petrol rationing has already been introduced with heavy penalties for "black marketeers" (→ 8/1/40).

Commando training in Scotland.

1940

Britain, 1 January. Two million men between the ages of 20 and 27 are called up.

Dublin, 3 January. The government takes emergency powers to combat the IRA (→ 7/2).

Britain, 8 January. Food rationing begins with controls over butter, sugar and bacon (→ 1/6/41).

London, 6 February. Ministers launch a campaign against gossip under the slogan "careless talk costs lives".

Birmingham, 7 February. Two men are hanged after being convicted of planting the bomb at Coventry which killed five people in August 1939 (→ 19/4).

Los Angeles, 1 March. The British actress Vivien Leigh wins an Oscar for her performance in *Gone with the Wind.*

North Sea, 8 April. Royal Navy ships begin to lay mines in Norwegian waters just as Germany begins to invade Denmark and Norway (→ 3/7).

Eire, 19 April. A hunger strike begun in February by nine IRA prisoners is called off after a second man dies within four days (→ 27/5/41).

Western Europe, 10 May. German forces attack France and the Low Countries (→ 4/6).

Rome, 10 June. Italy declares war on the Allies (→ 13).

Algeria, 3 July. British ships attack the French fleet at anchor in Mers-el-Kebir to stop their former ally's vessels being used by Germany (→ 26/10).

Britain, 23 July. The Local Defence Volunteers are renamed the Home Guard.→

London, 20 August. Winston Churchill praises RAF pilots, saying that "never ... was so much owed by so many to so few" (→ 7/9).

London, 7 September. The codeword "Cromwell" for an imminent invasion is issued as London is bombed (→ 15).

Tokyo, 27 September. Japan joins the Axis powers (→ 26/7/41).

Coventry, 15 November. The cathedral and much of the city are destroyed by German bombers; 568 people are killed (→ 30/12).

London, 10 December. Two Germans are hanged after being convicted of spying.

Winston Churchill is new war premier

Allies are forced to pull out of Norway

Trondheim, Norway, 3 May
The Allied attempt to force the German invaders out of Norway is going badly. The 13,000 British, French and Polish troops who were landed in Norway to take Trondheim have been defeated by 2,000 Germans and have been evacuated from Namsos and Andalsnes. The Allied forces were ill equipped for fighting in Arctic conditions and found themselves up against highly trained mountain troops.

They were also inadequately supported from the air and suffered constant attack from Ju87 Stuka dive-bombers operating from captured Norwegian airfields. After Major-General Sir Adrian Carton de Wiart, one of the British commanders, had asked for permission to evacuate, the rearguard got away from Namsos early this morning.

One allied force remains in Norway. Assigned to take the northern town of Narvik, it failed to attack when the Germans were vulnerable and now faces a hard slog. The only aspect of this campaign which provides any satisfaction is that the Norwegian coastal batteries and the Royal Navy have inflicted crippling losses on the German fleet (→ 10).

The man of the hour: Winston Churchill becomes prime minister.

All-party coalition to rule the country

London, 10 May 1940
Winston Churchill is to be Britain's new prime minister at the head of a coalition government. Summoned to Buckingham Palace tonight, he told King George VI that he would build an all-party team to achieve victory against Hitler.

Two senior members of the new government will be Clement Attlee, the Labour leader, and his deputy, Arthur Greenwood; they effectively put Churchill in power by making it clear that they would join a coalition only if it was led by Churchill rather than Lord Halifax, the foreign secretary, who critics say has a record of appeasement.

Churchill's appointment follows two of the most turbulent days in the history of Britain's parliament. When the Commons met after the defeat in Norway, Leo Amery, a senior Tory, flung Oliver Cromwell's words at Neville Chamberlain: "You have sat too long for any good you have been doing. Depart, I say, and let us have done with you. In the name of God, go!"

Chamberlain, who sought peace, has gone. In his place is the pugnacious Churchill. He has no intention of seeking peace, only victory.

Mosley is detained as the government takes emergency powers

London, 31 May
Sir Oswald Mosley, his wife and 32 other leading British fascists including Captain A M Ramsay, the Tory MP for Peebles, were arrested tonight under Defence Regulation 18B which gives the home secretary the power to detain members of organizations which may be used for "purposes prejudicial to national security". The move has been greeted with much satisfaction.

All German subjects in Britain are also being interned despite the fact that nearly all of them are Jews who have fled from Hitler's terror squads and most of the remainder were political opponents of the Nazi regime. As such, they are unlikely to perform actions "prejudicial to national security", and many are distinguished scientists working on defence projects; however, the fear of a "fifth column" of traitors is so great they have all been rounded up. Posters urge people to beware of gossip.

These dictatorial measures have been adopted by the government in order to fight the war. On 22 May parliament took under three hours to pass the Emergency Powers Act – arguably the most drastic legislation in British history. It gives the government almost unlimited power over the life, liberty and property of every person in the land. The most sweeping powers have been granted to Ernest Bevin, the former trade union leader who is now minister of labour in the coalition government (→ 1/12/43).

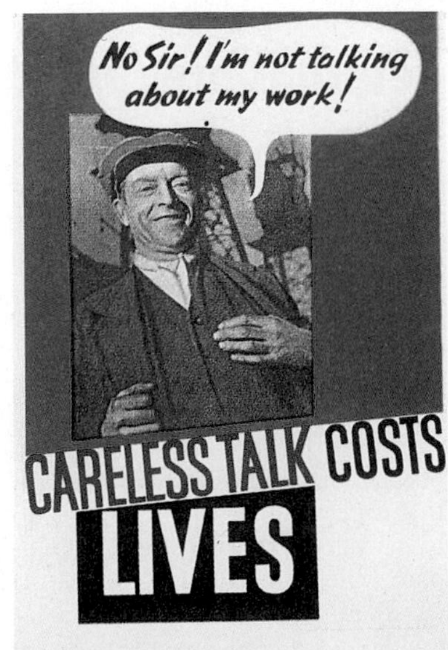

No Sir! I'm not talking about my work!
CARELESS TALK COSTS
LIVES

Posters warn against gossip.

Luftwaffe attacks to prepare for German invasion

London, 16 August
The fierceness of the aerial battles over southern England increases daily as the Luftwaffe tries to win air superiority so that Hitler can launch an invasion across the English Channel. The young Spitfire and Hurricane pilots have no intention of being swept aside, however, and they are battling Goering's fighters and bombers in the skies.

The battle raged all along the east coast from Tyneside to Kent and then west along the Channel to Devon yesterday as German planes took off from airfields ranging from Norway to Brittany. The day belonged to the RAF, which shot down 90 planes for the loss of 42. The Germans returned today, flying 1,700 sorties, and received the same medicine, losing 44 to the RAF's 24. But they concentrated their efforts on the defenders' airfields and Radio Direction Finding [radar] stations and caused great damage. According to the invasion timetable these attacks ought to have brought the Luftwaffe within sight of victory, but it has still not won air superiority.

Winston Churchill followed the progress of the battle from the "ops room" of No. 11 Group at Uxbridge, west of London. As he was driven home, the prime minister said: "Don't speak to me. I have never been so moved" (→20).

Scramble: RAF fighter pilots race to their airplanes after another alert.

Allies escape from Dunkirk bombardment

A wounded soldier limps home.

Dunkirk, 4 June
Operation Dynamo, the evacuation of British and other Allied forces from Dunkirk, was completed today in spite of intense aerial bombardment and shellfire. In all, some 338,226 men of the army which had been forced to retreat to this Channel port have been transported to safety. Around 800 civilian "little ships" and 222 naval vessels took part in an operation which Winston Churchill describes as "a miracle of deliverance".

Perversely, the British are defiantly looking on the evacuation as a victory rather than a defeat, even though most of its army's heavy equipment has been lost (→10).

Channel Islands fall to invading Germans

Guernsey, 13 June
The Channel Islands have fallen to the Germans without a shot being fired. The government decided earlier this month that they could not be defended without a huge loss of civilian lives. British nationals drew their money from the banks, shot their cats and dogs and crowded onto the evacuation boats.

The Germans gave their orders for the surrender of the islands in canvas bags dropped from aircraft. Today every house displays a white sheet, and the Germans are landing in force. The only incident so far has been a pub fight between an Irish worker and a German soldier. The Irishman won (→27/4/41).

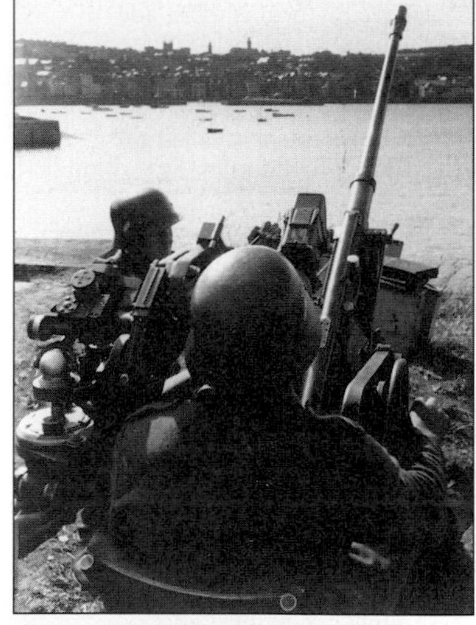

German guns at Guernsey harbour.

Veterans are 'proud to do their bit' and enrol in Home Guard

London, 23 July
Britain's Local Defence Volunteer force, now over a million strong, was officially renamed the Home Guard today. Veterans of the Great War, anxious to "do their bit", are flocking to join this nationwide force. Generals and admirals with several rows of medals are serving in the ranks. The veterans are short of weapons and uniforms; many of them are drilling with broom handles, while farmers with shotguns patrol their land on horseback, prepared to fight the invaders. So far they have only had to cope with shot-down enemy pilots.

A Home Guard unit drills in a high street "somewhere in England".

'Lord Haw-Haw' is new voice of Berlin

London, 1 March
William Joyce, a Briton who now lives in Hamburg, has become the voice of German propaganda. Research just completed for the BBC shows that two-thirds of the adult population in Britain have listened to his propaganda talks, with one in six apparently being regular members of his audience. Joyce's drawling nasal voice has earned him the nickname of "Lord Haw-Haw" as he sneers at claims made by British politicians and newspapers about the war (→26/6/45).

RAF claims victory after the 'battle of Britain'

London, 15 September
RAF Fighter Command withstood everything the Luftwaffe could throw at it today and chased the Germans back across the English Channel, leaving southern England littered with the burning wrecks of enemy aircraft. This was probably the most crucial day of the "battle of Britain", the day on which the German air minister, Goering, had planned finally to sweep aside what he told his pilots were Britain's few remaining Hurricanes and Spitfires and so clear the path for Hitler's "Operation Sealion" – Germany's invasion of Britain.

It did not happen like that. As the blips of the attacking force showed on the RDF [radar] sets this fine, sunny morning, Air Vice Marshal Keith Park, commanding 11 Group, sent up 11 squadrons, about a hundred fighters, to harry the German formations as they headed for London. Over the capital they were met by Douglas Bader, the "legless ace", at the head of his "big wing" of five squadrons.

Four Hurricane squadrons met the German bombers head-on, breaking up their formation so that their bombs were scattered over a wide area. The fight raged all the way from the coast and back again with British fighters chasing crippled bombers and fuel-short Messerschmitt 109 fighters at wave-top height. The Germans came back in the afternoon, with 150 bombers preceded by fighters. This tactic did not work either.

Air Chief Marshal Sir Hugh Dowding, who has been conducting the RAF's battle with a fine economy, was warned of their impending arrival by decoded German signals and his young pilots were ready to pounce on the Germans as they crossed the coast. Those who did get through were once again met over London by the daunting sight of Bader's 60 machines tearing in at them.

The RAF's victory today was brought about not only by the courage and skill of the pilots and the careful husbanding of men and machines but also by a Luftwaffe error in switching its attacks from airfields and radar stations to London in retaliation for an an RAF raid on Berlin on 25 August. If Goering had maintained the assault on the airfields, he might still have won, but by striking at London he gave the fighter pilots some rest.

Even so there were anxious moments today. Winston Churchill, visiting an RAF operations HQ at Uxbridge, watched the commander feeding squadrons into the fray. As the battle reached a ferocious climax Churchill asked: "What other reserves have we?" He was told: "There are none" (→ 15/11).

British cities 'blitzed' by German air war

What was once a street in Bristol lies devastated after a November raid.

London, 30 December
The City of London is still smouldering this morning after a series of fire raids in which over 22,000 incendiary bombs and 127 tons of high explosive were dropped by 136 bombers. Many of the City's finest buildings were destroyed, among them the Guildhall, eight Wren churches and three hospitals. St Paul's Cathedral, although damaged, stands proudly among the gutted shells of its neighbours.

These raids were among the most ferocious and damaging inflicted on the capital by the almost continuous bombardment which has been maintained since that first terrible afternoon of 7 September when the Luftwaffe switched its attacks from the RAF's airfields to the streets and houses of Britain's cities.

Since then thousands of civilians have died, 3,700 this month alone, in what has come to be known as "the Blitz". Coventry has had its heart ripped out, and many of Britain's major cities have been severely damaged. For the moment there seems little that the RAF can do to counter the night bombers, which are directed to their targets by beams. Scientists are working on airborne RDF [radar], but until it is ready the nightfighters are blind and bombs rain down (→ 2/1/41).

U-boats step up attacks to block Atlantic

A U-boat on patrol: hunting in "wolf packs" in the Atlantic war.

London, 26 October
Germany's U-boats are waging a ferocious war to sever Britain's Atlantic lifeline. Despite the British system of sending boats in convoys, the U-boats, using new tactics devised by their commander, Admiral Karl Dönitz, are sinking ship after ship. Allied shipping losses this week total 88,000 tons, more than eight times greater than the average losses at the beginning of the year.

The U-boats operate in "wolf packs", forming a patrol line and then gathering when one of the boats spots a convoy and signals its position and course. When gathered they often outnumber the convoy's armed escorts and steam into the convoy, picking off their targets with the escorts unable to protect the vulnerable merchant ships.

One of the problems is that the escort's detection equipment can only spot the U-boats when they are submerged, so the Germans attack on the surface at night, virtually invisible with their low silhouettes. The defenders are also hampered by a lack of long-range aircraft, while the Germans fly from French airfields to lead the wolf packs to their prey. So effective is this that 30 ships from two convoys were sunk in just two days earlier this month (→ 27/5/41).

1941

Eire, 2 January. German planes bomb southern Ireland despite the government's neutrality in the war (→ 16/4).

Thames estuary, 5 January. Amy Johnson, the pioneering airwoman, is feared dead after the plane she was flying for the Air Transport Auxiliary crashed into the Thames.

Britain, 3 February. Doctors complete the first effective treatment using penicillin since it was discovered in 1928 (→ 31/12/43).

Washington, DC, 11 March. President Roosevelt signs the Lend-Lease Bill to help Britain to obtain war supplies, with payment deferred until later (→ 14/8).

Westminster, 17 March. Plans are announced to conscript 20 and 21-year-old women for jobs in industry and auxiliary forces (→ 4/12).

Athens, 27 April. British troops are forced to evacuate Greece as Germans advance (→ 1/6).

London, 11 May. The House of Commons is destroyed in the Luftwaffe's most devastating raid on the capital; over 1,400 people are killed (→ 28/3/42).

Atlantic Ocean, 27 May. The German battleship *Bismarck* is scuttled after being hit by torpedoes (→ 10/7/42).

Westminster, 27 May. Plans to extend conscription to Northern Ireland are dropped after Eire protests (→ 31/12).

Westminster, 1 June. Clothes are to be rationed (→ 31/12).

USSR, 20 June. A two-front war in Europe begins as Germany attacks its former ally, the Soviet Union (→ 12/7).

Moscow, 12 July. Britain and the Soviet Union sign a pact to fight Germany (→ 15/8/42).

London, 26 July. Britain and the US freeze Japanese economic assets (→ 8/12).

London, 23 September. General Charles de Gaulle forms a Free French government-in-exile.

Westminster, 8 December. Britain declares war on Japan one day after American ships at Pearl Harbor were attacked, bringing the United States into the war (→ 31).

USA, 26 December. Winston Churchill addresses Congress during a visit to plan Allied war strategy (→ 26/1/42).

Civilians learn to cope on front line

January: a bomb near the Bank of England rips London's streets apart.

March: school lessons continue in an air raid shelter in Bermondsey.

April: rescue workers salvage belongings after raids on Belfast.

How blitzed cities struggle through

London, 16 April
German bombers have renewed the Blitz on the cities of the United Kingdom after the bad weather of the winter. Early this morning it was the turn of Belfast, where more than 700 people are feared to have died in what was one of the most concentrated raids of the war to date. Fire brigades were sent from Eire as well as Northern Ireland.

Major industrial centres and ports have been the principal targets of the Luftwaffe, but the bombs are hitting all classes and all regions. Buckingham Palace was hit on the night of 8/9 March, and the Café de Paris nightclub was destroyed in the same attack. Terrible damage was inflicted on Clydeside on 13 March – with only seven houses left undamaged in the shipbuilding town of Clydebank. The raid left 1,100 dead in Scotland's worst raid so far. Bristol, Cardiff, Plymouth, Birmingham, Merseyside and Portsmouth figure in the long list of places battered.

There have been instances of panic, but people are learning to "live with the bomb". In London thousands take shelter in the Underground. The government, which originally tried to prevent the use of the Underground system as shelters, is now fitting bunks and sanitary facilities. Regulars are given tickets for specific bunks. In Portsmouth many shelter in the tunnels of Portsdown Hill, and there is an exodus from Plymouth every night as people head for the safety of the countryside pushing treasured possessions in carts and prams.

Yet, despite the death and destruction, the Blitz appears to be bolstering the nation's resolve. Even in Coventry, where the damage was so great that the army wanted to impose martial law, people soon returned to the factories, and production actually rose. The RAF is also gaining the upper hand in its struggle with the German bombers. New nightfighters equipped with RDF [radar] are, as Churchill says, "clawing the Hun out of the sky" (→ 11/5).

Nazi troops tighten grip on Europe

Crete is abandoned by the Allied forces

Crete, 1 June
After a week of some of the fiercest fighting yet seen in this war the Allied forces on Crete have been defeated, and the Royal Navy, under incessant attack from the air, is endeavouring to evacuate as many as possible. It is almost exactly a year since it performed the same task at Dunkirk.

The battle started following the fall of Greece when Germany's General Kurt Student's paratroopers established a bridgehead on the island and flocks of JU52 transports laden with airborne troops were sent in. Many were shot out of the sky, and Student's élite force has suffered appalling casualties.

It was touch and go despite the Germans' total air supremacy – the few RAF planes on the island were withdrawn rather than suffer annihilation – but "Creforce" was disposed to face an attack from the sea rather than the air and the Germans were able to take Malame airfield and pour in reinforcements.

So far the Royal Navy has taken off 18,000 men – but at great cost, losing three cruisers and nine destroyers, with 17 other ships crippled and 2,011 men dead (→ 14/11).

A British merchant ship under attack by a German commerce raider.

Air cover goes as 'Ark Royal' capsizes

Gibraltar, 14 November
Constant German claims to have sunk the aircraft carrier *Ark Royal* became reality when the ship capsized and sank at 6.13 am today. She was torpedoed by a U-boat yesterday, but it was hoped that she could be saved. However, as she was towed towards Gibraltar, 25 miles away, fire broke out, her list increased, and she was abandoned.

With the *Illustrious* and the *Formidable* under repair in the US, the Mediterranean Fleet is left without air cover at a time when Hitler is transferring bombers from the USSR to Sicily to step up the attack on Malta. It is not all bad news from the Mediterranean, however: the cruisers *Aurora* and *Penelope* have sunk two Italian destroyers and ten merchant ships.

There is also good news for Britain in the battle of the Atlantic to follow the success in May when the much feared battleship *Bismarck* sank. The United States has now decided that it will escort convoys carrying lend-lease materials as far east as Iceland (→ 19/8/42).

Churchill and US sign 'Atlantic Charter'

Washington, 14 August
President Roosevelt and Winston Churchill have signed an "Atlantic Charter", an historic declaration of Anglo-American aims and principles. It declares that neither country seeks territorial gains from the war and that both look forward to a lasting peace and the end of the use of force. It also says that it hopes all nations will cooperate economically after the war.

The charter, stemming from the US president's wish that the Western democracies should make their aims clear to the Soviet Union, was signed during a series of meetings over the past five days on the US cruiser *Augusta* and the British battleship *Prince of Wales* at Placenta Bay off Newfoundland (→ 26/12).

Churchill: the voice of Britain.

Desert armies face winter campaigns

Western Desert, 13 November
The North African armies fighting under the leadership of Generals Erwin Rommel and Claude Auchinleck are both preparing decisive winter campaigns. The Germans are planning to take Tobruk, cut off for nine months, and then crash into Egypt. However, Auchinleck knows of Rommel's plans through intercepted German signals and intends to forestall him.

The Allies outnumber the Germans two to one in tanks and aircraft, but no Eighth Army tanks can withstand the German 88mm gun. The British also have to face the superb generalship of Rommel, "the Desert Fox" (→ 21/6/42).

Women called up to meet wartime labour shortages

Westminster, 4 December
Unmarried women in their 20s now face the call-up. Female conscription was announced today by Winston Churchill as one of a series of moves to combat a critical labour shortage. The government is also requiring married women up to the age of 40 and single women in their 30s to register as labour which can be directed to industries.

Men are not forgotten in this new extension of conscription – the call-up comes down to 18 years and six months, with men in their 40s also now liable for military service – but it is the powers over women which are unprecedented. Single women in their 20s will be sent to join the police, fire service or to non-combat roles in the forces.

Since last April they have had to register for war work. In many cases this has meant filling the places left in industry and other occupations vacated by the men now serving in the forces, although Britain had entered the war with a higher proportion of its female population in the total workforce than any other European country. Taking account of certain exemptions (as exist for men in reserved occupations and for conscientious objectors), the new conscription will cover nearly 1.7 million single women (→ 6/2/48).

Women at work in a factory.

US joins war after Pearl Harbor raid

Hong Kong falls to Japanese offensive

South-east Asia, 31 December
Japanese forces have struck with devastating speed since 7 December when they stunned the United States by attacking the Pearl Harbor base in Hawaii. The next day the US declared war on Japan, as did Britain. Other declarations of war came almost daily, but the most significant came when Germany and Italy, supporting their Axis ally of Japan, declared war on the United States.

Winston Churchill is privately delighted, having long sought US support. But the potential long-term benefits of US participation in the war have been offset by short-term reverses as Japanese forces sweep across the Pacific and south-east Asia. In Malaya, Japan is pushing towards Kuala Lumpur and Singapore. Burma is under attack, and there have been landings in the Philippines, Wake and Guam.

Britain has already suffered serious losses. Two warships, the *Repulse* and the *Prince of Wales*, have been sunk, and on Christmas Day Hong Kong became the first British possession to see the Union Jack replaced by the emblem of the Rising Sun. Sir Mark Young, its governor, ordered all 11,000 troops under British command to lay down their arms following 18 days of fighting with intense air and artillery bombardment (→ 11/1/42).

Japanese troops enter Hong Kong after the British colony's surrender.

Indian troops fighting with Britain cross a river in Burma near Mandalay.

Make Do and Mend is the motto for the British housewife

Britain, 31 December
This has been the year when the upper classes have found themselves facing the kind of problem only too common in working-class families. A special "Make Do and Mend" department has been set up in the board of trade to publicize suggestions for patching clothes and mending curtains and bed-linen instead of replacing them with new items.

Travelling exhibitions are being planned to show how worn stockings can be cut into "clips" and made into rugs (an old tradition in northern industrial towns), prewar golfing plus-fours can be made up into overcoats, and scarves can be used to make children's frocks. Jumble sales have suddenly become popular, so much so that admission tickets are being issued for some sales. The Women's Voluntary Service is arranging "clothing exchanges" for mothers to trade in items their children have outgrown.

Wartime deprivation has found comic relief in radio programmes such as *ITMA* starring Tommy Handley. *It's That Man Again*, to give the show its full title, pokes fun at officialdom with Handley as the minister of aggravation and mysteries. "I have several hundred irritating restrictions to impose on you," said Handley in a show which proves that whatever Britons have lost during the war it is not their sense of humour (→ 3/3/42).

Now the war spreads around the world

London, 11 December
A year ago Britain and its empire stood alone against Hitler and his Italian ally, Mussolini; now, after the German invasion of the Soviet Union and Japan's attack on Pearl Harbor, the war has become one that girdles the whole globe.

In the battle of the Atlantic, US warships are already escorting convoys as far as Iceland, where the Royal Navy takes over; shipping losses of 400,000 tons a month have fallen to 100,000 tons this year.

The Italians have been expelled from Ethiopia, but in the western desert of North Africa neither Britain's Eighth Army ("the Desert Rats") nor the Axis forces under General Rommel have been able to deliver a decisive blow. Germany's drive into the Soviet Union may at last have been halted, however. Five days ago Soviet forces counter-attacked, pushing the enemy back from Moscow, though Leningrad remains besieged.

Churchill told MPs today that, though a "hard period" lies ahead, the US entry into the war ensures that Britain will receive a vast increase in munitions and aid.

De Valera spurns a plea to join Allies

Dublin, 31 December
Eamon de Valera, the Eire leader, continues to maintain Irish neutrality even though the United States, the country to which he looks for traditional support, has entered the war. Believing that he would alter his stance, Winston Churchill sent a personal message to de Valera – the first since the war began – urging him to join the Allies. But the Eire premier has interpreted this as yet another move towards unity and has rejected it (→ 1/5/43).

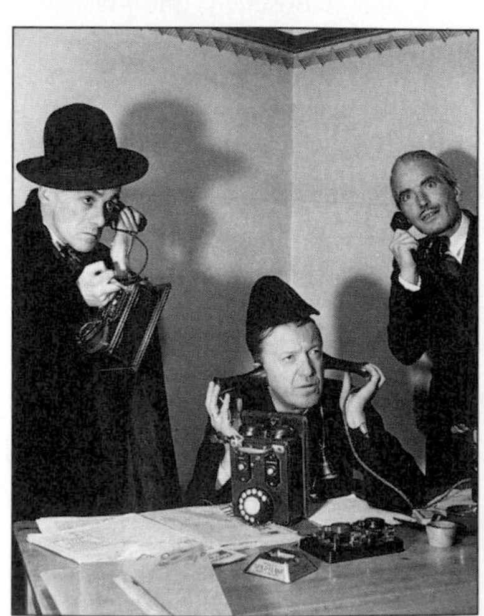

Tommy Handley (centre), the star of radio's hit show "ITMA".

1942

Malaya, 11 January. Kuala Lumpur, the capital, falls to the Japanese army (→ 15/2).

Belfast, 26 January. The first US troops in Europe since the First World War land in Northern Ireland (→ 5/2).

Derry City, 5 February. A US naval base is established (→ 14/1/43).

Westminster, 17 March. Coal, gas and electricity are to be rationed, MPs are told (→ 26/7).

Germany, 28 March. RAF Bomber Command signals a new policy by launching a concerted attack by 200 planes against Lübeck (→ 24/4).

New Delhi, 28 March. Indian leaders are told by the British government that they will be offered independence after the war (→ 19/9/45).

Devon, 24 April. German planes bomb Exeter in retaliation for the RAF raid on Lübeck last month (→ 5/5).

Germany, 30 May. The RAF launches its first 1,000-bomber raid, with Cologne the target (→ 31).

Oxford, 1 July. A charity to provide aid for people suffering from famine is formed.

Britain, 26 July. Rationing of sweets begins today (→ 1/2/44).

Moscow, 15 August. Winston Churchill holds his first summit meeting with Joseph Stalin, the Soviet Union's leader (→ 21/2/43).

Russia, 18 September. The largest convoy yet arrives with 27 out of 40 ships intact, two months after the disastrous PQ-17 convoy (→ 22/5/43).

North Africa, 24 October. The Eighth Army under General Bernard Montgomery launches a major offensive at El Alamein (→ 30/10).

Bordeaux, 12 December. British commandos travelling in canoes blow up six moored ships (→ 10/7/43).

Britain, 15 December. A campaign to halt the increase in venereal disease that has occurred since the war began.

London, 17 December. In a joint statement with its allies the British government condemns the anti-Semitic atrocities which it says are being perpetrated by Germany.

Burma, 19 December. British forces begin a cautious advance against Japanese troops (→ 24/3/44).

German bombers target 'Baedeker' cities

The cup that cheers: a fireman pauses during the rescue work at Exeter.

Exeter, 5 May
In the latest of the "Baedeker" raids on lightly defended English towns of historic interest, the Luftwaffe mounted a second attack on Exeter last night but with markedly less success than on the first occasion.

As well as Exeter, the Germans have hit Bath, Norwich and York with devastating effect, using high explosive, incendiaries and machine-gun fire guided by a new electronic targeting beam. The RAF has responded by transmitting a radio signal which misleads the Luftwaffe beam. In the latest raid only 13 per cent of German bombs found their target, against 50 per cent previously.

The German raids on towns featured in the Baedeker guidebook are Hitler's retaliation for the RAF's fire-bombing of Lübeck and Rostock in the last six weeks. These raids were Bomber Command's trial runs for its new policy of bombing cities in a bid to destroy German workers' morale (→ 30/5).

Allies driven back by Rommel's forces

Tobruk, Libya, 21 June
Axis forces today captured the vital North African port of Tobruk. Its loss – along with 35,000 Allied soldiers and 70 tanks – is the biggest single blow to Britain since the fall of Singapore. General Rommel's Afrika Korps has been pushing the Eighth Army back deeper into Egypt but surprised the Allies by turning back towards Tobruk in Libya. A heavy bombardment by air and artillery yesterday signalled the assault with the infantry and Panzers completing the port's capture this afternoon. The German advance is now set to continue across the desert as Rommel, "the Desert Fox", moves closer to Cairo and the Suez Canal(→ 24/10).

Maltese honoured

Valletta, Malta, 16 April
The tiny island of Malta, which has endured over a thousand German and Italian air raids in the past four months, was today awarded the George Cross – the civilian equivalent of the Victoria Cross – by King George VI in recognition of the heroism and devotion of its people. The island is less than a hundred miles (160km) from Sicily.

Singapore, the 'impregnable' naval base, surrenders to Japan

Singapore, 15 February
The Singapore base surrendered to Japan today after several confused and ineffective counter-attacks by British and Indian troops. It is the greatest military defeat in British history. The base was reputedly impregnable, but its great guns were pointing out to sea as the invaders came by land.

Unknown to the British, the Japanese, after a lightning advance down the Malay peninsula, were almost out of ammunition, though they had supremacy in the air and at sea. Lt-Gen Arthur Percival, responsible for a million civilians and 130,000 troops, was told that water supplies were running out and so surrendered to General Tomoyuki Yamashita, who has now acquired a massive arsenal of guns and ammunition (→ 19/12).

Lt-Gen Percival (second left) marches to surrender Singapore to Japan.

Battles intensify on land, sea and in the air

Air war: RAF stages 1,000-bomber raid

Germany, 31 May
More than a thousand aircraft were sent aloft by the RAF last night to devastate the city of Cologne; 1,455 tons of bombs were dropped in 90 minutes, 2,300 separate fires were started and over 3,000 buildings destroyed. Vital machine-tool and chemical plants have been crippled, and over 45,000 civilians are thought to be homeless.

Air Marshal Arthur Harris made use of every last plane in Bomber Command, from new Lancasters to ancient Whitleys; the 6,500 crewmen of the 1,047 aircraft included many who had not completed their training. The raid is seen as a test of saturation bombing tactics designed to bring the reality of total war home to Germans.

In a message to Harris, Churchill says: "This proof of the growing power of Britain's bomber force is also a herald of what Germany will receive, city by city, from now on." A message smuggled out of the Warsaw ghetto says Jews rejoiced when they heard of the raid. They see it as vengeance on Germany for Hitler's persecution of the Jews in Nazi-occupied Europe (→30/1/43).

The detritus of defeat: helmets and guns left by the Allies at Dieppe.

Land war: heavy Allied losses at Dieppe

Dieppe, 19 August
In just nine hours of fighting along an 11-mile stretch of the French coast at Dieppe, a 6,100-strong force of Canadians, British, Americans and Free French today lost 1,000 men killed and 2,000 taken prisoner; all their tanks and equipment were abandoned. The Royal Navy's casualties were 75 dead, 206 wounded and 269 missing; a destroyer and 33 landing craft were sunk. The RAF lost 106 planes, the Germans 48. Enemy casualties included 314 killed, 294 wounded and 37 taken prisoner and brought to England. The raid, officially no more than a "reconnaissance in force", was a disaster. Hitler, however, told his commanders: "We must realize that we are not alone in learning a lesson from Dieppe. The British have also learned. We must reckon with a totally different mode of attack and at a quite different place" (→12/12).

Sea war: convoy is shattered in Arctic

USSR, 10 July
The Allied convoy PQ-17 is limping into the Soviet Union's Arctic port of Murmansk after losing 24 ships of the 39 which sailed from, Iceland on 27 June with vital munitions for the USSR. Of 156,492 tonnes of cargo, 99,316 tonnes were lost, including 430 of the 594 tanks on board, 210 of 297 warplanes and 3,350 of 4,246 vehicles.

The disaster has been attributed to an order which assumed that a powerful task force, headed by Germany's biggest battleship, the *Tirpitz*, had sailed to attack PQ-17. The Allies had long known of the plan for such an attack, codenamed Operation Rasselsprung [Knight's Move], and were extremely apprehensive. When the admiralty failed to get confirmation that the *Tirpitz* force was still in Norwegian ports, the order to scatter was given.

In fact Hitler, anxious not to put his most powerful ships at risk, had ordered them back to port while U-boats and dive-bombers were sent into action. For three nights and days the planes caused havoc among the defenceless merchantmen. But Sir Dudley Pound, the first sea lord, says that had the convoy not scattered the *Tirpitz* might have continued, and then all the merchant ships would have been sunk (→18/9).

Skirts get shorter as material gets scarce

Britain, 3 March
Skirts are several centimetres shorter than peace-time styles, and the number of buttonholes, pleats and seams has been severely restricted by new Utility regulations. After clothes rationing was introduced last year, manufacturers with limited quotas of material maximized their profits by concentrating on higher-priced items. Board of trade regulations now limit the range of materials and styles and control the level of retail prices.

A woman's tweed winter coat sells for £4/3/11 [£4.20]. For just a bit more, a man can buy a suit (if he has enough coupons), but the trousers lack turn-ups, and the jacket is single-breasted. Five centimetres (2 inches) have disappeared from shirt tails (→17/3).

A "Utility" suit – for 18 coupons.

Churchill wins MPs' vote of confidence

Westminster, 2 July
Accusing his critics in the House of Commons of "nagging and snarling", Churchill tonight demanded a rousing vote of confidence – and received it by 476 to 25, with 30 abstentions. He was greatly helped by the ineptitude of his chief critic, the old Chamberlainite Tory Sir John Wardlaw Milne, who called for King George VI's younger brother, the duke of Gloucester, to be appointed commander-in-chief of the army, "without, of course, administrative duties". MPs roared with derisive laughter. Churchill is none the less relieved by the vote, as there has been serious criticism of his leadership following the recent German victories in North Africa.

Sun rays compensate for shelter life for these London children.

El Alamein victory turns tide for Allies

A wounded gunner is helped as the battle rages in the African desert.

Montgomery: the new British hero.

El Alamein, 30 October
After five days locked in ferocious combat on a 40-mile (64km) front, Field Marshal Rommel's mighty Afrika Korps lies battered and demoralized, its last reserves used up and its tank force shattered as Lt-Gen Bernard Montgomery, the new British commander of the Eighth Army, prepares a new offensive – Operation Supercharge.

The Eighth Army had opened its offensive on the evening of 23 October with a 15-minute artillery barrage by 1,000 guns. Then the infantry went in – the 51st Highland and the South African and New Zealand Divisions – to clear a way through the minefield for the armour. The British XXX Corps has lost 200 tanks driving a wedge into German lines, but the weight of Allied armour and the infantry's determination is winning the war of attrition. Montgomery has also been greatly helped by allied codebreaking which revealed Rommel's plans – and his weaknesses.

The fate of the Afrika Korps was, in fact, sealed seven weeks ago when Montgomery stopped Rommel in a seven-day battle at Alam Halfa ridge, near El Alamein. Until then Rommel had enjoyed three months of triumphs that caused near panic at British GHQ in Cairo, where mountains of confidential papers were burnt. Churchill had arrived in person in August to install new men, General Harold Alexander as C-in-C Middle East and Montgomery to lead the Eighth Army, with orders to destroy the enemy "at the earliest opportunity" (→ 7/11).

Allied troops storm ashore in massive invasion of North Africa

Algiers, 7 November
The most formidable amphibious invasion force ever mounted – 300 warships, 370 merchant ships and 107,000 men – tonight descended upon the coast of French North Africa in an Allied bid to trap Rommel's Afrika Korps in a giant nutcracker. Operation Torch is commanded by Lt-Gen Dwight D Eisenhower, and most of his troops are also American; two British destroyers off Algiers are flying the Stars and Stripes. By playing down the British role it is hoped that the the Vichy French forces in North Africa will be cooperative, but early reports suggest the Allied troops are meeting resistance at Algiers, Oran and Casablanca (→ 13/5/43).

Allied troops land as Operation Torch steps up the attack on Rommel.

Welfare proposed for everyone 'from cradle to grave'

Britain, 1 December
A "welfare state" caring for people "from the cradle to the grave" is proposed in a report published today. Social planning is seen as the means to build on the solidarity forged by battle and to conquer what the report identifies as the "five giants" of Want, Ignorance, Squalor, Idleness and Disease.

Sir William Beveridge, the economist who headed the committee which produced the report, wants a system of social insurance with contributions from workers, employers and the state to provide benefits for unemployment, sickness, pensions and everything from maternity to funeral grants. Family allowances would be paid to offset poverty, and "national assistance" to people who fall outside other benefits. A major element in the Beveridge vision is the creation of a "national health service".

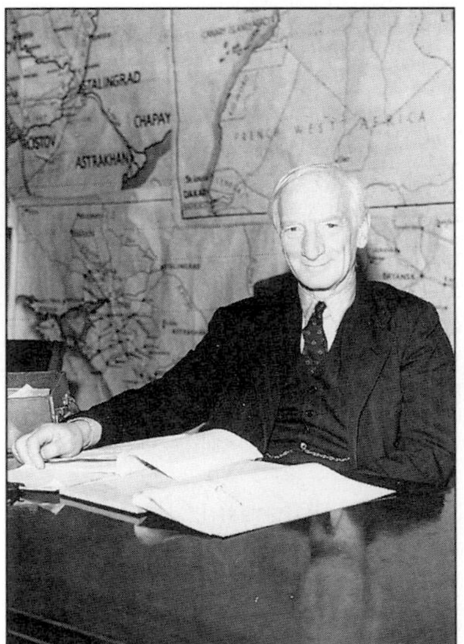

Beveridge: a visionary for peace.

The proposals have been warmly welcomed and build on a growing social consensus and concern that the unity shown in war should be maintained in peace. Magazines such as *Picture Post*, books, church leaders, academics and professional groups such as those representing doctors have all outlined ideas not dissimilar to those published today. The coalition government promises to give the report earnest consideration (→ 18/2/43).

1943

Morocco, 14 January. Winston Churchill meets President Roosevelt at Casablanca to discuss war strategy with their military advisers; invasion of Italy is to precede a second front in western Europe.

Germany, 30 January. RAF planes make the first daytime bombing raid on Berlin (→ 6/3).

Westminster, 18 February. The Commons vote in principle to accept the "welfare state" proposals of the Beveridge Report published last year (→ 17/2/44).

Britain, 21 February. Britons celebrate "Red Army Day" to congratulate the Soviet Union on its victory at Stalingrad last month.

London, 3 March. An accident at Bethnal Green tube station kills 178 people.

Germany, 6 March. Allied air forces step up the bombing campaign against the Ruhr (→ 17/5).

Belfast, 1 May. Sir Basil Brooke becomes prime minister of Northern Ireland (→ 2/5/45).

Tunisia, 13 May. German and Italian forces in North Africa surrender to the Allies.

Germany, 17 May. A special "Dambuster" squadron of the RAF attacks three dams in the Ruhr with bouncing bombs (→ 31/7).

Lisbon, 1 June. The actor Leslie Howard is among the passengers feared dead after a plane flying from here to Eire goes missing.

Sicily, 10 July. British and American forces land (→ 9/9).

Italy, 9 September. Allied forces land in three areas of southern Italy one day after the Italian government announces its surrender.→

Britain, 23 September. Income tax is to be collected by a new "pay as you earn" (PAYE) scheme announced today.

London, 19 October. The rapid rise in venereal disease is blamed on "moral laxity" in a statement by the archbishops of Canterbury and York.

Germany, 19 November. RAF Bomber Command begins its winter campaign against Berlin.

Westminster, 2 December. Ernest Bevin, the labour minister, says some conscripts will have to work in the mines and industry.→

German shipyards and factories reduced to a pile of rubble after bombing raids

A woman weeps in Hamburg after identifying a victim of the bombing.

Germany, 31 July
Close on one million terrified citizens have fled Germany's biggest port, Hamburg, after three devastating night raids by RAF bombers in the last five days. Over 7,000 tonnes of bombs have obliterated 25,000 sq metres (6,200 acres) of buildings and severely damaged U-boat construction yards. Water, gas and electricity supplies failed, and over 40,000 people died, many of them being sucked into the centre of firestorms rising to 1,000 degrees Celsius (1,832 degrees Fahrenheit).

The Hamburg raids came as a climax to seven months of concentrated bombing directed at a dozen cities in Germany's industrial heartland, the Ruhr. At the beginning of this year the RAF had only 260 heavy bombers. Now upwards of 700 aircraft are regularly dispatched on a single night raid.

Special bombs have been devised for specific targets. Barnes Wallis of Vickers Armstrong designed a bomb that bounces over water. This was used to breach the Mohne and Eder dams, which supply water to Ruhr industries. Over 300 million gallons of water were lost.

Pathfinder aircraft are now being used to identify the target city and drop marker bombs for the main force. Then masses of aluminium foil strips are released to confuse the enemy radar. The RAF's bombing offensive has forced Hitler to order Luftwaffe squadrons to withdraw from the eastern front; little more than 20 per cent of the Luftwaffe force is now deployed in the Soviet Union.

German sources admit that the RAF offensive has hit morale. Colonel Adolf Galland says of the Hamburg raids: "A wave of terror radiated from the suffering city and spread throughout Germany ... After Hamburg in the wide circle of the political and military command could be heard the words "the war is lost"." Albert Speer, Hitler's minister for war production, is reported to have said that six more raids on the Hamburg scale could bring Germany to its knees (→ 13/6/44).

Testing the "bouncing bomb".

U-boats withdrawn as Allies hit back in Atlantic battle

North Atlantic, 22 May
After a month of disastrous losses, Grand Admiral Karl Dönitz has ordered his U-boats to pull out of the North Atlantic. Only three days ago his son, Peter, perished when an RAF Liberator bomber operating from Iceland sank the U954.

In recent months, British, Canadian and American naval and air units have steadily gained the upper hand. In 1942 eight million tonnes of shipping were lost, and even as recently as March this year losses were running at almost 600,000 tonnes a month.

But now attacks on convoys by Dönitz's "Wolf Packs" are repulsed with heavy U-boat losses. Last week five of 33 U-boats were sunk in an unsuccessful attack on convoy SC-130. The Allies are operating a new short-wave radar system which is able to detect a U-boat surfacing several miles away to recharge its batteries. More powerful depth charges are also being used.

Dropping a depth charge at sea.

These measures have been backed up by more Allied successes in breaking German codes, including one used by U-boats to communicate with their central command. The Royal Navy's codebreakers, just 24 before the war, now number 1,000 and include historians, mathematicians and linguists, some of them German refugees. Listening posts to intercept enemy signals are scattered across Britain and British territories overseas.

Italy gives up the fight

Salerno, Italy, 9 September
Allied troops aboard ships which had left Sicily for an unknown destination heard today that Italy had surrendered unconditionally – and that they were about to go ashore at Salerno, south of Naples.

These dramatic announcements came after a week of secret contacts in Lisbon between the Allies and representatives of King Victor Emmanuel and Marshal Pietro Badoglio, who ousted Mussolini in July. The British were represented by General Carton de Wiart, who had been freed from an Axis prisoner-of-war camp. An armistice was signed in Sicily a week ago but kept secret until today's amphibious operation began.

Hitler, taking an afternoon nap at his HQ in east Prussia, was roused and told the BBC had broadcast news of Italy's surrender. He ordered the disarming of Italian troops and their deportation to Germany for forced labour. As the Germans entered Rome, Badoglio and the Italian king fled to territory occupied by the Allies (→ 31/1/44).

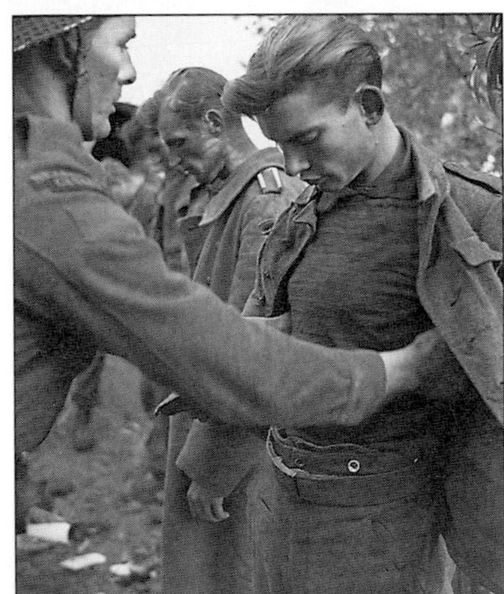

An Axis prisoner is searched.

'Wonder drug' is used in army hospitals

London, 31 December 1943
A life-saving drug which was used to treat Churchill's pneumonia earlier this month and is now in use in military hospitals is being imported from the United States, despite the fact that it was discovered by a British scientist, Alexander Fleming, in 1928. The patent for penicillin was lost when war came, and a shortage of microbiologists held up the drug's large-scale development. It was first used in Britain in 1941 to treat a policeman for blood poisoning; he died because not enough was available. Factories to manufacture the drug are being built in Britain, but it may be some two years before home-produced supplies exceed imports from the US. However, enough of another "wonder drug" for treating infections, sulphanilamide, is being produced for Britain to be self-sufficient.

Row as sick Mosley is released from jail

Protests over Mosley's release.

Westminster, 1 December
After noisy protests by a group of Labour MPs, the Commons today endorsed by a substantial majority the decision by Herbert Morrison, the home secretary, to release Sir Oswald Mosley, the founder of the British Union of Fascists, who is suffering from thrombo-phlebitis. Mosley, who was interned in 1940, is back in his Oxfordshire home but must report regularly to the police. Morrison said he had been advised by doctors that Mosley's life could be put at risk by continued imprisonment. The fascist leader conducted anti-Semitic marches through Jewish parts of London's East End in the 1930s.

How the home fires keep burning as the long years of wartime just drag on

Britain, 2 December
After four years of war Britain is running out of men and women to fill the ranks of the services and run the factories. Numbers registered as unemployed in 1939 – 1,250,000 – have fallen to fewer than 60,000.

To fill a manpower gap of two million, the minister of labour, Ernest Bevin, has extended the call-up downwards to 18-year-olds and upwards to men aged 51. Conscription of women has also been extended beyond those in their twenties to women up to 50, although they can still choose between industry and service with the armed forces.

Bevin: extending the call-up.

Today Bevin went further and announced that 30,000 men under 25 called up for national service will be directed to work in coal mines; they are to be selected by ballot. Coal output has fallen below the critical level of 200 million tons a year. Coal rationing was announced and then found to be unworkable; people are meanwhile urged to save fuel by bathing in no more than five inches of water.

Income tax collection began running into problems as the number of manual workers liable for tax rose from under one million before the war to over seven million. Deduction of the tax from pay packets seemed to be the answer until it was discovered that taking the tax in arrears, based on the previous year's assessment, could cause hardship if overtime diminished. So now it is being based on each week's pay – Pay As You Earn.

Even Christmas turkeys will be hard to find this year: each butcher with 800 registered customers will be allocated just 15 birds. Beer remains unrationed, but it has been so reduced in strength that a drinker must put down about twice as much by volume in order to keep up his alcohol intake. Still, it is not all grim news: the suicide rate has fallen from a pre-war 12.9 per 100,000 to below nine today.

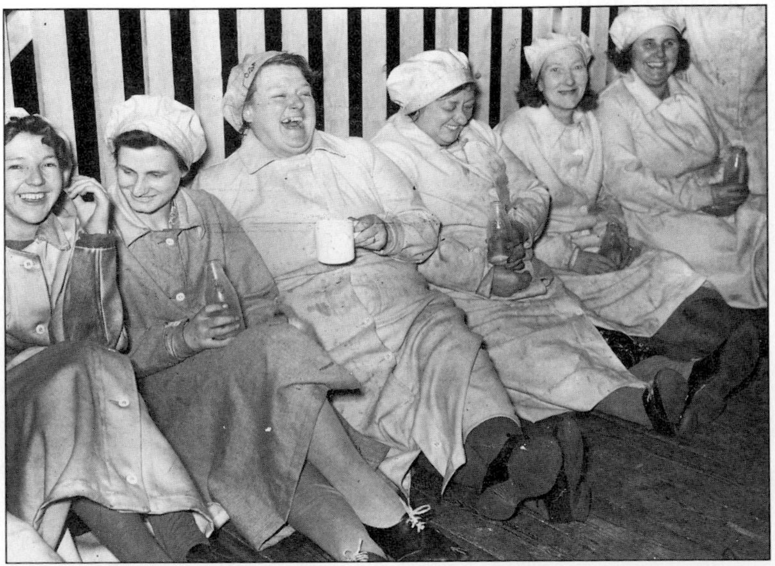

Women munitions workers take a break from life on the production line.

1944

Britain, 18 January. The first batch of conscripts sent down the pits (nicknamed "Bevin Boys" after the minister of labour) start their training.

Britain, 1 February. Clothing restrictions are lifted (→ 7/2/46).

Westminster, 17 February. Ministers announce plans for a post-war national health service and an Education Bill that will raise the school leaving age to 15 (→ 27/1/48).

Eire, 23 February. Grants are to be paid for third and further children under the Children's Allowances Act.

South Wales, 8 March. Strikes by miners are spreading, with 156 out of 200 pits idle.

Britain, 12 March. Travel to Eire is banned because of fears that German diplomats in Dublin could discover information about the proposed Allied landings.

France, 19 April. Railway lines and river bridges become key targets in an Allied bombing campaign in advance of the anticipated invasion (→ 6/5).

London, 30 April. The first "prefabricated" home goes on show; at least 500,000 are planned to provide temporary homes to replace those damaged during the war.

Devon, 6 May. Allied forces stage invasion rehearsals at Slapton Sands (→ 15/5).

Normandy, 12 June. Winston Churchill visits Allied troops six days after the D-Day invasion of occupied Europe.

France, 13 June. A new weapon, the V1 rocket, is launched at London (→ 18/7).

London, 18 July. V1 rocket attacks are causing a new wave of evacuation of mothers and children (→ 8/9).

Belgium, 8 September. British troops are among the first to enter Brussels, two weeks after Paris was liberated (→ 27).

London, 8 September. A new and more powerful rocket, the V2, lands at Chiswick (→ 10/11).

Netherlands, 27 September. British paratroopers surrender at Arnhem as a plan to seize key bridges over the Rhine fails (→ 14/10).

Athens, 14 October. British troops return to Greece to liberate Athens (→ 22/12).

London, 13 December. A series of "ring roads" and "green belts" are proposed.

'Forgotten army' strikes back in Burma

British jungle fighters in Burma: some attacked by land, some by air.

Imphal, India, 24 March
British, Indian and Gurkha forces have this month struck deep into Burma behind the Japanese lines, blowing up railways and bridges. In one encounter 100 Japanese were killed for the loss of one Gurkha. A glider-borne Allied force of 9,000 men, known as "Chindits" from the Burmese for "mighty lion", are being joined by Americans, Chinese and Gurkhas marching overland.

"We have inflicted complete surprise on the enemy," said Major-General Orde Wingate. "All our columns are inside the enemy's guts. The time has come to reap the fruit of the advantage we have gained." Tragically, soon after he made this statement his plane crashed in bad weather and he was killed.

The Chindits were Wingate's brainchild. British operations on the India/Burma front had had few successes, and the force became known as the "forgotten army". Wingate, described by Churchill as a "man of genius and audacity", put the Burmese theatre of war back in the headlines (→ 3/5/45).

Allied invasion of Europe draws near

London, 15 May
King George VI, with Winston Churchill and South Africa's prime minister, Field Marshal Jan Smuts, went to school today – St Paul's in London, where allied commanders have been planning Operation Overlord, the invasion of Nazi-occupied Europe. The visitors were shown a gigantic map of the Normandy beaches as General Montgomery ("Monty") explained the plan for putting eight divisions, five seaborne and three airborne, ashore in the first 48 hours.

The Germans have 60 divisions deployed along the coast to defend the Netherlands, France and Belgium. The Overlord strategy depends upon an elaborate deception operation aimed at the enemy. An entirely phantom army has been "stationed" in England opposite the Calais coast and kept busy with radio traffic for the enemy to monitor. In Stockholm, British agents have been manipulating the stock exchange to send up the value of Norwegian shares. And the day before "Monty" set out the true invasion plan he received a decrypt of Field Marshal Rommel's report to the German high command that Allied bombing of railways in northern France was disrupting supplies and his troop movements to reinforce the Calais defences (→ 6/6).

Allied forces open the road to Rome with landings at Anzio

Anzio, Italy, 31 January
When British and American forces went ashore in landing craft here last week they found the Italian coastal town of Anzio, 32 miles (51 km) south of Rome, completely deserted. The Italians had been evacuated, and the Germans had pulled out. The Allies put ashore 50,000 men and 3,000 vehicles with only 13 casualties from mines.

By landing behind enemy lines the Allies seem to have a clear road to Rome, but the US commander, Major-General John Lucas, has insisted on building up his beach defences before pushing inland as the British urge. This seems likely to give the Germans an opportunity to mobilize reserves and pin down the beach-head with artillery (→ 19/4).

British soldiers shelter in a German trench while awaiting reinforcements.

'D-Day' sees the biggest-ever seaborne invasion

The second front opens at last: Royal Marine commandos wade ashore on the beaches of Normandy to set in motion the greatest-ever invasion.

Normandy, 6 June
By dawn today 18,000 British and American airborne troops had landed in Normandy, seizing bridges and disrupting German communications. The BBC was broadcasting coded messages to the French Resistance to cut rail links, and 1,000 RAF planes were dropping 5,000 tons of bombs on German batteries.

As darkness gave way to a dull grey morning, a vast armada of 6,000 ships – men-of-war, merchantmen, barges and landing craft – could be seen rolling and heaving in the heavy seas. The Allies were going ashore to establish five beach-heads between Le Havre and the Cotentin peninsula.

This is Operation Overlord, the long-awaited Allied assault against Nazi Germany's Fortress Europe. Even at this late hour, though, the Germans still believed the "real" invasion would take place in the Pas de Calais, where Field Marshal von Rundstedt, C-in-C West, has concentrated his most powerful Panzer formations. Along with Rommel, his field commander, von Rundstedt has been duped by an elaborate deception operation, a phantom army in southern England and a stream of misleading reports from German agents who have been "turned" to serve the Allies.

On the beaches there were mixed fortunes. The British pushed inland from **Sword Beach** after repelling a Panzer attack, but their drive towards Caen was held up by tanks and trucks jamming the narrow roads. At **Juno Beach**, on Sword's right flank, the Canadians drove inland after fierce street fighting in the small town of Courseulles. The British, at **Gold Beach**, captured a pillbox and found a breakfast of sausage and hot coffee abandoned by the fleeing Germans. Further west, on **Utah Beach**, the Americans lost only six dead in clearing the beach, and the German defenders could scarcely wait to give themselves up.

But it was very different at **Omaha Beach**, where tanks were lost in heavy seas and men who reached the beach came under intense mortar and machine-gun fire. After hours of confusion the Americans recovered, and the Germans, lacking reserves, were forced to give way. By midnight, the Allies had put 155,000 troops ashore for the loss of 9,000 men.

Von Rundstedt has 60 divisions strung out across France, Belgium and the Netherlands. The Allies can muster only 37. The decisive factor will be the speed with which each side can build up its forces. Here, the Allies reckon they have the advantage with their absolute command at sea and in the air.

At this critical point, the Allies have acquired a vital piece of information. British Intelligence has decoded a Luftwaffe message reporting a critical shortage of aviation fuel. Churchill has ordered RAF Bomber Command's attacks to be diverted to Germany's vital oil installations (→8/9). ▷

Strikes soar to mar life on home front

London, 3 December
The Home Guard mustered for its final parade in London today. King George VI took the salute as the Londoners cheered the volunteers whose disbandment symbolizes the belief that victory will be achieved.

Another emblematic change this year has been the replacement of the "black-out" of lights by the "dim-out". While servicemen are still fighting, politicians have been looking forward. A major house-building programme has been promised and an Education Act passed which creates a three-tier system of secondary education with the school-leaving age raised to 15.

Less welcome, though, has been a wave of strikes which seems certain to give 1944 a worse record for industrial unrest than many peacetime years. Three times as many days are likely to be lost this year as in 1939 – and two-thirds of all strikes were in the coal mines.

Most of the miners' grievances related to pay and conditions. In spite of their crucial role in fuelling the war industries they were, until recently, some of the worst paid workers, coming 81st in the national league table of average industrial earnings. Today, after long battles with the colliery owners and repeated government interventions, the miner is among the best paid. After the miners, workers in the engineering industry were the most strike-prone in 1944, with disputes often arising over pay scales for women performing skilled or semi-skilled jobs once reserved for men.

Nazi rockets bring new terror to London

A victim of a V1 attack on Clapham, London, is pulled from the rubble.

London, 10 November
A terrifying new weapon is being aimed at the capital and south-eastern England. Josef Goebbels, the Nazi propaganda chief, gleefully proclaims it to be Germany's second *Vergeltungswaffe*, or reprisal weapon. The V2 is a 12-tonne rocket with a speed of 3,600mph, a range of 200 miles (320 km) and a one-tonne bomb. It arrives without warning and creates widespread devastation.

The first two came down two months ago, on Friday, 8 September, at Chiswick and Epping, and thereafter began to arrive at the rate of four to six a day. But the news was suppressed; in a bid to mislead the Germans it was put about that the mysterious explosions were caused by leaks of domestic gas.

Only today has Churchill admitted to MPs that almost a hundred V2s have come down in built-up areas, after having been fired from launchers in the Netherlands. "The damage and casualties have not so far been heavy," Churchill said.

His words were not entirely reassuring. Like the V1 flying bomb, or "doodlebug" as Londoners dubbed it, the V2 is a weapon of random destruction. The first V1s arrived last June; between then and mid-September 6,725 were spotted over Britain, and 3,500 were destroyed by fighter planes or anti-aircraft guns. The death toll was a relatively low 5,475, but in London some 25,000 houses were destroyed, leading to a new wave of evacuation for the capital's children that was greater than that in the early years of the war. The V1 menace finally ended when Allied forces progressively captured the launch sites across the Channel.

Ardennes breakout surprises the Allies

Belgium, 22 December
The Allied forces on the lightly defended Ardennes front in Belgium were sent scattering in panic and confusion last week when the Germans mounted a surprise attack with two Panzer and four infantry divisions – 250,000 men and 950 tanks against 83,000 Americans with 420 tanks.

The Germans punched a huge bulge in the US lines at Bastogne and then, lunging towards the coast at Antwerp, threatened to cut off Field Marshal Montgomery's 21st Army Group from General Bradley's 12th US Army Group. To Bradley's chagrin, his forces trapped north of the bulge have been placed under Montgomery.

Though the German forces' initial thrust was devastatingly successful, it is doubtful whether they can keep up the momentum. They lack reinforcements, are hampered by fuel shortages, and the sleet and low cloud which protected them from Allied planes are clearing.

Winter war in the Ardennes.

General George S Patton with the US Third Army, which has been engaged on the Saar front, has now swung north and is racing for Bastogne with his Sherman tanks. He reckons he can lift the siege by Christmas day. Inside the town, General Anthony C McAuliffe received a message from the Germans inviting him to surrender. He took the paper and scrawled on it: "NUTS" (→9/1/45).

A prison camp at East Ham in London provides a temporary home for Germans captured on the western front.

1945

Belgium, 9 January. The German counter-offensive in the Ardennes is defeated (→ 2/1945).

Crimea, 11 February. Winston Churchill, Franklin Roosevelt and Joseph Stalin meet at Yalta to redraw the map of post-war Europe as the Red Army advances into Germany.

Germany, February. Over 50,000 people are thought to have died in RAF raids which devastated Dresden this month (→ 24/3).

Germany, 24 March. Allied troops cross the Rhine in large numbers (→ 17/4).

Britain, 26 March. David Lloyd George, prime minister in the First World War, dies at the age of 82.

Germany, 17 April. British troops are shocked the by piles of corpses and emaciated survivors at the Belsen concentration camp (→ 30).

San Francisco, 25 April. Delegates from 46 countries meet to plan a new "United Nations" organization.

Berlin, 30 April. Adolf Hitler commits suicide (→ 7/5).

Dublin, 2 May. Eamon de Valera calls on the German envoy to condole officially on Hitler's death (→ 16).

Westminster, 23 May. The wartime coalition government resigns; a general election will take place on 5 July (→ 26/7).

Eire, 16 June. Sean Kelly is elected president (→ 6/7/46).

Denmark, 26 June. William Joyce, known for his "Lord Haw-Haw" propaganda broadcasts, is arrested and faces trial for treason.

Britain, 26 July. Labour wins a landslide victory in the general election; the result was delayed to count votes of servicemen overseas (→ 21/8).

Singapore, 12 September. Japanese forces in south-east Asia formally surrender to Lord Louis Mountbatten, the supreme Allied commander south-east Asia.

Westminster, 19 September. It is announced that India will have home rule (→ 16/5/46).

Britain, 5 November. A dock strike ends after seven weeks.

USA, 27 December. Britain is among the signatories to agreements setting up an International Monetary Fund and World Bank.

Jubilant Britons are victors in Europe

London, 8 May
After waiting all yesterday for the announcement of victory, the British people heard at 7.40 last night that today is VE (Victory in Europe) day. Dense crowds waited in the streets around Whitehall and Buckingham Palace for the prime minister's 3pm broadcast that "the German war is at an end". Hostilities would end at midnight. Sirens and hooters sounded all over the country, while bonfires were built and fancy-dress parades for children were improvised. Churches and pubs were filled to the doors. There were flags everywhere, and the government announced that bunting could be bought without coupons.

In London Churchill's car was lost in a sea of people on the way to the House of Commons. Later he appeared on a ministry balcony above Whitehall for an impromptu speech. "This is *your* victory," he told the crowds, "God bless you all!" Beside him Labour's Ernest Bevin led the crowd's singing of *For He's a Jolly Good Fellow.*

On the palace balcony King George VI and Queen Elizabeth appeared with the princesses, Elizabeth and Margaret, to a rapturous crowd. There were eight balcony appearances – some of which Churchill joined – and at nightfall the king allowed his daughters to join the throng.

The euphoria of victory: civilians and service personnel celebrate VE day.

At night the palace, Big Ben and the Houses of Parliament were floodlit, and searchlights illuminated the sky. Like everywhere else in Britain, London had a party mood. The streets were full of dancing and singing, and chains of people doing the "Hokey-Cokey" or "Knees Up, Mother Brown" tailed behind anyone with a musical instrument. At midnight, when Big Ben sounded the hour of the official ceasefire, a roar went up, fireworks exploded, and Thames tugs did the V-sign on their sirens. All across Britain bonfires blazed, bells pealed and people embraced complete strangers in a very unBritish manner (→ 9).

Twin advances on Berlin reveals horrors of Nazi 'death camps'

Rheims, France, 7 May
The final surrender of all forces under German command was signed here at 2.40am by General Jodl before General Bedell Smith of Eisenhower's Allied command. The surrender covers not only the western front, which has commanded most attention in Britain, but also the eastern front where the Soviet forces powered through Poland and into Germany in January.

It was the Red Army which first discovered the true bestial horror of Hitler's war when it liberated a Nazi "death camp" for Jews at Auschwitz. Allied leaders had known from codebreaking that the Nazis were persecuting Jews on a massive scale, with millions apparently murdered. But the reality seen at Auschwitz, and again last month at Belsen when it was liberated by British troops, shocked even the most hardened of soldiers.

The final crunch that destroyed the Third Reich began on 24 March when Montgomery's armies crossed the Rhine while the Red Army, commanded by Marshal Zhukov, crossed the Oder, poised to attack Berlin. Soviet forces were first to reach Hitler's capital, which had been subjected to sustained attack by Allied bombers. Other German cities were also hit, including Dresden, where a controversial raid and the resulting firestorm are believed to have killed over 50,000 people.

Hitler retreated to his chancellery bunker on 16 April. He committed suicide with his wife Eva Braun, formerly his mistress, on 30 April, two days after Mussolini was shot by Italian partisans (→ 8). ▷

British troops recapture city of Rangoon

Troops of the 14th Army negotiate a river as they advance in Burma.

Rangoon, Burma, 3 May
Men of the British 14th Army today marched into Burma's capital, Rangoon – in a reminder to their fellow countrymen that, while the war may be over in Europe, it continues against Japan. The recapture of Rangoon – three years after it fell – ends General William Slim's campaign to liberate Burma, which began in February. Mandalay fell in March, and the advance has continued at lightning pace.

Elsewhere in the war against Japan the US is stepping up the offensive which it began last October with the first landing in the Philippines by an invasion force of 250,000. The Japanese counterattack led to a three-day battle with the US Third and Seventh Fleets in and around the islands. It ended in a knock-out victory in which the Japanese lost 28 ships – including two battleships and all four remaining aircraft carriers.

In February Manila was surrounded, but 20,000 Japanese fell in its fanatical defence. Landings on Mindanao in March and Okinawa in April were accompanied by huge firebomb raids on Tokyo, Osaka and Kobe, now within range of the US's B29 Superfortresses. Japan is critically short of oil, yet there is no sign of surrender (→ 14/8).

Atom bomb ends war

Tokyo, 14 August
Emperor Hirohito today ordered all Japanese commanders to surrender their arms after two atomic bombs – the most powerful bombs the world has ever known – were dropped on Japanese cities. On 6 August Hiroshima was totally destroyed by an atomic bomb dropped by a B29 Superfortress of the US Air Force, and three days later Nagasaki was obliterated. To compound Japan's agony, the Soviet Union declared war on 9 August and attacked.

Harry Truman, who succeeded Franklin Roosevelt as US president in April, threatened other Japanese with "a rain of ruin from the air, the like of which has never been seen on this earth". The bomb, whose explosion is powered by a chain of nuclear fission in atoms of uranium 235, has the force of more than 20,000 tons of TNT. Japan claims that more than 70,000 people perished immediately, many of whom were burnt to cinders where they stood. Both cities were covered by a giant mushroom cloud of radioactive dust.

The bomb was developed by British and American scientists working in secrecy at Los Alamos, New Mexico under the codename "Manhattan Project". Research work was transferred there from Britain after the US entered the war (→ 15).

VJ Day: six years of war really are over

Londoners celebrate in Piccadilly.

London, 15 August
The surrender of Japan was announced by Clement Attlee, the new prime minister [*see opposite page*], on the wireless at midnight, with a two-day holiday to celebrate VJ day. King George VI and Queen Elizabeth, going to parliament in an open carriage, were soaked by rain. Later they made repeated appearances on the palace balcony. The crowds, bonfires, street parties and flag-decked displays of rejoicing were the equal of VE day in May, but with added thankfulness that the British, who have been fighting for six years less two weeks, have no more enemies to fight (→ 12/9).

De Valera defends Eire's war record

Dublin, 16 May
Eamon de Valera, the Irish prime minister, has given a calm and dispassionate reply to the angry attack on Eire's neutrality launched by Winston Churchill in his victory broadcast. De Valera gave credit to Churchill for successfully resisting the temptation to violate Irish neutrality, thereby advancing the cause of international morality. But he stressed that Eire's neutral stance resulted from its being a small nation which had stood alone for several hundred years against massacres and aggression (→ 16/6).

Channel Islands return to British forces after German occupation

British troops (and a policeman) return to cheers on liberated Jersey.

St Helier, Jersey, 9 May
A German soldier climbed a crane in Jersey harbour to fly a Union Jack in place of the *swastika* as the German occupation of the only British home soil to be captured during the war came to an end. The Channel Islands, which were surrendered without a shot being fired, were host to 10,000 German troops whose commander, Vice-Admiral Huffmeier, threatened to fight on. His men took no notice of his order to give only the Nazi salute to British officers. In recent weeks the islands have come close to starvation. People have been stewing rabbit skins and cabbage.

Churchill loses to a Labour landslide

Attlee is confronted by economic crisis

London, 21 August
Clement Attlee's Labour government had its rejoicings over the party's sweeping election victory last month cut short today by a body blow from the new American president, Harry S Truman. Britain faces its gravest economic crisis because, without warning, the president has put an end to the US Lend-Lease agreement with Britain, under which Britain has been receiving food imports from the US without down payment in cash.

As a result Britain now faces austerity even fiercer than that of wartime, with food, tobacco and petrol imports reduced, and British products largely reserved for export to pay for our imports. Rationing will be prolonged indefinitely; Britain's reserves are all but exhausted.

Labour won a landslide victory in last month's poll with 393 seats to 213 for the Tories, 12 Liberals and 22 Independents. The result was a surprise to all but the armed forces, who voted overwhelmingly for Labour. Their regard for Winston Churchill as a war leader was outweighed by the desire for social changes in peace. The wartime coalition government had broken up on 23 May, and in an election broadcast on 4 June Churchill turned on Labour leaders who had supported him all through the war, and declared that "no socialist system can be established without a political police ... some form of Gestapo". This did more harm to the Conservatives than to Labour. People thought it ridiculous to accuse men like Attlee and Ernest Bevin, the wartime labour minister, of being no better than the Nazis.

Labour's programme for a "welfare state", with a free national health service, and for state ownership of industries such as coal and the railways reflects the discussions of post-war aims since the Beveridge Report of 1942 on how to achieve social security and a later report on full employment.

However, Labour politicians are faced with the fact that the war has bankrupted Britain. The economist J M Keynes, who is advising the treasury, calls it "a financial Dunkirk" – £4,000 million of our foreign investments have gone, exports are below half the pre-war level, civilian industries and shipping are gravely run down, and 700,000 houses in London alone need bomb damage repaired (→ 12/9).

Clement Attlee, the new prime minister after five years as number two.

Britain counts human, and economic, cost of its 'finest hour'

Singapore, 12 September
With the final surrender of Japanese forces in south-east Asia today, an estimate of war casualties can be given. Britain lost 420,000 members of the armed forces killed, compared with the US figure of 292,000 and the USSR's 13 million. Enemy dead are put at 3,500,000 for Germany and 2,600,000 for Japan. British civilian casualties in air raids were around 60,000 killed and 86,000 badly injured.

This, then, is the price of victory. Winston Churchill called the time when Britain stood alone its "finest hour". But now the US and the Soviet Union have emerged as the "superpowers", with Britain economically crippled – another price of victory (→ 12/1946).

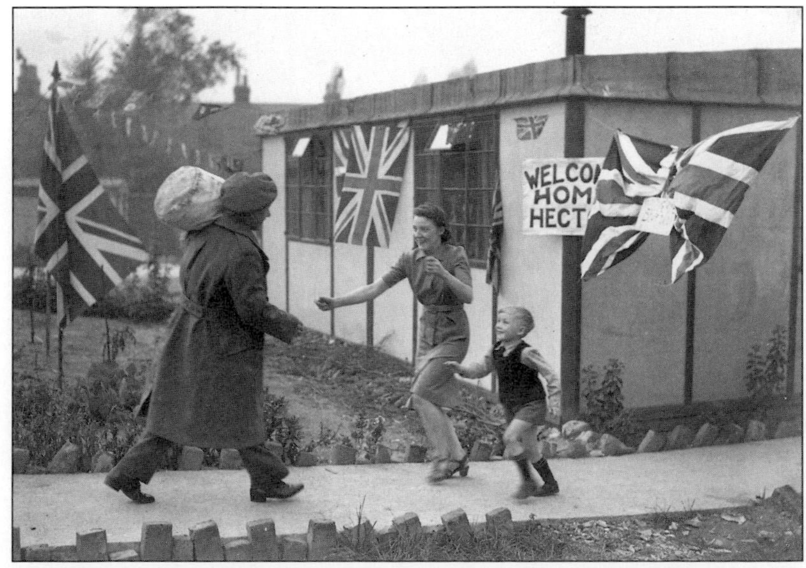

One of the lucky ones: a joyful reunion for one soldier and his family.

Radio and music offer antidote to rigours of war

Britain, 31 December
The First World War is recalled as a time that inspired great poetry. "Where are the poets?" was a question much asked in the early stages of the war that ended this year. War poetry did emerge – through new names such as Keith Douglas (killed in action) and established figures such as Louis MacNeice – but there was no romanticism in this mechanized war of conscripts.

Yet the arts and entertainment played important roles in the war as escapism or inspiration. In popular terms, radio was the dominant medium of entertainment – not just comedy such as *ITMA* but cerebral programmes such as the *Brains Trust* and J B Priestley's talks. *Music While You Work* also became a national institution.

The cinema was the focus of entertainment and propaganda. The crown film unit produced documentaries such as *Target for Tonight* and *Western Approaches*, which drew enormous audiences. Laurence Olivier and Noël Coward were among major stars who gave their work a patriotic tinge in *Henry V* and *In Which We Serve* respectively.

For millions the weekly trip to the cinema was an important antidote to rationing and other wartime deprivations. So, too, was the dance hall. The arrival of US servicemen brought with it a new kind of music – the big band sound epitomized by Glenn Miller. But the most popular singer of the war was Britain's own Vera Lynn, whose songs, such as *The White Cliffs of Dover*, established her as the "forces' sweetheart".

More serious music also prospered, with record audiences for the Prom concerts and Dame Myra Hess's lunchtime recitals at the National Gallery. In the world of visual art Henry Moore painted people sheltering in the tube; he was one of over a hundred artists commissioned as official war painters.

1946

Middlesex, 1 January. Test flights begin at Heathrow, near Hounslow, which is to be a major new civilian airport (→ 4/7/48).

Far East, 27 January. More than 2,000 airmen strike in protest at the slow pace of demobilization.

Westminster, 7 February. Food rations are to be cut in response to world shortages (→ 8/3).

London, 1 March. The Bank of England is nationalized.

USA, 5 March. In a speech at Fulton, Missouri, Winston Churchill warns of the "iron curtain" of communism falling across Europe (→ 19/9).

London, 8 March. Bananas are available at Covent Garden for the first time since the war (→ 25/8).

Westminster, 28 March. Plans are announced for free school milk and dinners.

Westminster, 20 May. Student grants are to be introduced.

Dublin, 6 July. Clann na Poblachta, a republican party with a left-wing social policy, is formed with Sean MacBride as its leader (→ 13/8).

Jerusalem, 22 July. Jewish terrorists blow up the British Army HQ in the King David Hotel, killing 42 with 52 people missing and 53 injured.

Calcutta, 19 August. Riots between Moslems and Hindus over British plans for Indian independence cause the deaths of thousands (→ 20/2/47).

Britain, 25 August. A "black market" in chocolate, nylons and perfumes is flourishing (→ 27/12).

Zurich, 19 September. Winston Churchill calls for a "United States of Europe".

London, 29 September. BBC Radio launches its "Third Programme".

Southampton, 16 October. The *Queen Elizabeth* makes her first commercial voyage after service as a troopship.

Westminster, 28 November. The House of Lords is told that there is a "tidal wave" of divorce sweeping Britain (→ 27/3/47).

Westminster, 18 December. MPs vote to approve the nationalization of the railways, road haulage and the ports; plans were also announced this year for nationalizing the iron and steel industry (→ 1/1/47).

'New towns' offer hope for war homeless

"New towns" and estates are needed to house workers and boost industry.

Westminster, December

Up to 20 "new towns" are being planned as part of the Labour government's programme to provide more housing and to revitalize industry. The New Towns Act passed this year authorizes development corporations to be formed which will create communities supposedly self-sufficient in terms of houses, jobs and public services.

Several new towns are expected to be built in south-east England to relieve pressure upon London – Stevenage, Basildon and Harlow are among possible sites. But others are intended primarily to tempt new industries to areas threatened by economic decline. Aycliffe in Darlington is likely to be the centre of one such new town with developments also planned for south Wales and central Scotland.

However it is unlikely that the first new residents will move into any of the planned developments before 1948 or 1949. In the meantime the government and local authorities face more immediate problems of housing people in cities scarred by bomb damage from the war. Hull, for instance, is estimated to need 30,000 new houses. For many, home will be one of the temporary pre-fabricated houses (known as "prefabs") now being erected in most of Britain's bomb-damaged cities (→ 18/12).

UN refuses to give membership to Eire

Ireland, 13 August

Eire has been refused admission to the United Nations Organization because of opposition from the Soviet Union. This further emphasizes the country's isolation from world affairs. The war years, known in neutral Eire as the "Emergency", have resulted in agricultural and economic crises, strikes, inflation and rising emigration. Given the state's small and ageing population, there are growing fears that the situation can only get worse.

Dissatisfaction with the Fianna Fáil government is widespread and has resulted in a proliferation of small political parties such as Clann na Talmhan, the farmers' party, which is calling for a new system of allocating land (→ 4/2/48).

Boost for the arts

London, August

The wartime funding of the arts by government will continue under the Arts Council of Great Britain, which is to be set up with a budget of £230,000. The council is the brainchild of the economist, the late Lord Keynes, who campaigned for it. Its twin objectives are to increase knowledge of the arts and to make them more accessible on the principle of "the best for the most".

'GI brides' leave Britain to begin a new life in the United States

An estimated 50,000 British GI brides were shipped out to the USA.

New York, 10 February

The first "GI brides" arrived here today to begin their new lives in the United States. As many as 50,000 British women are believed to have become engaged or married to American servicemen who were stationed in Britain during the war. "Overpaid, over-sexed and over here" was the complaint of British males. The first group of GI brides assembled at a special transit camp in Hampshire last month. There were 344 women – the youngest only 16 years old – and their 116 children. Mothers slept three to a room at the camp, with their babies beside them, before sailing in the *Queen Mary*. It is expected to take until July to transport all the women and children.

Britain's economic crisis gets worse

Housewives queue for food and coal

Britain, 27 December
Twelve cotton mills closed today and a four-day working week was announced for many factories in the English Midlands as a fuel shortage intensified. Lack of coal is forcing manufacturers to close production lines already hit hard by lack of raw materials. With queues for coal and many basic foodstuffs still rationed, it has been a bleak Christmas with little prospect of economic improvement.

A world food shortage has meant a return to wartime rations and, in some cases, tougher restrictions than were imposed during the war. In February the government announced that butter, margarine and cooking fat rations were to be reduced from eight to seven ounces per person per week. Then, in May, bread was rationed for the first time. The controls, which led to a booming black market in food and other rationed goods, were attacked by the Tory opposition leader Winston Churchill as "socialist incapacity". Labour counters by pointing to global shortages, factories and shipping destroyed by war, compounded by a lack of foreign currency (→22/1/47).

Petrol can be tested for a trace chemical absent from illegal supplies.

Bread was never rationed during the war, but now there are queues.

Cinemas boom with Britons rivalling Americans as stars

Britain, December
Cinema-going expanded hugely in the war to an average of 30 million admissions a week and the habit has stuck: a third of the population is now goes once a week, even though cinemas still have a run-down wartime look and their neon lights are banned to save fuel.

British films continue to rival American in popularity. A poll of cinemagoers names as many British stars as American in the top ten: James Mason and Stewart Granger head the actors, Margaret Lockwood the actresses, with Anna Neagle, Vivien Leigh and Patricia Roc high on the list. Hitchcock, Wilcox, Asquith, Korda and Lean head the directors. Last year's hits, *The Way to the Stars* and *Brief Encounter* are now being equalled by *A Matter of Life and Death* and *Great Expectations*(→11/4/47).

Bolton football tragedy: 33 die as barriers collapse at cup-tie

Police control the crowds while ambulancemen take away one of the victims.

Bolton, 9 March
Thirty-three football fans were killed and 500 others were badly hurt today when steel barriers collapsed at the Bolton Wanderers' ground, Burden Park, after thousands of supporters broke down fencing to get into a packed enclosure to watch the FA cup-tie with Stoke City. The home secretary, Chuter Ede, is expected to order an enquiry.

Police, who closed entrance gates nearly an hour before the trouble, were overwhelmed by the surging crowd who broke down perimeter fencing to get in. Several fans were crushed to death but further casualties were avoided when officers let fans escape by pulling down fencing around the pitch.

Full independence promised to India

London, 16 May
A plan for a united and independent India was unveiled today by Clement Attlee, the prime minister. The announcement came while Sir Stafford Cripps was in India at the head of a British mission to seek a deal that will contain the bitter divisions between the Hindu Congress and the Moslem League.

In 1935 a Government of India Bill, fiercely opposed by the Tories, virtually gave self-government to the provinces and proposed a new federal assembly at the centre, but the war has made full independence inevitable. The surrender of Singapore in February 1942 shattered British authority in India beyond repair. Although the Indian army stayed loyal, the leading nationalists, Nehru and Gandhi, were among those imprisoned for mounting a hugely popular "Quit India" campaign of civil disobedience.

If the threat of more unrest were not enough, the British have been under growing American pressure to implement the ideal of self-determination (→19/8).

1947

Britain, 8 January. Troops are called in to move supplies as transport strikes bite.

Britain, 13 January. Top radio shows are *Radio Forfeits*, *Dick Barton* and *Woman's Hour*.

Britain, 22 January. Meat rations are reduced – again (→28).

Britain, 28 January. Power is cut as freezing temperatures bring much of the country to a standstill (→26/2).

London, 20 February. Lord Louis Mountbatten is named to be the last viceroy of India (→23/5).

Eire, February. Prolonged cold weather and fuel shortages bring industry to a virtual standstill.

Britain, March. Many towns are hit by floods when the big freeze finally ends; farming casualties include an estimated two million sheep and 500,000 acres of wheat (→7/1947).

Westminster, 27 March. Public money for the Marriage Guidance Council is promised in a bid to stem the growing number of divorces (→12/1947).

Britain, 11 April. James Mason and Margaret Lockwood are voted top British film stars (→25/3/49).

Eire, 21 April. Shannon airport becomes a customs-free zone.

Westminster, 23 May. The cabinet agrees to partition India into two states – one Hindu, one Moslem (→15/8).

USA, 5 June. George Marshall, the US secretary of state, outlines an aid plan to help European nations recover from the ravages of war.

Britain, 15 August. The country's first atomic reactor starts up at Harwell.

Westminster, 27 August. A package of "austerity cuts" is announced by the government to tackle the economic crisis with reduced rations and new currency controls (→30/9).

New York, 26 September. Britain tells the UN that it intends to leave Palestine.

Britain, 30 September. Women are urged by the government to avoid the trend to longer skirts in order to save cloth (→9/9/48).

Westminster, 13 November. Hugh Dalton, the chancellor of the exchequer, resigns after leaking details of budget tax proposals to a journalist.

Britons struggle against big freeze

Gangs of workers clearing snow from London's Smithfield meat market.

Dinner by candlelight becomes compulsory as shortages continue to bite.

Belts tightened as food crisis deepens

Britain, 26 February

Coal rationing is one of the options being considered by the government today as the "big freeze" goes into its fifth week. The coldest winter since 1880-81 has exacerbated fuel shortages which have already brought short-time working to many factories and steel mills. Lack of coal has also curbed supplies of electricity and gas, making over four million workers idle through power cuts. Yet coal is now piling up at the pits, unable to be moved along roads and rail lines blocked by snow.

Many shivering domestic consumers of coal have been without heat or light during the daytime for much of February. Yet some are even worse off. In Lincolnshire, Norfolk and Yorkshire the RAF is dropping food supplies for stranded villagers as well as livestock. The towns of Buxton and Bridlington have been cut off. Snowdrifts as high as 20 feet have blocked roads – the Great North Road is impassable for 22 miles – and railways. Blizzards have stopped shipping in the Channel and kept fishing fleets in port, worsening food shortages.

Emergency regulations sought to keep industry working, while offices, shops and even pubs carry on by candlelight. Weather forecasters offer no sign of an end to the subzero temperatures (→3/1947).

School leaving age is raised to fifteen

Britain, September

The new school year now beginning will not be the final year for the current generation of 14-year-olds. The minimum age to leave school is now 15, as one of the reforms of the 1944 Butler Education Act is implemented. The Act envisages raising the school leaving age to 16 at some point in the future, but no date has been set. Until now, a 1918 Act had made 14 the minimum leaving age – and most 14-year-olds did leave then (→26/4/48).

Planning becomes the post-war vogue

Britain, July

An Economic Planning Council has been set up this month in a move to give more coherent direction to a British economy battered by fuel shortages last winter and a run on currency reserves this summer. Its creation reflects the government's faith in "planning" as a means to combat the difficulties of the postwar years. But there is also faith in planning as a positive tool to fashion a new role for the state.

The Town and Country Planning Act requires larger local authorities to prepare comprehensive plans for their areas with powers of compulsory purchase. Local authorities will have powers to preserve historic buildings, and the government plans to levy a development charge on any increase in land values by developing the land.

The legislation stems from Labour's view that the public sector must play a greater role in shaping the economy and society than was the case before the war. Another instance of this belief is this year's Agriculture Act, which guarantees minimum prices to farmers for their products (→27/8).

Labour nationalizes the coal industry

London, 1 January
Cabinet ministers gathered at the headquarters of the new National Coal Board today to celebrate the fulfilment of a Labour dream: nationalization of the coal industry. But the dream could hardly have been realized at a less opportune time. The industry is struggling to meet demand, with too few miners and antiquated machinery producing too little coal. Low output, as well as low productivity, has already caused some cotton mills to begin short-time working because of fuel shortages. But Emmanuel Shinwell, the minister of fuel, insists there is no crisis (→ 1/1/48).

Coal industry under new colours.

Britain closes door on Indian empire

New Delhi, 15 August
British rule in India ended here after 163 years on the stroke of midnight last night as two new dominions, Pakistan and India, were born. A conch shell was blown in the Constituent Assembly and, as the clock ticked away the seconds to full independence, its members cheered and then pledged themselves to serve India and her people.

Lord Mountbatten, the last viceroy, immediately became governor-general of the new dominion of India. He has been rewarded with an earldom for his part in managing Britain's withdrawal.

Bells ring out for Elizabeth and Philip

The marriage of Princess Elizabeth brightens an otherwise grey outlook.

London, 20 November
The grey realities of rationing were forgotten today when Princess Elizabeth married the Duke of Edinburgh in a glittering ceremony. The bridegroom, listed as Lieutenant Philip Mountbatten on the order of service, was made Prince Philip, Duke of Edinburgh, a little earlier. Huge crowds cheered the state coach as the princess, in an ivory dress embroidered with flowers of beads and pearls, was escorted by the Household Cavalry resplendent in scarlet tunics. After a simple service and a wedding breakfast the newlyweds left to begin their honeymoon in Hampshire (→ 14/11/48).

Edinburgh plays host to new arts festival

Edinburgh, 24 August
The first international arts festival in Britain was launched here today as a defiant gesture in the face of the prevailing austerity. Under the directorship of Rudolf Byng, the Scottish capital, decked with flags, is playing host to 800 artists from 20 countries performing music and drama. They include the Vienna Philharmonic Orchestra under conductor Bruno Walter and the Jean-Louis Barrault theatre company from Paris. Individual stars invited include Kathleen Ferrier, pianist Artur Schnabel, and the string virtuosi Josef Szigeti, William Primrose and Pierre Fournier.

Compton sweeps into cricket record books

Compton: also a top footballer.

London, 20 September
A record-breaking summer has ended today for Denis Compton, the Middlesex and England batsman. He has scored more runs (3,816) and more centuries (18) in a single season than any other cricketer in history. His teammate, Bill Edrich, scored 3,539 runs in a hot summer which the Middlesex pair made even more uncomfortable for bowlers. Compton's cavalier attacking style captivated the crowds as much as his run-scoring. He is also a professional footballer when England's cricket team is not on tour. He plays for Arsenal and won several wartime international caps.

Divorce and babies are on the increase

Britain, December
This has been a record-breaking year in family life. Divorces have hit a new peak of 60,000 cases this year – ten times the pre-war maximum. And the birth rate has produced a "baby boom" with 20.5 births per thousand people – up a fifth over the 1939 figure.

Hasty marriages contracted during the war are now being dissolved at a rate that has alarmed church leaders. The archbishop of Canterbury blamed reforms in the divorce law while the bishop of London singled out the immoral influence of Hollywood films. Government ministers have generally adopted a more constructive approach, increasing aid to bodies such as the Marriage Guidance Council in a bid to stem the flood of divorces. Marriage itself is not declining in popularity: three in four of all people who are divorced take the plunge again.

Tired of the drab wartime Utility clothing, women love Dior's New Look, but to achieve the outer hour-glass shape it needs, they sometimes require inside help.

1948

London, 27 January. Medical consultants threaten to boycott the national health service due to begin this year (→ 5/7).

India, 30 January. Mahatma Gandhi is assassinated.

Ireland, 4 February. De Valera loses an overall majority in the Irish general election (→ 18).

Westminster, 6 February. MPs vote to make the ATS and WAAF permanent; they will be known as the Women's Royal Army Corp and the Women's Royal Air Force.

Westminster, 16 February. The government warns Argentina not to challenge British rule in the Falkland Islands.

Westminster, 15 March. Communists and fascists are to be banned from civil service jobs vital to state security.

Brussels, 17 March. Britain joins France and the Benelux countries in forming a new defence pact.

Britain, 1 April. The electricity industry is nationalized (→ 1/5/49).

London, 26 April. A new General Certificate of Education examination is announced for England and Wales (→ 9/1948).

Britain, 13 May. Figures show the birth rate last year was the highest for 26 years.

Berlin, 30 June. The RAF joins an airlift of supplies to beat the Russian blockade of the former German capital (→ 12/5/49).

Middlesex, 4 July. Thirty-nine people die when two passenger aircraft collide near Northolt airport in Britain's worst aircraft disaster to date (→ 27/7/49).

Britain, 9 September. Footwear rationing ends (→ 15/3/49).

Westminster, 23 September. For the second session running, the House of Lords rejects the Parliament Bill curbing its powers.

Westminster, 4 November. Harold Wilson, the president of the board of trade, says many government controls over industry will be lifted.

London. 14 November. Prince Charles is born.

Dublin, 17 November. The Dáil gives a first reading to a bill under which Eire will leave the Commonwealth.

De Valera ousted after 16 years in office

Ireland, 18 February

John Costello today became head of a new coalition government, following the narrow defeat of Eamon de Valera after 16 years as Eire's prime minister.

The Fianna Fáil party faced the electorate burdened by rising emigration and a disastrous economic situation which they had done little to rectify. But de Valera's chief fear was the growing strength of the new party Clann na Poblachta. Led by Sean MacBride, a former chief of staff of the IRA, it offered an attractive blend of radical republicanism and social and economic reform, similar in fact to that offered by Fianna Fáil in 1932. De Valera appears to have taken fright at the threat posed to the ideological heartland of his own party, which lacked the energy and initiative and a vision of the future shown by MacBride.

Despite his handsome majority, de Valera decided to go to the country early in the hope of depriving Clann na Poblachta of the opportunity to improve its electoral chances in the current period of severe austerity. This error of judgement led to his defeat, although Fianna Fáil remains the largest party and Clann na Poblachta with ten seats is the junior partner in the coalition government with Fine Gael and Labour (→ 30/1/49).

Eamon de Valera badly miscalculates and loses the election to MacBride.

Troops called in to combat dock strike

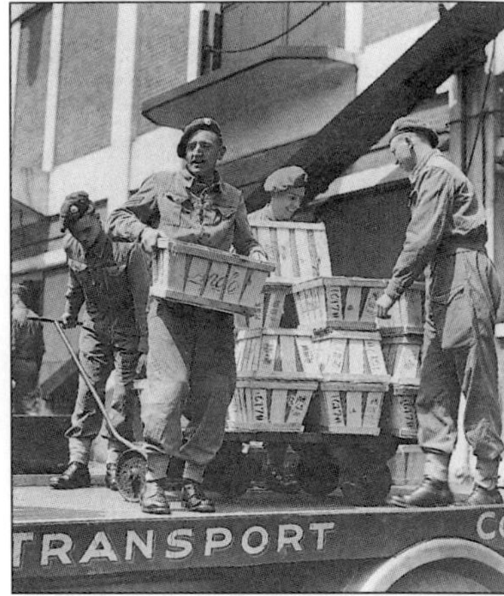

Troops unload food at the docks.

Britain, 28 June

Draconian action was taken last night to deal with the dock strike when King George signed an order-in-council giving the government emergency powers to bring in troops to unload ships.

In a broadcast just before the 9 o'clock news Clement Attlee, the prime minister, said: "We must see the people are fed." He went on to rebuke the strikers: "This strike is not against capitalists and employers. It is a strike against your mates."

About 230 ships are held up by the 19,000 unofficial strikers who have been disowned by their union. Last week the ration was reduced to 6d [2.5p] worth of fresh meat and 6d worth of canned meat.

State takes over control of railways

Britain, 1 January

The passengers may not notice much difference, but from today all Britain's railways are owned by the state. Mergers had reduced the 19th-century plethora of private companies to four regional groupings by the 1920s and two world wars have left the railways increasingly dependent upon state finance to keep going. The railways were a prime target for enemy bombing in the last war and need massive investment and modernization which ministers say are way beyond the capacity of private companies to provide (→ 1/4).

'Comprehensives' aim to beat the 11-plus

London, September

A new school year is beginning and so is a new type of school. The first pupils have started term in three "comprehensive" schools now established by Middlesex County Council on the outskirts of London at Hillingdon and Potter's Bar. Other local authorities, notably the London County Council, are planning similar schools.

Comprehensive schools aim to cater for all secondary age pupils, regardless of academic ability. Elsewhere in England and Wales – the Scots have a different education system – children take an exam in the final year at primary school which determines which secondary school they attend. A varying minority of the more academically able children who "pass the 11-plus" go to grammar schools with the remainder going to secondary modern or technical schools.

A spokesman for the Middlesex County Council says: "At 11 a child may not have an examination temperament, and may fail dismally. That failure may penalize him or her for a long time, not only in denying the child grammar school and university education but shattering his or her confidence."

Another educational innovation this year was the announcement of a new General Certificate of Education (GCE) exam for 16-year-olds.

Labour constructs the 'welfare state'

Britain, December
The centrepiece of the Labour government's programme – the "welfare state" – is now in place. This year has seen the introduction of the National Health Service [*see below*], a National Assistance Act and a National Insurance scheme. Although the latter builds on 40 years' worth of social security provision, the insurance system and the health service are distinguished by a crucial new hallmark, that of "universality". Previous schemes for unemployment or sickness insurance have hinged upon payments reflecting contributions or, if these were inadequate, a "means test" to determine assistance.

Contributions to the National Insurance scheme will still be made by employees, employers and the state, but direct taxation will be used to ensure that neither financial help in times of need nor medical care will depend upon contributions. The principle of universality means that the new services will be open to all without any variation.

National Insurance and health care are the most visible expressions of the welfare state principle that government take a greater role in social problems. This year's Children's Act on the duties of local authorities for homeless children is another manifestation, as are policies for housing, education and legal aid (→ 9/5/51).

National Health Service aims to offer free medical care to all

Britain, 5 July
The National Health Service came into operation today as the flagship of the Labour government's "welfare state". It promises free health care from the cradle to the grave with treatment offered according to medical need rather than ability to pay. Dental services are included in the scheme, as is the provision of free glasses. Medicines will be prescribed free of charge.

Although the National Health Service Act became law in the autumn of 1946, it has taken until today to realize the vision of a health service open to all without charge. Aneurin Bevan, the health minister, faced strong opposition from the British Medical Association over what the doctors perceived as constraints on their freedom. Although doctors will be refused permission to establish practices in wealthy areas which have more GPs per population than poorer areas, doctors can continue their private practices.

Hospitals have also been, in effect, nationalized with control to be exercised through a network of 14 regional hospital boards in England and Wales and management committees for the individual hospitals. A similar system is being introduced in Scotland.

The medical profession has been much exercized by questions of organization, but a more immediate problem could be finance. Until now medicines, dental care and appropriate spectacles have been luxuries for many families. Demand for these services, now that they are free, is expected to be high and, some fear, limitless (→ 12/1948).

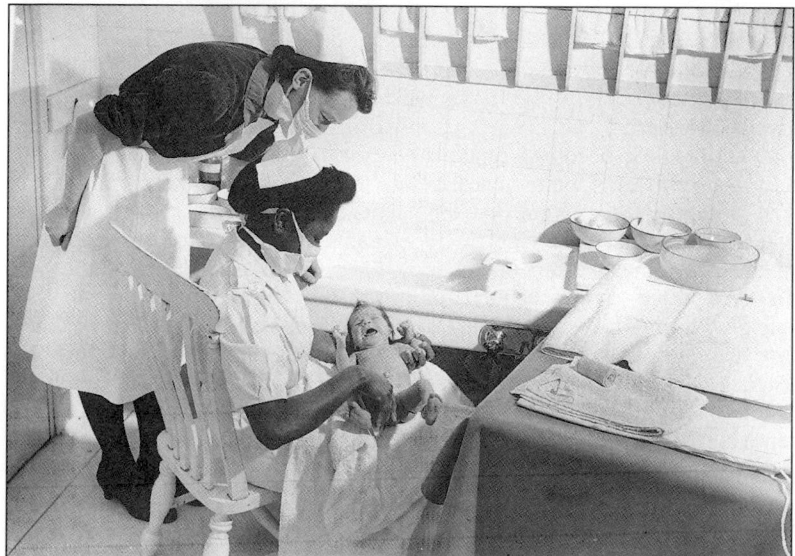

The new National Health Service offers care from cradle to grave.

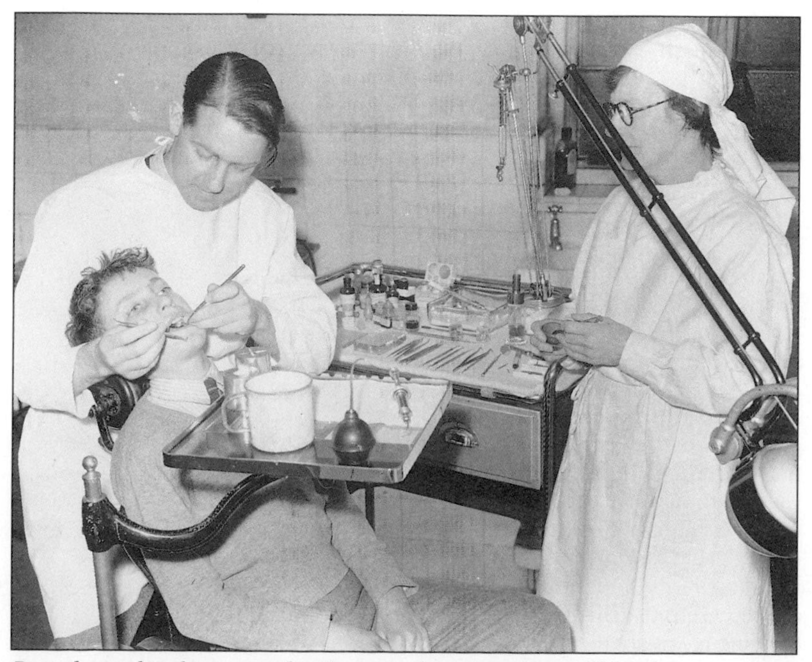

Dental care has been rare for the poor; from now on it will be free.

Britain stages the Olympics, but has few gold medallists

John Mark carries the flame.

Wembley, 12 August
They were called the "austerity Olympics". The first games since the flamboyantly Nazi Olympiad of 1936 in Berlin were held without ostentation – and without new stadiums. Henley, Cowes and Bisley were used for rowing, yachting and shooting with Wembley's stadium and Empire Pool hosting the athletics and swimming. Huge crowds filled Wembley, but they had no native gold-medallists to cheer. British golds were confined to rowing (two) and yachting.

Second vote taken from businessmen

Westminster, December
The principle of one man, one vote, (and one woman, one vote) has now been accepted for Westminster parliaments. The Representation of the People Act passed this year ends the double voting of businessmen and some university graduates. Previously businessmen could vote in the constituencies where they lived and in the constituencies where their business was located. Universities also lose their separate seats – to be elected by graduates with their second vote – as does the City of London. However, 17 additional constituencies are to be created under the Act to reflect population movements.

1949

Eire, 30 January. Collections are made at all Catholic churches for an "anti-partition" fund backed by all political parties (→ 8/2).

Dublin, 8 February. The government refuses to join the planned North Atlantic Treaty Organization (Nato) while Ireland is divided (→ 18/4).

Europe, 18 March. Britain is among eight countries which agree to form Nato next month.

Los Angeles, 25 March. *Hamlet* becomes the first British film to win the Oscar for the year's best movie; its director, Laurence Olivier, was also named best actor.

Britain, 24 April. Chocolate and sweets rationing ends (→ 14/7).

Britain, 1 May. The gas industry is nationalized (→ 24/2/50).

Europe, 5 May. The Council of Europe is formed with Britain and Eire among its members.

London, 9 May. Britain's first "launderette" opens for a six-month trial in Bayswater.

Westminster, 11 May. Britain formally recognizes the new Republic of Ireland (→ 2/6).

Berlin, 12 May. The USSR ends the blockade (→ 25/5/51).

Westminster, 2 June. The Ireland Act confers special status on the republic, whose citizens are not to be regarded as aliens (→ 6/6/50).

Ireland, 10 July. The last tramcar runs in Dublin.

Britain, 14 July. More rationing is announced in moves to deal with the dollar shortage (→ 26/5/50).

Britain, 4 September. The Bristol Brabazon, at 130 tons the largest airliner in the world, makes its maiden flight (→ 12/3/50).

London, 3 November. The BBC buys the Rank film studios at Shepherd's Bush to make television programmes (→ 31/12).

Westminster, 29 November. The Parliament Bill, curbing the delaying powers of the Lords, is rejected by peers, but it becomes law as MPs have passed it three times.

Britain. A Legal Aid Act passed this year helps people to obtain legal advice in and out of court.

Eire to become the Republic of Ireland

The new republic puts on a show of force after the announcement in Dublin.

Ireland, 18 April
Eire has formally become a republic and has left the Commonwealth. The prime minister, John A Costello, leader of the Fine Gael party in the coalition government, made an unexpected announcement of this plan during his visit to Canada last year, surprising his cabinet colleagues who were unaware of his intentions. With the inaugural Easter Monday parade today, the republic comes into being.

There are thought to have been several reasons for Costello's decision. He is known to have disliked the ambiguity of de Valera's External Relations Act of 1936, which left Ireland a republic in her own internal affairs while retaining the British king as a sleeping partner in external relations.

Perhaps more important, the new republic has stolen Fianna Fáil's thunder since its members have always considered themselves the only true republicans. By behaving in a manner so out of character with the performance of the party for more than a decade, Fine Gael may now be able to retrieve its fading image and appear to be a serious party concerned with the real business of politics and power.

Ireland's departure from the Commonwealth has been regretted by some, though it will probably make little difference. Britain will still treat Irish immigrants as Commonwealth citizens (→ 11/5).

Clothes rationing is not all the fashion

Britain, 15 March
Clothing rationing – imposed in 1941 – ended today. Clothing coupons can be consigned to the "appropriate salvage channel", Harold Wilson, the president of the board of trade, told the Commons.

The Utility scheme – in which ready-to-wear clothes are made under a cloth quota system – will continue. Price controls on clothing, however, will stay and the government has said it is ready to freeze prices if traders start to increase them.

The end of rationing will involve a direct saving of 10,000 workers, Mr Wilson said, as department stores made hurried overnight preparations for "celebratory sales" tomorrow (→ 24/4).

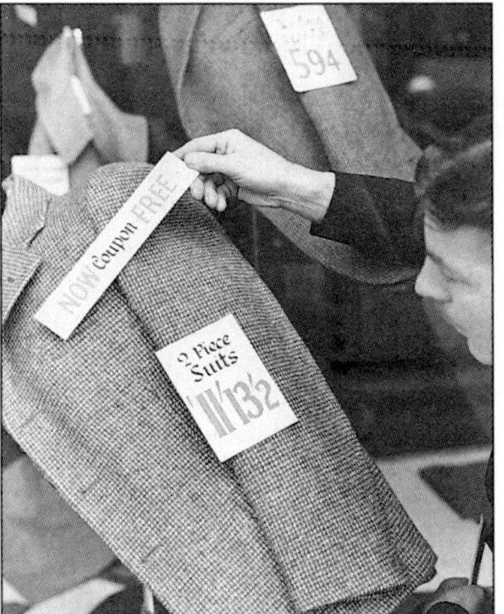

Clothes come off the ration at last.

Jitterbugging is the latest dance craze

Britain, December
The American GIs may have gone home, but their legacy lives on in the dance halls and popular music. It was US servicemen who brought the "swing" sound of big bands such as Glenn Miller and Tommy Dorsey to Britain during the war. Now young Britons remain in a US groove with the current craze for the "jitterbug". The more stately waltz and quickstep are not entirely out of fashion, but the jitterbug and "jiving" have grown dramatically in popularity among younger dancers. In most British towns only the cinema rivals the dance hall as a place for an evening out.

Jitterbugging and the New Look.

British warship in a dash for freedom

Hong Kong, 30 July
The British frigate *Amethyst* has docked here after a 140-mile [224km] dash down the Yangtse river to flee Mao Tse-tung's Communists. Caught up in the Chinese civil war between Mao and Chiang Kai-shek's Nationalists, the *Amethyst* was shelled by Communist batteries four months ago, with the loss of 43 crewmen. With fuel and rations running low, the commander, Lt-Cdr J S Kerans, had to break out. Safely home, he has signalled the Admiralty: "No damage or casualties. God Save the King."

The pound is devalued

London, 18 September
Sterling is to be devalued by 30 per cent, the treasury announced tonight. From tomorrow one pound will be worth $2.80 as against $4.03. City firms had expected a devaluation for several weeks, as Britain's trading position worsened during the summer. The dollar deficit has grown, and in the second quarter of this year alone Britain lost £160 million of gold. However, the size of the devaluation was greater than forecast and will increase the cost of living by around 5 per cent. Banks and the stock market will be closed tomorrow by a royal proclamation which is intended to avoid panic selling.

A frantic dealer signals the cut.

Comet jets into the history of aviation

Hertfordshire, 27 July
The world's first passenger jet airliner took to the skies today after years of secret development work. The de Havilland Comet made its maiden flight from the company's works at Hatfield. The tests had begun as ground handling operations, but on his third taxi down the runway Group Captain John Cunningham allowed the aircraft to take off. BOAC has ordered 16 of the Comets (→4/9).

Tories blast African project as 'Nuts'

Westminster, 21 November
Conservative MPs tonight accused the government of wasting millions of pounds of taxpayers' money on a scheme for ground nuts in East Africa. The scheme is promoted by the government's Overseas Food Corporation. The ground nuts are meant to yield vegetable oils, thereby helping the colonies and giving Britain cheap imports, but the scheme's Tory critics claim that it costs millions more than it yields.

The Lake District becomes a national park

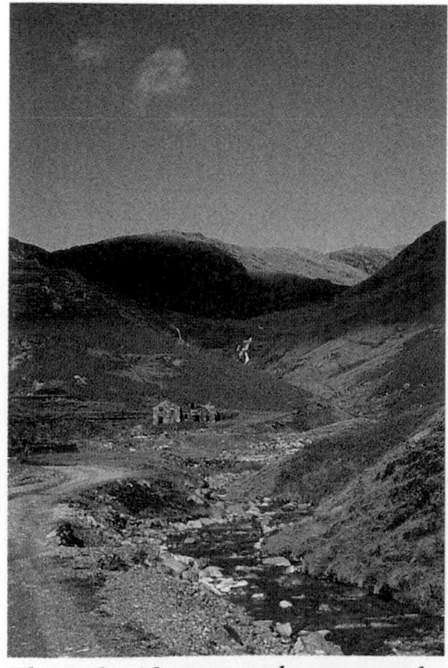

The Lakes' beauty: to be preserved.

Westminster, 1 April
Twelve national parks are proposed in legislation announced today in the National Parks and Access to the Countryside Bill. The parks would cover approximately 9 per cent of England and Wales – none are envisaged for Scotland or Northern Ireland. The objectives of the parks will be the potentially conflicting goals of preserving and enhancing natural beauty while also promoting public enjoyment.

It is not yet clear whether the parks will have their own planning authorities or be administered by local authorities. The relationship with farmers is also uncertain; agricultural grants to increase output could undermine the preservation of landscapes or wildlife.

British films win plaudits of Hollywood, but television poses longer-term threat

Britain, 31 December
The award of five "Oscars" to the film adaptation of William Shakespeare's famous tragedy *Hamlet* sets the seal on the new success of Britain's film industry. No British production has ever before won an Academy Award for best film, and Sir Laurence Olivier, who produced and directed it, also received the best actor award for the title role. Another British entry, *The Red Shoes*, made by Michael Powell and Emeric Pressburger, won three more awards.

Hollywood's accolade has come at a propitious time for the industry, which has recently been granted what it regards as an inadequate loan of £5 million of government money through the National Film Finance Corporation. The quota of films of British origin which the government lays down that cinemas must show was raised to 45 per cent this year.

Last year brought the director Carol Reed to prominence with *The Fallen Idol*. This year he and the writer he worked with on the earlier film, Graham Greene, followed it up with *The Third Man*, a brilliant extension of the thriller genre into high drama precisely set amid the squalor of war-battered Vienna. Two Americans, Orson Welles and Joseph Cotten, took the lead roles.

Meanwhile, under the guidance of Michael Balcon, Ealing Studios reached the heights of their own

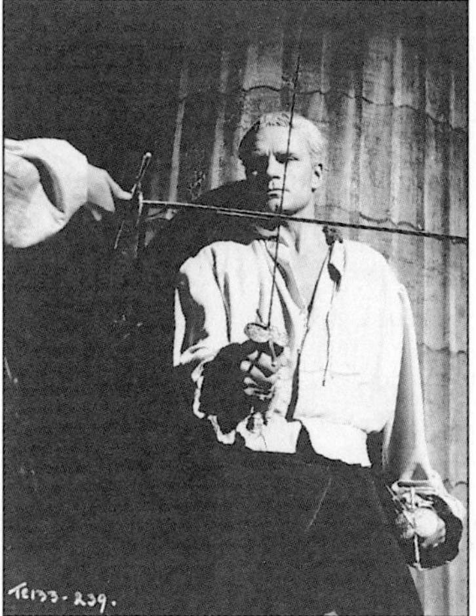

Olivier triumphs in the title role of his award-winning "Hamlet".

invention in a genre now called "Ealing comedy". This summer saw three hilarious scripts, T E B Clarke's *Passport to Pimlico*, Compton Mackenzie's *Whisky Galore!* and Robert Hamer's *Kind Hearts and Coronets*. All three provide a feast of character acting by such stars as Stanley Holloway and Alec Guinness.

But there is competition on the horizon. When the BBC's transmitters now being built are complete, television will reach 75 per cent of the population. Viewing hours and the availability of sporting events and films to TV are still limited, but this year the BBC bought Rank's Lime Grove film studios for making programmes (→27/8/50).

Barbara Murray and Stanley Holloway star in "Passport to Pimlico".

1950

London, 4 January. Britain asks the US for a stockpile of atomic weapons.

Thames estuary, 12 January. Sixty seamen are feared dead after their submarine, HMS *Truculent*, was in collision with a Swedish merchant ship.

Ireland, 19 January. The first peat-fired power station begins operations at Portarlington, Co Leix.

Britain, 8 March. The last Lancaster bomber leaves RAF service.

Britain, 21 March. A survey shows that only 46 per cent of households have a bathroom.

Britain, 26 May. Petrol rationing ends (→27/1/51).

Britain, May. Twenty people fly to Corsica for the first "package holiday"; the two-week holiday organized by Horizon costs £32 10s.

Dublin, 6 June. The Labour Party and National Labour Party are to unite (→9/7).

South-east Asia, 28 June. Royal Navy ships are to join US forces in a United Nations operation against the invasion of South Korea three days ago by Communist North Korea (→26/7).

Ireland, 9 July. The Dublin and Belfast governments announce agreement on control of Lough Foyle fisheries in a rare instance of inter-governmental cooperation (→30/5/51).

Westminster, 26 July. British troops are to fight in Korea under UN orders (→8/12).

London, 31 July. The first self-service grocery store is opened by J Sainsbury.

France, 27 August. The BBC transmits television pictures from overseas for the first time with a two-hour programme from Calais (→31/12/51).

Derbyshire, 28 September. Eighty miners are killed in a colliery fire at Creswell.

Westminster, 19 October. Hugh Gaitskell takes over as chancellor from Sir Stafford Cripps, retiring on health grounds.

London, 26 October. King George VI opens the restored House of Commons, destroyed in a bomb raid in 1941.

Cleveland, 9 November. ICI is to build a factory at Redcar to manufacture a new fabric, "Terylene".

Labour clings to power

Labour prime minister Clement Attlee addresses an election meeting.

Westminster, 24 February
Labour has clung to power in the general election yesterday, but only just. The final result emerged after hours of suspense as votes were counted in one of the closest contests for 100 years. Clement Attlee has seen his government's overall majority fall to just five – despite increasing Labour's total vote to its highest-ever figure of 13,266,592. The results are 315 Labour, 298 Conservatives. nine Liberals and three MPs from other parties.

There was an 84 per cent turnout for the poll – higher than ever before. It was a day of disaster for the Liberal Party, with 319 out of their 475 candidates losing their deposit, in what was overwhelmingly a two-horse race for power. Winston Churchill, the Conservative leader, believes that another election cannot be long delayed. "Parliament will be in an unstable condition now," he said today.

Attlee has made no public comment, but he seems likely to shelve some of the more controversial elements of the Labour programme, such as the nationalization of the cement, sugar, water and shipping industries. However, Labour is determined to complete the nationalization of iron and steel begun in the last parliament (→26/10/51).

Eighty die in worst ever civil air crash

South Wales, 12 March
A Tudor V airliner bringing rugby fans home from the Wales/Ireland international has crashed just outside Cardiff. Eighty of the 83 passengers and crew are feared dead, the highest ever death toll for a civil aircraft disaster. Sixty ambulances took the bodies to the RAF station of St Athan. No one can as yet explain the crash: the weather was clear when the Tudor V took off, only to stall and nosedive into a field shortly afterwards. It had flown without trouble, on the Berlin airlift (→2/5/52).

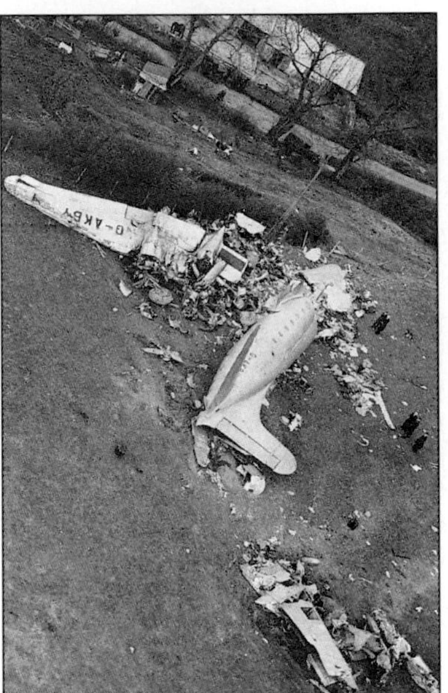

The wreck of the Tudor airliner.

Fuchs, atomic scientist, jailed for spying

Britain, 3 February
A top nuclear scientist, Dr Klaus Fuchs, was today charged with giving Russian agents secret information about how to build atomic bombs. If convicted he faces up to 14 years in prison.

Fuchs, aged 38, a German-born Communist, has been given full access to British and American research bases for seven years. It was only shortly before his arrest that the FBI of America discovered his betrayal and tipped off MI5.

The prosecution will allege that Fuchs is guilty of the "grossest treachery" and that by his betrayal he has saved the Russians years of research.

The accused scientist Klaus Fuchs.

English football is humiliated by USA

Brazil, 28 June
The nation that gave football to the world today suffered its greatest sporting embarrassment: the English football team lost 1-0 to the United States. Ironically, the US is almost the only significant country where football has not become the most popular sport. But its team of multi-national immigrants was still able to defeat the cream of English football – including Tom Finney and Billy Wright – at Belo Horizonte, Brazil, to send England crashing ignominiously out of the first World Cup competition it has deigned to enter.

Playwright George Bernard Shaw dies

Ireland, 2 November
The playwright and Nobel prize-winner George Bernard Shaw has died at the age of 94. Born in Dublin in 1856, he began his literary career by ghosting musical criticism and writing five unsuccessful novels. He scored his first popular success with his play *John Bull's Other Island*, which was performed in London in 1904. He went on to write over 50 plays, many of which were controversial and many of which are still regularly performed, the best known being *Pygmalion*, *Man and Superman*, *Mrs Warren's Profession*, *The Devil's Disciple*, and *Heartbreak House*.

In his plays Shaw often dealt with contemporary social and moral problems. An active member of the Fabian Society, he supported women's rights, the abolition of private property and campaigned for a radical change in the voting system and the reform of the English alphabet. His unorthodox views, his humour and his love of paradox have become an institution and he was still writing plays up to the time of his death.

He was awarded the Nobel prize for literature in 1925.

George Bernard Shaw: died today.

Traffic jams are signs of motoring boom

Britain, 30 May
Record traffic jams on this Whit bank holiday were reported tonight by the motoring organizations. It is the first bank holiday since petrol rationing ended and motor manufacturers are predicting that there will now be a boom in car sales.

The number of private cars on the roads has been growing steadily since the war. There were just over two million cars and vans registered in 1948 – little more than there had been ten years earlier – but this year's equivalent total will be between 2.25 and 2.5 million.

Petrol had been rationed for ten years and motorists celebrated its end by tearing up their coupons. But prices are expected to rise.

The post-war boom has ended petrol rationing, but started traffic jams.

Attlee warns Truman against the use of the atomic bomb in the Korean conflict

British troops march to the front line in Korea to relieve their US allies.

Washington, 8 December
Clement Attlee has won assurances from the United States that there is no intention to use the atomic bomb in the war in Korea. The British prime minister flew to meet President Harry Truman after a press conference on 30 November in which the US president appeared to consider deploying nuclear weapons in south-east Asia.

Britain has backed the US-led United Nations force which has been defending South Korea since the North Korean invasion last June. But Attlee has been alarmed by the potential escalation of the conflict since Chinese "volunteers" entered the fray last month in support of North Korea. He demanded urgent talks with President Truman in order to argue against the use of nuclear weapons.

A bland communiqué at the end of five days of talks conceals a diplomatic triumph for the British prime minister. The text commits the US to consult its allies on the use of nuclear weapons. British sources say privately that Truman has assured Attlee that he has no plans to use the A-bomb (→ 1/5/53).

Britons are tops in newspaper league

London, December
Britons read more newspapers than any other nation in the world. Sales of national daily papers this year have reached a new record of just under 17 million copies. This is a higher proportion per head of population than in any other country and is in addition to the papers published in cities outside London and Manchester. The national distribution of newspapers – unlike, for instance, the United States where papers are generally confined to one city – gives press barons such as Beaverbrook, Rothermere and Kemsley great political power.

Coronation stone is stolen from abbey

London, 25 December
The Coronation stone, a sandstone slab weighing over 205 kg (450 pounds), was stolen today from Westminster Abbey. Scottish nationalists have claimed responsibility. Detectives in Scotland are searching for a man and woman with Scottish accents, reportedly seen near the abbey last night.

The stone, which lay underneath the Coronation Chair behind the high altar, was dragged out through a small door. It was taken from Scone in Scotland by Edward I in 1296. Historians say that England promised to return it (→ 11/4/51).

1951

Britain, 27 January. Meat rations are reduced to the lowest levels yet – the equivalent of four ounces of rump steak a week (→ 3/7/54).

Westminster, 9 March. Herbert Morrison replaces the ailing Ernest Bevin as foreign secretary.

Scotland, 11 April. The Stone of Scone is recovered at Forfar.

Britain, 14 April. Ernest Bevin dies, aged 70.

English Channel, 16 April. The 75-man crew of the submarine HMS *Affray* are feared dead after the sub went missing.

Dublin, 8 May. An Arts Council is set up in Ireland.

Westminster, 9 May. Old age pensions will be paid at the ages of 65 and 60 for men and women respectively, not 70 and 65 as originally planned.

London, 19 May. Britain warns Iran not to seize British oil properties; eight Britons died in riots there last month (→ 23/8).

London, 25 May. Diplomats Guy Burgess and Donald Maclean disappear (→ 7/6).

Ireland, 30 May. A general election gives Fianna Fáil 69 seats, Fine Gael 40 and others 38 (→ 13/6).

Dublin, 13 June. Eamonn de Valera becomes prime minister again (→ 18/5/54).

Tehran, 23 August. British oil companies and their workers prepare to leave Iran.

London, 23 September. King George has his left lung removed in an operation at Buckingham Palace (→ 6/2/52).

Ireland, September. The Waterford Glass company begins production.

Egypt, 19 October. British troops seize the Suez Canal zone in a dispute with the Egyptian government (→ 4/12).

Ireland, 21 October. The first Wexford opera festival begins.

Britain, 24 November. Motor manufacturers Austin and Morris announce a merger.

Kent, 4 December. A bus ploughs into Royal Marine cadets at Chatham, killing 23.

Egypt, 4 December. British forces come under attack during anti-British riots; servicemen's families were evacuated last month (→ 27/7/54).

Missing diplomats suspected of spying

Donald Maclean: a Soviet spy?

Guy Burgess: another Soviet spy?

London, 7 June

Two British diplomats who served in sensitive posts in the Washington embassy have vanished in circumstances suggesting they may have been undercover Soviet spies.

Donald Maclean, aged 38, was first secretary in Washington before becoming head of the American department of the Foreign Office. Guy Burgess, aged 40, was for eight months second secretary in Washington. They disappeared from London two weeks ago. Police in Europe are looking for the men, paying special attention to the border between the British and Soviet zones in Austria. The Foreign Office has refused to speculate on their whereabouts, saying only that they have been suspended for being absent without leave.

But the US press makes no bones about the Soviet connection. The *Journal-American* predicts that the diplomats' disappearance will cause a furore over communist sympathizers in government (→ 18/9/55).

Ministers quit over new health charges

Westminster, 22 April

Aneurin Bevan, the minister of labour, today resigned from the government in protest at the decision to impose on adults half the cost of glasses or false teeth prescribed for them under the National Health Service. He will be joined on the back benches by Harold Wilson, until today the president of the board of trade, and John Freeman, a junior war office minister. The health charges were among measures introduced by the chancellor, Hugh Gaitskell, to meet increased defence spending (→ 30/9/52).

Bevan walks out of government.

A woman's work is done in 15 hours!

London, 10 July

The average housewife works an astonishing 75-hour week – and still has to put in overtime on weekends. This picture has been built up by a Mass Observation study which looked at 700 working-class homes in the London area. It reports that "Mrs Average Housewife" has a normal working day of 15 hours. She cooks, cleans and looks after the children, and spends a quarter of her day in the kitchen. Most women do their shopping on Fridays, spending between ten shillings [50 pence] and £2. When she does get some free time, the housewife spends it reading, enjoying the radio or television or visiting the cinema (→ 16/5/52).

The Stone of Scone, on which monarchs are traditionally crowned, turned up in Scotland four months after being stolen from Westminster Abbey, London, by Scottish nationalists. Scots say it was stolen from them in the 12th century. Tradition says the stone cries out against unlawful kings.

Minister ousted in church-state clash

Ireland, 11 April
Dr Noel Browne, the minister of health, has been forced to resign from the government following a clash between himself and the Catholic hierarchy over his controversial "Mother and Child" scheme.

A member of the recently formed Clann na Poblachta party, Browne became a minister on his first day in parliament, aged 32. He quickly proposed to introduce free ante- and post-natal care for mothers, as well as free medical care for all children under 16. The Catholic bishops objected at once, claiming that Catholic mothers might be exposed to gynaecological information from non-Catholic doctors. Many doctors themselves were opposed to the scheme believing that it heralded the introduction of socialized medicine.

Browne's political naivety had serious consequences. He failed to secure cabinet approval for details of his scheme, or to satisfy the demands of the hierarchy who were making strong protests to the prime minister. Finally, he decided to abide by a decision of the bishops on the compatibility of his scheme with Catholic morality.

However, the bishops denounced the scheme as being in conflict with Catholic social teaching; the prime minister, John Costello, tiring of the whole business, immediately sought Browne's resignation.

Churchill becomes premier at age of 77

Winston Churchill has never before been voted into office by the electorate.

Westminster, 26 October
At the age of 77, Winston Churchill has won his first election as prime minister. The Conservatives have been returned to office in yesterday's general election despite winning 231,067 fewer votes than Labour – 48 per cent of the poll compared to Labour's 48.8 per cent. The number of MPs for the parties is 321 Conservative, 295 Labour, 6 Liberals and 3 from other parties.

Labour used fear of unemployment and Churchill's alleged "war mongering" as weapons in its bid to retain power. The Tories countered by promising lower taxes, fewer controls and more houses. In the event, Churchill was helped by the collapse of the Liberals, who fielded candidates in only one constituency in six. Most Liberals appear to have switched to the Tories, leaving the party which led Britain into the First World War with just a handful of seats.

Labour recriminations have already begun, with left-wingers accusing the outgoing premier, Clement Attlee, of betraying socialism. But Attlee's government was exhausted as well as split. Many of its senior members had been in government for ten years and had run out of steam (→ 11/1951).

More Britons tune in to television age

Britain, 31 December
Television has spread this year to the north-west of England with the opening of a transmitter in the Manchester area. With broadcasts to Scotland due to begin next year, the fledgling sibling of radio is set for years of rapid expansion. The BBC began the world's first regular TV service in 1936, but until the opening of a Midlands transmitter two years ago viewers were confined to the London area. By last year some 344,000 homes had TV sets. This year manufacturers plan to produce 250,000 sets. By this time next year four in five of the population will be in reach of television, threatening the popularity of the cinema and radio (→ 1/5/53).

Tory plan for steel

Westminster, November
The new Conservative government plans to denationalize the iron and steel industry, which Labour took under state control earlier this year. Road haulage is also set for denationalization, but the Tories appear to have accepted the other major acts of nationalization undertaken by the post-war Labour government. Labour had begun to take iron and steel into state ownership before last year's election and, despite its small majority, completed the process in February (→ 5/4/55).

Festival promises to be a national tonic

The Festival of Britain adds light, and fun, to the heart of London.

London, 4 May
"This is no time for despondency," said King George VI as he opened the Festival of Britain on London's South Bank. One of the prime purposes of the exhibition is to dispel the gloom caused by the continuing postwar austerities. Its director, Sir Gerald Barry, calls the festival "a tonic to the nation".

A fantasy world has been created on 11 hectares [27 acres] of cleared bombsites. A "Dome of Discovery" dominates the scene and the "Skylon" hangs aloft apparently unsupported, resembling an aluminium exclamation mark. The decorative styles of the pavilions, fountains and concourses are designed to create a sense of "fun, fantasy and colour" such has not been seen in Britain since before the war. The cafés and exhibits employ furniture and fabrics in the style known as "contemporary" with bent and moulded shapes, tapering spindly legs and ball-feet.

The Royal Festival Hall gave its opening concert last night. The interior of the building has angled projecting boxes along both sides of the auditorium and forests of indoor plants – innovations that have provoked much comment. Up river at Battersea park are open-air sculpture exhibits and a funfair.

1952

London, 31 January. Princess Elizabeth leaves for a tour of Africa (→ 6/2).

Windsor, 16 February. King George VI is buried (→ 8/12).

Britain, 21 February. Identity cards are abolished.

Westminster, 26 February. Winston Churchill tells MPs that Britain has developed its own atomic bomb (→ 3/10).

Britain, 30 April. The pharmaceutical industry decides to sell its products in metric units.

Wembley, 3 May. Newcastle United becomes the first team since 1891 to win the FA Cup in successive seasons, beating Arsenal 1-0.

Westminster, 16 May. Equal pay for men and women civil servants is accepted in principle by the government.

Britain, 20 June. Pedestrian crossings are to be marked by blinking orange beacons.

Dublin, 3 July. Bord Failte is established to promote tourism in the Republic of Ireland.

London, 5 July. The capital says goodbye to its last tram.

Britain, 11 July. Further details from last year's census show that one household in three lacks a bath and one in 20 has no piped water.

Northern Ireland, 26 August. A Canberra bomber returns to Aldergrove airport after the first transatlantic round-trip in a single day; it took 7 hours 59 minutes (→ 6/9).

Hampshire, 6 September. A prototype jet aircraft crashes at the Farnborough air show, killing 28 people (→ 3/4/53).

Loch Ness, 29 September. John Cobb, holder of the world land-speed record, dies in an attempt on the water-speed record.

Britain, 30 September. Left-wing supporters of Aneurin Bevan win six out of seven constituency seats on Labour's national executive (→ 11/11).

Britain, 11 November. Herbert Morrison beats Aneurin Bevan for the deputy leadership of the Labour Party (→ 14/4/54).

London, 8 December. Queen Elizabeth gives permission for next year's coronation to be televised (→ 24/3/53).

Britain. The first British film shot in Technicolor, *Genevieve*, has its première.

Nation mourns the king

Sandringham, 6 February

King George VI is dead and for the first time in half a century Britain is to be ruled by a queen, his elder daughter Princess Elizabeth.

As the nation mourns the man who, but for his brother Edward VIII's abdication, would have lived out his life as the duke of York, the princess, who has been holidaying in Kenya with her husband the duke of Edinburgh, is heading for home and her new responsibilities.

Born 56 years ago, the second son of King George V and christened not George but Albert, the late king had been one of the unknowns of the royal family. Unlike his flamboyant elder brother, he had an undistinguished childhood, a naval career plagued by illness and a persistent stammer that dogged his attempts at public speaking.

Yet he grew quickly into the role which had been thrust upon him, and provided a much-needed stability after King Edward's brief but turbulent reign. King George and Queen Elizabeth further endeared themselves to the public by their stalwart conduct during the Second World War.

A heavy smoker, the king was suffering from lung cancer. However it was a heart attack, not cancer, that killed him some time in the early hours of this morning (→ 16/2).

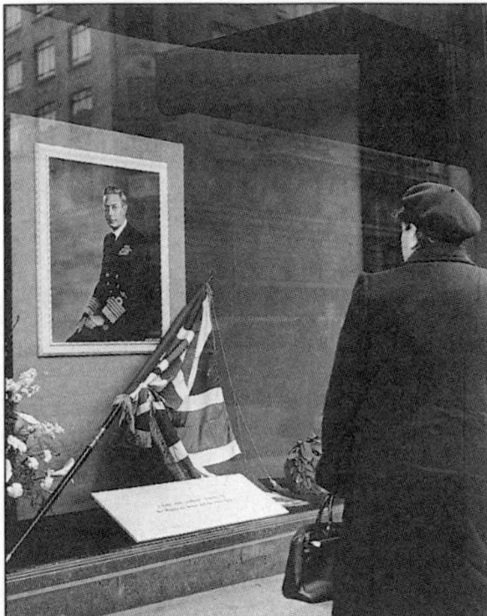

Smoking cut short the king's life.

Comet begins first scheduled jet service

Comets put Britain ahead of the world with the first passenger jets.

London, 2 May

An historic first was achieved today when the British Overseas Airways Corporation (BOAC) inaugurated its passenger jet service between London and Johannesburg. This is the world's first regular scheduled airline service to be operated by a turbojet-powered aircraft – the de Havilland Comet.

The aircraft is in itself a record-maker, being the first of its kind to win a certificate of airworthiness. At 3.12pm the Comet took off from runway 5 at London's Heathrow airport and climbed swiftly on its way to Rome, where it will make its first stop-over in the 23-hour flight to South Africa. Among those witnessing the take-off were Sir Geoffrey de Havilland and the Comet's designers, R E Bishop and R M Clarkson, all confident that today's flight puts British civil aviation ahead of its US and French competition (→ 26/8).

Immigration grows from West Indies

Britain, January

Increasing numbers of people are arriving to make a new life in Britain from the West Indies, India and Pakistan. As British citizens, they have free right of entry and the total arriving this year is expected to be the highest since the current wave of immigration began in 1948. A third of the new immigrants are settling in London, but there are also communities beginning to develop in parts of the West Midlands and Yorkshire.

In some cases, immigrants have been lured to Britain by the prospect of jobs in public transport and the health service. Employers such as London Transport have looked to the West Indies to overcome labour shortages for jobs such as bus conductors and station staff.

Skipper abandons battle to save ship

Falmouth, 10 January

Captain Henrik Carlsen, who for 12 days has fought to save his sinking freighter, the *Flying Enterprise*, was forced to abandon ship today. Forty minutes later the vessel vanished beneath the waves. Carlsen's ordeal began on Christmas Day when the ship began to break up in mountainous seas. Ordering the crew and passengers to safety, the captain and a young mate stayed. But the storms did not abate and today they too had to leave.

Carlsen clings to the railings.

Britain explodes its first atomic bomb

Australia, 3 October
Britain joined the atomic superpowers today when scientists exploded the first British atomic bomb at a site on the Monte Bello islands, north-west Australia. The bomb has been developed in secret over the last five years. Unlike the usual mushroom cloud that has marked US tests, the home-grown atomic weapon produced more of a raggedy-edged shape, but in all other respects it resembled its American peers.

Specialists and servicemen observed the explosion from nearby warships, and observers on a hill 100 miles away also saw it. One said, "We felt no ground shock wave, but a heavy air pressure pulse smacked the mainland four minutes and 15 seconds after the flash."

'Mousetrap' opens

London, 24 November
The noted crime writer, Agatha Christie, presented a new mystery to baffle her admirers tonight when her play *The Mousetrap* opened in London's West End. In the play, eight characters are stranded in a snowbound house; one of them is the killer, and Miss Christie keeps the audience at the Ambassadors Theatre guessing until the final scene.

Freak flash floods destroy Devon village

Workmen attempt to clear the centre of Lynmouth after the disaster.

Devon, 16 August
North Devon, well known for its holiday resorts, suffered far from summer weather today when a freak flood hit a large part of the area. Some 36 people have died, and thousands more have lost their homes as the flood devastated some 250 square miles.

Worst hit was the resort of Lynmouth – much of which was submerged when, after 23cm (9 inches) of rain fell in a single day, nearby rivers burst their banks and poured down the surrounding hills. As mud, rocks and debris smashed into their houses, many of the victims had no time to escape and were buried in their own homes.

Others died too, including three boy scouts, whose camp was overrun, a postman on his rounds and two girl hikers. The Red Cross has already begun bringing in emergency supplies of food and fresh water. Lynmouth has been declared a disaster area and a special fund has been set up for nationwide contributions to help rebuild the shattered town.

Bentley to hang for killing of policeman

London, 11 December
Derek Bentley, aged 19, will hang for the murder of a policeman, even though his accomplice Christopher Craig fired the fatal shots. At 16 Craig is too young to hang, and will be detained at "Her Majesty's pleasure" while Bentley – who allegedly urged on his partner, shouting, "Let him have it Chris!" – will face the gallows. The two men were arrested after police surrounded them on the roof of a Croydon warehouse during a bungled robbery attempt. It was then that shots were fired and PC Sidney Miles was killed (→28/1/53).

Bentley: sentenced to be hanged.

At least 112 are killed in three-train collision outside Harrow

Harrow, 8 October
One hundred and twelve people died today in Britain's second worst railway disaster, when the Perth to London express ploughed into the 7.31am commuter train at Harrow and Wealdstone station in north-west London. Seconds later a second express travelling north from Euston smashed into the wreckage.

The station was obliterated and emergency services fought their way through piles of debris as they battled to save the injured. Some 200 people were treated, many of whom had been crowding the platforms for the morning rush hour. Smashed carriages were piled 50 feet high; special cutting gear was used to free trapped passengers.

Rescuers hunt for survivors among the tangled wreckage of three trains.

British forces sent to fight 'Mau Mau'

Kenya, 21 October
British troops flew into the Kenyan capital of Nairobi today, an advance guard for a full-scale security operation designed to suppress the increasing violence of the country's "Mau Mau" terrorists.

Mau Mau attacks, aimed to drive the colonial government out of Kenya, have escalated sharply in recent weeks: some 40 people – both black and white – have been murdered by the self-styled freedom fighters. Social life is at a standstill, and there is some justified concern, but residents believe that the troops will right a deteriorating situation.

1953

Paris, 5 January. *Waiting for Godot* by Samuel Beckett has its first performance.

London, 28 January. Derek Bentley is hanged at Wandsworth prison.

Westminster, 5 February. Plans are announced for a Central African Federation.

Britain, 25 February. An inquest into last month's loss of the *Princess Victoria* hears that the car ferry sailed with its doors open.

London, 24 March. Queen Mary, the widow of King George V, dies, aged 85 (→2/6).

London, 25 March. Police launch a hunt for John Christie after the remains of three women are found in his former house in Notting Hill (→25/6).

Britain, 3 April. Air travel is up 20 per cent on last Easter (→11/1/54).

Wiltshire, 1 May. British prisoners of war return to Lyneham from Korea.

Ireland, 1 May. The first television broadcasts are made in Ireland from a BBC transmitter near Belfast (→2/6).

India, 2 May. Forty-three people die when a BOAC Comet crashes near Calcutta.

England, 11 June. Len Hutton becomes the first professional cricketer to captain England (→19/8).

London, 23 June. Winston Churchill is partially paralysed by a stroke (→1/12).

London, 15 July. John Christie is hanged, one day after a government tribunal maintains that Timothy Evans was rightly convicted of his wife's murder in Christie's house.

London, 19 August. England's cricketers win back the Ashes for the first time since 1933.

Britain, 13 November. A commercial television channel to rival the BBC is announced (→6/6/54).

Britain, 1 December. A record number of more than 300,000 new houses has been built this year.

Stockholm, 10 December. Winston Churchill wins the Nobel prize for literature (→30/11/54).

Britain. Top radio programmes this year include *The Goons, Educating Archie* and *Take It From Here.*

Hundreds die as east coast is flooded

Floods have inundated eastern England; Canvey Island above is badly hit with 125 dead and 500 missing.

Eastern England, 3 February
Hurricane-force winds combined with high tides today to swamp the sea defences along England's east coast from Lincolnshire to Kent. At least 280 people are known to have been drowned and thousands more are homeless. A major operation has been launched to save people trapped on rooftops by 2.4 metres (8 feet) of water, some in villages eight kilometres (5 miles) inland. Damage is estimated in hundreds of millions of pounds.

At Canvey Island in Essex 125 people have drowned, 500 are missing and 13,000 have been evacuated. Near Clacton, holiday chalets are under 12 feet of water and survivors are falling from rooftops into the floodwater from exhaustion.

Mablethorpe and Sutton-on-Sea have been evacuated, with hundreds still awaiting rescue: in Suffolk boats were rowed into a church to rescue 40 trapped children.

The flooding comes hard on the heels of another disaster – the January storms which caused widespread havoc.

Car ferry sinks as waves smash doors

Stranraer, 31 January
One hundred and twenty-eight people died tonight when the Irish Sea car ferry, the 2,694-ton *Princess Victoria*, sank after mountainous waves smashed in through the cargo doors. Of the 44 survivors ten were crewmen. The master, Captain James Ferguson, went down with his ship, saluting as the waves covered his head.

While the death toll is of immediate concern, an inquiry will be launched to discover just how the doors burst open. Some critics maintain that so poor was their design that this disaster was simply waiting to happen.

Further questions will cover the *Princess Victoria's* lack of proper communications equipment – she had only a limited ship-to-shore radio – and of lifeboats. Many passengers died in their life jackets after being forced to jump overboard and swim through the waves to life rafts (→25/2).

British climbers conquer Mount Everest

Safely down: Edmund Hillary (left), John Hunt and Norgay Tensing.

Nepal, 1 June
Mount Everest, at 29,028 feet the world's highest peak, has been conquered at last. Two days ago, at 11.30am, New Zealander Edmund Hillary and Sherpa Norgay Tensing stood on the summit, planted their respective flags, plus that of the United Nations, and spent 15 minutes taking photographs and eating mint cake. The British expedition, led by Sir John Hunt, had made one earlier attempt, which was defeated by bad weather. Now the peak has been scaled – a fitting prelude to tomorrow's coronation.

Elizabeth II crowned at Westminster

Huge crowds cheer the young monarch

PLondon, 2 June
Vivat Regina! A new Elizabethan age began today with the coronation of Queen Elizabeth II in Westminster abbey. Crowds thronged the London streets, defying the rain for a glimpse of their new young monarch, and the abbey itself brimmed with heads of state, prime ministers and other dignitaries gathered from every corner of the earth. London was witnessing its greatest celebration since the end of the Second World War.

In a ceremony dating back to the Middle Ages, Princess Elizabeth was anointed with holy oil by the archbishop of Canterbury, then presented with the symbols of her authority – the orb, the sceptre, the rod of mercy and the ring of sapphires and rubies. Then the archbishop raised the crown of St Edward above her head, lowered it and proclaimed, "God save the Queen".

As the peers and dignitaries echoed the cry, and trumpets and bells echoed across the capital, the guns of the Tower of London fired their salute. Then Prince Philip led forward his fellow peers in the formal act of homage to the woman who is not only his Queen but also his wife. Afterwards the crowd had its reward – a procession of carriages that took the Queen to Buckingham Palace (→ 3/2/54).

A new Elizabethan age begins: the queen is crowned in Westminster abbey.

Pomp and ceremony captured on television

London, 2 June
Thousands packed the streets of London today to watch the coronation, but tens of thousands more, many of them viewing for the first time, saw the ceremony on that new technological miracle – the television. Indeed, at a time when the monarchy, as much as any institution, must come to terms with the modern world, the televising of the coronation has been heralded as a practical step in that direction.

Television, invented in the 1920s, was launched as a public service in the 1930s but suspended during the Second World War. Since then the BBC has relaunched its service, but the purchase of sets has remained gradual. The coronation changed all that. It has captured the public interest more than any other post-war event, and the decision to permit cameras into the abbey was welcomed by the thousands who would have had no other chance to witness the pageantry and ceremony. Britain, it is said, is a democracy; television will undoubtedly make it even more so (→ 13/11).

Christie to hang for murder of his wife and three others

London, 25 June
John Christie was sentenced to death today for strangling four women, one of them his wife, and hiding their bodies in his house at 10 Rillington Place in Notting Hill. Three of the women were prostitutes with whom he had attempted sexual intercourse after making them unconscious with coal gas.

The balding, bespectacled clerk's plea of insanity was dismissed by the jury. The judge described the case as a "horrible one and a horrifying one".

Three years ago Christie was the key witness against Timothy Evans, who was hanged for his wife's murder. Now Evans's family has asked for a review (→ 15/7).

Christie: did he kill Evans's wife?

At last! Newly knighted jockey Sir Gordon Richards finally wins the Derby at his 28th attempt.

At last! After years of trying, Stanley Matthews finally wins the FA Cup with Blackpool.

Scientists discover the secrets of DNA

Cambridge, 25 April
The British bio-physicist Francis Crick and the American virochemist James Watson, have identified what many are describing as the secret of life itself: the genetic material DNA, or deoxyribonucleic acid; its molecule, the carrier of genetic inheritance, bears the shape of a double helix. The discovery comes as the climax of years of work by a whole community of international scientists, but much of the credit must go to these two inspired young scientists.

Hard-drinking poet dies at age of 39

New York, 9 November
Dylan Thomas died at the age of 39 here today at the beginning of a lecture tour. His wild, hard-drinking behaviour has made him better known for his life than for his poems. Just before leaving London for the United States he delivered the manuscript of a radio script, after losing it and then retrieving it from a Soho pub. Called *Under Milk Wood*, it is the account of a day in the life of a sleepy Welsh seaside village. His *Collected Poems* came out last year.

1954

Britain, 1 January. Flashing indicator lights become a legal requirement on motor vehicles (→25/6).

Britain, 11 January. All Comet jets are grounded following a crash of one of the airliners off Elba (→9/4).

Britain, 12 February. An official committee links smoking with lung cancer.

London, 24 February. Billy Graham, the American evangelist, arrives to begin a three-month "crusade".

London, 22 March. The gold market opens in the City for the first time since 1939.

Britain, 9 April. Comets are grounded again after another crash; they had returned to service after modifications in February (→20/7).

Britain, 22 April. The RSPCA sets out proposals for a safer Grand National after the deaths of four horses this year.

Westminster, 6 May. Sir David Maxwell Fyfe, the home secretary, says that the problem of "Teddy Boys" is not widespread (→28/5/55).

Ireland, 18 May. Fianna Fáil loses its majority in the Irish general election (→2/6).

Europe, 6 June. The pope is the first person to appear on British television screens by means of a new "Eurovision" link (→22/9/55).

London, 25 June. Doctors urge tougher tests on suspected drunk drivers than having to recite "tongue twisters" or walk in a straight line (→8/12).

Strathclyde, 8 July. Plans are unveiled for a new steel plant near Motherwell.

Ireland, 19 July. The first outbreak of myxomatosis is reported in the republic.

Sussex, 20 July. A public inquiry approves the expansion of Gatwick airport (→19/10).

Egypt, 27 July. It is agreed that British troops will leave the Suez Canal zone by 1956 (→12/6/56).

Britain, 20 October. A dock strike cuts sea trade by half.

Westminster, 30 November. Sir Winston Churchill is upset by an 80th birthday portrait of him by Graham Sutherland.

Britain, 8 December. Parking meters are to be introduced under a new Road Traffic Act (→30/8/56).

Costello forms his second Irish coalition

John Costello receives his seal of office from President Sean O'Kelly.

Ireland, 2 June
John Costello, the Fine Gael leader, has put together his second coalition government after preventing the return of Fianna Fail at the polls. The outgoing administration had pursued a deflationary economic programme that was deeply unpopular. Its finance minister, Sean McEntee, had been seen as the natural successor to Eamon de Valera, whose days as leader of Fianna Fail are numbered; but, as a result of the electoral defeat, McEntee has given way to Sean Lemass.

The new administration is made up of members of Fine Gael, Labour and Clann na Talmhan, a traditional party representing farmers which has intermittently enjoyed a minority representation in the Dáil. It also has the tacit support of Clann na Poblachta, an active participant in Costello's first coalition government, formed in 1948.

Significantly, Costello's former finance minister, Patrick McGilligan, has taken the job of attorney general, and Gerard Sweetman, a vigorous conservative, has gone to the department of finance.

Ireland faces a serious balance of payments problem, isolation from markets in Europe and America, a stagnant manufacturing sector, and a general lack of confidence. These difficulties, together with rampant emigration, present the new coalition government with a formidable challenge (→14/12/55).

Bevan quits in row over foreign policy

London, 14 April
Aneurin Bevan resigned from the shadow cabinet today in protest at Labour's support for the rearming of West Germany. Often regarded as a maverick, the Welsh firebrand is not alone in his opposition to the creation of a new Wehrmacht. He has more than 100 parliamentary supporters and there is a general feeling of uneasiness in the country about giving guns back to the Germans so soon after their "permanent" demobilization.

However, the rearmament issue is only part of a growing internal conflict facing the Labour Party. In addition to the "Bevanites" in parliament, Bevan has strong support within constituency parties, trade unions and the party's national executive committee for more left-wing policies.

Rabbits wiped out

Britain, 1 July
Britain's rabbits are on the road to extinction. Over the last year the virus myxomatosis has infected 90 per cent of burrows in southern England alone. Farmers say that the virus is a vital aid to pest control, since rabbits destroy crops worth £50 million each year. Scientists, however, are warning that this epidemic, if unchecked, will badly disturb the balance of nature (→19).

Bannister runs a record four-minute mile

Oxford, 6 May
Roger Bannister, a medical student aged 25, entered the history books this afternoon when he became the first man to run a mile in under four minutes. The four-minute mile had become the most sought-after goal for middle-distance athletes, with intense competition to be the first to break the barrier. Australia's John Landy had come close – and so today Bannister, aided by his pacemakers Chris Chataway and Chris Brasher, set out to try to break the record. In spite of a cool wind at Oxford University's Iffley Road track, they succeeded in achieving their target: Bannister broke the tape at three minutes 59.4 seconds.

Roger Bannister runs into history.

British troops open fire on Greek riots

Cyprus, 18 December
British troops shot dead two Cypriot youths today when nationalist demonstrators campaigning for union with Greece besieged the police station at Limassol. At the height of the protests, which spread across the island, the Union Jack outside the police station was torn down and briefly replaced by the Greek flag. In all, 42 Greek Cypriots were arrested. The riots followed an announcement by the United Nations that it has put off a demand by the Athens government that Cyprus be allowed to exercise the right of self-determination (→13/9/55).

Books go up in flames as rationing ends

Not only ration books went up: women celebrated with balloons.

London, 3 July
Men and women ceremonially tore up their ration books in Trafalgar Square last night as the government announced the end of all rationing after 14 years. Clothes and sweet rationing were ended in 1949. Meat was the last to go; already the butchers are predicting price rises.

Smithfield market opened at midnight, instead of 6am, for the first time since the war and porters handled huge sides of beef, some weighing 400 pounds. "We haven't seen the like since 1939," a market spokesman said. "It's extraordinarily good quality, too." When the rationing of clothes ended, the government threatened to freeze prices if they began to increase. Now regulation has been left to the National Federation of Housewives, whose members were seen patrolling butchers' shops with notebooks today. "If we find that prices are not falling we will hold protest meetings," they warned.

At several Conservative Association meetings ration books were burned as relics of the dark days of 1947 when an economic crisis forced rationing back to wartime levels and the meat ration was reduced to a shilling a week.

Eighteen-year-old Lester Piggott is led in after winning the Derby.

Metal fatigue was cause of jet deaths

Farnborough, 19 October
Experts based at the Royal Aircraft Establishment here may have identified the cause of a series of recent disasters involving Comet jets.

Wreckage from a jet that crashed off the island of Elba on 11 January – after which all Comets were grounded – shows that metal fatigue weakened the cabin roof containing the radio direction-finding aerial. The roof broke up in flight, bringing about the accident, which left 35 people dead. Today's report will be passed to investigators of two other crashes involving Comets – that of 2 May last year at Calcutta, which claimed 43 lives, and that of 9 April this year near Naples, in which 14 passengers and crew were killed (→17/3/57).

Building of houses breaks all records

Britain, 31 December
In what is seen as a triumph for the housing minister, Harold Macmillan, a record number of new houses – 354,000 – have been constructed this year. Three years ago the Conservative Party conference called for 300,000 houses to be built annually; the total in 1951 was just over 200,000 and falling.

Macmillan introduced a range of measures to encourage all forms of housing, including higher subsidies and fewer restrictions on obtaining mortgages. But in particular he put much greater emphasis on private house-building than had been the case under the Labour government. Almost 30 per cent of new houses completed this year were built by the private sector.

Royal tour comes up trumps down under

The Queen and Duke are warmly received on their first tour of Australia.

Australia, 3 February
The Queen arrived in sun-drenched Sydney this morning for the first visit to Australia by a reigning British monarch. She was accompanied by the duke of Edinburgh. Their liner, the *Gothic*, edged into the harbour through a line of some 500 small craft. The Queen was clearly excited by the warmth of the welcome as she stood on the bridge waving to port and starboard. As the *Gothic* dropped anchor at Athol Bight, the headlands were covered with cheering, flag-waving people.

In the past month she has enjoyed equally rapturous receptions in New Zealand. "I want to show that the crown is not merely an abstract symbol of our unity but a personal and living bond between you and me," she said in her Christmas Day broadcast – the first to be delivered from outside Britain.

1955

Britain, 25 January. Details are released of a £1,240 million plan to electrify the railways; new motorways are also being planned (→ 6/3/56).

Westminster, 17 February. A defence white paper reveals that Britain is making a hydrogen bomb.

Westminster, 18 February. Anthony Wedgwood Benn, a Labour MP, fails in a bid to renounce his family's peerage (→ 8/5/61).

Birmingham, 8 March. Bus crews in West Bromwich reimpose a colour bar that has already led to strikes.

Westminster, 5 April. Winston Churchill resigns as prime minister; he is succeeded by Sir Anthony Eden (→ 26/5).

Britain, 21 April. National newspapers reappear after a strike by electricians and maintenance engineers which began on 26 March.

Italy, 1 May. Stirling Moss becomes the first Briton to win the Mille Miglia road race.

Britain, 14 June. The rail strike that began on 29 May is called off, but the dock strike continues (→ 1/7).

Britain, 1 July. Dockers call off their strike (→ 23/7/57).

London, 13 July. Ruth Ellis is hanged at Holloway prison.

Cumbria, 23 July. Donald Campbell sets a new water-speed record of 202.32mph (over 325kph) on Ullswater.

London, 14 August. Record crowds attend the Royal Academy summer exhibition to see the portrait of the Queen by Pietro Annigoni (→ 28/1/57).

Britain, August. A fashion for denim "jeans" becomes popular this summer.

London, 18 September. The Foreign Office says that Guy Burgess and Donald Maclean, who disappeared in 1951, were Soviet spies (→ 11/11).

London, 11 November. Harold "Kim" Philby denies claims that he was the "third man" who tipped off Burgess and Maclean (→ 18/4/56).

Cyprus, 28 November. British authorities declare a state of emergency here after more terrorist attacks (→ 12/1/56).

Westminster, 14 December. Hugh Gaitskell is elected Labour Party leader (→ 9/1/57).

London. Mary Quant opens a clothes shop in Chelsea.

Eden leads Tories to election victory

Anthony Eden salutes the crowds.

Westminster, 26 May 1955

Sir Anthony Eden – who succeeded Sir Winston Churchill as prime minister on 6 April – has led the Conservatives to victory in a general election. The handsome Eden, who has long lived in the shadow of the great warrior-statesman, is now prime minister in his own right. With an overall majority of 58 seats, he has broken the stalemate created by the close results of the 1950 and 1951 elections.

Eden appears to have got his timing right, winning a confidence vote from the nation that will allow him to attack the economic problems and the industrial unrest, which grow more menacing every day. He has also been given a strong mandate for the East-West diplomatic talks scheduled for this summer.

One of the pleasures of the election has been to see the 80-year-old Churchill, relieved of the cares of office, successfully defending his Woodford constituency with boyish enjoyment. There is less joy for the defeated Labour Party, however, with rumours abounding of a bitter rift over the right of succession to the ageing Clement Attlee, who prefers Hugh Gaitskell to the deputy leader, Herbert Morrison. Others favour the radical Aneurin Bevan (→ 7/12).

Troops on stand-by as strikes worsen

London, 31 May

Troops are to be put on stand-by following the granting of emergency powers to the government to cope with the worsening effects of the rail and dock strikes. Privy councillors were summoned to Balmoral today for a special meeting at which the Queen signed the proclamation of a state of emergency.

Gwilym Lloyd George, the home secretary, insisted tonight that the emergency powers will not be used to break the strikes but will enable the government to maintain public order and to make sure that food supplies get through. A total of 125,000 men are now on strike and travel, exports and the unloading of food are severely affected (→ 14/6).

Air will be cleaner in smokeless zones

Westminster, 27 July

The Clean Air Bill is published today. It is an attempt to banish forever the London pea-souper whose last major appearance in December 1952 brought the capital to a halt and killed 4,000 people. If passed, the bill will restrict the use of coal on domestic fires, establish smokeless zones and raise the chimneys of power stations. It should cut dramatically deaths from bronchitis and other respiratory complaints.

Attlee steps down as leader of Labour Party

Sir Winston Churchill, now in his eighties, finally departs from office.

Clement Attlee decides to resign.

London, 7 December

Within eight months the two wartime leaders Winston Churchill and Clement Attlee have left frontline politics. Churchill resigned as premier in April and today his wartime deputy and peacetime opponent, Attlee, announced his departure in typically modest fashion.

"Before you turn to important business I have a personal statement," he told Labour colleagues. "I want to end uncertainty over the future leadership. I am resigning." He is 72 and his greatest legacy is perhaps the "welfare state" forged during his premiership between 1945 and 1951 (→ 14).

Toothpaste ad heralds new age of TV

London, 22 September
Amid much speechifying and trumpeting, commercial television started broadcasting tonight, providing London viewers with an alternative to BBC television for the first time.

Offerings from the two London commercial contractors, Associated Rediffusion and the Associated Broadcasting Company, included such standard fare as a variety show, drama excerpts linked by the actor Robert Morley, and a boxing match from Shoreditch.

The real difference lay in the six minutes of advertisements, which, as the first to be screened on TV, were the target of much controversy. In the event they proved tasteful if anticlimactic. They began with one for Gibbs SR toothpaste.

The BBC went on air half an hour earlier. Its answer to commercial television's opening speeches from the Guildhall was *The Donald Duck Story*. But what really stole its rival's thunder was a drama on steam radio – the death in a fire of Grace Archer, a leading character in *The Archers*. The timetabling on ITV's big night, the BBC would have its audience believe, was sheer coincidence (→ 11/12/56).

Cleaner teeth, and a clean break with the past for commercial TV.

The romance is over: Princess Margaret announces she will not marry Townsend

London, 31 October
The threat of a scandal within the royal family was laid to rest tonight when Princess Margaret announced that her romance with Group Captain Peter Townsend is at an end. While the princess, at 25, has the right to marry whomever she wishes, she has chosen to place national duty before personal emotion. It is less than 20 years since her uncle, Edward VIII, chose a very different course; his niece has other priorities. Her love for the former Battle of Britain hero became public two years ago. No one doubted their affection, nor were there any criticisms of the character of the 40-year-old former equerry to King George VI.

But Townsend is a divorced man, and as such is ineligible to marry a royal princess. Margaret could have chosen a civil marriage, but that would have effectively placed her outside her family. To general relief, her head has triumphed over her heart (→ 6/5/60).

Before the end: Townsend stands unobtrusively behind Princess Margaret.

Ireland is admitted to the United Nations

Ireland, 14 December
The Republic of Ireland has been admitted to membership of the United Nations. It is felt that the timing of Ireland's entry will enable it to play an active part in influencing the United Nations policy of general decolonization.

This significant change in Ireland's status, comparable in importance, perhaps, to the declaration of Ireland as a republic in 1949, occurs during the second inter-party government under the premiership of John Costello. His minister for external affairs, Liam Cosgrave, the son of the country's first leader after independence, has made a dignified and impressive speech to the assembly. He will receive able support from several outstanding officials in his department, including Conor Cruise O'Brien and F H Boland (→ 12/12/56).

Ex-model to hang for lover's murder

London, 21 June
Ruth Ellis, the blonde model who has been convicted of the murder of her boyfriend David Blakely, a racing driver, will hang for her crime. An Old Bailey jury of ten men and two women took only 25 minutes to find Ellis guilty, rejecting her defence that it was a "crime of passion", and affirming that jealousy can never justify murder. Ellis displayed no emotion as she heard the verdict, although she plans an appeal. Women are rarely hanged in Britain, and the case will give fresh impetus to the campaign against capital punishment (→ 13/7).

Swaggering 'Teddy Boys' invite trouble

"Teds": setting a new fashion.

Bath, 28 May
Groups of raucous "Teddy Boys" are attracting attention across Britain. But their flamboyant imitation of "Edwardian" fashion – slicked-back hair, long coats with velvet collars and "drainpipe" trousers – is not the only cause of interest. Several cities have reported disturbances as violence flares between rival gangs of teenage youths. In Bath, for instance, 16 "Teds" were arrested tonight after trouble at a dance hall. Their behaviour often matches their extravagant clothes, but the swaggering "Teds" say they are being blamed for trouble which others provoke. The older generation is not amused.

Crisis in Cyprus is worsened by strike

Cyprus, 13 September
The crisis in the British colony of Cyprus escalated today when the nationalist group EOKA brought out the island's workers on a general strike. Illegal processions and demonstrations and fighting between the Greek and Turkish communities stretched police and military resources, and hundreds were arrested. Orders to shoot to kill if necessary did not have to be used, although soldiers of the Royal Inniskillings used bayonets to disperse a huge mob that had erected a barricade on the road between Lysi and Nicosia (→ 29/11).

1956

Cyprus, 12 January. More British troops arrive (→9/3).

Britain, 8 February. Malaya is promised independence by August 1957 (→18/9).

Britain, 6 March. British Railways says that steam will be replaced by electric services between London, Liverpool and Manchester (→3/6).

Liverpool, 24 March. The Queen Mother's horse Devon Loch collapses mysteriously 100 yards from victory in the Grand National steeplechase.

Westminster, 17 April. Premium bonds offering prizes of up to £1,000 are announced by the chancellor, Harold Macmillan.

London, 18 April. Soviet leaders Nikolai Bulganin and Nikolai Khrushchev begin a visit to Britain (→14/5).

Cork, 21 May. An international film festival begins in the city.

Britain, 3 June. Third-class rail carriages are abolished.

Egypt, 12 June. British troops leave the Suez Canal zone (→26/7).

Egypt, 26 July. The Anglo-French Suez Canal company is nationalized (→29/8).

Mediterranean, 29 August. Britain and France build up forces as part of their pressure against Egypt (→31/10).

Britain, 30 August. The introduction of traffic wardens is planned to enforce parking controls (→16/6/58).

Britain, September. Screenings of the film *Rock Around the Clock* cause riots in cinemas.

Cumbria, 17 October. Britain's first nuclear power station opens at Calder Hall (→17/10/57).

Egypt, 31 October. British and French forces launch attacks, after Egypt fails to heed an ultimatum to withdraw from the Suez Canal (→3/11).

Egypt, 21 November. British troops hand over to UN forces.

Britain, 11 December. Television broadcasting is allowed between 6 and 7pm (→9/1/57).

Northern Ireland, 12 Dec. Twelve attacks by the IRA signal the start of a new terrorist campaign (→4/1/57).

London, 14 December. The premier, Sir Anthony Eden, returns from his convalescence in Jamaica (→9/1/57).

Makarios deported by British authorities

Cyprus, 9 March

Archbishop Makarios, the leader of the Greek Cypriot community, was deported to the Seychelles today by the British authorities. Described by the governor, Sir John Harding, as "a major obstacle to a return to peaceful conditions", Makarios is the figurehead of his people's demands for independence, as important as the elusive General Grivas, the head of the terrorist organization EOKA. Indeed, Makarios is regarded as the inspiration for and a leading member of EOKA, which has threatened a massive bombing campaign in retaliation for the deportation (→9/8/57).

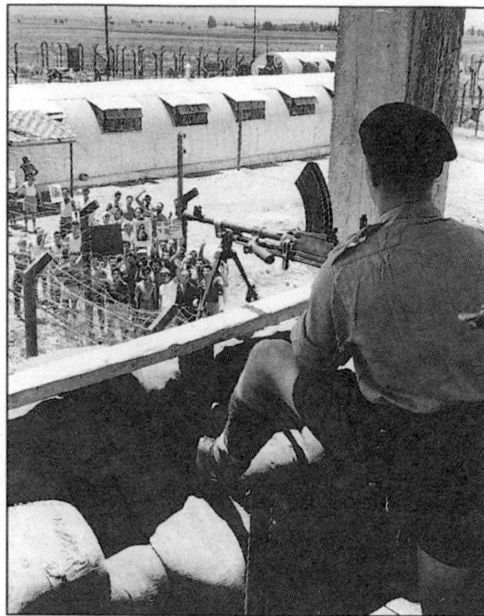

EOKA suspects under guard.

Controversial play shakes up the stage

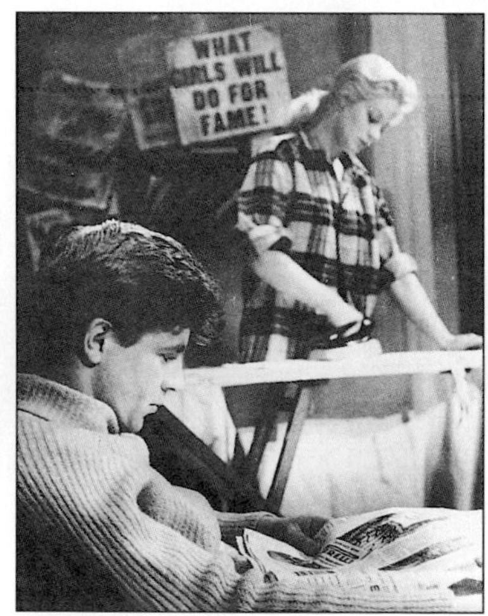

Kitchen sink drama has arrived.

London, 13 May

Look Back In Anger, written by an unknown actor, John Osborne, is hailed today by the critic Kenneth Tynan as "the best young play of its decade" and its hero, the ranting Jimmy Porter, as "the completest young pup since Hamlet" and the spokesman for the generation now in its twenties. The play is one of the first to be staged at the Royal Court theatre under the new regime of George Devine, after some 25 theatres had turned it down. The theatre's publicity names Osborne as one of the "Angry Young Men". Older critics have asked what he and his hero are so angry about.

Britain mourns its first movie mogul

London, 23 January

Sir Alexander Korda, the nearest thing Britain has known to a movie mogul in the Hollywood style, died today aged 62. A Hungarian, he began making films in a shed in his twenties but failed in Hollywood before creating London Films in 1932. He gambled everything on *The Private Life of Henry VIII* – which made his and Charles Laughton's fortunes. He built Denham studios in 1936 and produced H G Wells's *Things to Come*, *The Ghost Goes West*, *The Scarlet Pimpernel*, *The Four Feathers*, and after 1945 *Anna Karenina* and *Richard III*. He made and lost £2 million in films.

First African colony promised freedom

London, 18 September

The Gold Coast is to be Britain's first black colony in Africa to win its freedom. It was announced today that the colony will become independent on 6 March next year. The first leader of the new nation will be Kwame Nkrumah, the head of the Convention People's Party, who led his party to victory in elections in 1951. Nigeria and Sierra Leone are two other West African colonies expected to follow the Gold Coast towards independence. Their peaceful progress contrasts with the continuing violence in Kenya and uncertainty in the Central African Federation (→6/3/57).

Missing frogman near Soviet ship, government admits

Britain, 14 May

The British government said today that a frogman missing since last month had been doing "underwater tests" near the cruiser carrying the Soviet leaders Nikita Khrushchev and Nikolai Bulganin during their visit to Britain. The government had earlier denied that any such activity had been in progress near the *Ordzhonikdze* and two escort ships in Portsmouth harbour, but has now agreed that Commander Lionel "Buster" Crabbe was testing "certain equipment". Crabbe disappeared during the operation and is presumed drowned. Soviet newspapers have accused Britain of "shameful underwater espionage" and "dirty work by enemies of international cooperation".

The Soviet delegation spent eight days here for talks about "peaceful coexistence". Bulganin is the Soviet premier, but most interest was focused on the ebullient Khrushchev. In March he electrified the Soviet Communist Party's 20th congress by a speech in which he denounced his predecessor, Joseph Stalin, as a despotic and criminal murderer. During his British visit Khrushchev clashed with George Brown, a Labour leader. "I'd vote Tory," the Soviet leader said afterwards (→26/6/57).

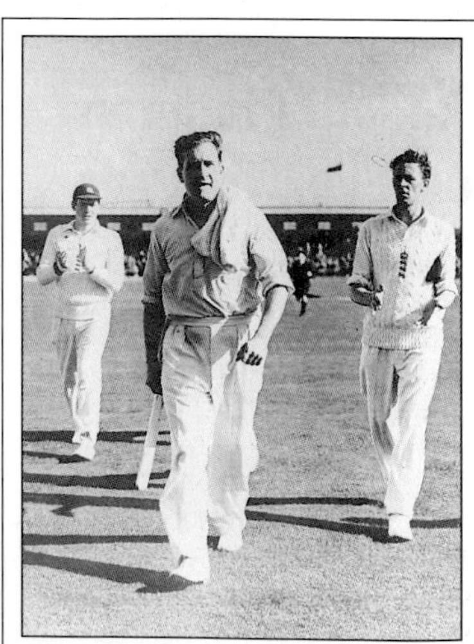

July 27. Jim Laker walks off at Old Trafford as the first cricketer to take all ten wickets in a test innings, finishing with 19 for 88 in the match against Australia.

British opinion divided as crisis erupts in Suez

Nasser sees off Britain and France.

London, 3 November
The Suez invasion begun by Anglo-French forces on 31 October has divided opinion in Britain. Two junior ministers, Anthony Nutting and Edward Boyle, have resigned and, while there have been no resignations from the cabinet, R A ("Rab") Butler and Sir Walter Monckton are said to have been opposed to the attack on Egypt.

The Labour Party has joined the Liberals and dissident Tories to mount an attack on the government under the slogan "Law not War". Hugh Gaitskell, the Labour leader, has been passionate in his criticism of the prime minister, Sir Anthony Eden, and in a broadcast tonight appealed for his overthrow. But there has been equally fierce criticism of Labour for allegedly damaging national unity at a time when the forces are risking their lives.

The Foreign Office, alarmed by international criticism, is opposed to the invasion. The Treasury is fearful of US hostility. The newspapers are split: most support Eden, but the *Observer* and the *Manchester Guardian* describe his actions as "gangsterism" (→8).

Sir Eden blunders over Suez.

US forces Allies to cease fire in Suez

Suez Canal Zone, 8 November
The Anglo-French attempt to seize the Suez Canal from Egypt and topple Colonel Nasser from power has failed. All military operations were halted at midnight under the terms of the ceasefire imposed by the United Nations.

There is no doubt that the invading force could have gone on to take the entire canal zone – most of the Egyptian air force has been destroyed and those army units that resisted have been pushed aside – but Britain was unable to withstand American pressure. In spite of what Sir Anthony Eden understood to be the tacit approval of John Foster Dulles, the US secretary of state, President Eisenhower reacted furiously to the invasion. His ministers and diplomats have put enormous pressure on Britain to withdraw, and the Americans were crucial in forcing through the ceasefire resolution at the UN.

Even more important, "Ike", for so long a friend of Britain, made it clear that sterling, under attack from all sides, would receive no support from the United States. The crunch came yesterday when the Treasury informed the chancellor, Harold Macmillan, that Britain needed a loan of a billion dollars if the pound was not to be devalued.

Washington's answer to his plea for help was emphatic: no money without a ceasefire. The cabinet had no choice but to accept. Britain is no longer a world power (→19).

Buildings are set ablaze as the British and French storm into Port Said.

With the fighting over, British paras patrol unconcerned through Port Said.

Strain of Suez crisis takes toll on Eden

London, 19 November
Sir Anthony Eden, worn out by the strain of the Suez affair, is to fly to Jamaica and rest there for three weeks. A communiqué, issued at midnight by the prime minister's office, announced that the leader of the House of Commons, "Rab" Butler, will run the cabinet while Sir Anthony is away.

The question that must be asked is: will he ever return to power? He has suffered a terrible international disaster and has inflicted divisive wounds on Britain. There is no doubt about his moral and physical courage, but even before Suez there were signs that his health was giving way.

In 1953 he suffered an attack of the jaundice that has troubled him for some time; he had three gall-bladder operations that year. There is speculation that his ill-health may have undermined his political judgement. Certainly, he became obsessed with toppling Nasser, regarding the Egyptian strongman as a Middle Eastern Hitler. It was an obsession that clouded his thinking at a dangerous time.

His departure will do little to ease the controversy provoked by Suez. Despite the denials of the foreign secretary, Selwyn Lloyd, many people in the United States believe that Britain and France colluded with Israel to allow the Israeli army to invade Egypt and so give Britain and France the excuse to intervene (→21).

1957

Limerick, 4 January. The funeral takes place of Sean South, killed in an IRA raid on a Northern Ireland police station three days ago (→5/3).

Britain, 9 January. The Post Office introduces detector vans to fight TV-licence dodging (→13/8).

London, 28 January. Prince Charles starts at a prep school in Knightsbridge (→18/10).

London, 7 February. The US rock star Bill Haley gives his first British concert.

Ireland, 5 March. Fianna Fáil wins the general election with 78 seats; Fine Gael wins 40 seats, other parties 25 (→20).

West Africa, 6 March. Gold Coast becomes the first black British colony in Africa to achieve independence; it will be renamed Ghana (→30/9/60).

Dublin, 20 March. Eamon de Valera becomes Irish premier again, at the age of 75 (→5/7).

Britain, 4 April. National Service is to end in 1960.

London, 23 May. The Church of England says that remarried divorcees can take the sacraments, if a bishop allows.

Britain, 26 June. A Medical Research Council report says smoking is a direct cause of lung cancer (→27/5/59).

Sussex, 26 June. The headless body of missing frogman Commander Crabb is found in Chichester harbour (→21/2/59).

Bradford, 20 July. Harold Macmillan tells Tories that "most of our people have never had it so good" (→7/1/58).

Britain, 23 July. Violence breaks out on picket lines as a national bus strike takes effect.

Cyprus, 9 August. The state of emergency ends (→23/2/59).

Britain, 13 August. BBC figures show audiences for radio falling as those for television soar (→21/1/59).

Washington, DC, 18 October. The Queen meets President Eisenhower during the first visit by a British monarch to the White House (→19/11/59).

Britain, 12 November. The Post Office announces plans to introduce postal codes.

London, 14 November. The Queen says that debutantes will not be presented at court after next year (→3/7/58).

Cheshire. The Jodrell Bank space telescope is inaugurated (→14/3/60).

Macmillan replaces Eden as Tory leader

Surprise choice: Macmillan, seen here with the chief whip, Edward Heath.

Westminster, 9 January
The ailing Sir Anthony Eden, his once glittering career ruined by the Suez débâcle, has resigned as prime minister, and the chancellor, Harold Macmillan, aged 62, has been appointed to succeed him.

While Eden's departure had been expected, the appointment of Macmillan had not. It is the outcome of a bitter struggle within the Tory Party. The man marked down to succeed was "Rab" Butler, Eden's deputy, but he was strongly opposed by some Tory MPs because of his lack of enthusiasm for the Suez enterprise.

Butler is deeply disappointed but would only comment in his usual enigmatic fashion that "if my services are of value, they will be at Mr Macmillan's disposal". At first hawkish over Suez, the new prime minister's attitude changed to that of a dove when the financial situation became serious. He has good personal and business connections in the United States and he sees the repair of Anglo-American relations as his first task (→20/7).

IRA maintains new violence campaign

Dublin, 5 July
Eamon de Valera, who became the Irish premier again after the general election in March, has today moved against the Irish Republican Army by using part of the Offences Against the State Act of 1940.

Tough emergency measures will involve using the Curragh military camp as a detention centre. However it is by no means clear that this will stem the IRA's renewed campaign of violence against military targets in Northern Ireland which began last December. De Valera's decision was in part politically motivated. In the election, Sinn Féin emerged from the wilderness and won four seats (→9/10/58).

Britain says 'No' to Common Market

Rome, 25 March
The European Economic Community came into being today with the signing of the Treaty of Rome by "the Six": France, West Germany, Italy, Belgium, Holland and Luxembourg. The aim of this "Common Market" is the free movement of people, goods and money among the member states.

Britain has decided not to join for traditional British reasons: its ties to the Commonwealth and its suspicion of European entanglements. It also fears that the EEC will develop a supra-national authority that will erode Britain's sovereignty over domestic affairs. The government is hoping to establish a wider, but less formalized European Free Trade Area (→20/11/59).

Airliners grounded

Manchester, 17 March
Following a crash last week at Manchester's Ringway airport, in which 22 people died, British European Airways has grounded all its oldest Viscount turbo-prop airliners. Passengers due to fly out on five scheduled flights from London have been left stranded. Experts are now blaming the recent crash on a mechanical fault in the Viscount's wing flaps (→4/10/58).

One way of trying to acquire riches is to invest in the new premium bonds; prizes of up to 1,000 are on offer, picked by a machine called "Ernie".

Legalization urged of homosexual acts

Britain, 4 September
Homosexual acts between consenting adults should no longer be a criminal offence, according to a government report published today. The committee, chaired by Sir John Wolfenden, also proposes new laws on soliciting to clear prostitutes from the streets, but does not seek to ban "the oldest profession". Sir John, who is vice-chancellor of Reading University, argues that the law should allow individual freedom of choice and action in matters of private morality. By "adult" the committee means anyone over the age of 21. Reform of the homosexual laws would remove a common cause of blackmail. The government will await public reaction before initiating any legislation.

Death toll mounts as Asian flu hits UK

Britain, 23 September
The Ministry of Health has tried to allay public alarm over the present outbreak of Asian influenza, stressing that it is a mild one. But attacks have been complicated by pneumonia and bronchitis. Deaths from influenza in 160 large towns in England and Wales rose from 8 to 47 in the week ending 14 September. Children are particularly vulnerable and many are staying away from school.

Lewisham train crash kills more than 90

A scene of unutterable chaos greets rescuers at the site of the crash.

London, 4 December
Two trains packed with commuters and Christmas shoppers crashed in thick fog at Lewisham, south London, this evening. It is feared that over 90 people are dead and some 200 injured, many still trapped in the wreckage. It appears that the driver of the 4.56 steam express from Cannon Street to Ramsgate failed to see two stop signals. His fireman shouted a warning and he applied the emergency brake – but it was too late. His locomotive slammed into the rear of the stationary 5.18 Charing Cross to Hayes electric train.

The electric train, its brakes on, telescoped and, while the steam locomotive stayed on the tracks, its tender reared up and brought down the supports of a bridge carrying a loop line over the track. The 350-ton bridge crashed onto the already mangled carriages. Two minutes later the driver of another train on the loop line, moving slowly up to a red light, saw a gaping hole in the track. He halted with his leading coach tilted over the wreckage.

Tonight heavy lifting gear looms through the fog as members of the emergency services and the Royal Engineers struggle to lift girders and untangle the telescoped carriages, while stretcher-bearers carry away the dead and injured. This accident will boost the campaign for the introduction of an automatic warning system.

Severe fire causes nuclear plant scare

Cumberland, 17 October
Britain's fledgling atomic industry has suffered its most serious accident to date. Fuel rods in one of the 152-metre (500-foot) chimneys at the Windscale atomic works overheated, releasing large amounts of radioactive material into the atmosphere. The Atomic Energy Authority stresses that no one was injured and that most of the radioactive material has been blown out to sea. The chimney where the fire began has been shut down, while the rest of the plant, which makes plutonium for the military, is back in production. None the less sales of milk from a large area around Windscale have been banned, since the milk contains up to six times the legal limit of radioiodine.

Women among 'life peers' to join Lords

London, 30 October
Women will be included in a new category of "life peers" to be admitted to the House of Lords, it was announced today by the leader of the upper house, the earl of Home. Formerly, entrance to the house has been restricted to male bearers of hereditary titles, but it will now be revitalized by an infusion of new blood. Other reforms will streamline the day-to-day procedures of the Lords (→21/10/58).

The latest music rocks around the clock

Haley is good, but rather old.

London, December
A craze for "rock and roll" has swept Britain this year. Its birthplace was the coffee bars of London's Soho district. Tommy Hicks, a 20-year-old merchant seaman, acquired a new surname (Steele) and a new career (singer) after being discovered singing in the "Two I's" coffee bar. Hits such as *Singing the Blues* demonstrated that Britons could rock just as well as the Americans who inspired the new musical fashion.

Television has recognized and exploited the popularity of rock with the BBC's *Six-Five Special*, but the major stars remain American. Bill Haley and his group, the Comets, were enthusiastically mobbed when he toured Britain in February; his audiences jived in the aisles, just as they had done during the first rock films. Elvis Presley – well known from such films as *Loving You* – has been the biggest record-seller.

A distinctive variant of rock has emerged in the "skiffle" sound of the former jazzman Lonnie Donegan. Cheap guitars and even washboards have enabled hundreds of amateurs to form their own skiffle or rock groups.

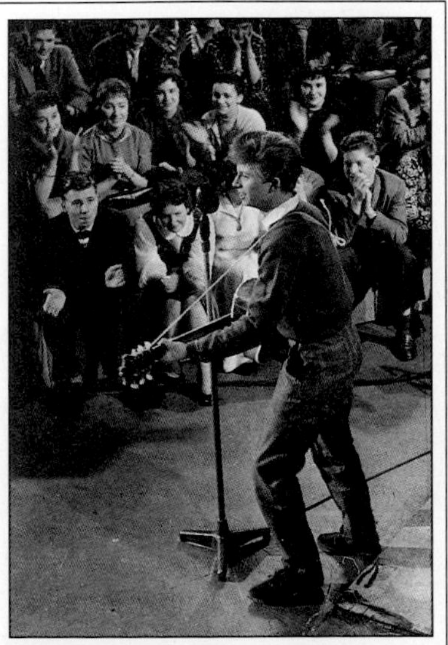

Steele is good, and younger.

1958

London, 17 February. A group called the Campaign for Nuclear Disarmament is formed (→ 7/4).

Munich, 21 February. England football star Duncan Edwards dies of injuries from the plane crash 15 days ago (→ 3/5).

London, 26 March. Parking tickets are issued for the first time in Britain (→ 16/6).

Wembley, 3 May. Three months after the Munich disaster, Manchester United lose 2-0 to Bolton Wanderers in the FA Cup final.

London, 16 June. Yellow "no waiting" lines come into force on the capital's roads; the first parking meters are to begin trials on 10 July (→ 5/12).

Cardiff, 18 July. Prince Philip opens the Empire Games.

Britain, 21 July. A large increase in polio vaccination is announced.

Britain, 25 August. The Midland Bank is the first bank to offer personal loans, from next month.

Nottingham, 30 August. Fighting breaks out between police and local youths (→ 31).

London, 31 August. Clashes occur in the Notting Hill district between black and white youths (→ 9/9).

London, 1 September. Surrey win cricket's county championship for the seventh consecutive year.

London, 15 September. Nine youths are jailed for four years each for attacking blacks in the recent disturbances (→ 1/11/61).

London, 4 October. BOAC launches the first scheduled transatlantic jet service (→ 17/11/59).

Belfast, 9 October. Protestants object when the City Hall flag flies at half-mast on the death of Pope Pius XII (→ 8/1/59).

Westminster, 21 October. The first women peers take their seats in the House of Lords.

Britain, 12 November. A government report warns against the increasing use of sedatives and tranquillizers.

Lancashire, 5 December. The first stretch of motorway in Britain, a five-mile Preston by-pass, opens (→ 18/8/59).

Britain, 31 December. Fears are expressed that birth defects are linked to a drug called thalidomide, widely prescribed for sickness in pregnancy.

'Busby Babes' die in plane tragedy

The wrecked plane in which England's finest football team was travelling.

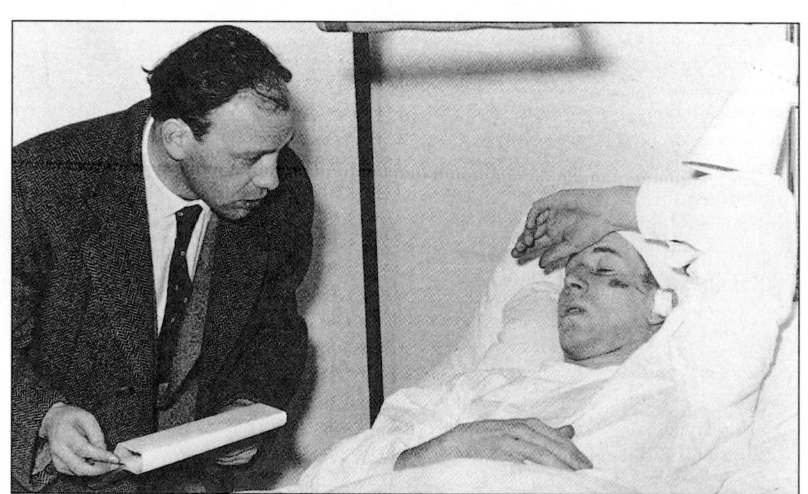

Young star Bobby Charlton talks to pressmen from his hospital bed.

Munich, 6 February
Manchester United football club's bid for the European Cup has ended in tragedy. Seven members of arguably the finest team in England – nicknamed the "Busby Babes" after their manager Matt Busby – have been killed in a plane crash at Munich airport. The tragic accident, in which eight journalists and three of the club's staff also died, happened as the team began the last leg of its journey home from Belgrade, where they qualified for the European Cup semi-finals.

The Munich runway was covered with snow, and the pilot of the BEA Ambassador had to abort his first take-off. At the second attempt the plane failed to gain height, hitting a fence and then an airport building before breaking in two. The survivors, many of them badly injured, have been taken to a Munich hospital. Among the most seriously hurt are Busby himself, the England left-half Duncan Edwards and fellow England player John Berry.

Of the players reported killed four were full internationals. They were the Manchester captain Roger Byrne (28), Tommy Taylor (25) and David Pegg (22), who played for England; and Bill Whelan (22), who had four caps for the Irish Republic (→ 21).

Nuclear disarmers march 50 miles to weapons headquarters

Aldermaston, 7 April
To the sounds of a skiffle group playing "When The Saints Go Marching In" 3,000 people marched past the gates of the Atomic Weapons Research Establishment at Aldermaston today and called for Britain, Russia and the United States to stop the manufacture, testing and storage of nuclear weapons.

The Campaign for Nuclear Disarmament, formed this year, claimed that 12,000 supporters attended the final rally and that 600 hardcore marchers had walked the entire 50 miles from London.

There were speeches from Stuart Morris of the Peace Pledge Union and the US pacifist Beyard Rustin. At one point marchers attacked a car of people who accused them, through a loudspeaker, of "playing Khrushchev's game" (→ 3/10/60).

Footsore anti-nuclear marchers hope to influence government policy.

Treasury ministers quit in benefits row

Westminster, 7 January
The chancellor of the exchequer, Peter Thorneycroft, and his two junior treasury ministers, Enoch Powell and Nigel Birch, resigned yesterday when their proposals to slash expenditure to curb inflation were turned down by the cabinet. Their proposals, which included abolishing the family allowance for the second child, were said by the prime minister to be "neither politically nor socially desirable". As he set out on a Commonwealth tour this morning, Macmillan was asked about the loss of his treasury team. He replied: "I thought that the best thing to do was to settle up these little local difficulties and then turn to the wider vision of the Commonwealth" (→ 8/10/59).

Britain and Iceland start war over cod

North Sea, 2 September
Britain and Iceland are at loggerheads over fishing rights in the North Sea after two Icelandic gunboats seized a Grimsby trawler today. Although the Royal Navy has freed the trawler, the *Northern Foam*, this "cod war" is unlikely to end here. The Reykjavik government is determined to maintain its newly declared 12-mile (19.2-km) limit around Iceland (→ 6/5/59).

'Grand Old Man' of English music dies

London, 26 August
Dr Ralph Vaughan Williams, the most "English" composer of his time, went on producing important works to the end. His last four symphonies were written between the ages of 76 and 85 – the last, his ninth, premiered only four months before his death today. He loved and used English folk song but also wrote for films such as *Scott of the Antarctic*. His "Fantasias" were popular, but he departed from the pastoral vein in his tough and dissonant fourth symphony. "I don't know whether I like it," he said. "But that is what I meant."

Race riots break out in two English cities

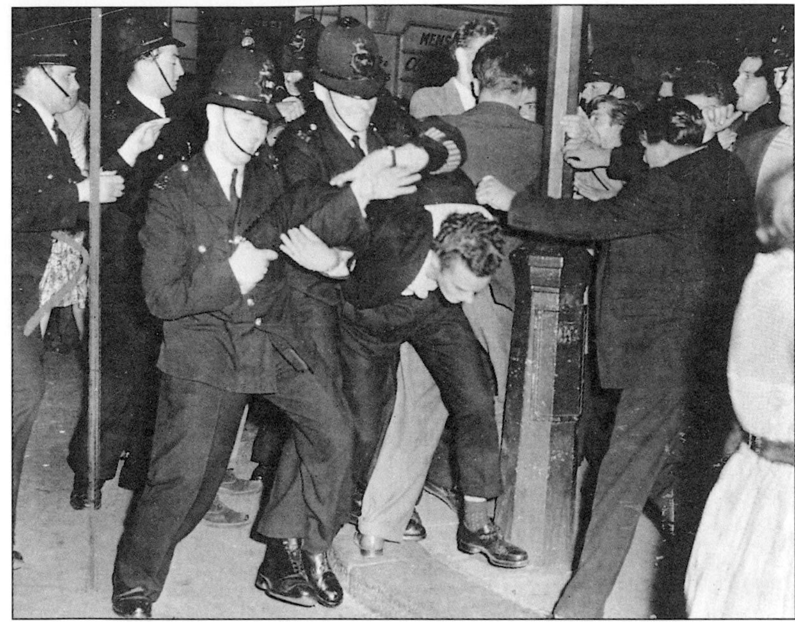

Policemen struggle with crowds as racial violence flares in Notting Hill.

London, 9 September
Petrol bombs and thousands of milk bottles were thrown at police in London last night, after white youths taunted black immigrants with racist slogans. Several people were badly hurt and 59 are being charged with weapons offences.

A white gang had been abusing black people at a house in Blenheim Crescent, Notting Hill Gate, when the immigrants replied with a hail of milk bottles and a petrol bomb. Several black men then attacked the whites with iron bars. In nearby Bayswater black men were ambushed leaving a club. Police detectives from the Special Branch think that right-wing extremists may have started the trouble.

In another incident today, at a Nottingham magistrates' court, a television cameraman was accused of starting a riot which led to a clash between white and black communities in Ann's Well Road and five people being imprisoned. The prosecution said the cameraman had attempted to reconstruct a previous fight. After he lit a magnesium flare "the mock fight, presumably staged for the benefit of the cameras, developed into something more serious" (→ 15).

The last debs are presented to the Queen

The palace feels debs are archaic.

Edinburgh, 3 July
A youthful, if perhaps archaic, ritual came to an end today when the Queen received the last debutantes to be presented at court. Miss Fiona Macrae curtseyed her way into royal history at Holyrood Palace, four months after the last debutantes had been presented at Buckingham Palace. Debs' dances, debs' delights and the whole paraphernalia of "coming out", so much a part of upper-class life, are unlikely to vanish, but this rite of passage will now have to do without royal patronage. The duke of Edinburgh played a part in ending the tradition, which he believes conflicts with the modern image sought by royalty.

LP, STD and Zeta: useful inventions enter British life

Britain, December
It has been an exciting year for scientific developments in Britain. The year opened with the announcement of experiments with a machine called "Zeta", which is reported to offer the possibility of harnessing atomic power to provide cheap or even free energy.

It is too soon to say whether this attractive theoretical vision is realistic. However, some other innovations of 1958 are already in production – including long-playing 33rpm records (LPs), a Lotus car with a glassfibre shell, and the "stereophonic" record players or amplifiers. A different kind of revolution in communications was initiated this month when the Queen made the first telephone call in a new "subscriber trunk dialling" (STD) system. On 5 December she dialled directly from Bristol to Edinburgh without her call having to be made via an operator. The Post Office says that the whole of Britain will be connected to the new STD system.

Potentially the most spectacular development is what is called a "hovercraft". This is a new form of vehicle that floats above the ground on a cushion of air and can therefore travel across water or land. It was invented by Christopher Cockerell, a Suffolk boat-builder (→ 16/4/59).

Trying out the new "stereo".

1959

Dublin, 8 January. Eamon de Valera says he will quit as prime minister and run for the Irish presidency (→ 23/6).

Surrey, 22 January. Mike Hawthorn, the British world champion racing driver, dies in a car crash at Guildford.

Britain, 22 January. New figures show that two-thirds of Britons now have television sets (→ 17/9).

Moscow, 21 February. Harold Macmillan, the British prime minister, arrives for talks with Soviet leaders (→ 29/3/60).

London, 23 February. A peace agreement is reach on the future government of Cyprus (→ 27/10).

Southern Rhodesia, 27 Feb. A state of emergency is declared in the British colony.

Britain, 27 May. Filter-tip cigarettes have helped tobacco manufacturers maintain sales after recent reports linking smoking and lung cancer.

Ireland, 23 June. Sean Lemass becomes head of the government (→ 25).

London, 7 July. Hugh Carleton-Greene is chosen to be BBC director-general.

Norwich, 28 July. The first postal codes and postal sorting machines are introduced.

Birmingham, 18 August. The "Mini" motor car is launched (→ 8/11).

London, 24 August. The House of Fraser wins a takeover battle with Debenham's for Harrod's department store.

Westminster, 27 October. The Queen's speech opening parliament promises independence for Cyprus and Nigeria (→ 16/8/60).

London, 19 November. The Queen's head is to appear on bank notes for the first time (→ 8/2/60).

Scotland, 17 November. Duty-free areas are introduced at Prestwick and Renfrew airports; Heathrow plans similar facilities (→ 22/2/60).

Stockholm, 20 November. The European Free Trade Association (EFTA) is formed by Britain and six other nations as an alternative to the six-nation European Economic Community, or Common Market (→ 14/1/63).

Westminster. The National Insurance Act introduces a graduated pension scheme.

De Valera becomes president of Ireland

Dublin, 25 June

After a lifetime in active politics, Eamon de Valera has been elected president of the Republic of Ireland. Under the constitution which he created, he moves now to a non-political, head-of-state position.

Sean Lemass replaced Eamon de Valera as leader of Fianna Fáil and head of the government two days ago, advocating a change of focus towards a more pragmatic set of priorities mainly concerned with trade and the economy. Inevitably, there will be less emphasis on civil war politics, on the reunification of Ireland and on the restoration of the Irish language (→ 6/10/61).

De Valera: the new Irish president.

Invention takes off on a cushion of air

Isle of Wight, 16 April

The hovercraft – a revolutionary vehicle that travels on a cushion of air – has just floated off the drawing board and into reality.

Unveiled last year by its inventor, the Suffolk boat-builder Christopher Cockerell, the hovercraft at once attracted the interest of the National Research and Development Corporation. Now a two-ton hovercraft is under construction by Saunders Roe on the Isle of Wight. Future plans include a 100-ton vehicle for passengers and one of 10,000 tons for freight (→ 20/7/62).

Film industry suffers as television booms

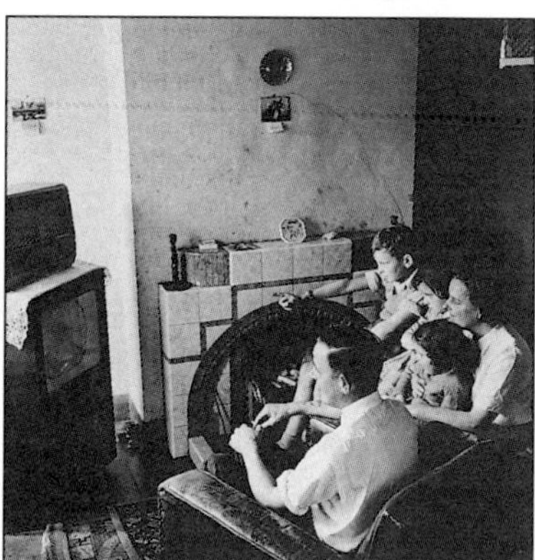

The goggle-box takes over Britain.

Britain, 17 September

The British cinema industry is being hit hard by TV. The people who used to take pleasure in going out to lose themselves in the glamour and the adventure of the movies now stay at home and watch the "goggle-box". The Rank Organization revealed today that cinema attendances slumped from 1.396 million in 1950 to 1.101 million in 1956 and they are still dwindling. Even fiercer competition is promised by the BBC's purchase of 20 American films for TV (→ 8/2/61).

Icelandic cod war hits stormy waters

North Sea, 6 May

The so-called "cod war" between Britain and Iceland is becoming increasingly violent. During a recent stand-off 20 live rounds were fired by an Icelandic gunboat at a Hull trawler, the *Arctic Viking*. Though they were just warning shots, one shell missed the trawler by a mere 3 yards. Britain has today protested vigorously to the Icelandic government about this "dangerous and unseamanlike" action.

Over five million teenagers make their mark on the decade

Britain, January

Most areas of Britain have enjoyed more affluence during this decade than ever before – and among the beneficiaries are the nation's teenagers. As a group, "teenagers" did not exist before the 1950s. Now there are fashions, music and consumer products produced specifically for a teenage market said to be worth £500 million a year.

Many of the first influences were American – actors such as Marlon Brando and James Dean or singers such as Elvis Presley. But native stars such as Cliff Richard through TV shows like *Oh Boy* have built on the earlier trad jazz and skiffle crazes to eclipse most of the Americans, at least in the home market. Films such as *Expresso Bongo* highlight the distinctive teenage culture that is emerging in Britain.

Oh Boy! Worth £500 million a year, Britain's young are taken seriously.

Mac's majority keeps the Tories in power

Westminster, 8 October
Harold Macmillan, campaigning on the slogan "You've never had it so good", has brought the Tories home with a thumping majority of 102 in the general election. The result is unique this century as the Tories have increased their majority twice in a row: from 20 in 1951 to 62 in 1955 and 102 today. The final tally of seats is expected to be Conservatives and Unionists 365, Labour 258, Liberals 6, Others 1.

"Supermac" is highly delighted with the result, although he has dismissed it offhandedly, saying: "It has gone off rather well." It did not go off at all well for the Liberals, who had such high hopes of success under their new leader, Jo Grimond. They doubled their votes but failed to win any more seats. Among their candidates were two former presidents of the Oxford Union, Jeremy Thorpe, who was elected, and Robin Day, who lost.

The Labour Party ended the day in disarray, racked with divisions and totally defeated. Hugh Gaitskell conceded defeat early in the vote-counting, bitterly blaming the squabbling between the left and right of his party. Privately he agreed with the prime minister, who commented: "I think the class war is now obsolete."

The election has, in fact, been a triumph for the unflappable prime minister, who, although patrician in style, has learnt how to appeal to the man in the street as well as to the City of London (→3/11/60).

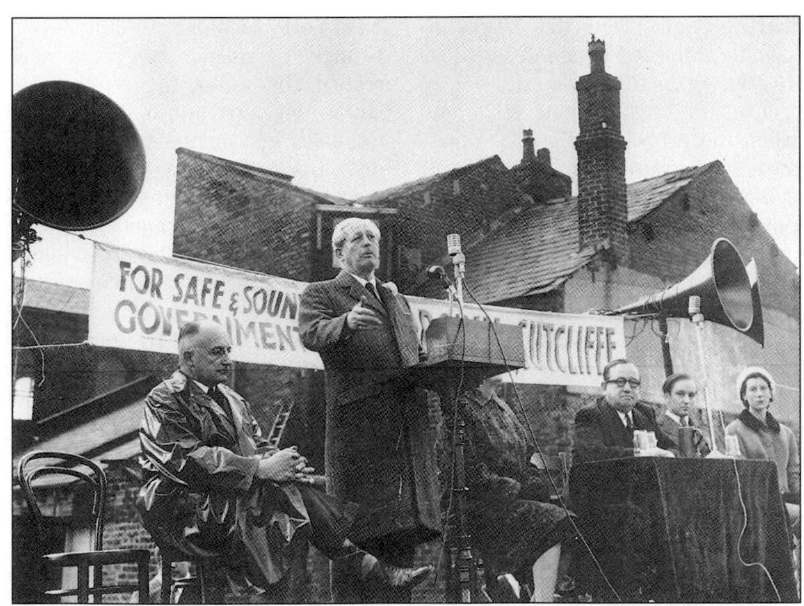
Macmillan on the stump: affluent voters have returned him to power.

Irish trade unions form new group

Dublin, 24 September
The Irish Congress of Trade Unions held its inaugural conference today. Last February the Congress of Irish Unions and the Irish Trade Union Congress voted to unite.

This represents the healing of a rift in the trade union movement that has existed since 1945 when the Irish Transport and General Workers' Union, together with a number of smaller unions, seceded from the ICTU to establish their own Congress of Irish Unions.

Report slams new buildings as 'ugly'

London, 18 December
The "drabness", "mediocrity" and "deplorably low standards" of modern inner-city architecture were attacked in the annual report of the Royal Fine Art Commission today. Ugly nuclear power stations in regions of natural beauty and spreading suburbs were also targets for criticism. The commission, whose members include John Betjeman and Henry Moore, concluded that without a plan the outlook for cities was "poor"(→2/6/60).

Motoring boom fuelled by first motorway and the introduction of the £500 'Mini'

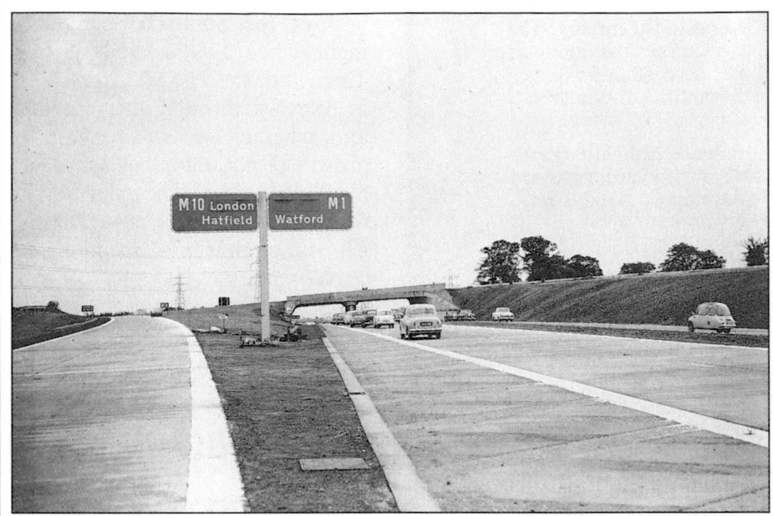

Motorways seem certain to become part of the new British landscape.

Britain, 8 November
Sightseers flocked to Britain's new motorway, the M1, on the first Sunday since it opened last week. An eight-mile by-pass for Preston was opened last year as the first stretch of motorway in Britain, but the new M1 north of Watford towards the Midlands is the first extensive stretch of proper motorway.

Its completion marks the climax of a decade of astonishing growth in motoring, which has seen the number of private cars and vans in Britain more than double from the total of 2,307,000 that were registered in 1950. This growth was boosted still further by the launch this year of the British Motor Corporation's new "Mini" car. It went on sale in August at no more than £500 including purchase tax. Its designer, Alec Issigonis, has produced a revolutionary design by mounting the engine sideways.

In many ways the Mini is an austere creation – instruments are sparse, doors are opened by strings, windows slide open – but the sprightly engine and the car's smallness make it a highly convenient vehicle for driving in town. Less welcome consequences of motoring's boom years are the introduction of parking restrictions such as yellow lines (→3/1/61).

Designer Alec Issigonis with two of the first of his revolutionary Minis.

1960

Westminster, 20 January. The government announces curbs on the sale of "pep pills".

London, 8 February. The Queen says the family name of her descendants will be Mountbatten-Windsor (→ 7/6/67).

Britain, 22 February. A supersonic airliner is to be developed, possibly in collaboration with France (→ 11/12/67).

London, 14 March. Plans are announced for a Thames barrier against floods.

Washington, DC, 29 March. Harold Macmillan reaches agreement with US leaders on a nuclear test ban treaty to be put to the USSR (→ 8/1/61).

Britain, 30 April. The Blue Streak missile project is abandoned.

London, 9 May. South Africa's apartheid policies cause a big row at the Commonwealth Conference (→ 15/3/61).

London, 2 June. Planners give details of ways in which they aim to combat the spread of high-rise buildings.

Britain, 7 June. The first NHS hearing aids are issued.

Coventry, 19 June. Jaguar takes over the Daimler motor company.

Cyprus, 16 August. The former British colony becomes independent (→ 30/9).

London, 19 August. Penguin Books is prosecuted for obscenity over its plans to publish the novel *Lady Chatterley's Lover* (→ 2/11).

London, 27 September. Europe's first moving pavement or "Travelator" goes into service at Bank station.

Nigeria, 30 September. Independence becomes effective (→ 15/3/61).

London, 17 October. It is announced that the *News Chronicle* is to close and merge with the *Daily Mail*.

Westminster, 3 November. Hugh Gaitskell sees off Harold Wilson's challenge for the Labour leadership (→ 15/3/62).

Britain, 10 November. The initial print run of 200,000 copies of *Lady Chatterley's Lover* sells out on the first day of publication.

Stratford-upon-Avon. The Royal Shakespeare Company is formed under director Peter Hall with the Aldwych theatre as its London home.

PM's talk of change angers South Africa

Cape Town, 3 February
Harold Macmillan angered members of the South African parliament when he declared in Cape Town today: "The wind of change is blowing through this continent and, whether we like it or not, this growth of national consciousness is a political fact." They did not like it at all, and many accused the British prime minister of meddling.

Now at a crucial stage of his African tour, Macmillan said that the great issue was whether Asia and Africa swung to communism or to the West and he urged South Africa to adopt policies to promote racial equality. The premier, Hendrik Verwoerd, was loudly applauded when he retorted: "There has to be justice not only for the black man but also for the white man." Britain has been bending with the "winds of change". Ghana is due to become a republic this year, Nigeria is to be independent and Kenya will be given a power-sharing constitution. Since 1945 some 500 million people in former British colonies have become self-governing (→ 9/5).

Space-tracking station sets a new record

Jodrell Bank telescope sets record.

Cheshire, 14 March
The radio telescope at Jodrell Bank has set a record in space-tracking, making contact with the American satellite Pioneer 5 over a distance of 407,000 miles (651,000km).

The first contact came yesterday when the probe was 350,000 miles away. A spokesman said: "We sent a signal out at 2pm which switched on the transmitter in the satellite and we tracked it for the next half-hour before turning it off."

The previous record – about 290,000 miles – was achieved when the Soviet Union contacted Lunik 3, which photographed the dark side of the moon last year.

Atlantic record set by lone yachtsman

Francis Chichester nears New York.

New York, 21 July
Francis Chichester has set a new record for sailing across the Atlantic. He arrived in New York today in his yacht *Gypsy Moth II* just 40 days after starting his solo voyage from Plymouth. Chichester, who is 58 years old and has had lung cancer for the last two years, was often beset by hurricane-force winds. Clothes kept in the lockers were tossed about so much that holes were worn in them. The dinner jacket he planned to wear in the evenings went mouldy (→ 27/8/66).

New talent revives Irish film industry

Ireland, 5 February
President Eamon de Valera and the Irish prime minister, Sean Lemass, have both attended the première this evening of the first full-length feature film to be made in the Irish language. It is entitled *Mise Eire* (*I am Ireland*).

The creation of George Morrison – an international film archivist of some distinction – with Irish folk music orchestrated by Sean O'Riada, *Mise Eire* will give Irish audiences their first opportunity to see a film about their recent past. The period covered is the civil war and the war of independence. It is also hoped that the film, which was made in collaboration with Gael-Linn, will help in a campaign to promote the Irish language.

May 6. Princess Margaret waves to the crowds from the balcony of Buckingham Palace following her wedding to the photographer Antony Armstrong-Jones, here standing between the Queen and Queen Mother.

Irish soldiers killed in Congo troubles

Ireland, 8 November
Ireland's involvement in United Nations peacekeeping in the Congo has resulted in the tragic deaths of ten soldiers in an ambush at Niemba. A wave of sadness, mingled with pride, has swept Ireland at this first international sacrifice in the cause of world peace. It is widely seen as the mark of Ireland's emergence from its isolation after the Second World War.

The decision to commit military forces to the peacekeeping effort in central Africa, which required special Dáil legislation, also involved General Sean MacEoin, and, at the diplomatic level, the controversial work in Katanga of Conor Cruise O'Brien (→1/12/61)

Surge in gambling

Britain, December
The passing of the Betting and Gaming Act, designed to set the British love of a flutter within a legal framework, has led to a great surge in gambling, with betting shops and gambling clubs springing up to replace the street-corner bookies. The growing craze for bingo is astonishing. Many disused churches and cinemas are being converted into bingo halls.

'Lady Chatterley' is cleared of obscenity

Queues form to buy "Lady Chatterley's Lover" after the jury's decision.

London, 2 November
Lady Chatterley's Lover, the long-banned novel by D.H. Lawrence, has emerged from the shadows and into the bookshops, thanks to today's landmark decision by an Old Bailey jury, who declared that the work, prosecuted under last year's Obscene Publications Act, was not obscene. As of today copies of the 3/6d [17.5p] Penguin paperback will be freely available.

The "Lady C" trial has been a test case for the new act, the first of its kind since 1857, and is designed to draw a line between "filth" and work that, though controversial, is of real literary merit. Too often, the literary baby has been washed away with the "dirty" bathwater.

In many ways the trial pitted the old Britain against the new, with experts from both sides putting forward their own sincerely held beliefs. It has not only been a case of what makes "literature", but of the direction of national morality. The old brigade may complain, but the Old Bailey jury has voted for the future (→10).

National Service's passing-out parade

Britain, 31 December
National service – a rite of passage that has been losing its popularity among British males – came to an end today when 2,049 young men became the last to receive their call-up cards. Since national service began in 1939, 5,300,000 scruffy civilians have been squarebashed into men by bellowing sergeants. All but 50 of today's batch are destined for the army; others will join the RAF. The privates will discover the joys of Brasso and blanco on two weeks' basic training in Aldershot, while the RAF recruits will fall in at Cardington, Bedfordshire.

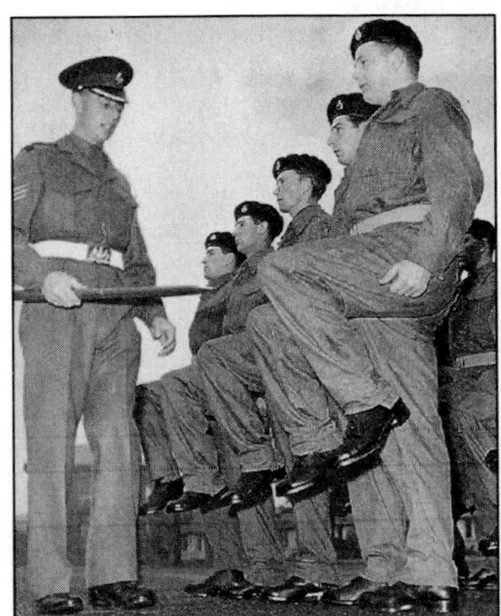
The last of the batch go on parade.

Working-class realism takes the centre stage in films and plays

London, December
Working-class realism, pioneered at the Royal Court theatre, has all but ousted traditional drawing room comedy from the West End, banishing "posh" diction in favour of regional accents and manners.

The Court has produced Arnold Wesker's plays *Roots*, which focuses on farmworkers in Norfolk, and *The Kitchen*, set below stairs in a restaurant. Harold Pinter with *The Caretaker*, about a devious tramp, Shelagh Delaney with *A Taste of Honey*, set in deprived Salford, and Keith Waterhouse with *Billy Liar*, the dreams of a Leeds undertaker's assistant, are among the new wave of playwrights, while the cinema has produced *Room at the Top* and *Saturday Night and Sunday Morning* in the same vein.

Albert Finney on the make in "Saturday Night and Sunday Morning".

Labour leaders are split over the bomb

Scarborough, 3 October
A furious row erupted at the Labour Party conference here today over nuclear disarmament. During the debate the party leader, Hugh Gaitskell, launched a fierce attack on the supporters of the Campaign for Nuclear Disarmament, calling them "pacifists, unilateralists and fellow travellers". Close to tears, he told a largely hostile conference: "There are some of us who will fight, fight and fight again to bring back sanity and honesty to the party we love." Despite his plea, the major unions voted with the unilateralists to "ban the bomb". Ignoring all other differences, the party is now split from top to bottom on this one issue (→12/9/61).

1961

Britain, 3 January. The one millionth Morris Minor is produced (→ 10/7/62).

Britain, 8 January. Five people, including the Canadian businessman Gordon Lonsdale, are arrested as spies (→ 8/5/).

Britain, 30 January. An oral contraceptive pill becomes available in Britain (→ 4/12).

Ireland, 31 January. The West Clare railway, made famous in song by Percy French, closes.

London, 8 February. The BBC says it is to drop the radio programme *Children's Hour* because television has cut its audiences (→ 31/12).

London, 15 March. South Africa says it will leave the Commonwealth after becoming a republic in May (→ 24/10).

Paris, 28 April. It is revealed that Britain has applied to join the Common Market (→ 4/8).

Wembley, 6 May. Tottenham Hotspur become the first team this century to complete the league and FA Cup "double".

Britain, 18 May. New universities are to be built at Colchester, Canterbury and Coventry.

Canterbury,27 June. Michael Ramsey becomes the 100th archbishop of Canterbury.

London, 28 June. A judge says that a ballot by the Electrical Trades Union was illegal because it was rigged by communists.

London, 14 July. Yuri Gagarin, the first spaceman, receives an ecstatic welcome from crowds as he begins a visit to Britain.

Westminster, 4 August. MPs approve the government's bid to join the Common Market.

Sussex, 28 August. The earliest known Roman mosaics are uncovered at Fishbourne, near Chichester.

London, 12 September. Nobel prize winner Bertrand Russell and playwright Arnold Wesker are jailed for inciting a breach of the peace in their campaign for nuclear disarmament (→ 18).

Malta, 24 October. The island becomes independent (→ 27/10/64).

Britain, 4 December. The oral contraceptive pill is to become available on the NHS (→ 12/1967).

Dublin, 31 December. Radio Eireann begins a television service (→ 27/6/62).

Mass arrests at big ban-the-bomb demo

London, 18 September

More than 800 people were arrested today in the biggest, most violent ban-the-bomb demonstration so far seen in London. Among those held by police were Canon John Collins, the chairman of the Campaign for Nuclear Disarmament, the playwright John Osborne, the jazz singer George Melly and the actress Vanessa Redgrave.

At one point over 15,000 protestors jammed Trafalgar Square, on a day that saw the Russians explode the 12th nuclear bomb in the present series of tests. The clashes came as 3,000 police struggled to arrest demonstrators staging "sit-down" protests. Last week the Nobel prizewinning philosopher Bertrand Russell, a prominent member of CND, was jailed for inciting a breach of the peace.

Formed just over three and a half years ago, CND has gained the support of between a quarter and a third of the public, according to opinion polls. Last year it was a major factor in persuading the Labour Party's annual conference to back unilateral nuclear disarmament. But the determination of the Tory government to maintain its independent deterrent has led some CND supporters to form a Committee of 100, which urges civil disobedience rather than seeking to woo political parties (→ 20/2/62).

Part of a crowd estimated at 15,000 stage a "sit-down" nuclear protest.

Labour peer battles for Commons seat

Benn fights against being a peer.

Westminster, 8 May

Anthony Wedgwood Benn, who has just doubled his majority in the by-election at Bristol South-east, was refused admission to the House of Commons today when he arrived to claim his seat. His problem is that the by-election was caused by his own elevation to the peerage as Viscount Stansgate on the death of his father last year. As a peer, he cannot sit in the Commons.

The reluctant Labour lord was barred from the Commons by the principal doorkeeper, a formidable former regimental sergeant major, who told him that, if necessary, force would be used to keep him out. He must now await the passage of a law enabling peers to renounce their titles (→ 30/5/63).

Brainwashed spy is jailed for 42 years

London, 8 May

An ex-diplomat was given a record 42-year jail term at the Old Bailey today. For nine and a half years the self-confessed spy, 38-year-old George Blake, is said to have passed all the documents he could to the Russians while working in Germany and the Lebanon. Lord Chief Justice Parker said his treachery had "rendered much of this country's efforts useless". Blake was captured by the communists in the Korean war when he was vice-consul in Seoul. He was held for three years and is thought to have been brainwashed (→ 22/10/62).

English women finalists at Wimbledon

Mortimer (right) wins Wimbledon.

Wimbledon, 8 July

For the first time since 1914 the All-England Lawn Tennis and Croquet Club of Wimbledon today staged an all-English final for its ladies' singles championship. It ensured the first home win since Dorothy Round's in 1937.

Christine Truman, just 20, was favoured to beat her compatriot, Angela Mortimer, for the title. But Mortimer's patience eventually won the day against the greater power of Truman, who appeared to have been hampered by a fall in the first half of a closely fought match. Mortimer, in her second Wimbledon singles final, finally won in three sets by 4-6, 6-4, 7-5.

Government tightens immigration control

Westminster, 1 November
The government, concerned about the ability of Britain to absorb the increasing number of immigrants from the Commonwealth, is to introduce a Commonwealth Immigration Bill which will impose some restrictions on their numbers. More than 21,000 arrived last year and 100,000 are expected this year.

Under the terms of the bill Commonwealth citizens will be able to apply for an entry voucher if they have a job to come to, or if they possess skills or educational qualifications likely to be useful in the United Kingdom. They may also be allowed to enter as part of a quota, the size of which will be decided at any given time by the government. There will be no restrictions on immigrants who can support themselves by private means.

The bill, seen against the background of the racial disturbances in Nottingham and London's Notting Hill, is bound to cause great political controversy. The Labour and Liberal parties are certain to oppose it on the ground of racial discrimination because it will hardly affect white Commonwealth immigrants. At the same time the Labour Party is bound to be embarrassed by the hostile attitude of its working-class supporters to coloured immigrants who are seen to be competing for jobs and houses (→2/7/62).

Seeking a new life: West Indian immigrants arrive in Southampton.

Irish diplomat sacked

Conor Cruise O'Brien talks to Irish UN troops in breakaway Katanga.

Ireland, 1 December
In an atmosphere of intense controversy, the secondment of Conor Cruise O'Brien from the department of external affairs to the United Nations, as special representative in Katanga, has been ended. He has been recalled to the Irish foreign service by the minister for external affairs, but is unlikely to accept this move, and will almost certainly resign.

He has been the victim of personal vilification, mainly directed at his left-wing views, in an attempt to prevent him from implementing the United Nations mandate in the Congo – part of which involved the removal of all foreign military and paramilitary personnel, including mercenaries and foreign political advisers.

Although complex, the situation has involved at least two countries, France and Britain, in activities designed deliberately to frustrate the objectives of the UN while at the same time maintaining formal support for that organization. They allowed United Nations resolutions aimed at ending the conflict to pass, but then took action to stop their implementation. They also actively worked to ensure the removal of Conor Cruise O'Brien from the key position he occupied, a move to which the Irish government has reluctantly agreed.

'Beyond the Fringe' is satirical success

Britain, December
Four university graduates, appearing on stage without scenery or special costumes, have brought a new brand of satirical humour to London's West End this year with their revue, *Beyond the Fringe*. The quartet – Alan Bennett, Peter Cook, Jonathan Miller and Dudley Moore – find humour in politics, the Church, the Second World War and even death. The revue's successful transfer from the Edinburgh Festival has been followed by the launch of a new satirical magazine, *Private Eye*, which revives the tradition of lampooning public figures.

Sean Lemass set to head minority rule

Ireland, 6 October
In his first electoral test as leader of Fianna Fáil, Sean Lemass has demonstrated that he is an indifferent votegetter, but he has managed to form a minority government with the support of independents.

After the baleful years of the fifties, with high emigration, serious balance of payments problems and poor economic growth, the country is beginning to show signs of recovery and Sean Lemass, widely regarded as having the right mixture of business opportunism and caution, is seen as the right leader for the new decade (→26/2/62).

Eighty-two people were killed in Ireland's worst air crash, when this chartered DC6 of President Air Lines crashed into the Shannon estuary.

1962

Liverpool, January. The Beatles, a local rock group, are refused a contract by the Decca record company (→4/11/63).

Essex, 11 February. A schoolboy claims a world record after dancing "the Twist" nonstop for 33 hours.

London, 17 February. James Hanratty is sentenced to death for murdering Michael Gregsten on the A6 last year, after the longest murder trial in British history.

London, 20 February. Six anti-nuclear protesters are jailed under the Official Secrets Act (→8/8/63).

Northern Ireland, 26 February. The IRA announces a ceasefire after a five-year campaign of violence (→25/3/63).

Kent, 15 March. The Liberals overturn a huge Tory majority to win the Orpington by-election (→13/7).

London, 2 April. The first push-button-controlled pedestrian "Panda" crossings are introduced.

West Sussex, 23 April. Stirling Moss, the racing driver, is seriously injured in a crash at Goodwood.

Brighton, 3 June. The first legal casino in Britain opens.

Britain, 27 June. A second BBC television channel is urged by a government committee (→11/7).

Belfast, 10 July. A motorway opens to Lisburn, the first in Ireland (→22/8/63).

Cornwall, 11 July. The first live television pictures are beamed across the Atlantic via the Telstar satellite and a terminal at Goonhilly Downs (→19/1/63).

London, 9 August. Sir Laurence Olivier is named as the first director of the National Theatre (→22/10/63).

Britain, 19 September. A royal commission recommends the creation of a "press council".

London, 8 October. Judge Elizabeth Lane becomes the first female judge to sit in the High Court (→1970).

Westminster, 8 November. A junior minister, Thomas Galbraith, resigns after his letters to the spy, William Vassall, are published (→11/5/63).

Bermuda, 21 December. The US agrees to sell Polaris missiles to Britain.

Mac purges his cabinet

Westminster, 13 July

Harold Macmillan, renowned as "Supermac", is now being called "Mac the Knife" after his ruthless purge of his ministers tonight. The prime minister has sacked seven of his most senior colleagues – one-third of the cabinet. It is a blood-letting on a scale without equal in modern political life.

The casualties, headed by Selwyn Lloyd, the chancellor of the exchequer, Lord Kilmuir, the lord chancellor, and Harold Watkinson, the minister of defence, seem to have had little notice of their dismissals, which followed 24 hours after another huge Tory voting collapse in by-election polling.

The view in Westminster is that the prime minister, normally so unflappable, has been panicked into extreme action in order to save his government, which is under pressure from many quarters. Rising unemployment, the pay pause, Britain's failure to keep up with her economic rivals, especially resurgent Germany and Japan, have all eroded Tory support among its traditional sympathizers.

It was the Orpington by-election in March, when a Tory majority of nearly 15,000 was turned into a Liberal win by 7,800, which sounded the alarm. There is a smell of Tory fear in the air and it is doubtful if Macmillan's explanation of his purge – "we need a broad reconstruction" – will wash. Observers see it more as a firing squad to encourage the others (→14/2/63).

"Mac the Knife" draws blood.

Civil servant spy jailed for 18 years

London, 22 October

A 38-year-old admiralty clerk and son of a vicar, who was "entrapped by his lust", was jailed for 18 years today for spying for the USSR.

While working at the British embassy in Moscow, William Vassall was photographed at a homosexual party and blackmailed. Back in London he used a tiny camera to photograph "highly important" documents and was paid enough to double his salary. The Attorney-General, Sir John Hobson, said: "Entrapped by his lust he had neither the moral fibre nor the patriotism to alter his conduct" (→8/11).

Sporting changes

London, July

The Gentlemen and the Players will meet this month for the 137th, and last, time. The annual match between the nation's top amateur and professional cricketers has been ended by the cricket authorities at Lord's on the grounds that it is anachronistic. In another portent of professional dominance, players in the most popular winter game, football, have won their campaign against the minimum wage.

Britten's 'War Requiem' marks the opening of Coventry Cathedral

The interior of the new Coventry Cathedral, risen from the ashes of 1940.

Coventry, 30 May

Benjamin Britten's sombre new *War Requiem* was given its first performance here tonight as part of the inauguration of Coventry's new cathedral. The stone building, joined to the black ruins of the old, which was destroyed by German bombers in November 1940, was designed by Sir Basil Spence and is dominated by works by contemporary artists: a vast window of richly coloured glass by John Piper, a giant tapestry of Christ Enthroned by Graham Sutherland and, beside the entrance steps, Jacob Epstein's huge sculpture of St Michael, the cathedral patron saint, triumphing over the Devil. Building took six years. Britten's setting of the requiem mass alternating with First World War poems by Wilfrid Owen has already been hailed as a major masterpiece (→4/12/76).

First hovercraft passenger service opens

The first passengers reach the shore after a hover trip at up to 56mph.

Rhyl, 20 July
The world's first ever passenger hovercraft service opened today, running from Rhyl to Wallasey across the estuary of the River Dee. It carried 24 passengers, plus 8,000 letters and cards. The hovercraft was invented in 1953 by Christopher Cockerell, who was knighted for his efforts. Designed to operate over water, rough or swampy ground, or flat land surfaces, the craft rides on a cushion of air, generated by downwards-directed fans and driven by a gas turbine or diesel engine. It is hoped that their commercial use may be extended to longer journeys (→ 30/4/66).

Immigrants rush to beat midnight deadline

Westminster, 2 July
The new rules restricting the right of Commonwealth citizens to enter the United Kingdom became effective at midnight last night. The advent of the restrictions has led to a last-minute flood of immigrants and there have been some remarkable scenes at ports and airports. Among the luckiest were 74 Jamaicans without the newly required work permits whose plane was delayed by bad weather. They landed at Belfast 56 minutes after the new rules were applied but were allowed to stay. Others were less lucky. Three Pakistanis were sent home from London and several Indians and Adenis are being held awaiting repatriation (→ 22/2/68).

007 James Bond makes his screen debut

The name is Bond, James Bond.

London, 30 October
The exotic adventures and hair's-breadth escapes from implausible villains by novelist Ian Fleming's hero, James Bond, might have been thought unfilmable. But *Dr No* is proving that assumption wrong.

The terrors of the Caribbean island of Crab Key, where Dr No resides, are handled with nonchalant ease by Sean Connery as Agent 007. The direction by Terence Young is smooth and efficient, above the average for British thrillers. Fleming has written 12 James Bond novels and plans are afoot to film *From Russia With Love* and *Goldfinger*.

1963

Paris, 14 January. President de Gaulle dashes Britain's hopes of joining the European Economic Community (→ 16/5/67).

London, 18 January. Hugh Gaitskell, the Labour leader, dies aged 56 (→ 14/2).

London, 4 February. Two journalists are jailed for refusing to disclose the sources of their stories.

Westminster, 22 March. John Profumo, the war minister, tells MPs there was "no impropriety" in his friendship with a model, Christine Keeler (→ 5/6).

Belfast, 25 March. Captain Terence O'Neill becomes prime minister of Northern Ireland (→ 28/10/64).

Moscow, 11 May. Greville Wynne, a British businessman, is jailed for spying (→ 1/7).

Westminster, 30 May. A Peerage Bill is published which will enable peers such as Viscount Stansgate (Anthony Wedgwood Benn) to renounce their titles.

London, 9 July. Ninety-four people are arrested after protests against a visit by the Greek king and queen.

Westminster, 22 July. An independent commission into slum housing is announced.

Moscow, 8 August. A treaty is signed banning nuclear tests in the atmosphere (→ 17/6/80).

London, 26 September. A report on the Profumo scandal by top judge Lord Denning says security had not been endangered but criticizes how ministers handled the affair.→

Scarborough, 3 October. Harold Wilson commits Labour to a new scientific revolution.

Westminster, 10 October. Harold Macmillan announces his resignation as prime minister because of illness (→ 18).

Westminster, 20 October. Iain Macleod and Enoch Powell refuse to serve in the cabinet under Lord Home (→ 8/11).

Kinross, 8 November. Sir Alec Douglas-Home, having renounced his earldom, wins a by-election in order to join the House of Commons (→ 16/10/64).

London, 6 December. Christine Keeler is jailed for perjury and conspiracy to pervert the course of justice.

Wilson elected as new Labour leader

Westminster, 14 February
Harold Wilson has today emerged the victor in a bruising battle for the leadership of the Labour Party following the death of Hugh Gaitskell. After James Callaghan was eliminated from the contest in a preliminary vote, the choice was between the wily Wilson and the temperamental George Brown, who was the deputy leader of the party under Mr Gaitskell. After much infighting Wilson eventually won comfortably with 144 votes against 103. Aged 46, he is the youngest leader in the history of the Labour Party. "My mandate", he says, "is to lead the party to victory in the coming election and that is what I intend to do" (→ 10/10).

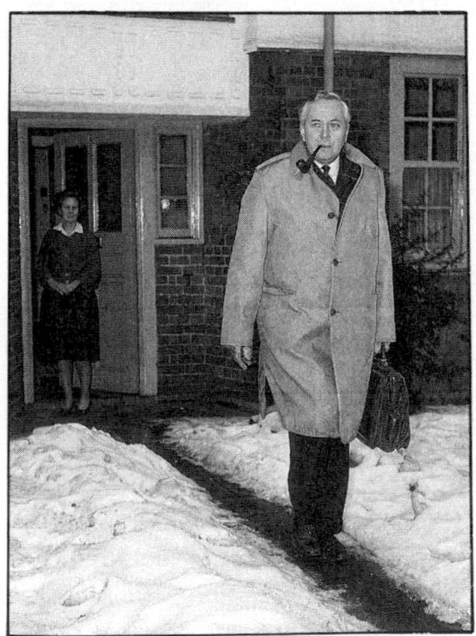

Harold Wilson is Labour's choice.

Politicians upset by lampooning 'TW3'

Britain, 19 January
Public houses will empty earlier than usual tonight, conversation will stop in millions of homes. The reason? A late-night, live television show called *That Was The Week That Was*. Its brand of irreverent humour has upset politicians and troubled the BBC governors but also attracted audiences of up to 12 million since it began last month. Religion, royalty, politics and sex were previously taboo in comedy shows on TV, but they are staple ingredients of "TW3", which is fronted by David Frost (→ 17/1/64). ▷

War minister quits after sex and spy revelations

Profumo, dressed for state pomp.

London, 5 June
John Profumo, the secretary of state for war, resigned from office today, confirming one detail of a long-simmering scandal involving sex, high society and national security. He admitted "with deep remorse" that ten weeks ago he lied to the Commons in saying that there had been "no impropriety whatever" in his relationship with attractive young "model" Christine Keeler, at the time a missing witness in an Old Bailey trial.

For months there have been hints, like this version of "She Was Poor But She Was Honest" on the satirical TV show TW3: "See him in the House of Commons/Making laws to put the blame/While the object of his passion/Walks the street to hide her shame."

The scandal now rocking Mr Macmillan's government first emerged when a West End osteopath and artist, Stephen Ward, facing charges of living off immoral earnings, claimed that Profumo had used his flat to meet Keeler. Ward had a country cottage on Lord Astor's Cliveden estate and it was there, Ward claimed, that Profumo first saw 21-year-old Keeler naked in the swimming pool.

But the scandal does not just involve sex and high society – after Profumo's first statement he and and his wife, the actress Valerie Hobson, went to the races with the Queen Mother – spying is said to be involved, too. Another of Keeler's lovers is the Soviet naval attaché Captain Eugene Ivanov and there are rumours that Ward is in the pay of MI5.

To spice this brew still further another of Keeler's lovers recently attempted to shoot her, and her flatmate is Ward's mistress, an 18-year-old blonde model Mandy Rice Davies, who was previously mistress to the notorious slum landlord Peter Rachman.

Mr Macmillan has written to Profumo saying: "This is a great tragedy for you." He hopes the confession and resignation will end the matter. It seems unlikely (→3/8).

Keeler, undressed for the camera.

Ward takes fatal overdose after vice trial

London, 3 August
Dr Stephen Ward, the artist and osteopath at the centre of the high-society sex scandal, is dead. He had been in a coma for three days after overdosing on sleeping pills on the final day of his trial.

While unconscious he was found guilty of living off immoral earnings, a charge he firmly denied. He claimed he was a victim of a campaign of vilification and that the authorities were determined to destroy him for his part in the Profumo affair.

The trial revealed a twilight world where the rich and famous consort with drug addicts, callgirls like Christine Keeler and others of dubious morality. Members of the public queued for hours to hear details of orgies, two-way mirrors and black magic rituals.

Ward, the son of a vicar, admitted to being a connoisseur of love-making and a "thoroughly immoral man" but strenuously denied he had ever taken money for prostitution. However, in his hour of need, high society deserted him (→26/9).

Ward, deserted by his high-society friends, hemmed in by officials.

Sex scandal investigated by Lord Denning

Mandy Rice-Davies leaves the Old Bailey after giving evidence.

London, 26 September
It must have been the first time ever that hundreds of people scrabbled for copies of a government report when it went on sale at midnight. But this was the Denning report on the Profumo affair and there was always hope of fresh revelations. Who, for example, was the eminent figure who served at dinner parties naked except for a mask?

Sensation-seekers, however, had to content themselves with learning that Harold Macmillan and his ministers were condemned for failing to deal with the affair even when it was affecting public confidence, but that security was not endangered. The man in the mask was interviewed but Denning declared he was not a minister.

Fall-out from the affair continues. Police are investigating the confessions of two prostitutes, Vicky Barrett and Ronna Ricardo, that they lied when giving evidence against Stephen Ward; evidence of perjury has also emerged in the trial of "Lucky" Gordon, Christine Keeler's boyfriend (→6/12).

Train robbers steal more than a million

Buckinghamshire, 8 August
A gang of highly organized thieves netted the biggest haul ever taken in a British robbery today when they stopped a Royal Mail train and stole 120 mailbags holding well over £1 million worth of banknotes. At least 15 men, armed and masked, carried out what has been dubbed the Great Train Robbery, but police suspect that so carefully planned a crime must have had inside help. No firearms were used but the driver, Jack Mills, aged 58, was severely beaten during the raid, which depended on split-second timing (→ 27/3/64).

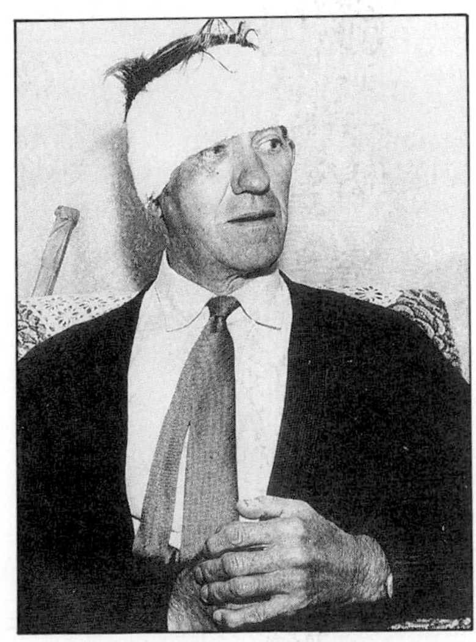

Driver Jack Mills was clubbed.

Complete outsider becomes new Tory PM

Westminster, 18 October
The unlikely figure of the 14th Earl of Home is to be Britain's next prime minister. His name emerged from the mysterious Tory process of "consultation" following the resignation of the ailing, dispirited Harold Macmillan during the party conference at Blackpool last week. Lord Home, a cricket-loving Old Etonian, will renounce his title in order to sit in the Commons.

Behind the smooth announcement that he has been appointed by the queen on the advice of Mr Macmillan and after consulting Sir Winston Churchill and other elder statesmen, lies a tale of intrigue and skulduggery. It was expected that "Rab" Butler, the deputy premier, would get the job but Macmillan, an old foe of the urbane Butler, plotted from his hospital bed to have him excluded.

Lord Hailsham and Reginald Maudling were also found wanting by the Tory "magic circle" and Macmillan produced Alec Douglas Home, as he will be called, like a rabbit from a hat (→ 20).

Home: like a rabbit from a hat.

Nuffield, the creator of Morris cars, dies

London, 22 August
Lord Nuffield, the farmer's son who became to Britain what Henry Ford was to America, has died at the age of 84. His was a remarkable success story. Born William Morris, he worked in a cycle repair shop in Oxford, set up his own business and then turned to making cycles. He progressed to motorcycles and, in 1912, produced his first car. He saw the potential of the family car and made a fortune from classics like the Morris Oxford. His MG sports cars enjoyed worldwide acclaim.

In later life he developed a second career, giving away the £27 million he had accumulated in the first. His greatest gift was the Nuffield Foundation (→ 24/11/65).

Rail branch lines axed by Beeching

London, 27 March
The nation's rail network is to be savagely pruned under proposals contained in *The Reshaping of British Railways*, by Dr Beeching, who was brought in as chairman of the British Railways Board to increase efficiency. The proposed cuts are certain to raise fierce opposition. They will slash the rail network by a quarter, close 2,128 stations, scrap 8,000 coaches and axe 67,700 jobs. There will be no passenger services north of Inverness and most branch lines in north and central Wales and the West Country will close (→ 16/2/65).

Report urges spread of higher education

Westminster, 23 October
A massive expansion of higher education is called for in a report published today by a government-appointed committee under Lord Robbins. The report says that higher education should be available to all those qualified to benefit from it. It proposes six new universities – in addition to the four approved two years ago – and the expansion of existing universities, plus university status for ten colleges of advanced technology (→ 1/1965).

Screaming pop fans go wild as 'Beatlemania' sweeps Britain

London, 4 November
The indisputable stars of the Royal Variety Show tonight were four young men from Liverpool. "Rattle your jewels," said John Lennon as the Beatles rocked their way to another triumph. Their first record made only a modest impact last year, but this year has seen a string of number ones such as *She Loves You* and *I Wanna Hold Your Hand.*

Most of their songs are composed by two members of the group, John Lennon and Paul McCartney – but the music can rarely be heard above the screams of fans in the grip of "Beatlemania". Roads and airports have been blocked by fans clamouring to see the "Fab Four", who next year plan to take their music to America (→ 8/2/64).

The "Fab Four" celebrate the news that "She Loves You" has sold a million.

Bishop of Woolwich causes unholy row

London, 31 December
The press, secular and religious alike, has been unusually riven with arguments about the nature of God ever since the Bishop of Woolwich, Dr John Robinson, published a slim paperback entitled *Honest to God* earlier this year. In it he says the traditional ways of conceiving of God, as "up there" above the clouds and later "out there" beyond the universe, like a mental vision of an Old Man in the Sky, are nowadays obstacles to faith. God as "a sort of celestial Big Brother" must give way to God as "ultimate reality" and the ground of all being. But as to how this is to be imagined, the bishop remains obscure.

▷

'Third Man' named in spy controversy

London, 1 July

The government admitted today in a House of Commons statement that "Kim" Philby, the former foreign office colleague of the traitors Burgess and Maclean, was, after all, the "Third Man". It was he who tipped off Maclean, through Burgess, that he had been discovered. Both then fled to the Soviet Union.

Philby was named by Labour MP Marcus Lipton in 1955 but he was cleared by Harold Macmillan, then foreign secretary. Philby was forced to resign from the Foreign Office in 1951 and became a foreign correspondent in Beirut. He vanished in January and is now assumed to be in Moscow (→ 22/4/64).

Philby: Moscow's secret servant.

Curtain goes up on 'National' actors

London, 22 October

The National Theatre Company's first performance took place tonight at its temporary home, the Old Vic. Laurence Olivier directed *Hamlet* with Peter O'Toole in the title role leading a company mainly of young actors who have yet to make their names. It is nearly 60 years since the first practical proposals for a national theatre: after many false starts an architect, Denys Lasdun, has been appointed and a site – the fifth – has been chosen, on the South Bank. Parliament in 1949 voted £1 million to build the theatre.

1964

London, 13 January. Designer Mary Quant says Paris fashions are out of date (→ 12/1964).

Britain, 17 January. The top TV programme is *Steptoe and Son* (→ 21/4).

London, 6 February. Britain and France agree to build a Channel tunnel (→ 20/1/75).

New York, 8 February. The Beatles arrive at the start of their first US tour (→ 30/6/67).

Ireland, 20 March. Playwright Brendan Behan dies.

Aylesbury, 27 March. Ten men are convicted for their part in last year's Great Train Robbery.

Britain, 28 March. Radio Caroline begins pop music transmissions from a ship in the North Sea.

London, 31 March. Single service ministries are abolished and become part of the ministry of defence.

London, 9 April. Labour wins the first elections for the new Greater London Council.

Britain, 21 April. BBC-2 goes on the air; *Play School* is its first programme (→ 8/2/65).

Berlin, 22 April. Greville Wynne is freed by the Russians in a spy swap deal for Gordon Lonsdale (→ 23/7/65).

Co Down, 2 July. The Ulster Folk Museum opens at Cultra.

Westminster, 28 July. Winston Churchill leaves the House of Commons for the last time (→ 24/1/65).

Britain, 29 July. The first clinic offering family planning advice to unmarried women opens (→ 12/1967).

London, 21 August. Three women are found guilty of indecency for wearing "topless" dresses.

South-east Asia, 3 September. Britain agrees to back Malaysian forces against Indonesian aggression.

Britain, 15 September. The *Daily Herald* ceases publication, to be replaced by *The Sun*.

Belfast, 28 October. Rioting begins in Catholic areas after a republican flag is removed by the police (→ 9/2/65).

London, 27 October. Harold Wilson warns Southern Rhodesia against a unilateral declaration of independence (→ 11/11/65).

Mods and Rockers run riot on South Coast

Mods charge across Margate sands in pursuit of the retreating Rockers.

Margate, 18 May

Rival gangs of teenage Mods and Rockers clashed again this weekend at a number of South Coast resorts. Members of the teen cults fought, terrorized holidaymakers and ran riot in an orgy of vandalism that brought chaos and violence to the Whitsun break.

Fights broke out in Southend, Bournemouth and Clacton, but the resorts worst hit were Brighton, where police dispersed a mob of 600 youths and arrested 76, and Margate, where two teenagers were stabbed and 51 arrests were made.

Jailing four of the rioters, and imposing fines that totalled £1,900, the magistrate echoed the views of many when he dismissed the brawlers as "little sawdust Caesars". One paid his fine by cheque, a gesture that seemed to sum up what many see as a culture that gives its youngsters too much money and too little responsibility.

Mods – sharp-suited, scooter-riding, and consumers of "purple hearts", that is, amphetamines – and Rockers – who prefer leather jackets, motorcycles and alcohol – have hit the headlines this summer with a series of beachfront battles. This weekend has seen the worst violence yet, and Home Secretary Henry Brooke has promised action.

Press baron Beaverbrook dies, aged 85

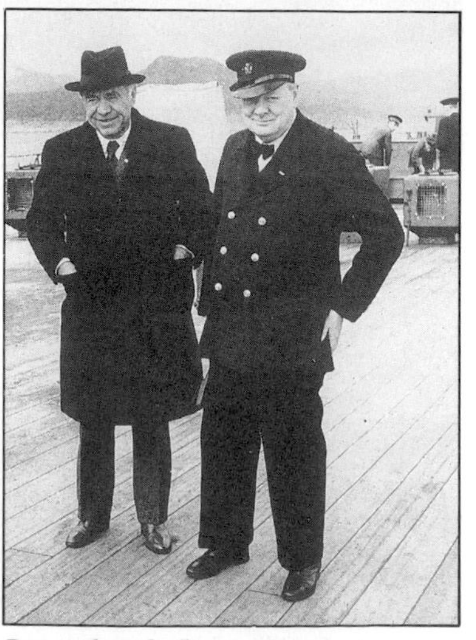

Beaverbrook (l): newspaper tycoon.

London, 9 June

Lord Beaverbrook, the Canadian-born press baron, died of cancer today. He was 85. A bishop's son, he made his first fortune with deals which owed more to buccaneering zeal than evangelical spirit. He arrived in London like a whirlwind, throwing himself into politics and using his *Express* newspapers to "cause trouble".

He knew he was dying and met death with customary bravery. Two weeks ago he made a supreme effort to attend his birthday party at the Dorchester. He moved his friends to tears when he said he would soon become an apprentice again, whether in heaven or hell he did not know.

Labour back in power

Westminster, 16 October
The Labour Party has won the general election – but by the thinnest of margins. Labour has 317 seats, the Tories 303, the Liberals 9. Counting the Speaker's seat this gives the new prime minister, Harold Wilson, an overall majority of only 4. It was uncertain until the last votes were counted late this afternoon which party would emerge the victor.

But Wilson is delighted. "Nice place we've got here," he said as he stepped inside 10 Downing Street. He led his party to victory with the promise of "purposive planning" and benefited from his pipe-puffing wisdom, which came over well on the new electoral weapon of television. His rival's cadaverous features showed up to poor advantage and he could not rid himself of the tag of "14th earl of Home" despite his neat retaliatory crack that his opponent was presumably the 14th Mr Wilson.

What remains to be seen now is whether Wilson, with such a small majority, can run the country in the face of hostile opposition in the House of Commons (→22/7/65).

Harold Wilson and George Brown had high hopes despite a slim majority.

Vocal younger generation cuts loose to forge a fashionable, swinging Britain

Britain, December
Whether it is a reaction to the austerity of the years after the Second World War, the growth of the baby boom generation, or the flowering of Mr Macmillan's "never had it so good" society, today the keyword is youth. And Britain, often seen as a backwater in the face of the ever-faster spread of American culture, is setting the pace.

Traditionalists may (and do) decry what they see as an increasingly permissive society, but it is the young, whose spending power has made them an unprecedentedly important force in the market place, who are calling all the cultural and social shots.

Mary Quant, with the architect, Alexander Plunket Greene.

Britain's new standards can be seen in every walk of life. In the world of rock music the fabulously successful Beatles have exported their own brand of charm to the United States, where it has taken the country by storm and paved the way for what Americans are already calling the "British invasion". In fashion, where Mary Quant's designs have made every smart young (and not so young) woman into a "swinging dolly-bird", Britain is setting the rules.

Carnaby Street, for many people as much a concept of trendy living as a sidestreet in London's West End, is equally popular among the boys, with designers like John Stephen showing that staid old Savile Row has no monopoly on fashionable tailoring. The new developments represent an end to the drabness of the Fifties. The old conformity has been replaced by a new way of life, dictated not by the old establishment, but by a more vocal, energetic and creative young.

Pop culture is the new thing. The outrageous styles which are on display in the boutiques, the pacy lyrics of the new rock songs, the irreverent pirate radio stations, the discotheques filled with what the press are calling a "new aristocracy" of pop stars, model girls, photographers and other young and chic professionals, lively shops such as Habitat, providing a short-cut to the latest lifestyles – everything is combining to promote a new, "swinging" Britain.

Dancing to "Sounds Incorporated" on the TV show "Ready Steady Go".

Doors close at the 'Ever-open' Theatre

London 31 October 1964
The permissive society, as it is being called, has made the once-naughty Windmill Theatre redundant. The home of stage nudity since before the Second World War, its proud boast throughout the wartime air raids was "We Never Closed". Now its nude tableaux are not titillating enough to save it.

The Windmill's great days were immediately after the war when a new wave of comedians, including Peter Sellers and Tony Hancock, appeared between the nude scenes attempting to distract the patrons from the Windmill girls.

Capital punishment is to be abolished

Westminster, 21 December
In a free vote today the House of Commons abolished the death penalty for murder by the overwhelming majority of 355 to 170. This does not mean there will never be another hanging in Britain, for the effect of the measure will be reviewed in five years' time and there are certain offences, such as treachery, for which death remains the penalty. The House of Lords also has to give its decision on the bill, but such is the anti-hanging feeling in the Commons that it is unlikely the trap will ever be sprung on another murderer (→18/12/69).

1965

Belfast, 14 January. Sean Lemass and Terence O'Neill stage the first meeting on Irish soil between the premiers of the north and south (→ 9/2).

Gibraltar, 3 February. Spanish forces begin a blockade of the British colony.

Britain, 16 February. Details of rail closures based on the Beeching Report are released.

Westminster, 25 February. The Conservative Party says future leaders will be elected by MPs.

Surrey, 14 May. The queen dedicates a field at Runnymede to John Kennedy, the US president shot in 1963.

Westminster, 24 May. Britain is to switch to metric systems.

Westminster, 2 June. The Speaker's casting vote approves a bill to impose corporation tax on company profits.

Britain, 18 June. An alcohol limit is to be set for drivers (→ 21/3/68).

London, 23 June. The USSR rejects a Vietnam peace mission proposed by Harold Wilson (→ 17/3/68).

Westminster, 22 July. Sir Alec Douglas-Home resigns as Conservative leader (→ 27).

Moscow, 23 July. Gerald Brooke, a university lecturer, is jailed for smuggling leaflets into the USSR (→ 22/10/66).

London, 26 July. The Post Office says that telephones will have numbers only in future.

Britain, 30 July. *Coronation Street* is the top TV show (→ 29/11).

London, 7 October. The Post Office Tower is opened; at 186 metres (620 feet), it is the tallest building in Britain.

Cork, 31 October. The opera house reopens, having been destroyed by fire in 1955.

Britain, 5 November. The fashion for mini-skirts results in new Customs rules to prevent women avoiding taxes by buying children's sizes.

Westminster, 16 November. Emergency legislation is rushed through Parliament to impose sanctions on Rhodesia (→ 6/12/66).

Britain, 24 November. An experimental 70mph (112 kph) speed limit is introduced for motorways (→ 1/3/76).

London and Dublin, 14 Dec. An Anglo-Irish trade agreement is signed (→ 8/3/66).

Historic Irish meetings

The first meeting between the Irish prime ministers of the north and south.

Dublin, 9 February
In the second of two historic meetings between the prime ministers of Northern Ireland and the Irish Republic, Sean Lemass here met Captain Terence O'Neill to continue discussions begun last month when he paid a visit to Stormont Castle.

Lemass's motives, in responding to O'Neill's cross-border initiative, are essentially economic. Setting aside completely the united Ireland objectives of his predecessor, he is seeking to achieve modest cooperation in trade, energy and tourism. Captain O'Neill, although more cautious in his view of the political wisdom of meeting his opposite number in the south, has continued with the talks in the belief that a new and more liberal climate must develop between north and south. But he faces a hardline attitude from northern Unionists and is unlikely to win the support of the Catholic minority who believe themselves to be victims of sectarian discrimination (→ 16/11).

Labour backs one education for all

Westminster, January
The 11-plus exam is to end. Tony Crosland, the education secretary, this month asked local authorities to produce plans for "comprehensive" secondary schools to cater for pupils of all abilities.

Labour has long campaigned for an end to the 11-plus exam, which allocates children to grammar or secondary modern schools. One in ten pupils in England and Wales attend comprehensive schools already, but the government wants the schools to cater for a majority of pupils within a decade. Several forms of comprehensives are being mooted, but none will appease Tory critics who want to preserve the grammar schools (→ 10/9/66).

TV curbs smoking

London, 8 February
Cigarette advertising is to vanish from the television screen, health minister Kenneth Robinson announced today. Although critics call the ban illogical – press and billboard advertising are to continue as usual – the government has singled out television as especially effective in targetting the young and vulnerable (→ 30/7).

World bids a sad farewell to Winston Churchill with state funeral

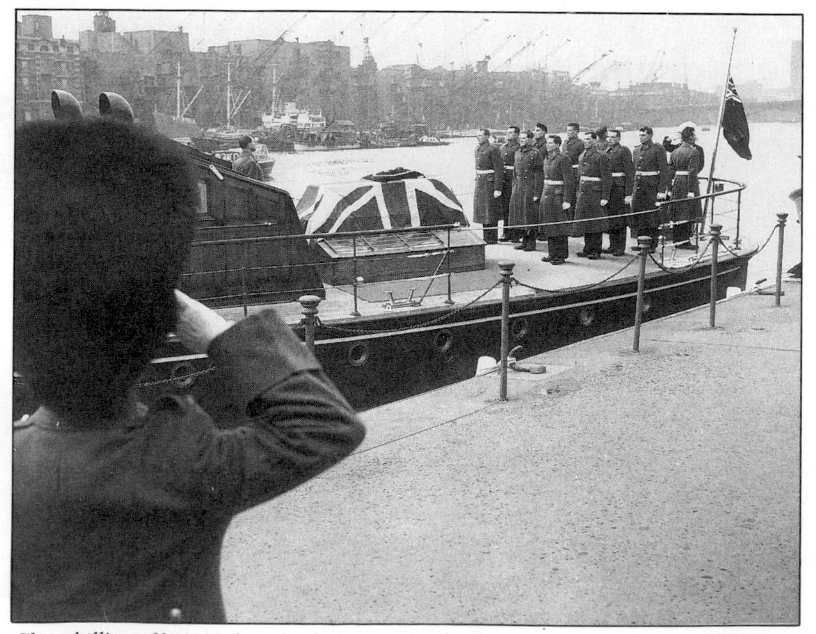

Churchill's coffin is taken by barge on his last journey along the Thames.

Oxfordshire, 30 January
Sir Winston Churchill, who died six days ago at the age of 90, has been laid to rest in a village churchyard near his family's home at Blenheim Palace. Today's modest graveside ceremony stood in stark contrast to the last few days of national mourning on the grand scale, led by Queen Elizabeth II.

Hundreds of thousands of people filed past Sir Winston's coffin over the three days that he lay in state in Westminster Hall, whilst representatives of 110 nations attended the state funeral service in St Paul's Cathedral, London. Some 350 million people in Europe alone watched on television. Tributes have meanwhile poured in from around the world to the man whom the Pope, for one, has called the "indefatigable champion of freedom".

Edward Heath elected as new Tory leader

London, 27 July
The Tory Party today elected Edward Heath as its new leader in place of Sir Alec Douglas-Home. Heath owes much to his predecessor – for Sir Alec, appalled at the plotting that led to his own "emergence" as leader, instituted the system by which Heath was elected.

Heath received 150 votes against 133 for the favourite, Reginald Maudling, and 15 for Enoch Powell. At 49 years, he is the youngest Tory leader for a century. A grammar school boy, he represents a shift to the middle class in the leadership of the Tory Party, which has for so long been an aristocratic prerogative (→31/3/66).

Mr Heath collects a bouquet.

Child murder on the Moors shocks nation as crimes of violence soar to new levels

Cheshire, 28 October
Two people have been charged with the murder of Lesley Ann Downey, a ten-year-old girl whose body was found on Saddleworth Moor 13 days ago. Angry crowds tried to attack the cars carrying Ian Brady, aged 27, and Myra Hindley, aged 23, as they left court after the hearing today. A police search continues for other bodies on the moors. The "moors murder" is a case that has shocked the nation.

It is part of an upward spiral of violence in Britain over the last ten years. Until the mid-1950s violent crime increased by around six per cent a year; since then, the rate of increase has been 11 per cent. The number of offences of violence has rocketed from 5,869 in 1955 to 15,976 last year. And the percentage increases among young people between the ages of 14 and 21 has been proportionately greater than in the population as a whole.

"Law and order" is becoming a more prominent political issue. By a piquant irony, the Murder Bill to abolish the death penalty for a trial period of five years completed its final parliamentary stages today. Its measures are expected to become law next month (→6/5/66).

Last African colony rebels against Britain

Rhodesia, 11 November
Rhodesia, Britain's last colony in Africa, is on a war footing tonight after Ian Smith, the prime minister, issued a long-expected unilateral declaration of independence.

Echoing the 18th-century American Declaration he said: "It may become necessary for a people to assume .... the separate and equal status to which they are entitled ..." But in this case the "people" are not the four million Africans in the colony but the 220,000 whites.

Smith has been threatening UDI since last year but it became inevitable after the May election when there was a 30 per cent swing in favour of the "cowboy" Rhodesian Front party, committed to keeping power in white hands in order to maintain "civilized standards".

Mr Smith has assumed wide powers to impose rationing and censorship and has sacked the governor, Sir Humphrey Gibbs. Britain has cut all ties with the rebel regime and promises to impose sanctions but is in a dilemma. Commonwealth countries are calling for decisive action to crush the rebel regime but a majority of the British might well oppose such measures against their "kith and kin" (→16).

Volunteers help with the search for more bodies on Saddleworth Moor.

The Beatles received MBE's from the Queen for their services to music. Unknown to her they smoked cannabis in the Buckingham Palace loo.

First Irish premier, 'WT', dies aged 89

Ireland, 16 November
Ireland's first prime minister, William Thomas Cosgrave, has died. Born in Dublin in 1880, he fought in the 1916 rebellion and was later imprisoned.

He supported the 1921 treaty, was minister for local government in the first Dail and president of the second Dail. After the deaths of Arthur Griffith and Michael Collins, he was effectively head of the government and led each administration until Fianna Fail came to power in 1932. A conservative and hardline leader, he never again achieved power. He retired from politics in 1944 (→14/12).

Housewife launches a 'clean-up' of TV

Birmingham, 29 November
Mrs Mary Whitehouse, whose "Clean Up TV" campaign has been combating what she sees as immorality on television for the past 18 months, launched a new pressure group today. The National Viewers' and Listeners' Association is to pursue identical aims to CUTV, targeting what Mrs Whitehouse calls the "bad taste and irresponsibility" of the BBC. The corporation dismisses her as at best a self-appointed censor, and at worst a crank, but Mrs Whitehouse says she has 500,000 supporters, dedicated to fighting the evils of today's "permissive society" (→3/7/67).

1966

Britain, 8 February. An airline for the package holiday market is set up by Freddie Laker.

Dublin, 8 March. A bomb destroys the Nelson Pillar (→ 10/4).

Cheltenham, 17 March. The Gold Cup is won for the third successive year by Arkle.

London, 27 March. The World Cup trophy, stolen seven days ago, is found in a garden by a dog called Pickles.

Britain, 31 March. Labour wins the general election with 363 seats to 253 Tory, 12 Liberal and 2 others (→ 18/1/67).

Ireland, 10 April. Commemoration of the 50th anniversary of the Easter Rising begins (→ 2/6).

Ramsgate, 30 April. A hovercraft service begins to Calais.

Westminster, 23 May. A state of emergency is declared in response to a seamen's strike.

Dublin, 2 June. De Valera is re-elected as president (→ 6).

Belfast, 6 June. The Ulster Volunteer Force is banned (→ 20/7).

Britain, 29 June. Barclaycard, the first British credit card, is introduced (→ 27/6/67).

Ireland, 20 July. Rev Ian Paisley is jailed for breaching the peace at a church assembly in June (→ 9/11).

Britain, 28 July. Florence Nagle, aged 70, becomes the first woman racehorse trainer.

Plymouth, 27 August. Francis Chichester embarks on a lone round-the-world voyage (→ 28/5/67).

Ireland, 10 September. Free post-primary education will be introduced in 1967.

London, 10 September. The musical *Oliver!* ends a record-breaking six-year run.

London, 30 September. Lord Thomson buys *The Times*.

London, 18 October. The hanged Timothy Evans wins a posthumous royal pardon.

London, 22 October. Soviet spy George Blake escapes from prison (→ 24/7/69).

Britain, 31 October. Strikes against redundancies close all British Motor Corporation factories.

Gibraltar, 6 December. Talks to resolve the dispute over Rhodesian UDI break down.

England surge to dramatic World Cup win

Hurst leaps above the goalkeeper on his way to a World Cup hat trick.

Wembley, 30 July
England won football's World Cup in a pulsating match at Wembley stadium today. The nation where football began has thus won the sport's supreme international competition for the first time.

Sixteen nations competed in the finals, which were staged in England for the first time. Matches were held in several parts of the country before today's Wembley final. It was Portugal whom England had to overcome to reach the final – and they did so in a classic encounter starring two of the tournament's top stars, Bobby Charlton and Eusebio. West Germany were the other finalists, having beaten the Soviet Union in the second semi-final.

The Germans took an early lead in today's final, but goals from the West Ham pair, Geoff Hurst and Martin Peters, put England into a lead that they held until the dying seconds. Then a West German equalizer took the game into extra time – and controversy. A shot by Hurst bounced down from the bar just behind the line, according to the linesman but not the Germans. However, a third goal by Hurst dispelled the doubts to seal England's triumph, 4-2. Even the laconic manager, Alf Ramsey, smiled.

Church heads meet after 400-year rift

Rome, 23 March
The heads of the Roman Catholic and Anglican communions today met officially for the first time in 400 years. Pope Paul VI received Dr Michael Ramsey, the Archbishop of Canterbury, with the "kiss of peace" in the Sistine Chapel and talked of "a bridge of respect, of esteem and of charity" being rebuilt between the two confessions. During his visit Ramsey will discuss various issues that still divide Canterbury and Rome in the hope of moving towards greater unity. But opponents are never far away: three British ministers here have dubbed Dr Ramsey "a traitor to Protestant Britain".

Archbishop meets pope in Rome.

Economic troubles hit the newly elected Labour government

Wilson playing street football; some critics see his policies as an own goal.

London, 20 July
The worsening economic situation has forced the government to impose a freeze on pay and dividends. It will last for six months and be followed by another six months of severe restraint. Announcing these and other crisis measures today, Harold Wilson said that "the time has come to call a halt" to runaway inflation.

While the prime minister's actions may make economic sense, they have created political turmoil. The cabinet is split and the unions furious. George Brown is threatening to join Frank Cousins, the former transport workers' leader, in resigning. Cousins was formerly the minister of technology (→ 19/11/67).

Coal tip buries Welsh schoolchildren

Aberfan, 27 October
Aberfan, the Welsh mining village that has lost a whole generation of children in a disaster that has appalled the world, today began the task of burying its dead. The funeral was held of 82 of the 116 children and 28 adults who died on 21 October when the massive, waterlogged coal tip that for decades had hung precariously above the village engulfed the local school, leaving a trail of destruction in its wake.

A ten-year-old survivor recalled the scene: "We heard a noise and saw all the stuff flying about. The desks were falling about and the children were shouting and screaming. We couldn't see anything." No-one yet knows exactly why the tip collapsed – the best guess is that an underground spring loosened the piles of waste, creating what Lord Robens, the Coal Board chairman, called "a water bomb" – but around midmorning the huge pile began its fatal slide towards the school. Tens of thousands of tons of slurry, which had collected over years of mining, rolled over the school, demolishing it in a matter of seconds. A high-level inquiry into the incident has been ordered.

Hundreds of rescuers, many of them parents, fought to uncover the victims. The headmistress was among the lucky survivors; the deputy head was found dead, the bodies of five children in his arms. As prime minister Harold Wilson, who visited the site, put it, "I don't think any of us can find words to describe this tragedy."

The Aberfan school was directly in line with the avalanche of slurry.

Jack Lynch, former footballer, is voted new Irish premier

Dublin, 9 Nov 1966
Sean Lemass, the Irish prime minister, has resigned as the leader of the Fianna Fail party and has been succeeded in the post by his minister for finance, Jack Lynch. Born in Cork and a former footballer, the softly-spoken Lynch was not considered to be a likely candidate for prime minister. But he emerged as a practical compromise choice between the two more aggressive candidates, Charles Haughey and George Colley.

The personalities and political styles of the three men are very different but their policies are firmly those of their erstwhile leader, Sean Lemass. Lynch is expected to be a quietist leader, with no strong views on policy. This was epitomised in his winning style – an outsider quietly romping home on the rails (→ 6/2/67).

Jack Lynch takes over as premier.

Moors Murderers are to be jailed for life

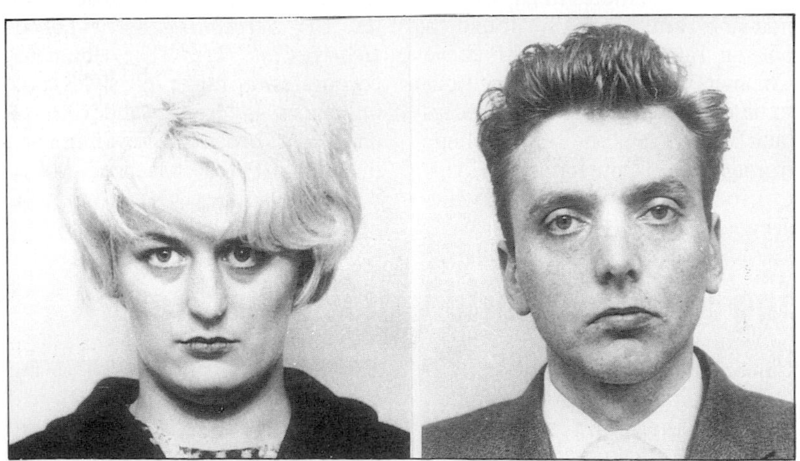

Hindley and Brady tortured and murdered young children for pleasure.

Chester, 6 May
A man and a woman were sentenced to life imprisonment today for the torture and murder of two children and a teenage boy. The all-male jury was visibly harrowed by a recording of the torments one of the victims was subjected to before she was killed.

Known as the Moors Murderers because the bodies were buried on the Pennine moors, the killers – Myra Hindley, aged 24, and Ian Brady, aged 28 – were found out when Hindley's brother-in-law called the police after he saw Edward Evans, aged 17, killed with an axe.

Nude photographs of the victims and tape-recordings of the killings were traced through a left-luggage ticket found in Hindley's prayer-book. The two other victims were Lesley Ann Downey, aged ten, and John Kilbride, aged 12.

First Nationalist MP is elected in Wales

Westminster, 21 July
Gwynfor Evans, the first Welsh Nationalist member of the House of Commons, took his seat today as victor in the by-election at Carmarthen. There was a nice bit of by-play when he was sworn in. He had been expected to refuse to take the oath in English but did so without demur. However, he then asked if he could repeat the ceremony in Welsh. Mr Speaker refused. Why not? asked Evans. Because other people would not know what you were saying, said Mr Speaker.

Biggest gas field discovered in North Sea

London, 2 June
Philips Petroleum today claimed to have "struck it rich" in the North Sea, drilling into a huge gas field off the mouth of the Humber. A test well is showing a gas flow of up to 480,000 cubic metres (17 million cubic feet) a day, which is 3.5 per cent of Britain's daily gas needs. This discovery, taken in conjunction with a Shell/Esso announcement last month of a "significant" find in a nearby area means that this region is as rich in gas as the BP field further north. If trade expectations are fulfilled all Britain's gas will one day be provided from the North Sea (→ 20/6/69).

1967

Buckinghamshire, 12 January. Plans are announced for a new city – "Milton Keynes".

Westminster, 18 January. Jeremy Thorpe is to be Liberal leader to succeed Jo Grimond (→ 15/3/68).

Northern Ireland, 6 February. A newly formed Civil Rights Association states its aims (→ 6/10/68).

Britain, 10 February. Emil Savundra, the head of an insurance company, is arrested on fraud charges.

London, 13 March. Students at the London School of Economics stage a sit-in to protest at the suspension of two student leaders (→ 31/5/68).

Britain, March. A star grading system for petrol begins.

Britain, 1 April. Sir Edmund Compton begins work as the country's first ombudsman.

Plymouth, 28 May. Sir Francis Chichester returns from his lone voyage around the world.

London, 7 June. The duchess of Windsor meets the queen in public for the first time at the unveiling of a plaque for Queen Mary (→ 20/9).

London, 27 June. Barclays introduces the world's first cash dispensing machine at a branch in Enfield .

Britain, 3 July. ITV launches *News at Ten*; two days ago colour television began on BBC2 (→ 2/12/82).

Westminster, 18 July. British forces are to withdraw from areas east of Suez by the mid-1970s, it is announced.

Britain, 15 August. Pirate radio stations are closed by a new act of Parliament (→ 30/9).

Britain, 21 August. Majority jury verdicts are to be allowed in court.

Glasgow, 20 September. The *Queen Elizabeth II* (or *QE2*) liner is launched by the Queen at Clydebank (→ 7/6/77).

Britain, 30 September. Radios One, Two, Three and Four replace the previous Home, Light and Third Programmes.

Westminster, 25 October. The Abortion Bill is passed by Parliament (→ 12/1967).

Westminster, 29 November. Roy Jenkins succeeds James Callaghan as chancellor.

Britain, November. Over 130,000 animals have been slaughtered during an outbreak of foot-and-mouth disease.

Leaking oil tanker bombed to save coast

Land's End, 30 March
Fighter aircraft blasted the wreck of the oil tanker *Torrey Canyon* again today in a final attempt to burn off the oil that has fouled 100 miles of coastline in what has been described as "the greatest peacetime threat to Britain". Fighters have dropped 48 incendiary bombs and some 5,500 litres (1,200 gallons) of napalm on the remains of the 61,000-tonne tanker, which was wrecked on the Seven Stones Reef between Land's End and the Scilly Isles, carrying 100,000 tonnes of oil. Tomorrow divers will check that no oil remains on board.

The prime minister, Harold Wilson, held a mini-cabinet meeting to deal with this threat to the West Country tourist industry.

The broken wreck has been bombed.

Wilson snubbed by de Gaulle over EEC

Paris, 16 May
President de Gaulle of France told members of the press today that there are "formidable obstacles" to Britain's application to join the European Economic Community (EEC). France will say "oui" only when the British prove that they have begun to think like good Europeans. Apparently it would also help if the "special relationship" between England and the US ceased. The prime minister, Harold Wilson, has put a brave face on this. He told MPs that the application will be vigorously pursued. After all, his government secured a huge majority in favour of this move: 488 votes for and only 62 against.

Scotland's Celtic clinch European Cup win

Lisbon, 25 May
Scottish pride was triumphantly reasserted tonight when Glasgow Celtic became the first football team from the British Isles to win the European Champions' Cup. So Scotland, smarting from the English triumph at last year's World Cup, has won the supreme soccer competition between the league champions of all the major European countries.

On a sweltering night in the Portuguese capital, Celtic were soon one goal adrift in their final against Internazionale of Milan. The Scots conceded an early penalty and were faced with a struggle against a team renowned for one of the strongest defences in Europe. However, with nearly 60 minutes gone, Tommy Gemmell equalized and the Scots pressed home their attacks against a team that could no longer rely solely on defence.

With eight minutes to go, Celtic's non-stop attack finally found a hole in Inter's defence with Steve Chalmers claiming what turned out to be the winning goal. Celtic's captain Billy McNeill hoisted the huge trophy and Lisbon tonight belongs to Jock Stein's green-and-white army of fans.

'Sergeant Pepper' is success for Beatles

Liverpool, 30 June
The Cavern, where the Beatles first honed their musical skills, may have become a shrine for their fans, but the simple rock tunes of those years are another world compared to the virtuosity of the group's latest LP, *Sergeant Pepper's Lonely Hearts' Club Band*. The album incorporates a range of styles and influences – from vaudeville to drugs – to produce a revolutionary thematic LP that has been widely praised by critics. The group gave up touring last year (→ 1/1968).

Campbell dies attempting to break world water speed record

Donald Campbell: "She's going!"

Cumbria, 4 January
Donald Campbell's brave attempt to break the world water speed record has ended in tragedy. His craft, the jet-powered *Bluebird*, somersaulted and disintegrated today on Coniston Water as Campbell chased his own record of 276.33 mph (442 kph). His last words on the radio link were: "She's going – she's going. I'm almost on my back." He was within a fraction of a second of achieving his goal. Frogmen have recovered Campbell's helmet, shoes, oxygen mask and teddy bear mascot, but there is no sign of the body. The search has now been called off.

"Bluebird" plunges into the water.

The pound is devalued

Westminster, 19 November
The government, facing economic disaster with labour troubles, a massive foreign trade deficit and a heavy run on sterling, has been forced to devalue the pound. It goes down from 2.80 dollars to 2.40, a fall of 14.3 per cent. This move is a blow for James Callaghan, the chancellor, who said that devaluation was "a flight into escapism".

The prime minister, on the other hand, seems positively chirpy. In a television address he presented devaluation and the tightening of the credit squeeze as the key to economic expansion. The move does not mean, he said, "that the pound here in Britain in your pocket or purse or in your bank has been devalued".

James Callaghan, the chancellor.

Flower power blooms among the hippies

London, 31 December
It has been the year of "flower power". It has bloomed at hippy festivals, such as that at Woburn in August, and has its own language, fashions and lifestyles. Drugs are part of this world, and icons, including some members of the Rolling Stones, have fallen foul of the law. If the rest of the world finds the drugs, the music and the notion of "love" as a cure for the world's ills somewhat hard to take, then the "hippies" who preach this new gospel are equally convinced that they are right. The hippie revolution springs from the USA. Now it is here too, fuelled by the psychedelic hallucinogen LSD and serenaded by rock music. The generation gap has never been wider (→27/9/68).

Rolling Stones Mick Jagger (l) and Keith Richards: drugs charges.

Abortion and sex laws made more liberal

Britain, December
The more liberal and permissive attitudes to sexual behaviour that have characterized the 1960s have culminated in three significant new acts of Parliament becoming law this year.

The first was the Abortion Act, piloted through Parliament by a young Liberal MP, David Steel, but backed by the government and many Conservatives. This allows women to have abortions if two doctors confirm that this is necessary on medical or psychological grounds. The National Health Service (Family Planning) Act, which allows local authorities to provide contraceptives and contraceptive advice, was the second. Birth control clinics now anticipate that increasing numbers of women will choose the contraceptive "pill", which is becoming more widely available.

The third was the Sexual Offences Act, which (in England and Wales) allows homosexual acts to take place between two consenting adults in private. Previously, these had been criminal acts. However, the age of consent for homosexuals is to be 21, not the 16 allowed for heterosexual intercourse (→1/4/74).

Hippy pop festivals have a fair share of fights and drugs among the love.

As traffic increases so does the need for extra road safety. The breathalyser is the latest attack on drunks behind the wheel.

Scots join the bandwagon of nationalism

Scotland, 2 November
Scotland, officially part of the United Kingdom since the 1707 Act of Union, showed that lust for independence never dies, even after nearly three centuries, when the Scottish Nationalist Party (SNP) today won its first seat in Westminster since 1945. In the by-election at Hamilton, Winifred Ewing took the seat for the SNP, which was formed in 1934 with the aim of separating Scotland from the UK and establishing a national assembly.

British troops leave Aden after 128 years

Aden, 30 November
Exultant Arabs celebrated in the streets of the port city of Aden today as the last British troops left for home. Few will regret leaving a posting that for the last year has become increasingly hostile. It was the final chapter in a 128-year-old story, which started when in 1839 the British East India Company seized the port to protect its routes to the East and has ended with the creation of the People's Republic of South Yemen.

Goodbye to steam, but hello Concord

Toulouse, 11 December
In the year that Britain bade farewell to its last steam-hauled mainline passenger trains, the nation has taken a significant step towards a new era of air travel. The first prototype of the world's first faster-than-sound passenger airline was rolled out of its hangar today at Toulouse in France. The Concord (or Concorde to the French) is a triumph of international collaboration as well as aviation technology; it is being developed jointly by aircraft manufacturers in France and Britain (→9/4/69).

1968

Surrey, 1 January. Five Surbiton typists start an "I'm Backing Britain" campaign.

Westminster, 15 January. A new bill makes "irretrievable breakdown of marriage" the sole grounds for divorce (→ 13/6/69).

Britain, 17 January. The British Leyland Motor Corporation is formed.

London, January. The "Apple" boutique is opened by the Beatles (→ 9/4/70).

Hull, 5 February. Nineteen men die when their trawler sinks off Iceland, making 60 trawler deaths in a month.

Westminster, 20 February. Provision of free milk is to end in secondary schools.

Westminster, 22 February. Emergency legislation is planned to cut Asian immigration from East Africa (→ 21/4).

London, 17 March. Police and Vietnam war demonstrators clash in Grosvenor Square.

Britain, 21 March. Figures show that road deaths fell by 23 per cent in the three months after the introduction of breath tests.

Birmingham, 21 April. Tory MP Enoch Powell attacks immigration policies (→ 6/5).

London, 3 May. The first heart transplant operation is performed in Britain.

Australia, 24 June. Comedian Tony Hancock commits suicide in Sydney.

Wimbledon, 6 July. The men's title in the first championships open to professionals is won by Rod Laver of Australia.

Britain, 13 September. Banks announce plans to close on Saturdays.

Britain, 16 September. A two-tier post service comes into operation – at 5d and 4d.

Co Londonderry, 1 October. The New University of Ulster opens at Coleraine.

London, 16 October. The foreign and commonwealth offices merge.

Belfast, 22 November. The Ulster government announces reforms to meet demands by the Civil Rights Association (→ 4/1/69).

Britain, 26 November. The Race Relations Act banning a colour bar in employment comes into force (→ 1/1/69).

Powell speech stirs row over immigration

London, 6 May
Enoch Powell's views on the danger of Britain being flooded by immigrants won support today from a Gallup poll which showed that 74 per cent of the population is broadly sympathetic to his argument that Britain must be "mad, literally mad as a nation" to allow 50,000 dependants of immigrants into the country each year.

Powell was sacked from his position as Tory shadow defence minister by the Opposition leader, Edward Heath, last week following an apocalyptic speech in Birmingham in which Powell said: "As I look ahead I am filled with foreboding. Like the Roman, I seem to see the River Tiber foaming with much blood."

The classical allusion may have made Powell's warning excessively dramatic but he insists he chose his words carefully and denies he is being irresponsible or seeking to incite racial prejudice. The speech took other senior Tories by surprise, although a number of them share his views, and reaction to it was immediate, triggering a fierce controversy over race relations that is still raging some time later.

Powell has been condemned as a racist, both by liberals and representatives of the immigrant communities, but there have been marches and demonstrations in his support and politicians of all parties are uneasily aware that he reflects the fears of very many people (→ 26/11).

Smithfield porters show support.

Enoch Powell: rivers of blood.

George Brown quits the foreign office

Westminster, 15 March
George Brown, the tempestuous deputy leader of the Labour Party, today carried out what he has often threatened – he quit the government. He departed blaming Harold Wilson for running a dictatorial administration, although most of his former colleagues think the prime minister has shown great patience. Brown, who lost a leadership contest to Wilson in 1963, was initially the minister for economic affairs before becoming foreign secretary. A man of undoubted energy and originality, his fiery personality and sometimes erratic behaviour have led to his departure (→ 18/5/70).

Twice world motor racing champ dies

West Germany, 7 April
Champion racing driver Jim Clark was killed instantly in a horrifying crash on the Hockenheim circuit today when he lost control of his Lotus on a fast straight and slammed into trees at 125 mph. Clark, son of a farmer from the Scottish border country, won the Formula One championship twice and was leading this year's championship. He won a remarkable 25 races in only seven seasons and was regarded by his fellow drivers as the best of his generation.

Three die as London tower block collapses

Ronan Point after the collapse.

London, 16 May
One of London's newest tower blocks, the 22-storey Ronan Point, in Newham, east London, collapsed today, killing three residents. The immediate cause of the disaster was a gas explosion in a flat built on the corner of the 18th floor, but poor building work coupled with essential design faults in the fast-track "system building" design – used in many of London's modern towers – meant that every single flat on the corner crumbled. It was as if a house of cards had been dislodged. A full-scale inquiry has been ordered and the Greater London Council is considering banning any further "system-built" blocks.

The wreckage of Jim Clark's car.

Police break up Ulster civil rights march

Derry, 6 October
Rioting broke out in the Catholic Bogside area of Londonderry overnight after police dispersed a banned march staged by the Northern Ireland Civil Rights Association. The Unionist government objected to the provocative route, from a Protestant area into the walled city, and when police baton-charged the marchers, Gerry Fitt, the Westminster MP for West Belfast, was one of 88 people injured.

Only about 400 attended the march, which was mainly to protest against the Unionist city council's failure to provide Catholic housing, but there was anger throughout the nationalist community at what was seen as police over-reaction. The marchers offered little resistance as police attacked them with batons and the first water-cannon to be deployed on the streets of Ulster. While most photographers fled, an Irish television cameraman continued filming, capturing scenes of RUC brutality which have alerted world opinion to the Ulster civil rights campaign (→22/11).

RUC men club a demonstrator.

'Hair' is well and truly let down in the West End after censorship laws abolished

London, 27 September
Tonight, one day after the censorship of the Lord Chamberlain over the theatre was abolished, the hippie musical *Hair* did not so much open as hit London like a "happening". The show is a deafening, "tribal love-rock musical" that celebrates "doing your own thing".

The cast, when they were not swinging from the balconies or the proscenium or pelting the audience with confetti or with a resounding fusillade of *the* four-letter word, swung to the tribal rock beat of Galt MacDermot's exciting score, in numbers like "Good morning Starshine!" At the first-act curtain they took all their clothes off under a huge blanket and stood there confronting the audience. It demonstrated that once they had taken their clothes off, there was not much more even they could do.

The show was created by two New York actors, Gerome Ragni and James Rado, inspired by seeing a flower-people's "Be-in" in Central Park, against the war in Vietnam. It was first staged in New York's East Village. One song is in praise of:

Hair like Jesus wore it
Hallelujah I adore it. (→21/9/69)

"Hair" explodes onto the London stage with fun, songs and full nudity.

Student sit-ins spread across the country

Students at Hornsey College of Art demand a say in running the college.

London, 31 May
As student sit-ins spread through universities and colleges, the latest flashpoint emerged in north London today when angry students at the Hornsey College of Art have declared "a state of anarchy".

Following the example of such institutions as the London School of Economics, which in turn has echoed a movement first seen in the USA and, earlier this month, the bloody clashes on the streets of Paris, the Hornsey students have abandoned debate, turning instead to direct action in their bid to revolutionize the way in which their college is administered.

They want a complete shake-up both of teaching in the college and of the way student affairs are conducted. They have taken over the college buildings, evicted the principal, Harold Shelton, and declared that they will sit in until all their demands are met (→3/2/69).

South Africa blocks cricket tour by MCC

Bloemfontein, 17 September
John Vorster, South Africa's prime minister, has cancelled this winter's MCC tour of South Africa because Basil D'Oliviera, England's Cape Coloured all-rounder, has been chosen to replace the injured Tom Cartwright. In a statement read out at a meeting of the Nationalist Party here today, Vorster claimed that the touring party was "no longer a cricket team but a team of trouble-makers for South Africa's separate development policies". The omission of D'Oliviera from the team chosen last month was greeted by protests from both anti-apartheid groups and cricket fans; when Cartwright fell out, his selection became inevitable (→5/11/69).

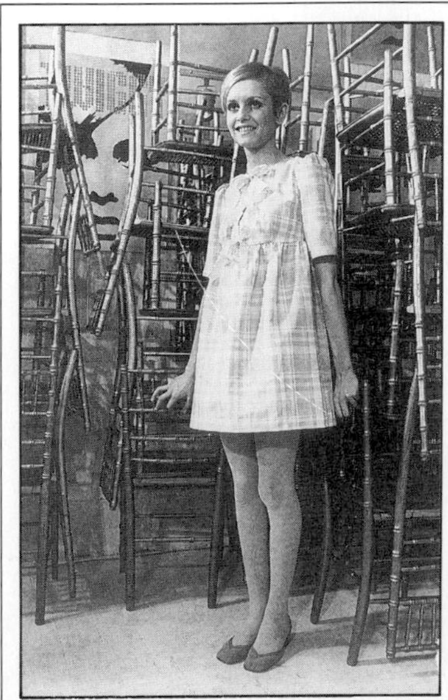
Top fashion model Twiggy is thin, pale, gauche and young. Her look seems to sum up an era and millions of girls copy it.

1969

London, 1 January. Rupert Murdoch wins a takeover battle against Robert Maxwell for the *News of the World.*

Kenya, 1 January. Thousands of Asians holding UK passports are expected to leave for Britain shortly.

Westminster, 23 January. A proposal to cut legal penalties for smoking cannabis is rejected by the government.

London, 3 February. Student protests close the London School of Economics.

Northern Ireland, 24 February. In a general election Unionist supporters of the pro-reform premier, Terence O'Neill, win 27 seats compared to 12 for his Unionist opponents (→ 18/4).

Northern Ireland, 18 April. Nationalist Bernadette Devlin wins a Mid-Ulster by-election at the age of 21 (→ 1/5).

Northern Ireland, 1 May. James Chichester-Clark becomes prime minister (→ 16/8).

North Sea, 20 June. High-grade crude oil is found (→ 19/10/70).

Lancashire, 12 July. Tony Jacklin becomes the first British golfer to win the Open championship since 1951.

Moscow, 24 July. Jailed Briton Gerald Brooke is freed in a swap for two Soviet spies (→ 24/9/71).

Isle of Wight, 31 August. Bob Dylan stars in a pop festival that draws 150,000 fans.

London, 16 September. "Biba", a fashionable boutique, opens as a department store.

London, 21 September. Police storm a hippie "squat" at 144 Piccadilly.

Belfast, 28 September. Troops erect a "peace wall" between the warring communities (→ 12/10).

Twickenham, 5 November. Anti-apartheid demonstrators invade the pitch during a game by the touring South African Springboks (→ 22/5/70).

London, 13 November. A woman has quintuplets after fertility drug treatment.

Westminster, 18 December. The experimental ban on capital punishment is made permanent.

Westminster, 18 December. The formation of a part-time Ulster Defence Regiment is approved (→ 29/3/70).

Concorde makes supersonic maiden flight

"Wizard flight": Britain's Concorde prototype takes off for the first time.

Bristol, 9 April
The British Concorde has made its first flight. Concorde 002, the fruit of £360 million of investment, took off from Filton, Bristol, on a 21-minute flight in which the supersonic aircraft's four Rolls-Royce Olympus engines managed a modest 202 mph (323 kph). Brian Trubshaw, today's pilot, was none the less delighted and said he had a "wizard flight". Britain and France – whose own Concorde (001) took off a month ago – hope to sell 400 of the craft, netting some £4,000 million by the 1980s. The lucrative United States market could prove a problem, however: noise levels recorded today were twice those permitted in the US (→ 23/1/70).

Derry marchers are caught in ambush

Londonderry, 4 January
Defenceless students dived through hedges and jumped into a river to escape stones and screaming loyalist attackers at Burntollet bridge, south of Derry today, as they neared the end of their four-day civil rights march across Northern Ireland. Although the 70 marchers had a heavy police escort, no effective action was taken against the ambush by about 200 Protestants blocking the main road and occupying the hillside. Sweeping reforms of housing and local government were announced last month (→ 24/2).

Labour backs down over union reforms

Westminster, 18 June
Harold Wilson has been forced to abandon the Industrial Relations Act in the face of opposition within the cabinet and the trade union movement. The act, designed to implement the recommendations of the employment secretary Barbara Castle's white paper, *In Place of Strife*, would have given the government legal powers to cope with strikes. Opposition to it, led by James Callaghan, has proved too strong and at a meeting today the prime minister was forced to agree to the formula of a "solemn and binding agreement" by which the TUC will monitor disputes.

East End Kray twins face long jail term

London, 5 March
Gangland twins Ronald and Reginald Kray, who were said to have terrorized the East End, were given life sentences today for murder. Mr Justice Melford Stevenson said they should not be released for 30 years. Four members of their "firm" were also convicted.

The 35-year-old brothers gained a reputation for violence, as well as a cult following in the club world. They were arrested after George Cornell, aged 38, was shot in the head at the Blind Beggar pub and Jack "The Hat" McVitie, also 38, was lured to a flat and then stabbed in the face, chest and throat.

Easier end planned for unhappy couples

London, 13 June
An easier end to unhappy marriages came a step nearer today when the Divorce Reform Bill was given its third reading. It will mean that a divorce can be obtained after two years' separation with mutual consent or after five years apart without. Opposition to the bill has centred on fears for the financial position of women – Lady Summerskill has called it a "Casanova's Charter" – and it will not be implemented before further legislation has been passed giving women a bigger stake in matrimonial assets.

July 5. The Beatles may have stopped performing, but Mick Jagger struts on, leading the Rolling Stones in a free concert at London's Hyde Park.

British troops are deployed to control Ulster riots

Rioters and police confront each other near a Catholic barricade in Belfast.

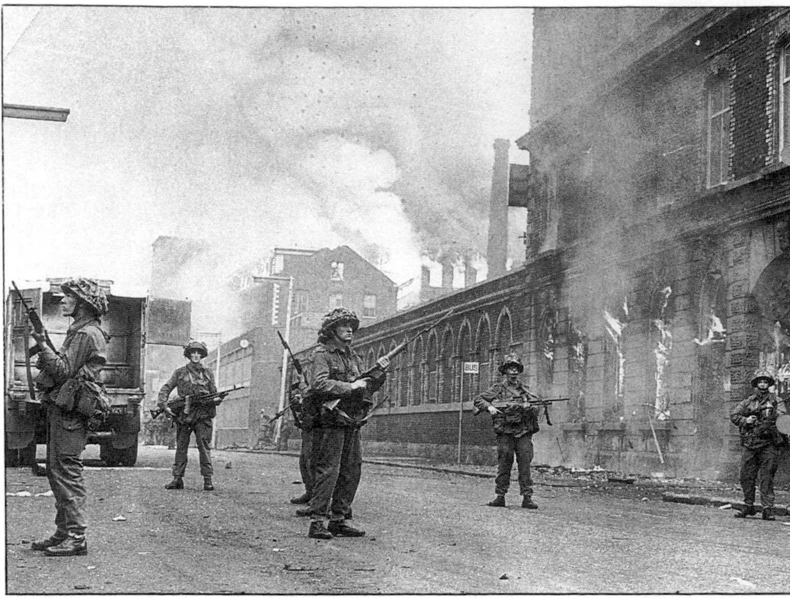

With little idea what has caused the riots, British troops stand bemused.

Northern Ireland, 16 August
British troops have been welcomed in Catholic areas of Londonderry and Belfast, standing in for a police force exhausted by sectarian riots. Ten people have been killed and over 100 wounded by gunfire in two days that recall the worst periods of the 1920s.

Housewives offered cups of tea as 600 soldiers of the Light Infantry mounted guard moved in to the Catholic Falls Road district of Belfast, which had been attacked by armed Protestant gangs. The IRA could only muster six guns in west Belfast and were taunted in graffiti: "IRA – I Ran Away". Altogether 500 houses, mostly belonging to Catholics, were destroyed.

Riots flared in Londonderry on 12 August after a controversial decision to permit the annual Apprentice Boys' parade by Protestants near the Catholic Bogside. Barricades were erected, marking out a "Free Derry" area, and a panic reaction to the threatened deployment of the partisan "B Special" police reservists drove matters to a head. As agreed by Stormont and Westminster, 400 men of the Prince of Wales' Own Yorkshire regiment took up positions around the Bogside at 5pm on 14 August. They remain, under the army GOC, General Ian Freeland, as part of a "temporary" operation, with instructions to act impartially.

Fears for the safety of Catholics led the Irish prime minister, Jack Lynch, to broadcast a statement in which he said that Dublin "can no longer stand by". In practice, this has meant ordering field hospitals to the border, near Derry; but hopes and fears have been raised on all sides (→ 28/9).

Army uses tear gas on Protestant crowd

Northern Ireland, 12 October
Three people were killed – including the first security force victim in the current violence – and 66 were injured in a weekend of Protestant mayhem, following an announcement that the "B Special" police reserves were to be abolished and the Royal Ulster Constabulary reorganized. Protestant reaction was quick and violent. Shots rang out during angry confrontations in the Shankill district yesterday and Constable Victor Arbuckle fell dead, the 11th victim of the violence. After 20 soldiers were hurt during attacks with petrol bombs, the army was issued with instructions to shoot back at snipers and bombers. At the height of the riots, tear gas was fired at a stone-throwing mob of 500 Protestants. Further troop reinforcements have brought their numbers to 9,000 (→ 12/12).

Some rioters wore gas masks.

Nationalist MP jailed for inciting a riot

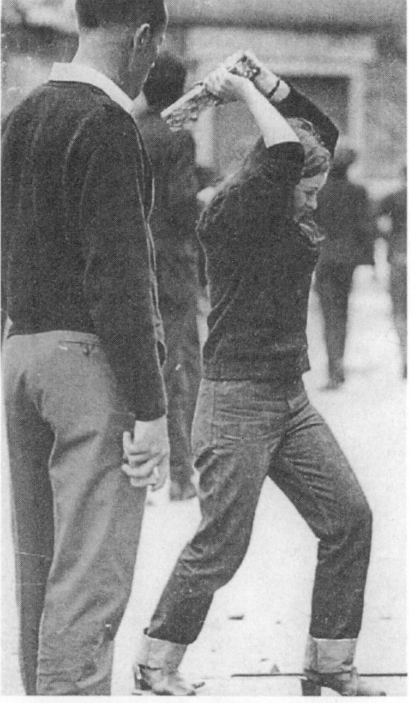

Devlin MP breaks rocks to throw.

Londonderry, 12 December
Bernadette Devlin, who in April became at 22 the youngest MP for nearly 200 years, was today sentenced to six months' imprisonment in Derry for incitement to riot during "the battle of the Bogside" in August. She was freed on bail pending an appeal.

A diminutive figure in a miniskirt, she was cheered from the courthouse by supporters singing "We Shall Overcome". Her lawyer claimed that she had acted from the highest motives, comparable to "the roles of Joan of Arc and Florence Nightingale", with concern for the safety of women and children. She won a by-election as an anti-Unionist unity candidate by 4,000 votes, but is bitterly disliked by Protestants who are unhappy about police reforms introduced by the British government (→ 18).

1970

Britain, 9 January. "Hong Kong flu" claims 2,850 lives this week.

London, 23 January. The first "jumbo" jet, a Boeing 747 of Pan Am, lands at Heathrow airport (→21/1/76).

Britain, 2 February. Bertrand Russell, the passionate liberal philosopher, dies aged 97.

Westminster, 9 February. Parliament says that men and women will receive equal pay by 1976 (→6/3/71).

Britain, 16 March. The *New English Bible*, published today, is a sell-out.

Derry City, 29 March. Troops seal off the Catholic Bogside area after riots (→16/4).

Northern Ireland, 16 April. Britain announces plans to send an extra 500 troops to join the 6,000 already here; the Unionist Reverend Ian Paisley wins the Bannside by-election (→31/7).

London, 18 May. A general election is called (→19/6).

London, 22 May. The MCC, under government pressure, cancels the South African cricket tour of England.

Dublin, 28 May. Charles Haughey and Neil Blaney, former cabinet ministers of the Republic, face arms smuggling charges (→23/10).

Britain, 22 June. Female ministers are to be ordained in the Methodist Church.

Luxembourg, 30 June. Britain, Ireland, Denmark and Norway open talks on entry into the Common Market (→24/6/71).

London, 17 July. A new sex comedy by Kenneth Tynan, *Oh! Calcutta!*, opens.

Westminster, 20 July. Iain MacLeod, the chancellor of the exchequer, dies suddenly.

Belfast, 2 August. The army begins using rubber bullets.

Cumbria, 24 August. A part of Windscale nuclear power station is closed due to a radioactive leak.

Beirut, 30 September. The British government exchanges Leila Khaled, a Palestinian terrorist, for British hostages seized by Palestinian hijackers.

North Sea, 19 October. BP has struck oil (→3/11/75).

Germany, 26 December. The 22-year-old Olympic athlete Lillian Board dies of cancer in a Bavarian clinic.

Damages paid to thalidomide victims

London, 23 March

Damages totalling £370,000 were awarded in the high court today to 18 children born with defects caused by their mothers taking the drug thalidomide while pregnant. The judgement was against Distillers (Biochemicals), which sold the drug under licence to Germany.

The amounts awarded depend on the severity of the disability, with five children born with tiny "flipper" arms winning £28,800 each. The figure includes damages to parents for shock and loss of earnings.

The case follows a long investigation and campaign by the *Sunday Times* which was fiercely contested through the courts by the Distillers company (→29/11/72).

Jacklin wins the US Open championship

Minneapolis, USA, 21 June

Tony Jacklin drove, chipped and putted his way into golfing history today when he became only the third player to hold the British and US Open championships at the same time. His victory in the US Open today – the first by a Briton for 50 years – follows success in the British one last July.

Jacklin won by seven strokes in sweltering heat. He was the only golfer to beat par in all four rounds of the tournament. His prize is £12,500 but is worth far more in terms of commercial contracts that await the new double champion.

Jacklin in the rough on the 17th.

Election win for Heath

Edward Heath, the jubilant winner.

Westminster, 19 June

After a big political upset, Edward Heath arrived at Downing Street tonight as Britain's new prime minister. The Conservatives confounded opinion pollsters to achieve 68 net gains in yesterday's general election, sweeping to office with a 4.7 per cent swing from a shell-shocked Labour Party. Until the campaign's final days Harold Wilson had appeared to be heading for a third successive election victory.

Labour had recovered from the rows over union policy last year and edged into an opinion poll lead last month. This lead soared to as high as 12.5 per cent at one point during a campaign fought mostly in warm sunshine.

Wilson mounted a relaxed, almost presidential campaign. Heath doggedly battled away on rising prices and union power, with few signs of encouragement until a balance of payments deficit announced 72 hours before polling day took the gloss off Labour's claims to economic recovery. Then the final opinion poll became the first to show a swing to the Tories.

Labour apathy was as much a factor as any late swing to the Conservatives, however, with voter turn-out down to 70 per cent. Final figures are 330 Conservatives, 287 Labour, 6 Liberals and 1 Scottish Nationalist (→4/3/74).

'Women's Lib' becomes a powerful force

Britain

Women's rights made two tangible advances this year in terms of law reform while finding a new champion in Germaine Greer, the author of *The Female Eunuch*.

The legal advances came in the form of two acts of parliament. The Matrimonial Property Act laid down that a wife's work – whether in jobs outside the home or as a housewife within it – was to be regarded as an equal contribution with that of the husband if, in the event of divorce, the family home had to be divided.

The Equal Pay Act also passed through its parliamentary stages this year. It does not come fully into practice for five years, and even then there are loopholes, but it does finally establish the principle of equal pay for equal work.

Feminists have welcomed both of these new acts, which continue a process of reform which gathered momentum during the Sixties in areas such as abortion, divorce and contraception. The availability of the contraceptive pill came to symbolize a new liberation for women, which Germaine Greer advances in her bestselling book. A university lecturer, she challenges the masculine world with an erudite critique of the way it stereotypes women's roles. Even so, "women's lib" as a movement is in its infancy here compared with more strident campaigns in the United States (→9/2).

Ardent feminist: Germaine Greer.

'Fabulous four' to go separate ways

Liverpool, 9 April
Sad-faced youngsters dressed in mourning black here today at the news that this city's favourite sons – the Beatles – are splitting up and going their separate ways. The sadness will be echoed wherever the fabulous four's music is played – that is, in every corner of the globe.

Paul McCartney – who is now reputed to be at loggerheads with his co-Beatle John Lennon – issued in the high court the writ that ended the partnership, which had recently been under strain from business squabbles within the Beatles' multi-million pound Apple Corporation (→8/12/80).

Kidnappers release British diplomat

Toronto, 13 December
For the British diplomat James Cross the ordeal by kidnap ended today when he was released by French-Canadian terrorists of the Quebec Liberation Front (FLQ). Cross had been held for two months – and there were grave concerns for his safety when the body of Pierre Laporte, the Quebec minister of labour, who had been kidnapped at the same time, was found in the boot of a car. Cross is with a Cuban diplomat until his kidnappers reach Havana, under an agreement reached with the Canadian police. He told the Canadian prime minister, Pierre Trudeau, by telephone: "The nightmare is over."

Northern Ireland erupts in chaos

Army's honeymoon with Catholics ends

Belfast, 31 July
The killing by troops of an alleged petrol bomber, Danny O'Hagan, during rioting in north Belfast has marked the conclusion of a year-long honeymoon between the British Army and the Roman Catholic community. O'Hagan was the first to die following a warning by General Ian Freeland, the army GOC, that petrol bombers would be shot.

Relations have worsened since the jailing on 26 June of Bernadette Devlin, the civil rights leader, for her part in the August 1969 riots in Derry, and a 35-hour curfew of the Lower Falls area this month after six Protestants and a Catholic had been killed in skirmishes.

A house-to-house search involving 3,000 soldiers turned up 107 firearms, 250 pounds of explosives, 100 home-made bombs and 21,000 rounds of ammunition. It was regarded as counter-productive, however, in terms of antagonizing an entire Catholic population.

The deteriorating relations have been exploited by the Provisional IRA which was formed in January, having split from the Official IRA in a clash over political or military strategies. The new "provisional" executive has dedicated itself to making Northern Ireland ungovernable, and with finance from overseas, as well as from the Republic, has already been responsible for more than 40 bombings (→21/8).

British military police patrol the Falls Road area after a night of violence.

Gerry Fitt leads new Ulster reform party

Belfast, 21 August
A new party for moderate nationalists, the Social Democratic and Labour Party (SDLP), was launched today by Gerry Fitt, the Westminster MP for West Belfast, and six prominent Stormont MPs, including John Hume. The party is a radical supporter of civil rights, believing that the unity of Ireland can be achieved only through the consent of the majority of the people.

The new party reflects the volatility of politics here. In April the Rev Ian Paisley and a Democratic Unionist colleague won Stormont by-elections, followed by Paisley's election to Westminster in June. And in April the Alliance Party was formed, aimed at liberal Protestants and Catholics (→9/2/71).

Ian Paisley: Protestant Unionist.

January 9. Flames and smoke, fanned by gale-force winds, cause serious damage to the Starlight theatre on Eastbourne's 100-year-old pier.

Haughey is not guilty in Irish gun trial

Dublin, 23 October
The former government minister Charles Haughey, together with three other defendants, has been acquitted of conspiring to import arms into the republic. It was alleged that their intention – not sanctioned by the government – was to send the arms to the beleaguered Roman Catholic minority in the north of Ireland. Immediately after the verdict, Haughey issued a challenge to the Fianna Fáil party leader, Jack Lynch, whose action in dismissing Haughey from his government last May had led to the trial. The case has attracted enormous public attention. Charges against a second former senior minister, Neil Blaney, were dropped at a preliminary hearing. The trial which followed was aborted, due to inadmissible evidence about one of the defendants, and a new trial was ordered. During that, conflict of evidence between Charles Haughey and his former government colleague James Gibbons clearly indicated that one of the two men was committing perjury.

1971

Uruguay, 8 January. The British ambassador, Geoffrey Jackson, is kidnapped by left-wing terrorists (→ 9/9).

Britain, 20 January. Postal workers strike for the first time, in pursuit of a 19.5 per cent pay rise (→ 8/3).

Britain, 4 February. Rolls-Royce, the luxury car manufacturer, goes bankrupt.

Northern Ireland, 9 February. A British soldier is shot dead in violent rioting (→ 10/3).

London, 6 March. The biggest ever women's liberation march is staged (→ 31/12/75).

Britain, 8 March. The postal strike ends; workers vote 14-1 to return to work.

Belfast, 10 March. Three more British soldiers are shot dead in an outbreak of sectarian violence (→ 11/8).

Belfast, 20 March. James Chichester-Clark resigns as prime minister of Northern Ireland (→ 21).

Westminster, 15 June. The education secretary, Margaret Thatcher, plans to end free school milk (→ 25/1/75).

Plymouth, 11 August. Edward Heath, the prime minister, skippering *Morning Cloud*, leads the British team to victory in the Admiral's Cup.

Belfast, 16 August. The IRA threatens to step up its bombing campaign on the mainland (→ 7/10).

Uruguay, 9 September. The kidnapped British envoy, Geoffrey Jackson, is freed after eight months' captivity.

London, 24 September. Ninety Russian diplomats are expelled after a KGB defector gives secret information on spying in Britain (→ 8/10).

Northern Ireland, 7 October. A further 1,700 troops are sent to the province (→ 16/11).

London, 9 October. Crowds greet a visit by Emperor Hirohito of Japan in silence.

Westminster, 28 October. MPs vote by 356-244 to join the Common Market (→ 22/1/72).

London, 5 November. Princess Anne is named Sportswoman of the Year (→ 14/11/73).

Ulster, 20 December. The IRA begins a Christmas bombing campaign (→ 30/1/72).

Britain, 31 December. Beer-lovers found the Campaign for Real Ale.

'Angry Brigade' bombs minister's home

London, 14 January

An anonymous letter sent to several Fleet Street newspapers claims that an extremist group calling itself the Angry Brigade was responsible for planting two terrorist bombs at the home of a cabinet minister two days ago. The bombs exploded outside the Hertfordshire home of Robert Carr, the employment secretary. He and his wife and younger daughter were in the house at the time. They escaped unhurt, but windows were shattered, and the front door was blown out.

The Angry Brigade has previously claimed responsibility for three other terrorist attacks in London – the machine-gunning of the Spanish embassy and bombs at the Miss World contest and the department of employment offices in Westminster. Robert Carr, although a liberal Tory, has been at the centre of controversy because he is spearheading the proposals of Edward Heath's government for curbing trade union power. Leaders of all political parties have condemned the attacks.

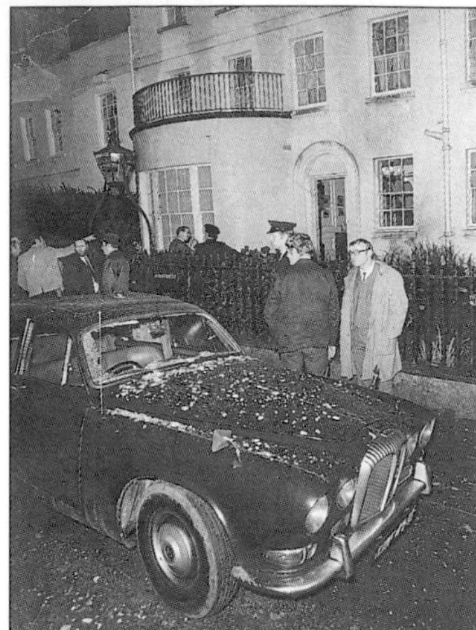

Carr's Daimler after the blast.

Faulkner becomes Stormont premier

Belfast, 21 March

Brian Faulkner was elected today as prime minister of Northern Ireland after Major James Chichester-Clark had resigned "in order to underline the seriousness of the situation". Faulkner, a former commerce minister, takes over at a time of turmoil, after the murder of three off-duty Scottish soldiers and a march by shipyard men demanding the introduction of internment without trial. London's agreement to send 1,000 more troops was insufficient to save Chichester-Clark, who was regarded as too soft in his dealings with Westminster.

Brian Faulkner selects his cabinet.

Football crowd barriers collapse, killing 66

The buckled barriers at Ibrox Park, where 66 people were crushed to death.

Glasgow, 2 January

Crowd barriers collapsed today at Ibrox Park stadium, sending football fans tumbling down terraces amid a tangle of twisted metal. Sixty-six people died and hundreds were injured in Britain's worst soccer disaster – and the second at Ibrox Park this century. In 1902 20 people died when a terrace collapsed during an international.

Today's tragedy occurred shortly after Glasgow Rangers, the home team, had equalized against their closest and fiercest rivals, Glasgow Celtic. As the capacity crowd pushed forwards, some barriers gave way, hurling fans onto those at the front. Some fans found safety on the pitch, but others were crushed by the weight of bodies falling helplessly on top of them.

An inquiry into safety at major sporting venues seems certain to be announced by either central or local government.

British currency gets decimal point

Britain, 15 February

Britons bade a reluctant farewell to the venerable system of pounds, shillings and pence today and began the struggle to understand decimal coinage. Gone are the half-crown [12.5p] and the florin [10p], and the wholly illogical system in which 240 pennies equal one pound.

The chairman of the decimal currency board, Lord Fiske, is content that things are going well; but many are finding it hard to cope with the new currency which includes a minute and anachronistic half-pence piece, which is roughly the equivalent of the chunky and trusted old copper penny.

Soviets oust Britons in tit-for-tat move

Moscow, 8 October
Five Britons are to be expelled from the USSR, the Soviet authorities announced today. A further 13 have been refused entry into the country.

The move comes as no surprise. On 24 September the foreign secretary, Sir Alec Douglas-Home, announced the expulsion of 100 Soviet diplomats and officials – who, he said, had turned London into a "hive of Russian intelligence activity". A tit-for-tat response by the other side is usual in these cases.

The British move was taken at a time of strained Anglo-Soviet ties, partly prompted by the decision in June to grant asylum to the Soviet space expert Anatol Fedoseyev, a big prize for the West. The revelations of another defector, the KGB agent Oleg Lyalin, led to the September expulsions (→21/11/79).

Britain agrees to terms to join EEC

Westminster, 24 June
After a year of negotiations, the government announced today that it had agreed terms to join the European Economic Community (EEC) or Common Market. "We have a very satisfactory deal," said Geoffrey Rippon, the minister in charge of the EEC negotiations.

Rippon told MPs that transitional arrangements would safeguard the interests of both British and Commonwealth farmers. And he defended the annual cost of membership – £100 million in 1973 rising to £200 in 1977. The European policy is a linchpin of Edward Heath's strategy. It was the British prime minister's talks with President Pompidou of France last month which resolved many of the difficulties. Now Heath has to win the consent of parliament (→28/10).

Riots flare in Ulster after IRA suspects are interned in massive terrorist crackdown

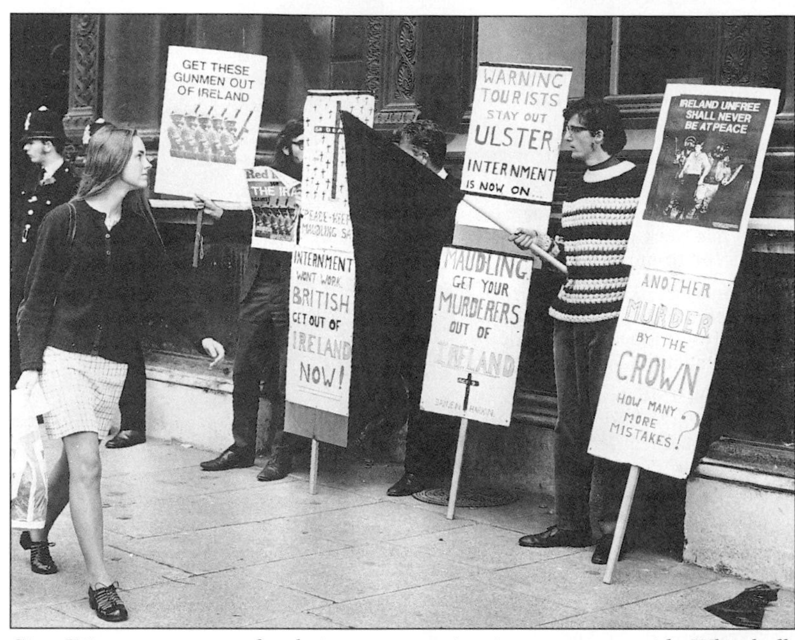

Sinn Féin supporters make their protest against internment outside Whitehall.

Northern Ireland, 11 August
Violence has erupted on the streets of Belfast in the 48 hours following the re-introduction of internment without trial. Twenty-one civilians – including a priest giving the last rites – and two soldiers have been killed and some 300 houses destroyed by fire. An estimated 7,000 refugees have fled to the Republic.

All 342 terrorist suspects seized on 9 August were nationalists. Of these 116 have already been released, many of them non-violent civil rights activists. Even though the round-up, code-named Operation Demetrius, was brought forward a day as a consequence of riots, many IRA leaders escaped the net. The Northern Ireland prime minister, Brian Faulkner, claimed success in his efforts to "flush out the gunmen". But it has also provoked the moderate Social Democratic and Labour Party to boycott all government bodies in protest (→16).

Shipbuilding hit by 'lame duck' policy

Glasgow, 14 June
No government money is to be made available to help Upper Clyde Shipbuilders stave off liquidation. The announcement was made today by John Davies, the trade and industry secretary. His declaration was attacked in the House of Commons by Tony Benn, who as Labour's technology minister had put £20 million into the company.

Edward Heath's government was elected on a manifesto promising non-intervention in industry; it was made clear that "lame ducks" would not be saved. Although ministers back-tracked from this policy following the collapse of Rolls-Royce in February, no reprieve is envisaged for the shipbuilders. Davies insists that public money should not be pumped into ailing or bankrupt industries.

Four thousand jobs are directly threatened at Upper Clyde Shipbuilders, and there is talk of a "work-in" by a labour force convinced that the yard – where many of Britain's most famous ships were built – can still be profitable.

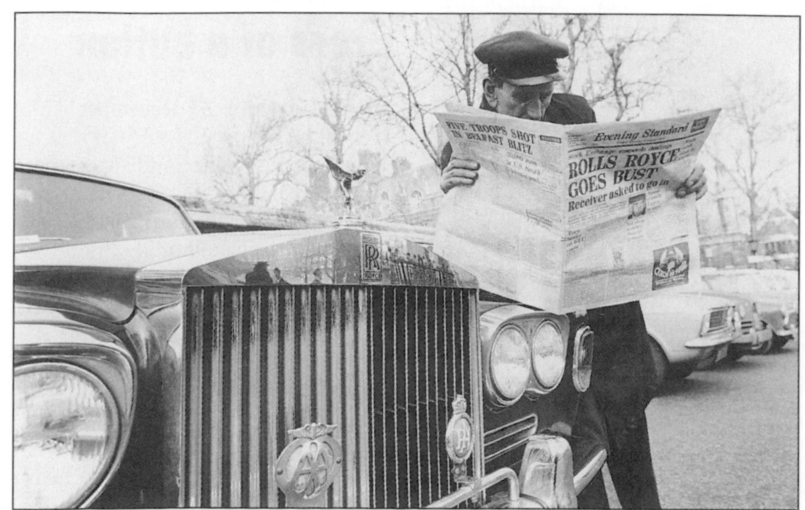

British engineering takes a bashing with the collapse of Rolls-Royce.

Suspects face rough internment in Ulster

Belfast, 16 November
Nationalists reacted angrily today to the findings of the Compton commission, appointed to investigate allegations of torture of internees in Northern Ireland. Sir Edmund Compton, the ombudsman, found no evidence of brutality by police interrogators. Five interrogation techniques developed by the army in Aden and Cyprus were investigated, involving hooding of suspects, exposure to continuous noise, standing against a wall supported by the fingertips and deprivation of sleep and food. All the detainees except one refused to give evidence, on the grounds that the commission sat in private (→20/12).

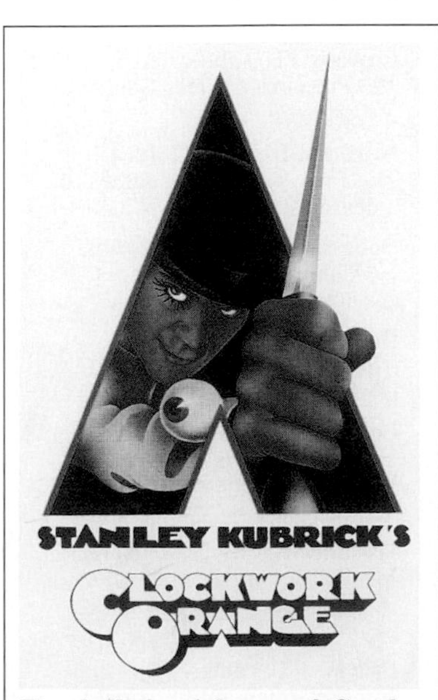

The balletic violence of Stanley Kubrick's "Clockwork Orange" has been thrilling cinemagoers.

1972

Britain, 9 January. The government plans to ration coal as miners go on strike (→ 16/2).

Britain, 20 January. Unemployment figures reach one million (→ 21/8/75).

Dublin, 2 February. The British embassy is destroyed in anti-British protests (→ 22).

Westminster, 18 February. A £6 per week pay increase is offered to miners (→ 25).

Hampshire, 22 February. Seven die in an IRA attack on the 16th Parachute Brigade at Aldershot (→ 24/3).

Britain, 25 February. The miners vote 27-1 in favour of a pay settlement (→ 28).

Birmingham, 28 February. Striking miners riot at the Saltley coke depot (→ 13/11/73).

Belfast, 28 March. Over 100,000 Protestants march against direct rule (→ 19/4).

Westminster, 11 April. Roy Jenkins resigns as deputy leader of the Labour Party over plans for a referendum on membership of the EEC.

London, 19 April. An inquiry into the "Bloody Sunday" killings finds that troops were provoked but then fired recklessly (→ 22/6).

Oxford, 27 April. Five university colleges admit women for the first time.

Ireland, 11 May. A referendum backs membership of the European Economic Community (→ 1/1/73).

Paris, 28 May. The duke of Windsor – who, as King Edward VIII, abdicated in 1936 to marry Wallis Simpson – dies, aged 77.

Northern Ireland, 22 June. The Provisional IRA agrees to a ceasefire (→ 14/7).

Belfast, 14 July. Four die as IRA abandons its two-week ceasefire (→ 31).

Belfast, 9 August. British troops clash with Protestant Ulster Defence troops (→ 1/12).

London, 10 October. After Cecil Day Lewis's death in May, John Betjeman is made poet laureate.

Westminster, 29 November. More thalidomide victims are to receive compensation payments (→ 5/1/73).

Dublin, 1 December. The Dáil votes in tough anti-terrorist laws.→

All-out miners' strike puts Britain in dark

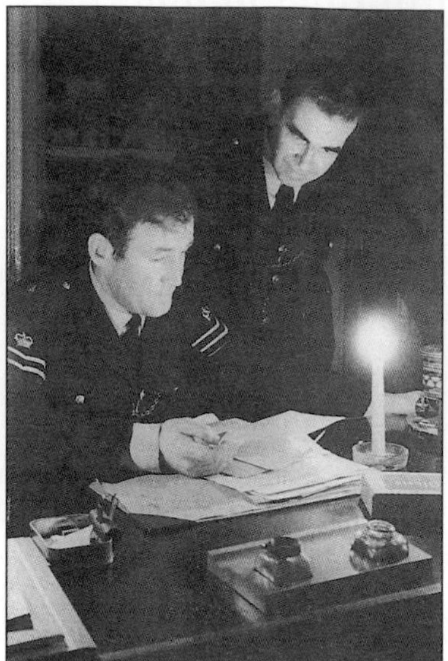

Police work goes on by candlelight despite the cuts in power supply.

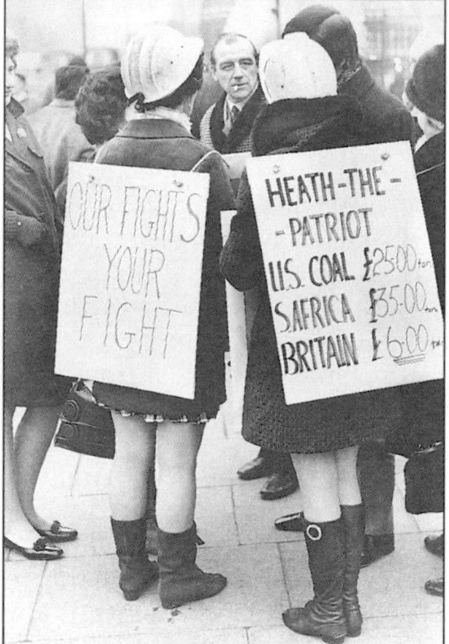

Miners' wives join the protest, which has led to nationwide blackouts.

London, 16 February
With most power stations working below capacity and 12 completely shut down by fuel shortages, Britain has been hit by electricity blackouts lasting nine hours. Militant miners are picketing power stations in order to impede deliveries; at Longannet, near Edinburgh, three policemen were injured on Monday when 2,000 miners fought police to stop deliveries of oil. In London, miners have hired boats to picket Thames-side power stations.

Operating under the government's state of emergency, which was proclaimed last week, industry is working a three-day week, and families are being urged to heat only one room in their homes. It is reckoned that industry has laid off over one million workers.

In a move widely interpreted as a sign of the government's weakening resolve, Edward Heath, the prime minister, has appointed a high court judge, Lord Wilberforce, to lead a three-man inquiry into the miners' claim for a pay increase which would be substantially above the Coal Board's pre-strike offer of £2 a week (→ 18).

Britain signs on dotted line to join EEC

Brussels, 22 January
Britain, Ireland, Denmark and Norway signed a treaty here today agreeing to join the European Economic Community next January. Although the European Community Bill has yet to be accepted by the British parliament, MPs backed the principle of membership last October by a majority of 112. Opponents from both sides of the house plan to fight the bill all the way, with Labour more seriously split than the Conservatives. Edward Heath, the prime minister, remains confident of success. Ten years ago President de Gaulle thwarted his negotiations to join. Today, not even a bag of printer's ink thrown at him by a demonstrator could mar his satisfaction (→ 11/5).

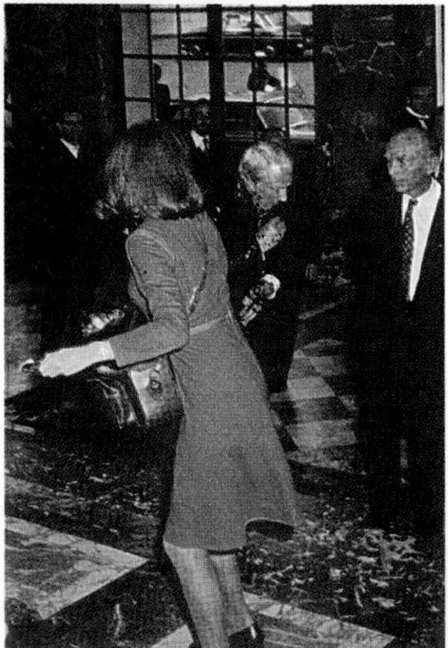

An ink-spattered Edward Heath.

Maudling quits in financial scandal

Westminster, 18 July
Reginald Maudling, the home secretary, resigned today because of his connection with a Yorkshire architect, John Poulson, who is facing corruption charges. Bankruptcy hearings have raised wider allegations of corruption. With a police inquiry inevitable, Maudling decided that he had to quit, since the home secretary has ministerial responsibility for the police. It has not been alleged that Maudling has done anything improper, but he was involved with a Poulson company during his time in opposition. Although he received no payment himself, his children and a theatre charity with which his wife is connected did benefit.

Allegations force Maudling to quit.

Calculations at the press of a button

Cambridgeshire, 31 December
It weighs 70 grams (2.5 oz), it is 50mm (2in) wide and less than 10mm thick, and it is, says its inventor, Clive Sinclair, the world's first true pocket calculator. He is off to New York to put the £79 Sinclair Executive on sale there for $195. Sinclair, who left school with "A" levels in maths and physics, has turned out a whole string of innovations in his works, an old flour mill, at St Ives. The Executive has four tiny mercury cells, as used in hearing aids, which drive a 7,000-unit micro-chip.

Wages frozen and price rises halted

Westminster, 6 November
Wages and prices are to be frozen for 90 days, the prime minister told MPs today. The standstill, which also covers dividends and rents, could be extended for a further 60 days under emergency legislation which amounts to a major U-turn by the Heath government.

Edward Heath was elected on a platform that included the rejection of statutory wage controls, but rising prices, a worsening balance of payments deficit and increasing numbers of strikes produced a sterling crisis this summer. Talks with unions and industry have failed to produce a voluntary agreement to curb inflation (→ 1/5/73).

Civil rights marchers are shot dead

Derry City, 30 January
Paratroopers opened fire on an illegal civil rights march in Derry today, killing 13 civilians and injuring 29 in what has already been dubbed another "Bloody Sunday". Army claims that the soldiers were fired upon, and that some of the victims were carrying nail bombs, have been hotly disputed.

About 15,000 took part in the march against internment. Near the city centre, water cannon and tear gas were used before men of the 1st Paratroop Regiment opened fire on fleeing marchers. The killings followed an intense IRA bombing campaign in Belfast. In reprisal, a Protestant bomb in December killed 15 in a Catholic pub (→ 2/2).

Two of the victims of "Bloody Sunday" lie dead on a deserted Bogside street.

Amin expels Asians

Kampala, 6 August
Uganda's industrious and prosperous Asians were faced with imminent expulsion to Britain today when the country's brutal military dictator, General Idi Amin, alleged that they were "sabotaging the economy" and said that he was getting rid of all those with British passports, an estimated 50,000, or virtually the whole community. When Uganda, Kenya and Tanganyika became independent ten years ago, the Asians were reassured by being given British passports, although without the automatic right to come to Britain.

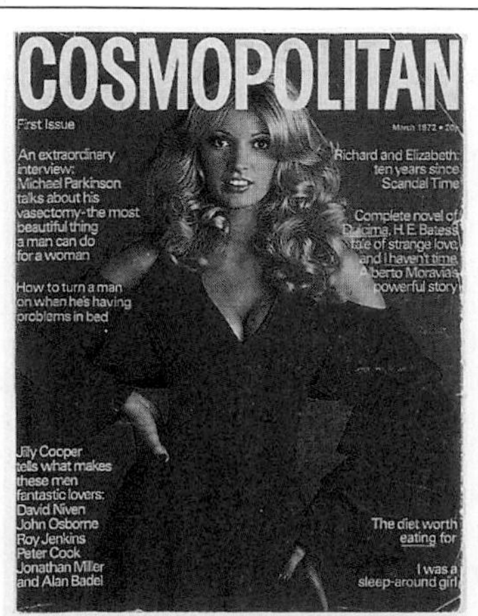

Women rush to buy the first issue of "Cosmopolitan", a monthly magazine promising articles on life, love, sex and money.

Direct rule imposed in Northern Ireland

Shipyard workers in Belfast protest at the imposition of direct rule for Ulster.

Belfast, 24 March
The Northern Ireland government of Brian Faulkner resigned today in protest at Edward Heath's demand for security responsibility to be transferred to Westminster. Stormont will be suspended from 28 March, and William Whitelaw has been appointed secretary of state for the province, ending 51 years of self-government.

London is responding to increasing signs that Stormont is losing the war against the paramilitaries. On 4 March two women died in the bombing of the Abercorn restaurant in Belfast, and after six people had died in a Donegal Street blast loyalists threatened all-out warfare against the IRA. Summoned to London, Faulkner was stunned by Heath's demands for a referendum on the border, steps to end internment and moves towards power-sharing, but only refused to give way on security. The Heath government has distanced itself from Stormont ever since Bloody Sunday [*see above*], and security chiefs believed that their policies would not be acceptable as long as they were associated with the Unionist regime (→ 28).

British army ends IRA 'no-go' areas

Derry City, 31 July
Army bulldozers today demolished barricades which had turned parts of Derry into "no-go" areas for a year. Some 5,000 of the 21,000 troops in Northern Ireland assisted in the operation, in which two civilians died. There was little resistance from the IRA, many of whose leaders are in the Republic. The show of force followed a "Bloody Friday" in Belfast on 21 July, when 11 died in 21 IRA explosions. Two weeks earlier a 14-day IRA truce had broken down (→ 9/8).

Anti-terrorist laws extended in Ireland

Dublin, 1 December
Two bombs have exploded in the centre of the city, one outside Liberty Hall and the other in Marlborough Street, killing two people and injuring 127. The explosions occurred during a parliamentary debate on an amendment to the Offences Against the State Act, giving greater powers of arrest and detention to the police. It was expected that the Fianna Fáil government would be defeated, leading to a general election. In the event Fine Gael dropped its opposition, and the legislation was passed (→ 28/1/73).

1973

Europe, 1 January. Britain and Ireland join the Common Market (→ 6/6/75).

Derry City, 28 January. Troops fire plastic bullets to break up an anniversary riot to mark "Bloody Sunday" (→ 7/2).

Northern Ireland, 7 February. Unionists call a one-day general strike (→ 8/3).

Ireland, 1 March. After 16 years in office Fianna Fáil loses an election to the Fine Gael-Labour coalition.

Northern Ireland, 9 March. In a referendum, 90 per cent opt to stay within the UK; most Catholics refused to vote (→ 20).

Northern Ireland, 20 March. Trials without jury are to be introduced to deal with suspected terrorists (→ 16/4).

Jamaica, 26 March. Noël Coward, the playwright and actor, dies aged 73.

Dublin, 16 April. Sean MacStiofain, the IRA chief, is freed from jail (→ 31/7).

North Sea, 24 April. An Icelandic gunboat opens fire on two British trawlers (→ 21/5).

Britain, 1 May. A TUC one-day strike in protest at pay restraints is supported by 1.6 million (→ 17/12).

Westminster, 24 May. Two government ministers, Lord Lambton and Earl Jellicoe, resign amid a sex scandal.

Wimbledon, 22 June. Tennis stars boycott Wimbledon in a row over contracts.

Belfast, 31 July. The first, stormy, meeting of the Ulster assembly takes place (→ 31/10).

Dublin, 31 October. Three Provisional IRA leaders escape prison by helicopter (→ 22/11).

Westminster, 13 November. The government calls a state of emergency as power workers and miners strike (→ 6/3/74).

Westminster, 14 November. Princess Anne marries Captain Mark Phillips (→ 20/3/74).

Northern Ireland, 22 November. Catholics and Protestants agree to share power (→ 9/12).

Westminster, 5 December. As the Middle East crisis worsens, a 50-mph speed limit is imposed on the roads to conserve fuel (→ 17).

London, 30 December. Joseph Sieff, the head of Marks and Spencer and strong Zionist, is recovering after an Arab terrorist fired shots at him.

London devastated by IRA bombing

London, 8 March

The IRA brought its bombing campaign to the heart of London today when cars parked outside the Old Bailey and Scotland Yard exploded, killing one man and injuring 244. Most injuries were caused by flying glass which sliced through the busy streets. There would have been many more casualties if the police had not acted on a telephoned warning and defused two other car bombs.

It is thought that the bombs were planted to mark the referendum being held in Northern Ireland to decide if the people want to remain part of the United Kingdom. Most Catholics are boycotting the poll, but the IRA's actions leave no doubt about its intention not only to continue its campaign of violence in Ireland but also to spread it to the mainland.

It is pointed out that last year's attack on the Parachute Regiment's mess at Aldershot was carried out by the Official IRA as a specific act of revenge for "Bloody Sunday", when the "Paras" shot dead 13 demonstrators in Derry. Today's bombs were planted by the Provisional IRA, which is responsible for most of the current violence. Ten people have been arrested tonight at Heathrow airport (→ 9).

Council of Ireland created at Sunningdale

Faulkner (l) and Cosgrave making history as north and south are linked.

Berkshire, 9 December

An historic four-day conference at Sunningdale was concluded today with an agreement between the British, Irish and Northern Ireland governments to set up a council of Ireland, a consultative body linking Belfast and Dublin for the first time since partition.

The council provides an Irish dimension, as demanded by nationalists, to the accord reached on 21 November between the Northern Ireland parties and the Ulster secretary William Whitelaw on a new power-sharing executive for the province. The Sunningdale agreement ties the Republic to recognition of the fact that there can be no change in Northern Ireland's status without majority consent.

The council, consisting of seven ministers from Belfast and Dublin, will be mainly concerned with co-operative ventures in areas like trade and tourism. But loyalist politicians, absent from the conference, have promised to resist any Dublin involvement in the affairs of Northern Ireland (→ 22/1/74).

Thirty holidaymakers die as flames destroy Isle of Man complex

Holidaymakers watch in horror as flames and smoke engulf Summerland.

Douglas, Isle of Man, 2 August

The £2 million Summerland entertainment complex at Douglas, on the Isle of Man, was packed with holidaymakers when fire broke out in the upper storeys tonight. Within minutes the restaurant, solarium, discothèque and theatre were engulfed in a raging inferno that killed 30 people and injured at least 80 others. Many have severe burns; others were trampled in the panic. "I was knocked down in the stampede," a woman survivor said. "I was flat on my stomach, and there was a kiddie underneath me."

Hours after the fire had been extinguished a pall of black smoke hung over the devastation. Fire investigators are seeking to establish both the cause of the fire and the reason why it spread so fast.

Distillers is banned from supermarkets in thalidomide row

London, 5 January
In a new twist to the dispute over the controversial thalidomide drug, goods produced by the Distillers Company, the drink and pharmaceuticals giant, are being banned from some supermarket shelves because of the delay in settling compensation claims. The boycott, by David Greig and Redmans, will affect well known brands of whisky, gin, vodka and brandy.

Cases involving Distillers (Biochemicals), which marketed the drug in Britain, are still before the courts, but Distillers has offered £11.25 million to thalidomide victims and their families, and the government has given £3 million to help cover the cost of home care.

The drug had been in use for several years before it was discovered that when it was taken as a sedative during pregnancy a woman was at risk of giving birth to a deformed baby.

Three-day working week introduced

Westminster, 17 December
Most British workers face a three-day week in the New Year under a package of measures announced today to combat what the government called "the gravest situation by far since the end of the war". Public spending will be cut, a speed limit of 50mph imposed, television blacked-out at 10.30pm and credit controls will be tightened in a mini-budget which comes barely one month after last month's state of emergency and rises in bank rate.

Edward Heath's government is under attack both at home and abroad. At home, industrial unrest over stage three of the government's prices and incomes policy has been compounded by more particular grievances. Power workers, miners and railwaymen are among groups currently imposing overtime bans or other restrictions. Coal supplies to power stations are already down 40 per cent.

These difficulties have been intensified by the Arab-Israeli war last October. Supplies of oil – which provides 50 per cent of Britain's energy – have been cut by 15 per cent, causing long queues for petrol and the distribution of ration books. More ominous for the government is the prospect of the import bill for oil quadrupling at a time when the balance of payments is already grim. If the industrial rows are not solved quickly, it is likely that the Conservatives will call an election (→26/6/74).

Motorists join the queue for petrol as the shortage of oil worsens.

Britain and Iceland clash in fishing row

An Icelandic boat pulls alongside a British fishing vessel as a warning.

Reykjavik, 21 May
The British frigate *Cleopatra* and the Icelandic gunboat *Thor* spent much of today shadow-boxing in the disputed 50-mile (80-km) fishing zone around Iceland.The *Thor*, which had been shadowing the British fishing fleet, suddenly made off to harass a West German trawler, and the *Cleopatra* followed. With only 4 miles between the two ships, the *Thor* spun round and headed for the *Cleopatra*; when she came within a quarter of a mile, the *Cleopatra* made off. The *Thor* later reappeared and, closing to 100 yards (91m), sent a large wave against the *Cleopatra's* starboard side. As darkness fell the two ships were still dodging and weaving (→19/2/76).

BBC feels waves as rival radio goes on air

London, 8 October
The BBC's 50-year-old monopoly of radio broadcasting was broken today when the all-news station LBC – the London Broadcasting Company – went on the air using a temporary aerial slung from the smoke stacks of a Thames-side power station and studios off Fleet Street in a square near Dr Samuel Johnson's house, now a museum.

Tomorrow Capital Radio, a pop music station to rival the BBC's Radio One, will start broadcasting. Both will look to advertising for revenue. LBC has set out to build up a newsgathering network of contributors at home and overseas, but doubts have been expressed as to whether it can pull in the £1 million a year gross on which its ambitious plans are based.

May 5. A triumphant Bobby Kerr, captain of second division Sunderland, lifts the FA cup after their shock 1-0 victory over mighty Leeds United.

1974

Belfast, 22 January. The Northern Ireland Assembly collapses amid protests over power-sharing (→ 4/2).

Bradford, 4 February. An IRA bomb explodes on a coach carrying servicemen and their families; 11 people die (→ 11/3).

Britain, 6 March. Miners end their strike after the offer of a 35 per cent pay rise (→ 13/2/75).

Dublin, 11 March. Kenneth and Keith Littlejohn, allegedly MI6 spies inside the IRA, escape from prison (→ 20/4).

London, 20 March. An attempt to kidnap Princess Anne fails (→ 12/6/87).

Britain, 1 April. Free family planning is now available on the National Health Service.

Belfast, 20 April. A Catholic man becomes the thousandth person to die in the present "troubles" (→ 17/5).

Canterbury, 14 May. Dr Donald Coggan is made archbishop of Canterbury (→ 25/3/80).

Dublin, 17 May. An IRA car bomb kills 23 people in the rush hour (→ 28).

Westminster, 17 June. An IRA bomb hurts 11 people and causes great damage (→ 5/10).

Westminster, 26 June. The government agrees a "social contract" with the TUC to restrain pay increases (→ 13/5/75).

Britain, 14 August. The collapse of Clarksons and Horizon Holidays leaves 100,000 without holidays and over 5,000 stranded abroad.

London, 1 October. The first McDonald's hamburger restaurant in Britain opens.

Guildford, Surrey, 5 October. Five die and 65 are injured when IRA bombs explode in two pubs (→ 16).

Britain, 10 October. Labour wins the general election (→ 11).

Belfast, 16 October. Republican prisoners set fire to the Maze prison (→ 21/11).

London, 4 November. Judith Ward is jailed for the coach bombing on the M62 in which 11 people died.

Westminster, 29 November. The Prevention of Terrorism Act becomes law (→ 18/12).

Northern Ireland, 18 December. The government agrees to pay £42,000 compensation to the victims of "Bloody Sunday" (→ 16/1/75).

Labour in power after two elections

Heath loses after miners' challenge

Westminster, 4 March
Harold Wilson is back in Downing Street tonight, promising to put Britain back to work. He heads a minority government after the general election held on 28 February rebounded on the outgoing prime minister, Edward Heath, who had run an anti-union campaign on the issue of "Who governs Britain?".

Not the Conservatives, came the answer, although for four days the fate of Heath's government hung in the balance as he sought a pact with Jeremy Thorpe's resurgent Liberals. In the election, Labour won 301 seats, the Conservatives 297 and the Liberals 14; nine went to Scottish and Welsh Nationalists and 12 to Northern Ireland.

Talks between Heath and Thorpe failed, in spite of the offer of a cabinet post for the Liberal leader, so Harold Wilson begins his third term as premier. He is expected to end the four-week pit strike and to lift the state of emergency, including the three-day week. Tory hopes in the campaign were undermined by a disclosure that official figures for miners' pay were incorrect, improving the cause of the strikers and of Labour, which argued that it was best able to end the rash of industrial disputes (→ 10/10).

Harold Wilson congratulating his staff at Labour Party headquarters.

Tiny majority returns Wilson to No 10

Westminster, 11 October
Harold Wilson has won his fourth general election out of five contests, but his majority is just three seats over all other parties in yesterday's poll. The totals are Labour 319, Conservatives 276, Liberals 13, Nationalists 14 and others 13.

Labour had ruled for seven months as a minority government, using the time to promote an aura of stability after the trauma of the three-day week and miners' strike. A voluntary "social contract" with the unions was cited as an alternative to the Tory reliance on legislation to curb inflation and strikes. Denis Healey, the new chancellor, boosted pensions and said that difficulties with the balance of payments had eased. Edward Heath warned about rising inflation but failed to shake off the legacy of last winter. Now he faces trouble within his party, after three defeats in four as Conservative leader (→ 11/2/75).

Huge explosion kills 29 at the Flixborough chemical plant

The acrid smoke and rubble are all that remain of the chemical plant.

Humberside, 2 June
At 4.35 this afternoon the village of Flixborough (population 200) was devastated by violent explosions at a nearby chemical plant which for years has been the community's main source of employment.

Twenty-nine people were killed, about a hundred stone-built cottages were wrecked, the factory was left a grotesque tangle of blackened steel girders, and an acrid cloud is drifting across the countryside. All those who died were working close to the central control room when a red warning light came on, and the factory hooter sounded. The next moment two tremendous blasts tore the factory apart.

Counties all change for a more efficient local government

London, 1 April
The biggest shake-up in local government for almost a century comes into effect today with the redrawing of almost all county boundaries along the lines set out by Lord Redcliffe-Maud and his commission. Town charters dating from the Middle Ages and counties recorded in the Domesday Book have had their ancient identities erased. Only ten of 45 English counties and one of 13 in Wales remain unchanged.

Yorkshire and Lincolnshire, England's two largest counties, lose their distinctive ridings ("thirdings", from Old Norse). Part of Yorkshire's East Riding is joined to part of Lincolnshire over the river Humber to become Humberside. Four English counties disappear completely: Cumberland, Huntingdonshire, Westmorland and Rutland, the smallest (pop 19,000), which is joined to Leicestershire.

Another innovation is the creation of "metropolitan counties" – conurbations based on six large cities. The wide-ranging reforms are accompanied by new regulations for the payment of councillors for attending meetings and carrying out other council duties. It is claimed that local government will become more efficient, but cynics point out that today is April Fools' Day (→ 31/3/86).

IRA blasts Birmingham

One of the busy pubs bombed by the IRA in a night of carnage and destruction.

Birmingham, 21 November
The IRA's three-year-long mainland bombing campaign moved into a new dimension of terror tonight when two Birmingham pubs packed with young drinkers were wrecked; 17 people were killed and more than 120 injured.

When the timed bombs went off simultaneously in the Mulberry Bush and the Tavern in the Town, tons of rubble crashed down on the drinkers. Firemen worked with bare hands to extricate the hundreds trapped beneath beams and masonry. Passing taxis joined ambulances to ferry the injured to the city's hospitals. It is believed that the outrage was planned as revenge for the authorities' ban on the staging of a "hero's" funeral for James McDade, who blew himself up in Coventry last week while putting together a home-made bomb.

In Northern Ireland intelligence sources reported in August 1971 that the IRA was believed to be planning to bring the bombing campaign to England. Two months later the observation platform of the Post Office Tower in London was wrecked by a bomb. Since then all parts of the tower have been closed to the public (→ 29).

'Lucky' Lord Lucan wanted for murder

London, 12 November
A distraught young woman appeared in the doorway of a Belgravia pub crying: "He's murdered my nanny! My children! My children!" The woman, suffering from head injuries, was Lady Lucan, the wife of Richard John Bingham, the earl of Lucan, known ironically as "Lucky Lucan" for his heavy losses at London's gaming tables. Lady Lucan said that her husband had battered the nanny, Sandra Rivett, aged 29, in the basement of their home and then attacked her when she came into the room. Lucan is being sought by police to face a murder charge (→ 19/6/75).

Lucky Lucan: wanted by police.

Morecambe and Wise: the inimitable comedy duo whose zany sense of fun and the ridiculous pulls in television audiences of at least 20 million.

Strike puts an end to power-sharing

Belfast, 28 May
Northern Ireland's power-sharing executive collapsed today after a 14-day strike by loyalists opposed to the inclusion of nationalists in the government and to the Council of Ireland [*see page 1172*]. There had been fears that power cuts could lead to sewage in the streets. The executive's leader, Brian Faulkner, quit after failing to persuade SDLP colleagues to negotiate with the strikers. London gave little support to the executive. On 25 May Harold Wilson called the strikers "spongers" on British democracy, which hardened their resolve (→ 17/6).

Missing MP found alive down under

Sydney, Australia, 24 December
Britain's missing Labour MP, John Stonehouse, is being questioned by police here. He vanished after an inquiry began into the affairs of a Bangladeshi bank of which he was chairman. Later his clothes were found on a Miami beach. But it was not long before stories emerged from Australia about a man resembling Stonehouse, said to be accompanied by the MP's secretary, Sheila Buckley. Police arrested him, saying that they had seized a false passport. Stonehouse says that he had wanted to start a new life down under.

1975

London, 16 January. The IRA ends its 25-day truce (→ 5/4).

London, 20 January. The government abandons plans for a Channel tunnel (→ 20/1/86).

Britain, 13 February. Miners accept a pay rise of 35 per cent.

Glasgow, 15 March. Troops clear the 70,000 tonnes of refuse which have built up during the nine-week dustmen's strike.

Britain, 3 April. The National Health Service admits that over half of the 5,000 paying beds in hospitals have been closed in an attempt to phase out private patients.

Belfast, 5 April. Nine people die and 79 are injured in bomb blasts (→ 4/5).

Westminster, 26 April. Members of the Labour Party vote 2-1 to leave the European Economic Community.

Northern Ireland, 4 May. Ulster Unionists win in elections to the Ulster Convention (→ 29/8).

Britain, 13 May. Inflation reaches 21 per cent (→ 11/7).

St Ives, Cornwall, 21 May. Barbara Hepworth, the sculptor, dies in a fire at her studio, at the age of 72.

Westminster, 9 June. Proceedings in the House of Commons are broadcast live on radio for the first time (→ 21/11/89).

London, 19 June. A jury finds the missing peer, Lord Lucan, guilty of the murder of Sandra Rivett, his children's nanny.

Britain, 21 August. Unemployment figures reach 1.25 million (→ 22/4/80).

Northern Ireland, 2 October. Protestant revenge killings for IRA atrocities leave 11 people dead (→ 3).

Dublin, 3 October. The Irish government refuses to free three imprisoned IRA members in exchange for the Dutch businessman Tiede Herrema, who was kidnapped today (→ 31).

Belfast, 31 October. The provisional Sinn Fein leader Seamus McCusker is shot dead by the official IRA (→ 7/11).

North Sea, 1 November. Three people die and six are injured in a blaze aboard the Ekofisk A oil rig.

Co Kildare, 7 November. Tiede Herrema is freed after being held for 36 days (→ 12/12).

Thatcher is first woman to lead party

Westminster, 11 February
Margaret Thatcher today became the first woman to lead a British political party. She beat four rivals to clinch the leadership of the Conservative Party, but the real battle was a week ago. It was then that the 49-year-old former education secretary unexpectedly beat Edward Heath by 130 votes to 119. That vote was too close to be decisive, except for Heath, who stood down after more than nine years as leader. William Whitelaw joined the race, but Mrs Thatcher's momentum was unstoppable; she won 146 votes to Whitelaw's 79. Nobody else got more than 20 (→ 5/4/76).

A triumphant Margaret Thatcher.

Inflation reaches a record 25 per cent

Britain, 11 July
Pay rises are to be limited to £6 a week under a policy unveiled today. People earning more than £8,500 a year will get nothing at all, and firms will be penalized if they pass on higher wage costs in higher prices. Harold Wilson, the prime minister, called the plans "rough justice" but said they were essential to cut inflation, now running at 25 per cent a year. The "social contract" with the unions has failed to curb huge pay rises, which have taken over from imports as the main cause of inflation (→ 13/7/77).

Thirty-four passengers killed in Underground crash at Moorgate

Firemen struggle to find survivors in the wreckage of the underground train.

London, 28 February
In the worst ever accident on the London Underground, 34 passengers and a driver were killed at Moorgate station when a crowded train crashed at full speed into a dead-end tunnel. The driver, Leslie Newson, aged 56, was bringing his 8.37am train from Drayton Park alongside platform nine when, instead of braking, he accelerated into a 72-metre (80-yard) blind tunnel, crashed through sand piles and overrode the buffers. The first three of the train's six coaches crumpled into a tangled mass of steel; 4.5 metres of the leading carriage were compacted into 60 centimetres. Teams of doctors and firemen spent the day in the dust and heat of the wreckage struggling to reach those who were still alive (→ 18/11/87).

Women win important rights on equality

London, 31 December
Britain has marked International Women's Year, which ends today, with two major pieces of legislation to advance the status of women. The Sex Discrimination Act makes it an offence to discriminate against women in employment, education, training and trade union activities, and in the supply of goods, facilities and services.

A potentially controversial aspect of the act is the ban on discrimination in advertisements for job vacancies. It seems certain that it will no longer be possible to advertise for, say, a fireman, a doorman or even a female secretary. Some occupations – in mining, prisons, religious orders and midwifery – have been exempted. An equal opportunities commission has been set up to look for offenders and take them to court.

The Equal Pay Act is the latest in a number of measures over the years which have sought to remove pay differentials between men and women, with varying degrees of success. The new act does not give women equality in pensions, taxes or social security (→ 18/11/87).

Charlie Chaplin swaps his bowler for a top hat and a knighthood.

Britons vote to stay in Common Market

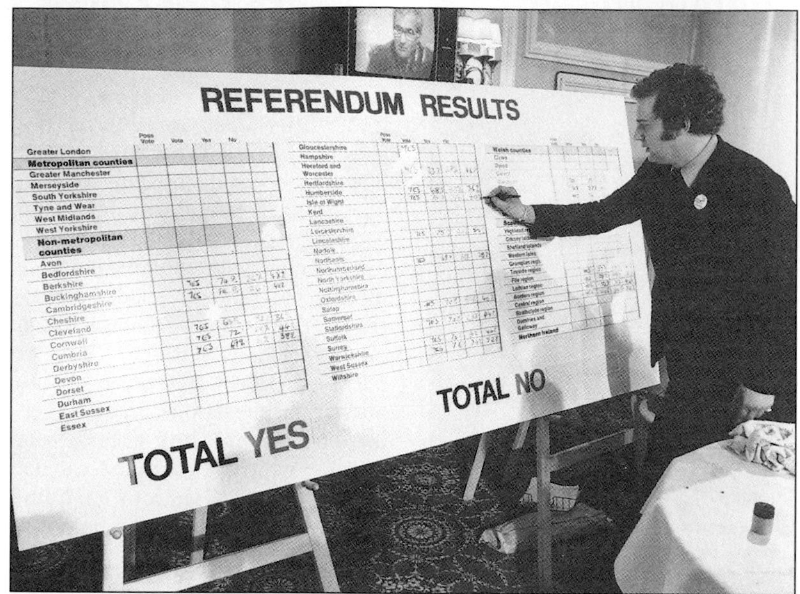

The first results of the referendum are shown at London's Waldorf hotel.

Britain, 6 June
The people of Britain have voted overwhelmingly to stay in the European Economic Community. Final figures released tonight show that in yesterday's unprecedented referendum those voting "Yes" to Europe totalled 67.2 per cent of the poll. There were pro-European majorities in all parts of the United Kingdom, with only the Shetlands and Western Isles saying "No".

It was the first referendum in British history. It also saw the abandonment of collective cabinet responsibility as ministers were allowed to campaign for opposing policies. The official government line was to recommend a vote in favour on the basis of what Harold Wilson called the improved terms of membership which he had negotiated at an EEC summit in Dublin. But seven of the 23-strong cabinet backed opposition to membership, as Wilson knew they would; the referendum was designed as much to keep Labour intact as to offer a democratic right to vote. The campaign cut across party lines, with the former Tory premier Edward Heath sharing platforms with Labour's Roy Jenkins and other pro-Europeans against such unlikely political bedfellows as Tony Benn and Enoch Powell (→ 3/1/77).

British elms struck by a deadly fungus

London, 30 October
A devastating fungus is spreading through the forests of England, destroying the country's elm trees. Already, according to the Forestry Commission, 6.5 million trees have died. Known as Dutch elm disease, it was identified in France in 1918, in the United States in 1933 and in Britain in the 1960s. The fungus is believed to be transmitted by the elm bark beetle, and there is no known cure; to prevent, or slow down, the spread of the disease, infected trees are cut down and then burnt. The elm is a valuable timber tree, being a tough, durable hardwood favoured by carpenters.

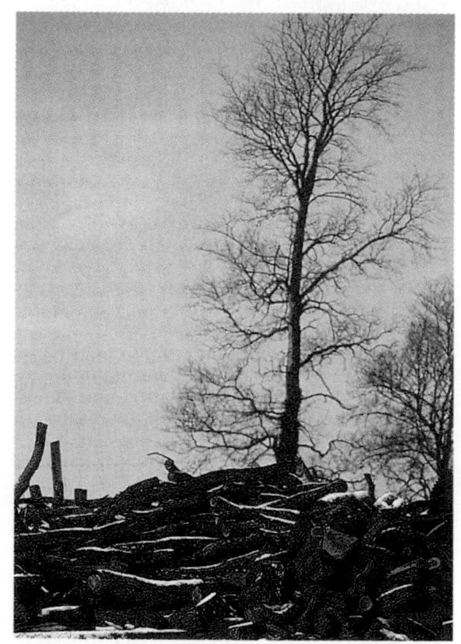

Thousands of elm trees are felled.

North Sea gold is just flowing ashore

Britain's first production platform.

Edinburgh, 3 November 1975
Britain's currency took the first step towards becoming a "petro-pound" today, when the Queen inaugurated an underwater pipeline to bring North Sea oil ashore from BP's Forties Field. The pipeline runs for 100 miles (160km) on the seabed and then 127 miles underground to the Grangemouth refinery on the Firth of Forth. When the Forties comes into full production the pipeline will carry 400,000 barrels a day, about one quarter of the country's oil needs. Proved reserves are valued at £200,000 million; to exploit them engineers are operating in rough seas and harsh conditions on so far unexplored frontiers of technology (→ 30/4/77).

'Dev', a nationalist first and last, dies

Dublin, 29 August
Eamon de Valera, the former president of Ireland – the man who, in his life and character, had become the embodiment of Ireland in the first half of the 20th century – died today, aged 92. The fact that he was born in New York, the son of a Spanish father and an Irish mother, saved him from execution in 1916, though he was a leader of the Easter rising. He went on to become an astute and vigorous Irish republican leader, and from the time of his accession to power in 1932 until his death he overshadowed Irish public life (→ 2/10/75).

IRA gunmen hold husband and wife hostage in Balcombe Street

Armed police cover the flat which was under siege in Balcombe Street.

London, 12 December
IRA gunmen who had been holding a middle-aged couple hostage in their Balcombe Street home for six days surrendered peacefully today as members of the SAS prepared to storm the flat. The siege began when the four men, believed to have been part of the gang which has been terrorizing the West End, burst into Mr and Mrs Matthews' flat, following a car chase in which shots were fired when the gang was recognized by one of the policemen swamping London. They are now being questioned about the murders of a policeman and of Ross McWhirter, the editor of the *Guinness Book of Records* (→ 7/1/76).

1976

Ireland, 5 January. John Costello, a former premier, dies.

Co Armagh, 7 January. In an attempt to combat the latest wave of violence, Special Air Service (SAS) troops arrive; 15 Protestants and Catholics have died in the last week (→ 5/3).

Britain, 12 January. Dame Agatha Christie, the queen of detective fiction, dies aged 85.

London, 21 January. Supersonic travel takes off with Concorde's first commercial flight, from London to Bahrain (→ 26/9/77).

Birmingham, 2 February. The Queen opens the £45 million National Exhibition Centre.

Iceland, 19 February. Iceland breaks all links with Britain as a "cod war" begins.

Westminster, 1 March. Parliament passes the Road Traffic Bill; the wearing of seat belts is to be compulsory.

Belfast, 5 March. Merlyn Rees, the secretary of state for Northern Ireland, dissolves the Ulster convention (→ 29/1/77).

London, 19 March. Princess Margaret and her husband, the earl of Snowdon, announce plans to separate (→ 10/5/78).

London, 26 May. Politicians are angry at the resignation honours list of Sir Harold Wilson, the former prime minister.

Epsom, Surrey, 2 June. The racing jockey Lester Piggott wins the Derby for a record seventh time.

London, 7 June. The government receives a joint loan of £3,000 million from ten nations in support of sterling (→ 28/9).

Wimbledon, 3 July. Bjorn Borg, aged 20, beats Ilie Nastase to win the men's tennis singles; he is the youngest player to win in the past 45 years (→ 1/7/77).

Yorkshire, 1 September. As the drought worsens, water to 750,000 homes is delivered by communal standpipes.

London, 27 November. Over 30,000 join the Ulster women's peace march (→ 10/10/77).

London, 3 December. The Sex Pistols, a "punk rock" group, run riot on BBC radio's *Today* show (→ 31/12/78).

Suffolk, 4 December. Benjamin Britten, the first composer to be made a peer, dies aged 63.

James Callaghan, 64, is elected by Labour Party as the successor to Harold Wilson

Wilson resigns as prime minister.

Callaghan takes over at No 10.

Westminster, 5 April
James Callaghan is the new prime minister. Just three weeks after Harold Wilson unexpectedly announced his resignation, he gives way to an older man – the 64-year-old Callaghan, who held off a strong challenge from Michael Foot by 176 votes to 137. Previous rounds in the contest had eliminated Roy Jenkins, Tony Crosland, Tony Benn and Denis Healey.

No major change in government policy is expected, with Healey staying at the treasury to deal with the worsening economic crisis. Sterling is fragile, but the political cost of harsh economic medicine could be high. The government has a wafer-thin majority which could be eroded altogether through by-election losses. The strong leadership challenge of Michael Foot also indicates the growing strength of Labour's left-wing.

However, speculation about the cabinet is still secondary at Westminster to that concerning the reasons for Wilson's resignation. He says that he told the Queen last December, and had decided to go back in March 1974. Thirty years on the front bench was enough, he said, but voluntary retirement from the top in apparently full health is very rare in politics (→ 24/3/77).

Thorpe quits amid homosexual claims

Westminster, 10 May
Jeremy Thorpe has quit as Liberal leader after weeks of Westminster gossip. Thorpe, who is 47, said today that he could no longer stand "a sustained press witchhunt and campaign of denigration". He denied claims by an unemployed male model that they had had a homosexual relationship. "No man can effectively lead a party if the greater part of his time has to be devoted to answering allegations and countering plots and intrigues," said Thorpe, who was offered a cabinet post by Edward Heath in 1974 during moves to form a coalition government (→ 27/10/77).

Jeremy Thorpe: forced to resign.

UK guilty of torture

Strasbourg, France, 2 September
Britain was accused today of "inhumane treatment and torture" in its war against terrorist violence in Northern Ireland. A commission set up under the European Economic Community found that the "deep interrogation" techniques routinely used during the questioning of IRA suspects constituted a clear breach of human rights.

The British government has reacted angrily to reports that the Irish Republic plans to press these charges further. Dublin is asking that all allegations of torture should be heard by the European court of human rights (→ 19/1/78).

Oct 24. James Hunt: world motor-racing champion by a point.

Scots drink all day

Glasgow, 16 December
Although MPs today voted their approval "in principle" for the setting up of separate Scots and Welsh parliaments, few expect that these changes will ever be enacted. But for citizens north of the border, at any rate, there is one consolation prize: from now on, unlike the English, they will have the right to drink all day. As a result of section 64, subsection 3, of the Licensing (Scotland) Act, which is now safely on the statute book, pubs in certain places where there is strong local demand and no pressing official objections will be free to stay open from 11am to 11pm (→ 2/3/79).

Belfast women launch a peace campaign

Women and children of Belfast march for an end to the violence in their city.

Belfast, 8 August
The deaths of three Catholic children, run down by a hijacked car in west Belfast, has inspired the so-called "Peace People" to launch a campaign against violence from all sides. Mairéad Corrigan, the sister of the children's injured mother, Anne Maguire, joined Betty Williams and a journalist, Ciaran McKeown, to organize a peace march to the Shankhill Road, the traditional home of Belfast unionism.

The hijacked car's IRA driver had been shot dead by his army pursuers. Because of the tragic circumstances the peace women have won enormous public sympathy at a time when the political situation in the province looks gloomy. The constitutional convention, elected last year to advise on new political structures for Northern Ireland, broke up in March after MPs rejected a majority report calling for a reversion to an old-style Stormont, without power-sharing. On 21 July the new British ambassador to Dublin, Sir Christopher Ewart-Biggs, and his secretary died when an IRA landmine exploded under his armoured Jaguar (→27/11).

Britain borrows to prop up the pound

Blackpool, 28 September
James Callaghan bluntly warned the Labour party conference here today that Britain could no longer cut taxes and boost public spending. "You cannot spend your way out of a recession," said the prime minister, just 24 hours after the slide in the value of sterling had forced Denis Healey, the chancellor, to turn back at Heathrow from a planned trip to an international finance conference.

Despite swingeing public spending cuts and higher interest rates announced in July, sterling has continued to fall, plummeting by four cents against the dollar on Monday to a record low of $1.63. Alerted by the Bank of England to the run on reserves, Healey returned to the treasury where he is orchestrating an application for a massive loan of £2.3 billion from the International Monetary Fund (IMF).

The chancellor was later given a rough reception at the party conference, but this is just a foretaste of battles to come. The IMF loan to prop up the pound will entail further public spending cuts, much to the dismay of Labour left-wingers who accuse Healey and Callaghan of betraying socialism by implementing monetarist policies (→22/5/85).

Scorching hot sun breaks all records

Cooling off in Trafalgar Square.

London, 31 August
Cricket-loving crowds at Lord's cheered today when rain briefly stopped play in a crucial county match. It was the first break for weeks in Britain's cloudless, record-breaking summer. The heatwave, unrivalled since accurate records began, has delighted most people, filling parks and beaches with sunbathers. But it has forced the government to give the popular sports minister, Denis Howell, a second job: "minister for drought". Millions in Wales and the southwest are without water (→1/9).

National Theatre opens on South Bank

London, 25 October 1976
Britain's new National Theatre building was opened by the Queen tonight – the culmination of a campaign that began in 1907, when the actor-playwright Harley Granville-Barker and the critic William Archer published their *Scheme for a National Theatre* and won support from campaigners like Bernard Shaw. Denys Lasdun, the new building's architect, was the fifth to draw up plans for national theatres on as many sites. The result is a concrete structure resembling a liner and containing three auditoriums: the open-stage Olivier, the proscenium Lyttleton theatre and the Cottesloe studio space.

The Queen was welcomed by Sir Laurence Olivier (a peer who refuses to use his title in the theatre) on the stage which bears his name. He created the National Theatre as an illustrious company at the Old Vic in 1963 and gave way to Peter Hall as director in 1973 after much ill-health. "To those who follow I wish joy eternal of all of it," he said in what may be his last appearance on the stage.

The first productions in the two main auditoriums were *Hamlet* in the Lyttleton and *Tamburlaine the Great* in the Olivier, both starring Albert Finney and directed by Peter Hall. The building is not yet finished, and the Cottesloe is due to open next spring. The total cost of the building, met by the government and the Greater London Council, is running at £16 million, and the finishing and equipping of it is plagued by union disputes.

The sky is lit up with fireworks as the long-awaited National Theatre opens.

1977

Brussels, 3 January. Roy Jenkins, the home secretary and former Labour deputy leader, is appointed president of the European Economic Community (→30/11/79).

London, 29 January. Seven IRA bombs explode in the West End (→4/2).

Liverpool, 4 February. Police discover an IRA bomb factory (→16/5).

London, 8 May. Seven nations attend an economic summit.

London, 13 May. A deal is revealed between an Australian publisher, Kerry Packer, and 35 of the world's best cricketers to play in a series of internationals (→3/8).

Northern Ireland, 16 May. The IRA claims to have kidnapped, interrogated and killed a SAS officer (→17/2/78).

Dublin, 23 June. Liam Cosgrave resigns as prime minister of Ireland (→26).

Britain, 2 July. Miners seek £135 for a four-day week.

Westminster, 13 July. The government abandons its "social contract" of 1974 with the TUC as wages rise (→21/7/78).

London, 3 August. Kerry Packer takes the English cricket authorities to court (→25/11).

Leeds, 11 August. The cricketer Geoff Boycott scores his 100th century against Australia (→19/6/78).

London, 13 August. Police use Ulster riot shields against anti-National Front rioters (→15).

Birmingham, 15 August. Anti-National Front protesters clash with police (→24/4/79).

Oslo, 10 October. Betty Williams and Mairéad Corrigan, the co-founders of the Ulster peace movement, are presented with the Nobel peace prize for 1976.

London, 27 October. Jeremy Thorpe, the former Liberal leader, denies homosexual links with the unemployed model Norman Scott (→3/6/78).

Yorkshire, October. Police are searching for a vicious killer of women known as "the Yorkshire Ripper" (→4/4/79).

Oslo, 10 December. Amnesty International is awarded the 1977 Nobel peace prize.

Switzerland, 25 December. The British-born film star Charlie Chaplin dies aged 88.

Liberals honour deal with Labour Party

David Steel, the Liberal leader.

Westminster, 24 March

Thirteen Liberal MPs tonight kept alive the Labour government by opposing a motion of "no confidence" tabled by the Conservatives. The vote was the first fruit of a "Lib-Lab pact" agreed between James Callaghan and David Steel, who succeeded Jeremy Thorpe as Liberal leader last year. It helps the government to buy time until the economy improves, and it gives the Liberals a toehold in government. Liberals will have a veto, in theory, over future cabinet proposals.

The pact dashed Tory hopes, which had soared when Nationalist MPs declared their intention to vote against Labour. By-election losses have cut the government's overall majority to just one, excluding the speaker and his deputies. Margaret Thatcher, the Conservative leader, mocked her party rivals as "timid men fearful of the fate they know awaits them". David Steel backs the pact as both a means of achieving greater influence for his party and a move towards electoral reform. But with his party in the electoral doldrums, he is also playing for time (→25/5/78).

Oil rig blows sky high in North Sea

Attempts to quell the fire continue.

Aberdeen, 30 April

Eight days after the Bravo oil rig blew up in Norway's Ekofisk Field, a huge 1,000-square-mile slick is threatening wildlife and fishing along most of Scotland's eastern coastline. Only wind change now looks likely to avert a major ecological disaster. Over a hundred platform workers were safely evacuated when oil gushed 45 metres (150 feet) into the air during an attempted drilling-valve change. Twenty-eight million litres of crude then escaped before experts succeeded in applying an effective seal. Norway has called it the worst pollution catastrophe since North Sea oil-prospecting began (→27/6/78).

Fianna Fáil party wins Irish elections

Ireland, 26 June

In the most substantial election reversal in Irish political history, Fianna Fáil, led by Jack Lynch, has been returned to power while the former coalition government has suffered a humiliating defeat. Three outgoing ministers (among them Conor Cruise O'Brien) have lost their seats. Liam Cosgrave has resigned as leader of Fine Gael, and Brendan Corish has resigned as leader of the Labour Party. The Fianna Fáil party worked hard for its victory, and fought a hard, intelligent and carefully prepared campaign. A detailed manifesto included specific promises. The most attractive, to a population crippled by inflation, was the removal of the rates paid by householders. Jack Lynch's personal appeal to voters was also a major factor in securing the result (→7/12/79).

Pickets turn violent at Grunwick strike

North London, 20 June

Police came under vicious attack today as they moved in to arrest 17 bottle-throwing pickets at the Grunwick film-processing laboratories, where a long-running strike has been fanned by left-wing political groups into a focus for increasingly violent protest.

Initially the dispute was about achieving union recognition for the plant's poorly paid, mainly Asian workforce. That has now become a secondary issue as TV teams arrive from all over the world to film the daily confrontations.

April 2. Red Rum, the crowd's favourite, returns to the winner's enclosure after becoming the first horse to win the Grand National hat trick.

Queen celebrates her silver jubilee

London, 7 June
The Queen lit a giant bonfire in Windsor Great Park tonight to launch a week of celebrations for her silver jubilee. As the flames leapt high above the trees, 100 other congratulatory beacons, from Land's End in Cornwall to Saxavord in the Shetland Isles, sparked into life. Many were on the same sites as the fires commanded in 1588 by Elizabeth I to mark the defeat of the Spanish Armada.

But although the country is almost universally happy to congratulate Elizabeth II on completing the first quarter-century of her reign, there is widespread recognition that not everything has gone well for Britain in the 25 years since she ascended the throne.

During that period virtually all the former colonies that made up the British Empire have achieved independence, and although Britain remains a nuclear power and, after a couple of false starts, is now confirmed as a member of the European Community, few would yet argue that this provides a fully satisfactory alternative role.

Although the country basked in unparalleled prosperity during the 1950s and 1960s, it has undoubtedly slipped several places down the world's economic league tables and is currently suffering very high unemployment, inflation and idle production capacity (→ 30/6/81).

The Queen and the lord mayor of London on a jubilee "walkabout".

Laker's 'no-frills' Skytrain leaves runway

The first Skytrain, Gatwick to New York, is waved off by Freddie Laker.

Gatwick airport, 26 September
More than 270 passengers queued for 24 hours to buy seats on the first cut-price Skytrain service to New York. They paid just £59 for a "no-frills" flight, while the cheapest regular single fare is £186.

As they filed on board, Freddie Laker, the man who made it all possible, personally thanked them all for "helping to prove me right" in his belief that there is a profitable mass market in air travel at rock-bottom prices.

For an extra £1.75 they were able to enjoy a meal of paté, beef, apple pie, cheese and a small bottle of red wine. Although Laker has now successfully got his airline off the ground, the big carriers are expected to redouble their efforts to put him out of business (→ 7/2/82).

Economic statistics show steep decline

Birmingham, 31 December
For the first time since the invention of the internal combustion engine, Britain imported more cars this year than it made itself. This depressing statistic marks yet another significant milestone in the long history of industrial decline.

The drastic oil-price rise in the early 1970s and the resulting worldwide recession cruelly exposed the weaknesses of the country's manufacturing base. In trade after trade, from textiles and shoes through steel and heavy engineering to the new growth sectors of electronics and computers, the once dominant British market share has steadily dwindled. In many sectors, imports now dwarf home production.

Government efforts to reverse this trend have had only limited success. Despite the stepping up of governmental "trade and industry" support by 44 per cent this decade, to its present annual level of £2.6 billion, there is little sign of widespread revival. Nearly two million people are currently without work, a figure not seen since the 1930s.

Cricket crisis as Packer wins case

London, 25 November
Cricket's establishment today lost a legal battle to punish top players for joining a series of unofficial internationals planned by the Australian publisher Kerry Packer. The high court in London ruled that a proposed ban on players taking part in Packer's "cricket circus" was an unreasonable, and therefore illegal, restraint of trade.

Tony Greig and Ian Chappell, two former captains of England and Australia, head 35 test cricketers who have signed contracts with Packer for a series of matches in Australia this winter. This private venture is seen as a direct challenge to the future of test cricket.

Jubilant Wade wins glory at Wimbledon

Wimbledon, 1 July
The Queen's silver jubilee year saw an appropriate victory for patriots in the ladies' tennis final at Wimbledon today. Virginia Wade recovered from losing the first set to Betty Stove of the Netherlands to become the first British champion since Ann Jones in 1969. The Queen was present to witness her country's triumph in Wimbledon's own centenary year. Another Briton led the parade of former winners – Kitty Godfree, who was the champion in 1924 (→ 8/7/78).

Wade well on her way to winning.

1978

Belfast, 25 February. In the wake of last week's restaurant bombing, the leading republican Gerry Adams is charged with membership of the IRA (→6/9).

London, 25 March. Oxford win the Boat Race after the Cambridge boat sinks a mile from the finish (→4/4/81).

London, 25 May. David Steel, the Liberal leader, says that the Lib-Lab pact will end with the current parliamentary session (→4/5/79).

Devon, 3 June. Jeremy Thorpe, the former Liberal leader, is interviewed by detectives investigating a plot to kill a former male model, Norman Scott (→4/8).

Wimbledon, 8 July. Bjorn Borg wins his third Wimbledon singles title (→7/7/85).

Westminster, 21 July. The government announces a new pay-increase guideline of 15 per cent; the unions reject it as unrealistic (→11/1978).

Somerset, 4 August. Jeremy Thorpe is accused with three others of plotting to kill Norman Scott (→20/11).

Manchester, 31 August. The *Express* newspaper group announces plans to launch a new national daily, possibly to be called the *Daily Star*.

Belfast, 6 September. Gerry Adams is released from jail after a judge rules that there is insufficient evidence to prove that he is a member of the IRA (→17/12).

London, 29 September. A Bulgarian defector, Georgi Markov, who died after being stabbed by an umbrella point, is believed to have been poisoned.

London, 23 October. The government plans to replace GCE "O" Level and CSE examinations with a single exam, the GCSE (→29/7/88).

Somerset, 20 November. Committal proceedings against Jeremy Thorpe, for allegedly plotting to murder Norman Scott, begin at Minehead (→13/12).

London, 30 November. Publication of *The Times* and the *Sunday Times* is suspended indefinitely, owing to industrial action.

London, 17 December. Police step up security as the IRA begins a Christmas bombing campaign (→30/3/79).

Britain found guilty of inhumane action

Strasbourg, France, 19 January
Britain has been found guilty of using interrogation techniques that were "inhumane and degrading, in breach of Article 3 of the Human Rights Convention" in Northern Ireland. But the judges of the European Court of Human Rights threw out, by 13 votes to four, the much more serious charges of torture which the government of the Irish Republic has been trying to establish for the past two years. Dublin reacted angrily to the decision and issued a long statement justifying its acrimonious pursuit of the case, on which it is believed to have spent over £300,000.

Cricket newcomer Ian Botham a star

Botham is the hero of the test.

London, 19 June
English cricket has a new star. In the test against Pakistan which ended at Lord's today, Ian Botham achieved the finest all-round performance ever recorded by an England player. Botham, who is 22, struck his third century in seven test matches before his medium-fast swing bowling produced figures of eight wickets for 34 runs in Pakistan's second innings: the best analysis since Jim Laker took all ten Australian wickets in an innings in 1956. The Somerset all-rounder has now captured five wickets in an innings five times in his first seven test matches (→21/7/81).

World's first 'test-tube baby' is delivered

Manchester, 26 July
The world's first "test-tube baby" was born just before midnight tonight at Oldham General Hospital, in Greater Manchester. The baby girl's successful delivery, by Caesarean section, marks a potentially enormous step forward in the ability of medical science not only to treat infertility, which was the immediate objective, but also, more controversially, to establish much greater control over the whole process of human reproduction.

Meanwhile Dr Patrick Steptoe, who was responsible for both the delivery and a large part of the 12-year research programme which made it possible, said: "All examinations showed that the baby is quite normal." Mrs Lesley Brown, her mother, was said to be "enjoying a well earned sleep".

The embryo which became baby Louise had been implanted in Mrs Brown's womb last November after one of her eggs was fertilized under laboratory conditions by her husband's sperm. Mrs Brown was sterile because of blocked fallopian tubes (→26/3/82).

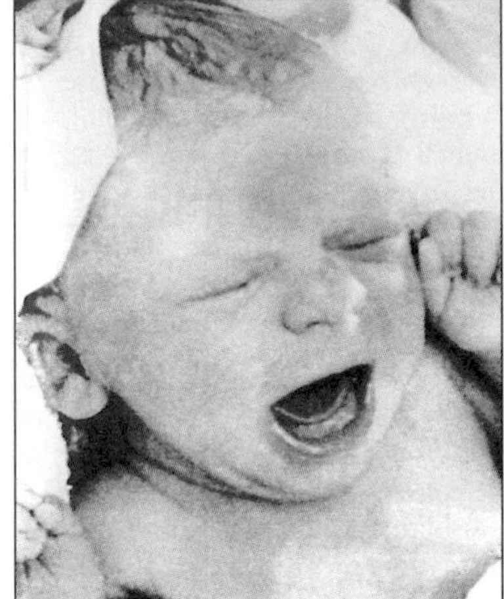
Louise Brown screams healthily.

Belfast bomb kills at least 14 in restaurant

Northern Ireland, 18 February
Twenty IRA suspects were arrested in Belfast today following yesterday's terrorist attack on the Le Mons restaurant, ten miles east of the city. Blast incendiaries turned the restaurant into an inferno, killing 14 people at a dog-club dinner and injuring many more. Unusually, the IRA issued an abject apology, accepting that its nine-minute warning was "totally inadequate". But it went on to claim that "all killings stem from British ... denial of Irish sovereignty".

Several hotels in Northern Ireland were attacked during a two-week IRA blitz before Christmas aimed at destroying the remaining tourist trade (→25).

Mrs Bridges (Angela Baddeley), Hudson (Gordon Jackson), Rose (Jean Marsh): below-stairs stars of the ITV series "Upstairs Downstairs".

North Sea gives UK oil self-sufficiency

Aberdeen, 27 June
Oil output from the North Sea has exceeded one million barrels a day for the first time. The latest monthly production figures show that Britain is now the 16th biggest oil-producing nation and is set to become totally self-sufficient within two years. Current liftings, running at the rate of 56 million tonnes a year, represent 60 per cent of demand. But new discoveries are being made all the time, and Britain will soon be able not only to meet all its own needs but also to become a substantial exporter (→ 27/3/80).

Princess announces intention to divorce

The royal couple in happier times.

London, 10 May
Princess Margaret, the Queen's younger sister, is seeking a divorce from her husband, the earl of Snowdon. The couple have been separated for the past two years, and it is expected that the two children of the marriage will continue, as at present, to live with their mother.

Under the proposed settlement Lord Snowdon will receive a house in central London. He has already resumed his former career as a successful photographer. The princess plans to continue her public engagements. Her official position will be unaffected by the split.

Former Liberal leader goes on trial

Jeremy Thorpe, looking drawn and tired, takes a walk with his wife, Marion.

Minehead, Somerset, 13 December
Jeremy Thorpe, the former leader of the Liberal Party, was today committed for trial at the Old Bailey charged, with three other men, with conspiracy and incitement to murder. The alleged victim of the conspiracy and murder plot was Norman Scott, a former male model who has alleged that he and Thorpe once had a homosexual relationship. Thorpe, who has always denied this allegation, said in court: "I plead not guilty and will vigorously defend this matter."

The magistrates told that Thorpe allegedly paid £5,000 for Scott to be shot, decided that there was a *prima facie* case to be answered. Thorpe resigned as party leader in 1976 because of press speculation about Scott (→ 22/6/79).

Union clashes with government over a 15 per cent pay rise

Dagenham, Essex, November
A 17 per cent pay rise has been agreed by the Ford motor company, effectively torpedoing the government's hopes of imposing a 15 per cent pay norm on British industry this year. This policy was rejected by both the TUC and the Labour Party conferences this autumn, although the Labour government had already signalled that it was determined to maintain its tough anti-inflationary stance.

Car workers at Ford were the first major group to challenge the policy, with a claim for a minimum pay rise of £20 a week. By the end of September all 23 plants were at a standstill. The 17 per cent pay deal conceded by the Ford management sets a benchmark for other industries far in excess of what the government insists will be imposed on public sector workers. The success of the Ford strike will encourage other workers to adopt militant tactics. James Callaghan, the prime minister, said this month that this winter will be "make or break" for his government (→ 14/2/79).

More seek sun, fun and cheap holidays

Heathrow airport, 31 December
Airlines, charter firms, package-tour operators, cross-Channel ferries and the whole range of travel agents all report yet another near-record year as more and more Britons seek their annual dose of sea, sun and getting away from it all.

Officially a holiday is defined as any four nights or more away from home that are not spent on business. On that basis Britons took 48 million of them in 1978, almost equalling the 49 million peak recorded in 1973. An ever-increasing number of holidays are spent abroad. Some nine million holidaymakers crossed the Atlantic, the North Sea or the Channel this year – up from seven million in 1971, and from just two million in 1951. By far the most popular destination is still Spain, which attracts 30 per cent of all these tourists.

Punk faces the future without Sex Pistols

Britain, 31 December
The outlook for punk is not good: the year ends amidst persistent rumours that the archetypal punk band, the Sex Pistols, is soon to split up. Things certainly look bleak for their bassist, Sid Vicious, currently facing police charges in New York for the murder of his girlfriend, Nancy Spungen, last October.

Maybe punk can survive the Pistols' demise: it has, after all, been around for a while. It first hit the headlines in 1976 and has since won the notoriety that it always craved. Its acolytes like their music simple, loud, fast and aggressive. One- or two-minute songs are thrashed out by the likes of the Clash, Sham 69 and Generation X with a commitment and fury totally at odds with the disco music of the charts.

Yet punk is more than the music alone. It offers teenagers what they have always sought from rock: a vehicle for their wish to rebel. Committed to "anarchy", punks set out to shock, with their dyed Mohican hairstyles, torn mohair sweaters, bondage gear and spitting at the stage during gigs – and that is just the girls.

Punks dressed in all their finery.

1979

Britain, 5 January. A lorry drivers' strike causes severe shortages (→ 15).

Britain, 15 January. A series of one-day rail strikes begins (→ 24).

Britain, 24 January. A 24-hour public employees' strike hits hospitals and schools (→ 12/2).

Britain, 12 February. Over a thousand schools close because of lack of heating oil caused by the lorry drivers' strike (→ 14).

Westminster, 2 March. The Scots vote in favour of devolution, while the Welsh vote against (→ 28).

Cardiff, 17 March. Wales beat England 27-3 to win rugby's Triple Crown for the fourth year in a row.

Westminster, 29 March. James Callaghan calls a general election for 3 May (→ 4/5).

Westminster, 30 March. Airey Neave, a Tory MP and an aide to Margaret Thatcher, is killed by an IRA car bomb (→ 17/4).

West Yorkshire, 4 April. "The Yorkshire Ripper" kills for the 11th time, at Halifax; for the first time the victim is not a prostitute (→ 2/9).

Northern Ireland, 17 April. Four policemen are killed by a 1,000-lb bomb, the IRA's most powerful yet (→ 27/8).

London, 24 April. Police are investigating the death of a schoolteacher, Blair Peach, during yesterday's National Front rally.

London, 22 June. Jeremy Thorpe is found not guilty of murder (→ 10/10).

Yorkshire, 2 October. Police launch a £1 million publicity campaign to find "the Yorkshire Ripper" (→ 19/10/80).

Devon, 10 October. Jeremy Thorpe announces that he will not stand for parliament again.

Dublin, 23 November. Thomas McMahon is jailed for life for murdering Lord Mountbatten (→ 27/10/80).

Dublin, 30 November. Margaret Thatcher demands a a £1,000 million rebate for Britain from the EEC (→ 30/5/80).

London, 21 December. A settlement is agreed whereby Zimbabwe-Rhodesia will revert to British colonial rule as a transitional step to black majority government (→ 18/4/80).

Britain in grip of political turmoil

Britons suffer harsh winter of discontent

London, 14 February

Union leaders and ministers today announced a St Valentine's day agreement in a bid to end the "winter of discontent" caused by a rash of strikes. What began in January as a strike by lorry drivers for a 25 per cent claim escalated into a wave of action that has seen rubbish pile up in streets, food and petrol supplies disrupted, patients turned away from hospitals and even the dead left unburied.

The settlement of the strike by petrol-tanker drivers only opened the floodgates for others, as the drivers' 14 per cent pay deal shattered the government's 5 per cent pay norm. Disputes spread to the public sector, causing widespread chaos. With James Callaghan, the prime minister, at a summit in the West Indies, Margaret Thatcher, the Tory leader, moved to attack union power. "A boneless wonder" was her verdict on today's deal.

Piles of uncollected rubbish fill the streets as the strike continues.

Labour is doomed by devolution issue

Westminster, 28 March

Two Irish MPs abstained tonight and brought down the Labour government. James Callaghan lost a no-confidence motion by a single vote – 311 to 310 – and becomes the first prime minister to be defeated on such a motion since 1924.

Callaghan's parliamentary problems became acute on 2 March when devolution referendums were held in Wales and Scotland. Since the ending of the Lib-Lab pact last year the government had relied on Nationalist MPs for its majority. Voters in Wales rejected devolution and while those in Scotland were narrowly in favour of a Scottish Assembly they failed to achieve the required 40 per cent figure. When the government rejected pleas by Scottish Nationalist MPs to push ahead regardless, the Nationalists withdrew their support. With one Labour MP absent through illness, the government was doomed (→ 29).

Thatcher victorious in general election

London, 4 May

Margaret Thatcher today became the first woman to be prime minister of Britain. She moved into Downing Street following the Conservatives' victory in yesterday's election, promising that "where there is discord may we bring harmony". The final figures are Conservatives 339, Labour 269, Liberal 11, Nationalists 4, others 13.

Labour has slumped to 36.9 per cent of the vote – its lowest since 1931. The Tories had two million more voters with 43.9 per cent of the poll, with particularly high swings in their favour in southern England. Although the Tory lead in the opinion polls was cut during the campaign, the legacy of the "winter of discontent" proved impossible for James Callaghan, the outgoing premier, to shake off (→ 12/6).

Winning wave from Mrs Thatcher.

Change of direction signalled at No 10

Westminster, 12 June

Margaret Thatcher's government has lost little time in signalling a change in economic direction. The first budget introduced today by Sir Geoffrey Howe, the chancellor of the exchequer, slashes income tax, boosts indirect taxes such as VAT and attacks public spending. Controls on pay, prices and dividends are to be scrapped, while a range of measures is planned to offer incentives to businessmen. The budget has the hallmark of the "enterprise culture" espoused by monetarist Tories such as Sir Keith Joseph.

Mrs Thatcher believes that her election victory last month is a watershed in post-war politics. The old Keynesian primacy of public spending, the power of the unions and the corporatism of the welfare state are all blamed for contributing to economic decline (→ 10/10/80).

Oil-tanker blast kills 49 in Ireland

Bantry Bay, Co Cork, 8 January
A series of explosions tore apart an oil tanker early this morning, claiming the lives of 49 people. The ship, owned by the Total oil company, was unloading her 120,000-ton cargo when the first blast turned her into a fireball and shook the whole town. Seven of the victims were shore-workers. Witnesses said that the tanker had discharged half her load when she exploded without warning. Tugs fought the blaze but were forced to retreat by spreading patches of burning oil. Total officials are mystified as to the possible cause of the disaster.

Charles Haughey is elected as Irish PM

Ireland, 7 December
Charles Haughey, the former minister of health, has defeated George Colley for leadership of the Fianna Fáil party, following the surprise resignation of Jack Lynch, and is now prime minister. A controversial figure, he stood trial in 1970 for importing arms, and was acquitted.

Haughey remained on the back benches of the party until 1975, when Jack Lynch, then in opposition, was persuaded to bring him on to the front bench as spokesman on health (→ 30/6/81).

IRA kills public figures

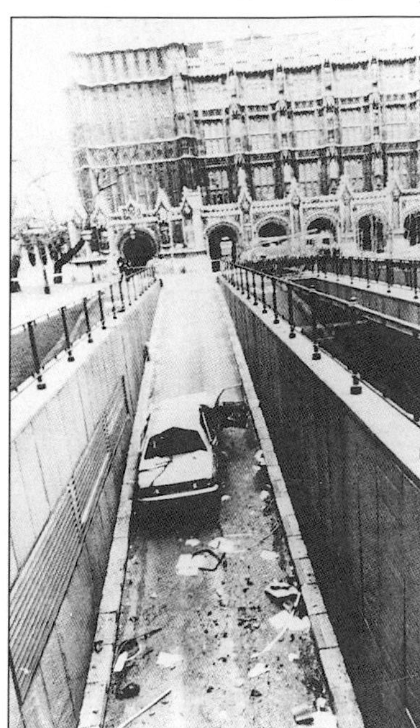

Airey Neave's car, blown up as it left the House of Commons' car park.

Mullaghmore, Co Sligo, 27 August
Shock and outrage have greeted the murder today of Earl Mountbatten of Burma, formerly supreme Allied commander in South-east Asia, the last viceroy of India and a cousin of the Queen. In a day of horrific IRA carnage 15 soldiers also died in a massive blast at Warrenpoint, Co Down. The 79-year-old earl, who was holidaying at his Irish home, Classiebawn Castle, died instantly when an IRA bomb ripped apart his boat, the *Shadow V*. His grandson Nicholas, aged 14, and a boatman of 17 also died in the blast. For the second time in five months a respected public figure has died at the hands of the IRA. On 30 March Airey Neave, the hardline Tory spokesman on Northern Ireland who was a close aide of Margaret Thatcher, died when a bomb blew up under his car as it left the Commons's car park (→ 23/11).

'Yorkshire Ripper' claims his twelfth victim

Bradford, 2 September
The murder of Barbara Leach, aged 20, a student at Bradford University, brings to 12 the total of women killed by the man known as "the Yorkshire Ripper". The grisly nickname derives from the bizarre way in which he mutilates his victims' bodies. The body of the Ripper's 12th victim was found on the borders of the city's red-light district, but unlike most of the previous victims in a reign of terror that has lasted four years, Barbara Leach was not a prostitute. Detectives leading one of the biggest manhunts ever mounted in Britain warn that after this seemingly random attack no woman can be safe alone on the streets at night (→ 2/10).

Royal art adviser was 'Fourth Man'

Anthony Blunt – the fourth man.

Westminster, 21 November
Sir Anthony Blunt, the art adviser to the Queen and a guru to generations of art students, was a Russian spy, the prime minister told shocked members of parliament today. In a written answer, Margaret Thatcher named Blunt as the fourth man in the Burgess, Maclean and Philby spy ring. She said that he had been investigated in 1964 and after being granted immunity from prosecution had admitted his role as a long-term Soviet agent, talent-spotting for the KGB in pre-war Cambridge. Blunt, who is in hiding abroad, has been stripped of his knighthood (→ 26/3/83).

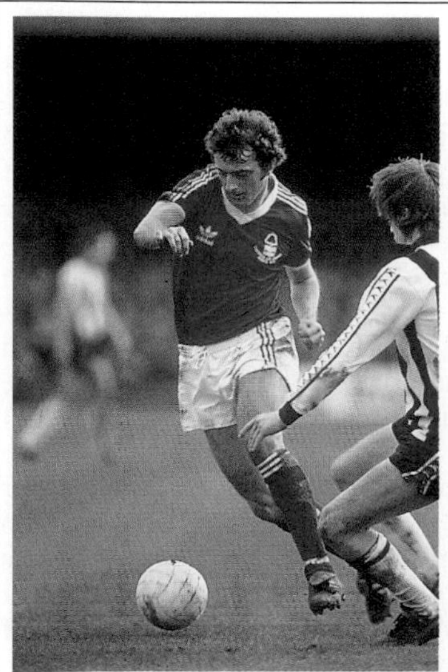

February 9: Trevor Francis joins Nottingham Forest as the first ever £1 million footballer.

Irish Catholics rejoice as the pope makes a peace visit to Ireland

Dublin, 30 September
No pop star could have expected a more rousing welcome than that which Pope John Paul II received today from the Irish nation. One and a quarter million people came to Phoenix Park to watch his plane arrive at Dublin airport. Two hours later he said Mass in the park with 40 cardinals and bishops. He then conducted a huge service outside Drogheda where the congregation included 250,000 from Northern Ireland. The pope's message was peace. "On my knees I beg you," he said, "to turn away from violence. Further violence will only drag down to ruin the land you claim to love and the values you claim to cherish" (→ 29/5/82).

Pope John Paul II brings his message of peace to the Catholics of Ireland.

1980

Britain, 2 January. Steelworkers call a national strike (→ 17/3).

Wales, 17 January. British Steel announces that it will axe 11,287 jobs by the end of March (→ 15/2).

Wiltshire, 18 January. Sir Cecil Beaton, the photographer and designer, dies at his home at Broadchalke, aged 76.

Britain, 15 February. As the steel strike continues, British Steel's middle management passes a vote of no confidence in the board of executives (→ 1/4).

Canterbury, 25 March. Robert Runcie, the bishop of St Albans, is enthroned as archbishop of Canterbury.

Britain, 1 April. The steel strike ends.

Southern Africa, 18 April. The Prince of Wales hands over sovereignty of Rhodesia, the last British colony in Africa, to President Canaan Banana of Zimbabwe, the newest African nation.

Britain, 22 April. Unemployment figures reach 1.5 million (→ 24/6).

London, 30 April. Five gunmen, calling for freedom for 91 Arabs in Iran, seize 20 hostages at the Iranian embassy (→ 5/5).

Britain, 16 May. Inflation rises to 21.8 per cent.

Europe, 30 May. Britain wins a big cut in payments to the EEC.

Turin, Italy, 12 June. English soccer fans run riot at England's opening game in the European championship (→ 29/5/85).

Britain, 12 June. Sir William Butlin, the founder of Butlin's Holiday Camps, dies aged 80.

Britain, 24 June. Unemployment figures reach 1.6 million (→ 27/8).

Britain, 27 August. Unemployment figures reach 2 million (→ 23/4/81).

Westminster, 15 October. James Callaghan announces his resignation as leader of the Labour Party (→ 10/11).

Leeds, 19 October. "The Yorkshire Ripper" kills his 13th victim, Jacqueline Hill, another student (→ 5/1/81).

Belfast, 27 October. Seven IRA prisoners at the Maze prison go on hunger strike for political status (→ 16/1/81).

Oil-rig tragedy kills 100

The huge oil rig topples and sinks as one of the five supporting legs gives way.

North Sea, 27 March
An oil platform capsized in stormy seas today, leaving half the 200 men aboard feared dead. It took just 15 minutes for the Alexander Kielland, a semi-submersible platform, to disappear beneath the waves after one of its five massive air-filled steel legs was broken, presumably by a wave. It was a floating hotel for North Sea rig workers, about 50 of whom were in the cinema at the time. Many must have drowned, but rescuers hope some will have survived in air pockets.

Phillips Petroleum, the owners of the Alexander Kielland, said: "We fear a great disaster." Helicopters, planes and at least 13 ships have gone to the rescue. Seven people are known to have died, and bodies have been seen hundreds of metres away. Some survivors were flown ashore, others given emergency treatment on a production platform nearby. Tom Greenwood, a survivor, saw disaster strike at 6.30pm: "Metal screeched as it began to keel over. Suddenly men were cut and bleeding" (→ 6/7/88).

Fury as missile base opens in Greenham

Berkshire, 17 June
Anti-nuclear protesters, mostly women, are gathering in response to the news that US-owned cruise missiles are to be based at the US Air Force airfield at Greenham, and later at Molesworth in Cambridgeshire. The missiles are among 160 to be based in Britain after NATO's decision to counter the Soviet SS-20 rockets being moved into Eastern Europe. Britain is the first NATO country to accept cruise missiles on its land (→ 12/12/82).

Heart attack kills chiller master Hitch

Bel Air, California, 29 April
Alfred Hitchcock, the Leytonstone greengrocer's son who became one of film's great masters of suspense, died today, aged 80. He made the first British talkie, *Blackmail*, in 1929, and successes such as *The Lady Vanishes* and *The Thirty-Nine Steps* followed. He moved to Hollywood and won an Oscar for his first film there, *Rebecca*. Later chillers included *Rear Window*, *Psycho* and *The Birds*. "Hitch", knighted four months ago, could be glimpsed briefly in most of his films.

Thatcher says 'the lady's not for turning' as ministers squabble

Strikers, including "flying pickets" from Corby, are pushed aside at the steel stockists John Lee Co in Grantham, Lincs – Mrs Thatcher's home town.

Brighton, 10 October
Margaret Thatcher today made clear her determination not to abandon her tough economic policies in the face of rising unemployment and increasing divisions within the cabinet. She told the Tory conference here that there would be no policy U-turns like those of Edward Heath in the 1970s. "You turn if you like," she said. "The lady's not for turning."

Unemployment is now over two million, and there have been bitter strikes involving steelworkers, who are in one of the heavy industries most hit by the current recession. More liberal (or "wet") members of the cabinet, such as James Prior, Peter Walker and Francis Pym, are resisting treasury demands – backed by Mrs Thatcher – for savage cuts in public spending (→ 15).

Iranian embassy stormed by SAS

Kensington, London, 5 May
Television viewers watched a real-life thriller this evening as the Special Air Service stormed the terrorist-held Iranian embassy and released 19 hostages. Cameras had been trained on the elegant Regency terrace overlooking Hyde Park since the siege began six days ago, when five gunmen captured the embassy staff and demanded the release of political prisoners in Iran. Suddenly, the news emerged that the terrorists had shot dead one hostage and were threatening to kill another every half-hour.

Within minutes, men in black uniforms and balaclavas, carrying sub-machine guns, had leapt onto the balcony and attached explosives to the windows, while their comrades abseiled from the roof to break in from the rear. When the charge went off, the SAS men ran inside, threw stun grenades and hunted down the terrorists, who had opened fire on their captives. One Iranian diplomat was killed and another badly wounded.

The terrorist leader would have killed one SAS man had he not been tackled by PC Trevor Lock, who had been on duty when the gunmen first invaded the embassy. Four of the five terrorists were shot dead by the SAS, who bundled the hostages to safety. The fifth survived after women hostages had pleaded for his life.

The SAS gives cover as a hostage is guided to safety during the siege.

Foot leads the way for Labour Party

Westminster, 10 November
Michael Foot tonight became the new leader of the Labour Party, following the resignation of the former premier, James Callaghan, last month. Foot, a 67-year-old left-winger, defeated Denis Healey, the combative standard-bearer of the right in Labour's increasingly bitter sectarian divisions, by 139 votes to 129 in a ballot of Labour MPs. Tory ministers are surprised and delighted. Foot, a former Fleet Street editor, is an engaging, cultured man, but they believe that as a nuclear disarmer with relatively limited experience of high office he is a vulnerable opponent. Healey is a former chancellor and defence secretary with a populist appeal that the Tories feared (→ 9/5/83).

Foot gives a wave as the new leader.

Obsessive fan shoots John Lennon at point-blank range

New York, 8 December
John Lennon, whose music inspired a generation, was shot dead tonight by a crazed fan. The former Beatle, aged 40, had been at a recording session and was walking into the Dakota building with his wife Yoko Ono when Mark Chapman, to whom Lennon had given his autograph earlier in the day, came up to him and fired five shots at point-blank range from a .38 revolver.

As word of the shooting spread, fans began a vigil outside the Dakota. Lennon was rushed to Roosevelt hospital for surgery but never recovered. His killer, meanwhile, read *The Catcher in the Rye* while waiting to be arrested. He is being held under high security in Tombs prison. Police say that Chapman flew from Hawaii, where he bought the gun, and stalked Lennon for three days before shooting him.

Golding steals Booker prize from Burgess

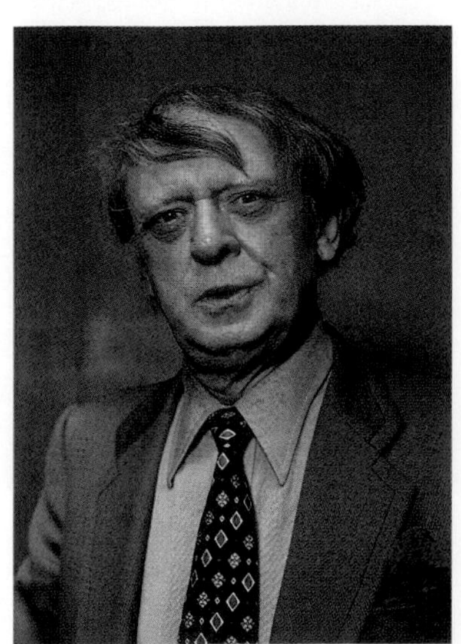

Burgess: a master of language.

London, 21 October
Two of Britain's small number of literary titans fought it out for this year's Booker prize for fiction. William Golding, a veteran of 69 with *Lord of the Flies* and *Free Fall* to his credit, published *Rites of Passage*, the account of a voyage to Australia in a converted wooden warship, written by a young man setting out for a colonial post. The writing in period idiom is a *tour de force.* Against it was ranged the latest meaty novel from the prolific Anthony Burgess. *Earthly Powers* is also a *tour de force* about an attempt to canonize a pope, narrated by a homosexual novelist. It was a close contest between top-class entries. Golding just won.

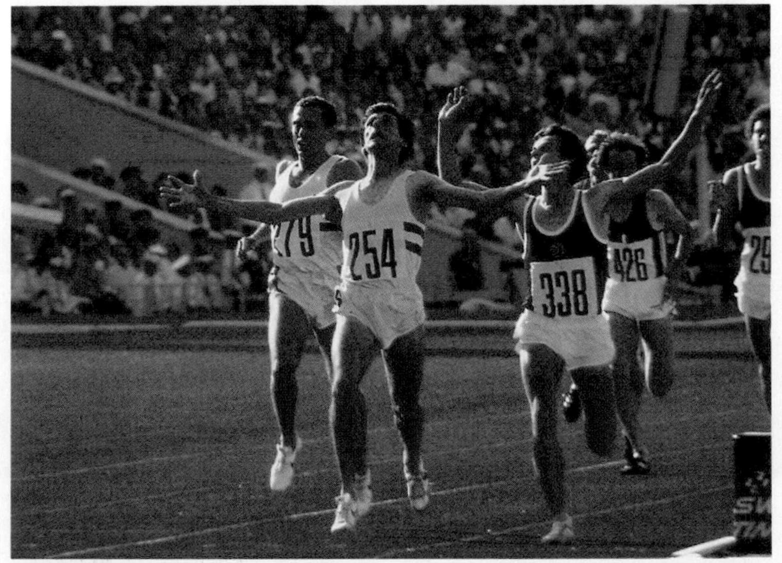

Sebastian Coe (c), disappointed by a silver medal in the Olympic 800m, pushes himself to his limit to win the gold medal in the 1,500m final.

1981

Sheffield, 5 January. Peter Sutcliffe, a 35-year-old long-distance lorry-driver, is charged with "the Yorkshire Ripper" murders (→29/4).

Ulster, 16 January. Bernadette McAliskey, née Devlin, a former MP, is shot by three loyalist gunmen (→1/3).

South Wales, 17 February. Miners threaten to strike over the proposed pit closures (→18).

Westminster, 18 February. Margaret Thatcher, the prime minister, promises more money for the miners in an attempt to avert a strike (→8/12).

Belfast, 1 March. IRA prisoners begin a second hunger strike (→15).

Belfast, 15 March. Bobby Sands, an IRA hunger striker, stands as the Republican candidate for the Fermanagh and South Tyrone by-election (→11/4).

Liverpool, 4 April. Bob Champion, who recovered from cancer, rides Aldaniti to win the Grand National at Aintree.

London, 4 April. Sue Brown, the first woman cox in the Oxford and Cambridge Boat Race, leads Oxford to victory.

Belfast, 11 April. Bobby Sands wins the by-election (→5/5).

Britain, 23 April. Unemployment reaches 2.5 million (→26/1/82).

Belfast, 5 May. Bobby Sands dies (→12).

Belfast, 12 May. The city erupts in rioting after the deaths of the hunger strikers Bobby Sands and Francis Hughes (→19/7).

Northern Ireland, 19 July. Efforts by the Red Cross to end the hunger strike in the Maze prison fail (→3/10).

Britain, 21 July. Ian Botham, who resigned as captain, leads the English cricket team to victory over Australia.

London, 17 September. Plans to close the Royal Docks are finalized.

Belfast, 3 October. The hunger strike ends after seven months and ten deaths.→

Belfast, 14 November. IRA gunmen kill Robert Bradford, the Unionist MP for Belfast South (→20/7/82).

Britain, 8 December. Arthur Scargill is elected president of the National Union of Mineworkers (→12/3/84).

Britain suffers worst riots of century

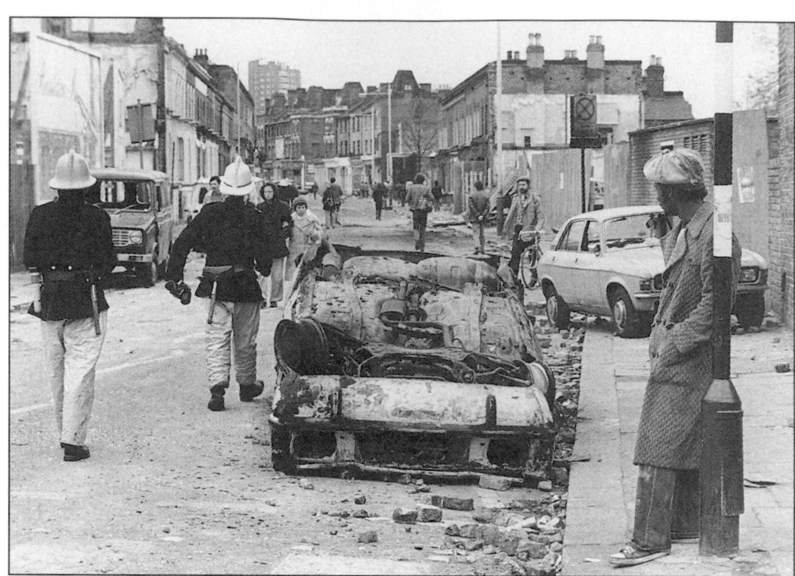

All is quiet on Mayall Road, Brixton, after a night of violence and terror.

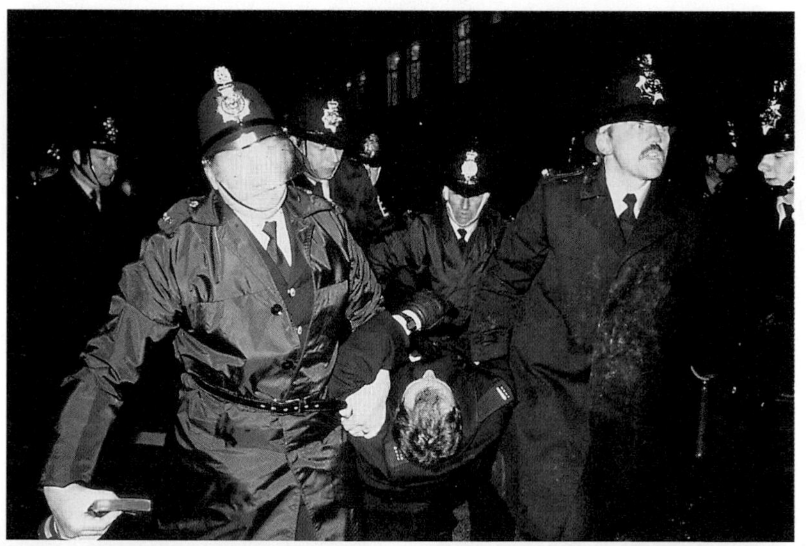

Police struggle with a rioter as the streets of Toxteth erupt in violence.

Liverpool, 13 July
As shopkeepers in Liverpool, London, Hull, Wolverhampton, Reading, Birmingham, Preston and Chester shovel up the broken glass from their shopfronts, and bulldozers clear the barricades of cars and rubbish from the streets, Britain reflects on its worse week of rioting this century.

Trouble began in the Liverpool ghetto of Toxteth on 4 July when black and white youths attacked the police. Next day the police withdrew from the area, admitting that the mob had got "out of control". By the week's end there was rioting and looting in eleven different inner city areas, reaching its climax on 10 July, "Britain's night of anarchy".

This week's riots were far more extensive than April's riot at Brixton, in south London, when what began as a confrontation between black youths and police cracking down on street crime turned into a two-night orgy of looting, vandalism and arson as young blacks and whites – mostly unemployed – attacked the police.

Government spokesmen affirm that they will not permit any "no-go" areas – where police cannot go in Britain – and dismiss the political significance of much of this week's anarchy as "copy-cat" riots. Community leaders disagree, pointing to the high levels of poverty and unemployment and to the perception of young blacks that they are harassed by the police for being both young and black (→29/9/85).

SDP takes shape

London, 25 January
At Limehouse today a time-bomb was placed under British politics by four former Labour cabinet ministers. "The gang of four", as Roy Jenkins, Shirley Williams, David Owen and William Rodgers are nicknamed, issued a statement attacking Labour for drifting towards extremism. They were stung into action by a special Labour Party conference this month at Wembley which gave more power to unions and party activists in selecting leaders and MPs. The proposed Council for Social Democracy could become a fully fledged party.

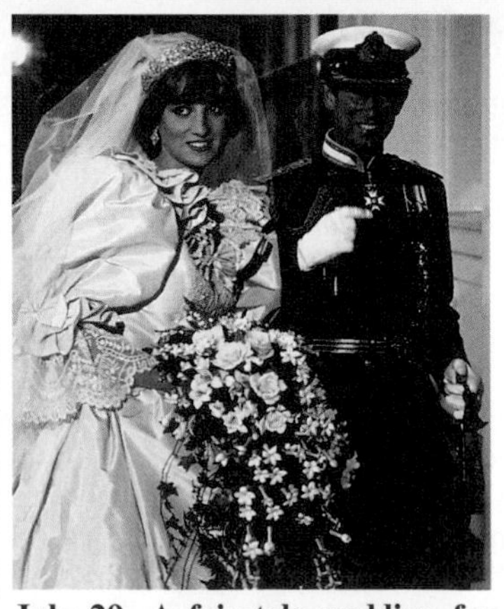

July 29. A fairytale wedding for the Prince of Wales, who married Lady Diana Spencer in St Paul's Cathedral today (→21/6/82).

Disco fire kills 49

Dublin, 14 February
Ireland is in shock and mourning after 49 Dubliners, mostly teenagers, burnt to death in a disco fire during a St Valentine's day dance. A further 130 who survived are in hospital with severe burns. The ceiling of the Stardust Club was made of plastic, the emergency exit doors were blocked, and there were iron bars on the windows to prevent people from coming in without paying. Once the ceiling caught fire the flames spread. The ceiling melted onto the victims, who were trapped in the building, as the exit was blocked by panicking crowds.

FitzGerald is new premier of Ireland

Ireland, 30 June
Following a general election, Dr Garret FitzGerald has taken office as prime minister at the head of a precarious Fine Gael/Labour Party coalition government which depends on the support of three Independent deputies.

It has been a troubled year for the out-going Fianna Fáil government, beset by difficulties caused by the IRA prisoners' hunger strike in Northern Ireland. Added to this has been the exposure of serious deficiencies in economic forecasting, reinforcing vigorous criticism by the opposition of the government's prodigality (→ 12/1982).

IRA hunger strike ends

Belfast, 3 October
Six republicans ended a seven-month hunger-strike campaign in the Maze prison today as it became clear that their families would intervene to save their lives. There were also signs that the government would concede some of their demands. The campaign began after the withdrawal in 1976 of the special status for terrorists. Prisoners refused to wear uniform and smeared excrement around their cells. Bobby Sands, aged 27, began his fast on 1 March. Sands, elected as Sinn Féin MP for Fermanagh and South Tyrone on 9 April, became the first striker to achieve IRA martyrdom on 5 May (→ 14/11).

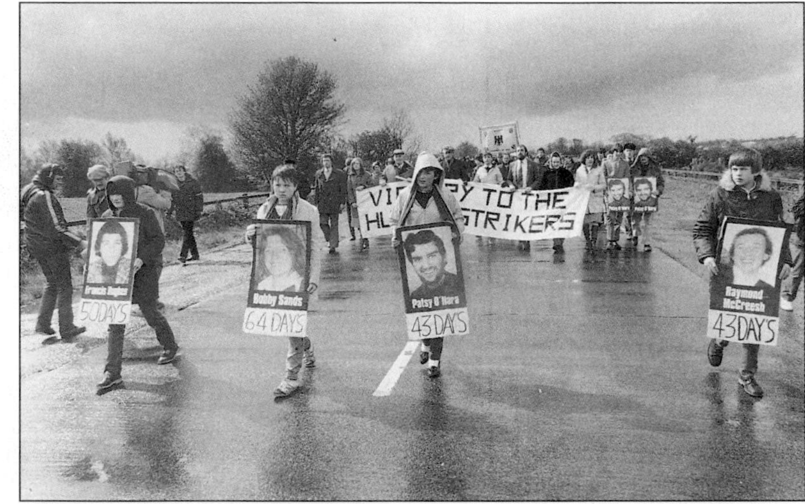

Marchers rally in support of the IRA hunger strikers in the Maze prison.

Sutcliffe confesses to 'Ripper' murders

London, 29 April
Peter Sutcliffe, a 34-year-old Bradford lorry driver with a neat beard and an impassive stare, stood in the dock at the Old Bailey today and admitted that he was "the Yorkshire Ripper". In his four-year reign of terror he had killed 13 women and attempted to kill another seven, mostly prostitutes. He denies murder but admits manslaughter on the grounds of diminished responsibility. Behind him sat two survivors of his attacks. In front of Sutcliffe were laid out the Ripper's tools: knives, drills, hammers and screwdrivers. His wife, Sonia, only a metre away, looked as impassive as her husband (→ 24/5/89).

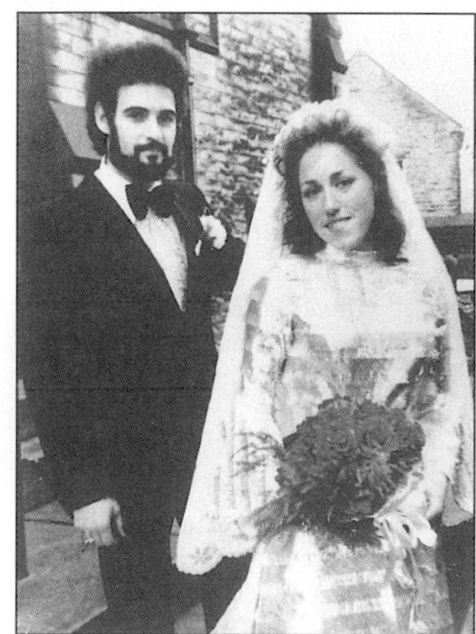
Peter Sutcliffe on his wedding day.

Blank shots fired at Queen in the Mall

London, 30 June
As the Queen rode side-saddle down the Mall for the Trooping of the Colour, six shots range out from the crowd, fired by an unemployed youth, Marcus Sargeant. Police and guardsmen disarmed him while the Queen, recovering from the shock, patted her black mare Burmese on the neck to reassure her, then continued on to Horseguards' Parade.

The shots, it later turned out, were blanks. Sargeant – who has been charged under the Treason Act – told Special Branch officers that his action was a protest against unemployment (→ 7/7/82).

Penlee lifeboatmen perish in rescue bid

Cornwall, 20 December
Eight lifeboatmen – all unpaid volunteers – perished today off Land's End with four shipwrecked sailors whom they had rescued. The lifeboat was launched from the tiny fishing village of Mousehole, two miles from Penzance, into hurricane-lashed seas to answer an SOS call from the 1,400-tonne coaster *Union Star*, dashed on rocks.

Though the men took four crew members off the stricken ship, the lifeboat was crushed against the *Union Star* by 18-metre (60-foot) waves before it could take off the remaining eight.

Crippled Irish novelist Christy Brown dies

The talented artist Christy Brown.

Co Kerry, 7 September
Christy Brown, one of Ireland's authentic novelists despite having cerebral palsy from birth, died here today at the age of 48. He was one of a family of 13 and had the full use of only one of his limbs, his left foot. He grew up in Dublin, where his father was a bricklayer. He learned to draw and paint with his foot before he could talk. In 1954 he wrote the moving account of his struggles, *My Left Foot*, and in 1970 an autobiographical novel, *Down All Our Days*, which had all the tang and unsentimentality of the Dublin slums.

July. The Humber Bridge, the world's longest single-span suspension bridge, under construction since January 1980, is officially opened.

1982

Britain, 26 January. Unemployment reaches three million (→ 3/2/83).

Belfast, 19 February. John De Lorean's luxury car plant goes into receivership (→ 19/10).

London, 4 March. The Barbican arts centre opens.

Glasgow, 25 March. Roy Jenkins, a founder-member of the SDP, wins the Hillhead by-election (→ 2/7).

Cambridge, 26 March. The first test-tube twins are born.

Falkland Islands, 2 April. Argentinian troops invade (→ 4).

South Atlantic, 4 April. The Argentinians take South Georgia (→ 5).

Plymouth, 5 April. The Royal Navy sails for the Falklands (→ 12).

Falklands Islands, 12 April. The Argentinians evacuate their forces as the British-imposed 200-mile war zone comes into force (→ 25).

South Atlantic, 25 April. The British seize South Georgia (→ 4/5).

Brussels, 13 May. The EEC bans the rubber bullets used by the British Army in Northern Ireland.

Falkland Islands, 22 May. British troops land at San Carlos on East Falkland (→ 25).

Falkland Islands, 25 May. Over 24 men die when HMS *Coventry* is hit by an Exocet missile (→ 14/6).

London, 21 June. The Princess of Wales gives birth to a son, William Arthur Philip Louis (→ 15/9/84).

Westminster, 2 July. Roy Jenkins is elected as leader of the SDP.

London, 20 July. Eight servicemen are killed by IRA bombs in two incidents (→ 13/12).

Falkland Islands, 22 July. Britain lifts the 200-mile exclusion zone.

Solent, 11 October. King Henry VIII's flagship, the *Mary Rose*, which sank on her maiden voyage, is raised after 400 years.

Belfast, 19 October. The De Lorean car plant closes, with the loss of 1,500 jobs.

London, 13 December. The GLC's invitation to members of Sinn Féin, the political wing of the IRA, causes an uproar in parliament (→ 5/8/83).

Britain at war in the Falkland Islands

The "General Belgrano" lists and sinks after the British submarine attack.

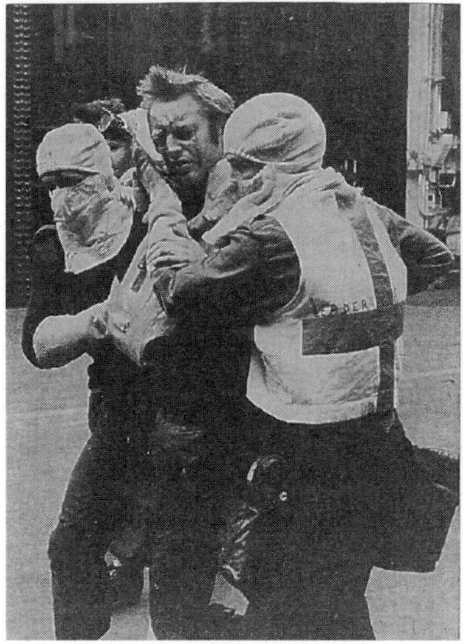
A survivor from HMS "Sheffield".

South Atlantic, 4 May
The harsh realities of modern war were brought home to the British task force today when the destroyer HMS *Sheffield* sank after being hit by an Exocet missile which had been launched from a Super Etendard fighter flying beneath the fleet's radar screen. Captain James "Sam" Salt only had time to shout "Take cover" before the missile struck.

The rocket's unexpended fuel set fire to the *Sheffield's* plastic and aluminium fittings, and the "Shiny Sheff" was blotted out by poisonous black fumes. Other ships sent their fire-fighting teams, but the fires were too fierce. The battle to save her went on for five hours; she was taken in tow, but, as if tired of the struggle, she rolled over and sank. Twenty of her crew were killed.

This setback is a major blow to Britain's attempt to regain the Falkland Islands – long claimed by their nearest neighbour, Argentina, and invaded last month. It follows the sinking of the Argentinian cruiser *General Belgrano* by the nuclear-powered submarine HMS *Conqueror*, and the recapture of South Georgia, a Falklands dependency, by Royal Marine commandos. When Margaret Thatcher, the prime minister, announced the news that South Georgia had been taken she cried "Rejoice", but the threat of the radar-guided Exocets, which can be launched more than 20 miles (32km) from their targets and skim the waves at speeds of 700mph (1,125kph), will ensure that regaining the Falklands will be no walkover despite the great success of the Harrier jump-jets in protecting the task force.

Politically, the sinking of the *Sheffield* – the first loss of a major British warship for 37 years – has sent tremors round Westminster, with some Tory MPs demanding the bombing of Argentina. Cooler heads argue that this would harm the justice of Britain's cause (→ 22).

Argentinians surrender as British forces regain Port Stanley

Port Stanley, 14 June
Fighting in the Falklands ended today with the surrender of Major-General Menendez, the Argentinian commander, and tonight the Union flag flies over Port Stanley once more. The end came when British troops, fighting hand to hand, broke through the last ring of defences at Tumbledown mountain, and the Argentinians began to leave their well prepared defences and stream back to the port.

White flags were blossoming like flowers, and a Spanish-speaking British officer got through to Menendez by radio and convinced him of the hopelessness of his situation. Shortly afterwards Major-General Jeremy Moore, Land Forces Commander, signalled London: "The Falkland Islands are once more under the government desired by their inhabitants. God save the Queen."

His news was received with rejoicing in the House of Commons, and Margaret Thatcher said that the victory had been won by an operation which was "boldly planned, bravely executed and brilliantly accomplished". However, there can be no doubt that this campaign, fought 8,000 miles away, was balanced on a knife edge. The loss of the *Atlantic Conveyor* and her supplies was a disaster, and it is unlikely that the task force could have continued the fight much longer. The known death toll is 255 British and 652 Argentinian (→ 22/7).

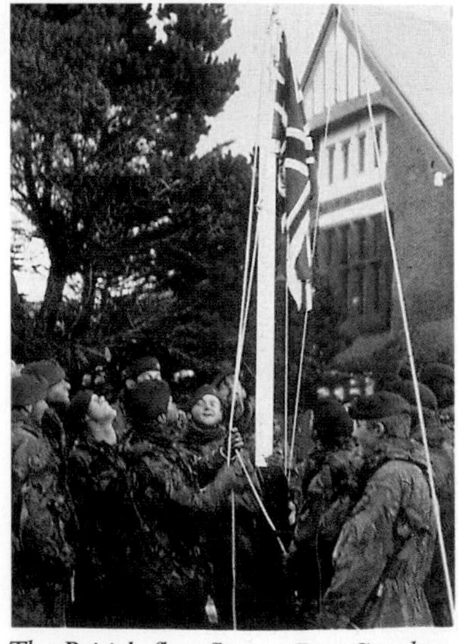
The British flag flies at Port Stanley.

Pope's visit to Britain ends 450-year rift

Canterbury, 29 May
Pope John Paul II, on an historic visit to Britain, prayed in Canterbury Cathedral today with the archbishop of Canterbury, Dr Robert Runcie. It was the most dramatic gesture of reconciliation between the Anglican and Roman Catholic Churches since Henry VIII's split with Rome 450 years ago.

One of Henry's descendants, the Prince of Wales, was there to represent the Queen, the supreme head of the Church of England, and emotions spilt over in tears and applause as the pope stepped out of the sunshine into the cool nave to a fanfare of trumpets. The pope and the archbishop announced the creation of a commission to study the reunification of the churches.

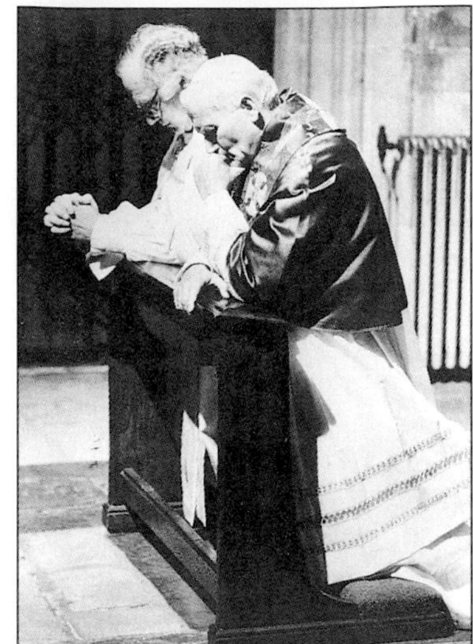

Historic moment: Archbishop Robert Runcie (l) prays with the pope.

FitzGerald returns as PM after hectic year

Ireland, December
Following the second of two elections this year, political stability has been restored by a coalition between Fine Gael and the Labour Party, with Garret FitzGerald as prime minister.

The first election took place in March after a particularly harsh budget brought in by the 1981/2 coalition government, also led by Dr FitzGerald. Neither of the two main parties achieved a majority, but Charles Haughey managed to secure the support of left-wing deputies, and he and his Fianna Fáil party were therefore able to form a government.

That administration then faced a period of severe economic crisis and was weakened by political scandals, dissension, the death of one deputy and the serious illness of another. Defeat in a no-confidence motion brought about by FitzGerald ended one of the unhappiest years in Irish politics (→ 10/3/87).

Haughey campaigning in Dublin.

Uninvited visitor in Queen's bedroom

London, 7 July
Michael Fagan, a 35-year-old unemployed Irishman, climbed into Buckingham Palace early today, took a bottle of wine and made his way to the Queen's bedroom, where he woke her by drawing the curtains and then sitting on her bed to chat about his family.

He sat there for at least eight minutes, and it was not until he asked for a cigarette that the Queen was able to alert the switchboard. Fagan was then escorted from the bedroom by a footman and arrested by embarrassed policemen. Heads will undoubtedly roll (→ 12/10/86).

Women lead peaceful anti-missile protest at Greenham Common

Non-violent protesters plan the next move outside the missile base.

Berkshire, 12 December
Greenham Common airbase was ringed by 20,000 women holding hands today to "embrace the base" in protest at the proposed siting there of 96 US cruise missiles. The women, mostly from the "Peace Camp" they have established on common ground outside the base, have been staging a vigil here since September. The council has twice tried to evict them but has failed.

Their demonstration went off peacefully today, with stirring anti-war songs and a great shout of "Freedom" as the circle was completed. Tomorrow they plan to blockade the base and confront US servicemen (→ 1/4/83).

Laker's dream dies as airline collapses

Gatwick airport, 7 February
Sir Freddie Laker, the pioneer of cut-price air travel, is "in a state of misery" following the collapse three days ago of Laker Airways. He cannot even take heart from the offers of help which are pouring in. One businessman, who argued that Sir Freddie has done more for enterprise in Britain than anyone else in the past 25 years, offered £1 million. Prince Michael of Kent sent a telegram offering his support. But the banks have decided otherwise.

TV's fourth channel sparks early row

London, 2 December
The new ITV Channel Four has run into trouble only a month after it started transmitting. William Whitelaw, the home secretary, tonight expressed concern at the "bad language, political bias and many other undesirable qualities" which he says that people have found in its programmes. The channel was set up to cater for minorities, but some viewers are shocked by explicit discussion of subjects such as homosexuality and feminism (→ 17/1/83).

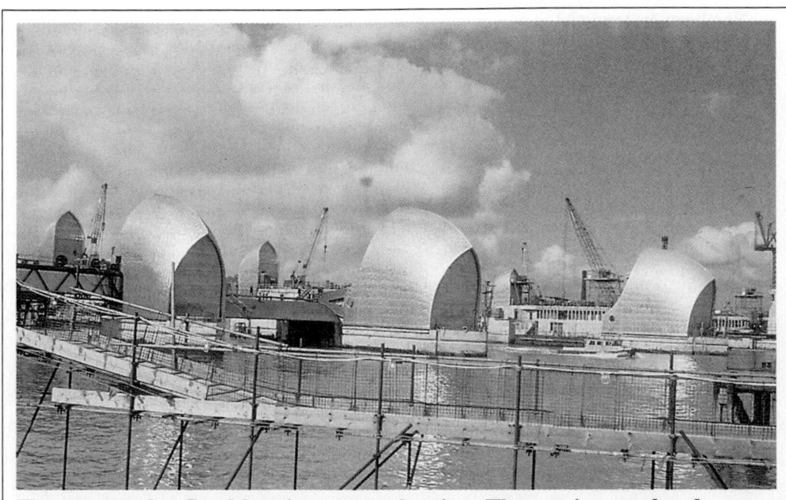

The spectacular flood barrier across the river Thames is completed.

1983

Britain, 1 February. ITV's breakfast television programme, TV-am, goes on the air (→ 5/4/87).

Britain, 3 February. Unemployment figures reach an all-time high of 3,224,715 (→ 18/6/87).

London, 26 March. Anthony Blunt, the Queen's former art adviser and a Russian spy, dies.

Berkshire, 1 April. Thousands of CND supporters form a 14-mile-long human chain linking Greenham to Burghfield in protest at the cruise missile base.

Westminster, 9 May. Margaret Thatcher calls a general election for 9 June (→ 10/6).

Westminster, 12 June. Michael Foot resigns as leader of the Labour Party (→ 13).

Westminster, 13 June. Roy Jenkins resigns as leader of the SDP; he suggests Dr David Owen as his successor (→ 2/10).

Westminster, 14 September. John Selwyn Gummer succeeds Cecil Parkinson as chairman of the Conservative Party (→ 5/10).

Westminster, 2 October. Neil Kinnock is the new leader of the Labour Party; his deputy is Roy Hattersley.→

London, 5 October. Cecil Parkinson admits having had a relationship with his secretary, Sara Keays (→ 14).

Westminster, 16 October. Norman Tebbit succeeds Cecil Parkinson as secretary for trade and industry.

Belfast, 12 November. Gerry Adams is elected leader of Sinn Féin (→ 22).

Liverpool, 18 November. Janet Walton, a 31-year-old, gives birth to sextuplets, all girls.

Northern Ireland, 22 November. The Unionist Party pulls out of the Ulster Assembly after three church elders were shot dead in South Armagh last Sunday (→ 4/12).

London, 26 November. Over £25 million in gold bars is stolen from Heathrow airport in one of the UK's biggest robberies.

Northern Ireland, 4 December. Allegations of a "shoot-to-kill" policy are raised after the deaths of two IRA gunmen in an SAS ambush (→ 17).

London, 17 December. The IRA steps up its Christmas bombing campaign with a bomb in Harrods (→ 14/3/84).

Thatcher back in power

Westminster, 10 June

The Conservative vote fell in the general election yesterday, but Margaret Thatcher is back in power with the Tories' largest majority since 1935 – 144 over all other parties. The scale of her triumph was largely the result of a split in the anti-Tory vote, with the Liberal-Social Democratic Alliance on 25.4 per cent of the poll coming close to pipping Labour (27.6 per cent) as runner-up. But the Alliance was better at securing votes than seats. The final results are Conservatives 397, Labour 209, Alliance 23, Nationalist 4, Others 17.

In spite of high unemployment, a victory for the Tories never seemed in doubt during the campaign. The Tory party managers contrasted Mrs Thatcher, the Falklands victor, with Michael Foot, the CND-supporting Labour leader. Labour's manifesto did little to deflect attacks on its alleged extremism, promising to leave the Common Market and more nationalization. The result is a disaster for Labour – its worst share of the vote since the 1920s, and virtually wiped out in southern England. Foot and Roy Jenkins, the Social Democratic leader, intend to resign (→ 12).

Mrs Thatcher campaigning on home ground in Finchley in the election run-up.

Irish wonder-horse Shergar is snatched

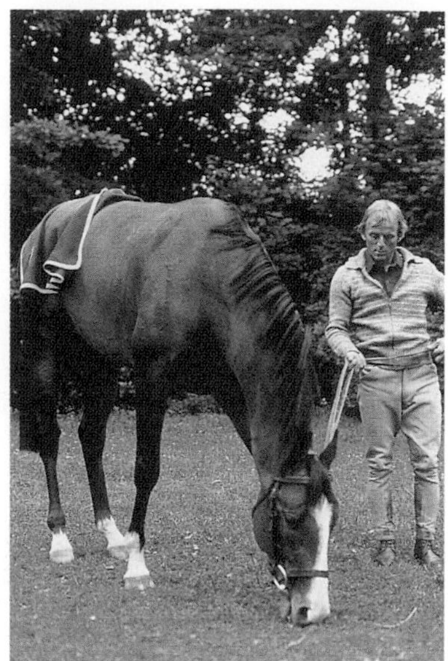

Shergar: where is he now?

Co Kildare, 9 February

Shergar, the winner of the Epsom and Irish Derbies and worth more than £10 million at stud, has been stolen from the Ballymany Stud near Newbridge. Details of the theft are unclear, and the mystery is not made easier by the fact that nine hours elapsed before the police were alerted.

There are rumours both that he has been killed and that he has been seen in dozens of little villages. It is known, however, that a ransom demand for £2 million has been made by telephone. Suspicion is hardening that the wonder-horse, owned by a syndicate headed by the Aga Khan, has been taken not by a man of the turf but by the IRA.

Cereal, eggs, toast and breakfast TV

London, 17 January

Early-morning television began today with the BBC's "Breakfast Time", presented by Selina Scott and Frank Bough. Despite some moans that people do not want, or need, TV with their cornflakes, the BBC is confident that breakfast TV is here to stay. Next month ITV's early morning show, TV-am, headed by "the Famous Five" – David Frost, Robert Kee, Angela Rippon, Anna Ford and Michael Parkinson – goes on the air (→ 1/2).

IRA hurt at hands of Belfast 'supergrass'

Belfast, 5 August

The longest – 117 days – and most expensive trial in Irish legal history ended today with the conviction of 35 IRA members on the word of Christopher Black, aged 29, a north Belfast man who turned "supergrass". He gave police extensive inside details of the IRA which seriously undermined its activity.

Black is one of six "converted terrorists", both republican and loyalist, who have named their accomplices in return for immunity and new identities for themselves and their families. So far about 80 have been convicted, and up to 220 suspects are in custody awaiting trial on the evidence of about 14 new "supergrasses" (→ 25/9).

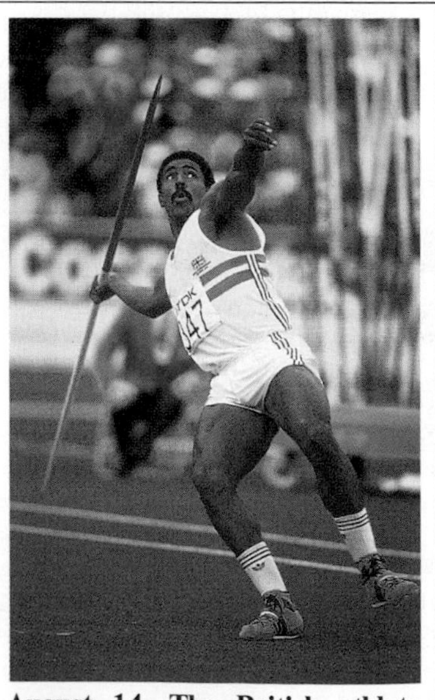

August 14. The British athlete Daley Thompson wins the gold medal in the first World Championship decathlon in Helsinki.

Over 130 break out of Belfast prison

Belfast, 25 September
One hundred and thirty-four jailed IRA members escaped today from the high security Maze prison, 12 miles south of Belfast. It is the biggest jailbreak in British history. A prison warder was stabbed to death, another was shot in the head, and a policeman and a prisoner were wounded. Official sources said that 15 prisoners were recaptured near the prison.

Prisoners on cleaning duty in one of the H-blocks produced guns and overpowered warders before hijacking a meals lorry and driving to the main gates in warders' uniforms. A warder was stabbed during a struggle, and the prisoners made off on foot or in hijacked cars. Locals said that five were recaptured almost immediately, and four were caught trying to cross the river Lagan. Prison staff are unarmed, although H-blocks have the highest proportion of "lifers" in the world – 230 out of 850. Three-quarters of the province's 2,500 prisoners are classified as terrorists (→12/11).

Irish people vote to restrict abortions

Ireland, September
A referendum to ensure that abortion would never be legalized, by approving the insertion of a clause into the constitution giving the foetus equal rights to that of the mother, has been carried. Support for it came largely from rural areas.

The so-called "pro-life" amendment is the result of a long, bitter and divisive campaign. It began when members of a right-wing "pro-life" group approached the leaders of the two main political parties, Charles Haughey and Garret FitzGerald, seeking assurances by way of a national referendum that abortion (already illegal) could never be introduced. Both agreed.

Through three divisive general elections the matter remained unresolved. Finally Dr FitzGerald, as prime minister, concluded the business by giving in to pressure and agreeing to a definitive wording which the most eminent lawyers of the day argued over for some time. Eventually an amendment was put before the people and carried.

Kinnock and Owen plot Tories' downfall

Brighton, 2 October
Neil Kinnock, a 41-year-old left-winger who has never held office in government, was today chosen to be the Labour Party's new leader. His defeated rival, Roy Hattersley, is to become deputy leader in what the party hopes will be the "dream ticket" to recover from the débâcle of its second successive general election defeat. But Kinnock faces major internal and external problems. The Labour Party is still split between left and right, with constituency activists – and some unions – markedly to the left of the parliamentary leaders. And he also has the challenge of the Social Democrats, now led by the former Labour foreign secretary David Owen, who succeeded Roy Jenkins after the election (→27/1/86).

A new future for Labour: Kinnock (center) and Hattersley (left) taste victory.

Burrell collection finds striking new home

The Burrell gallery: both the building and its contents have won awards.

Glasgow
The Burrell collection, which has been waiting for a home since 1944 when it was presented to the city by Sir William Burrell, has one at last. The new gallery, which won a competition for its architects Britt Andreson, John Munier and Barry Gasson, has already won awards as both a museum and a building. The Burrell collection is mainly of artefacts from ancient civilizations and mediaeval Europe. It furthers the revival of Glasgow as a home of the arts. The Citizens' theatre in the Gorbals has won international renown under Giles Havergal for its revivals of classic plays.

Parkinson quits in secretary sex scandal

Lancashire, 14 October
Cecil Parkinson, who as party chairman was the architect of the Conservative election victory in June, has resigned from the cabinet following revelations of an affair with his secretary, Sara Keays. She is expecting his child in January, and this week, during the party conference at Blackpool, she gave *The Times* an interview in which she claimed that Parkinson had broken a promise to marry her. He had told Margaret Thatcher of the scandal in June; she saw no reason for him to quit and appointed him trade and industry secretary. Now that it is public he has decided to go (→16).

Cecil Parkinson and Sara Keays – no longer romantically involved.

1984

East Anglia, 5 March. Scientists warn of a "greenhouse effect" caused by excessive amounts of carbon dioxide.

Britain, 12 March. A national miners' strike begins (→9/4).

Belfast, 14 March. The Sinn Féin leader Gerry Adams is shot by Loyalists (→12/10).

Derbyshire, 9 April. Over a hundred miners are arrested in some of the worst outbreaks of violence of the strike (→29/5).

London, 27 April. The government expels 30 Libyan diplomats (→6/2/85).

Cornwall, 19 May. Sir John Betjeman, the poet laureate, dies aged 78 (→19/12).

Gloucestershire, 29 May. Eric Morecambe, the comedian, aged 58, dies of a heart attack at Tewkesbury.

South Yorkshire, 30 May. Arthur Scargill, the NUM president, is arrested and charged with obstruction at Orgreave (→7/6).

Westminster, 7 June. Over 250 miners are arrested for rioting at a mass lobby (→9/9).

London, 12 July. Robert Maxwell buys the *Mirror* newspaper for £113.4 million (→5/11/91).

Edinburgh, 9 September. Ian MacGregor, the chairman of the NCB, arrives for talks with Arthur Scargill (→21).

London, 15 September. The Princess of Wales gives birth to her second son, Henry Charles Albert David (→10/3/88).

South Yorkshire, 21 September. Maltby Colliery at Rotherham is hit by the worst violence so far in the miners' strike (→10/10).

London, 10 October. The high court fines Scargill £1,000 and the NUM £200,000 for contempt of court (→5/11).

Britain, 5 November. Over 800 miners return to work (→6).

Dublin, 6 November. The high court rules to freeze the funds of the NUM (→20).

Wales, 20 November. The North Wales branch of the NUM ends its strike (→25/2/85).

Britain, 14 December. Rock stars led by Bob Geldof, the lead singer of the Boomtown Rats, form "Band Aid" to raise money for the famine in Ethiopia (→13/6/85).

Violence sours pit strike

Riot police charge to disperse the pickets at Orgreave coking plant.

South Yorkshire, 29 May
In the bitterest confrontation yet of the three-month-old coal strike, 41 policemen and 28 miners were injured today outside the Orgreave coking plant here. The police wore full riot gear for the first time and only restored order after repeated mounted charges.

The picketing miners were trying to stop convoys of lorries taking coke from the plant to a steelworks. The NUM president, Arthur Scargill, claimed that South Yorkshire was like a "police state which you might expect to see in Chile but not here". The strike began in opposition to a 5.2 per cent pay offer and a programme of pit closures. Much of the violence so far has been concentrated in Nottinghamshire, where the miners have continued working in defiance of "flying pickets" of Yorkshire miners who in turn were defying a high-court injunction restricting them to their own area. The personal animosity between the coal board's chairman, Ian MacGregor, and Scargill, as well as the gulf between their positions – 20 pit closures and 20,000 job losses against no closures and no job losses – makes a speedy end to the strike unlikely (→30).

Fire from the skies sets off York blaze

York, 9 July
A thunderbolt, traditionally a sign of divine wrath, struck 700-year-old York Minster today, causing fire damage estimated at £1 million. The archbishop of York dismissed the suggestion that the wrath was directed at the liberal and controversial Dr David Jenkins, who was consecrated last week as bishop of Durham, and Dr Robert Runcie, the archbishop of Canterbury, saw a miracle in that only the south transept was destroyed, and the famous Rose Window survived. Many of the treasures were saved, and insurance will cover rebuilding costs.

Flames engulf York Minster.

Hong Kong part of Anglo-Chinese deal

Beijing, 26 September
An agreement was initialled here today which allows China to resume sovereignty of the British colony of Hong Kong in 1997 when the lease negotiated in the 19th century expires. The communist leaders of China have promised that the free-enterprise system and lifestyle established in Hong Kong will "remain unchanged for 50 years" after the date of the transfer of power. Hong Kong is to be a special administrative region of the People's Republic of China, with various rights and individual freedoms which will be enshrined in a new "basic law" (→22/12/89).

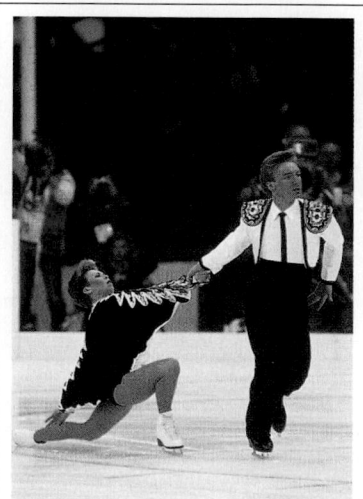

Britain's ice-dancing duo, Jayne Torvill and Christopher Dean, skate superbly to win the Olympic gold for ice-dancing.

Concern grows over spread of HIV virus

Tyne and Wear, 18 November
Two people have died of Aids after being infected by blood transfusions. One was Terence McStay, a haemophiliac who received contaminated American plasma. The 35-year-old laboratory worker was treated in Newcastle. Homosexuals, hard-drug users and other high-risk groups will now be banned as blood donors; within 12 months blood imports will end, and blood tests for Aids are being developed. In April it was announced that the virus which causes Aids, HIV, had been independently identified by American and French researchers (→15/3/85).

IRA bomb blasts Tory conference HQ

The bomb-shattered Grand hotel.

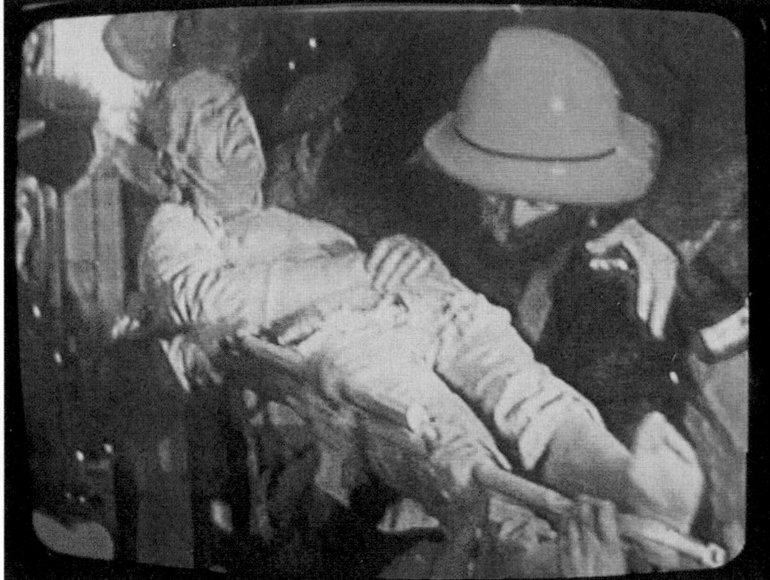
Fireman carry Norman Tebbit, the trade and industry minister, to safety.

Brighton, 12 October
Margaret Thatcher today made a defiant speech to the Conservative conference just hours after she had narrowly escaped death when an IRA bomb ripped apart the Grand hotel in the early hours of the morning. Five people were killed, including one MP, Sir Anthony Berry, and the wife of the party's chief whip, John Wakeham. More than 30 people were injured, many seriously, after being pulled from the rubble by firemen. The bomb exploded at 2.54am in the hotel, which was being used by most members of the cabinet during this week's party conference. It ripped a huge gash down the front of the building on the seafront. Four floors of the hotel were shattered by the blast, caused by a bomb weighing 9 kilos (20 pounds).

The prime minister had a lucky escape. She was still awake, having been working on today's speech to the conference. Two minutes before the bomb exploded she had been in a bathroom which was to be wrecked by the explosion. Some of her colleagues were less fortunate. Norman Tebbit, the industry minister, was pulled from the wreckage by firemen after several hours. His wife was also hurt. The IRA admitted responsibility for the bomb, adding: "Today we were unlucky, but remember we have only to be lucky once" (→ 28/2/85).

Innocent woman PC shot dead by Libyans outside embassy

Shots from the Libyan embassy leave Yvonne Fletcher fatally wounded.

London, 22 April
The anonymous Libyan who shot dead Yvonne Fletcher, the young policewoman, has seven days to leave the country, together with the rest of the students and professional diplomats living in the embassy in St James's Square. WPC Fletcher was killed five days ago while on duty at a demonstration outside the "People's Bureau"; however, her abandoned hat remains on the pavement, a poignant reminder for the millions who have followed this siege on TV.

Britain has now severed diplomatic relations with Colonel Gadaffi's Libya, and British diplomats in Tripoli have been warned to "consider their safety". As the Libyans are likely to remove vital evidence, the identity of WPC Fletcher's killer may never be known (→ 27).

Scientists face a difficult future as funding cuts bite

Britain
Science is in crisis. While a cost-cutting government demands that funding is concentrated on areas which promise practical benefits, its popularity is slipping. Science's transformation of daily life is now taken for granted, and it is increasingly seen as the source of many current problems, from acid rain to the vanishing ozone layer.

The power of science can be seen in the achievements of molecular biology. On the one hand it promises cures for genetically based diseases like sickle-cell anaemia, and the cheap production of insulin; on the other loom spectres like sheep being engineered to produce pharmaceuticals in their milk.

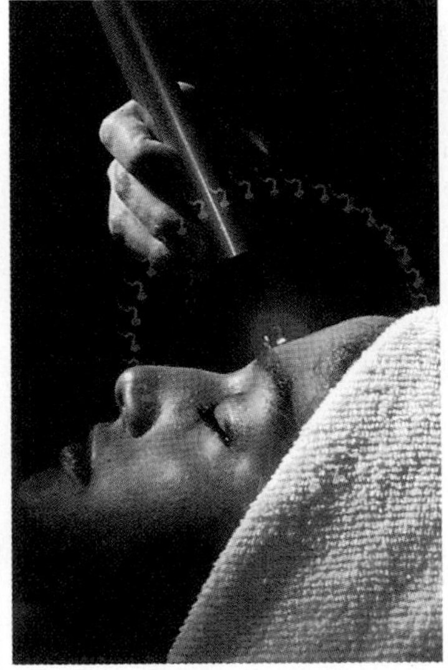
Lasers revolutionize surgery.

Science has been the victim of successful developments like the computer's silicon chip, which first appeared on the mass market about ten years ago, powering a pocket calculator that cost around £70. Now it is in everything, from nuclear weapons to watches, and the same computing power costs £7.

Science may have caused pollution, but it alone can clear it up, maybe using discoveries made by financially starved pure researchers.

1985

Britain, 10 January. Sir Clive Sinclair unveils the Sinclair C5, an electric tricycle (→ 15/10).

Dublin, 20 February. The sale of contraceptives is made legal.

Britain, 22 February. The pound is at an all-time low of $1.0765.

Britain, 25 February. 3,807 miners end their strike; 51 per cent are still on strike (→ 6/3).

Co Armagh, 28 February. Nine RUC men are killed in an IRA attack on Newry police station (→ 7/8).

Britain, 15 March. Blood donors are to be tested for the Aids virus (→ 11/4).

Westminster, 1 April. The government bans alcohol from selected football grounds.

Britain, 11 April. An 18-month-old boy is the first British baby to die of Aids (→ 26/9).

Birmingham, 11 May. A man is killed as fans run riot at a Leeds United-Birmingham City football match (→ 29).

Brussels, 30 May. British soccer teams are banned from Belgium after yesterday's Heysel tragedy (→ 31).

London, 31 May. The FA bans all English clubs from playing in Europe next season (→ 29/4/89).

Wimbledon, 7 July. Boris Becker, the 17-year-old German, is the youngest player to win the men's singles final.

Britain, 7 August. BBC journalists are on strike over the government's intervention to cancel the programme *Real Lives* in which a film interview with Sinn Féin's Martin MacGuiness is shown (→ 15/11).

Birmingham, 15 September. The European golf team win the Ryder Cup from America.

London, 26 September. The government announces a £1 million plan to help counter the spread of Aids (→ 21/11/86).

London, 29 September. Over 209 people have been arrested in two days of rioting in Brixton (→ 1/10).

Liverpool, 1 October. Riots break out in Toxteth (→ 7).

Britain, 15 October. Sir Clive Sinclair, the maker of the C5 electric tricycle, is forced to call in financial receivers.

Belfast, 11 December. Police and loyalists clash at the first Anglo-Irish conference (→ 24/1/86).

Twin tragedies shake British football

Onlookers watch horrified as the stands at Bradford City go up in flames.

People lie dead or dying in the wake of rioting by Liverpool soccer fans.

Brussels, 29 May

Forty-one Italian and Belgian soccer supporters were killed tonight when Liverpool fans went on the rampage against followers of the rival Juventus team at Heysel stadium, and a wall and a safety fence at the stadium collapsed. The disaster comes only 18 days after a fire swept through the main stand of Bradford City football club during a match against Lincoln City, killing 40 people. At Bradford, as at Heysel, most of the dead were trampled in the panic.

With the tragedy at Heysel, Britain's reputation in European football has reached its nadir. Even as Belgian police and ambulance personel tried to revive victims, Liverpool fans were still attacking the Italian supporters with bottles, iron bars and flagpoles. In the end police commanders had to call in mounted police and paratroopers.

The image of drunken and chauvinistic British football hooligans is familiar to every European country, and many now expect that British teams will be banned from European football.

The prime minister, Margaret Thatcher, who watched today's events live on televison, said that those responsible had brought "shame and dishonour" to the community. Some of her opponents argue that Mrs Thatcher's own brand of anti-European chauvinism has done as much to contribute to the hooliganism as the beer (→ 30).

Church 'diplomat' wins release of hostages

Tripoli, 6 February

Four Britons held prisoner in Libya for eight months have been freed. They were handed over today to Terry Waite, the archbishop of Canterbury's special envoy. All four – Robin Plummer, a British Telecom engineer; Michael Berdinner, a university lecturer; Alan Russell, an English teacher, and Malcolm Anderson, an engineer – were arrested last May in reaction to the "siege" of the Libyan embassy in London, following the shooting of a policewoman and several protesting Libyan exiles. Only two – Anderson and Russell – have been charged, Russell receiving a three-year sentence for "breaches of security".

There were fears that Waite's mission would fail after Jana, the Libyan news agency accused Mrs Thatcher of trying to hamper the release by unveiling a memorial to WPC Yvonne Fletcher and going ahead with the trial in Manchester of four Libyans on bomb charges. But Libya now says that the releases will go ahead as planned.

For Terry Waite – a gentle giant – the releases are seen as a triumph for his own personal brand of unofficial diplomacy, at a time when Britain has no diplomatic contacts with Libya (→ 21/1/87).

July 4. First-class maths honours for Ruth Lawrence, aged 13, who took her degree in two years.

Miners' strike ends to cries of 'scab!'

The year-long national strike is over.

South Wales, 6 March
Welsh miners marched back to work today to the sound of brass band after their year-long strike against redundancies. It is the end of their industry, but like their English and Scottish comrades they display dignity in defeat. It was not only the longest coal strike in British history but also the most bitter. The early violence at the Orgreave coking plant in South Yorkshire, where one miner died and hundreds were injured and arrested, set the tone. To add to the bitterness – and the violence – Nottinghamshire miners refused to strike and formed a rival to the National Union of Mineworkers: the Union of Democratic Mineworkers.

'Live Aid' rocks to help feed the world

London, 13 July
£40 million was raised for the hungry of Ethiopia today at the biggest rock concert ever produced. The concert, Live Aid, was organized by the Dublin-born rock star Bob Geldof, whose Band Aid single *Do They Know It's Christmas?* raised tens of thousands of pounds for Ethiopia's starving people.

Live Aid was held at two venues, Wembley stadium in London and the JFK stadium in Philadelphia. Over one and a half billion people in some 160 countries watched on television while the giants of rock, Mick Jagger, David Bowie, Queen and Dire Straits, urged fans to donate their cash (→17/7).

Thousands pack Wembley stadium.

Anglo-Irish deal signed

Ulster Unionists demonstrating against the Anglo-Irish agreement.

Belfast, 15 November
The prime ministers of the United Kingdom and of the Republic of Ireland today signed an agreement that all sides regard as momentous. The Anglo-Irish Agreement allows the Irish government the right to discuss virtually all aspects of life in Northern Ireland and sets up a secretariat to be staffed by civil servants from London and Dublin.

Unionist politicians in Northern Ireland have reacted with fury to the agreement, failing to be mollified by the Dublin government's acknowledgement that Irish unity could be achieved only "with the consent of a majority of the people of Northern Ireland". Mass demonstrations are planned in Belfast in protest at the agreement, which was signed today at Hillsborough by Margaret Thatcher and Garret FitzGerald. Some Irish Nationalists are also unhappy, castigating the Dublin government for giving up its traditional belief in Irish unity.

Mrs Thatcher said today that the agreement recognizes the interests of both the Protestant majority and the Catholic minority in Northern Ireland. The failure to make political headway within Northern Ireland, and increasing cooperation between security forces on both sides of the border, provided the background to today's deal. Talks at an inter-governmental council had also brought the two governments closer together (→11/12).

Holiday tragedy at Manchester airport

Manchester, 22 August
Fifty-four passengers were killed today when an engine on a British Airtours Boeing 737 exploded and the plane burst into flames just as it was about to take off. The pilot attempted to abort take-off after the explosion, but in vain. Eighty passengers escaped down the chutes; the rest died in the inferno.

The crash has turned this August into the worst month for airline crashes ever recorded. So far 711 passengers have died: 517 in Tokyo, 140 at Dallas, Texas, and now 54 at Manchester.

PC is hacked to death in Tottenham riots

London, 7 October
A former community policeman was hacked to death on a north London housing estate today, in the most vicious rioting that British police have ever experienced.

The riots – on the Broadwater Farm estate in Tottenham, an inner city council project that belies its name – were sparked off by the death of a middle-aged black woman, Mrs Cynthia Jarrett, who died of a heart attack during a police raid. Within hours police had been called to the estate by fake "999" calls and been ambushed by a hail of bricks and petrol bombs, and – for the first time in an inner city riot – by gunshots. From 6.30pm until long after midnight both black and white youths fought bloody battles with more than 500 police in riot gear. The dead policeman has been named as PC Keith Blakelock, aged 40. Four more policeman have been wounded by gunshots, and over two hundred others have been injured.

A Tory MP, John Wheeler, dismissed claims that the riot stemmed from either social deprivation or insensitive policing. The Labour home affairs spokesman, Gerald Kaufman, has called for a full inquiry. "This is not the England we should be living in," he said.

Sir Clive Sinclair test drives his latest invention, the C5.

1986

Northern Ireland, 24 January. Unionists are re-elected in 14 of 15 seats contested on the Anglo-Irish agreement (→23/6).

Westminster, 28 January. The rates system will be replaced with a "community charge" (→20/9/89).

London, 16 February. Police clash with pickets at the new News International plant at Wapping. The trouble is over the move of the production of the *Sunday Times* and *News of the World* there (→5/2/87).

Australia, 2 March. The Queen signs the Australia Bill severing constitutional ties with Britain.

London, 29 March. The first test-tube quintuplets are born.

Lebanon, 17 April. Three British hostages are murdered in retaliation for British participation in the US air strike against Libya.

Belfast, 24 June. The Reverend Ian Paisley is forcibly removed from the Ulster Assembly after it is dissolved (→12/7).

Atlantic Ocean, 29 June. Richard Branson in the *Virgin Atlantic Challenger II* completes a record crossing.

Northern Ireland, 12 July. Over a hundred are injured in Orange day clashes between Catholics and Protestants (→13/8).

Westminster, 23 July. Prince Andrew, the duke of York, marries Sarah Ferguson.

Dublin, 13 August. Gerard O'Reilly, an IRA suspect, is freed because of an error in his extradition warrant (→8/5/87).

Sunderland, 8 September. Nissan, the Japanese car manufacturers, opens a factory.

China, 12 October. The Queen begins the first state visit by a British monarch.

Westminster, 21 November. A "safe-sex" campaign is launched in a bid to stop the spread of Aids (→4/5/87).

London, 1 December. A department of trade and industry inquiry opens into the shares of Guinness, the beer and spirits group (→9/1/87).

Manchester, 19 December. John Stalker resigns from the police force.

Britain, 29 December. Harold Macmillan, the earl of Stockton and a former prime minister, dies aged 92.

Leon Brittan resigns as trade and industry secretary over leaks in 'Westland' affair

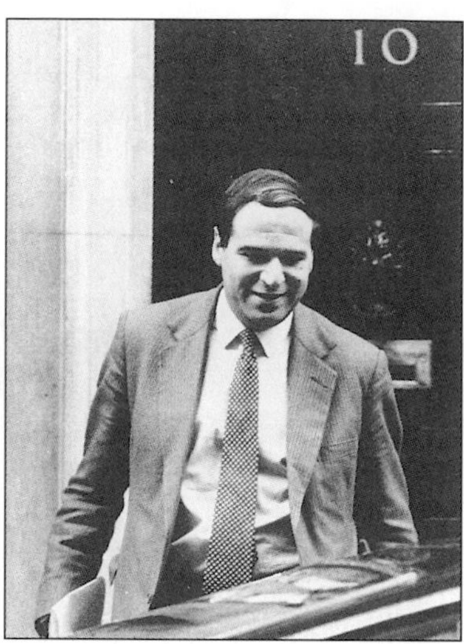

Leon Brittan resigns over a leak ...

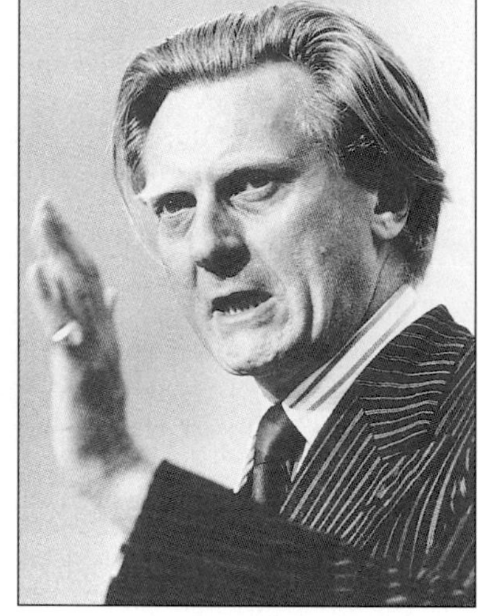

... and so does Michael Heseltine.

Westminster, 27 January
Margaret Thatcher has survived the greatest threat so far to her 11-year leadership of the Conservative Party. After a month in which two cabinet ministers have resigned – ostensibly over the future of the Westland helicopter company but in reality about her style of government – the prime minister has survived a debate today in the Commons which even she had thought could end in her resignation.

The fuse in the Westland affair was lit by Michael Heseltine, who walked out of a cabinet meeting on 9 January to announce his resignation. The defence secretary had been locked in an increasingly public dispute with Leon Brittan, the trade and industry secretary, about official policy towards the Yeovil-based Westland company. But then Heseltine widened the assault by talking of "a breakdown of constitutional government".

Three days ago Brittan resigned, taking responsibility for the role of his press secretary in leaking part of a letter from a government law officer that had been critical of Heseltine. The role of Downing Street staff in the leak is what made Mrs Thatcher vulnerable (→12/6/87).

Northern Ireland is to lose its assembly

London, 23 June
The government has today dissolved the Northern Ireland assembly, which had degenerated after four years into a unionist forum for attacking the Anglo-Irish Agreement signed last year [*see page 1197*].

The Northern Ireland secretary, James Prior, wanted the assembly to be the basis of "rolling devolution" leading to self-government. Any application for devolution needed the support of 70 per cent of the membership – 55 out of 78 – so that unionists needed nationalist backing. The SDLP won 14 assembly seats, to Sinn Féin's five, but never took them up because Prior's plan had no role for Dublin (→24).

Irish reject divorce

Dublin, 26 June
A referendum to amend the constitution and allow a limited form of divorce has been overwhelmingly defeated. Opinion polls predicted a "yes" vote, but in the closing stages of the campaign it became clear that the opposition of the Roman Catholic Church, coupled with apparent confusion about the benefits to which the divorced wife would be entitled, had caused the public – particularly women – to change its mind.

Britain and France move a little closer as 'Chunnel' gets go-ahead

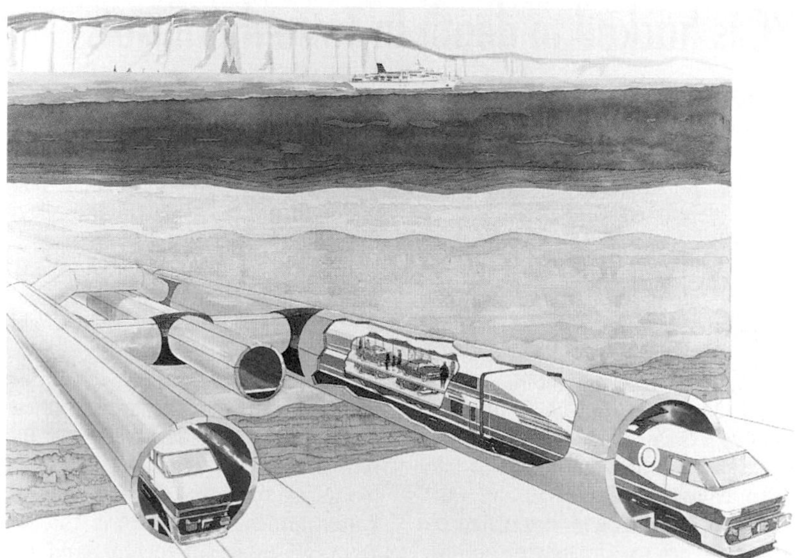

Pipe-line dreams become a reality as Britain and France agree to a tunnel.

Lille, France, 20 January
After nearly two hundred years of bickering and false starts, Britain and France have finally agreed to link their two countries with a pair of undersea rail tunnels, expected to cost around £5 billion. The first passengers through the Channel tunnel from Folkestone to Sangatte are scheduled to make the London/Paris trip in April 1993. Margaret Thatcher and President François Mitterrand made the historic announcement today in Lille.

The all-rail solution was decided on after various alternatives, like a multi-lane road bridge, were rejected as too hazardous or too expensive. But it is hoped that it may be possible to add a road tunnel early in the 21st century (→8/3/89).

Greater London loses its local council

The staff of the former Greater London Council (GLC) pose for a last photo.

London, 31 March
The Greater London Council, which always claimed to be the world's largest local authority, was abolished tonight, along with the metropolitan county councils of Greater Manchester, Merseyside, Tyne & Wear, South Yorkshire, West Yorkshire and West Midlands. Responsibility for planning, coordinating and servicing large parts of Britain's capital city will in future be divided among its 42 constituent boroughs.

This decision brings to an end a long simmering conflict between the prime minister, Margaret Thatcher, and the GLC's outspoken and irreverent chairman, Ken Livingstone, who deliberately set out to become the voice of the ultra-radical (or, as most Conservatives put it, "loony") left wing of the Labour Party. He delighted in both mocking and flouting government intentions at every turn.

But it was his attitude to spending public money that set him on the final collision course with central authority. Local government budgets, of which London's was by far the largest, account for up to a quarter of national expenditure, and during the early 1980s the treasury became determined to bring this under effective ministerial control. The final straw was Livingstone's popular "Fares Fair" cheap fare policy for London Transport, which involved lavish subsidies. When the courts declared these illegal, the GLC's fate was sealed.

Manchester deputy is taken off inquiry

Belfast, 30 June
John Stalker, Manchester's deputy chief constable, has been suspended from duty pending investigation of his alleged association with "known criminals". This further clouds the future of the controversial inquiry he has been conducting for the past two years into the possible existence of a deliberate police "shoot-to-kill" policy in Northern Ireland.

Stalker's attempts to clarify the deaths of various IRA suspects have frequently brought him into conflict with the Royal Ulster Constabulary. He is believed to have been on the verge of significant discoveries in May when he was sent on indefinite leave (→19/12).

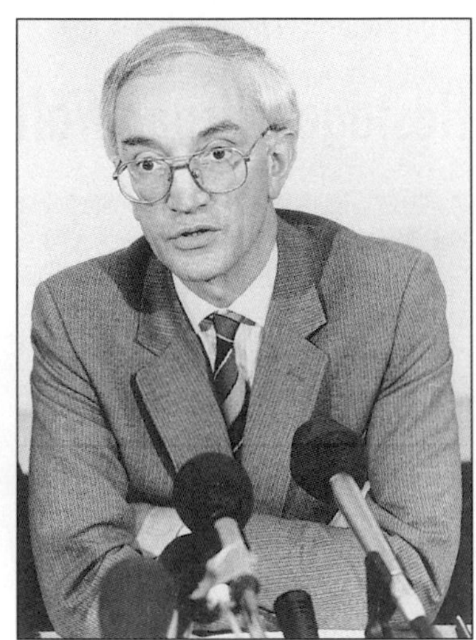

John Stalker: policy investigation.

Moore, poet of the human figure, dies

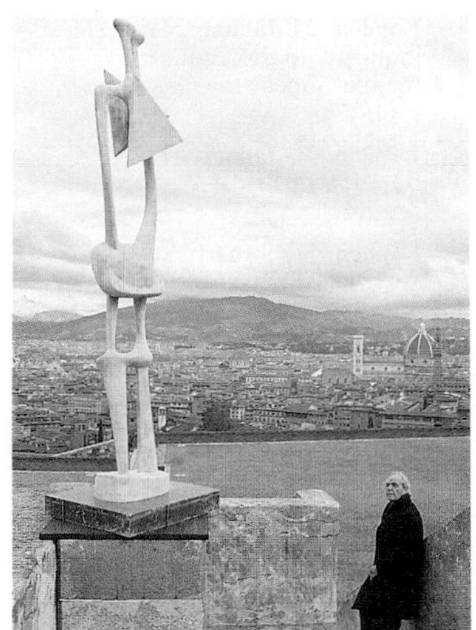

Henry Moore: international fame.

Hertfordshire, 31 August
Henry Moore, the sculptor who has the biggest international reputation of any living British artist, died today at his home in the village of Much Hadham.

Born a Yorkshire miner's son, he carved directly in stone and enjoyed what he called the "hard navvying" involved. He sought inspiration not from Graeco-Roman sculpture but from primitive, particularly Mexican, art, which suggested the theme of the reclining figure which he explored all his life. He sometimes set his works in the open landscape. His drawings of people sleeping in the London Underground during the Blitz first made him popular.

"Big Bang": new technology comes to the floor of the Stock Exchange.

Rich pickings for 'Yuppies' in City boom

London, 27 October
"Big Bang" day, marking the wholesale deregulation of London's many interlocking financial markets, started with a damp squib. The £20 million of new stock-market computers broke down under the early flood of orders.

But that failure, which was quickly corrected, only momentarily obscured the extent of the revolution undergone by the City. From a network of small, gentlemanly firms and partnerships, where the wealth enjoyed by the favoured participants was protected by a centuries-old system of price-fixing agreements and cartels, it has become overnight an international casino where many of the world's most astute (and highly paid) brains compete for profits.

In preparation for this opportunity, a formidable roster of international banks and brokerage firms has set up shop in Britain, often paying astronomical sums in both salaries and purchase fees to buy the way in. The resulting proliferation of bright young people earning six- and even seven-figure salaries has necessitated a new collective noun: these "Yuppies" (from the acronym YUP – Young Urban Professional) now confidently expect to rule the world.

1987

London, 9 January. Ernest Saunders resigns as the chief executive of Guinness (→ 21).

London, 21 January. The DTI inquiry into the Guinness scandal shocks the City (→ 17/7).

London, 30 January. The flotation of British Airways begins.

London, 5 February. SOGAT calls off its picket of Rupert Murdoch's Wapping plant.

Dublin, 10 March. Charles Haughey is elected as prime minister for the third time (→ 7/1989).

Co Armagh, 8 May. Eight IRA men die when an attack on an RUC post in Loughgall fails (→ 8/11).

London, 12 June. Princess Anne is given the title "princess royal" (→ 31/8/89).

Britain, 18 June. Unemployment figures fall below three million.

London, 17 July. Ernest Saunders, a former director of Guinness, is ordered to repay £5 million to Guinness (→ 13/10).

Paris, 26 July. The Tour de France is won by the Irish cyclist Stephen Roche.

Edinburgh, 28 July. Nick Faldo wins the Open golf championship at Muirfield (→ 27/9).

Westminster, 6 August. The SDP votes to merge with the Liberal Party; Dr David Owen resigns as SDP leader (→ 27/8).

Britain, 10 August. The latest figures reveal that one person dies of Aids every day (→ 11/1/90).

Westminster, 27 August. The Scottish MP Robert Maclennan is the new leader of the SDP (→ 23/1/88).

Ohio, 27 September. The US fail to regain golf's Ryder Cup at Muirfield Village.

London, 13 October. Gerald Ronson, the director of Heron, is charged with the theft of £6 million from Guinness (→ 15).

London, 15 October. Roger Seelig, a Morgan Grenfell director, is arrested for stealing £2.95 million from Guinness (→ 28/8/90).

Birmingham, 5 December. David Barber, the seven-week-old baby whose hole-in-the-heart operation 11 days ago caused a furore in the NHS, dies.

Car ferry sinks; 200 die

Zeebrugge, Belgium, 6 March
Disaster was inevitable when the bow doors of a car ferry were left open, allowing the sea to flood into the car deck as the ship left this Belgian port tonight. The *Herald of Free Enterprise* rolled over and sank, drowning 200 passengers and crew in the North Sea.

Disaster came so swiftly that there was no time for a "Mayday" distress call to be sent out, but Dutch and Belgian helicopters were swiftly on the scene, plucking many passengers from the sea. Survivors told of horror and heroism as victims clung to fixed furniture before slipping into the water; of selfless acts of courage by the crew; and of a man who formed a human bridge to allow passengers to climb to safety through broken windows.

Rescue workers search for survivors.

Hostage-rescuer Waite is seized in Beirut

Fears are growing for the safety of Terry Waite, the archbishop's envoy.

Beirut, 21 January
Terry Waite, the archbishop of Canterbury's special representative in Lebanon, failed to return from a mission to rescue hostages here today and is now believed to be a hostage himself. The tall, bearded Waite dismissed his Druze escorts before setting off to negotiate with Hezbollah ("the Party of God") which is thought to be holding the hostages. He insisted that he was safe and would be taken to see Westerners being held prisoners.

The Druze are concerned for his safety. Their leader, Walid Jumblatt, has contacted the Shia Moslems asking for news. With no sign of Waite's return, most Western observers are convinced that Waite is now a "star hostage".

More knowledgeable experts believe that Waite's name is tainted in the Middle East by his involvement in the "Irangate" affair. In Hezbollah thought he is associated with Colonel Oliver North and the CIA, and more than likely he is being held, like the other hostages, in a terrorist cell in the teeming downtown quarter of this war-torn and divided city (→ 30/8/90).

Thatcher is elected for her third term

Westminster, 12 June
Margaret Thatcher has become the first prime minister this century to win three successive general elections. Despite some jitters, and a glitzy campaign by Neil Kinnock's red-rose-wearing Labour Party, the Conservatives yesterday won an overall majority of 100. The final results: Conservatives 375, Labour 229, Alliance 22, Nationalists 6, Others 18. One consolation for Kinnock is that Labour is further ahead of the Alliance, with 30.8 per cent of the votes against 22.6. David Steel, the Liberal leader, plans to call for a merger with the other half of the Alliance, the Social Democrats led by David Owen (→ 6/8).

U2 recalls the glory days of British rock

United States, April
The Dublin-based band U2 has scaled another rock-music peak by appearing on the cover of *Time* this month, an accolade shared only with the Beatles and The Who.

Gone are the heady days of the Sixties when British bands dominated the American charts, although three years ago the English seemed back on top when Culture Club, Duran Duran and The Police all received Grammy Awards.

Two years ago the baton of acclaim crossed the Irish Sea when *Rolling Stone* hailed U2 as "the band of the eighties".

Dublin's greatest export: U2.

'Black Monday' hits the financial world

London, 19 October
London's Stock Exchange reeled under a tidal wave of selling today as more than £50 billion was wiped off the value of shares in publicly quoted companies. Selling continued from the moment that dealers reached their desks at 7am today, and the Exchange was still in tumult at the close.

London's disastrous day echoed a similar panic on Wall Street last Friday and heavy selling in Tokyo. The Hong Kong market is to remain closed all week. In New York, the Dow Jones industrial average fell 508 points to 1,739, wiping 22.5 per cent off share values. The fall was almost double that experienced on the first day of the great crash of 1929 and was described by the chairman, John Phelan, as "the nearest thing to a financial meltdown I've ever come across."

The crash is blamed on the United States budget, trade deficits, rising interest rates and computerized "program trading".

England lashed by worst storm of century

The morning after the storm the full extent of the damage can be seen.

Southern England, 16 October
A full-scale hurricane hit southern England today, killing at least 17 people and leaving a swathe of damage and destruction from Dorset to East Anglia. Damage is estimated at £300 million: roads and railway lines have been blocked by countless fallen trees, hotels and houses have collapsed, and thousands of homes are without power and likely to remain so for days. In London, the hospital casualty wards were crowded with victims of flying debris; the fire brigade dealt with 6,000 emergency calls, and Kew Gardens lost a third of its trees. The meteorological office is under fire for having failed to predict the extraordinary storm. Only hours before the disaster hit the country, a TV forecaster laughed off what turned out to be an accurate prediction by an anxious viewer.

IRA bombers blast Armistice parade

Co Fermanagh, 8 November
The IRA exploded a huge bomb in a disused school at Enniskillen this morning, killing 11 people as they assembled for the annual Armistice day parade. A further 63 were injured, several critically. A claim by the IRA that the army triggered off the bomb with a scanning device was dismissed contemptuously by the Northern Ireland secretary, Tom King. Gordon Wilson, aged 60, was buried under the rubble with his daughter Marie. Father and daughter held hands, but Marie died five hours after being freed. Even so, her father was prepared to forgive her killers. "I shall pray for those people," he said (→28/1/88).

Enniskillen mourns its dead.

North-south divide widens as southern house prices soar sky high

London, 24 September
Never was the "north-south divide" in Britain better demonstrated than in a review of house prices published today showing that the price of a typical semi-detached house in London has leapt by 26.8 per cent – £53 a day – in the past year. Such is the escalation in property values that any northerner or midlander finding work in London will need a pay rise of at least 25 per cent to maintain living standards.

House prices in London now cost five and a half times salaries; in the midlands two and a half; in the north two and a third. Some hard-pressed southerners are now commuting to London from newly bought homes in the north.

Gunman runs amok in Berkshire town

Berkshire, 20 August
Bearing an automatic rifle and other weapons from his collection, Michael Ryan, aged 27, walked almost casually through the sleepy market town of Hungerford today, leaving 14 people dead and 15 wounded before, cornered by police in his old school, he shot himself.

Ryan's orgy of slaughter began in nearby Savernake Forest, where he shot a woman who was with her two children. He drove home and shot his mother and set light to their home before he set out again on foot, killing indiscriminately – anyone who came in his sights.

Thirty killed in an horrific Underground blaze at King's Cross

The horrifying reality of the fire damage is seen at King's Cross Underground.

London, 18 November
Commuters heading home for the weekend were engulfed in a blazing inferno when a flash fire ripped through King's Cross tube station tonight, killing 30 people. The ferocity of the blaze was such that only seven survivors were treated in nearby University College hospital for severe flash burns.

The fire began on a wooden escalator which carried travellers into the blazing ticket hall. An accumulation of inflammable fluff under the escalator is being blamed, together with staff cuts and poor training. Despite a previous recommendation, no sprinkler system is in operation at King's Cross.

1988

Manchester, 7 January. Nurses go on strike for more pay (→ 21/4).

Westminster, 23 January. David Steel, the Liberal Party leader, announces that he will not stand for leadership of the merged Liberal/SDP (→ 28/7).

London, 28 January. The Old Bailey rejects an appeal by six Irishmen convicted of the 1974 Birmingham pub bombings (→ 7/3).

Channel Ports, 4 February. An all-out ferry strike brings chaos to British ports (→ 15/3).

Switzerland, 10 March. The Prince of Wales escapes death when his ski-ing party is hit by an avalanche (→ 28/10).

Dover, 15 March. P&O European Ferries announces that 2,300 striking Dover seamen will lose their jobs.

Belfast, 16 March. Three people die and 50 are wounded when a loyalist gunman fires on an IRA funeral (→ 19).

Belfast, 19 March. Two British soldiers are lynched and killed by members of an IRA funeral cortège (→ 20/8).

Westminster, 21 April. Nurses are offered pay rises averaging 15 per cent.

Liverpool, 26 May. The Tate Gallery opens a new wing in the renovated Albert Dock.

London, 5 July. The Church of England votes to go ahead with the ordination of women (→ 1/8).

London, 16 July. Thousands of fans turn out at Wembley for Michael Jackson's sell-out tour.

Westminster, 28 July. Paddy Ashdown, a former Royal Marine commando, is the new leader of the Social and Liberal Democrats (→ 26/10/89).

Northern Ireland, 20 August. Six British soldiers die when a landmine explodes their bus (→ 13/12).

Britain, 7 September. Almost all sorting offices have ceased work in the postal strike.

Ireland, 13 December. Irish officials refuse to extradite Patrick Ryan, the priest accused of terrorism, on the grounds that he would not get a fair trial (→ 20/3/89).

Westminster, 16 December. Edwina Currie, the junior health minister who said that all egg production was infected with salmonella, resigns.→

IRA bomb trio gunned down by SAS team

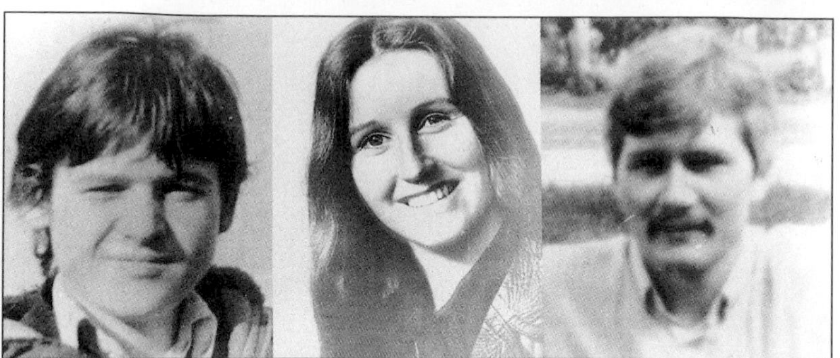

Sean Savage (l), Mairéad Farrell (c) and Danny McCann: all shot dead.

Gibraltar, 7 March 1988
Three well-known IRA terrorists, Sean Savage, Danny McCann and Mairéad Farrell, were shot dead here today by undercover SAS men. The three, admitted by the IRA in Belfast tonight to be an "active service unit", had been trailed across the Spanish border, and it is believed that they were planning to bomb the Changing of the Guard ceremony, which is watched by large crowds. In the House of Commons, Sir Geoffrey Howe, the foreign secretary, said that when the three were challenged "they made movements which led the military personnel operating in support of the Gibraltar police to conclude that their own lives and the lives of others were under threat. In the light of this response, they were shot dead." This version is disputed by some eye-witnesses of the event, who say that the SAS men opened fire without warning (→ 16).

Death toll mounts to 150 in oil rig blaze

North Sea, 6 July
It is feared that more than 150 men died tonight when the Piper Alpha oil rig positioned 120 miles east of Wick blew up with an explosion which one survivor said was "like an atom bomb going off". Only about 70 of the rig's workers are thought to have survived the blast and the inferno which brought the sea near to boiling-point.

One man told how some gave up and waited for death while others jumped 12 metres into the scalding sea to be picked up by rescue boats, themselves in danger of bursting into flames. Many men were trapped in the crew's quarters which now lie on the seabed in a tangle of wreckage. Survivors speak of a scream of gas before the explosion.

Fires still rage on Piper Alpha.

Prince Charles slams modern architecture

London, 28 October
Prince Charles lambasted Britain's modern architects tonight in an *Omnibus* TV programme which he wrote and narrated himself. He did not pull his punches. The British library, he said, was "like an academy for secret police"; the National Theatre, like "a nuclear power station in the middle of London"; and St Paul's was surrounded by a "jostling scrum of skyscrapers". He said that he had discovered on his travels that many people are "appalled by what we have done to so many of our towns since the war". Architects, still smarting under his description of the proposed extension to the National Gallery as a "monstrous carbuncle", will take no comfort from this new attack, although laymen might.

Licensing laws give drinkers more time

London, 20 May
There will be celebratory drinks for those who hate to hear a landlord call "time, gentlemen, please", for under the Licensing Act, which received the royal assent today, 65,000 pubs in England and Wales will be able to stay open from 11am to 11pm on weekdays, with more restricted hours on Sundays. How many pubs will take advantage of the new freedom remains to be seen. Many publicans are unhappy at the thought of all the extra wages they will have to pay to keep their houses open for such long hours.

Physicist interprets the 'History of Time'

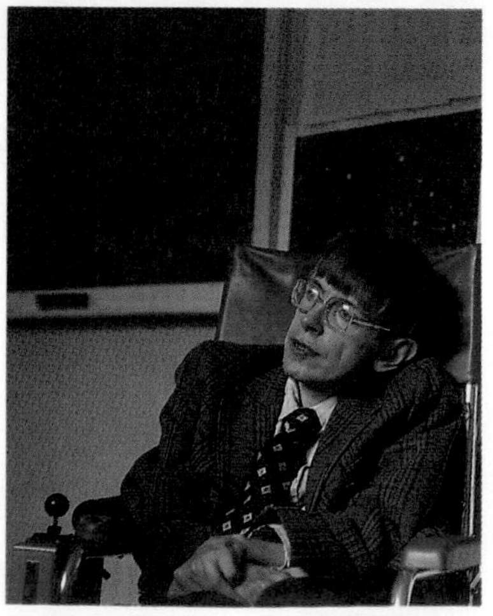

Stephen Hawking: time historian.

Cambridge, 31 December
Stephen Hawking, possibly the greatest physicist since Einstein, has seen his layman's guide to the mystery of time and the universe top the non-fiction bestseller list every week since it was published. This is despite the fact that *A Brief History of Time* is no easy reading. Dr Hawking, who is 46, is professor of mathematics at Cambridge University. For the last 20 years he has been confined to a wheelchair by motor neurone disease. He lectures, dictates and converses by means of a computer with synthetic voice operated by two fingers of one hand – all that he can move.

Anglicans debate women bishops

London, 1 August
The bitterness and confusion which persists among Anglicans over the position of women within the church was demonstrated by two contrary votes at the Lambeth conference today. The assembled bishops first agreed overwhelmingly, by 423 votes to 28, that the consecration of women as bishops could not be prevented. But the archbishop of Sydney then found much support for another motion arguing that it would "destroy our unity" and "the credibility of the office of bishop". He lost by 277 to 187, but his supporters point out that if the votes of the American delegation are discounted a majority of bishops in the rest of the world is against the consecration of women.

Edwina quits with egg on her face

Westminster, 16 December
Edwina Currie, the junior health minister, resigned today after two weeks of controversy caused by her claim that most British eggs are infected with salmonella. Egg sales plummeted, flocks were slaughtered and farmers outraged. Today she bowed to the storm and left; it had been one rumpus too far for a controversial politician. As a health minister she had said that northerners died of "ignorance and crisps" and that cervical cancer was the result of being too sexually active – "nuns don't get it," she said.

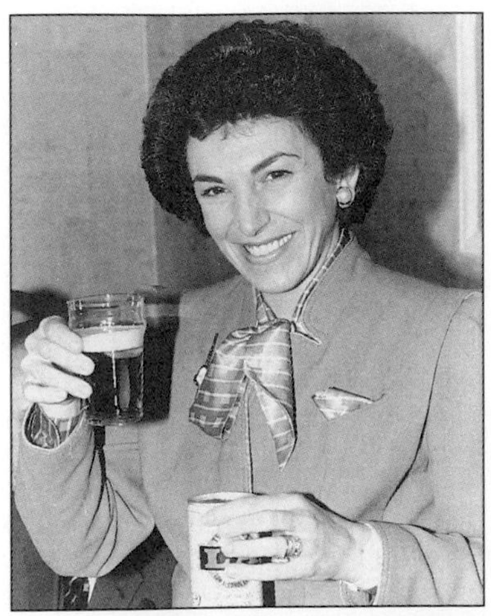

Outspoken Edwina is forced to quit.

Pan Am jet disaster over Lockerbie

Dumfries and Galloway, 22 Dec
A Pan American jumbo jet blew up in mid-air last night, raining debris on a swathe of border country. The fuselage crashed into the heart of the quiet market town of Lockerbie, vaporizing several houses and gutting others. All 259 passengers and crew died, along with 11 people on the ground. Shocked citizens spoke of a fireball falling from the sky. "The whole sky lit up and it was virtually raining fire," said one, Mike Carnahan.

Flight 103 had originated in Frankfurt, and after stopping at Heathrow was on its way to New York. Most of the passengers were Americans, among them servicemen and 38 students from Syracuse University, flying home to join their families for Christmas.

There has been no official explanation yet for the tragedy, but the suddenness of the catastrophic break-up of an aircraft as strong as a Boeing 747 – it simply vanished from the radar screens – points to sabotage by bomb. Ever since the US cruiser *Vincennes* mistakenly shot down an Iranian Airbus last July killing 286 people, a revenge attack has been feared and expected. It has emerged that US embassies had been warned that a Pan Am flight could be the target for a terrorist bomb attack.

Lockerbie surveys the damage and loss of life after last night's horrific plane crash over the town. All that remains of one street is a huge charred crater.

National curriculum imposed in schools

Westminster, 29 July
Schools in England and Wales face their biggest shake-up since the 1944 Education Act. Under the Education Reform Bill which received the royal assent today a national curriculum will be laid down for all state schools detailing not only which subjects must be taught but also the elements within those subjects. The new curriculum will be introduced progressively over the next few years and will be backed by attainment targets and regular testing for children at the ages of seven, 11, 14 and 16. This represents an unprecedented shift towards centralized power in education, away from the classroom and local authorities.

The role of local education authorities is certainly under attack with provision for schools to opt out of councils' control. Ministers see this power – to be decided by parental ballot – as a counter to what they regard as the "loony left" policies of Labour councils. Similar opting-out provisions are to be introduced in Scotland.

Train crash tragedy at Clapham Junction

Rescue workers battle to free trapped passengers from the twisted wreckage.

London, 12 December
Two trains packed with rush-hour commuters ran into each other this morning at Clapham Junction, the world's busiest junction. Seconds later an empty train piled into the wreckage, and only instant reaction by a guard stopped a fourth train adding to the carnage of Britain's worst railway disaster for more than 20 years. The death toll has reached 36, and more than a hundred are injured. Rescue workers had to prise the mangled trains apart to get to trapped passengers. Doctors crawled through wreckage administering transfusions and painkillers to the injured until they could be cut free.

Signal failure seems to have been the cause of the tragedy. British Rail admits: "The fail-safe mechanism did not work." There is to be a public inquiry.

1989

England, 11 January. It emerges that the pilot of the Boeing 737 which crashed in the midlands two days ago shut down the wrong engine.

London, 8 March. The proposed Channel tunnel rail route through south London and Kent causes angry protests (→ 31/10).

Belfast, 20 March. The IRA kills two RUC officers (→ 22/9).

Dunoon, Strathclyde, 14 April. Kelly Lynch, aged 11, is savaged to death by two pet rottweilers.

Brussels, 29 April. Fourteen Liverpool fans get jail sentences for their part in the 1985 Heysel stadium disaster.

London, 24 May. Sonia Sutcliffe, the wife of "the Yorkshire ripper" Peter Sutcliffe, wins record libel damages of £600,000 against *Private Eye*.

London, 28 June. A second national one-day rail strike coincides with a shutdown of London Underground (→ 24/7).

Britain, 24 July. Rail workers accept a pay offer and call off their one-day strikes.

England, 4 August. A report on the recent Hillsborough tragedy blames the police.

Birmingham, 14 August. The West Midlands serious crimes squad is disbanded on allegations of corruption.

Britain, 13 September. Ambulance staff ban overtime in a pay dispute (→ 23/10).

Deal, Kent, 22 September. An IRA bomb kills ten Royal Marine bandsmen (→ 8/10).

Belfast, 8 October. At least 28 UDR members are held in connection with leaks about republican suspects (→ 26).

West Germany, 26 October. The IRA kills an RAF corporal and his child (→ 28/5/90).

London, 31 October. Plans for a new rail link to the Channel tunnel are shelved.

Westminster, 21 November. Proceedings in the House of Commons are televised for the first time.

Britain, 21 November. Ambulance crews ban all work but accidents and emergencies (→ 13/1/90).

Westminster, 22 December. The government splits over a plan to admit 250,000 Hong Kong citizens to the UK.

Thirty die when jet hits motorway just short of the airport

The wreckage of the Boeing 737.

Leicestershire, 9 January

Motorists on the M1 watched terrified tonight as a Boeing 737 airliner smashed into an embankment, scattering burning debris across three lanes. The crash took place near the village of Kegworth, between Nottingham and Leicester.

The new British Midland plane, on a flight from Heathrow to Belfast, had already reported engine difficulties and was heading for an emergency landing at East Midlands airport. At least 30 of the 125 passengers and crew have died, but 70 have been rescued, some after being trapped for two hours (→ 11).

Death threat to Rushdie

Tehran, 14 February

The execution of a British author, Salman Rushdie, was ordered here today by the Iranian leader Ayatollah Khomeini. In a radio broadcast he declared: "I inform the proud Moslem people of the world that the author of *The Satanic Verses* book, which is against Islam, the Prophet and the Koran, and all those involved in its publication who were aware of its content, are sentenced to death."

The novel, published last year, has sold 40,000 copies and been publicly burnt in Britain at large rallies, and last weekend five people died in a demonstration against it in Pakistan. Its title refers to verses cut from the Koran by the Prophet as Satan-inspired; in one, prostitutes play out a fantasy that they are the Prophet's wives.

Rushdie, a Booker prize-winner who was born in India but lives in Britain, said: "It is not true that this book is a blasphemy against Islam. I doubt very much that Khomeini has read it. It concerns the struggle between the secular and the religious views of life." He is seeking police protection.

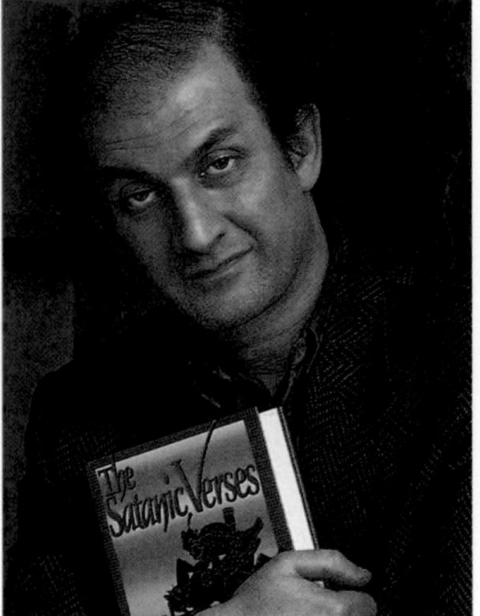

A death threat hangs over Rushdie.

Thousands of Scots fail to pay 'poll tax'

Strathclyde, 20 September

The community charge is meeting severe problems in Scotland. Today almost 300,000 people in the large Strathclyde region were said not to have paid it. The "poll tax" was introduced here, but not in England and Wales, in April. In Glasgow almost almost one in three adults are in arrears. These difficulties with a tax championed by Margaret Thatcher in the face of widespread opposition are a source of glee for the Scottish Nationalists and other political opponents. But Labour's Scottish spokesman, Donald Dewar, scorned the idea that the defaulters were "a determined army marching in support of a non-payment campaign". They were, he said "the victims of circumstance, oppressed by poverty" (→ 2/3/90).

Pact helps Haughey to survive again

Dublin, July

Charles Haughey has finally been elected prime minister, with the support of the Progressive Democrats, and his Fianna Fáil party has entered into its first coalition government. The results of the election held on 15 June had been inconclusive, with no one party able to form a government. Mr Haughey, having failed for the fifth time to gain an overall majority, was unwillingly forced into coalition discussions with the Progressive Democrats, a party led by Fianna Fáil dissidents (→ 9/11/90).

Lives at risk as ambulance crews strike

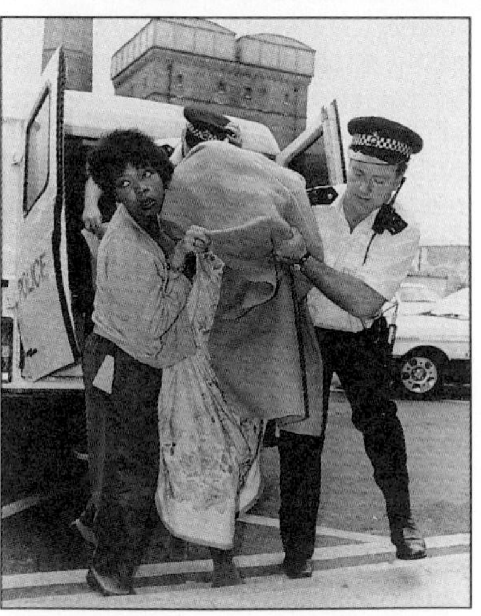

Police take over as ambulance men.

London, 23 October

Londoners calling for an ambulance are likely to get the police from today. This morning ambulance crews began a work-to-rule in support of a pay claim, and management promptly stopped their pay and declared them "off duty".

The union accused the management of being intimidated by the government, while the management claims that the crews are in breach of contract. Both sides say that they want talks before someone dies. Although the police are supported by the Red Cross and St John's Ambulance Brigade, their equipment and training are vastly inferior (→ 21/11).

Disaster hits FA Cup semi-final

Sheffield, 15 April
The city of Liverpool is in deep mourning tonight after the death of 94 Liverpool football fans, one aged only ten, in Britain's worst-ever sporting disaster. The tragedy happened at an FA Cup semi-final between Liverpool and Nottingham Forest when the police ordered one of the gates of the Hillsborough stadium in Sheffield to be opened to allow more Liverpool fans onto terraces that were already packed. As they rushed in those at the front were crushed; as well as the dead, 170 were injured.

One shocked supporter, Wayne Adams, aged 17, said: "I realized it was serious when I saw one of the lasses standing near me just turn blue. She went down. She was dead. That was it." Badly injured supporters were passed over the fence to the pitch; some lucky ones scrambled to safety on the balcony above.

Within minutes play had stopped, and the pitch became like a battlefield with police, ambulancemen and fans working frantically to revive the dying and cope with countless broken arms and legs. Nottingham and Liverpool supporters alike willed the rescuers on. Applause broke out as a man seemed to stir as he was given the kiss of life while an ambulanceman pummelled his heart, but it died away as his head sagged in death (→4/8).

Some fans are hauled to safety and escape the desperate crush which follows.

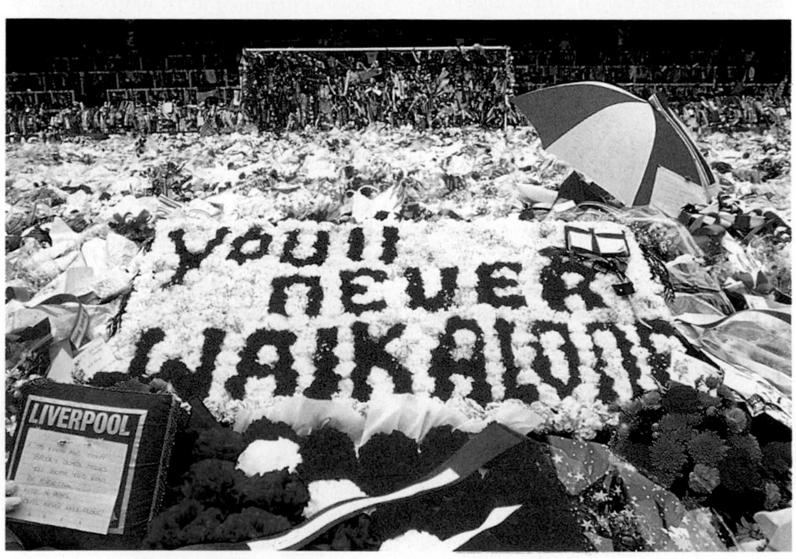

Over two million pay their respects at Anfield in a week of mourning.

Lawson resigns in a bitter public clash with prime minister

Westminster, 26 October
Nigel Lawson tonight resigned as chancellor of the exchequer after a day of drama at Westminster. The man whom Margaret Thatcher had called her "brilliant" and "unassailable" chancellor walked out after two confrontations with the prime minister at Downing Street.

In the morning Lawson told her that his position was being undermined by sniping from Sir Alan Walters, her personal economic adviser. Sack him or I go, Lawson warned. Mrs Thatcher answered questions in the House of Commons in the afternoon about Sir Alan's position, but pointedly declined to disown Sir Alan's criticisms of her chancellor.

It was the final straw for the chancellor, who, after seeing the prime minister once more, handed in his resignation. "Successful conduct of economic policy is possible only if there is full agreement between the prime minister and the chancellor of the exchequer," says Lawson in his letter of resignation, with the obvious implication that this was not so with Mrs Thatcher. The two had disagreed in particular over Lawson's support for Britain joining the European monetary system as soon as possible.

Revellers drown on Thames river boat

London, 20 August
An all-night birthday party on a Thames pleasure boat ended in tragedy in the early hours of this morning, with at least 26 drowned.

It was just before 2am when the 90-tonne pleasure cruiser *Marchioness* was hit by an 1,880-tonne ocean-going dredger, the *Bowbelle*, and sank within seconds. "It was like a tank running over a mini" said Ken Dwan, a director of the owners of the *Marchioness*.

There were about 150 fashionable young people on the boat – photographers, models and City workers; so far 76 of them are known to have survived, but the final death toll could top 60.

Free after 14 years: 'the Guildford Four' walk away from prison

London, 19 October
Four alleged terrorists, found guilty in 1975 of a pub bombing in Guildford, had their convictions overturned by the court of appeal today on the grounds that the evidence against them had been based on police lies and fabricated confessions.

Known as "the Guildford Four", Gerard Conlon, aged 35, Carole Richardson, aged 32, Patrick Armstrong, aged 39, and Paul Hill, aged 35, had been the focus of a lengthy campaign. In January the appeal court was ordered to review their convictions, and in May inquiries by the Avon and Somerset police showed that detectives had tampered with evidence. Another bombing case – that of the Maguires – also involves dubious evidence.

Gerard Conlon, free after 14 years, raises a fist to the ecstatic crowd.

1990

Westminster, 9 January. The government allocates £2.2 million to research bovine spongiform encephalopathy (BSE), "mad cow disease".

Britain, 11 January. Aids claimed 1,612 victims last year (→ 11/12).

London, 13 January. Over 50,000 support the ambulance workers' strike.

Glasgow, 2 March. The Queen inaugurates the city's year as "cultural city of Europe".

London, 2 March. The borough of Wandsworth sets the lowest poll tax – £148 per head (→ 31).

Iraq, 15 March. An Iranian-born British journalist, Farzad Bazoft, is executed as a spy (→ 11/4).

Cleveland, 11 April. Customs officers at Teesport seize parts of a huge cannon bound for Iraq (→ 23/8).

London, 25 April. Parliament reduces the time limit for abortions from 28 to 24 weeks.

Netherlands, 28 May. The IRA kills two Australians, believing them to be British servicemen (→ 26/6).

Westminster, 3 June. Dr David Owen dissolves the SDP (→ 14/11).

London, 26 June. The IRA bombs the Carlton Club (→ 30/7).

Italy, 7 July. England lose 2-1 to Italy to take fourth place in the football World Cup.

East Sussex, 30 July. An IRA car bomb kills the Tory MP Ian Gow (→ 7/2/91).

London, 28 August. British troops join a multinational force against Iraq (→ 23/10).

Europe, 5 October. Britain applies to join the European exchange rate mechanism.

Iraq, 23 October. Edward Heath, a former British prime minister, secures the release of 33 British hostages (→ 22/11).

London, 22 November. Another 15,000 British troops are to be sent to the Gulf (→ 17/1/91).

Westminster, 22 November. Margaret Thatcher announces her resignation as prime minister (→ 27).

Westminster, 11 December. The government provides £42 million in compensation for 1,200 haemophiliacs infected with the Aids virus by blood transfusions.

Prison erupts in an 'explosion of evil'

Manchester, 6 April

The mutiny at Strangeways prison, now in its sixth day with prisoners still occupying two wings of the vast Victorian prison was described today by its Governor, Brendan O'Friel, as "an explosion of evil". He said that the destruction within the prison was of a magnitude hard to comprehend. Fires have been started, roof slates ripped off for use as missiles and facilities destroyed. The riot, obviously planned, erupted in the prison chapel. The rioters are protesting about overcrowding and being "banged up" for as long as 23 hours a day in their cells.

Western hostages take the centre stage as British troops move into Persian Gulf

Persian Gulf, 23 August

The build-up of troops comprising the "Desert Shield" force to combat Saddam Hussein's aggression in the Gulf is taking place slowly but surely. The Americans already have 30,000 soldiers plus aircraft in Saudi Arabia. Warships are moving into position in the Gulf. One RAF squadron of Tornadoes has arrived, and more men, ships and planes are in the pipeline.

Meanwhile Saddam is twisting and turning in his attempt to avoid conflict with the United Nations while holding on to Kuwait. His latest ploy is to appear on Baghdad television with British hostages. Describing them as his "guests", he said that they were "heroes of the peace" who would prevent a war by their presence in Iraq. Dressed in a grey civilian suit, he was all oleaginous charm as he attempted to ruffle the hair of six-year-old Stuart Lockwood and ask him if he was getting enough cornflakes. Stuart, arms folded defiantly, squirmed at the dictator's touch. Saddam appears to have thought that he could allay fears for the hostages' safety, but his handling of a frightened little boy has served only to underline their peril (→ 28).

Guinness sentences

London, 28 August

The Guinness takeover scandal ended with fines and prison sentences for three of Britain's top businessmen today. Ernest Saunders, the former chairman of the brewing company, was jailed for five years for "dishonesty on a massive scale". The stockbroker Tony Parnes, who collapsed in the dock, received 18 months. Gerald Ronson, the garage and property tycoon, was jailed for a year and fined £5 million. Sir Jack Lyons, who was also found guilty, was judged to be too ill to be sentenced today.

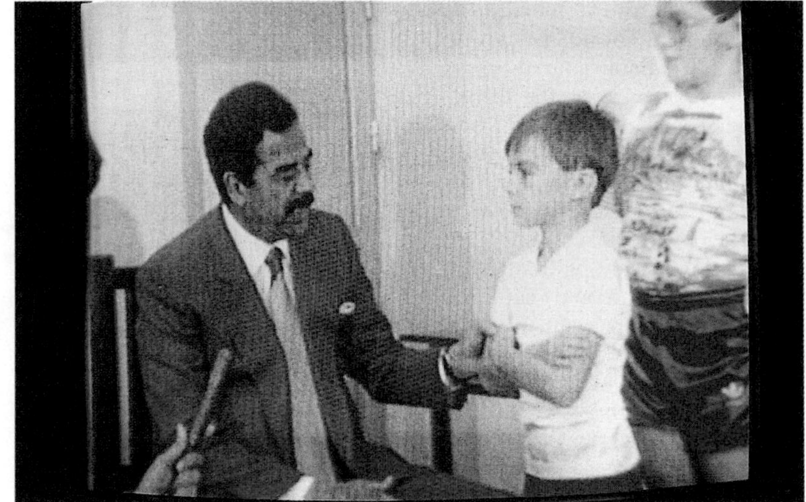

Young Stuart Lockwood shies away from Iraq's President Saddam Hussein.

Poll-tax protesters do battle with police on streets of London

Police in riot gear clash with political extremists on the poll-tax march.

London, 31 March

A full-scale riot raged through the West End last night, following a rally in Trafalgar Square by some 300,000 people protesting against the introduction of the poll tax. The demonstrators chanted: "We won't pay" and listened to the Labour MP Tony Benn call for civil disobedience to make it unworkable.

Trouble broke out when violent elements in the largely peaceful crowd clashed with the police. Cars and buildings were set on fire and shopfronts smashed, and, as mounted police dispersed the crowds, the rioting moved on to Soho where tourists were caught up in the violence, which lasted until midnight. Many people were injured, and 341 arrests were made (→ 1/3/91).

Hostile challenge ousts Thatcher as Tory leader

Howe and Heseltine take up the challenge

Turning against his team captain: Sir Geoffrey in the House of Commons.

Westminster, 14 November
Michael Heseltine today declared his intention to fight Margaret Thatcher for the leadership of the Conservative Party. His challenge came within 24 hours of an outspoken attack on the Thatcher style of government by the man who had been her longest serving cabinet minister, Sir Geoffrey Howe.

Sir Geoffrey had resigned as deputy prime minister on 1 November, and yesterday he told MPs that Mrs Thatcher had a "nightmare" vision of Europe which was running "increasingly serious risks for the future of our nation". He said that colleagues were undermined and added: "It's rather like sending your opening batsmen to the crease only for them to find, the moment the first balls are bowled, that their bats have been broken before the game by the team captain."

Heseltine cites cabinet disunity and Europe as reasons for his challenge, nearly four years after he quit the cabinet in the "Westland" crisis. He plans to make reform of the poll tax an issue (→22).

Thatcher resigns; enter Hurd and Major

Westminster, 22 November
Shortly after nine o'clock this morning Britain's first woman prime minister announced her intention to resign. "It's a funny old world," said Margaret Thatcher just two days after she had failed by only four votes to win a sufficient margin of victory over Michael Heseltine. She was attending a summit in Paris when the result of the first ballot was announced and initially signalled her determination to fight on. Frantic discussions went on all day yesterday, with a majority of cabinet colleagues saying that they no longer felt she could beat her former defence secretary. Douglas Hurd, the foreign secretary, and John Major, the chancellor, have now joined the fight for the succession (→27).

The boy from Brixton makes it to the top

Westminster, 27 November
John Major is to be Britain's next prime minister. At 47, he is the youngest this century and has had a meteoric rise; he became an MP in 1979 and only joined the cabinet three years ago. He also has an unlikely background for a Tory leader: he left school at 16, without any O-levels, and was out of work for a time in Brixton, south London, before beginning a banking career.

Major won 185 votes for the Tory leadership against 131 for Michael Heseltine and 56 for Douglas Hurd. It was two votes short of outright victory under party rules, but Heseltine said that he would withdraw in the interests of party unity, and so did Hurd (→28/6/91).

John Major, the new prime minister.

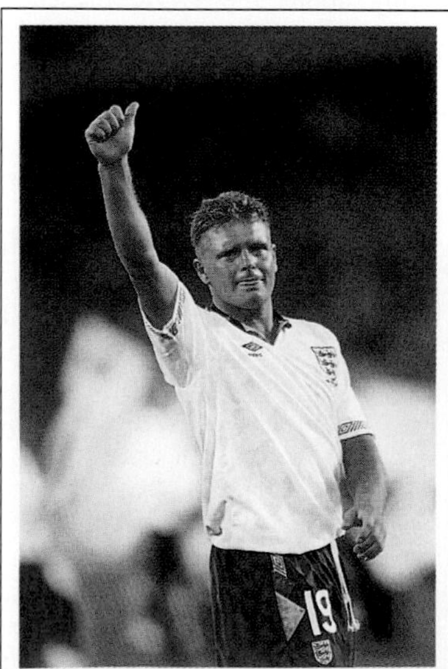

July 4. Tears of despair from Paul "Gazza" Gascoigne as England's World Cup chances are dashed when Germany win 4-3.

Hostage is freed from 'ultimate despair'

Dublin, 30 August 1990
Brian Keenan, freed after four years and four months as a hostage of Islamic Jihad terrorists in Beirut, came home to a joyous reception today bearing the news that at least one of the British hostages, John McCarthy, is alive. Keenan said that it was McCarthy's sense of humour which kept them sane.

The 39-year-old teacher, pale and haggard and on the verge of tears, gave a moving description of the ordeal he shared with his fellow captives: "Hostage is a crucifying aloneness ... it is a silent screaming slide into the bowels of ultimate despair. Hostage is a man hanging by his fingernails over the edge of chaos, feeling his fingers slowly straightening" (→19/11/91).

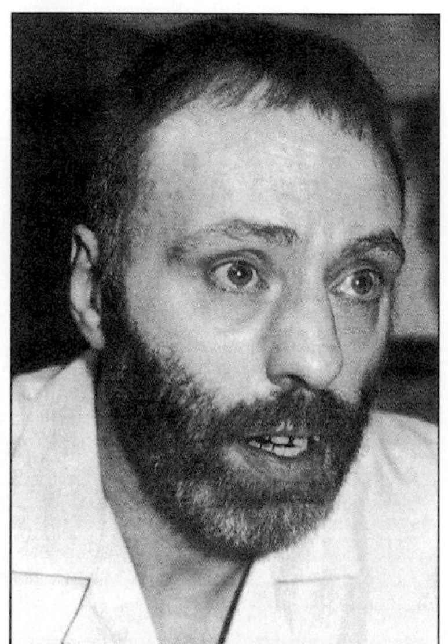

Brian Keenan: glad to be free.

Irish get their first woman president

Dublin, 9 November
Mary Robinson has become the first woman president of Ireland. A doctor's daughter from Ballina, in Co Mayo, she had a distinguished academic career and later became one of the country's best known constitutional lawyers. Elected to the senate at the age of 25, she campaigned for the introduction of family planning legislation – a controversial issue at the time.

Many people see her victory as representing the image of a new Ireland. She is seen to speak not only for women but also for minority groups and the disadvantaged, for whom much of her work as a lawyer has been carried out.

1991

Dublin, 1 January. Dublin is Europe's "city of culture".

Britain, 15 January. Over 10,000 NHS beds are prepared for Gulf War casualties.

London, 18 February. An IRA bomb at Victoria Station leaves one man dead and 43 people injured (→14/3).

London, 1 March. The lowest poll tax, £136 per head, is set by Wandsworth Council (→23).

Canterbury, 6 March. Dr George Carey is enthroned as archbishop of Canterbury.

Westminster, 23 March. The government will abandon the poll tax to win voters.

Belfast, 25 March. Unionist leaders agree to talks with the British and Irish governments (→3/6).

Luxembourg, 8 April. John Major plans to provide a "safe haven" for Kurds in Iraq.

Westminster, 21 May. The import of American pit bull terriers is banned after the latest attack.

Co Tyrone, 3 June. Three IRA terrorists are shot dead in an SAS dawn raid (→18).

Britain, 4 June. Government cuts reduce army manpower.

Leeds, 10 June. England win a home test match against the West Indies for the first time for 22 years, at Headingley.

Belfast, 18 June. The Ulster peace talks, headed by Peter Brooke, the Northern Ireland secretary, begin (→4/7).

Westminster, 28 June. Margaret Thatcher is to retire as an MP.

Belfast, 4 July. Loyalist paramilitaries call off their cease-fire as talks collapse (→17/8).

London, 5 July. The Bank of England closes the Bank of Commerce and Credit International (BCCI).

London, 17 August. The case of Judith Ward, convicted of an IRA bombing in 1974, goes to the court of appeal (→15/11).

London, 21 August. A boxer, Michael Watson, faces brain surgery; he collapsed after a world-title fight against Chris Eubank.

England, 2 November. Australia beat England 12-6 at Twickenham to win the Rugby World Cup.

Britain, 1 December. Retailers defy the Sunday trading laws.

British troops move into Gulf war zone

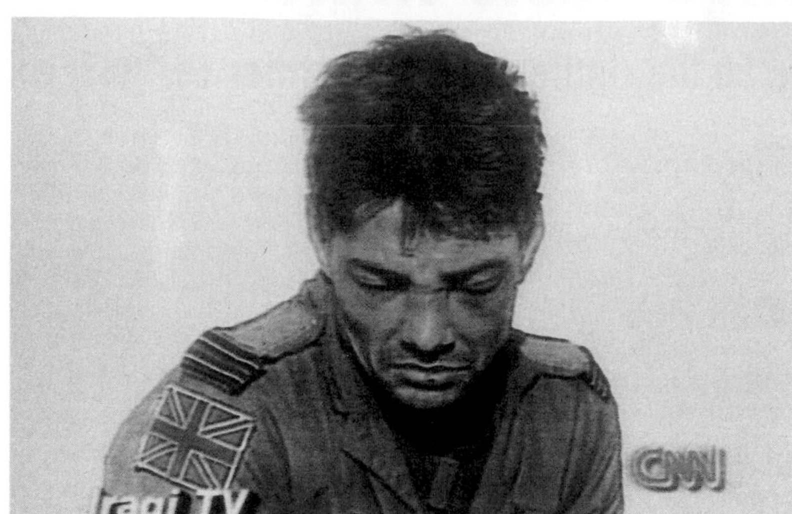

Lieutenant John Peters, a captured RAF pilot, as seen on Iraqi television.

Saudi Arabia, 17 January
The awesome power of modern weaponry was unleashed on the Iraqi capital, Baghdad, last night as the talking ended, the deadlines ran out, and Operation Desert Storm was launched with the aim of retaking Kuwait from Saddam Hussein.

A single F-117 Stealth fighter began the attack by destroying a telecommunications centre with a 2,000-lb (909-kg) "smart" bomb. This was followed by Tomahawk cruise missiles, bombers, radar-jamming planes, Wild Weasel missiles and RAF Tornadoes which made dangerous, low-level sorties against Iraqi airfields. Britain has contributed 25,000 men to the 700,000-strong Allied force, about half of which is American, as well as four warships and 60 strike aircraft. "It is a battle that must be fought," said John Major (→8/4).

'Birmingham Six' cheered as they walk free

A jubilant "Birmingham Six" greet the crowds outside the Old Bailey.

London, 14 March
For 16 years six men were imprisoned for the IRA-inspired bombing of a pub in Birmingham. Today they walked free into the arms of their ecstatic supporters after the appeal court acknowledged that they had been convicted on faulty scientific evidence and forced confessions. The release of "the Birmingham Six" – Hugh Callaghan, Richard McIlkenny, Paddy Hill, Billy Power, Gerry Hunter and Johnny Walker – has led to calls for the resignation of Lord Lane, who denied their appeal three years ago. The home secretary, Kenneth Baker, has acknowledged that this is the third gross injustice involving Irish people in 18 months (→25).

Downing Street hit by IRA mortar bomb

London, 7 February
The IRA attempted to assassinate John Major and the cabinet today when it fired a mortar bomb into the garden of No 10 Downing Street. It exploded just 12 metres from where the prime minister was chairing a war cabinet meeting.

The mortars – two others fell harmlessly 100 metres away – were fired through the roof of a white Transit van parked in Whitehall just after a man had jumped out and escaped on a motorcycle.

"I think we had better start again somewhere else," Mr Major is said to have remarked (→18).

Belfast is patrolled

Belfast, 15 November
Hundreds of extra troops have been drafted into Belfast to combat a new wave of sectarian murders. Seven people have been killed in 36 hours, prompting fears of an IRA and loyalist paramilitary tit-for-tat campaign before Christmas. Most of the loyalist murders are claimed by the outlawed Ulster Defence Association (UDA).

British troop numbers have been boosted by 300, including 100 sent from England, plus 1,400 part-time members of the Ulster Defence Regiment (UDR). Nationalists are unhappy about the UDR presence, saying that they are mistrusted by Roman Catholics and should be confined to loyalist streets.

Britain's first woman astronaut, Helen Sharman, out of orbit.

World watches as Western hostages freed

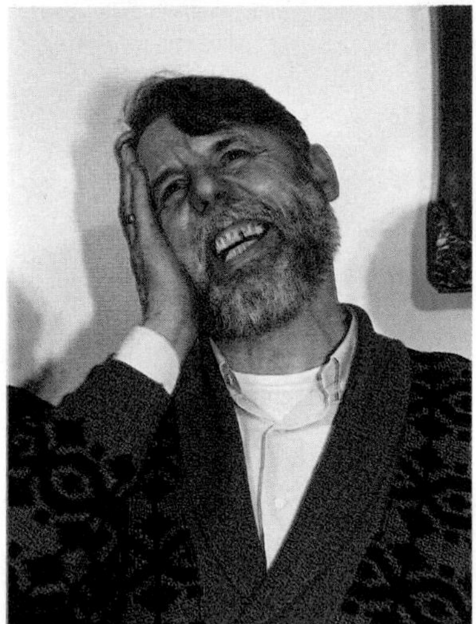

A sigh of relief as Waite is freed.

McCarthy waves: glad to be free.

Wiltshire, 19 November
A big man came home today. Five years ago Terry Waite, as special envoy for the archbishop of Canterbury, was working to free Western hostages held in Lebanon. Then he was kidnapped himself.

He limped down the plane steps at RAF Lyneham – the effect of being chained to a wall for nearly five years – but his forceful and moving account of his captivity showed that his spirit and his Christian faith were unbroken. He told of how in his darkest days he had been sustained by a postcard from an unknown well-wisher, showing a picture of an earlier imprisoned Christian – John Bunyan. Waite is the sixth hostage to be released this year since the freeing of the journalist John McCarthy (held for five years) in August. McCarthy came out with the news that Waite and others were well and a letter from the Islamic Jihad for the UN secretary, Javier Perez de Cuellar. It became clear that Israel held the key to breaking the Western hostage log-jam, since Hizbollah wanted its people out of Israeli jails.

No one is revealing the backstage deals, but gradually the hostages were freed, including the courageous Jacke Mann, a 77-year-old Spitfire pilot who survived two-and-a-half years on a chain. Three Americans are still held in Beirut, including Terry Anderson who has been there for six years.

Longest post-war recession grips UK

Britain, 19 December
A rise in German interest rates announced by the Bundesbank today was not the Christmas present which British ministers wanted. Several other European countries raised their rates in line with those of Germany, thus intensifying the pressure on sterling while making it more difficult for Britain to reduce interest rates to boost the economy.

Norman Lamont, the chancellor, has spent much of the year saying that recovery was just around the corner, and in August the Bank of England agreed that the worst of the recession was over. But recovery has proved elusive, and the current recession has now lasted longer than any other since the slump of the 1930s.

In this week alone there have been figures showing that manufacturing output fell again in October; that unemployment has risen to more than 2.5 million; and that housing repossessions, as people are unable to pay their mortgages, are expected to rise to 80,000 this year. A gloomy forecast from the previously upbeat Confederation of British Industry, and few signs of a Christmas boom in the shops, have dented hopes that consumer demand would spearhead economic recovery. Exports, too, are flagging as economic problems mount in the United States and Germany.

Indebted publisher meets watery end

DAILY Mirror

MAXWELL DIES AT SEA

THE MAN WHO SAVED THE DAILY Mirror

Publisher in yacht tragedy

A GREAT BIG EXTRAORDINARY MAN

Maxwell: the "Mirror's" hero is dead.

Canary Islands, 5 November
Did he jump or was he pushed? That is the question that may never be answered about the dead publishing tycoon Robert Maxwell, whose naked body was found today floating in the sea 20 miles south-east of Tenerife a few hours after disappearing from his luxury yacht *Lady Ghislaine*.

Those favouring suicide point to the increasing problems facing his debt-laden empire, which owes the banks an estimated £2.6 billion. Others claim that he was far too arrogant to take his own life and favour a murder scenario.

Flamboyant Freddie succumbs to Aids

London, 24 November
One of the most extravagant figures in the pop world died of Aids today. Freddie Mercury, the lead singer of Queen, was the driving force behind a band that stayed at the top throughout the 1970s and 1980s. Despite being firmly in the high-risk category for Aids, as both a bisexual and a heavy drug user, he shrugged off his alarming weight-loss of recent months and denied having Aids until yesterday.

Queen produced the first video to promote a single – *Bohemian Rhapsody* – in 1975 and embarked on a series of flamboyant tours; in 1985 it stole the show at the Live Aid concert. A bright light has gone out in the pop firmament.

Flamboyant Freddie on stage.

Major makes stand at Maastricht talks

Netherlands, 11 December
John Major, the prime minister, today hailed an agreement between European leaders as "game, set and match" for Britain. Leaders of the 12 nations in the European Community finally reached agreement on closer economic and monetary union in the early hours of today at their summit in Maastricht. Britain was allowed to defer a decision on a single currency and to opt out of a proposed "social chapter" of the treaty. But the Maastricht treaty still moves to what it calls "ever closer union" and extends central powers of the commission. It has to be ratified by each country.

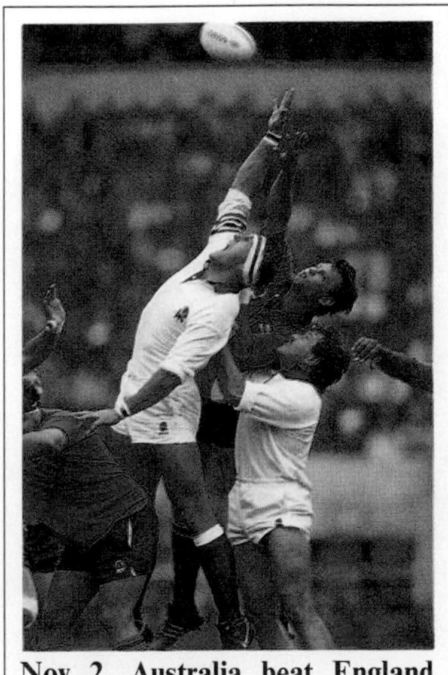

Nov 2. Australia beat England 12-6 to win the Rugby World Cup in a fiercely fought contest.

Some of the most memorable moments of 1992

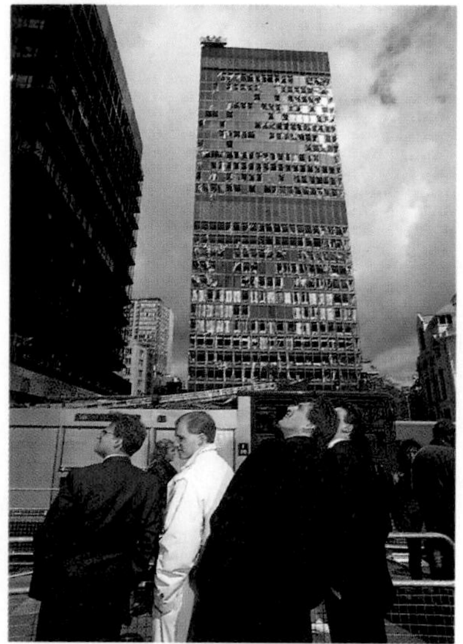

An IRA bomb explodes in the City of London, claiming three lives.

The duke and duchess of York relax before their decision to separate.

John Major, who succeeded Margaret Thatcher as prime minister in 1990, is congratulated after his return to office with a much reduced majority.

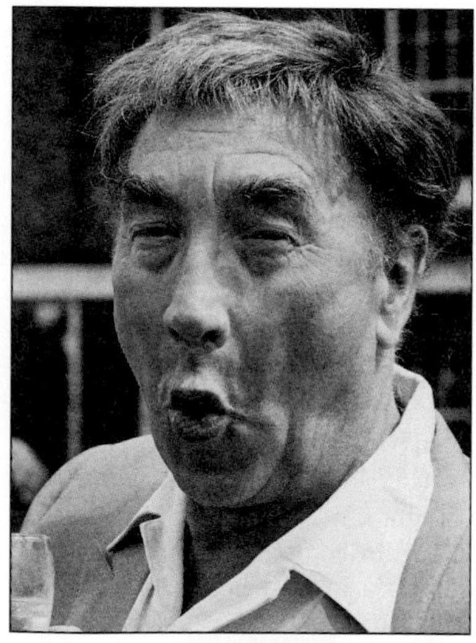

"Oooh!": catchphrase of comedian Frankie Howerd, who died in April.

Albert Reynolds, the Irish prime minister (second left), at a news conference after Ireland's vote in favour of the Maastricht treaty on European union.

Andrew Morton's book on the life of the Princess of Wales creates a stir.

Arrested for fraud: Kevin Maxwell, the son of the late tycoon, Robert.

Baroness Thatcher of Kesteven is introduced into the House of Lords.

John Smith and Margaret Beckett celebrate their election as leader and deputy leader of the Labour Party, following the resignation of Neil Kinnock.

The Prince and Princess of Wales decide to separate.

British sportsmen and women win glory

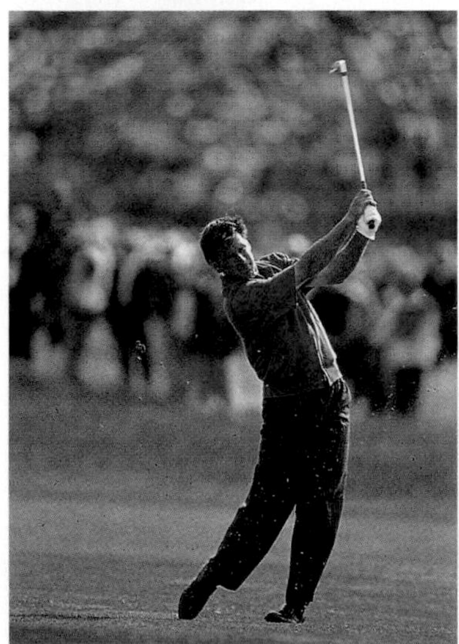

Nick Faldo triumphs at the 121st Open golf tournament at Muirfield.

Linford Christie wins Olympic gold in the 100 metres at Barcelona.

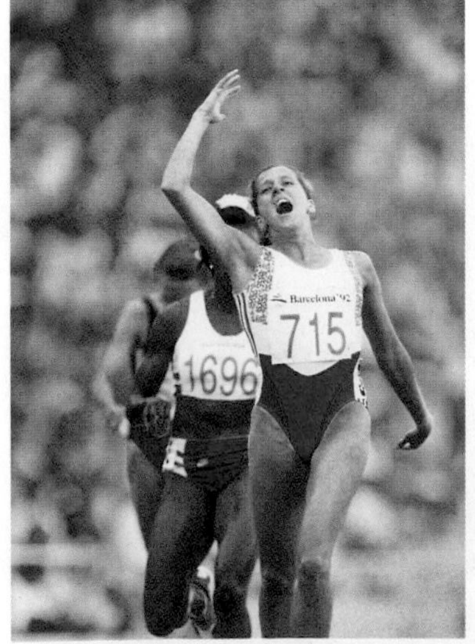

Joy for Sally Gunnell after a gold in the Olympic 400-metres hurdles.

Nigel Mansell on his way to becoming world motor-racing champion.

Debate continues to rage over closer ties with Europe as tunnel nears completion

The mighty British lion flees from the belligerent French cock: a humorous view of the fears of a possible invasion by means of a Channel tunnel.

Britain and Ireland

As the second millennium looms into view, the prospect of ever-closer links with Europe dominates the political and social agenda in Britain and Ireland. In 1993 Britain is set to see the end of several thousand years of physical isolation from the continent of Europe with the opening of the Channel tunnel, and border restrictions will be removed with the completion of the single European market.

While the fears of military invasion that attended many of the past plans for a tunnel may have receded, debate continues to rage about the future of national sovereignty within the wider European community. As opposition to the idea of a "European superstate" grows, the British and Irish governments are concerned about the fate of the 1991 Maastricht treaty on closer European union. With Britain still deep in economic recession, doubts have also arisen about the country's position in the exchange rate mechanism (ERM) of the European monetary system. Membership of the ERM restricts the freedom of national governments to stimulate their economies by adjusting interest rates, and to some this represents one more step on the road to "government from Brussels".

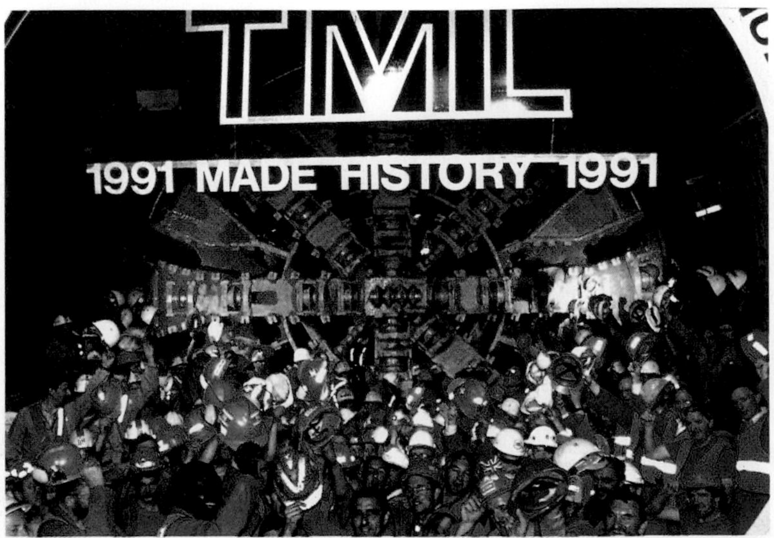

Workers celebrate as the British and French ends of the tunnel are joined.

Postwar decades reap a rich harvest in the arts

Abiding legacy of a literary generation

In the past 30 years Britain has lost the leading writers of the generation which had made its name by the Second World War. When T S Eliot died in 1965 his fame rested as much on the mystical *Four Quartets* as on the shock of *The Waste Land.* W H Auden was adding to his short colloquial poems up to his death in 1973. Robert Graves (d.1985) was the best loved poet of his time. Sir John Betjeman was made poet laureate in 1972 but then produced little before his death in 1984. Philip Larkin, who came to fame later, died the following year.

Three top novelists laid down their pens. The satirist Evelyn Waugh ended with the *Sword of Honour* trilogy about wartime Britain. His fellow-Catholic Graham Greene (d.1991), whose novels and "entertainments" were uncannily topical, produced late works like *The Honorary Consul* and *Monsignor Quixote* which dealt in religious doubt. J B Priestley (d.1984) won fame as a novelist, critic and playwright, but his best work was in essay form. Somerset Maugham (d.1965) was another novelist-dramatist but endures best in his laconic short stories. With Anthony Powell almost silent since his *Dance to the Music of Time* novel sequence, the mantle of social comedy fell on Kingsley Amis. Amis's son Martin became the *enfant terrible* among a vigorous generation of younger novelists, including Julian Barnes, William Boyd and Peter Ackroyd. Among notable women writers have been Doris Lessing, Iris Murdoch, Beryl Bainbridge and Angela Carter (d.1992).

Three authors whose readers are counted in millions also died. P G Wodehouse, who introduced Jeeves in 1919 and Blandings Castle in 1923, was still writing about them in his 90s. J R R Tolkien (d.1973) became a cult in his 70s after the publication of *The Lord of the Rings*. Agatha Christie's Hercule Poirot first appeared in 1926 and had just solved his last case when she died in 1976, the richest writer whom Britain has yet produced.

Britten in front of the Maltings, Snape: home to the Aldeburgh music festival.

Britten and Tippett at height of powers

Benjamin Britten rose to a pre-eminent position in British classical music in the decades after the war. His operas *A Midsummer Night's Dream* (1960) and *Death in Venice* (1973) were major events, and his friendship with Rostropovich produced a series of cello works. He was the first composer to be made a peer – in 1976, the year in which he died. His death left Sir Michael Tippett as the "grand old man" of British music. Tippett has produced four operas, the latest, *New Year*, when he was 85, with typical jazzlike passages. His choral work *The Mask of Time* (1984) was immediately popular.

Among the next generation, Sir Peter Maxwell Davies and Harrison Birtwhistle have been widely acclaimed. John Tavener's religious music, drawing on his experiences since his conversion to the Orthodox Church, has found an appreciative audience in the last few years.

Ashton leads Royal Ballet to success

The 1960s and 70s were golden years for the Royal Ballet under Sir Frederick Ashton, who succeeded Dame Ninette de Valois as director in 1963. He created hits like *La Fille Mal Gardée* (1960) and *The Dream* (1964) and gave new roles to Dame Margot Fonteyn as well as to Antoinette Sibley and Anthony Dowell. Sir Kenneth MacMillan took over in 1970.

In this period many young dancers dedicated themselves to modern dance. Under Robert Cohan the London Contemporary Dance Theatre, with its own school, had a good deal of success. The Ballet Rambert – formed in the 1920s by Marie Rambert – was reorganized in 1966 to concentrate primarily on modern dance. One acclaimed contemporary choreographer, Christopher Bruce, trained with the Rambert. His *Ghost Dances* (1981) examined attitudes to death in Latin America and was widely acclaimed. In recent years, the anarchic shows of Michael Clarke have won ringing praise.

Artists' uncompromising vision shows suffering of human body

The painter Francis Bacon (d.1992) achieved international repute equal to that of the sculptor Henry Moore (d.1986). Self-taught, and indifferent to honours or money, Bacon commanded astronomic prices – £3.9 million was paid for a triptych. He painted the figure hemmed in, often naked or screaming, as if violently bruised by the brush, conveying the shock of panic and helplessness. Lucian Freud conducts a similarly clinical scrutiny of the naked body in detail, but David Hockney paints the surfaces of things with carefree enjoyment.

Graham Sutherland (d.1980) was much admired for his almost malevolent portraits of the famous – Maugham, Beaverbrook, Helena Rubinstein. But his portrait of Churchill aged 80, commissioned by parliament in 1954, so preyed on the statesman's mind that Lady Churchill had it destroyed.

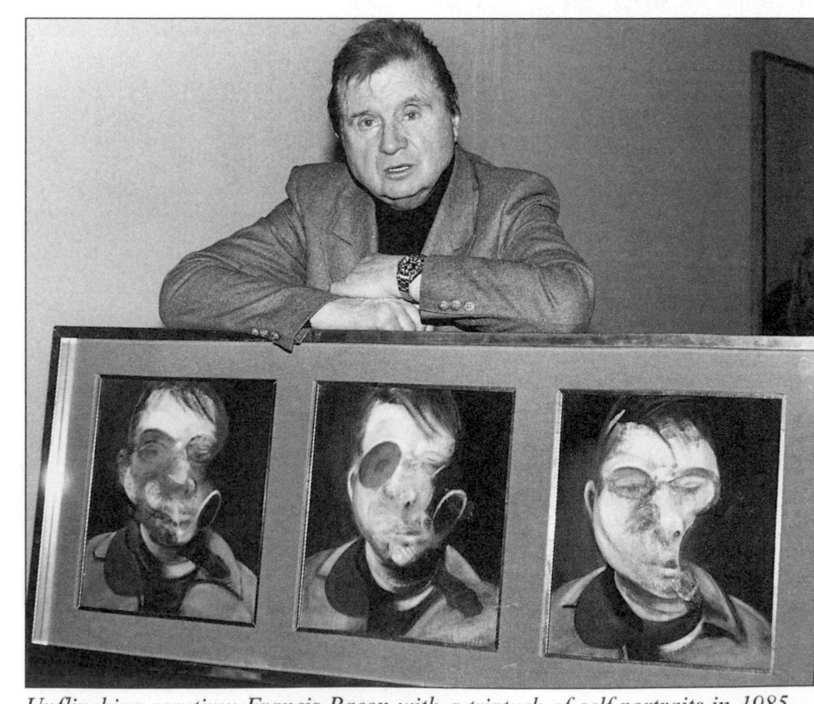

Unflinching scrutiny: Francis Bacon with a triptych of self-portraits in 1985.

From 'kitchen sink' plays to the era of high-cost musicals

The Royal Court revolution, led by John Osborne with *Look Back in Anger* and *The Entertainer* in the 1950s and *Luther* (1961), brought new talent in the 1960s: Arnold Wesker, John Arden, David Storey, Edward Bond and Joe Orton flourished there, while Peter Shaffer and Tom Stoppard were at the National theatre. The West End had annual comedies by Alan Ayckbourn, from *Relatively Speaking* (1967) to *Man of the Moment* (1990). Samuel Beckett (d.1990), the Irish dramatist, was in a class of one: *Waiting for Godot* (1955), *Endgame* (1958) and *Happy Days* (1961) are inimitable, but Harold Pinter echoed him in *The Caretaker* (1960) and *No Man's Land* (1975). Brian Friel, at Dublin's Abbey theatre, showed in *Dancing at Lughnasa* (1990) none of the exhaustion that has silenced many English playwrights.

Lloyd Webber: true star of the show.

Time put an end to an exceptional era of theatre with the deaths of Sir Noël Coward (1973), Sir Ralph Richardson (1983), Richard Burton (1984), Sir Michael Redgrave (1985) and Dame Peggy Ashcroft (1991). Sir John Gielgud's swansong was the remarkable Shakespearean film *Prospero's Books*.

From *Jesus Christ Superstar* (1976) to *Phantom of the Opera* (1986), Andrew Lloyd Webber dominated the musical. He was knighted in 1992.

Tougher British films reflect social change

English through and through: Peggy Ashcroft in "A Passage to India".

The 1960s saw British films, for once, on top. *Room at the Top* (1959) began their liberation from gentility as working-class youth, bent on sex as well as money, took over. Jack Clayton's breakthrough won Oscars, followed by Karel Reisz's *Saturday Night and Sunday Morning* (1960), Tony Richardson's *Tom Jones* (1963), Lindsay Anderson's *This Sporting Life* (1963), John Schlesinger's *Darling* (1965), *Billy Liar* and *Alfie* (Lewis Gilbert, 1967). Their quality came from raw, abrasive new stars like Richard Harris, Albert Finney, Tom Courtenay, Glenda Jackson, Julie Christie and Michael Caine.

But the boom did not outlast the US dollars that financed it. *Chariots of Fire* (1981), *Gandhi* (1983), *A Passage to India* (1985) and *A Room with a View* (1987) won Oscars, but financing British films remained as precarious as ever despite talented directors like David Lean (d.1991), Sir Richard Attenborough and James Ivory, and of Oscar-winning actors like Ben Kingsley, Dame Peggy Ashcroft (d.1991), Daniel Day-Lewis, Jeremy Irons and Anthony Hopkins.

Period dramas win British TV wide acclaim

A scene from life "downstairs".

Television drama, from the 1970s, was much devoted to the drama series, especially set in earlier, more picturesque periods of the century. *Upstairs, Downstairs* (1975) revealed the appetite for a more ordered world. Sherlock Holmes, Bertie Wooster, Hercule Poirot and Miss Marple held audiences with their period look and manners. The epics of the 1980s, *Brideshead Revisited* and *The Jewel in the Crown*, were exotic versions of English life, as was *The Darling Buds of May*. All were adapted from books. Only purpose-written TV dared be up to date: *The Boys from the Blackstuff, G B H*, the comedy series *Fawlty Towers, Yes Prime Minister, Rumpole of the Bailey* or Alan Bennett's *Talking Heads*. TV films, especially on Channel Four, gave outlets to directors like Apted, Frears, Greenaway, Jarman, Leigh and Roeg and to Peter Brook's epic *Mahabharata*.

Modern architects come under fire from a royal critic

After the orgy of development in the 1960s and 70s, with its legacy of tower-blocks, shopping centres and office slabs, the 80s brought the first twinges of doubt. The Prince of Wales, as the public's critic, struck a very popular note in his speeches and his TV programme and book *A Vision of Britain*, declaring that architects were ruining cities.

It was too late to stop the National theatre (1976), the NatWest tower (1980) and the Barbican (1982), and the Lloyds of London of Richard Rogers (1986) was exempted. But after the prince complained that a plan for the National Gallery extension was "a monstrous carbuncle on the face of a well-loved friend", the gallery acquired a quietly matching new wing. He was caustic about the new precinct planned beside St Paul's. It was replaced by a classical scheme by Terry Farrell. A huge wave of office building culminated in 1991 with Canary Wharf in Docklands. Its 240-metre tower by César Pelli sank its developers into bankruptcy at a time when London was awash with unlet office space.

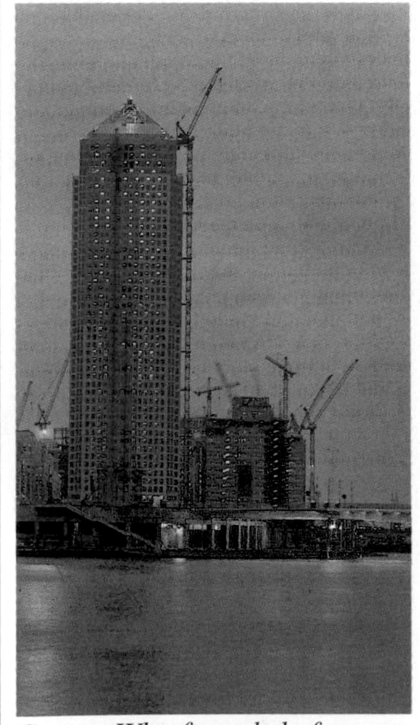

Canary Wharf: symbol of an era.

APPENDIX

* *Tables on p.1230 & 1231; graph ("Divorce: UK, 1961–89") and text on divorce on p.1231; pie chart ("Household expenditure: UK & Ireland, 1988–89") on p.1232; table ("Consumer durables: GB 1990") and text on modern spending patterns on p.1233 all © Central Statistical Office 1992.*

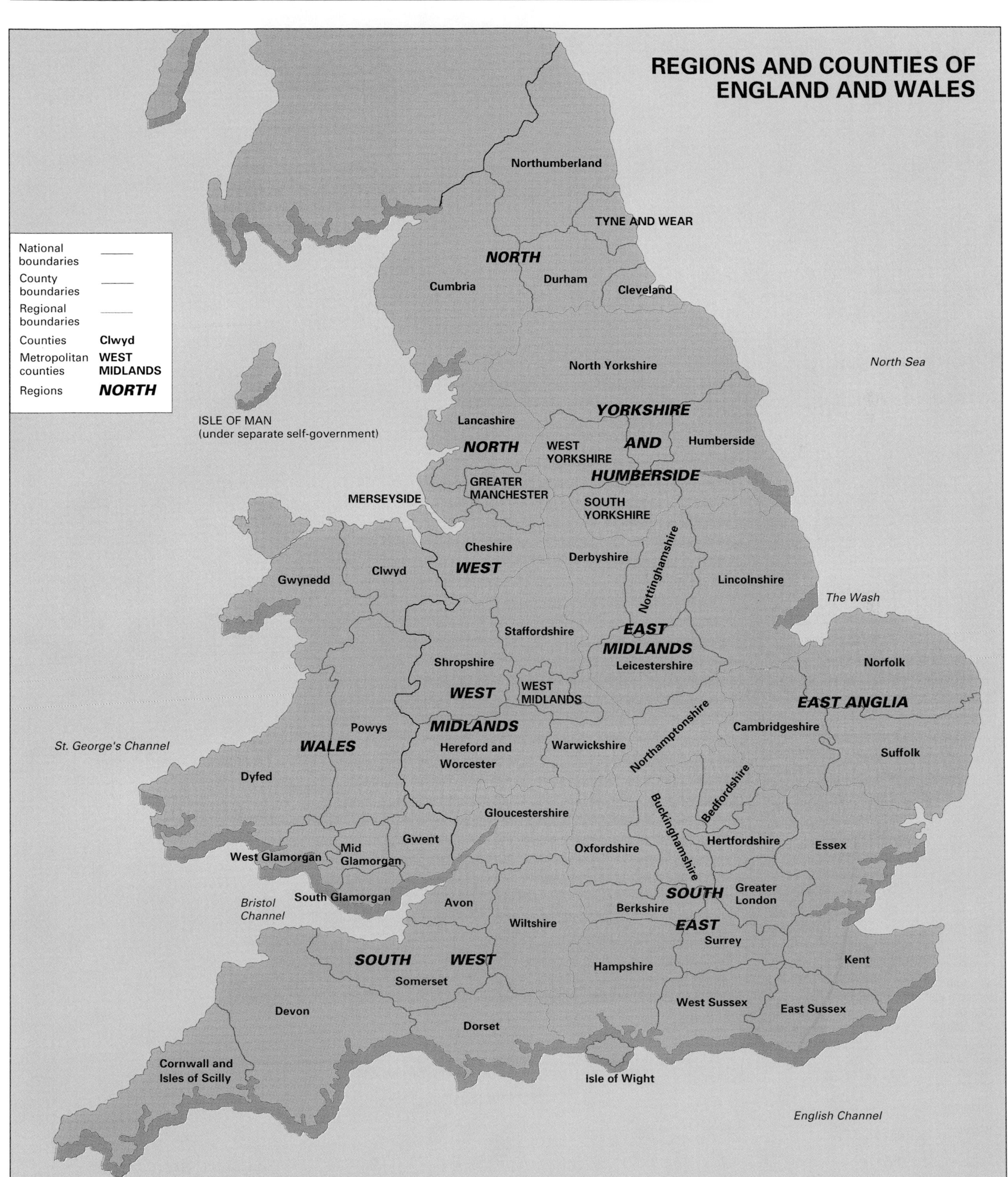

REGIONS AND COUNTIES OF ENGLAND AND WALES
National boundaries
County boundaries
Regional boundaries
Counties Clwyd
Metropolitan counties WEST MIDLANDS
Regions NORTH
ISLE OF MAN (under separate self-government)
North Sea
St. George's Channel
Bristol Channel
The Wash
English Channel
NORTH
YORKSHIRE AND HUMBERSIDE
WEST MIDLANDS
EAST MIDLANDS
EAST ANGLIA
WALES
SOUTH EAST
SOUTH WEST
Northumberland
TYNE AND WEAR
Cumbria
Durham
Cleveland
North Yorkshire
Lancashire
WEST YORKSHIRE
Humberside
GREATER MANCHESTER
MERSEYSIDE
SOUTH YORKSHIRE
Cheshire
Derbyshire
Nottinghamshire
Lincolnshire
Gwynedd
Clwyd
Staffordshire
Leicestershire
Shropshire
WEST MIDLANDS
Norfolk
Powys
Hereford and Worcester
Warwickshire
Northamptonshire
Cambridgeshire
Suffolk
Dyfed
Gloucestershire
Bedfordshire
Buckinghamshire
Gwent
Mid Glamorgan
West Glamorgan
South Glamorgan
Oxfordshire
Hertfordshire
Essex
Greater London
Avon
Berkshire
Wiltshire
Surrey
Kent
Somerset
Hampshire
West Sussex
East Sussex
Devon
Dorset
Cornwall and Isles of Scilly
Isle of Wight

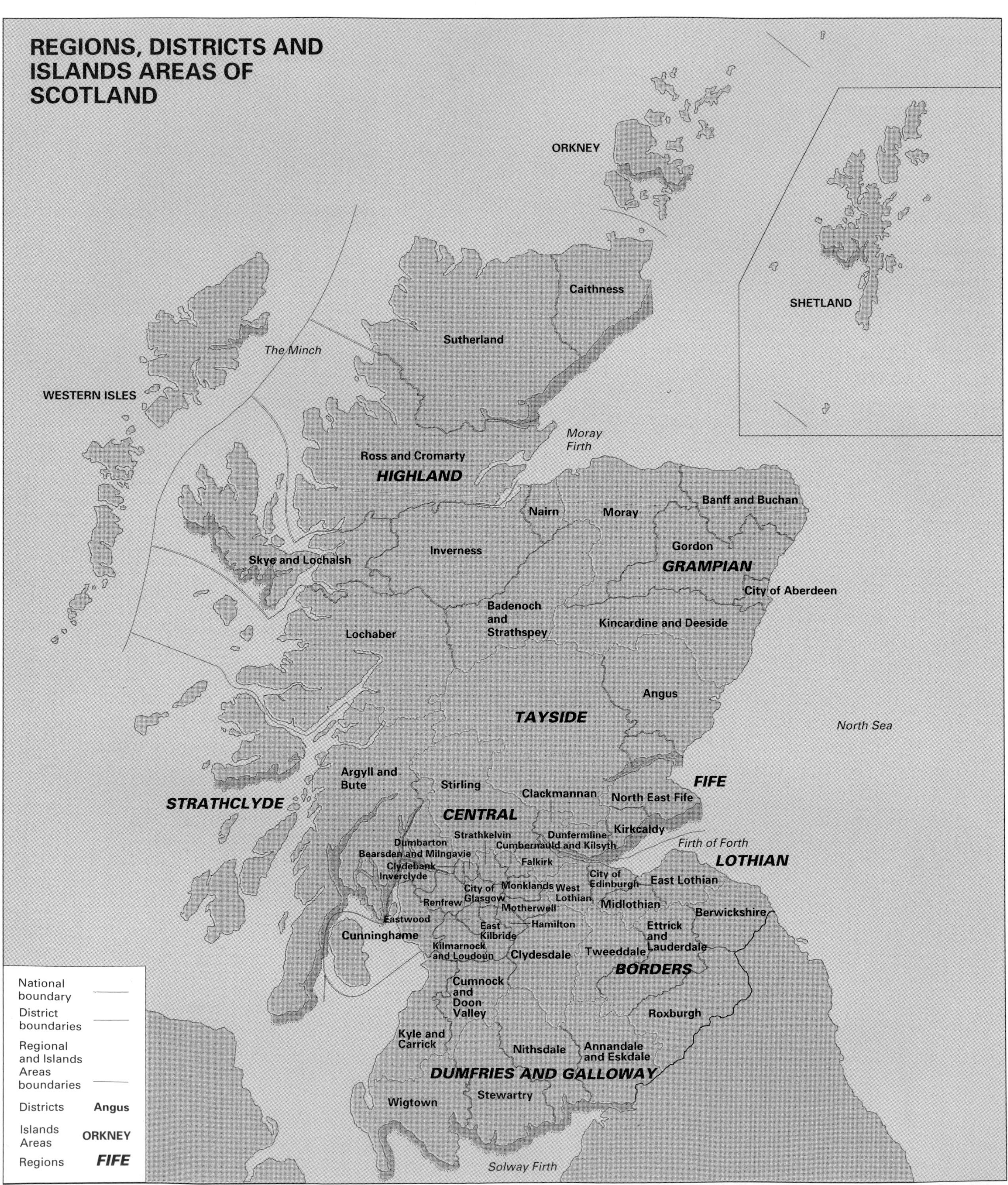
REGIONS, DISTRICTS AND ISLANDS AREAS OF SCOTLAND
ORKNEY
SHETLAND
Caithness
Sutherland
The Minch
WESTERN ISLES
Moray Firth
Ross and Cromarty
HIGHLAND
Banff and Buchan
Nairn
Moray
Gordon
Inverness
Skye and Lochalsh
GRAMPIAN
City of Aberdeen
Badenoch and Strathspey
Kincardine and Deeside
Lochaber
Angus
TAYSIDE
North Sea
Argyll and Bute
Stirling
Clackmannan
North East Fife
FIFE
STRATHCLYDE
CENTRAL
Kirkcaldy
Dumbarton
Strathkelvin
Dunfermline
Bearsden and Milngavie
Cumbernauld and Kilsyth
Firth of Forth
LOTHIAN
Clydebank
Falkirk
Inverclyde
City of Edinburgh
East Lothian
City of Glasgow
Monklands
West Lothian
Renfrew
Motherwell
Midlothian
Berwickshire
Eastwood
East Kilbride
Hamilton
Ettrick and Lauderdale
Cunninghame
Kilmarnock and Loudoun
Clydesdale
Tweeddale
BORDERS
Cumnock and Doon Valley
Roxburgh
Kyle and Carrick
Nithsdale
Annandale and Eskdale
DUMFRIES AND GALLOWAY
Wigtown
Stewartry
Solway Firth
National boundary
District boundaries
Regional and Islands Areas boundaries
Districts Angus
Islands Areas ORKNEY
Regions FIFE

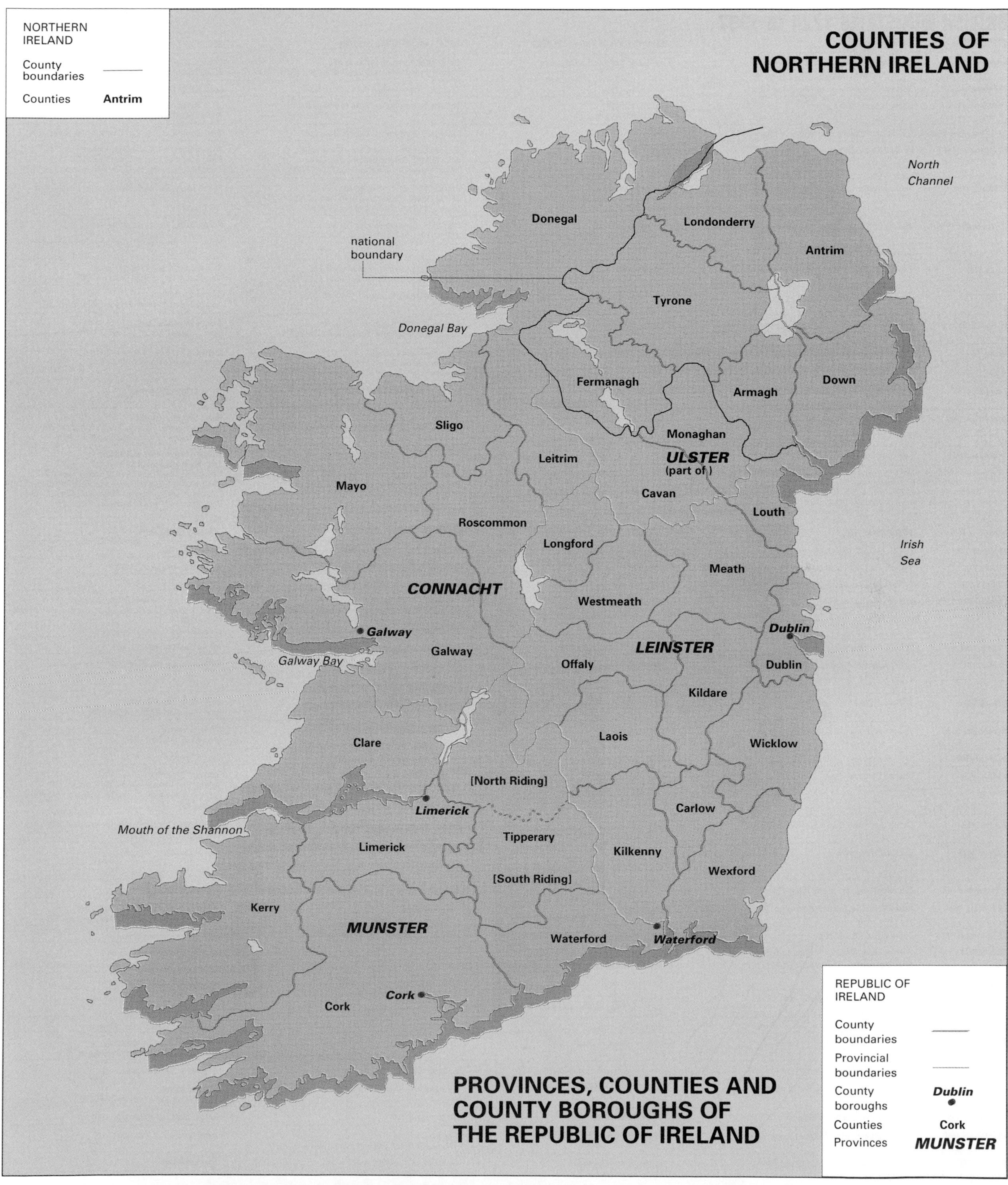

NORTHERN IRELAND
County boundaries
Counties Antrim
COUNTIES OF NORTHERN IRELAND
North Channel
Donegal
Londonderry
Antrim
national boundary
Tyrone
Donegal Bay
Fermanagh
Armagh
Down
Sligo
Monaghan
Leitrim
ULSTER (part of)
Mayo
Cavan
Louth
Roscommon
Longford
Irish Sea
Meath
CONNACHT
Westmeath
Galway
Dublin
Galway
LEINSTER
Galway Bay
Offaly
Dublin
Kildare
Clare
Laois
Wicklow
[North Riding]
Limerick
Carlow
Mouth of the Shannon
Tipperary
Limerick
Kilkenny
Wexford
[South Riding]
Kerry
MUNSTER
Waterford
Waterford
Cork
Cork
REPUBLIC OF IRELAND
County boundaries
Provincial boundaries
County boroughs Dublin
Counties Cork
Provinces MUNSTER
PROVINCES, COUNTIES AND COUNTY BOROUGHS OF THE REPUBLIC OF IRELAND

BRITISH MINISTRIES 1721 to 1992

MINISTRY FORMED	PRIME MINISTER	CHANCELLOR OF THE EXCHEQUER	SECRETARY OF STATE (SOUTH)	SECRETARY OF STATE (NORTH)
3 April 1721	Sir Robert Walpole, Earl of Orford (Whig)	Sir Robert Walpole, Earl of Orford	John, Baron Carteret, Earl Granville Thomas Pelham-Holles, Duke of Newcastle (April 1724)	Charles, Viscount Townshend William Stanhope, Earl of Harrington (June 1730)
16 February 1742	Spencer Compton, Earl of Wilmington (Whig)	Samuel Sandys	Thomas Pelham-Holles, Duke of Newcastle	John, Baron Carteret, Earl Granville
25 August 1743	Henry Pelham (Whig)	Samuel Sandys Henry Pelham (Dec 1743)	Thomas Pelham-Holles, Duke of Newcastle	John, Baron Carteret, Earl Granville William Stanhope, Earl of Harrington (Nov 1744)
10–12 February 1746	Sir William Pulteney, Earl of Bath (Whig)	Henry Pelham	Thomas Pelham-Holles, Duke of Newcastle	John, Baron Carteret, Earl Granville (10-14 Feb 1746)
12 February 1746	Henry Pelham (Whig)	Henry Pelham	Thomas Pelham-Holles, Duke of Newcastle John Russell, Duke of Bedford (Feb 1748) Robert Darcy, Earl of Holdernesse (June 1751)	William Stanhope, Earl of Harrington (Feb 1746) Philip Stanhope, Earl of Chesterfield (Oct 1746) Thomas Pelham-Holles, Duke of Newcastle (Feb 1748)
16 March 1754	Thomas Pelham-Holles, Duke of Newcastle (Whig)	Henry Pelham Henry Bilson Legge (April 1754) Sir George Lyttleton (Nov 1755)	Robert Darcy, Earl of Holdernesse Sir Thomas Robinson, Lord Grantham (23 March 1754) Henry Fox, Baron Holland of Foxley (Nov 1755)	Robert Darcy, Earl of Holdernesse (23 March 1754)
16 November 1756	William Cavendish, Duke of Devonshire (Whig)	Henry Bilson Legge William Murray, Earl of Mansfield (April 1757)	Henry Fox, Baron Holland of Foxley William Pitt [the Elder], Earl of Chatham (Dec 1756)	Robert Darcy, Earl of Holdernesse
8–12 June 1757	James Waldegrave	Unable to form a ministry		
2 July 1757	Thomas Pelham-Holles, Duke of Newcastle (Whig)	Henry Bilson Legge William Wildman, Viscount Barrington (March 1761)	William Pitt (the Elder), Earl of Chatham Charles Wyndham, Earl of Egremont (Oct 1761)	Robert Darcy, Earl of Holdernesse John Stuart, Earl of Bute (March 1761)
29 May 1762	John Stuart, Earl of Bute (Tory)	Sir Francis Dashwood (June 1762)	Charles Wyndham, Earl of Egremont	George Grenville George Montagu-Dunk, Earl of Halifax (Oct 1762)
15 April 1763	George Grenville (Whig)	George Grenville	Charles Wyndham, Earl of Egremont George Montagu-Dunk, Earl of Halifax (Sept 1763)	George Montagu-Dunk, Earl of Halifax John Montagu, Earl of Sandwich (Sept 1763)
10 July 1765	Charles Watson-Wentworth, Marquis of Rockingham (Whig)	William Dowdeswell	Henry Seymour-Conway Charles Lennox, Duke of Richmond (May 1766) William Petty, Marquis of Lansdowne (July 1766)	Augustus Fitz Roy, Duke of Grafton Henry Seymour-Conway (May 1766)
2 August 1766	William Pitt [the Elder], Earl of Chatham (Whig)	Charles Townshend William Murray, Earl of Mansfield (Sept 1767)	William Petty, Marquis of Lansdowne	Henry Seymour-Conway
September 1767	Augustus Fitz Roy, Duke of Grafton (Whig)	Frederick, Lord North, Earl of Guilford	William Petty, Marquis of Lansdowne Thomas Thynne, Viscount Weymouth (Oct 1768)	Henry Seymour-Conway Thomas Thynne, Viscount Weymouth (Jan 1768) William Nassau, Earl of Rochford (Oct 1768)
6 February 1770	Frederick, Lord North, Earl of Guilford (Tory)	Frederick, Lord North, Earl of Guilford	Thomas Thynne, Viscount Weymouth William Nassau, Earl of Rochford (Dec 1770) Thomas Thynne, Viscount Weymouth (Nov 1775) Wills Hill, Earl of Hillsborough (Nov 1779)	William Nassau, Earl of Rochford John Montagu, Earl of Sandwich (Dec 1770) George Montagu-Dunk, Earl of Halifax (Jan 1771) Henry Howard, Earl of Suffolk and Berkshire (June 1771) Thomas Thynne, Viscount Weymouth (March 1779) David Murray, Viscount Stormont (Oct 1779)

Dates after ministers' names (e.g. April 1724) refer to when they took up an appointment. The Secretaries of State for the South and the North looked after both foreign and home affairs. The Southern Department took care of France, Spain, Portugal, Switzerland, Italy, Turkey and, from c.1700, Ireland; the Northern handled Germany, the United Provinces of the Netherlands, Denmark, Sweden, Russia and Poland. The Secretaryships for the North and South were changed to Home and Foreign in March 1782. Politicians' aristocratic and honorific titles are not necessarily contemporary with a particular office but those held at the end of their careers.

Offices abolished 1782

MINISTRY FORMED	PRIME MINISTER	CHANCELLOR OF THE EXCHEQUER	HOME SECRETARY	FOREIGN SECRETARY
27 March 1782	Charles Watson-Wentworth, Marquis of Rockingham (Whig)	Lord John Cavendish	William Petty, Earl of Shelburne, Marquis of Lansdowne	Charles James Fox
13 July 1782	William Petty, Earl of Shelburne, Marquis of Lansdowne (Whig)	William Pitt [the Younger]	Thomas Townshend, Viscount Sydney	Thomas Robinson, Baron Grantham
4 April 1783	William Bentinck, Duke of Portland (Coalition)	Lord John Cavendish	Frederick, Lord North, Earl of Guilford	Charles James Fox
19 December 1783	William Pitt [the Younger] (Tory)	William Pitt [the Younger]	Frederick, Lord North, Earl of Guilford Thomas Townshend, Viscount Sydney (23 Dec 1783) William Wyndham, Baron Grenville (June 1789) Henry Dundas, Viscount Melville (April-June 1791)	George Grenville, Earl Temple, Marquis of Buckingham Francis Godolphin-Osborne, Marquis of Carmarthen, Duke of Leeds (23 Dec 1783) William Wyndham, Baron Grenville (June 1791)
11 July 1794	William Pitt [the Younger] (Tory)	William Pitt [the Younger]	William Bentinck, Duke of Portland	William Wyndham, Baron Grenville
21 March 1801	Henry Addington, Viscount Sidmouth (Tory)	Henry Addington, Viscount Sidmouth	William Bentinck, Duke of Portland Thomas, Lord Pelham, Earl of Chichester (July 1801) Charles Philip Yorke (July 1803)	Robert Jenkinson, Earl of Liverpool
10 May 1804	William Pitt [the Younger] (Tory)	William Pitt [the Younger]	Robert Jenkinson, Earl of Liverpool	Dudley Ryder, Earl of Harrowby Henry Phipps, Earl of Mulgrave (Jan 1805)
10 February 1806	William Wyndham, Baron Grenville (Whig)	Lord Henry Petty	George Churchill, Earl Spencer	Charles James Fox Charles, Earl Grey (Sept 1806)
24 March 1807	William Bentinck, Duke of Portland (Tory)	Spencer Perceval	Robert Jenkinson, Earl of Liverpool	George Canning
4 October 1809	Spencer Perceval (Tory)	Spencer Perceval	Robert Jenkinson, Earl of Liverpool Richard Ryder (Nov 1809)	Henry, Earl Bathurst Richard Colley-Wellesley, Marquis Wellesley (Dec 1809) Robert Stewart, Viscount Castlereagh, Marquis of Londonderry (March 1812)
9 June 1812	Robert Jenkinson, Earl of Liverpool (Tory)	Nicholas Vansittart Frederick Robinson, Earl of Ripon (1823)	Henry Addington, Viscount Sidmouth Sir Robert Peel (Jan 1822)	Robert Stewart, Viscount Castlereagh, Marquis of Londonderry George Canning (Sept 1822)
30 April 1827	George Canning (Tory)	George Canning	William Sturges-Bourne Henry Petty, Earl of Shelburne, Marquis of Lansdowne (July 1827)	John William Ward, Earl Dudley
8 September 1827	Frederick Robinson, Earl of Ripon (Tory)	John Charles Herries	Henry Petty, Earl of Shelburne, Marquis of Lansdowne	John William Ward, Earl Dudley
26 January 1828	Arthur Wellesley, Duke of Wellington (Tory)	Henry Goulburn	Sir Robert Peel	John William Ward, Earl Dudley George Hamilton-Gordon, Earl of Aberdeen (June 1828)
24 November 1830	Charles, Earl Grey (Whig)	John Charles Spencer, Viscount Althorpe	William Lamb, Viscount Melbourne	Henry Temple, Viscount Palmerston
13 July 1834	William Lamb, Viscount Melbourne (Whig)	John Charles Spencer, Viscount Althorpe	John Ponsonby, Viscount Dungannon, Earl of Bessborough	Henry Temple, Viscount Palmerston
	After Melbourne's resignation in Nov 1834 the Duke of Wellington held the offices of prime minister & first lord of the treasury, home secretary, & foreign secretary. Lord Denman was chancellor. Peel was appointed prime minister in Dec 1834.			
26 December 1834	Sir Robert Peel (Tory)	Sir Robert Peel	Henry Goulburn	Arthur Wellesley, Duke of Wellington
18 April 1835	William Lamb, Viscount Melbourne (Whig)	T Spring Rice Sir Francis Thornhill Baring, Baron Northbrook (1839)	John, Earl Russell Constantine Henry Phipps, Marquis of Normanby (Aug 1839)	Henry Temple, Viscount Palmerston
6 September 1841	Sir Robert Peel (Tory)	Henry Goulbourn	Sir James Graham	George Hamilton-Gordon, Earl of Aberdeen
6 July 1846	John, Earl Russell (Whig)	Charles, Viscount Wood	Sir George Grey	Henry Temple, Viscount Palmerston Granville Leveson-Gower, Earl Granville (Dec 1851)
28 February 1852	Edward Stanley, Earl of Derby (Tory)	Benjamin Disraeli, Earl of Beaconsfield	Spencer Walpole	James Harris, Earl of Malmesbury
28 December 1852	George Hamilton-Gordon, Earl of Aberdeen (Peelite)	William Ewart Gladstone	Henry Temple, Viscount Palmerston	John, Earl Russell George Villiers, Earl of Clarendon (Feb 1853)
5 February 1855	Henry Temple, Viscount Palmerston (Whig)	William Ewart Gladstone	Sir George Grey	George Villiers, Earl of Clarendon
19 February 1858	Edward Stanley, Earl of Derby (Conservative)	Benjamin Disraeli, Earl of Beaconsfield	Spencer Walpole Thomas Sotheron-Estcourt (March 1859)	James Harris, Earl of Malmesbury
18 June 1859	Henry Temple, Viscount Palmerston (Whig)	William Ewart Gladstone	Sir George Cornewall Lewis Sir George Grey (July 1861)	John, Earl Russell

BRITISH MINISTRIES 1721 to 1992

MINISTRY FORMED	PRIME MINISTER	CHANCELLOR OF THE EXCHEQUER	HOME SECRETARY	FOREIGN SECRETARY
6 November 1865	John, Earl Russell (Whig)	William Ewart Gladstone	Sir George Grey	George Villiers, Earl of Clarendon
6 July 1866	Edward Stanley, Earl of Derby (Conservative)	Benjamin Disraeli, Earl of Beaconsfield	Spencer Walpole Gathorne Hardy, Earl of Cranbrook (March 1867)	Edward Henry Stanley, Earl of Derby
27 February 1868	Benjamin Disraeli, Earl of Beaconsfield (Conservative)	G Ward Hunt	Gathorne Hardy, Earl of Cranbrook	Edward Henry Stanley, Earl of Derby
9 December 1868	William Ewart Gladstone (Liberal)	Robert Lowe William Ewart Gladstone (1873)	Henry Bruce, Lord Aberdare Robert Lowe, Viscount Sherbrooke (Aug 1873)	George Villiers, Earl of Clarendon Granville Leveson-Gower, Earl Granville (July 1870)
21 February 1874	Benjamin Disraeli, Earl of Beaconsfield (Conservative)	Sir Stafford Northcote, Earl of Iddesleigh	Sir Richard Cross, Viscount Cross	Edward Henry Stanley, Earl of Derby Robert Gascoyne-Cecil, Marquis of Salisbury (March 1878)
28 April 1880	William Ewart Gladstone (Liberal)	William Ewart Gladstone Hugh Childers (1882)	Sir William Vernon-Harcourt	Granville Leveson-Gower, Earl Granville
24 June 1885	Robert Gascoyne-Cecil, Marquis of Salisbury (Conservative)	Sir Michael Hicks Beach	Sir Richard Cross, Viscount Cross	Robert Gascoyne-Cecil, Marquis of Salisbury
6 February 1886	William Ewart Gladstone (Liberal)	Sir William Vernon-Harcourt	Hugh Childers	Archibald Philip Primrose, Earl of Rosebery
3 August 1886	Robert Gascoyne-Cecil, Marquis of Salisbury (Conservative)	Lord Randolph Churchill George Joachim Goschen (1887)	Henry Matthews, Viscount Llandaff	Sir Stafford Northcote, Earl of Iddlesleigh Robert Gascoyne-Cecil, Marquis of Salisbury (Jan 1887)
18 August 1892	William Ewart Gladstone (Liberal)	Sir William Vernon-Harcourt	Herbert Henry Asquith, Earl of Oxford	Archibald Philip Primrose, Earl of Rosebery
15 March 1894	Archibald Primrose, Earl of Rosebery (Liberal)	Sir William Vernon-Harcourt	Herbert Henry Asquith, Earl of Oxford	John Wodehouse, Earl of Kimberley
2 July 1895	Robert Gascoyne-Cecil, Marquis of Salisbury (Conservative)	Sir Michael Hicks Beach	Sir Matthew White-Ridley, Viscount Ridley Charles Ritchie (Nov 1900)	Robert Gascoyne-Cecil, Marquis of Salisbury Henry Petty-Fitzmaurice, Marquis of Lansdowne (Nov 1900)
12 July 1902	Arthur James, Earl of Balfour (Conservative)	Charles Ritchie Austen Chamberlain (1903)	Aretas Akers-Douglas, Viscount Chilston	Henry Petty-Fitzmaurice, Marquis of Lansdowne
5 December 1905	Sir Henry Campbell-Bannerman (Liberal)	Herbert Henry Asquith, Earl of Oxford	Herbert Gladstone, Viscount Gladstone	Sir Edward, Viscount Grey of Fallodon
8 April 1908	Herbert Henry Asquith, Earl of Oxford (Liberal)	David Lloyd George, Earl of Dwyfor	Herbert Gladstone, Viscount Gladstone Sir Winston Churchill (Feb 1910)	Sir Edward, Viscount Grey of Fallodon
10 December 1910	Herbert Henry Asquith, Earl of Oxford (Liberal)	David Lloyd George, Earl of Dwyfor	Sir Winston Churchill Reginald McKenna (Oct 1911)	Sir Edward, Viscount Grey of Fallodon
25 May 1915	Herbert Henry Asquith, Earl of Oxford (Coalition)	Reginald McKenna	John, Viscount Simon Herbert, Viscount Samuel (Jan 1916)	Sir Edward, Viscount Grey of Fallodon
7 December 1916	David Lloyd George, Earl of Dwyfor (War Cabinet)	Andrew Bonar Law Austen Chamberlain (Jan 1919)		Arthur James, Earl of Balfour
November 1919	David Lloyd George, Earl of Dwyfor (Coalition)	Austen Chamberlain Robert, Viscount Horne of Slamannen (1921)	Edward Shortt	George, Baron Curzon of Kedleston
16 November 1922	Andrew Bonar Law (Conservative)	Stanley Baldwin, Earl of Bewdley	W C Bridgeman	George, Baron Curzon of Kedleston
22 May 1923	Stanley Baldwin, Earl of Bewdley (Conservative)	Stanley Baldwin, Earl of Bewdley Neville Chamberlain (1923)	W C Bridgeman	George, Baron Curzon of Kedleston
22 January 1924	James Ramsay MacDonald (Labour)	Philip, Viscount Snowden	Arthur Henderson	James Ramsay MacDonald
4 November 1924	Stanley Baldwin, Earl of Bewdley (Conservative)	Sir Winston Churchill	Sir William Joynson-Hicks	Austen Chamberlain
7 June 1929	James Ramsay MacDonald (Labour)	Philip, Viscount Snowden	Joseph Robert Clynes	Arthur Henderson
25 August 1931	James Ramsay MacDonald (Coalition)	Philip, Viscount Snowden	Herbert, Viscount Samuel	Marquis of Reading
28 October 1931	James Ramsay MacDonald (Coalition)	Neville Chamberlain	Herbert, Viscount Samuel Sir J Gilmour (1932)	John, Viscount Simon
7 June 1935	Stanley Baldwin, Earl of Bewdley (Conservative)	Neville Chamberlain	John, Viscount Simon	Sir Samuel John Gurney Hoare Anthony Eden, Earl of Avon (1935)
28 May 1937	Neville Chamberlain (Coalition)	John, Viscount Simon	Sir Samuel John Gurney Hoare	Anthony Eden, Earl of Avon Edward Wood, Earl of Halifax (1938)
3 September 1939	Neville Chamberlain (War Cabinet)	John, Viscount Simon	Sir Samuel John Gurney Hoare (to 1939)	Edward Wood, Earl of Halifax
11 May 1940	Sir Winston Churchill (War Cabinet)	Sir Howard Kingsley Wood	Herbert, Baron Morrison of Lambeth	Edward Wood, Earl of Halifax Anthony Eden, Earl of Avon
23 May 1945	Sir Winston Churchill (Caretaker Cabinet)	John Anderson, Viscount Waverley	Sir Donald Bradley Somervell	Anthony Eden, Earl of Avon
26 July 1945	Clement Richard, Earl Attlee (Labour)	Hugh, Baron Dalton of Forest and Frith Sir Richard Stafford Cripps (1947) Hugh Gaitskell (1950)	James Chuter Ede	Ernest Bevin Herbert, Baron Morrison of Lambeth (1951)
26 October 1951	Sir Winston Churchill (Conservative)	Richard Austen, Baron Butler of Saffron Walden	Sir David Maxwell-Fyfe, Earl of Kilmuir Gwilym Lloyd George (1954)	Anthony Eden, Earl of Avon
6 April 1955	Sir Anthony Eden, Earl of Avon (Conservative)	Richard Austen, Baron Butler of Saffron Walden Maurice Harold Macmillan, Earl of Stockton (Dec 1955)	Gwilym Lloyd George	Maurice Harold Macmillan, Earl of Stockton John, Baron Selwyn Brooke (1955)
13 January 1957	Maurice Harold Macmillan, Earl of Stockton (Conservative)	Peter, Baron Thorneycroft Derick Heathcoat, Viscount Amory (1958)	Richard Austen, Baron Butler of Saffron Walden	John, Baron Selwyn Brooke
9 October 1959	Maurice Harold Macmillan, Earl of Stockton (Conservative)	Derick Heathcoat, Viscount Amory	Richard Austen, Baron Butler of Saffron Walden	Sir Alexander Frederick Douglas-Home, Baron Home of the Hirsel
19 October 1963	Sir Alexander Frederick Douglas-Home, Baron Home of the Hirsel (Conservative)	Reginald Maudling	Henry Brooke	Richard Austen, Baron Butler of Saffron Walden
16 October 1964	James Harold, Baron Wilson of Rievaulx (Labour)	Leonard James, Baron Callaghan of Cardiff	Sir Frank Soskice Roy, Baron Jenkins of Hillhead	Patrick Gordon Walker Michael, Baron Stewart of Fulham (Jan 1965)
1 April 1966	James Harold, Baron Wilson of Rievaulx (Labour)	Leonard James, Baron Callaghan of Cardiff Roy, Baron Jenkins of Hillhead	Roy, Baron Jenkins of Hillhead Leonard James, Baron Callaghan of Cardiff (Nov 1967)	Michael, Baron Stewart of Fulham George Brown, Baron George-Brown (Aug 1966) Michael, Baron Stewart of Fulham (March 1968)
19 June 1970	Sir Edward Richard George Heath (Conservative)	Iain Mcleod Anthony, Baron Barber of Wentbridge (July 1970)	Reginald Maudling Leonard Robert Carr, Baron of Hadley (1972)	Sir Alexander Frederick Douglas-Home, Baron Home of the Hirsel
4 March 1974	James Harold, Baron Wilson of Rievaulx (Labour)	Denis Healey	Roy, Baron Jenkins of Hillhead	Leonard James, Baron Callaghan of Cardiff
11 October 1974	James Harold, Baron Wilson of Rievaulx (Labour)	Denis Healey	Roy, Baron Jenkins of Hillhead	Leonard James, Baron Callaghan of Cardiff
5 April 1976	Leonard James, Baron Callaghan of Cardiff (Labour)	Denis Healey	Merlyn Rees	Anthony Crosland David, Lord Owen (May 1977)
4 May 1979	Margaret Hilda, Baroness Thatcher of Kesteven (Conservative)	Sir Richard Edward Geoffrey Howe	William Whitelaw, Viscount of Penrith	Peter Carington, Lord Carrington Francis, Baron Pym of Sandy (April 1982)
10 June 1983	Margaret Hilda, Baroness Thatcher of Kesteven (Conservative)	Nigel Lawson	Sir Leon Brittan Douglas Hurd (Sept 1985)	Sir Richard Edward Geoffrey Howe
12 June 1987	Margaret Hilda, Baroness Thatcher of Kesteven (Conservative)	Nigel Lawson John Major (Oct 1989)	Douglas Hurd David, Lord Waddington (Oct 1989)	Sir Richard Edward Geoffrey Howe John Major (July 1989) Douglas Hurd (Oct 1989)
27 Nov 1990	John Major (Conservative)	Norman Lamont	Kenneth Baker	Douglas Hurd
9 April 1992	John Major (Conservative)	Norman Lamont	Kenneth Clarke	Douglas Hurd

The parliamentary system of the United Kingdom

From Saxon wise men to modern MPs

An aerial view of the Palace of Westminster, home to Britain's parliament.

The British parliamentary system boasts of being the "mother of parliaments", for its evolution can be traced all the way back to the *witenagemot*, or "council of wise men", of the Anglo-Saxon kings. William I [the Conqueror] (1066-87) and his successors adapted this system, summoning the leading men of the kingdom to a great council three or four times a year to settle matters of state.

As control of the land became concentrated in the hands of the monarchy, it became necessary to set up another body, the king's court, composed of officers of the royal household, to manage the efficient running of the nation. The great council was still summoned to give advice and make laws, but it was the king's court that administered them.

This was the system that governed the country until that historic day at Runnymede in 1215 when the barons compelled King John (1199-1216) to sign *Magna Carta*. Originally, the "Great Charter" was a selfish document, meant to protect the barons' feudal rights from the king's grasp, but over the years it came to enshrine the rights of the people against the crown.

The other significant development in the 13th century led to the formation of the two-chamber system, with a House of Lords and a House of Commons. This came about because the monarchy was expected to meet all expenses from its own pocket. Often unable to do so, kings summoned the great council to enact new taxation, but in order to get general support they were obliged to summon the representatives of counties and towns – the Commons – as well as the tenants-in-chief summoned by name – the Lords.

The great council with its two constituent bodies and the king eventually came to be called "parliament", a word that originally meant a meeting where people "parleyed" or discussed.

By using the weapon of taxation the Commons gradually won more and more power. Inevitably this led to the confrontation between parliament and the crown that resulted in the Civil War (1642-48) and the execution of Charles I (1625-49). Although the monarchy was restored under Charles II (1660-85) the parliamentary victory led to the Bill of Rights (1689), which confirmed parliament's control of taxation and legislation, as well as the right of members to freedom of speech and debate. Then, just three years later, came the Act of Settlement. This neatly secured the Protestant succession to the throne at the same time as it established the supremacy of parliament. Britain is still governed, however, in the sovereign's name.

A tale of Tories, Whigs and 'whippers-in'

The television image of the House of Commons, with the government and the opposition baying at one another across the green leather benches, may give the impression that the party system is as old as parliament itself. In fact, although the pejorative terms "Whig" and "Tory" go back to the 17th century, political parties are relatively new, dating chiefly from the early 19th century. Before then the House consisted not of organized parties but of groups of men who formed alliances to support or oppose the ministers appointed by the sovereign.

This worked because the right to vote was held by only a small number of people – only about 500,000 out of an adult population of ten million in 1830 – and the influence of the candidate up for election was more important than the policy of any group to which he belonged.

Everything changed after the succession of Reform Acts and the institution of the secret ballot. The mass of new voters demanded to be represented not by individuals but by parties with a coherent policy based on recognized principles. Such parties needed nationwide organizations outside parliament and disciplined behaviour inside. Hence the party system grew, as much parliamentary business has, by pragmatic evolution.

The Conservative Party (originally the Tories) has been a major party from the beginning, opposed first by the Liberal Party (previously the Whigs) and then by the socialist Labour Party. Smaller parties have always been represented, but part of the strength of the system is that one or other of the major parties has usually been able to form a viable government.

The daily business of the parties in the House of Commons is run largely by the whips, powerful officials who take their name from the "whippers-in" of fox-hunting who prevent the hounds from straying. They send out a weekly circular to MPs of their party informing them of parliamentary business and its relative importance. If a debate is underlined three times – a "three-line whip" – it must be attended.

One of the aspects of the party system not easily appreciated by watching debates is that parliament could not function without the co-operation of "her majesty's opposition". It is as much a part of the government of the country as the government itself.

Elections: first past the post is victorious

General elections in the United Kingdom have to be held every five years – or less, if the government of the day decides to "go to the country" – and are settled by simple majorities in the 651 constituencies into which the nation is divided. The vote is by the secret ballot of the citizens of Britain, as well as of the citizens of other Commonwealth countries or of the Irish Republic resident in the United Kingdom. All voters must be 18 years old and be registered on the electoral roll of a constituency.

Not quite everyone is allowed to vote, however. Those excluded are: members of the House of Lords; aliens; patients detained under mental health legislation; convicted offenders detained in custody; and anyone convicted within the previous five years of illegal election practices.

The laws governing elections are very strict in order to make them as fair as possible. The old days of rich candidates buying votes are long gone. All expenses must be accounted for, and no candidate may spend more than £4,144 plus 3.5 pence for each elector in borough constituencies or 4.7 pence in the larger county constituencies.

Voting is supervised by a returning officer, who has also to announce the result. Provision is made for proxy voters and postal votes for people in special circumstances, such as soldiers serving abroad. When all the results are in, the party with the most members returned is asked by the sovereign to form a government.

Parliament and the EC: uneasy alliance

Britain's relations with the European Community are the source of passionate parliamentary debate, cutting across party lines, between the "Europeans" who believe that Britain's future lies in the Community and the "Euro-sceptics" who fear that parliament is losing its hard-won sovereignty to foreign civil servants in Brussels.

Britain's entry into the EC in 1973 has entailed the acceptance of a good deal of Community legislation, such as "regulations", which are legally binding on all member states, and "directives", which require countries to achieve certain results but allow each government to decide how to go about it.

A close eye is kept on EC matters at Westminster. Members are kept informed, and proposals for Community legislation are scrutinized – and also fiercely debated. Both Houses have established select committees to examine such legislation, and legal advice is given by the government's law officers.

Britain sends 81 representatives, elected on party lines, to the European parliament, which debates major EC policy issues and can question both the commission and the council of ministers. The European parliament is, however, something of a mystery to British voters.

Laws: the long road to the royal assent

The laws that govern the life of the country come into force when they receive the royal assent from the sovereign, but before that auspicious occasion they undergo a long, critical and often heated examination by both the Commons and the Lords. A public bill starts life as part of a government's policy programme. Both its implications and practicality will be considered, and interested parties consulted, before it is drafted for presentation.

A bill may be introduced in either House, where it goes through various stages. There is a first reading – a formality to introduce it to the House – and then, between one day and several weeks later, its first real scrutiny comes in the second reading, when its general principles are debated and voted on.

Once past this test the bill goes to the committee stage, where it is examined clause by clause in a standing committee of between 16 and 50 members. Some bills, especially those dealing with constitutional matters, are heard by the whole House sitting as a committee. This is the stage at which the bill may be considerably amended – as long as the changes do not affect the principles agreed in the second reading.

Once the committee is finished, the bill is returned to the House for the report stage. Here the committee's amendments are debated, and further amendments may be proposed. Only the amendments (not the clauses) may be discussed. The third reading comes next, to review its final form. Substantive amendments can no longer be made, and the reading is usually short.

Whichever House it started in, the bill now passes to the other, where it goes through the same procedure. Relations can now become delicate between the two Houses, for any new amendments have to be considered by the House in which the bill originated and may not be accepted. If the Houses find it impossible to agree, the bill fails. The Commons can, however, override the Lords because they have the right to present their bills for royal assent after one year, whatever the Lords' objections. The bill then becomes an act of parliament and part of the law of the land.

Private members can also introduce bills. At the start of each session in the Commons individual members draw lots for the right to introduce his or her own bill on one of the Fridays set specially aside. The first 20 picked out are allowed so to do. Some members are happy enough to withdraw their bills if the government promises to introduce similar legislation or set up an inquiry, while others fight passionately for their bills to become law. A few are even successful.

Parliament and the British citizen

Members of the House of Commons are elected by the people and, ultimately, parliament reflects the will of the people. While a member is not bound to consult his constituents on his speeches or the way he votes on a day-to-day basis, he knows that they have the sanction of voting against him at the next election – when he might be left with ample time to rue the fact that he had not taken more notice of their wishes. The official parliamentary record, Hansard, will give any interested citizen an account of proceedings in the House.

MPs represent all their constituents at Westminster no matter how they voted and, when necessary, should fight for all their interests. Members listen to constituents' problems in "surgeries" and can refer them to the appropriate government department or else raise the matter in the House by means of a parliamentary question or by asking for an adjournment debate.

MPs can also refer a grievance to the parliamentary commissioner, better known as the ombudsman, who is an officer of the House of Commons, not of the government, and whose function is to investigate complaints of maladministration where there is no other way of obtaining redress.

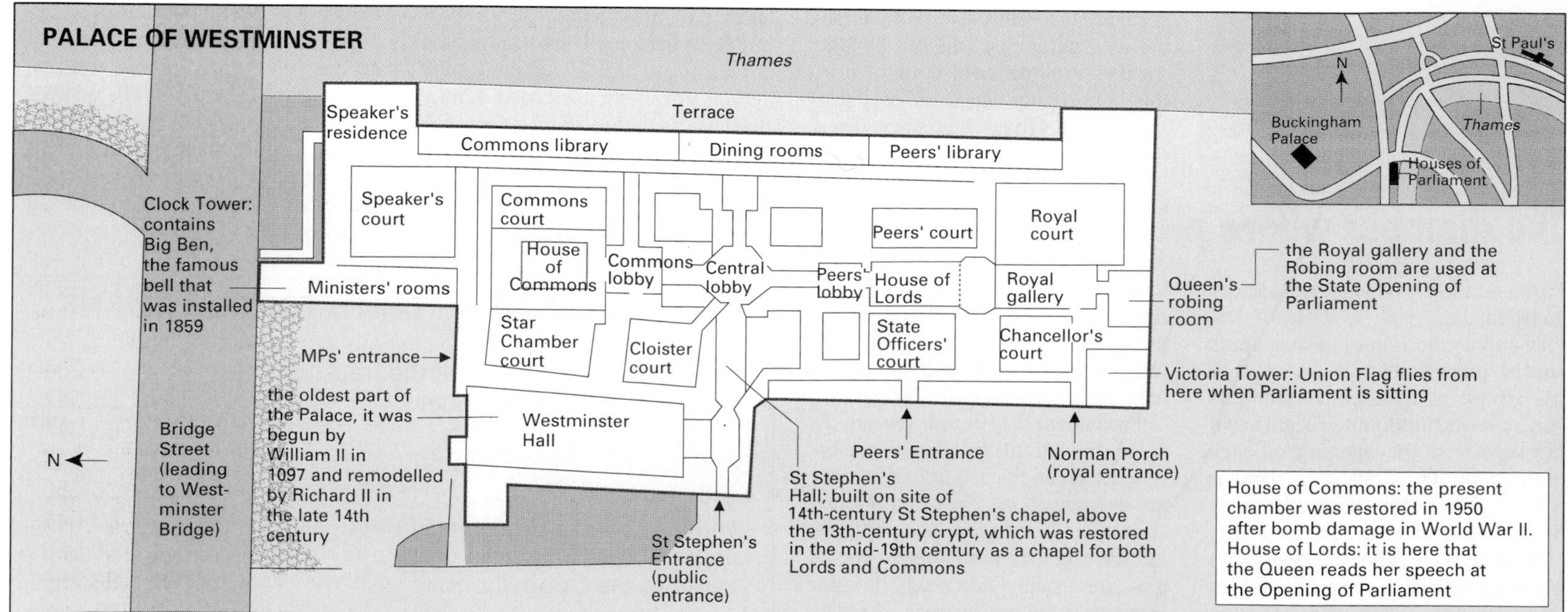

The Commons originally met not at the palace of Westminster (above) but in Westminster Abbey; from 1547 to 1834, when fire destroyed much of the palace, they met in St Stephen's Chapel. The present building owes its appearance chiefly to the Victorian architects Sir Charles Barry and AW Pugin.

Inside the House of Commons: how it all works

Life at the top of the Commons heap

The office of prime minister, now the elected leader of the majority party in the House of Commons, emerged gradually with the increasing reliance of the Hanoverian dynasty in the 18th century on the lord treasurer, who became recognized as the chief or "prime" minister of state. Sir Robert Walpole (in power 1721-42) is often called the first prime minister, but it is only with Sir Robert Peel's ministry (1841-46) that the office becomes truly recognizable in modern terms.

The occupant is the most powerful person in the country, able to appoint or sack ministers, conduct the nation's affairs, and act as the link between the Houses of parliament and the sovereign. Yet this power lasts only so long as the prime minister has the confidence of the electorate and his own colleagues.

Madam speaker: Ms Boothroyd.

The leader of the opposition presents a mirror image. Although he has no official function under parliamentary rules, the post carries a salary, and without the holder's cooperation the Commons could not function properly. He appoints a "shadow cabinet" and can himself be elected or replaced according to the rules of his party.

The office of speaker, recently occupied by a woman, Betty Boothroyd, for the first time in Westminster's history, is quite different. Originally the Commons' representative chosen to "speak" to the king, the speaker maintains that ceremonial function but more importantly presides over the House and ensures that members conduct themselves according to its rules.

Chosen by the Commons and ceremonially dragged to the speaker's chair with feigned reluctance, the speaker has to be absolutely impartial. Once elected, he or she avoids all party contacts, not even eating in the Commons dining-room. The speaker stands not as a party member at general elections but as "the speaker seeking re-election". It is this impartiality which ensures that a turbulent House will obey when the speaker calls "Order! Order!".

The chamber where privilege is sacred

Parliamentary privilege is jealously guarded; it is with a sense of history and a determination to keep its special powers that the speaker of the House of Commons claims its "ancient and undoubted rights and privileges" at the opening of each parliament. The highest of these is freedom of speech, controlled only by parliament's own rules of order.

Members can speak in the Commons without fear of being sued for libel or prosecuted for sedition. This has led to outraged demands for members to repeat what they have said outside the House – and risk being sued. The point of the privilege is, however, not to protect members but to allow them to defend the interests of the people.

Parliament can punish those guilty of breach of privilege or contempt against the House. Offenders are brought to the bar of the House – literally a wooden pole barring entrance to the floor. Their apologies are usually accepted, but the House has the power to expel members or imprison others – usually journalists – who offend.

The power games that politicians play

Inside the Commons: Tories (government) left, Labour (opposition) right.

Parliament, which is the supreme law-making authority within the United Kingdom, is an alliance of the sovereign, the House of Commons and the House of Lords. Although they only meet together on certain ceremonial occasions, the agreement of all three branches is needed to pass legislation.

It enjoys enormous powers. Unfettered by a written constitution, it is able to pass any legislation which it sees fit to do. Parliament may declare war or sue for peace; it may enact laws, change them or abolish them; it may legalize that which was unlawful, and make unlawful – and therefore punishable – that which was legal when it was done. It may extend its own term of office beyond the stipulated five years, as it did in both World Wars. In certain circumstances it may even hold secret sessions.

There are, however, checks and balances, with public opinion, common law, precedent, the opposition and indeed the sovereign acting as powerful restraints. Few governments persist with legislation so unpopular that it would ensure defeat at the following election. An example from the early 1990s was the "poll tax", whose unpopularity brought rapid changes. Parliament had the power to enforce this legislation but was forced to abandon it by the weight of public opinion.

THE SALARIES OF BRITAIN'S TOP POLITICIANS

	£
Prime minister, first lord of the treasury	76,234
Chancellor of the exchequer	63,047
Secretary for home affairs	63,047
Secretary for foreign affairs	63,047
Lord chancellor	106,750
Leader of the House of Commons	63,047
Leader of the House of Lords	50,558
Leader of the Opposition	59,736
The speaker	65,008
Ordinary members of the House of Commons	30,854

Britain's feudal present: the House of Lords

Peers of the realm and men of honour

Members of the House of Lords debate live on television for the first time.

The House of Lords is a unique mixture of feudal privilege and modern pragmatism that in theory cannot work effectively but in practice works extremely well. It is, moreover, admirably suited to the British temperament. It consists of the "lords spiritual" and the "lords temporal", and although it lost the struggle for power with the Commons long ago it is still referred to as the "upper house".

The "lords spiritual", a throwback to pre-Reformation days when spiritual peers were in the majority, now consist of the archbishops of Canterbury and York, the bishops of London, Durham and Winchester and the 21 next most senior bishops of the Church of England.

There are three types of "lords temporal": all hereditary peers and peeresses over the age of 21 who have not disclaimed their peerages; all life peers and peeresses created under the Life Peerages Act; and the law lords, who are made life peers to help the House in its function as the final court of appeal.

This eclectic body numbers nearly 2,000, but many of the hereditary "backwoodsmen" do not attend, so that the average daily attendance is around 320. Except for those such as the law lords who receive salaries, peers who attend are entitled to expenses of £68 for overnight subsistence, £26 for day subsistence and incidental travel, and £27 for office costs. This, with membership of "the best club in London", makes the Lords an attractive place for peers to pass their time.

There are peers, however, who prefer to be in the "lower house"; Tony Benn, the Labour MP, is one such. When his succession to the title of Viscount Stansgate barred him from the Commons he fought for and won the right of peers to disclaim their titles.

This works two ways, for while the majority of ministers are members of the Commons, the government must be fully represented in the Lords so that its policies can be properly presented – and criticized. This means that politically efficient hereditary peers can be made ministers, and senior members of the Commons can, contrariwise, be made life peers.

To maintain a balance of working peers, opposition parties submit their own lists of candidates for life peerages, adding to the mixture of experience and abilities. It also adds to the variety of business interests represented in the House. However, while members of the Commons must disclose their interests and may not vote on matters affecting those interests, members of the Lords are permitted to decide for themselves if it is within the bounds of "honourable" behaviour for them to speak or vote.

The Lords enjoy a range of subtle powers

Over the years the House of Lords, once more powerful than the Commons, has lost much of that power. It is, for example, now agreed that both the prime minister and the chancellor of the exchequer have to be members of the Commons. Another such restriction is that a bill designated a "money bill" become law within one month of having been passed by the Commons and be sent to the Lords even if the Lords have not passed it.

The power that the Lords enjoy today is more subtle than in the past, stemming from the ability and extensive experience of their active members, whose civilized debates often have a more profound influence on legislation than the sometimes more robust proceedings over in the House of Commons.

Where the Lords have actual power is as the final court of appeal. In theory all members of the House are entitled to attend when it is sitting as a court but in practice appeals are heard by the law lords only. These are: the lords of appeal in ordinary, specifically appointed to hear appeals, and salaried; other lords who hold or have held high judicial office and whose expert knowledge is required; and, from time to time, the lord chancellor.

One ancient privilege a member of the Lords might still claim is to be tried by his peers and, if found guilty of a capital charge, to be hanged with a silken rope.

The Queen reads her speech in the Lords at each opening of parliament.

'Strangers' can queue to watch the action

The essence of parliamentary proceedings is that they are conducted openly, and the public has a right to watch what is being done from the "strangers' galleries" in either House. This is in fact a popular tourist attraction, and the galleries are often full. Visitors can join the appropriate queue at St Stephen's Entrance [*see graphic on page 1221*] but are better advised to obtain tickets, seven or eight weeks in advance, through their MP's office. When in session the Commons sit from 2.30pm Monday to Thursday and 9.30am on Fridays. The Lords sit from 2.30pm on Tuesdays, Wednesdays and most Mondays, from 3.00pm on Thursdays and from 11.00am on Fridays when business is heavy. Overseas visitors may apply to their embassy or high commission for admission cards, but these do not ensure a seat for prime minister's question time, "the best show in town".

The parliamentary system of the Irish Republic

The three-fold form of Irish democracy

The *Oireachtas* [national parliament] of the Republic of Ireland, meeting in Dublin, consists of two Houses: the *Dail Eireann* and *Seanad Eireann*, and a president. It has the sole power of law-making for the state – a power exercised, since 1972, within the framework provided by Ireland's membership of the European Community. Government policy is scrutinized in both Houses, but the constitution provides for the overriding authority of the Dail in the making of laws.

Members of the Dail are elected to represent a given constituency. At present there are 166 members – *Teachtai Dala* or TDs – returned by the 41 constituencies into which the country is divided. Members may represent no more than 30,000 people and no fewer than 20,000, and at least once every 12 years both Houses are required to hold a review of the constituencies in order to ensure that there is a fair elected member:population ratio.

The Seanad has 60 members or senators. Of these, 11 are nominated by the *Taoiseach* [prime minister]. Forty-three are elected from five panels of candidates; each panel consists of the names of persons knowledgeable or experienced in a given field. The panels are concerned with culture and education, agriculture, labour, industry and commerce, and administration. At present the other six members of the Seanad are elected by certain universities. The election of these six members has been open to revision since 1979.

Any citizen over 21 years of age (with the exception of certain employees and functionaries of the state) may stand for either the Dail or the Seanad. Membership of both Houses at the same time is, however, not permitted.

The maximum term of the Dail is five years, the president setting the dates for dissolution and reconvening. Candidates for election to the Dail may nominate themselves or be nominated by a single registered voter – who can be any citizen over 18 who is not disqualified by law from voting. This right can be also extended to people resident in Ireland who are citizens of other states. Voting is by secret ballot, and the system used is proportional representation by means of a single transferable vote.

Candidates for the 43 elected places in the Seanad may be nominated by four members of the two Houses or by a registered nomination body associated with a panel. Members may only nominate one candidate. The Seanad is reconstituted soon after the election of a new Dail, and the electorate for the 43 panel places consists of the members of the newly elected Dail, the members of the outgoing Seanad and members of local government.

The centre of Ireland's democracy: the Dail Eireann in Dublin.

Taoiseach and president: power partners

The *Taoiseach* [prime minister] is nominated by the Dail and appointed by the president – who is elected by the people. Any citizen of 35 years or over is eligible for office. On 9 November 1990 history was made when Mary Robinson became the first woman to hold this post. Once elected, the president acts on the advice and authority of the government of the day.

The *Taoiseach* nominates the other members of government for the approval of the Dail, and assigns them to particular departments. One such nomination is that of *Tanaiste* [deputy prime minister] and another, the attorney-general, for appointment by the president. The *Taoiseach* also advises the president to summon or dissolve the Dail as appropriate, and his department provides a secretariat to the government.

The *Taoiseach* has to keep the president informed on matters of domestic and international policy, and it is on the authority and advice of the government that the president is permitted to exercise executive powers in international affairs. The president has, furthermore, certain discretionary powers. He or she may, for instance, refer a bill to the supreme court for vetting, and may decline to sign a bill if a majority of the Seanad and a third or more of the Dail request it – bills need the president's signature to become law. The people's will is then sought in a referendum. The president may also call a meeting of either or both Houses of the *Oireachtas* [national parliament].

LEADERS OF IRELAND, FROM 1922 TO 1992

FF = Fianna Fáil
FG = Fine Gael
SF = Sinn Féin

THE IRISH FREE STATE (6 Dec 1922 – 29 Dec 1937)

Governor-general	President of the Executive Council
Timothy Michael Healy Dec 1922 – Dec 1927	Arthur Griffith (SF) Jan – 12 Aug 1922
James McNeill Dec 1927 – Oct 1932	Michael Collins (SF) 12 Aug – 22 Aug 1922
Donal Buckley Nov 1932 – Dec 1936	William Thomas Cosgrave Sept 1922 – March 1932
Post abolished Dec 1936	Eamon de Valera (FF) March 1932 – Dec 1937

THE REPUBLIC OF IRELAND (Éire 29 Dec 1937 – 2 June 1949; thereafter the Republic of Ireland)

President	Taoiseach
Presidential Commission Dec 1937 – June 1938	Eamon de Valera (FF) Dec 1937 – Feb 1948
Dr Douglas Hyde (appointed with the agreement of all parties) June 1938 – June 1945	John Aloysius Costello (inter-party coalition) Feb 1948 – June 1951
Séan Thomas O'Kelly (FF) June 1945 – June 1959	Eamon de Valera (FF) June 1951 – June 1954
	John Aloysius Costello (FG) June 1954 – March 1957
	Eamon de Valera (FF) March 1957 – June 1959
Eamon de Valera (FF) June 1959 – June 1973	Sean Francis Lemass (FF) June 1959 – Nov 1966
	John Mary Lynch (FF) Nov 1966 – March 1973
Erskine Childers (FF) June 1973 – Nov 1974	Liam Cosgrave (FG/Labour coalition) March 1973 – July 1977
Cearbhall Ó Dálaigh (FF) Dec 1974 – Oct 1976	John Mary Lynch (FF) July 1977 – Dec 1979
Dr Patrick John Hillery (FF) Dec 1976 – Nov 1990	Charles Haughey (FF) Dec 1979 – June 1981
	Dr Garret Fitzgerald (FG/Labour coalition) June 1981 – Feb 1982
	Charles Haughey (FF) March 1982 – Dec 1982
	Dr Garret Fitzgerald (FG) Dec 1982 – Feb 1987
	Charles Haughey (FF/Progressive Democrat coalition) Feb 1987 – June 1989 July 1989 – Jan 1992
Mary Robinson (independent member of Seanad) Nov 1990 –	Albert Reynolds (FF/Progressive Democrat coalition) Feb 1992 –

The government

The executive powers of the Irish state are exercised by the government, which consists of between seven and 15 ministers. Of these no more than two may be members of the Seanad. The *Taoiseach* [prime minister], *Tanaiste* [deputy prime minister] and the minister for finance must be members of the Dail.

The government bears collective responsibility to the Dail, so the resignation of the *Taoiseach* means in effect the resignation of the government. Ministers have a right to be heard in both houses and, usually, each minister heads one of the state departments.

A shared history: Britain and the Commonwealth

Free association grew out of empire

Britain may not have an empire any more, but it does have the Commonwealth. A free association of 50 sovereign states which has evolved from the former Empire, the Commonwealth originated in a report of 1839 that spoke of discontent in the Canadian colonies. Britain feared that Canada might follow the example of the other North American colonies that seceded in the 1770s to form the US. The report suggested that the governor of Canada should appoint ministers who had the confidence of the local assembly, and that he should accept its views – unless they touched on relations with Britain. In 1847 this practice of "responsible government" was in force in Canada.

There were of course limits on the independence of the Canadian and other "dominions", or self-governing colonies, especially in foreign relations, trade and constitutional change. In 1914, for instance, Britain declared war on behalf of the Empire without consulting the dominions. Yet their autonomy was gradually increased. Under the Statute of Westminster of 1931 they were described as "autonomous communities within the ... Empire, equal in status, in no way subordinate one to another in any respect of their domestic or external affairs, though unified by a common allegiance to the crown". Most member states joined the Commonwealth after 1945, following Britain's decision to guide its dependent territories to full independence. This process began with the independence of India and Pakistan in 1947.

Nowadays being a member of the Commonwealth entails no legal or constitutional demands, but Queen Elizabeth II is still acknowledged as its head. For 17 member countries she is in any case the head of state. In each of these – apart from Britain – the Queen is represented by a governor-general, who is wholly independent of the British government and is appointed on the recommendation of the government of the country concerned.

Ghanaian women sorting rice: cash crops are vital to the Commonwealth.

Links with the EC: conflict of loyalties?

Commitment to the European Community is a major element in Britain's foreign policy – the EC is, after all, the world's largest trading unit. Yet there was concern when Britain joined the EC in 1973 that its membership should not be at the cost of the Commonwealth states, many of whose economies are dependent on the export to Britain of certain commodities. The Treaty of Accession therefore offered 20 Commonwealth countries several forms of association with the EC, including the chance to join with other associate countries in negotiating an agreement on trade and aid.

In 1975 the Lomé Convention marked the acceptance of this by 46 countries in Africa, the Caribbean and the Pacific – the so-called ACP states. The current convention (Lomé IV) runs to the year 2000 and focuses on rural development and improved access for agricultural products. Other forms of commercial cooperation exist with non-ACP states.

THE BRITISH COMMONWEALTH:
MEMBER STATES AND YEAR OF JOINING

Member states	Year	Member states	Year
Australia, Britain, Canada, New Zealand	1931	Bangladesh	1972
India, Pakistan	1947	The Bahamas	1973
Sri Lanka	1948	Grenada	1974
Ghana, Malaysia	1957	Papua New Guinea	1975
Nigeria	1960	Seychelles	1976
Cyprus, Sierra Leone	1961	Dominica, Solomon Islands, Tuvalu	1978
Jamaica, Trinidad and Tobago, Uganda	1962	Kiribati, St Lucia, St Vincent and the Grenadines	1979
Kenya	1963	Vanuatu, Zimbabwe	1980
Malawi, Malta, Tanzania, Zambia	1964	Antigua and Barbuda, Belize	1981
The Gambia, Singapore	1965	Maldives	1982
Barbados, Botswana, Guyana, Lesotho	1966	St Christopher and Nevis	1983
Mauritius, Nauru, Swaziland	1968	Brunei	1984
Tonga, Western Samoa	1970	Namibia	1990

Aid and education in Commonwealth

The Commonwealth offers Britain a unique opportunity to aid development and stability in the Third World. Among the many ways that it does so, the most obvious are the provision of financial aid and educational cooperation.

Bilateral aid for developing countries in the Commonwealth stood at £371 million in 1990 (total gross bilateral aid in 1990 was £1,042 million). Aid is concentrated on the world's poorest countries, with the emphasis on promoting long-term social and economic development.

Set up in 1948, the Commonwealth Development Corporation (CDC) promotes economic development by investing in developing countries. Much of the CDC's funding is in the form of loans allocated from the official aid programme at special concessionary rates.

International debt is an immense problem, and Britain's proposals at the 1990 Commonwealth Finance Ministers' Conference aimed at reducing the burden that has weighed so hard on poor countries, including some in the Commonwealth, since the 1980s. Yet in addition to money, it is necessary to pass on knowledge. Britain complements its financial aid to Commonwealth countries with technical cooperation. This means passing on skills as well as providing equipment. The Commonwealth Fund for Technical Co-operation is the organization that specializes in so-called "technology transfer" between developing countries.

Educational cooperation is also important, based on a common use of English and similarities in the educational systems among members, as well as on professional ties. The aim of the Commonwealth Education Conferences is to promote various programmes, such as the professional development of school teachers and initiatives to encourage higher education, while British bilateral aid supports schemes assisting educational institutions. The Commonwealth Institute in London is the British centre for Commonwealth education and culture.

The Imperial State Crown, shown here, belongs to the regalia, or crown jewels; that worn in the coronation is St Edward's Crown. Kept in the Tower of London, almost all the jewels on display there date from after the Restoration (1660); the previous regalia was destroyed during the Commonwealth of 1649-53.

The role played by the monarchy in British life

Queen Elizabeth II did not expect to come to the throne. Born on 21 April 1926 to the duke and duchess of York, she grew up confident in the knowledge that her "Uncle David", the prince of Wales, would be king. But when, as Edward VIII, he abdicated in 1936 to marry the twice-divorced Mrs Simpson, Elizabeth's father reluctantly became George VI (1936-52).

Elizabeth came to the throne on 6 February 1952, following George VI's death. Elizabeth was at the time in Kenya with her husband, Lieutenant Philip Mountbatten, now Prince Philip, the duke of Edinburgh. She has ruled the country ever since, earning the thanks of prime ministers for her wisdom and the admiration of the nation. In recent years, however, the much publicized marital difficulties of the Queen's children have shown that the royal family, like any other, has its share of problems.

The Queen's functions are various. She is assumed to be the fountain of both justice and of honour; as such she pardons criminals and appoints government ministers and judges. Titles and honours are also granted by her. As commander-in-chief of the armed forces she appoints officers, and as head of the Church of England it is she who appoints bishops. But all these things the Queen does on the advice of her government.

It is in her relations with the prime minister of the day that the Queen's real power lies. She has seen them come and go, from Sir Winston Churchill to Lady Thatcher, and has learnt from each of them. All cabinet papers pass before her, and she receives copies of important foreign and commonwealth office telegrams. She also sees the prime minister once a week, and her advice is rarely ignored. This is the reality behind her public appearances, but these too are of great importance, binding the relationship with her subjects – and boosting the tourist trade.

The authority of the modern monarchy

Queen Elizabeth II: the living symbol of a thousand years of history.

The monarchy in the United Kingdom has evolved over a thousand years of warfare and politics, during which time the sovereign's status and authority have constantly changed – and they are still changing. As a result of the union of England and Scotland in 1707, the union with Ireland in 1801 and the emergence of the Commonwealth from the old Empire [*see report on page 1225*], the Queen's title in the United Kingdom is: "Elizabeth the Second, by the Grace of God, of the United Kingdom of Great Britain and Northern Ireland and of Her other Realms and Territories Queen, Head of the Commonwealth, Defender of the Faith."

Her right to this title derives from the common-law rules of heredity and from legislation such as the Act of Settlement (1700), which stipulates that only Protestant descendants of Electress Sophia of Hanover, the granddaughter of James I (1603-25), may succeed to the throne. Under the Statute of Westminster (1931) the succession can only be altered if all the nations of the Commonwealth which recognize the Queen as sovereign consent to the change. Unless that happens, the eldest son of the sovereign automatically succeeds to the throne, followed by his own descendants, with sons taking precedence over daughters. As in the case of the present Queen, if a daughter succeeds she becomes "queen regnant" and has the same powers as if she were king.

One anomaly is that while the wife of a king takes her husband's rank and style as queen, the husband of a queen regnant is entitled to no special title under the constitution. In practice, however, he is granted honours by the crown, and the Queen has certain honours, such as the Royal Victorian Order, which are in her personal gift.

The sovereign succeeds to the throne immediately on the death of his or her predecessor. In the past this was done to avoid bloodshed, and so the cry went up: "The king is dead – long live the king!" Today the new sovereign is proclaimed at an accession council and is subsequently crowned in Westminster Abbey by the archbishop of Canterbury in a ceremony that has remained virtually the same for more than a thousand years. It is this sense of continuity that helps to vest the sovereign with true status and authority.

Money: how the nation funds the royals

The Queen, reputed to be the richest woman in the world, pays no taxes. This is part of the complicated arrangement whereby she surrenders the revenue from the crown estate to the exchequer. In recent years this has amounted to around £55 million.

In return, the cost of running the royal household, any other expenses for the Queen's official duties, and payments to other members of the royal family are made out of public funds through the Queen's civil list [*see table below*]. Other expenses incurred by the Queen are paid by the privy purse, which is financed from the revenues of the 21,000 hectares (52,000 acres) owned by the duchy of Lancaster.

The Queen meets her personal expenses from her own resources, but some 80 per cent of the costs involved in the official duties of the royal family is still paid for by public departments. This includes the costs of the royal yacht, the Queen's flight, the royal train, the maintenance of the various royal palaces and state visits abroad.

THE CIVIL LIST OF PAYMENTS TO THE ROYAL FAMILY, 1991–2000

	£
Queen Elizabeth II	7,900,000
Queen Elizabeth, the Queen Mother	640,000
Prince Philip, the duke of Edinburgh	360,000
Prince Andrew, the duke of York	250,000
Prince Edward	100,000
Princess Anne, the princess royal	230,000
Princess Margaret	220,000
Princess Alice, the duchess of Gloucester	90,000
Prince Charles, the prince of Wales	none

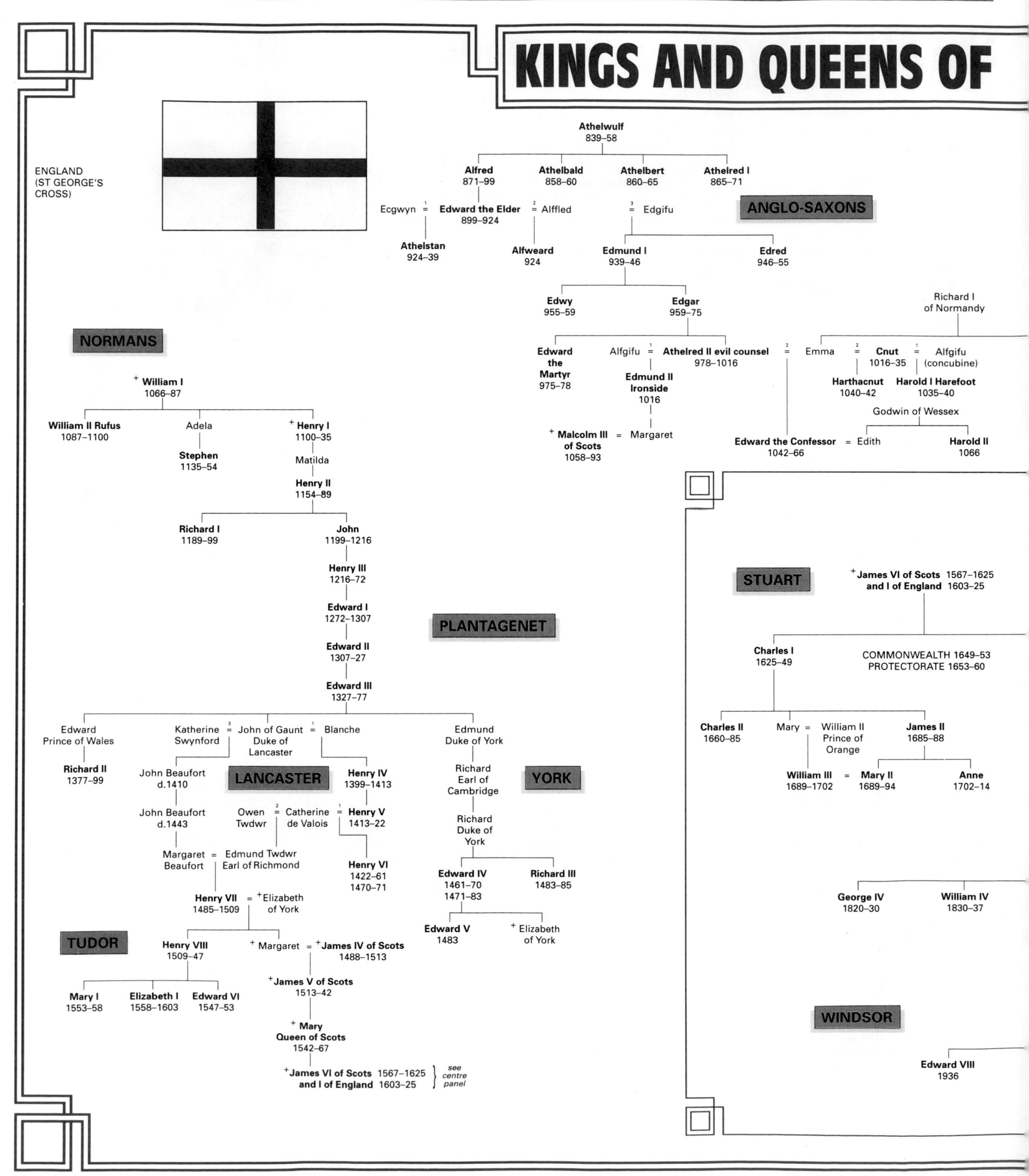
KINGS AND QUEENS OF
ENGLAND (ST GEORGE'S CROSS)
ANGLO-SAXONS
Athelwulf 839–58
Alfred 871–99
Athelbald 858–60
Athelbert 860–65
Athelred I 865–71
Ecgwyn = Edward the Elder 899–924 = Alffled
= Edgifu
Athelstan 924–39
Alfweard 924
Edmund I 939–46
Edred 946–55
Edwy 955–59
Edgar 959–75
Edward the Martyr 975–78
Alfgifu = Athelred II evil counsel 978–1016 = Emma = Cnut 1016–35 = Alfgifu (concubine)
Richard I of Normandy
Edmund II Ironside 1016
Harthacnut 1040–42
Harold I Harefoot 1035–40
Godwin of Wessex
+ Malcolm III of Scots 1058–93 = Margaret
Edward the Confessor 1042–66 = Edith
Harold II 1066
NORMANS
+ William I 1066–87
William II Rufus 1087–1100
Adela
+ Henry I 1100–35
Stephen 1135–54
Matilda
Henry II 1154–89
Richard I 1189–99
John 1199–1216
Henry III 1216–72
Edward I 1272–1307
PLANTAGENET
Edward II 1307–27
Edward III 1327–77
Edward Prince of Wales
Katherine Swynford = John of Gaunt Duke of Lancaster = Blanche
Edmund Duke of York
Richard II 1377–99
John Beaufort d.1410
LANCASTER
Henry IV 1399–1413
Richard Earl of Cambridge
YORK
John Beaufort d.1443
Owen Twdwr = Catherine de Valois = Henry V 1413–22
Richard Duke of York
Margaret Beaufort = Edmund Twdwr Earl of Richmond
Henry VI 1422–61 1470–71
Edward IV 1461–70 1471–83
Richard III 1483–85
Henry VII 1485–1509 = + Elizabeth of York
Edward V 1483
+ Elizabeth of York
TUDOR
Henry VIII 1509–47
+ Margaret = + James IV of Scots 1488–1513
Mary I 1553–58
Elizabeth I 1558–1603
Edward VI 1547–53
+ James V of Scots 1513–42
+ Mary Queen of Scots 1542–67
+ James VI of Scots 1567–1625 and I of England 1603–25
see centre panel
STUART
+ James VI of Scots 1567–1625 and I of England 1603–25
Charles I 1625–49
COMMONWEALTH 1649–53
PROTECTORATE 1653–60
Charles II 1660–85
Mary = William II Prince of Orange
James II 1685–88
William III 1689–1702 = Mary II 1689–94
Anne 1702–14
George IV 1820–30
William IV 1830–37
WINDSOR
Edward VIII 1936

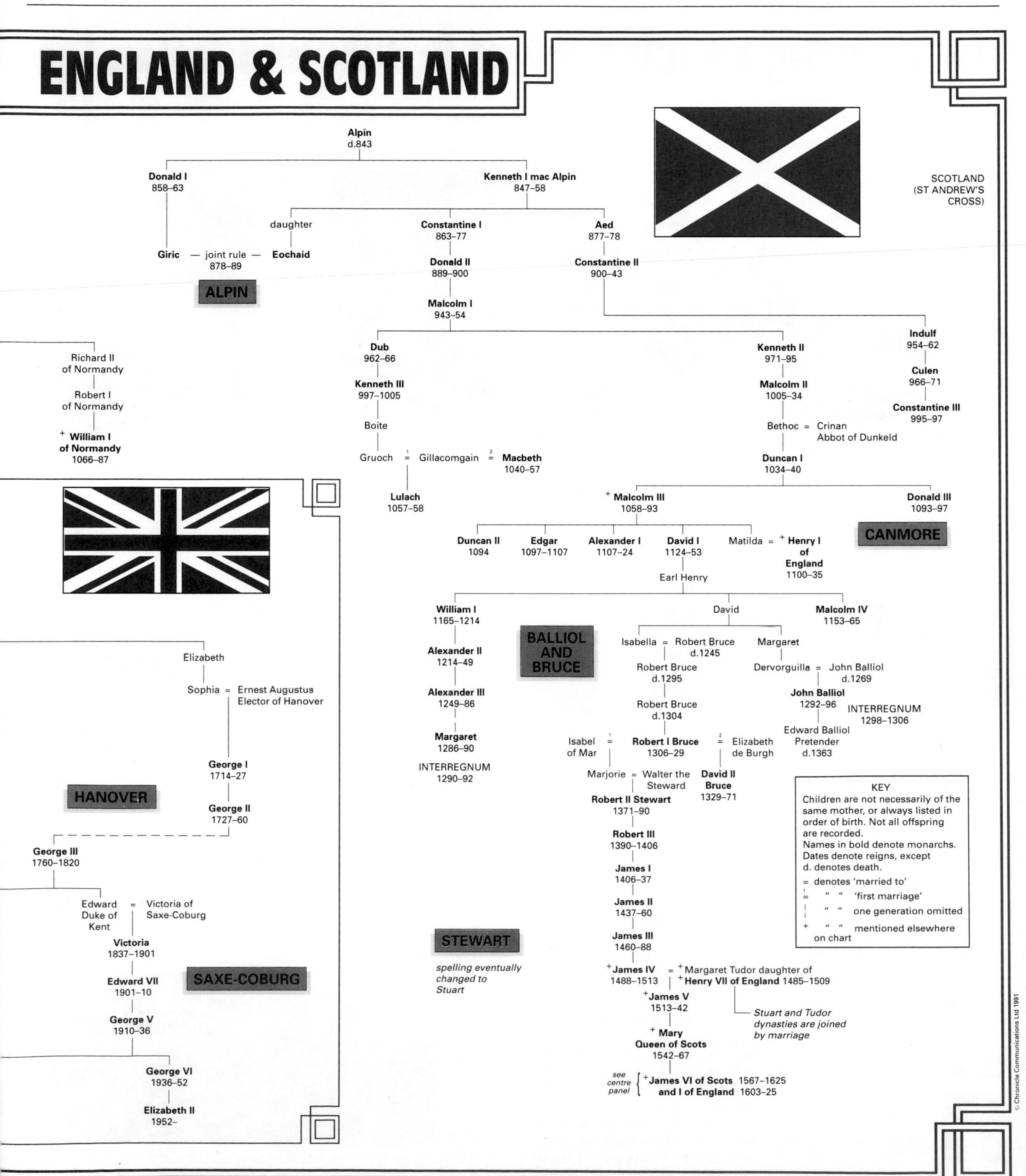

ENGLAND & SCOTLAND
SCOTLAND (ST ANDREW'S CROSS)
Alpin d.843
Donald I 858–63
Kenneth I mac Alpin 847–58
daughter
Constantine I 863–77
Aed 877–78
Giric — joint rule — Eochaid
878–89
Donald II 889–900
Constantine II 900–43
ALPIN
Malcolm I 943–54
Indulf 954–62
Dub 962–66
Kenneth II 971–95
Culen 966–71
Kenneth III 997–1005
Malcolm II 1005–34
Constantine III 995–97
Boite
Bethoc = Crinan Abbot of Dunkeld
Gruoch = Gillacomgain = Macbeth 1040–57
Duncan I 1034–40
Lulach 1057–58
+ Malcolm III 1058–93
Donald III 1093–97
CANMORE
Duncan II 1094
Edgar 1097–1107
Alexander I 1107–24
David I 1124–53
Matilda = + Henry I of England 1100–35
Earl Henry
William I 1165–1214
David
Malcolm IV 1153–65
BALLIOL AND BRUCE
Isabella = Robert Bruce d.1245
Margaret
Alexander II 1214–49
Robert Bruce d.1295
Dervorguilla = John Balliol d.1269
Alexander III 1249–86
John Balliol 1292–96
Robert Bruce d.1304
INTERREGNUM 1298–1306
Margaret 1286–90
Edward Balliol Pretender d.1363
INTERREGNUM 1290–92
Isabel of Mar = Robert I Bruce 1306–29 = Elizabeth de Burgh
Marjorie = Walter the Steward
David II Bruce 1329–71
Robert II Stewart 1371–90
Robert III 1390–1406
James I 1406–37
James II 1437–60
James III 1460–88
STEWART
spelling eventually changed to Stuart
+James IV 1488–1513 = +Margaret Tudor daughter of +Henry VII of England 1485–1509
+James V 1513–42
Stuart and Tudor dynasties are joined by marriage
+ Mary Queen of Scots 1542–67
see centre panel
+James VI of Scots 1567–1625
and I of England 1603–25
KEY
Children are not necessarily of the same mother, or always listed in order of birth. Not all offspring are recorded.
Names in bold denote monarchs.
Dates denote reigns, except d. denotes death.
= denotes 'married to'
= " " 'first marriage'
¦ " " one generation omitted
+ " " mentioned elsewhere on chart
Richard II of Normandy
Robert I of Normandy
+ William I of Normandy 1066–87
Elizabeth
Sophia = Ernest Augustus Elector of Hanover
George I 1714–27
HANOVER
George II 1727–60
George III 1760–1820
Edward Duke of Kent = Victoria of Saxe-Coburg
Victoria 1837–1901
Edward VII 1901–10
SAXE-COBURG
George V 1910–36
George VI 1936–52
Elizabeth II 1952–
© Chronicle Communications Ltd 1991

The growing populations of Britain and Ireland

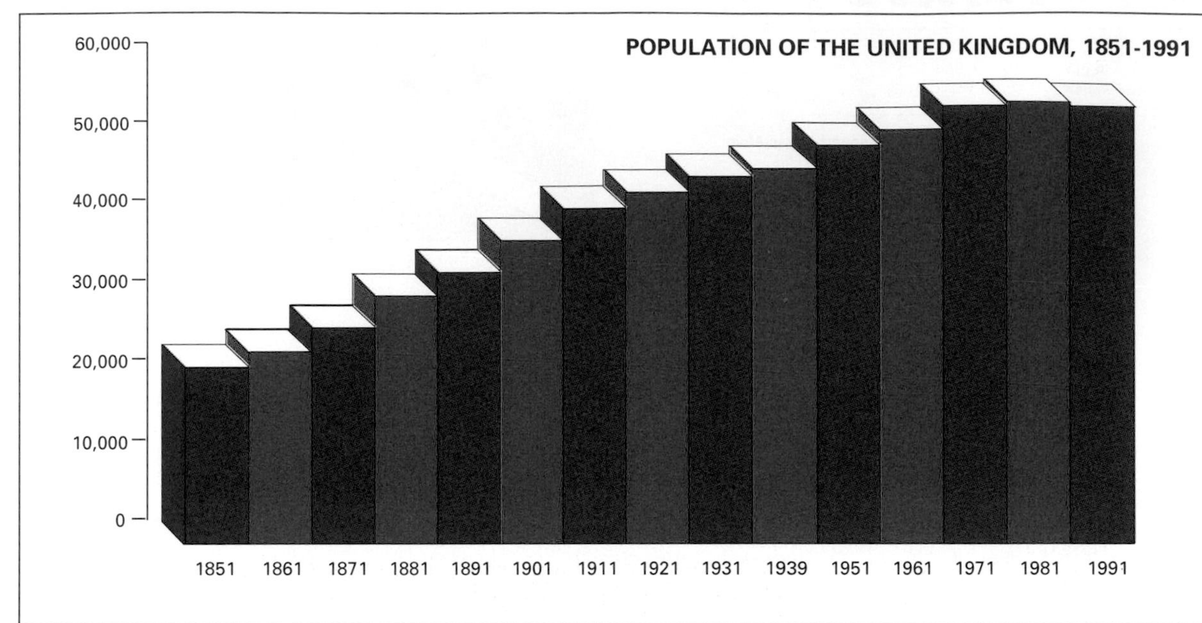

The crush of commuters in cities is symptomatic of our rising numbers.

City-dwellers crammed into trains and buses cannot help but be reminded every day that our national populations are growing. The bar chart above shows how, for instance, the population of the United Kingdom has more than doubled since 1851. In that year there were 22.4 million people; the figure from the 1991 census stands at 55.7 million. The bar chart for Ireland [*below right*] starts, for obvious reasons, a lot later than the UK one, at 1926. The total population for the Irish Free State (as it was called) then stood at just below 2.8 million, whereas that of the present-day Republic has reached 3.5 million, a rise of 20 per cent over 65 years. Over a similar period (1931-91) the United Kingdom's population rose from about 46.2 million to 55.7 million – an increase of 17 per cent.

The small table below shows one very dramatic difference between the British and Irish situations: population density. The population of the Republic is – as an average – spread far more thinly than it is on the other side of the Irish Sea. In fact, the United Kingdom is more densely populated than any other EC country – with the exception of the Netherlands and Belgium.

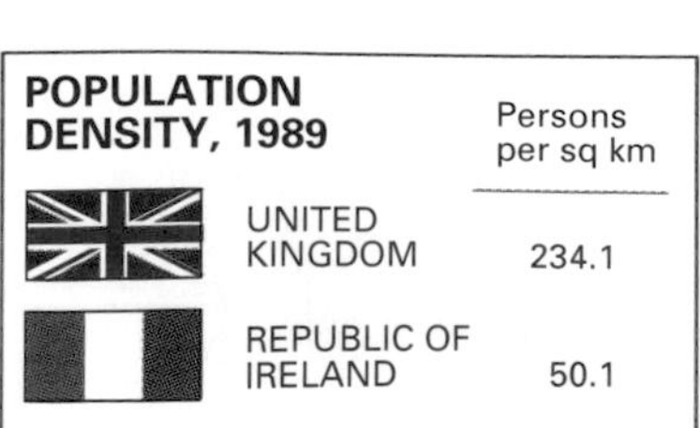

POPULATION DENSITY, 1989

	Persons per sq km
UNITED KINGDOM	234.1
REPUBLIC OF IRELAND	50.1

If time travel were actually possible, one of the things that might strike us most would be the comparatively small populations of previous centuries. Going back to, say, the middle of the 16th century, we would find only about 2.8 million people living in England – which as approximately the same number of people today living in Wales. Even a hundred years later, around 1650, the figure was still only 5.5 million. To put that in some kind of context, the population of Greater London is at the present day just under 6.4 million.

All kinds of factors affect population size. Better housing, better food and more widely available medical care combine to help more people to survive. Under these favourable conditions babies and young children stand a much better chance of making it into adulthood, while the adult population itself lives longer.

Life expectancy has increased dramatically over the centuries. An Englishman born in 1600 could have expected to live no longer – on average – than his late thirties. Nowadays he should, all things being equal, make it into his early seventies. Similarly an Irishman born in the 1870s might have lived to be about 50 years old. He should now survive to about 70. Paradoxically, when in previous times there were fewer people around there were more babies born. Now that there are more people, birth-rates are falling – indeed, in the United Kingdom there will be more deaths than births within about 40 years' time if current trends continue.

In the past – as in the contemporary Third World – couples had more children because there was less chance that all would live to be adults. The more children you had, the greater chance there was that a few would survive to look after you in your old age. It is estimated that in the late 16th century, for instance, there were about 40 births per 1,000 of the population for England and Wales. In the late 20th century that figure stood at just under 13 births. Records for Ireland suggest a similar pattern: in the middle of the last century there were about 39 births per 1,000 of the population. By the early 1980s that had dropped by nearly 50 per cent to just 21 births.

In many ways, however, the Republic of Ireland offers a situation quite unlike that in the United Kingdom. The Irish have a relatively high proportion of young people. A major reason for this is that so many Irish still leave their country to seek a better life abroad. This leads to the strange situation that, although the number of births in Ireland still exceeds the number of deaths, the population actually decreased slightly between 1986 and 1991, the date of the last census.

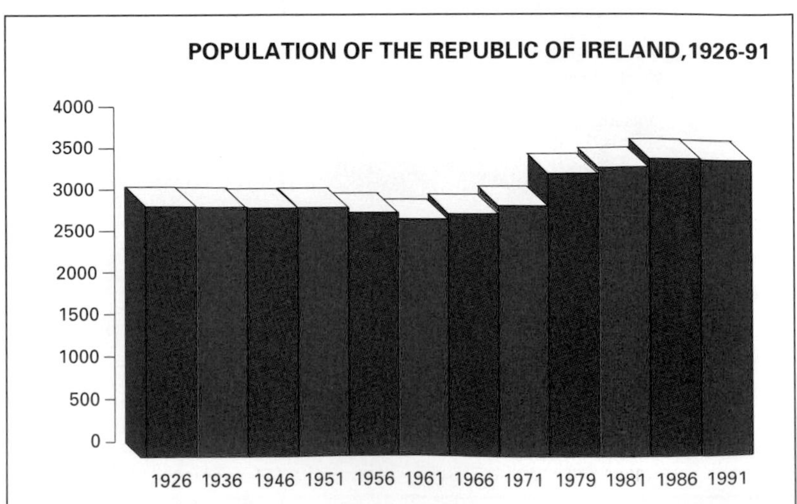

Marriage and divorce in Britain and Ireland

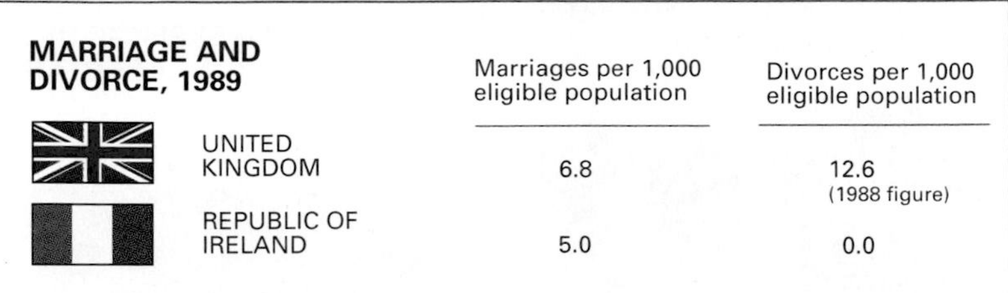

MARRIAGE AND DIVORCE, 1989	Marriages per 1,000 eligible population	Divorces per 1,000 eligible population
UNITED KINGDOM	6.8	12.6 (1988 figure)
REPUBLIC OF IRELAND	5.0	0.0

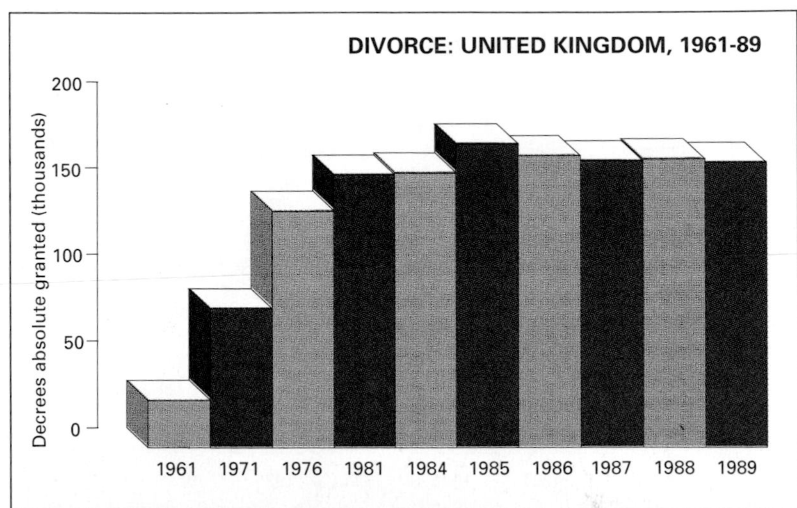

Samuel Butler (1612-80) once put the rhyming question:

... in what stupid age or nation
Was marriage ever out of fashion?

The table above shows that both the United Kingdom and Ireland are nations in which marriage remains very much in fashion. The higher rate for the former should not cause any surprise: the UK marriage rates are amongst the highest in Europe. Sadly, the same can also be said for its divorce rates. In the Republic, however, divorce is not allowed – one of the many signs of the influence of the Roman Catholic Church over the country.

To judge, also, from the bar charts below for marriage rates, the answer to Butler's question appears to be that marriage has stayed about as popular as it ever was. In the England of 1601 the rate was 8.5 persons per 1,000; in 1971 it was 8.3 and a decade later not much less, at 7.1. In Ireland the rate stood at 7.2 in 1871 and in 1981 was 7.0.

People's motives and expectations may, however, differ from age to age. In past centuries marriage was basically an economic union as well as the necessary social and religious sanction for having children. In the late 20th century people lay greater stress on the emotional commitment. As for having children, more and more people – in the United Kingdom, at least – are no longer choosing to do so within a traditional marriage. Up until the early 1960s the percentage of illegitimate births was about 4 to 5 per cent of the total. Since then it has shot up dramatically: births outside marriage in 1990 stood at 28 per cent of all births.

The graph above right shows the dark side of the equation: the dramatic rise in the UK divorce statistics. Some 27,000 decrees absolute were granted in 1961; that number had risen by 1989 to 164,000 – a staggering rise of over 600 per cent. Yet no matter how many actual divorces there are, they tend to occur at the same point in a marriage and to partners in a particular age group. Whether in 1961 or 1989, the people most likely to get divorced were those whose marriages had lasted between five and nine years – in apparent vindication of the theory of the "seven-year itch" – and those who were aged between 25 and 29.

The flares and platform heels readily identify this as a 1970s wedding.

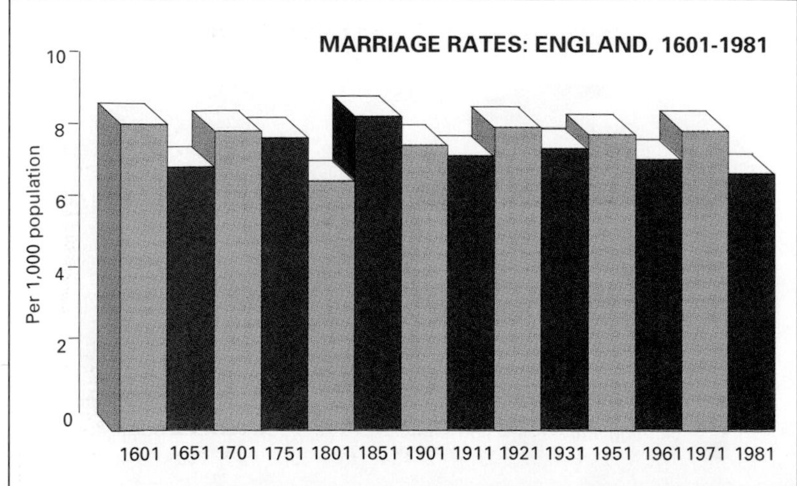

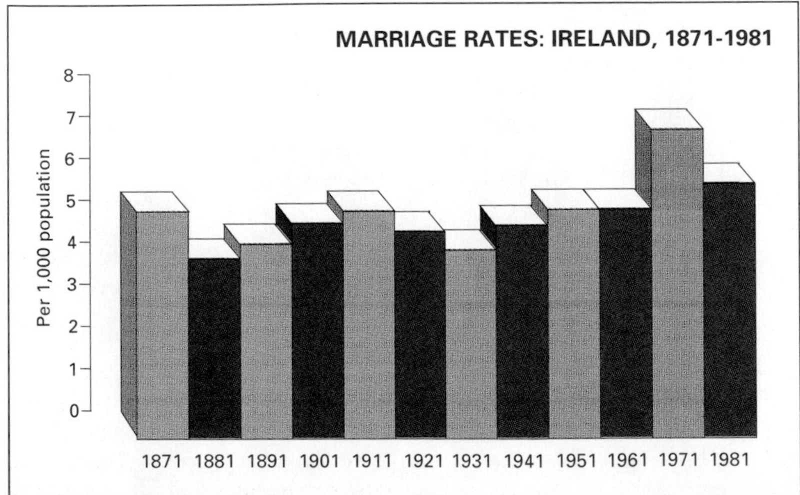

Intimations of mortality

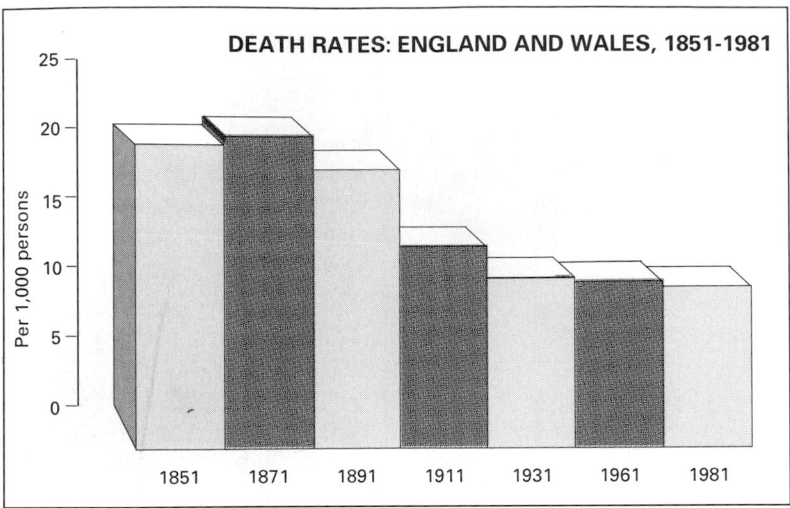

The Grim Reaper comes for us all eventually – but at least his visits now come less frequently for the population as a whole than once they did. The bar charts above and below give an indication of how death rates have generally declined. The rate per 1,000 persons in England and Wales in 1851 was 22; this has now been nearly halved to just over 11. In Ireland 17.5 persons per 1,000 died in 1881; a century later the rate had dropped, again by about half, to 9.6.

The overall picture is clear: for all the threats of war and ecological catastrophe, people living in contemporary Britain and Ireland are much more likely to survive into old age than their ancestors. In Shakespeare's time (the late 16th and early 17th centuries), for instance, the death rate was probably about 28 persons per 1,000. Infant mortality has also dropped considerably, especially over recent decades. Other important factors in the declining death rate are improved health care and water supplies. Some diseases, such as typhoid and cholera, have been virtually wiped out, while others, such as poliomyelitis, are at least kept at bay with vaccination programmes.

A glance at the statistics can provide some startling reading. About 266 deaths per 100,000 of the Irish population were put down to tuberculosis in 1871. Just over a century later, in 1979, that figure was 5.6. Diphtheria and croup accounted for 32 Scottish deaths per 100,000 of the population in 1855; in 1951 that had shrunk to 0.01. Yet the death toll from some other diseases has increased. One such is cancer: 32 Scots per 100,000 died of cancer in 1855, but by 1981 the number was just under 137, a frightening rise of 428 per cent.

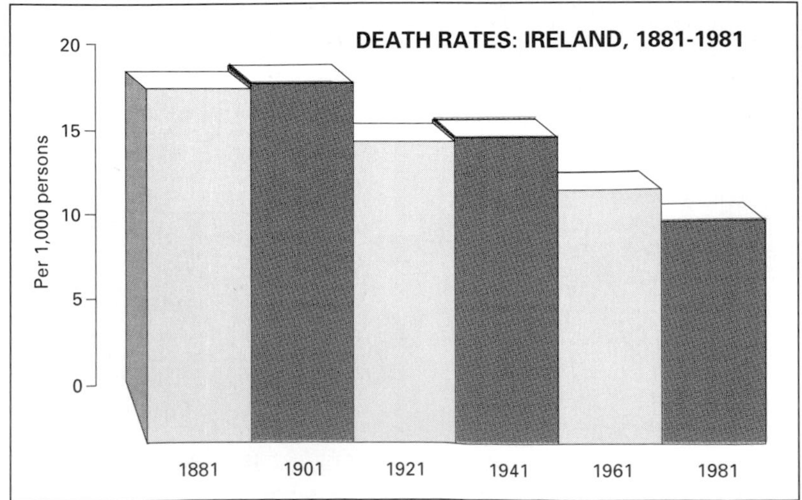

Spending on the basics

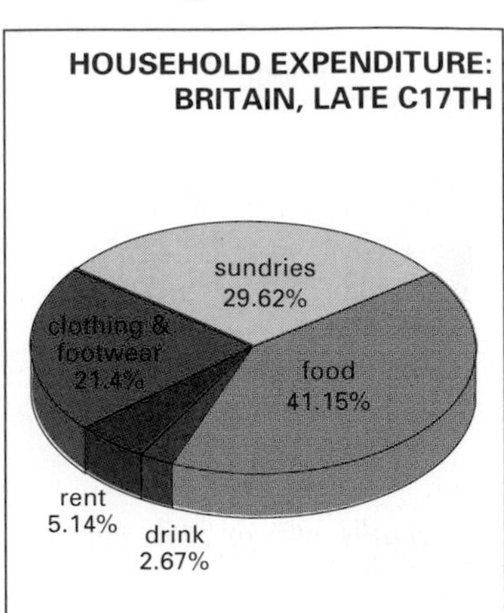

Man cannot live by bread alone – but it helps: food takes up the lion's share of family budgets now (left) just as it did 300 years ago (right).

A comparison of the pie chart above right with those below reveals that although a smaller proportion of our total income goes on food and drink than in previous times, it is still the largest proportion. The Irish seem to be especially big spenders – proportionately – when it comes to food, drink and tobacco. These take up nearly 40 per cent of the family budget. This is not only a higher proportion than that among UK families but also the highest in the European Community. The Irish also outspend the UK in clothing and footwear, household equipment, medical care, recreation and entertainment.

Certain other items have increased considerably as a proportion of spending in both countries over the years. British households used to spend about 6 to 7 per cent of their money on transport in the 1930s and 1940s. Since the early 1960s that has jumped to nearly 18 per cent. Ireland has witnessed a similar pattern. In the early 1950s transport accounted for about 4 per cent of the family's budget. That has now more than trebled to 12.6 per cent. Naturally the wider use of the motor car is partly to blame, as well as increased fuel prices making buses and trains more expensive.

Most – perhaps all – of the items presented here might be classed as necessities: we cannot do without food, clothing, medicine. The picture would be incomplete, however, without looking at our "luxuries", too [*see page 1233*].

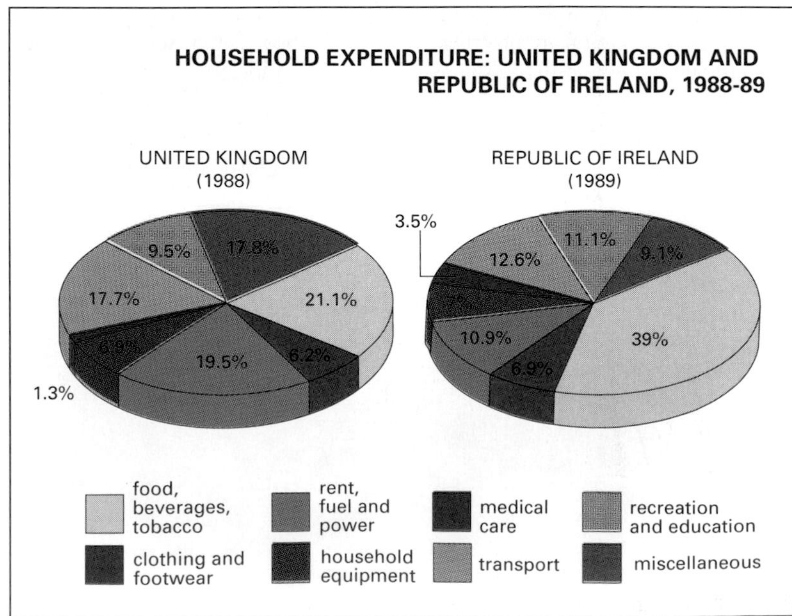

Spending on durables

Those of us who have spent good money on hardware that breaks down within weeks of being purchased might find the term "consumer durables" grimly ironic. However that may be, more and more people feel that items which were once considered luxuries, such as washing machines, televisions and videos, are essential to the modern home. The tables below show the percentage of households possessing various kinds of consumer durable. In both Britain and Ireland the most popular item is the television – beyond the reach of all but a few when first developed, it is now a *sine qua non* of modern life.

The tables do not show, however, what well-off and rather less well-off families prefer to own. While a majority of British unskilled manual and skilled manual households can run to the expense of a video, for instance, very few indeed have dishwashers – owned by a third of professional households. Just one in ten unskilled manual households owns a home computer, yet 44 per cent of professional ones do.

In the 17th century a well furnished home had little more than the basic artefacts of stools, pots and basins. The following century, however, saw more and more folk able to buy the luxuries of the day: clocks, mirrors, silver spoons and copper saucepans. Today mass-production methods and consumer credit allow a greater proportion of people to fill their homes with gadgets inconceivable to past ages.

HOUSEHOLDS POSSESSING CONSUMER DURABLES: GREAT BRITAIN, 1990

GOODS	% OF HOUSEHOLDS
Deep-freezers	80
Washing machine	86
Tumble drier	45
Microwave oven	47
Dishwasher	12
Telephone	87
Television	98
Video	60
Home computer	19
CD player	16

HOUSEHOLDS POSSESSING CONSUMER DURABLES: IRELAND, 1981

GOODS	% OF HOUSEHOLDS
Central heating	36.2
Washing machine	66.3
Fridge	88.2
Deep-freezers	16.4
Television	93.1
Telephone	38.7

Buy now, pay later: manufacturers compete to sell us "vital" hardware.

The drift to the towns

Rural heritage: carrying the harvest home, Spalding, Lincs., c.1900.

It is perhaps appropriate at the end of a history book such as this to look at one enormous contrast between the present and the past: the move from land to town. For most of the time covered in this book the people of Britain and Ireland lived in close contact with the land and the seasons. Yet many of us looking at a photograph such as the one above are struck with nostalgia for a way of life of which we have, ironically, no direct experience.

The two pie charts below show how great the change has been over the last 200 years. Even in Ireland, whose image abroad is still that of a predominantly rural country, the proportion of people working in agriculture has dropped greatly since the last century. In Britain the decline is even bigger.

For many years the populations of both countries have been shifting from the country to the towns. In 1850 only about 17 per cent of the Irish lived in towns; a century later this had risen to over 40 per cent. Figures for Scotland over the same period show a rise from about 36 to 70 per cent, and for England and Wales a rise from 30 to 80 per cent.

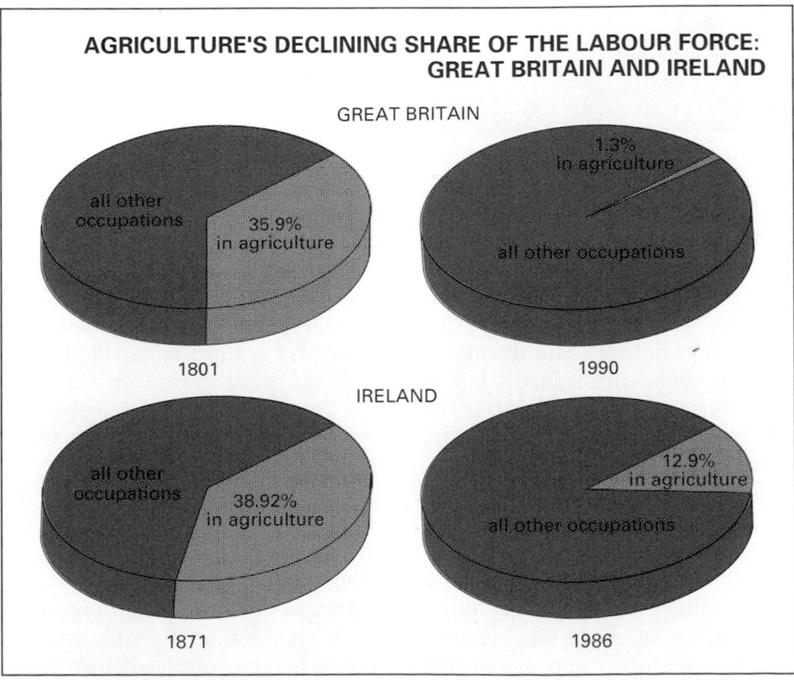

Worsening environment is major issue of concern

Awareness increases, but problems remain

In the late 1980s people suddenly started to wake up to environmental – or "green" – issues. Drivers began using unleaded petrol, and bottle banks sprang up everywhere. The phrases "global warming", "ozone layer" and "greenhouse effect" came out of the laboratories and onto everyone's lips.

Concern does not always, however, translate into action. Although membership of the pressure group Friends of the Earth rocketed from 8,000 in 1981 to 110,000 in 1990, environmental issues wield little political clout. In the 1992 British general election, the Green Party won a pitifully small percentage of the votes.

Environmental worries extend far beyond Britain and Ireland. The destruction of the South American rain forests, industrial pollution in eastern Europe and carbon dioxide emissions from the entire industrialized world affect us all. Pollution, as the Chernobyl disaster in 1987 showed, knows no frontiers. Yet there is hope: Green consumerism. More and more of us avoid "ecologically unsound" goods. The people power that has found little political expression may yet force industry, and governments, to think again.

A cause of growing public fear: smoke belching out of an industrial plant.

A hard choice – clean air or more cars?

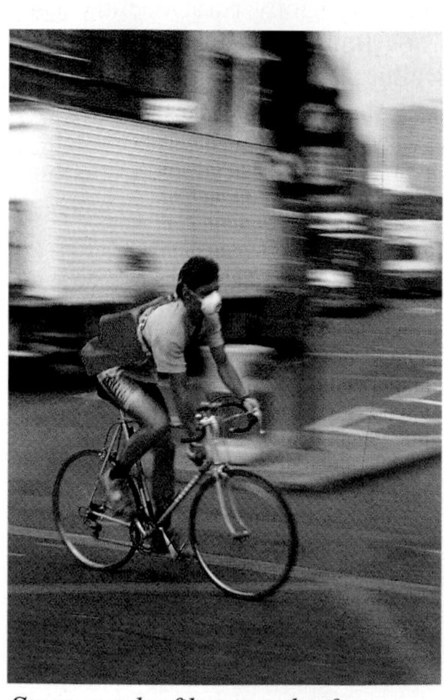

Smog masks filter out the fumes.

The air we *need* consists mainly of oxygen and nitrogen. The air we *get* is tainted with smoke, carbon monoxide, carbon dioxide, sulphur dioxide and nitrous oxides – all products of industry and the motor car. The main culprit in the UK is road transport, responsible for 88 per cent of carbon monoxide and about half of the nitrogen oxides.

Carbon monoxide is thought to cause certain cancers; other emissions from cars react with the sunlight to produce low-atmosphere ozone which irritates the lungs, eyes and throat. Then there is lead, added to petrol to improve engine performance. It has been proved that lead in the atmosphere can damage the brains and nervous systems of children. Unheeding of such reports, most British car owners (58 per cent in 1991) still prefer leaded petrol or diesel, even though a simple adjustment to most petrol cars enables them to run on unleaded. Yet going unleaded does not solve the problem; the carbon emissions are just as high, and to make up for the loss in fuel performance manufacturers are adding more known carcinogens, such as benzene and toluene. The only solution, it seems, is to use our cars less.

In Britain, however, transport policy since the 1960s has strongly favoured private transport while running down the buses and railways. Between 1982 and 1989 tax subsidies and expenditure on roads and cars stood at more than £33 billion, while less than £20 billion was spent on public transport. The average width of British roads has grown by a third since 1960, and over the same period an extra 17 per cent (in terms of length) has been added to the network. Over 150 officially designated sites of special scientific interest, such as Twyford Down, are threatened by the ministry of transport's current road-building plan. But get off the roads we must, or resign ourselves to air pollution on the same scale as Tokyo or Los Angeles before long.

Recycling and the 'disposable society'

In 1990 members of the British public threw about 130,000 tonnes of glass into over 4,600 bottle banks. Patting themselves on the back, they felt that they had done their bit for the environment. Glass recycling is indeed a British success story: 14 per cent of our glass containers are made into new ones. Even so, nearly 1,900,000 tonnes of glass is still thrown in the bin to be ploughed into landfill sites. The Dutch put both the British and the Irish to shame by recycling an astonishing 62 per cent of their glass.

It is, clearly, wise to use glass again: our milk and beer bottles, which are indeed used over and over, set a proud example, even though soft-drink manufacturers have long since withdrawn the deposit scheme which ensured that they could reuse their own bottles.

Yet glass is just the highly visible tip of an iceberg composed of solid waste. Our efforts as individuals make little difference: household refuse makes up just 3 per cent of our total waste. Around 75 per cent of Britain's waste originates from mines, quarries and farms. In this context the target set by London to recycle by the year 2000 half of all its domestic waste that it is possible to recycle seems insignificant.

Industry does its bit: 60 per cent of copper, tin and lead is recycled. But the benefits of recycling are outweighed by the relentless drive to make new goods. The irony is that the disposable society seems to be here to stay.

Cars dumped amidst green fields: just rubbish – or a potential resource?

Aquatic dumping-grounds grow dirtier

Every day, millions of litres of sewage are poured into our seas. About three-quarters of that is raw – in other words, not treated chemically to remove harmful bacteria. The sewage finds its way to the sea directly – in Britain there are over 400 outfalls straight into bathing waters – or via the rivers. In 1989 nearly a quarter of 440 UK beaches failed to reach the European Community's minimum standards for bathing water quality. Exactly the same number failed in 1991.

The UK government appears reluctant to respond and has adopted only the EC minimum guidelines in its clean-up targets. By contrast, the Irish government has taken a much firmer stance and aims to have a coast that is twice as clean.

Plans to end short outfalls pumping sewage near to the coast, and to ensure that all sewage discharged is at least treated so that solid waste is held back, are to be implemented over a very long timescale. Britain dumps sewage sludge – that is, the residue after treatment – straight into the North Sea and will continue to do so until 1998. The water companies want to spread the cost to the consumer of meeting generally accepted pollution standards, estimated at £7,000 million, over as long a period as possible.

Britain's rivers have a different set of problems, although only 2,500 miles (4,000km) of its 26,000 miles of waterway are officially classified as "badly polluted". Industrial and agricultural effluent has in fact made many stretches of water poisonous. River pollution is getting steadily worse: 480 miles of river were more polluted in 1991 than they were in 1985. The National Rivers Authority, which has the responsibility for monitoring and enforcing pollution controls, says that industry is cleaning up its act, while farm pollution has become the principal cause of new problems. Intensive farming, with its reliance on fertilizers and pesticides, has succeeded in polluting some of Britain's most remote waterways. Farm sewage is a serious threat: it is 100 times more polluting than the human variety. A single escape of slurry – 114,000 litres (25,000 gallons) of it – from a farm tank wiped out a breeding-ground for salmon in the river Tamar in 1991.

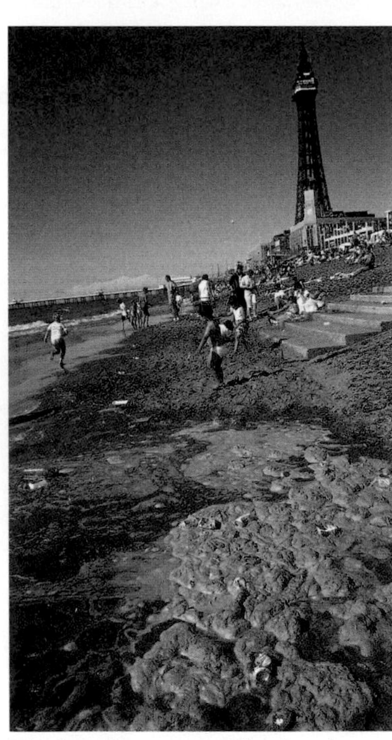

Blackpool's not-so-golden beaches.

Conservationists campaign to preserve the countryside from the urban sprawl

Langdale Pikes, Cumbria: an idyllic scene, but vulnerable to developers.

Countrymen tend to believe that nature conservation, like hunt sabotage, is the fad of London or Dublin busybodies blithely ignorant of how the rural economy works. Townies might, however, be forgiven for saying that the countryside belongs to us all: it is an amenity that, like our cities, has to be managed.

Organizations such as Friends of the Earth, the Woodland Trust and the Worldwide Fund for Nature saw their membership mushroom in the 1980s. It was bodies like this which drew attention to the way that plantations of alien conifers were ousting native trees such as the oak, beech and lime.

Britain's beauty spots are designated in various categories, of which the best known are the National Parks (covering 10 per cent of the UK), Areas of Outstanding Natural Beauty (38 regions covering a further 13 per cent of England and Wales) and Green Belts around major conurbations, designed to prevent them sprawling into the next city.

These and other measures can help wildlife to survive by offering them "security of tenure". Yet British wildlife remains vulnerable. Butterfly and spider populations have dropped significantly, and 63 species of native bird (out of a total of 519 native species) are in danger of extinction. Like everyone else, especially in the developed world, the British and the Irish need to take ever greater care to retain the best in their natural surroundings.

Care for environment begins at home

One of the great environmental disaster areas in Britain and Ireland is – the average home. It is draughty, poorly insulated and heated by an inefficient system, and no small amounts of fossil fuels have to be burnt to heat these conservationist's nightmares. We pay for it in terms of the environment as well as in high fuel bills. More efficient insulation and boilers would cut 5 per cent off our requirements.

The beauty of insulating our homes is that we can save the planet and lots of money at the same time. Steps such as draught-proofing, low-energy lightbulbs, heavier curtains, or cellophane to "double-glaze" windows all work – and they soon pay for themselves. Turning down a central heating thermostat by just one degree centigrade cuts 10 per cent off heating bills.

Every kilowatt hour of electricity generated from fossil fuel releases a whole kilogram (2.2 pounds) of carbon dioxide – the principal "greenhouse gas". Some simple economies at home could do a lot to reduce global warming.

The (so far) unspoilt beauty of the Kerry coast in the Republic of Ireland.

General Index

As this book is about the component parts of the British Isles, the names Britain, England, Ireland, Scotland and Wales are not used as headings in the index. The dates of entries are those of the datelines of the reports in which the events are recorded, nor necessarily of the events themselves. Page numbers in bold italic type refer to main reports; those in roman italic refer to the chronology summaries. People with more than one name – for example, before and after receiving peerages – are indexed under the best known form of name, which is usually the latest, with reference(s) from the other form(s). The index also includes many other "see" and "see also" references and should be used in conjunction with the cross-referencing system which is explained in "How to use this book" on page 4, where there is also a general note on the styles used for the names of both people and places.

A

B

C

D

F

G

I

L

M

N

O

METRIC AND IMPERIAL MEASUREMENTS

INCHES : to convert to centimetres, multiply by 2.54

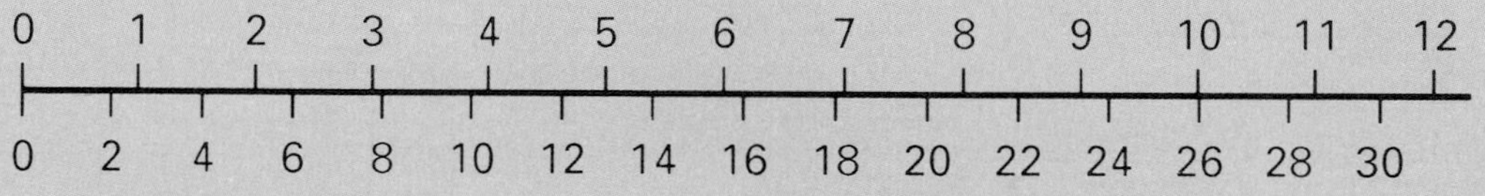

0 1 2 3 4 5 6 7 8 9 10 11 12

0 2 4 6 8 10 12 14 16 18 20 22 24 26 28 30

CENTIMETRES : to convert to inches, multiply by 0.39

FEET : to convert to metres, multiply by 0.3

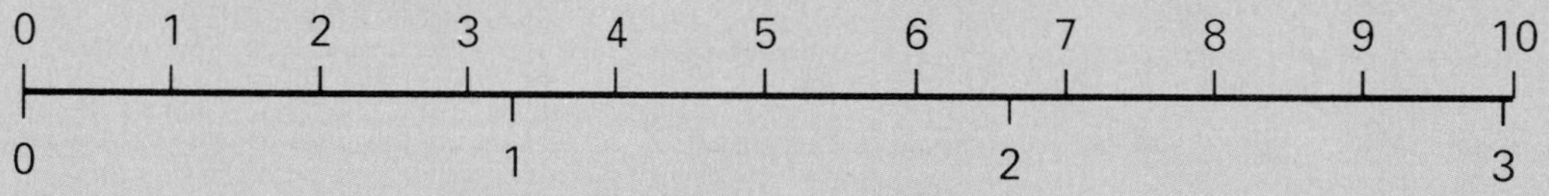

0 1 2 3 4 5 6 7 8 9 10

0 1 2 3

METRES : to convert to feet, multiply by 3.28

to convert yards to metres, multiply by 0.9;
to convert metres to yards, multiply by 1.09

MILES : to convert to kilometres, multiply by 1.6

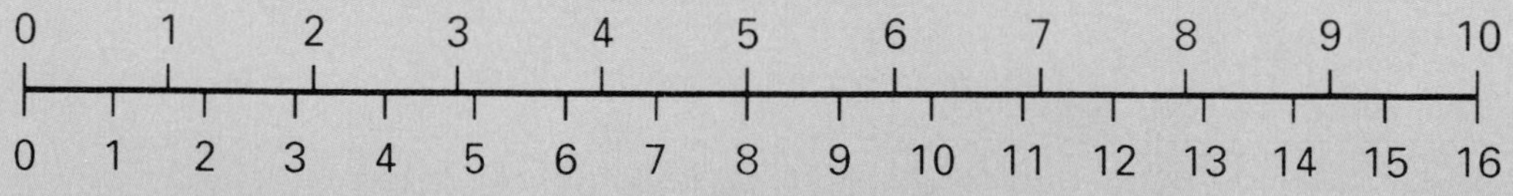

0 1 2 3 4 5 6 7 8 9 10

0 1 2 3 4 5 6 7 8 9 10 11 12 13 14 15 16

KILOMETRES : to convert to miles, multiply by 0.62

ACRES : to convert to hectares, multiply by 0.4

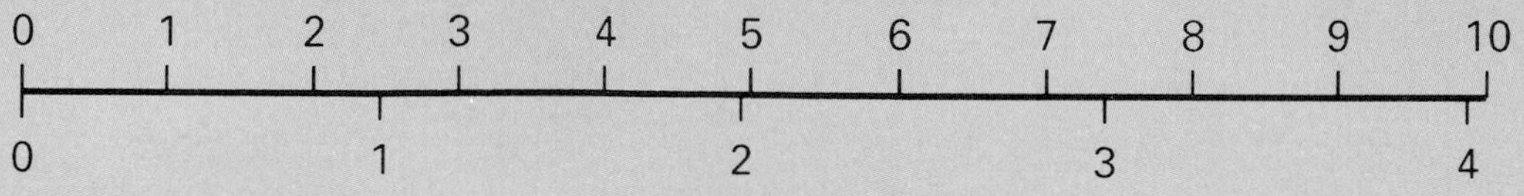

0 1 2 3 4 5 6 7 8 9 10

0 1 2 3 4

HECTARES : to convert to acres, multiply by 2.47

POUNDS : to convert to kilograms, multiply by 0.45 [1 lb = 16 oz]

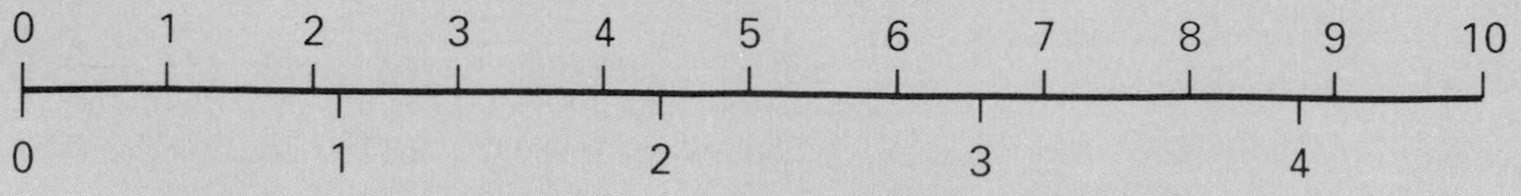

0 1 2 3 4 5 6 7 8 9 10

0 1 2 3 4

KILOGRAMS : to convert to pounds, multiply by 2.2

Picture credits

Jacket

1: Michael Holford – 2: Central Office of Information – 3: E T Archive – 4: Kobal Collection – 5: Bridgeman Art Library – 6: Peter Newark's Historical Pictures – 7: Timothy Woodcock – 8: Rex Features – 9: Bridgeman Art Library – 10: Michael Holford – 11: Popperfoto – 12: Timothy Woodcock – 13: Mary Evans Picture Library – 14: Edinburgh Photographic Library – 15: Mary Evans Picture Library – 16: Tim Woodcock – 17: Bridgeman Art Library – 18: Bridgeman Art Library – 19: Susan Griggs Agency – 20: E T Archive – 21: Topham Picture Library – 22: Bridgeman Art Library – 23: Bridgeman Art Library – 24: Timothy Woodcok – 25: Rex Feature – 26: Michael Holford – 27: Michael Holford – 28: Michael Holford

1 2 3 4 5 6 7 8 9

Chronicle of Britain

10 13 15 18 20 23 25 27

11 12 Back 14 16 17 Spine 19 21 22 Front 24 26 28

Agencies

Some agency names have been abbreviated in this index.
The list below provides full names of the picture agencies:

AAAC: Ancient Art and Architecture Collection
Bridgeman: Bridgeman Art Library
CCL: Chronicle Communication Ltd
Dean: Dean and Chapter of Durham
Evans: Mary Evans Picture Library
Heritage: English Heritage
Harding: Robert Harding Picture Library
Holford: Michael Holford
Hulton: Hulton Deutsch
Love: Billie Love Collection
Master: Master & Fellows of Corpus Christi College, Cambridge
Newark: Peter Newark's Pictures
NLI: National Library of Ireland
NMI: National Museum of Ireland
NTPL: National Trust Photographic Library
Portrait: National Portrait Galery
Rex: Rex Features
Topham: Topham Picture Library
Weidenfeld: Weidenfeld Archives
Werner: Werner Forman Archive
Woodcock: Timothy Woodcock

The position of the pictures is indicated by a combination of two letters: B: Bottom, T: Top, M: Middle, L: Left, R: Right, X: Middle Left, Y: Middle Right. FP indicates that the picture fills the entire page.

While every effort has been made to trace the copyright of the photographs and illustrations used in this publication, there may be an instance where an error has been made in the picture credits. If this is the case, we apologise for the mistake and ask the copyright holder to contact the publisher so that it can be rectified.

Picture credits

Front endpaper – Harding c 96/193
Back endpaper – Topham C C00788210
6 – TL Harding – ML, BL Holford – BR National Maritime Museum, Greenwich
7 – TR Sir Alexander Gibb and Partners – MR Bridgeman – BL E T Archive – BR Science Photo Library
8 – FP National Trust Photo Library/Upton House/Angelo Hornak
10 – MR CCL
11 – TM, MM British Museum (Natural History) – MR Mark Roberts
12 – TL National Museums and Galleries on Merseyside – TR, BL British Museum (Natural History) – ML British Museum – MR Illustrated London News
13 – All pictures from National Museum of Wales
14 – TR C M Dixon – BY British Museum (Natural History) – BR British Museum – ML Holford
15 – TY Bruce Coleman – TR Woodcock – MX Holford – MR Alan Sorrell
16 – SP David Lyons
18 – TR CCL – MM David Lyons
19 – TM Pictorial Colour Slides – MM Mick Sharp – MR CCL
20 – TY British Museum – MX Heritage – MR Corinium Museum
21 – TR David Lyons – TL Mick Sharp – MR E T Archive – MY Pictorial Colour Slides
22 – TM Janet and Colin Bord – BX, BY C M Dixon
23 – ML Committee for Aerial Photography (Cambridge Uni) – TR Mick Sharp – BR CCL
24 – TM Mick Sharp – BX AAAC – BY, MR National Museum of Scotland
25 – TL, BL National Museum of Scotland – TR C M Dixon – MR AAAC
26 – TL Mick Sharp – TR Alan Sorrell – BR Heritage
27 – TM Fotomas Index – MX Heritage – MY Fay Godwin's Photo Files – BL C M Dixon
28 – TM C M Dixon – BY Cornwall Archaeology Unit
29 – TL, TY, TR, BR National Museum of Scotland – BL, BX E T Archive
30 – TY, TR E T Archive – ML British Museum – MR Norwich Castle Museum – BR AAAC
31 – TR Committee for Aerial Photography (Cambridge Uni) – MX CCL – BL British Museum
32 – TX Royal Pavilion, Art Gallery and Museum, Brighton – TR CCL – BX E T Archive – BR Somerset County Council
33 – TL Frank Lane Picture Agency – TR CCL – ML National Museum of Wales – MR Pictorial Colour Slides
34 – TM Dundee Art Galleries and Museum – MR National Maritime Museum, Greenwich – BY Heritage
35 – TL National Museum of Wales – MR Museum of London – BL NMI
36 – TM National Museum of Wales – MR City of Plymouth Museums and Art Gallery – BY C M Dixon
37 – TL Popperfoto – MR Heritage – BL British Museum – BR Committee for Aerial Photography (Cambridge Uni)
38 – TM, TR Mick Sharp (Courtesy Peter Reynolds) – MR Werner
39 – TY Royal Institute of Cornwall – ML C M Dixon – MR, BX, BY, BR Werner
40 – TY Werner – BM Somerset Levels Project
41 – TL C M Dixon – TR Werner – BL Mick Sharp – BR AAAC
42 – SP Harding
44 – TR C M Dixon – MY Evans
45 – TM Evans – BM CCL
46 – TR Professor M. Fulford – BR British Museum
47 – TL Lesley East – TR Werner – BR Susan Griggs Agency
48 – TX Hulton – TR Lesley East – MX Harlow Museum – BR C M Dixon
49 – TM Topham – MM CCL – BR AAAC
50 – TM Bridgeman – MY Heritage – BR C M Dixon
51 – TR Lesley East – MX Mansell Collection – BL Werner – BR C M Dixon
52 – TL National Museum of Wales – MR Colchester and Essex Museum – BL Holford
53 – TR Newark – MY C M Dixon – MR Hulton
54 – TL Museum of London – TR AAAC – BY British Museum
55 – TL, TM, TX Lesley East – MY Evans – BX C M Dixon
56 – TM Mick Sharp – MY Hulton – BY CCL – BR C M Dixon
57 – TM C M Dixon – MR Pictorial Colour Slides – BM Museum of London
58 – TX Newark – TY CCL – MR Hulton – BY Werner
59 – TR Fishbourne Roman Palace/Sussex Arch. Trust – BR C M Dixon
60 – TR Scala – MR British Museum – MX C M Dixon
61 – TX E T Archive – TR Bridgeman – MM AAAC – MR Holford
62 – TX Heritage – MR CCL
63 – TL Heritage – TR C M Dixon – BL Robert Estall – BY National Museum of Scotland – BR Holford
64 – TR NTPL/Howard Philips – BX C M Dixon
65 – TM Heritage – BL E T Archive – BR Holford
66 – FP CCL
67 – TR, BY Heritage – ML British Museum – BR Holford
68 – MR Frank Graham – BX Heritage
69 – TL Woodcock – TR Museum of London – ML C M Dixon
70 – MX, MR, MY Holford – MR Heritage
71 – TL C M Dixon – TR Mansell Collection – BY, BR Holford
72 – TY Bridgeman – MM Museum of London – MR Lesley East
73 – TR Holford – MX Robert Estall – MR Lesley East
74 – TR Bridgeman – MM Holford – BM British Museum
75 – TR Mansell Collection – MR British Museum – BR Editions Larousse
76 – TR C M Dixon – BX, BR Museum of London – BY Holford
77 – TM Evans – BM David Lyons
78 – TX, TY C M Dixon – MY Grosvenor Museum, Chester
79 – TL AAAC – TR Lesley East – BM Heritage – BR National Museum of Wales
80 – TR Pictorial Colour Slides – MY, MR British Museum
81 – TL Holford – MR Patrick Thurston – BX C M Dixon
82 – TR C M Dixon – MX Mick Sharp – MR Hulton
83 – TM Mick Sharp/Dave Longley – MY Mansell Collection – BR C M Dixon
84 – TM Bridgeman
85 – TX AAAC – TR Bridgeman – ML Museum of London – BR Holford
86 – MX C M Dixon – TR AAAC – MR AAAC
87 – MX Committee for Aerial Photography (Cambridge Uni) – TR C M Dixon – BL C M Dixon – BR C M Dixon
88 – TY Bridgeman – MR Woodcock
89 – ML Museum of London – TR, MR Roman Research Trust – BR Patrick Thurston
90 – TR C M Dixon – MX British Museum – TY AAAC
91 – ML Museum of London – MR CCL
92 – SP Holford
94 – TR Heritage – BR Mansell Collection
95 – TR National Museum of Scotland – TL, MM C M Dixon
96 – TR Patrick Thurston – MX C M Dixon
97 – ML C M Dixon – BX Rob Moore – BL Pictorial Colour Slides – TY Norwich Castle Museum – TR CCL
98 – TY NMI
99 – TL, BX C M Dixon – TR Carmarthen Museum – MY Bridgeman
100 – TR CCL – TX Evans – BX C M Dixon
101 – BL E T Archive – TX Bridgeman – TY National Museums and Galleries of Merseyside – BY Norwich Castle Museum
102 – TY AAAC – BX National Museum of Scotland
103 – BX CCL – TL AAAC – BY Heritage – TR Bridgeman – BR Pictorial Colour Slides
104 – TM, BX C M Dixon – MR Bede Monastery Museum
105 – TX Cardiff City Council – MR Kent County Record Office – BM C M Dixon
106 – MM Holford – BR C M Dixon
107 – All pictures from Holford
108 – TR Topham – BR CCL
109 – TL Alan Sorrell – TR British Museum – BR Bridgeman
110 – TY CCL – MM Popperfoto
111 – TX Dean – BR Bridgeman – TR Heritage – BL C M Dixon
112 – TX, BX Holford – TR AAAC – BR Bridgeman
113 – TY Norwich Castle Museum – MX Heritage – BR British Museum
114 – BL Janet and Colin Bord – TR Artephot – BX Bridgeman
115 – TM C M Dixon – BL Musée de Chelles – BR Holford
116 – BR Topham – MY David Lyons
117 – TR CCL – TL Bede Monastery Museum – MX Dean – BX Patrick Thurston
118 – MR C M Dixon – TM Evans
119 – BL, MY Heritage – MX Dean – TR AAAC
120 – TM Norwich Castle Museum – BM Pictorial Colour Slides – MR British Museum
121 – TX Bridgeman – TR British Library – BR AAAC
122 – MX AAAC – TR Holford – MX C M Dixon
123 – All pictures from Bridgeman
124 – TX Popperfoto – BX C M Dixon – MR Department of Environment and Culture/Florence – MR Topham
125 – TL AAAC – TR C M Dixon – BR C M Dixon
126 – TR Bede Monastery Museum – TY E T Archive
127 – TX CCL – TR C M Dixon – BX Lesley East
128 – TR CCL – MR C M Dixon
129 – TL Holford – TR NMI – BY, BR C M Dixon
130 – TR C M Dixon – MX Dean
131 – TL Janet and Colin Bord – TR CCL – BY AAAC
132 – TY Woodcock – TR Bridgeman – BY C M Dixon -BR Royal Comm. on Anc. and Hist. Mons. of Scotland
133 – ML Lesley East – BX Bridgeman – TR Board of Trinity College, Dublin – BR Topham
135 – FP CCL
136 – TY C M Dixon – BR AAAC
137 – TL Mick Sharp – MR Bridgeman
138 – TX C M Dixon – MR Bridgeman
139 – TL Hulton – TY Lesley East – MR Board of Trinity College, Dublin – BY Evans
140 – TR Museum of London – MR Werner – BX AAAC – BR C M Dixon
141 – ML C M Dixon – TR Werner – BR CCL
142 – TR Edinburgh Photographic Library – BR C M Dixon
143 – TL Sheffield City Museum – TR Mick Sharp – BR Hulton
144 – TR British Library – BM Bridgeman – MR Bridgeman
145 – MX Topham – TY, BL British Museum – TR C M Dixon – BR AAAC
146 – TY, TR Bridgeman – MM E T Archive
147 – ML Holford – TM Bodleian Library MS Junius XI fol. 81 – BR C M Dixon
148 – MM Evans – TY Patrick Thurston
149 – ML Holford – BX Woodcock – TR CCL
150 – TR AAAC – BR Newark – TX Lesley East
151 – TR NMI – ML Werner – TL Bridgeman – BR C M Dixon
152 – TR Bridgeman – ML British Museum – BL Yorkshire Museum – BR National Museum of Scotland
153 – TL National Museum of Scotland – TY, TR, MR C M Dixon – ML Heritage – BL Bridgeman – BY Holford – BR British Museum
154 – MX Lesley East – TR, TX Dean
155 – TY C M Dixon – ML British Library – MR York Archaeological Trust
156 – MR Bridgeman – TY CCL – MY Lesley East – BY Woodcock
157 – TL C M Dixon – MX CCL – MY Topham – MR Love
158 – TY British Library – MY Hulton
159 – All pictures from Bridgeman
160 – TX CCL – TR C M Dixon – MY, MR Bridgeman
161 – TR Evans – BY Lesley East – BL Bridgeman
162 – TL British Library – MR Topham
163 – MX Hulton – TY British Library – TR Bridgeman BR British Museum
164 – TL CCL – MY Lesley East – TR British Museum
165 – TR NMI – MM AAAC – ML Werner
166 – TM C M Dixon – BR Werner
167 – TL C M Dixon – TR CCL – BX Holford
168 – TM, TR C M Dixon – BR Bridgeman
169 – TL British Library – TR AAAC
170 – TX C M Dixon – TY Evans – MR Bridgeman
171 – TL British Library – TR Topham
172 – MX AAAC – TR C M Dixon – BR Woodcock
173 – ML Werner – TR, MR Bridgeman
174 – BX Evans – TY C M Dixon – MR Aspect Picture Library
175 – TX E T Archive – BR E T Archive – BL CCL
176 – TY Scottish Development Department – TX Central Office of Information Picture Library – MR Holford – BY C M Dixon
177 – MX Evans – TR British Library – TL NMI
178 – TX AAAC – TR Artephot – MR C M Dixon
179 – TL, TX, MR C M Dixon – TR AAAC
180 – TR Evans – BR CCL
181 – TL, BL Holford – BR CCL
182 – TM Heritage – MM, BM Holford – BL Topham
183 – TM Holford – BR Love – BL AAAC
184 – TR Corporation of London Records Office – MR Holford
185 – ML Holford – TR Burrell Collection – BY Evans – BL British Library
186 – TX C M Dixon – BL Holford – MX C M Dixon – BR David Lyons
187 – TL Bridgeman – MY AAAC BR Bodleian Library MS 569. fol. 1
188 – MX Holford – MR Cadw Welsh Historic Monuments
189 – TL, ML E T Archive – MR, MR CCL
190 – TY British Museum – MM Topham
191 – TL Newark – MR C M Dixon
192 – TM Holford – BM Fine Art Photographic Library – MR British Library
193 – ML British Library – TR Evans – MX Holford
194 – TR CCL – BY Gloucester City Museum – ML NMI
195 – TR AAAC – BX Heritage
196 – All pictures from British Library
197 – TL, BL British Library – TR HMSO/Public Record Office – MX CCL
198 – TX AAAC – TR Lesley East – MR, BX C M Dixon
199 – TY AAAC – BR Dean – MX Love
200 – TL Topham – TR Hulton – BY, BR C M Dixon
201 – TX Dean – MR Cadw Welsh Historic Monuments
202 – MR Dean – TY Bodleian Library MS 271, fol. 2v – BM C M Dixon
203 – ML Bridgeman – BR Evans – TY Weidenfeld
204 – TM Evans – BR Woodcock
205 – TL Museum of London – TR Holford – BR British Library
206 – All pictures from Bridgeman
207 – TR Hulton – ML City Sights of London – BR Bridgeman
208 – TY Hulton – BX NMI
209 – TL, BL AAAC – MR Evans
210 – BR Bridgeman – MX C M Dixon
211 – TL British Library – BR Alan Sorrell
212 – TX J. Charmet – TR Great Scot Pictures – BR E T Archive
213 – TY Topham – MR Bodleian Library/Bridgeman MS Ash. 1462 fol. 9v – BL Holford
214 – TM CCL – BR Herzog August Bibliothek
215 – TY British Library – BL Hulton – BR NMI
216 – TY Pictorial Colour Slides – BR Topham
217 – TL Trinity College, Cambridge – BL CCL – BR Mick Sharp – TR Weidenfeld
218 – TX Bridgeman – TR NMI – BR Master
219 – BL C M Dixon – TR Patrick Thurston – BR, BY Harding
220 – TR Bridgeman – BR Holford
221 – TL CCL – TY British Library – ML British Museum – BR Holford
222 – TY Evans – MM CCL
223 – TR Woodcock – BX Bridgeman – BL C M Dixon
224 – TM British Library – MR Lesley East – BM CCL
225 – TR, ML Heritage – BY AAAC – BR Harding
226 – BX Janet and Colin Bord – MY AAAC – BR Susanna Harrison
227 – TX, TR CCL – MX, BY British Library
228 – TM Weidenfeld – MR Hulton
229 – TX AAAC – TY CCL – BL Topham – ML C M Dixon – MX Bridgeman
230 – SP Holford
232 – BM CCL – TM Tallandier
233 – MX Heritage – BR Bridgeman
234 – TY Holford – BR Bridgeman
235 – MX Woodcock – TL, TR C M Dixon – BL Heritage
236 – TY Love – BR CCL
237 – TL NMI – MR Bridgeman – BL Holford
238 – TR AAAC – MR C M Dixon – MR Bridgeman
239 – TR CCL – MR Evans – ML Museum of London
240 – TR CCL – TX Evans – BR Woodcock
241 – BL Evans – MR Holford – TL Patrick Thurston
242 – TY Woodcock – MR NLI
243 – TL Alan Sorrell – BR E T Archive
244 – TM Topham – MX Lesley East – BR Bridgeman
245 – ML Topham – TM Dean – MR Hulton
246 – TR British Library – MY Evans
247 – FP CCL
248 – BY Evans – TR Topham
249 – TR, MR Bridgeman – TX Love
250 – TM E T Archive
251 – All pictures from Bridgeman
252 – TY Woodcock – MX C M Dixon – MY AAAC
253 – TM CCL – BX Evans
254 – TL Hulton – TR Newark – BL AAAC
255 – TM Topham – MR, MY Bridgeman
256 – TR AAAC
257 – TL Bridgeman – MR Woodcock – BL Mick Sharp
258 – BR Bodleian Library MS Ash. 1511, fol. 105 – MM Bodleian Library MS Laud Misc 165, fol. 149v
259 – ML Bridgeman – TM British Library – MR Hulton – BY C M Dixon
260 – MY Dean – MM Hulton – TR C M Dixon
261 – MY National Museum of Wales – TL Love – BL C M Dixon
262 – MR Master – BX Hulton – TX Great Scot Pictures
263 – BL Newark – TM E T Archive – BR Bridgeman
264 – TR CCL – MR Bridgeman
265 – TR Master – ML CCL – MR Heritage
266 – TY AAAC – MM, BR Bridgeman
267 – TY British Library – MR Bridgeman
268 – TM Mick Sharp/Dave Longley – BY NLI – MR British Library
269 – MX Hulton – TL E T Archive – BR Cadw Welsh Historic Monuments
270 – MY C M Dixon – TY Topham
271 – TL Mick Sharp – ML Love – TR Bridgeman – MR Evans
272 – All pictures from Master
273 – TM AAAC – BR CCL BL Woodcock
274 – TX British Library – MR Bridgeman
275 – TL, MR Topham – TR Holford – BL, BR STB/Still Moving Picture Company – BM Edinburgh Photographic Library
276 – TR Newark – MR AAAC – BR By kind permission of Her Majesty the Queen
277 – TM CCL – MX Fitzwilliam Museum – BR Bridgeman
278 – TM Heritage – BM Bridgeman
279 – TL Heritage – TY AAAC – BM Master
280 – All pictures from Newark
281 – MR Hulton – TX Dean – ML Evans
282 – All pictures from Newark
283 – TM Evans – BX AAAC – BY Topham
284 – TY Evans – BX Topham – BR Bridgeman
285 – TM AAAC – BL Bridgeman – BR Heritage
286 – TR Holford – MY Heritage
287 – TX Love – ML, MY Topham – MR, BR Newark
288 – TM Bridgeman – BR AAAC
289 – TM Holford – BM Museum of London
290 – TR CCL – BR Newark
291 – TY Evans – BM Heritage
292 – TR National Gallery of Scotland
293 – TR Love – TL Newark – MR Bridgeman
294 – TR Newark – MR CCL – BR Heritage – TL, BL AAAC – BX Topham
295 – MR AAAC – TX National Library of Scotland
296 – MX Bridgeman – TR Evans
297 – TM Paisley Museum
298 – TM CCL
299 – TR Bridgeman – MM Hulton – BM Newark
300 – TM Scottish National Portrait Gallery – BR Love
301 – TL Evans – TR, BR Topham
302 – TY Love – BR Newark
303 – TM Newark
304 – TY Newark – BY Holford – BR Woodcock
305 – TM CCL – TL AAAC – BR Bridgeman
306 – All pictures from AAAC
307 – MR Evans – TL Topham – BL Norwich Castle Museum
308 – TX Evans – MR Bridgeman – BX City Sights of London
309 – TL Evans – TR Love – MM Woodcock
310 – TX Love – BR Evans
311 – TL Newark – BM Bridgeman
312 – TR Evans – BY Edinburgh Photographic Library
313 – TX Portrait – TR Evans – BR CCL – BL Bridgeman
314 – TR Topham – MX Holford – BR AAAC
315 – ML, TM Evans – BR Topham
316 – TM Bridgeman – BX Topham – BR Love
317 – ML Bibliotheque Nationale de Paris – TR Bridgeman – BR Love
318 – TR Hulton – MY Bridgeman – BL AAAC
319 – TM Topham – MY, MR Evans
320 – TR, MX Evans – BL CCL
321 – TY, ML Evans – BM Topham – BR Bridgeman
322 – TL Newark – TR, MR Evans
323 – TR Board of Trinity College, Dublin
323 – TX Bridgeman
324 – TY, BX Bridgeman – TR CCL – BR AAAC
325 – TR Holford – TL National Library of Scotland – BY Bodleian Library MS Douce 104, fol. 46
326 – All pictures from Bridgeman
327 – TR Bridgeman – MR Newark
328 – All pictures from Bridgeman
329 – ML City Sights of London – MR, BR Evans – BL David Lyons
330 – All pictures from Bridgeman
331 – TM, BL Love – BR Heritage
332 – MM Evans
333 – TL Newark – BX Holford – TR Heritage – MR Bridgeman – BR Museum of London
334 – All pictures from Evans
335 – TL Evans – TR Topham – BM Bridgeman – BR AAAC
336 – MX Victoria and Albert Museum – TR Evans – BR British Library
337 – All pictures from Bridgeman
338 – TL Holford – TR, ML Bridgeman – BL Topham – BY AAAC – BR Museum of London
339 – TX, MR, BX Evans – BR Newark
340 – TX Love – TR Evans – MR City Sights of London
341 – MX Bodleian Library MS Laud Misc 165, fol. 5r – TR AAAC – BR Bridgeman – BX C M Dixon
342 – TY Evans – MM Newark
343 – TX Holford – TR, MR British Library – MY Bridgeman
344 – TR Love – BX Norwich Castle Museum
345 – TR, BL Bridgeman – MR CCL
346 – All pictures from Evans
347 – TR C M Dixon – ML City Sights of London
348 – TX Topham – TR Scala
349 – TL British Library – TR Love – BX C M Dixon
350 – BR Topham – TM Hulton
351 – TL, BL Bridgeman – MR Giraudon
352 – MM Bodleian Library/Bridgeman MS Douce 208 fol. 120v – BR Newark
353 – TR, MX Bridgeman – TL Evans
354 – TM Popperfoto – BY Evans
355 – TL Bridgeman – TR National Library of Wales – BL Woodcock
356 – TR Evans
357 – TR Love – TL Evans – BL British Library – BR Holford
358 – TX, BX Evans – TR National Monuments Record
359 – TL British Library – TY CCL – MR Evans – BL Bridgeman
361 – TM Newark – BR Woodcock
362 – TY, BM Hulton – MR Bridgeman
363 – TR CCL – BL Topham
364 – TR AAAC – MR Evans
365 – TM Bodleian Library MS Jesus Coll. 124 (R) Top – MM Newark – BM CCL
366 – TR AAAC – BR Evans
367 – TL Hulton – TR Evans – BR C M Dixon
368 – TY E T Archive – MR AAAC
369 – TL British Library – TR Evans – MX Portrait – BM Fotomas Index
370 – TX Lesley East – MR Evans
371 – ML CCL – TY Bridgeman – MR E T Archive
372 – TY Topham – MM Love
373 – ML Evans – TR British Library – TM Woodcock – BR Mansell Collection
374 – TM Evans – BR Newark
375 – TX Bodleian Library MS Arch. Seld. B10 fol. 184r – TR, BR C M Dixon – MR Hulton
376 – TM C M Dixon – MR Evans – BY Weidenfeld
377 – TL Portrait – BM Evans
378 – TX E T Archive – TX AAAC – BR Bridgeman
379 – BL Bridgeman – TM Newark
380 – SP National Maritime Museum, Greenwich
382 – TM, MX Lesley East – MR Holford
383 – TL Board of Trinity College, Dublin – TY Bridgeman – BR National Museum of Scotland
384 – All pictures from Evans
385 – TL Topham -TR Newark – BR Robert Estall
386 – TL, BR Evans – TR Woodcock – BL Newark
387 – TL E T Archive – TR C M Dixon – BL Holford – BR AAAC
388 – TX Evans – TY Bridgeman
389 – TM Topham – MM Evans – BR Bridgeman
390 – TY Evans – MM Bridgeman – BR Woodcock
391 – TX Evans – TR National Library of Scotland – MM Hulton
392 – TX AAAC – MR Hulton
393 – TM Topham – MR Bridgeman – BM Evans
394 – TM Werner – BX Bridgeman – BY Holford
395 – TM, BR Bridgeman – MM Evans
396 – TR Mansell Collection – BX Evans
397 – All pictures from Bridgeman
398 – Holford

399 – TL AAAC – TR Evans – MX, BL Bridgeman

400 – TM Bridgeman – MR Hulton

401 – TY Bridgeman – MY AAAC – BR Evans – BX Hulton

402 – TX, BR Evans – TR Bridgeman

403 – TX Mansell Collection – MR Patrick Thurston – BY Portrait

404 – MM E T Archive – TR C M Dixon

405 – TL Hulton – BL Evans – MR Robert Estall – BR Holford

406 – TM Hulton – BR Bridgeman

407 – ML, TX, TY Evans – MR Bridgeman

408 – ML Hulton – TR Scottish National Portrait Gallery – MR Mansell Collection

409 – MM Heritage – TR Evans

410 – TR Belvoir Castle

411 – TR Edinburgh Photographic Library – MX Bridgeman – BR Mansell Collection

412 – TY Portrait – MR Hulton

413 – TM Hulton – BX Evans – BR Bridgeman

414 – TY, BY Hulton – MR Portrait

415 – TL Evans – MY Hulton – BL Bridgeman

416 – TM Hulton – MR Heritage

417 – TR CCL – TL, MM Hulton

418 – TL Hulton – BR CCL

419 – TX Newark – MY Heritage – BR Bridgeman

420 – TY British Library – MY Evans

421 – TL Fotomas Index – TR Mick Sharp/Dave Longley – MY Giraudon – MR Giraudon – BR Heritage

422 – BM Bridgeman – TY Hulton

423 – TY Hulton – TL Evans – MR Bridgeman – BL Victoria and Albert Museum

424 – TR Newark – MX National Library of Scotland

425 – TY Evans – MY Hulton – BL Bridgeman

426 – MR Bridgeman – TY Hulton

427 – TR Love – MX AAAC – BR Evans

428 – TM E T Archive – BY Hulton – MR Bridgeman

429 – TL Royal Comm. on Historical Monuments of England – TR STB/Still Moving Picture Company/Paul Tomkins – BX Mansell Collection

430 – TR Bridgeman – MM Newark

431 – TX, MR Evans – BL Portrait

432 – TX Evans – BR CCL

433 – TL Newark – MR Hulton – BX Evans

434 – TM Bridgeman – MM Evans

435 – TR, ML, MR Bridgeman – TL Evans

436 – TM Evans – BM Patrick Thurston

437 – TL Newark – BL Bridgeman – TR, BR Evans

438 – TX Topham – TY, MY Evans – MR Bridgeman

439 – TX Bridgeman – MX Archives Nationales de France – TR AAAC – BR Fotomas Index

440 – MX C M Dixon – MY NTPL/Mike Williams – BR Fotomas Index

441 – TL, ML Bridgeman – MR AAAC

442 – TX, MM Bridgeman – MR E T Archive

443 – TL Holford – TR E T Archive – BL Weidenfeld – BR NTPL/Roy Fox

444 – TM Evans – MR Bridgeman – MY AAAC

445 – TL Love – ML Hulton – MY Woodcock – BR E T Archive – BL Evans

446 – TX Lesley East – TR Weidenfeld – MX Love – MR Hulton

447 – TX, BL Bridgeman – MR E T Archive

448 – TM British Library – TR Portrait – MR E T Archive

449 – TM Great Scot Pictures – MY Edinburgh Photographic Library – BR Evans

450 – TR Great Scot Pictures – MR Portrait

451 – TM Fine Art Photographic Library – MM Bridgeman – BL Evans

452 – TR Portrait – MM Hulton

453 – TL, TR, BL Bridgeman – BR Weidenfeld

454 – TR Heritage – MR Wallace Collection – BY AAAC

455 – ML Hulton – TM Fine Art Photographic Library – BM Holford

456 – TR Bridgeman – BM Evans

457 – ML Fotomas Index – TR E T Archive – BL Evans – BR Newark

458 – TR Bridgeman – BR Edinburgh Photographic Library

459 – ML Evans – TR Love – MM Weidenfeld

460 – TM Love – BR Evans

461 – TR Hulton – ML Weidenfeld – BR Heritage – BX Evans

462 – TM Evans – MR AAAC – MM Portrait

463 – TL Fotomas Index – TR Newark – BY Bridgeman – BL Evans

464 – TY Bridgeman – MR E T Archive – BM E T Archive

465 – TL Weidenfeld – TR Bridgeman – MR Angelo Hornak

466 – TR Newark – BR AAAC

467 – ML Fotomas Index – TR Weidenfeld – MR AAAC – BY Weidenfeld – BR Weidenfeld – TX AAAC

468 – TX Hulton – TR Bridgeman – BR Evans

469 – ML Evans – TR Bridgeman – MR Weidenfeld

470 – TY Love – MR Evans – BX Scottish National Portrait Gallery

471 – TM Hulton – MR Evans – BL Bridgeman – BR Bridgeman

472 – TM Hulton – BM Bridgeman – MR NTPL

473 – TX Evans – MR By kind permission of Viscount de L'Isle from his collection at Penshurst Place/Angelo Hornak – BL Evans

474 – TM Edinburgh Photographic Library – MR Evans – BR Fotomas Index

475 – MX Weidenfeld – TR Evans – BR AAAC

476 – TM Hulton – BY Bridgeman

477 – TX CCL – TR, BR Bridgeman – ML Love

478 – TM Holford – BR Bridgeman

479 – ML Evans – TR Newark – BX Hulton

480 – TR Scottish National Portrait Gallery – MR Portrait – BX Evans

481 – TY Hulton – TR Fotomas Index – ML Bridgeman – BR Angelo Hornak

482 – TR Bridgeman – MR Newark – MR E T Archive – BR Mansell Collection

483 – TM Weidenfeld – BR CCL

484 – TX Evans – MR Bridgeman – BL Evans

485 – TY Scottish National Portrait Gallery – TR Portrait – BX Holford – BR Evans

486 – TR, MX Newark – BR Trustees of the Earl of Scarbrough Settlement/Angelo Hornak

487 – ML Evans – TR Museum of London – MR, BR AAAC

488 – TL Love – ML Evans – MR Newark

489 – TY Portrait – MR Evans – BM Newark

490 – TY NTPL/E. Leigh – BX Evans – MR Bridgeman

491 – TR Mansell Collection – BL Bridgeman – MM Fotomas Index – BR Weidenfeld

492 – TM Evans – MR Portrait – BR Bridgeman

493 – TL Hulton – TR Bridgeman – BY Weidenfeld

494 – TR Evans – BX Woodcock – BR Angelo Hornak

495 – TR Weidenfeld – BR Fotomas Index – ML Hulton

496 – TY E T Archive – BX Evans – BR Newark

497 – TL Hulton – TR By kind permission of the Marquess of Tavistock – MR Newark – BY Bridgeman – BR Bodleian Library/Bridgeman MS C.17.48 (9)

498 – TY NTPL – BR E T Archive – BX NTPL/John Bethell

499 – TM Hulton – MR Portrait

500 – SP E T Archive

502 – MM E T Archive – BR AAAC

503 – TR National Library of Scotland – ML CCL – BR NTPL/John Bethell

504 – TR Portrait – BY C M Dixon

505 – TM AAAC – TR Fotomas Index – ML Mansell Collection – BR Edinburgh Photographic Library

506 – All pictures from Hulton

507 – TL Bridgeman – TR E T Archive – MR National Library of Scotland – BL Evans

508 – TM Weidenfeld – MR, BY Evans

509 – MX Love – TR Glasgow District Library – BL Portrait – BR Werner

510 – TX, TY Weidenfeld – BM Mansell Collection

511 – TX Fotomas Index – MR E T Archive – BL, BR Weidenfeld

512 – TX Newark – TR Weidenfeld – BM Evans

513 – TR By kind permission of Her Majesty the Queen – ML Holford – BR E T Archive – BL Bridgeman

514 – TM E T Archive – BR Hulton

515 – TL Hulton – TX Heritage – TR Evans – BR Bridgeman

516 – TX Love – TR Bridgeman – MR Weidenfeld

517 – ML Fotomas Index – TR, BY Woodcock – MR Angelo Hornak – BR Edinburgh Photographic Library

518 – TR Popperfoto – BL Weidenfeld – MX Mander & Mitchenson Theatre Collection – MR E T Archive

519 – TX Weidenfeld – ML, BR Mander & Mitchenson Theatre Collection – R Master – MR Portrait

520 – TM Bridgeman – BX Portrait – MR Evans

521 – TM, BY Weidenfeld – MR Bridgeman

522 – MX Evans – TR Weidenfeld – BY, BR Angelo Hornak

523 – TL, MR Bridgeman – TR Newark – BL AAAC

524 – TX Bridgeman – BX Weidenfeld – MR Evans

525 – TR, BR Evans – BL Weidenfeld

526 – TX Newark – MR Scottish National Portrait Gallery – BY Evans

527 – TL Portrait – TR Evans – MR Weidenfeld

528 – TM, BM Evans – MR Weidenfeld

529 – TY Bridgeman – BM Weidenfeld

530 – TL Heritage – BL Newark – TR Topham – BR Fotomas Index

531 – TR Evans – MX Bridgeman – BL Angelo Hornak – BR Love

532 – MX, MR Bridgeman – TY Evans

533 – ML Evans – TR E T Archive – MX Portrait

534 – TR Bridgeman – MX Evans

535 – TL Love – TY Evans – TR Hulton – BR Bridgeman

536 – MM By kind permission of Her Majesty the Queen – BR Evans

537 – TR, BR Bridgeman – MR Evans

538 – TY Canadian High Commission – BY Angelo Hornak

539 – TL Weidenfeld – MX, MR Portrait – BY Newark

540 – TM Topham – MY Weidenfeld – BR Fotomas Index

541 – TL Bridgeman – TR Woodcock – BL Weidenfeld – BR City Art Gallery Manchester

542 – TR Weidenfeld – MX Evans – BR Bridgeman

543 – TM Evans – BM Bridgeman

544 – TM, MR Hulton – BY Evans

545 – TM E T Archive

546 – TM, BL Newark – BR Weidenfeld

547 – ML, MY Bridgeman – TR C M Dixon – MR Woodcock

548 – TM Evans – BM Fotomas Index

549 – ML AAAC – TX, TR Hulton – MR Portrait – BX, BR Evans

550 – TL, MR Weidenfeld – TX, BX Portrait – BL Evans – MY Hulton

551 – All pictures from Bridgeman

552 – TL, BL Hulton – MR Newark – MX Evans

553 – TM Mansell Collection – BL Hulton – BR C M Dixon

554 – TY, BM Hulton – MR AAAC

555 – BL Evans – TR CCL

556 – TR Topham – TL NTPL – MM Evans

557 – TY Mansell Collection – BM Hulton – MR Bridgeman

558 – TR Bridgeman

559 – ML Newark – TY Bridgeman – TR Portrait – BR Scottish National Portrait Gallery

560 – All pictures from Weidenfeld

561 – ML Newark – TR CCL

562 – TL Portrait – ML CCL – TR Evans – BY Newark

563 – MX NTPL/C. Hurst – TY Newark – TR E T Archive – BR Fotomas Index

564 – TR, MM Bridgeman – MY Hulton – BL Woodcock

565 – TM, BY Evans – MR Portrait

566 – TM, BX Hulton – BR Weidenfeld

567 – ML, BM Newark – TR Hulton

568 – TM Bridgeman – BY Weidenfeld

569 – TL, BL Bridgeman – MY Hulton

570 – TL Hulton – BR Weidenfeld – BL E T Archive

571 – TM Newark – MR CCL – BM Bridgeman

572 – TL, TR Evans – BY Hulton

573 – ML NTPL/J. Whitaker – BX Edinburgh Photographic Library – BY, BR STB/Still Moving Picture Company – TR Holford

574 – MX Weidenfeld – TR Mansell Collection – BY E T Archive

575 – MX Angelo Hornak – TR Newark – BL Love – BR Evans

576 – TR AAAC – BY Evans

577 – TL Newark – TR Topham – BR Holford

578 – TR Weidenfeld – MR, ML Evans – BL Evans

579 – TX, TR Evans – MY Bridgeman

580 – All pictures from Evans

581 – TX AAAC – MX E T Archive – TR Weidenfeld – MR Portrait

582 – TM Bridgeman – MR Hulton – BY AAAC

583 – TL Hulton – TR, MR Portrait – BL Fotomas Index

584 – TR Weidenfeld – BM AAAC

585 – TR Fotomas Index – MR E T Archive – BM Portrait

586 – MX Evans – TR Great Scot Pictures

587 – MR Topham – TL Hulton – ML Bridgeman – BM E T Archive

588 – TY, BM Evans – MR Newark

589 – TM Newark – BL Love – BR Bridgeman

590 – TM, BX, BY Hulton – MR Evans

591 – TM Weidenfeld – BL CCL – BM Evans – MR Bridgeman

592 – TL, MY Bridgeman – MX Newark – BR Evans

593 – TM Tate Gallery, London – MM E T Archive

594 – MR Bridgeman – MX Portrait – BR Fotomas Index

595 – TL, MR E T Archive – BR C M Dixon

596 – MX Weidenfeld – TR Fotomas Index – BY By kind permission of Her Majesty the Queen

597 – TM Weidenfeld – ML Evans – BR NTPL/Mike Williams

598 – TR Newark – MR C M Dixon – MX Bodleian Library/Bridgeman MS Ash. 971. fol. 14v

599 – TM Hulton – BL Evans – BY Bridgeman – MR Weidenfeld

600 – TY Portrait – BR Bridgeman

601 – ML Hulton – TR, BR Bridgeman – MR Evans

602 – TY Hulton – MY Portrait – BR Newark

603 – TL Fotomas Index – MY Newark – MX Weidenfeld – MR Evans

604 – All pictures from Bridgeman

605 – TL Newark – TY Topham – TR Fotomas Index – BM Evans

606 – TY Topham – MM Evans

607 – TX Love – MY Portrait – TR Hulton – BL Evans

608 – MR E T Archive – BR Hulton

609 – TL Portrait – TR Fotomas Index – MR Portrait

610 – TY Portrait – MR Newark – BX Evans

611 – TL Evans – MR E T Archive – BL Hulton

612 – TR Fine Art Photographic Library – MR Weidenfeld

613 – TM Hulton – BM AAAC – MR Bridgeman

614 – TY Bridgeman – MY Bridgeman – BR Hulton

615 – TM Hulton – MR AAAC – MM Evans

616 – TR Bridgeman – BM CCL

617 – TM Hulton – MM CCL – BL Evans – BR Bridgeman

618 – BX Bridgeman – TR Weidenfeld – BR Fotomas Index

619 – ML Weidenfeld – BX Love – TR PSA/Department of Environment

620 – TR Newark – MR E T Archive – BM Hulton

621 – TL AAAC – TR CCL – BL Bridgeman

622 – TR Mick Sharp/Jean Williamson – BR Bridgeman

623 – ML, MR Newark – TY Evans – BY Hulton

624 – MX, TR Hulton – BR Bridgeman

625 – ML Portrait – TY Evans – MR Bridgeman

626 – TM Weidenfeld – BR Hulton

627 – ML, BM Evans – TR Weidenfeld

628 – All pictures from Bridgeman

629 – TY Evans – BR Bridgeman – BL NTPL/Ben Rice

630 – TX, MR Portrait – TY Evans – BY Bridgeman

631 – BR C M Dixon – TM National Library of Scotland

632 – MX Newark – TR Weidenfeld – BR Evans

633 – TR, ML, MR Portrait – MX Evans

634 – TM AAAC – MR Evans – MM Topham

635 – TL Weidenfeld – MR Hulton – BL Love

636 – TL, MR Bridgeman – BR Evans – BX Newark

637 – MX Duke of Hamilton/On loan to Scottish National Portrait Gallery – TR Hulton – BR E T Archive

638 – ML AAAC – TM Bridgeman – MR Holford

639 – TX Evans – TR NTPL – MR Bridgeman – BR Fotomas Index

640 – SP Sir Alexander Gibb and Partners

642 – TX Weidenfeld – MM Evans – BR Bridgeman

643 – TM Hulton

644 – TR Newark – MY Evans

645 – TM, ML, MR Hulton – BM NTPL

646 – TY Hulton – MR Portrait – BX Bridgeman

647 – TL, MY Bridgeman – MX Portrait – TR Fotomas Index

648 – TM Weidenfeld – BL Hulton – BR Evans

649 – TR Bridgeman – MM Newark

650 – TL Love – TY Bridgeman – ML Holford – MY, BY Woodcock – BL Angelo Hornak

651 – TL Bridgeman – TY Weidenfeld – TR Newark – BR Portrait – ML Fotomas Index

652 – TR Weidenfeld – BY Love

653 – TR Bridgeman – BL NTPL/Andrew Haslam – BM NTPL/John Bethell – BR NTPL/Erik Pelham

654 – TR, BX Weidenfeld – MR Bridgeman

655 – TX Bridgeman – TR Portrait – MR CCL – BL NTPL/J. Whitaker

656 – TX Weidenfeld – MY Portrait

657 – TR E T Archive – MY, BM Weidenfeld – MR CCL

658 – TM Hulton – MR Weidenfeld – BR NTPL/Erik Pelham

659 – TX Evans – MX, MR Weidenfeld – BL Angelo Hornak

660 – TY Portrait – MM Weidenfeld – BR Heritage

661 – TL, MR Bridgeman – TR Newark – BL Evans

662 – TM Topham – BY Evans

663 – TR, MR His Grace the Duke of Marlborough/Angelo Hornak – ML Bridgeman

664 – TY Evans – ML Scotish National Portrait Gallery – BR Newark

665 – TM, BM E T Archive – BR Evans

666 – TY Lesley East – TR Weidenfeld – BR Portrait

667 – TX NTPL – TR Weidenfeld – MM Woodcock

668 – TR Fotomas Index – BR AAAC – BX Evans

669 – TY Newark – ML Bridgeman – MR Topham

670 – TR Angelo Hornak – MR Hulton – BM Evans

671 – TX Mrs Maxwell Scott of Abbotsford – MR Fotomas Index – BY Evans – BL Bridgeman

672 – TL Evans – MM, BM Bridgeman

673 – TR Fotomas Index – MR Evans – MX Great Scot Pictures – MR Hulton

674 – TM Weidenfeld

675 – TL Hulton – MY, BR Bridgeman

676 – TM E T Archive – MR Bridgeman – BY Topham

677 – TX NTPL/John Bethell – TR Evans – MY Angelo Hornak – MR Architectural Association/Valerie Bennett – BR Bridgeman – BL Irish Tourist Board

678 – TM Evans – MR, BR Bridgeman

679 – TL, TX, TR Evans – BR Bridgeman

680 – All pictures from Evans

681 – TM Hulton – BR Evans

682 – TR Evans – MR Hulton – BL E T Archive

683 – All pictures from Bridgeman

684 – TX Newark – TR NTPL/Jerry Harper – ML Evans – BR National Trust Photographic Library/John Bethell

685 – TM, MY Newark – MR E T Archive

686 – TR Bridgeman – MR Edinburgh Photographic Library – ML Portrait

687 – ML Holford – TR Evans – BR E T Archive

688 – MX Evans – TR NTPL/G. Shakeley – BR Bridgeman

689 – TM E T Archive – MR Bridgeman – BR Hulton

690 – TL Bridgeman – TR E T Archive – BR Weidenfeld – MM Hulton

691 – TM E T Archive – BR Portrait – BL Fotomas Index

692 – MX Evans – TR Bridgeman – BR Newark

693 – TM Hulton – MR Portrait – BR NTPL/Mike Williams

694 – TX E T Archive – MR Bridgeman – TR E T Archive – BX Evans

695 – BR, MR Evans – TM Holford

696 – TM E T Archive – MM Bridgeman – BM Evans

697 – TR Bridgeman – BL CCL – MM Evans

698 – MX, MR Newark – TR Bridgeman

699 – TM Weidenfeld – MR Portrait – MM Hulton

700 – All pictures from MM Evans

701 – ML Weidenfeld – TM, BL Bridgeman – MR E T Archive – BR Woodcock

702 – All pictures from Bridgeman

703 – TL Holford – TM Weidenfeld – TR, ML, MR, BM Bridgeman – BL NTPL/Mark Fiennes – BR NTPL/Nick Carter

704 – TR Hulton – MY STB/Still Moving Picture Company

705 – TX Evans – TR CCL – MR Bridgeman – BL E T Archive

706 – MX Bridgeman – TR Hulton – MR Evans

707 – ML Evans – TX Weidenfeld – TR, BY Hulton – MR, BR E T Archive

708 – TM Evans – MR Bridgeman – MY Newark

709 – TL, TR Portrait – BL CCL – BX Newark – MR Bridgeman

710 – TM Evans

711 – TL Evans – MX E T Archive – TR Bridgeman – BR Newark

712 – TM Newark – MM CCL – BL Woodcock – BY Hulton

713 – TR, MY Bridgeman – BR Evans

714 – TL Bridgeman – BL E T Archive – MR Weidenfeld

715 – TR Hulton – BL Woodcock – MR Bridgeman

716 – TY, TR Bridgeman – BR Evans

717 – ML Weidenfeld – TR E T Archive – BR Angelo Hornak

718 – TY Portrait – TL, BM Evans

719 – TR Evans – BR CCL

720 – TM E T Archive – MM Evans – BL Holford – BR Bridgeman

721 – ML Bridgeman – TR Hulton – TX Newark

722 – MX Evans – TR Newark – MR Edinburgh Photographic Library

723 – TX Bridgeman – MR Portrait – BL Northern Ireland Tourist Board – BR NTPL/John Bethell

724 – TY Portrait – MX, MR Evans

725 – BL National Trust for Scotland – TM Bridgeman – BR Evans

726 – TR, MM Evans – MR Holford

727 – TM, BX Bridgeman – ML Evans

728 – BY Evans – MX Holford – TR Mansell Collection

729 – TM Newark – MM Portrait – BL, BR Bridgeman

730 – TL Holford – TM Newark – MR, BL Evans

731 – MY Newark – TR Evans

732 – TY, MR Evans – BX Werner

733 – TR India Office Library – MX Weidenfeld – MY NTPL/Andrew Haslam – BR Hulton

734 – TX, TR Newark – MR Evans – BL E T Archive

735 – ML, TR Evans – BR CCL

736 – TM, MX Evans – BR Fotomas Index

737 – ML AAAC – TX Bridgeman – BR Newark

738 – TM Bridgeman – BY Portrait – MR Holford

739 – TL Bridgeman – BX E T Archive – MR Evans

740 – TR Bridgeman – ML Weidenfeld – BY Edinburgh Photographic Library

741 – TM, BR Newark – BX Love

742 – TM, MM Evans – MR Portrait

743 – TR E T Archive – BR Weidenfeld

744 – TL Bridgeman – TR Evans – MM Newark

745 – TM CCL – MY Newark – BM Evans

746 – TR Evans – MR Bridgeman – ML Great Scot Pictures

747 – TM Weidenfeld – MM E T Archive – MX Newark

748 – TM, MR Newark – BY NTPL/Angelo Hornak

749 – TX Portrait – TR Weidenfeld – ML Hulton – BR Fotomas Index

750 – TR Fotomas Index – BR Hulton

751 – TM Weidenfeld – BR Evans – ML David Lyons

752 – TR Weidenfeld – BR E T Archive

753 – TR Museum of London – ML, BR E T Archive

754 – TY E T Archive – MR, BM Evans

755 – TM E T Archive – BR Weidenfeld – BL STB/Still Moving Picture Company

756 – TY Bridgeman – MM Newark

757 – TM, MR Hulton – BL Bridgeman

758 – MX Portrait – TR Hulton – MR Evans

759 – TM Weidenfeld – BX C M Dixon – BR Bridgeman

760 – TX, MR Weidenfeld – TR Bridgeman – BR Topham

761 – TR Newark – BM Fotomas Index

762 – MX Bridgeman – TM, BR Hulton

763 – TM Edinburgh Photographic Library – MR Fotomas Index – BX Holford

764 – TR, MX Bridgeman – BR Evans

765 – TL, MR Hulton – TR Weidenfeld – BX Weidenfeld

766 – TY Evans – BM Bridgeman

767 – ML Hulton – TM Bridgeman – BL Edinburgh Photographic Library – BR NTPL/Rupert Truman

768 – TR Portrait – MX E T Archive

769 – ML, BR E T Archive – TR Evans – BL Topham

770 – TM Newark – MR Evans – BR Hulton

771 – TL E T Archive – TR Evans – MX Bridgeman – MR Newark

772 – TY, MX Bridgeman – BR Fotomas Index

773 – TL Portrait – MX Evans – TR Fotomas Index – BR NTPL/Angelo Hornak

774 – TX Evans – TR Bridgeman – BM Topham/The Antman Archives

775 – ML Bridgeman – TR, MR Weidenfeld – BR Bridgeman

776 – TL, MM Bridgeman – TR Evans

777 – TM E T Archive – BL AAAC

778 – All pictures from Evans

779 – TR Evans – BR E T Archive – BL Bridgeman

780 – TM Weidenfeld – MM Evans – MR C M Dixon

781 – TL Hulton – MR, BL Bridgeman – BR E T Archive

782 – TM Evans – MR Newark – BY E T Archive

783 – ML E T Archive – TR, MR Great Scot Pictures

784 – TX Bridgeman – TR Weidenfeld – MY Hulton – BL Holford

785 – TR, ML Bridgeman – BL Hulton

786 – SP Bridgeman

788 – TX, TY CCL – BM Weidenfeld

700 – TX Weidenfeld – MY Evans – TR Love – BL David Lyons

790 – TR Evans/Bruce Castle Museum – BR Bridgeman

Picture credits

791 – ML Evans – TM Love – MR, BM Weidenfeld
792 – TM, MR Evans – BM Newark
793 – TR Evans – BL Weidenfeld – BR E T Archive
794 – TR Hulton – MR Mick Sharp/Jean Williamson – BM Evans
795 – TM, BL Bridgeman – MR Evans
796 – TY Portrait – MM Bridgeman – BR E T Archive
797 – TL, BX Bridgeman – MR Hulton
798 – TM Mansell Collection – MR Hulton
799 – MR Hulton – TM Bridgeman – BL Evans
800 – TM Weidenfeld – MR NTPL/Roy Fox
801 – TM Hulton – BL, BR Newark
802 – TY Evans – BR Bridgeman
803 – TL AAAC – TY, MR E T Archive
804 – ML Evans – TM, BM Bridgeman
805 – TM, BR Hulton – BX Portrait
806 – TY Evans – MR Weidenfeld – MM Mick Sharp
807 – TL, TR Evans – MR Bridgeman
808 – TY Portrait – MR Newark
809 – ML Hulton – TM E T Archive – MR, BR Evans
810 – TM Weidenfeld – MM E T Archive – BR Evans
811 – TM, BM Evans – MM Bridgeman
812 – TM Bettmann Archive – BR Evans
813 – All pictures from Evans
814 – MX, TR Evans – BR Hulton
815 – TM, BL E T Archive – MM CCL
816 – TR Bridgeman – BM Evans
817 – TR Hulton – MR CCL – BY, BL E T Archive
818 – TR Mansell Collection – BR Holford
819 – TR Fotomas Index – ML Portrait – BM Hulton
820 – TR Bridgeman – MR E T Archive
821 – ML Portrait – TM, MR Bridgeman – BR Hulton
822 – MY Evans – TR, BR Bridgeman
823 – ML Hulton – TR Evans – MR AAAC – MR Angelo Hornak – BR National Trust Photographic Library/John Bethell
824 – TR Hulton – MR Evans
825 – TX Weidenfeld – TR Bridgeman – BR Holford
826 – TY Topham – MM, MR David Lyons
827 – ML Evans – TR Weidenfeld – BY Hulton
828 – TY Newark – MM John Frost Historical Newspaper Archive – MR Evans
829 – All pictures from Evans
830 – TY, MR Evans – BM Bridgeman
831 – TL Fotomas Index – MR Love – MR C M Dixon – BR CCL
832 – TR, BR Evans – MM Bridgeman
833 – TM Love – MR Evans – BM E T Archive
834 – TY Evans – MR AAAC – MM Hulton
835 – TL, BR Bridgeman – MY Evans – TR Hulton
836 – TR E T Archive – BY Evans
837 – TM Bridgeman – MM Evans
838 – TM Mick Sharp/Jean Williamson – BR Weidenfeld
839 – ML AAAC – TM Evans – BM E T Archive – MR Portrait
840 – TY Hulton – MM Love
841 – TL E T Archive – TR, BR Topham – ML Bridgeman
842 – TY Evans – BR Bridgeman
843 – ML Hulton – TM Bridgeman – BM Evans
844 – TM Hulton – BR E T Archive
845 – ML Hulton – TX Evans – MR, BR Bridgeman
846 – All pictures from Evans
847 – TX Weidenfeld – TR Bridgeman – MR Evans
848 – TL Weidenfeld – TY Evans – ML Bridgeman
849 – TL, BX Evans – TR Newark – MR Weidenfeld
850 – TL, TR E T Archive – MR, BL Bridgeman
851 – TM, MM Bridgeman – BL, BR Portrait
852 – TY Hulton – MM Holford – BR Bridgeman
853 – TR Bridgeman – MM Evans
854 – TM Hulton – BR Bridgeman
855 – TL Portrait – TR, MR Bridgeman
856 – All pictures from Bridgeman
857 – TX Hulton – MM Evans – TR E T Archive – BL, BR Hulton
858 – TM Bridgeman – MR STB/Still Moving Picture Company – BR Evans
859 – TL Portrait – MM, TR Hulton – BR Evans
860 – TY, BR Bridgeman – MM Weidenfeld
861 – TM, BR Bridgeman – MR Weidenfeld – ML E T Archive
862 – TM Bridgeman – BM Hulton
863 – TX, BL Evans – MY Bridgeman – TR Portrait
864 – TM, BM Weidenfeld – MR Bridgeman
865 – TL E T Archive – MR, MY Weidenfeld – MX Newark
866 – TR, BR Bridgeman – MR Weidenfeld
867 – TX Evans – MX Hulton – MR NTPL/A. C. Cooper
868 – ML AAAC – TX, TR Bridgeman – MR CCL
869 – TM Weidenfeld – MR Evans – BY E T Archive
870 – TL Hulton – ML NTPL/Nick Carter – MR Weidenfeld
871 – TM, BR E T Archive – BL Hulton
872 – TM Bridgeman – BY Evans
873 – TL, TR, MR Evans – ML Topham
874 – All pictures from Bridgeman
875 – ML, MY Evans – TY Mansell Collection – BR Portrait
876 – TX Portrait – MR AAAC – BR Bridgeman
877 – TM Weidenfeld – MM, MR Evans – BM Topham
878 – MX, BR Bridgeman – TR Newark
879 – ML Hulton – TY, BL Evans – BR Bridgeman
880 – TR Evans – BR Bridgeman
881 – ML NTPL/Roy Fox – TR Hulton – BR NTPL/K. Richardson
882 – TM Bridgeman – MR Weidenfeld – MM E T Archive
883 – TY Hulton – MR Evans – BL Love
884 – ML, BY Weidenfeld – TY Hulton – BL NTPL/John Bethell
885 – TM Evans – MM Hulton – MR Weidenfeld
886 – TX Portrait – BY, BL Weidenfeld
887 – ML, MM Evans – TR, MR Hulton
888 – MX, TR Hulton – BR Evans
889 – ML Evans – TX, BY Hulton – TR Weidenfeld
890 – TR Evans – BR Portrait
891 – ML, TM Bridgeman – MR E T Archive
892 – TM E T Archive – BX Hulton
893 – TM, MR Evans – BM Hulton
894 – TY Newark – MM Bridgeman
895 – ML, BL Weidenfeld – TR Hulton
896 – MX Love – TR, BY Evans
897 – TM Fotomas Index – MR Evans – BL E T Archive
898 – TL Fotomas Index – TR Bridgeman – BM Hulton
899 – TM Hulton – BL Bridgeman
900 – TM Weidenfeld – MM Hulton – BM Evans
901 – TL Bridgeman – TR Evans – BR CCL
902 – TY Weidenfeld – MM, BR Bridgeman
903 – TR Hulton – ML Newark – BR Bridgeman
904 – TR, MM Evans – BR Weidenfeld
905 – ML, MR Evans – TR E T Archive
906 – TM Evans – BM Love
907 – TM, BR Newark – TL CCL
908 – TY Weidenfeld – MM Love – BR Bridgeman
909 – ML Hulton – TR Evans – MR E T Archive
910 – TR Weidenfeld – BX CCL – MR Evans
911 – TM, BL Evans – MR Weidenfeld
912 – TM Evans – BR Hulton
913 – TM Bridgeman – BL, BR Evans
914 – TY Hulton – MR Evans – BM Bridgeman
915 – TR, MR Bridgeman – BL Evans
916 – TR Fotomas Index – MR Hulton – TL Bridgeman – ML, BL E T Archive
917 – MX Weidenfeld – TR Holford – MR Hulton – BR E T Archive
918 – TM, BR Evans – MR Hulton
919 – TM Evans – MX Newark – BR Hulton
920 – TM Hulton – MR Evans – BY Weidenfeld
921 – TM Evans – MR Love – BX Bridgeman
922 – TR Evans – MR Hulton
923 – TM Newark – TR Hulton – BM E T Archive
924 – TR Hulton – MR Evans
925 – TM Hulton – MR E T Archive – MM, BL Evans
926 – TY Hulton – MM E T Archive – BR Bridgeman
927 – MX Portrait – TR, BR Evans
928 – MX Weidenfeld – TR Evans – BY Topham
929 – ML Hulton – TR Weidenfeld – MY Bridgeman
930 – TY E T Archive – MR Bridgeman – BR Evans
931 – TX, TR Evans – BX E T Archive – MR Love
932 – TR Newark – MR CCL – BM Portrait
933 – TY E T Archive – MY Evans – BX, BR Hulton
934 – TM Hulton – BR, ML, MY Weidenfeld
935 – TM Hulton – MR Newark – BR Hulton
936 – TM Fotomas Index – BL, MR Hulton
937 – All pictures from Evans
938 – TL Love – TR Hulton – BR Evans – BL Woodcock
939 – TY Portrait – MM Evans – BR Bridgeman
940 – TL Holford – TR, BR Hulton – BL Love
941 – TM Evans – MM Weidenfeld – BM The Mistress and Fellows, Girton College, Cambridge
942 – TR NTPL – BY Evans
943 – TX Bridgeman – TR Hulton – BM Evans
944 – TX Newark – TR, BR Evans – MM Love
945 – TM Evans – MR Portrait – ML C M Dixon
946 – TY Topham – BR Newark
947 – ML, BR Evans – TM Hulton – MY CCL – BX Bridgeman
948 – TY, TR Hulton – BM Bridgeman
949 – MX, BL Evans – TR Hulton
950 – MX Bridgeman – TR Evans – BY Woodcock
951 – ML Hulton – TR, BR Evans
952 – TY Evans – MR Newark
953 – TL Bridgeman – MR Evans – BL NTPL/John Bethell – BY Woodcock
954 – TR, BR Evans – MM Holford
955 – ML, TY Evans – TX, BR Hulton – BY Bridgeman
956 – TY, TR Hulton – BM Evans
957 – TX Hulton – TR E T Archive – ML Bridgeman – BR Evans
958 – TY Bridgeman – MY Weidenfeld – BX Holford – BR Hulton
959 – ML, TR Hulton – MR Bridgeman
960 – TR Weidenfeld – MM, BR Hulton
961 – ML Portrait – TM, MR Evans – TR Hulton
962 – MR Hulton – TL, BL Evans
963 – TR Hulton – BR Weidenfeld
964 – BL, TM Newark – MR E T Archive
965 – TL, TR Evans – BX NTPL/J Gibson – BR Bridgeman
966 – TR Hulton – BR Love
967 – All pictures from Bridgeman
968 – BX Evans – TR Hulton
969 – TX, TR, ML Evans – BR Newark
970 – TL, BL Evans – TR Fotomas Index
971 – TM, MR Hulton – BR Newark
972 – TL E T Archive – TR, MX, MR Hulton
973 – TM Newark – TR E T Archive – BR NTPL/Jerry Harper
974 – TY Hulton – MX Newark – MR Evans – BL E T Archive
975 – TL Evans – MR Bridgeman – BL City of Plymouth Museums and Art Gallery
976 – MX Evans – TR, BR Hulton
977 – TX, BM Hulton – TY, MM E T Archive
978 – TM, MR Hulton – MY, BL Evans
979 – TR Evans – BM BTA/ETB/SI
980 – TM Evans – MX Portrait – MY Weidenfeld – BR Bridgeman
981 – TR Hulton – ML Love – BR Edinburgh Photographic Library
982 – MX Topham – TR Evans – BY Bridgeman
983 – MR CCL
984 – TL Newark – TY Topham – MM Hulton
985 – MX Evans – TR Hulton – BR E T Archive
986 – TL, BL Hulton – MR Evans
987 – TM Evans – TR Hulton – BM Topham
988 – MX John Frost Historical Newspaper Archive – TY Hulton – TR Evans – BR Edinburgh Photographic Library
989 – TY, BM Evans – MR Newark
990 – ML Evans – TY Weidenfeld – BR Hulton
991 – All pictures from Evans
992 – TY Weidenfeld – ML E T Archive – BR Evans
993 – All pictures from Hulton
994 – ML, TX, MR Hulton – BM Harding
995 – All pictures from Evans
996 – TM Heritage – MM, BL Evans – BR Hulton
997 – TL, MR, BY Hulton – MX Evans
998 – TY, MR Hulton – MX Evans
999 – TL Evans – MX, TR Hulton – MR John Hannavy Collection – BR Bridgeman
1000 – MX Portrait – TX, BR Evans – TR Topham
1001 – TR Newark – MR Hulton – ML Love – BX Evans
1002 – TX, ML NTPL – TR Hulton – BR Northern Ireland Tourist Board
1003 – All pictures from Evans
1004 – TL Bridgeman – MY Hulton – TR, BL Evans
1005 – TM Hulton – BX Evans – MR, BR Bridgeman
1006 – TX Topham – TR Bridgeman – MR, BR Hulton
1007 – ML Hulton – TY, TR, MR, BR Evans
1008 – TR Hulton – MM Evans – MR Mansell Collection
1009 – TM, BR Evans – MX Hulton
1010 – TM, BL Bridgeman – TR, MR Portrait – AAAC – MY Evans – BX NTPL/J Gibson
1011 – TM Fotomas Index – MR Hulton – BR Northern Ireland Tourist Board
1012 – TL, ML E T Archive – TR, BR Hulton
1013 – TM Evans – BL E T Archive – BY Newark
1014 – All pictures from CCL
1015 – TR CCL
1016 – TM Newark – MM CCL – BR Hulton
1017 – All pictures from BL Hulton
1018 – SP Science Photo Library
1020 – TR Heritage – MR Hulton
1021 – ML, TR Newark – BR Topham
1022 – TY Topham – BY Evans
1023 – ML, TX, TY Evans – BR Topham
1024 – TY Hulton – BM Popperfoto
1025 – TM Popperfoto – BX Hulton – BR Topham
1026 – TY Evans – BR Topham
1027 – TL Hulton – MM Love – TR NLI – BR Topham
1028 – TY Topham – BY Hulton
1029 – TX, TR Topham – BL Mander & Mitchenson Theatre Collection – BR Hulton
1030 – TM Topham – BR Hulton
1031 – TL Hulton – TR Topham – BR Popperfoto
1032 – TY Museum of London – MR Newark – BM NLI
1033 – TM Hulton – ML Evans – BR Topham
1034 – TX, TY, MR Hulton – BY Newark
1035 – TY, BR Hulton – ML Evans
1036 – TM Hulton – BX Evans – BR Newark
1037 – TX, BL Hulton – TR Newark – BR Architectural Association/Barry Capper
1038 – TR Hulton – MY Newark
1039 – TL Topham – TR, BM Hulton
1040 – TM, BR Hulton – BX Topham
1041 – TL, BX Evans – BR Tate Gallery, London
1042 – TX, MR Newark – MX Hulton
1043 – TM, BL Hulton – MR John Frost Historical Newspaper Archive
1044 – MY Evans – TM Popperfoto
1045 – TX Topham – MR Hulton – BL Newark
1046 – All pictures from Hulton
1047 – TM Syndication International – BM CCL
1048 – TY Imperial War Museum – MX Newark
1049 – All pictures from Hulton
1050 – All pictures from Popperfoto
1051 – All pictures from Newark
1052 – TR Imperial War Museum
1053 – TM Hulton – BM Imperial War Museum
1054 – TM, BM Imperial War Museum – MR Newark
1055 – TM Hulton – MR Popperfoto
1056 – TR Robert Hunt Library – ML, BR Hulton
1057 – All pictures from Hulton
1058 – TM Hulton – BR Popperfoto
1059 – TL, BX Topham – MM, BR Hulton
1060 – TM Hulton – BR Popperfoto
1061 – TL Hulton – TR Topham – BY Popperfoto
1062 – TY Popperfoto – BM Hulton
1063 – MM Hulton – BL Popperfoto
1064 – TY Popperfoto – MR Evans – BM Newark
1065 – TM, BX Popperfoto – BY Topham
1066 – TY Newark – BM Topham
1067 – TL Hulton – TY Popperfoto – BR Bridgeman
1068 – All pictures from Topham
1069 – TX Topham – BX, BR Hulton – TR Sygma/Illustration
1070 – TR Newark – MM Hulton
1071 – TM CCL – BL Popperfoto – BR Evans
1072 – TR Hulton – MR Popperfoto
1073 – TR Popperfoto – BR Newark
1074 – TL Popperfoto – TY, BR Hulton
1075 – All pictures from Hulton
1076 – TX Topham – BL Evans – MR Hulton
1077 – All pictures from Hulton
1078 – ML Ronald Grant Archive – TM Hulton – MR Topham – BY Evans
1079 – TM, MR Mander & Mitchenson Theatre Collection – BM Popperfoto
1080 – TY, BR Topham – BX Popperfoto
1081 – TL, BM Hulton – MR Evans
1082 – TM Topham – BR Museum in Docklands
1083 – MM Popperfoto – TM Hulton
1084 – TR Hulton – MR Popperfoto
1085 – TX Popperfoto – BM Hulton
1086 – TM Hulton – BY Evans
1087 – ML Topham – TR, BR Hulton
1088 – TM Topham – BY, BR Hulton
1089 – TL, BR Hulton – TY Topham – BL Evans
1090 – TY Popperfoto – BR Hulton
1091 – TL, BL Topham – MR Hulton
1092 – All pictures from Hulton
1093 – TY Newark – BY Hulton – ML Love
1094 – TY Hulton – BR Angelo Hornak
1095 – TX Topham – TR Royal Opera House, London – BR Popperfoto – BL Evans
1096 – TR Topham – BM Popperfoto
1097 – TM Hulton – BL National Railway Museum – BR Robert Opie
1098 – All pictures from Hulton
1099 – MM Hulton – BM Popperfoto
1100 – TM Topham – BR Popperfoto – BR Hulton
1101 – TY Topham – BR Newark
1102 – TR Robert Hunt Library – ML Popperfoto – MR, BM Topham
1103 – ML Associated Press – MR Robert Hunt Library
1104 – TM, MM Hulton – BM Associated Press
1105 – TM Hulton – BX Newark – BR Popperfoto
1106 – TM Robert Hunt Library – MM, BR Popperfoto
1107 – TM Hulton – BR Popperfoto
1108 – TM, BX Topham – BR Popperfoto
1109 – TL Newark – TY Imperial War Museum – MR AP/Topham – BM Robert Hunt Library
1110 – TM Robert Hunt Library – BY Topham – MR Popperfoto
1111 – TX National Archives of Canada – BL Popperfoto – TR Hulton – BR Topham
1112 – TM Robert Hunt Library – BR Popperfoto
1113 – TM Topham
1114 – TM Imperial War Museum – MR, BL Popperfoto
1115 – TR Popperfoto
1116 – TL, MY Popperfoto – BM Hulton
1117 – TM AP/Topham – BM Hulton
1118 – TM Topham – BM Popperfoto
1119 – TM PA/Topham – MM Topham – BL Hulton
1120 – TM Hulton – MM Popperfoto
1121 – ML, BX Hulton – TM Popperfoto – BR Topham
1122 – MM PA/Topham – TR Topham
1123 – TR Popperfoto – MM, BM Topham
1124 – TM, MR Topham – BY PA/Topham
1125 – TX, BL Topham – TR Hulton – BR Ronald Grant Archive
1126 – TM Hulton – MR Topham – BY Popperfoto
1127 – TX, BL Popperfoto – TR Hulton
1128 – TX AP/Topham – TY Topham – TM, MR, BR, BL Popperfoto
1130 – All pictures from Popperfoto
1131 – TM, BM Popperfoto – MR Topham
1132 – TR PA/Topham – MR Topham
1133 – TM Hulton – MR AP/Topham – BL, BX Popperfoto
1134 – All pictures from Topham
1135 – TL, MR Topham – BL Hulton
1136 – TX AP/Topham – MR Topham – BY Popperfoto
1137 – TX Robert Opie – MR Topham – BX Popperfoto
1138 – TY Hulton – MX, BR Topham
1139 – TL, TR Hulton – MM, BM Topham
1140 – TM Popperfoto – BR Topham
1141 – TM Hulton – BL Topham – BR Popperfoto
1142 – TM Popperfoto – MM Hulton – BR Topham
1143 – TM, BR Hulton – BX Topham
1144 – TY PA/Topham – MX Hulton – BR Topham
1145 – ML, TR Topham – BR Popperfoto
1146 – TR, MX Topham – BR Hulton
1147 – TM, MR Topham – BM Kobal Collection
1148 – MM Popperfoto – TR PA/Topham – BY Topham
1149 – ML Topham – TR, BR Popperfoto
1150 – TY Topham – BM Popperfoto
1151 – All pictures from Popperfoto
1152 – TL Popperfoto – TR, BY Topham – BX Hulton
1153 – ML Topham – TY, BM Popperfoto
1154 – ML Popperfoto – TR Topham – BY Hulton
1155 – ML, TR Topham – BR Hulton
1156 – TM PA/Topham – BM Popperfoto
1157 – TX PA/Topham – MR Popperfoto – BL AP/Topham
1158 – TM AP/Topham – MR, BM Topham
1159 – TM, ML PA/Topham – MR Topham
1160 – TY Topham – BX Hulton – BR PA/Topham
1161 – TX, TR, BL Hulton – MR Topham
1162 – TY Topham – MY, BX Hulton – BR AP/Topham
1163 – TX, MR, BR Topham – ML PA/Topham
1164 – TM Popperfoto – BR Topham
1165 – TL PA/Topham – TR, BX, BY Popperfoto
1166 – TY, BX Hulton – MR Popperfoto
1167 – TR Popperfoto – MR, BL Hulton
1168 – TY Popperfoto – MR Topham – MM Hulton
1169 – TR, BL Popperfoto – BR Kobal Collection
1170 – TX, BY Popperfoto – TY Hulton – MR Topham
1171 – TR Magnum Photos – MM Hulton – BL Cosmopolitan
1172 – All photos from Hulton
1173 – TR Popperfoto – ML AP/Topham – BR Allsport
1174 – TR Hulton – BM AP/Topham
1175 – TM Rex – MR Topham – BL Hulton
1176 – TY, MM Hulton – BR PA/Topham
1177 – TL, TR Hulton – MY Topham – BM Rex
1178 – TX, MR, BY Hulton – TY Topham
1179 – TL Rex – TR Topham – BR Hulton
1180 – TX Hulton – TR Rex – BR Allsport
1181 – TM, ML Hulton – BR Allsport
1182 – TR Popperfoto – MX Hulton – BR Ronald Grant Archive
1183 – TM, ML Hulton – MR Topham
1184 – TR Rex – MR AP/Topham
1185 – TX Popperfoto – TR Hulton – BR Topham – BL Allsport
1186 – TM Rex – BM Hulton
1187 – TM Impact – MR Popperfoto – BL Topham – BR AP/Topham
1188 – TM Popperfoto – MM Rex – BY Topham
1189 – TR Rex – MX, BR Topham – BL Popperfoto
1190 – TM AP/Topham – TR Hulton – BR Rex
1191 – TX PA/Topham – TR Topham – MM Rex – BR AP/Topham
1192 – TX Allsport – MR Topham – BR Allsport
1193 – MR Rex – ML Topham – BR AP/Topham
1194 – TM Network – MR AP/Topham – BY Allsport
1195 – TL, BL Rex – TM Topham – MR Sygma
1196 – All pictures from Rex
1197 – TL, MX, BR Rex – TR AP/Topham
1198 – TX PA/Topham – TY, BM Popperfoto
1199 – TL, TR Topham – MY PA/Topham – BL Rex
1200 – TY, MM AP/Topham – BR Topham
1201 – All pictures from Rex
1202 – TM PA/Topham – MR AP/Topham – BY Topham
1203 – TR AP/Topham – BL PA/Topham – MR Rex
1204 – TX, BY PA/Topham – TR Rex
1205 – TM, MM Rex – BR Popperfoto
1206 – MR AP/Topham – BM PA/Topham
1207 – TL Rex – MR, BY Popperfoto – BL Allsport
1208 – TM Rex – MM PA/Topham – BR AP/Topham
1209 – TL, TX Popperfoto/AFP – TR PA/Topham -BX Popperfoto – BR Allsport
1210 – TL, TX, ML, BL, BR Rex – TR PA/Topham – MR Rex – BX Topham
1211 – TL Sipa Press – ML, MX, BL, BX Allsport – TR Mansell Collection – BR Sipa Press
1212 – TM Topham – BR Popperfoto
1213 – ML Popperfoto – TM, BX Ronald Grant Archive – MR Topham
1215 – FP CCL
1216 – FP CCL
1217 – FP CCL
1218 – SP CCL
1220 – TL AP/Topham
1221 – B CCL
1222 – ML, TR Central Office of Information Picture Library – BR CCL
1223 – TL Topham – MR House of Commons Public Information Office
1226 – FP Crown Copyright. By Permission of the Controller of her Majesty's Stationery Office
1227 – BL CCL – TR Rex
1234 – TR Bruce Coleman – ML The Environmental Picture Library – BR Ardea
1235 – MX The Environmental Picture Library – TR Bruce Coleman – BR Ardea

RD – 40/336/2